Lab Safety

Safety symbol	What it means	What to do in the event of an accident
Eye protection	Wear safety goggles anytime there is the slightest chance that your eyes could be harmed.	If anything gets into your eyes, notify your teacher immediately and flush your eyes with running water for 15 minutes.
Clothing protection	Wear your apron whenever you are working with chemicals or whenever you are instructed to do so.	If you spill a corrosive chemical onto your clothing, rinse it off immediately by using a faucet or the safety shower and remove the affected clothing while calling to your teacher.
Hand safety	Wear appropriate protective gloves when working with an open flame, chemicals, or plants. Your teacher will provide the type of gloves necessary for a given activity. Wash your hands with soap and hot water at the end of every lab.	If any chemical gets on your hands, rinse it off immediately with water for at least 5 minutes while calling to your teacher. Report any burn of the hands to your teacher no matter how minor it seems.
Safety with Gases	Do not inhale any gas or vapor unless directed to do so by your teacher. Handle materials that emit vapors or gases in a well-ventilated area.	Notify your teacher immediately if you have inhaled a gas or vapor, or if your eyes, nose, or throat become irritated.
Hygienic Care	Keep you hands away from your face, hair, and mouth while you are working on any activity. Wash your hands thoroughly before you leave the lab or when you finish any activity. Remove contaminated clothing immediately.	Notify your teacher immediately if you spill corrosive substances on your skin or clothing no matter how minor it seems. Use the safety shower or faucet to rinse. Remove affected clothing while you are under the shower and call to your teacher.
Sharp/pointed object safety	Use knives and other sharp objects with extreme care. Place objects on a suitable work surface for cutting.	Notify your teacher immediately in the event of a cut or puncture no matter how minor it seems.
Animal care and safety	Handle animals only as your teacher directs. Treat animals carefully and respectfully. Wash your hands thoroughly after handling any animal.	Notify your teacher immediately if you injure yourself or any live specimen no matter how minor the injury seems.
Glassware Safety	Inspect glassware before use; do not use chipped or cracked glassware.	Notify your teacher immediately if a piece of glassware or a light bulb breaks.
Electrical safety	Do not place electrical cords where they could trip someone or cause equipment to fall. Do not use equipment with damaged cords. Do not use electrical equipment near water or when your clothing or hands are wet. Make sure that electrical equipment is in the "off" position before plugging it in. Turn off and unplug electrical equipment when you have finished using it.	Notify your teacher immediately if you notice any abnormal or potentially dangerous equipment. In the event of an electric shock, notify your teacher no matter how minor it seems.
Chemical safety	Wear safety goggles, an apron, and gloves whenever working with chemicals.	If a chemical spills onto your skin, rinse it off immediately by using the faucet or safety shower for at least 5 minutes while calling to your teacher.
Proper waste disposal	Dispose of contaminated materials in special containers only as directed by your teacher. Dispose of sharp objects in the appropriate sharps container as directed by your teacher. Clean and sanitize all work surfaces and personal protective equipment after each lab period.	Notify your teacher immediately if a piece of glassware or a light bulb breaks. Dispose of broken glass in the appropriate container as directed by your teacher. Notify your teacher immediately if you spill a chemical or culture of microorganisms. Follow your teacher's instructions for clean up.
Heating safety	Wear safety goggles when using a heating device or flame. Wear heat-resistant gloves when instructed to do so. When heating materials in a test tube, angle the test tube away from yourself and others.	Notify your teacher immediately in the event of a burn or fire no matter how minor it seems.
Plant safety	Do not eat any part of a plant or plant seed. When in nature, do not pick any wild plants unless your teacher instructs you to do so. Wash your hands thoroughly after handling any part of a plant.	Notify your teacher immediately if any potentially dangerous plant material comes into contact with your skin or if any plant matter is inhaled or ingested no matter how minor the event seems.

Commonly Used Word Parts

Word Parts

Word part	Definition	Example
amphi-	both	amphibian: a type of vertebrate that lives both on land and in water
ante-	before	anterior: front of an organism
anti-	against	antibiotic: substance, such as penicillin, capable of killing bacteria
arche-	ancient	Archaeopteryx: an ancient, fossilized bird
arthro-	joint	arthritis: a painful disease affecting the joints
bio-	life	biology: the study of life
chloro-	green	chlorophyll: green pigment in plants; needed for photosynthesis
chondro-	cartilage	Chondrichthyes: fish whose skeletons are made of cartilage
cyte-	cell	cytology: the study of cells
derm-	skin	dermatology: the study of the skin
ecto-	outer, outside	ectoderm: the outer tissue layer in many organisms
endo-	inner, inside	endoderm: the inner tissue layer in many organisms
gastro-	stomach	gastritis: inflammation of the stomach or stomach lining
gen-	produce	generate: to make, produce, or bring into being
hemi-	half	hemisphere: half of a sphere
hetero-	different	heterogeneous: made of unrelated or various parts
homeo-	the same	homeostasis: maintaining steady internal conditions
hydro-	water	hydroponics: growing plants in water instead of soil
hyper-	above, over	hypertension: blood pressure that is higher than normal
hypo-	below, under	hypothermic: body temperature that is below normal
inter-	between, among	interpersonal: relationships between or among people
intra-	within	intracellular: inside a cell
-logy	study of	biology: the study of life
macro-	large	macromolecule: large molecule, such as DNA or a protein
mega-	large	megaspore: a large spore produced by some ferns and flowering pants
meta-	change	metamorphosis: change in form
micro-	small	microscope: a tool for looking at very small objects
morph-	form	morphology: the study of the form of an organism
neo-	new	neonatal: newborn
para-	near, on	parasite: organism that lives on and feeds on another organism
peri-	around	pericardium: the membrane around the heart
photo-	light	phototropism: bending of plants toward light
-phyte-	plant	epiphyte: plant that lives on another plant, as in the branches of trees
poly-	many	polypeptide: many amino acids joined together to make a protein
pre-	before	prediction: a forecast of events before they take place
semi-	partially	semitransparent: allowing some, but not all, light to pass through
sub-	under	submarine: a boat that travels underwater
syn-	with	synapse: a place where two or more nerves come together
trans-	across	transcontinental: going across a continent

HOLT

Biology

DeSalle • Heithaus

HOLT, RINEHART AND WINSTON

A Harcourt Education Company

Orlando • Austin • New York • San Diego • London

Authors

Rob DeSalle, Ph.D.

is a curator in the Division of Invertebrate Zoology at the American Museum of Natural History in New York City. He is an adjunct professor at Columbia University and City University of New York and is a Distinguished Research Professor at New York University. His current research focuses on molecular evolution in various organisms, including pathogenic bacteria and insects. He coauthored *Welcome to the Genome: A User's Guide to the Genetic Past, Present, and Future* (Wiley) and *The Science of Jurassic Park and the Lost World* (HarperCollins), and he edited *Epidemic! The World of Infectious Diseases* (W. W. Norton), which are all aimed at nontechnical readers.

Michael R. Heithaus, Ph.D.

is an assistant professor of biological sciences at Florida International University and a former host of National Geographic's *Crittercam* television program. He currently works with the National Geographic Channel to develop programming and educational materials and to give talks to students. His current research centers on predator-prey interactions among marine vertebrates. Mike's research in animal behavior has taken him all over the world to deploy Crittercam on a host of marine and terrestrial animal species, including dolphins, sharks, seals, sea turtles, whales, lions, hyenas, and, most recently, penguins.

Contributing Authors

Wayne Moorehead, MS, F-ABC
is a forensic scientist in Orange County, California. He teaches classes in forensic science at various colleges. He is a fellow of the American Board of Criminalistics.

Linda K. Gaul, Ph.D.
is an epidemiologist at the Texas Department of State Health Services. She conducts surveillance and epidemiological investigations related to infectious diseases. She has taught both biology and epidemiology at the college level.

David Haig, Ph.D.
is a professor of organismic and evolutionary biology at Harvard University. His current research focuses on genomic imprinting—the differential contributions of maternal and paternal genes to offspring—in plants and animals.

Sidney Rogers
is a science teacher at Cerritos High School in Cerritos, California. He teaches classes in forensic science to elementary, junior high, and high school students.

Shubha Govind, Ph.D.
is a professor of biology at City College, New York. Her current research focuses on the function of proteins as cellular signaling molecules in the immune response and in animal development.

Ann S. Lumsden, Ph.D.
is a professor of biological science at Florida State University, where she is the coordinator of biology classes for nonmajors. She is a former president of the National Association of Biology Teachers.

Erika Zavaleta, Ph.D.
is an assistant professor in the Environmental Studies Department of the University of California, Santa Cruz. Her current research centers on how changes in levels of biodiversity affect society.

Daniel Rozen, Ph.D.
Post-doctoral Fellow
Emory University
Department of Biology
Atlanta, Georgia

Miles R. Silman, Ph.D.
Associate Professor of Biology
Wake Forest University
Biology Department
Winston-Salem, North Carolina

Richard Storey, Ph.D.
Professor of Biology
University of Montana, Western
Dillon, Montana

Gerald Summers, Ph.D.
Associate Professor of Biological Sciences
The University of Missouri
Division of Biological Sciences
Columbia, Missouri

Billie J. Swalla, Ph.D.
Associate Professor of Biology
University of Washington
Biology Department
Seattle, Washington

Sean Veney, Ph.D.
Assistant Professor
Kent State University
Biological Sciences
Kent, Ohio

Elizabeth Wenk, Ph.D.
Adjunct Faculty
Cerro Coso Community College
Science Department
Bishop, California

Mary K. Wicksten, Ph.D.
Professor of Biology
Texas A&M University
Department of Biology
College Station, Texas

James Young, Ph.D.
President of the American Academy of Forensic Science and former Chief Coroner of Ontario, Canada
Colorado Springs, Colorado

Teacher Reviewers

Robert S. Akeson
Biology Teacher
Boston Latin School
Boston, Massachusetts

Janet B. Barnett
Biology Teacher
Columbus North High School
Columbus, Indiana

Bob Baronak
Biology Teacher
Donegal High School
Mount Joy, Pennsylvania

Angelique Biehl
IB Biology Teacher
Portage Northern High School
Portage, Michigan

Ellen Feuerman Cohen
Science Department Chair
Marjory Stoneman Douglas High School
Parkland, Florida

Jacqueline B. Curley
Teacher
Academy of Science
Loudoun County Public Schools
Sterling, Virginia

Martha M. Day, Ed.D.
Science Department Chairperson
Whites Creek High School
Nashville, Tennessee

Alan Eagy
Biology Teacher
The Dalles Wahtonka High School
The Dalles, Oregon

Benjamin D. Ebersole
Biology and Chemistry Teacher
Donegal High School
Mount Joy, Pennsylvania

Yolanda Michelle Harman
Biology Teacher; Science Chairperson
Northern Garrett High School
Accident, Maryland

Jason Hook
7th Grade Science Teacher
Kealing Middle School
Austin, Texas

Nancy Kossover
Biology Teacher
Leadership High School – Hayward
Hayward, California

Andrew M. Larson
Biology Teacher
Columbus North High School
Columbus, Indiana

Tammie Niffenegger
Science Chair and Teacher
Port Washington High School
Port Washington, Wisconsin

Amy K. Ragan
Biology Teacher
Cedar Park High School
Austin, Texas

Tami Reardon
Biology Teacher
Columbus North High School
Columbus, Indiana

Dale Simon
Biology Teacher
Central High School
Camp Point, Illinois

Bert Wartski
Biology and AP Biology Teacher
Chapel Hill High School
Chapel Hill, North Carolina

Tyson Yager
Biology Teacher
Wichita High School East
Wichita, Kansas

Kathy A. Yorks
Anatomy and Physiology Teacher
Central Mountain High School
Mill Hall, Pennsylvania

Patricia Arnett Zeck, M.A.
Biology Teacher and Science Department Facilitator
Northwestern High School
Kokomo, Indiana

Safety in the Laboratory xxiv
How to Use Your Textbook xxviii

Unit 1 Introduction 2
Chapter 1 Biology and You 4
Chapter 2 Applications of Biology 26
Chapter 3 Chemistry of Life 48

Unit 2 Ecology 74
Chapter 4 Ecosystems 76
Chapter 5 Populations and Communities 100
Chapter 6 The Environment 122

Unit 3 Cells 146
Chapter 7 Cell Structure 148
Chapter 8 Cells and Their Environment 172
Chapter 9 Photosynthesis and Cellular
           Respiration 194
Chapter 10 Cell Growth and Division 220

Unit 4 Heredity 242
Chapter 11 Meiosis and Sexual Reproduction 244
Chapter 12 Mendel and Heredity 264
Chapter 13 DNA, RNA, and Proteins 290
Chapter 14 Genes in Action 316
Chapter 15 Gene Technologies and
           Human Applications 342

Unit 5 Evolution 370
Chapter 16 Evolutionary Theory 372
Chapter 17 Population Genetics and Speciation .. 396
Chapter 18 Classification 420
Chapter 19 History of Life on Earth 444

Unit 6 Microbes 466
Chapter 20 Bacteria and Viruses 468
Chapter 21 Protists 494
Chapter 22 Fungi 518

Unit 7 Plants 538
Chapter 23 Plant Diversity and Life Cycles 540
Chapter 24 Seed Plant Structure and Growth 570
Chapter 25 Plant Processes 596

Unit 8 Animals 618
Chapter 26 Introduction to Animals 620
Chapter 27 Simple Invertebrates 652
Chapter 28 Mollusks and Annelids 676
Chapter 29 Arthropods and Echinoderms 698
Chapter 30 Fishes and Amphibians 726
Chapter 31 Reptiles and Birds 754
Chapter 32 Mammals 782
Chapter 33 Animal Behavior 810

Unit 9 Humans 834
Chapter 34 Skeletal, Muscular, and
           Integumentary Systems 836
Chapter 35 Circulatory and Respiratory Systems . 862
Chapter 36 Digestive and Excretory Systems 888
Chapter 37 The Body's Defenses 912
Chapter 38 Nervous System 936
Chapter 39 Endocrine System 968
Chapter 40 Reproduction and Development 990
Chapter 41 Forensic Science 1014

Appendix 1042
Reading Toolbox 1044
Skills Appendix 1050
Reference 1062
Answers to Reading Checks 1066
Glossary 1075
Index 1126

Safety in the Laboratory xxiv
How to Use You Textbooks xxviii

UNIT 1 Introduction

2

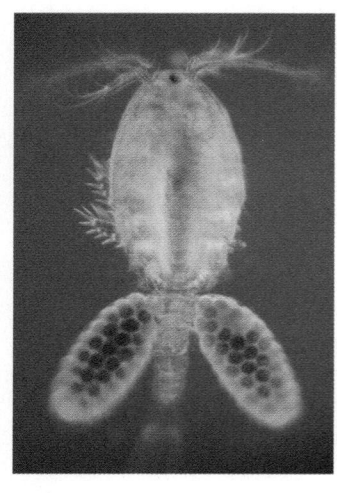

Chapter 1 Biology and You 4

Section 1 The Nature of Science 7
Section 2 Scientific Methods 10
Section 3 Tools and Techniques 14
Section 4 What is Biology? 17
Standardized Test Prep 25

> **Why It Matters** Biology in the Wild 18

> **Labs** Make a Prediction 5
> Evaluate a Scientific Claim 9
> The pH of Common Substances 11
> Practice Staining Techniques 15
> SI Units 20

Chapter 2 Applications of Biology 26

Section 1 Health in the 21st Century 29
Section 2 Biology, Technology, and Society 33
Section 3 Biology and the Environment 38
Standardized Test Prep 47

> **Why It Matters** Bio Bots 41

> **Labs** Artificial Shark Skin 27
> Model a Low-Tech Solution 31
> Biomimetic Engineering 34
> Microbe Growth 42

Chapter 3 Chemistry of Life 48

Section 1 Matter and Substances 51
Section 2 Water and Solutions 55
Section 3 Carbon Compounds 59
Section 4 Energy and Metabolism 64
Standardized Test Prep 73

> **Why It Matters** Water Wonders 58

> **Labs** Yeast Activity 49
> Atom Models 53
> Telltale Cabbage 57
> Brown Paper Test 61
> Enzymes in Detergents 68

Chapter 4 Ecosystems 76

Section 1 What Is an Ecosystem? 79
Section 2 Energy Flow in Ecosytems 86
Section 3 Cycling of Matter 90
Standardized Test Prep 99

> **Why It Matters** Maintained by Fire 85

> **Labs** Water Cycle 77
> Biodiversity Evaluation 80
> The Carbon Cycle 93
> Ecosystem Change 94

> **Math Skills** Energy Pyramid 88

Chapter 5 Populations and Communities 100

Section 1 Populations 103
Section 2 Interactions in Communities 109
Section 3 Shaping Communities 112
Standardized Test Prep 121

> **Why It Matters** Growth in Asia 108

> **Labs** Population Size 101
> Population Growth 105
> The Effects of Herbivores on a Plant Species 110
> Changes in a Realized Niche 113
> Yeast Population Growth 116

Chapter 6 The Environment 122

Section 1 An Interconnected Planet 125
Section 2 Environmental Issues 128
Section 3 Environmental Solutions 134
Standardized Test Prep 145

> **Why It Matters** Cars of the Future 139

> **Labs** The Greenhouse Effect 123
> Contaminated Water 127
> Soil Erosion 131
> Recycled Paper 135
> Effects of Acid Rain on Seeds 140

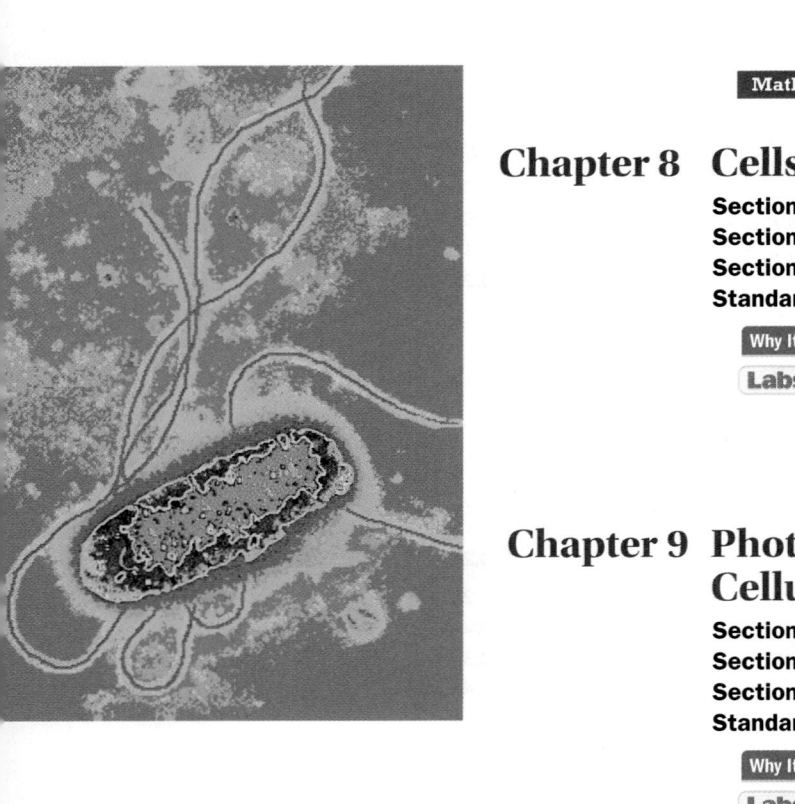

Chapter 7 **Cell Structure** **148**

Section 1 Introduction to Cells **151**
Section 2 Inside the Eukaryotic Cell **156**
Section 3 From Cell to Organism **162**
Standardized Test Prep **171**

Why It Matters Cell Shape 152

Labs Is It Alive? 149
Cell Parts Model 160
Colonies on the Move 165
Plant Cell Observation 167

Math Skills Ratio of Surface Area and Volume 153

Chapter 8 **Cells and Their Environment** **172**

Section 1 Cell Membrane **175**
Section 2 Cell Transport **178**
Section 3 Cell Communication **184**
Standardized Test Prep **193**

Why It Matters Heady Effects 187

Labs Salty Cells 173
Osmosis 181
Sensitive Plants 185
Cell Size and Diffusion 188

Chapter 9 **Photosynthesis and Cellular Respiration** **194**

Section 1 Energy in Living Systems **197**
Section 2 Photosynthesis **202**
Section 3 Cellular Respiration **208**
Standardized Test Prep **219**

Why It Matters Life in a Biosphere 214

Labs Stored Energy 195
Product of Photosynthesis 198
Photosynthetic Rate 205
Cellular Respiration 215

Chapter 10 **Cell Growth and Division** **220**

Section 1 Cell Reproduction **223**
Section 2 Mitosis **228**
Section 3 Regulation **233**
Standardized Test Prep **241**

Why It Matters Replacement Parts 227

Labs Whitefish Cells 221
Chromosome Package 224
Number of Cells Resulting from Mitosis 229
UV and Sunblock 234
Mitosis in Plant Cells 236

Chapter 11 Meiosis and Sexual Reproduction 244

Section 1 Reproduction 247
Section 2 Meiosis 250
Section 3 Multicellular Life Cycles 256
Standardized Test Prep 263

> **Why It Matters** Girls, Girls, Girls 255

> **Labs** Pollen Up-Close 245
> Crossing-Over Model 253
> Chromosome Combinations 257
> Meiosis Model 259

Chapter 12 Mendel and Heredity 264

Section 1 Origins of Hereditary Science 267
Section 2 Mendel's Theory 272
Section 3 Modeling Mendel's Laws 276
Section 4 Beyond Mendelian Heredity 282
Standardized Test Prep 289

> **Why It Matters** Amazing Mutants 271

> **Labs** What Are the Chances? 265
> Mendel's Ratios 270
> Dominant and Recessive Traits 273
> Testcross 277
> Probabilities 278
> Pedigree Analysis 281
> Plant Genetics 285

> **Math Skills** Probability of Two Independant Events 279

Chapter 13 DNA, RNA, and Proteins 290

Section 1 The Structure of DNA 293
Section 2 Replication of DNA 300
Section 3 RNA and Gene Expression 304
Standardized Test Prep 315

> **Labs** Code Combinations 291
> DNA's Structure 297
> DNA Replication Rate 303
> Genetic Code of Keratin 310
> DNA Extraction from Wheat Germ 311

Chapter 14 Genes in Action 316

Section 1 Mutation and Genetic Change 319
Section 2 Regulating Gene Expression 325
Section 3 Genome Interactions 330
Standardized Test Prep 341

Why It Matters Forensic Genealogy 335

Labs Where Is the Protein? 317
Make a Model of Mutations 321
A Model of Introns and Exons 328
Protein Detection 336

Chapter 15 Gene Technologies and Human Applications 342

Section 1 The Human Genome 345
Section 2 Gene Technologies in Our Lives 350
Section 3 Gene Technologies in Detail 355
Standardized Test Prep 369

Why It Matters Cleanup Microbes 349

Labs Code Comparison 343
Forensic DNA Fingerprints 347
Gel Electrophoresis Model 356
DNA Fingerprint Analysis 364

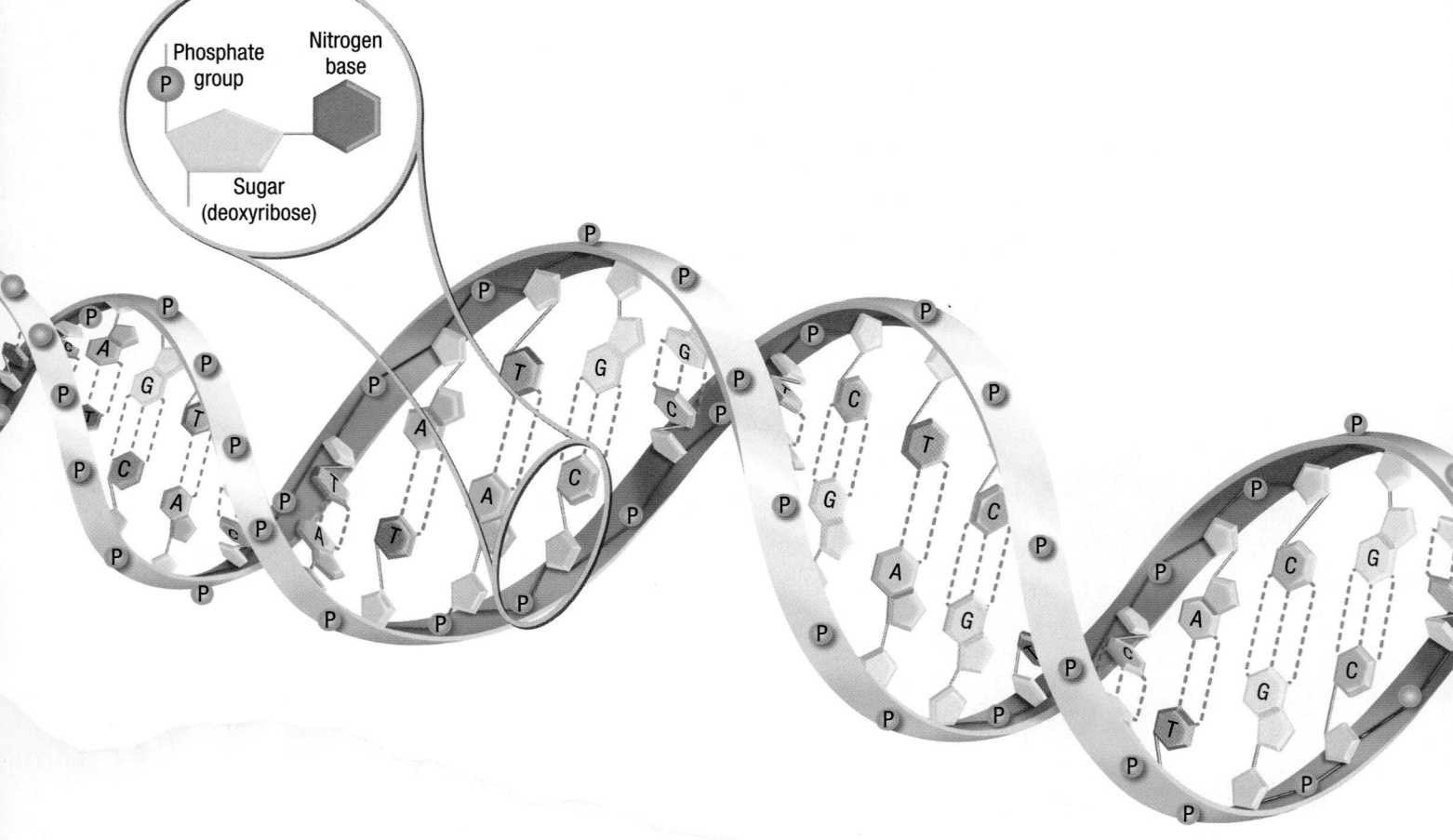

Phosphate group

Nitrogen base

Sugar (deoxyribose)

Chapter 16 Evolutionary Theory 372

Section 1 Developing a Theory 375
Section 2 Applying Darwin's Ideas 380
Section 3 Beyond Darwinian Theory 386
Standardized Test Prep 395

Why It Matters Breeding 377

Labs Scientific Inference 373
Two Kinds of Growth 378
Selection Model 387
Natural Selection Simulation 390

Chapter 17 Population Genetics and Speciation 396

Section 1 Genetic Variation 399
Section 2 Genetic Change 404
Section 3 Speciation 411
Standardized Test Prep 419

Why It Matters Wild Laboratories 410

Labs Normal Variation 397
Alleles: The Next Generation 403
Genetic Risk Assessment 407
Genetic Drift 415

Math Skills Histograms and Distributions 401
Hardy-Weinberg Equation 405

Chapter 18 Classification 420

Section 1 The Importance of Classification 423
Section 2 Modern Systematics 427
Section 3 Kingdoms and Domains 433
Standardized Test Prep 443

Why It Matters New Species 432

Labs What's Your System? 421
Cladogram Construction 430
Field Guides 435
Dichotomous Keys 438

Chapter 19 History of Life on Earth 444

Section 1 How Did Life Begin? 447
Section 2 The Age of Earth 450
Section 3 Evolution of Life 454
Standardized Test Prep 465

Why It Matters Nearing the End 460

Labs Logical Order 445
Radioactive Decay 452
Timeline of Earth 457
Model of Rock Strata 461

Chapter 20 Bacteria and Viruses **468**

Section 1 Bacteria **471**
Section 2 Viruses **476**
Section 3 Bacteria, Viruses, and Humans **481**
Standardized Test Prep **493**

Why It Matters Tiny Terrors 487

Labs Bacterial Observation 469
Model Bacterial Growth 474
How Small Are Nanometers? 480
Emergence of Bird Flu 486
Bacterial Staining 488

Chapter 21 Protists **494**

Section 1 Characteristics of Protists **497**
Section 2 Groups of Protists **501**
Section 3 Protists and Humans **507**
Standardized Test Prep **517**

Why It Matters Protist Plague 509

Labs Pond Water World 495
Diatom Observation 505
Everyday Algae 511
Protistan Responses to Light 512

Chapter 22 Fungi **518**

Section 1 Characteristics of Fungi **521**
Section 2 Groups of Fungi **524**
Section 3 Fungi and Humans **529**
Standardized Test Prep **537**

Why It Matters Salem Witch Trials 532

Labs Mushroom Dissection 519
Mold 523
Fungal Factor 530
Yeast and Fermentation 533

Chapter 23 Plant Diversity and Life Cycles **540**

Section 1 Introduction to Plants **543**
Section 2 Seedless Plants **547**
Section 3 Seed Plants **553**
Section 4 Flowering Plants **559**
Standardized Test Prep **569**

Labs Plant Cells 541
Cuticle Modeling 545
Fern Gametophytes 552
Pine Gametophytes 558
The Arrangement of Parts of a Flower 560
Fruit or Vegetable? 563
Plant Diversity 565

Chapter 24 Seed Plant Structure and Growth **570**

Section 1 Plant Tissue Systems **573**
Section 2 Roots, Stems, and Leaves **579**
Section 3 Plant Growth and Development **585**
Standardized Test Prep **595**

Why It Matters Extreme Plants 584

Labs Function of Plant Parts 571
Behavior of Stomata 575
Internal Structures of Roots and Stems 581
The Effect of Cold on Seed Germination 587
Monocot and Dicot Seeds 590

Chapter 25 Plant Processes **596**

Section 1 Nutrients and Transport **599**
Section 2 Plant Responses **603**
Standardized Test Prep **617**

Why It Matters Plants in Space 611

Labs Capillary Action 597
Transpiration Rate 601
Effects of Ethylene on a Plant 606
Seed Dormancy and Germination 609
Cultivation Techniques 612

Chapter 26 Introduction to Animals **620**

Section 1 Characteristics of Animals 623
Section 2 Animal Body Systems 627
Section 3 Evolutionary Trends in Animals 632
Section 4 Chordate Evolution 638
Standardized Test Prep 651

Why It Matters SuperCroc 645

Labs Animal Characteristics 621
Filtration Rate in the Kidney 628
Symmetry 633
The Notochord and Nerve Cord 639
Embryonic Development 646

Chapter 27 Simple Invertebrates **652**

Section 1 Sponges 655
Section 2 Cnidarians 658
Section 3 Flatworms 663
Section 4 Roundworms 667
Standardized Test Prep 675

Why It Matters Rain Forest of the Sea 662

Labs Body Symmetry 653
Coral Skeletons 660
Planarian Behavior 665
Parasite Identification 670
Hydra Behavior 671

Chapter 28 Mollusks and Annelids **676**

Section 1 Mollusks 679
Section 2 Annelids 686
Standardized Test Prep 697

Why It Matters Creepy Leeches 691

Labs Garden Snails 677
Open Circulatory System 681
An Annelid in Cross-Section 687
Clam Characteristics 692

Chapter 29 Arthropods and Echinoderms **698**

Section 1 Arthropods 701
Section 2 Arachnids and Crustaceans 706
Section 3 Insects 712
Section 4 Echinoderms 717
Standardized Test Prep 725

Why It Matters Come and Get It! 716

Labs Larval Life 699
Jointed Appendages 702
Bee Wing 713
Butterfly Metamorphosis 720

Chapter 30 Fishes and Amphibians 726

Section 1 The Fish Body 729
Section 2 Groups of Fishes 734
Section 3 The Amphibian Body 739
Section 4 Groups of Amphibians 744
Standardized Test Prep 753

> **Labs** Water Breathing 727
> Ion Excretion in Fish 732
> Modeling Frog Inhalation 741
> Amphibian Leg Structure 745
> Live Frog Observation 748

Chapter 31 Reptiles and Birds 754

Section 1 The Reptile Body 757
Section 2 Groups of Reptiles 762
Section 3 The Bird Body 766
Section 4 Groups of Birds 772
Standardized Test Prep 781

> **Labs** Amniotic Eggs 755
> Identity of Ectotherms 758
> Model of Watertight Skin 763
> Average Bone Density 767
> Webbed Feet 775
> Bird Digestion 776

Chapter 32 Mammals 782

Section 1 Characteristics of Mammals 785
Section 2 Groups of Mammals 791
Section 3 Evolution of Primates 797
Standardized Test Prep 809

> **Why It Matters** A New Species? 803

> **Labs** Heat Loss and Hair 783
> Mammalian Bones 786
> Taxonomic Key to Mammals 792
> Opposable Thumbs 798
> Mammalian Characteristics 804

Chapter 33 Animal Behavior 810

Section 1 The Nature of Behavior 813
Section 2 Classes of Behavior 821
Standardized Test Prep 833

> **Why It Matters** Proud as a Peacock 820

> **Labs** A Ball of Armor 811
> Learned Behavior 816
> Safety in Darkness 823
> Territorial Behavior 828

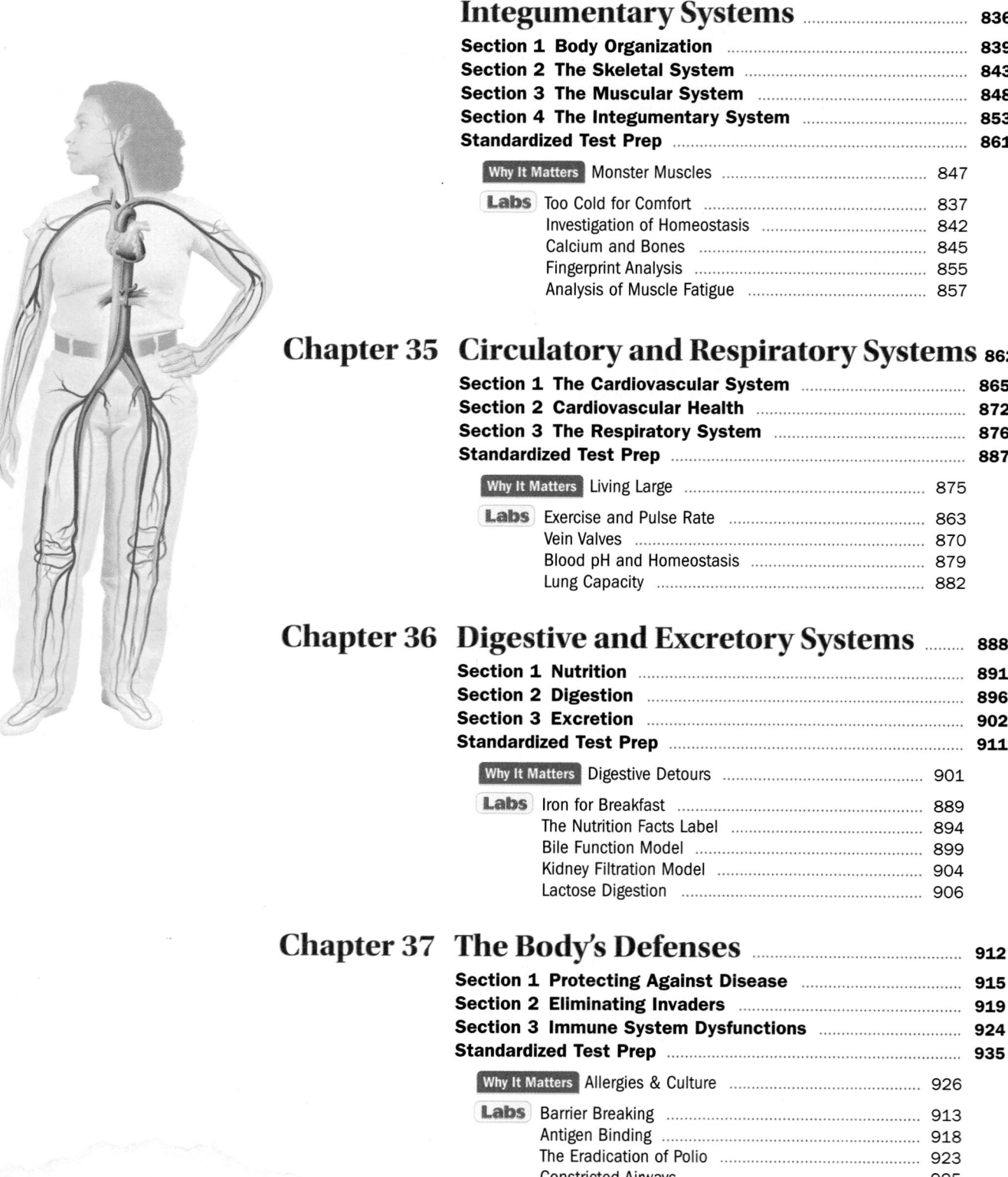

Chapter 34 Skeletal, Muscular, and Integumentary Systems 836

Section 1 Body Organization 839
Section 2 The Skeletal System 843
Section 3 The Muscular System 848
Section 4 The Integumentary System 853
Standardized Test Prep 861

Why It Matters Monster Muscles 847

Labs Too Cold for Comfort 837
Investigation of Homeostasis 842
Calcium and Bones 845
Fingerprint Analysis 855
Analysis of Muscle Fatigue 857

Chapter 35 Circulatory and Respiratory Systems 862

Section 1 The Cardiovascular System 865
Section 2 Cardiovascular Health 872
Section 3 The Respiratory System 876
Standardized Test Prep 887

Why It Matters Living Large 875

Labs Exercise and Pulse Rate 863
Vein Valves 870
Blood pH and Homeostasis 879
Lung Capacity 882

Chapter 36 Digestive and Excretory Systems 888

Section 1 Nutrition 891
Section 2 Digestion 896
Section 3 Excretion 902
Standardized Test Prep 911

Why It Matters Digestive Detours 901

Labs Iron for Breakfast 889
The Nutrition Facts Label 894
Bile Function Model 899
Kidney Filtration Model 904
Lactose Digestion 906

Chapter 37 The Body's Defenses 912

Section 1 Protecting Against Disease 915
Section 2 Eliminating Invaders 919
Section 3 Immune System Dysfunctions 924
Standardized Test Prep 935

Why It Matters Allergies & Culture 926

Labs Barrier Breaking 913
Antigen Binding 918
The Eradication of Polio 923
Constricted Airways 925
Disease Transmission Model 930

Chapter 38   Nervous System   936

Section 1 Structures of the Nervous System   939
Section 2 Neurons and Nerve Impulses   944
Section 3 Sensory Systems   950
Section 4 Nervous System Dysfunction   956
Standardized Test Prep   967

> **Why It Matters** Your Amazing Brain   955

> **Labs** Pass it On   937
> Knee-Jerk Reflex   943
> The Action Potential   948
> Your Blind Spot   951
> Impaired Senses   957
> Reaction Times   962

Chapter 39   Endocrine System   968

Section 1 Hormones   971
Section 2 Major Endocrine Glands   978
Standardized Test Prep   989

> **Why It Matters** Diabetes   983

> **Labs** Fight, Flight, or Speech?   969
> Observing Solubilities   973
> Epinephrine and Heart Rate   984

Chapter 40   Reproduction and Development   990

Section 1 The Male Reproductive System   993
Section 2 The Female Reproductive System   996
Section 3 Human Development   1001
Section 4 Sexually Transmitted Infections   1005
Standardized Test Prep   1013

> **Why It Matters** Seeing Double   1008

> **Labs** A Closer Look at Gametes   991
> Hormone Secretions   1000
> An Amniotic Shock Absorber   1003
> STI Rates   1006
> Sonography   1009

Chapter 41   Forensic Science   1014

Section 1 Introduction to Forensics   1017
Section 2 Inside a Crime Lab   1022
Section 3 Forensic Science in Action   1032
Standardized Test Prep   1041

> **Why It Matters** King Tut Unmasked   1021

> **Labs** A Thread of Evidence   1015
> The Forged Signature   1019
> Toolmarks Analysis   1025
> Estimate Time of Death   1033
> The Counterfeit Drugs   1038

Appendix   1042
Glossary   1075
Index   1126

Why It Matters

Have you ever wondered why you should care about learning biology? These short articles show how science relates to your everyday life and to what you might do in the future.

Real World

Biology in the Wild	18
Maintained by Fire	85
Growth in Asia	108
Breeding	377
Wild Laboratories	410
New Species	432
Tiny Terrors	487
Protist Plague	509
Rain Forest of the Sea	662
Proud as a Peacock	820
Living Large	875
Digestive Detours	901
Allergies & Culture	926
Diabetes	983
Seeing Double	1008

Biotechnology

Bio Bots	41
Life in a Biosphere	214
Forensic Genealogy	335
Cleanup Microbes	349
Plants in Space	611
Monster Muscles	847
King Tut Unmasked	1021

Weird Science

Water Wonders	58
Cars of the Future	139
Cell Shape	152
Heady Effects	187
Replacement Parts	227
Girls, Girls, Girls	255
Amazing Mutants	271
Nearing the End	460
Salem Witch Trials	532
Extreme Plants	584
SuperCroc	645
Creepy Leeches	691
Come and Get It!	716
A New Species?	803
Your Amazing Brain	955

READING TOOLBOX

The tools we show you in the **Reading Toolbox** can be used throughout to help you remember what you read and to mentally organize the concepts. Find the ones that work best for you.

Analogies	266, 344, 838
Booklet	572, 970
Cause and Effect	222, 470, 572, 654, 970
Cause and Effect Maps	812
Classification	542, 678, 700, 890
Comparisons	246, 520, 728, 756
Comparison Table	50, 318, 678
Concept Map	542, 728
Describing Space	196, 598, 622
Describing Time	292, 446
Double-Door Fold	756
Everyday Words in Science	6, 50, 398, 678, 812
Finding Examples	174, 318, 1016
Finding Main Ideas	938
Four-Corner Fold	174
General Statements	398, 496
Hypothesis, or Theory?	6, 124, 374
Idea Wheel	6
Key Term Fold	196, 246, 374, 470, 700, 890, 938
Layered Book	78, 784
Mnemonics	422, 914
Outlining	398, 700
Pattern Puzzles	196, 222, 344, 890, 914
Phylogenetic Tree	422
Predictions	28, 102, 812
Prefixes	318
Process Chart	150, 446, 470, 520, 654
Punnet Squares	266
Pyramid	992
Quantifiers	50
Recognizing Main Ideas	864, 992
Similes	150
Spider Maps	622, 938, 1016
Summarizing Notes	374
Three-Panel Flip Chart	28, 292, 864
Two-Column Notes	246
Tri-Fold	598
Venn Diagrams	102, 124, 496, 838
Word Families	78, 992, 1016
Word Origins	102, 422, 496, 572, 784
Word Parts	28, 124, 150, 174, 222, 266, 292, 344, 446, 520, 542, 598, 622, 654, 728, 756, 838, 864, 914, 970
Word Problems	78, 784

Up **Close**

Some things are worth looking at in detail. You'll see features that are common and aspects that are unique.

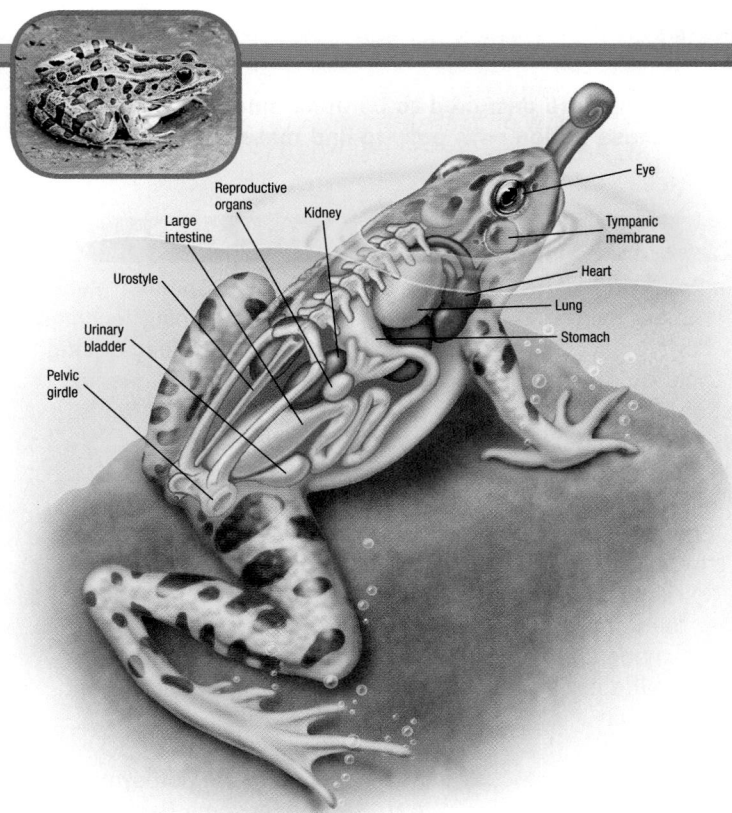

Bacteria **473**
HIV Reproduction **479**
Paramecium **503**
Vascular Plant **577**
Planarian **664**
Earthworm **689**
Arachnid **710**
Insect **711**
Bony Fishes **737**
Frogs **746**
Snakes **764**
Birds **773**
Mammals **789**
Bones **844**

Image labels: Reproductive organs, Large intestine, Kidney, Eye, Tympanic membrane, Urostyle, Heart, Urinary bladder, Lung, Stomach, Pelvic girdle

Interactive Art

go.hrw.com
✳ **interact online**

Many illustrations in the textbook are more easily understood by watching them move and react to you in an online animation. These will be marked by the Interact Online logo and a keyword to use.

Common SI Units **14**
Ionic Bonding in Salt **53**
Enzyme Action **67**
Water Cycle **90**
Exponential Growth **104**
Water Pollution **130**
Making and Exporting Proteins **159**
Facilitated Diffusion **179**
Sodium-Potassium Pump **182**
Photosynthesis and Cellular Respiration **199**
Electron Transport Chains of Photosynthesis ... **204**
Calvin Cycle **206**
Glycolysis **209**
Electron Transport Chain **211**
Stages of Mitosis **230**
Stages of Meiosis I **250**
Three Steps of Mendel's First Experiment ... **269**
Hershey-Chase Experiment **295**
DNA Replication **301**
Transcription **306**

Translation **308**
Kinds of Mutations **320**
Chain Termination Sequencing **359**
Recombinant Cloning **360**
The Theory of Evolution by Natural Selection ... **381**
Population Size and Genetic Drift **406**
Cladogram **429**
Tree of Life **436**
Endosymbiotic Theory **456**
Koch's Postulate **482**
Life Cycle of Chlamydomonas **498**
Life Cycle of Ulva **499**
Life Cycle of Zygote Fungi **525**
Water Movement in Plants **600**
Pressure-Flow Model **602**
Went's Experiment **604**
Early Embryonic Development **634**
The Steps in Muscle Contraction **851**
Transport of Oxygen and Carbon Dioxide **878**
Kidney Structure **903**
Inflammation **916**
The Action Potential **947**
Action of Amino Acid-Based Hormones **974**
Action of Steroid Hormones **975**

Quick Labs

These short labs are designed to be done quickly during any class period with easy-to-find materials.

Inquiry

Make a Prediction 5
Artificial Shark Skin 27
Yeast Activity 49
Water Cycle 77
Population Size 101
The Greenhouse Effect 123
Is It Alive? 149
Salty Cells 173
Stored Energy 195
Whitefish Cells 221
Pollen Up Close 245
What Are the Chances? 265
Code Combinations 291
Where Is the Protein? 317
Code Comparison 343
Scientific Inference 373
Normal Variation 397
What's Your System? 421
Logical Order 445
Bacterial Observation 469
Pond-Water World 495
Mushroom Dissection 519
Plant Cells 541
Function of Plant Parts 571
Capillary Action 597
Animal Characteristics 621
Body Symmetry 653
Garden Snails 677
Larval Life 699
Water Breathing 727
Amniotic Eggs 755
Heat Loss and Hair 783
A Ball of Armor 811
Too Cold for Comfort 837
Exercise and Pulse Rate 863
Iron for Breakfast 889
Barrier Breaking 913
Pass it On 937
Fight, Flight, or Speech? 969
A Closer Look at Gametes 991
A Thread of Evidence 1015

Hands-On

The pH of Common Substances   11
Practice Staining Techniques 15
Model a Low-Tech Solution 31
Biomimetic Engineering 34
Atom Models 53
Telltale Cabbage 57
Brown Paper Test 61
Biodiversity Evaluation 80
The Carbon Cycle 93
Contaminated Water 127
Soil Erosion 131
Recycled Paper 135
Cell Parts Model 160
Colonies on the Move 165
Osmosis 181
Sensitive Plants 185
Product of Photosynthesis 198
Chromosome Package 224
UV and Sunblock 234
Crossing-Over Model 253
DNA's Structure 297
Make a Model of Mutations 321
A Model of Introns and Exons .. 328
Gel Electrophoresis Model 356
Two Kinds of Growth 378
Selection Model 387
Alleles: The Next Generation 403
Field Guides 435
Radioactive Decay 452
Timeline of Earth 457
Model Bacterial Growth 474
How Small Are Nanometers? ... 480
Diatom Observation 505
Everyday Algae 511
Mold 523
Cuticle Modeling 545
Fern Gametophytes 552
Pine Gametophytes 558
The Arrangement of
    Parts of a Flower 560
Fruit or Vegetable? 563
Behavior of Stomata 575
Internal Structures of
    Roots and Stems 581

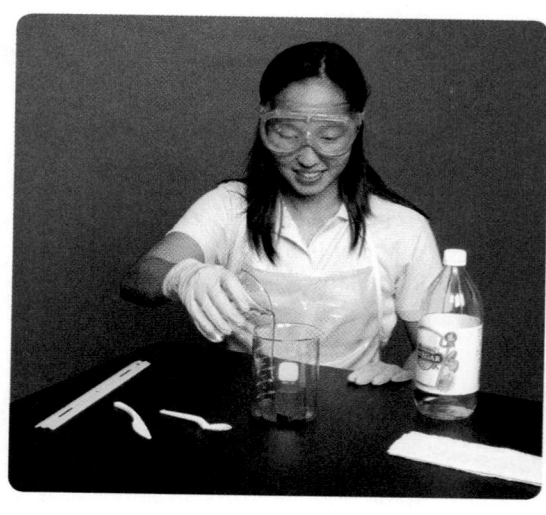

Effects of Ethylene on a Plant .. 606
Symmetry 633
The Notochord and Nerve Cord 639
Coral Skeletons 660
Planarian Behavior 665
Open Circulatory System 681
An Annelid in Cross Section 687
Jointed Appendages 702
Bee Wing 713
Modeling Frog Inhalation 741
Amphibian Leg Structure 745
Model of Watertight Skin 763
Webbed Feet 775
Mammalian Bones 786
Opposable Thumbs 798
Learned Behavior 816
Safety in Darkness 823
Investigation of Homeostasis .. 842
Calcium and Bones 845
Fingerprint Analysis 855
Vein Valves 870
Blood pH Homeostasis 879
Bile Function Model 899
Kidney Filtration Model 904
Antigen Binding 918
Constricted Airways 925
Knee-Jerk Reflex 943
Your Blind Spot 951
Impaired Senses 957
Observing Solubilities 973
An Amniotic Shock Absorber .. 1003
The Forged Signature 1019
Toolmarks Analysis 1025

Chapter **Labs**

Each chapter includes an in-depth, hands-on lab that lets you see how science is really done. You'll learn the scientific method in practice, as well as fundamental experimental skills.

Data

Evaluate a Scientific Claim **9**
Population Growth **105**
The Effects of Herbivores
   on a Plant Species **110**
Changes in a Realized Niche ... **113**
Photosynthetic Rate **205**
Number of Cells Resulting
   from Mitosis **229**
Chromosome Combinations **257**
Mendel's Ratios **270**
Dominant and Recessive Traits **273**
Testcross **277**
Probabilities **278**
Pedigree Analysis **281**
DNA Replication Rate **303**
Genetic Code of Keratin **310**
Forensic DNA Fingerprints **347**
Genetic Risk Assessment **407**
Cladogram Construction **430**
Emergence of Bird Flu **486**
Fungal Factor **530**
The Effect of Cold on Seed
   Germination **587**
Transpiration Rate **601**
Seed Dormancy and
   Germination **609**
Filtration Rate in the Kidney **628**
Parasite Identification **670**
Ion Excretion in Fish **732**
Identity of Ectotherms **758**
Average Bone Density **767**
Taxonomic Key to Mammals **792**
The Nutrition Facts Label **894**
The Eradication of Polio **923**
The Action Potential **948**
Hormone Secretions **1000**
STI Rates **1006**
Estimate Time of Death **1033**

Skills Practice

SI Units **20**
Microbe Growth **42**
Yeast Population Growth **116**
Cellular Respiration **215**
Mitosis in Plant Cells **236**
Meiosis Model **259**
DNA Extraction from
   Wheat Germ **311**
Protein Detection **336**
DNA Fingerprint Analysis **364**
Natural Selection Simulation **390**
Dichotomous Keys **438**
Model of Rock Strata **461**
Bacterial Staining **488**
Plant Diversity **565**
Monocot and Dicot Seeds **590**
Cultivation Techniques **612**
Embryonic Development **646**
Hydra Behavior **671**
Clam Characteristics **692**
Butterfly Metamorphosis **720**
Live Frog Observation **748**
Bird Digestion **776**
Mammalian Characteristics **804**
Lung Capacity **882**
Disease Transmission Model ... **930**
The Counterfeit Drug **1036**

Inquiry

Enzymes in Detergents **68**
Ecosystem Change **94**
Effects of Acid Rain
   on Seeds **140**
Plant Cell Observation **168**
Cell Size and Diffusion **188**
Plant Genetics **285**
Genetic Drift **415**
Protistan Responses to Light ... **512**
Yeast and Fermentation **533**
Territorial Behavior **828**
Analysis of Muscle Fatigue **857**
Lactose Digestion **906**
Reaction Times **962**
Epinephrine and Heart Rate **984**
Sonography **1009**

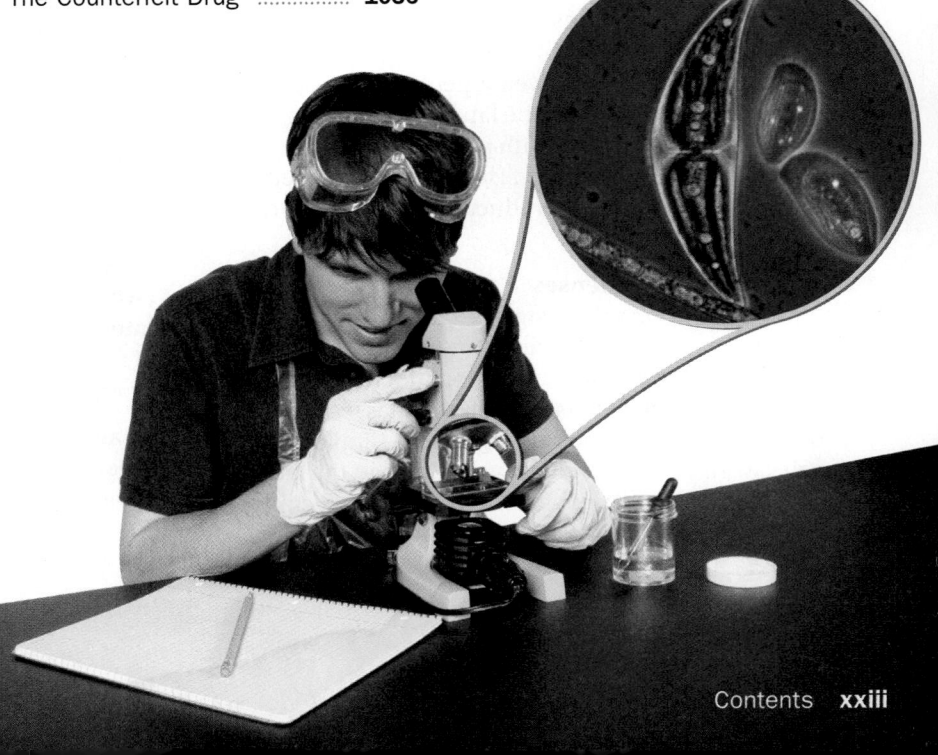

In the laboratory or in the field, you can engage in hands-on explorations, test your scientific hypotheses, and build practical lab skills. However, while you are working, it is your responsibility to protect yourself and your classmates by conducting yourself in a safe manner. You will avoid accidents by following directions, handling materials carefully, and taking your work seriously. Read the following safety guidelines before working in the lab or field. Make sure that you understand all safety guidelines before entering the lab or field.

Before You Begin

- **Read the entire activity before entering the lab.** Be familiar with the instructions before beginning an activity. Do not start an activity until you have asked your teacher to explain any parts of the activity that you do not understand.

- **Student-designed procedures or inquiry activities must be approved by your teacher before you attempt the procedures or activities.**

- **Wear the right clothing for lab work.** Before beginning work, tie back long hair, roll up loose sleeves, and put on any required personal protective equipment as directed by your teacher. Remove all jewelry, and confine all clothing that could knock things over, catch on fire, contact electrical connections, or absorb chemical solutions. Wear pants rather than shorts or skirts. Protect your feet from chemical spills and falling objects. Do not wear open-toed shoes, sandals, or canvas shoes in the lab. In addition, chemical fumes may react with and ruin some jewelry, such as pearl jewelry. Do not apply cosmetics in the lab. Some hair care products and nail polish are highly flammable.

- **Do not wear contact lenses in the lab.** Even though you will be wearing safety goggles, chemicals could get between contact lenses and your eyes and could cause irreparable eye damage. If your doctor requires that you wear contact lenses instead of glasses, then you should wear eye-cup safety goggles—similar to goggles worn for underwater swimming—in the lab. Ask your doctor or your teacher how to use eye-cup safety goggles to protect your eyes.

- **Know the location of all safety and emergency equipment used in the lab.** Know proper fire-drill procedures and the location of all fire exits. Ask your teacher where the nearest eyewash stations, safety blankets, safety shower, fire extinguisher, first-aid kit, and chemical spill kit are located. Be sure that you know how to operate the equipment safely.

While You Are Working

- **Always wear a lab apron and safety goggles.** Wear these items while in the lab, even if you are not working on an activity. Labs contain chemicals that can damage your clothing, skin, and eyes. Aprons and goggles also protect against many physical hazards. If your safety goggles cloud up or are uncomfortable, ask your teacher for help. Lengthening the strap slightly, washing the goggles with soap and warm water, or using an anti-fog spray may help the problem.

- **NEVER work alone in the lab.** Work in the lab only when supervised by your teacher.

- **NEVER leave equipment unattended while it is in operation.**

- **Perform only activities specifically assigned by your teacher.** Do not attempt any procedure without your teacher's direction. Use only materials and equipment listed in the activity or authorized by your teacher. Steps in a procedure should be performed only as described in the activity or as approved by your teacher.

- **Keep your work area neat and uncluttered.** Have only books and other materials that are needed to conduct the activity in the lab. Keep backpacks, purses, and other items in your desk, your locker, or other designated storage areas.

- **Always heed safety symbols and cautions listed in activities, listed on handouts, posted in the room, provided on equipment or chemical labels (whether provided by the manufacturer or added later), and given verbally by your teacher.** Be aware of the potential hazards of the required materials and procedures, and follow all precautions indicated.

- **Be alert, and walk with care in the lab.** Be aware of others near you and your equipment, and be aware of what they are doing.

- **Do not take food, drinks, chewing gum, or tobacco products into the lab.** Do not store or eat food in the lab. Either finish these items or discard them before coming into the lab or beginning work in the field.

- **NEVER taste chemicals or allow them to contact your skin.** Keep your hands away from your face and mouth, even if you are wearing gloves. Only smell vapors as instructed by your teacher and only in the manner indicated.

- **Exercise caution when working with electrical equipment.** Do not use electrical equipment with frayed or twisted wires. Check that insulation on wiring is intact. Be sure that your hands are dry before using electrical equipment. Do not let electrical cords dangle from work stations. Dangling cords can catch on apparatus on tables, can cause you to trip, and can cause an electric shock. The area under and around electrical equipment should be dry; cords should not lie in puddles of spilled liquid, under sink spigots, or in sinks themselves.

- **Use extreme caution when working with hot plates and other heating devices.** Keep your head, hands, hair, and clothing away from the flame or heating area. Never leave a heating device unattended when it is in use. Metal, ceramic, and glass items do not necessarily look hot when they are hot. Allow all items to cool before storing them.

- **Guard against complacency.** Remember that it is human nature to become careless when doing routine things. As you become familiar with apparatus and procedures, remain alert and pay attention.

- **Do not fool around in the lab.** Take your lab work seriously, and behave appropriately in the lab. Lab equipment and apparatus are not toys; never use lab time or equipment for anything other than the intended purpose. Be considerate and be aware of the safety of your classmates as well as your safety at all times.

Emergency Procedures

- **Follow standard fire-safety procedures.** If your clothing catches on fire, do not run; WALK to the safety shower, stand under it, and turn it on. While doing so, call to your teacher.

- **Report any accident, incident, or hazard—no matter how trivial—to your teacher immediately.** Any incident involving bleeding, burns, fainting, nausea, dizziness, chemical exposure, or ingestion should also be reported immediately to the school nurse or to a physician. If you have a close call, tell your teacher so that you and your teacher can find a way to prevent it from happening again.

- **Report all spills to your teacher immediately.** Call your teacher rather than trying to clean a spill yourself. Your teacher will tell you whether it is safe for you to clean up the spill; if it is not safe, your teacher will know how to clean up the spill.

- **If you spill a chemical on your skin, wash the chemical off in the sink and call your teacher.** If you spill a solid chemical onto your clothing, using an appropriate container, brush it off carefully without scattering it onto somebody else and call your teacher. If you spill corrosive substances on your skin or clothing, use the safety shower or a faucet to rinse. Remove affected clothing while you are under the shower, and call to your teacher. (It may be temporarily embarrassing to remove clothing in front of your classmates, but failure to thoroughly rinse a chemical off your skin could result in permanent damage.)

- **If you get a chemical in your eyes, walk immediately to the eyewash station, turn it on, and lower your head so that your eyes are in the running water.** Hold your eyelids open with your thumbs and fingers, and roll your eyeballs around. You have to flush your eyes continuously for at least 15 minutes. Call your teacher while you are flushing your eyes.

When You Are Finished

- **Clean your work area at the conclusion of each lab period as directed by your teacher.** Broken glass, chemicals, and other waste products should be disposed of in separate, special containers. Dispose of waste materials as directed by your teacher. Put away all material and equipment according to your teacher's instructions. Report any damaged or missing equipment or materials to your teacher.

- **Even if you wore gloves, wash your hands with soap and hot water after each lab period.** To avoid contamination, wash your hands at the conclusion of each lab period and before you leave the lab.

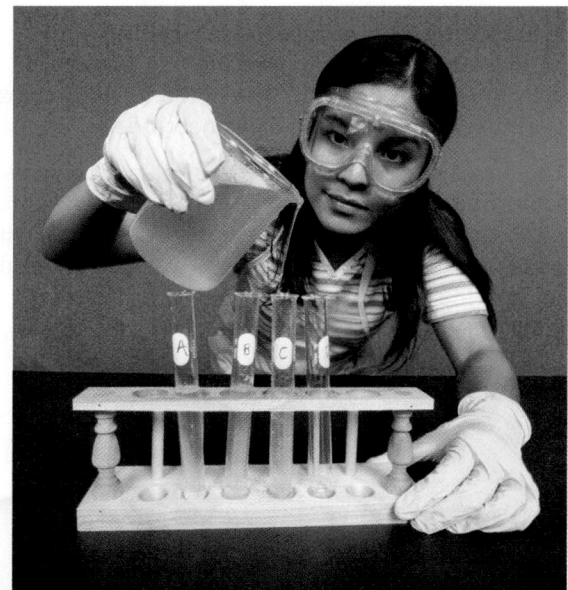

Before you begin working on an activity, familiarize yourself with the following safety symbols, which are used throughout your textbook, and the guidelines that you should follow when you see these symbols.

 ## Eye Protection

- **Wear approved safety goggles as directed.** Safety goggles should be worn in the lab at all times, especially when you are working with a chemical or solution, a heat source, or a mechanical device.

- **If chemicals get into your eyes, flush your eyes immediately.** Go to an eyewash station immediately, and flush your eyes (including under the eyelids) with running water for at least 15 minutes. Use your thumb and fingers to hold your eyelids open, and roll your eyeballs around. While doing so, call your teacher or ask another student to notify your teacher.

- **Do not wear contact lenses in the lab.** Chemicals can be drawn up under a contact lens and into the eye. If you must wear contacts prescribed by a physician, tell your teacher. In this case, you must also wear approved eye-cup safety goggles.

- **Do not look directly at the sun or any intense light source or laser.** Do not reflect direct sunlight to illuminate a microscope. Such action concentrates light rays to an intensity that can severely burn your retinas and cause blindness.

 ## Clothing Protection

- **Wear an apron or lab coat at all times in the lab to prevent chemicals or chemical solutions from contacting skin or clothes.**

- **Tie back long hair, secure loose clothing, and remove loose jewelry so that they do not knock over equipment or come into contact with hazardous materials or electrical connections.**

- **Do not wear open-toed shoes, sandals, or canvas shoes in the lab.** Splashed chemicals directly contact skin or quickly soak through canvas. Hard shoes will not allow chemicals to soak through as quickly, and they provide more protection against dropped or falling objects.

 ## Hand Safety

- **Wear appropriate protective gloves when working with a heat source, chemicals, solutions, or wild or unknown plants.** Your teacher will provide the type of gloves necessary for a given activity.

 ## Sharp-Object Safety

- **Use extreme care when handling all sharp and pointed instruments, such as scalpels, sharp probes, and knives.**

- **Do not cut an object while holding the object in your hand.** Cut objects on a suitable work surface. Always cut in a direction away from your body.

- **Do not use double-edged razor blades in the lab.**

 ## Glassware Safety

- **Inspect glassware before use; do not use chipped or cracked glassware.** Use heat-resistant glassware for heating materials or storing hot liquids, and use appropriate tongs or a heat-resistant mitt to handle this equipment.

- **Notify your teacher immediately if a piece of glassware or a light bulb breaks.** Do not attempt to clean up broken glass or remove broken bulbs unless your teacher directs you to do so.

 ## Chemical Safety

- **Always wear safety goggles, gloves, and a lab apron or coat to protect your eyes and skin when you are working with any chemical or chemical solution.**

- **Do not taste, touch, or smell any chemicals or bring them close to your eyes unless specifically instructed to do so by your teacher.**

- **Know where the emergency lab shower and eyewash stations are and how to use them.** If you get a chemical on your skin or clothing, wash it off while calling to your teacher.

- **Handle chemicals or chemical solutions with care.** Check the labels on bottles, and observe safety procedures. Label beakers, flasks, test tubes, or other temporary storage vessels containing chemicals.

- **For all chemicals, take only what you need.** Do not return unused chemicals to their original containers.

- **NEVER take any chemicals out of the lab.**

- **Do not mix any chemicals unless specifically instructed to do so by your teacher.** Check the labels to make sure that you picked up the correct chemicals before you mix them. Otherwise harmless chemicals can be poisonous or explosive if combined.

- **Report all spills to your teacher immediately.** Clean up spills promptly as directed by your teacher.

Electrical Safety

- **Do not use equipment with frayed electrical cords or loose plugs.** Do not attempt to remove a plug tine if it breaks off in the socket. Notify your teacher, and stay away from the outlet.

- **Fasten electrical cords to work surfaces by using tape.** Doing so will prevent tripping and will ensure that equipment will not fall or be pulled off the table.

- **Do not use electrical equipment near water or when your clothing or hands are wet.**

- **Hold the plug housing when you plug in or unplug equipment.** Do not touch the metal prongs of the plug, and do not pull on the cord.

Heating Safety

- **Avoid using open flames.** If possible, work only with hot plates that have an on/off switch and an indicator light. Turn off hot plates and open flames when they are not in use.

- **Never leave a hot plate unattended while it is turned on or while it is cooling off.**

- **Know the location of lab fire extinguishers and fire-safety blankets.**

- **Use tongs or appropriate insulated holders when handling heated objects.** Heated objects often do not appear to be hot. Do not pick up an object with your hand if the object could be warm.

- **Keep flammable substances away from heat, flames, and other ignition sources.**

- **Allow all equipment to cool before storing it.**

- **Wear chemical splash goggles when working with liquids hotter than 60° C.**

Animal Care and Safety

- **Handle animals only as directed by your teacher.** Mishandling or abusing animals will not be tolerated.

- **Always get your teacher's permission before bringing any animal (including pets) into the school building.**

- **Do not approach or touch any wild animals.** When working outdoors, be aware of poisonous or dangerous animals in the area.

- **Dispose of specimens only as instructed by your teacher.**

Plant Safety

- **Do not ingest any plant part used in the laboratory (especially commercially sold seeds).** Do not touch any sap or plant juice directly. Always wear gloves.

- **Wear disposable polyethylene gloves when handling any wild plant.**

- **Wash hands thoroughly after handling any plant or plant part (particularly seeds).** Avoid touching your face and eyes.

- **Do not pick wildflowers or other plants unless instructed to do so by your teacher.**

Hygienic Care

- **Keep your hands away from your face, hair, and mouth while you are working on any activity.**

- **Wash your hands thoroughly before you leave the lab or when you finish any activity.**

- **Remove contaminated clothing immediately.** If you spill corrosive substances on your skin or clothing, use the safety shower or a faucet to rinse. Remove affected clothing while you are under the shower, and call to your teacher. (It may be temporarily embarrassing to remove clothing in front of your classmates, but failure to thoroughly rinse a chemical off your skin could result in permanent damage.)

- **Use the proper technique demonstrated by your teacher when you are handling bacteria or other microorganisms.** Treat all microorganisms as if they are pathogens. Do not open Petri dishes to observe or count bacterial colonies.

Proper Waste Disposal

- **Clean and sanitize all work surfaces and personal protective equipment after each lab period as directed by your teacher.**

- **Dispose of contaminated materials (biological or chemical) in special containers only as directed by your teacher.** Never put these materials into a regular waste container or down the drain.

- **Dispose of sharp objects (such as broken glass) in the appropriate sharps or broken glass container as directed by your teacher.**

How to Use Your Textbook

You might notice that there are many unique elements in this text-book. By reading the next few pages, you will learn how the different parts of this textbook will help you to become a successful science student. You may be tempted to skip this section, but you should read it. This textbook is an important tool in your exploration of science. Like any tool, the more you know about how to use this textbook, the better your results will be.

Step into Science

The beginning of each chapter is designed to get you involved with science. You will immediately see that science matters!

Chapter Outline You can get a quick overview of the chapter by looking at the chapter's outline. In the outline, the section titles and the topics within that section are listed.

Inquiry Lab This lab gives you a chance to get some hands-on experience right away. It is designed to help you start thinking about what you will learn in the chapter.

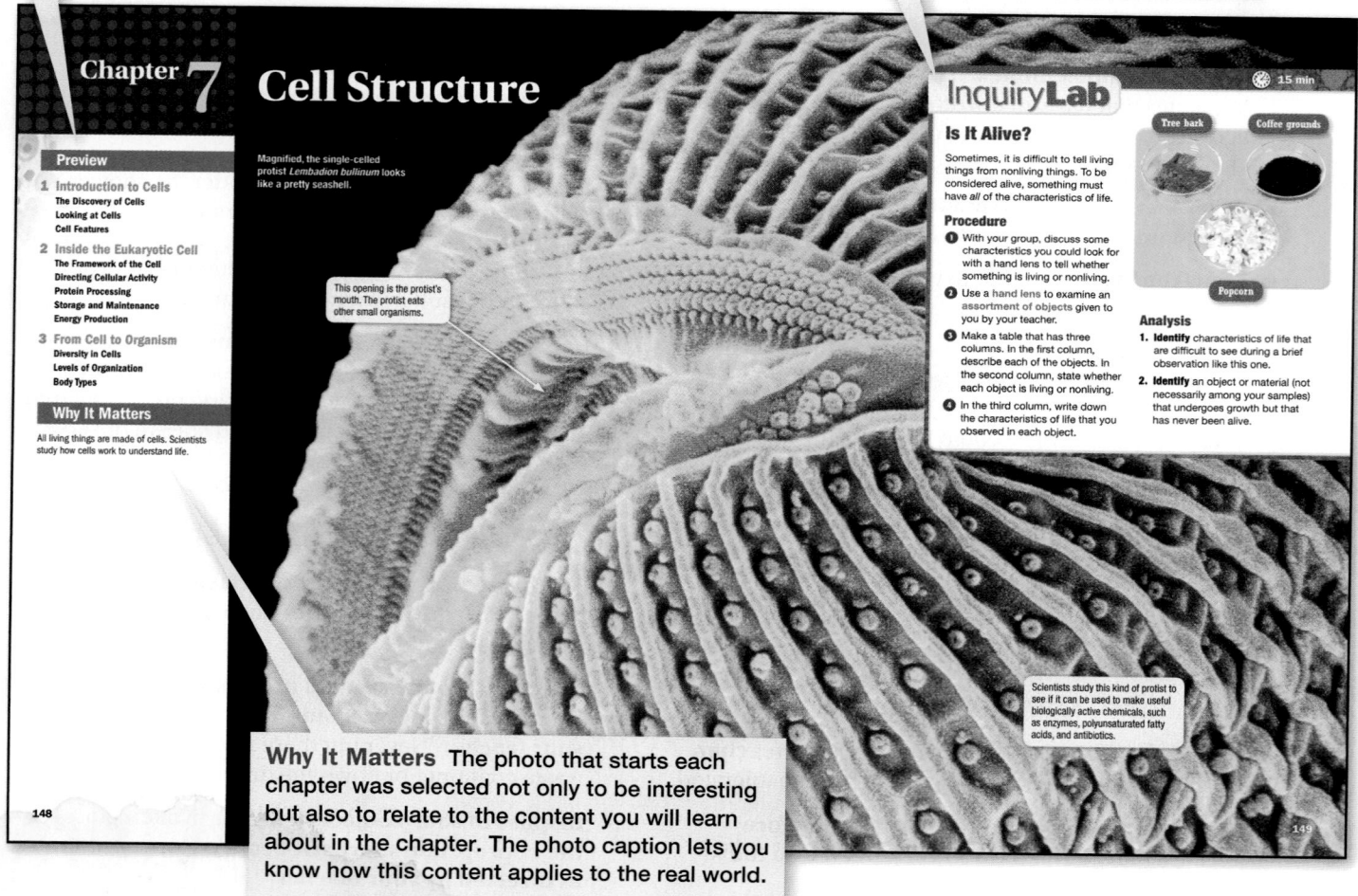

Chapter 7 — Cell Structure

Preview

1 Introduction to Cells
   The Discovery of Cells
   Looking at Cells
   Cell Features

2 Inside the Eukaryotic Cell
   The Framework of the Cell
   Directing Cellular Activity
   Protein Processing
   Storage and Maintenance
   Energy Production

3 From Cell to Organism
   Diversity in Cells
   Levels of Organization
   Body Types

Why It Matters

All living things are made of cells. Scientists study how cells work to understand life.

Magnified, the single-celled protist *Lembadion bullinum* looks like a pretty seashell.

This opening is the protist's mouth. The protist eats other small organisms.

Inquiry Lab ⏱ 15 min

Is It Alive?

Sometimes, it is difficult to tell living things from nonliving things. To be considered alive, something must have *all* of the characteristics of life.

Procedure

1. With your group, discuss some characteristics you could look for with a hand lens to tell whether something is living or nonliving.

2. Use a hand lens to examine an assortment of objects given to you by your teacher.

3. Make a table that has three columns. In the first column, describe each of the objects. In the second column, state whether each object is living or nonliving.

4. In the third column, write down the characteristics of life that you observed in each object.

Tree bark   Coffee grounds

Popcorn

Analysis

1. **Identify** characteristics of life that are difficult to see during a brief observation like this one.

2. **Identify** an object or material (not necessarily among your samples) that undergoes growth but that has never been alive.

Scientists study this kind of protist to see if it can be used to make useful biologically active chemicals, such as enzymes, polyunsaturated fatty acids, and antibiotics.

Why It Matters The photo that starts each chapter was selected not only to be interesting but also to relate to the content you will learn about in the chapter. The photo caption lets you know how this content applies to the real world.

148

149

Read for Meaning

At the beginning of each chapter you will find tools that will help you grasp the meaning of what you read. Each section also introduces what is important in that section and why.

The **Key Ideas** ask the important questions that you will be able to answer after learning about the science in each section.

The **Key Terms** are science words that you may not be familiar with but that are important to understanding the section. Pay special attention when you see them highlighted in the pages that follow.

Each **Reading Toolbox** contains a variety of learning tools that will help you better understand the content of the chapter.

Why It Matters This gives at least one reason that you might be interested in the subject of the section. In some cases, this topic is covered in more detail with an article.

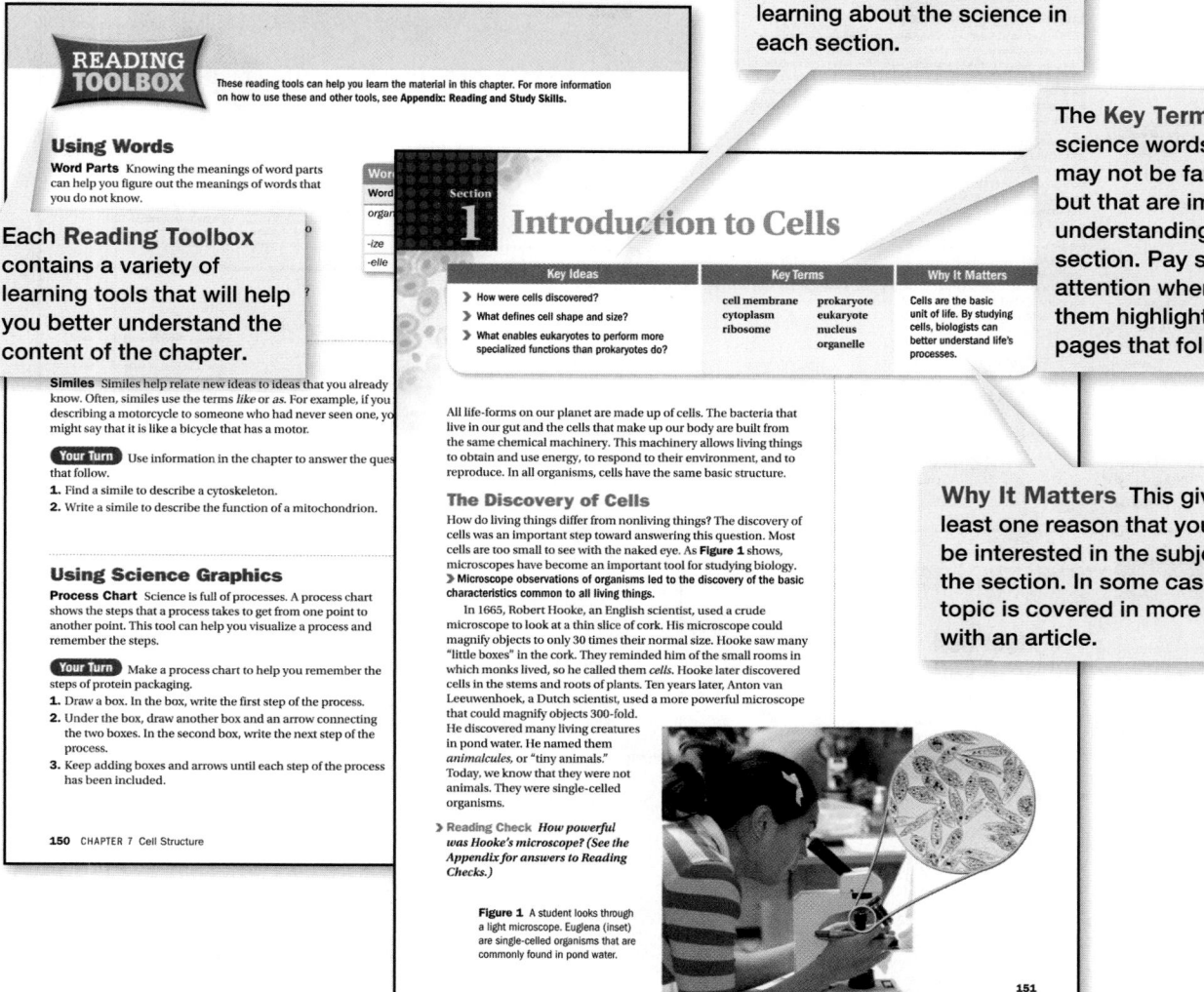

Keep an Eye on Headings

Notice that the headings in this textbook are different sizes and different colors. The headings help you organize your reading and form a simple outline, as shown below.

Green: Section titles

Blue: Key-idea heading

Black: ❯ Key-idea statements

The paragraphs under each blue heading contains a sentence that answers a **Key Idea** question from the section opener. These key-ideas are indicated with a blue pointer and are printed in bold.

Science Is Doing

You will get many opportunities throughout this textbook to actually do science. After all, doing is what science is about.

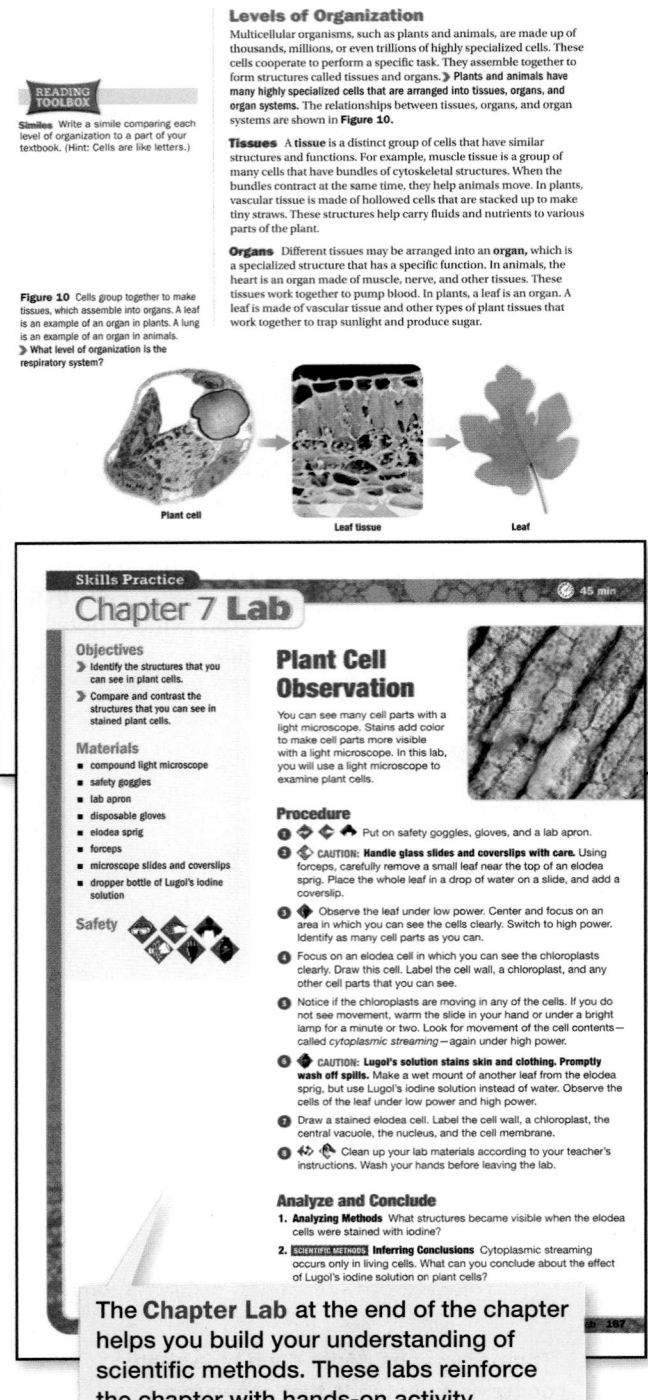

Levels of Organization

Multicellular organisms, such as plants and animals, are made up of thousands, millions, or even trillions of highly specialized cells. These cells cooperate to perform a specific task. They assemble together to form structures called tissues and organs. ▶ **Plants and animals have many highly specialized cells that are arranged into tissues, organs, and organ systems.** The relationships between tissues, organs, and organ systems are shown in **Figure 10.**

READING TOOLBOX

Similes Write a simile comparing each level of organization to a part of your textbook. (Hint: Cells are like letters.)

Tissues A **tissue** is a distinct group of cells that have similar structures and functions. For example, muscle tissue is a group of many cells that have bundles of cytoskeletal structures. When the bundles contract at the same time, they help animals move. In plants, vascular tissue is made of hollowed cells that are stacked up to make tiny straws. These structures help carry fluids and nutrients to various parts of the plant.

Organs Different tissues may be arranged into an **organ,** which is a specialized structure that has a specific function. In animals, the heart is an organ made of muscle, nerve, and other tissues. These tissues work together to pump blood. In plants, a leaf is an organ. A leaf is made of vascular tissue and other types of plant tissues that work together to trap sunlight and produce sugar.

Figure 10 Cells group together to make tissues, which assemble into organs. A leaf is an example of an organ in plants. A lung is an example of an organ in animals. ▶ What level of organization is the respiratory system?

Plant cell   **Leaf tissue**   **Leaf**

Skills Practice
Chapter 7 Lab
⏱ 45 min

Objectives
▶ Identify the structures that you can see in plant cells.
▶ Compare and contrast the structures that you can see in stained plant cells.

Materials
- compound light microscope
- safety goggles
- lab apron
- disposable gloves
- elodea sprig
- forceps
- microscope slides and coverslips
- dropper bottle of Lugol's iodine solution

Safety ◆◆◆◆

Plant Cell Observation

You can see many cell parts with a light microscope. Stains add color to make cell parts more visible with a light microscope. In this lab, you will use a light microscope to examine plant cells.

Procedure
1 ◆◆◆◆ Put on safety goggles, gloves, and a lab apron.
2 ◆ **CAUTION: Handle glass slides and coverslips with care.** Using forceps, carefully remove a small leaf near the top of an elodea sprig. Place the whole leaf in a drop of water on a slide, and add a coverslip.
3 ◆ Observe the leaf under low power. Center and focus on an area in which you can see the cells clearly. Switch to high power. Identify as many cell parts as you can.
4 ◆ Focus on an elodea cell in which you can see the chloroplasts clearly. Draw this cell. Label the cell wall, a chloroplast, and any other cell parts that you can see.
5 Notice if the chloroplasts are moving in any of the cells. If you do not see movement, warm the slide in your hand or under a bright lamp for a minute or two. Look for movement of the cell contents—called *cytoplasmic streaming*—again under high power.
6 ◆ **CAUTION: Lugol's solution stains skin and clothing. Promptly wash off spills.** Make a wet mount of another leaf from the elodea sprig, but use Lugol's iodine solution instead of water. Observe the cells of the leaf under low power and high power.
7 Draw a stained elodea cell. Label the cell wall, a chloroplast, the central vacuole, the nucleus, and the cell membrane.
8 ◆◆◆ Clean up your lab materials according to your teacher's instructions. Wash your hands before leaving the lab.

Analyze and Conclude
1. **Analyzing Methods** What structures became visible when the elodea cells were stained with iodine?
2. **SCIENTIFIC METHODS** **Inferring Conclusions** Cytoplasmic streaming occurs only in living cells. What can you conclude about the effect of Lugol's iodine solution on plant cells?

The **Chapter Lab** at the end of the chapter helps you build your understanding of scientific methods. These labs reinforce the chapter with hands-on activity.

Almost every section in the textbook has at least one **Quick Lab** to help you get real hands-on experience doing science.

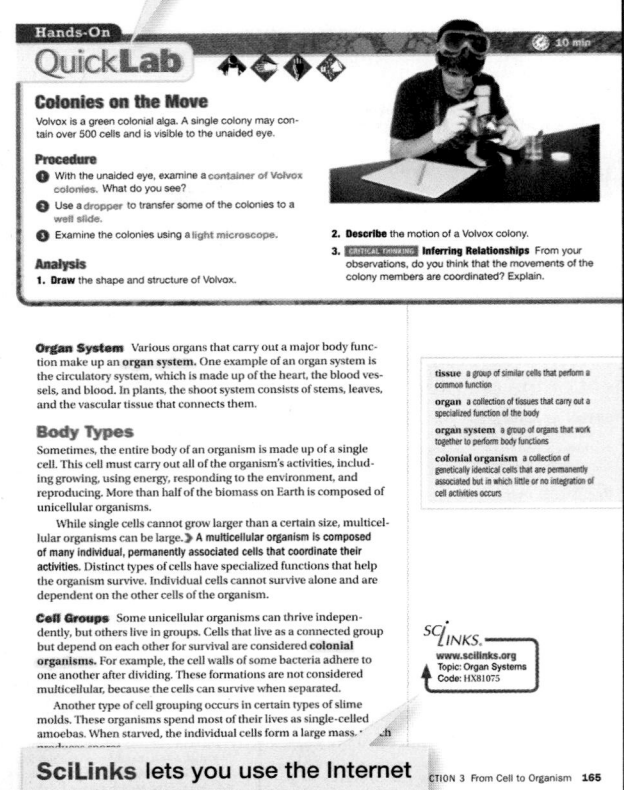

Hands-On
QuickLab
⏱ 10 min

Colonies on the Move
Volvox is a green colonial alga. A single colony may contain over 500 cells and is visible to the unaided eye.

Procedure
1 With the unaided eye, examine a container of *Volvox* colonies. What do you see?
2 Use a dropper to transfer some of the colonies to a well slide.
3 Examine the colonies using a light microscope.

Analysis
1. **Draw** the shape and structure of Volvox.
2. **Describe** the motion of a Volvox colony.
3. **CRITICAL THINKING** **Inferring Relationships** From your observations, do you think that the movements of the colony members are coordinated? Explain.

Organ System Various organs that carry out a major body function make up an **organ system.** One example of an organ system is the circulatory system, which is made up of the heart, the blood vessels, and blood. In plants, the shoot system consists of stems, leaves, and the vascular tissue that connects them.

Body Types
Sometimes, the entire body of an organism is made up of a single cell. This cell must carry out all of the organism's activities, including growing, using energy, responding to the environment, and reproducing. More than half of the biomass on Earth is composed of unicellular organisms.

While single cells cannot grow larger than a certain size, multicellular organisms can be large. ▶ **A multicellular organism is composed of many individual, permanently associated cells that coordinate their activities.** Distinct types of cells have specialized functions that help the organism survive. Individual cells cannot survive alone and are dependent on the other cells of the organism.

Cell Groups Some unicellular organisms can thrive independently, but others live in groups. Cells that live as a connected group but depend on each other for survival are considered **colonial organisms.** For example, the cell walls of some bacteria adhere to one another after dividing. These formations are not considered multicellular, because the cells can survive when separated.

Another type of cell grouping occurs in certain types of slime molds. These organisms spend most of their lives as single-celled amoebas. When starved, the individual cells form a large mass, which produces spores.

tissue a group of similar cells that perform a common function

organ a collection of tissues that carry out a specialized function of the body

organ system a group of organs that work together to perform body functions

colonial organism a collection of genetically identical cells that are permanently associated but in which little or no integration of cell activities occurs

SCLINKS.
www.scilinks.org
Topic: Organ Systems
Code: HX81075

SciLinks lets you use the Internet to link to interesting topics and activities related to the section.

SECTION 3 From Cell to Organism **165**

Throughout the book, **interact online** markers on figures indicate that an animated, interactive version of the diagram is available online.

go.hrw.com
interact online
Keyword: HX8CSFF5

Making and Exporting Proteins

Figure 5 The cell manufactures many proteins. Some proteins are used outside the cell that makes them. Many organelles play a role in producing, processing, and packaging these proteins.

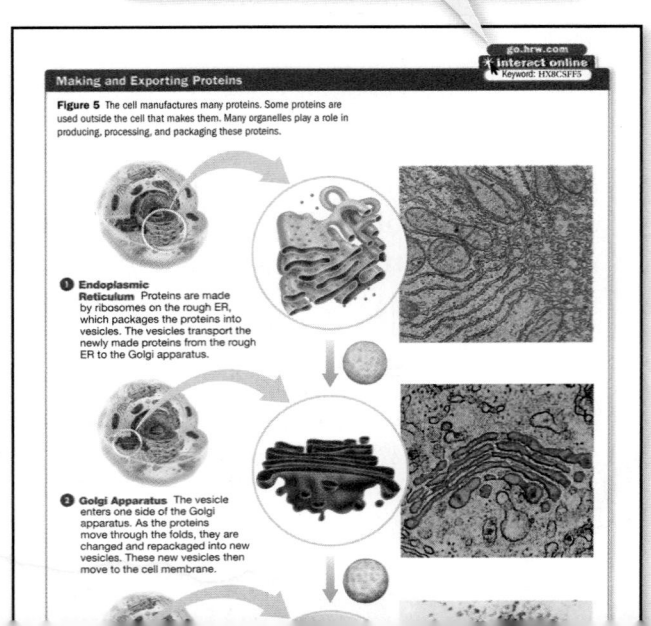

1 **Endoplasmic Reticulum** Proteins are made by ribosomes on the rough ER, which packages the proteins into vesicles. The vesicles transport the newly made proteins from the rough ER to the Golgi apparatus.

2 **Golgi Apparatus** The vesicle enters one side of the Golgi apparatus. As the proteins move through the folds, they are changed and repackaged into new vesicles. These new vesicles then move to the cell membrane.

Review What You Have Learned

You can't review too much when learning science. To help you review, a **Section Review** appears at the end of every section and a **Chapter Summary** appears at the end of every chapter. Following that are even more review questions. All of this not only helps you study for tests but also deepens your understanding of the content.

Just a few clicks away, each **Super Summary** gives you even more ways to review and study for tests using a computer and the Internet.

Mastering science standards takes practice. The end of each chapter has more practice questions about the chapter. To help you be ready, they are in a format similar to formats you will see on standardized tests or exams.

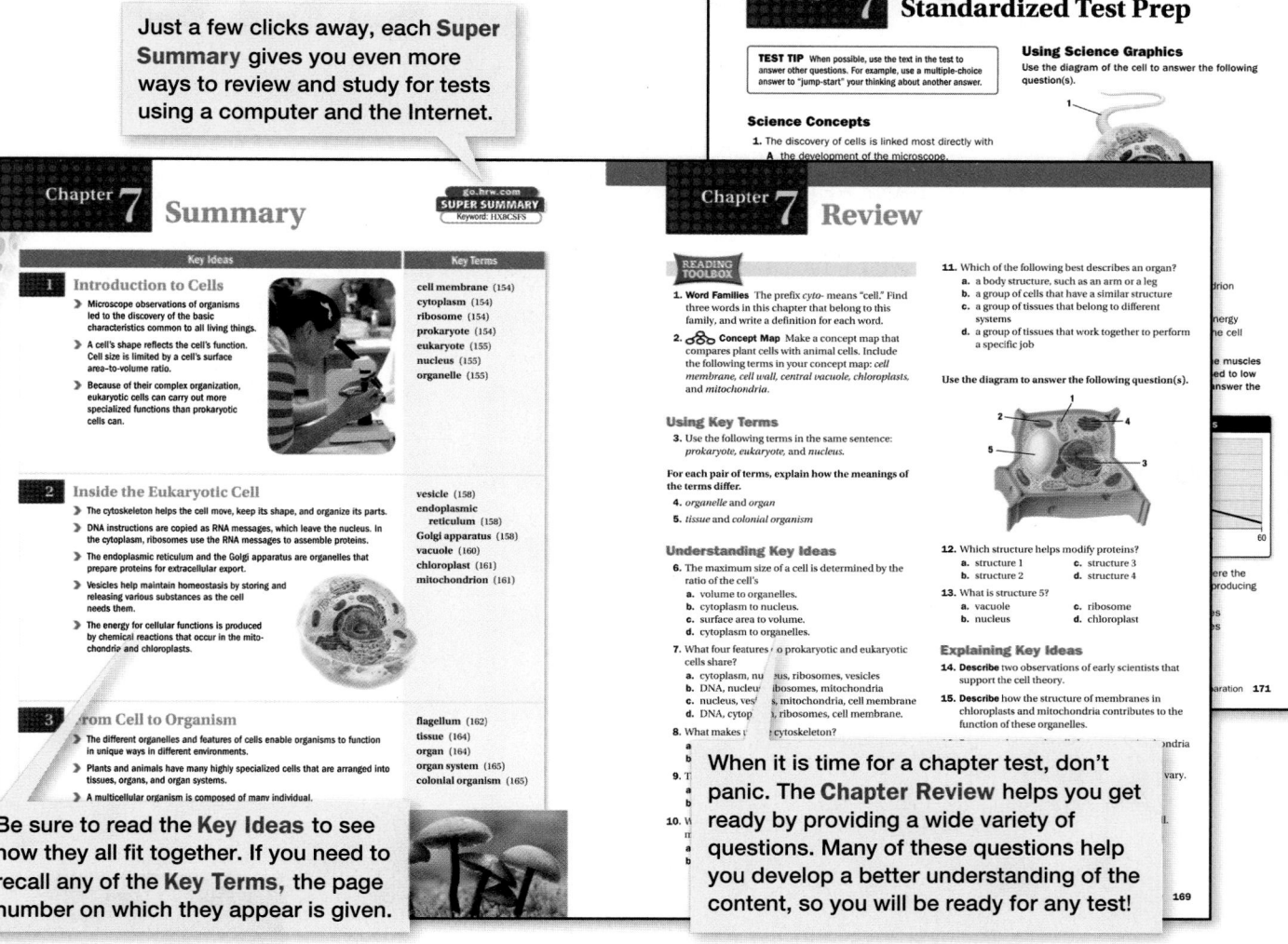

Be sure to read the **Key Ideas** to see how they all fit together. If you need to recall any of the **Key Terms,** the page number on which they appear is given.

When it is time for a chapter test, don't panic. The **Chapter Review** helps you get ready by providing a wide variety of questions. Many of these questions help you develop a better understanding of the content, so you will be ready for any test!

↗ Be Resourceful—Use the Web!

More Resources

There are plenty of resources online for you. When you see a SciLinks code in the book, just go to **scilinks.org** and type the code in for information and activities on a topic. When you see **Super Summary** or **Interact Online** in the book, go to **go.hrw.com** snd type in the keyword for study helps and interactive art.

Your Online Textbook

If your teacher gives you a special password to log onto the **Holt Online Learning** site, you will find your complete textbook on the Web. In addition, you will find some great learning tools and interactive materials. You can now access your textbook anywhere and anytime via the Internet.

Take a Test Drive

How well can you use this book now? Take Chapter 1 out for a spin and see how you do. Log onto **go.hrw.com** and enter the keyword **HX8 TEST DRIVE** for a short list of questions that will test your ability to navigate this book.

UNIT 1 Introduction

1 Biology and You

2 Applications of Biology

3 Chemistry of Life

Researcher with
Nassau grouper

Giant panda cub with
caretaker at Wolong
Nature Reserve in China

2

Ecological survey of
mountain eucalyptus

DISCOVERIES IN SCIENCE

Milestones in Biology

1489

Leonardo da Vinci applies architectural techniques to anatomical drawing. His detailed drawings of the human skull revolutionize scientific illustration.

Statue of Leonardo da Vinci in Italy

1811

At 12 years old, Mary Anning, a British fossil collector, discovers the first complete fossil skeleton of an ichthyosaur. Other scientists use her discoveries to support the theory that fossils are evidence of extinct species.

1898

Marie Curie, a scientist born in Poland, demonstrates that isotopes of certain elements, such as radium and polonium, are the source of radioactive energy in radioactive rocks.

Marie Curie in her laboratory

1910

Alex Carrel publishes a paper reporting his success in using cold storage to preserve blood vessels for long periods of time before transplanting them. His work, related to developing organ-transplant processes, earns him the Nobel Prize in physiology or medicine in 1912.

1918–1919

An influenza epidemic kills between 20 million and 40 million people worldwide. In less than a year, about 675,000 Americans die of the disease, 10 times the number of Americans who died in World War I.

1927

George Washington Carver, American inventor and botanist, patents a process for making paints from soybean extracts.

George Washington Carver

1971

Louis Leaky sponsors Biruté Mary Galdikas to study the orangutans of Borneo. In 1975, Galdikas begins publishing articles about her observations of orangutan behavior. Many articles and lectures follow. Her work helps educate the public about the need to preserve wild habitats.

1996

David Ho is recognized as *Time* magazine's Man of the Year for his pioneering work developing "cocktails" of medicines that fight HIV.

David Ho

Mason wasp with prey

BIOLOGY CAREER

Forensic Scientist
Wayne Moorehead

Wayne Moorehead is a forensic scientist. Forensic scientists use scientific processes to investigate legal matters. Moorehead works with the Trace Evidence and Fire Division of the Orange County Sheriff–Coroner Crime Laboratory in California. He specializes in forensic microscopy, trace evidence, and the analysis of explosives, fire debris, and unusual evidence. Moorehead enjoys his work, especially using critical thinking to answer questions about crimes.

Moorehead traces his interest in forensic science back to his childhood, when he enjoyed using a chemistry set and microscope and reading forensic science books. He still collects books in his field.

Moorehead enjoys using forensic science in criminal investigations but considers his greatest accomplishment to be teaching forensic science to high school students, college students, professors, and the public.

Yellow crinoid and reef fish on a coral reef

Biology and You

Biologists are curious about living things. This biologist was curious enough about seabirds to climb to the top of this high cliff.

This scientist is taking measurements of a puffin chick to estimate its age. This information will help the scientist predict when the chick will leave its burrow and head out to sea.

One mystery that biologists have yet to solve about puffins is how the chicks, who leave their burrow when they are only 50 days old, are able to return to the same spot many years later to have their own chicks.

Preview

1 The Nature of Science
Scientific Thought
Universal Laws
Science and Ethics
Why Study Science?

2 Scientific Methods
Beginning a Scientific Investigation
Scientific Experiments
Scientific Theories

3 Tools and Techniques
Measurement Systems
Lab Techniques
Safety

4 What Is Biology?
The Study of Life
Properties of Life

Why It Matters

Biology, the study of life, directly applies to your health, life, and future in ways as simple as making daily food choices or as complex as deciding which career to pursue.

InquiryLab

Make a Prediction

Making predictions is an important part of scientific thought. To make a prediction, you use observations to foretell what will happen in a given situation. In this lab, you will practice making predictions.

Procedure

1. Open a **Petri dish with agar,** and streak your finger across the agar.

2. Replace the lid, and seal it with **tape.** Label the dish with your name and the number "1."

3. Seal the **second Petri dish with agar** without removing the lid. Label this Petri dish with your name and the number "2."

4. Write a prediction about what will happen in each dish. Store your dishes as your teacher directs. Record your observations.

Analysis

1. **Restate** your prediction.

2. **List** the evidence that you can cite to support your prediction.

3. **Explain** whether you would change your testing method or your prediction if you did not obtain the results that you predicted.

4. **Evaluate** the importance of obtaining a result that does not support your prediction.

Scientists rely on tools to make accurate measurements. This tool is called a *Vernier caliper.* It was invented in 1631 by the French scientist Pierre Vernier. Now, there is a street in Paris named after him.

5

READING TOOLBOX

These reading tools can help you learn the material in this chapter. For more information on how to use these and other tools, see **Appendix: Reading and Study Skills.**

Using Words

Everyday Words in Science Many words that we use every day have special meanings in science. For example, "matter" in everyday use is an issue or problem. In science, matter is the substance of which all things are made.

Your Turn Make a table like the one shown here.
1. Before you read, write in your own words the everyday meaning of the terms in the table.
2. As you read, fill in the science meaning for the terms in the table.

Everyday Words in Science		
Word	Everyday Meaning	Science Meaning
theory		
reproduction		
control		
conclude		

Using Language

Hypothesis or Theory? In everyday language, there is little difference between a *hypothesis* and a *theory*. But in science, the meanings of these words are more distinct. A *hypothesis* is a specific, testable prediction for a limited set of conditions. A *theory* is a general explanation for a broad range of data. A theory can include hypotheses that have been tested and can also be used to generate new hypotheses. The strongest scientific theories explain the broadest range of data and incorporate many well-tested hypotheses.

Your Turn Use what you have learned about the difference between a hypothesis and a theory to answer the following questions.
1. What is the difference between a hypothesis and a theory?
2. Propose a testable hypothesis to explain why the chicken crossed the road.

Using Graphic Organizers

Idea Wheel An idea wheel is an effective type of visual organization. Ideas in science can be divided up into topics around a central, or main, idea.

Your Turn Create an idea wheel like the one shown here to help you organize your notes about tools and techniques used in science.
1. Draw a circle. Draw a larger circle around the first circle.
2. Divide the ring between the circles into sections by drawing lines from the center circle to the outer circle.
3. Write the main idea *Tools and Techniques* in the smaller circle.
4. Label each section of the ring with a topic that falls under the main idea.
5. In each section of the ring, include notes about each topic.

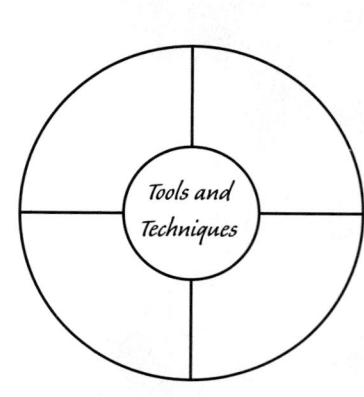

The Nature of Science

Key Ideas	Key Terms	Why It Matters
❯ How can someone practice scientific thought? ❯ What are universal laws in science? ❯ How do ethics apply to science? ❯ Why should someone who is not planning to become a scientist study science?	skepticism	Thinking like a scientist helps you solve problems and think critically about the world around you.

The goal of science is to help us understand the natural world and improve people's lives. Thinking like a scientist can help you solve problems and think critically about your world.

Scientific Thought

❯ Scientific thought involves making observations, using evidence to draw conclusions, being skeptical about ideas, and being open to change when new discoveries are made.

Questioning Ideas Scientists carefully observe the world. They then ask questions about what they observe. Often, the questions that they ask lead to even more questions. This process is the cornerstone of scientific thought. Scientific thought also requires **skepticism**—a questioning and often doubtful attitude. Scientists question everything. They require evidence, not opinions, to support ideas. Many great discoveries have been made when scientists doubted conventional wisdom. For example, people once thought that stress caused stomach ulcers. However, a group of researchers found the bacteria *Helicobacter pylori* in the stomachs of people with ulcers. Studies confirmed that the bacteria, shown in **Figure 1,** caused ulcers.

skepticism a habit of mind in which a person questions the validity of accepted ideas

Discovery and Change As scientists challenge old claims and make new discoveries, they change the way that people view the world. Many scientific discoveries lead to new technologies and medical treatments. For example, discovering that bacteria cause stomach ulcers led to prescribing antibiotics for patients with ulcers. Through the ongoing cycle of challenge and discovery, scientific knowledge grows.

Helicobacter pylori **bacterium**

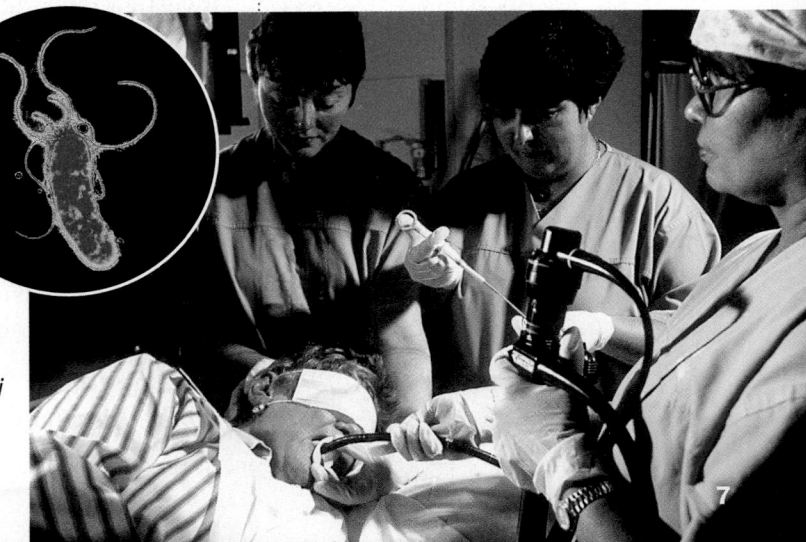

Figure 1 Doctors once thought that stress caused stomach ulcers. However, in 1982, scientists discovered that *Helicobacter pylori* bacteria were the actual cause.

Figure 2 All objects in the universe, from birds to stars, are affected by gravity. Birds must overcome gravity to fly. Stars are formed when gravity pulls a mass of gases together.

ACADEMIC
VOCABULARY

aspect the way in which an idea or situation is viewed

www.scilinks.org
Topic: Scientific
Discoveries
Code: HX81356

Universal Laws

❯ Science is governed by truths that are valid everywhere in the universe. These truths are called *universal laws*. Though branches of science address different aspects of the natural world, universal laws such as the law of gravity, the law of conservation of energy, and the laws of planetary motion apply to all branches of science and to every person. A biologist studying the flight of the bird in **Figure 2** is studying how animals have adapted to overcome the force of gravity. A biologist studying the habits of nocturnal animals is studying the way that animal behavior has adapted to take advantage of the regular pattern of day and night caused by Earth's rotation on its axis.

Science and Ethics

Ethics are a system of moral principles and values. ❯ Because scientific experimentation and discovery can have serious ethical implications, scientific investigations require ethical behavior. Scientists performing investigations must report only accurate data and be willing to allow their peers to review their work. All scientists rely on the work of other scientists. If the data or claims of one scientist are misleading or false, many other scientists may waste time and resources conducting investigations that are based on that unethical work.

Many other people also rely on scientists to be ethical. For example, if a scientist falsely claims to have discovered a cure for diabetes, people with diabetes may change how they manage their condition to take advantage of the discovery. Because the findings are false, the people relying on the discovery could be in danger.

Scientists must also obey laws and behave ethically with people involved in scientific investigations. Ethical scientists adhere to strict guidelines to ensure that no one involved in medical experiments is coerced, exploited, or involuntarily exposed to a known danger.

❯ **Reading Check** *Why is it important that scientific investigations be done ethically? (See the Appendix for answers to Reading Checks.)*

Quick**Lab**

🕐 15 min

Evaluate a Scientific Claim

As a consumer, you need to make wise decisions. Often, your buying choices depend on evaluating claims made by the manufacturer. Are the claims accurate? What can you really expect from the products?

Analysis

1. **CRITICAL THINKING** **Evaluating Conclusions** Suppose that two television commercials claim that their own product is the fastest-acting acne medicine. Design a strategy that could be used to compare the brands. How would you compare their effectiveness?

2. **CRITICAL THINKING** **Determining the Validity of a Claim** New automobiles are sold with a window sticker displaying the expected miles per gallon. Are these manufacturers' estimates realistic and repeatable by consumers? How would you find out?

Why Study Science?

Scientific thinking is not just for scientists. The same critical-thinking process that scientists use is a tool that you can use in your everyday life. ❯ **An understanding of science can help you take better care of your health, be a wiser consumer, and become a better-informed citizen.** For example, you may read an article claiming that riding a bike for 30 minutes a week can lower your blood pressure. How will you know if the claim is accurate? You can investigate the claim by using scientific thought. Ask questions about the claim, be skeptical about what you read, and be ready for discovery and change.

You can also use science to improve the world around you. You may see a problem in your town, such as a struggling recycling program or a dangerous crosswalk. You can investigate these problems with skepticism and creativity to discover helpful solutions. By applying scientific thinking to these problems, you can help yourself and your community.

READING TOOLBOX

Everyday Words in Science In your own words, write the everyday meaning for the word *law*. How does the everyday meaning compare to the science meaning of *law*?

Section **1** Review

❯ KEY IDEAS

1. **Describe** the processes involved in practicing good scientific thought.
2. **Identify** two universal laws.
3. **Explain** how ethics apply to science.
4. **Relate** how science has already helped you in your everyday life.

CRITICAL THINKING

5. **Making Inferences** Most animals have solid bones. However, most birds have bones with hollow spaces. Explain how this feature of birds is related to one of the universal laws.

6. **Evaluating Claims** Two brands of yeast claim to produce a fast-rising dough. Design a strategy that could be used to compare the brands. What would you measure?

WRITING FOR SCIENCE

7. **Persuasive Writing** Write a letter to a younger brother or sister explaining the importance of studying science. Give at least three reasons to support your explanation.

Scientific Methods

Key Ideas	Key Terms	Why It Matters
❯ How do scientific investigations begin? ❯ What are two types of experiments that scientists can use to test hypotheses? ❯ What is the difference between a theory and a hypothesis?	observation hypothesis experiment control group theory	Scientific thinking can help you understand and analyze information that you come across in your daily life.

All scientists have a certain way of investigating the world. Studying an actual scientific investigation is an exciting way to learn how science is done. Our story begins with a population of Canada geese.

Beginning a Scientific Investigation

For many years, the number of Canada geese around Chicago, shown in **Figure 3,** had been rising rapidly. Scientist Charles Paine of the Max McGraw Wildlife Foundation was studying this population growth when he noticed that the number of geese was no longer increasing. Why was the population boom over?

Making Observations ❯ Most scientific investigations begin with observations that lead to questions. **Observation** is the act of noting or perceiving objects or events by using the senses. Scientists must use both direct and indirect observation to study the world around them. Many things, like the Canada geese, can be seen. This means they can be directly observed. Other things, like the force of gravity, cannot be seen. Gravity is observed indirectly by observing the effects of gravity on objects that can be directly observed.

Formulating a Hypothesis To find out what was happening to the population of Canada geese, Paine needed to form a hypothesis. A **hypothesis** is a possible explanation that can be tested by observation or experimentation. Hypotheses are not guesses. Possible hypotheses to explain Paine's observations included these:

• The geese were being killed by predators.

• Many of the geese had become infertile.

• The geese were migrating out of the area.

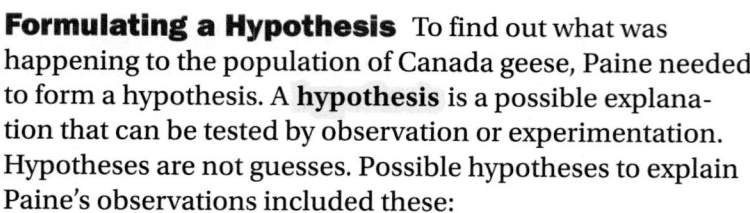

Figure 3 Chicago's Canada goose population had risen rapidly for several years. After making observations, Charles Paine discovered that the population was now increasing by only about 1% per year.

Hands-On
Quick**Lab**

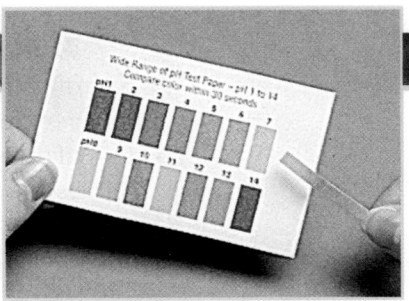

 15 min

The pH of Common Substances

You can use pH indicator paper to determine the pH of various solutions. The pH indicator paper changes color when it is exposed to a solution. The change in color indicates how acidic or basic the solution is.

Procedure

❶ Make a data table with three columns. Add these headings: "Solution," "Predicted pH," and "Measured pH." Make a row for **five solutions** to be tested.

❷ Predict the pH (acid or base) of each solution, and record your predictions in your data table.

❸ **Test** each solution with **pH paper,** and record the results in the appropriate row in your data table.

Analysis

1. **Summarize** your findings in two sentences.

2. **Compare** your results with those of the rest of the class. Explain any differences.

3. **List** the scientific methods that you followed in doing this activity.

4. **CRITICAL THINKING** **Analyzing Results** Were the predictions that you made correct? Explain any differences between your predictions and your results.

Scientific Experiments

An **experiment** is a procedure that is carried out under controlled conditions to test a hypothesis. ❯ Scientists conduct controlled experiments or perform studies in order to test a hypothesis.

Controlled Experiments A controlled experiment is a procedure that tests one factor at a time and that uses a control group and an experimental group. A **control group** serves as a standard of comparison because the group receives no experimental treatment. Experimental groups are identical to the control group except for one factor, or *variable.* The single factor that scientists change in an experiment is called the *independent variable.* Factors that may change in response to the independent variable are called *dependent variables.* Scientists analyze changes to the dependent variables to understand how the independent variable affects the system that they are studying.

Study Without Experimentation There are often cases in which experiments are not possible or not ethical. For example, researchers are trying to find out if the bacteria that cause dental plaque also contribute to heart disease. It is not ethical to ask a group of people not to brush their teeth for years in order to find out if they will develop heart disease. Instead, researchers look for connections in data gathered from patients who have heart disease. However, many factors can contribute to heart disease. Researchers try to reduce the number of variables that may affect their data. For example, smoking leads to heart disease. If a person who has heart disease smokes and has dental plaque, determining which factor caused the patient's heart disease is impossible.

observation the process of obtaining information by using the senses

hypothesis a testable idea or explanation that leads to scientific investigation

experiment a procedure that is carried out under controlled conditions to discover, demonstrate, or test a fact, theory, or general truth

control group in an experiment, a group that serves as a standard of comparison with another group to which the control group is identical except for one factor

www.scilinks.org
Topic: Scientific
 Investigations
Code: HX81358

READING TOOLBOX

Hypothesis or Theory? List the hypotheses that were proposed to explain the decrease in Canada geese in Chicago. Identify which hypothesis was supported by evidence.

Analyzing Results To test his hypothesis, Paine put radio collars on the adult Canada geese. He tracked the geese and learned that very few of the adult geese were being killed by predators. The results of an experiment may support a hypothesis or prove that a hypothesis is not true. After Paine analyzed his results, he had to change his hypothesis. Paine now hypothesized that the eggs, not the adult geese, were being eaten by predators. He discussed his ideas with his colleague Stan Gehrt, who was studying predators in the Chicago area. Gehrt had recently discovered an amazing fact: Chicago was home to about 2,000 coyotes! Gehrt had observed that coyotes, such as the one in **Figure 4,** sometimes ate the eggs of Canada geese.

Drawing Conclusions and Verifying Results Scientists draw conclusions that explain the results of their experiments. Working together, Paine and Gehrt concluded that urban coyotes were controlling the Canada goose population by eating the eggs. How could Paine and Gehrt verify their conclusions? Scientists verify their conclusions by conducting experiments and studies many times. They also check to see if other scientists have found similar results. In this case, urban coyotes have been found in many large cities. Paine and Gehrt could try to find out if these coyotes also eat goose eggs.

Considering Bias Scientists are human and have particular points of view, or biases. Scientists work hard to prevent bias from affecting their work, but bias can still influence an experiment. Also, a conflict of interest could affect a scientific study. For example, an investigation funded by a company may be biased in favor of that company's products or services. For this reason, you should view all scientific claims in their context and question them. Remember that skepticism is an important part of scientific thought, even when considering research done by qualified scientists.

Figure 4 Coyotes like this one have adapted to city life. ❯ **How do coyotes most likely control Chicago's Canada goose population?**

Scientific Theories

When related hypotheses are well supported and explain a great amount of data, these hypotheses may be put together to form a **theory.** ❯ The main difference between a theory and a hypothesis is that a hypothesis is a specific, testable prediction for a limited set of conditions and a theory is a general explanation for a broad range of data. Some examples of scientific theories include the quantum theory, the cell theory, and the theory of evolution. As you study science, remember that the word *theory* is used very differently by scientists and by the general public. People may say, "It's just a theory," suggesting that an idea is untested, but scientists view a theory as a highly tested, generally accepted principle that explains a vast number of observations and experimental data.

Constructing a Theory **Figure 5** summarizes the steps in the development of a theory. Constructing a theory often involves considering contrasting ideas and conflicting hypotheses. Argument, disagreement, and unresolved questions are a healthy part of scientific research. Scientists routinely evaluate and critique one another's work. Once a scientist completes an investigation, he or she often writes a report for publication in a scientific journal. Before publication, the research report is reviewed by other scientists. These reviewers ensure that the investigation was carried out with the appropriate controls, methods, and data analysis. The reviewers also check that the conclusions reached by the author are justified by the data obtained. Publishing an investigation allows other scientists to use the information to form their hypotheses. They can also repeat the investigations and confirm the validity of the conclusions.

If the results of an experiment can be reproduced many times, the scientific research may help develop a new theory. However, the possibility always remains that future evidence will cause a scientific theory to be revised or even rejected. Challenging old theories is how scientific understanding grows.

❯ **Reading Check** *How does the scientific use of the word* theory *differ from how it is used by the general public?*

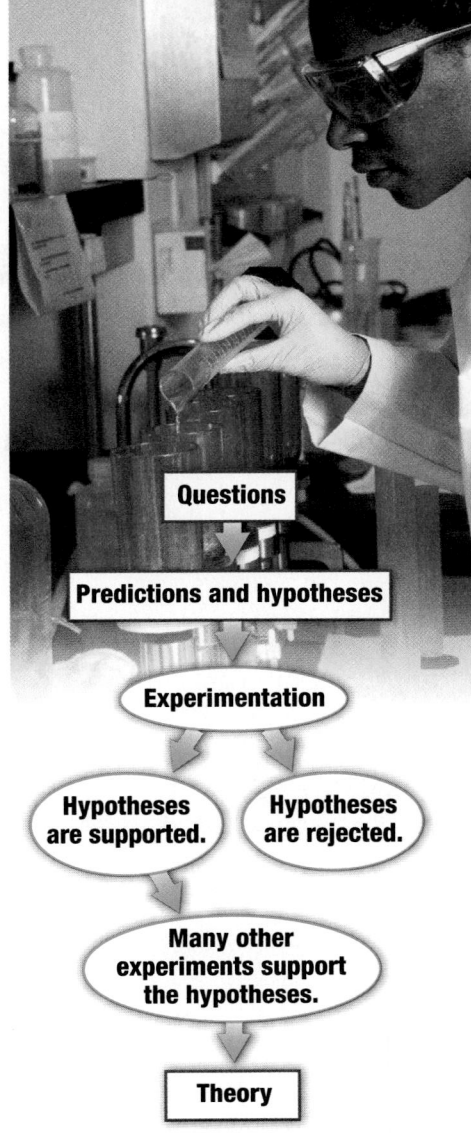

Figure 5 Scientists build theories from questions, predictions, hypotheses, and experimental results. ❯ How can an experiment lead to a theory?

Section 2 Review

❯ KEY IDEAS

1. **Summarize** the processes that scientists often use when beginning scientific investigations.
2. **Describe** two ways that scientists test hypotheses.
3. **Explain** the difference between a hypothesis and a theory.

CRITICAL THINKING

4. **Analyzing Methods** Provide one example of a case in which an experiment would not be possible and one example in which an experiment would not be ethical.
5. **Forming Hypotheses** A friend notices that her dog is getting thinner even though she has not changed how much she feeds him. Propose three testable hypotheses to explain the dog's weight loss.

METHODS OF SCIENCE

6. **Designing an Experiment** Suppose that Paine had hypothesized that the Canada geese in Chicago were not reproducing at a normal rate. What experiment could he use to test whether the geese in Chicago were less fertile than geese elsewhere?

Tools and Techniques

Key Ideas	Key Terms	Why It Matters
❯ Why do scientists use SI units for measurement? ❯ What are some tools and techniques that scientists use in the laboratory? ❯ What can you do to stay safe during an investigation?	SI	Understanding the tools and techniques that scientists use can help you work safely and effectively in the lab.

Scientists use various units of measurements, tools, and lab techniques to help them make observations and gather and record data.

Measurement Systems

Measurements taken by scientists are expressed in the International System of Units (**SI**), which is the official name of the metric system. ❯**The International System of Units is used by all scientists because scientists need to share a common measurement system. SI is also preferred by scientists because it is scaled in multiples of 10, which makes the system easy to use.** Like the U.S. monetary system, SI is a decimal system, so all relationships between SI units are based on powers of 10. Most SI units have a prefix that indicates the relationship of that unit to a base unit. For example, the SI base unit for length is the meter. The prefix *kilo-* means 1,000. Thus, a kilometer is equal to 1,000 meters. **Figure 6** shows other common SI units.

❯ **Reading Check** *How are prefixes used in names of SI units?*

go.hrw.com
✳**interact online**
Keyword: HX8BIOF6

Figure 6 How many dimes are in a dollar? The question is easy to answer because our monetary system, like SI, is built on powers of 10. ❯ **How many pennies are there in $10?**

 0.01  0.1  1  10

Common SI Units

Prefix	Factor	Volume	Length	Mass
kilo-	1,000	1 kiloliter = 1,000 L	1 kilometer = 1,000 m	1 kilogram = 1,000 g
—	1	1 liter (L)	1 meter (m)	1 gram (g)
centi-	0.01	1 centiliter = 0.01 L	1 centimeter = 0.01 m	1 centigram = 0.01 g
milli-	0.001	1 milliliter = 0.001 L	1 millimeter = 0.001 m	1 millligram = 0.001 g

Hands-On

QuickLab

 15 min

Practice Staining Techniques

The parts (organelles) of a typical cell are mostly transparent. In a technique called *staining,* color is added to cell parts to help identify and distinguish them.

Procedure

1. Use forceps to remove a thin layer of onion skin, and place it in the center of a glass slide. Add a drop of water, and place a coverslip over the specimen.

2. Examine the onion skin with a light microscope. Draw what you see.

3. Place a drop of iodine stain along one edge of the coverslip. Touch a piece of paper towel to the opposite edge to draw the water. When the skin is stained, examine it with the microscope.

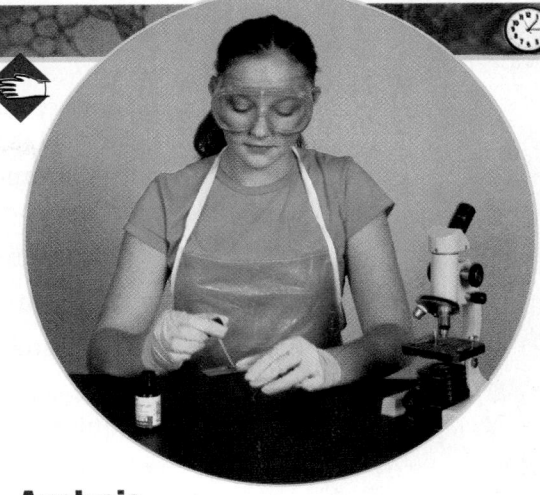

Analysis

1. **Describe** how the stain affected the onion skin.

2. CRITICAL THINKING **Analyzing Information** What is the advantage of using the paper to draw the stain across the field of view?

Lab Techniques

❯ In the lab, scientists always keep detailed and accurate notes and perform precise measurements. Many scientists also use specialized tools, such as microscopes, and specialized procedures, such as sterile technique.

Microscopy Many organisms, such as bacteria, are too small to see with the unaided eye. Microscopes help magnify these organisms. Two common kinds of microscopes are light microscopes and electron microscopes. In a light microscope, light passes through one or more lenses to produce an enlarged image of an object. An electron microscope forms an image of an object by using a beam of electrons to magnify extremely small objects.

Sterile Technique Scientists who study cells need to be able to grow cells in a controlled setting. Because bacteria live everywhere on Earth, scientists must use sterile technique when growing cells. Sterile technique is a method of keeping unwanted microorganisms out of a lab to minimize the risk of contamination. The tools of sterile technique include an autoclave for sterilizing equipment, sterilized dishes and pipets, a laminar-flow hood, and latex gloves.

Collecting Data Remotely As electronic technology has advanced, more tools have become available for scientists to use. Remote tracking devices to attach to released animals, data collected from satellites, and technology based on the global positioning system (GPS) have enabled scientists to conduct investigations that would have been impossible just a few decades ago.

❯ **Reading Check** *When might sterile technique be used in a lab?*

SI the International System of Units, which is the measurement system that is accepted by scientists worldwide

ACADEMIC VOCABULARY

technique a way of doing something

SCiLINKS.
www.scilinks.org
Topic: History of
Standard Units
Code: HX80747

Figure 7 Using proper safety equipment is necessary during every scientific investigation. For example, this scientist must use a special suit to protect his skin from the extreme heat coming from this volcano vent.

Safety

As you can see in **Figure 7,** studying science is exciting, but it can also be dangerous. ❯ **Scientists must use caution when working in the lab or doing field research to avoid dangers such as chemical burns, exposure to radiation, exposure to infectious disease, animal bites, or poisonous plants.** Here are some guidelines for working safely in the lab:

- Listen carefully to your teacher, and follow all instructions.
- Read your lab procedure carefully before beginning the lab.
- Do not take any shortcuts in your lab procedure.
- Always wear your safety goggles and any other needed safety equipment when working in the lab.
- Measure chemicals precisely.
- Never taste or smell any materials or chemicals that you use in a lab unless your teacher instructs you to do so.
- Do not use any damaged or defective equipment.
- Keep your lab area clean and free from clutter.
- When you place something onto the lab bench, make sure that the object sits securely on the bench and will not fall or tip over.
- Pay attention to where you are walking.
- If you are working outside, be aware of your surroundings. Avoid poisonous plants and animals that live in the area. Wear sunscreen and a hat that shades your neck and ears.

Accidents If an accident does occur, remain calm. Make sure that you are safe and that no one else is in danger. Then, inform your teacher right away. Follow all of the instructions that your teacher gives you. Know the location and proper operation of all lab safety equipment before it is needed. A review of lab safety equipment before labs begin can save valuable time if an accident happens in your lab. For more information about lab safety and how to respond to accidents in the lab, read *Lab Safety* at the front of this book.

❯ **Reading Check** *List at least five actions that you can take in the laboratory to ensure your safety.*

Section 3 Review

❯ **KEY IDEAS**

1. **Explain** why scientists use SI units for measurement.
2. **Describe** two kinds of microscopes.
3. **Summarize** the steps that you should take if an accident occurs in the lab.

CRITICAL THINKING

4. **Inferring Conclusions** In general, measurement systems that are based on powers of 10 are the easiest for people to use. Infer why these systems are easiest to use.
5. **Analyzing Information** Why is reading the lab procedure before starting an experiment considered an important part of lab safety?

MATH SKILLS

6. **Performing Conversions** A scientist pours 3.48 milliliters (mL) of hydrochloric acid into a beaker. How many liters of hydrochloric acid did the scientist pour into the beaker?

What Is Biology?

Key Ideas	Key Terms	Why It Matters
❯ What are some of the branches of biology? ❯ What are seven characteristics that all living things share?	biology reproduction cell heredity homeostasis evolution metabolism	All living things on Earth are tied together by common traits and rely on one another for their common survival.

The giant sequoia shown in **Figure 8** is very different from the man standing below it. But both organisms have much in common. Studying living organisms is what the science of biology is all about.

The Study of Life

Biology is the study of life. Life is extremely diverse. It would be impossible for one person to become an expert in all aspects of biology, so scientists specialize. There are many branches of biology.
❯ **Biology includes biochemistry, ecology, cell biology, genetics, evolutionary theory, microbiology, botany, zoology, and physiology.** Biochemistry is the study of the chemistry of life. Ecology is the study of how organisms interact with each other and with their environment. The study of life on the cellular level is called cell biology. Genetics is the study of how organisms pass traits to their offspring. Evolutionary theory is the study of changes in types of organisms over time. The study of microscopic organisms is called microbiology. The study of plants is called botany. Zoology is the study of animals. Physiology is the study of the human body. As you read, you will learn about each of these fields. You will also have the opportunity to practice techniques that are used in careers in each of these fields.

biology the scientific study of living organisms and their interactions with the environment

Figure 8 Both the man and the sequoia tree that he is standing on are living organisms.
❯ Which branches of biology would study both humans and trees?

Properties of Life

All living organisms share certain properties. ❯ **The seven properties of life are cellular organization, homeostasis, metabolism, responsiveness, reproduction, heredity, and growth.** Life is characterized by the presence of all seven properties at some stage in an organism's life.

Cellular Organization A cell is the smallest unit capable of all life functions. A **cell** is a highly organized, tiny structure that is enclosed in a thin covering called a *membrane*. The basic structure of cells is the same in all organisms.

Why It Matters

Biology in the Wild

REAL WORLD

A biologist who studies organisms in their natural habitat is called a field biologist. These scientists study life in every kind of habitat. They may tag polar bears near the North Pole or climb into caves deep underground. By studying organisms in their natural habitat, field biologists can learn about life in the wild.

Hanging Around for Science

Sometimes, field biologists hang around in interesting places. Scientists who study the biology of cave-dwelling organisms are called speleologists. This scientist is hanging over a cave called the Well of the Birds. This sinkhole is more than 200 meters deep and growing.

Life Under Water This marine biologist has to go underwater to study manatees in their habitat. Manatees are an endangered species. Scientists hope that by learning about manatees, we may be able to prevent the extinction of this species.

Research Use library or Internet sources to learn more about jobs that are available for field biologists.

Homeostasis All living organisms must maintain a stable internal environment in order to function properly. The maintenance of stable internal conditions in spite of changes in the external environment is called **homeostasis.**

Metabolism Living things carry out many chemical reactions in order to obtain energy. **Metabolism** is the sum of all of the chemical reactions carried out in an organism. Almost all of the energy used by living things originally comes from sunlight. Plants, algae, and some bacteria capture this energy and use it to make molecules. These molecules serve as the source of energy, or food, for other organisms.

Responsiveness In addition to maintaining a stable internal environment, living organisms also respond to their external environment. Plants bend toward sunlight. Birds fluff their feathers to insulate their bodies during cold weather. Students, shown in **Figure 9,** also respond to their environment.

Reproduction Most living things can reproduce. **Reproduction** is the process by which organisms make more of their own kind from one generation to the next. Because no organism lives forever, reproduction is an essential part of life.

Heredity When an organism reproduces, it passes on its own traits to its offspring in a process known as **heredity.** Heredity is the reason that children tend to look like their parents. Inherited characteristics change over generations. This process is called **evolution.**

Growth All living organisms grow . Some one-celled organisms only grow briefly, during the time that they are reproducing. Other living things, like the giant sequoia, grow for thousands of years and reach an enormous size. As organisms grow, many change. This process is called *development.* Frogs begin as eggs, develop into tadpoles, and eventually develop into frogs. Development differs from evolution because development refers to change in a single individual during that individual's life.

❯ Reading Check *How is heredity related to evolution?*

Figure 9 These students are responding to the rain by using raincoats. ❯ Can you think of a way that you have responded to your environment today?

---

cell in biology, the smallest unit that can perform all life processes

homeostasis the maintenance of a constant internal state in a changing environment

metabolism the sum of all chemical processes that occur in an organism

reproduction the process of producing offspring

heredity the passing of genetic traits from parent to offspring

evolution the process of change by which new species develop from preexisting species over time

---

Section 4 Review

❯ KEY IDEAS

1. **Explain** what biology is.
2. **Describe** nine fields that are part of the science of biology.
3. **Name** the basic unit of life.
4. **Discuss** the seven properties all living organisms share.
5. **Define** homeostasis.

CRITICAL THINKING

6. **Recognizing Verifiable Facts** If you find an object that seems alive, how might you determine if the object is indeed an organism?
7. **Elaborating** Give an example of one way that you are interdependent on another type of organism.
8. **Analyzing Information** Relate five of the characteristics of life to an organism familiar to you.

ALTERNATIVE ASSESSMENT

9. **Interview a Biologist** Choose a field of biology that interests you. Locate a biologist working in that field, and conduct an interview by phone or e-mail. Ask the biologist how he or she became interested in his or her field and what the scientist's work is like. Report your findings to the class.

Chapter 1 **Lab**

Objectives

❯ Express measurements in SI units.

❯ Read a thermometer.

❯ Measure liquid volume by using a graduated cylinder.

❯ Measure mass by using a balance.

❯ Determine the density (mass-to-volume ratio) of two liquids.

Materials

- graduated cylinder, 100 mL
- sand, light colored, 75 mL
- cups, plastic, (2)
- sand, dark colored, 75 mL
- thermometers, Celsius, alcohol filled (2)
- gloves, heat resistant
- ring stand or lamp support
- light source
- stopwatch or clock
- balance
- corn oil, 25 mL
- water, 25 mL
- cup, clear plastic
- graph paper

Safety

SI Units

Most scientists use SI units for all of the measurements that they take. In this lab, you will practice making measurements in SI units.

Procedure

Measure Sand Temperature

❶ In your lab report, prepare a data table similar to the table below.

❷ Put on safety goggles, gloves, and a lab apron. Using a graduated cylinder, measure 75 mL of light-colored sand, and pour it into one of the small plastic cups. Repeat this procedure with the dark-colored sand and another plastic cup.

❸ Level the sand by placing the cup on your desk and sliding the cup back and forth. Insert one thermometer into each cup.

❹ Using a ring stand or lamp support, position the lamp approximately 9 cm from the top of the sand, as shown in the figure. Make sure that the lamp is evenly positioned between the two cups.

❺ Before turning on the lamp, record in your data table the initial temperature of each cup of sand.

❻ ◈ CAUTION: **Wear heat-resistant gloves when handling the lamp. The lamp will become very hot and may burn you.** Note the time or start the stopwatch when you turn on the lamp. The lamp will become hot and warm the sand. Check the temperature of the sand in each container at 1-minute intervals for 10 minutes. In your data table, record the temperature of the sand after each minute.

Sand Temperature		
	Temperature (degrees C)	
Time (min)	Dark-colored sand	Light-colored sand
Start		
1		
2		
3		
4		
5		

Compare the Density of Oil and Water

7 In your lab report, prepare a data table similar to the Density of Two Liquids table.

8 Label one clean plastic cup "Oil," and label another "Water." Using a balance, measure the mass of each plastic cup, and record the value in your data table.

9 Put on an apron. Using a clean graduated cylinder, measure 25 mL of corn oil, and pour it into the plastic cup labeled "Oil." Using a balance, measure the mass of the plastic cup containing the corn oil, and record the mass in your data table.

10 Repeat step 9 with water and the plastic cup labeled "Water."

11 To find the mass of the oil, subtract the mass of the empty cup from the mass of the cup and the oil together.

12 To find the density of the oil, divide the mass of the oil by the volume of the oil, as shown in the equation below.

$$Density\ of\ oil = \frac{mass\ of\ oil}{volume\ of\ oil} = \underline{\hspace{1cm}}\ g/mL$$

13 Repeat steps 11 and 12 to find the mass and density of water.

14 Combine the oil and water in the clear cup, and record your observations in your lab report.

15 Clean up your materials according to your teacher's instructions. Wash your hands before leaving the lab.

Density of Two Liquids

a. Mass of empty oil cup	g
b. Mass of empty water cup	g
c. Mass of cup and oil	g
d. Mass of cup and water	g
e. Volume of oil	25 ml
f. Volume of water	25 ml
Calculating Actual Mass	
Oil Item c – Item a =	g
Water Item d – Item b =	g
g. Density of oil	g/ml
h. Density of water	g/ml

Analyze and Conclude

1. Graphing Data Use graph paper or a graphing calculator to graph the data that you collected in the first part of the lab. Plot time on the *x*-axis and temperature on the *y*-axis.

2. SCIENTIFIC METHODS Interpreting Data Based on your graph, what is the relationship between color and heat absorption?

3. Inferring Conclusions How might the color of the clothes that you wear affect how warm you are on a sunny day?

4. SCIENTIFIC METHODS Making Systematic Observations In the second part of the lab, what did you observe when you combined the oil and water? Relate your observation to the densities that you calculated.

5. SCIENTIFIC METHODS Using Evidence to Make Explanations What could you infer about the value for the density of ice if you observe it floating in water?

Extensions

6. Understanding Relationships How would your calculated density values be affected if you misread the volume measurement on the graduated cylinder?

7. Experimental Design Pumice is a volcanic rock that has a density less than 1.00 g/cm^3. How would you prove this density if you did not have a balance to weigh the pumice? (Hint: The density of water is 1.00 g/cm^3.)

Key Ideas	Key Terms

1 The Nature of Science

> Scientific thought involves making observations, using evidence to draw conclusions, being skeptical about ideas, and being open to change when new discoveries are made.

> Science is governed by truths that are valid everywhere in the universe. These truths are called *universal laws*.

> Scientific investigations require ethical behavior.

> An understanding of science can help you take better care of your health, be a wiser consumer, and become a better-informed citizen.

skepticism (4)

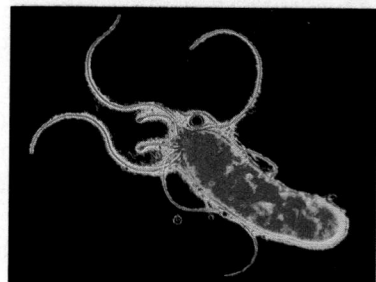

2 Scientific Methods

> Most scientific investigations begin with observations that lead to questions.

> Scientists can conduct controlled experiments and qualitative studies in order to test a hypothesis.

> The main difference between a theory and a hypothesis is that a hypothesis is a specific, testable prediction for a limited set of conditions and a theory is a general explanation for a broad range of data.

observation (10)
hypothesis (10)
experiment (11)
control group (11)
theory (13)

3 Tools and Techniques

> The International System of Units (SI) is used by all scientists because scientists need to share a common measurement system. SI is scaled in multiples of 10, which makes the system easy to use.

> In the lab, scientists always keep detailed and accurate notes and perform precise measurements. Many scientists also use specialized tools, such as microscopes, and specialized procedures, such as sterile technique.

> Scientists must use caution when working in the lab or doing field research to avoid dangers such as chemical burns, exposure to radiation, exposure to infectious disease, animal bites, or poisonous plants.

SI (14)

4 What Is Biology?

> Biology includes biochemistry, ecology, cell biology, genetics, evolutionary theory, microbiology, botany, zoology, and physiology.

> The seven properties of life are cellular organization, homeostasis, metabolism, responsiveness, reproduction, heredity, and growth.

biology (17)
cell (18)
homeostasis (19)
metabolism (19)
reproduction (19)
heredity (19)
evolution (19)

Chapter 1 Review

1. Hypothesis or Theory? Write a statement that summarizes the difference between a hypothesis and a theory.

2. Concept Mapping Make a concept map that outlines scientific investigations in biology. Try to include the following words: *biology, observation, communication, hypotheses, predictions, experiments,* and *theories.*

Using Key Terms

Use each of the following terms in a separate sentence.

3. *skepticism*

4. *control group*

For each pair of terms, explain how the meanings of the terms differ.

5. *hypothesis* and *theory*

6. *homeostasis* and *metabolism*

7. *reproduction* and *heredity*

Understanding Key Ideas

8. To support claims, scientists require
  a. evidence.
  c. technology.
  b. opinions.
  d. photographs.

9. Though scientists study the world from differing perspectives, what must all scientists take into account?
  a. universal laws
  b. animal behavior
  c. temperature differences
  d. the importance of biology

10. Which of the following observations is qualitative, described in words rather than numbers?
  a. surveying the size of the goose population
  b. observing the nocturnal behavior of coyote populations
  c. recording the date when goose migration begins every year
  d. counting the number of goose nests that are robbed of eggs in an area

11. What is true of all hypotheses?
  a. They are true.
  b. They are false.
  c. They are testable.
  d. They are indisputable.

12. In an experiment, what happens to the control group?
  a. It receives no experimental treatment.
  b. It receives experimental treatment last.
  c. It receives experimental treatment first.
  d. It receives more experimental treatments than the other groups.

13. Which of the following units of measure would be most appropriate for determining the mass of an apple?
  a. gram
  b. kilogram
  c. milligram
  d. centigram

14. How does a microscope help scientists observe objects?
  a. It measures objects.
  b. It magnifies images.
  c. It performs calculations.
  d. It stains transparent objects.

15. Some toads that live in a hot, dry environment bury themselves in the soil during the day. What characteristic of living things does this behavior describe?
  a. heredity
  c. metabolism
  b. reproduction
  d. responsiveness

Explaining Key Ideas

16. Summarize the four key steps to practicing good scientific thought.

17. Explain why the study of science is important.

18. Infer why scientists try to limit the number of independent variables in an experiment.

19. Identify 10 things that you can do to stay safe during scientific investigations.

Using Science Graphics

This diagram shows a breakdown of the types of municipal solid waste, by weight, generated in the United States. Use the chart and your knowledge of science to answer the following questions.

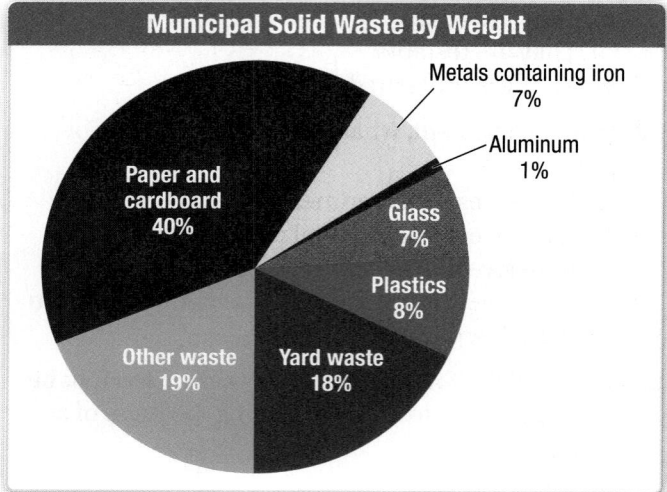

Municipal Solid Waste by Weight

Metals containing iron 7%
Aluminum 1%
Paper and cardboard 40%
Glass 7%
Plastics 8%
Yard waste 18%
Other waste 19%

20. According to the diagram, which makes up the greatest proportion of waste?
 a. paper and cardboard
 b. metals containing iron
 c. yard waste, glass, and plastics
 d. other waste

21. If each type of solid waste were recycled, which type would have the biggest impact on conserving trees?
 a. aluminum   **c.** plastics
 b. glass   **d.** paper and cardboard

22. Which of these types of waste could be turned into compost?
 a. glass
 b. plastics
 c. yard wastes
 d. metal containing iron

Critical Thinking

23. Forming Reasoned Opinions The law of conservation of matter states that matter cannot be created or destroyed. How does this universal law relate to biology?

24. Recognizing Relationships The development of science and technology is closely linked. Explain how the invention of the microscope led to the development of the sterile technique. List at least one other technology that most likely resulted from the invention of the microscope.

25. Inferring Relationships The most rigorous form of peer review is blind peer review, in which the scientists reviewing the work do not know the identity of the scientists who authored the work. Why might blind peer review be more rigorous than other forms of peer review?

Technology Skills

26. Computer Presentation Find out more about the differences between theories, laws, and hypotheses. Create a computer presentation that uses examples and illustrations to show the differences between each.

Methods of Science

27. Analyzing Methods Scientists collect both quantitative and qualitative data. Quantitative data can be expressed in numbers. Qualitative data must be expressed in words. If you were observing a pride of lions, what are some examples of quantitative and qualitative data that you could collect?

Alternative Assessment

28. Homeostasis Display Research five ways that your body maintains homeostasis. Then, create a poster-board display that illustrates how each of these responses functions.

Math Skills

29. Estimating The diagram below shows the relationship between the Fahrenheit and the Celsius temperature scales. If the air temperature is 60°F, estimate the air temperature in Celsius.

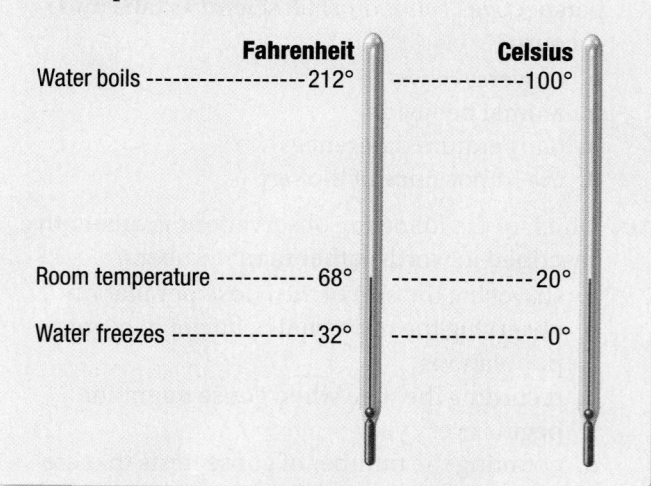

	Fahrenheit	Celsius
Water boils	212°	100°
Room temperature	68°	20°
Water freezes	32°	0°

Standardized Test Prep

Science Concepts

1. A scientist is investigating a new treatment for a disease that affects thousands of people. Many people with this disease volunteer to be part of the study. Which of the following is an ethical concern that the scientist must address before conducting the study?

   A The scientist must ensure that the treatment will be effective.

   B The scientist must ensure that the study's results will not be shared with other scientists.

   C The scientist must inform the volunteers about the potential dangers of participating in the study.

   D The scientist must demonstrate the treatment on him or herself.

2. Which of the following is an example of scientific skepticism?

   F A scientist investigates how a universal law affects many fields of study.

   G A scientist falsely claims to have discovered a cure for diabetes.

   H A scientist conducts an experiment that supports the conclusions of another scientist.

   J A scientist questions another scientist's conclusions and develops an experiment to test an alternative hypothesis.

Math Skills

3. Calculate The strength of a light microscope is determined by multiplying the strength of the eyepiece by the strength of the objective lens. Light microscopes often have several objective lenses. Suppose that a microscope has an eyepiece that magnifies by 10 and two objective lenses, one that magnifies by 10 and one that magnifies by 40. Calculate the total magnification for each objective lens used with the eyepiece.

Using Science Graphics

Use the diagram to answer the following question.

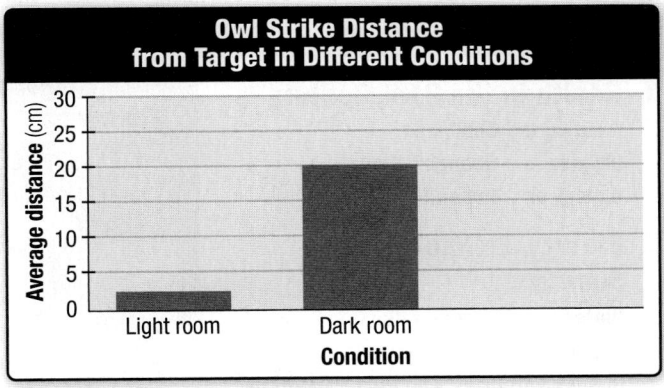

4. In which room does an owl strike a target most accurately?

   A dark room   **C** heated room

   B light room   **D** dark and lighted room

Use the diagram to answer the following question.

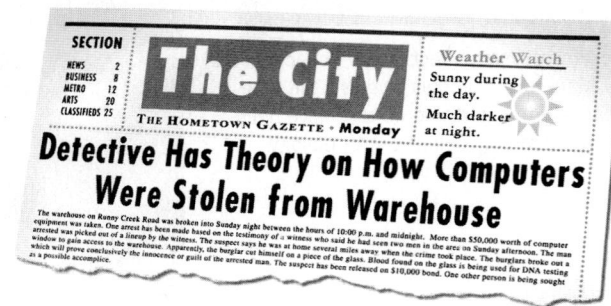

5. Which of the following words most accurately reflects the use of the term *theory* in the newspaper headline above?

   F law   **H** hypothesis

   G fact   **J** experiment

Writing Skills

6. Evaluating Statements Write a short paragraph that expresses your opinion on the following statement: "The lengthy drug-approval process costs hundreds of lives every year. Doctors have a moral obligation to provide potentially life-saving drugs to terminally ill patients, even if the drugs have not been scientifically tested."

Chapter 2
Applications of Biology

Preview

1 Health in the 21st Century
Meeting the Challenge
Disease in a Changing World
Biology and Human Potential

2 Biology, Technology, and Society
Biotechnology Around Us
Applications of Biological Research
Biology, Forensics, and Public Safety
The Ethics of Biotechnology

3 Biology and the Environment
A Lost World
Technology in Environmental Science
Citizen Scientists

Why It Matters

Biological research affects many aspects of our lives. Many of the products we use, the food we eat, and the medicine we take have been improved through applications of biology.

A robotic instrument in your blood vessels—is this possible? Not yet, but someday doctors may be able to use tiny robots to fix problems inside your body.

This tiny instrument has captured a disease-ridden cell and is destroying it. Though this technology does not exist yet, it may be developed in the near future.

When biologists and engineers work together to solve problems that affect our lives, amazing inventions can result.

InquiryLab

⏱ 15 min

Artificial Shark Skin

Shark skin contains small channels that offer paths that water easily flows through around a shark's body. With reduced water resistance, the animal moves more quickly—a quality that competitive swimmers desire.

Procedure

1. Examine a **prepared slide of shark skin** under low power on a **microscope.**

2. Switch to higher magnification. Move through the entire depth of the field. Vary the fine focus in order to examine the full depth of the specimen.

3. Select several overlapping scales. Sketch their pattern.

4. Observe a **swatch of Fastskin® fabric** used in the manufacture of competitive swimsuits. Compare this fabric to the shark skin.

Analysis

1. **Propose** how the arrangement of scales produces channels in the shark skin.

2. **Describe** how the Fastskin® fabric resembles the shark skin.

3. **Explain** how the Fastskin® might give an advantage to swimmers.

READING TOOLBOX

These reading tools can help you learn the material in this chapter. For more information on how to use these and other tools, see **Appendix: Reading and Study Skills.**

Using Words

Word Parts You can tell a lot about a word by taking it apart and examining its prefix, root, and suffix.

Your Turn Use the table to hypothesize the meanings of the following words.

1. *biometrics*
2. *genetics*
3. *biome*
4. *genome*

Word Parts		
Part	**Type**	**Meaning**
bio-	prefix	life
metric	root	measurement
-ic	suffix	having to do with
-ome	suffix	all parts of something
gen	root	born; to become; to produce

Using Language

Predictions A prediction is a statement about what might happen in the future. You can identify predictions in the material you read by locating terms such as *might, impossible,* and *likely.*

Your Turn Read the following sentences, and write the author's prediction.

1. Scientists agree that the birdcall heard on the tape is likely a bird thought to be extinct.
2. With enough funding and effort, humans might travel to Mars one day.

Using FoldNotes

Three-Panel Flip Chart A three-panel flip chart is useful when you want to compare the characteristics of three topics. The three-panel flip chart can help you organize the characteristics of the three topics side by side under the flaps. Similarities and differences between the three topics can then be easily identified.

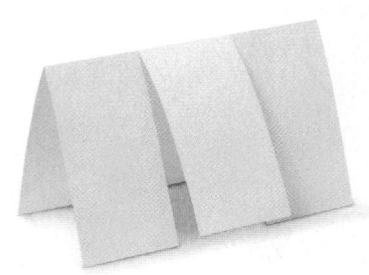

Your Turn Create a flip chart that compares areas of biological research such as epidemiology, genetics, and environmental science.

1. Fold a piece of paper in half from the top to the bottom.
2. Fold the paper in thirds from side to side. Then, unfold the paper so that you can see the three sections.
3. From the top of the paper, cut along each of the vertical fold lines to the fold in the middle of the paper. You now have three flaps.

Health in the 21st Century

Key Ideas	Key Terms	Why It Matters
❯ How are biologists working to eliminate major diseases that affect human populations? ❯ How has our understanding of the biological nature of disease changed over time? ❯ How might medical advances improve and extend human lives?	epidemiology vaccination genetics genome	Studying how diseases spread and developing ways to prevent and treat diseases can help reduce human suffering.

Biological research in the 20th century led to incredible advances in the prevention and treatment of disease. Yet, despite this progress, we still have more to learn and understand about how diseases affect humans. One of the great challenges of biology is to apply our understanding of the natural world to these issues.

Meeting the Challenge

❯ **Biologists combine research and data from many different fields of science to help reduce the spread of disease.** For example, biologist Rita Colwell has applied biological research, data from the ocean, and chemistry to reduce the number of outbreaks of cholera. Cholera is a disease that is caused by ingesting food or water that contains the cholera bacterium. This bacterium is a *pathogen,* that is, an agent that causes disease. Normally, a person must ingest millions of cholera bacteria to contract the disease. However, Colwell and her students found that tiny animals called *copepods* give the bacteria an advantage. The bacteria cluster around the mouthparts and egg casings of female copepods, which are shown in **Figure 1.** The copepods benefit from this behavior because the bacteria help burst the copepods' egg casings and release the copepod eggs. Then, the bacteria feed on the broken egg casings. Copepods feed on plankton—microscopic plant and animal life—in ocean water. When the amount of plankton in the water increases, the number of copepods (and, thus, bacteria) in the water increases and a cholera outbreak could occur.

❯ **Reading Check** *Why is the cholera bacterium a pathogen? (See the Appendix for answers to Reading Checks.)*

SCI*LINKS*
www.scilinks.org
Topic: Disease Prevention
Code: HX80414

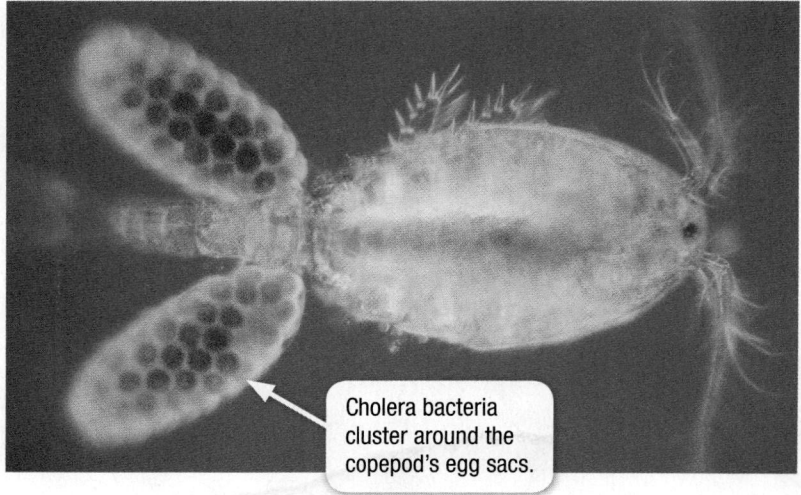

Cholera bacteria cluster around the copepod's egg sacs.

Figure 1 This micrograph illustrates two egg sacs (left, dark yellow) that are attached to a copepod (right, light yellow). The cholera bacteria is spread in part when the egg sacs rupture.

Figure 2 Colwell analyzed satellite data of the ocean to predict cholera outbreaks. In this image, warm colors such as red represent warmer water temperatures.

Figure 3 Today, many people use saris to filter water. This low-tech solution has greatly reduced the frequency of cholera outbreaks.

Solving the Riddle After Colwell established a link between cholera and copepods, she focused on some interesting data. Cholera outbreaks occurred regularly in water that tested negative for cholera bacteria. As a result, researchers assumed that the bacteria were not present in the water. However, Colwell was convinced that the bacteria existed in a form that could not be detected by the tests.

Colwell developed a more sensitive test that relied on the chemical properties of the bacteria's cell wall. She used this new test to detect cholera bacteria in water that had previously tested negative for the bacteria. This research suggested that cholera bacteria exist in a dormant state in cold water and that they become active when water temperature increases.

Using Models Colwell was able to predict cholera outbreaks with much greater accuracy because she now understood the role of water temperature in the cholera life cycle. She used satellite data, shown in **Figure 2,** to study the characteristics of ocean water and to predict cholera outbreaks. These predictions allowed health workers to anticipate cholera outbreaks and save lives. Even so, warm water is only one of many factors that play a role in cholera outbreaks.

A Low-Tech Solution Although researchers could predict cholera outbreaks, it was still difficult to prevent the spread of the disease. So Colwell focused on a low-tech solution to reduce the spread of cholera. Cholera bacteria attach to copepods that are much larger by comparison. The researchers demonstrated that the copepods could be filtered from water by using a folded piece of cotton cloth, such as a *sari*. A sari is a traditional garment worn by Indian woman and is shown in **Figure 3.** In some areas, these simple filters have reduced cases of cholera by almost 50%. Colwell's work is just one example of how biological research can make a huge difference in people's lives.

❯ **Reading Check** *Relate water temperature to cholera outbreaks.*

Model a Low-Tech Solution

Procedure

① Put on gloves, a lab apron, and goggles. Use an eyedropper to put a copepod from a copepod culture onto a well slide. Examine the specimen under a microscope. Record your observations.

② Stretch a piece of dark cotton cloth over the mouth of a beaker. Secure the fabric with a rubber band.

③ Pour the copepod culture onto the fabric. Examine a sample of the strained liquid under the microscope, and record your observations. Return any strained copepods and the culture solution to the culture jar.

④ Repeat steps 2 and 3, but replace the cloth with a funnel lined with filter paper.

Analysis

1. **Compare** the pore size of the cotton cloth with that of the filter paper.

2. **Determine** which filter(s) strains out the copepods.

3. **CRITICAL THINKING** **Inferring Relationships** From your observation, is the filter with the smallest pore size the most practical to use for obtaining drinking water? Explain.

Disease in a Changing World

Rita Colwell's work is an example of **epidemiology**—the study of how diseases spread. ❯ As scientists learn more about the nature of disease, our ability to prevent and treat diseases has improved.

Disease "Conquered" by Biology In 1979, scientists announced that they had destroyed the smallpox virus. Smallpox is a disease that causes terrible scarring and even death. Vaccination, a technique first developed during the 1800s, played an important role in getting rid of smallpox. A **vaccination** is a medical procedure that allows a person to resist infection by a disease. During this procedure, genetic information from a dead or weakened pathogen is introduced into the body. As a result, the body's immune system "learns" to fight the pathogen. Today, the development of vaccinations and global health programs have nearly succeeded in getting rid of many other diseases.

New Insights into Disease Discoveries in the field of genetics have produced many new tools to study and treat diseases that are caused by abnormalities in a person's genes. **Genetics** is the science of heredity and the study of how traits are passed on to offspring. Genetics research will benefit greatly from discoveries made by the Human Genome Project. In 2003, the project finished sequencing the entire human genome. A **genome** is the complete set of genetic information for an organism. Now, researchers can begin to study single genes in order to understand their role in genetic diseases.

❯ **Reading Check** *How do vaccination programs prevent diseases?*

Predictions Scientists use observations to make predictions. Make a list of the predictions in this section and the hypotheses that they address.

epidemiology (EP uh DEE mee AHL uh jee) the study of the distribution of diseases in populations and the study of factors that influence the occurrence and spread of disease

vaccination (VAK suh NAY shuhn) the administration of treated microorganisms into humans or animals to induce an immune response

genetics (juh NET iks) the science of heredity and of the mechanisms by which traits are passed from parents to offspring

genome (JEE NOHM) the complete genetic material contained in an individual or species

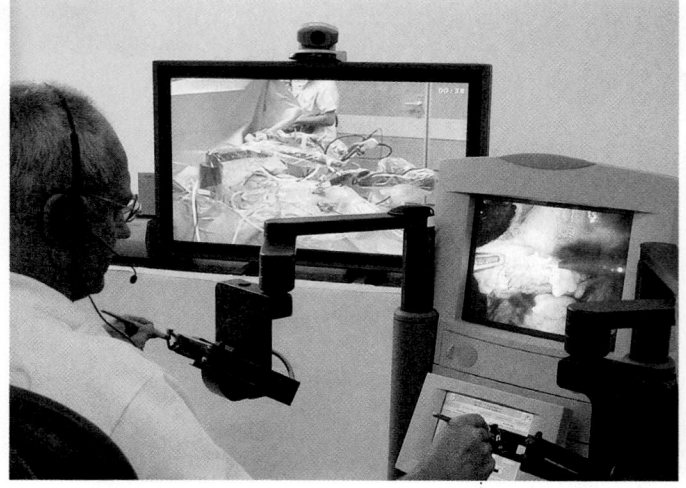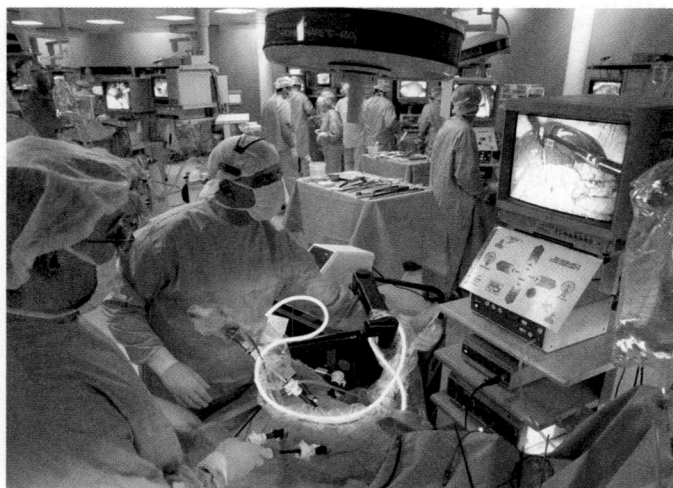

Figure 4 Advances in battlefield medicine include remote surgery. The doctor on the left is performing a surgery from a remote site. The surgery is aided by nurses, such as those on the right.

Biology and Human Potential

The length of human lives in developed countries has nearly doubled in the past century. ❯ **As our understanding of medicine, biology, and science in general increases, humans will live longer and healthier lives.**

Assistive Technologies People who have injuries, diseases, or disabilities can use assistive technology products to help them accomplish everyday tasks. These products include bionic limbs and computer interfaces, and can help a person speak, see, or hear. They can also help a person coordinate his or her movements.

Battlefield Medicine Battlefield medicine is a new field of medicine which includes remote surgery, as shown in **Figure 4.** This field also includes new products designed for use in battle. For example, heavy blood loss is a common cause of death in war zones. Researchers have developed a bandage that can stop the flow of blood from serious wounds in a short period of time, before massive blood loss occurs. This <u>device</u> might eventually be used in hospitals to treat patients with gunshot wounds and other injuries.

❯ **Reading Check** *Give an example of an assistive technology.*

ACADEMIC VOCABULARY

device a piece of equipment made for a specific use

Section 1 Review

❯ **KEY IDEAS**

1. **Describe** ways in which biologists are "meeting the challenge" to reduce the spread of diseases.

2. **Describe** how our understanding of the nature of disease has changed over time.

3. **Explain** how advances in biology have improved human potential.

CRITICAL THINKING

4. **Forming Hypotheses** Rita Colwell's success in tracking cholera outbreaks was due to her open-minded approach to the available data. What were her assumptions, and how did they differ from assumptions of other scientists? Explain your answer.

5. **Expressing an Opinion** What is the future of battlefield medicine? Explain your answer.

WRITING FOR SCIENCE

6. **Writing an Essay** Write an essay that explains your thoughts on why humans would be able to live longer, healthier lives as our understanding of biology increases. Include examples of technologies that would enable humans to live longer lives.

Biology, Technology, and Society

Key Ideas	Key Terms	Why It Matters
❯ What is one way that genetic engineering affects our lives? ❯ How has biotechnology provided new tools for scientists to understand biological processes? ❯ How are biological factors used to verify an individual's identity and to ensure public safety? ❯ What ethical issues are raised by the use of biotechnology?	genetic engineering biometrics	Understanding the potential applications of biotechnology will help you make ethical decisions about its use.

What do hook-and-loop fasteners, a database of fingerprints, and a pet fish that glows in the dark have in common? They are all examples of how biological research affects society.

Biotechnology Around Us

Biotechnology affects many aspects of our lives, including our food sources. Genetic engineering is one of the most common examples of biotechnology. **Genetic engineering** is a technology in which the genetic material of a living cell is changed. ❯ **In agriculture, genetic engineering is used to create crops that yield more product or are resistant to pests.** For example, **Figure 5** shows a genetically modified type of corn called Bt corn. Bt corn has been altered to contain a gene from a naturally occurring soil bacterium called *Bacillus thuringiensis*. This gene allows the corn to make a toxin that kills a crop pest called the European corn borer. The use of Bt corn has raised crop yields and lowered the amount of pesticides that farmers use to control European corn borers.

genetic engineering (juh NET ik EN juh NIR ing) a technology in which the genome of a living cell is modified for medical or industrial use

Figure 5 The use of Bt corn reduces the amount of pesticides that farmers use to control pests. However, its use is controversial.

QuickLab

⏱ 15 min

Biomimetic Engineering

Bony fishes have a swim bladder that controls their buoyancy. This structure fills with gas to make the fish more buoyant. To become less buoyant, gas is released from the bladder. Engineers modeled submarines after this principle. In this lab, you will model a swim bladder and relate its structure and function to that of a submarine.

Procedure

❶ Fill a **basin** about two-thirds full with **water**. Use **tape** to secure a **metal spoon** to a **cup**. Put the cup in the water (the cup should sink).

❷ Link **three straws** together to form a long tube. Tape the straw "pipe" inside the mouth of a **large balloon**.

❸ Secure the balloon in the cup, and put the cup in the water. Blow into the straws to add air to the balloon.

Analysis

1. **Describe** what happens when you blow air into the model bladder and when you let air escape.

2. **Assess** how the volume of the inflated balloon affects the overall buoyancy of the model.

3. **CRITICAL THINKING** **Relating Concepts** What structures of the swim bladder relate to the parts of a submarine?

ACADEMIC
VOCABULARY

process a set of steps, events, or changes

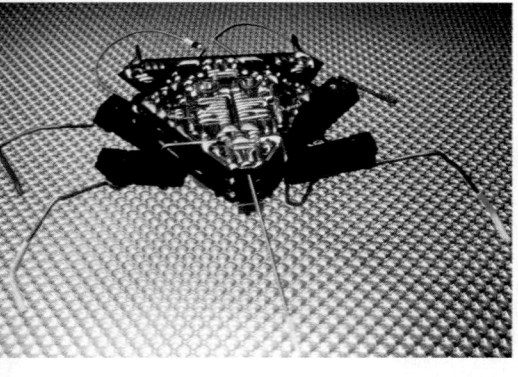

Figure 6 Nanotechnology often takes the form of tiny robotic items that look like animals. This robot was formed from a computer microchip.

Applications of Biological Research

Biotechnology is also used to produce medicines, to perform scientific research, and to develop new materials. ❯ **Tools such as genetic engineering, nanotechnology, and computer models have expanded the potential applications of biological research.**

Biotechnology and Scientific Research Scientists often use genetic engineering tools to study biological processes. For example, Nigel Atkinson is a biologist who studies the effects of alcohol and other compounds on fruit flies. To do this, he uses genetically modified fruit flies to determine if certain genes help the flies form resistance to the effects of alcohol. This research may help other scientists develop new methods of treating alcoholism in humans.

Scientists also take advantage of gene technology to make vaccines and medical products such as insulin. Insulin is a hormone that controls the metabolism of sugar as well as carbohydrates, fats, and proteins from the diet. Some people who have diabetes must take regular doses of insulin because their bodies cannot produce enough of the hormone. Before genetic engineering, insulin was obtained from pigs and cows. Now, it is made from bacteria that are changed so that they contain the human gene that produces insulin.

Nanotechnology Biological research has also gained from advances in nanotechnology. One application of this technology is shown in **Figure 6**. Nanotechnology is the science of creating products by changing individual atoms or molecules. For example, the release of a drug can be controlled by putting the drug compound inside a shell of atoms. Nanotechnology can also help repair damaged body tissue. For example, researchers are developing a very small, biodegradable template that may help damaged brain cells grow back after an injury.

Biomolecular Materials Some cells and organisms have amazing ways of putting together organic compounds, or *biomolecules.* These methods inspire scientists to develop new, synthetic, biomolecular materials. For example, new types of ceramics are based on the process that clams use to form their own shells. Scientists are trying to create a stronger glue by studying how bacteria stick to rocks in fast-moving streams. Artificial spider silk is being used to make a new lightweight, strong fabric.

Biomimetics New products are also based on larger-scale biological structures and processes. *Biomimetics* (BIE oh muh ME tiks) is the application of biological processes and systems to solve design and engineering problems. Hook-and-loop fasteners, originally made by the company Velcro®, are one of the most familiar biomimetic products. These fasteners were modeled after prickly burrs that attach to animal fur or clothing. Another example is the submarine, which was modeled after the swimbladder of bony fishes. Studies of animal eyes have helped astronomers design new telescopes such as the lobster-eye telescope, which collects and focuses X-rays. Other amazing products are being developed every day!

Adapting Tools and Methods Tools and methods that are developed for one purpose are often adapted for other uses. For example, computerized axial tomography (CAT) scanning technology was originally developed to help doctors make detailed three-dimensional images of internal organs. Biologists can now use CAT scans to create models of fossils and of living organisms. **Figure 7** shows one of these kinds of models. Now, scientists can study specimens without dissecting them.

❯ **Reading Check** *How is the lobster-eye telescope unique from other types of telescopes?*

READING TOOLBOX

Word Parts Using your knowledge of word parts, write a definition in your own words for *nanotechnology, biotechnology,* and *biomolecules.*

Figure 7 Digital scanning technology combines CAT scans and digital imaging to create three-dimensional models of organisms.

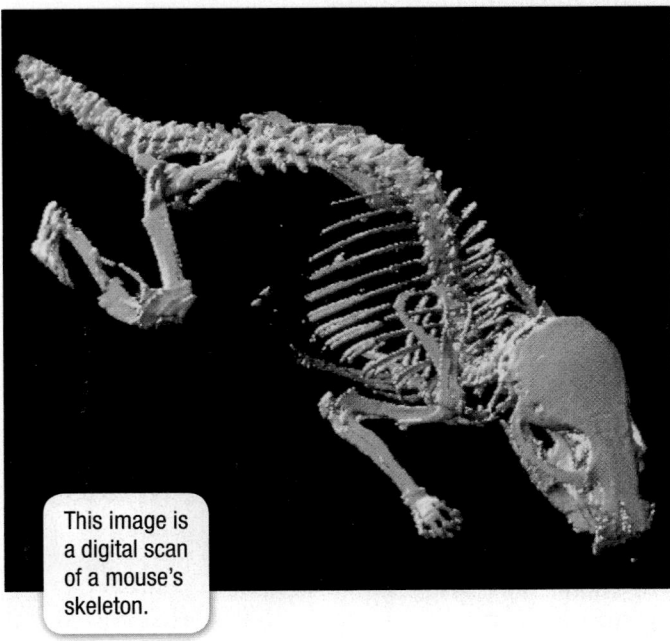

This image is a digital scan of a mouse's skeleton.

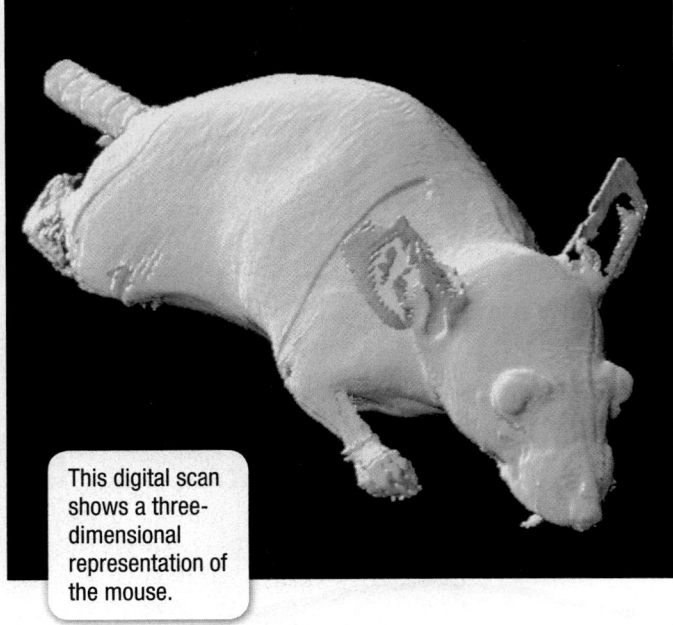

This digital scan shows a three-dimensional representation of the mouse.

Biology, Forensics, and Public Safety

Biological research is also used in criminal investigations and to make sure that the public is safe. ❯ **Because biological factors such as fingerprints, iris patterns, and genetic material are unique, they can be used to identify individuals.** The use of biological traits to determine a person's identity is called **biometrics.**

Two Types of Fingerprinting Fingerprints are one of the most common forms of evidence used in criminal investigations. For example, the FBI fingerprint database is the largest database of its kind in the world. A fingerprint scanner is shown in **Figure 8.** Another method of identification is called *DNA fingerprinting.* A DNA fingerprint has nothing to do with a person's actual finger but rather is a unique pattern of DNA that represents the total of a person's genetic material. Evidence such as hair or skin cells that are left behind at a crime scene can be identified by using DNA fingerprinting.

Other Forms of Biometric Identification Improved computer processing power has led to the development of many new biometric technologies. For example, **Figure 8** shows examples of different iris patterns. Iris scans are very fast and reliable, and are as unique as a fingerprint. These scans can also detect changes in a person's iris. Other software programs can tell the difference between human faces, or can analyze brain waves and speech patterns.

❯ **Reading Check** *What is DNA fingerprinting, and how is it used to identify someone?*

biometrics (BIE oh ME triks) the statistical analysis of biological data; the measurement and analysis of unique physical or behavioral characteristics to verify the identity of a person

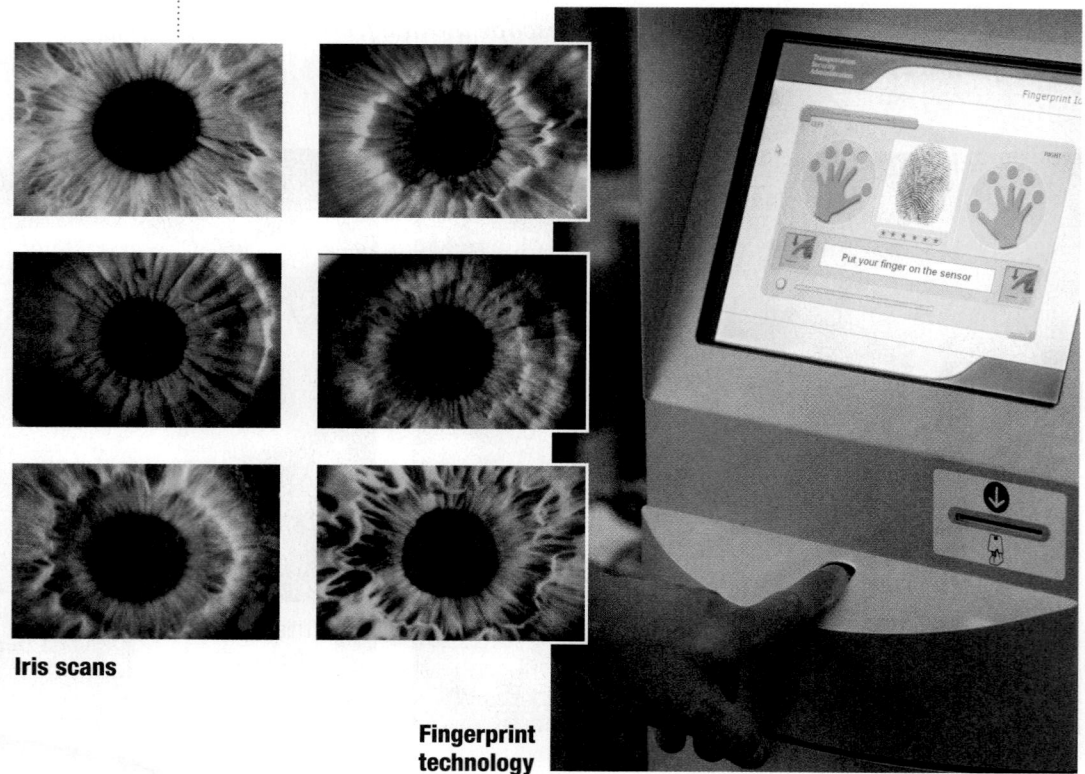

Figure 8 Iris scans (left) show ridges, strings of tissue, and tiny pits in the iris. These features make every person's iris unique. The fingerprint scan (right) is also used to identify people.

Iris scans

Fingerprint technology

Preventing Bioterrorism Biologists and other scientists are working to develop new ways to detect and prevent the use of biological agents by terrorists. After the events of September 11, 2001, people have become more concerned about the possibility of a bioterrorist attack. Drills such as the one shown in **Figure 9** help people prepare for such an event. Handheld probes have been developed that can quickly detect common biological agents. Other research focuses on making vaccines and new antibiotic treatments for victims of anthrax or other biological weapons.

The Ethics of Biotechnology

Although biotechnology has great potential to improve our lives, its use also raises many ethical concerns. ❯Advances in biotechnology raise ethical concerns that must be addressed, both by individuals and by society.

Manipulating DNA People have many concerns about genetic engineering. Some people worry that putting genetically engineered organisms into an ecosystem could harm the environment. Others worry that eating food that is made from genetically modified organisms might be harmful to their health. Some people object to the idea of changing an organism's DNA, or to techniques such as cloning, or to the use of human stem cells in research. Others feel that limiting the kinds of scientific research that might save lives and cure diseases is unethical.

Personal Security Putting biometric identification methods to use also raises ethical issues. Many people feel that databases of personal, biological information represents an invasion of privacy. The concern is that governments or other organizations could use this information improperly.

❯ **Reading Check** *What are some ethical concerns faced by society that relate to genetically modified organisms?*

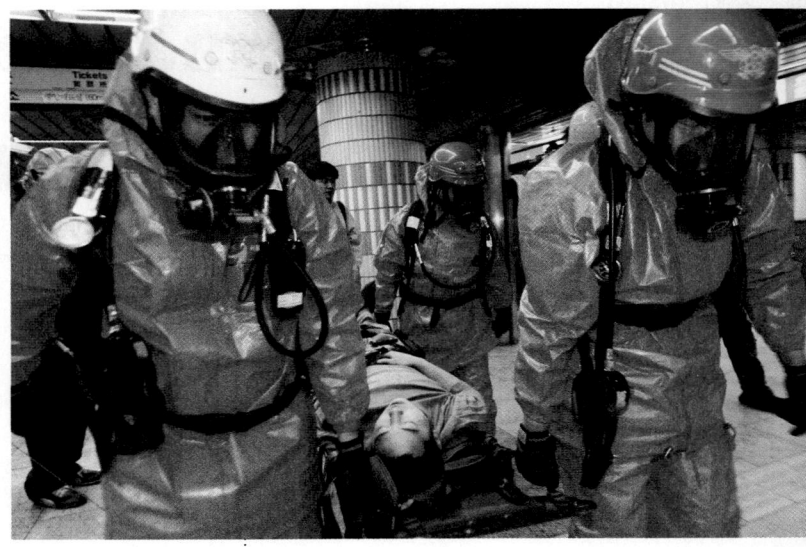

Figure 9 Bioterrorism drills such as this one can help populations prepare for bioterrorist attacks.

SC/*LINKS*®
www.scilinks.org
Topic: Biological Weapons
Code: HX81692

Section 2 Review

❯**KEY IDEA**

1. **Describe** briefly how genetic engineering has improved agricultural crops.
2. **Explain** how biotechnology research has affected modern life.
3. **Describe** the biological features that are considered to be unique to an individual's identity.

4. **State** an example of an ethical issue that is brought up by advances in biotechnology.

CRITICAL THINKING

5. **Applying Information** Explain how crime investigators use biometrics to determine who is and who is not the perpetrator of a crime.
6. **Applying Information** Why should both individuals and society address ethical concerns? Explain your reasoning.

ALTERNATIVE ASSESSMENT

7. **Product Design** Biomimetics is described as "the abstraction of good design from nature." What does *biomimetics* mean? Describe an example of the type of product that would exemplify the abstraction of good design from nature. Be specific in your example.

Key Ideas	Key Terms	Why It Matters
❯ How does biological research help protect the environment? ❯ How do new technologies help us study the environment? ❯ How do biologists rely on the contributions of community members to develop solutions for environmental problems?	ecology environmental science	Studying the environment will help us make wise choices about the conservation and protection of natural resources.

The study of the interactions of living organisms with one another and with their environment is called **ecology.** The study of ecology and the environment, or **environmental science,** is one of the most important applications of biology.

A Lost World

In February 2006, an international team of biologists announced an amazing discovery. In a mountainous region of western New Guinea, the researchers discovered a "lost world" that appeared untouched by humans. During just two weeks of fieldwork, the team discovered more than 40 species of plants and animals. **Figure 10** shows a few of the species that were discovered by the team.

The discovery of the lost world stresses the fact that parts of the world still exist that we know little about. Therefore, the need to study and protect these areas is very important. ❯ **Biological research helps us understand, value, and protect the environment. We learn how to protect the environment by learning more about what affects it.** The environment provides natural resources such as water, food, and energy sources that are vital to human societies and to all organisms. Biologists are working to protect areas such as the lost world in New Guinea and to find ways that Earth's resources can continue to meet the needs of growing human populations.

Figure 10 These photographs show the habitat of New Guinea and examples of two species that were recently discovered there.

This biologist is tracking the fish's behavior.

The mola is the largest bony fish in the world.

Figure 11 Biologists use satellite tagging to help protect the mola. ❯ **What information can you learn about a fish by tracking its location?**

Technology in Environmental Science

Biologists are using many new technologies to study the environment. ❯ **Tools such as satellite tagging, geographic information systems (GISs), and genetics are used to study and protect the environment.**

Satellite Tagging The scientist in **Figure 11** is part of a research team that is tracking the movements of molas, some of the largest fish in the world. In this study, molas are tagged with a transmitter that sends data about the fish's movements to a satellite. The data will help the team understand the mola's behavior, such as its role in ocean food webs. By keeping track of individual fish, the team also hopes to find out if the molas are overfished. Satellite tagging is used in many other kinds of wildlife studies, such as to track polar bears and sea turtles. This technology gives scientists the information they need to plan conservation strategies.

Geographic Information Systems Satellite data can be used in computer modeling programs called *geographic information systems* (GIS). A GIS is a powerful tool in environmental research because it allows biologists to compare different kinds of data. For example, mola researchers could use a GIS to map the relationship between ocean temperature, the location of food sources, and the movement of the mola. A GIS also allows researchers to have access to data from many different studies so that they can work together.

Genetic Tools Scientists use genetics in many ways to study and protect the environment. For example, many species of endangered wildlife are killed for their body parts. Wildlife agents are using DNA fingerprinting to identify the remains of endangered animals and to identify the people who killed the animals. Biologists are also collecting DNA samples from endangered animals so that they can still be studied if the animals become extinct. In the future, DNA samples could possibly be used to clone extinct animals.

❯ **Reading Check** *How does a GIS allow scientists to work together?*

Three-panel Flip Chart Construct a three-panel flip chart to compare satellite tagging, GIS technology, and genetic tools in the study of environmental science.

ecology (ee KAHL uh jee) the study of the interactions of living organisms with one another and with their environment

environmental science (en VIE ruhn MENT'l) the study of the air, water, and land surrounding an organism or a community, which ranges from a small area to Earth's entire biosphere

Figure 12 The Raptor Rehabilitation Center is one of the most exciting projects that the students of the SWCC take part in. At the center, students help care for injured and orphaned birds of prey such as eagles, hawks, and owls.

ACADEMIC VOCABULARY

contribution a part given toward a whole

SCiLINKS.

www.scilinks.org
Topic: Environmental
Decision Making
Code: HX80525

Citizen Scientists

❯ **Biologists rely on the contributions of individuals and communities to help develop solutions for environmental problems.** These "citizen scientists" make valuable <u>contributions</u> to biological research and environmental conservation.

Environmental Clubs Many high schools have clubs that involve students in environmental research and conservation. For example, **Figure 12** shows members of the Southwestern High School Conservation Club (SWCC) in Somerset, Kentucky. SWCC's mission is to help other students understand the natural world through hands-on activities. This project is just one example of how biology students can become involved in environmental science.

Getting Involved If your school does not have an environmental club, find a teacher who can help you start one. Begin by working with other students to create a list of local environmental issues. Then, discuss some ways that your science class can learn more about these issues. You never know where environmental research can lead you, so keep an open mind and get involved!

❯ **Reading Check** *What is the mission of the SWCC?*

Section 3 Review

❯ KEY IDEA

1. **Evaluate** how the study of biology protects the environment.
2. **State** some tools that are used to protect the environment.
3. **Explain** why biologists rely on citizens to develop solutions to environmental problems.

CRITICAL THINKING

4. **Forming Reasoned Opinions** Why should biologists work on solutions that both protect fragile areas and support human needs? Explain your answer.
5. **Analyzing Methods** How can information gained from GIS technology aid environmental research? Explain your answer.

ALTERNATIVE ASSESSMENT

6. **New Species Table** Conduct Internet research on the "lost world" recently discovered by scientists in New Guinea. Make a table that includes at least five new species. Name each organism, and describe its characteristics. Why is the discovery of new species important in biology?

Bio Bots

BIOTECHNOLOGY

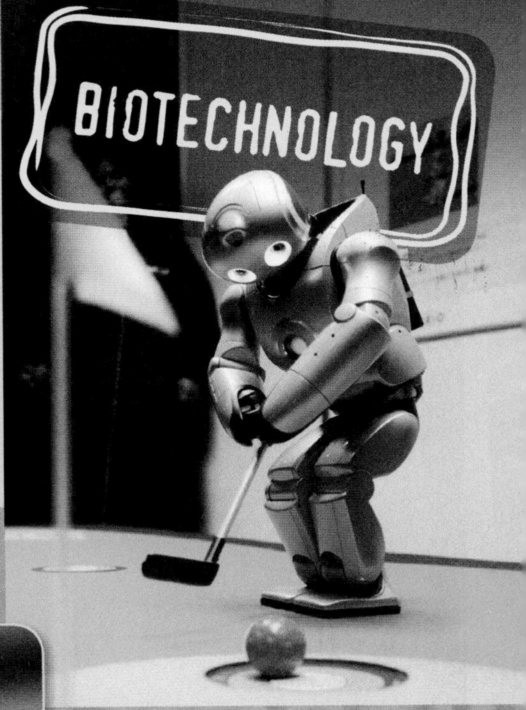

A robot that can play miniature golf? The boundary between living things and mechanical devices is not as clear as it used to be. These boundaries are being tested at every level, from biochemistry to intelligent behavior. Many fields of science and technology have been brought together to develop *bionics* (combinations of biological organisms and electronic devices) and *artificial intelligence* (computers that can learn and make decisions).

Bugs in the Machine

Insects are particularly popular subjects for bionic and artificial-intelligence work. One reason is because insects are easy to study in terms of both anatomy and behavior. Another reason is that many insects have "swarm" behaviors, which means that group behaviors emerge from the independent decisions of individuals. Scientists are using computer software to study and model these kinds of behaviors, and this software is being used in applications that range from environmental management to computer games.

Bug Bots A wide variety of "bug bots" have been developed. Some bug bots can be remotely controlled by insects, such as this roach.

Bionics Robotic limbs, such as this model of a human hand, almost eliminate the need for more traditional prosthetic limbs.

Quick Project Ask 10 people to define what being "alive" and being "intelligent" mean. (Do not tell them your reason for asking until after you record their answers.) Make a graphic organizer that compares the responses, and then write your own response.

Chapter 2 **Lab**

Objectives

❯ Observe the effect of sterile and nonsterile conditions on the growth of microbes.

❯ Make daily observations, and organize data.

❯ Hypothesize about the conditions under which microbes grow.

Materials

- test tubes, sterile (4)
- pencil, wax
- test-tube rack
- broth, nutrient
- rubber stoppers, sterile (4)
- water, sterilized
- test-tube holder
- gloves, heat-resistant
- water bath, boiling

Safety

Microbe Growth

To prepare for field research, Rita Colwell, a biologist, read that cholera, like other infectious diseases, was caused by a particular microbe. Thus, a person would need to be exposed to the disease-causing microbe to become infected with cholera. Colwell developed a low-tech method of sterilization, in which living organisms are removed, to prevent disease.

There are millions of different microbes. Not all of them cause disease, but many can interfere with scientific experiments. How do scientists keep laboratories free of such organisms? Sterile techniques, though common today, were not always common in the laboratory. Scientists such as Francesco Redi, Lazzaro Spallanzani, and Louis Pasteur demonstrated the importance of sterilization in preventing the growth of the microbes. In this lab, you will explore conditions under which microbes grow, and you will ask questions about the variables that might affect the microbes' growth.

Procedure

Prepare the Lab Materials

❶ Work with a partner. Review all safety procedures, including sterile techniques and safe handling of microbe cultures, with your teacher.

❷ ♦ ♦ ♦ Put on a lab apron, safety goggles, and disposable gloves.

❸ ♦ CAUTION: **Handle glass test tubes carefully.** Obtain four sterilized test tubes and a test-tube rack. Use a wax pencil to label the tubes "A" through "D," and place the tubes in the test-tube rack.

Observations of Microbe Growth								
	Tube Contents	**Day 1**	**Day 2**	**Day 3**	**Day 4**	**Day 5**	**Day 6**	**Day 7**
Tube A	sterile broth							
Tube B	broth exposed to air							
Tube C	exposed broth, then sterilized							
Tube D	sterilized water, exposed to air							

4. Fill tubes A, B, and C halfway with sterile nutrient broth solution.

5. Insert a sterile rubber stopper into the mouth of tube A. For now, leave the other broth-filled tubes unsealed.

6. Fill tube D halfway with sterilized water and add the tube to the test-tube rack.

7. Make a table for your observations of microbe growth. Observe the appearance of the broth in all four test tubes, and record your observations in the column labeled "Day 1."

8. Once you have recorded your observations, place the test-tube rack in an area where it will not be disturbed for 24 hours.

Make Observations on Day Two

9. Put on a lab apron, safety goggles, and disposable gloves.

10. Observe the appearance of the solution in each of the four test tubes. Record your observations in the column labeled "Day 2."

11. ◆ CAUTION: **Review the safety procedures associated with heating and electrical safety.** Put on heat-resistant gloves. With your teacher's guidance, use a test-tube holder to move tube C into a boiling water bath. Keep the test tube in the bath for 10 min.

12. Use the test tube holder to remove tube C from the water. Allow the tube to cool, and return it to the test-tube rack.

13. Insert a sterile rubber stopper into the mouth of tubes B, C, and D.

14. Place the rack with all four sealed test tubes in an area where it will not be disturbed for several days.

Make Continued Observations

15. Each day for the next 5 days, put on safety goggles and gloves. Carefully examine the contents of each tube. (Note: Make sure that the stopper remains in place, sealing the tube's opening.)

16. Write down your observations of the broth. Note any changes in the clarity of the solution. Also, look for changes in the appearance of the broth surface.

17. ◆ ◆ Clean up your materials according to your teacher's instructions. Wash your hands before leaving the lab.

Analyze and Conclude

1. **Summarizing Data** Did you observe any changes in the appearance of the tube contents over time? Describe your results for each of the four test tubes.

2. **Using Evidence to Make Explanations** If any of the tubes remained unchanged, explain why they did not support microbe growth.

3. SCIENTIFIC METHODS **Formulating Scientific Questions** Why was keeping all of the tubes sealed throughout the experiment essential?

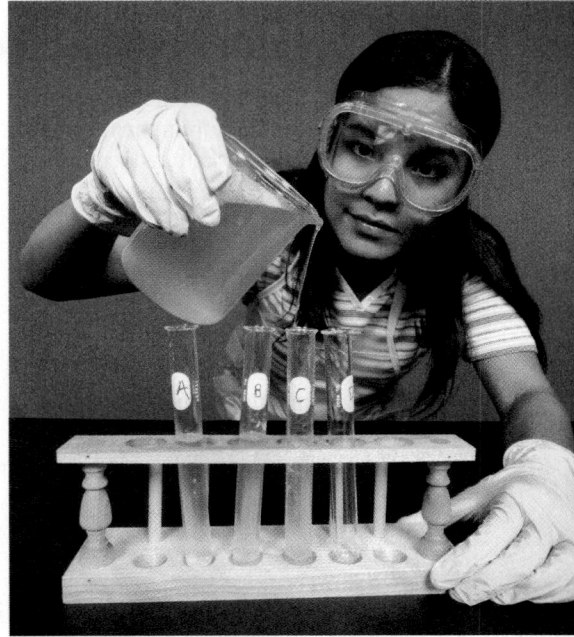

www.scilinks.org
Topic: Microbes
Code: HX80956

Extensions

4. **Further Inquiry** Does temperature affect microbe growth? How could you find out? Based on this investigation, design an experiment that would uncover any relationship between microbe growth and temperature. Share your experimental design with your teacher. With your teacher's permission, perform the investigation.

go.hrw.com
SUPER SUMMARY
Keyword: HX8APBS

Key Ideas	Key Terms

1 Health in the 21st Century

> Biologists combine research and data from many different fields to help reduce the spread of disease.

> As scientists learn more about the nature of disease, our ability to prevent and treat diseases has improved.

> As our understanding of medicine, biology, and science in general increases, humans will live longer and healthier lives.

epidemiology (31)
vaccination (31)
genetics (31)
genome (31)

2 Biology, Technology, and Society

> Genetic engineering is used to create crops that yield more product or are resistant to pests.

> Tools such as genetic engineering, nanotechnology, and computer models have expanded the potential applications of biological research.

> Because biological factors such as fingerprints, iris patterns, and genetic material are unique, they can be used to determine an individual's identity.

> Advances in biotechnology raise ethical concerns that must be addressed by individuals and by society.

genetic engineering (33)
biometrics (36)

3 Biology and the Environment

> Biological research helps us understand, value, and protect the environment. We learn how to protect the environment by learning more about what affects it.

> Tools such as satellite tagging, geographic information systems, and genetics are used to study and protect the environment.

> Biologists rely on the contributions of individuals and communities to help develop solutions for environmental problems.

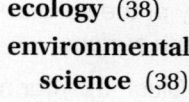

ecology (38)
environmental science (38)

Chapter 2 Review

READING TOOLBOX

1. **Three-panel Flip Chart** Organize three examples of ethical issues that face society today in a three-panel flip chart.

2. **Concept Map** Construct a concept map that describes some applications of biology. Try to include the following terms in your concept map: *genetics, ecology, environmental science, vaccination, epidemiology,* and *genome.*

Using Key Terms

Use each of the following terms in a separate sentence.

3. *environmental science*

4. *genetic engineering*

Write a definition for each of the following terms.

5. *vaccination*

6. *ecology*

Understanding Key Ideas

7. Cholera bacteria cluster
   a. around the plankton where the copepods feed in the ocean water.
   b. throughout the shells of both the male and female copepods.
   c. only around the mouthparts of both male and female copepods.
   d. around the mouthparts and egg casings of female copepods.

8. Define *battlefield medicine.*
   a. amputation during surgery
   b. the treatment of soldiers in or near an area of combat
   c. the vaccination of soldiers prior to being deployed to a battlefield
   d. the term used for military hospitals

9. What area of biology applications does genetic engineering *not* represent?
   a. bioscience
   b. biotechnology
   c. biometrics
   d. bioagriculture

10. Criminal investigators use biological factors for all of the following *except*
   a. to determine a person's identity.
   b. to determine how to keep the public safe.
   c. to make detailed three-dimensional images of internal organs.
   d. to determine the pattern of bands that would result in a fingerprint.

Use the graph to answer the following question.

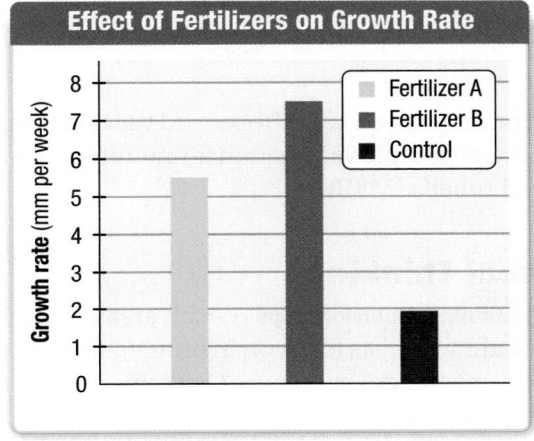

Effect of Fertilizers on Growth Rate

11. Which of the following is the dependent variable in the experiment?
   a. control
   b. fertilizer A
   c. fertilizer B
   d. growth rate

Explaining Key Ideas

12. **Describe** why Rita Colwell focused on a low-tech solution to reduce the spread of cholera.

13. **Explain** the function of a vaccination in the human body.

14. **Investigate** the purpose for assistive technology.

15. **Describe** how biomolecular materials have influenced research studies.

16. **Describe** how to get an environmental club started at your school.

17. **Describe** how genetics is used to study and protect endangered animals.

18. **Describe** the impact of Bt corn when the corn is grown by farmers.

Using Science Graphics

Use the graph to answer the following question.

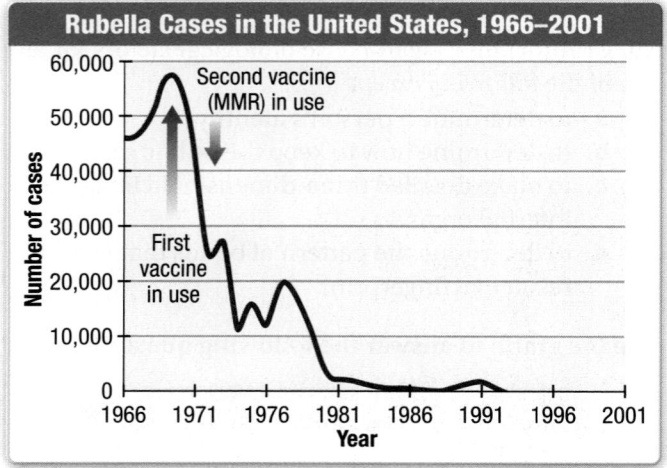

Rubella Cases in the United States, 1966–2001

19. What happened after the second vaccine license became a triple vaccination for mumps, measles, and rubella (MMR)?

Critical Thinking

20. **Explaining Relationships** Which areas of the world should scientists focus on in order to identify and prevent cholera epidemics? Explain why you think this is the case.

21. **Predicting Consequences** Future breakthroughs in science may alter the genes that affect aging in humans, and might allow some people to live longer lives. What are some possible environmental consequences if this type of technology is developed? What are some possible social consequences of this technology?

22. **Logical Reasoning** Insect populations may develop resistance to pesticides or other chemical compounds. When a population is resistant, the chemical can no longer kill the insect pest. Could insect populations develop resistance to Bt corn? If so, what could scientists do to control the resistant populations?

23. **Finding Evidence** What kind of scientific experiments would you want to perform in order to ensure that a genetically modified crop was safe for people and the environment?

24. **Applying Information** Describe how new technologies could be used to manage and protect an endangered species like the timber wolf.

25. **Forming Hypotheses** Describe how iris scans are considered a more reliable form of biometric identification than fingerprint analysis is. Explain your reasoning.

26. **Cholera and Technology** What kind of new technology would be most useful for studying the connection between cholera and ocean temperatures? Explain your answer.

Alternative Assessment

27. **Design a Product** Develop a new product that is based on one aspect of an organism or biological system. Create a brochure that describes the product and shows how it works. In the brochure, also describe how the product's design is inspired by nature.

Writing for Science

28. **Outline Ethical Issues** Create an outline that summarizes the many ethical issues surrounding the use of biometric technology for public safety. Then, write a letter to your congressperson to express your concerns about or support for this technology.

Methods of Science

29. **Forming Models** A geographic information system (GIS) uses computerized map layers to compare data. Construct a paper model that shows how a GIS would compare the areas that are important to you (such as your house, school, natural areas, and shopping areas) to the areas that are important to a friend and the areas that are important to one of your caregivers.

Math Skills

30. **Using Percentages** Filtering water through a few layers of sari cloth can reduce the number of cholera bacteria by 99%. If a sample of water contained 2.5 million cholera bacteria, how many bacteria would be left in the water after filtration?

> **TEST TIP** Carefully read the instructions, the question, and the answer options before choosing an answer.

Science Concepts

1. Which of the following is the study of how diseases spread?

A epidemiology

B biology

C genetics

D Human Genome Project

2. What is the area of science that creates products by manipulating individual atoms or molecules?

F biodegradable   **H** nanotechnology

G biotechnology   **J** nanodegradable

3. What is the most commonly used form of biometric evidence?

A skin cells   **C** hair follicles

B fingerprints   **D** DNA fragments

4. What three natural resources does the environment provide to all organisms?

F water, food, and air

G soil, food, and energy sources

H water, food, and energy sources

J food, energy sources, and minerals

5. What are members of the public called when they give observations to professional scientists?

A citizen scientists

B biological researchers

C environmental scientists

D environmental conservationists

6. In 1979, scientists announced that they had successfully eliminated a disease. Which of the following diseases was eliminated?

F chicken pox   **H** smallpox

G German pox   **J** polio

7. What is another term for genetic engineering?

A ecosystem DNA

B studying DNA structures

C manipulating DNA structures

D biological research of DNA strands

Using Science Graphics

The following diagram depicts the global distribution of paralytic polio cases in 1994. Use the diagram to answer the following questions.

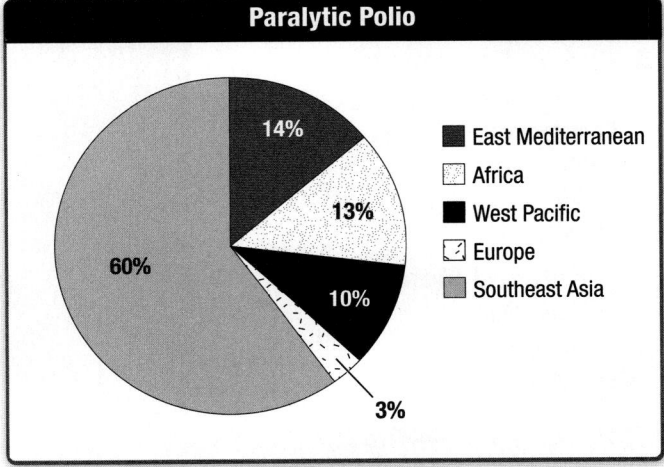

Source: Centers for Disease Control and Prevention, 1994.

8. Where were the greatest number of paralytic polio cases in the world?

F Africa   **H** West Pacific

G Europe   **J** Southeast Asia

9. Where were the least number of paralytic polio cases in the world?

A Africa   **C** Southeast Asia

B West Pacific   **D** Europe

10. If the number of paralytic polio cases in Southeast Asia were 1,950, what would be the number of cases in the East Mediterranean?

F 164   **H** 455

G 437   **J** 273

Writing Skills

11. Short Response Write an essay to describe why the study of ecology is considered an important application of biology.

Chemistry of Life

What do people and igloos have in common? Both are made from matter that has a very precise structure.

Preview

1 Matter and Substances
Atoms
Chemical Bonds
Polarity

2 Water and Solutions
Properties of Water
Solutions

3 Carbon Compounds
Building Blocks of Cells
Carbohydrates
Lipids
Proteins
Nucleic Acids

4 Energy and Metabolism
Changing Matter
Chemical Reactions
Biological Reactions

Why It Matters

The chemicals that make up living things are more complex than those in nonliving things. Learning the chemical basis of biology can help you understand how processes occur and how living things respond to their environment.

Igloos are built from blocks of compressed snow. Snow is nonliving matter made up of simple water molecules.

The fire inside the igloo gives off heat energy in a chemical reaction. Living things also produce heat in chemical reactions to stay alive.

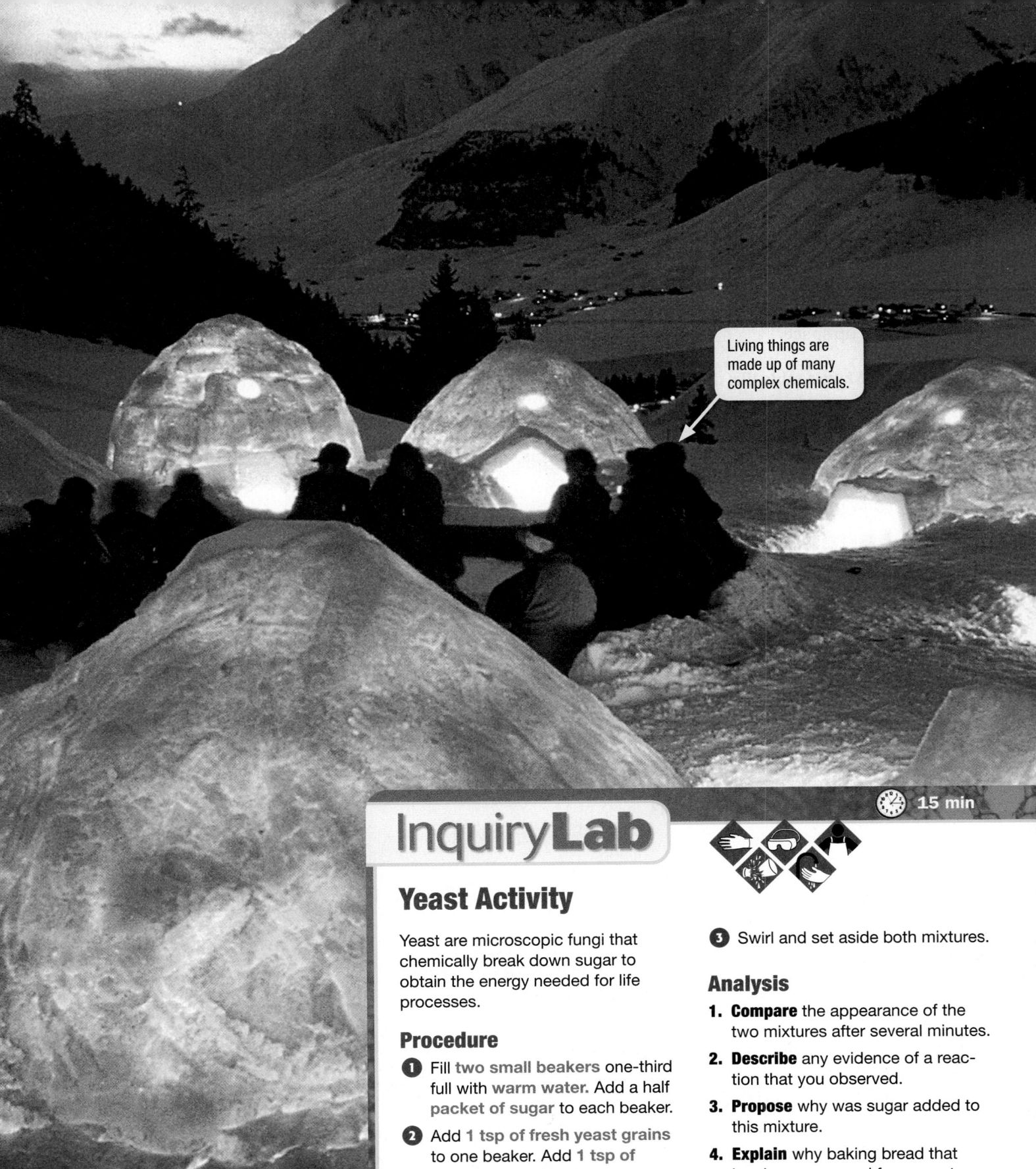

Living things are made up of many complex chemicals.

InquiryLab

⏱ 15 min

Yeast Activity

Yeast are microscopic fungi that chemically break down sugar to obtain the energy needed for life processes.

Procedure

1. Fill **two small beakers** one-third full with **warm water.** Add a half **packet of sugar** to each beaker.

2. Add **1 tsp of fresh yeast grains** to one beaker. Add **1 tsp of deactivated yeast grains** to the other.

3. Swirl and set aside both mixtures.

Analysis

1. **Compare** the appearance of the two mixtures after several minutes.

2. **Describe** any evidence of a reaction that you observed.

3. **Propose** why was sugar added to this mixture.

4. **Explain** why baking bread that has been prepared from yeast-containing dough rises.

Using Words

Everyday Words in Science Many words that we use every day have special meanings in science. For example, *matter* in everyday use is "an issue or problem." In science, matter means "anything that has mass and takes up space."

Everyday Words in Science		
Word	**Everyday meaning**	**Scientific meaning**
compound		
solution		
energy		

Your Turn Make a table like the one shown here.

1. Before you read, write in your own words the everyday meaning of the terms in the table.

2. As you read, fill in the scientific meaning for the terms in the table.

Using Language

Quantifiers Quantifiers are words that describe how much, how large, and how often. Quantifiers can also describe the order in which things occur. Words that describe an order include *first, second, third, fourth, primary, secondary, tertiary,* and *quaternary.*

Your Turn Use what you have learned about quantifiers to answer the following questions.

1. Place the following months in order of fourth, third, second, and first: January, March, April, February.

2. Would a student attending primary school be younger or older than a student attending secondary school?

Taking Notes

Comparison Table A comparison table is useful for comparing characteristics of topics in science. All topics in a table are described in terms of the same characteristics. This approach helps you compare several topics at one time.

	Carbohydrates	Lipids
Structure		
Function		
Energy Content		

Your Turn Make a comparison table to compare carbohydrates and lipids.

1. Draw a table like the one shown here.

2. In the top row, write the topics *Carbohydrates* and *Lipids.*

3. In the left column, write the general characteristics *Structure, Function,* and *Energy Content.* As you read the chapter, fill in the characteristics for each topic in the appropriate cells.

1 Matter and Substances

Key Ideas	Key Terms	Why It Matters
❯ What makes up matter? ❯ Why do atoms form bonds? ❯ What are some important interactions between substances in living things?	atom element valence electron compound molecule ion	All living things are made of matter, so understanding the structure and behavior of matter can help you understand how your body works.

Every living and nonliving thing is made of matter. Matter is anything that has mass and takes up space. To understand how living things work and interact, you must first understand the structure of matter.

Atoms

What does all matter have in common? It is made of very small particles called atoms. An **atom** is the smallest unit of matter that cannot be broken down by chemical means. ❯ **All matter is made up of atoms. An atom has a positively charged core surrounded by a negatively charged region.**

Atomic Structure Atoms are made of three types of particles. *Protons* have a positive charge, *electrons* have a negative charge, and *neutrons* have no charge. Atoms have no overall charge because each atom has as many electrons as protons. Protons and neutrons have about the same mass and make up the core, or nucleus, of an atom. Electrons have very little mass and move around the nucleus in a region called the *electron cloud*, which is much larger than the nucleus.

atom the smallest unit of an element that maintains the chemical properties of that element

element a substance that cannot be separated or broken down into simpler substances by chemical means

Elements An **element** is a substance made up of atoms that have the same number of protons. For example, each atom of the element carbon has six protons, as **Figure 1** shows. Atoms of an element may have different numbers of neutrons. These atoms are called *isotopes* of elements.

❯ **Reading Check** *What is a proton? (See the Appendix for answers to Reading Checks.)*

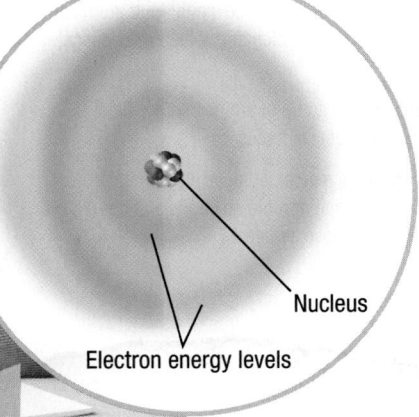

Figure 1 The graphite in pencil lead is made of atoms of the element carbon.
❯ If an uncharged carbon atom (inset) has six protons in its nucleus, how many electrons does it have?

Nucleus

Electron energy levels

Figure 2 A water molecule consists of an oxygen atom covalently bonded to two hydrogen atoms. The electron cloud model (left) shows the interaction between the atoms of the molecule. The space-filling model (right) shows the three-dimensional structure of a molecule.

Electron cloud model

Space-filling model

valence electron an electron that is found in the outermost shell of an atom and that determines the atom's chemical properties

compound a substance made up of atoms of two or more different elements joined by chemical bonds

molecule a group of atoms that are held together by chemical forces

ion an atom, radical, or molecule that has gained or lost one or more electrons and has a negative or positive charge

Chemical Bonds

The electron cloud of an atom may have levels. The innermost level can hold only two electrons. Levels farther from the nucleus can usually hold eight electrons. Electrons in the outermost level, or shell, are called **valence electrons.** Atoms tend to combine with each other such that eight electrons will be in the valence shell.

When atoms combine, a force called a *chemical bond* holds them together. ❯ Chemical bonds form between groups of atoms because most atoms become stable when they have eight electrons in the valence shell. However, the smallest atoms, such as hydrogen, are stable when they have only two valence electrons. When atoms of different elements bond, a compound forms. A **compound** is a substance made of the bonded atoms of two or more different elements.

Covalent Bonding One way that atoms bond is by sharing valence electrons to form a *covalent bond*. A **molecule** is a group of atoms held together by covalent bonds. Not all substances that have covalent bonds are compounds. The oxygen in the air you breathe consists of molecules made of two oxygen atoms sharing electrons in a covalent bond. To represent an oxygen molecule, write "O_2," not "O." A carbon dioxide molecule has two oxygen atoms bonded to a single carbon atom, so its formula is CO_2.

Water: A Covalent Compound As **Figure 2** shows, a water molecule, H_2O, forms when an oxygen atom combines with two hydrogen atoms. The atoms form chemical bonds by sharing electrons in a way that gives oxygen eight valence electrons, making it stable. The hydrogen atoms become stable because sharing gives each two valence electrons.

❯ **Reading Check** *What is a chemical bond?*

QuickLab

 15 min

Atom Models

Scientists use models to represent their understanding of things that they cannot directly observe.

Procedure

❶ Using assorted materials provided by your teacher, work in groups to make model atoms for hydrogen, carbon, oxygen, sodium, and chlorine.

❷ Model the covalent bonds in a water molecule.

❸ Model an ionic bond in sodium chloride.

Analysis

1. **Model** the covalent bonds in a carbon dioxide molecule, CO_2. How many electrons are shared?

2. CRITICAL THINKING **Critiquing Models** Exchange models with another group. What is accurate and useful about those models? What could be improved? Write down your comments for the other group.

Ionic Bonding Atoms can achieve a stable valence level in another way—by losing or gaining electrons. This results in a positive or negative charge. An **ion** is an atom or group of atoms that has an electric charge because it has gained or lost electrons. The attractive force between oppositely charged ions is an *ionic bond.*

Table Salt: An Ionic Compound One familiar example of an ionic compound is table salt, NaCl, shown in **Figure 3.** A sodium atom has one valence electron, while a chlorine atom has seven. ❶ Sodium readily gives up its electron, while chlorine readily accepts an electron. ❷ The sodium atom is now a sodium ion, Na^+. The chlorine atom is now a chloride ion, Cl^-. ❸ The positively charged sodium ion and negatively charged chloride ion attract each other and form sodium chloride, NaCl. ❹ The attractive forces between several sodium ions and chloride ions form a crystal of table salt.

Figure 3 Salt crystals in sodium chloride, NaCl, are formed by the interaction between sodium ions, Na^+, and chloride ions, Cl^-. ❯ How many electrons are in the valence shell of a chloride ion?

go.hrw.com
✳ interact online
Keyword: HX8BCMF3

Ionic Bonding in Salt

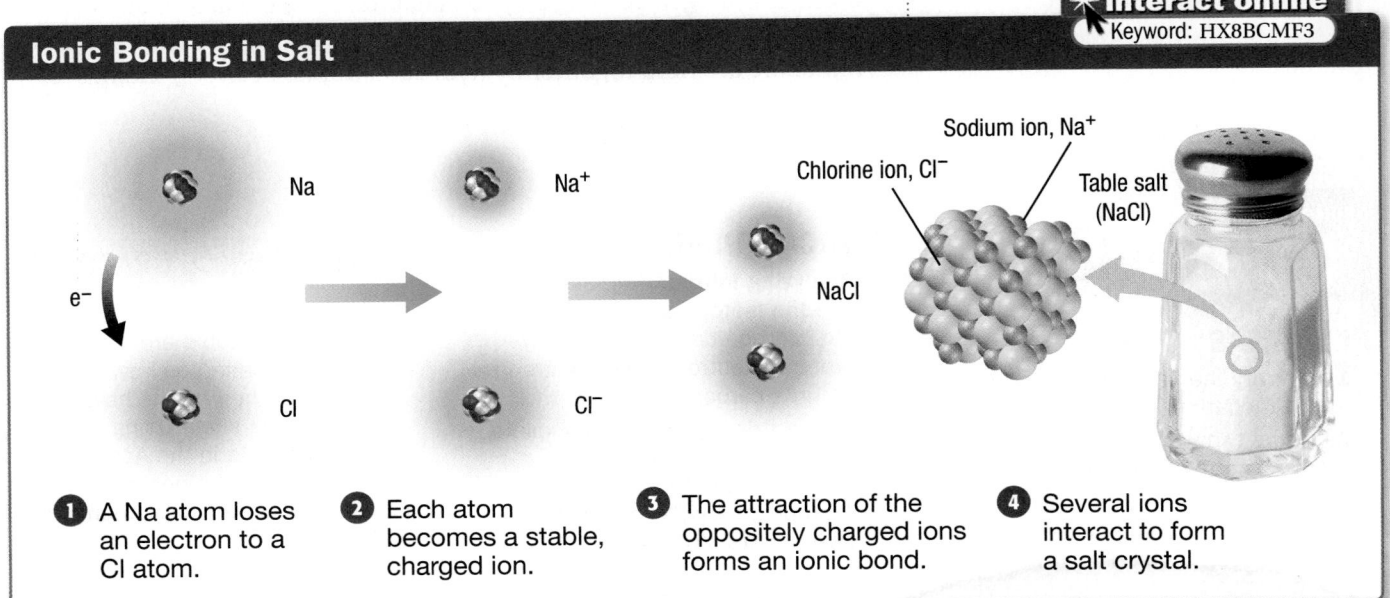

❶ A Na atom loses an electron to a Cl atom.

❷ Each atom becomes a stable, charged ion.

❸ The attraction of the oppositely charged ions forms an ionic bond.

❹ Several ions interact to form a salt crystal.

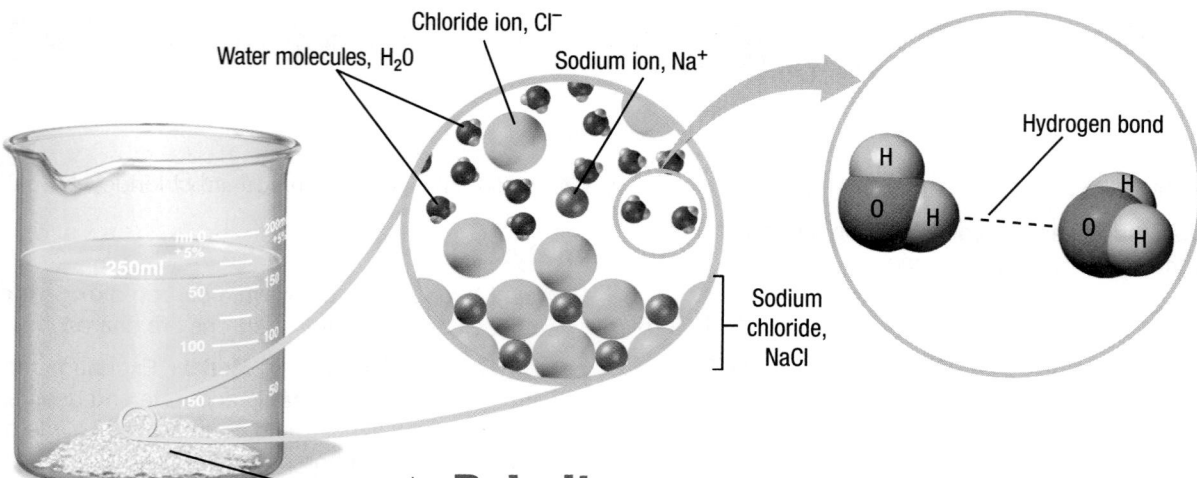

Water molecules, H$_2$O
Chloride ion, Cl$^-$
Sodium ion, Na$^+$
Hydrogen bond
Sodium chloride, NaCl
NaCl

Figure 4 Water dissolves ionic compounds. When sodium chloride, NaCl, is dissolved in water, sodium ions, Na$^+$, and chloride ions, Cl$^-$, become surrounded by water molecules, H$_2$O.

Polarity

In some covalent bonds, the shared electrons are attracted more strongly to one atom than to the other. As a result, one end, or pole, of the molecule has a partial negative charge, while the opposite end has a partial positive charge. Molecules with partial charges on opposite ends are said to be *polar*. The water molecule is polar.

Solubility The partially charged ends of polar molecules attract opposite charges. Because of this behavior, water can dissolve polar molecules, such as sugar, and ionic compounds, such as the salt in **Figure 4.** Nonpolar substances, such as oil, grease, and wax, do not dissolve well in water. Instead, they remain together in clumps or a separate layer. The reason is that water molecules are more attracted to each other than to the nonpolar molecules.

Hydrogen Bonds When bonded to an oxygen, nitrogen, or fluorine atom, a hydrogen atom has a partial charge nearly as great as a proton's charge. It attracts the negative pole of other nearby molecules. This attraction, called a *hydrogen bond*, is stronger than attractions between other molecules, but not as strong as a covalent bond. ❯ Hydrogen bonding plays an important role in many of the molecules that make up living things. For example, the two strands of a DNA molecule are held together by hydrogen bonds between the bases.

❯ **Reading Check** *Why does salt dissolve in water?*

Section 1 Review

❯ KEY IDEAS

1. **Identify** the parts of atoms and their locations.
2. **Name** two ways that atoms can combine to become more stable in compounds.
3. **Explain** how charges cause salt and sugar to dissolve in water.

CRITICAL THINKING

4. **Analyzing Information** Scientists use the isotope carbon-14 in radiocarbon dating. How many protons, neutrons, and electrons are in a carbon-14 atom?
5. **Recognizing Differences** Explain the difference between polar and nonpolar molecules. Give an example of a polar molecule, and describe its structure.

USING SCIENCE GRAPHICS

6. **Periodic Table** Elements on the periodic table are arranged in groups based on how many electrons their atoms have in the valence shell. Using the periodic table in the Appendix, propose why the noble gases in Group 18 rarely form chemical bonds.

Humans can survive for a few weeks without food but only a few days without water. In fact, all life on Earth depends on this simple substance.

Properties of Water

Water has many unique properties that make it an important substance for life. ❯ **Most of the unique properties of water result because water molecules form hydrogen bonds with each other.**

- **Ice floats.** When water freezes, hydrogen bonds lock water molecules into a crystal structure that has empty spaces. This structure makes water less dense as a solid than as a liquid, so ice floats. Floating ice prevents rivers, lakes, and oceans from freezing solid, so life can exist in the water under the ice.

- **Water absorbs and retains heat.** Hydrogen bonds are constantly breaking and forming between water molecules. Because of this, water can absorb a large amount of heat without changing temperature. It is also why water takes a long time to cool. Large bodies of water can help keep temperatures on Earth from changing too fast. This property of water can also help organisms maintain a constant internal temperature.

- **Water molecules stick to each other.** Hydrogen bonds hold water molecules together in much the same way holding hands keeps a crowd of people together. Thus small drops, such as the dewdrops on the flower in **Figure 5,** are pulled into a ball shape. **Cohesion** is the attraction of particles of the same substance. Water is a liquid at ordinary temperatures because such forces keep it from evaporating easily.

- **Water molecules stick to other polar substances.** Attraction between particles of different substances is called **adhesion.** As **Figure 5** shows, a combination of adhesion and cohesion causes water to move upward through the stem of a plant from the roots to the leaves.

cohesion the force that holds molecules of a single material together

adhesion the attractive force between two bodies of different substances that are in contact with each other

Figure 5 Cohesion and adhesion contribute to the upward movement of water from the roots of plants.

Inside of stem

55

Figure 6 A hydronium ion, H_3O^+, and a hydroxide ion, OH^-, form when a hydrogen ion, H^+, separates from a water molecule and bonds to another. This reaction can also re-form two water molecules from a hydronium ion and a hydroxide ion.

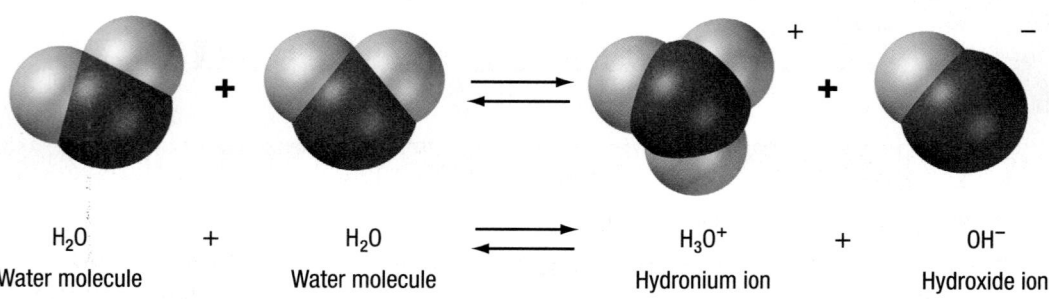

H₂O	+	H₂O	⇌	H₃O⁺	+	OH⁻
Water molecule		Water molecule		Hydronium ion		Hydroxide ion

Solutions

A **solution** is a mixture in which ions or molecules of one or more substances are evenly distributed in another substance. Many substances are transported throughout living things as solutions of water. Dissolved substances can move more easily within and between cells. Water dissolves many ionic and polar substances but does not dissolve nonpolar substances.

Acids and Bases Some water molecules break apart to form ions, as **Figure 6** shows. In pure water, hydronium ions and hydroxide ions are present in equal numbers. ❯ In solutions, some substances change the balance of these ions. **Acids** are compounds that form extra hydronium ions when dissolved in water. Your stomach uses a solution of hydrochloric acid, HCl, to digest food.

In contrast, **bases** are compounds that form extra hydroxide ions when dissolved in water. Many bases contain hydroxide ions. An example is sodium hydroxide, NaOH, which is used to remove clogs from drains. Other bases react with water molecules. For example, ammonia, NH_3, reacts with a water molecule, H_2O, to form an ammonium ion, NH_4^+, and a hydroxide ion, OH^-.

When acids and bases are mixed, the extra hydronium and hydroxide ions react to form water. Depending on the amounts of extra ions, the solution will be either less acidic, less basic, or neutral.

solution a homogeneous mixture throughout which two or more substances are uniformly dispersed

acid any compound that increases the number of hydronium ions when dissolved in water

base any compound that increases the number of hydroxide ions when dissolved in water

pH a value that is used to express the acidity or alkalinity (basicity) of a system

buffer a solution made from a weak acid and its conjugate base that neutralizes small amounts of acids or bases added to it

Figure 7 The pH scale is based on the concentration of hydronium ions in a solution. ❯ **How does an antacid relieve acid indigestion?**

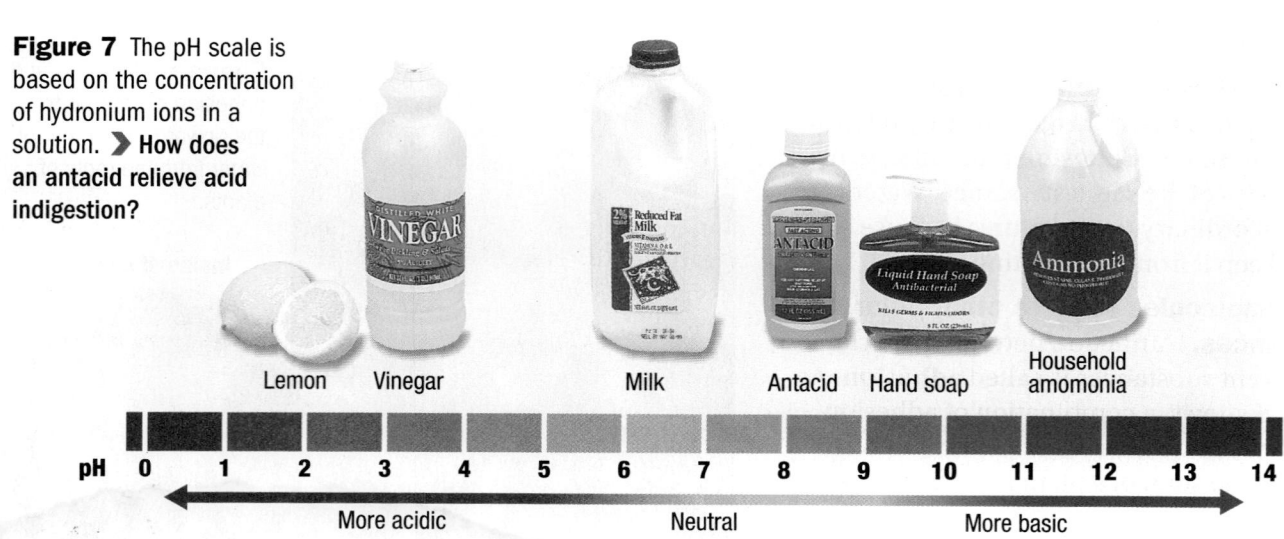

Lemon Vinegar Milk Antacid Hand soap Household amomonia

pH 0 1 2 3 4 5 6 7 8 9 10 11 12 13 14

More acidic ← Neutral → More basic

Hands-On

QuickLab

Telltale Cabbage

Red cabbage contains a natural indicator that can be used to identify how acidic or basic a solution is.

Procedure

1. Cut up a **cabbage leaf** into very tiny clippings by using **scissors.**

2. Put on **safety goggles.** Place the clippings in a **beaker** of **warm water.** Swirl the mixture. Wait several minutes until the water changes color.

3. Add several drops of **lemon juice.** Note any changes in appearance.

4. Add about **1/4 tsp of baking soda.** Note any changes in appearance. Continue adding small amounts of baking soda, and observe additional color changes.

Analysis

1. **Describe** what happened when the leaf clippings were placed in warm water.

2. **Describe** what happened when lemon juice (an acid) was added to the indicator solution.

3. **Describe** what happened when the baking soda was added to the acidic solution.

4. **CRITICAL THINKING** **Inferring Relationships** From your observations, what probably happened when the baking soda was added to the acidic solution?

---

pH and Buffers pH is a measure of how acidic or basic a solution is. The pH scale is shown in **Figure 7.** Each one-point increase in pH represents a 10-fold decrease in hydronium ion concentration. So, the H_3O^+ concentration in a solution of pH 2 is 10 times as great as it is in a solution of pH 3. Pure water has a pH of 7. Acidic solutions have a pH below 7, and basic solutions have a pH above 7.

❯ **The pH of the solutions in living things must be stable.** The pH of human blood is about 7.4. If the pH goes down to 7.0 or up to 7.8, an individual will die within minutes. For a stable pH to be maintained, the solutions in living things contain buffers. A **buffer** is a substance that reacts to prevent pH changes in a solution. An important buffer in living things is the bicarbonate ion, HCO_3^-.

READING TOOLBOX

Everyday Words in Science Write a sentence that uses the everyday meaning of the word *basic.* Then, write a sentence that uses the scientific meaning of the word *basic.*

Section 2 Review

❯ KEY IDEAS

1. **Identify** four unique properties of water that make life on Earth possible.

2. **Differentiate** between acids and bases.

3. **Explain** the role of buffers in maintaining homeostasis.

CRITICAL THINKING

4. **Recognizing Relationships** Cells contain mostly water. If cells contained mostly oil, how would an organism's ability to maintain homeostasis be affected?

5. **Applying Information** The active ingredient in aspirin is acetylsalicylic acid. Why would doctors recommend buffered aspirin, especially for people with a sensitive stomach?

MATH SKILLS

6. **Exponents** The pH of solution A is 2. The pH of solution B is 4. Which solution has the greater concentration of hydronium ions? The concentration of that solution is how many times the concentration of the other solution?

Water Wonders

A water spider can live underwater by capturing air bubbles at the surface. Most of the life cycle of this "bubble breather" occurs below the water surface. All organisms depend on water. Water has many unique properties that make life on Earth possible.

WEIRD SCIENCE

Bergy Bits

An iceberg is a floating mass of freshwater ice that has broken off from a glacier or an ice sheet. Icebergs vary greatly in size. Very large tabular icebergs are known as *ice islands*. Icebergs that are about the size of a small house are called *bergy bits*. Because freshwater ice is slightly less dense than sea water, only a small portion of an iceberg projects above water.

Walking on Water This water strider can run across the surface of water! Its feet are covered with fine, water-repellent hairs that enable the insect to "skate" over the surface film of water.

Ice Hotel Winter travelers to Canada, Alaska, China, and Sweden can spend the night at a hotel that is entirely chiseled from chunks of ice and snow!

Research Find out the difference between icebergs and four other types of ocean ice: sea ice, pack ice, ice floes, and fast ice.

Carbon Compounds

Suppose that you are building a house. You need wood for framing and metal for nails, screws, and electrical wiring. You also need concrete for the foundation, glass for windows, and drywall siding. This complex structure is made of a few basic materials that must be assembled in a highly organized way. The same is true of the molecules that make up living things.

Building Blocks of Cells

The parts of a cell are made up of large, complex molecules, often called *biomolecules.* ❯ **Large, complex biomolecules are built from a few smaller, simpler, repeating units arranged in an extremely precise way.** These simple units are like the toy blocks in **Figure 8,** which connect to build the large sculpture. Not all of the blocks are exactly the same, but they all connect with other blocks in a few different ways.

Carbon Compounds The basic units of most biomolecules contain atoms of carbon. Carbon atoms have four valence electrons, so they can form covalent bonds with as many as four other atoms. Carbon atoms can bond with each other to form chains or rings. The carbon atoms in these chains and rings can also connect with atoms of other elements to form the basic units of most biomolecules.

❯ **Reading Check** *What element is the basis of biomolecules?*

Figure 8 Large, complex structures can be built from a few basic units arranged in a precise way. ❯ **Describe two shapes that you could make from these five blocks.**

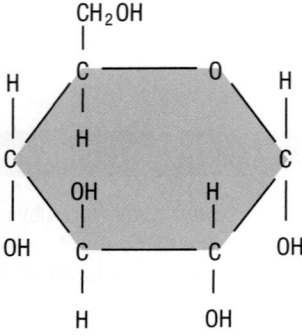

Figure 9 The sugar glucose, $C_6H_{12}O_6$, is made from carbon, hydrogen, and oxygen atoms. Sugars are the building blocks of carbohydrates.

carbohydrate a class of molecules that includes sugars, starches, and fiber; contains carbon, hydrogen, and oxygen

lipid a fat molecule or a molecule that has similar properties, including waxes and steroids

ACADEMIC
VOCABULARY

vary to make a minor or partial change in

Carbohydrates

You may have heard about carbohydrates in foods such as grains, fruits, and vegetables. **Carbohydrates** are molecules made of sugars. A sugar contains carbon, hydrogen, and oxygen in a ratio of 1:2:1. **Figure 9** shows the ring structure of glucose, a common sugar found in grape juice. Glucose is a *monosaccharide,* or "single sugar."

Two sugars can be linked to make a *disaccharide.* Examples of disaccharides are sucrose (table sugar) and lactose (found in milk). Many sugars can be linked together to make a *polysaccharide.* Starch consists of hundreds of glucose units bonded together. Glycogen (found in animals) consists of many branched chains of glucose.

Monosaccharides and disaccharides are considered simple carbohydrates. Polysaccharides are considered complex carbohydrates. **Figure 10** shows an example of each carbohydrate. ❯ **Cells use carbohydrates for sources of energy, structural materials, and cellular identification.**

Energy Supply Carbohydrates are a major source of energy for many organisms, including humans. Plants store the sun's energy for future use by making glucose and converting it to starch. Organisms release chemical energy for cell activities by breaking down glucose.

Structural Support *Chitin* and *cellulose* are two complex carbohydrates that provide support. The shells of crabs, lobsters, and insects are made of chitin. Chitin is also found in the cell walls of mushrooms and molds. The cell walls of plants are made of cellulose. Bundles of cellulose are stiff enough to hold plants upright.

Cell Recognition Cells may have short, branched chains of varying sugar units on their outer surface. In a complex organism, cells recognize neighboring cells by these carbohydrates. Carbohydrates on the outside of invading cells allow the body to recognize them as not being part of the body so that they can be destroyed.

❯ **Reading Check** *What is the basic unit of a carbohydrate?*

Figure 10 Milk contains lactose, a simple carbohydrate. Cereal grains contain starch, a complex carbohydrate. ❯ **Which of these carbohydrates is a disaccharide?**

Starch (from cereal)
Complex carbohydrate

Lactose (from milk)
Simple carbohydrate

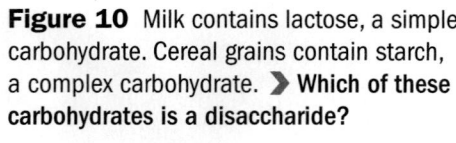

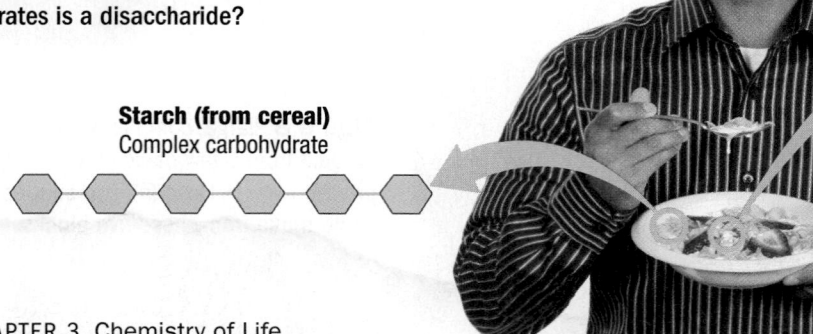

Lipids

Lipids are another class of biomolecules, which includes fats, phospholipids, steroids, and waxes. Lipids consist of chains of carbon atoms bonded to each other and to hydrogen atoms. This structure makes lipids repel water. **>The main functions of lipids include storing energy and controlling water movement.** Lipids also include steroid hormones, used as signaling molecules, and some pigments, which absorb light.

Energy Stores The main purpose of fats is to store energy. Fats can store energy even more efficiently than carbohydrates. Many animals, such as the dormouse in **Figure 11,** can survive without a steady diet because of fat storage. When food is plentiful, the animal converts the excess food into fats for long-term energy storage. When food is scarce, the animal can break down the fat molecules to release energy for life processes. Plant oils are stored in seeds to provide energy to start the growth of a new plant.

Water Barriers The cell's boundary is made of phospholipids. One end of this molecule is attracted by water molecules. The other end, which is made of long carbon chains, is not. You will learn more about the behavior of these molecules when you study the structure of cell membranes.

The stems and leaves of many plants are covered with a thin layer of wax, another type of lipid. This wax helps prevent the evaporation of water from the cells at the surface of a plant. Waxy feathers can also help keep ducks and other aquatic birds dry. One type of wax molecule found on bird feathers is shown in **Figure 11.**

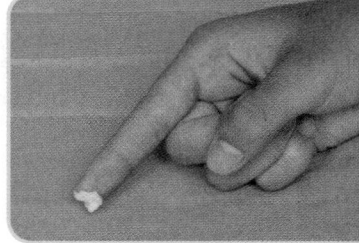

Hands-On
Quick**Lab**

🕐 15 min

Brown Paper Test

You can test substances for fats by using ordinary brown paper. Oils are fats that are liquid at room temperature. This test also works for oils.

Procedure

❶ Place a drop of water in one area of your brown paper. Place a drop of oil in another area. Rub a spot of butter into a third area.

❷ Fan the paper to evaporate any of these substances. Hold the stained paper to the light. What do you see?

❸ Now, test other substances provided by your teacher.

Analysis

1. **Compare** how the butter, oil, and water affected the paper.

2. **Describe** how each of the other substances that you tested affected the paper. Which ones contained lipids?

Figure 11 Many fat molecules have three long chains of carbons. Waxes may be composed of chains of about 24 to 34 carbon atoms.

Dormouse

Fat molecule

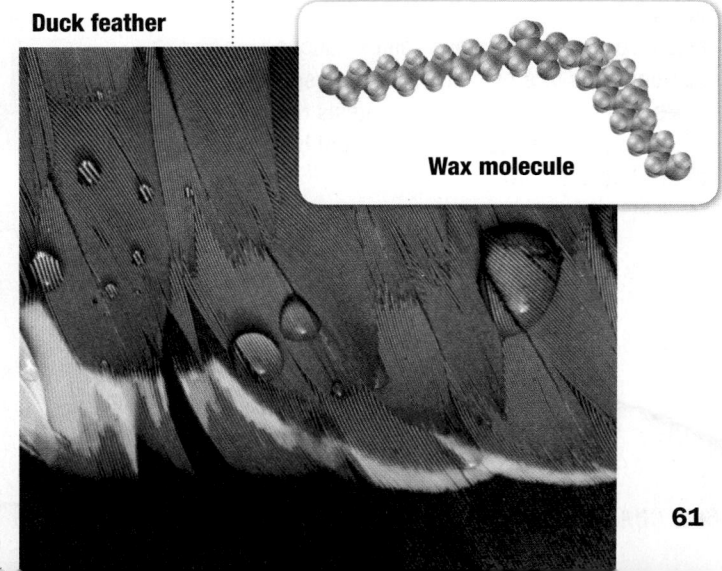

Duck feather

Wax molecule

protein an organic compound that is made of one or more chains of amino acids and that is a principal component of all cells

amino acid a compound of a class of simple organic compounds that contain a carboxyl and an amino group and that combine to form proteins

SCLINKS

www.scilinks.org
Topic: Proteins
Code: HX81241

Proteins

Proteins are the workhorse molecules of all living things. There are many types of proteins that perform many types of functions. ❯ **Proteins are chains of amino acids that twist and fold into certain shapes that determine what the proteins do.** Some proteins provide structure and support. Others enable movement. Some proteins aid in communication or transportation. Others help carry out important chemical reactions.

Amino Acids A **protein** is a molecule (usually a large one) made up of **amino acids,** building blocks that link to form proteins. **Figure 12** shows the basic structure of an amino acid. Every amino acid has an amino group (-NH_2), a carboxyl group (-COOH), and a variable side group. The carboxyl group of one unit can link to the amino group of another. This link is a *peptide bond.*

The side group gives an amino acid its unique properties. Twenty different amino acids are found in proteins. In order to build proteins, the body requires a supply of the correct amino acids. The body can make many amino acids from other substances, but a few amino acids must be included in the diet. To get these amino acids, your body breaks apart the proteins in the foods you eat.

Levels of Structure For each type of protein, amino acids are arranged in a specific order. This order is the protein's primary structure. The various side groups interact to bend and twist the chain. Portions of the chain may form coils and folds. These patterns are known as the protein's secondary structure.

Some small proteins consist of only one chain, but most proteins consist of two or more chains. The tertiary structure of proteins is the overall shape of a single chain of amino acids. The quaternary structure is the overall shape that results from combining the chains to form the protein. This shape suits the function of each protein.

❯ **Reading Check** *What is a protein's primary structure?*

Figure 12 Proteins are chains of amino acids linked by peptide bonds. An amino acid (top) has a side group (blue). Various combinations of amino acids result in specific types of proteins, such as the proteins that make up the muscles, hair, horns, and hooves of this highland cow.

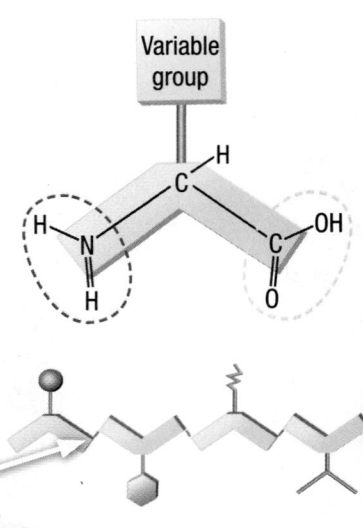

Variable group

A *peptide bond* (orange) forms between the carboxyl group (yellow) of one amino acid and the amino group (red) of another.

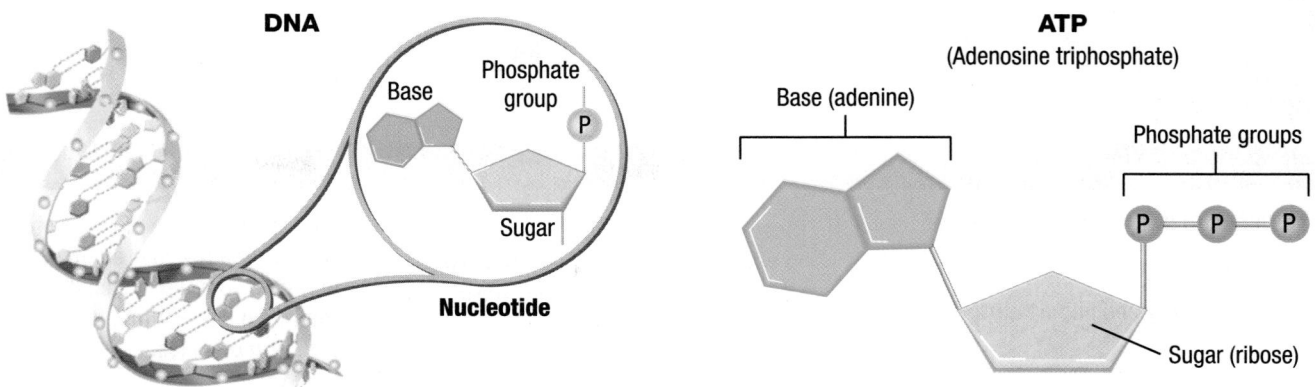

DNA

Base

Phosphate group

P

Sugar

Nucleotide

ATP
(Adenosine triphosphate)

Base (adenine)

Phosphate groups

P   P   P

Sugar (ribose)

Figure 13 DNA is made of two strands of multiple nucleotides (inset) linked by hydrogen bonds. ATP is also a nucleotide and is made up of a sugar, a base, and three phosphate groups. ❯ **What is the function of ATP?**

Nucleic Acids

All of your cells contain nucleic acids. A **nucleic acid** is a long chain of nucleotide units. A **nucleotide** is a molecule made up of three parts: a sugar, a base, and a phosphate group. Nucleotides of deoxyribonucleic acid, or **DNA,** contain the sugar deoxyribose. Nucleotides of ribonucleic acid, or **RNA,** contain the sugar ribose.

Hereditary Information DNA molecules act as "instructions" for the processes of an organism's life. These instructions, called the *genetic code,* depend on the order of bases in the nucleotides of the DNA molecule. DNA consists of two strands of nucleotides that spiral around each other, as **Figure 13** shows. The bases in one strand of nucleotides form hydrogen bonds with the bases on the other to hold the DNA molecule together and protect the code. RNA also interacts with DNA to help decode the information. ❯ **Nucleic acids store and transmit hereditary information.**

Energy Carriers Some single nucleotides have other important roles. Cells need a steady supply of adenosine triphosphate, or **ATP,** to function. ATP, shown in **Figure 13,** is a nucleotide that has three phosphate groups. Energy is released in the reaction that breaks off the third phosphate group. Other single nucleotides transfer electrons or hydrogen atoms for other life processes.

nucleic acid an organic compound, either RNA or DNA, whose molecules are made up of one or two chains of nucleotides and carry genetic information

nucleotide an organic compound that consists of a sugar, a phosphate, and a nitrogenous base

DNA deoxyribonucleic acid, the material that contains the information that determines inherited characteristics

RNA ribonucleic acid, a natural polymer that is present in all living cells and that plays a role in protein synthesis

ATP adenosine triphosphate, an organic molecule that acts as the main energy source for cell processes

---

❯ **KEY IDEAS**

1. **Discuss** how one type of atom (carbon) can be the basis of so many types of biomolecules.
2. **List** three major functions of carbohydrates.
3. **Describe** two functions of lipids.

4. **Explain** how two different proteins will have two different shapes.
5. **Summarize** the role of nucleic acids in a cell.

CRITICAL THINKING

6. **Applying Information** Before a long race, runners often "carbo load." In other words, they eat substantial quantities of carbohydrates. How might this practice help their performance?

METHODS OF SCIENCE

7. **Identifying Unknown** Analysis of an unknown substance shows that that the substance contains carbon, hydrogen, and oxygen and is soluble in oil, but not in water. Which of the four types of biomolecules could this substance be?

Key Ideas	Key Terms	Why It Matters
❯ Where do living things get energy? ❯ How do chemical reactions occur? ❯ Why are enzymes important to living things?	energy enzyme reactant substrate product active site activation energy	All living things need energy to survive. You get that energy by breaking complex molecules from food you eat into simpler, stabler molecules.

Changes constantly occur in living things. In fact, you could say that a key feature of life is change. The ability to move or change matter is called **energy.** Energy exists in many forms—including light, heat, chemical energy, mechanical energy, and electrical energy—and can be converted from one form to another. The athlete in **Figure 14** is using mechanical energy to move the basketball.

Changing Matter

Living things are made of matter, which consists of a substance with a form. A physical change occurs when only the form or shape of the matter changes. The substances that make up the matter do not change into different substances. When you pour sugar into iced tea and stir, the sugar crystals disappear. The sweet taste shows that the sugar is still there but has changed form.

A chemical change occurs when a substance changes into a different substance. In a chemical change, the identity of the matter changes. When wood burns, the carbohydrates in the wood fibers combine with oxygen, O_2, in the air. The wood fibers change to different substances: carbon dioxide, CO_2, and water vapor, H_2O.

Figure 14 This athlete uses energy to move the basketball. ❯ **What form of energy is used to move the basketball?**

Conservation of Mass Matter is neither created nor destroyed in any change. The same mass is present before and after the wood burns and the sugar dissolves. This observation is called the *law of conservation of mass.*

Conservation of Energy Every change in matter requires a change in energy. Energy may change from one form to another, but the total amount of energy does not change. This observation is called the *law of conservation of energy.* In some changes, energy is taken in from the surroundings. In others, energy is released into the surroundings. The total amount of *usable* energy decreases because some energy is given off to the surroundings as heat. ❯ **Living things use different chemical reactions to get the energy needed for life processes.**

❯ **Reading Check** *What is a chemical change?*

Chemical Reactions

Changing a substance requires a chemical reaction. During this process, bonds between atoms are broken, and new ones are formed. A **reactant** is a substance that is changed in a chemical reaction. A **product** is a new substance that is formed. Scientists summarize reactions by writing equations in the following form:

$$\text{Reactants} \longrightarrow \text{Products}$$

The arrow means "changes to" or "forms." For example, carbon dioxide and water can react to form carbonic acid, H_2CO_3, in your blood. The following equation represents this reaction:

$$CO_2 + H_2O \rightleftharpoons H_2CO_3$$

The double arrow indicates that the products can reform reactants. In this example, carbonic acid changes back to carbon dioxide and water in your lungs.

Activation Energy Chemical reactions can occur only under the right conditions. To form new bonds, particles must get close enough to share electron clouds. However, even though the particles move constantly, as they get close, their negatively charged electron clouds tend to push them apart. To react, the particles must collide fast enough to have kinetic energy to overcome the repulsion between them. The **activation energy** of the reaction is the minimum kinetic energy that colliding particles need to start a chemical reaction.

Alignment Even if enough energy is available, the product still may not form. When the reactant particles collide, the correct atoms must be brought close together in the proper orientation, as **Figure 15** shows. Otherwise, the product will not form. ❯ **Chemical reactions can occur only when the activation energy is available and the correct atoms are aligned.** In living things, chemical reactions occur between large, complex biomolecules. Life can only exist if these molecules collide in the correct orientation.

❯ **Reading Check** *What causes particles to repel other particles?*

energy the capacity to do work

reactant a substance or molecule that participates in a chemical reaction

product a substance that forms in a chemical reaction

activation energy the minimum amount of energy required to start a chemical reaction

ACADEMIC VOCABULARY

orientation the relative position or direction of something

Reaction Conditions

Reactants	Conditions	Result	Products
	not enough energy	no reaction	none
	enough energy; wrong orientation	no reaction	none
	enough energy; proper orientation	reaction	

Figure 15 Chemical reactions can occur only under the right conditions. The correct atoms of reactants must be aligned, and they must collide with enough energy. ❯ What term describes the minimum amount of energy needed for a reaction to occur?

go.hrw.com
✴ interact online
Keyword: HX8BCMF15

Biological Reactions

Living things carry out many chemical reactions that help maintain a stable internal environment. Many of these reactions require large activation energies. Often, the reactants are large biomolecules that must collide in a very specific orientation. Many of these reactions would not occur without the help of enzymes.

Enzymes An **enzyme** is a molecule that increases the speed of biochemical reactions. Enzymes hold molecules close together and in the correct orientation. This way, the molecules do not have to depend on random collisions to react. An enzyme lowers the activation energy of a reaction, as **Figure 16** shows. ❯ **By assisting in necessary biochemical reactions, enzymes help organisms maintain homeostasis.** Without enzymes, chemical reactions would not occur quickly and easily enough for life to go on.

Enzyme Activity Enzymes fit with reactants like a lock fits a key. As **Figure 17** shows, each enzyme has an **active site,** the region where the reaction takes place. The shape of the active site determines which reactants, or **substrates,** will bind to it. Each different enzyme acts only on specific substrates.

Step ❶ Two substrates bind to an enzyme's active site. The substrates fit in a specific position and location, like a key in a lock.

Step ❷ Binding of the substrates causes the enzyme's shape to change slightly. The substrates fit more tightly in the enzyme's active site. The change in shape causes some bonds in the substrates to break and new bonds to form.

Step ❸ The chemical reaction is complete when the product, a new substance, is formed. The unchanged enzyme releases the product, and can then be reused for another reaction.

Conditions Many enzymes are proteins. Changes in temperature and pH can change a protein's shape. If an enzyme changes shape, it won't work well. Most enzymes need a certain range of temperatures and pH.

---

enzyme a molecule, either protein or RNA, that acts as a catalyst in biochemical reactions

active site on an enzyme, the site that attaches to a substrate

substrate the reactant in reactions catalyzed by enzymes

www.scilinks.org
Topic: Enzymes
Code: HX80531

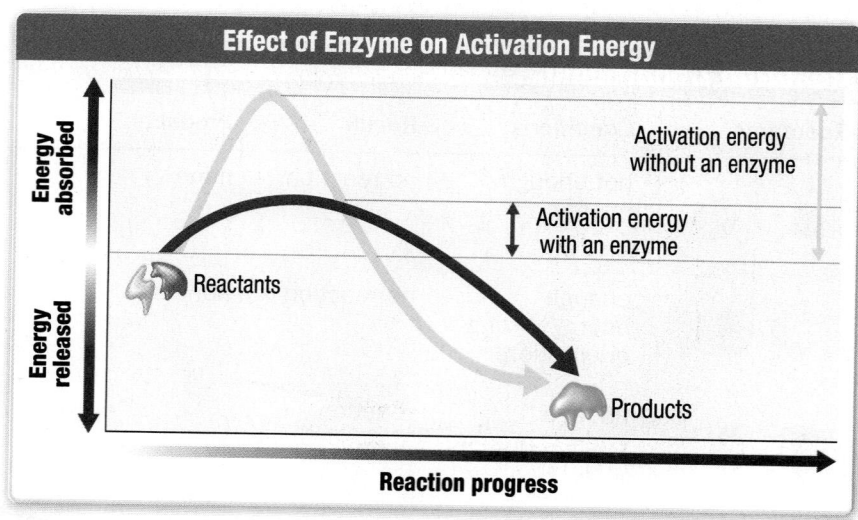

Figure 16 Enzymes decrease the amount of energy needed to start a chemical reaction without changing the amount of energy contained in either the reactants or the products.

Enzyme Action

1 The substrates bind to the enzyme's active site.

Substrates

Active site

Enzyme

2 The enzyme changes shape, which catalyzes the chemical reaction between the substrates.

3 The product is released when the reaction is complete.

Product

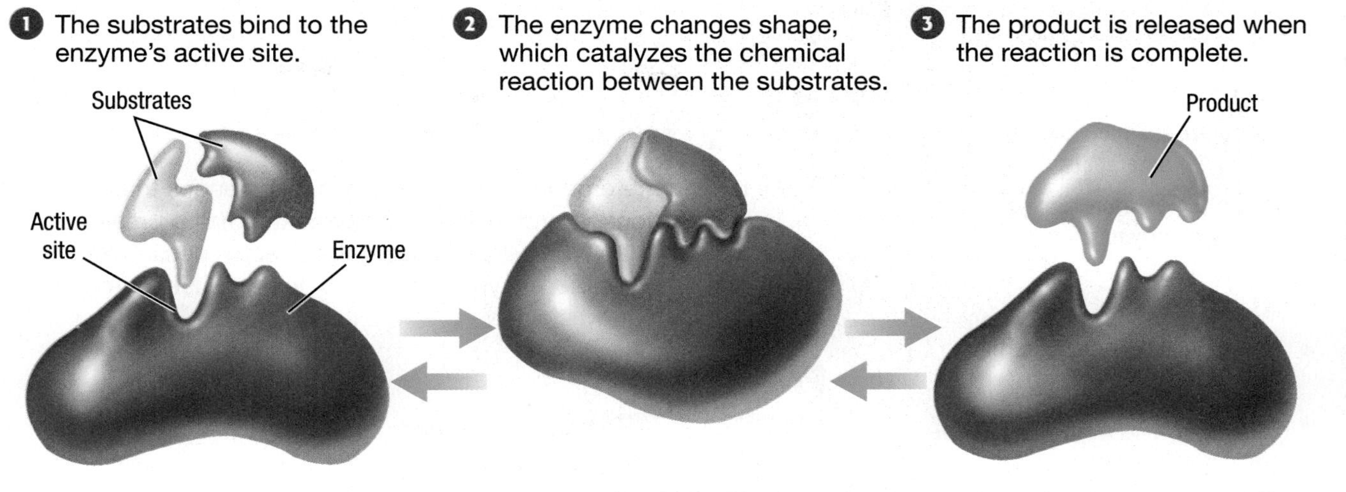

Figure 17 Enzymes catalyze specific reactions between specific reactants.
> **How would a change in the shape of the active site affect the enzyme's activity?**

Metabolism Your cells get most of the energy needed for metabolism from the food you eat. When food is digested, it is broken into small molecules that can enter the blood, which delivers them to cells. Here, chemical reactions release energy by breaking down these food molecules so that cells can use it. The release of energy from food molecules involves many steps and many enzymes.

Consider the breakdown of sugar to release energy. You can use a match to supply enough activation energy to set fire to cellulose, a polysaccharide, when you burn wood. However, the match flame is hot, and the reaction of glucose with oxygen gets even hotter because it is so fast. Living things also "burn" sugars, but they use enzymes to do so. The enzymes reduce the activation energy so much that only a little energy is needed to start the reaction. Then, a series of enzymes carries out the reaction in a slower, step-by-step manner so that the energy can be captured in the form of ATP molecules. In this process, very little heat is produced.

> **Reading Check** *Why is the shape of an enzyme important?*

Section 4 Review

> **KEY IDEAS**

1. **Explain** the importance of chemical reactions in living things.
2. **Describe** two conditions necessary for a chemical reaction to occur.
3. **Relate** enzymes and homeostasis.

CRITICAL THINKING

4. **Applying Information** Explain the difference between usable energy and the total amount of energy. How is this difference accounted for in living organisms?
5. **Recognizing Relationships** Your body breaks down starch into glucose molecules. In this reaction, which substance is the reactant, and which is the product?

WRITING FOR SCIENCE

6. **Predicting Outcomes** Research the enzyme carbonic anhydrase. Explain its role in maintaining homeostasis in the human body. How might a molecule that interferes with the action of carbonic anhydrase affect your body?

Objectives

> Recognize the function of enzymes in laundry detergents.

> Relate temperature and pH to the activity of enzymes.

Materials

- lab apron, safety goggles, and disposable gloves
- balance
- graduated cylinder
- stirring rod, glass
- beaker, 150 mL
- gelatin, instant, regular (18 g) or sugar-free (1.8 g)
- $NaHCO_3$ (0.1 g)
- tongs or a hot mitt
- boiling water, 50 mL
- thermometer
- pH paper
- test tubes (6)
- test-tube rack
- pipet with bulb
- plastic wrap
- tape
- beakers, 50 mL (6)
- distilled water, 50 mL
- detergent, laundry, powdered, five brands (1 g of each)
- wax pencil
- metric ruler

Safety

Enzymes in Detergents

Some laundry detergents contain enzymes, substances that speed up chemical reactions. A protease is an enzyme that helps break down proteins. In this lab, you will investigate the effectiveness of laundry detergents that contain enzymes. To do so, you will use a protein mixture to simulate food stains.

Preparation

1. **SCIENTIFIC METHODS** **State the Problem** How can you determine if a detergent contains proteases?

2. **SCIENTIFIC METHODS** **Form a Hypothesis** Form a testable hypothesis that explains how a protein mixture might be affected by a detergent that contains protease.

Procedure

Make a Protein Substrate

1 Put on a lab apron, safety goggles, and gloves.

2 **CAUTION: Use tongs or a hot mitt to handle heated glassware.** Put 18 g of regular gelatin in a 150 mL beaker. Slowly add 50 mL of boiling water to the beaker, and stir the mixture with a stirring rod. Test and record the pH of this solution.

3 ☠ Very slowly add 0.1 g of $NaHCO_3$, baking soda, to the hot gelatin while stirring. Note any reaction. Test and record the pH of this solution.

4 Place six test tubes in a test-tube rack. Pour 5 mL of the gelatin-$NaHCO_3$ mixture into each tube. Use a pipet to remove any bubbles from the surface of the mixture in each tube. Cover the tubes tightly with plastic wrap and tape. Cool the tubes, and store them at room temperature until you begin your experiment.

5 ⬦ ⬡ Clean up your lab materials according to your teacher's instructions. Wash your hands before you leave the lab.

Design an Experiment

6 Design an experiment that tests your hypothesis and that uses the materials listed for this lab. Predict what will happen during your experiment if your hypothesis is supported.

7 Write a procedure for your experiment. Identify the variables that you will control, the experimental variables, and the responding variables. Construct any tables you will need to record your data. Make a list of all safety precautions you will take. Have your teacher approve your procedure before you begin the experiment.

Conduct Your Experiment

8 ⬦ ⬡ ⬢ Put on a lab apron, safety goggles, and gloves.

9 ⬦ ☠ Make a 10% solution of each laundry detergent by dissolving 1 g of detergent in 9 mL of distilled water.

10 Carry out your experiment. Observe the test tubes after 24 h. Record your data in a data table.

11 ⬦ ⬡ Clean up your lab materials according to your teacher's instructions. Wash your hands before you leave the lab.

Analyze and Conclude

1. **SCIENTIFIC METHODS** **Analyzing Methods** Suggest a reason for adding $NaHCO_3$ to the gelatin solution.

2. **SCIENTIFIC METHODS** **Summarizing Data** Make a bar graph of your data. Plot the amount of gelatin that has broken down (change in the depth of the gelatin) on the y-axis. Plot detergent on the x-axis.

3. **SCIENTIFIC METHODS** **Inferring Conclusions** What conclusions did your group infer from the results? Explain.

4. **Designing an Experiment** How can you test the effect of pH and temperature on action of enzymes in detergents?

5. **Further Inquiry** Write a new question about enzymes in detergents that could be explored in another investigation.

SCI LINKS
www.scilinks.org
Topic: Enzymes
Code: HX80531

Extensions

6. **Relating Concepts** What other active ingredients are present in laundry detergents, and how do they help clean clothes?

7. **Applying Information** What other household products contain enzymes, and what types of enzymes do they contain?

Key Ideas	Key Terms

1 Matter and Substances

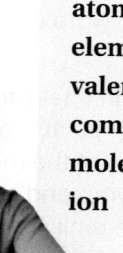

➤ All matter is made up of atoms. An atom has a positively charged nucleus surrounded by a negatively charged electron cloud.

➤ Chemical bonds form between groups of atoms because most atoms become stable when they have eight electrons in the valence shell.

➤ Polar attractions and hydrogen bonds are forces that play an important role in many of the molecules that make up living things.

Key Terms:
atom (51)
element (51)
valence electron (52)
compound (52)
molecule (52)
ion (53)

2 Water and Solutions

➤ The hydrogen bonding between water molecules explains many of the unique properties that make water an important substance for life.

➤ Acids and bases change the concentration of hydronium ions in aqueous solutions. The pH of solutions in living things must be stable.

Key Terms:
cohesion (55)
adhesion (55)
solution (56)
acid (56)
base (56)
pH (57)
buffer (57)

3 Carbon Compounds

➤ Large, complex biomolecules are built from a few smaller, simpler, repeating units arranged in an extremely precise way.

➤ Cells use carbohydrates for sources of energy, structural materials, and cellular identification.

➤ The main functions of lipids include storing energy and controlling water movement.

➤ Proteins are chains of amino acids that twist and fold into shapes that determine what the protein does.

➤ Nucleic acids store and transmit hereditary information.

Key Terms:
carbohydrate (60)
lipid (61)
protein (62)
amino acid (62)
nucleic acid (63)
nucleotide (63)
DNA (63)
RNA (63)
ATP (63)

4 Energy and Metabolism

➤ Living things use different chemical reactions to get the energy needed for life processes.

➤ An activation energy is needed to start a chemical reaction. The reactants must also be aligned to form the product.

➤ By assisting in necessary biochemical reactions, enzymes help organisms maintain homeostasis.

Key Terms:
energy (64)
reactant (65)
product (65)
activation energy (65)
enzyme (66)
active site (66)
substrate (66)

Chapter 3 Review

READING TOOLBOX

1. **Comparison Table** Make a comparison table to compare proteins and nucleic acids.

2. **Concept Map** Make a concept map that illustrates the structure of matter. Include the following terms in your map: *atom, element, compound, molecule,* and *ion.*

Using Key Terms

3. Explain the relationship between *reactant, product,* and *substrate.*

For each pair of terms, explain how the meanings of the terms differ.

4. *cohesion* and *adhesion*

5. *nucleic acid* and *nucleotide*

Understanding Key Ideas

6. What are the three components of atoms?
   a. matter, electrons, and ions
   b. matter, compounds, and ions
   c. nucleus, electrons, and isotopes
   d. protons, electrons, and neutrons

7. Water dissolves ionic compounds because water molecules
   a. are nonpolar.
   b. do not contain atoms.
   c. have a pH of 14 or greater.
   d. have partially charged ends.

8. An aqueous solution that contains extra hydroxide ions is a(n)
   a. gas   c. acid
   b. base   d. solid

9. How many electrons are in the valence shell of a carbon atom?
   a. 1   c. 4
   b. 2   d. 6

10. The order of amino acids is a protein's
    a. primary structure.   c. tertiary structure.
    b. secondary structure.   d. quaternary structure.

11. A new substance that forms as the result of a chemical reaction is a(n)
    a. gas.   c. reactant.
    b. product.   d. element.

12. Why do living things depend on enzymes?
    a. Enzymes produce energy.
    b. Enzymes change the temperature.
    c. Enzymes speed up chemical reactions.
    d. Enzymes prevent the formation of wastes.

This diagram is a model of a nucleotide. Use the diagram to answer the following question(s).

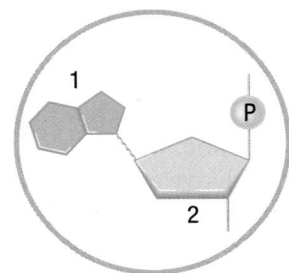

13. What does Structure 1 represent?
    a. a base   c. a steroid
    b. a sugar   d. a phosphate

14. What does Structure 2 represent?
    a. a base   c. a steroid
    b. a sugar   d. a phosphate

Explaining Key Ideas

15. **Describe** how forming compounds affects the stability of atoms.

16. **Identify** an example of adhesion and an example of cohesion.

17. **Compare** the structure of a simple carbohydrate with that of a complex carbohydrate.

18. **Identify** an important characteristic of waxes in living things.

19. **Differentiate** between a physical change and a chemical change.

20. **Explain** why a product might not form even if the activation energy is available.

Using Science Graphics

This graph shows the relationship between pH and the activity of two digestive enzymes, pepsin and trypsin. Use the graph to answer the following question(s).

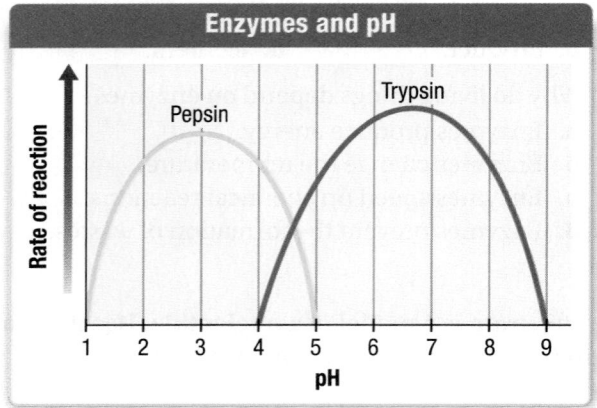

Enzymes and pH

21. At what pH does pepsin work best?

22. Pepsin works in the stomach, while trypsin works in the small intestine. What does the graph indicate about the relative acidity of the stomach and small intestine?

Critical Thinking

23. **Applying Information** Given that elements are pure substances, how many types of atoms make up the structure of a single element? Explain your answer.

24. **Analyzing Concepts** In nature, the elements oxygen and hydrogen are usually found as gases with the formulas O_2 and H_2. Why? Are they compounds? Are they molecules?

25. **Recognizing Differences** What are two differences between ionic bonds and covalent bonds?

26. **Inferring Relationships** When salt is added to water, the freezing point of the water decreases. Explain why.

27. **Applying Concepts** Based on what you know about carbohydrates, lipids, and proteins, why is a balanced diet important?

28. **Making Inferences** Animals that live in freezing climates often store body fat as oil. What would be the adaptive advantage of storing body fat as oil instead of as a solid?

29. **Recognizing Relationships** High temperatures can weaken bonds within a protein molecule. How might this fact explain the effects of using a hot curling iron or rollers in one's hair?

30. **Analyzing Concepts** Living things need a constant supply of energy. Explain why.

31. **Inferring Conclusions** Outline a reason why a slight change in the pH of solutions in living things could result in the death of the organism.

Why It Matters

32. **Surface Tension** Using what you have learned about the properties of water, explain how some insects, such as water striders, can stand on the surface of water.

Alternative Assessment

33. **Evaluating Promotional Claims** Analyze the ingredients of various packaged foods. For each food, record the percentage of the food that carbohydrates, fats, and proteins make up. List any additives that the products contain. Research whether the additives are natural or artificial, and find out why they are added to particular foods. Compare these data to advertising claims about the products that you analyzed.

Writing for Science

34. **Extended Response** Pure water contains equal numbers of hydronium ions and hydroxide ions and is therefore neutral. What is the initial cause of the dissociation of water molecules into hydrogen and hydroxide ions? Explain the process. After water dissociates, hydronium ions form. Explain this process.

35. **Short Response** In an experiment that a student conducted, the rate of an enzyme-catalyzed reaction did not increase, even though the student increased the substrate concentration. Deduce why the reaction rate does not change even though more of the reactant is available.

Science Concepts

1. The way in which elements bond to form compounds depends on which of the following?

    A the size of the electrons

    B the shape of the nucleus

    C the number of neutrons in each atom

    D the electrons in the atoms of the elements

2. In what type of bond are electrons shared?

    F ionic   **H** covalent

    G nuclear   **J** hydrogen

3. What weak bond holds together the two strands of nucleotides in a DNA molecule?

    A ionic   **C** covalent

    B nuclear   **D** hydrogen

4. When an unknown substance is dissolved in water, hydronium ions form. What can you conclude about the substance?

    F The substance is a gas.

    G The substance is a base.

    H The substance is an acid.

    J The substance is a carbohydrate.

This diagram shows a type of biomolecule. Use the diagram to answer the following question(s).

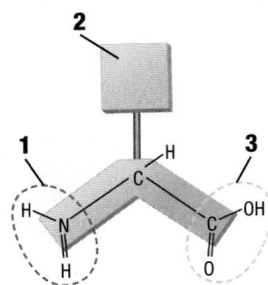

5. A bond can form between Group 1 of this type of molecule and Group 3 of another type of this molecule. What is this bond called?

    A ionic bond   **C** double bond

    B peptide bond   **D** triple bond

6. Carboxypeptidase is an enzyme that catalyzes reactions in the small intestine. The products of these reactions are amino acids. What are the substrates of carboxypeptidase?

    F lipids   **H** nucleic acids

    G proteins   **J** carbohydrates.

Using Science Graphics

This graph shows the energy in a catalyzed chemical reaction as the reaction progresses. Use the graph to answer the following question(s).

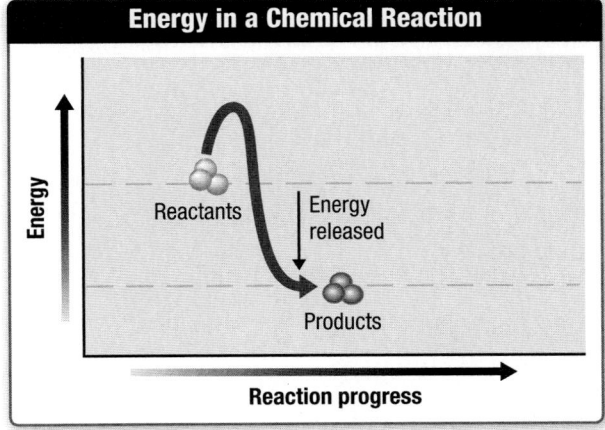

7. The amount of energy needed for this chemical reaction to begin is shown by the line rising from the reactants. What is this energy called?

    A chemical energy   **C** activation energy

    B electrical energy   **D** mechanical energy

8. Suppose that this reaction needs a catalyst to proceed. In the absence of a catalyst, the activation energy would be which of the following?

    F larger than what is shown

    G the same as what is shown

    H smaller than what is shown

    J very similar to what is shown

Math Skills

9. Protein A is a chain of 660 amino acids. Protein B is a chain of 11 amino acids. How many times as many amino acids as Protein B does Protein A have?

    A 6   **C** 60

    B 16   **D** 66

UNIT 2 Ecology

4 Ecosystems

5 Populations and Communities

6 The Environment

Atlantic puffins

Plastic bottles for recycling

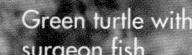

Green turtle with
surgeon fish

The Changing Environment

AROUND 250

Mayan farmers build terraces to control the flow of water to crops. The irrigated terraces greatly increase crop yields and enable farmers to make use of farmland on steep hillsides.

1791

A canal for Washington D.C. is designed to connect the James and Tiber Creeks. The canal drains wet areas of the city and provides a new commercial transportation route.

Washington, D.C., capital of the United States

1890

John Muir and others successfully persuade Congress to create Yosemite National Park, the first national park in the world.

Half Dome, Yosemite National Park

1936

The captive thylacine, or Tasmanian tiger, dies in a zoo in Hobart, Tazmania. Sightings in the wild continue but are rare. The population dwindles because of predation by humans and dogs. The thylacine is declared extinct in 1986.

1962

Rachel Carson's book, *Silent Spring*, which describes the careless use of pesticides and their damage to the environment, is published.

Rachel Carson

1986

In the Ukraine, an accident at the Chernobyl nuclear power plant releases large amounts of nuclear radiation. The area around the power plant becomes one of the most highly radioactive places on Earth. A cloud of radioactive fallout travels as far as the eastern United States.

1990

Three large tuna companies announce that they will sell only tuna that is caught using nets that do not trap dolphins. This change is attributed to a successful consumer boycott of tuna caught using conventional nets that can trap and drown dolphins.

1999

Hybrid cars, which run on gas and electricity, hit the mass market in the United States.

Prototype Daihatsu UFE II hybrid

Ant removing butterfly eggs from a leaf

BIOLOGY CAREER

Ecologist
Erika Zavaleta

Erika Zavaleta is an assistant professor in the Environmental Studies department of the University of California, Santa Cruz. Her current research focuses on changes in levels of biodiversity in biological communities and ecosystems that result from environmental challenges and changes.

A high school science teacher, Dr. Roberts, inspired Zavaleta to become a scientist. Roberts used scientific nonfiction and an inquiry-based approach to inspire her students. Zavaleta still loves to read and engage scientific problems with a creative and open mind.

Zavaleta considers her greatest accomplishment in science to be bridging scientific disciplines to explore changes from many angles. These changes include climate change, the invasive species, the ecological and socioeconomic implications of losing biodiversity, and woodland restoration.

Apart from science, Zavaleta enjoys traveling, reading, and outdoor activities such as surfing, bodyboarding, bicycling, hiking, and backpacking.

Hamster and grasshopper predator-prey relationship

Chapter 4 Ecosystems

Preview

1 What Is an Ecosystem?
Ecosystems
Succession
Major Biological Communities
Terrestrial Biomes
Aquatic Ecosystems

2 Energy Flow in Ecosystems
Trophic Levels
Loss of Energy

3 Cycling of Matter
Water Cycle
Carbon and Oxygen Cycles
Nitrogen Cycle
Phosphorus Cycle

Why It Matters

An ecosystem is a community of organisms that interact with one another and their physical environment. Humans are part of ecosystems and are dependent on healthy ecosystems. However, humans can disrupt ecosystems, and the disruption may harm the organisms of the ecosystems and humans themselves.

Organisms in ecosystems interact with each other. This small fish has an unusual predator—a spider. This fishing spider from French Guiana waits at the surface of the water for its prey.

Some species of fishing spiders can walk on the water's surface, aided by fine hairs on the legs which trap air and act as buoys.

Like most spiders, the fishing spider has eight eyes.

The unlucky prey is nearly as large as its predator.

InquiryLab

Water Cycle

The cycling of water in an ecosystem is necessary for the organisms that are part of the ecosystem. In this activity, you will model the water cycle.

Procedure

1. Place a **small, dark-colored bowl** inside a **large, sealable, plastic freezer bag.** Position the bag so that the opening is at the top.

2. Fill the bowl halfway with **water.** Place three drops of **red food coloring** in the water. Seal the bag.

3. Place the bowl and bag under a strong and warm light source, such as a **lamp** or direct sunlight.

4. Leave the bag in the light for one hour. Observe the bag at regular intervals.

Analysis

1. **Describe** how your model mimics the behavior of water in the environment

2. **Predict** how organisms such as plants would be affected if water did not cycle through the environment.

READING TOOLBOX

These reading tools can help you learn the material in this chapter. For more information on how to use these and other tools, see **Appendix: Reading and Study Skills.**

Using Words

Word Families Word families include words that can be combined to create a meaning that differs from the meaning of each word in the combination. The names of natural cycles of Earth are formed from word families that you will find in this chapter.

Your Turn Use the information in the table to answer the following questions.
1. What do you think happens in the carbon, water, and phosphorus cycles?
2. How do the three cycles differ?

Word Parts		
Word part	**Type**	**Meaning**
carbon	noun	an element common to all living things
water	noun	a liquid necessary for life
phosphorus	noun	a chemically reactive, nonmetallic element
cycle	noun	a circular process

Using Language

Word Problems Read word problems several times before trying to solve them. After you understand what the problems are asking, write down all of the relevant information on a piece of paper. Then, use the mathematical processes that apply to the situation.

Your Turn Solve the following word problem about energy.
1. When a snake a eats a mouse, only about 10% of the energy stored in the mouse's body is stored in the snake. If the body of a mouse contains 2000 kcal of energy, how much energy is stored in the snake?

Using FoldNotes

Layered Book A layered book is a useful tool for taking notes as you read a chapter. The four flaps of the layered book can summarize information into four categories. Write details of each category on the appropriate flap to create a summary of the chapter.

Your Turn Create a layered book FoldNote.
1. Lay one sheet of paper on top of another sheet. Slide the top sheet up so that 2 cm of the bottom sheet is showing.
2. Holding the two sheets together, fold down the top of the two sheets so that you see four 2 cm tabs along the bottom.
3. Using a stapler, staple the top of the FoldNote.
4. On each tab, write the category of the information that will appear on that layer.

What Is an Ecosystem?

Key Ideas	Key Terms	Why It Matters
➤ What are the parts of an ecosystem? ➤ How does an ecosystem respond to change? ➤ What two key factors of climate determine a biome? ➤ What are the three major groups of terrestrial biomes? ➤ What are the four kinds of aquatic ecosystems?	community ecosystem habitat biodiversity succession climate biome	Ecosystems are important units of the natural world. Humans are part of ecosystems and depend on ecosystems for food and many products. Without healthy ecosystems, humans would be in trouble!

When you walk through a forest, you see many different organisms. There are trees, birds, ants, mushrooms, and much more. You may not see many of these organisms interact. But all organisms, including humans, that live together are interdependent.

Ecosystems

A species never lives alone. A group of various species that live in the same place and interact with one another is called a **community.** The group, along with the living and nonliving environment, make up an **ecosystem.** ➤ An ecosystem includes a community of organisms and their physical environment.

Community of Organisms A community of organisms is a web of relationships. One relationship is that of a predator eating its prey. For example, some fish eat spiders, as **Figure 1** shows. Some species help each other. For example, some bacteria fix nitrogen into a form that plants can use to grow. Relationships between organisms are examples of biotic factors that affect an ecosystem. *Biotic* describes living factors in an ecosystem. Biotic factors also include once-living things, such as dead organisms and the waste of organisms.

> **community** a group of various species that live in the same habitat and interact with each other
>
> **ecosystem** a community of organisms and their abiotic environment

Chhops

Figure 1 In this relationship, the fish is the predator, and the spider is the prey. ➤ **Give another example of a relationship between two species in a community.**

Hands-On

QuickLab

 30 min

Biodiversity Evaluation

By making simple observations, you can draw some conclusions about biodiversity in an ecosystem.

Procedure

CAUTION: Follow your teacher's instructions about sun protection handling organisms. Prepare a list of biotic and abiotic factors to observe around your home or in a nearby park, and record your observations.

Analysis

1. **Identify** the habitat and community that you observed.

2. **Calculate** the number of different species as a percentage of the total number of organisms that you saw.

3. **Rank** the importance of biotic factors within the ecosystem that you observed.

4. **Infer** what the relationships are between biotic factors and abiotic factors in the observed ecosystem.

---

habitat a place where an organism usually lives

biodiversity the variety of organisms in a given area, the genetic variation within a population, the variety of species in a community, or the variety of communities in an ecosystem

succession the replacement of one type of community by another at a single location over a period of time

---

Physical Factors The physical or nonliving factors of an environment are called *abiotic factors*. Examples of abiotic factors are oxygen, water, rocks, sand, sunlight, temperature, and climate. These physical factors shape organisms. For example, plants and animals in deserts are small because deserts do not have enough water to support large organisms. Water supply also affects the number of individuals and variety of species that an ecosystem can support. A crop of corn will have a higher yield in a wetter habitat than in a drier habitat. A **habitat** is the place where an organism lives.

Biodiversity Suppose you counted the various species in a pine forest. Then, you counted the number of species in a tropical rain forest. Do you think the number of species in each ecosystem would be the same? No, a tropical rain forest has many more species than a pine forest does. The variety of organisms in a given area is called **biodiversity.**

Physical factors can have a big influence on biodiversity. In places that have very high or very low temperatures, biodiversity is often lower. Limited water and food also cause lower biodiversity. The biodiversity of habitats and ecosystems varies greatly. The vast expanse of the open ocean has very low biodiversity. In contrast, rain forests and coral reefs have very high biodiversity. When ecosystems have high biodiversity, they are often more able to resist damage. Damage to ecosystems can be caused by severe weather events or human activities. Systems with low biodiversity can be severely damaged easily. When biodiversity decreases in any ecosystem, that ecosystem is not as healthy as it could be.

❯ **Reading Check** *List three examples of physical parts of an ecosystem. (See the Appendix for answers to Reading Checks.)*

Succession

When we observe an ecosystem, it may look like an unchanging feature of the landscape. However, all ecosystems change. As an ecosystem changes, the kinds of species that the ecosystem supports change. The replacement of one community by another at a single place over a period of time is called **succession.**

Change in an Ecosystem When a volcano forms a new island or a fire burns the vegetation of an area, new opportunities are made for organisms. The first organisms to appear in a newly made habitat are called *pioneer species*. Pioneer species are often small, fast-growing plants that reproduce quickly. They change the habitat in such a way that other species can live in the ecosystem. For example, pioneer species such as lichens and mosses will break down volcanic rock on a new island to help form soil. Other species can then grow on the soil. For example, after lichens and mosses have formed soil, grasses and weeds may then cover a volcanic island. Even later, shrubs and trees often outcompete and replace the grass. Then, the grassland turns into a forest. **Figure 2** shows an example of succession in response to the receding of a glacier.

Equilibrium If a major disruption strikes a community, many of the organisms may be wiped out. But the ecosystem reacts to the change. ❯ **An ecosystem responds to change in such a way that the ecosystem is restored to equilibrium.** When a tree falls down in a rain forest, for example, the newly vacant patch proceeds through succession until the patch returns to its original state. Sometimes, the ecosystem will find an equilibrium in which different species dominate after a change. In the grasslands of Africa, for example, weather conditions can lead to succession. When there is a lot of rain in the grasslands, one species of grass dominates the savanna. But when conditions are drier, a drought-resistant species of grass will dominate.

❯ **Reading Check** *Why are pioneer species helpful to other species?*

Figure 2 At Glacier Bay in Alaska, a receding glacier makes succession possible.

Pioneer species quickly modify the land recently exposed after a glacier has receded.

Alders, grasses, and shrubs take over from the pioneer plants and help form more soil.

As the amount of soil increases, spruce and hemlock trees become plentiful.

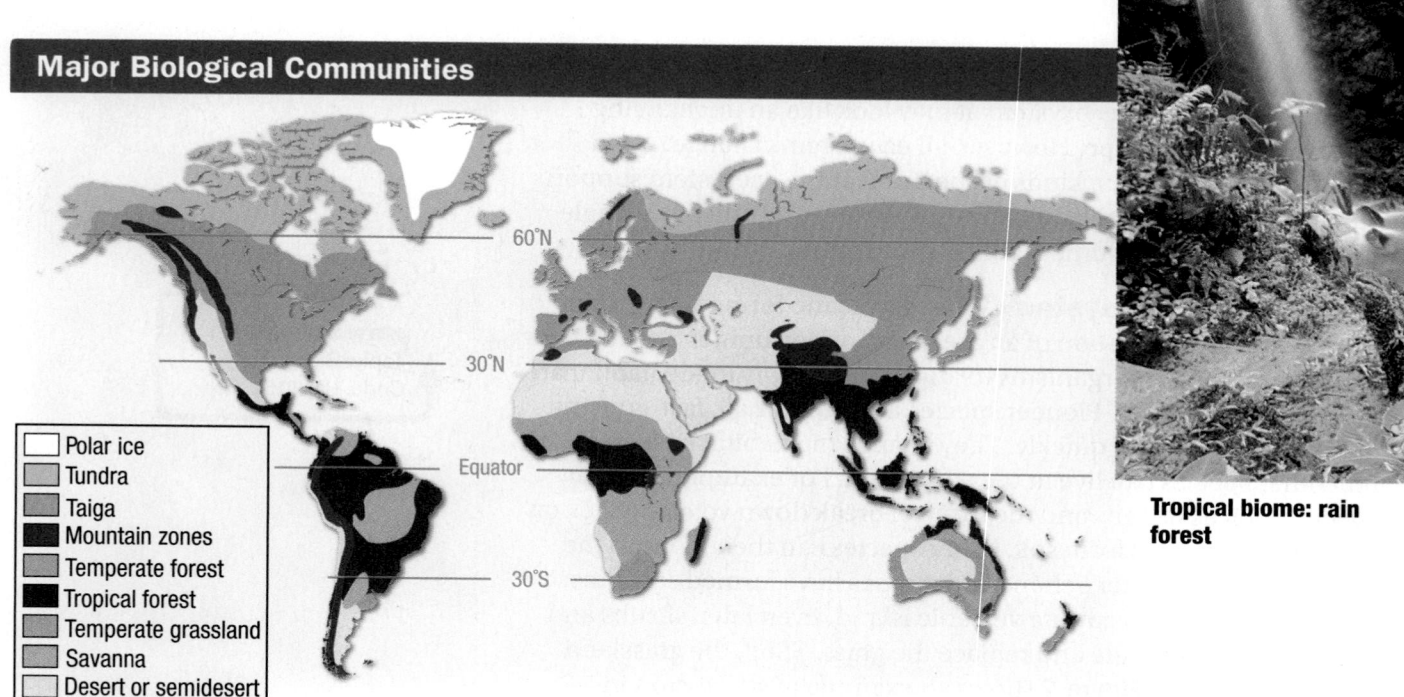

Major Biological Communities

Tropical biome: rain forest

Figure 3 Biomes cover most of Earth's land surface. Because mountainous areas do not belong to any one biome, they are given their own designation. Polar ice covers Greenland and Antarctica, which is not shown in the map. ❯ **Identify the biome that you live in.**

Map legend:
- Polar ice
- Tundra
- Taiga
- Mountain zones
- Temperate forest
- Tropical forest
- Temperate grassland
- Savanna
- Desert or semidesert

ACADEMIC VOCABULARY

range a scale or series between limits

climate the average weather conditions in an area over a long period of time

biome a large region characterized by a specific type of climate and certain types of plant and animal communities

Major Biological Communities

If you drive across the United States, you notice a change in the kinds of plants and animals. The kinds of species that live in a particular place are determined partly by climate. **Climate** is the average weather conditions in an area over a long period of time. At places near the North Pole, you may see polar bears. Polar bears have thick, white fur and insulating fat that keep them warm on the frozen tundra. The same adaptations that help polar bears in the tundra would hurt polar bears in a tropical forest. Polar bears must live in a biome to which they are adapted. A **biome** is a large region characterized by a specific kind of climate and certain kinds of plant and animal communities.

❯ **Two key factors of climate that determine biomes are temperature and precipitation.** Most organisms are adapted to live within a particular range of temperatures and cannot survive at temperatures too far above or below that range. Precipitation also determines the kinds of species that are found in a biome. In biomes where precipitation is low, for example, the vegetation is made up mostly of plants that need little water, such as cactuses.

Terrestrial Biomes

There are many different biomes on land. ❯ **Earth's major terrestrial biomes can be grouped by latitude into tropical, temperate, and high-latitude biomes.** As **Figure 3** shows, tropical biomes are generally near the equator. For the most part, temperate biomes are between 30° and 60° latitude. High-latitude biomes are at latitudes 60° and higher. Latitude affects the amount of solar energy that a biome receives and thus affects a biome's temperature range.

Temperate biome: temperate grasslands

Polar biome: taiga

Tropical Biomes Because they are located at low latitudes near the equator, all tropical biomes are warm. However, each tropical biome receives a different amount of rain. *Tropical rain forests* receive large amounts of rain and are warm all year. They have the greatest biodiversity of any land biome. At least half of Earth's species of land organisms live in tropical rain forests. *Savannas* are tropical grasslands. They get less rain than tropical rain forests do. Savannas also have long dry seasons and shorter wet seasons. The most well-known savannas are in eastern Africa, where zebras, giraffes, lions, and elephants roam the grasslands. *Tropical deserts* get very little rain. Because the deserts have less water, they have fewer plants and animals than other biomes do.

Temperate Biomes Biomes at mid-latitudes have a wide range of temperatures throughout the year. *Temperate grasslands* have moderate precipitation and cooler temperatures than savannas do. Temperate grasslands are often highly productive when used for agriculture. Herds of grazing animals, like bison, used to live on the temperate grasslands of North America. *Temperate forests* grow in mild climates that receive plenty of rain. Trees of the temperate deciduous forests shed their leaves in the fall because of the cold winters. Trees of temperate evergreen forests do not lose their leaves or needles during the winter. Temperate forests are home to deer, bears, beavers, and raccoons. Like tropical deserts, *temperate deserts* receive little precipitation. However, unlike tropical deserts, temperate deserts have a wide temperature range throughout the year.

High-Latitude Biomes Biomes at high latitudes have cold temperatures. Coniferous forests in cold, wet climates are called *taiga*. Winters are long and cold. Most of the precipitation falls in the summer. Moose, wolves, and bears live in the taiga. The *tundra* gets very little rain, so plants are short. Much of the water in the soil is not available because the water is frozen for most of the year. Foxes, lemmings, owls, and caribous live in the tundra.

SCLINKS.
www.scilinks.org
Topic: Biomes
Code: HX80158

❯ **Reading Check** *In what latitudes are savannas found?*

Figure 4 A bayou, such as this one in Louisiana, is an example of a wetland. The coral reef is an example of a marine ecosystem.

Aquatic Ecosystems

The diverse regions in the world's bodies of water are not usually called *biomes*. They are often called *aquatic ecosystems.* ❯ **Aquatic ecosystems are organized into freshwater ecosystems, wetlands, estuaries, and marine ecosystems.**

Freshwater ecosystems are located in bodies of fresh water, such as lakes, ponds, and rivers. These ecosystems have a variety of plants, fish, arthropods, mollusks, and other invertebrates.

Wetlands provide a link between the land and fully aquatic habitats. Water-loving plants dominate wetlands. This ecosystem supports many species of birds, fishes, and plants, as shown in **Figure 4.** Wetlands are important because they moderate flooding and clean the water that flows through them.

An *estuary* is an area where fresh water from a river mixes with salt water from an ocean. Estuaries are productive ecosystems because they constantly receive fresh nutrients from the river and the ocean.

Marine ecosystems are found in the salty waters of the oceans. Kelp forests, seagrass communities, and coral reefs are found near land. The open ocean, far from land, has plankton and large predators, such as dolphins, whales, and sharks.

❯ **Reading Check** *Which aquatic ecosystems have salt water?*

Section 1 Review

❯ KEY IDEAS

1. **Describe** the difference between an ecosystem and a community.
2. **Explain** how an ecosystem responds to change.
3. **Identify** the three major groups of terrestrial biomes.
4. **Describe** the four types of aquatic ecosystems.
5. **Identify** two factors of climate that determine a biome.

CRITICAL THINKING

6. **Relating Concepts** If two areas on separate continents have similar climates, do they have similar communities? Explain your answer.

WRITING FOR SCIENCE

7. **Essay** Identify a biome in which the plants are short and require little water and the animals are small. Then, write a one page description of this biome.

Why It Matters

Maintained by Fire

When a fire sweeps through a forest, the fire destroys just about everything in its path. But did you know that fire can actually be a good thing for certain communities? In fact, fire is important for preserving many plant communities and the animals that depend on them.

Fire Lovers

Some plants benefit from fire. Fireweed, a plant with purple flowers as shown in this burned forest in Alaska, is one such plant. Fireweed gets its name because it quickly colonizes burned land without competition from other species. Other species of plants need fire in order to reproduce! The jack pine is one such species. The jack pine can release seeds only after it is exposed to the intense heat of a fire.

Ecosystem on Fire
Firefighters often light fires on purpose. This firefighter in South Dakota is setting a controlled fire because burned vegetation helps bring nutrients to the soil.

Research Find out more about controlled fires. Why must controlled fires be set in some ecosystems? What are the advantages and disadvantages of controlled fires?

Energy Flow in Ecosystems

Key Ideas	Key Terms	Why It Matters
❯ How does energy flow through an ecosystem? ❯ What happens to energy as it is transferred between trophic levels in a community?	producer consumer decomposer trophic level energy pyramid	The way in which energy flows through an ecosystem is critical to the ecosystem's productivity and ability to support its species. By understanding this flow of energy, we can learn how to develop food more efficiently.

Everything that organisms do requires energy. Running, breathing, and even sleeping require energy. Every species must somehow get food for energy. A zebra grazes on savanna grass. A lion chases down the zebra and eats it. The lion eventually dies and is eaten by scavengers. The rest of the carcass is decomposed by bacteria and other microbes. At each step in this process, energy flows through the ecosystem.

Trophic Levels

An organism eating another organism is the most obvious interaction in a community. This interaction transfers energy through an ecosystem. The way in which energy flows through an ecosystem determines how many species and individuals live in the ecosystem.

The primary source of energy for an ecosystem is the sun. Photosynthetic organisms, such as plants and algae, change light energy from the sun into energy that they can use to grow. These photosynthetic organisms are **producers,** the basic food source for an ecosystem. **Consumers** are organisms that eat other organisms instead of producing their own food. **Decomposers,** such as bacteria and fungi, are organisms that break down the remains of animals. ❯ **In an ecosystem, energy flows from the sun to producers to consumers to decomposers.** Each step in the transfer of energy through an ecosystem is called a **trophic level. Figure 5** shows the trophic levels through which energy passes to a blue jay.

❯ **Reading Check** *Where do consumers get their energy?*

SCI LINKS.
www.scilinks.org
Topic: Food Webs
Code: HX80600

Figure 5 Each step in the transfer of energy through an ecosystem is called a *trophic level.*

The sun is the primary energy source.

Producers use energy from the sun to produce their own food.

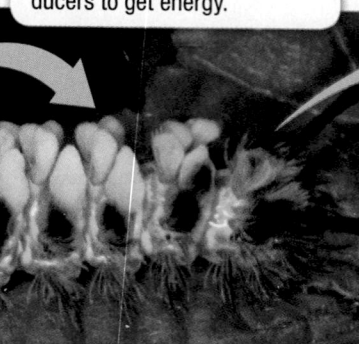

Some consumers eat producers to get energy.

Some consumers eat other consumers.

Food Chains In ecosystems, energy flows from one trophic level to the next, forming a *food chain.* The first trophic level of ecosystems is made up of producers. Plants, algae, and some bacteria use the energy in sunlight to build energy-rich carbohydrates. The second trophic level of a food chain is made up of *herbivores,* which eat producers. Cows are an example of an herbivore. The third trophic level includes animals that eat herbivores. Any animal that eats another animal is a *carnivore.* Some carnivores are on the third trophic level because they eat herbivores. For example, small birds eat caterpillars, which feed on plant leaves. Other carnivores are on the fourth trophic level or an even higher trophic level because they eat other carnivores. For example, hawks eat small birds. *Omnivores,* such as bears, are animals that are both herbivores and carnivores.

Food Web In most ecosystems, energy does not follow a simple food chain. Energy flow is much more complicated. Ecosystems almost always have many more species than a single food chain has. In addition, most organisms eat more than one kind of food. For example, hawks eat fish, small birds, and rabbits. Rabbits are food not only for hawks but also for wolves, mountain lions, and many other carnivores. This complicated, interconnected group of food chains, such as the group in **Figure 6,** is called a *food web.*

producer a photosynthetic or chemosynthetic autotroph that serves as the basic food source in an ecosystem

consumer an organism that eats other organisms or organic matter instead of producing its own nutrients or obtaining nutrients from inorganic sources

decomposer an organism that feeds by breaking down organic matter from dead organisms

trophic level one of the steps in a food chain or food pyramid

Figure 6 A food web shows a more complete picture of the feeding relationships in an ecosystem. The arrows show the direction in which energy travels. ❯ **In the diagram, identify the animals that receive energy from the rabbit.**

Figure 7 This girl is eating producers, which form the base of an energy pyramid.

Loss of Energy

When a zebra eats 20 lb of grass, the zebra does not gain 20 lb. A lot of the energy that was stored in the grass is lost. Where did the energy go? ❯ **Energy is stored at each link in a food web. But some energy that is used dissipates as heat into the environment and is not recycled.**

The Ten Percent Rule When a zebra eats grass, some of the energy in the grass is stored in the zebra. The energy may be stored as fat or as tissue. However, most of the energy does not stay in the zebra. As the zebra uses energy from the grass to run and grow, the energy is changed into heat energy. Then, the heat energy is dispersed into the environment. Thus, the zebra does not keep 90% of the energy that it gets from the grass. Only about 10% of the energy in the grass becomes part of the zebra's body. This amount of stored energy is all that is available to organisms at the next trophic level that consume the zebra. For example, a 100 kg lion needs 1,000 kg of zebras. And combined, the zebras need 10,000 kg of plants!

By understanding energy flow between trophic levels, we can learn how to feed more people. If people eat big fish that are in the third trophic level, it takes 1,000 kg of producers to build 1 kg of human. If people eat cows that are in the second trophic level, 100 kg of producers are needed for 1 kg of human. If people, such as the girl in **Figure 7,** eat producers—such as vegetables, fruits, and grains— only 10 kg of producers are needed to produce 1 kg of human.

❯ **Reading Check** *When energy is transferred from one trophic level to another, where does 90% of the energy go?*

Math Skills ⟩ Energy Pyramid

This energy pyramid shows the trophic levels in a marine ecosystem. You can use the pyramid to help you understand how energy is transferred from one trophic level to another.

The base of a pyramid is the producer, which contains the most energy. Phytoplankton is the base of this pyramid. As energy is transferred from one trophic level to the next trophic level, 90% of the energy is lost. Only 10% of the energy is available to the next trophic level.

If the phytoplankton level has 10,000 units of energy, the amount of energy stored in the copepod level can be calculated as follows:

10,000 units of energy × 10% = 1,000 units of energy

The amount of energy stored in the herring level can be calculated as follows:

1,000 units of energy × 10% = 100 units of energy

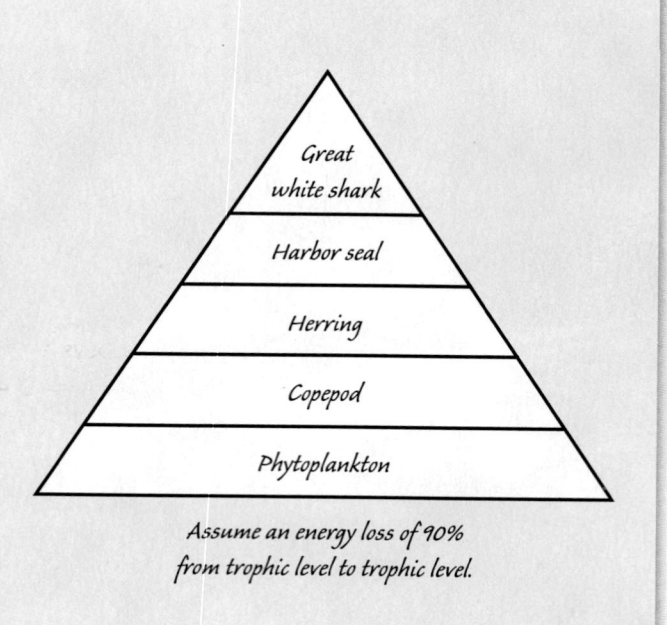

Great white shark

Harbor seal

Herring

Copepod

Phytoplankton

Assume an energy loss of 90% from trophic level to trophic level.

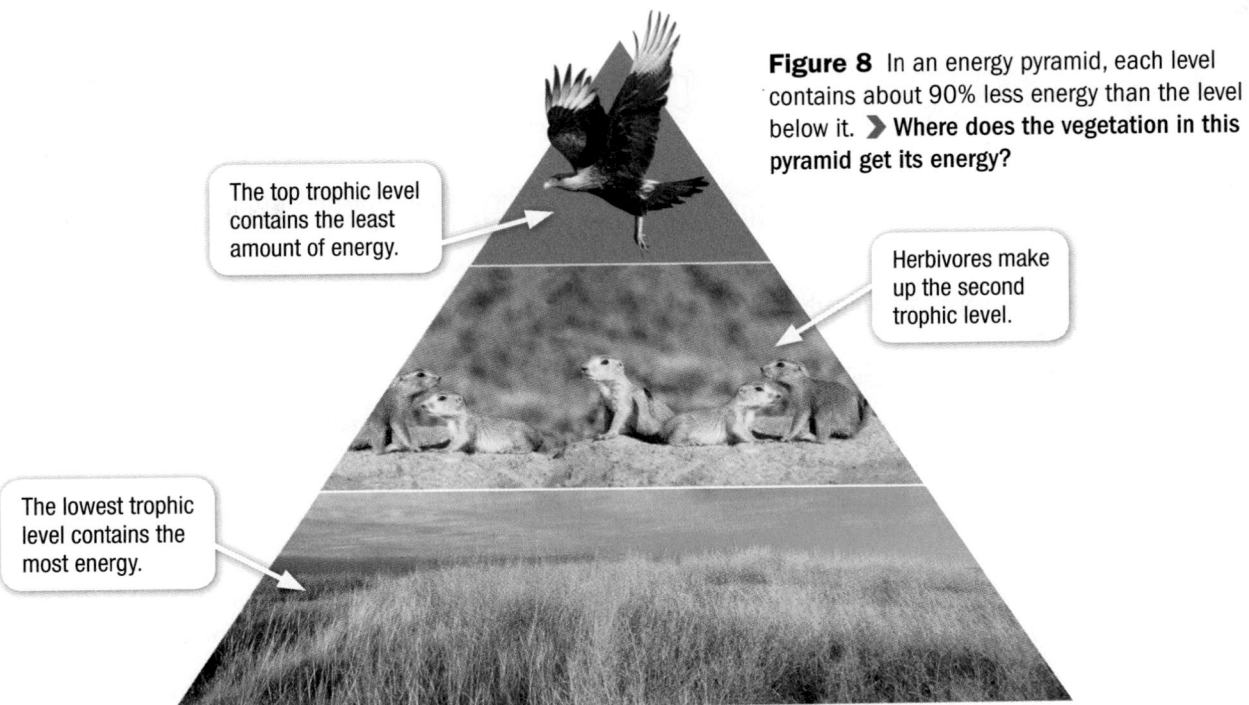

Figure 8 In an energy pyramid, each level contains about 90% less energy than the level below it. ❯ **Where does the vegetation in this pyramid get its energy?**

The top trophic level contains the least amount of energy.

Herbivores make up the second trophic level.

The lowest trophic level contains the most energy.

Energy Pyramid A triangular diagram that shows an ecosystem's loss of energy, which results as energy passes through the ecosystem's food chain, is called an **energy pyramid.** An energy pyramid is shown in **Figure 8.** Each layer in the energy pyramid represents one trophic level. Producers form the pyramid's base, which is the lowest trophic level. The lowest level has the most energy in the pyramid. Herbivores have less energy and make up the second level. Carnivores that feed on herbivores make up the higher level. The energy stored by the organisms at each trophic level is about one-tenth the energy stored by the organisms in the level below. So, the diagram takes the shape of a pyramid.

Big predators, such as lions, are rare compared to herbivores. Big predators are rare because a lot more energy is required to support a single predator than a single herbivore. Many ecosystems do not have enough energy to support a large population of predators.

energy pyramid a triangular diagram that shows an ecosystem's loss of energy, which results as energy passes through the ecosystem's food chain

READING TOOLBOX

Word Problem If the prairie dog level in a food pyramid contains 35,000 units of energy, how much of that energy can be stored in the eagle level of the food pyramid?

Section 2 Review

❯ **KEY IDEAS**

1. **Describe** how energy flows in an ecosystem.
2. **Explain** why only 10% of energy is transferred from one trophic level to the next.
3. **Describe** the difference between a herbivore, a carnivore, and an omnivore.

CRITICAL THINKING

4. **Justifying Conclusions** What limits the length of food chains in an ecosystem?
5. **Evaluating an Argument** Explain why scientists believe that most animals would become extinct if all plants died.
6. **Analyzing Data** Which trophic level contains more energy: a trophic level of herbivores or a trophic level of carnivores? Why?

USING SCIENCE GRAPHICS

7. **Creating Diagrams** Draw a diagram of a food web that has four trophic levels and at least one species that is an omnivore. Be sure to label producers, consumers, omnivores, and top predators. Label each trophic level.

Cycling of Matter

Key Ideas	Key Terms	Why It Matters
❭ What is the water cycle? ❭ Why are plants and animals important for carbon and oxygen in an ecosystem? ❭ Why must nitrogen cycle through an ecosystem? ❭ Why must phosphorus cycle through an ecosystem?	carbon cycle respiration nitrogen cycle phosphorus cycle	Water, carbon, phosphorus, and nitrogen are critical resources for organisms, including humans. Natural cycles of these resources are important to ecosystems, but humans can disrupt these cycles.

Water, carbon, oxygen, nitrogen, and phosphorus are five of the most important substances for life. An ecosystem must be able to cycle these kinds of matter in order to support life.

Water Cycle

Life could not exist without the *water cycle.* ❭ **The water cycle continuously moves water between the atmosphere, the land, and the oceans.** As **Figure 9** shows, water vapor *condenses* and falls to Earth's surface as *precipitation.* Some of this water *percolates* into the soil and becomes groundwater. Other water runs across the surface of Earth into rivers, lakes, and oceans. Then, the water is heated by the sun and reenters the atmosphere by *evaporation.* Water also evaporates from trees and plants in a process called *transpiration.*

go.hrw.com
✳ interact online
Keyword: HX8ECOF9

Figure 9 Water cycles through ecosystems by the processes of transpiration, evaporation, condensation, precipitation and percolation.

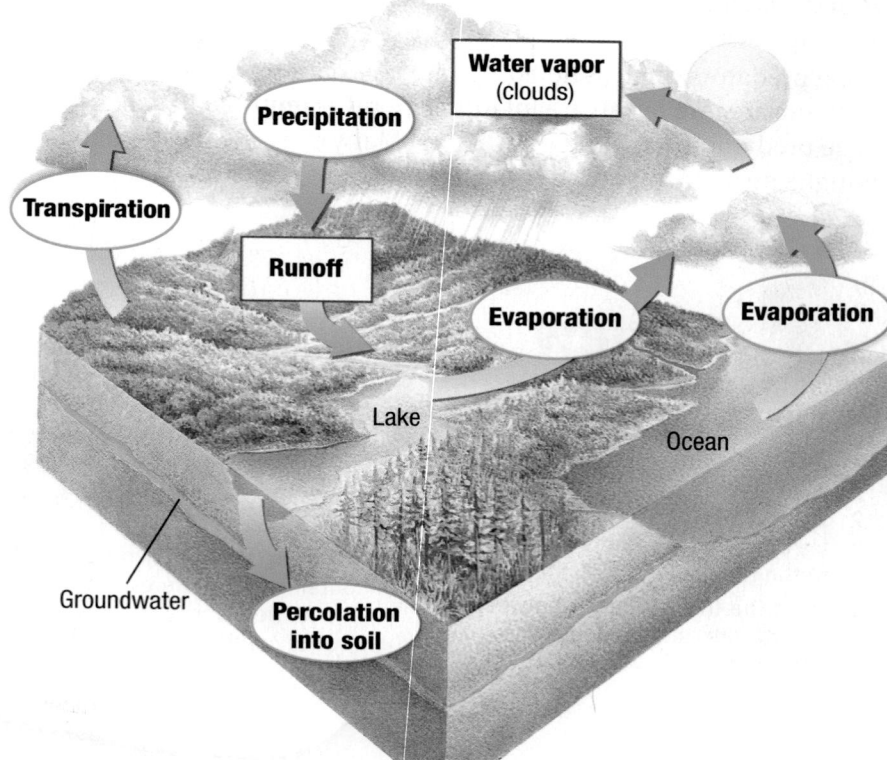

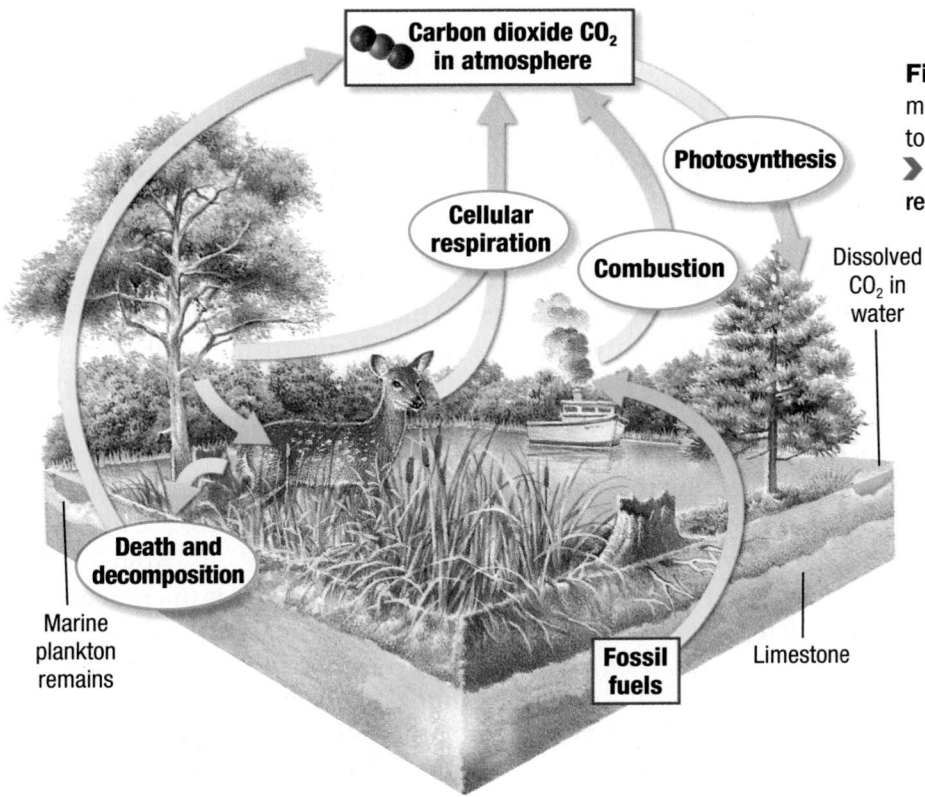

Carbon dioxide CO$_2$ in atmosphere

Photosynthesis

Cellular respiration

Combustion

Dissolved CO$_2$ in water

Death and decomposition

Marine plankton remains

Fossil fuels

Limestone

Figure 10 In the carbon cycle, carbon moves from organisms to the atmosphere, to the soil, and to other living things.
❯ How is the carbon in fossil fuels released into the atmosphere?

www.scilinks.org
Topic: Carbon Cycle
Code: HX80216

Carbon and Oxygen Cycles

Carbon and oxygen are critical for life on Earth, and their cycles are tied closely together. The **carbon cycle** is the continuous movement of carbon from the nonliving environment into living things and back. The carbon cycle is shown in **Figure 10.**

❯ Animals, plants, and other photosynthesizing organisms play an important role in cycling carbon and oxygen through an ecosystem. Plants use the carbon dioxide, CO$_2$, in air to build organic molecules during the process of photosynthesis. During photosynthesis, oxygen is released into the surroundings. Many organisms, such as animals, use this oxygen to help break down organic molecules, which releases energy and CO$_2$. Then, plants can use the CO$_2$ in photosynthesis. The process of exchanging oxygen and CO$_2$ between organisms and their surroundings is called **respiration.**

Carbon is also released into the atmosphere in the process of combustion. *Combustion* is the burning of a substance. All living things are made of carbon. When living things or once-living things are burned, they release carbon into the atmosphere. For example, the burning of trees releases carbon into the atmosphere as CO$_2$. Fossil fuels are formed from the remains of dead plants and animals. Thus, the burning of fossil fuels releases CO$_2$ into the atmosphere. Humans burn fossil fuels to generate electricity and to power vehicles. Examples of fossil fuels that humans burn are oil and coal.

❯ **Reading Check** *How does respiration play a role in cycling carbon and oxygen through an ecosystem?*

carbon cycle the movement of carbon from the nonliving environment into living things and back

respiration the exchange of oxygen and carbon dioxide between living cells and their environment

READING TOOLBOX

Word Families Explain how the carbon cycle and the oxygen cycle are similar. Explain how they are different.

Nitrogen Cycle

All organisms, including you, need nitrogen. ❯ **Nitrogen must be cycled through an ecosystem so that the nitrogen is available for organisms to make proteins.** The **nitrogen cycle** is the process in which nitrogen circulates among the air, soil, water, and organisms in an ecosystem. The nitrogen cycle is shown in **Figure 11.**

The atmosphere is about 78% nitrogen gas, N_2. But most organisms cannot use nitrogen gas. It must be changed into a different form. A few bacteria have enzymes that can break down N_2. These bacteria supply the nitrogen that all other organisms need. The bacteria split N_2 and then bind nitrogen atoms to hydrogen to form ammonia, NH_3. The process of combining nitrogen with hydrogen to form ammonia is called *nitrogen fixation*. Nitrogen may be fixed by lightning. But more nitrogen is fixed by bacteria. Nitrogen-fixing bacteria live in the soil and on the roots of some plants. Nitrogen is also fixed when humans burn fuels in vehicles and industrial plants.

Plants get nitrogen by assimilation. *Assimilation* is the process in which plants absorb nitrogen. When an animal eats a plant, nitrogen compounds become part of the animal's body. During *ammonification,* nitrogen from animal waste or decaying bodies is returned to the soil by bacteria. Ammonia is then <u>converted</u> to nitrite and then nitrate by the process of *nitrification*. Finally, in *denitrification,* nitrate is changed to nitrogen gas, N_2, which returns to the atmosphere.

❯ **Reading Check** *Explain the role of bacteria in the nitrogen cycle.*

nitrogen cycle the cycling of nitrogen between organisms, soil, water, and the atmosphere

phosphorus cycle the cyclic movement of phosphorus in different chemical forms from the environment to organisms and then back to the environment

Figure 11 Bacteria carry out many of the important steps in the nitrogen cycle, including the conversion of atmospheric nitrogen into a usable form, such as ammonia.

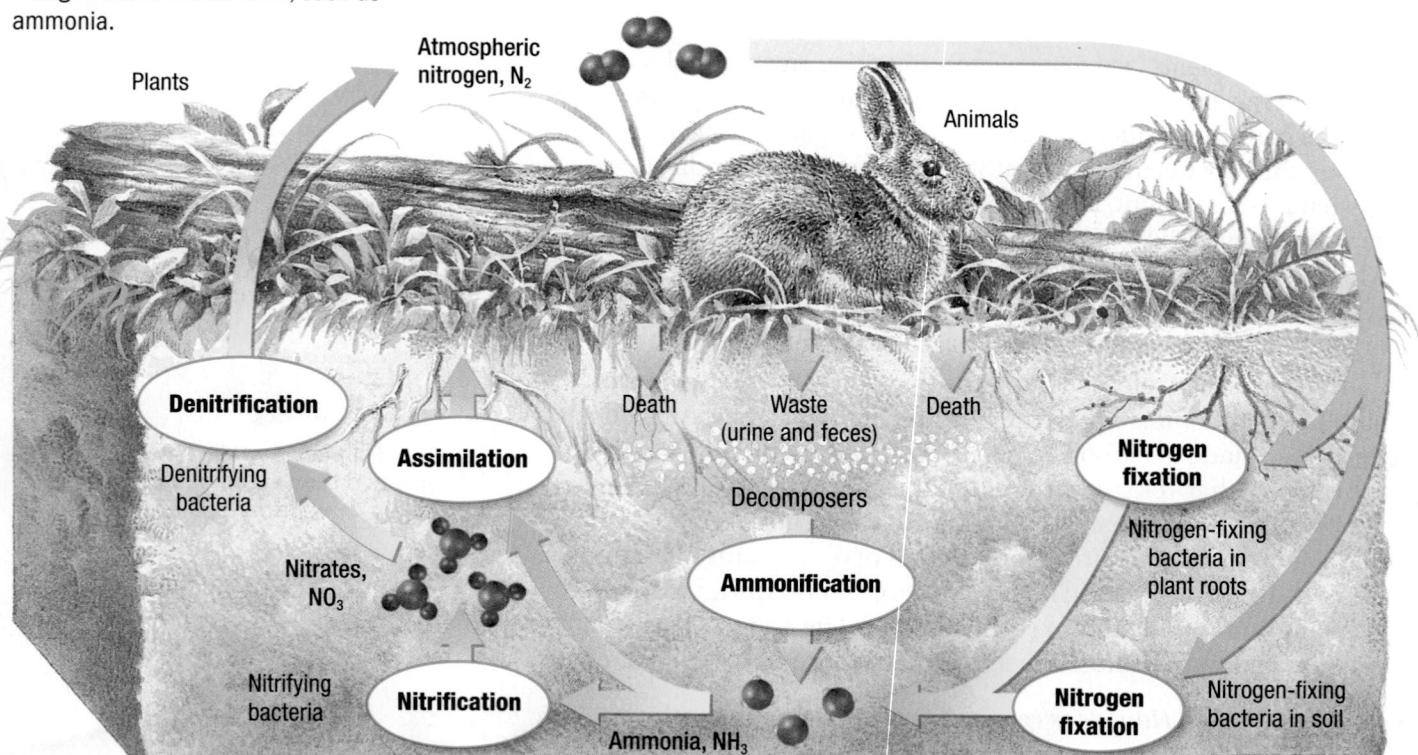

QuickLab

🕐 15 min

The Carbon Cycle

You are part of the carbon cycle. Every time that you exhale, you release CO_2 into the atmosphere. But the CO_2 does not stay as CO_2 for very long.

Procedure

1 Pour **100 mL of water** into a **250 mL beaker.** Add **several drops of bromthymol blue** to the water. Add enough drops to make the solution dark blue.

2 ☠ **CAUTION: Be sure not to inhale or ingest the solution.** Exhale through a **straw** into the solution until the CO_2 in your breath turns the solution yellow.

3 Pour the yellow solution into a **large test tube** that contains a **sprig of Elodea.**

4 Use a **stopper** to seal the test tube. Then, place the test tube in a sunny location.

5 Observe the solution in the test tube after 15 min.

Analysis

1. **CRITICAL THINKING** **Inferring Conclusions** What do you think happened to the carbon dioxide that you exhaled into the solution?

2. **CRITICAL THINKING** **Analyzing Methods** How do plants, such as the *Elodea,* affect the carbon cycle?

Phosphorus Cycle

❯ **Phosphorus is an important part of ATP and DNA and must be cycled in order for an ecosystem to support life.** The **phosphorus cycle** is the movement of phosphorus in different chemical forms from the surroundings to organisms and then back to the surroundings. Phosphorus is often found in soil and rock as calcium phosphate, which dissolves in water to form phosphate. The roots of plants absorb phosphate. Humans and animals that eat the plants reuse the organic phosphorus. When the humans and animals die, phosphorus is returned to the soil.

❯ **Reading Check** *How is phosphorus passed from soil to plants?*

Section

3 Review

❯ KEY IDEAS

1. **Explain** how carbon and oxygen are cycled through an ecosystem.

2. **Describe** why nitrogen must cycle through an ecosystem.

3. **Explain** why it is important that phosphorus be cycled through an ecosystem.

4. **Summarize** the steps of the water cycle.

CRITICAL THINKING

5. **Making Connections** Explain why the oxygen and carbon cycles are tied so closely together.

6. **Predicting Outcomes** Describe what would happen if matter could not cycle through ecosystems.

7. **Analyzing Processes** Defend the argument that nutrients can cycle but energy cannot.

METHODS OF SCIENCE

8. **Designing an Experiment** Design an experiment in which you would determine whether nitrogen-fixing bacteria really help plants grow faster.

Chapter 4 **Lab**

Objectives

▶ Construct an ecosystem model.

▶ Observe interactions of organisms in an ecosystem model.

▶ Compare an ecosystem model with a natural ecosystem.

Materials

- goggles, gloves, and lab apron
- coarse sand or pea gravel
- terrarium or glass jar, large, with a lid
- soil
- grass seeds, a pinch of
- clover seeds, a pinch of
- water, 150 mL
- rolled oats
- mealworms (beetle larvae)
- mung bean seeds
- earthworms
- isopods (pill bugs)
- crickets

Safety

Ecosystem Change

Organisms in an ecosystem interact with one another and with their environment. Feeding is one interaction that occurs among the organisms in an ecosystem. A food web describes the feeding relationships among the organisms in an ecosystem. In this lab, you will use a terrarium or a jar to model a closed ecosystem. A *closed ecosystem* is a system that allows energy to enter but that is closed to the transfer of matter.

Preparation

1. **SCIENTIFIC METHODS** **State the Problem** How might the different organisms interact in an ecosystem model?

2. **SCIENTIFIC METHODS** **Form a Hypothesis** Form a testable hypothesis about how the number of individuals of each species in an ecosystem model will change over time.

Procedure

Build an Ecosystem in a Jar

❶ ◈ **CAUTION: Glassware is fragile. Notify your teacher promptly of any broken glass or cuts. Do not clean up broken glass or spills that contain broken glass unless your teacher tells you to do so.** Place 5 cm of sand or pea gravel in the bottom of a large, clean, glass jar that has a lid. Cover the gravel with 5 cm of soil.

❷ Sprinkle the seeds of two or three kinds of small plants, such as grasses and clovers, onto the surface of the soil. Add about 150 mL of water. Put the lid on the jar loosely, and place the jar in indirect sunlight. Let the jar remain undisturbed for one week.

❸ ◈ **CAUTION: Handle animals carefully.** Do not allow animals to escape from containers. After one week, place a handful of rolled oats into the jar. Place the mealworms in the oats. Then, place the other animals into the jar, and replace the lid. Place the lid on the jar loosely so that air can enter the jar.

Design an Experiment

4 Work with the members of your lab group to design an experiment that will test the hypothesis that you recorded previously. Design your experiment to use the ecosystem model that you built.

5 Write a procedure for your experiment. Make a list of all of the safety precautions that you will take. Have your teacher approve your procedure and safety precautions before you begin the experiment.

6 Set up your group's experiment. Conduct your experiment for at least 14 days.

Cleanup and Disposal

7 ⟨⟩ Dispose of solutions, broken glass, and other materials in the designated waste containers. Do not put lab materials in the trash unless your teacher tells you to do so.

8 🧤 Clean up your lab materials according to your teacher's instructions. Wash your hands before you leave the lab.

Analyze and Conclude

1. **Summarizing Results** Make graphs showing how the number of individuals of each species in your ecosystem changed over time. Be sure to count both plants and animals. Plot time on the *x*-axis and the number of organisms on the *y*-axis.

2. **SCIENTIFIC METHODS** **Analyzing Data** Compare your results with your hypothesis. Explain any differences.

3. **Inferring Conclusions** Construct a food web for the ecosystem that you observed.

4. **SCIENTIFIC METHODS** **Recognizing Relationships** Does your ecosystem model resemble a natural ecosystem? Explain your answer.

5. **Analyzing Methods** How can you build an ecosystem model that better represents a natural ecosystem?

6. **Critiquing Models** Was your ecosystem model truly a closed ecosystem? List your model's strengths and weaknesses as a closed ecosystem.

7. **Analyzing Data** List the biotic and abiotic factors in your ecosystem model.

www.scilinks.org
Topic: Ecosystems
Code: HK80466

Extensions

8. **Further Inquiry** Write a new question to explore with another investigation using an ecosystem model.

9. **Making Comparisons** Use the library or Internet to learn about Biosphere 2. What problems did the Biosphere 2 crew encounter during the 1991–1993 project?

go.hrw.com
SUPER SUMMARY
Keyword: HX8ECOS

Key Ideas	Key Terms

1 What Is an Ecosystem?

> An ecosystem is a community of organisms and their abiotic environment.

> An ecosystem responds to change in such a way that the ecosystem is restored to equilibrium.

> Two key factors of climate that determine biomes are temperature and precipitation.

> Earth's major terrestrial biomes can be grouped by latitude into tropical, temperate biomes, and high-latitude.

> Aquatic ecosystems are organized into freshwater ecosystems, wetlands, estuaries, and marine ecosystems.

community (79)
ecosystem (79)
habitat (80)
biodiversity (80)
succession (81)
climate (82)
biome (82)

2 Energy Flow in Ecosystems

> In an ecosystem, energy flows from the sun to producers to consumers to decomposers.

> Energy is stored at each link in a food web, but some energy that is used dissipates as heat into the environment and is not recycled.

producer (86)
consumer (86)
decomposer (86)
trophic level (86)
energy pyramid (89)

3 Cycling of Matter

> The water cycle is the continuous movement of water between the atmosphere, the land, and the oceans.

> Animals, plants, and other photosynthesizing organisms play an important role in cycling carbon and oxygen through an ecosystem.

> Nitrogen must be cycled through an ecosystem so that the nitrogen is available for organisms to make proteins.

> Like water, carbon, oxygen, and nitrogen, phosphorus must be cycled in order for an ecosystem to support life.

carbon cycle (91)
respiration (91)
nitrogen cycle (92)
phosphorus cycle (93)

1. **Layered Book** Create the layered book FoldNote. Use the layered book to summarized the information you learned in this chapter.

2. **Concept Map** Make a concept map that describes the flow of energy through an ecosystem. Try to include the following terms: *trophic level, food web, food chain, producer, consumer, carnivore, decomposer,* and *herbivore.*

Using Key Terms

Use each of the following terms in a separate sentence.

3. *respiration*

4. *biodiversity*

5. *decomposer*

For each pair of terms, explain how the meanings of the terms differ.

6. *climate* and *biome*

7. *ecosystem* and *community*

8. *producer* and *consumer*

Understanding Key Ideas

9. Which of the following is a biotic factor?
   a. rainfall
   b. predators
   c. air temperature
   d. the availability of nitrogen

10. Which kind of organism converts the sun's energy into energy that can be used to grow?
    a. consumers   c. omnivores
    b. producers   d. decomposers

11. Which of the following biomes has a wide range of temperatures and is located at mid-latitudes?
    a. taiga   c. temperate forest
    b. savanna   d. tropical rain forest

12. Which of the following is not a step in the nitrogen cycle?
    a. nitrification   c. percolation
    b. denitrification   d. ammonification

13. Which of the following processes describes the loss of water from leaves to the atmosphere?
    a. transpiration   c. precipitation
    b. condensation   d. percolation

14. What percentage of the energy in a rabbit is stored in a coyote that eats the rabbit?
    a. 0%   c. 90%
    b. 10%   d. 100%

Use the diagram to answer the following question(s).

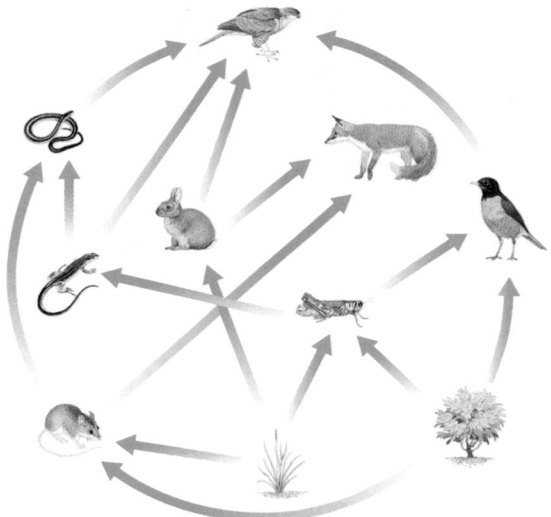

15. How would this food web be affected if the plants were eliminated?
    a. Herbivores would become carnivores.
    b. The herbivores would move to another trophic level.
    c. The carnivores would survive, but the herbivores would not survive.
    d. The herbivores would die because of the lack of food. Then, the rest of the animals would die because of the loss of the herbivores.

Explaining Key Ideas

16. **Describe** what eventually happens to the pioneer species in an ecosystem.

17. **Summarize** the steps of energy flow through an ecosystem by creating food chain diagram.

18. **Explain** the process of nitrogen fixation, and describe where it occurs.

Using Science Graphics

Use the diagram of the food chain to answer the following question(s).

19. Which organisms are consumers?
  a. the leaf and bird
  b. the tree and leaf
  c. the bird and caterpillar
  d. the tree and caterpillar

Use this diagram to answer the following question(s).

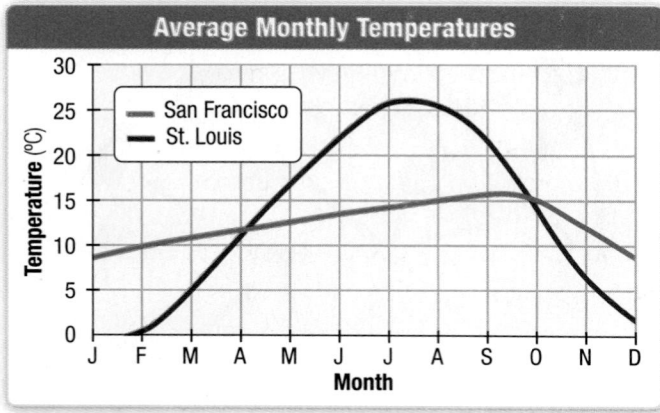

20. Estimate the difference between the average temperatures of San Francisco and St. Louis in July.

Critical Thinking

21. Predicting Outcomes What would happen to an ecosystem if all of the decomposers disappeared?

22. Analyzing Processes Which component of the carbon cycle removes carbon dioxide from the atmosphere?

23. Drawing Conclusions Why might wetlands be considered economically and environmentally important?

24. Evaluating Information For deciduous trees, compare the benefits and possible disadvantages of shedding leaves in the fall.

25. Forming Reasoned Opinions A friend says that the idea of food chains is silly because almost no ecosystems have simple food chains. Is your friend correct? Explain why or why not.

26. Forming Hypotheses Speculate what might happen to a plant if you sprinkle some nitrogen in a usable form on the soil near the plant.

Writing for Science

27. Advertisement Create an ad explaining how understanding the flow of energy through an ecosystem can help humans feed more people or put less pressure on ecosystems.

Methods of Science

28. Designing an Investigation You are asked to determine the biodiversity inside a local park. How will you measure the park's biodiversity? Explain why you chose this particular method.

Alternative Assessment

29. Research Find information about organisms that live in marine ecosystems. Compare deep-sea organisms with organisms that live near the surface. What are the major abiotic factors that influence the organisms at particular depths? Why don't animals near the surface also live deep below the surface? What is the source of food for animals in the deep sea?

30. Nature Study Spend the afternoon at a park. For every organism that you see, write down what the organism is and how it gets its energy (a butterfly, for example, is a herbivore that gets its energy from flowers). Create two bar graphs. Make one show the number of species in each trophic level and the other show the number of individuals for each trophic level. Explain the patterns that you find.

31. Research Find information on the eutrophication of freshwater ecosystems. Write an essay explaining what happens during this process and how the disruption of the phosphorus cycle affects the ecosystem.

Math Skills

32. Energy Pyramid Assume that 1 energy unit is required to support a great white shark. If an ecosystem has 1,000,000 units of energy at the phytoplankton level, how many great white sharks could this ecosystem support?

> **TEST TIP** For multiple-choice questions, try to eliminate any answer choices that are obviously incorrect. Then, consider the remaining answer choices.

Science Concepts

1. Which of the following is an abiotic factor?

  A the presence of ample food

  B the presence of trees where birds can nest

  C the presence of strong currents around a reef

  D the presence of a cleaner shrimp that can help fish get rid of parasites

2. Which of the following biomes is the coldest and driest biome?

  F taiga   **H** savanna

  G tundra   **J** desert

3. In what form is carbon released during respiration?

  A calcium carbonate   **C** carbohydrate

  B carbon dioxide   **D** water vapor

4. Where do animals get their supply of phosphorus?

  F plants   **H** soil

  G water   **J** the atmosphere

5. Which of the following situations describes a carnivore and a herbivore?

  A A horse eats an apple.

  B A rabbit eats a dandelion.

  C A mountain lion eats a rabbit.

  D A fungus breaks down a dead oak tree.

6. Which term applies to most humans?

  F herbivore   **H** omnivore

  G carnivore   **J** decomposer

7. Which of the following does not fix nitrogen?

  A trees   **C** bacteria

  B lightning   **D** burning fuels

Using Science Graphics

Use the diagram to answer the following question(s).

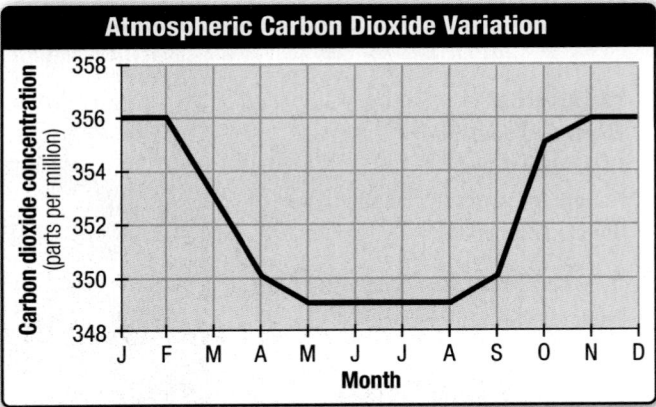

Atmospheric Carbon Dioxide Variation

8. During which of the following months is the rate of photosynthesis greatest?

  F January   **H** May

  G March   **J** September

Use the diagram of a food chain to answer the following question(s).

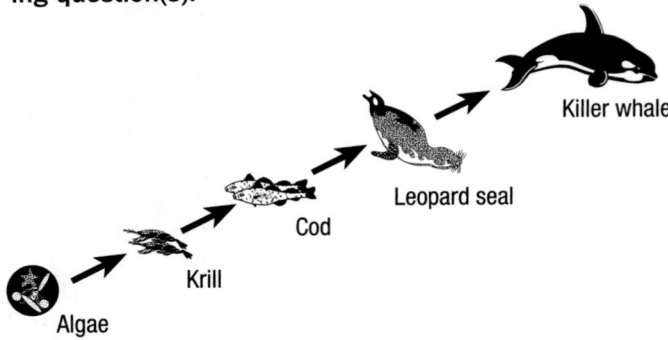

9. What is the role of the krill in this food chain?

  A producers   **C** detritivores

  B consumers   **D** decomposers

Writing Skills

10. Creative Writing Write a short story about an old abandoned farm that experiences succession over a 70-year period.

Chapter 5

Populations and Communities

Preview

1 Populations

What Is a Population?
Population Growth
Factors That Affect Population Size
Human Population

2 Interactions in Communities

Predator-Prey Interactions
Other Interactions

3 Shaping Communities

Carving a Niche
Competing for Resources
Ecosystem Resiliency

Why It Matters

How many species are in an area, how their populations grow, and how they interact with other species, including humans, are major factors that shape ecosystems and the environment's resources.

This crab and iguana have a relationship in which both benefit. The crab eats the iguana's dead skin. The iguana gets the irritating, dead, flaky skin removed, and the crab gets a meal.

The sally lightfoot crab is a scavenger and will feed on just about anything, including dead skin.

InquiryLab

Population Size

In this activity, you will model the change in size of a population.

Procedure

1. Using **110 g of dry beans,** count out five beans to represent the starting population of a species.

2. Assume that each year, 20% of the beans have two offspring. Also, assume that 20% of the beans die each year.

3. Calculate the number of beans to add or subtract for 1 year.

4. Add to or remove beans from your population as appropriate. Record the new population size.

5. Continue modeling your population changes over the course of 10 years. Record the population size for each year.

Analysis

1. **Calculate** the final population size after 10 years.

2. **Graph** your data. Describe the changes in your population.

The marine iguana and the sally lightfoot crab live on the Galápagos Islands in the Pacific Ocean.

The marine iguana is the only true saltwater lizard. It is an excellent swimmer and feeds on marine algae.

READING TOOLBOX

These reading tools can help you learn the material in this chapter. For more information on how to use these and other tools, see **Appendix: Reading and Study Skills.**

Using Words

Word Origins Many common English words derive from Greek or Latin words. Learning the meanings of some Greek or Latin words can help you understand the meaning of many modern English words.

Word Origins		
Word	**Origin**	**Meaning**
niche-	Latin (nidus)	nest
para-	Greek	beside
-site	Greek	food

Your Turn Answer the following questions.

1. Why might an organism's role be called its *niche?*
2. Why might a tick on a dog be considered a parasite?

Using Language

Predictions Some predictions are conditional: Something might happen, but only if something else happens first. For example, if the temperature drops below freezing, snow might fall. The prediction is that snow might fall tonight. But snow might fall under one condition. First, the temperature has to drop below freezing.

Your Turn In the following sentences, identify the condition and the prediction.

1. After the deer population reaches 600 individuals on the island, the deer will eat most of the vegetation, and the number of deer will decrease.
2. If the otters are removed from the ecosystem, the sea urchins will eat all of the kelp.

Using Graphic Organizers

Venn Diagram A Venn diagram is a useful tool for comparing two or three topics in science. A Venn diagram shows which characteristics are shared by the topics and which characteristics are unique to each topic.

Your Turn Create a Venn diagram that compares the characteristics of communities, ecosystems, and populations.

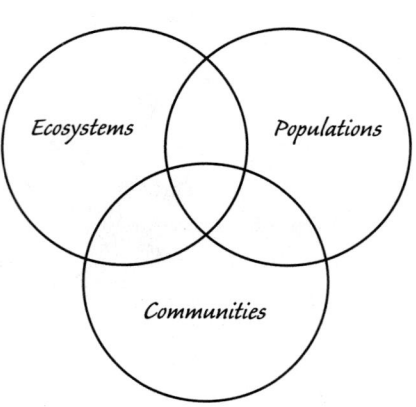

1. Draw a diagram like the one shown here. Draw one circle for each topic. Make sure that each circle partially overlaps the other circles.
2. In each circle, write a topic that you want to compare with the topics in the other circles.
3. In the areas of the diagram where circles overlap, write the characteristics that the topics in the overlapping circles share.
4. In the areas of the diagram where circles do not overlap, write the characteristics that are unique to the topic of the particular circle.

Key Ideas	Key Terms	Why It Matters
❯ Why is it important to study populations? ❯ What is the difference between exponential growth and logistic growth? ❯ What factors affect population size? ❯ How have science and technology affected human population growth?	population carrying capacity	Understanding how populations grow and shrink is critical to managing agricultural pests and diseases and also for knowing how to protect ecosystems.

In the 1850s, about two dozen rabbits from Europe were introduced into Australia. The rabbits had plenty of vegetation to eat, no competition, and no predators. Their numbers increased rapidly. By the 1950s, there were 600 million rabbits! The rabbits ate so much vegetation that the numbers of native plants and animals declined and crops were damaged.

What Is a Population?

As Australia learned, understanding populations is important for protecting ecosystems. A **population** is made up of a group of organisms of the same species that live together in one place at one time and interbreed. **Figure 1** shows members of a zebra population. As new zebras are born, the population size increases. As other zebras fall prey to predators, the population decreases. Hundreds of miles away, there may be another zebra population that lives together and interbreeds.

Populations can be small or large. Some populations stay at nearly the same number for years at a time. Some populations die out from lack of resources. Other populations grow rapidly, such as the rabbit population in Australia. The rapid growth of the rabbit population caused problems with Australia's ecosystems, other species, and farmland. ❯ **Understanding population growth is important because populations of different species interact and affect one another, including human populations.**

> **population** a group of organisms of the same species that live in a specific geographical area and interbreed

❯ **Reading Check** *What distinguishes one zebra population from another zebra population? (See Appendix for answers to Reading Checks.)*

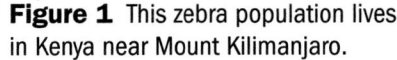
Figure 1 This zebra population lives in Kenya near Mount Kilimanjaro.

go.hrw.com
✴ **interact online**
Keyword: HX8COMF2

Figure 2 Exponential growth is characterized by a J-shaped curve. Rabbits and bacteria are two examples of populations that can grow exponentially.

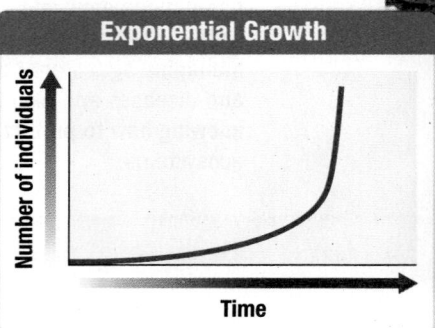

Exponential Growth

Number of individuals

Time

carrying capacity the largest population that an environment can support at any given time

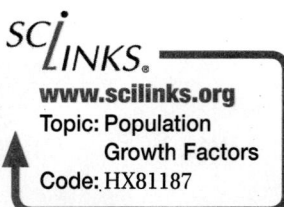

www.scilinks.org
Topic: Population Growth Factors
Code: HX81187

Population Growth

One of the most basic questions ecologists ask is "How do populations grow and shrink?" To help answer this question, biologists make population models. A population model attempts to show key growth characteristics of a real population.

Whether a population grows or shrinks depends on births, deaths, immigration, and emigration. *Immigration* is the movement of individuals into a population. *Emigration* is the movement of individuals out of a population. So, a simple population model describes the rate of population growth as the difference between birthrate, death rate, immigration, and emigration. Plotting population changes against time on a graph creates a model in the form of a curve. Two major models of population growth are *exponential growth* and *logistic growth*.

Exponential Growth One important part of a population model is the growth rate. When more individuals are born than die, a population grows. In exponential growth, there are always more births than deaths. As time goes by, more and more individuals enter the population. ❯ *Exponential growth* occurs when numbers increase by a certain factor in each successive time period. This type of increase causes the J-shaped curve of exponential growth seen in **Figure 2.**

In exponential growth, population size grows slowly when it is small. But as the population gets larger, growth speeds up. Bacteria are an example of a population that can grow exponentially. Populations of bacteria grow very fast. A single bacterial cell that divides every 30 minutes will have produced more than 1 million bacteria in 10 hours. Some populations, such as the rabbits shown in **Figure 2,** may grow exponentially for a while. If they continued to grow exponentially forever, the world would fill up with rabbits!

❯ **Reading Check** *What are the characteristics of a population that grows exponentially?*

Quick Lab

Population Growth

You can learn a lot about a population by plotting its changes on a graph. In this activity, you will plot the growth of a deer population.

Procedure

1 On a graph, plot the data from the table.

2 Title the graph. Then, label the *x*-axis and the *y*-axis.

Analysis

1. **Identify** the dependent and independent variables.

2. **Describe** the growth curve. Does the population increase logistically or exponentially?

3. **Identify** the point at which the population is growing fastest.

4. **CRITICAL THINKING** **Analyzing Results** Are you able to determine the carrying capacity from this graph? If so, label it on the graph. What is its value?

Year	Number of individuals
1930	30
1935	50
1940	98
1945	175
1950	250
1955	273
1960	201
1965	159
1970	185
1975	205
1980	194
1985	203

Logistic Growth Populations do not grow unchecked forever. Factors such as availability of food, predators, and disease limit the growth of a population. Eventually, population growth slows and may stabilize.

An ecosystem can support only so many organisms. The largest population that an environment can support at any given time is called the **carrying capacity.** *Density-dependent factors* are variables affected by the number of organisms present in a given area. An example of a density-dependent factor is the availability of nesting sites. As the number of adult birds increases, there are no longer enough nesting sites for the entire population. So, many birds will not have young, and growth of the population is limited. *Density-independent factors* are variables that affect a population regardless of the population density. Examples of density-independent factors are weather, floods, and fires.

The logistic model takes into account the declining resources available to populations. ❯ *Logistic growth is population growth that starts with a minimum number of individuals and reaches a maximum depending on the carrying capacity of the habitat.* When a population is small, the growth rate is fast because there are plenty of resources. As the population approaches the carrying capacity, resources become scarce. Competition for food, shelter, and mates increases between individuals of a population. As a result, the rate of growth slows. The population eventually stops growing when the death rate equals the birthrate. On a graph, logistic growth is characterized by an S-shaped curve, as **Figure 3** shows. Most organisms, such as the macaws shown in **Figure 3,** show a logistic growth pattern.

Figure 3 Logistic growth is characterized by an S-shaped curve.

Logistic Growth

Population size — Carrying capacity

Time

**READING
TOOLBOX**

Word Origins Write down the definitions of the words *biotic* and *abiotic*. Then, write down what you think that *bio-* means. Use a dictionary to check your answer.

Figure 4 Climate is an abiotic factor that affects the population size of these emperor penguins in Antarctica. ❯ **Name another abiotic factor that may affect the population size of these penguins.**

Factors That Affect Population Size

Most populations increase or decrease. Some change with the seasons. Others have good years and bad years. Many factors cause populations to grow and shrink. ❯ Water, food, predators, and human activity are a few of many factors that affect the size of a population.

Abiotic Factors Nonliving factors that <u>affect</u> population size are called *abiotic factors*. Weather and climate are the most important abiotic factors. For example, the population size of the penguins shown in **Figure 4** is affected by the climate of Antarctica. Unusually low temperatures can reduce the number of young penguins that survive. The amount of water available can also influence populations. Kangaroo populations in Australia grew when farmers gave water to their livestock that was also available for kangaroos to drink.

Biotic Factors A factor that is related to the activities of living things is called a *biotic factor*. Food, such as grass or other animals, is a biotic factor. When there is plenty of food, populations tend to grow. When food is scarce, populations decline. Predators are another kind of biotic factor. When populations of Canadian lynx grow, they eat a lot of snowshoe hares. The population of hares is then reduced. Diseases and parasites, when they infect many individuals, can also cause populations to decline. Biotic factors are often density dependent because they can have a stronger influence when crowding exists. As the density of a population increases, the effects of starvation, predators, and disease often also increase.

Humans affect populations of many species. Most of the time, humans cause populations to drop by disrupting habitats, introducing diseases, or introducing nonnative species. But some organisms do better around humans. Elk thrive near some Canadian towns because wolves will not come close to humans.

❯ **Reading Check** *Describe the difference between biotic and abiotic factors.*

Human Population

Today, the world population is more than 6 billion people and is increasing. ❯Better sanitation and hygiene, disease control, and agricultural technology are a few ways that science and technology have decreased the death rate of the human population. As more humans live on the planet, more resources will be needed to support them. As demand for resources increases, more pressure will be put on Earth's ecosystems.

Historic Growth For most of human history, there have been fewer than 10 million people. Once agriculture was developed, the population began to grow, but relatively slowly. Two thousand years ago, there were only 10 million people. Around the time of the Industrial Revolution, the human population started to accelerate rapidly. **Figure 5** shows the human population accelerating exponentially starting in the late 1700s. Now, there are more than 6 billion people, and some scientists think that the population will grow to 9 billion in 50 years. How many people Earth can support depends in part on science and technology.

Science and Technology Science and technology are major reasons why the human population is growing so rapidly. Advances in agricultural technology have allowed efficient production of crops and other foods. More food supports more people. As a result, the human population has begun to grow faster. Medical advances have also allowed the human population to increase. Vaccines have lowered the death rate. More children are surviving to adulthood. Other medical advances have allowed adults to live longer lives.

❯ **Reaching Check** *How have advances in technology allowed the human population to grow faster?*

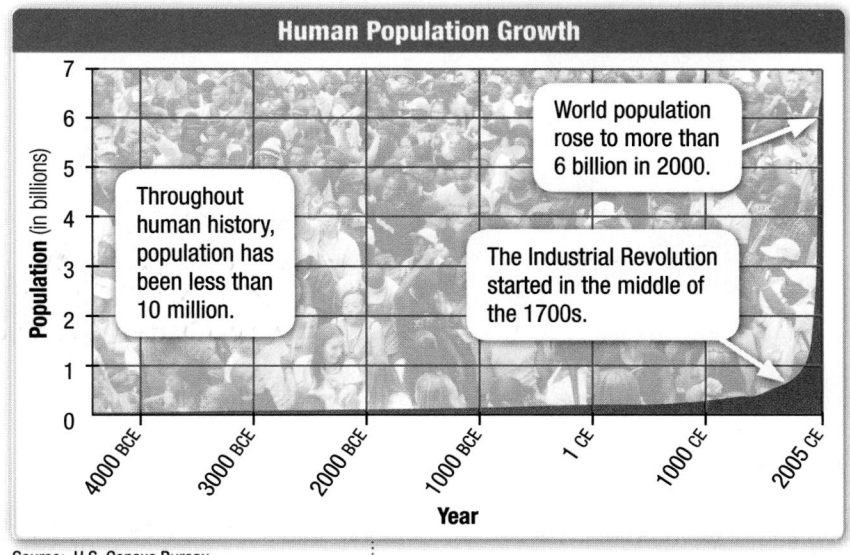

Human Population Growth

Throughout human history, population has been less than 10 million.

World population rose to more than 6 billion in 2000.

The Industrial Revolution started in the middle of the 1700s.

Source: U.S. Census Bureau.

Figure 5 During the last 200 years, the human population has grown exponentially.

❯**KEY IDEAS**

1. **Explain** the importance of studying populations.
2. **Compare** exponential growth with logistic growth.
3. **Identify** an abiotic factor that affects populations.
4. **Explain** how science and technology have affected human population growth.

CRITICAL THINKING

5. **Relating Concepts** A small species of mouse lives in a desert in Arizona. What factors do you think influence the size of this mouse population?
6. **Predicting Outcomes** Identify a biotic factor that could affect the size of the human population. Predict the effect of this biotic factor.

USING SCIENCE GRAPHICS

7. **Making Graphs** Draw a graph with a growth curve for a population that starts at 10 individuals and experiences exponential growth. Draw a second graph with a growth curve for a population that starts with 10 individuals and undergoes logistic growth. The second graph should have a carrying capacity of 100 individuals.

Growth in Asia

REAL WORLD

The world population is more than 6 billion and growing by about 9,000 people per hour. Most of the growth is coming from Asia. Because Asia's current population is already so large, one child per couple in Asia adds more to the world population than two children per couple in other areas of the world. As the world population continues to grow, pressure will increase on availability of food, energy, livable space, and landfill space.

A Recycling Society

As landfills quickly approach full capacity, the Japanese government has become a world leader in waste-recycling measures. Japan recycles refrigerators, washing machines, televisions, and even air conditioners. By 2015, Japan plans to recycle 95% of discarded cars. In the United States, 60% to 70% of waste is sent to landfills. In Japan, only 16% of waste is sent to landfills!

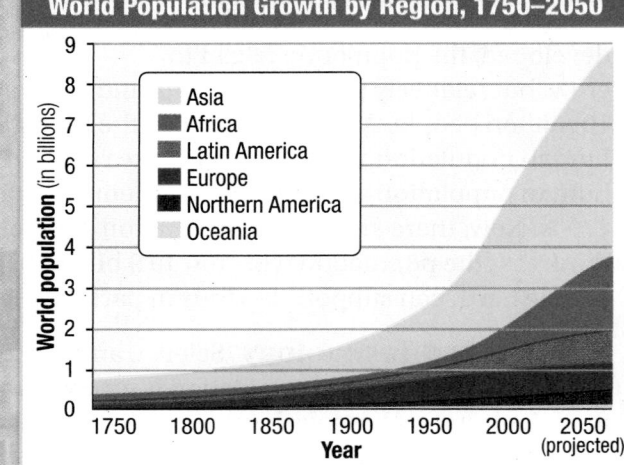

World Population Growth by Region, 1750–2050

Legend:
- Asia
- Africa
- Latin America
- Europe
- Northern America
- Oceania

Y-axis: World population (in billions) 0–9

X-axis: Year 1750, 1800, 1850, 1900, 1950, 2000, 2050 (projected)

Source: National Geographic

Old to New These workers in Tokyo, Japan, are dismantling computers and sorting the parts for recycling.

Crowed City With 6,380 people per square kilometer, Hong Kong, China, shown here, is one of the most densely populated regions of the world.

Research Identify four strategies used by various countries to slow the rate of population growth.

2 Interactions in Communities

Key Ideas	Key Terms	Why It Matters
❯ How do predator-prey interactions influence both predators and prey? ❯ What are two other types of interaction in a community?	predation coevolution parasitism symbiosis mutualism commensalism	Interactions between organisms are the basis of communities and are shaped by evolution.

Interactions in communities can take many forms. Predators and prey are locked in a struggle for survival. Organisms with the same needs compete for food. Parasites and hosts try to get ahead of one another. Some organisms even depend on one another for survival.

Predator-Prey Interactions

One of the most common interactions in communities is that between predators and their prey. **Predation** is the act of one organism killing another for food. As **Figure 6** shows, predators try to get a meal, and prey do their best not to become one! We often think of predators as big animals, such as lions chasing zebras or sharks eating fish. Predators come in all sizes. Even microscopic organisms can be predators. In fact, most animals are both predators and prey. Only a few species, such as killer whales, are not hunted by any other animals.

Many interactions between species are the result of a long evolutionary history. Evolutionary changes in one species can result in changes in another species. ❯**Species that involve predator-prey or parasite-host relationships often develop adaptations in response to one another.** For example, predators evolve to be more cunning to catch their prey. In response, prey evolve to be faster runners to escape more easily. Back-and-forth evolutionary adjustment between two species that interact is called **coevolution.**

> **predation** an interaction between two organisms in which one organism, the predator, kills and feeds on the other organism, the prey
>
> **coevolution** the evolution of two or more species that is due to mutual influence

Figure 6 This lion is hoping to have the zebra for lunch.

QuickLab

⏲ 15 min

The Effects of Herbivores on a Plant Species

Background

Some plant species, such as *Gilia,* respond to grazing by growing new stems. Consider the three images of *Gilia* to the right. Then, answer the statements below.

Analysis

1. **Identify** the plant that is likely to produce more seeds.

2. **Explain** how grazing affects this plant species.

3. **Evaluate** the significance to its environment of the plant's regrowth pattern.

4. **Hypothesize** how this plant species might be affected if individual plants did not produce new stems in response to grazing.

Ungrazed plant   Grazed plant   Regrowth after grazing

Venn Diagram Make a Venn diagram to help you compare the similarities and differences between predators, parasites, and herbivores.

---

parasitism a relationship between two species in which one species, the parasite, benefits from the other species, the host, which is harmed

symbiosis (SIM bie OH sis) a relationship in which two different organisms live in close association with each other

mutualism a relationship between two species in which both species benefit

commensalism a relationship between two organisms in which one organism benefits and the other is unaffected

---

Parasitism In **parasitism,** one organism feeds on another organism called a *host.* The host is almost always larger than the parasite and is usually harmed but not killed. Parasites often live on or in their host. Therefore, the parasite depends on its host not only for food but for a place to live as well. For example, tapeworms live in the digestive system of their hosts. Fleas that live on the skin of their host are another example.

Hosts try to keep parasites from infecting them. Hosts can defend themselves with their immune systems or behaviors such as scratching. In response, parasites may evolve ways to overcome the host's defenses.

Herbivory Herbivores are animals that eat plants. Unlike predators, herbivores do not often kill the plants. But plants do try to defend themselves. Some plants have thorns or spines that cause pain for herbivores that try to eat them. Other plants have chemical compounds inside them that taste bad. Some chemical compounds can make an herbivore sick or kill the herbivore.

Some herbivores have evolved ways to overcome plant defenses. For example, monarch butterfly caterpillars feed on milkweed, which is a plant that is toxic to many herbivores. Not only can the caterpillars survive eating the toxic milkweed but the plant toxins then make the monarch butterfly inedible to bird predators.

❯ **Reading Check** *Identify one way in which herbivores and plants coevolve.*

Cleaner fish eat parasites from the eel's mouth.

Orchids receive more sunlight when attached to trees.

Other Interactions

Not all interactions between organisms result in a winner and a loser. **Symbiosis** is a relationship in which two species live in close association with each other. In some forms of symbiosis, a species may benefit from the relationship. ❯ **Mutualism and commensalism are two kinds of symbiotic relationships in which at least one species benefits.**

Mutualism A relationship between two species in which both species benefit is called **mutualism.** Some shrimp and fishes on coral reefs clean the bodies of large fish and turtles. The cleaners even venture into the mouths of big predators that could easily swallow them, as **Figure 7** shows. Why don't the cleaners become an easy meal? The reason is that the big fish is having parasites removed by the cleaner. Because the cleaner gets a meal, both species win.

Commensalism In **commensalism,** two species have a relationship in which one species benefits and the other is neither harmed nor helped. **Figure 7** shows an example of commensalism between orchids and trees. In thick, tropical forests, little sunlight reaches the forest floor. Orchids need sunlight to survive. To reach the sunlight, orchids get a boost from the forest trees. Orchids will attach themselves and grow on the trunks of the trees. In this way, the orchids move up off the dark forest floor and closer to the sunny canopy.

❯ **Reading Check** *Compare mutualism and commensalism.*

Figure 7 This yellow-edged moray eel is getting its mouth cleaned by a humpback cleaner shrimp. Orchids avoid the dark forest floor by attaching themselves to the trunks of trees. ❯ **Name another symbiotic relationship.**

SC*I*INKS.
www.scilinks.org
Topic: Symbiosis
Code: HX81486

❯ KEY IDEAS

1. **Explain** how predator-prey interactions influence both predators and prey.
2. **Define** symbiosis.
3. **Describe** two types of relationships in a community.

CRITICAL THINKING

4. **Analyzing Results** The cookie-cutter shark feeds by taking a bite of flesh out of whales and large fish. The shark does not kill the larger fish it feeds on. Is the shark a predator or a parasite? Why?

5. **Relating Concepts** In commensalism, would both species coevolve?

WRITING FOR SCIENCE

6. **Essay** In a report, explain what might happen to an ecosystem if one species in a mutualistic relationship disappeared. What would happen if a new predator were introduced to prey with which it has not coevolved?

Shaping Communities

Key Ideas	Key Terms	Why It Matters
❯ How does a species' niche affect other organisms? ❯ How does competition for resources affect species in a community? ❯ What factors influence the resiliency of an ecosystem?	niche fundamental niche realized niche competitive exclusion keystone species	The interactions among organisms in communities shape the ecosystem and the organisms that live there.

No organism can live everywhere. Each organism has its own set of conditions where it can live and where it does best. Some plants, such as cactuses, can survive in deserts, but other plants need a lot of water. The desert plants cannot live in areas that have a lot of water because other plants outcompete them.

Carving a Niche

Think of your favorite plant or animal. How does it use the physical environment? How does it interact with other species? The unique position occupied by a species, both in terms of its physical use of its habitat and its function in an ecological community, is called a **niche.** A niche is not the same as a habitat. A *habitat* is the place where an organism lives. ❯ **A niche includes the role that the organism plays in the community. This role affects the other organisms in the community.** For example, the beaver shown in **Figure 8** cuts down trees with its sharp teeth. The beaver then uses the trees to make dams that divert, or redirect, water flow in rivers and streams. These actions directly affect the trees by killing the trees. These actions also affect organisms that depend on the trees for shelter or food. However, some plants would benefit: fewer trees would allow the plants access to more sunlight. Diverting water flow in a stream could be beneficial to some forms of aquatic life. For others, a dam in a stream could prevent them from traveling upstream to mating grounds. The beaver's role affects many other organisms. If you took the beaver out of this ecosystem, the community would be very different.

❯ **Reading Check** *How is a niche different from a habitat?*

Figure 8 Beavers build dams from trees and tree branches that they cut with their sharp, powerful teeth. ❯ **How might these dams affect other organisms in the community?**

Changes in a Realized Niche

This graph shows the location where species A feeds and the size of its preferred prey. The darkest shade in the center of the graph indicates the prey size and feeding location most frequently selected by species A.

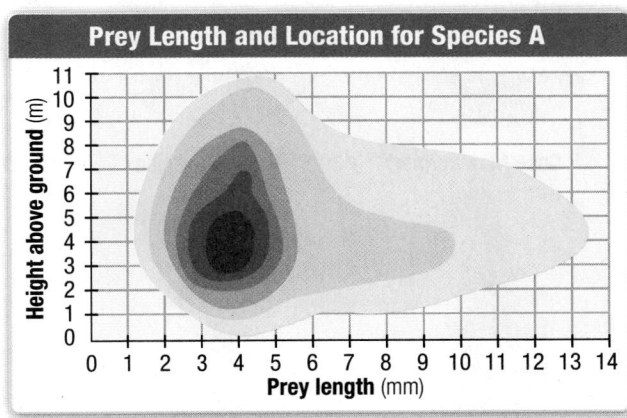

Prey Length and Location for Species A

(graph: y-axis "Height above ground (m)" ranging 0–11; x-axis "Prey length (mm)" ranging 0–14)

Analysis

1. **State** the range of lengths of prey on which species A prefers to feed.

2. **Identify** the maximum height above ground at which species A feeds.

3. **Describe** what the palest shade at the edge of the contour lines represents.

4. **CRITICAL THINKING** **Predicting Outcomes** Species B is introduced into species A's ecosystem. Species B has the same feeding preferences but hunts at a different time of day. How might this affect species A?

5. **CRITICAL THINKING** **Interpreting Graphics** Species C is now introduced into species A's feeding range. Species C feeds at the same time of day as species A but prefers prey that are between 10 and 13 mm long. How might this change affect species A?

Competing for Resources

The entire range of conditions where an organism or species could survive is called its **fundamental niche.** Many species share parts of their fundamental niche with other species. Sometimes, species compete for limited resources. Because of this competition, a species almost never inhabits its entire fundamental niche. ❯ **Competition for resources between species shapes a species' fundamental niche.** The actual niche that a species occupies in a community is called its **realized niche.**

Sometimes, competition results in fights between rivals. Hyenas and lions will even steal food from one another. The stealing of food is called *kleptoparasitism.* Many competitive interactions do not involve direct contests. But when one individual takes a resource, the resource is no longer available for another individual. Many plants compete fiercely for access to light. Some do so by growing quickly to get above other plants. Other plants can tolerate periods of shade and grow slowly. As the slow-growing plants become larger, they eventually shade out other plants.

Competition has several possible outcomes. Sometimes, one species wins, and the other loses. The loser is eliminated from the habitat. Other times, competitors can survive together in the same habitat. They are able to survive together because they divide the resources.

❯ **Reading Check** *Why do organisms rarely occupy their entire fundamental niche?*

niche the unique position occupied by a species, both in terms of its physical use of its habitat and its function within an ecological community

fundamental niche the largest ecological niche where an organism or species can live without competition

realized niche the range of resources that a species uses, the conditions that the species can tolerate, and the functional roles that the species plays as a result of competition in the species' fundamental niche

SCILINKS.
www.scilinks.org
Topic: Habitats and Niches
Code: HX80707

Cape May warbler   Blackburnian warbler   Black-throated warbler   Bay-breasted warbler   Myrtle warbler

Figure 9 Each of these five warbler species feeds on insects in a different portion of the same tree, as indicated by the five colors shown in the figure.

competitive exclusion the exclusion of one species by another due to competition

keystone species a species that is critical to the functioning of the ecosystem in which it lives because it affects the survival and abundance of many other species in its community

ACADEMIC VOCABULARY

potential possible

Competitive Exclusion No two species that are too similar can coexist. Why? If species are too similar in their needs, one will be slightly better at getting the resources on which they both depend. The more successful species will dominate the resources. The less successful species will either die off or have to move to another ecosystem. Eventually, the better competitor will be the only one left. One species eliminating another through competition is called **competitive exclusion.**

Competitive exclusion is seen in many places. When there are no predators around, mussels take over all of the space on rocks in the surf zone. The mussels eliminate barnacles from the surf-zone rocks that are part of the mussels' fundamental niche. Introduced species can also competitively exclude native species. When introduced species multiply quickly, they can use up all of the available resources. When resources are used up, other species that depend on the resources may become extinct.

Dividing Resources Sometimes, competitors eat the same kinds of food and are found in the same places. How do these species live together? Some competitors divide resources by feeding in slightly different ways or slightly different places. The five warblers shown in **Figure 9** are all potential competitors. All five species feed on insects in the same spruce trees at the same time. But they divide the habitat so that they do not compete. Each species feeds in a different part of the tree. Every one of the warbler species would feed everywhere in the tree if it had the tree to itself. Therefore, all the warbler species have the same fundamental niche. But when they are all present in the tree, they each have a smaller realized niche.

❯ **Reading Check** *How might two different species divide resources?*

Ecosystem Resiliency

Ecosystems can be destroyed or damaged by severe weather, humans, or introduced species. Some factors can help keep an ecosystem stable. ❯ **Interactions between organisms and the number of species in an ecosystem add to the resiliency of an ecosystem.**

Predation and Competition Predation can reduce the effects of competition among species. Many aquatic species compete for space in the intertidal zone along the Pacific coast. Mussels are fierce competitors that can take over that space. All other species are excluded. However, sea stars eat mussels. When sea stars eat the mussels, a variety of species can live in the intertidal zone.

Predators can influence more than their prey. Sea otters, as shown in **Figure 10,** eat sea urchins. Sea urchins eat kelp. When sea otters are present, lush kelp forests grow along the west coast of North America. These kelp forests provide habitat for many fishes and aquatic animals. When sea otters disappeared because of overhunting, the sea urchins ate all of the kelp. All of the species that depended on the kelp also disappeared. Sea otters are an example of a keystone species. A **keystone species** is a species that is critical to an ecosystem because the species affects the survival and number of many other species in its community.

Biodiversity and Resiliency One community has 50 species. Another community has 100 species. If a severe drought affected both communities equally, the community with 100 species would be more likely to recover quickly. The reason is that higher biodiversity often helps make an ecosystem more resilient. Predation helps increase biodiversity. The sea stars prevented the mussels from excluding other species. In response, the inter tidal zone had a higher biodiversity.

❯ **Reading Check** *List two factors that contribute to the resiliency of an ecosystem.*

Figure 10 Sea otters off the coast of California are a threatened species. The decrease in their population has affected the stability of the ecosystem. ❯ **Why is the sea otter considered a keystone species?**

Predictions Using the term *keystone species*, write a sentence with a prediction based on a condition.

Section 3 Review

❯ KEY IDEAS

1. **Explain** why an organism's role is important for a community.
2. **Describe** one example of how competition for resources affects species in a community.
3. **Explain** how predation can help make an ecosystem resilient.
4. **Compare** niche and habitat.

CRITICAL THINKING

5. **Inferring Conclusions** Two predators feed on small antelope. One predator weighs 100 kg, and the other weighs 35 kg. Explain what might happen if the two predators share the same area.
6. **Evaluating Results** Wolves are reintroduced into a park. As a result, the vegetation changes. Explain how the changes to the vegetation happened.

ALTERNATIVE ASSESSMENT

7. **Essay** Search the Internet to find out about the niche of wolves in their community. Determine if they are a keystone species. Then, write a one-page essay describing their role in their ecosystem.

Chapter 5 Lab

Objectives

> Observe the growth and decline of a population of yeast cells.

> Determine the carrying capacity of a yeast culture.

Materials

- lab apron, safety goggles, and gloves
- yeast cell culture
- test tube (2)
- pipets, 1 mL (2)
- methylene blue solution, 1%
- microscope slide, ruled
- coverslip
- microscope, compound

Safety

Yeast Population Growth

You have learned that a population will keep growing until limiting factors slow or stop this growth. In this lab, you will observe the changes in a population of yeast cells. The cells will grow in a container and have limited food over several days.

Procedure

Collecting Data

1 ☠ **CAUTION: Do not touch or taste any chemicals. Know the location of the emergency shower and eyewash station and how to use them. Methylene blue will stain your skin and clothing.** Transfer 1 mL of yeast culture to a test tube. Add two drops of methylene blue to the test tube. The methylene blue will remain blue in dead cells but will turn colorless in living cells.

2 Make a wet mount by placing 0.1 mL, or about one drop, of the yeast culture and methylene blue mixture on a ruled microscope slide. Cover the slide with a coverslip.

3 Observe the wet mount under low power of a compound microscope. Notice the squares on the slide. Then, switch to high power. (Note: Adjust the light so that you can clearly see both stained and unstained cells.) Move the slide so that the top left-hand corner of one square is in the center of your field of view. This area will be area 1, as shown in the diagram.

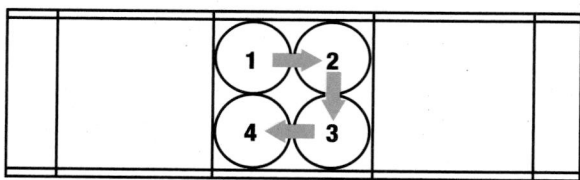

4 Make two data tables like the one shown. One table will contain your observations of living cells. The other table will contain your observations of dead cells.

Number of cells							
Time (h)	1	2	3	4	5	6	Average
0							
24							
48							
72							
96							

Methylene blue stains the dead yeast cells.

5 Count the live (unstained) cells and the dead (stained) cells in the four corners of a square by using the pattern shown in the diagram in step 3. Record the number of live cells and dead cells that you counted in the entire square.

6 Repeat step 5 until you have counted all six squares on the slide.

7 ⚠ ⚠ Clean up your lab materials according to your teacher's instructions. Wash your hands before leaving the lab.

Compiling Data

8 Refer to your first data table. Find the total number of live cells in the six squares. Divide this total by 6 to find the average number of live cells per square. Record this number in your data table. Repeat this procedure for the dead cells.

9 Repeat steps 1 through 5 each day for four more days.

Analyze and Conclude

1. Evaluating Methods Explain why several areas were counted and averaged each day.

2. Analyzing Data Graph the changes in the numbers of live yeast cells and dead yeast cells over time. Plot the number of cells in 1 mL of yeast culture on the *y*-axis and the time (in hours) on the *x*-axis.

3. Evaluating Results Describe the general population changes that you observed in the yeast cultures over time.

4. SCIENTIFIC METHODS **Inferring Conclusions** Did the yeast population appear to reach a certain carrying capacity? What limiting factors probably caused the yeast population to decline?

SC*I*LINKS.

www.scilinks.org
Topic: Characteristics
of Populations
Code: HX80260

Extensions

5. Designing an Investigation Write a question about population growth that could be explored in another investigation. Design an investigation that could help answer that question.

go.hrw.com
SUPER SUMMARY
Keyword: HX8COMS

Key Ideas	Key Terms

1 Populations

> Understanding population growth is important because populations of different species interact and affect one another, including human populations.

> Exponential growth occurs when numbers increase by a certain factor in each successive time period. Logistic growth is population growth that starts with a minimum number of individuals and reaches a maximum depending on the carrying capacity of the habitat.

> Water, food, predators, and human activity are a few of many factors that affect the size of a population.

> Better sanitation and hygiene, disease control, and agricultural technology are a few ways that science and technology have decreased the death rate of the human population.

population (103)
carrying capacity (105)

2 Interactions in Communities

> Species that involve predator-prey or parasite-host relationships often develop adaptations in response to one another.

> Mutualism and commensalism are two types of symbiotic relationships in which one or both of the species benefit.

predation (109)
coevolution (109)
parasitism (110)
symbiosis (111)
mutualism (111)
commensalism (111)

3 Shaping Communities

> A niche includes the role that the organism plays in the community. This role affects the other organisms in the community.

> Competition for resources between species shapes a species' fundamental niche.

> Interactions between organisms and the number of species in an ecosystem add to the stability of an ecosystem.

niche (112)
fundamental niche (113)
realized niche (113)
competitive exclusion (114)
keystone species (115)

Chapter 5 Review

READING TOOLBOX

1. **Venn Diagram** Make a Venn diagram to help you compare the similarities and differences between niche, realized niche, and fundamental niche.

2. **Concept Map** Draw a concept map that shows characteristics of a population. Try to include the following words in your map: *mutualism, commensalism, predation, abiotic factors, biotic factors, population, parasitism, carrying capacity, logistic growth,* and *exponential growth.*

Using Key Terms

Use each of the following terms in a separate sentence.

3. *population*

4. *competitive exclusion*

For each pair of terms, explain how the meanings of the terms differ.

5. *exponential growth* and *logistic growth*

6. *immigration* and *emigration*

Understanding Key Ideas

7. Which of the following is an abiotic factor that could influence population size?
   a. amount of food
   b. amount of water
   c. presence of predators
   d. presence of competitors

8. Which of the following has *not* been a factor in decreasing the death rate of the human population?
   a. vaccine
   b. disease
   c. Industrial Revolution
   d. agricultural technology

9. Which of the following describes a relationship between two species in which one species benefits and the other is unaffected?
   a. predation
   b. mutualism
   c. parasitism
   d. commensalism

10. Which of the following is *not* an example of coevolution?
    a. Prey evolve faster running to escape, and predators evolve to be smarter at catching prey.
    b. Predators evolve heavy jaws to crunch the bones of herbivores, and herbivores evolve thick fur for warmth.
    c. Plants evolve chemical defenses, and herbivores evolve ways to neutralize the chemicals.
    d. Insects evolve green wings to blend into the environment, and predators evolve better eyesight to find the prey.

11. Which of the following describes an organism's role in a community?
    a. niche
    b. abiotic factor
    c. habitat
    d. coevolution

12. Which of the following may help stabilize an ecosystem?
    a. severe weather
    b. invasive species
    c. low biodiversity
    d. high biodiversity

13. Which region of the world will contribute the least to world population in 2050?

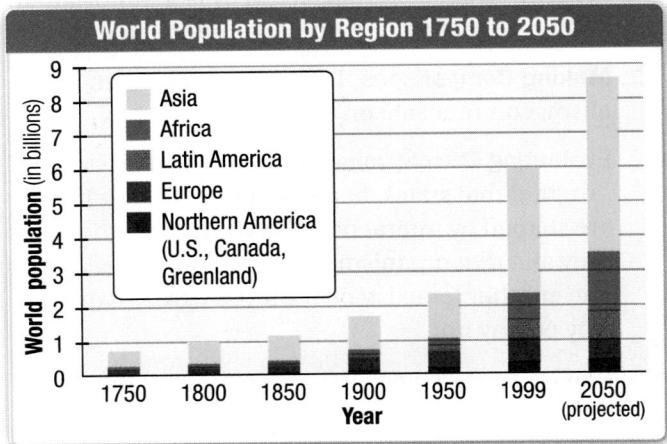

Explaining Key Ideas

14. **List** three factors that could affect population size.

15. **Describe** what has happened to the human population since the Industrial Revolution.

16. **Explain** how predators and parasites differ in their effect on the organisms on which they feed.

Chapter Review **119**

Using Science Graphics

Use the diagram to answer the following questions.

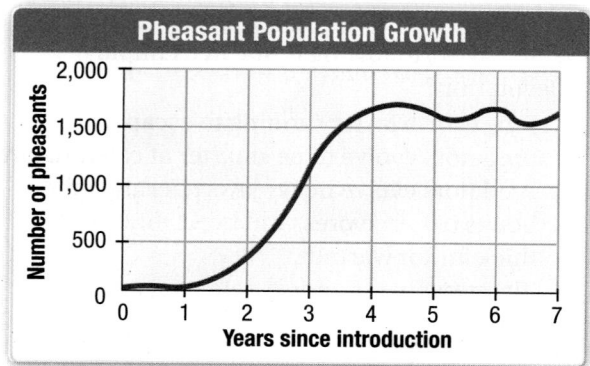

Pheasant Population Growth

17. Biologists introduced pheasants onto an island in Washington State in the 1930s. Using the data in the graph, estimate the number of pheasants on the island two years after they were first introduced.

18. Estimate the island's carrying capacity for pheasants.

Critical Thinking

19. **Evaluating an Argument** A classmate tells you that the boundaries of human populations are at the borders of countries. Is your classmate correct? Explain why or why not.

20. **Forming Reasoned Opinions** Why is it important to know and understand human population growth?

21. **Making Comparisons** Differentiate between mutualism, commensalism, and symbiosis.

22. **Evaluating Conclusions** You watch a television program that states that biological communities are shaped by interactions between predators and prey and that organisms must always struggle with one another for existence. Do you agree? Explain why or why not.

23. **Predicting Outcomes** How might population size influence the chances that a population will grow, shrink, or become extinct?

24. **Evaluating Models** Is a population growth model that is based on exponential growth more or less realistic than a population growth model that is based on logistic growth? Explain your answer.

Writing for Science

25. **Comparing Relationships** Write an essay describing several examples of how humans can influence the size of populations.

26. **Analyzing Results** In an essay, explain why few populations grow exponentially for long periods of time. Include in your argument factors that influence population growth.

Methods of Science

27. **Forming Hypotheses** You measure the conditions under which a species, cattail, can survive when there are no competitors around. Next, you introduce another species of closely related cattail in the same area. Hypothesize what will happen to the niche of the first cattail.

28. **Designing an Experiment** You want to find out how a highway cut through a forest would affect the biodiversity of the forest. You decide to compare the biodiversity of two similar forests, one with a highway and one without. Design an investigation that measures and compares the number and types of species in each forest.

Alternative Assessment

29. **Recognizing Relationships** Use Internet resources to find out about the niche of your favorite organism. Write an essay describing this organism's role in an ecosystem. Include a description of the organism's fundamental niche and realized niche.

30. **Forming Hypotheses** Formulate a hypothesis about human population growth. Then, use library or Internet resources to find estimates of the current rate of human population growth and forecasts for future growth. Predict trends from the data, and communicate your conclusions in the form of a report to your class.

Math Skills

31. **Problem Solving** A population of bacteria has two individuals. If the population doubles in size with each generation, how many bacteria will there be in the eighth generation? Assume that there are no deaths.

Science Concepts

1. Which of the following is a biotic factor that could influence population growth?

A water

B climate

C temperature

D the presence of predators

2. What is the human population projected to be 50 years from now?

F 3 billion

G 6 billion

H 9 billion

J 50 billion

3. Which of the following describes the actual role of a species in a community in response to competition?

A niche

B actual niche

C realized niche

D fundamental niche

4. When two closely matched competitors occupy the same area, what happens to the size of their fundamental niches?

F Both increase.

G Both decrease.

H Both stay the same.

J One increases, and one decreases.

5. What do you call a species that has a huge impact on an ecosystem even if the species is not very abundant?

A parasite

B competitor

C top predator

D keystone species

6. Which of the following is a density-independent factor?

F food

G water

H predators

J hurricanes

Using Science Graphics

The diagram below shows the size of a particular population over time. Use the diagram to answer the following question.

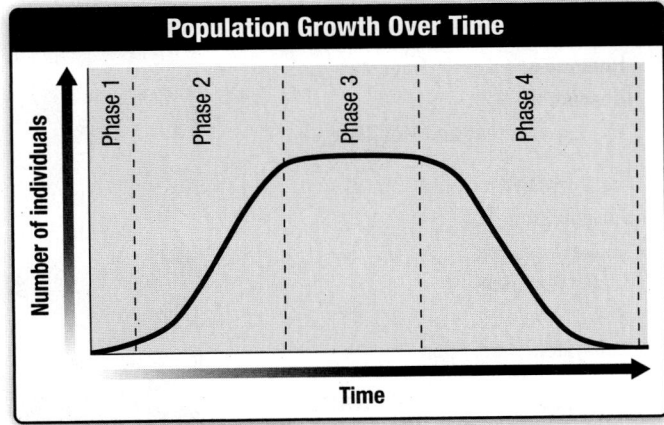

Population Growth Over Time

7. Which time period shows negative growth of the population?

A phase 1

B phase 2

C phase 3

D phase 4

The diagram below shows the growth of a population of fruit flies over time. Use the diagram to answer the following question.

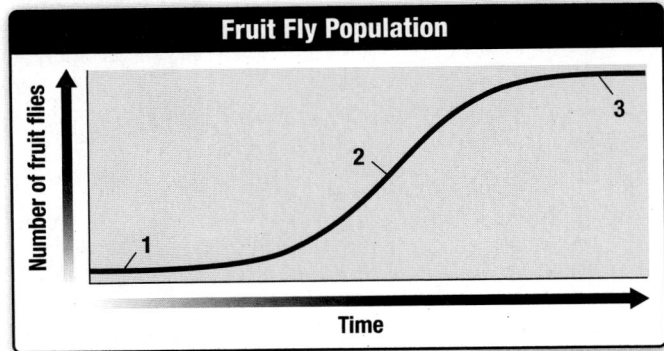

Fruit Fly Population

8. At which point would a density-dependent factor have a greater impact on the population?

F point 1

G point 2

H point 3

J points 1 and 3

Writing Skills

9. Essay In the Fruit Fly Population diagram, explain why the population stops increasing after it reaches point 3 on the curve.

Chapter 6

The Environment

The Neversink Pit in Alabama has recently been bought by local cavers who plan to preserve its ecosystem.

Neversink is an open air pit that is 162 ft deep.

A rare species of fern lives in the Neversink Pit.

Preview

1 An Interconnected Planet
Humans and the Environment
Resources
The Environment and Health

2 Environmental Issues
Air Pollution
Global Warming
Water Pollution
Soil Damage
Ecosystem Disruption

3 Environmental Solutions
Conservation and Restoration
Reducing Resource Use
Technology
Environmental Awareness
Planning for the Future

Why It Matters

The environment provides the basic support system for all life on Earth, including humans. By taking care of the environment, we take care of ourselves and all other life on Earth.

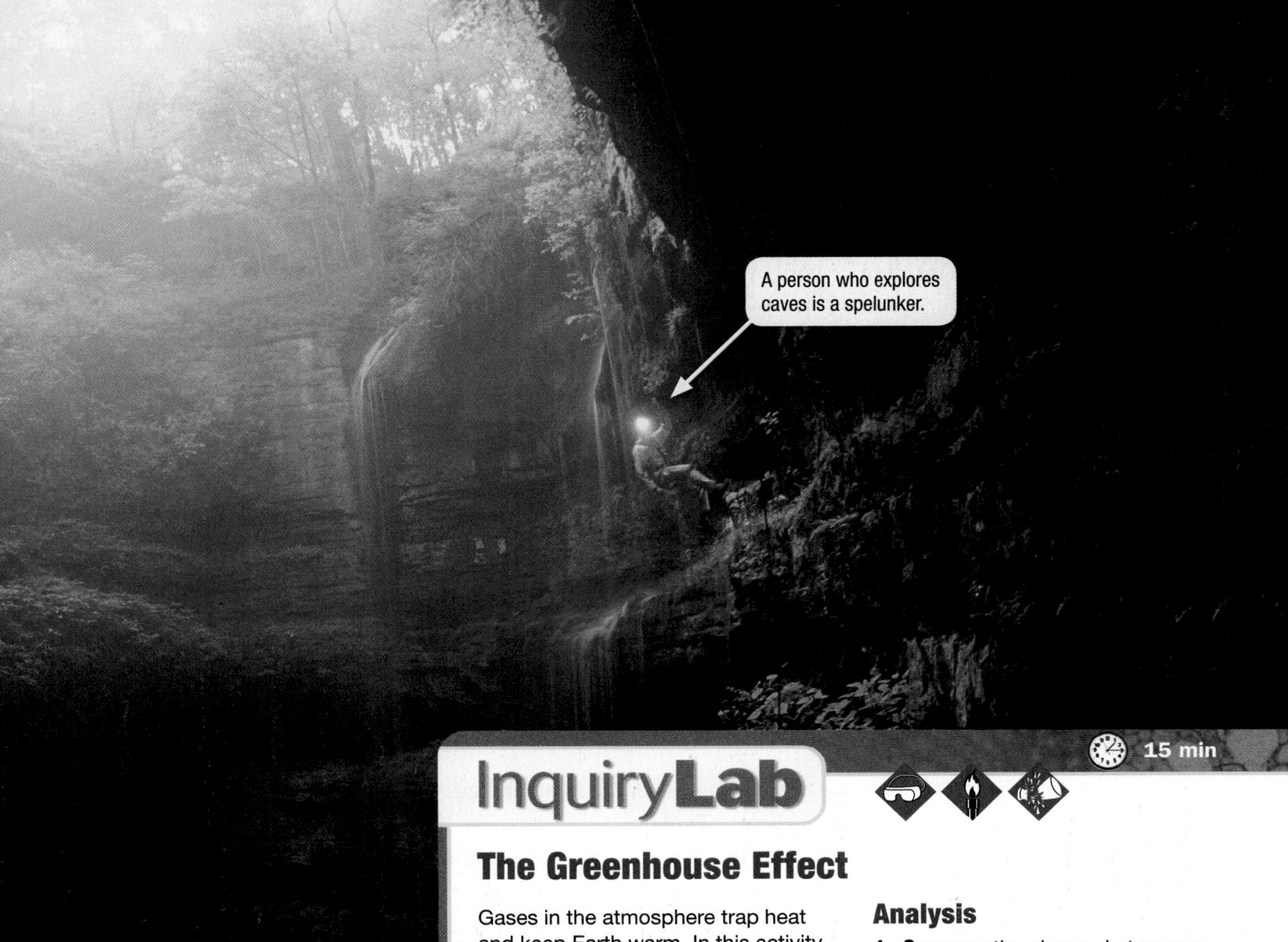

A person who explores caves is a spelunker.

Inquiry Lab

⏱ 15 min

The Greenhouse Effect

Gases in the atmosphere trap heat and keep Earth warm. In this activity, you will model this process called the *greenhouse effect*.

Procedure

1. ⚠ **CAUTION: Handle the glass thermometer and jar with care.** Insert a **thermometer** through a hole in the lid of a **quart jar.** Tape the thermometer in place.

2. Place the jar about 30 cm from a **heat source,** such as a sunlit window.

3. Record the temperature inside and outside the jar every 30 s for 5 min.

4. Remove the jar from the heat source. Record the temperature inside and outside the jar every 30 s for another 5 min.

Analysis

1. **Compare** the change in temperature inside the jar with the change in temperature outside the jar.

2. **Identify** the part of your model that represents the gases in the atmosphere.

3. **Explain** a possible reason why global temperatures on Earth have increased. Include what you learned from your model of the greenhouse effect.

READING TOOLBOX

These reading tools can help you learn the material in this chapter. For more information on how to use these and other tools, see **Appendix: Reading and Study Skills.**

Using Words

Word Parts You can tell a lot about a word by taking it apart and examining its prefix, root, and suffix.

Your Turn Use the information in the table to define the following words.

1. biodiversity
2. deforestation

Word Parts		
Word Part	**Type**	**Meaning**
bio-	prefix	life
versi	root	various
de-	prefix	remove
-ation	suffix	a state of being

Using Language

Hypothesis or Theory? To scientists, a theory is a well-supported scientific explanation that makes useful predictions. The main difference between a theory and a hypothesis is that a hypothesis has not been tested, and a theory has been tested repeatedly and seems to correctly explain all the available data.

Your Turn Use information from the chapter to answer the following questions.

1. Is the greenhouse effect a hypothesis or theory? Explain.
2. Write your own hypothesis that explains the increase in global temperatures.

Using Graphic Organizers

Venn Diagrams A Venn diagram is a useful tool for comparing two or three topics in science. A Venn diagram shows which characteristics the topics share and which characteristics are unique to each topic.

Your Turn Create a Venn diagram that describes the characteristics of renewable and nonrenewable resources.

1. Draw a diagram like the one shown here. Draw one circle for each topic. Make sure that each circle partially overlaps the other circles.

2. In each circle, write a topic that you want to compare with the topics in the other circles.

3. In the areas of the diagram where circles overlap, write the characteristics that the topics in the overlapping circles share.

4. In the areas of the diagram where circles do not overlap, write the characteristics that are unique to the topic of the particular circle.

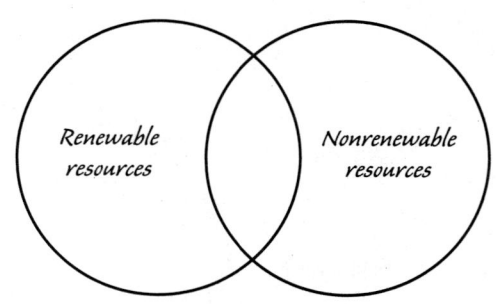

An Interconnected Planet

Key Ideas	Key Terms	Why It Matters
❯ How are humans and the environment connected? ❯ What is the difference between renewable resources and nonrenewable resources? ❯ How can the state of the environment affect a person's health and quality of life?	fossil fuel	The environment provides the resources that we need to live. When the environment is damaged, our resources are damaged.

We depend on the environment for food, water, air, shelter, fuel, and many other resources. However, human actions can affect the quality and availability of these important resources. The study of the impact of humans on the environment is called *environmental science*.

Humans and the Environment

10,000 years ago, there were only about 5 million people on Earth. The development of dependable food supplies, sanitation, and medical care have allowed the population to grow to more than 6 billion. The population will likely exceed 10 billion before it stabilizes. All 10 billion of these people will need a place to live. Humans now live in almost every kind of ecosystem on Earth. **Figure 1** shows one type of ecosystem in which humans live. As human population increases, the impact of humans on the environment increases. ❯ **Humans are a part of the environment and can affect the resilience of the environment.** The more that the human population grows, the more resources from the environment we will need to survive. Today's humans consume more resources than their ancestors did. The environment does not have an infinite amount of resources with which to meet humans' demand.

Earth is an interconnected planet: we depend on the environment, and the environment is affected by our actions. Learning about this connectedness helps us care for the environment and helps ensure that the environment will continue to support us and other species on Earth.

❯ **Reading check** *How is Earth an interconnected planet? (See the Appendix for answers to Reading Checks.)*

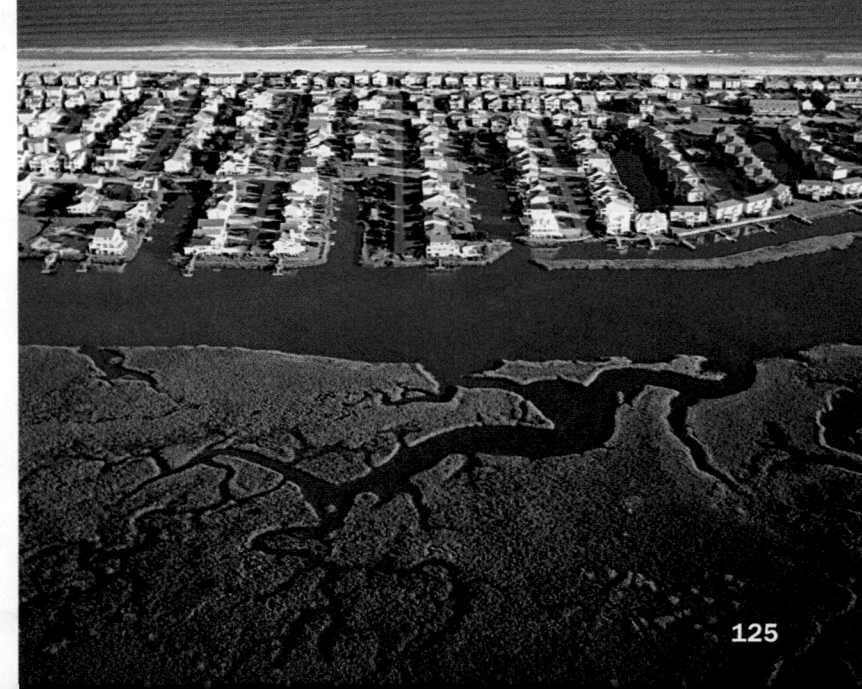

Figure 1 This housing development lies in the marshlands along Myrtle Beach, South Carolina. ❯ **Can you describe another ecosystem that humans live in?**

125

www.scilinks.org
Topic: Renewable and
nonrenewable
resources
Code: HX81290

fossil fuel a nonrenewable energy resource
formed from the remains of organisms that lived
long ago; examples include oil, coal, and natural gas

Resources

What would your day be like if you didn't have water to drink or electricity to provide lighting and heat? Water and fuel that generates electricity are two of Earth's many <u>resources</u>. Earth's resources are described as renewable or nonrenewable, as shown in **Figure 2**.

Renewable Resources Fresh water, solar energy, and fish are examples of renewable resources. ❯ *Renewable resources are natural resources that can be replaced at the same rate at which they are consumed.* A renewable resource's supply is either so large or so constantly renewed that it will never be used up. However, a resource can be renewable but still be used up if it is used faster than it can be renewed. For example, trees are renewable. But, some forests are being cut down faster than new forests can grow to replace them.

Nonrenewable Resources Many resources that we depend on, such as minerals, coal and oil, are nonrenewable resources. ❯ *Nonrenewable resources are resources that form at a rate that is much slower than the rate at which they are consumed.* Most of our energy today comes from fossil fuels. **Fossil fuels** are nonrenewable energy resources that formed from the remains of organisms that lived long ago. Examples of fossil fuels are coal, oil, and natural gas. Coal, oil, and natural gas are nonrenewable resources because it takes millions of years for them to form. They form from the remains of organisms that were buried by sediment millions of years ago. As sediment accumulated over the remains, heat and pressure increased. Over time, the heat and pressure caused chemical changes that changed the remains into oil and natural gas. We use fossil fuels at a rate that is faster than the rate at which they form. So, when these resources are gone, millions of years will pass before more have formed.

❯ **Reading check** *Explain why natural gas is a nonrenewable resource.*

Figure 2 Windmills produce renewable wind energy, while the oil rig extracts a nonrenewable energy resource. ❯ **Can you think of another example for each renewable and nonrenewable resource?**

Renewable Resources
- wind energy
- solar energy
- fresh water
- trees

Nonrenewable Resources
- oil
- coal
- natural gas

Contaminated Water

In this activity, you will learn how contaminated water can spread an infectious disease.

Procedure

1  **CAUTION: Do not taste or touch the fluids used in this lab.** Obtain one **test tube** of **fluid** from your teacher. Some test tubes contain pure water. One test tube contains water that has been "contaminated".

2 Pour half your fluid into the test tube of a classmate. Your classmate will then pour an equal amount back into your test tube. Exchange water with three classmates in this way.

3 Your teacher will now put a small amount of a **test chemical** into your test tube. If your water turns cloudy, you have been "contaminated."

Analysis

1. **CRITICAL THINKING** **Analyzing Conclusions** Who had the test tube that started the "infection?"

2. **Identify** a disease that could be spread in water.

The Environment and Health

Our health and quality of life are affected by the state of the environment. ❯ **Pollution and habitat destruction destroy the resources we need to live, such as the air we breathe, the water we drink, and the food we eat.** Air pollution can cause headaches, sore throats, nausea, and upper respiratory infections. Air pollution has also been connected to lung cancer and heart disease. Some chemical pollutants in drinking water can lead to birth defects and cancer. Many infectious diseases, such as cholera, are spread by water polluted by sewage. Habitat destruction can also affect our safety. The root networks of trees help hold soil in place. Cutting down trees increases the number of landslides and floods, which can cause deaths and injuries.

READING TOOLBOX

Word Parts Look up the suffix *-tion* in the dictionary. Also, look up the words *pollute* and *destroy* in a dictionary. Then, write your own definition for *pollution* and *destruction*.

Section 1 Review

❯ KEY IDEAS

1. **Explain** how human population affects the environment.
2. **Describe** the difference between renewable resources and nonrenewable resources.
3. **State** a nonrenewable resource that you used today.
4. **State** three ways that environmental problems may affect human health.

CRITICAL THINKING

5. **Inferring relationships** Events such as floods and landslides are commonly called *natural disasters.* Explain how both natural events and human actions might have contributed to a natural disaster that you have learned about.
6. **Analyzing data** Consider a 1,000-year-old forest and a 30-year-old tree farm. How do differences between these resources affect how renewable the resources are?

WRITING FOR SCIENCE

7. **Evaluating viewpoints** A classmate argues that pollution is a necessary evil to produce food, jobs, and a high standard of living. Write a one-page paper describing your opinion of your classmates argument. Support your opinion with facts.

Environmental Issues

Key Ideas	Key Terms	Why It Matters
❯ What are the effects of air pollution? ❯ How might burning fossil fuels lead to climate change? ❯ What are some sources of water pollution? ❯ Why is soil erosion a problem? ❯ How does ecosystem disruption affect humans?	acid rain global warming greenhouse effect erosion deforestation biodiversity extinction	In the course of meeting their basic needs, humans can unintentionally damage the global environment.

Human activities can affect every ecosystem on Earth. Understanding these effects and the problems that they can cause is the first step to successfully solving them.

Air Pollution

Have you ever breathed air that smelled bad or made your lungs burn? The bikers in **Figure 3** have. Natural processes, such as volcanic activity, can affect air quality. However, most air pollution is caused by human activities. Industries, power plants, and vehicles must burn fossil fuels for energy. The burning of fossil fuels releases the pollutants carbon dioxide (CO_2), sulfur dioxide (SO_2), and nitrogen oxides (NO_2 and NO_3) into the air. ❯ **Air pollution causes respiratory problems for people, results in acid rain, damages the ozone layer, and may affect global temperature.**

Acid rain is precipitation that has an unusually high concentration of sulfuric or nitric acids, which is caused by pollution. Acid rain damages forests and lakes. The ozone layer protects life on Earth from the sun's damaging ultraviolet (UV) rays. The ozone layer has been damaged by *chlorofluorocarbons (CFCs)*. CFCs are human-made chemicals that are used as coolants in refrigerators and air conditioners and as propellants in spray cans. Global temperature may be affected by air pollutants. **Global warming** is the gradual increase in the average global temperature.

Figure 3 Workers leaving the steel mill in Baotou, China, wear masks to avoid breathing in the pollution.

② Some heat radiates away from Earth into the atmosphere. Some heat escapes into space.

③ Greenhouse gases also absorb some of the sun's energy and radiate it back toward Earth's surface.

① Solar radiation passes through the atmosphere and warms Earth's surface.

Global Warming

What does it feel like to climb into a car on a hot, sunny day? The inside of the car is hot because the sun's energy passes through the glass windows. The inside of the car absorbs the solar energy and changes it to heat energy. The heat energy cannot easily pass back through the glass windows. Therefore, the heat is trapped and makes the inside of the car hot. The atmosphere traps heat and warms the Earth in a similar way. The **greenhouse effect** is the warming of the surface and lower atmosphere of Earth that happens when greenhouse gases in the air absorb and reradiate heat. Examples of greenhouse gases are CO_2 and water vapor. **Figure 4** shows how this process works.

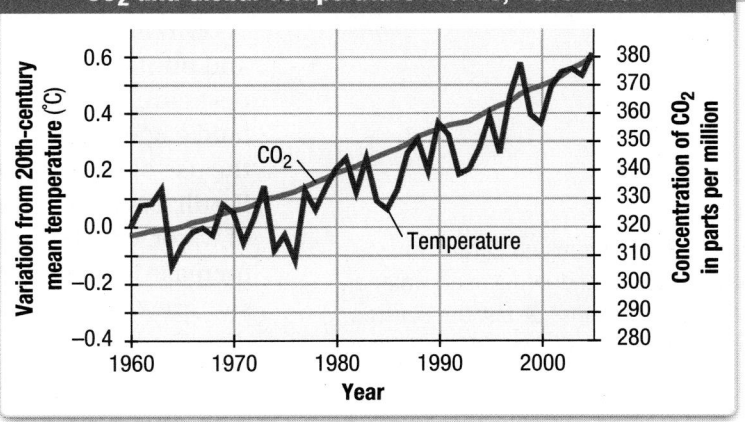

CO₂ and Global Temperature Trends, 1960–2005

Source: Scripps Institute of Oceanography and National Oceanic & Atmospheric Administration.

The greenhouse effect is necessary to keep Earth's temperatures stable. However, Earth's global temperatures have been rising steadily for many decades. Most scientists think that this increase in temperatures is caused by an increase in CO_2. ❯ **Burning fossil fuels increases the amount of CO_2 in the atmosphere. Increases in atmospheric CO_2 may be responsible for an increase in global temperatures.**

Effects of Global Warming A continued increase in global temperatures has the potential to cause a number of serious environmental problems. For example, ice sheets over Antarctica and Greenland have already started to melt. If these ice sheets continue to melt, they could raise sea levels around the world. Coastal ecosystems would be destroyed. People who live along a coast could lose their homes. Global weather patterns would also be affected. For example, warmer oceans make hurricanes and typhoons more intense and could make such storms more common. Droughts could become more frequent, causing damage to crops. The equilibrium in ecosystems could be altered. Migration patterns of some birds have already changed.

❯ **Reading check** *How might the burning of fossil fuels affect climate?*

Figure 4 The greenhouse effect is a natural process that keeps Earth warm.
❯ **How does the increase in CO_2 relate to global warming?**

acid rain precipitation that has a pH below normal and has an unusually high concentration of sulfuric or nitric acids, often as a result of chemical pollution of the air from sources such as automobile exhausts and the burning of fossil fuels

global warming a gradual increase in the average global temperature

greenhouse effect the warming of the surface and lower atmosphere of Earth that occurs when carbon dioxide, water vapor and other gases in the air absorb and reradiate infrared radiation

Water Pollution

Every person needs 20–70 L (5–18 gal) of clean water each day to meet his or her drinking, washing, and sanitation needs. Unfortunately, many sources of water are polluted. **Figure 5** shows major sources of water pollution. **› Water pollution can come from fertilizers and pesticides used in agriculture, livestock farms, industrial waste, oil runoff from roads, septic tanks, and unlined landfills.** Pollution enters groundwater when polluted surface water percolates down through the soil. Oil on roads can be washed into the ground by rain. Pesticides, fertilizers, and livestock waste seep into the ground in a similar way. Landfills and leaking underground septic tanks are also major sources of groundwater pollution.

When pollutants run off land and into rivers, both aquatic habitats and public water sources may be contaminated. For example, the pesticide, DDT, harmed many species, such as the bald eagle. The bald eagle was in danger of becoming extinct until the U.S. restricted the use of DDT in 1972. Pollution can also affect ecosystems. Fertilizers from farms, lawns, and golf courses can run off into a body of water, which increases the amount of nutrients in the water. An increase in some nutrients in a body of water can lead to an excessive growth of algae called a "bloom." Algal blooms can deplete the dissolved oxygen in a body of water. Fish and other organisms then suffocate in the oxygen-depleted water.

› Reading check ***List three sources of water pollution.***

SCILINKS.
www.scilinks.org
Topic: Chemical Pollution
Code: HX80272

Figure 5 Pollutants on Earth's surface run off the land and into ground water and other water systems. **› List the sources of water pollution that might occur in your neighborhood.**

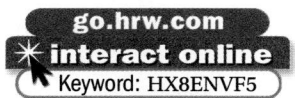

go.hrw.com
interact online
Keyword: HX8ENVF5

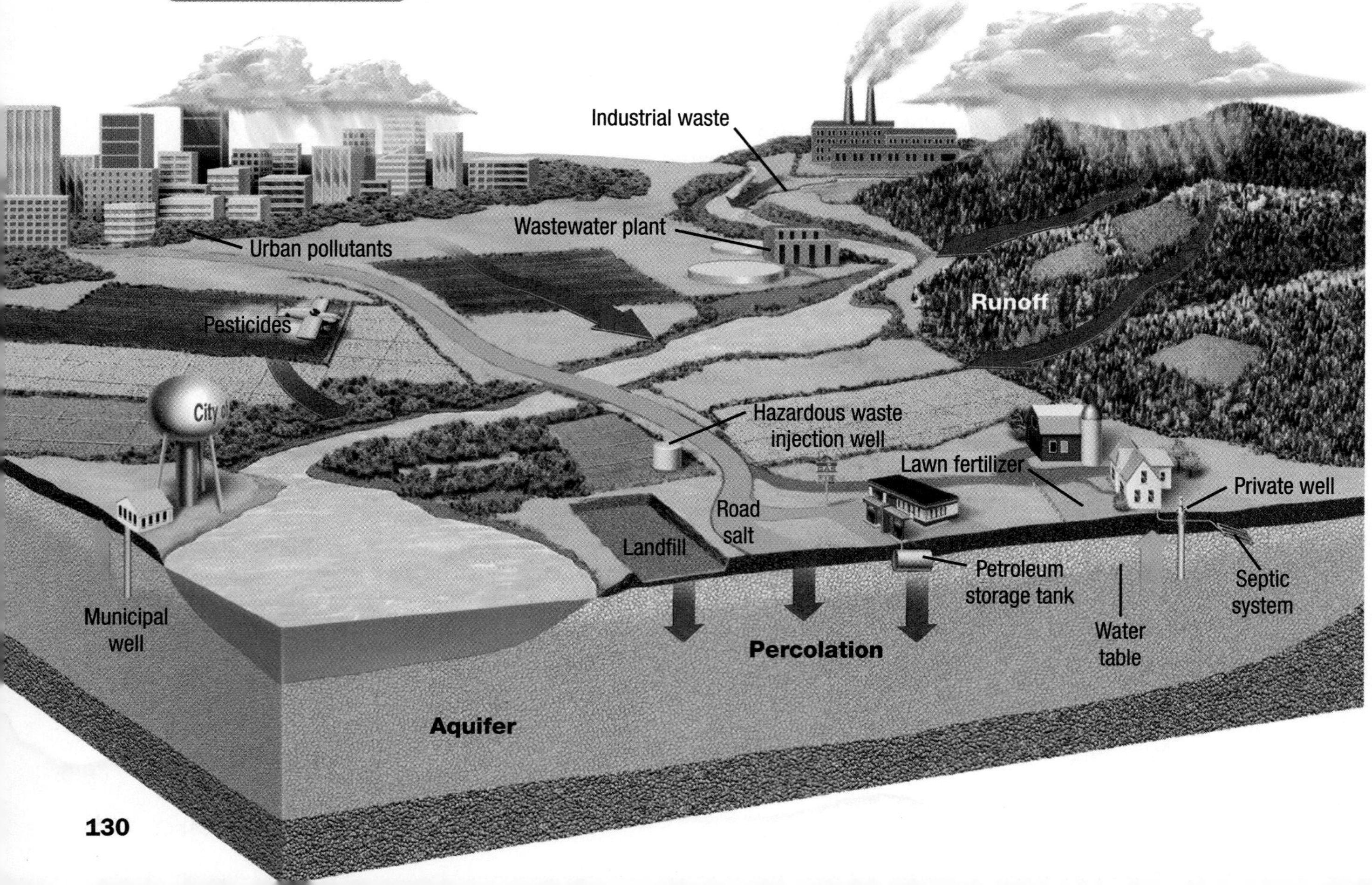

Industrial waste
Wastewater plant
Urban pollutants
Pesticides
Runoff
City of
Hazardous waste injection well
Lawn fertilizer
Private well
Road salt
Landfill
Petroleum storage tank
Septic system
Municipal well
Percolation
Water table
Aquifer

Hands-On
Quick Lab

Soil Erosion

In this lab you will investigate factors that affect erosion.

Procedure

1 Fill **three trays:** one with **sod,** one with **topsoil,** and one with a type of **mulch.**

2 Place each tray at an angle on a "hill" of stacked **textbooks.** Place the same type of **large bowl** at the bottom of each tray to catch the runoff.

3 Pour **2 L of water** slowly and evenly on each tray to simulate heavy rainfall.

4 Use a **scale** to weigh the runoff of soil and water that collected in each bowl.

Analysis

1. Determine which tray had the most soil erosion and water runoff. Which tray had the least? Why?

2. **CRITICAL THINKING** **Inferring Conclusions** What does this lab demonstrate about soil erosion?

Soil Damage

Fertile soil allows agriculture to supply the world with food. The United States is one of the most productive farming countries, largely because of its fertile soils. Fertile soil forms from rock that is broken down by weathering. Nutrients that make soil fertile come from the weathered rock as well as from bacteria, fungi and the remains of plants and animals. The processes that form just a few centimeters of fertile soil can take thousands of years. Without fertile soil, we cannot grow crops to feed ourselves or the livestock we depend on.

Soil Erosion The greatest threat to soil is soil erosion. **Erosion** is a process in which the materials of Earth's surface are worn away and transported from one place to another by wind, gravity, or water.
❭ **Soil erosion destroys fertile soil that we need in order to produce food.**
Roots from plants and trees help hold soil together and protect it from erosion. When vegetation is removed, soil is left vulnerable to erosion. Many farming methods can lead to soil erosion. Plowing loosens the topsoil and removes plants that hold the soil in place. The topsoil can then be washed away by wind or rain.

Soil Conservation Sustainable agricultural practices can help conserve fertile soil. For example, *terracing* changes a steep field into a series of flat steps that stop gravity from eroding the soil. Planting a *cover crop,* such as soybeans, restores nutrients to the soil. *Crop rotation,* or planting a different crop every year, slows down the depletion of nutrients in the soil. In *contour plowing,* rows are plowed in curves along hills instead of in straight lines. The rows then act as a series of dams, which prevent water from eroding the soil.

❭ **Reading check** *How does erosion damage soil?*

erosion a process in which the materials of Earth's surface are loosened, dissolved, or worn away and transported from one place to another by a natural agent, such as wind, water, ice, or gravity

Hypothesis or Theory? A lake in your state has had hundreds of dead fish wash up on shore. Write your own hypothesis that might explain why so many fish in the lake died.

Ecosystem Disruption

We share Earth with about 5 million to 15 million species. We depend on many of these species for fulfillment of our basic needs. We get food, clothing, medicines, and building material from many plants and animals. Yet as the human population has grown and affected every ecosystem, this wondrous diversity of life has suffered. ❯ **Ecosystem disruptions can result in loss of biodiversity, food supplies, potential cures for diseases, and the balance of ecosystems that supports all life on Earth.** We cannot avoid disrupting ecosystems as we try to meet the needs of a growing human population. But we can learn about how our actions affect the environment so that we can create ways to conserve it.

Habitat Destruction Over the last 50 years, about half of the world's tropical rain forests have been cut down or burned. The forests have been cleared for timber, pastureland, or farmland, as shown in **Figure 6.** This process of clearing forests is called **deforestation.** Many more thousands of square miles of forest will be destroyed this year. Some of the people who cut down the trees are poor farmers trying to make a living. The problem with deforestation is that as the rain forests and other habitats disappear, so do their inhabitants. In today's world, habitat destruction and damage cause more extinction and loss of biodiversity than any other human activities do.

Loss of Biodiversity Ecosystem disruption decreases the number of Earth's species. Biodiversity affects the stability of ecosystems and the sustainability of populations. **Biodiversity** is the variety of organisms in a given area. Every species plays an important role in the cycling of energy and nutrients in an ecosystem. Each species either depends on or is depended on by at least one other species. When a species disappears, a strand in a food web disappears. If a keystone species disappears, other species may also disappear. The species that disappears may be one that humans depend on.

There are many ways in which humans benefit from a variety of life forms on Earth. Humans have used a variety of organisms on Earth for food, clothing, shelter, and medicine. At least one-fourth of the medicines prescribed in the world are derived from plants. Fewer species of plants could mean fewer remedies for illnesses.

deforestation the process of clearing forests

biodiversity the variety of organisms in a given area, the genetic variation within a population, the variety of species in a community, or the variety of communities in an ecosystem

extinction the death of every member of a species

Figure 6 This forest in Brazil was slashed and burned to provide land for cattle and crops. ❯ **How does deforestation decrease biodiversity?**

Figure 7 The zebra mussel (left) is an invasive species that has disrupted the ecosystems of the Great Lakes region. The red panda (right) is an endangered species because its habitat, located in China and Myanmar, is being disrupted. ❯ **Name another example of an invasive species. Name three other endangered species.**

Invasive Species Humans have disrupted ecosystems by intentionally and unintentionally introducing nonnative species. One example of an invasive species is the zebra mussel, shown in **Figure 7.** In the 1980s, the zebra mussel was unintentionally introduced to the Great Lakes by ships traveling from the Black and Caspian Seas. The zebra mussel disrupted the Great Lakes ecosystem, causing some species to struggle while others flourished. Zebra mussels have also had a negative impact on humans. Zebra mussels clog the pipes of water treatment facilities which costs the public millions of dollars a year.

Extinction Many species are on the edge of extinction. **Extinction** is the death of every member of a species. One species that is at risk of extinction is the red panda. A red panda is shown in **Figure 7.** When a species becomes extinct, we lose forever the knowledge and benefits that we might have gained from the species. For example, two anticancer drugs have been developed from the rosy periwinkle, a flower in Madagascar that is threatened by deforestation. If this flower becomes extinct, a possible source of new drugs is gone.

❯ **Reading Check** *How has the introduction of the zebra mussel into the Great Lakes affected humans?*

Section

2 Review

❯ **KEY IDEAS**

1. **Identify** the affects of air pollution.
2. **Explain** how the burning of fossil fuels, such as oil, might lead to climate change.
3. **Identify** five sources of water pollution.
4. **Explain** why soil erosion is a problem.

5. **List** four ways ecosystem disruption affects humans.

CRITICAL THINKING

6. **Evaluating Viewpoints** A classmate asserts that extinction is not a problem because everything goes extinct eventually. Explain how extinction can be both a natural process and a current problem for society.

USING SCIENCE GRAPHICS

7. **Predicting Patterns** Using the chart, "CO_2 and Global Temperature Trends, 1960–2005," predict temperature and CO_2 levels for the year 2020. Describe how the temperature you predict would affect humans.

3 Environmental Solutions

Key Ideas	Key Terms	Why It Matters
❯ How do conservation and restoration solve environmental issues? ❯ What are three ways that people can reduce the use of environmental resources? ❯ How can research and technology affect the environment? ❯ How do education and advocacy play a part in preserving the environment? ❯ Why is it important for societies to consider environmental impact when planning for the future?	recycling ecotourism	Everyone can play an important role in sustaining a healthy environment for all of us.

Protecting the environment is critical to human well-being. With new technologies and the effort of individuals and governments, many environmental problems can be solved.

Conservation and Restoration

Two major techniques for dealing with environmental problems are conservation and restoration. ❯ **Conservation involves protecting existing natural habitats. *Restoration* involves cleaning up and restoring damaged habitats.** The best way to deal with environmental problems is to prevent them from happening. Conserving habitats prevents environmental issues that arise from ecosystem disruption. For example, parks and reserves protect a large area in which many species live.

Restoration reverses damage to ecosystems. Boston Harbor, shown in **Figure 8,** is one restoration success story. Since the colonial period, the city dumped sewage directly into the harbor. The buildup of waste caused outbreaks of disease. Beaches were closed. Most of the marine life disappeared and as a result, the shellfish industry shut down. To solve the problem, the city built a sewage-treatment complex. Since then, the harbor waters have cleared up. Plants and fish have returned, and beaches have been reopened.

❯ **Reading check** *What is the difference between restoration and conservation?*

Figure 8 Once considered one of the most polluted harbors in the world, Boston Harbor has been cleaned up as part of a restoration project.
❯ Name a restoration project or natural preserve in your state.

Hands-On
Quick Lab

30 min

Recycled Paper

In this activity, you will learn how to recycle paper.

Procedure

1. Tear **two sheets of used paper** into small pieces.

2. Put the pieces in a **blender** with **1 L of water.** Cover and blend until the mixture is soupy.

3. Fill a square **pan** with **2–3 cm of water.** Place a **wire screen** in the pan.

4. Pour 250 mL of the paper mixture onto the screen and spread the mixture evenly.

5. Lift the screen and paper mixture out of the water.

6. Place the screen inside a section of **newspaper.** Close the newspaper and turn it over so that the screen is on top of the mixture.

7. Cover the newspaper with a **flat board** and press on the board to squeeze out the water.

8. Open the newspaper and let your paper dry overnight.

Analysis

1. **Evaluate** whether the paper you made is as strong as the paper that it was made from.

2. **CRITICAL THINKING Analyzing Methods** How might you improve your technique to produce stronger paper?

Reduce Resource Use

The impact of humanity on the environment depends on how many resources we use. We can decrease our impact by using fewer resources. ❯ **We can reduce our use of resources, such as water and fossil fuels for energy. We can reuse goods rather than disposing of them. Furthermore, we can recycle waste to help protect the environment.**

Reduce One of the best ways that you can help solve environmental problems is by reducing the amount of energy that you use and the amount of waste that you produce. You can use ceramic plates instead of a disposable paper plate. Low-flow toilets and shower heads can decrease the amount of water used.

Reuse The reuse of goods saves both money and resources. Many things are thrown away and wasted though they are still useful. Plastic bags and utensils can be used several times, rather than only once before disposal.

Recycle The process of reusing things instead of taking more resources from the environment is called **recycling.** Recycling existing products generally costs less than making new ones from raw materials does. For example, recycling aluminum uses about 95 percent less energy than mining and processing the aluminum from Earth does. Recycling also prevents pollution. For example, recycling motor oil keeps toxic substances out of landfills.

❯ **Reading Check** *What are three ways that you can reduce your use of resources?*

ACADEMIC VOCABULARY

impact the effect of one thing on another

recycling the process of recovering valuable or useful materials from waste or scrap

Technology

Advances in technology have lead to the production of cars and the development of industry. Both of these processes have contributed to the problem of pollution. But, technology brings not only problems but also environmental solutions. ❯ **Research and technology can help protect our environment by providing cleaner energy sources, better ways to deal with waste, and improved methods for cleaning up pollution.**

Solar panels, shown in **Figure 9,** hybrid cars, and scrubbers are examples of advances in technology. Hybrid cars use a combination of electricity and gasoline as their source of energy. Hybrid cars designed to be fuel-efficient, burn less gasoline and release less pollution into the atmosphere than the average car. Scrubbers are devices that reduce harmful sulfur emissions from industrial smoke-stacks. Scrubbers have decreased emissions of sulfur dioxide, carbon monoxide, and soot by more than 30%!

Researching Solutions Researchers must determine the cause of an environmental problem before they can provide a solution to it. Researching such problems requires the use of scientific methods. Scientists make observations and collect data. After analyzing the data, a scientist may propose a solution to the environmental problem that was studied. Proposals should take into account the costs, risks, and benefits of implementing the solution. Mario Molina is a scientist who researched the effects of CFCs on the ozone layer of the atmosphere. He determined that CFCs damage the ozone layer, which protects us from the sun's harmful ultra-violet radiation. His research convinced the nations of the world to limit the use of CFCs.

Research by students can also help solve environmental problems. **Figure 9** shows students trying to find out why the dwarf wedge mussel is disappearing from rivers.

❯ **Reading Check** *How can fuel-efficient hybrid cars help solve environmental problems?*

SCI LINKS.
www.scilinks.org
Topic: Environment
Code: HX80524

Figure 9 Students at Keene High School in New Hampshire do field research on dwarf wedge mussels (left). Solar panels in California generate energy without producing pollution (right).

Figure 10 From a skybridge, ecotourists learn about the unique ecosystems at Monteverde Biological Cloud Forest Preserve in Costa Rica, without disturbing wildlife.

Environmental Awareness

Addressing environmental issues requires cooperation among conservation groups, individuals, and governments. Education and advocacy help more individuals take an active role in this process.
❯ Education makes people more aware of environmental issues. Education also shows people how they can help address such issues. Expressing support, or *advocating,* for efforts to protect the environment can help get more people involved in these efforts.

Advocacy Many environmental problems have been solved because of the efforts of those who advocate for a solution. Conservation groups make efforts to educate people, protect land, and influence laws through advocacy. Some organizations work on an international level. Others work on local environmental problems. Some groups help farmers, ranchers, and other landowners ensure the long-term conservation of their land.

Individuals and the media also play an important role in raising awareness of environmental issues. With her 1962 book *Silent Spring,* biologist Rachel Carson made millions of people aware of the dangers of pesticides. Her efforts contributed to the restriction on the use of the dangerous pesticide DDT.

Education Educating the public about the environment helps gain public support for solving environmental issues. Environmental education can enrich people's experience of their world and empower them to care for it. Ecotourism is one way to educate the public about the environment. **Ecotourism** is a form of tourism that supports conservation of the environment. **Figure 10** shows ecotourists in Costa Rica. Ecotourists may learn about the particular environmental problems of an area. Often, an ecotourist is given an opportunity to help solve environmental problems as part of his or her tour.

❯ **Reading check** *How can advocacy and education help solve environmental problems?*

READING TOOLBOX

Venn Diagram Make a Venn diagram to help you compare the similarities and differences between advocacy and education relating to environmental science.

ecotourism a form of tourism that supports the conservation and sustainable development of ecologically unique areas

Figure 11 The Fresh Kills landfill (left) occupies 2,200 acres on Staten Island. To the right is the plan for the Fresh Kills of tomorrow. ❯ **In what ways does your community plan to conserve or restore the environment?**

www.scilinks.org
Topic: Solving
        Environmental
        Problems
Code: HX81424

Planning for the Future

What will our planet look like in 50 years? Will it still supply the basic needs and quality of life that we enjoy today, or will we lack the resources we need? ❯ **Careful planning for the future can help us avoid damaging the environment and can help us solve the environmental issues that we face.** If we want a safe, healthy, bright future, we need to actively aim for it. **Figure 11** shows how Staten Island is planning for the future by turning a landfill into a park.

Society can plan by noting the effects of certain activities, such as development and resource use. For example, if a builder wants to develop an area that is near an aquifer's recharge zone, the local government may evaluate the effects of development on the aquifer. After analyzing risks, costs, and benefits to the community, the government may choose to enforce limitations on the development. When governments plan for the future, they can protect resources for the community for years to come.

❯ **Reading check** *Why do we need to evaluate effects of development before following through with the development?*

Section
3 Review

❯ KEY IDEAS

1. **Explain** how conservation might help an endangered species.
2. **Describe** three ways you can reduce the use of environmental resources.
3. **Describe** how research and technology affect the environment.

4. **Explain** how education on the resources that we use can help preserve the environment.
5. **Describe** how planning can prevent damage to the environment.

CRITICAL THINKING

6. **Analyzing Methods** To join a global agreement to fight climate change, the United States must reduce CO_2 levels by 10%. What would be the positive and negative effects on society of such a reduction in CO_2?

METHODS OF SCIENCE

7. **Predicting Outcomes** A land manager proposes planting shrubs to help restore land damaged by erosion. Describe a study or experiment that you could carry out to evaluate whether this proposal will work.

Cars of the Future

WEIRD SCIENCE

For many Americans, a car is a necessity. People rely on cars to get to work, to school, and to run errands. However, most cars are the main contributor of pollutants, such as CO_2, in the atmosphere. To help reduce the amount of pollutants released into the atmosphere, scientists have been developing cars that use nonpolluting forms of energy.

Different Forms of Energy

Scientists have developed many cars of the future that are more fuel efficient than other cars of today or that use nonpolluting forms of energy. The hybrid, a type of car that is becoming popular in the United States, uses electricity as well as gasoline. Some cars of the future run on only solar power! Solar-car races, as shown in the image above right, inspire advancements in car technology through friendly competitions. The FIA Alternative Energies Cup in Japan has solar cars compete in an eight-hour endurance race. Scientists have also developed cars that can run on ethanol and hydrogen. Some day, you may be riding in one of these cars.

Research Many technical universities have teams that compete in solar car races. Conduct Internet research and investigate some of the more successful teams. Create a Web site or poster supporting one of the teams you learn about.

Obvio!—Gas or Ethanol This fuel-efficient Brazilian minicar can run on either gas or ethanol. Ethanol produces less pollution than gas and is renewable. Ethanol is formed from biomass, such as corn or potatoes.

Toyota Fine-N Fuel Cell Hybrid (FCHV) The FCHV doesn't burn fossil fuels. It gets its energy from a fuel cell that produces chemical energy by combining oxygen and hydrogen. The best thing about the fuel cell is that it doesn't produce any pollution. The only byproduct of the fuel cell is water!

Chapter 6 Lab

Objectives

▶ Simulate an environmental condition in the laboratory.

▶ Measure the difference between treated and untreated seedlings.

▶ Analzye the effects of acidic conditions on plants.

Materials

- seeds (50)
- beaker (250 mL)
- mold inhibitor (20 mL)
- water, distilled
- paper towels
- solutions of various pH
- pencil, wax (or marker)
- bags, plastic, resealable
- metric ruler
- graph paper

Safety

Effects of Acid Rain		
Solution	Date	Observations

Effects of Acid Rain on Seeds

Living things, such as salamander embryos, can be damaged by acid rain at certain times during their lives. In this lab, you will design an experiment to investigate the effects of acidic solutions on seeds. To do this, you will germinate seeds under various experimental conditions that you determine.

Preparation

1. **SCIENTIFIC METHODS** **State the Problem** How does acid rain affect plants?

2. **SCIENTIFIC METHODS** **Form a Hypothesis** Form a testable hypothesis that explains how a germinating plant might be affected by acid rain. Record your hypothesis.

Procedure

Design an Experiment

1 Design an experiment that tests your hypothesis and that uses the materials listed for this lab. Predict what will happen during your experiment if your hypothesis is supported.

2 Write a procedure for your experiment. Identify the variables that you will control, the experimental variables, and the responding variables. Construct any tables that you will need to record your data. Make a list of all of the safety precautions that you will take. Have your teacher approve your procedure before you begin.

Conduct Your Experiment

3 Put on safety goggles, gloves, and a lab apron.

4 CAUTION: **The mold inhibitor contains household bleach, which is a toxic chemical and a base.** Place your seeds in a 250 mL beaker, and slowly add enough mold inhibitor to cover the seeds. Soak the seeds for 10 minutes, and then pour the mold inhibitor into the proper waste container. Gently rinse the seeds with distilled water, and place them on clean paper towels.

5 CAUTION: **Solutions that have a pH below 7.0 are acids.** Carry out your experiment for 7–10 days. Make observations every 1–2 days, and note any changes. Record your observations each day in a data table, similar to the one shown.

6 Clean up your lab materials according to your teacher's instructions. Wash your hands before leaving the lab.

Analyze and Conclude

1. **Summarizing Results** Describe any changes in the look of your seeds during the experiment. Discuss seed type, average seed size, number of germinated seeds, and changes in seedling length.

2. **Analyzing Results** Were there any differences between the solutions? Explain.

3. **Analyzing Methods** What was the control group in your experiment?

4. **Analyzing Data** Make graphs of your group's data. Plot seedling growth (in millimeters) on the *y*-axis. Plot number of days on the *x*-axis.

5. SCIENTIFIC METHODS **Interpreting Data** How do acidic conditions appear to affect seeds?

6. **Predicting Outcomes** How might acid rain affect the plants in an ecosystem?

7. SCIENTIFIC METHODS **Critiquing Procedures** How could your experiment be improved?

8. SCIENTIFIC METHODS **Formulating Scientific Questions** Write a new question about the effect of acid rain that could be explored with another investigation.

SCI *LINKS*.

www.scilinks.org
Topic: Acid Rain
Code: HX80008

Extensions

9. **Inferring Relationships** Research to identify the parts of the United States that are most affected by acid rain. Explain why acid rain affects these areas more than it affects other areas.

10. **Analyzing Methods** Describe how factories have changed to reduce the amount of acid rain.

go.hrw.com
SUPER SUMMARY
Keyword: HX8ENVS

Key Ideas	Key Terms

1 An Interconnected Planet

> Humans are a part of the environment and can affect the resilience of the environment.

> Renewable resources are natural resources that can be replaced at the same rate at which they are consumed.

> Nonrenewable resources are resources that form at a rate that is much slower than the rate at which they are consumed.

> Pollution and habitat destruction destroy the resources we need to live, such as the air we breathe, the water we drink, and the food we eat.

fossil fuel (126)

2 Environmental Issues

> Air pollution causes respiratory problems for people, results in acid rain, damages the ozone layer, and affects global temperature.

> Burning fossil fuels increases the amount of CO_2 in the atmosphere. Increases in atmospheric CO_2 may be responsible for an increase in global temperatures.

> Water pollution can come from fertilizers and pesticides used in agriculture and from livestock farms, industrial waste, oil runoff from roads, septic tanks, and unlined landfills.

> Soil erosion destroys fertile soil that we need in order to produce food.

> Ecosystem disruptions can result in loss of biodiversity, food supplies, potential cures for diseases, and the balance of ecosystems that supports all life on Earth.

acid rain (128)
global warming (128)
greenhouse effect (129)
erosion (131)
deforestation (132)
biodiversity (132)
extinction (133)

3 Environmental Solutions

> Conservation involves protecting existing natural habitats. Restoration involves cleaning up and restoring damaged habitats.

> We can reduce our use of natural resources, such as water and fossil fuels for energy. We can reuse goods rather than disposing of them. Furthermore, we can recycle waste to help protect the environment.

> Research and technology can help protect our environment by providing cleaner energy sources, better ways to deal with waste, and improved methods for cleaning up pollution.

> Education makes people more aware of environmental issues and of ways that they can help. Expressing support, or *advocating,* for efforts to protect the environment can help get more people involved.

> Careful planning for the future can help us avoid damaging the environment and solve environmental issues that we currently face.

recycling (135)
ecotourism (137)

1. **Word Parts** Copy each of the following words: *biodiversity* and *extinction*. Write down other words that have the same word parts. Then, look in the dictionary for the definitions of the words.

2. **Concept Map** Make a concept map on how human activity affects climate. Try to use the following terms in your map: *greenhouse effect, carbon dioxide, greenhouse gases, global warming, CFCs, ozone layer, acid rain,* and *sulfur dioxide.*

Using Key Terms

Use each of the following terms in a separate sentence.

3. *fossil fuel*

4. *recycle*

For each pair of terms, explain how the meaning of the terms differ.

5. *global warming* and *greenhouse effect*

6. *erosion* and *deforestation*

Understanding Key Ideas

Use the the figure to answer the following question(s).

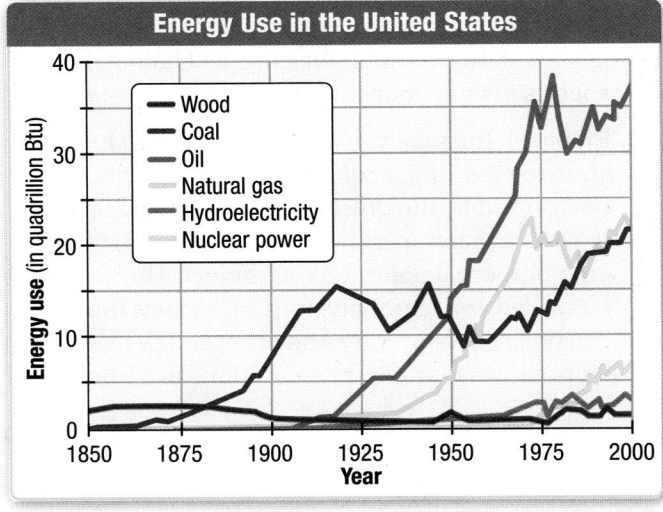

Energy Use in the United States

Legend: Wood, Coal, Oil, Natural gas, Hydroelectricity, Nuclear power

Y-axis: Energy use (in quadrillion Btu) — 0, 10, 20, 30, 40
X-axis: Year — 1850, 1875, 1900, 1925, 1950, 1975, 2000

7. Which form of energy use has increased the most in the U.S. since 1850?

8. Which of the following damages the ozone layer?
   a. CO_2
   b. SO_2
   c. NO_3
   d. CFCs

9. Which of the following is not a source of water pollution?
   a. CFCs
   b. oil runoff
   c. pesticides
   d. industrial waste

10. Which of the following is a result of ecosystem disruption?
    a. acid rain
    b. global warming
    c. greenhouse effect
    d. loss of biodiversity

11. Which of the following is a technology used to harness a renewable resource?
    a. benzene
    b. hybrid cars
    c. solar panels
    d. smokestack scrubbers

12. Rachel Carson's book *Silent Spring* educated readers about what environmental threat?
    a. pesticide use
    b. invasive species
    c. CFC production
    d. burning fossil fuels

13. Which of the following is an example of conservation?
    a. creating a nature preserve
    b. cleaning up a polluted stream
    c. planting trees on an eroding slope
    d. reintroducing endangered species

14. Which of the following is an example of planning for the future to avoid environmental damage?
    a. creating a landfill
    b. cleaning up an oil spill
    c. mining aluminum from Earth's crust
    d. evaluating potential effects of development

Explaining Key Ideas

15. **Describe** one way in which the environment affects human health.

16. **Explain** how increasing CO_2 in Earth's atmosphere might lead to climate change.

17. **Explain** the difference between conservation and restoration.

Using Science Graphics

Use the diagram to answer the following question(s).

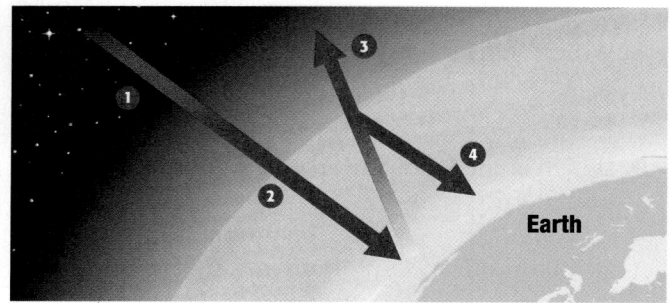

Earth

18. Which arrow represents a flow of heat that will increase as atmospheric CO_2 rises?

   a. 1   **c.** 3

   b. 2   **d.** 4

19. Which arrow represents a flow of heat that will decrease as atmospheric CO_2 rises?

   a. 1   **c.** 3

   b. 2   **d.** 4

Critical Thinking

20. Constructing Explanations Fossil fuel burning and the clearing of forests each contribute large amounts of CO_2 to the atmosphere. How might deforestation lead to this release of CO_2?

21. Proposing Solutions Your state is experiencing a shortage of electrical power on hot summer days when many air conditioners are on. You are asked to propose measures that might solve this shortage problem without increasing electricity supplies. Propose one such measure, and explain how it would address the problem.

22. Analyzing Information What do environmental scientists mean by *interdependence?* Give an example of interdependence from this chapter.

23. Analyzing Processes Propose two steps that scientists might take to speed restoration of a river damaged by a major toxic spill.

24. Predicting Outcomes How would stopping all pesticide use likely affect rates of food production and incidence of diseases, such as malaria, that are spread by insects?

25. Inferring Relationships Describe how some species would be affected by global warming.

Connecting Key Ideas

26. Analyzing Processes Humans need clean, fresh water. Environmental scientists think that fresh water may become a limiting factor for human population growth. Explain how you could estimate Earth's carrying capacity for humans based on the availability of fresh water. What information would you need to make this estimate?

Alternative Assessment

27. Field Trip Plan Develop a lesson plan for a 30-minute class or field trip about one environmental issue that students in your class could do something about. Include the issue to be covered, an outline of points to discuss, and description of activities, location, or materials you would need.

28. Waste Investigation Find out where household waste goes in your community. How far is the waste taken from your home? Is the waste close to other homes or to important water sources for your area? Write a short summary of your findings.

Writing for Science

29. Speech Imagine that your town is holding a public hearing on whether to build a diesel bus depot next to your school. Use the library or the Internet to write a two-minute speech on why you support or oppose the project.

30. Research Obtain a list of the plants and animals that are endangered in your state. Find out where these species live, and mark the locations on a map of your state. Research the effects of habitat loss on species in your county or in surrounding areas.

31. Proposal Imagine you are a scientist who has been studying the subject of global warming. You have been asked by the President of the United States to write a recommendation for the president's environmental policy on the subject. The President has asked you to provide important facts that can be used to promote the proposed policies. Summarize your recommendations in a brief letter.

TEST TIP For a question involving experimental data, determine the constants, variables, and control before answering the questions.

Science Concepts

1. What is the term for the natural ability of Earth's atmosphere to trap energy from the sun?

A global warming

B ozone depletion

C greenhouse effect

D biological magnification

2. Which of the following terms means "liquid precipitation that has a low pH and that results from sulfur emissions reacting with water"?

F acid rain   H greenhouse gas

G sulfuric acid   J thermal pollution

3. What does Earth's ozone layer shield Earth's inhabitants from?

A solar heating   C ultraviolet rays

B meteor impacts   D ozone depletion

4. Which of the following describes the variety of species in an area?

F biodiversity

G species richness

H species evenness

J bioindicator species

5. Which of the following is a renewable resource?

A coal   C gasoline

B trees   D natural gas

6. Which of the following is a process in which materials of Earth's surface are worn away and transported from one place to another by wind, gravity, or water?

F erosion   H disruption

G terracing   J deforestation

Using Science Graphics

Use the graph to answer the following question(s).

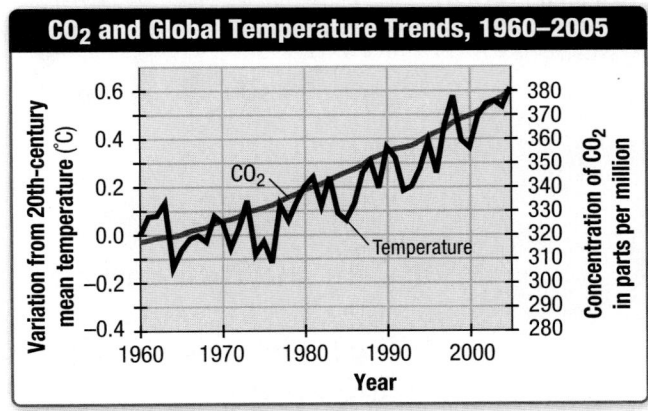

Source: Scripps Institute of Oceanography and National & Atmospheric Administration.

7. What is the term commonly used to describe the trend shown in this graph?

A water pollution   C ozone depletion

B global warming   D biodiversity crisis

Use the table to answer the following question(s).

	United States	Japan	Indonesia
Number of people per square mile	78	829	319
Garbage produced per person per year (kg)	720 kg	400 kg	43 kg

8. Which country has the most people per square mile?

F Japan   H Indonesia

G United States   J Japan and Indonesia

9. Which country produces the greatest amount of garbage per square mile?

A Japan   C Indonesia

B United States   D Japan and Indonesia

Math Skills

10. Making Conversions An oil tanker hit a coral reef and spilled 800,000 mL of oil into the ocean. If the oil spread evenly over 100 km², how many liters of oil does each square kilometer contain?

UNIT 3 Cells

7 Cell Structure

8 Cells and Their Environment

9 Photosynthesis and Cellular Respiration

10 Cell Growth and Division

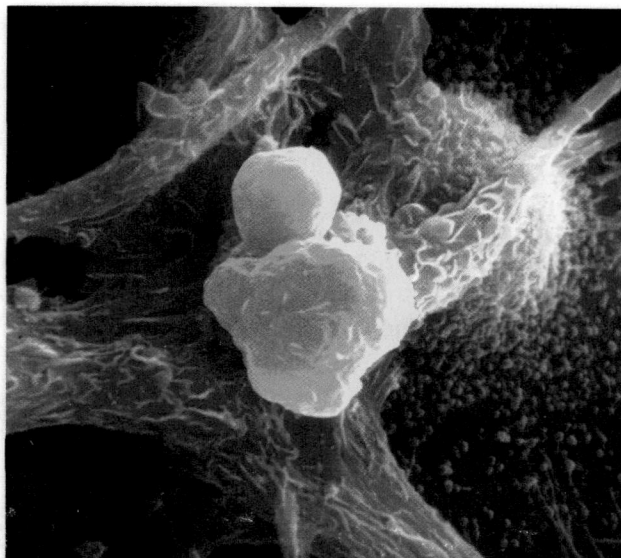

Macrophage (purple) attack on a cancer cell (yellow)

Sex chromosomes of a human male: Y (left) and X (right)

Human motor neuron

Cell Biology

1665

Robert Hooke builds a microscope to look at tiny objects. He discovers cells after observing a thin piece of cork under a microscope. He also finds cells in plants and fungi.

Hooke's microscope

1772

British clergyman and chemist, Joseph Priestly, presents his paper, *On Different Kinds of Air,* in which he describes his discovery of oxygen and other previously-unknown gases found in air. He also demonstrates that oxygen is produced by plants.

1839

Theodor Schwann shows that all animal tissue is made of cells. With plant biologist, Matthias Schleiden, Schwann identifies cell components, such as membranes and a nucleus common, to many eukaryotic cells.

1855

Rudolf Virchow publishes a theory stating that all cells come from another cells. He explains, "Where a cell exists, there must have been a preexisting cell."

Animal cells
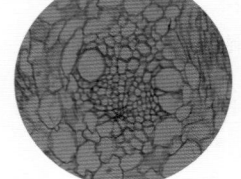

1945

Keith R. Porter, Albert Claude, and Ernest F. Fullam publish the first electromicrograph of a cell. Small organelles, such as the endoplasmic reticulum and the Golgi apparatus, are visible for the first time.

LATE 1950s

Canadian scientists Ernest McCulloch and James Till begin research on stem cells in rodents. Bone marrow stem cells can produce several types of blood cells.

Bone marrow stem cell

1971

Lynn Margulis proposes the endosymbiotic theory of the origins of cell organelles. This theory states that chloroplasts and mitochondria in eukaryotes evolved from prokaryotes.

Lynn Margulis

2004

Richard Axel, and Linda Buck earn the Noble Prize in Medicine or Physiology for their discovery of how olfactory cells detect odors and how the brain processes information to provide a sense of smell.

Microtubules (green) and chromosomes (blue) in a dividing cell

146B

BIOLOGY CAREER

Cell Biologist
Shubha Govind

Shubha Govind is a professor of biology at City College, City University of New York. Govind considers her most important scientific contribution to be developing a model system for using genetic tools to study the molecular basis of host-parasite interaction in fruit flies. She is studying how blood cells of fruit flies are formed and how they guard against infections when flies are attacked by parasites. She is also studying how parasites have evolved to overcome the immune reactions of the fly.

Govind grew up in India, and her family traveled a lot. As she traveled, she was impressed with the diversity of flora and fauna in different parts of the country. By the time she reached middle school, she knew that she wanted to be a biologist.

Apart from science, Govind enjoys reading, listening to music and spending time with family and friends.

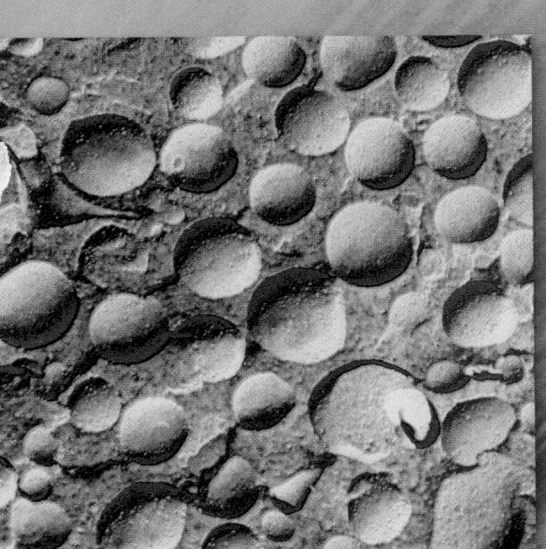

Freeze fracture of cell

Chapter 7

Cell Structure

Preview

1 Introduction to Cells
The Discovery of Cells
Looking at Cells
Cell Features

2 Inside the Eukaryotic Cell
The Framework of the Cell
Directing Cellular Activity
Protein Processing
Storage and Maintenance
Energy Production

3 From Cell to Organism
Diversity in Cells
Levels of Organization
Body Types

Why It Matters

All living things are made of cells. Scientists study how cells work to understand life.

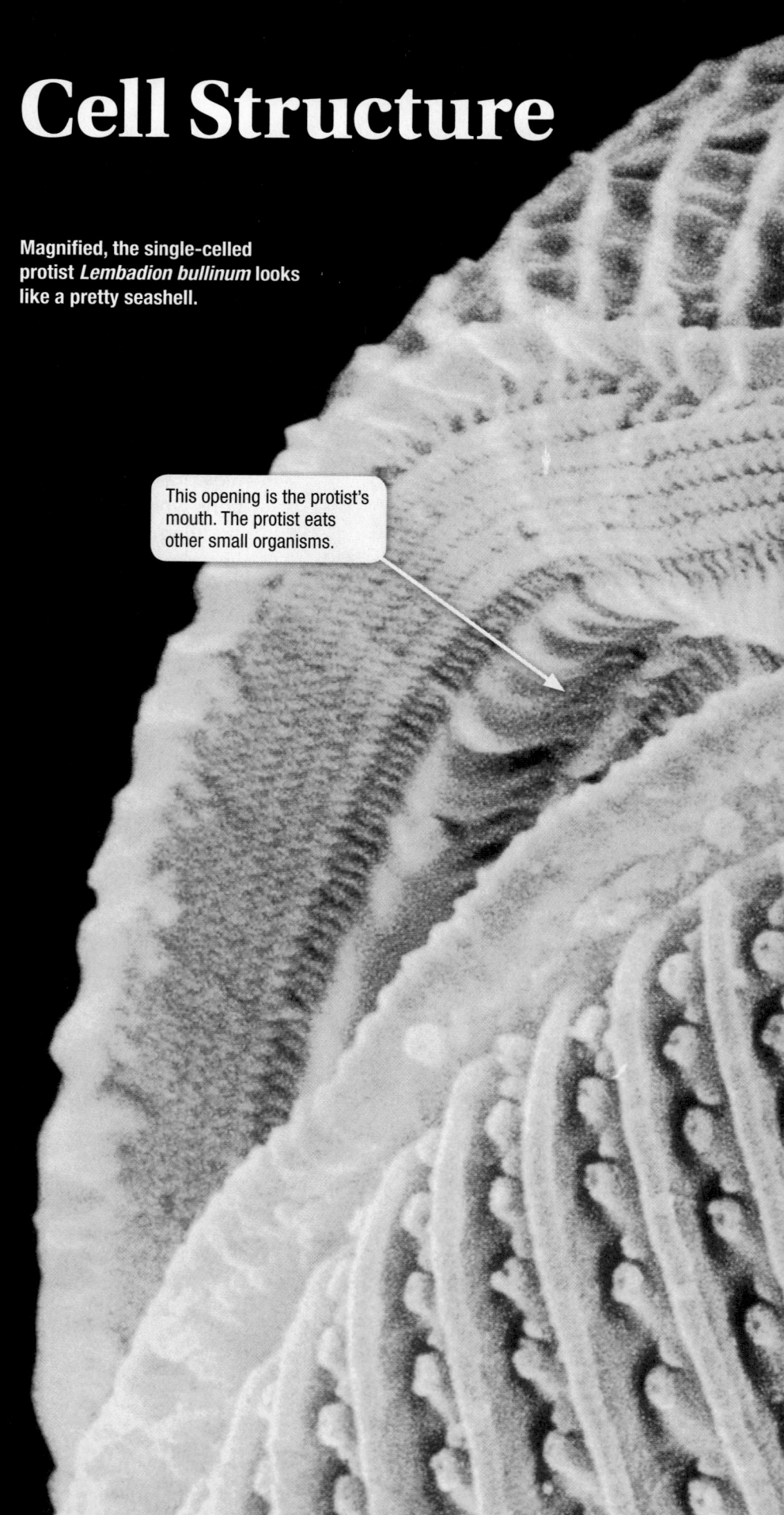

Magnified, the single-celled protist *Lembadion bullinum* looks like a pretty seashell.

This opening is the protist's mouth. The protist eats other small organisms.

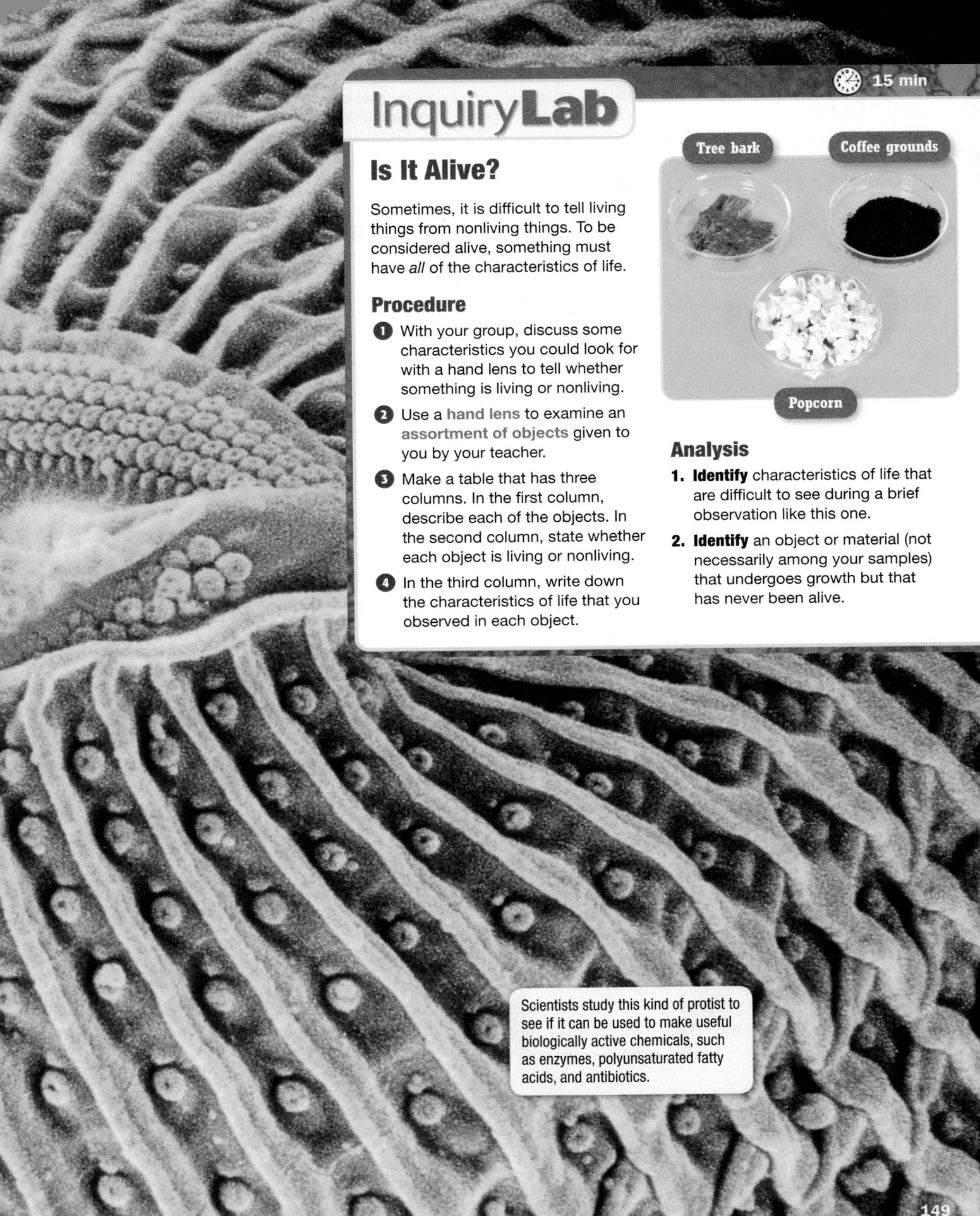

InquiryLab

⏱ 15 min

Tree bark **Coffee grounds**

Popcorn

Is It Alive?

Sometimes, it is difficult to tell living things from nonliving things. To be considered alive, something must have *all* of the characteristics of life.

Procedure

1. With your group, discuss some characteristics you could look for with a hand lens to tell whether something is living or nonliving.

2. Use a **hand lens** to examine an **assortment of objects** given to you by your teacher.

3. Make a table that has three columns. In the first column, describe each of the objects. In the second column, state whether each object is living or nonliving.

4. In the third column, write down the characteristics of life that you observed in each object.

Analysis

1. **Identify** characteristics of life that are difficult to see during a brief observation like this one.

2. **Identify** an object or material (not necessarily among your samples) that undergoes growth but that has never been alive.

Scientists study this kind of protist to see if it can be used to make useful biologically active chemicals, such as enzymes, polyunsaturated fatty acids, and antibiotics.

READING TOOLBOX

These reading tools can help you learn the material in this chapter. For more information on how to use these and other tools, see **Appendix: Reading and Study Skills.**

Using Words

Word Parts Knowing the meanings of word parts can help you figure out the meanings of words that you do not know.

Your Turn Use the information in the table to answer the questions that follow.

1. Use the table to write your own definition for *organize.*

2. What do you think an organelle does in a cell?

Word Parts		
Word part	Type	Meaning
organ	root	a group of parts that work together
-ize	suffix	to make or become
-elle	suffix	small part

Using Language

Similes Similes help relate new ideas to ideas that you already know. Often, similes use the terms *like* or *as.* For example, if you were describing a motorcycle to someone who had never seen one, you might say that it is like a bicycle that has a motor.

Your Turn Use information in the chapter to answer the questions that follow.

1. Find a simile to describe a cytoskeleton.

2. Write a simile to describe the function of a mitochondrion.

Using Science Graphics

Process Chart Science is full of processes. A process chart shows the steps that a process takes to get from one point to another point. This tool can help you visualize a process and remember the steps.

Your Turn Make a process chart to help you remember the steps of protein packaging.

1. Draw a box. In the box, write the first step of the process.

2. Under the box, draw another box and an arrow connecting the two boxes. In the second box, write the next step of the process.

3. Keep adding boxes and arrows until each step of the process has been included.

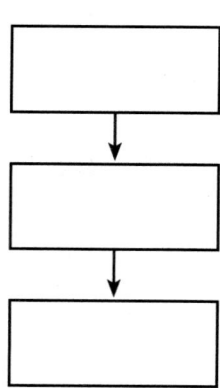

Introduction to Cells

Key Ideas	Key Terms	Why It Matters
❯ How were cells discovered? ❯ What defines cell shape and size? ❯ What enables eukaryotes to perform more specialized functions than prokaryotes do?	cell membrane prokaryote cytoplasm eukaryote ribosome nucleus organelle	Cells are the basic unit of life. By studying cells, biologists can better understand life's processes.

All life-forms on our planet are made up of cells. The bacteria that live in our gut and the cells that make up our body are built from the same chemical machinery. This machinery allows living things to obtain and use energy, to respond to their environment, and to reproduce. In all organisms, cells have the same basic structure.

The Discovery of Cells

How do living things differ from nonliving things? The discovery of cells was an important step toward answering this question. Most cells are too small to see with the naked eye. As **Figure 1** shows, microscopes have become an important tool for studying biology.
❯ **Microscope observations of organisms led to the discovery of the basic characteristics common to all living things.**

In 1665, Robert Hooke, an English scientist, used a crude microscope to look at a thin slice of cork. His microscope could magnify objects to only 30 times their normal size. Hooke saw many "little boxes" in the cork. They reminded him of the small rooms in which monks lived, so he called them *cells*. Hooke later discovered cells in the stems and roots of plants. Ten years later, Anton van Leeuwenhoek, a Dutch scientist, used a more powerful microscope that could magnify objects 300-fold. He discovered many living creatures in pond water. He named them *animalcules,* or "tiny animals." Today, we know that they were not animals. They were single-celled organisms.

❯ **Reading Check** *How powerful was Hooke's microscope? (See the Appendix for answers to Reading Checks.)*

Figure 1 A student looks through a light microscope. Euglena (inset) are single-celled organisms that are commonly found in pond water.

Cell Theory It took more than 150 years for scientists to fully appreciate the discoveries of Hooke and Leeuwenhoek. By the 1830s, microscopes were powerful enough to resolve structures only 1 μm apart. In 1838, Matthias Schleiden, a German botanist, concluded that cells make up every part of a plant. A year later, Theodor Schwann, a German zoologist, discovered that animals are also made up of cells. In 1858, Rudolph Virchow, a German physician, proposed that cells come only from the division of existing cells. The observations of Schleiden, Schwann, and Virchow form the *cell theory:*

- All living things are made up of one or more cells.
- Cells are the basic units of structure and function in organisms.
- All cells arise from existing cells.

The cell theory has withstood the rigorous examination of cells by scientists equipped with today's high-powered microscopes. As new tools and techniques are invented, scientists will learn more about the characteristics of cells.

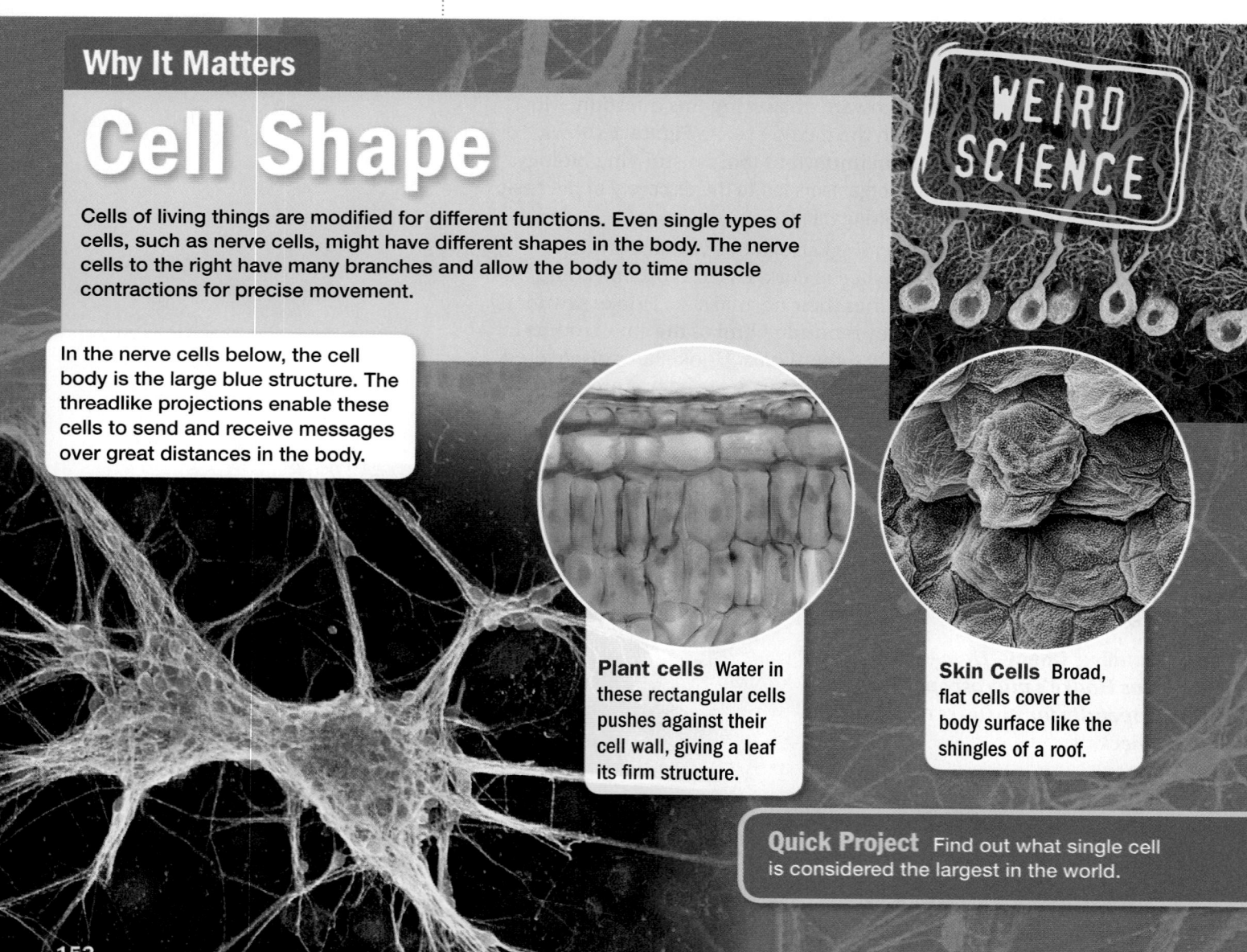

Why It Matters

Cell Shape

Cells of living things are modified for different functions. Even single types of cells, such as nerve cells, might have different shapes in the body. The nerve cells to the right have many branches and allow the body to time muscle contractions for precise movement.

In the nerve cells below, the cell body is the large blue structure. The threadlike projections enable these cells to send and receive messages over great distances in the body.

WEIRD SCIENCE

Plant cells Water in these rectangular cells pushes against their cell wall, giving a leaf its firm structure.

Skin Cells Broad, flat cells cover the body surface like the shingles of a roof.

Quick Project Find out what single cell is considered the largest in the world.

152

A ratio compares two numbers by dividing one number by the other number. A ratio can be expressed in three ways:

$$x \text{ to } y \qquad \frac{x}{y} \qquad x:y$$

You can improve your understanding of a cell's surface area–to-volume ratio by practicing with cubes of various sizes. What is the surface area–to-volume ratio of a cube that has a side length (l) of 4 mm?

❶ Find the surface area of the cube. A cube has six square faces. The surface area of one face is $l \times l$, or l^2.
- total surface area of cube = $6 \times l^2$
- total surface area of cube = $6 \times (4 \text{ mm})^2 = 96 \text{ mm}^2$

❷ Find the volume of the cube.
- volume of cube = l^3
- volume of cube = $(4 \text{ mm})^3 = 64 \text{ mm}^3$

Surface Area and Volume

Side length	Surface area	Volume	Surface area–to-volume
1 mm	6 mm²	1 mm³	6:1
2 mm	24 mm²	8 mm³	3:1
4 mm	96 mm²	64 mm³	3:2

❸ Divide the total surface area by volume:

- $surface\ area\text{–}to\text{-}volume\ ratio = \dfrac{total\ surface\ area}{volume}$

Reduce both numbers by their greatest common factor:

- $surface\ area\text{–}to\text{-}volume\ ratio = \dfrac{(96 \div 32)}{(64 \div 32)} = \dfrac{3}{2}$

Looking at Cells

Cells vary greatly in size and in shape. **❯ A cell's shape reflects the cell's function.** Cells may be branched, flat, round, or rectangular. Some cells have irregular shapes, while other cells constantly change shapes. These differences enable different cells to perform highly specific functions in the body. There are at least 200 types of cells. The human body is made up of about 100 trillion cells, most of which range from 5 to 20 μm in diameter. Why are cells so small?

Cell Size All substances that enter or leave a cell must pass through the surface of the cell. As a cell gets larger, it takes up more nutrients and releases more wastes. These substances must move farther to reach their destination in a larger cell. **❯ Cell size is limited by a cell's surface area–to-volume ratio.**

Scientists can estimate a cell's ability to exchange materials by calculating the cell's surface area–to-volume ratio. Cells with greater surface area–to-volume ratios can exchange substances more efficiently. When cells that are the same shape as one another are compared, the smaller cells have greater surface area–to-volume ratios than larger cells do.

Cell Shape Larger cells often have shapes that increase the surface area available for exchange. A cell may grow large in one or two dimensions but remain small in others. For example, some skin cells are broad and flat. Some nerve cells are highly extended and can be more than 10,000 times as long as they are thick. In both of these types of cells, the surface area-to-volume ratio is larger than it would be if the cells were spheres.

ACADEMIC VOCABULARY

dimension a measurement in a particular direction

❯ Reading Check *How does a cell's size affect the cell's function?*

Figure 2 The cytoplasm of a prokaryotic cell (left) is made up of everything that is inside the cell membrane, including ribosomes and a loop of DNA. The cytoplasm of a eukaryotic cell (right) is made up of many different structures that are surrounded by membranes.

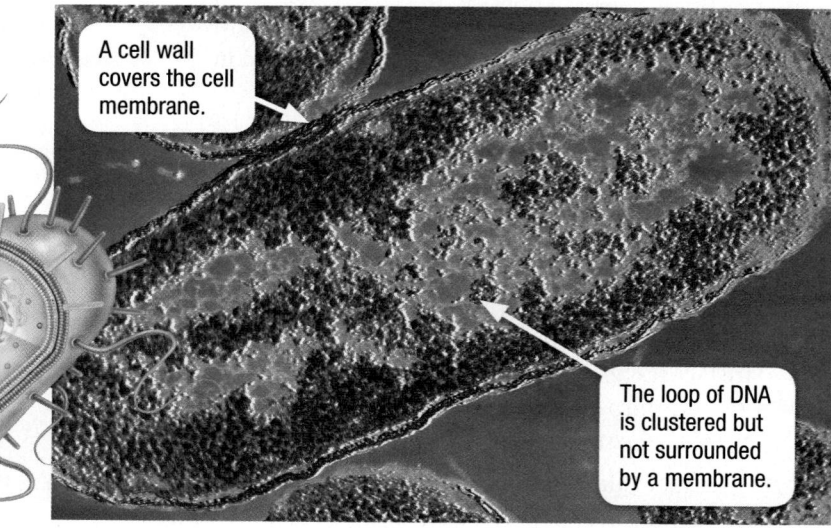

A cell wall covers the cell membrane.

The loop of DNA is clustered but not surrounded by a membrane.

Bacterium (Prokaryotic cell)

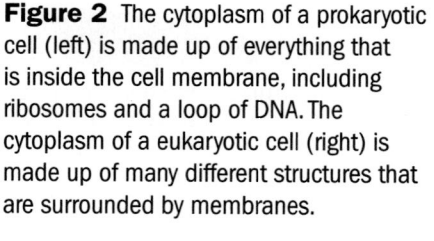

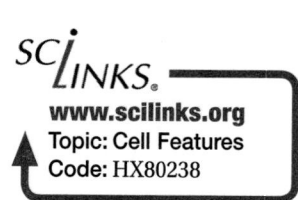

www.scilinks.org
Topic: Cell Features
Code: HX80238

cell membrane a phospholipid layer that covers a cell's surface and acts as a barrier between the inside of a cell and the cell's environment

cytoplasm (SIET oh PLAZ uhm) the region of the cell within the membrane

ribosome (RIE buh SOHM) a cell organelle where protein synthesis occurs

prokaryote a single-celled organism that does not have a nucleus or membrane-bound organelles

eukaryote an organism made up of cells that have a nucleus and membrane-bound organelles

nucleus in a eukaryotic cell, a membrane-bound organelle that contains the cell's DNA

organelle one of the small bodies that are found in the cytoplasm of a cell and that are specialized to perform a specific function

Cell Features

All cells—from bacteria to those in a berry, bug, or bunny—share common structural features. All cells have a cell membrane, cytoplasm, ribosomes, and DNA. The **cell membrane** is the cell's outer boundary. It acts as a barrier between the outside environment and the inside of the cell. The *cytosol,* the fluid inside the cell, is full of dissolved particles. The **cytoplasm** includes this fluid and almost all of the structures that are suspended in the fluid. Many ribosomes are found in the cytoplasm. A **ribosome** is a cellular structure on which proteins are made. All cells also have DNA, the genetic material. DNA provides instructions for making proteins, regulates cellular activities, and enables cells to reproduce.

Features of Prokaryotic Cells The bacterium shown in **Figure 2** is an example of a **prokaryote,** an organism that is a single prokaryotic cell. A prokaryotic cell is quite simple in its organization. The genetic material is a single loop of DNA, which looks like a tangled string and usually lies near the center of the cell. Ribosomes and enzymes share the cytoplasm with the DNA.

Prokaryotic cells have a cell wall that surrounds the cell membrane and that provides structure and support. Some prokaryotic cell walls are surrounded by a *capsule,* a structure that enables prokaryotes to cling to surfaces, including teeth, skin, and food.

Scientists think that the first prokaryotes may have lived 3.5 billion years ago or more. For millions of years, prokaryotes were the only organisms on Earth. They were very simple and small (1 to 2 μm in diameter). Like their ancestors, modern prokaryotes are also very small (1 to 15 μm), and they live in a wide range of habitats. Prokaryotes make up a very large and diverse group of cells.

❯ **Reading Check** *What is a ribosome?*

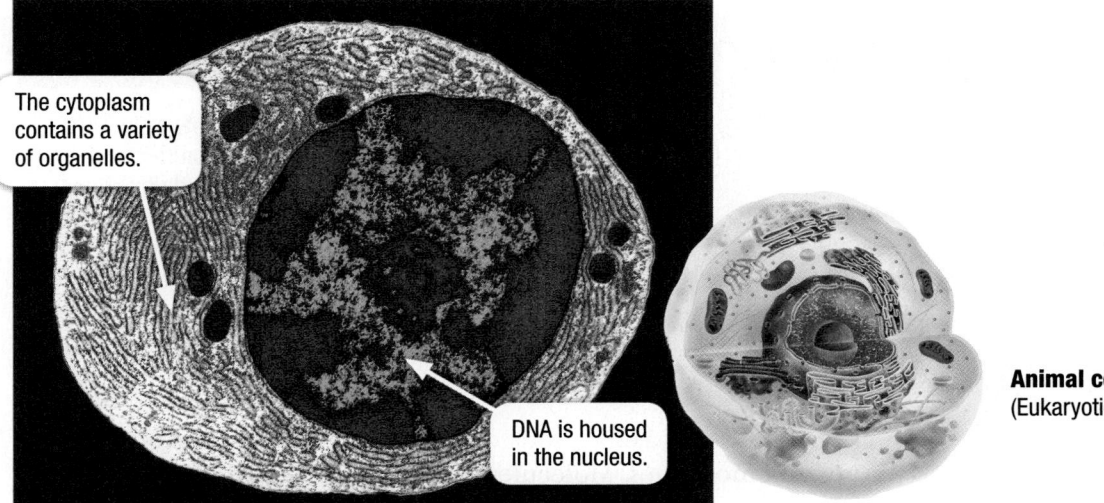

The cytoplasm contains a variety of organelles.

DNA is housed in the nucleus.

Animal cell
(Eukaryotic cell)

Features of Eukaryotic Cells A **eukaryote** is an organism that is made up of one or more eukaryotic cells. Some eukaryotes live as single cells. Others are multicellular organisms. In fact, all multicellular organisms are made up of eukaryotic cells. ❯ **Because of their complex organization, eukaryotic cells can carry out more specialized functions than prokaryotic cells can.**

Primitive eukaryotic cells first appeared about 1.5 billion years ago. As shown in the animal cell in **Figure 2,** a eukaryotic cell contains compartments that are separated by membranes. The cell's DNA is housed in an internal compartment called the **nucleus.**

In addition to having a membrane, cytoplasm, ribosomes, and a nucleus, all eukaryotic cells have membrane-bound organelles. An **organelle** is a structure that carries out specific activities inside the cell. The animal cell in **Figure 2** shows many of the organelles found in eukaryotic cells. Each organelle performs distinct functions. Many organelles are surrounded by a membrane. Some of the membranes are connected by channels that help move substances within the cell.

READING TOOLBOX

Word Parts The root *kary* means "kernel," which describes the nucleus. *Eu-* means "true," so a eukaryotic cell has a true nucleus. If *pro-* means "before," what does prokaryotic mean?

Section 1 Review

❯ **KEY IDEAS**

1. **List** the three parts of the cell theory.
2. **Describe** the importance of a cell's surface area–to-volume ratio.
3. **Compare** the structure of a eukaryotic cell with that of a prokaryotic cell.

CRITICAL THINKING

4. **Explaining Relationships** The development of the cell theory is directly related to advances in microscope technology. Why are these two developments related?
5. **Making Comparisons** How do the membrane-bound organelles of a eukaryotic cell act in a manner similar to the organs in a multicellular organism?

METHODS OF SCIENCE

6. **Extraterrestrial Cells** You are a scientist with NASA. Some samples of extraterrestrial material containing living things have arrived on your spaceship. Your first job is to determine if the samples contain prokaryotic or eukaryotic cells. How will you proceed?

Inside the Eukaryotic Cell

Key Ideas	Key Terms	Why It Matters
❯ What does the cytoskeleton do? ❯ How does DNA direct activity in the cytoplasm? ❯ What organelles participate in protein production? ❯ What is the role of vesicles in cells? ❯ How do cells get energy?	vesicle endoplasmic reticulum Golgi apparatus vacuole chloroplast mitochondrion	Knowing how cells work helps you understand how your body functions and what goes wrong when you get sick.

The cytoplasm of a eukaryotic cell is packed with all sorts of structures and molecules. Molecules can be concentrated in certain parts of the cell because of the membranes that divide the cytoplasm into compartments. This organization enables each organelle to perform highly sophisticated and specialized functions.

The Framework of the Cell

The *cytoskeleton* is a web of protein fibers, shown in **Figure 3,** found in eukaryotic cells. The cytoskeleton supports the cell in much the same way that bones support your body. ❯ **The cytoskeleton helps the cell move, keep its shape, and organize its parts.** There are three kinds of cytoskeleton fibers.

Microfilaments are long, thin fibers that are made of the protein actin. Some are attached to the cell membrane. They contract to pull the membrane in some places and expand to push it out in others. *Microtubules* are thick, hollow fibers that are made of the protein tubulin. Information molecules move through these tubes to various parts of the cell. *Intermediate fibers* are moderately thick and mainly anchor organelles and enzymes to certain parts of the cell.

Figure 3 The cytoskeleton's network of protein fibers anchors cell organelles and other components of the cytoplasm. ❯ **What are the three types of cytoskeleton fibers?**

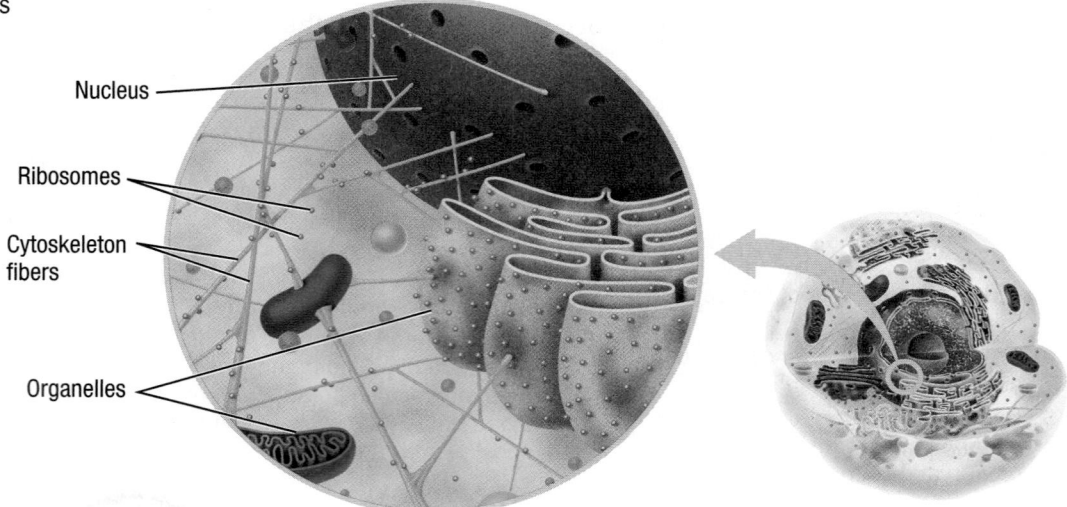

Nucleus

Ribosomes

Cytoskeleton fibers

Organelles

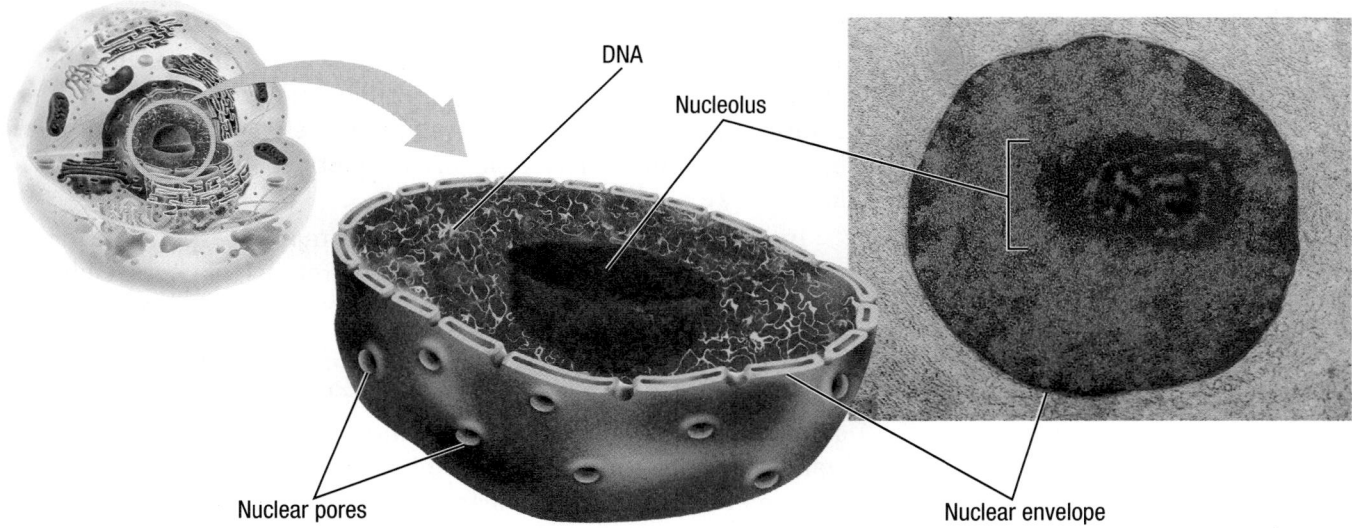

DNA

Nucleolus

Nuclear pores

Nuclear envelope

Figure 4 The nucleus stores the cell's DNA. The nuclear envelope is a double membrane that surrounds the nucleus of a cell. Ribosomes are made in the nucleolus. ❯ **How do molecules move from the nucleus to the cytoplasm?**

Directing Cellular Activity

Almost all cellular activity depends on the proteins that the cell makes. The instructions for making proteins are stored in the DNA. In a eukaryotic cell, the DNA is packed into the nucleus. This location separates the DNA from the activity in the cytoplasm and helps protect the information from getting lost or destroyed. ❯ **DNA instructions are copied as RNA messages, which leave the nucleus. In the cytoplasm, ribosomes use the RNA messages to <u>assemble</u> proteins.**

Nucleus As **Figure 4** shows, the nucleus is surrounded by a double membrane called the *nuclear envelope*. The nuclear envelope has many nuclear pores. Nuclear pores are small channels that allow certain molecules to move into and out of the nucleus. Even though the inside of the nucleus appears to be quite jumbled, the DNA is very organized. Within the nucleus is a prominent structure called the *nucleolus*. The nucleolus is the region where ribosome parts are made. These "preassembled" parts of ribosomes pass through the nuclear pores into the cytoplasm. Outside the nucleus, the parts are assembled to form a complete ribosome.

Ribosomes Each ribosome is made of RNA and many proteins. Some ribosomes in a eukaryotic cell are suspended in the cytosol, as they are in prokaryotic cells. These "free" ribosomes make proteins that remain inside the cell, such as proteins that build new organelles or enzymes to speed chemical reactions. Other ribosomes are attached to the membrane of another organelle. These "bound" ribosomes make proteins that are exported from the cell. Some of these proteins are important in cell communication. Bound ribosomes also make proteins that must be kept separate from the rest of the cytoplasm. Ribosomes can switch between being bound or free depending on the kind of protein that the cell needs to make.

❯ **Reading Check** *What kind of protein do "free" ribosomes make?*

ACADEMIC VOCABULARY

assemble to fit together parts or pieces; to build

www.scilinks.org
Topic: Proteins
Code: HX81241

Process Chart Make a process chart that shows how the cell digests food particles.

Protein Processing

The proteins produced by cells have many uses. The proteins that are sent outside the cell must be kept separate from the rest of the cytoplasm. To achieve this separation, the cell packages the proteins in vesicles. A **vesicle** is a small, often spherical-shaped sac that is formed by a membrane.

In a eukaryotic cell, two structures are mainly responsible for modifying, packaging, and transporting proteins for use outside the cell. ❭ **The endoplasmic reticulum and the Golgi apparatus are organelles that prepare proteins for extracellular export.**

Endoplasmic Reticulum The **endoplasmic reticulum** (ER) is a system of internal membranes that moves proteins and other substances through the cell. The membrane of the ER is connected to the outer membrane of the nuclear envelope.

Rough ER Ribosomes are attached to some parts of the surface of the ER. This *rough ER* has a bumpy appearance when viewed with an electron microscope, as shown in **Figure 5.** ❶ As proteins are made, they cross the ER membrane, entering the ER. Then, the ER membrane pinches off to form a vesicle around the proteins.

Smooth ER The rest of the ER, called *smooth ER,* has no attached ribosomes. Thus it appears smooth when viewed with an electron microscope. Enzymes of the smooth ER performs various functions, such as making lipids and breaking down toxic substances.

Golgi Apparatus The **Golgi apparatus** is a set of flattened, membrane-bound sacs. Cell products enter one side of the Golgi apparatus, which modifies, sorts, and packages them for distribution.

Repackaging Vesicles that contain newly made proteins move through the cytoplasm from the ER to the Golgi apparatus. ❷ The vesicle membrane fuses with the Golgi membrane. Inside the Golgi apparatus, enzymes modify the proteins as they move through the organelle. On the other side, the finished proteins are enclosed in new vesicles that bud from the surface of the Golgi apparatus.

Exporting Many of these vesicles then migrate to the cell membrane. ❸ As the vesicle membrane fuses with the cell membrane, the completed proteins are released to the outside the cell.

Storage and Maintenance

Vesicles have many functions in the cell. Some transport materials within the cell. Others have important storage roles. ❭ **Vesicles help maintain homeostasis by storing and releasing various substances as the cell needs them.**

Lysosome A lysosome is a vesicle that contains specific enzymes that break down large molecules. These enzymes can digest food particles to provide nutrients for the cell. They also help recycle materials in the cell by digesting old, damaged, or unused organelles. Lysosomes work by fusing with other vesicles. Lysosomes, made by the Golgi apparatus, prevent the enzymes from destroying the cell.

Figure 5 The cell manufactures many proteins. Some proteins are used outside the cell that makes them. Many organelles play a role in producing, processing, and packaging these proteins.

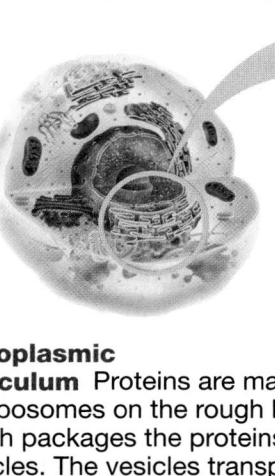
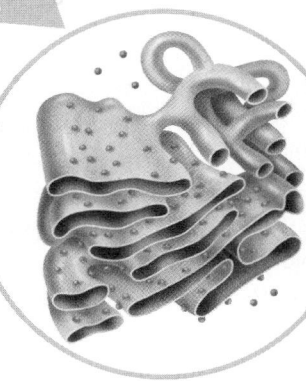
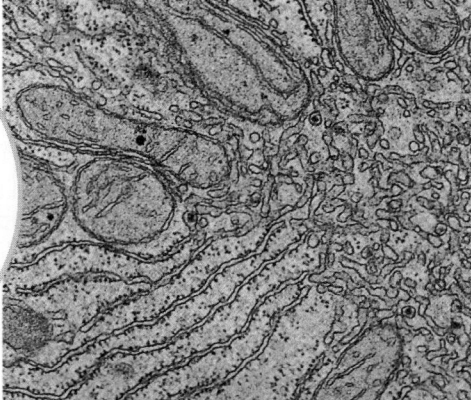

1 **Endoplasmic Reticulum** Proteins are made by ribosomes on the rough ER, which packages the proteins into vesicles. The vesicles transport the newly made proteins from the rough ER to the Golgi apparatus.

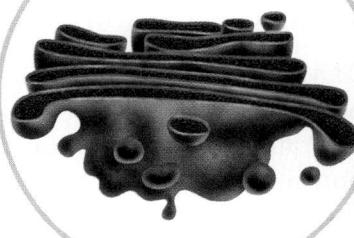
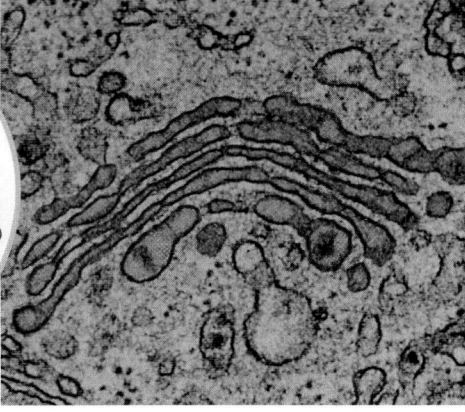

2 **Golgi Apparatus** The vesicle enters one side of the Golgi apparatus. As the proteins move through the folds, they are changed and repackaged into new vesicles. These new vesicles then move to the cell membrane.

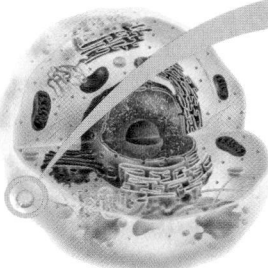
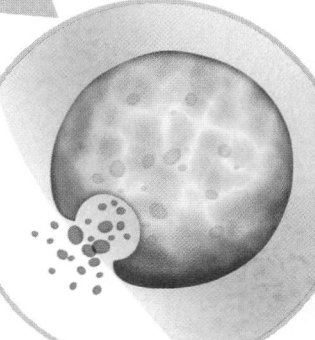
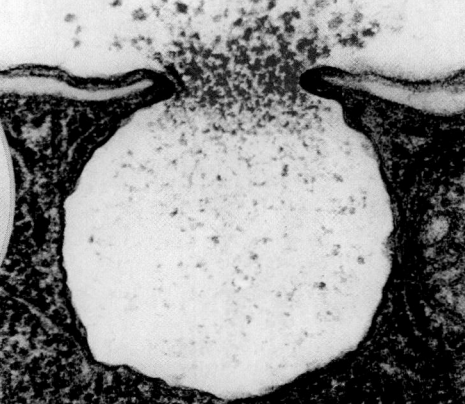

3 **Cell Membrane** The vesicles move to the cell membrane and release their contents (modified proteins) outside the cell. The vesicle membrane becomes part of the cell membrane.

Cell Parts Model

No space is wasted inside a cell. Packed into the cell are all parts essential to its survival.

Procedure

❶ Fill a **sealable plastic sandwich bag** halfway with **tap water**. Add several drops of **blue food dye.** Before you seal the bag, push out any remaining air.

❷ Roll this water-filled bag into a cylindrical shape. Use two long strips of **tape** to secure this shape.

❸ Fill **two smaller jewelry bags** with water. Before sealing the bags, add several drops of **green food dye** to each bag.

❹ Place the large rolled bag and the two smaller jewelry bags into a second **large plastic bag.**

❺ Fill this outer bag two-thirds full with water. Push out any remaining air, and seal the bag.

Analysis

1. **State** what each plastic bag in this model represented.

2. **Describe** how the "central vacuole" affects the contents of your cell model.

3. CRITICAL THINKING **Predicting Outcomes** Explain how removing water from the model's central bag might affect the tension and shape of the outer plastic bag.

Central Vacuole Many plant cells contain a large, membrane-bound compartment called the central **vacuole.** This large vacuole stores water, ions, nutrients, and wastes. It can also store toxins or pigments. When water fills the central vacuole, as shown in **Figure 6,** it makes the cell rigid, allowing the plant to stand upright. When the vacuole loses water, the cell shrinks, and the plant wilts.

Other Vacuoles Some protists have contractile vacuoles, which pump excess water out of the cell. This process controls the concentration of salts and other molecules and helps the cell maintain homeostasis. Another type of vacuole forms when the cell membrane surrounds food particles outside the cell and pinches off to form a vesicle inside the cell. When the food vacuole later fuses with a lysosome, the enzymes that digest the stored food are released.

Figure 6 A plant cell may have a large central vacuole and several chloroplasts. When filled, the central vacuole pushes the other organelles against the membrane. ❯ **In which organelle does photosynthesis occur?**

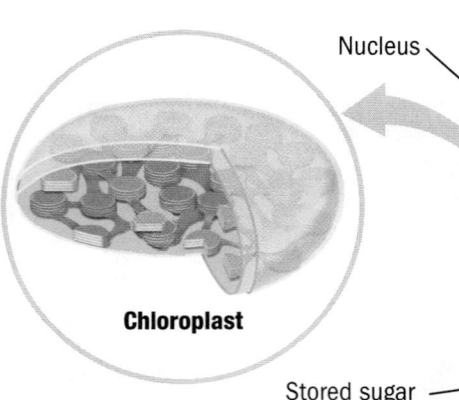

Nucleus

Central vacuole

Chloroplast

Stored sugar

Plant cell

Energy Production

Cells need a constant source of energy. ❯ **The energy for cellular functions is produced by chemical reactions that occur in the mitochondria and chloroplasts.** Nearly all eukaryotic cells contain mitochondria. Chloroplasts are found in plants and some plant-like protists, such as seaweed, but not in animal cells. In both organelles, chemical reactions produce adenosine triphosphate (ATP), the form of energy that fuels almost all cell processes.

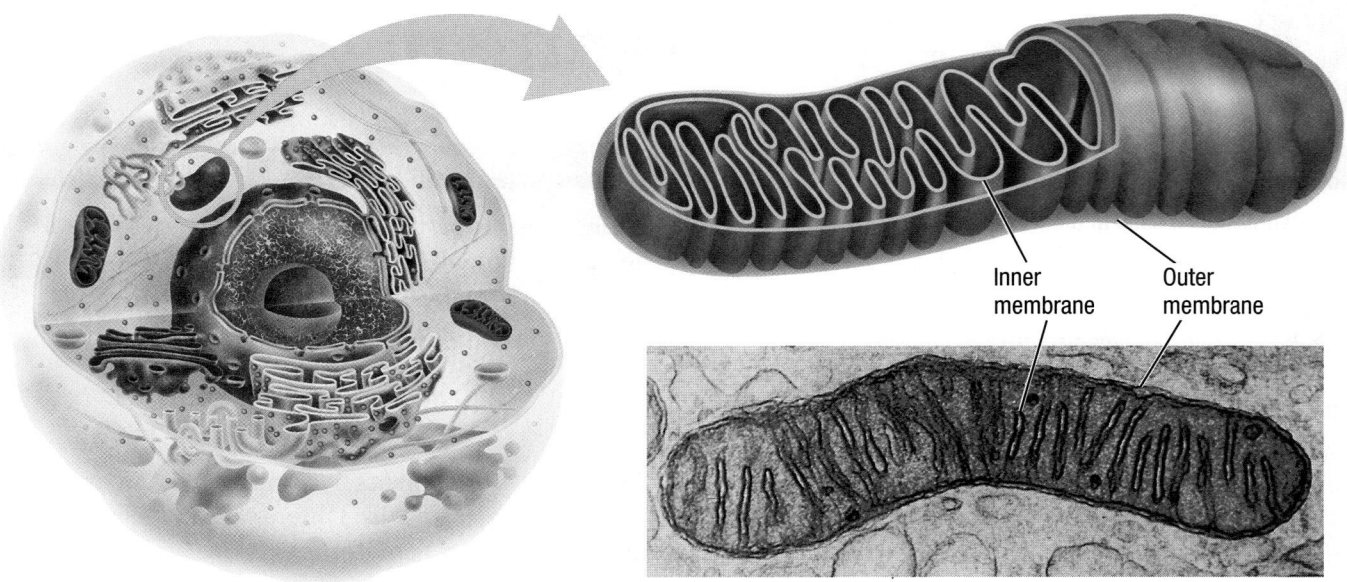

Inner membrane   Outer membrane

Chloroplasts A **chloroplast** is an organelle that uses light energy to make sugar from carbon dioxide and water. As **Figure 6** shows, plant cells may have several chloroplasts. Each chloroplast is surrounded by a pair of membranes. Inside the inner membrane are many stacks of flattened sacs. The ATP-producing chemical reactions take place on the membranes of these sacs.

Mitochondria A **mitochondrion** is an organelle that uses energy from organic compounds to make ATP. Although some ATP is made in the cytosol, most of a cell's ATP is made inside mitochondria. Cells that have a high energy requirement, such as muscle cells, may contain hundreds or thousands of mitochondria. As **Figure 7** shows, a mitochondrion has a smooth outer membrane. It also has a greatly folded inner membrane, which divides the organelle into two compartments. Many ATP-producing enzymes are located on the inner membrane.

❯ **Reading Check** *In what kinds of cells are mitochondria found?*

vacuole (VAK yoo OHL) a fluid-filled vesicle found in the cytoplasm of plant cells or protists

chloroplast an organelle found in plant and algae cells where photosynthesis occurs

mitochondrion (MIET oh KAHN dree uhn) in eukaryotic cells, the cell organelle that is surrounded by two membranes and that is the site of cellular respiration

---

Section
2 **Review**

❯ **KEY IDEAS**

1. **Compare** the functions of the three types of cytoskeletal fibers.
2. **Describe** the nucleus.
3. **Trace** a protein's path through the cell, from assembly to export.
4. **Contrast** vesicles and vacuoles.

5. **Compare** the role of mitochondria and chloroplasts.

CRITICAL THINKING

6. **Constructing Explanations** Is it accurate to say that organelles are floating freely in the cytosol? Why or why not?
7. **Real World** Research Tay-Sachs disease, and explain what goes wrong in diseased cells.

ALTERNATIVE ASSESSMENT

8. **Analogy** Compare the organelles of a eukaryotic cell to the parts of a city. For example, the lysosome could be a recycling center.

From Cell to Organism

Key Ideas	Key Terms	Why It Matters
❯ What makes cells and organisms different? ❯ How are cells organized in a complex multicellular organism? ❯ What makes an organism truly multicellular?	flagellum organ system tissue colonial organ organism	Diverse organisms have unique cells and cellular organization.

More than 50 million types of organisms live on Earth. Each organism is made up of different types of cells. Differences in cells enable organisms to adapt to their natural environments.

Diversity in Cells

Prokaryotes are always unicellular and limited in size. Eukaryotes are often larger and can be either unicellular or multicellular. Prokaryotic cells lack a nucleus and membrane-bound organelles, which are found in eukaryotic cells. Within both types, cells can have a variety of shapes and structures. Recall that a cell's shape reflects its function. ❯ **The different organelles and features of cells enable organisms to function in unique ways in different environments.**

Diversity in Prokaryotes Prokaryotes can vary in shape, the way that they obtain and use energy, the makeup of their cell walls, and their ability to move. Many prokaryotes have **flagella**—long, threadlike structures that rotate to quickly move an organism through its environment. Many prokaryotes have pili. Pili are short, thick outgrowths that allow prokaryotes to attach to surfaces or to other cells. These features are shown in **Figure 8.**

flagellum a long, hairlike structure that grows out of a cell and enables the cell to move

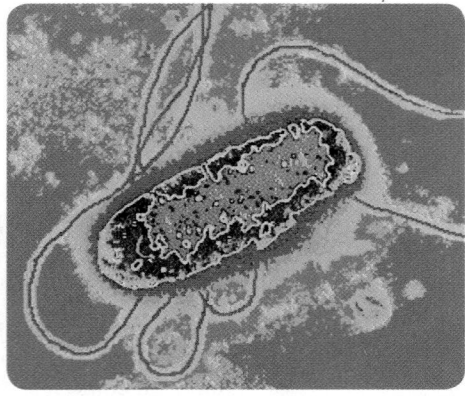

Figure 8 The bacterium *Escherichia coli* is a rod-shaped prokaryote that has both pili and flagella. ❯ **What do flagella enable prokaryotic cells to do?**

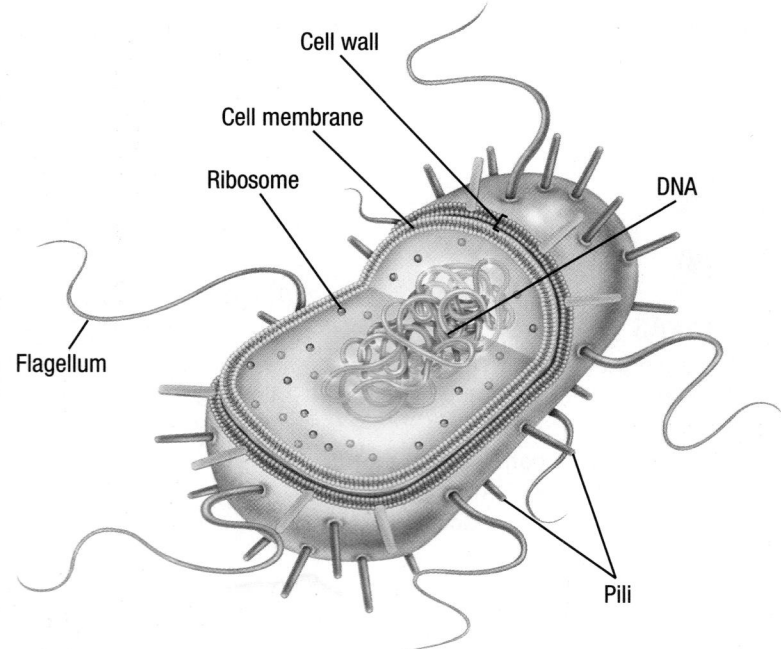

Cell wall

Cell membrane

Ribosome

DNA

Flagellum

Pili

Diversity in Eukaryotic Cells Animal and plant cells are two types of eukaryotic cells, as **Figure 9** shows. Both have many of the same organelles, but plant cells also have chloroplasts, a large central vacuole, and a cell wall that surrounds the cell membrane.

Like prokaryotic cells, eukaryotic cells vary in structure according to their function. Also, some organelles are more prominent in some cell types. By varying in their internal makeup, cells can become specialized for certain functions. For example, muscle cells, which use large amounts of energy, have many mitochondria.

❯ **Reading Check** *What are flagella?*

Eukaryotic Cells

Figure 9 Most eukaryotic cells contain all of the organelles shown here. Depending on their function, cells may have different shapes and different amounts of certain organelles. ❯ **What are three features that plant cells have, but animal cells lack?**

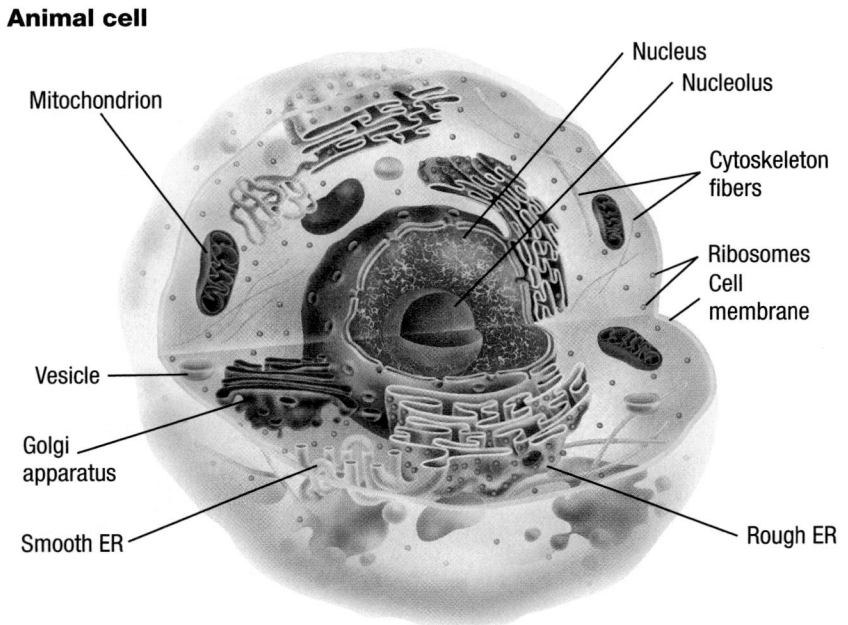

Animal cell

- Mitochondrion
- Nucleus
- Nucleolus
- Cytoskeleton fibers
- Ribosomes
- Cell membrane
- Vesicle
- Golgi apparatus
- Smooth ER
- Rough ER

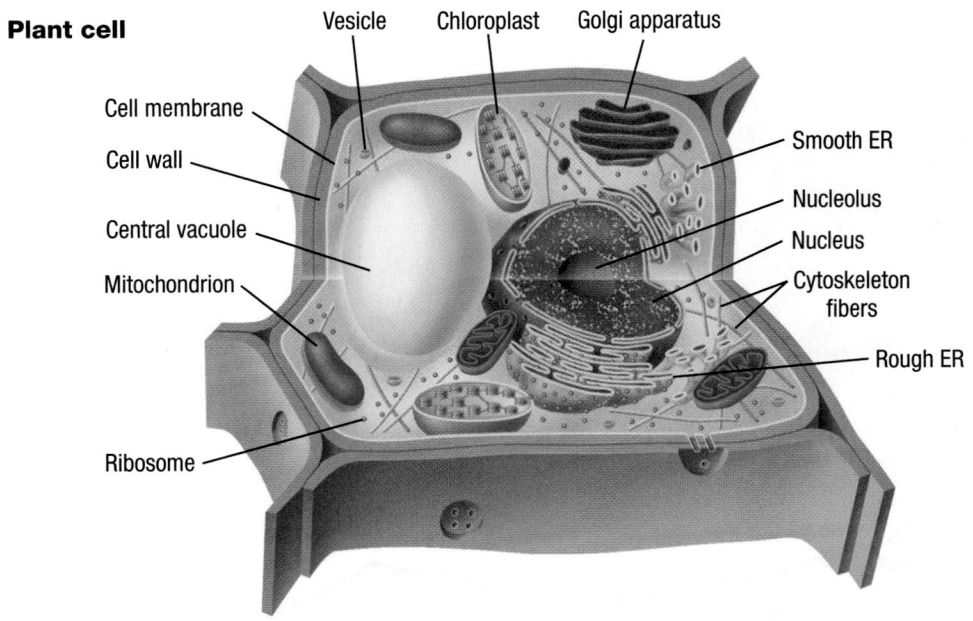

Plant cell

- Vesicle
- Chloroplast
- Golgi apparatus
- Cell membrane
- Cell wall
- Central vacuole
- Mitochondrion
- Smooth ER
- Nucleolus
- Nucleus
- Cytoskeleton fibers
- Rough ER
- Ribosome

Similes Write a simile comparing each level of organization to a part of your textbook. (Hint: Cells are like letters.)

Levels of Organization

Multicellular organisms, such as plants and animals, are made up of thousands, millions, or even trillions of highly specialized cells. These cells cooperate to perform a specific task. They assemble together to form structures called tissues and organs. ❯ **Plants and animals have many highly specialized cells that are arranged into tissues, organs, and organ systems.** The relationships between tissues, organs, and organ systems are shown in **Figure 10.**

Tissues A **tissue** is a distinct group of cells that have similar structures and functions. For example, muscle tissue is a group of many cells that have bundles of cytoskeletal structures. When the bundles contract at the same time, they help animals move. In plants, vascular tissue is made of hollowed cells that are stacked up to make tiny straws. These structures help carry fluids and nutrients to various parts of the plant.

Organs Different tissues may be arranged into an **organ,** which is a specialized structure that has a specific function. In animals, the heart is an organ made of muscle, nerve, and other tissues. These tissues work together to pump blood. In plants, a leaf is an organ. A leaf is made of vascular tissue and other types of plant tissues that work together to trap sunlight and produce sugar.

Figure 10 Cells group together to make tissues, which assemble into organs. A leaf is an example of an organ in plants. A lung is an example of an organ in animals.
❯ **What level of organization is the respiratory system?**

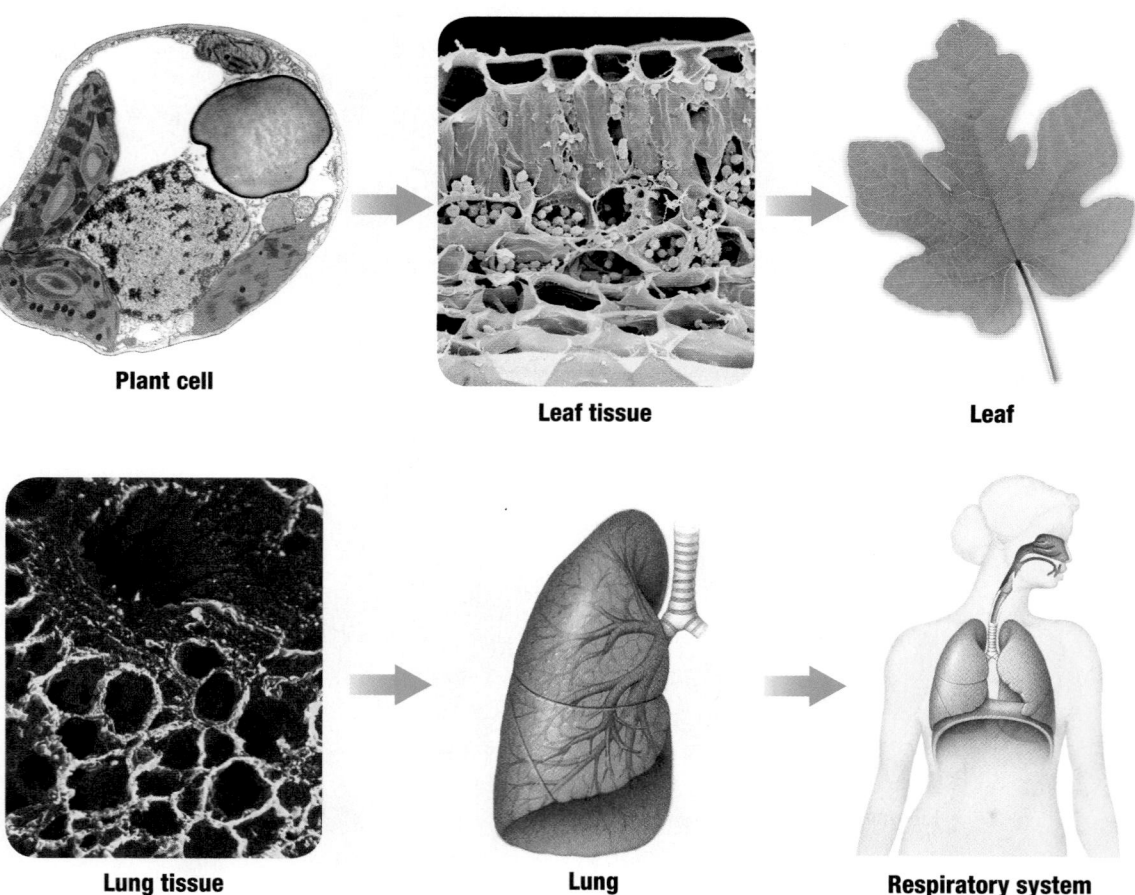

Plant cell

Leaf tissue

Leaf

Lung tissue

Lung

Respiratory system

QuickLab

🕐 10 min

Colonies on the Move

Volvox is a green colonial alga. A single colony may contain over 500 cells and is visible to the unaided eye.

Procedure

1 With the unaided eye, examine a container of Volvox colonies. What do you see?

2 Use a dropper to transfer some of the colonies to a well slide.

3 Examine the colonies using a light microscope.

Analysis

1. Draw the shape and structure of Volvox.

2. Describe the motion of a Volvox colony.

3. CRITICAL THINKING **Inferring Relationships** From your observations, do you think that the movements of the colony members are coordinated? Explain.

Organ System Various organs that carry out a major body function make up an **organ system.** One example of an organ system is the circulatory system, which is made up of the heart, the blood vessels, and blood. In plants, the shoot system consists of stems, leaves, and the vascular tissue that connects them.

Body Types

Sometimes, the entire body of an organism is made up of a single cell. This cell must carry out all of the organism's activities, including growing, using energy, responding to the environment, and reproducing. More than half of the biomass on Earth is composed of unicellular organisms.

While single cells cannot grow larger than a certain size, multicellular organisms can be large. ❯ **A multicellular organism is composed of many individual, permanently associated cells that coordinate their activities.** Distinct types of cells have specialized functions that help the organism survive. Individual cells cannot survive alone and are dependent on the other cells of the organism.

Cell Groups Some unicellular organisms can thrive independently, but others live in groups. Cells that live as a connected group but do not depend on each other for survival are considered **colonial organisms.** For example, the cell walls of some bacteria adhere to one another after dividing. These formations are not considered multicellular, because the cells can survive when separated.

Another type of cell grouping occurs in certain types of slime molds. These organisms spend most of their lives as single-celled amoebas. When starved, the individual cells form a large mass, which produces spores.

> **tissue** a group of similar cells that perform a common function
>
> **organ** a collection of tissues that carry out a specialized function of the body
>
> **organ system** a group of organs that work together to perform body functions
>
> **colonial organism** a collection of genetically identical cells that are permanently associated but in which little or no integration of cell activities occurs

www.scilinks.org
Topic: Organ Systems
Code: HX81075

Protist

Plant

Fungus

Animal

Figure 11 The giant kelp is a multicellular protist. Mushrooms are multicellular fungi. All plants and animals are multicellular organisms. ❯ **Can prokaryotes be multicellular?**

Multicellularity True multicellularity occurs only in eukaryotes, such as the organisms shown in **Figure 11.** Some protists, most fungi, and all plants and animals have a multicellular body. The cells of a multicellular body perform highly specific functions. Some cells protect the organism from predators or disease. Others may help with movement, reproduction, or feeding.

Most multicellular organisms begin as a single cell. For example, as a chicken develops from an egg, new cells form by cell division. These cells then grow and undergo differentiation, the process by which cells develop specialized forms and functions. The specialized cells are arranged into tissues, organs, and organ systems, making up the entire organism.

❯ **Reading Check** *What is differentiation?*

Review

❯ **KEY IDEAS**

1. **Relate** the structure of a cell to the cell's function.
2. **Describe** the four levels of organization that make up an organism.
3. **Explain** what makes a group of cells a truly multicellular organism.

CRITICAL THINKING

4. **Comparing** Describe how the circulatory system in animals is similar to the vascular system in plants.
5. **Making Inferences** How would the formation of bacterial colonies be affected if bacterial cells did not contain pili?

WRITING FOR SCIENCE

6. **Cell Group Therapy** Write a short play set in a therapy group that contains cells belonging to a unicellular colony and cells belonging to a multicellular organism. Have the cells discuss issues such as communication and individuality.

Chapter 7 Lab

45 min

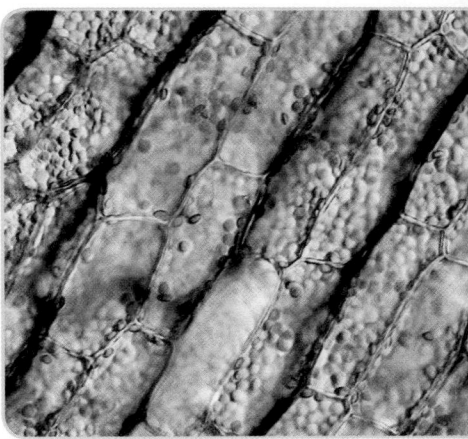

Objectives

▶ Identify the structures that you can see in plant cells.

▶ Investigate factors that influence the movement of cell contents.

Materials

- compound light microscope
- elodea sprig
- forceps
- microscope slides and coverslips
- lamp, incandescent
- dropper bottle of Lugol's iodine solution

Safety

Plant Cell Observation

When you look at cells under a microscope, you often can observe cytoplasmic streaming, or movement of cell contents. This effect occurs only in living cells. In this lab, you will investigate factors that influence cytoplasmic streaming.

Preparation

1. **SCIENTIFIC METHODS** **State the Problem** How do heat and an iodine solution influence cytoplasmic streaming?

2. **SCIENTIFIC METHODS** **Form a Hypothesis** Form testable hypotheses that explain how heat and iodine influence cytoplasmic streaming.

Procedure

1. Put on safety goggles, gloves, and a lab apron.

2. **CAUTION: Handle glass slides and coverslips with care.** Using forceps, remove a small leaf near the top of an elodea sprig. Place the whole leaf in a drop of water on a slide, and add a coverslip.

3. Observe the leaf under low power. Switch to high power.

4. Focus on a cell in which you can see the chloroplasts clearly. Draw this cell. Label the cell parts that you can see.

5. If chloroplasts are not moving in any of the cells, briefly warm the slide under a lamp. Look for movement again under high power.

6. **CAUTION: Lugol's solution is toxic and stains skin and clothing. Promptly wash off spills.** Make a wet mount of another leaf with Lugol's iodine solution. Observe the cells under low and high power.

7. Draw a stained elodea cell and label all visible parts.

8. Clean up your lab materials according to your teacher's instructions. Wash your hands before leaving the lab.

Analyze and Conclude

1. **Inferring Relationships** What effect did warming the slide have on the movement of cell contents? Why do you think this is so?

2. **SCIENTIFIC METHODS** **Inferring Conclusions** What can you conclude about the effect of Lugol's iodine solution on plant cells?

go.hrw.com
SUPER SUMMARY
Keyword: HX8CSFS

Key Ideas	Key Terms

1 Introduction to Cells

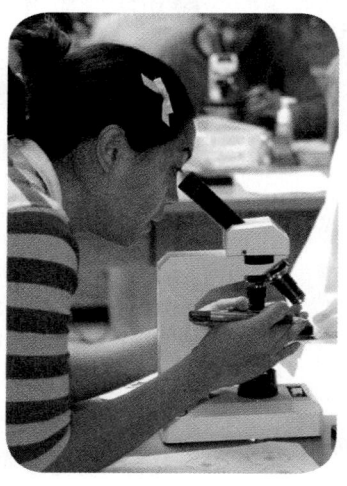

> Microscope observations of organisms led to the discovery of the basic characteristics common to all living things.

> A cell's shape reflects the cell's function. Cell size is limited by a cell's surface area–to-volume ratio.

> Because of their complex organization, eukaryotic cells can carry out more specialized functions than prokaryotic cells can.

cell membrane (154)
cytoplasm (154)
ribosome (154)
prokaryote (154)
eukaryote (155)
nucleus (155)
organelle (155)

2 Inside the Eukaryotic Cell

> The cytoskeleton helps the cell move, keep its shape, and organize its parts.

> DNA instructions are copied as RNA messages, which leave the nucleus. In the cytoplasm, ribosomes use the RNA messages to assemble proteins.

> The endoplasmic reticulum and the Golgi apparatus are organelles that prepare proteins for extracellular export.

> Vesicles help maintain homeostasis by storing and releasing various substances as the cell needs them.

> The energy for cellular functions is produced by chemical reactions that occur in the mito-chondria and chloroplasts.

vesicle (158)
endoplasmic reticulum (158)
Golgi apparatus (158)
vacuole (160)
chloroplast (161)
mitochondrion (161)

3 From Cell to Organism

> The different organelles and features of cells enable organisms to function in unique ways in different environments.

> Plants and animals have many highly specialized cells that are arranged into tissues, organs, and organ systems.

> A multicellular organism is composed of many individual, permanently associated cells that coordinate their activities.

flagellum (162)
tissue (164)
organ (164)
organ system (165)
colonial organism (165)

1. **Word Families** The prefix *cyto-* means "cell." Find three words in this chapter that belong to this family, and write a definition for each word.

2. **Concept Map** Make a concept map that compares plant cells with animal cells. Include the following terms in your concept map: *cell membrane, cell wall, central vacuole, chloroplasts,* and *mitochondria.*

Using Key Terms

3. Use the following terms in the same sentence: *prokaryote, eukaryote,* and *nucleus.*

For each pair of terms, explain how the meanings of the terms differ.

4. *organelle* and *organ*

5. *tissue* and *colonial organism*

Understanding Key Ideas

6. The maximum size of a cell is determined by the ratio of the cell's
   a. volume to organelles.
   b. cytoplasm to nucleus.
   c. surface area to volume.
   d. cytoplasm to organelles.

7. What four features do prokaryotic and eukaryotic cells share?
   a. cytoplasm, nucleus, ribosomes, vesicles
   b. DNA, nucleus, ribosomes, mitochondria
   c. nucleus, vesicles, mitochondria, cell membrane
   d. DNA, cytoplasm, ribosomes, cell membrane.

8. What makes up the cytoskeleton?
   a. bones   c. proteins
   b. flagella   d. cellulose

9. The function of ribosomes is to
   a. copy DNA.   c. organize the nucleus.
   b. assemble proteins.   d. store genetic material.

10. Which specialized structures allow prokaryotes to move quickly through their environment?
    a. pili   c. flagella
    b. nuclei   d. mitochondria

11. Which of the following best describes an organ?
    a. a body structure, such as an arm or a leg
    b. a group of cells that have a similar structure
    c. a group of tissues that belong to different systems
    d. a group of tissues that work together to perform a specific job

Use the diagram to answer the following question(s).

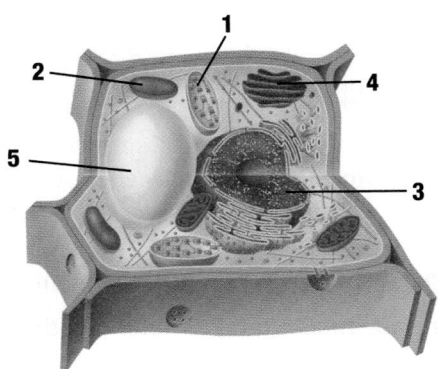

12. Which structure helps modify proteins?
    a. structure 1   c. structure 3
    b. structure 2   d. structure 4

13. What is structure 5?
    a. vacuole   c. ribosome
    b. nucleus   d. chloroplast

Explaining Key Ideas

14. **Describe** two observations of early scientists that support the cell theory.

15. **Describe** how the structure of membranes in chloroplasts and mitochondria contributes to the function of these organelles.

16. **Propose** why muscle cells have more mitochondria than other kinds of eukaryotic cells do.

17. **List** four ways in which prokaryotic cells may vary.

18. **Explain** how a unicellular organism and a multicellular organism differ in the way life processes are carried out by an individual cell.

Using Science Graphics

This graph shows the relationship between cell size and surface area–to-volume ratio. Use the graph to answer the following question(s).

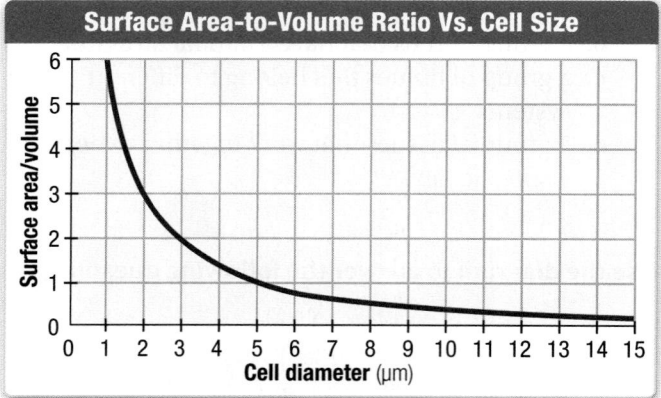

Surface Area-to-Volume Ratio Vs. Cell Size

19. By what percentage does the surface area–to-volume ratio change when a cell grows from 1 μm to 2 μm in diameter?
    a. 10 percent
    b. 20 percent
    c. 50 percent
    d. 90 percent

20. What is the maximum diameter that this cell could reach before the surface area–to-volume ratio would fall below 1?
    a. 2 μm
    b. 5 μm
    c. 10 μm
    d. 15 μm

Critical Thinking

21. **Making Connections** Connective tissue in the human body holds organs in place. Which structure within a cell is similar to connective tissue?

22. **Predicting Outcomes** What would happen if the nuclear pores of the cell became blocked?

23. **Constructing Explanations** Some ribosomes are bound to rough ER, while other ribosomes float freely in the cytoplasm. How would the products of these two types of ribosomes likely differ in appearance, and why?

24. **Making Comparisons** Compare and contrast the functions of the endoplasmic reticulum and the Golgi apparatus.

25. **Explaining Relationships** Describe how a food vacuole and lysosome work together to capture and digest food.

26. **Comparing Functions** Identify the structural elements that hold the shape of a prokaryotic cell, an animal cell, and a plant cell.

27. **Applying Information** Drugs that rid the body of eukaryotic parasites often have more side effects and are harder on the body than drugs that act on bacterial parasites. Suggest a reason for this difference.

28. **Evaluating Hypotheses** One of your classmates states a hypothesis that all organisms must have organ systems. Is your classmate's hypothesis valid? Explain your answer.

Methods of Science

29. **Technology** Explain how the development of the microscope has contributed to the study of biology. Describe how the discovery of cells led to the advancements in technology.

Alternative Assessment

30. **Owner's Manual** Pick an organ system in the human body. Draw a poster that shows the levels of organization. Write an owner's manual explaining what each part is and how the parts fit together.

31. **Advertisement** Imagine that you have the ability to convert unicellular organisms into multicellular organisms. Make an advertisement that sells your service to unicellular organisms. Be sure to include at least three advantages of being multicellular.

Math Skills

Volume Suppose that a cube-shaped multicellular organism exists. Each of its cells is a cube that has a volume of 1 cm³. Each side of the organism is 3 cm long.

32. What is the total volume of this organism?

33. How many cells does this organism have?

34. If each side of the organism doubles in length, how many 1 cm³ cells will the organism have?

Science Concepts

1. The discovery of cells is linked most directly with

  A the development of the microscope.

  B early investigations of causes of disease.

  C observations of large, unicellular organisms.

  D efforts to reproduce organisms in the laboratory.

2. Eukaryotic cells differ from prokaryotic cells in that eukaryotic cells

  F have a nucleus.   **H** lack ribosomes.

  G lack organelles.   **J** have a cell wall.

3. Which organelle produces proteins that are exported from the cell?

  A nucleolus   **C** free ribosome

  B rough ER   **D** bound ribosome

4. Which structure helps a plant stand upright?

  F lysosome   **H** central vacuole

  G chloroplast   **J** contractile vacuole

5. Ribosome : protein synthesis :: mitochondria :

  A cell support   **C** nutrient storage

  B energy release   **D** protein transport

6. Tissues are composed of distinct types of

  F cells.   **H** organelles.

  G organs.   **J** cytoskeleton fibers.

7. The process by which cells become specialized in form and function during development is called

  A association.   **C** coordination.

  B aggregation.   **D** differentiation.

Math Skills

8. Proportions The Dutch scientist Anton van Leeuwenhoek used a microscope that made objects appear 300 times as large as they were. If a cell appeared to be 6 mm long under the microscope, how long was the cell in real life?

  F 0.02 mm   **H** 0.05 mm

  G 0.20 mm   **J** 0.50 mm

Using Science Graphics

Use the diagram of the cell to answer the following question(s).

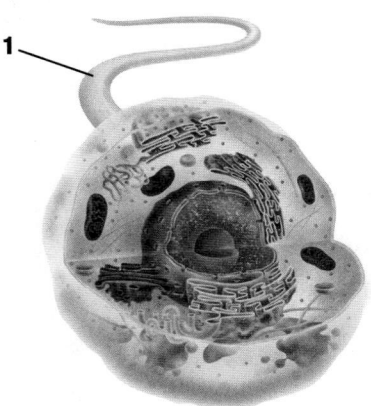

9. What is structure 1?

  A pilum   **C** flagellum

  B cilium   **D** mitochondrion

10. What is the function of structure 1?

  F to make ATP   **H** to store energy

  G to grab food   **J** to move the cell

This graph shows the amount of ATP in the muscles of a squid after the squid had been exposed to low oxygen concentrations. Use the graph to answer the following question(s).

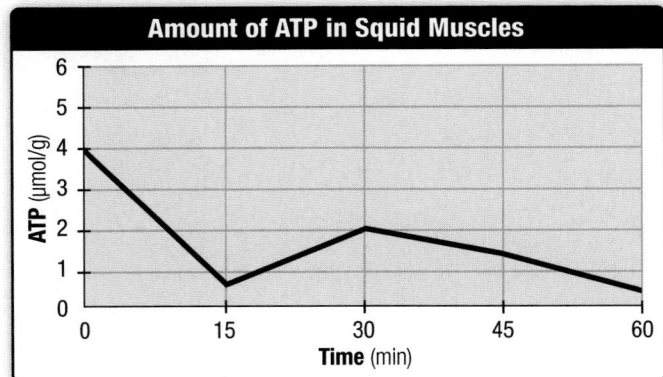

11. At what time during the experiment were the mitochondria in the squid's muscles producing the most energy?

  A 0 minute   **C** 30 minutes

  B 15 minutes   **D** 45 minutes

Chapter 8

Cells and Their Environment

Preview

1 Cell Membrane
Homeostasis
Lipid Bilayer
Membrane Proteins

2 Cell Transport
Passive Transport
Osmosis
Active Transport

3 Cell Communication
Sending Signals
Receiving Signals
Responding to Signals

Why It Matters

Cells interact with their environment to exchange nutrients and wastes and to coordinate activities over long distances.

Did you know that cells drink? This blood capillary cell wraps its cell membrane around the surrounding fluid and takes in a big gulp.

The lumen (blue) is the hollow part of a capillary.

A row of vesicles forms in the upper cell membrane (purple) and moves toward the bottom of the capillary. These vesicles help transport serum.

InquiryLab

🕐 10 min

Salty Cells

The movement of substances in a living cell can produce observable changes in the cell's appearance.

Procedure

1. Make **two wet mounts** of the **epidermis of a red onion.** Use **distilled water** for one and **saline solution** for the other.

2. Examine both slides under low power. Carefully switch to high power.

3. Make drawings of representative cells from each slide.

Analysis

1. **Compare** the appearance of the cells in the two wet mounts.

2. **Predict** what might cause the observed difference in cell appearance.

3. **Infer** whether the onion's cell wall is permeable to water.

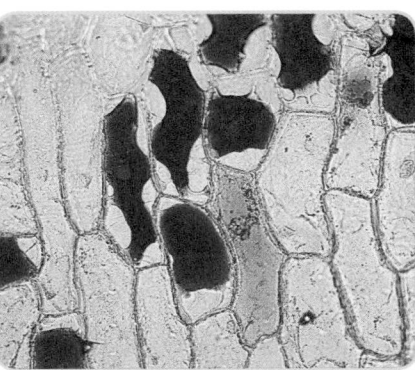

This is the nucleus of the cell that lines the inside of a capillary.

READING TOOLBOX

These reading tools can help you learn the material in this chapter. For more information on how to use these and other tools, see **Appendix: Reading and Study Skills.**

Using Words

Word Parts You can tell a lot about a word by taking it apart and examining its prefix and root.

Your Turn Use the information in the table to predict the meaning of the following words:
1. *phospholipid*
2. *exocytosis*

Word Parts

Word part	Type	Meaning
phospho-	prefix	containing phosphorus
lipid	root	a fat
exo-	prefix	outside
cyto	root	cell

Using Language

Finding Examples Concrete examples often help clarify new information. Certain words and phrases can help you recognize examples. These words include *for example, such as, like,* and *including.*

Your Turn Use what you have learned about examples to answer the following questions.
1. Find the examples in the following sentence: Some cells also use exocytosis to remove infecting microbes, such as bacteria or fungal spores.
2. Find the examples in the introductory paragraph above.

Using FoldNotes

Four-Corner Fold A four-corner fold is useful when you want to compare the characteristics of four topics. The four-corner fold can organize the characteristics of the four topics side by side under the flaps. Similarities and differences between the four topics can then be easily identified.

Your Turn Make a four-corner fold to help you learn about four topics in this chapter.
1. Fold a sheet of paper in half from top to bottom. Then, unfold the paper.
2. Fold the top and bottom of the paper to the crease in the center.
3. Fold the paper in half from side to side. Then, unfold the paper.
4. Using scissors, cut the top flap creases made in step 3 to form four flaps.

Cell Membrane

Key Ideas	Key Terms	Why It Matters
❯ How does the cell membrane help a cell maintain homeostasis? ❯ How does the cell membrane restrict the exchange of substances? ❯ What are some functions of membrane proteins?	phospholipid lipid bilayer	A simple defect in a cell membrane protein can make a life-or-death difference. In people who have cystic fibrosis, the cell membrane is does not work properly.

Every cell is surrounded by a cell membrane. The cell membrane protects the cell and helps move substances and messages in and out of the cell. By regulating transport, the membrane helps the cell maintain constancy and order.

Homeostasis

All living things respond to their environments. For example, we sweat when we are hot and shiver when we are cold. These reactions help our bodies maintain homeostasis. Recall that homeostasis is the maintenance of stable internal conditions in a changing environment. Individual cells, as well as organisms, must maintain homeostasis in order to live. ❯ **One way that a cell maintains homeostasis is by controlling the movement of substances across the cell membrane.**

Like the swimmer and the jellyfish in **Figure 1,** cells are suspended in a fluid environment. Even the cell membrane is fluid. It is made up of a "sea" of lipids in which proteins float. By allowing some materials but not others to enter the cell, the cell membrane acts as a gatekeeper. In addition, it provides structural support to the cytoplasm, recognizes foreign material, and communicates with other cells. These functions also contribute to maintaining homeostasis.

❯ **Reading Check** *What are some roles of the cell membrane? (See the Appendix for answers to Reading Checks.)*

www.scilinks.org
Topic: Homeostasis
Code: HX80753

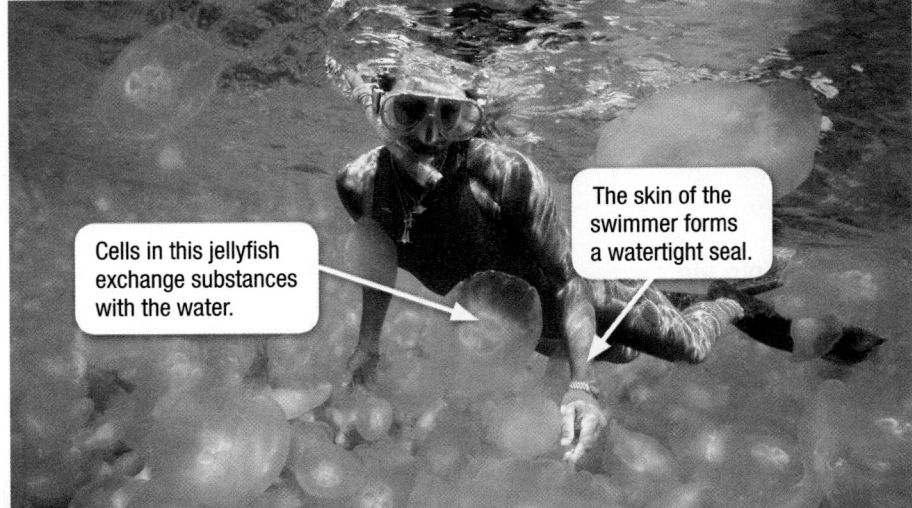

Cells in this jellyfish exchange substances with the water.

The skin of the swimmer forms a watertight seal.

Figure 1 The cells of the jellyfish exchange materials more freely with the sea water than do the cells of the swimmer.

175

Lipid Bilayer

The cell membrane is made of a "sea" of phospholipids. As **Figure 2** shows, a **phospholipid** is a specialized lipid made of a phosphate "head" and two fatty acid "tails." The phosphate head is polar and is attracted to water. In contrast, the fatty acid tails are nonpolar and are repelled by water.

Structure Because there is water inside and outside the cell, the phospholipids form a double layer called the **lipid bilayer.** The nonpolar tails, repelled by water, make up the interior of the lipid bilayer. The polar heads are attracted to the water, so they point toward the surfaces of the lipid bilayer. One layer of polar heads faces the cytoplasm, while the other layer is in contact with the cell's immediate surroundings.

Barrier Only certain substances can pass through the lipid bilayer. **❯The phospholipids form a barrier through which only small, nonpolar substances can pass.** Ions and most polar molecules are repelled by the nonpolar interior of the lipid bilayer.

Membrane Proteins

Various proteins can be found in the cell membrane. Some proteins face inside the cell, and some face outside. Other proteins may stretch across the lipid bilayer and face both inside and outside.

Proteins in Lipids What holds these proteins in the membrane? Recall that proteins are made of amino acids. Some amino acids are polar, and others are nonpolar. Nonpolar portions of a protein are attracted to the interior of the lipid bilayer but are repelled by water on either side of the membrane. In contrast, polar parts of the protein are attracted to the water on both sides of the lipid bilayer. These opposing attractions help hold the protein in the membrane.

❯ **Reading Check** *Why can't ions pass through the lipid bilayer?*

phospholipid (FAHS foh LIP id) a lipid that contains phosphorus and that is a structural component in cell membranes

lipid bilayer (LIP id BIE LAY uhr) the basic structure of a biological membrane, composed of two layers of phospholipids

Figure 2 The membrane that surrounds the cell is made of a lipid bilayer, a double layer of phospholipids.

The lipid bilayer is the foundation of the cell membrane.

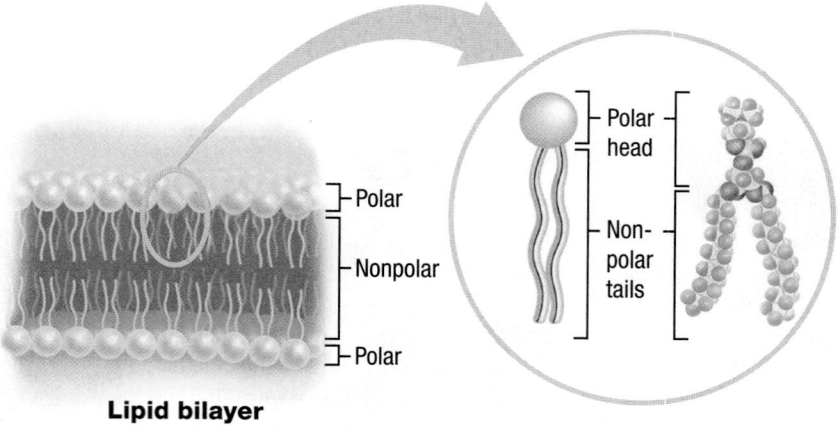

Lipid bilayer

The arrangement of phospholipids in the lipid bilayer makes the cell membrane selectively permeable.

A phospholipid's "head" is polar, and its two fatty acid "tails" are nonpolar.

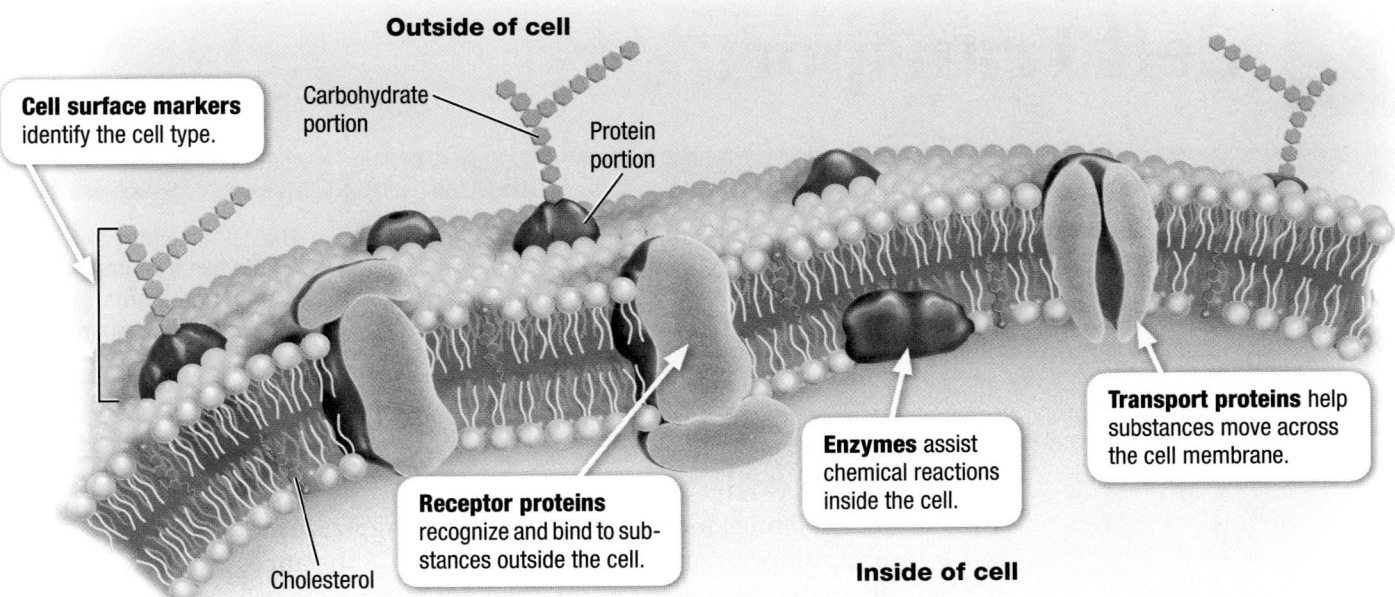

Outside of cell

Cell surface markers identify the cell type.

Carbohydrate portion

Protein portion

Receptor proteins recognize and bind to substances outside the cell.

Cholesterol

Enzymes assist chemical reactions inside the cell.

Transport proteins help substances move across the cell membrane.

Inside of cell

Types of Proteins As **Figure 3** shows, membranes contain different types of proteins. ❯ Proteins in the cell membrane include cell-surface markers, receptor proteins, enzymes, and transport proteins.

- **Cell-Surface Markers** Like a name tag, a chain of sugars acts as a marker to identify each type of cell. Liver cells have a different chain of sugars from heart cells. These sugars (carbohydrates) are attached to the cell surface by proteins called *glycoproteins*. Glycoproteins help cells work together.

- **Receptor Proteins** Receptor proteins enable a cell to sense its surroundings by binding to certain substances outside the cell. When this happens, it causes changes inside the cell.

- **Enzymes** Many proteins in the cell membrane help with important biochemical reactions inside the cell.

- **Transport Proteins** Many substances that the cell needs cannot pass through the lipid bilayer. Transport proteins aid the movement of these substances into and out of the cell.

Figure 3 The cell membrane contains various proteins that have specialized functions.

READING TOOLBOX

Four-Corner Fold Make a four-corner fold to compare four types of proteins found in the cell membrane.

Section **1** **Review**

❯ **KEY IDEAS**

1. **Relate** the functions of the cell membrane to homeostasis.
2. **Describe** the types of substances that can pass through the lipid bilayer of the cell membrane.
3. **Outline** four functions of proteins within the cell membrane.

CRITICAL THINKING

4. **Applying Logic** What would happen if the cell membrane were fully permeable to all substances in the cell's environment?
5. **Predicting Outcomes** What would happen if the cell were exposed to a drug that disabled the transport proteins in the cell membrane?

ALTERNATIVE ASSESSMENT

6. **Making Models** Create a model of the lipid bilayer, including its associated proteins. Your model may be made of clay or household items. Present your model to the class. Indicate the role of each type of protein in maintaining homeostasis.

Cell Transport

Key Ideas	Key Terms	Why It Matters

❯ What determines the direction in which passive transport occurs?
 	
❯ Why is osmosis important?
 	
❯ How do substances move against their concentration gradients?
	equilibrium
	concentration
	  gradient
	diffusion
	carrier protein
	
	osmosis
	sodium-
	  potassium
	  pump
		The cell's membrane is a little like a country's border. Both barriers regulate who or what enters and who or what leaves.

The cell must move substances of varying size, electrical charge, and composition into and out of the cell. Substances may enter and leave the cell in a variety of ways. Sometimes the cell must use energy to move a substance across the cell membrane. In *active transport,* the cell is required to use energy to move a substance. In *passive transport,* the cell does not use energy.

Passive Transport

In a solution, randomly moving molecules tend to fill up a space. When the space is filled evenly, a state called **equilibrium** is reached. The amount of a particular substance in a given volume is called the *concentration* of the substance. When one area has a higher concentration than another area does, as **Figure 4** shows, a **concentration gradient** exists. Substances move from an area of higher concentration to an area of lower concentration. This movement down the concentration gradient is called **diffusion.**

The cell membrane separates the cytoplasm from the fluid outside the cell. Some substances enter and leave the cell by diffusing across the cell membrane. The direction of movement depends on the concentration gradient and does not require energy. ❯ **In passive transport, substances cross the cell membrane down their concentration gradient.** Some substances diffuse through the lipid bilayer. Others diffuse through transport proteins.

Figure 4 If people acted like molecules, they would fill up the space in this room evenly over time. ❯ **What area of this room has a high concentration of people?**

Simple Diffusion
Small, nonpolar molecules can pass directly through the lipid bilayer. This type of movement is called *simple diffusion.* As **Figure 5** shows, oxygen diffuses into the cell through the lipid bilayer. The concentration of oxygen is higher outside the cell than it is inside. Thus, oxygen moves down its concentration gradient into the cell. In contrast, the concentration of carbon dioxide is often higher inside the cell than it is outside. So, carbon dioxide diffuses out of the cell. Natural steroid hormones, which are nonpolar and fat soluble, can also diffuse across the lipid bilayer.

Facilitated Diffusion
Many ions and polar molecules that are important for cell function do not diffuse easily through the nonpolar lipid bilayer. During *facilitated diffusion,* transport proteins help these substances diffuse through the cell membrane. Two types of transport proteins are channel proteins and carrier proteins.

Channel Proteins
Ions, sugars, and amino acids can diffuse through the cell membrane through channel proteins. These proteins, sometimes called *pores,* serve as tunnels through the lipid bilayer. Each channel allows the diffusion of specific substances that have the right size and charge. For example, only sodium ions can pass through the sodium ion channel shown in **Figure 5.**

Carrier Proteins
Carrier proteins transport substances that fit within their binding site, as **Figure 6** shows. A carrier protein binds to a specific substance on one side of the cell membrane. This binding causes the protein to change shape. As the protein's shape changes, the substance is moved across the membrane and is released on the other side.

❯ **Reading Check** *Why does oxygen diffuse into the cell?*

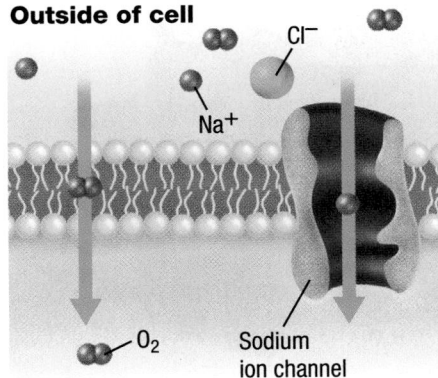

Figure 5 Nonpolar molecules, such as O_2, diffuse through the lipid bilayer. Channel proteins allow certain ions, such as Na^+, to diffuse through the cell membrane. Cl^- ions cannot pass through the sodium ion channel.

equilibrium a state that exists when the concentration of a substance is the same throughout a space

concentration gradient a difference in the concentration of a substance across a distance

diffusion the movement of particles from regions of higher density to regions of lower density

carrier protein a protein that transports substances across a cell membrane

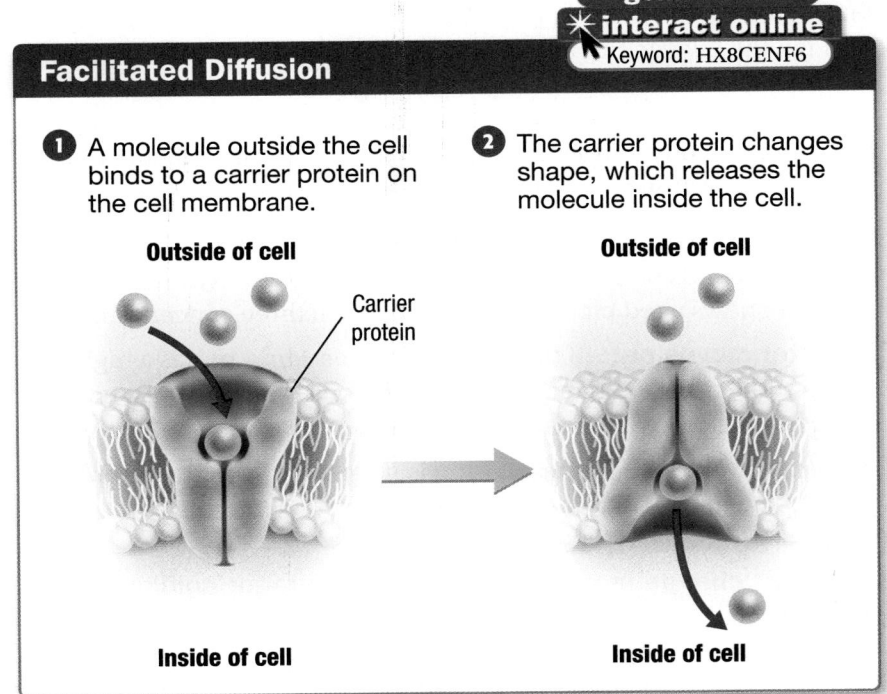

go.hrw.com
✳ **interact online**
Keyword: HX8CENF6

Facilitated Diffusion

1 A molecule outside the cell binds to a carrier protein on the cell membrane.

2 The carrier protein changes shape, which releases the molecule inside the cell.

Outside of cell

Carrier protein

Inside of cell

Outside of cell

Inside of cell

Figure 6 Carrier proteins allow the diffusion of specific molecules by binding the molecules on one side of the cell membrane and releasing them on the other side.
❯ Which side of this membrane has a higher concentration of molecules?

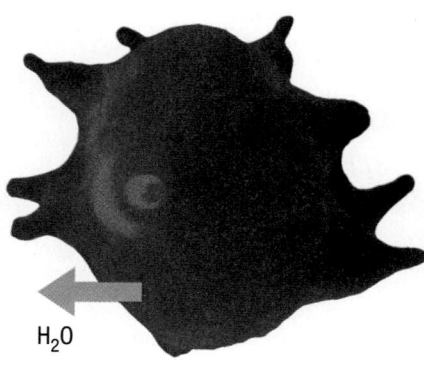

H_2O

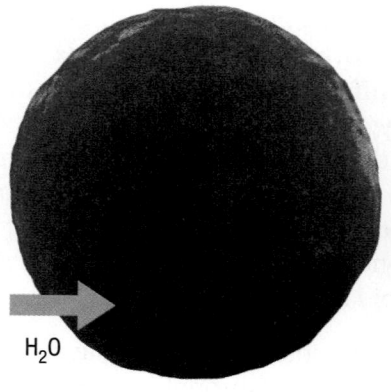

H_2O

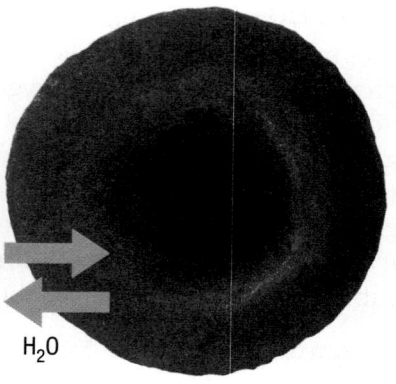

H_2O

> **Hypertonic Solution** The fluid outside is more concentrated. As water moves out of the cell, the cell shrinks.

> **Hypotonic Solution** The fluid outside is less concentrated. As water moves into the cell, the cell swells.

> **Isotonic Solution** Water moves into and out of the cell at the same rate. The cell stays the same size.

Figure 7 Red blood cells change shape due to the movement of water. The direction of water movement depends on the difference between the concentration of the solution outside the cell and the concentration of the cytosol.

Word Parts The prefix *hyper-* means "higher than," and *hypertonic* means "higher concentration." If *hypo-* means "lower than," what does *hypotonic* mean?

osmosis the diffusion of water or another solvent from a more dilute solution (of a solute) to a more concentrated solution (of the solute) through a membrane that is permeable to the solvent

Osmosis

Water can diffuse across a selectively permeable membrane in a process called **osmosis.** Osmosis is a type of passive transport that is very important to keeping cells functional. ❯ **Osmosis allows cells to maintain water balance as their environment changes.**

When ions and polar substances dissolve in water, they attract and bind some water molecules. The remaining water molecules are free to move around. If a concentration gradient exists across a membrane for solutes, a concentration gradient also exists across the membrane for free water molecules. Osmosis occurs as free water molecules move down their concentration gradient into the solution that has the lower concentration of free water molecules.

Water Channels Polar water molecules do not diffuse directly through the bilayer. But the cell membrane contains channel proteins that only water molecules can pass through. Thus, osmosis in cells is a form of facilitated diffusion. In humans, water channels help in the regulation of body temperature, in digestion, in reproduction, and in water conservation in the kidneys.

Predicting Water Movement The direction of water movement in a cell depends on the concentration of the cell's environment. **Figure 7** shows a red blood cell in solutions of three concentrations.

1. Water moves out. If the solution is *hypertonic,* or has a higher solute concentration than the cytoplasm does, water moves out of the cell. The cell loses water and shrinks.

2. Water moves in. If the solution is *hypotonic,* or has a lower solute concentration than the cytoplasm does, water moves into the cell. The cell gains water and expands in size.

3. No net change in water movement occurs, or equilibrium is reached. If the solution is *isotonic,* or has the same solute concentration that the cytoplasm does, water diffuses into and out of the cell at equal rates. The cell stays the same size.

Hands-On

QuickLab

MULTI-DAY 🕐 15 min

Osmosis

You will observe the movement of water into or out of a grape under various conditions.

Procedure

1. Make a data table with four columns and three rows.

2. Fill **one jar** with a **sugar solution**. Fill a **second jar** with **grape juice**. Fill a **third jar** with **tap water**. Label each jar with the name of the solution that it contains.

3. Use a **balance** to find the mass of each of **three grapes**. Place one grape in each jar, and put the lids on the jars.

4. Predict whether the mass of each grape will increase or decrease over time. Explain your predictions.

5. After 24 h, remove each grape from its jar, and dry the grape gently with a **paper towel**. Using the balance, find each grape's mass again. Record your results.

Analysis

1. **Identify** the solutions in which osmosis occurred.

2. **CRITICAL THINKING** **Evaluating Conclusions** How did you determine whether osmosis occurred in each of the three solutions?

3. **CRITICAL THINKING** **Evaluating Hypotheses** Did the mass of each grape change as you had predicted? Why or why not?

Effects of Osmosis If left unchecked, the swelling caused by a hypotonic solution could cause a cell to burst. The rigid cell walls of plants and fungi prevent the cells of these organisms from expanding too much. In fact, many plants are healthiest in a hypotonic environment, as **Figure 8** shows. Some unicellular eukaryotes have *contractile vacuoles,* which collect excess water inside the cell and force the water out of the cell. Animal cells have neither cell walls nor contractile vacuoles. However, many animal cells can avoid swelling caused by osmosis by actively removing solutes from the cytoplasm. The removal of dissolved solutes from a cell increases the concentration of free water molecules inside the cell.

Figure 8 Plant cells are healthiest in a hypotonic environment. When its cells swell, the plant stands rigid. In an isotonic environment, a plant wilts. ❯ **What would happen if you added water to the plant on the right?**

Hypotonic

Isotonic

Active Transport

Sometimes, cells must transport substances against their concentration gradients. This movement is called *active transport* because the cell must use energy to move these substances. ❯ **Active transport requires energy to move substances against their concentration gradients.** Most often, the energy needed for active transport is supplied directly or indirectly by ATP.

Pumps Many active transport processes use carrier proteins to move substances. In facilitated diffusion, the carrier proteins do not require energy. In active transport, the carrier proteins do require energy to "pump" substances against their concentration gradient.

One of the most important carrier proteins in animal cells is the **sodium-potassium pump,** shown in **Figure 9.** Sodium ions inside the cell bind to the carrier protein. A phosphate group from ATP transfers energy to the protein. The protein changes shape and releases the sodium ions outside the cell membrane. Outside the cell, potassium ions bind to the pump. As a result, the phosphate group is released from the pump. The pump returns to its original shape and releases the potassium ions inside the cell membrane. For every three sodium ions taken out, two potassium ions are brought inside.

This pump prevents sodium ions from building up in the cell. Osmosis results when sodium ion levels are high. The cell could swell or even burst if too much water enters. The concentration gradients of sodium ions and potassium ions also help transport other substances, such as glucose, across the cell membrane.

sodium-potassium pump a carrier protein that uses ATP to actively transport sodium ions out of a cell and potassium ions into the cell

Figure 9 The sodium-potassium pump actively transports both Na⁺ and K⁺ ions across the cell membrane. ❯ **In this figure, is the concentration of sodium ions higher inside the cell or outside the cell?**

Sodium-Potassium Pump

1 Three sodium ions bind to the pump. A phosphate from ATP also binds, which transfers energy.

2 The pump changes shape, releasing the three sodium ions on the other side of the membrane.

3 Two potassium ions bind to the pump and are tranported across the cell membrane.

4 The phosphate group is released. The pump returns to its original shape, releasing the two potassium ions.

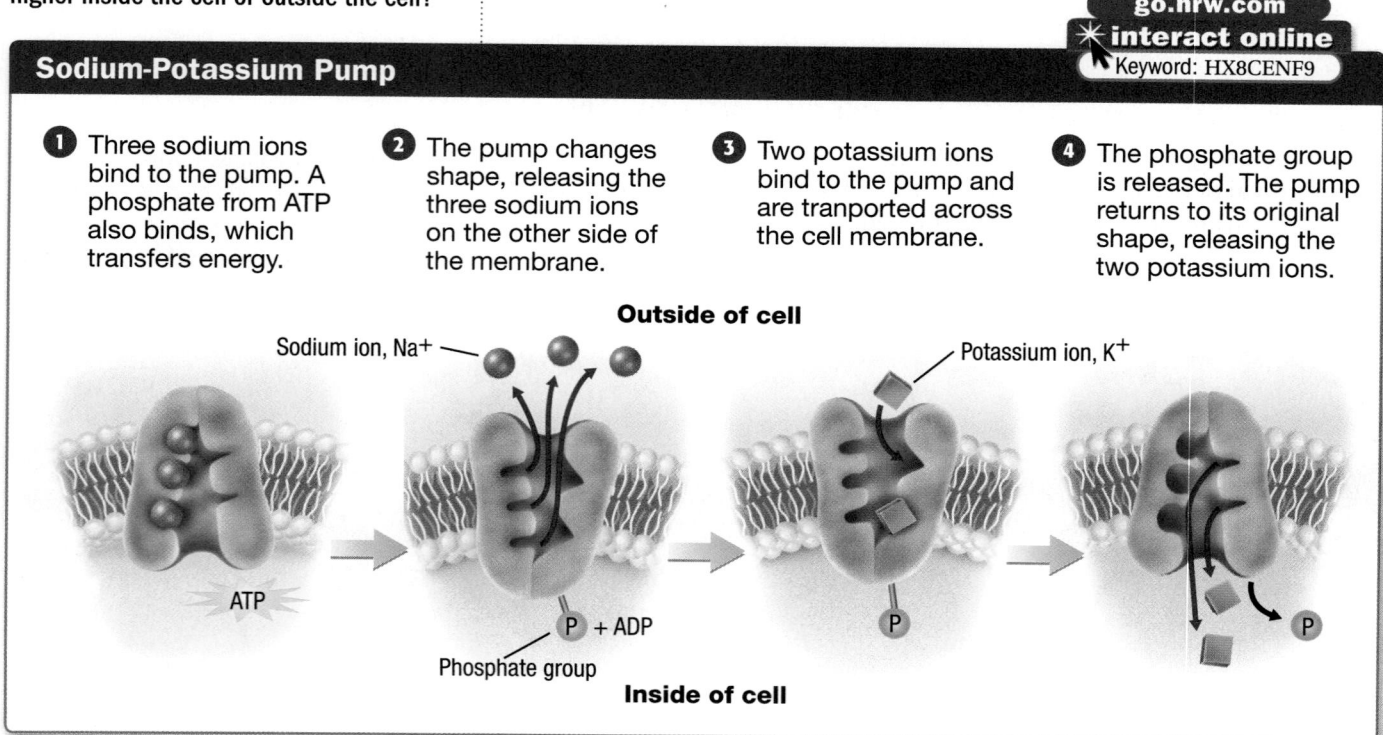

Sodium ion, Na⁺

Outside of cell

Potassium ion, K⁺

ATP

P + ADP

Phosphate group

P

P

Inside of cell

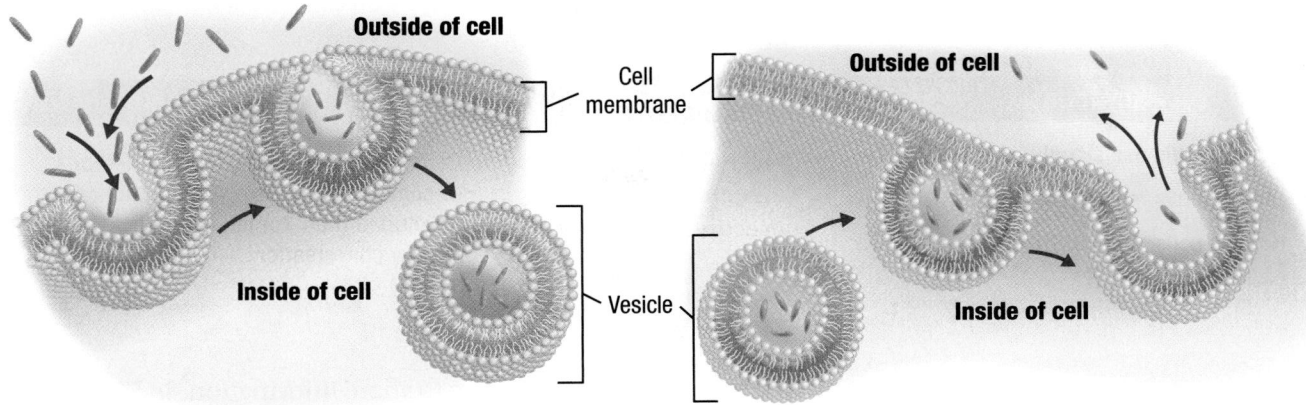

Endocytosis

Outside of cell

Cell membrane

Inside of cell

Vesicle

Exocytosis

Outside of cell

Inside of cell

Vesicles Many substances, such as proteins and polysaccharides, are too large to be transported by carrier proteins. Instead, they cross the cell membrane in vesicles. Recall that vesicles are membrane-bound sacs. The vesicle membrane is a lipid bilayer, like the cell membrane. Therefore, vesicles can bud off from the membrane, fuse with it, or fuse with other vesicles.

The movement of a large substance into a cell by means of a vesicle is called *endocytosis*. During endocytosis, shown in **Figure 10,** the cell membrane forms a pouch around the substance. The pouch then closes up and pinches off from the membrane to form a vesicle inside the cell. Vesicles that form by endocytosis may fuse with lysosomes or other organelles.

The movement of material out of a cell by means of a vesicle is called *exocytosis*. During exocytosis, shown in **Figure 10,** vesicles inside the cell fuse with the cell membrane. From the cell membrane, the contents of the vesicle are <u>released</u> to the outside of the cell. Cells use exocytosis to export proteins modified by the Golgi apparatus. Some protists release their waste products through this process. Some cells also use exocytosis to remove bacteria or other microbes.

❯ Reading Check *What is the structure of the vesicle membrane?*

Figure 10 A cell moves large substances or large amounts of materials in vesicles. Vesicles can fuse with the cell membrane to take in and release substances.

ACADEMIC VOCABULARY

release to set free

Section 2 Review

❯ KEY IDEAS

1. **Compare** the functions of channel proteins and carrier proteins in facilitated diffusion.

2. **Explain** why the presence of dissolved particles on one side of a membrane results in diffusion of water across the membrane.

3. **List** two ways that a cell can move a substance against its concentration gradient.

CRITICAL THINKING

4. **Applying Logic** Based on have learned about homeostasis and osmosis, why should humans avoid drinking sea water?

5. **Predicting Outcomes** If a cell were unable to make ATP, how would the cell membrane's transport processes be affected?

METHODS OF SCIENCE

6. **Designing an Experiment** What data would a biologist need to collect to determine whether a specific molecule is transported into cells by diffusion, by facilitated diffusion, or by active transport?

Key Ideas	Key Terms	Why It Matters
❯ How do cells use signal molecules? ❯ How do cells receive signals? ❯ How do cells respond to signaling?	signal receptor protein second messenger	Cells developed sophisticated methods of communication long before humans developed the Internet, cell phones, or even regular conversation.

We communicate in many ways to share information. In **Figure 11,** one person is surfing the Internet, another is talking on her cell phone, and two are having a face-to-face conversation. All of these are forms of communication. To coordinate activities, information must be shared. Cells in multicellular organisms depend on the activities of other cells to survive. Even unicellular organisms need to communicate—for example, to find a mate.

Sending Signals

You use different methods to communicate in different ways. You may whisper a secret to a trusted friend, or you may shout a warning to several people nearby. You may phone a friend who is far away, or you may put an ad in the newspaper for everyone to see.

Cells also use various methods of communication. These methods vary depending on whether the target is specific or general. They also depend on whether the target is nearby or far away. ❯ **Cells communicate and coordinate activity by sending chemical signals that carry information to other cells.** A *signaling cell* produces a **signal,** often a molecule, that is detected by the *target cell.* Typically, target cells have specific proteins that recognize and respond to the signal.

Targets Neighboring cells can communicate through direct contact between their membranes. Short-distance signals may act locally, a few cells away from the originating cell. Long-distance signals are carried by hormones and nerve cells. Hormones are signal molecules that are made in one part of the body. Hormones are distributed widely in the bloodstream throughout the body, but they affect only specific cells. Nerve cells also signal information to distant locations in the body, but their signals are not widely distributed.

Environmental Signals While most signal molecules originate within the body, some signals come from outside. For example, light has a great effect on the action of hormones in plants. The length of the day determines when some plants flower.

❯ **Reading Check** *Compare the targets of signaling hormones and nerve cells.*

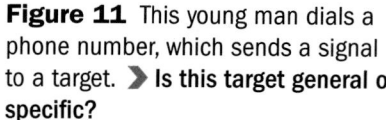

Figure 11 This young man dials a phone number, which sends a signal to a target. ❯ Is this target general or specific?

Hands-On
Quick**Lab**

🕐 10 min

Sensitive Plants

The sensitive plant *(Mimosa pudica)* reacts to touch. This reaction results from rapid cell-to-cell communication.

Procedure

1 Observe and sketch the extended leaves on the *Mimosa* plant branch.

2 Touch the tip of the end leaf on this branch. Observe the plant's reaction.

3 Make a sketch showing the branch's new appearance.

Analysis

1. Identify what stimulus produced the plant's response.

2. Describe the plant's response.

3. Explain whether the reaction behavior was communicated beyond the leaf that was touched.

4. CRITICAL THINKING **Making Inferences** Plants can respond to touch, although they lack a nervous system. Propose a mechanism for the response you observed.

Receiving Signals

A target cell is bombarded by hundreds of signals. But it recognizes and responds only to the few signals that are important for its function. This response to some signals, but not to others, is made possible by **receptor proteins,** such as the ones in the cell's membrane.

Binding Specificity A receptor protein binds specific substances, such as signal molecules. The outer part of the protein is folded into a unique shape, called the *binding site.* ❯ A receptor protein binds only to signals that match the specific shape of its binding site. As **Figure 12** shows, only signal molecules that have the "right" shape can fit into the receptor protein. Signal molecules that have the "wrong" shape have no effect on that particular receptor protein. A cell may also have receptor proteins that bind to molecules in its environment. Some cells may have receptor proteins that can detect and respond to light. Receptor proteins enable a cell to detect its environment.

Effect Once it binds the signal molecule, the receptor protein changes its shape in the membrane. This change in shape relays information into the cytoplasm of the target cell.

signal anything that serves to direct, guide, or warn

receptor protein a protein that binds specific signal molecules, which causes the cell to respond

SC*i*LINKS.
www.scilinks.org
Topic: Receptor Proteins
Code: HX81274

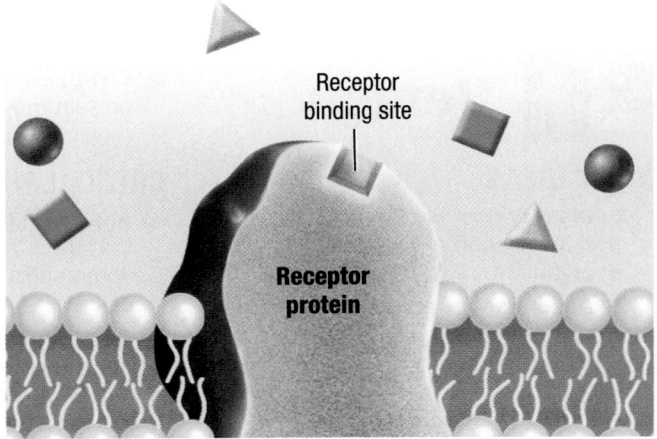

Receptor binding site

Receptor protein

Figure 12 The binding site of this receptor protein has a specific shape to which only one type of signal molecule can bind. ❯ **Which of these molecules would bind with the receptor?**

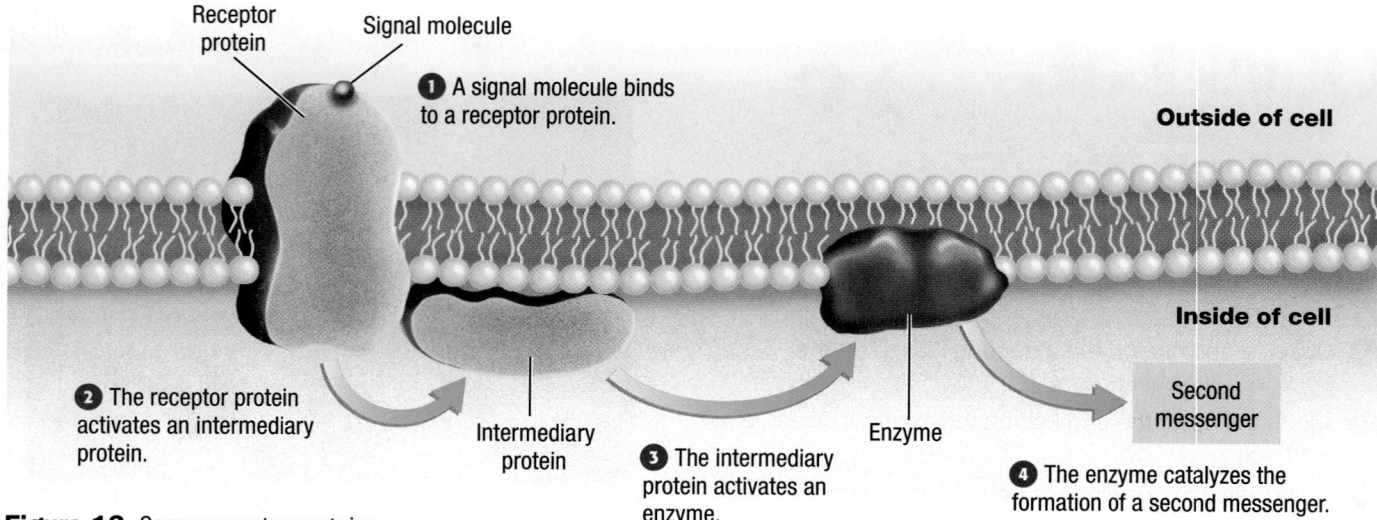

① A signal molecule binds to a receptor protein.

Receptor protein

Signal molecule

Outside of cell

Inside of cell

② The receptor protein activates an intermediary protein.

Intermediary protein

③ The intermediary protein activates an enzyme.

Enzyme

Second messenger

④ The enzyme catalyzes the formation of a second messenger.

Figure 13 Some receptor proteins trigger the production of second messengers.

Finding Examples Search the text on this page to find an example of the function of a transport protein.

second messenger a molecule that is generated when a specific substance attaches to a receptor on the outside of a cell membrane, which produces a change in cellular function

Responding to Signals

When a signal molecule binds to a receptor protein, the protein changes shape, which triggers changes in the cell membrane. ❯ **The cell may respond to a signal by changing its membrane permeability, by activating enzymes, or by forming a second messenger.**

- **Permeability Change** Transport proteins may open or close in response to a signal. For example, a nerve impulse may result when ion channels in nerve cells open after receiving a signal.

- **Enzyme Activation** Some receptor proteins activate enzymes in the cell membrane. Some receptors are enzymes themselves and are activated by the binding of a signal molecule. Enzymes trigger chemical reactions in the cell.

- **Second Messenger** Binding of a signal molecule outside the cell may cause a second messenger to form, as **Figure 13** shows. The **second messenger** acts as a signal molecule within the cell and causes changes in the cytoplasm and nucleus.

❯ **Reading Check** *How does membrane permeability change?*

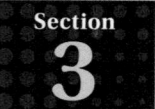

Section 3 Review

❯ **KEY IDEAS**

1. **Identify** one function of signal molecules in a multicellular organism.
2. **Describe** the relationship between receptor proteins and signal molecules.
3. **List** three ways that a receptor protein may respond when a signal molecule binds to it.

CRITICAL THINKING

4. **Applying Logic** Why do you think that there are many forms of communication between body cells?
5. **Applying Logic** Why is specificity between a receptor protein and a signal molecule important?

WRITING FOR SCIENCE

6. **Finding Information** Use library or Internet resources to research a human disease that results from problems in the transport of molecules across the cell membrane. Describe the disease's symptoms and treatments. Summarize your findings in a written report.

Heady Effects

Many people start their day with a hot cup of coffee. Coffee contains a chemical stimulant, caffeine, that produces a feeling of heightened alertness.

Caffeine

The shape of the caffeine molecule is similar to the shape of a signal molecule that your body produces naturally. Receptor proteins respond to this signal in a chain of events that increases heart rate, blood flow, and the amount of sugar in the bloodstream.

Wacky Webs Most spider webs look like the one on the left. This web was created by a common garden spider, *Araneus diadematus*. The web on the right was created by the same spider after it was fed caffeine-dosed flies.

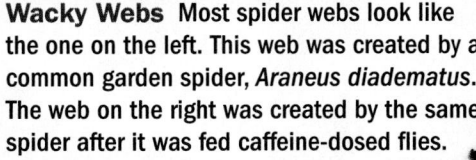

Quick Project Find out the average caffeine content in milligrams (mg) of coffee, tea, cola drinks, energy drinks, chocolate milk, dark chocolate, and milk chocolate.

Objectives

▶ Relate a cell's size to its surface area–to-volume ratio.

▶ Predict how the surface area–to-volume ratio of a cell will affect the diffusion of substances into the cell.

Materials

- safety goggles
- lab apron
- disposable gloves
- block of phenolphthalein agar (3 cm × 3 cm × 6 cm)
- knife, plastic
- ruler, metric
- beaker, 250 mL
- vinegar, 150 mL
- spoon, plastic
- paper towel

Safety

Cell Size and Diffusion

Substances enter and leave a cell in several ways, including by diffusion. Substances that a cell needs must come from outside the cell to the cell's center. How easily a cell can exchange substances depends on the ratio of its surface area to its volume (surface area ÷ volume). Surface area is a measure of the exposed outer surface of an object. Volume is the amount of space that an object takes up.

In this lab, you will design an experiment to investigate how a cell's size affects the diffusion of substances into the cell. To do so, you will make cell models using agar that contains phenolphthalein. Phenolphthalein is an indicator that changes color in the presence of an acidic solution.

Preparation

1. SCIENTIFIC METHODS **State the Problem** How does a cell's size affect the delivery of substances via diffusion to the center of the cell?

2. SCIENTIFIC METHODS **Form a Hypothesis** Form a testable hypothesis that explains how a cell's size affects the rate of diffusion of substances from outside the cell.

Procedure

Design an Experiment

❶ Design an experiment that tests your hypothesis and that uses the materials listed for this lab. Predict what will happen during your experiment if your hypothesis is correct.

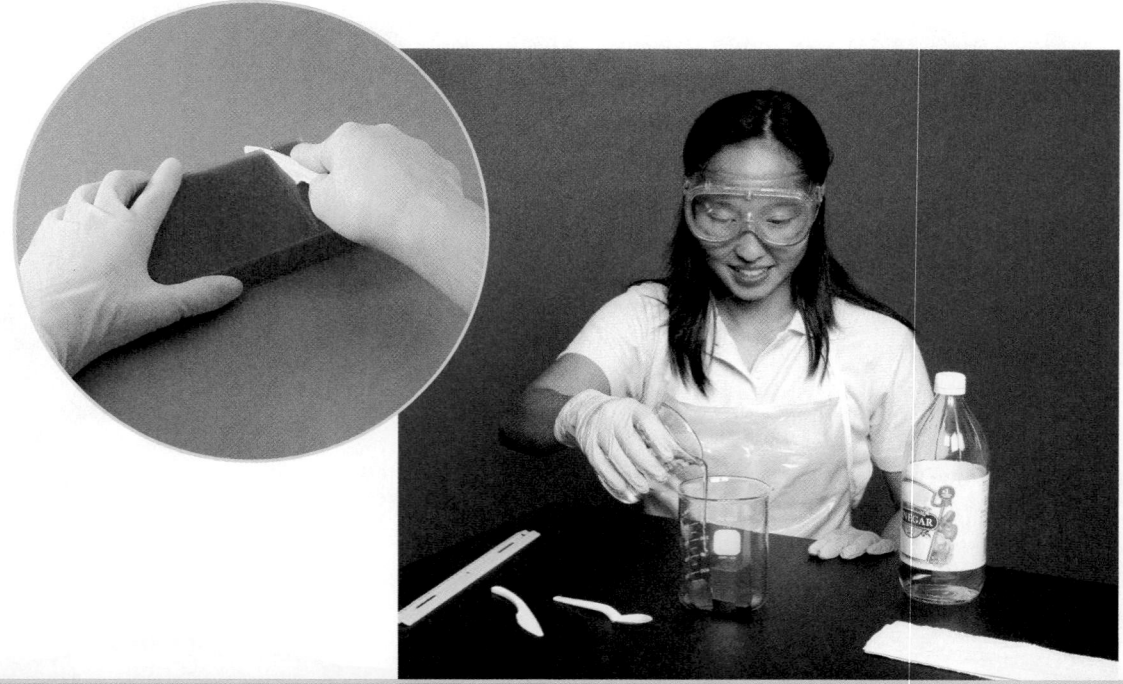

2 Write a procedure for your experiment. Identify the variables that you will control, the experimental variables, and the responding variables. Construct any tables that you will need to record your data. Make a list of all safety precautions that you will take. Have your teacher approve your procedure before you begin.

Diffusion in Cubes		
Size (cm)	Ratio	Distance (mm)

Conduct Your Experiment

3 Put on safety goggles, gloves, and a lab apron.

4 Carry out your experiment. Record your observations in your data table.

5 Follow your teacher's instructions for cleaning up your lab materials. Wash your hands before leaving the lab.

Analyze and Conclude

1. **Interpreting Observations** Describe any changes in the appearance of the agar cubes. Explain why these changes occurred.

2. **Summarizing Results** Make a graph labeled "Diffusion distance (mm)" on the vertical axis and "Surface area–to-volume ratio" on the horizontal axis. Plot your group's data on the graph.

3. **SCIENTIFIC METHODS Analyzing Results** Using the graph you made in item 2, make a statement relating the surface area–to-volume ratio and the distance that the substance diffuses.

4. **Summarizing Results** Make a second graph using your group's data. Label the vertical axis "Rate of diffusion (mm/min)" (distance that vinegar moved ÷ time). Label the horizontal axis "Surface area–to-volume ratio." Plot your group's data on the graph.

5. **Analyzing Results** Referring to the graph that you made in item 4, write a statement that relates the surface area–to-volume ratio and the rate at which the substance diffuses.

6. **SCIENTIFIC METHODS Evaluating Methods** In what ways do your agar models simplify or fail to simulate the features of cells?

7. **Calculating** Calculate the surface area and the volume of a cube that has a side length of 5 cm. Calculate the surface area and volume of a cube that has a side length of 10 cm. Determine the surface area–to-volume ratio of each cube. Which cube has the greater surface area–to-volume ratio?

8. **SCIENTIFIC METHODS Evaluating Conclusions** How does the size of a cell affect the rate at which substances diffuse into the cell?

9. **Further Inquiry** Write a new question about cell size and diffusion that could be explored in another investigation.

SC*L*INKS®

www.scilinks.org
Topic: Diffusion
Code: HX80406

Extensions

10. How does cell transport in prokaryotic cells differ from cell transport in eukaryotic cells?

11. Which of the following can diffuse across the cell membrane without the help of a transport protein: water, carbohydrates, lipids, or proteins?

Key Ideas	Key Terms

1 Cell Membrane

> One way that a cell maintains homeostasis is by controlling the movement of substances across the cell membrane.

> The lipid bilayer is selectively permeable to small, nonpolar substances.

> Proteins in the cell membrane include cell-surface markers, receptor proteins, enzymes, and transport proteins.

phospholipid (176)
lipid bilayer (176)

2 Cell Transport

> In passive transport, substances cross the cell membrane down their concentration gradient.

> Osmosis allows cells to maintain water balance as their environment changes.

> Active transport requires energy to move substances against their concentration gradients.

equilibrium (178)
concentration gradient (178)
diffusion (178)
carrier protein (178)
osmosis (180)
sodium-potassium pump (182)

3 Cell Communication

> Cells communicate and coordinate activity by sending chemical signals that carry information to other cells.

> A receptor protein binds only to the signals that match the specific shape of its binding site.

> The cell may respond to a signal by changing its membrane permeability, by activating enzymes, or by forming a second messenger.

signal (184)
receptor protein (185)
second messenger (186)

1. **Four-Corner Fold** Make a four-corner fold to compare methods cells use to transport substances across their membranes.

2. **Concept Map** Make a concept map that shows how cells maintain homeostasis. Try to include the following terms in your map: *concentration gradient, diffusion, osmosis,* and *carrier protein.*

Using Key Terms

3. Differentiate between *diffusion* and *osmosis.*

Use each of the following terms in a separate sentence.

4. *equilibrium*

5. *concentration gradient*

Understanding Key Ideas

6. In the cell membrane, the fatty acid tails of phospholipid molecules point
   a. toward each other.
   b. away from each other.
   c. toward the cytoplasm.
   d. toward the outside of the cell.

7. What keeps membrane proteins within the cell membrane?
   a. the pressure of the cytoskeleton against the proteins in the membrane
   b. the pressure of the phospholipids in the lipid bilayer against the proteins in the membrane
   c. the pressure of the cytoplasm against the proteins in the membrane
   d. the attractions between the polar and nonpolar portions of the proteins and the lipid bilayer

8. What does the sodium-potassium pump do?
   a. It moves sodium and potassium into the cell.
   b. It moves sodium and potassium out of the cell.
   c. It moves sodium into the cell and potassium out of the cell.
   d. It moves sodium out of the cell and potassium into the cell.

9. A cell that produces a signal molecule is called a
   a. target cell.
   c. recipient cell.
   b. marker cell.
   d. signaling cell.

10. Signal molecules bind to
    a. carbohydrates.
    c. marker proteins.
    b. phospholipids.
    d. receptor proteins.

Use the diagram to answer the questions that follow.

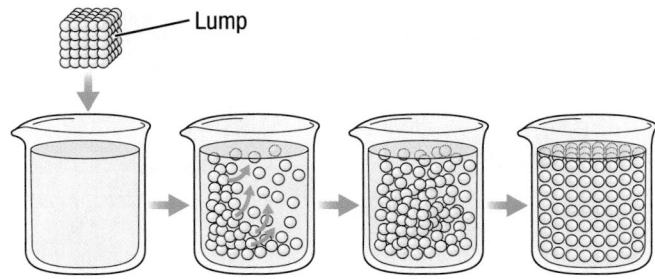
Lump

11. What process does the diagram show?
    a. osmosis
    c. active diffusion
    b. diffusion
    d. facilitated diffusion

12. In this process, the substance moves
    a. down its concentration gradient.
    b. independently of its concentration.
    c. against its concentration gradient.
    d. from an area of lower concentration to an area of higher concentration.

Explaining Key Ideas

13. **Explain** why the cell needs a selectively permeable barrier.

14. **Describe** the structure of the lipid bilayer of the cell membrane.

15. **Relate** osmosis and diffusion.

16. **Contrast** the action of carrier proteins in facilitated diffusion and active transport.

17. **Explain** how the sodium-potassium pump contributes to homeostasis in an animal.

18. **Compare** two ways that the binding of a signal molecule to a receptor protein causes a change in the activity of the receiving cell.

Using Science Graphics

The amounts of protein, lipid, and carbohydrate found in the cell membrane differ depending on the type of cell. The two diagrams show the composition of the cell membrane of a human red blood cell and the cell membrane of an amoeba, a single-celled protist. Use the diagrams to answer the questions that follow.

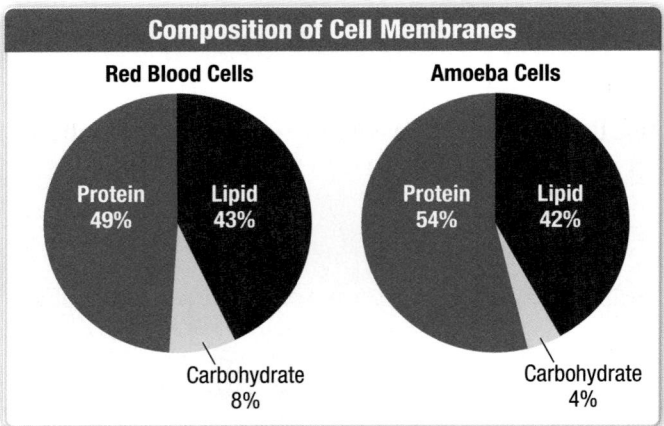

Composition of Cell Membranes

Red Blood Cells — Protein 49%, Lipid 43%, Carbohydrate 8%

Amoeba Cells — Protein 54%, Lipid 42%, Carbohydrate 4%

19. **Identify** the type of cell in which the percentage of the cell membrane made up of proteins is larger.

20. **Identify** the type of cell in which the ratio of carbohydrate to lipid is smaller.

Critical Thinking

21. **Recognizing Relationships** How does the arrangement of phospholipids influence the permeability of the lipid bilayer?

22. **Applying information** Using what you know about osmosis, explain what would happen to a jellyfish if it were placed in a freshwater lake.

23. **Applying Information** During exercise, potassium ions tend to accumulate in the fluid that surrounds muscle cells. Which protein in the cell membrane helps muscle cells counteract this tendency? Explain your answer.

24. **Inferring Relationships** When a cell takes in substances through endocytosis, the outside of the cell membrane becomes the inside of the vesicle. What might this transformation suggest about the structure of the cell membrane?

25. **Making Inferences** What would happen if all receptor proteins were removed from the membranes of all liver cells?

Alternative Assessment

26. **Cellular Conversation** When a physician taps your knee, your leg automatically jerks. Use Internet or library resources to learn about the rapid cell signaling that is involved in this knee-jerk reflex. Write a "conversation" that could occur between these cells. Create a comic strip, a short story, or a skit based on the conversation, and present it to your class.

Why It Matters

27. **Research** The molecular structure of caffeine is similar to the structure of a signal molecule that your body produces naturally. Find out what this signal molecule is, and compare its structure to caffeine's. Propose some properties of the binding site of the receptor protein to which caffeine binds.

Methods of Science

28. **Evaluating Models** A student wants to model osmosis by placing a mesh bag in a solution of salt water. The bag fills up with a saltwater concentration that is the same as the concentration of the solution outside of the bag. Is this model a good model for osmosis?

29. **Connecting Concepts** Transport proteins in the membrane of a lysosome move hydrogen ions into the lysosome. Use this information to predict whether digestive enzymes in a lysosome work best in a neutral, basic, or acidic environment.

Math Skills

30. **Concentration** The concentration of a solution in Beaker A is 0.4 g/mL. Beaker B contains 8 mL of water. Two milliliters of the solution in Beaker A is poured into Beaker B. When the solution in Beaker B reaches equilibrium, what is its concentration?

31. **Ratios** Suppose a sodium-potassium pump transports 12 sodium ions out of the cell. How many potassium ions did this pump transport into the cell?

Science Concepts

1. Why are phospholipids ideal for making up the selectively permeable cell membrane?
   A They repel small ions.
   B They react readily with water molecules.
   C They form triple layers that insulate the cell.
   D They have a nonpolar and a polar region.

2. The membrane-bound proteins that identify a cell type are
   F enzymes.
   G glycoproteins.
   H receptor proteins.
   J transport proteins.

3. Which substance crosses the cell membrane by facilitated diffusion?
   A oxygen
   B sugar
   C sodium ion
   D chloride ion

4. The concentration of molecule X is greater inside a cell than it is outside the cell. If the cell acquires X from its surroundings, X must cross the cell membrane by means of
   F exocytosis.
   G active transport.
   H receptor proteins.
   J second messengers.

5. A cell begins to swell when it is placed in an unknown solution. What can you conclude about the solution?
   A The solution is isotonic.
   B The solution is hypotonic.
   C The solution is saturated.
   D The solution is hypertonic.

6. Which proteins transmit information into a cell by binding to signal molecules?
   F end proteins
   G marker proteins
   H channel proteins
   J receptor proteins

Math Skills

7. What will happen to a cell (1% salt) that is placed in a 5% salt solution?
   A Salt moves in.
   B Salt moves out
   C Water moves in.
   D Water moves out.

Using Science Graphics

This graph shows the rate of glucose transport across a cell membrane versus the concentration gradient. Use the graph to answer the question that follows.

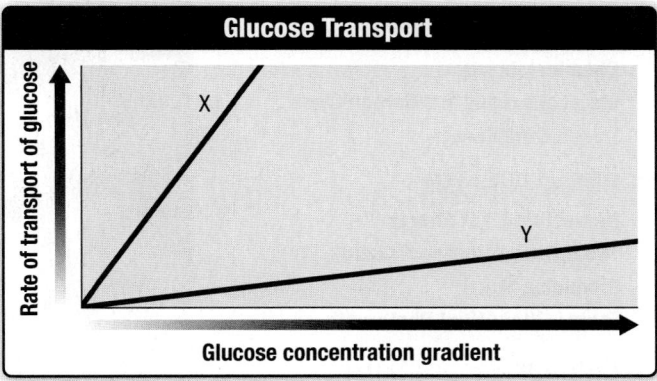

8. If Line X represents the facilitated diffusion of glucose, what could Line Y represent?
   A diffusion of glucose through osmosis
   B diffusion of glucose through the lipid bilayer
   C diffusion of glucose through carrier proteins
   D active transport of glucose through carrier proteins

This diagram shows a cellular process that occurs at the cell membrane. Use the diagram to answer the question that follows.

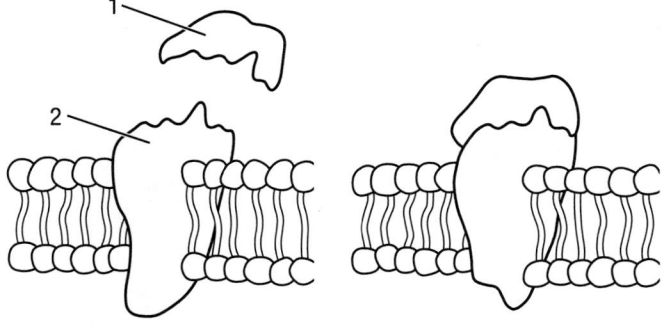

9. What happens immediately after structure 1 binds to structure 2?
   F Structure 1 is destroyed.
   G Structure 2 becomes larger.
   H Structure 2 changes in shape.
   J Structure 1 is released from the membrane.

Photosynthesis and Cellular Respiration

Preview

1 Energy in Living Systems
Chemical Energy
Metabolism and the Carbon Cycle
Transferring Energy

2 Photosynthesis
Harvesting Light Energy
Two Electron Transport Chains
Producing Sugar
Factors that Affect Photosynthesis

3 Cellular Respiration
Glycolysis
Aerobic Respiration
Fermentation

Why It Matters

Everything you do—from moving, to breathing, to thinking—requires energy. The energy your body uses is mostly derived from the processes of photosynthesis and cellular respiration.

A saturniid caterpillar feeds on a leaf. The leaf provides the energy the caterpillar needs to grow and undergo metamorphosis.

The caterpillar gets the organic compounds it needs for cellular respiration from the leaf. Caterpillars, like other animals, are *heterotrophs*.

Carbohydrates and oxygen are produced in leaves by photosynthesis. A green pigment called *chlorophyll* gives plants their characteristic green color.

 15 min

InquiryLab

Stored Energy

Have you ever used a hot pack? The way the hot pack works has to do with energy storage and the release of stored heat energy during a chemical reaction.

Procedure

1. Fill a **plastic foam cup** halfway with **tap water**.

2. Measure and record the water's temperature.

3. Examine the **reusable hot pack.** Then, activate it according to your instructor's directions. Quickly place the pack into the water-filled cup.

4. Measure and record the water's temperature at intervals of 30 s.

Analysis

1. **Describe** what happened when the hot pack was activated.

2. **Explain** how the activated hot pack affected the temperature of the water.

3. **Explain** where the observed heat energy came from.

4. **Speculate** whether the hot pack can be restored to its activated state by placing the hot pack in direct sunlight.

The veins in leaves are part of a vascular system. Sugars produced by photosynthesis are transported through the veins in leaves to the stems and roots by special tissues called *vascular tissues*.

READING TOOLBOX

These reading tools can help you learn the material in this chapter. For more information on how to use these and other tools, see **Appendix: Reading and Study Skills.**

Using Words

Key-Term Fold A key-term fold is useful for studying definitions of key terms in a chapter. Each tab can contain a key term on one side and its definition on the other side.

Your Turn Make a key-term fold for the terms in this chapter.

1. Fold a sheet of lined notebook paper in half from left to right.

2. Using scissors, cut along every third line from the right edge of the paper to the center fold to make tabs.

Using Language

Describing Space As you read the chapter, look for language clues that answer the question, "Where does this process take place?" Words such as *inside, outside,* and *between* can help you learn where these processes happen. Knowing where these processes take place can help you better understand them.

Your Turn Describe as precisely as you can where the following processes happen.

1. photosynthesis

2. cellular respiration

Using Graphic Organizers

Pattern Puzzles You can use pattern puzzles to help you remember information. Exchanging puzzles with a classmate can help you study.

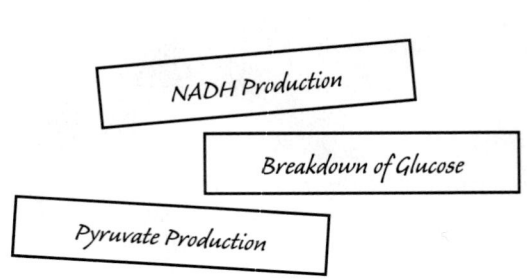

NADH Production

Breakdown of Glucose

Pyruvate Production

Your Turn Make pattern puzzles for the steps of glycolysis.

1. Write down the steps of the process. On a sheet of notebook paper, write down one step per line. Do not number the steps.

2. Cut the sheet of paper into strips with only one step per strip of paper. Shuffle the paper strips so that they are out of sequence.

3. Place the strips in the correct sequence. Confirm the order of the steps of the process by checking your text or class notes.

Energy in Living Systems

Key Ideas	Key Terms	Why It Matters
❯ What type of energy is used in cells, and what is the ultimate source of this energy? ❯ How is an organism's metabolism related to the carbon cycle? ❯ How is energy released in a cell?	photosynthesis cellular respiration ATP ATP synthase electron transport chain	Plants convert sunlight into chemical energy. This chemical energy can be used for biological processes in nearly all living things.

Imagine an abandoned house that is falling apart. The house, like almost everything else in the universe, breaks down over time. Restoring order to the house would require an input of energy, such as the energy needed to apply a fresh coat of paint. Living things also need energy in order to stay in good repair, or maintain their *homeostasis.* Remember that homeostasis is the process of maintaining internal order and balance even when the environment changes. Every organism must maintain homeostasis as long as it lives. Therefore, organisms require a constant source of energy.

Chemical Energy

❯ **Organisms use and store energy in the chemical bonds of organic compounds. Almost all of the energy in organic compounds comes from the sun.** Solar energy enters living systems when plants, algae, and certain prokaryotes use sunlight to make organic compounds from carbon dioxide and water through the process of **photosynthesis.** Organisms that are able to perform photosynthesis, such as the wheat plants shown in **Figure 1,** are *autotrophs.* Autotrophs make organic compounds that serve as food for them and for almost all of the other organisms on Earth.

Most autotrophs have a supply of food as long as sunlight is available. But how do other organisms get food molecules? To survive, organisms that cannot make their own food must absorb food molecules made by autotrophs, eat autotrophs, or eat organisms that consume autotrophs. Food molecules that are made or consumed by an organism are the fuel for its cells. Cells use these molecules to release the energy stored in the molecules' bonds. The energy is used to carry out life processes.

❯ **Reading Check** *Why do organisms need a constant supply of energy? (See the Appendix for answers to Reading Checks.)*

photosynthesis the process by which plants, algae, and some bacteria use sunlight, carbon dioxide, and water to produce carbohydrates and oxygen

Figure 1 Food crops such as wheat supply humans and other animals with the chemical energy needed to carry out life processes.

Product of Photosynthesis

Plants use photosynthesis to produce food. One product of photosynthesis is oxygen. In this activity, you will observe the process of photosynthesis in elodea.

Procedure

1 Add **450 mL of baking-soda-and-water solution** to a **beaker**.

2 Put **two or three sprigs of elodea** into the beaker. The baking soda will provide the elodea with the carbon dioxide it needs for photosynthesis.

3 Place the wide end of a **glass funnel** over the elodea. The elodea and the funnel should be completely submerged in the solution.

4 Fill a **test tube** with the remaining solution. Place your thumb over the end of the test tube. Turn the test tube upside down, taking care that no air enters. Hold the opening of the test tube under the solution, and place the test tube over the small end of the funnel.

5 Place the beaker setup in a well-lit area near a lamp or in direct sunlight, and leave it overnight.

Analysis

1. **Describe** what happened to the solution in the test tube.

2. **CRITICAL THINKING** **Predicting Patterns** Explain what may happen if an animal, such as a snail, were put into the beaker with the elodea sprig.

---

cellular respiration the process by which cells produce energy from carbohydrates

ATP adenosine triphosphate, an organic molecule that acts as the main energy source for cell processes; composed of a nitrogenous base, a sugar, and three phosphate groups

Metabolism and the Carbon Cycle

❯ Metabolism involves either using energy to build organic molecules or breaking down organic molecules in which energy is stored. Organic molecules contain carbon. Therefore, an organism's metabolism is part of Earth's carbon cycle. The carbon cycle not only makes carbon compounds continuously available in an ecosystem but also delivers chemical energy to organisms living within that ecosystem.

Photosynthesis Energy enters an ecosystem when organisms use sunlight during photosynthesis to convert stable carbon dioxide molecules into glucose, a less stable carbon compound. In plant cells and algae, photosynthesis takes place in chloroplasts. **Figure 2** summarizes the process by which energy from the sun is converted to chemical energy in chloroplasts.

Cellular Respiration Organisms extract energy stored in glucose molecules. Through the process of **cellular respiration,** cells make the carbon in glucose into stable carbon dioxide molecules and produce energy. Thus, stable and less stable compounds alternate during the carbon cycle and provide a continuous supply of energy for life processes in an ecosystem.

The breakdown of glucose during cellular respiration is summarized in **Figure 2.** The inputs are a glucose molecule and six oxygen molecules. The final products are six carbon dioxide molecules and six water molecules. Energy is also released and used to make **ATP** (adenosine triphosphate), an organic molecule that is the main energy source for cell processes.

❯ **Reading Check** *How is solar energy related to the carbon cycle?*

go.hrw.com
interact online
Keyword: HX8PHRF2

Photosynthesis and Cellular Respiration

Figure 2 Photosynthesis and cellular respiration are major steps in the carbon cycle. **Compare the end results of photosynthesis and cellular respiration.**

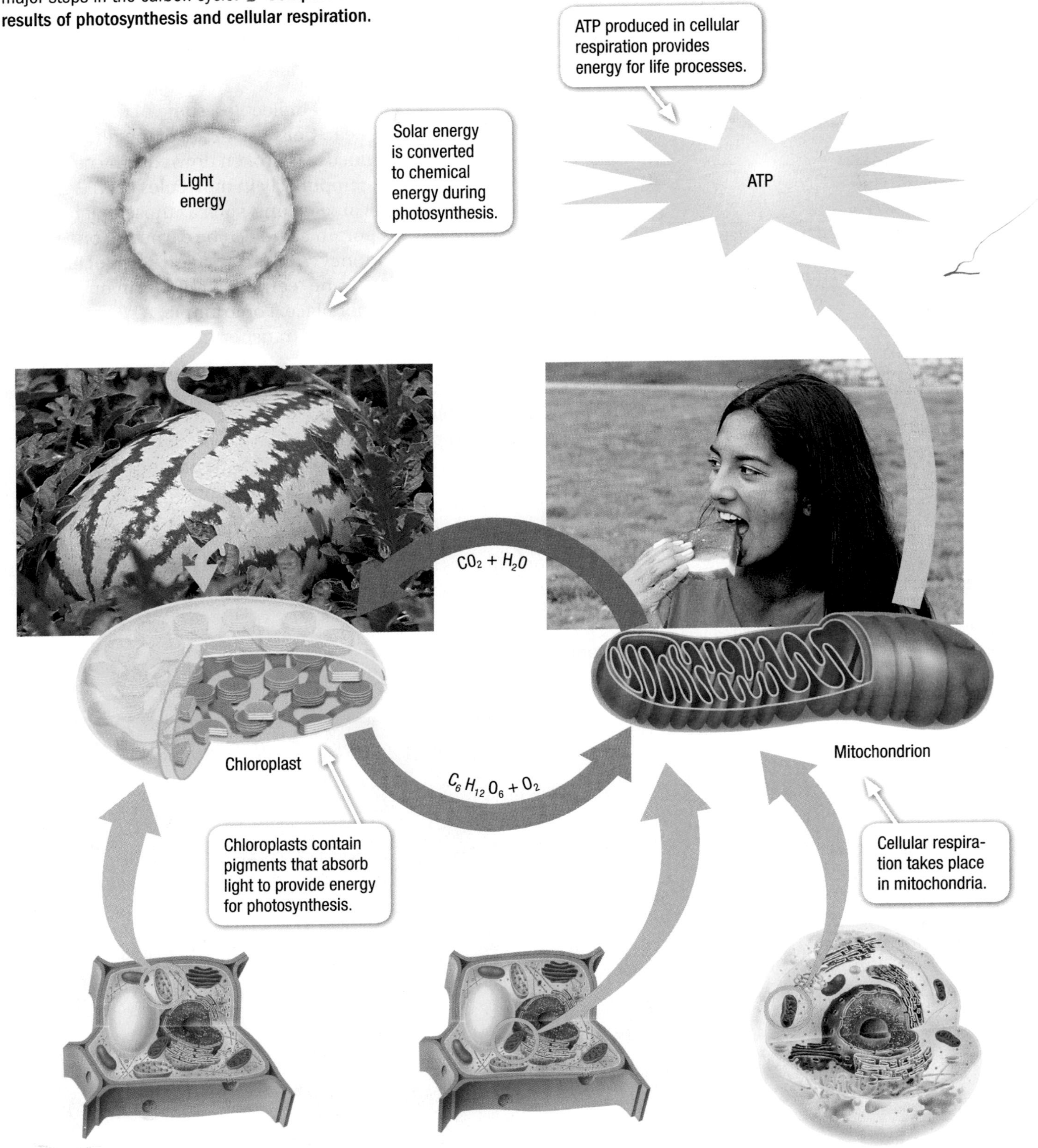
ATP produced in cellular respiration provides energy for life processes.
Solar energy is converted to chemical energy during photosynthesis.
Light energy
ATP
$CO_2 + H_2O$
Chloroplast
$C_6H_{12}O_6 + O_2$
Mitochondrion
Chloroplasts contain pigments that absorb light to provide energy for photosynthesis.
Cellular respiration takes place in mitochondria.

Transferring Energy

In chemical reactions, energy can be absorbed and released during the breaking and forming of bonds. For example, when a log burns, the energy stored in wood molecules is released in a burst of heat and light. ❯ **In cells, chemical energy is gradually released in a series of chemical reactions that are assisted by enzymes.** Recall that enzymes are proteins that act as catalysts in biochemical reactions.

ATP When cells break down food molecules, some of the energy in the molecules is released as heat. Cells use much of the remaining energy to make ATP. When glucose is broken down during cellular respiration, energy is stored temporarily in molecules of ATP. ATP can be used to power chemical reactions, such as those that build molecules. Paper money is portable and can be earned in one place and spent in another. Like money, ATP is a portable form of energy "currency" inside cells. ATP can be "earned," or made, in one place and "spent," or used, in another place. For example, ATP can be used to contract a muscle cell, to actively transport protein, or to help make more ATP.

ATP is a nucleotide made up of a chain of three phosphate groups. This chain is unstable because the phosphate groups are negatively charged and thus repel each other. When the bond of the third phosphate group is broken, energy is released. This produces adenosine diphosphate, or ADP. The equation below summarizes the process.

$$ATP \longrightarrow ADP + P + energy$$

The reaction in which ATP is converted to ADP requires a small input of energy. But much more energy is released than is used during the reaction.

❯ **Reading Check** *How is ATP used inside a cell?*

READING TOOLBOX

Key-Term Fold On the back of your key-term fold, write a definition in your own words for each key term in this section.

ACADEMIC VOCABULARY

process a set of steps, events, or changes

Figure 3 The energy of falling water can turn a water wheel, which provides energy to do work. In ATP synthase, the movement of hydrogen ions provides energy to convert ADP to ATP.

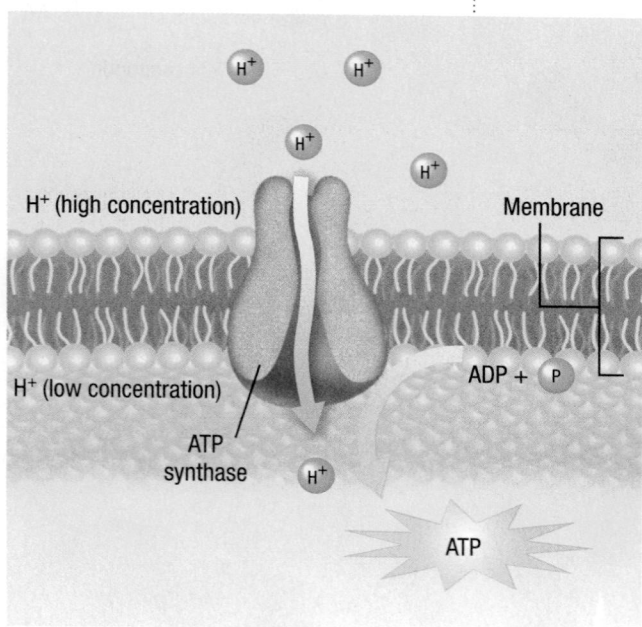

H⁺ (high concentration)

H⁺ (low concentration)

ATP synthase

Membrane

ADP + P

ATP

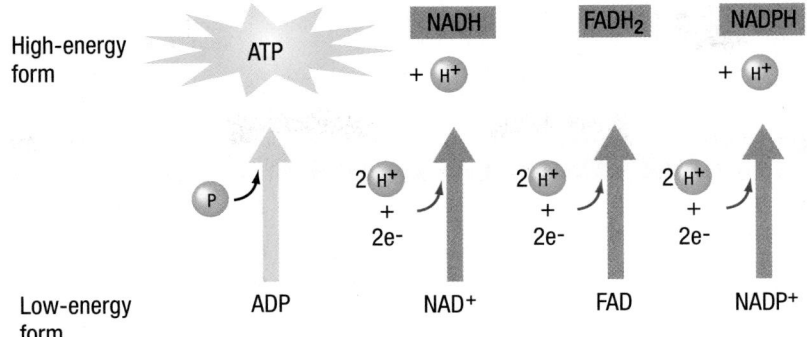

High-energy form

ATP

NADH + H^+

$FADH_2$

NADPH + H^+

P

2 H^+ + 2e⁻

2 H^+ + 2e⁻

2 H^+ + 2e⁻

Low-energy form

ADP

NAD^+

FAD

$NADP^+$

Figure 4 Electron carriers store energy by bonding with hydrogen, just as ATP stores energy by bonding a third phosphate group. ❯ **Where is the electron transport chain found in animal cells?**

ATP Synthase In many cells, **ATP synthase,** an enzyme that catalyzes the synthesis of ATP, recycles ADP by bonding a third phosphate group to the molecule. As **Figure 3** shows, ATP synthase acts as both an enzyme and a carrier protein for hydrogen (H^+) ions. The flow of H^+ ions through ATP synthase powers the production of ATP. You can think of the H^+ ions moving through ATP synthase to produce ATP as falling water turning a water wheel to produce power. As H^+ ions flow, ATP synthase catalyzes a reaction in which a phosphate group is added to a molecule of ADP to make ATP.

Hydrogen Ion Pumps Recall how diffusion across cell membranes works. Particles of a substance diffuse through a membrane from a region of higher concentration to a region of lower concentration. The inner mitochondrial membrane allows H^+ ions to diffuse through only ATP synthase. When glucose is broken down during cellular respiration, NAD^+ (nicotinamide adenine dinucleotide) accepts electrons and hydrogen ions, which changes NAD^+ to NADH. As **Figure 4** shows, NADH enters an **electron transport chain,** a series of molecules in the inner membrane of a mitochondrion. The electron transport chain allows electrons to drop in energy as they are passed along and uses the energy released to pump H^+ ions out of a mitochondrion's inner compartment. This action increases the concentration of H^+ ions in the outer compartment. The ions then diffuse back into the inner compartment through ATP synthase.

ATP synthase an enzyme that catalyzes the synthesis of ATP

electron transport chain a series of molecules, found in the inner membranes of mitochondria and chloroplasts, through which electrons pass in a process that causes protons to build up on one side of the membrane

SCI*LINKS.*

www.scilinks.org
Topic: ATP
Code: HX80123

Section 1 Review

❯ **KEY IDEAS**

1. **Identify** the primary source of energy that flows through most living systems.

2. **Explain** how an organism's metabolism is related to Earth's carbon cycle.

3. **Describe** how energy is released from ATP.

CRITICAL THINKING

4. **Analyzing Patterns** Explain how life involves a continuous flow of energy.

5. **Inferring Relationships** How can the energy in the food that a fox eats be traced back to the sun?

6. **Summarizing Information** What is the difference between cellular respiration and the process by which energy is released from a burning log?

WRITING FOR SCIENCE

7. **Career Connection** Research the educational background that a person needs to become an enzymologist. List the courses required, and describe additional degrees or training that are recommended for this career. Write a report on your findings.

Key Ideas	Key Terms	Why It Matters
> What is the role of pigments in photosynthesis? > What are the roles of the electron transport chains? > How do plants make sugars and store extra unused energy? > What are three environmental factors that affect photosynthesis?	thylakoid pigment chlorophyll Calvin cycle	Nearly all of the energy for life processes comes from the sun and is stored in organic molecules during the process of photosynthesis.

Plants, algae, and certain prokaryotes capture about 1% of the energy in the sunlight that reaches Earth and convert it to chemical energy through photosynthesis. Photosynthesis is the process that provides energy for almost all life.

Harvesting Light Energy

The cells of many photosynthetic organisms have chloroplasts, organelles that convert light energy into chemical energy. Study the diagram of a chloroplast in **Figure 5.**

A chloroplast has an outer membrane and an inner membrane. Molecules diffuse easily through the outer membrane. The inner membrane is much more selective about what substances enter and leave. Both membranes allow light to pass through.

The space inside the inner membrane is the stroma. Within the stroma is a membrane called the *thylakoid membrane.* This membrane is folded in a way that produces flat, disc-like sacs called **thylakoids.** These sacs, which contain molecules that absorb light energy for photosynthesis, are arranged in stacks. The first stage of photosynthesis begins when light waves hit these stacks.

> **Reading Check** *Describe the structure of a chloroplast.*

Figure 5 Pigments, as well as other molecules that participate in photosynthesis, are embedded in thylakoids. **> Where are thylakoids located?**

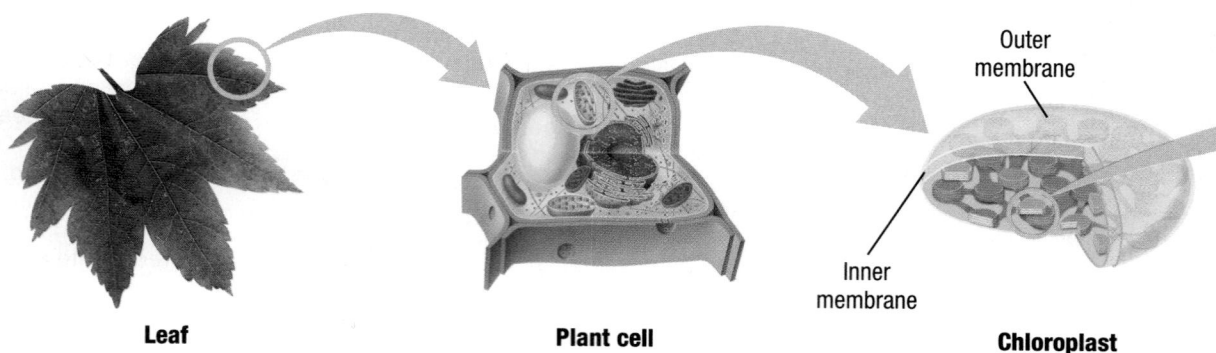

Leaf   **Plant cell**   Outer membrane / Inner membrane / **Chloroplast**

Electromagnetic Radiation

Light is a form of electromagnetic radiation, energy that can travel through empty space in the form of waves. Radio waves, X-rays, and microwaves are also forms of electromagnetic radiation. The difference between these forms of radiation is that they have different wavelengths. Each wavelength corresponds to a certain amount of energy. The wavelength is the distance between consecutive wave peaks. Sunlight contains all of the wavelengths of visible light. You see these wavelengths as different colors.

Pigments

What makes the human eye sensitive to light? Cells in the back of the eye contain pigments. A **pigment** is a substance that absorbs certain wavelengths (colors) of light and commonly reflects all of the others. ❯ **In plants, light energy is harvested by pigments that are located in the thylakoid membrane of chloroplasts. Chlorophyll** is a green pigment in chloroplasts that absorbs light energy to start photosynthesis. It absorbs mostly blue and red light and reflects green and yellow light, which makes plants appear green. Plants have two types of chlorophyll: chlorophyll *a* and chlorophyll *b*. Plants also have pigments called *carotenoids*. Carotenoids absorb blue and green light, and they reflect yellow, orange, and red light. When chlorophyll fades away in the fall, the colors of carotenoids are exposed. Carotenoids aid photosynthesis by allowing plants to absorb additional light energy. **Figure 6** shows the wavelengths of light that are absorbed by chlorophyll *a*, chlorophyll *b*, and carotenoids—the pigments found in thylakoid membranes.

Electron Carriers

When light hits a thylakoid, energy is absorbed by many pigment molecules. They all funnel the energy to a special chlorophyll molecule in a region called the *reaction center*, where the energy causes the electrons to become "excited" and to move to a higher energy level. These electrons are transferred quickly to other nearby molecules and then to an electron carrier.

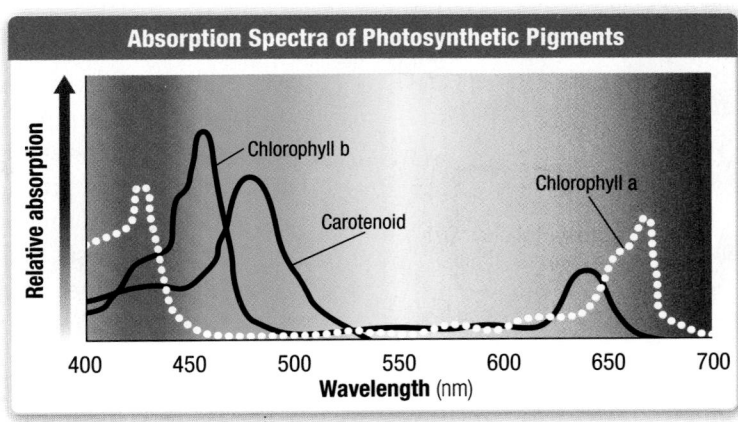

Absorption Spectra of Photosynthetic Pigments

Figure 6 This graph shows the colors of light that three different pigments absorb. Where a curve peaks, much of the light at that wavelength is absorbed. Where a curve dips, much of the light at that wavelength is reflected or transmitted.

thylakoid (THIE luh KOYD) a membrane system found within chloroplasts that contains the components for photosynthesis

pigment a substance that gives another substance or a mixture its color

chlorophyll (KLAWR uh FIL) a green pigment that is present in most plant and algae cells and some bacteria, that gives plants their characteristic green color, and that absorbs light to provide energy for photosynthesis

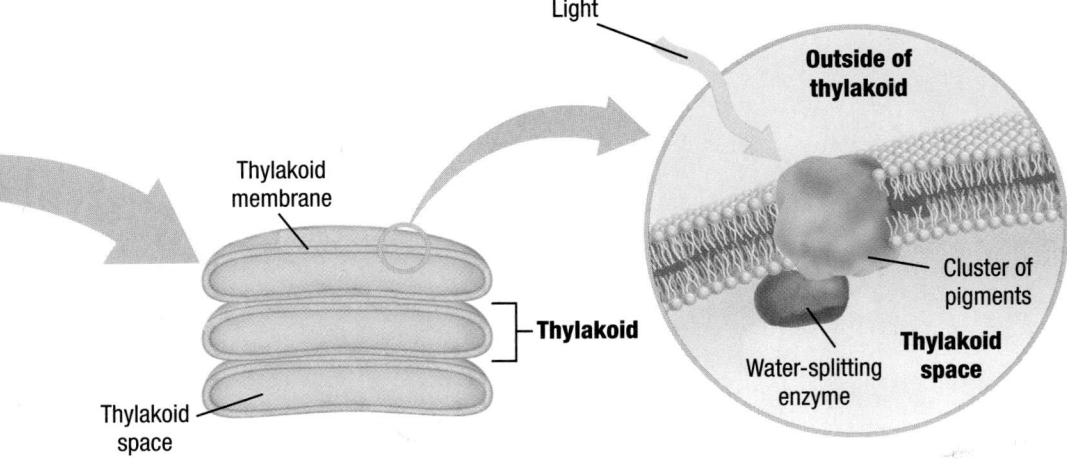

SCiLINKS®
www.scilinks.org
Topic: Photosynthesis
Code: HX81140

Two Electron Transport Chains

Electrons from the electron carrier are used to produce new molecules, including ATP, that temporarily store chemical energy. The carrier transfers the electrons to the first of two electron transport chains in the thylakoid membrane. Trace the path taken by the electrons in the electron transport chains shown in **Figure 7.** ❭ **During photosynthesis, one electron transport chain provides energy to make ATP, while the other provides energy to make NADPH.** Both chains use energy from electrons excited by light.

Producing ATP In mitochondria, electron transport chains pump H^+ ions through a membrane, which produces a concentration gradient. This process also happens in chloroplasts.

Step ❶ Water Splitting The excited electrons that leave chlorophyll molecules must be replaced by other electrons. Plants get these replacement electrons from water molecules, H_2O. During photosynthesis, an enzyme splits water molecules inside the thylakoid. When water molecules are split, chlorophyll molecules take the electrons from the hydrogen atoms, H, which leaves H^+ ions. The remaining oxygen atoms, O, from the split water molecules combine to form oxygen gas, O_2. This oxygen gas is not used for any later steps of photosynthesis, so it is released into the atmosphere.

Figure 7 Photosynthesis converts light energy to chemical energy. This figure shows key molecules involved in the capture of light, electron transport, and synthesis of ATP and NADPH. ❭ **What causes H^+ ions to move through the carrier protein that produces ATP?**

go.hrw.com
✴ **interact online**
Keyword: HX8PHRF7

Electron Transport Chains of Photosynthesis

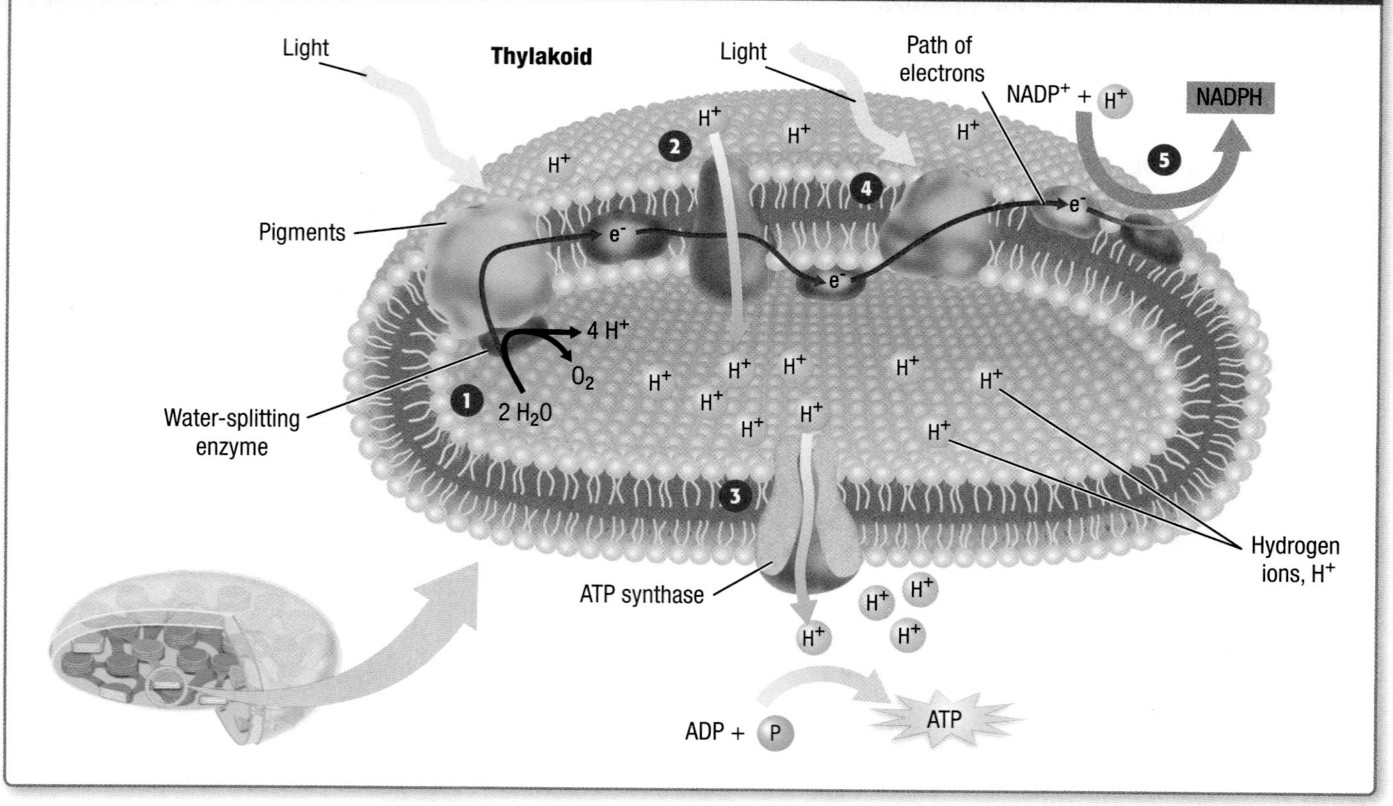

QuickLab

🕐 15 min

Photosynthetic Rate

Changes in a plant's surroundings influence photosynthetic rate. The two graphs illustrate how photosynthetic rate responds to changes in light intensity and temperature. Use the graphs to answer the following questions.

Analysis

1. **Describe** how increasing light intensity affects the rate of photosynthesis.

2. **Explain** whether continuing to increase light intensity will increase the rate of photosynthesis.

3. **Describe** how increasing temperature affects the rate of photosynthesis.

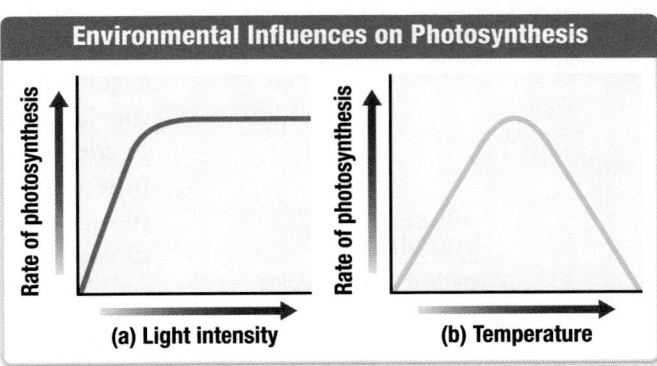

Environmental Influences on Photosynthesis

(a) Light intensity

(b) Temperature

4. **CRITICAL THINKING** **Inferring Relationships** Explain how a global temperature increase could affect plants.

Step ❷ Hydrogen Ion Pump A protein acts as a membrane pump. Excited electrons transfer some of their energy to pump H⁺ ions into the thylakoid. This process creates a concentration gradient across the thylakoid membrane.

Step ❸ ATP Synthase The energy from the diffusion of H⁺ ions through the carrier protein is used to make ATP. These carrier proteins are unusual because they function both as an ion channel and as the enzyme ATP synthase. As hydrogen ions pass through the channel portion of the protein, ATP synthase catalyzes a reaction in which a phosphate group is added to a molecule of ADP. The result of the reaction is ATP, which is used to power the final stage of photosynthesis.

Producing NADPH While one electron transport chain provides energy used to make ATP, a second electron transport chain receives excited electrons from a chlorophyll molecule and uses them to make NADPH. The second electron transport chain is to the right of the second cluster of pigment molecules in **Figure 7**.

Step ❹ Reenergizing In this second chain, light excites electrons in the chlorophyll molecule. The excited electrons are passed on to the second chain. They are replaced by the de-energized electrons from the first transport chain.

Step ❺ Making NADPH Excited electrons combine with H⁺ ions and an electron acceptor called NADP⁺ to form NADPH. NADPH is an electron carrier that provides the high-energy electrons needed to store energy in organic molecules. Both NADPH and the ATP made during the first stage of photosynthesis will be used to provide the energy to carry out the final stage of photosynthesis.

❯ **Reading Check** *Summarize how ATP and NADPH are formed during photosynthesis.*

READING TOOLBOX

Describing Space Use spatial language to describe production of ATP and NADPH during photosynthesis.

Figure 8 The Calvin cycle is the most
common method of carbon dioxide
fixation. ❯ **What is formed when the three
six-carbon molecules split during step 2
of the Calvin cycle?**

Producing Sugar

The first two stages of photosynthesis depend directly on light
because light energy is used to make ATP and NADPH. ❯ **In the final
stage of photosynthesis, ATP and NADPH are used to produce energy-storing
sugar molecules from the carbon in carbon dioxide.** The use of carbon
dioxide to make organic compounds is called *carbon dioxide fixation,*
or *carbon fixation.* The reactions that fix carbon dioxide are light-
independent reactions, sometimes called *dark reactions.* Among
photosynthetic organisms, there are several ways in which carbon
dioxide is fixed. The most common <u>method</u> of carbon dioxide fixation is the **Calvin cycle,** which is described in the following steps:

Step ❶ Carbon Fixation In carbon dioxide fixation, an enzyme
adds a molecule of carbon dioxide, CO_2, to a five-carbon compound.
This process occurs three times to yield three six-carbon molecules.

Step ❷ Transferring Energy Each six-carbon compound splits
into two three-carbon compounds. Phosphate groups from ATP and
electrons from NADPH are added to the three-carbon compounds to
form higher energy three-carbon sugars.

Step ❸ Making Sugar One of the resulting three-carbon sugars
leaves the cycle and is used to make organic compounds—including
glucose, sucrose, and starch—in which energy is stored for later use
by the organism.

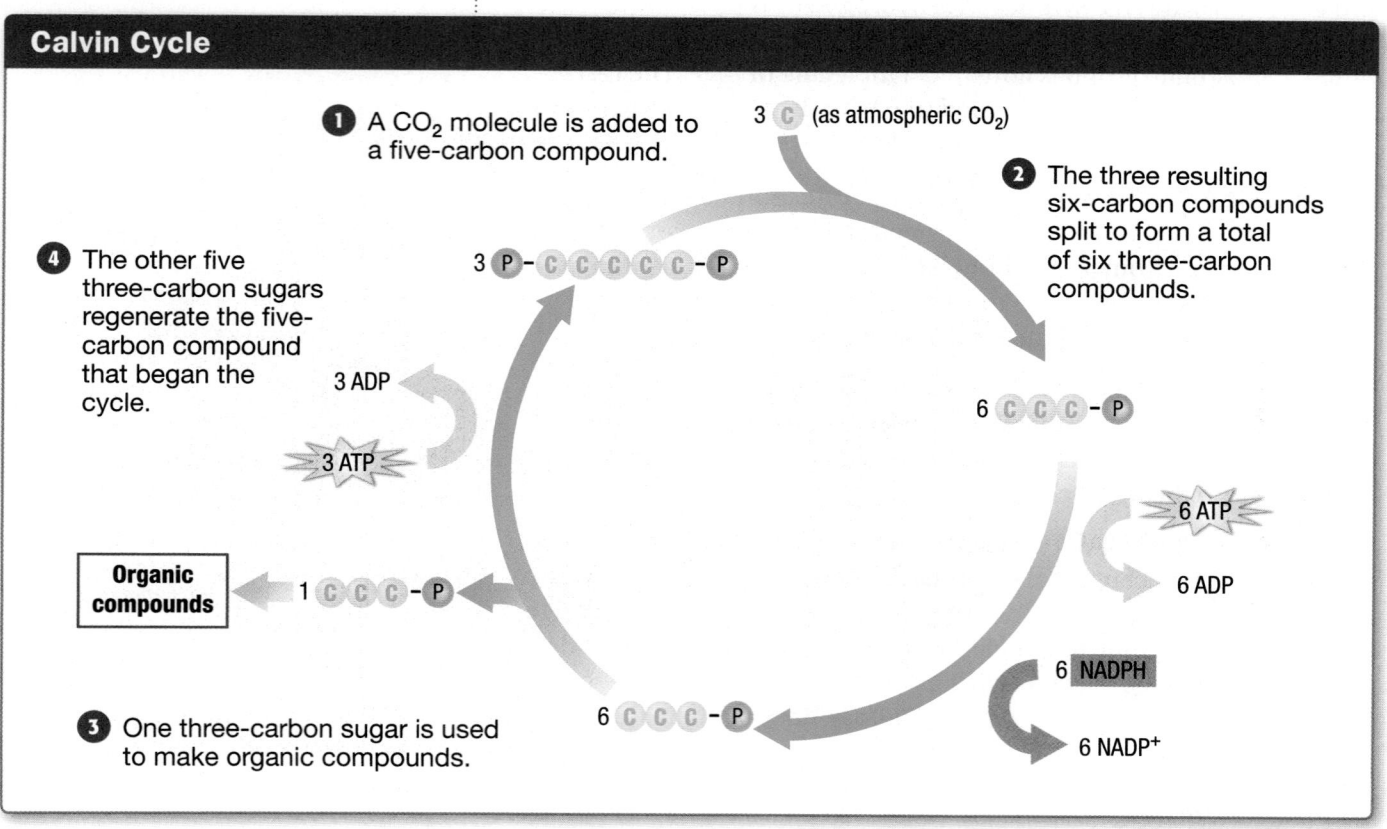

Calvin Cycle

❶ A CO_2 molecule is added to a five-carbon compound.

3 C (as atmospheric CO_2)

❷ The three resulting six-carbon compounds split to form a total of six three-carbon compounds.

❹ The other five three-carbon sugars regenerate the five-carbon compound that began the cycle.

3 P - C C C C C - P

3 ADP

3 ATP

6 C C C - P

6 ATP

6 ADP

Organic compounds

1 C C C - P

6 NADPH

6 NADP⁺

❸ One three-carbon sugar is used to make organic compounds.

6 C C C - P

Figure 9 Some plants, such as a cactus (left), grow in extremely sunny, dry environments. Others, such as the bromeliad (right), are able to grow in shady areas.

Step ❹ Recycling The remaining five three-carbon sugars are rearranged. Using energy from ATP, enzymes reform three molecules of the initial five-carbon compound. This process completes the cycle. The reformed compounds are used to begin the cycle again.

Factors that Affect Photosynthesis

❯ **Light intensity, carbon dioxide concentration, and temperature are three environmental factors that affect photosynthesis.** The most obvious of these factors is light. **Figure 9** shows plants that are adapted to different levels of light. In general, the rate of photosynthesis increases as light intensity increases until all of the pigments in a chloroplast are being used. At this saturation point, the rate of photosynthesis levels off because the pigments cannot absorb more light.

The concentration of carbon dioxide affects the rate of photosynthesis in a way similar to light. Once a certain concentration of carbon dioxide is present, photosynthesis cannot proceed any faster.

Photosynthesis is most efficient in a certain range of temperatures. Like all metabolic processes, photosynthesis involves many enzyme-assisted chemical reactions. Unfavorable temperatures may inactivate certain enzymes so that reactions cannot take place.

❯ **Reading Check** *How does temperature affect photosynthesis?*

Section 2 Review

❯ **KEY IDEAS**

1. **Summarize** how autotrophs capture the energy in sunlight.
2. **Compare** the roles of water molecules and H⁺ ions in electron transport chains.
3. **Describe** the role of the Calvin cycle in photosynthesis.
4. **Name** the three main environmental factors that affect the rate of photosynthesis in plants.

CRITICAL THINKING

5. **Organizing Information** Make a table in which you identify the role of each of the following in photosynthesis: light, water, pigments, ATP, NADPH, and carbon dioxide.

METHODS OF SCIENCE

6. **Inferring Relationships** How do you think photosynthesis will be affected if the sun's rays are blocked by clouds or by smoke from a large fire? How might the levels of atmospheric carbon dioxide and oxygen be affected? What experiments could scientists conduct in the laboratory to test your predictions?

3 Cellular Respiration

Key Ideas	Key Terms	Why It Matters
❯ How does glycolysis produce ATP? ❯ How is ATP produced in aerobic respiration? ❯ Why is fermentation important?	glycolysis anaerobic aerobic Krebs cycle fermentation	Cellular respiration is the process used by humans and most other organisms to release the energy stored in the food they consume.

Where do the students shown in **Figure 10** get energy? Most of the foods we eat contain energy. Much of the energy in a hamburger, for example, is stored in proteins, carbohydrates, and fats. But before you can use that energy, it must be released and transferred to ATP. Like cells of most organisms, your cells transfer the energy in organic compounds, especially the glucose made during photosynthesis, to ATP through cellular respiration, which begins with glycolysis.

Glycolysis

The primary fuel for cellular respiration is glucose, which is formed when carbohydrates, such as starch and sucrose, are broken down. If too few carbohydrates are available to meet an organism's energy needs, other molecules, such as fats, can be broken down to make ATP. In fact, one gram of fat releases more energy than two grams of carbohydrates do. Proteins and nucleic acids can also be used to make ATP, but they are usually used for building important cell parts.

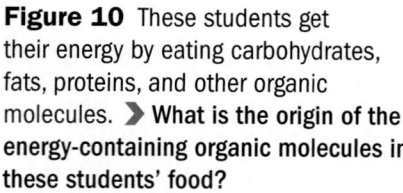

Figure 10 These students get their energy by eating carbohydrates, fats, proteins, and other organic molecules. ❯ What is the origin of the energy-containing organic molecules in these students' food?

Glycolysis

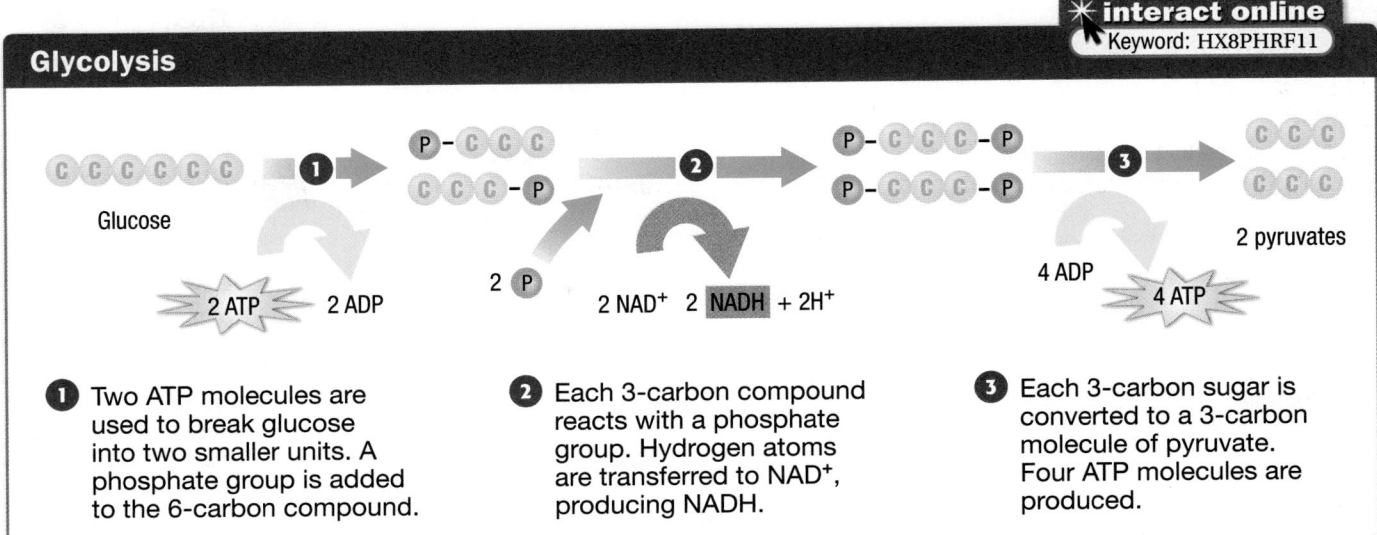

Glucose

2 ATP → 2 ADP

2 P

2 NAD⁺   2 NADH + 2H⁺

4 ADP

4 ATP

2 pyruvates

1 Two ATP molecules are used to break glucose into two smaller units. A phosphate group is added to the 6-carbon compound.

2 Each 3-carbon compound reacts with a phosphate group. Hydrogen atoms are transferred to NAD⁺, producing NADH.

3 Each 3-carbon sugar is converted to a 3-carbon molecule of pyruvate. Four ATP molecules are produced.

Steps of Glycolysis In the first stage of cellular respiration, glucose is broken down in the cytoplasm by glycolysis. In **glycolysis,** enzymes break down one six-carbon molecule of glucose into two three-carbon pyruvate molecules, as **Figure 11** shows. Most of the energy that was stored in the glucose molecule is stored in the pyruvate.

Step ❶ Breaking Down Glucose In the first stage of glycolysis, two ATP molecules are used to break glucose into two smaller units. This stage has four steps with four different enzymes. A phosphate group from ATP is added to the six-carbon compound. This makes the molecule reactive so that an enzyme can break it into two three-carbon sugars, each with a phosphate group. ATP is produced in the next two stages.

Step ❷ NADH Production In the second stage, each three-carbon compound reacts with another phosphate group (not from ATP). As the two three-carbon sugars react further, hydrogen atoms, including their electrons, are transferred to two molecules of NAD⁺, which produces two molecules of the electron carrier NADH. NADH is used later in other cell processes, where it is recycled to NAD⁺.

Step ❸ Pyruvate Production In a series of four reactions, each three-carbon sugar is converted into a three-carbon molecule of pyruvate. This process produces four ATP molecules. ❭ **Thus, the breaking of a sugar molecule by glycolysis results in a net gain of two ATP molecules.**

Glycolysis is the only source of energy for some prokaryotes. This process is **anaerobic,** so it takes place without oxygen. Other organisms use oxygen to release even more energy from a glucose molecule. Metabolic processes that require oxygen are **aerobic.** In aerobic respiration, the pyruvate product of glycolysis undergoes another series of reactions to produce more ATP molecules.

❭ **Reading Check** *What are the three products of glycolysis?*

Figure 11 Glycolysis uses two ATP molecules but produces four ATP molecules. The process results in a net gain of ATP. ❭ **What is the starting material in glycolysis?**

glycolysis (glie KAHL i sis) the anaerobic breakdown of glucose to pyruvate, which makes a small amount of energy available to cells in the form of ATP

anaerobic (AN uhr OH bik) describes a process that does not require oxygen

aerobic (er OH bik) describes a process that requires oxygen

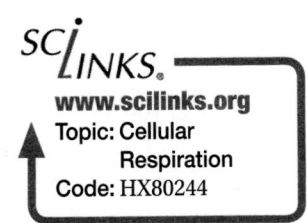

*SCI*LINKS.
www.scilinks.org
Topic: Cellular Respiration
Code: HX80244

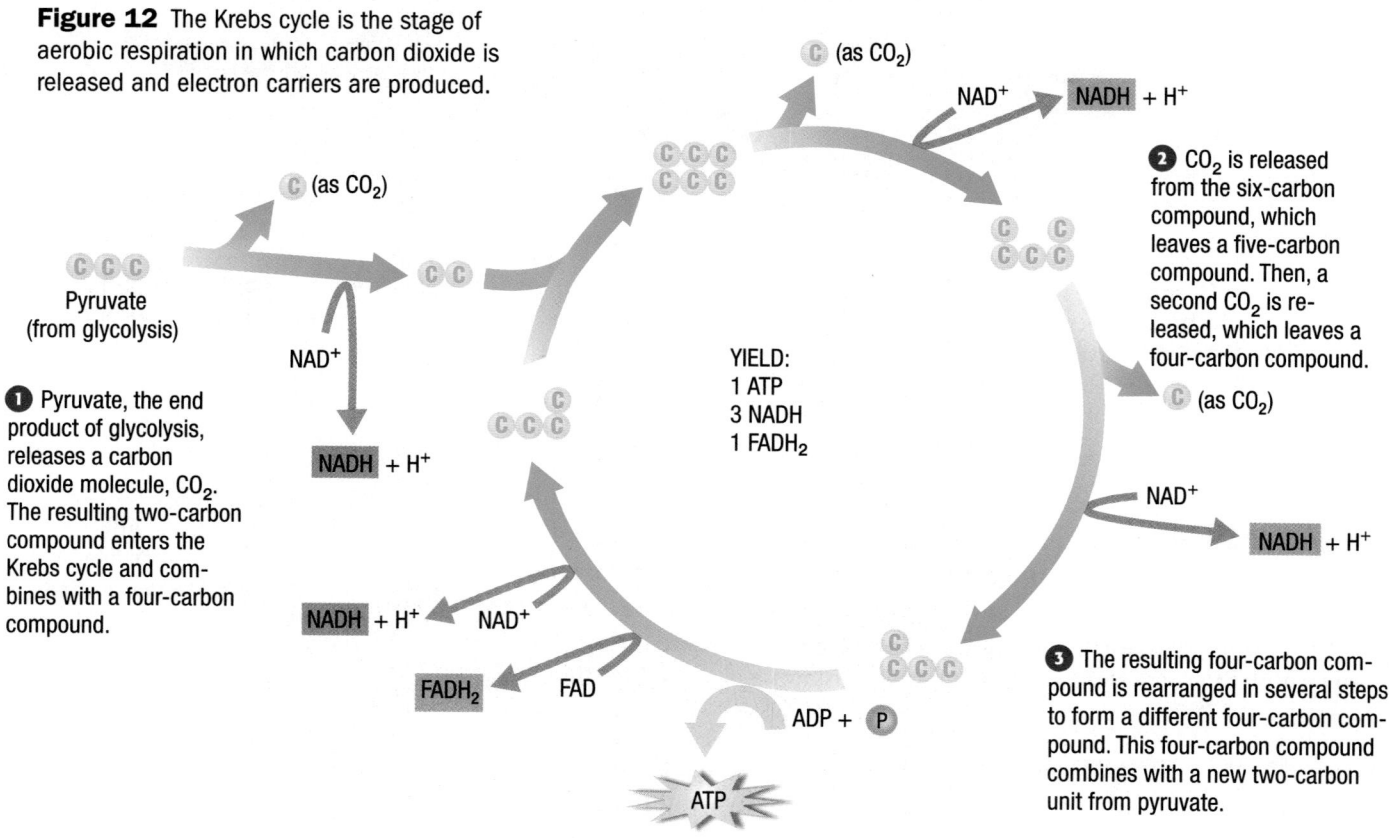

Figure 12 The Krebs cycle is the stage of aerobic respiration in which carbon dioxide is released and electron carriers are produced.

Ⓒ (as CO₂)

NAD⁺ NADH + H⁺

❷ CO₂ is released from the six-carbon compound, which leaves a five-carbon compound. Then, a second CO₂ is re-leased, which leaves a four-carbon compound.

Ⓒ (as CO₂)

Pyruvate (from glycolysis)

Ⓒ (as CO₂)

❶ Pyruvate, the end product of glycolysis, releases a carbon dioxide molecule, CO₂. The resulting two-carbon compound enters the Krebs cycle and com-bines with a four-carbon compound.

NAD⁺

NADH + H⁺

YIELD:
1 ATP
3 NADH
1 FADH₂

NAD⁺

NADH + H⁺

NADH + H⁺ NAD⁺

FADH₂ FAD

ADP + ⓟ

ATP

❸ The resulting four-carbon com-pound is rearranged in several steps to form a different four-carbon com-pound. This four-carbon compound combines with a new two-carbon unit from pyruvate.

Aerobic Respiration

Organisms such as humans can use oxygen to produce ATP effi-ciently through aerobic respiration. Pyruvate is broken down in the **Krebs cycle,** a series of reactions that produce electron carriers. The electron carriers enter an electron transport chain, which powers ATP synthase. Up to 34 ATP molecules can be produced from one glucose molecule in aerobic respiration.

Krebs Cycle The first stage of aerobic respiration, the Krebs cycle, is named for Hans Krebs, a German biochemist. He was awarded the Nobel Prize in 1953 for discovering it. As **Figure 12** shows, the Krebs cycle begins with pyruvate, which is produced during glycolysis. Pyruvate releases a carbon dioxide molecule to form a two-carbon compound. An enzyme attaches this two-carbon compound to a four-carbon compound and forms a six-carbon compound.

The six-carbon compound releases one carbon dioxide molecule and then another. Energy is released each time, which forms an electron carrier, NADH. The remaining four-carbon compound is converted to the four-carbon compound that began the cycle. This conversion takes place in a series of steps that produce ATP, then FADH₂, and another NADH. The four-carbon compound combines with a new two-carbon unit from pyruvate to continue the cycle.

Krebs cycle a series of biochemical reactions that convert pyruvate into carbon dioxide and water

Products of the Krebs Cycle Each time the carbon-carbon bonds are rearranged or broken, energy is released. ❯ **The total yield of energy-storing products from one time through the Krebs cycle is one ATP, three NADH, and one FADH$_2$.** Electron carriers transfer energy through the electron transport chain, which ultimately powers ATP synthase.

Electron Transport Chain The second stage of aerobic respiration takes place in the inner membranes of mitochondria. Recall that electrons pass through a series of molecules called an *electron transport chain,* as **Figure 13** shows. **❶** The electrons that are carried by NADH and FADH$_2$ pass through this chain. Energy is transferred into each molecule through which the electrons pass. Some of the molecules are hydrogen ion pumps. **❷** Energy from the electrons is used to actively transport hydrogen ions, H$^+$, out of the inner mitochondrial compartment. As H$^+$ ions accumulate in the outer compartment, a concentration gradient across the inner membrane is created.

ATP Production The enzyme ATP synthase is also present on the inner membranes of mitochondria. **❸** Hydrogen ions diffuse through a channel in this enzyme. This movement provides energy, which is used to produce several ATP molecules from ADP.

The Role of Oxygen At the end of the electron transport chain, the electrons have given up most of their energy. **❹** An oxygen atom combines with these electrons and two H$^+$ ions to form two water molecules, H$_2$O. If oxygen is not present, the electron transport chain stops. The electron carriers cannot be recycled, so the Krebs cycle also stops. Without oxygen, a cell can produce ATP only by glycolysis.

❯ **Reading Check** *Why is glycolysis important to the Krebs cycle?*

READING TOOLBOX

Pattern Puzzles Make a pattern puzzle to help you remember the steps in aerobic respiration.

Figure 13 Along the inner mitochondrial membrane, an electron transport chain produces a hydrogen ion gradient. The diffusion of hydrogen ions provides energy for the production of ATP by ATP synthase.

go.hrw.com
✳ **interact online**
Keyword: HX8PHRF13

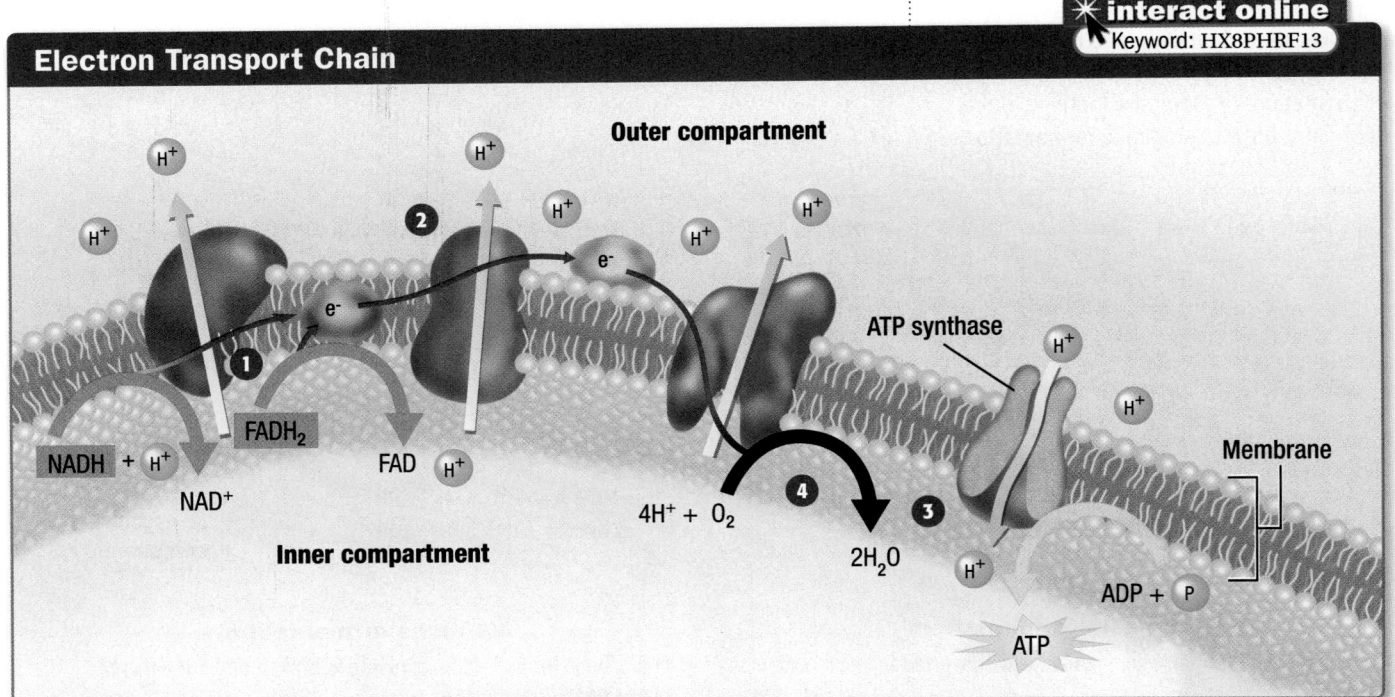

Electron Transport Chain

Outer compartment

ATP synthase

Membrane

NADH + H$^+$ FADH$_2$ FAD   H$^+$

NAD$^+$

Inner compartment

4H$^+$ + O$_2$ 2H$_2$O   ADP + P

ATP

Fermentation

ACADEMIC
VOCABULARY

transfer to carry or
remove something from
one thing to another

fermentation the breakdown of carbohydrates by enzymes, bacteria, yeasts, or mold in the
absence of oxygen

Many prokaryotes live entirely on the energy released in glycolysis. Recall that glycolysis produces two ATP molecules and one molecule of the electron carrier NADH. The NADH must be able to <u>transfer</u> its electrons to an acceptor so that NAD^+ is continuously available. Under anaerobic conditions, the electron transport chain, if present, does not work. Organisms must have another way to recycle NAD^+. So, electrons carried by NADH are transferred to pyruvate, which is produced during glycolysis. This process in which carbohydrates are broken down in the absence of oxygen, called **fermentation,** recycles the NAD^+ that is needed to continue making ATP through glycolysis. ❯ Fermentation enables glycolysis to continue supplying a cell with ATP in anaerobic conditions. Two types of fermentation are lactic acid fermentation and alcoholic fermentation.

Lactic Acid Fermentation Recall that the end products of glycolysis are three-carbon pyruvate molecules. In some organisms, pyruvate accepts electrons and hydrogen from NADH. Pyruvate is converted to lactic acid in a process called *lactic acid fermentation,* as **Figure 14** shows. Lactic acid fermentation also occurs in the muscles of animals, including humans. During vigorous exercise, muscle cells must operate without enough oxygen. So, glycolysis becomes the only source of ATP as long as the glucose supply lasts. For glycolysis to continue, NAD^+ is recycled by lactic acid fermentation.

Alcoholic Fermentation In other organisms, an enzyme removes carbon dioxide from the three-carbon pyruvate to form a two-carbon molecule. Then, a second enzyme adds electrons and hydrogen from NADH to the molecule to form ethanol (ethyl alcohol) in a process called *alcoholic fermentation*. In this process, NAD^+ is recycled and glycolysis can continue to produce ATP.

❯ **Reading Check** *Explain how fermentation recycles NAD^+.*

Figure 14 When oxygen is not present, cells recycle NAD^+ through fermentation. ❯ Compare lactic acid fermentation with alcoholic fermentation.

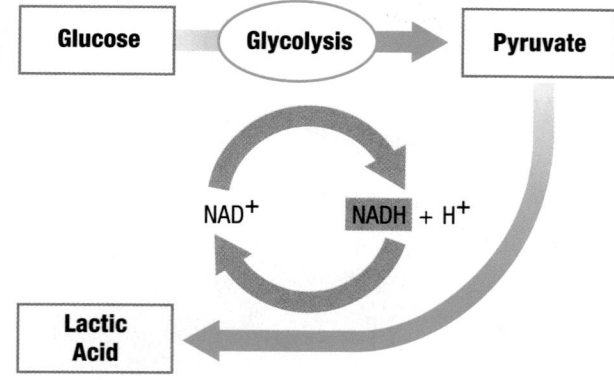

Lactic acid fermentation

In lactic acid fermentation, pyruvate is converted to lactic acid.

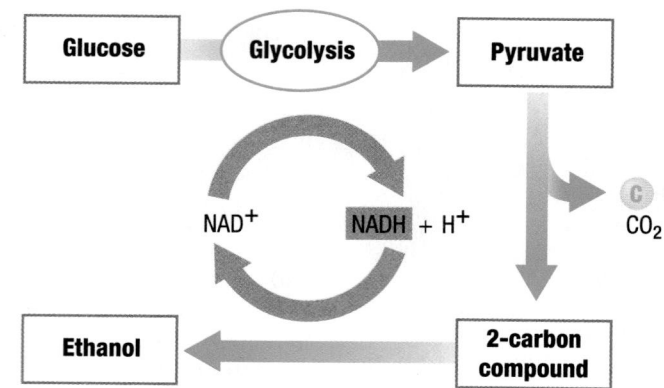

Alcoholic fermentation

In alcoholic fermentation, pyruvate is broken down to ethanol, releasing carbon dioxide.

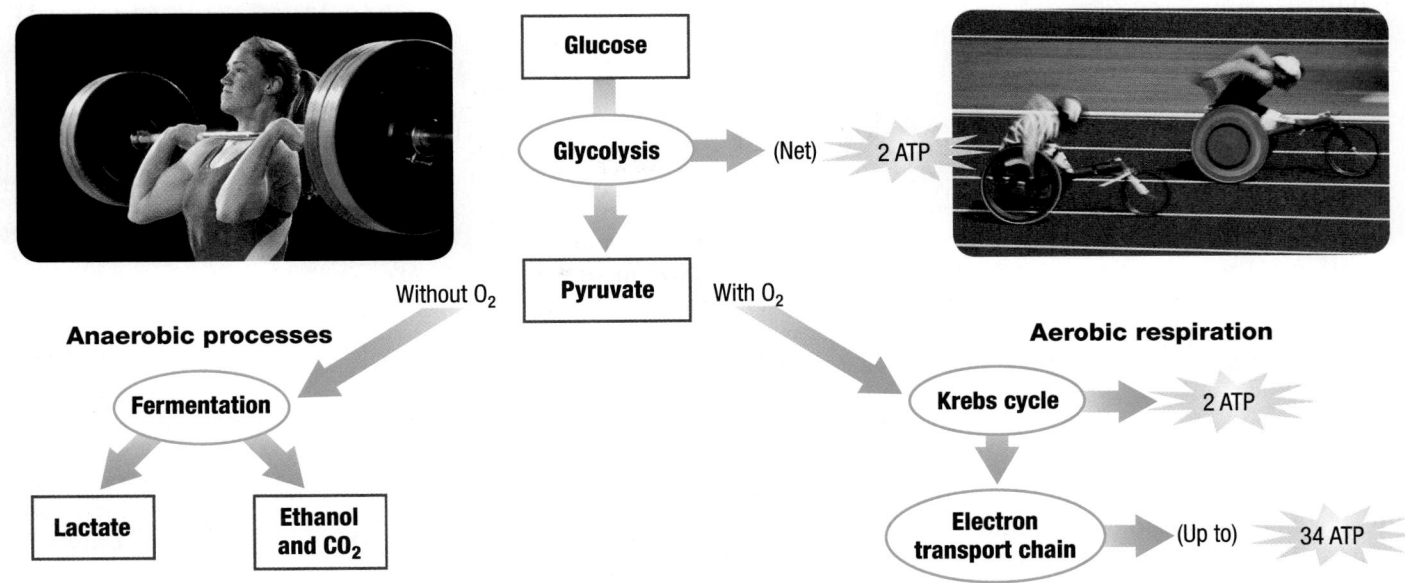

Efficiency of Cellular Respiration The total amount of ATP that a cell harvests from each glucose molecule depends on the presence or absence of oxygen. **Figure 15** compares the amount of ATP produced in both cases.

In the first stage of cellular respiration, glucose is broken down to pyruvate during glycolysis. Glycolysis is an anaerobic process, and it results in a net gain of two ATP molecules.

In the second stage of cellular respiration, pyruvate either passes through the Krebs cycle or undergoes fermentation. When oxygen is not present, fermentation occurs. The NAD^+ that is recycled during fermentation allows glycolysis to continue producing ATP.

Cells release energy most efficiently when oxygen is present because they make most of their ATP during aerobic respiration. For each molecule of glucose that is broken down, as many as two ATP molecules are made during the Krebs cycle. The Krebs cycle feeds NADH and $FADH_2$ to the electron transport chain. The electron transport chain can produce up to 34 ATP molecules.

Figure 15 Most ATP is produced during aerobic respiration. ❯ **Which cellular respiration process produces ATP molecules most efficiently?**

Section 3 Review

❯ KEY IDEAS

1. **List** the products of glycolysis, and explain the role of each of these products in both aerobic respiration and anaerobic respiration.

2. **Summarize** the roles of the Krebs cycle and the electron transport chain during aerobic respiration.

3. **Describe** the role of fermentation in the second stage of cellular respiration.

CRITICAL THINKING

4. **Inferring Conclusions** Excess glucose in your blood is stored in your liver as glycogen. How might your body sense when to convert glucose to glycogen and glycogen back to glucose again?

ALTERNATIVE ASSESSMENT

5. **Analyzing Methods** Research ways that fermentation is used in food preparation. Find out what kinds of microorganisms are used in cultured dairy products, such as yogurt, sour cream, and some cheeses. Research the role of alcoholic fermentation by yeast in bread making. Prepare an oral report to summarize your findings.

Life in a Biosphere

BIOTECHNOLOGY

The Biosphere 2 research facility has seven ecosystems that mirror those on Earth, including a desert, a savannah, a saltwater ocean that contains a million gallons of water, an Amazonian rain forest, a mangrove marsh, an area of intensive agriculture, and a habitat for humans. The giant, self-contained system of Biosphere 2 is a miniature version of the flows and balances that occur on Earth. But in Biosphere 2, they are occurring at a much faster pace.

A World Under Glass

Located on 3.15 acres in southern Arizona, this miniature, airtight world is sealed on the bottom by a stainless steel liner and on the top by a steel and glass structure. The seven ecosystems were built from scratch with soils, water, and plant and animal life from around the world. Biosphere 2 has more than 1,000 sensors that monitor the vital statistics of this living laboratory by measuring temperature, humidity, oxygen, carbon dioxide, and other qualities of the air and soil.

Biospherians Eight researchers, known as *biospherians,* lived entirely within the facility. They controlled the technical systems and gathered results for more than 60 research projects, including studies of carbon dioxide and oxygen cycles, soil composition, coral reef health, agricultural pest management, and waste and water recycling.

Quick Project Biosphere 2 research is being used to help develop environmental technologies for use in space. Find out details about the Mars on Earth Project and its connection to Biosphere 2.

Biosphere 2 The research facility opened in 1991 as an ecological experiment designed for research, education, and the development of environmental technologies.

Chapter 9 **Lab**

⏱ 45 min

Objectives

> Demonstrate how carbon dioxide affects bromothymol blue when added to the indicator solution.

> Describe the effect of temperature on carbon dioxide production by yeast.

Materials

- safety goggles
- disposable gloves
- lab apron
- plastic cups, clear (4)
- room temperature water
- bromothymol blue
- drinking straw, plastic
- warm water
- ice water
- baker's yeast
- ¼ teaspoon
- hand lens
- sugar

Safety

Cellular Respiration

In cellular respiration, sugar is broken down and energy is released. This energy is harnessed and used to produce ATP. In addition to releasing energy, respiration generates reaction byproducts such as carbon dioxide gas. Carbon dioxide readily dissolves in water to produce a mild acid. This change to an acid can be confirmed through the use of an acid-base indicator, such as bromothymol blue. In this activity, you will use bromothymol blue to confirm respiration, and you will explore how temperature may affect this metabolic process.

Procedure

1 ◇ ◇ ◆ Put on safety goggles, gloves, and a lab apron. Fill a clean plastic cup halfway with room temperature water. Add several drops of bromothymol blue to the water. Swirl to mix the solution. ◆ **CAUTION: Bromothymol blue is a skin and eye irritant.**

2 Insert a clean straw into the solution. Gently blow a steady stream of air through the straw. Note any changes in the solution's appearance. **CAUTION: Be careful not to accidentally drink the solution while blowing into the straw.**

3 Label three plastic cups, "A," "B" and "C."

4 Fill cup A with ice water, fill cup B with room temperature water, and fill cup C with warm water. Add several drops of bromothymol blue solution to each cup to ensure a uniform appearance.

5 Add ¼ teaspoon of baker's yeast to each cup. Swirl the cups, and observe the appearance of the solutions every 30 s. After 5 min, examine the surface of each solution with a hand lens.

6 ◇ ◆ Clean up your lab materials according to your teacher's instructions. Wash your hands before leaving the lab.

Analyze and Conclude

1. **Drawing Conclusions** What happened to the indicator as exhaled air bubbled through the solution? What caused this change?

2. **SCIENTIFIC METHODS** **Evaluating Results** Did the yeast produce a similar color change? Explain your answer.

3. **SCIENTIFIC METHODS** **Evaluating Results** Did temperature affect the yeast's production of carbon dioxide? Explain your answer.

4. **SCIENTIFIC METHODS** **Summarizing Results** What did you observe on the surface of the solutions?

5. **Predicting Outcomes** Will adding sugar to the yeast solution affect the respiration rate? Make a guess. Then, design a method for inquiry that would test the effects of various sugar concentrations on yeast metabolism.

go.hrw.com
SUPER SUMMARY
Keyword: HX8PHRS

Key Ideas	Key Terms

1 Energy in Living Systems

> Organisms use and store energy in the chemical bonds of organic compounds.

> Metabolism involves either using energy to build organic molecules or breaking down organic molecules in which energy is stored. Organic molecules contain carbon. Therefore, an organism's metabolism is part of Earth's carbon cycle.

> In cells, chemical energy is gradually released in a series of chemical reactions that are assisted by enzymes.

photosynthesis (197)
cellular respiration (198)
ATP (198)
ATP synthase (201)
electron transport chain (201)

2 Photosynthesis

> In plants, light energy is harvested by pigments located in the thylakoid membrane of chloroplasts.

> During photosynthesis, one electron transport chain provides energy used to make ATP, while the other provides energy to make NADPH.

> In the final stage of photosynthesis, chemical energy is stored by being used to produce sugar molecules from the carbon in the gas carbon dioxide.

> Light intensity, carbon dioxide concentration, and temperature are three environmental factors that affect photosynthesis.

thylakoid (202)
pigment (203)
chlorophyll (203)
Calvin cycle (206)

3 Cellular Respiration

> The breaking of a sugar molecule by glycolysis results in a net gain of two ATP molecules.

> The total yield of energy-storing products from one time through the Krebs cycle is one ATP, three NADH, and one $FADH_2$. Electron carriers transfer energy through the electron transport chain, which ultimately powers ATP synthase.

> Fermentation enables glycolysis to continue supplying a cell with ATP in anaerobic conditions.

glycolysis (209)
anaerobic (209)
aerobic (209)
Krebs cycle (210)
fermentation (212)

1. **Describing Space** Use spatial language to describe what takes place along the electron transport chain during aerobic respiration.

2. **Concept Map** Make a concept map that shows how photosynthesis and cellular respiration are related. Try to include the following terms in your map: *glycolysis, Krebs cycle, electron transport chain, Calvin cycle, fermentation,* and *NADH.*

Using Key Terms

In your own words, write a definition for each of the following terms.

3. *ATP*

4. *Calvin cycle*

5. *aerobic*

6. *Krebs cycle*

7. *fermentation*

Use each of the following pairs of key terms in the same sentence.

8. *photosynthesis* and *thylakoid*

9. *pigment* and *chlorophyll*

10. *glycolysis* and *anaerobic*

Understanding Key Ideas

11. Energy flows through living systems from
    a. the sun, to heterotrophs, and then to autotrophs.
    b. the environment, to heterotrophs, and then to autotrophs.
    c. the sun, to autotrophs, and then to heterotrophs.
    d. autotrophs, to the environment, and then to heterotrophs.

12. The products of photosynthesis that begin cellular respiration are
    a. ATP and water.
    b. NADP⁺ and hydrogen.
    c. carbon dioxide and water.
    d. organic compounds and oxygen.

13. Which of the following occurs in lactic acid fermentation?
    a. Oxygen is consumed.
    b. Lactic acid is converted into pyruvate.
    c. NAD^+ is regenerated for use in glycolysis.
    d. Electrons pass through the electron transport chain.

14. Aerobic respiration involves all of the following *except*
    a. ATP.   c. mitochondria.
    b. glycolysis.   d. the Krebs cycle.

Use the graph to answer the following question.

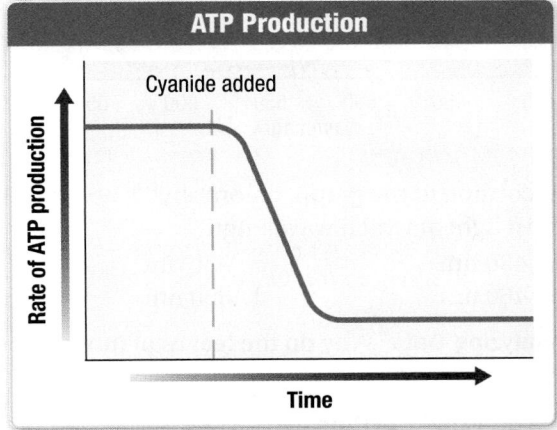

15. **Interpreting Graphics** The graph shows the rate of ATP production by a culture of yeast cells over time. At the time indicated by the dashed line, cyanide was added to the culture. Cyanide blocks the flow of electrons to O_2 from the electron transport chain in mitochondria. Explain why adding cyanide affects ATP production in the way shown by the graph.

Explaining Key Ideas

16. **Differentiate** between autotrophs and heterotrophs.

17. **Identify** the primary source of energy for humans.

18. **Predict** what might happen to photosynthesis if ATP were not produced in the light reactions.

19. **Relate** the rate of photosynthesis to light levels.

20. **Compare** the two stages of cellular respiration.

21. Define the role that oxygen plays in the electron transport chain.

22. Compare the efficiency of glycolysis with the efficiency of aerobic respiration.

Using Science Graphics

The graph shows the colors of light that three different photosynthetic pigments absorb. Use the graph to answer the following questions.

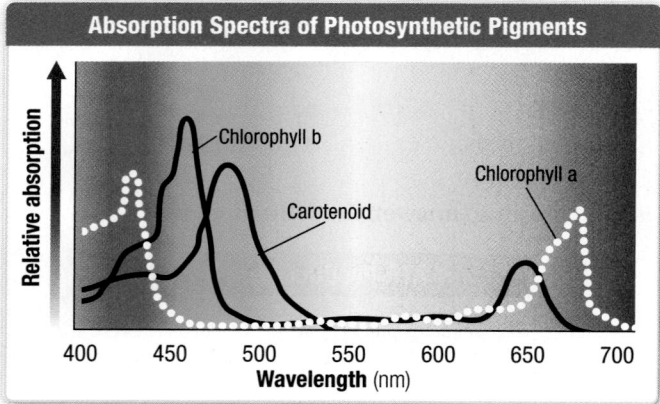

Absorption Spectra of Photosynthetic Pigments

Relative absorption

Chlorophyll b

Chlorophyll a

Carotenoid

400   450   500   550   600   650   700
Wavelength (nm)

23. According to the graph, chlorophyll *b* absorbs the most light at which wavelength?
a. 430 nm   **c.** 530 nm
b. 460 nm   **d.** 650 nm

24. Analyzing Data Why do the leaves of most plants appear green?

25. Recognizing Relationships How is the color of fall leaves related to the pigments in chloroplasts?

Critical Thinking

26. Evaluating Viewpoints State whether you think the following viewpoint can be supported, and justify your answer. "If Earth's early atmosphere had been rich in oxygen, photosynthetic organisms would not have been able to evolve."

27. Evaluating Differences Compare the energy flow in photosynthesis to the energy flow in cellular respiration.

28. Comparing Functions Explain why cellular respiration is more efficient when oxygen is present in cells than when oxygen is not present in cells.

29. Inferring Relationships What combination of environmental factors affects the rate of photosynthesis?

30. Evaluating Results Some yeast cells can use fermentation or cellular respiration. These yeast cells consume glucose much more slowly if oxygen is present than if oxygen is absent. Explain this observation.

31. Inferring Relationships How does cellular respiration depend on photosynthesis?

Writing Skills

32. Organizing Information Many plants have pores called *stomata* that take in CO_2 at night and release it during the day. These plants are called *CAM plants,* and some examples include cactuses and pineapple trees. Write a report about these types of plants, and summarize why this adaptation is an advantage for plants living in a hot, dry climate.

Alternative Assessment

33. Finding and Communicating Information Use the library or Internet resources to research how exercise physiologists regulate the diet and training of athletes. Find out how diets vary according to the needs of each athlete. Research the relationship between exercise and metabolism. Present your findings to your class.

34. Using Graphing Skills Create a poster that illustrates how an organism's metabolism is part of Earth's carbon cycle. Make drawings, create images on a computer, or use photos from magazines or online resources to illustrate your poster. Display your poster in the classroom.

Science Concepts

1. What pigment causes a plant to look green?

  A NADH   **C** carotenoid

  B NAPH   **D** chlorophyll

2. What is the product of the electron transport chains of photosynthesis?

  F water   **H** pyruvate

  G glucose   **J** ATP and NADPH

3. The oxygen that is produced during photosynthesis comes directly from the

  A absorption of light.

  B mitochondrial membranes.

  C splitting of water molecules.

  D splitting of carbon dioxide molecules.

Use the diagram of a chloroplast to answer the following question.

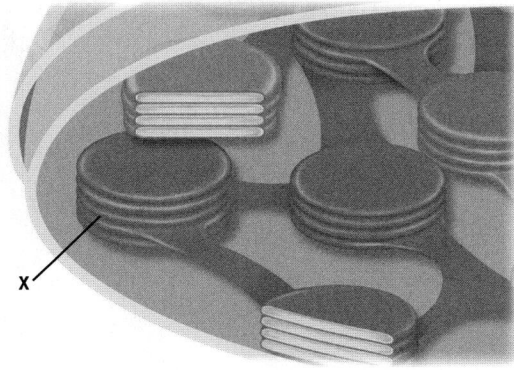

4. Which of the following correctly identifies the structure marked *X* and the activities that take place there?

  F stroma—Calvin cycle

  G thylakoid—Calvin cycle

  H stroma—light reactions

  J thylakoid—light reactions

5. Which of the following is involved in the aerobic part of cellular respiration?

  A ATP   **C** lactic acid

  B glycolysis   **D** fermentation

6. Which of the following is *not* a product of the Krebs cycle?

  F CO_2 **H** $FADH_2$

  G ATP   **J** ethyl alcohol

Using Science Graphics

The graph shows data on photosynthesis in one type of plant. Use the graph and your knowledge of science to answer the following question.

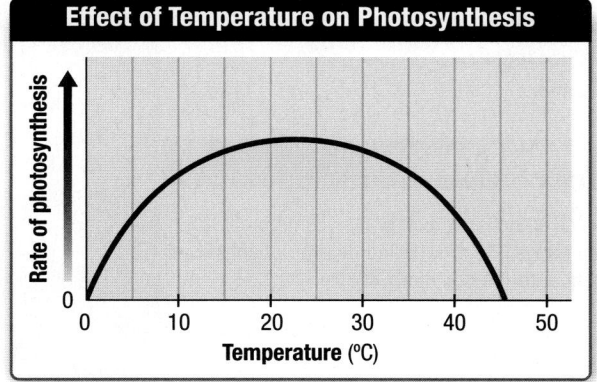

7. Which statement is supported by the data?

  A Photosynthesis does not occur at 0 °C.

  B The rate of photosynthesis at 40 °C is greater than the rate at 20 °C.

  C The optimum temperature for photosynthesis is approximately 46 °C.

  D The rate of photosynthesis increases as temperature increases from 25 °C to 30 °C.

Writing Skills

8. Short Response The inner membrane of a mitochondrion is folded. These folds are called *cristae*. How might cellular respiration be different if the inner mitochondrial membrane were not folded?

Chapter 10

Cell Growth and Division

Preview

1 Cell Reproduction
Why Cells Reproduce
Chromosomes
Preparing for Cell Division

2 Mitosis
Eukaryotic Cell Cycle
Stages of Mitosis
Cytokinesis

3 Regulation
Controls
Checkpoints
Cancer

Why It Matters

The cell is the basic unit of life—common to all living things. The growth and division of cells is essential to the continuity of life.

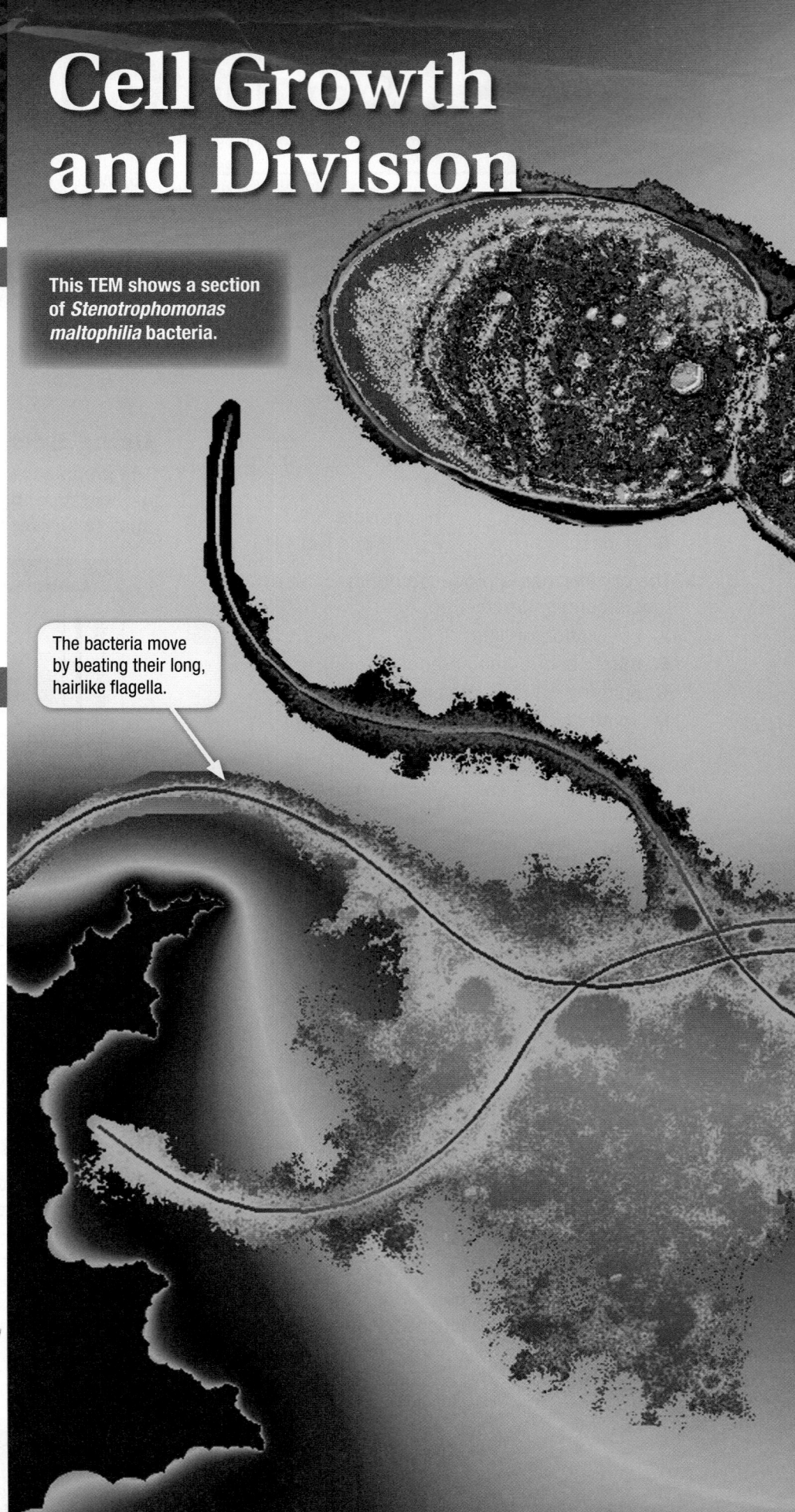

This TEM shows a section of *Stenotrophomonas maltophilia* bacteria.

The bacteria move by beating their long, hairlike flagella.

Inquiry Lab

15 min

Whitefish Cells

As an embryo develops, its cells divide rapidly. Few of these cells remain in a resting state, so when observing them, you will see groups of these cells in various stages of division.

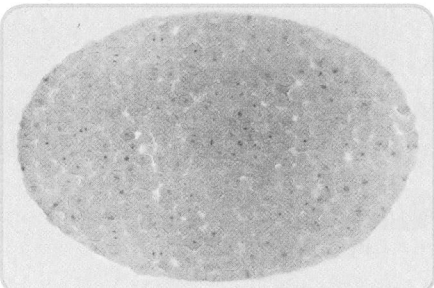

Procedure

1. Place a slide of whitefish cells on the stage of a microscope. Examine the cells under low power. Do all of the cells look alike? If not, how do they differ? Draw several representative cells.

2. Carefully switch to high power. Slowly scan the slide, and look for obvious differences between cells. Pay particular attention to the appearance of the nuclei.

3. Make a sketch of each distinct pattern of cells that you see.

Analysis

1. **Describe** any differences you observed in the nuclei of these cells.

2. **Determine** whether all the cells you observed had a distinct nucleus. Explain.

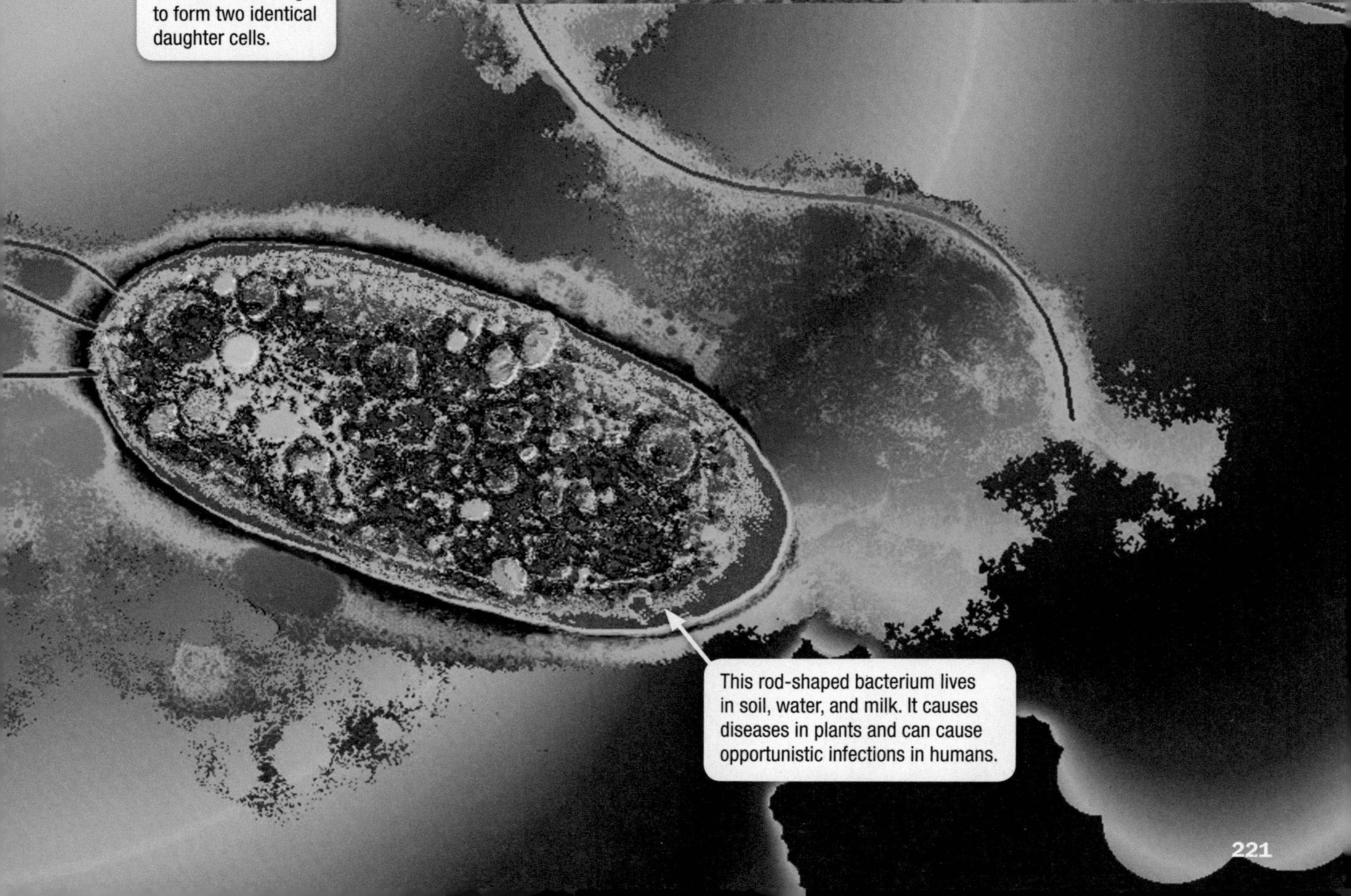

This cell is dividing to form two identical daughter cells.

This rod-shaped bacterium lives in soil, water, and milk. It causes diseases in plants and can cause opportunistic infections in humans.

221

READING TOOLBOX

These reading tools can help you learn the material in this chapter. For more information on how to use these and other tools, see **Appendix: Reading and Study Skills.**

Using Words

Word Parts You can tell a lot about a word by taking it apart and examining its prefix and root.

Your Turn Use the information in the table to define the following terms.
1. *chromosome*
2. *mitosis*

Word Parts		
Word part	**Type**	**Meaning**
mito-	prefix	thread
chromo-	prefix	color
-osis	suffix	condition or process
-some	root	body

Using Language

Cause and Effect In biological processes, one step leads to another step. When reading, you can often recognize these cause-and-effect relationships by words that indicate a result, such as *so, consequently, if-then,* and *as a result.*

Your Turn Identify the cause and effect in the following sentences.
1. People often shiver as a result of being cold.
2. The light got brighter, so the pupil of the eye got smaller.
3. If the cell passes the G_2 checkpoint, then the cell may begin to divide.

Using Graphic Organizers

Pattern Puzzles You can use pattern puzzles to help you remember sequential information. Exchanging puzzles with a classmate can help you study.

Your Turn Make a pattern puzzle for the stages of mitosis.
1. Write down the steps of the process. On a sheet of notebook paper, write down one step per line. Do not number the steps.
2. Cut the sheet of paper into strips so that each strip of paper has only one step. Shuffle the paper strips so that they are out of sequence.
3. Place the strips in their proper sequence. Confirm the order of the process by checking your text or class notes.

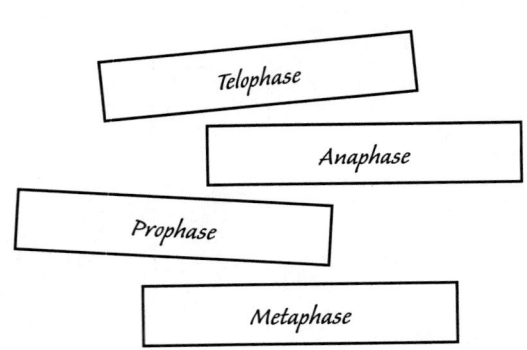

Key Ideas	Key Terms	Why It Matters
❯ Why do cells divide? ❯ How is DNA packaged into the nucleus? ❯ How do cells prepare for division?	gene nucleosome chromosome chromatid chromatin centromere histone	Cells are busy making more cells. The reproduction of cells allows you to grow and heal.

The adult human body produces roughly 2 trillion cells per day. The new cells are exact copies of the cells they replace. This process is called *cell reproduction*. Some cells, such as hair and skin cells, are replaced frequently throughout your life. Other cells, such as brain and nerve cells, are rarely produced after infancy.

Why Cells Reproduce

As the body of a multicellular organism grows larger, its cells do not also grow large. Instead, the body grows by producing more cells. New cells are needed to help tissues and organs grow. Even after organisms reach adulthood, old cells die and new cells take their place. This replacement and renewal is important for keeping the body healthy. New cells also replace damaged cells. As **Figure 1** shows, the body repairs a wound by making more cells.

Cell Size A cell grows larger by building more cell products. To do this, the cell must take in more nutrients, process them, and get rid of wastes. Recall that a cell's ability to exchange substances is limited by its surface area–to-volume ratio. As a cell gets larger, substances must travel farther to reach where they are needed.

Cell Maintenance The work of cells is done by proteins. As a cell gets larger, more proteins are required to maintain its function. Recall that the instructions for making these proteins are copied from the cell's DNA. If the cell gets too large, DNA instructions cannot be copied quickly enough to make the proteins that the cell needs to support itself. Thus, cell size is also limited by the cell's DNA.

Making New Cells Cell division can solve the problems of cell size. Each "daughter" cell has a higher surface area–to-volume ratio than its parent does. Each new cell also gets an entire copy of the cell's DNA. ❯ **Because larger cells are more difficult to maintain, cells divide when they grow to a certain size.**

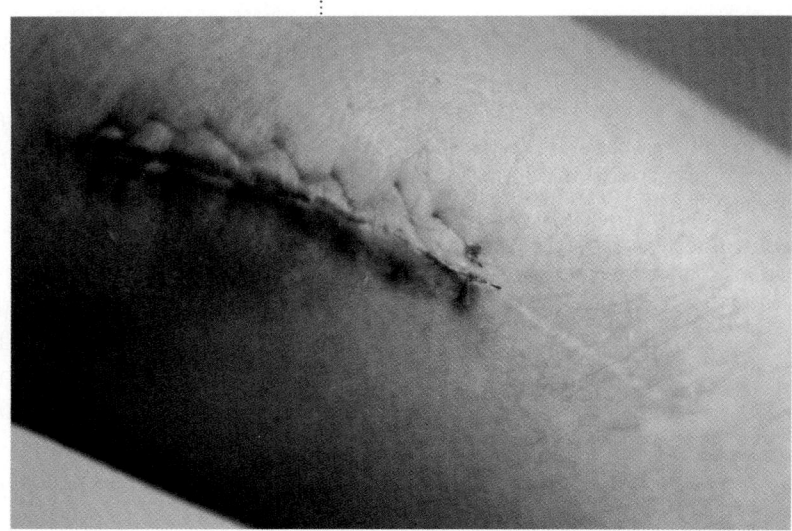

Figure 1 When these stitches are removed, this cut will be healed. Cell division enables the body to repair a wound.

QuickLab

⏰ 15 min

Chromosome Package

DNA is condensed to reduce the space that it occupies in the cell. In eukaryotic cells, the linear DNA molecule is condensed by being wrapped around a core of proteins.

Procedure

❶ Scrunch a **1 m length of kite string** into a wad. Cover this wad with a piece of **plastic wrap.**

❷ Wind another **1 m length of string** tightly and uniformly around a **paper clip.** Cover this shape with another piece of plastic wrap.

Analysis

1. **Identify** what the string, the plastic wrap, and the paper clip represent in each model.

2. **Compare** the volumes of space that the two models occupy.

3. **CRITICAL THINKING** **Evaluating Models** Describe an object that would be more effective than a paper clip as a core to wrap the string around. Explain your answer.

---

gene a unit of heredity that consists of a segment of nucleic acid that codes for a functional unit of RNA or protein

chromosome in a eukaryotic cell, one of the structures in the nucleus that are made up of DNA and protein; in a prokaryotic cell, the main ring of DNA

chromatin the substance of which eukaryotic chromosomes are composed

histone a type of protein molecule found in the chromosomes of eukaryotic cells but not prokaryotic cells

nucleosome (NOO klee uh SOHM) a eukaryotic structural unit of chromatin that consists of DNA wound around a core of histone proteins

chromatid one of the two strands of a chromosome that become visible during meiosis or mitosis

centromere the region of the chromosome that holds the two sister chromatids together during mitosis

Chromosomes

Recall that a cell's activity is directed by its DNA. The large molecule of DNA is organized into hereditary units called **genes.** A gene is a segment of DNA that codes for RNA and protein. The simplest organisms have thousands of genes. Each cell has a large amount of DNA that must be condensed into a very small volume. DNA is organized and packaged into structures called **chromosomes.**

Prokaryotic Chromosome A prokaryotic cell has a single circular molecule of DNA. This loop of DNA contains thousands of genes. A prokaryotic chromosome is condensed through repeated twisting or winding, like a rubber band twisted upon itself many times.

Eukaryotic Chromosome The challenge of packaging DNA into the eukaryotic nucleus is much greater. Eukaryotic cells contain many more genes arranged on several linear DNA molecules. A human cell contains 46 separate, linear DNA molecules that are packaged into 46 chromosomes. ❯ Eukaryotic DNA is packaged into highly condensed chromosome structures with the help of many proteins. The DNA and proteins make up a substance called **chromatin.**

Forms of Chromatin The first level of packaging is done by a class of proteins called **histones.** A group of eight histones come together to form a disc-shaped histone core. As **Figure 2** shows, the long DNA molecule is wound around a series of histone cores in a regular manner. The structure made up of a histone core and the DNA around it is called a **nucleosome.** Under an electron microscope, this level of packaging resembles beads on a string. The string of nucleosomes line up in a spiral to form a cord that is 30 nm in diameter.

Packaging During Cell Division During most of a cell's life, its chromosomes exist as coiled or uncoiled nucleosomes. As the cell prepares to divide, the chromosomes condense even further. This ensures that the extremely long DNA molecules do not get tangled up during cell division. The 30-nm fiber (the nucleosome cord) forms loops that are attached to a protein scaffold. These looped domains then coil into the final, most highly condensed form of the chromosome. Many dense loops of chromatin form the rod-shaped structures that can be seen in regular light microscopes.

Chromosome Structure A fully condensed, duplicated chromosome is shown in **Figure 2.** Each of the two thick strands, called a **chromatid,** is made of a single, long molecule of DNA. Identical pairs, called *sister chromatids,* are held together at a region called the **centromere.** During cell division, the sister chromatids are separated at the centromere, and one ends up in each daughter cell. This ensures that each new cell has the same genetic information as the parent cell.

❯ **Reading Check** *What is a chromatid? (See the Appendix for answers to Reading Checks.)*

Word Parts The prefix *tel-* means "end." If *centromere* means a "central part," what do you think *telomere* means?

Figure 2 A eukaryotic chromosome consists of DNA tightly coiled around proteins. As a cell prepares to divide, the duplicated chromosomes are condensed. ❯ **Why do chromosomes condense during cell division?**

Eukaryotic Chromosome Structure

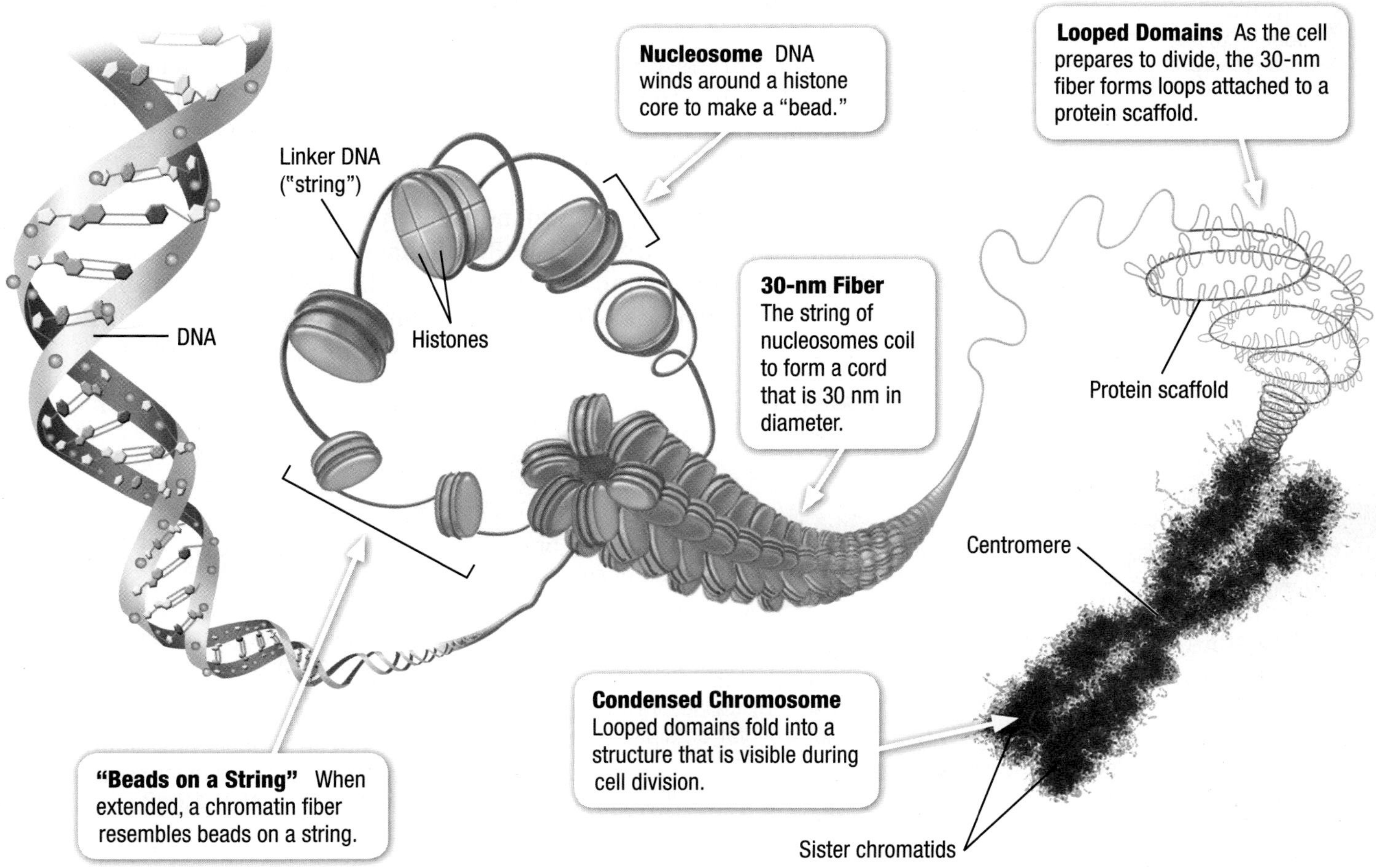

Nucleosome DNA winds around a histone core to make a "bead."

Linker DNA ("string")

DNA

Histones

Looped Domains As the cell prepares to divide, the 30-nm fiber forms loops attached to a protein scaffold.

30-nm Fiber The string of nucleosomes coil to form a cord that is 30 nm in diameter.

Protein scaffold

Centromere

Condensed Chromosome Looped domains fold into a structure that is visible during cell division.

"Beads on a String" When extended, a chromatin fiber resembles beads on a string.

Sister chromatids

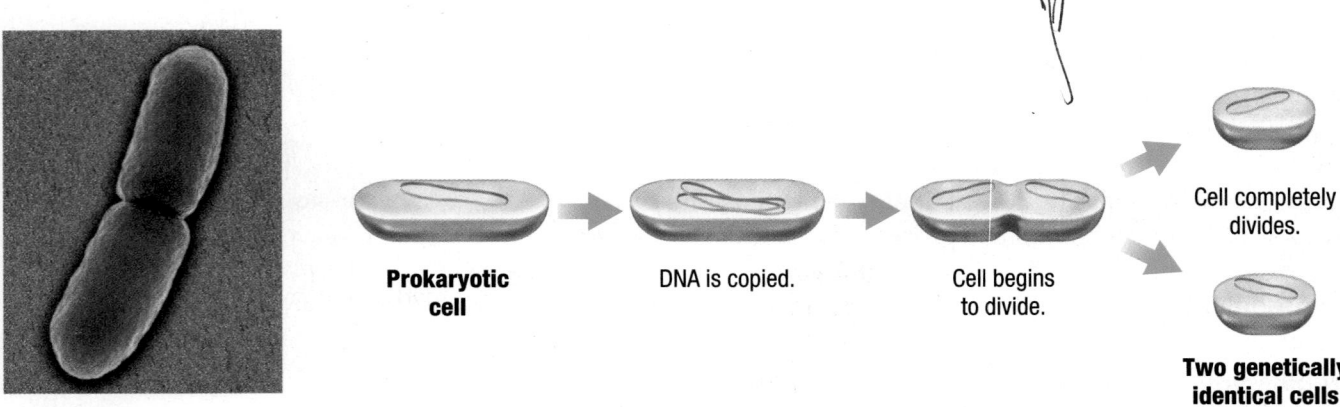

Prokaryotic cell → DNA is copied. → Cell begins to divide. → Cell completely divides. → Two genetically identical cells

Cell dividing

Figure 3 A prokaryotic cell divides by copying its single, circular chromosome and building a cell membrane between the two copies. A new cell wall forms around the membrane, squeezing the cell. Eventually it pinches off into two independent daughter cells.

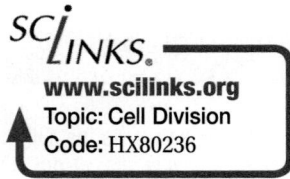

www.scilinks.org
Topic: Cell Division
Code: HX80236

ACADEMIC VOCABULARY

complex having many parts or functions

Preparing for Cell Division

All new cells are produced by the division of preexisting cells. The process of cell division involves more than cutting a cell into two pieces. Each new cell must have all of the equipment needed to stay alive. ❯ **All newly-formed cells require DNA, so before a cell divides, a copy of DNA is made for each daughter cell.** This way, the new cells will function in the same way as the cells that they replace.

Prokaryotes In prokaryotic cells, the circular DNA molecule is attached to the inner cell membrane. As **Figure 3** shows, the cytoplasm is divided when a new cell membrane forms between the two DNA copies. Meanwhile the cell continues to grow until it nearly doubles in size. The cell wall also continues to form around the new cell membrane, pushing inward. The cell is constricted in the middle, like a long balloon being squeezed near the center. Eventually the dividing prokaryote is pinched into two independent daughter cells, each of which has its own circular DNA molecule.

Eukaryotes The reproduction eukaryotic cells is more complex than that of prokaryotic cells. Recall that eukaryotic cells have many organelles. In order to form two living cells, each daughter cell must contain enough of each organelle to carry out its functions. The DNA within the nucleus must also be copied, sorted, and separated.

❯ **Reading Check** *Where does a prokaryotic cell begin to divide?*

Section 1 Review

❯ **KEY IDEAS**

1. **List** two reasons for cell reproduction in multicellular organisms.
2. **Describe** three levels of structure in the DNA packaging system found within a eukaryotic nucleus.

3. **Explain** why daughter cells are identical to the parent cell.

CRITICAL THINKING

4. **Evaluating Conclusions** If cells constantly double in number each time they divide, why doesn't a multicellular organism continue to grow in size?
5. **Inferring Relationships** Why do chromosomes condense before they divide?

MATH SKILLS

6. **Exponents** Imagine you are observing a cell that divides once every hour for 12 h. Assume that none of the cells die during this period. How many cells would exist after each hour? How many cells would exist after 12 h?

Replacement Parts

WEIRD SCIENCE

If you look closely at the camouflaged green anole lizard at right, you will see that it appears to be growing a new tail. The process by which an organism replaces or restores a lost or amputated body part is called *regeneration.* A series of rapid cell divisions allows certain organisms to regenerate certain lost parts.

Sea Star Comets

To keep sea stars from destroying oyster beds, oyster fishermen used to chop up sea stars and throw the pieces back into the sea. Unfortunately, this practice increased the number of sea stars! Some sea stars can regenerate their entire bodies from just a small piece of arm. Specimens such as the one shown below are sometimes called "comets." The regeneration of these sea stars is possible because they keep their vital organs in their arms.

Tail Regeneration Lizards, such as the gecko at left, are well known for their ability to "release" their tails. Lizards use this ability as a defense mechanism to escape predators. The broken piece of tail twists and wiggles, which diverts the attention of the predator while the lizard escapes. When the tail regenerates, it is made up of cartilage, rather than bone.

Research Investigate and explain compensatory hypertrophy, a process in mammals that is similar to the regeneration of body parts. Identify an organ in humans that is capable of compensatory hypertrophy.

Sea star "comet"

Key Ideas	Key Terms	Why It Matters
❯ What are the phases of the eukaryotic cell cycle? ❯ What are the four stages of mitosis? ❯ How does cytokinesis occur?	cell cycle cytokinesis interphase spindle mitosis centrosome	The events of the cell cycle ensure that new cells will be just like the old cell.

Unlike prokaryotic cells, eukaryotic cells cannot simply be pinched into two new cells. The physical division of one cell into two cells requires many preparations.

Eukaryotic Cell Cycle

The **cell cycle** is a repeating sequence of cellular growth and division during the life of a cell. ❯ **The life of a eukaryotic cell cycles through phases of growth, DNA replication, preparation for cell division, and division of the nucleus and cytoplasm.** The cell cycle is made up of five phases, shown in **Figure 4.** The first three phases together are known as **interphase.** The remaining two phases make up cell division.

Interphase During interphase, the cell is not dividing. It is growing and preparing to divide. Different types of cells spend different amounts of time in interphase. Cells that divide often, such as skin cells, spend less time in interphase. Cells that divide seldom, such as nerve cells, spend most of their time in interphase.

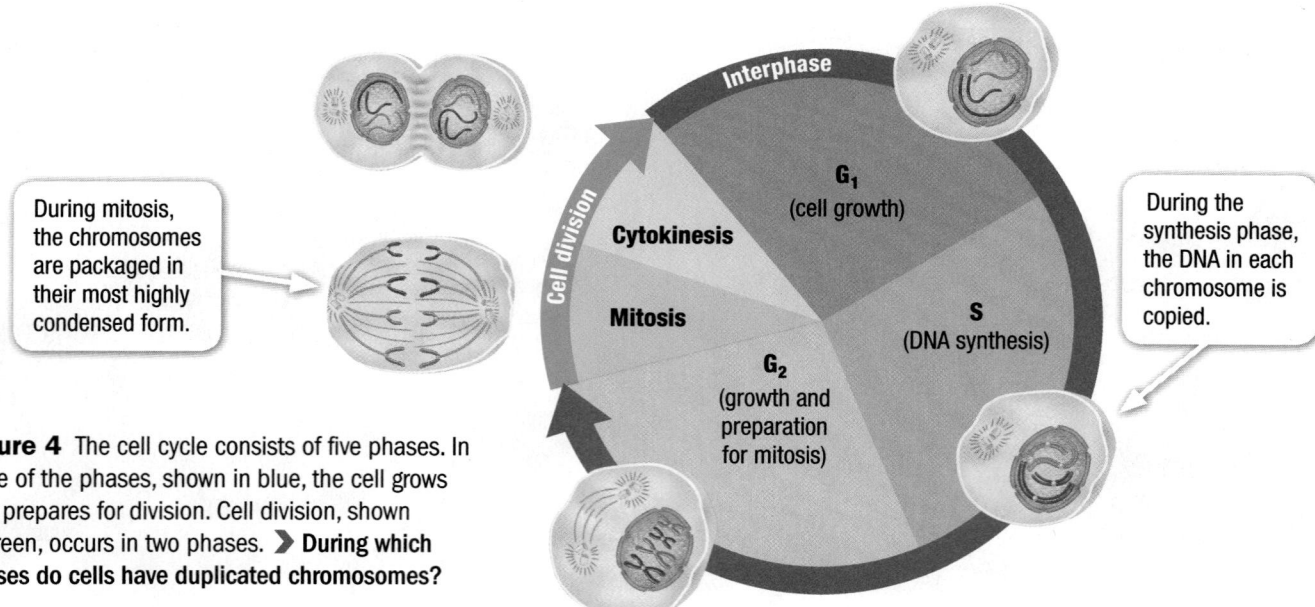

During mitosis, the chromosomes are packaged in their most highly condensed form.

During the synthesis phase, the DNA in each chromosome is copied.

Figure 4 The cell cycle consists of five phases. In three of the phases, shown in blue, the cell grows and prepares for division. Cell division, shown in green, occurs in two phases. ❯ **During which phases do cells have duplicated chromosomes?**

QuickLab

 5 min

Number of Cells Resulting from Mitosis

In the human body, the rate of mitosis is about 25 million (2.5×10^7) cells produced per second. By using this rate, you can calculate the number of cells produced by mitosis in a given amount of time.

Procedure

1 Calculate the number of cells produced by mitosis in the time given. For example, to find the number of cells produced in 3 min, determine how many seconds are in 3 min (because the rate is given in seconds).

$$\frac{60 \text{ seconds}}{1 \text{ minute}} \times 3 \text{ minutes} = 180 \text{ seconds}$$

2 Multiply the rate of mitosis by the time (in seconds) given in the problem (180 s).

$$\frac{2.5 \times 10^7 \text{ cells}}{\text{second}} \times 180 \text{ seconds} = 4.5 \times 10^9 \text{ cells}$$

$$4.5 \times 10^9 \text{ cells} = 4{,}500{,}000{,}000 \text{ cells} = 4.5 \text{ billion cells}$$

Analysis

1. **Calculate** the number of cells that would be produced in 1 h.

2. **Calculate** the number of cells that would be produced in 1 day.

3. **CRITICAL THINKING** **Predicting Patterns** Identify factors that might increase or decrease the rate of mitosis.

- **G₁** During the *first gap phase* (G_1), a cell grows rapidly as the cell builds more organelles. For most organisms, this phase occupies the major portion of the cell's life. Cells that are not dividing remain in the G_1 phase.

- **S** During the *synthesis phase* (S), a cell's DNA is copied. At the end of the S phase, the cell's nucleus has twice as much DNA as it did in the G_1 phase. Each chromosome now consists of two identical chromatids that are attached at the centromere.

- **G₂** During the *second gap phase* (G_2), the cell continues to grow and prepares to divide. The cell forms some special structures that help the cell divide. Hollow protein fibers called *microtubules* are organized in the cytoplasm during G_2 in preparation for division.

Cell Division Each new cell requires a complete set of organelles, including a nucleus. The process of dividing the nucleus into two daughter nuclei is called **mitosis.** The process of separating the organelles and the cytoplasm is called **cytokinesis.**

- **Mitosis** During mitosis, the nucleus divides to form two nuclei. Each nucleus contains a complete set of the cell's chromosomes. The nuclear membrane breaks down briefly. The two sister chromatids of each chromosome are pulled to the opposite sides of the dividing cell.

- **Cytokinesis** As the nucleus divides, the cytoplasm also begins to divide. Each daughter cell receives about half of the original cell's organelles. During cytokinesis, the two daughter cells are physically separated.

›Reading Check *What phases are included in interphase?*

cell cycle the life cycle of a cell

interphase the period of the cell cycle during which activities such as cell growth and protein synthesis occur without visible signs of cell division

mitosis in eukaryotic cells, a process of cell division that forms two new nuclei, each of which has the same number of chromosomes

cytokinesis the division of the cytoplasm of a cell

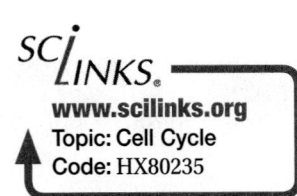

www.scilinks.org
Topic: Cell Cycle
Code: HX80235

Stages of Mitosis

Although mitosis is a continuous process, biologists traditionally divide it into four stages, as shown in **Figure 5.** ❯ Mitosis is a continuous process that can be observed in four stages: prophase, metaphase, anaphase, and telophase.

Stage ❶ Prophase Within the nucleus, chromosomes begin to condense and become visible under a light microscope. The nuclear membrane breaks down. Outside the nucleus, a special structure called the **spindle** forms. The spindle is made up of several spindle fibers. Each spindle fiber in turn is made up of an individual microtubule—a hollow tube of protein. Microtubules organize into a spindle that runs at a right angle to the cell's equator.

Cells have an organelle called the **centrosome,** which helps assemble the spindle. In animal cells, the centrosome includes a pair of centrioles, shown in **Figure 5.** Each centriole is made up of nine triplets of microtubules arranged as a short, hollow tube. Before mitosis, the cell's centrosome is duplicated. During prophase, the centrosomes move to opposite poles of the cell.

Figure 5 During mitosis, the copies (sister chromatids) of each chromosome are separated into two nuclei. ❯ **What is the role of the spindle fibers?**

Stages of Mitosis

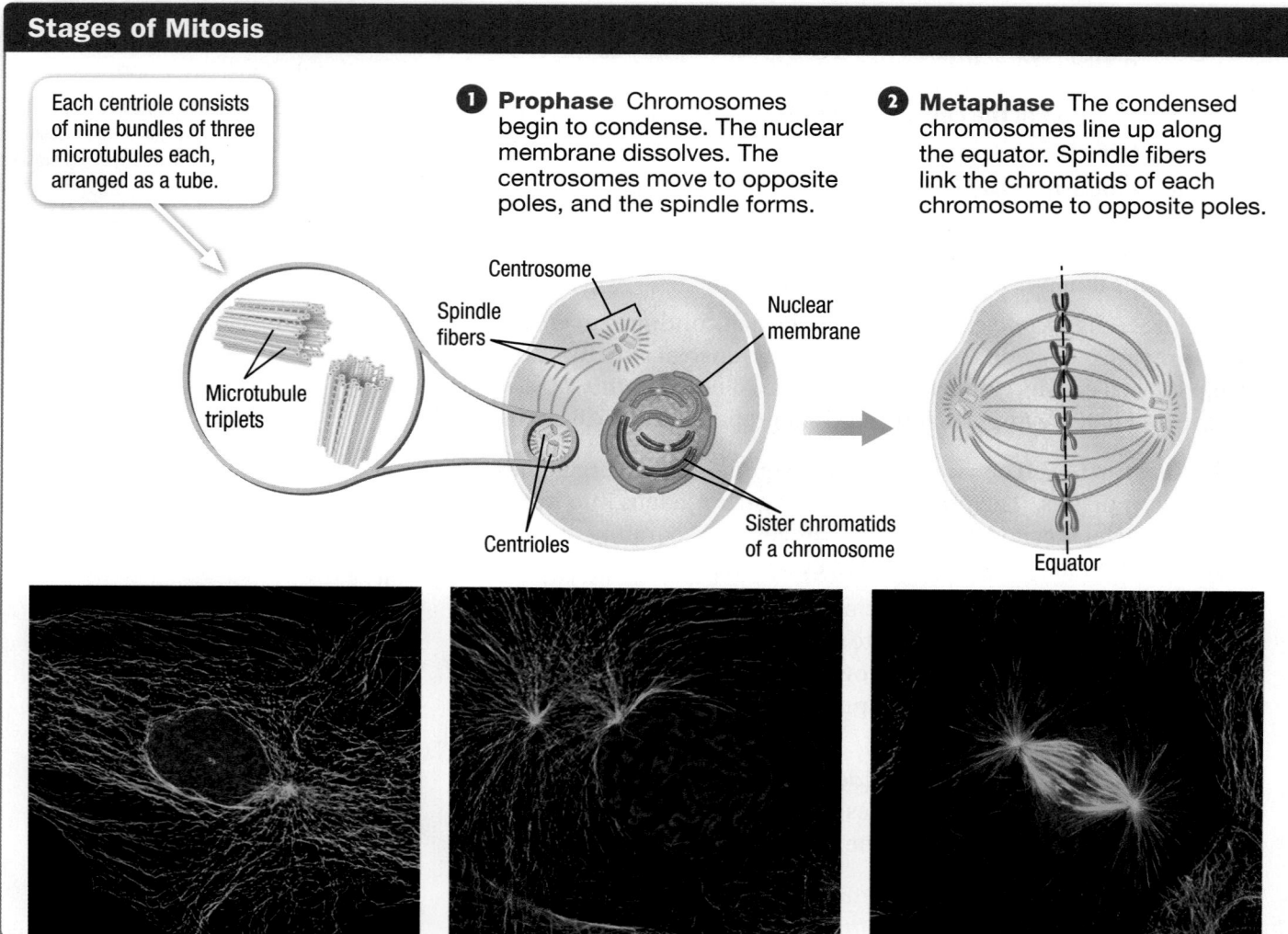

Each centriole consists of nine bundles of three microtubules each, arranged as a tube.

Microtubule triplets

❶ **Prophase** Chromosomes begin to condense. The nuclear membrane dissolves. The centrosomes move to opposite poles, and the spindle forms.

❷ **Metaphase** The condensed chromosomes line up along the equator. Spindle fibers link the chromatids of each chromosome to opposite poles.

Centrosome
Spindle fibers
Nuclear membrane
Centrioles
Sister chromatids of a chromosome
Equator

Stage ❷ Metaphase During metaphase, the chromosomes are packaged into their most condensed form. The nuclear membrane is fully dissolved, and the condensed chromosomes move to the center of the cell and line up along the cell's equator. Spindle fibers form a link between the poles and the centromere of each chromosome.

Stage ❸ Anaphase Once all of the chromosomes are lined up, the spindle fibers shorten. The spindle fibers shorten by breaking down the microtubules bit by bit. Sister chromatids move toward opposite poles as the spindle fibers that are attached continue to shorten. Each pole now has a full set of chromosomes.

Stage ❹ Telophase A nuclear envelope forms around the chromosomes at each pole of the cell. Chromosomes, now at opposite poles, uncoil and change back to their original chromatin form. The spindle dissolves. The spindle fibers break down and disappear. Mitosis is complete.

❯ **Reading Check** *What is the spindle composed of?*

READING TOOLBOX

Pattern Puzzles Cut each piece of the pattern puzzle that you made for the stages of mitosis so that each strip describes one of the events that occurs. Shuffle the strips and match the events with the correct stage.

go.hrw.com
* interact online
Keyword: HX8CRPF5

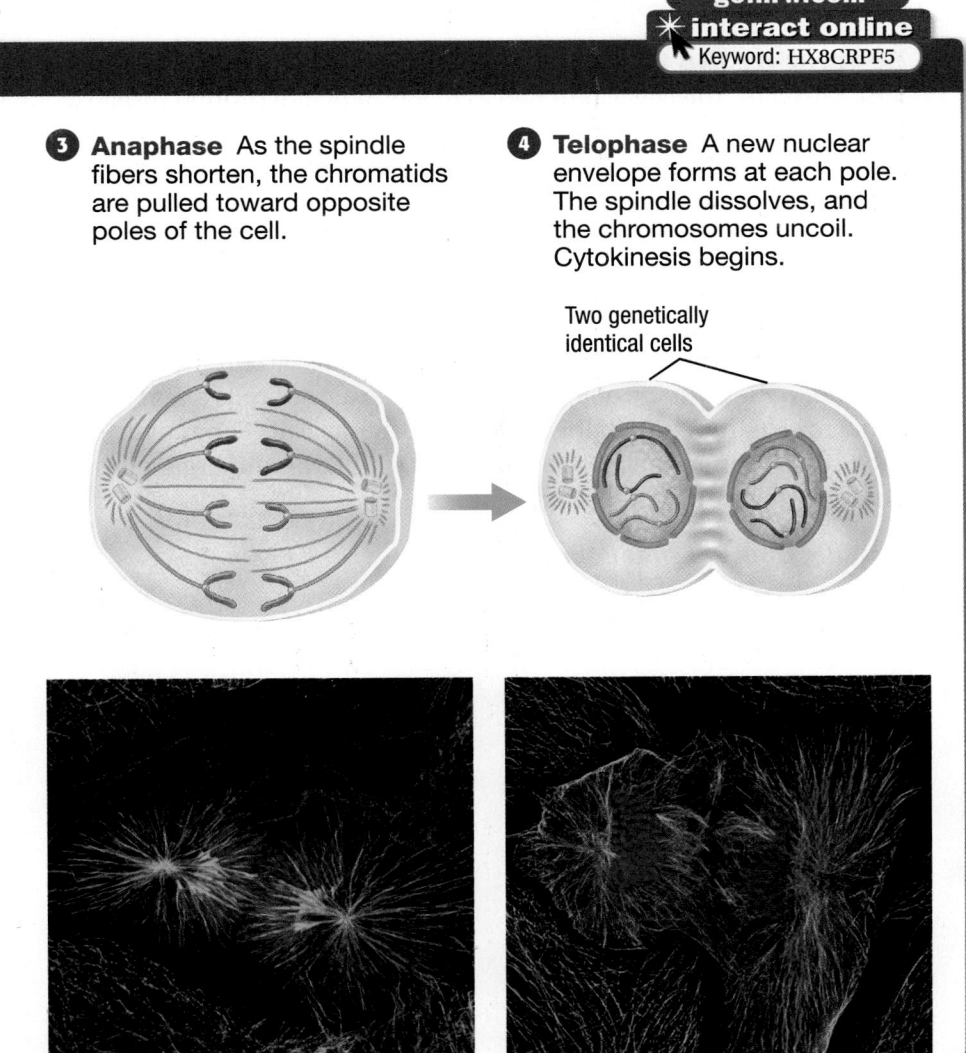

❸ Anaphase As the spindle fibers shorten, the chromatids are pulled toward opposite poles of the cell.

❹ Telophase A new nuclear envelope forms at each pole. The spindle dissolves, and the chromosomes uncoil. Cytokinesis begins.

Two genetically identical cells

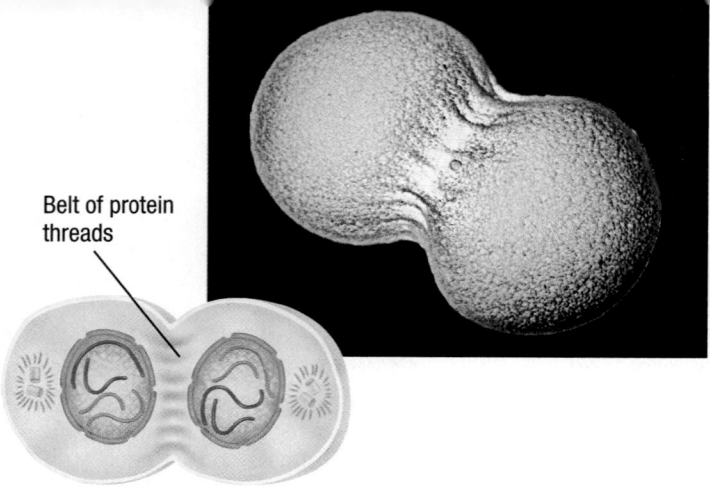
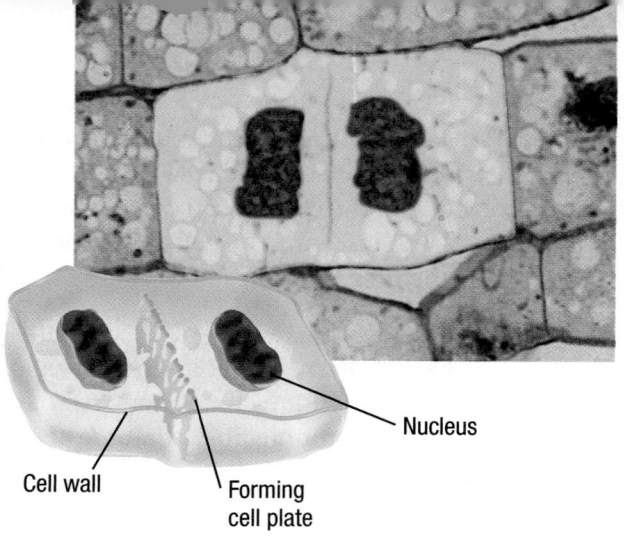

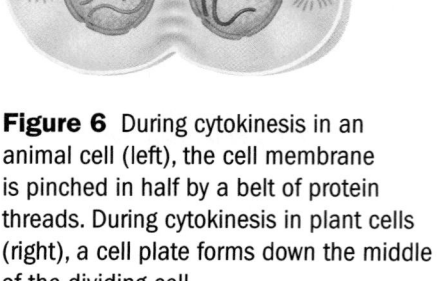

Belt of protein threads

Cell wall

Nucleus

Forming cell plate

Figure 6 During cytokinesis in an animal cell (left), the cell membrane is pinched in half by a belt of protein threads. During cytokinesis in plant cells (right), a cell plate forms down the middle of the dividing cell.

ACADEMIC VOCABULARY

rigid stiff, firm, inflexible

Cytokinesis

As mitosis ends, cytokinesis begins. The cytoplasm is separated, and two cells are formed. ❯ **During cytokinesis, the cell membrane grows into the center of the cell and divides it into two daughter cells of equal size. Each daughter cell has about half of the parent's cytoplasm and organelles.** The end result of mitosis and cytokinesis is two genetically identical cells in place of the original cell.

Separating the Cytoplasm In animal cells and other cells that lack cell walls, the cell is pinched in half by a belt of protein threads, as **Figure 6** shows. In plant cells and other cells that have rigid cell walls, the cytoplasm is divided in a different way. Vesicles holding cell wall material line up across the middle of the cell. These vesicles fuse to form a large, membrane-bound cell wall called the *cell plate*, shown in **Figure 6.** When it is completely formed, the cell plate separates the plant cell into two new plant cells.

Continuing the Cell Cycle After cytokinesis is complete, each cell enters the G_1 stage of interphase. The daughter cells are about equal in size—about half the size of the original cell. The activity of each cell continues because each has its own DNA and organelles. The cell cycle continues for each new cell.

❯ **Reading Check** *What is a cell plate?*

Section 2 Review

❯ **KEY IDEAS**

1. **Describe** the five phases of the cell cycle.

2. **List** in order the four stages of mitosis and the changes that occur during each stage.

3. **Compare** the products of cytokinesis.

CRITICAL THINKING

4. **Evaluating Information** Why are individual chromosomes more difficult to see during interphase than they are during mitosis?

5. **Predicting Results** What would happen if the cell did not have spindle fibers?

6. **Making Connections** Compare cell division in prokaryotic cells with cell division in eukaryotic cells.

ALTERNATIVE ASSESSMENT

7. **Animated Flipbook** Make a series of drawings that show the cell cycle of a plant cell. Be sure to include the five phases of the cell cycle and the four stages of mitosis.

Key Ideas	Key Terms	Why It Matters
❯ What are some factors that control cell growth and division? ❯ How do feedback signals affect the cell cycle? ❯ How does cancer relate to the cell cycle?	cancer tumor	Understanding how to control cell growth could be the key to curing cancer!

Your body grows when more cells are added to the tissues and organs that make up the body. To stay healthy, cells continue to divide as needed to replace or renew tissues. How is the cell cycle regulated?

Controls

Scientists study the cell cycle by observing cells in a culture medium. When a few healthy cells are placed in a dish with plenty of nutrients, they divide rapidly. But when they come in contact with one another or with the edge of the dish, the cells stop dividing.

These observations apply to real life. For example, when you cut your skin or break a bone, your cells start growing and dividing more rapidly to repair the wounds. The cells shown in **Figure 7** will begin dividing to replace the cells cut by the scalpel. As more cells form, the new cells come into contact with each other and close the wound. When the wound is healed, the cells slow down or stop dividing.

Cell division is highly controlled. ❯ **Cell growth and division depend on protein signals and other environmental signals.** Many proteins within the cell control the phases of the cell cycle. Signals from surrounding cells or even from other organs can also regulate cell growth and division. Environmental conditions, including the availability of nutrients, also affect the cell cycle.

❯ **Reading Check** *What are two factors that affect the cell cycle?*

Figure 7 The cells surrounding this surgical incision will begin dividing more often to fill in the gap. ❯ What signals the cells to stop dividing when the wound is healed?

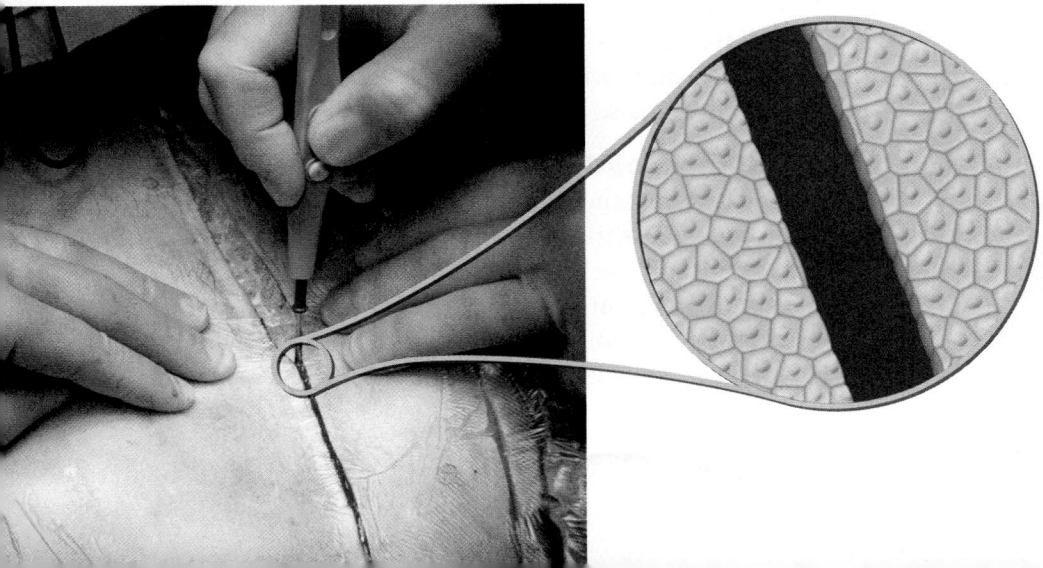

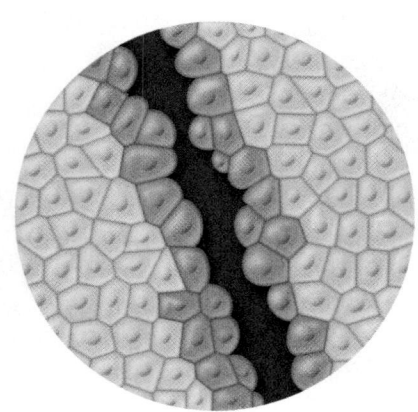

Hands-On
QuickLab

UV and Sunblock

Prolonged exposure to the sun's UV radiation can damage DNA, disrupting the cell cycle and causing skin cancer.

Procedure

1 In a dimly lit room, expose UV-sensitive beads to a bright, incandescent light source. Record any changes that you observe.

2 Thoroughly coat five beads in a thick covering of sunblock. Place these beads on one side of a paper plate. Place five uncoated beads on the other side.

3 Expose the plate to direct sunlight for a moment. Examine the beads in dim surroundings. Record any changes that you observe.

Analysis

1. **Describe** the appearance of the beads before they were exposed to bright light sources.

2. **Determine** whether exposure to the artificial light source affected their appearance.

3. **Describe** how direct sunlight affected the beads.

4. **CRITICAL THINKING** **Making Inferences** How can using sunblock protect you from getting cancer?

READING TOOLBOX

Cause and Effect At each checkpoint, identify a cause that would result in a delay of the next phase of the cell cycle.

Figure 8 The eukaryotic cell cycle has three checkpoints. Many proteins play a role in controlling the cell cycle.

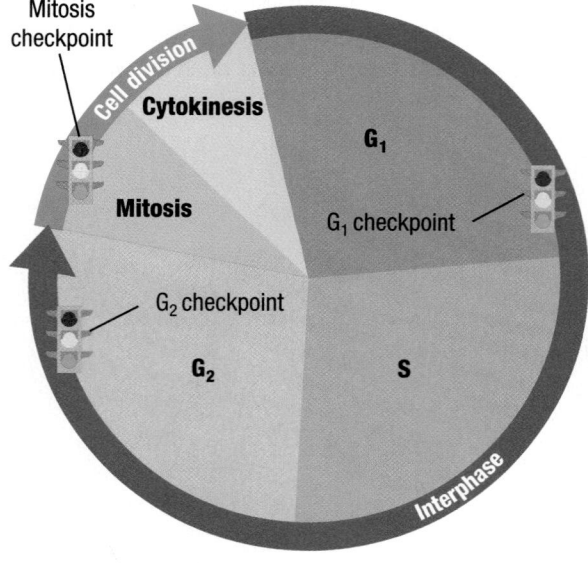

Checkpoints

During the cell cycle, a cell undergoes an inspection process to ensure that the cell is ready for the next phase in the cell cycle. ▶ Feedback signals at key checkpoints in the cell cycle can delay or trigger the next phase of the cell cycle. There are three main checkpoints in the cell cycle, as **Figure 8** shows.

G_1 Checkpoint Before the cell copies its DNA, the cell checks its surroundings. If conditions are favorable and the cell is healthy and large enough, the cell enters the synthesis phase. If conditions are not favorable, the cell goes into a resting period. Certain cells, such as some nerve and muscle cells, remain in this resting period for a long time. They do not divide very often.

G_2 Checkpoint Before mitosis begins, the cell checks for any mistakes in the copied DNA. Enzymes correct mistakes that are found. This checkpoint ensures that the DNA of the daughter cells will be identical to the DNA of the original cell. Proteins also double-check that the cell is large enough to divide. If the cell passes the G_2 checkpoint, then the cell may begin to divide. Once past this checkpoint, proteins help to trigger mitosis.

Mitosis Checkpoint During the metaphase stage of mitosis, chromosomes line up at the equator. At this point, the cell checks that the chromosomes are properly attached to the spindle fibers. Without this point, the sister chromatids of one or more chromosomes may not separate properly. This checkpoint ensures that the genetic material is distributed equally between the daughter cells.

▶ **Reading Check** *What happens at the G_2 checkpoint?*

Cancer

Each year, more than 1 million Americans are diagnosed with cancer. **Cancer** is a group of severe and sometimes fatal diseases that are caused by uncontrolled cell growth. ❯ **Uncontrolled cell growth and division can result in masses of cells that invade and destroy healthy tissues.** Preventing or curing cancer requires an understanding of how a healthy person's cells can become cancerous.

Loss of Control Normally, a cell responds properly to signals and controls. However, damage to a cell's DNA can cause the cell to respond improperly or to stop responding. The cell cycle can no longer be controlled. The defective cell divides and produces more defective cells, such as the cells in **Figure 9.** Eventually, these cells can form a mass called a **tumor.**

Development A *benign tumor* does not spread to other parts of the body and can often be removed by surgery. A *malignant tumor* invades and destroys nearby healthy tissues and organs. Malignant tumors, or cancers, can break loose from their tissue of origin and grow throughout the body. This process is called *metastasis*. Once a cancer has metastasized, it becomes more difficult to treat.

Treatment Some cancers can be treated by using drugs that kill the fast-growing cancer cells. Because drugs are chemicals, this method of treatment is called *chemotherapy*, or "chemo" for short. Some cancers can be treated by surgery to remove the affected organ. In radiation therapy, high-energy rays are focused on an area in order to destroy cancerous cells. Doctors choose the most effective treatment for a particular kind of cancer.

Prevention The best way to prevent cancer is to avoid things that can cause cancer. Ultraviolet radiation in sunlight can damage genes that control the cell cycle. Chemicals in cigarette smoke also affect how cell growth and division is regulated.

❯ **Reading Check** *What causes cells to lose control of the cell cycle?*

Figure 9 A doctor often can see a lung tumor on an X ray. Tumors are masses of cells (inset) that divide out of control.

cancer a group of diseases characterized by uncontrolled growth and spread of abnormal cells

tumor a growth that arises from normal tissue but that grows abnormally in rate and structure and lacks a function

---

Section 3 Review

❯ KEY IDEAS

1. **Describe** the effect of environmental conditions on the cell cycle.
2. **Summarize** the events of each of the three checkpoints of the cell cycle.
3. **Distinguish** between a benign tumor and a malignant tumor.

CRITICAL THINKING

4. **Applying Concepts** Propose an example of a situation in which an environmental condition might signal cell division in an organism.
5. **Logical Reasoning** The three checkpoint steps that a cell goes through allow the cell cycle to proceed correctly. What would happen if these steps did not function properly?

WRITING FOR SCIENCE

6. **Research** Use library resources or the Internet to research factors that increase the risk of cancer and the types of cancer that they could lead to. Why are factors in lifestyle or the environment difficult to identify? How can people protect themselves from exposure to known risk factors?

Chapter 10 Lab

Objectives

▶ Examine the dividing root-tip cells of an onion.

▶ Identify the phase of mitosis that each cell in an onion root tip is undergoing.

▶ Determine the relative length of time each phase of mitosis takes in onion root-tip cells.

Materials

- compound light microscope
- prepared microscope slide of a longitudinal section of *Allium* (onion) root tip

Safety

Mitosis in Plant Cells

Look at the photograph of a longitudinal section of an onion root tip. In the tips of plant roots and shoots, mitosis is ongoing in growth regions called *meristems.* Mitosis occurs in four phases: prophase, metaphase, anaphase, and telophase. In this lab, you will determine the relative length of time each phase of mitosis takes in onion root-tip cells. To do this, you will count the number of cells undergoing each phase of mitosis in the meristem of an onion root section.

Procedure

Identify the Phases of Mitosis

❶ 🔷 🔷 🔷 **CAUTION: Put on safety goggles, gloves, and a lab apron.**

❷ 🔷 **CAUTION: Handle glass slides and cover slips with care.** Using low power on your microscope, bring the meristem region on your slide into focus.

❸ Examine the meristem carefully. Choose a sample of about 50 cells. Look for a group of cells that appear to have been actively dividing at the time that the slide was made. The cells will appear to be in rows, so it should be easy to keep track of them. The dark-staining bodies are the chromosomes.

❹ For each of the cells in your sample, identify the stage of mitosis. Make a data table of the relative duration of each phase of mitosis. Record your observations in the data table.

Relative Duration of Each Phase of Mitosis				
Phase of mitosis	Tally marks	Count	Percentage of all cells	Time (min)
Prophase				
Metaphase				
Anaphase				
Telophase				

Calculate the Relative Length of Each Phase

❺ When you have classified each cell in your sample, count the tally marks for each phase and fill in the "Count" column. In which phase of mitosis was the number of cells the greatest? In which phase of mitosis was the number of cells the fewest?

6. Calculate what percentage of all cells were found in each phase. Divide the number of cells in a phase by the total number of cells in your sample, and multiply by 100%. Enter these figures under the "Percentage" column.

$$\text{Percentage} = \frac{\text{number of cells in phase}}{\text{total number of cells in sample}} \times 100\%$$

7. The percentage of the total number of cells that are found in each phase can be used to estimate how long each phase lasts. For example, if 25% of the cells are in prophase, then prophase takes 25% of the total time that a cell takes to undergo mitosis. Mitosis in onion cells takes about 80 min. Using this information and the percentages you have just determined, calculate the time for each phase and record it in your data table.

$$\text{Duration of phase (in minutes)} = \frac{\text{percentage}}{100} \times 80 \text{ min}$$

8. Make another table to record the data for the entire class. Collect and add the counts for each phase of mitosis for the entire class. Fill in the percentage and time information by using these data.

9. Clean up your lab materials according to your teacher's instructions. Wash your hands before leaving the lab.

Class Data			
Phase of mitosis	Count	Percentage of all cells	Duration (min)
Prophase			
Metaphase			
Anaphase			
Telophase			

Analyze and Conclude

1. **Identifying Structures** What color are the chromosomes stained?

2. **Recognizing Relationships** How can you distinguish between early and late anaphase?

3. **SCIENTIFIC METHODS** **Making Systematic Observations** According to your data table, which phase takes the least amount of time? Which phase of mitosis lasts the longest? Why might this phase require more time than other phases of mitosis do?

4. **SCIENTIFIC METHODS** **Summarizing Data** How do your data compare with the data of the entire class?

5. **SCIENTIFIC METHODS** **Critiquing Procedures** In this investigation, you assumed that the percentage of the total time that any given phase takes is equal to the percentage of the total number of cells in that phase at any moment. Why might this not be true for very small samples of cells?

Extensions

6. **Applying Methods** Cancerous tissue is composed of cells undergoing uncontrolled, rapid cell division. How could you develop a procedure to identify cancerous tissue by counting the number of cells undergoing mitosis?

go.hrw.com
SUPER SUMMARY
Keyword: HX8CRPS

Key Ideas	Key Terms

1 Cell Reproduction

> Because larger cells are more difficult to maintain, cells divide when they grow to a certain size.

> Many proteins help package eukaryotic DNA into highly condensed chromosome structures.

> All newly-formed cells require DNA, so before a cell divides, a copy of its DNA is made for each daughter cell.

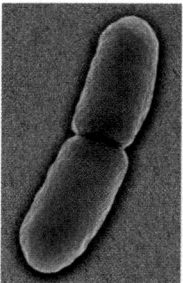

gene (224)
chromosome (224)
chromatin (224)
histone (224)
nucleosome (224)
chromatid (225)
centromere (225)

2 Mitosis

> The life of a eukaryotic cell cycles through phases of growth, DNA replication, preparation for cell division, and division of the nucleus and cytoplasm.

> Mitosis is a continuous process that can be observed in four stages: prophase, metaphase, anaphase, and telophase.

> During cytokinesis, the cell membrane grows into the center of the cell and divides it into two daughter cells of equal size. Each daughter cell has about half of the parent's cytoplasm and organelles.

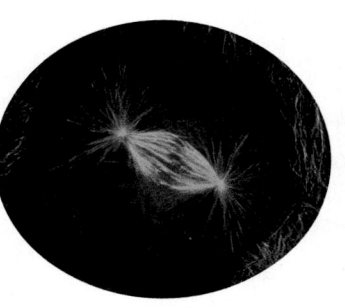

cell cycle (228)
interphase (228)
mitosis (229)
cytokinesis (229)
spindle (230)
centrosome (230)

3 Regulation

> Cell growth and division depend on protein signals and other environmental signals.

> Feedback signals at key checkpoints in the cell cycle can delay or trigger the next phase of the cell cycle.

> Uncontrolled cell growth and division results in tumors, which can invade surrounding tissues and cause cancer.

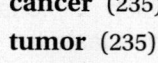
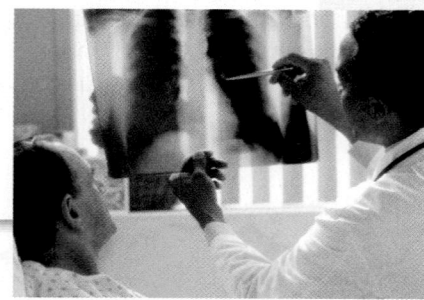

cancer (235)
tumor (235)

1. **Word Parts** Find out the meaning of the prefixes *ana-, meta-, pro-,* and *telo-*.

2. **Concept Map** Make a concept map that shows the events in the cell cycle. Try to include the following words in your map: *cell cycle, interphase, synthesis phase, chromosomes, cytokinesis, mitosis, second gap phase,* and *first gap phase.*

Using Key Terms

3. Explain the relationship between *gene* and *chromosome*.

4. Use the following terms in the same sentence: *tumor* and *cancer*.

For each pair of terms, explain how the meanings of the terms differ.

5. *chromatin* and *chromatid*

6. *centromere* and *centrosome*

Understanding Key Ideas

7. Which of the following is a reason that the size of a cell is limited?
   a. Larger cells are easier for an organism to produce than smaller cells.
   b. The cell's ability to exchange substances is limited by its surface area–to-volume ratio.
   c. The larger the cell becomes, the easier it is for substances to reach where they are needed.
   d. The size of a cell has no relationship to the cell's function in a multicellular organism.

8. What is a gene?
   a. a large molecule of chromosomes
   b. a protein that directs the activity of a cell
   c. a segment of DNA that codes for RNA and protein
   d. a segment of RNA that moves from the nucleus to the cytoplasm

9. During which stage of mitosis do the chromosomes line up along the equator?
   a. anaphase
   b. metaphase
   c. prophase
   d. telophase

10. What factors can cause cells to divide in a culture medium?
    a. protein signals
    b. lack of nutrients
    c. contact with other cells
    d. contact with the edge of the dish

11. What is the importance of feedback signals at key checkpoints within the cell cycle?
    a. to indicate the end of the cycle
    b. to indicate the presence of proteins
    c. to identify the meiosis and mitosis indicators
    d. to delay or trigger the next phase of the cycle

Use this diagram to answer the following question(s).

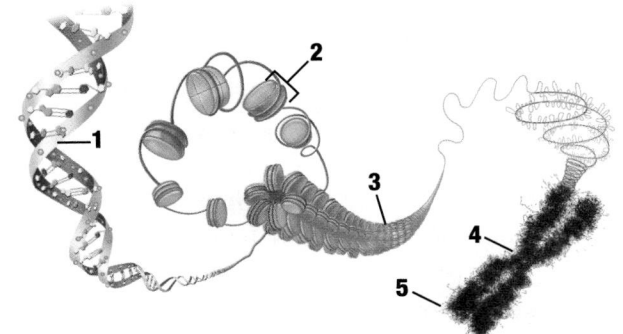

12. Which structure is a nucleosome?
    a. Structure 1   c. Structure 3
    b. Structure 2   d. Structure 4

13. What is Structure 5 called?
    a. histone   c. chromatid
    b. spindle   d. scaffold protein

Explaining Key Ideas

14. **Propose** why a new cell would need an entire copy of the old cell's DNA.

15. **Define** the importance of mitosis and cytokinesis in the life cycle of a eukaryotic cell.

16. **Contrast** cytokinesis in animal and plant cells.

17. **Identify** the events that occur at the G_2 checkpoint.

18. **Summarize** how normal cells can become cancerous.

Using Science Graphics

The graph shows the relative mass of DNA and chromosome number for a cell undergoing mitosis. Use the graph to answer the following questions.

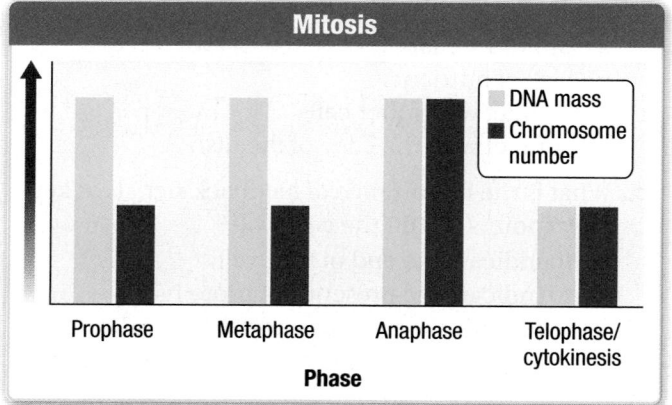

19. In which phase of mitosis do chromatids separate and become individual chromosomes?
- **a.** prophase
- **b.** metaphase
- **c.** anaphase
- **d.** telophase/cytokinesis

20. What process occurs that leads to the decrease in the cell's DNA mass?
- **a.** prophase
- **b.** metaphase
- **c.** anaphase
- **d.** telophase/cytokinesis

Critical Thinking

21. Evaluating Conclusions Damage to the brain or spinal cord is usually permanent. Use your knowledge of the cell cycle to explain why damaged cells in the brain or spinal cord are not replaced.

22. Analyzing Information Mitosis is similar in plants and animals, although plants lack centrioles. How might the absence of centrioles in plant cells have influenced scientists' thinking about the function of centrioles in mitosis?

Writing for Science

23. Communicating Information Scientists have determined that telomeres (the tips of chromosomes) are shaved down slightly every time a cell divides. When its telomeres become too short, a cell may lose its ability to divide. Find out what scientists have recently discovered about the relationship between telomere length, cell division and cancer. Prepare a written report to share with your class.

Methods of Science

Yeast cells are frequently used to study how cancer cells can form. Exposing cells to ultraviolet light during formation of new cells can affect new cell growth. Use the data in the table to answer the questions that follow.

Yeast colony identification code	Length of exposure to UV light (min)	Surviving yeast colonies
A	2	18
B	10	10
C	15	11
D	30	9
E	40	5
F	50	2
G	60	0

24. Identify the independent variable in this experiment.
- **a.** length of darkness (time)
- **b.** light intensity (brightness)
- **c.** yeast cell colonies (number)
- **d.** length of exposure to light (time)

25. Identify the dependent variable in this experiment.
- **a.** length of darkness (time)
- **b.** light intensity (brightness)
- **c.** yeast cell colonies (number)
- **d.** length of exposure to light (time)

26. Using the data in the table, construct a graph that plots surviving yeast colonies versus length of exposure.

27. Describe what happens to the yeast cell colonies when they are exposed to UV light.

Math Skills

28. Cell A has 3 times as many chromosomes as cell B has. Cell B undergoes mitosis, and has 6 chromosomes before cytokinesis is completed. How many chromosomes does cell A have?

Standardized Test Prep

Science Concepts

1. Prokaryotic chromosomes
  A have two chromatids.
  B are connected at the centromere.
  C consist of a circular DNA molecule.
  D are made of DNA wrapped around histone proteins.

2. In what stage of the cell cycle is the DNA copied?
  F G_1
  G S
  H G_2
  J mitosis

3. Mitosis could not proceed if a mutation interrupted the assembly of the
  A cell wall.
  B spindle fibers.
  C cell membrane.
  D nuclear envelope.

4. What might happen if cytokinesis were omitted from the cell cycle?
  F The daughter cells would die.
  G The cell would lose its mitochondria.
  H The daughter cells would not have nuclei.
  J The cell would not divide into two daughter cells.

5. G_1 checkpoint : DNA replication :: G_2 checkpoint :
  A mitosis
  B cell size
  C cytokinesis
  D mistakes in DNA

Using Science Graphics

This diagram shows a model of cell division. Use the diagram to answer the following question(s).

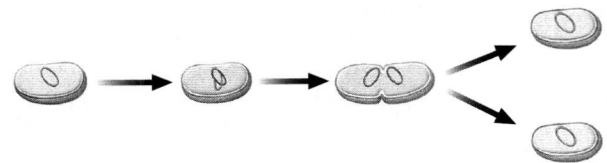

6. What type of cell undergoes this type of cell division?
  F a plant cell
  G an animal cell
  H a eukaryotic cell
  J a prokaryotic cell

The graph shows the number of cigarettes smoked per capita per year between 1920 and 2000 and the annual incidence of lung cancer among women. Use the graph to answer the following question(s).

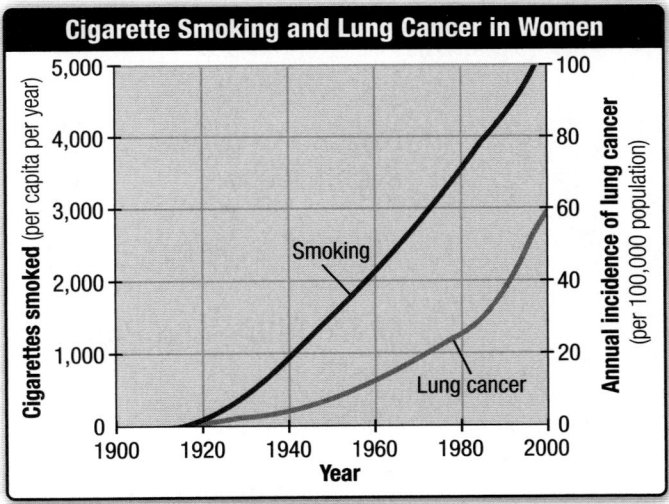

Cigarette Smoking and Lung Cancer in Women

7. What was the relationship between the number of cigarettes smoked and the incidence of lung cancer?
  A There was no relationship between cigarette smoking and lung cancer.
  B As the number of cigarettes smoked decreased, the incidence of lung cancer increased.
  C As the number of cigarettes smoked increased, the incidence of lung cancer increased.
  D As the number of cigarettes smoked increased, the incidence of lung cancer decreased.

Writing Skills

8. Extended Response For a cell to function efficiently, its surface area must be high relative to its volume. Explain how cell division maintains the relationship between surface area and volume. How does a stable ratio of surface area to volume help maintain proper cell functioning?

UNIT 4 Heredity

11 Meiosis and Sexual Reproduction

12 Mendel and Heredity

13 DNA, RNA, and Proteins

14 Genes in Action

15 Gene Technology and Human Applications

Eggs of the red-eyed tree frog stuck to the underside of a leaf

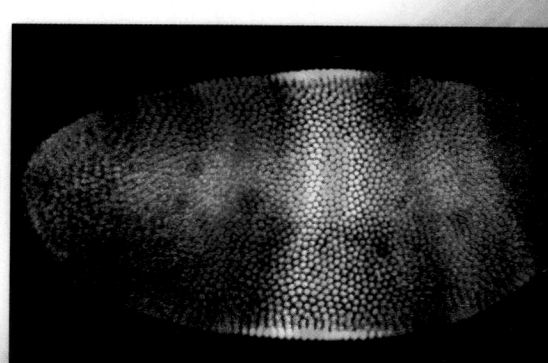

Fruit fly embryo, marked to show pattern of genes being expressed

BIOLOGY CAREER

Genetics Researcher
Rob Desalle

Rob DeSalle is a curator in the Division of Invertebrate Zoology at the American Museum of Natural History in New York City. His current research focuses on molecular evolution in a variety of organisms, including pathogenic bacteria and insects.

DeSalle studies molecular evolution through comparative genomics, which is the study of similarities and differences between the genomes of various species or strains within species. Comparing the genomes of species can help determine how the species are related.

DeSalle also helped found the Conservation Genetics Program at the American Museum of Natural History. This program uses the tools of molecular genetics to help protect wildlife around the world. For example, DeSalle helped develop a genetic test to determine if caviar sold in the United States was illegally harvested from endangered species of sturgeon in the Caspian Sea.

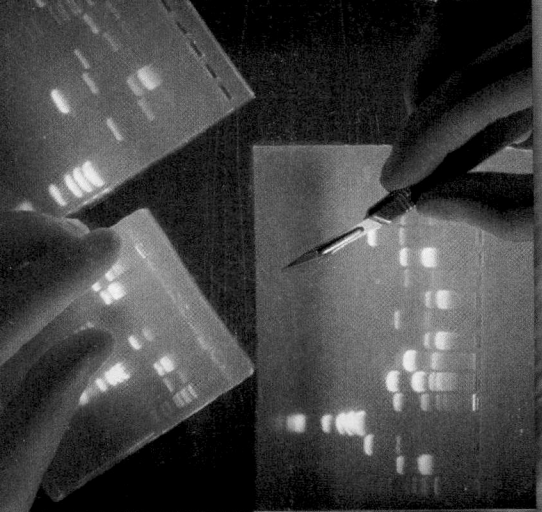

Genetic analysis by gel electrophoresis

Meiosis and Sexual Reproduction

Preview

1 Reproduction
Asexual Reproduction
Sexual Reproduction
Chromosome Number

2 Meiosis
Stages of Meiosis
Comparing Mitosis and Meiosis
Genetic Variation

3 Multicellular Life Cycles
Diploid Life Cycle
Haploid Life Cycle
Alternation of Generations

Why It Matters

You know that in sexual reproduction, an egg and a sperm combine to form a new organism. But how are eggs and sperm produced? In this chapter, you will learn about a special type of cell division called *meiosis.*

Like many organisms, the daddy long-legs spider reproduces sexually. Meiosis is a process that forms the eggs and sperm that make sexual reproduction possible for the daddy longlegs spiders.

A mother daddy longlegs spider will watch over her newly hatched young for nine days. After nine days, the young shed their skin and leave the web to build their own webs.

244

The newly hatched spiders, or *prenymphs,* may all look alike. However, because they formed from sexual reproduction, they are all genetically different.

⏱ 30 min

Inquiry Lab

Pollen Up Close

Pollen is produced in the male reproductive part of a flower called the *anther.* Pollen develops from cells called *microspores.* The mature pollen grain encloses two nuclei. Each nucleus contains half of the number of chromosomes found in most cells of the mature, flower-producing plant.

Procedure

❶ CAUTION: **Handle glass slides with care.** Place a prepared slide of a lily anther on the microscope stage. Examine the slide under low power.

❷ Identify the large chambers called *pollen sacs.* How many can you find in your cross-sectional view? Are they whole or broken? Make a sketch of what you see.

❸ Depending upon the stage of development, the pollen sacs will contain either clustered cells in various stages of division or mature grains of pollen. You can identify a pollen grain by its two stained nuclei and textured coat. Select several representative cells within the pollen sac. Make a sketch of each cell.

Analysis

1. **Describe** the structure of the lily anther.

2. **Determine** whether the observed pollen sacs contain dividing cells, pollen grains, or both.

3. **Describe** the appearance of the nuclei in either the dividing cells or the pollen grains.

4. **Explain** what advantage is achieved by halving the chromosome number in pollen nuclei.

READING TOOLBOX

These reading tools can help you learn the material in this chapter. For more information on how to use these and other tools, see **Appendix: Reading and Study Skills.**

Using Words

Key-Term Fold A key-term fold is a useful tool for studying definitions of key terms in a chapter. Each tab can contain a key term on one side and its definition on the other.

Your Turn Make a key-term fold for the terms of this chapter.

1. Fold a sheet of lined notebook paper in half from left to right.

2. Using scissors, cut along every third line from the right edge of the paper to the center fold to make tabs.

Using Language

Comparisons Comparing is a way of looking for the similarities between different things. Contrasting is a way of looking for the differences. Certain words and phrases can help you determine if things are being compared or contrasted. Comparison words include *and, like, just as,* and *in the same way.* Contrast words include *however, unlike, in contrast,* and *on the other hand.*

Your Turn In the following sentences, find the things that are being compared or contrasted.

1. Like mitosis, meiosis is a process that reproduces new cells.

2. In contrast to many other reptiles, the Burmese python does not reproduce sexually.

Taking Notes

Two-Column Notes Two-column notes can help you summarize the key ideas of a topic, chapter, or process. The left column of the table contains key ideas. The right column contains details and examples of each main idea.

Your Turn As you read the chapter, create two-column notes that summarize the key ideas of this chapter.

1. Write the key ideas in the left-hand column. The key ideas are listed in the section openers. Include one key idea in each row.

2. As you read the section, add detailed notes and examples in the right-hand column. Be sure to put these details and examples in your own words.

Meiosis and Sexual Reproduction	
Key Ideas	Details and Examples

Reproduction

> In asexual reproduction, how does the offspring compare to the parent?

> In sexual reproduction, how does the offspring compare to the parent?

> Why are chromosomes important to an organism?

gamete
zygote
diploid
haploid
homologous chromosomes

Living organisms produce offspring. How closely the offspring resemble their parents depends on how the organism reproduces.

Reproduction is the process of producing offspring. Some offspring are produced by two parents, and others are produced by just one parent. Some organisms look exactly like their parents, and others look very similar. Whether an organism is identical or similar to its parent is determined by the way that the organism reproduces.

Asexual Reproduction

In *asexual reproduction*, a single parent passes a complete copy of its genetic information to each of its offspring. > An individual formed by asexual reproduction is genetically identical to its parent.

Prokaryotes reproduce asexually by a kind of cell division called *binary fission.* Many unicellular eukaryotes also reproduce asexually. Amoebas reproduce by splitting into two or more individuals of about equal size. Some multicellular eukaryotes, such as starfish, go through fragmentation. *Fragmentation* is a kind of reproduction in which the body breaks into several pieces. Some or all of these fragments regrow missing parts and develop into complete adults.

Other animals, such as the hydra shown in **Figure 1,** go through *budding.* In budding, new individuals split off from existing ones. Some plants, such as potatoes, can form whole new plants from parts of stems. Other plants can reproduce from roots or leaves. Some crustaceans, such as water fleas, reproduce by parthenogenesis. *Parthenogenesis* is a process in which a female makes a viable egg that grows into an adult without being fertilized by a male.

> **Reading Check** *What is fragmentation? (See the Appendix for answers to Reading Checks.)*

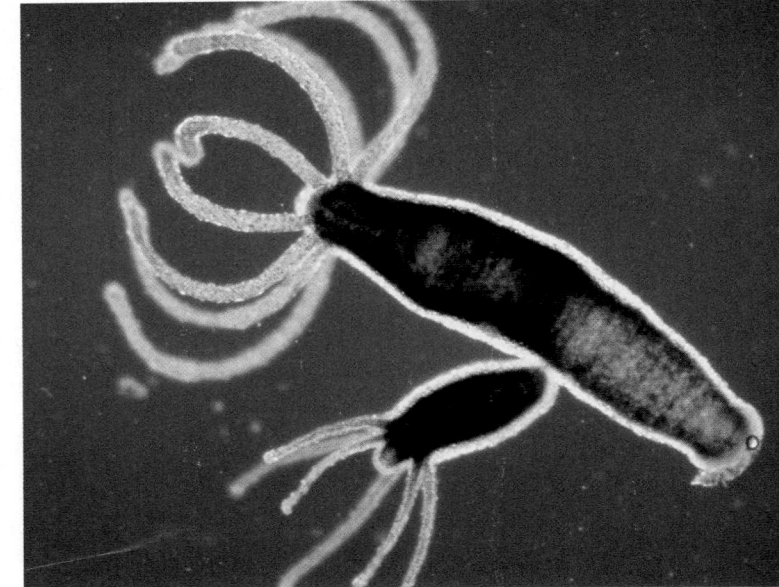

Figure 1 This hydra is in the process of reproducing asexually. The smaller hydra budding from the parent is genetically identical to the parent.

Sexual Reproduction

Most eukaryotic organisms reproduce sexually. ❯ **In** *sexual* **reproduction, two parents give genetic material to produce offspring that are genetically different from their parents.** Each parent produces a reproductive cell, called a **gamete.** A gamete from one parent fuses with a gamete from the other parent, as **Figure 2** shows. The resulting cell, called a **zygote,** has a combination of genetic material from both parents. This process is called *fertilization*. Because both parents give genetic material, the offspring has traits of both parents but is not exactly like either parent.

Germ Cells and Somatic Cells Recall that the cells of a multi-cellular organism are often specialized for certain functions. Muscle cells, for example, contract and move your body. Cells that are specialized for sexual reproduction are called *germ cells*. Only germ cells can produce gametes. Other body cells are called *somatic cells*. Somatic cells do not participate in sexual reproduction.

Advantages of Sexual Reproduction Asexual reproduction is the simplest, most efficient method of reproduction. Asexual reproduction allows organisms to produce many offspring in a short period of time without using energy to make gametes or to find a mate. But the genetic material of these organisms varies little between individuals, so they may be at a disadvantage in a changing environment. Sexual reproduction, in contrast, produces genetically diverse individuals. A population of diverse organisms is more likely to have some individuals that survive a major environmental change.

Chromosome Number

Genes are located on chromosomes. ❯ **Each chromosome has thousands of genes that play an important role in determining how an organism develops and functions.** Each species has a characteristic number of chromosomes. As shown in **Figure 3,** mosquitoes have only 6 chromosomes in each cell. Chimpanzees have 48 chromosomes in each cell. Some ferns have more than 500! An organism must have exactly the right number of chromosomes. If an organism has too many or too few chromosomes, the organism may not develop and function properly.

In humans, each cell has two copies of 23 chromosomes for a total of 46. When fertilization happens, two cells combine to form a zygote, which still has only 46 chromosomes. Why is the number the same? The gametes that form a zygote have only *one* copy of each chromosome, or one set of 23 chromosomes. This reduction of chromosomes in gametes keeps the chromosome number of human somatic cells at a constant 46.

❯ **Reading Check** *What kind of cells do germ cells produce?*

gamete (GAM eet) a haploid reproductive cell that unites with another haploid reproductive cell to form a zygote

zygote (ZIE GOHT) the cell that results from the fusion of gametes

diploid a cell that contains two haploid sets of chromosomes

haploid describes a cell, nucleus, or organism that has only one set of unpaired chromosomes

homologous chromosomes (hoh MAHL uh guhs) chromosomes that have the same sequence of genes, that have the same structure, and that pair during meiosis

SCI**LINKS**®

www.scilinks.org
Topic: Sexual and
         Asexual
         Reproduction
Code: HX81386

Figure 2 Two gametes, an egg and a sperm, combine during fertilization to form a zygote. ❯ **What types of cells produce gametes?**

Haploid and Diploid Cells A cell, such as a somatic cell, that has two sets of chromosomes is **diploid**. A cell is **haploid** if it has one set of chromosomes. Gametes are haploid cells. The symbol *n* is used to represent the number of chromosomes in one set. Human gametes have 23 chromosomes, so *n* = 23. The diploid number in somatic cells is written as 2*n*. Human somatic cells have 46 chromosomes (2*n* = 46).

Homologous Chromosomes Each diploid cell has pairs of chromosomes made up of two homologous chromosomes. **Homologous chromosomes** are chromosomes that are similar in size, in shape, and in kinds of genes that they contain. Each chromosome in a homologous pair comes from one of the two parents. In humans, one set of 23 chromosomes comes from the mother, and one set comes from the father. Homologous chromosomes can carry different forms of genes. For example, flower color in peas is determined by a gene on one of its chromosomes. The form of this gene can be white or purple. The cells of each pea plant will have two flower-color genes, one on each of the chromosomes that carry the flower-color gene. Both could be genes for white flower color, or both could be genes for purple flower color. Or one gene could be for white color, and the other could be for purple color.

Autosomes and Sex Chromosomes *Autosomes* are chromosomes with genes that do not determine the sex of an individual. *Sex chromosomes* have genes that determine the sex of an individual. In humans and many other organisms, the two sex chromosomes are referred to as the *X* and *Y chromosomes*. The genes that cause a zygote to develop into a male are located on the Y chromosome. Human males have one X chromosome and one Y chromosome (XY), and human females have two X chromosomes (XX).

Chromosome Number of Various Organisms	
Organism	**Number (2*n*) of chromosomes**
Penicillium	1–4
Saccharomyces (yeast)	16
Mosquito	6
Housefly	12
Garden pea	14
Corn	20
Fern	480–1,020
Frog	26
Human	46
Orangutan	48
Dog	78

Figure 3
Different species have different numbers of chromosomes.

Key-Term Fold On the back of your key-term fold, write a definition in your own words for the key terms in this section.

Review

> **KEY IDEAS**

1. **Compare** the offspring in asexual reproduction with the parent.
2. **Describe** how the offspring in sexual reproduction compares genetically with its parent.
3. **Compare** the number of sets of chromosomes between a haploid cell and a diploid cell.
4. **Explain** why chromosomes are important for organisms.

CRITICAL THINKING

5. **Inferring Relationships** Why are haploid cells important in sexual reproduction?
6. **Forming Reasoned Opinions** Do you agree or disagree that homologous chromosomes occur in gametes? Explain.

METHODS OF SIENCE

7. **Evaluating Hypotheses** A student states that organisms that reproduce asexually are at a disadvantage in a stable environment. If you agree with this hypothesis, name one or more of its strengths. If you disagree, name one or more of its weaknesses.

Key Ideas	Key Terms	Why It Matters
❯ What occurs during the stages of meiosis? ❯ How does the function of mitosis differ from the function of meiosis? ❯ What are three mechanisms of genetic variation?	meiosis crossing-over independent assortment	Meiosis allows genetic information from two parents to combine to form offspring that are different from both parents.

Most cells that divide and produce new cells form two offspring cells that have the same number of chromosomes as the parent cell. How do haploid gametes form from a diploid germ cell? **Meiosis** is a form of cell division that produces daughter cells with half the number of chromosomes that are in the parent cell.

Stages of Meiosis

Before meiosis begins, the chromosomes in the original cell are copied. Meiosis involves two divisions of the nucleus—meiosis I and meiosis II. ❯ **During meiosis, a diploid cell goes through two divisions to form four haploid cells.** In meiosis I, homologous chromosomes are separated. In meiosis II, the sister chromatids of each homologue are separated. As a result, four haploid cells are formed from the original diploid cell. **Figure 4** illustrates the steps of meiosis.

Stages of Meiosis I

1 Prophase I
Chromosomes condense. The nuclear envelope breaks down.

2 Metaphase I
Pairs of homologous chromosomes move to the cell's equator.

3 Anaphase I
Homologous chromosomes move to the cell's opposite poles.

4 Telophase I
Chromosomes gather at the poles. The cytoplasm divides.

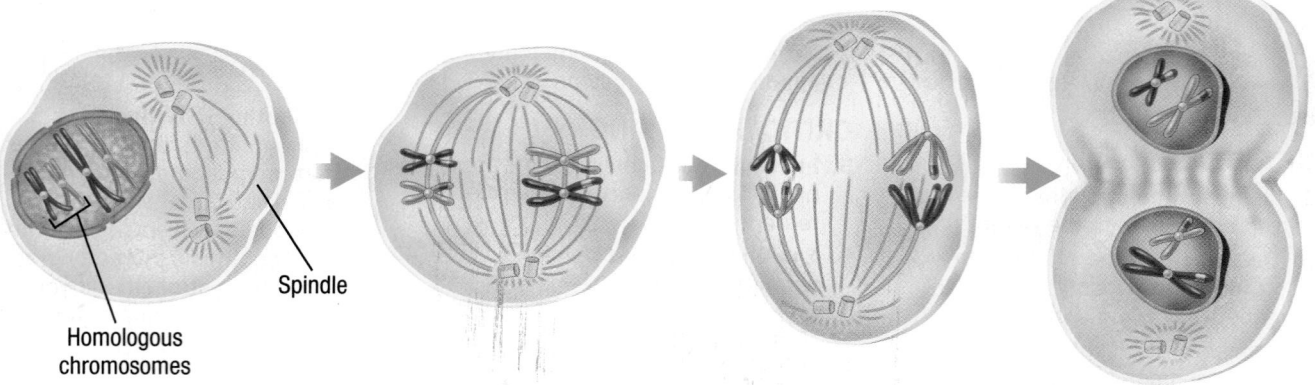

Spindle

Homologous chromosomes

Meiosis I Meiosis begins with a diploid cell that has copied its chromosomes. The first phase is prophase I. **①** During prophase I, the chromosomes condense, and the nuclear envelope breaks down. Homologous chromosomes pair. Chromatids exchange genetic material in a process called **crossing-over.** **②** In metaphase I, the spindle moves the pairs of homologous chromosomes to the equator of the cell. The homologous chromosomes remain together. **③** In anaphase I, the homologous chromosomes separate. The spindle fibers pull the chromosomes of each pair to opposite poles of the cell. But the chromatids do not separate at their centromeres. Each chromosome is still made of two chromatids. The genetic material, however, has recombined. **④** During telophase I, the cytoplasm divides (cytokinesis), and two new cells are formed. Both cells have one chromosome from each pair of homologous chromosomes.

Meiosis II Meiosis II begins with the two cells formed at the end of telophase I of meiosis I. The chromosomes are not copied between meiosis I and meiosis II. **⑤** In prophase II, new spindles form. **⑥** During metaphase II, the chromosomes line up along the equators and are attached at their centromeres to spindle fibers. **⑦** In anaphase II, the centromeres divide. The chromatids, which are now called *chromosomes,* move to opposite poles of the cell. **⑧** During telophase II, a nuclear envelope forms around each set of chromosomes. The spindle breaks down, and the cell goes through cytokinesis. The result of meiosis is four haploid cells.

❯ **Reading Check** *In what phase of meiosis is genetic material exchanged?*

meiosis a process in cell division during which the number of chromosomes decreases to half the original number by two divisions of the nucleus, which results in the production of sex cells (gametes or spores)

crossing-over the exchange of genetic material between homologous chromosomes during meiosis

Figure 4 During meiosis, four haploid cells are produced from a diploid cell.
❯ *What is the difference between anaphase I and anaphase II?*

go.hrw.com
✳ **interact online**
Keyword: HX8MEIF4

Stages of Meiosis II

⑤ Prophase II
A new spindle forms around the chromosomes.

⑥ Metaphase II
Chromosomes line up at the equators.

⑦ Anaphase II
Centromeres divide, and chromatids move to opposite poles.

⑧ Telophase II
A nuclear envelope forms around each set of chromosomes. The cells divide.

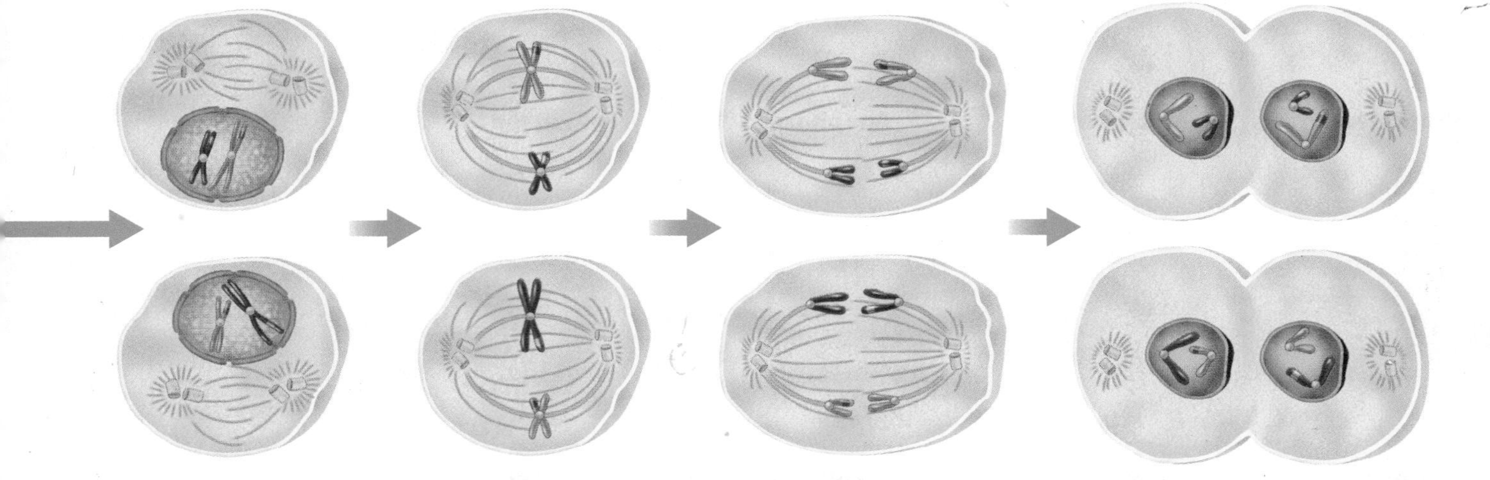

Comparisons Write two sentences that compare and two sentences that contrast meiosis and mitosis.

Comparing Mitosis and Meiosis

The processes of mitosis and meiosis are similar but meet different needs and have different results. ❯ **Mitosis makes new cells that are used during growth, development, repair, and asexual reproduction. Meiosis makes cells that enable an organism to reproduce sexually and happens only in reproductive structures.** Mitosis produces two genetically identical diploid cells. In contrast, meiosis produces four genetically different haploid cells. The haploid cells produced by meiosis contain half the genetic information of the parent cell. When two such cells, often an egg cell and a sperm cell, combine, the resulting zygote has the same number of chromosomes as each of the parents' cells.

If you compare meiosis and mitosis, as shown in **Figure 5,** you may think that they are alike. For example, in metaphase of mitosis and metaphase I of meiosis, the chromosomes move to the equator. However, there is a major difference that happens in an earlier stage.

In prophase I of meiosis, every chromosome pairs with its homologue. A pair of homologous chromosomes is called a *tetrad.* As the tetrads form, different homologues exchange parts of their chromatids in the process of crossing-over. The pairing of homologous chromosomes and the crossing-over do not happen in mitosis. Therefore, a main difference between meiosis and mitosis is that in meiosis, genetic information is rearranged. The rearranging of genetic information leads to genetic variation in offspring. Crossing-over is one of several processes that lead to genetic variation.

❯ **Reading Check** *How are cells formed by mitosis different from cells formed by meiosis in relation to number of chromosomes?*

Figure 5 Mitosis produces two diploid daughter cells that are identical to the parent cell. Meiosis produces four haploid cells from a diploid cell. ❯ *What is the difference between anaphase in mitosis and anaphase I in meiosis I?*

Comparing Mitosis and Meiosis

Mitosis

Prophase → Metaphase → Anaphase → Telophase → 2 identical diploid cells

Meiosis

Prophase I → Metaphase I → Anaphase I → Telophase I → Meiosis II → 4 nonidentical haploid cells

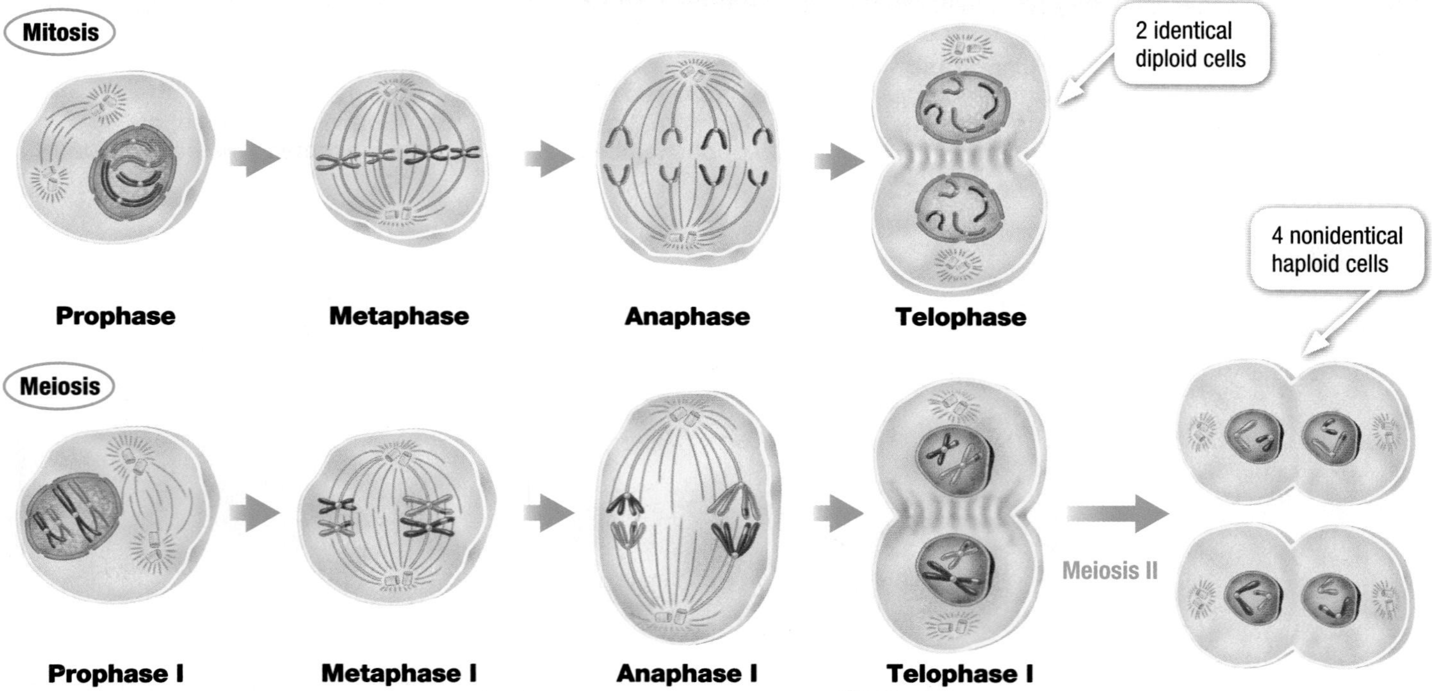

Crossing-Over Model

You can use paper strips and pencils to model the process of crossing-over.

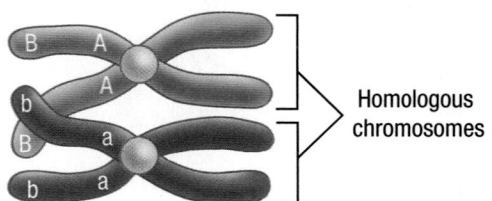

Homologous chromosomes

Procedure

1. Use a **colored pencil** to write "A" and "B" on **two paper strips.** These two strips will represent one of the two homologous chromosomes shown.

2. Use a **second colored pencil** to write "a" and "b" on **two paper strips.** These two strips will represent the second homologous chromosome shown.

3. **CAUTION: Handle scissors with care.** Use your chromosome models, **scissors,** and **tape** to demonstrate crossing-over between two chromatids.

Analysis

1. **Determine** what the letters *A, B, a,* and *b* represent.

2. **Making Inferences** Explain why the chromosomes that you made are homologous.

3. **Compare** the number of different types of chromatids (combinations of *A, B, a,* and *b*) before crossing-over with the number after crossing-over.

4. CRITICAL THINKING **Analyzing Information** How does crossing-over relate to genetic recombination?

Genetic Variation

Genetic variation is advantageous for a population. Genetic variation can help a population survive a major environmental change. For example, in the Arctic, if temperatures drop below average, those polar bears with genes that make thicker fur will survive. Polar bears without the genes for thicker fur may die out. The polar bears with the genes for thicker fur reproduce, and the population grows. Now, suppose that all of the individuals in the population have the same genes, but none of the genes are for thicker fur. What do you think will happen if the temperature drops below average? The entire population of polar bears may die out.

Genetic variation is made possible by sexual reproduction. In sexual reproduction, existing genes are rearranged. Meiosis is the process that makes the rearranging of genes possible. Fusion of haploid cells from two different individuals adds further variation. ❯ **Three key contributions to genetic variation are crossing-over, independent assortment, and random fertilization.**

Crossing-Over During prophase I, homologous chromosomes line up next to each other. Each homologous chromosome is made of two sister chromatids attached at the centromere. Crossing-over happens when one arm of a chromatid crosses over the arm of the other chromatid, as illustrated in the QuickLab. The chromosomes break at the point of the crossover, and each chromatid re-forms its full length with the piece from the other chromosome. Thus, the sister chromatids of a homologous chromosome no longer have identical genetic information.

❯ **Reading Check** *How can crossing-over increase genetic variation?*

www.scilinks.org
Topic: Genetic Variation
Code: HX80658

ACADEMIC VOCABULARY

exist to occur or be present

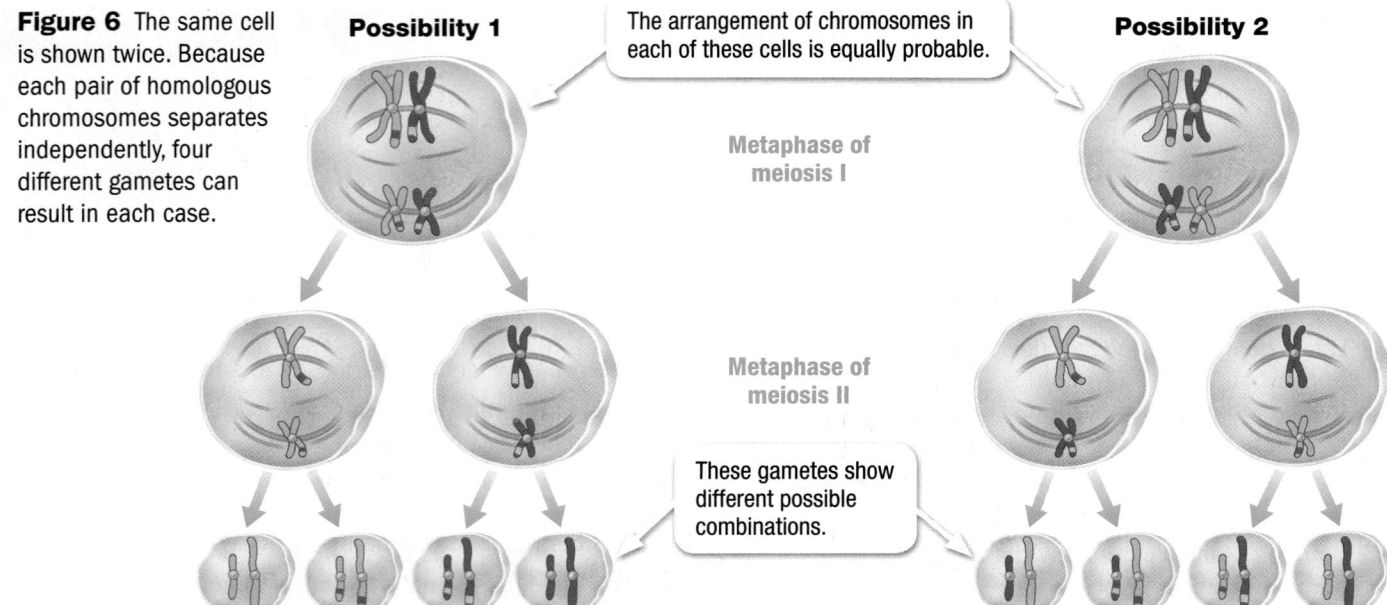

Figure 6 The same cell is shown twice. Because each pair of homologous chromosomes separates independently, four different gametes can result in each case.

Possibility 1

The arrangement of chromosomes in each of these cells is equally probable.

Possibility 2

Metaphase of meiosis I

Metaphase of meiosis II

These gametes show different possible combinations.

independent assortment the random distribution of the pairs of genes on different chromosomes to the gametes

Independent Assortment During metaphase I, homologous pairs of chromosomes line up at the equator of the cell. The two pairs of chromosomes can line up in either of two equally probable ways. This random distribution of homologous chromosomes during meiosis is called **independent assortment.** The four haploid cells formed in possibility 1 in **Figure 6** have entirely different combinations of chromosomes than do the four cells made in possibility 2.

In humans, each gamete receives one chromosome from each of 23 pairs of homologous chromosomes. Each of the 23 pairs of chromosomes separates independently. Thus, there are 2^{23} (more than 8 million) different possibilities for the gene combinations in gametes that form from a single original cell.

Random Fertilization Fertilization is a random process that adds genetic variation. The zygote that forms is made by the random joining of two gametes. Because fertilization of an egg by a sperm is random, the number of possible outcomes is *squared*. In humans, the possibility is $2^{23} \times 2^{23}$, or about 70 trillion, different combinations!

Section 2 Review

> **KEY IDEAS**

1. **Summarize** the different phases of meiosis.
2. **Explain** how the function of meiosis differs from the function of mitosis.
3. **Describe** three mechanisms of genetic variation.

CRITICAL THINKING

4. **Comparing Functions** Compare the processes of crossing-over and independent assortment. How does each contribute to genetic variation?
5. **Inferring Conclusions** Why might sexual reproducers better adapt to a changing environment than asexual reproducers?

ALTERNATIVE ASSESSMENT

6. **Word Problem** If one cell in a dog ($2n = 78$) undergoes meiosis and another cell undergoes mitosis, how many chromosomes will each resulting cell contain?

Girls, Girls, Girls

Did you know that some species, such as the predatory brush cricket to the right, and the lupin aphid below, have only females? These species, with only females, reproduce asexually.

WEIRD SCIENCE

Parthenogenesis

In animals, the process of a female producing an egg that can grow into a new individual without being fertilized by a male is called *parthenogenesis*. The major advantage of parthenogenesis is that every individual can reproduce and the population can grow quickly. The disadvantage is that every individual has the same genes. The animals may not have the genes that produce the traits that are necessary for adaptation. If a species cannot adapt, it could become extinct.

Apomixis Asexual reproduction in plants in which embryos develop in the absence of fertilization by pollen is called *apomixis*. There are more than 300 apomictic plant species, such as dandelions. Apomictic plants still produce seeds, and the offspring are genetically identical to the mother plant.

New Discovery Until recently, scientists believed that all snakes reproduced sexually. However, this Burmese python is parthenogenetic. Scientists discovered that the Burmese python was parthenogenetic only after an isolated female in a zoo had offspring.

Research Some species of mango and of cereals are apomictic. Conduct Internet research, and investigate how these species can benefit humans.

Multicellular Life Cycles

Key Ideas	Key Terms	Why It Matters
› What is a diploid life cycle? › What is a haploid life cycle? › What is alternation of generations?	life cycle sperm ovum	Some life cycles are mainly diploid, others are mainly haploid, and still others alternate between haploid and diploid phases.

All of the events in the growth and development of an organism until the organism reaches sexual maturity are called a **life cycle.** All organisms that reproduce sexually have both diploid stages and haploid stages.

Diploid Life Cycle

Most animals have a diploid life cycle. **Figure 7** illustrates this type of life cycle. Most of the life cycle is spent in the diploid state. All of the cells except the gametes are diploid.

A diploid germ cell in a reproductive organ goes through meiosis and forms gametes. The gametes, the sperm and the egg, join during fertilization. The result is a diploid zygote. This single diploid cell goes through mitosis and eventually gives rise to all of the cells of the adult, which are also diploid. **› In diploid life cycles, meiosis in germ cells of a multicellular diploid organism results in the formation of haploid gametes.**

Figure 7 Humans and most other animals have a life cycle dominated by a diploid individual. **› *What are the only haploid cells in a diploid life cycle?***

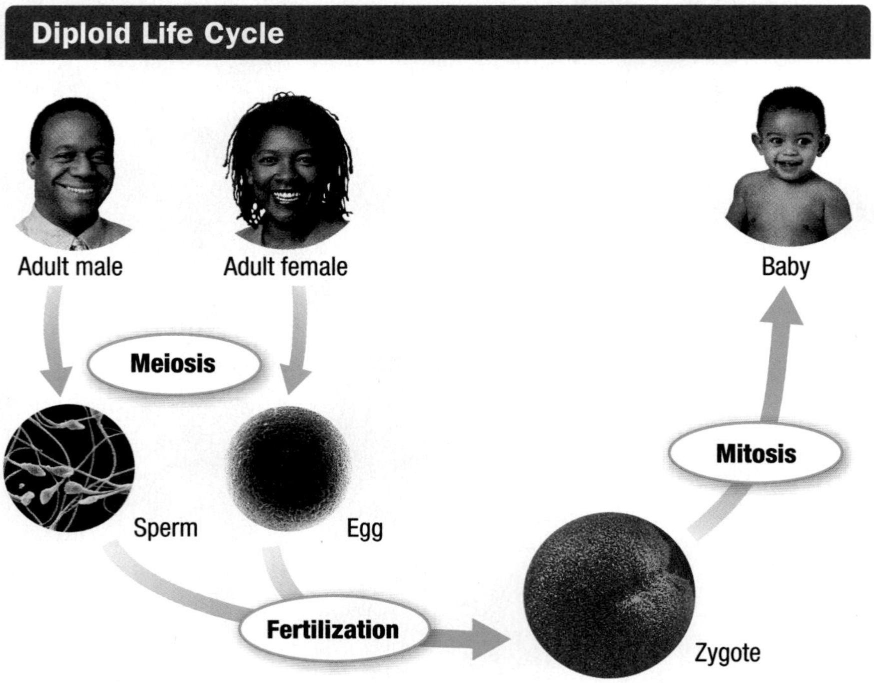

life cycle all of the events in the growth and development of an organism until the organism reaches sexual maturity

sperm the male gamete (sex cell)

ovum a mature egg cell

Diploid Life Cycle

Adult male   Adult female   Baby

Meiosis

Mitosis

Sperm   Egg

Fertilization   Zygote

Meiosis and Gamete Formation

Male animals produce gametes called **sperm.** As **Figure 8** illustrates, a diploid germ cell goes through meiosis I. Two cells are formed, each of which goes through meiosis II. The result is four haploid cells. The four cells change in form and develop a tail to form four sperm.

Female animals produce gametes called eggs, or ova (singular, **ovum**). A diploid germ cell begins to divide by meiosis. Meiosis I results in the formation of two haploid cells that have unequal amounts of cytoplasm. One of the cells has nearly all of the cytoplasm. The other cell, called a *polar body,* is very small and has a small amount of cytoplasm. The polar body may divide again, but its offspring cells will not survive. The larger cell goes through meiosis II, and the division of the cell's cytoplasm is again unequal. The larger cell develops into an ovum. The smaller cell, the second polar body, dies. Because of its larger share of cytoplasm, the mature ovum has a rich storehouse of nutrients. These nutrients nourish the young organism that develops if the ovum is fertilized.

❯ **Reading Check** *How many gametes are formed from one female germ cell?*

Data

Quick**Lab**

 15 min

Chromosome Combinations

When a sperm and egg fuse, two sets of chromosomes are combined. In this lab, you will model this cross between two sets of chromosomes.

Procedure

❶ **Write** "F1F2 X M1M2" on a sheet of paper. F1 and F2 represent the father's chromosomes. M1 and M2 represent the mother's chromosomes.

❷ **Determine** all of the possible chromosome combinations in the zygote that forms from the fusion of the gametes with the chromosomes that you wrote in step 1.

Analysis

1. **Calculate** the number of chromosome combinations that are possible in the zygote.

2. CRITICAL THINKING **Analyzing Data** List all of the possible chromosome combinations.

Figure 8 Meiosis of diploid germ cells results in haploid gametes.

Meiosis in Male and Female Animals

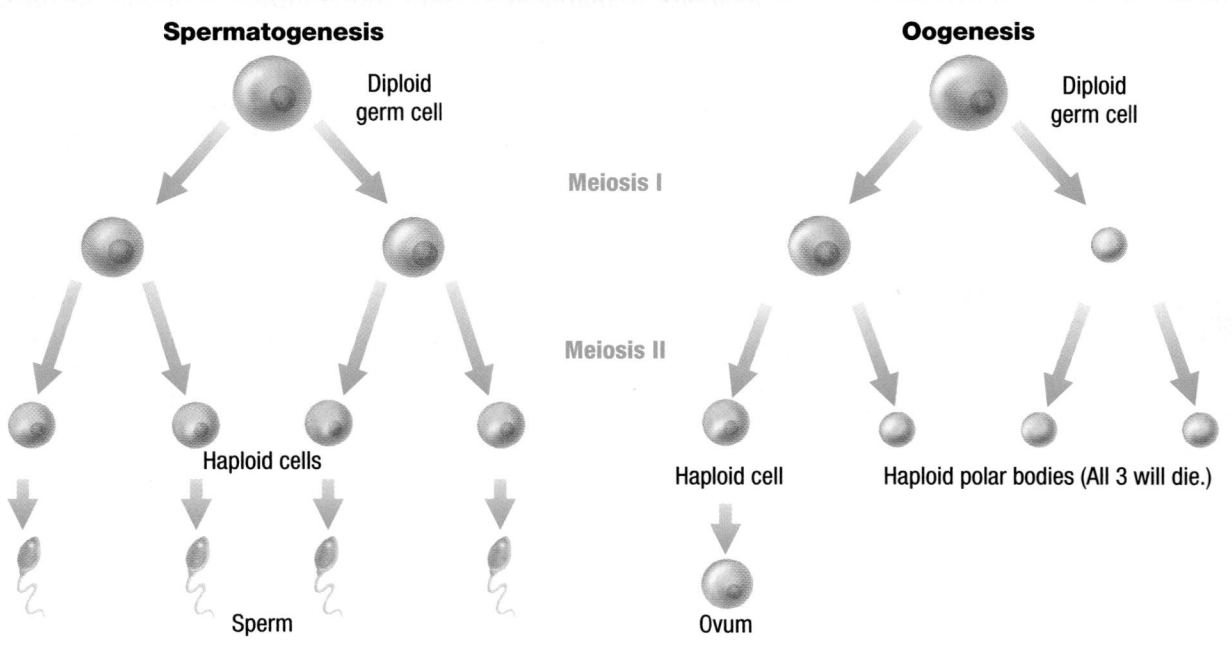

Spermatogenesis

Diploid germ cell

Meiosis I

Meiosis II

Haploid cells

Sperm

Oogenesis

Diploid germ cell

Haploid cell

Haploid polar bodies (All 3 will die.)

Ovum

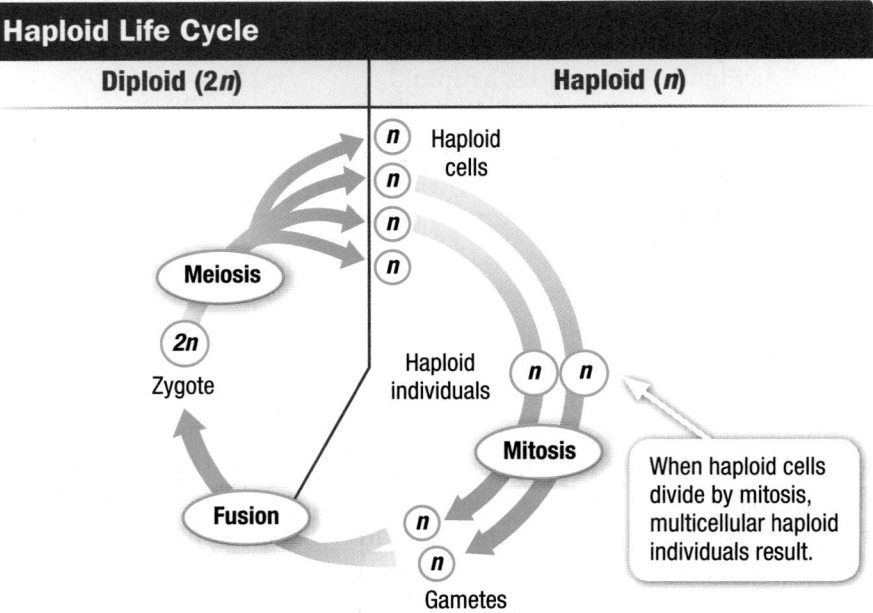

Figure 9 Some organisms, such as fungi, have haploid cells as a major portion of their life cycles.

Haploid Life Cycle

Haploid Life Cycle

Diploid (2*n*)	Haploid (*n*)

n Haploid cells

n

n

n

Meiosis

2n
Zygote

Haploid individuals

n *n*

Mitosis

Fusion

n

n
Gametes

When haploid cells divide by mitosis, multicellular haploid individuals result.

The haploid life cycle, shown in **Figure 9,** happens in most fungi and some protists. Haploid stages make up the major part of this life cycle. The zygote, the only diploid structure, goes through meiosis immediately after it is formed and makes new haploid cells. The haploid cells divide by mitosis and give rise to multicellular haploid individuals. ❯ **In haploid life cycles, meiosis in a diploid zygote results in the formation of the first cell of a multicellular haploid individual.**

Alternation of Generations

❯ **Plants and most multicellular protists have a life cycle that alternates between a haploid phase and a diploid phase called** *alternation of generations.* In plants, the multicellular diploid phase in the life cycle is called a *sporophyte.* Spore-forming cells in the sporophyte undergo meiosis and produce spores. A spore forms a multicellular gameto-phyte. The *gametophyte* is the haploid phase that produces gametes by mitosis. The gametes fuse and give rise to the diploid phase.

READING TOOLBOX

Two-column notes Use two-column notes to summarize the stages and details of the haploid life cycle.

Section
3 Review

❯ **KEY IDEAS**

1. **Summarize** the process in a diploid life cycle.

2. **Describe** what happens in a haploid life cycle.

3. **Describe** what happens to the polar bodies formed during meiosis of a female diploid cell in animal.

4. **Explain** the alternation of generations life cycle.

CRITICAL THINKING

5. **Evaluating Processes** How does the formation of sperm through meiosis of a diploid germ cell differ from the formation of an ovum from a diploid germ cell?

6. **Analyzing Information** What type of cell or structure is the first stage of every sexual life cycle?

WRITING IN SCIENCE

7. **Lesson Plan** Write a lesson plan that you can use to teach a classmate the difference between a haploid and a diploid life cycle. In your own words, write a summary of each. Include diagrams with your explanation.

Chapter 11 Lab

⏱ 45 min

Objectives

> Model the stages of meiosis.

> Describe the events that occur in each stage of the process of meiosis.

> Compare your meiosis model to meiosis stages in a set of prepared slides of lily anther microsporocytes.

Materials

- beads, wooden (40)
- index cards (8)
- marker
- microscope
- microscope slides of lilium anther, 1st and 2nd meiotic division
- scissors
- tape, masking
- yarn

Safety

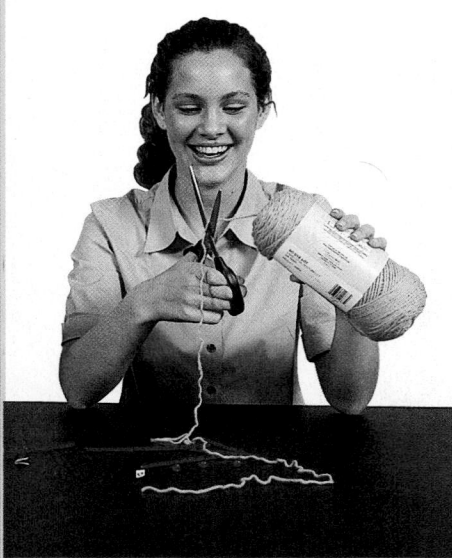

Meiosis Model

In this laboratory, you will work with a partner to develop a meiosis model. You will also have the opportunity to compare your model to the stages of meiosis found in the sacs of a lily anther.

Procedure

Build a Model

1. Work in a team of two. Review the stages of meiosis I and meiosis II. Note the structures and organization that are characteristic of each stage. Pay particular attention to the appearance and behavior of the chromosomes.

2. Work with your partner to design a model of a cell by using the materials listed for this lab. Select and assign a different material to represent each cell structure and keep this consistent in all models. Have your teacher approve the plan.

3. Label each of eight index cards with a specific stage of meiosis, such as "Prophase II."

4. Using your model plan that you designed in step 2, you or your partner will construct a set of models representing the four stages of meiosis I. The other team member will construct another set of models representing the four stages of meiosis II.

5. Once you have completed your set of models, position the cards in two horizontal rows. The top row illustrates the stages of meiosis I. The bottom row illustrates the stages of meiosis II. Compare and contrast the corresponding stages.

Observe Meiosis

6. ⚠ CAUTION: Handle glass slides with care. Obtain a set of prepared slides of lily anther microsporocytes that include a variety of meiotic stages.

7. Use your microscope to view each slide. Locate the various stages of meiosis within the anther sacs.

8. Compare what you observe in the prepared slides to the models that you have constructed.

Analyze and Conclude

1. **Analyzing Processes** Identify and label each stage of meiosis as a haploid stage or a diploid stage.

2. **Comparing Functions** How does anaphase I differ from anaphase II?

3. **SCIENTIFIC METHODS Critiquing Models** Based upon the observations of real cells, evaluate your model. How would you improve your model?

Key Ideas	Key Terms

1 ## Reproduction

> An individual formed by asexual reproduction is genetically identical to its parent.

> In sexual reproduction, two parents give genetic material to produce offspring that are genetically different from their parents.

> Each chromosome has thousands of genes that play an important role in determining how an organism develops and functions.

gamete (248)
zygote (248)
diploid (249)
haploid (249)
homologous chromosomes (249)

2 ## Meiosis

> During meiosis, a diploid cell goes through two divisions to form four haploid cells.

> Mitosis produces cells that are used during growth, development, repair, and asexual reproduction. Meiosis makes cells that enable an organism to reproduce sexually and it only happens in reproductive structures.

> Three key contributions to genetic variation are crossing-over, independent assortment, and random fertilization.

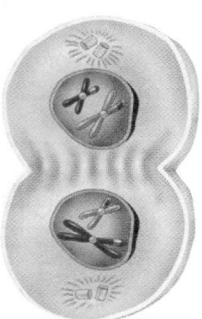

meiosis (250)
crossing-over (251)
independent assortment (254)

3 ## Multicellular Life Cycles

> In diploid life cycles, meiosis in germ cells of a multicellular diploid organism results in the formation of haploid gametes.

> In haploid life cycles, meiosis in a diploid zygote results in the formation of the first cell of a multicellular haploid individual.

> Plants and most multicellular protists have a life cycle that alternates between a haploid phase and a diploid phase called *alternation of generations*.

life cycle (256)
sperm (257)
ovum (257)

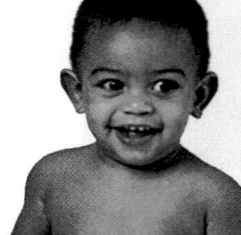

1. **Two-Column Notes** Use two-column notes to summarize the phases of meiosis. Label the left column "Phases of meiosis" and the right column "Details."

2. **Concept Mapping** Make a concept map that shows the three sexual life cycles in multicellular organisms. Include the following words in your map: *meiosis, gametes, spores, zygote, haploid, gametophyte, sporophyte,* and *diploid.*

Using Key Terms

3. Use the following terms in the same sentence: *meiosis, crossing-over,* and *chromatids.*

For each pair of terms, explain how the meanings of the terms differ.

4. *haploid* and *diploid*

5. *sperm* and *ovum*

Understanding Key Ideas

6. Cells that undergo meiosis are
   a. zygotes.
   c. germ cells.
   b. gametes.
   d. somatic cells.

Use the diagram to answer the following question(s).

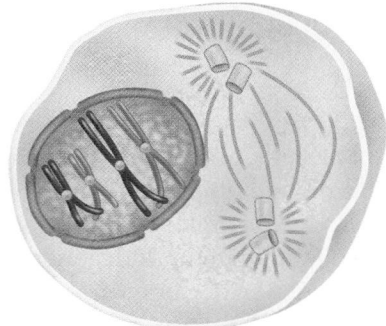

7. Which phase in meiosis is represented in the diagram?
   a. anaphase I
   c. anaphase II
   b. prophase I
   d. telophase I

8. Genes are exchanged between homologous chromosomes during
   a. mitosis.
   c. fertilization.
   b. meiosis II.
   d. crossing-over.

9. Which of the following is not directly produced by a germ cell?
   a. egg
   c. zygote
   b. sperm
   d. gamete

10. Which is *not* a form of asexual reproduction?
    a. budding
    b. binary fission
    c. fragmentation
    d. alternation of generations

11. Homologous chromosomes move to opposite poles during
    a. prophase I.
    c. prophase II.
    b. anaphase I.
    d. anaphase II.

12. Chromosomes that have the same shape, size, and type of genes, but not necessarily the same form of these genes, are called
    a. autosomes.
    c. chromatids.
    b. homologues.
    d. sex chromosomes.

13. Which of the following is a difference between a sporophyte and a gametophyte?
    a. A sporophyte is diploid, and a gametophyte is haploid.
    b. A sporophyte is a plant, and a gametophyte is an animal.
    c. A sporophyte is multicellular, and a gametophyte is unicellular.
    d. A sporophyte undergoes only mitosis, and a gametophyte undergoes both mitosis and meiosis.

Explaining Key Ideas

14. **Explain** the difference between a diploid life cycle and a haploid life cycle.

15. **Distinguish** mitosis from meiosis.

16. **Identify** what type of organisms have a life cycle that alternates between diploid and haploid.

17. **Describe** the process of alternation of generations.

Using Science Graphics

Use the diagram below to answer the following question(s).

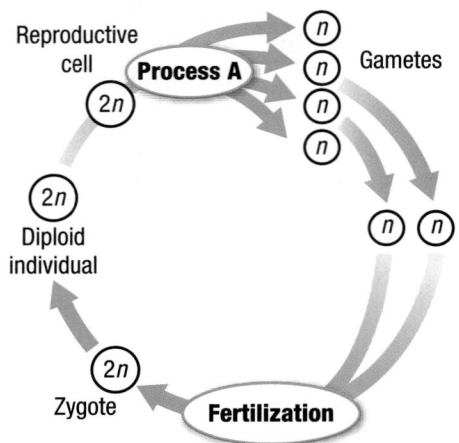

18. What occurs at Process A?

19. What organisms typically have the life cycle shown in this diagram?

Critical Thinking

20. Recognizing Patterns Which feature of an alternation of generations life cycle distinguishes this life cycle from both a diploid life cycle and a haploid life cycle?

21. Evaluating Results What would be the result of crossing-over between chromatids of the same homologous chromosome?

22. Analyzing Results Occasionally, homologous chromosomes fail to separate during meiosis I. Using the hypothetical example of an adult organism that has two pairs of chromosomes, describe the chromosomal makeup of the eggs that would result from this error in meiosis.

23. Evaluating Results If a cell begins meiosis with two pairs of homologous chromosomes, how many chromatids will be in each cell that is produced at the end of meiosis I?

24. Forming Reasoned Opinions Is there a relationship between the number of chromosomes and the complexity of an organism? Give support for your answer.

Connecting Key Ideas

25. Constructing Explanations The unicellular protist *Paramecium* can reproduce asexually by binary fission. How would binary fission in this eukaryote differ from binary fission in a prokaryote?

Alternative Assessment

26. Research Use the Internet to investigate captive-breeding programs for endangered species in zoos. Compare the genetic variation of captive-bred animals with the genetic variation of wild animals. What can researchers do to help maintain genetic diversity in breeding programs?

27. Building Models Collect materials to use in building models of the different stages of meiosis and mitosis. Attach your models to poster boards, and label each stage and the structures present in meiosis and mitosis.

Writing for Science

28. Report Write a brief report that summarizes the effects of various treatments for infertility. Find out how the production of gametes may be affected in some people who are infertile.

Math Skills

29. Making Calculations If the diploid chromosome number of a species is 24, how many chromosomes would a haploid cell have?
a. 12
b. 24
c. 36
d. 48

30. Problem Solving Consider a hypothetical species with a diploid number of 4 chromosomes. What would be the diploid chromosome number of the offspring in the 10th generation after meiotic production of gametes?

> **TEST TIP** If you are unsure of the answer to a particular question, put a question mark beside it and go on to the next question. If you have time, go back and reconsider any question that you skipped. (Do not write in this book.)

Science Concepts

1. Which of the following sex chromosomes do most human females have?

A XY   **C** YY

B XX   **D** XN

2. If the diploid chromosome number of a species is 24, then a cell with 12 chromosomes would be

F a zygote.   **H** a haploid cell.

G a polyploid cell.   **J** a diploid cell.

3. The random distribution of homologous chromosomes during meiosis is called

A fission.

B budding.

C crossing-over.

D independent assortment.

4. In addition to the genetic variability produced during meiosis, sexual reproduction generates genetic variability as a result of

F mitosis.

G spore formation.

H random fertilization.

J harsh environments.

5. Sperm formation produces

A four diploid cells.

B four haploid cells.

C four polar bodies.

D two haploid cells.

6. In a haploid sexual life cycle, meiosis occurs

F at any stage in the life cycle.

G in cells of multicellular individuals.

H immediately after a zygote is formed.

J at the time when an individual reaches its mature size.

Using Science Graphics

The graph shows chromosome number for different animals. Use the diagram to answer the following question(s).

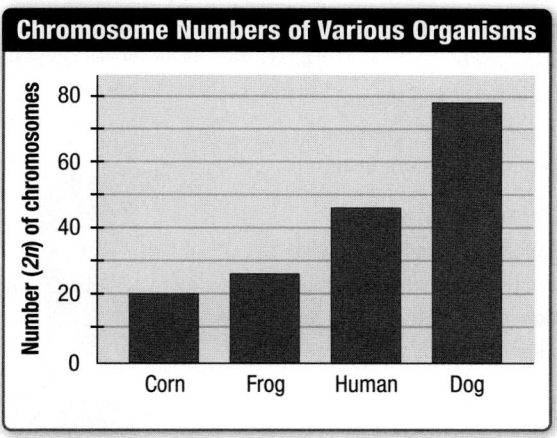

Chromosome Numbers of Various Organisms

7. How many chromosomes are in a frog gamete?

A 13   **C** 26

B 20   **D** 62

8. Which organism has 10 chromosomes in one of its gametes?

F dog   **H** corn

G frog   **J** human

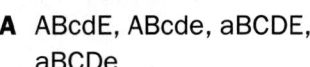

The diagram shows crossing over of two chromatids. Use the diagram to answer the following question(s).

9. After crossing-over as shown, what would the sequence of genes be for each of the chromatids?

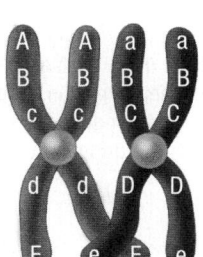

A ABcdE, ABcde, aBCDE, aBCDe

B ABEcd, ABcde, aBCDE, aBCDe

C ABcdE, ABcde, aBCDE, aBCdeE

D ABcdE, ABcdE, aBCDE, aBCde

Writing Skills

10. Essay Write a one-page report explaining why meiosis is important in sexual reproduction.

Chapter 12

Mendel and Heredity

The common corn snake (*Elaphe guttata*) is a popular pet. Snake breeders have discovered many variations of colors and patterns in this species.

This color pattern is common in wild corn snakes. It is a combination of black, red, and yellow skin colors.

Preview

1 Origins of Hereditary Science
Mendel's Breeding Experiments
Features of Pea Plants
Mendel's First Experiments
Ratios in Mendel's Results

2 Mendel's Theory
Explaining Mendel's Results
Random Segregation of Alleles
Mendel's Findings in Modern Terms
Mendel's Second Experiments

3 Modeling Mendel's Laws
Using Punnett Squares
Using Probability
Using a Pedigree

4 Beyond Mendelian Heredity
Many Genes, Many Alleles
Genes Affected by the Environment
Genes Linked Within Chromosomes

Why It Matters

Your genetic makeup influences your appearance, your personality, your abilities, and your health. We now know that many human traits, such as talents and diseases, have their origins in genes. As we come to understand how traits are inherited, we can use this information to better our lives.

InquiryLab

15 min

What Are the Chances?

Do you think you can predict the result of a coin toss? What if you flip the coin many times? In this activity, you will test your predictions.

Procedure

1 Read steps 2 and 3. Predict the results, and write down your prediction.

2 Flip a **coin,** and let it land. Record which side is up (heads or tails). Repeat this step 10 times.

3 Calculate what fraction of the total number of flips resulted in heads. Calculate what fraction of flips resulted in tails.

4 Read steps 5 and 6. Predict the results, and write down your prediction.

5 Tally the flip results of the entire class.

6 Calculate the fraction of heads and the fraction of tails in step 5.

Analysis

1. **Compare** your predictions from steps 1 and 4 with the results in steps 3 and 6.

2. **Compare** your own results in step 3 to those of other individuals in your class. Identify how closely each individual result matches the total class results.

This corn snake lacks the ability to produce red skin color.

This corn snake lacks the ability to produce black skin color.

READING TOOLBOX

These reading tools can help you learn the material in this chapter. For more information on how to use these and other tools, see **Appendix: Reading and Study Skills.**

Using Words

Word Parts Knowing the meanings of word parts can help you figure out the meaning of words that you do not know.

Your Turn Use the table to answer the following.

1. Heritage is something handed down from one's ancestors. What do you think *heredity* is?
2. Use the meaning of the prefix *phen-* and the suffix *-type* to figure out what *phenotype* means.

Word Parts		
Word part	**Type**	**Meaning**
gen-	prefix	born; to become; to produce
her-	prefix	heir; remains; to be left behind
phen-	prefix	to show
-type	suffix	form; mark; kind

Using Language

Analogies An analogy question asks you to analyze the relationship between two words in one pair and to identify a second pair of words that have the same relationship. Colons are used to express the analogy for this type of question. For example, the analogy "up is to down as top is to bottom" is written "up : down :: top : bottom. In this example, the relationship between the words in each pair is the same.

Your Turn Use information in the chapter to complete this analogy.

allele : gene :: trait : _____

(Hint: Finding out how alleles and genes are related will help you figure out which word to use to fill in the blank.)

Using Science Graphics

Punnett Squares A Punnett square is a tool that is used to figure out possible combinations when combining items from a group. For example, if you have a red shirt, a green shirt, and a yellow shirt that you could wear with either blue jeans or shorts, how many combinations could you make?

Your Turn Finish filling in the Punnett square shown here to answer the following questions.

1. How many combinations include a red shirt?
2. What combination of shirt and pants do you find in the bottom right corner of this Punnett square?
3. How many combinations would you have if you added a pair of brown pants to the group?

	Red shirt	Green shirt	Yellow shirt
Blue jeans	Red shirt with blue jeans		
Shorts		Green shirt with shorts	

Origins of Hereditary Science

Key Ideas	Key Terms	Why It Matters
❯ Why was Gregor Mendel important for modern genetics? ❯ Why did Mendel conduct experiments with garden peas? ❯ What were the important steps in Mendel's first experiments? ❯ What were the important results of Mendel's first experiments?	character trait hybrid generation	Our understanding of genetics, including what makes us unique, can be traced back to Mendel's discoveries.

Since they first learned how to breed plants and animals, people have been interested in heredity. In the 1800s, one person figured out some of the first key ideas of genetics. Recall that *genetics* is the science of heredity and the mechanism by which traits are passed from parents to offspring.

Mendel's Breeding Experiments

A monk named Gregor Johann Mendel lived in the 1800s in Austria. Mendel did breeding experiments with the garden pea plant, *Pisum sativum,* shown in **Figure 1.** Farmers had done similar experiments before, but Mendel was the first person to develop rules that accurately predict the patterns of heredity in pea plants. ❯ **Modern genetics is based on Mendel's explanations for the patterns of heredity in garden pea plants.**

As a young man, Mendel studied to be a priest. Later, he went to the University of Vienna. There, he learned how to study science through experimentation and how to use mathematics to explain natural events. Mendel lived the rest of his life in a monastery, where he taught high school and cared for a garden. It was in this garden that he completed his important experiments.

Most of Mendel's experiments involved crossing different types of pea plants. In this case, the word *cross* means "to mate or breed two individuals." Mendel crossed a type of garden pea plant that had purple flowers with a type that had white flowers. All of the offspring from that cross had purple flowers. However, when two of these purple-flowered offspring were crossed, some offspring had white flowers and some had purple flowers.

The white color had reappeared in the second group of offspring! Mendel decided to investigate this strange occurrence. So, he carefully crossed different types of pea plants and recorded the numbers of each type of offspring. He did this experiment many times.

❯ **Reading Check** *How did Mendel experiment with pea plants? (See the Appendix for answers to Reading Checks.)*

Figure 1 To cross plants that each had flowers of a different color, Mendel controlled the pollen that fertilized each flower.

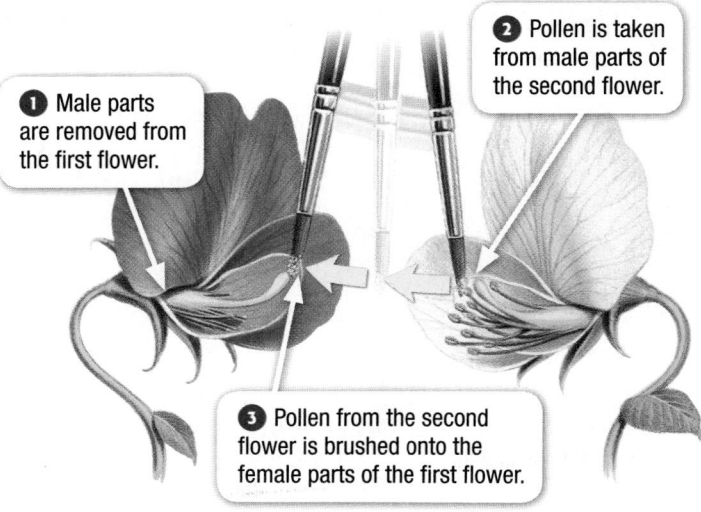

1 Male parts are removed from the first flower.

2 Pollen is taken from male parts of the second flower.

3 Pollen from the second flower is brushed onto the female parts of the first flower.

Features of Pea Plants

Mendel studied seven features in his pea plants, as **Figure 2** shows. **❯The garden pea plant is a good subject for studying heredity because the plant has contrasting traits, usually self-pollinates, and grows easily.**

Contrasting Traits In the study of heredity, physical features that are inherited are called **characters.** Several characters of the garden pea plant exist in two clearly different forms. The plant's flower color is either purple or white—there are no intermediate forms. A **trait** is one of several possible forms of a character. Purple is one of two possible traits for the flower-color character in pea plants. Other contrasting traits of pea plants are shown in **Figure 2.** (For some characters, more than two traits may be possible). Mendel wanted to see what would happen when he crossed individuals that have different traits. In such a cross, the offspring that result are called **hybrids.**

Self-Pollination In garden pea plants, each flower contains both male and female reproductive parts. This arrangement allows the plant to *self-pollinate,* or fertilize itself. Pea plants can also reproduce through *cross-pollination.* This process occurs when pollen from the flower of one plant is carried by insects or by other means to the flower of another plant. To cross-pollinate two pea plants, Mendel had to make sure that the plants could not self-pollinate. So, he removed the male parts (which produce pollen) from some of the flowers. But he did not remove the female parts (which produce eggs, fruit, and seeds). Then, he dusted the female parts of one plant with pollen from another plant.

Easy to Grow The garden pea is a small plant that needs little care and matures quickly. Also, each plant produces many offspring. Thus, many results can be compared for each type of cross. Recall that collecting repeated data is an important scientific method.

❯ Reading Check ***What is the difference between a trait and a character?***

ACADEMIC VOCABULARY

contrast to show differences when compared.

character a recognizable inherited feature or characteristic of an organism

trait one of two or more possible forms of a character; a recognizable feature or characteristic of an organism

hybrid the offspring of a cross between parents that have contrasting traits

generation the entire group of offspring produced by a given group of parents

Figure 2 In the experiments in his garden, Mendel grew and studied many kinds of pea plants. **❯ Why did Mendel study pea plants?**

Seven Characters with Contrasting Traits Studied by Mendel

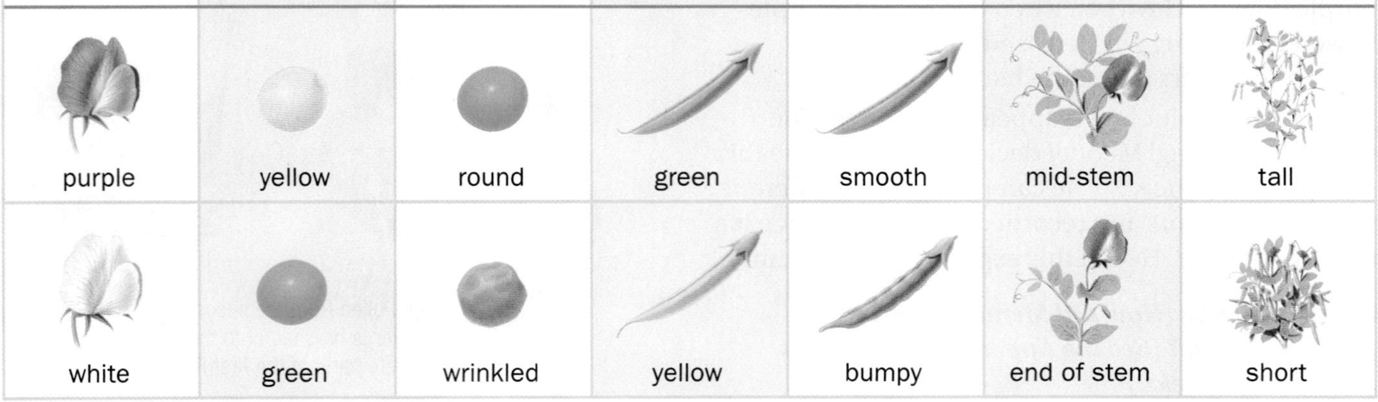

Flower color	Seed color	Seed shape	Pod color	Pod Shape	Flower position	Plant height
purple	yellow	round	green	smooth	mid-stem	tall
white	green	wrinkled	yellow	bumpy	end of stem	short

Three Steps of Mendel's First Experiments

1 Producing a true-breeding P generation

Self-pollination

P generation

Self-pollination

P generation

2 Producing an F₁ generation

Cross-pollination

F₁ generation
All purple

3 Producing an F₂ generation

Self-pollination

F₂ generation
705 purple : 224 white

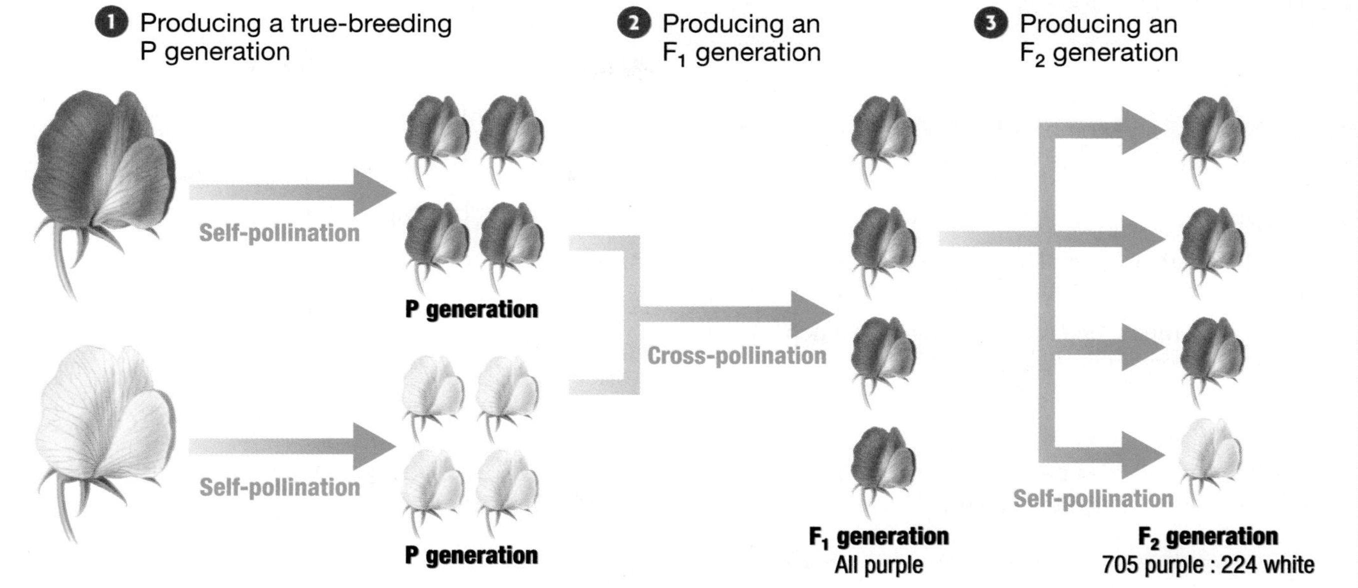

Figure 3 In his garden experiments, Mendel carefully selected and grew specific kinds of pea plants. ❯ **What is the relationship between each generation in these experiments?**

Mendel's First Experiments

A *monohybrid cross* is a cross that is done to study one pair of contrasting traits. For example, crossing a plant that has purple flowers with a plant that has white flowers is a monohybrid cross. ❯ **Mendel's first experiments used monohybrid crosses and were carried out in three steps.** The three steps are shown in **Figure 3.** Each step involved a new generation of plants. A **generation** is a group of offspring from a given group of parents.

Step 1 Mendel allowed plants that had each type of trait to self-pollinate for several generations. This process ensured that each plant always produced offspring of the same type. Such a plant is said to be *true-breeding* for a given trait. For example, every time a true-breeding plant that has purple flowers self-pollinates, its offspring will have purple flowers. Mendel used true-breeding plants as the first generation in his experiments. The first group of parents that are crossed in a breeding experiment are called the *parental generation,* or *P generation.*

Step 2 Mendel crossed two P generation plants that had contrasting traits, such as purple flowers and white flowers. He called the offspring of the P generation the *first filial generation,* or *F₁ generation.* He recorded the number of F₁ plants that had each trait.

Step 3 Mendel allowed the F₁ generation to self-pollinate and produce new plants. He called this new generation of offspring the *second filial generation,* or *F₂ generation.* He recorded the number of F₂ plants that had each trait.

❯ **Reading Check** *What is a monohybrid cross?*

Word Parts The word *filial* is from the Latin *filialis,* which means "of a son or daughter." Thus, F (filial) generations are all of the generations that follow a P (parental) generation. What do you think *filiation* means?

QuickLab

⏱ 10 min

Mendel's Ratios

You can calculate and compare the F₂ generation ratios that Mendel obtained from his first experiments.

Procedure

❶ Copy this partially complete table onto a separate **sheet of paper**. Then, fill in the ratios of F₂ traits.

❷ Simplify the ratios, and round the terms in each ratio to the nearest hundredth digit.

Analysis

1. **Identify** the similarities between the ratios by rounding each term to the nearest whole number.

Character	Traits in F₂ generation		Ratio
Flower color	705 purple	224 white	705:224 or 3.15:1.00
Seed color	6,022 yellow	2,001 green	
Seed shape	5,474 round	1,850 wrinkled	
Pod color	428 green	152 yellow	
Pod shape	882 smooth	299 bumpy	
Flower position	651 mid-stem	207 end of stem	
Plant height	787 tall	277 short	

2. **CRITICAL THINKING** **Analyzing Data** Why weren't all of the ratios exactly the same?

Ratios in Mendel's Results

www.scilinks.org
Topic: Gregor Mendel
Code: HX80698

All of Mendel's F₁ plants expressed the same trait for a given character. The contrasting trait had disappeared! But when the F₁ plants were allowed to self-pollinate, the missing trait reappeared in some of the F₂ plants. Noticing this pattern, Mendel compared the ratio of traits that resulted from each cross.

When F₁ plants that had purple flowers were crossed with one another, 705 of the F₂ offspring had purple flowers and 224 had white flowers. So, the F₂ ratio of purple-flowered plants to white-flowered plants was 705:224, or about 3:1. Mendel's studies of the other characters gave a similar pattern. ❯ **For each of the seven characters that Mendel studied, he found a similar 3-to-1 ratio of contrasting traits in the F₂ generation.** As you will learn, Mendel tried to explain this pattern.

❯ **Reading Check** *What was the important difference between Mendel's F₁ and F₂ generations?*

Section 1 Review

❯ KEY IDEAS

1. **Identify** Gregor Mendel's contribution to modern genetics.

2. **Describe** why garden pea plants are good subjects for genetic experiments.

3. **Summarize** the three major steps of Mendel's first experiments.

4. **State** the typical ratio of traits in Mendel's first experiments.

CRITICAL THINKING

5. **Using Scientific Methods** Why did Mendel record the results of so many plant crosses?

6. **Predicting Outcomes** Squash plants do not usually self-pollinate. If Mendel had used squash plants, how might his experiments have differed?

WRITING FOR SCIENCE

7. **Technical Writing** Imagine that you are Gregor Mendel and you need to document your first experiments for a science magazine. Write out your procedure for breeding pea plants. Be sure to explain how you controlled variables and assured that data was reliable.

Amazing Mutants

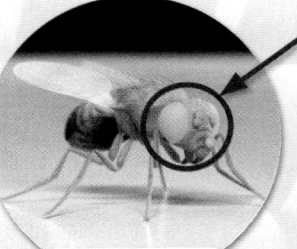
WEIRD SCIENCE

Fruit flies are widely used in genetic research because "mutant" forms provide clues about how genes work. One fly species, *Drosophila melanogaster,* has been studied so much that scientists understand its genes better than those of most other organisms. Still, there are many bizarre mutations yet to be understood.

Popular in the Lab

Fruit flies are popular with scientists because the flies are easy to breed and raise in a laboratory. The flies grow and reproduce quickly and reproduce in large numbers. Also, the flies have been used in important genetic experiments since 1910.

Many Mutations

Most scientists who study fruit flies are interested in genetic variation and mutations. Thousands of "mutant" forms that have unique *alleles* (versions of a gene) have been observed in species of the genus *Drosophila*. Databases on the Internet are used to share information on over 14,000 fruit fly genes. Just a few of the many kinds of fruit fly "mutants" are described here.

Research Find out more about *Drosophila,* such as its life cycle, size, and use in research.

Normal "wild" fruit fly

Fly lacking eye color

Different Colors Differences in color are easy to recognize in a lab. Some fruit fly mutations affect eye color and body patterns. Some of the genes for coloration in flies show simple inheritance patterns, like the patterns that Mendel observed in garden pea plants.

Malformed Body Parts Some genes control the development of body parts. Mutations in such genes often cause body parts to develop improperly, as did the malformed wings shown here. This particular trait is seen only when a fly has a normal allele paired with the malformed-wing allele. A fly that has two such alleles will not survive.

Fly with malformed wings

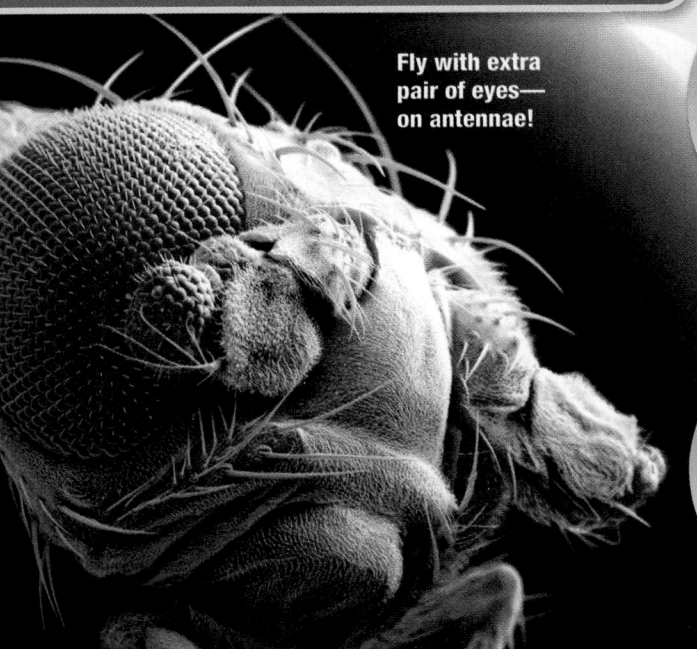
Fly with extra pair of eyes— on antennae!

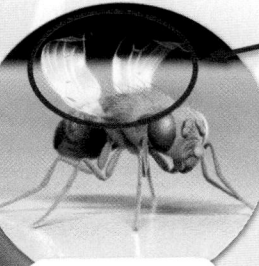
Fly with legs in place of antennae

Misplaced Body Parts Imagine growing legs from your head! Some mutations cause legs, antennae, mouthparts, and wings to grow in various places on a fly's body. By studying these oddities, scientists have begun to understand the genes that control the arrangement of body parts in insects and other animals.

Section 2

Mendel's Theory

Key Ideas	Key Terms	Why It Matters
❯ What patterns of heredity were explained by Mendel's hypotheses? ❯ What is the law of segregation? ❯ How does genotype relate to phenotype? ❯ What is the law of independent assortment?	allele phenotype dominant homozygous recessive heterozygous genotype	Mendel's theory explains why you have some, but not all, of the traits of your parents.

Explaining Mendel's Results

Mendel developed several hypotheses to explain the results of his experiments. His hypotheses were basically correct but have been updated with newer terms and more-complete knowledge. Mendel's hypotheses, collectively called the *Mendelian theory of heredity,* form the foundation of modern genetics. ❯ **Mendelian theory explains simple patterns of inheritance. In these patterns, two of several versions of a gene combine and result in one of several possible traits.**

Alternate Versions of Genes Before Mendel's experiments, many people thought that the traits of offspring were always a blend of the traits from parents. If this notion were true, a tall plant crossed with a short plant would result in offspring of medium height. But Mendel's results did not support the blending hypothesis. Mendel noticed that his pea plants would express only one of two traits for each character, such as purple or white flower color. Today, scientists know that different traits result from different versions of genes. Each version of a gene is called an **allele.**

❯ **Reading Check** *What is the "blending" hypothesis?*

Figure 4 Each individual has two alleles for a given character. A single gamete carries only one of the two alleles. ❯ **In pea plants, how many alleles for seed color does each parent pass on to each offspring?**

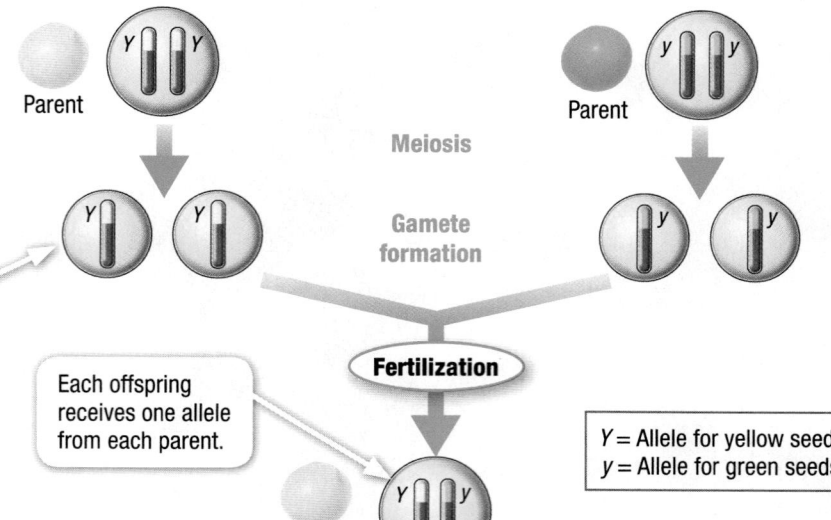

Each gamete receives one allele from the parent.

Each offspring receives one allele from each parent.

Parent   Meiosis   Parent

Gamete formation

Fertilization

Offspring

Y = Allele for yellow seeds
y = Allele for green seeds

QuickLab

15 min

Dominant and Recessive Traits

Can you find Mendelian patterns in humans? Look for ratios between these contrasting traits.

Freckles

Dimples

Procedure

1 On a separate sheet of paper, draw a table like the one shown here. For each character, circle the trait that best matches your own trait.

2 Tally the class results to determine how many students in your class share each trait.

Dominant trait	Recessive trait
freckles	no freckles
no cleft	cleft chin
dimples	no dimples

Analysis

1. **Summarize** the class results for each character.

2. **Calculate** the ratio of dominant traits to recessive traits for each character.

3. **CRITICAL THINKING Mathematical Reasoning** Are each of the ratios the same? Why is this unlikely to happen?

4. **CRITICAL THINKING Analyzing Results** For which traits must a person who has the given trait receive the same allele from both parents? Explain your answer.

One Allele from Each Parent Mendel also noticed that traits can come from either parent. The reason is related to meiosis, as **Figure 4** shows. When gametes form, each pair of alleles is separated. Only one of the pair is passed on to offspring.

Dominant and Recessive Alleles For every pair of traits that Mendel studied, one trait always seemed to "win" over the other. That is, whenever both alleles were present, only one was fully expressed as a trait. The other allele had no effect on the organism's physical form. In this case, the expressed allele is called **dominant.** The allele that is not expressed when the dominant allele is present is called **recessive.** Traits may also be called *dominant* or *recessive*. For example, in pea plants, the yellow-seed trait is dominant, and the green-seed trait is recessive.

Random Segregation of Alleles

Mendel did not understand how chromosomes separate during meiosis, but he learned something important about this process. Because chromosome pairs split up randomly, either one of a pair of homologous chromosomes might end up in any one gamete. As **Figure 4** shows, offspring receive one allele from each parent. But only chance decides which alleles will be passed on through gametes. Mendel showed that segregation is <u>random</u>, and he stated his hypothesis as a law. ❯ In modern terms, the *law of segregation* holds that when an organism produces gametes, each pair of alleles is separated and each gamete has an equal chance of receiving either one of the alleles.

allele (uh LEEL) one of two or more alternative forms of a gene, each leading to a unique trait

dominant (DAHM uh nuhnt) describes an allele that is fully expressed whenever the allele is present in an individual

recessive (ri SES iv) describes an allele that is expressed only when there is no dominant allele present in an individual

ACADEMIC VOCABULARY

random without aim

genotype (JEE nuh TIEP) a specific combination of alleles in an individual

phenotype (FEE noh TIEP) the detectable trait or traits that result from the genotype of an individual

homozygous (HOH moh ZIE guhs) describes an individual that carries two identical alleles of a gene

heterozygous (HET uhr OH ZIE guhs) describes an individual that carries two different alleles of a gene

Mendel's Findings in Modern Terms

Although Mendel did not use the term allele, he used a code of letters to represent the function of alleles. Today, scientists use such a code along with modern terms, as shown in **Figure 5.** A dominant allele is shown as a capital letter. This letter is usually the first letter of the word for the trait. For example, purple flower color is a dominant trait in pea plants, so the allele is written as *P*. A recessive allele is shown as a lowercase letter. The letter is usually the same as the one used for the dominant allele. So, white flower color is written as *p*.

Genotype and Phenotype Mendel's experiments showed that an offspring's traits do not match one-to-one with the parents' traits. In other words, offspring do not show a trait for every allele that they receive. Instead, combinations of alleles determine traits. The set of alleles that an individual has for a character is called the **genotype.** The trait that results from a set of alleles is the **phenotype.** In other words, ❯ genotype determines phenotype. For example, if the genotype of a pea plant is *pp,* the phenotype is white flowers. If the genotype is *Pp* or *PP,* the phenotype is purple flowers, as shown in **Figure 5.**

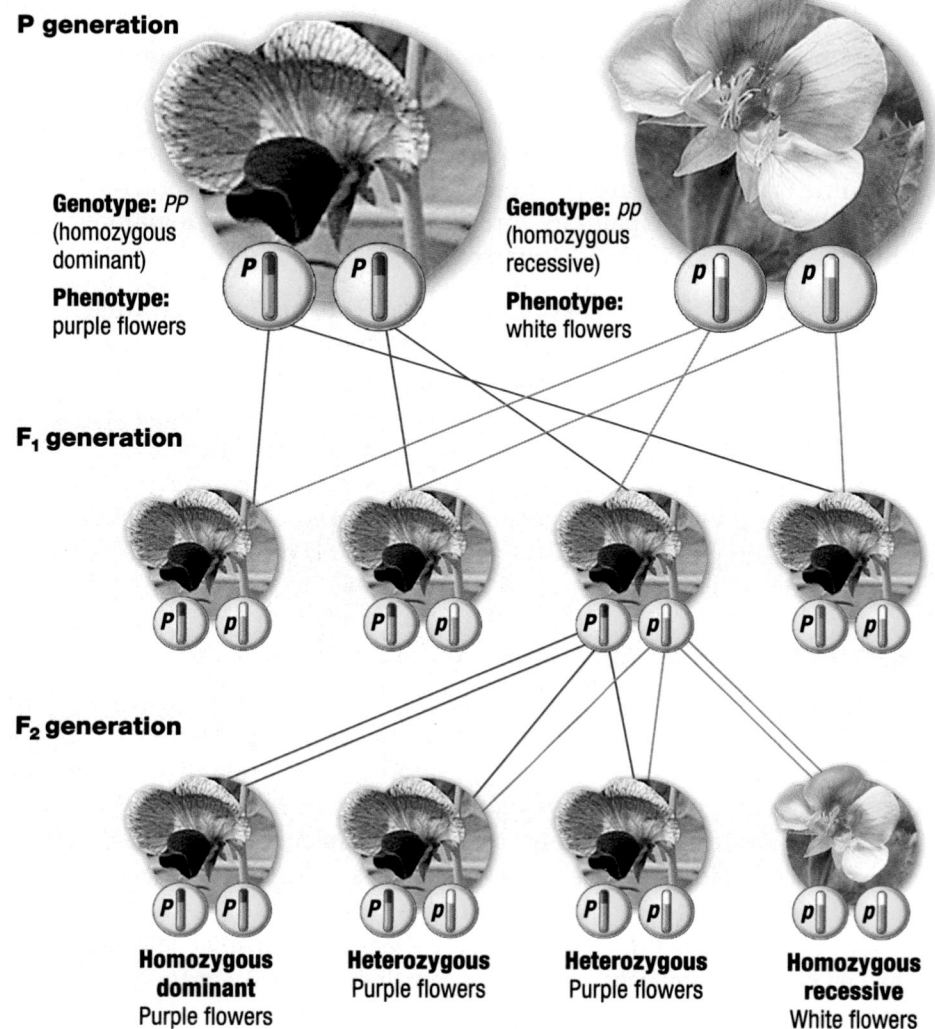

P generation

Genotype: *PP*
(homozygous dominant)

Phenotype:
purple flowers

Genotype: *pp*
(homozygous recessive)

Phenotype:
white flowers

F₁ generation

F₂ generation

Homozygous dominant
Purple flowers

Heterozygous
Purple flowers

Heterozygous
Purple flowers

Homozygous recessive
White flowers

Figure 5 Mendel's first experiments demonstrated dominance, segregation, genotype, and phenotype. ❯ **What is the relationship between the genotypes and phenotypes in each generation shown here?**

Homozygous and Heterozygous If an individual has two of the same alleles of a certain gene, the individual is **homozygous** for the related character. For example, a plant that has two white-flower alleles (*pp*) is homozygous for flower color. On the other hand, if an individual has two different alleles of a certain gene, the individual is **heterozygous** for the related character. For example, a plant that has one purple-flower allele and one white-flower allele (*Pp*) is heterozygous for flower color. In the heterozygous case, the dominant allele is expressed. This condition explains Mendel's curious results, as **Figure 5** shows.

Mendel's Second Experiments

Mendel not only looked for patterns, he also looked for a lack of patterns. For example, the round-seed trait did not always show up in garden pea plants that had the yellow-seed trait. Mendel made dihybrid crosses to study these results. A *dihybrid cross*, shown in **Figure 6,** involves two characters, such as seed color and seed shape.

Independent Assortment In these crosses, Mendel found that the inheritance of one character did not affect the inheritance of any other. He proposed another law. ❯ **In modern terms, the *law of independent assortment* holds that during gamete formation, the alleles of each gene segregate independently.** For example, in **Figure 6,** the alleles for seed color (*Y* and *y*) can "mix and match" with the alleles for seed shape (*R* and *r*). So, round seeds may or may not be yellow.

Genes Linked on Chromosomes Mendel's second law seems to say that each gene has nothing to do with other genes. But we now know that many genes are linked to each other as parts of chromosomes. So, genes that are located close together on the same chromosome will rarely separate independently. Thus, genes are said to be *linked* when they are close together on chromosomes. The only genes that follow Mendel's law are those that are far apart.

❯ **Reading Check** *What is a dihybrid cross?*

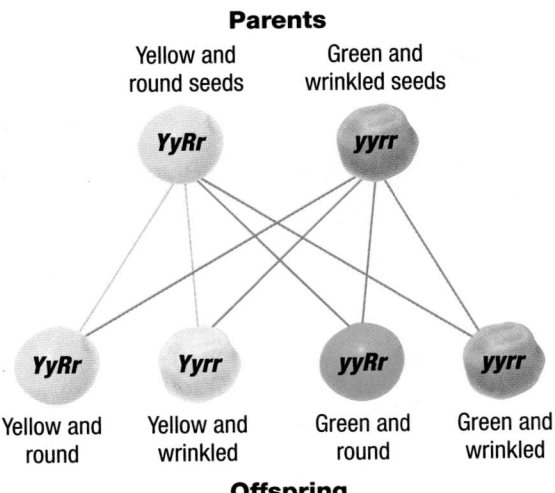

Parents

Yellow and round seeds — **YyRr**

Green and wrinkled seeds — **yyrr**

YyRr Yellow and round

Yyrr Yellow and wrinkled

yyRr Green and round

yyrr Green and wrinkled

Offspring

Figure 6 Mendel used dihybrid crosses in his second experiments. He found that the inheritance of one character, such as seed color, did not affect the inheritance of another character, such as seed shape.
❯ What law did Mendel propose to explain these findings?

www.scilinks.org
Topic: Mendel's Laws
Code: HX80938

Section 2 Review

❯ KEY IDEAS

1. **Describe** the patterns that Mendelian theory explains.
2. **Summarize** the law of segregation.
3. **Relate** genotype to phenotype, using examples from Mendel's experiments with pea plants.
4. **Summarize** the law of independent assortment.

CRITICAL THINKING

5. **Analyzing Data** The term *gene* did not exist when Mendel formed his hypotheses. What other genetic terms are used today that Mendel did not likely use?
6. **Arguing Logically** Would it be correct to say that a genotype is heterozygous recessive? Explain.
7. **Critiquing Explanations** Identify the strengths and weaknesses of Mendel's law of independent assortment.

METHODS OF SCIENCE

8. **Testing an Hypothesis** How did Mendel test his hypothesis that the inheritance of one character does not affect the inheritance of another character?

3 Modeling Mendel's Laws

Key Ideas	Key Terms	Why It Matters
❯ How can a Punnett square be used in genetics? ❯ How can mathematical probability be used in genetics? ❯ What information does a pedigree show?	Punnett square probability pedigree genetic disorder	Mendel's laws can be used to help breed exotic pets, thoroughbred livestock, and productive crops.

Why are Mendel's laws so important? Mendel's laws can be used to predict and understand the results of certain kinds of crosses. Farmers, gardeners, animal keepers, and biologists need to make predictions when they try to breed organisms that have desired characteristics. Medical professionals need to know about the inheritance of traits in their patients. Graphical models that can help with these tasks include Punnett squares and pedigrees.

Using Punnett Squares

A **Punnett square** is a model that predicts the likely outcomes of a genetic cross. The model is named for its inventor, Reginald Punnett.
❯ **A Punnett square shows all of the genotypes that could result from a given cross.**

The simplest Punnett square consists of a square divided into four boxes. As **Figure 7** shows, the possible alleles from one parent are written along the top of the square. The possible alleles from the other parent are written along the left side. Each box inside the square holds two letters. The combination of letters in each box represents one possible genotype in the offspring. The letters in each box are a combination of two alleles—one from each parent.

Punnett square (PUHN uht SKWER) a graphic used to predict the results of a genetic cross

Figure 7 Each of these Punnett squares shows a monohybrid cross involving seed color in peas. ❯ How does a Punnett square predict the outcome of a cross?

YY = homozygous dominant

Yy = heterozygous

yy = homozygous recessive

Homozygous Cross In a cross of homozygous parents that have contrasting traits, 100% of the offspring will be heterozygous and will show the dominant trait.

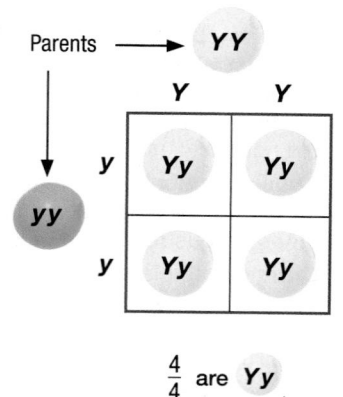

$\frac{4}{4}$ are **Yy**

Heterozygous Cross In a cross of heterozygous parents that have the same traits, the ratio of genotypes will be 1:2:1. The ratio of phenotypes will be 3:1.

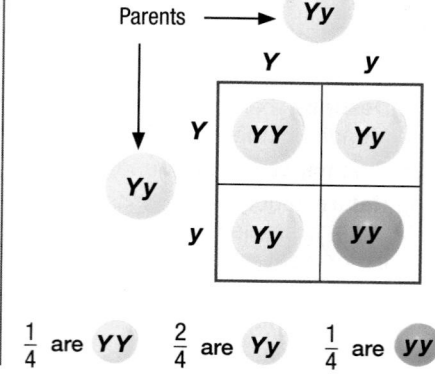

$\frac{1}{4}$ are **YY** $\frac{2}{4}$ are **Yy** $\frac{1}{4}$ are **yy**

Quick**Lab**

🕐 **10 min**

Testcross

When genotypes are known, Punnett squares can be used to predict phenotypes. But can genotypes be determined if only phenotypes are known?

Suppose a breeder has a rabbit that has a dominant phenotype, such as black fur (as opposed to recessive brown fur). How could the breeder know whether the rabbit is homozygous (*BB*) or heterozygous (*Bb*) for fur color? The breeder could perform a testcross.

A *testcross* is used to test an individual whose phenotype for a characteristic is dominant but whose genotype is not known. This individual is crossed with an individual whose genotype is known to be homozygous recessive. In our example, the breeder would cross the black rabbit (*BB* or *Bb*) with a brown rabbit (*bb*).

Procedure

On a separate **sheet of paper**, copy the two Punnett squares shown here. Write the appropriate letters in the boxes of each square.

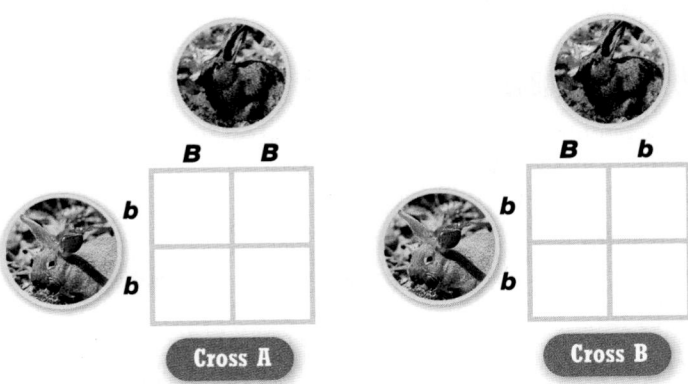

Cross A   **Cross B**

Analysis

1. **Label** what each pair of letters represents in each of the Punnett squares.

2. **Identify** which figure represents a testcross involving a heterozygous parent.

3. **Identify** which figure shows a cross in which all offspring will have black fur.

4. **CRITICAL THINKING** **Applying Models** If half of the offspring in a testcross have brown fur, what is the genotype of the parent that has black fur?

Analyzing Monohybrid Crosses Two kinds of monohybrid crosses are shown in **Figure 7.** A simple Punnett square can be used to analyze a monohybrid cross. Recall that this cross involves parents who each have a trait that <u>contrasts</u> with the trait of the other parent. The parents may be homozygous or heterozygous.

Monohybrid Homozygous Crosses Consider a cross between a pea plant that is homozygous for yellow seed color (*YY*) and a pea plant that is homozygous for green seed color (*yy*). The first Punnett square in **Figure 7** shows that all of the offspring in this type of cross will be heterozygous (*Yy*) and will express the dominant trait of yellow seed color. Other results are not possible in this case.

Monohybrid Heterozygous Crosses The second Punnett square in **Figure 7** predicts the results of a monohybrid cross between two pea plants that are heterozygous (*Yy*) for seed color. This cross is more complex than a homozygous cross. About one-fourth of the offspring will be *YY*. About two-fourths (or one-half) will be *Yy*. And about one-fourth will be *yy*. Another way to express this prediction is to say that the genotypic ratio will be 1 *YY* : 2 *Yy* : 1 *yy*. Because the *Y* allele is dominant, three-fourths of the offspring will be yellow (*YY* or *Yy*) and one-fourth will be green (*yy*). Thus, the phenotypic ratio will be 3 yellow : 1 green.

ACADEMIC VOCABULARY

contrast different when compared

READING TOOLBOX

Analogies Use the information on this page to solve the following analogy.

yy : Yy :: Homozygous : _____

❯ **Reading Check** *Explain the boxes inside a Punnett square?*

QuickLab

Probabilities

Some people are born with extra fingers or toes. This condition, known as *polydactyly,* is rare. However, it is usually the result of a dominant allele.

Procedure

Draw Punnett squares to represent all possible combinations of alleles for each the crosses discussed below. Use *Z* to represent a dominant allele and *z* to represent a recessive allele.

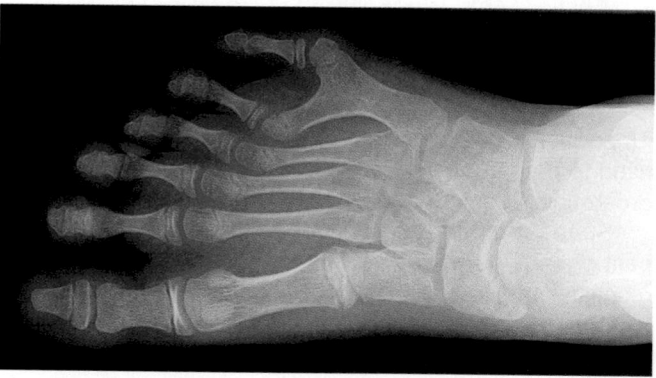

▲ Polydactyly (extra fingers or toes) is usually a dominant trait.

Analysis

1. **Calculate** the probability that a cross of two heterozygous (*Zz*) parents will produce homozygous dominant (*ZZ*) offspring.

2. **Determine** the probability that a cross of a heterozygous parent (*Zz*) and a homozygous recessive *(zz)* parent will produce heterozygous offspring.

3. **Calculate** the probability that a cross of a homozygous dominant parent and a homozygous recessive parent will produce heterozygous offspring.

4. **Determine** the probability that a cross between a heterozygous parent and a homozygous recessive parent will produce homozygous dominant offspring.

Using Probability

Punnett squares allow direct and simple predictions to be made about the outcomes of genetic crosses, but those predictions are not certain. A Punnett square shows the possible outcomes of a cross, but it can also be used to calculate the probability of each outcome. **Probability** is the likelihood that a specific event will <u>occur</u>.

Calculating Probability Punnett squares are one simple way to demonstrate probability. Probability can be calculated and expressed in many ways. Probability can be expressed in words, as a decimal, as a percentage, or as a fraction. For example, if an event will definitely occur, its probability can be expressed as either 1 out of 1 (in words), 100 % (as a percentage), 1.0 (as a decimal), or $\frac{1}{1}$ (as a fraction). If an event is just as likely to occur as to not occur, its probability can be expressed as either 1 out of 2, 50 %, 0.5, or $\frac{1}{2}$. Probability can be determined by the following formula:

$$probability = \frac{number\ of\ one\ kind\ of\ possible\ outcome}{total\ number\ of\ all\ possible\ outcomes}$$

Consider the example of a coin tossed into the air. The total number of possible outcomes is two—heads or tails. Landing on heads is one possible outcome. Thus, the probability that the coin will land on heads is $\frac{1}{2}$. Likewise, the probability that it will land on tails is $\frac{1}{2}$. Of course, the coin will not land on tails exactly half of the time, but it will tend to do so. The average number of total flips that result in tails will tend to be $\frac{1}{2}$.

ACADEMIC VOCABULARY

occur to take place

probability (PRAHB uh BIL uh tee) the likelihood that a specific event will occur; expressed in mathematical terms

Probability of a Specific Allele in a Gamete Recall the law of segregation, which states that each gamete has an equal chance of receiving either one of a pair of alleles. If a pea plant has two alleles for seed color, only one of the two alleles (yellow or green) can end up in a gamete. ❯ **Probability formulas can be used to predict the probabilities that specific alleles will be passed on to offspring.** For a plant that has two alleles for seed color, the total number of possible outcomes is two—green or yellow. The probability that a gamete from this plant will carry the allele for green seed color is $\frac{1}{2}$. The probability that a gamete will carry the allele for yellow seed color is also $\frac{1}{2}$.

Probability in a Heterozygous Cross The possible results of a heterozygous cross are similar to those of flipping two coins at once. Consider the possible results of a cross of two pea plants that are heterozygous for seed shape (Rr). Either parent is equally likely to pass on a gamete that has either an R allele or an r allele. So, the chance of inheriting either allele is $\frac{1}{2}$. Multiplying the probabilities for each gamete shows that the probability that the offspring will have RR alleles is $\frac{1}{4}$. The probability that the offspring will have rr alleles is also $\frac{1}{4}$. The combination Rr has two possible outcomes, so the probability that the offspring will have Rr alleles is $\frac{2}{4}$, or $\frac{1}{2}$.

❯ **Reading Check** *What is the probability that a heterozygous cross will produce homozygous recessive offspring?*

SC*L*INKS.
www.scilinks.org
Topic: Probability
Code: HX81217

Math Skills — Probability of Two Independent Events

Because two parents are involved in a genetic cross, both parents must be considered when predicting the probable outcomes. Consider the example of tossing two coins at the same time. The probability that a penny will land on heads is $\frac{1}{2}$, and the probability that a nickel will land on heads is $\frac{1}{2}$. How one coin falls does not affect how the other coin falls.

What is the probability that the nickel and the penny will both land on heads at the same time? To find the probability that a specific combination of two independent events will occur, multiply the probabilities of each event. Thus, the probability that both coins will land on heads is

$$\frac{1}{2} \times \frac{1}{2} = \frac{1}{4}$$

What about the probability that one coin will land on heads while the other coin lands on tails? Because the combination of heads and tails has two possible outcomes, the probabilities of each possible combination are added together:

$$\frac{1}{4} + \frac{1}{4} = \frac{2}{4} = \frac{1}{2}$$

Each coin has the same probability of landing on heads or tails.

	Heads $\frac{1}{2}$	Tails $\frac{1}{2}$
Heads $\frac{1}{2}$	Heads Heads $\frac{1}{4}$	Tails Heads $\frac{1}{4}$
Tails $\frac{1}{2}$	Heads Tails $\frac{1}{4}$	Tails Tails $\frac{1}{4}$

The green boxes have the same combination (heads and tails), so these two probabilities can be added together.

Figure 8 Albinism is a genetic disorder carried by a recessive allele. Because of this disorder, this baby koala's skin and hair cells do not produce pigments, so the baby is mostly white. The pedigree (top right) shows the presence of the albinism trait in a family.

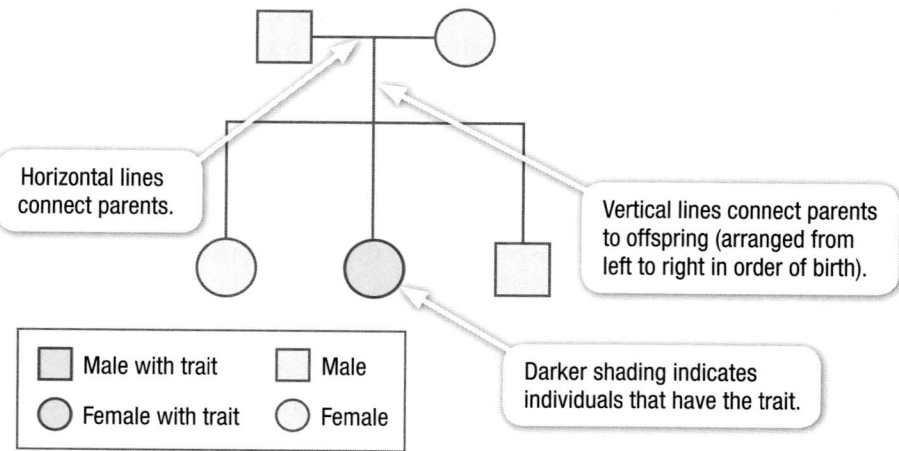

Horizontal lines connect parents.

Vertical lines connect parents to offspring (arranged from left to right in order of birth).

Darker shading indicates individuals that have the trait.

| ☐ Male with trait | ☐ Male |
| ○ Female with trait | ○ Female |

Using a Pedigree

Mendel observed several generations of pea plants to see patterns in the inheritance of traits. A simple way to model inheritance is to use a pedigree. A **pedigree** is a family history that shows how a trait is inherited over several generations. A healthcare worker may use a pedigree to help a family understand a genetic disorder. A **genetic disorder** is a disease or disorder that can be inherited. If a family has a history of a genetic disorder, the parents may want to know if their children could inherit the disorder. Some parents are carriers. Carriers have alleles for a disorder but do not show symptoms. Carriers can pass the allele for the disorder to their offspring.

Figure 8 shows a pedigree for a family in which albinism is present. A body affected by the genetic disorder albinism is unable to produce the pigment that gives dark color to skin, eyes, and hair. Without this pigment, the body may appear white or pink. A recessive allele causes albinism. The pedigree helps show how this trait is inherited. ❯A pedigree can help answer questions about three aspects of inheritance: sex linkage, dominance, and heterozygosity.

Sex-Linked Gene The sex chromosomes, X and Y, carry genes for many characters other than gender. A *sex-linked gene* is located on either an X or a Y chromosome, but most are located on the X chromosome. Because it is much shorter than the X chromosome, the Y chromosome holds fewer genes. Females usually have two X chromosomes. A recessive allele on one of the X chromosomes will often have a corresponding dominant allele on the other. Thus, the trait for the recessive allele is not expressed in the female. Males, on the other hand, usually have an X chromosome and the much shorter Y chromosome. Because it has few genes, the shorter Y chromosome may lack an allele that corresponds to a recessive allele on the longer X chromosome. So, the trait for the single recessive allele will be expressed in the male. Traits that are not expressed equally in both sexes are commonly sex-linked traits. Colorblindness is an example of a sex-linked trait that is expressed more in males than in females.

❯ **Reading Check** *How can one identify a sex-linked trait?*

pedigree (PED i GREE) a diagram that shows the occurrence of a genetic trait in several generations of a family

genetic disorder an inherited disease or disorder that is caused by a mutation in a gene or by a chromosomal defect

Data

Quick**Lab**

🕐 15 min

Pedigree Analysis

You will practice interpreting a pedigree. The pedigree to the right shows the presence or absence of a specific trait in several generations of a family.

Analysis

1. **Determine** whether the trait is dominant or recessive. Explain your reasoning.

2. **Determine** if Female A could be heterozygous for the trait. Do the same for Female B.

3. **CRITICAL THINKING** **Applying Information** Suppose that Female B is homozygous and produces children with Male C. If Male C is heterozygous, what is the probability that the children will have the trait?

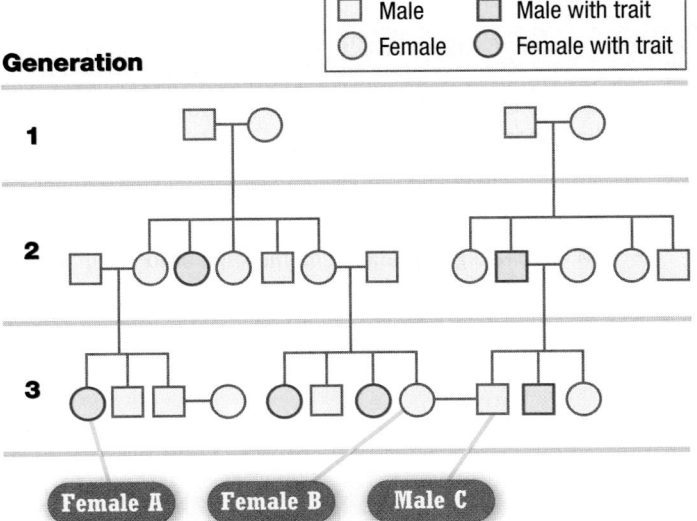

Generation

| ☐ Male | ☐ Male with trait |
| ○ Female | ○ Female with trait |

Dominant or Recessive? If a person has a trait that is autosomal and dominant and has even one dominant allele, he or she will show the trait. A dominant allele is needed to pass on the trait. If a person has a recessive trait and only one recessive allele, he or she will not show the trait but may pass it on. So, if a trait appears in a child whose parents lack the trait, it is most likely recessive.

Heterozygous or Homozygous? If a person is either heterozygous or homozygous dominant for an autosomal gene, his or her phenotype will show the dominant trait. If a person is homozygous recessive, his or her phenotype will show the recessive trait. Heterozygous parents can produce a child who is homozygous recessive. Thus, a recessive trait in the child shows that both parents were heterozygous carriers of the recessive allele.

Section 3 Review

> **KEY IDEAS**

1. **Describe** how a Punnett square is used in genetics.

2. **List** ways to express mathematical probability in genetics.

3. **Sketch** a pedigree for an imaginary family of three generations and describe what the pedigree shows.

CRITICAL THINKING

4. **Scientific Methods** How can you determine the genotype of a pea plant that has purple flowers?

5. **Mathematical Reasoning** If you flip two coins at once, will at least one coin land on heads? Explain.

6. **Analyzing Graphics** When analyzing a pedigree, how can you determine if an individual is a carrier (heterozygous) for the trait being studied?

USING SCIENCE GRAPHICS

7. **Pedigree** Some kinds of colorblindness are sex-linked traits carried on the X chromosome. So, males can inherit the trait from mothers that are not colorblind. Draw a pedigree that demonstrates this pattern of inheritance.

Beyond Mendelian Heredity

Key Ideas	Key Terms	Why It Matters
❯ Are there exceptions to the simple Mendelian pattern of inheritance? ❯ How do heredity and the environment interact to influence phenotype? ❯ How do linked genes affect chromosome assortment and crossover during meiosis?	polygenic character codominance linked	Some inheritance is more complex than Mendel showed. This complexity helps explain the large variety of human traits.

Suppose a horse that has red hair mates with a horse that has white hair. The offspring of the horses has both red and white hair on its body. How can this be? Shouldn't the colt's hair be one color or the other? Not always! In fact, most characters are not inherited in the simple patterns identified by Mendel. Although Mendel was correct about the inheritance of the traits that he studied, most patterns of inheritance are more complex than those that Mendel identified.

Many Genes, Many Alleles

If you look at people and animals around you, you will notice a variety of physical features, as **Figure 9** shows. Why do so few of these features have only two types? First, not all genes have only two alleles. Second, not all characters are controlled by one gene. ❯ **The Mendelian inheritance pattern is rare in nature; other patterns include polygenic inheritance, incomplete dominance, multiple alleles, and codominance.**

Polygenic Inheritance When several genes affect a character, it is called a **polygenic character.** For example, eye color is affected by several genes. One gene controls the relative amount of greenness of the eye, and another gene controls brownness. (The recessive condition in both cases is blue eyes.) Other genes also affect eye color. Sorting out the effects of each gene is difficult. The genes may be on the same or different chromosomes. Other examples of polygenic characters in humans are height and skin color. In fact, most characters are polygenic.

Incomplete Dominance Recall that in Mendel's pea-plant crosses, one allele was completely dominant over the other. In some cases, however, an offspring has a phenotype that is intermediate between the traits of its two parents. This pattern is called *incomplete dominance.*

Figure 9 A physical feature—such as height, weight, hair color, and eye color—is often influenced by more than one gene.

Possible alleles

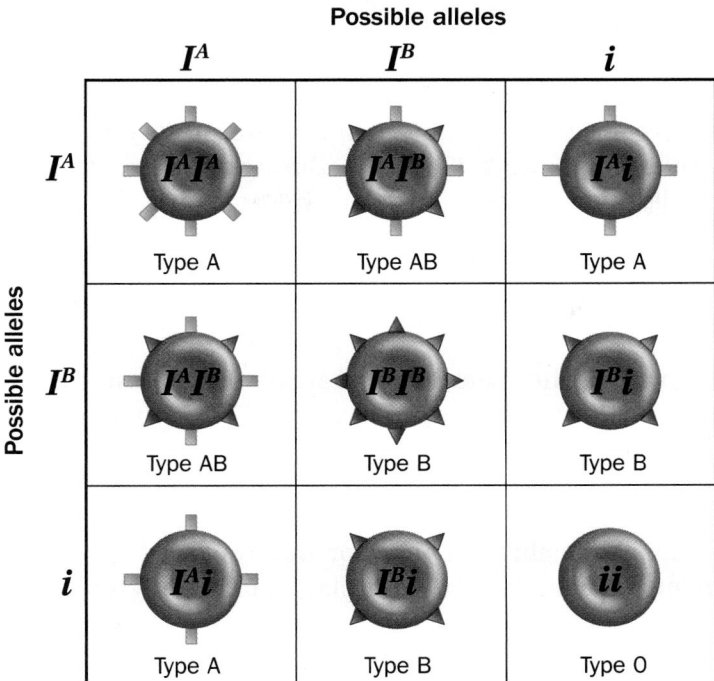

	I^A	I^B	i
I^A	$I^A I^A$ Type A	$I^A I^B$ Type AB	$I^A i$ Type A
I^B	$I^A I^B$ Type AB	$I^B I^B$ Type B	$I^B i$ Type B
i	$I^A i$ Type A	$I^B i$ Type B	ii Type O

Possible alleles

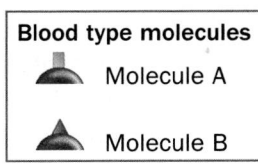

Blood type molecules
Molecule A
Molecule B

Figure 10 Multiple alleles control the ABO blood groups. Different combinations of three alleles (I^A, I^B, and i) result in four blood phenotypes (A, AB, B, and O). For example, a person who has the alleles I^A and i has type A blood. **❯ What is another kind of inheritance pattern demonstrated by the ABO blood groups?**

When a snapdragon that has red flowers is crossed with a snapdragon that has white flowers, the offspring have pink flowers. Neither the red allele nor the white allele is completely dominant over the other. The pink flowers simply have less red pigment than the red flowers do.

Multiple Alleles Genes that have three or more possible alleles are said to have *multiple alleles*. For example, multiple alleles exist for hair color in cats. Still, only two alleles for a gene can be present in one individual. The determination of dominance may be complex.

In humans, the ABO blood groups (blood types) are determined by three alleles: I^A, I^B, and i. **Figure 10** shows how <u>various</u> combinations of the three alleles can produce four blood types: A, B, AB, and O. The I^A and I^B alleles cause red blood cells to make certain molecules. The letters *A* and *B* refer to the two kinds of molecules. The *i* allele does not cause either molecule to be made. So, both the I^A and I^B alleles are dominant over *i*. But I^A and I^B are not dominant over each other. So, a person who has both I^A and I^B alleles has type AB blood. A person who has two *i* alleles has type O blood.

Codominance For some characters, two traits can appear at the same time. **Codominance** is a condition in which both alleles for the same gene are fully expressed.

The genetics of human blood groups, which was discussed above, is also an example of codominance. A person who has $I^A I^B$ alleles will have type AB blood because neither allele is dominant over the other. Type AB blood cells make both A-type and B-type molecules.

❯ Reading Check *How does codominance differ from incomplete dominance?*

polygenic (PAHL uh JEN ik) **character** a character that is influenced by more than one gene

codominance (KOH DAHM uh nuhns) a condition in which both alleles for a gene are fully expressed

ACADEMIC VOCABULARY

various many kinds of

SCi LINKS.
www.scilinks.org
Topic: Mendelian
Genetics
Code: HX80940

Figure 11 Many Arctic mammals, such as the Arctic fox, develop white fur during the winter and dark fur during the summer. ❯ **What does this change indicate about the character for fur color in these animals?**

linked in genetics, describes two or more genes that tend to be inherited together

Genes Affected by the Environment

Genes are the key to life, but there is more to life than genes. ❯ **Phenotype can be affected by conditions in the environment, such as nutrients and temperature.** For example, temperature affects the fur color of the Arctic fox, shown in **Figure 11.** During summer, genes in the fox's skin cells cause pigments to be made. These pigments make the fox's coat darker. Dark fur color helps the fox blend in with grass or woods. But during cold weather, the genes stop causing pigment to be made. Then, the fox's fur grows white, and the fox can blend in with the winter snow.

In humans, many of the characters that are partly determined by heredity are also affected by the environment. For example, a person's height is partly hereditary. Tall parents tend to produce tall children. But nutrition also affects height. A person who has an unhealthy diet may not grow as tall as he or she could have. Many aspects of human personality and behavior are strongly affected by the environment, but genes also seem to play an important role.

Genes Linked Within Chromosomes

Many traits do not follow Mendel's laws, but Mendel's pea traits did. Why? One reason is that Mendel studied the simplest kinds of heredity: characters determined by one gene that has two alleles. Also, he studied characters that are determined by independent genes.

Recall how meiosis relates to the *law of independent assortment*. If genes are on different chromosomes, the alleles for each gene can be sorted independently. Then, each set of alleles can be recombined in any way. For example, in the pea plants, the two alleles for seed color could be combined in any way with the two alleles for seed shape.

Some genes are close together on the same chromosome. ❯ **During meiosis, genes that are close together on the same chromosome are less likely to be separated than genes that are far apart.** Genes that are close together, as well as the traits that they determine, are said to be **linked.**

❯ **Reading Check** *What term describes genes that are close together on the same chromosome and that are unlikely to be separated?*

Section 4 Review

❯ **KEY IDEAS**

1. **List** exceptions to the Mendelian pattern of one character controlled by two alleles.
2. **Describe** the relationship between heredity and the environment.
3. **Relate** gene linkage to chromosome assortment and crossover during meiosis.

CRITICAL THINKING

4. **Evaluating an Argument** A classmate states that Mendel's hypotheses are incorrect because they do not consider intermediate forms of a character. Evaluate this argument.
5. **Applying Concepts** Propose another example of a character in humans that seems to be partly affected by heredity and partly affected by environment. Explain your reasoning.

USING SCIENCE GRAPHICS

6. **Punnett Square** Predict the ratios of each of the ABO blood groups in an average population. Use a Punnett square like the one shown in Figure 10 and explain your results. Assume that the population has equal numbers of I^A, I^B, and i alleles.

Chapter 12 **Lab**

Objectives

▶ Develop a hypothesis to predict the yield of a corn crop.

▶ Design and conduct an experiment to test your hypothesis.

▶ Compare germination and survival rates of three lots of corn seeds.

Materials

- lab apron, disposable gloves
- corn seeds, normal (10 from lot A and 10 from lot B)
- corn seeds, 3:1 mix of normal and albino (10 from lot C)
- plant tray or pots
- soil, potting (3 kg)
- water

Safety

Plant Genetics

In plants, albinism is characterized by the failure to produce chlorophyll, a plant pigment necessary for photosynthesis. Because the trait is recessive, parent plants with the normal phenotype may produce offspring (seeds) that carry the alleles for albinism. In this lab, you will investigate a question about albinism alleles in plants.

Preparation

1. **SCIENTIFIC METHODS** **State the Problem** What might happen to a seed that has one or more albinism alleles?

2. **SCIENTIFIC METHODS** **Form a Hypothesis** Form a hypothesis about how albinism affects the success of plants grown from seed.

Procedure

Design an Experiment

1 Design an experiment that will determine the germination and survival rates of three lots of corn seeds. Write out a procedure for your experiment on a separate sheet of paper. Be sure to include safety procedures, and construct tables to organize your data. Have your teacher approve your plan before you begin.

2 Predict the outcome of your experiment, and record this prediction.

Conduct Your Experiment

3 **CAUTION: Wear gloves and a lab apron whenever handling soil, seeds, or plants.**

4 Follow your written procedure. Make note of any changes.

5 Record all data in your tables. Also record any other observations.

6 At the end of the experiment, present your results to the class. Devise a way to collect the class data in a common format.

7 Clean up your lab materials according to your teacher's instructions. Wash your hands before leaving the lab.

Analyze and Conclude

1. **SCIENTIFIC METHODS** **Evaluating Experimental Design** Did you get clear results? How might you improve your design?

2. **SCIENTIFIC METHODS** **Analyzing Results** Did your results support your hypothesis? Explain your answer.

3. **Analyzing Data** Use the class data to calculate the average germination rate and survival rate for each lot of corn seeds. Describe any patterns that you notice.

go.hrw.com
SUPER SUMMARY
Keyword: HX8GENS

Key Ideas	Key Terms
1 Origins of Hereditary Science ❯ Modern genetics is based on Mendel's explanations for the patterns of heredity that he studied in garden pea plants. ❯ The garden pea plant is a good subject for studying heredity because the plant has contrasting traits, usually self-pollinates, and grows easily. ❯ Mendel's first experiments used monohybrid crosses and were carried out in three steps. ❯ For each of the seven characters that Mendel studied, he found a similar 3-to-1 ratio of contrasting traits in the F_2 generation.	**character** (268) **trait** (268) **hybrid** (268) **generation** (269)
2 Mendel's Theory ❯ Mendelian theory explains simple patterns of inheritance in which each possible combination of alleles results in one of several possible traits. ❯ In modern terms, the *law of segregation* holds that when an organism produces gametes, each pair of alleles is separated and each gamete has an equal chance of receiving either one of the alleles. ❯ Genotype determines phenotype. ❯ In modern terms, the *law of independent assortment* holds that during gamete formation, the alleles of each gene segregate independently.	**allele** (272) **dominant** (273) **recessive** (273) **genotype** (274) **phenotype** (274) **homozygous** (275) **heterozygous** (275)
3 Modeling Mendel's Laws ❯ A Punnett square shows all of the genotypes that could result from a given cross. ❯ Probability formulas can be used to predict the probabilities that specific alleles will be passed on to offspring. ❯ A pedigree can help answer questions about three aspects of inheritance: sex linkage, dominance, and heterozygosity.	**Punnett square** (276) **probability** (278) **pedigree** (280) **genetic disorder** (280)
4 Beyond Mendelian Heredity ❯ Mendelian inheritance is rare in nature; other patterns include polygenic inheritance, incomplete dominance, multiple alleles, and codominance. ❯ Phenotype can be affected by conditions in the environment, such as nutrients and temperature. ❯ Genes that are close together on the same chromosome are linked. 	**polygenic character** (282) **codominance** (283) **linked** (284)

READING TOOLBOX

1. **Punnet Square** Create a Punnet square of a cross between a heterozygous parent and a homozygous parent. Determine the ratio of genotypes and phenotypes.

2. ○○○ **Concept Map** Make a concept map that describes Mendel's experiments and results. Try to include the following words: *pea plants, alleles, P generation, F_1 generation, F_2 generation, dominant trait, recessive trait, segregation,* and *independent assortment.*

Using Key Terms

Use each of the following terms in a separate sentence.

3. *character*

4. *Punnett square*

5. *codominance*

For each pair of terms, explain how the meanings of the terms differ.

6. *genotype* and *phenotype*

7. *trait* and *allele*

8. *homozygous* and *heterozygous*

9. *incomplete dominance* and *codominance*

Understanding Key Ideas

10. The scientist whose studies formed the basis of modern genetics is
    a. T.A. Knight.
    b. Gregor Mendel.
    c. Louis Pasteur.
    d. Robert Hooke.

11. In Mendel's first experiments with pea plants, the average ratio of contrasting traits in the F_2 generation was
    a. 1:0.
    b. 1:1.
    c. 2:1.
    d. 3:1.

12. Each alternate version of a gene is called a(n)
    a. trait.
    b. allele.
    c. genotype.
    d. phenotype.

13. Some people are born with an extra finger or toe. People who have this trait have inherited either one or two of the same allele. So, the trait is
    a. recessive.
    b. dominant.
    c. phenotypic.
    d. independent.

14. The phenotype of an organism
    a. cannot be seen.
    b. exactly matches its genotype.
    c. is the physical result of its genes.
    d. occurs only in true-breeding organisms.

15. Mendel obtained his P generation by forcing pea plants to
    a. segregate.
    b. self-pollinate.
    c. cross-pollinate.
    d. assort independently.

16. What law states that the inheritance of one trait has no effect on the inheritance of another?
    a. the law of dominance
    b. the law of segregation
    c. the law of universal inheritance
    d. the law of independent assortment

17. Which of the following can help determine if an inherited trait is sex-linked?
    a. a ratio
    b. a testcross
    c. a pedigree
    d. a Punnett square

18. What is the expected phenotypic ratio resulting from a cross of a homozygous dominant parent with a heterozygous parent? Assume complete dominance.
    a. 1:3:1
    b. 1:2:1
    c. 2:1
    d. 1:0

Explaining Key Ideas

19. **Summarize** the design of Mendel's plant studies.

20. **State** the law of segregation in your own words.

21. **Describe** the information that a pedigree shows.

22. **Describe** incomplete dominance.

Using Science Graphics

Use the diagram of a dihybrid cross Punnett square to answer the following question(s).

Possible gametes from each parent

Yellow and round

	RY	Ry	rY	ry
RY	RRYY	RRYy	RrYY	RrYy
Ry	RRYy		RrYy	
rY	RrYY	RrYy		
ry	RrYy			

Yellow and round

23. Copy the Punnett square onto a separate piece of paper. Then, fill in the missing possible genotypes of offspring.

24. When homologous chromosomes are separated during meiosis, only chance determines which of the pair is passed into any given gamete. This finding is known as the
   a. law of chance.
   b. law of segregation.
   c. law of universal inheritance.
   d. law of independent assortment.

Critical Thinking

25. **Evaluating Methods** Mendel based his conclusion about inheritance patterns on experiments involving large numbers of plants. Why is it important to study many individuals when studying patterns of inheritance?

26. **Justifying Conclusions** A classmate states that a person cannot have type ABO blood. Is this statement true? Explain your answer.

27. **Forming Reasoned Opinions** Do you think that human behavior is determined by genes? Explain your answer.

28. **Justifying Conclusions** A 20-year-old man who has cystic fibrosis has a sister who is planning to have a child. The man encourages his sister to see a genetic counselor. Why do you think the man gave his sister this advice?

Writing for Science

29. **Summarizing** The Hopi, a Native American people, have an unusually high ratio of persons who have the albinism trait. Research current hypotheses explaining why albinism is more common in people of Hopi ancestry than in other populations. Write a short summary of your findings.

Methods of Science

30. **Designing an Experiment** In tomato plants, tallness is dominant over dwarfness, and hairy stems are dominant over hairless stems. You can buy true-breeding (homozygous) plants that are tall and have hairy stems or that are dwarf and have hairless stems. Design an experiment to determine whether the genes for height and hairiness of the stem are closely linked on chromosomes.

Alternative Assessment

31. **Speech** Imagine that you have just been awarded the Nobel Prize in medicine for your research in human genetics and heredity. Write and perform an acceptance speech describing how Gregor Mendel influenced your work.

Math Skills

32. **Probability** The mathematics of independent assortment applies to any set of independent events, such as the numbers drawn in a lottery. For example, suppose 10 balls are marked from 0 to 9 and placed in a jar. If the balls are mixed thoroughly and one is taken out, the chances are 1 in 10 that a particular number will be drawn. If two jars are used, the chances of the same number being drawn from both jars is

$$\frac{1}{10} \times \frac{1}{10} = \frac{1}{100}$$

or 1 in 100. Suppose you enter a lottery that uses four jars that each contain 10 numbered balls. A number is drawn from each jar in sequence to make a four-digit number. If you choose the number 9,999, what is the chance that your number will be drawn?

TEST TIP If a question uses terms that seem unfamiliar or that you may have forgotten, skip it temporarily. Mark the item, continue with the test, and come back to the item later. Other items on the test may refresh your thinking.

Science Concepts

1. The passing of traits from parents to offspring is called

  A heredity.   **C** assortment.

  B probability.   **D** reproduction.

2. In a breeding experiment, what are the offspring of true-breeding parents called?

  F F_1 generation   **H** dominant generation

  G F_2 generation   **J** recessive generation

3. What characteristic is described in the statement "The dog's coat is brown"?

  A pedigree   **C** phenotype

  B genotype   **D** dominance

4. What term describes a gene with two dominant alleles that are expressed at the same time?

  F polygenic

  G mutational

  H codominant

  J incompletely dominant

5. The owner of a pet store wants to breed more animals that have a certain color of fur. What tool might the pet-store owner use to predict which animals have inherited the fur color gene?

  A pedigree   **C** karyotype

  B mutation   **D** microscope

6. What does the law of segregation state?

  F The two alleles for a gene separate when gametes are formed.

  G A species can have a variety of different alleles that code for a single characteristic.

  H The alleles of different genes separate independently from one another during gamete fromation.

  J Populations of a single species divided geographically will change over time to form two separate species.

Using Science Graphics

Use the diagram of a Punnett square to answer the following question(s).

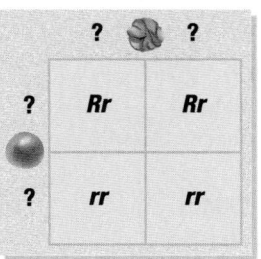

7. What are the genotypes of the parents represented in this cross?

  F *Rr* and *Rr*   **H** *Rr* and *rr*

  G *RR* and *rr*   **J** *rr* and *rr*

8. What genotypic ratio is expected in the offspring of this cross?

  A 1:1   **C** 1:3

  B 1:2   **D** 1:4

Use the table to answer the following question(s).

Experimental group	Dominant trait	Recessive trait
Group 1	77	23
Group 2	74	26
Group 3	75	25
Group 4	73	27

9. What is the approximate average ratio of dominant traits to recessive traits?

  F 1:0   **H** 1:2

  G 2:1   **J** 3:1

10. What kind of cross would result in these ratios?

  A two heterozygous parents

  B two homozygous recessive parents

  C two homozygous dominant parents

  D one heterozygous parent and one homozygous recessive parent

Writing Skills

11. Short Response Write a paragraph that summarizes the relationship between chromosomes and genes.

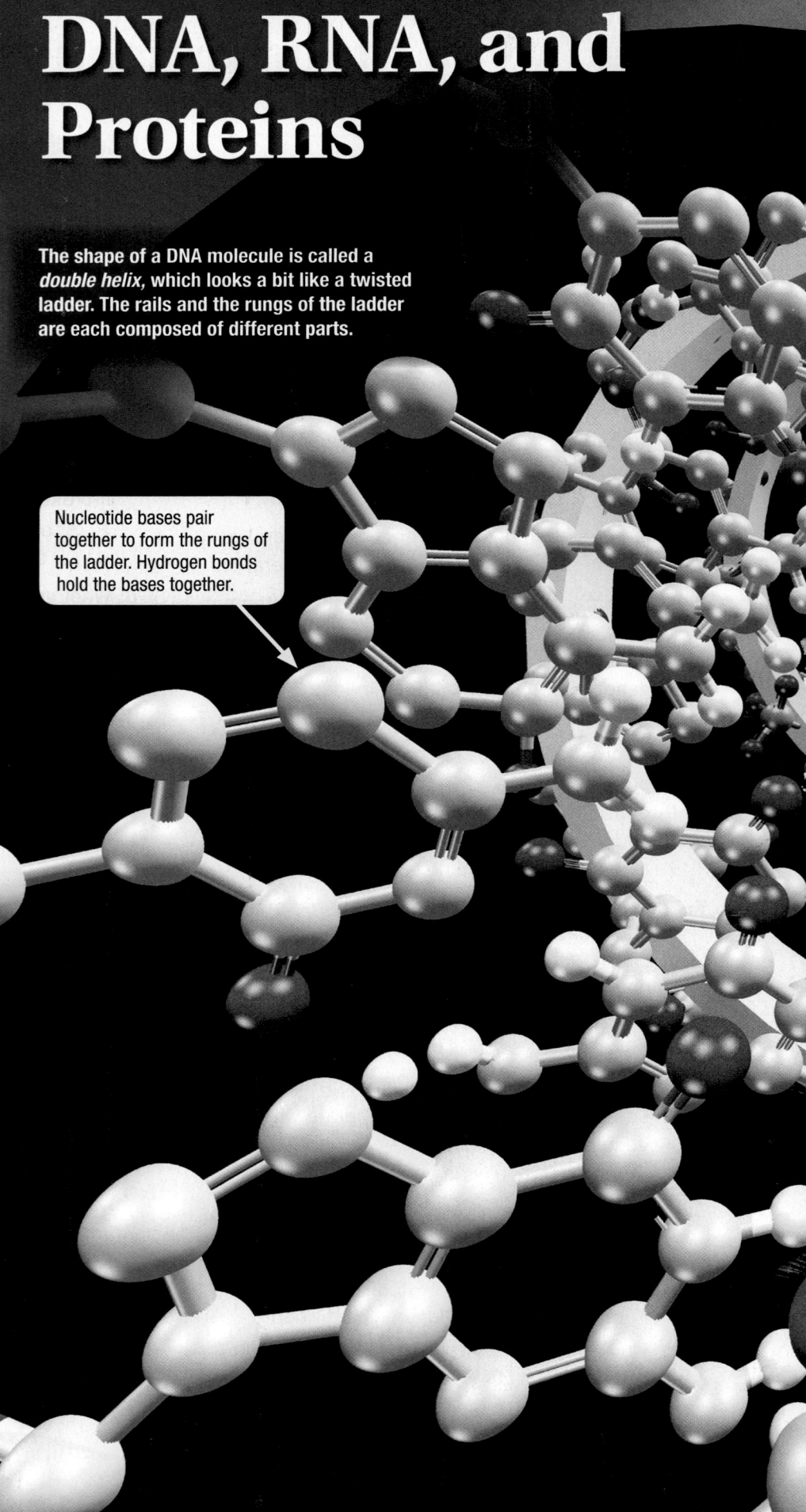

Chapter **13**

Preview

1 The Structure of DNA
DNA: The Genetic Material
Searching for the Genetic Material
The Shape of DNA
The Information in DNA
Discovering DNA's Structure

2 Replication of DNA
DNA Replication
Replication Enzymes
Prokaryotic and Eukaryotic Replication

3 RNA and Gene Expression
An Overview of Gene Expression
RNA: A Major Player
Transcription: Reading the Gene
The Genetic Code: Three-Letter "Words"
Translation: RNA to Proteins
Complexities of Gene Expression

Why It Matters

Did you know that DNA is found in the cells of all organisms? A unique set of genes makes one organism different from another, but DNA is the universal molecule found in all genes.

DNA, RNA, and Proteins

The shape of a DNA molecule is called a *double helix*, which looks a bit like a twisted ladder. The rails and the rungs of the ladder are each composed of different parts.

Nucleotide bases pair together to form the rungs of the ladder. Hydrogen bonds hold the bases together.

InquiryLab

Code Combinations

Have you ever used a secret code to send a message? The people who knew the code could translate your message into something that made sense. Cells also store information in a code. Although this code is relatively simple, it can store the "blueprints" for many substances.

Procedure

1 Obtain **four colors of paper clips.** You will need two each of the four different colors.

2 Place any two of the eight paper clips side by side. Record the color sequence from left to right.

3 Create new pairs of paper clips to produce as many color combinations as you can. Record all of the color sequences.

4 Now, place three paper clips side by side to form a triplet. Make paper clip triplets to produce as many color combinations as you can. Record all of the color sequences.

Analysis

1. Decide how many unique color pairs were assembled by using the four possible color options.

2. Determine how many unique color triplets were assembled by using the four possible color options.

3. Calculate whether a code that is based on pairs of paper clips could represent 20 different pairs using only four color options.

The rails of the ladder provide the backbone of the DNA molecule. They are composed of sugar and phosphate molecules.

READING TOOLBOX

These reading tools can help you learn the material in this chapter. For more information on how to use these and other tools, see **Appendix: Reading and Study Skills.**

Using Words

Word Parts Knowing the meanings of word parts can help you figure out the meanings of unknown words.

Your Turn Use the table to answer the following questions.

1. The root *-ptera* means "wing." What familiar machine is named for its spiral wing?
2. *Helicobacter* is a genus of bacteria. What shape is a bacterium of this genus?
3. In your own words, write a definition for *bacteriophage.*

Word Parts		
Part	**Type**	**Meaning**
bacterio	root	involving bacteria
helic	root	spiral
-ase	suffix	enzyme
phage	root	to eat or destroy

Using Language

Describing Time Certain words and phrases can help you understand when something happened and how long it took. These words and phrases are called *specific time markers.* Specific time markers include words and phrases such as *first, next, 1 hour, yesterday, the twentieth century,* and *30 years later.*

Your Turn Read the sentences below and write down the specific time markers.

1. Early in the morning, before the sun rises, Emilio gets up to take his dogs for a walk.
2. Before a cell can divide, it must first make a copy of its DNA.

Using FoldNotes

Three-Panel Flip Chart A three-panel flip chart is useful when you want to organize notes about three topics. It can help you organize the characteristics of the topics side by side.

Your Turn Make a three-panel flip chart to organize your notes about DNA structure and replication.

1. Fold a piece of paper in half from the top to the bottom.
2. Fold the paper in three sections from side to side. Unfold the paper so that you can see the three sections.
3. From the top of the paper, cut along the vertical fold lines to the fold in the middle of the paper. You will now have three flaps.
4. Label the flaps of the three-panel flip chart "Identifying the Genetic Material," "The Structure of DNA," and "The Replication of DNA."
5. Under each flap, write your notes about the appropriate topic.

Key Ideas	Key Terms	Why It Matters
❯ What is genetic material composed of? ❯ What experiments helped identify the role of DNA? ❯ What is the shape of a DNA molecule? ❯ How is information organized in a DNA molecule? ❯ What scientific investigations led to the discovery of DNA's structure?	gene DNA nucleotide purine pyrimidine	DNA is the "blueprint" from which all living things are made, so understanding DNA is key to understanding life.

Unless you have an identical twin, you—like the sisters in **Figure 1**—share some, but not all, characteristics with family members.

DNA: The Genetic Material

In the 1800s, Gregor Mendel showed that traits are passed from parents to offspring. Many years later, scientists have discovered how these traits are passed on. The instructions for inherited traits are called **genes.** Before the 1950s, however, scientists did not know what genes were made of. We now know that genes are made of small segments of deoxyribonucleic acid, or **DNA.** ❯ **DNA is the primary material that causes recognizable, inheritable characteristics in related groups of organisms.**

DNA is a relatively simple molecule, composed of only four different subunits. For this reason, many early scientists did not consider DNA to be complex enough to be genetic material. A few key experiments led to the discovery that DNA is, in fact, genetic material.

❯ **Reading Check** *What are genes composed of? (See Appendix for answers to Reading Checks.)*

gene a segment of DNA that is located in a chromosome and that codes for a specific hereditary trait

DNA deoxyribonucleic acid, the material that contains the information that determines inherited characteristics

Figure 1 These sisters share many traits but also have differences. ❯ **What role do genes play in passing traits from parents to offspring?**

Searching for the Genetic Material

Once scientists discovered DNA, they began to search for its location. By the 1900s, scientists had determined that genetic material was located in cells, but they did not know exactly where. ❯ **Three major experiments led to the conclusion that DNA is the genetic material in cells. These experiments were performed by Griffith, Avery, Hershey, and Chase.**

Griffith's Discovery of Transformation

In 1928, Frederick Griffith was working with two related strains of bacteria. The S strain causes pneumonia and is covered by a capsule of polysaccharides. The R strain has no capsule and does not cause pneumonia. Mice that are infected with the S bacteria get sick and die. Griffith injected mice with heat-killed S bacteria. The bacteria were dead, but the capsule was still present. The mice lived. Griffith concluded that the S bacteria cause disease.

However, when harmless, live R bacteria were mixed with the harmless, heat-killed S bacteria and were injected into mice, the mice died. Griffith had discovered *transformation,* which is a change in genotype that is caused when cells take up foreign genetic material. Griffith's experiments, shown in **Figure 2,** led to the conclusion that genetic material could be transferred between cells. But no one knew that this material was DNA.

Avery's Experiments with Nucleic Acids

In the 1940s, Oswald Avery wanted to determine whether the transforming agent in Griffith's experiments was protein, RNA, or DNA. Avery and his colleagues used enzymes to destroy each of these molecules in heat-killed S bacteria. They found that bacteria that were missing protein and RNA were able to transform R cells into S cells. However, bacteria that were missing DNA did not transform R cells. The scientists concluded that DNA is responsible for transformation in bacteria.

In 1952, Alfred Hershey and Martha Chase thought that they could support Avery's conclusions by showing how DNA and proteins cross the cell membrane. Their experiment would determine how DNA affected other cells.

READING TOOLBOX

Describing Time Use specific time markers and **Figure 2** to describe Griffith's experiment.

Figure 2 Griffith discovered that harmless bacteria could cause disease when they were mixed with killed disease-causing bacteria. ❯ **What were the variables in Griffith's experiments?**

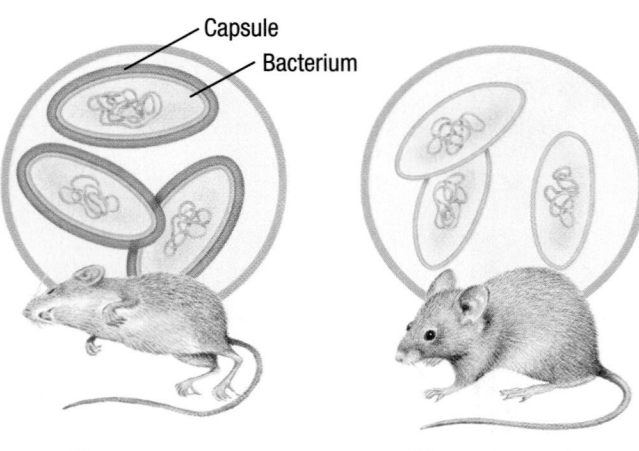

Capsule
Bacterium

❶ S bacteria kill the mouse.

❷ R bacteria do not kill the mouse.

❸ Heat-killed S bacteria do not kill the mouse.

❹ R bacteria and heat-killed S bacteria kill the mouse.

Hershey-Chase Experiment

Experiment 1

Bacteriophage

^{35}S-labeled protein

Phage proteins

Bacteria

Result
^{35}S radioactivity did not enter bacterial cell.

Conclusion
Protein is not the hereditary material.

Experiment 2

^{32}P-labeled DNA

Phage proteins

Bacteria

Result
^{32}P radioactivity entered bacterial cell.

Conclusion
DNA is the hereditary material.

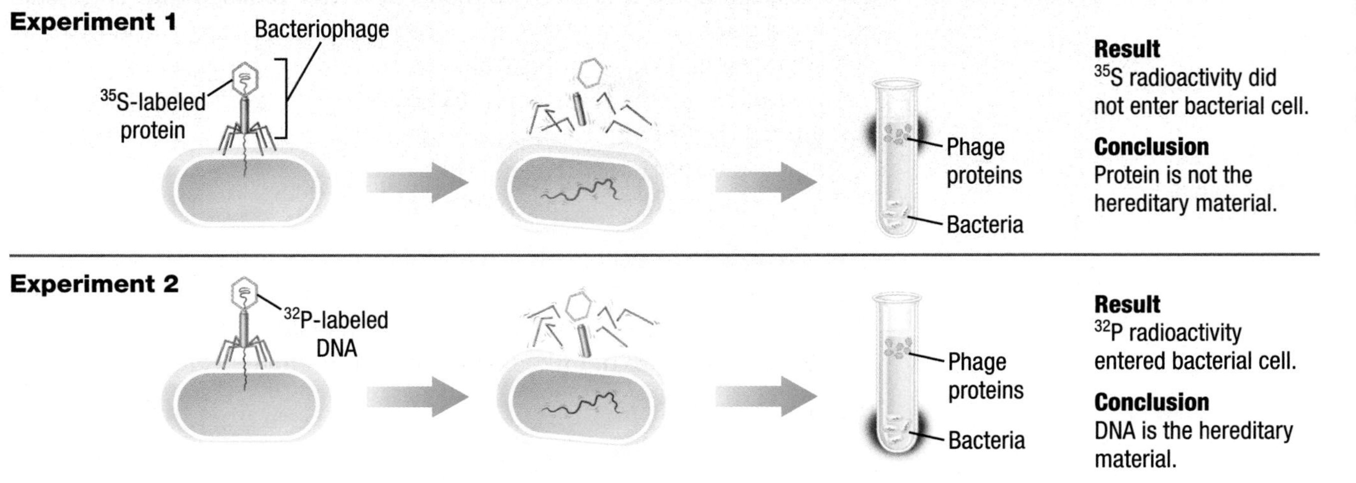

❶ Bacteriophages were labeled "^{35}S" or "^{32}P" and were used to infect separate batches of bacteria.

❷ A blender removed the virus's coat from the surface of the bacterial cells. The mixture was spun in a centrifuge to separate heavier bacteria from the lighter bacteriophages.

❸ ^{35}S radioactivity did not enter bacterial cells, but ^{32}P radioactivity did enter bacterial cells.

Figure 3 Bacteriophages were used to show that DNA, not protein, is the genetic material in viruses.

Hershey-Chase Experiment Hershey and Chase studied bacteriophages, viruses that infect bacterial cells and cause the cells to produce viruses. Bacteriophages are made up of proteins and DNA, but which of these two molecules is the genetic material in viruses? **Figure 3** illustrates their experiment.

Step ❶ First, Hershey and Chase knew that proteins contain some sulfur but no phosphorus and that DNA contains phosphorus but no sulfur. The scientists grew two sets of viruses in environments that were enriched with different radioactive isotopes. One set of viruses had radioactive sulfur (^{35}S) atoms attached to proteins. The other set had radioactive phosphorus (^{32}P) atoms attached to DNA.

Step ❷ Second, each set of viruses was allowed to infect separate batches of nonradioactive bacteria. Because radioactive elements release particles that can be detected with machines, they can be tracked in a biological process. Each of the batches was then separated into parts that contained only bacteria or only viruses.

Step ❸ The infected bacteria from the ^{35}S batch did not contain radioactive sulfur, so proteins could not have infected the bacteria. However, the infected bacteria from the ^{32}P batch did contain radioactive phosphorus. DNA had infected the bacteria.

Hershey and Chase concluded that only the DNA of viruses is injected into bacterial cells. The injected DNA caused the bacteria to produce viral DNA and proteins. This finding indicated that rather than proteins, DNA is the hereditary material, at least in viruses.

The Shape of DNA

After the important experiments in the early 1950s, most scientists were convinced that genes were made of DNA, but nothing was known about DNA's structure. The research of many scientists led James Watson and Francis Crick, two young researchers at Cambridge University, to piece together a model of DNA's structure. Knowing the structure of DNA allowed scientists to understand how DNA could serve as genetic material.

A Winding Staircase ❯ A DNA molecule is shaped like a spiral staircase and is composed of two parallel strands of linked subunits. This spiral shape is known as a *double helix,* as **Figure 4** shows. Each strand is made up of linked subunits called nucleotides.

Parts of the Nucleotide Subunits Each **nucleotide** is made up of three parts: a phosphate group, a five-carbon sugar molecule, and a nitrogen-containing base. **Figure 4** shows how these three parts are arranged to form a nucleotide. The phosphate groups and the sugar molecules of nucleotides link together to form a "backbone" for a DNA strand. The five-carbon sugar in DNA is called *deoxyribose,* from which DNA gets its full name, *deoxyribonucleic acid.* The bases of nucleotides pair together to connect the two strands.

www.scilinks.org
Topic: DNA
Code: HX80418

Figure 4 Watson and Crick's model of DNA is a double helix that is composed of two nucleotide chains. The chains are twisted around a central axis and are held together by hydrogen bonds.

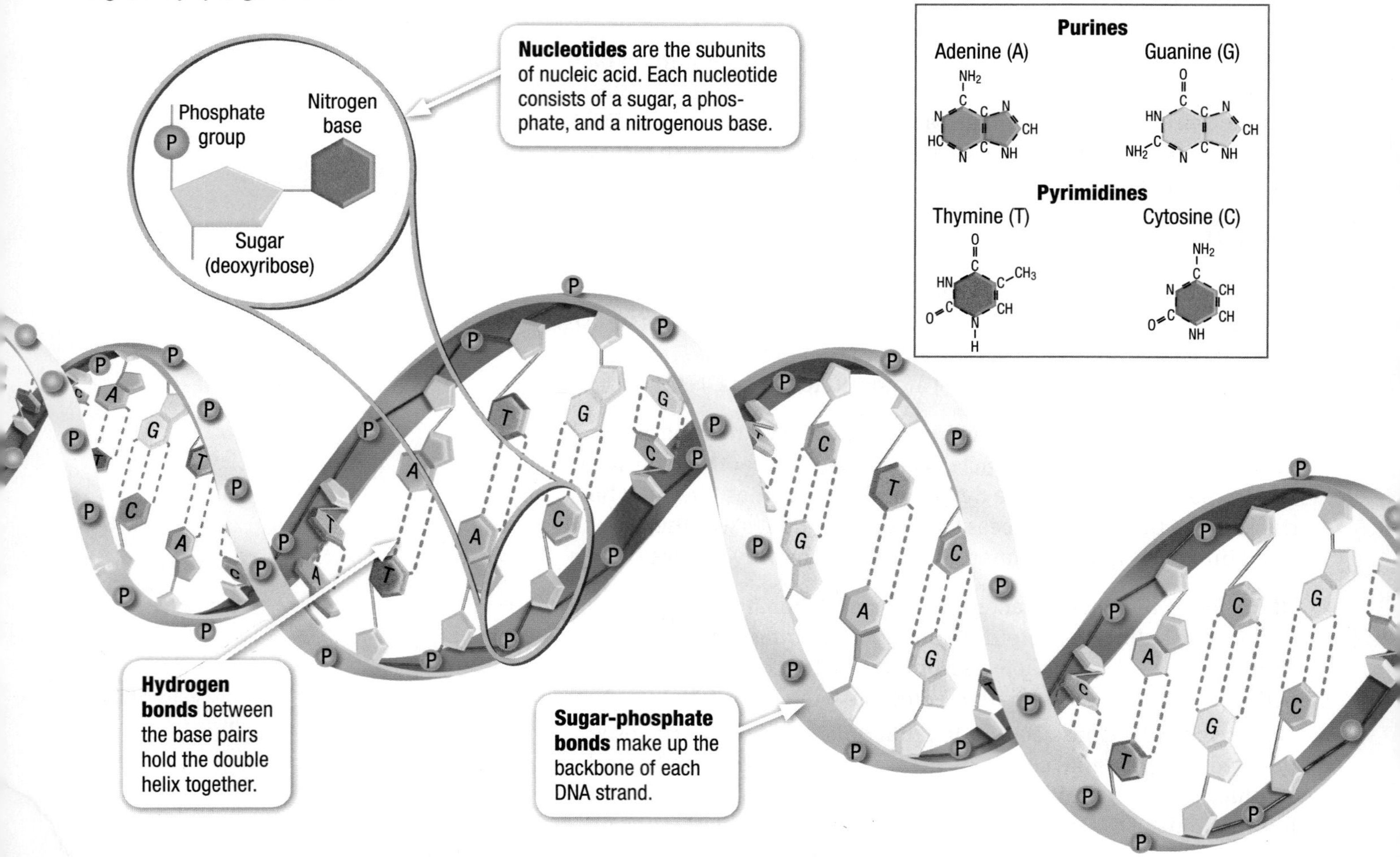

Nucleotides are the subunits of nucleic acid. Each nucleotide consists of a sugar, a phosphate, and a nitrogenous base.

Phosphate group

Nitrogen base

Sugar (deoxyribose)

Purines

Adenine (A)

Guanine (G)

Pyrimidines

Thymine (T)

Cytosine (C)

Hydrogen bonds between the base pairs hold the double helix together.

Sugar-phosphate bonds make up the backbone of each DNA strand.

296 CHAPTER 13 DNA, RNA, and Proteins

Hands-On
QuickLab

🕐 **15 min**

DNA's Structure

Build a model to help you understand the structure of DNA.

Procedure

1 Use the following materials to build a model of DNA: **plastic straws** cut into 3 cm sections, a **metric ruler, scissors, pushpins (four different colors),** and **paper clips.** Your model should have at least 12 nucleotides on each strand.

2 As you design your model, decide how to use the straws, pushpins, and paper clips to represent the three components of a nucleotide and how to link the nucleotides together.

Analysis

1. Describe your model by using words or drawings. Are the two strands in your model identical? Explain why or why not.

2. Explain how you determined which nucleotides were placed on each strand of DNA in your model.

3. `CRITICAL THINKING` **Inferring Relationships** How might the structure of DNA be beneficial when a cell copies its DNA before cell division?

The Information in DNA

The structure of DNA is very important in the transfer of genetic information. ❯ **The information in DNA is contained in the order of the bases, while the base-pairing structure allows the information to be copied.**

Nitrogenous Bases In DNA, each nucleotide has the same sugar molecule and phosphate group, but the nucleotide can have one of four nitrogenous bases. The four kinds of bases, shown in **Figure 4,** are *adenine* (A), *guanine* (G), *thymine* (T), and *cytosine* (C). Bases A and G are classified as **purines.** Purines have two rings of carbon and nitrogen atoms per base. Bases T and C are **pyrimidines.** Pyrimidines have one ring of carbon and nitrogen atoms per base.

Base-Pairing Rules A purine on one strand of a DNA molecule is always paired with a pyrimidine on the other strand. More specifically, adenine always pairs with thymine, and guanine always pairs with cytosine. These *base-pairing rules* are dictated by the chemical structure of the bases. The structure and size of the nitrogenous bases allow for only these two pair combinations. The base pairs are held together by weak hydrogen bonds. Adenine forms two hydrogen bonds with thymine, while cytosine forms three hydrogen bonds with guanine. The hydrogen bonds are represented by dashed lines in **Figure 4.** The hydrogen bonds between bases keep the two strands of DNA together.

❯ **Reading Check** *How are base-pairs held together?*

nucleotide (NOO klee oh TIED) in a nucleic acid chain, a subunit that consists of a sugar, a phosphate, and a nitrogenous base

purine (PYOOR EEN) a nitrogenous base that has a double-ring structure; adenine or guanine

pyrimidine (pi RIM uh DEEN) a nitrogenous base that has a single-ring structure; in DNA, either thymine or cytosine

Complementary Sides **Figure 5** shows a simpler way to represent base-pairing. Paired bases are said to be <u>complementary</u> because they fit together like puzzle pieces. For example, if the sequence of nitrogen bases on one strand is TATGAGAGT, the sequence of nitrogen bases on the other strand must be ATACTCTCA. The pairing structure ensures that each strand of a DNA molecule contains the same information. However, the information on one strand is in reverse order from that on the other strand.

Discovering DNA's Structure

How were James Watson and Francis Crick able to determine the double-helical structure of DNA? ❯ **Watson and Crick used information from experiments by Chargaff, Wilkins, and Franklin to determine the three-dimensional structure of DNA.**

Observing Patterns: Chargaff's Observations In 1949, biochemist Erwin Chargaff made an interesting observation about DNA. His data showed that for each organism that he studied, the amount of adenine always equaled the amount of thymine (A = T). Similarly, the amount of guanine always equaled the amount of cytosine (G = C). **Figure 6** shows some of Chargaff's data. Watson and Crick used this information to determine how nucleotides are paired in DNA.

Using Technology: Photographs of DNA The significance of Chargaff's data became clear when scientists began using X rays to study the structures of molecules. In 1952, Rosalind Franklin, shown in **Figure 6,** and Maurice Wilkins developed high-quality X-ray diffraction images of strands of DNA. These photographs suggested that the DNA molecule resembled a tightly coiled helix and was composed of two chains of nucleotides.

Figure 5 The diagram of DNA below the double helix simplifies the base pairing that occurs between DNA strands.

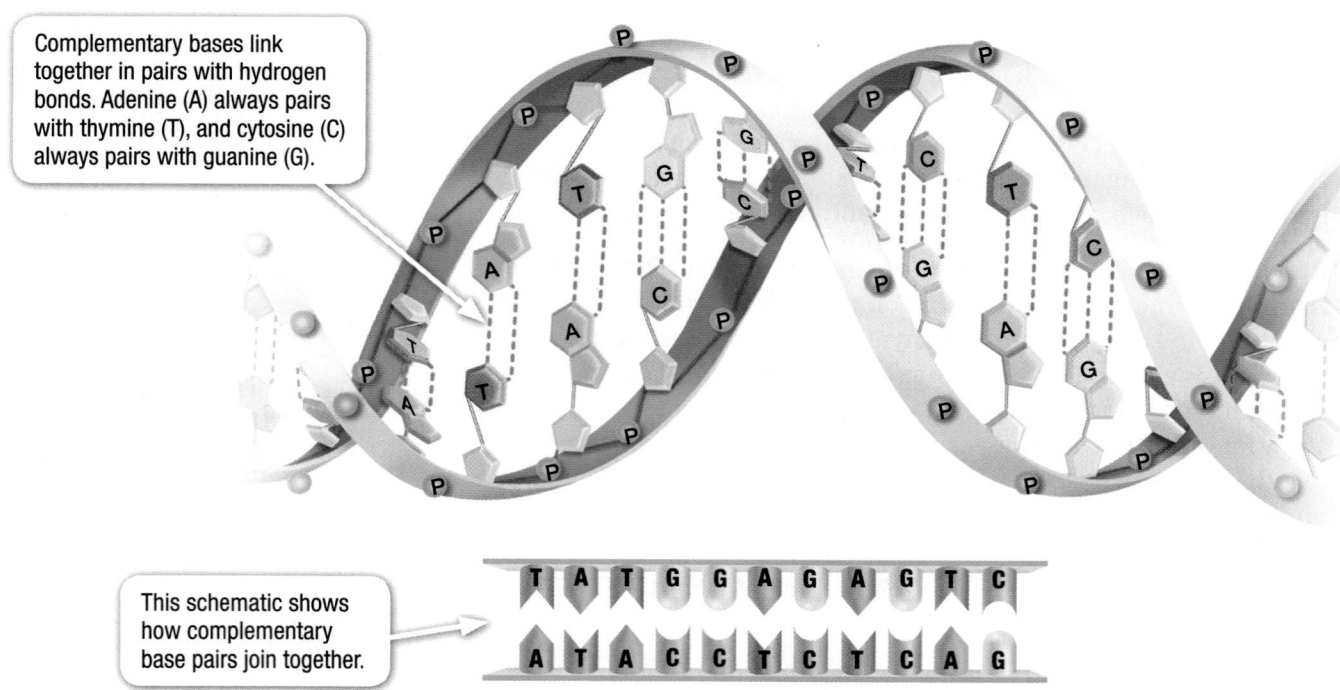

Complementary bases link together in pairs with hydrogen bonds. Adenine (A) always pairs with thymine (T), and cytosine (C) always pairs with guanine (G).

This schematic shows how complementary base pairs join together.

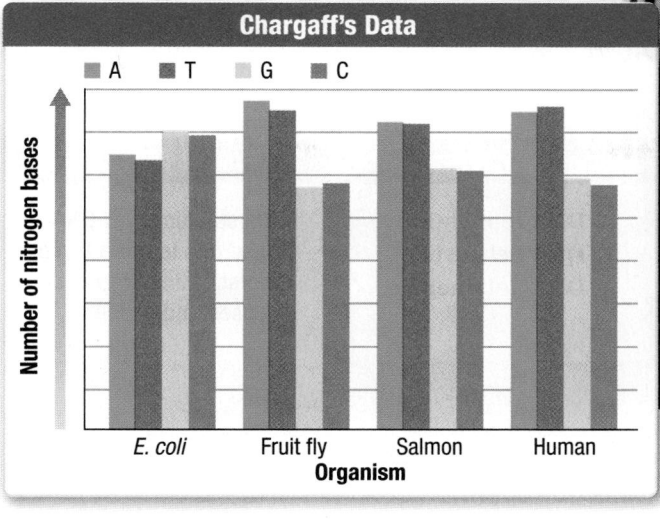

Chargaff's Data

A ■ T ■ G ■ C

Number of nitrogen bases

E. coli   Fruit fly   Salmon   Human
Organism

Watson & Crick

Franklin

Figure 6 Chargaff's data and Franklin's X-ray diffraction studies were instrumental in the discovery of DNA's structure. Watson and Crick are shown with their tin and wire model of DNA.

Watson and Crick's Model of DNA To determine the three-dimensional structure of DNA, Watson and Crick set out to build a model of DNA. They knew that any model would have to take into account both Chargaff's data and the findings from Franklin's X-ray diffraction studies. In 1953, Watson and Crick used these findings, along with knowledge of chemical bonding, to create a complete three-dimensional model of DNA. By using paper models of the bases, Watson and Crick worked out the pairing structure of purines with pyrimidines. Then, they built a large model of a DNA double helix by using tin, wire, and other materials. Their model showed a "spiral staircase" in which two strands of nucleotides twisted around a central axis. **Figure 6** shows Watson and Crick with their model.

Nine years later, in 1962, the Nobel Prize was awarded to Watson, Crick, and Wilkins for their discovery. Rosalind Franklin died in 1958 and was not named in the award.

❯ **Reading Check** *How was X-ray diffraction used to model the structure of DNA?*

Section 1 Review

❯ **KEY IDEAS**

1. **Identify** the substance that makes up genetic material.
2. **Name** the experiments that identified the role of DNA.
3. **Draw** the shape of a DNA molecule.
4. **Relate** the structure of DNA to the function of DNA as a carrier of information.
5. **Name** the studies that led to the discovery of DNA's structure.

CRITICAL THINKING

6. **Applying Information** If a DNA strand has the nucleotide sequence of CCGAGATTG, what is the nucleotide sequence of the complementary strand?
7. **Applying Information** What might Hershey and Chase have concluded if they had found ^{35}S instead of ^{32}P in bacterial cells? Explain your answer.

USING SCIENCE GRAPHICS

8. **Evaluating Graphics** Look at the graph of Chargaff's data in **Figure 6.** How do the amounts of adenine compare with the amounts of thymine across species? How do the amounts of cytosine and guanine compare? How did these data lead to the discovery of the base-pairing rules by Chargaff? How was this discovery used to determine DNA's structure?

Key Ideas	Key Terms	Why It Matters
❯ How does DNA replicate, or make a copy of itself? ❯ What are the roles of proteins in DNA replication? ❯ How is DNA replication different in prokaryotes and eukaryotes?	DNA replication DNA helicase DNA polymerase	Understanding how DNA is copied has led to a better understanding of genetic diseases and cancer.

When cells divide, each new cell contains an exact copy of the original cell's DNA. How is this possible?

DNA Replication

Remember that DNA is made of two strands of complementary base pairs. Adenine always pairs with thymine, and guanine always pairs with cytosine. If the strands of DNA are separated, as shown in **Figure 7,** each strand can serve as a pattern to make a new complementary strand. This separation allows two exact copies of DNA to be made from the original DNA molecule. Copying the DNA before cell division allows each new cell to have DNA identical to the original cell's.

The process of making a copy of DNA is called **DNA replication.** ❯ **In DNA replication, the DNA molecule unwinds, and the two sides split. Then, new nucleotides are added to each side until two identical sequences result.** DNA replication occurs before a cell divides so that each cell has a complete copy of DNA. The basic steps of DNA replication are described below and are illustrated in **Figure 8** on the next page.

Step ❶ Unwinding and Separating DNA Strands Before DNA replication can begin, the double helix unwinds. The two complementary strands of DNA separate from each other and form Y shapes. These Y-shaped areas are called *replication forks.* **Figure 7** shows two replication forks in a molecule of DNA.

Step ❷ Adding Complementary Bases At the replication fork, new nucleotides are added to each side and new base pairs are formed according to the base-pairing rules. For example, if one of the original strands has thymine, then adenine will be paired with thymine as the new strand forms. Thus, the original two strands serve as a template for two new strands. As more nucleotides are added, two new double helixes begin to form. The process continues until the whole DNA sequence has been copied.

Step ❸ Formation of Two Identical DNA Molecules This process of DNA replication produces two identical DNA molecules. Each double-stranded DNA helix is made of one new strand of DNA and one original strand of DNA. The nucleotide sequences in both of these DNA molecules are identical to each other and to the original DNA molecule.

Figure 7 When the two strands of the DNA helix separate, Y-shaped replication forks form.

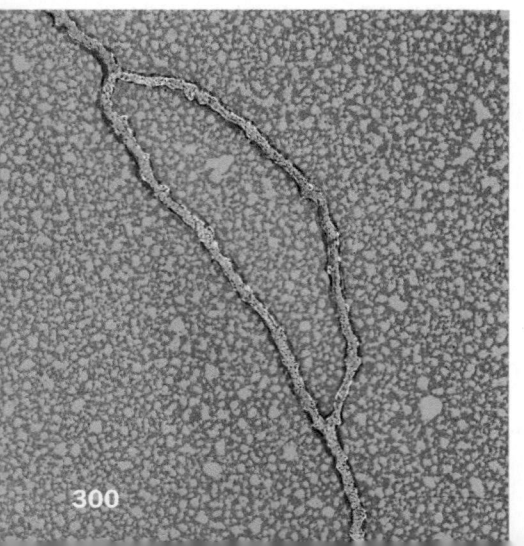

DNA Replication

1 Proteins called *helicases* separate the two original DNA strands.

2 Complementary nucleotides are added to each strand by DNA polymerases.

3 Two DNA molecules are formed that are identical to the original DNA molecule.

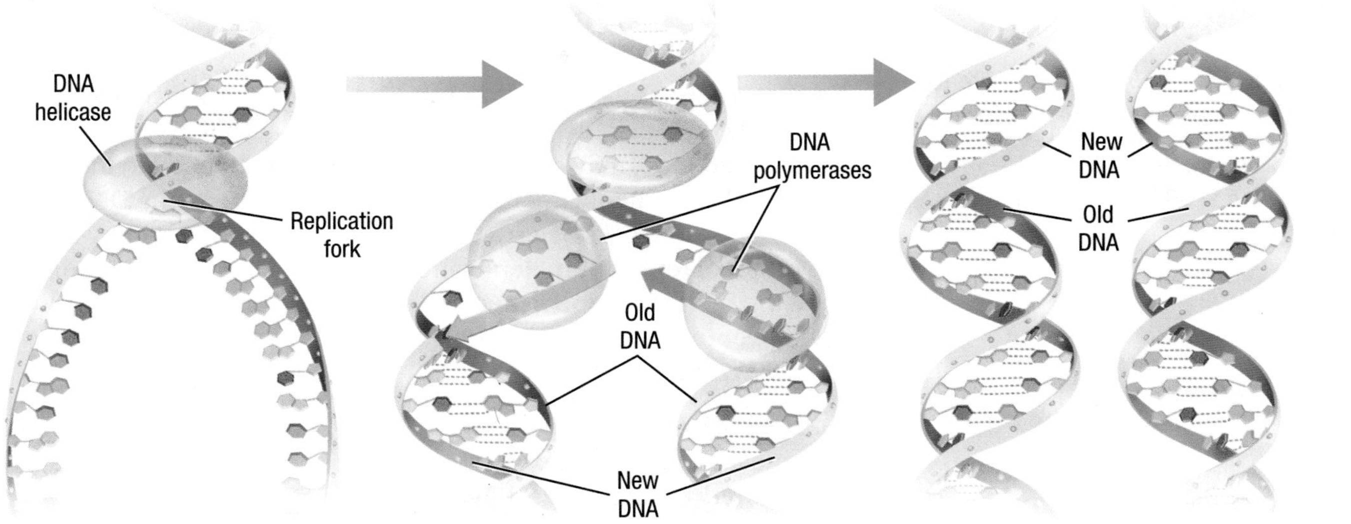

DNA helicase

Replication fork

DNA polymerases

Old DNA

New DNA

New DNA

Old DNA

Figure 8 DNA replication results in two identical DNA strands.

Replication Proteins

❯ **During the replication of DNA, many proteins form a machinelike complex of moving parts.** Each protein has a specific function.

DNA Helicase Proteins called **DNA helicases** unwind the DNA double helix during DNA replication. These proteins wedge themselves between the two strands of the double helix and break the hydrogen bonds between the base pairs. This process causes the helix to unwind and forms a replication fork, as **Figures 7** and **8** show. Additional proteins keep the two strands separated so that replication can occur.

DNA Polymerase Proteins called **DNA polymerases** catalyze the formation of the DNA molecule. At the replication fork, DNA polymerases move along each strand. The polymerases add nucleotides that pair with each base to form two new double helixes. After all of the DNA has been copied, the polymerases are released.

DNA polymerases also have a "proofreading" function. During DNA replication, errors sometimes occur, and the wrong nucleotide is added to the new strand. DNA polymerases cannot add another nucleotide unless the previous nucleotide is correctly paired with its complementary base. If a mismatch occurs, the DNA polymerase can backtrack, remove the incorrect nucleotide, and replace it with the correct one. Proofreading reduces the replication errors to about one per 1 billion nucleotides.

❯ **Reading Check** *Why is proofreading critical during replication?*

DNA replication the process of making a copy of DNA

DNA helicase (HEEL uh KAYS) an enzyme that unwinds the DNA double helix during DNA replication

DNA polymerase (puh LIM uhr AYS) an enzyme that catalyzes the formation of the DNA molecule

Prokaryotic and Eukaryotic Replication

Both prokaryotes and eukaryotes replicate their DNA to reproduce and grow. Recall that the packaged DNA in a cell is called a *chromosome*. All cells have chromosomes, but eukaryotes and prokaryotes replicate their chromosomes differently. ❯ **In prokaryotic cells, replication starts at a single site. In eukaryotic cells, replication starts at many sites along the chromosome.**

Prokaryotic DNA Replication Prokaryotic cells usually have a single DNA molecule, or chromosome. Prokaryotic chromosomes are a closed loop, may contain protein, and are attached to the inner cell membrane. Replication begins at one place along the DNA loop. Two replication forks begin at that single point, which is known as the origin of replication. Replication occurs in opposite directions until the replication forks meet on the opposite side of the DNA loop and the entire molecule has been copied. **Figure 9** shows prokaryotic DNA replication.

Eukaryotic DNA Replication While prokaryotes have a single chromosome, eukaryotic cells often have several chromosomes. Eukaryotic chromosomes differ from the simple, looped chromosomes found in prokaryotic cells. Eukaryotic chromosomes are linear, and they contain both DNA and protein. Recall that the long molecules of DNA are tightly wound around proteins called *histones* and are packaged into thick chromosome fibers.

By starting replication at many sites along the chromosome, eukaryotic cells can replicate their DNA faster than prokaryotes can. As in prokaryotic replication, two <u>distinct</u> replication forks form at each start site, and replication occurs in opposite directions. This process forms replication "bubbles" along the DNA molecule. The replication bubbles continue to get larger as more of the DNA is copied. As **Figure 9** shows, they eventually meet to form two identical, linear DNA molecules. Because multiple replication forks are working at the same time, an entire human chromosome can be replicated in about eight hours. Then, the cell will be ready to divide.

Figure 9 Prokaryotic and eukaryotic DNA have different numbers of replication forks. ❯ **Why does replication in eukaryotes involve more replication forks?**

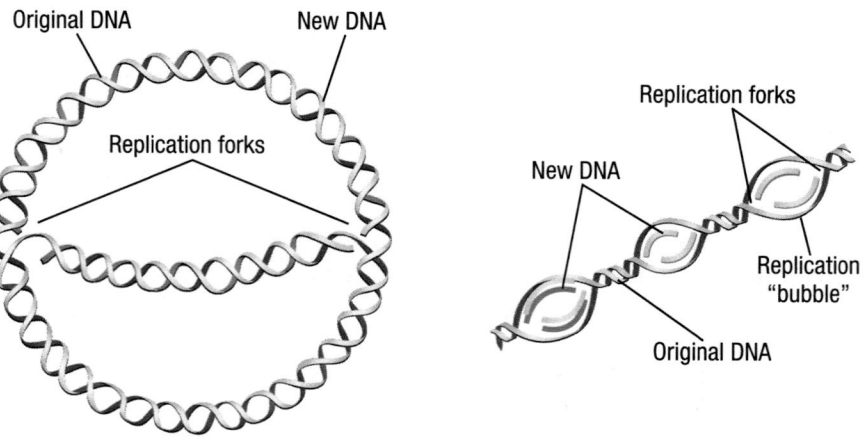

Original DNA   New DNA

Replication forks

Prokaryotic DNA

Replication forks

New DNA

Replication "bubble"

Original DNA

Eukaryotic DNA

QuickLab

🕐 15 min

DNA Replication Rate

Cancer is a disease caused by cells that divide uncontrollably. Scientists studying drugs that prevent cancer often measure the effectiveness of a drug by its effect on DNA replication. During normal DNA replication, nucleotides are added at a rate of about 50 nucleotides per second in mammals and 500 nucleotides per second in bacteria.

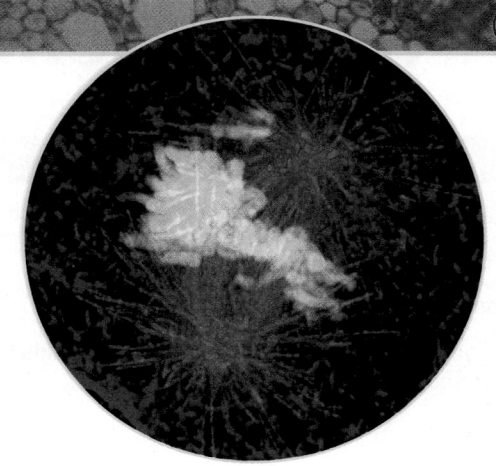

Analysis

1. **Calculate** the time it would take a bacterium to add 4,000 nucleotides to one DNA strand undergoing replication.

2. **Calculate** the time it would take a mammalian cell to add 4,000 nucleotides to one DNA strand undergoing replication.

3. **CRITICAL THINKING** **Predicting Outcomes** How would the total time needed to add the 4,000 nucleotides be affected if a drug that inhibits DNA polymerases were present? Explain your answer.

Size of Eukaryotic DNA The smallest eukaryotic chromosomes are often 10 times the size of a prokaryotic chromosome. If a scientist took all of the DNA in a single human cell and laid the DNA in one line (that is, laid the DNA from all 46 chromosomes end to end), the line would be 2 m long. In contrast, if the scientist laid out the DNA from one bacterial chromosome, the line would be only about 0.25 cm long. In fact, the length of eukaryotic chromosomes is so long that replication of a typical human chromosome would take 33 days if there were only one origin of replication.

Each human chromosome is replicated in about 100 sections that are 100,000 nucleotides long, each section with its own starting point. With multiple replication forks working in concert, an entire human chromosome can be replicated in about 8 hours.

SCILINKS
www.scilinks.org
Topic: DNA Replication
Code: HX80420

❯ **Reading Check** *How is a "replication bubble" formed?*

Section 2 Review

❯ **KEY IDEAS**

1. **Describe** the steps of DNA replication.
2. **Compare** the roles of DNA helicases and DNA polymerases.
3. **Compare** the process of DNA replication in prokaryotes and in eukaryotes.

CRITICAL THINKING

4. **Inferring Relationships** What is the relationship between DNA polymerases and mutations in DNA?
5. **Relating Concepts** Cancer is a disease caused by cells that divide uncontrollably. Scientists are researching drugs that inhibit DNA polymerase as potential anti-cancer drugs. Why would these drugs be useful against cancer?

ALTERNATIVE ASSESSMENT

6. **Replication Model** Conduct research on the shapes of prokaryotic and eukaryotic chromosomes. Draw a model of each type of chromosome. How does the structure of chromosomes in prokaryotic cells and eukaryotic cells affect the DNA replication processes in a cell?

RNA and Gene Expression

Key Ideas	Key Terms	Why It Matters
❯ What is the process of gene expression? ❯ What role does RNA play in gene expression? ❯ What happens during transcription? ❯ How do codons determine the sequence of amino acids that results after translation? ❯ What are the major steps of translation? ❯ Do traits result from the expression of a single gene?	RNA gene expression transcription translation codon	Traits, such as eye color, are determined by proteins that are built according to instructions coded in DNA.

Proteins perform most of the functions of cells. DNA provides the original "recipe," or information, from which proteins are made in the cell. However, DNA does not directly make proteins. A second type of nucleic acid, ribonucleic acid, or **RNA,** is essential in taking the genetic information from DNA and building proteins.

An Overview of Gene Expression

Gene expression is the manifestation of genes into specific traits.
❯ Gene expression produces proteins by transcription and translation. This process takes place in two stages, both of which involve RNA. **Figure 10** illustrates the parts of the cell that play a role in gene expression.

Transcription: DNA to RNA The first stage of gene expression, which is making RNA from the information in DNA, is called **transcription.** You can think of transcription as copying (transcribing) notes from the board (DNA) to a notebook (RNA).

RNA ribonucleic acid, a natural polymer that is present in all living cells and that plays a role in protein synthesis

gene expression the manifestation of the genetic material of an organism in the form of specific traits

transcription the process of forming a nucleic acid by using another molecule as a template

translation the portion of protein synthesis that takes place at ribosomes and that uses the codons in mRNA molecules to specify the sequence of amino acids in polypeptide chains

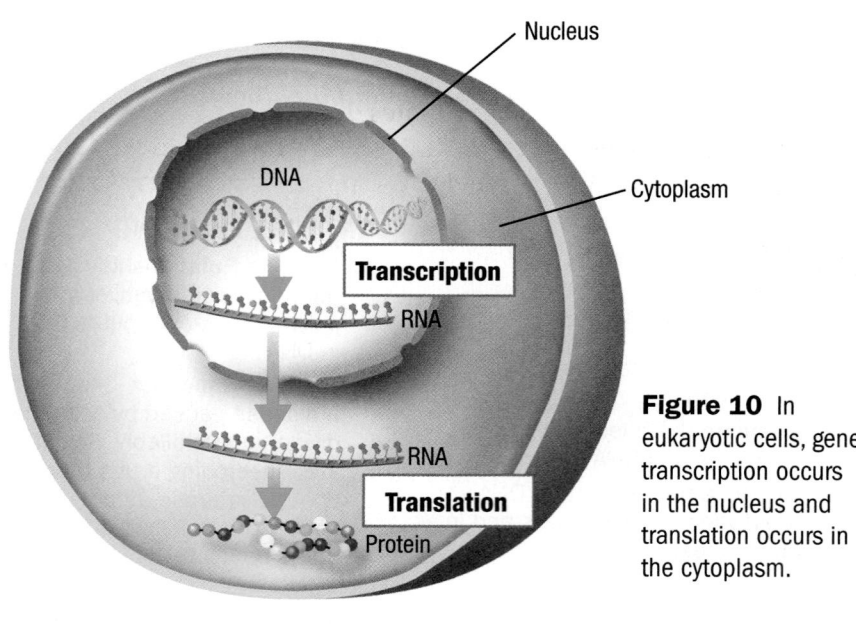

Figure 10 In eukaryotic cells, gene transcription occurs in the nucleus and translation occurs in the cytoplasm.

Translation: RNA to Proteins The second stage of gene expression, called **translation,** uses the information in RNA to make a specific protein. Translation is similar to translating a sentence in one language (RNA, the nucleic acid "language") to another language (protein, the amino acid "language").

RNA: A Major Player

All of the steps in gene expression involve RNA. Several types of RNA are used in transcription and translation. ❯ **In cells, three types of RNA complement DNA and translate the genetic code into proteins.** But what exactly is RNA, and how does it compare to DNA?

RNA Versus DNA Like DNA, RNA is a nucleic acid—a molecule made of nucleotide subunits linked together. Like DNA, RNA has four bases and carries information in the same way that DNA does.

RNA differs from DNA in three ways. First, RNA usually is composed of one strand of nucleotides rather than two strands. The structural difference between the two nucleotides is shown in **Figure 11.** Second, RNA nucleotides contain the five-carbon sugar *ribose* rather than the sugar deoxyribose. Ribose contains one more oxygen atom than deoxyribose does. And third, RNA nucleotides have a nitrogenous base called *uracil* (U) instead of the base thymine (T). Although no thymine (T) bases are found in RNA, the other bases (A, G, and C) are identical to the bases found in DNA. In place of thymine, uracil (U) is complementary to adenine (A) whenever RNA pairs with another nucleic acid.

Types of RNA There are several types of RNA. Three main types of RNA play a role in gene expression. These types are messenger RNA, transfer RNA, and ribosomal RNA.

Messenger RNA When DNA is transcribed into RNA, *messenger RNA* (mRNA) is the type of RNA that is produced. mRNA is complementary to the DNA sequence of a gene. The mRNA carries instructions for making a protein from a gene and delivers them to the site of translation.

Transfer RNA During translation, *transfer RNA* (tRNA) "reads" the mRNA sequence. Then, tRNA translates the mRNA sequence into a specific sequence of protein subunits, or amino acids. tRNA molecules have amino acids attached to them, and the tRNA molecules act as decoders by matching the mRNA sequence and placing the amino acids on growing protein chains.

Ribosomal RNA Protein production occurs on cellular structures called *ribosomes*. Ribosomes are made up of about 80 protein molecules (ribosomal proteins) and several large RNA molecules. The RNA that is found in ribosomes is called *ribosomal RNA* (rRNA). A cell's cytoplasm contains thousands of ribosomes. In eukaryotic cells, ribosomes are attached to the endoplasmic reticulum (ER), which transports proteins as the proteins are produced.

❯ **Reading Check** *What are the structural differences between RNA and DNA?*

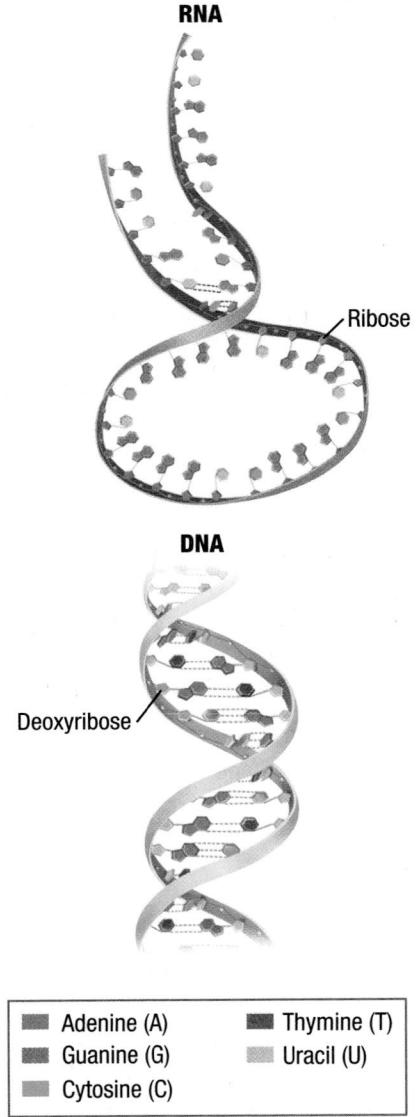

RNA

Ribose

DNA

Deoxyribose

Adenine (A)	Thymine (T)
Guanine (G)	Uracil (U)
Cytosine (C)	

Figure 11 Both RNA (top) and DNA (bottom) are nucleic acids.

① RNA polymerase binds to the gene's promoter.

② The two DNA strands unwind and separate.

③ Complementary RNA nucleotides are added.

RNA polymerase

Promoter site on DNA

RNA

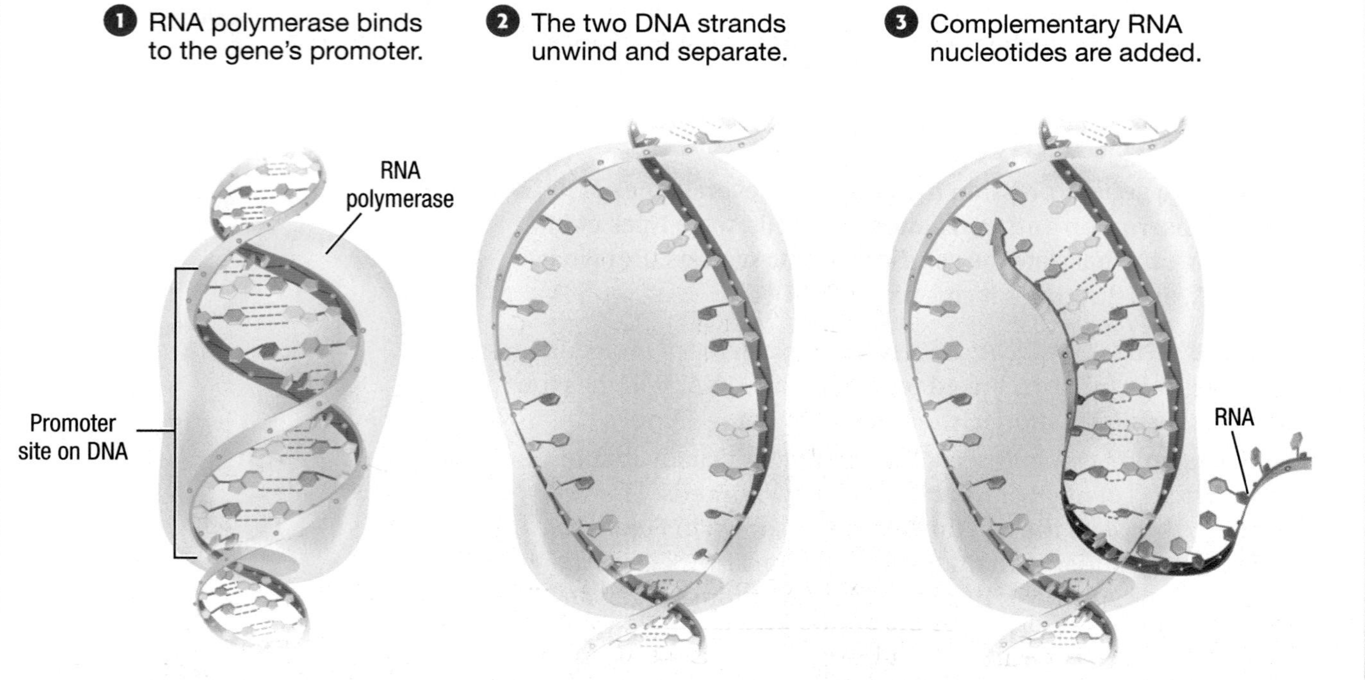

Figure 12 Transcription is the process in which mRNA is made to complement the DNA of a gene.

READING TOOLBOX

Three-Panel Flip Chart Make a three-panel flip chart to help you compare the roles of the three types of RNA used in gene expression.

Transcription: Reading the Gene

❯ **During transcription, the information in a specific region of DNA (a gene) is transcribed, or copied, into mRNA.** Transcription is carried out by a protein called *RNA polymerase*. The steps of transcription are described below and are shown in **Figure 12.**

Step ① Transcription begins when RNA polymerase binds to the specific DNA sequence in the gene that is called the *promoter*. The promoter site is the "start" location.

Step ② RNA polymerase then unwinds and separates the two strands of the double helix to expose the DNA bases on each strand.

Step ③ RNA polymerase adds and links complementary RNA bases as it "reads" the gene. RNA polymerase moves along the bases on the DNA strand in much the same way that a train moves along a track. Transcription follows the base-pairing rules for DNA replication except that in RNA, uracil—rather than thymine—pairs with adenine. As RNA polymerase moves down the DNA strand, a single strand of mRNA grows. Behind the moving RNA polymerase, the two strands of DNA close up and re-form the double helix.

The RNA polymerase eventually reaches a "stop" location in the DNA. This stop signal is a sequence of bases that marks the end of each gene in eukaryotes or the end of a set of genes in prokaryotes. The result is a single strand of mRNA.

❯ **Reading Check** *What is the role of a promoter?*

Transcription Versus Replication Like DNA replication, transcription uses DNA as a template for making a new molecule. In transcription, a new molecule of RNA is made from the DNA. However, in DNA replication, a new molecule of DNA is made from the DNA. Also, in DNA replication, both strands of DNA serve as templates. In contrast, during transcription only part of one of the two strands of DNA (a gene) serves as a template for the new RNA.

The Genetic Code: Three-Letter "Words"

A gene can be thought of as a "sentence" of "words" that is first transcribed and then translated into a functional protein. Once a section of a gene is transcribed into mRNA, the words can be carried from the nucleus to ribosomes in the cytoplasm. There, the words are translated to make proteins.

Codons of mRNA Each of the words in mRNA is made up of three adjacent nucleotide bases. Each three-nucleotide sequence is called a **codon.** Each codon is matched to 1 of 20 amino acids or acts as a start or stop signal for the translation stage. **Figure 13** shows this matching system for each of the possible 64 mRNA codons. For example, the codon GCU specifies the amino acid alanine. Notice that each codon specifies only one amino acid but that several amino acids have more than one codon. This system of matching codons and amino acids is called the *genetic code.* ❯ **The genetic code is based on codons that each represent a specific amino acid.**

codon in DNA and mRNA, a three-nucleotide sequence that encodes an amino acid or signifies a start signal or a stop signal

Figure 13 The amino acid coded for by a specific mRNA codon can be determined by following the three steps below. ❯ What amino acid does the codon GAA code for?

❶ Find the first base of the mRNA codon in this column of the table.

❷ Follow that row to the column that matches the second base of the codon.

❸ Move up or down in that box until you match the third base of the codon with this column of the chart.

Codons in mRNA

First base	Second base				Third base
	U	**C**	**A**	**G**	
U	UUU ⎤ Phenylalanine UUC ⎦ UUA ⎤ Leucine UUG ⎦	UCU ⎤ UCC ⎥ Serine UCA ⎥ UCG ⎦	UAU ⎤ Tyrosine UAC ⎦ UAA ⎤ Stop UAG ⎦	UGU ⎤ Cysteine UGC ⎦ UGA–Stop UGG–Tryptophan	U C A G
C	CUU ⎤ CUC ⎥ Leucine CUA ⎥ CUG ⎦	CCU ⎤ CCC ⎥ Proline CCA ⎥ CCG ⎦	CAU ⎤ Histidine CAC ⎦ CAA ⎤ Glutamine CAG ⎦	CGU ⎤ CGC ⎥ Arginine CGA ⎥ CGG ⎦	U C A G
A	AUU ⎤ AUC ⎥ Isoleucine AUA ⎦ AUG–Start	ACU ⎤ ACC ⎥ Threonine ACA ⎥ ACG ⎦	AAU ⎤ Asparagine AAC ⎦ AAA ⎤ Lysine AAG ⎦	AGU ⎤ Serine AGC ⎦ AGA ⎤ Arginine AGG ⎦	U C A G
G	GUU ⎤ GUC ⎥ Valine GUA ⎥ GUG ⎦	GCU ⎤ GCC ⎥ Alanine GCA ⎥ GCG ⎦	GAU ⎤ Aspartic acid GAC ⎦ GAA ⎤ Glutamic acid GAG ⎦	GGU ⎤ GGC ⎥ Glycine GGA ⎥ GGG ⎦	U C A G

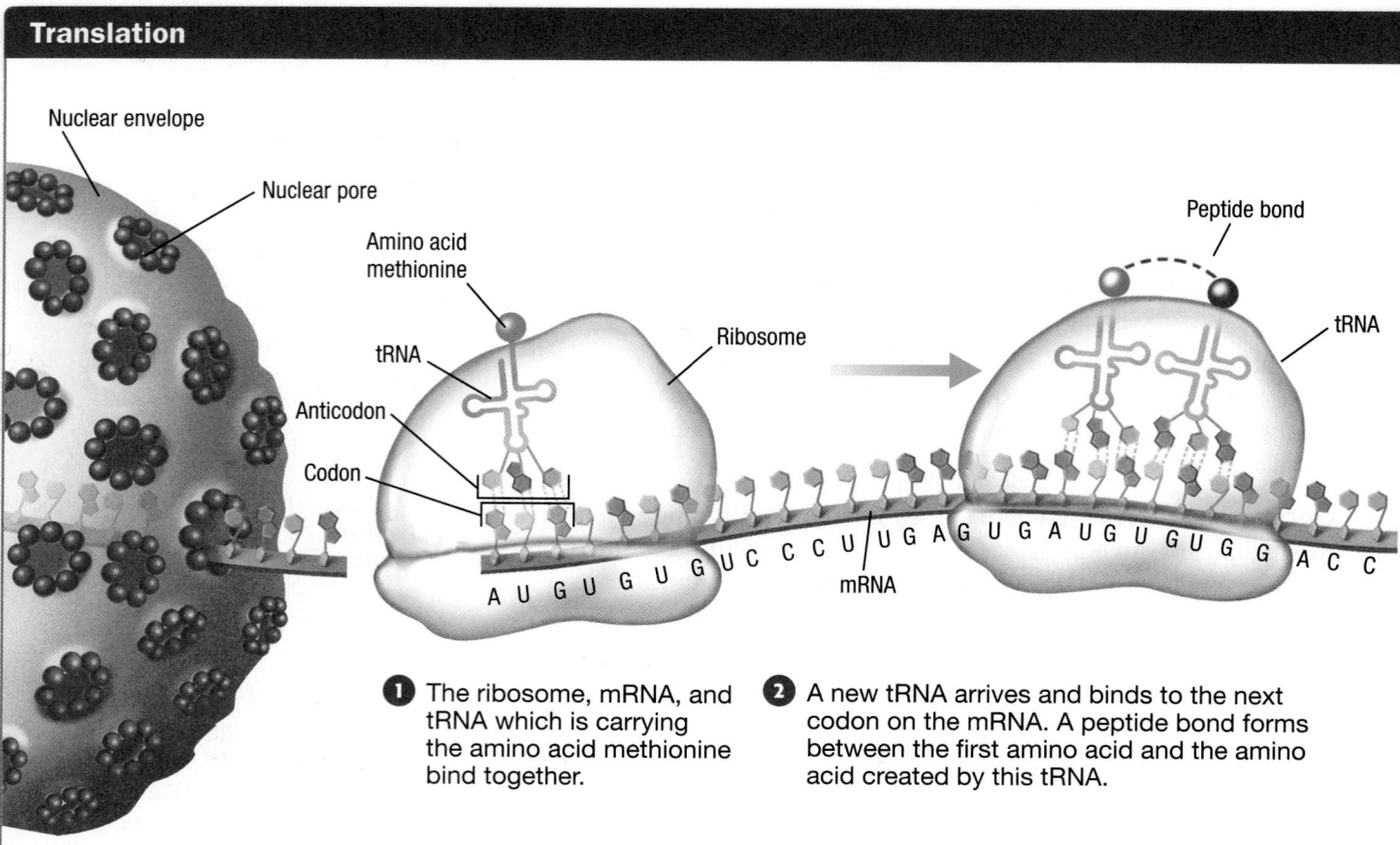

① The ribosome, mRNA, and tRNA which is carrying the amino acid methionine bind together.

② A new tRNA arrives and binds to the next codon on the mRNA. A peptide bond forms between the first amino acid and the amino acid created by this tRNA.

Figure 14 During translation, amino acids are assembled from information encoded in mRNA. As the mRNA codons move through the ribosome, tRNAs add specific amino acids to the growing polypeptide chain. This process continues until a stop codon is reached and the newly made protein is released.

Translation: RNA to Proteins

Translation is the process of converting the "language" of RNA (nucleotide sequences) into the "language" of proteins (amino acid sequences). ❯ **Translation occurs in a sequence of steps, involves three kinds of RNA, and results in a complete** *polypeptide.* In the cytoplasm, ribosomes are formed as tRNA, rRNA, and mRNA interact to assemble amino acid sequences that are based on the genetic code. The process of translation is summarized below and in **Figure 14.**

Step ① Each tRNA is folded into a compact shape, as **Figure 15** shows. An amino acid is added to one end of each tRNA. The other end of the tRNA has an anticodon. An *anticodon* is a three-nucleotide sequence that is complementary to an mRNA codon. Each tRNA molecule carries the amino acid that corresponds with the tRNA's anticodon. After leaving the nucleus, the mRNA joins with a ribosome and tRNA. The mRNA start codon, AUG, signals the beginning of a protein chain. A tRNA molecule carrying methionine at one end and the anticodon, UAC, at the other end binds to the start codon.

Step ② A tRNA molecule that has the correct anticodon and amino acid binds to the second codon on the mRNA. A peptide bond forms between the two amino acids, and the first tRNA is released from the ribosome. The tRNA leaves its amino acid behind.

Large ribosomal subunit

Small ribosomal subunit

Newly made polypeptide

mRNA

3 U U A A U G U G U G U C C C C U U G A G U G U A G A U U G G A C C G C A C A U U U A

Stop codon

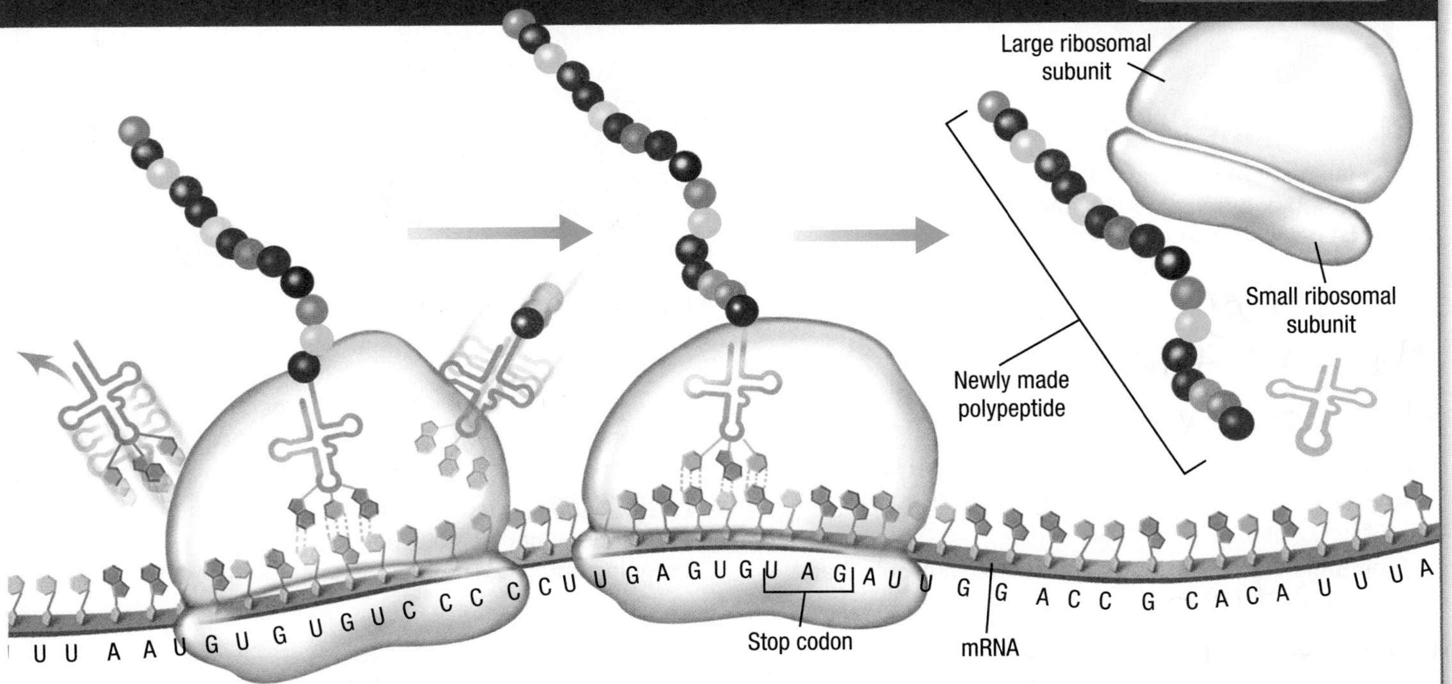

3 The first tRNA detaches and leaves its amino acid. With each new tRNA, the amino acid chain grows.

4 The process ends when a stop codon is reached.

5 The amino acid chain is released, and the ribosome complex falls apart.

Step 3 The ribosome moves one codon down the mRNA. Because the anticodon remains attached to the codon, the tRNA molecule and the mRNA molecule move as a unit, which leaves the next mRNA codon open and ready to receive the next tRNA and its amino acid. The amino acid chain continues to grow as each new amino acid binds to the chain and the previous tRNA is released.

Step 4 This process is repeated until a stop codon is reached. A *stop codon* is one of three codons: UAG, UAA, or UGA. No tRNAs have anticodons for these stop codons, so protein production stops.

Step 5 The newly made polypeptide falls off the ribosome. The ribosome complex falls apart. The last tRNA leaves the ribosome, and the ribosome moves away from the mRNA. The ribosome is then free to begin translation again on the same mRNA or on another mRNA.

Repeating Translation Like replication, translation needs to happen quickly and often. As a segment of mRNA moves through a ribosome, another ribosome can form on the AUG codon on the same mRNA segment and can begin a new translation process. Thus, several ribosomes can translate the same mRNA at the same time, which allows many copies of the same protein to be made rapidly from a single mRNA molecule.

❯ Reading Check *How do codons and anticodons differ?*

Figure 15 tRNA folds into this shape such that an anticodon is on one end and a binding site for amino acids is on the other end.

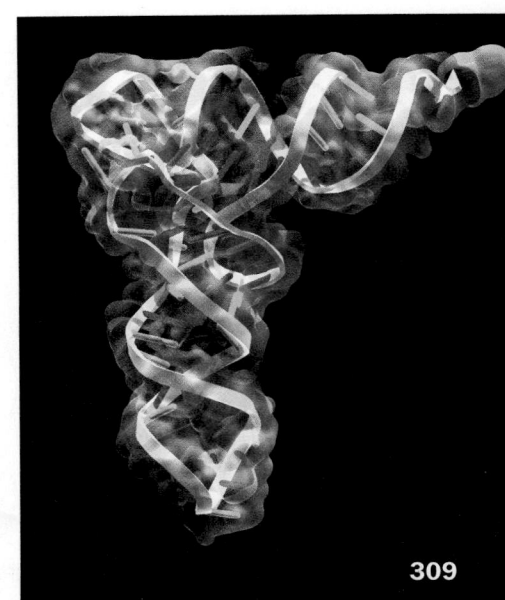

QuickLab

Genetic Code of Keratin

Keratin is one of the proteins in hair. The gene for keratin is transcribed and translated by certain skin cells. The sequence below is part of the mRNA molecule that is transcribed from the gene for keratin.

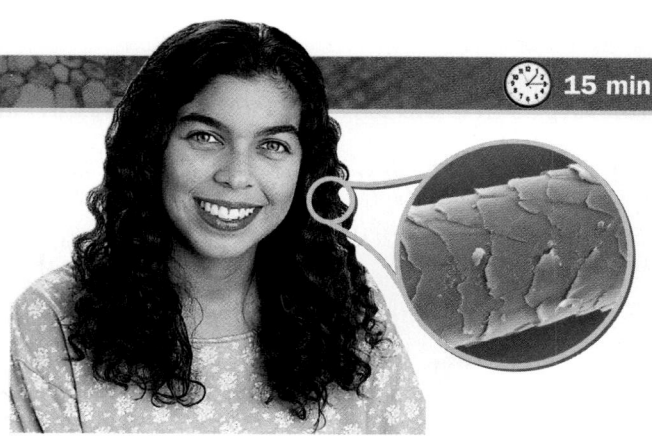

🕐 15 min

U C U C G U G A A U U U U C C

Analysis

1. **Determine** the sequence of amino acids that will result from the translation of the segment of mRNA above. Use the genetic code in **Figure 13**.

2. **Determine** the anticodon of each tRNA molecule that will bind to this mRNA segment.

3. **CRITICAL THINKING** **Recognizing Patterns** Determine the sequence of nucleotides in the segment of DNA from which this mRNA strand was transcribed.

4. **CRITICAL THINKING** **Recognizing Patterns** Determine the sequence of nucleotides in the segment of DNA that is complementary to the DNA segment that is described in item 3.

Complexities of Gene Expression

❯ **The relationship between genes and their effects is complex. Despite the neatness of the genetic code, every gene cannot be simply linked to a single outcome.** Some genes are expressed only at certain times or under specific conditions. Some traits result from the expression of multiple genes. Variations, mistakes, feedback, and other complex interactions can occur at each of the steps in replication and expression. The final outcome of gene expression is affected by the environment of the cells, the presence of other cells, and the timing of gene expression.

Overall, knowledge of the basic process of gene expression has allowed scientists to better understand the workings of all organisms. The next chapters delve into the exciting results of applying this knowledge.

Section 3 Review

❯ KEY IDEAS

1. **Describe** gene expression.
2. **Explain** the role of RNA in gene expression.
3. **Summarize** transcription.
4. **Explain** how codons determine the amino acid sequence of a protein.
5. **Describe** the steps of translation.
6. **Identify** a complexity of gene expression.

CRITICAL THINKING

7. **Inferring Relationships** Multiple codons can produce the same amino acid. What is the advantage of this redundancy?

8. **Relating Concepts** What amino acid is coded for by the mRNA codon CCU?

ALTERNATIVE ASSESSMENT

9. **Gene Poster** Research two methods used to sequence the nucleotides in a gene. Compare the two methods. Give examples of how this technology might be used in a clinical setting. Prepare a poster to summarize the two methods that you researched.

Chapter 13 Lab

Objectives

❯ Extract DNA from wheat germ.

❯ Explain the role of detergents, heat, and alcohol in the extraction of DNA.

Materials

- wheat germ, raw (1 g)
- test tube or beaker (50 mL)
- water, hot tap (55°C, 20 mL)
- salt, table
- soap, liquid dishwashing (1 mL)
- isopropyl alcohol, cold (15 mL)
- glass rod, 8 cm long
- inoculating loop
- glass slide

Safety

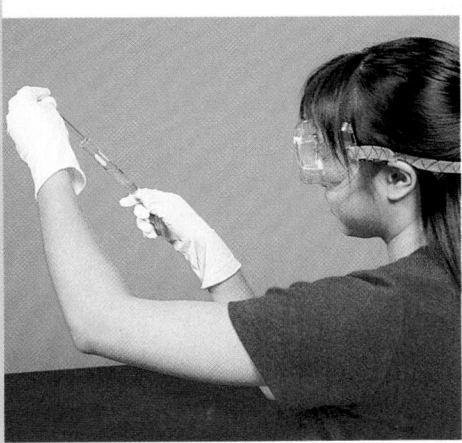

DNA Extraction from Wheat Germ

The extraction and purification of DNA are the first steps in the analysis and manipulation of DNA. Very pure DNA can be easily extracted from cells in a research laboratory, and somewhat less pure DNA can be extracted with some simple techniques easily performed in a classroom.

The first step in extracting DNA from a cell is to lyse, or break open, the cell. Cell walls, cell membranes, and nuclear membranes are broken down by physical smashing, heating, and the addition of detergents. In water, DNA is soluble. When isopropyl alcohol is added, the DNA uncoils and precipitates, leaving behind many other cell components that are not soluble in isopropyl alcohol. The DNA can be then spooled, or wound onto an inoculating loop, and pulled from the solution. In this lab, you will extract the DNA from wheat germ. Wheat germ is simply the ground-up cells of wheat kernels, or seeds.

Procedure

1. Put on safety goggles, lab apron, and gloves.

2. **CAUTION: Glassware, such as a test tube, is fragile and can break.** Place 1 g of wheat germ into a clean test tube.

3. Add 20 mL hot (55°C) tap water and stir with glass rod for 2 to 3 min.

4. Next, add a pinch of table salt, and mix well.

5. Add a few drops (1 mL) of liquid dishwashing soap. Stir the mixture with the glass rod for 1 min until it is well mixed.

6. **CAUTION: Isopropyl alcohol is flammable. Bunsen burners and hot plates should be removed from the lab.** Slowly pour 15 mL cold isopropyl alcohol down the side of the tilted tube or beaker. The alcohol should form a top layer over the original solution. Note: Do not pour the alcohol too fast or directly into the wheat germ solution.

7. Tilt the tube upright, and watch the stringy, white material float up into the alcohol layer (this result should occur after 10 to 15 min). This material is the DNA from the wheat germ.

8. Carefully insert the inoculating loop into the white material in the alcohol layer. Gently twist the loop as you wind the DNA around the loop. Remove the loop from the tube, and tap the DNA onto a glass slide.

9. Clean up your lab materials according to your teacher's instructions. Wash your hands before leaving the lab.

Analyze and Conclude

1. **Describing Events** Describe the appearance of the DNA on the slide.

2. **Interpreting Information** Explain the role of detergent, heat, and isopropyl alcohol in the extraction of DNA.

3. SCIENTIFIC METHODS **Comparing Structures** How do the characteristics of your DNA sample relate to the structure of eukaryotic DNA?

4. SCIENTIFIC METHODS **Designing Experiments** Design a DNA extraction experiment in which you explore the effect of changing the variables.

Key Ideas	Key Terms

1 The Structure of DNA

> DNA is the primary material that causes recognizable, inheritable characteristics in related groups of organisms.

> Three major experiments led to the conclusion that DNA is the genetic material in cells. These experiments were performed by Griffith, Avery, Hershey, and Chase.

> A DNA molecule is shaped like a spiral staircase and is composed of two parallel strands of linked subunits.

> The information in DNA is contained in the order of the bases, while the base-pairing structure allows the information to be copied.

> Watson and Crick used information from experiments by Chargaff, Wilkins, and Franklin to determine the three-dimensional structure of DNA.

Key Terms

gene (293)
DNA (293)
nucleotide (296)
purine (297)
pyrimidine (297)

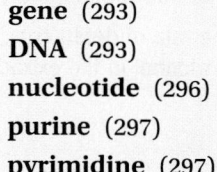

2 Replication of DNA

> In DNA replication, the DNA molecule unwinds, and the two sides split. Then, new bases are added to each side until two identical sequences result.

> The replication of DNA involves many proteins that form a machinelike complex of moving parts.

> In prokaryotic cells, replication starts at a single site. In eukaryotic cells, replication starts at many sites along the chromosome.

DNA replication (300)
DNA helicase (301)
DNA polymerase (301)

3 RNA and Gene Expression

> Gene expression produces proteins by transcription and translation. This process takes place in two stages, both of which involve RNA.

> In cells, three types of RNA complement DNA and translate the genetic code into proteins.

> During transcription, the information in a gene is transcribed, or copied, into mRNA.

> The genetic code is based on codons that each represent a specific amino acid.

> Translation occurs in a sequence of steps, involves three kinds of RNA, and results in a complete polypeptide.

> Despite the neatness of the genetic code, every gene cannot be simply linked to a single outcome.

RNA (304)
gene expression (304)
transcription (305)
translation (305)
codon (307)

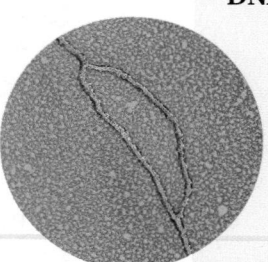

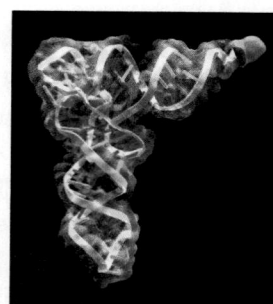

1. **Word Parts** Use the Word Parts exercise to identify and then understand the enzymes described in this chapter.

2. **Concept Mapping** Make a concept map that shows the structure of DNA and the way that DNA replicates. Try to include the following words in your concept map: *nucleotides, purine, pyrimidine, double helix, replication, transfer RNA, ribosomal RNA, gene expression, DNA polymerases,* and *gene.*

Using Key Terms

Use each of the following terms in a separate sentence.

3. *nucleotide*

4. *DNA replication*

For each pair of terms, explain how the meanings of the terms differ.

5. *transcription* and *translation*

6. *gene* and *DNA*

7. *DNA helicase* and *DNA polymerase*

Understanding Key Ideas

8. What is the function of DNA?
   a. DNA creates genetic material.
   b. DNA controls all of the aspects of an organism's behavior.
   c. DNA enables organisms to pass on genetic information to their offspring.
   d. DNA enables organisms to produce offspring that are identical to their parents.

9. If the sequence of nitrogenous bases in one strand of DNA is GAGTC, what is the sequence of bases in the complementary strand of DNA?
   a. AGACT   c. ATACG
   b. TCTGA   d. CTCAG

10. Which of the following bases pairs with uracil in an RNA molecule?
    a. adenine   c. thymine
    b. guanine   d. cytosine

11. What was the significance of Frederick Griffith's experiments with DNA?
    a. Griffith showed that DNA has a double-helix structure.
    b. Griffith disproved the idea that DNA contained genetic material.
    c. Griffith discovered that genetic material could be transferred between cells.
    d. Griffith demonstrated that viruses could inject their DNA into bacterial cells.

12. What does the process of transcription produce?
    a. tRNA   c. mRNA
    b. RNA   d. DNA

Use the diagram to answer the following question.

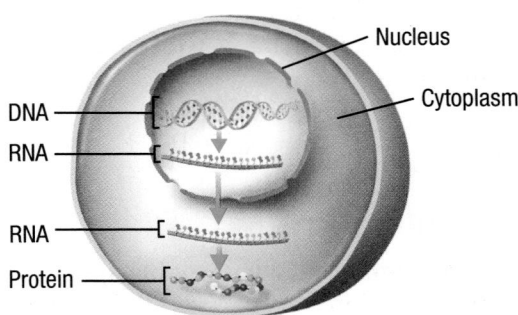

13. This illustration shows a eukaryotic cell. Where does translation occur in this cell?
    a. in the DNA   c. in the nucleus
    b. in the cytoplasm   d. in the ribosome

Explaining Key Ideas

14. **Identify** the roles that proteins play in DNA replication.

15. **Compare** the structure of RNA with that of DNA.

16. **Determine** the kinds of events that can cause complications in gene expression.

17. **Relate** the role of codons to the sequence of amino acids that results after translation.

Using Science Graphics

Use the table to answer the following question.

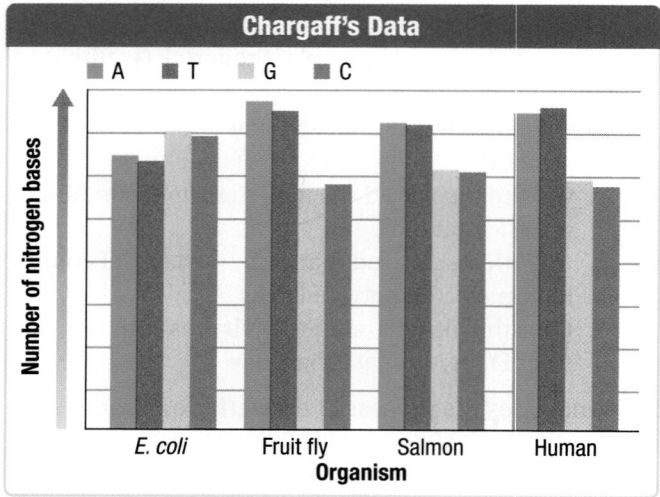

Chargaff's Data

■ A   ■ T   ■ G   ■ C

Number of nitrogen bases

E. coli   Fruit fly   Salmon   Human
Organism

18. Chargaff collected data involving bases in DNA. Which of the following ratios most accurately expresses the relationship between adenine and thymine in DNA?

   a. 1:2   **c.** 2:1
   b. 1:1   **d.** 1:4

Critical Thinking

19. Predicting Outcomes What would happen if the enzymes that keep DNA strands separated during the replication process were not present?

20. Recognizing Relationships How might the process of DNA replication in eukaryotic cells lead to more errors than the process of DNA replication in prokaryotic cells does?

21. Relating Concepts How does a replication fork enable the process of DNA replication?

22. Justifying Conclusions Why does DNA replication in eukaryotic cells involve multiple replication forks?

23. Contrasting Functions Contrast the roles of mRNA and tRNA in the process of protein synthesis.

24. Evaluating Viewpoints How did Watson and Crick build on the discoveries of other scientists to determine the structure of DNA?

25. Proposing Alternative Hypotheses Propose one possible exception to the formula of "one gene ⟶ one protein ⟶ one trait."

Writing for Science

26. Speech Writing Imagine that you are asked to introduce Watson, Crick, and Wilkins at the Nobel Prize ceremony in 1962. Write a speech that details the work that contributed to the discovery of the structure of DNA.

Methods of Science

27. Forming Hypotheses Recall that mRNA has one start codon and three stop codons. Based on what you know about the process of gene expression, hypothesize why it would be beneficial to have only one start codon but three stop codons involved in this process.

Alternative Assessment

28. Brochure Human blood types are examples of the complex results of genes. Make a brochure entitled "A Guide to Human Blood Types for Blood Donors." Use reference sources to find out about the major blood types. Be sure to find out and explain why each blood type matters for blood-donating purposes and what the genetic determinants of each blood type are.

Math Skills

Use the table to answer the following questions.

Percentage of Each Nitrogen Base				
	A	T	G	C
Human	30.4	30.1	19.6	19.9
Wheat	27.3	27.1	22.7	22.8
E. coli	24.7	23.6	26.0	25.7

29. Ratios What is the ratio of purines to pyrimidines?

30. Percentages Within each organism, which nucleotides are found in similar percentages?

31. Do the ratio and percentages in the previous two questions follow Chargaff's rule?

Science Concepts

1. During protein synthesis, transfer RNA (tRNA)
   A produces a new RNA molecule.
   B acts as a start signal for protein synthesis.
   C produces protein subunits by translating the codons on mRNA.
   D delivers the instructions for protein synthesis to the site of translation.

2. Erwin Chargaff's data on nitrogenous bases
   F suggested that DNA bases are paired.
   G suggested that DNA is a tightly coiled helix.
   H suggested that certain bases are found in equal amounts in DNA.
   J proved that DNA's structure is similar to a twisted ladder.

3. The immediate result of a mistake in transcription would most likely be a
   A different cell.
   B different gene.
   C different protein.
   D different set of alleles.

4. Which part of a nucleotide contains genetic information?
   F sugar molecules
   G nitrogen base pairs
   H phosphate molecules
   J deoxyribose molecules

Math Skills

5. **Calculating Percentages** DNA analysis reveals that adenine makes up 40% of a piece of DNA. What percentage of the DNA bases in the piece of DNA is guanine?
   A 20%   C 40%
   B 60%   D 10%

Using Science Graphics

Use the diagram to answer the following question.

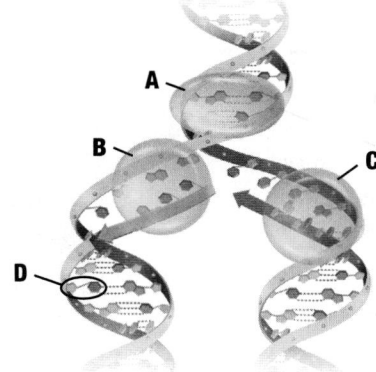

6. What is the function of the structure labeled "A"?
   F separating DNA strands
   G reconnecting DNA strands
   H checking the new DNA strands for errors
   J adding nucleotides to make new DNA strands

Use the diagram to answer the following questions.

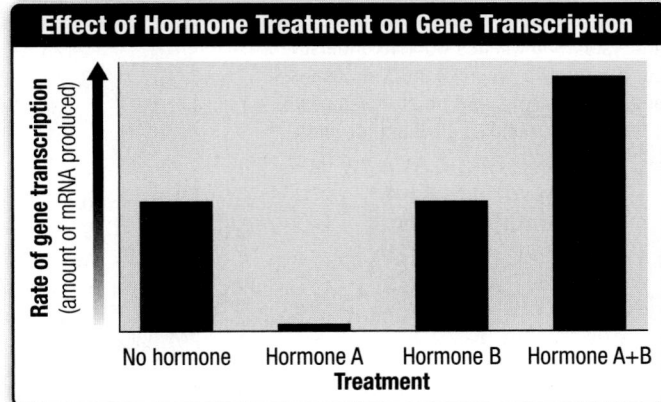

Effect of Hormone Treatment on Gene Transcription

7. What is the control variable in this experiment?
   A No Hormone   C Hormone B
   B Hormone A   D Hormone A+B

8. What can you conclude about the effect Hormone B has on the rate of gene transcription compared to the control treatment?
   F It increases gene transcription rate.
   G It decreases gene transcription rate.
   H It does not change gene transcription rate compared to the control.
   J It has a smaller effect on transcription rate than Hormone A does.

Chapter 14 Genes in Action

Preview

1 Mutation and Genetic Change
Mutation: The Basis of Genetic Change
Several Kinds of Mutations
Effects of Genetic Change
Large-Scale Genetic Change

2 Regulating Gene Expression
Complexities of Gene Expression
Gene Regulation in Prokaryotes
Gene Regulation in Eukaryotes
The Many Roles of Proteins

3 Genome Interactions
Genomes and the Diversity of Life
Moving Beyond Chromosomes
Multicellular Development and Aging

Why It Matters

Knowing the genetic code is not enough to understand how genes work. To understand our own bodies, we must study thousands of genes, proteins, and other molecules that interact as our bodies grow and develop.

These frogs have extra legs! When many mutated or deformed organisms are found in one area, scientists want to find out why.

Scientists have found several factors that increase the numbers of deformities in frogs. These factors include UV radiation, pesticides, and parasites. Parasites invade the frogs' bodies and may disrupt development.

InquiryLab

🕐 15 min

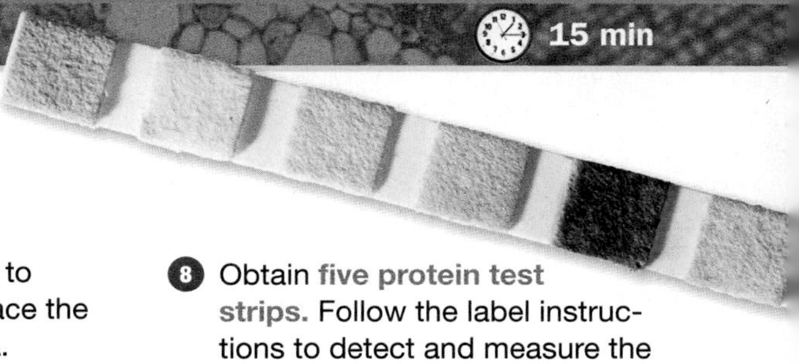

Where Is the Protein?

Protein test strips are inexpensive and easy-to-use measuring tools. Sold in local pharmacies, these strips are purchased by individuals who must monitor the concentration of protein in their urine. The strips can also be used to confirm the presence of protein in various foods.

Procedure

❶ Work with a partner. Label **five small cups** "A," "B," "C," "D," and "E."

❷ Use a **mortar and pestle** to crush **20 lentil beans**. Place the crushed beans into cup A.

❸ Place **1 g of instant oatmeal** into cup B.

❹ Pour **10 mL of water** into cups A and B. Swirl each cup to mix its contents.

❺ Pour **10 mL of water** into cup C.

❻ Pour **10 mL of milk** into cup D.

❼ Pour **10 mL of fruit juice** into cup E.

❽ Obtain **five protein test strips.** Follow the label instructions to detect and measure the presence of protein in each cup.

Analysis

1. **Identify** the cups in which protein was present.

2. **Identify** the cups that had the most and least amounts of protein.

3. **Identify** the control group in this experiment. Explain its purpose.

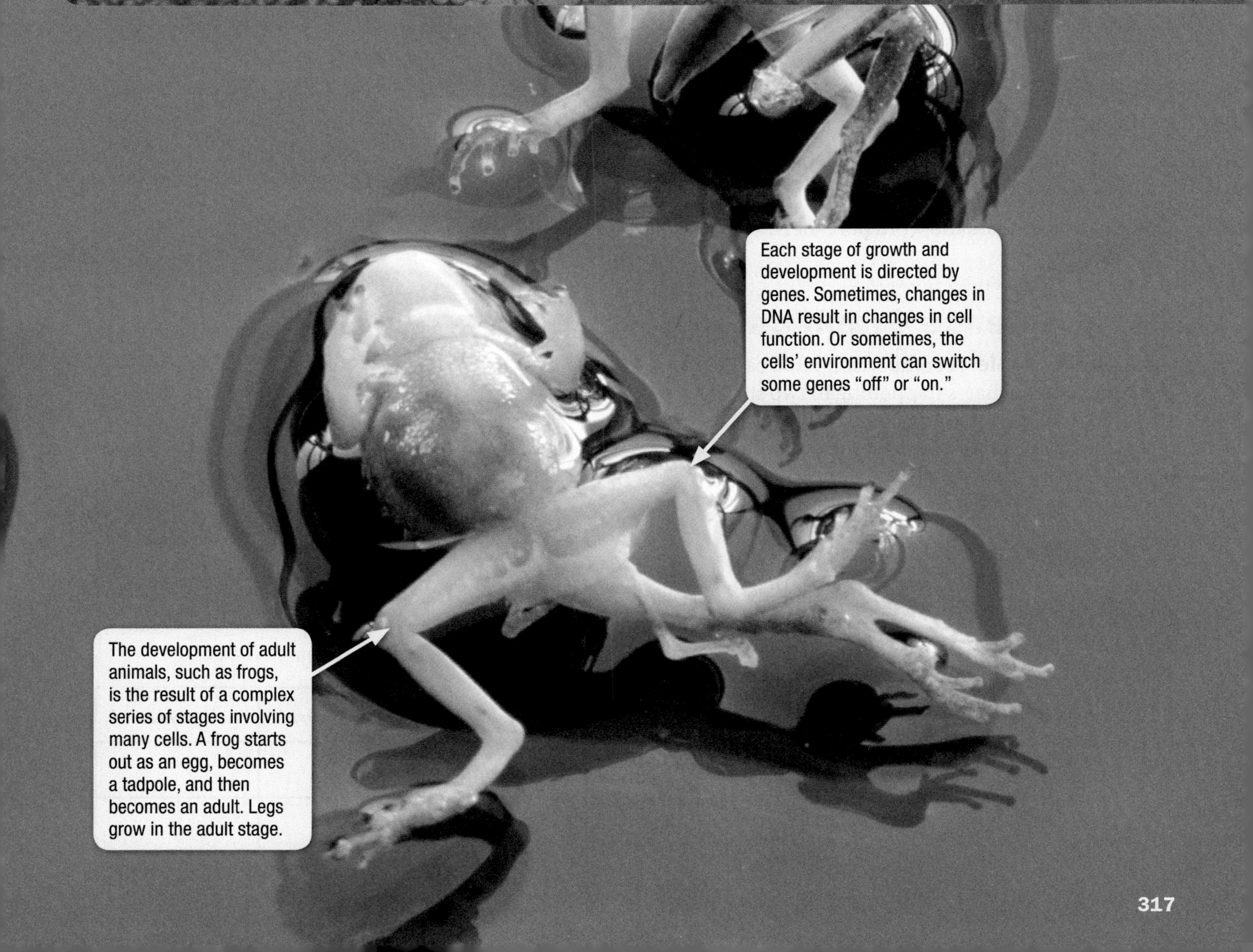

Each stage of growth and development is directed by genes. Sometimes, changes in DNA result in changes in cell function. Or sometimes, the cells' environment can switch some genes "off" or "on."

The development of adult animals, such as frogs, is the result of a complex series of stages involving many cells. A frog starts out as an egg, becomes a tadpole, and then becomes an adult. Legs grow in the adult stage.

READING TOOLBOX

These reading tools can help you learn the material in this chapter. For more information on how to use these and other tools, see **Appendix: Reading and Study Skills.**

Using Words

Prefixes A prefix is a word part that is attached to the beginning of a word. Prefixes add to the meaning of words. For example, the prefix *im-* means "not." So, *immovable* means "not able to be moved." This table shows some additional prefixes that you may see in this chapter.

Prefixes	
Prefix	**Meaning**
in- or *im-*	not
mut-	change
trans-	cross
homeo-	the same

Your Turn Use the table to answer the questions that follow.
1. In your own words, define *immutable.*
2. What do you think the word *transmutation* means?

Using Language

Finding Examples When you are reading scientific explanations, finding examples can help you put a concept into practical terms. Thinking of your own examples will help you remember what you read.

Your Turn For each category of items below, brainstorm as many examples as you can think of that could fit into the category.
1. hereditary traits
2. words that include the word part *-her-.*

Using Science Graphics

Comparison Table A comparison table can help you understand what is happening in two similar situations. For example, this graphic shows the effect of lactose on specific genes in some prokaryotic cells. If you compare the two situations shown, you will find similarities and differences.

Your Turn Make a comparison table like the one shown here to compare what happens when lactose is present and when lactose is absent.
1. Draw a table with two columns.
2. Label the first column "Lactose absent."
3. Label the second column "Lactose present."
4. Use the graphic as a reference as you list the structures and events that are similar or different.

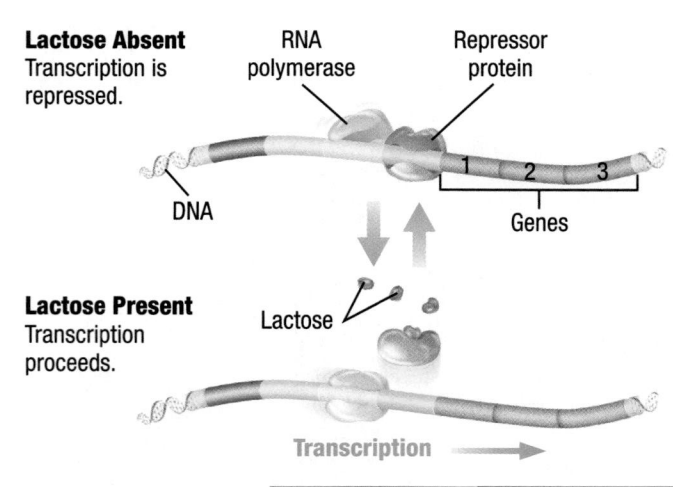

Lactose Absent Transcription is repressed.

RNA polymerase

Repressor protein

DNA

Genes

Lactose Present Transcription proceeds.

Lactose

Transcription

	Lactose absent	Lactose present
Similarities		
Differences		

Mutation and Genetic Change

Key Ideas	Key Terms	Why It Matters
❯ What is the origin of genetic differences among organisms? ❯ What kinds of mutations are possible? ❯ What are the possible effects of mutations? ❯ How can genetic change occur on a larger scale?	mutation nondisjunction polyploidy	Understanding mutation is key to understanding the differences among organisms over time.

In general, *mutation* simply means "change," and any organism that has changed from some previous or normal state can be called a *mutant*. So, a frog that has extra legs may be called a *mutant,* although the extra legs may or may not have a genetic cause.

Mutation: The Basis of Genetic Change

In genetics, a **mutation** is a change in the structure or amount of the genetic material of an organism. A genetic *mutant* is an individual whose DNA or chromosomes differ from some previous or normal state. ❯ **For the most part, genetic differences among organisms originate as some kind of genetic mutation.** Every unique allele of every gene began as a mutation of an existing gene.

Causes of Mutations Mutations occur naturally as accidental changes to DNA or to chromosomes during the cell cycle. Recall that enzymes repair most DNA that is mismatched during replication, but rarely, some DNA is not repaired. Other kinds of mistakes are possible, as you will learn. Also, the rate of mutation can be increased by some environmental factors. Such factors, called *mutagens,* include many forms of radiation and some kinds of chemicals.

Effects of Mutations Because of the way DNA is translated, a mutation can have many possible effects. A small change in DNA may affect just one amino acid in the protein that results from a gene. However, as you will see, other results are possible. A mutation may have no effect, or may harm or help in some way. The effect depends on where and when the mutation occurs. We notice mutations when they cause an unusual trait or disease, such as *sickle cell anemia,* shown in **Figure 1.** However, many mutations may go unnoticed.

❯ **Reading Check** *Where do new alleles come from?*
(See the Appendix for answers to Reading Checks.)

mutation a change in the structure or amount of the genetic material of an organism

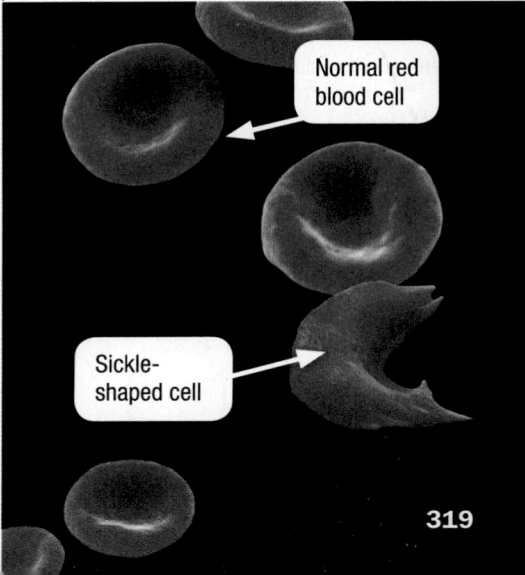

Normal red blood cell

Sickle-shaped cell

Figure 1 One out of 500 African Americans has sickle cell anemia, which is caused by a mutation in the gene that produces hemoglobin. Blood cells with the defective hemoglobin tend to bend, rupture, and get stuck.

Several Kinds of Mutations

DNA and chromosomes are involved in many processes, so there are many kinds of mutations. Most mutations involve a misplacement of a nucleotide in a DNA segment. A mutation may change the results of a gene (when the gene is translated and transcribed), but not all mutations do so. ❯ **Different kinds of mutations are recognized as either changes in DNA or changes in the results of genes, as shown in Figure 2.**

Mutations as Changes in DNA During DNA replication, the wrong nucleotide may be paired or placed in a sequence.

Point Mutation A *point* mutation is a change of a single nucleotide in a sequence from one kind of base to another.

Insertion or Deletion Rarely, errors in replication can cause the *insertion* or *deletion* of one or more nucleotides in a sequence.

Mutations as Changes in Results of Genes Changes in a DNA sequence may affect the results of genes in many ways.

Silent Mutation A mutation is *silent* when it has no effect on a gene's function. Point mutations are often silent because the genetic code is redundant (each amino acid has multiple codons).

Missense Mutation A *missense* mutation results when a codon is changed such that the new codon codes for a different amino acid. This kind of mutation is also called a *replacement* mutation.

Frameshift Mutation Recall that the genetic code is "read" in "words" of three letters each (codons). The *reading frame* of a sequence depends on the starting point for reading. An insertion or deletion can shift the reading frame, or cause a *frameshift*. In this case, the remaining sequence may be "read" as different codons.

READING TOOLBOX

Finding Examples Use the phrase "the cat ate" to create examples of mutations. For example, a point mutation could change the letter *c* to *b* and would result in "the bat ate." The new phrase is also a missense mutation. Use the original phrase to make examples of an insertion, a deletion, and a nonsense mutation.

Figure 2 A mutation is a change, insertion, or deletion of one or more nucleotides in a gene. The change may or may not result in a different amino acid sequence within a protein.

go.hrw.com
✳ **interact online**
Keyword: HX8GNXF2

Kinds of Mutations

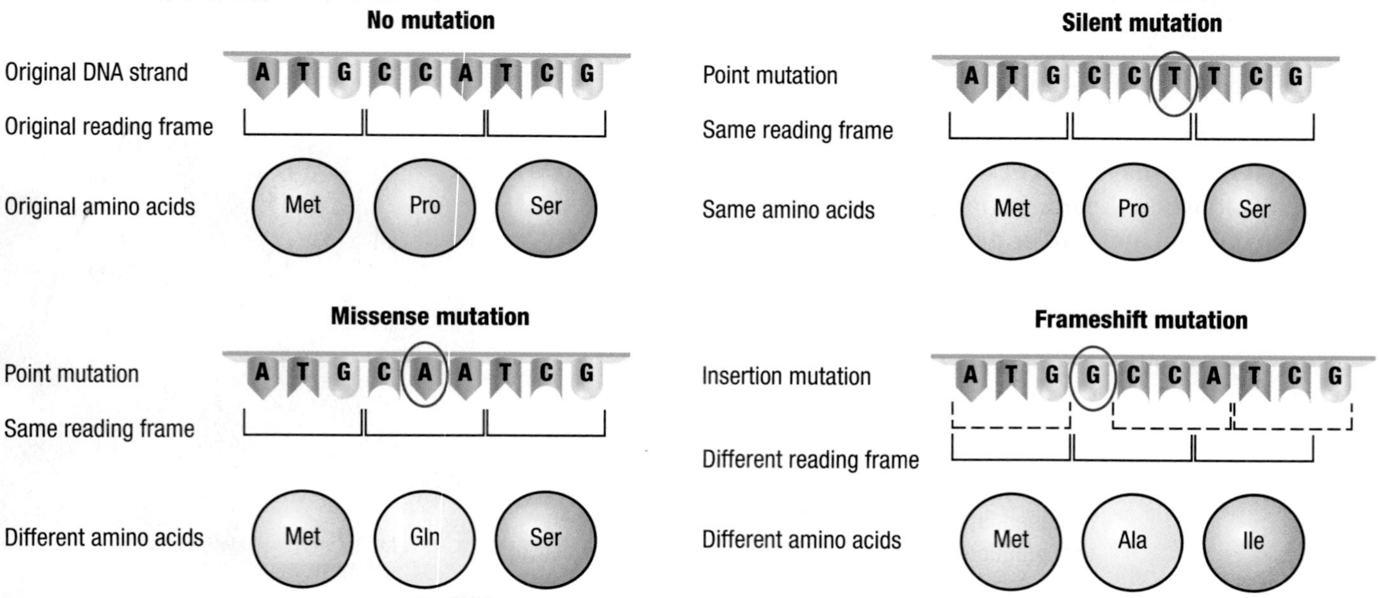

No mutation

Original DNA strand: A T G C C A T C G
Original reading frame
Original amino acids: Met Pro Ser

Silent mutation

Point mutation: A T G C C T T C G
Same reading frame
Same amino acids: Met Pro Ser

Missense mutation

Point mutation: A T G C A A T C G
Same reading frame
Different amino acids: Met Gln Ser

Frameshift mutation

Insertion mutation: A T G G C C A T C G
Different reading frame
Different amino acids: Met Ala Ile

QuickLab

Make a Model of Mutations

You have learned about (and may have built models of) DNA replication and gene expression. Now, challenge yourself to build (or add to) a model that demonstrates each type of mutation described in this section.

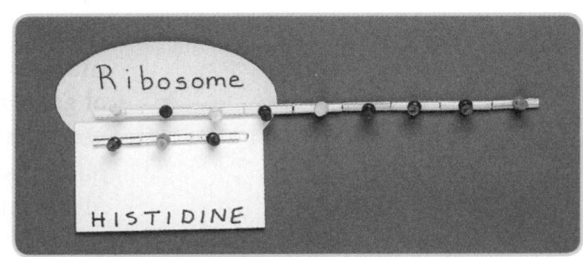

Analysis

1. **List** each mutation type on **12 separate sheets of paper.** Work with a partner.

2. **Demonstrate** each mutation type by using **assorted materials** (or models that you have built previously).

3. **Draw** the "before" and "after" state for each mutation.

4. **CRITICAL THINKING** **Critiquing Models** Trade your drawings with another group. What is accurate and useful about their model? What could be improved? Write down your comments for the other group.

Nonsense Mutation A *nonsense* mutation results when a codon is changed to a "stop" signal. In this case, the resulting string of amino acids may be cut short, and the protein may fail to function.

More or Fewer Amino Acids If an insertion or deletion is a multiple of 3, the reading frame will be preserved. However, the protein that results may have a few more or less amino acids in it. An insertion or deletion of many codons is likely to disrupt the resulting protein's structure and function.

Chromosomal Mutations ❯ In eukaryotic cells, the process of meiosis creates the chance of mutations at the chromosomal level. Recall that during this process, chromosomes pair up and may undergo *crossover*. Usually, the result is an equal exchange of alleles between homologous chromosomes. But errors in the exchange can cause *chromosomal mutations*, as shown in **Figure 3.**

Deletion A *deletion* occurs when a piece of a chromosome is lost. At the end of meiosis, one of the cells will lack the genes from that missing piece. Such deletions are usually harmful.

Duplication A *duplication* occurs when a piece remains attached to its homologous chromosome after meiosis. One chromosome will then carry both alleles for each of the genes in that piece.

Inversion An *inversion* occurs when a piece reattaches to its original chromosome, but in a reverse direction.

Translocation A *translocation* occurs when a chromosome piece ends up in a completely different, nonhomologous chromosome.

Gene Rearrangement A chromosomal mutation can move an entire gene to a new location. Such a change, called a *gene rearrangement,* is likely to disrupt the gene's function in other ways, as you will learn.

❯ **Reading Check** *Why are point mutations often silent?*

Figure 3 Four kinds of chromosomal mutations can result from errors in crossover during meiosis. ❯ **How are the types of chromosomal mutations similar to the types of smaller-scale mutations?**

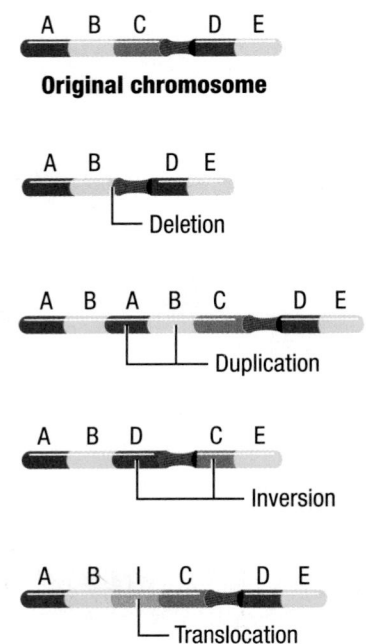

Effects of Genetic Change

Many genetic changes will cause no change in the appearance or function of organisms. Moreover, many changes in the DNA of cells may not be passed on to other cells by mitosis or meiosis. ❯ **The results of genetic change may be harmful, beneficial, or neutral; most changes are neutral and may not be passed on to offspring.** Mutations that occur in gametes can be passed on to offspring, but mutations in body cells affect only the individual in which they occur.

Heritable or Not Multicellular eukaryotes have two primary cell types: germ cells and somatic cells. *Germ cells* make up gametes, and *somatic cells* make up the rest of the body. Mutations can occur in either type of cell. However, if a mutation occurs in a somatic cell, that genetic change will be lost when the owner of the cell dies. For example, a mutation in a person's lung cell could cause the cell to grow into lung cancer. The mutated genes in the cancer cells will not be transferred to the person's children.

Only a mutation in a germ cell may be passed on to the next generation. However, any such mutation may be silent or have little effect. Only rarely do mutations cause <u>dramatic</u> changes in future generations.

If a mutation occurs in a somatic cell, the change may be silent or it may change the function of the cell. Recall that most tissues are derived from a few parent cells. So, if a mutation occurs in a parent cell, all cells that arise by mitosis from that cell will have copies of the mutation. If the new cells can function at all, each will have the altered structure or function caused by the mutation. If the other parent cells were normal, the resulting tissue may include both normal tissue and mutant tissue.

ACADEMIC VOCABULARY

dramatic vivid or striking

Figure 4 Melanoma is a type of skin cancer caused by mutations in melanocytes, the cells that make skin pigment. Melanoma is an example of a somatic cell cancer. ❯ **Can this kind of cancer be passed on to offspring?**

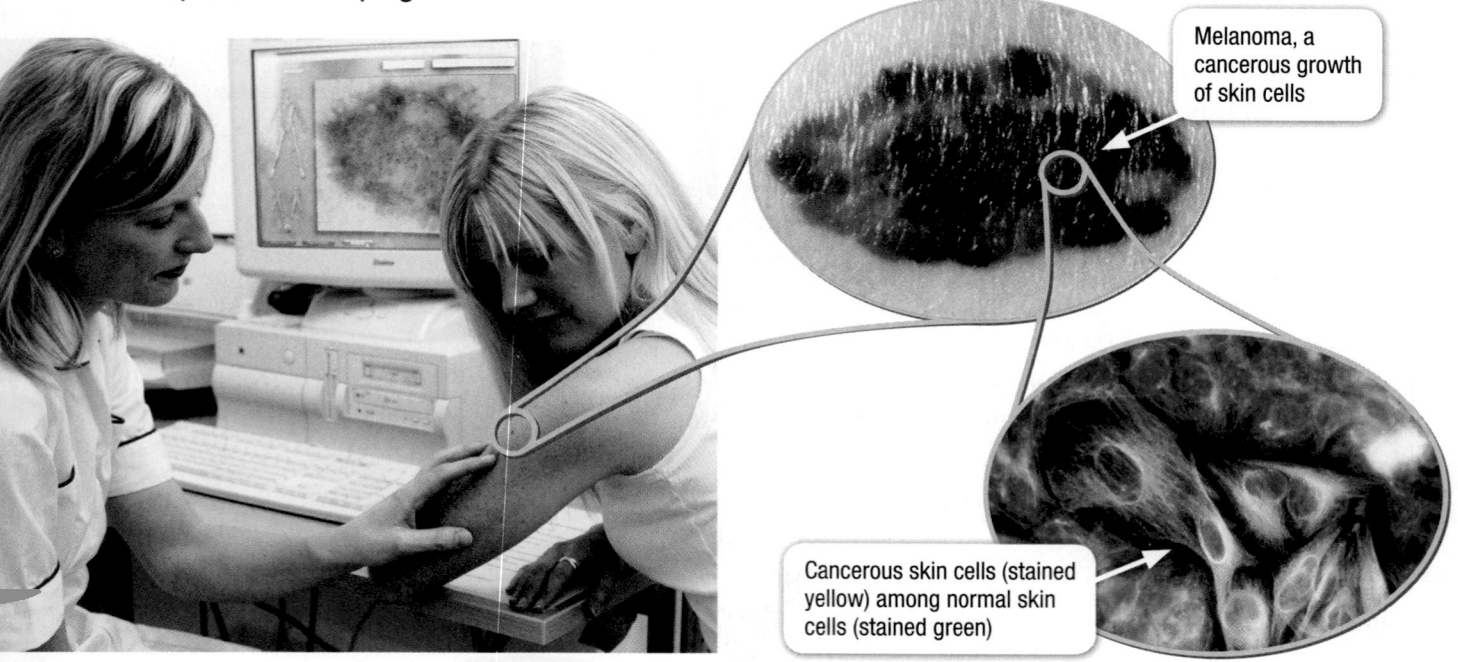

Melanoma, a cancerous growth of skin cells

Cancerous skin cells (stained yellow) among normal skin cells (stained green)

Some Human Genetic Disorders

Disorder	Inheritance pattern	Major physical symptoms	Genetic effect of mutant allele	Number of cases (United States)
Sickle cell anemia	recessive	poor blood circulation; pain; damage to organs such as liver, kidney, lungs, and heart	abnormal hemoglobin in red blood cells	72,000
Tay-Sachs disease	recessive in most cases	deterioration of central nervous system; death in early childhood	defective form of an enzyme in nerve cells	< 100
Cystic fibrosis	recessive	mucus buildup in organs such as lungs, liver, and pancreas; difficulty breathing and digesting; shortened life span	defective form of an enzyme in secretory cells	30,000
Hemophilia A (classical)	recessive, sex-linked	failure of blood to clot; excessive bleeding and bruising when injured	defective form of a protein for blood clotting	18,000
Huntington disease	dominant	gradual deterioration of brain tissue in middle age; shortened life expectancy	abnormal protein in brain cells	30,000

Tumors and Cancers Certain genes control the normal growth, division, and specialization of cells in bodies. Mutations in these genes can cause a normal somatic cell to "lose control" and begin growing and dividing abnormally. The group of cells that grows will become a *tumor*. If the tumor cells begin to invade other parts of the body, they become a form of *cancer*. An example of a somatic cell tumor is shown in **Figure 4.** Note that although cancers result from somatic cell mutations, not all somatic cell mutations cause cancer.

New Alleles You previously learned that for any given gene, many alleles, or variations, may exist. Now, you should see that any new allele must begin as a mutation of an existing allele. Most new alleles are simply the result of silent mutations, so these changes make little difference to the organisms in which they occur. However, sometimes a new allele can cause a change in a gene's function. Depending on the gene, the result may be harmful or beneficial to the organism.

Genetic Disorders Harmful effects produced by inherited mutations (defective alleles) are called *genetic disorders*. Several human genetic disorders are summarized in **Figure 5.** Often, such a disorder results because a mutation has altered the normal function of a gene. However, a person may still have one allele of the original, functioning gene. For this reason, many disorders are recessive—that is, the disorder develops only in a person who is homozygous for the mutated allele. So, two heterozygous people may be healthy, yet have children who develop a genetic disorder. A person who is heterozygous for such an allele is said to be a *carrier* of the disorder.

❯ **Reading Check** *How are mutations related to cancer?*

Figure 5 Genetic disorders are caused by inherited mutations that disrupt the normal function of a gene. ❯ **Why are genetic disorders relatively rare?**

SCI*LINKS*.

www.scilinks.org
Topic: Genetic Disorders
Code: HX80652

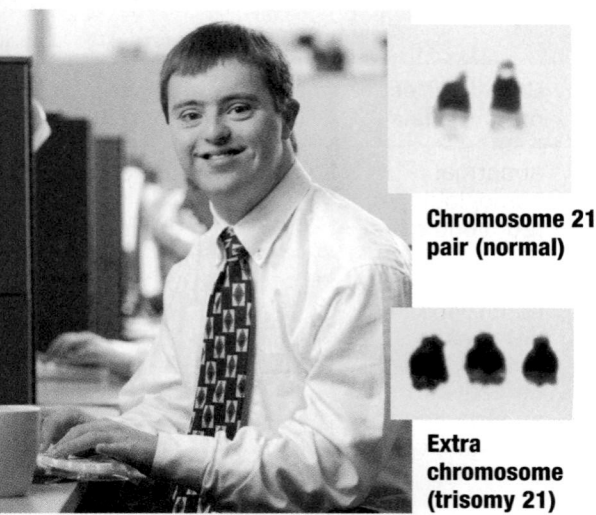

Chromosome 21
pair (normal)

Extra
chromosome
(trisomy 21)

Figure 6 Most people with Down syndrome have an extra copy of chromosome 21. The extra chromosome can be seen in a karyotype. ❯ What other conditions can result from accidents in chromosome sorting?

nondisjunction (NAHN dis JUHNK shuhn) a failure of homologous chromosomes to separate during meiosis I or the failure of sister chromatids to separate during mitosis or meiosis II

polyploidy (PAH lee PLOY dee) an abnormal condition of having more than two sets of chromosomes

Large-Scale Genetic Change

At another scale, accidents can happen to entire sets of chromosomes. ❯ **Very large-scale genetic change can occur by misplacement, recombination, or multiplication of entire chromosomes.**

Recombination During Crossover Genetic recombination through sexual reproduction has many important consequences. Recall that during the *crossover* step of meiosis, the alleles from one parent are recombined with the alleles from the other parent. So, meiosis creates new combinations of alleles in offspring. Over time, sexual reproduction and meiotic recombination maintain genetic variety within a population.

Errors in Sorting Chromosomes Each of your chromosomes has thousands of genes. Together, these genes control cell structure and function. So, all 46 chromosomes (23 pairs) are needed for your body to develop and function normally. Human embryos with missing chromosomes rarely survive. Humans with an extra chromosome may survive but do not develop normally.

Nondisjunction Recall that when gametes form by meiosis, each pair of chromosomes separates in the step called *disjunction*. When the pairs fail to separate properly, the error is called **nondisjunction.** For example, nondisjunction of chromosome 21 can lead to a disabling condition called *Down syndrome*, or *trisomy 21*, as shown in **Figure 6.** In this case, one of the parent's gametes received both copies of chromosome 21 instead of one. When that gamete joined with a normal gamete, the child received three copies instead of two.

Polyploidy The largest scale of genetic change can happen if the entire genome is duplicated. Such duplication can occur—rarely—during meiosis, by nondisjunction of *all* chromosomes. The result is a cell with multiple sets of chromosomes, a condition known as **polyploidy.** A polyploid cell has genetic material "to spare." In future offspring, mutations can happen in some genes without losing the functions of the original genes. Thus, polyploidy is another way that organisms can change over time. Polyploidy is common in plants.

❯ **Reading Check** *How can a child be born with extra chromosomes?*

Section 1 Review

❯ **KEY IDEAS**

1. **Identify** the primary mechanism for genetic change and differences among organisms.
2. **List** the kinds of mutations.
3. **Relate** the possible kinds of mutations to their effects.
4. **Relate** changes in chromosome number to possible results.

CRITICAL THINKING

5. **Evaluating Significance** Compare DNA mutations with chromosomal mutations in terms of the severity of the results of each.
6. **Justifying Conclusions** You read in a magazine that all mutations are bad. Do you agree? Explain.

USING SCIENCE GRAPHICS

7. **Visualizing** Look at **Figure 2** in this section. Notice that it shows only a single strand of the original DNA sequence and a final amino acid sequence. Sketch the matching DNA and RNA strands for the steps in between. Review the steps of gene expression if needed.

Key Ideas	Key Terms	Why It Matters
❯ Can the process of gene expression be controlled? ❯ What is a common form of gene regulation in prokaryotes? ❯ How does gene regulation in eukaryotes differ from gene regulation in prokaryotes? ❯ Why are proteins so important and versatile?	operon transcription factor intron exon domain	Understanding gene regulation may enable us to treat or prevent diseases that were previously unbeatable.

How do butterflies develop from caterpillars? We now know that genes determine traits such as patterns on butterfly wings, as shown in **Figure 7.** And we know that every cell in an individual starts with the same genes. So, in a butterfly's lifetime, every trait of every gene is not always "at work."

Complexities of Gene Expression

Scientists have learned that gene expression (transcription and translation) can be regulated. It is now clear that not all genes are expressed in every cell, nor are many genes expressed all of the time. ❯ **Cells have complex systems that regulate whether or not specific genes are expressed. Expression depends on the cell's needs and environment.**

Through *gene regulation,* a given genetic sequence can be expressed in different ways—in different bodies or tissues, under different conditions, or at different times. Thus, gene regulation accounts for changes during development as well as differences among organisms that have similar genes. One benefit of gene regulation is that cells can use energy and materials efficiently.

Recall that many steps take place in the expression of a gene. Also, other molecules play a role in the processes. Because complex interactions happen at each step, there are many opportunities to regulate gene expression. So, nearly every step in the process of gene expression can be regulated or controlled.

A molecular system that controls the expression of a specific gene is called a *genetic switch.* Like a light switch, a genetic switch can be turned "on" or "off." Often, the switch is triggered by factors or conditions outside the cell. Also, the product of one gene may serve to regulate another gene in the same organism.

Figure 7 Gene regulation causes changes in traits between a butterfly larva (caterpillar) and its adult form.

❯ **Reading Check** *Are all genes expressed all of the time?*

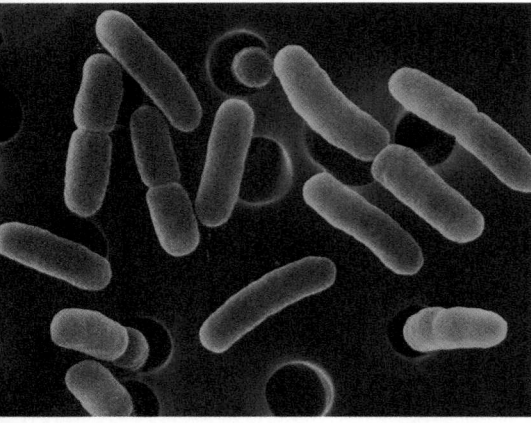

Figure 8 The *lac* operon controls the genes that code for the proteins that help a bacterium use lactose. The operon "turns on" and expresses the genes only in the presence of lactose. ▶ **How common are operons?**

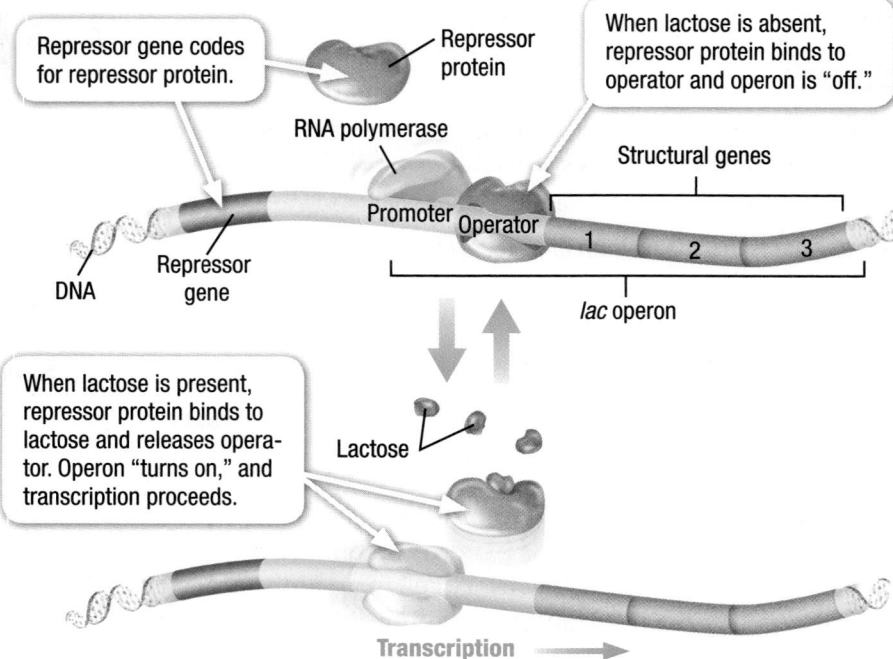

Repressor gene codes for repressor protein.

Repressor protein

When lactose is absent, repressor protein binds to operator and operon is "off."

RNA polymerase

Structural genes

Promoter Operator

1   2   3

DNA

Repressor gene

lac operon

When lactose is present, repressor protein binds to lactose and releases operator. Operon "turns on," and transcription proceeds.

Lactose

Transcription ⟶

READING TOOLBOX

Comparison Table Make a comparison table to compare **Figure 8** and **Figure 9.** Which roles do proteins have in the eukaryotic system but not in the prokaryotic system?

Gene Regulation in Prokaryotes

Scientists have studied and compared gene expression in prokaryotes and eukaryotes. Each has very different ways of regulating how genes are expressed. One reason for the differences can be found in the structure of genes in the two kinds of organisms.

▶ **The major form of gene regulation in prokaryotes depends upon operons that respond to environmental factors.** An **operon** is a gene-regulation system in which adjacent DNA segments control the expression of a group of genes with closely related functions. Operons are common in bacteria but uncommon in eukaryotes.

Interactions with the Environment Recall that bacteria are single cells that must get food directly from the environment. Given a stable environment, a bacterium will need a steady supply of proteins and will tend to keep expressing the same genes in the same way. But if the environment changes, a cascade of changes in gene expression may result. In a way, the environment "flips a switch."

The *lac* Operon Example An example of gene regulation is found in the bacterium *Escherichia coli*. Usually, when you eat or drink a dairy product, the chemical lactose ("milk sugar") is digested by *E. coli* cells living in your gut. These cells can use the lactose for energy or for other needs. But first, the cells must attach to, absorb, and then break down the lactose. These tasks require three different enzymes, each of which is coded for by a different gene.

The system that involves the *lac* genes is called the *lac operon* and is shown in **Figure 8.** This system includes the three genes plus a *promoter* site and an *operator* site. When lactose is available, the system "turns on" and the three genes are transcribed. When lactose is absent, the system "turns off" and transcription is blocked.

Gene Regulation in Eukaryotes

Eukaryotic cells, too, must turn genes on and off in response to signals from their environment. However, **gene regulation in eukaryotes is more complex and variable than gene regulation in prokaryotes.** To begin with, gene expression in eukaryotes involves more steps and interactions than gene expression in prokaryotes.

As you shall see, regulation can occur before transcription, after transcription, or after translation. Furthermore, in eukaryotes, a nuclear membrane separates these processes. So, each process can be regulated separately.

Eukaryotic gene regulation is unique in other ways. Operons are very rare in eukaryotic cells. Also, groups of genes with related functions may be scattered on different chromosomes and controlled by multiple factors. Finally, much of the DNA in eukaryotes may never be transcribed, and even less is ultimately translated into proteins.

Controlling Transcription Like prokaryotic cells, eukaryotic cells have proteins that regulate transcription. But many more proteins are involved, and the interactions are more complex. Most often, the genetic switch involves the first step of transcription, when RNA polymerase binds to the promoter region. The proteins involved in this kind of genetic switch are called **transcription factors.**

As shown in **Figure 9,** transcription factors interact with RNA polymerases around promoter regions of DNA. A given gene can be influenced by many transcription factors. Some transcription factors act as *activators,* and some act as *repressors.*

One kind of DNA sequence that can be bound by an activator is called an *enhancer.* Enhancers are often located thousands of bases away from the promoter. A loop in the DNA forms as the factors interact at the promoter site. Each factor may also affect other factors.

> **Reading Check** *Which parts of gene expression can be regulated?*

operon (AHP uhr AHN) a unit of adjacent genes that consists of functionally related structural genes and their associated regulatory genes

transcription factor an enzyme that is needed to begin and/or continue genetic transcription

ACADEMIC VOCABULARY

regulate to control, direct, or govern; to adjust

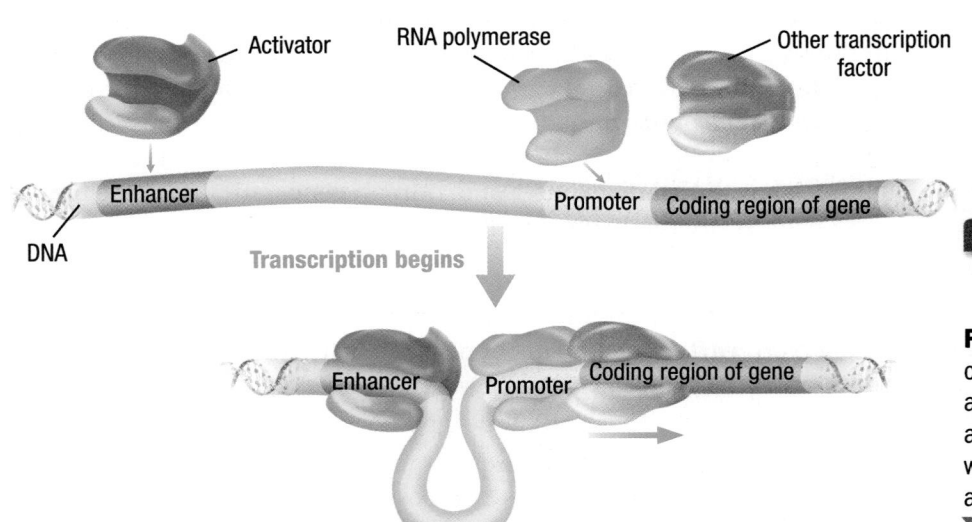

go.hrw.com
* interact online
Keyword: HX8GNXF9

Figure 9 Control of transcription is complex in eukaryotes. For example, an activator may bind to an enhancer site and also to RNA polymerase. This action will activate another transcription factor, and finally transcription will begin.
> Why is gene regulation more complex in eukaryotes than in prokaryotes?

A Model of Introns and Exons

appropriately joined

You can model introns and exons with masking tape.

Procedure

❶ Place a **15 to 20 cm strip of masking tape** on your desk. The tape represents a gene.

❷ Use **two colored pens** to write letters on the tape, exactly as shown in the example here. Space the letters to take up the entire length of the tape. The segments in one color represent introns; those in the other color represent exons.

❸ Lift the tape. Working from left to right, use **scissors** to cut apart each group of letters of the same color.

❹ Stick the pieces of tape to your desk as you cut them. Make two strips of matching colors, and join the pieces in their original order.

Analysis

1. **Determine** from the resulting two strips which strip represents "introns" and which represents "exons."

2. **CRITICAL THINKING** **Predicting Results** What might happen to the protein if an intron were not removed?

Figure 10 After transcription in eukaryotes, the entire new mRNA segment may not be translated into proteins. Instead, introns are removed, and only exons are translated.

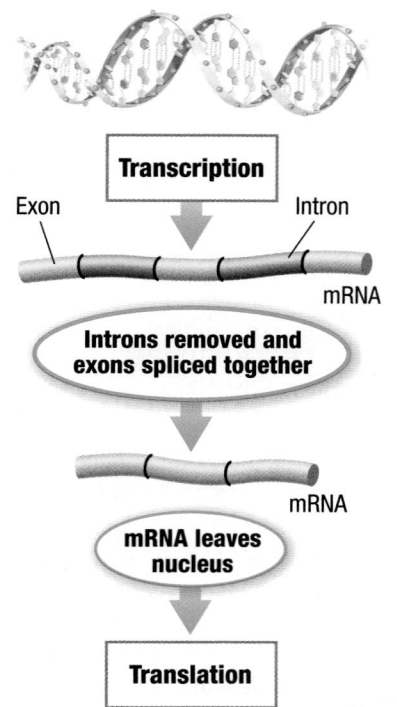

Processing RNA After Transcription It is simplest to think of a gene as a string of nucleotides that code for a protein. However, this simple arrangement is usually found only in prokaryotes. In eukaryotes, many genes contain *noncoding* sequences, or segments of code that will not be translated into amino acids. The noncoding segments are called **introns,** while those portions of the gene that *do* code for amino acids and will be translated are called **exons.**

RNA Splicing Exons and introns are handled in a process called *RNA splicing,* as shown in **Figure 10.** After a eukaryotic gene is transcribed, the introns are removed with the help of certain proteins. The exons that remain are *spliced,* or rejoined together, to form a smaller mRNA molecule. Finally, the spliced mRNA leaves the nucleus and is then translated.

Alternative Splicing The splicing of eukaryotic genes creates additional opportunities for variation over time. Because each exon encodes a different part of a protein, cells can occasionally shuffle exons between genes and thus make new proteins. The thousands of proteins in human cells appear to result from shuffling and recombining a few thousand exons. Some human genes, such as those for hemoglobin, are made up of multiple copies of similar exons.

Processing Proteins After Translation After translation, a chain of amino acids is formed, but the protein may not go directly into action. Further chemical changes may alter the structure and function of the protein. Such changes may affect the protein's shape, stability, or interactions with other molecules.

Final Destination A newly made protein may be needed in a specific location within the cell. The process of getting proteins to their correct destination is called *protein sorting.* Protein sorting occurs in many parts of the cell, such as the Golgi apparatus.

Sorting Signals Protein sorting is often directed by *sorting signals*, small parts of a protein that bind to other molecules within the cell. Some signals bind the protein to its final location in the cell. Some signals bind proteins to ribosomes while translation is in progress, and sends them together to the ER for further processing. This variation is another example of the complexity of genes.

The Many Roles of Proteins

Recall that proteins are complex strings of amino acids that do much of the work in cells. The diversity of protein structures relates to the many functions that proteins serve in cells. These functions range from forming the cell's shape to regulating gene expression. Proteins range in size from about 50 amino acids to more than 25,000 amino acids. The average protein is about 250 amino acids.

Protein Structure Because they can form many shapes, proteins can serve many roles. ❯ **The sequence of amino acids in a protein determines its three-dimensional structure and chemical behavior.** In turn, this folding determines the function of the protein, as shown in **Figure 11.** Some parts of a protein that have a specific chemical structure and function are protein **domains.** A protein may have several domains, each with a specific function. In eukaryotes, each domain is usually the result of a specific exon. Finally, large proteins may be made up of several smaller proteins, or *subunits*.

Proteins in Gene Expression Proteins serve important roles in gene expression. For example, several forms of RNA polymerase function to make mRNA, tRNA, and rRNA. Other proteins serve as *regulatory proteins* by binding to genetic switches in specific genes.

Because transcription is more complex in eukaryotes than in prokaryotes, more proteins are involved in the process. Likewise, more enzymes and structural proteins are required for translation in eukaryotes. Even after translation, additional steps may be needed to make a protein fully active in its proper place in a cell.

❯ **Reading Check** *What determines a protein's shape?*

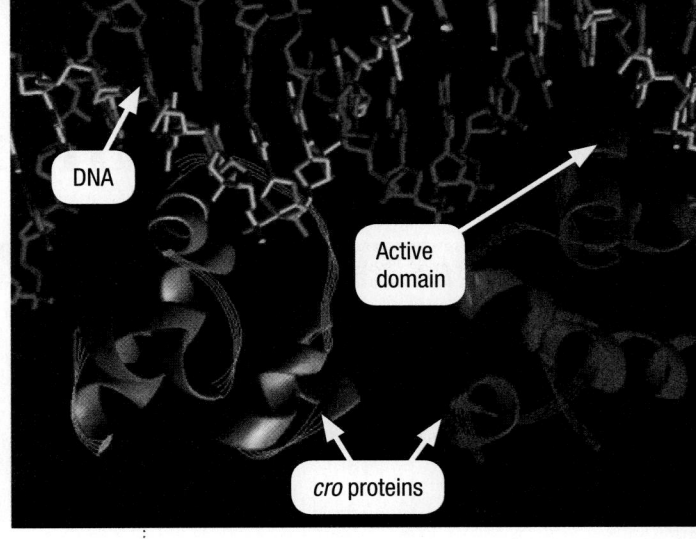

DNA

Active domain

cro proteins

Figure 11 Many of the proteins involved in gene regulation have a shape that fits closely with DNA or RNA molecules. The example shown here is a model of two molecules of bacterial *cro* protein (orange and red) binding to a molecule of DNA (blue and purple). The parts of the protein molecules that are chemically active are called *active domains*.

---

intron a nucleotide sequence that is part of a gene and that is transcribed from DNA into mRNA but not translated into amino acids

exon one of several nonadjacent nucleotide sequences that are part of one gene and that are transcribed, joined together, and then translated

domain in proteins, a functional unit that a has a distinctive pattern of structural folding

---

Section 2 Review

❯ KEY IDEAS

1. **Generalize** the ways that gene expression can be regulated.
2. **Describe** an example of gene regulation in prokaryotes.
3. **Identify** how gene regulation in eukaryotes is unique.
4. **Relate** protein structure to function in gene expression and regulation.

CRITICAL THINKING

5. **Proposing Mechanisms** Propose one other mechanism, not yet mentioned, for gene regulation in either prokaryotes or eukaryotes.
6. **Using Models** Use letters and words to show how a sequence could be spliced in several ways.

ALTERNATIVE ASSESSMENT

7. **Electronic Research** Use electronic resources to find three-dimensional computer models of proteins. Be sure that the models are based on scientific research. Make a display of several models.

Genome Interactions

Key Ideas	Key Terms	Why It Matters
❯ What can we learn by comparing genomes? ❯ Can genetic material be stored and transferred by mechanisms other than chromosomes? ❯ What are the roles of genes in multicellular development?	genome plasmid transposon cell differentiation apoptosis	We can understand how our own bodies work by comparing our genetic systems to those of other organisms.

Do you share genes with bacteria? In a way, you do. About 10% of human genes are nearly identical to bacterial genes. **Figure 12** shows the similarity between human genes and genes of other organisms.

Genomes and the Diversity of Life

Studying genomes has revolutionized how we look at gene regulation and gene expression. Recall that a **genome** is all of the DNA that an organism or species has within its chromosomes. A genome contains all the genes needed to make more of that organism. Today, the genomes of hundreds of organisms have been extensively studied.
❯ **Comparisons among the genetic systems of many organisms reveal basic biological similarities and relationships.**

Universal Code With few exceptions, the genetic code is the same in all organisms. For example, the codon GUC codes for the amino acid valine in bacteria, in eagles, in plants, and in your own cells. For this reason, the genetic code is often described as being universal. However, some exceptions exist to the universal aspects of the genetic code. For example, some bacteria use a slightly different set of amino acids in making proteins.

Figure 12 This graph shows the ratios of human genes that are nearly identical to genes in each of these species. ❯ What can we learn from such comparisons?

  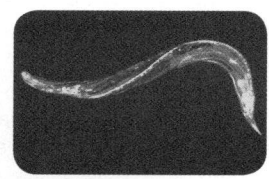 

Slime mold 16%

Mouse-ear cress 17%

Nematode 31%

Fruit fly 39%

Genome Sizes Genome size can be measured as an amount of DNA or a number of genes. Either way, genome size is only roughly related to complexity. Genomes in microbes range from 400,000 to millions of base pairs and include from 400 to 9,300 genes. Eukaryote genomes range from 100 million to more than 3 billion base pairs with 6,000 to 100,000 genes. The human genome has about 25,000 genes. Some plants have more than 100,000 genes.

DNA Versus Genes Not all DNA in a cell is part of a gene or even part of a chromosome. Special kinds of DNA include the following:

- **Plasmids in Prokaryotes** Recall that bacterial DNA is usually stored in one long, circular chromosome. However, most bacteria have extra pieces of DNA called **plasmids.** These small, circular DNA segments are replicated independently and can be transferred between cells. So, plasmids are an important source of genetic variation in bacteria.

- **Noncoding DNA in Eukaryotes** Eukaryotes have a great deal of *noncoding* DNA. For example, introns are transcribed but never translated. Also, long stretches of repeating sequences exist that are never transcribed. The function of most noncoding DNA is unclear.

- **DNA in Cell Organelles** Recall that mitochondria and chloroplasts, shown in **Figure 13,** are organelles that have special roles in eukaryotic cells. Chloroplasts enable plants to harvest energy from sunlight. Mitochondria act as the source of energy for cell function. Each of these organelles has its own small genome that is separate from that in the nucleus. These genomes code for proteins and RNAs (rRNA and tRNA) that assist in the function of each organelle.

Endosymbiotic Theory Why do mitochondria and chloroplasts have their own DNA? Scientists suspect that each organelle had its origin in ancient bacterial cells. This idea is known as the *endosymbiotic theory*. For example, chloroplast-like bacteria could have been engulfed, but not killed, by larger cells. Each kind of cell may have benefited from this relationship. Over time, the cells would live together in a close relationship called *symbiosis*.

❯ **Reading Check** *What kinds of organisms have large genomes?*

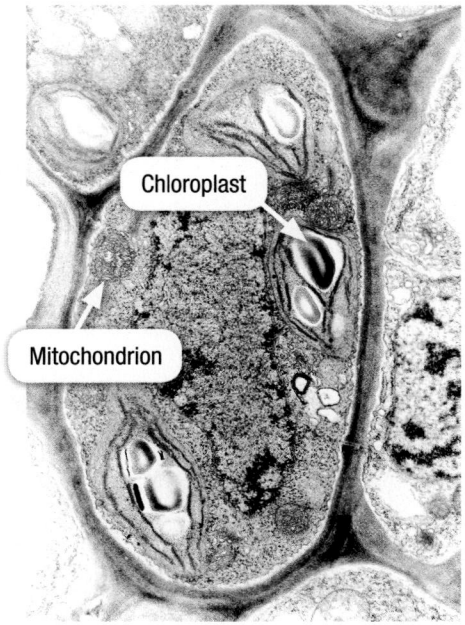

Figure 13 Chloroplasts and mitochondria have their own DNA. Each organelle's genome is stored and replicated separately from the chromosomes of the cell.

genome (JEE NOHM) the complete genetic material contained in an individual or species

plasmid (PLAZ mid) a genetic structure that can replicate independently of the main chromosome(s) of a cell

Zebra fish 63%
Chicken 67%
Dog 81%

Human (all genes compared to others)

Moving Beyond Chromosomes

We now know that cells can interact at the genetic level. And we know that genetic material exists outside of chromosomes. The closer we study genetics, the more complexities we find. ❯ Small bits of genetic material can be stored, moved, and changed by a variety of interactions.

Mobile Genetic Elements Plasmids are just one kind of *mobile genetic element (MGE)*. MGEs are units of DNA or RNA that are sometimes *transposed,* or moved as a functional unit, from one place to another in a genome. Other MGEs are transposons and viruses.

Transposons Sets of genes that are transposed randomly are *jumping genes,* or **transposons.** When a transposon moves to a new place, it may inactivate a nearby gene, much like an operon does. All organisms seem to have transposons in their genomes. Some bacteria have transposons that jump between plasmids and chromosomes.

Viruses In terms of structure and function, transposons are similar to viruses. *Viruses* are very small, nonliving particles that consist of DNA or RNA inside a protein coating. Viruses infect cells by using the cells' own replication processes to make new virus copies. Sometimes, viruses take away copies of the cells' DNA or leave some DNA behind. Thus, viruses can move genetic material between cells. Certain kinds of RNA viruses, called *retroviruses,* produce DNA that becomes part of the host cell's genome.

Genetic Change The discovery of MGEs has helped us further understand genetic change. It has also enabled us to manipulate genetic change for our own purposes, as you will learn. MGEs cause genetic change by bringing together new combinations of genes. Furthermore, MGEs can transfer genetic material between individuals and even between species. For example, the genome of *Escherichia coli* (common gut bacteria) is about 15% similar to that of *Salmonella* (food-borne, illness-causing bacteria). Scientists suspect that the similar genetic sequences are the result of MGEs being passed between the species.

Antibiotic Resistance Like mutations, transpositions may have helpful or harmful effects. And what helps one organism may harm another. An effect that is helpful to bacteria but harmful to humans is the evolution of antibiotic resistance. Antibiotic chemicals are often used to prevent or combat bacterial infections, as shown in **Figure 14.** But if just one bacterial cell has a gene that makes the cell resist the effect of a particular antibiotic, that cell may survive and reproduce. Furthermore, the gene could be passed to other bacteria as part of an MGE. Scientists fear that this process is indeed happening, because increasing numbers and kinds of bacteria are becoming resistant to each of the antibiotics that have been produced.

❯ **Reading Check** *How are transposons and viruses similar?*

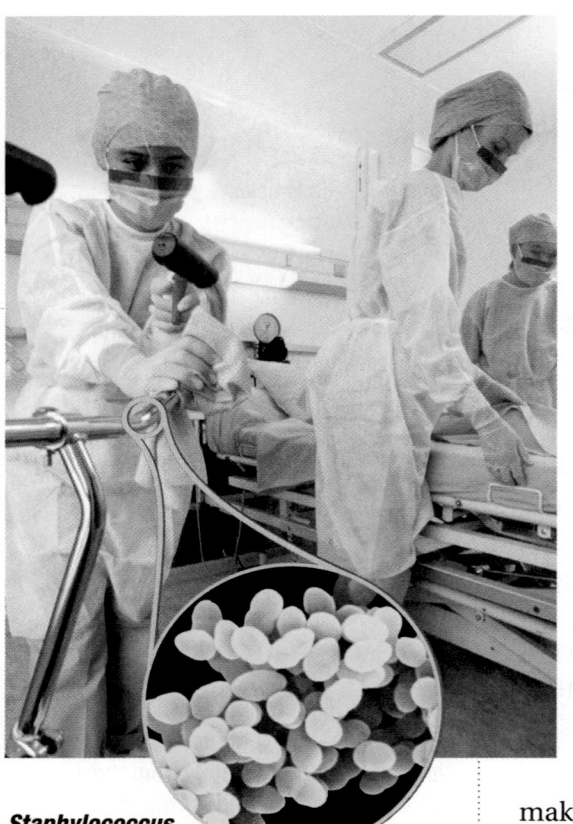

***Staphylococcus* bacteria**

Figure 14 We use antibiotic chemicals in drugs and cleaning products in an attempt to kill bacteria. However, some bacteria have become resistant to most antibiotics. ❯ What is the role of mobile genetic elements in antibiotic resistance?

SC*i*LINKS.

www.scilinks.org
Topic: Antibiotic
    Resistance
Code: HX80081

Multicellular Development and Aging

You have learned that external or environmental cues can regulate gene expression in cells. In multicellular eukaryotes, gene regulation can also happen because of internal cues. In particular, the development of an embryo involves complex gene regulation. Many cells will develop from one beginning cell. And different kinds of cells will develop to have different functions in different parts of the body. ❯ Each cell within a developing body will express specific genes. Gene expression depends on the cell's age and location within the body.

Cell Differentiation In the process of **cell differentiation,** each new cell is modified and specialized as the cells multiply to form a body. Gene regulation plays an important role in this process. *Homeotic* genes are examples of genes that regulate differentiation. Scientists first discovered these genes in fruit flies. Mutations in these genes can cause one body part, such as a leg, to develop in place of another body part, such as an antenna.

As scientists studied many genomes, they found that many kinds of organisms have homeotic genes. And these genes always seem to control similar developmental processes by similar mechanisms. All homeotic genes code for proteins that regulate the expression of other genes. Many homeotic genes contain a similar sequence of 180 bases. This sequence, called a *homeobox,* codes for a DNA-binding domain in the resulting protein.

In general, the genetic regulation of development seems to be similar in all animals. A specific set of homeotic genes, called *hox,* is found in all animals that have a head end and a tail end. Hox genes direct development relative to body position, as shown in **Figure 15.**

❯ **Reading Check** *What is a homeobox?*

transposon (trans POH ZAHN) a genetic sequence that is randomly moved, in a functional unit, to new places in a genome

cell differentiation the process by which a cell becomes specialized for a specific structure or function during multicellular development

READING TOOLBOX

Prefixes The prefix *homeo-* is used several times on this page. Use the Reading Toolbox page to find the meaning of the prefix *homeo-*. Write a definition for *homeotic* and *homeobox* in your own words.

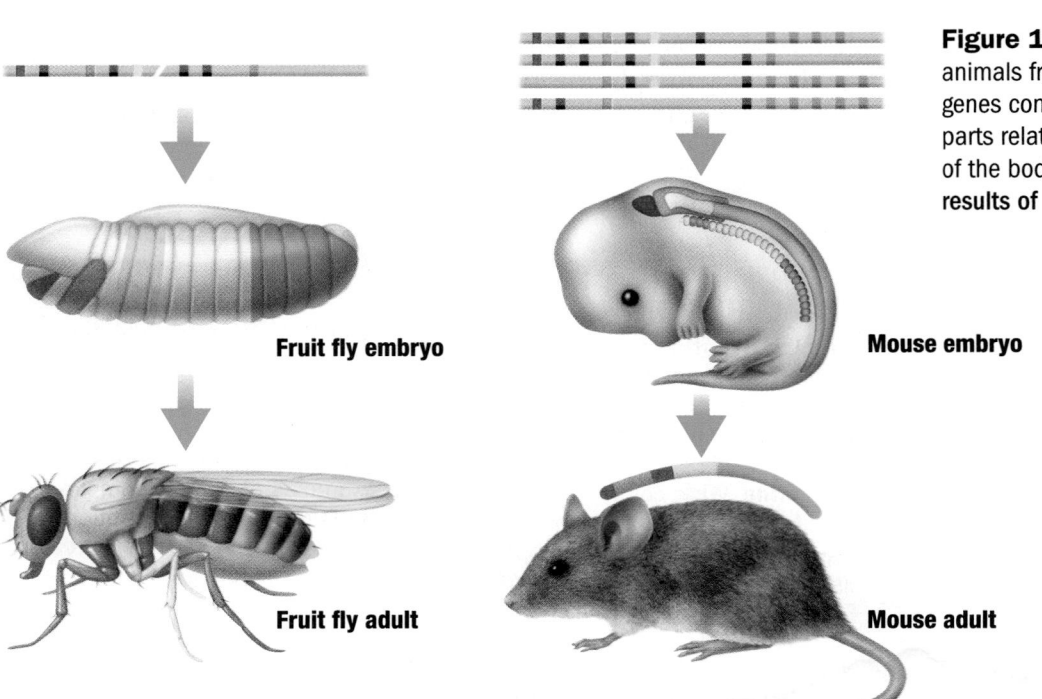

Figure 15 *Hox* genes are found in animals from insects to mammals. These genes control the development of body parts relative to the head and tail ends of the body. ❯ **What are some possible results of mutations in these genes?**

Fruit fly embryo

Mouse embryo

Fruit fly adult

Mouse adult

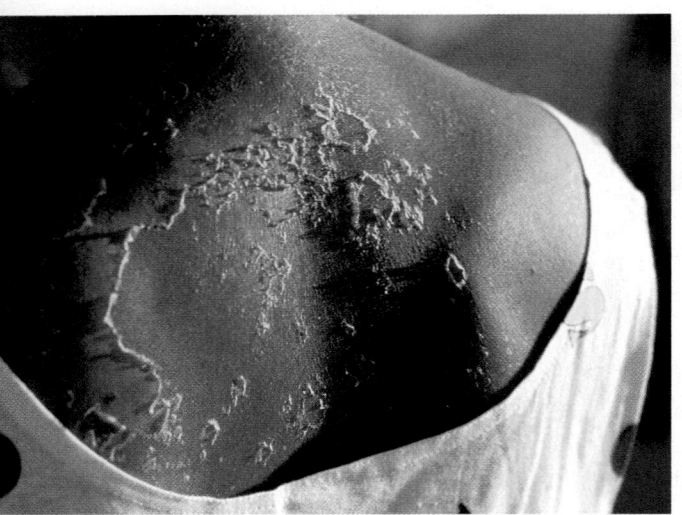

Figure 16 Sunburn is the result of apoptosis—or cell suicide. When skin cells are heavily damaged by over-exposure to the sun, a genetic switch in the cells may signal the cells to stop functioning. ❯ **Why is apoptosis important in multicellular organisms?**

apoptosis (AP uhp TOH sis) in multicellular organisms, a genetically controlled process that leads to the death of a cell; programmed cell death

Cell Growth and Maintenance Although scientists have long been aware of the *cell cycle*, only recently have they begun to understand how genes regulate the cell cycle and cell growth. In 2001, three scientists received the Nobel Prize for discovering the genetic systems that regulate the cell cycle. The scientists identified two kinds of proteins that regulate the cell cycle: *CDK* and *cyclin*. These proteins are present in all eukaryotes and drive the cell cycle forward. The CDK molecules function like an engine, and the cyclins function like gears. Together, they control the speed of the cell cycle. Cancer results when control of cells has been lost because either the "engine" or the "gears" malfunction.

Cell Death and Aging In multicellular organisms, all cells have arisen from the division of other cells. But most of these cells stop dividing once the organism is mature. In fact, almost all body cells are "programmed" to age and die. At some point, the cell will simply shut down all functioning, gradually shrink, and eventually fall apart. This process of cellular "suicide" is known as **apoptosis.** Apoptosis seems to occur in consistent steps, much like other cellular processes, such as mitosis. Scientists are still studying the genetic systems that may control apoptosis.

Function of Apoptosis Why do some cells need to die? In some cases, the full development of a body part requires the removal of some cells. For example, apoptosis is responsible for the loss of a tadpole's tail as the tadpole becomes an adult. Likewise, human fingers and toes are formed through the loss of in-between tissue in the embryonic limbs. Also, apoptosis is at work when sunburned skin begins to peel off, as shown in **Figure 16.**

Telomeres Aging has many effects on cells. An example is the effect of aging on the ends of chromosomes (called *telomeres*). As cells divide repeatedly, the telomeres lose nucleotides and become shortened. In older cells, this shortening may cause mishandling of the chromosomes during mitosis and thus result in nonfunctioning cells. However, telomere shortening is not the only cause of aging.

❯ **Reading Check** *What are the roles of proteins in the cell cycle?*

Section 3 Review

❯ **KEY IDEAS**
1. **Justify** comparing the genetic systems of various life-forms.
2. **List** mechanisms other than chromosomes by which genetic material may be stored and moved.
3. **Relate** gene expression to multicellular development.

CRITICAL THINKING
4. **Forming Hypotheses** Could any other cell organelles have arisen through endosymbiosis? If so, what findings may support such a hypothesis?
5. **Predicting** What could be the result of a mutation in a hox gene?
6. **Logical Reasoning** Is apoptosis a useful mechanism for prokaryotes? Explain your answer.

ALTERNATIVE ASSESSMENT
7. **Gallery of Genetic Curiosities** Create a poster, slide show, or other display that exhibits mutants and other interesting examples of genetic complexity. Be sure to provide a caption and a reference source for each of your images.

Forensic Genealogy

BIOTECHNOLOGY

Genealogy (JEE nee AHL uh jee) is the study of family histories. Forensic genealogy can involve finding lost relatives, identifying bodies, or confirming a claim of parenthood.

Clues in DNA

Because DNA is passed from parents to offspring, scientists can use DNA to find hereditary links between people. Samples of DNA can be analyzed to find similarities and differences. People who are related by birth will share at least some of the DNA of their common ancestors. DNA can be extracted from living cells and from dead cells in hair or bone.

Mother's or Father's DNA

Every cell in a person's body contains DNA from both parents. However, chromosome recombination makes it hard to tell which DNA came from which parent. But two kinds of DNA are unique. One kind is the DNA in a Y chromosome in males. The Y chromosome always comes from the father.

Mitochondrial DNA is also unique. The DNA in the mitochondria of cells is unrelated to the DNA in the nucleus. In humans, the mitochondria in all cells have been copied from the mother's egg cell. So, your mitochondrial DNA is the same as your mother's.

Analyses of these two kinds of DNA have solved crimes and mysteries. In some cases, people have been able to learn their true family history. In other cases, the identity of a dead body has been confirmed (or not) based on DNA comparisons with living or dead relatives.

Who is buried here? This tomb in the Cathedral of Seville, Spain, is supposed to contain the remains of Christopher Columbus. But the history of the remains is disputed, and some people claim that the true remains lie elsewhere. DNA analysis may solve the case.

Whose coffin is this? In 2005, Hurricane Katrina caused disastrous flooding in areas along the coast of the Gulf of Mexico. Many coffins floated out of burial sites. To help find the living or dead relatives of unidentified bodies, scientists could compare DNA samples. For example, mitochondrial DNA will be identical among siblings.

Quick Project Find out the latest findings from DNA analyses of the supposed remains of Christopher Columbus.

Chapter 14 **Lab**

Objectives

➤ Perform a protein assay to detect the results of gene expression.

➤ Use gel electrophoresis and staining to detect size differences.

➤ Infer the presence of similar genes in different species.

Materials

- lab apron, safety goggles, and disposable gloves
- fish muscle samples (3 to 6 unknowns)
- microtubes, flip-top or screw-top (6 to 12)
- protein buffer solution with dye
- water bath
- precast gel for electrophoresis chamber
- micropipettes or tips, sterile, disposable (3 to 6)
- electrophoresis chamber with power supply and wires
- running buffer solution
- gel staining tray
- protein stain solution
- water, distilled

Safety

Protein Detection

Because genes code for proteins, the presence of specific proteins in cells indicates the presence of specific genes. In this lab, you will detect the presence of specific proteins in several species of fishes. You will separate the different proteins by using gel electrophoresis.

Electrophoresis relies on a simple fact of biochemistry: opposite charges attract one another, and like charges repel. So, molecules that have a charge can be pulled around by an electric field. To separate molecules by electrophoresis, the molecules can be pulled through a microscopic "obstacle course" that will slow down larger molecules. If the "course" is "run" for a time, the molecules will be sorted by size.

In *gel electrophoresis*, the "obstacle course" is a slab of jellylike material, simply referred to as a *gel*. Several types of gels can be used to separate samples of DNA, RNA, or proteins. The samples can be stained to see where the parts ended up.

Procedure

Prepare Protein Samples

1 Put on a lab apron, safety goggles, and gloves. Read all procedures, and prepare to collect your data. For each sample of fish muscle, record the type of fish, and assign it a code letter. Then, mark the letter onto two microtubes.

2 CAUTION: **Never eat or taste food in the lab.** Obtain a small piece of each fish muscle sample. Place each piece in a microtube that has the correct code label.

3 CAUTION: **Never taste chemicals or allow them to contact your skin.** For each sample, add enough protein buffer solution to cover the sample piece. Cap the tube, then gently flick it to mix the contents. The buffer will cause some of the proteins from each fish muscle sample to become suspended in the solution.

4 Let the tubes sit at room temperature for 5 min. Then, pour just the liquid from each into the second tube with the matching label. Keep the samples on ice until used.

5 CAUTION: **Use extreme caution when working with heating devices.** Heat the samples in the water bath at 95 °C for 5 min. The heat will cause the proteins from each fish muscle sample to denature.

Separate Proteins by Gel Electrophoresis

6 Examine the gel that is precast within its chamber. Note the row of small wells along one edge. These wells are where you will place the samples to be separated. Keep the gel level as you work.

7 Slowly add running buffer solution to the chamber. Add just enough to flood the wells and to cover the gel surface with buffer about 2 mm deep. Be careful not to damage the gel while pouring.

8 Using a clean micropipette, transfer 10 μL of one sample solution into one well. Be careful not to overflow the well or puncture the gel with the pipette tip. Record the sample's "lane" position.

9 Repeat step 8 for each sample. Make sure to use a clean pipette for each transfer.

10 ◆ CAUTION: **Use caution when working with electrical equipment.** Assemble the electrophoresis chamber and power source as directed by your teacher. With your teacher's approval, connect the power supply to the chamber electrodes. The negative terminal should be connected to the electrode closest to the wells, and the positive terminal should be connected to the opposite electrode.

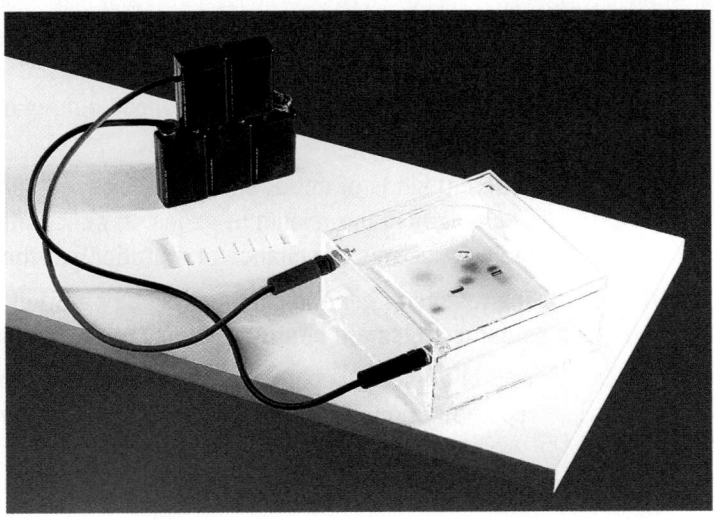

11 Leave the chamber running but undisturbed for the amount of time specified by your teacher. During this time, the samples and dye should move toward the positive side of the gel.

View the Separated Proteins

12 When the moving front of the dye has migrated across the entire gel, disconnect the electrodes from the power source. Gently transfer the gel to the staining tray.

13 ◆ CAUTION: **Dispose of materials as directed by your teacher.** Gently pour off the buffer solution into an appropriate container as directed by your teacher.

14 Slowly pour the protein stain solution over the staining tray, and then wait for the amount of time specified by your teacher.

15 Destain the gel by soaking and rinsing it several times in distilled water. Dispose of the rinse water as directed by your teacher. Some of the stain will remain on the proteins in the gel. Draw, photograph, or photocopy the gel for analysis.

16 ◆ ◆ Clean up and dispose of your lab materials and waste according to your teacher's instructions. Wash your hands before leaving the lab.

Analyze and Conclude

1. SCIENTIFIC METHODS **Organizing Data** On your picture of the gel, mark the position of each visible band in each lane of the unknown samples.

2. SCIENTIFIC METHODS **Analyzing Data** Compare the numbers and positions of visible bands among all lanes. Identify which bands of the unknown samples appear to match each other. Identify which of the samples share the most similarities.

SCILINKS®
www.scilinks.org
Topic: Gene
     Expression
Code: HX80642

Extension

3. Evolutionary Relationships Make a table to compare the protein bands from each fish. Use the table to infer which fish are most closely related by heredity and which are least related. Try to draw a "family tree" showing the evolutionary relationships among these fish.

go.hrw.com
SUPER SUMMARY
Keyword: HX8GNXS

Key Ideas	Key Terms

1 Mutation and Genetic Change

❯ For the most part, genetic differences among organisms originate as some kind of mutation.

❯ Different kinds of mutations are recognized as either changes in DNA or changes in the results of genes. In eukaryotic cells, the process of meiosis creates the chance of mutations at the chromosome level.

❯ The results of genetic change may be harmful, beneficial, or neutral; most changes are neutral and may not be passed on to offspring.

❯ Very large-scale genetic change can occur by misplacement, recombination, or multiplication of entire chromosomes.

mutation (319)
nondisjunction (324)
polyploidy (324)

2 Regulating Gene Expression

❯ Cells have complex systems that regulate whether or not specific genes are expressed, depending on the cell's needs and environment.

❯ The major form of gene regulation in prokaryotes depends upon operons that respond to environmental factors.

❯ Gene regulation in eukaryotes is more complex and variable than gene regulation in prokaryotes.

❯ The sequence of amino acids in a protein determines its three-dimensional structure and chemical behavior.

operon (326)
transcription factor (327)
intron (328)
exon (328)
domain (329)

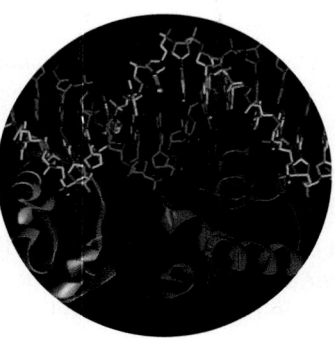

3 Genome Interactions

❯ Comparisons among the genetic systems of many organisms reveal basic biological similarities and relationships.

❯ Small bits of genetic material can be stored, moved, and changed by a variety of interactions.

❯ Each cell within a developing body will express specific genes, depending on the cell's age and location within the body.

genome (370)
plasmid (331)
transposon (332)
cell differentiation (333)
apoptosis (334)

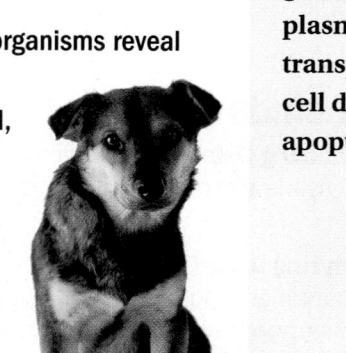

1. **Prefixes** Use a dictionary to look up the meanings of the prefixes *non-* and *dis-* and the word *junction*. Use this information to explain the meaning of the term *nondisjunction*.

2. **Concept Map** Construct a concept map that differentiates the many kinds of mutation. Try to use the following terms: *mutation, point, insertion, deletion, silent, missense, frameshift, nonsense, amino acids, chromosomal, deletion, duplication, inversion, translocation,* and *gene rearrangement*.

Using Key Terms

3. Use the following terms in the same sentence: *gene regulation, operon, transcription factor, prokaryote,* and *eukaryote.*

In each of the following sentences, replace the incorrect term(s) with the correct key term(s).

4. New alleles arise from *gene regulation.*

5. *Mutation* is the condition of having multiple sets of chromosomes.

Understanding Key Ideas

6. All genetic differences among organisms originate as some kind of
   a. DNA.
   b. gene.
   c. mutation.
   d. amino acid.

7. A point mutation occurs when
   a. a gene's location changes.
   b. long segments of a gene are lost.
   c. gametes are forming during meiosis.
   d. one nucleotide is replaced with a different nucleotide.

8. How does the karotype of a person with Down syndrome differ from a normal karotype?
   a. It lacks a chromosome.
   b. It has two sex chromosomes.
   c. It has twice the number of chromosomes.
   d. It has an extra copy of a single chromosome.

9. The *lac* operon shuts off the production of lactose enzymes when
   a. lactose is present.
   b. lactose is absent.
   c. glucose is present.
   d. glucose is absent.

10. Which of the following is found primarily in eukaryotic genomes?
    a. introns
    b. operons
    c. operators
    d. promoters

11. Plasmids are
    a. long pieces of eukaryotic DNA.
    b. circular pieces of bacterial DNA.
    c. broken pieces of large chromosomes.
    d. pieces of viral RNA that move between species.

12. An example of a mobile genetic element is
    a. a transposon.
    b. a bacterium.
    c. a cancer cell.
    d. a hox gene.

13. Programmed cell death is called
    a. aging.
    b. cyclin.
    c. apoptosis.
    d. transposition.

Explaining Key Ideas

14. **Explain** how a genetic disorder can result from a mutation.

15. **Summarize** the role of genetic switches in gene expression.

16. **Outline** the roles of proteins in gene expression.

17. **List** ways that genetic material can be transferred by mechanisms other than chromosomes.

This image shows that specific genes regulate the development of specific parts of animal bodies. Use the image to answer the following question(s).

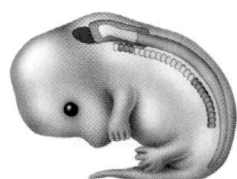

18. **Describe** the role of *hox* genes in development.

19. **Identify** which kind(s) of mutation could result in a group of homeotic genes being duplicated.

Using Science Graphics

This image shows a specific type of mutation. Use the image to answer the following question.

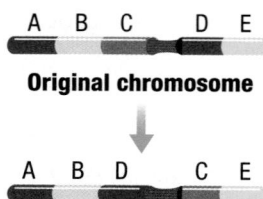

Original chromosome

20. What type of mutation is shown in the image?
    a. chromosomal deletion
    b. chromosomal inversion
    c. chromosomal duplication
    d. chromosomal translocation

21. Use this table to make a graph. Be sure to choose the appropriate graph type and to add labels.

Genetic Similarity Between Humans and Other Species*		
Common name	**Genus name**	**Similarity**
Dog	*Canis*	81%
Mouse	*Mus*	79%
Rat	*Rattus*	70%
Chicken	*Gallus*	67%
Pufferfish	*Takifugu*	65%
Zebrafish	*Danio*	63%
Fruit fly	*Drosophila*	39%
Bee	*Apis*	33%
Nematode	*Caenorhabditis*	31%
Mouse-ear cress	*Arabidopsis*	17%
Rice	*Oryza*	15%
Slime mold	*Dictyostelium*	16%
Yeast	*Saccharomyces*	11%
Bacterium	*Escherichia*	10%

* percentage of human genes that are similar to genes in each of these species

Critical Thinking

22. **Applying Logic** What are the possible effects of a point mutation on the results of a gene? Starting with the same codon, give specific examples.

23. **Applying Related Information** Can genetic changes due to nondisjunction occur in bacteria?

24. **Evaluating an Argument** A classmate states that damage to introns is very likely to affect the synthesis of a protein but damage to exons is not. Argue against this statement.

25. **Analyzing Language** Scientists often state that the genetic code is universal. Explain what this statement means.

26. **Inferring Relationships** What does the presence of similar homeotic gene sequences among many eukaryotes suggest about evolutionary relationships among these organisms?

Connecting Key Ideas

27. **Genomes and Reproduction** In what ways do mobile genetic elements and sexual reproduction have similar functions?

28. **Genomes and Ecology** What is the main difference between the symbiosis of lichen and the endosymbiosis that is thought to have led to mitochondria and chloroplasts?

29. **Genomes and Evolution** Antibiotic resistance in bacteria is often used as an example of coevolution. Explain the connection.

Methods of Science

30. **Experimental Setup** The scientist who first suspected, and later discovered, the existence of transposons was Barbara McClintock. She conducted her main experiments by using corn kernels that were the product of many generations of self-fertilization of the same corn plants. Why did she use this kind of corn?

Writing for Science

31. **Writing for an Audience** Draft a lecture for younger students entitled "Are We Controlled by DNA?"

Technology Skills

32. **Using Computer Graphics** Use library or Internet resources to find information about technologies for three-dimensional modeling and visualization of complex biological molecules. Bring or show examples to your class of three-dimensional models of DNA, RNA, and proteins.

Science Concepts

1. Which mutation can happen only to a chromosome?

A point

B silent

C deletion

D frameshift

2. Somatic cell cancer is the result of damage to

F genes that are found only in skin cells.

G genes that are found only in germ cells.

H genes that control head-to-tail orientation.

J genes that control the ability of cells to divide.

3. In the bacterium *Escherichia coli,* the *lac* operon causes the bacterium to produce certain enzymes only in the presence of lactose. The operon system is an example of

A gene mutation.

B gene regulation.

C gene duplication.

D gene differentiation.

Using Science Graphics

This diagram is a model of processes in a cell. Use the diagram to answer the following question(s).

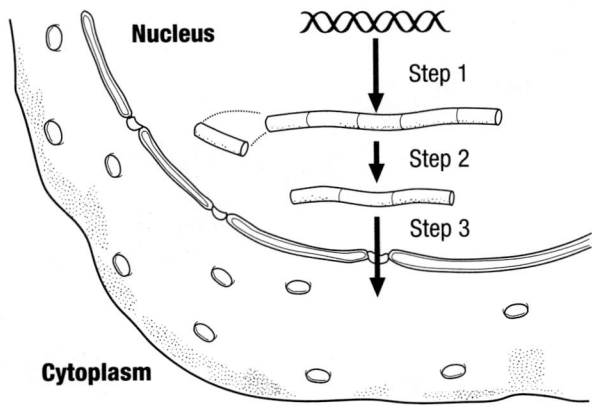

4. If step 1 is transcription and step 3 is translation, what is happening at step 2?

F mutation of DNA

G copying of DNA

H splicing of RNA

J copying of RNA

5. The cell shown must belong to a(n)

A bacterium.

B eukaryote.

C gamete.

D prokaryote.

This table shows the genetic code, or codons of RNA that are translated into specific amino acids. Use the table to answer the following question(s).

First base	Second base				Third base
	U	C	A	G	
U	Phe	Ser	Tyr	Cys	U
	Phe	Ser	Tyr	Cys	C
	Leu	Ser	stop	stop	A
	Leu	Ser	stop	Trp	G
C	Leu	Pro	His	Arg	U
	Leu	Pro	His	Arg	C
	Leu	Pro	Gln	Arg	A
	Leu	Pro	Gln	Arg	G
A	Ile	Thr	Asn	Ser	U
	Ile	Thr	Asn	Ser	C
	Ile	Thr	Lys	Arg	A
	Met	Thr	Lys	Arg	G
G	Val	Ala	Asp	Gly	U
	Val	Ala	Asp	Gly	C
	Val	Ala	Glu	Gly	A
	Val	Ala	Glu	Gly	G

6. Which of the following pairs of codons demonstrates the redundancy of the genetic code?

F AAC and AAA

G AUA and AUG

H ACA and ACG

J UGA and UGG

7. Suppose that the third base in the codon CUC is accidentally changed from C to G so that the codon is now CUG. What kind of mutation has occurred?

A a silent mutation

B a missense mutation

C a nonsense mutation

D a frameshift mutation

Writing Skills

8. Extended Response Write a brief essay entitled "The Pros and Cons of Genetic Mutation." Be sure to organize your essay logically, and provide examples to support your points.

Chapter 15

Gene Technologies and Human Applications

Preview

1 The Human Genome
Secrets of the Human Genome
Applications of Human Genetics
Ongoing Work

2 Gene Technologies in Our Lives
Manipulating Genes
Manipulating Bodies and Development
Ethical and Social Issues

3 Gene Technologies in Detail
Basic Tools for Genetic Manipulation
Major Gene Technology Processes
Exploring Genomes

Why It Matters

Gene technologies aid the study of basic biology. They have many other applications, such as producing food and treating disease.

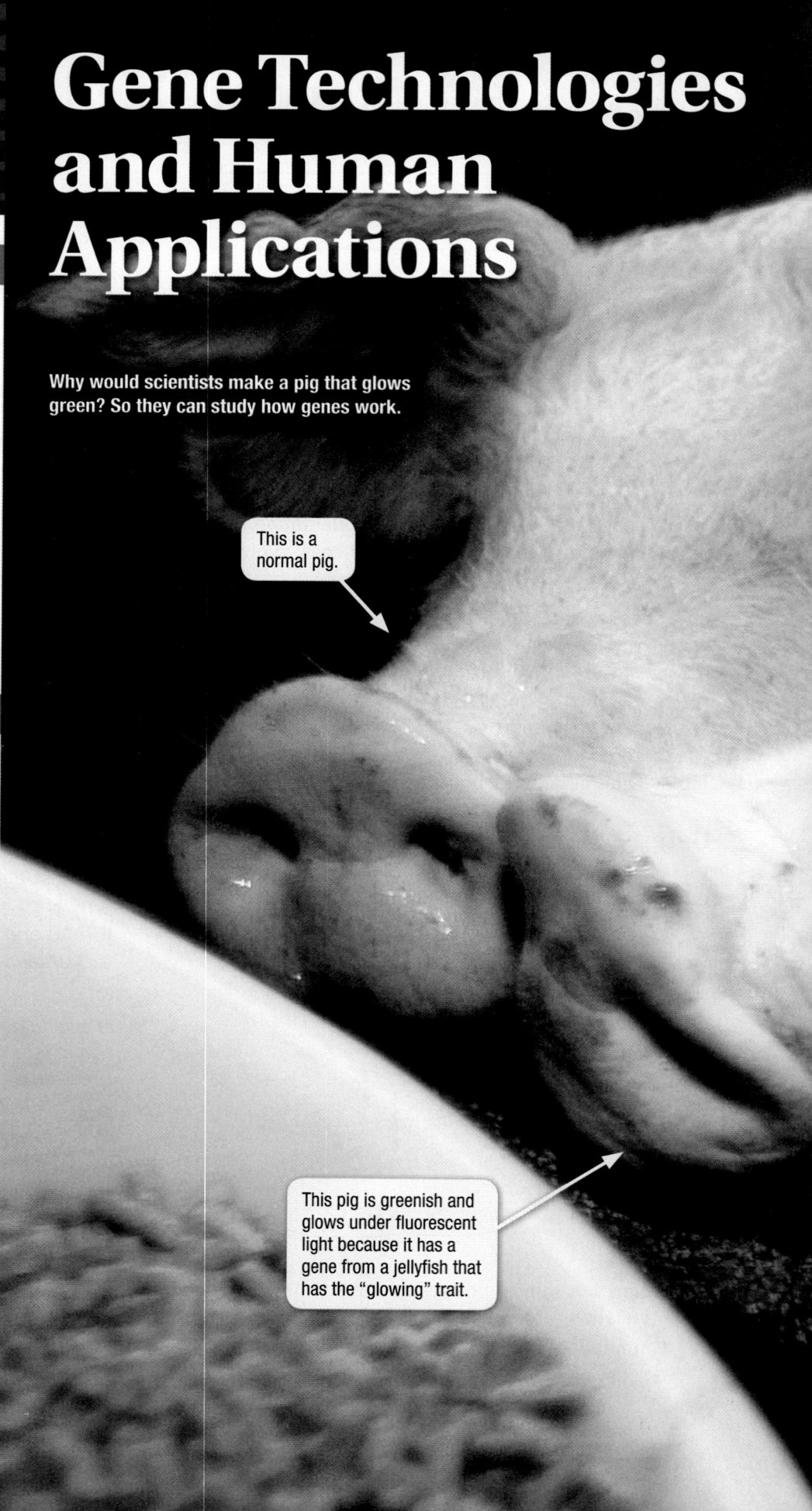

Why would scientists make a pig that glows green? So they can study how genes work.

This is a normal pig.

This pig is greenish and glows under fluorescent light because it has a gene from a jellyfish that has the "glowing" trait.

InquiryLab

Code Comparison

All humans have very similar DNA, with slight individual variations. The differences that are easiest to observe are among DNA stretches that have many short, repeating base sequences, as shown below. Different people have different numbers of repeats.

GATATATAGACTACTACTACTA

AGATATAGACTACTACTGACTT

GATATAGACTACTACTACTAGC

Procedure

❶ Copy and then examine the three DNA sequences shown here.

❷ Mark the portions of the code that include repeating bases.

Analysis

1. **Identify** what the four letters in the code sequences represent.

2. **State** how many kinds of repeating sequences you find.

3. **Identify** the basic repeating unit(s) among all segments.

4. **Explain** how each person can have a unique genetic code, even though some people may share an identical pattern of repeating base sequences.

The green-glowing gene was inserted into cloned pig cells by scientists using modern gene technologies. This gene is often used as a "marker" in genetic experiments because it is easy to see if the gene is present in an organism.

READING TOOLBOX

These reading tools can help you learn the material in this chapter. For more information on how to use these and other tools, see **Appendix: Reading and Study Skills.**

Using Words

Word Parts You can tell a lot about a word by taking it apart and examining its parts, such as the prefix and root.

Your Turn Use the information in the table to define the following terms:

1. *electrophoresis*

2. *microarray*

Word Parts	
Word Part	**Meaning**
electro-	using electricity
phore	to carry
micro-	very small
array	orderly arrangement

Using Language

Analogies Analogies compare words with similar relationships. You can write analogies with words or with colons. For example, the analogy "up is related to down in the same way that top is related to bottom" can be written "up : down :: top : bottom." To answer an analogy problem, you must figure out how the words are related. In this example, up is above down, and top is above bottom.

Your Turn Use information found in prior chapters to complete the following analogy:

transcription : RNA :: translation : ___.

Using Graphic Organizers

Pattern Puzzles You can use pattern puzzles to help you remember sequential information. Exchanging puzzles with a classmate can help you study.

Your Turn Make a pattern puzzle for the steps of a recombinant gene cloning process, as shown in this chapter.

1. Write the steps of the process on a sheet of notebook paper, one step per line. Do not number the steps.

2. Cut the paper so that there is one step per strip of paper.

3. Shuffle the paper strips so that they are out of sequence.

4. Try to place the strips in their proper sequence.

5. Check your sequence by consulting your textbook, class notes, or a classmate.

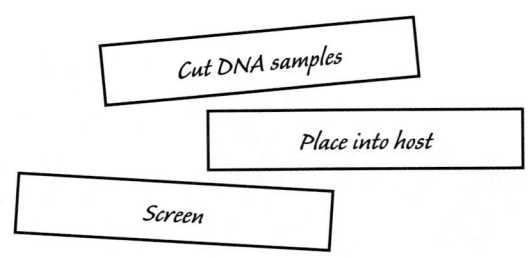

The Human Genome

Key Ideas	Key Terms	Why It Matters
❯ Why is the Human Genome Project so important? ❯ How do genomics and gene technologies affect our lives? ❯ What questions about the human genome remain to be studied?	genomics microarray DNA fingerprint	Many diseases may someday be cured by genetic technologies.

In 2000, headlines announced that scientists had deciphered the "book of life" by listing almost the entire sequence of bases in human DNA. This major feat was only the beginning of a new era.

Secrets of the Human Genome

The term *genome* refers to all of the genetic material in an organism, population, or species. **Genomics** is the study of entire genomes, especially by using technology to compare genes within and between species. A major part of genomics is to *sequence* genomes, or to identify every DNA base pair that makes up each genome. Only recently has it been possible to sequence the human genome.

The *Human Genome Project* (HGP) was an international cooperative effort to sequence the human genome. More than 20 laboratories in six countries worked together to sequence the 2.9 billion DNA base pairs that make up the human genome. ❯ **The sequencing of the human genome has advanced the study of human biology yet created new questions.**

Surprising Findings The major draft of the human genome sequence was completed and reported in 2003. Scientists were surprised and excited by findings such as these:

- **Humans have few genes.** Scientists expected to find 120,000 genes but found only about 25,000.

- **Most human DNA is noncoding.** Less than 2% of human DNA seems to code for proteins. The rest is either introns or is not yet fully explained.

- **Many human genes are identical to those of other species.** Much of what we learn about mice and flies can be used to understand ourselves.

- **All humans are genetically close.** If the DNA of any two people is compared, 99.9% is identical.

❯ **Reading Check** *How big is the human genome? (See the Appendix for answers to Reading Checks.)*

genomics (juh NOH miks) the study of entire genomes, especially by using technology to compare genes within and between species

Figure 1 Despite differences in appearance, the DNA of any two humans is 99.9% similar.

Applications of Human Genetics

Studying the human genome opens new doors to understanding our bodies. In addition, we have new ways to apply this knowledge. *Gene technologies* allow us to find genes, copy them, turn them on or off, and even move them between organisms. ❯ **Genomics and gene technologies have many applications in human healthcare and society.**

A major part of gene technologies is *genetic engineering,* which usually refers to the transfer of genes from one organism to another. For example, the human gene for insulin has been inserted into bacteria. Insulin is lacking in people with some forms of diabetes. So, the engineered bacteria are used to produce insulin to treat diabetes.

Diagnosing and Preventing Disease The first challenge to fighting disease is simply to diagnose, or identify, the problem. Modern gene technologies can help. For example, a **microarray,** shown in **Figure 2,** shows which genes are being actively transcribed in a sample from a cell. Some patterns of gene activity can be recognized as signs of genetic disorders or cancer.

Although most genetic disorders cannot be cured, they may be avoided in the future. For example, a person with a family history of genetic disorders may wish to undergo genetic counseling before becoming a parent. *Genetic counseling* informs people about the risk of genetic problems that could affect them or their offspring.

Many viral diseases are best prevented by vaccination. However, vaccines can be dangerous because they are made from disease-causing agents. Vaccines made through genetic engineering may limit such dangers by being more carefully designed. Various vaccines are now produced through genetic engineering. Some of these vaccines prevent diseases that were not preventable before.

❯ **Reading Check** *When might a person seek genetic counseling?*

microarray (MIE kroh uh RAY) a device that contains a micro-scale, orderly arrangement of biomolecules; used to rapidly test for the presence of a range of similar substances, such as specific DNA sequences

DNA fingerprint a pattern of DNA characteristics that is unique, or nearly so, to an individual organism

Figure 2 A microarray contains an assortment of gene sequences, each set in a dot. The colors indicate whether a sample of genetic material has bound to the sequence at that dot. Thus, a pattern of gene expression can be seen. ❯ **What conditions could be detected this way?**

QuickLab

⏱ 15 min

Forensic DNA Fingerprints

DNA "fingerprinting" is useful in forensics because it can be performed on a sample of DNA from body tissues such as hair or blood. Samples can be compared to find genetically identical or closely related people. Identical segments of DNA will form identical patterns of bands in the columns of a DNA fingerprint, as shown here.

Analysis

1. **Identify** the number of individuals whose DNA samples are being analyzed in this DNA fingerprint.

2. **CRITICAL THINKING** **Interpreting Graphics** Identify the suspect sample that matches the sample from the crime scene.

3. **CRITICAL THINKING** **Analyzing Methods** Column 6 shows an array of DNA segments sorted by increasing length. Propose a purpose for these columns in this method.

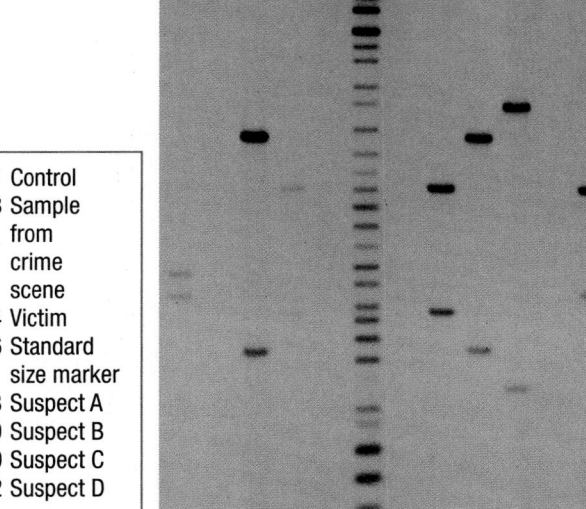

1	Control
3	Sample from crime scene
4	Victim
6	Standard size marker
8	Suspect A
9	Suspect B
10	Suspect C
12	Suspect D

Treating Disease Many genetic disorders occur when a specific protein, such as insulin, is missing or malformed because a gene has been mutated. So, the disorder can often be treated by supplying the needed protein. Many drug companies are now genetically engineering organisms to produce specific proteins for human use.

Another possible treatment for genetic disorders is to insert a functional "replacement" gene into a person's cells by using a genetically engineered virus. This technique is called *gene therapy.* However, gene therapy has had limited success because the human body has many protections against the invasion and genetic change that viruses cause.

The use of genomics to produce drugs is called *pharmaco-genomics.* Currently, most drugs are made to combat diseases in a broad way. The drugs are generally effective for many people but not tailored to individuals. Soon, drugs could be custom-made for individuals based on a personal genetic profile. Such a profile could be produced by technologies that rapidly sequence a person's DNA.

Identifying Individuals Each person (other than identical twins) has some parts of the DNA sequence that are unique. So, samples of DNA can be compared to determine if the samples came from the same person or from people related by ancestry. These samples of DNA are cut, sorted, and "tagged" to produce a pattern of banding called a **DNA fingerprint.** DNA fingerprints are now used regularly to confirm the identity of criminals, family members, or dead bodies.

Word Parts The prefix *pharma-* means "medicine" or "drug." Use this information to analyze the meaning of the term *pharmacogenomics.*

❯ **Reading Check** *Why is insulin used to treat genetic diabetes?*

Figure 3 The human genome contains as much information as 180 phone books from different major cities.

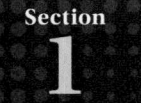
www.scilinks.org
Topic: Human Genome
Project
Code: HX80770

Ongoing Work

Making a list of all of the bases in the human genome was only a first step. Understanding this "book of life" will take much more work. First, a huge amount of information is involved, as **Figure 3** shows. Second, although we know how to read the "letters" of this "book," we do not understand most of its meaning. We have compiled a long list of genes, but we do not know what many of the genes actually do. ❯ **Many important questions about the human genome remain to be investigated or decided.** These questions include the following:

- **How do our genes interact?** To understand how genes interact, scientists are looking closely at the processes of gene expression. For example, they study how the protein that results from one gene may regulate the expression of other genes.

- **How unique are we?** Scientists are increasingly comparing our genome to those of other organisms to find out how small differences in genomes result in different species. Genome projects for many other species have been completed or are under way.

- **Can genetics help us live longer?** Gene technologies and genomics are thus leading to increased knowledge of how we could live longer, healthier lives. We are just beginning to find genetic clues about complex conditions such as asthma, obesity, schizophrenia, cancer, and aging. These conditions are affected by complex interactions between many genes as well as our environment. For many disorders, we are not likely to find a single cause, much less a simple cure.

- **How should we deal with ethical issues?** With so much information about human DNA being recorded, many questions arise that cannot be answered by scientific lab work. For example, Who should get the information? Who owns it? Should it be used to make decisions about individuals? Scientists and governments expect these issues to arise. In the United States, a portion of the federal funds for the HGP are dedicated to a special program of the HGP called *Ethical Legal and Social Implications* (ELSI).

❯ **Reading Check** *Why is asthma difficult to cure?*

Section 1 Review

❯ KEY IDEAS

1. **Describe** the major findings of the Human Genome Project.

2. **Identify** some applications of genomics and genetic engineering that benefit humans.

3. **List** remaining questions about the human genome.

CRITICAL THINKING

4. **Proposing Explanations** Propose some possible explanations for the large volume of noncoding DNA in the human genome.

5. **Applying Logic** Scientists say that knowing the sequence of nucleotides in the human genome is only the first step in understanding the genome. What are some possible next steps?

WRITING FOR SCIENCE

6. **Genetics on Trial** When were gene technologies first used as evidence in criminal cases? Research the early history of this field, and summarize your findings in a news-style oral report.

Cleanup Microbes

BIOTECHNOLOGY

Using microbes for environmental cleanup is called *bioremediation*. For example, oil-devouring microbes are used to help clean up oil spills. Increasingly, genetically modified organisms (GMOs) are being engineered for use in bioremediation.

Oil Spills

Spills of fuel oil can be devastating to environments because the oil is toxic, floats on water, and soaks into soils. Fortunately, scientists have found that some marine bacteria are capable of using oil as food. Some of the first genetically modified (GM) microbes were derived from such bacteria. In fact, the first organism to be patented was an oil-eating, genetically engineered bacterium.

Radioactive Waste

Nuclear waste is another bioremediation challenge with which GM microbes may help. Water near nuclear waste dumps may become polluted with radioactive substances. Again, bacteria naturally exist that can break down most of these substances, but those bacteria cannot survive high levels of radiation. So, scientists have turned to another kind of bacteria that can withstand 3,000 times the normal radiation levels. They hope to engineer a solution by transferring genes between these species.

An impossible job? Cleaning oil and dangerous chemical spills out of sand or soil can be nearly impossible for humans, even with tools. However, this cleanup is simple work for a microbe.

An Enormous Mess Oil spills at sea are dangerous to wildlife, dangerous to the people involved in fighting them, and difficult to contain.

Quick Project Find out the date that the first patent for a GMO was awarded in the United States. Also find out the name of the scientist to whom it was awarded.

Gene Technologies in Our Lives

Key Ideas	Key Terms	Why It Matters
❯ For what purposes are genes and proteins manipulated? ❯ How are cloning and stem cell research related? ❯ What ethical issues arise with the uses of gene technologies?	genetic engineering recombinant DNA clone stem cell	Gene technologies have many applications in modern life, but ethical issues exist for each of these applications.

Recall that a gene has a DNA sequence that is translated into the sequence of amino acids in a protein. In a sense, proteins are the "actors" in biology, and genes are the "directors." To understand how genes work, scientists have studied both the instructions in the genes and the actions of the proteins. Meanwhile, some have tried to modify the instructions to change the actions that result.

Manipulating Genes

Gene technologies include a wide range of procedures that analyze, decode, or manipulate genes from organisms. ❯ **Gene technologies are now widely applied to study organisms in new ways, to alter organisms for human use, and to improve human lives.** Gene technologies have rapidly changed over the past two decades, yet the basic applications are not so new. Human beings have been influencing the lives and genes of organisms for thousands of years. The first farmers and herders did so when they selected plants and animals to breed. But today, we have more specific knowledge, molecular tools, and the ability to move genes between organisms.

Genetic Engineering The application of science for specific purposes is often referred to as *engineering*. **Genetic engineering** is the deliberate alteration of the genetic material of an organism. The process often involves inserting copies of a gene from one organism into another. DNA that has been recombined by genetic engineering is called **recombinant DNA.** Organisms with recombinant genes may be called *recombinant, transgenic,* or *genetically modified*. In everyday use, they are often referred to as *genetically modified organisms* (GMOs). An example of a GMO is shown in **Figure 4.**

Many applications of gene technologies have become part of our everyday lives, from food to healthcare. In some ways, we are starting to depend on gene technologies, just as we depend on electricity and telephones. As with other technologies, gene technologies raise new social and ethical issues.

❯ **Reading Check** *What is a GMO?*

Figure 4 These fish "glow" because scientists have copied a gene from a naturally "glowing" jellyfish and inserted it into the fishes' genomes.

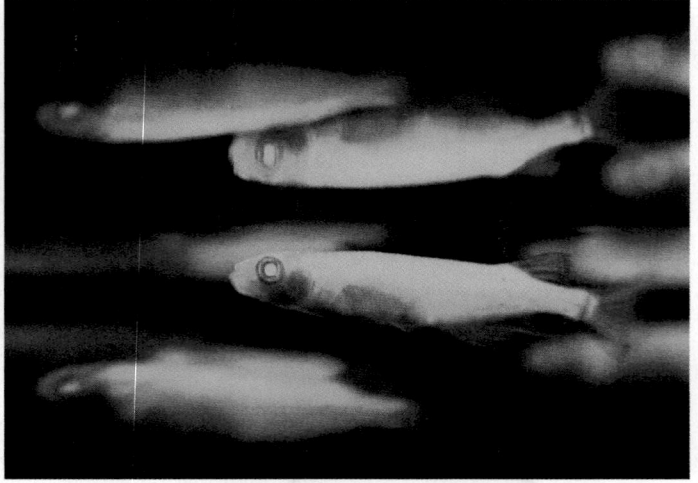

Everyday Applications Genetic engineering was first applied to bacteria, viruses, and plants and is now applied to many life-forms. Today, GMOs are widely used in agriculture, medicine, industry, and basic research. Following are examples of the many uses of GMOs.

- **Food Crops** Most corn and soybean products sold in grocery stores in the United States are made from GMOs. In many cases, the crops have a gene added from the bacterium *Bacillus thuringiensis* (*Bt*). The gene produces an insecticide and thus benefits the crop grower. Many food crops are engineered to be easier to grow or to be more nutritious.

- **Livestock** New breeds of livestock are being engineered to grow faster or to have more muscle or less fat. Some are made to produce milk with specific proteins. Some GMOs are sold as unusual pets.

- **Medical Treatment** As you have learned, many genetic disorders, such as hemophilia and diabetes, result from a missing or abnormal protein. If the normal human gene for needed protein has been identified, the gene can be spliced into bacterial cells. Then, the recombinant bacteria will rapidly produce the human protein in large quantities. People with hemophilia and diabetes are being treated with proteins produced in this way.

- **Basic Research Tools** A variety of GMOs have been made just for laboratory research. Some plants and animals have been engineered with genes from other organisms that "glow." Often, this engineering is done so that researchers can study another, less obvious gene. In this case, the two foreign genes are spliced into the GMO at the same time. The "glow" gene then serves as a "marker" of the presence of the second gene being studied.

Manipulating Cell Interactions Gene technologies involve more than just inserting genes. Cells and bodies are affected by when and where each gene is expressed. So, gene technologies are also used to control the expression of genes or to redirect the products.

The study of how proteins interact within cells is called *proteomics* (PROH tee OHM iks). As you have learned, these interactions are very complex. Gene technologies can be used to manipulate the production of specific proteins at specific times and in specific cells, tissues, organs, or individuals. This manipulation can be done for medical treatment or simply for research.

One way to study the actions of genes in cells is to work with living tissues. To do so, scientists can remove living cells from an organism and grow them in a laboratory as tissue culture, as **Figure 5** shows. Then, the cells can be studied closely and experimentally controlled.

❯ **Reading Check** *What is the* Bt *gene used for?*

> **genetic engineering** a technology in which the genome of a living cell is modified for medical or industrial use

> **recombinant DNA** (ree KAHM buh nuhnt) DNA molecules that are artificially created by combining DNA from different sources

Figure 5 Tissue culture is often used to study living cells. ❯ **What can we learn about genes from tissue culture?**

Manipulating Bodies and Development

Biologists still have much to learn about the development of multi-cellular organisms. To do so, they must study cells in the process of multiplying and differentiating into the many types of cells found in a body. ❯ **Cloning and stem cell techniques are used in research on animal development and have potential for treating certain diseases.**

Cloning A **clone** is an organism or piece of genetic material that is genetically identical to one that was preexisting. Making a clone in a lab is called *cloning,* but the process does occur in nature. Organisms clone themselves whenever they reproduce asexually. Single-celled organisms clone themselves by simple division. Multicellular organisms may clone themselves by budding off parts, as some plants and fungi do, or by self-fertilization, as many plants and some animals do.

Very few large animals can clone themselves. Also, animals have complex processes of fertilization and embryo development. So, scientists are still experimenting with cloning animals. The first such experiments made clones from eggs or embryos. Then, a clone was made from an adult mammal, as **Figure 6** shows. The clone was made using a process called *somatic-cell nuclear transfer* (SCNT). In this process, the nucleus of an egg cell is replaced with the nucleus of an adult cell. Then, the egg begins to develop into an embryo.

Problems with Cloning Although scientists have successfully cloned many kinds of animals, only a few of the cloned offspring have survived for long. In some cases, the fetuses have grown beyond normal size. Many have failed to develop normally with age. Because of such problems and because of ethical issues, efforts to clone humans are illegal in most countries.

Genomic Imprinting Some problems with cloning may be related to the ways that eggs and sperm normally develop. Chemicals in the reproductive system turn "on" or "off" certain genes in the developing gametes. These genes later affect development from embryo to adult. Such an effect, called *genomic imprinting,* is altered when animals are cloned in a lab. So, different genes may be activated early on, and the remaining development may be altered.

clone an organism, cell, or piece of genetic material that is genetically identical to one that was preexisting; to make a genetic duplicate

stem cell a cell that can divide repeatedly and can differentiate into specialized cell types

SC*LINKS*®
www.scilinks.org
Topic: Cloning
Code: HX80303

Figure 6 Dolly, a cloned sheep, was born in 1997. Dolly was the first successful clone produced from the nucleus of an adult somatic cell.

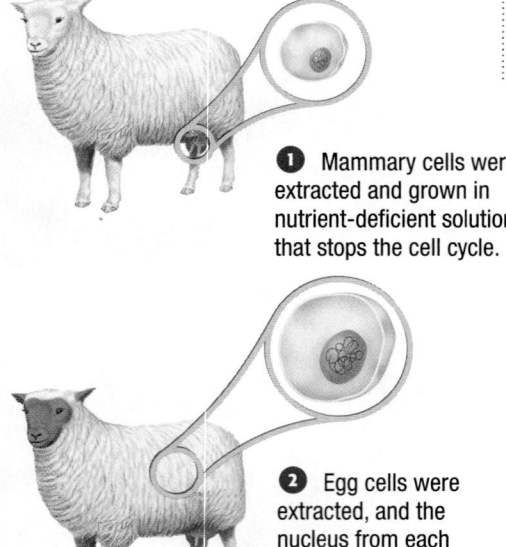

❶ Mammary cells were extracted and grown in nutrient-deficient solution that stops the cell cycle.

❷ Egg cells were extracted, and the nucleus from each was removed and discarded.

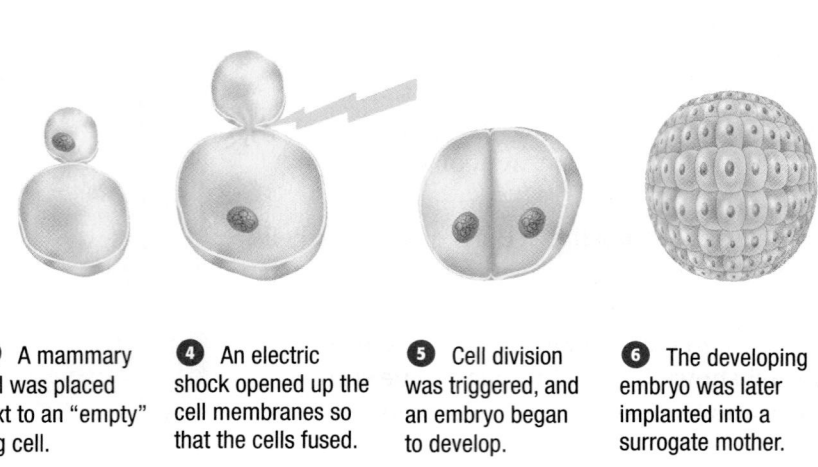

❸ A mammary cell was placed next to an "empty" egg cell.

❹ An electric shock opened up the cell membranes so that the cells fused.

❺ Cell division was triggered, and an embryo began to develop.

❻ The developing embryo was later implanted into a surrogate mother.

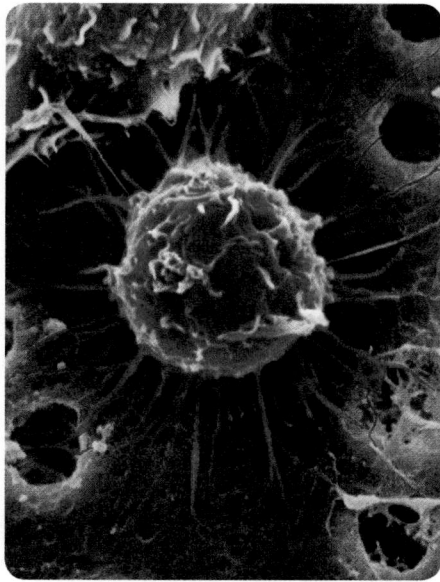

① An adult stem cell can be removed from a specific tissue, such as bone marrow.

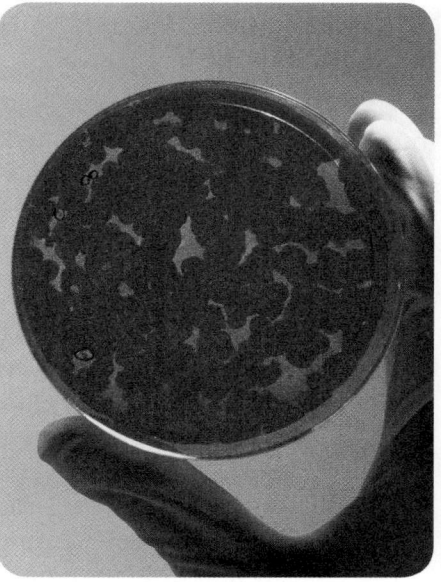

② The cell can be grown in tissue culture to produce more cells of a specific tissue type.

③ The cells can be re-implanted into a patient whose tissues are lacking or damaged.

Figure 7 Adult stem cells can be removed and used to grow more cells of specific tissue types. This kind of therapy can replace tissue that is damaged or deficient due to disease or other medical treatment. ❯ **How do adult stem cells differ from embryonic stem cells?**

Using Stem Cells

A **stem cell** is a cell that can continuously divide and differentiate into various tissues. Some stem cells have more potential to differentiate than others. *Totipotent* cells can give rise to any cell or tissue type, *pluripotent* cells can give rise to all types except germ cells, and *multipotent* cells can give rise to just a few other cell types. The state of the cell depends on the stage of development of the body and the tissue of which the cell is part.

Adults' bodies have some multipotent cells, such as bone marrow cells, that give rise to various blood cells. These cells can be removed, frozen or cultured, and used for medical treatments, as **Figure 7** shows. The cells of new embryos have more potential uses. These cells are totipotent at first and pluripotent during development.

Issues with Stem Cell Research

The first major source of human embryos for stem cell research was fertility clinics. Such clinics help people have children, often by uniting people's gametes and culturing embryos in a lab. Many extra embryos are stored in a frozen state in clinics. In some cases, the parents have given scientists permission to use the embryos for research. But such uses of human embryos pose ethical problems. In the United States, there have been strong debates about the use of federal funds for this kind of research.

Stem Cells from SCNT

A newer source of embryonic stem cells is through cloning using SCNT. Some people believe that using this kind of stem cell for medical research and treatment should be ethically acceptable. One reason is that an embryo made through SCNT does not have true parents. Another reason is that the cells of the embryo are separated early in its development, so there is no chance of the embryo developing further.

❯ **Reading Check** *What are the two main types of stem cells?*

READING TOOLBOX

Analogies Use the information in this section to help you write an analogy that relates adult stem cells to embryonic stem cells. Try to use the terms *pluripotent* and *multipotent* in your analogy.

Ethical and Social Issues

<u>Ethical</u> issues involve differing values and perspectives. For example, the use of GMOs is prohibited or tightly controlled by laws in some countries. In others, GMOs are widely used, and GM foods are sold with few restrictions. ❯ **Ethical issues can be raised for every use of gene technologies.**

Safety One danger of GMOs is that they can "escape" and have unforeseen effects. For example, the *Bt* toxin gene from GM corn crops, such as those in **Figure 8,** has been transferred to other plants. In addition, the toxic corn pollen seems to be harming populations of the monarch butterfly. Ecologists worry that we do not know enough to safely manipulate genes on a large scale.

Figure 8 This corn has been genetically modified to carry the *Bt* gene, which causes the corn plant to produce an insect-killing chemical. As with any use of pesticides, this practice presents risks. An additional danger is that the gene may be transferred to other plants.

Human Rights Being able to predict disease before it happens is a major achievement of modern medicine. Today, the DNA of individuals can be tested to find the risk of genetic disorders. But what should we do with this information? Many decisions could be influenced by such genetic information, such as whom to marry or what to eat. Who should have this information? Who should make these decisions? How can future probabilities be weighed against current human needs and rights? There are no easy answers to these ethical questions, but the questions need to be considered carefully.

Property Laws Gene technologies have also created new issues for old laws, especially those related to intellectual property and patents. Intellectual property (IP) is the ownership of the ideas or plans that a person creates. A patent is a specific set of rights that allows an inventor to control and profit from the uses of his or her idea. In the 1980s, the first patent for a GMO was awarded to a scientist who had engineered an oil-eating bacterium. Before this event, living organisms were considered a part of nature and, as such, were not patentable. Now, specific DNA sequences can be patented.

❯ **Reading Check** *What issues does the use of genetic testing raise?*

ACADEMIC
VOCABULARY

ethical conforming to moral standards

Section 2 Review

❯ **KEY IDEAS**

1. **Identify** applications of manipulating genes and proteins.
2. **Relate** stem cell research to the potential use of cloning.
3. **Describe** a specific ethical issue related to a gene technology.

CRITICAL THINKING

4. **Inferring Relationships** How can manipulating gene expression help advance the study of proteomics?
5. **Evaluating Risks** Given the difficulties that researchers have had with raising cloned animals, do you think it is safe to grow tissues or organs from cloned embryonic stem cells for the purpose of transplanting? Explain.

ALTERNATIVE ASSESSMENT

6. **Debate** Suppose that genetic analysis could predict a person's ability in sports, math, or music. Should genetic screening be used to determine the course selections and team assignments of every student in school? Prepare and conduct a formal debate on the subject.

3 Gene Technologies in Detail

Key Ideas	Key Terms	Why It Matters
❯ What are the basic tools of genetic manipulation? ❯ How are these tools used in the major processes of modern gene technologies? ❯ How do scientists study entire genomes?	restriction enzyme DNA polymorphisms electrophoresis polymerase chain reaction (PCR) DNA sequencing bioinformatics genome mapping genetic library	Humans now have the ability to identify and manipulate genes in many organisms.

How do you find a needle in a haystack? This phrase is often used to speak of a nearly impossible task. But if the haystack is a genome and the needle is a gene, the task is now possible!

Basic Tools for Genetic Manipulation

Molecular biologists spent many years developing tools and methods to manipulate genetic material. The methods continue to be used and adapted for a wide range of applications, but the basic tools are similar. ❯ **The basic tools of DNA manipulation rely on the chemical nature of genetic material and are adapted from natural processes discovered in cells.** These tools include restriction enzymes, polymorphisms, gel electrophoresis, denaturation, and hybridization. For example, the first GMOs were made by using plasmids and enzymes that are naturally present in some bacterial cells.

Restriction Enzymes Among the first tools used to manipulate DNA were enzymes that are made by bacteria as a defense. The enzymes serve to slice up any invading DNA sequences or genes from other organisms. These **restriction enzymes** recognize a specific sequence of DNA, called a *restriction site*. The enzymes will cut DNA strands at all such sites, as **Figure 9** shows.

These enzymes are useful in two ways. First, different enzymes recognize different sequences, so the enzymes can be used to cut up a DNA sample in specific ways. Second, the cuts of most restriction enzymes create sticky ends. A *sticky end* has a few bases on one strand that are unpaired but complementary to unpaired bases on other sticky ends. So, sticky ends will easily bind to one another.

❯ **Reading Check** *Which basic genetic tools were used to make the first GMOs?*

restriction enzyme an enzyme that cuts double-stranded DNA into fragments by recognizing specific nucleotide sequences and cutting the DNA at those sequences

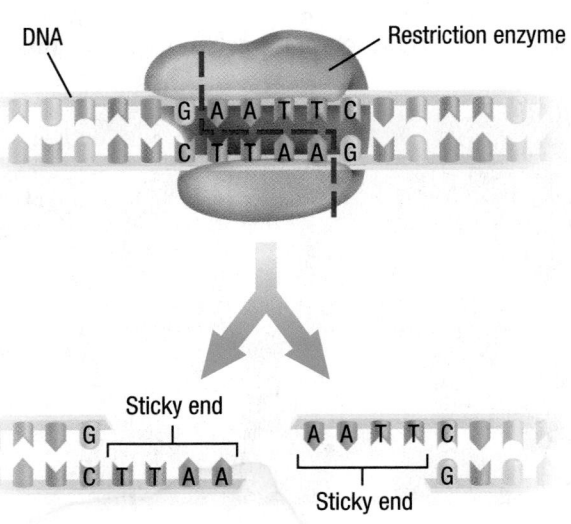

Figure 9 Restriction enzymes recognize and cut DNA at specific sequences. Usually, complementary ("sticky") ends are created. ❯ **In what ways are restriction enzymes useful?**

QuickLab

15 min

Gel Electrophoresis Model

You can use beads to model how DNA fragments are separated in a gel during electrophoresis.

Procedure

1 Fill a **large jar** with the largest of **three sets of beads** (each set should be a different size and different color). The filled jar represents a gel.

2 Mix the smaller sets of beads in a **plastic cup,** and then pour them slowly on top of the "gel." The smaller beads represent DNA fragments.

3 Observe the flow of the beads through the "gel." Lightly agitate the jar if the beads do not flow easily.

Analysis

1. **Identify** which beads flowed through faster.

2. **Relate** this model to how electrophoresis works.

3. **CRITICAL THINKING** **Using Models** Why did the beads identified in item 1 pass through the "gel" more quickly?

Polymorphisms Differences between the DNA sequences of individuals are called **DNA polymorphisms.** These differences may be slight but can be compared and analyzed for several purposes, as you will learn. Differences of just one nucleotide are called *single nucleotide polymorphisms* (SNPs). SNPs result from point mutations and are usually unique to individuals or populations. At a broader level, each species has a unique pattern of restriction sites. When different DNA samples are cut with the same restriction enzyme, the segments that result will have different lengths. These differences are called *restriction fragment length polymorphisms* (RFLPs).

Gel Electrophoresis DNA carries an electric charge, so an electric current can be used to push or pull DNA fragments. This process is called **electrophoresis.** Often, the DNA fragments are forced though a *gel,* a semisolid that allows molecules to move slowly through it. When a current is applied, shorter fragments will move faster through the gel than longer fragments will. The result is a lane of fragments sorted by size, as shown in **Figure 10.** If the fragments separate clearly, each lane is called a *ladder*. If the fragments have overlapping sizes and do not separate clearly, each lane is called a *smear*.

There are many types of electrophoresis. Different kinds of gels are used to sort different sizes of DNA fragments, and other methods are used to sort RNA or proteins. Newer methods use tiny tubes of gel to sort tiny samples that can then be "read" by a machine and analyzed by a computer.

Figure 10 Gel electrophoresis separates samples of molecules, such as DNA or proteins, into bands that are ordered by size. ❯ **What is the role of the gel?**

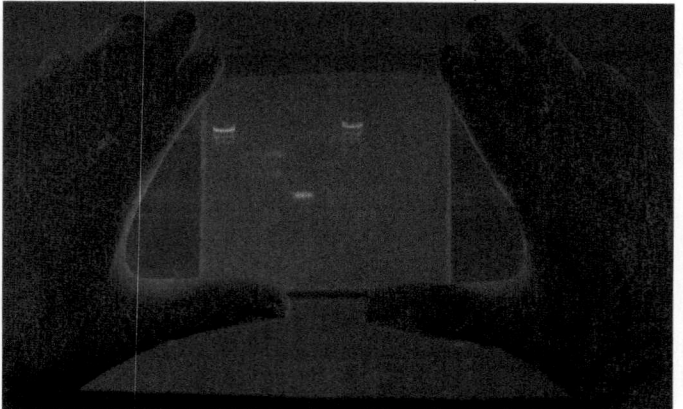

❯ **Reading Check** *What property of a gel does gel electrophoresis depend upon?*

Denaturation Recall that DNA in cells is usually double stranded, twisted, and often associated with proteins. Some conditions, such as heat or strong chemicals, can cause DNA to denature, or untwist and split into single strands. Scientists can easily denature and renature DNA and use the single strands for further manipulations.

Hybridization When single-stranded segments of DNA or RNA are mixed together under the right conditions, complementary segments will bind together, or hybridize. Genetic tools that take advantage of this natural process include the following:

- **Primers** *Primers* are short, single strands of DNA that will hybridize with a specific sequence. For this use, the sequence is one that will be recognized by an enzyme, such as DNA polymerase. Thus, primers can be used to initiate replication of single strands of DNA.

- **Probes** When DNA samples are sorted in a gel, probes are used to "tag" and find specific sequences. Probes are much like primers but carry radioactive or fluorescent materials that can be detected.

- **cDNA** Complementary DNA (cDNA) is DNA that has been made to match mRNA from cells. Recall that this mRNA is the result of transcription and has exons removed. So, making cDNA is a shortcut to getting just the expressed DNA of complete genes.

Major Gene Technology Processes

❯ **The major methods for working with genes use some combination of the basic tools and mechanisms of cellular machinery.** These methods include PCR, blotting, DNA sequencing, and gene recombination.

Polymerase Chain Reaction (PCR) The **polymerase chain reaction (PCR)** process is widely used to clone DNA sequences for further study or manipulation. PCR imitates the normal process of DNA replication in cells. So, using PCR is as simple as combining the right components in a test tube and then controlling the temperature, as **Figure 11** shows. The process is called a *chain reaction* because it is repeated over and over.

DNA polymorphisms (PAHL ee MAWR FIZ uhmz) variations in DNA sequences; used as a basis for comparing genomes

electrophoresis (ee LEK troh fuh REE sis) the process by which electrically charged particles suspended in a liquid move through the liquid because of the influence of an electric field

polymerase chain reaction (puh LIM uhr ays) a technique that is used to make many copies of selected segments of DNA (abbreviation, PCR)

Figure 11 PCR rapidly produces many copies of a DNA sample. The process can make 1 billion copies of a DNA sample within a few hours!

Polymerase Chain Reaction (PCR)

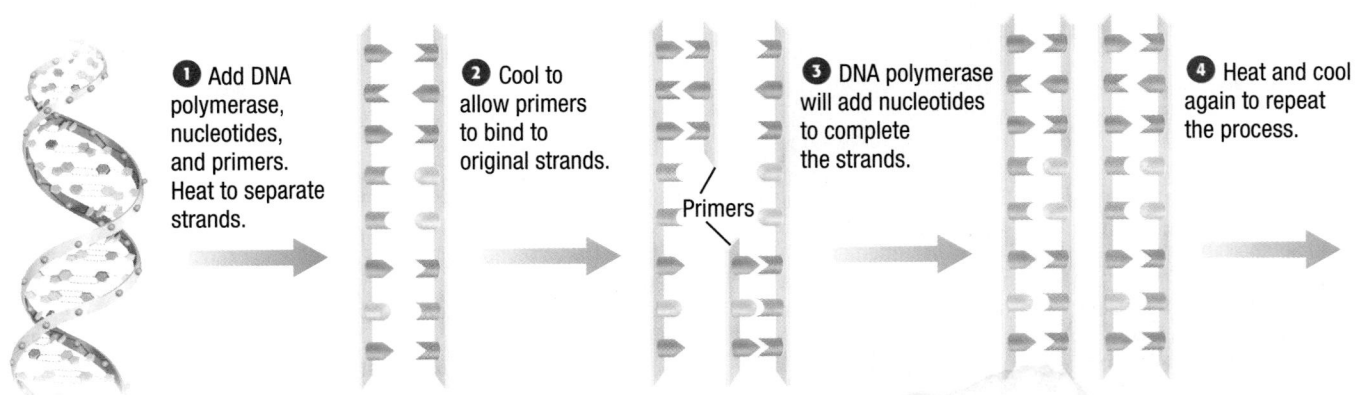

❶ Add DNA polymerase, nucleotides, and primers. Heat to separate strands.

❷ Cool to allow primers to bind to original strands.

Primers

❸ DNA polymerase will add nucleotides to complete the strands.

❹ Heat and cool again to repeat the process.

Blotting Processes and Applications Several gene technologies use a combination of restriction enzymes, gel electrophoresis, and hybridization with probes. The goal is to find or compare sequences of DNA or RNA. Many include a blotting step in which sorted segments are preserved by transferring from the gel to another surface or grid (such as a sheet of special paper). Then, probes are used to reveal the location of specific sequences.

Southern Blot The Southern blot process, shown in **Figure 12,** is used specifically for DNA, and especially for DNA fingerprints. The process may vary by using either different restriction enzymes on one DNA sample or different DNA samples with the same enzyme.

Fingerprints and Bar Codes DNA polymorphisms can be used to identify individuals or species. When restriction fragments are sorted through a Southern blot process, each person's DNA will have a unique pattern of banding called a *DNA fingerprint*. Similarly, a *DNA bar code* can be made to help identify species.

Northern Blot The Northern blot process differs from Southern blot in that the sample fragments are mRNA instead of DNA. Recall that mRNA in cells comes from genes being transcribed. So, Northern blot can be used to tell which genes in a cell are "turned on" (being expressed) or to tell the size of the expressed parts of a gene (after exons are removed).

Microarrays A *microarray* is a device that enables thousands of tiny Northern blots to be done at once. Microarrays can be used to show patterns of gene expression. For example, a cancer cell will have certain genes turned on or off. The pattern of gene activity seen in a microarray can help identify specific kinds of cancer.

Figure 12 In this example, a DNA sample is analyzed by using the Southern blot process. ❯ **Which basic genetic tools are used as part of this process?**

❯ **Reading Check** *What does "blotting" refer to?*

Southern Blot Process

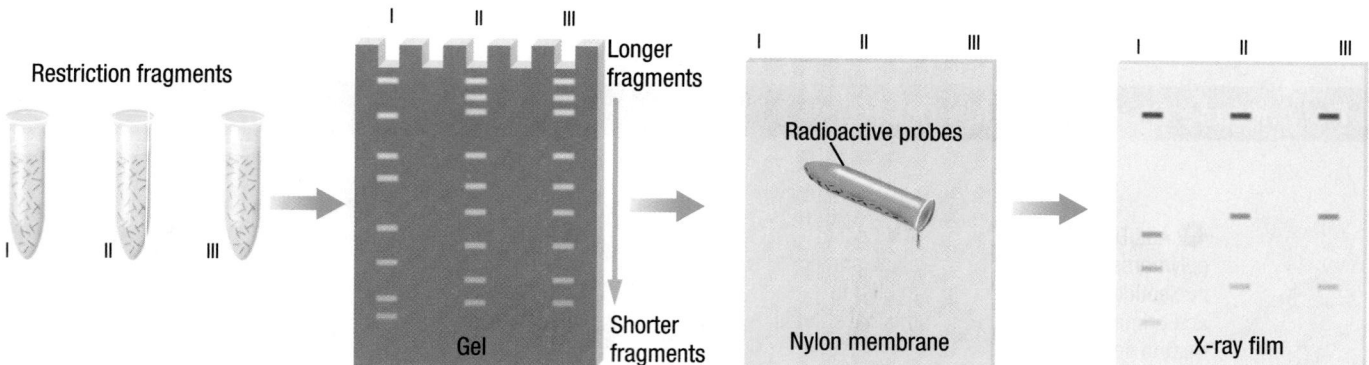

❶ The Southern blot process begins with a sample of DNA. The DNA is cut into fragments using restriction enzymes. A unique enzyme may be used to create several batches of sample DNA.

❷ The DNA fragments are sorted by gel electrophoresis. One lane in the gel is used for each batch. Then, a chemical splits all fragments into single-stranded form.

❸ The DNA strands are transferred (blotted) onto a piece of nylon paper. A solution containing probes is applied to the nylon paper. The probes bind to specific sites on the single strands.

❹ The exposure of photographic or X-ray film to the nylon paper reveals the location of those sample strands that hybridized with the probe. Each person's DNA will make a unique pattern.

Chain Termination Sequencing

1 Copy The unknown DNA sequence is copied, denatured, and incubated with specific genetic molecules.

2 Terminate New copies of the original sequence begin to form, but some are terminated randomly by tagged nucleotides.

3 Sort The resulting strands are denatured and sorted in a gel. The color-coded bands in the gel will match the orginal sequence.

"Template" sequence strand of original

Original, unknown DNA sequence

Short, known part of sequence

Copies of "template" sequence

"Free" DNA nucleotides

DNA polymerase

Primers

Color-tagged "terminator" nucleotides

DNA Sequencing Among the great achievements of modern biology are DNA sequencing methods. **DNA sequencing** is the process of determining the exact order of every nucleotide in a gene. The major modern method is *chain termination sequencing*, as shown in **Figure 13.** This method has been improved over time.

Step 1 Start Copying a Template The gene (DNA segment) of interest is copied (using PCR) and split into single strands. The copies are placed in solution with primers, DNA polymerase, and an assortment of bases. The primers will bond to the "template" strand, and then DNA polymerase will begin to add bases to the "copy" strand, as in normal DNA replication.

Step 2 Randomly Terminate the Copies Some of the bases act as "terminator" bases. When one of these bases is placed in one of the growing copy strands, copying will stop on that strand. Thus, an assortment of randomly "cut-off" sequence copies is produced.

Step 3 Sort the Copies by Size At this point, the sequence of bases can be deduced by sorting the segments by size. When sequencing was first developed, scientists would use four batches of radioactively tagged "terminators" (one for each base type). Then, they would perform electrophoresis in four lanes, side by side, which would reveal the relative order of each end-base. Today, scientists use color-coded fluorescent tags (one color for each base type) and run a single batch through a tiny tube of gel. A machine with a laser can detect the wavelengths of the tags and thus "read" the sequence.

❯ **Reading Check** *When are primers used in DNA sequencing?*

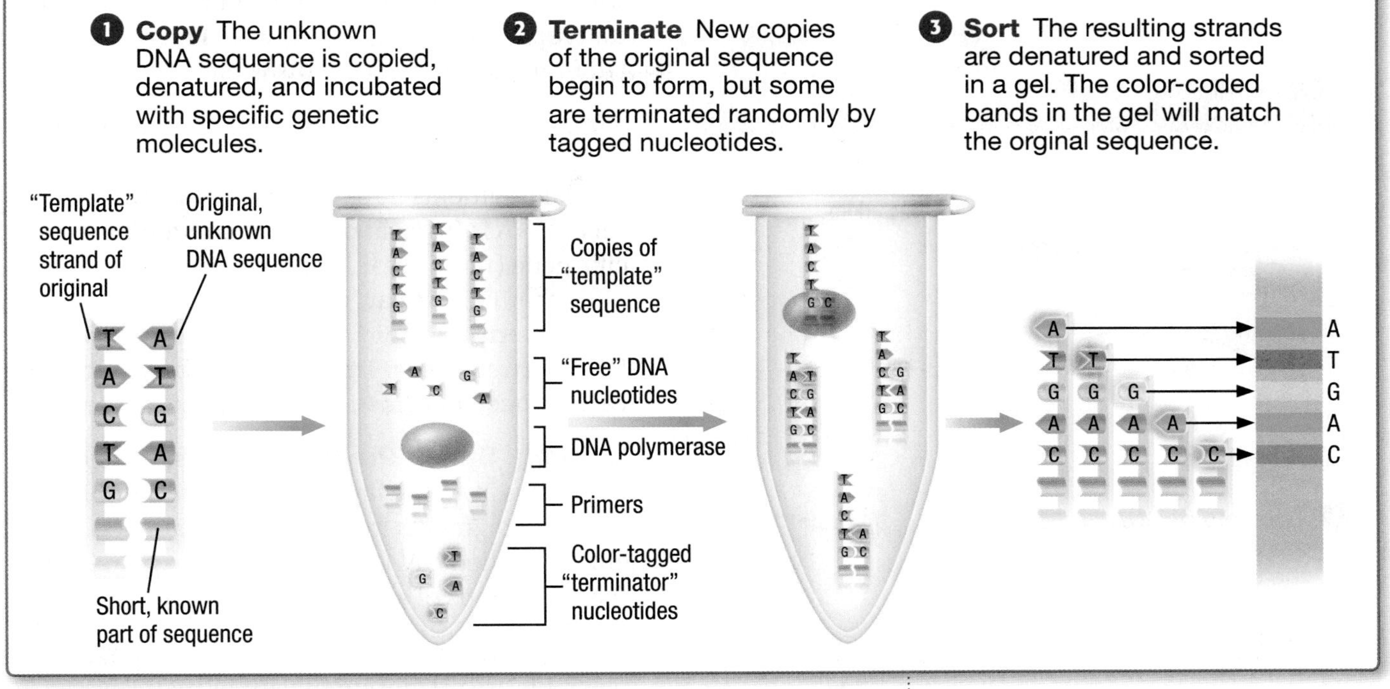

Figure 13 Chain termination sequencing modifies DNA replication processes in order to deduce a DNA sequence. ❯ **Why is this method so important?**

DNA sequencing (SEE kwuhns ing) the process of determining the order of every nucleotide in a gene or genetic fragment

Figure 14 The earliest gene cloning and recombination methods used the steps shown here. The first GMOs were produced in this way.

go.hrw.com
✴ **interact online**
Keyword: HX8GTCF14

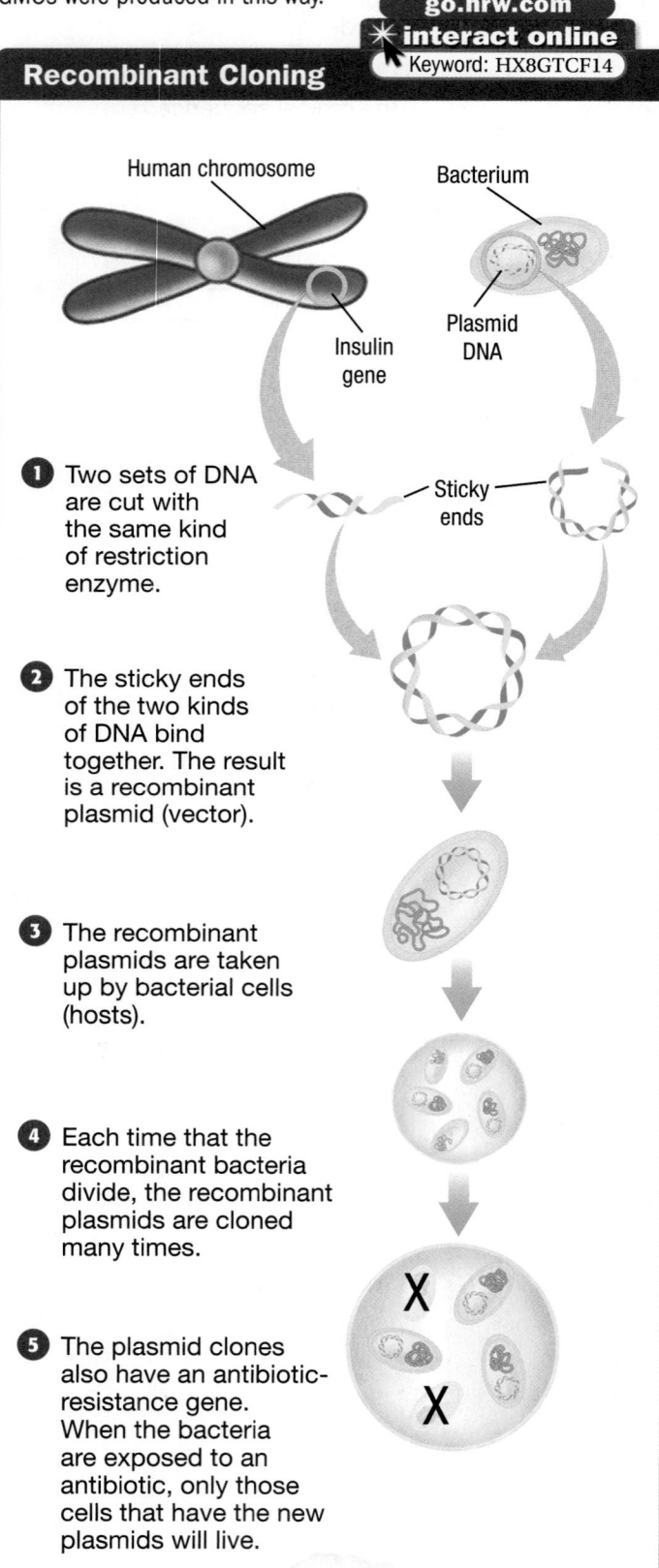

Recombinant Cloning

Human chromosome

Bacterium

Insulin gene

Plasmid DNA

❶ Two sets of DNA are cut with the same kind of restriction enzyme.

Sticky ends

❷ The sticky ends of the two kinds of DNA bind together. The result is a recombinant plasmid (vector).

❸ The recombinant plasmids are taken up by bacterial cells (hosts).

❹ Each time that the recombinant bacteria divide, the recombinant plasmids are cloned many times.

❺ The plasmid clones also have an antibiotic-resistance gene. When the bacteria are exposed to an antibiotic, only those cells that have the new plasmids will live.

Gene Recombination and Cloning The first attempts at gene recombination and cloning were done by inserting a gene into an organism that replicates easily, as shown in **Figure 14.** Other methods may use similar steps.

Step ❶ Cut DNA Samples Two sets of DNA are cut by the same kind of restriction enzyme so that all fragments have matching sticky ends. One set of DNA is from an organism containing a specific gene (in this case, the human insulin gene). The other DNA is part of a vector, such as a virus or a bacterial plasmid, that can carry or move DNA between cells. The vector will be replicated when placed in a host, such as a bacterial cell.

Step ❷ Splice Pieces Together The DNA fragments from the first organism are combined with the fragments from the vector. Then, an enzyme called *DNA ligase* is added to help bond the sticky ends of all the fragments together.

Step ❸ Place into Host At this point, some plasmids are recombinant with human DNA. When the plasmids are placed in a culture of bacteria, some cells take up the plasmids. The cells are allowed to replicate normally.

Step ❹ Replicate Gene Each time that a bacterial cell divides, its plasmids are copied many times. In a few generations, the cells make millions of clones of the recombinant plasmids.

Step ❺ Screen for Gene At this point, only some of the bacterial cells contain the recombinant plasmids. These cells must be identified in some way. One clever solution is to use vectors that contain another gene that is easy to detect. In this example, the original plasmids contained a gene that makes bacteria resistant to an antibiotic chemical. When the bacteria from step 4 are exposed to that chemical, only the cells that have taken up the vectors will survive.

These steps are just the beginning of genetic-engineering applications. Before PCR, this process of recombination was the main way to clone genes for further research. Another use is simply to produce a protein, such as insulin, from a cloned gene. As you have learned, recombinant organisms are created for many applications, from agriculture to medicine.

❯ **Reading Check** *What is a vector?*

Exploring Genomes

Until recently, the human genome was largely "unexplored." But now, specific genes are being identified and their locations "mapped." These first steps lead to understanding how each gene works. Like geographic maps, maps of genetic data can have different levels of detail or scale. For example, one can view a map of an entire nation or "zoom in" to view a particular state, city, neighborhood, or street. In a similar way, ❯ **one can explore and map a genome at many levels, including species, individual, chromosome, gene, or nucleotide.**

Managing Genomic Data Your school library has a system for organizing and keeping track of books, as **Figure 15** shows. Similarly, scientists need systems for managing the vast amounts of data in a genome. Today, they use information technologies. The application of information technologies in biology is **bioinformatics.** ❯ **Genomic bioinformatics starts with the mapping and assembly of the many parts of each genome.** The major stages of this work include the following:

- **Mapping and Assembly** Many genes have been "mapped" to reveal their location relative to other genes. In addition, large collections of sequences are being pieced together like a puzzle.

- **Organized Storage** Genomic information is stored in a logical system or database. This way, the information can be sorted and searched, and new information can be added easily.

- **Annotation** Each gene or sequence is named and categorized according to its location, structure, or function in each genome.

- **Analysis** The ultimate goal of genomics is to understand the exact function of each gene or sequence. This analysis includes studying the complex interactions among genes and proteins.

❯ **Reading Check** *What are the first steps of studying genomes?*

bioinformatics the application of information technologies in biology, especially in genetics

READING TOOLBOX

Learning Steps If you have not yet completed your pattern puzzle for **Figure 14,** do so now. Then, close your book, scramble the pieces, and see if you can put them in order.

Figure 15 Like a library full of books, genomic data must be organized in order to be useful. ❯ **What other actions are needed to manage genomic data?**

Mapping Methods **Genome mapping** is the process of determining the relative position of all of the genes on chromosomes in an organism's genome. To make a city map from scratch, you might start with landmarks that are easy to find and recognize. Similarly, genome mapping methods use *genetic markers,* or traits that can be easily detected, to trace the movement and location of genes. Examples are shown in **Figure 16.** Any detectable physical, behavioral, or chemical trait can be used as a marker. As the next step in making a map, you might try to determine the location of each thing relative to other things. Similarly, genome mapping uses several methods.

Linkage Mapping Linkage mapping methods identify the relative order of genes along a chromosome. Recall that the closer together that two genes are, the less frequently they will be separated during chromosome crossover. So, closely linked genes are more often associated, or found together, in the same individual. By comparing how often genes are associated, scientists can deduce their location relative to one another, as **Figure 16** shows.

Physical Mapping Physical mapping methods determine the exact number of base pairs between specific genes. These methods manipulate DNA to deduce exactly how close together genes are.

Human Chromosome Mapping Early attempts to map human genes used historical family records. By studying the patterns of inheritance of specific traits, scientists could infer which genes tend to be inherited together. This method was especially useful for initial mapping of the X chromosome. Such maps have since been filled in with data from physical mapping, as **Figure 16** shows.

Figure 16 Each of these maps shows the relative positions of genes on chromosomes. The physical map is more specific than the linkage map. ❯ Why was the X chromosome mapped more easily than other chromosomes?

Basic Genome Mapping

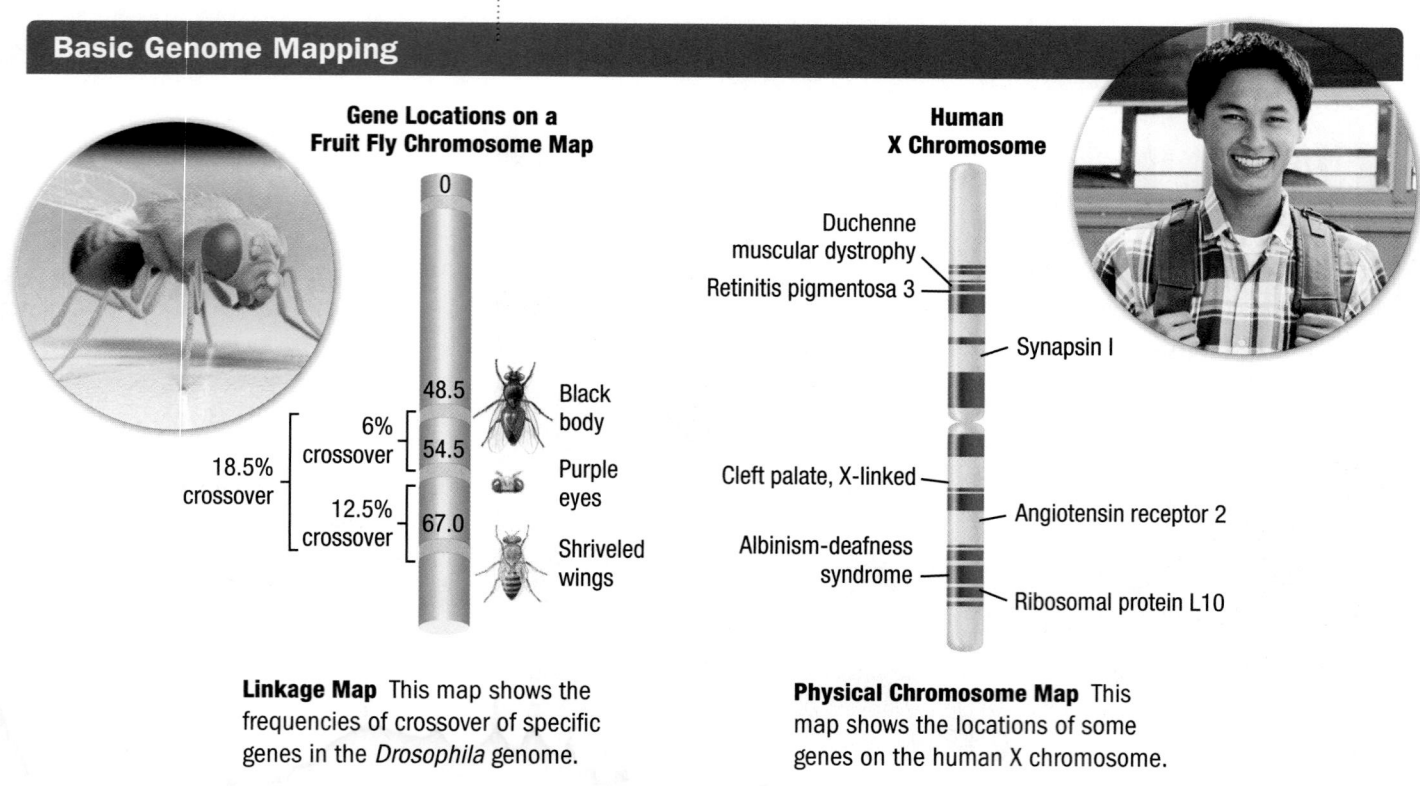

Gene Locations on a Fruit Fly Chromosome Map

0

18.5% crossover

6% crossover

48.5

54.5

12.5% crossover

67.0

Black body

Purple eyes

Shriveled wings

Linkage Map This map shows the frequencies of crossover of specific genes in the *Drosophila* genome.

Human X Chromosome

Duchenne muscular dystrophy

Retinitis pigmentosa 3

Synapsin I

Cleft palate, X-linked

Angiotensin receptor 2

Albinism-deafness syndrome

Ribosomal protein L10

Physical Chromosome Map This map shows the locations of some genes on the human X chromosome.

Genome Sequence Assembly As they zoom in on the map of genes, scientists want to record all of the nucleotide sequences in a genome. The process of deducing and recording the exact order of every base and gene in a genome is called *sequence assembly*. The process involves collecting, sorting, and comparing large samples of genetic material.

Genetic Libraries To study an entire genome, scientists break up the genome into small fragments and clone all of the fragments. A collection of clones that represent all of the genes in a given genome is called a **genetic library.** Two kinds of genetic libraries are made. A *genomic library* is made by cloning all of the DNA in a cell. A genomic library includes all functional genes as well as all noncoding DNA. An *expressed sequence tag* (EST) *library* starts with the mRNA that results from transcription. The mRNA is used to make cDNA segments, which are then cloned to make the library.

Using the Libraries Once the clones are assembled, they can be sequenced, sorted, and organized. Early methods involved sorting through libraries one gene at a time by repeated probing and deduction. More recently, a method called *shotgun sequencing* was developed. In this method, an entire genome is cut up randomly into segments of varying size. All resulting segments are cloned and sequenced. Then, by looking for overlapping parts, researchers put together the entire sequence like a puzzle. The resulting genome sequence is stored as data and can be searched for specific genes or sequences of any size.

Automated Sequencing Robotic devices are now used to sequence a genome in a fraction of the time that it took to complete such a project only decades ago. Automated sequencing devices can quickly "read" many tiny sequence gels at one time. In such a device, a laser beam scans each gel tube, and detectors identify each of the four kinds of tags. Finally, a computer compiles the data into a string of letters, as **Figure 17** shows.

❯ **Reading Check** *What are the two kinds of genetic libraries?*

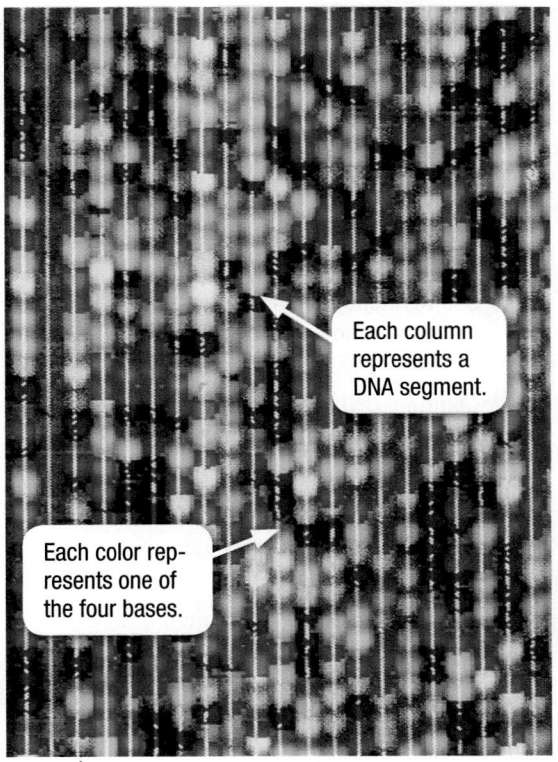

Each column represents a DNA segment.

Each color represents one of the four bases.

Figure 17 This computer screen shows the output of an automated sequencing device. The device "reads" DNA sequences by detecting color-coded, "tagged" bases in tiny gel-electrophoresis tubes. ❯ **What advantages do computers provide?**

Section 3 Review

❯ **KEY IDEAS**

1. **Identify** the basic tools of genetic manipulation.
2. **Outline** any one of the major processes of modern gene technologies.
3. **Identify** the major stages of the work of genomics, in terms of bioinformatics.

CRITICAL THINKING

4. **Relating Concepts** Differentiate between SNPs and RFLPs.
5. **Predicting Outcomes** If samples of nerve cells and bone cells from the same person were run through the same type of microarray, would the results differ? Explain.
6. **Analyzing Information** Why is *expressed sequence tag library* a fitting name for a collection of clones made from mRNA?

METHODS OF SCIENCE

7. **Choosing Appropriate Tools** Suppose that you are a genetic scientist who has been asked to help stop the illegal killing of some tropical bird species. These birds are being killed so that their feathers can be sold for fashionable hat decorations. Propose some ways that you could use gene technologies to help protect these birds.

Chapter 15 Lab

Objectives

▶ Model the forensic analysis of evidence from a crime scene.

▶ Use restriction enzymes, PCR, and gel electrophoresis to manipulate DNA samples.

▶ Compare DNA fingerprints to match identical DNA samples.

Materials

- lab apron, safety goggles, and disposable gloves
- marker, permanent, waterproof
- microcentrifuge tubes (5)
- micropipettes, sterile, disposable (25)
- DNA samples (5)
- restriction enzyme buffer
- restriction enzyme
- incubator or hot water bath
- ice, crushed
- cup, plastic-foam
- gel, agarose, precast for electrophoresis chamber
- electrophoresis chamber with power supply and wires
- running buffer
- loading dye
- bag, plastic, resealable
- DNA staining solution
- tray for staining gel
- water, distilled
- paper, white, or light table

Safety

DNA Fingerprint Analysis

Each person's DNA is unique. This fact can be used to match crime suspects to DNA samples taken from crime scenes. *DNA fingerprints* can be made by using restriction enzymes and gel electrophoresis to reveal unique patterns in each individual's DNA.

Procedure

Cut DNA with Restriction Enzyme

1. Read all procedures, and prepare to collect your data. Label each microcentrifuge tube with a code for each DNA sample provided. For example, label one tube "C" for "crime scene sample" and the remaining tubes "S1" to "S4," one for each suspect.

2. ⚠️ ⚠️ ⚠️ Wear a lab apron, safety goggles, and gloves during all parts of this lab.

3. ☠️ **CAUTION: Never taste chemicals or allow them to contact your skin.** Using a clean pipette each time, transfer 10 µL of each DNA sample to the microcentrifuge tube that has the matching label.

4. Using a clean pipette each time, transfer 2 µL of restriction enzyme buffer to each of the tubes.

5. Using a clean pipette each time, transfer 2 µL of restriction enzyme to each of the tubes. Close all of the tubes. Gently flick the bottom of each tube to mix the DNA and reagents.

6. 🔥 **CAUTION: Use caution when working with heating devices.** Transfer the tubes to the incubator or water bath set at 37 °C. Let the samples incubate for one hour.

7. Stand the tubes in crushed ice in the plastic-foam cup.

8. If you need to pause this lab at this point, store the cup at 4 °C.

Separate Fragments by Gel Electrophoresis

9. Place the precast gel on the level surface of the electrophoresis chamber. The wells in the gel should be closest to the black, or negative, electrode. Keep the gel level and flat at all times.

10. Fill the chamber with enough buffer to barely cover the gel. Do not pour the buffer directly onto the gel. Sketch a diagram of your gel in your lab notebook, as the sample diagram shows.

11. Using a clean pipette each time, transfer 2 µL of loading dye to each of the tubes. Gently flick the tubes to mix the contents.

12. Using a clean pipette, load the crime scene DNA into the well for Lane 1 of your gel. Be careful not to overflow or puncture the well.

13. Repeat step 12 for the remaining DNA samples and gel lanes. End with the DNA from Suspect 4. Use a clean pipette for each transfer.

14 ◆ **CAUTION: Use caution when working with electrical equipment; use only as directed by your teacher.** Make sure that everything outside the chamber is dry before proceeding. Attach the power connectors to the chamber and power supply as directed by your teacher. Set the power supply to the voltage determined by your teacher, and turn on the power supply.

15 Allow the gel to run undisturbed for the time directed by your teacher. Observe the gel periodically, and stop the process when the dye front is about 3 cm away from the end of the gel. At that point, turn off the power supply. Then, disconnect the power connectors from the power supply and chamber.

16 ◆ **CAUTION: Dispose of all waste materials as directed by your teacher.** Carefully remove the casting tray from the chamber. Pour off the running buffer according to your teacher's instructions.

17 If you need to pause this lab at this point, carefully slide the gel into a resealable bag. Add 2 mL running buffer, seal the bag, and store the bag in a refrigerator. Remember to keep the gel flat.

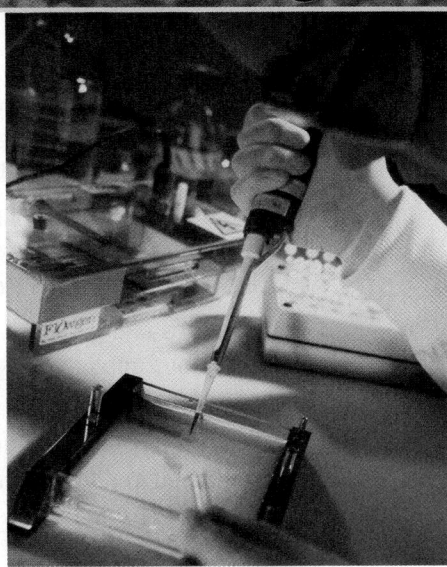

Loading the gel

View Separated DNA Fragments

18 Gently slide the gel onto the staining tray. Pour enough stain into the tray to barely cover the gel. Do not pour the stain directly onto the gel. Let the gel sit for at least 30 min.

19 Carefully pour off the stain as directed by your teacher.

20 Gently pour distilled water into the tray to cover the gel. Do not pour the water directly onto the gel. After 5 min, carefully pour off the water as directed by your teacher.

21 Repeat step 20 until bands are clearly visible on the gel.

22 Gently transfer the gel to a white sheet of paper or to a light table. Sketch and describe your observations in your lab notebook.

23 ◆ ◆ Clean up your lab materials according to your teacher's instructions. Wash your hands before leaving the lab.

Sample gel diagram

Analyze and Conclude

1. SCIENTIFIC METHODS **Organizing Data** Organize your data into a table. How many different fragment sizes resulted from the treatment of each DNA sample?

2. **Analyzing Data** Identify any bands of fragments that are the same size among any of the samples. Mark these bands on your sketch.

3. **Forming Conclusions** Use this evidence to determine which suspect most likely committed the crime. Explain your answer.

4. SCIENTIFIC METHODS **Evaluating Methods** Do these results provide enough evidence to convict the suspect? Explain your answer.

Extension

5. **Applying Concepts** Some bands appeared in the same position in several lanes. Propose an explanation for this result.

6. **Predicting Results** How might the results have been affected if a different restriction enzyme had been used? Explain your answer.

Chapter 15 Summary

go.hrw.com
SUPER SUMMARY
Keyword: HX8GTCS

Key Ideas	Key Terms

1 The Human Genome

> The sequencing of the human genome has advanced the study of human biology yet created new questions

> Genomics and gene technologies have many applications in human healthcare and society.

> Many important questions about the human genome remain to be investigated or decided.

genomics (345)
microarray (346)
DNA fingerprint (347)

2 Gene Technologies in Our Lives

> Today, gene technologies are widely applied to study organisms in new ways, to alter organisms for human use, and to improve human lives.

> Cloning and stem cell techniques are used in research on animal development and have potential for treating certain diseases.

> Ethical issues can be raised for every use of gene technologies.

genetic engineering (350)
recombinant DNA (350)
clone (352)
stem cell (353)

3 Gene Technologies in Detail

> The basic tools of DNA manipulation rely on the chemical nature of genetic material and are adapted from natural processes discovered in cells. These tools include restriction enzymes, polymorphisms, gel electrophoresis, denaturation, and hybridization.

> The major methods for working with genes use some combination of the basic tools of cellular machinery. These methods include PCR, blotting, DNA sequencing, and gene recombination.

> One can explore and map a genome at many levels, including species, individual, chromosome, gene, or nucleotide. Genomic bioinformatics starts with the mapping and assembly of the many parts of each genome.

restriction enzyme (355)
DNA polymorphisms (356)
electrophoresis (356)
polymerase chain reaction (PCR) (357)
DNA sequencing (359)
bioinformatics (361)
genome mapping (362)
genetic library (363)

1. Analogies Complete the following analogy:

genetic disorder : protein :: diabetes : ___

2. 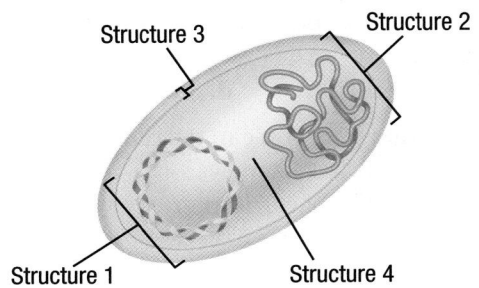 **Concept Map** Construct a concept map that differentiates the major processes of gene manipulation. Try to use the following terms: *cloning, genes, organisms, PCR, recombinant, engineering, SCNT,* and *asexual reproduction.*

Using Key Terms

3. Use the following terms in the same sentence: *restriction enzyme, DNA polymorphisms,* and *DNA fingerprint.*

Complete each of the following sentences by choosing the correct word from the word bank.

Genomics
Bioinformatics
Electrophoresis

4. ___ is the use of computers with biological data.

5. ___ is the separation of molecules using electricity.

6. ___ is the study of entire genomes.

Understanding Key Ideas

7. One of the surprising discoveries of the Human Genome Project was that
   a. the human genome consists of only about 25,000 genes.
   b. about 99% of the human genome codes for proteins.
   c. each gene encodes only a single protein.
   d. DNA is found in the nucleus of cells.

8. A DNA microarray is an important tool because it
   a. can cure cancer.
   b. identifies an individual.
   c. makes tumor cells glow green.
   d. shows which genes are active in a cell.

9. An organism that has been given a new gene through genetic engineering can be called any of the following *except*
   a. transgenic.   **c.** recombinant.
   b. sequenced.   **d.** genetically modified.

10. The Southern blot process is used to analyze
   a. RNA.   **c.** mRNA.
   b. DNA.   **d.** protein.

11. What do linkage mapping methods identify?
   a. only genes that are inherited together
   b. the exact nucleotide sequence of a chromosome
   c. the relative position of genes along a chromosome
   d. the exact number of base pairs between specific genes

This diagram shows a cell with recombinant DNA. Use the diagram to answer the following questions.

Structure 3   Structure 2

Structure 1   Structure 4

12. Which part of this cell is recombinant DNA?
   a. structure 1   **c.** structure 3
   b. structure 2   **d.** structure 4

13. The most appropriate term to describe this cell is
   a. *somatic.*   **c.** *transgenic.*
   b. *totipotent.*   **d.** *nongenetic.*

Explaining Key Ideas

14. Identify an application of gene technologies in human health care.

15. Describe how cloning can be used to produce embryonic stem cells.

16. Identify a risk associated with growing genetically modified cereal crops on farms.

17. Describe how a scientist could use gene recombination and cloning to produce a human protein.

18. Compare genomic libraries to EST libraries.

Using Science Graphics

This diagram shows two pieces of DNA that originated in two different organisms. Use the diagram to answer the following questions.

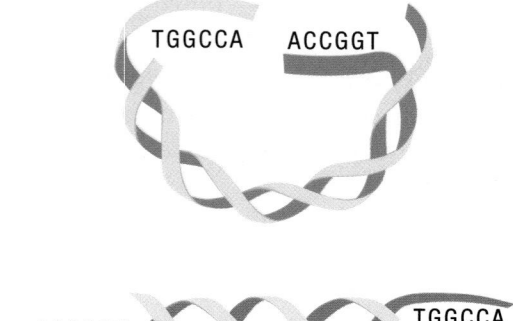

TGGCCA   ACCGGT

ACCGGT   TGGCCA

19. The single-stranded segments that stick out at the end of each DNA piece are called *sticky ends* because the strands form pairs that are
   a. identical.
   b. denatured.
   c. complementary.
   d. double stranded.

20. From the diagram, you can tell that each of these DNA segments has been
   a. taken up by a bacterium.
   b. cut by a restriction enzyme.
   c. denatured by a polymerase enzyme.
   d. recombined to make a genetically modified organism.

Critical Thinking

21. Forming Reasoned Opinions A student says that the Human Genome Project is a purely scientific pursuit and that there is no need to worry about ethical questions because science can answer any question. Do you agree with this statement? Explain.

22. Evaluating Complex Issues In the United States, government regulations require researchers to contain experimental GMOs inside a laboratory and to ensure that the organism cannot survive outside the lab. Why do you think that these strict regulations are in place?

23. Relating Concepts Scientists often use PCR before performing other DNA manipulation processes, such as Southern blot or sequencing. Why?

24. Making Inferences Should communication be an important aspect of bioinformatics? Explain.

Methods of Science

25. Critiquing Procedures The earlier method of DNA sequencing used four separate batches of radioactively tagged nucleotides. These nucleotides were added to four separate batches of the same DNA fragments, each of which were run through the termination and sorting steps. The newer method uses one mixture of four fluorescent, color-coded nucleotides mixed together and run in one batch. In what ways is the newer process more efficient?

Writing for Science

26. Script Your geneticist friend has just e-mailed you with exciting news: She has produced the first crop of glow-in-the-dark cotton! She has asked you to help think of ways to sell the cotton or to make new products from it. Help out your friend by writing a script for a television commercial that will help sell the cotton or products made from it.

Technology Skills

27. Visual Communication Create a slide show, cartoon, or animation that illustrates what happens in the PCR cycle. Present your project to your class, or display it on the internet.

Alternative Assessment

28. Veggie Invention Would people eat more broccoli if it were pink? Would they eat butter-flavored corn on the cob or orange-flavored spinach? Invent an idea for a new fruit or vegetable that could encourage people to eat more fruits and vegetables. Create an advertisement for your new item, and present it to your class. Be sure to consider the potential benefits of the new item and any negative reactions that people might have to it.

Math Skills

29. Rates Suppose a scientist wants to search for a specific gene from a complete genome sequence. Looking at printed sequences, a trained scientist can search through about 1,000 bases per minute. At this rate, estimate the amount of time it would take to search for a 1000-base-pair gene in the *Drosophila* genome, which contains 80,000,000 base pairs.

> **TEST TIP** When you encounter a question that involves graphics, pay close attention to any labels.

Science Concepts

1. The international effort to deduce the sequence of all of the DNA in human cells is called the

  A Human DNA Fingerprint.

  B Human Genome Project.

  C Polymerase Chain Reaction.

  D Global Genetic Engineering Program.

2. Which of the following is a molecule that contains DNA taken from two different organisms?

  F cDNA   **H** recombinant DNA

  G mRNA   **J** double-stranded DNA

3. The process that produces genetically identical embryos from adult somatic cells is called

  A adult stem cell culturing.

  B embryonic stem cell culturing.

  C totipotent cell transfer cloning.

  D somatic cell nuclear transfer cloning.

4. Protein molecules that cut DNA molecules at specific places are called

  F primers.   **H** restriction enzymes.

  G sticky ends.   **J** polymerase enzymes.

5. Complementary segments of DNA or RNA will spontaneously

  A hybridize.   **C** terminate.

  B denature.   **D** electrophorese.

Writing Skills

6. Extended Response It is becoming possible to identify some genetic factors that increase a person's risk of developing health problems such as asthma or cancer. Write a short essay supporting your answer to the following question: Should a health insurance company be able to use genetic analysis to assess the risks of insuring potential customers?

Using Science Graphics

This diagram shows the approximate location on an X chomosome of genes for some human traits. Use the diagram to answer the following question(s).

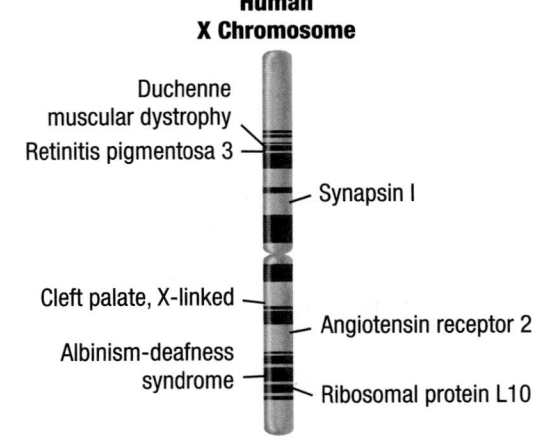

Human X Chromosome

7. This kind of information about genome is called a

  F chromosome map.   **H** genomic library.

  G genetic fingerprint.   **J** karyotype.

8. Many of these genes code for

  A typical traits.   **C** unlinked traits.

  B sex-linked traits.   **D** unexpressed traits.

This diagram shows the result of gel electrophoresis of DNA. The same DNA sample was run through each of the three lanes, but each lane is the result of a different kind of treatment of the DNA sample. Use the diagram to answer the following questions.

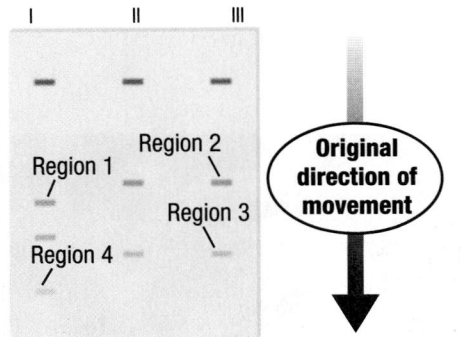

9. Which of the following regions contains longer DNA fragments than the other regions?

  F region 1   **H** region 3

  G region 2   **J** region 4

UNIT 5 Evolution

16 Evolutionary Theory

17 Population Genetics and Speciation

18 Classification

19 History of Life on Earth

Kingfisher male with courtship gift

Insect of the newly named order Mantophasmatodea

370

Poison dart frogs

Evolution and Life on Earth

1753

Carolus Linnaeus publishes the first of two volumes containing the classification of all known species. In doing so, Linnaeus establishes a consistent system for naming and classifying species. The system is widely used thereafter.

1859

Charles Darwin suggests that natural selection is the mechanism of evolution. Within months, public debates regarding the truth and significance of his theory ensue.

Galápagos tortoises

1907

In his book, *Plant Breeding,* Hugo de Vries, Dutch botanist, joins Mendel's laws of heredity with the newer theory of mutation. De Vries asserts that inheritable mutations are the mechanism by which species change and new species form.

1960

Mary and Jonathan Leakey discover fossil bones of a human ancestor, *Homo habilis,* in Olduvai Gorge, Tanzania.

Mary Leakey, paleoanthropologist

1974

Donald Johansen discovers a fossilized skeleton of one of the first hominids, *Australopithecus afarensis.* This specimen was nicknamed "Lucy."

Skull of *A. afarensis*

1980

Walter and Luis Alvarez, Frank Asaro, and Helen Michel publish a paper providing evidence that 65 million years ago, an asteroid collided with Earth and caused severe environmental changes. The changes may have led to the extinction of the majority of species that lived during that time.

1994

Reinhardt Kristensen and Peter Funch discover a tiny animal living on the lips of lobsters. They name the new species *Symbion pandora.* This species is so different from other animals that scientists classify it within a new phylum, Cycliophora, within kingdom Animalia.

2006

A team of biologists announces a study of Camiguin Island, the smallest island of the Philippines. They find 54 species of birds and 24 of species of mammals.

As-yet-unnamed parrot species

Beetles—one of the most diverse groups of animals on Earth

BIOLOGY CAREER

Museum Curator
Rob DeSalle

Rob DeSalle is a curator in the Division of Invertebrate Zoology at the American Museum of Natural History in New York City. He is an adjunct professor at Columbia University and City University of New York and is a Distinguished Research Professor at New York University. His current research focuses on molecular evolution in various organisms, including pathogenic bacteria and insects.

DeSalle enjoys being a scientist because he can investigate the diversity of life every day. He also enjoys the opportunity to serve as a mentor to students. Most of all, he enjoys the thrill of discovering something that no one else on the planet has found.

He considers his most significant accomplishment in science to be his work communicating scientific ideas through his writing and museum exhibitions.

Besides his work, DeSalle loves baseball and is a passionate fan of the Chicago Cubs.

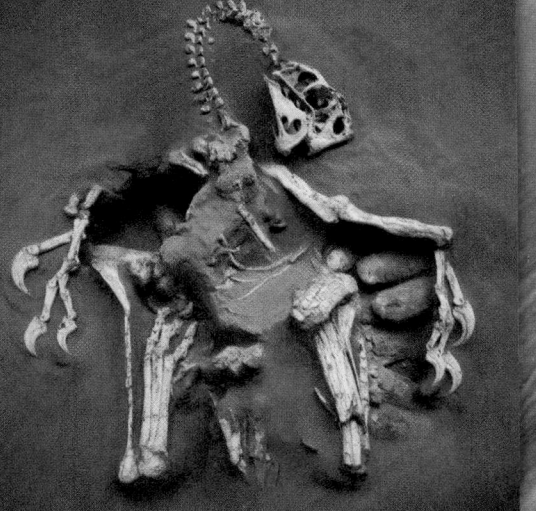

Fossil and eggs of dinosaur called *oviraptor*

Evolutionary Theory

Preview

1 Developing a Theory
A Theory to Explain Change over Time
Darwin's Ideas from Experience
Darwin's Ideas from Others

2 Applying Darwin's Ideas
Evolution by Natural Selection
What Darwin Explained
Evaluating Darwin's Ideas

3 Beyond Darwinian Theory
Darwin's Theory Updated
Studying Evolution at All Scales

Why It Matters

Modern evolutionary theory provides strong and detailed explanations for many aspects of biology, such as anatomy and behavior.

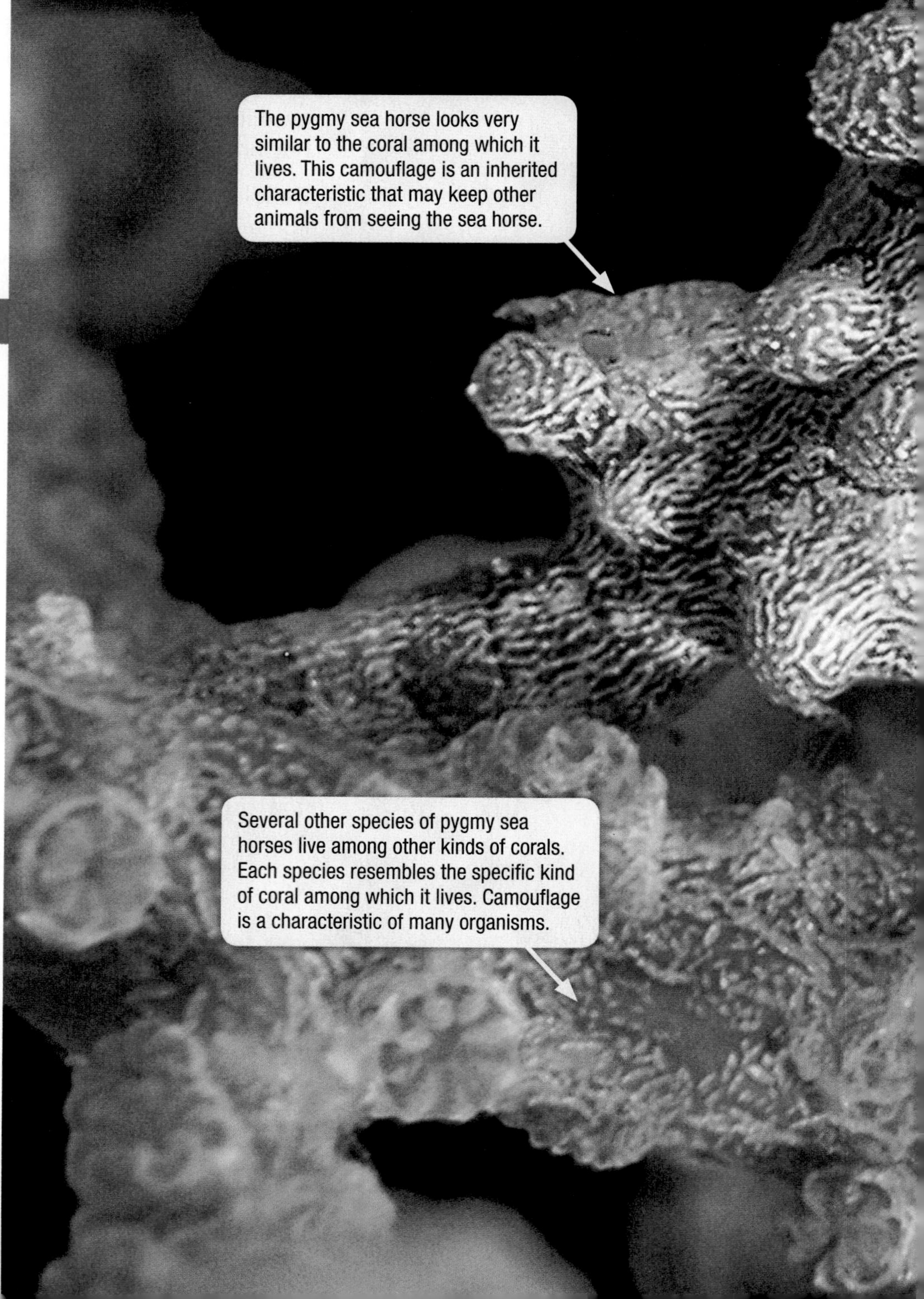

This pygmy sea horse is smaller than your fingernail. It lives exclusively among certain kinds of coral in coral reefs of the western Pacific Ocean.

The pygmy sea horse looks very similar to the coral among which it lives. This camouflage is an inherited characteristic that may keep other animals from seeing the sea horse.

Several other species of pygmy sea horses live among other kinds of corals. Each species resembles the specific kind of coral among which it lives. Camouflage is a characteristic of many organisms.

Charles Darwin's theory of evolution by natural selection provides an explanation for how characteristics such as camouflage can arise over time. Darwin's theory continues to be supported and expanded by modern scientists.

15 min

InquiryLab

Scientific Inference

Much of science is based on making inferences. Not all inferences can be supported by direct observation. Instead, many are tested by modeling, prediction, and experimentation. Doing so requires attention to detail and, sometimes, creative thinking.

Procedure

1. Break a **piece of flat-noodle pasta** into two smaller segments about 8 cm long and 3 cm long.

2. Erect two "walls" in the bottom of a **Petri dish** by securing the pasta pieces to the dish with **tape.**

3. Place a **ball bearing** in the dish.

4. Secure the lid onto the dish with tape. Keeping the dish upright, place it in a **brown paper bag.**

5. Exchange bags with another student. Without looking inside the bag, try to infer the arrangement of the pasta in the dish.

Analysis

1. **Describe** your inference, and explain how you formed it.

2. **Suggest** how your inference could be supported or confirmed.

READING TOOLBOX

These reading tools can help you learn the material in this chapter. For more information on how to use these and other tools, see **Appendix: Reading and Study Skills.**

Using Words

Key-Term Fold A key-term fold is useful for studying definitions of key terms in a chapter. Each tab can contain a key term on one side and the term's definition on the other.

Your Turn Prepare a key-term fold for the key terms in this chapter. Fill it in as you read. Use it later to quiz yourself on the definitions.

1. Fold a sheet of lined notebook paper in half from left to right.

2. Using scissors, cut along every third line from the right edge of the paper to the center fold to make tabs.

Using Language

Hypothesis or Theory? In everyday language, there is little difference between a *hypothesis* and a *theory*. But in science, the meanings of these words are more distinct. A *hypothesis* is a specific, testable prediction for a limited set of conditions. A *theory* is a general explanation for a broad range of data. A theory can include hypotheses that have been tested and can also be used to generate new hypotheses. The strongest scientific theories explain the broadest range of data and incorporate many well-tested hypotheses.

Your Turn Use what you have learned about a hypothesis and a theory to answer the following questions.

1. List some scientific theories that you have heard of.

2. Make a simple concept map or Venn diagram to show the relationship between hypotheses and theories.

3. The word *theory* may also be used to describe general trends and areas of active investigation in a scientific field. In this context, what does the term *evolutionary theory* mean?

Taking Notes

Summarizing Ideas Summarizing ideas helps you condense important information. When you summarize, use your own words and keep your sentences short. Focus on key ideas.

Your Turn Prepare to take notes for this chapter. Use this table as an example. As you read, be sure to summarize the following concepts:

1. natural selection

2. macroevolution

3. microevolution

Notes about Evolution		
Natural selection	Macroevolution	Microevolution

Developing a Theory

Key Ideas	Key Terms	Why It Matters
❯ Why is evolutionary theory associated with Charles Darwin? ❯ How was Darwin influenced by his personal experiences? ❯ How was Darwin influenced by the ideas of others?	evolution artificial selection	Many aspects of biology are best explained by evolutionary theory.

Recall that in biology, **evolution** is the process by which species change over time. The idea that life evolves is not new. Yet for centuries, scientists lacked clear evidence that evolution happens. They also lacked a strong theory to explain how evolution happens. In 1859, Charles Darwin pulled together these missing pieces. Darwin, shown in **Figure 1,** was an English naturalist who studied the diversity of life and proposed a broad explanation for it.

A Theory to Explain Change over Time

Recall that in science, a *theory* is a broad explanation that has been scientifically tested and supported. ❯ Modern evolutionary theory began when Darwin presented evidence that evolution happens and offered an explanation of how evolution happens. Like most scientific theories, evolutionary theory keeps developing and expanding. Many scientists since Darwin have tested and added to his ideas. Most of Darwin's ideas, including his main theory, remain scientifically supported.

❯ **Reading Check** *What does* evolution *mean in biology? (See the Appendix for answers to Reading Checks.)*

> **evolution** the process of change by which new species develop from preexisting species over time

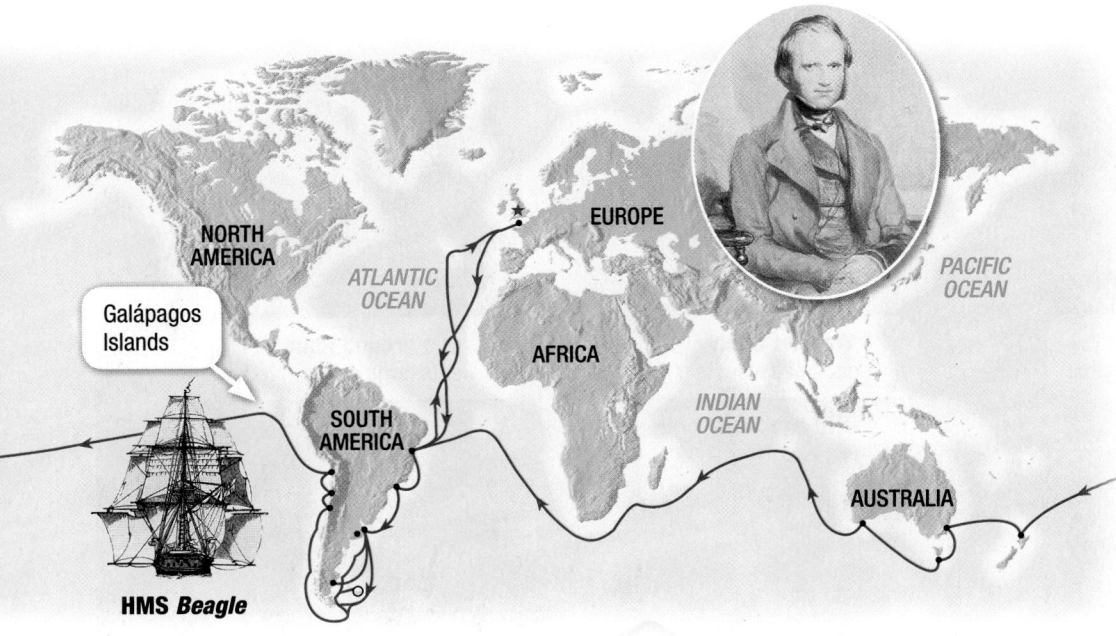

Figure 1 Charles Darwin took many years to publish his theory of evolution by natural selection. Many of his ideas were first inspired by his 1831 global voyage on a ship called the *Beagle*.

Darwin's Ideas from Experience

In Darwin's time, most people did not think that living things had changed over time. In fact, many doubted that Earth itself had ever changed. But Darwin saw evidence of gradual change. ❯ **Darwin's experiences provided him with evidence of evolution at work.**

The Voyage of the _Beagle_ Darwin's first evidence was gathered during a global voyage on a ship called the _Beagle_. As part of his work as a naturalist, Darwin collected natural objects from each place that he visited. For example, in South America, he collected fossils of giant, extinct armadillos. Darwin noticed that these fossils were similar, but not identical, to the living armadillos in the area.

Darwin also visited the Galápagos Islands in the Pacific Ocean. There, he collected several different species of birds called _finches_. Each of the finches are very similar, but differences can be seen in the size and shape of the bill (or beak), such as those shown in **Figure 2.** Each finch has a bill that seems suited to the finch's usual food.

Darwin noticed that many of the islands' plants and animals were similar, but not identical, to the plants and animals he saw in South America. Later, Darwin proposed that the Galápagos species had descended from species that came from South America. For example, he suggested that all of the finch species descended from one ancestral finch species that migrated from South America. Then, the descendant finches were modified over time as different groups survived by eating different types of food. Darwin called such change _descent with modification_. This idea was a key part of his theory.

Years of Reflection After returning from his voyage at the age of 27, Darwin spent years studying his data. He also continued studying many sciences. As he studied, his confidence grew stronger that evolution must happen. But Darwin did not report his ideas about evolution until much later. Instead, he took time to gather more data and to form a strong explanation for how evolution happens.

READING TOOLBOX

Key-Term Fold On the back half of your key-term fold, under each flap, write your own definition for the key terms in this section.

artificial selection the human practice of breeding animals or plants that have certain desired traits

Figure 2 Darwin eventually learned that all Galápagos finch species were similar to each other and to one particular South American finch. ❯ **What explanation did Darwin propose for this similarity?**

Cactus finch
eats insects and cactus

Warbler finch
eats small insects

Large ground finch
eats large seeds

Breeding and Selection Darwin took interest in the practice of breeding, especially the breeding of exotic pigeons. He bred pigeons himself and studied the work of those who bred other kinds of animals and plants, such as dogs, orchids, and food crops. Eventually, Darwin gained a new insight: breeders take advantage of natural variation in traits within a species. If a trait can be inherited, breeders can produce more individuals that have the trait. Breeders simply select individuals that have desirable traits to be the parents of each new generation. Darwin called this process **artificial selection** because the selection is done by humans and not by natural causes.

❯ **Reading Check** *When did Darwin first see evidence of evolution?*

ACADEMIC VOCABULARY

insight a clear understanding of something

Why It Matters

Breeding

REAL WORLD

The power of artificial selection can be seen today in the amazing variety of pets, show animals, and agricultural food crops. For example, more than 400 breeds of dogs exist today, from tiny Chihuahuas to Great Danes. All of these breeds, including wolves, are considered part of the same species (*Canis lupus*) because most can interbreed.

Dog Diversity

People have lived with dogs—or the wolf ancestors of dogs—throughout history. Over time, people learned to selectively breed dogs by choosing certain individuals to become parents. People have selected dogs that have various kinds of physical and behavioral traits. So today, each breed of dog is known for its appearance as well as its degree of playfulness, friendliness, watchfulness, or cleverness. Some breeds are also known for certain quirks or problems.

Quick Project Visit a local pet store, and ask which breeds are most popular or most expensive. Ask why.

QuickLab

⏱ 15 min

Two Kinds of Growth

Can you visualize the difference between linear growth and exponential growth?

Procedure

1. Place **grains of rice** in the cups of an **egg carton** in the following sequence: Place one grain in the first cup. Place two grains in the second cup. Place three grains in the third cup. In each of the remaining cups, place *one more* grain of rice than in the cup before.

2. Use a line graph to graph the results of step 1.

3. Repeat step 1, but use the following sequence: Place one grain in the first cup, two in the second cup, and four in the third cup. In each remaining cup, place twice as many grains as placed in the cup before.

4. Use a line graph to graph the results of step 3.

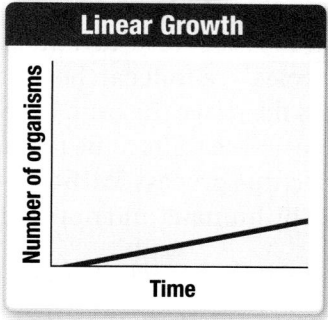

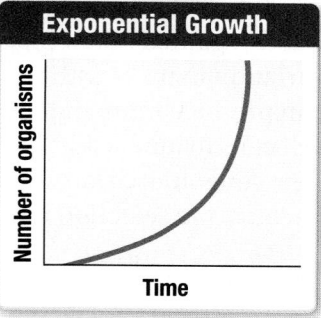

Analysis

1. **Match** your graphs to the graphs shown.

2. **CRITICAL THINKING** **Analyzing Terminology** Linear growth is also called *arithmetic growth,* and exponential growth is also called *geometric growth.* Propose an explanation for the use of these terms.

Darwin's Ideas from Others

In Darwin's time, most people—including scientists—believed that each species was created once and stayed the same forever. But this view could not explain fossils of organisms that no longer exist, such as dinosaurs. Some scientists tried to explain such observations by saying that species could die out but never change. Others, including Darwin's own grandfather, proposed various mechanisms to explain how species may change over time. ❯ **Darwin was influenced by ideas from the fields of natural history, economics, and geology.** The ideas of Lamarck, Malthus, Cuvier, and Lyell were especially important.

Lamarckian Inheritance In 1809, the French scientist Jean Baptiste Lamarck proposed an explanation for how organisms may change over generations. Like Darwin and others, Lamarck noticed that each organism is usually well adapted to its environment. He proposed, as Darwin would later, that organisms change over time as they adapt to changing environments.

However, Lamarck had an incorrect idea about inheritance. He proposed that changes due to use or disuse of a characteristic would be passed on to offspring. For example, he knew that a person's muscles may decrease in size because of disuse or may increase in size because of use, as shown in **Figure 3.** He believed that offspring inherited these kinds of changes. This idea was eventually disproved, but not in Darwin's time. Darwin once accepted this idea because it proposed a role for inheritance in evolution.

Figure 3 According to Lamarck's idea of inheritance, this baseball player's children would inherit strong arm muscles. ❯ **Why was this idea important to Darwin?**

Population Growth Another key influence on Darwin's thinking about evolution was an essay by Thomas Malthus. In 1798, this English economist observed that human populations were increasing faster than the food supply. Malthus pointed out that food supplies were increasing *linearly*. More food was being produced each year, but the amount by which the food increased was the same each year. In contrast, the number of people was increasing *exponentially*. More people were added each year than were added the year before. Malthus noted that the number of humans could not keep increasing in this way, because many people would probably die from disease, war, or famine.

Darwin simply applied Malthus's idea to all populations. Recall that a *population* is all of the individuals of the same species that live in a specific place. Darwin saw that all kinds of organisms tend to produce more offspring than can survive. So, all populations must be limited by their environments.

Geology and an Ancient Earth In Darwin's time, scientists had become interested in the study of rocks and landforms, and thus began the science of *geology*. In particular, scientists such as Georges Cuvier, James Hutton, and Charles Lyell studied fossils and rock layers, such as those shown in **Figure 4.** Cuvier argued that fossils in rock layers showed differences in species over time and that many species from the past differed from those of the present. But Cuvier did not see species as changing gradually over time. He thought that changes in the past must have occurred suddenly.

Hutton and Lyell, on the other hand, thought that geologic processes—such as those that wear away mountains and form new rocks and fossils—work gradually and constantly. Lyell carefully and thoroughly presented his ideas in a book, which Darwin read. Lyell's ideas fit well with Darwin's observations and showed that Earth's history was long enough for species to have evolved gradually.

> **Reading Check** *What idea did Darwin and Lamarck once share?*

Figure 4 Layers of rock contain evidence of changes occurring over millions of years in organisms and environments on Earth. Darwin realized that such evidence supported his ideas about evolution.

SC*I*LINKS.

www.scilinks.org
Topic: Charles Darwin
Code: HX80262

Section 1 Review

KEY IDEAS

1. **Describe** Darwin's relationship to modern evolutionary theory.
2. **Identify** personal experiences that contributed to Darwin's thinking about evolution.
3. **Identify** other scientists that influenced Darwin's thinking.

CRITICAL THINKING

4. **Applying Process Concepts** Darwin observed that artificial selection can produce specific traits. Suppose a farmer has a corn crop in which each ear of corn has some yellow kernels and some white kernels. Describe how the farmer could produce a variety of corn that has all white kernels.

METHODS OF SCIENCE

5. **Scientific Testing** According to Lamarck's idea of inheritance, an individual that developed an improved trait within its lifetime, especially through repeated use, could pass that trait on to its offspring. Propose a way to test the accuracy of this idea.

Key Ideas	Key Terms	Why It Matters
❯ What does Darwin's theory predict? ❯ Why are Darwin's ideas now widely accepted? ❯ What were the strengths and weaknesses of Darwin's ideas?	natural selection adaptation fossil homologous	The principles of evolution are used daily in medicine, biology, and other areas of modern life to understand, predict, and develop advancements in each area.

Darwin applied Malthus's idea to all species. Every living thing has the potential to produce many offspring, but not all of those offspring are likely to survive and reproduce.

Evolution by Natural Selection

Darwin formed a key idea: Individuals that have traits that better suit their environment are more likely to survive. For example, the insect in **Figure 5** is less likely to be seen (and eaten) than a brightly colored insect is. Furthermore, individuals that have certain traits tend to produce more offspring than others do. These differences are part of **natural selection.** Darwin proposed that natural selection is a cause of evolution. In this context, *evolution* is a change in the inherited characteristics of a population from one generation to the next.

Steps of Darwin's Theory Darwin's explanation is often called the *theory of evolution by natural selection.* ❯ **Darwin's theory predicts that over time, the number of individuals that carry advantageous traits will increase in a population.** As shown in **Figure 6,** this theory can be summarized in the following four logical steps:

Step ❶ Overproduction Every population is capable of producing more offspring than can possibly survive.

Step ❷ Variation Variation exists within every population. Much of this variation is in the form of inherited traits.

Step ❸ Selection In a given environment, having a particular trait can make individuals more or less likely to survive and have successful offspring. So, some individuals leave more offspring than others do.

Step ❹ Adaptation Over time, those traits that improve survival and reproduction will become more common.

Figure 5 This insect is well adapted to its environment. ❯ **How does Darwin's theory help explain this observation?**

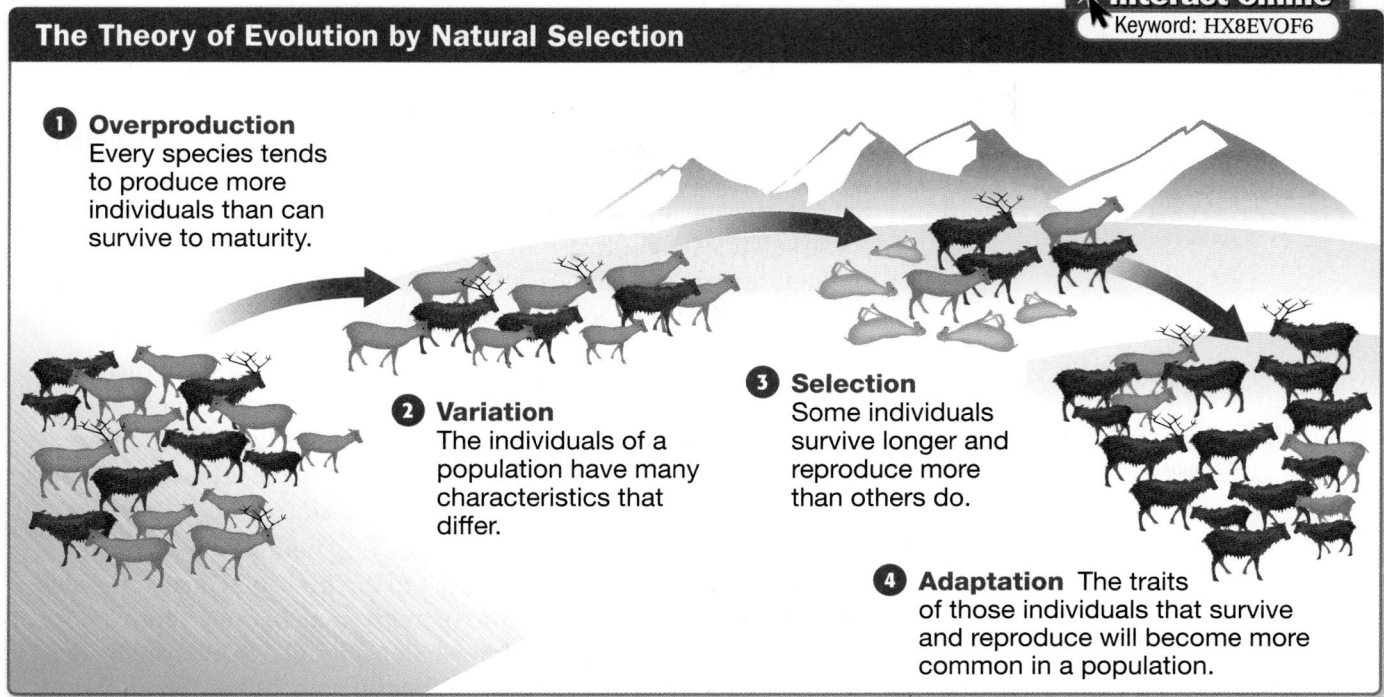

The Theory of Evolution by Natural Selection

❶ **Overproduction** Every species tends to produce more individuals than can survive to maturity.

❷ **Variation** The individuals of a population have many characteristics that differ.

❸ **Selection** Some individuals survive longer and reproduce more than others do.

❹ **Adaptation** The traits of those individuals that survive and reproduce will become more common in a population.

Figure 6 Darwin proposed a logical process by which evolution may occur.
❯ **Can this process act on individuals?**

Selection and Adaptation Darwin's theory explains why living things vary in form yet seem to fit their environment. Each habitat presents unique challenges and opportunities to survive and reproduce. So, each species evolves because of the "selection" of those individuals that survive the challenges or make best use of the opportunities. Put another way, each species becomes *adapted* to its environment as a result of living in it over time. An **adaptation** is an inherited trait that is present in a population because the trait helps individuals survive and reproduce in a given environment.

In sum, Darwin's theory explains evolution as a gradual process of adaptation. Note that Darwin's theory refers to *populations* and *species*—not *individuals*—as the units that evolve. Also, keep in mind that a species is a group of populations that can interbreed.

Publication of the Theory In 1844, Darwin finally wrote an outline of his ideas about evolution and natural selection. But he showed it only to a few scientists that he knew well. He was afraid that his ideas would be controversial. Then in 1858, he received a letter from another young English naturalist named Alfred Russel Wallace. Wallace asked for Darwin's opinion on a new theory—a theory much like Darwin's! Because of this similarity, Darwin and Wallace jointly presented their ideas to a group of scientists. Darwin was finally motivated to publish a full book of his ideas within the next year.

Darwin's book *On the Origin of Species by Means of Natural Selection* presented evidence that evolution happens and offered a logical explanation of how it happens. Biologists began to accept that evolution occurs and that natural selection helps explain it.

❯ **Reading Check** *Is natural selection the same thing as evolution?*

Hypothesis or Theory? Why isn't Darwin's explanation simply called *the theory of evolution*? Why isn't it called a *hypothesis*?

natural selection the process by which individuals that are better adapted to their environment survive and reproduce more successfully than less well adapted individuals do

adaptation a trait that improves an organism's ability to survive and reproduce; the process of becoming adapted

What Darwin Explained

Darwin's book was more than an explanation of his theory. It also included a thorough presentation of the evidence that living species evolved from organisms that lived in the past. Darwin had studied much of the data that was available in his time. ❯ **Darwin presented a unifying explanation for data from multiple fields of science.** Today, these sciences include geology, geography, ecology, developmental biology, anatomy, genetics, and biochemistry. Scientists continue to draw upon the power of Darwin's explanations.

The Fossil Record Have you ever looked at a series of historical maps of a city? You can <u>infer</u> that buildings and streets have been added, changed, or destroyed over time. Similarly, you can infer past events by looking at **fossils,** traces of organisms that lived in the past. All fossils known to science make up the *fossil record*.

Sometimes, comparing fossils and living beings reveals a pattern of gradual change from the past to the present. Darwin noticed these patterns, but he was aware of many gaps in the patterns. For example, Darwin suggested that whales might have evolved from a mammal that lived on land. But at the time, no known fossils were "in between" a land mammal and a whale.

fossil the trace or remains of an organism that lived long ago, most commonly preserved in sedimentary rock

ACADEMIC VOCABULARY

infer to derive by reasoning

Figure 7 Darwin once hypothesized that modern whales evolved from ancient, four-legged, land-dwelling, meat-eating mammals. Over the years since, scientists have collected a series of fossil skeletons that support this hypothesis.

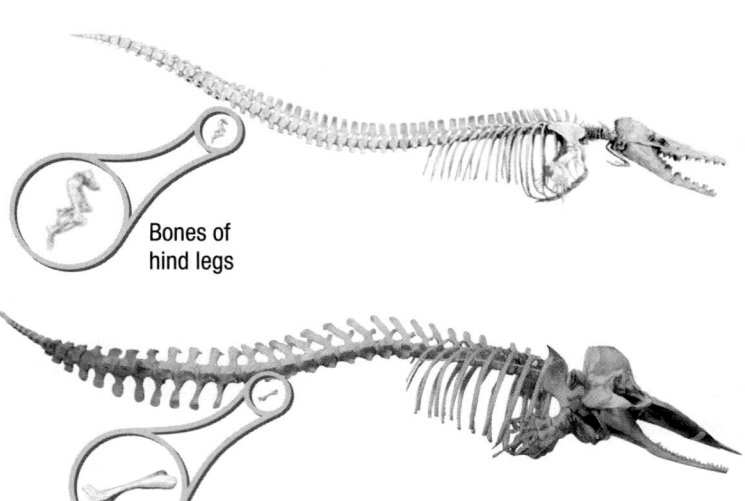

Bones of hind legs

Hip bones

❶ *Pakicetus* (PAK uh SEE tuhs) Scientists think that whales evolved from land-dwelling mammals such as those in the genus *Pakicetus*. The fossil skeleton of a pakicetid is shown here. These mammals lived about 50 million years ago, walked or ran on four legs, and ate meat.

❷ *Ambulocetus* (AM byoo loh SEE tuhs) Mammals of this genus lived in coastal waters about 49 million years ago. These mammals could swim by kicking their legs and using their tail for balance. They could also use their short legs to waddle on land. They breathed air through their mouth.

❸ *Dorudon* (DOHR oo DAHN) Mammals of this genus lived in the oceans about 40 million years ago. They resembled giant dolphins in the way that they swam and breathed. They had tiny hind limbs that were of no use in swimming.

❹ Modern Whales All modern whales have forelimbs that are flippers used for swimming. No whales have hind legs, but some toothed whales have tiny hipbones. All modern whales must come to the surface of the water to breathe through a hole at the top of their head.

Rhea (South America)

Ostrich (Africa)

Emu (Australia)

Darwin predicted that *intermediate forms* between groups of species might be found. And indeed, many new fossils have been found, such as those shown in **Figure 7.** But the conditions that create fossils are rare, so we will never find fossils of every species that ever lived. The fossil record will grow but will never be complete.

Biogeography *Biogeography* is the study of the locations of organisms around the world. When traveling, Darwin and Wallace saw evolution at work when they compared organisms and environments. For example, Darwin saw the similarity of the three species of large birds in **Figure 8.** He found each bird in a similar grassland habitat but on a separate continent. This finding was evidence that similar environments shape the evolution of organisms in similar ways.

Sometimes, geography separates populations. For example, a group of organisms may become separated into two groups living on two different islands. Over time, the two groups may evolve in different patterns. Generally, geologists and biologists have found that the movement of landforms in Earth's past helps to explain patterns in the types and locations of both living and fossil organisms.

Developmental Biology The ancestry of organisms is also evident in the ways that multicellular organisms develop from embryos. The study of such development is called *embryology.* This study is interesting because embryos undergo many physical and genetic changes as they develop into mature forms.

Scientists may compare the embryonic development of species to look for similar patterns and structures. Such similarities most likely derive from an ancestor that the species have in common. For example, at some time during development, all vertebrate embryos have a tail. *Vertebrates* are animals that have backbones.

❯ **Reading Check** *Why is the fossil record incomplete?*

Figure 8 Three unique bird species are shown here. Each of these is similar in size, shape, eating habits, and habitat. However, each species lives on a separate continent. ❯ **What does this pattern suggest about evolution?**

www.scilinks.org
Topic: Fossil Record
Code: HX80615

Figure 9 Although they look very different from one another on the outside, the forelimbs of most tetrapods (vertebrates that have four limbs) include a similar group of bones. ❯ **What hypothesis does this observation support?**

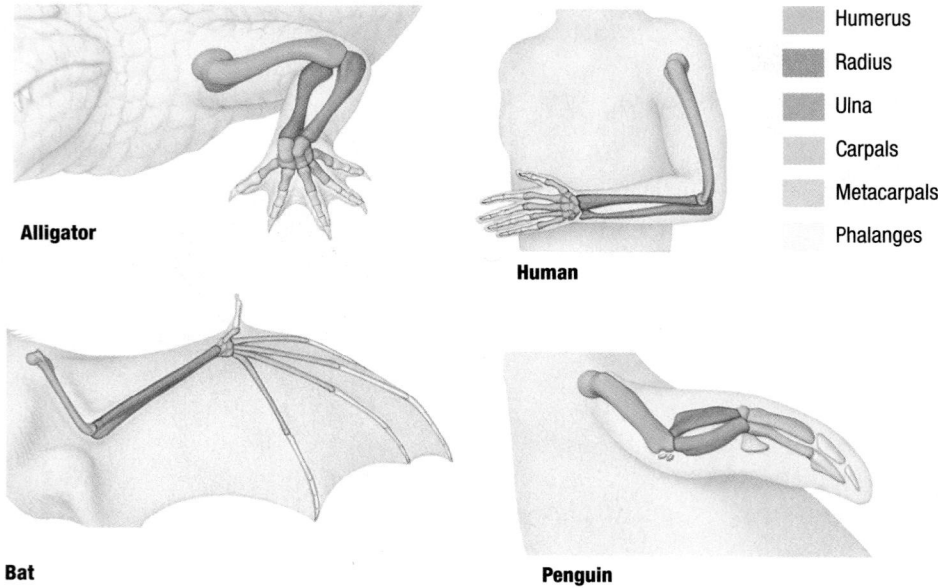

Humerus
Radius
Ulna
Carpals
Metacarpals
Phalanges

Alligator

Human

Bat

Penguin

Hemoglobin Comparison	
Animal with hemoglobin	Amino acids that differ from human hemoglobin
Gorilla	1
Rhesus monkey	8
Mouse	27
Chicken	45
Frog	67
Lamprey	125

Figure 10 Scientists have compared the amino acids that make up hemoglobin proteins in several species. Organisms that have fewer differences are more likely to be closely related. ❯ **How does this pattern relate to genetic change?**

Anatomy Another place to observe the results of evolution is inside the bodies of living things. The bodily structure, or *anatomy,* of different species can be compared. Many internal similarities are best explained by evolution and are evidence of how things are related.

For example, the hypothesis that all vertebrates descended from a common ancestor is widely accepted. Observations of the anatomy of both fossil and living vertebrates support this hypothesis. When modern vertebrates are compared, the difference in the size, number, and shape of their bones is clear. Yet the basic pattern of bones is similar. In particular, the forelimbs of many vertebrates are composed of the same basic groups of bones, as **Figure 9** shows. This pattern of bones is thought to have originated in a common ancestor. So, the bones are examples of **homologous** structures, characteristics that are similar in two or more species and that have been inherited from a common ancestor of those species.

Biochemistry To explain the patterns of change seen in anatomy, scientists make testable predictions. For example, if species have changed over time, the genes that determine their characteristics should also have changed. Recall that genes can change by mutation and that such change can make new varieties appear. Then, natural selection may "select against" some varieties and so "favor" others.

Scientists have observed that genetic changes occur over time in all natural populations. A comparison of DNA or amino-acid sequences shows that some species are more genetically similar than others. These comparisons, like those in anatomy, are evidence of hereditary relationships among the species. For example, comparing one kind of protein among several species reveals the pattern shown in **Figure 10.** The relative amount of difference is consistent with hypotheses based on fossils and anatomy.

❯ **Reading Check** *What explains similarities in bone structure?*

Evaluating Darwin's Ideas

Why was Darwin such an important scientist? ❯ **Darwin's work had three major strengths: evidence of evolution, a mechanism for evolution, and the recognition that variation is important.** Today, Darwin is given credit for starting a revolution in biology.

Strengths Darwin was *not* the first to come up with the idea that evolution happens, but he was the first to gather so much evidence about it. He described his most famous book as "one long argument" that evolution is possible. Before publishing, Darwin collected and organized many notes, observations, and examples, such as the illustration shown in **Figure 11.** So, one strength of Darwin's work is that it is supported by, and helps explain, so much data.

Darwin also presented a logical and testable mechanism that could account for the process of evolution. His theory of natural selection was well thought out and convincing to scientists of his time as well as today. It has since become a foundation of biology.

Finally, Darwin changed the way scientists thought about the diversity of life. Before Darwin, most scientists saw species as stable, unchanging things. They classified species based on average appearances and ignored variation. But Darwin showed that variation was everywhere and could serve as the starting point for evolution.

Weaknesses Darwin's explanations were incomplete in one major way: He knew very little about genetics. ❯ **Inherited variation was crucial to Darwin's theory of natural selection, yet his theory lacked a clear mechanism for inheritance.** At different times, Darwin proposed or accepted several ideas for such a mechanism, but none of them were correct. He thought about this problem for much of his life.

Darwin never knew it, but Gregor Mendel had begun to solve this problem. However, Mendel's findings about heredity were not widely published until 1900. Those findings opened the door to a new age in the study of evolution. Today, an understanding of genetics is essential to understanding evolution.

❯ **Reading Check** *What did Darwin do before publishing his ideas?*

Figure 11 This drawing of a rhea was printed in one of Darwin's books. Darwin collected and organized a large amount of data to help explain his ideas. ❯ **How else did Darwin support his main theory?**

homologous (hoh MAHL uh guhs) describes a character that is shared by a group of species because it is inherited from a common ancestor

---

Section 2 Review

❯ **KEY IDEAS**

1. **Outline** Darwin's theory of evolution by natural selection. Be sure to include four logical steps.
2. **List** the kinds of data that Darwin helped explain.
3. **Compare** the strengths and weaknesses of Darwin's ideas.

CRITICAL THINKING

4. **Applying Information** Use the theory of natural selection to explain how the average running speed of a population of zebras might increase over time.
5. **Elaborating on Explanations** Describe how a single pair of seed-eating bird species could have arrived on an island and evolved into an insect-eating species. (Hint: Consider the food available.)

USING SCIENCE GRAPHICS

6. **Process Cartoon** Create your own version of **Figure 6** in the form of a four-panel cartoon. Choose a unique type of organism to represent the population undergoing natural selection. Also, depict a unique set of traits and limiting conditions for the population.

Key Ideas	Key Terms	Why It Matters
❯ How has Darwin's theory been updated? ❯ At what scales can evolution be studied?	speciation	The study of evolution was new in Darwin's day, but it is essential to biology today.

Does modern evolutionary theory differ from Darwin's theory? Yes and no. Darwin observed and explained much about the large-scale patterns of biology, but some patterns have yet to be explained. He proposed a logical process (natural selection) for evolution, even though he could not explain evolution at the genetic level. Biology has made great progress since Darwin's time. Modern evolutionary theory relates patterns and processes at many levels.

Darwin's Theory Updated

Since Darwin's work was published, his theory has been thoroughly investigated. ❯ **Discoveries since Darwin's time, especially in genetics, have been added to his theory to explain the evolution of species.** Some parts of Darwin's theory have been modified, and new parts have been added. But mostly, Darwin's theory has been supported.

The first major advance beyond Darwin's ideas was the rediscovery, in 1900, of Mendel's *laws of heredity*. These ideas opened the door for a genetic explanation of evolution. By the 1940s, scientists began to weave Darwin's theory together with newer studies of fossils, anatomy, genetics, and more. This unification is called the *modern synthesis* of evolutionary theory.

In particular, biologists have learned that evolution can result from processes other than natural selection. For example, survival and reproduction can be limited by chance or by the way that genes work. In the modern view, any or all of these forces may combine with natural selection (as described by Darwin). This synthesis helps explain some of the patterns of evolution that were unexplained by natural selection alone.

Remaining Questions Some of the most important questions about evolution have been asked only recently. So, many questions are still being investigated, as shown in **Figure 12.** Modern biologists have tentative answers to the following questions:

• **Can an individual evolve?** Darwin correctly inferred that individuals do not evolve. They may respond to outside forces, but individuals do not pass on their responses as heritable traits. Rather, populations evolve when natural selection acts (indirectly) on genes.

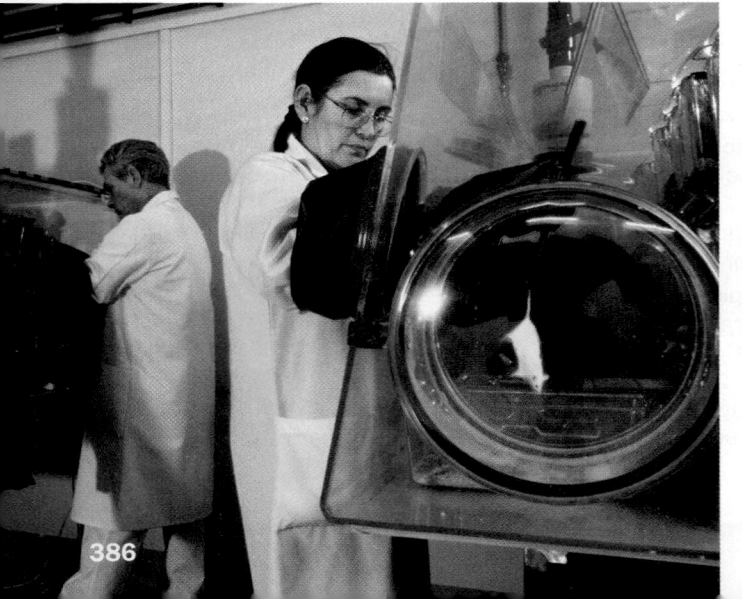

Figure 12 Modern genetic science and Darwin's theory have been united. ❯ **How could this genetic scientist study evolution?**

Hands-On
QuickLab

15 min

Selection Model

In this lab, you will model the process of natural selection. Can you predict the outcome?

Procedure

1. Work with a partner. Spread out a handful of small, colored candies onto a piece of cloth or paper that has a colorful design. One person should act as "predator" of the candies while the other uses a stopwatch to monitor time and then records the results.

2. The "predator" should use tweezers to try to "capture" as many candies as possible within 10 s.

3. Record the results, and switch roles. Repeat 10 times.

Analysis

1. **Graph** the total number of each color of candy that was "captured." Use a bar graph.

2. **CRITICAL THINKING** **Evaluating Results** Explain why some colors were "captured" more often than others.

3. **CRITICAL THINKING** **Forming Hypotheses** Predict the outcome if the background is changed to solid red.

- **Is evolution the survival of the fittest?** Natural selection can act only on the heritable variation that exists in a population. Chance variations do not always provide the best adaptation for a given time and place. So, evolution does not always produce the "fittest" forms, just those that "fit" well enough to leave offspring.

- **Is evolution predictable?** Evolution sometimes results in larger or more-complex forms of life, but this result cannot be predicted. Many forms of life are simple yet successful. For example, bacteria have been abundant for billions of years. In contrast, some complex organisms, such as dinosaurs, have appeared, been successful for a time, and then almost completely disappeared. Mostly, scientists cannot predict the exact path that evolution will take.

Studying Evolution at All Scales

> Because it affects every aspect of biology, scientists can study evolution at many scales. Generally, these scales range from microevolution to macroevolution, with speciation in between. Informally, *microevolution* refers to evolution as a change in the genes of populations, whereas *macroevolution* refers to the appearance of new species over time.

Speciation The link between microevolution and macroevolution is speciation. **Speciation,** the formation of new species, can be seen as a process of genetic change or as a pattern of change in the form of organisms. Recall that a *species* is a group of organisms that are closely related and that can mate to produce fertile offspring. So, speciation can begin with the separation of populations of the same species. For example, the two kinds of squirrels shown in **Figure 13** seem to be evolving from one species into two because of separation.

> **Reading Check** *At what scales can evolution be studied?*

speciation (SPEE shee AY shuhn) the formation of new species as a result of evolution

Figure 13 These squirrels are closely related but are almost different enough to be unique species. Their populations are separated by the Grand Canyon.

SECTION 3 Beyond Darwinian Theory **387**

ACADEMIC VOCABULARY

random without aim or plan; purposeless

Processes of Microevolution

To study microevolution, we look at the processes by which inherited traits change over time in a population. Five major processes can affect the kinds of genes that will exist in a population from generation to generation. These processes are summarized below. Notice that natural selection is only one of the five. You will learn more about these processes soon.

- **Natural Selection** As you have learned, natural selection can cause an increase or decrease in certain alleles in a population.

- **Migration** *Migration* is the movement of individuals into, out of, or between populations. Migration can change the numbers and types of alleles in a population.

- **Mate Choice** If parents are paired up randomly in a population, a <u>random</u> assortment of traits will be passed on to the next generation. However, if parents are limited or selective in their choice of mates, a limited set of traits will be passed on.

- **Mutation** Mutation can change the numbers and types of alleles from one generation to the next. However, such changes are rare.

- **Genetic Drift** The random effects of everyday life can cause differences in the survival and reproduction of individuals. Because of these differences, some alleles may become more or less common in a population, especially in a small population.

Patterns of Macroevolution

To study macroevolution, we look at the patterns in which new species evolve. We may study the direction, diversity, or speed of change. Patterns of change are seen when relationships between living and fossil species are modeled.

- **Convergent Evolution** If evolution is strongly directed by the environment, then species living in similar environments should evolve similar adaptations. Many examples of this pattern were observed by Darwin and can be seen today.

- **Coevolution** Organisms are part of one other's environment, so they can affect one another's evolution. Species that live in close contact often have clear adaptations to one another's existence, as shown in **Figure 14.**

Figure 14 This moth species and this orchid species have coevolved in a close relationship. The moth feeds exclusively on the orchid, and the orchid's pollen is spread by the moth.

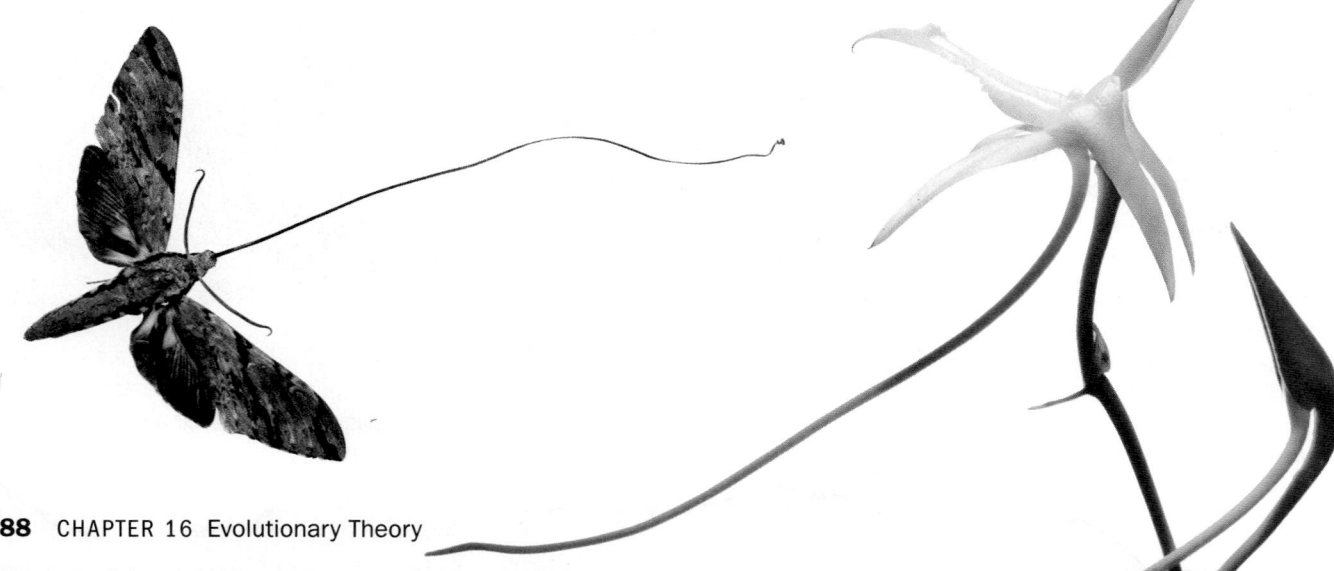

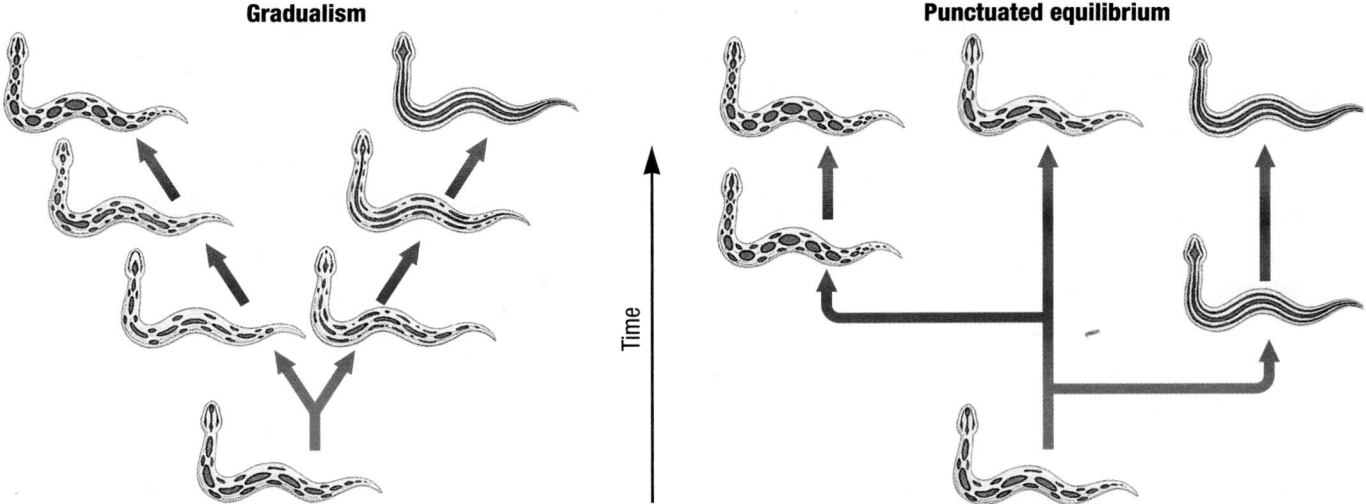

Gradualism

Punctuated equilibrium

Time

- **Adaptive Radiation** Over time, species may split into two or more lines of descendants, or *lineages*. As this splitting repeats, one species can give rise to many new species. The process tends to speed up when a new species enters an environment that contains few other species. In this case, the pattern is called *adaptive radiation*.

- **Extinction** If all members of a lineage die off or simply fail to reproduce, the lineage is said to be *extinct*. The fossil record shows that many lineages have arisen and radiated, but only a few of their descendants survived and evolved into the species present today.

- **Gradualism** In Darwin's day, the idea of slow, gradual change was new to geology as well as biology. Darwin had argued that large-scale changes, such as the formation of new species, must require many small changes to build up gradually over a long period of time. This model is called *gradualism* and is shown in **Figure 15.**

- **Punctuated Equilibrium** Some biologists argue that species do not always evolve gradually. Species may remain stable for long periods until environmental changes create new pressures. Then, many new species may "suddenly" appear. This model is called *punctuated equilibrium* and is shown in **Figure 15.**

Figure 15 Two differing models of the pace of evolution have been proposed. ❯ **Do these models show microevolution or macroevolution?**

READING TOOLBOX

Taking Notes Complete your notes summarizing the major concepts from this chapter. Be sure to include microevolution and macroevolution.

Section 3 Review

❯ **KEY IDEAS**

1. **Describe** how Darwin's ideas have been updated. Be sure to mention the role of natural selection in modern evolutionary theory.

2. **List** the scales at which evolution can be studied, and list the patterns and processes studied.

CRITICAL THINKING

3. **Arguing Logically** A classmate states that because land animals evolved from fishes and then flying things evolved from walking things, we can predict that future life will evolve to travel in outer space. Write a logical argument against this statement. Be sure to support your argument with examples.

ALTERNATIVE ASSESSMENT

4. **Who's Who** Make a brochure or poster entitled "Who's Who of Evolutionary Theory." Use reference sources to find basic facts about major evolutionary scientists that lived during or after Darwin's lifetime.

Chapter 16 **Lab**

Objectives

> Model natural selection.

> Relate favorable mutations to selection and evolution.

Materials

- construction paper
- meterstick or tape measure
- scissors
- cellophane tape
- soda straws
- marker, felt-tip
- penny or other coin
- die, six-sided

Safety

Natural Selection Simulation

In this lab, you will use a paper model of a bird to model the selection of favorable traits in a new generation. This imaginary bird, the Egyptian origami bird (*Avis papyrus*), lives in dry regions of North Africa. Imagine that the birds must fly long distances between water sources in order to live and reproduce successfully.

Procedure

Model Parental Generation

1 Cut a sheet of paper into two strips that are 2 cm × 20 cm each. Make a loop with one strip of paper. Let the paper overlap by 1 cm, and tape the loop closed. Repeat for the other strip.

2 Tape one loop 3 cm from one end of the straw and one loop 3 cm from the other end, as pictured. Use a felt-tip marker to mark the front end of the "bird." This bird represents the parental generation.

3 Test how far your parent bird can fly by releasing it with a gentle overhand pitch. Test the bird twice. Record the bird's average flight distance in a data table like the one shown.

Model First (F₁) Generation

4 Each origami bird lays a clutch of three eggs. Assume that one of the chicks is identical to the parent. Use the parent data to fill in your data table for the first new chick (Chick 1).

5 Make two more chicks (Chick 2 and Chick 3). Assume that these chicks have mutations. Follow Steps A through C for each chick to determine the effects of each mutation.

Data for All Generations									
Bird	Coin flip (H or T)	Die throw (1-6)	Anterior wing (cm)			Posterior wing (cm)			Average distance flown (m)
			Width	Circum.	Distance from front	Width	Circum.	Distance from back	
Parent	NA	NA	2	19	3	2	19	3	
Generation 1									
Chick 1									
Chick 2									
Chick 3									
Generation 2									
Chick 1									

Step A Flip a coin to find out which end is affected by the mutation.

  Heads = Front wing is affected.

  Tails = Back wing is affected.

Step B Throw a die to find out how the mutation affects the wing.

  ⚀ = Wing position moves 1 cm toward the end of the straw.

  ⚁ = Wing position moves 1 cm toward the middle.

  ⚂ = Wing circumference increases by 2 cm.

  ⚃ = Wing circumference decreases by 2 cm.

  ⚄ = Wing width increases by 1 cm.

  ⚅ = Wing width decreases by 1 cm.

Step C If a mutation causes a wing to fall off the straw or makes a wing's circumference smaller than the circumference of the straw, the chick cannot "survive." If such a mutation occurs, record it as "lethal," and then produce another chick.

6 For each new chick, record the mutation and the new dimensions of each wing.

7 Test each bird twice by releasing it with a gentle overhand pitch. Release the bird as uniformly as possible. Record the distance that each bird flies. The most successful bird is the one that flies the farthest.

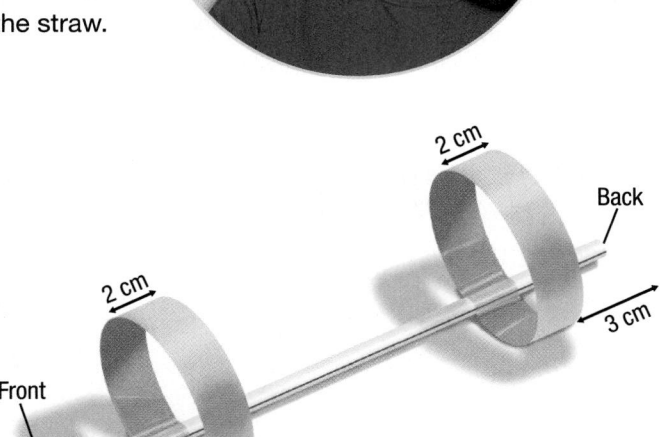

Model Subsequent Generations

8 Assume that the most successful bird in the previous generation is the sole parent of the next generation. Using this bird, repeat steps 4–7.

9 Continue to produce chicks and to test and record data for eight more generations.

Clean Up and Dispose

10 Clean up your work area and all lab equipment. Return lab equipment to its proper place. Dispose of paper scraps in the designated waste container. Wash your hands thoroughly before you leave the lab and after you finish all work.

Analyze and Conclude

1. Summarizing Results Describe any patterns in the evolution of the birds in your model.

2. Evaluating Models How well does this lab model natural biological processes? What are the limitations of this model?

3. Analyzing Data Compare your data with your classmates' data. Identify any similarities and differences. Try to explain any trends that you notice in terms of the theory of natural selection.

Extensions

4. Design an Experiment Propose a new hypothesis about natural selection that you could test by observing real organisms. Write a brief proposal describing an experiment that could test this hypothesis. Be sure to give your prediction, explain your methods, identify variables, and plan for control groups.

go.hrw.com
SUPER SUMMARY
Keyword: HX8EVOS

Key Ideas	Key Terms

1 Developing a Theory

> Modern evolutionary theory began when Darwin presented evidence that evolution happens and offered an explanation of how evolution happens.

> Darwin's experiences provided him with evidence of evolution at work.

> Darwin was influenced by ideas from the fields of natural history, economics, and geology.

evolution (375)
artificial selection (377)

2 Applying Darwin's Ideas

> Darwin's theory of evolution by natural selection predicts that over time, the number of individuals that carry advantageous traits will increase in a population.

> Darwin presented a unifying explanation for data from multiple fields of science.

> The strengths of Darwin's work—evidence of evolution, a mechanism for evolution, and the recognition that variation is important—placed Darwin's ideas among the most important of our time. However, Darwin lacked a mechanism for inheritance.

natural selection (380)
adaptation (381)
fossil (382)
homologous (384)

3 Beyond Darwinian Theory

> Discoveries since Darwin's time, especially in genetics, have been added to his theory to explain the evolution of species.

> Because it affects every aspect of biology, scientists can study evolution at many scales. Generally, these scales range from microevolution to macroevolution, with speciation in between.

speciation (387)

1. **Hypothesis or Theory?** Explain why Darwin's theory is not *the* theory of evolution.

2. **Concept Map** Make a concept map that describes the origins of Darwin's theory. Try to include the following words: *Darwin, ideas, evolution, experience, others, travels, reflection, breeding, Lamarck, Malthus,* and *Lyell.*

Using Key Terms

3. Explain the difference between the terms *natural selection* and *artificial selection.*

4. Use the following terms in the same sentence: *macroevolution, microevolution,* and *speciation.*

For each of the following terms, write a definition in your own words.

5. *evolution*

6. *homologous structures*

Understanding Key Ideas

7. After studying plant and animal life in South America and the Galápagos Islands, Darwin proposed that
   a. Galápagos species had descended from South American species.
   b. South American species had descended from Galápagos species.
   c. Galápagos species and South American species were unrelated.
   d. Galápagos species and South American species had descended from European species.

8. Darwin was influenced by Malthus's ideas about
   a. inheritance.   c. the fossil record.
   b. populations.   d. natural history.

9. Which of the following is a form of biochemical evidence that can be used to study evolution?
   a. speciation.
   b. intermediate forms.
   c. homologous structures.
   d. amino-acid similarities.

10. Which of the following was a weakness in Darwin's ideas about evolution?
   a. lack of evidence for evolution
   b. lack of a mechanism for evolution
   c. lack of a mechanism for inheritance of traits
   d. lack of recognition of the importance of variation

11. Modern evolutionary theory has incorporated most of Darwin's ideas except
   a. Darwin's laws of heredity.
   b. Darwin's theory of natural selection.
   c. Darwin's idea that species evolve gradually.
   d. Darwin's predictions of intermediate forms.

This image shows several species of finches that are related by evolution. Species 1 is from South America. Species 2–5 live in the Galápagos Islands. Use the image to answer the following question.

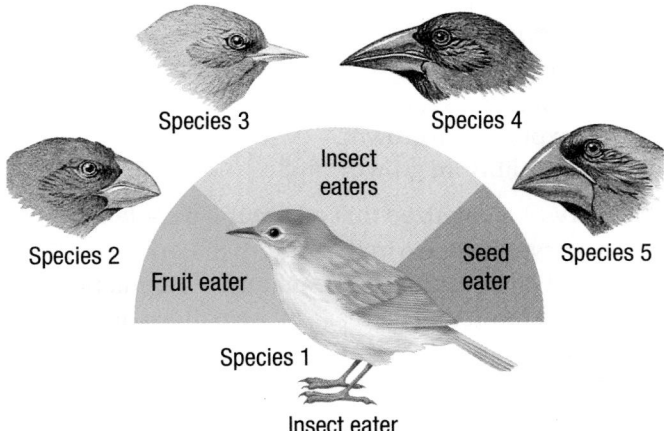

12. The ancestor of all Galápagos finches was probably
   a. a fruit eater.   c. a fish eater.
   b. a seed eater.   d. an insect eater.

Explaining Key Ideas

13. **Describe** the relationship between Darwin's ideas and modern evolutionary theory.

14. **List** the four steps of evolution by natural selection.

15. **Explain** how biogeography provides evidence for the influence of environment on evolution.

16. **Identify** two mechanisms other than natural selection that can affect the relative ratios of traits in populations of organisms.

Using Science Graphics

This graph shows the population growth of two different populations over the same period of time. Use the graph to answer the following question(s).

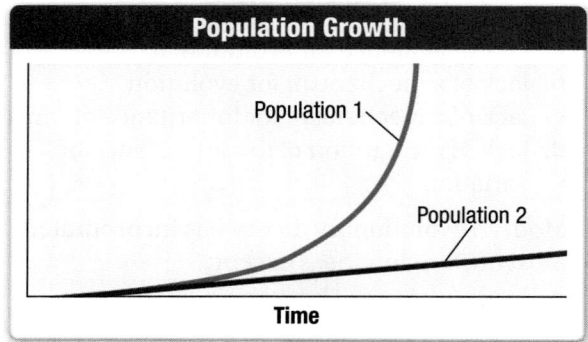

Population Growth

Population 1

Population 2

Time

17. From the graph, it is evident that Population 1 underwent
   a. no growth.
   b. linear growth.
   c. exponential growth.
   d. equilibrium growth.

18. From the graph, it is evident that Population 2 underwent
   a. no growth.
   b. linear growth.
   c. exponential growth.
   d. equilibrium growth.

19. Darwin recognized that all natural populations
   a. never increase in the pattern of Population 2.
   b. always increase in the pattern of Population 1.
   c. are limited to increase in the pattern of Population 2.
   d. have the potential to increase in the pattern of Population 1.

Critical Thinking

20. Criticizing an Argument According to Lamarck's ideas about inheritance, people who developed large muscles would pass on those large muscles directly to their offspring. Use another example to show that this conclusion cannot be correct.

21. Explaining Processes Propose a series of steps by which a pair of insect-eating birds could arrive on an island and then evolve into several species, each specializing on a different kind of food.

22. Analyzing Language Explain why the phrase "survival of the fittest" is misleading.

23. Explaining Relationships Why might there be more variation in a population in which individuals mate with random partners each mating season than in a population in which pairs of individuals mate for life?

Why It Matters

24. Applying Concepts Describe how relationships between humans and wolves in ancient history may have led to modern domestic dogs.

25. Quick Project Conduct a survey among any dog owners you know. Ask what breed of dog they have, if the breed is known. Also ask what traits, if any, influenced their selection of this breed.

Alternative Assessment

26. Lyrics Create a song, rap, or poem that explains the difference between everyday uses of the word *theory* and the scientific meaning of the word.

Writing for Science

27. Letter to Scientific Peers Pretend that you are Charles Darwin. Write a letter to one of the people who influenced your ideas about evolution (Lamarck, Malthus, Cuvier, or Lyell). Explain to that person how his ideas helped you understand how organisms evolve.

Math Skills

28. Compound Interest An example of exponential growth is a bank account that earns interest. Often, interest is added once per year, and the new total earns more interest the next year. Thus, the interest is *compounded* each year. The equation for this kind of interest is:

$$P = C(1 + r)^t$$

where P is the future value, C is the initial deposit, r is the interest rate (expressed as a decimal), and t is the number of years invested. Suppose you open an account with an initial deposit of $100.00 and a simple annual interest of 10% (or 0.10). This account would have $110.00 after one year and $121.00 after 2 years. Calculate the account balance over 10 years, and then draw a graph of this growth.

TEST TIP Watch out for words that qualify or put conditions on an answer option, such as "only," "always," "some," or "most." These qualifiers are important clues to choosing the correct answer.

Science Concepts

1. Which of the following is the best definition of a scientific theory?
   A a group of ideas about a scientific concept
   B an explanation that is accepted by most people
   C an explanation that has been scientifically tested and supported
   D a specific question that can be tested using the scientific method

2. In forming his theory of evolution, Darwin most lacked an adequate understanding of
   F geology.   H anatomy.
   G heredity.   J geography.

3. An inherited trait that helps an individual survive and reproduce in a particular environment is
   A an adaptation.   C a genetic trait.
   B a survival trait. D natural variation.

4. A human arm and a bat wing are each made up of a similar number and arrangement of bones. This similarity is evidence that humans and bats
   F evolved at the same time.
   G have the same parents.
   H have an ancestor in common.
   J once shared the same habitat.

5. Which of the following is a true statement about evolution?
   A Individuals cannot evolve, but populations can evolve.
   B Natural selection is the only mechanism for evolution.
   C Evolution always results in more complex forms of life.
   D Organisms always evolve to have the best adaptations for their environment.

Using Science Graphics

This diagram shows two contrasting models of the pace of evolution. Use the diagram to answer the following question(s).

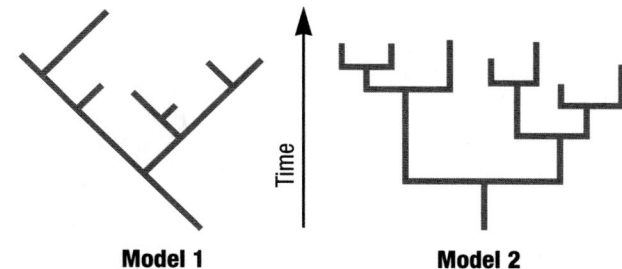

Model 1   Model 2

6. Model 1 is usually referred to as the model of
   F selection.
   G gradualism.
   H adaptive radiation.
   J punctuated equilibrium.

7. Model 2 is usually referred to as the model of
   A selection.
   B selectionism.
   C artificial selection.
   D punctuated equilibrium.

8. In Model 1, each point where one line splits into two lines represents
   F selection.   H adaptation.
   G speciation.   J punctuation.

This table shows the differences between the human hemoglobin protein and that of some animals. Use the table to answer the following question(s).

Animal with hemoglobin	Amino acids that differ from human hemoglobin
Mouse	27
Chicken	45
Frog	67
Lamprey	125

9. These data support the hypothesis that among the animals listed, the animal that is most closely related to humans by ancestry is the
   A mouse.   C frog.
   B chicken.   D lamprey.

Chapter 17

Population Genetics and Speciation

Preview

1 Genetic Variation
Population Genetics
Phenotypic Variation
Measuring Variation and Change
Sources of Genetic Variation

2 Genetic Change
Equilibrium and Change
Sexual Reproduction and Evolution
Population Size and Evolution
Natural Selection and Evolution
Patterns of Natural Selection

3 Speciation
Defining Species
Forming New Species
Extinction: The End of Species

Why It Matters

The fields of ecology, genetics, and evolutionary theory are brought together to understand how genetic changes in populations result in changes to species over time.

Every population, such as this group of banded wood snails, contains variation. Some of this variation can be seen, but much is hidden in DNA.

Physical variation in these snails includes variation in shell coloration, number of stripes, shell size, and shell thickness. Each trait may affect the survival and reproduction of individual snails.

Banding patterns can give the snails camouflage protection against predators, especially birds. Each pattern may provide better camouflage in some seasons or locations than in others.

Inquiry **Lab**

Normal Variation

Variation is normal and is evident in all populations. Just look down.

Procedure

1. Read step 2, and prepare a table for the class data.

2. Use a **ruler or tape-measure** to measure the length of one of **your shoes** to the nearest centimeter. Record this number, as well as your shoe size and gender. Share these data with the class.

3. Make a table of the shoe lengths of everyone in your class. In the first column, record the name of each student. In the second column, record each shoe length.

4. Make a tally of the numbers of each shoe size in your class.

Analysis

1. **Compare** the table that you made in step 3 to the tally that you made in step 4.

2. **Describe** how the table you made in step 3 could be converted into a tally like that of step 4.

3. **Propose** additional methods by which these kinds of data could be collected and analyzed.

4. **Predict** how the tally that you made in step 4 would change if the data for males were deleted.

Banded wood snails (also called *grovesnails*) eat plant parts and are very common in gardens and moist habitats.

READING TOOLBOX

These reading tools can help you learn the material in this chapter. For more information on how to use these and other tools, see **Appendix: Reading and Study Skills.**

Using Words

Everyday Words in Science Many words that we use every day have special meanings in science. For example, *matter* in everyday use is a topic, issue, or problem. In science, *matter* is the substance of which all things are made.

Your Turn Make a table like the one shown here.
1. Before you read, write in your own words the everyday meaning of the terms in the table.
2. As you read, fill in the scientific meaning for the terms in the table.

Everyday Words in Science

Word	Everyday Meaning	Science Meaning
normal		
distribution		
drift		
fitness		

Using Language

General Statements A general statement often summarizes the features of a group or describes an average or typical feature of members of the group. But if many features are summarized, some individuals in the group probably do not share all of those features. And if an average feature is described, some members of the group will not match the average. So, general statements may be true most of the time, but not always.

Your Turn Use what you know about general statements to complete the following tasks.
1. Write a general statement about apples, bananas, tomatoes, and peanuts.
2. List exceptions to the statement "Humans are bigger than monkeys."

Taking Notes

Outlining Outlining is a note-taking skill that helps you organize information. An outline can give you an overview of the topics in a chapter and help you understand how the topics are related.

Your Turn Create outlines for each section of this chapter. Start with the example shown here.
1. Copy all of the headings for a section, in order, on a piece of paper.
2. Leave plenty of space between each heading.
3. As you read the material under each heading of a section, write the important facts under that heading on your outline.

> Population Genetics and Speciation
> Genetic Variation
>   Population Genetics
>   Phenotypic Variation
>   Measuring Variation and Change
>   Studying Alleles
>   Allele Frequencies
>   Sources of Genetic Variation
> Genetic Change
>   Equilibrium and Change

Genetic Variation

Key Ideas	Key Terms	Why It Matters
❯ How is microevolution studied? ❯ How is phenotypic variation measured? ❯ How are genetic variation and change measured? ❯ How does genetic variation originate?	**population genetics** **normal distribution**	Without variation, evolution cannot occur.

One of Charles Darwin's contributions to biology was his careful study of variation in characteristics, such as the many flower colors shown in **Figure 1.** As you have learned, Darwin knew that heredity influences characteristics, but he did not know about genes. We now know a great deal about genes. We are able to study and predict the relationships between genotypes and phenotypes. We can also study the genetic variation and change that underlie evolution.

Population Genetics

Recall that evolution can be studied at different scales, from that of microevolution to macroevolution. And recall that *microevolution* is evolution at the level of genetic change in populations.
❯ **Microevolution can be studied by observing changes in the numbers and types of alleles in populations.** The study of microevolution in this sense is **population genetics**. Thus, the studies of genetics and evolution are advancing together. Furthermore, the link from microevolution to macroevolution—*speciation*—can be studied in detail.

❯ **Reading Check** *What do we now know about heredity that Darwin did not know? (See the Appendix for answers to Reading Checks.)*

population genetics the study of the frequency and interaction of alleles and genes in populations

Figure 1 Genetic variation is found in all living things and forms the basis on which evolution acts. ❯ **What kinds of variation can be seen in this photograph?**

Phenotypic Variation

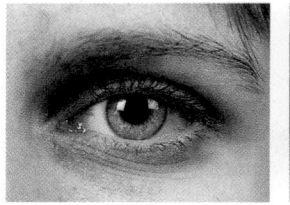
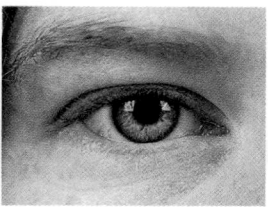
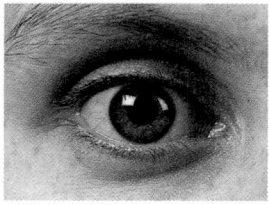
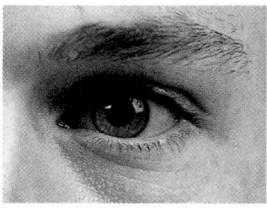
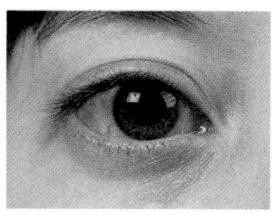

Figure 2 Eye color is a polygenic character. Different genes control different pigments, which combine to produce various shades of blue, green, or brown.

Before anyone understood genetics, the only kind of variation that could be observed and measured was phenotypic variation. Gregor Mendel was the first to suspect that some kind of inherited units determined the various phenotypes that he observed. (In Mendel's day, the term *phenotype* was not used.) We now know that the inherited units are alleles. Mendel used his data on phenotypes to mathematically deduce the ratio of alleles in each individual. Today, we call these ratios *genotypes*.

Mendel's work was made simple by the fact that he studied pea plants with only two phenotypes for each character. As you have learned, genetics is rarely so simple. For example, listing every possible phenotype for height in humans would be difficult. If you compare many humans, you find a range of possible heights, with many slight variations.

The variety of phenotypes that exist for a given character depends on how many genes affect that character. Recall that a character that is influenced by several genes is a *polygenic* character. Human height and human eye color, for example, are polygenic. Polygenic characters may exist as a variety of traits, as shown in **Figure 2,** or a range of trait values, as shown in **Figure 3.**

❯ Biologists study polygenic phenotypes by measuring each individual in the population and then analyzing the distribution of the measurements. A *distribution* is an overview of the relative frequency and range of a set of values. Mathematically, a distribution is a tally or a histogram with a smooth line to show the overall pattern of the values.

Often, some values in a range are more common than others. For example, suppose that you were to collect one shoe from each student in your class. If you ordered and grouped the shoes by size, you would probably form a hill-shaped curve such as the one shown in **Figure 3.** This pattern of distribution is called a **normal distribution** or a *bell curve.* "Normal" in this case simply means a tendency to cluster around an average value (mean, median, or mode).

Figure 3 Measurements of characters that have a wide range of variation, such as shoe size, can be arranged into a histogram and are likely to form a bell curve. ❯ **How do the number of genes for a character relate to its variation?**

❯ **Reading Check** *Why do polygenic characters vary so much?*

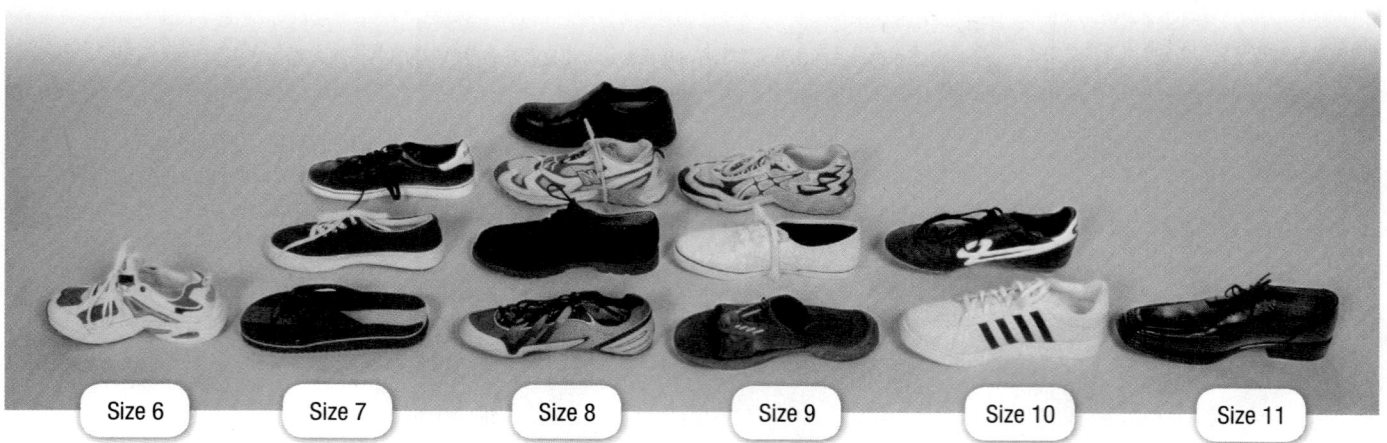

Size 6   Size 7   Size 8   Size 9   Size 10   Size 11

Suppose that you were to measure the height of every student in your school. You would probably gather a wide range of data. The best way to graph this data would be to use a histogram. A *histogram* is a special kind of bar graph for displaying a range of values. The histogram clearly shows the range of values as well as the values that are most common.

To make a histogram, list the values in order from smallest to largest. Then, determine the *range* from the smallest value to the largest. Draw the *x*-axis of the histogram to cover this range. Then, group the values into convenient intervals. For example, values for height in meters could be grouped into intervals of 0.2 m each, as shown here.

Next, count the number of values that fall within each interval. (Hint: Making a tally of the counts is helpful.) Draw the *y*-axis of the histogram to allow for the highest count in any one interval. Finally, draw bars to show the count for each interval. The bars should touch each other because the graph is showing a continuous range of data.

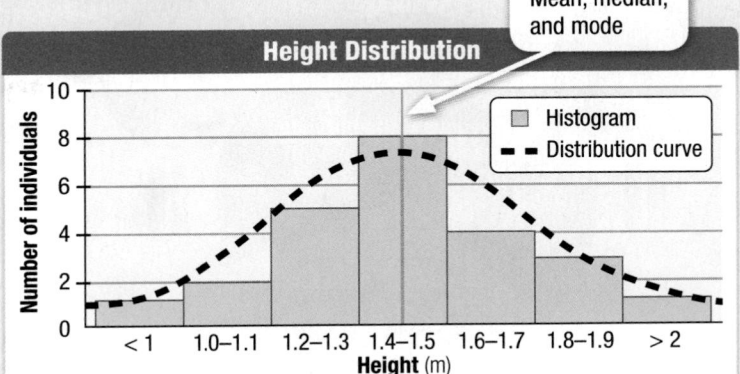

You can use math software to make a histogram and further analyze these kinds of data. For example, you can "fit a curve" to the data, adding a line through the bars to show the general shape, or *distribution*, of the data. You can group the data into smaller or larger intervals, or add or subtract values, and then see changes in the shape of the curve. Finally, you can find the mean, median, and mode(s) of the data. A *normal distribution* will have similar values for the mean, median, and mode.

Measuring Variation and Change

To study population genetics, we need to study how genes in populations change over time. To measure these changes, we must look at how alleles are passed on from generation to generation as organisms mate and produce offspring. The particular combination of alleles in a population at any one point in time makes up a *gene pool*.

Studying Alleles To study genetic variation, we need to estimate the number of alleles in a population. For characters with simple Mendelian inheritance, we can estimate by using simple math combined with our knowledge of genetics. For example, we may start by counting the number of individuals in the population and recording the phenotype of each. Then, we can deduce each genotype.

As you have learned, to keep track of alleles, we can represent alleles with letters. For example, a particular gene may have two alleles, R and r. In addition, we represent genotypes as combinations of alleles. So, if two alleles exist for a particular gene, then there are three genotypes: RR, Rr, and rr. To compare the numbers of alleles or genotypes, we measure or calculate the frequency of each. ❯ **Genetic variation and change are measured in terms of the frequency of alleles in the gene pool of a population.** A *frequency* is the proportion or ratio of a group that is of one type.

❯ **Reading Check** *What is the main measure of genetic variation?*

normal distribution a line graph showing the general trends in a set of data of which most values are near the mean

Everyday Words in Science The word *normal* in science and math is often used to describe measurements that fit within a normal distribution. What does a doctor mean when talking about "normal height" for a person of your age?

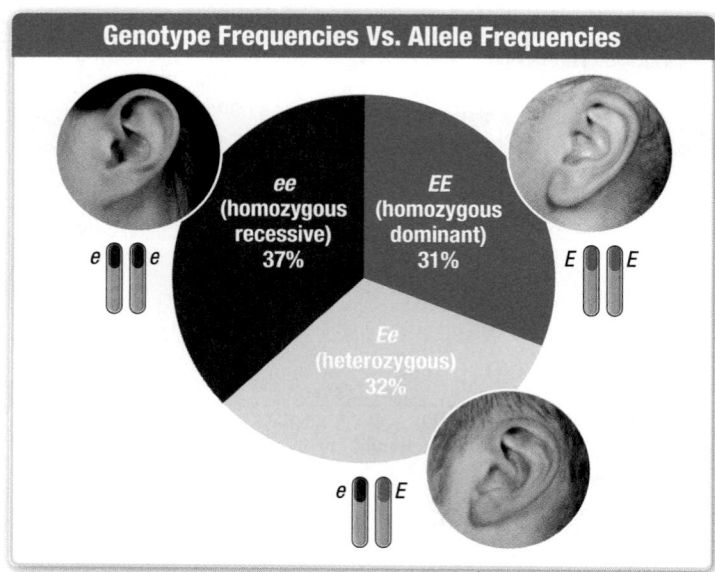

Genotype Frequencies Vs. Allele Frequencies

ee (homozygous recessive) 37%

EE (homozygous dominant) 31%

Ee (heterozygous) 32%

e | e

E | E

e | E

Figure 4 You cannot see alleles, and you cannot always tell genotype based on phenotype. You have to use math and know dominance patterns to calculate allele frequencies. ❯ **Is the dominant allele always the most frequent?**

Tracking Frequencies To study genetic change, biologists want to keep track of the frequency of each allele in a population over time. They can keep track in several ways. A direct way would be to detect and count every allele in every individual, which is rarely practical. An indirect way is to use mathematics along with a knowledge of how alleles combine. Recall that alleles combine to form genotypes that, in turn, produce recognizable phenotypes.

To understand the basic mathematics of allele frequencies, consider the simple example shown in **Figure 4.** Human ear lobes have two phenotypes: unattached (free hanging) or attached at the base. The ear lobe character is thought to be controlled by a single gene, and the unattached trait is thought to be dominant. So, the unattached allele is represented as *E,* and the attached allele is represented as *e.* People with attached ear lobes are homozygous recessive, or genotype *ee.* People with unattached ear lobes are either homozygous dominant (*EE*) or heterozygous (*Ee*).

Genotype Frequencies Notice how genotype frequencies differ from allele frequencies. Suppose that the population in **Figure 4** consists of 100 people. In this case, 37% of the population, or 37 people, are genotype *ee*; 32 are *Ee*; and 31 are *EE*. Keep in mind that in ratios and percentages, all of the parts add up to one whole, or 100%. So, the sum of genotype frequencies in a population should always be equal to 1 (or 100%). This fact leads to the following equation:

(frequency of *EE*) + (frequency of *Ee*) + (frequency of *ee*) = 1

Using the numbers in our example, the equation proceeds as follows:

$$0.31 + 0.32 + 0.37 = 1$$

Allele Frequencies Similarly, the sum of allele frequencies for any gene must equal 1, as in the following equation:

(frequency of *E*) + (frequency of *e*) = 1

or

$$\frac{(\text{count of } E)}{(\text{total})} + \frac{(\text{count of } e)}{(\text{total})} = 1$$

In our example population, there are 94 *E* alleles and 106 *e* alleles, and the total is 200 alleles. The equation proceeds as follows:

$$\frac{94}{200} + \frac{106}{200} = 0.47 + 0.53 = 1$$

As you can see, the frequency of the *E* allele is 0.47, and the frequency of the *e* allele is 0.53. Notice that the dominant allele is not necessarily the most frequent! Also keep in mind that you often cannot tell genotypes by looking at phenotypes. However, you will soon learn how these equations can be used to track changes in populations.

❯ **Reading Check** *What is the sum of all allele frequencies for any one gene?*

QuickLab

⏱ 15 min

Alleles: The Next Generation

Model the allele frequencies in a population over time.

Procedure

1 Work in a group, which will represent a population. Obtain **two colors of marbles (one pair) for each member in the group.** Each color will represent a unique allele. Choose one color to be "dominant."

2 Mix the marbles. Each member of the "population" should randomly take two "alleles." Record the resulting genotype and phenotype of each member.

3 Each member should hide one marble in each hand and then randomly exchange one of these "alleles" with another member. Record the resulting genotypes and phenotypes of each member.

4 Repeat the steps to model four more "generations."

Analysis

1. **Determine** the genotype and phenotype ratios for each "generation." Do the ratios change over time?

2. **Propose** a way to change the ratios in your population from one generation to the next. Propose a way that this change could happen in a real population.

Sources of Genetic Variation

Evolution cannot proceed if there is no variation. As you have learned, this variation must originate as new alleles. ❯ **The major source of new alleles in natural populations is mutation in germ cells.**

Mutation is important, but it generates new alleles at a slow rate. New alleles first arise in populations as changes to DNA in the sperm and ova (called *germ* cells) of individuals. If a germ cell with a mutation goes on to form offspring, then a new allele is added to the gene pool. Mutations can also occur in nongerm cells (called *somatic* cells), but these mutations are not passed on to offspring.

❯ **Reading Check** *Why is mutation so important?*

ACADEMIC VOCABULARY

generate produce; bring into being; cause to be

Section 1 Review

❯ **KEY IDEAS**

1. **Describe** the scope of population genetics.

2. **Explain** how polygenic phenotypes are studied.

3. **Describe** how genetic variation and change can be measured.

4. **Identify** the major source of genetic variation in a population.

CRITICAL THINKING

5. **Analyzing Concepts** Even in cases of simple Mendelian inheritance within a population, the ratio of phenotypes of a specific character is rarely the same as the ratio of alleles for that character. Explain why these ratios differ.

6. **Applying Logic** Can an individual organism evolve in the Darwinian sense? Explain your answer in terms of genetic variation within populations.

MATH SKILLS

7. **Distribution Curves** Suppose that **Figure 3** represents the distribution of shoe sizes in a class of twelfth graders. How might the distribution change if the shoes of a class of first graders were added to those of the twelfth graders? Explain your answer.

Genetic Change

Key Ideas	Key Terms	Why It Matters
❯ What does the Hardy-Weinberg principle predict? ❯ How does sexual reproduction influence evolution? ❯ Why does population size matter? ❯ What are the limits of the force of natural selection? ❯ What patterns can result from natural selection?	genetic equilibrium	The mathematics of genetics can be used to make predictions about future generations.

You might think that a dominant trait would always be the most common trait in a population. When biologists began to study population genetics, they found that this was not always true.

Equilibrium and Change

In 1908, the English mathematician G. H. Hardy and the German physician Wilhelm Weinberg began to model population genetics by using algebra and probabilities. They showed that in theory, the frequency of alleles in a population should not change from one generation to the next. Moreover, the ratio of heterozygous individuals to homozygous individuals (the genotype frequencies) should not change. Such a population, in which no genetic change occurred, would be in a state of **genetic equilibrium.**

Measuring Change Genetic change in a population can be measured as a change in genotype frequency or allele frequency. A change in one does not necessarily mean a change in the other. For example, as shown in **Figure 5,** the genotype frequencies changed between generations, but the allele frequencies did not.

Figure 5 Allele frequencies can remain stable while genotype frequencies change.

Allele Frequencies in Two Generations

Genotype frequency	Allele frequency	Generation
RR (red) = 0.5 *Rr* (pink) = 0.5 *rr* (white)= 0	*R* = 0.75 *r* = 0.25	1 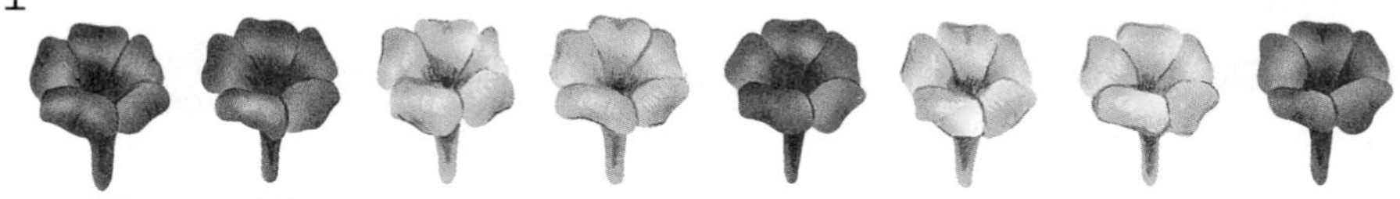 RR RR Rr Rr RR Rr Rr RR
RR (red) = 0.625 *Rr* (pink) = 0.25 *rr* (white)= 0.125	*R* = 0.75 *r* = 0.25	2  RR Rr rr RR RR Rr RR RR

The Hardy-Weinberg principle can be expressed as an equation that can be used to predict stable genotype frequencies in a population.

The equation is usually written as follows:

$$p^2 \quad + \quad 2pq \quad + \quad q^2 \quad = \quad 1$$

(frequency of *RR* individuals)   (frequency of *Rr* individuals)   (frequency of *rr* individuals)   (sum of all frequencies)

Recall that the sum of the genotype frequencies in a population must always equal 1.

By convention, the frequency of the more common of the two alleles is referred to as *p*, and the frequency of the rarer allele is referred to as *q*.

Individuals that are homozygous for allele *R* occur at a frequency of *p* times *p*, or p^2. Individuals that are homozygous for allele *r* occur at the frequency of *q* times *q*, or q^2.

Heterozygotes have one copy of *R* and one copy of *r*, but heterozygotes can occur in two ways—*R* from the father and *r* from the mother, or *r* from the father and *R* from the mother. Therefore, the frequency of heterozygotes is $2pq$.

Hardy-Weinberg Principle Hardy and Weinberg made a mathematical model of genetic equilibrium. This model is the basis of the *Hardy-Weinberg principle.* ❯ The Hardy-Weinberg principle predicts that the frequencies of alleles and genotypes in a population will not change unless at least one of five forces acts upon the population.

Forces of Genetic Change In reality, populations are subject to many forces and undergo genetic change constantly. ❯ The forces that can act against genetic equilibrium are gene flow, nonrandom mating, genetic drift, mutation, and natural selection.

Gene Flow *Gene flow* occurs when genes are added to or removed from a population. Gene flow can be caused by *migration,* the movement of individuals from one population to another, as shown in **Figure 6.** Each individual carries genes into or out of the population, so genetic frequencies may change as a result.

Nonrandom Mating In sexually reproducing populations, any limits or preferences of mate choice will cause nonrandom mating. If a limited set of genotypes mates to produce offspring, the genotype frequencies of the population may change.

Genetic Drift Chance events can cause rare alleles to be lost from one generation to the next, especially when populations are small. Such random effects on allele frequencies are called *genetic drift*. The allele frequencies are changed directly and genotype frequencies change as a result.

Mutation A mutation can add a new allele to a population. Allele frequencies are changed directly, if only slightly.

Natural Selection Natural selection acts to eliminate individuals with certain traits from a population. As individuals are eliminated, the alleles for those traits may become less frequent in the population. Thus, both allele and genotype frequencies may change.

❯ **Reading Check** *What can cause gene flow?*

> **genetic equilibrium** a state in which the allele frequencies of a population remain in the same ratios from one generation to the next

Figure 6 These caribou are migrating from one place to another. If they meet other groups of caribou and interbreed, gene flow may occur.

Figure 7 Sexual selection favors the development of extreme phenotypic traits in some species. The vibrant red stripe on the blue muzzle of this male mandrill baboon does not appear in females.

Figure 8 Alleles are more likely to be lost from smaller populations. So, variation tends to decrease over time in smaller populations but not in larger populations.

go.hrw.com
interact online
Keyword: HX8POPF8

Sexual Reproduction and Evolution

Recall that sexual reproduction creates chances to recombine alleles and thus increase variation in a population. So, sexual reproduction has an important role in evolution. **❯ Sexual reproduction creates the possibility that mating patterns or behaviors can influence the gene pool of a population.** For example, in animals, females sometimes select mates based on the male's size, color, ability to gather food, or other characteristics, as shown in **Figure 7.** This kind of behavior is called *sexual selection* and is an example of nonrandom mating.

Another example of nonrandom mating is *inbreeding*, in which individuals either self-fertilize or mate with others like themselves. Inbreeding tends to increase the frequency of homozygotes, because a smaller pool of alleles is recombined. For example, populations of self-fertilizing plants consist mostly of homozygotes. However, inbreeding does not change the overall frequency of alleles. Inbreeding is more likely to occur if a population is small.

Population Size and Evolution

Population size strongly affects the probability of genetic change in a population. **❯ Allele frequencies are more likely to remain stable in large populations than in small populations.** In a small population, the frequency of an allele can be quickly reduced by a chance event. For example, a fire or drought can reduce a large population to a few survivors. At that point, each allele is carried in a few individuals. The loss of even one individual from the population can severely reduce an allele's frequency. So, a particular allele may disappear in a few generations, as shown in **Figure 8.** This kind of change is called *genetic drift* because allele frequencies drift around randomly. The force of genetic drift is strongest in small populations. In a larger population, alleles may increase or decrease in frequency, but the alleles are not likely to disappear.

❯ Reading Check *What is the genetic effect of inbreeding?*

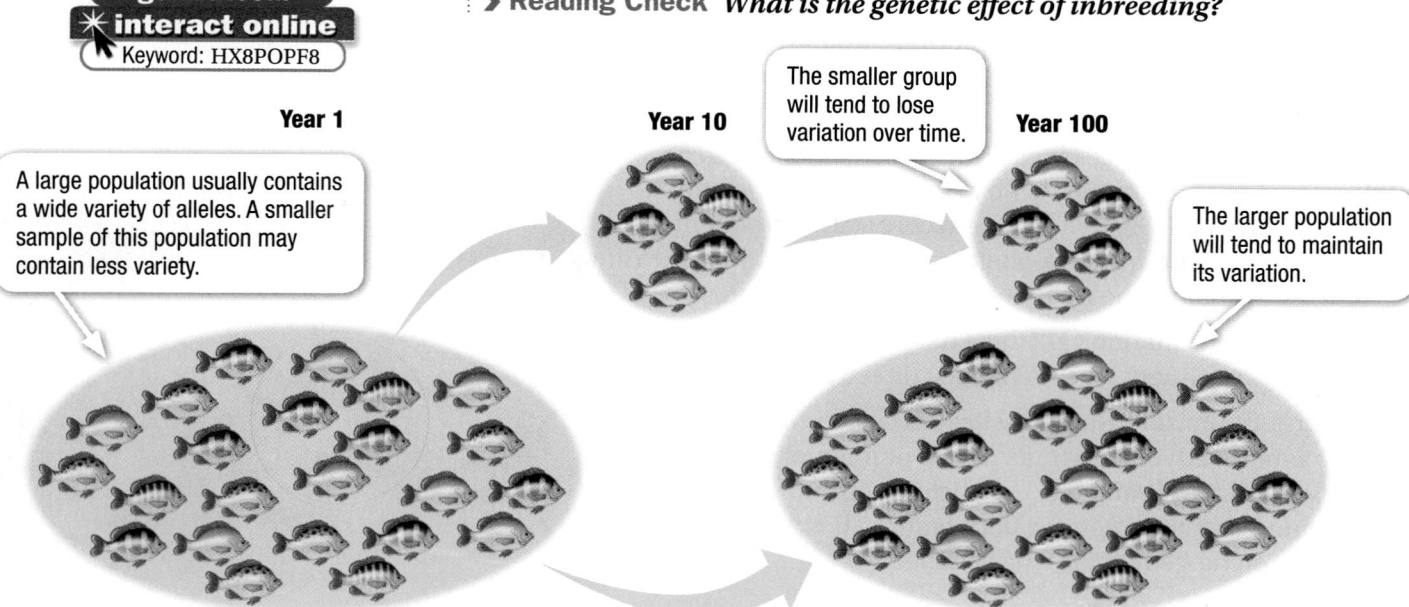

Year 1

Year 10

The smaller group will tend to lose variation over time.

Year 100

A large population usually contains a wide variety of alleles. A smaller sample of this population may contain less variety.

The larger population will tend to maintain its variation.

QuickLab

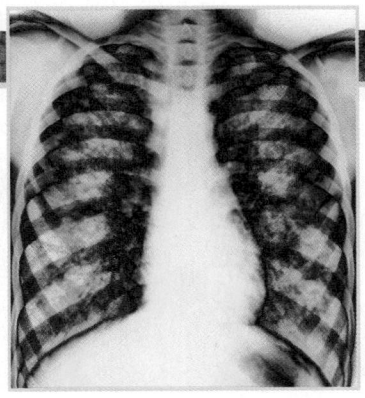

15 min

Genetic Risk Assessment

How can the Hardy-Weinberg equation be used? It can be used to predict the risk of genetic disorders in a population. For example, medical professionals may know how many people have been diagnosed with a genetic disorder. From this information, they can predict how many people are at risk of passing on the disorder.

Lungs of a person with cystic fibrosis

Procedure

❶ Consider these facts: Cystic fibrosis (CF) is a disorder that occurs in 1 out of every 2,500 Caucasians in North America. CF is caused by a recessive allele.

❷ Use the Hardy-Weinberg equation to predict the percentage of carriers of the allele that causes CF.

Analysis

1. **Calculate** the frequency of the recessive allele.

2. **Calculate** the frequency of the dominant allele.

3. **Calculate** the frequency of carriers (heterozygotes).

4. **Determine** how many of every 1,000 Caucasian North Americans are likely to carry the cystic fibrosis allele.

Natural Selection and Evolution

Recall that Charles Darwin proposed natural selection as a mechanism that could drive evolution. Scientists have studied many examples of natural selection in action.

How Selection Acts Keep in mind that the process of natural selection is a result of the following facts.

- **All populations have genetic variation.** Any population has an array of individuals that differ slightly from one another in genetic makeup. Although this variation may be obvious in humans, variation also exists in species whose members may appear identical, such as a species of bacteria.

- **Individuals tend to produce more offspring than the environment can support.** Individuals of a population often struggle to survive, whether competing with one another or not.

- **All populations depend upon the reproduction of individuals.** Some biologists have noted that "evolutionary fitness is measured in grandchildren." The statement means that an individual must survive to reproduce, and also produce offspring that can reproduce, to pass its genes on to future generations.

Genetic Results of Selection The result of natural selection is that the frequency of an allele may increase or decrease depending on the allele's effects on survival and reproduction. Natural selection causes <u>deviations</u> from genetic equilibrium by directly changing the frequencies of alleles. Although natural selection is not the only force of evolution, it is a powerful force.

❯ **Reading Check** *How is "fitness" measured in evolutionary terms?*

SC**LINKS.**
www.scilinks.org
Topic: Natural
Selection
Code: HX81016

ACADEMIC VOCABULARY

deviate to turn aside; to diverge or differ

Figure 9 Crayfish species exist in a variety of colorations. In many cases, the coloration helps the crayfish hide from predators or attract mates. But for crayfish species that live in lightless caves, having color gives no fitness advantage. ❯ **What might happen to a colorless crayfish placed in a well-lit pond?**

READING TOOLBOX

General Statements List possible exceptions to the statement "Natural selection removes unsuccessful phenotypes from a population."

Why Selection Is Limited The key lesson that scientists have learned about evolution by natural selection is that the environment does the selecting. If the environment changes in the future, the set of characteristics that are most adaptive may change. For example, each of the animals shown in **Figure 9** is adapted to a specific environment and may not be able to survive if placed in another environment.

Natural selection is limited by nature. ❯ **Natural selection acts only to change the relative frequency of alleles that exist in a population.** Natural selection cannot direct the creation of new alleles, nor will it necessarily delete every allele that is not adaptive. So, natural selection does not create perfectly adapted organisms.

Indirect Force Natural selection does not act directly on genes. It merely allows individuals who express favorable traits to reproduce and pass those traits on to their offspring. Darwin's idea of natural selection, stated in modern terms, is that ❯ **natural selection acts on genotypes by removing unsuccessful phenotypes from a population.** Biologists say that certain phenotypes are "selected against" and that certain genotypes are thus "favored."

Role of Mutation Think carefully about how natural selection might operate on a new allele that has arisen by mutation. At first, the mutation may make no difference. Even if the mutation results in a nonfunctional protein, the cell may have a functional copy of the original gene as its second allele. However, the new, nonfunctioning version could be passed on as a recessive allele. This kind of mutation is the probable origin of many recessive genetic disorders.

Only characteristics that are expressed can be targets of natural selection. Therefore, selection cannot operate against rare recessive alleles, even if they are unfavorable. A recessive allele must become common before two heterozygous individuals (carriers) are likely to mate and produce homozygous offspring. Only then does natural selection have an opportunity to act. And even then, selection will act only against homozygotes. For this reason, genetic disorders can persist in populations.

❯ **Reading Check** *How can unfavorable alleles persist?*

Patterns of Natural Selection

Recall that many traits, such as human height, have a bell-curve distribution in natural populations. When natural selection acts on polygenic traits, it essentially acts to eliminate some part of the bell curve.

❯ Three major patterns are possible in the way that natural selection affects the distribution of polygenic characters over time. These patterns are directional selection, stabilizing selection, and disruptive selection, as **Figure 10** illustrates.

Directional Selection In *directional selection,* the "peak" of a normal distribution moves in one direction along its range. In this case, selection acts to eliminate one extreme from a range of phenotypes. Thus, the alleles for the extreme phenotype become less common in the population. This pattern of selection is often seen in the evolution of single-gene traits, such as pesticide resistance in insects.

Stabilizing Selection In *stabilizing selection,* the bell-curve shape becomes narrower. In this case, selection eliminates individuals that have alleles for any extreme type. So, the ratio of intermediate phenotypes increases. In other words, this pattern of selection tends to "stabilize" the average by favoring a narrow range of phenotypes. Stabilizing selection is very common in nature.

Disruptive Selection In *disruptive selection,* the bell curve is "disrupted" and pushed apart into two peaks. In this case, selection acts to eliminate individuals with average phenotype values. Each peak is pushed in an opposite direction, away from the average. The result is increasingly distinct or variable phenotypes in the population. Mathematically, the new distribution is said to have two mode values, each of which differs from the mean value.

❯ **Reading Check** *Which form of selection increases the range of variation in a distribution?*

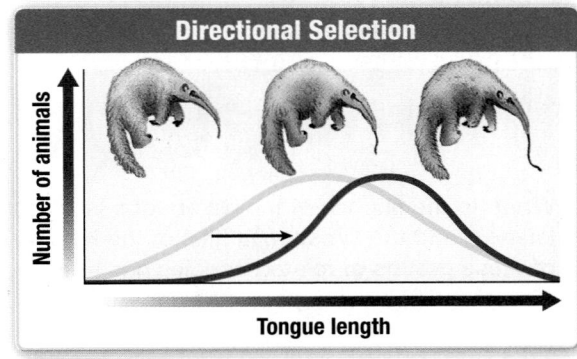

Directional Selection

Number of animals

Tongue length

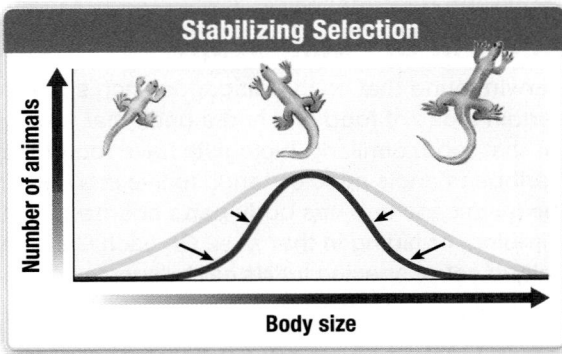

Stabilizing Selection

Number of animals

Body size

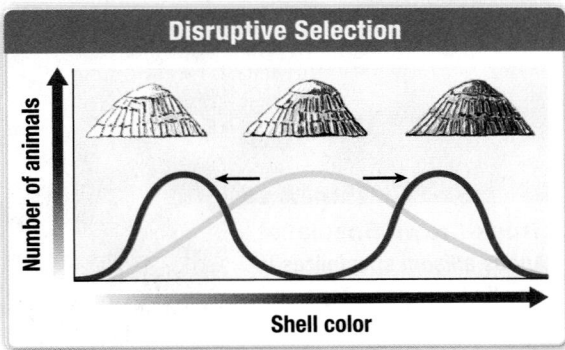

Disruptive Selection

Number of animals

Shell color

Figure 10 Selection can shift a distribution from an original bell curve (green) toward a new shape (purple).

Section 2 Review

❯ KEY IDEAS

1. **Restate** the Hardy-Weinberg principle in your own terms.
2. **Relate** sexual reproduction to evolutionary forces.
3. **Explain** why a small population is subject to genetic drift.
4. **Describe** the limits of the force of natural selection.
5. **List** the patterns that can result from natural selection acting on polygenic traits.

CRITICAL THINKING

6. **Comparing Concepts** In what way is the genetic effect of nonrandom mating similar to the genetic effect of gene flow?
7. **Reasoning Opinions** Are all organisms perfectly adapted for their habitat? Explain.

USING SCIENCE GRAPHICS

8. **Prediction** Redraw each of the graphs in **Figure 10.** Use as examples birds with a range of beak sizes. Describe possible situations that would cause each pattern of selection.

Wild Laboratories

REAL WORLD

What do the finches of the Galápagos Islands, the anole lizards of the Caribbean Islands, and the *Drosophila* flies of the Hawaiian Islands have in common? Each of these groups of related species has been extensively studied by evolutionary biologists. And each group has undergone a similar pattern of evolution on each group of islands.

Roles in the Landscape

Darwin found that each Galápagos finch species ate certain types of food and had a beak that was adapted for that food. Similarly, biologists have found that each Caribbean anole species tends to live in a certain part of the landscape and has body parts adapted for running, climbing, or hiding in that area. On each Caribbean island, a unique set of species fulfills each "specialist" role.

Trunk-Ground Specialist *Anolis lineatopus* specializes in running along tree trunks and the ground.

Trunk-Crown Specialist *Anolis allisoni* specializes in crawling along the tops and trunks of tropical plants.

Twig Specialist *Anolis angusticeps* specializes in clinging to twigs.

Quick Project Find out how many species of anoles have been identified in the Carribbean islands as compared with the total number of anole species worldwide. Likewise, find out the number of Hawaiian species of flies in the family Drosophilidae.

Grass-Bush Specialist *Anolis bahorucoensis* specializes in clinging to grass and stems.

Section 3 Speciation

Key Ideas
> How can species be defined?

> How do we know when new species have been formed?

> Why is studying extinction important to understanding evolution?

Key Terms
reproductive isolation
subspecies

Why It Matters
How we define species relates to how we study evolution and ecology.

All of the beetles in **Figure 11** belong to the same species, but each looks different. Identifying species or telling species apart is often difficult. Part of the difficulty lies in the very definition of *species*.

Defining Species

Since the days of Darwin, scientists have understood that species are not permanent, stable things. And thanks to Mendel, scientists have learned that genetics underlie the variation and change in species. With this knowledge, they have reconsidered the very definition of *species*. > Today, scientists may use more than one definition for *species*. The definition used depends on the organisms and field of science being studied. Increasingly, scientists want to do more than name and describe things—they want to know how things are related.

As you have learned, a *species* is generally defined as a group of natural populations that can interbreed. This definition is based on the *biological species concept*, which adds the requirement that the interbreeding produce healthy, fertile offspring. Applying this concept, any populations that do not share future offspring could be considered separate species.

However, the biological species concept cannot be applied to all organisms. It does not apply to those that reproduce asexually or that are known only from fossils. And any form of reproduction may be difficult to confirm. So, species may instead be defined based on their physical features, their ecological roles, and their genetic relatedness.

> **Reading Check** *Why is a species hard to define?*

Figure 11 How many species of beetles are in this photo? Just one!
> What problems arise when defining species based on appearances?

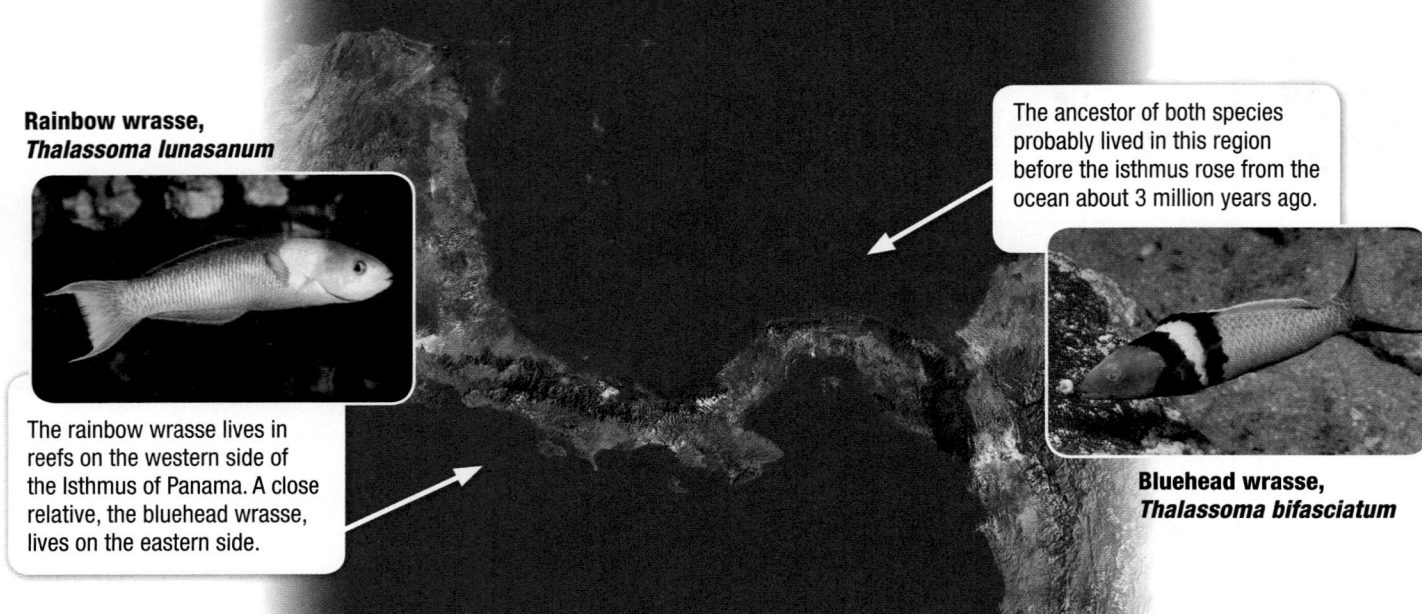

Rainbow wrasse,
Thalassoma lunasanum

The rainbow wrasse lives in reefs on the western side of the Isthmus of Panama. A close relative, the bluehead wrasse, lives on the eastern side.

The ancestor of both species probably lived in this region before the isthmus rose from the ocean about 3 million years ago.

Bluehead wrasse,
Thalassoma bifasciatum

Figure 12 These two species probably evolved from a single species that was separated into two groups by geographic change. ❯ **What other mechanisms can isolate species?**

reproductive isolation a state in which a population can no longer interbreed with other populations to produce future generations

subspecies a taxonomic classification below the level of species; refers to populations that differ from, but can interbreed with, other populations of the same species

Forming New Species

Each population of a single species lives in a different place. In each place, natural selection acts on the population and tends to result in offspring that are better adapted to the environment. If the environments differ, the adaptations may differ. The accumulation of differences between populations is called *divergence* and can lead to the formation of new species.

Recall that *speciation* is the process of forming new species by evolution from preexisting species. Speciation rarely occurs overnight; it usually occurs in stages over generations. ❯ **Speciation has occurred when the net effects of evolutionary forces result in a population that has unique features and is reproductively isolated.**

Reproductive Isolation Recall that the biological species concept defines species as interbreeding groups. Thus, if two groups stop interbreeding, they take a step toward speciation. **Reproductive isolation** is a state in which two populations can no longer interbreed to produce future offspring. From this point on, the groups may be subject to different forces, so they will tend to diverge over time.

Through divergence over time, populations of the same species may differ enough to be considered subspecies. **Subspecies** are simply populations that have taken a step toward speciation by diverging in some detectable way. This definition is imprecise because reproductive isolation is only apparent after the passage of time.

Mechanisms of Isolation Divergence and speciation can happen in many ways. Any of the following mechanisms may contribute to the reproductive isolation of populations.

• **Geography** A physical barrier, such as the one shown in **Figure 12,** may arise between populations. Such a barrier could prevent interbreeding. Over time, if the populations diverge enough, they will probably not interbreed even if the barrier is removed.

- **Ecological Niche** Recall that the *niche* of a species is the role that the species has in its environment, including all of its interactions with other species. Divergence can occur when populations use different niches. The divergence of multiple lineages into many new species in a specific area and time is called *adaptive radiation*.

- **Mating Behavior and Timing** Many species that sexually reproduce have specific behaviors for attracting mates, such as a pattern of sounds or actions. Some undergo mating at specific times or in response to environmental events. If two populations develop differences in these behaviors, they may no longer attract each other for mating. This mechanism seems to be responsible for the species divergence shown in **Figure 13.**

- **Polyploidy** Recall that a *polyploid* organism has received a duplicate set of chromosomes by accident. A polyploid individual may be reproductively isolated because it cannot pair gametes with others from the original population. However, it may reproduce by vegetative growth, self-fertilize, or find a polyploid mate. In these cases, a new species can arise rapidly. Polyploidy has been observed in many plant species.

- **Hybridization** In some cases, two closely related species may come back into contact with each other and attempt to mate. The offspring of such a mating are called *hybrids*. In cases in which the two parent species are sufficiently diverged from each other, their offspring may be sterile. For example, a mule is a sterile hybrid of a horse and a donkey. Another possibility is that hybrid offspring may not be well adapted to the environment of either parent. Finally, if the parents have many genetic differences, the offspring may not develop successfully. However, there are also many cases in which hybridization leads to new and successful species.

> **Reading Check** *Is hybridization always successful?*

Outlining Complete your outline for this chapter. Be sure to include each of the headings on this page, such as "Polyploidy" and "Hybridization." When you finish the chapter, review your outline and add notes to any heading whose meaning is unclear to you.

Figure 13 The pickerel frog and the leopard frog are closely related species. Differences in mating times may have caused their reproductive isolation. ❯ What other aspects of mating can push populations to diverge?

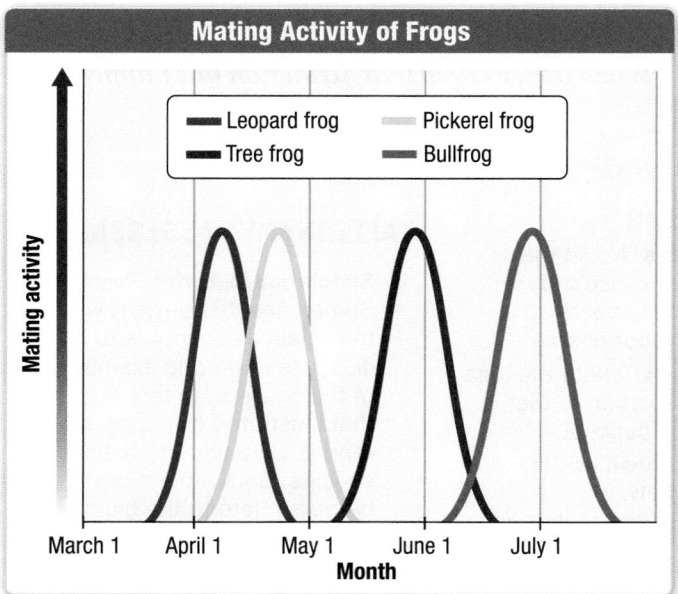

Pickerel frog, *Rana palustris*

Leopard frog, *Rana pipiens*

Figure 14 The Tasmanian wolf was driven to extinction by ranchers and dogs in Australia in the early 1900s. ❯ **What is the role of extinction in evolution?**

www.scilinks.org
Topic: Extinction
Code: HX80558

Extinction: The End of Species

Extinction occurs when a species fails to produce any more descendants. The animal in **Figure 14** is extinct. Extinction, like speciation, can be detected only after it is complete. And extinction is as much a part of evolution as speciation is. Scientists estimate that more than 99% of all of the species that have ever lived on Earth have become extinct. ❯ **The species that exist at any time are the net result of both speciation and extinction.** If you think of speciation as a branching of a "family tree," then extinction is like the loss of one of the branches.

As you will learn, many cases of extinction are the result of environmental change. Almost all of the dinosaurs died off because of some combination of meteorite impacts, volcanism, and climate change on Earth millions of years ago. Anytime that an environment changes, species that were once well adapted may become poorly adapted. If the environment changes more rapidly than new adaptations arise within a species, the species may be driven to extinction.

❯ **Reading Check** *When do we know that extinction has happened?*

Section 3 Review

❯ **KEY IDEAS**

1. **Identify** two definitions of *species* used in evolutionary biology.

2. **Summarize** a general process by which one species can evolve into two species.

3. **Relate** extinction to changes that occur in the numbers and types of species over time.

CRITICAL THINKING

4. **Making Inferences** Would the biological species concept be useful for classifying bacterial species? Explain your answer.

5. **Relating Concepts** Relate the idea of reproductive isolation to the biological species concept.

6. **Describing Relationships** Describe the relationship between speciation and extinction in terms of a "family tree" of descent.

ALTERNATIVE ASSESSMENT

7. **Speciation-in-Action Poster** Sometimes, the easiest way to explain a concept is to illustrate real-world examples of the concept. Create a poster that illustrates examples of reproductive barriers between species. Show how these barriers relate to the biological species concept. Present your poster to the class.

Objectives

➤ Investigate the effect of population size on genetic drift.

➤ Analyze the mathematics of the Hardy-Weinberg principle.

Materials

- buttons, blue (10 to 100)
- buttons, red (10 to 100)
- buttons, white (10 to 100)
- jar or beaker, large, plastic

Genetic Drift

Random chance affects the frequencies of alleles in a population over time. This effect, called *genetic drift,* also depends on population size.

Preparation

1. **SCIENTIFIC METHODS** **State the Problem** How does population size affect allele frequencies? Read the procedure to see how you will test this.

2. **SCIENTIFIC METHODS** **Form a Hypothesis** Form a hypothesis that predicts the results of this procedure for three different population sizes.

Procedure

1. Prepare to model the populations. First, assign each color button to one of the alleles (I^A, I^B, or i) of the ABO blood types. Notice how each possible pairing of alleles matches one of the four types (A, B, AB, or O). Then, choose three different population sizes. Also choose one ratio of alleles at which to start all three populations (for example, I^A:I^B:i = 2:2:1). Create tables for your data.

2. Represent the first population's alleles by placing the appropriate number of blue, red, and white buttons in a jar.

3. Randomly select two buttons from the jar to represent one person. Record this person's genotype and phenotype. Place the buttons back into the jar.

4. Repeat step 3 until you have modeled the appropriate number of people in the population. Tally the total number of each allele within this generation.

5. Empty the jar. Refill it with the number and color of buttons that matches the tallies recorded in step 4.

6. Repeat steps 3 through 5 until you have modeled four generations.

7. Repeat steps 2 through 6 to model two more populations.

Possible alleles

	I^A	I^B	i
I^A	I^AI^A Type A	I^AI^B Type AB	I^Ai Type A
I^B	I^AI^B Type AB	I^BI^B Type B	I^Bi Type B
i	I^Ai Type A	I^Bi Type B	ii Type O

Possible alleles

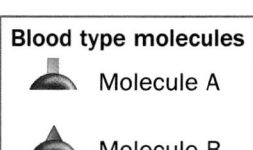

Blood type molecules

Molecule A

Molecule B

Analyze and Conclude

1. **Analyzing Data** Describe any changes in genotype and phenotype ratios within each population over time.

2. **Explaining Results** Did any population maintain genetic equilibrium? Explain how you can tell.

3. **SCIENTIFIC METHODS** **Analyzing Results** Which population showed the greatest amount of genetic drift? Explain.

go.hrw.com
SUPER SUMMARY
Keyword: HX8POPS

Key Ideas	Key Terms

1 Genetic Variation

> Microevolution can be studied by observing changes in the numbers and types of alleles in populations.

> Biologists study polygenic phenotypes by measuring each individual in the population and then analyzing the distribution of the measurements.

> Genetic variation and change are measured in terms of the frequency of alleles in the gene pool of a population.

> The major source of new alleles in natural populations is mutation in germ cells.

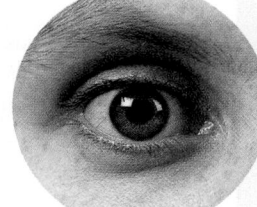

population genetics (399)
normal distribution (400)

2 Genetic Change

> The Hardy-Weinberg principle predicts that the frequencies of alleles and genotypes in a population will not change unless at least one of five forces acts upon the population. The forces that can act against genetic equilibrium are gene flow, nonrandom mating, genetic drift, mutation, and natural selection.

> Sexual reproduction creates the possibility that mating patterns or behaviors can influence the gene pool of a population.

> Allele frequencies are more likely to remain stable in large populations than in small populations.

> Natural selection acts only to change the relative frequency of alleles that exist in a population. Natural selection acts on genotypes by removing unsuccessful phenotypes from a population.

> Three major patterns are possible in the way that natural selection affects a distribution of polygenic characters over time. These patterns are directional selection, stabilizing selection, and disruptive selection.

genetic equilibrium (404)

3 Speciation

> Today, scientists may use more than one definition for species. The definition used depends on the organisms and field of science being studied.

> Speciation has occurred when the net effects of evolutionary forces result in a population that has unique features and is reproductively isolated.

> The species that exist at any time are the net result of both speciation and extinction.

reproductive isolation (412)
subspecies (412)

1. **Everyday Words in Science** Sometimes, words are used in science in ways that are not far from their everyday meanings, but the words need to be considered in context. For example, *drift* in the context of *genetic drift* means "to float about randomly." What does *pool* mean in the context of *gene pool*?

2. **Concept Map** Construct a concept map that describes the causes of genetic change. Try to include the following words in your map: *Hardy-Weinberg, genetic drift, nonrandom mating, natural selection, mutation,* and *gene flow.*

Using Key Terms

In your own words, write a definition for each of the following terms.

3. *normal distribution*

4. *genetic equilibrium*

Use each of the following terms in a separate sentence.

5. *gene pool*

6. *reproductive isolation*

Understanding Key Ideas

7. The sum of allele frequencies in a population should be
   a. equal to 1.
   b. less than 100.
   c. equal to the phenotype frequencies.
   d. one-half of the genotype frequencies.

8. In the Hardy-Weinberg equation, $p^2 + 2pq + q^2 = 1$, what does the term $2pq$ represent?
   a. frequency of heterozygous individuals
   b. frequency of individuals with two alleles
   c. frequency of homozygous recessive individuals
   d. frequency of homozygous dominant individuals

9. Genetic drift has the greatest impact on
   a. large populations.   c. growing populations.
   b. small populations.   d. migrating populations.

10. Which of the following is a reason why natural selection is limited in its influence on evolution?
    a. Natural selection cannot direct the creation of new alleles.
    b. All populations depend on the reproduction of individuals.
    c. Natural selection eliminates certain genotypes from populations.
    d. Individuals tend to produce more offspring than the environment can support.

11. In evolution, *extinction* describes the end of
    a. an allele.
    b. a single species.
    c. an individual organism.
    d. a population of organisms.

Explaining Key Ideas

12. **Describe** the role of population genetics in the study of microevolution.

13. **Identify** the major source of new alleles in natural populations.

14. **Relate** natural selection to changes in allele frequencies.

15. **Describe** the effect that directional selection has on the phenotypes in a population of organisms.

16. **Describe** the difficulty with defining species.

17. **Explain** how mating behavior can contribute to reproductive isolation.

Use the diagram to answer the following question.

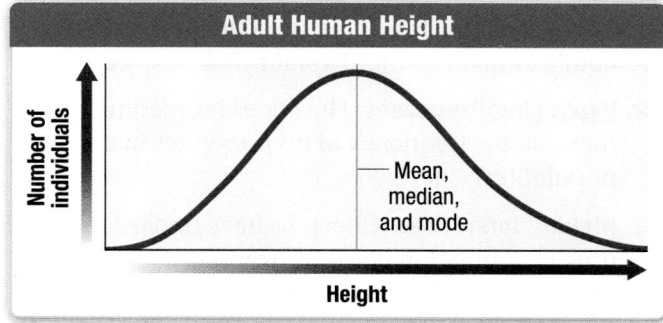

Adult Human Height

18. **Identify** the kind of characters in a population that will usually form a diagram like this one.

Using Science Graphics

Use the diagram to answer the following question.

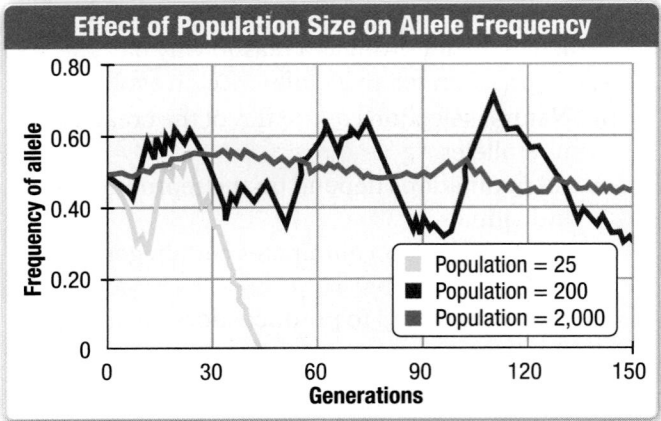

Effect of Population Size on Allele Frequency

- Population = 25
- Population = 200
- Population = 2,000

19. This diagram represents the effect of
  a. gene size.
  c. speciation.
  b. genetic drift.
  d. population growth.

This Punnett square shows how each part of the Hardy-Weinberg equation aligns to the possible combinations of two alleles.

	R (p)	r (q)
R (p)	RR (p^2)	Rr (pq)
r (q)	rR (pq)	rr (q^2)

20. The Hardy-Weinberg equation states that
$$p^2 + 2pq + q^2 = 1$$

Identify from the Punnett square what each part of the equation represents.

Critical Thinking

21. Applying Logic Is a population that is in genetic equilibrium evolving? Explain your answer.

22. Explaining Processes How does inbreeding increase the frequency of homozygotes in a population?

23. Making Inferences Cheetahs have undergone drastic population declines over the last 5,000 years. As a result, the cheetahs alive today are descendants of only a few individuals, and each cheetah is almost genetically uniform with other members of the population. Do you think that genetic drift has affected the cheetah population? Explain your answer.

24. Defining Concepts Propose a definition of *species* that encompasses more than one way that species could be defined.

25. Forming Reasoned Opinions In the laboratory, a scientist studied two identical-looking daisies that belong to the genus *Aster*. The two plants produce fertile hybrids in the laboratory, but they never interbreed in nature because one plant flowers only in the spring and the other flowers only in autumn. Do the plants belong to the same species? Explain.

Writing for Science

26. Speciation Narration Two species of antelope squirrel live on opposite sides of the Grand Canyon. *Ammospermophilus harrisi,* or Harris's antelope squirrel, lives on the south rim, and *Ammospermophilus leucrurus,* the white-tailed antelope squirrel, lives on the north rim. Imagine that you can speed up time and witness the speciation process ocurring with these squirrels. Write a running commentary—much like that heard at a sports event—on the process of speciation that occurred after the initial population of antelope squirrels became divided on both sides of the canyon. Read or act out your commentary to the class.

Why It Matters

27. Hawaiian Speciation Conduct research to identify another Hawaiian example of adaptive radiation.

Math Skills

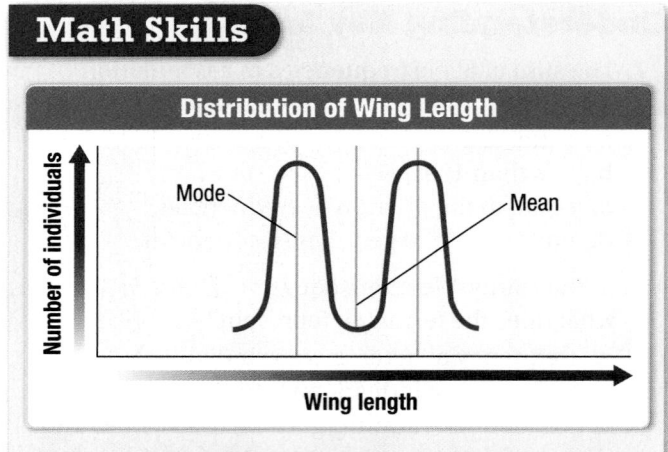

Distribution of Wing Length

Mode — Mean

Number of individuals

Wing length

28. Mean, Median, and Mode Describe this distribution in terms of mean, median, and mode.

29. Math Terminology This kind of distribution is sometimes called a *bimodal* distribution. Why?

TEST TIP For a question about a structure or process that has a complex name, write down the name and review its meaning before answering the question.

Science Concepts

1. Population genetics is the study of
- **A** how individuals evolve.
- **B** how populations interact.
- **C** how genes determine traits.
- **D** how alleles change within populations.

2. Phenotypic variations take the form of
- **F** genetic differences between organisms.
- **G** character differences between organisms.
- **H** molecular differences between organisms.
- **J** chromosomal differences between organisms.

3. The major source of new alleles in a natural population is
- **A** mutation.
- **B** polyploidy.
- **C** genetic drift.
- **D** natural selection.

4. Which of the following is an example of non-random mating?
- **F** Genes are removed from the population when individuals migrate.
- **G** A change in a populations' allele frequency is due to chance.
- **H** An individual chooses a mate that has the brightest coloration.
- **J** An individual is eliminated from the gene pool by natural selection.

5. Random change in allele frequency due to chance alone is called
- **A** gene flow.
- **B** genetic drift.
- **C** natural selection.
- **D** sexual selection.

Math Skills

6. The Hardy-Weinberg equation, $p^2 + 2pq + q^2 = 1$, describes a state of equilibrium among all alleles in a population. Expressed in terms of percentages, the sum of allele frequencies in a population would be
- **F** 1%
- **G** 2%
- **H** 50%
- **J** 100%

Using Science Graphics

Use the diagram to answer the following questions.

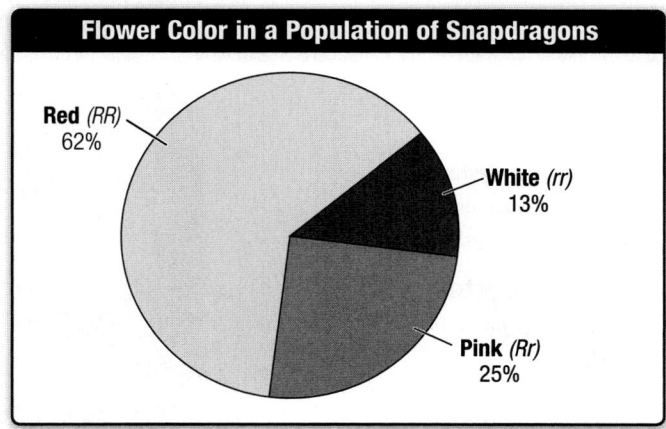

Flower Color in a Population of Snapdragons

Red *(RR)* 62%
White *(rr)* 13%
Pink *(Rr)* 25%

7. In this population, which genotype has the lowest frequency?
- **A** *RR*
- **B** *rr*
- **C** red
- **D** white

8. In this population, what is the frequency of heterozygotes?
- **F** 13%
- **G** 25%
- **H** 38%
- **J** 62%

Use the diagram to answer the following question.

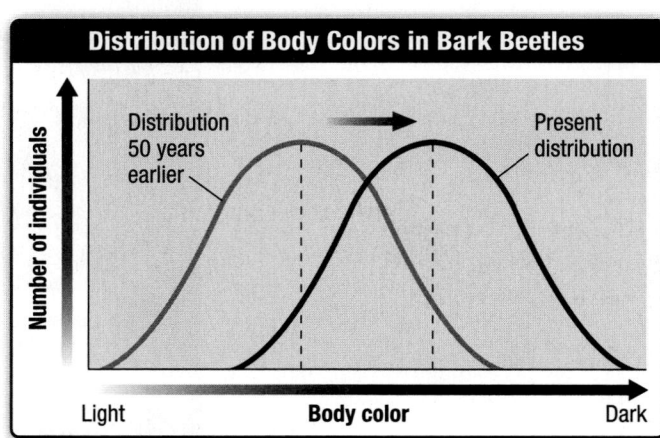

Distribution of Body Colors in Bark Beetles

Number of individuals

Distribution 50 years earlier

Present distribution

Light Body color Dark

9. The diagram represents which form of selection?
- **A** sexual selection
- **B** stabilizing selection
- **C** disruptive selection
- **D** directional selection

Chapter 18

Classification

Preview

1 The Importance of Classification
The Need for Systems
Scientific Nomenclature
The Linnaean System

2 Modern Systematics
Traditional Systematics
Phylogenetics
Cladistics
Inferring Evolutionary Relatedness

3 Kingdoms and Domains
Updating Classification Systems
The Three-Domain System

Why It Matters

More than one million species on Earth have been given scientific names, but many more species exist that have not been identified.

These butterflies look similar, but does that mean they are related? There is more to that answer than meets the eye.

Sometimes, butterflies that look different are actually members of the same species.

Scientists use systems for naming and grouping species. These butterflies have been classified as belonging to the family Pieridae.

Sometimes, two butterflies that look alike are *not* actually members of the same species.

🕐 **15 min**

Inquiry**Lab**

What Is Your System?

Often, more than one way exists to organize or group things. In this lab, you will work with others to decide on a system.

Procedure

1. Work with a partner. Examine the **assortment of objects** provided by your teacher.

2. Sort your objects into groups of "related" objects. Try to get every object into a group with at least one other object.

3. Choose a name for each group.

4. Choose one object from your collection, and trade it with an object from another pair of students.

5. Try to fit the new object into one of your groups.

Analysis

1. **List** and define each of your group names from step 3.

2. **Describe** how you classified the new object in step 4.

3. **Predict** whether another person would be able to "correctly" classify one of your objects by using your list of groups. Explain your reasoning.

READING TOOLBOX

These reading tools can help you learn the material in this chapter. For more information on how to use these and other tools, see **Appendix: Reading and Study Skills.**

Using Words

Word Origins Many scientific words derive their parts from Greek or Latin words. Learning the meanings of some Greek and Latin word parts can help you understand the meaning of many scientific words.

Your Turn Answer the following questions.
1. What do taxonomists probably do?
2. What role might nomenclature have in taxonomy?

Word Parts		
Word part	**Origin**	**Meaning**
tax	Greek	arrangement, order, movement
nom	Greek; Latin	law, order, system; name
clatur	Latin	calling, naming
clad	Greek	shoot, branch, twig
phyl	Greek	tribe, race, class, clan
gram	Greek	write, a written record
gen	Greek, Latin	birth, descent, origin, creation
morph	Greek	shape, form, appearance

Using Language

Mnemonics Mnemonic devices are tools that help you remember lists or parts in their proper order. Use the first letter of every word that you want to remember as the first letter of a new word in a memorable sentence. You may be more likely to remember the sentence if the sentence is funny.

Your Turn Create mnemonic devices that could help you remember all of the parts of the following groups of items.
1. the names of all of your teachers
2. the 12 months of the year

Using Science Graphics

Phylogenetic Tree A phylogenetic tree shows the relationships of different groups of organisms to each other. The groups that are most closely related appear on branches that lie close together. Branch points represent a point in time where groups became separated and speciation began. Time is represented as moving forward from the bottom (or trunk) toward the top (or branches) of the tree.

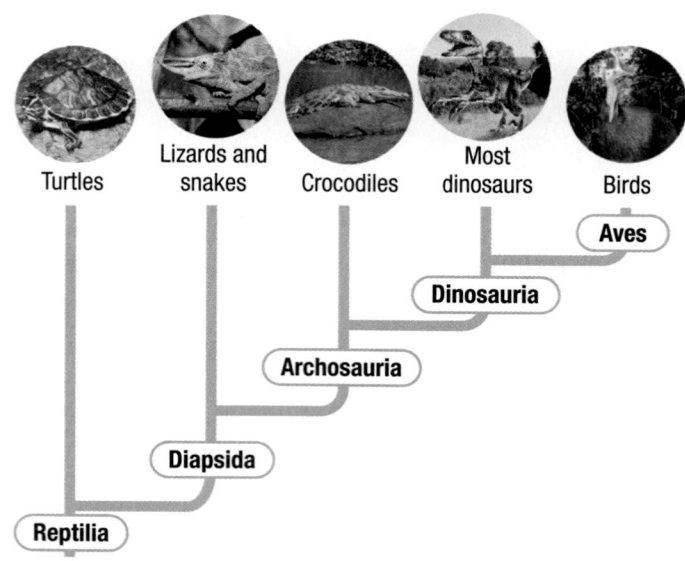

Your Turn Use this phylogenetic tree to answer the following questions.
1. Which group is most closely related to extinct dinosaurs?
2. Which group existed before the other groups did?

The Importance of Classification

Key Ideas	Key Terms	Why It Matters
❯ Why do biologists have taxonomic systems? ❯ What makes up the scientific name of a species? ❯ What is the structure of the modern Linnaean system of classification?	taxonomy genus binomial nomenclature	In order to study and make use of living things, we need a name for each specific thing.

The number of species that exist in the world is much greater than the number known. About 1.7 million species have been named and described by scientists. But scientists think that millions more are undiscovered. We have little knowledge of Earth's variety of species.

The Need for Systems

In biology, the practice of naming and classifying organisms is called **taxonomy.** Scientists use a logical system of classification to manage large amounts of information. Similarly, a library uses a system for organizing books. ❯ **Biologists use taxonomic systems to organize their knowledge of organisms. These systems attempt to provide consistent ways to name and categorize organisms.**

Common names of organisms are not organized into a system. One species may have many common names, and one common name may be used for more than one species. For example, the bird called a *robin* in Great Britain is a different bird from the bird called a *robin* in North America. To avoid confusion, biologists need a way to name organisms that does not depend on language or location.

Biologists also need a way to organize lists of names. A system that has categories is more efficient than a simple list. So, biologists group organisms into large categories as well as smaller and more specific categories. The general term for any one of these categories is a *taxon* (plural, *taxa*).

❯ **Reading Check** *What is the problem with common names of species? (See the Appendix for answers to Reading Checks.)*

taxonomy (taks AHN uh mee) the science of describing, naming, and classifying organisms

Figure 1 Museums are full of biological specimens, yet only a fraction of Earth's species have been scientifically named.

Common name: cheetah
Scientific name: *Acinonyx jubatus*

Common names: leopard, panther
Scientific name: *Panthera pardus*

Common names: lion, African lion
Scientific name: *Panthera leo*

Figure 2 Each species may have many common names but only one scientific name. The scientific name is made up of a genus name and a species identifier. Each genus is a group of closely related species. ❯ **To what genus do both lions and leopards belong?**

genus (JEE nuhs) a level of classification that contains similar species

binomial nomenclature (bie NOH mee uhl NOH muhn KLAY chuhr) a system for giving each organism a two-word scientific name that consists of the genus name followed by the species name

www.scilinks.org
Topic: Carl Linnaeus
Code: HX80226

Scientific Nomenclature

As biology became established as a science, biologists began to create systems for naming and classifying living things. A major challenge was to give each species a unique name.

Early Scientific Names In the early days of European biology, various naming systems were invented. Some used long, descriptive Latin phrases called *polynomials*. Names for taxa were inconsistent between these systems. The only taxon that was somewhat consistent was the **genus,** which was a taxon used to group similar species.

A simpler and more consistent system was developed by the Swedish biologist Carl Linnaeus in the 1750s. He wanted to catalog all known species. He wrote books in which he used the polynomial system but added a two-word Latin name for each species. His two-word system is called **binomial nomenclature.** For example, his two-part name for the European honeybee was *Apis mellifera*, the genus name followed by a single descriptive word for each species. **Figure 2** shows the binomial names of three other animals.

Naming Rules In the years since Linnaeus created his system, his basic approach has been universally adopted. The unique two-part name for a species is now called a *scientific name*. Scientific names must conform to rules established by an international commission of scientists. No two species can have the same scientific name.

❯ All scientific names for species are made up of two Latin or Latin-like terms. All of the members of a genus share the genus name as the first term. The second term is called the *species identifier* and is often descriptive. For example, in the name *Apis mellifera,* the term *mellifera* derives from the Latin word for "honey." When you write the scientific name, the genus name should be capitalized and the species identifier should be lowercased; both terms should be italicized.

❯ **Reading Check** *Why did Linnaeus devise a new naming system?*

The Linnaean System

In trying to catalog every known species, Linnaeus devised more than just a naming system. He devised a system to classify all plants and animals that were known during his time. His system formed the basis of taxonomy for centuries. **▶ In the Linnaean system of classification, organisms are grouped at successive levels of a hierarchy based on similarities in their form and structure.** Since Linnaeus's time, many new groups and some new levels have been added, as **Figure 3** shows. **▶ The eight basic levels of modern classification are domain, kingdom, phylum, class, order, family, genus, and species.**

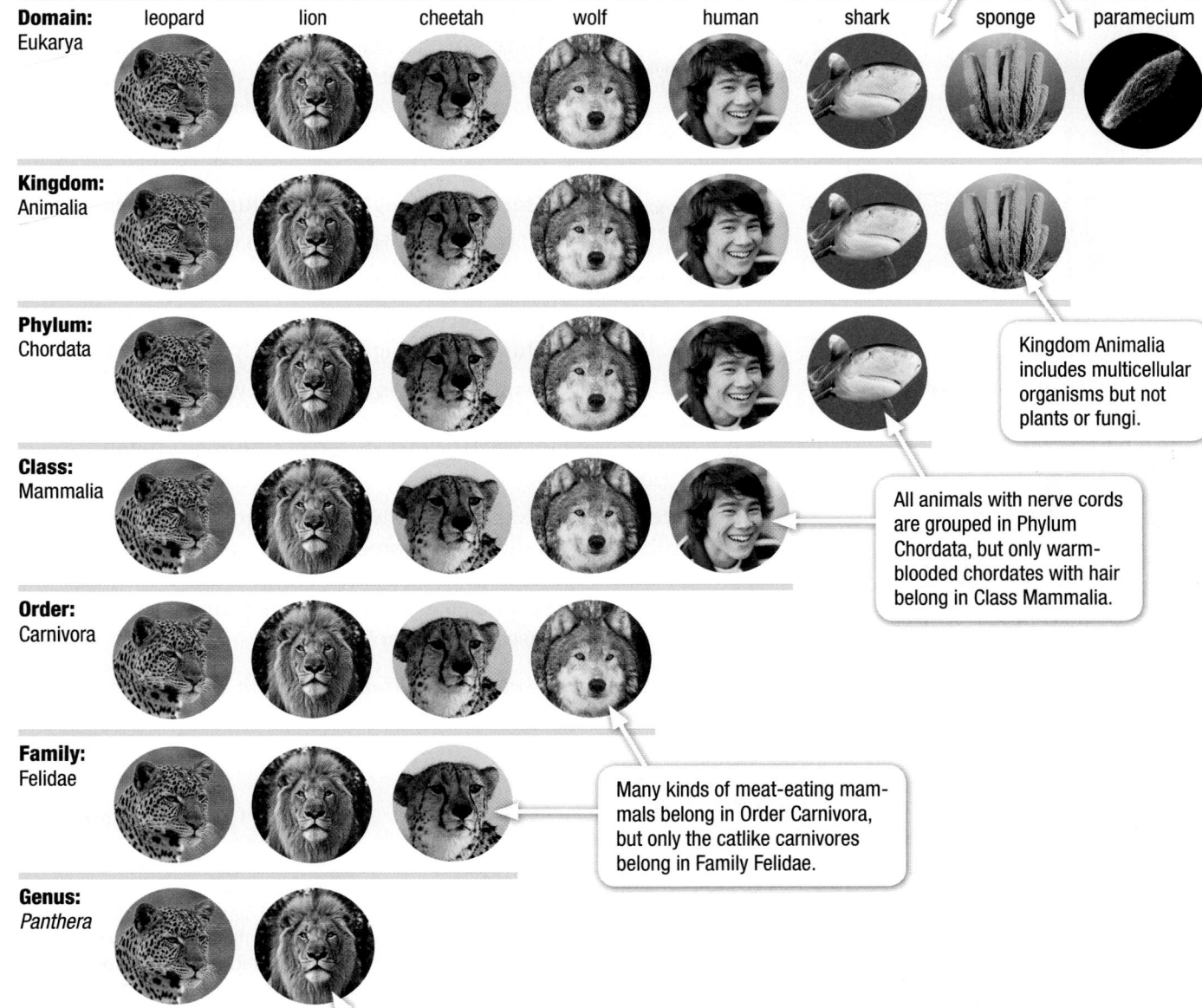

Domain Eukarya includes a wide diversity of eukaryotes but no prokaryotes.

Domain: Eukarya
leopard   lion   cheetah   wolf   human   shark   sponge   paramecium

Kingdom: Animalia

Kingdom Animalia includes multicellular organisms but not plants or fungi.

Phylum: Chordata

Class: Mammalia

All animals with nerve cords are grouped in Phylum Chordata, but only warm-blooded chordates with hair belong in Class Mammalia.

Order: Carnivora

Family: Felidae

Many kinds of meat-eating mammals belong in Order Carnivora, but only the catlike carnivores belong in Family Felidae.

Genus: *Panthera*

Species: *Panthera pardus*

The leopard is a unique species, but it is closely related to the lion. So, the two species are placed in Genus *Panthera*.

Figure 3 The Linnaean system has been updated and now includes eight levels, from domain to species. **▶ Which level includes the greatest number of species?**

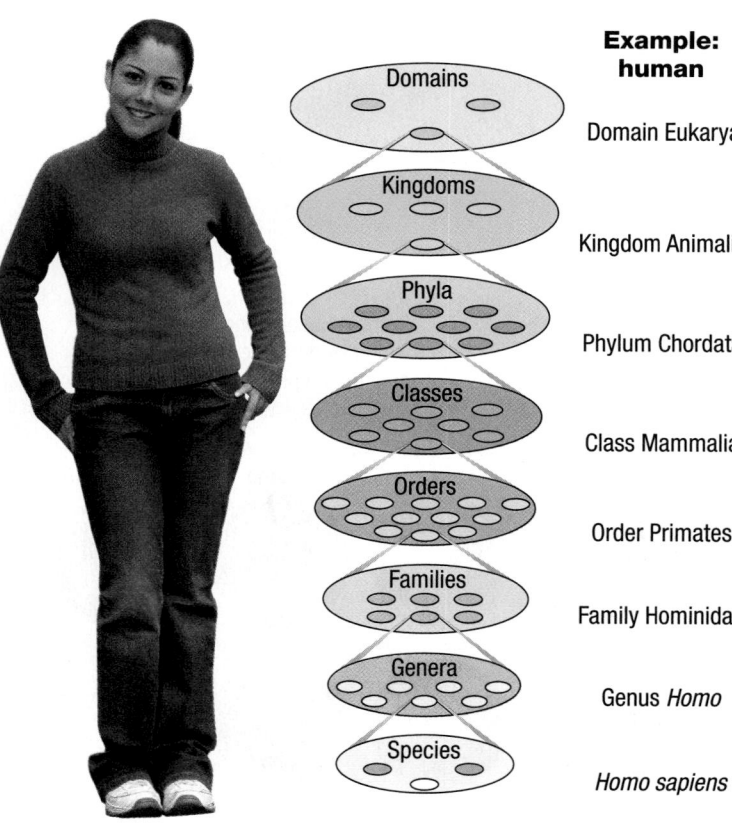

Example:
human

Domains

Domain Eukarya

Kingdoms

Kingdom Animalia

Phyla

Phylum Chordata

Classes

Class Mammalia

Orders

Order Primates

Families

Family Hominidae

Genera

Genus *Homo*

Species

Homo sapiens

Figure 4 A species can be classified at each level of the Linnaean system.

READING TOOLBOX

Mnemonics To remember the eight levels in their proper order, use a phrase, such as "Do Kindly Pay Cash Or Furnish Good Security," to represent *Domain, Kingdom, Phylum, Class, Order, Family, Genus,* and *Species.*

Levels of the Modern Linnaean System

Each level has its own set of names for taxa at that level. Each taxon is identified based on shared traits. Similar species are grouped into a genus; similar genera are grouped into a family; and so on up to the level of domain. **Figure 4** shows the classification of humans in this system.

- **Domain** Since Linnaeus's time, the category *domain* has been invented in order to recognize the most basic differences among cell types. All living things are now grouped into one of three domains. For example, humans belong to the domain Eukarya.

- **Kingdom** The category *kingdom* encompasses large groups such as plants, animals, or fungi. Six kingdoms fit within the three domains.

- **Phylum** A *phylum* is a subgroup within a kingdom. Many phyla exist within each kingdom. Humans belong to the phylum Chordata.

- **Class** A *class* is a subgroup within a phylum.

- **Order** An *order* is a subgroup within a class.

- **Family** A *family* is a subgroup within an order. Humans belong to the family Hominidae.

- **Genus** A *genus* (plural, *genera*) is a subgroup within a family. Each genus is made up of species with uniquely shared traits, such that the species are thought to be closely related. Humans belong to the genus *Homo.*

- **Species** A *species* is usually defined as a unique group of organisms united by heredity or interbreeding. But in practice, scientists tend to define species based on unique features. For example, *Homo sapiens* is recognized as the only living primate species that walks upright and uses spoken language.

❯ **Reading Check** *How many kingdoms are in the Linnaean system?*

Section

1
Review

❯**KEY IDEAS**

1. **Explain** why biologists have systems for naming and grouping organisms.

2. **Describe** the structure of a scientific name for a species.

3. **List** the categories of the modern Linnaean system of classification in order from general to specific.

CRITICAL THINKING

4. **Logical Reasoning** Describe additional problems that might occur for biologists without a logical taxonomic system.

5. **Anticipating Change** Although the basic structure of the system that Linnaeus invented is still in use, many aspects of this system have changed. Suggest some possible ways that the system may have changed.

ALTERNATIVE ASSESSMENT

6. **Classification Poster** Create a poster that shows the major levels of classification for your favorite organism. Write a description of the general characteristics of the organism at each level. For each level, include a list of other organisms that belong to the same taxon.

Modern Systematics

Key Ideas	Key Terms	Why It Matters
❯ What problems arise when scientists try to group organisms by apparent similarities? ❯ Is the evolutionary past reflected in modern systematics? ❯ How is cladistics used to construct evolutionary relationships? ❯ What evidence do scientists use to analyze these relationships?	phylogeny cladistics	Modern systematics unites evolutionary science with traditional studies of anatomy.

Have you ever wondered how scientists tell one species from another? For example, how can you tell a mushroom that is harmless from a mushroom that is poisonous? Identification is not easy, even for experts. The experts often revise their classifications as well as their procedures. This field of expertise is known as *systematics*.

Traditional Systematics

Linnaeus's system was based on his judgment of the importance of various similarities among living things. ❯ **Scientists traditionally have used similarities in appearance and structure to group organisms. However, this approach has proven problematic.** Some groups look similar but turn out to be distantly related. Other groups look different and turn out to be closely related. Often, new data or new analyses suggest relationships between organisms that were not apparent before.

For example, dinosaurs were once seen as a group of reptiles that became extinct millions of years ago. And birds were seen as a separate, modern group that was not related to any reptile group. However, fossil evidence has convinced scientists that birds evolved from one of the many lineages of dinosaurs. Some scientists now classify birds as a subgroup of dinosaurs, as described in **Figure 5**.

❯ **Reading Check** *What is systematics?*

Figure 5 In a sense, birds are dinosaurs. Scientists think that modern birds are descended from a subgroup of dinosaurs called *theropods*. This inference is based on thorough comparisons of modern birds and fossilized theropods.

Deinonychus This is a model of an extinct theropod dinosaur.

Cassowary This is a modern bird species.

Phylogenetics

Today, scientists who study systematics are interested in **phylogeny,** or the ancestral relationships between species. ❯ **Grouping organisms by similarity is often assumed to reflect phylogeny, but inferring phylogeny is complex in practice.** Reconstructing a species' phylogeny is like trying to draw a huge family tree that links ancestors and descendants across thousands or millions of generations.

Misleading Similarities Inferring phylogenies from similarities can be misleading. Not all similar characters are inherited from a common ancestor. Consider the wings of a bird and of an insect. Both types of wings enable flight, but the structures of the two kinds of wings differ. Moreover, fossil evidence shows that insects with wings existed long before birds with wings appeared. Through the process called *convergent evolution*, similarities may evolve in groups that are not closely related to one another, often because the groups become adapted to similar habitats or lifestyles. Similarities that arise through convergent evolution are called *analogous* characters.

Judging Relatedness Another problem is that grouping organisms by similarities is subjective. Are all characters equally important, or are some more important than others? Often, different scientists may give different answers to these questions.

For example, systematists historically placed birds in a separate class from reptiles, giving importance to characters such as feathers, as **Figure 6** shows. But more recently, fossil evidence and detailed studies of bird and dinosaur anatomy have changed the view of these groups. **Figure 6** shows that birds are now considered part of the "family tree" of dinosaurs. This family tree, or *phylogenetic tree,* represents a hypothesis of the relationships between several groups.

phylogeny the evolutionary history of a species or taxonomic group

cladistics a phylogenetic classification system that uses shared derived characters and ancestry as the sole criterion for grouping taxa

Figure 6 Traditional systematics grouped birds separately from other reptiles by emphasizing the unique features of birds. However, modern phylogenetics places birds as a subgroup of reptiles on a phylogenetic tree. ❯ **How do these two systems differ in structure?**

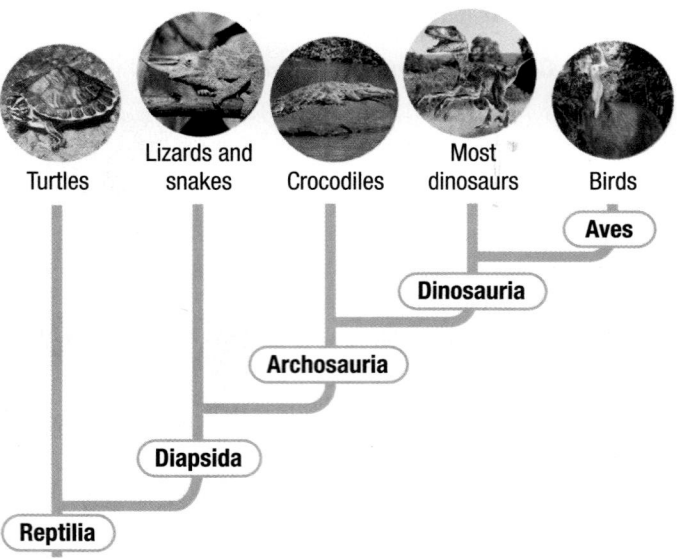

Linnaean Classification

Classes of Animals	
Class Reptilia	**Class Aves**
egg-laying, exothermic, scales	egg-laying, endothermic, feathers
lizards, snakes, turtles, crocodiles, and dinosaurs	birds

Modern Phylogeny

Turtles · Lizards and snakes · Crocodiles · Most dinosaurs · Birds

Aves · Dinosauria · Archosauria · Diapsida · Reptilia

Cladistics

To unite systematics with phylogenetics, scientists need an objective way to sort out relatedness. Today, the preferred method is cladistics. **Cladistics** is a method of analysis that infers phylogenies by careful comparisons of shared characters. ❯ **Cladistic analysis is used to select the most likely phylogeny among a given set of organisms.**

Comparing Characters Cladistics focuses on finding characters that are *shared* between different groups of organisms because of shared ancestry. With respect to two groups, a shared character is defined as *ancestral* if it is thought to have evolved in a common ancestor of both groups. In contrast, a *derived* character is one that evolved in one group but not in the other group. Cladistics infers relatedness by identifying shared derived and shared ancestral characters among groups while avoiding the use of analogous characters.

For example, consider the relationship between flowering plants and conifers. The production of seeds is a character that is present in all living conifers and flowering plants and in some prehistoric plants. So, it is a shared ancestral character among these groups. The production of flowers, however, is a derived character that is shared only among flowering plants. Flowers evolved in some ancestor of flowering plants but did not evolve in the group that led to conifers.

Constructing Cladograms Cladistics uses a strict comparison of many characters among several groups in order to construct a cladogram. A *cladogram* is a phylogenetic tree that is drawn in a specific way, as **Figure 7** shows. Organisms are grouped together through identification of their shared derived characters. All groups that arise from one point on a cladogram belong to a clade. A *clade* is a set of groups that are related by descent from a single ancestral lineage.

Each clade in a tree is usually compared with an *outgroup,* or group that lacks some of the shared characters. For example, **Figure 7** shows that flowering plants and conifers share a character with each other that they do not share with ferns. So, conifers and flowering plants form a clade, and ferns form the outgroup.

❯ **Reading Check** *What does a cladogram show?*

ACADEMIC VOCABULARY

objective independent of the mind; without bias

READING TOOLBOX

Word Origins The word root *clad* means "shoot, branch or twig" and the word root *gram* means "to write or record." Use this information to analyze the meaning of the term *cladogram.*

Figure 7 This cladogram organizes plants by using a strict comparison of the characters shown in the table. Each clade is united by a specific shared derived character. ❯ **Which groups are united by having seeds?**

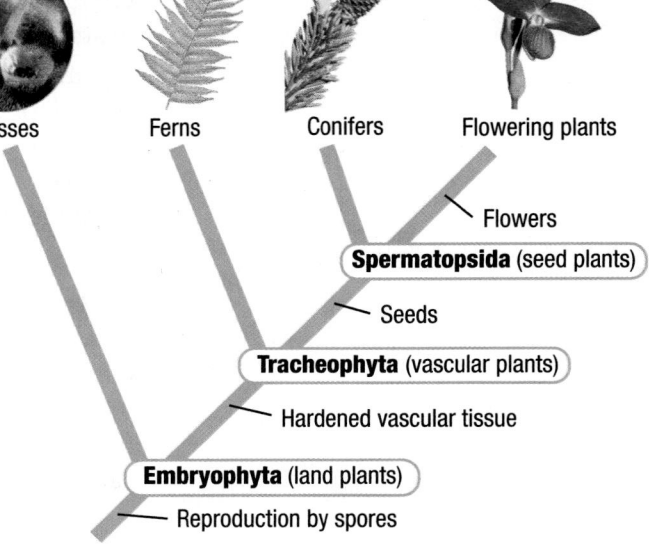

Mosses   Ferns   Conifers   Flowering plants

- Flowers
- **Spermatopsida** (seed plants)
- Seeds
- **Tracheophyta** (vascular plants)
- Hardened vascular tissue
- **Embryophyta** (land plants)
- Reproduction by spores

Characters in Plants			
Type of plants	**Vascular tissue**	**Seeds**	**Flowers**
Mosses	no	no	no
Ferns	yes	no	no
Conifers	yes	yes	no
Flowering plants	yes	yes	yes

QuickLab

Cladogram Construction

Use this table of shared characters to construct a cladogram. Use the other cladograms in this section to help you draw your cladogram.

Analysis

1. **Identify** the outgroup. The outgroup is the group that does not share any of the characters in this list. Draw a diagonal line and then a single branch from its base. Write the outgroup at the tip of this first branch.

2. **Identify** the most common character. Just past the "fork" of the first branch, write the most common derived character. This character should be present in all of the subsequent groups added to the tree.

Characters in Vertebrates

	Four legs	Amniotic egg	Hair
Tuna	no	no	no
Frog	yes	no	no
Lizard	yes	yes	no
Cat	yes	yes	yes

3. **Complete** the tree. Repeat step 2 for the second most-common character. Repeat until the tree is filled with all of the groups and characters from the table.

4. **CRITICAL THINKING** **Applying Concepts** What is a shared derived character of cats and lizards?

5. **CRITICAL THINKING** **Applying Concepts** What character evolved in the ancestor of frogs but not in that of fish?

www.scilinks.org
Topic: Phylogenetic Tree
Code: HX81141

Inferring Evolutionary Relatedness

As you have seen, phylogenetics relies heavily on data about characters that are either present or absent in taxa. But other kinds of data are also important. ❯ **Biologists compare many kinds of evidence and apply logic carefully in order to infer phylogenies.** They constantly revise and add details to their definitions of taxa.

Morphological Evidence *Morphology* refers to the physical structure or anatomy of organisms. Large-scale morphological data are most obvious and have been well studied. For example, the major characters used to define plant groups—vascular tissue, seeds, and flowers—were recognized long ago. But because convergent evolution can lead to analogous characters, scientists must consider many characters and look carefully for similarities and differences. For example, many animals have wings that are merely analagous.

An important part of morphology in multicellular species is the pattern of development from embryo to adult. Organisms that share ancestral genes often show additional similarities during the process of development. For example, in all vertebrate species, the jaw of an adult develops from the same part of an embryo. In many cases, studies of embryos bring new information to phylogenetic debates.

Molecular Evidence In recent decades, scientists have used genetic information to infer phylogenies. Recall that as genes are passed on from generation to generation, mutations occur. Some mutations may be passed on to all species that descend from a common ancestor. So, DNA, RNA, and proteins can be compared in the same manner as morphology is compared to infer phylogenies.

❯ **Reading Check** *What is an example of morphological data?*

Sequence Data Today, genetic sequence data are widely used for cladistic analysis. First, the sequence of DNA bases in a gene (or of amino acids in a protein) is determined for several species. Then, each letter (or amino acid) at each position in the sequence is compared. Such a comparison can be laid out in a large table, but computers are best able to calculate the relative similarity of many sequences.

Genomic Data At the level of genomes, alleles may be added or lost over time. So, another form of molecular evidence is the presence or absence of specific alleles—or the proteins that result from them. Finally, the relative timing between genetic changes can be inferred.

Evidence of Order and Time Cladistics can determine only the relative order of divergence, or branching, in a phylogenetic tree. To infer the actual time when a group may have begun to "branch off," extra information is needed. Often, this information comes from the fossil record. For example, by using cladistics, scientists have identified lancelets as the closest relative of vertebrates. The oldest known fossils of vertebrates are about 450 million years old, but the oldest lancelet fossils are 535 million years old. So, these two lineages must have diverged more than 450 million years ago.

More recently, scientists have noticed that most DNA mutations occur at relatively constant rates. So, genetic change can be used as an approximate "molecular clock," as **Figure 8** shows. Scientists can measure the genetic differences between taxa and then estimate the time at which the taxa began to diverge.

Inference Using Parsimony Modern systematists use the *principle of parsimony* to construct phylogenetic trees. This principle holds that the simplest explanation for something is the most reasonable, unless strong evidence exists against the simplest explanation. So, given two possible cladograms, the one that implies the fewest character changes between branch points is preferred.

❯ **Reading Check** *What kinds of molecular data inform cladistics?*

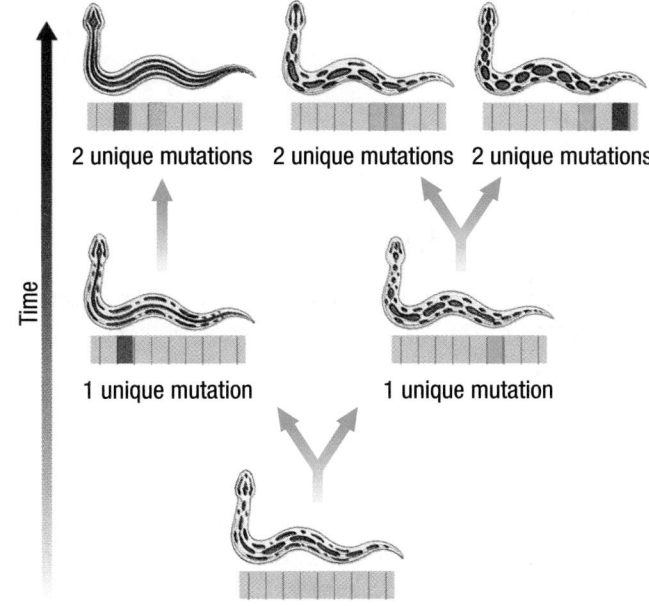

2 unique mutations   2 unique mutations   2 unique mutations

1 unique mutation   1 unique mutation

Genes in ancestral species

Time

Figure 8 Because mutation occurs randomly at any time, an average rate of mutation can be measured and used as a "clock" to estimate the time any two species took to accumulate a number of genetic differences.

Section 2 Review

❯ **KEY IDEAS**

1. **Identify** the kinds of problems that arise when scientists try to group organisms by similarities.
2. **Relate** classification to phylogeny.
3. **Describe** the method of cladistics.
4. **Identify** the kinds of evidence used to infer phylogenies.

CRITICAL THINKING

5. **Justifying Reasoning** Some scientists who study dinosaurs have stated that dinosaurs are not extinct. How could this statement be justified?
6. **Analyzing Relationships** Explain how the outgroup in a cladogram relates to the difference between ancestral and derived characters.

METHODS OF SCIENCE

7. **Taxonomic Challenge** In the past, mammals were identified as animals that have fur and give birth to live offspring, and reptiles were identified as animals that have scales and lay eggs. Then, an animal was found that has fur and lays eggs. How might this problem have been resolved?

New Species

The work of biology is never finished. Indeed, the work of finding, naming, and classifying all living species has barely begun. Scientists have estimated that 1 km² of rain forest may contain hundreds or thousands of species, most of which are currently unknown to science. In fact, new species are "discovered" all of the time, all around the world.

REAL WORLD

Mantophasmatodea—a new order of insects

When is a species "new"?

What does discovering a new species mean? Typically, it means collecting a specimen, giving it a name, and classifying it for the first time by using modern taxonomy. Although truly new species may be evolving at any time, most new species are simply new to science.

Big, Small, Far, Near
Undiscovered species are everywhere! Even mammals, such as this monkey, are still being discovered. Of course, we may never find all of the tiny bugs and microbes in the world.

Biodiversity Hot Spots
Some parts of the world, such as tropical rain forests, contain an extreme diversity of species. This frog is from a region of Sri Lanka that is home to many amphibian species.

Undiscovered Worlds
In 2005, an expedition went into a "lost world" of rain forest in New Guinea that was previously unexplored by scientists. The expedition quickly found dozens of new species, such as this honeyeater bird.

Lemur from Madagascar

Quick Project Find out if any new species have been discovered in your local area in the last few decades. Try to find the name of the new species, the story behind the name, and a photo of the species.

Kingdoms and Domains

Key Ideas	Key Terms	Why It Matters
❯ Have biologists always recognized the same kingdoms? ❯ What are the domains and kingdoms of the three-domain system of classification?	bacteria archaea eukaryote	The three-domain system is one of the latest revolutions in biology.

If you read old books or stories, you might read about plants and animals, or "flora and fauna," but probably not "fungi" or "bacteria."

Updating Classification Systems

For many years after Linnaeus created his system, scientists recognized only two kingdoms: Plantae (plants) and Animalia (animals). Relatively few of Earth's species were known, and little was known about them. ❯ **Biologists have added complexity and detail to classification systems as they have learned more.** Throughout history, many new taxa have been proposed and some groups have been reclassified.

For example, **Figure 9** shows sponges, which were first classified as plants. Then, the invention of the microscope allowed scientists to look at cells. Scientists learned that sponges have cells that are much more like animal cells than like plant cells. So today, sponges are classified as animals. The microscope prompted many such changes.

From Two to Five Kingdoms In the 1800s, scientists added Kingdom Protista as a taxon for unicellular organisms. Soon, they noticed the differences between prokaryotic cells and eukaryotic cells. So, scientists created Kingdom Monera for prokaryotes and left single-celled eukaryotes in Kingdom Protista. By the 1950s, five kingdoms were used: Monera, Protista, Fungi, Plantae, and Animalia.

Six Kingdoms In the 1990s, Kingdom Monera came into question. Genetic data suggested two major groups of prokaryotes. So, Kingdom Monera was split into two new kingdoms: Eubacteria and Archaebacteria.

❯ **Reading Check** *What were the original Linnaean kingdoms?*

Sponge cells with flagella

Figure 9 Early scientists classified sponges as plants because sponges are attached to the sea floor. Further study and microscopic views in particular led to a reclassification of sponges as animals. ❯ What features of sponges might have led to this reclassification?

433

Characteristics of Domains and Kingdoms

Domain	Bacteria	Archaea	Eukarya			
Kingdom	Eubacteria	Archae-bacteria	Protista	Fungi	Plantae	Animalia
Example	*Streptococcus pneumoniae*	*Staphylo-thermus marinus*	paramecium	spore cap mushroom	Texas paintbrush	white-winged dove
	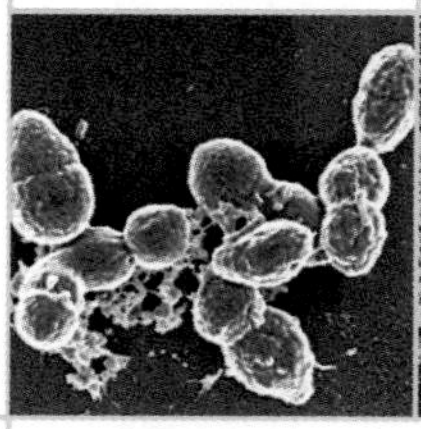	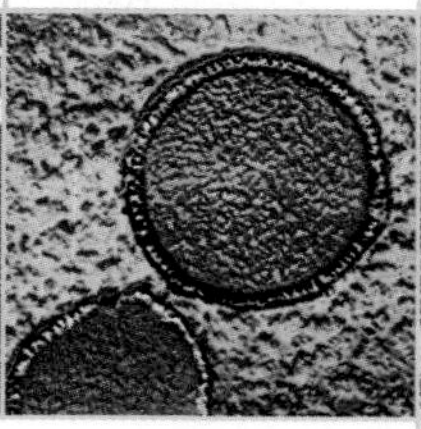	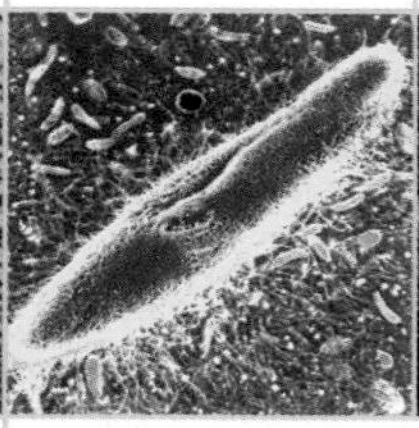			
Cell type	prokaryote		eukaryote			
Cell walls	cell walls with peptidoglycan	cell walls with unique lipids	some species with cell walls	cell walls with chitin	cell walls with cellulose	no cell walls
Number of cells	unicellular		unicellular or multicellular	mostly multicellular	mostly multicellular	multicellular
Nutrition	autotroph or heterotroph			heterotroph	autotroph	heterotroph

Figure 10 This table shows the major characteristics used to define the domains and kingdoms of the modern Linnaean system. ❯ **What other kind of characteristic differs between kingdoms?**

The Three-Domain System

As biologists began to see the differences between the two kinds of prokaryotes, they also saw the similarities among all eukaryotes. So, a new system was proposed that divides all organisms into three domains: Bacteria, Archaea, and Eukarya. ❯ **Today, most biologists tentatively recognize three domains and six kingdoms. Figure 10** shows the major characteristics of these taxa.

Major Characteristics Major taxa such as kingdoms are defined by major characteristics. These characteristics include:

- **Cell Type** The cells may be either *prokaryotic* or *eukaryotic*.
- **Cell Walls** The cells may either have a cell wall or lack a cell wall.
- **Body Type** An organism is either *unicellular* or *multicellular*.
- **Nutrition** An organism is either an *autotroph* (makes nutrients from inorganic materials) or a *heterotroph* (gets nutrients from other organisms). Some taxa have unique means of nutrition.
- **Genetics** As you have learned, related groups of organisms will have similar genetic material and systems of gene expression. So, organisms may have a unique system of DNA, RNA, and proteins.

Domain Bacteria ❯ Domain Bacteria is equivalent to Kingdom Eubacteria. The common name for members of this domain is *bacteria*. **Bacteria** are prokaryotes that have a strong exterior cell wall and a unique genetic system. However, bacteria have the same kind of cell membrane lipid as most eukaryotes do.

Field Guides

Have you ever used field guides to identify animals or plants? Do you know how these guides are organized? Take a few guides outside, and take a closer look.

Procedure

1 Gather **several different field guides** for plants or other organisms in your area. Also gather a **magnifying glass** and a **specimen jar.** Take these items with you to a **local natural area.**

2 ◈ CAUTION: **Do not touch or disturb any organisms without your teacher's permission; leave all natural items as you found them.** Try to find and identify at least two organisms that are listed in your field guides. Make notes to describe each organism.

Analysis

1. **Analyzing Methods** How difficult was identifying your organisms? How certain are you of your identification?

2. **Comparing Systems** How are the field guides organized? What other ways could they be organized?

All bacteria are similar in physical structure, with no internal compartments. Traditionally, bacteria have been classified according to their shape, the nature of their cell wall, their type of metabolism, or the way that they obtain nutrients. Bacteria are the most abundant organisms on Earth and are found in almost every environment.

Domain Archaea ▶ Domain Archaea is equivalent to Kingdom Archaebacteria. The common name for members of this domain is *archaea.* **Archaea** have a chemically unique cell wall and membranes and a unique genetic system. The genetic systems of archaea share some similarities with those of eukaryotes that they do not share with those of prokaryotes. Scientists think that archaea began to evolve in a separate lineage from bacteria early in Earth's history and that some archaea eventually gave rise to eukaryotes.

Archaea were first found by scientists in extreme environments, such as salt lakes, the deep ocean, or hot springs that exceed 100°C. These archaea are called *extremophiles.* Other archaea called *methanogens* live in oxygen-free environments. However, some archaea live in the same environments as many bacteria do.

Domain Eukarya ▶ Domain Eukarya is made up of Kingdoms Protista, Fungi, Plantae, and Animalia. Members of the domain Eukarya are **eukaryotes,** which are organisms composed of eukaryotic cells. These cells have a complex internal structure. This structure enabled the cells to become larger than the earliest cells and enabled the evolution of multicellular life. While eukaryotes vary in many fundamental respects, they share several key features.

▶ **Reading Check** *Which kingdoms are prokaryotic?*

bacteria (bak TIR ee uh) extremely small, single-celled organisms that usually have a cell wall and that usually reproduce by cell division; members of the domain Bacteria

archaea (ahr KEE uh) prokaryotes that are distinguished from other prokaryotes by differences in their genetics and in the makeup of their cell wall; members of the domain Archaea

eukaryote an organism made up of cells that have a nucleus enclosed by a membrane, multiple chromosomes, and a mitotic cycle; members of the domain Eukarya

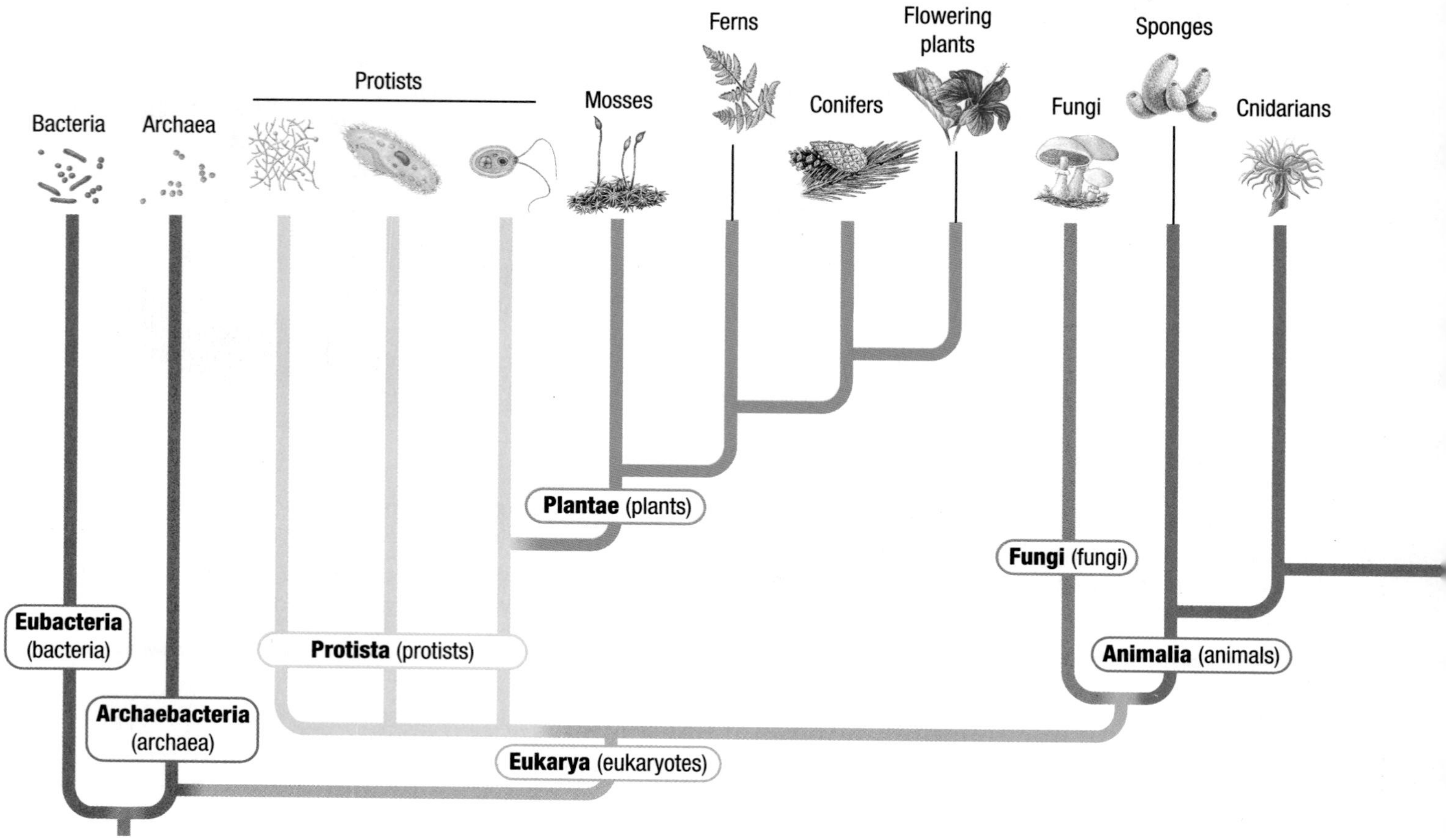

Figure 11 This tree of life shows current hypotheses of the relationships between all major groups of organisms. For updates on phylogenetic information, visit **go.hrw.com** and enter the keyword **HX8 Phylo.** ❯ Why might this type of model be revised?

Phylogenetic Tree Look carefully at **Figure 11.** Try to identify which groups are most closely related to each other. Which label includes lineages that do not share a unique common ancestor?

Characteristics of Eukaryotes Eukaryotes have highly organized cells. All eukaryotes have cells with a nucleus and other internal compartments. Also, true multicellularity and sexual reproduction occur only in eukaryotes. True multicellularity means that the activities of individual cells are coordinated and the cells themselves are in contact. Sexual reproduction means that genetic material is recombined when parents mate. Sexual reproduction is an important part of the life cycle of most eukaryotes.

Kinds of Eukaryotes The major groups of eukaryotes are defined by number of cells, body organization, and types of nutrition.

- **Plantae** Almost all plants are autotrophs that produce their own food by absorbing energy and raw materials from their environment. This process is *photosynthesis,* which occurs inside chloroplasts. The cell wall is made of a rigid material called *cellulose.* More than 270,000 known species of plants exist.

- **Animalia** Animals are multicellular heterotrophs. Their bodies may be simple collections of cells or highly complex networks of organ systems. Animal cells lack the rigid cell walls that plant cells have. More than 1 million known species of animals exist.

- **Fungi** Fungi are heterotrophs and are mostly multicellular. Their cell wall is made of a rigid material called *chitin.* Fungi are considered to be more closely related to animals than to any other kingdom. More than 70,000 known species of fungi exist.

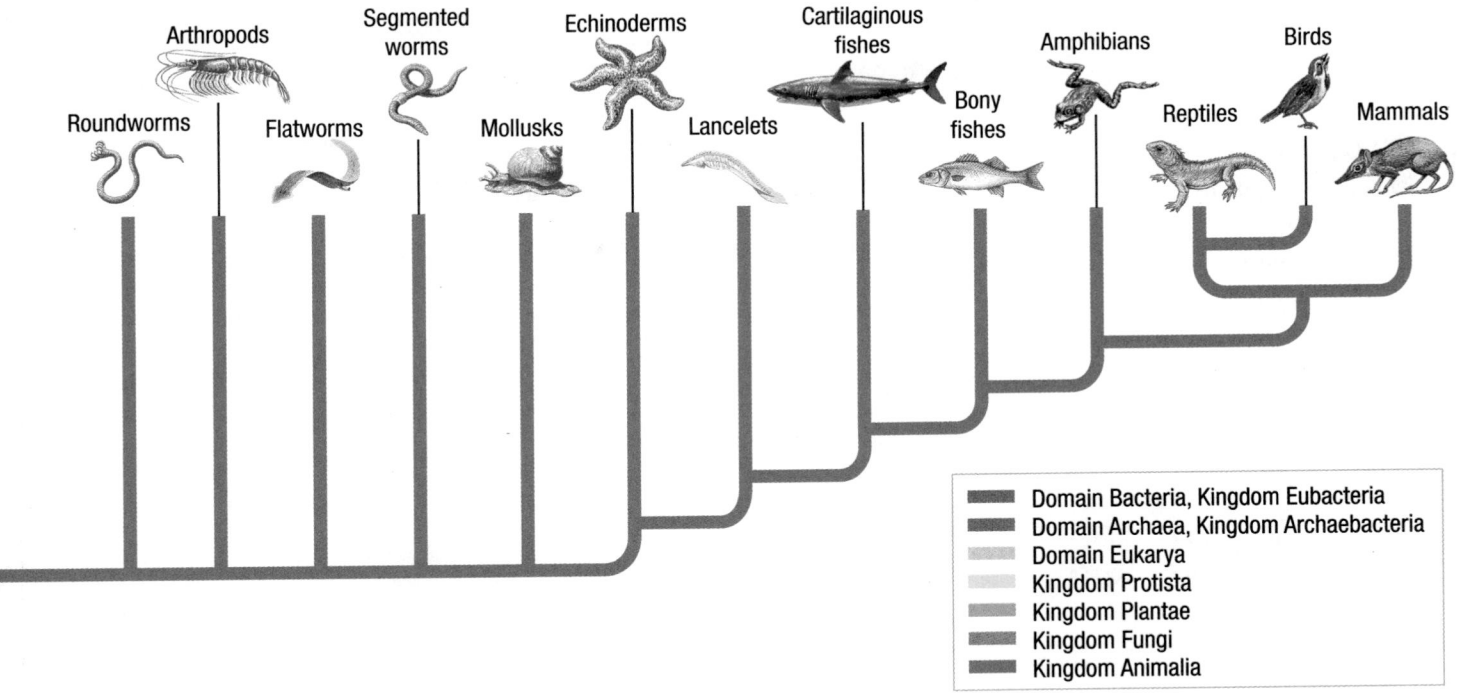

Roundworms
Arthropods
Flatworms
Segmented worms
Mollusks
Echinoderms
Lancelets
Cartilaginous fishes
Bony fishes
Amphibians
Reptiles
Birds
Mammals

■ Domain Bacteria, Kingdom Eubacteria
■ Domain Archaea, Kingdom Archaebacteria
▨ Domain Eukarya
░ Kingdom Protista
▒ Kingdom Plantae
▓ Kingdom Fungi
■ Kingdom Animalia

- **Protista** Kingdom Protista is a diverse group. Unlike the other three Kingdoms of Eukarya, Protista is not a natural group but rather a "leftover" taxon. Any single-celled eukaryote that is *not* a plant, animal, or fungi can be called a *protist*. Protists did not descend from a single common ancestor.

    For many years , biolgists recognized four major groups of protists: flagellates, amoebas, algae, and parasitic protists. More recently, biologists have proposed to replace Protista with several new kingdoms. These kingdoms would classify protists that seem to be unrelated to any other groups. However, some protists are being reclassified into other kingdoms. For example, algae that have chloroplasts are thought to be most closely related to plants, as shown in **Figure 11.** Biologists have not yet agreed how to resolve all of these issues.

❯ Reading Check *Which kingdoms contain only heterotrophs?*

go.hrw.com
✳ interact online
Keyword: HX8CLSF11

Section 3 Review

❯ KEY IDEAS

1. **Outline** how biologists have changed the major levels of the Linnaean system over time.

2. **List** the three domains, identify the kingdoms that align with each domain, and list the major characteristics of each kingdom.

CRITICAL THINKING

3. **Finding Evidence** The *theory of endosymbiosis* proposes that eukaryotes descended from a primitive combination of both archaea and bacteria. What evidence supports this theory?

4. **Science and Society** Microscopes led scientists to recognize new kingdoms. What other technology has impacted classification?

ALTERNATIVE ASSESSMENT

5. **Tree of Life Poster** Make a poster of the tree of life. At appropriate places on the tree, add images of representative organisms, along with labels. Include all domains and kingdoms as well as at least three major taxa within each kingdom.

Objectives

> Identify objects by using a dichotomous key.

> Design a dichotomous key for a group of objects.

Materials

- objects, common (6 to 10)
- labels, adhesive
- pencil

Safety

Dichotomous Keys

One way to identify an unknown organism is to use an identification key, which contains the major characteristics of groups of organisms. A dichotomous key is an identification key that contains pairs of contrasting descriptions. After each description, a key either directs the user to another pair of descriptions or identifies an object. In this lab, you will design and use a dichotomous key. A dichotomous key can be written for any group of objects.

Procedure

Use a Dichotomous Key

1. Work with a small group. Use the dichotomous key to identify the tree that produced each of the leaves shown here. Identify one leaf at a time. Always start with the first pair of statements (1a and 1b). Follow the direction beside the statement that describes the leaf.

2. Proceed through the key until you get to the name of a tree. Record your answer for each leaf shown.

A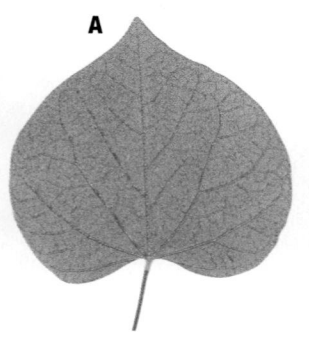

B

C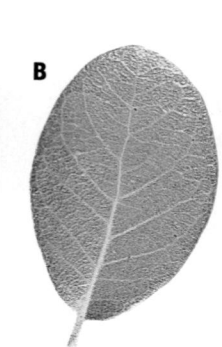

D

E

F

Key to Forest Trees		
1a	Leaf edge is smooth or barely curved.	go to 2
1b	Leaf edge has teeth, waves, or lobes.	go to 3
2a	Leaf has a sharp bristle at its tip.	shingle oak
2b	Leaf has no bristle at its tip.	go to 4
3a	Leaf edge has small, shallow teeth.	Lombardy poplar
3b	Leaf edge has deep waves or lobes.	go to 5
4a	Leaf is heart shaped.	eastern redbud
4b	Leaf is not heart shaped.	live oak
5a	Leaf edge has less than 20 large lobes.	English oak
5b	Leaf edge has more than 20 waves.	chestnut oak

Design a Dichotomous Key

3  Put on safety goggles, gloves, and a lab apron. Choose 6 to 10 objects from around the classroom or from a collection supplied by your teacher. Before you go to the next step, have your teacher approve the objects your group has chosen.

4 Study the structure and organization of the dichotomous key, which includes pairs of contrasting descriptions that form a "tree" of possibilities. Use this key as a model for the next step.

5 Work with the members of your group to design a new dichotomous key for the objects that your group selected. Be sure that each part of the key leads to either a definite identification of an object or another set of possibilities. Be sure that every object is included.

6 Test your key by using each one of the objects in your collection.

Exchange and Test Keys

7 After each group has completed the steps above, exchange your key and your collection of objects with another group. Use the key you receive to identify each of the new objects. If the new key does not work, return it to the group so that corrections can be made.

Cleanup

8 Clean up your work area and return or dispose of materials as directed by your teacher. Wash your hands thoroughly before you leave the lab and after you finish all of your work.

*SCI*LINKS.

www.scilinks.org
Topic: Classification
Code: HX80295

Analyze and Conclude

1. Summarizing Data List the identity of the tree for each of the leaves that you analyzed in step 2.

2. SCIENTIFIC METHODS Critiquing Procedures What other characteristics might be used to identify leaves by using a dichotomous key?

3. Analyzing Results What challenges did your group face while making your dichotomous key?

4. Evaluating Results Were you able to use another group's key to identify the group's collection of objects? Describe your experience.

5. SCIENTIFIC METHODS Analyzing Methods Does a dichotomous key begin with general descriptions and then proceed to more specific descriptions, or vice versa? Explain your answer by using examples.

6. SCIENTIFIC METHODS Evaluating Methods Is a dichotomous key the same as the Linnaean classification system? Explain your answer.

Extension

7. Research Do research in the library or media center to find out what types of methods, other than dichotomous keys, are used to identify organisms.

go.hrw.com
SUPER SUMMARY
Keyword: HX8CLSS

Key Ideas	Key Terms

1 The Importance of Classification

> Biologists use taxonomic systems to organize their knowledge of organisms. These systems attempt to provide consistent ways to name and categorize organisms.

> All scientific names for species are made up of two Latin or Latin-like terms.

> In the Linnaean system of classification, organisms are grouped at successive levels of a hierarchy based on similarities in their form and structure. The eight levels of modern classification are domain, kingdom, phylum, class, order, family, genus, and species.

taxonomy (423)
genus (424)
binomial nomenclature (424)

2 Modern Systematics

> Scientists traditionally have used similarities in appearance and structure to group organisms. However, this approach has proven problematic.

> Grouping organisms by similarity is often assumed to reflect phylogeny, but inferring phylogeny is complex in practice.

> Cladistic analysis is used to select the most likely phylogeny among a given set of organisms.

> Biologists compare many kinds of evidence and apply logic carefully in order to infer phylogenies.

phylogeny (428)
cladistics (429)

3 Kingdoms and Domains

> Biologists have added complexity and detail to classification systems as they have learned more.

> Today, most biologists tentatively recognize three domains and six kingdoms. Domain Bacteria is equivalent to Kingdom Eubacteria. Domain Archaea is equivalent to Kingdom Archaebacteria. Domain Eukarya is made up of Kingdoms Protista, Fungi, Plantae, and Animalia.

bacteria (434)
archaea (435)
eukaryote (435)

Chapter 18 Review

READING TOOLBOX

1. **Word Parts** Use the table of word parts at the beginning of this chapter to analyze the word *phylogeny*.

2. **Concept Map** Make a Venn diagram that shows the relationships between all major levels of the modern Linnaean classification system.

Using Key Terms

For each pair of terms, explain how the meanings of the terms differ.

3. *genus* and *species*

4. *bacteria* and *archaea*

Complete each of the following sentences by choosing the correct term from the word bank.

> *cladistics*   *taxonomy*
> *phylogeny*   *binomial nomenclature*

5. Scientists use ___ to name and classify organisms.

6. All modern scientific names are based on Linnaeus's original system of ___.

7. Today, biologists use ___ to analyze evolutionary relationships between groups of organisms.

8. Looking at obvious similarities is not always enough to infer ___.

Understanding Key Ideas

9. Which language is used for each scientific name?
   a. Greek
   b. Latin
   c. English
   d. French

10. Which classification level contains subgroups within orders?
    a. family
    b. class
    c. phylum
    d. domain

11. Which of the following pairs of characters are analogous but not homologous?
    a. eggs of a lizard and eggs of a snake
    b. feet of a dinosaur and feet of a bird
    c. wings of a butterfly and wings of a bat
    d. beak of a bluebird and beak of a blue jay

12. When constructing a cladogram, systematists use the principle of parsimony. This principle leads to cladograms that contain
    a. very few branch points.
    b. a few large branches, each with many smaller branches.
    c. the greatest number of character changes between branch points.
    d. the fewest number of character changes between branch points.

13. How do scientists use DNA sequences to infer which organisms share the most recent ancestry?
    a. They re-create fossil DNA to model ancient organisms.
    b. They compare all of the genes of every organism that exists.
    c. They look for organisms that share the most similar DNA sequences.
    d. They look for any organisms that have differences in DNA sequences.

Explaining Key Ideas

14. **Justify** the need for scientific nomenclature.

15. **Explain** why analogous characters, such as wings, should not be used to classify organisms.

16. **Differentiate** between the major characteristics of organisms in the domains Bacteria and Eukarya.

17. **Describe** this diagram. What does it represent? What does it tell us about an aster plant and a tomato plant as compared with a snapdragon?

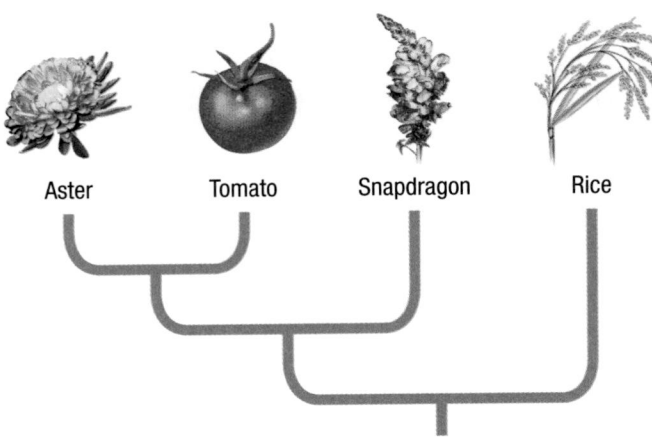

Aster   Tomato   Snapdragon   Rice

Using Science Graphics

This phylogenetic tree represents recent hypotheses about the major lineages of all life and relationships between each of these groups. In this diagram, the length of each branch represents the relative amount of divergence over time for each lineage. Use the diagram below to answer the following questions.

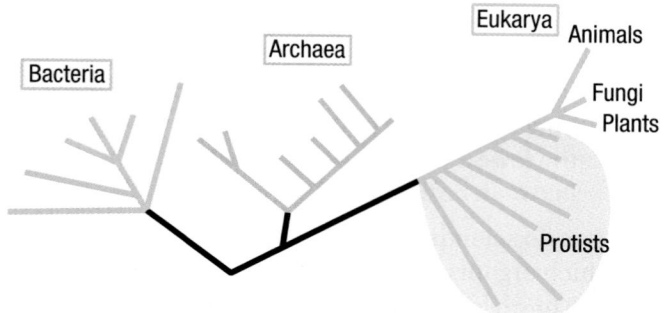

18. According to this model, which of the following two groups are most closely related?
  a. bacteria and plants **c.** archaea and eukarya
  b. animals and fungi **d.** fungi and protists

19. Which of the following statements is in agreement with this model?
  a. Protists do not make up a clade.
  b. Bacteria are descended from protists.
  c. Fungi should be reclassified as plants.
  d. Animals and protists form their own clade.

This table compares characters of several animals. Use the table to answer the following question.

Characters in Vertebrates			
	Amniotic sac	Mammary glands	Placenta
Trout	no	no	no
Hummingbird	yes	no	no
Koala	yes	yes	no
Gray squirrel	yes	yes	yes

20. Which organism in the table would be used as the outgroup in a cladogram that unites the other three organisms?
  a. trout
  b. hummingbird
  c. koala
  d. gray squirrel

Critical Thinking

21. Using Logical Systems In practice, taxonomists have invented many "in-between" levels for the Linnaean system, such as "subclass" or "superorder." Why might they have done this?

22. Analyzing Concepts Explain why ancestral characters are associated with the outgroup in a cladogram.

23. Constructing Explanations How could the presence of extra bones and a tail on a chicken embryo help scientists understand the evolutionary history of chickens?

24. Justifying an Opinion Given the the current characteristics of each kingdom in the six-kingdom system, would you split any of the kingdoms into new kingdoms? Explain your reasoning.

25. Comparing Features What similarities and differences exist between animals and fungi?

Why It Matters

26. New Species Will scientists ever finish classifying all species? Explain your answer.

Writing for Science

27. Lyrics Choose one of the six kingdoms, and write a song or poem about it.

Alternative Assessment

28. Linnaean Album Use library or Internet resources to make a picture album representing the six kingdoms. Find a picture of one species from each kingdom, and mount a copy of the picture in your album. Add a listing of each species' classification, using as many taxonomic levels as possible.

Math Skills

29. Rates Suppose that the amino acid sequence for gene Z of plant A has 10 bases that differ from those in the sequence for the same gene in plant B. Assume that mutations in this kind of gene occur at a rate of 2 mutations every 10,000 years. Estimate how long ago these two plants diverged from a common ancestor.

> **TEST TIP** After you finish writing your answer to a short-response item, proofread it for errors in spelling, grammar, and punctuation.

Science Concepts

1. Why do biologists have taxonomic systems?
   A to provide descriptive Latin names
   B to maintain a small number of taxa
   C to provide consistent ways to identify and classify organisms as they are being studied
   D to construct a family tree that predicts how many species may be discovered in the future

2. Which taxonomic system was developed by Carl Linnaeus in the 1750s and is used today?
   F cladistics
   G taxonomic phylogeny
   H the polynomial system
   J binomial nomenclature

This diagram shows the major levels of taxonomy in the modern Linnaean system. Use the diagram to answer the following questions.

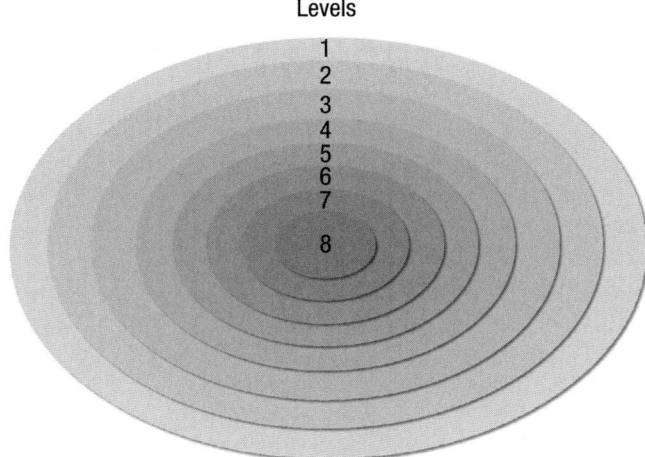

Levels
1
2
3
4
5
6
7
8

3. Which level represents the genus category?
   A level 1   C level 7
   B level 2   D level 8

4. Which level represents the kingdom category?
   F level 1   H level 7
   G level 2   J level 8

Using Science Graphics

This diagram shows the relationship between several types of plants. Use the diagram to answer the following questions.

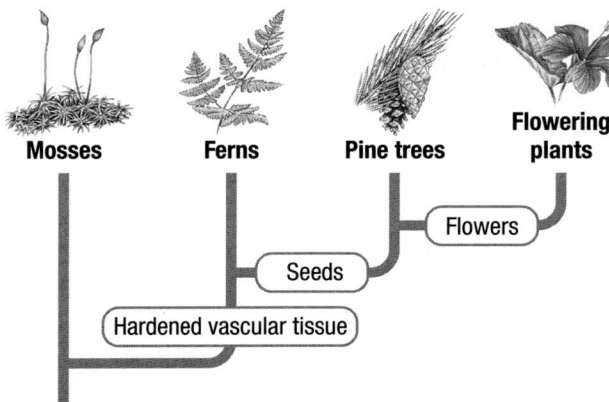

Mosses   Ferns   Pine trees   Flowering plants

Flowers

Seeds

Hardened vascular tissue

5. Which derived character is shared by pine trees and flowering plants but not ferns?
   A seeds   C mosses
   B flowers   D vascular tissue

6. Which of the following pairs of plant groups form a clade that is exclusive of all other plants?
   F mosses and ferns
   G ferns and pine trees
   H mosses and flowering plants
   J pine trees and flowering plants

7. What is the name of the domain that contains all of the organisms shown in the diagram?
   A Algae   C Eukarya
   B Plantae   D Bacteria

Writing Skills

8. **Short Response** Describe the origins of the modern Linnaean system of taxonomy.

9. **Extended Response** Write an essay that summarizes the historical development of scientific naming and classification systems. Include the reasons why such systems were invented, and describe the ways that modern systematics differs from earlier systems.

Chapter 19

History of Life on Earth

Preview

1 How Did Life Begin?
The Basic Chemicals of Life
Life's Building Blocks
The First Cells

2 The Age of Earth
The Fossil Record
Analyzing Fossil Evidence
Describing Geologic Time

3 Evolution of Life
Precambrian Time
Paleozoic Era
Mesozoic and Cenozoic Eras

Why It Matters

The history of life on Earth is like a puzzle; scientists continue to search for evidence and to put it together into a cohesive theory.

The Fly Geysers of the Black Rock Desert in Nevada are surrounded by a pool of water in which many different types of minerals are dissolved.

The geyser was created in the 1960s when farmers drilled into the earth to locate water. Boiling water spewed from the ground, and the molecules in the water created colorful deposits.

InquiryLab

Logical Order

By analyzing overlap in layers of sedimentary rock, scientists reassemble the relative order of much longer sequences of layers.

Procedure

1 Write the following sequence of letters on **six individual index cards** with a **marker**: WXQ, PNB, NBSF, RTK, SFVW, and TKLPN.

2 Look for overlaps in the sequences between individual cards. You can use this overlap to infer the order of the entire series.

Analysis

1. Sequence the most likely order of letters in the complete series.

2. Debate how the amount of overlap affected how you established this order.

3. Estimate how a newly discovered rock sample that had the sequence PNAPN would affect the assembled series.

Some of the colors in the deposits are caused by prokaryotes. Certain species can thrive in extreme environments.

READING TOOLBOX

These reading tools can help you learn the material in this chapter. For more information on how to use these and other tools, see **Appendix: Reading and Study Skills.**

Using Words

Word Parts You can tell a lot about a word by taking it apart and examining its prefix and root.

Your Turn Use the information in the table to write your own definition for the following terms.

1. *microsphere*
2. *lithosphere*
3. *paleolithic*

Word Parts		
Word part	Type	Meaning
micro-	prefix	small
paleo-	prefix	ancient
lith	root	rock, stone
sphere	root	ball-shaped object

Using Language

Describing Time Certain words and phrases can help you get an idea of when something happened and for how long it happened. These phrases are called *specific time markers*. Specific time markers include phrases such as 1 hour, yesterday, the 20th century, and 30 years later.

Your Turn Read the sentences below, and write the specific time markers.

1. Jennifer celebrated her 16th birthday on Saturday two weeks ago.
2. Dinosaurs became extinct about 65 million years ago, at the end of the Cretaceous Period.

Using Science Graphics

Process Chart Process charts show the steps that a process takes to get from one point to another point. Events in a process happen in a certain order. There are many words that can be used to describe the order in which things happen. Some of these words include *first, next, then,* and *last*.

Your Turn Use the diagram to answer the following questions.

1. Which event happens second?
2. Which event follows RNA self-replication?
3. Describe the process illustrated in this chart in paragraph form. Use sequence words to indicate in what order things happen.

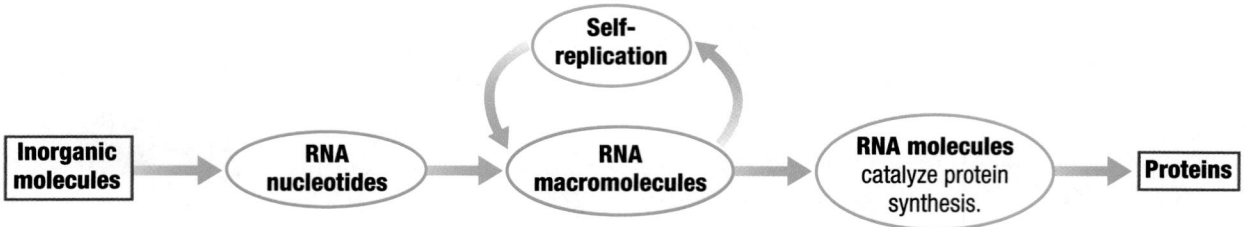

How Did Life Begin?

Key Ideas	Key Terms	Why It Matters
❯ What did the Miller-Urey experiment show about the formation of the basic molecules of life? ❯ What are two theories that propose where the building blocks of life originated on early Earth? ❯ How could molecules have become packaged into cells that contain heritable cellular instructions?	microsphere ribozyme	Studying the origin of life on Earth allows scientists to discover key biological and chemical processes.

Most scientists think that life on Earth evolved through natural processes. The point when life started likely involved simple chemicals.

The Basic Chemicals of Life

In the 1920s, Russian scientist Aleksandr I. Oparin and British scientist John B. S. Haldane suggested that Earth's early oceans contained large amounts of organic molecules. They proposed that these molecules formed spontaneously in chemical reactions that were activated by energy from the sun, volcanic eruptions, and lightning.

Oparin and American scientist Harold Urey, along with other scientists, hypothesized that the early atmosphere was rich in hydrogen gas, H_2, and hydrogen-containing gases, such as water vapor, H_2O, ammonia, NH_3, and methane, CH_4. They thought that if the atmosphere lacked oxygen gas, a variety of organic compounds made up of the elements found in these gases could form. This hypothesis was tested in the 1950s by Urey and American scientist Stanley Miller.

The Miller-Urey Experiment Urey and Miller placed the gases into a device like the one in **Figure 1.** To simulate lightning, they used electrical sparks. After a few days, they found organic molecules in the device, which included some of life's basic building blocks: amino acids, fatty acids, and other hydrocarbons (molecules made of carbon and hydrogen). ❯ **The Miller-Urey experiment showed that, under certain conditions, organic compounds could form from inorganic molecules.**

We now know that the molecules used in the Miller-Urey experiment could not have existed in abundance on early Earth. Four billion years ago, shortly after Earth formed, it did not have a protective layer of ozone gas. Ultraviolet radiation from the sun would have destroyed any ammonia and methane in the atmosphere when the ozone layer did not exist. When ammonia and methane gases are absent from the Miller-Urey experiment, key biological molecules are not made. However, the Miller-Urey experiment clearly shows that complex biological compounds can form from simple building blocks.

❯ **Reading Check** *What compounds were formed in the Miller-Urey experiment? (See the Appendix for answers to the Reading Checks.)*

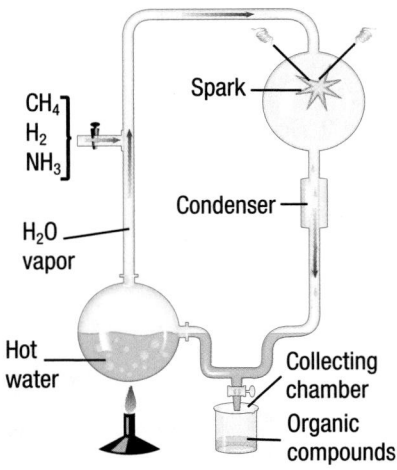

Figure 1 Urey and Miller simulated an atmosphere that Oparin and others incorrectly hypothesized as the atmosphere of early Earth. The experiment produced several organic compounds.

Life's Building Blocks

Scientists agree that the building blocks of life formed under special conditions. They research environments that could have made these molecules. ❯ **Among the hypotheses that address the origin of life, one states that early biological molecules formed close to hydrothermal vents. Organic molecules may also have arrived on early Earth in meteorites.**

Hydrothermal Vents Some scientists think that the chemical reactions that produced the first biological molecules occurred in the oceans of early Earth. The heat from hydrothermal vents, shown in **Figure 2,** could have provided energy for chemical reactions. Within the sea, biological molecules also would have been protected from potentially harmful solar radiation.

Space Some scientists think that organic molecules could have arrived on Earth on meteorites or comets. For example, the meteorite shown in **Figure 2** contains amino acids. Organic molecules likely arrived on early Earth from outside of our atmosphere. It is unknown, however, whether these chemicals influenced the history of life on Earth. But we know that such impacts were more frequent in the early history of Earth than they are now.

The First Cells

Research continues that might provide clues to how biological molecules first began to group together and become packaged into cells. For example, how did amino acids link to form proteins? There are major differences between simple organic molecules and the large organic molecules found in living cells. Research has shown that amino acids can form proteins under certain conditions.

Forming a Cell How did molecules become packaged together inside a cell membrane? To answer this question, scientists have studied the behavior of organic molecules in water. Lipids, which make up cell membranes, tend to combine in water. Certain lipids, when combined with other molecules, can form a tiny droplet that has a surface that resembles a cell membrane.

SCILINKS.

www.scilinks.org
Topic: Origin of Life
Code: HX81083

ACADEMIC VOCABULARY

impact collision

Figure 2 Scientists have suggested that the basic chemicals of life could have originated in deep-sea vents or from outside our atmosphere. ❯ **Why do scientists study the conditions around hydrothermal vents?**

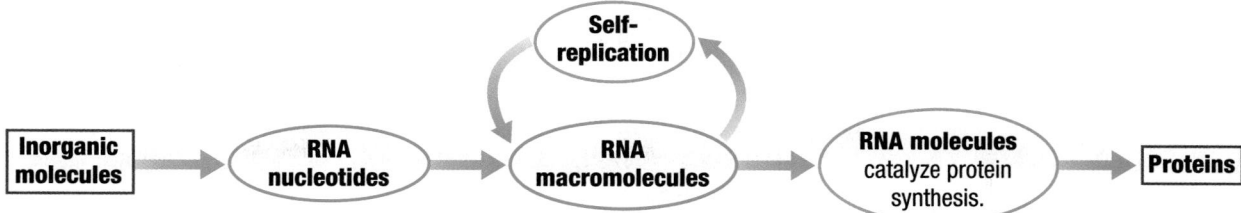

Further research has shown that, in water, lipids can form tiny spherical structures called **microspheres** that act like a membrane. ❯ **Many scientists think that the formation of microspheres may have been the first step toward cellular organization.** Microspheres could not be considered cells, however, unless they had characteristics of living things, including heredity.

Origin of Heredity How did heredity begin? Recall that our DNA contains instructions for making proteins. DNA is also passed on from one generation to the next. In the laboratory, scientists have not been able to make most proteins or DNA form spontaneously in water. However, scientists have been able to form short chains of RNA, the nucleic acid that helps carry out the instructions of DNA, in water.

Scientists now know that RNA molecules perform many tasks in a cell. There are several types of RNA that accomplish these tasks. Each type of RNA has a unique structure that relates to its function. In the 1980s, American scientists Thomas Cech and Sidney Altman found that a certain type of RNA molecule, called a **ribozyme,** can act like an enzyme. Also, they showed that RNA can form spontaneously in water, without DNA. Other scientists have hypothesized that RNA was the first self-replicating molecule that stored information and that catalyzed the formation of the first proteins. One idea of how RNA could have been involved in protein synthesis is shown in **Figure 3.** It was further hypothesized that RNA could have changed—evolved—from one generation to the next. Scientists hypothesize that DNA and proteins eventually took over these roles in the cell.

❯ **Reading Check** *Explain how RNA could have existed before DNA.*

Figure 3 In this proposed model of protein formation, chemical reactions between inorganic molecules formed RNA nucleotides. The nucleotides assembled into large RNA molecules which were able to replicate and to catalyze the formation of proteins.

Process Chart Use the process chart in **Figure 3** to understand the hypothesis about how proteins were created. What is the significance of the loop at the self-replication step?

microsphere (MIE kroh SFIR) a hollow microscopic spherical structure that is usually composed of proteins or a synthetic polymer.

ribozyme (RIE buh ZIEM) a type of RNA that can act as an enzyme

Section

1 Review

❯ **KEY IDEAS**

1. **State** what the Miller-Urey experiment demonstrated.
2. **Describe** two theories that address where the building blocks of life evolved.
3. **Explain** a prevailing theory of how cells evolved.

CRITICAL THINKING

4. **Evaluating Conclusions** People once believed fish could form from the mud in a pond that sometimes dried up. How could you demonstrate that this conclusion is false?
5. **Inferring Conclusions** How might the hypothesis about the origin of heredity change if DNA could form spontaneously in water?

USING SCIENCE GRAPHICS

6. **Analyzing Models** Using **Figure 1,** determine what changes to the apparatus used by Miller and Urey would be necessary to model the production of amino acids and other organic compounds near hydrothermal vents.

Key Ideas	Key Terms	Why It Matters
❯ How is the fossil record used to chronicle the history of life? ❯ How do paleontologists date fossils? ❯ What evidence was used to make the geologic time scale?	fossil record geologic relative dating time scale radiometric mass dating extinction half-life	The fossil record is used to understand the diversity of life on Earth.

Scientists think Earth formed more than 4.5 billion years ago. Fossil evidence indicates that for much of that long history, Earth has been the home of living things.

The Fossil Record

The **fossil record** includes all fossil remains of living things on Earth. ❯ **Both the geographical distribution of organisms and when they lived on Earth can be inferred from the fossil record. It chronicles the diversity of life on Earth.** The fossil record also provides evidence of intermediate forms of life and suggests how organisms are related to each other. Although our examination of the fossil record will never be complete, it presents strong evidence that evolution has taken place.

How Fossils Form Most fossils are found in sedimentary rock. These fossils form when organisms and traces of organisms are rapidly buried in fine sediments that are deposited by water, wind, or volcanic eruptions. The formation of one kind of fossil from a marine animal is shown in **Figure 4.** Environments that often cause fossil formation are wet lowlands, slow-moving streams, lakes, shallow seas, and areas near volcanoes that spew volcanic ash. However, many species have lived in environments where fossils do not form. Even if an organism lives in an environment where fossils can form, its dead body might not be buried in sediment before it decays or is eaten.

Figure 4 Fossils can form in several ways. The most common way is when an organism dies and is buried in sediment. ❯ **What happens when an organism is covered by sediment?**

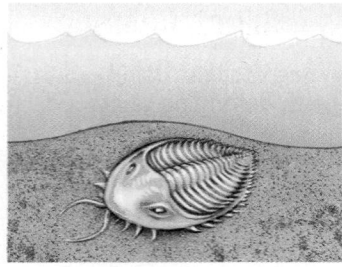

❶ This trilobite dies and becomes buried under layers of sediment that are deposited by water.

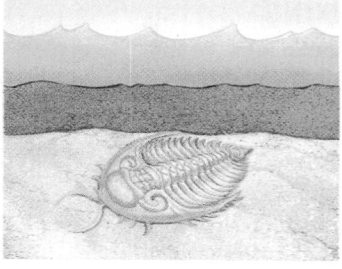

❷ The organism gradually dissolves and leaves a hollow impression, or mold, in the sediment.

❸ Over time, the mold may fill with minerals, which forms a cast of the organism.

Analyzing Fossil Evidence

Earth's surface changes constantly. Rocks are eroding and are laid down as sediment. This sediment forms layers of sedimentary rock called *strata,* shown in **Figure 5.** According to the *principle of superposition,* older strata are covered by younger strata. However, geologic events such as earthquakes can affect how the strata are arranged. ❯ **In order to analyze fossil evidence, paleontologists use both relative and absolute dating methods to date fossils.**

Types of Fossils The most common types of fossils are little-altered mineral shells of animals. In some cases, as shown in **Figure 4,** an organism breaks down, leaving a hollow space. This mold may fill with minerals. In other cases, the pores of the organism are filled with minerals, preserving the shape of the organism. An example of a mineralized fossil is shown in **Figure 5.** In rare cases, fossils are preserved in hardened plant sap, or amber. In these fossils, soft parts of the tissue are preserved in detail.

Relative Age A process called **relative dating** is used to estimate ages of fossils found within strata. Relative dating cannot reveal a fossil's age, in years. But it can reveal the order that strata and the fossils within them were laid down over time. Paleontologists organize fossils into a sequence based on the relative age of the strata in which the fossil was found.

Index Fossils An *index fossil* is a fossil of an organism that was common and had widespread geographical distribution during a certain time in Earth's history. Index fossils are used to estimate the age of other strata that contain the same type of fossil. Scientists have compared patterns of strata and the index fossils within them to make the geologic time scale.

❯ **Reading Check** *What is the principle of superposition?*

---

fossil record the history of life in the geologic past as indicated by the traces or remains of living things

relative dating a method of determining whether an event or object, such as a fossil, is older or younger than other events or objects

READING TOOLBOX

Word Parts The suffix *-ologist* means "one who studies." What do you think a paleontologist does?

Figure 5 Rock strata are easily visible in the Grand Canyon. Gastropod fossils like this one have been found in the region.

Strata on top formed more recently than strata beneath them.

Older strata are underneath younger strata.

Radioactive Decay

You can use pennies to model radioactive decay.

Half-life	Number of coins remaining
1	
2	
3	

Procedure

1 Work in pairs. Make a data table like the one shown.

2 Place **100 pennies** into a **box that has a lid.**

3 Shake the box gently. Remove the pennies showing heads. This process models one half-life. Record the number of coins remaining in the box.

4 Repeat step 3 until every coin has been removed.

5 Make a line graph of your data. Label "Half-life" on the x-axis and "Coins remaining" on the y-axis.

Analysis

1. Identify what "Number of coins remaining" represents.

2. Calculate the age of your sample if 25 coins remained. Assume that each half-life equals 5,730 years.

3. CRITICAL THINKING **Evaluating Models** Describe how this model illustrates radioactive decay.

---

radiometric dating a method of determining the absolute age of an object, often by comparing the relative percentages of a radioactive (parent) isotope and a stable (daughter) isotope

half-life the time required for half of a sample of a radioactive substance to decay

geologic time scale the standard method used to divide Earth's long natural history into manageable parts

mass extinction an episode during which large numbers of species become extinct

Absolute Age Relative dating can show only whether an object is older or younger than another object. **Radiometric dating** estimates the age in years of an object by measuring certain radioactive isotopes that the igneous rock that surrounds the object contains. An *isotope* is a form of an element whose atomic mass differs from that of other atoms of the same element. Radioactive isotopes, or *radioisotopes,* are unstable isotopes that break down and give off energy in the form of charged particles, or radiation. This breakdown is called *radioactive decay*.

When the radioactive isotope, called a "parent," decays, it produces new isotopes—*daughter* isotopes—that are smaller and more stable. The time required for half of a sample of parent radioisotope to decay into a daughter isotope is the isotope's **half-life. Figure 6** shows this concept. Each radioisotope has a specific half-life, and the rate at which a radioisotope decays is not affected by external factors.

Measuring Age As the parent radioisotope decays, the amount of the daughter radioisotope increases. By comparing the amounts of certain radioisotopes and their daughter isotopes, scientists can calculate how many half-lives have passed since a material formed. One radioisotope that is widely used to date organic materials, such as mummified remains, is carbon-14. The half-life of carbon-14 is relatively short—5,730 years. Carbon-14 is used to measure the age of carbon-containing materials that are younger than 75,000 years old. Older materials have too little isotope remaining for scientists to accurately measure the age of the materials. To find the age of the older materials, scientists have to measure other radioisotopes.

Figure 6 This graph shows the rate of decay of a radioactive isotope.

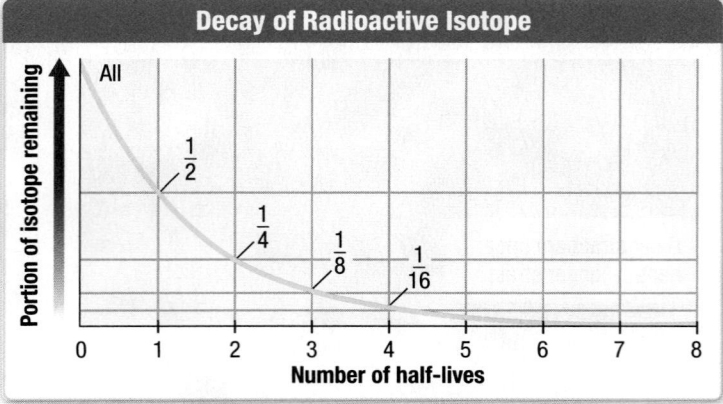

Decay of Radioactive Isotope

Portion of isotope remaining

All

$\frac{1}{2}$

$\frac{1}{4}$

$\frac{1}{8}$

$\frac{1}{16}$

0 1 2 3 4 5 6 7 8

Number of half-lives

Describing Geologic Time

The **geologic time scale** organizes geologic and evolutionary events. ❯ **The geologic time scale is based on evidence in the fossil record and has been shaped by mass extinctions.** A shortened geologic time scale is shown in **Figure 7.**

Divisions of Geologic Time Earth has existed for more than 4 billion years. From the beginning of Earth to about 542 million years ago is often referred to as Precambrian time. From the end of Precambrian time to the present, Earth's history is divided into three *eras*—the Paleozoic Era, the Mesozoic Era, and the Cenozoic Era. These three eras are further divided into periods. Humans appeared during the Quaternary Period.

Mass Extinction Recall that the extinction of a species is the death of all members of that species. When large numbers of species become extinct, the event is called a **mass extinction.** The fossil record indicates that many mass extinctions have occurred during Earth's history. Evidence indicates that world-wide geologic and climate changes are common factors that contribute to mass extinctions. Mass extinctions may have contributed to overall biodiversity on Earth. After a mass extinction, opportunities open for new life-forms to emerge.

Mass extinctions have been used to mark the divisions of geologic time. Large mass extinctions mark the boundaries between eras, as shown on **Figure 7.** For example, mass extinctions occurred at the end of Precambrian time, at the end of the Paleozoic Era, and at the boundary between the Mesozoic Era and Cenozoic Era. Smaller mass extinctions mark the divisions between periods.

❯ **Reading Check** *What evidence shows that mass extinctions occur?*

Geologic Time Scale

Era	Period	Time*
Cenozoic 	Quaternary	1.8
	Tertiary	65.5
MASS EXTINCTION		
Mesozoic 	Cretaceous	146
	Jurassic	200
	Triassic	251
MASS EXTINCTION		
Paleozoic 	Permian	299
	Carboniferous	359
	Devonian	416
	Silurian	444
	Ordovician	488
	Cambrian	542
MASS EXTINCTION		
Precambrian time 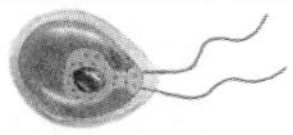	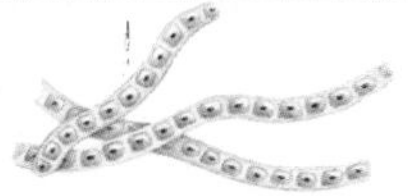	>4,500

*indicates how many millions of years ago the period began

Figure 7 The geologic time scale is based on fossil evidence. The time in the scale refers to the number of years ago that the time period started. ❯ **How long did the Permian period last?**

Section 2 Review

❯ KEY IDEAS

1. **Describe** how the fossil record chronicles the history of life.
2. **Explain** how dating methods are used to analyze fossil evidence.
3. **State** the evidence that scientists have used to create the geologic time scale.

CRITICAL THINKING

4. **Constructing Explanations** Why might the fossil record give an inaccurate picture of the history of biodiversity? Explain your answer.
5. **Explaining Relationships** How could index fossils in two different rock strata in a series help a paleontologist to estimate the absolute age of fossils in a layer of rock between them? Explain your reasoning.

METHODS OF SCIENCE

6. **Describing Methods** You are a paleontologist who is digging for fossils in a remote area. Describe the methods you would use on the dig to make sure that you could estimate the age of the fossils.

Key Ideas	Key Terms	Why It Matters
❯ What major evolutionary developments occurred during Precambrian time? ❯ What dominant organisms evolved during the Paleozoic Era? ❯ What dominant organisms evolved during the Mesozoic Era and the Cenozoic Era?	cyanobacteria endosymbiosis	Knowing the order in which life-forms evolved helps scientists form new hypotheses of how life forms are related.

When did life first evolve on Earth? To find out, scientists study fossils and other evidence of early life, such as "signatures" of certain isotopes in rock. These isotopes are associated with living things.

Precambrian Time

Precambrian time spanned between about 4.5 billion and 542 million years ago. Many critical events occurred during this long period of Earth's history. ❯ **Single-celled prokaryotes and later, eukaryotes, evolved and flourished in Precambrian time. The evolution of multicellular organisms set the stage for the evolution of modern organisms. The accumulation of atmospheric oxygen allowed organisms to become larger and live on land.**

Early Earth was a dangerous place. Meteors bombarded the planet in large numbers. This activity heated Earth's surface repeatedly and made our planet a hostile place for living things. Eventually, fewer meteor impacts occurred, which allowed early cells to evolve.

Prokaryotic Life Recall that organisms on Earth are divided into three groups: eukaryotes and Archaea and bacteria, the prokaryotes. Living examples from these two groups are shown in **Figure 8.** The close relationship of some eukaryotic genes to those of archaeans suggests that archaea played a role in eukaryote evolution.

cyanobacteria
(SIE uh noh bak TIR ee uh) bacteria that carry out photosynthesis; blue-green algae

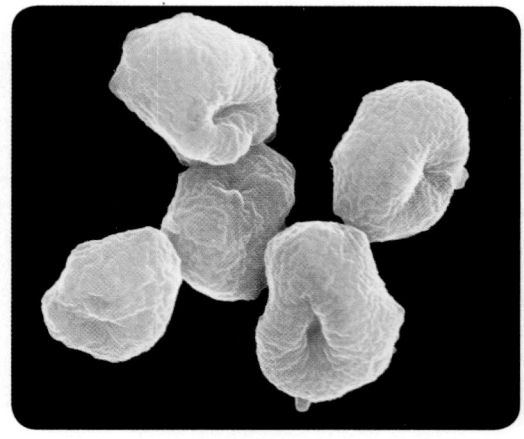 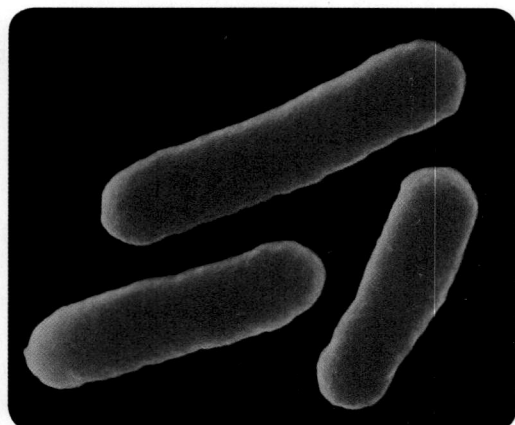

Figure 8 *Sulfolobus* (left) is a living example of archaea. *Escherichia coli* (right) is a living example of bacteria. Both archaea and bacteria are groups of organisms that have existed since ancient times.

Figure 9 Fossilized mats of cyanobacteria, called *stromatolites,* are the most common Precambrian fossils. These modern stromatolites are similar to stromatolites that existed during Precambrian time.

Recall that most prokaryotes are single-celled organisms that lack membrane-bound organelles. The oldest presumed fossils, which are microscopic fossils of prokaryotes, come from rock that is about 3.5 billion years old. The earliest common fossils are those of marine cyanobacteria. **Cyanobacteria** are photosynthetic prokaryotes. Modern cyanobacteria, clustered in layered structures called *stromatolites* are shown in **Figure 9.**

Formation of Oxygen About 2.4 billion years ago, the chemistry of rock layers changed markedly. Because of this, scientists think that cyanbacteria began adding oxygen to the atmosphere at this time. Before cyanobacteria appeared, oxygen gas was scarce on Earth. But as ancient cyanobacteria carried out photosynthesis, they released oxygen gas into Earth's oceans. This oxygen eventually escaped into the air. The increase of oxygen in the ocean destroyed many marine prokaryotes. These organisms had evolved to live without oxygen, which was a poison to them.

As oxygen reached Earth's upper atmosphere, the sun's rays caused some of the oxygen gas, O_2, to chemically react and form molecules of ozone, O_3. In the upper atmosphere, the ozone layer blocks some of the ultraviolet radiation of the sun. The sun provides life-giving light, but overexposure to ultraviolet radiation is dangerous to living things. Organisms on the very early Earth could not survive on land because ultraviolet radiation damaged their DNA. After millions of years however, enough ozone had <u>accumulated</u> to make land a safe place for organisms to live. The first organisms to live on land were prokaryotes.

Eukaryotic Life Later in Precambrian time, the first eukaryotes appeared. Most eukaryotic cells are much larger than prokaryotic cells are. Eukaryotes have a complex system of internal membranes, and their DNA is enclosed within a nucleus. Most eukaryotes have mitochondria. Plants and some protists also have chloroplasts, which carry out photosynthesis. Mitochondria and chloroplasts are the size of prokaryotes, and they contain their own DNA, which is similar to that of prokaryotes.

READING TOOLBOX

Describing Time Scientists describe events in Earth's history in terms of geologic time. Look for references to time in this section, and construct a table of their meanings.

ACADEMIC VOCABULARY

accumulate to collect, especially over a period of time

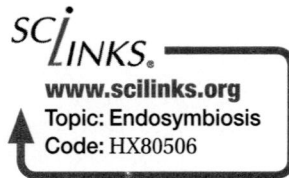

Figure 10 The theory of endosymbiosis states that energy-releasing organelles evolved from ancestors of bacteria.
❯ What genetic evidence supports the theory of endosymbiosis?

Origin of Energy-Releasing Organelles

Origin of Energy-Releasing Organelles Mitochondria and chloroplasts likely originated as described by the endosymbiotic theory proposed by Lynn Margulis, which is illustrated in **Figure 10**. **Endosymbiosis** is a mutually beneficial relationship in which one organism lives within another. Endosymbiotic theory proposes that larger cells engulfed smaller cells, which then began to live inside larger cells. According to this theory, mitochondria are the descendants of symbiotic, aerobic (oxygen-requiring) bacteria. Likewise, scientists think that chloroplasts are thought to be the descendants of symbiotic, photosynthetic bacteria. The following observations support the theory that mitochondria and chloroplasts descended from bacteria:

- **Size and Structure** Mitochondria are the same size as most bacteria. Chloroplasts are the same size as some cyanobacteria.
- **Genetic Material** Both chloroplasts and mitochondria contain genes that are different from those found in the nucleus of the host cell and that are closely related to bacterial genes.
- **Ribosomes** Mitochondrial and chloroplast ribosomes are similar in size and structure to bacterial ribosomes.
- **Reproduction** Like bacteria, chloroplasts and mitochondria reproduce by simple fission. This replication takes place independently of the cell cycle of the host cell.

Multicellularity *Volvox,* a colonial protist, is shown in **Figure 11**. Colonies differ from true multicellular organisms. In true multicellularity, cells communicate with one another and differentiate to form different cell types. The development of multicellular organisms marked an important step in the evolution of life-forms that are familiar to us. Multicellularity first developed in protists in Precambrian time. Scientists think that the first multicellular organisms began as clusters of single-celled organisms. Eventually these cells took on specialized functions.

Endosymbiotic Theory

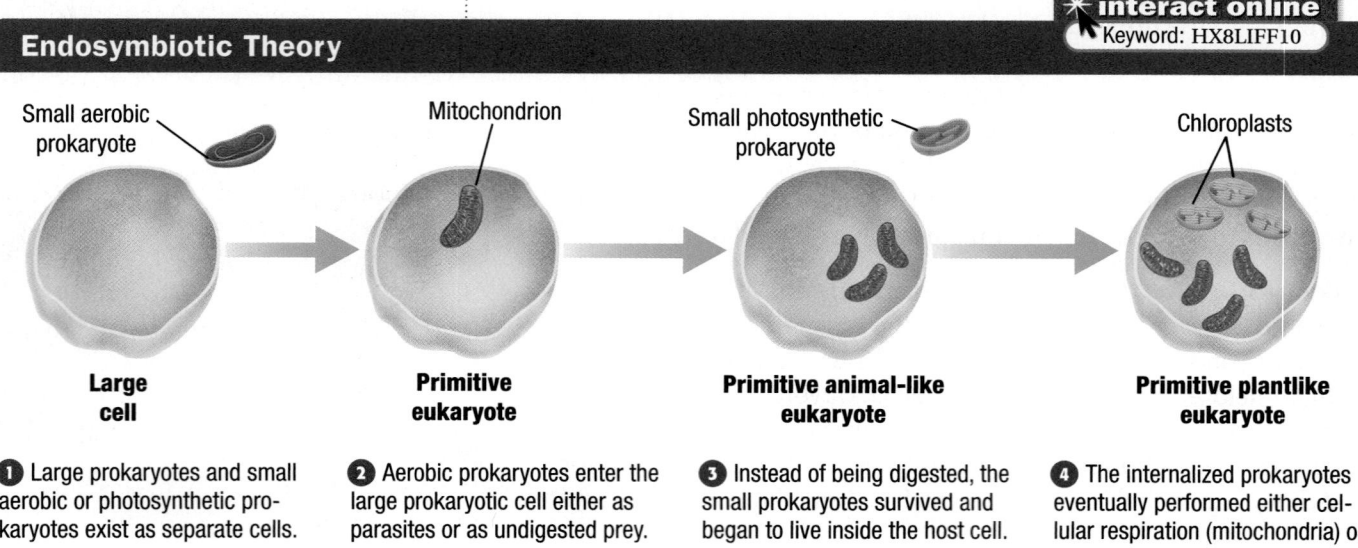

Small aerobic prokaryote

Mitochondrion

Small photosynthetic prokaryote

Chloroplasts

Large cell

Primitive eukaryote

Primitive animal-like eukaryote

Primitive plantlike eukaryote

1 Large prokaryotes and small aerobic or photosynthetic prokaryotes exist as separate cells.

2 Aerobic prokaryotes enter the large prokaryotic cell either as parasites or as undigested prey.

3 Instead of being digested, the small prokaryotes survived and began to live inside the host cell.

4 The internalized prokaryotes eventually performed either cellular respiration (mitochondria) or photosynthesis (chloroplasts).

Hands-On

QuickLab

⏱ 15 min

Timeline of Earth

Using some calculations, you can create your own time-line of Earth's history.

Procedure

1 Copy the table shown onto a piece of paper.

2 Complete the table by using this scale: 1 cm is equal to 10 million years.

3 Lay a 5 m strip of adding-machine paper flat on a hard surface. Use a meterstick, a metric ruler, and a pencil to mark off the beginning and end of Precambrian time according to the time scale that you calculated. Do the same for the three eras. Label each division of time, and make each a different color with colored pencils.

4 Refer to the geologic time scale shown in **Figure 7**. Using the same scale as in step 2, calculate the scale length for each period listed. Mark the boundaries of each period on the paper strip, and label them.

5 Decorate your strip by adding names or drawings of the organisms that lived in each division of time.

Analysis

1. **Identify** in which period humans appeared.

2. **Calculate** the length from the period in which humans appeared to the present.

3. **CRITICAL THINKING** **Interpreting Graphics** What percentage of the geologic time scale do these eras combined represent? What percentage of the geologic time scale does Precambrian time represent?

Era	Length of time (years)	Scale length
Precambrian	4,058,000,000	
Palezoic	291,000,000	
Mesozoic	185,500,000	
Cenozoic	65,500,000 (to present)	

Dominant Life For most of the end of Precambrian time, life probably was limited to prokaryotes and protists, which are eukaryotes. Recent evidence suggests that the oldest known fossils of multicellular eukaryotes have been found in rock that is about 1 billion years old. The first known fossils of true multicellular animals are about 600 million years old. Very early animal fossils are scarce because most animals at that time had soft body parts that did not fossilize well. Fossils of marine animals similar to modern jellyfishes and segmented worms are dated to late Precambrian time.

Mass Extinctions The first known mass extinction in Precambrian time occurred at the time of oxygen build-up and of extreme cold. This mass extinction killed many cyanobacteria as well as other types of bacteria. A second mass extinction, late in Precambrian time, killed off many animals that had recently evolved. This mass extinction opened up new ecological niches, and preceded a burst of diversification in animals. The animals, with their hard exoskeletons and shells, that evolved after this extinction have left a rich fossil record as evidence of evolution.

> **Reading Check** *Why is the evolution of colonial organisms an important step in evolution?*

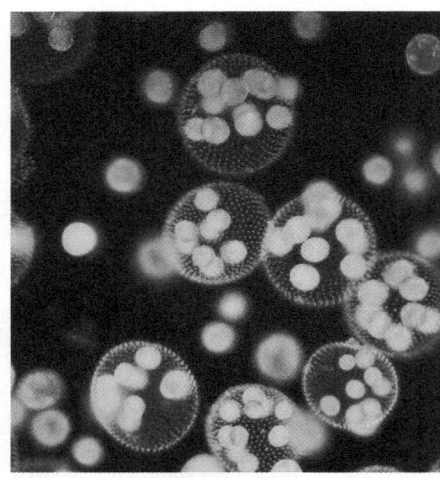

Figure 11 Multicellular protists were the first multicellular organisms. *Volvox* is an example of a multicellular protist.

Paleozoic Era

The Cambrian Period, the first period in the Paleozoic Era, was a time of great evolutionary expansion. The rapid diversification of animals that appeared in the fossil record is sometimes referred to as the "Cambrian explosion," though it occurred over several million years.

Dominant Life The Paleozoic Era was a time of great evolutionary expansion. ❯ **During the Paleozoic Era, marine invertebrates diversified, and marine vertebrates evolved. The first land plants evolved. Some arthropods, and then some vertebrates, left the oceans to colonize land.**

Plants and Fungi on Land The first multicellular organisms to live on land may have been fungi living together with plants or algae. Plants and fungi began living together on the surface of the land about 475 million years ago. Eventually, great forests, illustrated in **Figure 12,** covered much of Earth's landscape.

Plant life from the Paleozoic Era still has an impact on our lives. In the great coal swamps of the Carboniferous Period, organic materials were subjected to pressure from overlying earth. Over millions of years this produced fossil fuels—beds of coal and reservoirs of oil. Humans now burn both oil and coal to release stored energy.

Arthropods An arthropod is an animal that has a hard outer skeleton, a segmented body, and paired, jointed limbs. Although many arthropods continued to live in the oceans, the first animals to successfully live on land were also arthropods. An important terrestrial arthropod—the insect—evolved in the late Devonian.

Vertebrates A vertebrate is an animal with a backbone. According to the fossil record, the first vertebrates were small, jawless fishes that evolved in the oceans about 530 million years ago. Fishes that have jaws appeared about 430 million years ago. For over one hundred million years, vertebrates lived only in the sea. The first land vertebrates, amphibians, came out of the sea about 370 million years ago. Reptiles evolved from amphibian ancestors about 340 million years ago.

Figure 12 The Devonian Period, which began about 416 million years ago, was dominated by large forests, such as the one shown in this illustration.

Mass Extinctions The fossil record indicates that mass extinctions occurred both at the end of the Ordovician Period (440 million years ago) and just before the end of the Devonian Period (375 million years ago). These events eliminated about 70% of all of the species on Earth. The most devastating of all mass extinctions occurred at the end of the Permian Period, about 252 million years ago. More than 90% of all animals species living at the time became extinct.

Mesozoic and Cenozoic Eras

Many of the dominant life-forms on our planet diverged during the Mesozoic and Cenozoic Eras. ❯ **Reptiles, dinosaurs, and birds were the dominant animals during the Mesozoic Era, and mammalian animals dominated the Cenozoic Era.**

Figure 13 This woolly mammoth is an example of an animal that lived during the Quaternary Period. ❯ **Did woolly mammoths live before or after the K-T extinction?**

Dominant Life During the Mesozoic Era, dinosaurs and other reptiles evolved to be the dominant life-forms. Therapsids, which were mammal-like reptiles, gave rise to modern mammals at about the same time that dinosaurs evolved, during the Triassic Period. Scientists think that birds evolved from feathered dinosaurs during the Jurassic Period. Flowering plants evolved during the Cretaceous Period of the Mesozoic Era. The Cenozoic Era is the current era. During this era, mammals, such as the woolly mammoth shown in **Figure 13,** became the dominant life-form on land. The first hominids (early human ancestors) evolved during the Tertiary Period. Modern humans did not appear until the Quaternary Period.

Mass Extinction A mass extinction 65 million years ago included about two-thirds of all land species, including the dinosaurs. This mass extinction is often called the K-T extinction, because it marks the boundary between the Cretaceous Period (K) of the Mesozoic Era and the Tertiary Period (T) of the Cenozoic Era. Scientists think that this mass extinction was caused by a catastrophic event that had widespread effects.

Section 3 Review

❯ KEY IDEAS

1. **Describe** the major events that occurred during Precambrian time.
2. **Name** the types of life-forms that evolved during the Paleozoic Era.
3. **Describe** the dominant life-forms that evolved during the Mesozoic and Cenozoic eras.

CRITICAL THINKING

4. **Justifying Conclusions** A classmate states that mitochondria and chloroplasts descended from the same type of bacteria. Does the evidence support this? Explain your reasoning.
5. **Evaluating an Argument** Defend the argument that fossil fuels are *not* a renewable resource.

CONNECTING KEY IDEAS

6. **Evaluating Viewpoints** Several scientists have said that if a large asteroid struck Earth, the impact could result in a mass extinction. If an asteroid impact did not kill all organisms, would evolution continue or stop? Explain your reasoning.

Nearing the End

Sixty-five million years ago a mass extinction occurred on Earth. The dinosaurs and more than 50% of other species became extinct. What could have caused this worldwide extinction? In 1980, a group of scientists reported evidence that suggested that a huge asteroid 10 km in diameter struck Earth and triggered the mass extinction.

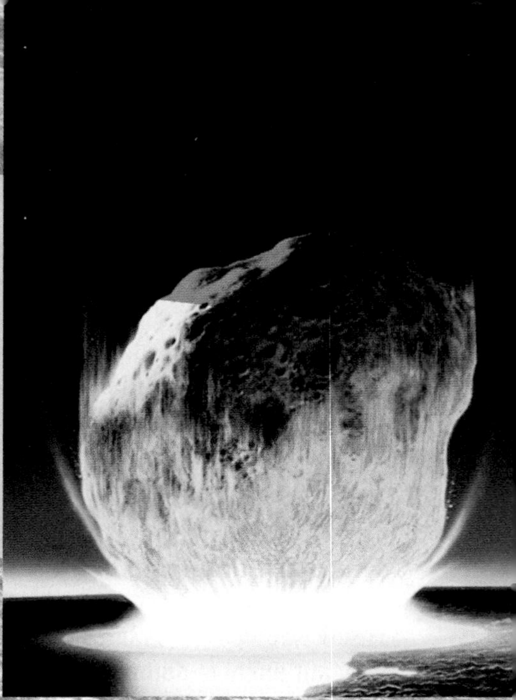

Effects of Impact

A 10 km asteroid would hit Earth with the force of 100,000 billion metric tons of TNT. This impact would generate an earthquake 1,000 times stronger than the strongest recorded earthquake and winds of more than 400 km/h. Long-term effects would be more deadly. Debris blasted upward would reenter the atmosphere at high speeds, heating it and igniting forest fires across the globe.

What Died? The most affected organisms were in the oceans, where 90% of the plankton was killed, which led to the collapse of the oceanic food chain. On land, dinosaurs became extinct but mammals and most non-dinosaur reptiles did not go extinct.

Research Conduct research on the Internet to discover why mammals and most non-dinosaur reptiles survived the KT extinction.

Chapter 19 Lab

Objectives

▶ Model the formation and analysis of strata.

▶ Apply the criteria used to identify index fossils to the strata model.

▶ Evaluate the effectiveness of the model to illustrate relative fossil age.

Materials

- graduated cylinder, 100 mL
- water, tap
- aquarium gravel, four distinct colors
- dish, small (8 per group)
- tablespoon
- beans, dried (navy, black, pinto)

Safety

Model of Rock Strata

Sedimentary strata are arranged so that, if they remain undisturbed, any layer is older than the strata on top of it but younger than the strata beneath it. One way to study strata and the fossils within them is to take core samples through the earth and compare them to samples taken at different locations. Paleontologists can determine the original order of strata by comparing multiple samples from many locations. In this lab, you will model how strata are formed and how they can be used to construct a record of Earth's geologic and biologic history.

Procedure

① Work in groups of three or four. Each student in the group should make a separate model. You will build up a series of layers in a column. You will model eight periods of time using different colors of gravel and different beans. The gravel represents sediment and the beans represent fossils. One tablespoon represents deposition that occurs over a 10,000-year period.

② ◆ **CAUTION: Glass items such as graduated cylinders are fragile and may break.** Add 30 mL of tap water to the graduated cylinder.

③ For the first time period, choose a color. Have each member of the group add 1 Tbsp of that gravel color to their column. Randomly choose one member of the group to omit this layer.

④ Repeat step 3 using another color of your choice until you have modeled eight time periods. At the third time period, insert some navy beans; at the fifth time period, insert pinto beans; at the seventh time period, insert black beans. Record the strata order used by your group. Keep this record as a key to your models.

⑤ Exchange the models from your group with those of another group. Try to determine the order of strata used by that group.

⑥ ◆ ◆ Clean up your lab materials according to your teacher's instructions. Wash your hands before leaving the lab.

Analyze and Conclude

1. **Recognizing Relationships** Explain how this model relates to how sedimentary strata are formed.

2. **SCIENTIFIC METHODS** **Analyzing Conclusions** Describe your success at inferring the other group's strata order.

3. **SCIENTIFIC METHODS** **Inferring Conclusions** Compare the occurrence of the three types of "fossils" across the models from each group. What is the significance of these fossils? Explain your reasoning.

4. **Analyzing Models** If the same fossils are contained within different kinds of strata, can they be classified as index fossils? Explain.

go.hrw.com
SUPER SUMMARY
Keyword: HX8LIFS

Key Ideas	Key Terms

1 How Did Life Begin?

> The Miller-Urey experiment showed that, under certain conditions, organic compounds could form from inorganic molecules.

> Among the scientific theories that address the origin of life, one suggests that life began close to hydrothermal vents, and another proposes that organic molecules arrived on early Earth from a meteorite.

> The formation of microspheres might have been the first step toward cellular organization.

microsphere (449)
ribozyme (449)

2 The Age of Earth

> Both the geographical distribution of organisms and when organisms lived on Earth can be inferred by examining the fossil record.

> In order to analyze fossil evidence, paleontologists use both relative and absolute dating methods to date fossils.

> The geologic time scale is based on evidence in the fossil record and has been shaped by mass extinctions.

fossil record (450)
relative dating (451)
radiometric dating (452)
half-life (452)
geologic time scale (453)
mass extinction (453)

3 Evolution of Life

> Prokaryotes and later, eukaryotes, evolved in the Precambrian. The evolution of multicellular life preceded the evolution of modern life-forms. Atmospheric oxygen allowed life to survive on land.

> During the Paleozoic Era, marine invertebrates diversified, and marine vertebrates evolved. The first land plants evolved. Some arthropods, and then some vertebrates, colonized the land.

> Reptiles, dinosaurs, and birds were the dominant animals in the Mesozoic Era, and mammalian animals were dominant in the Cenozoic Era.

cyanobacteria (455)
endosymbiosis (456)

Chapter 19 Review

1. **Describing Time** Describing time is an important skill when discussing historical events. Use this skill to organize the events of this chapter into a timeline.

2. **Concept Map** Construct a concept map that shows how life began based on information in the chapter. Include the following items in your map: *Miller-Urey experiment, hydrothermal vents, RNA, microspheres, strata,* and *radioactive isotopes.*

Using Key Terms

In your own words, write a definition for each of the following terms:

3. *microsphere*

4. *ribozyme*

5. *strata*

Use each of the following terms in a separate sentence.

6. *mass extinction*

7. *endosymbiosis*

8. *radiometric dating*

Understanding Key Ideas

9. Which gases did Oparin and Urey think were in the atmosphere of early Earth?
   a. water vapor, ammonia, and ozone
   b. oxygen gas, ozone, and water vapor
   c. hydrogen gas, ammonia, and methane
   d. methane, oxygen gas, and hydrogen gas

10. Which of the following can form spontaneously in water?
    a. DNA   c. lipids
    b. proteins   d. RNA

11. Where in the oceans do scientists think that life could have originated?
    a. in shallow bays
    b. near hydrothermal vents
    c. in areas filled with sediment
    d. in surface waters away from shore

12. The first multicellular organisms to invade land were
    a. reptiles.   c. amphibians.
    b. mammals.   d. fungi and plants.

13. A paleontologist can estimate the absolute age of an object by measuring the concentration of
    a. radioisotopes in the object.
    b. stable isotopes in the object.
    c. radioisotopes in rock surrounding the object.
    d. stable isotopes in rock surrounding the object.

14. Which ancient organisms were most likely responsible for the development of the ozone layer?
    a. protists   c. cyanobacteria
    b. sulfur bacteria d. plantlike eukaryotes

Use the diagram to answer the following question.

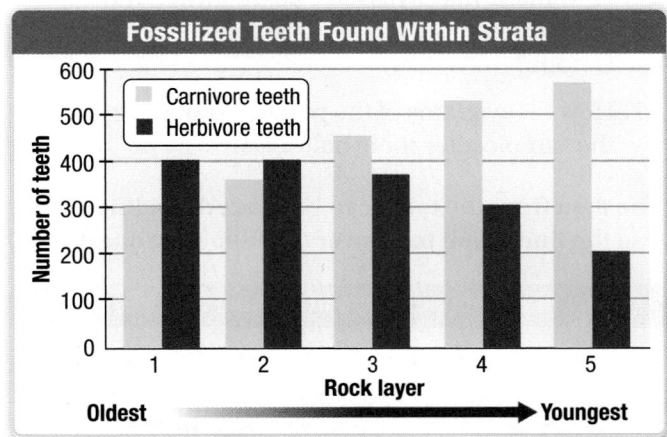

15. At what point did carnivore teeth begin to outnumber herbivore teeth?
    a. between layer 1 and layer 2
    b. between layer 2 and layer 3
    c. between layer 3 and layer 4
    d. between layer 4 and layer 5

Explaining Key Ideas

16. **Distinguish** between microspheres and cells.

17. **Describe** how fossils are formed in a lake.

18. **Explain** the law of superposition.

19. **Name** the dominant types of organisms that evolved during the Mesozoic and Cenozoic eras.

Using Science Graphics

Suppose the mass of a radioactive isotope is 100 kg, or 100,000 g. Use the table to answer the following questions.

Radioactive Isotope Half-Life		
Number of half-lives	Parent isotope	Daughter isotope
0	100,000 g	0 g
1	50,000 g	50,000 g
2	25,000 g	75,000 g
3	12,500 g	87,500 g
4	6,250 g	93,750 g
5	3,125 g	96,875 g

20. **How many half-lives have passed when there is three times more daughter isotope than parent isotope?**

21. **How many grams of the parent isotope are left in the sample after three half-lives?**

The data from the table can be plotted in a line graph. Use the line graph to answer the following questions.

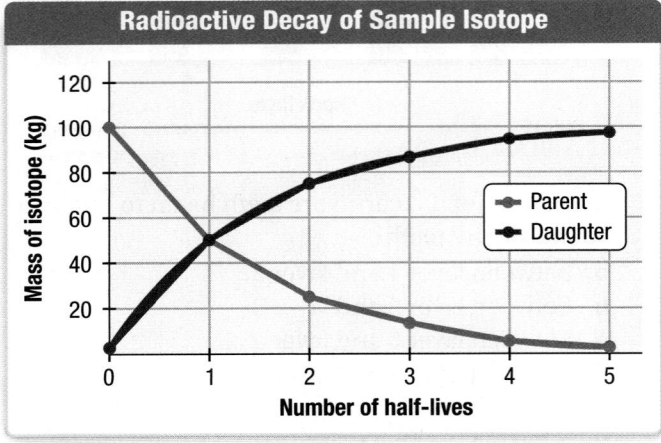

22. **Why is the line graph a curve instead of a straight line?**

23. **If a sample contained 94,000 g of the daughter isotope, where on the line graph would the sample be shown?**

Critical Thinking

24. **Making Inferences** If the building blocks for life came to Earth on a meteorite, under what conditions might those building blocks have formed in space?

25. **Judging Validity** A classmate states that birds are living dinosaurs. Is the classmate correct? Explain.

26. **Predicting Consequences** Some forms of air pollution reduce the thickness of Earth's ozone layer. How might this change affect modern life?

27. **Recognizing Relationships** Propose a hypothesis for the appearance of all animal phyla on Earth within a relatively short period during late Precambrian time and the early Cambrian Period.

28. **Justifying Conclusions** Justify the argument that today's organisms would not exist if mass extinctions had not occurred.

Methods of Science

29. **Forming Hypotheses** State the hypothesis that was tested in the Miller-Urey experiment.

Alternative Assessment

30. **Life Timeline** Create a timeline or visual display that shows the major events of life from Precambrian time to the Mesozoic and Cenozoic eras.

31. **Oral Report** Thomas Cech and Sidney Altman shared a Nobel prize in 1989 for their work on RNA. Research their work and the rewards associated with winning a Nobel prize. Present your findings in an oral report.

Math Skills

32. **Create a Graph** The half-life of the radioisotope lead-210 is about 22.3 years. Construct a line graph that shows how lead-210 decays over 120 years.

TEST TIP If time permits, take short mental breaks to improve your concentration during a test.

Science Concepts

1. In the Miller-Urey experiment, which of the following substances were formed after electricity activated chemical reactions?

   A ozone
   B methane
   C hydrocarbons
   D inorganic molecules

2. What is the function of a ribozyme?

   F to form microspheres
   G to catalyze protein assembly
   H to catalyze RNA formation
   J to store genetic information

3. Which of the following environments is least likely to cause fossil formation?

   A stream
   B desert plain
   C wet lowland
   D area near a volcano

4. In an area that has not been disturbed, which rock layer is the oldest?

   F the layer closest to Earth's surface
   G the layer right above Earth's crust
   H the layer deepest within Earth's crust
   J the layer that contains fossils

5. Most scientists believe that mitochondria are formed from

   A aerobic bacteria.
   B photosynthetic bacteria.
   C aerobic eukaryotes.
   D anaerobic archaea.

6. What were the first vertebrates?

   F reptiles
   G jawed fishes
   H amphibians
   J jawless fishes

7. What percentage of land species was eliminated during the mass extinction that occurred 65 million years ago?

   A about 45%
   B about 67%
   C about 70%
   D about 96%

Using Science Graphics

The table depicts the estimated abundance of certain elements on Earth and in meteorites. Use the table to answer the following questions.

Estimated Abundance of Elements		
Element	Percentage of total mass of Earth	Percentage of total mass of meteorites
Iron	36.0	27.2
Oxygen	28.7	33.2
Magnesium	13.6	17.1
Silicon	14.8	14.3
Sulfur	1.7	1.9

8. Which element is found in a greater abundance on Earth than in meteorites?

   F iron
   G sulfur
   H oxygen
   J magnesium

9. If this table is typical of the abundance of all elements on Earth, in meteorites, and on other planets, which statement would be supported?

   A Earth and meteorites have similar origins.
   B Earth and meteorites have different origins.
   C All meteorites formed from parts of Earth.
   D All elements on Earth come from meteorites.

Use the graph to answer the following question.

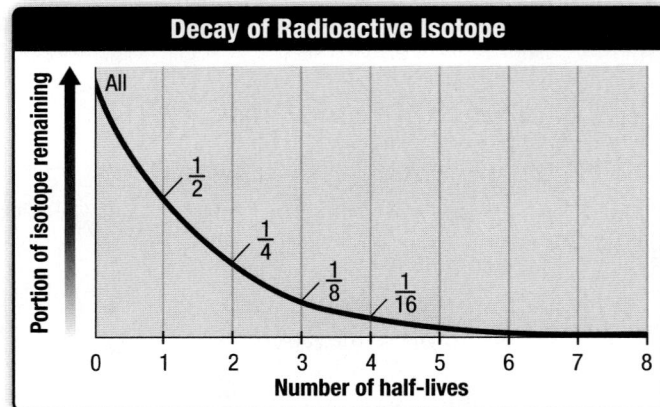

10. If the half-life of carbon-14 is 5,730 years, how many years would it take for 7/8 of the original amount of carbon-14 in the sample to decay?

    F 5,014 years
    G 11,460 years
    H 17,190 years
    J 22,920 years

UNIT 6 Microbes

20 Bacteria and Viruses

21 Protists

22 Fungi

Giant kelp

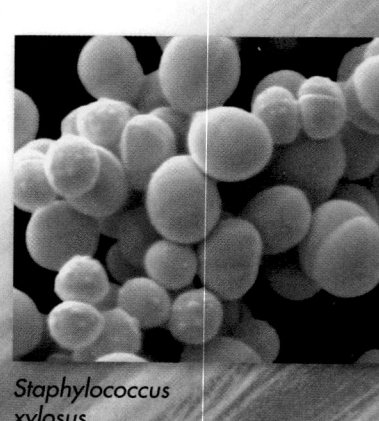

Staphylococcus xylosus

Fossilized diatoms

DISCOVERIES IN SCIENCE
Microbiology

1300

The bubonic plague kills 25 million people in Europe. The bacterium that causes the disease is carried by rats and transmitted to humans by fleas.

Rat, a carrier of the bubonic plague

1862

Louis Pasteur and Claude Bernard use heat to eliminate bacteria in liquid for the first time. The process of heating a liquid to kill bacteria is soon called pasteurization and helps prevent milk from spreading bacterial diseases.

1876

A botanical journal publishes Robert Koch's experiments and observations on anthrax bacilli. Koch demonstrates that the bacteria can still cause disease after growing for several generations in pure culture, without animal contact.

1901

Beatrix Potter, an amateur mycologist, finishes a portfolio of about 270 watercolor illustrations of fungi. Potter is best known as an author and illustrator of children's books, such as *The Tale of Peter Rabbit.*

Beatrix Potter with one of her dogs

1928

Alexander Fleming accidentally discovers antibiotics in his laboratory. He observes that *Penicillium notatum,* a mold that was contaminating culture plates, prevents the growth of a bacterium, *Staphylococcus aureus.*

1955

The United States Government permits the widespread use of the polio vaccine developed by Dr. Jonas Salk.

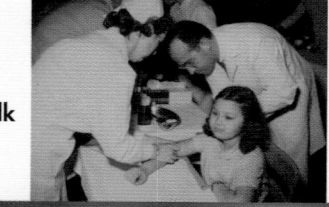

Jonas Salk

1983

Luc Montagnier of the Pasteur Institute in France identifies HIV as the virus that causes AIDS. This discovery made it possible to test blood for HIV.

Time **magazine cover on AIDS**

2003

In Northeast Oregon, an enormous fungus, *Armillaria ostoyae,* is discovered. The fungus covers 10 km^2, an area the size of 1,600 football fields. This fungus is believed to be the largest single organism on Earth.

Fungi on a moss-covered log

BIOLOGY CAREER

Epidemiologist
Linda Gaul

Linda Gaul is an epidemiologist at the Texas Department of State Health Services. She conducts surveillance and epidemiological investigations related to infectious diseases. She has also taught biology and epidemiology at the college level.

Gaul enjoys the process of scientific learning. She especially enjoys discovering connections between seemingly very different organisms that have adapted to a similar environmental constraint.

Gaul also loves teaching and helping others understand and appreciate the living world.

Gaul's father, who is a scientist, and Gaul's mother encouraged Gaul to be inquisitive about the world around her. Gaul credits their encouragement and several enthusiastic college professors for helping her decide to become a scientist.

Gaul also enjoys traveling with her family, gardening, and quilting.

Lichen on rocks

Bacteria and Viruses

Preview

1 Bacteria

What Are Prokaryotes?
Bacterial Structure
Obtaining Energy and Nutrients
Reproduction and Adaptation

2 Viruses

Is a Virus Alive?
Viral Structure
Reproduction
Viroids and Prions

3 Bacteria, Viruses, and Humans

Roles of Bacteria and Viruses
Koch's Postulates and Disease Transmission
Bacterial Diseases
Antibiotic Resistance
Viral Diseases
Emerging Diseases

Why It Matters

Most human diseases are caused by bacteria and viruses. Some of these diseases are incurable and others are becoming incurable.

Alien ships land on an unsuspecting planet. The aliens will soon take over and send more of their kind into the world. But these aliens are not from outer space.

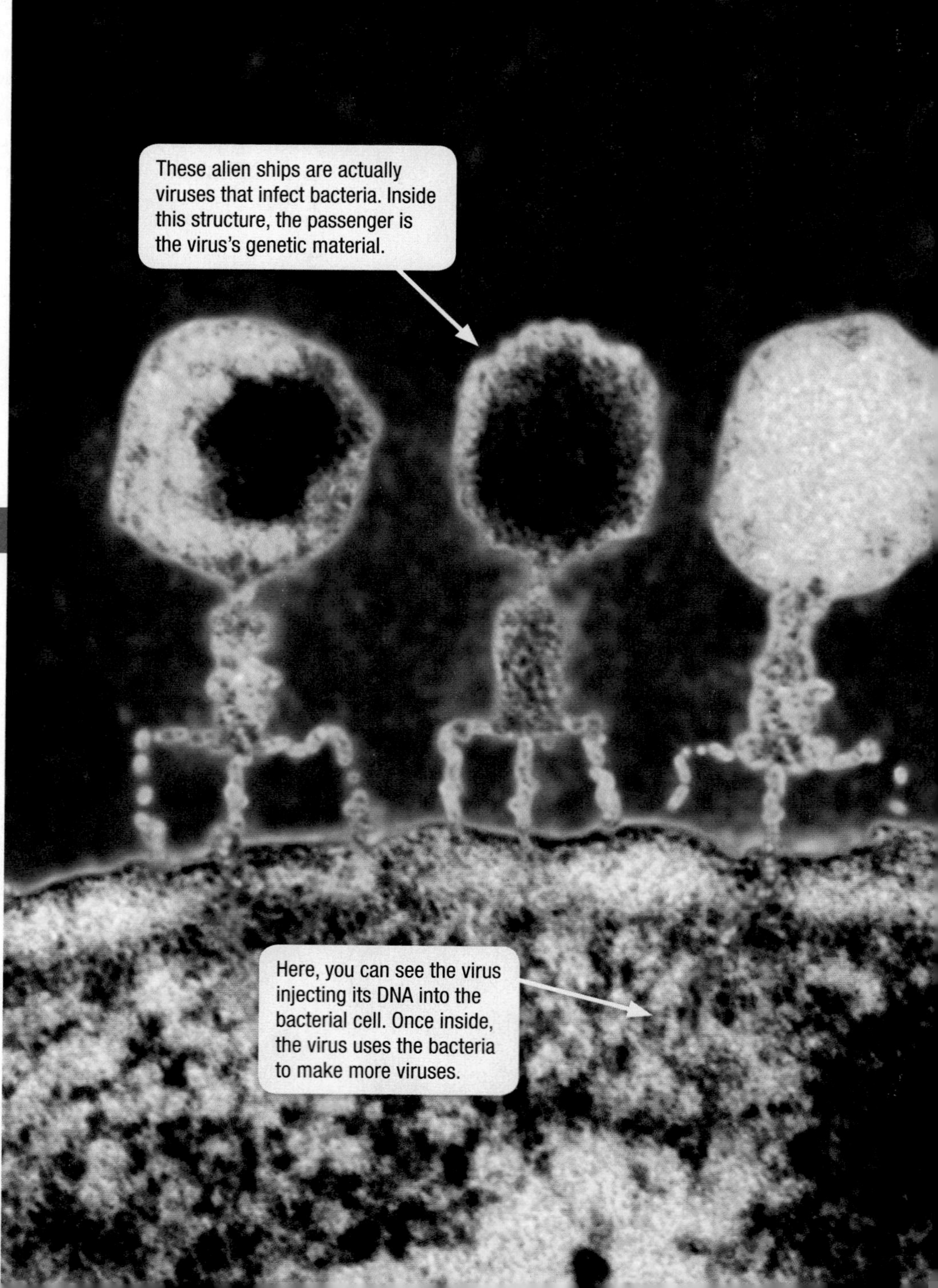

These alien ships are actually viruses that infect bacteria. Inside this structure, the passenger is the virus's genetic material.

Here, you can see the virus injecting its DNA into the bacterial cell. Once inside, the virus uses the bacteria to make more viruses.

Bacterial Observation

There are millions of kinds of bacteria, yet bacteria only appear in a few basic shapes.

Procedure

1. Using a **compound light microscope,** observe **prepared slides of bacteria.**

2. Draw each type of bacteria that you see.

Analysis

1. **Describe** the shapes of the bacteria that you saw.

2. **State** whether you saw a nucleus or organelles in any of the bacteria that you observed.

3. **Predict** whether bacterial cells are larger or smaller than animal cells.

Blast off! Once the DNA is inserted, the landing gear and pod detach and disintegrate. The bacterium is now doomed and will die.

READING TOOLBOX

These reading tools can help you learn the material in this chapter. For more information on how to use these and other tools, see **Appendix: Reading and Study Skills.**

Using Words

Key-Term Fold A key-term fold is a useful tool for studying definitions of key terms in a chapter. Each tab can contain a key term on one side and its definition on the other.

Your Turn Make a key-term fold to quiz yourself on the definitions of the key terms in this chapter.

1. Fold a sheet of lined notebook paper in half from left to right.

2. Using scissors, cut along every third line from the right edge to the center fold to make tabs.

Using Language

Cause and Effect In biological processes, one step leads to another step. When reading, you can recognize cause-and-effect relationships by words that indicate a cause or a result, such as *because, so, consequently,* and *as a result.*

Your Turn In the following sentences, identify the cause and the effect.

1. Disease spreads easily from one population to another because people travel frequently.

2. HIV infects white blood cells. Consequently, the immune system becomes vulnerable to disease.

Using Science Graphics

Process Chart Science is full of processes. Some processes are cycles that repeat the same steps. Some processes are two linked cycles. You can use two circular process charts to help you remember the order of the steps and where the cycles meet.

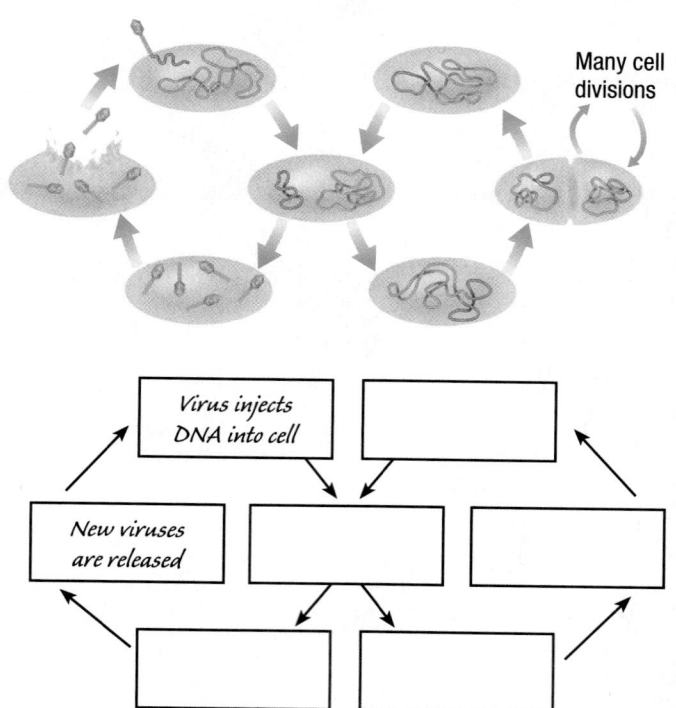

Your Turn Create two linked, circular process charts that illustrate the lytic cycle and the lysogenic cycle.

1. Draw a box. In the box, write the first step of the cycle.

2. To the right and slightly below the first box, draw a second box. Draw an arrow to connect the two boxes. In the second box, write the next step of the cycle.

3. Continue adding boxes in a circular pattern until each step of the cycle is written in a box.

4. Repeat steps 1 through 3 for the second cycle. Draw the second cycle right next to the first cycle.

5. Draw arrows showing where the two cycles are connected.

Key Ideas	Key Terms	Why It Matters
❯ What are the two major groups of prokaryotes? ❯ How are Gram-positive and Gram-negative bacteria different? ❯ How can bacteria be grouped by energy source? ❯ What are three ways that bacteria reproduce and adapt?	plasmid peptidoglycan Gram-positive Gram-negative conjugation transformation transduction endospore	Prokaryotes are everywhere, even in boiling hot springs to Antarctic lakes. These small, single-celled organisms can live where nothing else can survive.

Prokaryotes are the oldest living things on Earth. Fossil prokaryotes date back about 3.5 billion years! Over the millennia, prokaryotes have adapted to live in almost every environment.

What Are Prokaryotes?

Prokaryotes are single-celled organisms that do not have membrane-bound organelles. They are generally found in three shapes, as shown in **Figure 1:** a rod shape (*bacillus*), a sphere shape (*coccus*), and a spiral shape (*spirillum*). ❯ **Prokaryotes are divided into two major groups: the domain Archaea and the domain Bacteria.** Both groups are commonly referred to as *bacteria*.

Archaea Archaea are found in many places, including extreme environments such as salt lakes and hot springs. Archaea are structurally very different from Bacteria. Some Archaean molecules are more similar to those found in eukaryotes. Others are unique among living organisms.

Bacteria Most known prokaryotes are members of the domain Bacteria. Bacteria can be found virtually everywhere. One square inch of skin plays host to an average of 100,000 bacteria!

Figure 1 Prokaryotes are generally found in three shapes. The name of a prokaryote can sometimes tell you about its shape. ❯ **Which of these prokaryotes have names that reflect their shape?**

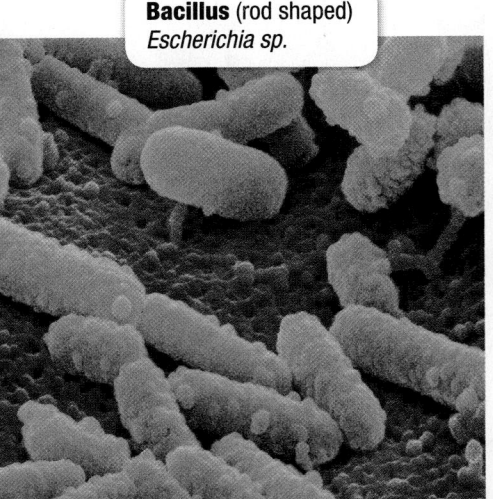

Bacillus (rod shaped)
Escherichia sp.

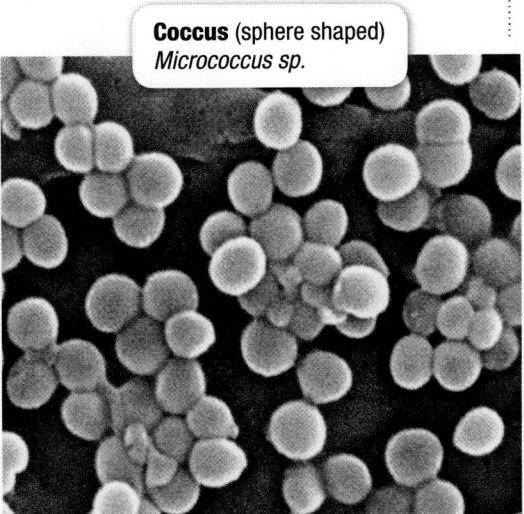

Coccus (sphere shaped)
Micrococcus sp.

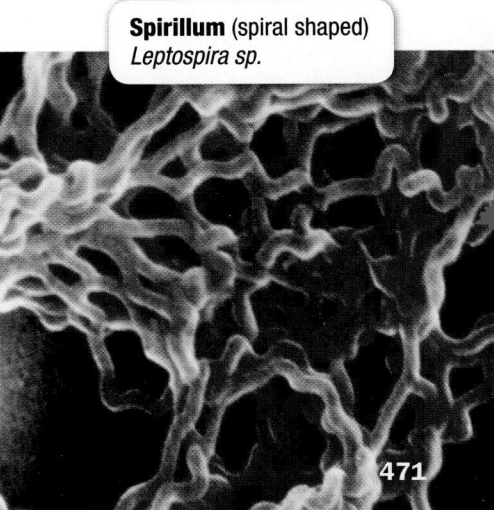

Spirillum (spiral shaped)
Leptospira sp.

Bacterial Structure

Although bacteria have no membrane-bound organelles, they do have many internal structures. Bacteria have genetic material in the form of DNA. Bacterial DNA is a single chromosome clustered in a mass called a *nucleoid*. Bacteria often have small extra loops of DNA called **plasmids.** Bacteria have ribosomes and many types of enzymes. Bacteria may also form granules of stored nutrients to be used if nutrients in the environment are in short supply.

Bacterial cell membranes are lipid bilayers. Outside the cell membrane, bacteria have rigid cell walls that can be one or two layers thick. The bacterial cell wall is made of a protein-carbohydrate compound called **peptidoglycan** and may also include a membrane covering the peptidoglycan layer. The presence of this membrane allows biologists to group bacteria into two categories using a technique called the *Gram stain*. ❯ **Gram-positive bacteria have a thick layer of peptidoglycan and no outer membrane. Gram-negative bacteria have a thin layer of peptidoglycan and have an outer membrane.**

Gram-Positive Bacteria The Gram stain involves two colors of dye. The first dye is dark purple. Gram-positive bacteria trap the dark purple dye because their peptidoglycan layer is very thick. The second, pink dye is also absorbed, but it cannot be seen because the purple dye is much darker. As a result, Gram-positive bacteria appear purple after staining, as **Figure 2** shows.

Gram-Negative Bacteria The thin peptidoglycan layer of Gram-negative bacteria does not trap the purple dye. When the pink dye is added, it is absorbed by the cell. Because the pink dye is the only dye present in Gram-negative bacteria, they appear pink after staining, as **Figure 2** shows. The outer membrane of Gram-negative bacteria makes them more resistant to host defenses and to medicines.

❯ **Reading Check** *Is E. coli (right) a Gram-positive or Gram-negative bacterium? (See the Appendix for answers to Reading Checks.)*

Figure 2 After Gram staining, the Gram-negative bacteria on the left appear pink. The Gram-positive cells on the right appear violet after staining.

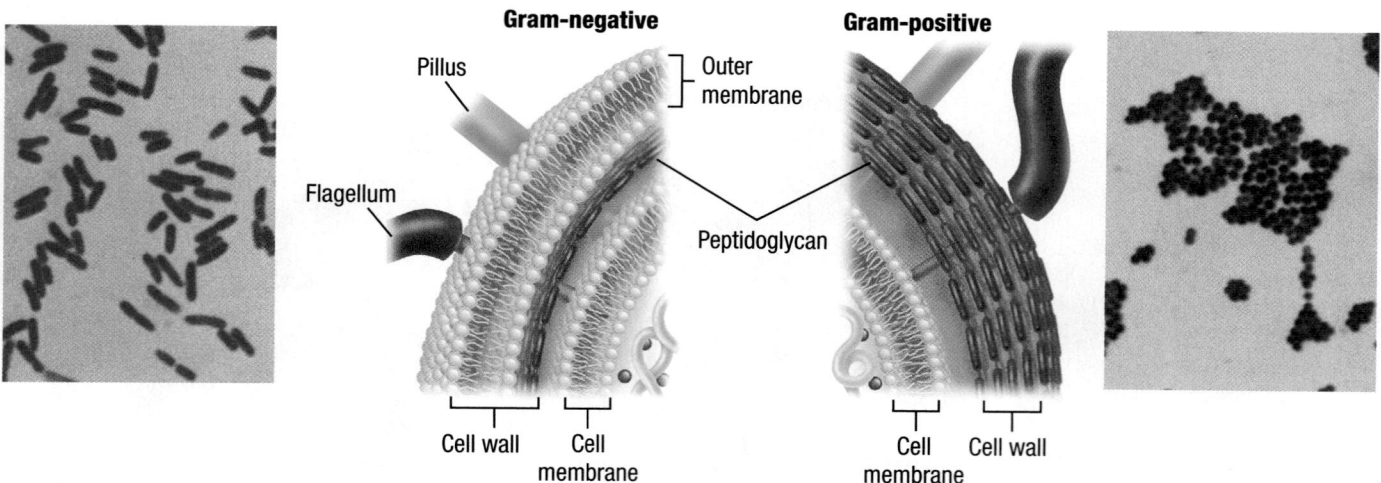

Up Close Bacteria

Escherichia (ESH uh RIK ee uh) *coli* is a Gram-negative bacterium. There are many strains of *E. coli.* Most are harmless residents of healthy human and animal intestines. One strain, *E. coli* O157:H7, produces a powerful toxin and can cause severe illness. About 73,000 people become ill and about 60 people die every year in the United States from *E. coli* O157:H7 poisoning.

E. coli

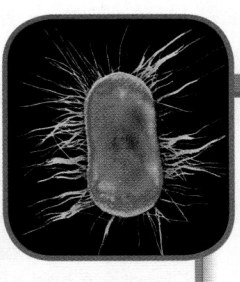

Scientific name: *Escherichia coli*
Size: up to 1 μm
Habitat: inhabits the intestines of many mammals
Mode of nutrition: heterotrophic
Diet: organic matter from living organisms or from the environment

Cell structure *E. coli* has a rigid cell wall composed of peptidoglycan. Outside the cell wall is an outer membrane composed of lipids and polysaccharides.

Cell wall

Outer membrane

Cell membrane

Genetic material Like all bacteria, *E. coli* has a single DNA molecule in the form of a loop. *E. coli* has approximately 5,000 genes.

Locomotion *E. coli* propels itself through its environment by rotating its whiplike flagella.

Ribosome

Reproduction Most bacteria reproduce by dividing into two identical new cells. *E. coli* can divide as often as every 20 minutes.

Peptidoglycan

Adherence *E. coli* has short, thin, protein tubes called *pili.* Pili adhere to surfaces, such as the intestinal lining, and join bacterial cells before bacteria exchange genetic information.

QuickLab

🕐 15 min

Model Bacterial Growth

You can estimate how many bacteria are present in a population if you know the growth rate of bacteria and how much time has passed.

Procedure

① Obtain a cupful of paper circles from a hole punch.

② Begin with a single circle, which represents a single bacterium.

③ Add a second circle to indicate one cycle of bacterial cell division.

④ Model another cycle of division by adding another circle for each of the bacteria in your population.

⑤ Repeat the procedure for four more cycles.

Analysis

1. **State** how many bacteria were present at the end of four cycles.

2. **Calculate** how many bacteria would be present at the end of six cycles.

3. **CRITICAL THINKING** **Predicting Outcomes** If your bacteria reproduce every 20 min, how many bacteria would you have at the end of 4 h, assuming that you begin with one bacterium?

Obtaining Energy and Nutrients

Bacteria differ in how they obtain energy and nutrients. ❯ **Grouping prokaryotes based on their energy source separates them into photoautotrophs, chemoautotrophs, and heterotrophs.**

Photoautotrophs Organisms that get their energy from sunlight through photosynthesis are called *photoautotrophs*. These bacteria include purple sulfur and nonsulfur bacteria, green sulfur bacteria, and cyanobacteria. Green and purple sulfur bacteria can grow only in oxygen-free environments. Cyanobacteria are abundant today and are a major component of the plankton that floats in the oceans. They produce a great deal of our oxygen and probably formed Earth's oxygen atmosphere.

Chemoautotrophs Prokaryotes called *chemoautotrophs* (KEE moh AWT oh TRAHFS) are the only organisms that can get their energy from inorganic sources. They use molecules that contain sulfur or nitrogen and simple organic molecules to obtain energy. In the presence of hydrogen-rich chemicals, chemoautotrophic bacteria can form all of their own amino acids and proteins.

Heterotrophs Most prokaryotes are *heterotrophs* and get both their energy and their nutrients from other organisms. Most absorb nutrients from dead organisms, but some are parasites or pathogens. Many heterotrophic bacteria live in the presence of oxygen, but some can live without it. *Rhizobium*, shown in **Figure 3,** is an important heterotrophic bacterium that converts nitrogen in the air into molecules that can be used by other organisms.

Figure 3 Bacteria of the genus *Rhizobium* live within these soybean root nodules. The bacteria fix nitrogen from the air into a form that both the bacteria and the plants can use.

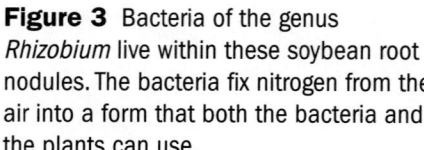

Rhizobium inside soybean nodules

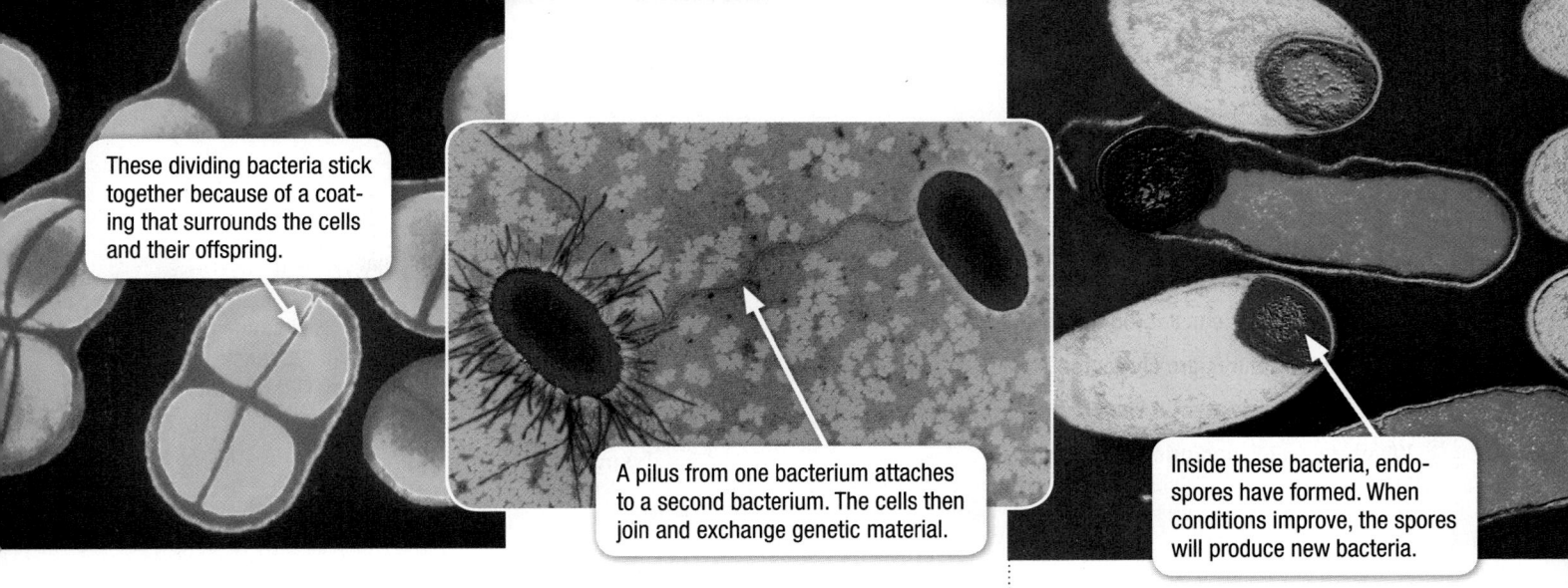

These dividing bacteria stick together because of a coating that surrounds the cells and their offspring.

A pilus from one bacterium attaches to a second bacterium. The cells then join and exchange genetic material.

Inside these bacteria, endospores have formed. When conditions improve, the spores will produce new bacteria.

Reproduction and Adaptation

❯ Prokaryotes reproduce by binary fission; exchange genetic material through conjugation, transformation, and transduction; and survive harsh conditions by forming endospores.

Binary Fission Prokaryotes usually reproduce asexually by binary fission. In this process, a single cell divides into two identical new cells, as **Figure 4** shows. Mutations do occur during prokaryotic reproduction, and new forms emerge frequently.

Genetic Recombination There are three ways that prokaryotes can form new genetic combinations. **Conjugation** occurs when two bacteria exchange genetic material. **Transformation** occurs when bacteria take up DNA fragments from their environment. **Transduction** occurs when genetic material, such as a plasmid, is transferred by a virus. Plasmids often convey antibiotic resistance.

Endospore Formation Some bacteria survive harsh conditions by forming thick-walled structures called **endospores.** Endospores form inside the bacteria. They surround the DNA and a small bit of cytoplasm. Endospores can survive boiling, radiation, and acid. They show no signs of life and can be revived after hundreds of years.

Figure 4 Bacteria can reproduce by binary fission, exchange DNA through conjugation, and survive harsh environments by spore formation.

conjugation a type of sexual reproduction in which two cells join to exchange DNA

transformation the transfer of genetic material in the form of DNA fragments

transduction the transfer of DNA from one bacterium to another through a virus

endospore a thick-walled structure that forms inside bacteria and resists harsh conditions

Section 1 Review

❯ KEY IDEAS

1. **Identify** the two major groups of prokaryotes.
2. **Explain** the difference between Gram-positive and Gram-negative bacteria.
3. **Describe** three ways that bacteria can obtain energy.

4. **Describe** how bacteria reproduce, exchange genetic information, and survive harsh conditions.

CRITICAL THINKING

5. **Predicting Outcomes** If Earth suddenly lost its light source but stayed at the same temperature, which organisms might survive?
6. **Applying Information** How do the products of binary fission, conjugation, and endospore germination differ from each other?

ALTERNATIVE ASSESSMENT

7. **Bacterial Meal** Research foods that are made by using prokaryotes. Prepare a menu, including recipes, for a meal made entirely of these foods. If possible, prepare the meal and share with your classmates. Or prepare the ingredients in small groups outside class, and bring the finished products to class to share.

Key Ideas	Key Terms	Why It Matters
❯ Why is a virus not considered a living organism? ❯ What two structures are characteristic of viruses? ❯ What are two ways that a virus can reproduce? ❯ What are viroids and prions?	capsid envelope bacteriophage lytic lysogenic	All viruses cause disease, and viral diseases are extremely difficult to treat.

Viruses are so small they can be seen only with an electron microscope. These tiny particles were discovered when material that had passed through a bacteria-trapping filter was found to cause disease.

Is a Virus Alive?

All living things are made of cells, are able to grow and reproduce, and are guided by information stored in their DNA. Viruses, in contrast, are pieces of nucleic acids contained in a protein coat. Biologists do not consider viruses to be living. ❯ **Viruses are not considered living because they are missing key characteristics of living organisms.** For example, viruses do have genetic material, but they cannot reproduce on their own. Viruses reproduce by infecting cells. Viruses use the cell's ribosomes, ATP, enzymes, and other molecules to make more viruses. Viruses do not grow. Instead, they are assembled into their full size within a cell. As **Figure 5** shows, viruses can have a variety of interesting shapes. Viruses do not carry out any metabolic activities, do not have any cytoplasm or organelles, and do not maintain homeostasis. However, even though viruses are not alive, they have a major impact on the living world.

Figure 5 Viruses can have a variety of sizes and interesting shapes.

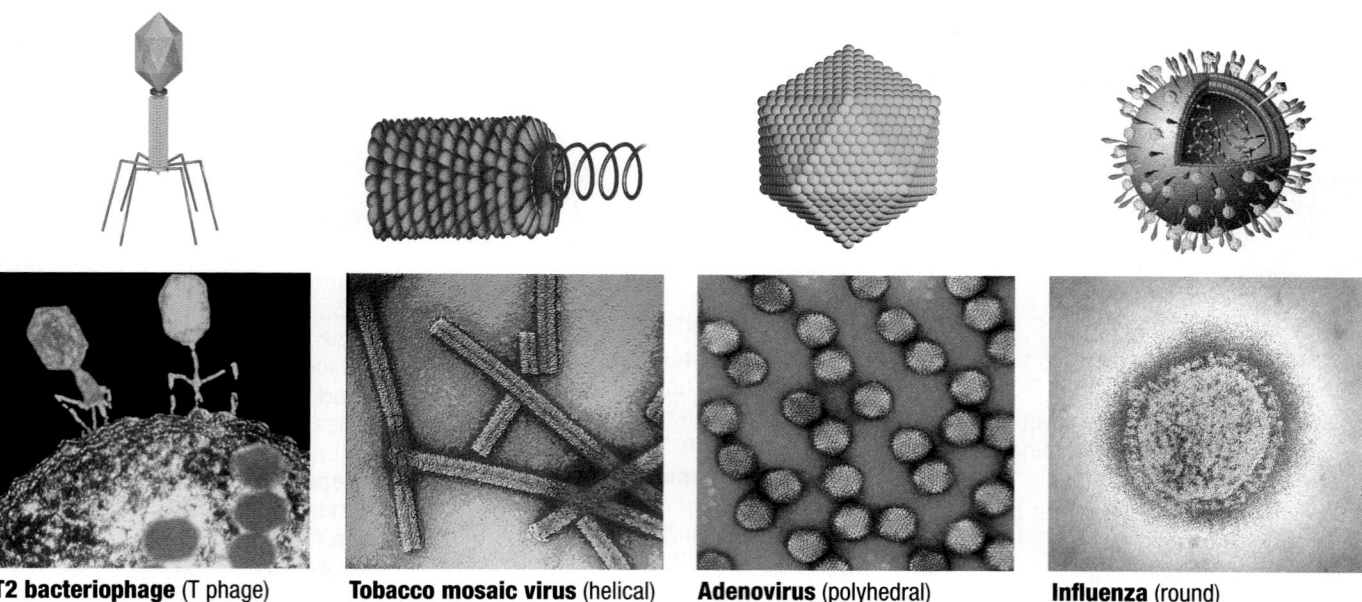

T2 bacteriophage (T phage) **Tobacco mosaic virus** (helical) **Adenovirus** (polyhedral) **Influenza** (round)

Viral Structure

The structure of a virus is relatively simple. There are two structures that are characteristic of all viruses. ❯ **All viruses have nucleic acid and a capsid.** In addition to a capsid, viruses may have an envelope or tail fibers.

Nucleic Acids The genetic material of a virus can be either RNA or DNA. Viral genetic material codes for the components of a virus.

DNA Viruses The genetic material of a DNA virus can become inserted into the host cell's DNA or may remain separate. The virus makes copies of its DNA by using the host cell's enzymes and nucleotides. Viral DNA also directs production of mRNA and proteins that are assembled into new viruses.

RNA Viruses When the genetic material of an RNA virus enters a host cell, reproduction can occur by one of two methods. In one method, the viral RNA may be used directly to make more viral RNA. In the second method, the viral RNA is transcribed into DNA, inserted into the host cell's DNA, and then transcribed into viral mRNA. Viruses that use this method of reproduction are called *retroviruses*. In both types of reproduction, viral mRNA is used to make new viral proteins that are assembled into new viruses.

Capsid The protein coat, or **capsid,** of a virus encloses its genetic material. Viruses recognize their hosts by specific proteins on a host cell's surface. The proteins on the host cell have to match proteins on the capsid of the virus, as a key matches a lock. Capsids are made from proteins and have a variety of shapes. **Figure 5** shows T phage, helical, polyhedral, and round viruses.

Envelope Many viruses, such as HIV, shown in **Figure 6,** have a membrane, or **envelope,** surrounding the capsid. The envelope gives the virus an overall spherical shape, but the capsid can have a very different shape. In the case of HIV, for example, the envelope surrounds an oval-shaped capsid. The envelope is studded with receptors that help the virus enter cells. The envelope is made of proteins, lipids, and *glycoproteins* (GLIE koh PROH teenz), which are proteins with attached carbohydrate molecules.

Tail Fibers Viruses that infect bacteria, called **bacteriophages** or just *phages,* have a complicated structure. A T2 bacteriophage, for example, has a capsid attached to a tail with tail fibers, as **Figure 5** shows. A long DNA molecule is coiled within the polyhedron. The tail and tail fibers function like a tiny syringe, which injects the viral DNA into its bacterial host.

❯ **Reading Check** *How does reproduction differ between DNA and RNA viruses?*

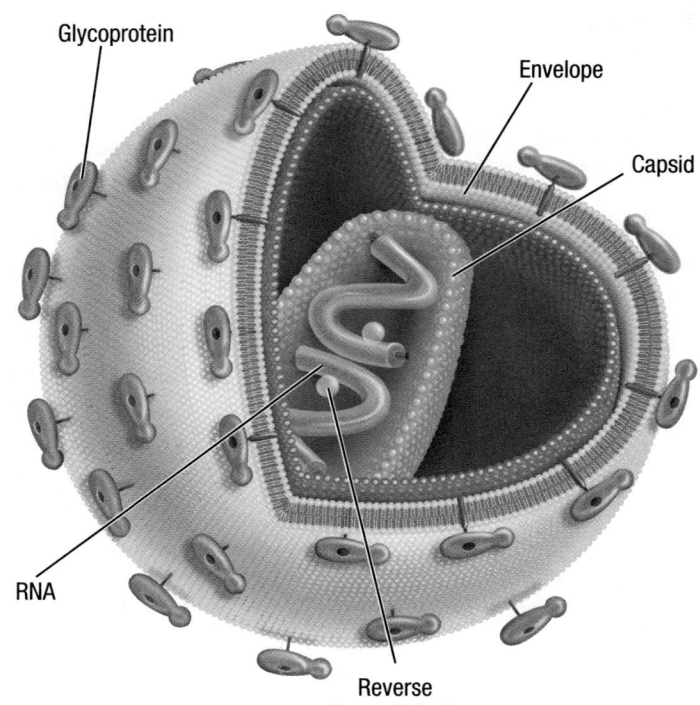

Glycoprotein

Envelope

Capsid

RNA

Reverse transcriptase

Figure 6 HIV is a spherical virus with an envelope surrounding its capsid. RNA is the genetic material. Along with the RNA, HIV has its own enzymes for converting RNA into DNA inside a cell.

---

capsid a protein sheath that surrounds the nucleic acid core in a virus

envelope a membranelike layer that covers the capsids of some viruses

bacteriophage a virus that infects bacteria

SC*i*LINKS.
www.scilinks.org
Topic: Viruses
Code: HX81607

Reproduction

A viral infection begins when the genetic material of a virus enters a host cell. Once inside the cell, a virus can reproduce by two different processes, shown in **Figure 7. ❯** Viruses can reproduce by a lytic life cycle and a lysogenic life cycle.

Lytic Cycle The cycle of viral infection, reproduction, and cell destruction is called the **lytic** cycle. Viral genetic material that has entered a cell remains separate from the host cell's DNA. The virus uses the host cell's organelles, enzymes, and raw materials to replicate the virus's DNA and to make viral proteins. The proteins are assembled with the replicated viral DNA to form complete viruses. The host cell breaks open, releases newly made viruses, and dies. The new virus particles can infect other host cells. The virus kills the host cells and further spreads the viral infection. Viruses that reproduce only by the lytic cycle are often called *virulent*.

Lysogenic Cycle When viral DNA becomes part of its host cell's DNA, the virus is called a *prophage*. When the host cell replicates its own DNA, the cell also replicates the provirus. New cells are produced that contain the provirus. New virus particles are not assembled, and the host cell is not destroyed. This process is called the **lysogenic** cycle. Many cells may be produced that contain the viral DNA. After days, months, or even years, the provirus may leave the host's DNA and enter a lytic cycle. If the virus never enters the lytic cycle, it may become a permanent part of its host's genome. A virus whose reproduction includes the lysogenic cycle is called a *temperate* virus.

READING TOOLBOX

Process Chart Use the information on this page to complete the process chart describing the lytic and lysogenic cycles of viral replication.

Figure 7 T4 is a bacterial virus that reproduces by using the lytic cycle and the lysogenic cycle.

Viral Replication in Bacteria

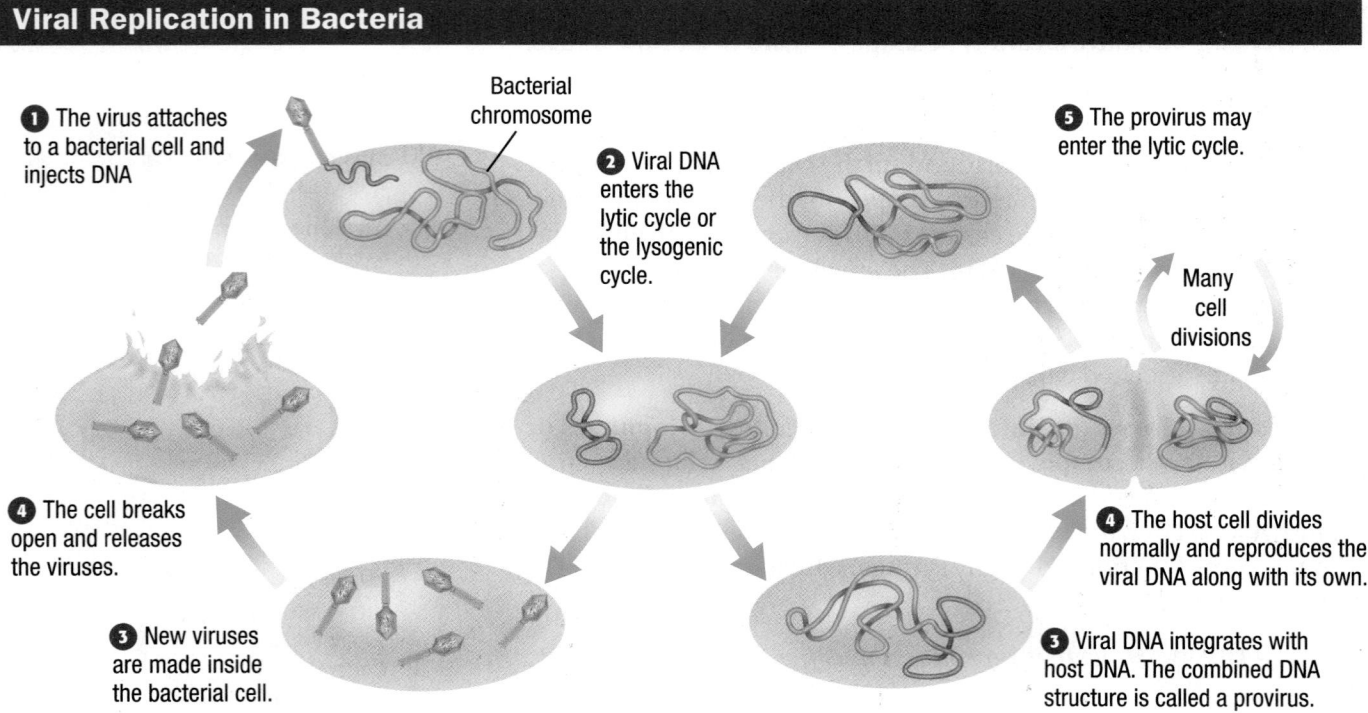

❶ The virus attaches to a bacterial cell and injects DNA

Bacterial chromosome

❷ Viral DNA enters the lytic cycle or the lysogenic cycle.

❺ The provirus may enter the lytic cycle.

Many cell divisions

❹ The cell breaks open and releases the viruses.

❸ New viruses are made inside the bacterial cell.

❹ The host cell divides normally and reproduces the viral DNA along with its own.

❸ Viral DNA integrates with host DNA. The combined DNA structure is called a provirus.

Up Close HIV Reproduction

Human immunodeficiency virus (HIV) is the virus that causes AIDS (acquired immune deficiency syndrome). HIV is considered to be a pandemic, a worldwide epidemic. About 22 million people have died as a result of AIDS. Currently, an estimated 33 million to 46 million people worldwide are living with HIV. There are several drugs used to treat HIV, but there is no cure.

HIV

Full name: human immunodeficiency virus
Size: 110–128 nm
Habitat: human CD4+ T lymphocyte and other cells that have the CD4 receptor including macrophages, B lymphocytes, and brain cells
Mode of nutrition: none

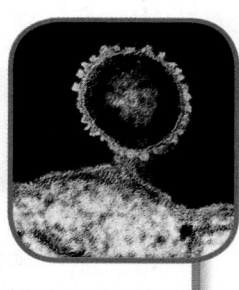

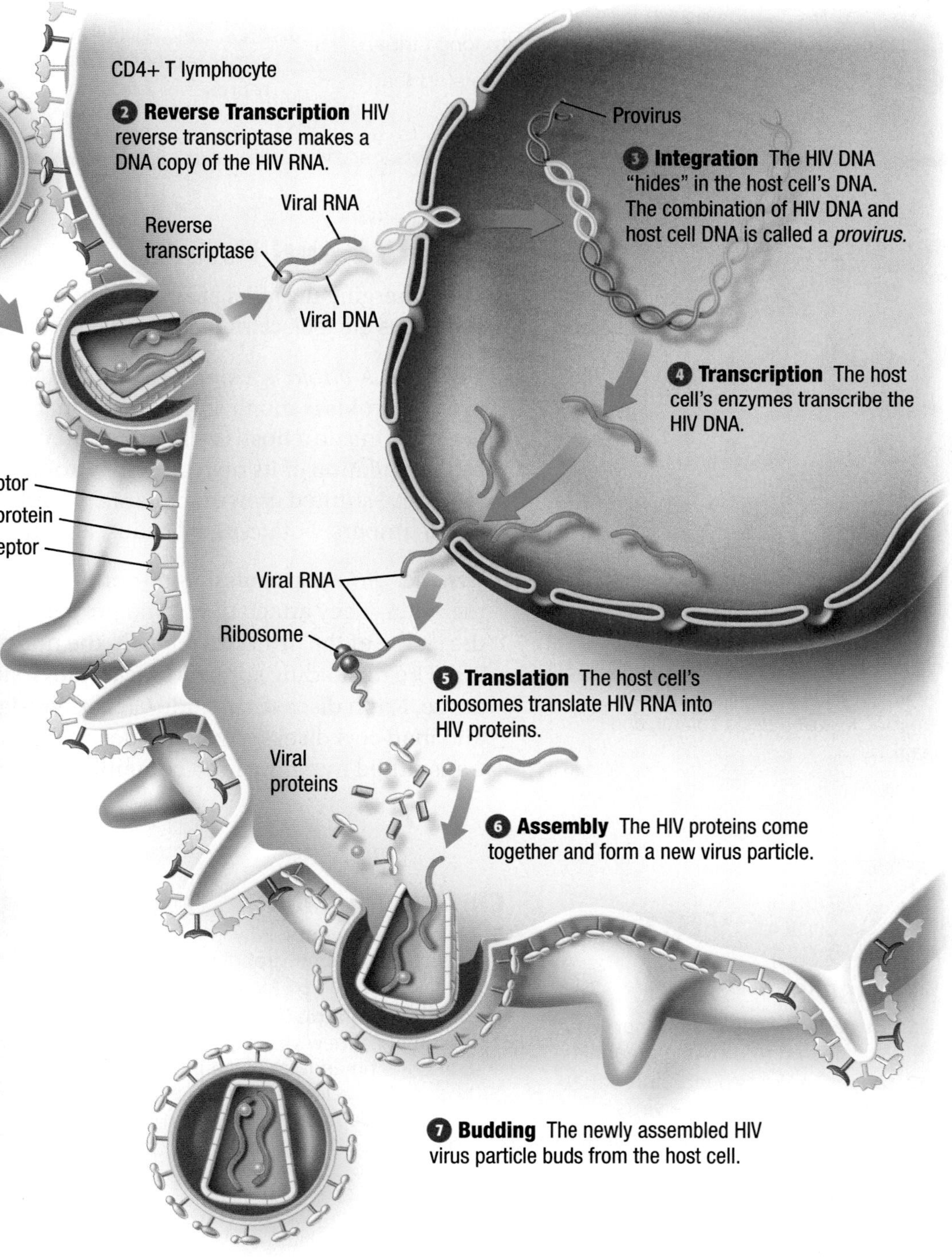

HIV particle

HIV surface glycoprotein

CD4+ T lymphocyte

1 Binding and Fusion The HIV virus binds to the CD4 receptor and one of the two co-receptors on a human CD4+ T lymphocyte. The HIV virus then fuses with the cell.

CCR5 co-receptor
CD4 receptor protein
CXCR4 co-receptor

2 Reverse Transcription HIV reverse transcriptase makes a DNA copy of the HIV RNA.

Reverse transcriptase

Viral RNA

Viral DNA

Provirus

3 Integration The HIV DNA "hides" in the host cell's DNA. The combination of HIV DNA and host cell DNA is called a *provirus*.

4 Transcription The host cell's enzymes transcribe the HIV DNA.

Viral RNA

Ribosome

5 Translation The host cell's ribosomes translate HIV RNA into HIV proteins.

Viral proteins

6 Assembly The HIV proteins come together and form a new virus particle.

7 Budding The newly assembled HIV virus particle buds from the host cell.

HIV budding

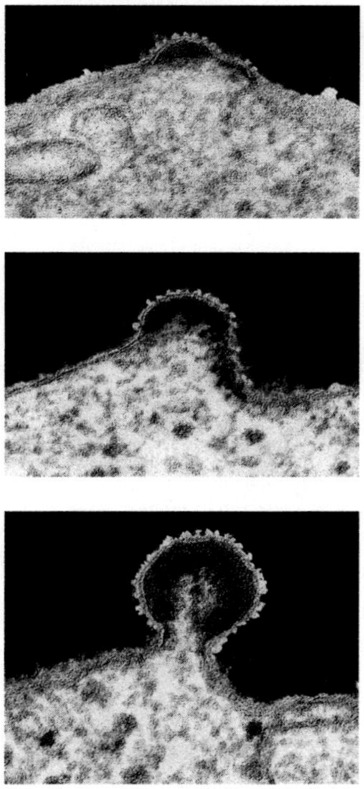

Hands-On

Quick**Lab**

 15 min

How Small Are Nanometers?

Viruses are extremely small. Most viruses are between 20 and 250 nm in length. One millimeter equals 1,000,000 nanometers. What would it look like if we could visually comparea nanometer to a millimeter?

Procedure

1 Using **scissors**, cut a piece of **paper** into long strips.

2 **Tape** the strips together until you have one strip that is 2 m long.

3 Use a **ruler** to label the strip of paper at the 2 mm, 2 cm, 20 cm, 1 m, and 2 m measurements.

Analysis

1. **Determine** how many millimeters are in 1 m.

2. **Determine** how many millimeters are in 2 m.

3. **CRITICAL THINKING** **Analyzing Data** If your entire strip of paper represents 2 mm, which mark on your paper represents 2,000 nm?

Figure 8 Mad cow disease damages a cow's brain and results in strange behavior, loss of muscle control, and death.

Viroids and Prions

Two emerging diseases are caused by nonliving particles. ❯ **Viroids and prions are molecules that are able to reproduce and cause disease.**

Viroids A *viroid* is a single strand of RNA that has no capsid. The RNA of viroids is much smaller than that of viruses. Viroids can replicate inside a host's cell to make new viroids. They disrupt a host cell's regulation of its own growth. Viroids cause abnormal development and stunted growth in plants. Viroids have affected plants such as cucumbers, potatoes, avocados, and oranges.

Prions *Prions* are misshapen versions of proteins that are found in the brain. They attach to normal proteins and cause them to take on the shape of the prion. As a result, the normal protein stops functioning. The misfolding spreads like a chain reaction and destroys brain tissue. Prion diseases include Creutzfeldt-Jakob disease in humans and mad cow disease, which is described in **Figure 8.** Prions can be transmitted by eating food contaminated with infected brain tissue.

Section 2 Review

❯ KEY IDEAS

1. **Explain** why viruses are not considered to be living organisms.

2. **Describe** the two structures that are characteristic of a virus.

3. **Differentiate** between reproduction by the lytic and lysogenic cycles.

4. **Describe** the structure of viroids and prions.

CRITICAL THINKING

5. **Relating Concepts** Why is it possible for some viral diseases remain undetected for years?

6. **Analyzing Information** The assembly of new viral particles can sometimes take place in the host cell's nucleus. However, such assembly does not occur with phage viruses. Why not?

WRITING FOR SCIENCE

7. **Article** Research mad cow disease. Write an article describing how the disease spread from sheep to cows, how it spread to humans, and what measures have been taken to prevent the disease in sheep, cows, and humans.

Bacteria, Viruses, and Humans

Key Ideas	Key Terms	Why It Matters
❯ What are three important roles of bacteria and viruses? ❯ What are the steps described in Koch's postulates? ❯ What are two ways that bacteria cause disease? ❯ How does antibiotic resistance develop? ❯ Why are viral diseases difficult to cure? ❯ What are four ways that a disease can emerge?	Koch's postulates pathogen toxin antibiotic resistance	Bacteria and viruses have a large impact on humans, from benefiting the environment to causing disease. Our world would not be the same without them.

When we think of bacteria and viruses, we usually think of disease. But bacteria and viruses are not all bad. Bacteria and viruses impact humans in many ways.

Roles of Bacteria and Viruses

❯ **Bacteria play important roles in the environment and in industry. Both bacteria and viruses are important in research.**

Bacteria and the Environment Bacteria play a vital role in all of Earth's ecosystems. Bacteria produce oxygen, make nitrogen available to other organisms, and help decompose dead organisms. Many form important symbiotic relationships. For example, *E. coli* lives in the large intestines of humans, where it produces vitamin K.

Bacteria and Industry Bacteria are important in a variety of industries. Many of the foods that we eat, such as pickles, soy sauce, and sourdough bread, are made by using bacteria. Bacteria are used to produce chemicals, such as acetone. Mining companies use bacteria to convert sulfur into a form that can be washed away to leave behind valuable minerals, such as copper and uranium. Bacteria are also used in cleaning up oil spills and in sewage treatment plants, as **Figure 9** shows.

Bacteria, Viruses, and Research Bacteria and viruses have been very important in genetic research. Their genetic material can be easily studied. They provide valuable information about DNA replication, transcription, and translation. Viruses are also used in gene therapy as a way to deliver genetic material directly to target cells.

Figure 9 Bubbles pumped into sewage provide oxygen to bacteria that break down organic molecules. Next, anaerobic bacteria break sewage down further and generate methane, which is used to power the plant.

481

Koch's Postulates and Disease Transmission

The German physician Robert Koch developed a technique for diagnosing the cause of an infection. His four-step procedure, described in **Figure 10,** is known as **Koch's postulates.** This technique is still used today to identify a disease-causing agent, or **pathogen.** ❯ The four main steps in Koch's postulates are finding and isolating the pathogen, growing the pathogen, infecting a healthy animal, and then isolating the same pathogen.

Step ❶ The pathogen must be found in an animal with the disease and not in a healthy animal.

Step ❷ The pathogen must be isolated from the sick animal and grown in a laboratory culture.

Step ❸ When the isolated pathogen is injected into a healthy animal, the animal must develop the disease.

Step ❹ The pathogen should be taken from the second animal, grown in the lab, and shown to be the same as the original pathogen.

Diseases that can spread from person to person are considered *contagious.* Some contagious diseases must be transmitted directly from one host to another by contact, such as by kissing or by animal and insect bites. Other diseases can survive outside a host for a period of time. These diseases can be transmitted through the air, in contaminated food or water, or on contaminated objects. Objects that often carry disease include utensils, toothbrushes, computer keyboards, kitchen sponges, and doorknobs.

❯ **Reading Check** *What are five ways diseases can be transmitted?*

Koch's postulates a four-stage procedure for identifying a pathogen

pathogen an organism or virus that causes disease; an infectious agent

toxin a substance that is produced by one organism that is poisonous to other organisms

Figure 10 Applying the four principles of Koch's postulates, scientists can identify the pathogen that causes an infectious disease. ❯ Why is it important for the pathogen to be grown from the second animal, as described in step 4?

go.hrw.com
✳ interact online
Keyword: HX8VBCF10

Koch's Postulates

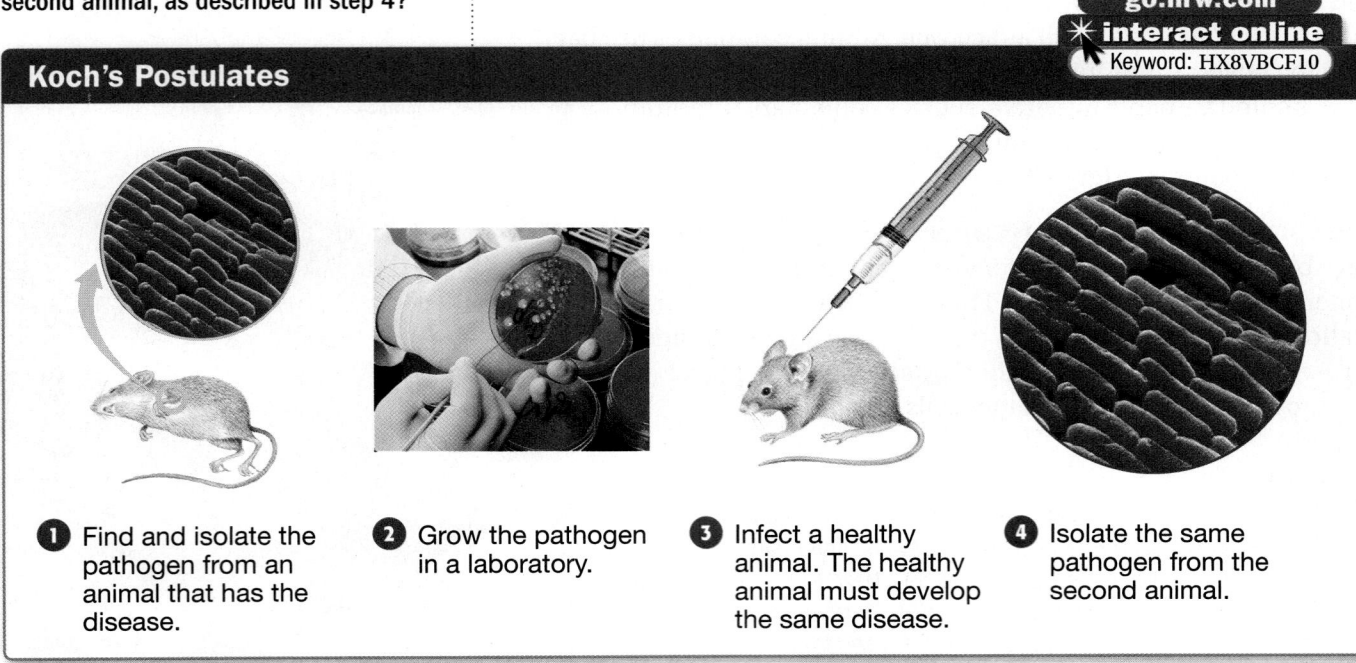

❶ Find and isolate the pathogen from an animal that has the disease.

❷ Grow the pathogen in a laboratory.

❸ Infect a healthy animal. The healthy animal must develop the same disease.

❹ Isolate the same pathogen from the second animal.

Bacterial Diseases

Bacteria	Disease	Symptoms
Escherichia coli O157:H7	food poisoning associated with undercooked meat	diarrhea, bloody stools; can cause kidney failure and death
Vibrio cholera	cholera	usually mild diarrhea, sometimes profuse watery diarrhea, vomiting, leg cramps, dehydration, death
Borrelia burgdorferi	Lyme disease	fever, headache, fatigue, and characteristic skin rash, untreated it can spread to joints, heart, and nervous system
Clostridium tetani	tetanus 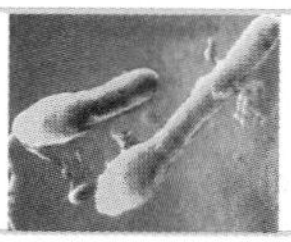	lockjaw, stiffness in neck and abdomen, difficulty swallowing, fever, high blood pressure, muscle spasms; if left untreated, death
Staphylococcus aureus	food poisoning, staph infections in wounds	nausea, vomiting, diarrhea; rarely fatal
Mycobacterium tuberculosis	tuberculosis	coughing up blood, chest pain, fever, fatigue, weight loss; and if left untreated, death
Helicobacter pylori	stomach ulcers	burning stomach pain; rarely nausea, vomiting, loss of appetite; with bleeding ulcer: anemia, weakness and fatigue
Neisseria meningitidis	bacterial meningitis 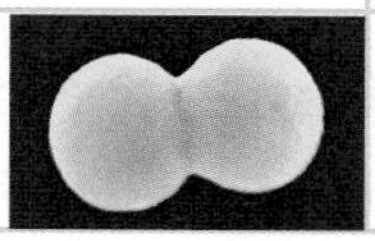 	high fever, headache, stiff neck, nausea, vomiting, sensitivity to light, confusion, possibly seizures; untreated may result in brain damage and hearing loss

Bacterial Diseases

Pathogenic bacteria cause disease in two ways. **❯ Bacteria can cause disease by producing toxins and by destroying body tissues.**

The most common way that bacteria cause disease is by producing poisonous chemicals, called **toxins.** Toxins may be released or stored inside the bacteria until the bacteria die. Foods contaminated with bacteria or with toxins can cause food poisoning. For example, botulism occurs when canned food is contaminated with endospores of the bacterium *Clostridium botulinum.* The bacteria multiply in the can, causing toxins to build up. Botulinum toxin destroys the tips of nerve cells. Symptoms of botulism include double vision and paralysis. Botulism can be fatal if the muscles involved in breathing become paralyzed. Botulinum toxin is also now used in cosmetic procedures that paralyze nerves in the face and reduce wrinkling of the skin.

A second way that bacteria cause disease is by producing enzymes that break down the host's tissues into nutrients that the bacteria can use. Tuberculosis, described in **Figure 11,** is an example of a bacterium that uses human tissue for nutrients. Group A streptococcus bacteria produce both toxins and digestive enzymes. These bacteria usually cause only mild illnesses, including strep throat and impetigo. However, when these bacteria get into muscle or skin tissue, necrotizing fasciitis can result. This is a severe and often deadly infection in which large areas of flesh die. For this reason, group A strep are sometimes called flesh-eating bacteria!

Figure 11 The scientific study of disease is called *pathology.* The table lists some bacterial pathogens, the disease caused by the bacterium, and symptoms of the disease.

READING TOOLBOX

Cause and Effect Make a two-column table. Title the left column "Cause" and the right column "Effect." In the "Effect" column, list all of the diseases discussed in this section. In the "Cause" column, list the pathogen that causes the disease, and note whether the pathogen is a bacterium or a virus.

❶ Genes in a few cells mutate.

❷ If antibiotic is absent, the mutant cell population will be outnumbered by the normal cells and will eventually disappear.

❸ Normal cells take over the population.

Normal staphylococcal cells

No antibiotic

Resistant cells take over the population.

If antibiotic is present, antibiotic-resistant bacteria survive and reproduce.

Antibiotic

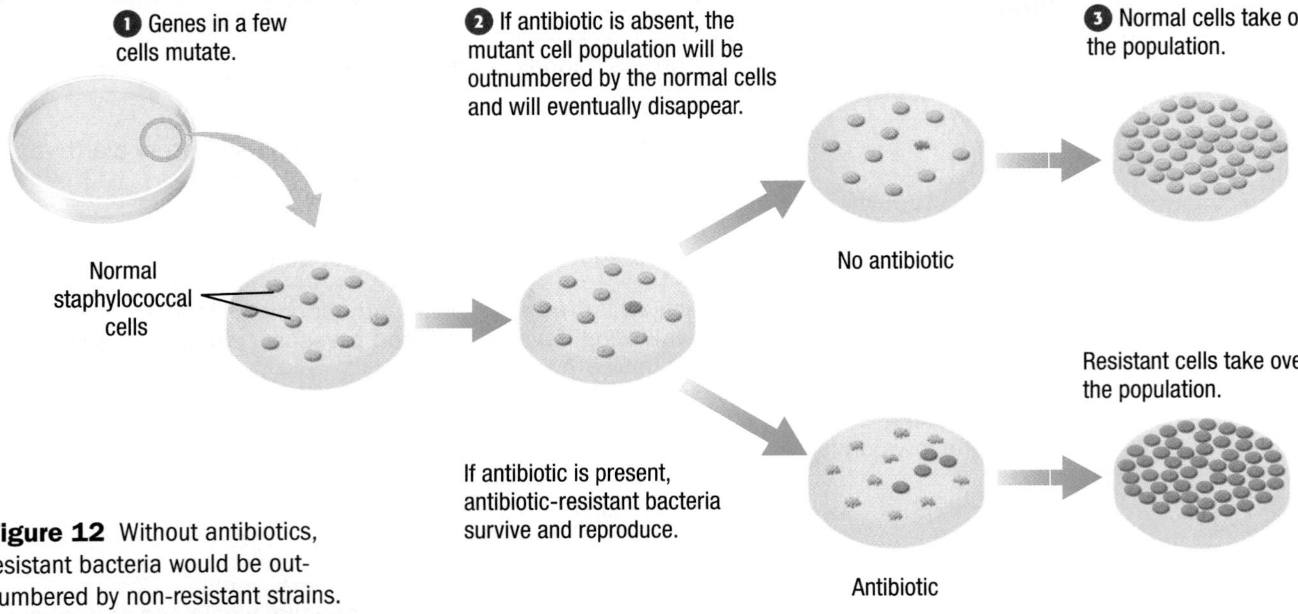

Figure 12 Without antibiotics, resistant bacteria would be out-numbered by non-resistant strains.
❯ **Should antibiotics be used in the process of treating viral diseases?**

antibiotic a substance that can inhibit the growth of or kill some microorganisms

resistance the ability of an organism to toler-ate a chemical or disease-causing agent

Antibiotic Resistance

Antibiotics are chemicals that inhibit the growth of or kill micro-organisms. Since the introduction of antibiotics, these drugs have reduced illness, suffering, and deaths from bacterial diseases.

Development of Resistance Over decades of antibiotic use, bacteria have developed resistance to these drugs. Antibiotic **resistance** is the ability of bacteria to tolerate antibiotics. Mutations for antibiotic resistance arise naturally and often in bacteria. Plasmids containing antibiotic-resistance genes can pass between bacteria during conjugation. When the antibiotic is present, vulner-able bacteria are killed. Resistant bacteria survive and reproduce. In this way, antibiotic-resistant bacteria become the dominant type in the population. **Figure 12** shows how antibiotic resistance can develop in a population of bacteria. ❯ **Antibiotic resistance spreads when sensitive populations of bacteria are killed by antibiotics. As a result, resistant bacteria thrive.**

Consequences of Resistance Today, nearly all bacterial pathogens are becoming resistant to one or more antibiotics. Diseases that were once easy to treat with antibiotics, such as staphylococcal infections, are now more difficult to treat because of resistance to multiple antibiotics. Widespread use of antibiotics promotes the spread of antibiotic resistance. As bacteria become resistant, physicians must switch to using different antibiotics. As new antibiotics are used, bacteria will probably develop resistance to those as well. For example, there are strains of tuberculosis in parts of South and Central America against which no antibiotics are <u>effective</u>. Many people fear that bacterial diseases will eventually become impossible to cure.

ACADEMIC VOCABULARY

effective able to have an effect

Viral Diseases

Viruses cause disease in bacteria, plants, and animals. Because viruses identify host cells by receptors on the cell surface, viruses are very specific. For example, the virus that causes colds infects cells of the upper respiratory tract. The virus that causes chickenpox and shingles, shown in **Figure 13,** affects nerve cells. **❯ Because viruses enter host cells to reproduce, it is difficult to develop a drug that kills the virus without harming the living host.**

Viruses can be transmitted by any action that brings virus particles into contact with a host cell. For this reason, certain viruses can be transmitted only by exchange of body fluids, whereas others can be transmitted through the air. Symptoms of a viral illness can be caused by several factors. Some viruses have toxic parts, such as envelope proteins. Other viruses cause the host cell to produce toxins. Some symptoms are caused by damage to the body's tissues as new viruses burst from host cells. Many symptoms of a viral infection, such as aches and fever, result from the body's response to infection.

Recently, viruses have been shown to cause some types of cancer. Viruses associated with human cancers include hepatitis B (liver cancer), Epstein-Barr virus (Burkitt's lymphoma), and human papilloma virus (cervical cancer). Many viral diseases can be prevented through vaccination. A *vaccine* is a weakened form of a pathogen that prepares the immune system to recognize and destroy the pathogen. **Figure 14** lists several common viruses, the disease caused by the virus, and the symptoms associated with the disease.

❯ Reading Check *What factors cause the symptoms of viral disease?*

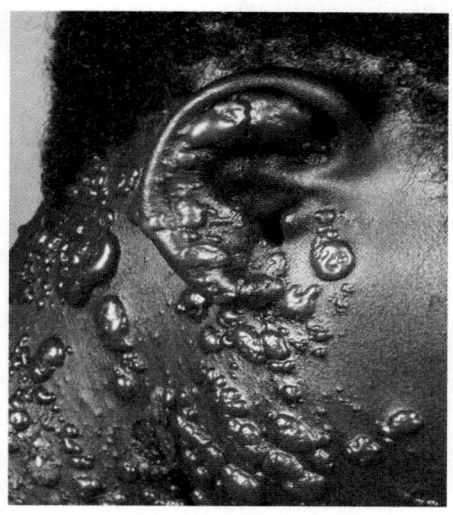

Figure 13 Shingles is caused by the same virus that causes chickenpox. It stays dormant until the immune system is stressed. Then, it travels along nerves and causes skin blisters and severe pain.

Figure 14 A virus is often named for the disease it causes. The table lists some viral diseases and their symptoms.

Viral Diseases

Virus	Disease	Symptoms
Influenza virus	flu	fever, headache, fatigue, muscle aches, cough
Varicella zoster virus	chickenpox, shingles	fever, tiredness, itchy or painful blisters
Measles virus	measles	fever, cough, runny nose, pink-eye, and a rash that covers the body
Mumps virus	mumps	fever, headache, muscle aches, tiredness, loss of appetite, swelling of salivary glands
Human immunodeficiency virus	AIDS/HIV	early symptoms: fever, tiredness, swollen lymph nodes; later symptoms: weight loss, Kaposi's sarcoma, opportunistic infections eventually resulting in death
Human papilloma virus	HPV infection, cervical cancer	usually no symptoms; occasionally genital warts; can cause cervical cancer and death
Hepatitis B virus	hepatitis, liver cancer	jaundice, fatigue, abdominal pain, nausea, joint pain, liver disease, liver cancer, death
West Nile virus	West Nile virus infection	fever, headache, bodyache; in rare cases coma, convulsions, numbness and paralysis

QuickLab

🕐 15 min

Emergence of Bird Flu

Although bird flu infection is rare in humans, the disease has emerged in several countries. This graph identifies the onset of new cases in the first half of 2006.

Analysis

1. **Identify** the countries in which new cases of humans infected with bird flu appeared in March 2006.

2. **Calculate** the total number of new cases that appeared in China between January and April 2006.

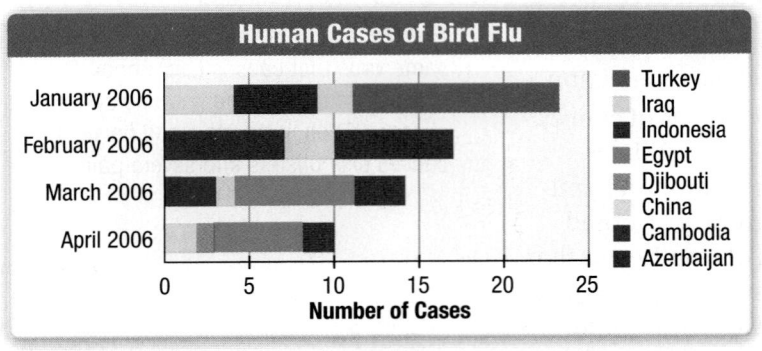

Human Cases of Bird Flu

Legend:
- Turkey
- Iraq
- Indonesia
- Egypt
- Djibouti
- China
- Cambodia
- Azerbaijan

(y-axis: January 2006, February 2006, March 2006, April 2006)
(x-axis: Number of Cases — 0, 5, 10, 15, 20, 25)

SCiLINKS.

www.scilinks.org
Topic: Emerging Viruses
Code: HX80499

Emerging Diseases

> Emerging diseases are infectious diseases that are newly recognized, that have spread to new areas or a new host, or that have reemerged when a disease that was once considered under control begins to spread.

In 2005, a new form of bird flu appeared in Asia and spread to other parts of the world. This newly recognized emerging disease was deadly to birds but not to humans. Health officials feared that the bird flu virus could mutate to become highly infectious to humans. The result could be a global flu pandemic.

Diseases can spread to new areas or a new host when people come into contact with a pathogen in a different way than in the past. For example, the use of exotic cats for meat in China resulted in the transmission of SARS (sudden acute respiratory syndrome) to humans.

Environmental changes can cause diseases to emerge. For example, in 1993, an abundance of pine nuts caused a rise in the population of rodents that carry hanta virus. An outbreak of hanta virus resulted. Human behavior plays an important role in emerging disease. Frequent use of antibiotics has resulted in the emergence of antibiotic-resistant pathogens. A decline in vaccination has allowed diseases such as whooping cough, measles, and diptheria to reemerge. And with the ease of global travel, health officials worry that emerging diseases will spread quickly and easily.

Section 3 Review

> ## KEY IDEAS

1. **Describe** the beneficial roles of bacteria and viruses in the environment, industry, and research.

2. **List** the four steps of Koch's postulates.

3. **Explain** two ways that bacteria cause disease.

4. **Describe** how antibiotic resistance spreads.

5. **Explain** why it is difficult to develop a cure for viral diseases.

6. **Describe** the three types of emerging diseases.

CRITICAL THINKING

7. **Proposing Solutions** In the search for medications to cure viruses, researchers try to find a way to target just the virus without damaging the host's cells. Propose a possible target for antiviral medication.

8. **Recognizing Relationships** The first antibiotic was discovered when the fungus *Penicillium* contaminated a laboratory dish of bacteria. Why might fungi naturally produce antibiotics?

ALTERNATIVE ASSESSMENT

9. **Brochure** Choose an exotic location that you would be interested in visiting on a vacation. Research infectious diseases that are common to the area. Make a travel brochure that will prepare tourists for diseases that they may encounter. Advise them about how they can avoid and recognize these diseases and about available treatment.

Tiny Terrors

The use of biological weapons is not new. During the Middle Ages, the dead bodies of plague victims were sent flying over the walls of besieged cities. In the 18th century, British forces decimated Native American populations by intentionally giving them blankets contaminated with smallpox. Today, biological weapons are becoming global news again.

Critical Biological Agents

The Centers for Disease Control and Prevention (CDC) has compiled a list of "critical biological agents." The list is divided into three categories (A, B, and C) based on the level of potential harm to the public. Category A agents have the greatest potential for harm because they can be easily distributed and can cause a large number of deaths. Diseases caused by category A agents include anthrax, smallpox, botulism, plague, and viral hemorrhagic fevers such as Ebola. The most likely way that a biological weapon would be used is as an aerosol, a fine particle released into the air. If a crop duster were used to spread anthrax spores over Washington, D.C., scientists estimate that the spores could cover 300 square miles and could kill 1 million to 3 million people.

Anthrax Inhalation anthrax results from breathing the spores of *Bacillus anthracis.* Once inside the lungs, the spores produce bacterial cells that multiply quickly. Early symptoms are similar to those of a cold and occur within seven days after exposure. If left untreated, anthrax results in suffocating pneumonia and death in only 24–36 hours after symptoms first appear.

Preparing for the Worst As biological weapons become more sophisticated, so must the response. Today, research strategies include enzyme detergents that can dissolve anthrax and aerosol vaccines that can immunize an entire population at once.

Research Research one of the six category A agents, and describe the incubation period, symptoms, and mortality rate of the disease.

Chapter 20 **Lab**

Objectives

➤ Prepare and stain smears of bacteria.

➤ Practice using sterile technique to avoid contaminating bacterial cultures.

Materials

- 70% isopropyl alcohol
- paper towels
- pencil, wax
- microscope slides (3)
- Bunsen burner with striker
- culture tubes of bacteria (3)
- test-tube rack
- sterile cotton swabs
- forceps or wooden alligator-type clothespin
- beaker, 150 mL
- water, 75 mL
- methylene blue stain in dropper bottle
- microscope, compound

Safety

Bacterial Staining

Bacteria are prepared for viewing by making a smear. A smear is a slide on which cells have been spread, dried, and usually stained. In this lab, you will practice staining and observing bacteria. To do so, you will make a smear from three cultures of bacteria.

Procedure

1 Put on safety goggles, gloves, and a lab apron.

2 **CAUTION: Alcohol is flammable. Do not use alcohol in the room when others are using a Bunsen burner.** Use alcohol and paper towels to clean the surface of your lab table and gloves. Allow the table to air-dry.

3 **CAUTION: Microscope slides are fragile and have sharp edges.** Use a wax pencil to label three microscope slides "A", "B", and "C".

4 **CAUTION: Keep combustibles such as alcohol-soaked paper towels away from flames. Do not light a Bunsen burner when others in the room are using alcohol.** Have your teacher light a Bunsen burner with a striker.

Part A: Making a Smear

5 Remove the cap from culture tube A. **CAUTION: Keep the cap in your hand.** To avoid contaminating your bacterial culture, do not place the cap on the table or other surface.

6 Pass the opening of the tube through the flame of a Bunsen burner to sterilize the end of the culture tube.

7 Use a sterile swab to collect a small sample of bacteria by lightly touching the tip of the swab to the bacterial culture.

8 Pass the opening of the tube through the flame again, and replace the cap.

9 Make a smear of bacterial culture A by rubbing the swab on the slide. Spread a thin layer of culture over the middle area of the slide. Cover about half of the total slide area and allow to dry.

10 Dispose of the swab in a proper container.

11 Repeat steps 5 through 10 for cultures B and C.

Part B: Staining Bacteria

12 Using microscope slide forceps, pick up each slide one at a time, and pass it over the flame several times. Let each slide cool.

13 Using microscope slide forceps, place one of your slides across the mouth of a 150 mL beaker half filled with water.

⑭ ◆ **CAUTION: Methylene blue will stain your skin and clothing.** Place 2 to 3 drops of methylene blue stain on the dried bacteria. Do not allow the stain to spill into the beaker.

⑮ Let the stain stay on the slide for 2 min.

⑯ Dip the slide into the water in the beaker several times to rinse it. Gently blot the slide dry with a paper towel. Do not rub the slide.

⑰ Repeat steps 14 through 17 for your other two slides.

⑱ Allow each slide to completely dry before observing your slides under the microscope.

Part C: Observing Bacteria

⑲ Observe each slide under the microscope on low and high power. Make a sketch of a few cells that you see on each slide.

⑳ ◆ ◆ Clean up your lab materials according to your teacher's instructions. Wash your hands before leaving the lab.

SC*LINKS*®
www.scilinks.org
Topic: Antibiotics
Code: HX80082

Analyze and Conclude

1. **Summarizing Results** Describe the shape and grouping of the cells of each type of bacteria that you observed.

2. **Drawing Conclusions** How did you classify the bacteria in cultures A, B, and C: as coccus, bacillus, or spirillum?

3. **CRITICAL THINKING** **Evaluating Viewpoints** Evaluate the following advice: Always use caution when handling bacteria, even if the bacteria are known to be harmless.

Extensions

4. **Further Inquiry** Write a question about bacteria that could be explored with another investigation using skills that you learned in this lab.

5. **On the Job** Microbiologists are scientists who study organisms too small to be seen by the unaided eye. Do research to find out about the kinds of work that microbiologists do and how microbiologists improve our lives.

| **Key Ideas** | **Key Terms** |

1 Bacteria

❯ Prokaryotes are divided into two major groups: the domain Archaea and the domain Bacteria.

❯ Gram-positive bacteria have a thick layer of peptidoglycan and no outer membrane. Gram-negative bacteria have a thin layer of peptidoglycan and have an outer membrane.

❯ Grouping prokaryotes based on their energy source separates them into photoautotrophs, chemoautotrophs, and heterotrophs.

❯ Prokaryotes can reproduce by binary fission, exchange genetic material through conjugation, transformation, and transduction, and survive harsh conditions by forming endospores.

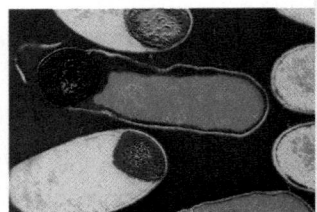

plasmid (472)
peptidoglycan (472)
Gram-positive (472)
Gram-negative (472)
conjugation (475)
transformation (475)
transduction (475)
endospore (475)

2 Viruses

❯ Viruses are not considered living because they do not grow, metabolize, or maintain homeostasis, and they cannot reproduce without a host cell.

❯ All viruses have nucleic acid and a capsid.

❯ Viruses can reproduce by a lytic life cycle and a lysogenic life cycle.

❯ Viroids and prions are nonliving pathogenic molecules that are able to reproduce.

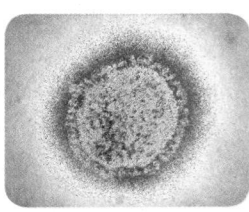

capsid (477)
envelope (477)
bacteriophage (477)
lytic (478)
lysogenic (478)

3 Bacteria, Viruses, and Humans

❯ Bacteria play important roles in the environment and in industry. Both bacteria and viruses are important in research.

❯ The steps of Koch's postulates are isolating the pathogen, growing the pathogen, infecting a healthy animal, and isolating the same pathogen.

❯ Bacteria cause disease by producing toxins and by destroying body tissues.

❯ Antibiotic resistance spreads when sensitive populations of bacteria are killed by antibiotics, allowing resistant bacteria to thrive.

❯ Because viruses reproduce inside host cells, it is difficult to develop a drug that kills the virus without harming the living host.

❯ Emerging diseases are infectious diseases that are newly recognized, that have spread to new areas or a new host, or that have reemerged when a disease that was once considered under control begins to spread.

Koch's postulates (482)
pathogen (482)
toxin (483)
antibiotic (484)
resistance (484)

1. **Key-Term Fold** Cut the tabs off your key-term fold. Shuffle the pieces that have the key terms written on them, and then try to match them with their definitions.

2. **Concept Map** Make a concept map that describes the relationships of bacteria and viruses to diseases. Include the following words in your map: *bacteria, viruses, pathogen, emerging diseases, antibiotics,* and *toxin.*

Using Key Terms

3. Use the following terms in the same sentence: *bacillus, coccus,* and *spirillum.*

For each pair of terms, explain how the meanings of the terms differ.

4. *capsid* and *endospore*

5. *lytic* and *lysogenic*

6. *Gram-positive* and *Gram-negative*

Understanding Key Ideas

7. What characteristic does the Gram stain indicate?
   a. energy source
   b. method of motility
   c. composition of cell wall
   d. form of genetic material

8. Bacteria that do not require sunlight and obtain energy from hydrogen-rich chemicals are called
   a. heterotrophs.
   b. cyanobacteria.
   c. chemoautotrophs.
   d. photosynthetic bacteria.

9. What shape is represented by organism 3?

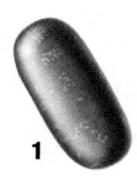 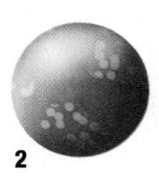 

   1 2 3

   a. coccus
   b. bacillus
   c. spirillum
   d. filamentous

10. Genetic recombination in bacteria can occur during which of the following processes?
    a. meiosis
    b. conjugation
    c. binary fission
    d. endospore production

11. Viruses differ from cells because viruses
    a. can grow.
    b. lack nucleic acids.
    c. have homeostasis.
    d. do not metabolize.

12. A virus kills its host cell during
    a. conjugation.
    b. a lytic cycle.
    c. a lysogenic cycle.
    d. assembly of the capsid.

13. Which is a pathogen composed only of protein?
    a. virus   c. viroid
    b. prion   d. prokaryote

14. Nitrogen fixation by bacteria is important to all other organisms because
    a. it does not take oxygen away from animals.
    b. it captures more energy than photosynthesis alone captures.
    c. it is necessary in order for dead organisms to be decomposed.
    d. it converts nitrogen gas into a form of nitrogen that plants can take up through their roots.

15. Botulism can be fatal because the toxin
    a. can poison the blood.
    b. can damage the heart.
    c. can paralyze the muscles used in breathing.
    d. can stress the body and enable other infectious agents to grow.

16. Antibiotic resistance arises in a population by
    a. mutation.
    b. crossing-over.
    c. Gram staining.
    d. endospore formation.

17. Viral diseases can be prevented by which of the following techniques?
    a. using antibiotics
    b. hospitalizing people who are infected
    c. using medicines that can destroy viruses
    d. vaccinating people before they become infected

Explaining Key Ideas

18. **Describe** the two major groups of prokaryotes.

19. **Compare** the characteristics of viruses with those of living organisms.

20. **Describe** how viruses, viroids, and prions differ from each other.

Critical Thinking

21. **Relating Concepts** Why might your doctor try to determine if the bacteria infecting your throat were Gram positive or Gram negative?

22. **Making Inferences** If cold viruses invade your body, your body's immune system may destroy most but not all of these viruses. How does your body's immune system affect the evolution of the cold virus?

23. **Evaluating Information** The drug azidothymidine (AZT) works by blocking the enzyme reverse transcriptase. Explain how AZT can help patients infected with HIV.

24. **Making Inferences** *Rhizobium* bacteria live inside the roots of certain plants. The bacteria provide the plants with nitrogen that the bacteria have fixed from the air. What benefit do the bacteria get from this association?

25. **Evaluating Results** In the 1520s, the Spanish explorer Cortez and his armies introduced smallpox to the Americas. The death rate among the Native Americans ranged from 50% to 90%, but the death rate was about 10% among people in Europe. What accounts for the difference in death rates?

Why It Matters

26. **Making Predictions** Would a virus that is transmitted through the bite of an insect be an agent that a bioterrorist would be likely to use? Explain your answer.

Alternative Assessment

27. **Phage Model** Use common household materials, such as hardware items or craft materials, to prepare a model of a bacteriophage. Your model must depict all of the structural characteristics of a bacteriophage. Display your model in the classroom.

Using Science Graphics

The diagram below shows human cases of bird flu from January to April 2006. Use the diagram to answer the following questions.

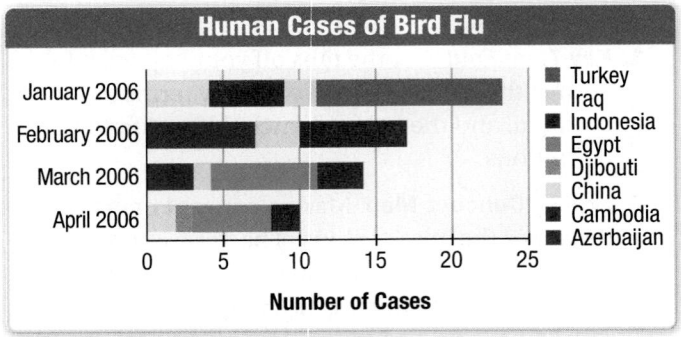

Source: European Union Communicable Diseases Network

28. Which country had the fewest cases of bird flu?
    a. China
    b. Djibouti
    c. Cambodia
    d. Azerbaijan

29. What was the total number of human cases of bird flu reported in Indonesia?
    a. 5
    b. 7
    c. 12
    d. 17

Methods of Science

30. **Germ Theory** Doctors have not always known that bacteria and viruses cause disease. Research the development of germ theory. Describe one or more alternative theories that explain the cause of disease. Discuss the research that scientists performed and how researchers proved that pathogens are the cause of disease.

Math Skills

31. **Unit Conversion** To convert a measurement from one unit to another, you need to know the relationship between the units. For example, there are 100 centimeters in a meter. So, to convert a measurement from meters to centimeters, you would multiply by 100. To convert a measurement from centimeters to meters, you would divide by 100.

How many centimeters are in 250 meters?

How many meters are in 250 centimeters?

TEST TIP When using a diagram to answer a question, study the diagram closely for evidence that supports your potential answer.

Science Concepts

1. Chemoautotrophic prokaryotes get their energy
  A from carbon dioxide.
  B from other organisms.
  C from inorganic molecules.
  D from fixing nitrogen.

2. *E. coli* is a
  F Gram-positive bacterium.
  G Gram-negative bacterium.
  H Gram-sensitive bacterium.
  J Gram-peptidoglycan bacterium.

3. In harsh conditions, *Clostridium bacteria* form
  A envelopes.   **C** endospores.
  B conjugation.   **D** endocapsids.

4. A virus is made up of
  F only protein.
  G only nucleic acid.
  H nucleic acid plus protein.
  J nucleic acid, protein, and organelles.

5. Viroids contain
  A only RNA.   **C** only protein.
  B only DNA.   **D** DNA and protein.

6. Environmental spills of petroleum are sometimes cleaned up by using
  F viroids.   **H** bacteria.
  G prions.   **J** bacteriophages.

7. HIV infects and destroys
  A skin cells.   **C** red blood cells.
  B bacterial cells.   **D** white blood cells.

Writing Skills

8. Short Response Write a paragraph that describes the process of Gram staining and the results obtained when staining Gram-positive and Gram-negative bacteria.

Using Science Graphics

The table below lists the response of bacteria to several antibiotics. A score of 0 means that the bacteria were not sensitive. Sensitivity increases as the score increases. Use the table to answer the following question(s).

Antibiotic	Sensitivity
Ampicillin	3
Bacitracin	0
Cephalosporin	0
Penicillin	0
Pifampin	0
Streptomycin	3
Tetracycline	2

9. Which of the following antibiotics killed bacteria most effectively?
  F penicillin   **H** tetracycline
  G bacitracin   **J** streptomycin

10. Which of the following antibiotics had no effect on the bacteria?
  A ampicillin   **C** streptomycin
  B tetracycline   **D** cephalosporin

The diagram shows the life cycle of a bacteriophage. Use the diagram to answer the following question(s).

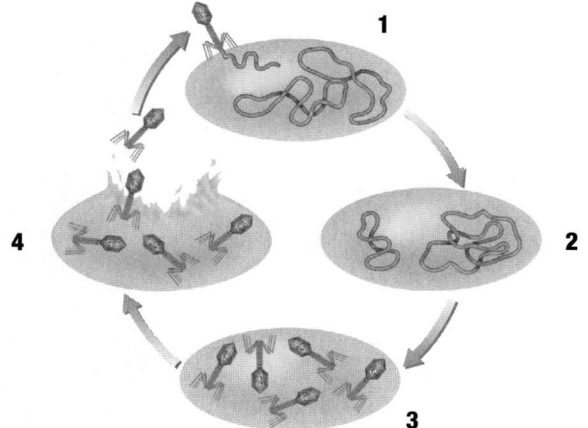

11. This bacteriophage would be considered
  F viral.   **H** temperate.
  G virulent.   **J** tempestuous.

Chapter 21 Protists

Preview

1 Characteristics of Protists
What Are Protists?
Reproduction
Classifying Protists

2 Groups of Protists
Grouping Protists
Animal-like Protists
Plantlike Protists
Funguslike Protists

3 Protists and Humans
Protists and Disease
Protists and the Environment
Protists and Industry

Why It Matters

Protists give us oxygen, gelatin, sparkly paint, and deadly diseases. Although most are microscopic, these organisms play a big part in our world.

Looking like bubbles inside bubbles, *Volvox* are small, beautiful, simple, and complex. These colonies of cells have an ability to coordinate their activities that we are just beginning to understand.

Only certain cells in a *Volvox* colony can reproduce. The signals that control which cells reproduce may give us clues about how our own cells communicate.

Daughter colonies grow inside the parent colony. Eventually, they burst out, as this one has done.

Inquiry**Lab**

Pond-Water World

Protists are everywhere. Even a single drop of water can hold an entire community of protists.

Procedure

❶ Place a drop of pond water in the center of a clean slide.

❷ Place a coverslip on the slide.

❸ Use a compound light microscope to observe the wet mount under both low power and high power.

❹ Place a drop of slowing agent at the very edge of the coverslip.

❺ Observe the wet mount under low power and high power again.

❻ Draw the organisms that you see.

Analysis

1. **State** how many types of organisms you could see before you added the slowing agent.

2. **Describe** the various types of organisms that you observed after you added the slowing agent.

3. **Propose** whether the organisms that you observed were prokaryotes or eukaryotes.

Each *Volvox* cell has two cilia that beat in unison like oars on a ship. No one knows how these movements are synchronized.

A *Volvox* colony has a front and a back. Cells at the front have one red eyespot and a light receptor. These cells can "see" where the colony is going.

READING TOOLBOX

These reading tools can help you learn the material in this chapter. For more information on how to use these and other tools, see **Appendix: Reading and Study Skills.**

Using Words

Word Origins Many of the words we use today come from Greek or Latin words. Knowing the meaning of Greek and Latin roots can help you figure out and remember the meaning of modern English words.

Your Turn Use the table to answer the following questions.

1. What do you think the word *cryptic* means?

2. Why might a writer use a pseudonym?

3. What do you think a pseudopod helps an organism do?

Word Origins		
Word part	**Origin**	**Meaning**
pseudo-	Greek	false, fake
-nym	Greek	name
-pod	Greek	foot
crypto-	Greek	hidden

Using Language

General Statements A general statement summarizes the features of a group or describes an average feature of members of the group. Some individuals in the group may not share all of the features. So, general statements may be true most of the time, but not always.

Your Turn Use what you know about general statements to answer the following questions.

1. Write a general statement that summarizes the features of baseballs, basketballs, tennis balls, soccer balls, and footballs.

2. Brainstorm exceptions to the general statement "In general, dogs have four legs, fur, and a tail and can bark."

Using Graphic Organizers

Venn Diagram A Venn diagram is useful for comparing topics in science. A Venn diagram shows which characteristics the topics share and which characteristics are unique to each topic.

Your Turn Make a Venn diagram to compare animal-like, plantlike, and funguslike protists.

1. Draw three circles, as shown here. Make sure that each circle partially overlaps the other circles.

2. Label one circle "Animal-like protists," another circle "Plantlike protists," and the third circle "Funguslike protists."

3. In the areas where the circles overlap, write the characteristics that the groups of protists share.

4. In the areas where the circles do not overlap, write the characteristics that are unique to each group of protists.

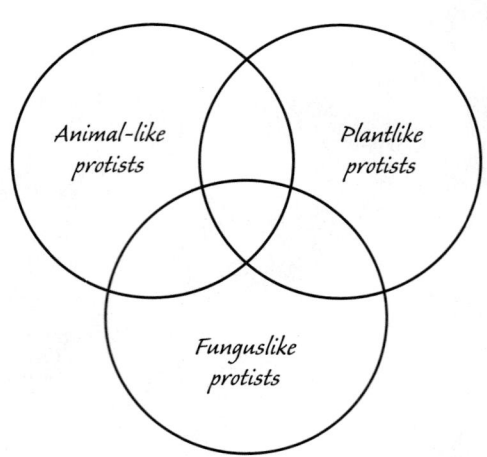

Characteristics of Protists

Key Ideas	Key Terms	Why It Matters
❯ What types of organisms are classified as protists? ❯ What methods of reproduction do protists use? ❯ Why is the classification of protists likely to change in the future?	gamete zygote zygospore alternation of generations	Protists offer clues about the evolution of fungi, plants, and animals.

From tiny glass stars that float in the ocean to slimy green fuzz that carpets rocks on the shore, a wide variety of organisms make up the group we call *protists*.

What Are Protists?

The kingdom Protista is made up of organisms that do not belong in any of the other kingdoms. As a result, the members of this kingdom are quite diverse, as **Figure 1** shows. But all protists have one thing in common: they are eukaryotic. ❯ **Protists are eukaryotic organisms that cannot be classified as fungi, plants, or animals.**

Several important characteristics evolved in protists. These characteristics include membrane-bound organelles, complex cilia and flagella, sexual reproduction with gametes, and multicellularity. Organelles, including mitochondria and chloroplasts, allow single cells to perform a wide variety of functions. Complex cilia and flagella like those found in protists are also found in many other types of cells. For example, the cells that keep particles out of our lungs use the same type of cilia as is found in protists. Sexual reproduction allows for greater genetic diversity than reproduction by binary fission does. Multicellularity allows cells to specialize, which in turn allows for the development of tissues, organs, and organ systems.

❯ **Reading Check** *What important characteristics arose among protists during their evolution? (See the Appendix for answers to Reading Checks.)*

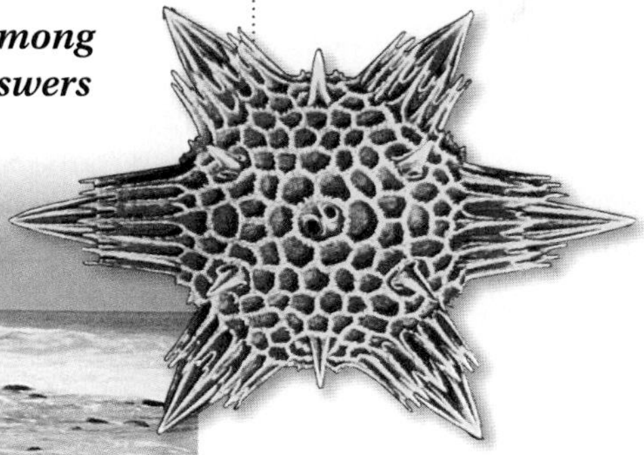

Figure 1 The radiolarian shown above is an example of a unicellular protist that captures and engulfs food. Algae, such as the kind growing on these rocks, contain chloroplasts and use photosynthesis to produce energy.

Reproduction

Asexual reproduction results in offspring that are genetically identical to the parent. Sexual reproduction results in offspring that are genetically different from either parent. Sexual reproduction involves the union of reproductive cells, usually called **gametes.** Gametes are haploid cells that join to form a diploid **zygote.** ❯ **Protists can reproduce asexually by binary fission, budding, and fragmentation. Protists can also reproduce sexually by fusion of gametes.**

Asexual Reproduction Asexual reproduction in protists occurs through binary fission, budding, or fragmentation.

Binary Fission *Binary fission* occurs when a unicellular organism reproduces by splitting in half after replicating its DNA. Binary fission is sometimes called mitosis. Mitosis is technically only the division of the nucleus. After the nucleus divides by mitosis, the cell generally divides in a process called cytokinesis. Prokaryotes lack nuclei and can undergo binary fission, but not mitosis. The cells of a multicellular organism reproduce by mitosis with cytokinesis, often simply called mitosis. Multicellular organisms do not undergo binary fission.

Budding Budding is a form of asexual reproduction in which a part of the parent organism pinches off and forms a new organism. This can occur in unicellular and multicellular organisms. Budding differs from binary fission in that the offspring is smaller than the parent.

Fragmentation In fragmentation, part of a multicellular organism breaks off and starts a new organism. Fragmentation differs from budding in that budding is an action that is performed by the organism itself. Fragmentation is the result of an action that is done to an organism. An accident can result in fragmentation, but not budding.

gamete (GAM eet) a haploid reproductive cell that unites with another gamete to form a zygote

zygote (ZIE GOHT) the cell that results from the fusion of gametes

zygospore (ZIE goh SPAWR) a thick-walled protective structure that contains a zygote

alternation of generations within the life cycle of an organism, the occurrence of two or more distinct forms that differ from each other in method of reproduction

Figure 2 Chlamydomonas reproduces both sexually and asexually. Sexual reproduction is triggered by environmental stress, such as drought.

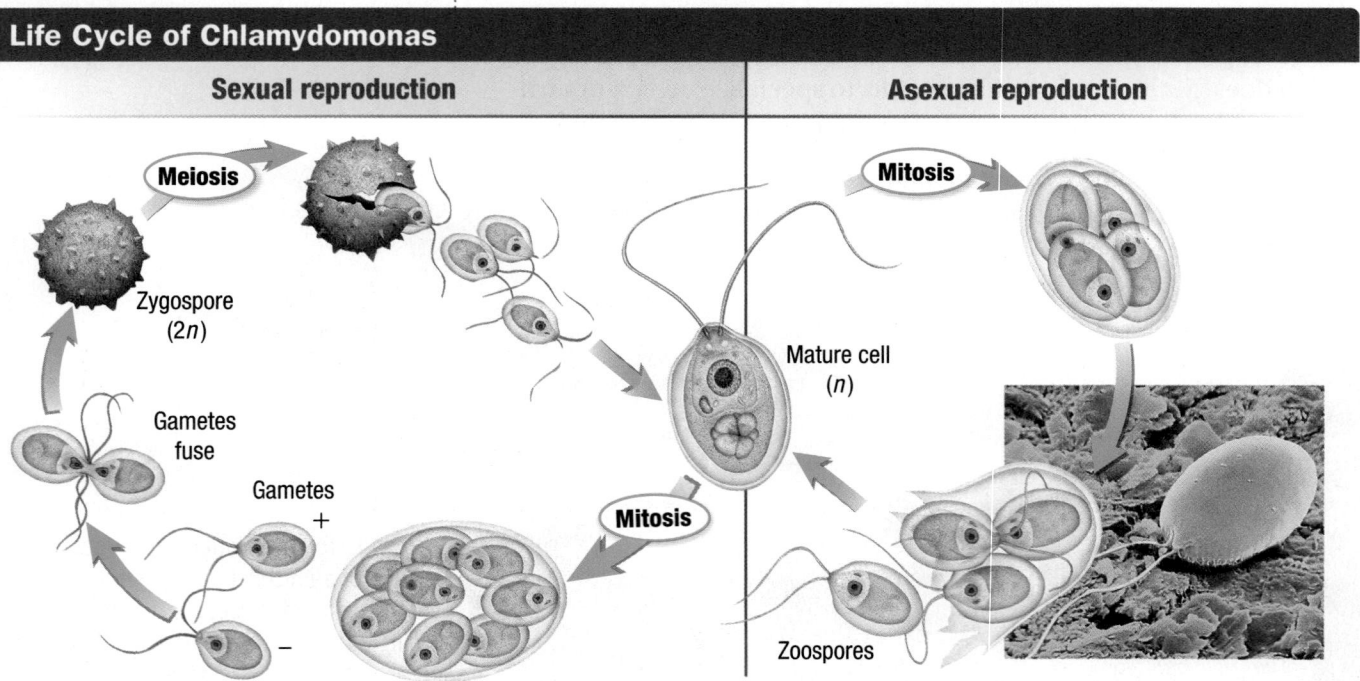

Life Cycle of Chlamydomonas

Sexual reproduction

Meiosis

Zygospore
(2*n*)

Gametes
fuse

Gametes
+

−

Mitosis

Asexual reproduction

Mitosis

Mature cell
(*n*)

Mitosis

Zoospores

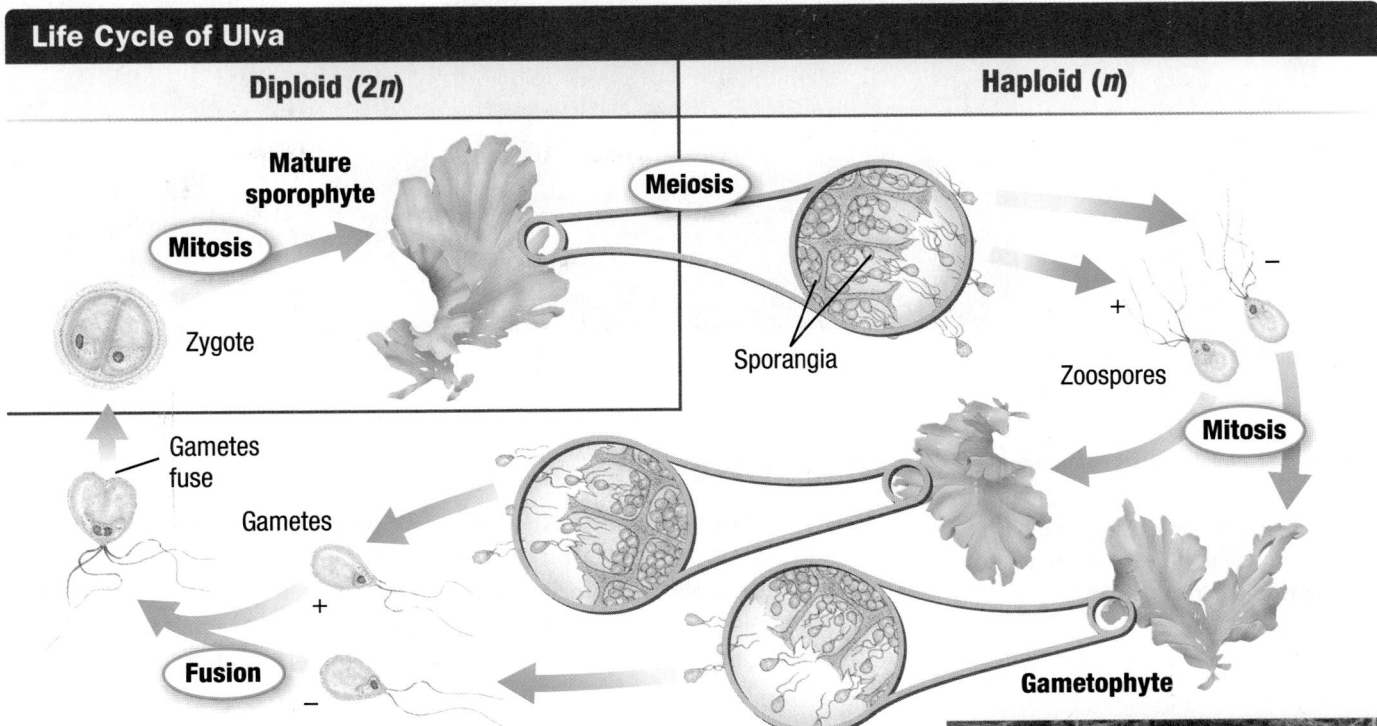

Life Cycle of Ulva

Diploid (2n) | **Haploid (n)**

Mature sporophyte

Mitosis

Zygote

Meiosis

Sporangia

Zoospores

Mitosis

Gametes fuse

Gametes

+

Fusion

−

Gametophyte

Sexual Reproduction In many protists, sexual reproduction occurs as a response to environmental stress. In some protists, the zygote secretes a tough outer coating and becomes a **zygospore.** Zygospores can survive freezing, drying, and UV radiation.

Sexual Reproduction in Unicellular Protists In most unicellular protists, such as the chlamydomonas shown in **Figure 2,** a mature organism is haploid. A haploid cell divides by binary fission to produce haploid gametes. Two gametes fuse to form a diploid zygote, which becomes a zygospore. When environmental conditions improve, meiosis occurs within the zygospore. Haploid cells break out of the zygospore and grow into mature cells.

Sexual Reproduction in Multicellular Protists Many multicellular protists can reproduce both sexually and asexually. This process, called **alternation of generations,** consists of two distinct forms that differ in method of reproduction. Ulva, shown in **Figure 3,** displays this kind of reproduction. The diploid, spore-producing phase is called the *sporophyte generation.* The adult sporophyte has sporangia, reproductive cells that produce haploid spores by meiosis. The spores grow into multicellular haploid organisms that produce gametes. The haploid, gamete-producing phase is called the *gametophyte generation.* The mature gametophyte produces haploid gametes by mitosis. Two gametes fuse and form a diploid zygote. The zygote divides to form a multicellular diploid organism. This step begins the first stage of a new sporophyte generation.

❱ **Reading Check** *How does alternation of generations differ from sexual reproduction in unicellular protists?*

Figure 3 Ulva, or sea lettuce, has a life cycle in which haploid and diploid individuals alternate.

Word Origins The Greek word root *phyte* means "plant." Using this information, propose your own definitions for *sporophyte* and *gametophyte.*

Dinoflagellate

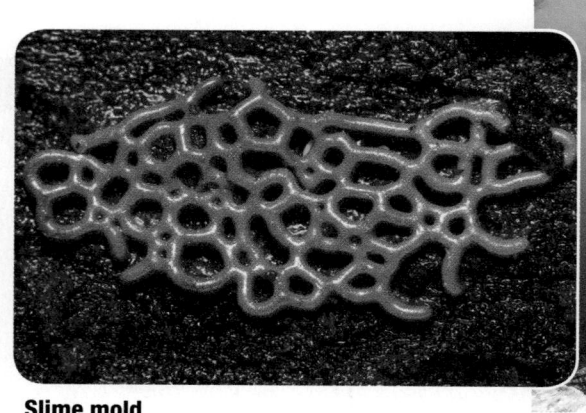
Slime mold

Giant kelp

Figure 4 Dinoflagellates, slime molds, and giant kelp are classified as protists. It is not yet clear how these and other protists are related to each other and to organisms in other kingdoms.

www.scilinks.org
Topic: Protists
Code: HX81245

Classifying Protists

Understanding the relationships between protists and developing a classification system that reflects these relationships are ongoing challenges. ❯ **The classification of organisms currently grouped in the kingdom Protista is likely to change as scientists learn more about how these organisms are related to each other and to members of other kingdoms.**

When living things are classified, relationships between groups are inferred from specific shared characteristics. Some protists share characteristics of plants or animals, while others are more like fungi, as **Figure 4** shows. The sequencing of DNA, RNA, and proteins has allowed scientists to infer relationships among groups of protists and between protists and other kingdoms. Molecular studies suggest that protists could be classified into up to 20 kingdoms!

The characteristics that protists share with plants, animals, and fungi provide information about the evolution of these organisms. For example, molecular evidence shows that green algae are more closely related to plants than to other algae. Studying green algae can offer clues about how plants evolved. Other protists that resemble cells found in sponges may help us understand the evolution of multicellular animals. The relationships between modern protists are still being discovered, and the classification of protists is uncertain. A new classification system for protists is currently being developed.

Section 1 Review

❯ KEY IDEAS

1. **Explain** which organisms are classified as protists.
2. **Compare** reproduction by binary fission, mitosis, budding, and fragmentation.
3. **Describe** sexual reproduction in unicellular and multicellular protists.
4. **Explain** how research may affect the classification of protists.

CRITICAL THINKING

5. **Evaluating Statements** A classmate tells you that he saw a unicellular organism through a microscope and concluded that it was a protist. Is his conclusion valid? What other information might be needed?

METHODS OF SCIENCE

6. **Classification** Using several sources, research the classification of protists. Note any differences in the ways in which the sources classify protists. Draw a phylogenetic tree that reflects the information that you find in your research.

Key Ideas	Key Terms	Why It Matters
❯ Why is it useful to group protists based on their methods of obtaining nutrition? ❯ What characteristic do animal-like protists share? ❯ What key characteristic do plantlike protists share? ❯ What characteristic makes funguslike protists similar to fungi?	pseudopodium plasmodium	The kingdom Protista includes an enormous diversity of life. You might be amazed to find out how many of the organisms you are familiar with are protists.

The group we call protists include snail-like creatures, giant kelp, yellow slime molds, and many other organisms. Its members have little in common. So, how do we discuss them in an organized way?

Grouping Protists

One common way to group protists is by their source of nutrition. ❯ **Grouping protists by the way they obtain nutrients helps us understand their ecological roles.** Using this method, we can divide protists into three groups, as shown in **Figure 5.** One group includes protists that, like plants, get energy by photosynthesis. Another group includes protists that, like animals, capture and eat other organisms. The third group includes protists that, like fungi, absorb nutrients from their environment. Keep in mind that discussing protists as plantlike, animal-like, and funguslike does not indicate anything about their relationship to each other or to plants, animals, and fungi. Also remember that for every generalization that is made about protists, there will be exceptions.

❯ **Reading Check** *What method can be used to group protists?*

Like fungi, yellow slime molds release spores and absorb nutrients from their environment, but they are not closely related to fungi.

Figure 5 Many protists resemble plants, animals, and fungi. ❯ Why might classifying protists based on their appearance be misleading?

Giant kelp obtain their energy through photosynthesis. The photosynthetic pigments in giant kelp differ from those in plants.

Foraminiferans can look just like small glass snails. However, a single amoeba-like cell lives in this shell.

Animal-like Protists

Animal-like protists are often called *protozoa,* which means "first animals." ❯ **Animal-like protists ingest other organisms to obtain energy.** Like animals, these protists are heterotrophic. All animal-like protists are unicellular, most can move, and most reproduce asexually by binary fission.

Amoeboid Protists Amoeboid protists include a wide variety of organisms that move by using extensions of their cells called **pseudopodia** (singular, *pseudopodium*). Pseudopodia are also used to surround and engulf food particles. Amoebas, such as the one in **Figure 6,** live in fresh water, in salt water, and in soil. Most amoebas are free-living, but some are parasites. Some amoeboid protists form outer shells called *tests.* These shells can be made of protein, calcium carbonate, silica, or mineral particles. Pseudopodia extend through holes in the tests to help amoebas move and catch prey.

Ciliates The ciliates include some of the most complex single-celled organisms. Most or all of the body of a ciliate is covered by a tough yet flexible outer covering and short, hairlike structures called *cilia.* Ciliates move and hunt for food by beating their cilia. Most ciliates are free-living and can be found in fresh water and salt water. Ciliates reproduce sexually by conjugation, in which two cells join temporarily and exchange one of their small nuclei with each other.

Flagellates Flagellates are protists that have whip-like structures called *flagella.* Some have one flagellum, while others have many. Some flagellates also have cilia or form pseudopodia. Many flagellates are free-living. Others, such as members of the genus *Leishmania,* shown in **Figure 6,** are parasites that cause disease.

Sporozoans Animal-like protists that form sporelike cells when they reproduce are called sporozoans. They lack flagella, cilia, and pseudopodia and thus do not move. All sporozoans are parasitic and cause disease. Sporozoans reproduce both asexually and sexually.

❯ **Reading Check** *Which group of protists is all parasitic?*

ACADEMIC VOCABULARY

variety a collection of things that are very different from each other; diversity

pseudopodium (soo doh POH dee uhm) a cytoplasmic extension that functions in food ingestion and movement

Figure 6 *Amoeba proteus* and *Leishmania* are two examples of animal-like protists.

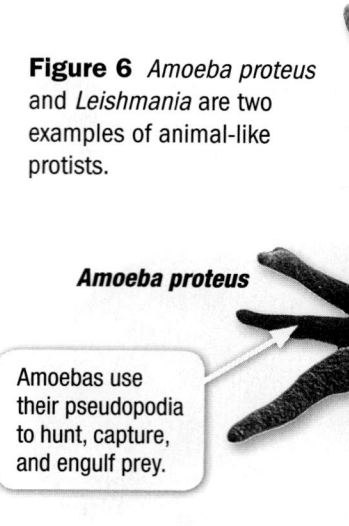

Amoeba proteus

Amoebas use their pseudopodia to hunt, capture, and engulf prey.

Leishmania

Leishmania is a parasitic flagellate that may cause oozing sores and fatal liver damage.

Up **Close** Protists

Paramecium caudatum is a ciliate protist. It is well known for its ability to avoid harm. If a paramecium encounters a negative stimulus, it will maneuver itself to escape. It may also fire a trichocyst, a sac that can eject a stinging filament to ward off predators or capture prey.

Paramecium

Scientific name: *Paramecium caudatum*
Size: microscopic; up to 1 mm long
Habitat: freshwater streams and ponds
Diet: bacteria, small protists, and organic debris

Nuclei Paramecia have two kinds of nuclei. The macronucleus controls routine cellular functions. The micronucleus functions in a sexual process called *conjugation*.

Cilia *P. caudatum* is covered with thousands of hairlike cilia that are arranged in rows along the cell. The cilia beat in waves that cause the protist to spin through the water.

Contractile Vacuole Like other freshwater protists, *P. caudatum* constantly absorbs water by osmosis. Excess water is removed by contractile vacuoles. These organelles fill with water. When they contract, they squeeze the water out of the cell.

Macronucleus

Micronucleus

Food vacuole

Oral Groove Cilia line the oral groove and create a "whirlpool" that draws in bacteria and other food. Food moves down the funnel-shaped groove and is engulfed in a food vacuole. Enzymes in the vacuole digest the food. *P. caudatum* can consume up to 5,000 bacteria per day!

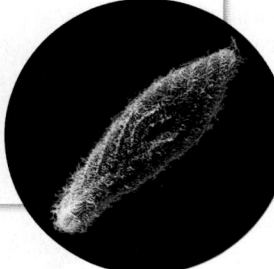

Genetic Variation *P. caudatum* generally reproduces asexually by binary fission. During conjugation, the micronuclei of two paramecia fuse, and their genes are recombined.

Plantlike Protists

Plantlike protists include the organisms commonly called *phytoplankton* and *algae.* ❯ **Plantlike protists obtain energy through photosynthesis.** They vary widely in the types of pigments that they use for photosynthesis and the types of molecules that they use to store energy. Some are very similar to plants and others are not.

Diatoms Diatoms are photosynthetic, unicellular protists with unique double shells. These shells are made of silica or calcium carbonate and have distinct patterns, as **Figure 7** shows. Diatom shells are like small boxes with lids. Individuals are diploid and usually reproduce asexually. The two halves of a "box" separate. Each half regenerates a new base that fits inside the lid. As a result, diatoms tend to get smaller with each generation. When they reach a certain minimum size, they shed their shells and begin a sexual reproductive cycle that produces full-sized offspring that have new shells.

Euglenoids Euglenoids are freshwater protists that have one or two flagella. Many euglenoids are photosynthetic. Some are both photosynthetic and heterotrophic. Others lack chloroplasts and ingest their food. Some, such as *Euglena,* for which the group is named, have an eyespot, a light-sensitive organ that helps them move toward light. A euglena is shown in **Figure 7.**

Dinoflagellates Dinoflagellates are unicellular protists that typically have two flagella. Most dinoflagellates are photosynthetic, but some are heterotrophic. Most dinoflagellates have protective cellulose coats that may become encrusted with silica. The silica coats give dinoflagellates unusual shapes, as **Figure 7** shows. A dinoflagellate's flagella beat in two grooves. One groove encircles the body like a belt; the other is perpendicular. As its flagella beat, a dinoflagellate spins through the water like a top.

❯ **Reading Check** *In which group of protists do the individuals get smaller every time they reproduce asexually?*

READING TOOLBOX

General Statements Write a general statement that describes plantlike protists. Then, find two exceptions to this generalization in the text.

Figure 7 Unicellular photosynthetic protists are part of a group commonly referred to as *phytoplankton.*

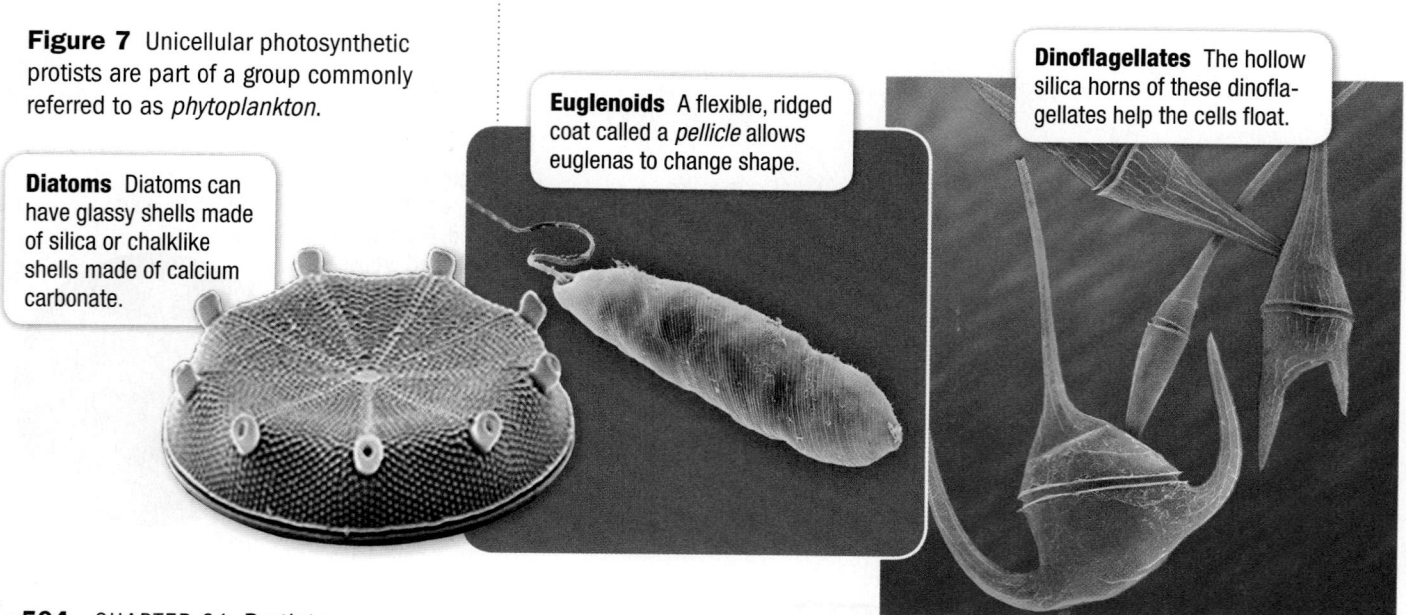

Diatoms Diatoms can have glassy shells made of silica or chalklike shells made of calcium carbonate.

Euglenoids A flexible, ridged coat called a *pellicle* allows euglenas to change shape.

Dinoflagellates The hollow silica horns of these dinoflagellates help the cells float.

Red Algae Most red algae are multicellular. These protists are usually found in warm ocean waters. The pigments in red algae can absorb the blue light that penetrates deep into water. As a result, red algae are able to grow at greater depths than other algae are. Some red algae, such as the one in **Figure 8**, have calcium carbonate in their cell walls. These coralline algae play an important role in the formation of coral reefs.

Brown Algae Brown algae are multicellular protists that are found in cool ocean environments. The largest brown algae are kelp that can reach 60 m (197 ft) in length. The body of a kelp has a rootlike structure called a *holdfast,* a stemlike structure called a *stipe,* and leaflike structures called *blades.* The blades often have air-filled sacs that help the algae float close to the surface of the ocean. Brown algae are the only algae that form more than one tissue type.

Green Algae Green algae are a very diverse group of protists. They form a major part of marine plankton. Some, such as algae of the genus *Acetabularia,* inhabit damp soil and resemble plants. Some are symbiotic within the cells of other organisms. Green algae are similar to plants in several ways. They use the same photosynthetic pigments that plants do, they use starch to store energy, and their cell walls contain cellulose. Green algae are thought to have given rise to the first true plants. Because they lack complex tissue layers, green algae are usually classified as protists. In the future, they may be classified as plants.

Hands-On QuickLab

10 min

Diatom Observation

If you look at diatomaceous earth, you can see why it is used to make fine abrasives, filters, and reflective paint.

Procedure

1. Mix a small amount of diatomaceous earth with a drop of water on a slide. Add a coverslip.
2. Using a compound microscope, observe your wet mount under low power and high power.
3. Turn off your microscope's light, and use a flashlight held at a 45° angle to light your slide.

Analysis

1. **Draw** each type of diatom that you observed.
2. **Describe** what you observed when the flashlight was shone on the slide.

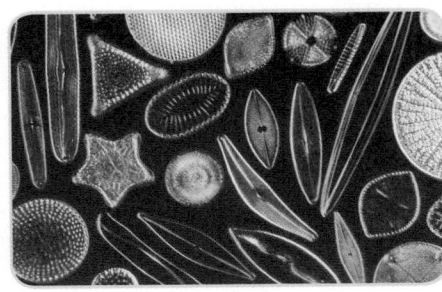

Figure 8 Red, green, and brown algae use different pigments for photosynthesis. These pigments give the algae their characteristic colors.

Green Algae *Acetabularia* are single celled organisms that have a hat, a stem, and a root-like structure.

Brown Algae *Fucus* often grow in intertidal zones, where they survive being battered by waves and dried out at low tide.

Red Algae Joints increase flexibility in coralline algae such as *Corallina.*

Physarum

Figure 9 Slime molds, such as *Physarum*, are often brightly colored. Some even glow in the dark. Water molds, like *Saprolegna*, can kill aquarium fish.

> **plasmodium** the multinucleate cytoplasm of a slime mold that is surrounded by a membrane and that moves as a mass

Saprolegna

Funguslike Protists

> Funguslike protists absorb nutrients from their environment and reproduce by releasing spores. Funguslike protists were once classified as fungi. However, according to molecular analyses, they are not closely related to fungi.

Slime Molds Slime molds are funguslike organisms that form spores and absorb nutrients from soil, decaying wood, or animal dung. Under normal conditions, cellular slime molds exist as single-celled amoebas. When food or water runs out, the cells release a chemical signal that causes them to form colonies and to release spores. A plasmodial slime mold, such as the one shown in **Figure 9,** is a **plasmodium,** a mass of cytoplasm that has many nuclei. If the plasmodium begins to dry out or starve, it divides into many small mounds and produces spores. Slime molds help researchers understand how cells interact and how cytoplasm moves within cells.

Water Molds and Downy Mildews Water molds and downy mildews typically form multicellular filaments that resemble fungi. Many of these protists decompose dead organisms. Others, such as the one shown in **Figure 9,** are common parasites of aquarium fish. In 1846, one type of water mold destroyed almost the entire potato crop in Ireland, which led to the Great Famine. In 1879, a downy mildew of grapes almost wiped out the French wine industry.

Section 2 Review

> **KEY IDEAS**

1. **Explain** why protists are grouped based on their source of nutrition.
2. **Identify** the characteristic that animal-like protists share.
3. **Name** the characteristics shared by plantlike protists.
4. **Describe** the characteristics of funguslike protists.

CRITICAL THINKING

5. **Recognizing Relationships** What characteristics of brown algae might cause people to think that brown algae should be classified as plants? Do you think that brown algae should be classified as plants? Explain why or why not.
6. **Analyzing Methods** What might be the major drawback of grouping protists based on their source of nutrition?

ALTERNATIVE ASSESSMENT

7. **Cookbook** Many types of algae are edible. Some are very important food sources in various parts of the world. Research edible algae, and construct a cookbook in which every recipe includes algae. Your cookbook should include an appetizer, a soup, a salad, a main course, and a dessert.

Protists and Humans

Key Ideas	Key Terms	Why It Matters
❯ What are seven diseases that protists cause? ❯ How do protists have a significant effect on the environment? ❯ What are five examples of ways that humans use protists in industry?	algal bloom	Some protists cause disease, but most have vital roles in ecosystems, and many provide useful products for humans.

Protists have significant effects on humans and other organisms. They can cause disease and alter ecosystems, and they are useful in industry and research.

Protists and Disease

❯ **Protists cause a number of human diseases, including giardiasis, amebiasis, toxoplasmosis, trichomoniasis, cryptosporidiosis, Chagas disease, and malaria.** Parasitic protists are a significant cause of illness and death, especially in the developing world.

Giardiasis Giardiasis is a disease caused by an intestinal parasite of the genus *Giardia,* shown in **Figure 10.** The parasite enters the body as a cyst. The cyst releases two flagellated protists that reproduce by binary fission. As the protists move through the intestine, they cause severe diarrhea and intestinal cramps that may last for two to six weeks. The disease is rarely fatal. When the cells reach the colon, they form cysts. A tough outer covering enables the cysts to survive for several months outside a host. Animals and humans can contaminate water with feces that contain cysts. Campers, hikers, and people who drink untreated water are at highest risk for infection. Infection can be prevented by boiling or filtering water.

Figure 10 *Giardia* attaches to the wall of the small intestine using a sucking disk. There they absorb nutrients from food passing through the small intestine.

Amebic Dysentery The parasite *Entamoeba histolytica* causes two forms of diarrheal illness. One form, amebiasis, is mild and can last a couple of weeks. Amebic dysentery is a severe form of amebiasis. Symptoms of amebic dysentery include pain, bloody diarrhea, and fever. In rare cases, amoebas travel to the liver, lungs, or brain and can be fatal. *E. histolytica* forms cysts that are transmitted in contaminated water, most commonly in countries that have poor sanitation. *E. histolytica* can also be transmitted on fruits, vegetables, and other foods that have been washed with contaminated water and eaten raw.

Here, *Giardia* are seen in their natural environment, the human intestine.

❯ **Reading Check** *In what form are* **Giardia** *and* **Entamoeba** *parasites transmitted?*

Toxoplasmosis Toxoplasmosis (TAHKS oh plaz MOH sis), caused by the protist *Toxoplasma gondii,* is spread by cats and by eating undercooked meat that contains cysts. Infected cats release spores in their feces for up to two weeks after infection. Adult humans who have a healthy immune system are usually not affected. A small number of people develop flulike symptoms. Rarely, infection causes nerve, brain, or eye damage. If a pregnant woman is infected, her fetus can suffer eye or brain damage. To avoid toxoplasmosis, cook meat fully and wash hands thoroughly after gardening or changing a cat's litter box. Pregnant women should avoid changing cat litter.

Trichomoniasis Trichomoniasis (TRIK oh moh NIE uh sis) is one of the most common sexually transmitted infections in the United States. It is caused by *Trichomonas vaginalis*, shown in **Figure 11.** Men often have no symptoms, but can still spread the infection. Women who are infected typically experience discolored discharge, genital itching, and the urge to urinate. If a pregnant women is infected, her infant may be born prematurely or with low birth weight. Trichomoniasis is easily treated with medication.

Cryptosporidiosis Cryptosporidiosis (KRIP toh spuh RID ee OH sis), commonly called *crypto,* is caused by protists of the genus *Cryptosporidium.* It can be spread by contaminated water or objects and in uncooked food. In 1993, water contaminated with crypto infected more than 400,000 people in Wisconsin. The most common symptoms of crypto are severe cramps and diarrhea that may last up to two weeks. Individuals who have weakened immune systems may suffer severe, prolonged cases of cryptosporidiosis.

Chagas Disease Chagas disease, or American trypanosomiasis (TRIP uh NOH soh MIE uh sis), is caused by the protist *Trypanosoma cruzi.* This disease occurs in South and Central America. It is spread by kissing bugs, shown in **Figure 11.** The early stage of infection has few or no symptoms. The chronic stage can result in heart disease, abnormal heartbeat, heart failure, heart attack, and enlargement of the esophagus and the large intestine.

Word Origins The word part *crypto-* means hidden. *Cryptosporidium* forms spores that can survive for long periods of time outside a host. Why might the name *crypto* be appropriate?

Figure 11 Trichomoniasis and Chagas disease are two common diseases caused by protists.

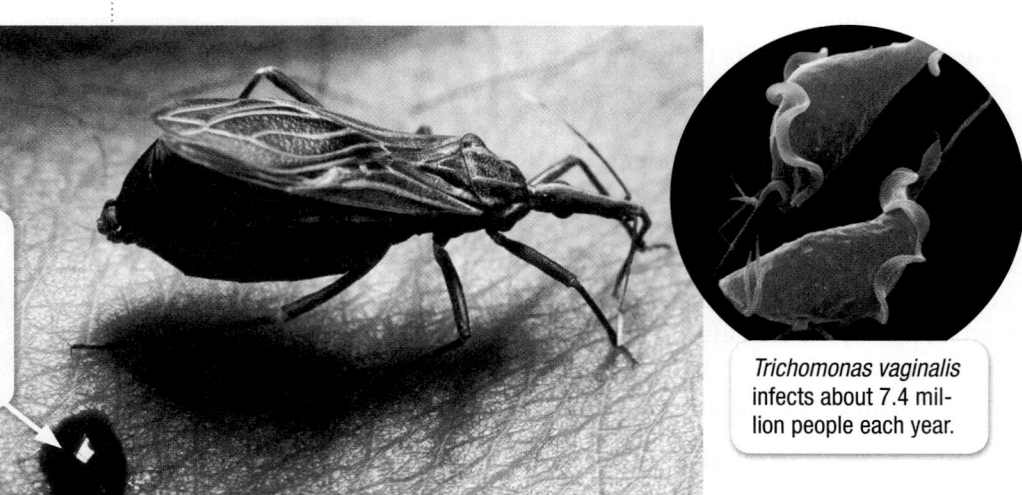

When a kissing bug bites its host it releases feces containing *Trypanosoma cruzi.* A person can become infected if the feces gets into an open wound or an eye.

Trichomonas vaginalis infects about 7.4 million people each year.

Protist Plague

Malaria was eradicated from the United States in the 1950s. Yet today it is the third most deadly disease in the world. Up to 500 million people are infected. Up to 3 million die every year. A child dies from malaria every 30 seconds.

Malaria

Malaria is caused by several types of sporozoans of the genus *Plasmodium.* It is spread by the bite of the *Anopheles* mosquito. When an infected mosquito bites a human, it injects saliva containing the parasite. The first stage of the malaria parasite, called a *sporozoite,* infects the liver. It invades liver cells, produces millions of parasites, and destroys the liver cells in the process. The second stage, called a *merozoite,* infects red blood cells. Inside a red blood cell, the parasite divides. It produces 8 to 24 merozoites that burst from the cell and destroy the red blood cell. The new merozoites invade and destroy more red blood cells in a cycle that repeats every 48 to 72 hours. As red blood cells die, malaria causes anemia and cycles of fever. If left untreated, malaria can cause rupture of the spleen, kidney failure, coma, brain damage, and death.

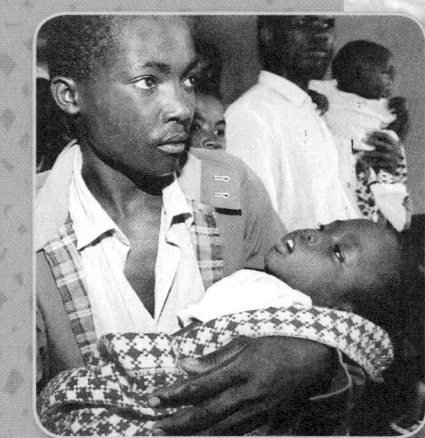

The Price of Life The cost of potentially life-saving treatment is as low as 13 cents per dose. However, medicines are not always available.

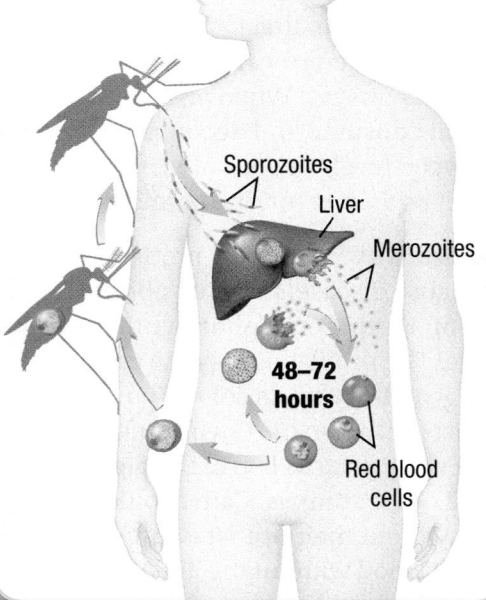

Sporozoites

Liver

Merozoites

48–72 hours

Red blood cells

Stopping a Killer Efforts to control malaria include distribution of insecticide-treated mosquito nets and fumigation to kill mosquitoes. Research is also underway to develop a malaria vaccine.

go.hrw.com
✳ **interact online**
Keyword: HX8PRTWIM

Research Use library and Internet sources to find out more about the efforts to eradicate malaria worldwide.

Protists and the Environment

> Protists produce oxygen, take up carbon dioxide, are important producers in aquatic food webs, can produce deadly blooms, serve as nutrient recyclers, and have symbiotic relationships with many animals and plants.

Oxygen Production and Nutrient Cycling Plantlike protists, along with photosynthetic cyanobacteria, produce at least half of Earth's oxygen. During photosynthesis, these protists also consume carbon dioxide, a greenhouse gas. By taking up carbon dioxide, protists may play an important role in reducing global warming. Other protists are important decomposers. They contribute to the recycling of nutrients, such as carbon, nitrogen, and other minerals.

Food Webs Photosynthetic protists, with cyanobacteria, and tiny arthropods form the base of almost all aquatic food chains. For example, protists make up a large percentage of the plankton in the oceans. Plankton are eaten by organisms such as anchovies. The anchovies are eaten by sea lions, and the sea lions become food for orcas. Many organisms depend solely on plankton for food. In fact, baleen whales, the largest animals on Earth, which can grow to up to 100 ft long, feed exclusively on tiny plankton in the ocean.

Algal Blooms During warm seasons, when nutrients in ocean water are abundant, algae populations can rise dramatically. An **algal bloom** is a rapid increase in the population of algae in an aquatic ecosystem. During a bloom, there may be as many as 20 million protists per liter of sea water. A *red tide,* such as the one in **Figure 12,** is caused by a bloom of dinoflagellates. Dinoflagellates produce powerful toxins.

Figure 12 Ciguatera is a combination of digestive, nerve, and cardiovascular disorders caused by eating fish that are contaminated with dinoflagellate toxins.
> Why might toxins become concentrated in fish and shellfish?

Humans can become ill if they eat fish or shellfish during a red tide. One genus of dinoflagellates, *Pfiesteria,* produces a powerful toxin that can become airborne. This toxin can cause memory and concentration problems as well as skin rashes. When an algal bloom dies, the bacteria that consume and decompose the algae deplete the oxygen levels in the water. As a result, large numbers of fish and other marine animals may die.

Protist Symbioses Symbiotic protists, including the ones that cause disease, make up about 15% of all of the species on Earth. Some photosynthetic protists live with corals. The protists supply the coral with nutrients and give the coral its color. The coral provides the protists with a stable environment, nitrogen, and minerals. Many protists live in the digestive tracts of humans and other animals. Cattle could not digest hay and grass without their protist symbionts. Termites could not digest wood without the aid of protists. Photosynthetic single-celled algae form an association with fungi that we call lichen.

> **Reading Check** *What are three ways in which protists affect ocean ecosystems?*

Everyday Algae

You may be surprised to learn how many products in your kitchen contain algae.

Procedure

1 Look at a group of **food products** that your teacher has placed on display.

2 Guess which products contain algae and which do not. Write down the names of the products that you think contain algae.

3 As your teacher reveals which products contain algae, note how many you got right.

Analysis

1. **State** how many of your guesses were correct.

2. **Identify** some common characteristics of the products that contain algae.

3. **CRITICAL THINKING** **Recognizing Relationships** Based on the similarities between products containing algae, what role do you think algae play in these products?

Protists and Industry

❯ **Protists are important in many foods, in industrial and consumer products, and in scientific research.** Many types of algae are eaten as vegetables. Algae produce substances that are used to thicken many food products. Carrageenan, agar, and alginate are used in foods such as ice cream, salad dressings, and gelatin desserts.

Agar is also used to grow bacteria in laboratories and to make gelatin capsules for medications. Carrageenan is used in paints, fire-fighting foam, and cosmetics. The empty shells of diatoms are used as abrasives in cleaning agents, such as toothpaste. They also add the reflective quality to roadway paint. Diatomaceous earth (DE) is sold as a natural product to control insect pests. DE absorbs oils from an insect's body, causing water loss, dehydration, and death.

Protists are important in biological research. They are used to study ribosomes, cell aging, and cell cycle control. Slime molds are studied as models of cell movement and cell signaling. They also help scientists understand how white blood cells fight disease.

Section
3 Review

❯ KEY IDEAS

1. **Name** seven diseases that are caused by protists.

2. **Explain** why a cycle of fever occurs when one has malaria.

3. **Describe** the roles that protists play in the environment.

4. **Identify** three ways that protists are used in industry.

CRITICAL THINKING

5. **Making Connections** Disease-causing protists often form cysts or spores before they leave a host. Does this fact indicate that these protists are closely related to each other? Why or why not?

6. **Forming Reasoned Opinions** The mosquitoes that transmit malaria live in warm climates. How might global warming affect the incidence of malaria?

WRITING FOR SCIENCE

7. **Persuasive Speaking** Imagine that you are speaking to Congress to request funding for malaria treatment. Write a persuasive speech stating why you should receive funding. Be sure to include data that support your position.

Chapter 21 Lab

Objectives

❯ Identify several types of protists.

❯ Compare the structures, methods of locomotion, and behaviors of several kinds of protists.

❯ Relate a protist's response to light to the protist's method of feeding.

Materials

- protist slowing agent
- plastic pipets with bulbs
- mixed culture of protists
- compound microscope
- microscope slides
- coverslips
- toothpicks
- construction paper, black
- paper, white
- paper punch
- scissors
- forceps
- sunlit windowsill or lamp

Safety

Protistan Responses to Light

Photosynthetic protists depend on light to make food. Consumers and decomposers do not require light. In this lab, you will observe live protists and test their responses to light. To do this, you will make a shade that you can place over a wet mount of protists to find out whether they move toward or away from light.

Preparation

1. **SCIENTIFIC METHODS** **State the Problem** How do protists respond to various amounts of light?

2. **SCIENTIFIC METHODS** **Form a Hypothesis** Form a testable hypothesis about how different protists will respond to various levels of light.

Procedure

Make a Wet Mount of Protists

❶ Put on safety goggles, gloves, and a lab apron.

❷ **CAUTION: Do not touch your face while handling microorganisms.** Place a drop of protist slowing agent on a microscope slide. Add a drop of liquid from the bottom of a mixed culture of protists. Add a coverslip.

❸ View the slide under low power and high power of a microscope.

❹ Make a drawing of each type of protist. Note whether the protist moves, and try to determine how it moves.

❺ Repeat step 1, but do not use the slowing agent. Note differences in the movement of the protists that you see.

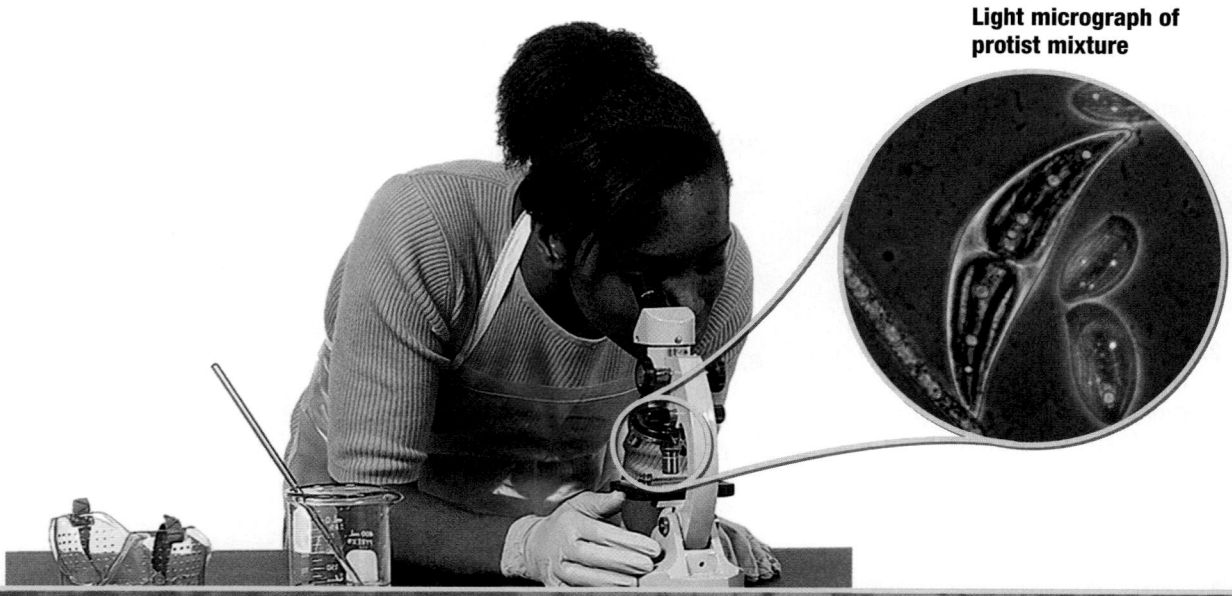

Light micrograph of protist mixture

Test Protistan Responses to Light

6 Place a wet mount of protists on a piece of white paper. Then, place the paper and the slide on a sunlit windowsill or under a table lamp.

7 Punch a hole in a piece of black construction paper that has a slight curl, as shown in the photo. Position the black paper on top of the slide so that the hole is in the center of the coverslip.

8 To examine the slide, first view the area in the center of the hole under low power. (Note: Do not disturb the black paper, and do not switch to high power. Switching to high power will move the paper.) Then, have a partner carefully remove the black paper with forceps while you observe the slide. Note any movement of the protists in response to the change in light.

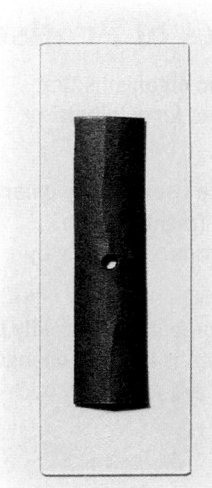

Design an Experiment

9 Design an experiment that tests your hypothesis and that uses the materials listed for this lab. Predict what will happen during your experiment if your hypothesis is supported.

10 Write a procedure for your experiment. Identify the variables that you will control, the experimental variables, and the responding variables. Construct any tables you will need to record your data. Make a list of all the safety precautions you will take. Have your teacher approve your procedure before you begin.

11 Set up and carry out your experiment.

12 Clean up your lab materials according to your teacher's instructions. Wash your hands before leaving the lab.

Analyze and Conclude

1. **Summarizing Results** Describe the various types of locomotion that you observed in protists, and give examples of each type.

2. **SCIENTIFIC METHODS** **Analyzing Results** Identify which protists were affected by light, and describe how they were affected.

3. **SCIENTIFIC METHODS** **Drawing Conclusions** How are a protist's response to light and the protist's method of feeding related?

Extensions

4. **Research** Investigate livestock diseases that are caused by parasitic protists. Which of these diseases are most common in the United States?

5. **Research** Find out how backpackers can avoid getting diseases that are caused by protists and transmitted in water.

go.hrw.com
SUPER SUMMARY
Keyword: HX8PRTS

Key Ideas	**Key Terms**

 1 Characteristics of Protists

> Protists are eukaryotic organisms that cannot be classified as fungi, plants, or animals.

> Protists can reproduce asexually by binary fission, budding, and fragmentation. Protists can also reproduce sexually by fusion of gametes.

> The classification of organisms currently grouped in the kingdom Protista is likely to change as scientists learn more about how these organisms are related to each other and to members of other kingdoms.

gamete (498)
zygote (498)
zygospore (499)
alternation of generations (499)

 2 Groups of Protists

> Grouping protists by the way they obtain nutrients helps us understand their ecological roles.

> Animal-like protists ingest other organisms to obtain energy.

> Plantlike protists obtain energy through photosynthesis.

> Funguslike protists absorb nutrients from their environment and reproduce by releasing spores.

pseudopodium (502)
plasmodium (506)

3 Protists and Humans

> Protists cause a number of human diseases, including giardiasis, amebic dysentery, toxoplasmosis, trichomoniasis, cryptosporidiosis, Chagas disease, and malaria.

> Protists produce oxygen, take up carbon dioxide, are important producers in aquatic food webs, can produce deadly blooms, serve as nutrient recyclers, and have symbiotic relationships with many animals and plants.

> Protists are important in many foods, in industrial and consumer products, and in scientific research.

algal bloom (510)

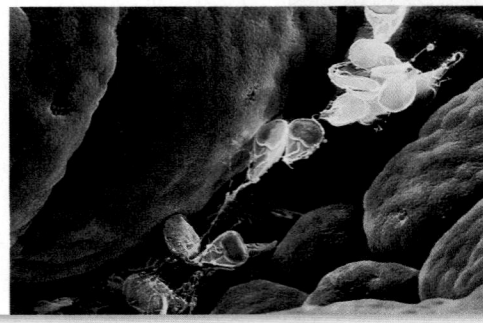

READING TOOLBOX

1. **Venn Diagram** Make a Venn diagram to summarize the similarities and differences between red algae, brown algae, and green algae.

2. **Concept Map** Make a concept map that describes protists. Try to include the following terms in your map: *red algae, malaria, slime mold, photosynthesis, plants, diseases, flagellates,* and *ciliates.* You may include additional terms.

Using Key Terms

Use each of the following terms in a separate sentence.

3. *alternation of generations*

4. *algal bloom*

5. *gamete*

For each pair of terms, explain how the meanings of the terms differ.

6. *zygote* and *zygospore*

7. *pseudopodium* and *plasmodium*

Understanding Key Ideas

8. The organisms in the kingdom Protista are grouped together because
   a. all of them are eukaryotic.
   b. all of them are closely related.
   c. all of them are microscopic and unicellular.
   d. they do not belong in the plant, fungi, or animal kingdoms.

9. Which process would *not* occur during asexual reproduction in protists?
   a. budding
   b. fragmentation
   c. binary fission
   d. fusion of gametes

10. Grouping protists by nutrition reflects their
    a. ancestry.
    b. ecological roles.
    c. importance to humans.
    d. evolutionary relationships.

11. Photosynthetic protists that have boxlike double shells are called
    a. kelp.   c. euglenoids.
    b. diatoms.   d. dinoflagellates.

12. Slime molds reproduce by forming
    a. slugs.   c. plasmodia.
    b. spores.   d. pseudopodia.

13. Which organism is responsible for transmitting Chagas disease?
    a. tsetse fly
    b. house cat
    c. kissing bug
    d. *Anopheles* mosquito

14. Photosynthetic protists affect the ecosystem in all but which of the following ways?
    a. They produce oxygen.
    b. They take up carbon dioxide.
    c. They consume harmful bacteria.
    d. They form the base of many aquatic food chains.

15. Which protists are used in cleaning agents, toothpaste, and reflective paint?
    a. kelp   c. red algae
    b. diatoms   d. dinoflagellates

16. To which group of protists does the organism shown belong?
    a. ciliates   c. sporozoans
    b. flagellates   d. amoeboid protists

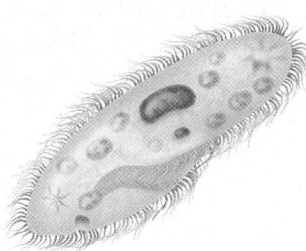

Explaining Key Ideas

17. **Differentiate** between the classification of protists and the relationships between protists.

18. **Name** two traits that evolved among protists.

19. **Sequence** the steps in the life cycle of *Ulva.* Begin with the zygote stage.

Critical Thinking

20. Predicting Outcomes The protist that causes malaria is rapidly developing resistance to drugs used to treat malaria. Would it be possible for drug-resistant malaria to become an epidemic in the United States? Explain your reasoning.

21. Making Connections How might agricultural fertilizer cause large numbers of fish to die?

22. Relating Form and Function Recall that sporozoans are animal-like protists that have no means of locomotion and are all parasitic. How does the lack of locomotion relate to a parasitic lifestyle?

23. Recognizing Relationships How could polluting the ocean affect global warming?

24. Forming Reasoned Opinions A classmate says that giant kelp should be classified as plants. Do you agree with your classmate? Why or why not?

Using Science Graphics

The table shows the number of new cases of amebiasis and malaria in the United States from 1986 to 1994. Use the table to answer the following questions.

Cases of Protist-Caused Diseases in the United States, 1986–1994		
Year	Amebiasis cases	Malaria cases
1986	3,532	1,123
1988	2,860	1,099
1990	3,328	1,292
1992	2,942	1,087
1994	2,983	1,229

25. How many more cases of malaria were reported in 1990 than were reported in 1986?
 a. 100
 b. 106
 c. 130
 d. 169

26. What is the difference between the average number of cases of amebiasis and the average number of cases of malaria between 1986 and 1994?
 a. 1,166
 b. 1,963
 c. 2,166
 d. 3,192

This diagram shows part of the life cycle of malaria. Use the diagram to answer the following question.

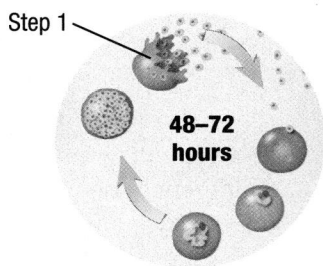

Step 1

48–72 hours

27. What event is taking place in step 1?
 a. mitosis
 b. meiosis
 c. release of spores
 d. release of merozoites

Why It Matters

28. Proposing Solutions Health agencies around the world are working to provide medicine to treat malaria as well as insecticide-treated mosquito nets, fumigation to kill mosquitoes, and a vaccine to prevent malaria. Can you think of other efforts that might be effective in the battle against malaria?

Methods of Science

29. Designing an Experiment Design an experiment to test whether protists respond to chemical signals such as food. Write a question, a hypothesis, and a procedure for your experiment. Include all safety precautions that you will take.

Math Skills

30. Calculating Speed Some protists move very quickly for their size. For example, if a protist of the genus *Strobilidium* were the same size as a cheetah, it would travel faster than a cheetah! Speed is calculated by dividing the distance an object travels by the time the object takes to travel that distance.

$$speed = distance/time$$

Suppose that a microscopic protist travels 3 cm in 1 s. You could express the speed of this protist as 3 cm/s.

If this protist keeps traveling at 3 cm/s, how far will it travel in 5 h? Express your answer in meters. (Hint: There are 100 cm in 1 m.)

Science Concepts

1. Which of the following features do protists, fungi, plants, and animals share but bacteria lack?

  A DNA   **C** reproduction

  B a nucleus   **D** a cell membrane

2. In which group of animal-like protists do organisms that have tests belong?

  F ciliates   **H** flagellates

  G amoebas   **J** sporozoans

3. How is amoebic dysentery spread?

  A by the bite of a mosquito

  B by eating overcooked meat

  C by the bite of a kissing bug

  D by drinking contaminated water

4. Which of the following items is produced without the use of protists?

  F soap   **H** roadway paint

  G ice cream   **J** fire-fighting foam

5. Which of the following processes can be found in both bacteria and protists?

  A mitosis   **C** binary fission

  B meiosis   **D** fusion of gametes

6. Which of the following is a sexually transmitted infection caused by a protist?

  F toxoplasmosis   **H** Chagas disease

  G trichomoniasis   **J** cryptosporidiosis

7. Which of the following protists are likely to be classified as plants in the future?

  A red algae   **C** brown algae

  B green algae   **D** dinoflagellates

Writing Skills

8. Short Response Describe the life cycle of *Plasmodium*, the protist that causes malaria.

Using Science Graphics

Use the diagram of the cycle of fever in a person who has malaria to answer the following question(s).

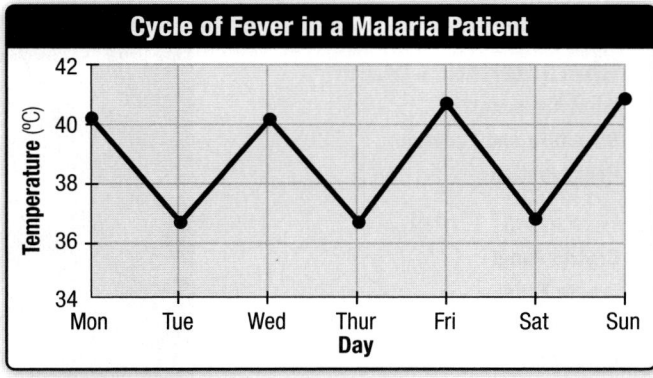

9. If the fever pattern continues, what will be the approximate temperature of the patient on the following Monday?

  F 37 °C   **H** 41 °C

  G 39 °C   **J** 45 °C

The diagram shows the percentage of animal-like protists belonging to each major group. Use the diagram to answer the following question(s).

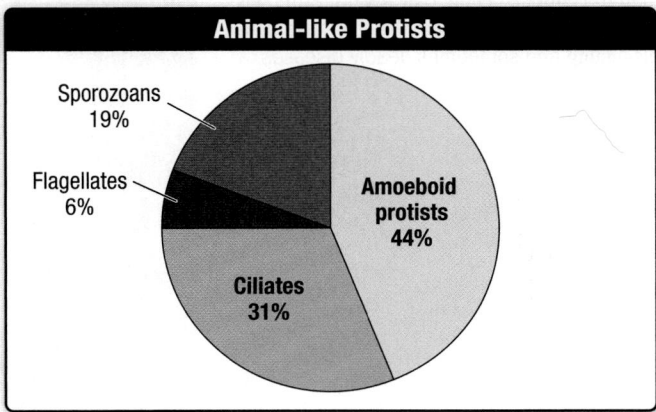

10. What percentage of animal-like protists are not able to move on their own?

  A 6%   **C** 31%

  B 19%   **D** 44%

11. What percentage of animal-like protists move by pseudopodia?

  F 6%   **H** 31%

  G 19%   **J** 44%

Chapter 22 Fungi

Preview

1 Characteristics of Fungi
What Are Fungi?
Structure and Function
Reproduction

2 Groups of Fungi
Chytrid Fungi
Zygote Fungi
Sac Fungi
Club Fungi
Fungal Partnerships

3 Fungi and Humans
Fungi and Industry
Fungi and the Ecosystem
Fungi and Disease

Why It Matters

When we think of fungi, we usually think of grocery-store mushrooms. But fungi are more than mushrooms. Fungi play several extremely important ecological roles. They can also cause disgusting and sometimes deadly diseases.

Fungi can grow in the most unexpected places. This ant was certainly not expecting to play host to the fungus that ate its body from the inside out.

The fungus *Cordyceps* entered this ant's body when the ant breathed in the spores. Don't worry. *Cordyceps* only infects invertebrates.

Now, *Cordyceps* begins a new life cycle as spores develop at the tip of this stalk. They will be released into the air and ready to find another unsuspecting victim.

   15 min

InquiryLab

Mushroom Dissection

Procedure

1. Identify the stalk, the cap, and the gills on a **mushroom.**

2. Carefully twist or cut off the cap. Use a **magnifying lens** to observe the gills. Look for spores.

3. Use the magnifying lens to observe the other parts of the mushroom. Try to find individual hyphae.

Analysis

1. **Sketch** the mushroom, and label its parts.

2. **Identify** the part of the mushroom that produces spores.

3. **Describe** the part of the mushroom that absorbs nutrients.

4. **Explain** how gills might help a fungus reproduce more efficiently.

Slowly the fungus absorbed nutrients from the ant's body, devouring it from the inside.

READING TOOLBOX

These reading tools can help you learn the material in this chapter. For more information on how to use these and other tools, see **Appendix: Reading and Study Skills.**

Using Words

Word Parts Knowing the meanings of word parts can help you figure out the meanings of words that you do not know.

Your Turn Use the table to write your own definitions for the following terms.

1. *basidiocarp*
2. *ascocarp*
3. *basidiomycete*

Word Parts		
Word part	Type	Meaning
basidio-	prefix	pedestal
asco-	prefix	a bag or sac
mycet	root	a fungus
carp	root	body

Using Language

Comparisons Comparing is a way of looking for the similarities between different things. Contrasting is a way of looking for the differences. Certain words and phrases can help you recognize when things are being compared or contrasted. Comparison words include *and, like, just as,* and *in the same way.* Contrast words include *however, unlike, in contrast,* and *on the other hand.*

Your Turn In the following sentences, find the things that are being compared or contrasted.

1. Fungi, like plants, have rootlike structures that anchor them.
2. Some mushrooms are edible; however, others are highly poisonous.
3. Unlike most types of fungi, chytrids are unicellular.

Using Graphic Organizers

Process Chart Science is full of processes. Some processes are cycles that repeat the same steps over and over. You can use a circular process chart to help yourself remember what order the steps follow and where the cycle begins again.

Your Turn Create a circular process chart illustrating the life cycle of a club fungus.

1. Draw a box. In the box, write the first step of the cycle.
2. To the right and slightly below the first box, draw a second box. Draw an arrow to connect the two boxes. In the second box, write the next step of the cycle.
3. Continue adding boxes in a circular pattern until each step of the cycle is written in a box. Draw an arrow to connect the last box and the first box.

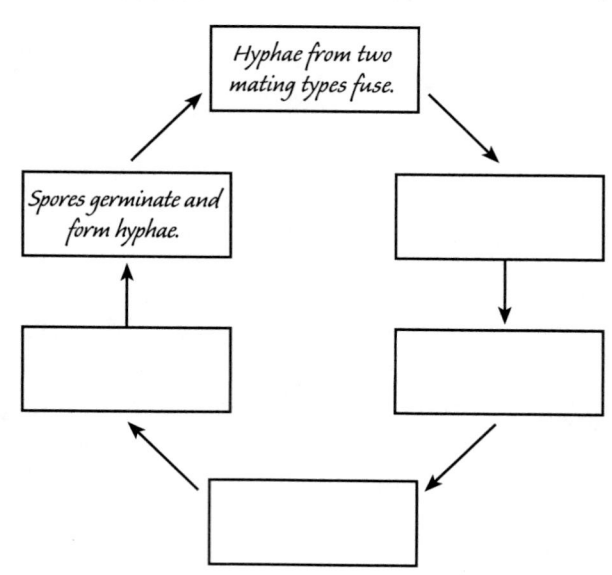

Characteristics of Fungi

Key Ideas	Key Terms	Why It Matters
❯ What are three characteristics that all fungi share? ❯ How is the structure of a fungus related to the way in which a fungus obtains nutrients? ❯ What is the difference between sexual and asexual production of spores in fungi?	chitin hypha mycelium rhizoid saprobe	Fungi are important decomposers, foods, and parasites.

A fungus grows in one place until its food source runs out. Before it dies, it produces millions of spores that float through the air or the water, find more food, and begin the cycle again.

What Are Fungi?

Fungi are a very diverse group of organisms, but all fungi share three characteristics. ❯ **Fungi have threadlike bodies, their cell walls are made of chitin, and they absorb nutrients from their environment.**

- **Fungi have threadlike bodies.** A fungus is made of long, slender filaments. Most of the fungal body is made of loosely woven filaments. The filaments weave more tightly to form reproductive structures, like the colorful mushrooms and brackets in **Figure 1.**

- **Fungal cell walls contain chitin.** The cells of fungi have walls made of chitin. **Chitin** is a tough carbohydrate that is also found in the hard outer covering of insects and other organisms.

- **Fungi are heterotrophic.** Fungi cannot make their own food or move to capture food. Instead, they obtain energy by breaking down organic and inorganic material in their environment and absorbing the nutrients.

chitin (KIE tin) a carbohydrate found in the cell walls of fungi and other organisms

Figure 1 Fungi get their color from chemicals that form during metabolic processes. Most of these colorful chemicals are toxic.

Hygrocybe conica

Laetiporus sulphureus

Entoloma virescens

Hygrocybe graminicolor

521

Structure and Function

The mushroom seen above ground is a small part of a fungus. Most of the fungus is hidden in the ground or in the substance that the fungus feeds on. **❯ A typical fungal body is made of filaments that allow the fungus to have a large surface area and to absorb nutrients efficiently.**

Body Structure Fungi have bodies made of threadlike strands called **hyphae** (singular, *hypha*). The cells of the hyphae are haploid, are almost identical, and generally perform the same functions. In some fungi, these cells do not have walls that separate the cells. In other fungi, the cells have partial walls, called *septa*, which are shown in **Figure 2.** Gaps in the septa allow cytoplasm, nutrients, and some organelles to flow through the hyphae. Hyphae form a tangled mass, often many meters long, called a **mycelium.** In some fungi, hyphae also form rootlike structures called **rhizoids.**

Obtaining Nutrients Fungi release enzymes that break down organic and inorganic matter into nutrients. Fungi absorb the nutrients across their cell walls. Fungi that absorb nutrients from dead organisms are called **saprobes.** Saprobes are a very important part of an ecosystem; they recycle nutrients that otherwise would stay trapped in the bodies of dead organisms. Fungi that absorb nutrients from living hosts are called *parasites*. In humans, fungal parasites sometimes cause diseases, such as athlete's foot and ringworm.

Reproduction

❯ In sexual reproduction, spores are produced by meiosis. In asexual reproduction, spores are produced by mitosis. Sexual reproduction results in genetic diversity. Asexual reproduction allows fungi to spread rapidly. Most fungi reproduce both sexually and asexually.

Sexual Reproduction Sexual reproduction occurs when hyphae from one fungus fuse with hyphae from a fungus of the opposite mating type. The fused hyphae then form a reproductive structure, such as the mushroom in **Figure 2.** Inside the structure, nuclei from the two mating types fuse. These newly formed diploid nuclei undergo meiosis and produce haploid spores that are released.

Asexual Reproduction Asexual reproduction in fungi is simpler than sexual reproduction is. Specialized hyphae produce long stalks. At the tips of these stalks, haploid spores are produced by mitosis. The fungi that develop from these spores are genetically identical to the parent. Fungi that do not have an observed sexual stage are grouped together and called *imperfect fungi*.

Figure 2 Hyphae are loosely woven through the soil and tightly packed in the body of the mushroom. **❯ How might a tall reproductive structure be beneficial?**

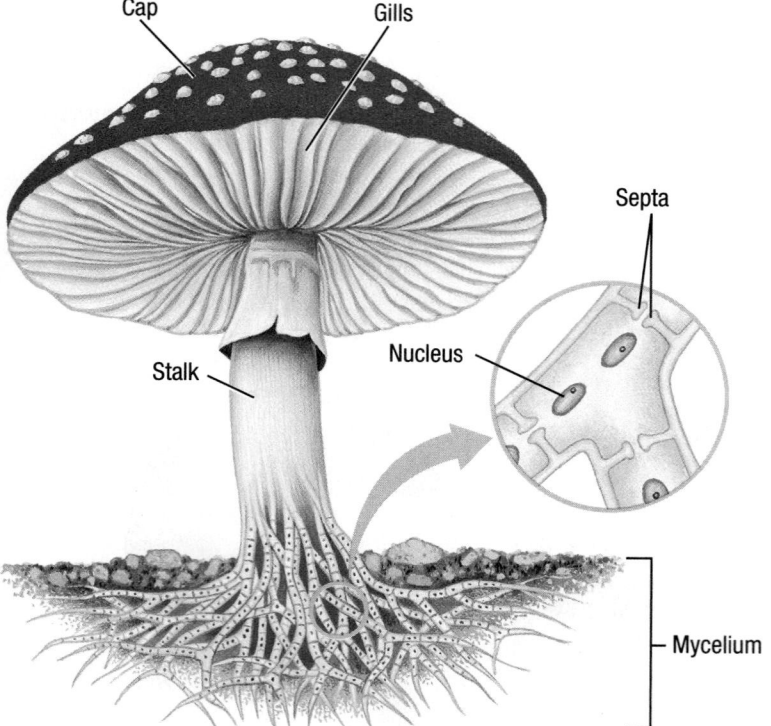

Cap

Gills

Septa

Stalk

Nucleus

Mycelium

Hands-On

QuickLab

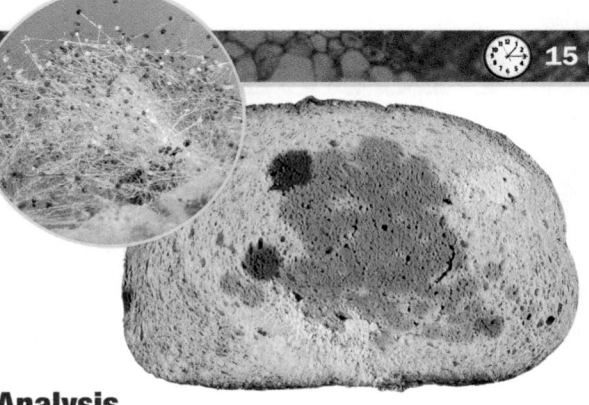

Mold

You can use a microscope to see the individual threads of cells that make up the body of a fungus.

Procedure

1 Examine a **slide of black bread mold** under a **microscope** at low power.

2 Move the slide until you can clearly see threadlike structures and round dark spores.

3 Draw the structures that you have observed.

Analysis

1. Explain where you would find each structure on the loaf of bread shown above.

2.  **Recognizing Relationships** Why do you think spores are produced at the tips of stalks?

Yeast and Mold Often, we think of yeasts and molds as distinct classes of fungi. In fact, the words *yeast* and *mold* refer to specific stages of the life cycle that are shared by several types of fungi.

Yeast Some species of fungi exist primarily in a unicellular state. The common name for this unicellular stage is *yeast*. Yeasts usually reproduce asexually by budding, a process in which part of the parent pinches off to form a new organism. Under very specific conditions, yeasts can form multicellular hyphae and may reproduce sexually.

Mold A mold is a rapidly growing, asexually reproducing stage of some types of fungi. The term *mold* refers only to the asexual phase. Some fungi that form molds have no observed sexual stage and are grouped with imperfect fungi. Other fungi that grow as molds also reproduce sexually and are classified according to their sexual reproductive structures.

❯ **Reading Check** *What is the difference between spores produced sexually and spores produced asexually in fungi? (See the Appendix for answers to Reading Checks.)*

READING TOOLBOX

Comparisons Write two sentences that compare and two sentences that contrast sexually and asexually produced spores.

*SCI*LINKS®

www.scilinks.org
Topic: Fungi
Code: HX80628

Section 1 Review

❯ KEY IDEAS

1. Identify three characteristics that fungi share.

2. Relate the structure of a fungal body to the way in which a fungus obtains nutrients.

3. Describe sexual and asexual production of spores in fungi.

CRITICAL THINKING

4. Recognizing Relationships How might the pores in septa be important to fungi?

5. Relating Concepts Certain fungi, such as those that form yeasts and molds, grow very rapidly. They reproduce sexually only under harsh conditions. How might this strategy benefit these fungi?

ALTERNATIVE ASSESSMENT

6. Baker's yeast, *Saccharomyces cerevisiae,* is a fungus that is used for making bread, beer, and wine. Research baker's yeast. Find out what conditions will cause baker's yeast to reproduce sexually.

Section 2 Groups of Fungi

Key Ideas	Key Terms	Why It Matters
› What group of fungi provides clues about the evolution of fungi? › Which reproductive structure characterizes the zygote fungi? › Which reproductive structure characterizes the sac fungi? › What is the name of the structure that produces spores in club fungi? › What two symbiotic partnerships do fungi form?	zygosporangium ascus basidium lichen mycorrhiza	Fungi spread rapidly and destroy harvested citrus because of the efficiency of the fungus life cycle.

Modern fungi are classified into four phyla: Chytridiomycota (chytrids), Zygomycota (zygote fungi), Ascomycota (sac fungi), and Basidiomycota (club fungi). They are classified based on the type of sexual reproductive structures that they form.

Chytrid Fungi

Fungi date back about 500 million years. Fossils show that the earliest fungi produced spores and gametes that had flagella. The ability of ancient fungi to swim suggests that fungi first appeared in water. Today, one group of modern fungi, the chytrids (KIE trids), still retains this ability. › **The chytrids are a group of aquatic fungi that provide clues about the evolution of fungi.**

Chytrids, shown in **Figure 3,** were once classified with protists because the two groups share two important characteristics. Like protists, many chytrids are unicellular and produce spores and gametes that have flagella. The similarities between chytrids and protists suggest that fungi may have evolved from protists that had flagella.

Chytrids are like all other fungi in several important ways. They have chitin in their cell walls. They digest food outside their bodies. Most produce hyphae that form rhizoids. These root-like structures hold chytrids in place and absorb nutrients. Finally, the sexual reproductive structures of chytrids contain spores.

Most chytrids are aquatic, although some live in moist places on land. They are mainly saprobes, which feed on dead algae or plants. Some chytrids are parasites that feed on protists, plants, animals, or even other fungi. Chytrids are common parasites of aquarium fish, and they are one of the reasons for the recent and continuing decline of amphibians in the wild.

› **Reading Check** *Which characteristics do chytrids share with protists, and which do they share with other fungi?*

zygosporangium (ZIE goh spoh RAN jee uhm) a sexual structure that contains zygotes

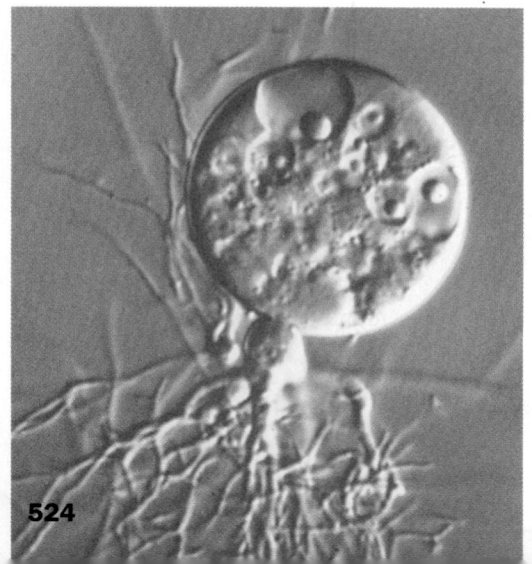

Figure 3 Chytrids are unicellular fungi that provide clues about early fungi and what they may have been like.

Life Cycle of Zygote Fungi

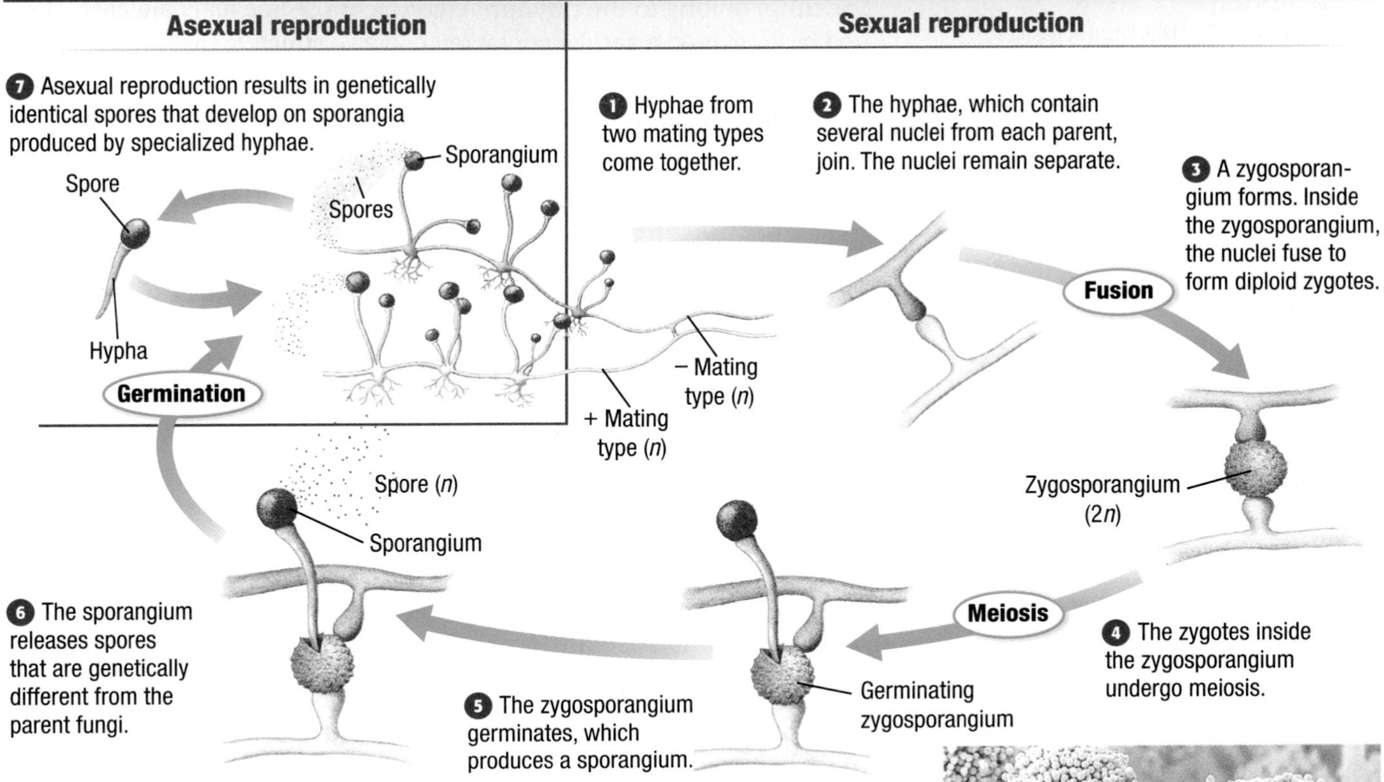

Asexual reproduction	**Sexual reproduction**

7 Asexual reproduction results in genetically identical spores that develop on sporangia produced by specialized hyphae.

Spore

Sporangium

Spores

Hypha

Germination

1 Hyphae from two mating types come together.

2 The hyphae, which contain several nuclei from each parent, join. The nuclei remain separate.

3 A zygosporangium forms. Inside the zygosporangium, the nuclei fuse to form diploid zygotes.

Fusion

− Mating type (*n*)

+ Mating type (*n*)

Zygosporangium (2*n*)

Spore (*n*)

Sporangium

6 The sporangium releases spores that are genetically different from the parent fungi.

5 The zygosporangium germinates, which produces a sporangium.

Germinating zygosporangium

Meiosis

4 The zygotes inside the zygosporangium undergo meiosis.

Zygote Fungi

Common black bread mold is a member of the phylum Zygomycota, which contains zygote fungi. ❯ **Zygote fungi are named for sexual reproductive structures that produce zygotes inside a tough capsule.**

Sexual reproduction in zygote fungi begins when hyphae from two mating types come together. In fungi, different mating types are not referred to as male and female, because they are physically <u>identical.</u> Instead, they are called "+" and "−." The hyphae join, but the nuclei remain separate. A tough capsule called a **zygosporangium** forms. Zygosporangia are resistant to hot, cold, and dry conditions. When conditions are right for growth, the nuclei fuse to form diploid (2*n*) zygotes. The zygotes undergo meiosis. The zygosporangium germinates, which produces a *sporangium* that releases haploid (*n*) spores.

Asexual reproduction is more common than sexual reproduction in zygote fungi. During asexual reproduction, haploid (*n*) spores are produced in sporangia at the tips of specialized hyphae, as **Figure 4** shows. The haploid spores are produced by mitosis. Spores are carried by the wind to new locations, where they grow into new fungi.

Species of *Rhizopus* and other zygote fungi usually live in the soil and feed on decaying plant and animal matter. However, some species of *Rhizopus,* including the one that grows on bread, have been found to cause cancer in humans.

❯ **Reading Check** *Where does meiosis take place in zygote fungi?*

Figure 4 Zygomycetes reproduce both sexually and asexually. Both types of reproduction result in spores produced in sporangia.

ACADEMIC VOCABULARY

identical looking exactly the same

Sac Fungi

ascus the microscopic structure that produces spores in sac fungi

basidium the microscopic structure that produces spores in club fungi

Sac fungi belong to the phylum Ascomycota. ❯ **Sac fungi are characterized by an ascus, a saclike sexual reproductive structure that produces spores.** The word *ascus* means "sac," and the plural form is *asci*.

Sexual reproduction of sac fungi, shown in **Figure 5,** is similar to that of zygote fungi in several ways. Hyphae of different mating types grow together. The hyphae fuse to form a bridge that connects them. Haploid nuclei from one mating type move into the tip of a hypha of the other mating type. The nuclei pair up, one "+" with one "−" nucleus. The cells—and the nuclei inside the cells—divide to form a mass of hyphae that contain two nuclei per cell. In most sac fungi, this mass of *dikaryotic* (having two nuclei) hyphae forms a structure called an *ascocarp*. Certain cells within the ascocarp become saclike asci. The nuclei inside the asci fuse and undergo meiosis. Haploid spores are released and grow into new sac fungi.

Sac fungi usually reproduce asexually. Asexual spores called *conidia* form by mitosis on specialized hyphae called *conidiophores*. Conidiophores are slightly different from the sporangia of zygote fungi. Asexual spores of zygote fungi form inside the tip of the sporangium. Conidia usually form in chains and are not covered. The spores are carried by wind and germinate to form new fungi.

Process Chart Draw a process chart that shows the steps of the life cycle of sac fungi. Draw separate loops for sexual and asexual reproduction.

❯ **Reading Check** *In sac fungi, which structure is dikaryotic?*

Figure 5 The life cycle of a typical sac fungus is shown below. Sac fungi can reproduce sexually or asexually.

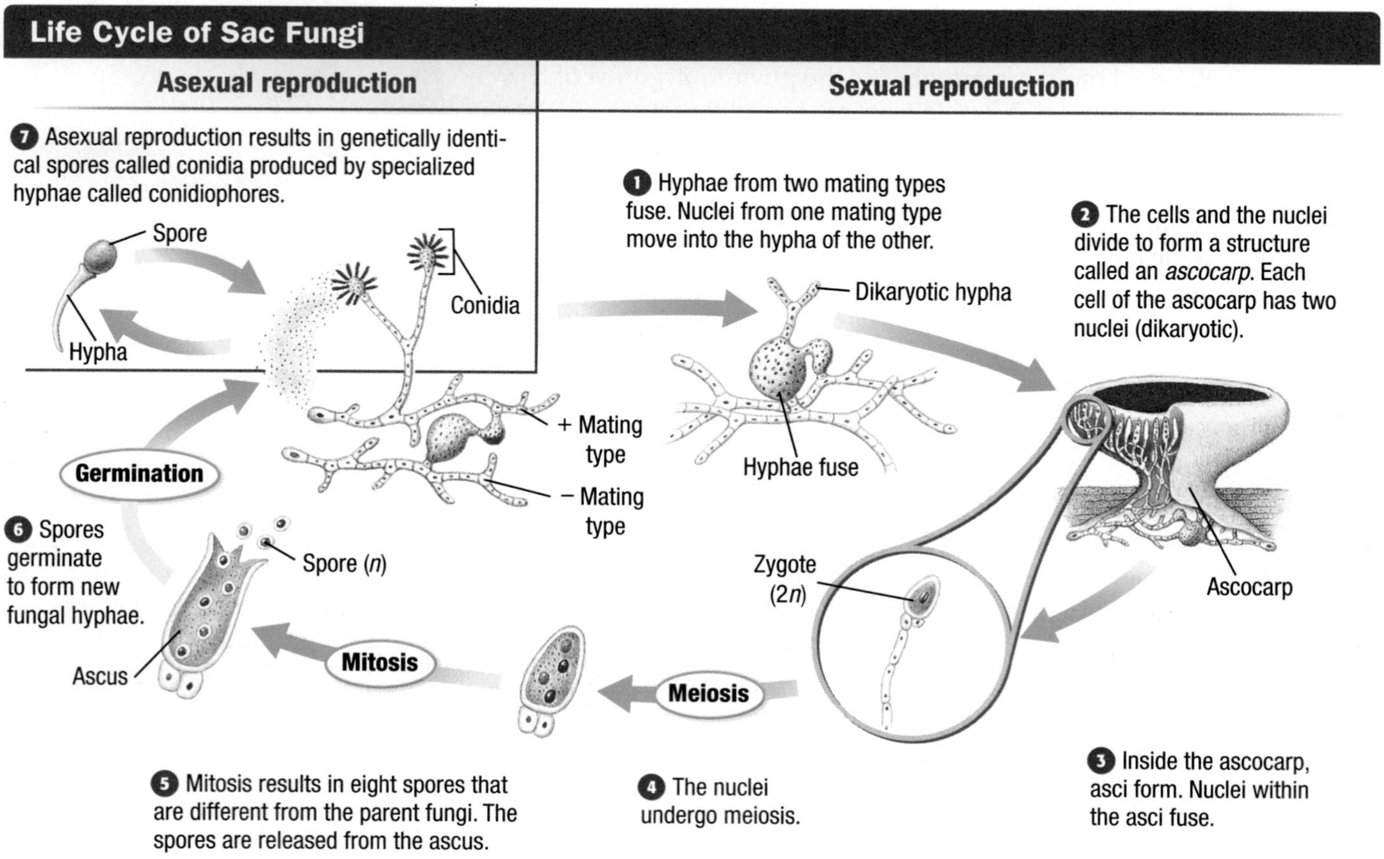

Life Cycle of Sac Fungi

Asexual reproduction

7 Asexual reproduction results in genetically identical spores called conidia produced by specialized hyphae called conidiophores.

Spore

Conidia

Hypha

Germination

6 Spores germinate to form new fungal hyphae.

Spore (*n*)

Ascus

Mitosis

5 Mitosis results in eight spores that are different from the parent fungi. The spores are released from the ascus.

Sexual reproduction

1 Hyphae from two mating types fuse. Nuclei from one mating type move into the hypha of the other.

Dikaryotic hypha

+ Mating type

− Mating type

Hyphae fuse

2 The cells and the nuclei divide to form a structure called an *ascocarp*. Each cell of the ascocarp has two nuclei (dikaryotic).

Zygote (2*n*)

Ascocarp

Meiosis

4 The nuclei undergo meiosis.

3 Inside the ascocarp, asci form. Nuclei within the asci fuse.

Life Cycle of Club Fungi

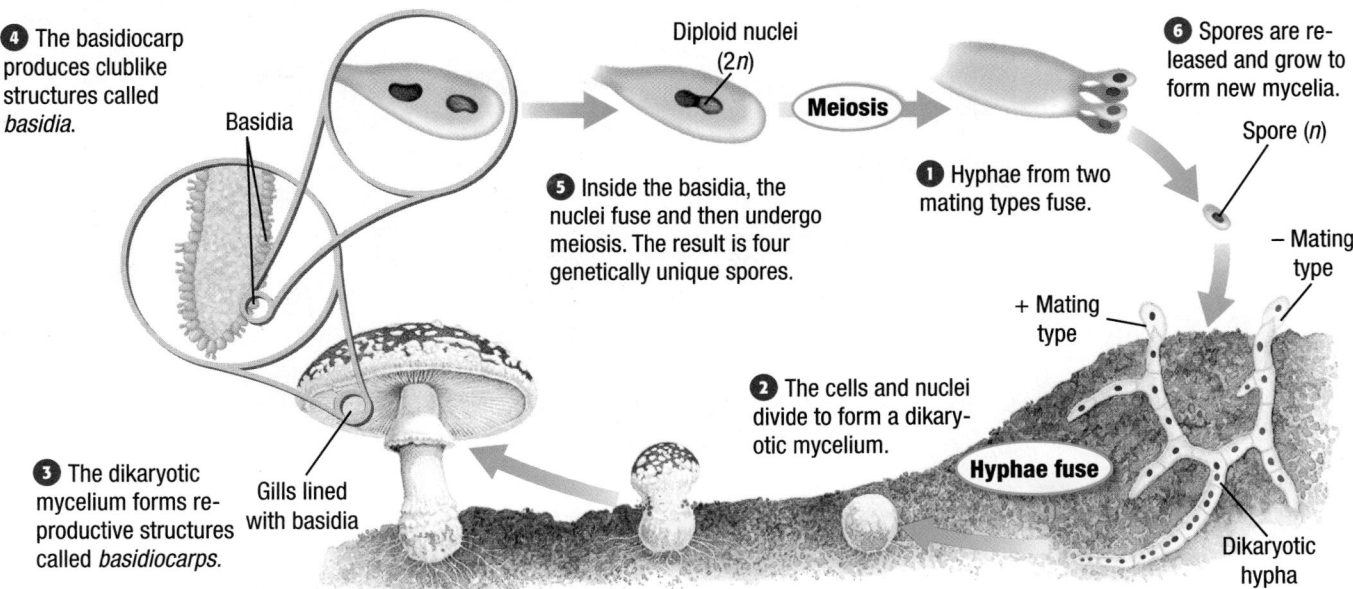

④ The basidiocarp produces clublike structures called *basidia*.

Basidia

Diploid nuclei (2*n*)

Meiosis

⑥ Spores are released and grow to form new mycelia.

Spore (*n*)

⑤ Inside the basidia, the nuclei fuse and then undergo meiosis. The result is four genetically unique spores.

① Hyphae from two mating types fuse.

– Mating type

+ Mating type

② The cells and nuclei divide to form a dikaryotic mycelium.

Hyphae fuse

③ The dikaryotic mycelium forms reproductive structures called *basidiocarps*.

Gills lined with basidia

Dikaryotic hypha

Figure 6 The life cycle of a typical club fungus is shown above. Club fungi usually reproduce sexually.

Club Fungi

Club fungi, which belong to the phylum Basidiomycota, include mushrooms, toadstools, puffballs, jelly fungi, shelf fungi, rusts, and smuts. ❯ **Club fungi are characterized by a basidium, a clublike sexual reproductive structure that produces spores.**

Sexual reproduction of club fungi is shown in **Figure 6.** Specialized hyphae of different mating types grow together. A hypha of one mating type fuses with a hypha of the opposite mating type to form a dikaryotic cell. The nuclei remain separate as the cell grows into a new mycelium in which each cell has two nuclei. The dikaryotic mycelium of a club fungus grows rapidly. When environmental conditions are right, the mycelia form a reproductive structure called a *basidiocarp*. A mushroom, such as the one in **Figure 7,** is an example of a basidiocarp. On the underside of a basidiocarp, club-shaped cells called *basidia* form. The two nuclei inside each basidium fuse. The diploid nucleus undergoes meiosis. Spores are produced and released from the basidium. The spores are carried by the wind and can grow into new club fungi. Asexual reproduction is rare among basidiomycetes but occurs in some rusts and smuts.

Basidiocarps often form at the outer edges of the large mycelial mats that club fungi produce. The mycelia grow out from a central starting point and form an expanding ring of hyphae. When the fungus reproduces sexually, a ring of mushrooms appears. Fungi can grow quite large. In fact, the largest known organism on the planet is a club fungus in Oregon that is 3.5 miles across.

❯ **Reading Check** *Which part of a club fungus is dikaryotic?*

Figure 7 Mushrooms produce spores on structures called gills. ❯ **What might be the reproductive advantage of having gills on the underside of the mushroom?**

Figure 8 Fungal hyphae surround an algal cell (below). Lichens like the British soldier lichen (middle) and wolf lichen (right) get their bright colors from pigments in their fungi.

Fungal Partnerships

Some fungi form important partnerships. ❯ **Fungi form mutualistic symbiotic associations to form lichens and mycorrhizae.** In a mutualistic relationship, both members benefit.

A **lichen,** shown in **Figure 8,** is an association between a fungus and a photosynthetic partner, such as a cyanobacterium or a green alga. The photosynthetic partner provides carbohydrates to the fungus. The fungus provides a protected environment as well as vitamins and minerals to the photosynthetic partner. Lichens can survive in extreme environments, such as on volcanic rock and arctic tundra. However, lichens can be damaged by chemical changes in their environment. They can serve as living indicators of air pollution.

A **mycorrhiza** is an association between fungi and the roots of nearly all plants. The fungal hyphae grow inside or around the plant root and out into the soil. The hyphae transfer phosphorus and other minerals from the soil to the roots of the plant. The plant supplies carbohydrates to the fungus.

lichen (LIE kuhn) a fungus in a symbiotic association with a photosynthetic partner

mycorrhiza (MIE koh RIE zuh) a symbiotic association between fungi and plant roots

---

Section 2 Review

❯ KEY IDEAS

1. **Identify** the characteristics of chytrids that provide clues about the evolution of fungi.
2. **Name** the sexual reproductive structure of zygote fungi.
3. **Identify** the two spore-producing structures in sac fungi.
4. **Describe** the function of the basidium in club fungi.
5. **Name** the two symbiotic partnerships formed by fungi.

CRITICAL THINKING

6. **Relating Concepts** The sexual reproductive structures of some sac fungi, such as truffles, are found underground. Truffles are eaten by animals and people. How might edible reproductive structures affect the spread of spores of these sac fungi?

USING SCIENCE GRAPHICS

7. Use the life cycles of zygote fungi, sac fungi, and club fungi to develop and draw a generalized life cycle of a fungus. Be sure to include both sexual and asexual reproductive stages.

Key Ideas	Key Terms	Why It Matters
> What are some common ways in which humans use fungi? > How are fungi ecologically important? > What are some diseases that fungi cause in humans?	dermatophyte	Fungi have huge effects—both good and bad—on humans and all other living things.

Fungi are in our food and medicines. They are in our labs, in our cars, and in our crops. They can be found on dead organisms and sometimes on living ones. Even though we rarely notice them, fungi play an important role in our world.

Fungi and Industry

Believe it or not, fungi have an enormous effect on industry. > **Fungi are used for food, medicines, research, alternative fuels, and pest control.**

Fungi are probably most familiar as food. White button, shiitake, and portabella mushrooms are common in grocery stores. Fungi provide the flavor and color of blue cheese, shown in **Figure 9.** Yeast is used in baking, brewing, and winemaking. Fungi also produce the citric acid that is used in soft drinks and candies. Some fungi, such as truffles, are delicacies that can sell for $1,000 per pound!

Fungi are an important part of the medical industry. They produce the antibiotics penicillin and cephalosporin. Black bread mold produces cortisone, a drug used to treat skin rashes and to reduce joint swelling. Yeast cells have been genetically engineered to make a vaccine for hepatitis B.

Fungi can also help us improve our environment and reduce pollution. Yeast produces gasohol, a fuel alternative to gasoline. The use of fungal insect parasites to kill crop-destroying insects helps reduce the use of harmful pesticides.

Figure 9 Morels (left) are considered a delicacy by many people. Fungi give blue cheese (middle) its characteristic color and flavor. Yeast is used to make bread rise (right).

QuickLab

10 min

Fungal Factor

Two groups of plants were planted in similar soils under similar conditions. Group A was grown in sterilized soil, and group B was grown in nonsterilized soil. After 18 weeks of growth, a photograph was taken of the roots of the plants. Use the photograph to answer the questions that follow.

A   B

Analysis

1. Compare the growth of the two groups of plants. Which group grew faster?

2. Explain why one group grew better than the other group.

3. **CRITICAL THINKING** **Inferring Relationships** Suggest a possible cause of slower growth in the smaller plants.

4. Recommend a course of action to restore growth in the stunted plants.

SCLINKS.

www.scilinks.org
Topic: Uses of Fungi
Code: HX81585

Figure 10 These mushrooms are decomposing a log. Fungi are one of the few types of organisms that can break down the tough fibers of wood. Fungi can also break down cloth, leather, and even some plastics!

Fungi and the Ecosystem

Fungi have a large effect on the world around them. ❯ **Fungi play important ecological roles by decomposing organic matter and by breaking down and absorbing minerals from rocks and soil.** The main role of fungi in ecosystems is decomposition of dead organisms. Fungi are among the few organisms that can break down wood, as shown in **Figure 10**. By doing this, fungi release nutrients which other organisms can then use. Without fungi, these nutrients might not be available to other organisms ever again. As part of lichens, fungi slowly break down rocks and prepare environments for other organisms. As part of mycorrhizae, fungi absorb minerals from the soil and transfer them to plant roots. Almost all plants have mycorrhizae. Some plants, such as orchids, could not survive without them.

❯ **Reading Check** *What is the primary role of fungi in ecosystems?*

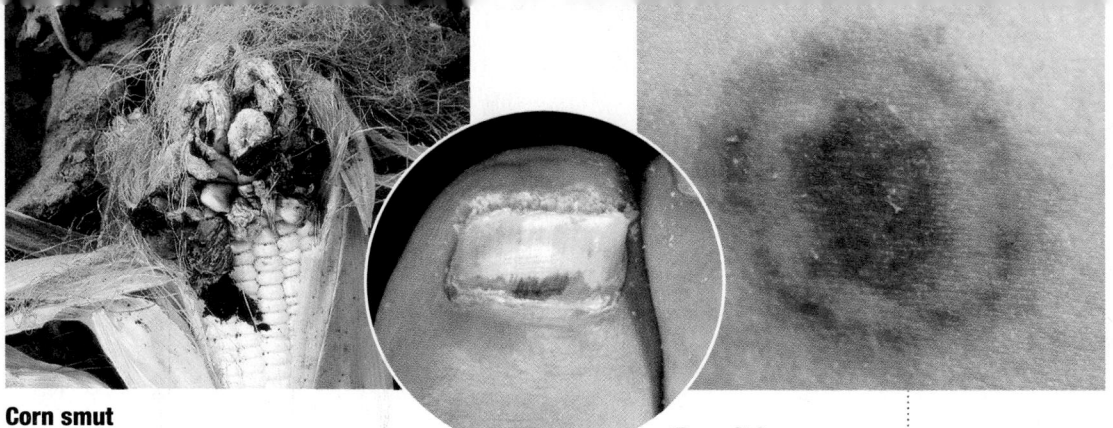

Corn smut

Toenail fungus

Ringworm

Fungi and Disease

Fungi cause may diseases in plants and animals. ❯ **Fungi cause disease by absorbing nutrients from host tissues and by producing toxins.**

Fungal Infections Fungi can grow on and inside tissues of the body. **Dermatophytes** are fungi that infect the skin and nails. They cause athlete's foot, toenail fungus, and ringworm. Toenail fungus and ringworm are shown in **Figure 11.** These fungi absorb nutrients and release metabolic wastes that irritate the skin. Yeast is a normal resident of the human body. Antibiotics, hormonal changes, or illness can cause yeast to grow too much. The result is a yeast infection. Yeast infections occur on tissues of the reproductive organs and in the mouth. Histoplasmosis is a lung infection caused by a fungus that grows in bat and bird feces. When its spores are inhaled, this fungus can cause severe respiratory illness in humans. The fungus sometimes spreads from the lungs to other organs. If untreated, it is fatal.

Because fungi grow within the tissues of their host, fungal infections can be difficult to cure. Surface treatments may only relieve the symptoms. Oral medication can cure an infection but can cause damage to the liver or other organs.

Fungal Toxins Many fungi produce dangerous toxins. Toxins in mushrooms can cause vomiting, diarrhea, liver damage, and even death. A type of fungus that contaminates corn, peanuts, and cottonseed produces *aflatoxins,* which can cause liver cancer. Indoor molds can aggravate allergies. Mold toxins may be linked with pulmonary bleeding in infants, but this link has not been proven.

Figure 11 Smut (left) is a fungus that destroys corn crops. Dermatophytes are a group of fungi that infect skin, hair, and nails, and cause athlete's foot, toenail fungus (middle), and ringworm (right).

dermatophyte a fungus that infects the skin, hair, or nails

Word Parts The prefix *histo-* means "a web." Explain why this prefix might be part of an appropriate name for a fungal disease.

Section 3 Review

❯ **KEY IDEAS**

1. **Describe** ways that fungi are used in industry.
2. **Explain** the roles of fungi in an ecosystem.
3. **Discuss** two ways that fungi can cause disease.

CRITICAL THINKING

4. **Making Predictions** What do you think would happen to an ecosystem if all of the fungi died?
5. **Relating Concepts** How do you think antibiotics and fungal toxins might be related?
6. **Connecting Concepts** What do you think might be the reason that yeast infections cause discomfort?

WRITING FOR SCIENCE

7. Imagine that you work for the health department. You have just been informed that a deadly strain of airborne fungus has been reported your area. Write a public service announcement warning people of precautions they should take.

Salem Witch Trials

WEIRD SCIENCE

It all began in December 1691 when a few young girls were suddenly afflicted with unusual symptoms. The girls claimed that they were possessed and began accusing townspeople of witchcraft. Soon, witchcraft hysteria had spread throughout the colony of Salem, Massachusetts. Over the next six months, 19 "witches" were hanged, one was pressed to death, several died in jail, and more than 150 townspeople were imprisoned.

Witches or Fungi?

Evidence now suggests that a small fungus may have started the madness that erupted in Salem. Ergot poisoning, or ergotism, results from eating grain infected with the fungus *Claviceps purpurea*. Warm, wet weather favors the growth of *C. purpurea*. Early rains, a warm spring, and a hot, stormy summer were the perfect conditions for ergot in Salem in 1691. The rye was harvested in August, stored in barns, and then processed in November. Bread baked from this rye was beginning to hit the tables in December. The children's first symptoms appeared in late December. Luckily for the people of Salem, 1692 turned out to be a dry year, so the rye was not contaminated. By late fall of 1692, the witchcraft crisis had come to an abrupt end.

A Mysterious Affliction Ergotism is characterized by seizures, crawling sensations in the skin, tingling in the fingers, vomiting, diarrhea, delirium, and hallucinations. All of these symptoms are described in the Salem court records and eyewitness accounts. The victims claimed that they were being tortured by witches.

Research The toxic chemicals that cause ergotism include lysergic acid and ergotamine. Use library or Internet resources to find out more about these chemicals and their current uses.

Chapter 22 **Lab**

Objectives

❯ Observe the process of fermentation by yeast.

❯ Investigate various energy sources and their effects on fermentation.

❯ Measure energy released by fermentation in the form of heat.

Materials

- vacuum flask, 500 mL
- rubber stopper, one-hole
- beaker, 250 mL
- sucrose (75 g)
- glucose (75 g)
- milk (50 mL)
- potato flakes (50 mL)
- packets of artificial sweetener (5)
- package of dry baker's yeast
- thermometer
- rubber tubing, 50 cm long

Safety

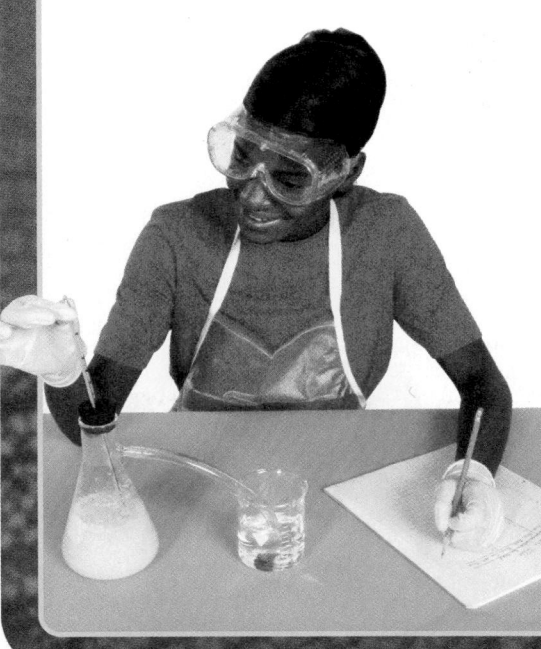

Yeast and Fermentation

Yeast releases energy stored in carbohydrates in a process called *fermentation*. In this investigation, you will measure energy released in the form of heat, observe CO_2 release during fermentation, and figure out which carbohydrate best supports yeast growth.

Preparation

1. **SCIENTIFIC METHODS** **State the Problem** Which carbohydrate does yeast use most efficiently as food for fermentation?

2. **SCIENTIFIC METHODS** **Form a Hypothesis** Form a testable hypothesis about which carbohydrate will promote yeast fermentation the best.

Procedure

1. Put on safety goggles, gloves, and a lab apron.

2. Mix 75 g or 50 mL of a carbohydrate of your choice in 400 mL of water.

3. **CAUTION: Do not touch your face when working with active yeast.** When your carbohydrate is thoroughly mixed, add one package of dry yeast and stir. Pour the yeast solution into a vacuum flask.

4. **CAUTION: Use extreme caution when working with glass.** Insert a thermometer into a one-hole rubber stopper. Place the stopper into the mouth of the bottle. Adjust the thermometer so that it extends into the yeast solution.

5. Attach a piece of rubber tubing to the side arm of your vacuum flask. Place the end of the tubing into a beaker of water so that you can observe bubbles of CO_2 produced during fermentation.

6. Record the temperature of the solution. Continue to record the temperature at regular intervals during the next two days.

7. Clean up your lab materials according to your teacher's instructions. Wash your hands before leaving the lab.

Analyze and Conclude

1. **Summarizing Data** Prepare a line graph of your data to illustrate the temperature of your solution over time.

2. **SCIENTIFIC METHODS** **Analyzing Data** Compare your graph to your classmates' graphs. Which carbohydrate best supported yeast growth?

3. **SCIENTIFIC METHODS** **Analyzing Methods** Design an experiment in which you measure CO_2 production in a different way.

Chapter 22 Summary

Key Ideas	Key Terms

1 Characteristics of Fungi

> Fungi have threadlike bodies, their cell walls are made of chitin, and they absorb nutrients from their environment.

> A typical fungal body is made of filaments that allow the fungus to have a large surface area and to absorb nutrients efficiently.

> In sexual reproduction in fungi, spores are produced by meiosis. In asexual reproduction in fungi, spores are produced by mitosis.

Key Terms

chitin (521)
hypha (522)
mycelium (522)
rhizoid (522)
saprobe (522)

2 Groups of Fungi

> The chytrids are a group of aquatic fungi that provide clues about the evolution of fungi.

> Zygote fungi are named for sexual reproductive structures that produce zygotes inside a tough capsule.

> Sac fungi are characterized by an ascus, a saclike sexual reproductive structure that produces spores.

> Club fungi are characterized by a basidium, a clublike sexual reproductive structure that produces spores.

> Fungi form mutualistic symbiotic associations to form lichens and mycorrhizae.

Key Terms

zygosporangium (525)
ascus (526)
basidium (527)
lichen (528)
mycorrhiza (528)

3 Fungi and Humans

> Fungi are used for food, medicines, research, alternative fuels, and pest control.

> Fungi play important ecological roles by decomposing organic matter and by breaking down and absorbing minerals from rocks and soil.

> Fungi cause disease by absorbing nutrients from host tissues and by producing toxins.

Key Terms

dermatophyte (531)

READING TOOLBOX

1. **Comparisons** Find the paragraphs in your text that discuss chytrids. Write down the sentences that compare protists, chytrids, and other fungi. Then, write down the sentences that contrast protists, chytrids, and other fungi.

2. **Concept Map** Construct a concept map that describes the structure and reproductive methods of zygote, sac, and club fungi. Use the following terms in your concept map: *zygosporangia, hyphae, ascus, spore, basidiocarp,* and *meiosis.*

Using Key Terms

For each pair of terms, explain how the meanings of the terms differ.

3. *hypha* and *mycelium*

4. *ascus* and *basidium*

5. *mycorrhiza* and *lichen*

Use each of the following terms in a separate sentence:

6. *saprobe*

7. *dermatophyte*

Understanding Key Ideas

8. The cell walls of fungi are made out of
   a. asci.
   b. chitin.
   c. rhizoids.
   d. cellulose.

9. What is a hypha?
   a. a small, lightweight reproductive cell
   b. a single filament that is part of a fungus body
   c. a toxin produced by poisonous mushrooms
   d. a group of filaments that make up a fungus body

10. A rapidly growing, asexually reproducing stage of a fungus is called a
    a. mold.
    b. yeast.
    c. parasite.
    d. zygote fungus.

11. Which fungi produce cells that have flagella?
    a. chytrids
    b. sac fungi
    c. club fungi
    d. zygote fungi

12. Zygote fungi usually reproduce
    a. sexually by spores.
    b. asexually by spores.
    c. by budding.
    d. by fragmentation.

13. The reproductive body of a sac fungus is a(n)
    a. zygospore.
    b. ascocarp.
    c. basidiocarp.
    d. zygocarp.

14. In the life cycle shown here, which step results in a diploid cell?

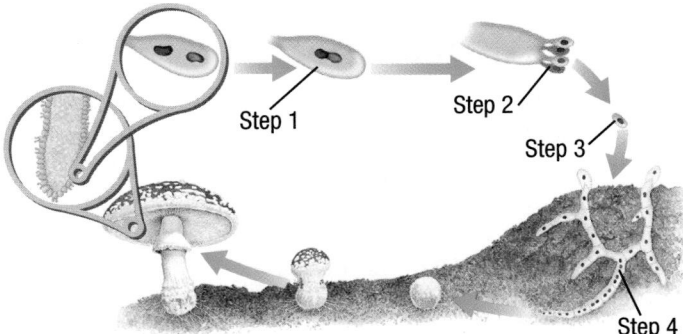

   a. Step 1
   b. Step 2
   c. Step 3
   d. Step 4

15. The association between a fungus and an alga in lichen is an example of
    a. predation.
    b. parasitism.
    c. mutualism.
    d. commensalism.

16. What is the main ecological role of fungi?
    a. parasites
    b. producers
    c. consumers
    d. decomposers

17. Which two fungal infections are caused by the same type of fungus?
    a. smut and thrush
    b. athlete's foot and thrush
    c. athlete's foot and ringworm
    d. yeast infections and liver cancer

Explaining Key Ideas

18. Name three ways that fungi are used in industry.

19. Describe the similarities and differences between protists, chytrid fungi, and other fungi.

20. Explain why people should not eat mushrooms found growing in the wild?

Critical Thinking

21. Recognizing Relationships In what way is the mycelium of a fungus a good adaptation for absorbing nutrients from the environment?

22. Applying Information Yeast cells break down simple sugars into carbon dioxide and ethanol in a process called *fermentation*. Explain how this process is used in bread making.

23. Predicting Outcomes If all fungi suddenly disappeared from Earth, what kinds of changes would you notice immediately? What kinds of changes would you notice over several years?

Methods of Science

24. Recognizing Relationships Imagine that you are a doctor in an emergency room. A patient comes in with a severe cough and difficulty breathing. A chest X ray reveals cloudy lungs, indicating a respiratory infection. How might you determine whether the infection is bacterial, viral, or fungal?

Using Science Graphics

The graph shows the growth rate of three types of yeast. Each type was grown in a separate container on the same variety of grapes. Use the graph to answer the question that follows.

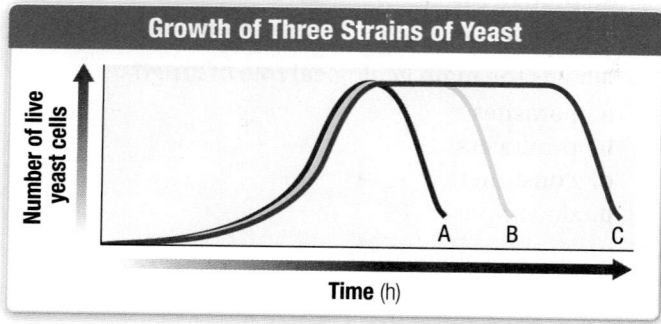

Growth of Three Strains of Yeast

Number of live yeast cells

Time (h)

25. Which of the following statements might explain the data in the graph?
  a. Strains B and C reproduced rapidly and ran out of food quickly.
  b. Strains A and B reproduced more slowly than strain C and therefore survived longer.
  c. Strain A produced more yeast cells than strains B and C did.
  d. Strain C was more tolerant of high alcohol concentrations than strains A and B were and survived longer.

The diagram shows the reproductive structures of a type of fungus. Use the graphic to answer the question that follows.

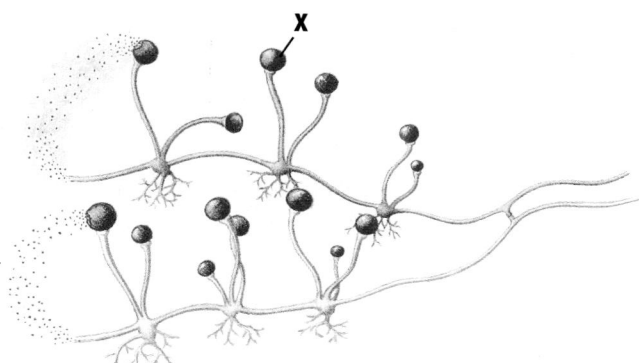

X

26. What is the structure labeled "X" called?
  a. a hypha
  b. a zygote
  c. a sporangium
  d. a zygosporangiospore

Writing for Science

27. Communicating Results In 1882, Pierre Millardet, a professor in France, made an important discovery. A mixture of copper sulfate, calcium oxide (lime), and water was used in France to make wine grapes unappetizing and to keep thieves from stealing them. Millardet noticed that this chemical also killed downy mildew, a fungus that destroys wine grape crops. Imagine that you are Pierre Millardet. Write a week of daily journal entries chronicling your observations and discovery.

Math Skills

28. Using Percentages An estimated 10% of the U.S. population is allergic to inhaled mold spores. In a population of 1,000, how many people will be allergic to mold? This can be calculated by multiplying 1,000 by 0.10, which gives you 100.

If 25% of the population were allergic to mold, how many individuals in a population of 1,000 would be allergic to mold?

If 25% of the population were allergic to mold, how many individuals in a population of 165,000 would be allergic to mold?

TEST TIP When studying for a test on the life cycles of fungi, organize the information into a table. It can be easier to recall information from a table than from a paragraph.

Science Concepts

Choose the letter of the answer choice that best answers the question.

1. The body of a fungus is called a
   - **A** stolon.
   - **B** mycelium.
   - **C** mycorrhiza.
   - **D** zygosporangium.

2. Fungi that absorb nutrients from dead organisms are called
   - **F** parasites.
   - **G** saprobes.
   - **H** mutualists.
   - **J** autotrophs.

3. During sexual reproduction in club fungi, which of the following steps happens first?
   - **A** Nuclei in the basidia fuse.
   - **B** Fused hyphae form a mushroom.
   - **C** Opposite mating types grow together.
   - **D** The zygote undergoes meiosis, which forms spores.

4. What does the word *basidiocarp* mean?
   - **F** zygote
   - **G** hyphae
   - **H** mushroom
   - **J** haploid nuclei

5. Which of the following is an association between a fungus and a plant?
   - **A** a lichen
   - **B** a rhizoid
   - **C** a mycorrhiza
   - **D** a microrhizoid

6. Which fungi generally reproduce only sexually?
   - **F** chytrids
   - **G** zygote fungi
   - **H** sac fungi
   - **J** club fungi

7. Which disease is caused by inhaled spores?
   - **A** thrush
   - **B** aflatoxins
   - **C** histoplasmosis
   - **D** dermatophytes

Writing Skills

8. **Short Response** Describe the general process of sexual reproduction in fungi.

Using Science Graphics

The graph below shows changes in truffle harvest in a certain oak forest over a 40-year period. Use the graph to answer the following question(s).

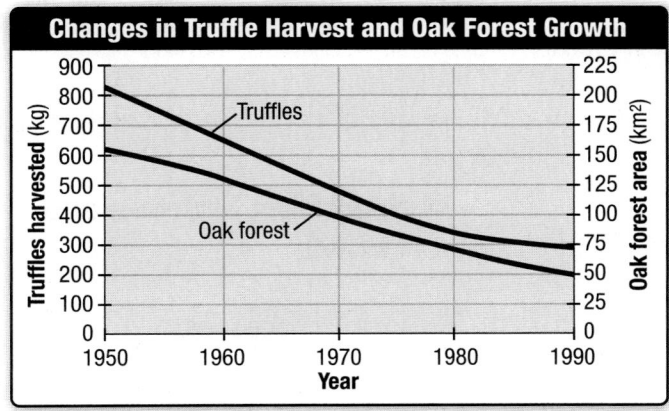

Changes in Truffle Harvest and Oak Forest Growth

9. Which of the following statements is supported by the data in the graph?
   - **F** The oak forest covered 125 km² in 1970.
   - **G** The truffle harvest decreased most rapidly between 1980 and 1990.
   - **H** The oak forest area decreased by 50 percent between 1955 and 1970.
   - **J** The truffle harvest decreased at a constant rate between 1950 and 1975.

The diagram below shows the reproductive structure of a club fungus. Use the diagram to answer the following question(s).

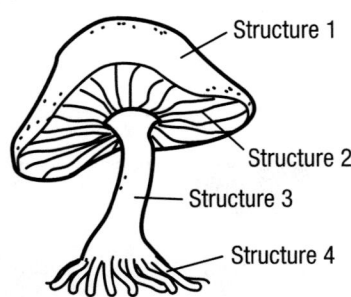

10. Which structure obtains nutrients for the fungus?
    - **A** Structure 1
    - **B** Structure 2
    - **C** Structure 3
    - **D** Structure 4

11. Which structure is the stalk?
    - **F** Structure 1
    - **G** Structure 2
    - **H** Structure 3
    - **J** Structure 4

UNIT 7 Plants

23 Plant Diversity and Life Cycles

24 Seed Plant Structure and Growth

25 Plant Processes

Lemon

Amazon water lily

Water drops on
passion flower
tendrils

DISCOVERIES IN SCIENCE

Plants

9400 BCE

Neolithic people in the Middle East grow figs by cultivating shoots from infertile fig trees. This may be the first food crop intentionally grown in human history. The fig trees grew about 1,000 years before the domestication of cereal crops such as wheat and barley in the Middle East.

1325 BCE

Plant products, including seeds, spices, olive oil, and barley are entombed with King Tutankhamen in Egypt.

Golden mask of King Tut

1493 CE

Christopher Columbus makes his second voyage across the Atlantic. This time, he brings sugar cane to plant in Santo Domingo. He also brings lemon, lime, and orange seeds to plant in Hispaniola.

1793

Eli Whitney invents the cotton gin, a machine that removes the seeds from cotton. Cotton production in the American South soars, along with the demand for slave labor.

Cotton gin

1845

An outbreak of potato blight, a fungal disease, destroys the potato crop in Ireland. About 1,000,000 people die of starvation, and about 1,500,000 more emigrate to North America and Britain.

Potatoes

1930

Dutch elm disease is introduced to the United States from Europe. Over time, the disease devastates American elms throughout the country, killing an estimated 77 million trees by 1970. Many urban areas, once lush with elms, are treeless.

1944

While studying corn genetics, Barbara McClintock discovers that pieces of DNA are mobile and can change position on chromosomes.

Barbara McClintock

1994

While hiking in a canyon in Australia, David Noble discovers a grove of pine trees, *Wollemia nobilis*, thought to have been extinct for 65 million years. The trees were discovered growing just 150 km from Sydney.

Sundew with fly

BIOLOGY CAREER

Evolutionary Biologist
David Haig

David Haig is a professor of organismic and evolutionary biology at Harvard University. His academic and postgraduate training was in the evolution of plant reproduction.

Haig enjoys being a scientist, especially learning about the natural world and solving puzzles. Watching birds in his native Australia as a child inspired Haig to become a scientist.

Haig's current research focuses on the evolution of conflicts within the genome and in parent-offspring relations. Haig's particular interest is in genes in which parental origin matters—genes inherited from the egg behave differently than genes inherited from the sperm.

In addition to science, Haig enjoys studying history.

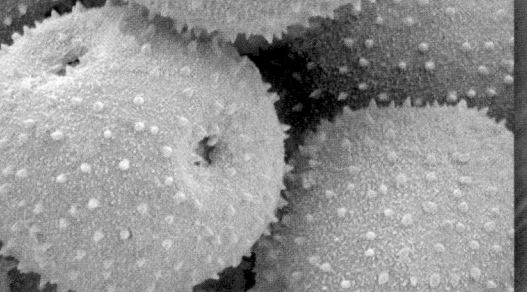

Pollen grains of ladybell flower

Chapter 23

Plant Diversity and Life Cycles

Preview

1 Introduction to Plants
What Is a Plant?
Establishment of Plants on Land
Plant Life Cycles

2 Seedless Plants
Nonvascular Plants
Reproduction in Nonvascular Plants
Seedless Vascular Plants
Reproduction in Seedless Vascular Plants

3 Seed Plants
Kinds of Seed Plants
Reproduction in Seed Plants
Gymnosperms
Life Cycle of a Conifer

4 Flowering Plants
Kinds of Angiosperms
Reproduction in Angiosperms
Pollination
Fruits
Vegetative Reproduction

Why It Matters

Imagine life on Earth without plants. Not only do they supply us with the oxygen we need to breathe, plants also provide us with food, clothing, building materials, and medicines.

A wasp in search of food visits a passion flower. Many flowering plants are pollinated by insects, which are attracted by the smell, color, or shape of the flowers.

Pollen is located on the downturned anthers. The pollen sticks to the wasp as it feeds on nectar at the center of the flower.

The wasp transfers pollen to the stigmas of this flower or to those of the next flower it visits.

InquiryLab

⏱ 15 min

Plant Cells

Have you ever cut open an onion? If so, you may have observed the tightly wrapped, see-through layers of onion skin. These delicate skin membranes are an ideal tissue in which to observe plant cells.

Procedure

1. Use **tweezers** to peel a thin, moist membrane from a freshly cut **onion slice.**

2. Place this membrane on a **slide.** Add several drops of water. Then, gently position a **coverslip** over the tissue specimen.

3. Examine the tissue by using low-power and medium-power objectives. Describe and draw what you observe.

4. Place a drop of **methylene blue solution** along the edge of the coverslip. Position a piece of **paper towel** at the opposite edge and draw the stain across the specimen.

5. Wait several moments and examine the tissue sample again. Describe and draw what you observe.

Analysis

1. **Identify** which features were easiest to observe in the unstained onion tissue.

2. **Describe** how adding the methylene blue solution affected your observations.

541

READING TOOLBOX

These reading tools can help you learn the material in this chapter. For more information on how to use these and other tools, see **Appendix: Reading and Study Skills.**

Using Words

Word Parts You can tell a lot about a word by taking it apart and examining its prefix and suffix.

Your Turn Use the table and information that you read in the chapter to define the following terms in your own words.

1. angiosperm

2. gymnosperm

Word Parts		
Word part	Type	Meaning
angio-	prefix	a vessel or box
gymno-	prefix	naked or bare
-sperm	suffix	seed

Using Language

Classification As you read the chapter, make distinctions between general words that describe categories and specific words that describe individuals within a category. Words that name categories are more general than words that describe individuals.

Your Turn Use information that you read in the chapter to answer the following questions.

1. What are two types of seedless vascular plants?

2. What is the general term identifying the category that includes mosses, liverworts, and hornworts?

Using Science Graphics

Concept Map Concept maps are useful when you are trying to identify how several ideas are related to a main concept. Concept maps may be based on vocabulary terms or on main topics from the text.

Your Turn As you read about angiosperms, look for terms that can be organized in a concept map.

1. Select a main concept. Place this concept at the top or center of a piece of paper.

2. Place other ideas under or around the main concept based on their relationship to the main concept. Draw a circle around each idea.

3. Draw lines between the concepts, and add linking words to the lines.

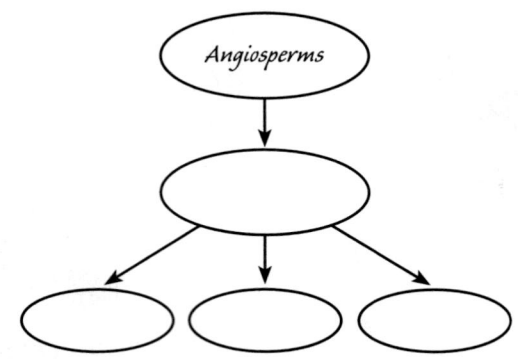

Introduction to Plants

Key Ideas	Key Terms	Why It Matters
❯ What are the key characteristics of plants? ❯ What adaptations helped plants live successfully on land? ❯ Why is a plant's life cycle referred to as "alternation of generations?"	cuticle spore sporophyte gametophyte	Most plants live on land, and they've adapted to a variety of habitats, including deserts, tundra, and tropical rainforests.

Humans depend on plants in many ways. All types of plant parts—roots, stems, leaves, flowers, fruits, and seeds—are eaten as food. Plants provide us with the oxygen that makes life possible. They also provide materials for buildings, paper, furniture, clothing, and medicines. Without plants, many other organisms could not exist.

What Is a Plant?

Plants are the dominant group of organisms on land, based on mass. The kingdom Plantae is a very diverse group. Individual plants range from less than 2 mm (0.08 in.) across to more than 100 m (328 ft) tall. But what is a plant and what do plants need? ❯ **Plants are multicellular eukaryotes whose cells have cell walls. Most plants are *autotrophs*—they produce their own food through photosynthesis.** Recall that photosynthesis is the process by which plants produce organic materials from inorganic materials by using energy from the sun and carbon dioxide. Photosynthesis occurs in *chloroplasts,* as shown in the plant cell in **Figure 1.** To survive, plants need sunlight, water, air, and minerals.

❯ **Reading Check** *What do plants need for photosynthesis? (See the Appendix for answers to Reading Checks.)*

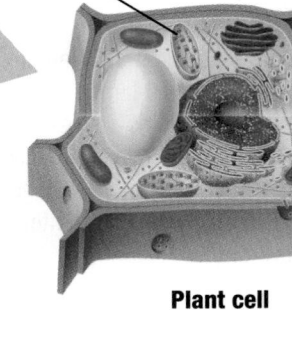

Chloroplast

Plant cell

Figure 1 Plants make their own food by capturing energy from sunlight. ❯ Where in the plant cell does photosynthesis occur?

Figure 2 Plants of genus *Cooksonia,* the oldest known type of vascular plant, lived about 410 million years ago.

ACADEMIC
VOCABULARY

transport to carry from one place to another

Establishment of Plants on Land

Plants probably evolved from multicellular aquatic green algae. On land, minerals, light, and carbon dioxide are available at the soil surface, but water may be in short supply. *Nonvascular plants* grow close to the soil surface. They photosynthesize when water is available but stop when the surface dries. Many nonvascular plants can survive the loss of most of the water from their bodies and can quickly resume photosynthesis when the surface is wet again.

Other plants can photosynthesize when the soil surface is dry because they have roots that obtain water from soil below the surface. These plants are *vascular plants.* Vascular tissue is a specialized tissue that transports water and mineral nutrients from roots to leaves where photosynthesis occurs. Vascular tissue also transports organic molecules produced by photosynthesis from leaves to roots. **❯ In order to thrive on land, plants had to be able to absorb nutrients from their surroundings, to survive dehydration or avoid drying out, and to have a way of dispersal—or way of scattering—that did not require water. Figure 2** shows the earliest known vascular plant, which was of the genus *Cooksonia.* **Figure 3** shows the relationship between plants and algae.

Absorbing Nutrients On land, most vascular plants absorb nutrients from the soil through their roots. Although the first plants lacked roots, fossils show that fungi lived on or within the underground parts of many such early plants. Botanists think that fungi may have helped early land plants get nutrients from Earth's rocky surface. Symbiotic relationships between fungi and plant roots are called *mycorrhizae.*

Preventing Water Loss A watertight covering, which reduces water loss, made it possible for plants to live in dry habitats. This covering, called the **cuticle,** is a waxy layer that covers the nonwoody aboveground parts of most plants. Roots obtain water from the soil and allow vascular plants to replace water lost to the atmosphere.

Figure 3 This phylogenetic diagram represents a hypothesis for the evolutionary relationships between plants and green algae. The earliest plants were nonvascular. For updates on phylogenetic information, visit **go.hrw.com.** Enter the keyword **HX8 Phylo.**

Nonvascular plants

Seedless vascular plants

Hardened vascular tissue

Reproduction by spores

Algal ancestors

Hands-On
QuickLab

Cuticle Modeling

You can use wax paper to model how a plant's cuticle helps to restrict the flow of water out of living tissues.

Procedure

1 Cut out two identical leaf shapes from construction paper. Use tape and two rectangles of wax paper to make a sleeve that is slightly larger than the "leaves."

2 Tape the two leaves side by side to a tabletop so that they extend off the table edge. Place a drop of alcohol in the center of each leaf.

3 Quickly, slip the wax paper sleeve over one of the leaves. Use a third sheet of paper to fan both leaves for several minutes. Observe the alcohol spots.

Analysis

1. Describe what happened to the alcohol spot on each of the two leaf models.

2. Propose a mechanism for the observed changes.

3. **CRITICAL THINKING** **Analyzing methods** Why was alcohol used instead of water?

Dispersal on Land Aquatic algae release cells that undergo dispersal by drifting in water currents or by active swimming. The earliest plants produced single cells called **spores** that could dry out and be dispersed to distant locations by wind. Some plants are still dispersed by spores. Seed plants produce a special kind of spore called *pollen* that is scattered across the land by wind or by animals. Pollen transports sperm cells to eggs. After a sperm fertilizes an egg, the zygote becomes an embryo that is dispersed in a seed.

> **Reading Check** *What is the waxy layer on the aboveground parts of most plants that helps prevent water loss called?*

cuticle a waxy or fatty and watertight layer on the external wall of epidermal cells

spore a reproductive cell or multicellular structure that is resistant to environmental conditions

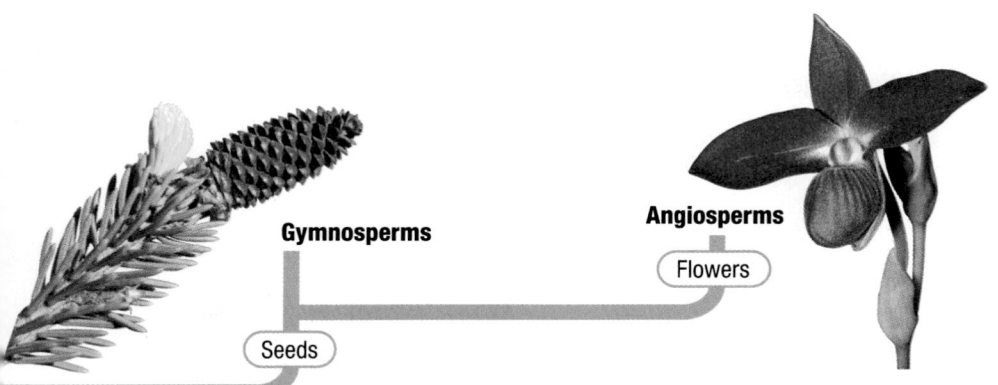

Gymnosperms

Angiosperms

Flowers

Seeds

SCiLINKS
www.scilinks.org
Topic: Plant
     Characteristics
Code: HX81158

Figure 4 In the life cycle of a plant, a diploid sporophyte generation alternates with a haploid gametophyte generation. ❯ **What structure produces gametophytes?**

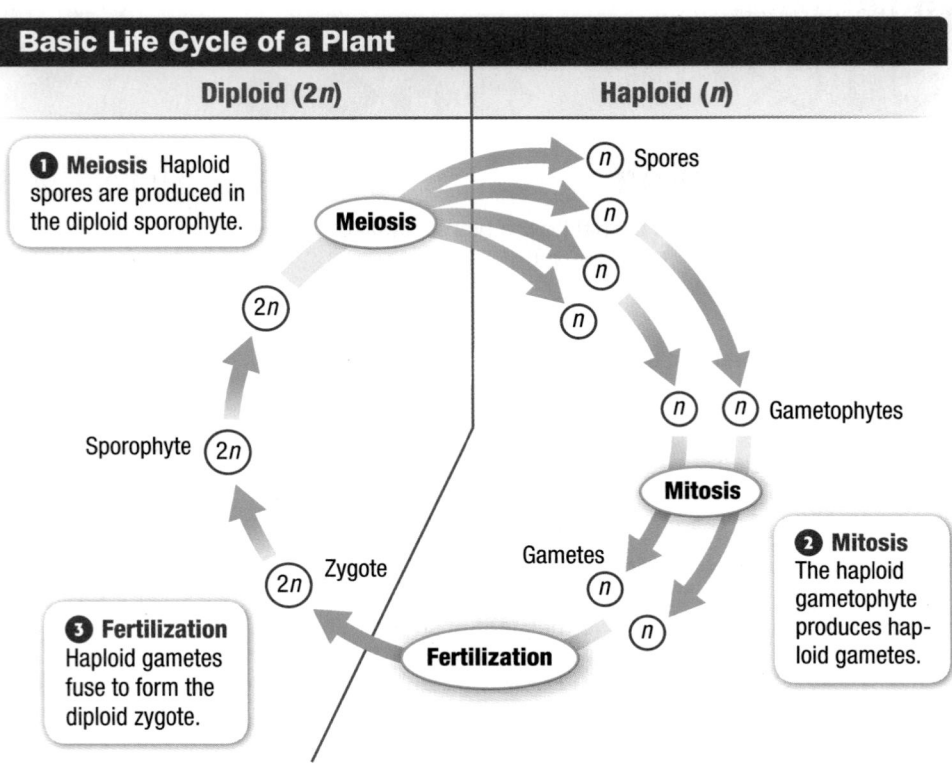

Basic Life Cycle of a Plant

| Diploid (2*n*) | Haploid (*n*) |

❶ **Meiosis** Haploid spores are produced in the diploid sporophyte.

n Spores

Meiosis

2*n*

Sporophyte 2*n*

n *n* Gametophytes

Mitosis

❷ **Mitosis** The haploid gametophyte produces haploid gametes.

2*n* Zygote

Gametes *n*

n

❸ **Fertilization** Haploid gametes fuse to form the diploid zygote.

Fertilization

sporophyte in plants and algae that have alternation of generations, the diploid individual or generation that produces haploid spores

gametophyte in alternation of generations, the phase in which gametes are formed; a haploid individual that produces gametes

Plant Life Cycles

Recall that plants probably evolved from multicellular green algae. In many algae, the zygote is the only diploid cell. It undergoes meiosis following fertilization. As a result of meiosis, the bodies of these algae consist of haploid cells. But in the ancestors of plants, meiosis was delayed. The zygote divided by mitosis and grew into a multicelled **sporophyte** that was diploid. This diploid sporophyte produced haploid spores by meiosis. Spores grew into multicelled **gametophytes** that were haploid and produced gametes by mitosis. ❯ **Plants have life cycles in which haploid gametophytes alternate with diploid sporophytes. A life cycle in which a gametophyte alternates with a sporophyte is called** *alternation of generations.* **Figure 4** shows the basic plant life cycle.

❯ **Reading Check** *Is a plant sporophyte diploid or haploid?*

❯ **KEY IDEAS**

1. **Identify** the key characteristics of plants.
2. **Describe** the adaptations that allowed plants to live on land.
3. **Outline** the life cycle of a plant.

CRITICAL THINKING

4. **Applying Information** Is a plant that is thriving in a dark underground cave likely to be an autotroph? Explain your answer.
5. **Applying Logic** Explain why, during fertilization, the diploid zygote cannot be formed from the fusing of two diploid cells.

ALTERNATIVE ASSESSMENT

6. **Creating a Documentary** Make a video showing pollination by insects such as bees, butterflies, and moths. Write a script that narrates the action and documents the process that you are showing.

Key Ideas	Key Terms	Why It Matters
❯ What are the characteristics of nonvascular plants? ❯ What characterizes reproduction in nonvascular plants? ❯ How do seedless vascular plants differ from nonvascular plants? ❯ How does reproduction in a seedless vascular plant compare to reproduction in a nonvascular plant?	archegonium antheridium sporangium rhizome frond sorus	Peat bogs are composed mainly of decayed sphagnum moss. Well-preserved bodies of humans that lived more than 2,000 years ago have been discovered in peat bogs in Europe.

When you think of a plant, what is the first thing that comes to mind? You may think of grass or a tree. Grasses and trees are examples of seed plants. Some plants do not produce seeds. Mosses and ferns are examples of seedless plants.

Nonvascular Plants

The brilliant green carpet of mosses shown in **Figure 5** is made up of thousands of individual plants. Mosses are most often found near streams, coastlines, and other moist places. Mosses are a type of *nonvascular plant.* ❯ **Nonvascular plants are small plants that reproduce by means of spores. They lack true roots, stems, and leaves, which are complex structures that contain vascular, or conducting, tissues.**

In nonvascular plants, water and nutrients are transported by osmosis and diffusion, which move materials short distances and very slowly. This method of transport greatly limits the size of a nonvascular plant's body. Thus, all nonvascular plants are relatively small.

❯ **Reading Check** *How is water transported in nonvascular plants?*

Figure 5 Mosses grow in tightly packed mats that may contain dozens of plants per square inch. ❯ Why are nonvascular plants usually small?

This carpet of mosses is made up of many individual plants.

Mosses are often found near streams or other moist places.

547

A moss of genus *Polytrichum*
(Phylum Bryophyta)

A spore capsule tops the stalk of the sporophyte.

A liverwort of genus *Marchantia*
(Phylum Hepatophyta)

Female gametophytes produce eggs.

Male gametophytes produce sperm.

A hornwort of genus *Anthoceros*
(Phylum Anthocerophyta)

Hornlike sporophytes grow from flattened gametophytes.

Figure 6 Mosses (left), liverworts (center), and hornworts (right) are all nonvascular plants.

ACADEMIC VOCABULARY

consist to be made up of

archegonium (AHR kuh GOH nee uhm) a female reproductive structure that produces a single egg and in which fertilization and development take place

antheridium (AN thur ID ee uhm) a reproductive structure that produces male sex cells in seedless plants

sporangium (spoh RAN jee uhm) a specialized sac, case, capsule, or other structure that produces spores

Mosses The mosses are the most familiar nonvascular plants. The seemingly leafy green plants that you recognize as mosses are gametophytes. Moss sporophytes, which are not green, grow from the tip of a gametophyte, as **Figure 6** shows. Each sporophyte consists of a bare stalk topped by a spore capsule. Most mosses have a cuticle, stomata, and simple conducting cells. Because these cells carry water only short distances, mosses never get very large.

Liverworts Like the mosses, liverworts grow in mats of many individual plants. Liverworts have no conducting cells, no cuticle, and no stomata. In some species, such as the common liverwort shown in **Figure 6**, the gametophytes are flattened and have lobes. Structures that resemble stems and leaves make up the gametophytes of most liverworts. The sporophytes of liverworts are very small and consist of a short stalk topped by a spore capsule.

Hornworts The hornworts are a small group of nonvascular plants that, like the liverworts, completely lack conducting cells. The sporophyte of a hornwort has both stomata and a cuticle. The gametophyte of a hornwort is green and flattened. Green hornlike sporophytes grow upward from the gametophytes, as shown in **Figure 6.**

Reproduction in Nonvascular Plants

Like all plants, nonvascular plants have a life cycle characterized by an alternation of generations. ❯ **In the life cycle of nonvascular plants, the gametophyte is the dominant generation. Gametophytes must be covered by a film of water in order for fertilization to occur.** Gametophytes produce gametes (eggs and sperm) in two separate structures. The structure that produces eggs is called an **archegonium.** The structure that produces sperm is called an **antheridium.** Sporophytes produce spores in a **sporangium.** The smaller sporophytes grow on the gametophytes and depend on them for nutrients.

Life Cycle of a Moss As you can see in **Figure 7,** a moss sporo-phyte grows from a gametophyte. The sporophyte consists of a bare stalk with a spore capsule, or sporangium, at its tip. Spores form by meiosis inside the spore capsule. Therefore, the spores are haploid. The spore capsule opens when the spores are mature, and the spores are carried away by wind or water. When a moss spore settles to the ground, it germinates and grows into a leafy-looking green gameto-phyte. Archegonia and antheridia form at the tips of the haploid gametophytes. Eggs and sperm form by mitosis inside the archegonia and antheridia. Moss gametophytes grow in tightly packed clumps. When water covers a clump of mosses, sperm can swim to nearby archegonia and fertilize the eggs inside them.

❯ **Reading Check** *Which structure produces male sex cells in nonvascular plants?*

www.scilinks.org
Topic: Nonvascular
Plants
Code: HX81045

Figure 7 In mosses, a sporophyte that consists of a spore capsule on a bare stalk alternates with a leafy-looking green gametophyte. ❯ How are spores dispersed in nonvascular plants?

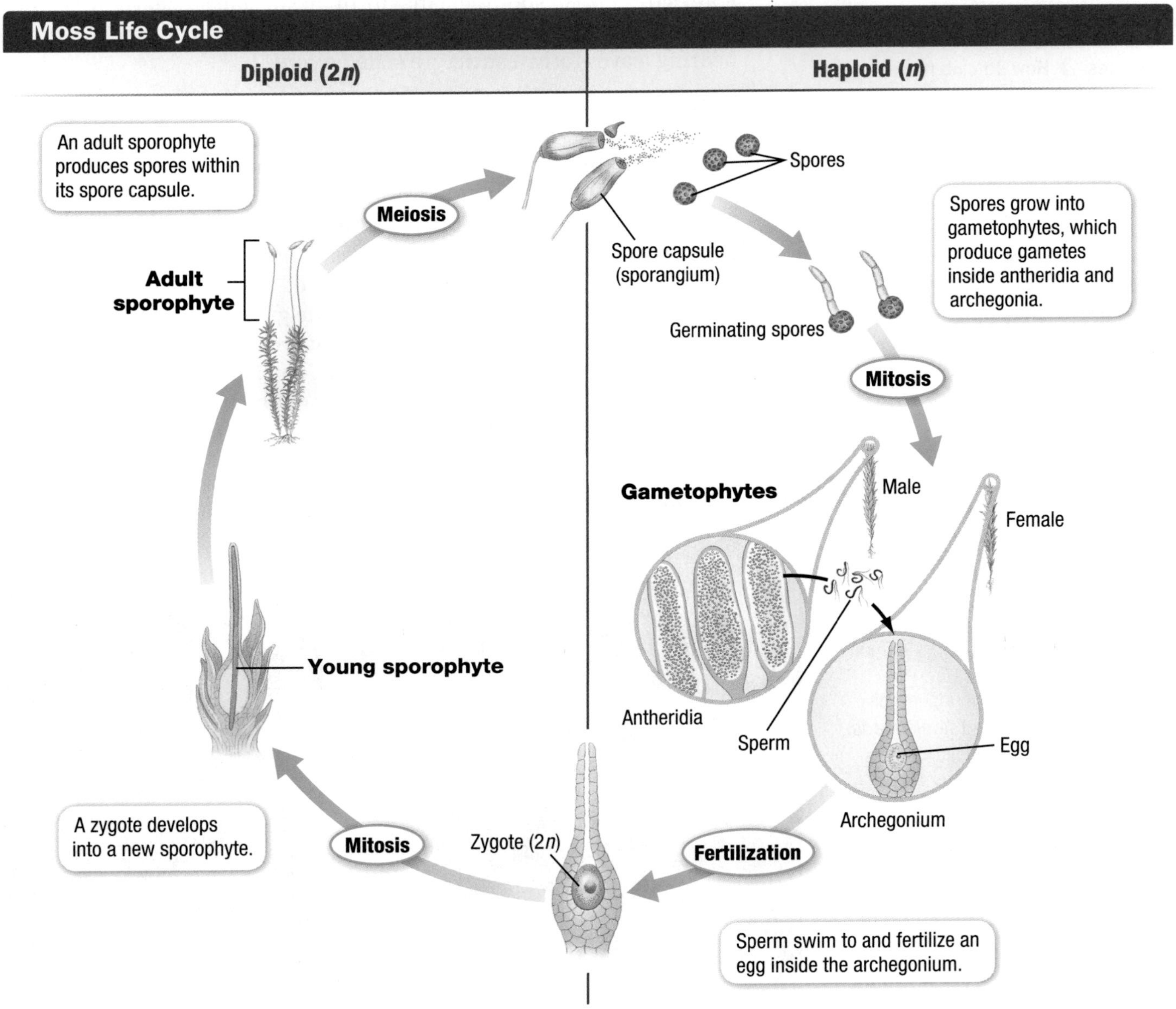

Moss Life Cycle

Diploid (2*n*)	Haploid (*n*)

An adult sporophyte produces spores within its spore capsule.

Meiosis

Adult sporophyte

Spore capsule (sporangium)

Spores

Spores grow into gametophytes, which produce gametes inside antheridia and archegonia.

Germinating spores

Mitosis

Gametophytes

Male

Female

Antheridia

Sperm

Egg

Archegonium

Young sporophyte

A zygote develops into a new sporophyte.

Mitosis

Zygote (2*n*)

Fertilization

Sperm swim to and fertilize an egg inside the archegonium.

Figure 8 Club mosses are sometimes known as *ground pines*. The tips of the aerial stems contain conelike structures. ❯ **How do club mosses differ from true mosses?**

Classification What are two types of seedless vascular plants?

Seedless Vascular Plants

Vascular plants that do not produce seeds are called *seedless vascular plants.* ❯ Sporophytes of seedless vascular plants have vascular tissue, but gametophytes lack vascular tissue. Because of their vascular system, vascular plants grow much larger than nonvascular plants and also develop true roots, stems, and leaves. The much smaller gametophytes of most seedless vascular plants develop on or below the surface of soil. As in nonvascular plants, water is needed for fertilization in seedless vascular plants. When enough water is on or in the soil, the sperm swim to eggs and fertilize them. There are two major groups of seedless vascular plants: club mosses (lycophytes) and ferns and related species (monilophytes).

Club Mosses Unlike true mosses, the club mosses have roots, stems, and leaves. Their leafy green stems branch from an underground **rhizome.** A rhizome is a horizontal, underground stem. Spores develop in sporangia that form on specialized leaves. In some species, such as the one seen in **Figure 8,** clusters of nongreen spore-bearing leaves form a structure called a *cone.*

Ferns and Fern Allies The ferns and fern allies, or relatives, are the most common and familiar seedless vascular plants. Ferns grow throughout the world, but they are most abundant in the tropics. The plants that you recognize as ferns are sporophytes. Most fern sporophytes have a rhizome that is anchored by roots and have leaves called **fronds.** The coiled young leaves of a fern, shown in **Figure 9,** are called *fiddleheads.* Spores are produced in sporangia that grow in clumps on the lower side of fronds. The gametophytes of ferns are flattened, heart-shaped green plants that are usually less than 1 cm (0.5 in.) across. Horsetails are related to ferns. The vertical stems of horsetails, which grow from a rhizome, are hollow and have joints. Whorls of scalelike leaves grow at the joints. Spores form in cones located at the tips of stems.

❯ **Reading Check** *Where do sporangia form on ferns?*

Figure 9 The coiled young leaves of a fern (left) are called *fiddleheads.* Horsetails (right) have hollow stems topped by cones.

Young fern fronds are called *fiddleheads.*

The hollow, jointed stems of horsetails are topped by cones.

Reproduction in Seedless Vascular Plants

> Like nonvascular plants, seedless vascular plants can reproduce sexually only when a film of water covers the gametophyte. Unlike nonvascular plants, seedless vascular plants have sporophytes that are much larger than their gametophytes. Some ferns have sporophytes that are as large as trees. On the other hand, the gametophytes of ferns are less than 1 cm (0.5 in.) across. The archegonia and antheridia develop on the lower surfaces of the gametophytes. In most species of seedless vascular plants, both eggs and sperm are produced by the same individual. In some species, however, eggs and sperm are produced by separate gametophytes. The life cycle of a fern is summarized in **Figure 10.**

> **Reading Check** *How large is a fern gametophyte?*

rhizome a horizontal, underground stem that provides a mechanism for asexual reproduction

frond the leaf of a fern or palm

Figure 10 In ferns, a large sporophyte with leaves called *fronds* alternates with a small, green, heart-shaped gametophyte. > **Which generation is dominant in the life cycle of a fern?**

Fern Life Cycle

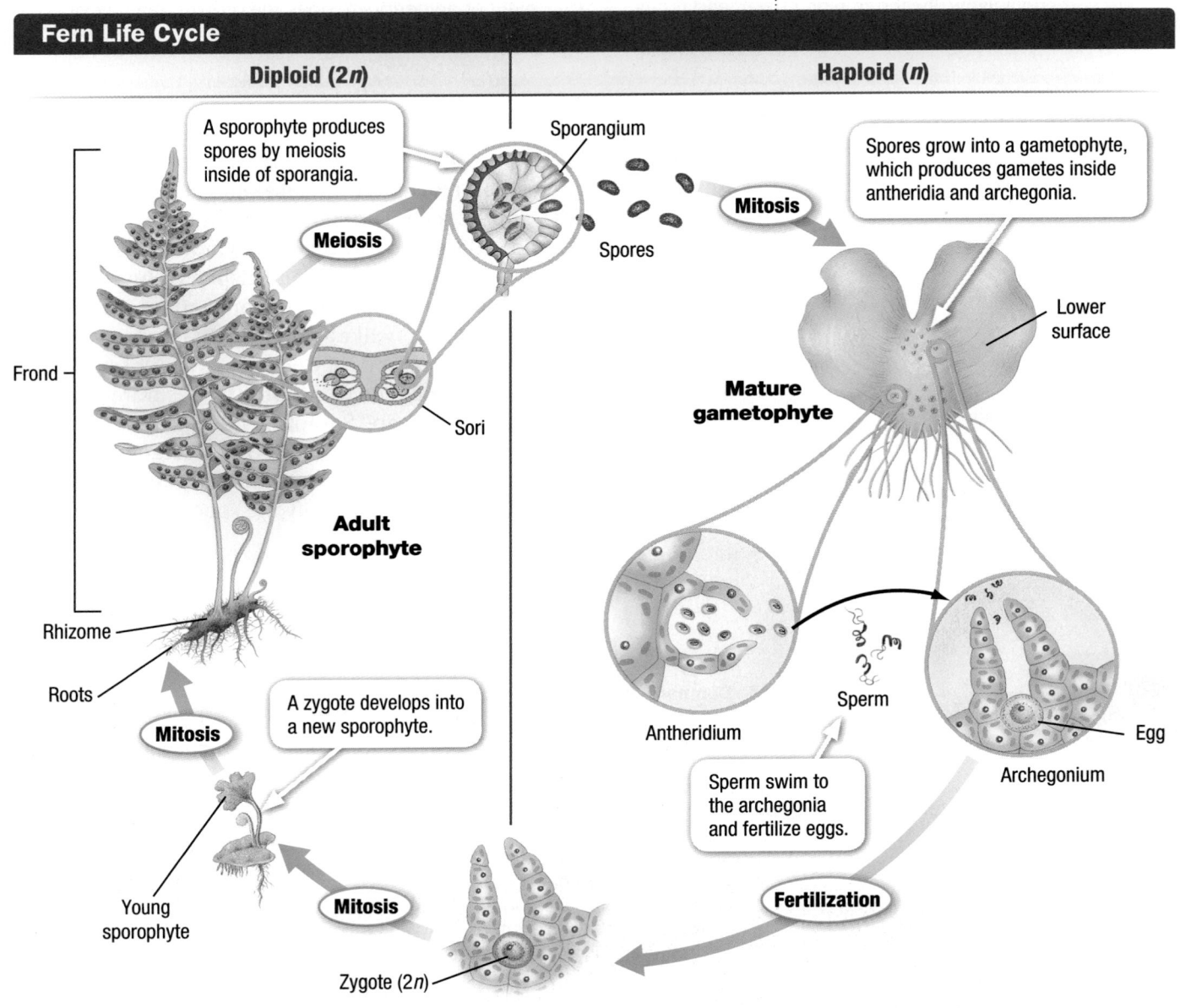

Diploid (2n) | **Haploid (n)**

A sporophyte produces spores by meiosis inside of sporangia.

Sporangium

Spores grow into a gametophyte, which produces gametes inside antheridia and archegonia.

Meiosis

Mitosis

Spores

Frond

Sori

Lower surface

Mature gametophyte

Adult sporophyte

Rhizome

Roots

A zygote develops into a new sporophyte.

Mitosis

Antheridium

Sperm

Egg

Archegonium

Sperm swim to the archegonia and fertilize eggs.

Young sporophyte

Mitosis

Fertilization

Zygote (2n)

Hands-On
QuickLab

🕐 15 min

Fern Gametophytes

You can observe the archegonia and antheridia of a fern gametophyte with a microscope.

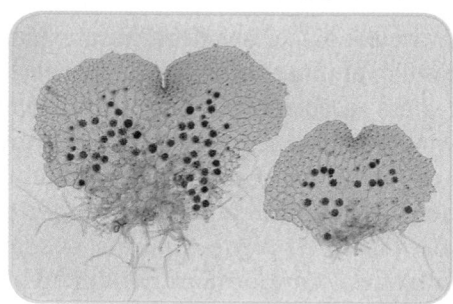

Procedure

1 Examine a slide of a fern gametophyte under low power of a microscope. Move the slide until you can see a cluster of archegonia. Now, switch to high power, and focus on one archegonium. Draw and label what you see.

2 Switch back to low power, and move the slide until you can see several egg-shaped structures. These are antheridia. Now, switch to high power, and focus on one antheridium. Draw and label what you see.

Analysis

1. Describe the appearance of an archegonium and an antheridium.

2. Drawing Conclusions In which structure, an archegonium or antheridium, does the growth of a new sporophyte begin? Explain.

---

sorus a cluster of sporangia

Spores Recall that a spore is a haploid reproductive cell. A spore is produced by meiosis and is capable of developing into an adult without fusing with another cell. The spores of seedless vascular plants have thickened walls that allow the spores to withstand drying and adverse conditions. The spores are easily dispersed by wind. Sporophytes produce spores in sporangia. In horsetails and club mosses, sporangia develop in conelike structures. In ferns, clusters of sporangia form on the lower surfaces of fronds. A cluster of sporangia on a fern frond is called a **sorus.** The word *sorus* comes from the Greek word *soros*, meaning "a heap." Sori often look like brownish dots on the lower surface of a fern frond, as shown in **Figure 10** on the previous page. Some fern fronds have distinctive patterns of sori. These patterns may be used to help identify the species of the fern.

❯ Reading Check *What is a cluster of sporangia on a fern frond called?*

Section 2 Review

❯ KEY IDEAS

1. Identify the characteristics of nonvascular plants.

2. Describe reproduction in nonvascular plants.

3. Describe how seedless vascular plants differ from nonvascular plants.

4. Compare reproduction in seedless vascular plants to reproduction in nonvascular plants.

CRITICAL THINKING

5. Making Inferences Ferns grow throughout the world, but they are most abundant in the tropics. Why might a fern have a better chance of reproducing in a tropical environment than in another environment? Explain your answer.

ALTERNATIVE ASSESSMENT

6. Finding and Communicating Information Mosses have a variety of commercial uses. Use the Internet or library resources to investigate some of these uses. Create a leaflet about the past and present uses of mosses that you can present to your class or display on a wall in your classroom.

Key Ideas	Key Terms	Why It Matters
❯ What are the two groups into which seed plants are classified? ❯ What characterizes reproduction in seed plants? ❯ What are the four major groups of living gymnosperms? ❯ What characterizes reproduction in a conifer?	gymnosperm angiosperm ovule seed pollen grain pollination	Conifers are extremely important economically. They provide softwood for construction and for the production of paper.

Most plants living today are seed plants—vascular plants that produce seeds. Seeds were an important terrestrial adaptation that enhanced survival and dispersal of offspring.

Kinds of Seed Plants

The first seed plants appeared about 380 million years ago. ❯ **Seed plants are traditionally classified into two groups—gymnosperms and angiosperms.** **Gymnosperms** are seed plants whose seeds do not develop within a fruit. The word *gymnosperm* comes from the Greek words *gymnos*, meaning "naked," and *sperma*, meaning "seed." The seeds of most gymnosperms develop within a cone, as shown in **Figure 11. Angiosperms** are seed plants whose seeds develop enclosed within a fruit, a specialized plant structure. The word *angiosperm* comes from the Greek words *angeion*, meaning "case," and *sperma*, meaning "seed." Fruits develop from part of a flower, another specialized plant structure. Therefore, angiosperms are flowering plants. Most species of seed plants are flowering plants.

❯ **Reading Check** *What is the difference between gymnosperms and angiosperms in terms of seed production?*

gymnosperm (JIM noh spuhrm) a vascular seed plant whose seeds are not enclosed by a fruit

angiosperm (AN jee oh spuhrm) a flowering plant that produces seeds within a fruit

Figure 11 Gymnosperms and angiosperms are both types of seed plants. Unlike the seeds of angiosperms, the seeds of gymnosperms do not develop within a fruit.

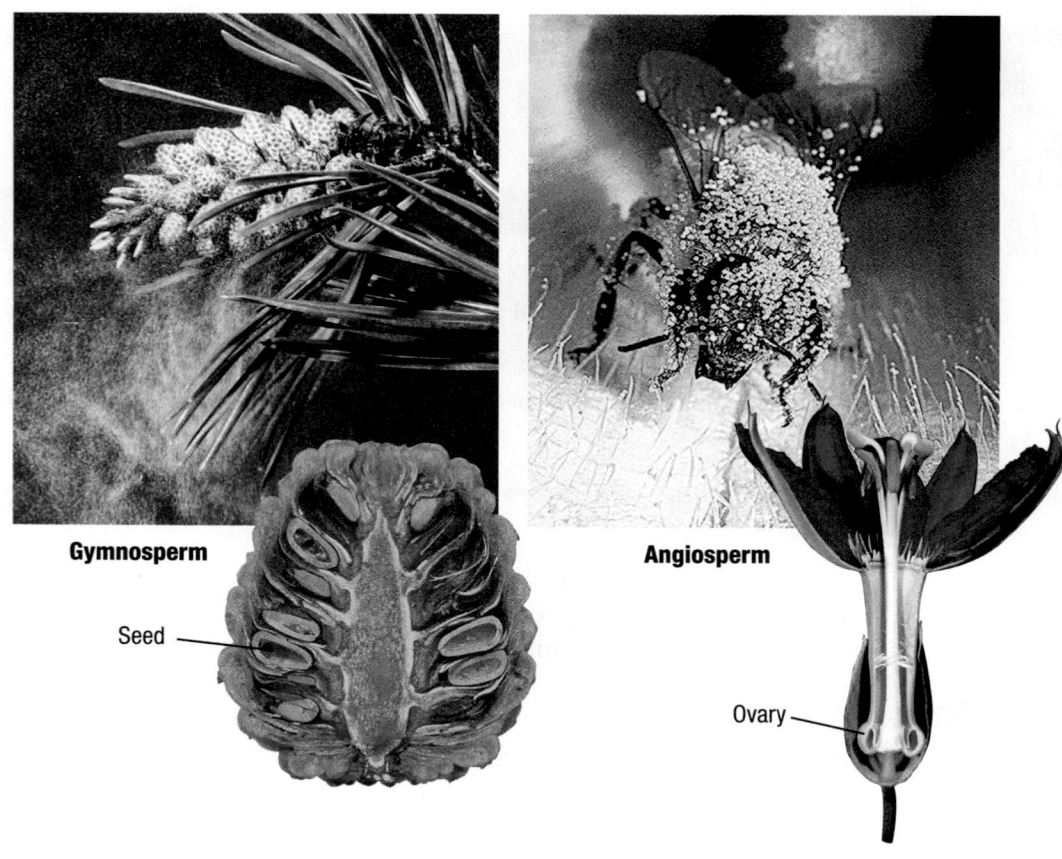

Figure 12 The pollen of gymnosperms is usually dispersed by wind (left). After fertilization, seeds develop inside cones. The pollen of many angiosperms is dispersed by insects (right). Seeds develop from ovules inside the ovary.

Gymnosperm

Angiosperm

Seed

Ovary

READING TOOLBOX

Concept Map Create a concept map based on what you learned about reproduction in seed plants.

Reproduction in Seed Plants

Reproduction in seed plants is quite different from reproduction in seedless plants. ❯ **Unlike seedless plants, seed plants do not require water to reproduce sexually. Reproduction in seed plants is also characterized by a greatly reduced gametophyte and a dominant sporophyte.** In fact, you often need a microscope to see the gametophytes of seed plants.

Sporophytes produce two kinds of spores that develop into two kinds of gametophytes—female gametophytes, which produce eggs, and male gametophytes, which produce sperm. A female gametophyte of a seed plant develops inside an **ovule,** which is a multicellular structure that is part of the sporophyte. Following fertilization, the ovule and its contents develop into a **seed.** The male gametophyte of seed plants develops inside a **pollen grain.**

Pollination and Fertilization The transfer of pollen grains from the male reproductive structures of a plant to the female reproductive structures of a plant is called **pollination.** Wind or animals transport pollen grains to the structures that contain ovules, as shown in **Figure 12.**

When a pollen grain reaches a compatible female reproductive structure, a tube emerges from the pollen grain. This tube, called a *pollen tube,* grows to the female gametophyte within an ovule and enables a sperm to pass directly to an egg. The fusion of an egg and sperm is called *fertilization.*

❯ **Reading Check** *Where do gametophytes develop in seed plants?*

Seed Formation After fertilization, the ovule is called a *seed* and contains an *embryo*. A seed is a complex structure. The outer cell layers of an ovule harden to form the seed coat as a seed matures. The tough seed coat protects the embryo in a seed from mechanical injury and from a harsh environment. The seed coat is formed from tissues of the mother sporophyte but contains an embryo which is an offspring sporophyte. Seeds also contain tissue that provides nutrients to plant embryos. In gymnosperms, this nutritious tissue develops from the female gametophyte. The seeds of some angiosperms contain a nutritious tissue called *endosperm*.

Seed Dispersal Seeds are dispersed, or scattered, from the parent plant to locations where the embryos in the seeds develop into new sporophytes. Dispersal may prevent competition for water, nutrients, light, and living space between parents and offspring. Many seeds have structures that help wind, water, or animals carry them away from their parent plant, as shown in **Figure 13.**

Dispersal by Wind Many conifer seeds have winglike structures that act like propellers as seeds fall to the ground. The fruits of maples also have wings. Dandelion and milkweed seeds are dispersed with the help of parachute-like structures that allow the seeds to drift in the wind and travel far from the parent plant.

Dispersal by Animals Fruits are important for seed dispersal by animals. Some fruits have hooks that cling to an animal's fur. Other fruits provide food for animals. Seeds are dispersed when they pass undigested through the animal's body.

> **ovule** (AHV YOOL) a structure of a seed plant that contains a female gametophyte and that develops into a seed after fertilization
>
> **seed** a plant embryo that is enclosed in a protective coat
>
> **pollen grain** the structure that contains the male gametophyte of seed plants
>
> **pollination** the transfer of pollen from the male reproductive structures (anthers) to the tip of a female reproductive structure (pistil) of a flower in angiosperms or to the ovule in gymnosperms

Figure 13 Some seeds, such as milkweed seeds and maple seeds, are dispersed by the wind. Other seeds are dispersed by animals. ❯ **How does seed dispersal benefit plants?**

Wind

Animal

Animal

Wind

Gymnosperms

Gymnosperms are among the most successful groups of plants. ❯ There are four major groups of gymnosperms—conifers, cycads, ginkgoes, and gnetophytes. Examples of each group appear in **Figure 14.**

Conifers The conifers are the most familiar gymnosperms. Conifers have leaves that are needle-like or that are reduced to tiny scales. Some of the tallest living plants, the redwoods of coastal California and Oregon, are conifers. The oldest trees in the world are thought to be bristlecone pines. Some bristlecone pines are about 5,000 years old. Large forests of conifers grow in cool, dry regions of the world. The pollen grains of most conifers are dispersed by wind.

Cycads The cycads have short stems and palmlike leaves. Cones that produce pollen and those that produce seeds develop on different plants. Cycads are widespread throughout the tropics. The pollen grains of most cycads are dispersed by insects.

Ginkgoes The only living species of ginkgo, or maidenhair tree, has fan-shaped leaves. The male and female gametophytes of ginkgoes develop on separate trees. Ginkgo seeds do not develop within a cone. Pollen grains are dispersed by wind.

Gnetophytes The gnetophytes are a diverse group of trees, shrubs, and vines that produce pollen and seeds in cones. One unusual gnetophyte is *Welwitschia,* a desert plant of southwestern Africa. Welwitschia has a short, wide stem and twisting leaves.

❯ **Reading Check** *Which gymnosperm has seeds that do not develop within a cone?*

Figure 14 The four living phyla of gymnosperms are made up of conifers, cycads, ginkgoes, and gnetophytes. ❯ **How is the pollen of most gymnosperms dispersed?**

Conifer

Cycad

Ginkgo

Gnetophyte

Life Cycle of a Conifer

Most gymnosperms are conifers, a group that includes pines.
❯ Reproduction in conifers is characterized by a dominant sporophyte, wind pollination, and the development of seeds in cones. You can trace the stages in the life cycle of a pine in **Figure 15.**

In pines, as in all plants, a diploid zygote results from the fertilization of an egg by a sperm. The zygote develops into an embryo, which then becomes dormant. The embryo and surrounding tissues form a seed. When their seeds are mature, seed cones open, and the seeds fall out. A seed of most pines has a wing that causes it to spin like the blade of a helicopter. Thus, pine seeds often travel some distance from their parent tree. When conditions are favorable, the scattered embryos grow into new sporophytes.

❯ **Reading Check** *What characteristic of pine seeds aids in dispersal of the seeds?*

ACADEMIC VOCABULARY

cycle a repeating series of changes

Figure 15 In conifers, a large sporophyte that produces cones alternates with tiny gametophytes that form on the scales of cones. ❯ Where is pollen produced in a conifer?

Conifer Life Cycle

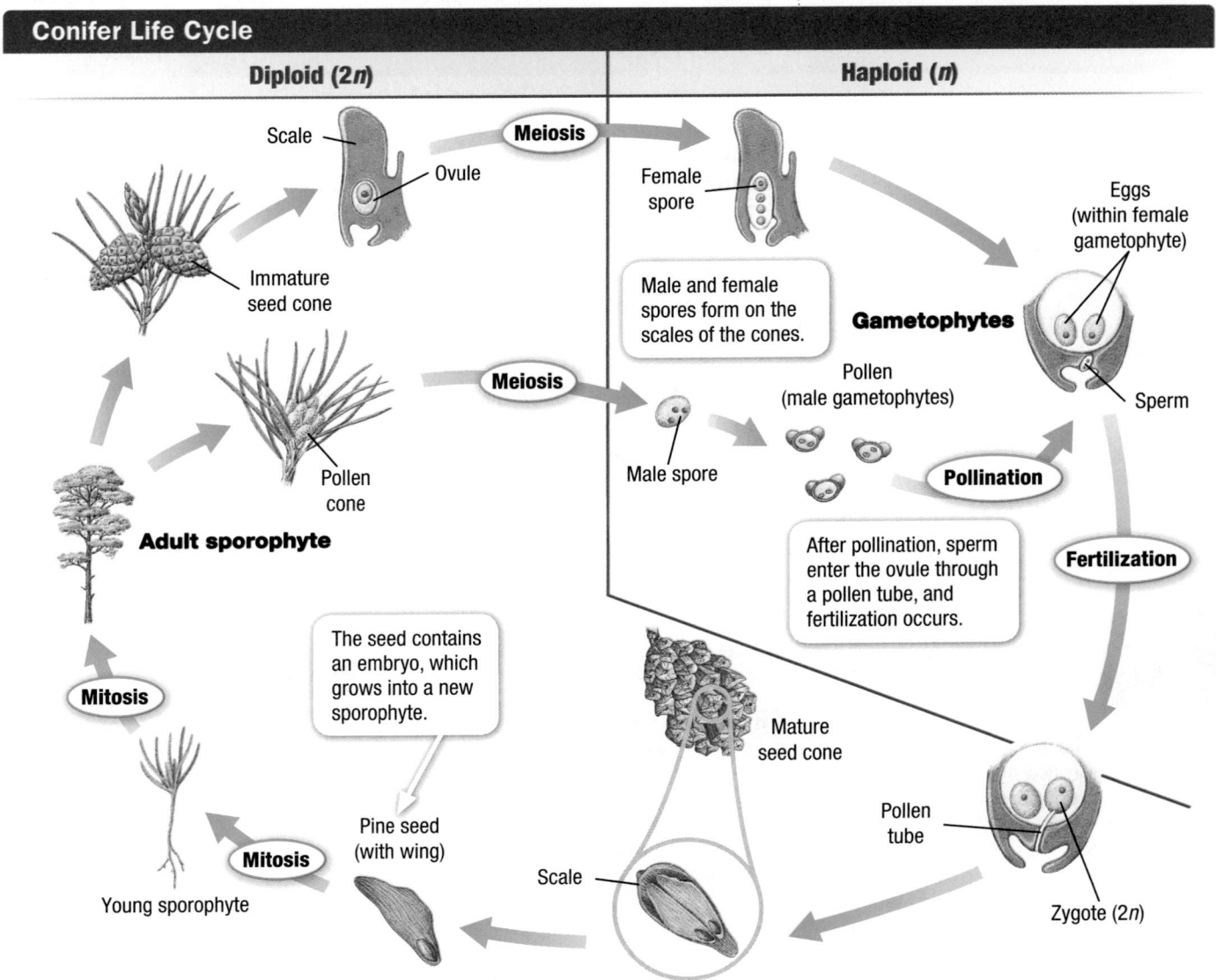

Diploid (2n) | **Haploid (n)**

Scale
Ovule
Meiosis
Female spore
Eggs (within female gametophyte)

Immature seed cone
Male and female spores form on the scales of the cones.
Gametophytes
Pollen (male gametophytes)
Sperm

Meiosis
Pollen cone
Male spore
Pollination

Adult sporophyte
After pollination, sperm enter the ovule through a pollen tube, and fertilization occurs.
Fertilization

The seed contains an embryo, which grows into a new sporophyte.
Mitosis
Mature seed cone
Pollen tube

Pine seed (with wing)
Mitosis
Scale
Zygote (2n)
Young sporophyte

Hands-On QuickLab

Pine Gametophytes

In pines, male gametophytes develop inside male cones, or pollen cones. Female gametophytes develop inside female cones, or seed cones. You can observe the gametophytes of a pine with a microscope.

Immature female pine cone

15 min

Procedure

1 Examine **prepared slides of male and female pine cones** first with a **hand lens** and then under the low power of a **microscope**.

2 Make a sketch of each type of pine cone, and label the structures that you recognize.

3 Examine a **prepared slide of a pine ovule** under the low power of a compound microscope. Compare what you see with the photo above.

4 Draw a pine ovule, and label the following structures: scale, ovule, egg, pollen tube (if visible).

Analysis

1. Compare the structure and contents of male pine cones to the structure and contents of female cones.

2. **CRITICAL THINKING** **Applying Information** It takes 15 months for a pine pollen tube to grow through the wall of a pine ovule. How would you describe the rate of pollen-tube growth in pines?

Cones The gametophytes of most gymnosperms develop in cones, which consist of whorls (circles) of modified leaves called *scales*. Gymnosperms produce two types of cones. Male cones, or pollen cones, produce pollen grains within sacs that develop on the surface of their scales. Female cones, or seed cones, produce ovules on the surface of their scales. Many gymnosperms produce both male and female cones on the same plant. In some gymnosperms, male and female cones form on separate plants. At the time of pollination, the scales of a female cone are open, exposing the ovules to pollen grains carried by the wind or by insects. Seed cones close up after pollination and remain closed until the seeds within them are mature.

> **Reading Check** *Are male and female cones always produced on separate plants?*

Section 3 Review

› KEY IDEAS

1. Name the two groups into which seeds plants are traditionally classified.

2. Describe how sexual reproduction in seed plants differs from sexual reproduction in seedless plants.

3. List the four major groups of living gymnosperms.

4. List three characteristics of a conifer's life cycle.

CRITICAL THINKING

5. Applying Logic A classmate states that there is an apple tree in the park that produces apples but never has any flowers. Is the classmate's statement logical? Explain your answer.

ALTERNATIVE ASSESSMENT

6. Mapping Skills Coniferous forests contain some of the tallest trees on Earth. Use the Internet or library resources to research the location and size of coniferous forests. Make a map of the globe showing where these forests are located.

Key Ideas	Key Terms	Why It Matters
❯ What are the names of the two subgroups of angiosperms? ❯ What is a flower, and how does it function in reproduction? ❯ How does a flower's structure relate to pollination? ❯ What is the primary function of a fruit? ❯ How do plants reproduce vegetatively?	monocot cotyledon dicot stamen anther pistil fruit	Flowering plants are the most important group of plants in agriculture. Grains such as corn, wheat, and rice are important food sources for humans and livestock.

The angiosperms, or flowering plants, are by far the most successful group of plants, with about a quarter of a million species alive today. In contrast, there are fewer than one thousand known species of gymnosperms.

Kinds of Angiosperms

Angiosperms range in size from tiny herbs to giant trees. ❯ **Botanists traditionally divide the angiosperms into two subgroups—monocots and dicots. Monocots** are flowering plants whose seeds have one seed leaf, or **cotyledon.** Most monocots have long, narrow leaves with parallel veins and produce flowers whose parts are in multiples of three. **Dicots** are flowering plants whose seeds have two seed leaves. Most dicots have leaves with branching veins and produce flowers whose parts are in multiples of four or five, as **Figure 16** shows.

❯ **Reading Check** *What are three characteristics of monocots?*

Comparing Monocots and Dicots

Plant type	Leaves	Flower parts	Examples
Monocots 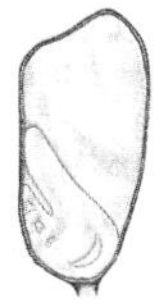	parallel venation 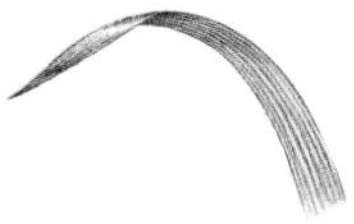	usually occur in threes 	lilies, irises, palms, orchids, coconut, onions, bananas, pineapples, tulips, bamboo, and grasses (including wheat, corn, rice, and oats)
Dicots 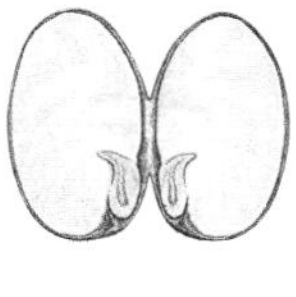	net venation 	usually occur in fours or fives 	beans, lettuce, oaks, maples, roses, carnations, elms, cactuses, and most broad-leaved forest trees

monocot an angiosperm that produces seeds that have only one cotyledon

cotyledon (KAHT uh LEED'n) the embryonic leaf of a seed

dicot an angiosperm that produces seeds that have two cotyledons

Figure 16 Angiosperms are divided into two subgroups—monocots and dicots. ❯ **What type of angiosperm has leaves with net venation?**

QuickLab

15 min

The Arrangement of Parts of a Flower

By dissecting flowers, you can see how the parts of flowers are arranged.

Procedure

1 Put on gloves. Examine a monocot flower and a dicot flower. Locate the sepals, petals, stamens, and pistil of each flower.

2 Separate the parts of each flower, and tape them to a piece of paper. Label each set of parts.

3 Count the number of petals, sepals, and stamens in each flower. Record this information below each flower.

Analysis

1. **Compare** the sepals and petals of the monocot flower to the sepals and petals of the dicot flower.

2. **CRITICAL THINKING** **Forming a Hypothesis** For each flower, suggest a function for the petals based on their appearance.

3. **CRITICAL THINKING** **Justifying Conclusions** Explain why each flower is from either a monocot or a dicot.

Reproduction in Angiosperms

❯ **A *flower* is a specialized reproductive structure of angiosperms. The male and female gametophytes of angiosperms develop within flowers, which promote pollination and fertilization more efficiently than do cones.** The female reproductive part of a flower provides a pathway that enables sperm to reach and fertilize eggs but does not require the sperm to swim through water.

Structure of Flowers The basic structure of a flower is shown in **Figure 17.** Flower parts are arranged in four concentric whorls, or circular swirls. The outermost whorl consists of *sepals,* which protect a flower from damage while it is a bud. The second whorl consists of *petals,* which attract pollinators. The third whorl consists of **stamens,** which produce pollen. Each stamen is made of a thread-like filament that is topped by a pollen-producing sac called an **anther.** The fourth and innermost whorl of a flower consists of one or more **pistils,** which produce ovules. Ovules develop in a pistil's swollen lower portion, which is called the *ovary.* Recall that after fertilization, ovules develop into seeds. Usually, a stalk, called the *style,* rises from the ovary. Pollen lands on and sticks to the stigma—the swollen, sticky tip of the style.

Kinds of Flowers Flowers may or may not have all four of the basic flower parts. A flower that has all four parts is a complete flower. A flower that lacks any one of the four types of parts is an incomplete flower.

❯ **Reading Check** *What is the function of a stamen?*

Figure 17 The four basic parts of a flower—sepals, petals, stamens, and pistils—are arranged in concentric whorls. ❯ **What is the function of sepals?**

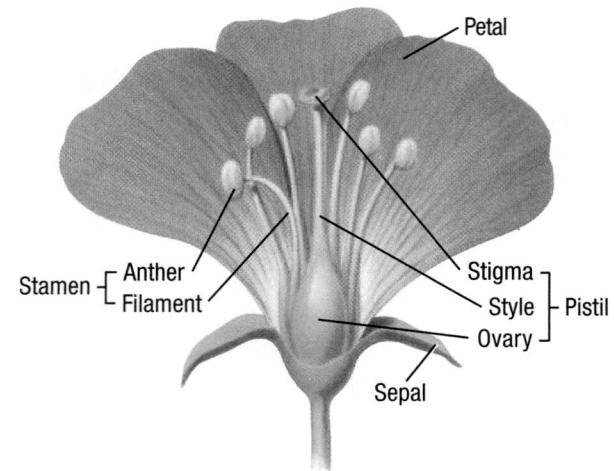

Petal

Stamen { Anther / Filament

Stigma ⎤
Style ⎬ Pistil
Ovary ⎦

Sepal

Life Cycle of an Angiosperm You can trace the life cycle of an angiosperm in **Figure 18.** Adult sporophytes produce haploid spores by meiosis. These spores grow into gametophytes. Female gametophytes grow inside ovules, which develop within the ovary of a pistil. Male gametophytes, or pollen grains, are produced in the anther of a stamen. Pollination occurs when a pollen grain is carried from an anther to a stigma. The pollen grain forms a pollen tube that grows down the style to the ovules in the ovary of a flower. The pollen tube releases two sperm cells into the female gametophyte within an ovule. One sperm fuses with the egg, forming the zygote. The zygote develops into an embryo that will grow into a new sporophyte. The other sperm fuses with two other haploid (n) nuclei to form a triploid ($3n$) cell that develops into endosperm. This is a process called *double fertilization.* The endosperm may form a nutrient store for growth of the embryo.

stamen (STAY muhn) the male reproductive structure of a flower that produces pollen and consists of an anther at the tip of a filament

anther the tip of a stamen, which contains the pollen sacs where pollen grains form

pistil the female reproductive part of a flower that produces seeds and consists of an ovary, style, and stigma

❯ **Reading Check** *What is the function of a pollen tube?*

Figure 18 In angiosperms, a large sporophyte alternates with a tiny gametophyte.

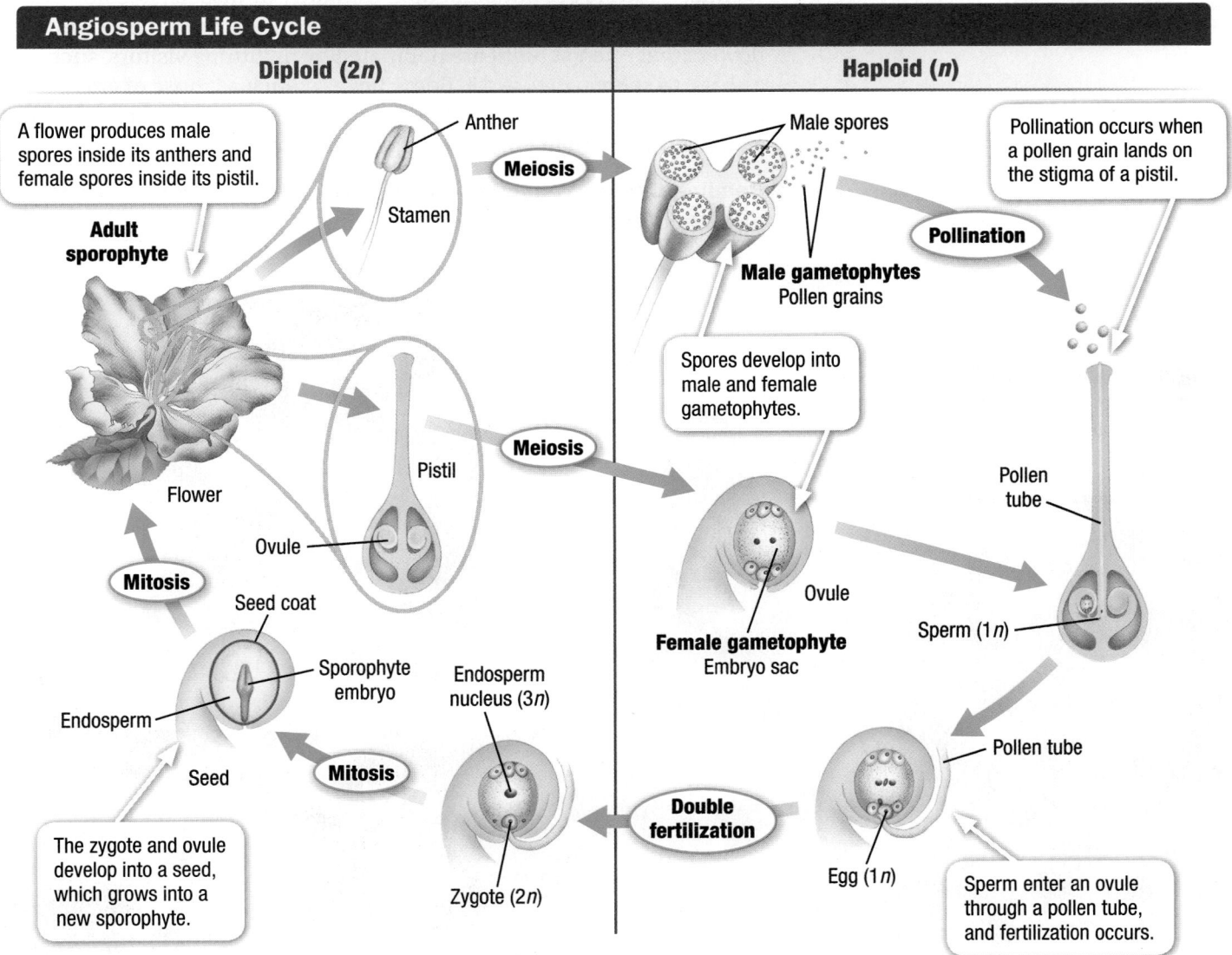

Angiosperm Life Cycle

Diploid (2*n*)	Haploid (*n*)

A flower produces male spores inside its anthers and female spores inside its pistil.

Anther

Male spores

Pollination occurs when a pollen grain lands on the stigma of a pistil.

Meiosis

Adult sporophyte

Stamen

Male gametophytes Pollen grains

Pollination

Spores develop into male and female gametophytes.

Meiosis

Pistil

Flower

Pollen tube

Ovule

Mitosis

Ovule

Female gametophyte Embryo sac

Sperm (1*n*)

Seed coat

Sporophyte embryo

Endosperm nucleus (3*n*)

Pollen tube

Endosperm

Seed

Mitosis

Double fertilization

The zygote and ovule develop into a seed, which grows into a new sporophyte.

Zygote (2*n*)

Egg (1*n*)

Sperm enter an ovule through a pollen tube, and fertilization occurs.

SCILINKS.
www.scilinks.org
Topic: Pollination
Code: HX81177

Pollination

Some plants have pollen that can fertilize the plant's own ovules. These plants can breed by *self-fertilization.* Often, a plant's pollen is unable to fertilize the plant's own ovules. These plants breed by *cross-fertilization.* **› The flowers of many angiosperms are adapted for pollination by wind or by animals.**

Flowers may have brightly colored petals, sugary nectar, strong odors, and shapes that attract animal pollinators. Flowers are a source of food for pollinators such as insects, birds, and bats. For example, bees eat nectar and collect pollen, which is a rich source of protein that they feed to their larvae. As a bee visits a flower, picks up pollen, and carries that pollen to other flowers, the bee gets coated with pollen. Bees locate flowers by scent first and then by color and shape. Bee-pollinated flowers are usually blue or yellow and often have markings that show the location of nectar. Moths feed at night and tend to visit heavily scented white flowers, which are easy to find in dim light. Flies may pollinate flowers that smell like rotten meat.

Many flowers are not pollinated primarily by insects. Red flowers, for example, may be pollinated by hummingbirds. Some large white flowers that open at night are pollinated by nighttime visitors, such as bats, as seen in **Figure 19.** Some flowers, such as those of grasses and oaks, are pollinated by wind. Wind-pollinated flowers are usually small and lack bright colors, strong odors, and nectar.

› Reading Check ***Name three characteristics of flowers that might attract pollinators.***

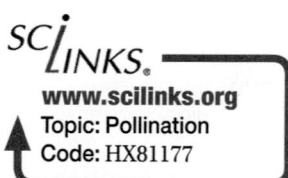

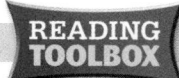

READING TOOLBOX

Classification List two characteristics of insect-pollinated flowers, then list two characteristics of wind-pollinated flowers.

Figure 19 Many flowers are adapted for pollination by wind or animals. Some species of orchids, such as the bee orchid shown at left below, have evolved to resemble their pollinators.

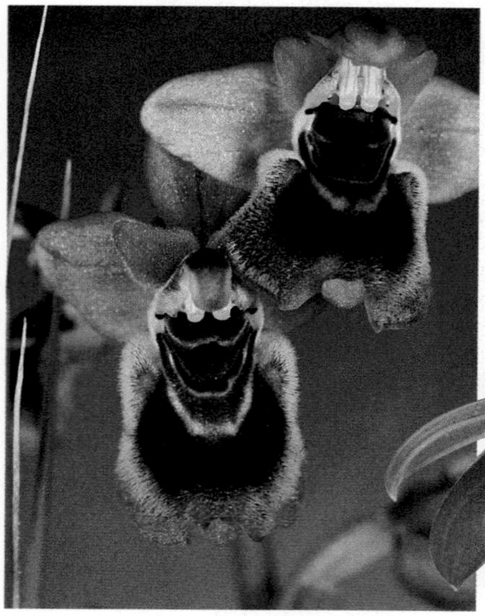

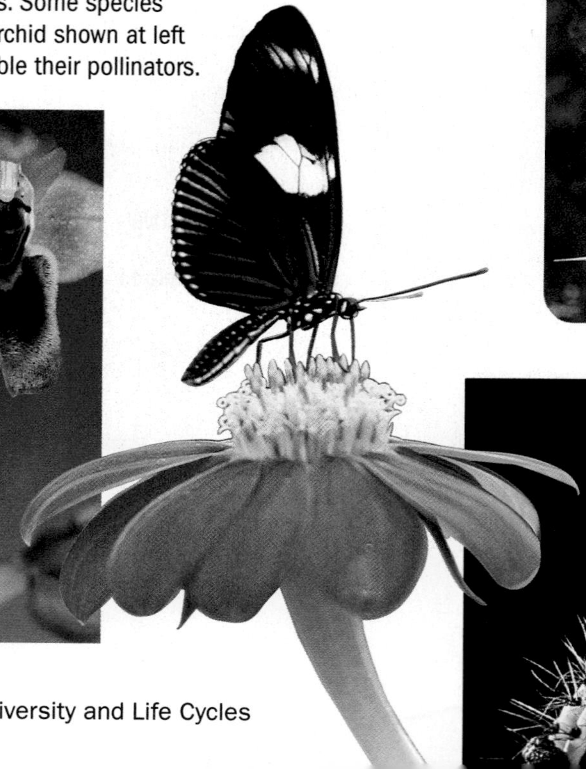

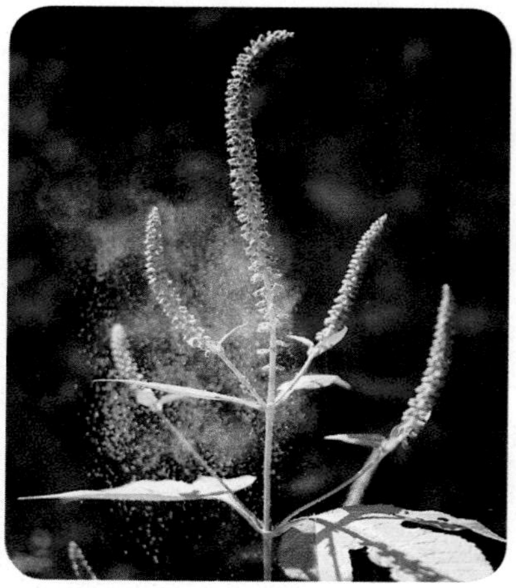

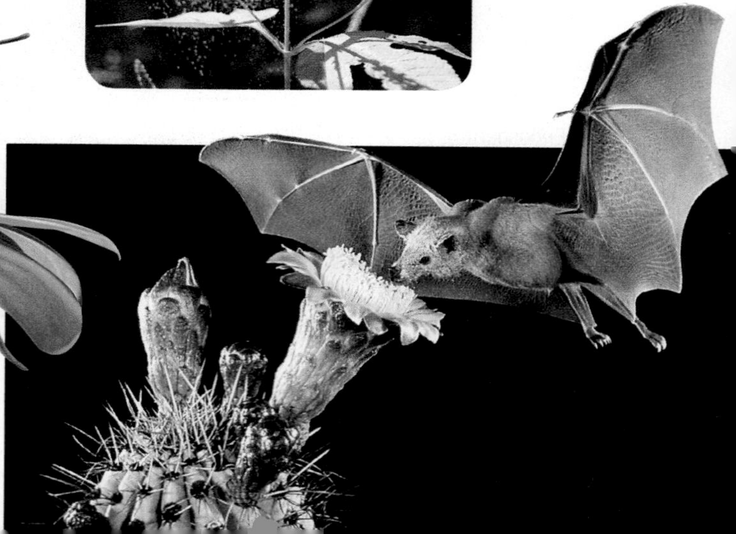

QuickLab

  15 min

Fruit or Vegetable?

Some of the foods that we think of as vegetables—parts of plants such as roots, stems, and leaves—are actually fruits. You can find out if a plant product is a fruit—the mature ovary of a flowering plant—by cutting the product open and examining its internal structure.

Procedure

❶ Look at several examples of common **fruits** and **vegetables.** Classify each one as either a fruit or a vegetable in the familiar sense.

❷ Use a **plastic knife** to cut open each fruit and vegetable.

❸ Look at the fruits and vegetables again. Classify each by its botanical function—either as a fruit or as a vegetative part.

Analysis

1. **Compare** the familiar and botanical classifications that you gave each fruit and vegetable.

2. **CRITICAL THINKING** **Analyzing Data** Which fruits and vegetables did you change the classification of?

3. **CRITICAL THINKING** **Analyzing Results** Defend the classifications that you made for item 2.

4. **CRITICAL THINKING** **Drawing Conclusions** Based on your observations, when is a vegetable a fruit?

Fruits

The ovary of a pistil is called a **fruit** after its ovules are fertilized. A fruit is a structure that develops from an ovary of a flower and contains seeds. This botanical meaning of *fruit* is different from the everyday meaning of *fruit*. A tomato is a fruit, a pumpkin is a fruit, a pea pod is a fruit, and a nut is a fruit. The thistledown of a dandelion is a fruit with a seed inside. ❯ **Although fruits provide some protection for developing seeds, they primarily function in seed dispersal.**

The angiosperms produce many types of fruits. **Figure 20** shows one example of a fruit. Many fruits are eaten by animals. The fruits' seeds are dispersed as they pass undigested through the animals. For example, the mesquite tree is thought to have been spread throughout the southwestern United States by cattle that ate the tree's sugary seed pods. Other fruits, such as the maple seed, have structures that help them float on wind or water. Some plants, such as the witch-hazel plant, forcefully eject their seeds.

❯ **Reading Check** *From which part of a flower does a fruit develop?*

> **fruit** a mature plant ovary; the plant organ in which the seeds are enclosed

Figure 20 The seeds of this pomegranate are enclosed inside a fruit. The fruit protects the seeds and aids in their dispersal. ❯ **How do you think pomegranate seeds are dispersed?**

Bulb

Tuber

Stolon

Figure 21 Plants can reproduce vegetatively through modified stems. Examples of modified stems include bulbs (left), tubers (center), and stolons (right). ❯ What is an advantage of vegetative reproduction?

Vegetative Reproduction

Many plants are able to reproduce asexually. The new individuals that result from asexual reproduction are genetically the same as the parent plant. ❯ **Plants reproduce asexually in a variety of ways that involve nonreproductive parts, such as stems, roots, and leaves. The reproduction of plants from these parts is called** *vegetative reproduction.* Many of the structures by which plants reproduce vegetatively are modified stems, such as bulbs, tubers, and stolons, as shown in **Figure 21.**

In most plants, vegetative reproduction is faster than sexual reproduction. By reproducing vegetatively, a single plant can spread rapidly in a habitat that is ideal for its growth. Therefore, a mass of hundreds or even thousands of individuals, such as a stand of grasses or ferns, may have come from one individual.

People often grow plants from vegetative parts that are specialized for vegetative reproduction. For example, in tubers such as potatoes, a single tuber can be cut or broken into pieces such that each piece has at least one bud. Each of these pieces can grow into new shoots.

❯ **Reading Check** *What are three types of modified stems by which plants can reproduce vegetatively?*

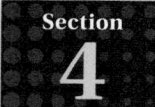

Section 4 Review

❯ KEY IDEAS

1. **Name** the two main subgroups of angiosperms.
2. **Describe** the role of a flower in angiosperm reproduction.
3. **List** three adaptations that flowers have developed to attract pollinators.
4. **Identify** the primary function of a fruit.
5. **List** three nonreproductive parts of a plant that may be involved in vegetative reproduction.

CRITICAL THINKING

6. **Predicting Outcomes** Explain how a significant reduction in the bird population of an area could affect the number of angiosperms growing in that area.

ALTERNATIVE ASSESSMENT

7. **Career Connection** Use the Internet or library resources to find out about the field of plant breeding. Write a report on your findings. Your report should include a job description, the training required, names of employers, growth prospects, and an average starting salary.

Objectives

❯ Identify similarities and differences among four phyla of living plants.

❯ Relate structural adaptations of plants to plants' success on land.

Materials

- live or preserved specimens of mosses, ferns, conifers, and angiosperms
- stereomicroscope or hand lens
- compound microscope
- prepared slides of fern gametophytes
- prepared slides of pine pollen

Safety

Plant Diversity

Most plants are photosynthetic organisms that live on land. In this lab, you will examine representatives of the four most familiar plant phyla.

Procedure

1 Visit the station for each of the plants listed below, and examine the specimens there. Record your observations.

2 **Mosses** Use a stereomicroscope or hand lens to examine a moss gametophyte that has a sporophyte attached to it. Draw what you see, and label the parts that you recognize.

3 **Ferns** Examine the sporophyte of a fern, and look for evidence of reproductive structures on the underside of the fronds. Use a compound microscope to examine a slide of a fern gametophyte. Draw what you see, and label any structures you recognize.

4 **Conifers** Draw a part of a branch of one of the conifers at this station. Label a leaf, stem, and cone (if present). Examine a prepared slide of pine pollen. Draw a few of the pollen grains.

5 **Angiosperms** Draw one of the representative angiosperms at this station. Label a leaf, stem, root, and flower (if present). Indicate the sporophyte and location of gametophytes.

6 ⬦ ◆ Clean up your lab materials according to your teacher's instructions. Wash your hands before leaving the lab.

Moss

Fern

Conifer

Angiosperm

Analyze and Conclude

1. **Recognizing Patterns** How do the gametophytes of gymnosperms and angiosperms differ from the gametophytes of mosses and ferns?

2. **Comparing Structures** What structures are present in both gymnosperms and angiosperms but absent in both mosses and ferns?

Chapter 23 Summary

Key Ideas	Key Terms

1 Introduction to Plants

> Plants are multicellular eukaryotes whose cells have cell walls made of cellulose. Most plants produce their own food through photosynthesis.

> In order to thrive on land, plants had to be able to absorb nutrients from their surroundings, to survive dehydration or avoid drying out, and to have a way of dispersal—or way of scattering—that did not require water.

> In plant life cycles, haploid gametophytes alternate with diploid sporophytes.

Key Terms:
cuticle (544)
spore (545)
sporophyte (546)
gametophyte (546)

2 Seedless Plants

> Nonvascular plants do not have a vascular system for transporting water and nutrients within their bodies.

> In the life cycle of nonvascular plants, the gametophyte is the dominant generation.

> Sporophytes of seedless vascular plants have vascular tissue. Because of their vascular system, vascular plants grow much larger than nonvascular plants and also develop true roots, stems, and leaves.

> In the life cycle of seedless vascular plants, the sporophyte is the dominant generation.

Key Terms:
archegonium (548)
antheridium (548)
sporangium (548)
rhizome (550)
frond (550)
sorus (552)

3 Seed Plants

> Seed plants are classified into two groups—gymnosperms and angiosperms.

> Reproduction in seed plants is characterized by a greatly reduced gametophyte and a dominant sporophyte.

> There are four major groups of gymnosperms—conifers, cycads, ginkgoes, and gnetophytes.

> Reproduction in conifers is characterized by a dominant sporophyte, wind pollination, and the development of seeds in cones.

Key Terms:
gymnosperm (553)
angiosperm (553)
ovule (554)
seed (554)
pollen grain (554)
pollination (554)

4 Flowering Plants

> Angiosperms are divided into two subgroups—monocots and dicots.

> In angiosperms, sexual reproduction takes place within a specialized structure called a *flower.*

> Flowers often have adaptations for pollination by wind or by animals.

> The primary function of fruits is to promote seed dispersal.

> Plants reproduce asexually by vegetative reproduction, which occurs by means of nonreproductive parts, such as stems, roots, and leaves.

Key Terms:
monocot (559)
cotyledon (559)
dicot (559)
stamen (560)
anther (560)
pistil (560)
fruit (563)

READING TOOLBOX

1. **Word Parts** Use what you know about word parts to define the words *monocot* and *dicot* in your own words.

2. **Concept Map** Make a concept map that shows how plants are classified. Try to include the following terms in your map: *vascular plants, nonvascular plants, ferns, angiosperms, gymnosperms, mosses, cones, vascular tissue, seeds,* and *flowers.*

Using Key Terms

In your own words, write a definition for each of the following terms.

3. *cuticle*

4. *sorus*

5. *pollen*

6. *sepal*

7. *anther*

8. *pistil*

For each pair of terms, explain how the meanings of the terms differ.

9. *sporophyte* and *gametophyte*

10. *archegonium* and *antheridium*

11. *gymnosperm* and *angiosperm*

Understanding Key Ideas

12. Most plants produce their own food through
    a. osmosis.
    b. diffusion.
    c. absorption.
    d. photosynthesis.

13. The cuticle of a plant functions as
    a. a primary location of cellular regeneration.
    b. a barrier around the roots to protect them from rotting.
    c. a special layer of tissue to transport water from roots to leaves.
    d. a watertight covering to reduce moisture loss and drying out.

14. The most familiar nonvascular plants that contain simple conducting cells are
    a. ferns.
    b. mosses.
    c. horsetails.
    d. ground pines.

15. The horizontal, underground stem found on most seedless vascular plants is called a
    a. cone.
    b. frond.
    c. rhizome.
    d. fiddlehead.

16. Seed plants whose seeds do not develop within a fruit are called
    a. monocots.
    b. angiosperms.
    c. gymnosperms.
    d. flowering plants.

Use the diagram of a flower to answer the following questions.

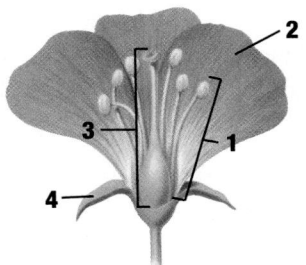

17. Which structure contains the ovules?
    a. Structure 1
    b. Structure 2
    c. Structure 3
    d. Structure 4

18. Which structure is made of an anther and a filament and produces pollen?
    a. Structure 1
    b. Structure 2
    c. Structure 3
    d. Structure 4

Explaining Key Ideas

19. **List** the three structures that club mosses have that true mosses do not.

20. **Identify** which group of gymnosperms includes the redwoods, some of the world's tallest living plants.

21. **Describe** how insects such as bees help with the cross-fertilization of many angiosperms.

Using Science Graphics

Use the graph showing annual pesticide use in California to answer the following questions.

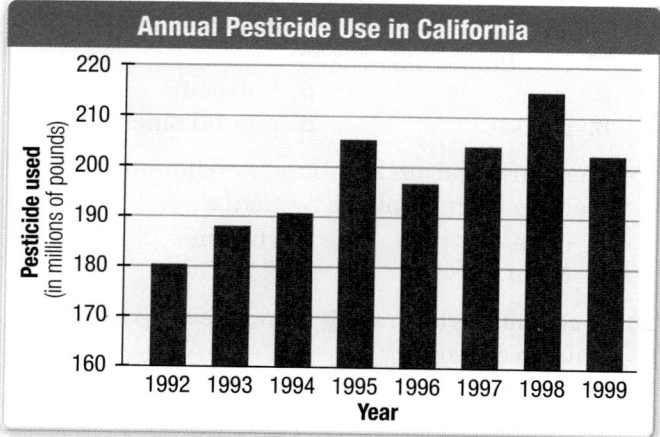

Annual Pesticide Use in California

Source: State of California Environmental Protection Agency, Department of Pesticide Regulation, February 2000.

22. **Identify** the year in which the most pesticide was used in California.

23. **Graphing Skills** Use the data on the graph to make a line graph titled *Amount of Pesticide Used in California*.

24. **Math Skills** Scientists estimate that less than 0.1% of applied pesticides stay on the intended target, while the remaining amount of pesticide becomes an environmental contaminant. For the year 1998, estimate how many pounds of pesticide stayed on the intended target, and then calculate how many pounds became environmental contaminants.

25. **Predicting Results** What effect do you think the overall increase in the amount of pesticide use shown in these data and the subsequent environmental contamination might have on the reproduction of many plants? Explain your answer.

Critical Thinking

26. **Explaining Relationships** Explain the relationship between the small size of most nonvascular plants and the means by which they transport water and nutrients.

27. **Applying Information** In the life cycle of a moss, a haploid spore may germinate in a location far from its parent plant. Explain how this might happen and why the availability of enough water will determine whether this moss will reproduce.

28. **Sequencing** Outline the sequence of events that takes place in the reproduction of seed plants from the time eggs and sperm are formed to the time of seed dispersal.

29. **Supporting Conclusions** A classmate shows you a large orange and yellow flower that has a heavy scent and tells you that the plant is probably pollinated by wind because it was found growing on a tall stem in an open field. Can you support your classmate's conclusion? Explain your answer.

Alternative Assessment

30. **Finding and Communicating Information** Visit a local garden center or nursery, and see how many plants you can identify as monocots or dicots. Take pictures of the flowers, and use the pictures to create a poster that shows examples of monocots and dicots. Include in your poster an explanation of the difference between each subgroup based on the number of flower parts. Are most of the plants for sale monocots or dicots? Present your poster to your class, and explain your findings.

Writing Skills

31. **Speech Writing** Imagine that your city council is planning to rezone 20 acres of heavily wooded land for commercial development. The land is located next to a large park and botanical gardens. Write a short speech giving the council your opinion about how destroying the habitat for all of the birds and insects in 20 acres might affect the reproduction and dispersal of the seed plants in the botanical gardens and park.

32. **Short Story** Paleobotany is a branch of paleontology dealing with the recovery and identification of plant remains from geological fossils. Imagine that you are a paleobotanist searching for evidence of the first trees, which many scientists believe to be the *Archaeopteris*. Write a short story describing how you recover and identify your first *Archaeopteris* specimen. Use the Internet or library resources to research paleobotany and *Archaeopteris* to help gather information for your story.

Science Concepts

1. Plants are
  A multi-celled eukaryotes.
  B multi-celled prokaryotes.
  C single-celled eukaryotes.
  D single-celled prokaryotes.

2. Nonvascular plants transport water and nutrients within their bodies by
  F absorption alone.
  G osmosis and diffusion.
  H specialized vascular tissue.
  J absorption and condensation.

3. The seeds of most gymnosperms develop within a
  A fruit.   **C** pistil.
  B cone.   **D** flower.

Using Science Graphics

Use the pie chart showing the distribution of plants by group to answer the following question.

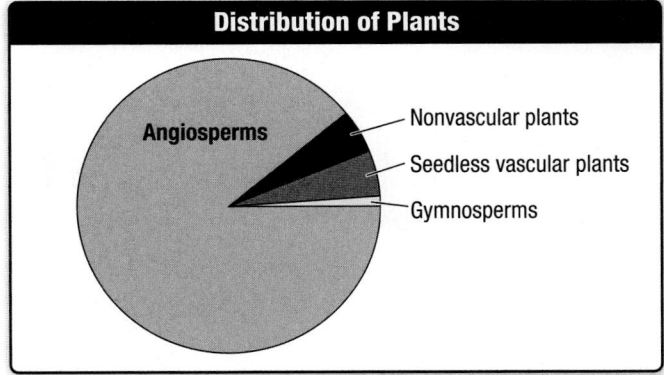

Distribution of Plants

Angiosperms

Nonvascular plants
Seedless vascular plants
Gymnosperms

4. If the total number of plant species is about 260,000, and gymnosperms make up 0.35% of the total, about how many species of gymnosperms are there?
  F 910   **H** 9100
  G 7429   **J** 91000

Use the diagram showing the basic life cycle of a plant to answer the following questions.

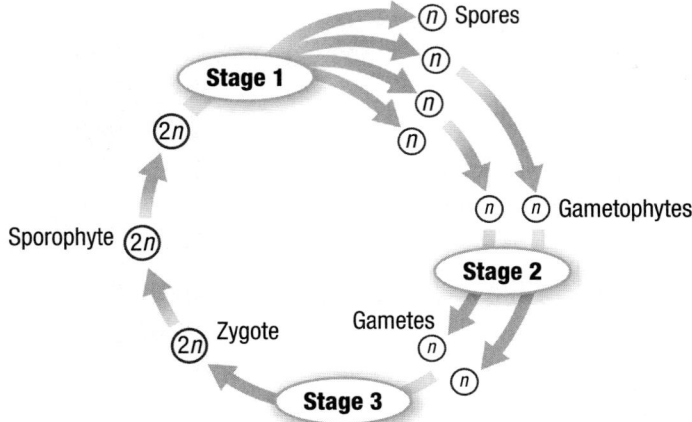

n Spores
Stage 1
$2n$
n
n
n
n
Sporophyte $2n$
n n Gametophytes
Stage 2
Gametes
$2n$ Zygote n
n
Stage 3

5. In the basic life cycle of a plant, what occurs at Stage 1?
  A Diploid zygotes are produced by mitosis.
  B Haploid spores are produced by mitosis.
  C Haploid spores are produced by meiosis.
  D Haploid gametes are produced by meiosis.

6. The correct order of events that take place at Stage 1, Stage 2, and Stage 3 is
  F mitosis, meiosis, and fertilization.
  G meiosis, fertilization, and mitosis.
  H meiosis, mitosis, and fertilization.
  J mitosis, fertilization, and meiosis.

Writing Skills

7. Extended Response All plants have a life cycle that alternates between haploid and diploid phases. Name the two phases of a plant life cycle and describe how they differ from each other. Describe the life cycle of one nonvascular plant and one vascular plant, including the relative sizes of the different forms and other characteristics.

Seed Plant Structure and Growth

Preview

1 Plant Tissue Systems
Plant Tissues
Dermal Tissue System
Vascular Tissue System
Ground Tissue System

2 Roots, Stems, and Leaves
Roots
Stems
Leaves

3 Plant Growth and Development
The Plant Embryo
Meristems
Primary Growth
Secondary Growth

Why It Matters

Like your body, a plant's body is made up of tissues, which make up organs. Seeds were an important terrestrial adaptation that enhanced survival and dispersal of plants.

A climber is supported by the strong roots of a tescalama tree. This tescalama, or rock fig, is growing on a stone wall in Mexico.

Roots anchor a plant to the spot where it grows. They also absorb water and minerals, which the plant needs to grow.

InquiryLab

⏱ **15 min**

Function of Plant Parts

How closely related are structure and function in a plant? Can you infer the function of a plant part by analyzing its structure?

Procedure

1 Without removing a **potted plant** from its container, examine the plant's outer appearance.

2 Carefully remove the plant from its container. Use a **cotton swab** to gently brush soil from the roots.

3 Locate the plant's leaves. Use a **hand lens** to closely examine these plant parts. Can you see small, veinlike vessels in the leaf?

4 Locate the main stem and the smaller stalks that connect the leaves to the stems.

5 Locate the roots. Use a hand lens to closely examine these plant parts. Can you see any small hairs that emerge from the main root parts?

6 Record your observations. Then, try to infer the function of each plant part based on its structure.

Analysis

1. **Explain** how the hand lens improved your observational skills.

2. **Describe** how the stem section that was below the soil differs from the stem section above the soil.

3. **Explain** how the root system is adapted to anchor the plant in soil.

The roots of this rock fig grow down the rock wall and eventually fuse, forming what looks like a wooden waterfall or lava flow. Rock figs are sometimes called *lava figs.*

READING TOOLBOX

These reading tools can help you learn the material in this chapter. For more information on how to use these and other tools, see **Appendix: Reading and Study Skills.**

Using Words

Word Origins Many of the words we use today come from Greek or Latin words. Knowing the meanings of Greek and Latin roots can help you figure out and remember the meanings of modern English words.

Your Turn Use the table to answer the following questions.

1. Where on a plant would you find dermal tissue?
2. Where on a plant would you find mesophyll?

Word Origins		
Word part	**Origin**	**Meaning**
derm	Greek	skin
vas	Latin	vessel
meso	Greek	middle
phyll	Greek	leaf

Using Language

Cause and Effect In biological processes, one step leads to another step. When reading, you can recognize cause-and-effect relationships by words that indicate a result, such as *so, consequently, next, then,* and *as a result.*

Your Turn Identify the cause and the effect in the following sentences.

1. Some seeds float on the wind, so they are often found far from the parent plant.
2. The substance that makes up plant cell walls is very strong. As a result, trees are able to grow very tall without breaking.

Using FoldNotes

Booklet A booklet is a useful tool for taking notes as you read a chapter. Each page of the booklet can contain a main topic from the chapter and the details that describe the main topic.

Your Turn Make a booklet to help you organize your notes for this chapter.

1. Fold a sheet of paper in half from top to bottom.
2. Fold the sheet of paper in half again, from left to right.
3. Fold the sheet of paper one more time, from top to bottom.
4. Completely unfold the paper.
5. Using scissors, cut a slit along the center crease of the sheet from the T made by the top fold to the T made by the bottom fold. Do not cut the entire sheet in half.
6. Fold the sheet of paper in half from top to bottom. While holding the bottom and top edges of the paper, push the bottom and top edges together so that the center collapses at the center slit. Fold the four flaps to form a four-page book.

Plant Tissue Systems

Key Ideas	Key Terms	Why It Matters
❯ What three types of tissue are found in vascular plants? ❯ What is the dermal tissue system? ❯ What are two types of vascular tissue? ❯ What is ground tissue?	dermal tissue guard cell vascular tissue xylem ground tissue phloem stoma	Did you know that plants, like animals, have tissues? Plant tissues perform functions such as protection, support, and transport.

Like your body, a plant's body is made of tissues. Plant tissues are arranged into systems, which are further organized into organs.

Plant Tissues

❯ Vascular plants have three tissue systems—the dermal tissue system, vascular tissue system, and ground tissue system. **Dermal tissue** forms the protective outer layer of a plant. **Vascular tissue** forms strands that conduct water, minerals, and organic compounds throughout a vascular plant. **Ground tissue** makes up much of the inside of the nonwoody parts of a plant, including roots, stems, and leaves. **Figure 1** shows how these three tissues are arranged in a nonwoody dicot. Each type of tissue contains one or more kinds of cells that are specialized to perform particular functions.

❯ **Reading Check** *Where on a plant is dermal tissue found? (See the Appendix for answers to Reading Checks.)*

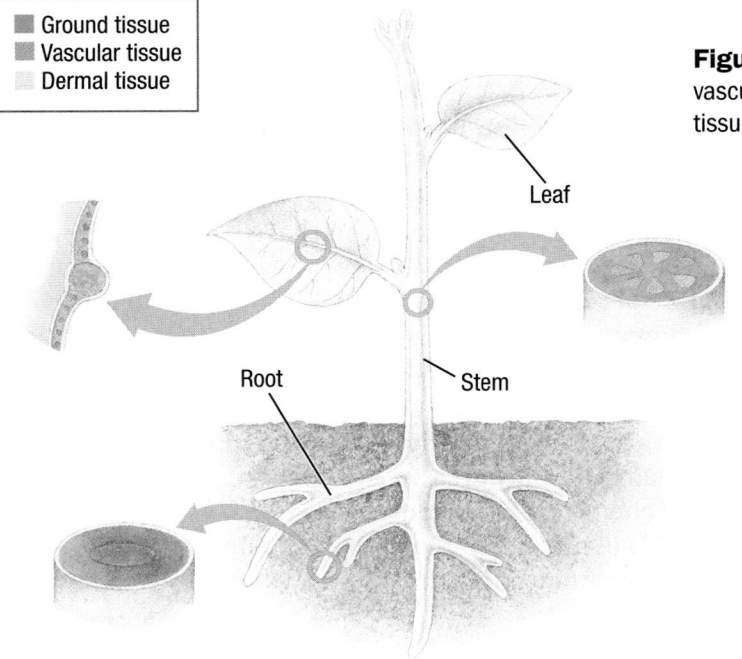

■ Ground tissue
■ Vascular tissue
□ Dermal tissue

Leaf

Root   Stem

Figure 1 The leaves, stems, and roots of a vascular plant contain all three kinds of plant tissues. ❯ **What is the function of vascular tissue?**

dermal tissue the outer covering of a plant

vascular (VAS kyuh luhr) **tissue** the specialized conducting tissue that is found in higher plants and that is made up mostly of xylem and phloem

ground tissue a type of plant tissue other than vascular tissue that makes up much of the inside of a plant

Water beads up on the waxy surface of the leaf.

Tiny hairs trap moisture and help reflect sunlight.

Figure 2 The waxy cuticle on water lily leaves (above) protects the leaves and repels water. Hairlike outgrowths of the epidermis of some plants (right) help reduce water loss from the leaves.

ACADEMIC
VOCABULARY

function use or purpose

Dermal Tissue System

❭ **Dermal tissue covers the outside of a plant's body. In the nonwoody parts of a plant, dermal tissue forms a "skin" called the *epidermis.*** The epidermis of most plants is made up of a single layer of flat cells. Often, the cells of the epidermis have hairlike extensions or other structures, as shown in **Figure 2.** Extensions of the epidermal cells on leaves and stems often help slow water loss by trapping moisture close to the surface of the leaf. Extensions of the epidermal cells on root tips, called *root hairs,* help increase water absorption.

The waxy cuticle coats the epidermis of stems and leaves. The cuticle protects the plant and prevents water loss. Recall that the development of a cuticle made it possible for plants to live in drier habitats. Some aquatic plants, such as the water lilies shown in **Figure 2,** also have a cuticle. The <u>function</u> of the cuticle in these plants is to protect the leaves and repel water.

The dermal tissue on woody stems and roots consists of several layers of dead cells that are referred to as *cork.* Cork cells contain a waterproof chemical and are not covered by a waxy cuticle. In addition to its role in protection, dermal tissue functions in gas exchange and in the absorption of mineral nutrients.

❭ **Reading Check** *What is the function of root hairs?*

QuickLab

🕐 15 min

Behavior of Stomata

You can use nail polish to see that a leaf has many stomata.

Procedure

1 Paint a thin layer of **clear nail polish** on a 1 × 1 cm area of a leaf on a **plant kept in light** and on a **plant kept in darkness.** Let the nail polish dry for 5 min.

2 Place a **4 to 5 cm strip of clear tape** over the nail polish on each leaf. Press the tape firmly to the nail polish.

3 Carefully pull the tape off each leaf. Stick each piece of tape to a **microscope slide.** Label the slides appropriately.

4 View each slide with a **microscope,** first under low power and then under high power.

5 Draw and label what you see on each slide.

Analysis

1. Describe any differences in the stomata of the two plants.

2. **CRITICAL THINKING** **Drawing Conclusions** Which plant will lose water more quickly? Explain.

Stomata Like the wax on a shiny car, the cuticle does not let gases pass through it. So, how does a plant obtain the carbon dioxide it needs for photosynthesis? Pores called **stomata** (singular, *stoma*) permit plants to exchange oxygen and carbon dioxide. Stomata, which extend through the cuticle and the outer layer of cells, are found on at least some parts of most plants. A pair of specialized cells called **guard cells** border each stoma, as seen in **Figure 3.** Stomata open and close as the guard cells change shape. When the stomata are open, a plant is able to gain carbon dioxide from the air, but the plant loses water vapor through the open stomata. When the stomata are closed, the plant conserves water, but photosynthesis slows down or stops because of a shortage of carbon dioxide.

Figure 3 The surface of a leaf has numerous stomata, each of which is surrounded by a pair of guard cells. ❯ Why does photosynthesis slow down when stomata are closed?

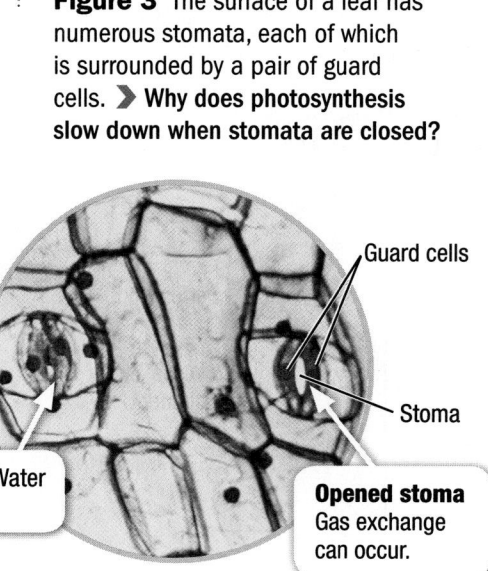

Spiderwort leaves

Guard cells

Stoma

Closed stoma Water is conserved.

Opened stoma Gas exchange can occur.

Figure 4 Both xylem and phloem contain strands of tubular conducting cells that are stacked end to end like sections of pipe. ❯ **Which kind of vascular tissue transports water and minerals?**

Vascular Tissue System

One of the most important changes as plants evolved was the development of vascular tissues. ❯ **Vascular plants have two kinds of vascular tissue, called *xylem* and *phloem*, that transport water, minerals, and nutrients throughout the plant.** These tissues are composed of cells that are stacked end to end like sections of pipe, as shown in **Figure 4.** Xylem and phloem allow most vascular plants to grow to much larger sizes than nonvascular plants, which do not have xylem and phloem.

Xylem Xylem is composed of thick-walled cells that conduct water and mineral nutrients from a plant's roots through its stems to its leaves. At maturity, xylem cells are dead, and all that is left of the cells is their strong cell walls. The two types of conducting cells in xylem are called *tracheids* and *vessel elements*. Water flows from one tracheid to the next through pits, or thin areas in the cell walls. Vessel elements link to form vessels. The vessel elements have large perforations in their ends that allow water to flow more quickly between vessel elements.

Phloem Phloem is made up of cells that conduct sugars and nutrients throughout a plant's body. The conducting cells of phloem have a cell wall, a cell membrane, and cytoplasm. These cells either lack organelles or have modified organelles. The conducting cells in phloem are called *sieve-tube members*. Sieve-tube members link to form sieve tubes. Pores in the walls between neighboring sieve-tube members connect the cytoplasms and allow substances to pass from cell to cell. Beside the sieve tubes are rows of companion cells, which contain organelles. Companion cells carry out cellular respiration, protein synthesis, and other metabolic functions for the sieve tubes.

❯ **Reading Check** *What are the conducting cells in phloem called?*

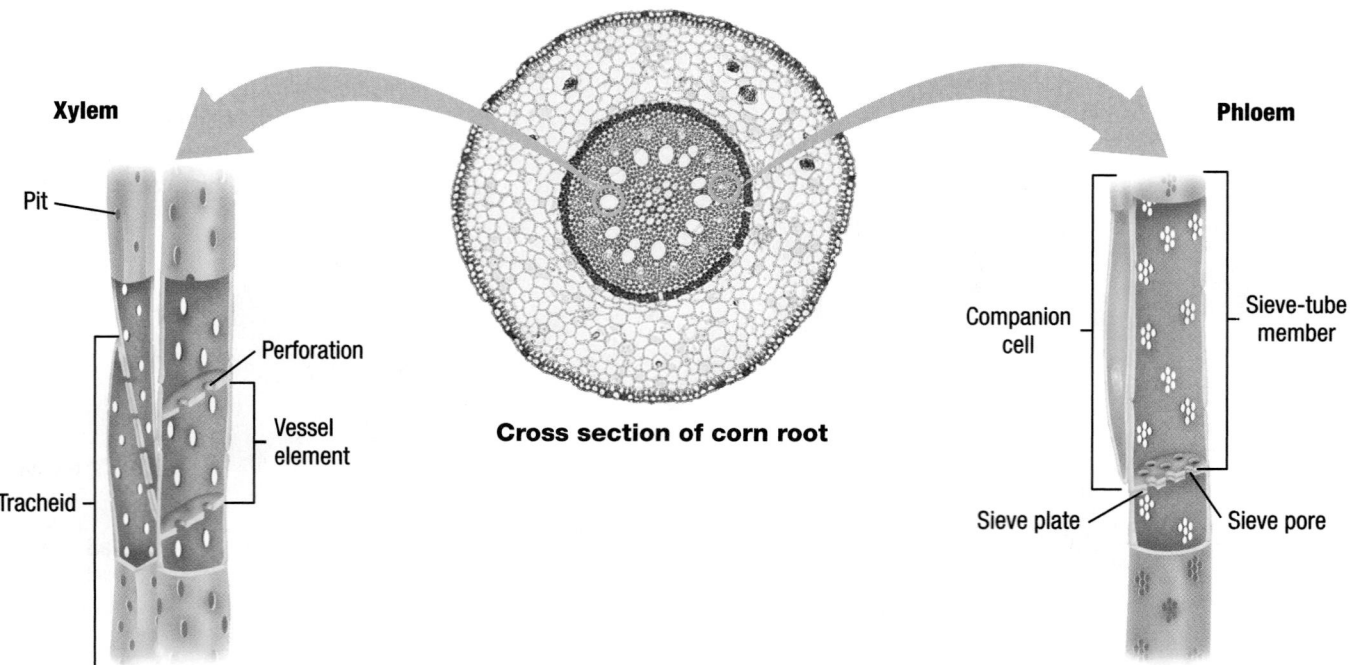

Cross section of corn root

Up Close Vascular Plant

Kalanchoes belong to the Crassulaceae family, a group of succulent plants that are adapted to hot climates. Kalanchoes can reproduce vegetatively by means of plantlets that develop on leaf margins. A plantlet that falls to the ground grows into a new plant.

Kalanchoe

Scientific name: *Kalanchoe daigremontiana*
Size: grows from 30 cm to 1 m (1 to 3 ft) tall
Range: native to southwestern Madagascar; cultivated worldwide
Habitat: semiarid tropical grassland with moist summers and well-drained, fertile soil
Importance: grown as indoor potted plants and as outdoor perennials in warm climates

Leaves The leaves are fleshy and have saw-toothed margins. Leaf blades range from 12 to 25 cm (4 to 10 in.) long.

Flowers A cluster of flowers forms on a flowering stalk that grows from the end of a stem. Flower parts occur in fours. Each flower produces many tiny seeds.

Plantlets Tiny new plants develop along leaf margins. These plantlets are a means of vegetative reproduction.

Air roots The roots that grow from the stems and from plantlets originate from the stem tissue.

Mesophyll cells

Central vacuole

Organelles

Leaf structure A thick cuticle covers the leaf, and the epidermis consists of several layers of cells. Relatively few, very small stomata dot the leaf surfaces.

Cuticle
Epidermis
Mesophyll
Epidermis

Stoma   Vascular bundle

Large central vacuole The cells inside a leaf, called *mesophyll cells*, have a large central vacuole that can hold a lot of water.

Characteristics of Plant Tissue Systems

Tissue system	Location	Function in roots	Function in stems	Function in leaves
Dermal tissue system	outermost layer(s) of cells	absorption, protection	gas exchange, protection	gas exchange, protection
Vascular tissue system	tubes throughout plant	transport, support	transport, support	transport, support
Ground tissue system	between dermal and vascular tissues in nonwoody plant parts	support, storage	support, storage	photosynthesis

Figure 5 All three plant tissue systems are found in the roots, stems, and leaves of vascular plants. ❯ **What is the primary function of ground tissue in leaves?**

Word Origins The root *vas* means vessel. Use this information and the table above to describe the function of vascular tissue.

Ground Tissue System

The third type of tissue in vascular plants is ground tissue. ❯ **Ground tissue makes up much of the inside of most nonwoody plants, where it surrounds and supports vascular tissue.** Most ground tissue consists of thin-walled cells that remain alive and keep their nucleus after they mature. But ground tissue also contains some thick-walled cells that lose their nucleus and cell contents when they mature.

Ground tissue contains many cell types, each with specific functions based on where the cells are located in a plant. In leaves, the ground tissue is composed of cells that are packed with chloroplasts. These cells are specialized for photosynthesis.

The ground tissue in stems and roots functions mainly in support and in the storage of water, sugar, and starch. Cells in these locations often contain large vacuoles for storage. In angiosperms, ground tissue makes up the flesh of fruits. Ground tissue is largely absent in the woody parts of plants. The characteristics of ground tissue, as well as the other types of plant tissue, are summarized in **Figure 5.**

❯ **Reading Check** *What is the primary function of ground tissue in roots and stems?*

Review

❯ KEY IDEAS

1. **Name** three types of tissue that make up vascular plants.
2. **Describe** the dermal tissue system and its functions.
3. **Name** two types of vascular tissue, and identify their functions.
4. **List** three functions of ground tissue.

CRITICAL THINKING

5. **Forming Reasoned Opinions** Guard cells are the only cells of the upper epidermis that have chloroplasts. Based on what you know about the function of guard cells, why do you think guard cells contain chloroplasts?
6. **Evaluating Results** Some herbicides (weed killers) contain a chemical that breaks down waxy substances. Explain why such a chemical may be useful in a herbicide.

WRITING FOR SCIENCE

7. **Comparing Structures** Write a paragraph comparing and contrasting the dermal tissue system of plants with the human integumentary system. In particular, compare and contrast the epidermis.

Key Ideas	Key Terms	Why It Matters
❯ What are roots, and what is their function? ❯ What are stems, and what is their function? ❯ What are leaves, and what is their function?	vascular bundle blade pith petiole heartwood mesophyll sapwood	What is in your salad? Likely, it is plant organs—roots, stems, and leaves of different plants.

The tissue systems of a plant make up the plant's organs. Plants have three basic kinds of organs—roots, stems, and leaves—and each organ contains all three tissue types.

Roots

❯ **Most plants are anchored to the spot where they grow by roots, which absorb water and mineral nutrients. In many plants, roots also function in the storage of organic nutrients, such as sugar and starch.** Most monocots, such as grasses, have a highly branched, *fibrous root* system, as shown in **Figure 6.** Many dicots, such as dandelions and radishes, have a large central root from which much smaller roots branch. This type of root system is called a *taproot* system.

A root has a central core of vascular tissue that is surrounded by ground tissue. The ground tissue surrounding the vascular tissue is called the *cortex.* Roots are covered by dermal tissue. An epidermis covers all of a root except the root tip. The epidermal cells just behind a root tip often produce root hairs, which increase the surface area of a root and its ability to absorb water. Recall that root hairs are actually extensions of the epidermal cells. A mass of cells called the *root cap* covers and protects the actively growing root tip.

❯ **Reading Check** *What are three functions of roots?*

SCLINKS.
www.scilinks.org
Topic: Root Structures
Code: HX81330

Fibrous roots

Taproots

Root hairs

Figure 6 Grasses (left) have highly branched fibrous roots. Radishes (right) have a large, central root called a *taproot.* Root hairs increase the surface area of a root and help it absorb water. ❯ **What type of root system do carrots have?**

Stems

The shoots of most plants consist of stems and leaves. ❯ **Stems support the leaves and house the vascular tissue, which transports substances between the roots and the leaves.** Many plants have stems that are specialized for other functions. For example, the stems of cactuses store water. Potatoes are stems that are specialized for nutrient storage and for asexual reproduction.

Leaves attach to a stem at points called *nodes.* The space between two nodes is called an *internode.* Buds that can grow into new branches are also located at the nodes on a stem. Look for these structures in **Figure 7.** Other features of a stem depend on whether the stem is woody or nonwoody.

Nonwoody Stems A plant with stems that are flexible and usually green is called a *herbaceous plant.* As **Figure 7** shows, the stems of herbaceous plants contain bundles of xylem and phloem called **vascular bundles.** The vascular bundles are surrounded by ground tissue. In monocot stems, such as those of irises, the vascular bundles are scattered in the ground tissue. In dicot stems, such as those of sunflowers, the vascular bundles are arranged in a ring. The ground tissue outside the ring of vascular bundles is called the *cortex.* The ground tissue inside the ring is called the **pith.** Herbaceous stems are covered by an epidermis.

❯ **Reading Check** *What is the name of the point where a leaf attaches to a stem?*

Figure 7 The vascular bundles are arranged differently in dicots (left) and monocots (right). ❯ **How are the vascular bundles arranged in a dicot stem?**

Node

Internode

Node

Cortex
Pith
— Ground tissue

Vascular bundle

Cross section of a dicot stem

Ground tissue

Vascular bundle

Cross section of a monocot stem

Internal Structures of Roots and Stems

You can use a microscope to see differences in the internal structure of roots and stems.

Procedure

1 View **cross sections of dicot and monocot roots** with a **compound microscope.** Draw and label what you see under low power. Then, look at the vascular tissue in each root under high power. Draw what you see in each root, and label the xylem and phloem.

2 View **cross sections of dicot and monocot stems** with a compound microscope. Draw and label what you see under low power. Then, look at a vascular bundle in each stem under high power. Draw each vascular bundle, and label the xylem and phloem.

Analysis

1. **Compare and contrast** the location of xylem and phloem in roots and stems.

2. **Compare and contrast** the arrangement and structure of the vascular bundles in monocot and dicot stems.

3. CRITICAL THINKING **Describe** the relationship between the structure and function of vascular tissue.

Woody Stems Trees, such as oaks, and shrubs, such as hollies, have woody stems. Woody stems are stiff and nongreen. Buds, which produce new growth, are found at the tips and at the nodes of woody stems. A young woody stem has a central core of pith and a ring of vascular bundles, which fuse into solid cylinders as the stem matures. Layers of xylem form the innermost cylinder and are the major component of wood. The cylinder of phloem lies outside the cylinder of xylem. Woody stems are covered by cork, which protects them from physical damage and helps prevent water loss. Together, the layers of cork and phloem make up the bark of a woody stem.

A mature woody stem, such as the one shown in **Figure 8,** contains many layers of wood and is covered by a thick layer of bark. The wood in the center of a mature stem or tree trunk is called **heartwood.** The xylem in heartwood can no longer conduct water. **Sapwood,** which lies outside the heartwood, contains vessel elements that can conduct water.

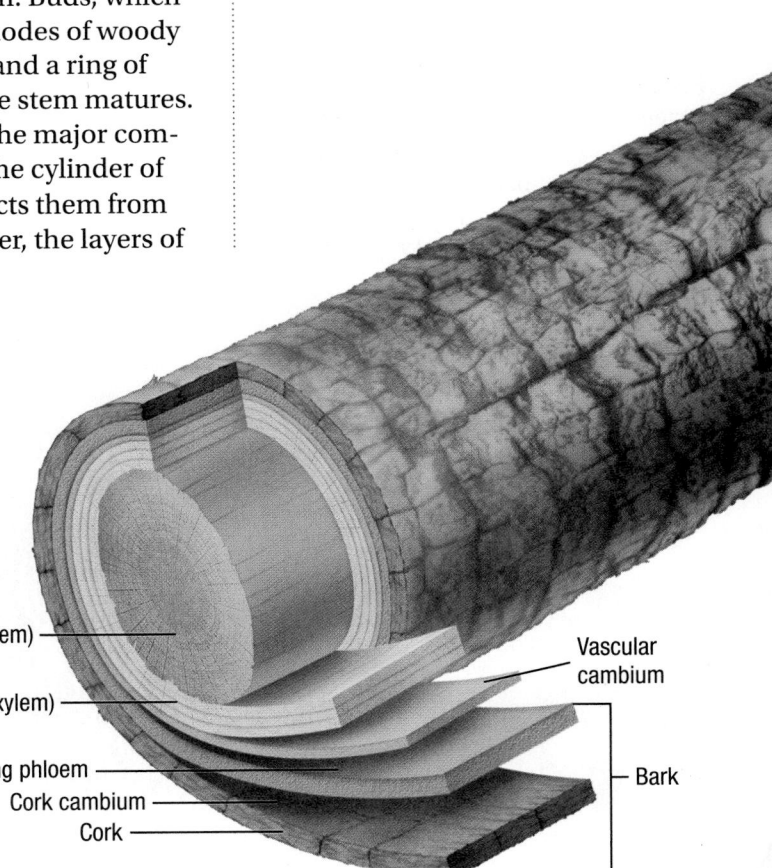

Heartwood (xylem)
Sapwood (xylem)
Living phloem
Cork cambium
Cork
Vascular cambium
Bark

Figure 8 In a mature woody stem, the xylem that makes up heartwood provides support but no longer conducts water. The xylem of sapwood functions in the transport of water and minerals.

Figure 9 Most leaves consist of a flattened blade and a petiole that attaches to a stem. ❯ **What type of leaf has an undivided blade?**

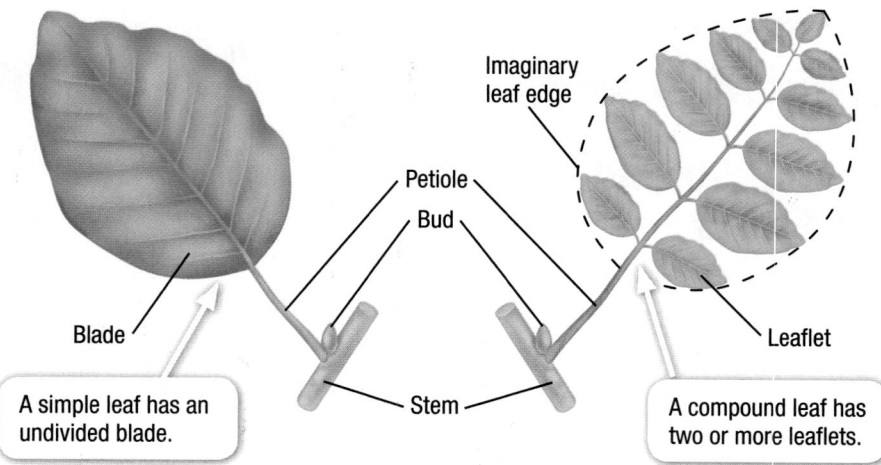

Imaginary leaf edge

Petiole

Bud

Blade

A simple leaf has an undivided blade.

Stem

Leaflet

A compound leaf has two or more leaflets.

READING TOOLBOX

Booklet Make a booklet to help you organize your notes on roots, stems, and leaves.

Figure 10 Cells from all three tissue systems are represented in a leaf. The epidermis is part of the dermal system, and the vascular bundle (vein) is part of the vascular system. The mesophyll is ground tissue, and it generally contains chloroplasts.

Leaves

❯ **Leaves are the primary photosynthetic organs of plants.** Most leaves have a flattened portion, the **blade,** which is usually attached to a stem by a stalk, called the **petiole.** A leaf blade may be divided into two or more sections, called *leaflets,* as shown in **Figure 9.** Leaves with an undivided blade are simple leaves. Leaves with two or more leaflets are compound leaves.

A leaf is a mass of ground tissue and vascular tissue covered by epidermis, as shown in **Figure 10.** A cuticle coats the upper and lower epidermis. Both xylem and phloem are found in the veins of a leaf. Veins are extensions of vascular bundles that run from the tips of roots to the edges of leaves.

In leaves, the ground tissue is called **mesophyll.** Mesophyll cells are packed with chloroplasts, where photosynthesis occurs. Most plants have leaves with two layers of mesophyll. One or more rows of closely packed, columnar cells make up the *palisade layer,* which lies just beneath the upper epidermis.

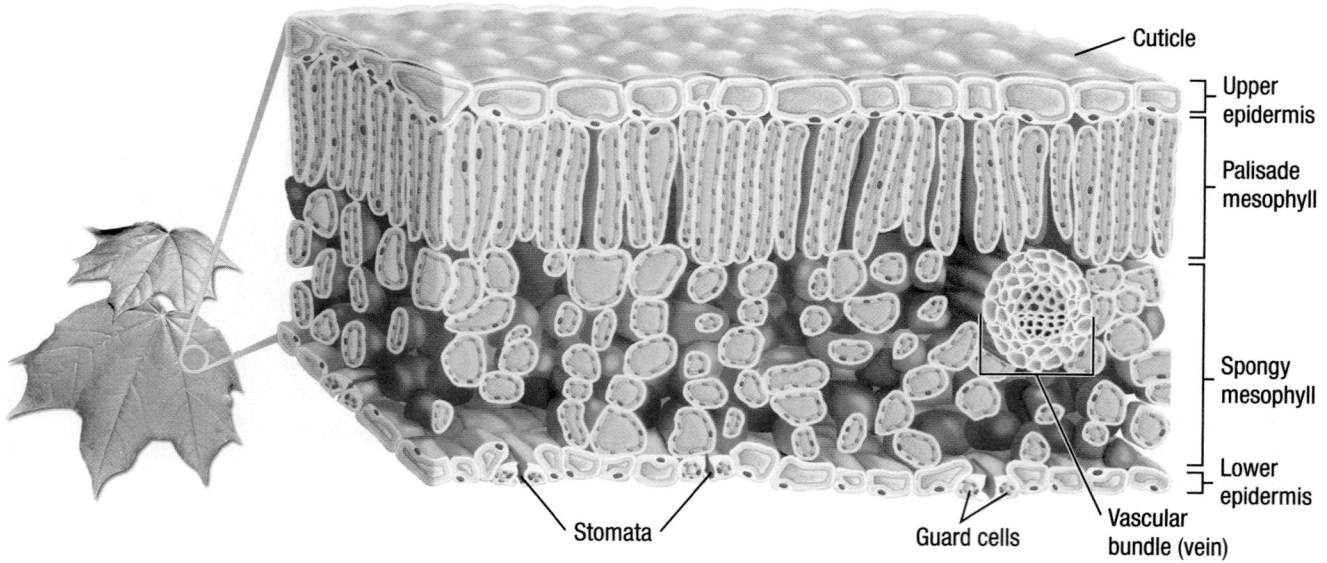

Cuticle

Upper epidermis

Palisade mesophyll

Spongy mesophyll

Lower epidermis

Stomata

Guard cells

Vascular bundle (vein)

Figure 11 The spines on a cactus (left) and the tendrils found on many vines (right) are specialized leaves. ❯ **What is one function of cactus spines?**

A layer of loosely packed cells, called the *spongy layer,* lies between the palisade layer and the lower epidermis. The spongy layer has many air spaces through which gases can travel. Stomata, the tiny holes in the epidermis, connect the air spaces to the outside air. Stomata are usually located in the lower epidermis of a leaf.

Specialized Leaves Many plants have modified leaves that are specialized for particular functions. For example, the leaves of a water lily are specialized for floating on the surface of ponds. Water lily leaves have stomata on their upper epidermis rather than on their lower epidermis. The leaves of a cactus, such as the one shown in **Figure 11,** have been modified as spines. Spines may help protect the plant from herbivores. Photosynthesis in a cactus takes place in the succulent stem rather than in leaves.

Some of the leaves of the garden pea have been modified to form tendrils that are specialized for climbing, as shown in **Figure 11.** The leaves of the Venus' flytrap have been modified to catch insects that are used by the plant as a <u>source</u> of nitrogen. These plants often grow in areas that are poor in mineral nutrients.

❯ **Reading Check** *What are two types of specialized leaves, and what are their functions?*

---

blade the broad, flat portion of a typical leaf

petiole (PEHT ee OHL) the stalk that attaches a leaf to the stem of a plant

mesophyll (MES oh FIL) in leaves, the tissue between epidermal layers, where photosynthesis occurs

ACADEMIC VOCABULARY

source the thing from which something else comes

Section 2 Review

❯ **KEY IDEAS**

1. **Describe** the function of roots, and name two types of root systems.
2. **Describe** the primary functions of stems in a vascular plant.
3. **Name** the primary function of leaves, and describe how leaf structure relates to this function.

CRITICAL THINKING

4. **Applying Logic** A general recommendation is that you should not remove a lot of the soil from the roots when transplanting plants. Why do you think that this recommendation is made?
5. **Applying Logic** A nail driven into the side of a tree will remain at exactly the same distance from the ground for the life of the tree. Explain.

ALTERNATIVE ASSESSMENT

6. **Organizing Information** Use library or Internet resources to learn about the many uses of wood. Prepare a poster that includes the types of trees that are common sources of lumber for items such as flooring, furniture, and paper.

Extreme Plants

Many plants have developed a variety of strategies to adapt to the unusual and sometimes extreme environments found on Earth. In tropical rainforests, for example, few tree roots penetrate the soil very deeply. This shallow rooting pattern increases the likelihood of trees toppling over, especially during heavy rainfall. Some trees, like the one at right, have special roots called *buttress roots* that grow radially outward from the lower part of the trunk. Buttress roots help stabilize the tree and keep it from toppling over.

Upside-Down Trees

Baobab trees are among the world's oldest and hardiest trees. They thrive in the harsh, arid environments of Africa. Their unusual barrel-like trunks can reach 9 m (30 ft) in diameter and act as a water tank that can store thousands of gallons of water. Their soft bark is spongy and has adapted to swell with absorbed water in the rainy season. Baobabs have thick, gnarly branches that look like old roots sticking up in the air. For this reason, the baobab has been called the upside-down tree. On the Kalahari Desert, human life would be almost impossible without the baobab. These hollow trees with moisture-rich wood provide sources of water where none otherwise exists. Baobabs are frequently referred to as *Africa's tree of life.*

Pitcher Plants Modified leaves form a "trap" for insects. Insects fall into a pool of liquid at the bottom of the pitcher and are digested by plant enzymes. The proteins from the digested insect supply nitrogen, which otherwise may be unavailable to these plants in the nutrient-poor soil where they grow.

Living Stones

The "pebbles" shown above are actually highly developed succulent plants called *living stones.* Native to South Africa, living stones are adapted to extreme heat and drought and can survive more than a year without water. Their pebble-shaped leaves minimize evaporation, and their spots and coloring serve as camouflage against herbivores.

Baobab trees

Research Find the scientific name for living stones, and explain its derivation.

Section 3 Plant Growth and Development

Key Ideas

> What are the characteristics of a seed plant embryo?

> How do meristems relate to plant growth?

> What is the result of primary growth on a plant?

> What is secondary growth, and what type of meristem is involved?

Key Terms

germination
meristem
primary growth
secondary growth
apical meristem
lateral meristem

Why It Matters

While animals stop growing when they reach maturity, plants continue to grow and develop throughout their lives.

As in animals, genes guide the development of plants, but the patterns of development in each are very different. Plants continuously make new cells, which differentiate and replace or add to existing tissues.

The Plant Embryo

Recall that a seed develops from an ovule and contains a plant embryo. **> The plant embryo possesses an embryonic root and an embryonic shoot. Leaflike structures called *cotyledons*, or seed leaves, are attached to the embryonic shoot.** The embryos of gymnosperms have two or more cotyledons. For example, pine embryos have eight cotyledons. In the flowering plants, or angiosperms, embryos have one or two cotyledons. Recall that flowering plants with a single cotyledon are called *monocots*. Corn and irises are examples of monocots. Flowering plants with two cotyledons are called *dicots*. Bean plants and sunflowers are examples of dicots. The structure of three types of seeds is shown in **Figure 12.**

> Reading Check *How many cotyledons does a bean seed have?*

Figure 12 Seeds contain the embryos of plants. **>** To which structure are cotyledons attached on the plant embryo?

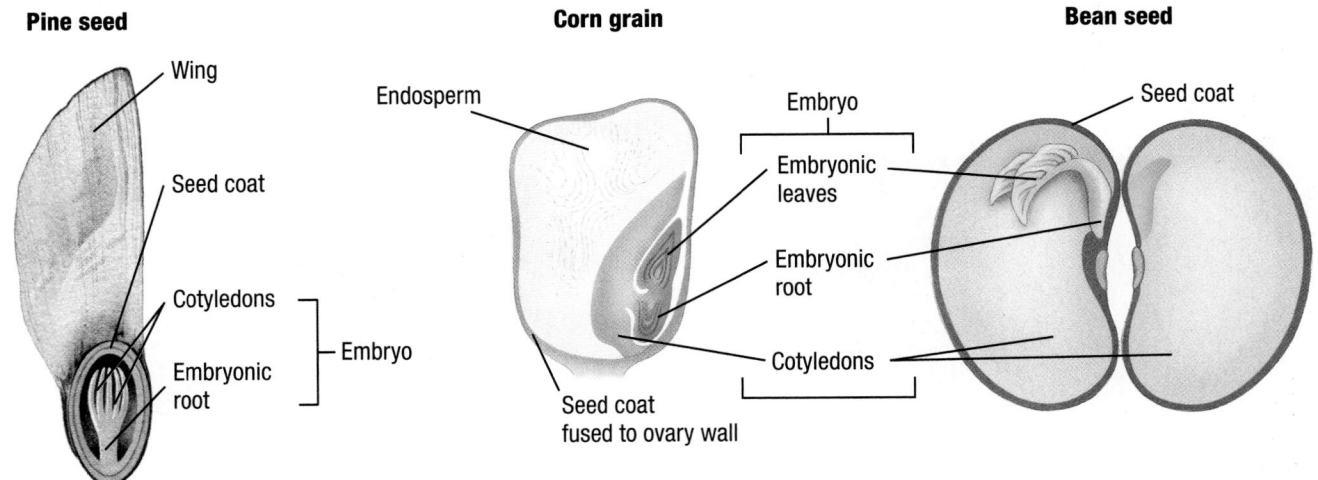

Pine seed — Wing, Seed coat, Cotyledons, Embryonic root, Embryo

Corn grain — Endosperm, Embryo, Embryonic leaves, Embryonic root, Cotyledons, Seed coat fused to ovary wall

Bean seed — Seed coat, Cotyledons

SECTION 3 Plant Growth and Development **585**

READING TOOLBOX

Cause and Effect Use cause and effect language to describe what happens when water penetrates a seed coat.

Figure 13 Beans and corn show two characteristic patterns of seed germination. ❯ How are young shoots protected in dicots and monocots?

Germination

The embryo within a seed is in a state of suspended animation, or *dormancy*. Some embryos can remain in suspended animation for thousands of years. The process by which a plant embryo resumes its growth is called **germination.** The first sign of germination is the emergence of the embryo's root. What happens next varies somewhat from one type of plant to another, as you can see in **Figure 13.** The young shoots of some plants, such as beans, form a hook. The hook protects the tip of the shoot from injury as it grows through the soil. The shoot straightens after the cotyledons emerge from the soil. The young shoots of other plants, such as corn, have a protective sheath around their shoots. The shoot grows straight up, but the cotyledon stays underground. After the shoot of a seedling emerges, its roots and shoots continue to grow throughout its life.

Breaking Dormancy

Seeds sprout in response to certain changes in the environment. These changes, such as rising temperature and increasing soil moisture, usually signal the start of favorable growing conditions. Many seeds must be exposed to cold before they can sprout. Otherwise, the seeds may sprout too early, such as during warm fall weather. The seed coats of other seeds must be damaged before they can sprout. Being exposed to fire, passing through the digestive system of an animal, and falling onto rocks are several natural ways that seed coats are damaged. A seed cannot sprout until water and oxygen penetrate the seed coat. When water enters a seed, the tissues in the seed swell and the seed coat breaks. If enough water and oxygen are available after the seed coat breaks, the young plant, or seedling, begins to grow.

❯ **Reading Check** *What are two ways in which the seed coat can be damaged so that the seed will be able to sprout?*

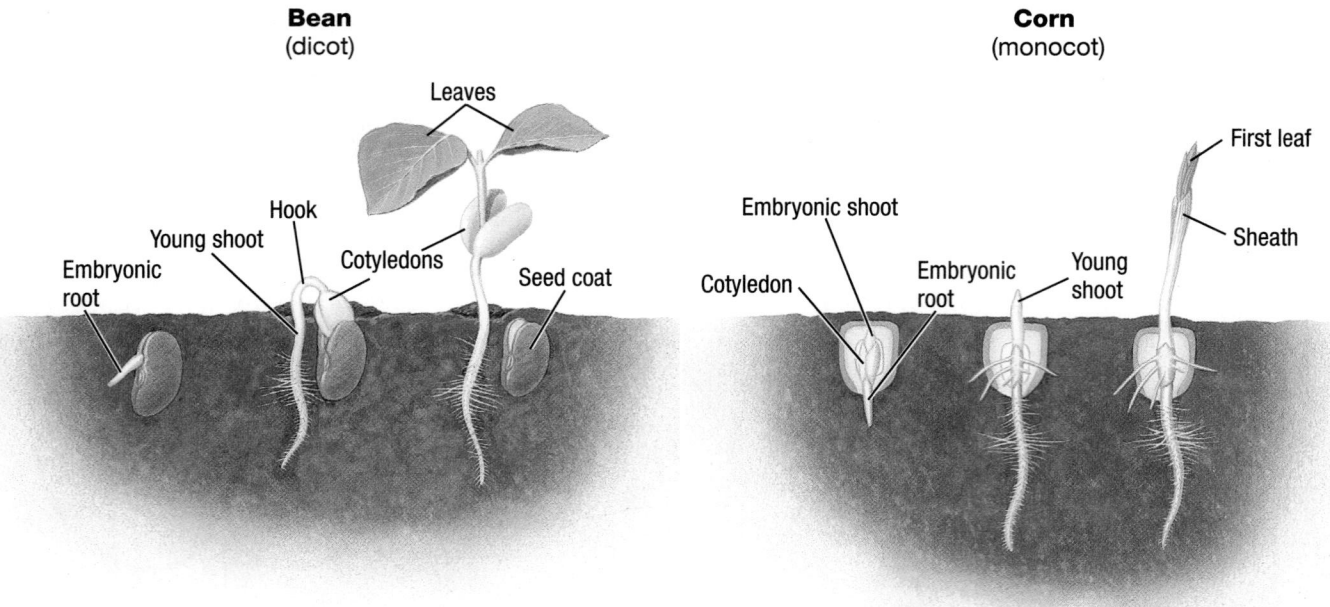

Bean
(dicot)

Leaves

Hook

Young shoot

Cotyledons

Embryonic root

Seed coat

Corn
(monocot)

First leaf

Sheath

Embryonic shoot

Cotyledon

Embryonic root

Young shoot

Quick**Lab**

⏱ 15 min

The Effect of Cold on Seed Germination

In some plants, a period of low temperatures is needed to break seed dormancy. Dormancy helps plants to survive by keeping seeds from germinating too early. The graph at right shows how storage at a low temperature (4 °C) affected the ability of apple seeds to germinate. Use the graph to answer the following questions.

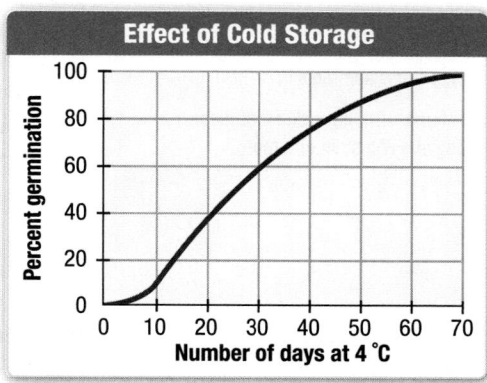

Effect of Cold Storage

Analysis

1. **Summarize** the overall effect of cold temperatures on the germination of apple seeds.

2. **Calculate** the number of weeks that apple seeds must be stored at 4 °C for at least 80% of the seeds to germinate.

3. **CRITICAL THINKING** **Interpreting Graphs** What percentage of seeds germinate after storage at 4 °C for 20 days?

4. **CRITICAL THINKING** **Predicting Patterns** What percentage of apple seeds will germinate after being stored at 4 °C for 80 days?

Meristems

Most seed plants have a body that consists of a vertical shaft from which specialized structures branch, as shown in **Figure 14.** The part of a plant's body that grows mostly upward is called the *shoot,* which consists of stems and leaves. The part of the body that grows downward is called the *root.* The vertical body form results as new cells are made at the tips of the plant body.

❯ **Plants grow by producing new cells in regions of active cell division called meristems. Meristems** are made up of undifferentiated cells that divide and can develop into specialized tissues.

Growth that increases the length or height of a plant is called **primary growth.** The tissues that result from primary growth are *primary tissues.* Many plants also become wider as they grow taller. Growth that increases the width of stems and roots is called **secondary growth.** The tissues that result from secondary growth are *secondary tissues.* After new cells are formed by cell division in meristems, the cells grow and undergo differentiation. Recall from your reading that differentiation is the process by which cells become specialized in form and function.

❯ **Reading Check** *How does primary growth differ from secondary growth?*

Figure 14 Most vascular plants have an above-ground shoot with stems and leaves and an underground root. Growth occurs in regions called *meristems.*

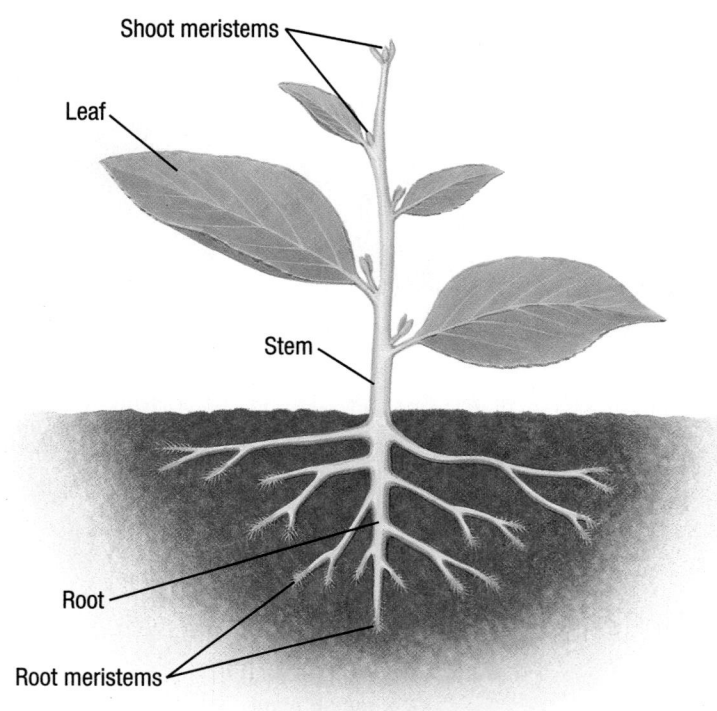

Primary Growth

Apical meristems, which are located at the tips of stems and roots, produce primary growth through cell division. The new cells produced by apical meristems differentiate into the primary tissues of roots, stems, and leaves. As shown in **Figure 15,** apical meristems are regions of small, undifferentiated cells. The plant embryo within a seed contains two apical meristems, one at the tip of the embryonic root and the other at the tip of the embryonic shoot.

To better understand how primary growth occurs in most plants, imagine a stack of dishes. As you add more dishes to the top, the stack grows taller but not wider. Similarly, the cells in the apical meristems of most plants add more cells to the tips of a plant's body. New cells are added through cell division. The cells then lengthen. ❯ Thus, primary growth makes a plant's stems and roots get longer without becoming wider.

Primary growth would end if all of the cells produced by an apical meristem differentiated. Some of the new cells produced in an apical meristem are used to replenish the meristem so that primary growth can continue. Other undifferentiated cells are left behind as stems and roots lengthen. These cells can produce new meristems. New apical meristems are found in *buds* at the base of leaves and within roots. When these apical meristems start dividing, the stem or root branches. Each branch of a stem and each branch of a root has its own apical meristem that produces new primary tissues as the branch grows.

❯ **Reading Check** *How many apical meristems does a plant embryo have?*

apical (AP i kuhl) **meristem** the growing region at the tips of stems and roots in plants

lateral meristem dividing tissue that runs parallel to the long axis of a stem or a root

SCI
LINKS.
www.scilinks.org
Topic: Primary Growth in Plants
Code: HX81215

Figure 15 Both shoot tips and root tips contain apical meristems, where cell division occurs. ❯ **What would happen if all the cells in an apical meristem differentiated?**

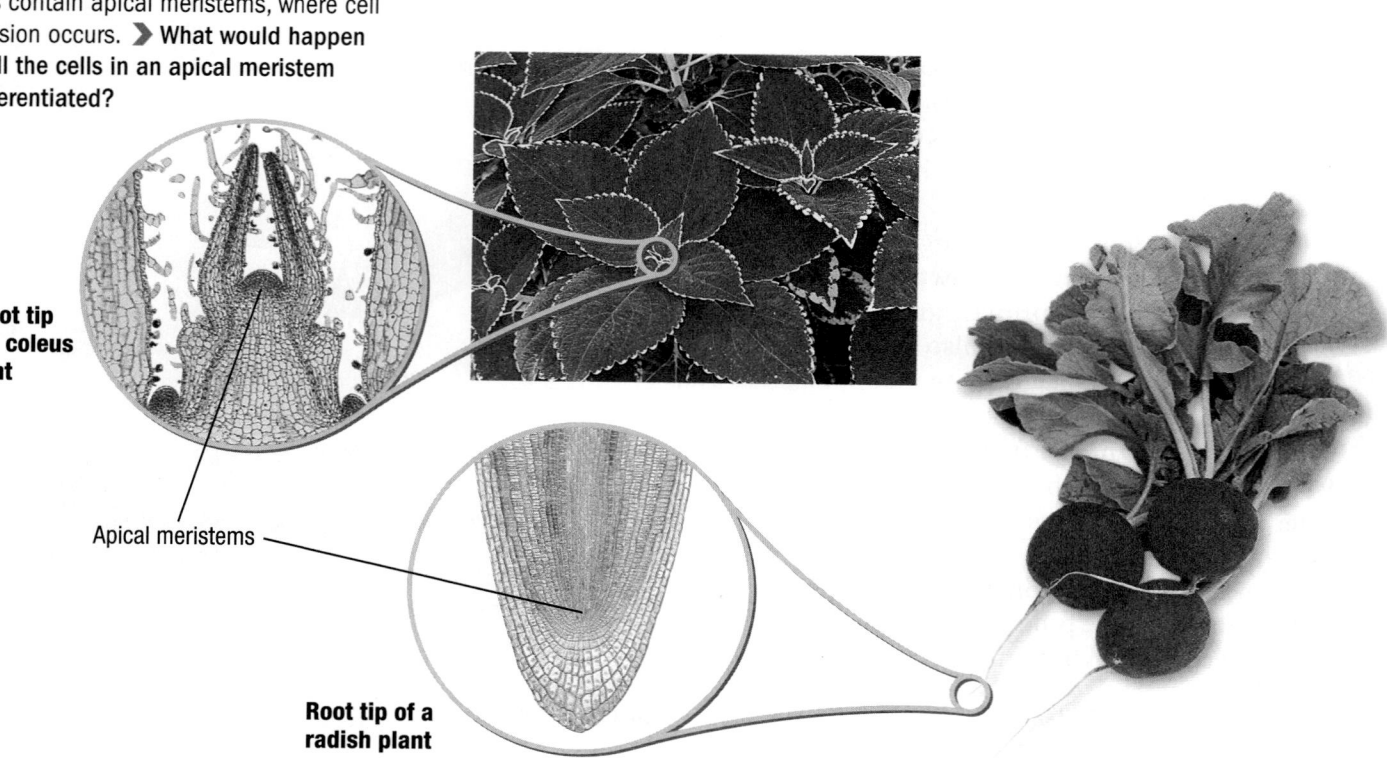

Shoot tip of a coleus plant

Apical meristems

Root tip of a radish plant

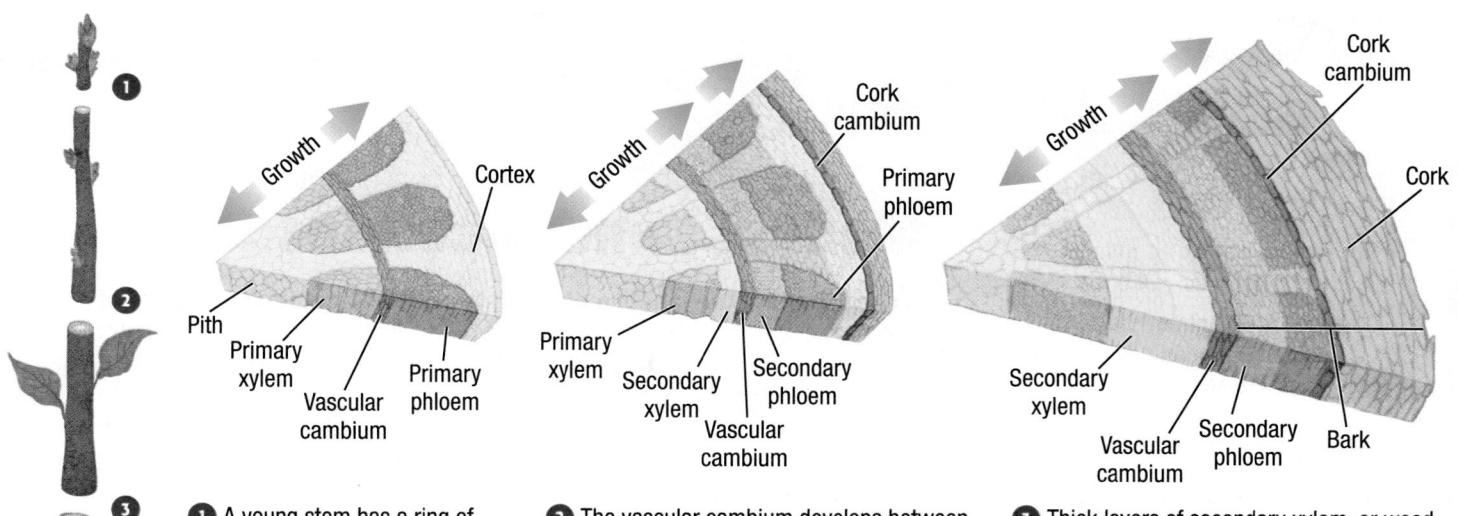

① A young stem has a ring of vascular bundles between the cortex and the pith. Each vascular bundle contains primary xylem and primary phloem.

② The vascular cambium develops between the primary xylem and the primary phloem in each vascular bundle. The cork cambium forms when the epidermis is stretched and broken as the stem grows in diameter.

③ Thick layers of secondary xylem, or wood, often form rings. Because one new ring is usually formed each year, the rings are called *annual rings.*

Figure 16 You can track the development of a woody stem by looking at sequentially older sections of the stem. ❯ **Where in a woody stem does the vascular cambium develop?**

Secondary Growth

Some of the undifferentiated cells that are left behind as stems and roots lengthen produce **lateral meristems.** ❯ **Lateral meristems are responsible for increases in the width of stems and roots. This increase is called** *secondary growth.* Secondary growth occurs in parts of many herbaceous plants, such as in carrot roots. However, it is most dramatic in woody plants. Secondary growth is produced by cell division in two lateral meristems, which form thin cylinders near the outside of woody stems and roots. One meristem, called the *cork cambium,* lies within the bark and produces cork cells. The other meristem, called the *vascular cambium,* lies just under the bark and produces secondary xylem and secondary phloem. **Figure 16** summarizes secondary growth in woody stems.

❯ **Reading Check** *What are the names of the two lateral meristems that are responsible for secondary growth?*

❯ **KEY IDEAS**

1. **Identify** the characteristics of a seed plant embryo.
2. **Summarize** the relationship between meristems and plant growth.
3. **Describe** the process of primary growth, and identify the type of meristem involved.

4. **Explain** how secondary growth increases the width of woody stems.

CRITICAL THINKING

5. **Forming Reasoned Opinions** How might seed dormancy be an evolutionary advantage?
6. **Inferring Conclusions** What would happen to a plant if apical meristems occurred on only one stem and one root of the plant?

ALTERNATIVE ASSESSMENT

7. **Organizing Information** Use library or Internet resources to research bonsai—the Asian art of growing miniature plants. Relate your findings in an illustrated report that explains plant growth and development in bonsai. Present your report to the class.

Chapter 24 **Lab**

Objectives

> Observe the structures of bean seeds and corn kernels.

> Compare and contrast the development of bean embryos as they grow into seedlings.

Materials

- bean seeds, soaked overnight (6)
- stereomicroscope
- corn kernels, soaked overnight (6)
- scalpel
- paper towels
- rubber bands (2)
- beakers, 150 mL (2)
- pen, glass-marking
- ruler, metric

Safety

Monocot and Dicot Seeds

A seed contains an inactive plant embryo. A plant embryo consists of one or more cotyledons, an embryonic shoot, and an embryonic root. Seeds also contain a supply of nutrients. In monocots, the nutrients are contained in the endosperm. In dicots, the nutrients are transferred to the cotyledons as seeds mature. A seed germinates when the embryo begins to grow and breaks through the protective seed coat. The embryo then develops into a young plant, or seedling. In this lab, you will examine bean seeds and corn kernels and then germinate them to observe the development of their seedlings.

Procedure

Observe Seed Structure

1 Remove the seed coat of a bean seed, and separate the two fleshy halves of the seed.

2 Locate the embryo on one of the halves of the seed. Examine the bean embryo with a stereomicroscope. Draw the embryo, and label the parts that you can identify.

3 CAUTION: **Put on goggles before you handle scalpels or glassware. Sharp or pointed objects may cause injury.** Handle scalpels carefully. Examine a corn kernel, and locate a small light-colored oval area. Use a scalpel to cut the kernel in half along the length of this area.

4 Locate the corn embryo, and examine it with a stereomicroscope. Draw the embryo, and label the parts that you can identify.

Observe Seedling Development

5 Fold a paper towel in half. Set five corn kernels on the paper towel.

6 Roll up the paper towel, and put a rubber band around the roll.

7 CAUTION: **Use glass beakers carefully.** Stand the roll in a beaker with 1 cm of water in the bottom.

8 Add water to the beaker as needed to keep the paper towels wet, but do not allow the corn kernels to be covered by water.

9 Repeat step 5 with five bean seeds.

10 After three days, unroll the paper towels, and examine the corn and bean seedlings.

11 Use a glass-marking pen to mark the roots and shoots of the developing seedlings. Starting at the seed, make a mark every 0.5 cm along the root of each seedling. Again, starting at the seed, make a mark every 0.5 cm along the stem of each seedling.

12 Draw a corn seedling and a bean seedling in your lab report. Label the parts of each seedling. Also, show the marks you made on each seedling, and indicate the distance between the marks.

13 Roll up the seeds in a fresh paper towel, place the rolls in the beakers, and add fresh water to the beakers.

14 After two more days, reexamine the seedlings. Measure the distance between the marks. Repeat step 8.

15 ✦ ✦ Clean up your lab materials according to your teacher's instructions. Wash your hands before leaving the lab.

Bean seedlings

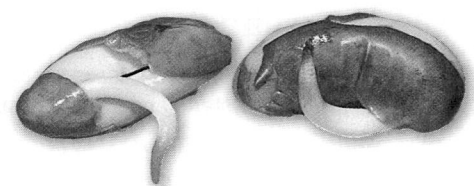

Corn seedlings

Analyze and Conclude

1. **Relating Concepts** Corn and beans are often cited as representative examples of monocots and dicots, respectively. Relate the seed structure of each to the terms *monocotyledon* and *dicotyledon*.

2. **SCIENTIFIC METHODS** **Summarizing Results** What parts of a plant embryo were observed in all seedlings on the third day?

3. **Drawing Conclusions** In which part or parts of bean seedlings and corn seedlings do the seedlings grow in length? Explain.

4. **SCIENTIFIC METHODS** **Forming Hypotheses** How are the tender young shoots of bean seedlings and corn seedlings protected as the seedlings grow through the soil?

5. **Evaluating Viewpoints** Defend the following statement: There are both similarities and differences in seed structure and seedling development in beans and corn.

SciLINKS.
www.scilinks.org
Topic: Seed
          Germination
Code: HX81366

Extensions

6. **Further Inquiry** Write a new question about seedling development that could be explored with another investigation.

7. **Career Connection** Plant physiology is the study of the processes that occur in plants. Do research to discover where plant physiologists work and what types of research are currently being conducted in the field of plant physiology.

go.hrw.com
SUPER SUMMARY
Keyword: HX8PSFS

Key Ideas	Key Terms

1 Plant Tissue Systems

> Vascular plants have three tissue systems—the dermal tissue system, vascular tissue system, and ground tissue system.

> Dermal tissue covers the outside of a plant's body. In the nonwoody parts of a plant, dermal tissue forms a "skin" called the *epidermis.*

> Vascular plants have two kinds of vascular tissue, called *xylem* and *phloem,* that transport water, minerals, and nutrients throughout the plant body.

> Ground tissue makes up much of the inside of most nonwoody plants, where it surrounds and supports vascular tissue.

Key Terms

dermal tissue (573)
vascular tissue (573)
ground tissue (573)
stoma (575)
guard cell (575)
xylem (576)
phloem (576)

2 Roots, Stems, and Leaves

> Most plants are anchored to the spot where they grow by roots, which absorb water and mineral nutrients.

> Stems support the leaves and house the vascular tissue, which transports substances between the roots and the leaves.

> Leaves are the primary photosynthetic organs of plants.

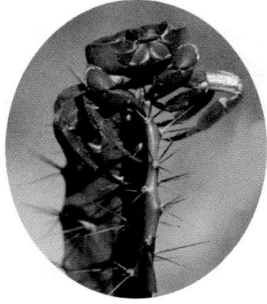

vascular bundle (580)
pith (580)
heartwood (581)
sapwood (581)
blade (582)
petiole (582)
mesophyll (582)

3 Plant Growth and Development

> The plant embryo possesses an embryonic root and an embryonic shoot. Leaflike structures called *cotyledons,* or seed leaves, are attached to the embryonic shoot.

> Plants grow by producing new cells in regions of active cell division called *meristems.*

> Apical meristems are reponsible for primary growth, which makes a plant's stems and roots get longer without becoming wider.

> Lateral meristems are responsible for increases in the width of stems and roots. This increase is called *secondary growth.*

germination (586)
meristem (587)
primary growth (587)
secondary growth (587)
apical meristem (588)
lateral meristem (589)

1. **Cause and Effect** Make a list of changes that may occur that cause seeds to break dormancy and germinate.

2. **Concept Map** Make a concept map that describes the organization of the vascular plant body. Try to include the following terms in your map: *cork, dermal tissue, epidermis, ground tissue, mesophyll, phloem, sieve tubes, tracheids, vascular tissue, vessels,* and *xylem.*

Using Key Terms

In your own words, write a definition for each of the following terms.

3. *vascular tissue*

4. *stomata*

5. *petiole*

6. *meristem*

For each pair of terms, explain how the meanings of the terms differ.

7. *heartwood* and *sapwood*

8. *primary growth* and *secondary growth*

9. *apical meristem* and *lateral meristem*

Understanding Key Ideas

10. Where is dermal tissue normally found in a plant?
    a. within the stem
    b. in the leaves only
    c. covering the outside
    d. in nonwoody plants only

11. Which of the following is *not* a part of the vascular system?
    a. xylem   c. tracheid
    b. phloem   d. stomata

12. Which of the following is the main function of ground tissue in stems and roots?
    a. storing nutrients
    b. moving water up the stem
    c. carrying out photosynthesis
    d. helping stomata open and close

13. Which of the following is a characteristic of herbaceous stems?
    a. They are stiff and woody.
    b. They contain heartwood.
    c. They are covered by cork.
    d. They are flexible and green.

14. What are cotyledons?
    a. embryonic leaves of seeds
    b. stalks that attach leaves to stems
    c. regions of undifferentiated plant cells
    d. protective layers of cells that cover root tips

15. Apical meristems located at the tips of stems and roots produce
    a. no growth.
    b. tertiary growth.
    c. primary growth.
    d. secondary growth.

Explaining Key Ideas

16. **Describe** the function of the cuticle.

17. **Compare** the internal structure of the monocot and dicot nonwoody stem.

18. **Identify** environmental changes that enable seeds to germinate.

The graph shows how storage at low temperatures affected the ability of apple seeds to germinate. Use the graph to answer the following question.

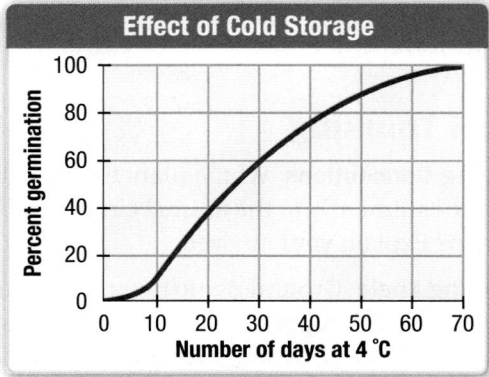

Effect of Cold Storage

19. **Calculate** the number of weeks that apple seeds must be stored at 4 °C for at least 60 percent of the seeds to germinate.

Using Science Graphics

Use the diagram of a leaf cross section to answer the following questions.

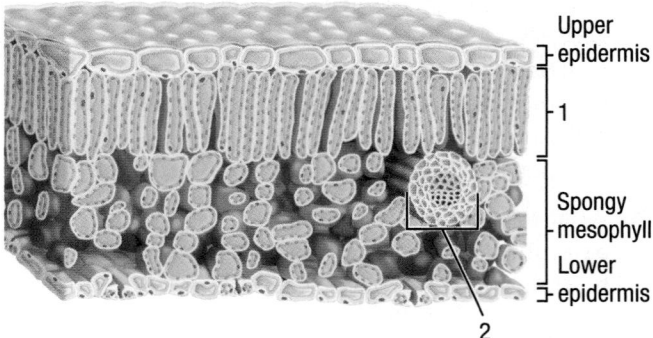

Upper epidermis

1

Spongy mesophyll

Lower epidermis

2

20. Structure 2 is
  a. epidermal tissue.
  b. vascular tissue.
  c. ground tissue.
  d. a strand of heartwood.

21. Which of the following events is likely to occur in structure 2?
  a. gas exchange
  b. manufacture of starch
  c. absorption of sunlight
  d. transport of water, minerals, and sugars

22. Most of the photosynthesis in a leaf occurs in
  a. the upper epidermis.
  b. structure 1.
  c. structure 2.
  d. the spongy mesophyll.

23. Stomata are found in
  a. structure 1.
  b. structure 2.
  c. the spongy mesophyll.
  d. the lower epidermis.

Critical Thinking

24. Making Connections Which plant tissue system functions similarly to the animal circulatory system? Explain your answer.

25. Applying Logic Ground tissue functions in nutrient storage and the support of plants. Ground tissue is made mostly of loosely packed, cube-shaped or elongated cells with a large central vacuole and thin, flexible cell walls. Outline how such a cell shape can aid these functions.

26. Developing Hypotheses The development of a vascular system has allowed vascular plants to grow much larger than nonvascular plants, such as mosses. Develop this hypothesis.

27. Applying Logical Thinking How would the meristems of grasses help them recover from being mowed by people or being grazed by animals?

Why It Matters

28. Making Inferences An unusual leaf modification occurs in carnivorous plants such as the pitcher plant. Pitcher plant leaves function as food traps. The plant receives its mineral nutrients by trapping and digesting insects and small animals. From this information, what can you tell about the type of soil environment in which pitcher plants live? Explain your answer.

29. Researching and Communicating Information Use library or Internet resources to learn about carnivorous plants, such as the Venus' flytrap, the sundew, and the pitcher plant. Prepare an illustrated oral presentation in which you describe the trapping process of each type of plant and the importance of insects to the plants.

Alternative Assessment

30. Using Graphics Skills Create a poster that illustrates the differences between and similarities of nonwoody stems and woody stems. Draw, create images on a computer, or use photos from magazine or online resources to illustrate your poster. Display your poster in the classroom.

31. Evolution in Action Use library or Internet resources to learn about mycorrhizae, the symbiotic relationship between plants and fungi. Prepare a report, poster, or slide presentation in which you explain the nature of the symbiosis and the frequency of this symbiotic relationship in nature. Present your findings to your class.

Science Concepts

1. Which of the following tissues conducts water, minerals, and organic compounds within plants?
   A ground tissue
   B dermal tissue
   C vascular tissue
   D secretory tissue

2. The dermal tissue on woody stems and roots is called
   F sap.
   G skin.
   H cork.
   J cuticle.

3. Grasses have which type of root system?
   A aerial
   B fibrous
   C taproot
   D underground

4. The primary photosynthetic organs of plants are the
   F roots.
   G stems.
   H leaves.
   J flowers.

5. Which of the following phrases describes the structure of a monocot stem?
   A contains vascular bundles that are scattered throughout the ground tissue
   B contains several layers of xylem that are surrounded by a ring of phloem
   C contains a ring of vascular bundles that surrounds a core of ground tissue
   D contains a core of vascular tissue that is surrounded by a ring of ground tissue

6. Primary growth causes
   F seeds to germinate.
   G an increase in the rate of photosynthesis.
   H an increase in the plant's length or height.
   J an increase in the width of stems and roots.

Using Science Graphics

Use the diagram of a seed to answer the following question.

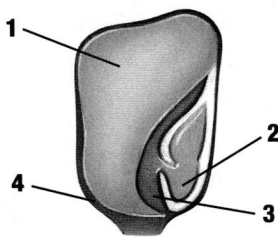

7. Which structure is the embryonic root?
   A 1
   B 2
   C 3
   D 4

Use the graph showing annual tree ring growth to answer the following questions.

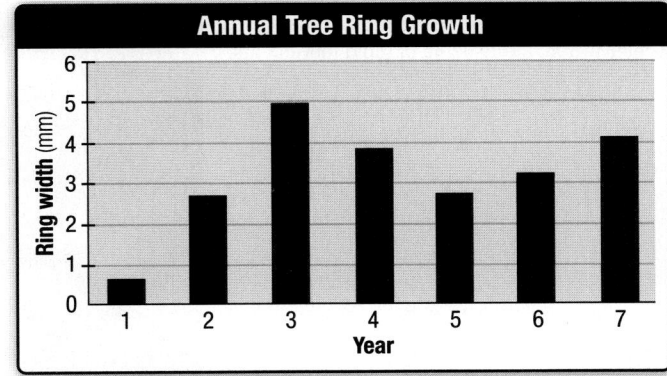

8. Which year showed the greatest growth?
   F 1
   G 3
   H 5
   J 7

9. Which 2 years showed nearly identical growth?
   A 2 and 3
   B 3 and 4
   C 2 and 5
   D 5 and 6

Writing Skills

10. **Short Response** The primary function of leaves is to carry out photosynthesis. Explain how a leaf's structure is an adaptation that allows intake of carbon dioxide with minimal water loss.

Chapter 25

Plant Processes

Preview

1 Nutrients and Transport
Nutrients
Transport of Water
Transport of Organic Compounds

2 Plant Responses
Plant Hormones
Tropisms
Seasonal Responses
Plant Movements

Why It Matters

It may seem like plants just sit around, but they can be very active. Some plants, such as the Venus' flytrap, are capable of rapid movements.

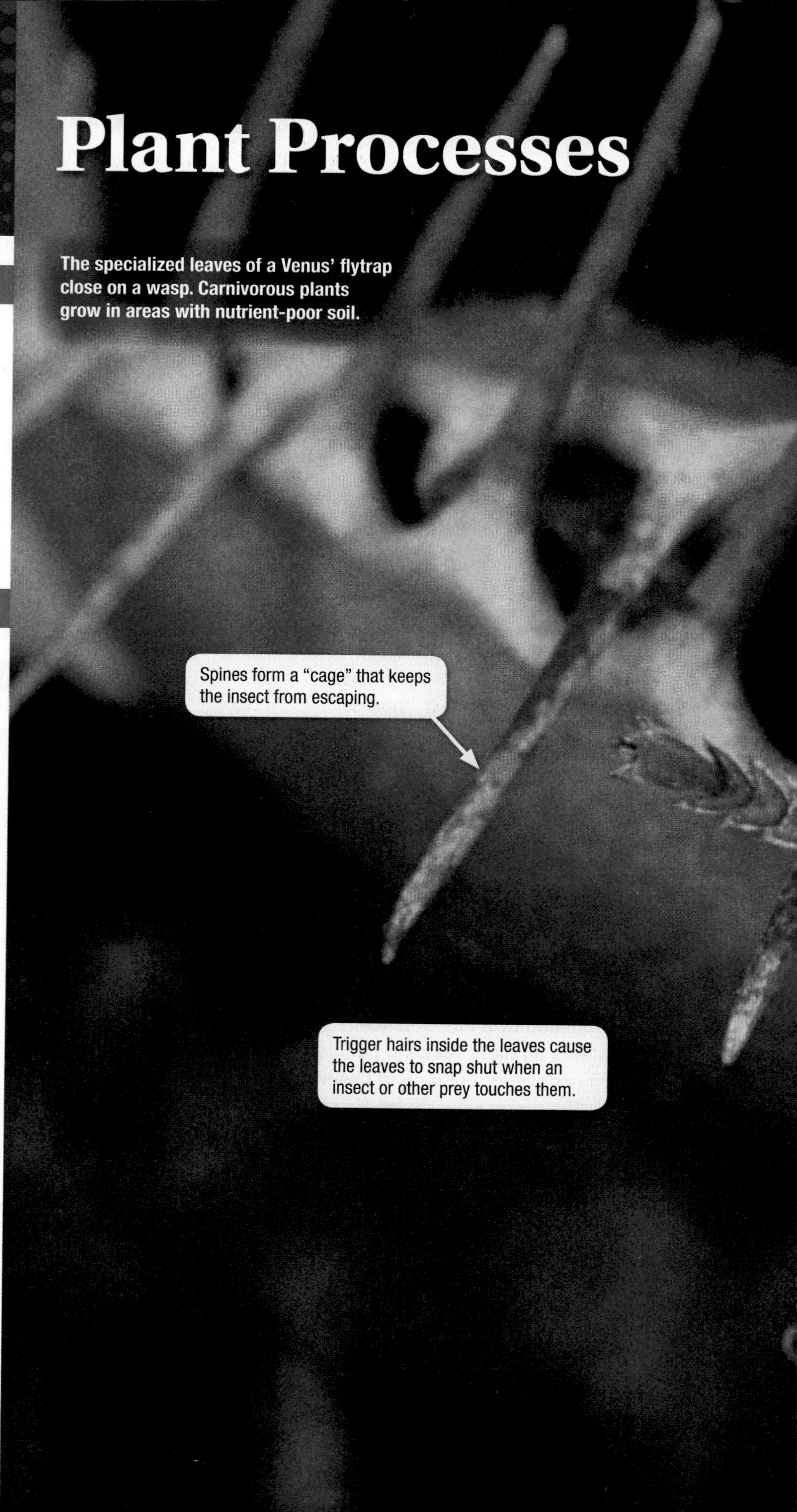

The specialized leaves of a Venus' flytrap close on a wasp. Carnivorous plants grow in areas with nutrient-poor soil.

Spines form a "cage" that keeps the insect from escaping.

Trigger hairs inside the leaves cause the leaves to snap shut when an insect or other prey touches them.

InquiryLab

⏱ 15 min

Capillary Action

In most vascular plants, water enters the plant through the root system. Water is transported upward by the adhesion of water molecules to the vertical surface of vessels in a process called *capillary action*.

Procedure

1. Predict whether capillary action will be stronger in a tube with a smaller or with a larger diameter.

2. Add **water** to a **small dish**. Insert a straight length of **laboratory glass tubing** in the water.

3. Observe the water's behavior. Use a **ruler** to measure the height to which the water rises.

4. Repeat step 2, but this time substitute a **capillary tube** for the length of laboratory glass tubing.

Analysis

1. **Identify** the tube in which the water rose to a greater height.

2. **Propose** a reason for this observed difference.

Digestive juices in the plant break down the insect's soft tissues, which provide nitrogen and other nutrients to the plant.

READING TOOLBOX

These reading tools can help you learn the material in this chapter. For more information on how to use these and other tools, see **Appendix: Reading and Study Skills.**

Using Words

Word Parts Knowing the meanings of word parts can help you figure out the meanings of words you do not know.

Your Turn Use the table to answer the following questions.

1. What does *phototropism* mean?
2. What does *thigmotropism* mean?
3. What does *gravitropism* mean?

Word Parts		
Word part	**Type**	**Meaning**
photo-	prefix	having to do with light
thigmo-	prefix	having to do with touch
gravi-	prefix	having to do with gravity
tropism	root	response to environmental stimuli

Using Language

Describing Space Understanding plant processes involves understanding what's happening inside the plant. When you read about transport within the plant, look for words such as *up* and *down* that indicate where things are moving. This kind of language is called *spatial language* because it describes how things are moving through space.

Your Turn Use spatial language to describe the following processes.

1. A train follows a path over the mountains.
2. Nutrients are transported through a plant.

Using FoldNotes

Tri-Fold A tri-fold can help you discover what you know and what you want to learn about plant processes.

Your Turn Make a tri-fold to help you track what you learn about plant processes in this chapter.

1. Fold a piece of paper in thirds from the top to the bottom.
2. Unfold the paper so that you can see the three columns.
3. In the first column, write what you know about plant processes. In the second column, write what you want to know about plant processes. In the third column, write information that you learn about plant processes.

Nutrients and Transport

Key Ideas	Key Terms	Why It Matters
❯ What substances do plants need, other than water, carbon dioxide, and oxygen, to survive? ❯ How does water move through a vascular plant? ❯ How do organic compounds move through a vascular plant?	transpiration	As plants adapted to land, long-distance transport of water, nutrients, and sugars became more important.

Like all multicellular organisms, plants grow by adding new cells through cell division. In order to grow, plants must have a steady supply of the raw materials they use to build new cells.

Nutrients

Recall that plants are autotrophs—they use energy from sunlight to make organic compounds. Plants need two raw materials, carbon dioxide and water, to make all of the carbohydrates in their tissues. As you learned earlier in this book, plants need carbon dioxide and water for photosynthesis. Plants also need oxygen for cellular respiration. ❯ **However, carbon dioxide, water, and oxygen do not satisfy all of a plant's needs for raw materials. Plants also require small amounts of at least 14 mineral nutrients, which are elements absorbed mainly as inorganic ions.** The six mineral nutrients that plants need in the greatest amounts are listed in **Figure 1**.

❯ **Reading Check** *What two raw materials do plants need to make carbohydrates? (See the Appendix for answers to Reading Checks.)*

Major Mineral Nutrients Required by Plants

Nutrient	Importance
Nitrogen	Part of proteins, nucleic acids, chlorophylls, ATP, and coenzymes; promotes growth of green parts
Phosphorus	Part of ATP, ADP, nucleic acids, phospholipids of cell membranes, and some coenzymes
Potassium	Needed for active transport, enzyme activation, osmotic balance, and stomatal opening
Calcium	Part of cell walls; needed for enzyme activity and membrane function
Magnesium	Part of chlorophyll; needed for photosynthesis and activation of enzymes
Sulfur	Part of some proteins and coenzyme A; needed for cellular respiration

Figure 1 The 6 mineral nutrients that plants need in the greatest amounts are found in most commercial fertilizers. ❯ **Why is magnesium important to plants?**

Transport of Water

Vascular plants obtain the water and mineral nutrients that they need for growth from the soil. ❯ **Water and mineral nutrients move up from a plant's roots to its leaves through xylem.**

Some trees have leaves that are more than 100 m (328 ft) above the ground. How do plants manage to get water so high? Water, as it evaporates from a plant's leaves, is pulled up through the plant. You can see this process in **Figure 2.**

Step ❶ Recall that the surfaces of leaves are covered with many tiny pores, or *stomata*. When the stomata are open, water vapor diffuses out of a leaf. This loss of water vapor from a plant is called **transpiration.** In most plants, more than 90% of the water taken in by the roots is eventually lost through transpiration.

Step ❷ The xylem contains a column of water that extends from the leaves to the roots. The cohesion of water molecules causes water molecules that are being lost by a plant to pull on the water molecules still in the xylem. This pull extends through the water in the xylem. Water is drawn upward in the same way that liquid is drawn through a siphon. As long as the column of water in the xylem does not break, water will keep moving upward as transpiration occurs.

Step ❸ Roots take in water from the soil by osmosis. This water, as it enters the xylem and moves up the stem, replaces the water lost through transpiration.

❯ **Reading Check** *What causes the upward pull on water molecules in xylem?*

READING TOOLBOX

Describing Space Use spatial language to describe the transport of water through a plant.

Figure 2 Transpiration drives the movement of water through a plant.
❯ How does water enter the roots of a plant?

go.hrw.com
✳ **interact online**
Keyword: HX8PGDF2

Water Movement in Plants

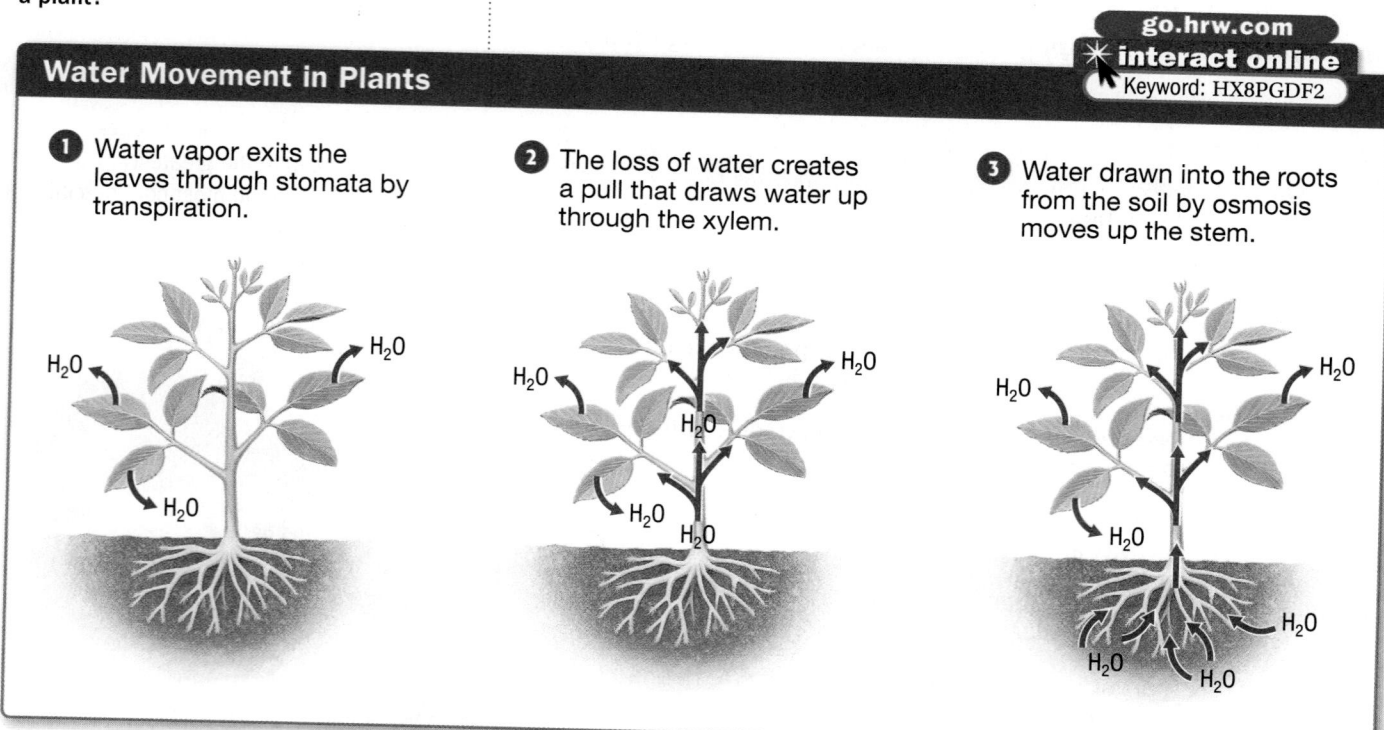

❶ Water vapor exits the leaves through stomata by transpiration.

❷ The loss of water creates a pull that draws water up through the xylem.

❸ Water drawn into the roots from the soil by osmosis moves up the stem.

QuickLab

Transpiration Rate

The graph shows the rate of water movement in a plant during periods of high humidity and of low humidity. The rate of water movement indicates the rate of transpiration. Use the graph to answer the following questions.

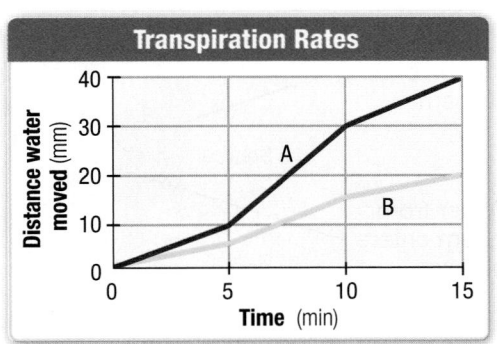

Transpiration Rates

Analysis

1. **Determine** how far the water had moved after 10 min under the condition represented by curve A.

2. **Determine** how far the water had moved after 10 min under the condition represented by curve B.

3. **CRITICAL THINKING** **Analyzing Results** How much farther had the water moved under condition A than under condition B after 15 min?

4. **CRITICAL THINKING** **Recognizing Relationships** Which curve indicates a lower transpiration rate?

5. **CRITICAL THINKING** **Inferring Conclusions** Which curve shows the transpiration rate during low humidity?

Guard Cells and Transpiration A stoma is surrounded by a pair of guard cells that are shaped like two cupped hands. Changes in water pressure within the guard cells cause the stoma to open or close, as **Figure 3** shows. When the guard cells take in water, they swell. However, extra cellulose strands in their cell walls permit the cells to increase in length but not in diameter. As a result, guard cells that take in water bend away from each other. So, the stoma opens, and transpiration proceeds. When water leaves the guard cells, they shorten and move closer to each other. So, the stoma closes, and transpiration stops. Thus, the loss of water from guard cells for any reason causes stomata to close, which stops further water loss.

❯ **Reading Check** *What happens to the guard cells and stoma when the guard cells take in water?*

Figure 3 Changes in the shape of guard cells cause stomata to open or close. ❯ What happens when water leaves the guard cells?

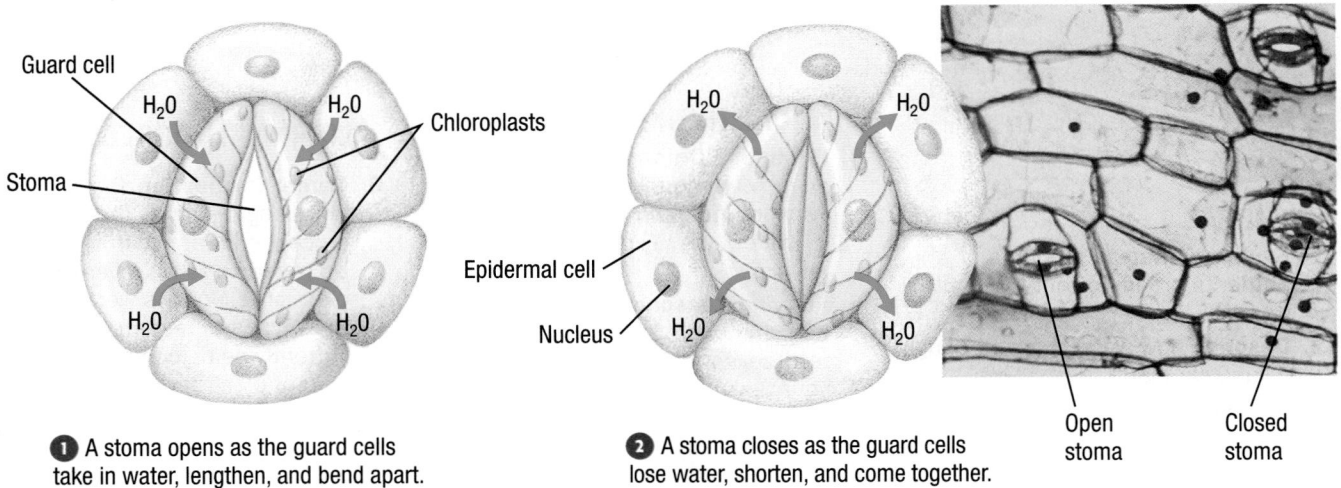

❶ A stoma opens as the guard cells take in water, lengthen, and bend apart.

❷ A stoma closes as the guard cells lose water, shorten, and come together.

Open stoma   Closed stoma

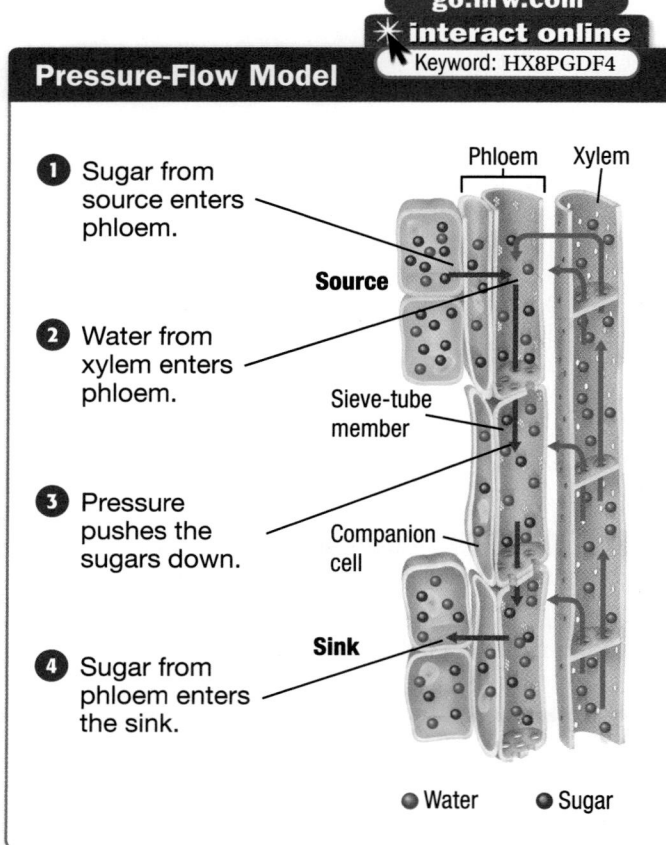

Pressure-Flow Model

go.hrw.com
✳ interact online
Keyword: HX8PGDF4

❶ Sugar from source enters phloem.

❷ Water from xylem enters phloem.

❸ Pressure pushes the sugars down.

❹ Sugar from phloem enters the sink.

Phloem   Xylem

Source

Sieve-tube member

Companion cell

Sink

● Water   ● Sugar

Figure 4 The pressure-flow model shows how organic compounds move in a plant. ❯ What is the term for a plant part to which organic compounds are delivered?

Transport of Organic Compounds

Plants produce organic compounds by the process of photosynthesis, usually within their leaves. ❯ **Organic compounds move through a plant within the phloem from a *source* to a *sink*.** Botanists use the term *source* to refer to a part of a plant that provides organic compounds for other parts of the plant. For example, a leaf is a source because it makes starch during photosynthesis. Botanists use the term *sink* to refer to a part of the plant to which organic compounds are delivered. Actively growing parts, such as root tips and developing fruits, are examples of sinks. Storage tissues, such as the roots of radishes, are also sinks.

Pressure-Flow Model The movement of organic compounds within a plant from a source to a sink is called *translocation.* The movement of organic compounds in a plant is more complex than the movement of water for three reasons. First, water flows freely through dead, empty xylem cells, but organic compounds must pass through the cytoplasm of living phloem cells. Second, water moves upward in xylem, but organic compounds move in all directions in phloem. Third, water can diffuse through cell membranes, but organic compounds cannot. The German botanist Ernst Münch proposed a model of translocation in 1924. **Figure 4** shows Münch's model, the *pressure-flow model.*

❶ Sugar from a source enters phloem cells by active transport. ❷ When the sugar concentration in the phloem increases, water from xylem enters the sieve tubes in phloem by osmosis. ❸ Pressure builds up inside the sieve-tube cells and pushes sugar through the sieve tubes. ❹ Sugar moves from phloem cells into a sink by active transport.

❯ **Reading Check** *What is an example of a sink?*

Section 1 Review

❯ **KEY IDEAS**

1. **Explain** why small amounts of nutrients are important for plant growth.
2. **Describe** how water moves through a vascular plant.
3. **Describe** the transport of organic compounds within a plant.

CRITICAL THINKING

4. **Predicting Outcomes** When the soil is dry and the temperature is very hot, how can a plant reduce its water loss? Explain your answer.
5. **Forming Reasoned Opinions** Why do commercial farmers often add fertilizer to their fields? Justify your reasoning based on the importance of nutrients.

ALTERNATIVE ASSESSMENT

6. **Career Connection** Plant physiologists study the processes that occur in plants. Do research to discover where plant physiologists work and what types of research are currently being conducted in the field of plant physiology.

Key Ideas

❯ Why are hormones important for plant growth and development?

❯ How do tropisms affect plants?

❯ What triggers seasonal change in plants?

❯ How do nastic movements affect plants?

Key Terms

tropism

phototropism

thigmotropism

gravitropism

photoperiodism

dormancy

nastic

movement

Why It Matters

Like animals, plants sense and respond to their environment. Hormones play a central role in plant responses.

Plants can sense changes in the environment and respond to these changes in adaptive ways. Some of these responses are rapid, such as the closing of stomata to conserve water. Other responses are slow, such as the growth of a shoot tip toward light. Plant hormones play an important role in plant responses.

Plant Hormones

A *hormone* is a chemical that is produced in one part of an organism and transported to another part, where it causes a response. ❯ **Plant hormones are produced in small amounts but may have large effects on the growth and development of plants. Hormones may stimulate or inhibit growth in a plant.** The same hormone may have a different effect on different tissues, or it may affect the same tissue in different ways, depending on the stage of development in the tissue. **Figure 5** shows the effect of one kind of hormone on fruit development.

Hormones are also important in plant responses to environmental stimuli. Plant responses often require the transfer of hormones from the part of a plant that detects a change to the part that responds to the change. Five major groups of plant hormones are discussed in this section.

❯ **Reading Check** *What are two ways in which hormones can affect the growth and development of a plant?*

Figure 5 Developing seeds contain the hormone auxin. A normal strawberry is shown at left. If all of the seeds are removed, the strawberry stops developing (center). Growth is inhibited in the area where a narrow band of seeds was removed (right).

Normal strawberry

Strawberry with all seeds removed

Strawberry with band of seeds removed

Auxins For centuries, people have known that plants bend strongly toward a light source as their shoots elongate. In the 1920s, the Dutch biologist Frits Went hypothesized that a chemical produced in the shoot tip of a grass causes this bending response. Went named the growth-promoting chemical that causes stems to bend *auxin*. The steps in Went's experiment are summarized in **Figure 6.**

Step 1 Went removed the tip of an oat shoot and placed the tip on an agar block. Auxin diffused from the tip into the block.

Step 2 Went then transferred the agar block to the cut end of a shoot. The shoot then grew straight upward.

Step 3 When Went placed an agar block containing auxin on either side of cut shoots, the shoots grew in the opposite direction.

Step 4 Went placed an agar block without auxin on the cut end of other shoots as a control. These shoots did not grow.

❯ Reading Check *What happened to the oat shoot when the agar block with auxin was applied to it?*

Figure 6 Frits Went's experiment showed that auxin stimulates cell elongation in oat shoots. **❯** Why does the shoot bend when the agar block with auxin is placed on one side of the cut shoot?

go.hrw.com
✳ **interact online**
Keyword: HX8PGDF6

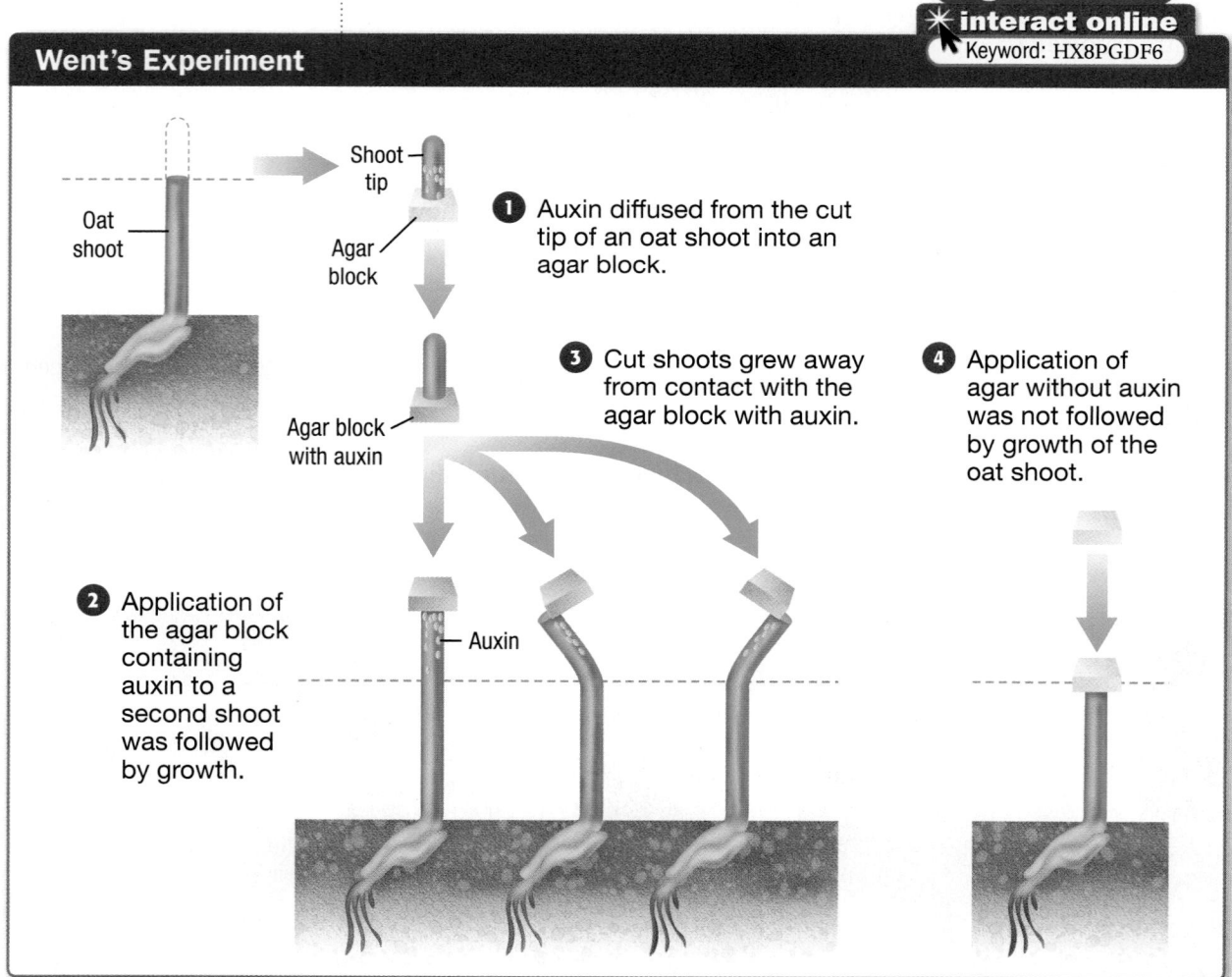

Went's Experiment

Oat shoot

Shoot tip

Agar block

❶ Auxin diffused from the cut tip of an oat shoot into an agar block.

Agar block with auxin

❷ Application of the agar block containing auxin to a second shoot was followed by growth.

Auxin

❸ Cut shoots grew away from contact with the agar block with auxin.

❹ Application of agar without auxin was not followed by growth of the oat shoot.

Gibberellins stimulate grapes to grow larger.

Ethylene causes tomatoes to ripen.

Gibberellins Gibberellins are produced in developing shoots and seeds. They stimulate stem elongation, fruit development, and seed germination. Gibberellins are used commercially to enlarge Thompson seedless grapes, as **Figure 7** shows. Other seedless fruits treated with gibberellins include apples, cucumbers, mandarin oranges, and peaches.

Cytokinins Cytokinins are named for their role in stimulating cell division. Recall that *cytokinesis* is the process during cell division in which the cytoplasm divides. Cytokinins are produced in root tips and other actively growing tissues. Cytokinins may slow the aging of some plant organs. Cytokinins are sprayed on cut flowers to keep them fresh and on fruits and vegetables to extend their shelf life.

Ethylene More than a century ago, citrus farmers discovered that they could cause citrus fruits to ripen by storing them in a room heated by a kerosene stove. The ripening was caused by ethylene, which is a gaseous organic compound produced when kerosene is incompletely burned. Plants, such as the tomatoes shown in **Figure 7,** produce ethylene. Today, ethylene is used commercially to promote the ripening of tomatoes, bananas, and other fruits that are harvested before they ripen. Ethylene also loosens the fruit of blueberries, cherries, and blackberries so that these crops are easier to harvest mechanically.

Abscisic Acid Unlike some other plant hormones, abscisic acid does not act as a growth stimulator but often slows growth in plants. It also plays a role in maintaining dormancy in seeds. Levels of the hormone increase during seed development and prevent germination from occurring too early. Additionally, abscisic acid helps plants withstand drought by causing stomata in leaves to close.

> **Reading Check** *What is one effect of each of the plant hormones discussed in this section?*

Figure 7 Gibberellins are used commercially to enlarge Thompson seedless grapes (left). Ethylene causes the ripening of tomatoes (right) and other fruits. **> How might plant hormones be used in agriculture?**

www.scilinks.org
Topic: Plant Hormones
Code: HX81161

QuickLab

🕐 **15 min**

Effects of Ethylene on a Plant

Ripe apples give off ethylene, a gaseous organic compound. Ethylene affects plants in many ways. You can use a ripe apple to see one of the effects of ethylene on plants.

Procedure

❶ **Place** one plant inside a 4 L plastic jar. Tightly secure the lid.

❷ **Place** a second plant and an apple inside a second 4 L glass jar. Tightly secure the lid.

❸ **Observe** both jars for several days. Record your observations.

Analysis

1. **Describe** any changes in the plant in each jar.

2. **CRITICAL THINKING** **Inferring Conclusions** A ripe apple gives off ethylene gas. Based on your observations, how does ethylene affect a plant?

Figure 8 The growth of these sprouts of flowering shamrock toward a light is an example of positive phototropism. Auxin stimulates the cells on the shaded side of the plant stem to elongate. ❯ **How can growing toward the light benefit a plant?**

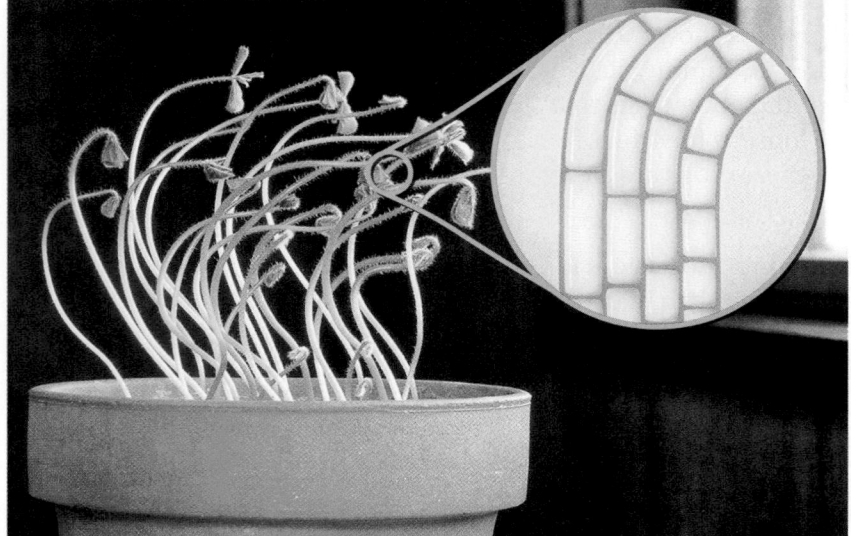

Tropisms

Because most plants are anchored in one spot, they cannot move from an unfavorable environment to a more favorable one, as animals do. Instead, plants respond to their environment by adjusting the rate and pattern of their growth. For example, a plant that receives plenty of water and mineral nutrients may grow much faster and larger than it would if it received very little water and mineral nutrients. Also, a plant grown in full sun may grow much faster and larger than it would if it were grown in the shade or indoors. So, the availability of light and nutrients affects the rate of plant growth. **Tropisms,** a plant's responses to environmental stimuli, are triggered by the hormones that regulate plant growth.

❯ A tropism is a response in which a plant grows toward or away from a stimulus. Plant hormones are responsible for producing tropisms. If a plant grows toward a stimulus, the response is called a *positive tropism.* **Figure 8** shows an example of a positive tropism. If a plant grows away from a stimulus, the response is called a *negative tropism.* Thus, a shoot that grows up out of the ground shows both a positive tropism (growing toward the light) and a negative tropism (growing away from the pull of gravity).

❯ **Reading Check** *What is a negative tropism?*

Heliotropism Sunflowers turn toward the sun as it moves across the sky.

Thigmotropism The tendrils on this grapevine wrap around the wire.

Gravitropism The upward growth of this tree trunk is a negative gravitropism.

Figure 9 Plants respond to environmental stimuli such as light (left), touch (center), and gravity (right).

Phototropism Directional movements in response to light are called **phototropisms.** Shoots usually show positive phototropism by growing toward a light source. Light causes auxin to accumulate on the shaded side of the shoot. Auxin is thought to cause cells to lengthen on the shaded side of the shoot. So, the shoot bends toward the side on which cells are shorter. As a result, the growing shoot bends toward the light.

A leaf can gather more light when the leaf's surface is directed toward the sun. The leaves of some plants track the sun as it moves across the sky. This is called *heliotropism,* or solar tracking. Leaves benefit from heliotropism because the light that is available for photosynthesis increases. Some plants have flowers that track the sun, such as the sunflowers shown in **Figure 9.** The advantage to flowers of tracking the sun is not clear. Some botanists think that warmer flowers may be more attractive to insects that carry pollen.

Thigmotropism Growth responses to touch are called **thigmotropisms.** Tendrils or stems of climbing plants bend when they touch an object. Touch appears to cause changes in the elasticity of cell walls. These changes may be regulated by auxin. A vine that climbs the stem of another plant can grow higher more rapidly because the vine does not need to support its own weight. Instead, the vine exploits the supporting tissues of the other plant. By this means, some vines are able to grow from shade to the high light levels at the tops of trees without having to grow thick stems.

Gravitropism Responses to gravity are called **gravitropisms.** Gravitropisms appear to be regulated by the accumulation of auxins on the lower sides of stems and roots. In stems, auxins cause increased cell elongation on the lower side. As a result, the stems bend up. In roots, auxins cause reduced cell elongation on the lower side, so the roots bend down. This example shows that different cells can respond to the same hormone in different ways.

READING TOOLBOX

Word Parts Use what you know about word parts to write a definition of the word *heliotropism.*

tropism (TROH PIZ uhm) the movement of all or part of an organism in response to an external stimulus

phototropism a plant growth movement that occurs in response to the direction of a source of light

thigmotropism a response of an organism or part of an organism to touch, such as the coiling of a vine around an object

gravitropism the growth of a plant in a particular direction in response to gravity

Seasonal Responses

In seasonal climates, some times of year are better for growing than others. Many responses to the seasons have evolved in plants. For example, many trees shed their leaves in fall and grow new leaves in spring. A tree that produces its new leaves too soon may lose them in a frost. But a tree that waits too long will have less time to grow. Timing is important. ❯ **The principal way in which plants time seasonal responses is by sensing changes in night length.**

Photoperiodism Certain plants bloom in the spring, and others bloom in the summer or fall. In many plants, seasonal patterns of flowering and other aspects of growth and development are caused by changes in the length of days and nights. The response of a plant to the length of days and nights is called **photoperiodism.**

In reference to photoperiodism, most plants can be <u>categorized</u> as one of three types. A plant that responds when days become shorter than a certain number of hours is a *short-day plant*. A plant that responds when days become longer than a certain number of hours is a *long-day plant*. Plants whose growth and development are not affected by day length are known as *day-neutral plants*. However, the length of the nights rather than the length of the days controls photoperiodism, as **Figure 10** shows.

Knowledge of photoperiodism is very important to the nursery and floral industries. The length of days and nights is controlled artificially in greenhouses where plants such as chrysanthemums and poinsettias are grown. Commercial growers force the plants to produce flowers at times of the year when they ordinarily would not. So, flowering chrysanthemums and poinsettias are now available year-round.

❯ **Reading Check** *What are plants whose growth is not affected by day length called?*

ACADEMIC VOCABULARY

categorize to put into groups or classes

Figure 10 Long-day plants flower when nights are short. Short-day plants flower when nights are long. If a flash of light interrupts a long night, long-day plants flower and short-day plants do not. ❯ **Why is knowledge of photoperiodism important to the nursery industry?**

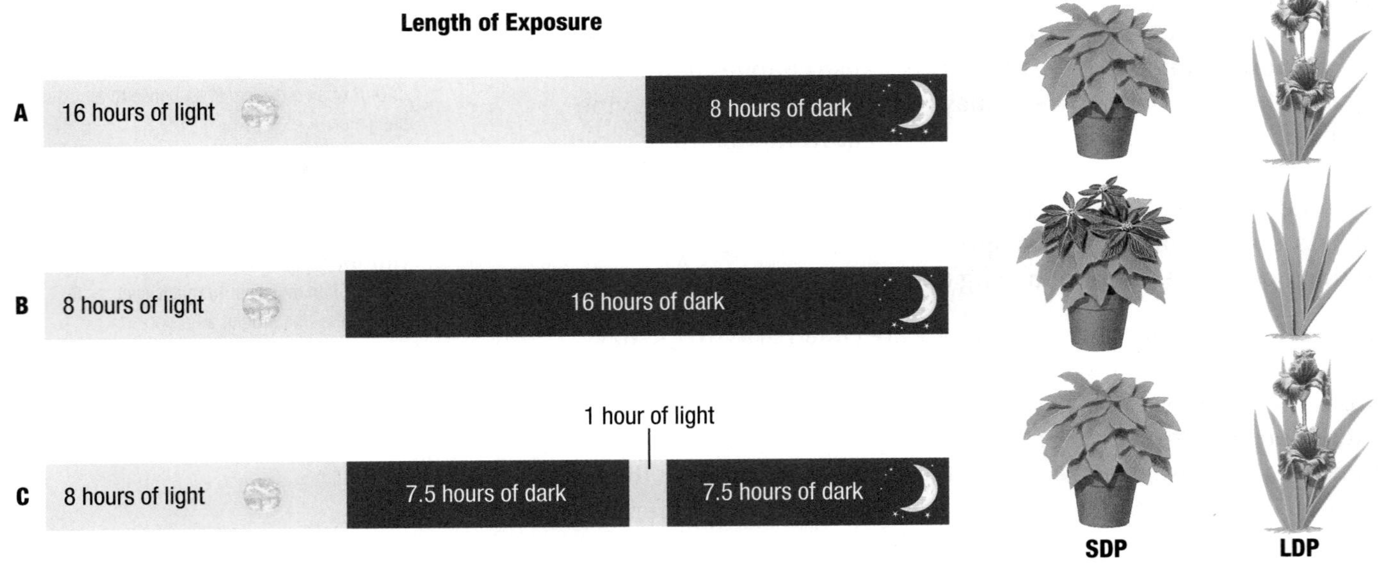

Length of Exposure

A 16 hours of light   8 hours of dark

B 8 hours of light   16 hours of dark

1 hour of light

C 8 hours of light   7.5 hours of dark   7.5 hours of dark

SDP   LDP

Quick**Lab**

Seed Dormancy and Germination

In some plants, a period of low temperatures is needed to break seed dormancy. When dormancy is broken, seeds can germinate. The graph shows how storage at a low temperature (4 °C) affected the ability of apple seeds to germinate. Use the graph to answer the following questions.

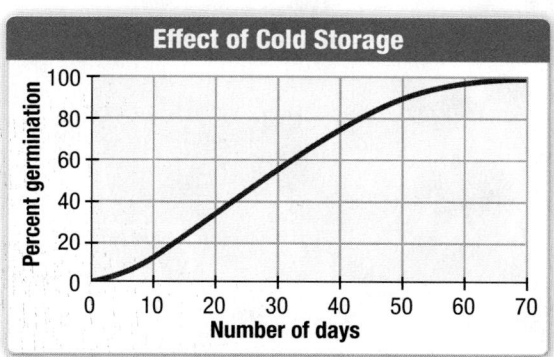

Effect of Cold Storage

Analysis

1. **Summarize** the overall effect of cold temperatures on the germination of apple seeds.

2. **Calculate** the number of weeks that apple seeds must be stored at 4 °C for at least 80% of the seeds to germinate.

3. **Determine** the percentage of apple seeds that germinated after being stored at 4 °C for 20 days.

4. **CRITICAL THINKING** **Predicting Patterns** What percentage of apple seeds will germinate after being stored at 4 °C for 80 days?

Responses to Temperature Temperature affects growth and development in many plants. For example, most tomato plants will not produce fruit if nighttime temperatures are too high. Many plants that flower in early spring will not produce flowers until the plants are exposed to cold temperatures for a certain number of hours. Most deciduous woody plants drop their leaves in the fall in response to cooler temperatures and shorter periods of daylight. Thick, protective scales develop around their buds, as **Figure 11** shows. After a period of low temperatures, the buds begin growing into new leaves or sections of woody stem.

Dormancy is the condition in which a plant or a seed remains inactive, even when conditions are suitable for growth. Many plants and seeds remain dormant until they have been exposed to low temperatures for at least several weeks. Dormancy helps plants survive by keeping buds from growing and seeds from germinating during warm periods before winter has ended.

photoperiodism the response of plants to seasonal changes in the relative length of nights and days

dormancy a state in which seeds, spores, bulbs, and other reproductive organs stop growth and development and reduce their metabolism, especially respiration

Figure 11 Thick scales cover the dormant buds on this twig. ❯ **What would happen to the plant if the buds were not protected?**

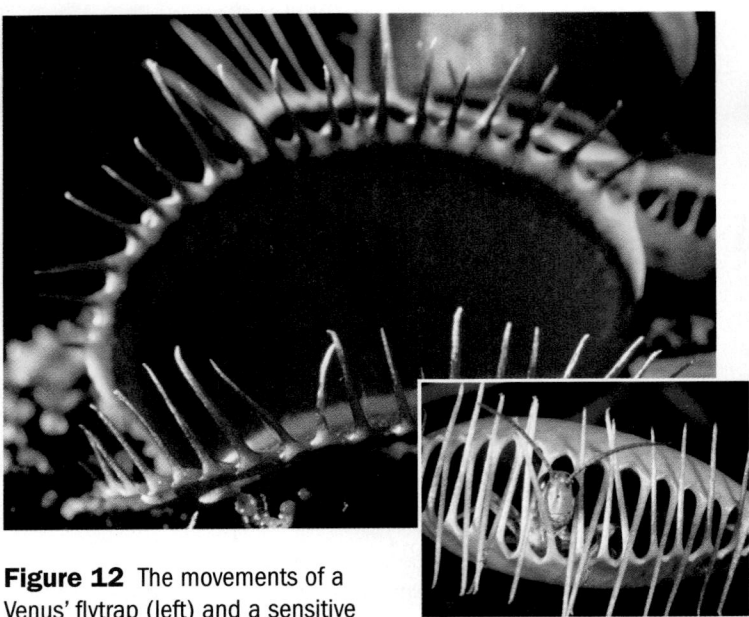

Figure 12 The movements of a Venus' flytrap (left) and a sensitive plant (right) are called *nastic movements*. ❯ **How could the closing of a sensitive plant's leaves benefit the plant?**

nastic movement a type of plant response that is independent of the direction of a stimulus

Plant Movements

Recall that tropisms are plant movements in which a part of a plant bends toward or away from a stimulus. Tropisms usually require changes in cell elongation or cell division. ❯ **Some plant movements respond to an environmental stimulus but are not influenced by the direction of the stimulus.** These movements are called **nastic movements.** Nastic movements are usually regulated by changes in the water content of special cells. The shape of these cells changes in response to changes in the water pressure against their cell wall. Examples of nastic movements include the rapid closing of the leaves of a Venus' flytrap to trap an insect and the closing of the leaves of a sensitive plant, as **Figure 12** shows. Some plants have flowers that open only in the morning, at midday, or at night. These nastic movements may allow a plant to "choose" its pollinators.

❯ **Reading Check** *How are nastic movements regulated at the cellular level?*

Section 2 Review

❯ KEY IDEAS

1. **Describe** how hormones affect the growth and development of plants.
2. **Define** *tropism,* and give an example of a positive tropism.
3. **Name** the principal factor affecting seasonal responses in plants.
4. **Define** *nastic movements,* and describe how they differ from tropisms.

CRITICAL THINKING

5. **Predicting Outcomes** Why is it an advantage for plant growth and development to be regulated by environmental stimuli?
6. **Inferring Relationships** The growth of most deciduous trees in the northern United States, where winters are severe, is regulated strictly by photoperiodism. That is, temperature plays no part in the regulation of the trees' yearly growing cycle. Explain why this fact is ecologically significant.

METHODS OF SCIENCE

7. **Evaluating Results** A student placed a green banana in each of 10 plastic bags. The student also placed a ripe pear in 5 of the bags and then sealed all of the bags. The bananas in the bags without pears took longer to ripen than the bananas in the bags with pears. Evaluate these experimental results.

Plants in Space

Life on Earth would be impossible without plants. Plants affect our lives every day. They supply oxygen for us to breathe, fibers for clothing, wood for houses, and food for us to eat. Scientists are experimenting with plants in space. But growing plants in space is not easy. How do scientists help plants cope with the rigors of space travel?

BIOTECHNOLOGY

A Different Environment

On Earth, plants get light and the materials they need to grow from their natural environment. In space, scientists must recreate an environment that fosters plant growth. Far away from Earth and without gravity, these plants must be provided with water, nutrients, and the proper kind of light.

To help both the plants and the humans aboard the International Space Station, scientists have experimented with a system that integrates the needs of the plants with the needs of the astronauts. Astronauts generate waste, such as wastewater and carbon dioxide. In the Advanced Life Support (ALS) system, this waste is used to provide plants with the substances they need to grow. In return, the plants provide food, oxygen, clean water, and waste removal for the astronauts.

Hydroponics This scientist is checking the growth of radishes being grown using hydroponic techniques. This type of research is important for future long-term space exploration.

Research Hydroponic gardening provides a solution of water and nutrients to the roots of plants, which eliminates the need for soil. Research the ancient history of this method of gardening, and write a brief report on it.

Chapter 25 **Lab**

Objectives

❯ Compare hydroponic plant-cultivation with conventional plant-cultivation techniques.

❯ Observe the germination of wheat seeds over a two-week period.

Materials

- pen, marking
- tape, labeling
- clear plastic cups (2)
- potting soil, 50 mL
- wheat seeds (12)
- plastic-foam floater that has 6 evenly spaced holes
- water, distilled, 10 mL
- graduated cylinder, 50 mL
- complete nutrient solution, 50 mL
- cheesecloth, large enough to cover the plastic-foam floater
- dropper, plastic
- ruler, metric

Safety

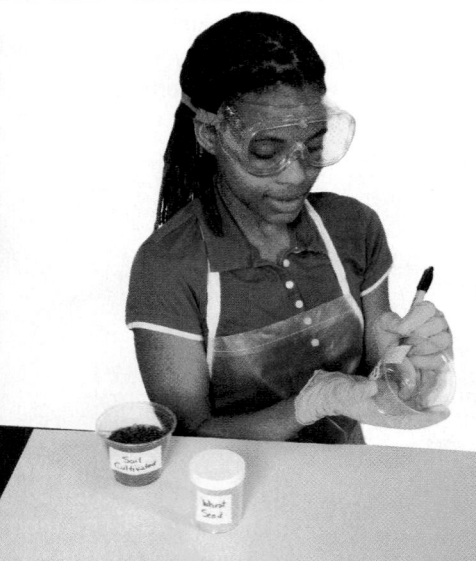

Cultivation Techniques

Hydroponic cultivation is a technique for growing plants in a solution that contains all of the inorganic nutrients that the plant needs. Plants that are grown hydroponically do not require soil. The beginning of growth in a seed is called *germination.* In this lab, you will compare plants grown hydroponically with plants grown in soil.

Procedure

Day 1

1 ✦ ✦ ✦ Put on a lab apron, safety goggles, and disposable gloves.

2 Using the marking pen and the labeling tape, label one plastic cup "Soil cultivated," and label the other plastic cup "Hydroponically cultivated."

3 Fill the cup labeled "Soil cultivated" halfway with moist potting soil. Place six wheat seeds on the surface of the soil; use the distance between the holes in the foam floater as a guide to determine the spacing of the wheat seeds. (Do not place the floater on the soil.)

4 Press the seeds into the soil until they are approximately 0.5 cm below the surface. Cover the seeds with soil, and press down firmly.

5 Water the seeds with 10 mL of distilled water.

6 Add 50 mL of complete nutrient solution to the cup labeled "Hydroponically cultivated," and place the plastic-foam floater on the surface of the solution.

7 Place the cheesecloth on top of the floater. Press lightly at the location of the holes in the floater to moisten the cheesecloth.

8 Place the remaining six wheat seeds on top of the cheesecloth in the cup labeled "Hydroponically cultivated." Position the seeds so that each one lies in an indentation formed by the cheesecloth in a hole in the floater. Press each seed lightly into the hole until the seed coat is moistened.

9 Place both cups in a warm, dry location. Water the soil-cultivated seeds as needed, and monitor the amount of water added. Aerate the roots of the hydroponic plants every day by using a clean plastic dropper to blow air into the nutrient solution.

10 In your lab report, prepare data tables similar to the ones on the next page. Write your observations of the seeds in your data tables.

11 ✦ ✦ Clean up your lab materials according to your teacher's instructions. Wash your hands before leaving the lab.

Observations of Soil-Grown Plants		
Day	Appearance of seedlings	Average height (mm)
1		
2		
3		
4		
5		

Observations of Hydroponically Grown Plants		
Day	Appearance of seedlings	Average height (mm)
1		
2		
3		
4		
5		

Days 2–14

12 Compare the contents of each cup every day for two weeks, and record the appearance of the wheat seedlings in your data tables. If you are unable to observe your seedlings over the weekend, be sure to note in your data tables that no observations were made on those days.

13 Each time that you observe the seedlings after they have begun to grow, measure their height and record in your data tables the average height of the seedlings in each cup. To find the average height for one cup, add the heights of each seedling in the cup together and divide by the number of seedlings.

14 After the seeds in the cup containing nutrient solution have germinated and formed roots, allow an air pocket to form between the floater and the surface of the nutrient solution. A portion of the roots should still be submerged in the nutrient solution. The air pocket allows the roots of the seeds to absorb the oxygen necessary for metabolic processes while continuing to absorb nutrients from the nutrient solution. Continue to observe and record the progress of the seedlings in each cup on a daily basis.

15 ♦ ☜ Clean up your lab materials according to your teacher's instructions. Wash your hands before leaving the lab.

Analyze and Conclude

1. **Analyzing Data** Based on the data that you recorded, which seeds germinated more quickly? Which seeds grew taller?

2. **SCIENTIFIC METHODS** **Analyzing Results** Compare your results with those of your classmates. Were the results the same for each group?

3. **SCIENTIFIC METHODS** **Analyzing Methods** Why do you think that you were instructed to plant six seeds instead of a single seed in each cup? Why is the use of more than one sample important?

Extensions

4. **Further Inquiry** The nutrient solution that you used in this investigation should have provided all of the inorganic nutrients that the wheat seeds needed for proper growth. How could you determine, by using hydroponic cultivation, exactly which inorganic nutrients a plant requires?

go.hrw.com
SUPER SUMMARY
Keyword: HX8PGDS

Key Ideas	Key Terms

1 Nutrients and Transport

> Carbon dioxide, water, and oxygen do not satisfy all of a plant's needs for raw materials. Plants also require small amounts of at least 14 mineral nutrients, which are elements absorbed mainly as inorganic ions.

> Water and mineral nutrients move up from a plant's roots to its leaves through xylem.

> Organic compounds move through a plant within the phloem from a source to a sink.

transpiration (600)

2 Plant Responses

> Plant hormones are produced in small amounts but may have large effects on the growth and development of plants. Hormones may stimulate or inhibit growth in a plant.

> A tropism is a response in which a plant grows toward or away from a stimulus. Plant hormones are responsible for producing tropisms.

> The principal way in which plants time seasonal responses is by sensing changes in night length.

> Some plant movements respond to an environmental stimulus but are not influenced by the direction of the stimulus. These movements are called *nastic movements.*

tropism (606)
phototropism (607)
thigmotropism (607)
gravitropism (607)
photoperiodism (608)
dormancy (609)
nastic movement (610)

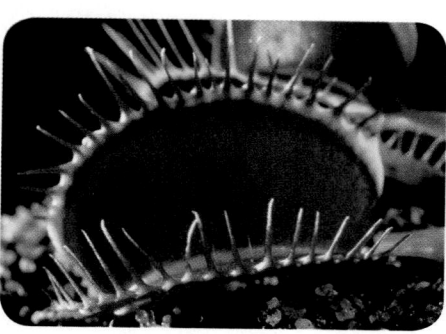

1. **Word Parts** *Photoperiodism* is a seasonal response of plants. Using the meaning of the word parts, state the principal factor affecting this response.

2. **Concept Map** Use the following terms to create a concept map that shows the major effects of some plant hormones: *auxin, cytokinin, gibberellin, gravitropism, plant hormone, phototropism,* and *thigmotropism.*

Using Key Terms

In your own words, write a definition for each of the following terms:

3. *transpiration*

4. *tropism*

5. *dormancy*

6. *nastic movement*

For each pair of terms, explain how the meanings of the terms differ.

7. *phototropism* and *photoperiodism*

8. *thigmotropism* and *gravitropism*

Understanding Key Ideas

9. Major mineral nutrients required by plants include all of the following except
   a. lead.
   b. nitrogen.
   c. potassium.
   d. phosphorus.

10. The column of water in a plant's xylem can remain unbroken because of the
   a. stiff fibers in the bark.
   b. strong walls in the xylem.
   c. cohesion of water molecules.
   d. repulsion between water molecules.

11. Auxin causes cells to
   a. develop lateral buds.
   b. bend away from light.
   c. have less flexible cell walls.
   d. elongate more as they grow.

12. When a vine reponds to the touch of a fence wire by growing a tendril around the wire, the vine is exhibiting
   a. gravitropism.
   b. phototropism.
   c. thigmotropism.
   d. photoperiodism.

13. The response of a plant to the length of days and nights is
   a. gravitropism.
   b. phototropism.
   c. thigmotropism.
   d. photoperiodism.

Use the diagram to answer the following questions.

Condition 1   **Condition 2**

Guard cell

Stoma

Epidermal cells

14. What caused the change from condition 1 to condition 2?
   a. Sugar moved into the stoma.
   b. Sugar moved into the guard cells.
   c. Water moved out of the guard cells.
   d. Water moved out of the epidermal cells.

15. How is the change from condition 1 to condition 2 beneficial to the plant?
   a. It promotes water transport.
   b. It reduces water loss from the plant.
   c. It prevents the plant from overheating.
   d. It stops the loss of sugar from the plant.

Explaining Key Ideas

16. **Describe** how translocation occurs in plants.

17. **Explain** how auxin causes a stem to grow toward a light source.

18. **Describe** an example of a negative gravitropism.

Using Science Graphics

Use the diagram showing three different growing conditions to answer the following question.

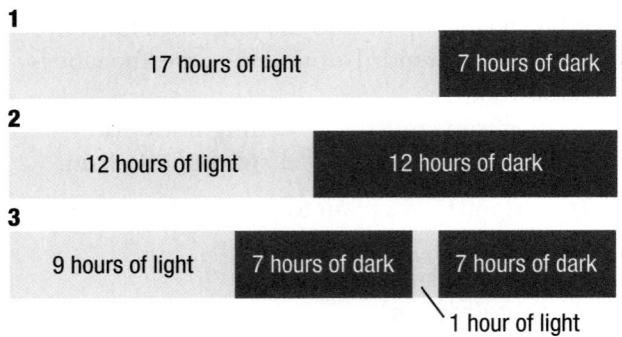

1

| 17 hours of light | 7 hours of dark |

2

| 12 hours of light | 12 hours of dark |

3

| 9 hours of light | 7 hours of dark | 7 hours of dark |

1 hour of light

19. In which of the conditions is a long-day plant most likely to flower?

    a. 1   **c.** 1 and 3

    b. 2   **d.** 2 and 3

Critical Thinking

20. Inferring Function When a plant wilts, its stomata close. How does wilting help a plant maintain homeostasis?

21. Evaluating Differences What adaptive advantages might the dead cells of xylem tissue provide over transporting cells that are alive?

22. Applying Information Why would an agricultural practice that eliminated transpirational water loss be disadvantageous to plants?

23. Predicting Results Would you expect a plant that had its shoot tip removed to exhibit phototropism? Why or why not?

24. Inferring Relationships Why aren't nastic movements regulated by hormones?

25. Evaluating Results Suppose that a friend who lives in North Dakota gives you a cutting from a flowering plant growing in his yard. You plant the cutting at your home in Georgia. The plant grows but does not produce flowers. Based on your knowledge of plant responses, what might be preventing the plant from flowering?

Why It Matters

26. Forming Reasoned Opinions Imagine trying to grow plants on a spacecraft or on the International Space Station. Many plants take up a lot of room. There is not much room in a spacecraft. What measures might scientists take to grow plants in space with little room?

27. Applying Information Scientists are experimenting with growing plants in space hydroponically. Without gravity, however, you cannot have water in open containers. In space, the water would leave the open container and float in the air. How might scientists provide water to plants without gravity?

Writing for Science

28. Finding and Communicating Information Use Internet resources to learn how commercial growers produce plants such as poinsettias and chrysanthemums that flower at times when they would not flower in nature. Summarize your findings in a written report.

29. Career Connection Agronomists study soil management and crop production. Write a report that includes a job description, training required, kinds of employers, growth prospects, and starting salary for an agronomist.

Alternative Assessment

30. Finding and Communicating Information Use library or Internet resources to find information about nastic movements in plants. Research different plant species that exhibit nastic movements, such as the Venus' flytrap, sensitive plant, and prayer plant. Summarize your findings in a poster that shows examples of these plants. Be sure to include information about the types of movements that occur and the adaptive advantages that these movements might provide a plant.

> **TEST TIP** If you are unsure of an answer, try to eliminate the answers that you know are wrong before choosing your response.

Science Concepts

1. Which of the following raw materials is *not* needed for plant growth?

  A water

  B oxygen

  C vitamins

  D carbon dioxide

2. Guard cells swell and become longer when

  F water moves into the cells.

  G oxygen moves into the cells.

  H water moves out of the cells.

  J carbon dioxide moves out of the cells.

3. Organic compounds move through phloem

  A by diffusion from a sink to a source.

  B by active transport within a sieve tube.

  C by diffusion from the leaves to the roots.

  D by the pressure created by the movement of water into the sieve tubes.

4. Which of the following plays a role in cell division in plants?

  F auxins

  G ethylene

  H cytokinins

  J abscisic acid

5. A thigmotropism is a response to

  A light.   **C** gravity.

  B touch.   **D** temperature.

6. Which statement describes the relationship between nastic movements and a stimulus?

  F Nastic movements occur toward a stimulus.

  G Nastic movements occur without a stimulus.

  H Nastic movements occur away from a stimulus.

  J Nastic movements occur independently of the direction of the stimulus.

Using Science Graphics

Use the graph to answer the following question.

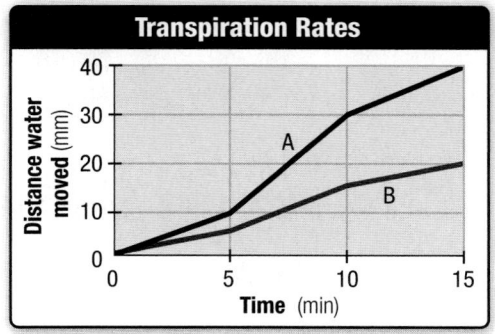

7. How far did water move after 5 min under the condition represented by curve A?

  A 5 mm   **C** 15 mm

  B 10 mm   **D** 20 mm

Use the diagram of a growing seedling to answer the following question.

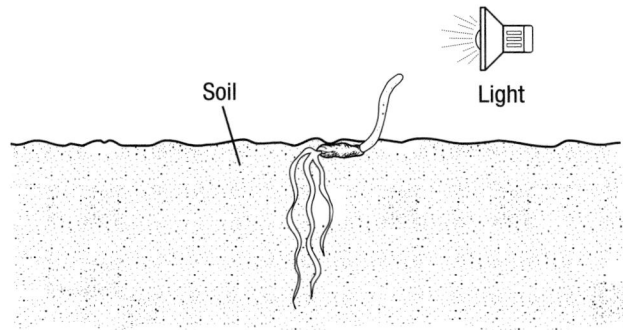

8. Which statement about this seedling is true?

  F The shoot is exhibiting negative phototropism.

  G The shoot is exhibiting positive phototropism.

  H The roots are exhibiting negative gravitropism.

  J The seedling is exhibiting negative thigmotropism.

Writing Skills

9. Extended Response A stem contains tissues that transport water, dissolved minerals, and sugars. Identify the cells that transport water, and describe how water moves through a plant. Identify the cells that transport sugar, and describe how sugars move through a plant.

UNIT 8 Animals

26 Introduction to Animals

27 Simple Invertebrates

28 Mollusks and Annelids

29 Arthropods and Echinoderms

30 Fishes and Amphibians

31 Reptiles and Birds

32 Mammals

33 Animal Behavior

Fish-eating anemone

Dog's eye

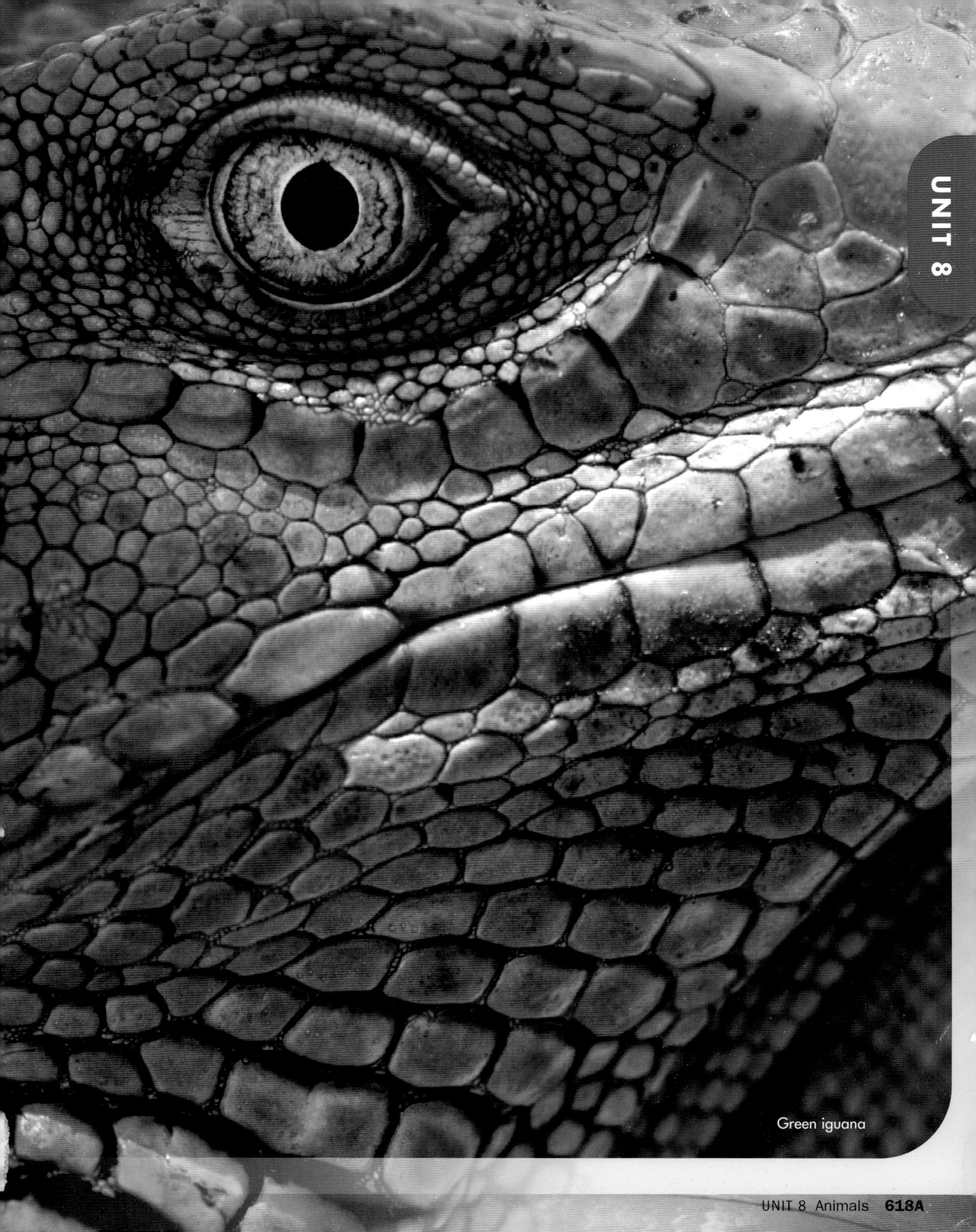

Green iguana

DISCOVERIES IN SCIENCE

Animals

350 BCE

Aristotle writes *Historia Animalium,* or "The History of Animals." The book categorizes animals by their mode of locomotion—flying, swimming, or walking.

Aristotle

1693 CE

The dodo, *Raphus cuculla-tus,* a large, flightless bird on the island of Mauritius, becomes extinct less than 100 years after its discovery. Reasons for the dodo's extinction include destruction of habitat by humans and predation by dogs and cats that were introduced to the island by explorers.

1827

John James Audubon publishes the first of four volumes of *Birds of North America.* Each set of books contains 435 hand-colored, life-size prints of birds.

Audubon print of Northern Cardinal

1860

Amos Root publishes plans for a radically new kind of honeybee hive. The hive uses carefully spaced frames that can be easily disassembled without upsetting the colony. Beekeeping becomes much more efficient and profitable.

1938

While investigating a pile of fish caught off the coast of South Africa, Marjorie Courtenay-Latimer, a museum curator, discovers a coelacanth. Coelacanths are a type of lobe-finned fish. This discovery disproves the theory that coelacanths have been extinct for 65 million years.

1960

Jane Goodall begins her study of chimpanzees in Tanzania. Among her many contributions to the field of primatology is the discovery that chimpanzees can make and use tools.

Jane Goodall with young chimpanzee

1965

Tu'i Malila, a female radiated tortoise estimated to be 188 years old, dies in Tonga. Tu'i Malila had been a gift to the royal family of Tonga by the explorer James Cook in 1777, and she lived with the royal family until her death.

1973

Konrad Lorenz earns the Nobel Prize in physiology or medicine for his lifelong study of animal behavior.

Konrad Lorenz with Greylag geese

Red-and-green macaw

BIOLOGY CAREER

Animal Behaviorist
Michael Heithaus

Mike Heithaus is an assistant professor of biological sciences at Florida International University. He hosted National Geographic's Crittercam television program and currently works with the National Geographic channel to develop programming and educational materials and to give talks to students. His current research focuses on how interactions between predators and prey affect entire communities, especially in marine ecosystems.

Heithaus enjoys being outside and working with some of the most fascinating animals on the planet. He also enjoys the problem-solving element of science, teamwork, and environmental protection. A childhood spent outdoors playing and fishing inspired Heithaus to prepare for his career in biological fieldwork. He still enjoys spending time outdoors with his family, exploring, swimming, and taking photographs.

Mandrill

Chapter 26

Introduction to Animals

Preview

1 **Characteristics of Animals**
General Features of Animals
Kinds of Animals

2 **Animal Body Systems**
Support
Digestive and Excretory Systems
Nervous System
Respiratory and Circulatory Systems
Reproduction

3 **Evolutionary Trends in Animals**
Tissues and Symmetry
Early Embryonic Development
Body Cavities
Segmentation and Jointed Appendages

4 **Chordate Evolution**
Characteristics of Chordates
Evolution of Fishes
Evolution of Amphibians
Evolution of Reptiles
Evolution of Birds
Evolution of Mammals

Why It Matters

We share the planet with a fantastic array of animal forms. Our lives intersect the lives of animals in both positive and negative ways.

A Giant Pacific octopus makes a meal of a spiny dogfish shark.

The Giant Pacific octopus is an example of an invertebrate. This animal is the largest species of octopus in the world.

InquiryLab

Animal Characteristics

Animals share many characteristics of structure and function. How many common features can you observe in classroom specimens?

Procedure

❶ Place a **pill bug** in a **small box** filled with a layer of moist **potting soil**. Place an **aquarium snail** in a **water-filled dish**.

❷ First, examine these animals by using just your eyes. Then, use a **hand lens** to examine the animals.

❸ Compile two lists. On one list, record all of the features that these animals have in common. On the other list, record all of the ways that these animals differ.

Analysis

1. **Describe** any differences in how your specimens move.

2. **Describe** any sense organs that the animals have, if any.

3. **Describe** any protection that the animals have against predators.

The spiny dogfish shark is an example of a vertebrate. This species often travels in schools of hundreds or even thousands of individuals.

Octopuses have eight arms that have suckers, which they use to grasp and pull apart prey.

READING TOOLBOX

These reading tools can help you learn the material in this chapter. For more information on how to use these and other tools, see **Appendix: Reading and Study Skills.**

Using Words

Word Parts You can tell a lot about a word by taking it apart and examining its prefix and root.

Your Turn Use the table to define the following words.
1. endoskeleton
2. exoskeleton

Word Parts		
Word part	**Type**	**Meaning**
endo-	prefix	inside
exo-	prefix	outside
skeleton	root	organ that protects, supports, and gives structure to the body

Using Language

Describing Space Describing an object accurately is not as easy as it may seem. Certain words, called *spatial* words, can help you describe the shape and position of an object. Spatial words include *perpendicular, parallel, diagonal, horizontal,* and *vertical.*

Your Turn Practice using spatial words by completing the activity below.
1. Look around your classroom, and choose an object to describe.
2. Without revealing what the object is, use spatial words to try to get a partner to draw the object you have chosen.

Using Science Graphics

Spider Map A spider map is an effective tool for classifying the details of topics in science. A spider map divides a topic into ideas and details.

Your Turn Use the spider map shown here to list details about each of the major animal body systems.
1. Draw a diagram like the one shown here. In the circle, write the main topic.
2. From the circle, draw legs to represent characteristics of animals. Draw one leg for each of the seven major animal body systems.
3. From each leg, draw horizontal lines. As you read the chapter, write details about each body system on the horizontal lines. To add more details, make the legs longer and add more horizontal lines.

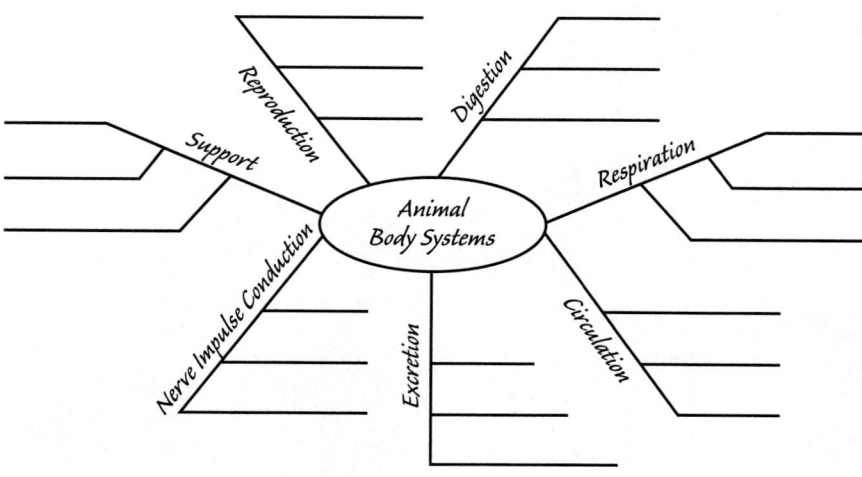

1 Characteristics of Animals

Key Ideas	Key Terms	Why It Matters
❯ What general features do all animals share? ❯ What two groups are animals informally classified into?	heterotroph invertebrate vertebrate	Animals are all around us, and we depend on many of them. Some animals provide food or companionship, while others may be harmful parasites or pests.

We are more familiar with animals than with any other type of organism. Not only do we live with and around animals—we are animals. When we first hear the word *animal,* we might think of cats, dogs, cows, or birds. Millions of types of animals exist today.

General Features of Animals

Some animals are so small we cannot see them without the help of a microscope. For example, small animals called *mites* live around us and even on us. Other animals, such as blue whales, are huge. Mites and blue whales are very different organisms, as **Figure 1** shows. Why are they grouped together as animals? ❯ **Animals are multicellular, heterotrophic organisms with cells that lack cell walls.** Recall that heterotrophs obtain food by eating other organisms or their byproducts.

The lives of humans and many other animals are connected. We depend on domestic animals, such as cows and chickens, for food. Cats and dogs are companions and pets. We even depend on tiny animals, such as insects. People may think of insects as pests that destroy crops or transmit diseases or as annoyances that bite or sting. But insects can also benefit humans. For example, honeybees not only produce honey but also help pollinate crops.

❯ **Reading Check** *List three ways in which humans depend on animals. (See the Appendix for answers to Reading Checks.)*

Figure 1 The blue whale is the largest living animal. A mite is often microscopic in size. ❯ **What features do blue whales and mites share?**

Figure 2 The Thompson's gazelle relies on speed and agility to try to escape a cheetah. Reaching speeds greater than 60 mi/h, cheetahs are the fastest land mammals.

Multicellularity Some organisms, such as bacteria, are made up of only one cell. Animals are *multicellular,* which means that they are made up of many cells. Most animals have many types of cells. Groups of cells take on special shapes and functions in order to work together. For example, the cells in our heart are different from the cells that form our stomach or our skin. Because cells specialize, animal cells depend on other cells. The cells of our skin cannot survive for long without all of our other cells doing their jobs. Unlike the cells of other multicellular organisms, animal cells do not have a rigid cell wall that surrounds them. Because animal cells lack a cell wall, animals have greater mobility than other organisms have.

Heterotrophy Animals are **heterotrophs,** organisms that cannot make their own food. So, unlike plants and other autotrophs, animals must obtain food from other sources. Most animals move around their <u>environment</u> to look for food. Once food is located, it is eaten and then digested inside the animal's body. Other animals, such as sponges and corals, do not move but instead catch particles of food that drift by in the water. These animals are *filter feeders.*

Movement Animals are unique among living things because animals can move rapidly and in complex ways. In addition, locomotion, the ability to move from place to place, is a big advantage for animals. It helps animals find food and favorable environments and helps them avoid predators, as **Figure 2** shows. Locomotion occurs when muscle cells contract with great force to move an animal's limbs or tail. Animals can swim, walk, run, and even fly. Not all animals move from place to place. Some animals, such as the sponges and corals described above, attach themselves to the ocean bottom or other submerged surface.

❯ **Reading Check** *What are three advantages of being able to move around the environment?*

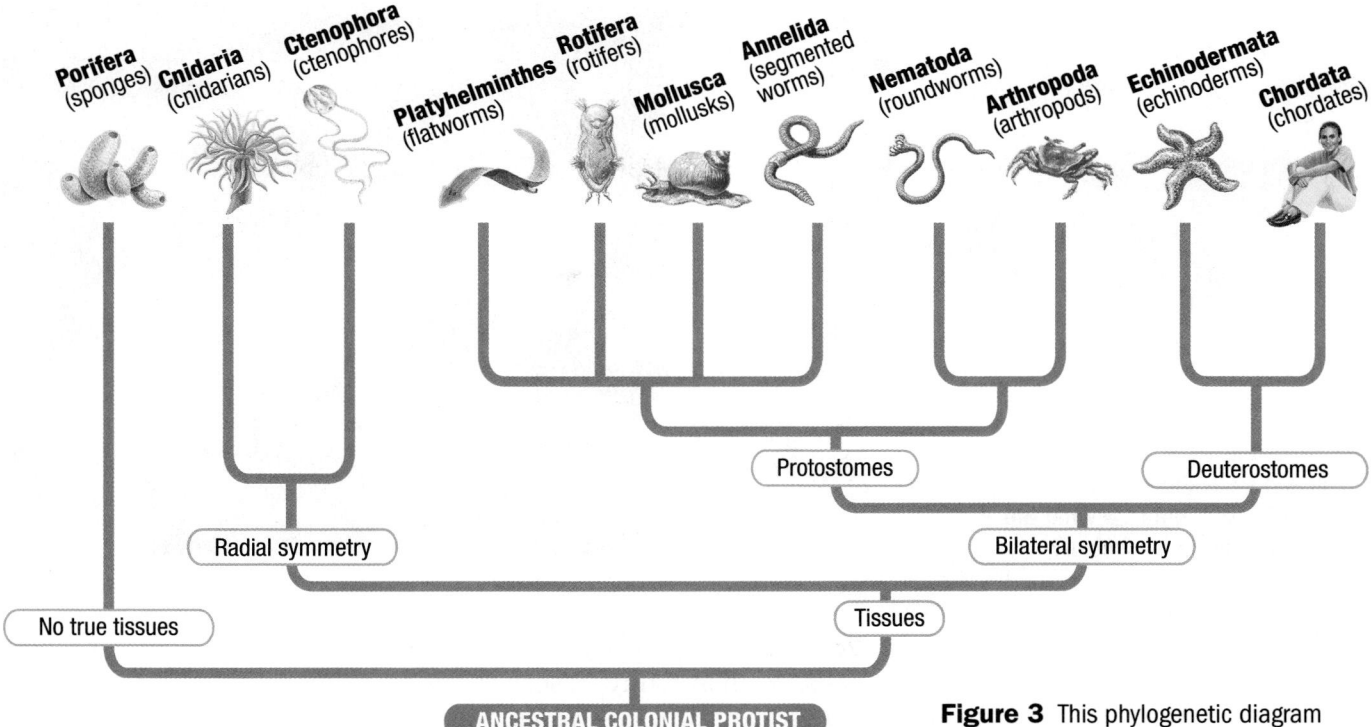

Figure 3 This phylogenetic diagram represents a hypothesis for the relationship between members of the animal kingdom based on rRNA analysis. For updates on phylogenetic information, visit **go.hrw.com**. Enter the keyword **HX8 Phylo.**

Kinds of Animals

Kingdom Animalia contains about 35 major divisions called *phyla* (singular, *phylum*). Animals are often classified according to developmental or body characteristics. **Figure 3** shows examples of 11 phyla. ❯Animals are often informally grouped as invertebrates or vertebrates, although vertebrates make up only a subgroup of one phylum—Chordata. The vast majority of animals are invertebrates.

Invertebrates Invertebrates include any animal that does not have a backbone. A variety of invertebrates exist, and many look completely different from one another. The most primitive animals, sponges, are invertebrates, but some advanced animals, such as ants and octopuses, are also invertebrates. Land invertebrates tend to be quite small because they do not have an internal skeleton to support them. In the ocean, a few invertebrates grow extremely large. For example, the giant squid can reach a length of 13 m (42 ft).

Some invertebrates form the basis of entire ecosystems. Corals are small invertebrates that look like upside-down jellyfish. Their skeletons form huge coral reefs made of limestone that provide a habitat for many other organisms. The largest structure built by organisms is not the Great Wall of China or anything else made by humans—it is the Great Barrier Reef, which stretches 2,300 km along the eastern coast of Australia. On land, invertebrates pollinate plants and decompose dead material so that this material can be recycled through the ecosystem.

❯ **Reading Check** *Explain why many invertebrates are small.*

Word Parts Use the meanings of the word parts in the term *invertebrate* to define the term in your own words.

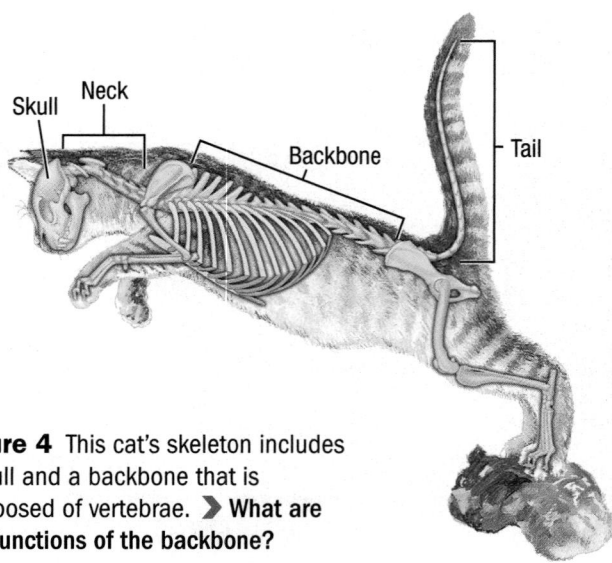

Figure 4 This cat's skeleton includes a skull and a backbone that is composed of vertebrae. ❯ **What are two functions of the backbone?**

Skull
Neck
Backbone
Tail

vertebrate (VUHR tuh brit) an animal that has a backbone; includes mammals, birds, reptiles, amphibians, and fish

SC*I*LINKS.
www.scilinks.org
Topic: Vertebrates
Code: HX81602

Vertebrates If you go to a zoo, many of the animals you see—the lions, elephants, turtles, snakes, and birds, for example—are vertebrates. Although these vertebrates may appear different from each other, they share many internal characteristics. What are the internal characteristics shared by vertebrates? In addition to having the characteristics common to all chordates, vertebrates have a cranium and have an internal skeleton composed of bone or cartilage. Thus, **vertebrates** are chordates that have a backbone. Their name comes from *vertebrae* (singular, *vertebra*), which are the individual segments that make up the backbone. You can see the structure of a cat's skeleton in **Figure 4.**

The backbone supports and protects a dorsal nerve cord. It also provides a site for muscle attachment. As animals evolved, these functions paved the way for the development of an internal skeleton. The complex skeleton of vertebrates allowed some species to grow much larger than their invertebrate ancestors.

❯ **Reading Check** *What are two characteristics that all vertebrates share?*

Section 1 Review

KEY IDEAS

1. **Name** three characteristics that all animals share.
2. **Identify** the two groups into which animals are often informally classified. What is the name of the phylum into which vertebrates are classified?

CRITICAL THINKING

3. **Justifying Conclusions** A classmate tells you that sponges are plants because they just attach themselves to the bottom of the ocean. Is your classmate correct? Explain your answer.
4. **Forming Reasoned Opinions** Your friend says that invertebrates are useless pests. Do you agree?

WRITING FOR SCIENCE

5. **Essay** Conduct an Internet search to discover the important roles that invertebrates play in our lives. Write an essay about your favorite invertebrate, and explain its importance to people.

Animal Body Systems

Key Ideas	Key Terms	Why It Matters
❯ Why is an animal's skeleton important? ❯ What are the functions of the digestive and excretory systems? ❯ What is the function of the nervous system? ❯ Why are the respiratory and circulatory systems important? ❯ What are two reproductive strategies of animals?	hydrostatic skeleton exoskeleton endoskeleton gastrovascular cavity	Body systems allow animals to grow and behave the way animals do and to breathe, feed, and react to the environment.

The body systems of animals allow animals to function. Animals do not always have every body system. The body systems of animal groups are shaped by the lifestyles that the animal groups have.

Support

One of the keys to the success of animals is animals' ability to move. In order to move, their body needs support. ❯ **An animal's skeleton provides a framework that supports the animal's body. The skeleton is also vital to an animal's movement.** Many soft-bodied invertebrates have a **hydrostatic skeleton,** which is a water-filled cavity that is under pressure. This skeleton is similar to a balloon filled with water. The jellyfish in **Figure 5** has a hydrostatic skeleton. Insects, clams, crabs, and many other familiar invertebrates have an exoskeleton. An **exoskeleton** is a rigid external skeleton that encases the body of an animal. The muscles of an animal with an exoskeleton are attached to the inside of the skeleton, which provides a surface for the muscles to pull against. An exoskeleton also protects an organism's soft internal parts. An **endoskeleton** is made of a hard material, such as bone, inside an animal. Humans and other vertebrates have endoskeletons.

❯ **Reading Check** *What are three types of skeletons?*

hydrostatic skeleton (HIE droh STAT ik SKEL uh tuhn) a cavity that is filled with water and that has a support function

exoskeleton (EKS oh SKEL uh tuhn) a hard, external, supporting structure that develops from the ectoderm

endoskeleton (EN doh SKEL uh tuhn) an internal skeleton made of bone and cartilage

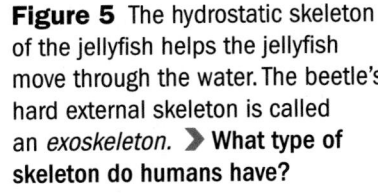

Figure 5 The hydrostatic skeleton of the jellyfish helps the jellyfish move through the water. The beetle's hard external skeleton is called an *exoskeleton.* ❯ **What type of skeleton do humans have?**

QuickLab

🕐 15 min

Filtration Rate in the Kidney

The human kidney filters fluid from the blood at the rate of about 125 mL/min. However, most of this fluid is reabsorbed by the kidneys and only a small percentage of the fluid is excreted as urine. Adult humans normally excrete between 1.5 and 2.3 L of urine a day. Use this information to answer the questions below.

Analysis

1. **Calculate** how many milliliters of fluid the human kidneys filter each hour.

2. **Calculate** how many milliliters of fluid the kidneys filter each day.

3. `CRITICAL THINKING` **Analyzing Data** Convert your answer in item 2 from milliliters to liters.

4. `CRITICAL THINKING` **Predicting Outcomes** What would happen if the kidneys could not return water to the body?

Digestive and Excretory Systems

Catching or gathering food is only the first step for animals. They still have to remove the useful parts of food and get rid of waste products. ❯ **The digestive system is responsible for extracting energy and nutrients from an animal's food, while the excretory system removes waste products from the animal's body.**

Digestive System Single-celled organisms and sponges do not have a digestive system. Instead, they digest their food within each of their body cells. All other animals digest their food outside of their body cells within a digestive cavity. Simple animals, such as the hydra shown in **Figure 6,** have a **gastrovascular cavity,** a digestive cavity with only one opening. Food comes in and wastes go out through the same opening. Every cell is exposed to all stages of food digestion, and there are no specialized digestive cells. Other animals have a digestive tract, or gut, with two openings, a mouth and an anus. In a digestive tract, food moves from mouth to anus. This one-way digestive system allows for specialization and more efficient digestion.

Excretory System Excretion is the removal of wastes produced by cellular metabolism. Waste products such as ammonia will hurt or kill an organism if they are not removed. Simple aquatic invertebrates and some fishes excrete ammonia into the water through their skin or gills. Excretion is effective, but it results in a loss of water. Terrestrial animals need to minimize water loss. Some have excretory systems that convert ammonia to less toxic chemicals, such as urea, before passing them out of the body. As the excretory system eliminates the wastes, water and other useful substances are returned to the body.

❯ **Reading Check** *How does a gastrovascular cavity of a hydra differ from a one-way digestive system?*

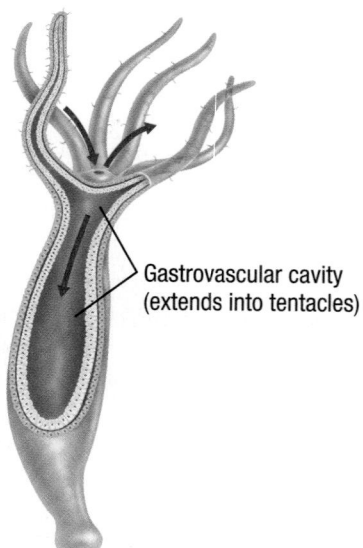

Figure 6 The gastrovascular cavity of the hydra has only one opening.

Gastrovascular cavity (extends into tentacles)

Nervous System

In order to survive, animals must sense the environment around them and then coordinate a response. **❯ The nervous system carries information about the environment through the body and coordinates responses and behaviors.** Not all animals have a complex nervous system, and some do not have a brain to coordinate the nervous system.

Simple Nervous Systems Nerve cells are specialized for carrying messages in the form of electrical impulses. These cells coordinate the activities in an animal's body, which enables the animal to sense and respond to its environment. All animals except sponges have nerve cells. **Figure 7** shows the arrangement of nerve cells in a hydra, a flatworm, and a grasshopper. The simplest arrangement of nerves, called a *nerve net,* is found in animals such as hydras and jellyfish. In a nerve net, nerve cells do not coordinate actions efficiently.

In contrast, many animals have clusters of nerve cells called *ganglia* (singular, *ganglion*) that can coordinate responses. In some animals, such as the flatworm, ganglia near the front of the animal are larger and more complex, similar to a brain.

Complex Nervous Systems More-complex invertebrates, such as the grasshopper, have a true brain with sensory structures, such as eyes, associated with it. These animals can interact with their environment in complex ways and are capable of sophisticated behaviors. Vertebrates have the most advanced nervous system. Vertebrates have a relatively large brain, and many species have special sensory systems that make these animals even better at catching food and avoiding predators than other animals are. For example, dolphins have a large brain that has a big part devoted to processing sounds that the dolphins use to "see" the world around them.

❯ Reading Check *What type of nervous system do jellyfish have?*

READING TOOLBOX

Describing Space Use spatial language to describe the nervous systems of the animals in **Figure 7.**

Figure 7 The hydra has a simple nerve net, while the flatworm and the grasshopper have more-complex nervous systems.

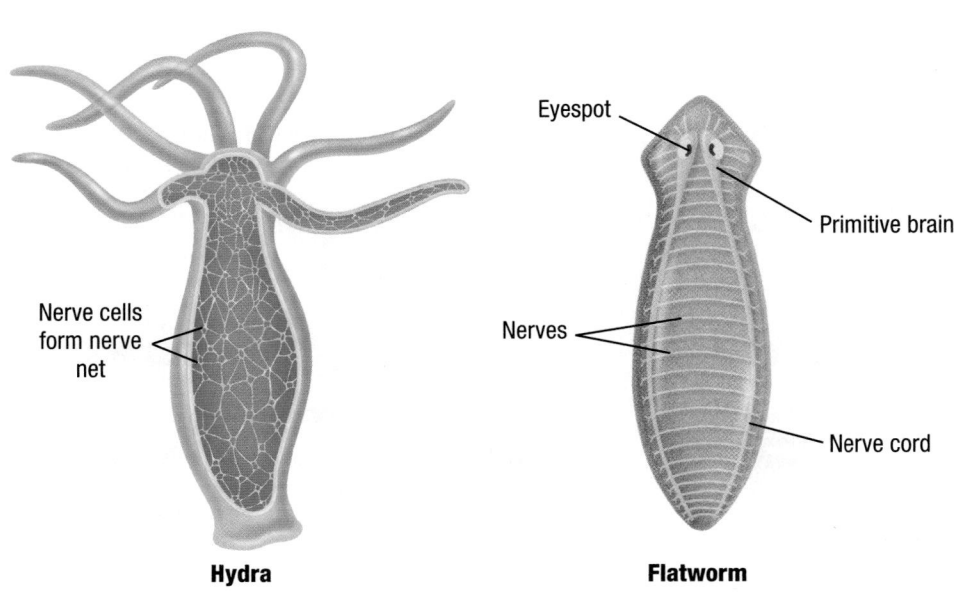

Nerve cells form nerve net

Hydra

Eyespot

Primitive brain

Nerves

Nerve cord

Flatworm

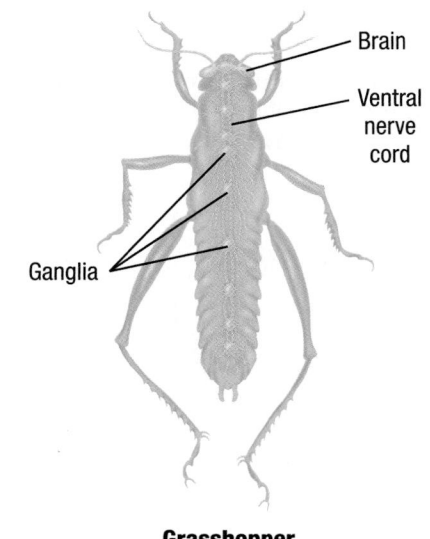

Brain

Ventral nerve cord

Ganglia

Grasshopper

Figure 8 The feathery gills of this salamander lie outside of its body and are supported by its watery environment.

ACADEMIC
VOCABULARY

transport to carry from one place to another

Respiratory and Circulatory Systems

The cells of a simple animal can exchange oxygen and carbon dioxide directly with the environment around them. Most animals need specialized systems for exchanging and transporting gases through the body. ❯ **The respiratory system is responsible for exchanging oxygen and carbon dioxide between the body and the environment. The circulatory system transports gases, nutrients, and other substances within the body.**

Respiratory System Respiration involves the uptake of oxygen and the release of carbon dioxide. Most animals have specialized respiratory systems. Aquatic animals, such as fish and some salamanders, respire by using thin projections of tissue called *gills,* as **Figure 8** shows. A variety of respiratory organs, including lungs, have evolved in terrestrial animals, which allow these animals to respire on land.

Circulatory System In some small, simple animals, cells can obtain oxygen and nutrients directly. Larger animals have cells that are located far from oxygen or nutrient sources. A circulatory system is needed to <u>transport</u> oxygen and nutrients to, and waste products from, these cells. **Figure 9** shows two types of circulatory systems.

In an *open circulatory system,* a heart pumps fluid containing oxygen and nutrients through a series of vessels into the body cavity. There, the fluid washes across the body's tissues, which supplies the tissues with oxygen and nutrients. The fluid collects in open spaces in the animal's body and flows back to the heart.

In a *closed circulatory system,* a heart pumps blood through a system of blood vessels. These blood vessels form a network that permits blood flow from the heart to all of the body's cells and back again. The blood remains in the vessels and does not come in direct contact with the body's tissues.

❯ **Reading Check** *What is the function of the circulatory system?*

Figure 9 In an open circulatory system, fluid leaves the blood vessels. In a closed circulatory system, blood remains inside the blood vessels. ❯ **What type of circulatory system do humans have?**

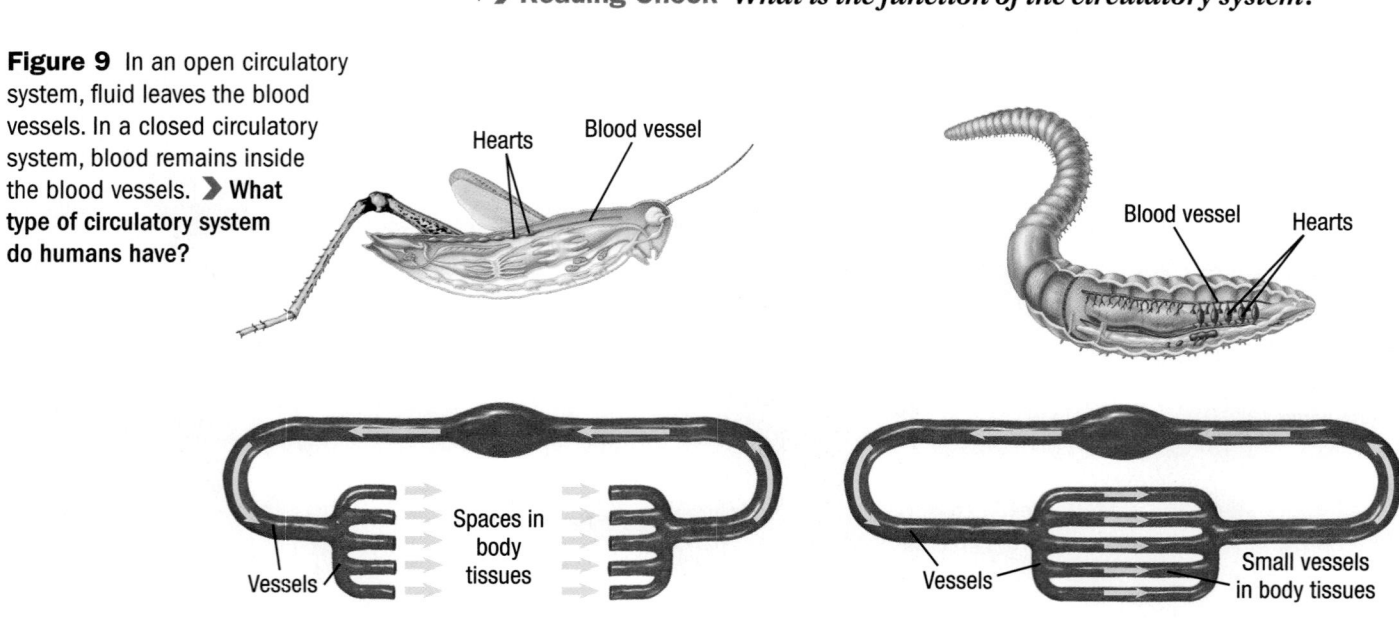

Open circulatory system

Closed circulatory system

A single arm has given rise to a whole new individual.

The egg sac of the nursery web spider may contain over 1,000 eggs.

Reproduction

While the reproductive system of an *individual* animal is not essential to survival, reproduction is necessary if the *species* is to survive.
> The two types of reproduction in animals are asexual and sexual.

Asexual Reproduction Asexual reproduction occurs when an individual produces exact copies of itself and does not mix its genes with those of another. **Figure 10** shows a sea star reproducing asexually by growing a new body from one arm. Even some vertebrates, such as some salamanders and fishes, reproduce asexually. In these species, a new individual develops from an unfertilized egg.

Sexual Reproduction In sexual reproduction, a new individual is formed by the union of a male and a female gamete. Gametes are produced in the sex organs. The testes produce the male gametes (sperm), and the ovaries produce the female gametes (eggs). A number of species can reproduce either sexually or asexually. For example, coral colonies grow larger through asexual reproduction, but new colonies are formed through sexual reproduction.

> **Reading Check** *Name an animal that can reproduce asexually.*

Figure 10 The large arm on the sea star (left) grows four new, small arms, which produces a new individual by asexual reproduction. The nursery web spider (right) reproduces sexually. The eggs are enclosed in an egg sac.

SC*L*INKS.
www.scilinks.org
Topic: Animal
          Reproduction
Code: HX80075

---

3 Evolutionary Trends in Animals

Key Ideas	Key Terms	Why It Matters
❯ What evolutionary trends in body structure do animals exhibit? ❯ What characterizes early embryonic development in animals? ❯ What types of internal body plans do animals have? ❯ What two body characteristics gave animals a greater ability to move and to be more flexible?	cephalization cleavage blastula gastrulation protostome deuterostome coelom	Through time, animals have evolved more-complex body plans and more sophisticated ways of sensing and reacting to the environment.

Scientists believe that animals first appeared in the oceans about 650 million years ago. These early animals were generally small and simple. Over time, more-complex groups of animals evolved, first in the world's oceans and eventually on land. No matter where animals live or how simple or complex they are, animals have evolved to be well adapted for their particular lifestyle and environment.

Tissues and Symmetry

An animal's *body plan* is the animal's shape, symmetry, and internal organization. ❯ **Through evolutionary time, animals have developed more-complex body plans, including true tissues and bilateral symmetry.** The most primitive animals have the simplest body plans and have few ways to sense and interact with the environment. Animal groups that have appeared more recently have complicated body plans and can interact with and modify their environment.

Tissues The cells of all animals except sponges are organized into units called *tissues*. Recall that tissues are groups of cells that have the same structure and that work together to perform a specific function. For example, the cells of muscle tissue are specialized to produce movement by contracting together. The cells of nerve tissue are specialized to conduct signals. In many animals, different tissues work together and are organized into structures called *organs,* which perform particular jobs. In some simple animals, such as the coral in **Figure 11,** tissues are not arranged into organs. The tissues and organs in your body help you do the things that you want to do, such as move around.

❯ **Reading Check** *What are tissues, and what is an example of a type of tissue?*

Figure 11 Corals are marine animals that belong to the phylum Cnidaria. The cells of cnidarians are organized into true tissues.

QuickLab

Symmetry

You can use the letters of the alphabet to better understand the nature of symmetry.

Procedure

1 Write each letter of the alphabet on an **index card,** and spread the cards on the table in front of you.

2 Sort the cards into groups based on the letters' symmetry; use the terms *asymmetry, radial symmetry,* and *bilateral symmetry.* For example, the letters *A* and *T* show bilateral symmetry. The letter *J* is asymmetrical.

Analysis

1. List any letters that you found difficult to classify, and explain why classifying these letters was difficult.

2. Identify the letters that show the kind of symmetry that sponges do.

3. Identify two or three animals that you might be familiar with that have the kind of symmetry that the letter *M* does.

4. CRITICAL THINKING **Evaluating Methods** What are some strengths and weaknesses of using symmetry to classify or describe organisms?

Body Symmetry Body symmetry describes how an animal's body can be divided into similar pieces, as **Figure 12** shows. Sponges are *asymmetrical,* which means that a sponge cannot be divided into similar pieces. Through evolutionary time, animals developed radial and bilateral symmetry. Animals with *radial symmetry* have body parts arranged around a central axis. Any plane that passes through the central axis divides the organism into roughly equal halves.

The bodies of other animals show *bilateral symmetry.* A plane that passes down the middle of an animal from head to tail divides the animal into mirror-image halves. Bilateral symmetry was a major evolutionary change in animals. Bilateral symmetry enabled parts of the body to become specialized in different ways. For example, most bilaterally symmetrical animals have an anterior concentration of sensory structures and nerves, which is called **cephalization.**

> **cephalization** (SEF uh li ZAY shuhn) the concentration of nerve tissue and sensory organs at the anterior end of an organism

Figure 12 The sponge lacks a consistent pattern of structure. The sea anemone displays radial symmetry. The butterfly displays bilateral symmetry and cephalization.

Asymmetry

Radial symmetry

Bilateral symmetry

Early Embryonic Development

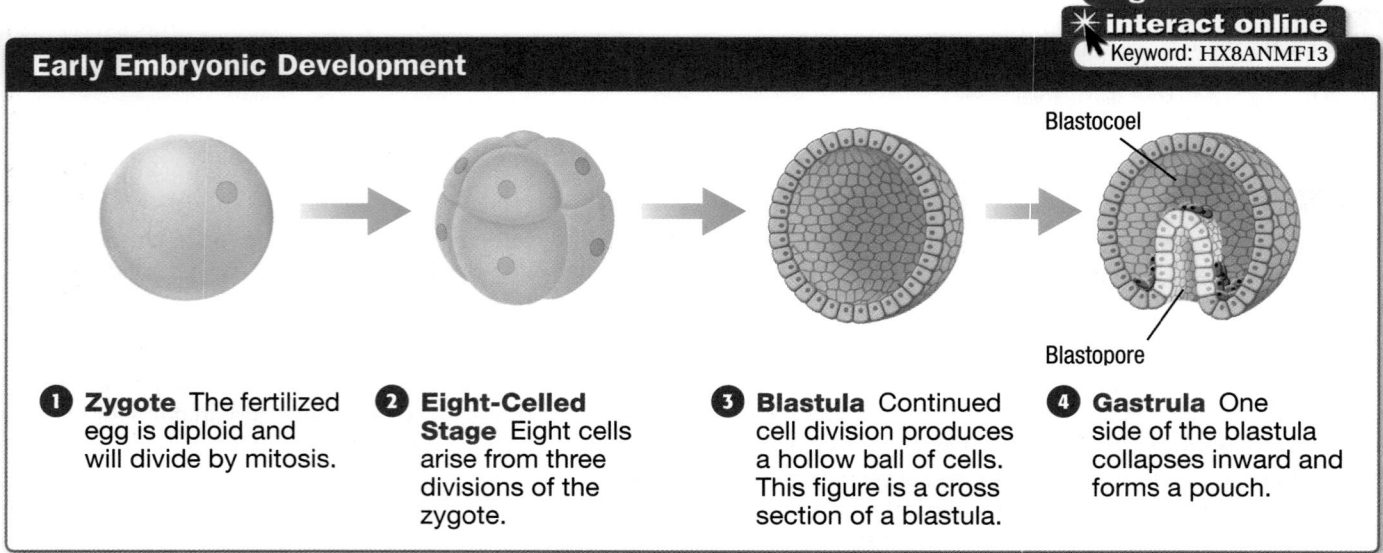

1. **Zygote** The fertilized egg is diploid and will divide by mitosis.

2. **Eight-Celled Stage** Eight cells arise from three divisions of the zygote.

3. **Blastula** Continued cell division produces a hollow ball of cells. This figure is a cross section of a blastula.

4. **Gastrula** One side of the blastula collapses inward and forms a pouch.

Blastocoel

Blastopore

Figure 13 Development of an animal's body starts with a zygote. Cleavage produces many cells from one original cell. ❯ **How many cells will be present after five cell divisions?**

cleavage (KLEEV IJ) a series of cell divisions that occur immediately after an egg is fertilized

blastula (BLAS tyoo luh) the stage of an embryo before gastrulation

gastrulation (GAS troo LAY shuhn) the transformation of the blastula into the gastrula or the formation of the embryonic germ layers

protostome (PROHD uh STOHM) an organism whose embryonic blastopore develops into the mouth

deuterostome (DOO tuh roh STOHM) an animal whose mouth does not derive from the blastopore

Early Embryonic Development

Most animals reproduce through sexual reproduction. ❯ **The zygote that is produced through the union of sperm and egg cells undergoes cell division and tissue development during cleavage, blastula formation, and gastrulation.**

Stage ❶ The diploid zygote is the first cell of a new individual. The zygote will undergo cleavage, a series of cell divisions by mitosis.

Stage ❷ Each cell division doubles the number of cells. Thus, the first division produces two cells, the second division produces four cells, and so on. The dividing cells do not grow during **cleavage.** Thus, the cell divisions of cleavage produce smaller and smaller cells.

Stage ❸ The end result of cleavage is a **blastula.** A blastula is a hollow ball formed by the growing mass of dividing cells. The fluid-filled interior of the blastula is called the *blastocoel.*

Stage ❹ During **gastrulation,** the blastula begins to collapse inward. Inside the hollow ball, now called a *gastrula,* is a pocket that makes the gastrula cup-shaped. The cells of the gastrula continue to divide, some more quickly than others.

Differentiation During differentiation, groups of dividing cells in the gastrula become increasingly different from each other. **Figure 13** and **Figure 14** show the three main cell types in different colors. These three cell types will form the primary tissue layers in the adult organism: the ectoderm, the endoderm, and the mesoderm. The ectoderm, shown in blue, will form the outer layer of the body, the sense organs, and the nervous system. The endoderm, shown in yellow, will form the gut, the respiratory system, and many glands. The mesoderm, shown in red, will form most of the skeleton, the muscles, the circulatory system, and the organs of reproduction and excretion.

❯ **Reading Check** *What are the three primary tissue layers?*

Patterns of Development The gastrula continues to change as it develops. The inward folding of the pocket (shown in yellow in **Figure 14**) becomes deeper. Eventually, the pocket breaks through the side of the gastrula opposite the blastopore. This process changes the pocket into a passage, lined with endoderm, which **Figure 14** shows. This passage is the gut of the developing embryo.

Animals develop from the gastrula in two major ways. These different ways can help us understand evolutionary relationships between animal groups. Animals in which the anus develops from or near the blastopore are called deuterostomes.

Protostomes In some animal groups, the mouth develops from the end of the embryo near the blastopore. The anus develops at the opposite end of the embryo. **Figure 14** shows the development of these animals, called **protostomes.** Protostomes include flatworms, earthworms, snails and clams, spiders and insects, and the relatives of these animals.

Deuterostomes In some animal groups, this pattern is reversed. The mouth develops from the end of the embryo opposite the blastopore. And as you might expect, the anus develops at or near the blastopore. **Figure 14** shows the development of these animals, called **deuterostomes.** Deuterostomes include sea stars and their relatives and vertebrates and their relatives.

The first deuterostomes were marine echinoderms that evolved more than 650 million years ago. Deuterostomes were also the first animals to develop an endoskeleton. Vertebrates are also deuterostomes and have an internal skeleton. If you look at a sea star, you might not realize that the sea star is more closely related to vertebrates than an octopus is. However, the similarity of development between a sea star and vertebrates implies that this is true.

❯ **Reading Check** *Where does the mouth form in protostomes?*

Spider Map Create a spider map to organize the information you learned about early embryonic development in animals.

Figure 14 The development of an animal embryo follows one of two patterns. ❯ **What are two examples of protostomes and two examples of deuterostomes?**

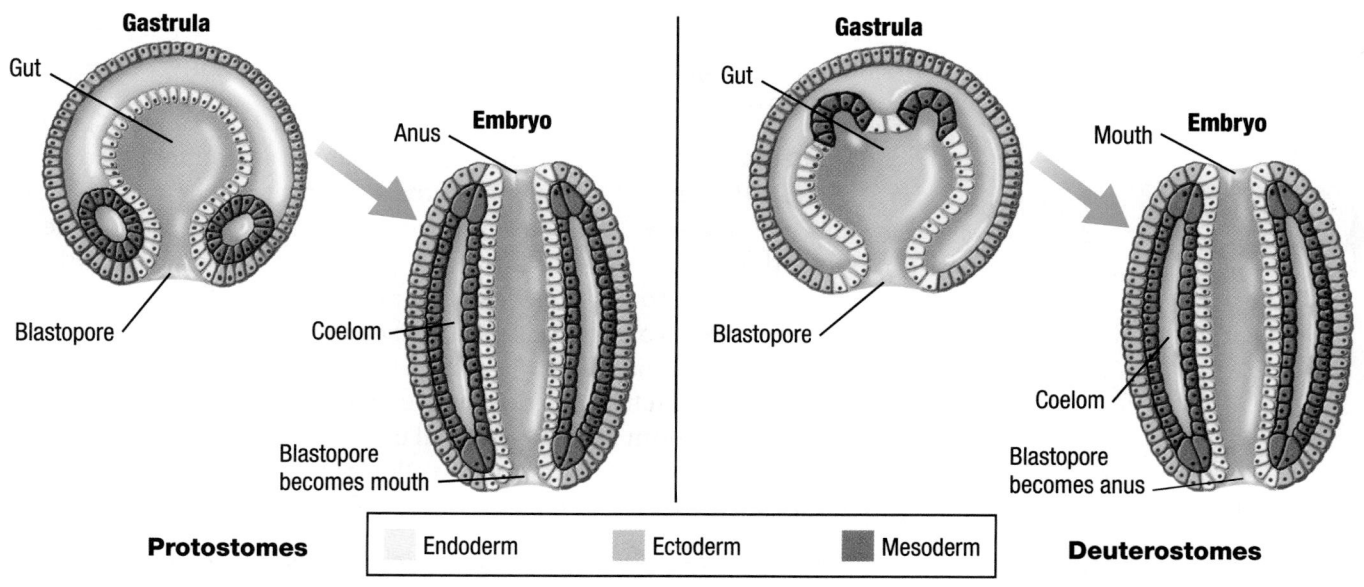

Protostomes / Deuterostomes

Gastrula — Gut — Blastopore — Embryo — Anus — Coelom — Blastopore becomes mouth — **Protostomes**

Gastrula — Gut — Blastopore — Embryo — Mouth — Coelom — Blastopore becomes anus — **Deuterostomes**

Endoderm ▪ Ectoderm ▪ Mesoderm

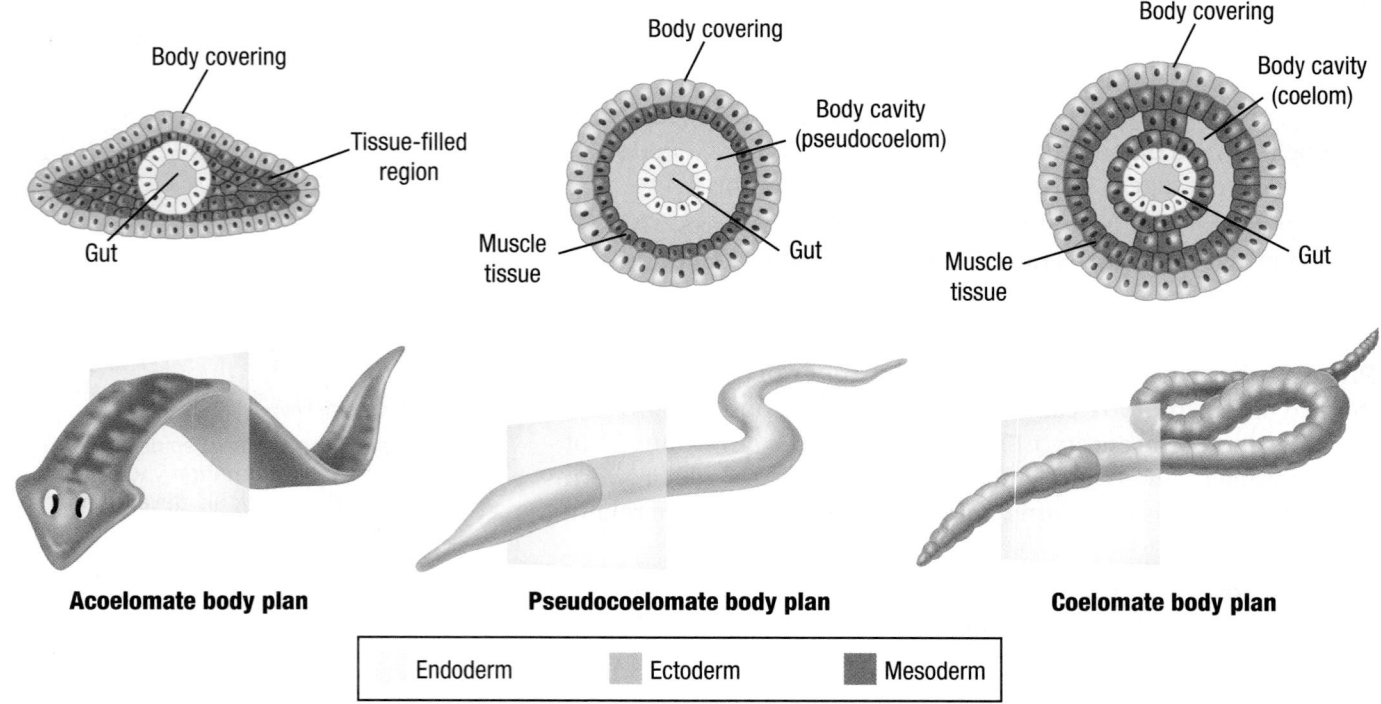

Body covering

Tissue-filled region

Gut

Acoelomate body plan

Body covering

Body cavity (pseudocoelom)

Muscle tissue

Gut

Pseudocoelomate body plan

Body covering

Body cavity (coelom)

Muscle tissue

Gut

Coelomate body plan

| Endoderm | Ectoderm | Mesoderm |

Figure 15 Bilaterally symmetrical animals have one of three basic body plans. ❯ What type of body cavity do humans have?

coelom (SEE luhm) a body cavity that contains the internal organs

www.scilinks.org
Topic: Body Cavity
Code: HX80180

Body Cavities

❯ **Animals with bilateral symmetry have one of three basic kinds of internal body plans. The body plan may include a body cavity, or** *coelom.* A **coelom** is a fluid-filled space found between the body wall and the gut. Humans and other vertebrates have a coelom. The coelom is lined with cells that come from mesoderm, as shown in **Figure 15.**

Animals with no body cavity are called *acoelomates.* The space between an acoelomate's body wall and its gut is completely filled with tissues. Flatworms are acoelomates.

Other animals, called *pseudocoelomates,* have a body cavity located between the mesoderm and endoderm. Their body cavity is called a *pseudocoelom,* or false coelom. This false coelom is filled with liquid that can act like a skeleton by providing support. Roundworms are pseudocoelomates.

A True Coelom Coelomates, which include segmented worms and all other more "advanced" animals, have a true coelom. Because the coelom is lined with mesoderm and wraps around the gut, the gut and other internal organs of coelomates are suspended within the coelom. A true coelom provides an internal space where mesoderm and endoderm can be in contact with each other during embryonic development. This contact was important for the evolution of complex organs, which are made of more than one type of tissue. The fluid-filled coelom protects internal organs from the movement of surrounding muscles. The coelom allows an animal to move without damaging its organs or interfering with the organs' functions.

❯ **Reading Check** *What is an example of a pseudocoelomate?*

Segmentation and Jointed Appendages

Recall that animals are unique in their ability to move rapidly and in complex ways. ❯ **Two major body characteristics evolved that gave animals a greater ability to move and to be flexible. These two evolutionary trends in animals are body segmentation and jointed appendages.**

Body Segmentation Besides mollusks, coelomate animals are composed of a series of repeating, similar units called *segments*. Segmentation is easy to see in some animals, such as earthworms or the caterpillar that **Figure 16** shows. Lobsters, spiders, and insects also show obvious body segments. In other animals, such as vertebrates, you cannot see segments except during early development. For example, the muscles of vertebrates develop from repeated blocks (segments) of tissue called *somites*. Also, the vertebral column consists of a stack of similar vertebrae.

Segmentation can allow great mobility and flexibility. For example, an earthworm can tie its body into knots. To move along a flat surface, the earthworm lengthens some segments of its body while shortening others. In highly segmented animals, such as earthworms, each segment repeats many of the organs in the adjacent segment.

Segmentation also offers evolutionary flexibility. A small change in an existing segment can produce a new type of segment with a different function. For example, some segments are modified for feeding or moving, and others are modified for reproduction.

Jointed Appendages Another evolutionary trend in animals is the appearance of jointed appendages. Arthropods were the first animals to have jointed appendages. Joints permit powerful movement and aid in locomotion. Jointed appendages became specialized in many ways, which helped create the vast diversity seen among the arthropods. Jointed appendages allow animals to perform complex movements, such as the defensive display of a mantis, which **Figure 16** shows.

❯ **Reading Check** *What is the name of the repeated blocks of tissue from which the muscles of vertebrates develop?*

Figure 16 This caterpillar displays clearly defined segments. Jointed appendages are visible on this mantis.
❯ **What are the advantages of body segmentation?**

Section 3 Review

❯ KEY IDEAS

1. **Describe** the evolutionary importance of tissues and bilateral symmetry.
2. **Describe** early embryonic development in animals.
3. **List** the three types of internal body plans that animals have, and give an example of each type.
4. **Name** two body characteristics that gave animals a greater ability to move and to be more flexible.

CRITICAL THINKING

5. **Forming Hypotheses** Radially symmetrical animals, such as hydras, are not found on land. However, bilaterally symmetrical animals live on land and in water. Propose a hypothesis to explain why radially symmetrical animals are best suited to aquatic life.

ALTERNATIVE ASSESSMENT

6. **Identifying Patterns** Use the Internet to find pictures of invertebrates from the Burgess Shale. These specimens are some of the earliest known invertebrates. What do you notice about their body plans? Why do you think that these animals were so successful?

Key Ideas	Key Terms	Why It Matters
❯ What are the key characteristics of chordates? ❯ What were the key evolutionary innovations in fish? ❯ What characteristics helped amphibians adapt to land? ❯ What major evolutionary innovations first appeared in reptiles? ❯ When did birds evolve, and what were the first birds like? ❯ When and from what group did mammals evolve?	notochord amniotic egg therapsid	We are chordates, and so are many of the species that we depend on for food and companionship. All vertebrates are chordates, but not all chordates are vertebrates.

We are all familiar with members of the phylum Chordata. Sharks, frogs, lizards, pigeons, cows, and humans are all chordates. The first chordates appeared in the oceans more than 500 million years ago.

Characteristics of Chordates

Even though a fish and a monkey look nothing alike, they share several characteristics that indicate that they have a common ancestor. ❯ At some point in their development, all chordates have a dorsal nerve cord, a notochord, pharyngeal pouches, and a postanal tail. **Figure 17** shows an example of a chordate.

Dorsal Nerve Cord Chordates have a single, hollow, dorsal nerve cord with nerves attached to it that travel to different parts of the body. In vertebrates, the dorsal nerve cord develops into the spinal cord and forms an important part of a complex nervous system.

Notochord During the development of the chordate embryo, a stiff rod called the **notochord** develops along the back of the embryo. In most vertebrates, the notochord is present only in the embryo.

Pharyngeal Pouches Chordates have a series of pouches in the throat called *pharyngeal pouches*. The pharyngeal pouches of aquatic chordate embryos develop into gill slits and portions of the gills. In land vertebrates, the pharyngeal pouches develop into different structures in the head and the neck, such as the parathyroid gland and the inner ear.

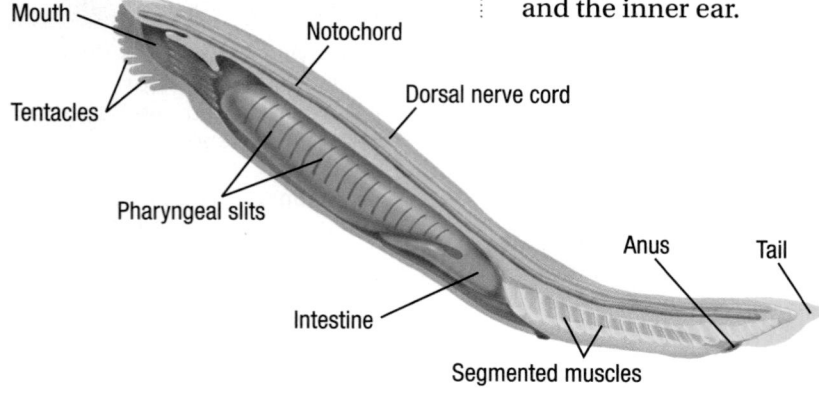

Mouth
Tentacles
Notochord
Dorsal nerve cord
Pharyngeal slits
Intestine
Segmented muscles
Anus
Tail

Figure 17 An adult lancelet possesses all of the characteristics of chordates. The pharyngeal slits in a lancelet function in filter feeding.

The Notochord and Nerve Cord

The notochord and the hollow nerve cord are two important characteristics of all chordates. While both structures are located on an animal's dorsal side, they differ in size, structure, and location. You can compare these two structures by viewing a cross section of an adult lancelet.

Procedure

1 Place a prepared slide of a cross section of an adult lancelet under the microscope.

2 Locate the notochord and the hollow nerve cord. Locate the intestine if it is visible.

3 Sketch the specimen, and label the dorsal (top) and ventral (bottom) sides, the notochord, the nerve cord, and the intestine.

Analysis

1. **Describe** the structure, size, and relative location of both the nerve cord and the notochord.

2. **Identify** the symmetry that the lancelet displays.

3. **CRITICAL THINKING** **Forming Hypotheses** In vertebrate chordates, the notochord is replaced by a backbone that encases the nerve cord. Why might this arrangement be an advantage for an animal?

Postanal Tail Another chordate characteristic is a postanal tail, which is a tail that extends beyond the anus. In many chordates, such as fish, the tail allows for rapid movements underwater. In other chordates, such as cats, the tail is used for maintaining balance while the cat chases prey. In some chordates, including humans, the tail is present only in the embryo.

Invertebrate Chordates The vast majority of chordate species belong to subphylum Vertebrata. Members of the other two subphyla do not have a backbone and are called *invertebrate chordates.* The two types of invertebrate chordates are tunicates and lancelets.

Tunicates Adult tunicates, such as the one that **Figure 18** shows, are filter feeders that live in the ocean. A tough sac, called a tunic, develops around the adult's body and gives tunicates their name. Adult tunicates do not have a nerve cord, notochord, or postanal tail. However, tunicate larvae have all four traits of chordates.

Lancelets Lancelets, such as the one shown in **Figure 17** on the previous page, get their name from their bladelike shape. Although lancelets may resemble fish, they are not fish. Lancelet fossils have been found in rocks more than 530 million years old, which makes lancelets older than any fish species is. Lancelets feed on microscopic protists that they filter out of the water.

The First Vertebrates Vertebrates first appeared about 500 million years ago. The first vertebrates were fish that had neither jaws nor paired fins. Also, the earliest fishes, called *agnathans,* did not have a backbone. They had a notochord that their muscles attached to, which allowed them to swim. When the agnathans first appeared, the ability to swim provided a major advantage over other animals.

❯ Reading Check *What are two types of invertebrate chordates?*

> **notochord** (NOHT uh KAWRD) the rod-shaped supporting axis found in the dorsal part of the embryos of all chordates, including vertebrates

Figure 18 A pouchlike pharynx with slits is the only chordate characteristic retained by adult tunicates. Larval tunicates have all four chordate characteristics, but they lose them during metamorphosis.

Figure 19 The great white shark is the largest predatory fish in the world. The development of jaws was a key evolutionary innovation. Jawed fishes were able to hold onto prey and to better compete for food.

Scientists believe that jaws evolved from gill arches.

SCi
LINKS.
www.scilinks.org
Topic: Evolution of Jaws
Code: HX80548

Figure 20 The fish *Tiktaalik roseae* lived 375 million years ago. It had bony fins that functioned as limbs. ❯ **What was an advantage of the bony fins of fish like** *Tiktaalik roseae*?

Evolution of Fishes

❯ Two important structures that first evolved in fish allowed them to become efficient underwater predators. Jaws and paired fins allowed fish to pursue and grasp prey. About 430 million years ago, the *acanthodians*, or spiny fishes, appeared. Spiny fishes had strong jaws with jagged, bony edges that served as teeth, which enabled the fish to hold onto prey. Jaws, such as the shark's jaws shown in **Figure 19,** probably evolved from gill arches made of cartilage, a lightweight, strong, flexible tissue. When jawed fishes appeared, they replaced most jawless fishes. Jawed fishes were better able to compete for food.

The spiny fishes had an internal skeleton composed mainly of cartilage along with some bone. Their scales also contained small plates of bone. Bone would come to play a much larger role in the descendant bony fishes.

About 20 million years after the spiny fishes appeared, the placoderms evolved. Placoderms were jawed fishes that had large heads covered with bony plates. By 350 million years ago, almost all of these early fishes had disappeared, replaced by faster swimmers—the sharks and bony fishes.

Transitional Forms The first vertebrates to emerge on land were probably similar to the fish shown in **Figure 20.** Instead of the spiny fins that familiar fishes such as trout and goldfish have, these early fishes had bony fins that functioned like primitive limbs and allowed these fishes to move in shallow water. **Figure 20** shows that these bony fins were much like the limb bones of four-legged vertebrates that now live on land. But these early fishes probably spent little time out of the water. They probably represent a transition between fishes that lived only in water and the first vertebrates to live primarily on land: the amphibians.

Evolution of Amphibians

The first amphibians appeared about 370 million years ago. Early amphibians were not like the familiar frogs and toads of today. Early amphibians had limbs that were not very efficient for moving. With new habitats and no competition from other predators, however, amphibians increased quickly in number and <u>diversity</u>.

Over time, the bodies of amphibians became better adapted to life on land. ❯ **Three major characteristics helped amphibians succeed on land. First, amphibians had lungs that could exchange gases outside of a water environment, where gills could not. Second, an amphibian's heart delivered more oxygen to the body than a fish's did. Finally, amphibians had strong limbs that supported their bodies and allowed movement from place to place.**

But amphibians still needed to keep their skin and eggs moist. Thus, they had to stay close to water or live in wet areas. Most modern amphibians are better at moving on land than their ancestors were. But many species are not well adapted to dry land. For example, amphibian eggs are not watertight. So, modern amphibians must seek out water or damp areas in which to reproduce.

Evolution of Reptiles

To truly conquer land, vertebrates needed to be able to reproduce away from water. The evolution of the watertight **amniotic egg** in a new group of animals, the reptiles, aided them. Amniotic eggs allowed reptiles to take over the land because reptiles were not tied to water for reproduction. Reptiles, birds, and mammals have amniotic eggs, though in most mammals the eggs remain inside of the mother.

❯ **The major evolutionary innovations that first appeared in reptiles include watertight, scale-covered skin and the amniotic egg.** You can see these characteristics in **Figure 21.** When reptiles evolved about 320 million years ago, the Earth was entering a long, dry period. Reptiles were better suited to dry conditions than amphibians were. Within 50 million years, reptiles had replaced amphibians as the dominant land vertebrates.

For hundreds of millions of years, reptiles dominated the land. One group of reptiles, the *pterosaurs,* took to the air long before birds did. Other reptile groups lived in the seas. Before whales and dolphins existed, huge seagoing reptiles roamed the seas. All of the flying reptiles and most of the large seagoing reptiles would become extinct along with the dinosaurs. Today, many smaller reptiles, such as snakes and crocodiles, are important predators in many ecosystems.

❯ **Reading Check** *Why are amphibians tied to water, despite their adaptations to life on land?*

ACADEMIC VOCABULARY

diversity variety

amniotic egg (AM nee AHT ik EG) a type of egg that is produced by reptiles, birds, and egg-laying mammals and that contains a large amount of yolk

Figure 21 The tough but porous shell of an amniotic egg provides protection while allowing the exchange of oxygen and carbon dioxide. The amniotic egg allows reptiles to reproduce in dry environments.

Dinosaurs Dinosaurs capture our imagination like few other groups of animals do. These animals grew to huge sizes and dominated life on land for more than 100 million years. Then, they seemingly vanished. The first dinosaurs appeared about 230 million years ago, but these animals were relatively small. We often think of dinosaurs as just large reptiles, but dinosaurs were special. Recent fossil evidence suggests that at least some dinosaurs were warmblooded.

Kinds of Dinosaurs Dinosaurs lived through three major time periods—the Triassic Period, the Jurassic Period, and the Cretaceous Period. Many of the dinosaurs we know best are from the Jurassic Period, which includes the largest land animals of all time, the plant-eating sauropods. **Figure 22** shows examples of dinosaurs from the Jurassic Period. By the late Jurassic Period, the carnivorous theropods were common. Theropods, like *Tyrannosaurus rex,* had a large head with teeth adapted for slicing, and some theropods had sickle-shaped claws on their feet for ripping open prey. Theropods were the dominant terrestrial predators until the end of the Cretaceous Period.

READING TOOLBOX

Word Parts Use a dictionary to find the meanings of the word parts in the terms *theropod* and *sauropod.*

Extinction of Dinosaurs Some debate still exists about what caused the extinction of dinosaurs at the end of the Cretaceous Period. From information based on geological formations, we know that massive volcanic eruptions occurred during this time, and a huge chunk of rock, 8 to 16 km (5 to 10 mi) in diameter, slammed into the Earth at the end of the Cretaceous Period. The huge asteroid created a crater 320 km (200 mi) wide off of the coast of Mexico's Yucatán Peninsula.

The material thrown into the air by this impact may have blocked out sunlight for a long time, and the amount of food for plant-eating dinosaurs would have dropped significantly. Also, these events probably changed the climate dramatically. The endothermic birds and mammals, which were relatively small and were insulated by feathers and fur, survived. Many smaller, coldblooded reptiles and amphibians also survived. Few large species survived.

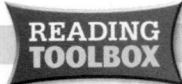

Figure 22 Dinosaurs of the Jurassic Period included the huge, plant-eating sauropod and theropods such as *Tyrannosaurus rex.*

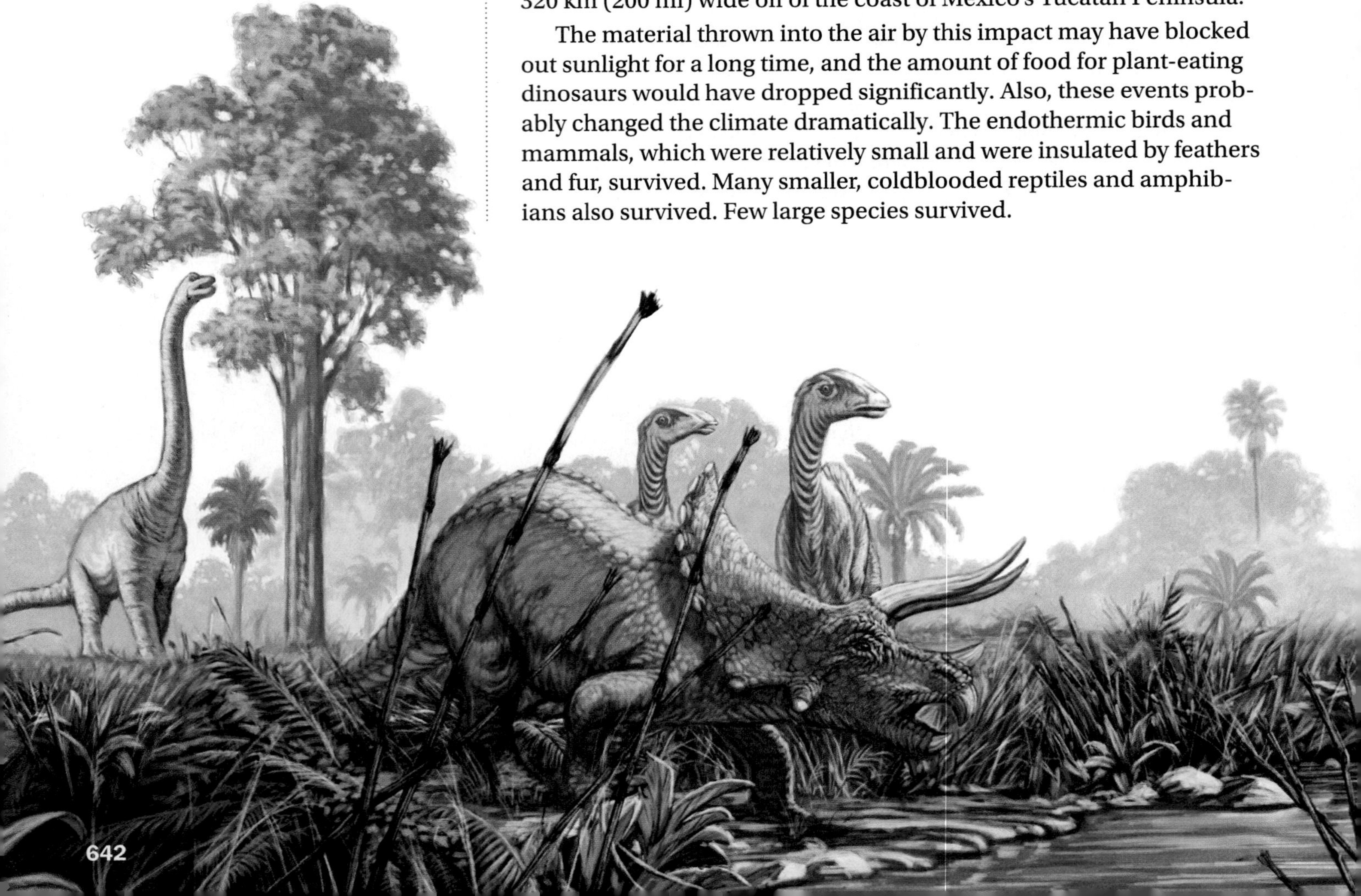

Evolution of Birds

❯ Birds first evolved about 150 million years ago from small, meat-eating dinosaurs. The first birds had a skeleton that looked almost exactly like that of a dinosaur. The first fossil found to show the link between dinosaurs and birds was that of *Archaeopteryx*. **Figure 23** shows *Archaeopteryx,* which was about the size of a crow and shared many features with its small, theropod ancestors. For example, it had a long reptilian tail, teeth, and arms with fingers and claws. *Archaeopteryx* did not have a breastbone to anchor its flight muscles, like modern birds have. Also, *Archaeopteryx* had solid bones instead of the hollow bones that modern birds have. Because of these dinosaur-like features, several *Archaeopteryx* fossils were thought to be the fossils of a dinosaur.

What makes *Archaeopteryx* fossils appear birdlike? First, *Archaeopteryx* had feathers on its wings and tail. It also had a fused collarbone—the wishbone—which dinosaurs did not have. Recent fossil discoveries in China have supported the view that dinosaurs are the ancestors of birds. These discoveries also suggest that flight probably evolved to help dinosaurs glide from trees.

Age of Birds While the dinosaurs went extinct at the end of the Cretaceous Period, birds survived and diversified rapidly. On some continents, a brief Age of Birds arose before mammals took over the land. During this time, huge birds ranged through the plains and forests, preying on small mammals. Many features that evolved in birds helped birds fly. For example, light, hollow bones have reduced birds' weight. Birds have also gained huge flight muscles and a breastbone for the attachment of these muscles. Birds have adapted to many habitats, including the oceans and the deserts.

❯ **Reading Check** *What characteristics of Archaeopteryx were similar to the characteristics of birds today?*

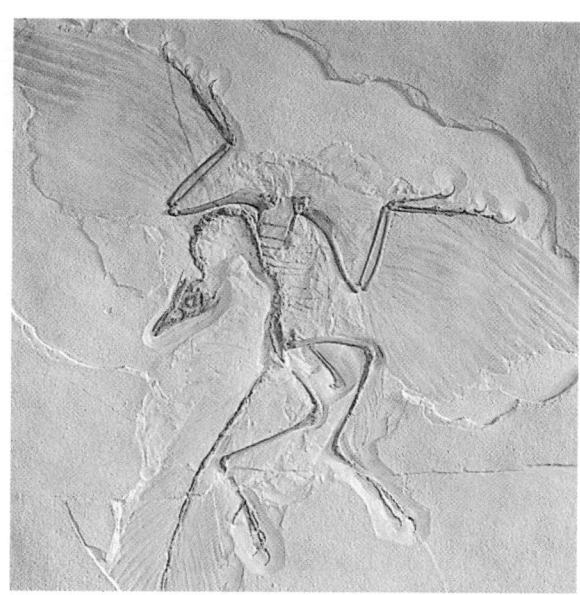

Figure 23 The *Archaeopteryx* fossil above shows clear impressions of feathers surrounding the wings. ❯ **What features did *Archaeopteryx* share with dinosaurs?**

Figure 24 The first mammals were probably small, insect-eating animals, much like this tree shrew. **❯ Did mammals exist during the time of the dinosaurs?**

therapsid (thuh RAP sid) a member of the extinct order of mammal-like reptiles that likely gave rise to mammals

Evolution of Mammals

❯ The first mammals appeared about 220 million years ago, not long after dinosaurs appeared. Mammals are descendants of the *therapsids.* **Therapsids** were an extinct order of mammal-like reptiles that enjoyed a brief period of dominance on land before the dinosaurs became dominant. Early mammals were tiny—about the size of mice. They were probably insect-eating tree dwellers that were active at night and perhaps resembled the tree shrew in **Figure 24.** Recent discoveries, however, show that some early mammals may have spent time in the water, like the beavers of today do.

For 155 million years, while the dinosaurs flourished, mammals were a minor group that changed little. The extinction of dinosaurs opened a huge opportunity for mammals. In the Tertiary Period, many new groups of mammals appeared and many species grew to large sizes and took over the ecological roles once filled by dinosaurs. About 10 million years after the dinosaurs and large marine reptiles disappeared, mammals took to the oceans, with the appearance of the ancestors of today's whales, dolphins, and sea cows.

Ice Age Mammals Today, almost all large land animals are mammals. However, many more large land mammals existed during the last ice age (about 2 million to 10,000 years ago). At that time, many species of enormous mammals roamed the Earth. Giant ground sloths weighed 3 tons and were as large as a modern elephant. Large, lionlike saber-toothed cats hunted with jaws that opened an incredible 120° to allow the cat to drive its huge upper pair of canine teeth into prey. The shoulders of Irish elk were over 2.1 m (7 ft) high, and the span of the antlers could be as large as 3.65 m (12 ft). All of these giant mammals are now extinct. Many disappeared because of changes in the climate, but hunting by early humans also played a role in the extinction of many large mammals around the world. Today, only elephants approach the size of the enormous mammoths that roamed Earth long ago.

❯ **Reading Check** *What were early mammals like?*

Section 4 Review

❯ KEY IDEAS

1. **List** the key characteristics of chordates.
2. **Name** two important evolutionary innovations in fish.
3. **Identify** three characteristics that helped amphibians adapt to land.
4. **Describe** two evolutionary innovations that first appeared in reptiles.
5. **Describe** the evolutionary link between birds and dinosaurs.
6. **Name** the group from which mammals evolved.

CRITICAL THINKING

7. **Evaluating a Hypothesis** Evaluate this statement: Amphibians are not fully adapted for life on land.
8. **Recognizing Relationships** In what ways are the adaptations of reptiles to land similar to the adaptations of plants to land?

WRITING FOR SCIENCE

9. **Essay** Dinosaurs changed dramatically from the Triassic to the Jurassic to the Cretaceous. Write an essay about why you think that the types of dinosaurs that dominated the land changed through time.

SuperCroc

WEIRD SCIENCE

Over 100 million years ago, during the Cretaceous period, a creature unlike any that exist today hunted and lived in and along the rivers of prehistoric, sub-Saharan Africa. It was 40 feet long (about as long as a school bus), weighed about 10 tons, and resembled modern-day crocodiles. Due to its size, paleontologists named the species *Sarcosuchus imperator,* which means "flesh crocodile emperor." This animal is the largest crocodilian that has ever lived and has rightfully earned the nickname SuperCroc.

Super Hunter

SuperCroc's skull possessed several adaptations that made it a magnificent hunter. Its jaws were 6 feet long and contained more than 100 thick, spike-like teeth. Powerful jaws allowed SuperCroc to eat very large prey. SuperCroc also had a bony bulb at the tip of the snout that enclosed a hollow cavity. This bulb, called a *bulla,* may have given SuperCroc an enhanced sense of smell, which it could use to locate prey. It may also have been a resonating chamber for sounds used to communicate with other SuperCrocs. The eye sockets of SuperCroc are tilted upward, which allowed SuperCroc to watch the river bank for food while it stayed camouflaged in the water.

Digging up bones Paleontologist Paul Sereno patiently digs up the fossilized bones of a SuperCroc. By studying the bones and how they fit together, paleontologists can determine how the animal used its environment and what kind of food it ate.

Quick Project SuperCroc had bony plates covering its body. Find out what these plates are called and how they were used.

Objectives

> Identify the stages of early animal development.

> Describe the changes that occur during early development.

Materials

- prepared slides of sea-star development, including:
  - unfertilized egg
  - zygote
  - 2-cell stage
  - 4-cell stage
  - 8-cell stage
  - 16-cell stage
  - 32-cell stage
  - 64-cell stage
  - blastula
  - early gastrula
  - middle gastrula
  - late gastrula
  - young sea-star larva
- compound light microscope
- paper and pencil

Safety

Embryonic Development

Most members of the animal kingdom (including sea stars and humans) begin life as a single cell—the fertilized egg, or zygote. The early stages of development are quite similar in different species. Cleavage follows fertilization. During cleavage, the zygote divides many times without growing. The new cells migrate and form a hollow ball of cells called a blastula. The cells then begin to organize into the three primary germ layers: endoderm, mesoderm, and ectoderm. During this process, the developing organism is called a gastrula.

Procedure

1 Obtain a set of prepared slides that show sea-star eggs at different stages of development. Choose slides labeled unfertilized egg, zygote, 2-cell stage, 4-cell stage, 8-cell stage, 16-cell stage, 32-cell stage, 64-cell stage, blastula, early gastrula, middle gastrula, late gastrula, and young sea-star larva. (Note: Blastula is the general term for the embryonic stage that results from cleavage. In mammals, a blastocyst is a modified form of the blastula.)

2 ◆ **CAUTION: Glassware is fragile.** Examine each slide using a compound light microscope. Using the microscope's low-power objective first, focus on one good example of the developmental stage listed on the slide's label. Then switch to the high-power objective, and focus on the image with the fine adjustment. Notify the teacher of broken glass or cuts. Do not clean up broken glass or spills with broken glass unless the teacher tells you to do so.

3 In your lab report, draw a diagram of each developmental stage that you examine (in chronological order). Label each diagram with the name of the stage it represents and the magnification used. Record your observations as soon as they are made. Do not redraw your diagrams. Draw only what you see; lab drawings do not need to be artistic or elaborate. They should be well organized and include specific details.

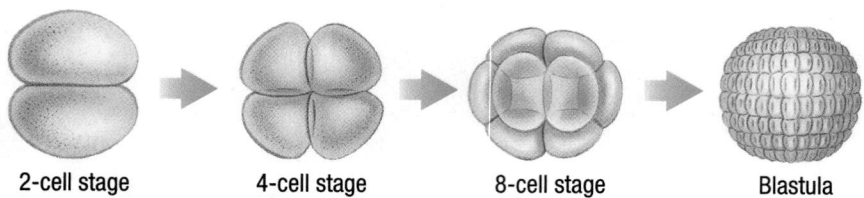

2-cell stage   4-cell stage   8-cell stage   Blastula

**Orange marble
sea star**

④ ⬧ ⬧ Clean up your lab materials according to your teacher's instructions. Wash your hands before leaving the lab.

Analysis and Conclusions

1. **Summarizing Results** Compare the size of the sea-star zygote with that of the blastula. At what stage does the embryo become larger than the zygote?

2. **Analyzing Data** At what stage do all of the cells in the embryo not look exactly like each other? How do cell shape and size change during successive stages of development?

3. **Drawing Conclusions** From your observations of changes in cellular organization, why do you think the blastocoel (the space in the center of the hollow sphere of cells of a blastula) is important during embryonic development?

4. **Predicting Patterns** How are the symmetries of a sea-star embryo and a sea-star larva different from the symmetry of an adult sea star? Would you expect to see a similar change in human development? What must happen to the sea-star gastrula before it becomes a mature sea star?

SCI
LINKS.
www.scilinks.org
Topic: Origin of Tissues
Code: HX81086

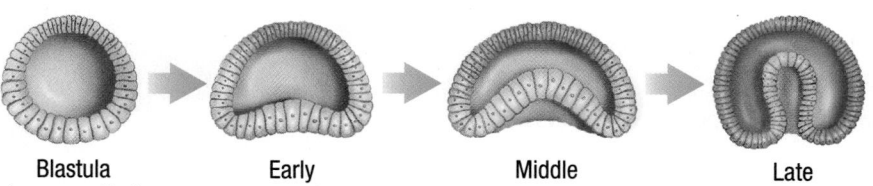

| Blastula (cross section) | Early gastrula | Middle gastrula | Late gastrula |

Extensions

5. **Further Inquiry** Using the procedure that you followed in this investigation, compare embryonic development in other organisms with embryonic development in sea stars. Which types of organisms would you expect to develop similarly to sea stars? Which types of organisms would you expect to develop differently from sea stars?

Chapter 26 Summary

Key Ideas	Key Terms

1 Characteristics of Animals

> Animals are multicellular, heterotrophic organisms with cells that lack cell walls.

> Animals are often informally grouped as invertebrates or vertebrates, although vertebrates make up only a subgroup of one phylum—Chordata.

Key Terms:
heterotroph (624)
invertebrate (625)
vertebrate (626)

2 Animal Body Systems

> An animal's skeleton provides a framework that supports its body and is vital to animal movement.

> The digestive system extracts energy and nutrients from an animal's food, while the excretory system removes waste products from the animal's body.

> The nervous system carries information about the environment through the body and coordinates responses and behaviors.

> The respiratory system is responsible for exchanging oxygen and carbon dioxide between the body and the environment. The circulatory system transports gases, nutrients, and other substances within the body.

> The two types of reproduction in animals are asexual and sexual.

Key Terms:
hydrostatic skeleton (627)
exoskeleton (627)
endoskeleton (627)
gastrovascular cavity (628)

3 Evolutionary Trends in Animals

> Through evolutionary time, animals have developed more-complex body plans, including true tissues and bilateral symmetry.

> The steps of early embryonic development in animals include cleavage, blastula formation, and gastrulation.

> Animals with bilateral symmetry have one of three basic kinds of internal body plans. The body plan may include a body cavity, or *coelom*.

> The evolution of body segmentation and jointed appendages gave animals a greater ability to move and to be flexible.

Key Terms:
cephalization (633)
cleavage (634)
blastula (634)
gastrulation (634)
protostome (635)
deuterostome (635)
coelom (636)

4 Chordate Evolution

> The key characteristics of chordates are a dorsal nerve cord, a notochord, pharyngeal pouches, and a postanal tail.

> The evolution of jaws and paired fins allowed fish to become efficient underwater predators.

> The major characteristics that helped amphibians succeed on land include lungs, limbs, and a more efficient heart.

> The major evolutionary innovations that first appeared in reptiles are watertight skin and the amniotic egg.

> Birds first evolved about 150 million years ago from small, meat-eating dinosaurs.

> The first mammals appeared about 220 million years ago, not long after dinosaurs appeared. Mammals are descendants of the *therapsids*.

Key Terms:
notochord (638)
amniotic egg (641)
therapsid (644)

1. **Word Parts** Use a dictionary to find the meanings of the word parts in the term *heterotroph*. Then, define the term in your own words.

2. **Concept Map** Construct a concept map that describes the characteristics of animals. Try to include the following terms in your concept map: *heterotrophic, multicellular, cell specialization, body plan, radial symmetry, bilateral symmetry, body system, open circulatory system, closed circulatory system,* and *sexual reproduction.*

Using Key Terms

In your own words, write a definition for each of the following terms.

3. *vertebrate*

4. *gastrovascular cavity*

5. *cephalization*

6. *cleavage*

7. *coelom*

8. *notochord*

9. *amniotic egg*

For each pair of terms, explain how the meanings of the terms differ.

10. *exoskeleton* and *endoskeleton*

11. *protostome* and *deuterostome*

Understanding Key Ideas

12. Which of the following is *not* a characteristic of all animals?
    a. multicellular
    b. heterotrophic
    c. have vertebrae
    d. cells lack cell walls

13. Which type of skeleton uses water pressure to provide support?
    a. spicuoles   c. endoskeleton
    b. exoskeleton   d. hydrostatic skeleton

14. Which body system coordinates responses and behavior?
    a. nervous system
    b. digestive system
    c. circulatory system
    d. respiratory system

15. Which of the following is a group of cells that have the same structure and that work together to perform a specific function?
    a. tissue   c. ganglion
    b. organ   d. organ system

Use the diagram showing one stage of early embryonic development to answer the following question.

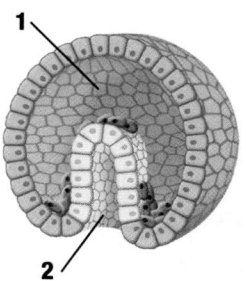

16. Structure 1 is the
    a. blastula.   c. blastopore.
    b. blastocoel.   d. endoderm.

17. What type of animal were the first vertebrates?
    a. fishes   c. amphibians
    b. lancelets   d. echinoderms

18. Which of the following are *not* amniotes?
    a. birds   c. mammals
    b. reptiles   d. amphibians

Explaining Key Ideas

19. **Describe** the functions of the digestive and excretory systems.

20. **List** the first three major steps in development after an animal's egg is fertilized.

21. **Describe** two benefits of having a segmented body.

22. **Explain** how the amniotic egg helped reptiles to replace amphibians as the dominant group of land vertebrates.

Using Science Graphics

Use the graph showing the makeup of the animal kingdom to answer the following questions.

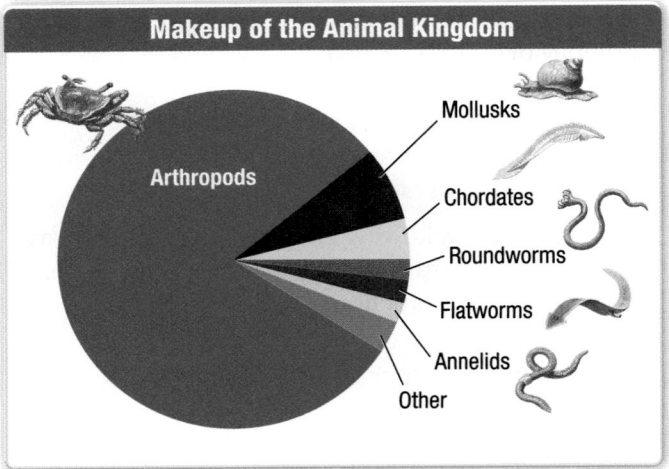

Makeup of the Animal Kingdom

Arthropods

Mollusks

Chordates

Roundworms

Flatworms

Annelids

Other

23. What percentage of animal species represented on the graph are vertebrates?
   a. 75%
   b. 50%
   c. 25%
   d. <10%

Critical Thinking

24. **Recognizing Relationships** Considering that an endoskeleton can support more weight than an exoskeleton, would a large-bodied animal with an exoskeleton be more likely to live in the water or on land? Explain your answer.

25. **Forming Reasoned Opinions** You dissect a jellyfish and an earthworm and notice that they have very different digestive systems. What is a benefit of the earthworm's digestive tract relative to the gastro-vascular cavity of the jellyfish?

26. **Justifying Conclusions** Your friend tells you that sponges are animals and they can sense and respond to the environment because, like all animals, they have a nervous system. Is your friend correct? Why or why not?

27. **Evaluating Hypotheses** Defend the position that cephalization gives terrestrial animals an advantage as they seek food.

28. **Justifying Conclusions** Support the argument that segmentation makes an animal more evolutionarily flexible.

29. **Recognizing Relationships** Explain why scientists think that vertebrates evolved from chordates in the sea.

30. **Forming Reasoned Opinions** Why do you think that amphibians quickly diversified shortly after they first evolved?

Alternative Assessment

31. **Finding and Communicating Information** Use the Internet to find the number of existing species of insects and the number of existing species of worms. Why do you think that there are so many species of insects relative to worms?

32. **Finding and Communicating Information** Use the Internet or library resources to learn what role public aquariums play in educating the public about aquatic life. Then, develop a poster presentation designed to convince the public to donate money to protect aquatic species.

33. **Recognizing Relationships** Vertebrates share several characteristics. Develop an illustrated guide that informs readers about these characteristics.

Writing for Science

34. **Career Connection** Zookeepers are responsible for the day-to-day care of animals in their charge. Research a zookeeper's responsibilities, and write a report that includes job description, training required, kinds of employers, growth prospects, and starting salary.

35. **Essay** Write an essay that describes the progression of dominant vertebrates on land and the evolutionary innovations that helped them take over the land.

36. **Finding and Communicating Information** Use the Internet to research ice-age mammals, and write a report about why these animals went extinct.

Science Concepts

1. Which of the following is a defining characteristic of heterotrophic organisms?

A They are capable of flight.

B They obtain food from their environment.

C They remain in one place throughout their lifetime.

D They make their own food from inorganic materials.

2. Skeletal systems provide all of the following *except*

F absorption of nutrients from food.

G protection for an animal's soft parts.

H a framework for supporting the body.

J a framework for muscles to pull against.

3. Where does gas exchange take place in many aquatic phyla?

A gut   **C** lungs

B gills   **D** kidneys

4. What developmental process leads to the formation of tissue layers?

F evolution

G fertilization

H gastrulation

J asexual reproduction

5. What were the earliest fishes called?

A agnathans

B therapsids

C thecodonts

D acanthodians

6. The first fully terrestrial vertebrates were

F frogs.   **H** dinosaurs.

G reptiles.   **J** mammals.

Using Science Graphics

The diagrams illustrate different organisms. Study the images to answer the following question.

  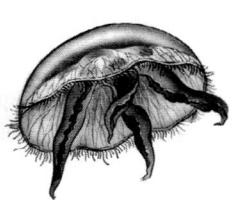

Sponge   Beetle   Jellyfish

7. Which of the organisms has radial symmetry?

A beetle

B sponge

C jellyfish

D both the beetle and the sponge

The graph shows the number of nonmarine tetrapod families over geologic time. Use the graph to answer the following question.

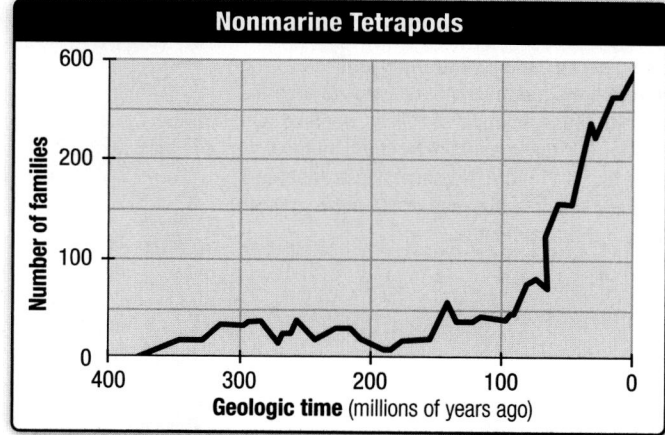

8. What conclusion can be drawn from the graph?

F Most nonmarine tetrapods went extinct.

G The number of nonmarine tetrapods went up.

H The diversity of nonmarine tetrapods went up.

J A mass extinction of nonmarine tetrapods occurred 300 million years ago.

Writing Skills

9. Extended Response Explain how acoelomates and pseudocoelomates differ from coelomates.

Chapter 27

Simple Invertebrates

Preview

1 Sponges
Characteristics of Sponges
Sponge Reproduction
Groups of Sponges

2 Cnidarians
Characteristics of Cnidarians
Groups of Cnidarians

3 Flatworms
Characteristics of Flatworms
Groups of Flatworms

4 Roundworms
Characteristics of Roundworms
Groups of Roundworms
Fighting Parasites

Why It Matters

Sponges, cnidarians, flatworms, and roundworms are the simplest types of animals. Despite these animals' simplicity, humans rely on many of these animals for food, medical products, and more. Humans also fear some of these animals because of the animals' toxic sting or parasitic nature.

These sea anemones may look like plants but are really meat-eating invertebrates.

A sea anemone looks harmless, but each of its tentacles is equipped with thousands of tiny harpoonlike stingers that are filled with poison. Anything that touches the tentacles will be injected with the stingers.

Sea anemones that live directly against each other must be genetically identical. If they are not identical, they will attack each other by using their tentacles until one anemone dies or retreats.

Inquiry Lab

Body Symmetry

Animals vary widely in basic body form. Nowhere is this difference in appearance more pronounced than across the invertebrate phyla.

Procedure

❶ In the center of **three paper squares**, draw a copy of each of the animals shown at right.

❷ Try to fold the drawings along different axes in order to produce halves that are mirror images of each other.

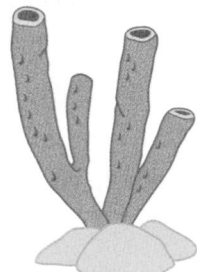

Sponge

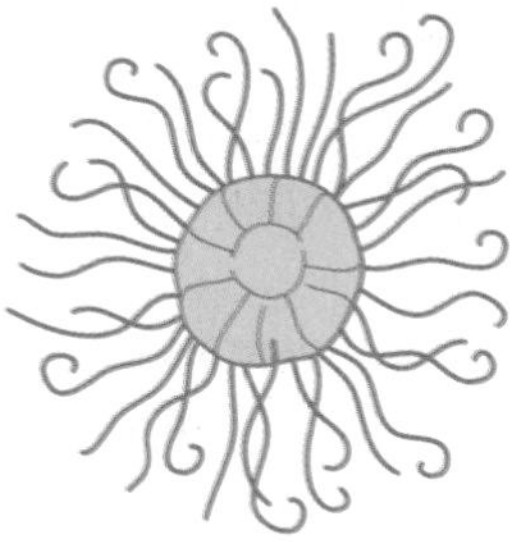

Jellyfish

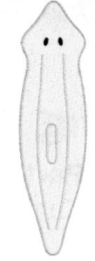

Flatworm

Analysis

1. **Identify** how many axes you can fold the drawings of the sponge, jellyfish, and flatworm along to produce halves that are mirror images.

2. **Research** the terms *asymmetry, radial symmetry,* and *bilateral symmetry.* Apply these terms to the animals shown here.

This sea anemone will eat almost any small animal that swims by, including fish, crabs, shrimps, and as you can see here, squids.

READING TOOLBOX

These reading tools can help you learn the material in this chapter. For more information on how to use these and other tools, see **Appendix: Reading and Study Skills**.

Using Words

Word Parts Knowing the meanings of word parts can help you figure out the meanings of words that you do not know.

Your Turn Use the table to answer the following questions.

1. Propose a definition in your own words for *amoebocyte.*

2. Based on the meanings of the word parts *choan-* and *cyte,* draw what you think a choanocyte might look like.

Word Parts		
Word part	**Type**	**Meaning**
choan-	prefix	funnel
amoebo-	prefix	moving like an amoeba
cyte	root	cell

Using Language

Cause and Effect In biological processes, one step leads to another step. When reading, you can recognize cause-and-effect relationships by looking for words that indicate a result, such as *consequently, next, then,* and *as a result.*

Your Turn Identify the cause and the effect In the following sentences.

1. Water moves forcefully in rivers. Consequently, it wears away the soil from the riverbanks.

2. Rising ocean temperatures may result in the death of coral reefs.

Using Graphic Organizers

Process Chart Science is full of processes. Some processes are cycles that repeat the same steps. You can use a circular process chart to help you remember what order the steps follow and where the cycle begins again.

Your Turn Create a circular process chart that illustrates the life cycle of a fluke.

1. Draw a box. In the box, write the first step of the cycle.

2. To the right and slightly below the first box, draw a second box. Draw an arrow to connect the two boxes. In the second box, write the next step of the cycle.

3. Continue adding boxes and arrows in a circular pattern until each step of the cycle is written in a box. Draw an arrow to connect the last box and the first box.

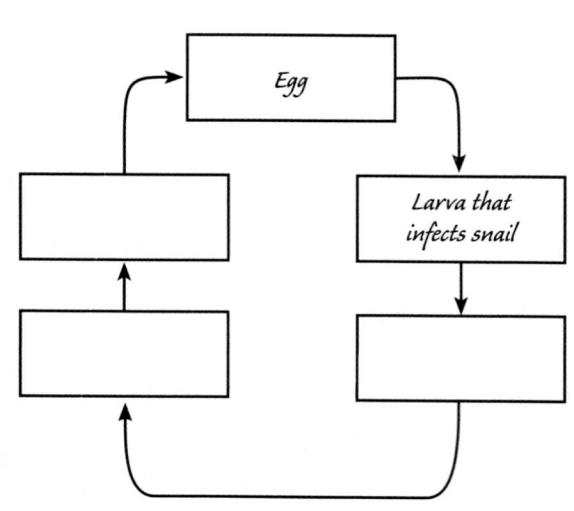

Sponges

Key Ideas	Key Terms	Why It Matters
❯ What are the key characteristics of sponges, and why are sponges considered to be animals? ❯ How do sponges reproduce? ❯ How are groups of sponges classified?	choanocyte amoebocyte spicule spongin	Sponges, with their simple body plan, are the most primitive animals and lack many characteristics we consider typical of animals.

Sponges are so unlike other animals that early naturalists classified them as plants. The body of most sponges has no symmetry and is basically a mass of cells stuck together by a gel-like substance.

Characteristics of Sponges

Sponges can be as small as 1 cm or as large as 2 m. Sponges are considered multicellular, but these animals have only a few types of cells. These cells are not organized into tissues or organs. ❯ **Sponges are classified as animals because they are multicellular, are heterotrophic, have no cell walls, and contain some specialized cells.**

Body Plan A sponge's body is a filter-feeding structure. As **Figure 1** shows, water enters a sponge through tiny pores called *ostia* (singular, *ostium*). Many sponges have one or more baglike chambers, each with an internal cavity. Lining the inside of a sponge is a layer of cells called **choanocytes,** or collar cells. The flagella of these cells extend into the body cavity. As the flagella beat, water is drawn into the ostia. Water exits through a large opening called an *osculum.*

choanocyte (koh AN uh SIET) any of the flagellate cells that line the cavities of a sponge

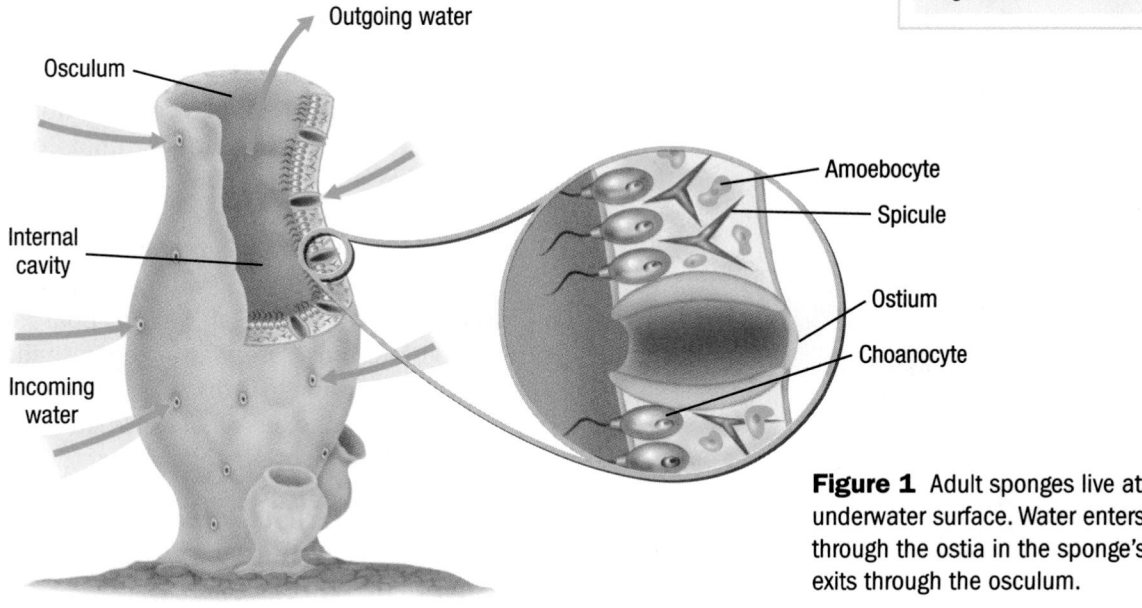

Figure 1 Adult sponges live attached to an underwater surface. Water enters the sponge through the ostia in the sponge's body wall and exits through the osculum.

Feeding The body of a sponge acts like a sieve as water passes through the body cavity. Choanocytes trap bacteria, plankton, and other tiny organisms in their small hairlike projections. The trapped organisms are pulled inside of the choanocytes, where the organisms are digested. Wastes are carried away by sea water exiting the sponge. The choanocytes release nutrients into the body wall of the sponge, where other specialized cells, called amoebocytes, pick up the nutrients. **Amoebocytes** are irregularly shaped, amoebalike cells that move around in the body wall. Amoebocytes supply the rest of the sponge's cells with nutrients and carry away wastes.

Sponge Reproduction

❯ **Sponges reproduce both asexually and sexually. Most sponges are hermaphrodites, which means they produce both eggs and sperm.** The eggs and sperm are produced at different times, which prevents self-fertilization. In most sponges, sperm cells are released from one sponge and are carried by sea water into another sponge's pores, as **Figure 2** shows. Choanocytes in the receiving sponge pass the sperm into the sponge's body wall, where the egg cells are located, and fertilization occurs. Fertilized eggs develop into larvae and then leave the parent sponge. After a short free-swimming stage, the larvae attach to a surface, such as a rock or a coral reef, and develop into adult sponges.

Asexual Reproduction Sponges can reproduce asexually by shedding fragments that are able to produce more cells and develop into a new individual. Some freshwater sponges, which are subjected to more widely varying conditions than marine sponges are, are able to reproduce asexually in a second way. When living conditions become harsh (cold or very dry), these freshwater sponges form clusters of amoebocytes that are encased in a protective coat. Ample food is sealed inside of the clusters of cells so that the cells can survive if the rest of the sponge dies. When conditions improve, the cells grow into a new sponge.

Regeneration A sponge's cells are not organized into tissues, as other animals' cells are. However, a sponge's cells do have a key property of all animal cells—self-recognition. Thus, the cells of a sponge are held together and are organized. A living sponge can be passed through a fine mesh, which separates the individual cells. Afterwards, the individual cells can recombine to form a new sponge. The regenerated sponge has all of the features and organization of the original sponge.

❯ **Reading Check** *Describe how a sponge can asexually reproduce. (See the Appendix for answers to Reading Checks.)*

READING TOOLBOX

Process Chart Draw a process chart showing how sponges can sexually reproduce.

Figure 2 In most species of sponges, sperm from one sponge fertilize eggs from another sponge. ❯ **After a sponge's egg is fertilized, what does it develop into?**

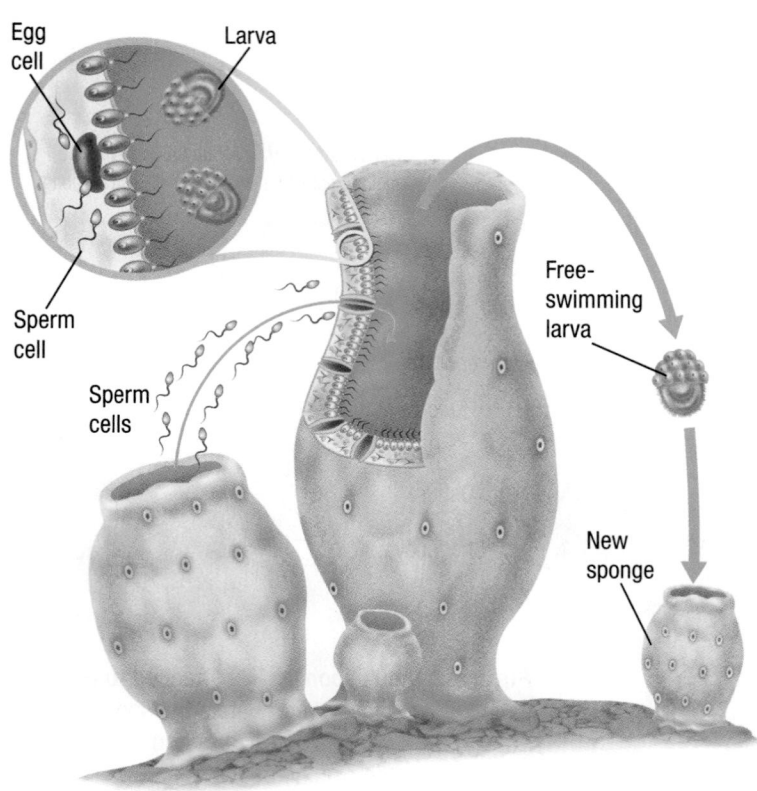

Egg cell

Larva

Sperm cell

Sperm cells

Free-swimming larva

New sponge

Calcareous sponge

Glass sponge

Demosponge

Groups of Sponges

Sponges live in warm, shallow sea water and in deep, cold areas of the ocean. A few species of sponges even live in fresh water. About 5,000 species of sponges are living today. **Figure 3** shows the three different main types of modern sponges.

Sponge Skeletons The skeleton of a sponge keeps the sponge from collapsing in on itself. A sponge's skeleton, however, does not have a fixed framework like a human skeleton does. Instead, the skeleton of most sponges is composed of spicules. A **spicule** is a tiny needle made of silica or calcium carbonate. A few sponges have a skeleton composed of a resilient, flexible protein fiber called **spongin.** Spicules, spongin, or both are found throughout a sponge's body wall. Each of the three groups of modern sponges has a skeleton made of one or more of these supportive structures.

Sponge Classification ❯ **The modern sponges are classified according to the composition of the skeleton in their body wall.** Calcareous sponges have a hard skeleton made of individual calcium carbonate spicules. Glass sponges have a latticelike skeleton made of silica spicules. Demosponges can have a skeleton made of loose silica spicules, spongin, a combination of silica spicules and spongin, or neither.

❯ **Reading Check** *Compare the three main types of sponge skeletons.*

Figure 3 Sponges have skeletons that are made of spicules, spongin, or both.
❯ Why do you think that glass sponges are named as they are?

---

amoebocyte (uh MEE boh SIET) in sponges and other invertebrates, an amoeba-like cell that moves through the body fluids, removes wastes, and participates in other processes

spicule a needle of silica or calcium carbonate in the skeleton of some sponges

spongin a fibrous protein that contains sulfur and makes up the skeleton of some sponges

---

Section 1 Review

❯ **KEY IDEAS**

1. **Describe** the characteristics that sponges share with other animals.
2. **Compare** asexual and sexual reproduction in sponges.
3. **Describe** the three types of sponge skeletons.

CRITICAL THINKING

4. **Inferring Conclusions** Individuals of a single sponge species vary greatly in appearance because of many different environmental factors, such as temperature and water depth. How might these factors make sponge classification difficult?

METHODS OF SCIENCE

5. **Forming Hypotheses** Adult sponges are sessile, which means that they do not move around. What advantage might a free-swimming larval stage provide to sponges?

Section 2
Cnidarians

Key Ideas	Key Terms	Why It Matters
❯ What are the two body forms that are found in the cnidarian life cycle? ❯ What are the three main groups of modern cnidarians?	medusa polyp cnidocyte nematocyst planula	Cnidarians have a simple but distinctive body plan and two body forms and are important organisms in aquatic environments.

Hydras, corals, jellyfish, and sea anemones belong to the phylum Cnidaria. Most cnidarians (ni DER ee uhns) live in the ocean.

Characteristics of Cnidarians

The cells of cnidarians, in contrast to the cells of sponges, are arranged into tissues. **Figure 4** shows that the cnidarian body has two tissue layers, an outer *epidermis* and an inner *gastrodermis*. Between these layers is a jellylike material called *mesoglea*. Cnidarians have a body that is radially symmetrical. In radial symmetry, an organism's body parts are arranged around a central axis, like the spokes of a wheel. ❯ Cnidarians have two basic body forms, called the *medusa* and the *polyp*. **Medusa** forms are free floating and are often umbrella shaped. **Polyp** forms are tubelike and attach to a rock or some other object. Many cnidarians exist only as medusas, others exist only as polyps, and still others alternate between these two forms.

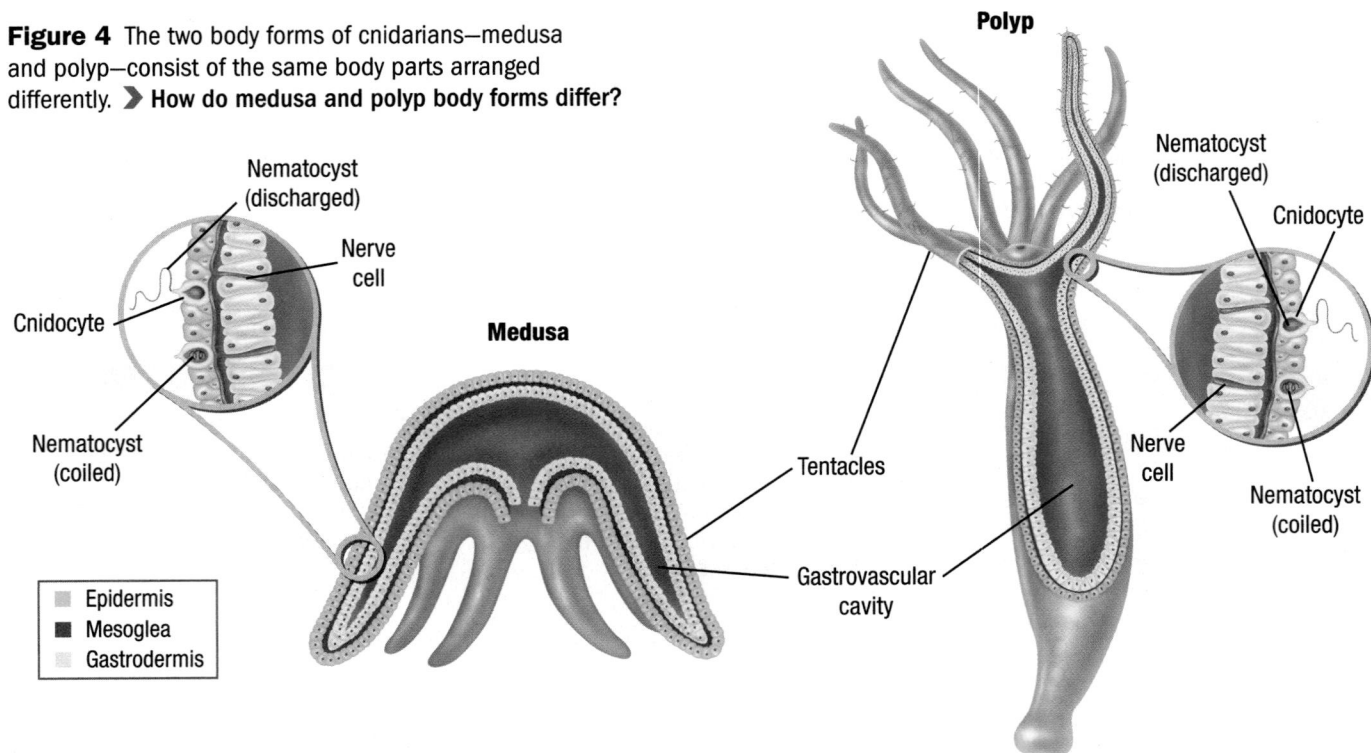

Figure 4 The two body forms of cnidarians—medusa and polyp—consist of the same body parts arranged differently. ❯ How do medusa and polyp body forms differ?

Polyp

Nematocyst (discharged)

Cnidocyte

Nerve cell

Nematocyst (coiled)

Nematocyst (discharged)

Nerve cell

Cnidocyte

Nematocyst (coiled)

Medusa

Tentacles

Gastrovascular cavity

■ Epidermis
■ Mesoglea
■ Gastrodermis

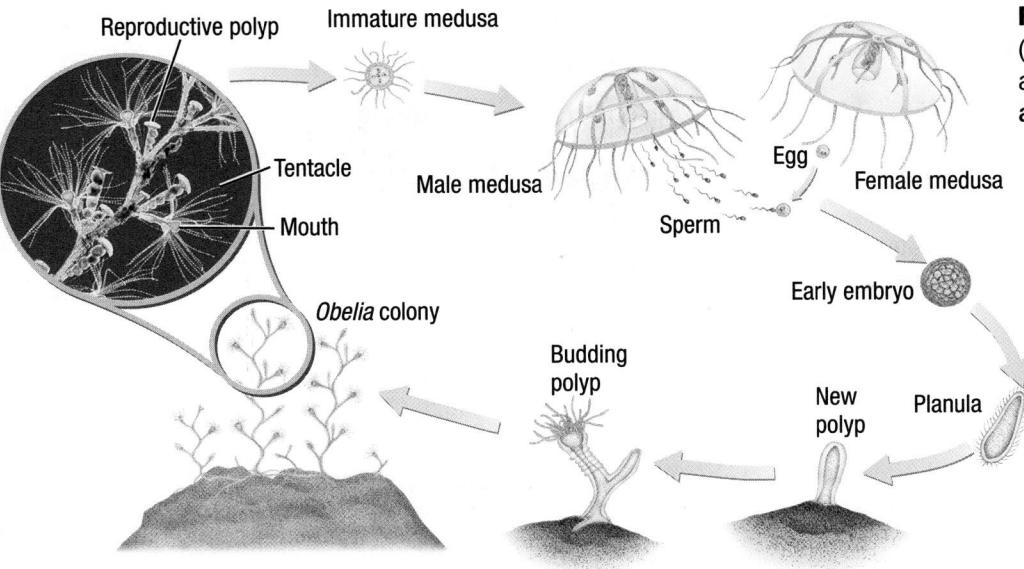

Reproductive polyp

Immature medusa

Tentacle

Mouth

Obelia colony

Male medusa

Sperm

Egg

Female medusa

Early embryo

Budding polyp

New polyp

Planula

Figure 5 In *Obelia*'s life cycle, the medusa (sexual) stage and the polyp (asexual) stage alternate. **❯ What does the fertilized egg of a medusa develop into?**

Movement and Response Cnidarians have nerve cells arranged into two nets, one in the epidermis and the other in the gastrodermis. Although cnidarians do not have a centralized structure that functions as a brain, the nerve nets coordinate sensory and motor activities. Sensory cells detect light, chemicals, and mechanical stimuli. Musclelike cells are involved in feeding, digestion, and other activities. These cells compress the mesoglea. The compressed mesoglea extends, which results in movement.

Feeding The cnidarian gastrovascular cavity has only one opening, which functions as both a mouth and an anus. Flexible fingerlike tentacles surround this opening. Located on the tentacles are stinging cells called **cnidocytes.** Cnidocytes are the distinguishing characteristic of the animals in the phylum Cnidaria. Within each cnidocyte is a threadlike organelle called a **nematocyst.** Nematocysts, which may contain toxins, are used for defense and to capture prey. When triggered, the nematocyst shoots out and sinks into the cnidarian's prey. The captured prey is then pushed by the tentacles into the cnidarian's gastrovascular cavity, where the prey is digested.

Reproduction Many cnidarians, such as *Obelia* shown in **Figure 5,** have a life cycle that alternates between a polyp and a medusa stage. Sexual reproduction occurs when the medusas release sperm or eggs into the water. The gametes fuse and produce zygotes that develop into free-swimming larvae called **planulae** (singular, *planula*). The planulae eventually settle on the ocean floor and develop into polyps. Each polyp gives rise to a colony by asexual budding. Reproductive polyps give rise asexually to male and female medusas. These medusae leave the polyps. Mature male and female medusas release gametes, and the life cycle is repeated. Reproduction in cnidarians varies widely, with sexual and asexual reproduction occurring in both the polyp and medusa forms.

❯ Reading Check *Summarize the life cycle of* **Obelia.**

medusa a free-swimming, jellyfish-like, and often umbrella-shaped sexual stage in the life cycle of a cnidarian

polyp a form of a cnidarian that has a cylindrical, hollow body and that is usually attached to a rock or to another object

cnidocyte (NIE doh SIET) a stinging cell of a cnidarian

nematocyst a stinging organelle that is used to inject a toxin into prey

planula the free-swimming, ciliated larva of a cnidarian

READING TOOLBOX

Word Parts Use the words *cnidocyte* and *nematocyst* in a sentence. How are these two words related?

QuickLab

Coral Skeletons

Some corals are colonial animals that secrete a rock-hard covering around their soft bodies. Like other skeletons, these structures are species specific and can be used to distinguish between coral types.

15 min

Procedure

❶ Examine several types of **coral skeletons** with a **hand lens.** Observe the distinct pits or channels in which the individual coral animals once lived.

❷ For each different coral skeleton, make a drawing of the skeleton's appearance.

Analysis

1. **Explain** whether the coral skeleton was once alive.

2. **Describe** how the structure of the coral skeleton complements the skeleton's function.

3. **CRITICAL THINKING** **Forming Hypotheses** Although a coral skeleton may be asymmetric, coral animals have radial symmetry. Explain the difference in symmetry.

Groups of Cnidarians

❯ **The three main groups of cnidarians are hydrozoans, scyphozoans, and anthozoans.** Hydrozoans are the most primitive type of cnidarian. Scyphozoans (SIE fuh ZOH uhns) are referred to as true jellyfish. Anthozoans, such as corals, are the largest group of cnidarians.

Hydrozoans Most hydrozoans are marine animals with a life cycle that includes both polyp and medusa stages. Often many individual hydrozoans live in colonies. Unlike the cells of most multicellular organisms, the cells of the colony are not interdependent. However, colony cells are specialized. For example, a Portuguese man-of-war colony (genus *Physalia*) has both medusae and polyps. A gas-filled float allows *Physalia* to float on the surface of the water. Long tentacles dangle below the float. These tentacles stun and entangle prey. *Physalia* has other specialized polyps and medusae, each of which carries out a unique function, such as feeding or sexual reproduction.

Freshwater hydrozoans are less common than marine hydrozoans. The freshwater hydra has no medusa stage. The hydra exists only as a polyp that can move along an underwater surface by tumbling, as **Figure 6** shows. Hydras live in quiet ponds, lakes, and streams.

Figure 6 Hydras attach themselves to a surface and stay in place for long periods of time. However, hydras can move by tumbling. ❯ **Infer why a hydra might move from one place to another.**

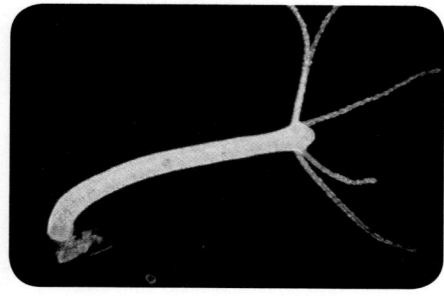

Scyphozoans Scyphozoans are also called *jellyfish.* Most jellyfish have a life cycle similar to that of the *Obelia* hydrozoan. But unlike *Obelia,* jellyfish spend most of their life as a medusa. Jellyfish are active predators. They trap their prey by using tentacles and then sting the prey by using nematocysts. Some jellyfish make toxins strong enough to kill a large animal. Jellyfish can be as small as a thimble or as large as a queen-size mattress!

Figure 7 The clownfish lives symbiotically among the tentacles of sea anemones. The anemone's stinging tentacles protect the clownfish from predators. The clownfish, in turn, drives away other fish that try to feed on the anemone.

Anthozoans The name *Anthozoa* means "flower animals," which is a fitting description for the more than 6,000 species in this group. Two examples of anthozoans are the brightly colored sea anemones, which **Figure 7** shows, and corals. Anthozoans exist only as polyps. Nearly all of the shallow-water species contain symbiotic algae. The anthozoans provide a place for the algae to live in exchange for some of the food that the algae produce. The brilliant color of most anthozoans actually comes from the algae living inside of them.

Sea anemones are found in coastal areas. Anemones attach themselves to rocks and other submerged objects. Sea anemones feed on fish and other marine animals that happen to swim within reach of the anemones' tentacles. When anemones are touched, they pull their tentacles into their body cavity and contract into a tight ball.

Most coral polyps live in colonies called *coral reefs*. The top layer of a coral reef contains living coral polyps. Each polyp secretes a tough, stonelike outer skeleton that is made of calcium carbonate and that is cemented to the skeletons of its neighbors. When the polyps die, their hardened skeletons remain and serve as the foundation for new polyps. Over thousands of years, these polyps build up the foundation of the reef. Coral reefs are found primarily in tropical regions of the world where the ocean is warm and clear. Coral reefs form a habitat for a wide diversity of life. Reefs also protect coastlines from wave erosion and provide food for fish.

> **Reading Check** *How is the foundation of a coral reef formed?*

www.scilinks.org
Topic: Coral Reefs
Code: HX80356

Section 2 Review

> **KEY IDEAS**

1. **Compare** the polyp and medusa body forms of cnidarians, and give an example of each.

2. **Summarize** the similarities and differences in the three main groups of modern cnidarians.

CRITICAL THINKING

3. **Forming Hypotheses** How might having two body forms give cnidarians an advantage over species with only one body form?

4. **Applying Information** A scientist announces the discovery of a new cnidarian species. What features would you expect this species to have?

USING SCIENCE GRAPHICS

5. **Understanding Diagrams** Examine the diagram of *Obelia*'s life cycle in this section. Identify the stage at which *Obelia* reproduces sexually.

Rain Forest of the Sea

Coral reefs are often called the *rain forests of the sea* because of the extraordinary amount of biodiversity found in these undersea ecosystems. Coral reefs may even exceed tropical rain forests as the most species-rich places on Earth. But like rain forests, reefs are a rapidly disappearing habitat.

More Than Just a Pretty Place

Coral reefs provide a protected habitat for an amazing diversity of life. Over 4,000 species of fish inhabit coral reefs. Reefs are home to many other organisms, such as sponges, jellyfish, crustaceans, mollusks, echinoderms, sea turtles, and sea snakes. Millions of people rely on fish found in coral reefs for food. Reefs attract millions of tourists each year. In addition, coral reefs provide medicines used to treat HIV, heart disease, and cancer.

At the current rate of destruction, 70% of coral reefs will be destroyed by the year 2050. Coral bleaching is one of the major problems. Rising ocean temperatures cause corals to lose their symbiotic algae. This process turns the coral white, and the coral usually dies.

Research Use library and Internet resources to find out how test-tube-baby coral may help save the coral reefs.

Threats to Reefs Humans are the single greatest threat to coral reefs. Overfishing disrupts the reef ecosystem and can result in damage to the reef itself. Fishing with dynamite or cyanide kills the fish and the coral reef in which the fish live.

Key Ideas	Key Terms	Why It Matters
❯ What are three important characteristics of flatworms? ❯ What are three groups of modern flatworms, and is each group free living or parasitic?	proglottid	Many flatworms are free-living marine animals that are predators of other small invertebrates, but others are serious parasites of humans and other vertebrates.

When you think of worms, animals with long, tubular bodies probably come to mind. Other types of worms, such as the flatworm shown in **Figure 8,** might be less familiar. Flatworms are the largest group of acoelomate worms—worms that lack a true body cavity, or *coelom.*

Characteristics of Flatworms

The flatworms are named for their thin, flat body, which is typically only a few cell layers thick. Although the flatworm body is relatively simple, it is a great deal more complex than the body of a sponge or cnidarian. ❯ **Flatworms have bilateral symmetry, three tissue layers, and cephalization—the concentration of nerve tissue at an animal's "head" end.**

Body Plan Flatworms are bilaterally symmetrical, which means that their body has right and left halves that are mirror images of each other. Flatworms also have a third embryonic tissue layer, the *mesoderm,* which is absent in sponges and cnidarians. And unlike sponges and cnidarians, flatworms have tissues that are organized into organs. Flatworms also have muscles, which are formed from mesodermal tissue. The gastrovascular cavity of flatworms is like that of cnidarians in that it has just a single opening.

Movement and Response Most of the sensory organs and nerve cells of flatworms are located at the "head" end of the body. This collection of cells forms a kind of primitive brain. In general, animals that have a head end move through their environment more easily than less-complex animals do. The flatworm's muscle tissue enables it to be more-active predators than cnidarians are.

Feeding Free-living flatworms are carnivores that take in food through the single opening of their gastrovascular cavity. This cavity is branched, and extensions of the cavity run through all of the worm's major tissues. These extensions give each cell ready access to food. Tapeworms, which are parasitic flatworms, have no gastrovascular system, but instead absorb nutrient molecules across their skin.

Figure 8 Flatworms are the simplest type of bilaterally symmetrical animal. ❯ Compare the body plan of this flatworm to the body plans of sponges and cnidarians.

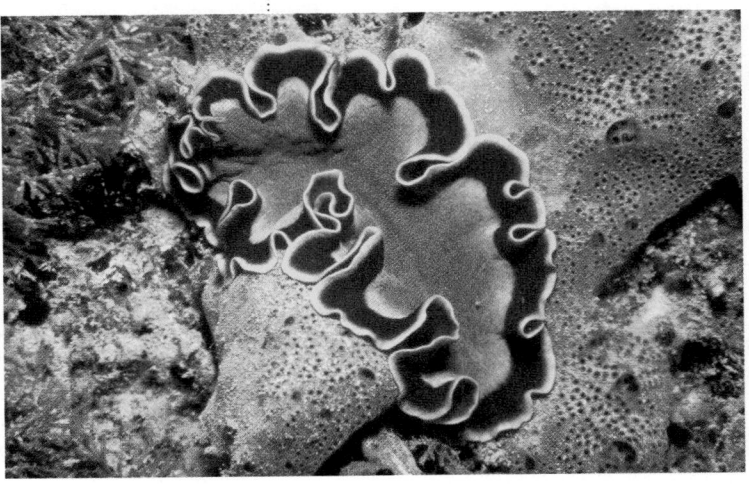

Respiration Flatworms have neither a respiratory nor a circulatory system. Each cell in the animal's body lies close to the exterior environment. This organization allows gases, such as oxygen, to pass efficiently through the flatworm's solid body by diffusion.

Reproduction Flatworms can generally reproduce sexually or asexually. Most species are hermaphroditic, but self-fertilization is not common. Some flatworms, including planarians, can reproduce asexually by fragmentation, so an entirely new individual can grow from a piece of another worm.

proglottid one of the many body sections of a tapeworm; contains reproductive organs

❯ **Reading Check** *How does a flatworm obtain oxygen?*

Up Close Planarian

Planarians are a type of turbellarian that has a three-branched gastrovascular cavity. The multiple branches of the gastrovascular cavity allow nutrients to pass near all of the flatworm's tissues. Some planarians are marine, but most, including *Dugesia,* live in freshwater environments.

Planarian

Scientific name: *Dugesia* sp.
Size: Average length of 3 mm to 15 mm
Range: Worldwide
Habitat: Cool, clear, permanent lakes and streams
Diet: Protozoans and dead and dying animals

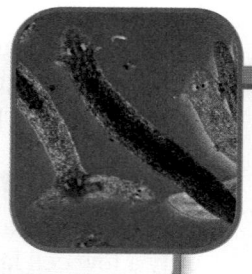

Nervous System Sensory information gathered by the brain is sent to muscles by two nerve cords that are cross-branched. Light-sensitive eyespots are connected to the brain.

Reproduction *Dugesia* reproduces asexually by attaching its tail to a stationary object and stretching until it breaks in two. Each piece will become a complete animal. *Dugesia,* which is hermaphroditic, also reproduces sexually. Two individuals transfer sperm to each other. Eggs of both individuals are fertilized and released.

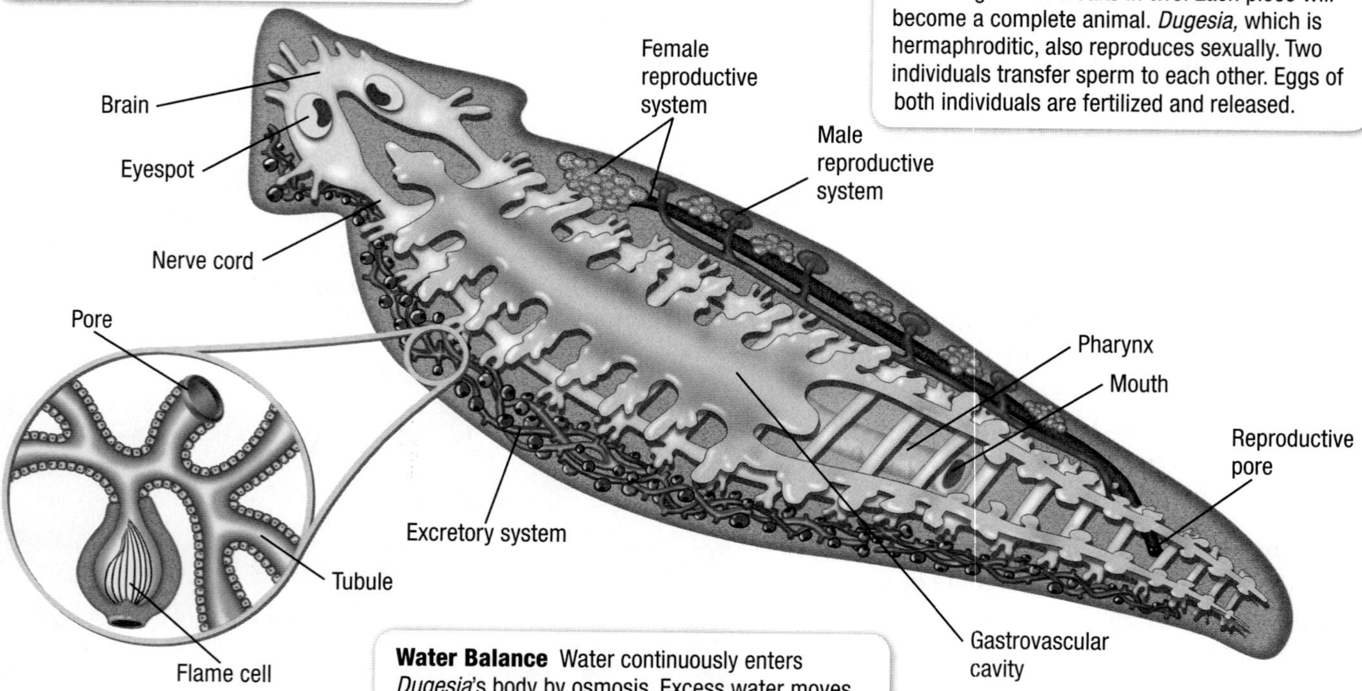

Brain

Eyespot

Nerve cord

Pore

Female reproductive system

Male reproductive system

Pharynx

Mouth

Reproductive pore

Excretory system

Tubule

Flame cell

Gastrovascular cavity

Water Balance Water continuously enters *Dugesia*'s body by osmosis. Excess water moves into a network of tiny tubules. Side branches are lined with flame cells—specialized cells with beating tufts of cilia. The beating cilia draw water through pores to the outside of the worm's body.

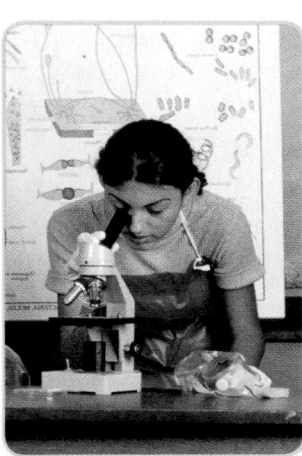

Planarian Behavior

In this lab, you will observe planarian behavior and body organization.

Procedure

❶ Put on **gloves.** Using an **eyedropper,** place a **planarian** in a **culture dish** with **pond water.**

❷ Place a piece of **liver** 1 cm behind the planarian. If the planarian approaches the liver, move the liver. Observe the planarian for 5 more minutes and move the liver periodically.

Analysis

1. **Describe** the planarian's means of locomotion and behavior.

2. **CRITICAL THINKING**
Making Inferences
Does having sensory organs concentrated in one end give planarians an advantage when feeding? Explain.

Groups of Flatworms

❯ Three major groups of modern flatworms include turbellarians, most of which are free-living, and tapeworms and flukes, which are parasitic. About 20,000 species of flatworms are known. Species <u>range</u> in size from less than 1 mm to many meters in length.

Turbellarians Most turbellarians are marine flatworms. These worms are typically predators, but some are herbivores or parasites. Larger turbellarians use their muscles to swim in wavelike motions, while smaller worms move by beating cilia on their lower body. The turbulence caused by the beating cilia gives this group its name. You can read more about turbellarians in the Up Close feature.

Tapeworms Tapeworms are parasitic flatworms. **Figure 9** shows the suckers and hooklike structures that tapeworms use to attach themselves to the inner wall of their host's intestines. Nutrients digested by the host's enzymes are then absorbed directly through the tapeworm's skin.

Tapeworms grow by continuously producing a string of rectangular body sections called **proglottids** immediately behind their head. Each proglottid is a complete reproductive unit that produces both sperm and eggs. Mature proglottids, containing fertilized eggs, break off of the parent worm and are shed in the feces of the host. New tapeworms grow in a host that eats food contaminated with the eggs. Tapeworms infect vertebrates, including humans.

ACADEMIC VOCABULARY

range the full extent covered by something

Figure 9 A tapeworm's body consists of a head and a series of proglottids.
❯ What type of reproduction do tapeworms use?

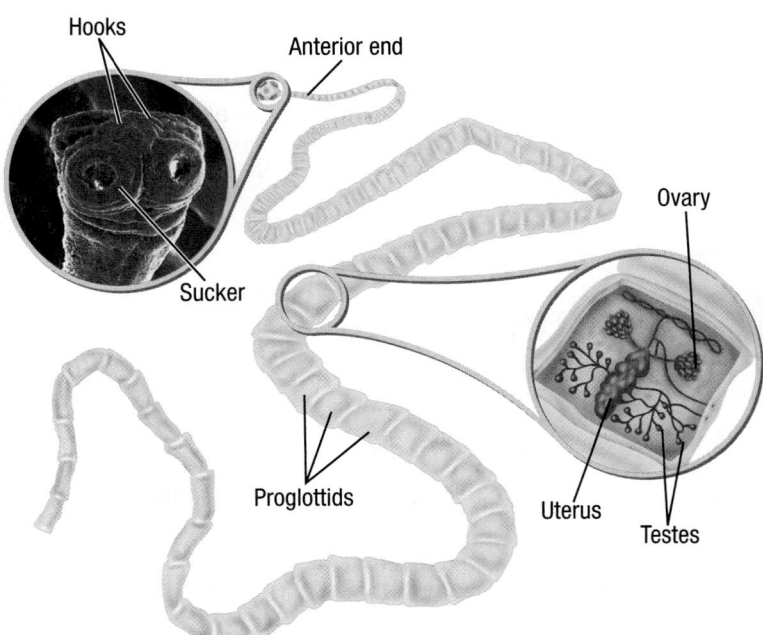

Hooks

Anterior end

Ovary

Sucker

Proglottids

Uterus

Testes

Life Cycle of a Fluke

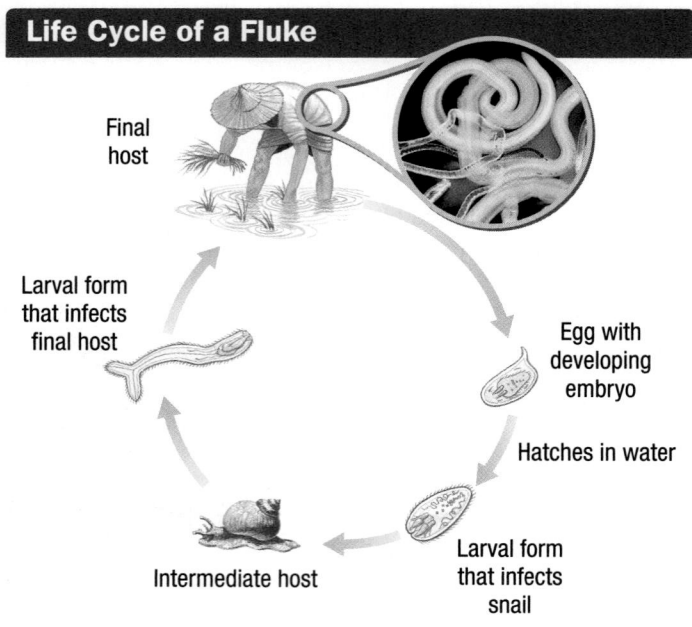

Final host

Egg with developing embryo

Hatches in water

Larval form that infects snail

Intermediate host

Larval form that infects final host

go.hrw.com
✱ interact online
Keyword: HX8SINF10

Figure 10 In the life cycle of blood flukes, snails are intermediate hosts and humans are final hosts.

Flukes The largest group of flatworms is made up of parasitic worms called *flukes.* Some flukes are *endoparasites,* or parasites that live inside their hosts. Endoparasites have a thick protective covering of cells called a *tegument,* which prevents the worm from being digested by its host. The tegument also makes the fluke resistant to the defenses of the host's immune system. Other flukes are *ectoparasites,* or parasites that live on the outside of their hosts. Ectoparasitic flukes infect aquatic hosts, such as fishes and frogs.

Flukes have a simple body plan with few organs. Flukes take their food directly from their host's body. Flukes have one or more suckers that they use to attach themselves to their host. Like tapeworms, ecotoparasitic flukes also have hooks to attach to their hosts. After attaching to a host, both types of flukes use their muscular pharynx to suck nourishment from the host's body fluids. Because of this feeding behavior, flukes do not need their own digestive system. However, flukes do have a highly developed reproductive system and a complex life cycle.

Fluke Life Cycle The life cycle of most flukes involves several hosts, one of which may be a human. Blood flukes of the genus *Schistosoma* are responsible for the disease called *schistosomiasis.* This disease is a major public health problem in Africa, Asia, South America, and some Caribbean islands. Infection occurs when people drink, bathe in, or wade in water containing *Schistosoma* larvae. The larvae bore through a person's skin and travel to blood vessels in the bladder or intestinal wall, where the larvae mature and the females lay eggs. The eggs block blood vessels in the intestinal wall and the liver, which results in bleeding and damage to these organs. The eggs are shed in urine or feces and hatch into larvae that can be picked up by the snail host, as **Figure 10** shows. The larvae reproduce asexually and develop into a form that can infect humans again.

❯ **Reading Check** *Why is a tegument important to endoparasites?*

Section 3 Review

❯ **KEY IDEAS**

1. **Explain** how flatworms differ from sponges and cnidarians.
2. **Name** the three groups of modern flatworms.
3. **Compare** the internal and external anatomy of a turbellarian with that of a tapeworm or a fluke.

4. **Summarize** the life cycle of a blood fluke.

CRITICAL THINKING

5. **Applying Information** Which animal would be most likely to have more water enter its body—a marine flatworm or a freshwater flatworm? Explain your answer.
6. **Recognizing Relationships** Why might it be an adaptive advantage for a parasite not to kill its host?

ALTERNATIVE ASSESSMENT

7. **Making Recommendations** Considering the life cycle of the *Schistosoma* blood fluke, recommend an effective way of controlling the spread of schistosomiasis.

Section 4 Roundworms

Key Ideas	Key Terms	Why It Matters
❯ What are three key characteristics of roundworms? ❯ What are four common types of parasitic roundworms? ❯ What steps can help people avoid roundworms and other parasites?	pseudocoelom	Most roundworms are beneficial decomposers in ecosystems, but others cause serious illness and death in people and destroy crops.

The Earth is literally covered with roundworms. More than 15,000 known species exists currently, and many experts estimate that more than half a million species are yet to be discovered. These worms reproduce so rapidly that some can lay 200,000 eggs in one day! Thousands of tiny roundworms can be found in a handful of soil.

Characteristics of Roundworms

Roundworms (nematodes) have a long, cylindrical body. Some roundworms grow to be a foot or more in length, but most species, such as the one that **Figure 11** shows, are only a few millimeters long. ❯ **Roundworms have three embryonic tissue layers, a pseudocoelom, and a digestive system with separate openings for feeding and waste elimination.**

Body Plan A roundworm's three embryonic tissue layers are the endoderm, the mesoderm, and the ectoderm. Roundworms are bilaterally symmetrical and have a body cavity called a **pseudocoelom** that is located between the mesoderm and the endoderm. In general, animals with pseudocoeloms can coordinate muscle movements more than acoelomate animals can. A roundworm has a long layer of muscles that pull against the body's outer covering and the pseudocoelom, whipping the worm's body from side to side. Like flatworms, roundworms have many nerve cells and sensory cells in the head and a pair of nerves that run the length of the body.

Digestion, Circulation, and Reproduction Free-living roundworms are active hunters that feed on bacteria, fungi, protists, or small invertebrates. Other species are parasites that feed on plants or animals. Food is digested in the tubular gut, and nutrients are taken up into the fluid of the pseudocoelom. Movement of the fluid in the pseudocoelom acts as a simple circulatory system. Oxygen taken up through the roundworm's outer covering and nutrients from the gut diffuse into the fluid and are distributed to the body cells. Cellular wastes pass into the fluid and then out of the body through the outer covering. Roundworms usually reproduce sexually, and the sexes are separate.

❯ **Reading Check** *List the functions of the pseudocoelom.*

pseudocoelom the type of body cavity that forms between the mesoderm and the endoderm in rotifers and roundworms

Figure 11 Most roundworms, including this *Caenorhabditis elegans*, are free living, and they play an important role in decomposition and nutrient recycling.

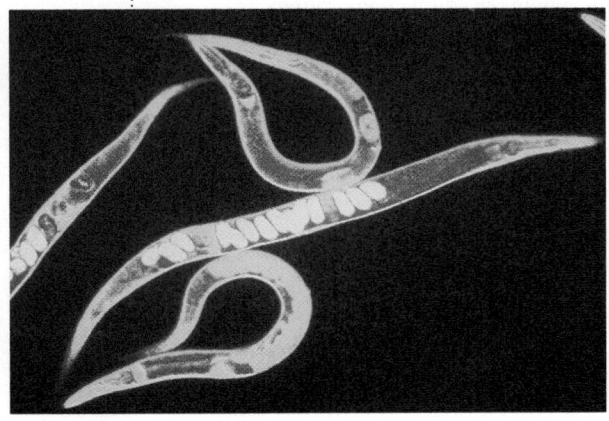

READING TOOLBOX

Cause and Effect Read the text about hookworms. What is the cause and effect that underlie becoming infected with a hookworm?

Groups of Roundworms

Most roundworms are free living, but many types of parasitic round-worms exist. Some of these worms infect humans and animals, while others cause serious damage to crops. ❯ **Common parasitic roundworms include pinworms, hookworms, filarial worms, and ascarids.**

Pinworms **Figure 12** shows a pinworm, which is an intestinal parasite of humans that lives in the rectum and is about 1 cm long. As many as 50% of preschool and school-age children are infected with pinworms. Many infected people have no symptoms. Itching around the anus and sleep disruption can occur. The symptoms are caused by the female pinworm, which moves out of the body during the night and lays her eggs on the host's skin.

Pinworms are spread easily by ingesting eggs found on objects that are contaminated with feces from an infected person. Infection is often discovered by finding adult worms in the feces. A pinworm infection is easily treated with medication and by washing sheets and blankets in hot water. Reinfection is common when many children in a school or child-care center are infected.

Hookworms Hookworms are another intestinal parasite that affect humans. About one-fifth of the world's population is infected with hookworms. The usual symptoms of infection are mild diarrhea and cramps. More serious infections can cause severe anemia.

Hookworms have a different route of infection and life cycle than pinworms have. Hookworms can infect people when they step barefooted on soil containing the worms' larvae. The larvae enter the body through the soles of the feet. They move into the blood vessels and are carried in the blood to the lungs. The larvae migrate through the lung tissue to the throat and are swallowed. After reaching the small intestine, the larvae mature into adults. Adult worms attach themselves to the lining of the small intestine and suck blood from the host. Eggs that are produced by the adults are passed in the host's feces. The larvae that hatch from the eggs can then infect other humans and repeat the cycle.

Figure 12 About 50 roundworm species are parasitic to humans, including pinworms, hookworms, filarial worms, and ascarids.

Hookworms

Pinworm

Filarial Worms Filarial worms are a group of long, thin round-worms that live as adults in the blood or other tissues of vertebrates. A number of these worms affect humans. Filarial worms that live in the lymphatic system cause the most serious infections. Infected mosquitoes transmit larvae to a human host. The larvae move to lymphatic vessels, where the larvae mature. Infection by this type of filarial worm can lead to a condition known as *elephantiasis,* which **Figure 13** shows. The symptoms of elephantiasis include swelling in the arms, legs, breasts, and male genitals due to the collection of fluids. The blocked vessels, as well as chemicals secreted by the worms, suppress the victim's ability to fight off other infections.

The dog heartworm, *Dirofilaria immitis,* is a filarial roundworm that lives as an adult in the heart and blood vessels leading to a dog's lungs. This worm occurs throughout most of the United States. Larvae of these worms are transmitted through the bite of an infected mosquito. The adult worms fill the heart, resulting in weakness and fatigue during exercise. Untreated infections can be fatal, and year-round preventive medication is recommended by veterinarians.

Ascarids Ascarids are roundworms that live in the intestines of pigs, horses, and humans. Ascarid infections are the most common human worm infections. Ascarids feed on food that passes through the intestines of their host. As **Figure 12** shows, the worms can become so numerous that they completely block the host's intestines if left untreated. One ascarid female can produce up to 200,000 eggs a day. The fertilized eggs leave the host's body in feces. The eggs can remain alive in the soil for years.

Ascarid eggs enter the body of another host when the host ingests contaminated food or water. The eggs develop into larvae in the intestines. The larvae bore their way into the bloodstream and are carried to the lungs and throat, where they develop further. The larvae are coughed up, swallowed, and returned to the intestines, where they mature and mate, completing the life cycle.

❯ **Reading Check** *Compare ascarids with hookworms.*

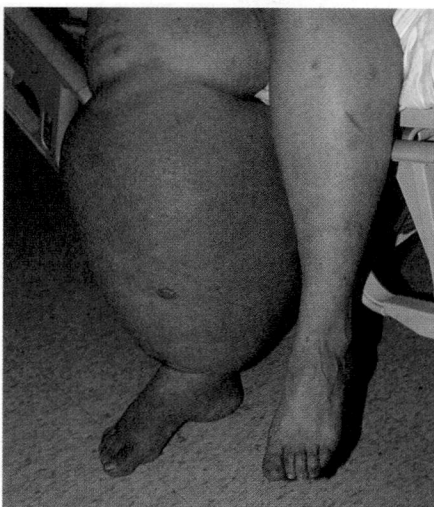

Figure 13 Elephantiasis results from the blockage of the lymphatic system by filarial worms. ❯ **Considering how elephantiasis affects the body, what do you think the function of the lymphatic system is?**

Filarial worms (dog heartworms)

Ascarids (in a pig intestine)

Quick**Lab**

🕐 15 min

Parasite Identification

This graph shows how two drugs affect the release of eggs in a human who is infected with two parasites—*Schistosoma* and an ascarid. Drug 1 works by killing adult parasites in the intestines. Drug 2 works by killing adult parasites in the blood vessels. Use the graph and your knowledge of roundworms to answer the questions.

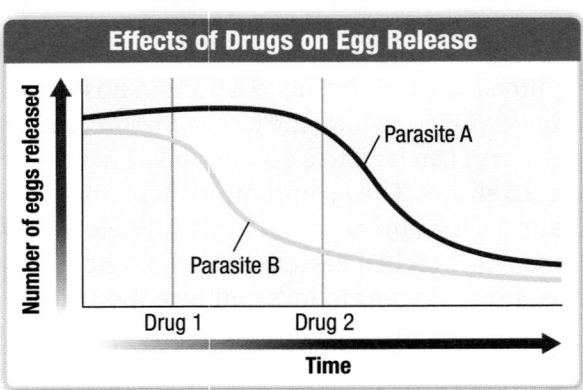

Effects of Drugs on Egg Release

Analysis

1. **Describe** the response of the parasites to the two different drug treatments.

2. **Identify** the main human organs and tissues infected by the adult stages of *Schistosoma* and an ascarid. Use your textbook if necessary.

3. **Identify** the curve on the graph that shows *Schistosoma* egg production and the curve on the graph that shows ascarid egg production.

4. **CRITICAL THINKING** **Justifying Conclusions** Explain the reason for your answers to item 3.

5. **CRITICAL THINKING** **Forming Hypotheses** *Schistosoma* spends part of its life cycle as a parasite of snails. Hypothesize a reason for an increase in the number of cases of schistosomiasis in villages near hydroelectric dams.

Fighting Parasites

Humans are hosts to a number of flatworm and roundworm parasites. These parasites cause billions of infections worldwide. a large part of the problem lies in the fact that about half of the world's population lives in areas with inadequate sewage systems. In addition, about 1 billion people do not have access to clean water. Also, in many areas it is difficult to control mosquitoes and other disease carriers. These factors are major contributors to the burden of parasitic diseases. ❯ **To prevent parasitic infections, people who live in or travel to places where parasites are common should wash their hands frequently, drink bottled or boiled water, eat only fully cooked meat, use insect repellent, wear protective clothing, and sleep under netting.**

ACADEMIC VOCABULARY

inadequate not good enough

Section 4 Review

❯ KEY IDEAS

1. **Describe** three key characteristics of roundworms.

2. **Name** four types of parasitic roundworms, and summarize their life cycles.

3. **List** three things that a person can do to avoid a parasitic infection.

CRITICAL THINKING

4. **Evaluating Conclusions** A student concludes that a *Schistosoma* infection is more difficult to prevent than a hookworm infection is. Evaluate this conclusion.

5. **Applying Concepts** Use what you have learned in this section to recommend a method of preventing the transmission of filarial worms.

WRITING FOR SCIENCE

6. **Writing Reports** Only a small percentage of roundworm species are parasitic. Many other roundworms are beneficial to humans. Research several beneficial roundworm species, and write a short report to describe their importance.

Chapter 27 **Lab**

⏱ 45 min

Objectives

➤ Observe a hydra finding and capturing prey.

➤ Determine how a hydra responds to stimuli.

Materials

- silicone culture gum
- microscope slide
- eyedroppers (2)
- *hydra* culture
- stereomicroscope
- filter paper, cut into pennant shapes
- forceps
- beef broth, concentrated
- *Daphnia* culture

Safety

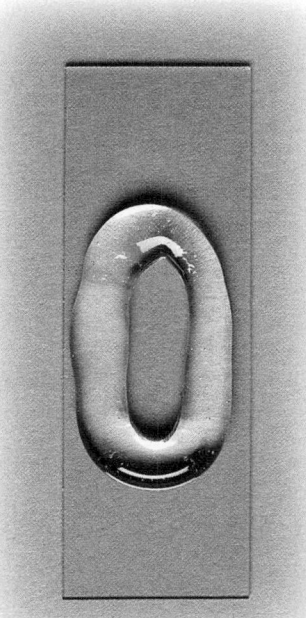

Hydra Behavior

Cnidarians are carnivorous animals. A common cnidarian is a hydra, which is a freshwater organism that feeds on smaller animals, such as water fleas (*Daphnia*). Hydras find food by responding to stimuli, such as chemicals and touch. In this lab, you will observe the feeding behavior of hydras to determine how they find and capture prey.

Procedure

① ⚠ **CAUTION: Handle glass slides carefully. Handle live organisms with care.** Arrange a piece of silicone gum to form a circular well on a microscope slide, as shown in the photo.

② 🔬 With an eyedropper, transfer a hydra from its culture dish to the well on the slide. Cover the animal in water. Examine the hydra under the microscope.

③ Hold a piece of filter paper with forceps and move the tip of the paper near, but not touching, the hydra's tentacles. Observe and record the hydra's response. Dip the same filter paper in beef broth and repeat the procedure.

④ Use the tip of a clean piece of filter paper to gently touch the hydra's tentacles, disk, and stalk. Record your observations.

⑤ Use the eyedropper to transfer live *Daphnia* to the well with the hydra on the microscope slide. Carefully observe the hydra under the microscope. Record your observations in a data table.

⑥ If the hydra does not respond, repeat steps 2–5 with another hydra.

⑦ ⚡ 🧤 Clean up your lab materials according to your teacher's instructions. Wash your hands before leaving the lab.

Analyze and Conclude

1. **Analyzing Results** Describe the hydra's response to touch, chemicals (beef broth), and prey *(Daphnia.)*

2. CRITICAL THINKING **Drawing Conclusions** How does a hydra detect its prey? Give evidence to support your conclusions.

3. CRITICAL THINKING **Making Predictions** Based on your observations, how do you think that a hydra behaves when it detects a threat in its natural habitat?

4. **Further Research** Find out what kinds of food hydras eat and how the feeding method of a hydra differs from that of a sponge.

Key Ideas	Key Terms

1 Sponges

> Sponges are classified as animals because they are multicellular, are heterotrophic, have no cell walls, and contain some specialized cells.

> Sponges reproduce both asexually and sexually. Most sponges are hermaphrodites, which means they produce both eggs and sperm.

> The modern sponges are classified according to the composition of the skeleton in their body wall.

choanocyte (655)
amoebocyte (656)
spicule (657)
spongin (657)

2 Cnidarians

> Cnidarians have two basic body forms called the medusa and the polyp.

> The three main groups of cnidarians are hydrozoans, scyphozoans, and anthozoans.

medusa (658)
polyp (658)
cnidocyte (659)
nematocyst (659)
planula (659)

3 Flatworms

> Flatworms have bilateral symmetry, three embryonic tissue layers, and cephalization.

> Three major groups of modern flatworms include turbellarians, most of which are free-living, and tapeworms and flukes, which are parasitic.

proglottid (665)

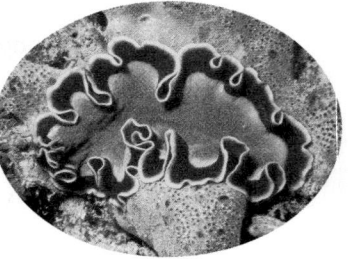

4 Roundworms

> Roundworms have three embryonic tissue layers, a pseudocoelom, and a digestive system with separate openings for feeding and waste elimination.

> Common parasitic roundworms include pinworms, hookworms, filarial worms, and ascarids.

> People who live in or travel to places where parasites are common should wash their hands frequently, drink bottled or boiled water, eat only fully cooked meat, use insect repellent, wear protective clothing, and sleep under netting.

pseudocoelom (667)

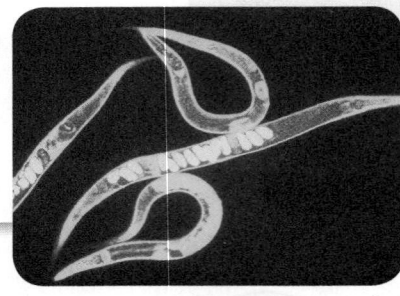

READING TOOLBOX

1. **Cause and Effect** What is the cause and effect of elephantiasis?

2. 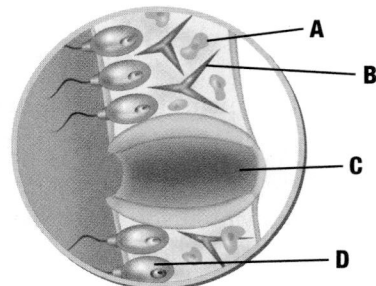 **Concept Mapping** Make a concept map that shows the major characteristics of sponges, cnidarians, flatworms, and roundworms. Include the following terms in your map: *choanocyte, spongin, medusa, polyp, cnidocyte, fluke, tegument,* and *proglottid.*

Using Key Terms

For each pair of terms, explain how the meanings of the terms differ.

3. *choanocyte* and *amoebocyte*

4. *spicule* and *spongin*

5. *medusa* and *polyp*

Use each of the following terms in a separate sentence.

6. *planula*

7. *proglottid*

Understanding Key Ideas

8. Which of the following is *not* a characteristic of sponges?
   a. body wall penetrated by many pores
   b. cells organized into tissues
   c. collar cells that trap food particles
   d. amoebocytes that transport food

9. What is one function of choanocytes in a sponge?
   a. supporting the body
   b. fertilizing eggs
   c. distributing nutrients
   d. moving water

10. Which of the following is the sequence of structures in the life cycle of a fluke?
    a. larva, egg, intermediate host, final host
    b. egg, larva, intermediate host, final host
    c. final host, larva, egg, intermediate host
    d. egg, larva, final host, intermediate host

11. In which way are corals different from most other cnidarians?
    a. They exist only in the medusa form.
    b. They secrete a tough outer skeleton.
    c. They reproduce only asexually.
    d. They are photosynthetic.

12. Which characteristic is found in roundworms but not in other simple invertebrates?
    a. a head end
    b. three tissue layers
    c. circulatory system
    d. tissues organized into organs

13. Which of the following roundworms leaves its host's body during the night to lay eggs?
    a. pinworm   c. hookworm
    b. schistosome   d. filarial worm

Use the diagram to answer the following question.

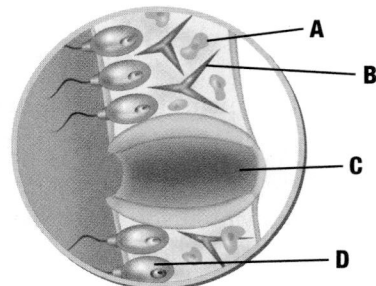

14. Which of the structures in the wall of a sponge provides structural support?
    a. structure A   c. structure C
    b. structure B   d. structure D

Explaining Key Ideas

15. **Summarize** how a sponge feeds and distributes nutrients.

16. **Relate** cnidocytes and nematocysts to the way that cnidarians gather food.

17. **Identify** the type of organism that lives symbiotically with corals, and explain the role of these organisms.

18. **Compare** tissue organization in sponges, cnidarians, flatworms, and roundworms.

Using Science Graphics

Use the table to answer the following questions.

Key of Simple Animal Phyla	
1. Cells are not organized into tissues	Phylum *W*
Cells are organized into tissues	Go to 2.
2. Tissues are not organized into organs	Phylum *X*
Tissues are organized into organs	Go to 3.
3. The body does not have a body cavity	Phylum *Y*
The body has a body cavity	Go to 4.
4. The body cavity is not a true coelom	Phylum *Z*
The body cavity is a true coelom	Go to a key of more complex animal phyla.

19. Which type of organism belongs in phylum *W*?
- **a.** ascarids
- **b.** hydra
- **c.** planarians
- **d.** sponges

20. Which type of organisms belong in phylum *Z*?
- **a.** coral
- **b.** jellyfishes
- **c.** roundworms
- **d.** tapeworms

21. Where on the key would you find a sea anemone?
- **a.** phylum *W*
- **b.** phylum *X*
- **c.** phylum *Y*
- **d.** phylum *Z*

Critical Thinking

22. Inferring Relationships The body wall of a sponge does not have a fixed framework as the bodies of most other animals do. How does this fact relate to the sponge's ability to regenerate from body fragments?

23. Applying Information The Portuguese man-of-war is often referred to as a jellyfish, and indeed it floats on the surface of the ocean as jellyfish do. In what ways is the Portuguese man-of-war different from typical jellyfish?

24. Analyzing Concepts How are the life cycles of filarial worms different from those of pinworms and hookworms?

25. Predicting Outcomes *Trichinella spiralis* is a roundworm that produces larvae that migrate to muscle tissue in pigs. How might people become infected with this roundworm, and how could such an infection be prevented?

Alternative Assessment

26. Making Models Research how one of the three different types of coral reefs—ringing, barrier, and atoll—is formed. Then, build a model of your reef type or make a map showing where such reefs are located. Set up an exhibit of your work, and use a tape recording to create a "tour."

27. Identifying Structures Make an anatomical drawing of the interior of a sponge, cnidarian, flatworm, or roundworm. Identify the species, and label at least 10 structures. Distribute copies of your drawing to your classmates.

28. Understanding Medicine Research current treatments for canine heartworms. Find out what medicines are used, how they are delivered, the prognosis after treatment, and any risks involved in the procedure. Summarize your findings in a report or an oral presentation.

Technology Skills

29. Technology and Agriculture Find out how new technologies have changed the methods and types of control measures being developed to combat crop losses due to nematodes (roundworms). Prepare an oral report, a written report, or a display that describes the newest methods and these new technologies.

Writing for Science

30. Jellyfish Toxins Conduct research at the library or on the Internet on jellyfish toxins and their effects on jellyfish prey and humans. Write a one-page report on your findings. Include information on the type of toxin, its general chemical composition, its physiological effects, the treatment for a sting, any lasting effects of a sting, and areas of the world where jellyfish that produce the toxin are found.

> **TEST TIP** On a test, take the time to read each question completely, including all the answer choices. Consider each possible choice before determining which answer is correct.

Science Concepts

1. Why are spongin and spicules important to a sponge?

  A They digest food.

  B They remove wastes.

  C They provide support.

  D They produce offspring.

2. In cnidarians, digestion occurs

  F only intracellulary.

  G only extracellularly.

  H only in a gastrovasculary cavity.

  J in a gastrovascular cavity and intracellulary.

3. Which is the sequence of structures in the life cycle of *Obelia*?

  A zygote, planula, polyp, medusa

  B medusa, polyp, zygote, planula

  C zygote, medusa, planula, polyp

  D medusa, planula, zygote, polyp

4. Where do blood flukes of the genus *Schistosoma* reproduce asexually?

  F in water

  G inside of a snail

  H inside of a cow's intestine

  J inside of a human's blood vessels

5. What is the best way to prevent hookworm infection?

  A wear shoes outside

  B get plenty of exercise

  C wash your hands often

  D thoroughly cook raw meat

6. Which of the following is an important factor contributing to parasitic diseases worldwide?

  F inadequate amounts of vaccine

  G lack of adequate sewage system

  H access to large amounts of water

  J infections are difficult to diagnose

Using Science Graphics

Use the diagram to answer the following question.

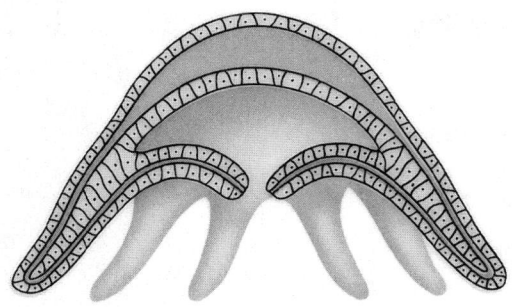

7. In which group of invertebrates is this body form dominant?

  A anthozoans **C** hydrozoans

  B choanocytes **D** scyphozoans

Use the diagram to answer the following questions.

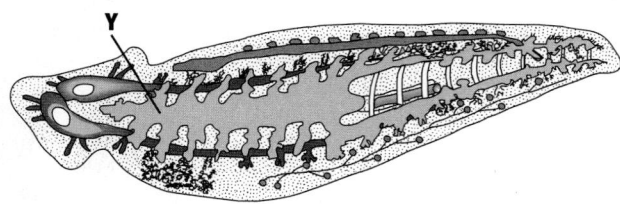

8. What type of animal is shown in the figure?

  F a flatworm **H** a roundworm

  G a tapeworm **J** a filarial worm

9. What is the structure labeled *Y*?

  A the eyespot

  B the mesoderm

  C the brain and nerve cord

  D the gastrovascular cavity

10. Which organ system is missing in this organism?

  F nervous system

  G digestive system

  H respiratory system

  J reproductive system

Writing Skills

11. Short Response Explain why it is important to avoid contact with soil in areas where parasites are common.

Chapter 28

Mollusks and Annelids

Preview

1 Mollusks

Characteristics of Mollusks

Mollusk Body Plan and Organ Systems

Mollusk Diversity

2 Annelids

Characteristics of Annelids

Annelid Diversity

Why It Matters

Mollusks and annelids benefit humans in a variety of ways by fertilizing garden soil, producing pearls, and providing nutritious food.

Garden snails, such as the white-lipped snails below, are some of the most common mollusks. An average yard has around 30,000 snails crawling around it!

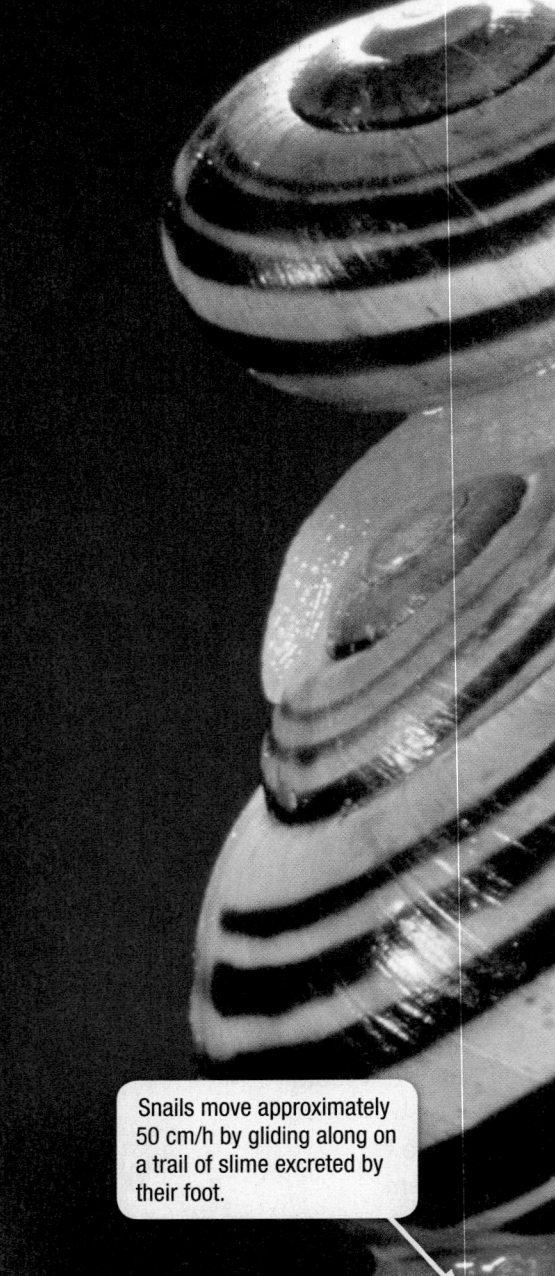

Snails move approximately 50 cm/h by gliding along on a trail of slime excreted by their foot.

Inquiry Lab

Garden Snails

If you explore a garden, you are likely to uncover a variety of snails. Snails are mollusks. By examining live specimens, you can learn firsthand about the biology of mollusks.

Procedure

1. While the garden snail is withdrawn in its shell, examine the shell with a hand lens. Observe features such as the shell's spiral and the seal at the shell's mouth.

2. Place the snail in the center of a Petri dish. After several moments, the animal will emerge. Observe the external features of the soft body. Use a pencil to make a drawing of your observations.

3. From the underside of the Petri dish, observe the animal. Can you identify its mouth? Make another drawing from this angle.

Analysis

1. **Determine** the function of the snail's shell, based on your observations.

2. **Describe** the snail's movement along the surface of the Petri dish.

3. **Describe** any sensory organs that the snail has.

4. **Explain** why drawings from two views might be useful.

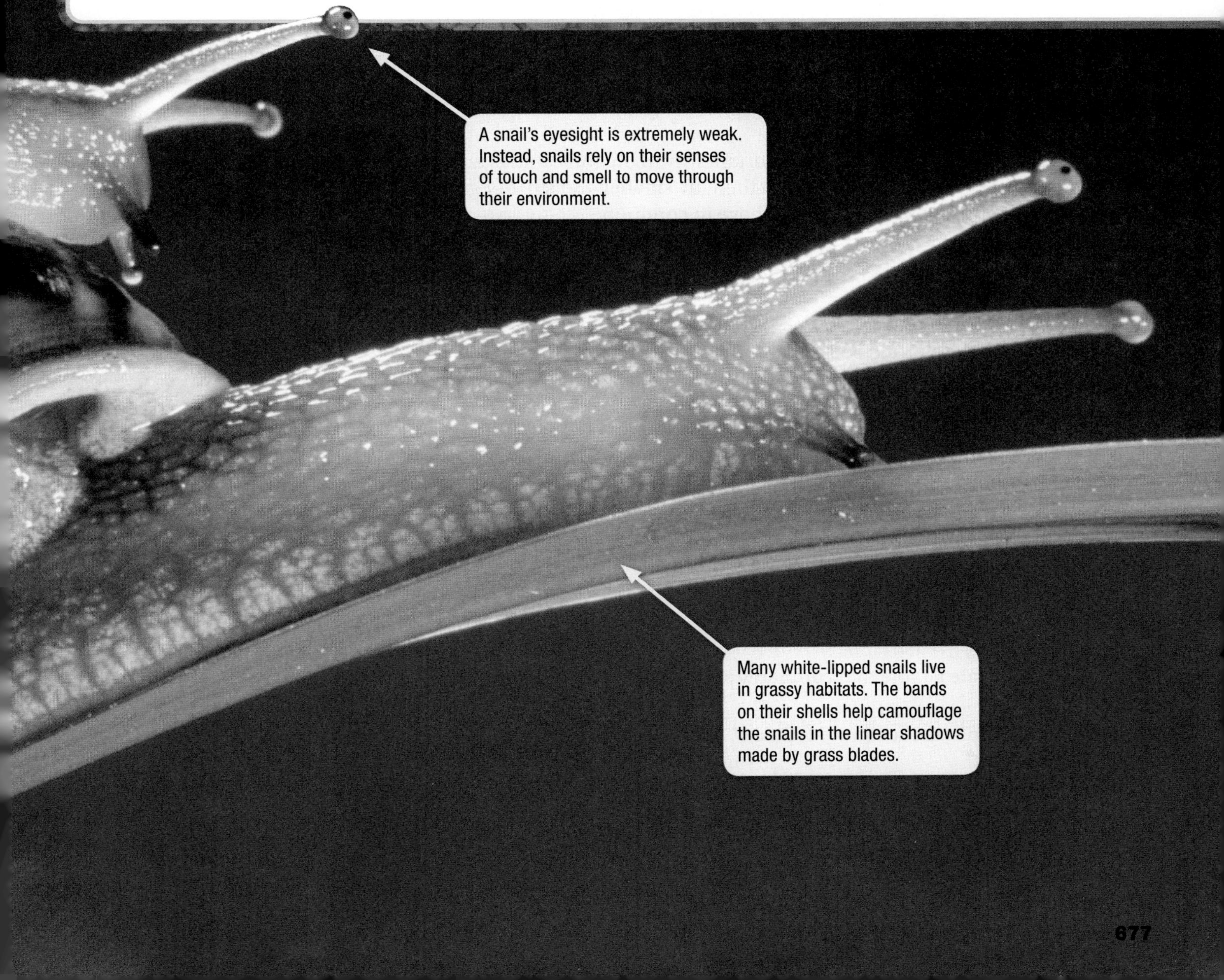

A snail's eyesight is extremely weak. Instead, snails rely on their senses of touch and smell to move through their environment.

Many white-lipped snails live in grassy habitats. The bands on their shells help camouflage the snails in the linear shadows made by grass blades.

READING TOOLBOX

These reading tools can help you learn the material in this chapter. For more information on how to use these and other tools, see **Appendix: Reading and Study Skills.**

Using Words

Everyday Words in Science Many words that we use every day have special meanings in science. For example, in everyday use, *matter* means "an issue or problem." In science, *matter* means the "substance that all things are made of."

Your Turn Use this table to help you understand the difference between the everyday meaning and the science meaning of words in this chapter.

1. Before you read, write the everyday meanings of the terms in the table.
2. As you read, fill in the science meanings for the terms in the table.

Everyday Words in Science		
Word	Everyday meaning	Science meaning
foot		
mantle		
siphon		
crop		

Using Language

Classification Classification is an important way to organize things and ideas. When you classify objects, you put them in smaller and smaller groups based on characteristics that the objects have in common.

Your Turn Brainstorm as many groups as you can think of that the following items could belong to.

1. *a, e, i, o,* and *u*
2. pants, shirts, sweaters, and socks
3. slugs, snails, squids, clams, and oysters

Taking Notes

Comparison Table A comparison table is useful when you want to compare the characteristics of two or more topics. Organizing information in a table helps you compare several topics at one time.

Your Turn Create a table that compares mollusks and annelids.

1. Draw two columns. Label one "Mollusks" and the other "Annelids."
2. In the Mollusks column, write general characteristics about mollusks.
3. In the Annelids column, write general characteristics about annelids.

Comparing Mollusks and Annelids	
Mollusks	Annelids

1 Mollusks

Key Ideas	Key Terms	Why It Matters
❯ What are the key characteristics of mollusks? ❯ What are the three parts of the mollusk body plan? ❯ What are the similarities of and differences between gastropods, bivalves, and cephalopods?	**visceral mass** **mantle** **foot** **radula** **trochophore** **siphon**	The largest known invertebrate is the colossal squid, a mollusk. These fearsome predators may grow up to 12 m (40 ft) long.

Snails, oysters, clams, octopuses, and squids all belong to the phylum Mollusca. Members of this phylum are called *mollusks*. The name *mollusk* comes from the Latin word *mollis,* which means "soft."

Characteristics of Mollusks

Despite their varied appearance, mollusks share a number of key characteristics, which **Figure 1** shows. ❯ **Mollusks are soft-bodied coelomates that have a three-part body plan. Mollusks also have bilateral symmetry, and most mollusks have a shell.** The body cavity in mollusks is a true coelom. Mollusks and all other animals except the simple invertebrates have a coelom. In animals that have a coelom, the gut and other internal organs are suspended from the body wall and are cushioned by the fluid within the coelom. A coelom allows the internal organs to fold over on themselves and to fill up, empty, and move past each other. Thus, the functional surface area and complexity of these organs are greatly increased compared with the organs of simple invertebrates. In most mollusks, the coelom is only a small area around the heart.

Figure 1 All mollusk bodies are composed of a visceral mass, a mantle, and a foot.

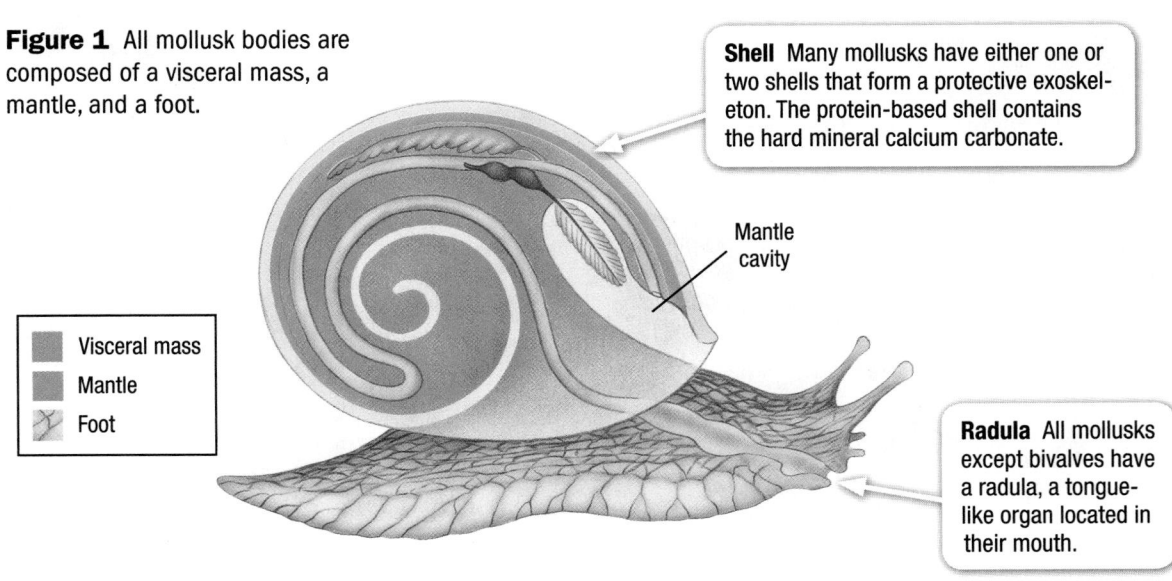

Shell Many mollusks have either one or two shells that form a protective exoskeleton. The protein-based shell contains the hard mineral calcium carbonate.

Mantle cavity

Radula All mollusks except bivalves have a radula, a tongue-like organ located in their mouth.

■ Visceral mass
■ Mantle
✖ Foot

Mollusk Body Plan and Organ Systems

Mollusks have a one-way digestive system similar to that of round-worms. However, mollusks are more complex than roundworms in that they have three major body sections. ❯ **The three parts that make up the basic mollusk body plan are the visceral mass, the mantle, and the foot.** The **visceral mass** is a central section that contains the mollusk's organs. The **mantle,** which is outside of the visceral mass, is a heavy fold of tissue that forms the outer layer of the body. A mollusk's shell is secreted by the mantle. Finally, every mollusk has a muscular region called a **foot,** which is used primarily for locomotion. In a few mollusks, the head, which contains the mouth and many sensory structures, and the foot are combined into one structure.

Feeding and Digestion   Some mollusks, such as clams, are filter feeders that do not move around much. Other mollusks, including snails, are slow-moving herbivores. And still other mollusks, such as squids and octopuses, are active predators. But regardless of their feeding habits, all mollusks except bivalves have a **radula. Figure 2** shows the radula, which has thousands of pointed, backward-curving teeth arranged in rows. When a mollusk feeds, it pushes its radula out of its mouth, and the teeth scrape fragments of food off of rocks or plant matter. Mollusks that are predators use their radula to attack their prey. Food is digested in the stomach and intestine of the one-way digestive tract. Wastes are passed out of the anus.

Excretion   A mollusk's coelom is a collecting place for waste-laden body fluids. The beating of cilia pulls the fluid from the coelom into tiny tubular structures called *nephridia* (singular, *nephridium*), which **Figure 2** shows. Nephridia recover useful materials (sugars, salts, and water) from the fluid. These materials are reabsorbed into the mollusk's body tissues. The remaining waste leaves the mollusk's body through a pore that opens into the mantle cavity. From the mantle cavity, the wastes are passed into the surrounding environment.

visceral mass   the central section of a mollusk's body that contains the mollusk's organs

mantle   in biology, a layer of tissue that covers the body of many invertebrates

foot   an appendage that some invertebrates use to move

radula   a rasping, tonguelike organ that is covered with teeth and that is used for feeding

Figure 2   Although mollusks vary greatly in body form, they all have similar organ systems. ❯ **How does the structure of the radula help a mollusk feed?**

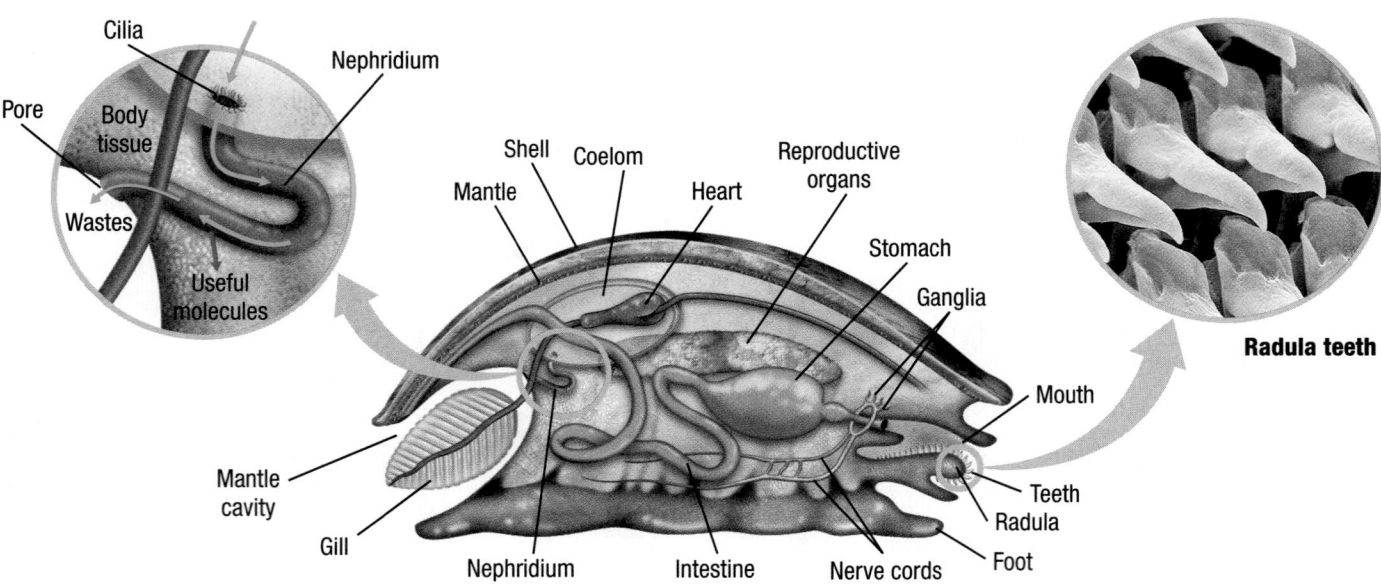

Quick**Lab**

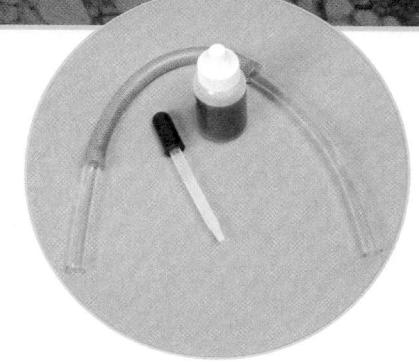

🕐 15 min

Open Circulatory System

You can model an open circulatory system by using simple items to represent the heart, blood vessels, blood, and body tissues of a living organism.

Procedure

1. Connect a **15-cm piece of surgical tubing** to a **15-cm piece and 7.5-cm piece of clear plastic tubing.**

2. Place the tubing into a **tray filled with water.** Allow the tubing to fill with water and rest on the bottom.

3. With the tubing still submerged, use an **eyedropper** to place **two drops of food coloring** into the short piece of clear plastic tubing.

4. By using your thumb and index finger, squeeze along the piece of surgical tubing to pump the food coloring through the system.

5. As you continue to pump, observe the movement of the food coloring.

Analysis

1. **Describe** what happened when you squeezed along the tubing.

2. **Identify** the body structures represented by the pan of water, the surgical tubing, and the clear plastic tubing.

3. **CRITICAL THINKING** **Evaluating Results** Evaluate your model's efficiency for pumping blood through the system.

4. **CRITICAL THINKING** **Analyzing Methods** How could you modify the model to make it more accurate?

Circulation In a mollusk circulatory system, blood carries nutrients and oxygen to tissues and removes wastes. Most mollusks have a three-chambered heart and an open circulatory system. The blood in an open circulatory system does not stay completely within vessels but instead fills spaces around the body organs. These blood-filled spaces take the place of the coelom. Octopuses and their relatives are exceptions because they have closed circulatory systems, in which blood remains entirely inside of the vessels.

Respiration Most mollusks respire with gills, which are located in the mantle cavity. The mantle cavity is a space between the mantle and the visceral mass. Mollusk gills extract 50% or more of the dissolved oxygen from the water that passes over them. Most terrestrial snails have no gills. Instead, the thin membrane that lines the snail's empty mantle cavity works like a primitive lung. This membrane must be kept moist for oxygen to diffuse across it. Therefore, terrestrial snails are most active at night or after rain when the air has a high moisture content. During dry weather, a terrestrial snail pulls back into its shell and plugs the opening with a wad of mucus to keep water in. Some sea snails and slugs also lack gills, and gas exchange takes place directly through their skin. For example, the featherlike structures on the outside of the sea slug, which **Figure 3** shows, act as gas-exchange organs.

❯ **Reading Check** *Describe a typical mollusk circulatory system. (See the Appendix for answers to Reading Checks.)*

Figure 3 The featherlike structures on this sea slug provide a large surface area for gas exchange to take place. ❯ **What are some advantages and disadvantages of having respiratory organs on the outside of the body?**

Gas-exchange organs

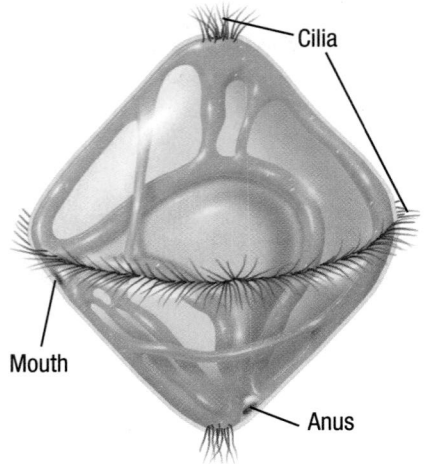

Figure 4 The microscopic trochophore larva has a belt of cilia that circles its body. The beating of the cilia propels the trochophore through the water.

Cilia

Mouth

Anus

Reproduction Most mollusks have distinct male and female individuals, although some snails and slugs are hermaphrodites. Certain species of oysters and sea slugs are able to change from one sex to the other and back again. Fertilization of eggs occurs externally in most aquatic mollusks and internally in terrestrial mollusks and in octopuses and their relatives. The fertilized eggs of most mollusks develop into a type of larva called a **trochophore,** which **Figure 4** shows. Many species of marine mollusks are moved from place to place as their trochophore larvae drift in the ocean currents. In other species, the trochophore is free swimming and propels itself through the water by the movement of cilia on its surface. The larval stage in some mollusks, such as octopuses, squids, and freshwater snails, occurs inside of an egg, and a juvenile mollusk hatches from the egg.

Mollusk Diversity

The phylum Mollusca is extremely diverse. Among the species in the kingdom Animalia, only the phylum Arthropoda has more species. Mollusks are abundant in almost all marine, freshwater, and terrestrial habitats. More species of terrestrial mollusks exist than species of terrestrial vertebrates do, but these mollusk species often go unnoticed because they are small and may come out only at night or in rainy weather.

Seven classes of mollusks make up the phylum Mollusca. The three major classes are Gastropoda (snails and slugs), Cephalopoda (octopuses and squids), and Bivalvia (clams, oysters, and scallops). ❯ Gastropods, cephalopods, and bivalves share the same basic organ systems and tissue layers, but they have different feeding strategies and body plans. In **Figure 5,** you can see how the basic mollusk three-part body plan differs in each class of mollusk. As you read about the three major classes of mollusks, you will see how the mollusk shell and foot are adapted for many different living conditions.

❯ **Reading Check** *What are the three major classes of mollusks?*

Figure 5 The arrangement of the visceral mass, the mantle, and the foot differ in the three major classes of mollusks. ❯ **Compare and contrast the body plans of gastropods, cephalopods, and bivalves.**

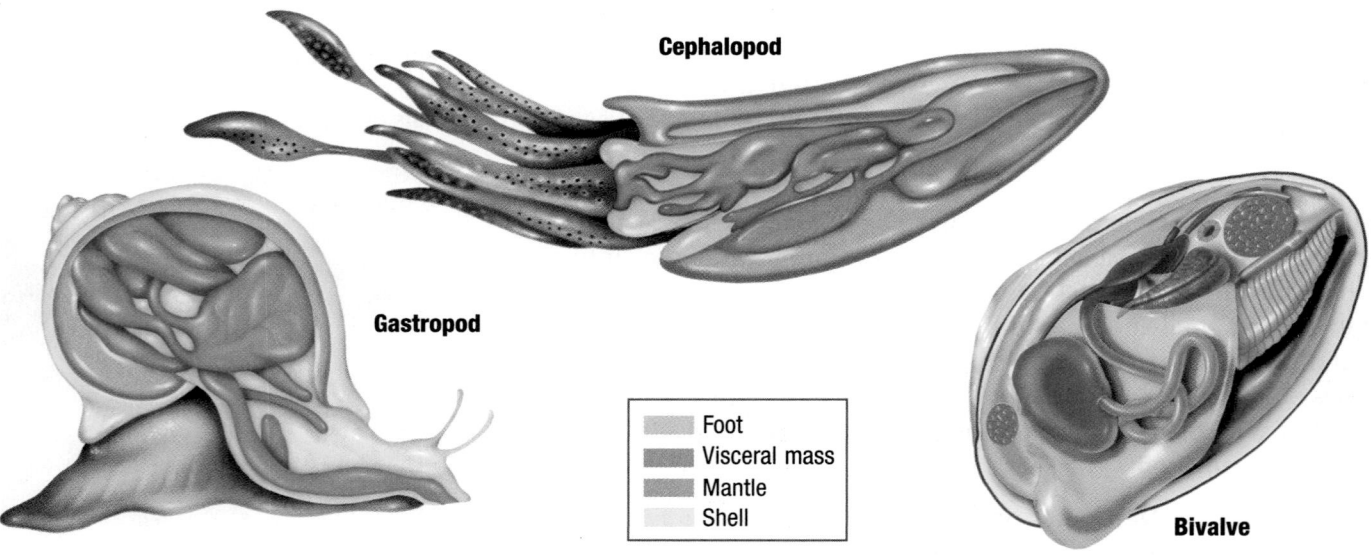

Cephalopod

Gastropod

| Foot |
| Visceral mass |
| Mantle |
| Shell |

Bivalve

White-lipped snail

Triton trumpet snail

Nudibranch

Figure 6 You are probably most familiar with terrestrial gastropods, but the majority of gastropods live in marine environments.

Gastropods Gastropods—snails and slugs—are primarily a marine group that also has members in freshwater and terrestrial habitats. They range in size from microscopic forms to the sea hare *Aplysia,* which reaches 1 m (almost 40 in.) in length. Most gastropods have a pair of tentacles on their head that have eyes located at the tips. If the gastropod feels threatened, it can retract the tentacles into its head. Most gastropods also have a single shell. Slugs and nudibranchs have no shell. **Figure 6** shows a terrestrial snail, a marine snail, and a nudibranch (sea slug).

Locomotion The foot of gastropods is adapted for locomotion. Terrestrial species secrete mucus from the base of their foot, which forms a slimy path that they can glide along. Some gastropods have unusual foot adaptations. For example, in pteropods, or "sea butterflies," the foot is modified into a winglike flap that is used for swimming rather than crawling.

Feeding Habits Gastropods have varied feeding habits. Many gastropods are herbivores that scrape algae off of rocks by using their radula. Some terrestrial snails can be serious garden and agricultural pests by using their radula to saw off leaves. Sea slugs and many other gastropods are active predators. For example, whelks and oyster drills use their radula to bore holes in the shells of other mollusks. Then, they suck out the soft tissues of their prey. In cone snails, the radula is modified into a kind of poison-tipped harpoon that is shot into prey. The poison paralyzes the prey, which is then swallowed whole. Nudibranchs can capture the nematocyst of a jellyfish or other cnidarian, move it through their body tissues to the mouth or other part, and then use it for their own defense or to capture prey.

❯ **Reading Check** *What are two feeding habits of gastropods?*

trochophore a free-swimming, ciliated larva of many worms and some mollusks

READING TOOLBOX

Classification Summarize how mollusks are classified.

ACADEMIC
VOCABULARY
_____
equip to supply with

siphon a hollow tube of mollusks used for
sucking in and expelling sea water

Cephalopods The squid, octopus, cuttlefish, and nautilus shown in **Figure 7** are all cephalopods. Most of a cephalopod's body mass is made up of a large head attached to tentacles (a foot divided into numerous parts). The tentacles are equipped with either suction cups or hooks for seizing prey. Squids have 10 tentacles, while octopuses have 8. The nautilus has 80 to 90 tentacles, although its tentacles are not nearly as long as those of the other cephalopods. Although cephalopods evolved from shelled ancestors, most modern cephalopods lack an external shell. The nautilus is the only living cephalopod species that still has an outer shell. Squids and cuttlefish have a small internal shell.

Brain and Sensory Organs Cephalopods are the most intelligent of all invertebrates. They have a complex nervous system that includes a well-developed brain. Cephalopods are capable of complex behaviors. Octopuses, for example, can be trained easily to distinguish between classes of objects, such as rectangles and triangles. They are some of the only invertebrates with this ability. The structure of a cephalopod eye is similar in many ways to that of a vertebrate eye, and some species have color vision.

Siphon Like many other aquatic mollusks, cephalopods draw water into their mantle cavity and expel it through a hollow tube called a **siphon.** In squids and octopuses, this system functions as a means of jet propulsion. When threatened, these animals close their mantle cavity quickly, which causes water to shoot forcefully out of the siphon. Squids and octopuses can also release a dark fluid that clouds the water and conceals the direction of their escape.

❯ **Reading Check** *How can some cephalopods escape predators?*

Figure 7 Octopuses and squids, like all cephalopods, are active predators. Cuttlefish are agile swimmers that hunt at night. The nautilus swims with its coiled shell positioned over its head.

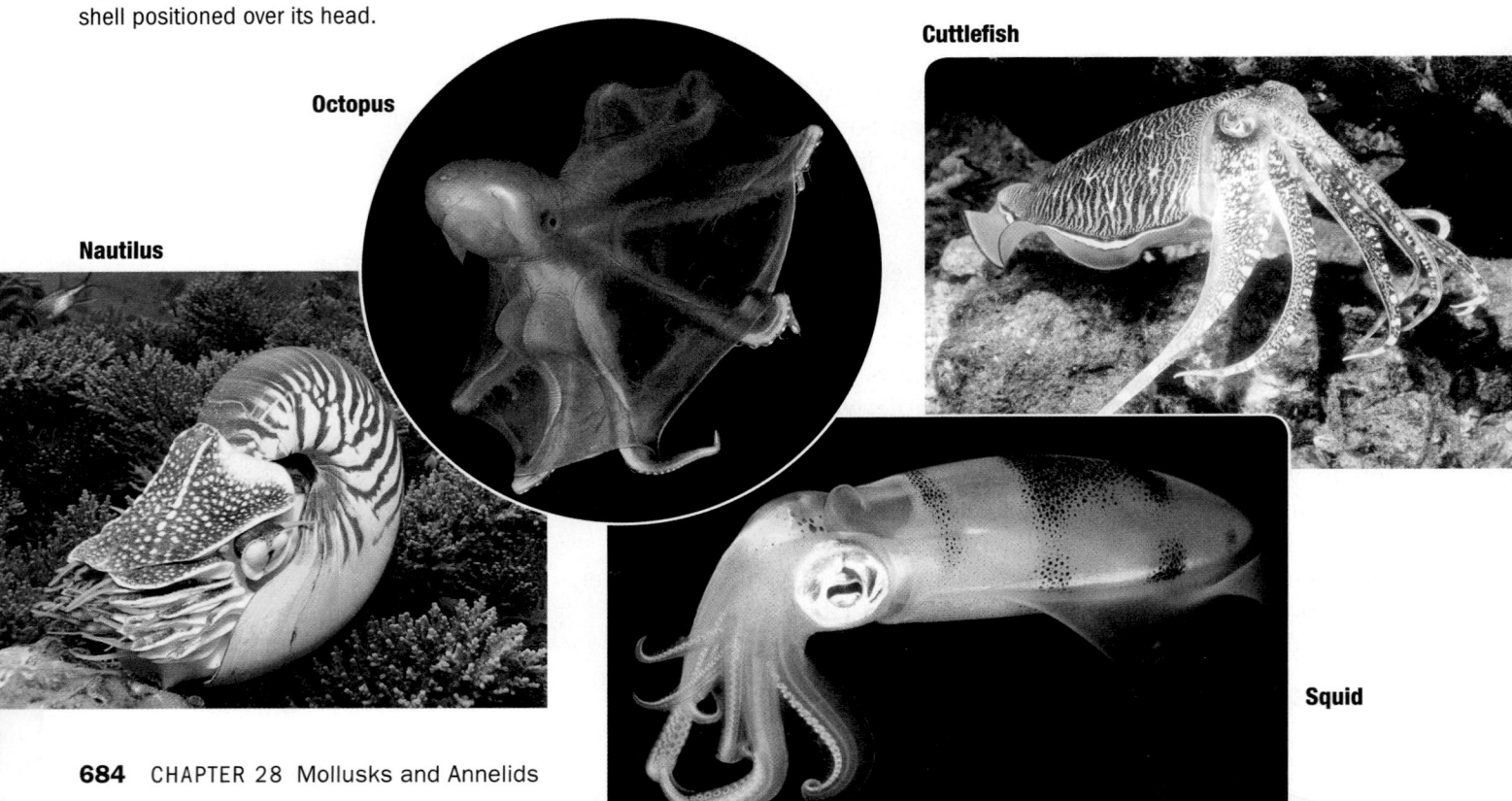

Cuttlefish

Octopus

Nautilus

Squid

Bivalves The bivalves are named for their two-part, hinged shell. The valves, or shells, are secreted by the mantle. Bivalves do not have a distinct head region or a radula, as other mollusks have. Their body is flattened between the two shells. Two thick muscles connect the valves. When these muscles are contracted, they cause the valves to close tightly. Most bivalves are sessile, but some can move quickly from place to place if necessary. For example, a swimming scallop opens and closes its valves rapidly. The jets of water released when the scallop's valves snap shut pushes the scallop along.

Feeding Habits Most bivalves, such as the scallops in **Figure 8,** are marine filter feeders. Some bivalves use their muscular foot to dig down into the sand. The cilia on the bivalve's gills draw in sea water through their siphons. The water moves down one siphon tube, over the gills, and out the other siphon tube. The gills are used for feeding as well as for respiration. As water moves over the gills, food particles are moved along by the cilia. The cilia carry the particles to a mucus-covered groove in the gills. The particles become trapped in the mucus and flow down to the bivalve's mouth. Some bivalves, such as oysters, are permanently attached to rocks in the open water, where they feed. Many scallops swim, and water passes over their gills as they move. Giant clams, which can reach 1.3 m (4.3 ft) in length, form a mutually beneficial partnership with algae. The algae provide the clams with food and are protected from grazing animals by the clams.

Pearl Production Many species of bivalves produce pearls. Pearls form when a tiny foreign object, such as a grain of sand, becomes lodged between the mollusk's mantle and shell. Bivalves respond by coating the object with thin sheets of *nacre,* or mother-of-pearl. Nacre is the hard, shiny substance that composes the inner surface of the shell. Many layers of nacre are added until the foreign body is completely enclosed in the newly formed pearl.

Figure 8 This flame scallop nests in sand and crevices of rocks. However, if it feels endangered, it can quickly scoot away by opening and closing its shell.
▶ **How do you think that flame scallops use their tentacles?**

SC LINKS.
www.scilinks.org
Topic: Mollusk
    Consumption
Code: HX80984

Section 1 Review

▶ **KEY IDEAS**

1. **Identify** two characteristics that all mollusks have in common.
2. **Summarize** the functions of the visceral mass, mantle, and foot.
3. **Describe** how a nephridium functions in waste removal.
4. **Compare** distinguishing features of each of the three major classes of mollusks.

CRITICAL THINKING

5. **Forming Hypotheses** A chemical pollutant accidentally spills into a bay. One of the effects of this chemical is that it paralyzes cilia. After a week, almost all of the oysters in the bay are dead. Develop a hypothesis that explains why the oysters died.
6. **Relating Concepts** Explain the significance of the evolution of a coelom in mollusks.

WRITING FOR SCIENCE

7. **Finding and Communicating Information** Compile a list of mollusks used by humans as a food source. For each mollusk listed, describe where it is harvested and which part of the mollusk is eaten. Prepare a brochure to summarize your findings. Include a visual aid that shows the reader the geographic location of the food source.

Key Ideas	Key Terms	Why It Matters
❯ What are the key characteristics of annelids? ❯ Which characteristics are used to classify annelids?	seta septum cerebral ganglion	The medicinal use of the blood-sucking annelid *Hirudo medicinalis* was once so common that doctors were often referred to as *leeches*.

While a snail may not seem to have much in common with an earthworm, these two animals are closely related. The most obvious difference between these two organisms, besides the snail's shell, is the presence of segments in the earthworm. Earthworms are coelomates that belong to the ancient phylum Annelida. Annelid fossils can be found in rock that is 530 million years old. Scientists think that annelids evolved in the sea, where two-thirds of today's annelid species live. Most other annelid species are terrestrial earthworms.

Characteristics of Annelids

Annelids, such as the fireworm that **Figure 9** shows, are easily recognized by their segments, which are visible as a series of ringlike structures along the length of their body. Annelids share a number of other characteristics. ❯ **In addition to segmentation, annelids are coelomates with highly specialized organ systems.** Most annelids have external bristles called **setae** (singular, *seta*). The large fluid-filled coelom is located entirely within the mesoderm. The organ systems of annelids show a high degree of specialization and include a closed circulatory system and nephridia for excretory structures. The gut has regions that perform different functions in digestion. Annelids have a trochophore larval stage that is similar to that of mollusks.

Figure 9 Like all annelids, this fireworm's body is made up of ringlike segments. ❯ What is the function of the bristles on the segments?

Segments Annelids were the first organisms to have a body plan based on repeated body segments.

Setae Most annelids have external bristles. The paired bristles located on each segment provide traction as the annelid crawls along.

Hands-On
QuickLab

⏱ 15 min

An Annelid in Cross Section

Earthworms, like all annelids, have a body composed of repeating segments that contain the worm's vital organs.

Procedure

1. Place a prepared slide of an earthworm on the stage of a microscope. Examine the cross section under low power. Make a drawing of what you see.

2. Identify the worm's outer covering and the muscle bands beneath this covering. The coelom is the clear region between the muscles and the central intestine.

3. Locate the dorsal and ventral blood vessels. These vessels are above and below the intestine, respectively. Locate the nephridia at the side of the intestine.

Analysis

1. **Identify** the significance of the worm having both a ventral and a dorsal blood vessel.

2. **Infer** why the nephridia look "chopped up."

3. **CRITICAL THINKING** **Making Predictions** How might the concentration of sensory organs in the head region affect the uniformity of an annelid's segments?

Segmentation Most of the body of an annelid is made up of repeating segments. These worms also have a head region and a tail-like region. Internal body walls, called **septa,** separate the segments of most annelids. Each segment has its own fluid-filled cavity, which contains a part of the animal's coelom. The cavity houses digestive, excretory, and circulatory organs, as well as organs involved in movement. Nutrients and other materials pass between the segments through the circulatory system. Segmentation of the annelid body and the body of all other segmented animals allows for greater freedom of movement and greater complexity of body organization.

Nervous System Well-developed **cerebral ganglia** form a primitive brain, which is located in the head region. The brain is connected to a nerve cord that runs along the underside of the worm's body. Sensory information is transported along the nerve cord from the segments to the brain, and motor signals are carried from the brain to each of the segments. Some of the segments are modified for specific functions, such as reproduction.

Reproduction and Development Annelids reproduce sexually. Both mollusks and annelids have a trochophore larval form that emerges from a fertilized egg and develops into the particular animal's adult form. The development of this larval form is quite different in annelids than it is in mollusks. In annelids, the lower part of the trochophore larva first lengthens. The elongated portion constricts into segments. The upper part of the larva becomes the head. Most annelids continue to add new segments at their tail end throughout their lifetime.

❯ **Reading Check** *Describe the body plan of an annelid.*

seta one of the external bristles or spines that project from the body of an animal

septum a dividing wall, such as the internal wall between an annelid's adjacent segments

cerebral ganglion one of a pair of nerve-cell clusters that serve as a primitive brain

READING TOOLBOX

Comparison Table As you read this section, complete a table in which you compare different classes of annelids.

Annelid Diversity

> Annelids are grouped into different classes based on the number of setae (bristles) that they have and the presence or absence of *parapodia*, which are flap-shaped appendages used for gas exchange and locomotion.

Marine Worms Marine segmented worms are members of the class Polychaeta, the largest group of annelids. Almost all polychaetes live in ocean habitats. They often have unusual forms and iridescent colors. Polychaetes have a pair of fleshy, paddlelike parapodia on most of their segments. The parapodia, which usually have setae, allow the worm to swim, burrow, or crawl. Parapodia also greatly increase the worm's body surface area, which enhances gas exchange between the animal and the water. Polychaetes usually have a well-developed head with eyes and other sensory structures.

Many polychaetes burrow in the ocean floor, but others live in protective tubes that are formed by hardened secretions. Tubeworms, such as the feather duster that **Figure 10** shows, stick only their head out of their tube. Featherlike head structures trap food particles from the water that passes over them. Other species of polychaetes feed by pumping water through their body. Free-swimming polychaetes are predators. They use their strong jaws to feed on small animals.

Earthworms Earthworms and some related freshwater worms are members of the class Oligochaeta. Oligochaetes have no parapodia and only a few setae on each segment. Earthworms lack the distinctive head region of polychaetes and have no eyes. They do, however, have light-sensitive and touch-sensitive organs located at each end of their body. They have other sensory cells that detect moisture.

Earthworms, such as the one featured in the Up Close "Earthworm," are scavengers that consume soil that contains organic matter. The ingested soil moves into a storage chamber called the *crop*. The soil then moves to an area called the *gizzard*, where grinding action breaks down the soil particles. After digested nutrient molecules have been absorbed into the blood, the unabsorbed wastes pass out through the anus in a form called *castings*. Earthworm castings are prized by gardeners as a soil fertilizer.

www.scilinks.org
Topic: Annelids
Code: HX80078

ACADEMIC VOCABULARY

region a specific surface or space

Figure 10 Feather dusters and star horseshoe worms filter feed by trapping food particles in their featherlike head structures.

Up Close | Earthworm

Earthworms may seem like simple animals, but they have a primitive brain that coordinates the muscular activity of each body segment. Their brain also processes sensory information from light-sensitive and touch-sensitive organs that are located at head and tail ends of the body.

Earthworm

Scientific name: *Lumbricus terrestris*
Size: grows up to 30 cm (12 in.) long
Range: Europe; eastern and northwestern North America
Habitat: damp soil
Diet: organic matter contained in soil

Tunneling The tunneling activity of earthworms breaks up soil, which allows air to penetrate. This process is important because many organisms in the soil need air to live.

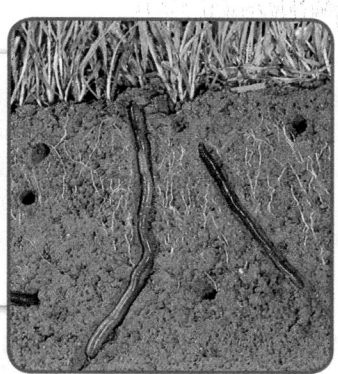

Movement of an Earthworm

1 Rear Anchor The earthworm anchors its rear segments by sinking its setae into the ground.

2 Elongation The worm contracts circular muscles in the anchored segments, which causes the front segments to elongate.

3 Front Anchor The worm anchors the setae in front of the stretched region, and the rear setae are released.

4 Pull The worm contracts its longitudinal muscles, which pulls the rear segments forward.

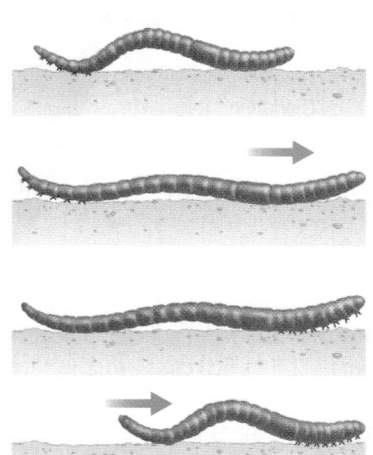

Digestion Earthworms "eat" soil, which is ground up in a thick, muscular gizzard. Food molecules pass across the walls of the intestine and are absorbed into the bloodstream.

Anus

Clitellum

Circular muscles

Longitudinal muscles

Dorsal blood vessel

Esophagus

Gizzard

Crop

Hearts

Pharynx

Mouth

Intestine

Nephridium

Ventral blood vessel

Ventral nerve cord

Setae

Reproductive organs

Cerebral ganglion (brain)

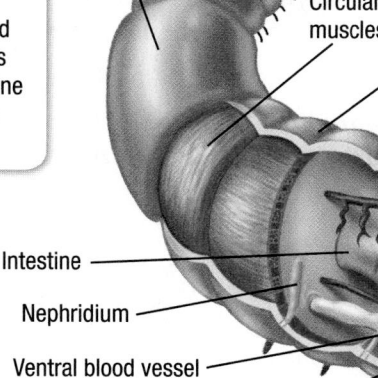

Reproduction Earthworms are hermaphrodites. Mating occurs when two earthworms join head to tail, exchanging sperm. During egg laying, the clitellum secretes a mucous cocoon that encloses the eggs. Young worms later emerge from the cocoon.

Respiration Oxygen and carbon dioxide diffuse through the earthworm's skin. This exchange can take place only if the worm's skin is kept moist.

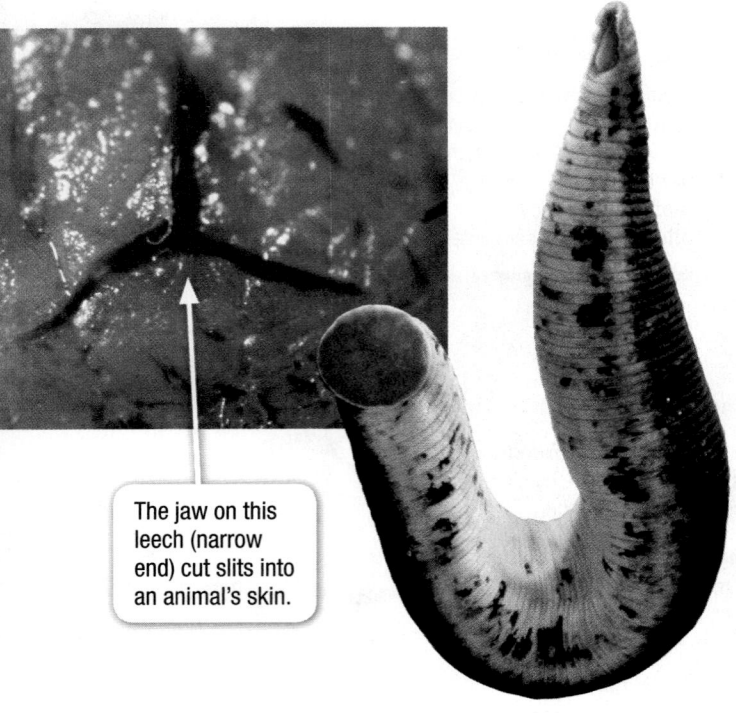

The jaw on this leech (narrow end) cut slits into an animal's skin.

Figure 11 Most species of leeches are small, 2.5 to 5.0 cm (1 to 2 in.) long, but leeches are able to expand to five or six times their normal size when feeding.

SCiLINKS.

www.scilinks.org
Topic: Leeches
Code: HX80867

Leeches Most leeches live in calm bodies of fresh water, but some species live among moist vegetation on land. When people hear the word *leech,* they usually associate it with bloodsucking, and for a good reason. A leech has suckers at both ends of its body. The body of a leech is flattened, and its segments are not separated internally, unlike other annelids. Leeches lack both setae and parapodia. By attaching the front sucker and then pulling the rest of the body forward, leeches can crawl along the ground. Aquatic leeches can also swim by undulating their body.

Most leeches are predators or scavengers. Only a small minority are parasites. **Figure 11** shows a parasitic leech, which attaches to a vertebrate host and cuts or digests a hole in the host's skin. The leech then secretes chemicals, called *anticoagulants,* into the host's blood. These chemicals keep the blood from clotting. Leeches also secrete an anaesthetic that prevents the host from feeling their presence. If undisturbed, a leech can ingest 10 times its own weight in blood.

Medical Use of Leeches For many centuries, people believed that an excess amount of blood was the cause of a wide range of illnesses, from a fever or headache to severe heart disease. A standard treatment for these conditions was bloodletting by using leeches. Physicians applied leeches to a patient's body and allowed the leeches to suck out the patient's "bad blood." Although doctors no longer believe in bad blood, leeches are making a comeback in the field of healthcare. For example, the strongest anticoagulant that leeches produce, called *hirudin,* is now being produced through genetic engineering. The synthetic hirudin is used in the treatment of some heart conditions. Other medical uses of leeches are discussed in the Why It Matters "Creepy Leeches."

❯ **Reading Check** *Explain how the chemicals that a leech's sucker secretes help a parasitic leech feed longer on its host.*

Section 2 Review

❯ **KEY IDEAS**

1. **Explain** how you could determine that a wormlike organism is an annelid.

2. **Describe** the major features of an earthworm's digestive system.

3. **Compare** the external appearance of marine annelids, earthworms, and leeches.

CRITICAL THINKING

4. **Recognizing Patterns** The gizzard of annelids that live in an aquatic environment is smaller and less muscular than that of terrestrial annelids, such as earthworms. How do the differences between the gizzards represent adaptations in aquatic and terrestrial feeding?

5. **Applying Information** Why do you see so many earthworms above ground after a long rainy period?

ALTERNATIVE ASSESSMENT

6. **Drawing Skills** Draw a "new" species of annelid. Label your "new" annelid's body parts. Make sure that the annelid that you invent has both the fundamental annelid traits as well as some adaptations to a particular environment.

Creepy Leeches

Leeches have been used by doctors for thousands of years for the purpose of leeching, or the application of a leech to the skin in order to deplete blood from the body. Leeching was not always a successful treatment, but with the advent of reconstructive microsurgery in the 1960s, leeching became a legitimate medical practice.

Medicinal Leeching

Leeching practices have been documented throughout the world for many centuries. Today, chemicals modeled after leech saliva are used to make the anticoagulant medicine hirudin. In addition, leeches are used in reconstructive surgery to reduce blood coagulation, relieve pressure from pooling blood, and stimulate circulation. The European medicinal leech, *Hirudo medicinalis,* is most commonly used because its jaws have hundreds of razor-sharp teeth. After attaching its head sucker to the skin, the leech uses its jaws and teeth to make a neat Y-shaped cut in the patient's skin.

Vein Congestion After a surgeon reattaches a severed body part, such as a finger or a toe, blood flow through the veins is often not completely restored at first. Blood in the reattached body part may become congested, and the reattached part could die. Leeches placed on the congested tissue remove excess blood and help keep the body part alive.

A leech for your headache? During the Middle Ages, leeching became such a common practice that physicians were commonly referred to as "leeches." Diseases treated with leeches included mental disorders, tumors, skin problems, whooping cough, obesity, teething, and headaches.

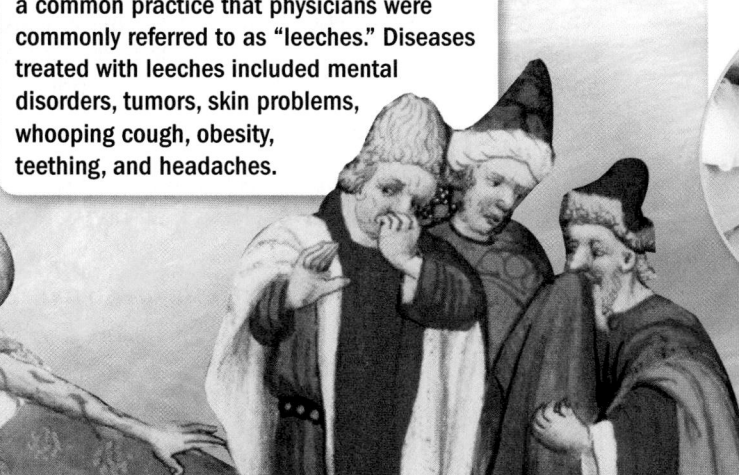

Research Find the first documented evidence of the use of leeches in medicine, and research the time and place in history when leeching was at its peak.

Chapter 28 **Lab**

Objectives

> Observe the behavior of a live clam.

> Examine the structure and composition of a clamshell.

Materials

- lab apron
- safety goggles
- disposable gloves
- clam, live
- beaker or dish, small
- eyedropper
- food coloring
- stirring rod, glass
- clamshell
- Petri dish
- hammer, small
- stereomicroscope
- HCl, 0.1 M

Safety

Clam Characteristics

Clams are mollusks, and they have a two-part shell. The body of a clam consists of a visceral mass and a muscular foot. A clam lacks a definite head. Two tubes, an incurrent siphon and an excurrent siphon, extend from the body on the side opposite from the foot. Like all mollusks, clams have a shell composed of calcium carbonate. The mantle lines the shell and forms successive rings of shell as a clam grows. The umbo is the oldest part of a clamshell. In this lab, you will examine live clams and clamshells.

Procedure

Observe a Live Clam

1 Put on a lab apron, safety goggles, and disposable gloves.

2 CAUTION: **Glassware is fragile. Notify the teacher of broken glass or cuts. Do not clean up broken glass or spills that contain broken glass unless the teacher tells you to do so.** Place a live clam in a small beaker or shallow dish of water.

3 CAUTION: **Do not touch or taste any chemicals. Know the location of the emergency shower and eyewash station and how to use them. If you get a chemical on your skin or clothing, wash it off at the sink while calling to the teacher. Notify the teacher of a spill. Spills should be cleaned up promptly, according to your teacher's directions.** Using an eyedropper, apply two drops of food coloring near the clam.

4 Observe and record what happens to the food coloring.

5 CAUTION: **Touch the clam gently to avoid injuring it. Remember that the clam is a live animal.** Using a stirring rod, touch the clam's mantle.

6 Observe and record the clam's response to touch.

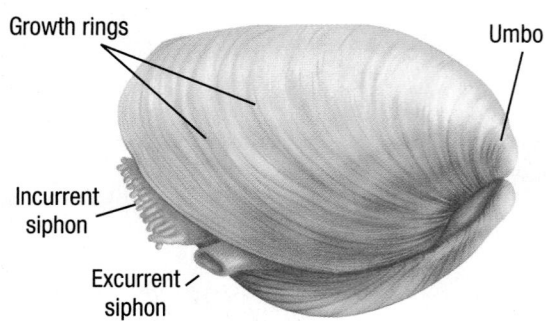

Growth rings

Umbo

Incurrent siphon

Excurrent siphon

Observe a Clamshell

7 Examine the surface of the clamshell. Locate the knob-shaped umbo on the shell. If you have difficulty finding the umbo, use the diagram of a clam as a guide. Take note of the concentric growth rings on the shell. Then, count and record the number of growth rings on the clamshell.

8 Place the clamshell in a Petri dish.

9 Use a small hammer to chip away part of the shell in order to expose the three layers of the shell. View the shell's layers by using a stereomicroscope. The outermost layer protects the clam from acids in the water. The innermost layer is mother-of-pearl, the material that forms pearls.

10 **CAUTION: Hydrochloric acid is corrosive and a poison. Avoid contact with skin, eyes, and clothing. Avoid breathing vapors.** The middle layer of the shell contains crystals of calcium carbonate. To test for the presence of this compound, place one drop of 0.1 M HCl on the middle layer of the shell. If calcium carbonate is present, bubbles of carbon dioxide will form in the drop. Record your observations.

11 Clean up your lab materials according to your teacher's instructions. Wash your hands before leaving the lab.

Analyze and Conclude

1. **SCIENTIFIC METHODS** **Analyzing Data** Find the incurrent and excurrent siphons of the clam in the diagram. Using this information, explain your observations in step 4.

2. **Drawing Conclusions** What is the purpose of a clam's shell?

3. **SCIENTIFIC METHODS** **Using Evidence to Develop Predictions** Based on your observations, how do you think clams respond when they are touched or threatened in their natural habitat?

4. **SCIENTIFIC METHODS** **Forming a Hypothesis** What does a clam take in from the water that passes through its body?

5. **Inferring Relationships** Water that enters a clam's incurrent siphon passes over the clam's gills. How does this help the clam respire?

Extensions

6. **Further Inquiry** Write a new question about clams that could be explored in another investigation.

7. **Designing an Investigation** Design an investigation that could answer the question that you wrote for the Further Inquiry extension exercise.

go.hrw.com
SUPER SUMMARY
Keyword: HX8MLAS

Key Ideas	Key Terms

1 Mollusks

> Mollusks are soft-bodied coelomates that have a three-part body plan. Mollusks also have bilateral symmetry, and most mollusks have a shell.

> The three parts that make up the basic mollusk body plan are the visceral mass, the mantle, and the foot.

> Gastropods, cephalopods, and bivalves share the same basic organ systems and tissue layers, but they have different feeding strategies and body plans.

> Gastropods—snails and slugs—are primarily a marine group that also has members in freshwater and terrestrial habitats.

> Squids, octopuses, cuttlefish, and nautiluses are all cephalopods. Most of their body is made up of a large head attached to tentacles (a foot that is divided into numerous parts).

> Bivalves do not have a distinct head region or a radula, as other mollusks have. Their body is flattened between the two shells.

Key Terms

visceral mass (680)
mantle (680)
foot (680)
radula (680)
trochophore (682)
siphon (684)

2 Annelids

> In addition to segmentation, annelids are coelomates with highly specialized organ systems. Most annelids have external bristles called setae.

> Annelids are grouped into classes based on the number of setae (bristles) that they have and the presence or absence of parapodia, which are flap-shaped appendages used for gas exchange and locomotion.

> Polychaetes have a pair of fleshy, paddlelike parapodia on most of their segments. The parapodia, which usually have setae, allow the worm to swim, burrow, or crawl.

> Earthworms lack the distinctive head region of polychaetes and have no eyes. They do, however, have light-sensitive and touch-sensitive organs located at each end of their body.

> Most leeches are predators or scavengers, but some are parasites. Parasitic leeches attach to a vertebrate host and cut or digest a hole in the host's skin.

seta (686)
septum (687)
cerebral ganglion (687)

1. **Classification** Make a dichotomous key that could be used to classify mollusks and annelids into the correct class.

2. **Concept Map** Make a concept map that shows the characteristics and diversity of mollusks. Include the following words in your map: *foot, visceral mass, mantle, radula, siphons, gastropod, bivalve, cephalopod, open circulatory system,* and *closed circulatory system.*

Using Key Terms

Use each of the following terms in a separate sentence.

3. *trochophore*

4. *septa*

For each pair of terms, explain how the meanings of the terms differ.

5. *mantle* and *visceral mass*

6. *radula* and *siphon*

7. *setae* and *parapodia*

Understanding Key Ideas

8. What characteristic do mollusks and annelids share?
   a. Both have a coelom.
   b. Both have a shell.
   c. Both have no larval form.
   d. Both have a visceral mass.

9. What is the structure shown below used for?
   a. excretion   c. respiration
   b. reproduction d. feeding

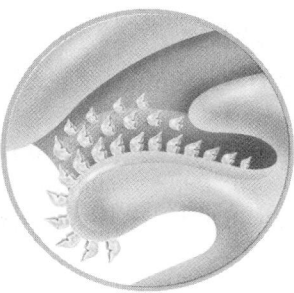

10. Which structure extracts useful molecules from coelomic fluid in mollusks?
    a. radula   c. nephridia
    b. ganglia   d. parapodia

11. What are the valves of bivalves connected by?
    a. siphons   c. mantle
    b. muscles   d. visceral mass

12. Earthworm movement requires all of the following *except*
    a. circular muscles.
    b. secretion of mucus.
    c. muscle contractions.
    d. traction provided by setae.

13. Blood in the circulatory system of an annelid
    a. flows into the body cavity.
    b. stays within the vessels.
    c. passes through the gills.
    d. delivers carbon dioxide to the tissues.

14. Which characteristic is used to classify annelids?
    a. number of setae on each segment
    b. presence or absence of a distinct head region
    c. method of movement
    d. presence or absence of a trocophore larva

15. An annelid can be distinguished from a roundworm in that annelids
    a. have a head end.
    b. are segmented.
    c. have a flat body.
    d. are symmetrical.

Explaining Key Ideas

16. **Compare** the distinguishing features of each of the three major classes of mollusks.

17. **Identify** two characteristics that mollusks and annelids have in common.

18. **Evaluate** the influence of segmentation on body movement in annelids.

19. **Name** the structure that functions as a primitive brain in annelids.

20. **Differentiate** between marine annelids, earthworms, and leeches by their external appearance.

Using Science Graphics

Use the diagram of a snail and your knowledge of science to answer the following questions.

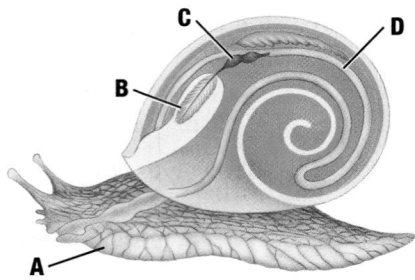

21. Which structure is part of the respiratory system?
- **a.** A
- **b.** B
- **c.** C
- **d.** D

22. Which structure is part of the digestive system?
- **a.** A
- **b.** B
- **c.** C
- **d.** D

23. One characteristic that is shown by this mollusk is
- **a.** cephalization.
- **b.** radial symmetry.
- **c.** body segmentation.
- **d.** a pseudocoelom.

Critical Thinking

24. Relating Concepts Explain the significance of the evolution of a coelom in mollusks.

25. Making Inferences Many mollusks are terrestrial animals, but they live in moist environments. Why do all mollusks require nearly constant exposure to water?

26. Justifying Conclusions Classification of organisms has traditionally been based on physical similarities. Given the physical differences of gastropods, bivalves, and cephalopods, how did these animals come to be grouped into the phylum Mollusca?

27. Finding Evidence Why should bivalves be cooked before they are eaten?

28. Making Connections Why is *poly-* an appropriate prefix for polychaete worms?

29. Drawing Conclusions Would you expect to find more earthworms in sandy soil or in soil rich in organic matter? Explain your answer.

Writing for Science

30. Preparing Reports Conduct library or Internet research on the use of mollusk fossils to determine the age of various sedimentary formations on Earth. Find out why mollusks are considered to be good index fossils. Prepare a half- to one-page report of your findings.

31. Summarizing Information Throughout history, people around the world have used mollusk shells for adornment and other purposes. Research some specific ways that humans have used shells, and prepare an oral or visual report of your findings.

Methods of Science

32. Controlling Variables A bivalve worm called a shipworm can do extensive damage to ocean pier pilings (supports) by burrowing into them. The worm burrows by scraping the pilings with its two shells and secreting acids. A scientist decides to determine if a new paint can reduce shipworm damage more than other paints can. What variables must the scientist control in order for the experimental results to be considered valid?

Alternative Assessment

33. Engineering Designs Conduct library or Internet research on composting through the use of earthworms. Use this information to design a compost bin that the class could build at your school. Consult with your teacher and other school officials to check on the feasibility of constructing the compost bin. Write a bulleted list of the benefits of composting.

34. Career Connection Research the field of worm farming, or raising segmented worms for use in research, as fishing bait, and for soil improvement. Your report should include a job description, types of training required, kinds of employers, growth prospects, and starting salary.

Technology Skills

35. Circle Graphs Use a computer graphing program to draw a pie chart of annelid classes by using the following information: Total number of annelid species, 9,000; Polychaeta species, 5,300; Oligochaeta species, 3,100; Hirudinea species, 500; Species in other classes, 100.

Standardized Test Prep

TEST TIP After you answer a test question in your mind, compare your answer with the answer choices. Choose the answer that most closely matches your own answer.

Science Concepts

Choose the letter of the answer choice that best answers the question.

1. How do terrestrial snails respire?
   A by using gills
   B by using a primitive lung
   C through their skin
   D through their siphon

2. Which of the following are the only mollusks with a closed circulatory system?
   F snails   H gastropods
   G bivalves   J cephalopods

3. How are bivalves different from all other mollusks?
   A They have a coelom.
   B They have a shell.
   C They lack a radula.
   D They lack a stomach.

4. A gastropod's nephridia are part of which of the following organ systems?
   F circulatory   H excretory
   G digestive   J respiratory

5. Annelids are divided into three classes based partly on the number of which of the following?
   A setae   C septa
   B segments   D aortic arches

6. Parapodia are a distinguishing characteristic of which group of annelids?
   F earthworms   H marine worms
   G leeches   J cephalopods

7. In which of the following ways do annelids differ from most mollusks?
   A Annelids lack a mantle.
   B Annelids have a coelom.
   C Annelids lack cerebral ganglia.
   D Annelids have trochophore larvae.

Using Science Graphics

Use the diagram showing the internal structure of a bivalve to answer the following questions.

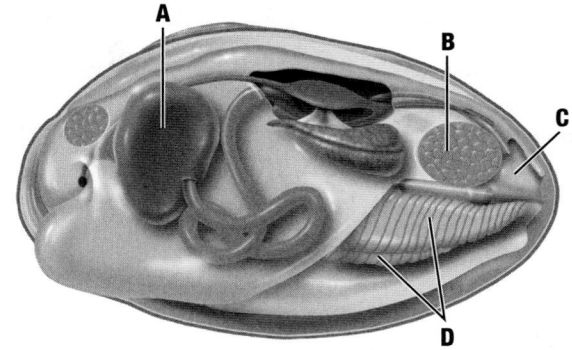

8. What is structure B?
   F a gill   H the mantle
   G a siphon   J a muscle

The graph plots the movement of the anterior end of an earthworm over time. Use the graph to answer the following question.

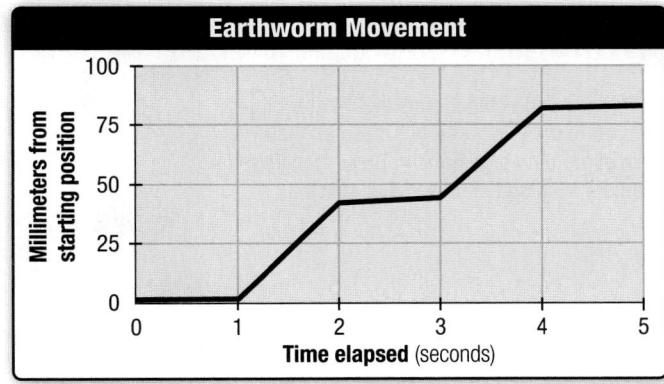

9. **Explaining Graphics** Was the anterior end moving or stationary during the periods represented by the horizontal sections of the graph? Which of the earthworm's sets of muscles were contracting during the periods represented by the horizontal sections? Explain.

Writing Skills

10. **Short Response** Summarize the seven characteristics that are common to most mollusks.

Arthropods and Echinoderms

Preview

1 Arthropods
Arthropod Characteristics
Arthropod Life Cycle
Groups of Arthropods

2 Arachnids and Crustaceans
Arachnids and Their Relatives
Crustaceans

3 Insects
Insect Characteristics
Adaptations for Flight
Insect Life Cycle
Social Insects
Centipedes and Millipedes

4 Echinoderms
Echinoderm Characteristics
Groups of Echinoderms

Why It Matters

Arthropods and echinoderms are different from each other in many ways, but these animals often share the same habitat. These two groups of animals include many familiar species.

A field of flowers under a cloudy sky? Look closely. This scientist is actually scuba diving and is examining a field of sea stars beneath the ice.

Various animals make breathing holes in the ice. Divers take advantage of these holes in the ice to study a variety of sea life.

InquiryLab

Larval Life

Larval life is unique in many aquatic crustaceans and echinoderms. Often, an animal's larval stage looks nothing like the adult organism into which the animal will develop.

Procedure

1. Examine a **prepared slide of crab larvae** on a **microscope** under both low and high power. Draw a picture of each distinct larval stage that you observe.

2. Examine a **prepared slide of starfish larvae** under low and high power on the microscope. Draw a picture of each distinct larval stage that you observe.

3. Examine a **prepared slide of zooplankton.** Identify any larvae that resemble crab or starfish larvae. Draw a picture of any unfamiliar larval forms.

Analysis

1. **Describe** how the crab larvae differ in form and structure from adult crabs.

2. **Describe** how the starfish larvae differ in form and structure from adult starfish.

3. **Describe** any other jointed-legged organisms that you saw in the zooplankton sample.

Sea stars and other sea creatures gather below these breathing holes to feed on dead animals and debris.

699

READING TOOLBOX

These reading tools can help you learn the material in this chapter. For more information on how to use these and other tools, see **Appendix: Reading and Study Skills.**

Using Words

Key-Term Fold A key-term fold is used to study definitions of key terms in a chapter. Each tab contains a key term on one side and the term's definition on the other.

Your Turn Use the key-term fold to quiz yourself on the definitions of the key terms in this chapter.

1. Fold a sheet of lined notebook paper in half from left to right.
2. Using scissors, cut along every third line from the right edge of the paper to the center fold to make tabs.

Using Language

Classification Categories are groups of things that have certain characteristics in common. Members of a category may differ from one another, but they share the characteristics that make them part of the same category. You can find members of a category by looking for words such as *include*, *such as*, and *are*.

Your Turn Read the following sentences. Identify the category and the members of that category in each sentence.

1. The Great Lakes include Huron, Ontario, Michigan, Erie, and Superior.
2. Most European countries, such as Germany, France, and Italy, use a currency called the *euro.*
3. Scorpions, mites, and spiders are chelicerates—relatives of insects.

Taking Notes

Outlining Outlining is a note-taking skill that helps you organize information. An outline gives you an overview of the topics in a chapter and helps you understand how the topics relate to each other.

Your Turn Create an outline for each section of this chapter.

1. Copy all of the section's headings, in order, on a piece of paper.
2. Leave plenty of space between each heading.
3. As you read the material under each heading in the section, write the important facts under the same heading in your outline.

> Section 1
> Arthropod Characteristics
> Jointed Appendages
> Segmented Body
> Exoskeleton

Arthropods

| Key Ideas | Key Terms | Why It Matters |

Key Ideas

> What are distinguishing features of arthropods?

> How is molting an important feature of the arthropod life cycle?

> What are the four main types of arthropods?

Key Terms

thorax
cephalothorax
appendage
trachea

spiracle
Malpighian tubule
compound eye
molting

Why It Matters

Arthropods are highly evolved animals that dominate both terrestrial and aquatic environments.

Arthropods are found in essentially every habitat on Earth. Humans are probably most familiar with the arthropods that live on land. Many land-dwelling arthropods, or insects, differ from most other invertebrate animals in that insects can fly. Though we often think of many arthropods as pests, these animals play many important roles in both land and sea environments. For example, many arthropods are natural enemies of pests. Some arthropods are a food source for other animals. Also, insects pollinate plants. Imagining a world without arthropods is difficult!

Arthropod Characteristics

Similar to annelids and mollusks, arthropods are protostomes. While arthropods are diverse, they share many internal and external features. > **Arthropods are characterized by having a segmented body, jointed appendages, and a hard external skeleton.** Most arthropods have an open circulatory system, and many arthropods have wings. Not every species displays every feature. However, these features are characteristic of the phylum as a whole.

Segmented Body In arthropods, individual body segments often exist only during the larval stage. For example, when you look at a butterfly larva (a caterpillar), you can easily see that it has many segments. However, if you look closely at an adult butterfly, or the dragonfly shown in **Figure 1,** you see only three body regions. In most arthropods the many body segments fuse during development to form three distinct regions—the head, the **thorax** (mid-body region), and the abdomen. In some arthropods, such as crabs, the head is fused with the thorax, which forms a body region called the **cephalothorax.**

thorax (THAWR AKS) in arthropods, the mid-body region

cephalothorax (SEF uh loh THAWR AKS) in arachnids and some crustaceans, the body part made up of the head and the thorax

Figure 1 The three main regions of an arthropod's segmented body can be seen on this dragonfly. > **What are the benefits of a segmented body?**

Head
Thorax
Abdomen

701

Jointed Appendages

Test your range of motion with and without bending your joints.

Procedure

❶ Work in pairs. Extend one arm, and place a meterstick along the inside of your arm, as shown in the figure. Your partner measures and records the distance along the meterstick that you can reach with extended (unbent) fingers.

❷ Bend only your fingers. Your partner measures and records the closest and farthest distances on the meterstick that you can reach with bent fingers.

❸ Bend your elbow. Your partner measures and records the closest and farthest distances on the meterstick that you can reach when your elbow is bent.

❹ Now, trade places with your partner, and repeat the exercise.

Analysis

1. **Calculate** the farthest distance that you could reach. Under which condition did you reach this distance?

2. **CRITICAL THINKING** **Inferring Relationships** Some arthropods have sense organs (eyes and odor detectors) on the ends of their jointed appendages. What advantages might these animals have over arthropods that do not have these adaptations?

3. **CRITICAL THINKING** **Predicting Outcomes** How might you eat breakfast differently if you did not have joints in your fingers and elbows?

Figure 2 This leaf-footed bug belongs to phylum Arthropoda. ❯ **Which arthropod characteristics does this insect have?**

Jointed Appendages Whether you are looking at a scorpion or a leaf-footed bug, as **Figure 2** shows, when you see an arthropod, you will probably notice its appendages. An **appendage** is a structure that extends from the arthropod's body wall. Unlike the parapodia and setae of annelids, arthropod appendages have joints that bend. The phylum name *Arthropoda* means "joint footed." A variety of jointed appendages are found in arthropods, including walking legs, sensory antennae, and several kinds of mouthparts.

Exoskeleton The rigid outer layer of the arthropod body is called an *exoskeleton,* which is composed primarily of the carbohydrate chitin. The exoskeleton provides protection against predators and helps prevent water loss. However, this outer layer is thin and flexible where the joints of the appendages are located. Muscles attached to the inside of the exoskeleton can pull against the exoskeleton, causing the animal's appendages to move.

The thickness and weight of an exoskeleton varies greatly in arthropods. Crustaceans such as lobsters have an especially thick, relatively inflexible exoskeleton. Ocean water supports the mass of a lobster's heavy exoskeleton. In contrast, the exoskeletons of insects and spiders are fairly soft and flexible. An exoskeleton does not grow; arthropods shed their exoskeleton periodically and form a new, larger one.

❯ **Reading Check** *What does arthropod mean? (See the Appendix for answers to Reading Checks.)*

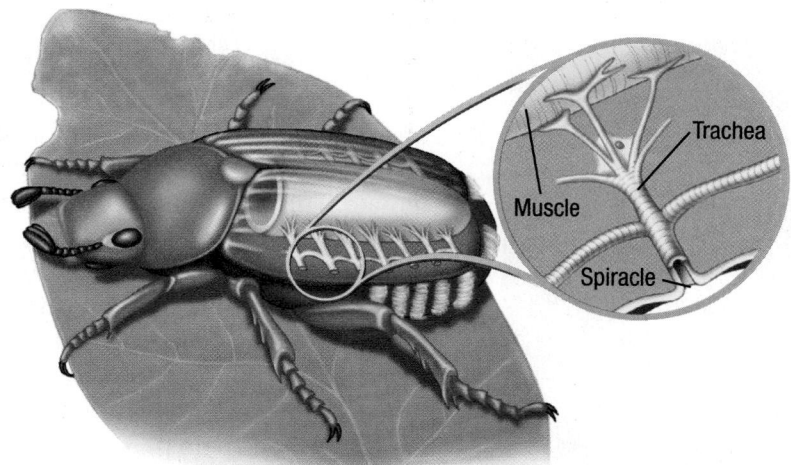

Figure 3 A series of hollow tubes called *tracheae* run through the body of most terrestrial arthropods. These tubes provide oxygen to the body. ❯ **How does air enter an arthropod's body?**

Trachea

Muscle

Spiracle

Respiration and Circulation Many land arthropods breathe through a network of fine tubes, which **Figure 3** shows. Each tube is called a **trachea.** Air enters the body through openings called **spiracles** and passes into the trachea, which delivers oxygen to the body. Other land arthropods breathe through book lungs, shown in the Up Close feature. Most aquatic arthropods breathe through gills.

The circulatory system of arthropods is open, which means that blood is not always contained within vessels. Most of an arthropod's internal organs are bathed in blood that flows through the body cavity. Blood returns to the heart and is recirculated through the body.

Feeding, Digestion, and Excretion The different arthropod groups have <u>varied</u> mouthparts and other appendages that are involved in obtaining and eating food. The intestinal tract extends from the mouth to the anus and contains structures that are specialized for storage, mechanical and chemical digestion, nutrient absorption, and elimination of digestive wastes.

The arthropod excretory system is composed of structures called Malpighian tubules. **Malpighian tubules** are narrow extensions from the arthropod's lower intestinal tract that are bathed in blood. Water and small, dissolved particles in the blood move through the tubules into the gut. As this fluid moves through the intestinal tract, most of the water, valuable ions, and metabolites from the fluid are absorbed into the body tissues. Metabolic wastes remain in the gut and eventually leave the body through the anus. Thus, terrestrial arthropods do not have to lose water to expel metabolic wastes.

Compound Eyes Many arthropods have compound eyes, which **Figure 4** shows. A **compound eye** is an eye that is composed of thousands of individual visual units. Each of these units collects information on a small field of view. The brain receives input from these units and then composes the image of an object. While the image is not very clear, the arthropod's compound eye is exceptionally good at detecting movement, which is why sneaking up on a fly is difficult. Some arthropods also have simple, single-lens eyes that do not form images but simply distinguish light from dark.

appendage a structure that extends from the main body, such as a limb, tentacle, fin, or wing

trachea (TRAY kee uh) in insects, myriapods, and spiders, one of a network of air tubes

spiracle (SPIR uh kuhl) an external opening in an insect or arthropod, used in respiration

Malpighian tubule (mal PIG ee uhn TOO BYOOL) an excretory tube that opens into the back part of the intestine of most insects and certain arthropods

compound eye an eye composed of many light detectors separated by pigment cells

ACADEMIC VOCABULARY

varied having more than one possible state

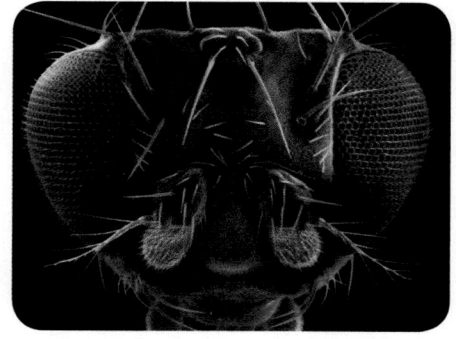

Figure 4 The compound eye of this housefly is made of 800 or more individual units.

Figure 5 This grasshopper emerges from its old exoskeleton and leaves the exoskeleton behind as a colorless ghost of itself.

molting the shedding of an exoskeleton, skin, feathers, or hair to be replaced by new parts

Key-Term Fold Make a key-term fold in order to learn the italicized words in this section. If you do not know the definitions of these words, look the words up in the dictionary.

Arthropod Life Cycle

Most arthropods reproduce only sexually, though some can produce offspring from unfertilized eggs. Fertilization of eggs by sperm is usually internal, in which a packet of sperm is deposited inside the female. This method of fertilization is more efficient than external fertilization and prevents the gametes from drying out. Many arthropods have specialized reproductive organs. Male and female structures in one species may fit together in the same way as a lock and key do. This fit helps ensure that mating does not occur between members of different species. Eggs are usually laid outside the female's body, and the immature animals that hatch from the eggs generally receive no parental care.

Molting A tough exoskeleton protects an arthropod from predators and helps prevent water loss. But an exoskeleton does not grow, so an arthropod cannot simply grow larger, as many other animals do. Imagine inflating a balloon inside a soft drink can. At a certain point, the balloon cannot get any bigger. Arthropods have the same problem. All arthropods must periodically shed their hard exoskeleton and grow a new one. In a process called **molting**, arthropods shed and discard their exoskeleton. ❯ **Molting allows the arthropod's body to grow larger.** This behavior is triggered by the release of certain hormones. Just before molting, a new exoskeleton forms beneath the old one. When the new exoskeleton is fully formed, the old one breaks open. The arthropod emerges in its new, still-soft exoskeleton, as **Figure 5** shows. The new exoskeleton expands before it hardens, which allows the animal to grow larger. Most arthropods molt several times before they reach their adult stage.

Groups of Arthropods

Living arthropods are traditionally divided into two groups—arthropods that have jaws and arthropods that have fangs or pincers. **Figure 6** shows that arthropods with jaws are further classified into subphylum Hexapoda (insects), subphylum Myriapoda (millipedes and centipedes), or subphylum Crustacea (lobsters and shrimps). Arthropods that have fangs or pincers, such as spiders, belong to the subphylum Chelicerata. Each of the four subphyla represents a distinct evolutionary line. ❯ **The four main arthropod groups (subphyla) are Hexapoda, Myriapoda, Crustacea, and Chelicerata.**

The Evolutionary Success of Arthropods The total number of arthropod species exceeds the number of all other animal species combined. More than 5 million species of arthropods may exist today! A number of factors contribute to the enormous evolutionary success of arthropods. Arthropods' exoskeleton provides a wonderful adaptation for life on land, where water is not always abundant. Arthropods are small, and they show a wide range of specialization in food sources and habitats. Other unique characteristics have also been important to the success of arthropods.

❯ **Reading Check** *How does an arthropod shed its exoskeleton?*

Figure 6 This phylogenetic tree illustrates hypothetical relationships among the arthropod subphyla. Two groups of arthropods exist: those with jaws and those with fangs or pincers. For updates on phylogenetic information, visit **go.hrw.com.** Enter the keyword **HX8 Phylo.**

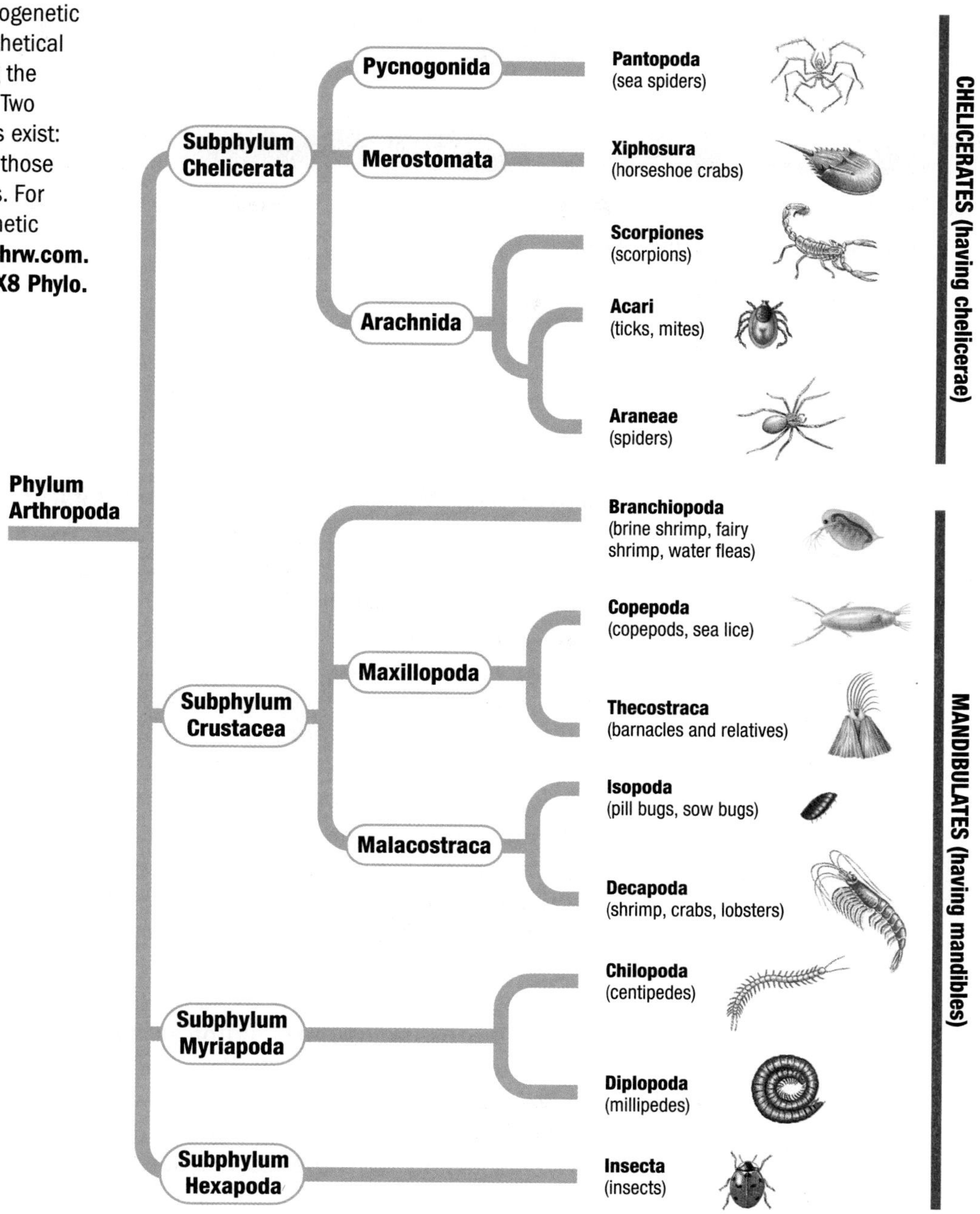

Phylum
Arthropoda

Subphylum
Chelicerata

Pycnogonida — Pantopoda (sea spiders)

Merostomata — Xiphosura (horseshoe crabs)

Arachnida
- Scorpiones (scorpions)
- Acari (ticks, mites)
- Araneae (spiders)

CHELICERATES (having chelicerae)

Subphylum
Crustacea

Maxillopoda
- Branchiopoda (brine shrimp, fairy shrimp, water fleas)
- Copepoda (copepods, sea lice)
- Thecostraca (barnacles and relatives)

Malacostraca
- Isopoda (pill bugs, sow bugs)
- Decapoda (shrimp, crabs, lobsters)

Subphylum
Myriapoda
- Chilopoda (centipedes)
- Diplopoda (millipedes)

Subphylum
Hexapoda — Insecta (insects)

MANDIBULATES (having mandibles)

> KEY IDEAS

1. **Name** the distinguishing features of arthropods.
2. **Describe** the arthropod life cycle and the molting process.
3. **List** the four main types of arthropods.

CRITICAL THINKING

4. **Relating Concepts** Draw a concept map of the four major subphyla of arthropods, and give an example of an animal in each group.
5. **Inferring Conclusions** How is the exoskeleton of a growing arthropod similar to a balloon that is inflated inside of a soft drink can? How does molting get around this limitation of the exoskeleton?

CONNECTING KEY IDEAS

6. **Arthropod Diseases** Conduct research in the library or on the Internet about diseases that are transmitted by arthropods. Develop a brochure to present your findings. Include photographs or diagrams of the arthropods and any visible symptoms of the diseases.

Arachnids and Crustaceans

Key Ideas	Key Terms	Why It Matters
❯ What adaptations have evolved in arachnids? ❯ What adaptations have evolved in crustaceans?	chelicera pedipalp spinneret	Numerous species of arachnids and crustaceans belong to the phylum Arthropoda. You likely recognize many of these species.

The many members of arthropod subphyla Chelicerata and Crustacea are diverse and are important to other organisms.

Arachnids and Their Relatives

The subphylum Chelicerata includes spiders, scorpions, mites and ticks, and horseshoe crabs. ❯ **The chelicerates are arthropods that have appendages called chelicerae, which are specialized for feeding.** **Chelicerae** (singular *chelicera*) are the first pair of appendages and are modified into pincers or fangs, as **Figure 7** shows. The second pair of appendages are **pedipalps,** which mostly catch and handle prey. Chelicerates have four pairs of appendages called *walking legs* and lack antennae. The chelicerate body is made up of a cephalothorax and an abdomen. Arachnids form the largest class of chelicerates.

All arachnids, except some mites, are carnivores, and most are terrestrial. Because arachnids do not have jaws, these animals are able to consume only liquid food. The arachnid first injects its prey with powerful enzymes that turn the prey's tissues into liquid. Then the arachnid sucks the liquid food into its stomach. Other internal features of arachnids are illustrated in the UpClose feature.

Perhaps no other group of animals is more disliked and feared by humans than arachnids are. While some spiders and scorpions are highly venomous, generally these animals do more good than harm. For example, many spiders are major predators of insect pests, and gardeners usually welcome spiders' pest-control expertise.

Figure 7 Arachnids, such as spiders, scorpions, ticks, and horseshoe crabs, form the subphylum Chelicerata.

Spider

Chelicerae

Scorpion

Spiders The chelicerae of spiders are modified into fangs. Poison glands that are located in the front part of the spider's body secrete a toxin through these fangs. The toxin kills or paralyzes the prey, and then the spider eats the prey. Spiders are important predators of insects in almost every terrestrial ecosystem. In the United States, two species of spiders that are poisonous to humans are the black widow and the brown recluse. Most spiders have **spinnerets,** appendages at the end of the abdomen that secrete sticky strands of silk. Some spinnerets do not produce silk. Instead, they secrete a sticky substance that the spider can use to make silk strands adhesive.

Scorpions, Mites, and Ticks Two other familiar groups of arachnids are scorpions and mites. Like spiders, both scorpions and mites have chelicerae and pedipalps, but these two structures are modified differently in each of these arachnid groups.

Scorpions Scorpions have a long, segmented abdomen that ends in a venomous stinger that is used to stun prey. **Figure 7** shows how the abdomen is usually folded over the rest of the scorpion's body. The pedipalps of scorpions are large, grasping pincers, which are used not for defense but for seizing food and during sexual reproduction.

Mites and Ticks Mites are by far the largest group of arachnids. Their head, thorax, and abdomen are fused into a single, unsegmented body. Mites such as chiggers and ticks are well known to humans because of their irritating bites. Most mites are not harmful, but some are plant and animal pests. While feeding, plant mites may pass viral and fungal infections to a plant. Blood-sucking ticks attach themselves to a host, often a human. Lyme disease is spread by bites from infected deer ticks, such as the one shown in **Figure 7.**

Horseshoe Crabs Horseshoe crabs, in spite of their name, are more closely related to spiders than to crabs. Like spiders, horseshoe crabs have chelicerae and pedipalps. Like crabs, these animals have a hard exoskeleton that covers most of the body, as **Figure 7** shows. Horseshoe crabs make up an ancient group of invertebrates that probably appeared on Earth about 400 million years ago.

❯ **Reading Check** *Name two types of spiders that are dangerous to humans.*

> **chelicera** (kuh LIS uhr uh) in arachnids, either of a pair of appendages used to attack prey
>
> **pedipalp** (PED i PALP) in certain arthropods, one of the second pair of appendages
>
> **spinneret** (SPIN uh RET) an organ that spiders and certain insect larvae use to produce silky threads for webs and cocoons

ACADEMIC
VOCABULARY

modify to change

Deer tick

Horseshoe crab

Pill bug

Barnacle

Crustaceans

While primarily marine, members of subphylum Crustacea also live in fresh water and in a few moist land habitats. Crustaceans share many features with other arthropods, but also differ in many ways.

> Many crustaceans have a cephalothorax and an abdomen. Like chelicerates, crustaceans have appendages on their abdomen. Unlike chelicerates, crustaceans have mandibles that are adapted for feeding and have two pairs of antennae. Crustaceans breathe by using gills.

The cephalothorax segments are hardened into a carapace. Almost all crustaceans have a distinctive larval form called a *nauplius.* Like the larval forms of insects, the nauplius undergoes a series of molts before the animal takes on its adult form.

Terrestrial Crustaceans **Figure 8** shows a pill bug, which is part of the largest group of terrestrial crustaceans, the isopods. These animals are the only crustaceans that are truly terrestrial. Another group, the sand fleas, is typically found along beaches. Land crabs are only partly adapted to terrestrial living. Their life cycle is tied to the ocean, where the larvae live until maturity.

Aquatic Crustaceans Some aquatic crustaceans are quite small. Common examples include fairy shrimps, water fleas, ostracods, and tiny copepods. Copepods are among the most abundant multicellular organisms on Earth and are a key part of marine food chains. **Figure 8** shows an example of a copepod. Another small marine crustacean, commonly known as krill, is the chief food source for many marine species.

Sessile Crustaceans Adult barnacles, shown in **Figure 8,** are sessile, which means that they are permanently attached to something. Free-swimming larvae attach themselves to a submerged object, where the larvae remain. The head end of the barnacle attaches to the hard surface. Glands on the first pair of antennae secrete a strong adhesive that hardens into a shell. This shell withstands pressure from moving water and resists bacterial decomposition.

READING TOOLBOX

Classification Using the classification skills that you practiced at the start of the chapter, classify arthropods into groups based on the types of appendages that the animals have.

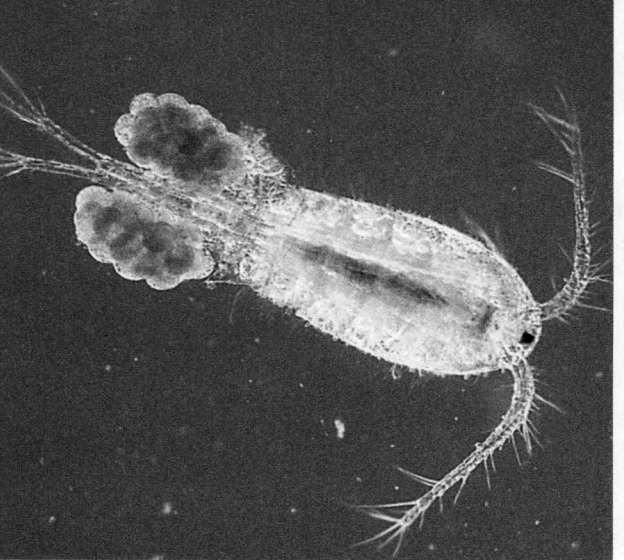

Copepod

Decapods have four pairs of walking legs.

Decapods use chelipeds to grab and eat food.

Crab

Figure 8 Crustaceans include pill bugs, barnacles, copepods, and decapods. ❭ **Do all crustaceans live in a marine environment?**

Hard plates that open and close help protect the barnacle's body from predators and wave action and from drying out. When feeding, barnacles extend their jointed feeding appendages through the open plates. The feathery, gill-tipped legs filter food, mostly plankton, from the water into the barnacle's mouth. Essentially, these animals stand on their head and kick food into their mouth!

Decapods Large crustaceans such as shrimps, crayfish, crabs, and lobsters have five pairs of legs and are often referred to as *decapods*. Almost one-quarter of all crustacean species are decapods. The head and thorax of decapods are fused into a cephalothorax, which is covered by a carapace that is especially thick on top. As shown in **Figure 8,** the anterior pair of legs is modified into large pincers called *chelipeds*. In decapods, the two pairs of antennae are sensory structures. In crayfish and lobsters, appendages called *swimmerets* are on the underside of the abdomen and are used in swimming and in reproduction. Flattened, paddlelike appendages called *uropods* are located at the end of the abdomen. Decapods can propel themselves through the water by forcefully flexing their abdomen.

❭ **Reading Check** *Which structures do decapods use to swim and to reproduce?*

Section 2 Review

❭ **KEY IDEAS**

1. **Describe** the features that distinguish chelicerates from other arthropods.
2. **Name** the features that crustaceans have in common with other arthropods.

CRITICAL THINKING

3. **Analyzing Logic** Explain how arachnids digest their food outside of their body. Why is this behavior beneficial to arachnids?
4. **Summarizing Information** Explain why a tick bite is more a cause for concern than the bite of most spiders is.

ALTERNATIVE ASSESSMENT

5. **Forming a Model** By using papier mâché or another material, make a model of a grasshopper or a spider. Present your model to the class, and describe the organism that you modeled.

Up Close Arachnid

The brown recluse spider is unaggressive toward humans, but has a highly venomous bite. Brown recluses are active at night. During the day, they hide in dark areas such as attics, woodpiles, or old boxes that are rarely opened.

Scientific Name: *Loxosceles reclusa*
Size: Females are up to 10 mm long; males are smaller.
Range: South-central United States, from central Texas to Alabama, north to southern Ohio
Habitat: Dark, dry sheltered sites outdoors or indoors
Diet: Small insects

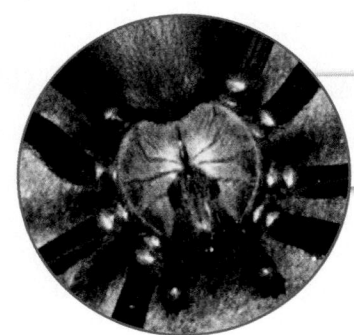

Identification The brown recluse can be recognized by the violin shape on its back.

Body Structure In arachnids, the head and thorax are fused into a cephalothorax. It contains simple eyes, pairs of chelicerae and pedipalps, and four pairs of legs. The abdomen contains most of the internal organs.

Reproduction During mating, the male uses its pedipalps modified into sperm storage organs to insert sperm into the female's body.

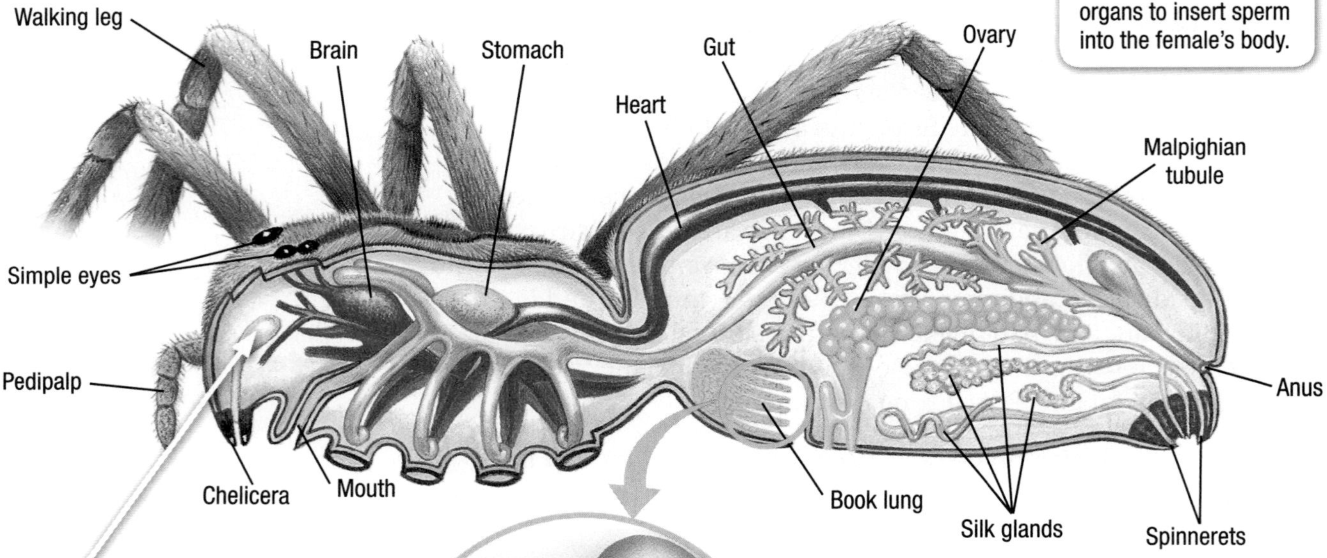

Walking leg

Brain

Stomach

Gut

Heart

Ovary

Malpighian tubule

Simple eyes

Pedipalp

Anus

Chelicera

Mouth

Book lung

Silk glands

Spinnerets

Poison Glands Poison glands are connected to the fanged chelicerae.

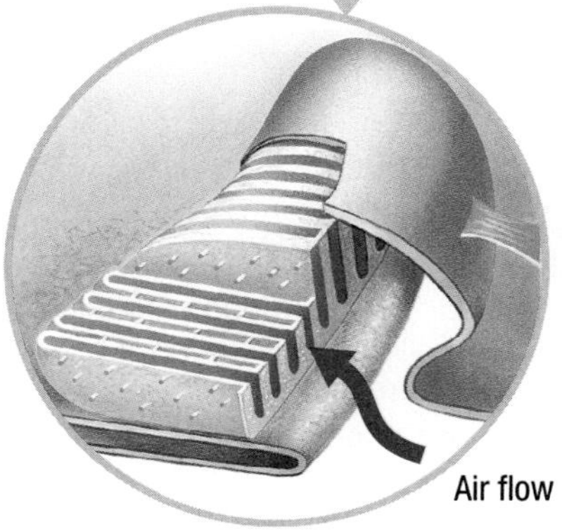

Air flow

Respiration Book lungs contain stacks of thin blood-filled plates of tissue. Air enters the book lungs through slits on the underside of the abdomen and passes over the lungs. Blood flowing through the plates picks up oxygen by diffusion.

Insect

Although the Eastern lubber grasshopper has wings, its wings are too short to be used in flight. Instead, the grasshopper moves by jumping. During the mating season, a male "sings" by rubbing a row of pegs on its jumping leg against ridges on its forewing.

Eastern Lubber Grasshopper

Scientific Name: *Romalea microptera*
Size: 5 cm to 6.5 cm in length
Range: Eastern United States
Habitat: Fields and meadows
Diet: Grasses and other leafy vegetation

Body Structure The head contains antennae, three light-detecting ocelli, and compound eyes. Three pairs of legs attach to the thorax. The thorax and abdomen contain most of the organ systems.

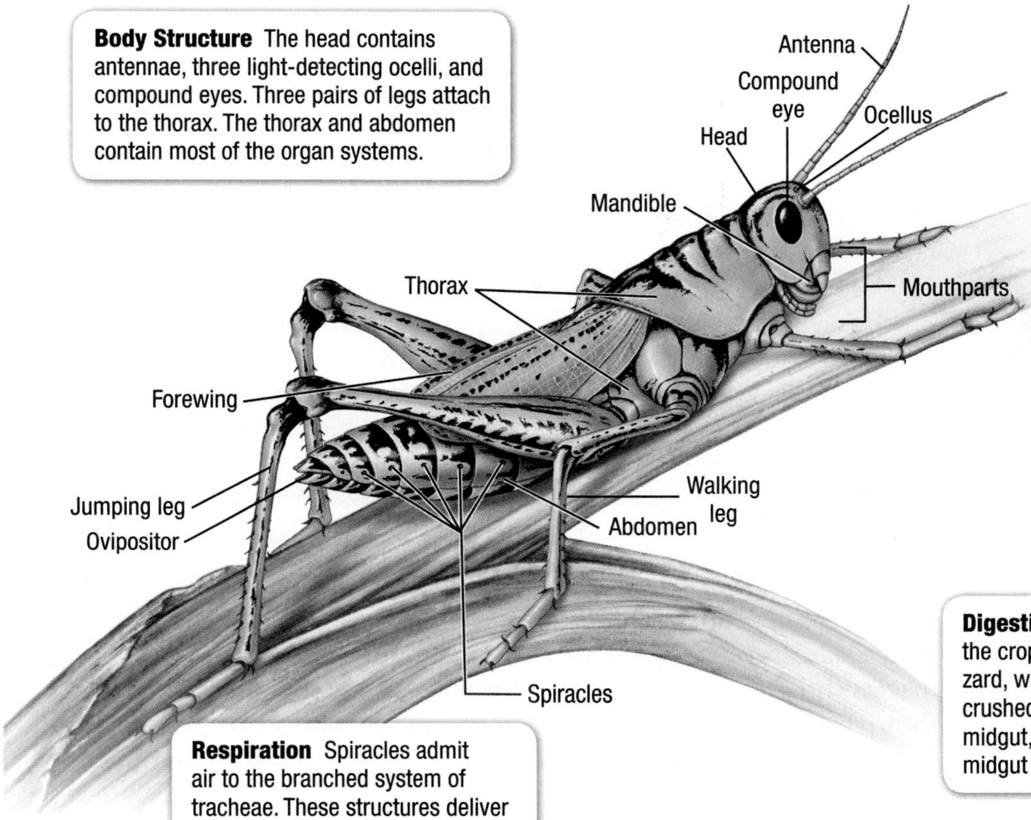

Molting Grasshoppers, like all arthropods, undergo molting. In this photo, the black exoskeleton has been shed during molting.

Antenna
Compound eye
Ocellus
Head
Mandible
Mouthparts
Thorax
Forewing
Jumping leg
Ovipositor
Walking leg
Abdomen
Spiracles

Respiration Spiracles admit air to the branched system of tracheae. These structures deliver oxygen throughout the body.

Digestion Chewed food enters the crop and passes to the gizzard, where it is shredded and crushed. Food is digested in the midgut, and passes through the midgut wall into the body fluid.

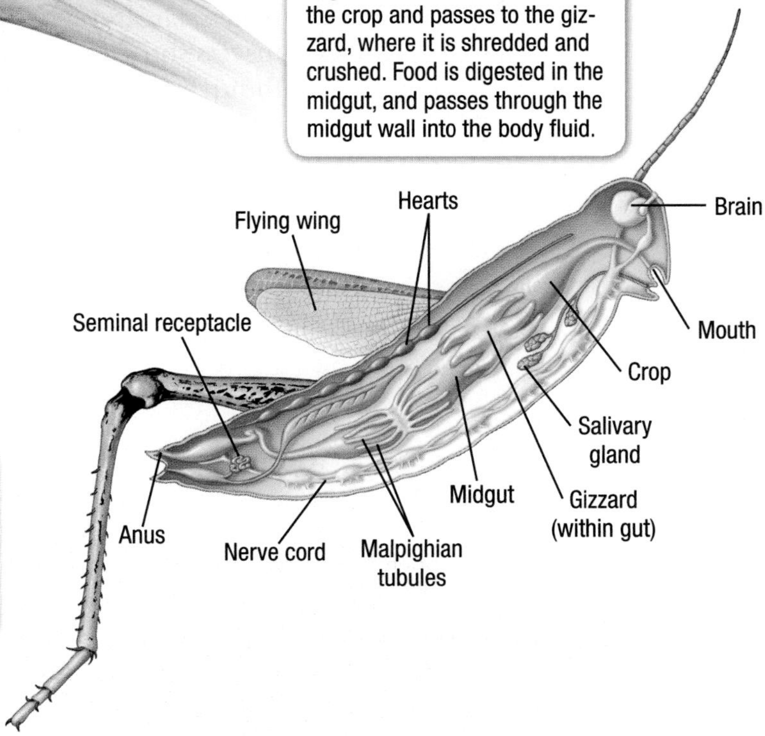

Hearts
Flying wing
Brain
Seminal receptacle
Mouth
Crop
Salivary gland
Anus
Nerve cord
Malpighian tubules
Midgut
Gizzard (within gut)

Reproduction The female stores sperm in a seminal receptacle. Later, the female digs a hole by using ovipositors. As she releases her eggs into the hole, the eggs are fertilized by the stored sperm.

Key Ideas	Key Terms	Why It Matters
❯ What are common insect characteristics? ❯ How are insects adapted for flight? ❯ How is insect development unique among arthropods? ❯ What are the characteristics of social insects? ❯ Which arthropods are known as myriapods?	mandible metamorphosis chrysalis pupa caste	Anyone who has ever been on a picnic does not have to be told that insects are numerous. The insects are by far the largest group of organisms on Earth.

Insects have specialized and often unique traits. Insects are highly adapted to their varied, mostly terrestrial environments.

Insect Characteristics

The insect body is similar to the body of other arthropods, with some specializations. The thorax is composed of three fused segments. Three pairs of jointed walking legs are attached to the thorax. Some insects, such as fleas, lice, and silverfish, lack wings. Other adult insects have one or two pairs of wings attached to the thorax. ❯ **Most insects share the same general body plan, specialized mouthparts for feeding, a unique life cycle, and the ability to fly.**

Adaptations for Feeding **Figure 9** shows that most insects have specialized mouthparts for eating called **mandibles.** Some insects pierce skin and suck blood, while others sponge up liquid. Some insects show little specialization in mouthparts. Other insects chew through wood (termites and carpenter ants) or hard seeds (harvester ants) or suck nectar from deep inside of a flower (various butterflies).

Grasshopper
(adapted for biting and chewing)

Mosquito
(adapted for piercing and sucking)

Fly
(adapted for sponging and lapping)

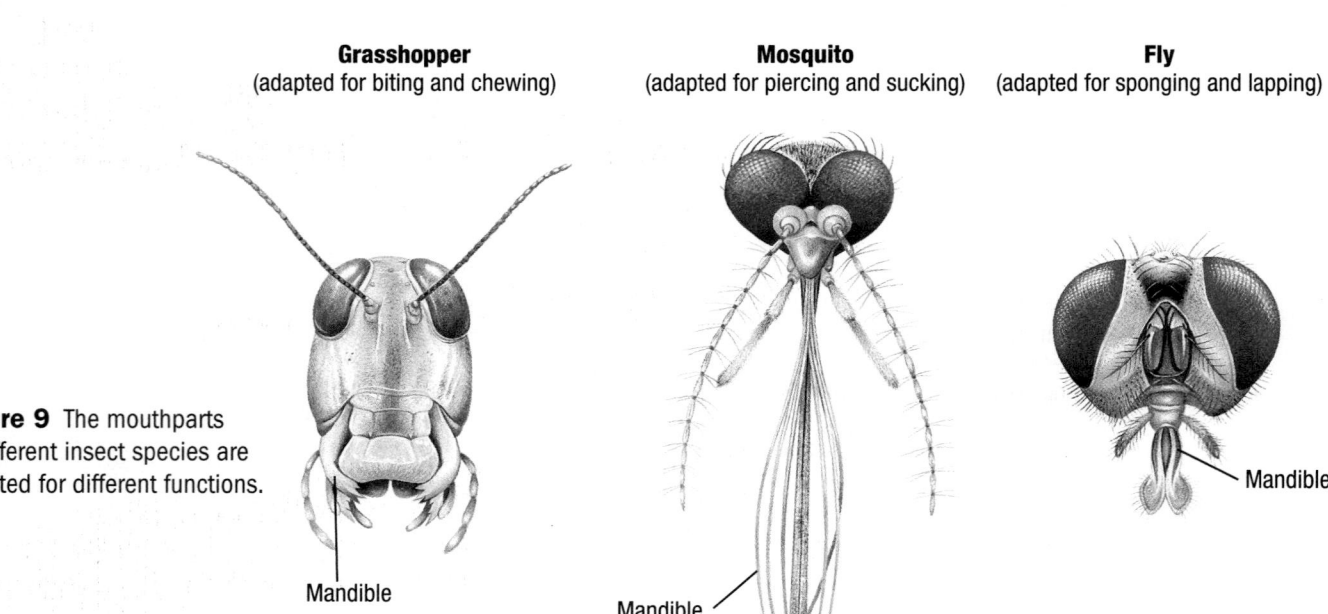

Figure 9 The mouthparts of different insect species are adapted for different functions.

Mandible

Mandible

Mandible

QuickLab

 15 min

Bee Wing

Like other flying insects, bees flap their wings in order to fly. To develop sufficient lift, bees add a propeller-like twist to the wings' movement. The overall vein pattern of the bee wing is species specific.

Procedure

1 Observe the slide of a bee wing on a microscope by using low power. Draw the wing structure.

2 Carefully switch to high power. Note the difference in the wing's appearance. Draw what you see.

3 Based on your observations, bend 25 cm of 22-gauge wire into the shape of the bee's wing.

4 Cover the wire frame with plastic wrap, and use tape to secure the wrap. Trim any excess wrap.

Analysis

1. **Describe** the appearance of the bee wing that you observed under the microscope.

2. **Analyze** whether your class viewed wings that were obtained from a single bee or several species of bees.

3. CRITICAL THINKING **Developing Hypotheses** By using your model, propose how a bee's wings might help the bee gain sufficient lift for flight.

Adaptations for Flight

Insects were the first animals to have wings. For more than 100 million years, until flying reptiles appeared, insects were the only flying organisms. Flight, illustrated in **Figure 10**, was a great evolutionary innovation. Flying insects were able to reach previously inaccessible food sources and to escape quickly from danger.

❯ **Insects are adapted for flight by having a lightweight body, wings, and strong muscles to power flight.** An insect's wings develop from saclike outgrowths of the body wall of the thorax. Most insects have two pairs of wings. The wings of adult insects are composed of chitin, strengthened by a network of veins. The veins carry air and a bloodlike substance. In most insects, the power stroke of the wing during flight is downward and is produced by strong flight muscles. The muscles are actually inside the insect's exoskeleton, and they move a wing by manipulating the exoskeleton near the wing's attachment point.

Flying Insects The "-ptera" ending of the insect order name means "wing." The beetles (order Coleoptera) have a shield-like first pair of wings that protect the flying wings when they are at rest. Flies and mosquitoes (order Diptera) fly using their first pair of wings. The second pair of wings is modified to help control stability during flight. Butterflies and moths (order Lepidoptera) also have two pairs of wings. The pairs are linked together and used in flight, and are covered with tiny scales. The ants, bees and wasps (order Hymenoptera), also fly using both pairs of wings. The two pairs of wings beat together, and both pairs fold over the abdomen at rest.

❯ **Reading Check** *What are some advantages of flight?*

mandible (MAN duh buhl) a type of mouthpart found in some arthropods that is used for eating

Figure 10 This stop-action series shows how an insect's wings move during flight.

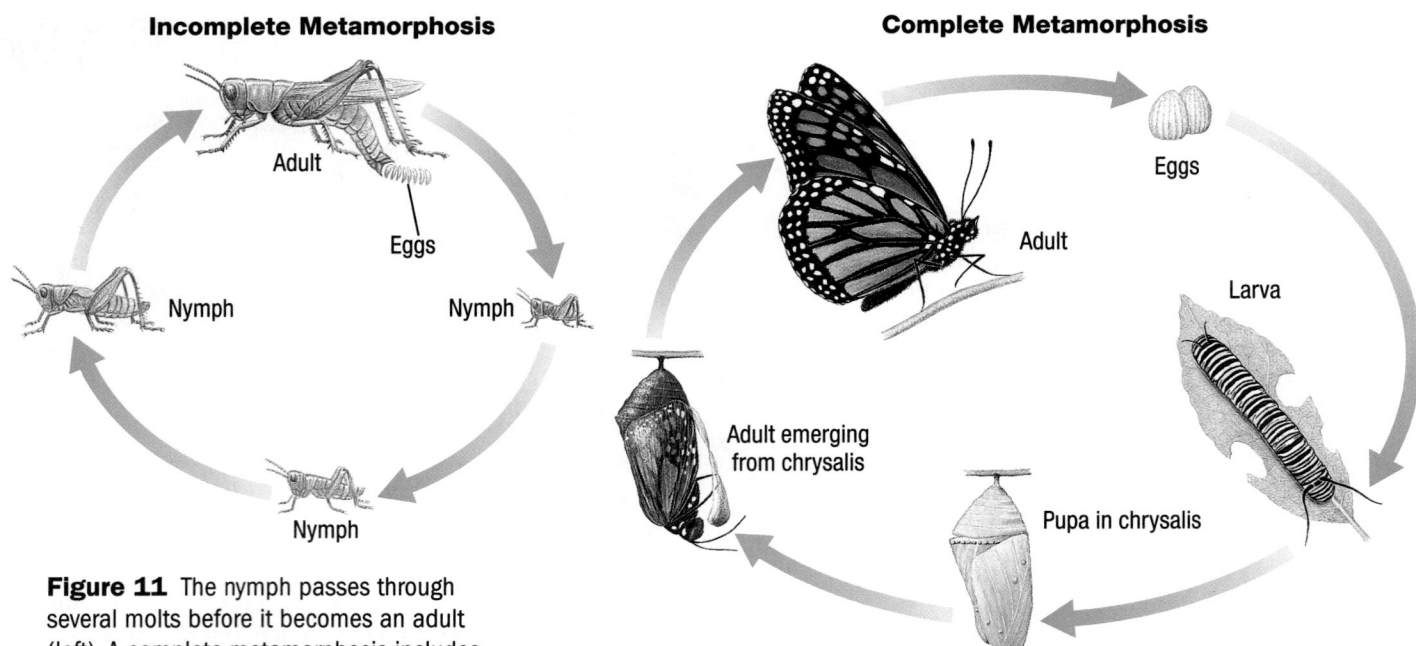

Incomplete Metamorphosis

Adult

Eggs

Nymph

Nymph

Nymph

Complete Metamorphosis

Eggs

Adult

Larva

Adult emerging from chrysalis

Pupa in chrysalis

Figure 11 The nymph passes through several molts before it becomes an adult (left). A complete metamorphosis includes a pupa stage, which takes place inside of a chrysalis (right).

go.hrw.com

* interact online

Keyword: HX8ARTF11

metamorphosis (MET uh MAWR fuh sis) a phase in the life cycle of many animals during which a rapid change from the immature organism to the adult takes place

chrysalis (KRIS uh lis) the hard-shelled pupa of certain insects, such as butterflies

pupa (PYOO puh) the immobile, nonfeeding stage between the larva and the adult of insects that undergo complete metamorphosis

caste (KAST) a group of insects in a colony that have a specific function

Insect Life Cycle

Insects vary widely in the extent of change that they undergo as they develop from larva to adult. **> Insects have a unique life cycle compared with other arthropods. During development, a young insect undergoes metamorphosis. Metamorphosis** is a dramatic physical change, which can be complete or incomplete.

Complete Metamorphosis Almost all insect species undergo complete metamorphosis, as **Figure 11** shows. In complete metamorphosis, the wingless larva grows in size and passes through a number of molts that are characteristic for its species. For example, fruit fly larvae molt twice. The larva then encloses itself within a protective capsule, which is called a **chrysalis** in some species. Inside the chrysalis, the larva passes through a **pupa** stage. The pupa is resistant to cold temperatures and dry conditions and does not feed. In the pupal stage, the larva changes into an adult. The larval tissues break down, and the adult form grows from cells that were present but inactive in the larva. Finally, the adult emerges from the chrysalis and flies away to reproduce. The four stages in a complete metamorphosis life cycle are the egg, the larva, the pupa, and the adult.

Incomplete Metamorphosis A smaller number of insect species develop into adults in a much less dramatic incomplete metamorphosis, as **Figure 11** shows. During incomplete metamorphosis, the egg hatches into a juvenile, or *nymph,* that looks like a small, wingless adult. The wings may be acquired in a later immature stage. After several molts, the nymph develops into a sexually mature adult.

> Reading Check *What is metamorphosis?*

Social Insects

Social insects live in highly organized groups of genetically related individuals. **❯ Social insects have elaborate social systems involving specialization of labor, parental care, and communication between individuals.** The role that an individual plays in a colony is called a **caste.** Caste is determined by a combination of heredity; diet, especially as a larva; hormones; and *pheromones,* hormonelike chemicals that are used for communication.

Honeybees A honeybee hive contains a queen, workers, and drone males. The honeybee queen usually is the only reproductive female in the hive. The workers care for the eggs, the larvae, the queen, and the drones. Workers also forage for food and maintain and defend the hive.

Termites Termite colonies are similar to colonies of honeybees and ants. However, termites have kings as well as queens, and the kings have functions in addition to reproduction. Only the king and queen reproduce. Workers gather the food, raise the young, and excavate tunnels. Larger soldiers use their immense jaws to defend the colony.

Centipedes and Millipedes

The subphylum Myriapoda means "many footed." **❯ Myriapods include centipedes and millipedes.** Myriapods are not considered insects, though they share certain characteristics. Centipedes, such as the one in **Figure 12,** and millipedes have similar bodies. Each myriapod has a head region that is followed by many similar segments. Each segment bears one or two pairs of legs. Centipedes have one pair of legs per segment and can have up to 173 segments. Millipedes have from 11 to 100 or more body segments, and most of these segments have two pairs of legs.

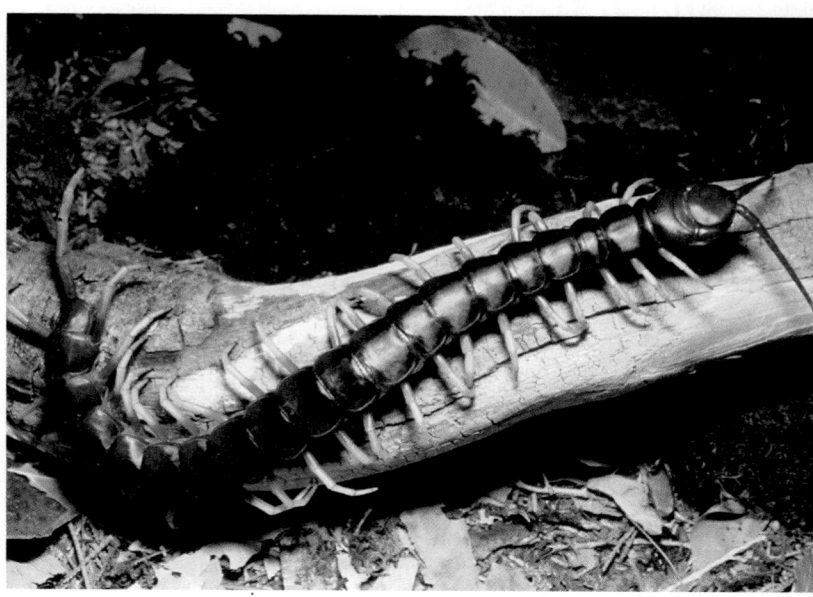

Figure 12 Centipedes and millipedes are relatives of insects and share many of the characteristics of insects.

SciLINKS.
www.scilinks.org
Topic: Honeybees
Code: HX80755

Section 3 Review

❯ KEY IDEAS

1. **Describe** the most common characteristics of insects.
2. **List** the adaptations that allow insects to fly.
3. **Define** the unique life cycle of an insect, and explain why this life cycle is unique among arthropods.
4. **Describe** the qualities of social insects.
5. **Classify** which arthropods are myriapods.

CRITICAL THINKING

6. **Inferring Conclusions** An unknown arthropod has three body regions, one pair of antennae, and three pairs of jointed legs. What kind of arthropod is it? Explain your answer.
7. **Making Inferences** A certain chemical does not kill crop-eating insect larvae but rather keeps them from pupating. Could this chemical be an effective insecticide? Explain your answer.

CONNECTING KEY IDEAS

8. **Report** Conduct research in the library or on the Internet about the historical and current importance of the study of the fruit fly *Drosophila melanogaster* to our understanding of genetics. Explain any unusual characteristics of this insect that made it particularly valuable for these genetic studies. Prepare a one-page report on your findings.

Come and Get It!

You communicate by using words, actions, and facial expressions. Animals such as dogs and whales communicate by using sounds or gestures. However, honeybees use a sophisticated dance called the *waggle dance* to direct other bees to a faraway food source (nectar). These directions are accurate and are easily understood by other bees.

WEIRD SCIENCE

Interpreting the Dance

Before performing the waggle dance, the honeybee "hands out" samples of the food she found. The waggle dance is composed of two loops and a straight run. The direction in which she begins the straight run is the direction of the nectar source from the hive. The frequency of the looping and the amount of buzzing the bee makes during the dance indicates how far away the nectar source is. The longer the bee buzzes, the farther away the food is. A honeybee can tell her hivemates about the location of food up to roughly 600 meters away!

The Dance When the bee performs this dance in the hive, her fellow bees often follow her rather than watch her from a distance. Bees can sense each other by using chemical signals.

Research Land mines often remain buried in a war zone long after the war is over. Bees are being used to help locate buried mines before the mines explode and cause injuries. Conduct research to find out how bees are helping find leftover land mines.

Echinoderms

Key Ideas	Key Terms	Why It Matters
❯ What characteristics do echinoderms share? ❯ What are the different classes of echinoderms?	ossicles water-vascular system tube foot skin gill	The five-arm body plan of adult echinoderms is a common sight in oceans, along shorelines, and in tidal pools.

Echinoderms are one of the most numerous of all marine phyla. Today, about 7,000 species of echinoderms are organized into 5 classes, but the fossil record reveals at least 15 additional classes of about 13,000 species that are now extinct.

Echinoderm Characteristics

While the arthropods are characterized by their jointed appendages, echinoderms are recognized by the spines that project from their internal skeleton through their outer covering. *Echinoderm*, in fact, means "spiny skinned." Also unlike arthopods, echinoderms are deuterostomes. The classes of echinoderms vary considerably in the details of their body plan. Despite apparent differences, however, all echinoderms share four basic characteristics. ❯ **All adult echinoderms have an internal skeleton, five-part radial symmetry, a water-vascular system, and the ability to breathe through their skin.**

Endoskeleton Echinoderms have a calcium-rich endoskeleton that is composed of individual plates called **ossicles.** Proteins mixed with minerals make the skeleton flexible. Even though the ossicles of adult echinoderms appear to be external, they are covered by a thin layer of skin. In adult sea stars, such as the one in **Figure 13,** a large number of these plates are fused together. The fused plates function much like an arthropod's exoskeleton does. They provide sites for muscle attachment and shell-like protection of the internal organs.

In most echinoderms, the plates of the endoskeleton bear spines that project outward through the skin.

ossicle (AHS i kuhl) one of the small, calcium carbonate plates that make up the endoskeleton of an echinoderm

❯ **Reading Check** *Why is an endoskeleton beneficial?*

Figure 13 A sea star's endoskeleton allows it to be more flexible than an arthropod can be.

The flexible sea star is preparing to eat the sea urchin.

Five-Part Radial Symmetry As larvae, all echinoderms have bilateral symmetry. As the larvae grow into adults, they develop five-part symmetry. All adult echinoderms, such as the sea star shown in **Figure 14,** have a five-part body plan with arms that radiate from a central point. However, the number of arms can vary.

Echinoderms have no head or brain. The nervous system consists of a central ring of nerves called the *nerve ring*, with branches extending into each of the arms. Most sensory perception in echinoderms occurs in the skin. Although echinoderms are capable of complex response patterns, each arm acts more or less independently.

Water-Vascular System Echinoderms have a water-filled system of interconnected canals with thousands of tiny, hollow tube feet that make up a **water-vascular system.** Water enters the system through a sievelike structure called a *madreporite*. The canals branch from a central ring canal that encircles the gut. The **tube feet** are tiny legs that can be used to move, grip surfaces, or manipulate objects. A structure called an *ampulla* contracts and forces water into the foot, extending it. Gas exchange and waste excretion also takes place through the thin walls of the tube feet.

Circulation and Respiration The body cavity, or coelom, functions as a simple circulatory and respiratory system. Particles and respiratory gases move freely throughout the large, fluid-filled coelom. Many echinoderms have skin gills that aid respiration and waste removal. **Skin gills** are small, fingerlike projections that grow among the echinoderm's spines. These projections create a larger surface area through which respiratory gases can be exchanged.

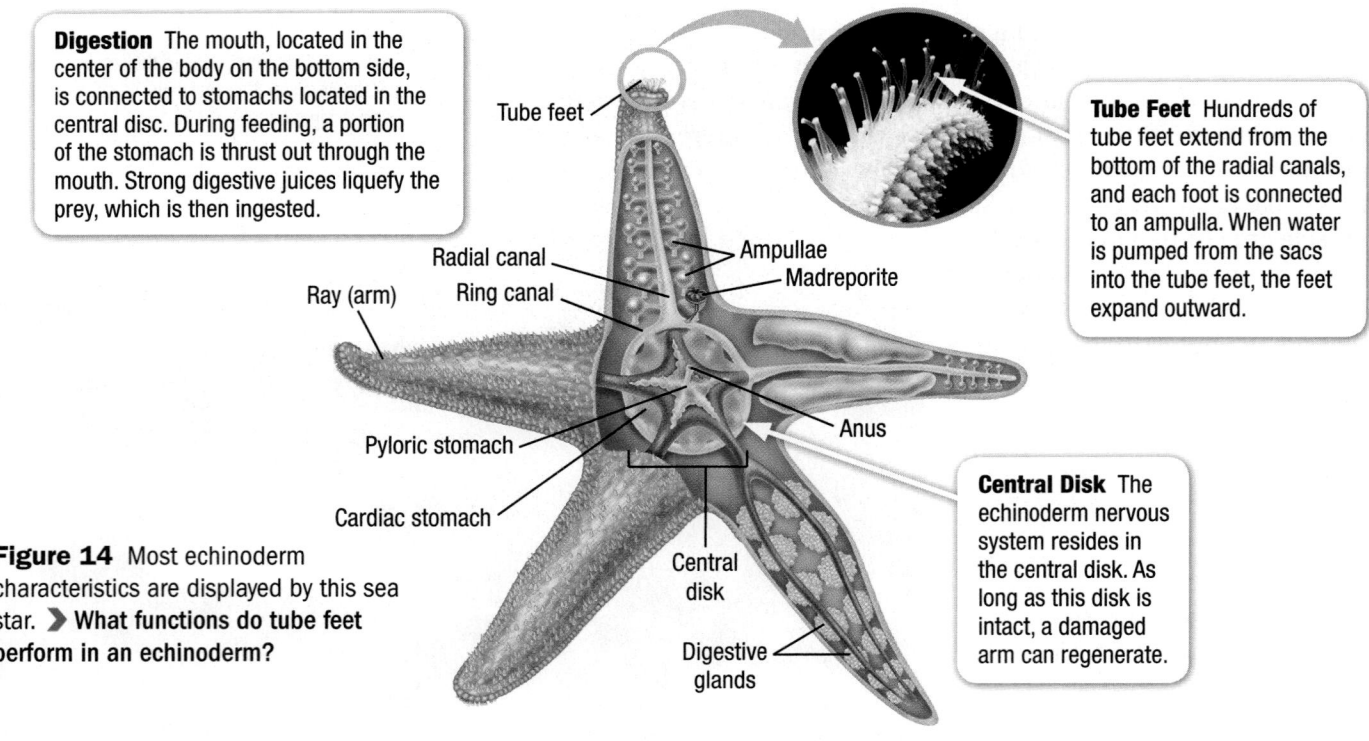

Digestion The mouth, located in the center of the body on the bottom side, is connected to stomachs located in the central disc. During feeding, a portion of the stomach is thrust out through the mouth. Strong digestive juices liquefy the prey, which is then ingested.

Tube feet

Radial canal

Ring canal

Ray (arm)

Ampullae

Madreporite

Tube Feet Hundreds of tube feet extend from the bottom of the radial canals, and each foot is connected to an ampulla. When water is pumped from the sacs into the tube feet, the feet expand outward.

Pyloric stomach

Cardiac stomach

Anus

Central disk

Central Disk The echinoderm nervous system resides in the central disk. As long as this disk is intact, a damaged arm can regenerate.

Digestive glands

Figure 14 Most echinoderm characteristics are displayed by this sea star. ▶ What functions do tube feet perform in an echinoderm?

Figure 15 Echinoderms make up a very diverse phylum. Brittle stars, sea cucumbers, and sea urchins are all echinoderms.

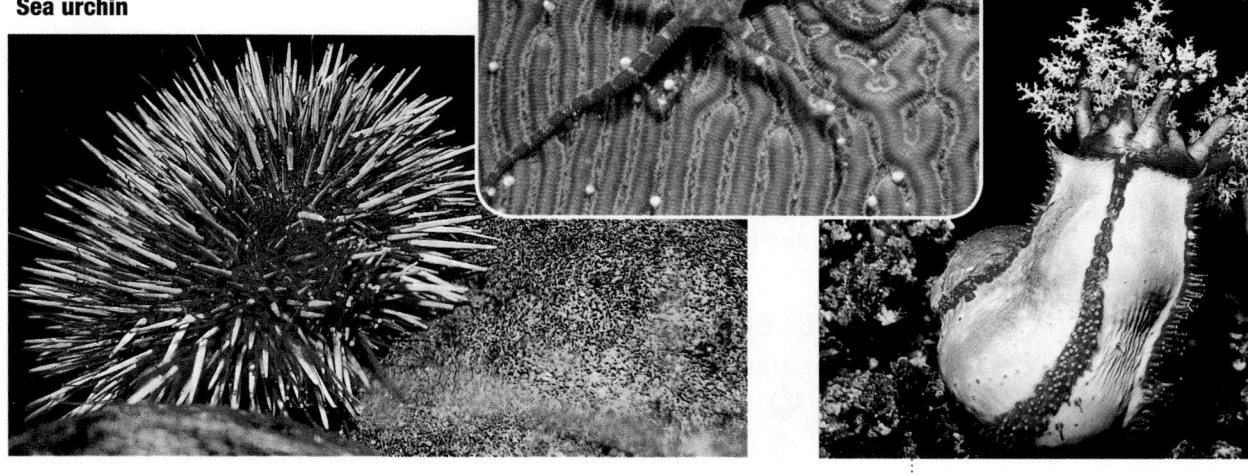

Brittle star

Sea cucumber

Sea urchin

Echinoderm Diversity

Figure 15 shows representatives of some echinoderm groups. ❯ **The living classes of echinoderms include sea stars, brittle stars and basket stars, sea lilies and feather stars, sea urchins and sand dollars, and sea cucumbers.** Sea stars, commonly called *starfish*, are perhaps the most familiar echinoderms. Brittle stars and basket stars are similar to sea stars, but the arms of brittle stars and basket stars are narrower and may be branched. Sea lilies and feather stars do not move around as most other echinoderms do. Their larvae, however, have the ability to swim, which allows them to disperse. Sea urchins and sand dollars lack arms. However, sea urchins have spines that provide protection from predators. Because of a sluglike shape and a lack of arms or spines, sea cucumbers look different from other echinoderms.

❯ **Reading Check** *Which echinoderms disperse as larvae?*

READING TOOLBOX

Outlining Use your outline of this section in order to write three sentences that relate the two key ideas to each other.

Section 4 Review

❯ **KEY IDEAS**

1. **Summarize** the four major characteristics of echinoderms.
2. **Summarize** the five major classes of echinoderms.
3. **Describe** which echinoderm structure carries out functions of a circulatory system.

CRITICAL THINKING

4. **Evaluating Conclusions** Sea cucumbers and sea lilies are relatively sessile as adults. Their larvae, however, are capable of swimming. Explain how swimming larvae provide an advantage for these echinoderms.
5. **Relating Concepts** Describe how sea stars use their water-vascular system to move along the sea floor.

METHODS OF SCIENCE

6. **Analyzing Data** A scientist collects several specimens of an unidentified animal. The scientist observes that they have tube feet, an endoskeleton, and a protostome pattern of embryonic development. Why is the classification of these organisms difficult?

Chapter 29 **Lab**

Objectives

▶ Create and maintain a habitat for caterpillars and butterflies.

▶ Observe the stages of metamorphosis in a butterfly.

▶ Observe the feeding behaviors of caterpillars and butterflies.

▶ Develop hypotheses about insect food preferences.

Materials

- disposable gloves
- caterpillars, painted lady (5)
- butterflies, adult painted lady
- plate, small
- hand lens
- dandelion greens
- lettuce
- shoe box
- packing box, large
- milk carton, small
- sugar, white
- scissors
- paper toweling
- mosquito netting
- tape

Safety

Butterfly Metamorphosis

Butterflies, like many arthropods and echinoderms, undergo a major change in body form as they develop into adults. This change is called *metamorphosis*. During their metamorphosis, butterflies are transformed from a caterpillar stage to a winged adult. In addition to changing physically, they change behaviorally. In this lab, you will explore the stages and process of metamorphosis in the common painted lady butterfly (*Vanessa cardui*).

Procedure

Observe Food Preferences in Caterpillars

1 Work in a small group. Put on disposable gloves.

2 CAUTION: **Exercise caution when using live animals.** Gently transfer a caterpillar that is at least 2 cm long to a small plate. Use a hand lens to observe this animal. Draw what you see.

3 Place several fresh dandelion greens on one side of a shoe box. Place a fresh lettuce leaf on the other side of the box.

4 Place four caterpillars in the box. Cover the box with mosquito netting, and tape into place. Place the box in a well-lit area, but not in direct sunlight. Maintain setup at room temperature.

5 Each day, record which food the caterpillars preferred in a table similar to the one shown. Then, replace the wilted food with fresh greens and leaves.

6 After about a week, you may observe that the caterpillars have secured themselves on the overhead netting and entered a new life stage. If so, let this hanging stage (called a *pupa*) remain undisturbed for 7 to 10 days. Go on to the next part of this activity.

Food Preference		
Insect	Type of food	Number of individuals
Caterpillar	Dandelion leaf	
	Lettuce	
Butterfly	Sugar solution	
	Experimental solution	

Maintain Adult Butterflies

7 Carefully poke a hole about the diameter of a pencil into the top of a small and clean milk carton.

8 Open the carton spout, and fill halfway with tap water. Add a packet of sugar. Close the spout, and swirl to mix the solution.

9 Twist a piece of paper towel into a tight roll. Insert this rolled towel through the carton hole so that it acts as a wick.

10 Undo the interwoven flaps forming the top and bottom of a large packing box. Use scissors to remove these eight cardboard flaps. Only a cardboard frame should remain.

11 Cut out two large rectangles of mosquito netting that can fit over each of the two openings. Stretch a piece of mosquito netting over one open side. Secure the fabric with tape.

12 Stand the box up on one of its sides. Set the milk carton feeder inside the frame on its base. Use the cardboard flaps to build structures on which the butterflies can perch inside the frame.

13 Begin securing the netting over the open side of the frame. Before completely sealing the chamber, introduce the adult butterflies.

14 Each day for five days, observe and record the butterfly feeding behavior. The butterflies should be exposed to sunlight for several hours each day.

Observe Food Preferences in Butterflies

15 Assemble an additional feeder station. Change the identity of the liquid (use various sugar concentrations or sugar substitutes) or appearance of this second station (add petal-like structures).

16 Offer both stations to the butterflies, and record the feeder around which the butterflies spend most of their time.

17 Clean up your lab materials according to your teacher's instructions. Wash your hands before leaving the lab.

Analyze and Conclude

1. Evaluating Results Did the caterpillars demonstrate a food preference? If so, what did you observe?

2. Recognizing Patterns Compare feeding in caterpillars and adult butterflies. Record similarities and differences.

3. SCIENTIFIC METHODS Identifying Variables What was the experimental variable that you used to explore food preferences in butterflies? What did you learn?

4. SCIENTIFIC METHODS Identifying Relationships Among Variables Why might the diet of the adult butterfly contain a concentrated energy source while the food preferred by the caterpillar be less energy intensive?

Extensions

5. Forming Reasoned Opinions How might the petal of a flower offer an advantage to a feeding butterfly?

6. Further Inquiry Many arthropods and echinoderms have preferences for certain foods. Conduct research in the library or on the Internet, and make a table that describes food preferences in at least five types of arthropods or echinoderms. Try to formulate a hypothesis that addresses why each animal has a particular food preference.

Chapter 29 Summary

go.hrw.com
SUPER SUMMARY
Keyword: HX8ARTS

Key Ideas	Key Terms
1 Arthropods	thorax (701)
❯ Arthropods are characterized by jointed appendages, a segmented body, and a hard external skeleton.	cephalothorax (701)
	appendage (702)
❯ In a process called molting, all arthropods periodically shed their hard exoskeleton and grow a new one.	trachea (703)
	spiracle (703)
	Malpighian tubule (703)
❯ The four main arthropod groups (subphyla) are Hexapoda, Myriapoda, Crustacea, and Chelicerata.	compound eye (703)
	molting (704)

2 Arachnids and Crustaceans	chelicera (706)
❯ The chelicerates are arthropods that have appendages called chelicerae, which are specialized for feeding.	pedipalp (706)
	spinneret (707)
❯ Like chelicerates, crustaceans have appendages on their abdomen. Unlike chelicerates, crustaceans have mandibles that are adapted for feeding and have two pairs of antennae. Crustaceans also breathe by using gills.	

3 Insects	mandible (712)
❯ Most insects share the same general body plan, specialized mouthparts for feeding, a unique life cycle, and the ability to fly.	metamorphosis (714)
	chrysalis (714)
❯ Insects are adapted for flight by having a lightweight body, wings, and strong muscles to power flight.	pupa (714)
	caste (715)
❯ Insects have a unique life cycle compared with other arthropods. During development, a young insect undergoes metamorphosis.	
❯ Social insects have elaborate social systems involving specialization of labor, parental care, and communication between individuals.	
❯ Myriapods include centipedes and millipedes.	

4 Echinoderms	ossicles (717)
❯ All adult echinoderms have an internal skeleton, five-part radial symmetry, a water-vascular system, and the ability to breathe through their skin.	water-vascular system (718)
	tube foot (718)
	skin gill (718)
❯ The living classes of echinoderms include sea stars, brittle stars and basket stars, sea lilies and feather stars, sea urchins and sand dollars, and sea cucumbers.	

READING TOOLBOX

1. **Key-Term Fold** Define each key term in your own words on the opposite side of your key-term fold.

2. **Concept Map** Construct a concept map that outlines the four major groups of arthropods and that gives the characteristics for each group. Try to include the following terms in your concept map: *appendages, cephalothorax, trachea, spiracles, chelicerae, complete metamorphosis, chrysalis,* and *pupa.*

Using Key Terms

For each pair of terms, explain how the meanings of the terms differ.

3. *thorax* and *cephalothorax*

4. *trachea* and *spiracle*

5. *chelicera* and *pedipalp*

Use each of the following terms in a sentence.

6. *caste*

7. *metamorphosis*

8. *water-vascular system*

Understanding Key Ideas

9. Which of the following has been important in the evolutionary success of arthropods?
   a. Most live in marine habitats.
   b. They have either fangs or pincers.
   c. They use a wide range of foods and habitats.
   d. Their endoskeleton enables them to live on land.

10. The adaptation seen in many terrestrial arthropods that delivers oxygen to body tissues is the
    a. blood.
    b. trachea.
    c. exoskeleton.
    d. Malpighian tubule.

11. Which is a feature of the arthropod body plan?
    a. radial symmetry
    b. an exoskeleton
    c. a nonsegmented body
    d. a hydrostatic support system

12. Molting
    a. reduces water loss.
    b. is the shedding of an exoskeleton.
    c. is the production of a new exoskeleton.
    d. occurs in insects but not in other arthropods.

13. In spiders, chelicerae are modified into
    a. legs.   c. spinnerets.
    b. fangs.   d. antennae.

14. All of the following are crustaceans *except* a
    a. lobster.   c. copepod.
    b. scorpion.   d. water flea.

15. A grasshopper's antennae contain sense organs for
    a. touch and smell.   c. hearing and vision.
    b. smell and hearing. d. vision and touch.

16. In adult insects,
    a. the abdomen has wings.
    b. there are two pairs of antennae.
    c. the legs are attached to the thorax.
    d. the first appendages are chelicerae.

Use the diagram to answer the following question.

17. During which of the stages in the life cycle of an insect do the most dramatic changes in body form occur?

a.   b.   c.   d.

Explaining Key Ideas

18. **Describe** a characteristic of arthropods that is not found in any other group of invertebrates.

19. **Name** the subphylum within the phylum Arthropoda that includes animals with fangs.

20. **Summarize** how fertilization occurs in most arthropods.

21. **Compare** the body plans of spiders, scorpions, and mites, and describe differences in appendages.

22. **Name** the only terrestrial group of crustaceans.

Using Science Graphics

Use the graph to answer the following questions.

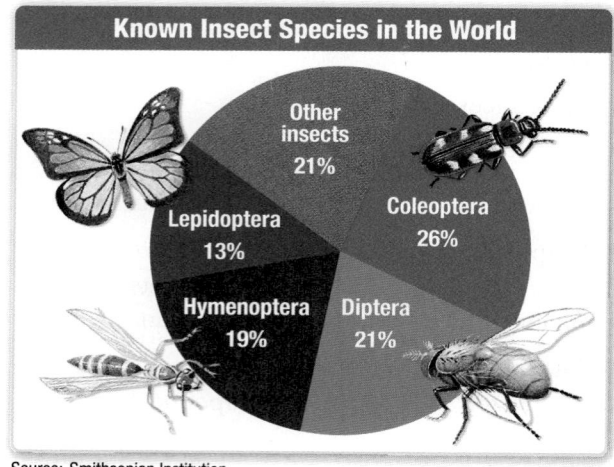

Known Insect Species in the World

Other insects 21%

Coleoptera 26%

Lepidoptera 13%

Diptera 21%

Hymenoptera 19%

Source: Smithsonian Institution.

23. Of the four groups of insects included in the diagram, which group has the largest percentage of known species?
- **a.** Lepidoptera
- **b.** Hymenoptera
- **c.** Diptera
- **d.** Coleoptera

24. If the total number of known insect species is 91,000, how many species does the group Diptera have?
- **a.** 23,700 species
- **b.** 19,110 species
- **c.** 17,500 species
- **d.** 11,500 species

Critical Thinking

25. Constructing Explanations In arthropods, what adaptive advantage might compound eyes offer over simple eyes?

26. Recognizing Relationships The wings of the atlas moth, *Attacus atlas*, look much like the head of a snake. How might a flying insect benefit by looking like a snake?

27. Making Inferences Provide a possible explanation for the observation that many arthropods go into hiding while they undergo a molt. How long do you think they would have to remain hidden? Explain your answer.

28. Evaluating Conclusions Is an animal that has grasping pincers, a segmented body, and two antennae correctly identified as a scorpion? Explain your answer.

29. Relating Concepts Compare the Eastern lubber grasshopper's body plan with the body plan of a typical insect.

30. Making Predictions Pill bugs respire by using gills. How might this type of respiration affect the distribution of pill bugs in an ecosystem?

31. Distinguishing Relevant Information List two ways in which barnacles are different from nearly all other crustaceans.

32. Recognizing Logical Inconsistencies A neighbor commented that there was an increased number of insects around her house and that she was killing every spider she saw. How might these actions affect the number of insects around the house?

Alternative Assessment

33. Insect Life-Cycle Diagram Conduct research on and prepare a diagram of the life cycle of an insect. Include information on the type of food eaten by the immature form of the insect, as well as the food eaten, if any, by the adult form. Annotate your diagram with this diet information. Include other information of interest, such as range and distribution, agricultural importance, and natural history.

34. Echinoderm Report Use the media center or Internet resources to learn more about the crown-of-thorns sea star, or *Acanthaster planci*. This animal is abundant on the Great Barrier Reef. Find out why this echinoderm poses such a threat to its environment, and prepare a report on your findings. Include steps being taken by the Australian government to reduce the threat.

Writing for Science

35. Insect Societies Report Conduct research in the library or on the Internet about a group of social insects. Collect information on the types of individuals and castes that are present in a colony, the genetic relatedness of the colony members, the length of time that a colony usually survives, the local conditions that are favored by the species, the natural and human-related enemies or dangers for the colony, the type of food that is collected and/or farmed, and any other information of interest. Write a brief report that details your findings. Include photographs or drawings if possible.

> **TEST TIP** Choose your answer to a question based on what you already know and what information is presented in the question.

Science Concepts

1. What is a caste in an insect society?
- **A** parental care of young
- **B** a specialized morphological form
- **C** an insect that defends the nest of a colony
- **D** an insect that develops from an unfertilized egg

2. The chief organ of excretion in insects is the
- **F** Malpighian tubule.
- **G** pedipalp.
- **H** trachea.
- **J** spiracle.

3. Arthropods molt because
- **A** their exoskeleton is damaged.
- **B** their exoskeleton cracks and lets in water.
- **C** their hard exoskeleton cannot grow larger.
- **D** their body grows faster than their exoskeleton.

4. Spinnerets are located on which part of a spider's body?
- **F** thorax
- **G** cephalothorax
- **H** abdomen
- **J** pedipalps

5. Although not all crustaceans are aquatic, which of the following structures is an adaptation that crustaceans developed in response to life in aquatic biomes?
- **A** gills
- **B** mandibles
- **C** antennae
- **D** walking legs

6. Which echinoderm does not show obvious five-part radial symmetry outside of its body?
- **F** sea star
- **G** sea urchin
- **H** sea lily
- **J** sea cucumber

Writing Skills

7. Ode to Tide-Pool Life Conduct research, and write an ode to invertebrates commonly found in tide pools (most prominent on the Pacific coast).

Using Science Graphics

Use the diagram to answer the following questions.

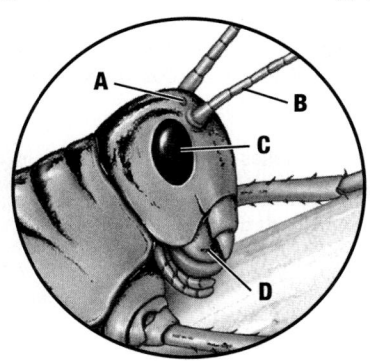

8. What type of environmental stimulus is structure A sensitive to?
- **A** touch
- **B** sound
- **C** light
- **D** odor

9. Structure D is specialized for
- **F** detecting light.
- **G** inhaling and exhaling air.
- **H** biting and chewing leaves.
- **J** catching and handling prey.

Use the diagram to answer the following questions.

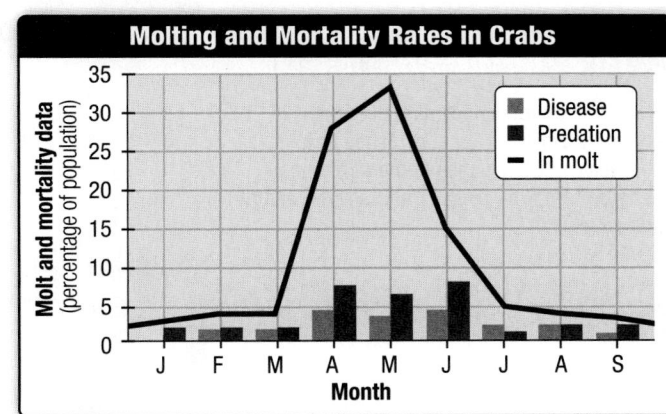

10. Crabs have a higher mortality rate in April, May, and June, which means that they have
- **A** died.
- **B** reproduced.
- **C** grown larger.
- **D** recently eaten.

11. Which of the following is the independent variable in this experiment?
- **F** month
- **G** disease
- **H** predation
- **J** molting rate

Chapter 30

Fishes and Amphibians

Black bass are bony fishes that live in streams and lakes around the world. Their diet includes minnows, insects, mice, ducklings, crayfish, and, as you can see here, frogs.

Most frogs, including this Iberian frog (*Rana iberica*), are able to jump about 20 times their own length. But that long leap doesn't always save them from predators.

Preview

1 The Fish Body
Characteristics of Fishes
Movement and Response
Respiration and Circulation
Excretion
Reproduction

2 Groups of Fishes
Jawless Fishes
Cartilaginous Fishes
Bony Fishes

3 The Amphibian Body
Characteristics of Amphibians
Movement and Response
Respiration
Circulation

4 Groups of Amphibians
Salamanders
Caecilians
Frogs and Toads

Why It Matters

All land vertebrates, including humans, ultimately evolved from early fishes and amphibians. Today, fishes and amphibians are important food sources and environmental indicators.

InquiryLab

Water Breathing

Although you can't see it, the watery environment of fishes and amphibians contains dissolved gases. Without these gases, fishes and young amphibians would suffocate. In this activity, you will look for evidence of dissolved gas in soda water.

Procedure

❶ Put on **safety goggles**. Observe a closed **bottle of soda water**. What do you see? Be careful not to shake the bottle.

❷ Slowly open the bottle of soda water. Pay attention to the sounds that you hear and the air movements that you feel. Record your observations.

❸ Place a **balloon** over the neck of the opened bottle. Secure the balloon with a **rubber band** to form an airtight seal. Gently shake the bottle. Then record your observations.

Analysis

1. **Describe** what you observed in step 1.

2. **Describe** what happened when you first opened the bottle.

3. **Describe** what you observed in step 3. Explain your observations.

4. **State** whether there was gas in the soda water. If so, why couldn't you see it in the capped bottle?

Black bass use their sense of touch to tell whether to swallow or spit out a potential snack. Bass also have five other senses—sight, hearing, smell, taste, and the ability to sense movements of the water.

READING TOOLBOX

These reading tools can help you learn the material in this chapter. For more information on how to use these and other tools, see **Appendix: Reading and Study Skills.**

Using Words

Word Parts A prefix is a word part that is attached to the beginning of a word. A prefix changes the meaning of the word. You probably already know that nonflammable means that something does not burn. The prefix "non-" means "not." The table shows some other prefixes you will encounter in this chapter.

Word Parts	
Prefix	**Meaning**
amphi-	both
counter-	against
re-	again
endo-	inside
ex-	out

Your Turn Use the table to answer the following questions.

1. Explain the difference between an endoskeleton and an exoskeleton.

2. Using what you know about frogs and other amphibians, explain why the prefix *amphi-* is appropriate for describing amphibians.

Using Language

Comparisons Comparing is a way of looking for the similarities between different things. Contrasting is a way of looking for the differences. Comparison words include *like, similar to,* and *also.* Contrast words include *unlike, however,* and *although.*

Your Turn In the following sentences, identify the things that are being compared or contrasted.

1. Like oranges, bananas have a thick peel. However, the seeds of bananas can be eaten easily.

2. Like fishes, frogs lay eggs in water. Unlike fishes, frogs do not have scales.

Using Graphic Organizers

Concept Map Concept maps are useful when you are trying to figure out how several ideas are related to a main idea or concept.

Your Turn Make a concept map to help you understand the relationships between key terms in this chapter.

1. Copy this concept map in your notebook

2. Use terms from the chapter to complete the concept map as you read.

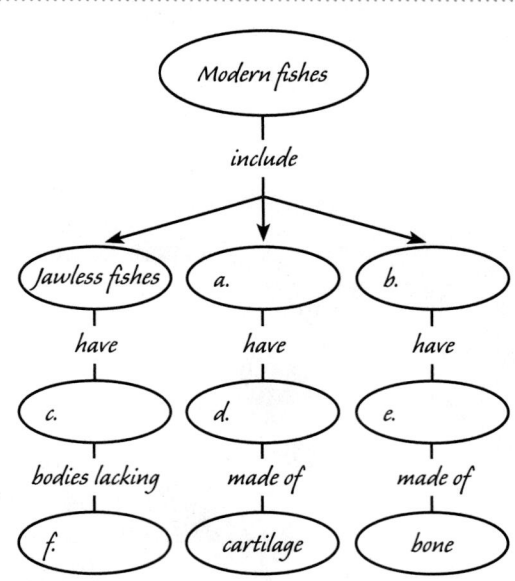

1 The Fish Body

Key Ideas	Key Terms	Why It Matters
❯ What are the main characteristics of fishes? ❯ What structures do fish use to swim and sense their environment? ❯ How do fish obtain oxygen from the environment? ❯ How do fish maintain their salt and water balance? ❯ How do fish reproduce?	swim bladder lateral line gill gill slit kidney	Fishes are the most abundant vertebrates and are an important source of food for humans. They also are key species in many marine and freshwater habitats.

Fishes are the most ancient vertebrates. There are about 25,000 species of fishes. Fish species can be found in almost every watery habitat, from the deep oceans to mountain streams and desert pools. Fishes have an amazing array of adaptations to these aquatic habitats. The smallest fishes could fit on your fingernail, yet some of the largest predators on Earth are also fishes.

Characteristics of Fishes

What makes a goldfish, such as the one shown in **Figure 1,** instantly recognizable as a fish? You may name its fins, gills, and scales as traits that contribute to the goldfish's "fishiness." But some fishes don't look quite so fishy. The diversity of fishes found today reflects various adaptations that enable fishes to live in the oceans and freshwater habitats around the world. Despite the variation seen among fishes, all share certain key characteristics. ❯ **Fishes have endoskeletons, gills, closed-loop circulation, and kidneys.**

❯ **Reading Check** *Why are fishes so diverse? (See the Appendix for answers to Reading Checks.)*

Caudal fin

Dorsal fin

Gill slit

Scales

Paired fins

Figure 1 This goldfish has scales and paired fins, but not all fishes share these features. ❯ **What characteristics does the goldfish have that are universal to all fishes?**

Movement and Response

> Fishes have many important structures for swimming and sensing their underwater environment, including endoskeletons, fins, swim bladders, and lateral lines. In addition, fishes' streamlined shape and a muscular tail allow them to move rapidly through the water.

Endoskeleton All fishes have an endoskeleton, or internal skeleton. In a few fishes, the endoskeleton is composed only of small pieces of cartilage along the dorsal nerve cord. But most fishes have a complete endoskeleton made of either cartilage or bone. Muscles that attach to the endoskeleton make strong movements possible.

Fins and Swim Bladder The fins on the backs and bellies of fishes increase stability. Some fishes use paired fins to help them turn, dive, or climb rapidly. Other fishes use paired fins to move forward, backward, sideways, and up and down. Many fishes regulate their vertical position in the water by controlling the amount of gas in their **swim bladder.** Sharks and stingrays don't have a swim bladder. Their buoyancy is increased by fat stored in their livers.

Sensory Organs Fishes have a variety of organs, such as those shown in **Figure 2,** that allow them to sense their environment. A fish's eyes sense light. One or two nostrils lead to olfactory sacs, which sense odors. To taste, fishes use taste buds in their mouths, as well as on their lips, fins, and skin. Fishes are able to hear sounds with their inner ears. Fishes also have a unique sense organ called a lateral line. The **lateral line** is a system of small canals in the skin. The canals are lined with cells sensitive to water vibrations caused by currents or pressure waves. Fishes use this sensory information to direct their movements as they swim.

> **Reading Check** *What is the function of the lateral line?*

Figure 2 Fishes have sensory organs that allow them to sense light, smells, tastes, sounds, and water vibrations.

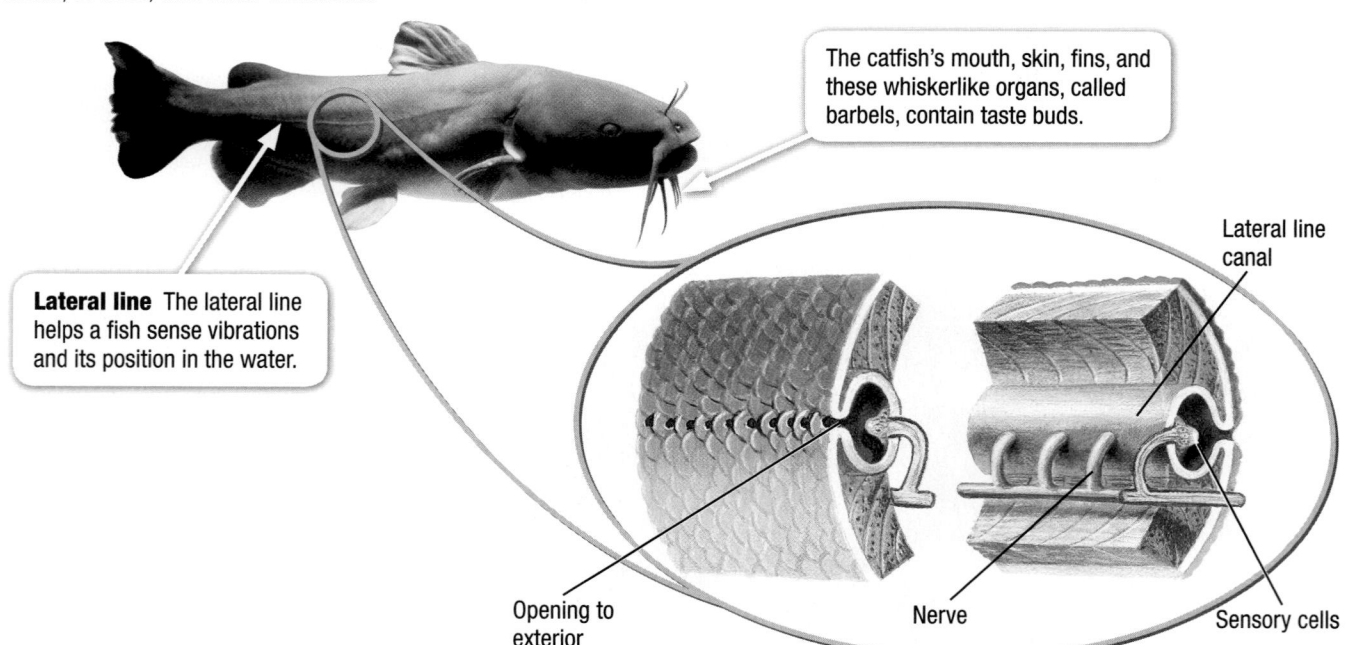

The catfish's mouth, skin, fins, and these whiskerlike organs, called barbels, contain taste buds.

Lateral line canal

Lateral line The lateral line helps a fish sense vibrations and its position in the water.

Opening to exterior

Nerve

Sensory cells

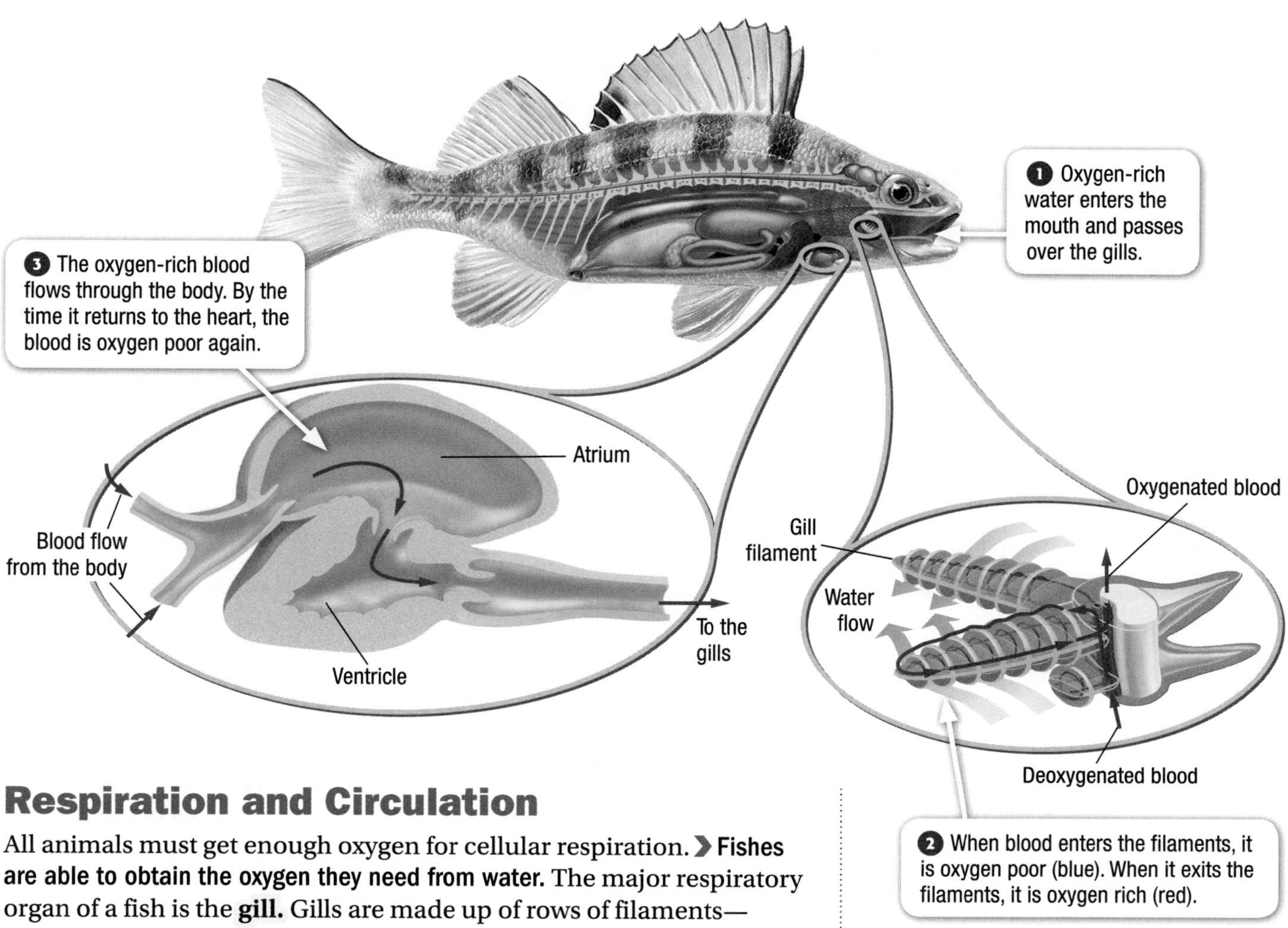

❸ The oxygen-rich blood flows through the body. By the time it returns to the heart, the blood is oxygen poor again.

❶ Oxygen-rich water enters the mouth and passes over the gills.

Atrium

Blood flow from the body

Ventricle

To the gills

Gill filament

Water flow

Oxygenated blood

Deoxygenated blood

❷ When blood enters the filaments, it is oxygen poor (blue). When it exits the filaments, it is oxygen rich (red).

Figure 3 A fish's gills and heart are directly behind its head.

go.hrw.com
✱ **interact online**
Keyword: HX8FSAF3

Respiration and Circulation

All animals must get enough oxygen for cellular respiration. ❱ **Fishes are able to obtain the oxygen they need from water.** The major respiratory organ of a fish is the **gill.** Gills are made up of rows of filaments—fingerlike projections through which gases enter and leave the blood. The filaments hang like curtains between a fish's mouth and cheeks. At the rear of the cheek is an opening called a **gill slit.**

Countercurrent Flow Have you ever seen a fish opening and closing its mouth while it swims, as if it were trying to eat water? This mouth movement helps pump a large amount of water over the gills and drive countercurrent flow, shown in **Figure 3.** In countercurrent flow, water passes over the gills in one direction as blood flows in the opposite direction through the gills' capillaries. Countercurrent flow allows oxygen to diffuse into the blood over the entire length of the gill capillaries. Due to this arrangement, gills are very efficient respiratory organs. Fish gills can extract up to 85% of the dissolved oxygen in the water passing over them.

Single-Loop Blood Circulation After blood leaves the gills' capillaries, it moves through vessels in the fish's body. The blood then enters the heart. In fishes, the tubular heart of invertebrates has been replaced with a simple chamber-pump heart. Blood collects in the heart's atrium. Then, the heart's ventricle pumps the blood back to the gills. In this way, the blood completes a single loop through the fish's body. All fishes, except lungfishes, have single-loop circulation.

❱ **Reading Check** *Describe how oxygen moves through a fish's body.*

READING TOOLBOX

Word Parts The prefix *counter* means "against." Write a definition in your own words for *countercurrent flow.*

QuickLab

Ion Excretion in Fish

A few species of fishes, such as salmon, are able to move between saltwater and freshwater environments. The graph at right shows the excreted ion concentration of a fish as it travels from one body of water to another. Examine the graph, and answer the analysis questions.

Analysis

1. **Determine** if the fish is losing or gaining ions by excretion as it travels.

2. **CRITICAL THINKING** **Inferring Conclusions** Is the fish traveling from fresh water to salt water or from salt water to fresh water?

3. **Summarize** the reasoning you used to answer item 2.

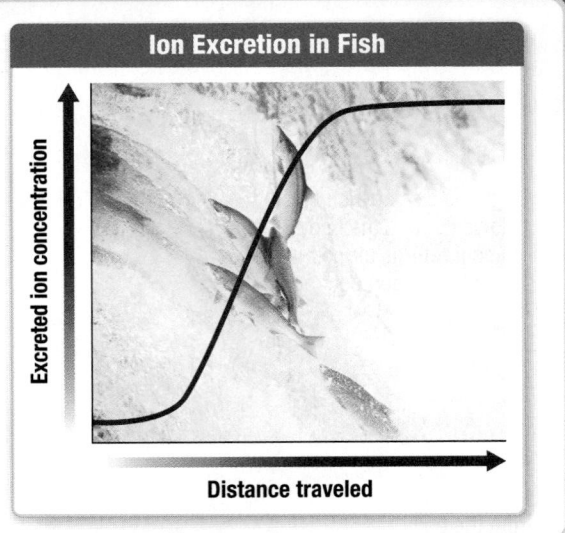

Ion Excretion in Fish

y-axis: Excreted ion concentration

x-axis: Distance traveled

Excretion

The body of most vertebrates is about two-thirds water. Vertebrates will die if they lose too much water. Therefore, minimizing water loss has been a key evolutionary challenge facing all vertebrates. Even fishes must cope with the problem of water loss. If it seems strange to you that fish have this problem, remember that osmosis causes a net movement of water through membranes, such as gills and skin, toward regions of higher ion concentration.

Salt and Water Balance The ion (salt) concentration of sea water is 3 times that of most marine fishes' tissues. As a result, these fishes lose water to the environment through osmosis. To make up for the lost water, the fishes drink sea water and pump out the excess salt through their gills. Freshwater fishes have the opposite problem. Their bodies contain more salt than the surrounding water, so they tend to take in water by osmosis. The additional water dilutes their body salts. Freshwater fishes regain salts by actively taking them in from their environment. Because of these two opposite challenges, few fishes can move between salt water and fresh water.

Kidneys ❯ Although the gills play a major role in maintaining a fish's salt and water balance, another key element is a pair of kidneys. A **kidney** is an organ that regulates the body's salt and water balance and removes metabolic wastes from the blood. Excess water and body wastes leave the kidneys in the form of a fluid called *urine*. To save water, marine fishes excrete only a small amount of urine, which has a high salt concentration. The rest of a marine fish's body waste is excreted through its gills. In contrast, freshwater fishes excrete very little waste from their gills. The majority of their body waste is excreted in large amounts of dilute urine.

❯ **Reading Check** *Compare marine and freshwater fish excretion.*

ACADEMIC VOCABULARY

minimize to make as small as possible

kidney one of the organs that filter water and wastes from the blood, excrete products as urine, and regulate the concentration of certain substances in the blood

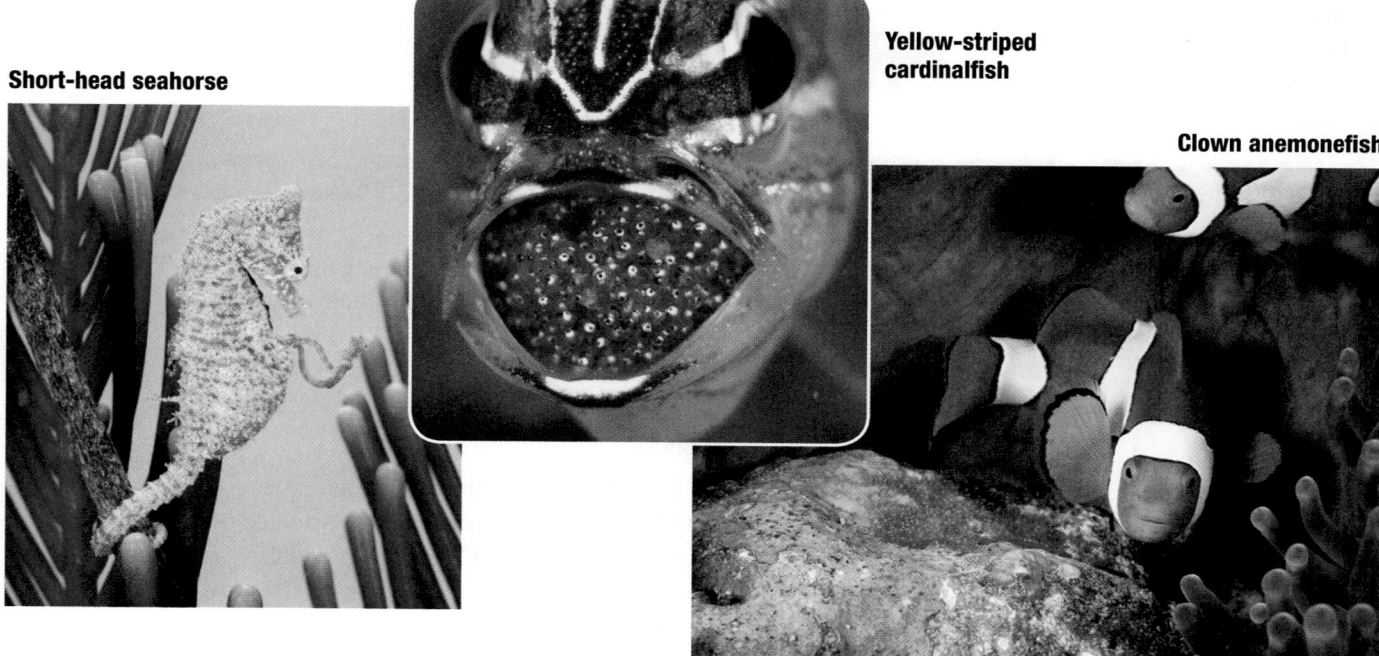

Short-head seahorse

Yellow-striped cardinalfish

Clown anemonefish

Reproduction

❯ **Most fishes reproduce sexually through external fertilization.** In a process called spawning, male and female gametes are released near one another in the water. Spawning may occur between two individuals, as with the clown anemonefish shown in **Figure 4,** or in large groups of males and females. Group spawning usually produces millions of fertilized eggs. Predators may eat many of these eggs and the resulting hatchlings, but the large number of eggs ensures that some individuals will survive.

In sharks, skates, and rays, eggs are fertilized inside the female's body. During mating, the male uses organs called *claspers* to insert sperm into the female. In most species, the eggs develop inside the female and the young are born live. These newborns are much larger than fishes that hatch from eggs. Because these offspring are large, they are less likely to be eaten by a predator.

❯ **Reading Check** *Describe the process of spawning.*

Figure 4 Fishes reproduce in a variety of ways. Male seahorses store eggs in a special pouch until they hatch (left). Male yellow-striped cardinalfish carry eggs in their mouths to protect the eggs from predators (center). Clown anemonefish spawn and then guard their eggs (right).

Section 1 Review

❯ **KEY IDEAS**

1. **Discuss** the key characteristics found in all fishes.
2. **Describe** how fishes use their fins.
3. **Summarize** how countercurrent flow helps a fish obtain oxygen.
4. **Explain** why freshwater fishes excrete more urine than marine fishes do.

5. **Contrast** reproduction in sharks with that of most other fishes.

CRITICAL THINKING

6. **Predicting Outcomes** The gills of fishes are made up of fingerlike projections called gill filaments through which gases enter and leave the blood. Explain a likely outcome if the gills were instead made up of a single, flat membrane.

ALTERNATIVE ASSESSMENT

7. **Making Models** Make a model of a fish that illustrates how its body is adapted to living in an aquatic environment. Choose five structures necessary or helpful for an animal in a water environment, and label them.

Groups of Fishes

Key Ideas	Key Terms	Why It Matters
❯ What are the characteristics of jawless fishes? ❯ What are the main traits of cartilaginous fishes? ❯ Why have bony fishes been so successful compared to the other groups of fishes?	operculum teleost	Fishes were the first vertebrates. Studying fishes can help scientists learn more about other vertebrates.

Modern fishes fall into three general groups: jawless fishes, cartilaginous fishes, and bony fishes. There are few species of jawless fishes, but they have unique lifestyles. Cartilaginous fishes are successful predators found mainly in the oceans. Bony fishes are the most diverse fish group. They are found in almost every aquatic habitat.

Jawless Fishes

Jawless fishes—hagfishes and lampreys—are primitive animals that have changed little during the past 330 million years. ❯ **Jawless fishes have skeletons made of cartilage, a strong fibrous connective tissue. They retain their notochord into adulthood. Jawless fishes are the only modern vertebrates without a backbone.** However, the notochord allows jawless fishes, shown in **Figure 5,** to swim with undulating movements.

Hagfishes Hagfishes are scavengers and predators that live at great depths on the ocean floor. When a fish or whale dies, hagfishes feed on the body. Hagfishes also eat small prey, such as worms. When threatened, a hagfish can produce huge quantities of slime. The sticky slime binds and suffocates the predator.

Lampreys Lampreys are parasitic. A lamprey uses its circular, suction-cuplike mouth to attach itself to a host. After attachment, the lamprey feeds on its host's blood and other body fluids.

❯ **Reading Check** *Compare the feeding methods of jawless fishes.*

Figure 5 Jawless fishes have scaleless, eel-like bodies with multiple gill slits and unpaired fins.

The lack of vertebrae makes this hagfish so flexible that it can tie itself into a knot.

This lamprey gouges out a wound in its host with these spines and its rough tongue.

Shark

Ray

Ratfish

Figure 6 Unlike jawless fishes, cartilaginous fishes have paired fins, jaws, and vertebral columns. ❯ **How is the body structure of a ray adapted to its lifestyle?**

Cartilaginous Fishes

Sharks, skates, rays, and ratfishes, shown in **Figure 6,** are cartilaginous fishes. ❯ **Cartilaginous fishes have paired fins and jaws. They also have skeletons made of cartilage strengthened by calcium carbonate (the material that makes up oyster shells).** Calcium carbonate is deposited in the outer layers of cartilage. It forms a thin layer that reinforces the cartilage. The result is a very light, yet strong skeleton.

Sharks The shark's light, streamlined body allows it to move quickly through the water in search of prey. Its skin is covered in triangular-shaped scales. The scales give the skin a rough texture but allow the shark to slide through the water easily. A shark's teeth are actually modified scales. They are triangular in shape and are arranged in 6 to 10 rows along the shark's jaw. The teeth in front, used for biting and cutting, are pointed and sharp. Behind the front teeth, rows of new teeth are growing. When a front tooth breaks or is worn down, a replacement tooth moves forward. One shark may use more than 20,000 teeth during its lifetime. This system of tooth replacement guarantees that the teeth being used are always new and sharp. Most sharks are predators of large marine animals. But the largest sharks, such as whale sharks, consume plankton.

Skates and Rays Skates and rays have flattened bodies that are well adapted to life on the sea floor. Rays are usually less than 1 m long, but skates are typically smaller. However, the giant manta ray may be as wide as 7 m. Most species of skates and rays have flattened teeth that are used to crush their prey, mainly small fishes and invertebrates. Manta rays and their relatives strain plankton from the water. Some rays can discharge a powerful electric shock that is used to stun prey or scare off predators.

❯ **Reading Check** *List three characteristics of cartilaginous fishes.*

www.scilinks.org
Topic: Sharks
Code: HX81389

ACADEMIC VOCABULARY

typically usually, most often

Bony Fishes

Together, there are about 1,000 species of jawless and cartilaginous fishes. In contrast, there are about 24,000 species of bony fishes. Bony fishes, shown in **Figure 7,** are perhaps the most successful vertebrates. ❯ **Bony fishes have a strong endoskeleton made completely of bone. Bony fishes also have structural adaptations, such as lateral lines, opercula, and swim bladders, that contribute to their success.**

Lateral Line Bony fishes have a fully developed lateral line system. As moving water presses against the fish's sides, nerve impulses from sensory cells in the lateral line go to the brain. So, the fish is aware of its position and rate of movement. The lateral line system also allows a fish to detect an object by the movement of water deflected by that object.

Gill Cover Most bony fishes have a hard plate, an **operculum,** that covers the gills on each side of the head. Movements of the opercula and nearby muscles draw water over the gills. The fish is thus able to take in oxygen. In this way, most bony fishes can move water over their gills while remaining in one place. Unlike many sharks, a bony fish doesn't have to swim forward with its mouth open to move water over its gills. The ability to take in oxygen without swimming allows a bony fish to conserve energy.

Swim Bladder A fish body is denser than water. So, to keep from sinking, bony fishes use their swim bladder. By adjusting the swim bladder's gas content, bony fishes can regulate their buoyancy. As the swim bladder fills, the fish rises. As it empties, the fish sinks. A swim bladder allows the fish to maintain or change its depth. Bony fishes do not have to swim to keep breathing and to keep from sinking, as sharks must do. Bony fishes also have highly mobile paired fins. These traits enable bony fishes to turn sharply and paddle backward.

SC_LINKS_®
www.scilinks.org
Topic: Anatomy of
Bony Fish
Code: HX80065

operculum (oh PUHR kyoo luhm) In fish, a hard plate that is attached to each side of the head, that covers the gills, and that is open at the rear

Figure 7 Bony fishes live in a diverse range of habitats. There is great variation in their appearance.

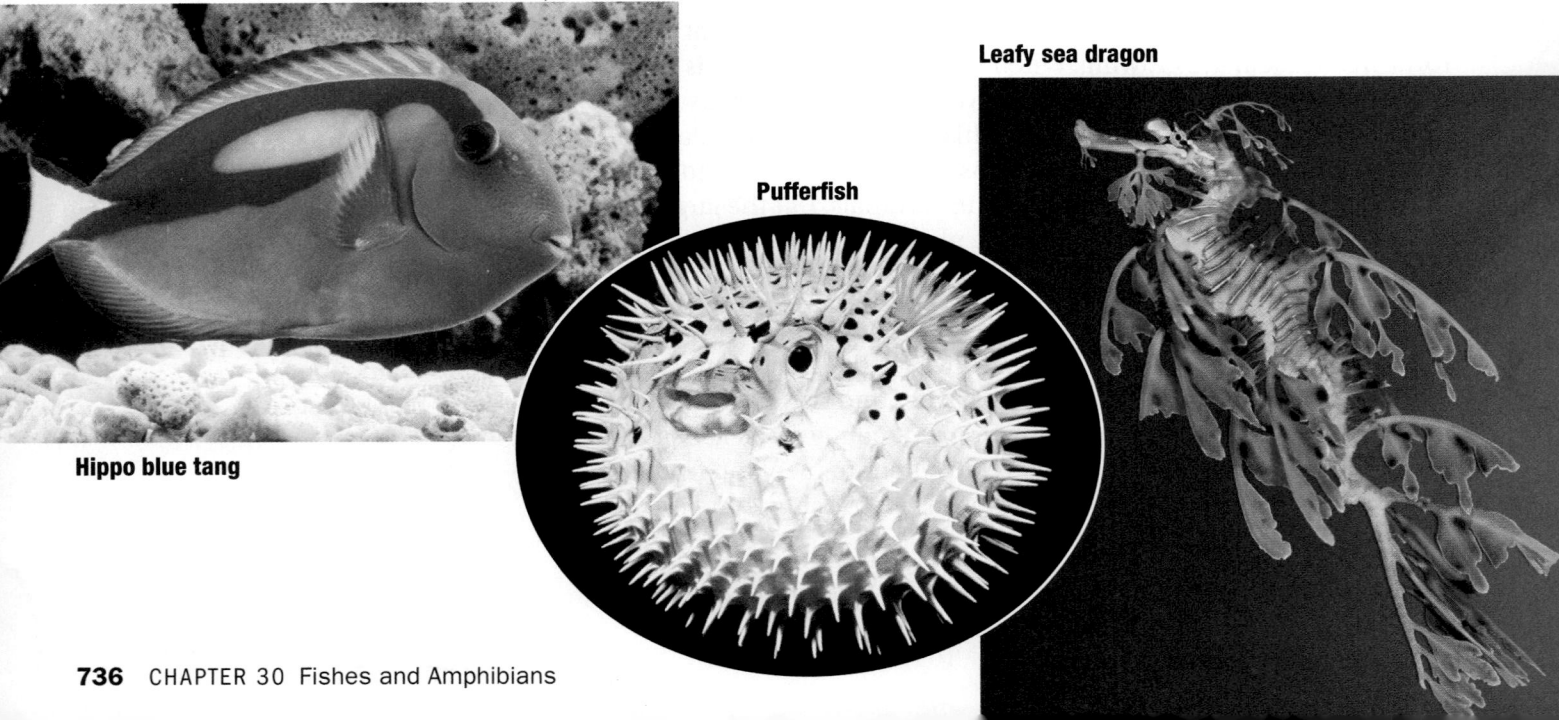

Leafy sea dragon

Pufferfish

Hippo blue tang

Up Close Bony Fishes

Although bony fishes vary greatly in size, color, and shape, a yellow perch is a typical example of this fish group. A yellow perch has a fully developed lateral line system that it uses to detect objects in its environment, including predators and prey. It also has caudal and dorsal fins. The caudal fin thrusts from side to side to propel the fish forward. The dorsal fins prevent the perch from rolling over as it swims.

Yellow Perch

Scientific name: *Perca flavens*
Size: About 0.3 m long and up to 2.3 kg
Range: Found in lakes and rivers from the Great Lakes to the Atlantic coast and as far south as South Carolina
Habitat: Lives concealed among vegetation
Diet: Feeds on insect larvae, crustaceans, and other fishes

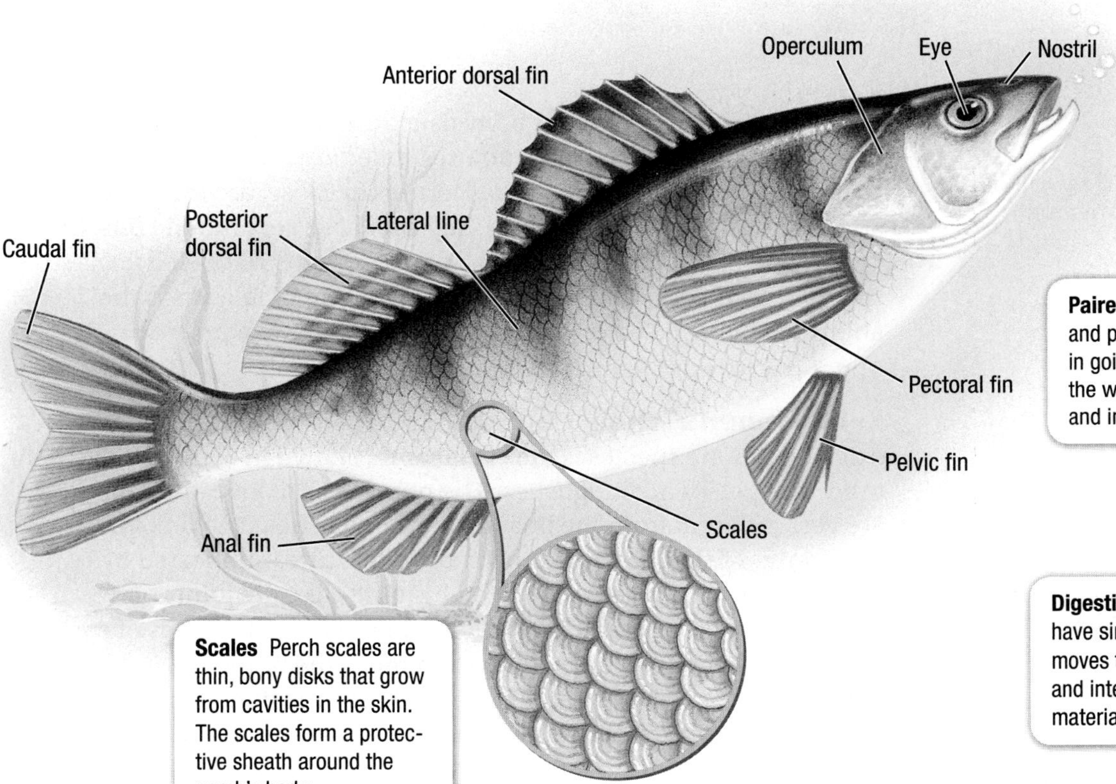

Anterior dorsal fin

Operculum   Eye   Nostril

Posterior dorsal fin

Caudal fin

Lateral line

Paired Fins Paired pectoral and pelvic fins assist the fish in going up or down through the water, in turning sharply, and in stopping quickly.

Pectoral fin

Pelvic fin

Anal fin

Scales

Scales Perch scales are thin, bony disks that grow from cavities in the skin. The scales form a protective sheath around the perch's body.

Digestive System All vertebrates have similar digestive systems. Food moves through the mouth, stomach, and intestines. The undigested material exits through the anus.

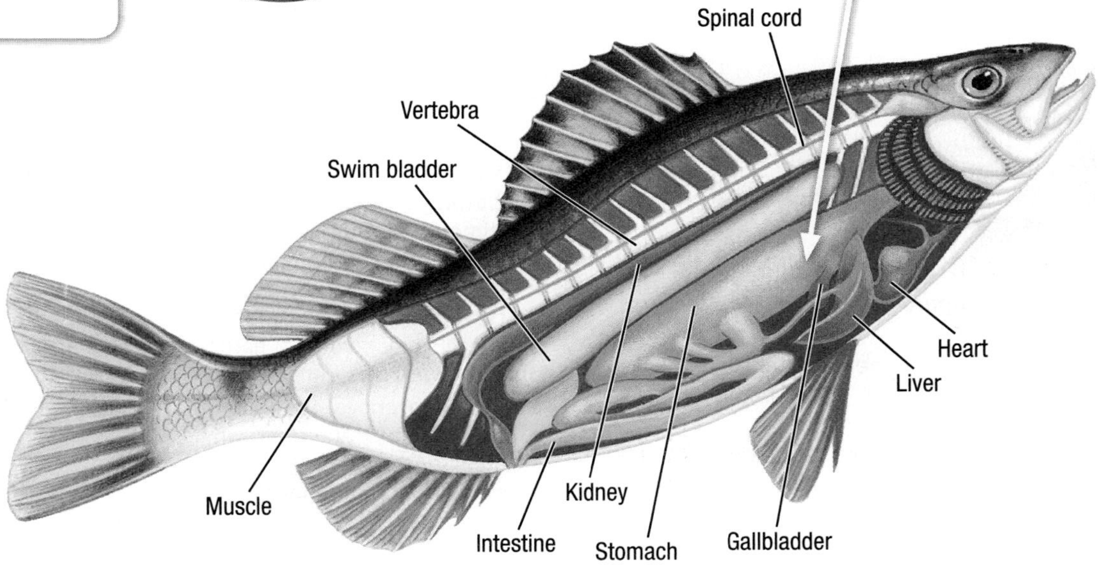

Spinal cord

Vertebra

Swim bladder

Heart

Liver

Reproductive Organs Female perch lay strings of eggs that are fertilized externally. The young hatch within days.

Muscle

Kidney

Intestine   Stomach   Gallbladder

Figure 8 Scientists thought coelacanths had been extinct for millions of years, until one was caught in 1938 off the coast of Africa. ❯ **How does a coelacanth differ from a ray-finned fish?**

Coelacanths have muscular fins with thick bones.

teleost (TEL ee ahst) a member of a group of ray-finned fishes that have a caudal fin, scales, and a swim bladder

READING TOOLBOX

Concept Map After reading this section, finish filling in the concept map that you made at the beginning of the chapter.

Ray-finned Fishes Most bony fishes are ray-finned fishes. Their fins are supported by bony structures called *rays*. **Teleosts,** such as the yellow perch shown in the feature Up Close, are the most advanced type of ray-finned fish. Teleosts have very mobile fins, thin scales, and completely symmetrical tails. About 95% of all living fish species are teleosts. One reason for the success of teleosts is their ability to suck food toward their mouth. The fish can protrude its upper jaw forward in order to grasp food.

Lobe-Finned Fishes Only seven species of lobe-finned fishes exist today. One species is the coelacanth, shown in **Figure 8.** The other six species are lungfishes. The paired fins of lobe-finned fishes are very different from the fins of ray-finned fishes. The fins of many lobe-finned fishes are fleshy, muscular structures supported by bones. These bones are connected by joints, like the joints between the bones in your hand. Bony rays are found only at the tips of each lobed fin. Muscles within each fin can move the bony rays independently of one another. A lobe-finned fish was the direct ancestor of amphibians and all other land vertebrates.

❯ **Reading Check** *How does the fin of a teleost compare with the fin of a lobe-finned fish?*

Section 2 Review

❯ **KEY IDEAS**

1. **Compare** jawless fishes with other fishes.
2. **List** the materials that make up the endoskeleton of bony fishes and sharks.
3. **Summarize** how the swim bladder can be viewed as an energy-saving mechanism.

CRITICAL THINKING

4. **Evaluating Conclusions** A fish specimen has rough skin, several rows of teeth, and no opercula. A student infers, based on these traits, that the fish has a swim bladder. Explain why you agree or disagree with this conclusion.
5. **Making Inferences** Propose an explanation for the reason why cartilaginous skeletons are not a characteristic of land-living vertebrates.

METHODS OF SCIENCE

6. **Forming a Hypothesis** Hagfishes do not have swim bladders. Write a hypothesis that could explain why the lack of a swim bladder is an adaptive advantage for hagfishes.

The Amphibian Body

Key Ideas	Key Terms	Why It Matters
❯ Which characteristics do most amphibians share? ❯ How do amphibians sense their environment? ❯ Which amphibian body structures work together to provide oxygen to body tissues? ❯ How does an amphibian circulatory system differ from those of most fishes?	tympanic membrane lung septum pulmonary vein	Ancient amphibian species gave rise to all other land vertebrates.

Amphibians were the first vertebrates to live on land. They developed many characteristics to survive in this harsh new habitat. The first amphibians, which descended from lobe-finned fishes, are the ancestors of all other land vertebrates.

Characteristics of Amphibians

Most people picture frogs when they think of amphibians. After all, the croaking and hopping of frogs make it difficult not to notice them. But frogs are not the only kind of amphibians. Frogs have quieter relatives that live nearby, hidden in damp habitats. These quieter amphibians include salamanders, newts, and caecilians. ❯ **Most of these amphibians share five key characteristics: legs, lungs, double-loop circulation, a partially divided heart, and cutaneous respiration.** These characteristics allow amphibians to thrive on land. However, because amphibian eggs are not watertight, amphibians need to reproduce in a wet area. Therefore, most amphibians, such as the salamander shown in **Figure 9,** must live in moist habitats.

❯ **Reading Check** *Why do most amphibians live in moist habitats?*

Amphibians can take in oxygen directly through their moist skin.

Legs help amphibians move around on land.

Figure 9 The earliest amphibians resembled this salamander.
❯ How is the body of a salamander similar to that of a fish? How is it different?

Movement and Response

Amphibians face environmental challenges different from those faced by fishes. Many of these challenges involve having to move differently on land. Also, not all sense organs work as well in air as in water. For example, the lateral line used by fishes to detect movement of the water works only in water. Thus, even though larval amphibians have a lateral line, it is usually lost by adulthood.

Skeleton Water supports the body of a fish against the force of gravity, but terrestrial vertebrates must rely on the support of their strong internal skeleton. Strong limbs support the body's weight as well as allow movement. Frog skeletons have several specializations for jumping and landing. In frogs, the bones of the lower limbs are fused into a single, thick bone. The hips also have thick bones with a sturdy structure that absorb the impact of landing.

Sense Organs ❯ The senses of sight and hearing are well developed in most amphibians. The primary sensory organs of amphibians are the eyes and ears. Vision is important in hunting and in avoiding predators. The eyes of amphibians are covered by a transparent, movable membrane called a *nictitating membrane.* The inner ear detects sound. Sounds are <u>transmitted</u> to the inner ear by the **tympanic membrane,** or eardrum, and a small bone that extends between the tympanic membrane and the inner ear. Sounds first strike the tympanic membrane, which is usually located on the side of the head, as shown in **Figure 10.** Vibrations of the tympanic membrane cause small movements that are transmitted to the fluid-filled inner ear. In the inner ear, sensitive hair cells change sound vibrations to nervous impulses. These impulses are then transmitted to the brain.

❯ **Reading Check** *Describe how amphibians hear sounds.*

ACADEMIC VOCABULARY

transmit to send from one place to another

Figure 10 The tympanic membrane of this frog transmits sound to the inner ear. The skeleton of the frog is adapted to absorb shocks when the frog jumps and lands.

Tympanic membrane

QuickLab

⏱ 15 min

Modeling Frog Inhalation

When a frog breathes in, its throat drops. This movement draws air into the mouth. The nostrils then close, and the throat moves up. So, air is forced into the lungs.

Procedure

❶ Use **scissors** to cut off the bottom of a **plastic bottle**. Use a **knife** to cut a 5 mm hole in the middle of the bottle. Secure a **balloon** over the bottle's neck.

❷ Cut a **second balloon** in half to form a circular section of balloon skin. Stretch this skin over the bottle's opened bottom. **Tape** the skin in place.

❸ Pull the balloon skin taut. Then, cover the hole and push the skin into the bottle. Observe what happens.

Analysis

1. **Determine** which parts of the frog anatomy are represented by the inside of the plastic bottle, balloon, stretched balloon skin, and hole in the bottle.

2. **CRITICAL THINKING** **Analyzing Results** Explain why the balloon attached to the bottle's neck inflated.

Respiration

One of the biggest challenges that amphibians faced when they left the water was gathering oxygen from the air. ❭ **In amphibians, the skin, lungs, double-loop circulation, and a partially divided heart work together to ensure that sufficient oxygen reaches the body tissues.**

Lungs Although larval amphibians have gills, most adult amphibians breathe with lungs. A **lung** is an internal, baglike organ that allows oxygen and carbon dioxide to be exchanged between the air and the bloodstream. The amount of oxygen that a lung can absorb depends on its internal surface area. The greater the surface area is, the greater the amount of oxygen that can be absorbed. In amphibians, the lungs are hardly more than sacs with folds on their inner membrane that increase their surface area. An amphibian breathes by changing the volume and pressure of air in its mouth while either opening or closing its nostrils. With each breath, fresh oxygen-rich air is drawn into the lungs. There, it mixes with a small volume of air that has already given up most of its oxygen. Due to this mixing, the respiratory efficiency of lungs is much less than that of gills. But lungs do not have to be as efficient as gills because air contains about 20 times as much oxygen as sea water does.

Skin Many amphibians also obtain oxygen through their thin, moist skin. This process is called cutaneous respiration. Cutaneous respiration has allowed one group of salamanders to live without lungs. In cutaneous respiration, gases and water pass directly through their skin. Because the skin must remain moist for the exchange of gases, amphibians have mucous glands to help keep the skin moist.

❭ **Reading Check** *What structures do amphibians use to breathe?*

tympanic membrane the eardrum

lung the central organ of the respiratory system in which oxygen from the air is exchanged with carbon dioxide from the blood

www.scilinks.org
Topic: Amphibians
Code: HX80058

Circulation

Much more energy is needed to walk on land than to swim. Land animals tend to have higher metabolic rates than aquatic animals. So the tissues of land animals require greater amounts of oxygen. ❯ **The structure of the amphibian circulatory system—including a partially divided heart and double-loop circulation—allows oxygen to be delivered to the body more efficiently than in fishes.**

Partially Divided Heart The chambers at the top of the amphibian heart are divided into left and right sides by a wall known as the **septum.** However, the heart's bottom chamber is not divided. For this reason, a mixture of oxygen-rich and oxygen-poor blood is delivered to the amphibian's body tissues.

As you can see in **Figure 11,** blood moves through an amphibian's heart in several steps. First, the oxygen-poor blood from the body is delivered to a chamber at the top of the heart, the right *atrium.* Oxygen-rich blood is carried by a vessel from the lungs directly to the heart's left atrium, which is separated from the right atrium by the septum. You cannot see the septum in **Figure 11** because it is beneath a large vessel, the conus arteriosus, which sends blood to the lungs and the body. The septum stops the total mixing of oxygen-rich and oxygen-poor blood as each enters the heart.

Both oxygen-rich and oxygen-poor blood empty into the *ventricle,* a large chamber at the bottom of the heart. Here, some mixing of the blood takes place. However, due to the shape of the ventricle, the two streams of blood remain somewhat separate. In the ventricle, oxygen-rich blood tends to stay on the side that directs blood toward the body. Oxygen-poor blood tends to stay on the side that directs blood toward the lungs. When the ventricle contracts, blood in both sides of the ventricle are pushed into vessels leading away from the heart.

septum the thick wall between the right and left chambers of the heart

pulmonary vein the vein that carries oxygenated blood from the lungs to the heart

Figure 11 These four steps show how blood flows through the heart of an amphibian. ❯ **How could an amphibian's heart be more efficient?**

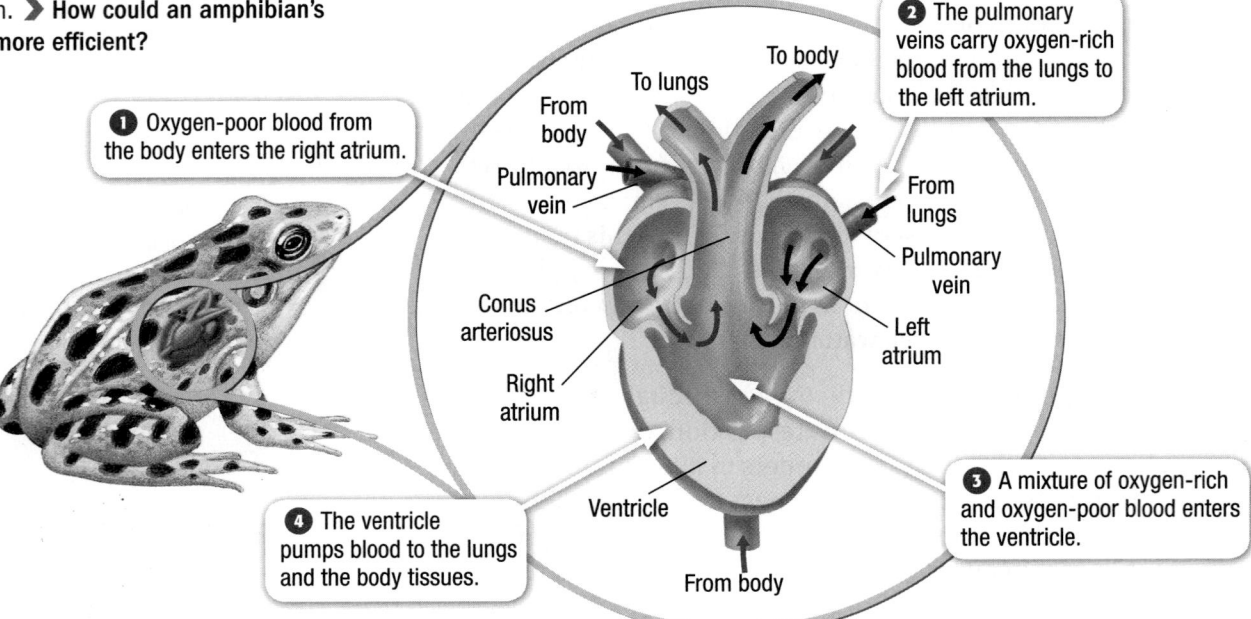

❶ Oxygen-poor blood from the body enters the right atrium.

❷ The pulmonary veins carry oxygen-rich blood from the lungs to the left atrium.

❸ A mixture of oxygen-rich and oxygen-poor blood enters the ventricle.

❹ The ventricle pumps blood to the lungs and the body tissues.

To lungs
To body
From body
Pulmonary vein
From lungs
Conus arteriosus
Pulmonary vein
Right atrium
Left atrium
Ventricle
From body

Spiral Valve Some amphibians have a spiral valve that divides the conus arteriosus. The spiral valve also helps keep the two streams of blood separate as they leave the heart. Even so, some oxygen-poor blood is delivered to the body's tissues. Recall, however, that amphibians also obtain oxygen through their skin. This extra oxygen partly makes up for the limitations of their circulatory system.

Double-Loop Circulation The path of circulation in amphibians is different from that in most fishes. As amphibians evolved, their circulatory system changed to support their life on land. The result was a second circulatory loop. This change allowed more oxygen to be delivered to their bodies. Examine **Figure 12,** and compare the single-loop circulation of most fishes with the double-loop circulation of amphibians.

Notice the circulatory loop that connects an amphibian's heart to its lungs. In this loop, amphibians have blood vessels that are not found in fishes—the pulmonary veins. The **pulmonary veins** are the vessels that carry the oxygen-rich blood from the amphibian's lungs directly back to its heart. An amphibian's second circulatory loop carries the oxygen-rich blood from the heart to the body. The advantage of this arrangement is that oxygen-rich blood can be pumped to the amphibian's tissues at a much higher pressure and speed than it can in fishes. (Recall that in fishes, blood is pumped through the narrow capillaries of the gills before reaching the body organs. Blood flow slows as it moves through the gill capillaries. As a result, much of the heartbeat's force is lost.)

❭ **Reading Check** *How is the circulatory system of amphibians different from the circulatory system of most fishes?*

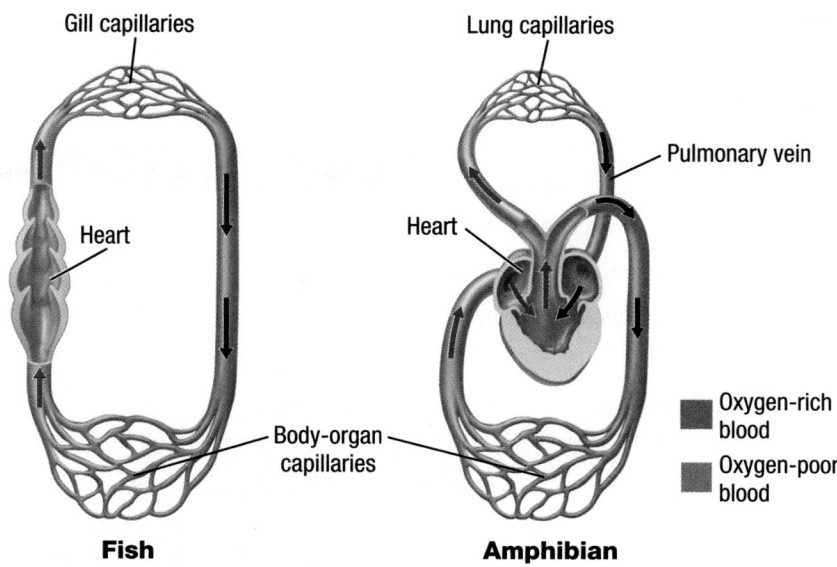

Gill capillaries
Lung capillaries
Pulmonary vein
Heart
Heart
Oxygen-rich blood
Oxygen-poor blood
Body-organ capillaries

Fish
Amphibian

Figure 12 Circulation in most fishes involves a single loop. Amphibians have a second loop that goes from the heart to the lungs and back to the heart.

READING TOOLBOX

Comparisons Using **Figure 12,** write two sentences that compare and two sentences that contrast fish and amphibian circulation.

Section 3 Review

❭ **KEY IDEAS**

1. **Describe** the key characteristics of amphibians.
2. **Identify** the function of the tympanic membrane.
3. **Summarize** how amphibians take in oxygen.
4. **Contrast** the single-loop circulation of fishes with the double-loop circulation of amphibians.

CRITICAL THINKING

5. **Justifying Conclusions** You read an article in a newspaper that states that amphibians are very vulnerable to pollutants in the water around them. Do you think this is likely? Why or why not?
6. **Comparing Structures** Which sense organ of a terrestrial amphibian resembles the fish's lateral line in function? Explain your answer.

WRITING FOR SCIENCE

7. **Writing News Articles** Use library resources and the Internet to research the worldwide decline in amphibian numbers that scientists have observed over recent years. Prepare a report on your findings in the form of a written news article or as a segment for a TV news program.

Groups of Amphibians

Key Ideas	Key Terms	Why It Matters
❯ What are the main characteristics of salamanders? ❯ What are the key traits of caecilians? ❯ What are the kinds of environments in which frogs and toads are adapted to live?	tadpole	Due to their porous skin, amphibians are especially sensitive to pollution. This trait makes them important environmental indicators.

Modern amphibians are divided into three main groups: salamanders, caecilians, and frogs and toads. Organisms belonging to these three groups are shown in **Figure 13.**

Salamanders

❯ Salamanders have elongated bodies; long tails; and smooth, moist skin. There are about 400 species of salamanders. They typically range from 10 cm to 0.3 m in length. Because salamanders need to keep their skin moist, most are unable to stay away from water for long periods. However, a few salamander species manage to live in dry areas by remaining inactive during the day. Like frogs, some salamanders have tongues that they can extend to catch prey.

Reproduction in Salamanders Salamanders lay their eggs in water or in moist places. Fertilization is usually external. A few species of salamanders have a type of internal fertilization. The female picks up a sperm packet that has been deposited by the male and places it in her body. The young that hatch from salamander eggs are carnivorous. They resemble small versions of the adults, except that the young usually have gills. A few species of salamanders retain their external gills when they become adults.

❯ **Reading Check** *How do most salamanders reproduce?*

Figure 13 Modern amphibians are a diverse group. Members of the three amphibian groups are shown here.
❯ How do the body plans of salamanders, caecilians, and frogs differ?

Salamander

Caecilian

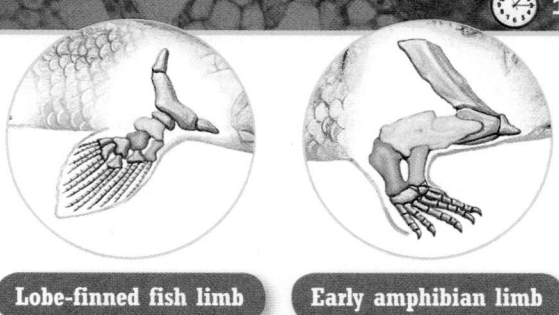

🕐 15 min

Lobe-finned fish limb   Early amphibian limb

Amphibian Leg Structure

Without limbs that could bear weight and walk, amphibians could not have adapted as readily to life on land.

Procedure

Study the diagram. Use modeling clay to shape models of each bone, and position them as shown in the picture.

Analysis

1. **Describe** how thicker limb bones and "finger bones" are an adaptation for life on land.

2. **CRITICAL THINKING** **Inferring Conclusions** Caecilians are a group of amphibians that lack limbs. Describe how this unique group of amphibians may have evolved.

Caecilians

❯ **Caecilians are a highly specialized group of burrowing amphibians with small, bony scales embedded in their skin.** These legless, wormlike animals are found in swamps in tropical regions. Caecilians grow to about 0.3 m long, although some species can grow to 1.2 m long. Most species burrow in soil, but some species are aquatic. Because they have very small eyes that are located beneath their skin or even under bone, most caecilians are blind. All species have teeth to help them catch and consume prey. They eat worms and other invertebrates. A caecilian detects its prey by using a tentacle on the side of its head that can sense chemicals given off by the prey.

Reproduction in Caecilians During breeding, a male caecilian deposits sperm directly into a female. Some species lay eggs, which the female guards until they hatch. In a few species, young are born alive. These caecilians provide nutrition to their developing embryos.

SCI
LINKS
www.scilinks.org
Topic: Salamanders
Code: HX81342

Frog

Toad

Up Close Frogs

Leopard frogs have many common amphibian traits, such as tympanic membranes and moist, porous skin. The leopard frog also has adaptations unique to frogs and toads. For example, the leopard frog's bulging eyes allow it to stay almost fully submerged in water while literally "keeping an eye out" for predators and prey above the water.

Leopard Frog

Scientific name: *Rana pipiens* and closely related species
Size: Body length (legs excluded) of 5 to 9 cm
Range: From California south to New Mexico and east to the Atlantic coast
Habitat: Lives in short grasses of meadows and around ponds
Diet: Feeds on crickets, mosquitoes, and other small animals

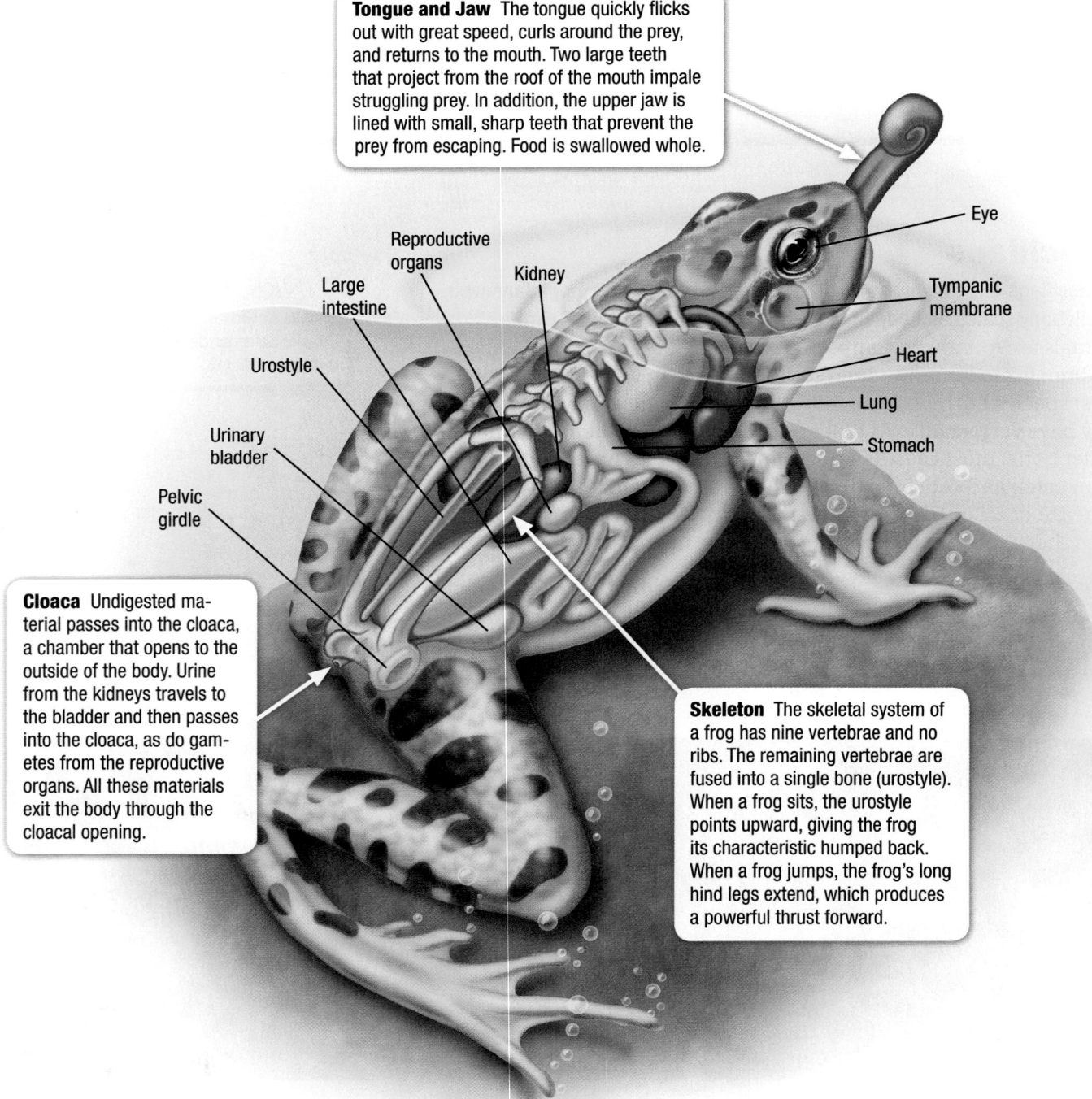

Tongue and Jaw The tongue quickly flicks out with great speed, curls around the prey, and returns to the mouth. Two large teeth that project from the roof of the mouth impale struggling prey. In addition, the upper jaw is lined with small, sharp teeth that prevent the prey from escaping. Food is swallowed whole.

Reproductive organs

Large intestine

Kidney

Urostyle

Urinary bladder

Pelvic girdle

Eye

Tympanic membrane

Heart

Lung

Stomach

Cloaca Undigested material passes into the cloaca, a chamber that opens to the outside of the body. Urine from the kidneys travels to the bladder and then passes into the cloaca, as do gametes from the reproductive organs. All these materials exit the body through the cloacal opening.

Skeleton The skeletal system of a frog has nine vertebrae and no ribs. The remaining vertebrae are fused into a single bone (urostyle). When a frog sits, the urostyle points upward, giving the frog its characteristic humped back. When a frog jumps, the frog's long hind legs extend, which produces a powerful thrust forward.

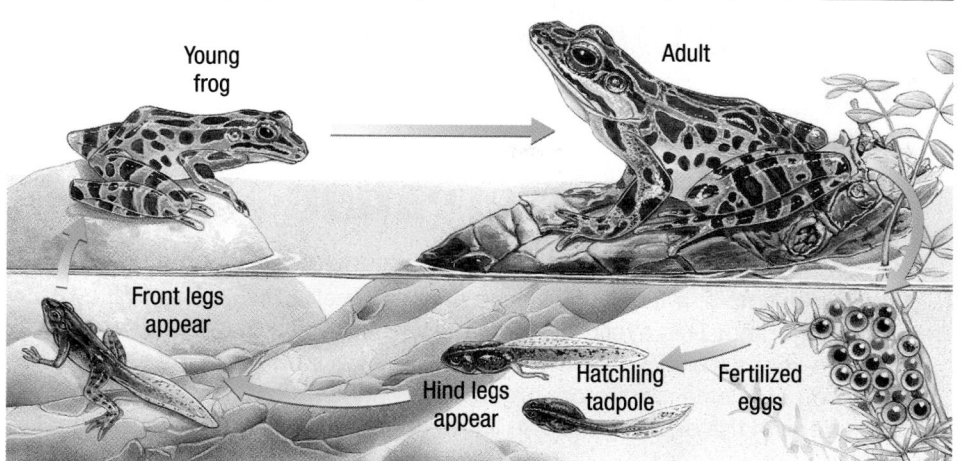

Young frog

Adult

Front legs appear

Hind legs appear

Hatchling tadpole

Fertilized eggs

Figure 14 The transition of a larval frog (tadpole) to an adult frog involves a complex series of external and internal body changes. ❯ What major physical change do tadpoles first undergo as they develop into an adult frog?

Frogs and Toads

❯ There are about 4,000 species of frogs and toads, also known as *anurans,* which live in environments ranging from deserts to rain forests, valleys to mountains, and ponds to puddles. Adult anurans are carnivores that eat a variety of small prey. Most frogs wait for prey to pass near them. They then catch the prey by using a long, sticky tongue that extends rapidly. The frog body, particularly its skeleton, is adapted for jumping, and its long muscular legs provide the power. Toads are very similar to frogs but have squat bodies and shorter legs. Their skin is not smooth like that of a frog but is covered with bumps.

Reproduction in Frogs Like most amphibians, frogs depend on water to complete their life cycle. The female releases her eggs into the water. A male's sperm fertilize them externally. The fertilized eggs hatch into swimming, fishlike larval forms called **tadpoles.** Tadpoles breathe with gills and feed mostly on algae. After a period of growth, hind legs appear on the tadpole. The tadpole continues to grow into an adult frog as its tail and gills disappear. This process of great physical change, shown in **Figure 14,** is called *metamorphosis.*

❯ **Reading Check** *How do the diets of adult and larval frogs differ?*

tadpole the aquatic, fishlike larva of a frog or toad

ACADEMIC VOCABULARY

cycle a recurring series of functional changes or events

Section 4 Review

❯**KEY IDEAS**

1. **Compare** salamander larvae with frog larvae.
2. **Contrast** the external characteristics of caecilians to those of other types of amphibians.
3. **Describe** a frog's adaptations for both aquatic and land environments.
4. **Summarize** the process of metamorphosis.

CRITICAL THINKING

5. **Analyzing Information** Frogs and toads inhabit a wider range of habitats than salamanders do. Why do you think this is the case?
6. **Inferring Relationships** Explain how the number of eggs produced by amphibians most likely relates to the amount of parental care invested.

WRITING FOR SCIENCE

7. **Report** Use library or Internet resources to find more information about caecilians. Your research should focus on what scientists already know about these amphibians and what scientists have yet to find out. Write a report that details what you discover.

Objectives

▶ Examine the external features of a frog.

▶ Observe the behavior of a frog.

▶ Explain how a frog is adapted to life on land and in water.

Materials

- lab apron, disposable gloves
- frog, live
- terrarium
- insects, live (crickets or mealworms)
- beaker, 600 mL
- aquarium
- dechlorinated water

Safety

Live Frog Observation

Frogs, which are amphibians, are adapted for living on land and in water. For example, a frog's eyes have an extra eyelid called the nictitating membrane. This eyelid protects the eye when the frog is underwater and keeps the eye moist when the frog is on land. The smooth skin of a frog acts as a respiratory organ by exchanging oxygen and carbon dioxide with the air or water. The limbs of a frog enable it to move both on land and in water.

In this lab, you will use observations to answer questions about a frog's body structure and its behavior. To do this, you will examine a live frog in both a terrestrial environment and an aquatic environment.

Procedure

1. Observe a live frog in a terrarium. Closely examine the external features of the frog. Then make a drawing of the frog. Label the eyes, nostrils, tympanic membranes, front legs, and hind legs.

2. Make a data table similar to the one shown. Watch the frog's movements as it breathes air into and out of its lungs. Record your observations.

3. Look closely at the frog's eyes, and note their location. Examine the upper and lower eyelids as well as a third transparent eyelid called a nictitating membrane. Describe how the eyelids move.

4. Study the frog's legs, and note the difference between the front and hind legs.

5. Place a live insect, such as a cricket or a mealworm, into the terrarium. Observe and record how the frog reacts.

6. Gently tap the side of the terrarium farthest from the frog, and observe the frog's responses. Record your observations.

Tadpole

Froglet

7 Put on gloves, and a lab apron.

8 **CAUTION: Handle live frogs gently. Frogs are slippery! Do not allow a frog to injure itself by jumping from a lab table to the floor.** Place a 600 mL beaker in the terrarium. Carefully pick up the frog, and examine its skin. How does it feel? Now place the frog in the beaker. Cover the beaker with your hand, and carry it to a freshwater aquarium. Tilt the beaker, and gently lower it into the water until the frog swims out.

9 Watch the frog float and swim. Notice how the frog uses its legs to swim. Also notice the position of the frog's head. As the frog swims, bend down to view the underside of the frog. Then look down on the frog from above. Compare the color on the dorsal and ventral sides of the frog.

10 Clean up your lab materials according to your teacher's instructions. Wash your hands before leaving the lab.

Data Table	
Behavior/structure	Observations
Breathing	
Eyes	
Legs	
Response to food	
Response to noise	
Skin	
Swimming behavior	

Analyze and Conclude

1. **Making Systematic Observations** How does a frog use its hind legs for moving on land and in water?

2. **Using Evidence to Develop Explanations** How does the position of a frog's eyes benefit the frog while it is swimming?

3. **SCIENTIFIC METHODS** **Using Evidence to Develop Predictions** What features of an adult frog provide evidence that it has an aquatic life and a terrestrial life?

4. **SCIENTIFIC METHODS** **Critiquing Explanations** Were you able to determine in this lab how a frog hears? Explain your reasoning.

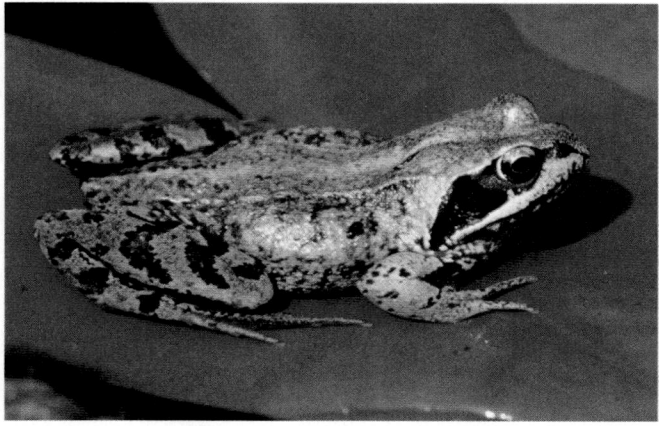

Adult Frog

Extensions

5. **Inferring Conclusions** What can you infer about a frog's field of vision from the position of its eyes?

6. **Forming Hypotheses** How is the coloration on the dorsal side of a frog an adaptive advantage?

7. **Further Inquiry** Write a new question about frogs that could be explored with another investigation.

8. **Careers in Science** Herpetology is the study of reptiles and amphibians. Do research to discover how herpetologists are working with the Declining Amphibian Task Force to solve the mystery of the worldwide decline in amphibian populations.

go.hrw.com
SUPER SUMMARY
Keyword: HX8FSAS

Key Ideas	Key Terms

1 The Fish Body

> Fishes have endoskeletons, gills, closed-loop circulation and kidneys.

> Fishes have many structures for swimming and sensing their underwater environment, including endoskeletons, fins, swim bladders, and lateral lines.

> Fishes are able to obtain the oxygen they need from water.

> Although gills play a major role in maintaining a fish's salt and water balance, another key element is a pair of kidneys.

> Most fishes reproduce sexually through external fertilization.

swim bladder (730)
lateral line (730)
gill (731)
gill slit (731)
kidney (732)

2 Groups of Fishes

> Jawless fishes have cartilaginous skeletons, but lack a backbone. They retain their notochord into adulthood.

> Cartilaginous fishes have paired fins and jaws. They also have skeletons made of cartilage strengthened by calcium carbonate (the material that makes up oyster shells).

> Bony fishes have a strong endoskeleton made completely of bone. Bony fishes also have structural adaptations, such as lateral lines, opercula, and swim bladders, that contribute to their success.

operculum (736)
teleost (738)

3 The Amphibian Body

> Most amphibians share five key characteristics: legs, lungs, double-loop circulation, a partially divided heart, and cutaneous respiration.

> The senses of sight and hearing are well developed in most amphibians. The primary sensory organs of amphibians are the eyes and ears.

> In amphibians, the skin, lungs, double-loop circulation, and a partially divided heart work together to ensure that sufficient oxygen reaches the body tissues.

> The structure of the amphibian circulatory system—including a partially divided heart and double-loop circulation—allows oxygen to be delivered to the body more efficiently than in fishes.

**tympanic
    membrane** (740)
lung (741)
septum (742)
pulmonary vein (743)

4 Groups of Amphibians

> Salamanders have elongated bodies; long tails; and smooth, moist skin.

> Caecilians are a highly specialized group of burrowing amphibians with small, bony scales embedded in their skin.

> There are about 4,000 species of frogs and toads, also known as anurans, which live in environments ranging from deserts to rain forests, valleys to mountains, and ponds to puddles.

tadpole (747)

Chapter 30 Review

READING TOOLBOX

1. **Comparisons** Write a paragraph that compares three key features of fishes and amphibians.

2. **Concept Map** Use the following terms to make a concept map describing the characteristics of jawless, cartilaginous, and bony fishes: *gills, countercurrent flow, cartilage, operculum,* and *teleosts.*

Using Key Terms

Use each of the following terms in a separate sentence.

3. *lateral line*

4. *swim bladder*

5. *tympanic membrane*

Use the following terms in the same sentence.

6. *lung* and *pulmonary vein*

7. *gill* and *countercurrent flow*

Understanding Key Ideas

8. Which of the following characteristics is *not* found in all three major groups of fishes?
   a. gills
   b. jaws
   c. endoskeleton
   d. single-loop circulation

9. In bony fishes, males and females release their gametes into the water in a process called
   a. courtship
   b. spawning
   c. copulation
   d. internal fertilization

10. Teleost fishes have been successful relative to all other bony fishes because they have
   a. a swim bladder.
   b. double-loop circulation.
   c. fins with a central core of bone.
   d. a jaw that is able to protrude forward.

11. Most adult amphibians respire
   a. through their skin only.
   b. through their lungs only.
   c. through their skin and gills.
   d. through their skin and lungs.

12. Which one of the following features is found in both cartilaginous and bony fishes?
   a. operculum
   b. paired fins
   c. bony skeleton
   d. swim bladder

13. Which of the following amphibian characteristics is not an adaptation especially for life on land?
   a. legs
   b. lungs
   c. efficient heart
   d. specialized eggs

14. Which of the following is not a characteristic of amphibians?
   a. heart with two ventricles
   b. lungs and moist skin
   c. cutaneous respiration
   d. double-loop circulation

15. Which of the following is true of salamander reproduction?
   a. The eggs are laid on dry land.
   b. Young salamanders are herbivores.
   c. The young resemble adults.
   d. Fertilization is always external.

Use the diagram to answer the following question(s).

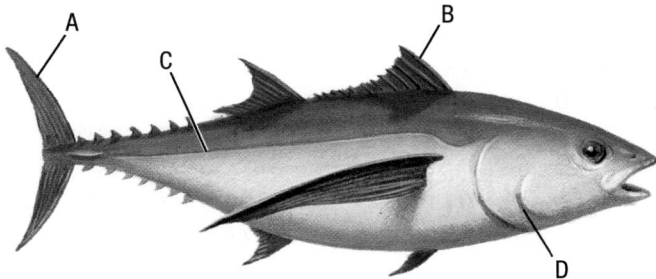

16. Which of the structures labeled on this fish allows the fish to sense vibrations in the water?
   a. structure A
   b. structure B
   c. structure C
   d. structure D

Explaining Key Ideas

17. **Explain** why some fishes, such as sharks, swim constantly with their mouth open.

18. **Describe** the function of paired fins in fishes.

19. **List** three structural adaptations that contribute to the success of bony fishes.

20. **Describe** how cutaneous respiration is beneficial to amphibians and why it limits their life on land.

Using Science Graphics

Use the diagram to answer the following question(s).

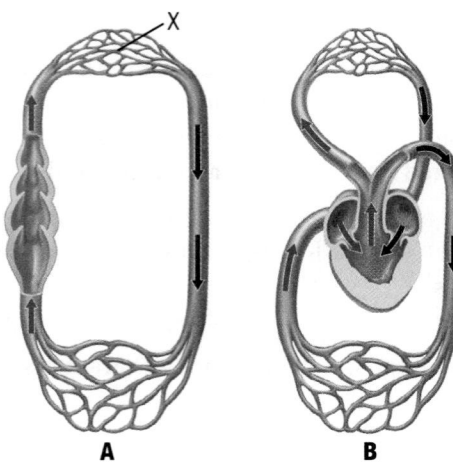

21. What is the location of the capillaries that are labeled *X* in the diagram?
  a. in the gills
  b. in the brain
  c. in the lungs
  d. in other body organs

22. In which environment would you be most likely to find an animal that has circulatory system B?
  a. deep ocean
  b. coral reef
  c. moist land habitat
  d. freshwater lake

23. Which statement applies to circulatory system A?
  a. Blood returns to the heart from the gills before being pumped to the rest of the body.
  b. The body organs receive fully oxygenated blood.
  c. A mixture of oxygen-rich and oxygen-poor blood is pumped to the gills.
  d. Blood is pumped to the body organs at a higher pressure than in circulatory system B.

Critical Thinking

24. Applying Information Determine whether the characteristics shared by all fish are mostly internal or external. Explain your answer.

25. Forming Reasoned Opinions You find a bizarre-looking animal that has washed up on an ocean beach. It might be a fish. How could you find out if it is a fish?

26. Predicting Results You catch two species of fish. One is streamlined and bullet shaped. The other is box shaped. Which of these fishes will swim faster? Explain your reasoning.

27. Justifying Conclusions Why do scientists think that the ancestor of amphibians was a lobe-finned fish rather than a ray-finned fish?

28. Applying Logic The word *amphibian* means "two lives". Explain why this term is appropriate for these animals.

29. Evaluating Statements You read in a magazine that a characteristic of all amphibians is a dramatic metamorphosis at some point in their life. Do you think that this statement is true? Why or why not?

30. Inferring Relationships What is the likely reason that most amphibians have small bodies?

Methods of Science

31. Forming a Hypothesis Form a hypothesis that explains why lungfishes have double-loop circulation instead of the single-loop circulation of all other fishes.

Writing for Science

32. Essay Writing Write a short essay explaining either why the swim bladder has helped bony fishes be more successful than cartilaginous fishes or why it is not important to their success.

33. Writing for an Audience Write a script for a short lecture to younger students about the three main groups of fishes. Be sure to describe how to identify each kind of fish.

Alternative Assessment

34. Anatomy Poster Use library resources and the Internet to compare the body shapes and dentition of two different types of cartilaginous fishes. Create a poster based on your research. Concentrate on showing the features that indicate how the fishes live and what they eat. If possible, present your poster to your classmates.

35. Ode to an Amphibian Write a short poem or song dedicated to your favorite amphibian. Try to explain why it is your favorite amphibian and describe the characteristics you would notice about it as it grows up.

Science Concepts

1. Amphibians must lay eggs in water primarily for what reason?
   A The eggs are not laid in nests.
   B The eggs need protection from predators.
   C The eggs do not have a shell to prevent water loss.
   D The eggs need to absorb oxygen and nutrients from water.

2. What is the function of a fish's lateral line system?
   F initiates spawning   H acts as camouflage
   G detects vibrations   J excretes wastes

3. Metamorphosis must take place before anurans are able to do what?
   A swim
   B live on land
   C respire with gills
   D feed themselves

4. Which of the following is not involved in controlling buoyancy in fishes?
   F a fat-filled liver
   G the lateral line
   H the swim bladder
   J continuous swimming

5. A shark's skeleton is
   A very dense.   C composed of bone.
   B quite rigid.   D composed of cartilage.

Writing Skills

6. **Short Response** Compare amphibian metamorphosis with insect metamorphosis.

Using Science Graphics

This diagram shows a cross section of a frog heart. Use the diagram to answer the following question(s).

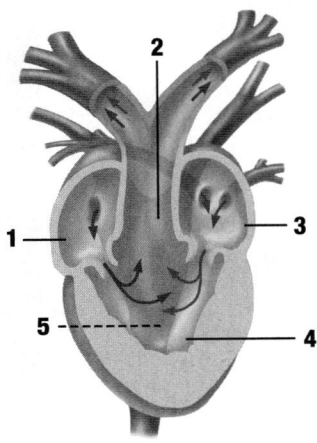

7. Identify the source of blood flow in the section of the heart labeled *1*.
   A the body   C the lungs
   B the aorta   D both lungs and body

Use the graph to answer the following question(s).

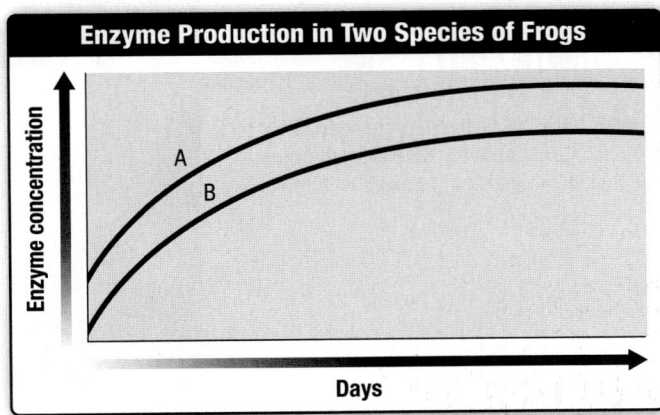

8. When tadpoles undergo metamorphosis, their bodies begin to produce an enzyme that converts ammonia into urea. The time that a tadpole takes to produce this enzyme varies among species. In the graph, the rate of enzyme production is shown for a species that inhabits a desertlike environment and a species that inhabits a forest environment. Which curve represents which frog? Explain.

Chapter 31

Reptiles and Birds

Preview

1 The Reptile Body
Characteristics of Reptiles
Movement and Response
Respiration and Circulation
Reproduction

2 Groups of Reptiles
Turtles and Tortoises
Tuataras
Crocodilians
Lizards and Snakes

3 The Bird Body
Characteristics of Birds
Adaptations of Birds
Respiration and Circulation
Reproduction

4 Groups of Birds
Terrestrial Birds
Aquatic Birds

Why It Matters

Reptiles were the first vertebrates capable of living in dry habitats. Birds evolved from reptiles and share many features with them.

This eyelash viper, a reptile, is close to making a meal out of the fleeing rufous-tailed hummingbird.

The snake hid behind this heliconia flower, a favorite feeding spot for hummingbirds. These tiny birds eat constantly. Their metabolism requires them to consume almost as many calories as an adult human consumes!

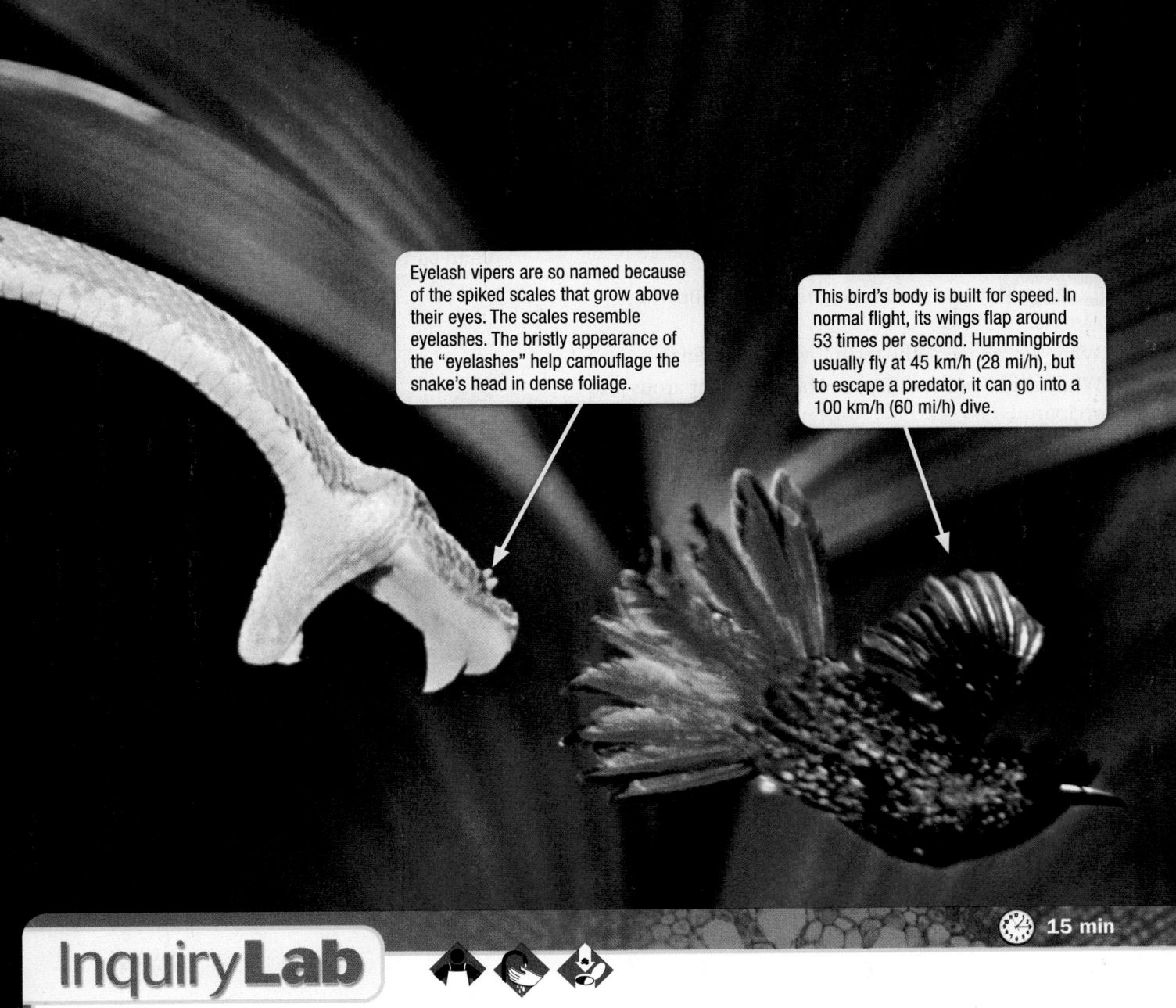

Eyelash vipers are so named because of the spiked scales that grow above their eyes. The scales resemble eyelashes. The bristly appearance of the "eyelashes" help camouflage the snake's head in dense foliage.

This bird's body is built for speed. In normal flight, its wings flap around 53 times per second. Hummingbirds usually fly at 45 km/h (28 mi/h), but to escape a predator, it can go into a 100 km/h (60 mi/h) dive.

InquiryLab

15 min

Amniotic Eggs

Both reptiles and birds produce amniotic eggs. In this lab, you will examine the structure of a familiar amniotic egg—a chicken egg.

Procedure

1. Examine a **chicken egg.** Set the egg on the floor. Push it gently, and observe how it moves.

2. Carefully crack the egg, and pour its contents into a **bowl.**

3. Examine a piece of the shell. Use a **forceps** to peel the shell away from its underlying membrane. With a **hand lens,** closely examine the shell and the membrane.

4. Use the hand lens to examine other membranes in the bowl. On the surface of the yolk, find a whitish spot about the size of a pinhead. This is the part of the egg that develops into an embryo.

Analysis

1. **State** whether the egg rolls in a straight line. How might its rolling behavior be an advantage?

2. **Explain** why the yolk and egg white don't mix freely.

3. **Infer** why a developing chick would require a yolk.

READING TOOLBOX

These reading tools can help you learn the material in this chapter. For more information on how to use these and other tools, see **Appendix: Reading and Study Skills.**

Using Words

Word Parts Knowing the meanings of word parts can help you figure out the meanings of words that you do not know.

Your Turn Use the table to answer the following questions.

1. What do you think the term "ovulate" means?
2. What might be the difference between oviparous and viviparous?
3. Can you guess what ovoviviparous means?

Word Meanings		
Word part	Part	Meaning
ovi-	prefix	egg
vivi-	prefix	alive, living
par	root	give birth to
-ous	suffix	of, having to do with

Using Language

Comparisons Comparing is a way of looking for the similarities between different things. Contrasting is a way of looking for the differences. Certain words and phrases can help you recognize when things are being compared or contrasted. Comparison words include *and, like, just as,* and *in the same way.* Contrast words include *however, unlike, in contrast,* and *on the other hand.*

Your Turn In the following sentences, find the things that are being compared or contrasted.

1. Unlike other reptiles, the bodies of turtles have a bony shell.
2. Lizards walk with a side-to-side motion, in the same way that salamanders do.
3. Like birds, turtles have beaks and lack teeth. However, unlike birds, turtles do not have feathers.

Using FoldNotes

Double-Door Fold A double-door fold is useful when you want to compare the characteristics of two topics. The double-door fold can organize characteristics of the two topics side by side under the flaps.

Your Turn Make a double-door fold to help you organize characteristics of reptiles and birds.

1. Fold a sheet of paper in half from the top to the bottom. Then unfold the paper.
2. Fold the top and bottom edges of the paper to the center crease.
3. Write "Reptiles" on the front of the top fold. Write "Birds" on the front of the bottom fold.
4. Write the characteristics of reptiles and birds under the fold for each group.

The Reptile Body

Key Ideas	Key Terms	Why It Matters
❯ What are the key characteristics that distinguish modern reptiles? ❯ Which characteristics allow reptiles to move through and sense terrestrial environments? ❯ How are a reptile's heart and lungs more efficient than an amphibian's? ❯ What structure is key to a reptile's success as a terrestrial animal?	Jacobson's organ ectothermic oviparous ovoviviparous	Reptiles were the first group of vertebrates to live completely on land. Birds and mammals evolved from reptiles.

Many people are afraid of reptiles, but these animals are important members of many ecosystems. Reptiles can help people by killing large numbers of insect pests and disease-spreading rodents.

Characteristics of Reptiles

Reptiles were the first vertebrates to live completely on land, thanks to an egg that doesn't dry out and a body that is covered with scales. These scales, visible in **Figure 1,** keep moisture inside. Reptiles dominated the land for millions of years, especially during the Age of Dinosaurs. Ancient reptiles came in all shapes and sizes and inhabited not only the land but also the air and the oceans.

Today, reptiles can be found in a range of habitats from deserts to tropical forests and even oceans, rivers, and lakes. However, reptiles are not found in very cold regions, where survival is impossible for a cold-blooded animal. All reptiles share certain characteristics that have been retained from the time when reptiles replaced amphibians as the dominant land vertebrates. ❯ **Modern reptiles have scales, clawed toes, and an ectothermic metabolism, and reptiles lack feathers or hair.** Reptiles also have dry, scaly skin that is virtually watertight. Internally, reptiles have a strong skeleton, well-developed lungs, and a heart with a partially divided ventricle. Reptiles reproduce by internal fertilization, and they lay amniotic eggs that are almost watertight.

❯ **Reading Check** *How are reptiles adapted to life on land? (See the Appendix for answers to Reading Checks.)*

Dry, scaly skin helps reptiles retain fluids.

Claws allow reptiles to get a good grip on the ground.

Figure 1 Reptiles have adaptations that free them from the water requirements of amphibians.
❯ How is this lizard different from an amphibian?

QuickLab

15 min

Identity of Ectotherms

The body temperature of all animals changes during the course of a day. The way that the body temperature changes can help you identify an animal as an ectotherm or an endotherm.

Analysis

1. **Analyze** the data, and determine which animal, Species A or Species B, is most likely an ectotherm. Explain your reasoning.

2. **Identify** the time of day that the animal you identified as an ectotherm reaches its lowest body temperature.

3. **Identify** the time of day that the animal you identified as an ectotherm reaches its highest body temperature.

4. **Propose** a reason why the ectotherm's body temperature is highest at this time.

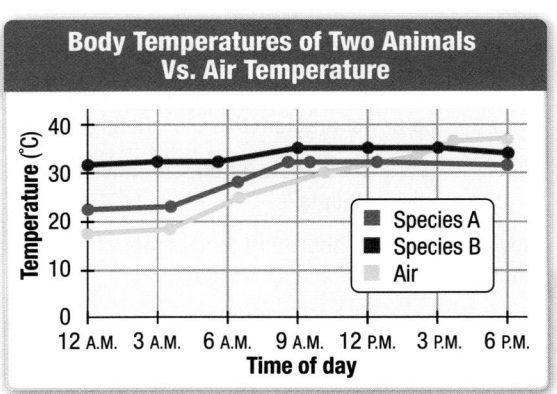

Body Temperatures of Two Animals Vs. Air Temperature

5. **CRITICAL THINKING** **Making Predictions** An endotherm is an animal that maintains its own body heat. Identify which species on the graph is an endotherm, and predict what its graph line would look like if it showed body temperature between 6 P.M. and midnight.

READING TOOLBOX

Word Parts Several words in this chapter begin with the prefixes *ecto-* and *endo-*. Use a dictionary to find the meanings of these prefixes.

Jacobson's organ an olfactory sac that opens into the mouth and is highly developed in reptiles

ectothermic describes the ability of an organism to maintain its body temperature by gaining heat from the environment

Movement and Response

To survive on land, an organism must move and respond to its environment differently than an organism living in water does. ❯ Reptiles have a strong skeleton, claws, legs positioned under the body, and highly developed vision. These adaptations help reptiles navigate dry environments. However, because reptiles are cold-blooded (ectothermic), the range of most reptile species is limited.

Endoskeleton Reptiles have a strong skeleton that is made of bone. Most reptiles have two pairs of limbs, but snakes and some lizards have no legs. The legs of reptiles are positioned more directly under the body than the limbs of amphibians are. Therefore, reptiles can move faster and more easily on land than amphibians can. However, reptiles' legs are not directly under their body in the way that mammals' legs are. As a result, reptiles are slower than most mammals are and lose energy more quickly. Unlike amphibians, reptiles have toes with claws, which are used for climbing and digging. Claws also allow reptiles to get a good grip on the ground, which enables reptiles to run quickly over short distances.

Sensory Systems Vision is an important sense for most reptiles. Many reptiles rely on their sense of sight to detect predators and prey. As **Figure 2** shows, the eyes of reptiles are usually large. Except for snakes and some geckos, reptiles have movable eyelids. Many species have keen vision. Some species, like geckos, are active at night and can see even when there is very little light. Hearing is also an important sense. As in amphibians, sound waves first strike the tympanum, or eardrum, and then are transmitted to the inner ear.

Snakes do not have a tympanum. They are able to detect ground vibrations by sensing the vibrations through the bones of their jaw. If you watch a snake or lizard, you may see it stick its tongue out and then pull it back into its mouth. When a reptile sticks its tongue out, the tongue collects small particles from the air. These particles come in contact with the Jacobson's organ when the tongue is drawn back into the mouth. The **Jacobson's organ** is a specialized sense organ in the roof of the mouth of many reptiles. The Jacobson's organ is sensitive to odors. So when a reptile flicks its tongue, it is "tasting" its environment! Some snakes can also sense the heat given off by warm-bodied prey, such as mammals and birds. These snakes have one heat-sensitive pit below each eye. These pit organs allow the snake to determine the direction of and distance to a warm object.

Body Temperature Control Reptiles are **ectothermic,** which means that they cannot heat their own body by using their metabolism. As a result, a reptile's body temperature is mostly <u>determined</u> by the temperature of the animal's environment. However, reptiles are not totally dependent on the climate. As **Figure 3** shows, many reptiles can change the temperature of their body by basking in the sun to warm up or seeking shade to cool down. A lizard can keep its body at a nearly constant temperature throughout the day by moving between sunlight and shade. At very low temperatures, most reptiles slow down and may not be able to function. This inability to tolerate cold weather limits the geographical range of most reptiles. In areas with warm summers but cold winters, reptiles are not active during winter.

> **Reading Check** *Why does being ectothermic limit reptiles' range?*

Figure 2 This gecko is keeping its vision clear by cleaning its eyes with its tongue. Geckos, like other reptiles, also use their tongue to smell their environment.

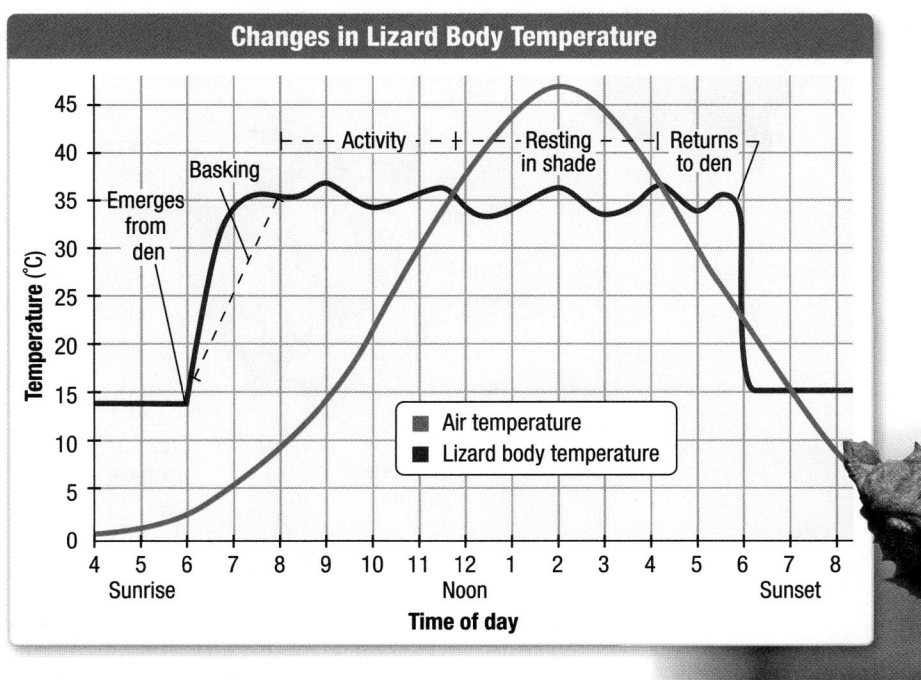

Changes in Lizard Body Temperature

- Activity
- Basking
- Resting in shade
- Returns to den
- Emerges from den

Temperature (°C): 45, 40, 35, 30, 25, 20, 15, 10, 5, 0

Time of day: 4 (Sunrise), 5, 6, 7, 8, 9, 10, 11, 12 (Noon), 1, 2, 3, 4, 5, 6, 7, 8 (Sunset)

- Air temperature
- Lizard body temperature

Figure 3 A lizard may regulate its body temperature by moving repeatedly between sun and shade. > **How do lizards increase their body temperature when they first emerge from their den in the morning?**

759

Respiration and Circulation

❯ **A reptile's lungs have a large surface area, and a reptile's heart is almost completely divided into four chambers.** These adaptations result in more-efficient respiration and circulation, which are necessary because reptiles are scale covered and cannot breathe through their skin as amphibians can.

Lungs As **Figure 4** shows, the lungs of most reptiles have many internal folds, which give the lungs a large surface area for oxygen exchange. So, reptiles can exchange more oxygen with each breath than amphibians can. Strong muscles in a reptile's rib cage move air into and out of the lungs quickly and thus maximize lung efficiency.

Heart Recall that the ventricle of an amphibian heart is not divided by a septum. So, some mixing of oxygen-poor blood and oxygen-rich blood occurs in the amphibian's ventricle. In most reptiles, the septum partly divides the ventricle into right and left halves. The septum enables a much better, but still incomplete, separation of oxygen-rich and oxygen-poor blood. As a result, oxygen is delivered to the body cells in reptiles more efficiently than it is in amphibians.

❯ **Reading Check** *Compare reptilian and amphibian circulation.*

oviparous (oh VIP uh ruhs) describes organisms that produce eggs that develop and hatch outside the body of the mother

ovoviviparous describes organisms that produce eggs that develop and hatch inside the body of the mother

www.scilinks.org
Topic: Characteristics of Reptiles
Code: HX80261

Figure 4 This reptile's lungs contain many internal folds, and its heart has a partially divided ventricle. ❯ **How would the surface area of the lungs change if the lungs did not have folds?**

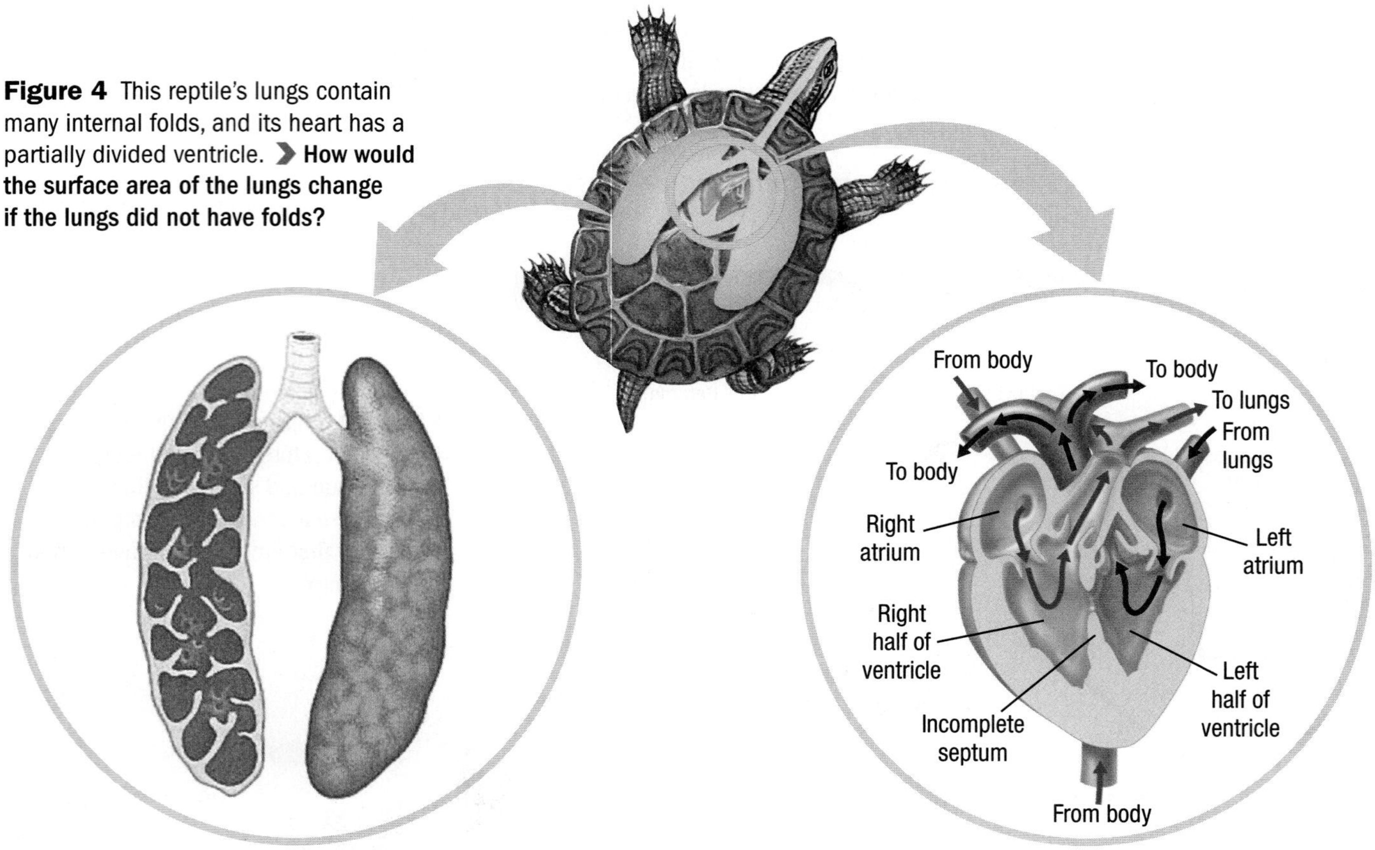

A reptile's scaly skin does not permit gas exchange. So reptiles, unlike amphibians, use only the lungs for respiration. The many folds in a reptile's lungs increase the lungs' surface area and thus their efficiency.

Oxygen-poor blood from the body enters the right atrium of a reptile's heart. The blood is pumped to the lungs. Oxygenated blood returns to the left atrium. From there, the blood moves into the left ventricle and then on to the body's tissues.

Reproduction

Reptilian eggs are fertilized inside the female through internal fertilization. Internal fertilization protects the gametes from drying out on land. Many reptiles are **oviparous,** which means that the young hatch from eggs that are laid outside of the mother's body. Most snakes and lizards and all turtles, tortoises, and crocodilians are oviparous. The eggs of most reptiles are not protected by the parents. However, mother alligators and crocodiles will guard their nests aggressively and care for their young. In addition, some snakes and lizards are **ovoviviparous,** which means that fertilized eggs remain inside the female's body for a long time and often hatch inside the mother. By keeping eggs inside their body, ovoviviparous reptiles protect their eggs from predators.

Amniotic Egg For a reptile living on dry land, reproduction presents a serious water-loss problem. Without a moist environment, eggs dry out. Recall that the amniotic egg, shown in **Figure 5,** solves this problem. ❯ **An amniotic egg contains both a water supply and a food supply and is key to a reptile's success as a terrestrial animal.** A tough shell makes the egg essentially watertight. Most reptiles, all birds, and three mammal species reproduce by using amniotic eggs.

In an amniotic egg, the shell and the albumen (egg white) protect and cushion the developing embryo. The albumen is also a source of nutrients for the embryo. Within the egg, four specialized membranes maintain a stable environment for the embryo. The amnion cushions the embryo in a watery environment. The yolk sac contains the embryo's main food supply. Blood vessels connect the embryo's gut to the yolk sac. The allantois stores waste and is the embryo's organ for gas exchange. The chorion allows oxygen to enter the egg and allows carbon dioxide to leave the egg.

❯ **Reading Check** *Summarize the structure of an amniotic egg.*

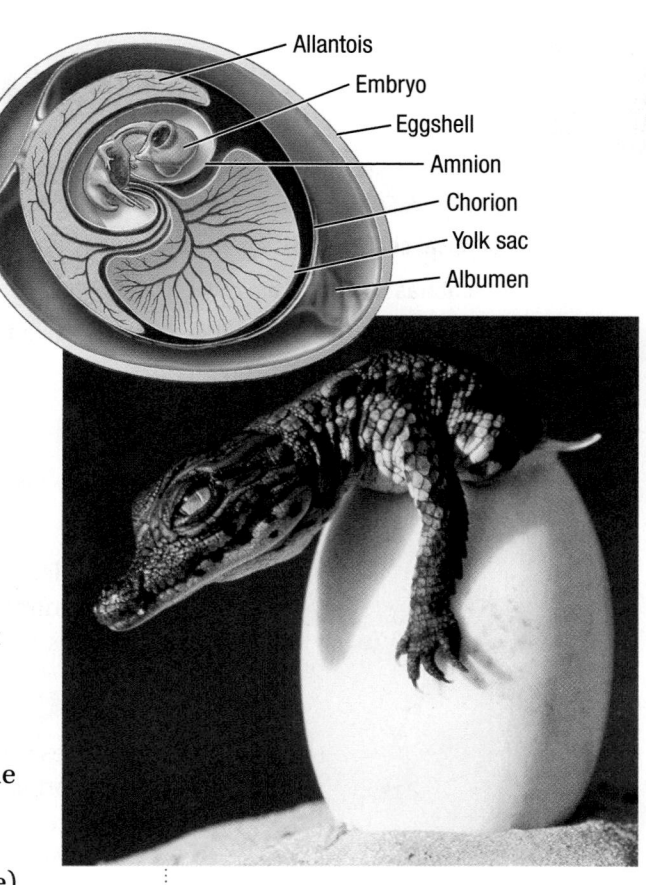

Allantois
Embryo
Eggshell
Amnion
Chorion
Yolk sac
Albumen

Figure 5 Reptiles and birds have very similar eggs. This bird's egg (left) shows the main structures of the amniotic egg. This young crocodile (right) used a tooth on the tip of its snout, called an *egg tooth,* to break open its egg.

Section 1 Review

❯ **KEY IDEAS**

1. **Identify** seven characteristics of reptiles.
2. **Describe** how being ectothermic influences a reptile's lifestyle.
3. **Explain** how reptiles meet their need for oxygen.
4. **Summarize** how the amniotic egg allows reptiles to live on land.

CRITICAL THINKING

5. **Drawing Conclusions** Crocodiles have a heart with a completely divided ventricle. How does this heart structure affect a crocodile's circulatory system?
6. **Making Inferences** Do you think that a reptile that cares for its young lays more or fewer eggs than a reptile that doesn't care for its young? Explain your answer.

METHODS OF SCIENCE

7. **Forming Hypotheses** Several species of ovoviviparous reptiles live in colder climates than most other reptiles do. Why might ovoviviparity be advantageous in such climates?

Groups of Reptiles

Key Ideas	Key Terms	Why It Matters
› Which physical characteristics make turtles unique? › How are tuataras different from other reptiles? › Why are crocodilian young more likely to survive than the young of other reptiles? › How are snakes and lizards similar?	carapace plastron constrictor	Reptiles are important in many aquatic and terrestrial habitats. Some species are sources of food, and some reptiles help farmers by keeping pest populations low.

Reptiles once ruled the land. Today, mammals have become the dominant land animals, but four groups of reptiles—turtles and tortoises, tuataras, crocodilians, and lizards and snakes—still exist.

Turtles and Tortoises

Turtles and tortoises are very different from other reptiles. › **Turtles and tortoises have a hard shell that covers their body, and their spine is fused to the top of their shell.** Many can pull their head and legs into their shell to avoid predators. Tortoises live on land, and most species have a dome-shaped shell. Most turtles, as **Figure 6** shows, live in water. Turtles have a streamlined shell that permits rapid movement in water. The shell is made of fused plates of bone covered with horny shields or tough skin. The shell consists of two parts. The **carapace** is the top part of the shell. The **plastron** is the bottom portion. The shell provides the support for all of the muscle attachments in the torso.

Turtles and tortoises lack teeth but have jaws covered by sharp plates. Many are herbivores, but some, such as the snapping turtle, are aggressive carnivores. Turtles and tortoises lay their eggs in the ground and do not care for their eggs or their young.

› **Reading Check** *Describe the structure of a turtle's shell.*

SCI
LINKS.
www.scilinks.org
Topic: Adaptations of
Reptiles
Code: HX80023

Turtles and Tortoises
Modern turtles and tortoises differ little from 200-million-year-old turtle fossils.

Figure 6 Modern reptiles live in diverse habitats and have a wide variety of body forms. › **How do the heads of these three reptiles compare with each other?**

Tuataras

The two living species of tuataras are native to New Zealand. Tuataras look like lizards, but they are a completely distinct group of ancient reptiles. ❯ **Unlike most other reptiles, tuataras are more active at low temperatures.** They burrow or bask in the sun during the day and feed on insects, worms, and other small animals at night. Tuataras are sometimes called *living fossils* because they have survived nearly unchanged for 150 million years.

Crocodilians

Crocodilians include crocodiles, alligators, caimans, and gavials. Crocodilians are aggressive carnivores. Some species are very large. Nile crocodiles can reach 6 m (20 ft) in length and can weigh 750 kg (1,650 lb). Crocodilians usually capture prey by ambush. Some crocodilians float just below the water's surface near the shore. When an animal comes to drink, the crocodilian explodes out of the water, seizes its prey, and then hauls the prey into the water to be drowned and eaten. The crocodilian's body is well adapted for this form of hunting. Its eyes are high on its head, and its nostrils are on top of its snout, so the crocodilian can see and breathe while nearly submerged in water. In addition, crocodilians have very sharp teeth. The teeth help them tear apart, rather than chew, their prey.

Reproduction in crocodilians is unique among reptiles. ❯ **Unlike most other reptiles, crocodilians care for their young.** For instance, an American alligator builds a nest of vegetation for her eggs. After the eggs hatch, the mother may tear open the nest to free the hatchlings. The young alligators remain under her protection for about a year.

Hands-On

QuickLab

🕐 **15 min**

Model of Watertight Skin

Unlike an amphibian's skin, a reptile's skin is almost watertight. You can use grapes to model water loss in different types of skin.

Procedure

❶ Use a **scale** to weigh one **grape**, and record its mass in a data table. Then, place the grape in an open **Petri dish.**

❷ Using a **forceps**, peel the skin from the **second grape.** Measure and record the mass of the peeled grape. Then, place it in the Petri dish, but do not let the two grapes touch.

❸ After 15 min, measure and record the grapes' masses again.

Analysis

1. **CRITICAL THINKING** **Proposing Explanations** Calculate the difference between the original and final masses of the grapes. Propose an explanation for any changes in mass.

2. **Determine** which grape represents an amphibian's skin and which represents a reptile's skin.

3. **Explain** why watertight skin is an adaptation to terrestrial life.

carapace a shieldlike plate that covers the cephalothorax of some crustaceans and reptiles

plastron the bottom, or ventral, portion of a turtle's shell

Tuataras
Tuataras grow very slowly. It takes 10–20 years for them to reach sexual maturity.

Crocodilians
This young crocodilian is about to have a tasty snack.

Up Close Snakes

Rattlesnakes, as their name suggests, have a rattle at the end of their tail. The rattle typically consists of five to seven interlocking rings, and when shaken, it produces a rattling sound that serves as a warning.

Timber Rattlesnake

Scientific Name: *Crotalus horridus*
Size: typical length 90 to 150 cm (36 to 60 in.); maximum length 189 cm (74 in.)
Range: eastern and central United States, from northern New York to northern Florida, and west to central Texas
Habitat: prefers thick brush, dense woodland, or swamp
Diet: primarily small mammals

Fangs Rattlesnakes have hollow fangs. When the snake strikes, these hinged fangs swing forward and inject venom deep into the prey. The venom contains hemotoxins, proteins that destroy red blood cells and cause internal bleeding.

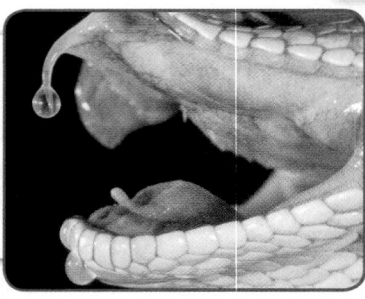

Jacobson's Organ A snake picks up particles in the air by flicking its tongue. The particles are carried to the roof of the mouth to the Jacobson's organ, which detects odors.

Tongue

Stomach

Trachea

Esophagus

Small intestine

Right lung

Left lung

Gallbladder

Internal Organs The internal organs are elongated, matching the snake's body shape. The left lung is nonfunctional.

Pancreas

Heart

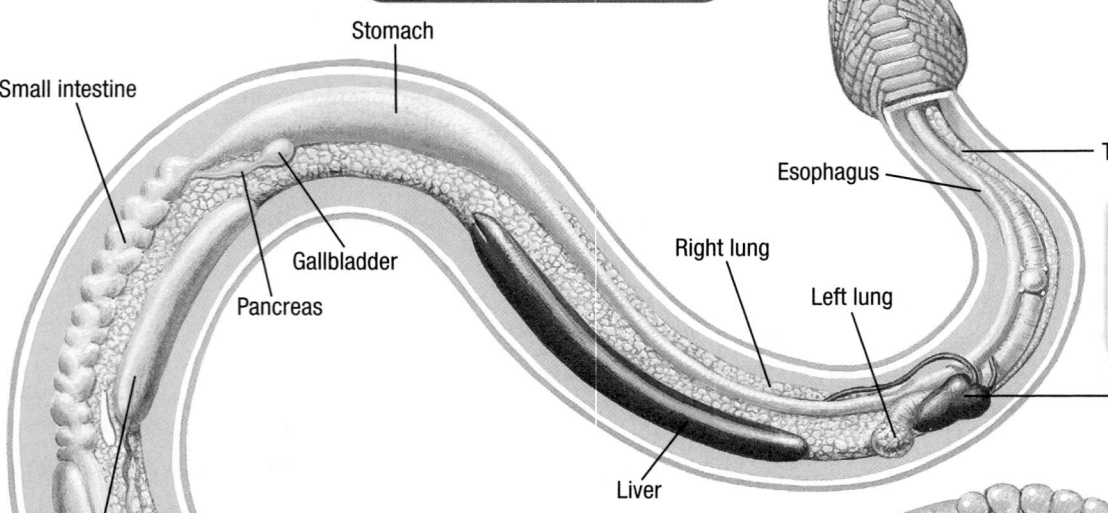

Liver

Large intestine

Kidneys

Testes

Cloaca

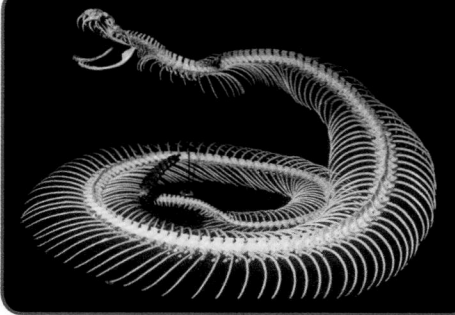

Reproductive Structures This male snake's testes produce sperm. Female rattlesnakes are ovoviviparous. After the eggs hatch in the mother's body, the young are ejected and must fend for themselves.

Spine A rattlesnake's spine is made up of several hundred vertebrae and ribs. It provides the framework for thousands of muscles that move not only the skeleton but also the snake's skin.

Lizards and Snakes

Snakes are close relatives of lizards; both reptiles evolved millions of years ago from an ancestor with legs. ❯ **Because lizards and snakes share a common ancestor, they have many features in common, including periodic molting and a jaw that is only loosely attached to the skull. This jaw allows the mouth to open wide enough to accommodate large prey.**

Lizards Common lizards include iguanas, geckos, anoles, and horned lizards (often mistakenly called *horny toads*). A few species of lizards are herbivores, but most are carnivores. Lizards are found in tropical forests and deserts. Some are fast runners, whereas others, such as the chameleon in **Figure 7,** are good climbers. Most lizards are small—less than 30 cm (1 ft) in length. The tail of some species of lizards breaks off easily, allowing the lizard to escape when attacked by a predator. Lizards can generate a new tail, but the new tail does not have any vertebrae in it. Some lizards are legless like snakes are. But unlike snakes, lizards have external ears and eyelids.

Snakes Snakes swallow their prey whole, but they still eat very large prey. The snake's jaw is very flexible because the jaw has five points of movement. (Your jaw has only one movement point.) In a snake, one of these points is the chin, where the halves of the lower jaw are connected by an elastic ligament. This ligament allows the lower jaw to spread apart when a large meal is being swallowed.

Many large snakes, such as boas and pythons, are constrictors. Some smaller species, such as king snakes, are also constrictors. **Constrictors** wrap their body around their prey, gradually squeezing tighter until the prey suffocates. The snakes then swallow their prey whole. Like all snakes' teeth, constrictors' teeth are not suited for cutting and chewing. Other snakes, such as cobras, vipers, and copperheads, kill their prey with venom. In most venomous snakes, <u>modified</u> salivary glands produce venom that is injected into the victim through grooved or hollow teeth.

Most snakes lay eggs. The mother may stay with the eggs until they hatch. Other snakes, such as the timber rattlesnake, featured in the UpClose feature, are ovoviviparous and give birth to live young.

❯ **Reading Check** *Describe the ways that snakes kill their prey.*

Figure 7 A chameleon changes its colors in response to variations in temperature, light, or even its mood!

---

constrictor a snake that kills its prey by crushing and suffocating it

ACADEMIC VOCABULARY

modify to change or make different

Section 2 Review

❯ KEY IDEAS

1. **Summarize** the ways turtles and tortoises differ from other reptiles.
2. **Compare** tuataras with lizards.
3. **Contrast** the parental care shown by alligators with that shown by most other reptiles.
4. **Describe** the characteristics shared by lizards and snakes.

CRITICAL THINKING

5. **Recognizing Relationships** How does a crocodile's nostril and eye position relate to its lifestyle?
6. **Making Inferences** When a lizard's tail breaks off, the tail may wiggle by itself. How is this adaptation advantageous for the lizard?

MATH SKILLS

7. **Problem Solving** About 8,000 snake bites occur in the United States each year. Around 0.15% of these bites are fatal. Approximately how many people die from snake bites in this country every year?

Key Ideas	Key Terms	Why It Matters
❯ What are the key characteristics of modern birds? ❯ How is a bird's body adapted for flight? ❯ How do birds meet their need for a large amount of oxygen? ❯ How does bird reproduction differ from reptilian reproduction?	endothermic contour feather down feather	Birds are masters of the air and are built perfectly for flight. By learning about birds' bodies, we can understand more about flight.

For many people, birds might be the most familiar animals seen in the wild. Birds' mastery of the air has allowed these animals to thrive in almost any environment from the open oceans to Antarctica, in dense tropical forests, deserts, and even cities. Many people enjoy watching the great range of colors, sizes, and behaviors of birds. Birds are the direct descendents of carnivorous dinosaurs and are close relatives of modern reptiles. The ancestors of birds were reptiles that most likely took flight in order to escape from predators and to find food, such as insects flying in the air.

Characteristics of Birds

Most people marvel at a bird's ability to fly, but there is more to birds than flight. In fact, some birds can't fly at all. Penguins have lost the ability to fly but have gained the ability to dive deep beneath the ocean's surface. The birds that you see today are the members of class Aves, but they have retained some reptilian characteristics. For instance, birds lay amniotic eggs that are very similar to those of reptiles, and the feet and legs of birds are covered with scales. But as you can see by looking at the bird in **Figure 8,** birds have many characteristics that are unique. Wings and a body covered by feathers are the most obvious characteristics that are different from reptiles. Also, birds have a beak that almost always lacks teeth, and their bony tail is much shorter than a reptile's tail is. Other differences include hollow bones, special lungs, and a warm-blooded (endothermic) metabolism. ❯ **The key characteristics of modern birds include feathers, wings, lightweight skeleton, endothermic metabolism, lungs with air sacs, and a beak.**

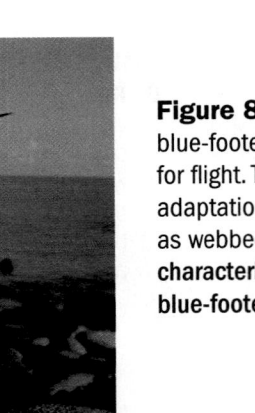

Figure 8 Like most birds, this blue-footed booby is well adapted for flight. This bird also has adaptations for swimming, such as webbed feet. ❯ **List several characteristics of birds that this blue-footed booby displays.**

QuickLab

🕐 10 min

Average Bone Density

Density is the ratio of an object's mass to the object's volume. Thus, you can calculate an object's density by dividing its mass by its volume. Several teams of students determined the density of bones from two different animals. You can use students' data, which is shown in the table at right, to practice calculating average bone density. Remember to express your answers in grams per cubic centimeter.

Bone type	Team 1	Team 2	Team 3	Team 4
Animal 1	1.6 g/cm^3	1.0 g/cm^3	1.2 g/cm^3	1.4 g/cm^3
Animal 2	2.3 g/cm^3	1.8 g/cm^3	1.8 g/cm^3	2.1 g/cm^3

Procedure

1. Add the densities of one bone type. For example, if three bone samples from an animal have densities of 3.0, 3.1, and 2.9 g/cm^3, their sum is 9.0 g/cm^3.

2. Divide the sum of the densities by the number of samples.

$$\frac{average}{density} = \frac{\text{sum of the densities}}{\text{number of samples}} = \frac{9.0 \text{ g/cm}^3}{3} = 3.0 \text{ g/cm}^3$$

Analysis

1. **Calculate** the average bone density for each of the two animals in the data table.

2. **CRITICAL THINKING** **Evaluating Methods** Why is it important to analyze several samples and obtain the average of your data?

3. **CRITICAL THINKING** **Drawing Conclusions** Based on your answer to item 1, which of the two animals is more likely to be a bird?

4. **CRITICAL THINKING** **Making Inferences** How is a bird's bone density an adaptation for flight?

Body Temperature and Control Birds are **endothermic,** which means that they generate enough heat through metabolism to maintain a high body temperature. As you can see in **Figure 9,** birds can maintain their body temperature even when their environment is very cold. Birds maintain body temperatures ranging from 40°C to 44°C (104°F to 111°F). These temperatures are significantly higher than the body temperature of most mammals. In comparison, your body temperature is about 37°C (98°F). These high temperatures in birds are due to a fast metabolism, which is needed to produce enough energy for flight.

The large amount of energy required to fly and regulate a bird's body heat is obtained by a quick and efficient digestive system. Some birds eat around one-half of their body weight in food every day. Food passes quickly through a bird's digestive system. For example, a thrush can eat blackberries, digest them, and excrete the seeds 45 minutes later. In contrast, food passes through the human digestive system in about 12 hours.

❯ **Reading Check** *How is a bird able to maintain a high body temperature even in an arctic environment?*

Figure 9 The endothermic nature of birds allows them to live in very cold habitats. Even so, birds such as this owl may roost in groups during the winter in order to conserve body heat. ❯ **In what other ways might a bird conserve body heat?**

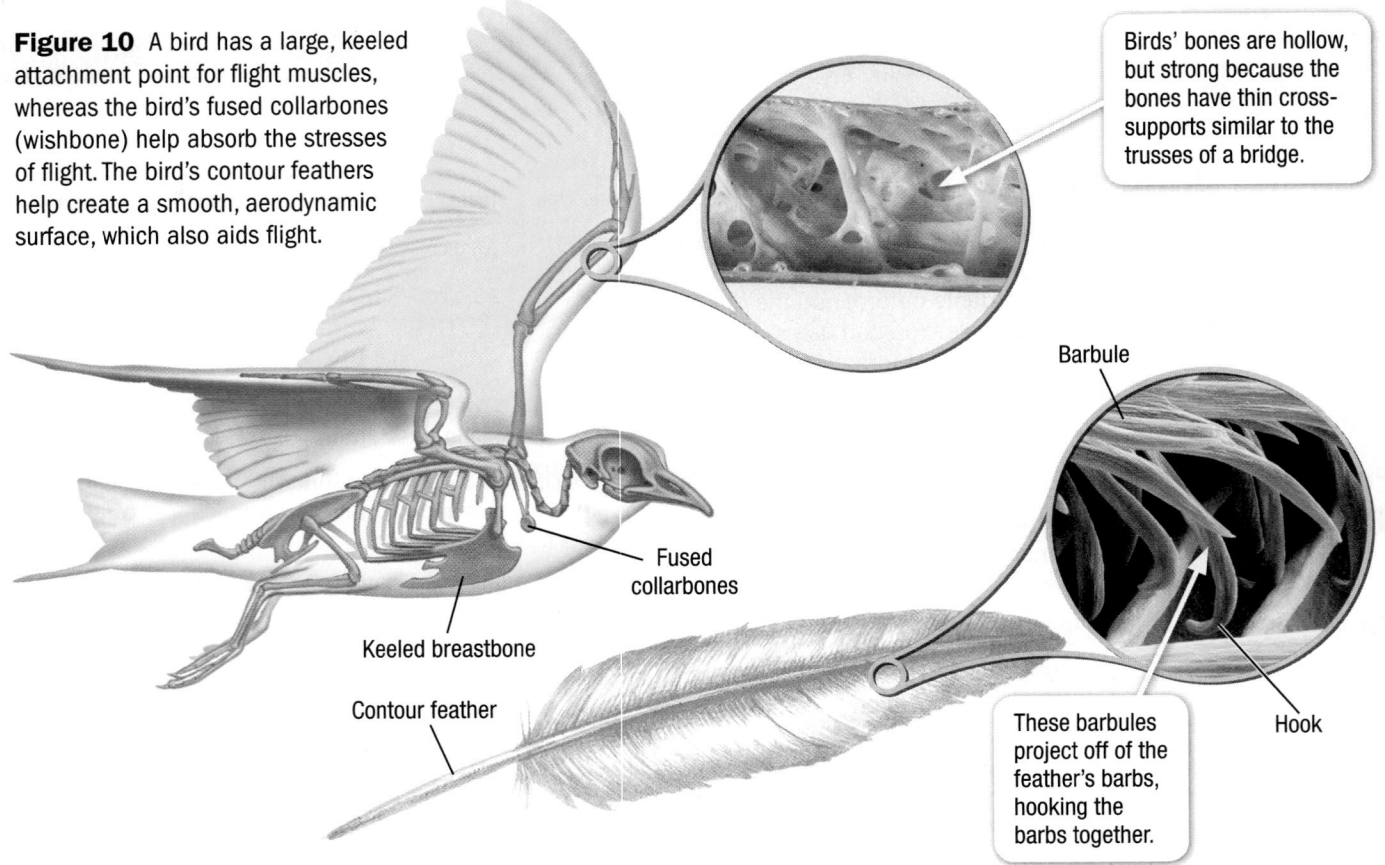

Figure 10 A bird has a large, keeled attachment point for flight muscles, whereas the bird's fused collarbones (wishbone) help absorb the stresses of flight. The bird's contour feathers help create a smooth, aerodynamic surface, which also aids flight.

Birds' bones are hollow, but strong because the bones have thin cross-supports similar to the trusses of a bridge.

Barbule

Fused collarbones

Keeled breastbone

Contour feather

These barbules project off of the feather's barbs, hooking the barbs together.

Hook

contour feather a type of feather that covers a bird and helps determine the bird's shape

down feather a type of soft feather that covers the body of young birds and provides insulation for adult birds

Adaptations of Birds

Flight requires a number of special adaptations. ❯ **Feathers and a strong, lightweight skeleton are critical to a bird's ability to fly.** In addition, a bird's beak and feet are adapted to the food that the bird eats and the environment that the bird lives in.

Feathers Birds have two main types of feathers: contour feathers and down feathers. **Contour feathers,** shown in **Figure 10,** cover an adult bird's body. Specialized contour feathers, called *flight feathers*, are found on a bird's wings and tail. These feathers help provide lift for flight. A contour feather has many branches called *barbs.* The barbs are linked together, giving the feather a smooth surface and a sturdy but flexible shape. **Down feathers** cover the body of young birds and are found beneath adult birds' contour feathers. The fluffy down feathers trap warm air, helping birds conserve body heat.

Lightweight Skeleton The bones of birds are thin and hollow. Many of the bones are fused, making a bird's skeleton more rigid than that of a reptile. The fused sections form a sturdy frame that anchors muscles during flight. The power for flight comes from large breast muscles that can make up 30% of a bird's body weight. These muscles stretch from the wing to the breastbone. The breastbone is very large and bears a prominent keel—like the V-shape of the bottom of a boat. Muscles are attached to the keel and to the fused collarbones. No other vertebrates have a keeled breastbone or fused collarbones.

Hummingbird

Toucan

Puffin

Figure 11 A bird's beak is adapted to the bird's diet. ❯ **How do you think that the toucan uses its beak to eat?**

Beaks and Feet Birds are adapted for different ways of life. Evolution has shaped birds' bodies to fit birds' various lifestyles. A person can learn a great deal about the diet and habits of a bird by simply examining the bird's beak, legs, and feet. Carnivorous birds, such as hawks, have curved talons for grabbing prey. These birds also have a razor sharp beak for tearing apart their meal.

Perching Birds and Flightless Birds Many species of birds have curved toes for holding onto branches. These birds are called perching birds. A canary is one example of a perching bird. A canary's beak is short and thick. This beak is perfect for crushing seeds, which are the mainstay of a canary's diet. Hummingbirds don't need to crush seeds. As you can see in **Figure 11,** hummingbirds have a long, thin beak for reaching into flowers to drink nectar. Some birds tend to have relatively long beaks for snatching insects out of the air. Woodpeckers have strong beaks for chipping through wood to expose insects living in trees. Some birds never land in trees—they can't even fly. These flightless birds, such as emus, have strong legs and feet with thick toes that are modified for running.

Marsh Birds and Water Birds Many birds live in marshes. Marsh birds have long toes that keep the bird from sinking into the mud and long legs to keep the bird's body above the water. These birds also have long beaks for catching fish or for digging in the mud for worms. Marsh birds are very clumsy when they try to land in a tree because their feet can't grip a branch very well. Also, water birds have trouble perching on branches because they have webbed feet for paddling, as **Figure 12** shows. Ducks are water birds that have rounded beaks for eating water plants. Water birds that eat fish have long beaks, and some birds have a hooked beak to grip slippery prey more easily. Other birds have sharp beaks that are used to spear fish.

❯ **Reading Check** *What type of beak does a seed-eating bird have?*

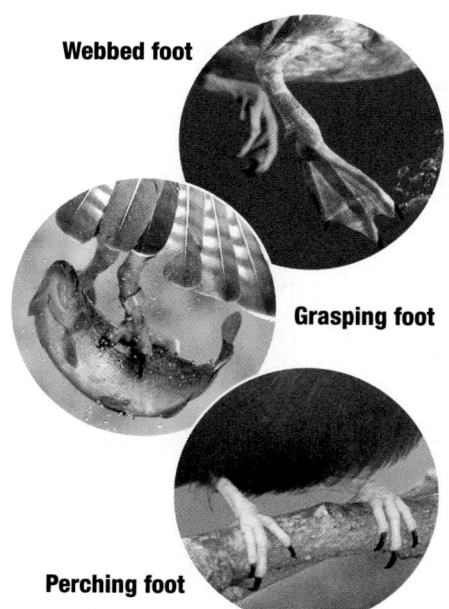

Webbed foot

Grasping foot

Perching foot

Figure 12 A bird's feet are adapted to the bird's lifestyle. Water birds have webbed feet for swimming. Birds of prey have grasping talons for seizing prey. Songbirds have perching feet for clinging to tree branches.

Respiration and Circulation

Birds use a huge amount of energy to fly. Because birds often fly for long periods of time, their cellular demand for energy <u>exceeds</u> that of even the most active mammals. ❯ **Birds have respiratory and circulatory structures, such as air sacs and a four-chambered heart, that improve the efficiency of oxygen intake and oxygen delivery and allow birds to get the energy that they need.**

Air Sacs Most vertebrates breathe in and then out, so there is a time period when fresh air is not flowing into the lung. Birds overcome this inefficiency by having air pass over a lung's surface in one direction only. One-way airflow is possible in birds because air sacs that are connected to a bird's lungs act as holding tanks for air, as **Figure 13** shows. There are two advantages to one-way airflow. First, the lungs are exposed only to fresh air, increasing the amount of oxygen that the lungs absorb. Second, the flow of blood in the lungs can run in a different direction than the flow of air does. This difference in direction increases oxygen absorption.

Four-Chambered Heart Blood from a bird's body enters the right atrium of the bird's heart. A small amount of specialized tissue lies in the muscular wall of the right atrium. This tissue is where the heartbeat originates and is known as the heart's pacemaker. A bird's heart rate can be extremely high in order to pump a large amount of oxygen to the bird's body. In addition to beating fast, a bird's heart works efficiently. The ventricle is completely divided by a septum. Oxygen-rich blood and oxygen-poor blood are kept separate, which means that oxygen is delivered to the body cells more efficiently.

❯ **Reading Check** *Describe the structure of a bird's heart.*

ACADEMIC VOCABULARY

exceed to be more than

READING TOOLBOX

Word Parts Examine Figure 13, which shows a bird's air sacs during inhalation and exhalation. What do you think the prefixes *in-* and *ex-* mean?

Figure 13 A bird's heart has a complete septum. A single breath of air stays in a bird's respiratory system for two cycles of inhalation and exhalation. ❯ **Summarize how one breath of air circulates through a bird's lungs.**

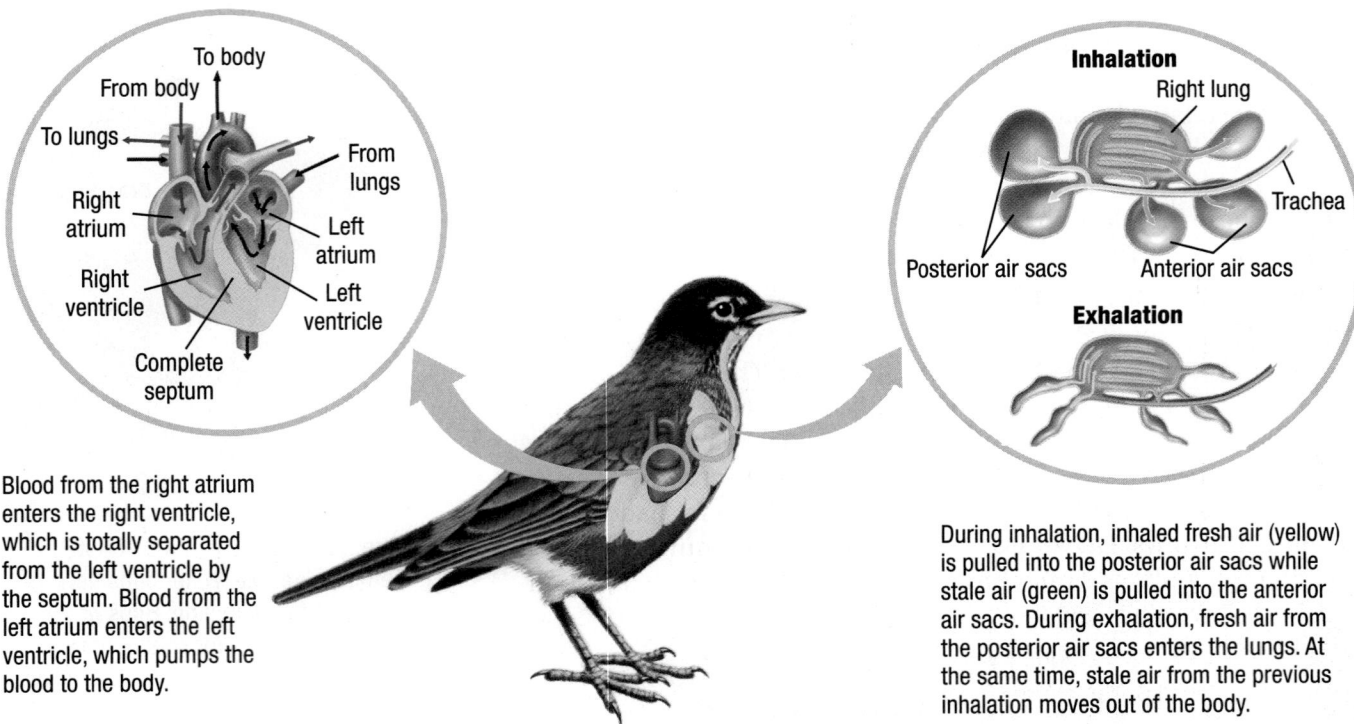

Blood from the right atrium enters the right ventricle, which is totally separated from the left ventricle by the septum. Blood from the left atrium enters the left ventricle, which pumps the blood to the body.

During inhalation, inhaled fresh air (yellow) is pulled into the posterior air sacs while stale air (green) is pulled into the anterior air sacs. During exhalation, fresh air from the posterior air sacs enters the lungs. At the same time, stale air from the previous inhalation moves out of the body.

Reproduction

Like reptiles, birds reproduce by using internal fertilization and an amniotic egg that resists drying out. Reptile eggs have a leathery shell, whereas bird eggs have a hard shell. During mating, the male bird presses his cloaca to the female's cloaca and releases sperm. A female may lay one egg or a clutch of several eggs.

Parental Care ❯ **Unlike most reptiles, most birds care for their eggs and for their young.** Birds usually lay their eggs in a nest. Nests hold the eggs, conceal young birds from predators, and provide shelter from the elements. Most birds build nests in well-hidden spots—ranging from holes in the ground to treetops. Woodpeckers, for example, nest in a hole that they have drilled in a tree. Orioles hang their nests from branches, well beyond the reach of predators. Birds construct their nests from almost any available material. Twigs, bark, grasses, feathers, and mud are common materials used in nests. One or both parents warm, or *incubate*, the eggs by sitting on them. Male emperor penguins incubate a single egg on top of their feet through the Antarctic winter.

Most species of birds form pairs that are made up of a male and a female. Sometimes a male and a female will spend their entire lives together and defend a territory. Even though the pair works together, the eggs laid by the female will commonly have several fathers and the male will fertilize eggs of other females. Once the eggs hatch, the young usually receive extensive parental care. In some cases, as with the African jacana shown in **Figure 14,** only one parent cares for the young. In other species, caring for hatchlings is an affair for the entire family, with the older siblings of the current chicks helping their parents feed the young. Some bird species, such as brown-headed cowbirds, do not care for their own young at all. Instead, they lay their eggs in the nest of another species, and let the other bird raise their chicks!

❯ **Reading Check** *Explain how different types of birds provide care for their young.*

Figure 14 After an African jacana female lays her eggs, the male incubates the eggs and cares for the young when they hatch. If a predator approaches, the father quickly scoops the young up under his wing and carries them to safety.

SC*I*LINKS.
www.scilinks.org
Topic: Characteristics
of Birds
Code: HX80255

Section 3 Review

❯ **KEY IDEAS**

1. **Summarize** how birds obtain the energy necessary for flight.
2. **Identify** a bird's adaptations for flight.
3. **Explain** the functions of the anterior and posterior air sacs.
4. **Describe** reproduction in birds.

CRITICAL THINKING

5. **Forming Reasoned Opinions** Some biologists have proposed that birds and reptiles should be grouped in the same class of vertebrates. Do you agree? Support your answer.
6. **Constructing Explanations** Why is it advantageous for birds to be oviparous rather than ovoviviparous?

ALTERNATIVE ASSESSMENT

7. **Making Observations** Design and build a bird feeder. Place the feeder where it can be easily observed. Keep a journal of your observations to share with your class. You may want to keep a bird field guide close to your journal so that you can identify unfamiliar bird species.

Key Ideas	Key Terms	Why It Matters
❯ How do the bodies of terrestrial birds reflect their lifestyle? ❯ What physical attributes characterize aquatic birds?	talon	Modern birds are important members of many ecosystems, and some birds help control insect populations.

Bird species are often categorized into six groups based on the birds' lifestyles. These groups include perching birds, birds of prey, flightless birds, water birds, wading birds, and diving birds.

Terrestrial Birds

Most perching birds, birds of prey, and flightless birds are terrestrial, which means that they live mainly on dry land. ❯ **Terrestrial birds have feet adapted to perching, hunting, or running and beaks adapted to eating fruits, seeds, insects, or small animals.**

Perching Birds Perching birds are by far the most common group of birds. In most perching birds, one toe on their foot points backward and the other toes point forward, which is perfect for getting a good grip on a branch. Some perching birds, like goldfinches, have thick, strong beaks for cracking seeds and nuts. Other species, such as the warbler shown in **Figure 15,** feed on insects and have long, thin beaks that are perfect for catching insects in the air or digging them out of the ground or tree trunks.

Birds of Prey Most birds of prey are hunters with keen vision. Eagles, hawks, and most of the smaller birds of prey hunt mainly during the day. Owls have huge eyes and hunt for small prey at night. Vultures, instead of using vision, use their amazing sense of smell to find dead animals. Most birds of prey have sharp, curved beaks for tearing flesh and curved **talons** that can grasp prey. Ospreys, for example, can dive into water and grab slippery fish with their talons. Peregrine falcons can snatch small birds out of the air. While most birds of prey hunt alone, some hunt in groups and flush prey toward their waiting partners. You can learn more about birds of prey in the UpClose feature.

talon claw of a bird of prey

Figure 15 Many perching birds, including this Blackburnian warbler, are called songbirds because the males chirp beautiful songs. The songs may warn away other males and attract females.

Up Close Birds

A bald eagle is a typical bird of prey. It has highly developed eyes with visual acuity that is about three to four times greater than a human's vision. The eagle's beak has a very sharp tip that is used to tear its prey into portions. The eagle's feet and talons are large—the hind talon may be 5 cm (2 in.) long. The talons are used to snatch prey when the eagle is flying. When the muscles of the legs contract, the tendons in the lower legs are pulled, and the talons lock together around the prey.

Bald Eagle

Scientific Name: *Haliaeetus leucocephalus*
Size: wingspan typically more than 2 m (6.5 ft) and body weight often exceeds 7 kg (15 lb)
Range: nearly all of North America, from Florida to northern Alaska
Habitat: forested areas near water that have tall trees for perching and nesting
Diet: fish, small mammals, birds, carrion

Digestive System Meals are first stored in the crop, which is the expandable lower esophagus. The food then passes into the stomach's first chamber, where acids begin digesting the food. The partially digested food then passes to the second chamber, the gizzard, where it is crushed. Undigested material is eliminated through the cloaca.

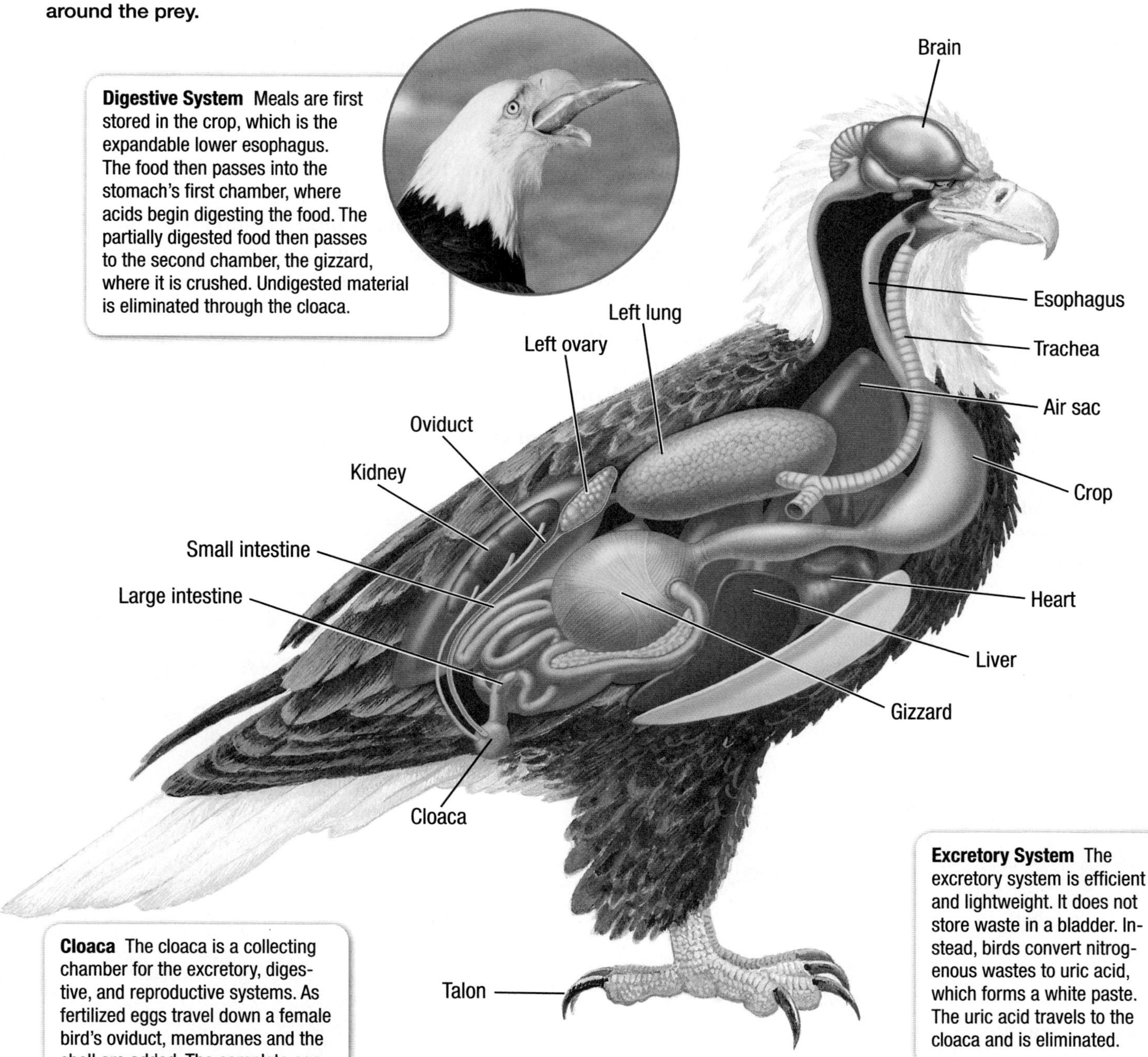

Brain

Left lung

Left ovary

Esophagus

Trachea

Oviduct

Air sac

Kidney

Crop

Small intestine

Large intestine

Heart

Liver

Gizzard

Cloaca

Cloaca The cloaca is a collecting chamber for the excretory, digestive, and reproductive systems. As fertilized eggs travel down a female bird's oviduct, membranes and the shell are added. The complete egg then passes out of the cloaca.

Talon

Excretory System The excretory system is efficient and lightweight. It does not store waste in a bladder. Instead, birds convert nitrogenous wastes to uric acid, which forms a white paste. The uric acid travels to the cloaca and is eliminated.

Double-Door Fold Use a double-door folded note to compare two or more different groups of birds.

maintain to keep as is or unchanged

Flightless Birds The world's largest birds are too big to fly. They have small wings and are built to run on land. The biggest flightless birds are ostriches, rheas, emus, and cassowaries. Ostriches are found in Africa and can be almost 3 m (10 ft) tall! As you can see in **Figure 16,** ostriches are very good high-speed runners. They have long, strong legs and can run up to 55 km/h. Ostriches have only two large, clawed toes on each foot. The cassowary, another large flightless bird, uses its powerful legs to deliver blows and uses its claws to tear at attackers. However, not all flightless birds are large. New Zealand's flightless kiwi grows to be only about the size of a chicken.

Aquatic Birds

Diving birds, water birds, and wading birds are aquatic, which means that they live mostly in water. ❯ Aquatic birds have feet adapted to paddling or wading and beaks adapted to eating aquatic organisms.

Diving Birds Not all flightless birds are found on land. Penguins are flightless; their wings and feet have been adapted for swimming. All 17 species of penguins live in the Southern Hemisphere. The penguin's wedge-shaped wings work as flippers, and the penguin's webbed feet can be used as paddles. Most penguins have a thick coat of feathers and a layer of fat beneath their skin, which allows them to live in freezing temperatures. A rich diet of fish and krill help penguins <u>maintain</u> this fat layer. Some diving birds are found in the Northern Hemisphere. But because their wings can still be used for flight, these diving birds cannot dive as well as penguins can.

❯ **Reading Check** *What structures does a penguin use to swim?*

Figure 16 Birds are extremely diverse because they live in a wide range of habitats and thus have a variety of lifestyles. ❯ Identify the bird group to which each of the pictured birds belongs.

Mallard duck

Ostriches

Emperor penguin

Sandhill crane and chicks

Hands-On QuickLab

⏱ 15 min

Webbed Feet

How much of an advantage do webbed feet give swimming water birds? In this lab, you will find out.

Procedure

1 Use a **knife** to cut the chevron shape shown above out of a piece of **foam core**. Stretch a **rubber band** across the cutaway end of the foam. Bend a **wire** that is 25 cm long into a Y shape at each end. Wrap the wire around the rubber band.

2 Wind up the wire. Place this device in a **pan** filled with **water,** and release the wire. What happens?

3 Completely cover both Y-shaped gaps at the ends of the wire with **aluminum foil.** Repeat step 2.

Analysis

1. Explain what the bent wire represented in the model. What did the aluminum foil represent?

2. CRITICAL THINKING **Making Inferences** Use your observations to explain how webbed feet give water birds an advantage.

Water Birds Swans, geese, and ducks are water birds, or birds found in or near the water. Water birds have webbed feet for paddling and long, flattened beaks with rounded tips. This beak is ideal for feeding on a variety of foods, from small insects and fish to grass. An unrelated group of birds, called *seabirds,* also exploits open waters, but these birds are found in the oceans. Like water birds, they have webbed feet. But unlike water birds, the beaks of seabirds are longer and are made for catching their typical meal of fish or squid.

Wading Birds Herons, storks, flamingos, and egrets are examples of wading birds. These birds feed in shallow waters that are rich with fish and invertebrates. In order to feed in a range of depths, wading birds have long, slender legs. Their long toes keep these birds from sinking into the mud. Many waders have spear-shaped beaks for fishing. Fishing waders often stand motionless as they wait for fish. When they see a fish, they quickly snatch it in their beak or they may even spear it. Waders that feed on invertebrates in the mud may have beaks that are built for stabbing into the mud to find their prey.

SC*L*INKS.

www.scilinks.org
Topic: Kinds of Birds
Code: HX80831

Section 4 Review

KEY IDEAS

1. Relate the bald eagle's methods of hunting and feeding to its external body features.

2. Compare and Contrast the foot structure of water birds and wading birds.

CRITICAL THINKING

3. Classifying Classify a bird that has delicate, curved feet with slender toes and a small, pointed beak.

4. Making Inferences Like most birds, penguins have large, keel-shaped sternums, but ostriches do not. Provide an explanation for this difference.

ALTERNATIVE ASSESSMENT

5. Synthesizing Information Pick a type of ecosystem, and design a bird that could successfully live in that ecosystem. Draw a picture of your bird, and write a short paragraph explaining your design.

Objectives

> Model the action of a glandular stomach

> Model the action of a muscular stomach

> Compare the stomach models.

Materials

- safety goggles
- lab apron
- disposable gloves
- glass beaker, small (2)
- graduated cylinder, 50 mL
- vinegar
- forceps
- dustless board chalk (broken into 1/4 sticks)
- sand paper
- felt (2 dark colored squares)
- aquarium gravel
- hand lens

Safety

Bird Digestion

To fuel their metabolism, birds need an efficient digestive system. At the bottom of the esophagus, many birds have a sack-like structure called a crop. The crop acts like a doggie bag. This way, the bird can eat-and-run, flying off to digest its meal in safety.

Birds also have a two-part stomach. The front part is a glandular chamber. It acts as a holding tank filled with a powerful acid. The acid is especially strong in predatory birds that swallow entire animals. The second chamber is a muscular pouch called the gizzard. Although the gizzard undergoes powerful contractions, these contractions are not enough to crack bones or hard grains. So, to increase the crunching power of the gizzard, these birds swallow small rocks! Powered by these muscular contractions, the rocks grind up tough food.

Now, it's your turn to explore digestion in birds. In this lab, you will compare the functions of the two types of stomachs found in birds. To do this, you will model the action of both the glandular stomach and the muscular stomach of birds.

Procedure

Model the Action of the Glandular Stomach

1 Put on safety goggles, a lab apron, and gloves.

2 CAUTION: **Use glass beakers with care.** Add about 50 mL of vinegar to two small beakers. Note: Vinegar is a weak acid. Exercise caution when using vinegar.

3 Use your forceps to carefully add a piece of chalk to the beaker. Observe and record any changes in the appearance of the chalk.

4 Use a piece of sand paper to grate the dustless chalk into small particles. Note: Do not inhale these particles.

5 Add the particles to the second beaker. Record your observations.

Model the Action of the Muscular Stomach

6 Place a piece of chalk in the center of a clean, square of felt. Close up the fabric around the chalk.

7 Squeeze and roll the chalk against a hard surface for 20 sec.

8 Open the fabric and examine the appearance of the chalk and felt. Use a hand lens to examine any particles that may have been produced.

9 Place a fresh piece of chalk in the center of the second felt square. Add a teaspoon of aquarium gravel and close up the fabric.

10 Squeeze and roll the chalk against a hard surface for 20 sec.

11 Open the fabric and examine the appearance of the chalk, gravel and felt. Use a hand lens to examine any particles that may have been produced.

12 Clean up your lab materials according to your teacher's instructions. Wash your hands before leaving the lab.

Analyze and Conclude

1. Identifying Variables In the first part of this activity, what did the chalk and vinegar represent?

2. Evaluating Results What happened when the chalk was added to the vinegar solution?

3. SCIENTIFIC METHODS Analyzing Methods How did grating the chalk into smaller particles affect the reaction?

4. Identifying Variables In the second part of this activity, what did the felt, gravel, and chalk represent?

5. SCIENTIFIC METHODS Using Evidence to Develop Explanations How did adding gravel to the chalk affect its breakdown?

6. Inferring Conclusions In some birds, the digesting food is often shifted back-and-forth between both stomachs. What advantage does this offer?

7. SCIENTIFIC METHODS Forming Reasoned Opinions Gizzard stones that become rounded and smooth often pass out of the stomach. The bird must then ingest more stones to replenish this load. What advantage might this have?

Extensions

8. Further Inquiry Write a new question about bird digestion that could be explored with another investigation.

9. Designing Models Choose another bird organ system, such as a bird's respiratory system or reproductive system. Research how the system functions and then describe how you could build a model of that system. Include a list of the materials you would need in your plan.

Key Ideas	Key Terms

1 The Reptile Body

> Modern reptiles have scales, clawed toes, an ectothermic metabolism, and reptiles lack feathers or hair.

> Reptiles have a strong skeleton, claws, legs positioned under the body, and highly developed vision.

> A reptile's lungs have a large surface area, and a reptile's heart is almost completely divided into four chambers.

> An amniotic egg is key to a reptile's success as a terrestrial animal.

Jacobson's organ (759)
ectothermic (759)
oviparous (761)
ovoviviparous (761)

2 Groups of Reptiles

> Turtles and tortoises have a hard shell that covers their body, and their spine is fused to the top of their shell.

> Unlike most other reptiles, tuataras are more active at low temperatures.

> Unlike most other reptiles, crocodilians care for their young.

> Because lizards and snakes share a common ancestor, they have many features in common, including periodic molting and a jaw that is only loosely attached to the skull. This jaw allows the mouth to open wide enough to accommodate large prey.

carapace (762)
plastron (762)
constrictor (765)

3 The Bird Body

> The key characteristics of modern birds include feathers, wings, lightweight skeleton, endothermic metabolism, lungs with air sacs, and a beak.

> Feathers and a strong, lightweight skeleton are critical to a bird's ability to fly.

> Birds have respiratory and circulatory structures, such as air sacs and a four-chambered heart, that improve the efficiency of oxygen intake and oxygen delivery and allow birds to get the energy that they need.

> Unlike most reptiles, most birds care for their eggs and for their young.

endothermic (767)
contour feather (768)
down feather (768)

4 Groups of Birds

> Terrestrial birds have feet adapted to perching, hunting, or running and beaks adapted to eating fruits, seeds, insects, or small animals.

> Aquatic birds have feet adapted to paddling or wading and beaks adapted to eating aquatic organisms.

talon (772)

READING TOOLBOX

1. **Word Parts** Use a chart to contrast the following groups of birds: perching birds, birds of prey, flightless birds, diving birds, water birds, and wading birds.

2. **Concept Map** Construct a concept map that describes the characteristics of both reptiles and birds. Include the following terms in your map: *ectotherm, endotherm, oviparous, ovoviviparous, scales, feathers, reptiles, snakes, lizards, tuataras, turtles, crocodilians, three-chambered heart,* and *four-chambered heart.*

Using Key Terms

Use the following terms together in a sentence.

3. *carapace* and *plastron*

For each pair of terms, explain how the meanings of the terms differ.

4. *contour feather* and *down feather*

5. *ectothermic* and *endothermic*

6. *oviparous* and *ovoviviparous*

Understanding Key Ideas

7. Which of the following is *not* a characteristic of reptiles?
   a. efficient respiration
   b. external fertilization
   c. strong skeleton
   d. watertight skin

8. Which of the following legs belongs to a reptile?

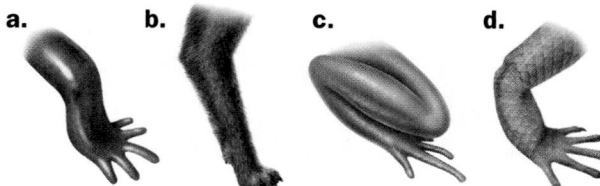

a.   b.   c.   d.

9. The heart of most reptiles has
   a. no septum.
   b. a fully divided ventricle.
   c. a partly divided ventricle.
   d. two pumping chambers.

10. Which of the following reptiles is more active at low temperatures?
    a. crocodiles   c. snakes
    b. lizards   d. tuataras

11. Which of the following characteristics distinguishes crocodilians from other reptiles?
    a. Crocodilians are ectothermic.
    b. Crocodilians have amniotic eggs.
    c. Crocodilians have dry, watertight skin.
    d. Crocodilians care for their young after hatching.

12. Which of the following is a characteristic of modern birds?
    a. ectothermic metabolism
    b. feet with scales and claws
    c. strong, heavy skeleton
    d. three-chambered heart

13. The feathers of most birds are well adapted for
    a. expelling heat and feeding.
    b. floating and protecting from predators.
    c. flying and insulating.
    d. swimming and repelling water.

14. Wading birds have which of the following characteristics?
    a. long legs and feet with splayed toes
    b. sharp, curved beak and talons
    c. short wings and thick toes
    d. webbed feet and a rounded beak

15. The bird pictured at right belongs to which of the following groups?
    a. birds of prey
    b. diving birds
    c. perching birds
    d. wading birds

Explaining Key Ideas

16. Summarize the benefits of the reptile's amniotic egg.

17. Explain how the septum of the reptile heart helps reptiles be more active on land than amphibians.

18. Describe two characteristics that help crocodiles ambush their prey.

19. List three differences between birds and reptiles.

20. Identify the beak and foot adaptations that help birds of prey feed.

21. Describe the feet and beak of a bird that dives to the bottom of ponds to eat water plants.

Using Science Graphics

This graph shows the normal ranges of body temperature in five groups of reptiles. Use the graph and your knowledge of science to answer the following questions.

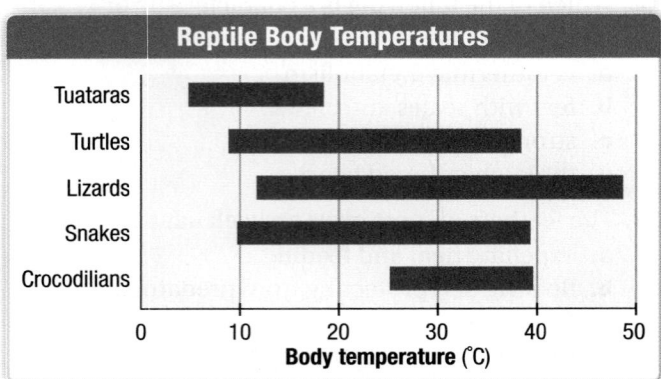

Reptile Body Temperatures

22. Which groups could probably best tolerate the temperature extremes found in deserts?
- **a.** turtles, snakes, and crocodilians
- **b.** turtles, lizards, and snakes
- **c.** tuataras, turtles, and snakes
- **d.** tuataras and crocodilians

23. Which of these statements is supported by the data in the chart?
- **a.** Crocodilians have a greater body temperature range than tuataras.
- **b.** Turtles and snakes have similar body temperature ranges.
- **c.** Lizards always have a higher body temperature than tuataras.
- **d.** Some tuataras can have a higher body temperature than some crocodilians.

24. If a bar showing the body temperature range of birds were added to this chart, the bar for birds would partially overlap with the bar for
- **a.** lizards.
- **c.** crocodilians.
- **b.** tuataras.
- **d.** turtles.

Critical Thinking

25. Judging Validity Reptiles have scales and more efficient respiration than amphibians do. A student speculates that having scales made it necessary for reptiles to develop more efficient respiration. Judge the validity of this conclusion.

26. Forming Reasoned Conclusions You collect data on the number of young lizards and young crocodiles that survive to adulthood. Young crocodiles are much more likely to survive. How would you explain this result?

27. Predicting Outcomes How might having a three-chambered heart, like that of most reptiles, affect a hummingbird in flight?

28. Classifying Your teacher tells you about a bird that weighs almost 100 lb and has long, strong legs with two thick toes. What type of lifestyle do you think that this bird has? Why?

Alternative Assessment

29. Identifying Patterns Go outside, and look for birds. Keep a list of the major types of birds that you see, based on the birds' beak, feet, and legs. Write a short essay about what these types of birds might eat and where they might live (for example, perching in trees, swimming in water).

Data Skills

30. Analyzing Information Research data on heart rates of at least three species of reptiles and three species of birds. Which group has a higher average heart rate? Propose a possible explanation for your findings.

Writing for Science

31. Speech Writing Write a speech about why reptiles were able to take over the land and drive many ancient species of amphibians into extinction.

Standardized Test Prep

Science Concepts

1. Which structure is part of the excretory, digestive, and reproductive systems of a bird?
   A kidney   C gizzard
   B cloaca   D ovary

2. The Jacobson's organs of a rattlesnake are senstive to which of the following?
   F airborne chemicals   H ground vibrations
   G faint sounds   J infrared radiation

3. What is the purpose of a lizard's ability to lose its tail and grow a new one?
   A to capture prey
   B to hide from predators
   C to escape from predators
   D to reduce its need for food

4. Long, legless bodies may have arisen as an adaptation that helped snakes do what?
   F catch prey
   G swallow large animals
   H absorb oxygen through their skin
   J burrow and move through thick vegetation

Use the diagram of a turtle heart to answer the following question.

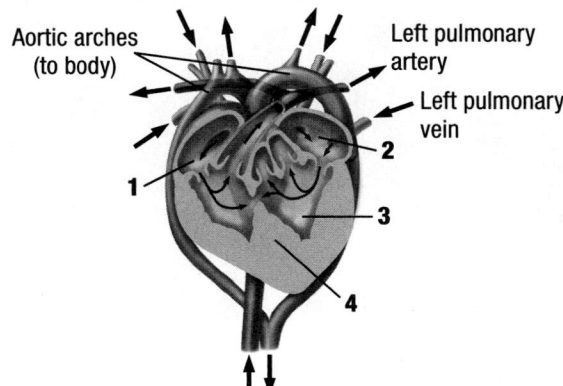

Aortic arches (to body)
Left pulmonary artery
Left pulmonary vein
1
2
3
4

5. Which feature of a turtle's heart structure is different from that of a crocodile?
   A 1   C 3
   B 2   D 4

Using Science Graphics

A clutch is the number of eggs laid by a bird at one time. The graph shows the effect of varying clutch sizes on the number of surviving offspring in one bird species. Use the graph to answer the following question.

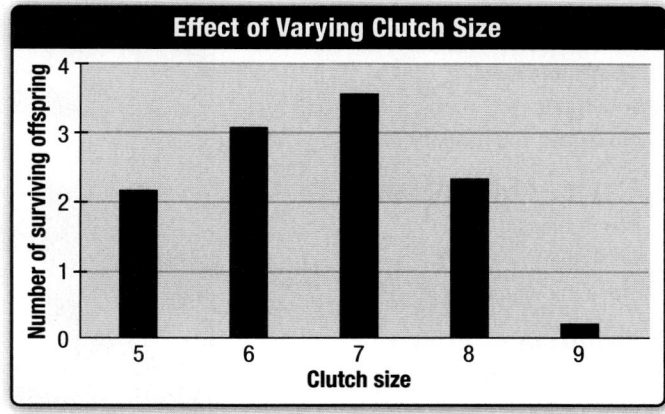

Effect of Varying Clutch Size

Number of surviving offspring

Clutch size

6. Based on the data in the graph, which of the following statements is true for this species?
   F The optimal number of eggs in a clutch is seven.
   G The greater the clutch size is, the greater the number of surviving offspring there are.
   H Nests with five eggs produced the fewest number of surviving offspring.
   J More offspring died in nests containing eight eggs than in nests containing nine eggs.

Writing Skills

7. **Short Response** Cowbirds lay their eggs in the nests of other birds. The young cowbirds hatch slightly earlier than the other birds do, and the cowbird hatchlings are slightly larger. Why might these characteristics be advantageous for young cowbirds?

Chapter 32

Mammals

Holding their arms out for balance, Coquerel's sifaka lemurs bound along the ground on their powerful hind limbs.

Sifakas, or dancing lemurs, live in heavily wooded areas in Madagascar.

Preview

1 Characteristics of Mammals
Key Characteristics of Mammals
Endothermy
Specialized Teeth
Parental Care
Movement and Response

2 Groups of Mammals
Monotremes
Marsupials
Placental Mammals

3 Evolution of Primates
Characteristics of Primates
Modern Nonhuman Primate Groups
Early Hominids
The Path to Humans
Modern Humans

Why It Matters

Human life has long been intertwined with the lives of other mammals. In terms of their diversity of size, anatomy, and habitat, mammals surpass all other vertebrates.

InquiryLab

⏱ 15 min

Heat Loss and Hair

Fur is an adaptation to keep in heat. Fur insulates by trapping air among densely packed hair shafts.

Procedure

1. Place **two empty 12 oz soda cans** side by side. Wrap one can with a **piece of fake fur,** and secure the fur with **tape.**

2. Put on **heat-resistant gloves.** Carefully fill both cans ¾ full with **hot tap water.**

3. Every 60 seconds, use a **thermometer** to measure the temperature of the water in both cans. Record this value.

Analysis

1. **Determine** if the temperature changed in the exposed can. If it did, how did it change?

2. **Determine** if the temperature changed in the can wrapped in fake fur. If it did, how did it change?

3. **Explain** any differences you observed between the two cans.

Sifakas are extraordinary climbers. They leap from one tree to another up to 10 m away, rotate through the leap, and catch the new perch with their hind legs.

Sifakas move through their territory (one or more hectares) several times a day as they forage for food.

READING TOOLBOX

These reading tools can help you learn the material in this chapter. For more information on how to use these and other tools, see **Appendix: Reading and Study Skills.**

Using Words

Word Origins Many common English words derive from Greek or Latin words. Learning the meanings of some Greek or Latin words can help you understand the meaning of many modern English words.

Word Origins		
Word part	**Origin**	**Meaning**
endo	Greek	inside
therm	Greek	heat
carn	Latin	flesh
vora	Latin	devour

Your Turn Use the table to answer the following questions.

1. What does *endothermic* mean?

2. Lions belong to the order Carnivora. What does the name *Carnivora* mean?

Using Language

Word Problems Solving word problems can seem tricky. A good place to begin is to figure out what the word problem is asking for. Here is an example: A pregnant whale weighs 136,000 kg. At birth, her calf weighs 2,700 kg. How much does the mother weigh after the calf is born?

You are looking for the weight of the mother whale. The beginning of the problem tells you how much the mother weighs, so something must happen to change her weight. She has a calf.

Your Turn Refer to the word problem to answer the questions below.

1. After having a calf, would the mother whale weigh more or less than she did before giving birth?

2. How would you solve the word problem above?

Using FoldNotes

Layered Book A layered book is a useful tool for taking notes as you read a chapter. The four flaps of the layered book can summarize information into four categories. Write details of each category on the appropriate flap to create a summary of the chapter.

Your Turn Create a layered book to organize your notes for this chapter.

1. Lay one sheet of paper on top of another sheet. Slide the top sheet up so that 2 cm of the bottom sheet is showing.

2. Holding the two sheets together, fold down the top of the two sheets so that you see four 2 cm tabs along the bottom.

3. Using a stapler, staple the top of the FoldNote.

Key Ideas	Key Terms	Why It Matters
❭ What are the key characteristics of mammals? ❭ How are the respiratory and circulatory systems of mammals adapted for endothermy? ❭ What do specialized teeth reveal about mammals? ❭ How do mammals differ from other vertebrates in terms of parental care? ❭ What types of locomotion do mammals exhibit?	mammary gland placenta gestation period echolocation	Mammals are some of the most familiar animals to us. We keep them as pets, use them to help us work, and use them as food. They are also familiar because we are mammals.

Mammals are the most obvious large animals in many places. Lions, elephants, and giraffes, such as the ones in **Figure 1,** are mammals. The largest animal that has ever lived, the blue whale, is a mammal. But most mammals are not large. Tiny mice, found all over the world, are mammals. So are bats, which rule the night skies.

Key Characteristics of Mammals

Mammals vary in shape and size. So, what makes a mammal a mammal? ❭ **Mammals are endothermic, they have hair and specialized teeth, and females produce milk in mammary glands to nourish their young.** Mammals are the only animals that have hair. Some mammals, such as dolphins and whales, may look as if they do not have any hair. But these mammals have a few small, sensitive hairs on their snouts.

The primary function of hair is insulation. But hair also has other roles. The color of a mammal's hair often can help the mammal blend in with its surroundings. For example, orange and black stripes conceal a Bengal tiger in the tall, orange-brown grass in which it hunts. The hair of some mammals, such as the arctic fox, changes from white in winter to brown in summer.

Sometimes, a mammal uses its hair for advertising. The black and white hair of a skunk warns predators to stay away. The mane of a male lion shows other males how big and strong the lion is.

In some mammals, specialized hairs serve a sensory function. The whiskers of cats and dogs are stiff hairs that are very sensitive to touch.

❭ **Reading Check** *What are three functions of hair? (See the Appendix for answers to Reading Checks.)*

Figure 1 Giraffes have all the key characteristics of mammals.

🕐 15 min

Mammalian Bones

When owls feed on small mammals, the owls regurgitate the indigestible parts, such as hair and bones, as pellets.

Procedure

❶ Work in teams of two. Put on **laboratory gloves.** Place an **owl pellet** on a **paper towel.**

❷ Use **forceps** and a **probe** to separate and remove the bones from the pellet.

❸ Use a **hand lens** to study any teeth and bones that you remove.

❹ When you are finished, dispose of the dissected pellet and gloves as directed by your instructor. Wash your hands thoroughly.

Analysis

1. **Estimate** the number of small mammals that are contained in the pellet.

2. **CRITICAL THINKING** **Comparing Functions** Based on structure, infer the function of the different types of teeth found in the pellet.

Endothermy

Like birds, mammals are *endotherms,* animals can maintain a constant body temperature despite temperature changes in the animal's environment. Unlike most amphibians and reptiles, mammals can live in very cold climates. Endothermy also enables mammals to be very active. Flying and running quickly for long periods of time require a lot of energy and a high metabolism. A high metabolic rate has a cost. A mammal needs to eat about 10 times as much food as an ectotherm of similar size does. Metabolizing food requires a lot of oxygen. ❯ **The respiratory and circulatory systems of mammals are adapted to endothermy. They acquire and distribute oxygen more efficiently than the respiratory and circulatory systems of ectotherms do.**

Respiratory System The lungs of mammals have a larger internal surface area than those of reptiles and amphibians do. Thus, mammals can exchange more oxygen and carbon dioxide in each breath than reptiles and amphibians can. Respiration in mammals is aided by the *diaphragm,* a sheet of muscle that separates the chest cavity from the abdominal cavity. When the diaphragm contracts, the chest cavity enlarges and air is drawn into the lungs.

Circulatory System Like birds, mammals have a four-chambered heart. A septum completely divides the ventricles, as **Figure 2** shows. The left ventricle pumps oxygen-rich blood to the body, while the right ventricle pumps oxygen-poor blood to the lungs. Only oxygen-rich blood is delivered to the tissues, a condition vital for meeting the oxygen needs of endotherms.

❯ **Reading Check** *Why does a mammal need to eat more food than a reptile of a similar size does?*

Figure 2 A mammal's four-chambered heart has ventricles that are completely separated by a septum. Blood pumped to the body has a higher oxygen content than the blood pumped to the body of a reptile or fish does. ❯ **What is the advantage of having a complete septum?**

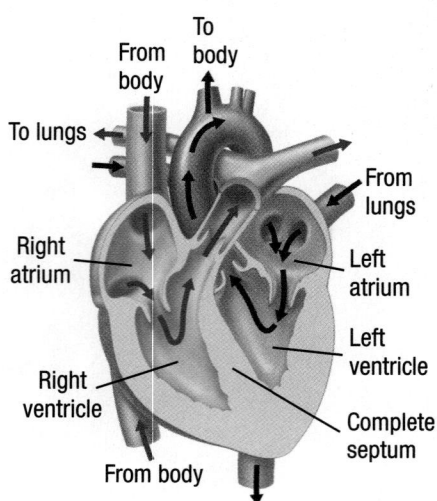

Specialized Teeth

Mammals eat many types of foods. Some mammals, such as zebras and elephants, are herbivores. Others, such as tigers and killer whales, are predators and feed on other animals. Still other mammals, such as raccoons and bears, eat both plants and animals.
> Mammals have specialized teeth that reflect the differences in their diets.

In most nonmammalian vertebrate groups, teeth are continually lost and replaced. Also, all of the teeth in the mouth look the same. Mammalian teeth are different. A mammal usually has only two sets of teeth during its life. The baby teeth, the first set, are replaced by permanent teeth, which are not replaced if lost or damaged.

Types of Teeth Most mammals have four types of teeth—incisors, canines, premolars, and molars. Each type of tooth performs a different function. Incisors, the front teeth, are used for biting and cutting. Behind the incisors are the canines, which are used for stabbing and holding. Lining the rest of the jaw are the premolars and molars, which are used in crushing and grinding food.

One can learn a lot about what a mammal eats by looking at its teeth. The differences between the teeth of a coyote (a carnivore) and the teeth of a deer (a herbivore) are shown in **Figure 3.** The coyote has long canine teeth that are suited for grasping prey, and its sharp premolars and molars can cut off pieces of flesh. In contrast, the deer has small, incisor-shaped canines. It uses its incisors and canines to nip off pieces of plant material. Its premolars and molars are flat and are covered with ridges that form a surface on which plant material can be ground.

> **Reading Check** *What type of tooth is used for stabbing and holding?*

READING TOOLBOX

Layered Book Create a layered book that summarizes what you learned about mammals' specialized teeth.

Figure 3 A mammal's teeth provide clues about its diet. > **How do the teeth of a coyote differ from those of a deer?**

Coyote

Molar Premolar Canine Incisor

Deer

Incisor

Molar Premolar Canine

SCLINKS.
www.scilinks.org
Topic: Monotremes
     and Marsupials
Code: HX80990

Parental Care

Mammals differ from other vertebrates in terms of parental care. ❯ Unlike the young of other vertebrates, young mammals depend on their mother for a relatively long period of time. They receive milk and other food, protection, and shelter from her. Mammals are unique in the way that they nourish their young after birth. Milk is produced in **mammary glands,** which are located on the female's chest or abdomen.

All mammals reproduce by internal fertilization, but mammals differ in how and where their fertilized eggs develop. Mammals are classified into three groups based on their pattern of development.

Monotremes Monotremes are *oviparous,* which means they reproduce by laying eggs. The eggs hatch quickly, and the mother stays with and nurses the young for several months. The only monotremes that are alive today are the duckbill platypus and echidnas.

Marsupials After fertilization, marsupial embryos remain inside their mother for only a few days or weeks. Then, the young crawl out of the mother, up the fur on her belly, and to her nipples, which are usually located inside a pouch. A young marsupial, such as the brushtail possum in **Figure 4,** completes its development inside the pouch, attached to its mother's nipple.

Placental Mammals Placental mammals complete their development inside the mother. A structure called the **placenta** attaches the fetus to the mother and allows the exchange of nutrients, oxygen, and wastes. The period of time between fertilization and birth is called the **gestation period.** Some placental mammals, such as the horses in **Figure 4,** can move around or even run shortly after birth.

❯ **Reading Check** *Which group of mammals lays eggs?*

Brushtail possum and young

Mare and foal

Figure 4 At birth, this young possum (left) looked like the pink, newborn possum (center), which is smaller than your thumb. Newborn foals (right) are on their feet and nursing within a couple of hours after birth. ❯ **Which of these mammals has a longer gestation period?**

Up Close Mammals

The name *grizzly* comes from silver-tipped hairs that are often sprinkled over the bear's head and back. Grizzlies have good hearing but relatively poor eyesight. They rely primarily on their excellent sense of smell to follow an odor trail or catch the scent of distant food. Grizzlies are extremely strong and have great endurance. Their paws are tipped with curved claws that are up to 10 cm (4 in) long.

Grizzly Bear

Scientific name: *Ursus arctos*
Size: males average 160 kg (350 lb) and can reach 1.2 m (4 ft) at the shoulder; females are smaller
Range: Alaska and western Canada, with small populations in Washington, Idaho, Montana, and Wyoming
Habitat: tundra and mountainous forests and meadows
Diet: omnivorous—eats vegetation; hunts insects, small mammals, and fish; eats carrion

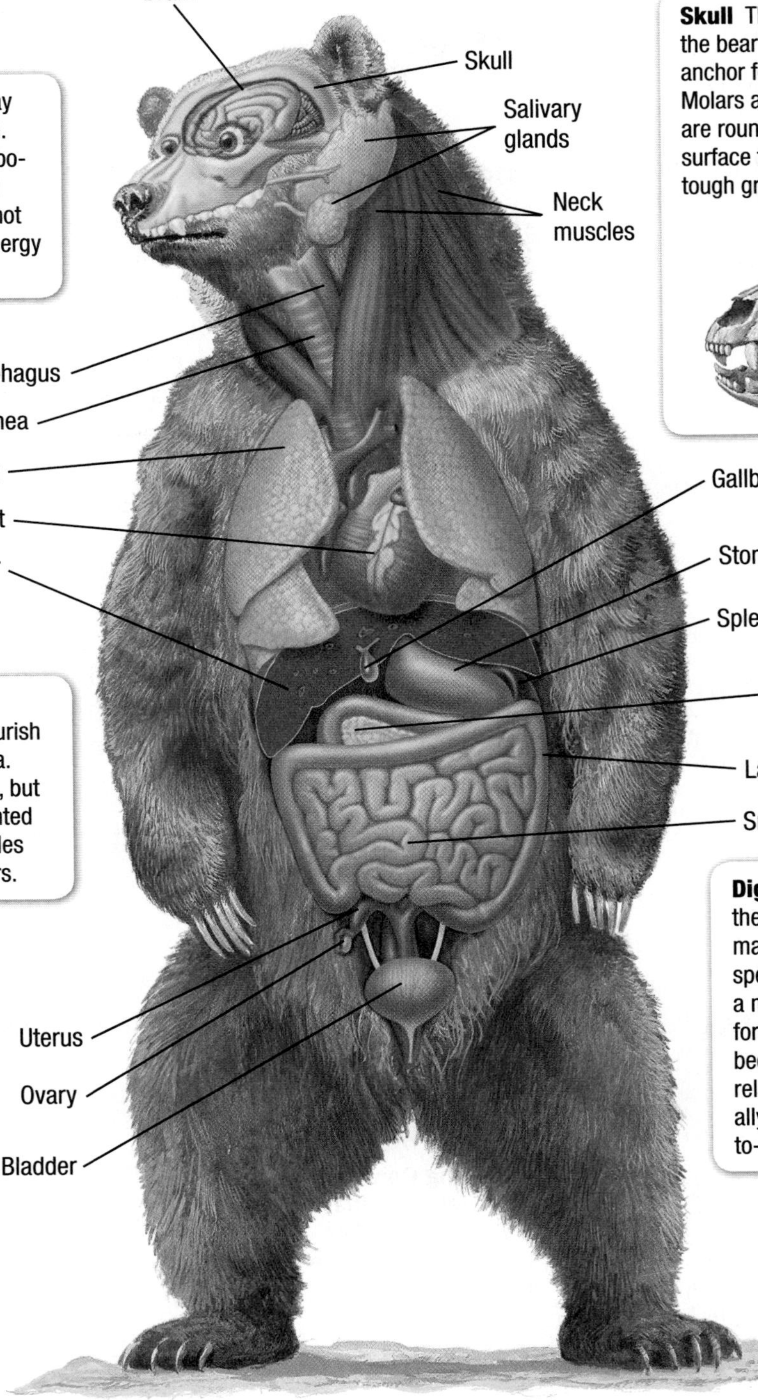

Brain

Skull

Salivary glands

Neck muscles

Fat Layer A grizzly snoozes away the winter in an underground den. During this time, the bear's metabolism slows, and its heart rate and breathing rate decrease. It does not eat or drink; it obtains all of its energy from a thick layer of stored fat.

Skull The long skull protects the bear's brain and serves as an anchor for the strong jaw muscles. Molars at the back of the jaw are rounded and have a wrinkled surface that is used for grinding up tough grasses and leaves.

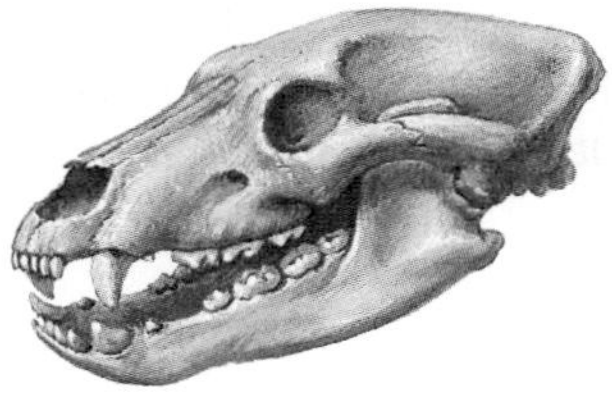

Esophagus

Trachea

Lung

Heart

Liver

Gallbladder

Stomach

Spleen

Pancreas

Large intestine

Small intestine

Reproductive System Like all placental mammals, grizzlies nourish their embryos through a placenta. Mating occurs from May to June, but the fertilized eggs are not implanted in the uterus until late fall. Females reproduce every two to four years.

Digestive System Although they eat large amounts of plant material, bears do not have specialized structures, such as a multichambered stomach, for digesting cellulose. But because their intestines are relatively long, bears are usually able to break down hard-to-digest plant material.

Uterus

Ovary

Bladder

Pumas are wide-ranging predators. Females have a home range of about 140 km² (54 mi²), and males have a home range about twice as large.

Bats are the only mammals that exhibit true flight. They use echolocation to help locate food.

Figure 5 Mammals are adapted to various modes of locomotion, including running and jumping (left) and flying (right). ❯ **Other than bats, which mammals use echolocation to find food?**

echolocation the process of using reflected sound waves to find objects

ACADEMIC VOCABULARY

process a set of steps, events, or changes

Movement and Response

❯ **Mammals use various modes of locomotion, including running, hopping, climbing, burrowing, flying, and swimming.** Adaptations in body structure help mammals move around in their particular environment. The mountain lion shown in **Figure 5** has powerful limbs for running and jumping. A bat's front limbs are modified into wings for flight. The limbs of dolphins and whales are adapted to swimming.

❯ **Mammals rely on their senses—vision, hearing, smell, taste, and touch—for survival. The importance of a given sense depends on a mammal's lifestyle and habitat.** Although bats and dolphins live in very different environments, both animals use sound to sense their environments. They make high-pitched clicks that spread into the air or the water. When sound waves hit an object, such as a moth or a fish, they bounce back to the bat or dolphin. The bat or dolphin can use these sound echoes to "see" their prey or obstacles in the environment. This process, called **echolocation,** allows a bat to navigate through a forest or catch a moth in total darkness, as **Figure 5** shows. Dolphins use echolocation to catch fish and navigate at sea.

❯ **Reading Check** *What are three types of locomotion that mammals use?*

Section 1 Review

❯ **KEY IDEAS**

1. **Name** three key characteristics of mammals.
2. **Relate** the mammal's heart and respiratory systems to its endothermic metabolism.
3. **Compare** the functions of different types of mammalian teeth.

4. **Describe** how mammals are unique in terms of parental care.
5. **Name** five types of locomotion that mammals use.

CRITICAL THINKING

6. **Justifying Conclusions** A classmate tells you that a mammal's metabolism makes it hard for the mammal to be active at night because of the cold. Is your classmate correct?

WRITING FOR SCIENCE

7. **Essay** Write an essay about how whales stay warm even though they have no hair and why seals can survive in cold climates with little hair. Compare how these mammals survive the cold with how other mammals do.

Key Ideas	Key Terms	Why It Matters
➤ What key characteristic sets monotremes apart from all other mammals? ➤ What are the key characteristics of marsupials? ➤ How common are placental mammals, and how does their development differ from the development of monotremes and marsupials?	monotreme	Mammals live in almost every environment on Earth and are the dominant species in many places. Many are critical species in their environments and maintain the diversity of life.

Mammals range in size from tiny shrews, which weigh about 1.5 g (< 0.1 oz), to blue whales, the largest animal that has ever lived, which can weigh up to 136,000 kg (150 tons). They inhabit more environments than any other vertebrates do. Modern mammals can be classified into three groups: monotremes, marsupials, and placental mammals.

Monotremes

Monotremes, such as the ones in **Figure 6,** are a small group of mammals found only in Australia and New Guinea. ➤ **Monotremes share more traits with reptiles than with other mammals. Monotremes are the only living mammals that lay eggs.** Like reptiles, monotremes have legs that sprawl to the side instead of being under the body. Also like reptiles, monotremes have a *cloaca,* a common passageway for the digestive, reproductive, and urinary systems. Finally, adult monotremes do not have teeth.

How are monotremes like other mammals? First, they have hair. Second, they produce milk to feed their young. However, female monotremes do not have nipples. Instead of nursing, the young lap up milk that oozes from glands located on their mother's belly.

➤ **Reading Check** *In what ways are monotremes more like reptiles than like other mammals?*

monotreme a mammal that lays eggs

Figure 6 The duckbill platypus (left) and the short-beaked echidna (right) are monotremes. ➤ In what part of the world are monotremes found?

A broad, flat tail and webbed feet make the platypus an excellent swimmer.

Echidnas have a long, beaklike snout and strong, sharp claws that are used for burrowing.

QuickLab

Taxonomic Key to Mammals

A taxonomic key is a tool used by scientists to classify and identify living things. Keys are assembled from pairs of contrasting statements. Using observations of a specimen, one selects the most correct statement and moves to the next step. This process is repeated until the organism is identified.

Procedure

1 Work with a partner. Review the operation of a taxonomic key as presented in the three statement pairs of this incomplete key.

2 Complete this mammal key. Begin with statements 4a and 4b. Develop all succeeding statement pairs and steps so that the completed key can be used to identify a kangaroo, an opossum, and five additional placental mammals that are shown on the next page.

Key to Mammals		
1a	Mammal lays eggs	go to 2
1b	Mammal does not lay eggs	go to 4
2a	Has duck-like bill and flat tail	platypus
2b	Lacks duck-like bill, has body with spines and fur	go to 3
3a	Has long beak, eats mostly worms and grubs	long-beaked echidna
3b	Has short beak, eats mostly ants and termites	short-beaked echidna

Analysis

1. **Identify** the two kinds of mammals distinguished in step 1 of the key.

2. **Identify** the characteristics shared by long-beaked echidnas and short-beaked echidnas.

3. **Speculate** how the key would change if there were more than one species of platypus.

Marsupials

Marsupials include not only the well-known kangaroos but also wombats, koalas, and opossums. ❯ **The females of most marsupials have a pouch, and their young spend most of their time developing inside this pouch while they nurse and grow.** Marsupials are the most diverse group of mammals in Australia. They are also found in South America, but only one species, the Virginia opossum, is native to North America.

Scientists believe that marsupials probably moved into Australia from South America before the breakup of Pangaea. At that time, South America and Australia were connected via Antarctica. After the continents separated, marsupials evolved and diversified in isolation from placental mammals.

The habitats and lifestyles of marsupials in Australia, New Zealand, and nearby islands are <u>similar</u> to those of placental mammals. Kangaroos and wallabies, such as the one in **Figure 7,** often live in large groups and, like deer, are herbivores. Much like monkeys, tree kangaroos are able to climb trees and jump from limb to limb. Gliders and possums are similar in habits to squirrels. Some marsupial predators are similar to small cats, and Tasmanian devils are similar to badgers in some ways. The Tasmanian tiger, a wolflike marsupial, was hunted to extinction in Australia by European settlers.

❯ **Reading Check** *What is an example of a marsupial whose ecological niche is similar to a deer's?*

ACADEMIC VOCABULARY

similar almost the same

Figure 7 For several months, young wallabies remain in their mother's pouch, where they receive milk and protection.

Placental Mammals

Placental mammals are the most familiar mammals. Cats, dogs, cows, horses, and humans are placental mammals. ❯ **Placental mammals make up nearly 95% of all mammalian species. The young of placental mammals develop inside the female's uterus, where they are nourished by nutrients from her blood.** Placental mammals have a longer period of internal development than marsupials do, and the young of most placentals are more developed at birth than the young of marsupials are. There are many types of placental mammals, which vary greatly in size, shape, diet, and habits. **Figure 8** shows the relationships of orders of placental mammals. **Figure 9** (on the next two pages) discusses the major orders of placental mammals.

SCiLINKS.
www.scilinks.org
Topic: Placental Mammals
Code: HX81150

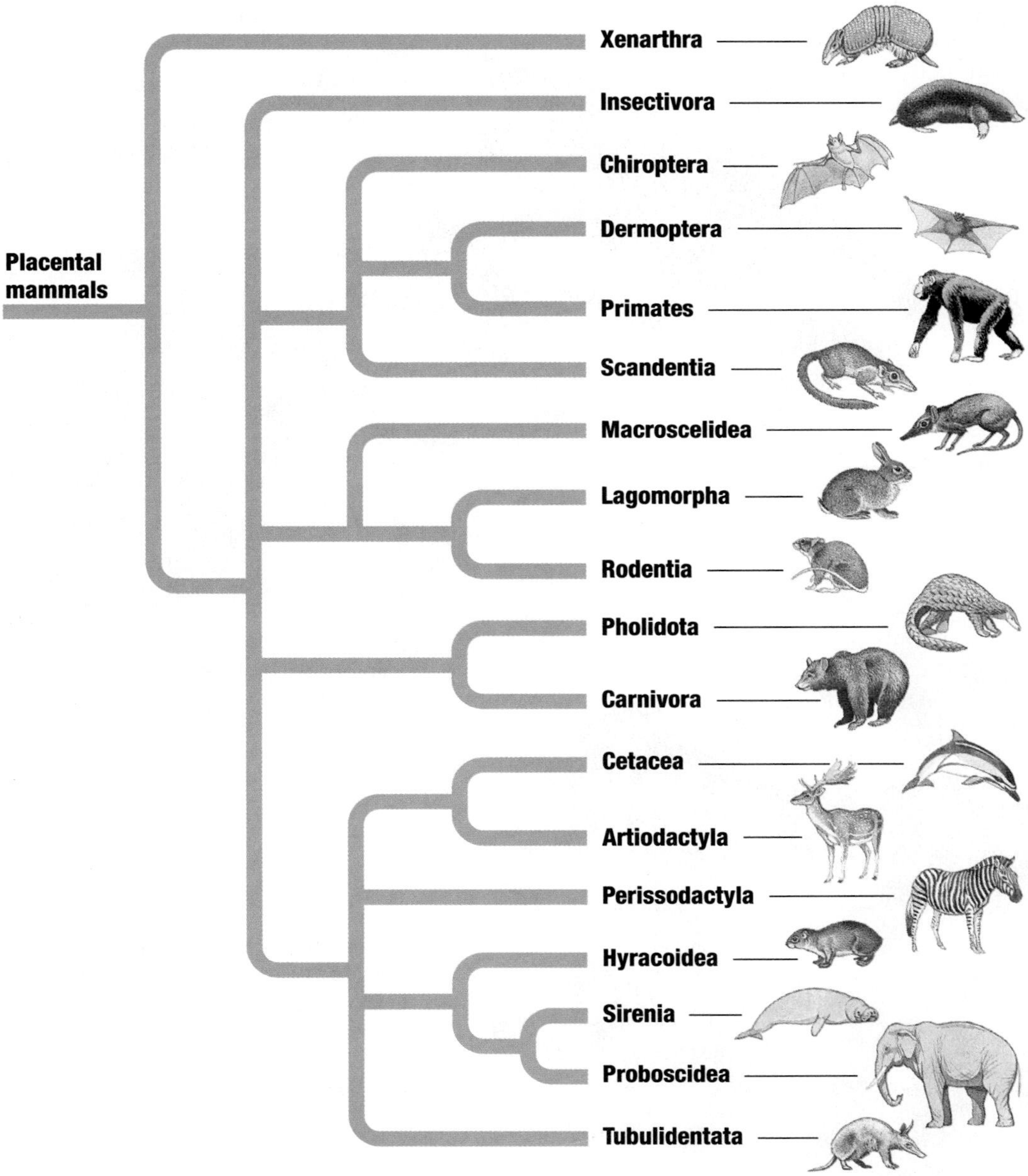

❯ **Reading Check** *In general, which group of mammals has a longer gestation period: marsupials or placental mammals?*

Xenarthra

Insectivora

Chiroptera

Dermoptera

Primates

Scandentia

Macroscelidea

Lagomorpha

Rodentia

Pholidota

Carnivora

Cetacea

Artiodactyla

Perissodactyla

Hyracoidea

Sirenia

Proboscidea

Tubulidentata

Placental mammals

Figure 8 This phylogenetic tree shows hypotheses of the evolutionary relationships between orders of placental mammals. For updates on phylogenetic information, visit **go.hrw.com.** Enter the keyword **HX8 Phylo.**

Figure 9 Placental mammals vary greatly in size, shape, diet, and habits. ❯ **Which orders have members that are primarily herbivores?**

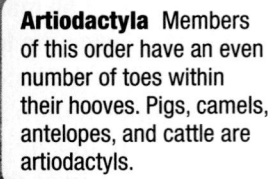

Artiodactyla Members of this order have an even number of toes within their hooves. Pigs, camels, antelopes, and cattle are artiodactyls.

Perissodactyla Members of this order have an odd number of toes within their hooves. They are grouped together with artiodactyls as *ungulates*. Horses, zebras, tapirs, and rhinoceroses are perissodactyls.

Cetacea Whales and dolphins are members of this order. Cetaceans have a streamlined body and move through the water with a powerful fluke. A layer of blubber keeps them warm.

Primates Humans, apes, lemurs, and monkeys are primates. Most primates are tree dwellers. They have grasping hands and feet and long arms and legs that aid in climbing. They have excellent eyesight and depth perception.

Rodentia More than 40% of all placental mammals are rodents. Rodents have teeth that are specialized for gnawing. Most rodents, such as mice and rats, are small, but some, such as beavers, can weigh 18 to 43 kg (40 to 95 lb).

Chiroptera Bats are the only mammals capable of true flight. Most bats are carnivorous and use echolocation to find insects, which they catch while in flight. Other bats eat fruit or nectar from night-blooming flowers. Some bats are impressive hunters that can catch fish or frogs.

Xenarthra Anteaters, sloths, and armadillos are members of this order. Anteaters lack teeth and use their long, sticky tongues to capture insects. Sloths eat mostly leaves. Most armadillos have simple teeth and are omnivorous.

Sirenia Dugongs and manatees are relatives of elephants. Their front limbs are flippers, and they use their flattened tail for swimming. Sometimes called *sea cows,* sirenians graze on aquatic plants.

Lagomorpha Rabbits, hares, and pikas are members of this order. Rabbits and hares have long hind legs and are specialized for hopping. Pikas have short limbs and live in mountainous areas of North America and in central Asia.

Insectivora Insectivores are small mammals that eat mainly insects. Shrews, hedgehogs, and moles are insectivores. Moles have adaptations for burrowing, which include short, powerful forelimbs with long claws.

Proboscidea The largest land animals alive today, elephants make up this order. The trunk of an elephant is an elongated nose and upper lip and is used for various tasks, including picking up food or water. An elephant's long, ivory tusks are modified upper incisors.

Carnivora Cats, dogs, foxes, bears, seals, and hyenas are carnivores. The long canine teeth of carnivores are specialized for capturing prey and tearing flesh. Some carnivores eat more than meat. Raccoons and bears are omnivores, while pandas are herbivores.

Figure 10 Humans domesticated dogs (left) and sheep (right) thousands of years ago. ❯ **Other than companionship, how are dogs useful to humans?**

READING TOOLBOX

Word Problems Australia is the world's leading producer of wool, producing about 27% of the global total. If Australia produces 475,000 kg of wool per year, what is the global production of wool?

Domestic Mammals Domestic animals, such as those in **Figure 10,** are animals that have been kept and bred by people for special purposes. Domestic animals may provide work, food, clothing, or companionship. Most domestic animals are placental mammals whose association with humans dates back up to 15,000 years or more. These animals include dogs, cats, cattle, horses, donkeys, mules, rabbits, sheep, goats, pigs, camels, llamas, and alpacas.

Various breeds of domestic mammals have been developed through selective breeding. For example, some breeds of goats produce more milk than others. Their milk is used to produce a variety of dairy products. Other goats, such as angora goats, are bred for their fine hair, which is spun into yarn. Some domestic mammals are hybrids of two species. Mules, for example, are the offspring of a female horse and a male donkey.

❯ **Reading Check** *What are three ways in which humans use domestic mammals?*

Section 2 Review

❯ KEY IDEAS

1. **Describe** how monotremes are like and unlike reptiles.
2. **Summarize** the importance of a marsupial's pouch in terms of development of young.
3. **Describe** how placental mammals differ from monotremes and marsupials in terms of development.

CRITICAL THINKING

4. **Forming Reasoned Opinions** You receive an e-mail from some friends who have taken a walk in the woods in Florida. They send you a grainy picture of a small animal, which they claim is a monotreme. Do you think that their claim is true? Why or why not?
5. **Relating Concepts** Speculate on why species of placental mammals make up almost 95% of mammalian species.

WRITING FOR SCIENCE

6. **Essay** Mammals are some of the most important animals to humans. Do some research on the Internet, and write an essay about domestic mammals and their close wild relatives. What characteristics do many domestic animals share?

Evolution of Primates

Key Ideas	Key Terms	Why It Matters
❯ What are two unique features of primates? ❯ What are the three groups of modern primates? ❯ How did early hominids differ from the primates that came before them? ❯ What does the hominid fossil record tell us? ❯ Where and when did modern humans evolve?	primate hominid	The study of primates is the study of ourselves, our past, and our closest relatives.

Fossil evidence indicates that small, insect-eating mammals with large eyes and small, sharp teeth appeared about 80 million years ago. These ancient mammals were the ancestors of the first primates.

Characteristics of Primates

A **primate** is a member of the mammalian order Primates. Modern primates include humans, monkeys and apes, and smaller animals such as lemurs and the tarsier in **Figure 11.** The first primates evolved more than 50 million years ago, and many species are now extinct. Primates were adapted for life in the trees, and two features have helped all groups of primates succeed. ❯ **All primates have grasping hands and most have grasping feet.** Their hands with flat nails instead of claws can hold and manipulate objects.

Unlike the eyes of their ancestors, which were located on the sides of the head, the eyes of primates are positioned at the front of the face. ❯ **The forward placement of the eyes give primates overlapping, binocular vision.** Binocular vision results in the ability to see depth. Some other mammals have binocular vision. But only primates have both binocular vision and grasping hands.

❯ **Reading Check** *When did the first primates evolve?*

primate a member of the order Primates, the group of mammals that includes humans, apes, and monkeys

Figure 11 This tarsier, a small primate from the South Pacific, has the key features of primates: eyes in the front of the head and grasping hands and feet.

Hands-On QuickLab

⏱ 15 min

Opposable Thumbs

If you make a fist, you can see that four of your fingers fold in together. The thumb, however, bends at a different angle. This opposing motion of the thumb allows you to grasp and finely manipulate objects.

Procedure

1. Work with a partner. Determine how long performing each of these tasks takes: tying a shoelace, writing your name, and inserting a button into its buttonhole. Record these times.

2. Use **tape** to secure the thumb of both hands to its neighboring index finger. Note: Do not wrap the tape too tightly. With your thumb taped, how long does performing each of the tasks take?

Analysis

1. **Explain** how removing the use of the thumb affected your performance on the three tasks.

2. **Predict** how taping the index finger to the middle finger would affect your performance.

3. **CRITICAL THINKING** **Forming Hypotheses** Why was an opposable thumb an important adaptation for mammals that lived in trees?

Modern Nonhuman Primate Groups

Many early primates are now extinct. ❯ **The three groups of primates alive today include lemurs and their relatives, tarsiers, and anthropoids—monkeys, apes, and humans.** Humans differ from these other primates in a number of ways.

Lemurs and Their Relatives This group include lemurs, lorises, and aye-ayes. All are small, mostly night-active primates that live in trees. Most species are found only on the island of Madagascar. Animals in this group first evolved more than 50 million years ago and probably most resemble early primates.

Tarsiers Tarsiers, such as the one shown on the previous page in **Figure 11,** live in Southeast Asia. Tarsiers were once grouped with the other small, night-active primates. Fossils indicate, however, that they are more closely related to monkeys and apes than to lemurs.

Monkeys and Apes Monkeys and apes are day active and generally have opposable big toes. An opposable digit stands at an angle from the other fingers or toes. It can be bent toward them to grasp objects, as **Figure 12** shows. There are two broad groups of monkeys. Old World monkeys live in Africa and Asia. Most Old World monkeys have opposable thumbs. New World monkeys live in Central America and South America. Many New World monkeys have opposable thumbs, and some have grasping tails.

Apes include the relatively small gibbons and the great apes—orangutans, gorillas, chimpanzees, and bonobos. Apes have larger brains with respect to their body size than monkeys do, and apes have no tails.

Figure 12 Primates have grasping hands and feet. This young orangutan is drinking rainwater from a pitcher plant. ❯ **How does an opposable thumb help an animal manipulate objects?**

Early Hominids

All early primates walked on all four limbs. According to the fossil record, primates that walked on two legs, called **hominids,** may have evolved as early as 7 million years ago. **❯ Hominids differ from other primates in that we are bipedal. Our spines are S-shaped, rather than C-shaped. We have relatively short arms and a bowl-shaped pelvis. Our thighs angle in under the body. Our spinal cord exits at the bottom of the skull. And our canine teeth are smaller than those of other primates.**

Bipedalism An early hominid is compared with a modern gorilla in **Figure 13.** Although a gorilla can stand erect, it uses all four limbs to walk. Why did hominids stand up and walk on two legs?

Some scientists think that climate played a role. Fifteen million years ago, Earth's climate began to cool. The great forests of Africa were largely replaced by grassy plains. Natural selection may then have favored primates adapted to living on the ground.

Studying Early Hominids Most of our information about early hominids comes from their fossilized bones. Fossils of hominids are usually incomplete skeletons. What can scientists tell from a collection of pieces of bones? First, bones are used to identify and classify the species. (Twenty or more species of hominids have been found so far.) Where and when the species lived also can be inferred.

If bones from more than one individual are found together, the species may have lived in a social group. Foot and leg bones and the skull are clues about whether the species was completely bipedal. (Some early hominids spent part of their time in trees.) The presence of stone tools and tool marks on animal bones are signs of tool use. Charred animal bone is a clue that fire was used for cooking.

hominid a member of the family Hominidae of the order Primates; characterized by bipedalism, relatively long lower limbs, and lack of a tail; examples include humans and their ancestors

READING TOOLBOX

Word Origins The Latin meaning of the species name *Homo erectus* is "upright man." Use a dictionary to find the meaning of the name *Homo sapiens.*

Figure 13 A gorilla's skeleton shows adaptations for walking on all four limbs. The skeleton of an early hominid shows adaptations for bipedalism.

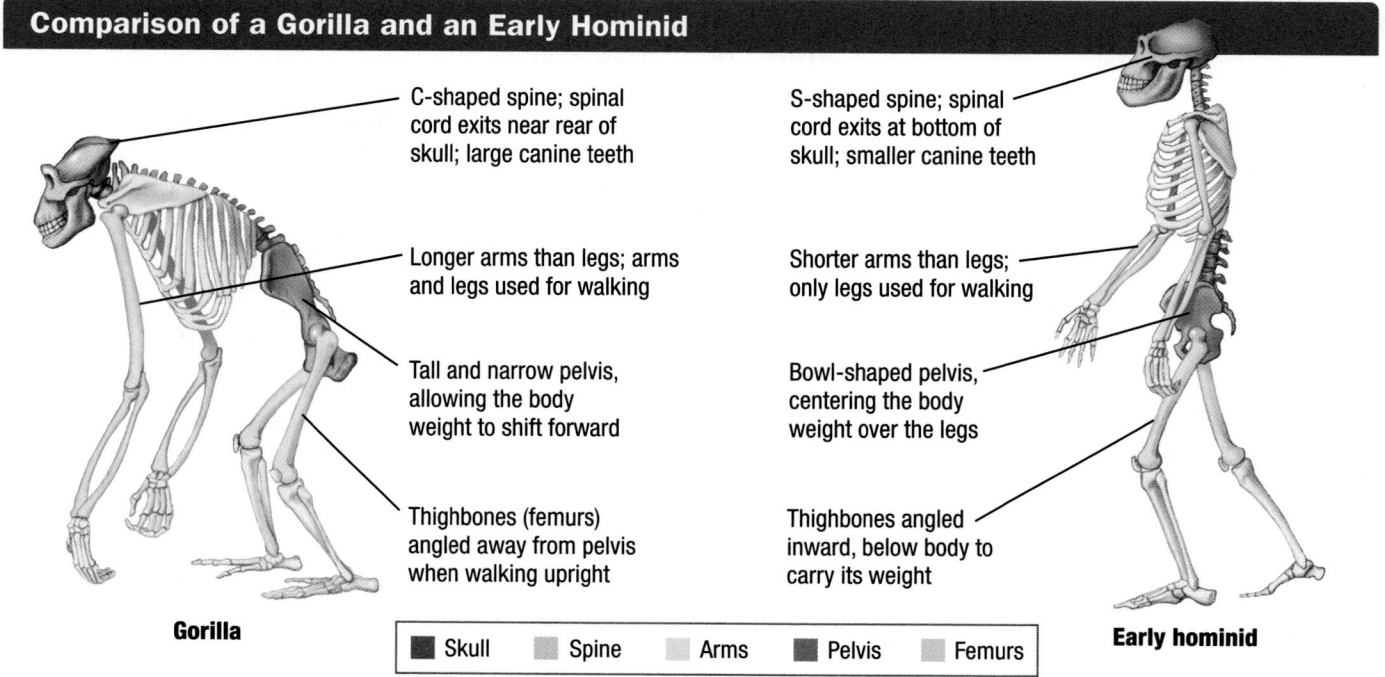

Comparison of a Gorilla and an Early Hominid

C-shaped spine; spinal cord exits near rear of skull; large canine teeth

Longer arms than legs; arms and legs used for walking

Tall and narrow pelvis, allowing the body weight to shift forward

Thighbones (femurs) angled away from pelvis when walking upright

S-shaped spine; spinal cord exits at bottom of skull; smaller canine teeth

Shorter arms than legs; only legs used for walking

Bowl-shaped pelvis, centering the body weight over the legs

Thighbones angled inward, below body to carry its weight

Gorilla

Early hominid

■ Skull   ■ Spine   ■ Arms   ■ Pelvis   ■ Femurs

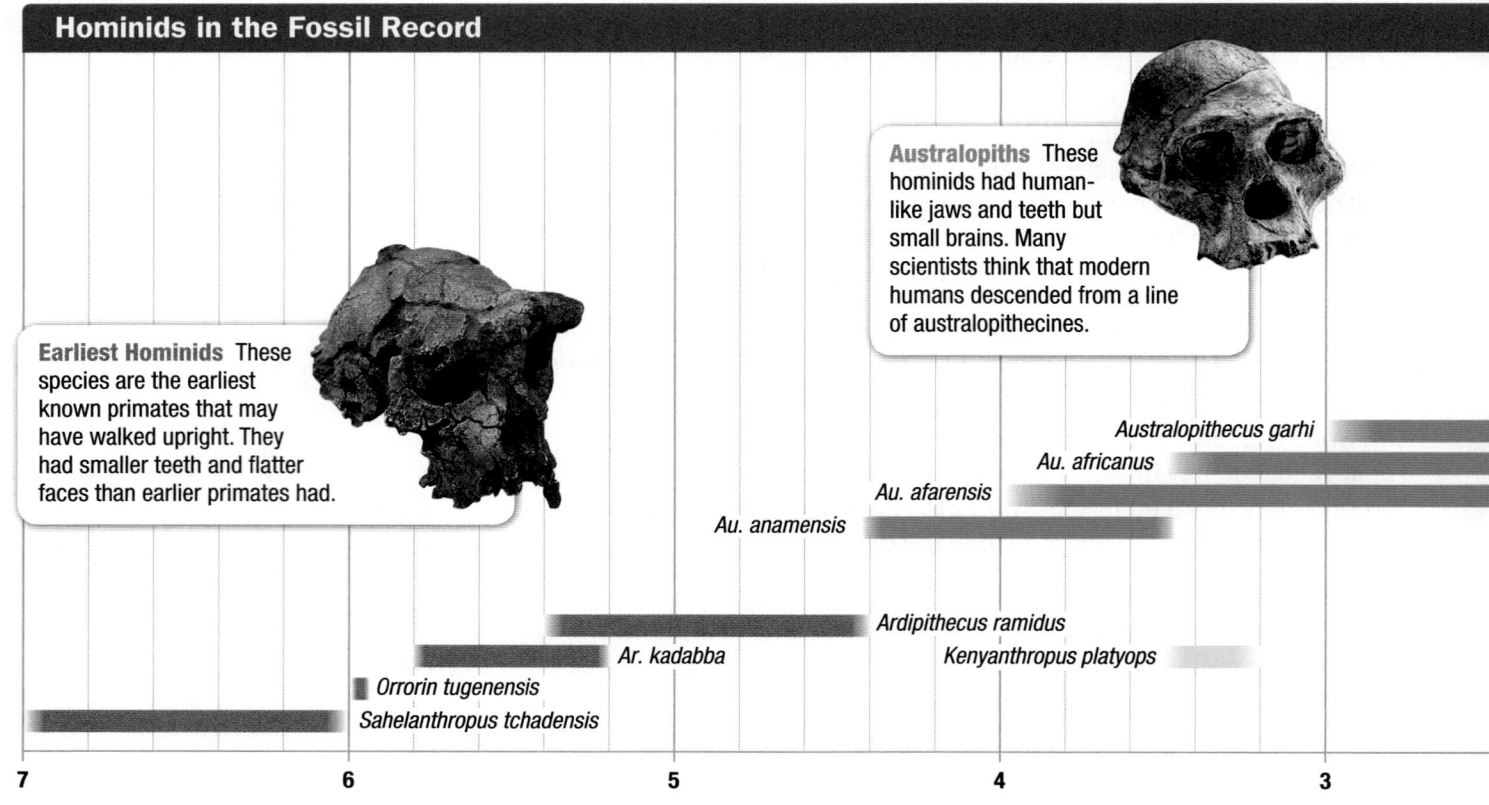

Hominids in the Fossil Record

Earliest Hominids These species are the earliest known primates that may have walked upright. They had smaller teeth and flatter faces than earlier primates had.

Australopiths These hominids had human-like jaws and teeth but small brains. Many scientists think that modern humans descended from a line of australopithecines.

Australopithecus garhi

Au. africanus

Au. afarensis

Au. anamensis

Ardipithecus ramidus

Ar. kadabba

Kenyanthropus platyops

Orrorin tugenensis

Sahelanthropus tchadensis

7   6   5   4   3

Estimated dates (millions of years ago)

The Path to Humans

The growing fossil record for hominids provides clues to our past. ❯ **Many different hominid species lived over the past 7 million years. And more than one species lived at the same time. Except for modern humans, all of these ancient hominid species died out.**

Earliest Hominids Four very old hominid species, shown in orange in **Figure 14,** have been found in the past 20 years. There is debate about the classification of all of these species as true hominids. They tended to have some hominid traits, such as small canine teeth, and some apelike traits, such as a relatively small brain.

Australopiths Fossils of the genus *Australopithecus,* shown in green in **Figure 14,** indicate that they walked upright on two legs. But they probably spent part of their days in trees. Their legs, arms, and teeth were more humanlike than earlier hominids. Their bodies were small, with small brains—about the size of a modern chimpanzee. The size of their brain implies that bipedalism did not result from the enlargement of the brain during evolution. Many scientists think that one of the australopith species was ancestral to modern humans.

Paranthropus Other hominids that lived later than most of the australopiths were larger, standing up to 5 ft tall. *Paranthropus,* shown in red in **Figure 14,** had very heavy jaws and skulls and relatively small brains. They are not thought to be human ancestors.

ACADEMIC VOCABULARY

imply to suggest

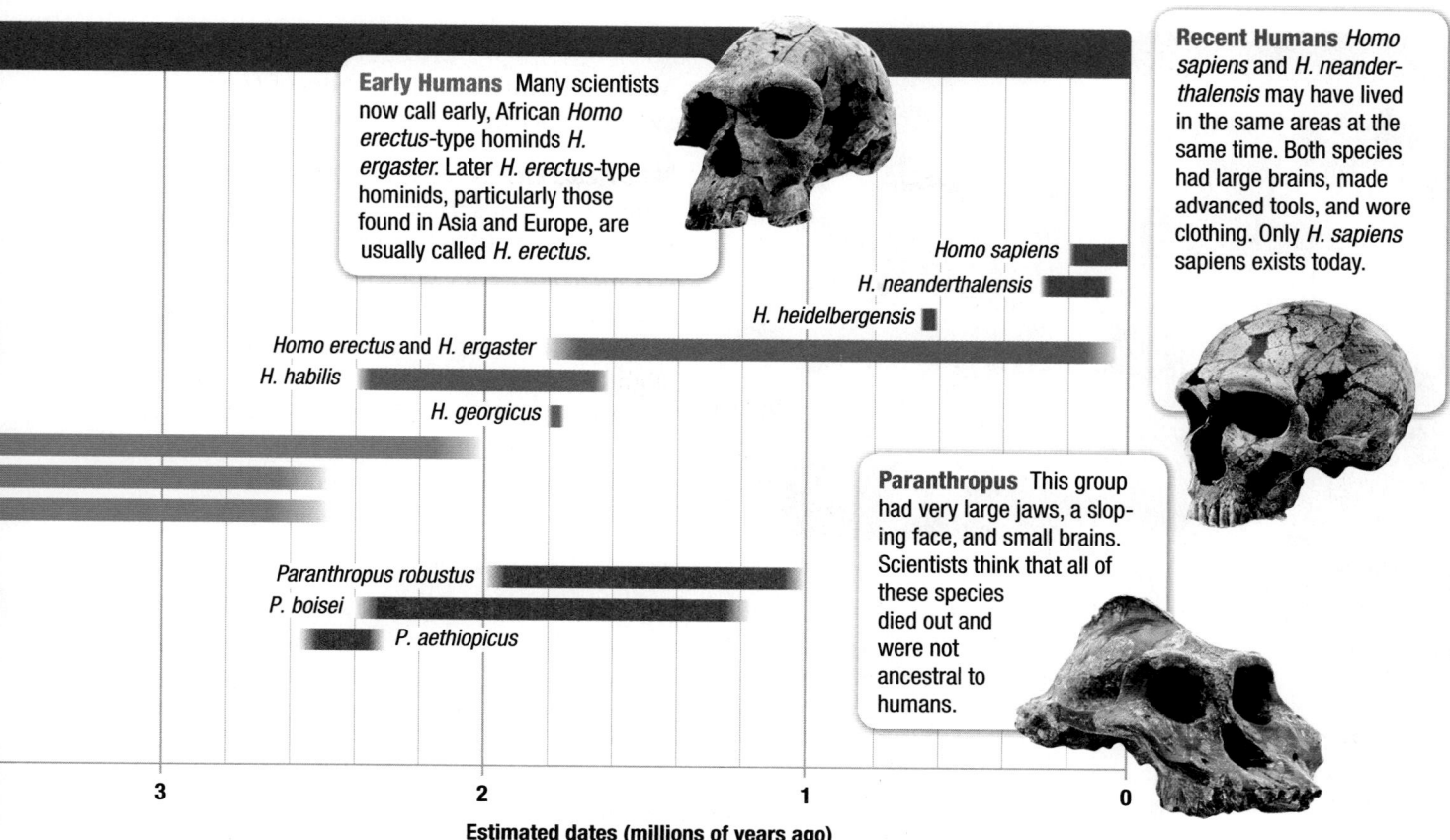

Early Humans Many scientists now call early, African *Homo erectus*-type hominds *H. ergaster.* Later *H. erectus*-type hominids, particularly those found in Asia and Europe, are usually called *H. erectus.*

Recent Humans *Homo sapiens* and *H. neanderthalensis* may have lived in the same areas at the same time. Both species had large brains, made advanced tools, and wore clothing. Only *H. sapiens* sapiens exists today.

Homo sapiens

H. neanderthalensis

H. heidelbergensis

Homo erectus and *H. ergaster*
H. habilis
H. georgicus

Paranthropus This group had very large jaws, a sloping face, and small brains. Scientists think that all of these species died out and were not ancestral to humans.

Paranthropus robustus
P. boisei
P. aethiopicus

| 3 | 2 | 1 | 0 |

Estimated dates (millions of years ago)

Homo habilis In the early 1960s, hominid bones were discovered near the site where australopith fossils had been found. Stone tools were scattered among the bones. This species stood up to about 1.27 m (5 ft) tall. Its brain was about 650 cm^3. This is larger than the australopith brain volume of 400 to 550 cm^3. Because of its association with tools, this hominid was named *Homo habilis,* which is Latin for "handy man." It was the first species of the human genus, *Homo.*

Homo ergaster and Homo erectus At least 1.8 million years ago, a new species replaced "handy man." As hominids evolved, their brains became larger. The brain of *Homo ergaster* was much larger— about 1,000 cm^3. The shape of its arms, hands, and legs suggests that it was more adapted to walking than to climbing trees. It made advanced stone tools and lived in social groups. Although it appeared after *H. habilis,* it may not have been descended from *H. habilis.*

The species now called *Homo ergaster* by many scientists was first called *Homo erectus.* And the name *H. erectus* is used for later, similar hominids that moved from Africa into Asia and Europe. Most scientists think that *H. erectus* or *H. ergaster* was the direct ancestor of our species, *Homo sapiens.* Often, scientists do not agree on the classification of hominid fossils. And some fossil discoveries are difficult puzzle pieces to place. For example, some scientists classify *H. georgicus* as *H. ergaster,* although *H. georgicus* was found in Asia.

❯ **Reading Check** *Which came first—a larger brain or bipedalism?*

Figure 14 Many species of hominids have lived during the past 7 million years. This diagram represents one hypothesis for the relationships between hominids. For updates on phylogenetic information, visit **go.hrw.com.** Enter the keyword **HX8 Phylo.**

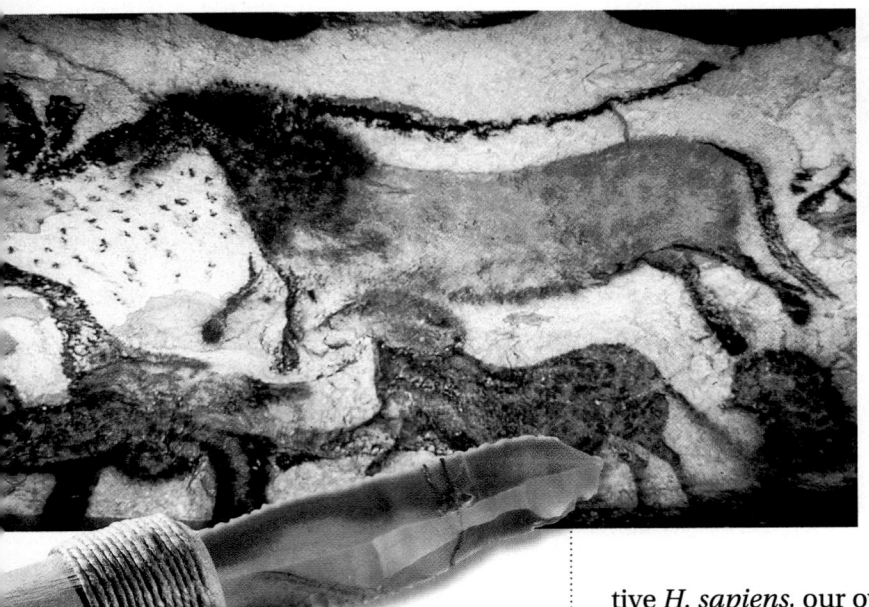

Figure 15 Early modern humans painted the walls of this cave (top) in France about 20,000 years ago. This early tool (bottom) was made from a brittle stone called *flint*.

SC*L*INKS.
www.scilinks.org
Topic: Evolution of Humans
Code: HX80550

Modern Humans

Modern humans are members of *Homo sapiens,* the only surviving species of hominid.

Neanderthals Fossils of an advanced hominid species, *Homo neanderthalensis,* were found in 1856 in Germany. Called *Neanderthals,* they were short and powerfully built. Their heavy skulls had large brow ridges. The average Neanderthal brain was slightly larger than that of a modern human. Neanderthals lived in Europe and Asia starting about 230,000 years ago. They cared for their injured and often buried their dead. They died out about 30,000 years ago.

Homo sapiens The oldest fossils of primitive *H. sapiens,* our own species, are about 500,000 years old. These fossils have much in common with *H. erectus* fossils and with modern humans. The earliest *H. sapiens* fossils of a truly modern type are about 195,000 years old and were found in eastern Africa. How did modern humans, which live all over Earth, arise? Did they evolve from *H. ergaster* and *H. erectus* populations at the same time in different locations? Or did they evolve in a single location?

❯ **Studies of fossils and the genes of modern populations indicate that modern humans evolved in Africa between 100,000 and 200,000 years ago.** They then probably migrated in waves to Europe and Asia. They may have reached North America from Asia as early as 15,000 years ago. As they populated Earth, modern humans replaced *H. erectus, H. ergaster,* Neanderthals, and other hominid species.

Several qualities unique to humans have contributed to our success. Humans can make and use tools. Humans can think abstractly, applying existing knowledge to new situations. Humans can plan for future events. And humans have symbolic communication: spoken and written language. Language allows for non-genetic communication. Concepts can be conveyed across space and through time, paving the way for a new kind of evolution: cultural evolution.

Section 3 Review

❯ KEY IDEAS

1. **Name** two unique features of primates.
2. **Name** the three groups of primates alive today.
3. **Describe** how early hominids differed from the primates that came before them.
4. **Explain** what the hominid fossil record tells us about the path to modern humans.
5. **State** where and when scientists think that modern humans evolved.

CRITICAL THINKING

6. **Explaining Relationships** How does the location of a primate's eyes help it live high above the ground in the branches of trees? Explain your answer.

ALTERNATIVE ASSESSMENT

7. **Group Project** Select a hominid described in this section, and write a report about who found the fossils and when the fossils were found. Be sure to include a map of where the fossils were found and a description of the fossils. Present your findings in the form of an oral report to the class.

A New Species?

WEIRD SCIENCE

Scientists announced in 2004 the discovery of a new species of hominid, *Homo floresiensis.* The 18,000-year old skeletal remains were found on the island of Flores, in Indonesia. The strangest characteristic of the nearly complete skeleton was its extremely small skull. It would have contained a brain about one-third the size of a normal *H. sapiens* brain. Members of the proposed new species have been referred to as the *hobbit people,* because they resemble the hobbits from J. R. R. Tolkien's book, *The Lord of the Rings.*

Flaws in the New Species Hypothesis

Further analysis of the skeletal remains indicates that they might not be those of a new species after all. The skull and other bones of the single adult specimen display many abnormalities. These included an unusual number of differences between the right and left sides of the skeleton and indications of poorly developed muscles. The small skull of the specimen may have been due to *microcephaly,* a condition in which the brain does not grow to normal size. The single skeleton came from a person who was smaller than other humans who lived on Flores and was about 1.5 m in height. Descendants of the ancient population live on the island today and make up one of many known pygmy populations in the world.

Research Find out more about the controversy surrounding the discovery of the "hobbit people." Why is it difficult to base the proposal of a new species on evidence from a single skeleton?

Hints to the Past A paleoarchaeologist examines a plaster model of the hominid skull originally thought to be from a new species, *H. floresiensis.* Scientists often have few and incomplete skeletons to compare with skeletal remains of other ancient organisms, including hominids, and draw conclusions about the history of a group of species.

A Small Mystery This cave, named Liang Bua, is where the skeleton was found that was proposed to characterize a new species. Archaeologists have unearthed fire pits, tools, and skeletons from the site that they are studying to learn more about the cave's inhabitants.

Chapter 32 Lab

Objectives

➤ Examine distinguishing characteristics of mammals.

➤ Infer the functions of mammalian structures.

Materials

- disposable gloves
- hand lens or stereomicroscope
- prepared slide of mammalian skin
- compound microscope
- mirror
- specimens or pictures of vertebrate skulls (some mammalian and some nonmammalian)

Safety

Mammalian Characteristics

Mammals are vertebrates that have hair, mammary glands, a single lower jawbone, and specialized teeth. Other characteristics of mammals include endothermy and a four-chambered heart. Mammals have oil (sebaceous) glands in their skin, and most have sweat glands. In this lab, you will examine some of the characteristics that distinguish mammals from other vertebrates.

Procedure

❶ Make a data table similar to the one below.

Mammalian Teeth				
Mammal	Incisors	Canines	Premolars	Molars
Human				

❷ Write a question that you would like to explore about the characteristics of mammals based on the objectives for this lab.

❸ Use a hand lens to look at several areas of your skin, including areas that appear to be hairless. Record your observations.

❹ Look at a prepared slide of mammalian skin under low power of a compound microscope. Notice the glands in the skin. Look for the oil (sebaceous) glands and the sweat glands. Draw and label an example of each type of gland.

❺ ⚠ CAUTION: **Wash your hands thoroughly with soap and water.** Use a mirror to look in your mouth. Identify the four kinds of mammalian teeth that are in your mouth.

❻ Count each kind of tooth on one side of your lower jaw. Multiply the number of each kind of tooth by 4, and record your results in the appropriate columns of your data table. Before continuing, wash your hands again.

❼ Look at the skulls of several mammals. Identify the kinds of teeth in each skull. For each skull, find the number of each kind of tooth. Record your results in your data table.

❽ Look at the skulls of several nonmammalian vertebrates, and compare nonmammalian teeth to mammalian teeth.

⑨ Compare the jaws of mammalian skulls to those of nonmammalian vertebrates. As you look at each skull, notice the structure of the lower jawbone and the way in which the upper jawbone and the lower jawbone connect.

⑩ ◈ ◈ Clean up your lab materials according to your teacher's instructions. Wash your hands before leaving the lab.

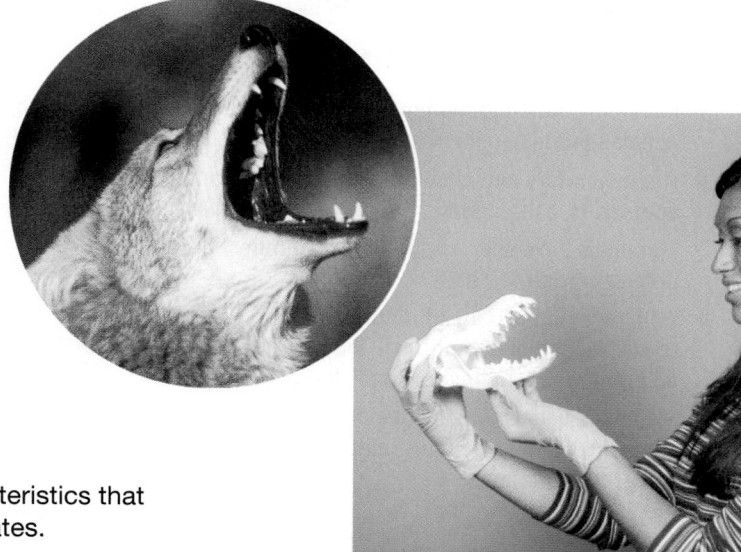

Analyze and Conclude

1. **Summarizing Information** List the characteristics that distinguish mammals from other vertebrates.

2. **Inferring Relationships** What role, if any, might hair or fur play in enabling mammals to be endotherms?

3. **SCIENTIFIC METHODS Forming Hypotheses** What roles other than the role identified in item 2 above do you think hair might play in mammals?

4. **Recognizing Patterns** Where are the oil (sebaceous) glands located in the skin of mammals?

5. **Comparing Structures** How does the mammalian jaw differ from nonmammalian jaws?

6. **SCIENTIFIC METHODS Inferring Conclusions** Given the shape of your teeth, would you classify humans as carnivores (meat eaters), herbivores (plant eaters), or omnivores (meat and plant eaters)? Explain.

7. **SCIENTIFIC METHODS Evaluating Conclusions** Justify the following conclusion: The kinds and shapes of a mammal's teeth can be used to determine the mammal's diet.

Extensions

8. **Further Inquiry** Write a new question about the characteristics of mammals that could be explored in a new investigation.

Chapter 32 Summary

Key Ideas	Key Terms

1 Characteristics of Mammals

> Mammals are endothermic, they have hair and specialized teeth, and females produce milk in mammary glands to nourish their young.

> The respiratory and circulatory systems of mammals are adapted to endothermy.

> Mammals have specialized teeth that reflect the differences in their diets.

> Young mammals depend on their mother for a relatively long period of time. They receive milk and other food, protection, and shelter from her.

> Mammals use various modes of locomotion, including running, hopping, climbing, burrowing, flying, and swimming.

mammary gland (788)
placenta (788)
gestation period (788)
echolocation (790)

2 Diversity of Mammals

> Monotremes share more traits with reptiles than with other mammals. Monotremes are the only living mammals that lay eggs.

> The females of most marsupials have a pouch, and their young spend most of their time developing inside this pouch while they nurse and grow.

> Placental mammals make up nearly 95% of all mammalian species. The young of placental mammals develop inside the female's uterus, where they are nourished by nutrients from her blood.

monotreme (791)

3 Evolution of Primates

> All primates have grasping hands and most have grasping feet. The forward placement of the eyes give primates overlapping, binocular vision.

> The three groups of primates alive today include lemurs and their relatives, tarsiers, and anthropoids—monkeys, apes, and humans.

> Early hominids differed from other primates in that they were bipdedal, they had relatively short arms, a bowl-shaped pelvis, and an S-shaped spine, and their spinal cord exited at the bottom of their skull rather than at the rear.

> Many different hominid species lived over the past 7 million years. And more than one species lived at the same time. Except for the direct ancestors of modern humans, all of these ancient hominid species died out.

> Studies of the genes of modern populations indicate that modern humans evolved in Africa about 160,000 years ago.

primate (797)
hominid (799)

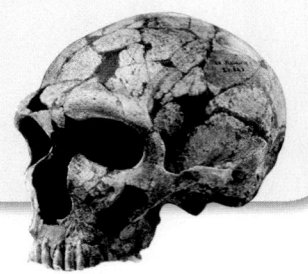

1. **Word Origins** Bats are mammals that belong to the order Chiroptera. Use a dictionary to find the meaning of the name Chiroptera.

2. **Concept Map** Make a concept map that describes the different methods of mammalian reproduction. Include the following terms in your map: *monotreme, marsupial, mammal, mammary gland, egg,* and *placenta.*

Using Key Terms

In your own words, write a definition for each of the following terms.

3. *mammary gland*

4. *echolocation*

5. *primate*

6. *hominid*

Use the following terms in the same sentence.

7. *gestation period* and *placenta*

Understanding Key Ideas

8. The primary function served by mammalian hair is
   a. defense.   c. insulation.
   b. sensory.   d. camouflage.

9. Which of the following mammals would you expect to have long canine teeth?
   a. tiger   c. buffalo
   b. giraffe   d. elephant

10. What characteristic of monotremes sets them apart from other mammals?
    a. They lay eggs.
    b. They have scales.
    c. The don't have hair.
    d. They don't have mammary glands.

11. Two unique features of primates are
    a. binocular vision and grasping hands.
    b. slow metabolic rate and binocular vision.
    c. grasping hands and two-chambered heart.
    d. two-chambered heart and slow metabolic rate.

Use the illustration of a grizzly bear and your knowledge of science to answer the following questions.

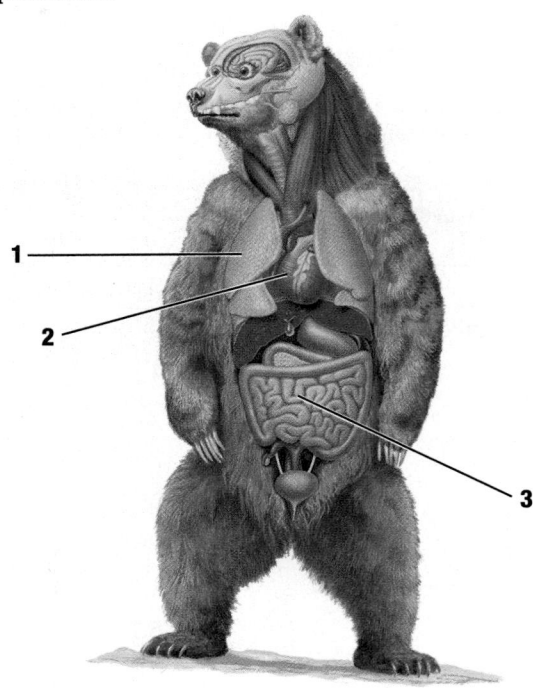

12. Which statement describes the function of structure 1?
    a. Milk is produced here.
    b. Air is drawn into structure 1.
    c. Fertilized eggs are implanted here.
    d. Nutrients and oxygen diffuse to a fetus through structure 1.

13. Which statement describes the function of structure 2?
    a. Two pumping chambers supply oxygen-rich blood to the lungs.
    b. Four pumping chambers supply oxygen-poor blood to the lungs.
    c. One pumping chamber supplies blood to the lungs and the body organs.
    d. One pumping chamber supplies oxygen-poor blood to the lungs, and one pumping chamber supplies oxygen-rich blood to the body organs.

Explaining Key Ideas

14. **Describe** the cost of having an endothermic metabolism.

15. **Identify** the ways that female mammals help their young after they are born, other than providing them with milk.

16. **Describe** three sets of marsupial and placental mammals that have similar lifestyles in different areas.

Interpreting Graphics

Use the table showing gestation periods in mammals to answer the following questions.

Gestation Periods in Mammals	
Mammal	Gestation period (days)
Chipmunk	31
Deer (white-tailed)	204
Elephant (Asian)	644
Gorilla	257
Kangaroo (red)	33
Lion	109
Monkey (rhesus)	166
Opossum (American)	12
Raccoon	63
Squirrel (fox)	44
Whale (blue)	330
Wolf (gray)	63

17. Which mammal has the shortest gestation period?
   a. lion   c. opossum
   b. gorilla   d. chipmunk

18. **Interpreting Data** Make a bar graph showing the gestation periods in mammals.

Critical Thinking

19. **Drawing Conclusions** How do hair and a high rate of metabolism help a mammal maintain homeostasis?

20. **Applying Information** A mammal must eat about 10 times as much food as an ectotherm of similar size. What role might the respiratory system play in this need?

21. **Evaluating Conclusions** Some mammal species must care for their young for many years before they reach maturity and can survive on their own. Can you conclude that all vertebrate young would benefit from this type of parental care? Explain why or why not.

22. **Assessing Significance** As Earth's climate began to cool millions of years ago, grassy plains began replacing many of the great forests. Explain why the loss of forests might have a significant affect on the characteristics seen in the early hominids.

23. **Supporting Conclusions** Some scientists think that Neanderthals were the first hominids to show evidence of abstract thought. Explain the archaeological evidence that seems to support this conclusion.

Alternative Assessment

24. **Creating a Documentary** Mammals are the only animals that have hair. But hair has functions other than to provide warmth and insulation. The color and pattern of a mammal's coat often enables it to blend in with its surroundings. Make a video showing the camouflage of different mammals in action. Write a script that narrates the action and describes how the mammals in your video have adapted to their specific surroundings.

25. **Creating an Animation** Mammals have a four-chambered heart that pumps blood to the lungs and to the body. Create an animation tracing the pathway of the flow of blood through the four chambers. Begin with oxygen-poor blood entering the right atrium, include the lungs in your pathway at the appropriate point, and finish with the oxygenated blood going to the entire body.

Writing for Science

26. **Recognizing Patterns** Find out more about how plate tectonics can explain the pattern of distribution of mammals on Earth. Analyze and critique the theory, and write a report on your findings. Include a description of how the breakup of Pangaea led to the predominance of placental mammals on all the continents except Australia.

TEST TIP Before looking at the answer choices for a question, try to answer the question yourself.

Science Concepts

1. Which of the following is *not* a key characteristic of mammals?

   A hair

   B specialized teeth

   C mammary glands

   D ectothermic metabolism

2. What is the function of a mammalian diaphragm?

   F enables efficient breathing

   G provides nourishment for young

   H carries the young inside the uterus

   J keeps oxygenated blood separate in heart

3. Bats and dolphins have a special way of sensing their environment using sound that is called

   A radar.   **C** gestation.

   B weaning.   **D** echolocation.

4. Which of these animals is a marsupial?

   F lion

   G echidna

   H opossum

   J duckbill platypus

5. Which of the following mammal groups accounts for 40% of placental mammals and has specialized teeth for gnawing?

   A bats   **C** carnivores

   B rodents   **D** artiodactyls

6. A primate's depth perception is produced by the

   F large frontal lobe of the brain.

   G rods and cones found in the retina.

   H position of the eyes at the front of the face.

   J the ability to see in bright light.

7. The only surviving species of our genus, *Homo*, is

   A *Homo habilis.*

   B *Homo erectus.*

   C *Homo ergaster.*

   D *Homo sapiens sapiens.*

Using Science Graphics

Use the illustration of the skulls of two different mammals to answer the following question.

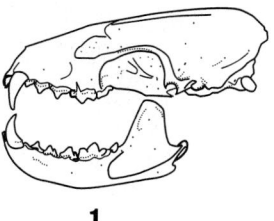   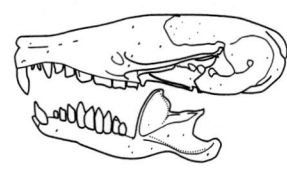

1   2

8. What can be inferred about these mammals?

   F Mammal 1 has more fat than mammal 2.

   G Mammal 1 has more hair than mammal 2.

   H Mammal 1 eats more meat than mammal 2.

   J Mammal 1 eats more grass than mammal 2.

Use the graph showing cranial capacity of hominids to answer the following question.

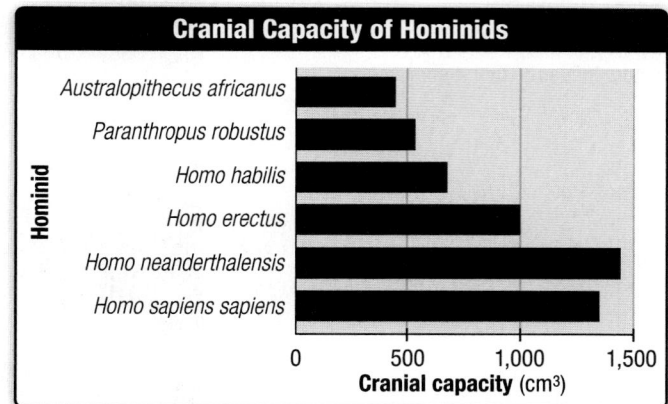

9. The hominid with the largest cranial capacity is

   A *Homo erectus.*

   B *Homo sapiens sapiens.*

   C *Homo neanderthalensis.*

   D *Australopithecus africanus.*

Writing Skills

10. Short Response Mammals and birds are endothermic vertebrates. Describe the functional costs and benefits of endothermy.

Chapter 33

Animal Behavior

It may not look like it, but these male stag beetles are fighting. Males of many species fight over desirable resources.

Preview

1 The Nature of Behavior
Questions About Behavior
Influences on Behavior
Evolution of Behavior
Innate Behavior
Learned Behavior

2 Classes of Behavior
Survival Strategies
Modes of Communication
Reproductive Strategies

Why It Matters

Did you know that most of our behavior is very similar to animal behavior? We can learn a lot about our own behavior by studying how animals interact with one another and what factors influence their behavior.

The male beetle on the bottom is using his front appendages (pincers) to lift his opponent high in the air.

The size of the beetle and the size of the beetle's pincers help determine the outcome of these fights.

Inquiry**Lab**

A Ball of Armor

In this lab, you will observe how pill bugs respond to a threat stimulus.

Procedure

1. Transfer several pill bugs to a small container.

2. Use a hand lens to examine these small arthropods. What features can you observe?

3. Gently poke a pill pug with the eraser end of a pencil. Observe the pill bug's behavior.

Analysis

1. **Describe** the features of a pill bug.

2. **Identify** the threat stimulus presented to the pill bug.

3. **Describe** how the pill bug reacted to the threat stimulus.

4. **Identify** how this change in appearance protects the animal.

READING TOOLBOX These reading tools can help you learn the material in this chapter. For more information on how to use these and other tools, see **Appendix: Reading and Study Skills.**

Using Words

Everyday Words in Science Several key terms in this chapter have everyday meanings that are different from the terms' scientific meanings.

Your Turn Make a table like the one shown.
1. Before you read, write in your own words the everyday meaning of the terms in the table.
2. As you read, fill in the science meaning for the terms in the table.

Everyday Words in Science		
Word	**Everyday meaning**	**Science meaning**
behavior		
conditioning		
signal		

Using Language

Predictions You are probably familiar with the phrase "It might rain today." There are many words that are used to make predictions. In science, words such as *rarely, often,* and *always* can offer clues about the likelihood that an event will happen. Analyze the statement "Cats rarely enjoy getting a bath." The statement tells you that most cats, but maybe not all cats, dislike baths.

Your Turn After reading your text, use *never, rarely, often,* or *always* to fill in the blank in the following sentences.
1. New males _____ kill all of the young cubs in the pride.
2. Territorial behavior _____ results in serious injuries.

Using Graphic Organizers

Cause-and-Effect Maps You can use a cause-and-effect map when you want to describe how, when, or why one event causes another. A cause-and-effect map can also be used to describe the relationship between a stimulus and a response in the production of behavior. The diagram shows one example of a cause-and-effect map.

Your Turn Create a cause-and-effect map to show the response to a stimulus. The first stimulus-and-response pair has been provided for you.
1. Draw two more boxes, and write a stimulus in each box.
2. Draw another box to the right of the stimulus box to represent a response.
3. One of the stimulus boxes is paired with more than one response. Make sure that the response is appropriate for each stimulus.

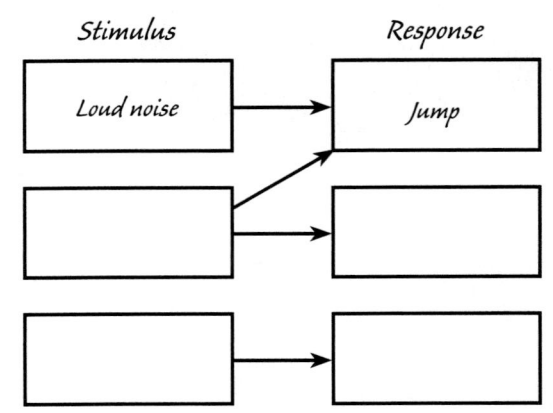

The Nature of Behavior

Key Ideas	Key Terms	Why It Matters
❯ What questions help scientists study behavior? ❯ What factors influence behavior? ❯ How does evolution shape behavior? ❯ What factors cause innate behavior? ❯ What are examples of learned behavior?	behavior learning stimulus reasoning response conditioning innate behavior imprinting fixed action pattern	Behavior shapes how animals interact with the environment and with each other.

We constantly interact with other people and our surroundings, and we change our behavior depending on who we are with and where we are. Many behaviors of animals are very similar to our behaviors.

Questions About Behavior

A squirrel buries a nut; a dolphin searches for fish; a hungry baby cries. These are all examples of behavior. A **behavior** is an action or series of actions performed by an organism in response to a stimulus.

A **stimulus** is something in the environment that an organism might respond to, such as a sound, a smell, a color, or another individual. The organism's reaction to the stimulus is the **response.** When the armadillo, shown in **Figure 1,** is frightened by a loud noise (a stimulus), it jumps high in the air (a response). Stimuli and responses can also be internal. For example, when the body detects the presence of foreign bacteria (a stimulus), it activates the immune system (a response).

How Vs. Why Questions Different questions address different aspects of behavior. ❯ Scientists studying behavior ask two kinds of questions—"how" questions and "why" questions. "How" questions ask how a behavior is triggered, controlled, and performed. For example, consider a squirrel. "How" questions about squirrel behavior might include "How does a squirrel select which nuts to bury?" and "How does it choose where to bury the nut?" Answers to "how" questions provide only a partial understanding of a behavior. "Why" questions address the evolution of behavior, such as "Why do squirrels bury nuts?"

❯ **Reading Check** *What is a response? (See the Appendix for answers to Reading Checks.)*

behavior an action that an individual carries out in response to a stimulus

stimulus (STIM yoo luhs) any action or agent that causes or changes an activity in an organism

response any biological reaction or behavior resulting from the application of a stimulus

Figure 1 This armadillo has clearly been frightened by something. Its behavior is a response to a stimulus.

813

How the Body Responds How do the many organ systems of animals coordinate to cause a behavior? Sensory systems gather information about the environment. This information triggers responses by the nervous system. The nervous system is one of the most important systems in the production of behavior. It sends very fast messages to the muscles to produce the behavior. Many behaviors involve other systems, such as the endocrine system.

Influences on Behavior

Many things influence the behaviors of an animal. Some influences are internal. When an animal is hungry, it looks for food. External factors also influence behavior. Sometimes, the physical environment is the external factor. When the water gets too cold, some sharks migrate to warmer water. Other animals may also influence behavior. Sperm whales form a defensive circle around their young when dangerous killer whales are nearby. Often, internal factors and external factors together influence behavior.

Genes, the Environment, and Behavior Animals are capable of very complex behaviors. For example, some European cuckoos perform a behavior known as *brood parasitism,* as **Figure 2** shows. The female cuckoo lays an egg in the nest of another bird. Once the cuckoo chick hatches, it reacts to any other object in the nest—an egg or chick—by pushing it out of the nest. As a result, the cuckoo chick receives all of the parental care from the surrogate parents. Soon, the chick outgrows the parent that is trying to feed it!

Nature Vs. Nurture It is misleading to ask whether genes (nature) or the environment (nurture) shapes behavior. **❯ Behavior is controlled by both genetic and environmental factors.** Genes may increase the likelihood that an individual will display a behavior, but the environment determines whether the behavior is displayed.

❯ Reading Check *What organ systems together produce behavior?*

Figure 2 The European cuckoo female often lays her eggs in the nests of other birds. This behavior has evolved to secure resources for the growing chick, which is raised by substitute parents.

A cuckoo chick pushes an egg from the nest.

The chick soon outgrows the parent.

Evolution of Behavior

Behaviors evolve in much the same way that physical traits do. ❯ Natural selection favors traits (such as behaviors) that increase an individual's reproductive success. Over time, traits that provide a reproductive advantage become more common in the population. Traits that do not provide an advantage become less common and may disappear from the population.

Natural Selection and Behavior Natural selection favors traits that contribute to the survival and reproduction of *individuals* (or an individual's relatives), not species. However, remember that only species can evolve, not individuals. Eventually, a change in selected individuals may cause the species to evolve.

For example, East African lions live in small groups, or prides. Each pride contains several adult females; several young lions, or cubs; and one or more adult males. Lions form prides for many reasons, but one reason lies with the behavior of the males. The adult males father all of the cubs in the pride. But a male or group of males controls a pride for only a couple of years. Then, they are forced out by younger males who take over the pride. When they take over, new males often kill all of the young cubs in the pride, as **Figure 3** shows.

At first glance, the killing of cubs seems to reduce the likelihood that the species will survive. However, remember that male lions behave in ways that are favorable for them, not for the pride as a whole. Killing the cubs benefits the new males. Female lions that have cubs will not breed until their cubs are grown, which may take more than two years. If a female's cubs die, however, the female will mate again almost immediately. By killing the cubs of males previously in control, a new male will be able to mate with the pride's females quickly. His reproductive success increases more than if he did not kill the cubs when he took over the pride. The selection of cub-killing behavior over time has contributed to the evolution of the lion species.

❯ **Reading Check** *What traits are favored by natural selection?*

Figure 3 After taking over a pride, a male lion often kills the young cubs in the pride. However, male lions are usually tolerant of their own cubs. ❯ Why would a male lion kill cubs that are not his own?

Everyday Words in Science The word *behavior* describes a phenotype, or trait of an organism. Use the word *behavior* in a sentence to illustrate its role as a trait, not just an action.

Hands-On QuickLab

Learned Behavior

Pill bugs must stay moist to survive. Can pill bugs learn to find moisture?

Procedure

1. Place a **moist paper wad** in the open end of the left side of a **T-maze,** and place the **dry paper wad** in the right side.

2. Place the **pill bug** at the bottom of the T. If it does not start to crawl, gently prod it with a **blunt probe.**

3. Observe what the pill bug does when it reaches the T section. Retrieve the pill bug. Perform as many trials as time allows. Record the results of each trial.

4. Use the same pill bug to repeat this procedure for three days.

Analysis

1. **Summarize** your pill bug's behavior.

2. **Describe** any trend in behavior that you observed.

3. **Determine** if your pill bug modified its behavior through learning. Use evidence to support your answer.

4. **CRITICAL THINKING** **Analyzing Methods** What is the value of performing a final trial in which the T-maze contains two dry paper wads?

Innate Behavior

For most animals, survival depends on being able to perform behaviors that they do not have a chance to learn. **Innate behaviors** are natural responses to stimuli that do not rely on experience in order to be produced. In mammals, for example, suckling is an innate behavior in response to a touch on the cheek. Sometimes, innate behavior is also called *instinctive behavior.* ❯ **Innate behaviors may be greatly influenced by genes, but these behaviors are not necessarily fixed. Some innate behaviors may be modified by experience.**

Fixed Action Pattern The spider shown in **Figure 4** builds her web the same way every time. There is little or no variation in what she does, and her offspring will build their webs in the same manner without being taught. This type of innate behavior is called a fixed action pattern because the action always occurs the same way. **Fixed action patterns** are innate behaviors that are triggered by a stimulus in the environment, and do not stop once the behavior has begun. For example, seeing another person yawn will trigger the person who sees it to yawn as well. It is very difficult to stop yawning once you have started.

Figure 4 Because web-building behavior is not learned and occurs the same way each time the web is created, web building is an example of a fixed action pattern.

Learned Behavior

Behaviors are influenced by genes but also by the environment and experience. The development of behaviors through experience is called **learning.** ❯ Learning can occur through habituation, problem solving, classical conditioning, and operant conditioning.

Habituation There are many stimuli in an animal's environment—many scents, sounds, actions, and other species. During *habituation,* an animal learns to no longer respond to a frequent, harmless, or unimportant stimulus. Some biologists use habituation to study animals. For example, chimpanzees are normally afraid of humans. But after biologists, such as Jane Goodall, spent hundreds of hours sitting quietly near them, the chimps learned to ignore them. This technique has allowed biologists to observe animals from close range and learn much about their behavior. You can probably think of many examples of habituation by humans. For example, people living near highways or airports habituate to the noise and can easily sleep through the night. However, a friend visiting from the country would likely be up all night because of the noise.

Problem Solving **Reasoning** is the act of drawing a conclusion from facts or an assumption. For example, in one experiment, a chimpanzee was placed in a room with some boxes and a banana hung high overhead. After many trials, the chimpanzee learned to stack up the boxes to reach the banana. This behavior required reasoning. In another experiment, ravens learned to use their beaks to retrieve food that dangled far below them on a string, as **Figure 5** shows. Some dolphins, such as the one shown in **Figure 5,** can find a tool and take it to a place to feed. It is unclear how many other types of animals show reasoning skills.

❯ **Reading Check** *What is the value of habituation?*

innate behavior (in NAYT) an inherited behavior that does not depend on the environment or experience

fixed action pattern a highly stereotyped pattern of innate behavior that is triggered by a simple sensory cue

learning the development of behaviors through experience or practice

reasoning the act of drawing a conclusion from facts or assumption

Figure 5 Reasoning skills are not restricted to humans and primates. The dolphin on the left and the raven on the right both are using reasoning to obtain food. ❯ **Does reasoning depend on learning?**

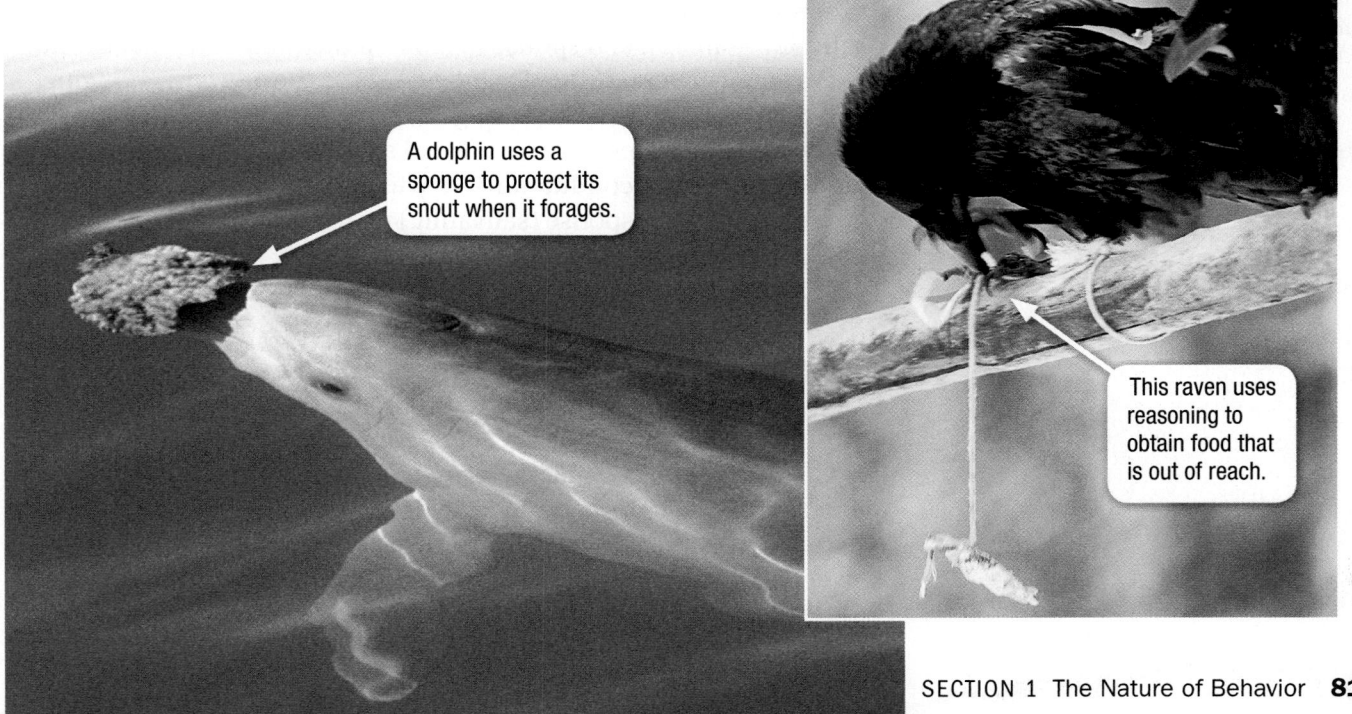

A dolphin uses a sponge to protect its snout when it forages.

This raven uses reasoning to obtain food that is out of reach.

❶ Before conditioning Pavlov gave the dog some food, and it salivated. When Pavlov later rang a bell, the dog did not salivate.

❷ During conditioning Pavlov then presented the food and rang the bell at the same time. He presented these two stimuli together many times. Each time, the dog salivated in the presence of the food.

❸ After conditioning Later, when the bell was presented alone, the dog salivated. It had learned to associate the bell with the appearance of food.

Figure 6 Pavlov first demonstrated that by a process of learning called *conditioning*, animals can learn to put two and two together. Humans also learn by association. ❯ **How is associative learning different from reasoning?**

go.hrw.com
✳ interact online
Keyword: HX8ABHF6

conditioning (kuhn DISH uhn ing) the process of learning by association

imprinting (im PRINT ing) learning that occurs early and quickly in a young animal's life and that cannot be changed once learned

Associative Learning To survive and reproduce successfully, animals must be able to "put two and two together." Associative learning is the process by which animals learn to relate stimuli and conditions in their environment through repeated experience with the same situation or events. Associative learning can be understanding the relationship between the presence of one stimulus and the presence or absence of another stimulus (classical conditioning) or understanding the consequences of one's actions (operant conditioning). Learning by association is called **conditioning**.

Classical Conditioning Conditioning was made famous by scientist Ivan Pavlov's work with dogs. **Figure 6** illustrates his experiment. When Pavlov presented meat powder to a hungry dog, the dog salivated—an innate response to food. At the same time that the dog received the meat powder, Pavlov presented the dog with a ringing bell. After repeated trials, the dog learned to associate the ringing bell with the meat powder and would salivate in response to the bell alone. This type of conditioning, in which an animal comes to associate an unrelated response (salivating) with a stimulus (the sound of a bell), is called *classical conditioning*.

Operant Conditioning Animals also learn by trial and error that performing a certain behavior will result in a reward or a punishment. For example, a dog may learn to avoid a particular cat after being scratched on the nose once or twice. Trial-and-error learning is often called *operant conditioning*. Psychologist B. F. Skinner studied learning in rats by placing them in a "Skinner box." Once inside, the rat would occasionally and accidentally press a lever that released a pellet of food. Eventually, the rat associated pressing the lever with getting the food reward and would perform the behavior more often.

Sensitive Periods Many behaviors develop and become fixed during a particular period of an animal's life. The song of male birds develops during a brief period early in life. The song develops from the bird's hearing its father's song and undergoing hormonal changes as the bird matures. Language in humans develops most rapidly in the first several years of life. The ability to learn new languages diminishes as we age. **Imprinting** occurs when an animal develops a particular response to an object or organism *only* during a brief period early in life. In this way, imprinting differs from other types of learning.

Imprinting Young geese and ducks have no innate recognition of their mother. These birds are genetically programmed to follow the first moving object they see during a short period immediately after they hatch. This behavior is highly adaptive; the young must follow their mother as she leads them to water, helps them find food, and keeps them out of danger. However, the young will follow any object they see during this period, just as they would their mother—including toy wagons, boxes, and balloons. Once the young birds imprint on an object, they prefer to follow it, even when given the opportunity to follow a member of their own species.

Scientist Konrad Lorenz observed imprinting when he raised a group of newly hatched goslings (young geese) by hand and found that they imprinted on *him*. **Figure 7** shows an extension of this experiment—an aircraft leading a "family" of cranes. The cranes' *ability* to imprint on an object is not a learned behavior; the ability is programmed into their genes. However, the *process* of imprinting is a form of learned behavior. Learning determines the final shape of this genetically based behavior.

❯ Reading Check *What are the benefits of imprinting behavior?*

Figure 7 These cranes imprinted on a researcher riding in this ultralight aircraft and followed it around as if the researcher were their mother.

ACADEMIC VOCABULARY

adaptive able to adjust to changes

Section 1 Review

❯ KEY IDEAS

1. **List** the two questions that help scientists study behavior.
2. **Describe** influences on behavior.
3. **Explain** how evolution shapes behavior.
4. **State** what influences innate behavior.
5. **List** the different types of learning.

CRITICAL THINKING

6. **Justifying Conclusions** Alcoholism runs in families. Does this mean that behavior is controlled only by genes? Why or why not?
7. **Justifying Conclusions** A newborn will turn toward a touch on the cheek and begin to suck. An older child will not. What two kinds of learning are demonstrated by this?

WRITING FOR SCIENCE

8. **Essay** Write a short essay about the costs and benefits of lions living together. Include in your argument the factors that influence the lions' behavior. Can you relate any of these costs and benefits to why humans usually live in groups?

Proud as a Peacock

Recognizing a potential mate is the first step in reproduction. But what if there are several potential mates? Males of many species have developed elaborate ways to attract females. Humans, on the other hand, are unique—both males and females use elaborate displays to attract potential mates.

Too Much of a Good Thing?

Sexual selection for traits that enhance a male's advertisement display is ultimately limited by the basic survival needs and fitness of the male. For example, peahens tend to prefer peacocks that have the longest tails. But the longer the peacock's tail is, the more the tail hampers his flight and maneuverability.

Bird The male ruff displays a special collar of raised feathers around his head and neck. Females lack the male plumage and coloring.

Beta Male betas bred in captivity have developed bright colors and very large fins to attract mates. Female betas have drab colors and small fins like those of their beta ancestors in the wild.

Crab Male fiddler crabs have one small claw and one enormous claw. Females have two small claws. The male waves his large claw in the air to attract females.

Research Investigate the meaning of *sexual dimorphism*, and give some examples.

Key Ideas	Key Terms	Why It Matters
❯ What behaviors are essential for survival? ❯ How do animals communicate with each other? ❯ How do animals maximize reproductive success?	foraging territorial migration behavior circadian courtship rhythm sexual selection communication	Foraging, antipredator, and reproductive behaviors are critical for an animal's survival. They determine how an animal interacts with individuals of its own and other species.

The two major challenges that an animal faces are survival and reproduction. By overcoming these challenges, an animal will achieve its ultimate "goal"—passing on its genes to the next generation.

Survival Strategies

Natural selection favors individuals with the highest reproductive success, and survival is a key part of achieving this success. ❯ **The survival of an individual depends on finding resources, such as food, and avoiding predators.**

Foraging Behavior Finding food is critical for survival. Animals have many behaviors, called **foraging,** that they use to find and gather food. Animals can be divided into two broad groups based on the range of food items that they eat. Specialists feed on one or very few kinds of food. Generalists, such as the grizzly bear shown in **Figure 8,** eat many kinds of food.

Predators have different strategies for finding food. Ambush predators, such as octopuses, wait for their prey to come close before quickly attacking. Stalking predators, such as lions, use stealth to get close to prey before attacking. Animals tend to prefer prey that maximizes the animals' energy intake but requires the least amount of foraging time. This approach is called *optimal foraging.* Natural selection favors the evolution of optimal-foraging behaviors.

foraging (FAWR ij ing) behavior associated with the search for, obtaining, and consumption of food

Figure 8 Grizzly bears are generalist foragers, so they eat a wide variety of different foods. ❯ **How does generalist foraging increase survival?**

migration (mie GRAY shuhn) in general, any movement of individuals or populations from one location to another

circadian rhythm (suhr KAY dee uhn RITH uhm) a biological daily cycle

communication (kuh MYOO ni KAY shuhn) a transfer of a signal or message from one animal to another that results in some type of response

SC**LINKS**.

www.scilinks.org
Topic: Animal
     Communication
Code: HX80071

Figure 9 Owls are nocturnal, so they are most active at night. ❯ **How does nocturnal behavior benefit some animals and not others?**

Antipredator Behavior Finding food is a challenge for animals but is not the only key to survival. Almost every animal must avoid becoming a meal for a predator. Even the world's largest animal, the blue whale, is eaten by much smaller killer whales. Some animals have physical defenses, such as the spines of a porcupine. Other animals have chemical defenses. Skunks spray a foul-smelling liquid at attacking predators that stings the eyes.

Some animals, such as opossums, play dead and hope a predator goes away. For others, running away is the best defense. Many prey, such as zebras, are fast runners. One of the most common defenses against predators is forming groups. Animal groups have more eyes to look for predators, and each individual has a lower chance of being the unlucky one when a predator does attack.

Cyclic Behavior Survival depends on being in the right place at the right time. For example, a bird that breeds in the Arctic during the summer would freeze there in the winter. A bat does not fly around during the day when it would be quickly eaten by a hawk. Because timing is important for survival, most animals organize their behavior into patterns that may repeat seasonally or daily.

Seasonal Behaviors Several types of behavior occur at the same time every year. For many species, reproductive behavior occurs only once a year during a short time period. **Migration** is a seasonal movement between widely spaced locations by a large proportion of the animals in a population. Migrations often involve movements between feeding areas and breeding areas. For example, humpback whales spend their summers in Alaska to focus on feeding and move to Hawaii during the winter to focus on mating and giving birth.

Some species that live in areas with long periods of cold weather become inactive, or hibernate. During *hibernation,* the animal's metabolic rate and body temperature drop dramatically. Some animals hibernate continuously for months, whereas other animals wake up several times during the winter. Hibernation helps animals conserve energy when little food can be found.

Circadian Rhythms A **circadian rhythm** is a cycle that occurs on a daily basis. Circadian rhythms occur in almost every animal. *Circadian* comes from the Latin words *circa,* meaning "about," and *diem,* meaning "day." Circadian rhythms are internal and are not tied to environmental signals. Many internal patterns are circadian rhythms. Body temperature, immune response, sleep patterns, and activity level all occur on a regular, cyclic basis. For example, some animals, such as the barn owl shown in **Figure 9,** are *nocturnal*—they sleep all day and are active at night. Other animals are *diurnal*—they sleep at night and are active during the day.

QuickLab

⏱ 15 min

Safety in Darkness

Mealworms, like many animals, avoid bright light. By remaining in dim or dark places, these beetle larvae are less likely to be detected by birds and other predators. Can you observe this behavior in the classroom?

Procedure

1 Cover one half of a **Petri dish lid** with **aluminum foil**.

2 Put on **disposable gloves**. Transfer **10 mealworms** to the **Petri dish bottom.** Use a **hand lens** to examine these larvae. Record your observations.

3 Place the dish in an area of bright light. Make sure that the mealworms are equally distributed.

4 Lower the lid over the dish bottom. Record the number of mealworms on the light side of the dish.

5 Wait 5 min. Then, record the number of mealworms remaining on the lit side.

6 Rotate the cover a half turn so that the exposed and covered sides of the dish bottom are reversed. Repeat steps 4 through 6.

Analysis

1. **Describe** how mealworms move.

2. **Explain** how the mealworms reacted to bright light. Can you give an explanation for this behavior?

3. **CRITICAL THINKING** **Identifying Functions** In step 6, why was the lid rotated so that its exposed and covered sides were switched?

Modes of Communication

You approach an unfamiliar dog, and it begins to bark. You know that if you go closer, the dog may bite you, so you stop and talk to it. The dog continues to bark but not so aggressively, and it begins to wag its tail. You and the dog have communicated with each other. **Communication** includes any behavior that contains information and involves a sender and a receiver.

A communication *signal* is sent and received through all of the senses familiar to us—sight, hearing, smell, touch, and taste—and some senses that are not, such as electrical sense. **❯ Animals use signals to influence the behavior of other animals. Many kinds of signals can be used for this purpose.** The behavior can be a sound, posture, movement, color, scent, facial expression, or even electric discharges.

Communication is absolutely necessary for social behavior. Because there are many social situations, animals use various signals. Many signals are suited to particular situations. Natural selection has shaped animal signals so that they reach the intended receiver efficiently and stimulate a response.

Sight Visual signals occur rapidly and are easy to produce. The caterpillar shown in **Figure 10** produces visual signals—bright colors and a false "face"—to deter a predator. If the signal is clearly visible, the receiver knows where the signaler is located. Visual signals do not always attract attention as easily as other signals. However, some visual signals, such as a firefly's light, are quite noticeable.

❯ Reading Check *How has natural selection shaped signals?*

Figure 10 A puss moth caterpillar displays its false face to warn off predators. Many animals use visual displays to appear threatening.

Chemical

Touch

Sound

Figure 11 Animals use different types of signals to communicate. Ants often communicate by using chemicals, and other animals may use touch or sound to communicate. ❯ **Why are different modes of communication beneficial?**

Chemicals Chemical signals last longer in the environment than other signals do and can even move long distances on a breeze. Many chemical signals, such as *pheromones,* are used in reproduction. When females of some species are ready to mate, they release chemical signals that males can follow for miles. Chemical signals are commonly used in marking the boundaries of territories. Ants, such as those shown in **Figure 11,** use chemicals to mark their paths.

Touch Touch has the advantage of conveying complex information that is easily interpreted and noticed. However, this form of communication is effective only when animals are in close proximity to one another. Many species, such as the prairie dogs shown in **Figure 11,** use touch to build social bonds and reassure members of their group.

Sound Sound is typically better than visual signals at getting attention or communicating over large distances. Whales may be able to communicate with sound over hundreds of miles! Sound does not convey as much information as visual signals, but it can convey a variety of messages. Animal calls, such as that of the mandrill shown in **Figure 11,** may provide information about the caller's identity or location. Calls may also signal the presence of food or predators or the motivation of the caller (angry, submissive, or content). Vocal communication appears to be most developed in primates and dolphins. Some primates have a "vocabulary" of calls that allows individuals to communicate the identity of specific predators.

Language Just as not all vocal communication is language, not all language involves vocalizations. Humans can teach chimpanzees and gorillas to recognize and use a large number of symbols to communicate abstract concepts. However, only humans combine symbols in novel ways to form language.

❯ **Reading Check** *Which signal is often used over large distances?*

Reproductive Strategies

Reproduction is the key to evolution and the success of an <u>individual</u>. ❯ **During a breeding period, animals perform mating and parenting behaviors. These behaviors, in different ways, maximize reproductive success.**

Reproductive behavior may include several steps. The first step is finding and choosing a mate. Choosing a mate may involve complex courtship behavior or intense competition among individuals. Once mating has occurred, species may either abandon their eggs or young or provide varying levels of care. One of the most important ways to increase reproductive success is to engage in social behavior.

Social Behavior *Social behavior* describes any interaction between individuals. There are many aggressive social behaviors, such as displays and fights, but also many friendly behaviors. For example, the elephants shown in **Figure 12** are protecting their young from a predator. Even though animals exhibit a variety of social behaviors, all the behaviors are the result of individuals doing their best to pass their genes to the next generation.

Territorial Behavior Animals defending a portion of habitat against other individuals of their species are exhibiting **territorial behavior.** Territorial behavior increases reproductive success because it helps secure resources (such as food or mates). The defense of territories may involve marking the territory with scent or sound, aggressive displays directed at intruders, or even fights. The impalas shown in **Figure 12** are fighting over a territory. However, fights are rare. Rather than risk injury, animals often display at one another to determine which individual is likely to win.

territorial behavior (TER uh TAWR ee uhl) the behavior pattern exhibited by an animal in defending its territory

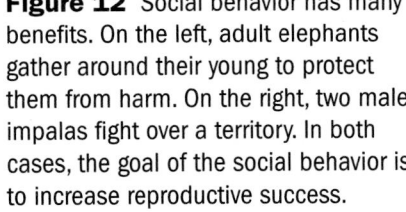

Figure 12 Social behavior has many benefits. On the left, adult elephants gather around their young to protect them from harm. On the right, two male impalas fight over a territory. In both cases, the goal of the social behavior is to increase reproductive success.

Courtship Behavior Before mating occurs, males and females must recognize one another as members of the same species. Usually, both must decide that they want to mate. **Courtship** is a behavioral ritual that precedes and helps lead to mating. Many courtship displays are meant to demonstrate the quality of the displaying male. Some species, such as the Western grebes and snails shown in **Figure 13,** have elaborate courtship displays that help in species recognition.

More than a century ago, Charles Darwin noticed that males often have extreme physical traits. For example, the peacock has a much longer tail than the female of the species, the peahen, does. Why did such differences between the sexes evolve? The long tail of the peacock cannot be essential for survival. The peahen survives well without a long tail. In fact, the long tail makes flying harder and probably reduces survival.

Sexual Selection Darwin recognized that extreme traits, such as the peacock's tail or bright coloration, could have evolved if they helped males attract or acquire mates. He proposed that sexual selection is the mechanism that accounts for such traits. **Sexual selection** occurs when females show a preference for a particular trait in males, and that trait may negatively affect the survival of the male. *Female preference* means that the female chooses to mate with one male instead of another, usually because the chosen male has the preferred trait.

Male Competition When females choose among males for a mate, males usually compete to gain the females' attention. In some species, traits that make a male more intimidating or better at combat are favored. Antlers in deer, horns in bighorn sheep, and manes in lions are all traits related to competition among males. Males that are not physically well matched rarely engage in serious fighting. In some species, males do not fight but instead provide gifts to females. The male that has the largest gift is usually chosen by the female.

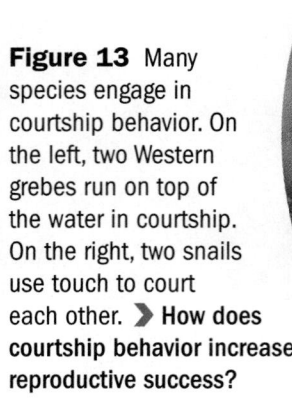

Figure 13 Many species engage in courtship behavior. On the left, two Western grebes run on top of the water in courtship. On the right, two snails use touch to court each other. ❯ **How does courtship behavior increase reproductive success?**

Parental Care As mammals, we are very familiar with the amount of care required for parents to raise their young. Parenting may include sheltering the young from danger and providing food, as the adult lemur is shown doing in **Figure 14.** Not all animals work as hard as humans and other mammals to bring up a family. Animals vary widely in the amount of care that they give their offspring. Nonetheless, raising young takes time and energy. A parent caring for its offspring reduces its own chances of survival and the number of offspring it could have later in life. So, parents trade their future survival and reproduction for the survival of their current offspring.

Parental care is most common in species that have few young or in species in which caring for young increases the offspring's chances for survival. Most fishes do not care for their young, but parents of some fish species keep their young close to protect them from predators. Young amphibians and most reptiles are on their own. In about 90% of bird species, both males and females give care. In mammals, a male cannot provide milk for the young, so the females usually care for offspring.

Cooperative Behavior An animal behaves to maximize its own reproductive success, not to ensure the survival of the species. But animals sometimes work together. Cooperative behavior occurs when two or more animals interact to mutual benefit in spite of the costs of working together. Female lions hunt together to catch large prey. They have to share the meat once it is caught, but without teamwork, they would never be able to catch large prey. Hyenas and wild dogs also cooperate to hunt large prey. Other cooperative acts involve breeding. In some bird and mammal species, mature offspring give up the chance to breed on their own and help their parents raise the next generation of offspring. This behavior indirectly passes some of the offspring's genes on to the next generation.

❯ **Reading Check** *How can parental care increase reproductive success?*

Figure 14 This adult lemur provides food and comfort to its young.

courtship (KAWRT ship) any behavior that leads to mating and the rearing of young

sexual selection an evolutionary mechanism by which a mate is chosen on the basis of a particular trait

---

Section 2 Review

❯ KEY IDEAS

1. **Define** the key skills for survival.
2. **Describe** how communication signals influence behavior.
3. **List** the types of behavior that increase reproductive success, and give an example of one type.

CRITICAL THINKING

4. **Predicting Outcomes** A monkey can smell intruders in its territory, but it cannot see them through the dense trees. What mode of communication will the monkey use to communicate its desire for the intruders to leave? Explain.
5. **Forming Reasoned Opinions** Do animals that live alone engage in social behavior? Why or why not?

ALTERNATIVE ASSESSMENT

6. **Poster** Use the Internet or library resources to learn more about how hibernation occurs and why it has developed. Create and present a poster to your class that explains the types of hibernation and the reason that bears are not considered "true" hibernators.

Objectives

❯ Recognize that territorial behavior is a type of social behavior.

❯ Observe how male crickets behave in close proximity to a defendable resource, such as food.

❯ Form hypotheses about the function of male territorial behavior in crickets.

Materials

- disposable gloves
- crickets (5 male and 5 female)
- colored paint, non-toxic, washable (5 colors)
- paint brushes, small, several
- aquarium
- cardboard tube
- cardboard, 5 cm square
- apple, slice
- potato, piece
- watch, with second hand

Safety

Territorial Behavior

A male cricket chirps to attract females and warn other males to stay away from his territory. Male crickets may also push and stroke others with their antennae. In this lab, you will design an experiment to investigate the signals that trigger territorial behavior in male crickets. To do this, you will observe male crickets in a variety of situations.

Preparation

1. **SCIENTIFIC METHODS** **State the Problem** Under what circumstances do male crickets chirp most often?

2. **SCIENTIFIC METHODS** **Form a Hypothesis** Form a testable hypothesis that explains how different situations and cues trigger chirping (territorial) behavior in a male cricket. Record your hypothesis.

Procedure

Observe Territorial Behavior

① Put on gloves.

② **CAUTION: Crickets are animals and should be handled with care.** With colored paint, mark the backs of 5 male crickets. Use a different color for each cricket. Place the crickets in an aquarium.

③ Place 5 unmarked female crickets in the aquarium.

④ Make two shelters. Construct the first shelter by turning the cardboard tube on its side. Construct the second shelter by folding the cardboard square in half to form a tent-like structure.

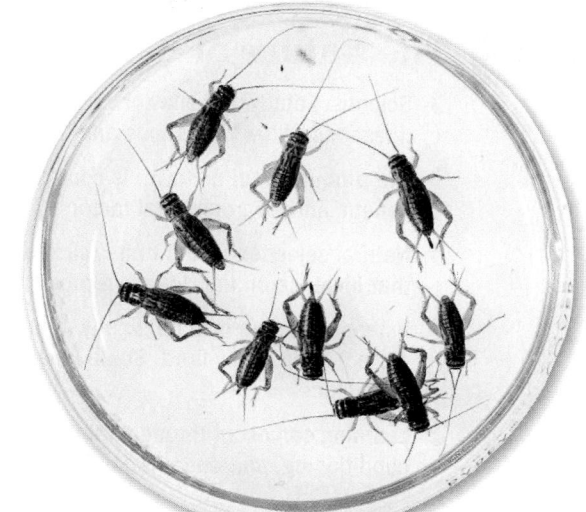

Cricket Behavior					
Cricket	Apple	Potato	Tube	Tent	Female
Blue					
Yellow					
Red					
Green					
White					

5 Place the shelters in different spots in the aquarium.

6 Place a slice of apple and a piece of potato in the aquarium.

7 Observe the crickets for 10 min. Look for territorial behaviors among the males, such as chirping, stroking others with antennae, and pushing others away.

Design an Experiment

8 Design an experiment that tests your hypothesis and that uses the materials listed for this lab. Predict what will happen during your experiment if your hypothesis is supported.

9 Write a procedure for your experiment. Identify the variables that you will control, the experimental variables, and the responding variables. Construct any tables you will need to record your data. Make a list of all safety precautions that you will take. Have your teacher approve your procedure before you begin.

Conduct Your Experiment

10 Put on gloves. Carry out your experiment. Record your observations in a data table.

11 Clean up your lab materials according to your teacher's instructions. Wash your hands before leaving the lab.

SCI**LINKS**.
www.scilinks.org
Topic: Animal Behavior
Code: HX80069

Analyze and Conclude

1. **SCIENTIFIC METHODS** **Analyzing Data** Were any crickets more aggressive than the others? Give evidence to support your answer.

2. **Describing Results** What were the circumstances in which most aggressive behavior occurred? Was your prediction correct?

3. **SCIENTIFIC METHODS** **Identifying Variables** What did the shelters and food represent to the male crickets?

4. **SCIENTIFIC METHODS** **Forming Hypotheses** For each aggressive behavior observed, form a hypothesis that explains the behavior's function.

Extensions

5. **Insect Behavior** Use the Internet to research the types of territorial behavior in other insects. Are the behaviors observed in the crickets typical for other insects?

go.hrw.com
SUPER SUMMARY
Keyword: HX8ABHS

Key Ideas

Key Terms

1 The Nature of Behavior

> Scientists studying behavior ask two kinds of questions—"how" questions and "why" questions.

> The production of behavior is controlled by both genetic and environmental factors.

> Natural selection favors traits (such as behaviors) that increase an individual's reproductive success.

> Innate behaviors may be greatly influenced by genes, but these behaviors are not necessarily fixed. Some innate behaviors may be modified by experience.

> Learning can occur through habituation, problem solving, classical conditioning, and operant conditioning.

behavior (813)
stimulus (813)
response (813)
innate behavior (816)
fixed action pattern (816)
learning (817)
reasoning (817)
conditioning (818)
imprinting (819)

2 Classes of Behavior

> The survival of an individual depends on finding resources, such as food, and avoiding predators.

> Animals use signals to influence the behavior of other animals. Many kinds of signals can be used for this purpose.

> During a breeding period, animals perform mating and parenting behaviors. These behaviors, in different ways, maximize reproductive success.

foraging (821)
migration (822)
circadian rhythm (822)
communication (823)
territorial behavior (825)
courtship (826)
sexual selection (826)

READING TOOLBOX

1. **Cause-and-Effect Map** Use "evolution of behavior" as your example in a new cause-and-effect map. Replace the terms as necessary.

2. ⚬⚬⚬ **Concept Map** Construct a concept map that describes animal behavior. Use the following terms in your map: *behavior, stimulus, innate behavior, fixed action pattern, learning, conditioning, reasoning,* and *imprinting*.

Using Key Terms

Use the following terms in the same sentence.

3. *behavior, stimulus,* and *response*

4. *conditioning* and *learning*

5. *hibernation* and *migration*

Use each of the following terms in a separate sentence.

6. *sexual selection*

7. *territorial behavior*

8. *courtship*

Understanding Key Ideas

9. Which type of question addresses the evolution of behavior?
   a. "how" question   c. "what" question
   b. "why" question   d. "when" question

10. Natural selection favors behaviors that increase
    a. the survival of an individual's family.
    b. the chance of survival of the species.
    c. the reproductive success of the individual.
    d. the reproductive success of the individual's group.

11. Which behavior is an example of a fixed action pattern?
    a. a person developing language
    b. a duckling following its mother
    c. a person yawning after seeing someone else yawn
    d. an animal learning to associate a particular call with food

12. Over time, pigeons in a park learn that they do not have to fly away each time that a person walks by, because not everyone is a threat. What type of behavior are the pigeons exhibiting?
    a. habituation
    b. social learning
    c. operant conditioning
    d. classical conditioning

13. Which factor controls circadian rhythms?
    a. temperature
    b. internal clock
    c. cycles of dark and light
    d. seasonal changes in weather and light level

Use the diagram to answer the following question.

14. What kind of behavior is depicted in the illustration?
    a. reasoning
    b. habituation
    c. conditioning
    d. innate behavior

Explaining Key Ideas

15. **List** the organ systems that are important in the control and production of behavior.

16. **Describe** why a male lion that has just taken over a pride would kill all the cubs in the pride.

17. **Identify** the type of behavior that does not depend on experience to be produced.

18. **Describe** the difference between operant conditioning and classical conditioning.

19. **List** three behaviors that animals can use to avoid being eaten by a predator.

Using Science Graphics

Use the diagram to answer the following questions.

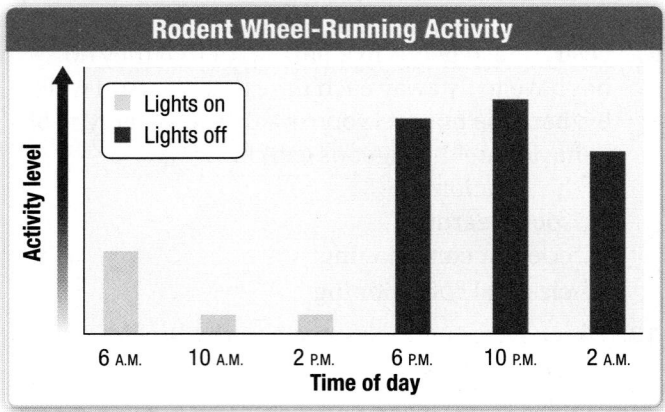

Rodent Wheel-Running Activity

Lights on
Lights off

Activity level

6 A.M.   10 A.M.   2 P.M.   6 P.M.   10 P.M.   2 A.M.
Time of day

20. Which kind of cyclic behavior does the graph describe?
  a. hibernation
  b. communication
  c. circadian rhythms
  d. antipredator behavior

21. The type of behavior shown on the graph is
  a. foraging.   **c.** diurnal behavior.
  b. migration.   **d.** nocturnal behavior.

22. What is the dependent variable in this experiment?
  a. time of day   **c.** lights off
  b. lights on   **d.** activity level

Critical Thinking

23. Predicting Outcomes Describe the one condition that is required for territorial behavior to occur. Typically, territorial behavior occurs in males. Can you think of a condition under which females might display territorial behavior?

24. Justifying Conclusions You see a group of young ducks following a person around as if the person were their parent. What learning process leads to this behavior, and how?

25. Forming Reasoned Opinions While walking around a local park, you notice that squirrels forage in areas very close to trees. Even though there is a lot of food far from the trees, the squirrels spend most of their time trying to find food near a tree. Are they foraging to get the most energy in the shortest time? Why do you think that the squirrels forage in this way?

Writing for Science

26. Essay Write a short essay about why cooperative behavior occurs. Why would an individual sacrifice its own interests to help another individual survive or reproduce?

27. Essay Write an essay that describes the costs and benefits of being a foraging generalist and of being a foraging specialist.

28. Speech Write a speech about why animals do not necessarily behave to ensure the survival of a species.

Why It Matters

29. Real World Whales communicate by using sounds that travel long distances in the ocean. How might loud noises caused by tankers and oil exploration influence these animals? Should we worry about such influences? Why or why not?

Graphing Skills

30. Bar Graph Go outside and find some birds to watch. For every behavior you see, mark whether it is a foraging behavior, an anti-predator behavior, a social behavior, or a reproductive behavior. Make a bar graph showing the number of behaviors in each category. Which is the most common type of behavior? Why do you think this is the case?

Math Skills

31. Analyzing Data Use the table to answer the following question.

Prey type	Time required to catch prey (hrs)	Relative energy content of prey
1	0.5	1
2	1	2.5
3	2	3
4	3	4

The data table shows how long a tiger takes to catch several types of prey and how much energy the tiger gets from each type of prey. Based on what you know about optimal foraging behavior, which type of prey should the tiger eat? Why?

TEST TIP When using experimental data to answer a question, determine the contents, variables, and control before answering the question.

Science Concepts

1. Which organ system releases hormones that can trigger behavior?

  A nervous system   **C** endocrine system

  B sensory system   **D** circulatory system

2. Which factor is an internal factor that influences behavior?

  F predators   **H** air temperature

  G hunger level   **J** prey abundance

3. What is another name for innate behavior?

  A habituation   **C** learned behavior

  B intuitive behavior   **D** instinctive behavior

4. What is the ability to use experience to develop an insight into how to solve a new problem?

  F reasoning

  G habituation

  H operant conditioning

  J classical conditioning

5. Which mode of communication lasts longest in the environment?

  A sound   **C** visual signal

  B touch   **D** chemical signal

6. Which of the following species have complex language?

  F only humans

  G apes and humans

  H dolphins and humans

  J dolphins, apes and humans

7. What name is given to the ritual that precedes mating and may help in species recognition?

  A courtship   **C** reproduction

  B mate choice   **D** sexual selection

Writing Skills

8. Short Response Write a short essay that describes the costs and benefits of communication through visual signals.

Using Science Graphics

Use the diagram to answer the following questions.

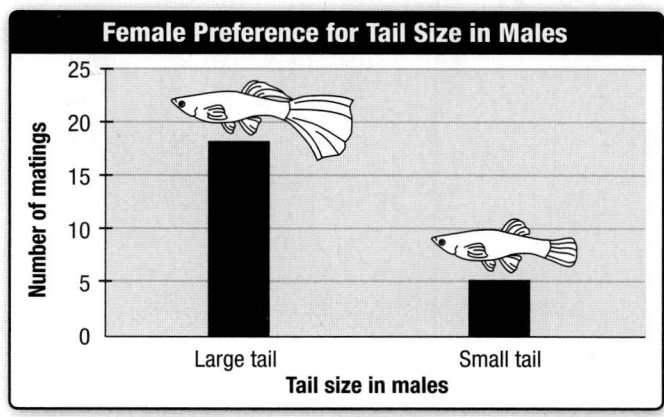

Female Preference for Tail Size in Males

(y-axis: Number of matings, 0 to 25; x-axis: Tail size in males — Large tail, Small tail)

9. Which of the following statements best describes the data presented in the graph?

  F females have no preference for tail size

  G more males have large tails than small tails

  H females prefer to mate with small-tailed males

  J females mate more often with large-tailed males than with small-tailed males

10. Which of the following best explains the fact that certain males have larger tails than other males?

  A imprinting   **C** courtship

  B habituation   **D** sexual selection

Use the table to answer the following questions.

Behavior	Number of years of reproduction	Number of offspring/ year of reproduction
1	1	2
2	1	4
3	2	3
4	3	1

11. Which behavior produces the highest number of offspring per year of reproduction?

  F 1   **H** 2

  G 3   **J** 4

12. Which behavior is favored by natural selection?

  A 1   **C** 2

  B 3   **D** 4

UNIT 9 Humans

34 Skeletal, Muscular, and Integumentary Systems

35 Circulatory and Respiratory Systems

36 Digestive and Excretory Systems

37 The Body's Defenses

38 Nervous System

39 Endocrine System

40 Reproduction and Development

41 Forensic Science

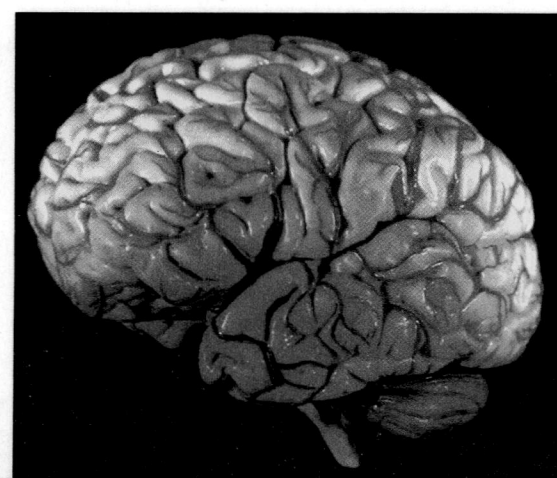

Magnetic resonance imaging (MRI) scan of a human brain

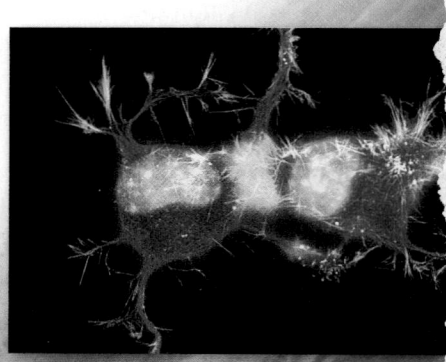

New growth (green) on nerve cells

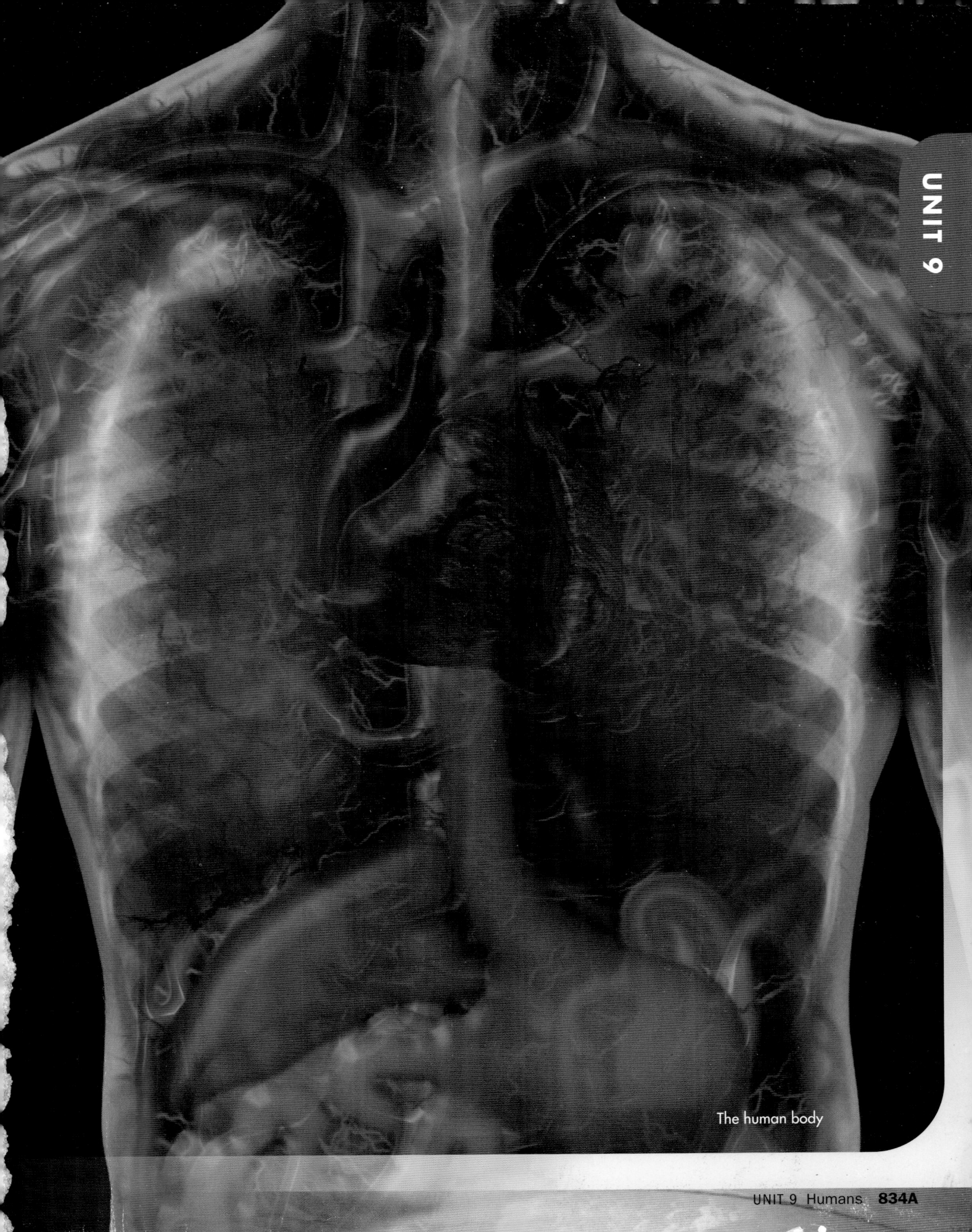

The human body

Medical Advances

400 BCE

Hippocrates writes the oath taken by physicians—to treat all patients with honesty, understanding, and confidentiality.

Hippocrates

910 CE

A Persian physician and pharmacist, al-Razi, known as Rhazes, publishes his comprehensive medical book, *Kitab-al-hawi*. The book includes the earliest description of smallpox and, once translated into Latin, becomes an influential medical text in Europe.

1552

An anonymous Aztec artist creates *The Badianus Manuscript*, which describes Aztec medical practices. The manuscript includes information about the effective uses of medicinal herbs; the cleaning, suturing, and dressing of wounds; preventive dental hygiene; and the setting of broken bones.

1628

William Harvey, an English physician, describes how blood circulates and how the heart acts as a pump. He challenges the belief that the liver creates blood from food.

Human heart

1846

In Boston, a dentist named W.T.G. Morton performs the first public demonstration of ether anesthesia on a person during a surgical procedure. Ether had been used as an anesthetic as early as 1842.

1895

X rays are discovered by Wilhelm Röntgen. The first "röntgenogram" ever taken was of Röntgen's wife's hand.

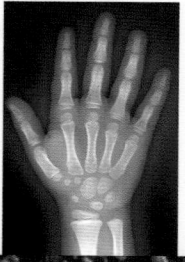

X ray

1982

Dr. William DeVries implants an artificial heart into Barney Clark. The heart, a Jarvik-7, is designed by Dr. Robert Jarvik. Barney Clark lives 117 days with the artificial heart.

2005

Claudia Mitchell becomes the first woman to be fitted with a computerized ("bionic") prosthetic arm.

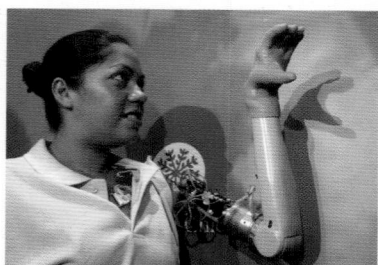

Claudia Mitchell using bionic limb

Thyroid (red) and thyroid hormone (orange)

BIOLOGY CAREER

High School Science Teacher
Sid Rogers

Sid Rogers is a science teacher at Cerritos High School in the ABC Unified School District in Cerritos, California. Rogers earned his certification in forensic science from California State University, Fullerton. He has developed courses in forensic science for his high school and teaches forensic science to elementary and junior high students in the summer through an enrichment program.

Rogers enjoys the challenge of making difficult material accessible and even enjoyable for students. He feels especially gratified when he helps struggling students work hard and become good students. Rogers is honored and flattered when students return years later and tell him that they pursued a science degree in college because of a class that they took with him.

Rogers also enjoys reading, photography, and being an active member of his church.

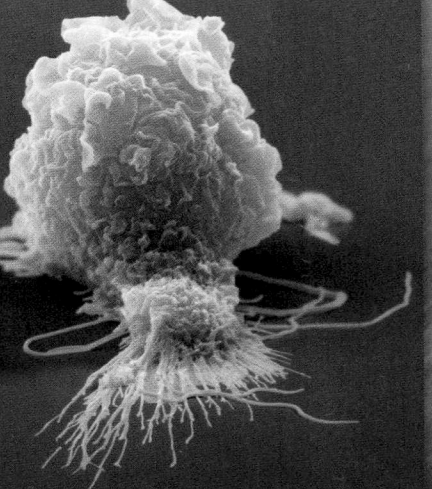

Macrophages (yellow) and bacteria (blue)

Chapter 34

Skeletal, Muscular, and Integumentary Systems

Preview

1 Body Organization
Cells
Tissue Types
Organs and Organ Systems
Homeostasis

2 The Skeletal System
The Skeleton
Bones
Joints

3 The Muscular System
Types of Muscles
Movement and Muscle
Structure of Muscles
Function of Muscles
Exercise and Muscle

4 The Integumentary System
Skin
Functions of Skin
Hair and Nails
Disorders of Skin

Why It Matters

The human body is extremely complex. Your skin, bones, and muscles work together to protect, support and move your body. Knowing how these body systems work can help you keep them strong and healthy.

Acrobats such as these Cirque de Soleil performers remind us of the amazing things the human body can do.

Strong muscles allow these acrobats to hang perfectly still in the air.

Bones give the body its shape and structure. There are 206 bones in an adult human body.

InquiryLab

Too Cold for Comfort

One of the ways your skin protects your body is by sensing pain.

Procedure

1. Hold a large ice cube tightly in one hand, and start a timer.
2. Allow the melting water to drip into a dish.
3. Hold the ice until the cold becomes uncomfortable.
4. Release the ice into the dish, and stop the timer.

Analysis

1. **State** how long it took for the ice to feel uncomfortable.
2. **Describe** what you noticed about the color of your skin where you held the ice.
3. **Explain** why holding something that is very cold causes pain after a certain amount of time.

When you look at another person, the first thing you see is the person's integumentary system—skin, hair, and nails.

READING TOOLBOX

These reading tools can help you learn the material in this chapter. For more information on how to use these and other tools, see **Appendix: Reading and Study Skills.**

Using Words

Word Parts Knowing the meanings of word parts can help you figure out the meanings of words that you do not know.

Your Turn Use the table to answer the following questions.

1. Hemoglobin is a protein found in blood. What do you think myoglobin is?
2. If the prefix *sub-* means "under", what might *subcutaneous* mean?

Word Parts		
Word part	**Type**	**Meaning**
epi-	prefix	on top of
homeo-	prefix	the same or similar
myo-	prefix	muscle
cut	root	skin

Using Language

Analogies Analogies compare words with similar relationships. You can write analogies with words or with colons. For example, the analogy "up is related to down the same way that top is related to bottom" can be written "up : down :: top : bottom". To answer an analogy problem you must figure out how the words are related. Up is above down, and top is above bottom.

Your Turn Use information found in the chapter to complete the following analogy.

bone : ligament :: muscle : _____

(Hint: Finding out how bones and ligaments are related will help you figure out which word to use to fill in the blank.)

Using Science Graphics

Venn Diagram In science, you often learn about what things are made of. Remembering how all of the parts fit together can be very confusing. A Venn diagram can help you simplify a graphic and make it easier to understand.

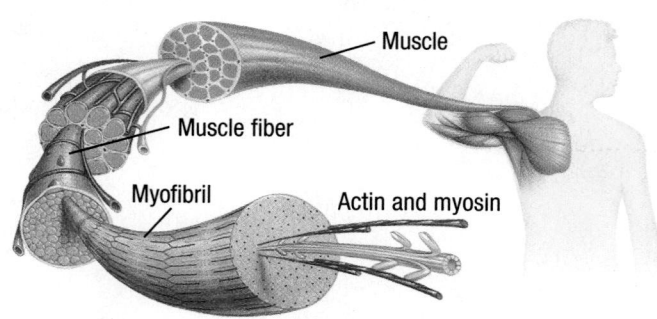

Your Turn Use a Venn diagram to help you understand the parts of muscle.

1. Draw four boxes by drawing each one inside the other.
2. Label the largest box "Muscle."
3. Label the smallest box "Actin and myosin."
4. Use the figure to label the other boxes.

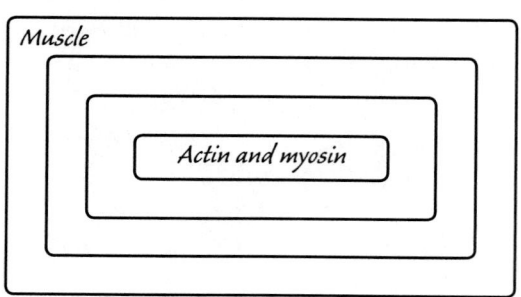

Body Organization

Key Ideas	Key Terms	Why It Matters
❯ What two properties make stem cells different from other body cells? ❯ What four types of tissues can be found in the human body? ❯ How are tissues, organs, and organ systems related? ❯ How does the body maintain homeostasis?	stem cell epithelial tissue nervous tissue connective tissue muscle tissue	For the human body to function properly, the cells, tissues, organs, and organ systems must work together.

Imagine what your body would look like if it were made up of one type of cell. Luckily, our bodies are made of many types of cells that work together.

Cells

Cells are the basic building blocks of every living organism. The human body contains more than 100 trillion cells and more than 100 types of cells. Each cell type performs a specific function in the body. Some cells produce chemicals, like the acid producing cells in the stomach. Other cells transmit nerve signals. Some cells become surrounded by the mineral calcium to protect the body. Our health depends on each of our cells performing their function.

Stem Cells Today, **stem cells** are an important focus of research. ❯ Stem cells are different from other cells of the body because they can divide repeatedly and can become more than one type of cell. The stem cells used in research, like the one in **Figure 1,** are either embryonic or adult cells. Embryonic stem cells are harvested from eggs that were fertilized in the laboratory and donated for research. Adult stem cells used in research are taken from adult tissue.

The use of embryonic and adult stem cells each has advantages and disadvantages. Embryonic stem cells can become any type of cell, are grown easily in the lab, and millions of cells can be produced from one embryo. Using these cells is controversial because a human embryo is destroyed to obtain them. Research suggests, however, that embryonic stem cells might be collected from an umbilical cord, which would not result in the destruction of an embryo.

Adult stem cells may be limited in the types of cells they can become, they are relatively rare in the body, and currently cannot be grown to produce large numbers of cells in the lab. This is important because large numbers of cells are needed for stem cell therapy. The advantage of using adult stem cells is that they can be taken from a patient's own body. As a result, the transplanted cells would not be rejected by the patient's immune system.

stem cell a cell that can develop into many different types of cells

Figure 1 This adult bone marrow stem cell can typically only produce blood, bone, and cartilage cells.

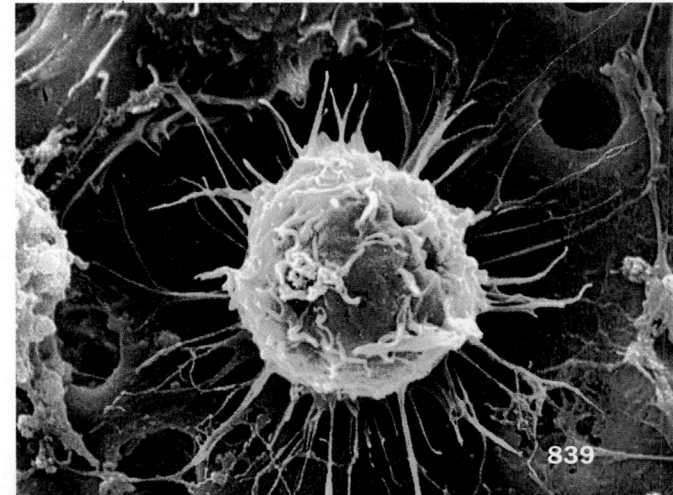

Figure 2 The three types of muscle tissue are shown on the left. Nervous, connective, and epithelial tissue are shown on the right.

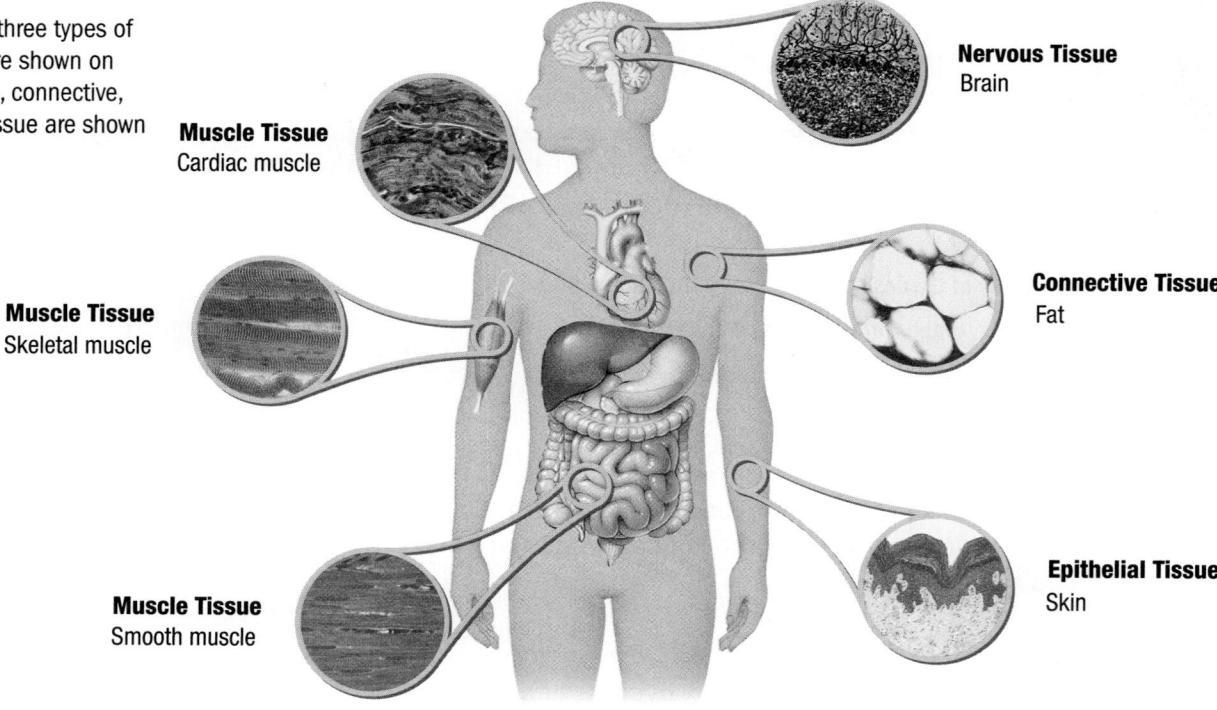

Muscle Tissue
Cardiac muscle

Muscle Tissue
Skeletal muscle

Muscle Tissue
Smooth muscle

Nervous Tissue
Brain

Connective Tissue
Fat

Epithelial Tissue
Skin

epithelial tissue tissue that covers a body surface or lines a body cavity

nervous tissue tissue of the nervous system, including neurons and their supporting cells

connective tissue a tissue that connects and supports other tissues

muscle tissue the tissue made of cells that can contract and relax to produce movement

Tissue Types

A tissue is a group of similar cells that work together to perform a common function. ❯ **The human body contains four types of tissues: epithelial, nervous, connective, and muscle tissue.** The four types of tissue (including three kinds of muscle tissue) can be seen in **Figure 2.**

Epithelial Tissue **Epithelial tissue** lines the body surfaces and protects the body from dehydration and damage. An epithelial layer can be one or many cells thick. Epithelial tissue is constantly being replaced as old cells die. Skin and the lining of the respiratory system are examples of epithelial tissue.

Nervous Tissue **Nervous tissue** is made up of neurons (nerve cells) and their supporting cells. The nervous system is made mostly of nervous tissue. Neurons carry information to all parts of the body.

Connective Tissue **Connective tissue** supports, connects, protects, and insulates the body. Connective tissue includes fat, cartilage, bone, tendons, and blood. Some connective tissue cells, such as those in bone, are densely packed. Others, such as those found in blood, are loosely connected to each other.

Muscle Tissue **Muscle tissue** is made up of cells that contract and relax to produce movement. There are three types of muscle tissue: skeletal, smooth, and cardiac muscle. Skeletal muscle is attached to bone, smooth muscle makes up the walls of the intestines and blood vessels, and cardiac muscle is only found in the heart.

❯ **Reading Check** *What are four types of tissues found in the body? (See the Appendix for answers to Reading Checks.)*

Organs and Organ Systems

Organs are structures made of two or more types of tissue that work together to perform a specific function. Each organ belongs to at least one *organ system*. An organ system is a group of organs that work together to carry out the major processes of the body. ❯ **Tissues that work together form organs. Organs that work together form organ systems.**

The heart is an organ made of cardiac muscle tissue, connective tissue, and nervous tissue working together to pump blood. The heart, along with the blood vessels and blood, make up the circulatory system. Some organs function in more than one system. The ovaries and testes function in both the endocrine and reproductive systems. The major organ systems and their structures are listed in **Figure 3.**

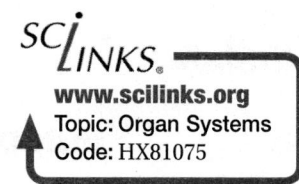
www.scilinks.org
Topic: Organ Systems
Code: HX81075

Figure 3 The table below lists the major structures and functions of the organ systems of the body. ❯ **Which organs function in more than one system?**

Major Organ Systems of the Body

System	Major structures	Functions
Cardiovascular system	heart, blood vessels, blood	to transport nutrients, wastes, hormones, water and gases
Digestive system	mouth, throat, esophagus, stomach, liver, pancreas, gall bladder and small and large intestines	to absorb nutrients from food; to remove wastes; to maintain water and chemical balances
Endocrine system	hypothalamus, pituitary gland, pancreas, testes, ovaries, and many other glands	to regulate body temperature, metabolism, development, and reproduction; to maintain homeostasis; to regulate other organ systems
Urinary system	kidneys, urinary bladder, ureters, and urethra	to remove wastes from blood; to regulate concentration of body fluids
Immune system	white blood cells, lymph nodes and vessels, and skin	to defend against pathogens and disease
Integumentary system	skin, nails, and hair	to protect against injury, infection, and fluid loss; to help regulate body temperature
Muscular system	skeletal, smooth, and cardiac muscle tissues; tendons	to move limbs and trunk; to move substances through the body; to provide structure and support
Nervous system	brain, spinal cord, nerves, and sense organs	to regulate behavior; to maintain homeostasis; to regulate all other organ systems; to control senses and movement
Reproductive system	testes, penis, ovaries, uterus, and breasts	to produce gametes (eggs and sperm) and offspring
Respiratory system	nose, mouth, trachea, bronchi, and lungs	to move air into and out of lungs; to control gas exchange between blood and lungs
Skeletal system	bones, ligaments, and cartilage	to protect and support the body and organs; to work with skeletal muscles; to produce red blood cells, white blood cells, and platelets

Hands-On
QuickLab

🕑 15 min

Investigation of Homeostasis

The human body maintains a fairly constant internal temperature of about 37 °C (98.6 °F). You can test this fact by taking your temperature in a variety of conditions.

Procedure

1 Use a **thermometer** to record the air temperature inside your classroom. Use an **oral thermometer** to take your temperature, and record it.

2 Move to a location that is warmer or colder than your classroom. Record the air temperature. After 10 min, take your temperature and record it.

Analysis

1. **Explain** what happened to your body temperature when you went from your classroom to a warmer or colder place.

2. **CRITICAL THINKING** **Recognizing Relationships** The body produces heat through metabolism. So, why can people freeze to death?

Homeostasis

Homeostasis is the steady internal environment that your body maintains, despite changes in the external environment. ❯ **The body maintains homeostasis by sensing and responding to changes in the internal environment.**

Negative Feedback Almost all body processes use a system called *negative feedback* to maintain homeostasis. Negative feedback is a system in which the results of a process provide the signal for the process to stop. One example of this is the regulation of body temperature.

Body Temperature Despite temperature changes in the environment, our bodies maintain a fairly constant internal temperature of about 37 °C. The body regulates its internal temperature using negative feedback, in much the same way that a thermostat works. When the body senses that its internal temperature has dropped below normal, a chemical signal causes the body to produce heat. The result is shivering, a process you are probably familiar with. When your body temperature returns to normal, the chemical signal is turned off, and you stop shivering. If your body temperature rises above normal, another chemical signal is sent. This signal tells the body to begin cooling itself through the evaporation of sweat and by increasing blood flow to small vessels below the skin. This releases heat and cools the body. Temperatures that are too high cause proteins to *denature* (change shape) and stop functioning. Temperatures too far below the normal range cause cellular processes to stop.

Section 1 Review

❯ **KEY IDEAS**

1. **Identify** the two characteristics that make stem cells different from other cells of the body.

2. **List** the four types of body tissue, and give an example of each type.

3. **Explain** the relationship between cells, tissues, organs, and organ systems.

4. **Describe** the system used to maintain homeostasis in most of the body's processes.

CRITICAL THINKING

5. **Inferring Relationships** How might developing a fever during illness be beneficial to the body?

6. **Forming Reasoned Opinions** Would you recommend that embryonic stem cell research be regulated by law? Explain your answer.

MAKING CONNECTIONS

7. **Predict** Recall that cytoplasm is the region inside a cell that includes the cell's fluid. Based on this information, would you expect the cells that form the surface of the skin to have more or less cytoplasm than fat cells have? Why or why not?

Key Ideas	Key Terms	Why It Matters
❯ What are five important functions of the skeletal system? ❯ What are the four layers that make up a bone? ❯ Which structures make up movable joints?	osteocyte bone marrow leukemia joint ligament	The skeletal system gives the body shape and makes movement possible. In addition, the skeletal system protects our organs, stores minerals and fat, and is where blood cells form.

What keeps your body from collapsing like a limp noodle? An internal skeleton made of strong bones gives the body shape and provides anchors for the muscles that move the body.

The Skeleton

❯ **The five important functions of the skeletal system are support, protection, movement, mineral storage, and blood cell formation.** Without our skeleton, our bodies would have no definite shape. The skeleton protects the internal organs. For example, the skull protects the brain. The skeleton is also important for movement. Muscles are attached to bones and pull on bones to cause movement. Bones store important minerals, such as calcium and phosphorus. Lastly, some bones make blood cells. The skeleton is divided into two major parts: the *axial skeleton* and the *appendicular skeleton*, shown in **Figure 4.**

Axial Skeleton The axial skeleton includes the skull, spine, ribs, and sternum. The axial skeleton forms the central axis of the body. The skull protects the brain. The spine supports the trunk. The ribs and sternum protect the heart and lungs.

Appendicular Skeleton The appendicular skeleton includes the appendages, which are the shoulders, arms, hips, and legs. The arms attach to the axial skeleton at the shoulders. The shoulder blades (scapulae) and the collar bone (clavicles) make up the pectoral girdle. The legs attach to the axial skeleton at the pelvic girdle. The pelvic girdle (hips) includes the bones of the pelvis: the ilium, ischium, and pubis.

❯ **Reading Check** *Which bones make up the pectoral girdle and which make up the pelvic girdle?*

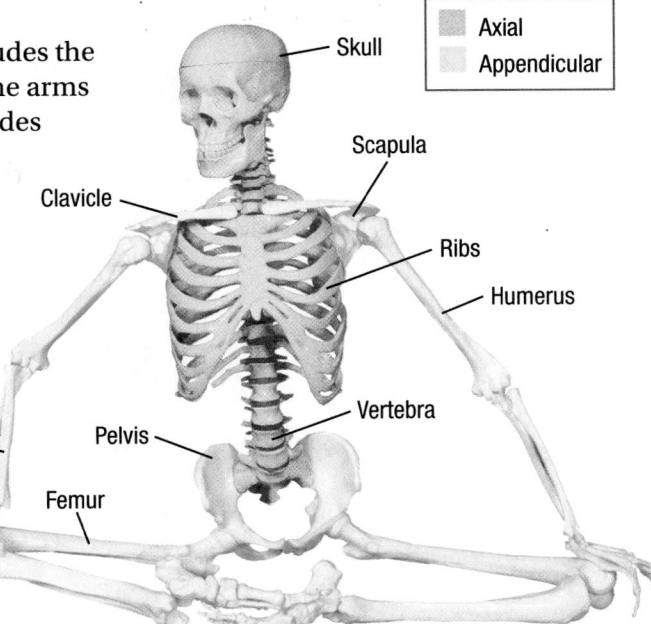

Figure 4 The skeleton is divided into two major parts. ❯ **When you sit on the floor, which bones are touching the floor: axial or appendicular bones?**

Bones

Your skeleton is made of bones. There are four basic bone shapes: long, short, flat, and irregular. Long bones are tube shaped, and include bones of the arms, legs, and fingers. Short bones are found in the wrists and ankles. Flat bones include the skull and sternum. Irregular bones include the bones of the spine.

Bone Structure ❯ A typical bone is made up of four layers: the periosteum, compact bone, spongy bone, and bone marrow. Bones are covered by a tough membrane called the *periosteum* (PER ee AHS tee uhm). Beneath the periosteum is a layer of compact bone. Compact bone is made of tightly packed mature bone cells called **osteocytes.** Inside the compact bone is a layer of spongy bone. Some of the spaces in spongy bone are filled with soft tissue called **bone marrow.** There are two types of bone marrow. Red bone marrow produces all blood cells. Yellow bone marrow is mostly fat, which stores energy.

Up Close Bones

Bones contain the four types of tissue: connective tissue in the form of cartilage and bone cells, nervous tissue, which is found in the nerves within bone, epithelial tissue in the periosteum, and muscle and epithelial tissue found in the blood vessels.

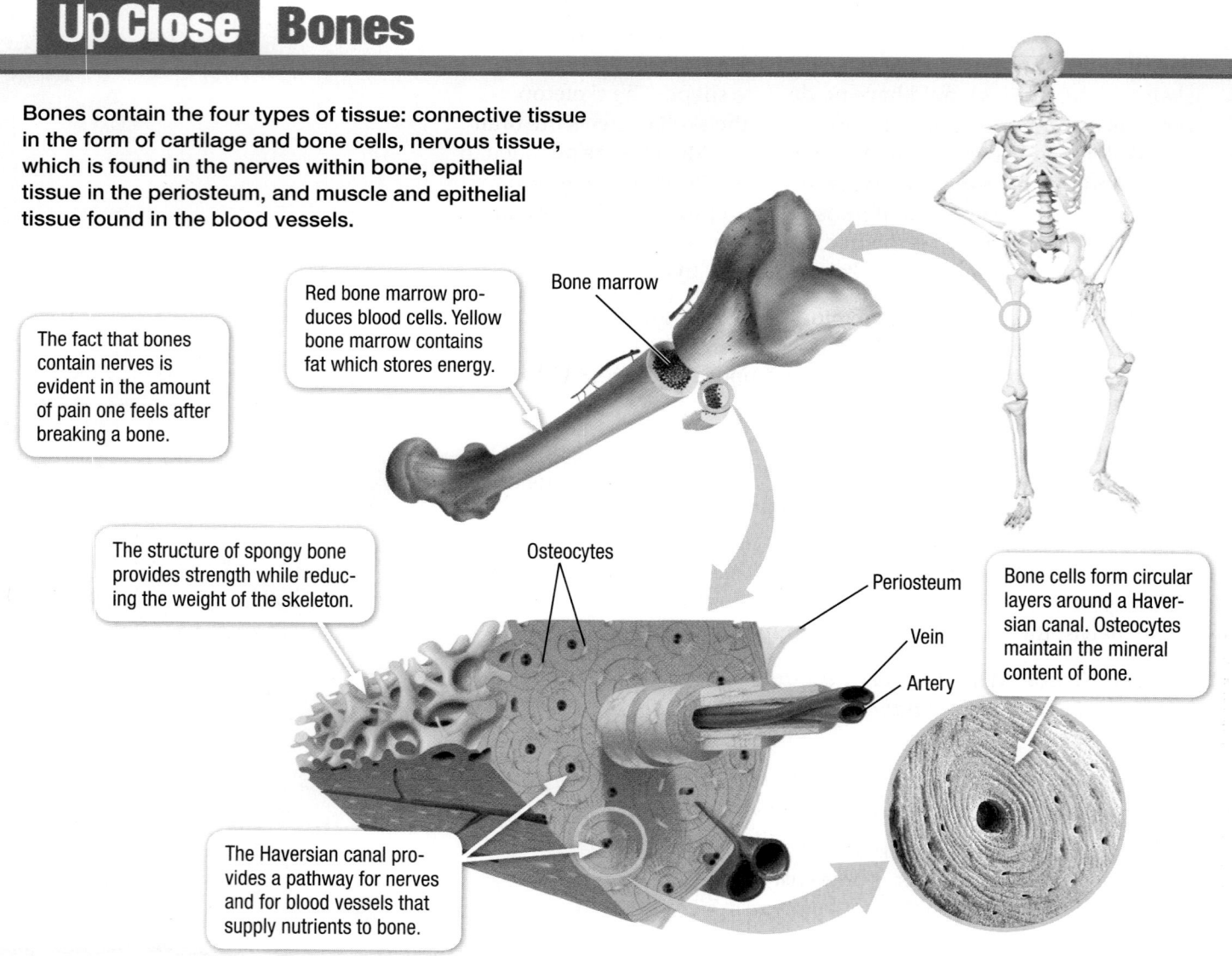

Bone marrow

Red bone marrow produces blood cells. Yellow bone marrow contains fat which stores energy.

The fact that bones contain nerves is evident in the amount of pain one feels after breaking a bone.

The structure of spongy bone provides strength while reducing the weight of the skeleton.

Osteocytes

Periosteum

Vein

Artery

Bone cells form circular layers around a Haversian canal. Osteocytes maintain the mineral content of bone.

The Haversian canal provides a pathway for nerves and for blood vessels that supply nutrients to bone.

Hands-On

QuickLab

 MULTI-DAY 🕐 20 min

Calcium and Bones

Calcium is a very important mineral in the body. It is required for building strong bones and teeth, blood clotting, sending nerve impulses, and regulating the heart beat. Ninety-nine percent of the calcium in your body is stored in your bones and teeth.

Procedure

Allow a clean chicken bone to soak in vinegar for five days. On the fifth day, remove the bone and try to bend it.

Analysis

1. **Describe** what happened to the bone.

2. **Identify** the mineral that was affected by vinegar.

3. **CRITICAL THINKING** **Predicting Outcomes** What do you think would happen if you placed the vinegar-soaked bone in a beaker of milk?

Bone Growth In infants, the skeleton is made mostly of cartilage. *Cartilage* is a type of connective tissue that cushions joints, makes up flexible body parts such as ears and noses, and serves as a template for bone formation. As bones grow, bone cells called *osteoblasts* deposit calcium and other minerals. Bones continue to become thicker and longer through adolescence as bone replaces cartilage. Eventually, almost all of the cartilage in the body is replaced by bone. In compact bone, new bone cells grow in tight layers around channels called *Haversian canals*. Haversian canals provide a passageway for blood vessels to deliver the nutrients to bone cells.

Bone Injuries and Disorders There are many kinds of injuries and disorders that can affect bone. Three common bone injuries and disorders are discussed below.

Fractures The most common injury to bones is a fracture. Fractures can range from hairline stress fractures, such as those from running or jumping on hard surfaces, to compound fractures in which the broken bone breaks through the skin.

Leukemia **Leukemia** is cancer of the tissues that produce blood cells. Leukemia results in large numbers of immature white blood cells. Because they are not fully developed, the cells do not function properly. The buildup of these cells also interferes with production of other types of blood cells. Bone marrow and stem cell transplants can produce healthy blood cells, but leukemia has no cure.

Osteoporosis As people age, the replacement of bone cells and of the minerals in bone becomes less efficient. Over time, bone tissue is lost. Severe bone loss can lead to *osteoporosis,* a condition in which bones become brittle and are easily broken. A healthy diet, regular exercise, and medication can help maintain bone density.

❯ **Reading Check** *How are osteocytes and osteoblasts different?*

www.scilinks.org
Topic: Joint Disorders
Code: HX80825

READING TOOLBOX

Venn Diagram Make a Venn diagram to help you remember the structure of bone. Figure out how many boxes you will need, and which labels will go in each box.

SECTION 2 The Skeletal System **845**

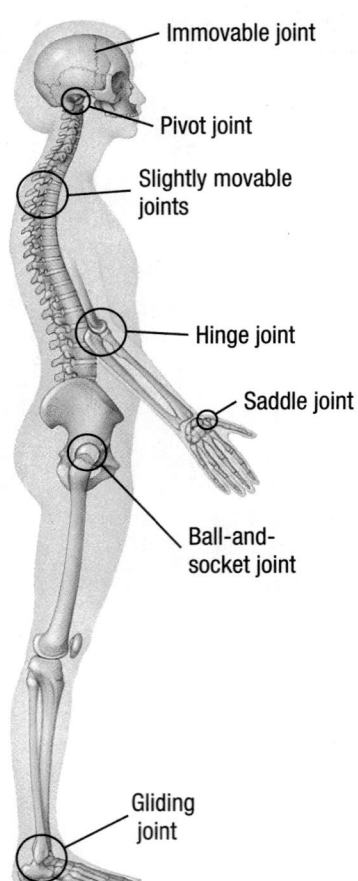

Immovable joint

Pivot joint

Slightly movable joints

Hinge joint

Saddle joint

Ball-and-socket joint

Gliding joint

Figure 5 Different types of joints allow varying degrees of motion in the body.

joint a place where two or more bones meet

ligament a type of connective tissue that holds together the bones in a joint

Joints

The skeletal system is linked by many types of joints, as shown in **Figure 5.** A **joint** is a place where two or more bones meet. Joints are grouped by their structure and by the way they move.

Types of Joints Immovable joints, such as those in the skull, do not allow the bones to move. Slightly movable joints, such as the joints of the spine and rib cage, allow only a small amount of movement. Freely movable joints allow the most movement. Most joints of the appendages are freely movable.

❯ **Movable joints are made up of bones, cartilage, and ligaments.** Pads of cartilage cushion the ends of bones and help movable joints withstand pressure and stress. Movable joints are held together by strong bands of connective tissue called **ligaments.** Ligaments help prevent joints from moving too far in any direction.

Joint Injuries and Disorders Joints are strong and flexible. However, joints are susceptible to certain kinds of injury and disease.

Sprain The most common injury to a joint is a sprain. A sprain occurs when a joint is bent too far or in the wrong direction. This incorrect movement damages the ligaments of the joint. Knees are especially vulnerable to sprains because of the amount of weight that the knees support.

Bursitis *Bursae* are fluid-filled sacs that help cushion and lubricate pressure points around joints. When joints are overused, bursae can become inflamed. *Bursitis* is a common disorder in athletes and musicians in which these sacs become swollen and painful.

Arthritis When the cartilage protecting joints is damaged, a disease called *arthritis* can result. There are two types of arthritis. Osteoarthritis occurs when the cartilage that covers the surfaces of bones wears away. The bones rub together, which causes pain. Rheumatoid arthritis occurs when cells of the immune system attack the tissues around joints. Rheumatoid arthritis is very painful and can result in damaged and deformed joints.

❯ **Reading Check** *What is the difference between osteoarthritis and rheumatoid arthritis?*

Section 2 Review

❯ **KEY IDEAS**

1. **List** the functions of the skeleton.
2. **Describe** the structure of a typical bone.
3. **Identify** the structures that are found in a movable joint.
4. **Describe** six injuries and disorders that affect bones and joints.

CRITICAL THINKING

5. **Relating Concepts** If a person's skeleton were not mostly cartilage at birth, how might the person's growth and development be affected?

6. **Recognizing Relationships** A runner on a track team has a stress fracture. What kinds of activities would you recommend to help the athlete continue to train while letting the fracture heal?

SCIENTIFIC METHODS

7. **Design an Experiment** Calcium can be removed from a chicken bone by soaking the bone in vinegar. Design an experiment to test whether calcium can be reabsorbed by the chicken bone from substances that contain calcium. Sources of calcium may include milk, yogurt, or dissolved antacid.

Monster Muscles

BIOTECHNOLOGY

They say "no pain, no gain," but these days, that saying is not really true. Selectively bred cattle and genetically modified mice provide clues about how muscle development and genetics are linked.

Build a Better Body Builder?

What do muscle-bound cattle and herculean mice have in common? The answer lies in what they don't have: the myostatin gene. Myostatin is a protein that tells muscles when to stop growing. A normal body has a limited number of muscle cells. Muscle growth from exercise is the result of growing larger muscle cells. But when the myostatin gene is gone, developing muscles don't know when to stop. They become packed with cells. About 20% more muscle cells are found in myostatin mutants than in normal myostatin animals. What does this mean for us? Now, it means more beef. In the future, who knows?

Research Is superhuman strength a possibility? Use library or Internet resources to find out more about myostatin mutations in humans.

The Real Mighty Mouse The mouse on the left is called a *knockout mouse*. A knockout animal has been genetically modified with a non-functioning version of a gene. In this way, scientists can study the role of a specific gene in the body.

Belgian Blue Cattle Beginning in the 1950s, the Belgian Blue was selectively bred for massive muscles. The muscle bulk is the result of a mutation in the myostatin gene.

The Muscular System

Key Ideas	Key Terms	Why It Matters
❯ What three types of muscles can be found in the human body? ❯ How do muscles produce energy for movement? ❯ What are the structures found in skeletal muscle? ❯ How do actin and myosin interact to cause muscle contraction? ❯ How can muscles be affected by exercise?	tendon flexor extensor muscle fiber myofibril sarcomere myosin actin	Muscles move blood through our veins, move food through our digestive system, and move the bones of our bodies.

Muscle cells are long, strong, thin cells that are filled with strands of protein. What makes muscle cells special is that they have the ability to become shorter, or to *contract.*

Types of Muscles

The muscles that move our bodies from place to place are not the only kind of muscle in the body. ❯ **The human body contains three types of muscle: skeletal muscle, smooth muscle, and cardiac muscle.** The three kinds of muscle are shown in **Figure 6.**

- **Skeletal Muscle** Skeletal muscle, also called *voluntary muscle,* is the only type of muscle that you can control. Skeletal muscles are attached to bones and are responsible for moving the body.

- **Smooth Muscle** Smooth muscle is often called *involuntary muscle* because you cannot control its movement. Smooth muscle lines the walls of blood vessels, digestive system organs, the uterus, and the bladder.

- **Cardiac Muscle** Cardiac muscle is involuntary muscle and is found in the heart. The powerful, rhythmic contractions of cardiac muscle pump blood to all body tissues.

Figure 6 The human body contains three types of muscles: skeletal muscle, smooth muscle, and cardiac muscle.

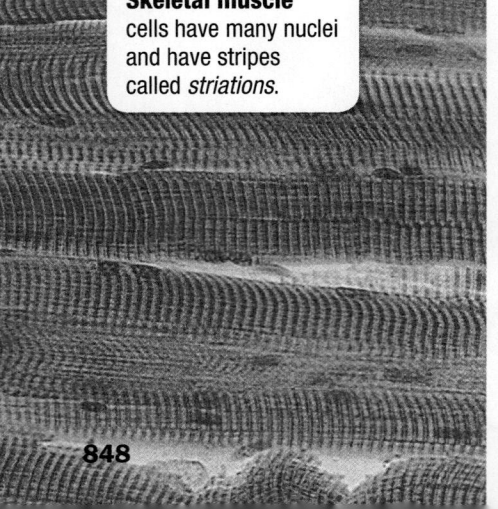

Skeletal muscle cells have many nuclei and have stripes called *striations*.

Smooth muscle cells are interlaced to form sheets. Each smooth muscle cell has one nucleus.

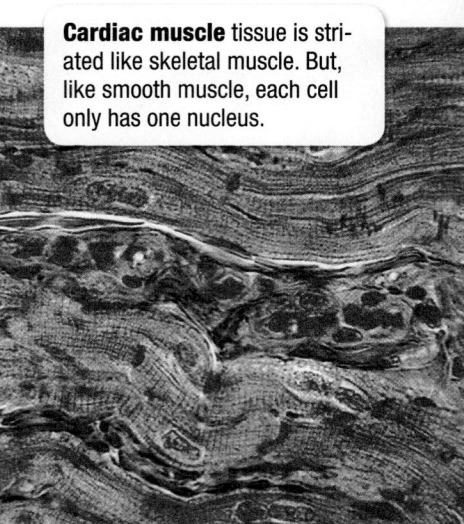

Cardiac muscle tissue is striated like skeletal muscle. But, like smooth muscle, each cell only has one nucleus.

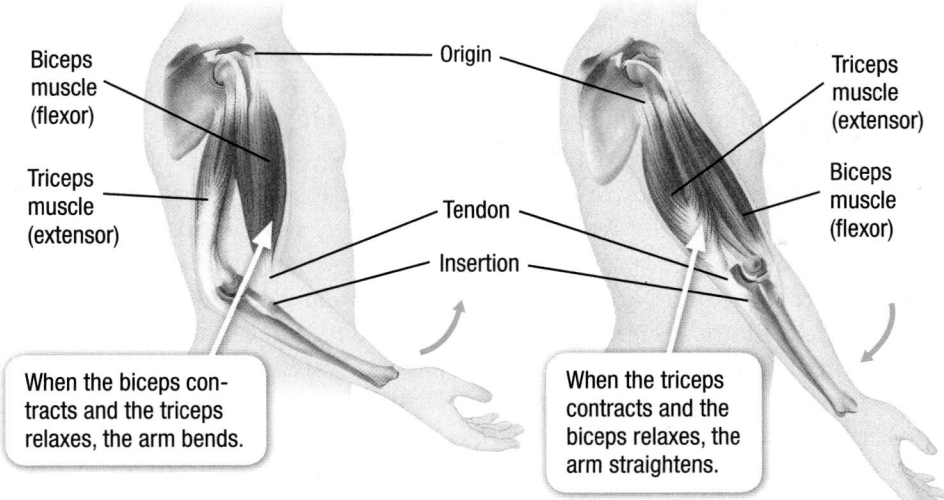

Biceps muscle (flexor)

Triceps muscle (extensor)

Origin

Tendon

Insertion

Triceps muscle (extensor)

Biceps muscle (flexor)

When the biceps contracts and the triceps relaxes, the arm bends.

When the triceps contracts and the biceps relaxes, the arm straightens.

Figure 7 Pairs of opposing muscles work together to move bones at joints. When one muscle in the pair contracts, the other muscle relaxes to produce movement. ❯ **Name another joint that is moved by a flexor and extensor pair.**

Movement and Muscle

Muscles move the body by pulling on bones of the skeleton. Muscles are attached to bones by strips of very strong, <u>flexible</u> connective tissue called **tendons.** One attachment of a muscle, the *origin*, is on a bone that does not move when the muscle contracts. The other attachment, the *insertion*, is on the bone that moves. In general, muscles are connected to bones in opposing pairs, as shown in **Figure 7.** One muscle pulls a bone in one direction, the other muscle pulls in the opposite direction. In the limbs, opposing pairs of muscle include a flexor muscle and an extensor muscle. A **flexor** is a muscle that causes a joint to bend. An **extensor** causes a joint to straighten.

Movement and Energy To contract, muscles need energy. Cells use the molecule adenosine triphosphate (ATP) as a power source. ❯ **Muscles switch between two processes to produce ATP, depending on the level of exercise and the presence of oxygen.**

Aerobic Respiration During normal, light activity, muscles produce ATP by a process called *aerobic respiration*. Aerobic respiration requires oxygen to break down fats and glucose and to make ATP. This process produces a large amount of ATP, but also requires a large amount of oxygen. As activity level increases, breathing rate increases in order to supply enough oxygen for aerobic respiration.

Anaerobic Respiration During vigorous exercise, oxygen cannot be delivered fast enough to keep up with the muscles' demand for ATP. When this happens, muscles switch to a process that does not use oxygen. This process, called *anaerobic respiration*, uses glucose and produces lactic acid and ATP. Very little ATP is produced, but anaerobic respiration is faster than aerobic respiration. This process can supply ATP for about 1 to 3 minutes. At this point, lack of glucose, lack of ATP, and the buildup of lactic acid in the muscles results in *muscle fatigue*, the inability of a muscle to contract.

❯ **Reading Check** *What are the advantages and disadvantages of aerobic and anaerobic respiration?*

ACADEMIC VOCABULARY

flexible able to bend easily without breaking

tendon a tough connective tissue that attaches a muscle to a bone

flexor a muscle that bends a joint

extensor a muscle that extends a joint

Structure of Muscles

Skeletal muscle cells are also called **muscle fibers.** Muscle fibers are held together by strong, stretchy membranes of connective tissue. A group of muscle fibers is called a *bundle,* and a group of bundles makes up an organ we call a muscle.

Inside each muscle fiber are small, cylinder-shaped structures called **myofibrils.** Myofibrils are made of the same kinds of protein that make up the cytoskeleton in other cells. In muscle cells these strands of protein are linked end-to-end. A single group of these protein filaments is called a **sarcomere.** Sarcomeres are the basic unit of contraction in skeletal and cardiac muscle. ❯ **Skeletal muscle tissue is made of cells called *muscle fibers*. Muscle fibers contain small cylinders called *myofibrils*. Myofibrils are made of sarcomeres linked end-to-end.** The place where sarcomeres attach to each other is called a *Z line*. Z lines and the filaments between them create light and dark bands that make skeletal and cardiac muscle appear striped.

Muscle Contraction

There are two types of protein grouped together in sarcomeres. The thick protein filaments are **myosin,** and the thin protein filaments are **actin.** Actin and myosin overlap each other, as shown in **Figure 8.** The ends of actin filaments are attached to the Z lines.

Muscle Contraction The overlapping arrangement of the protein filaments in a sarcomere enable muscles to contract. Muscle contraction usually begins when a muscle fiber receives a signal from a nerve cell. The steps below and those shown in **Figure 8** explain the process that results in muscle contraction.

Step ❶ Myosin attaches to a binding site on an actin filament. Calcium is required to make a binding site available for myosin.

Step ❷ The myosin head rotates and causes the actin filament to slide along the myosin filament. This sliding causes the filaments to overlap more, and the sarcomere becomes shorter.

Step ❸ After the myosin head has rotated as far as it can, it must let go of the actin fiber. ATP is required for myosin to detach from actin. The myosin head snaps back into its original position, using the energy in the ATP. The ATP becomes adenosine diphosphate (ADP) and releases a phosphate ion.

Step ❹ Calcium exposes a new actin binding site and myosin reattaches to actin. Steps 1 through 3 happen again.

In this way, the myosin heads walk along actin filaments and step at available binding sites. This grabbing and pulling action repeats, the sarcomere shortens, and the Z lines are pulled closer together. ❯ **Myosin filaments bind to actin filaments, actin filaments move inward, and sarcomeres shorten to cause muscle contraction.** This whole process occurs many times in the instant that you snap your fingers!

❯ **Reading Check** *How is ATP involved in muscle contraction?*

---

muscle fiber   a muscle cell

myofibril   a structure found in skeletal muscle cells that is made up of actin and myosin

sarcomere   the basic unit of contraction in skeletal and cardiac muscle

myosin   a protein that forms the thick filaments in muscle fibers

actin   a protein that forms the thin filaments in muscle fibers

READING TOOLBOX

Word Parts The word part *myo-* means "muscle." The word part *sarco-* means "flesh." Why might *myo-* and *sarco-* both be used to refer to muscle?

SCiLINKS.
www.scilinks.org
Topic: Muscle Contraction
Code: HX81004

The Steps in Muscle Contraction

Figure 8 The proteins actin and myosin work together to cause muscles to contract.

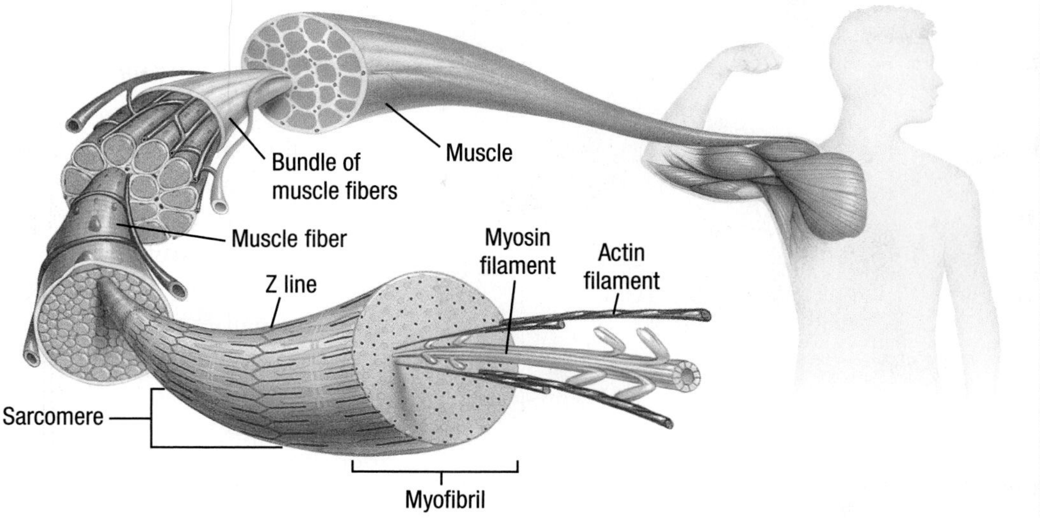

Bundle of muscle fibers

Muscle

Muscle fiber

Myosin filament

Actin filament

Z line

Sarcomere

Myofibril

Myofibril

Myosin

Actin

Sarcomere

Z line

① Myosin attaches to a binding site on an actin filament.

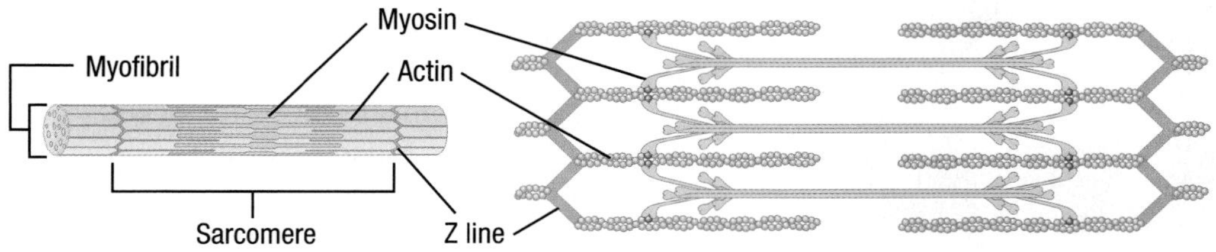

② The myosin head rotates and pulls the actin filaments closer together, making the sarcomere shorter.

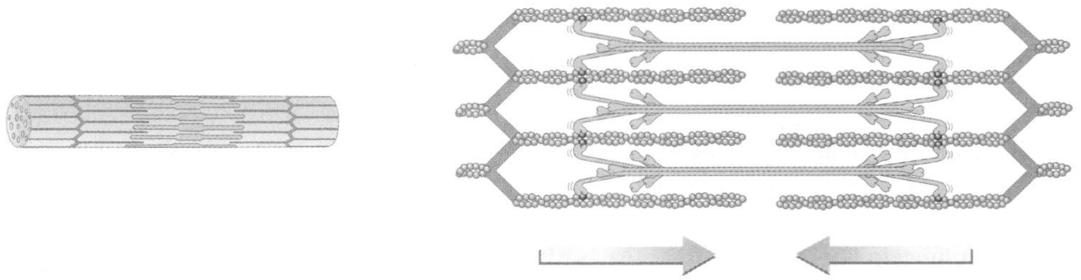

③ The myosin head releases from the actin filament. ATP is used in the process.

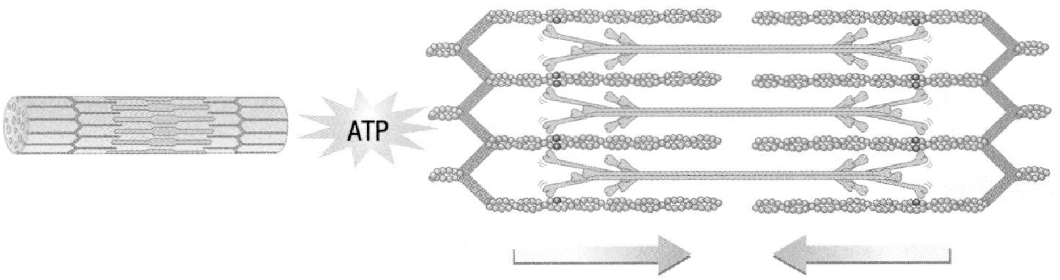

ATP

④ Steps 1 through 3 repeat until the sarcomere is fully contracted.

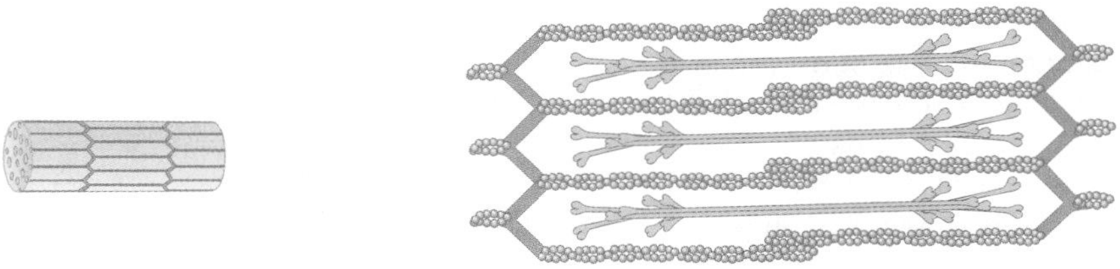

Exercise and Muscle

❯ Exercise can effect muscle strength, speed, and endurance. It can result in fatigue and injury. And lack of exercise can cause muscle atrophy.

Strength, Speed, and Endurance Two types of muscle fiber affect strength, speed, and endurance. *Slow-twitch* fibers are resistant to fatigue but produce relatively little force. *Fast-twitch* fibers produce large amounts of force but fatigue quickly. Slow-twitch fibers use aerobic respiration for energy, as long as enough oxygen is available. These fibers can increase their endurance by training for activities such as the marathon in **Figure 9.** Fast-twitch fibers depend on anaerobic respiration. They contain large stores of glucose that are used up quickly. These fibers become stronger or faster in response to short, intense activities. Most muscles contain both fiber types.

Fatigue During strenuous exercise, all of the ATP in muscle cells may be used. When all of the ATP is used, muscles cannot contract. Sometimes, muscles become locked in contraction, and a muscle cramp results. Muscle cramps eventually release as more ATP is generated in the cells.

Injury Muscles can tear if they are stretched too far during exercise. Muscles are also susceptible to overuse injuries. Overuse injuries can result from training that is too intense or that is done with poor technique. One common example is shin splints, a painful overuse injury to the small muscle of the shin. Tendons that are repeatedly stressed can also become inflamed. This is called *tendinitis.*

Atrophy The condition in which muscle mass is lost is called *atrophy.* Atrophy can occur when muscles do not get enough exercise, and in astronauts as a result of weightlessness. Atrophy can also occur as the result of an injury or disease. Examples include spinal cord injury, polio, Lou Gehrig's disease, and muscular dystrophy.

Figure 9 Aerobic exercises, such as jogging and swimming, increase endurance and improve cardiovascular health. Anaerobic exercises, such as weight lifing and jumping, build muscle strength and speed. ❯ Would you expect heart muscle to contain more slow-twitch or fast-twitch muscle fibers?

Section 3 Review

❯ KEY IDEAS

1. **Differentiate** between the three types of muscle tissue found in the human body.
2. **Describe** the role of oxygen in aerobic and anaerobic respiration.
3. **Name** the structures that make up skeletal muscle tissue.
4. **Explain** the roles of actin and myosin in muscle contractions.
5. **Identify** six ways that exercise can affect muscles.

CRITICAL THINKING

6. **Analyzing Information** Rigor mortis is a condition in which all of the body muscles become rigid shortly after a person dies. Why does rigor mortis develop?
7. **Connecting Concepts** When muscles lose mass as a result of atrophy, do you think they are losing muscle cells or do you think the cells are becoming smaller?

ALTERNATIVE ASSESSMENT

8. **Research** Isometric exercise involves holding muscles in one position until they become fatigued. It is currently not known why muscles tire even though they are not moving. Use the library or the Internet to find out more about research on isometric exercise and fatigue. Present your findings as a speech or poster.

Key Ideas	Key Terms		Why It Matters
❯ What is the structure of skin? ❯ What are four important functions of skin? ❯ How do hair and nails form? ❯ What are three possible causes of skin diseases and disorders?	epidermis dermis subcutaneous tissue	melanin keratin sebum	Your skin is the only thing between your internal organs and the rest of the world.

When you look in the mirror, the first thing you see is your skin. Skin makes up about 7% of your total body weight. The skin, along with the hair and nails, form the integumentary system.

Skin

Our skin is continuously scraped, ripped, worn away by friction, dried out, soaked, and exposed to radiation, as demonstrated by the swimmer in **Figure 10.** Your body deals with damage to the skin by replacing skin cells. Skin cells are shed about a month after they reach the surface of your body. ❯ **The structure of skin includes the epidermis, the dermis, and the subcutaneous tissue.**

Epidermis The **epidermis** is the outer layer of the skin. It is only about as thick as a sheet of paper. The epidermis is made of epithelial cells that are covered by a thin layer of flattened, dead cells. The flattened cells form a waterproof, protective barrier that covers the body. The epidermis also contains cells that produce pigment.

Dermis The **dermis** is the layer of skin under the epidermis. The dermis contains blood vessels, hair follicles, sweat glands, and oil glands. It also contains several types of nerve cells that sense heat, cold, pain, pressure, and touch. Connective tissue in the dermis makes skin tough and elastic.

Subcutaneous Tissue Subcutaneous **tissue,** located under the dermis, is a layer of connective tissue made mostly of fat. This tissue acts as a shock absorber, stores energy, and insulates the body. Subcutaneous tissue is not technically part of the skin, but the tissue anchors the skin to the body.

epidermis the outer surface layer of cells

dermis the layer of skin below the epidermis

subcutaneous tissue the layer of cells beneath the dermis

Figure 10 Skin is the largest organ of the body. The skin forms a waterproof barrier that keeps us from drying out. ❯ **What might happen to this swimmer if his skin were not waterproof?**

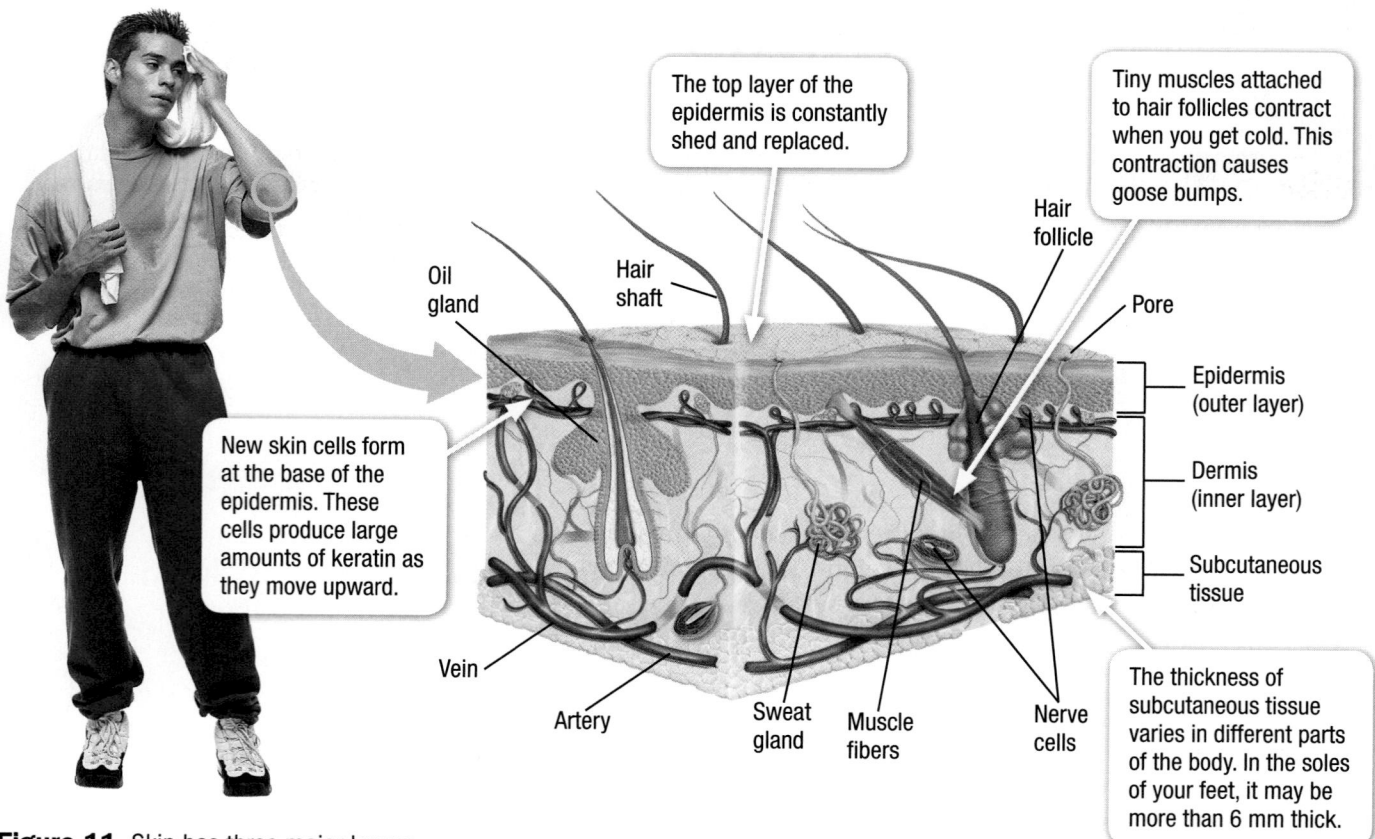

Oil gland

Hair shaft

The top layer of the epidermis is constantly shed and replaced.

Tiny muscles attached to hair follicles contract when you get cold. This contraction causes goose bumps.

Hair follicle

Pore

Epidermis (outer layer)

Dermis (inner layer)

Subcutaneous tissue

New skin cells form at the base of the epidermis. These cells produce large amounts of keratin as they move upward.

Vein

Artery

Sweat gland

Muscle fibers

Nerve cells

The thickness of subcutaneous tissue varies in different parts of the body. In the soles of your feet, it may be more than 6 mm thick.

Figure 11 Skin has three major layers: the epidermis, the dermis, and the subcutaneous tissue.

melanin a pigment that helps determine skin and hair color

keratin a hard protein that makes up hair and nails

sebum oily secretion of the sebaceous glands

Functions of Skin

The skin performs several important functions. ❯ **The skin protects the body from injury and UV radiation, defends against disease, helps regulate body temperature, and prevents the body from drying out.**

UV Protection The lower layers of the epidermis contain cells that produce the pigment **melanin.** Melanin absorbs ultraviolet radiation (UV radiation), which can damage DNA and cause skin cancer. When the skin is exposed to UV rays, skin cells produce more melanin. This process is called *tanning*.

Disease Prevention The top layer of skin, shown in **Figure 11,** forms a tight barrier that keeps bacteria out and protects the body from disease. Damage to large areas of skin allow bacteria to enter the body freely. This is one reason why severe burns are dangerous.

Temperature Regulation A network of blood vessels in the dermis brings nutrients to the living cells of the skin and helps regulate body temperature. Sweat glands in the dermis also help remove excess body heat through the evaporation of sweat. Most sweat is about 99% water and 1% dissolved salts and acids.

Waterproofing Keratin is a hard protein found in skin, hair, and nails. It makes skin tough and waterproof. Glands in the dermis release **sebum,** an oily secretion that lubricates the skin. Without the protection of keratin and sebum, our bodies would lose water through evaporation or absorb water from the environment.

Fingerprint Analysis

The skin on your hands and feet is covered with tiny grooves called *friction ridges*. These ridges produce the familiar pattern that we know as fingerprints.

Procedure

1 Rub a **pencil** on a piece of **paper** to form a 2 cm × 2 cm smudge of pencil graphite.

2 Rub the tip of your index finger in the smudge so that it becomes coated with graphite.

3 Place a piece of **transparent tape** onto the darkened finger tip.

4 Remove the tape, and stick it onto an **index card**.

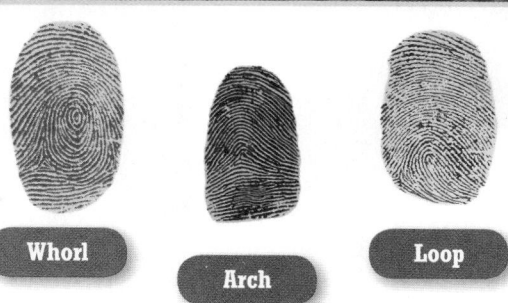

Whorl

Arch

Loop

Analysis

1. Determine whether your fingerprint contains a whorl, loop, or arch. Use the examples above.

2. Compare your fingerprint with fingerprints of other students in the class. Are any of the fingerprints the same?

3. CRITICAL THINKING **Predicting Results** Would you expect fingerprints from your right and left hands to have similar patterns? Explain.

Hair and Nails

Hair and nails, seen in **Figure 12,** are unique types of cells. ❭ **Hair and nails are formed by cells in the skin and made of keratin.**

Hair Hair helps protect and insulate the body. Hair begins in a part of the follicle called the *hair bulb*. Cells in the hair bulb divide faster than any other cells in the body. As new cells are produced, older cells are pushed upward through the skin. As the cells move farther from the root they die. The hair shaft is made of dead cells. Each hair on your head grows for several years. Then, the follicle enters a resting phase that lasts for several months. During this time, the hair that was growing from that follicle is shed. The color of hair comes from the pigment melanin, the same pigment found in skin. Blonde hair and red hair typically contain less melanin than brown hair and black hair contain.

Figure 12 Skin, hair, and nails are made of cells that contain protein that makes them strong. ❭ **Which protein makes hair and nails strong?**

Nails Fingernails and toenails grow from an area of the nail called the *lunula*. This is the light-colored, curved area at the base of each nail. The cells in the lunula are continually dividing. Nail cells fill with keratin as they are pushed outward by new cells. Our nails protect the tips of our fingers and toes.

❭ **Reading Check** *Which structures produce hair and nails?*

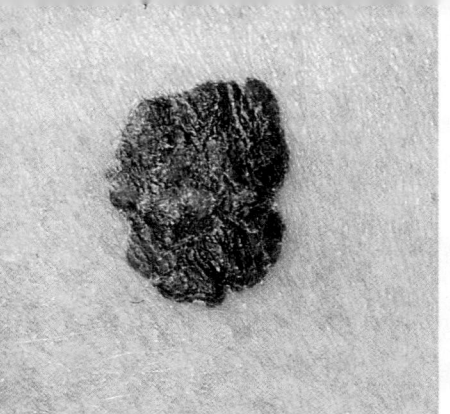
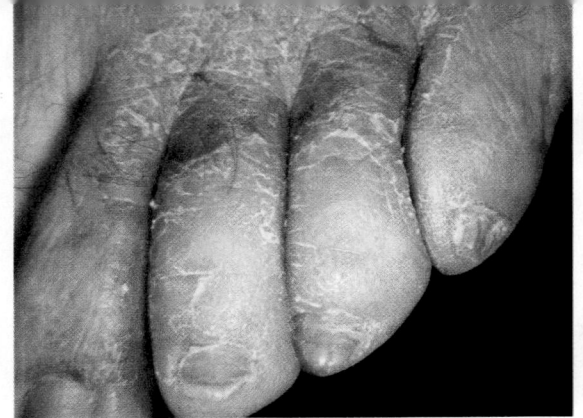
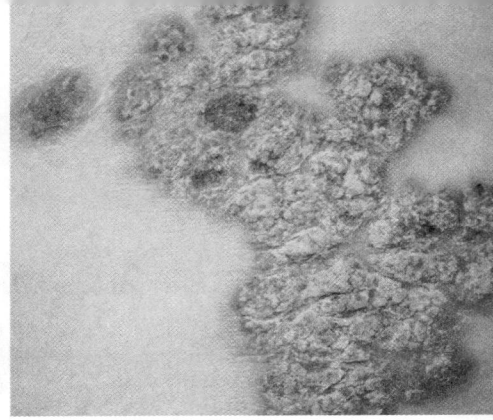

Figure 13 Skin disorders can have a variety of causes. Malignant melanoma (*left*) is usually caused by overexposure to UV radiation in sunlight. Athletes foot (*middle*) is caused by a fungus. Psoriasis (*right*) is a hereditary condition.

www.scilinks.org
Topic: Skin Cancer
Code: HX81401

READING TOOLBOX

Analogies Use information on this page to solve the following analogy.
skin cancer : radiation :: ringworm : ___

Disorders of Skin

Skin diseases and disorders have a variety of causes. ❯ **Skin disorders can be genetic, the result of infections or parasites, or a result of changes that occur within the body over time.** Some common skin disorders are shown in **Figure 13.**

Acne Oil glands are especially active during adolescence. Acne results when pores become clogged and infected with bacteria. These bacteria produce pus, which causes pimples. Often, acne can be controlled by washing gently twice a day and using a topical acne treatment. Serious acne may need to be treated with antibiotics.

Skin Cancer The most common types of skin cancer are carcinomas (KAHR suh NOH muhz), which develop in epidermal cells that do not produce melanin. Carcinomas can be treated if they are detected early. Cancer that occurs in pigment-producing epidermal cells are called *melanomas* (MEL uh NOH muhz). This type of cancer tends to grow very quickly and spread to other parts of the body. About 8 out of 10 skin cancer deaths are from malignant melanomas. Avoiding UV radiation can help reduce your risk of skin cancer.

Other Disorders Fungal infections of the skin include athlete's foot and ringworm. *Psoriasis* is a hereditary skin disorder that causes red, scaly patches. These patches tend to appear during cold weather, when the skin is irritated, or when the body's immune system is stressed.

Section 4 Review

❯ KEY IDEAS

1. **Describe** the structures found in each layer of skin.
2. **List** four important roles that skin plays in the body.
3. **Name** the structures that form hair and nails.
4. **Identify** four possible causes of skin diseases and disorders.

CRITICAL THINKING

5. **Making Inferences** Why can a third-degree burn, which destroys the epidermis and dermis of the skin, be a deadly injury?
6. **Evaluating Viewpoints** Your friend tells you that because she tans easily, she does not need to wear sunscreen. Evaluate this statement. Does this viewpoint seem valid? Why or why not?

USING SCIENCE GRAPHICS

7. **Pie Graph** About 7% of your body weight is skin. What percentage of your body weight is made up by the rest of your body's systems? Draw a pie graph to represent this information.

Chapter 34 **Lab**

⏱ **45 min**

Objective

- Relate muscle energy use and fatigue to the work muscles do.
- Observe the effects of fatigue on a muscle.

Materials

- hand grips, spring
- watch with second hand
- graph paper

Analysis of Muscle Fatigue

When muscles contract for a long period of time, ATP is used, lactic acid builds up, and fatigue results. In this lab you will investigate how fatigue affects the amount of work that muscles can do. Create a data table like the one below.

Preparation

1. **SCIENTIFIC METHODS** **State the Problem** How do dominant and non-dominant hands compare in the amount of work they can do?

2. **SCIENTIFIC METHODS** **Form a Hypothesis** Form a testable hypothesis that predicts the work that can be done by each hand.

Procedure

1. Design an experiment that tests your hypothesis and that uses the materials listed for this lab.

2. Write a procedure for your experiment. Identify the variables that you will control, the experimental variables, and the responding variables. Construct any tables that you will need. You can use the table shown here as an example.

3. Make a list of all safety precautions you will take. Have your teacher approve your procedure before you begin.

Analyze and Conclude

1. **Summarizing Results** Make a graph of your data. Use the x-axis for the number of the trials. Use the y-axis for the number of muscle contractions (squeezes).

2. **SCIENTIFIC METHODS** **Analyzing Results** Explain the differences in the amount of work done by the muscles during the three trials.

3. **SCIENTIFIC METHODS** **Drawing Conclusions** What is the relationship between the work muscles can do and fatigue?

4. **Comparing Functions** Compare the work done by the muscles in your hand to the work done by your heart muscle.

Trial	Squeezes
Trial 1	
Trial 2	
Trial 3	

Key Ideas	Key Terms

1 Body Organization

> Embryonic stem cells can become more than one type of cell.

> The human body contains four types of tissues: epithelial, nervous, connective, and muscle tissue.

> Tissues that work together form organs. Organs that work together form organ systems.

> The body maintains homeostasis, a steady internal environment.

stem cell (839)
epithelial tissue (840)
nervous tissue (840)
connective tissue (840)
muscle tissue (840)

2 The Skeletal System

> The five important functions of the skeletal system are support, protection, movement, mineral storage, and blood cell formation.

> The structure of a typical bone includes the periosteum, compact bone, spongy bone, and bone marrow.

> Movable joints are made up of bone, cartilage, and ligaments.

osteocyte (844)
bone marrow (844)
leukemia (845)
joint (846)
ligament (846)

3 The Muscular System

> The human body contains skeletal, smooth, and cardiac muscle.

> Muscles switch between two processes to produce ATP.

> Skeletal muscle is made of muscle fibers, myofibrils, and sarcomeres

> Actin filaments sliding inward along myosin filaments cause muscle contraction.

> Exercise affects strength, speed, endurance, fatigue, injury, and atrophy in muscles.

tendon (849)
flexor (849)
extensor (849)
muscle fiber (850)
myofibril (850)
sarcomere (850)
myosin (850)
actin (850)

4 The Integumentary System

> The structure of skin includes the epidermis, dermis, and subcutaneous layer.

> The skin protects the body and helps regulate body temperature.

> Hair and nails are made by cells in the skin.

> Skin disorders can be genetic, caused by infections, or the result of changes in the body.

epidermis (853)
dermis (853)
subcutaneous tissue (853)
melanin (854)
keratin (854)
sebum (854)

Chapter 34 Review

READING TOOLBOX

1. Analogies Read the analogy below. Describe the relationship between the words.

> bone : osteocyte :: muscle : muscle fiber

2. **Concept Map** Make a concept map that illustrates the body's four levels of structural organization. Try to include the following terms in your map: *muscle tissue, organ, organ system, nervous tissue, connective tissue,* and *epithelial tissue.*

Using Key Terms

For each pair of terms, explain how the meanings of the terms differ.

3. *ligament* and *tendon*

4. *dermis* and *epidermis*

5. *flexor* and *extensor*

Understanding Key Ideas

6. Which of the following is a characteristic of embryonic stem cells?
  a. They are difficult to grow in the lab.
  b. They can continue to divide endlessly.
  c. They come from the patient's own tissue.
  d. They are limited in what they can become.

7. Blood is an example of which type of tissue?
  a. muscle tissue
  b. nervous tissue
  c. epithelial tissue
  d. connective tissue

8. Which of the following is organized in order from smallest to largest?
  a. organs, organ systems, tissues, and cells
  b. tissues, cells, organs, and organ systems
  c. organ systems, organs, tissues, and cells
  d. cells, tissues, organs, and organ systems

9. Which of the following is a way that the body maintains homeostasis?
  a. using feedback
  b. being endothermic
  c. using temperature
  d. biosignaling

10. The skeletal system does all of the following *except*
  a. give support.
  b. provide protection.
  c. store minerals.
  d. circulate blood.

11. Which layer in long bones produces blood cells?
  a. marrow
  b. osteocyte
  c. spongy bone
  d. Haversian canal

12. Which type of joint is found in the hip?
  a. a hinge joint
  b. a gliding joint
  c. a saddle joint
  d. a ball-and-socket joint

13. Which step in muscle contraction requires ATP?
  a. when myosin reattaches to actin
  b. when the myosin head releases from actin
  c. when myosin attaches to a binding site
  d. when the myosin head rotates and pulls actin filaments closer

14. The dermis contains all of the following *except*
  a. nerves.
  b. melanin.
  c. hair follicles.
  d. sebaceous glands.

15. Which of the following helps regulate body temperature?
  a. sebum
  b. melanin
  c. keratin
  d. sweat glands

16. Where are fingernails and toenails made?
  a. in the lunula
  b. in the hair bulb
  c. in the nail bulb
  d. in subcutaneus tissue

17. Which of the following can cause skin cancer?
  a. parasites
  b. infections
  c. UV radiation
  d. inflammation

18. In this figure, which muscle is the flexor?

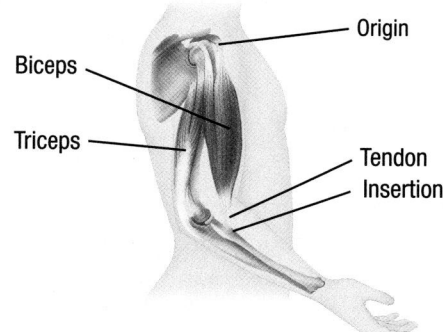

  a. origin
  b. biceps
  c. triceps
  d. insertion

Explaining Key Ideas

19. Why is it important to avoid UV radiation?

20. When you sprain an ankle, which part of the joint is damaged?

Critical Thinking

21. Applying Information The joints of an adult's skull are fused and thus are immovable. The joints of an infant's skull are not fused. Instead, the skull bones are connected by tough, fibrous tissue. What might be the advantages of having movable skull joints as infants and fused joints as adults?

22. Applying Logic Muscles that hold the body up and maintain posture are almost always contracted. What type of muscle fibers would you expect to find in these muscles?

23. Identifying Relationships Which of the following activities are anaerobic, and which are aerobic: walking, jogging, sprinting, weight lifting, boxing, playing baseball, and swimming? Explain your reasoning.

Using Science Graphics

The table shows the relationship between skin type, UV index, and sunburns. Use the table to answer the following question(s).

Relationship of UV Index and Sunburns

UV index	Minutes before Skin Type 1 burns	Minutes before Skin Type 4 burns
0–2	30	>120
3	20	90
5	12	60
7	8.5	40
9	7	33

24. Which statement about skin types is true?
  a. Skin type 4 will never sunburn.
  b. Skin type 1 will always burn in less than 20 min.
  c. Skin type 1 is less sensitive to UV exposure than skin type 4 is.
  d. Skin type 1 is more sensitive to UV exposure than skin type 4 is.

The bar graph shows the percentage of teen boys and girls who met the daily recommended intake for calcium between 1994 and 1996. Use the graph to answer the following question(s).

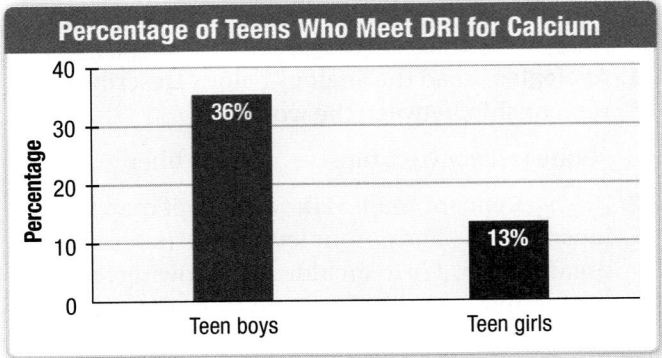

25. What percentage of boys did *not* consume enough calcium?
  a. 44%
  c. 64%
  b. 54%
  d. 74%

26. What is the difference between the percentage of girls and boys that did *not* consume enough calcium?
  a. 13%
  c. 33%
  b. 23%
  d. 36%

Writing for Science

27. Descriptive Writing Write a paragraph that describes the difference between voluntary and involuntary muscles and where on the body these muscles can be found.

Why It Matters

28. Relating Concepts In 1999, a German boy was born with unusually large muscles. Doctors discovered that he had a myostatin mutation. What might be some of the advantages and disadvantages of myostatin mutation in humans?

Alternative Assessment

29. Research Infants and children have more bones in their skeletons than adults do. Use library or Internet resources to learn about the changes that the skeleton and bones go through as the skeleton matures. Show how the structure of bones, including skull bones, changes as the bones mature. Display your results in a poster.

Science Concepts

1. Muscle cells are also known as
   - **A** myosin.
   - **B** myofibrils.
   - **C** sarcomeres.
   - **D** muscle fibers.

2. Which of the following is the protein that makes up hair and nails?
   - **F** sebum
   - **G** keratin
   - **H** melanin
   - **J** collagen

3. What is a melanoma?
   - **A** an infected skin pore
   - **B** a fungal infection of the skin
   - **C** a tumor that forms in pigment-producing skin cells
   - **D** a tumor that forms in skin cells that do not produce pigment

4. Tissues working together form
   - **F** cells.
   - **G** organs.
   - **H** colonies.
   - **J** organ systems.

5. A mature bone cell is called an
   - **A** osteon.
   - **B** osteo cell.
   - **C** osteocyte.
   - **D** osteoblast.

6. A myostatin knockout mouse has
   - **F** less muscle than a normal mouse.
   - **G** more muscle than a normal mouse.
   - **H** more myostatin than a normal mouse.
   - **J** more muscle producing genes than a normal mouse.

Writing Skills

7. **Short Response** Name the four types of tissues, and identify one place in the body where each type of tissue is found.

Using Science Graphics

The graph shows the number of men and women who have, or are predicted to have, osteoporosis. Use the graph to answer the following question.

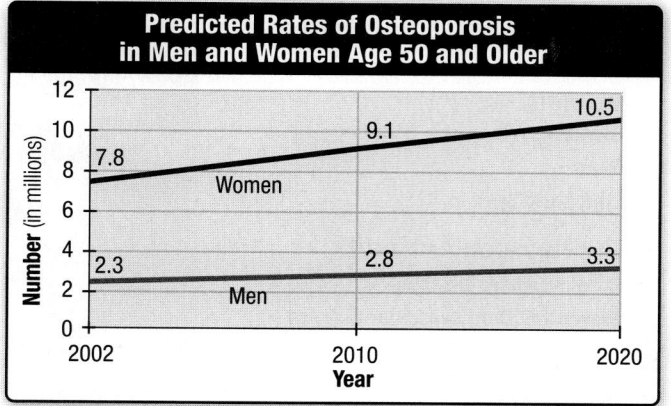

Predicted Rates of Osteoporosis in Men and Women Age 50 and Older

8. How many more women than men are predicted to have osteoporosis in the year 2020?
   - **A** 3.3 million
   - **B** 6.2 million
   - **C** 7.2 million
   - **D** 10.5 million

The graph shows the measurement of hair length over time. Use the graph to answer the following question(s).

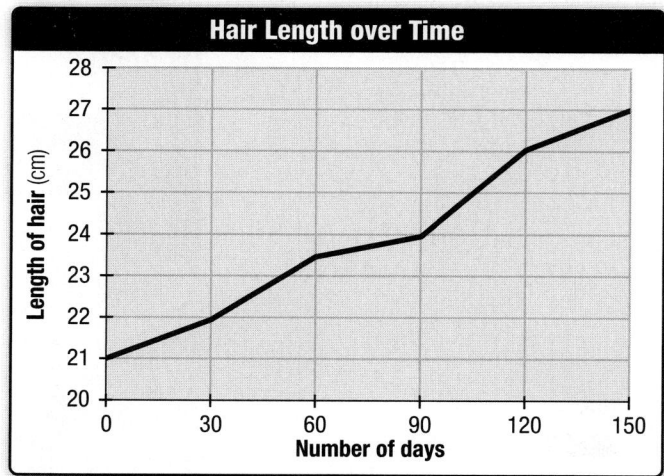

Hair Length over Time

9. How much did the person's hair grow between the beginning of the study and the end?
   - **F** 5 cm
   - **G** 6 cm
   - **H** 6 inches
   - **J** 26 cm

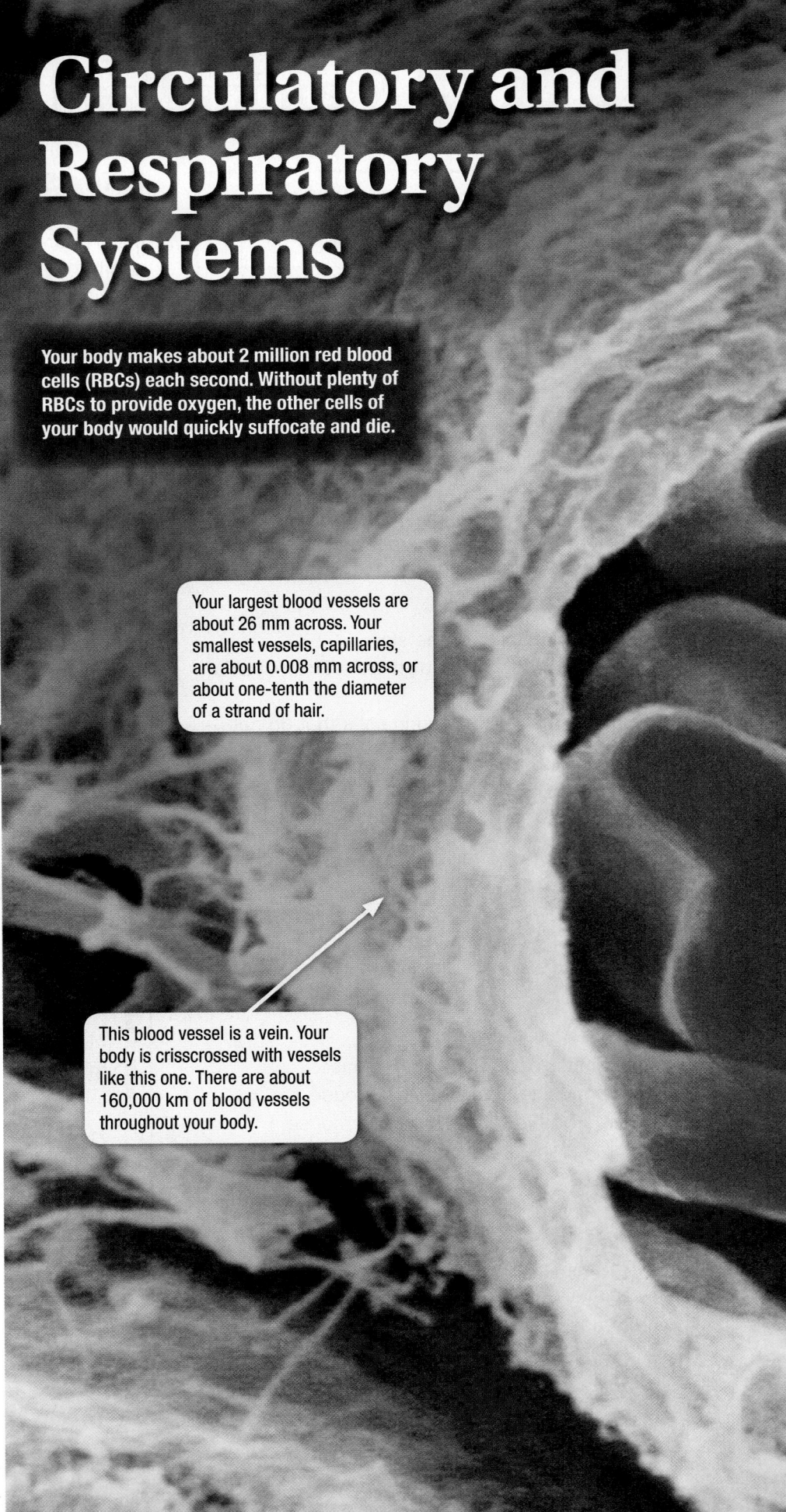

Chapter 35

Circulatory and Respiratory Systems

Preview

1 The Cardiovascular System
What Is the Cardiovascular System?
The Heart
Blood Vessels
Blood
Lymphatic System

2 Cardiovascular Health
Cardiovascular Disease
Preventing Cardiovascular Disease

3 The Respiratory System
The Path of Air
Breathing
Gas Exchange and Transport
Respiratory Diseases

Why It Matters

Your cells can survive only a few minutes without oxygen. It is the job of your respiratory system to obtain that oxygen. It is the job of your cardiovascular system to transport the oxygen throughout your body.

Your body makes about 2 million red blood cells (RBCs) each second. Without plenty of RBCs to provide oxygen, the other cells of your body would quickly suffocate and die.

Your largest blood vessels are about 26 mm across. Your smallest vessels, capillaries, are about 0.008 mm across, or about one-tenth the diameter of a strand of hair.

This blood vessel is a vein. Your body is crisscrossed with vessels like this one. There are about 160,000 km of blood vessels throughout your body.

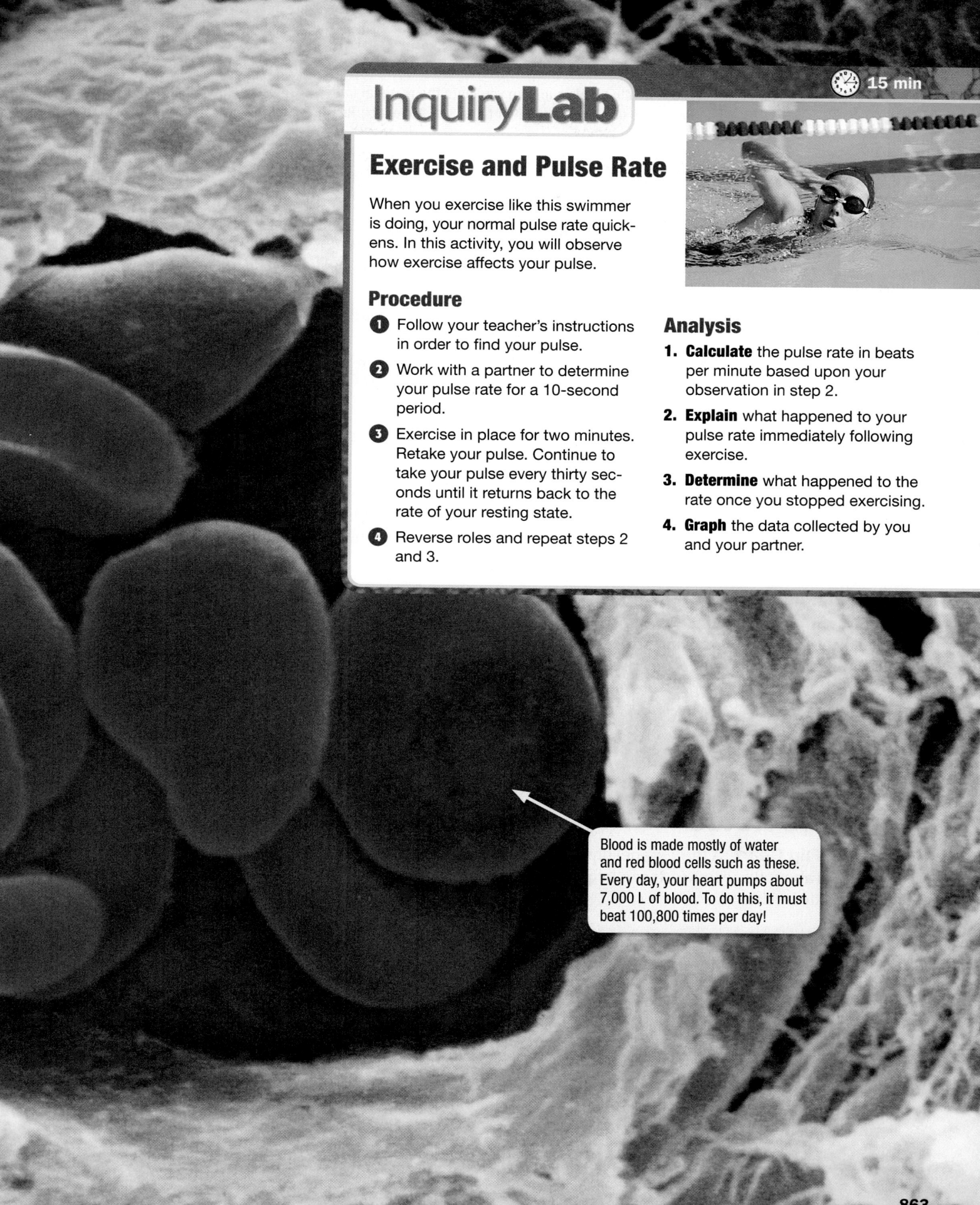

Inquiry**Lab**

⏱ 15 min

Exercise and Pulse Rate

When you exercise like this swimmer is doing, your normal pulse rate quickens. In this activity, you will observe how exercise affects your pulse.

Procedure

1. Follow your teacher's instructions in order to find your pulse.

2. Work with a partner to determine your pulse rate for a 10-second period.

3. Exercise in place for two minutes. Retake your pulse. Continue to take your pulse every thirty seconds until it returns back to the rate of your resting state.

4. Reverse roles and repeat steps 2 and 3.

Analysis

1. **Calculate** the pulse rate in beats per minute based upon your observation in step 2.

2. **Explain** what happened to your pulse rate immediately following exercise.

3. **Determine** what happened to the rate once you stopped exercising.

4. **Graph** the data collected by you and your partner.

Blood is made mostly of water and red blood cells such as these. Every day, your heart pumps about 7,000 L of blood. To do this, it must beat 100,800 times per day!

READING TOOLBOX

These reading tools can help you learn the material in this chapter. For more information on how to use these and other tools, see **Appendix: Reading and Study Skills.**

Using Words

Word Parts Knowing the meanings of word parts can help you figure out the meanings of words that you do not know.

Your Turn Use the table to answer the following questions.

1. Write a definition in your own words for bronchitis.

2. When air gets into the chest cavity, or thorax, the lungs collapse. What would you guess this condition is called?

Word Parts		
Part	**Type**	**Meaning**
bronchi-	prefix	the wind pipe
pneumo-	prefix	wind, air, the lungs
tuber-	prefix	a knot, knob, or swelling
-itis	suffix	inflammation

Using Language

Recognizing Main Ideas A main idea is a statement that tells you the main point of the paragraph. It summarizes what the paragraph is about. The main idea is often, but not always, one of the first few sentences of a paragraph.

Your Turn Find the main idea in the paragraph below.

Cardiovascular diseases include high blood pressure, clogged and hardened arteries, heart attack, and stroke. High blood pressure causes the heart to work harder than normal, weakening the heart. Clogged and hardened arteries raise blood pressure and can also lead to heart attack and stroke.

Using Fold Notes

Three-Panel Flip Chart A three-panel flip chart is useful when you want to organize notes about three topics. It can help you organize the characteristics of the topics side by side.

Your Turn Make a three-panel flip chart to organize your notes about the cardiovascular system, cardiovascular health, and the respiratory system.

1. Fold a piece of paper in half from the top to the bottom

2. Fold the paper in three sections from side to side. Unfold the paper so that you can see the three sections.

3. From the top of the paper, cut along the vertical fold lines to the fold in the middle of the paper. You will now have three flaps.

4. Label the flaps of the three-panel flip chart "Cardiovascular System", "Cardiovascular Health", and "Respiratory System".

5. Under each flap write your notes about each of the topics.

Key Ideas	Key Terms		Why It Matters

❯ What does the cardiovascular system do?
❯ How does the structure of the heart relate to its function?
❯ How are the structures of arteries, veins, and capillaries related to their functions?
❯ What are the functions of the key components of human blood?
❯ How does the lymphatic system work with the cardiovascular system?
	cardiovascular
	   system
	atrium
	ventricle
	pulse
	artery
	capillary
		vein
		plasma
		red blood cell
		white blood cell
		platelet
		lymphatic
		   system
			The cardiovascular system provides every cell of the body with the substances needed for survival.

The cardiovascular system, shown in **Figure 1,** is very much like a network of highways that transports chemicals to and from all of the cells in the body. Nearly every material needed by cells travels through this system.

What Is the Cardiovascular System?

The heart, blood vessels, and blood make up the **cardiovascular system.** ❯ The cardiovascular system carries nutrients, oxygen, hormones, and wastes through the body and distributes heat to maintain homeostasis.

Blood moves through the vessels of the cardiovascular system. Blood interacts with every body system, either by carrying products of the system or by bringing needed products to it. Blood also carries wastes, such as carbon dioxide, away from every system. In addition to carrying materials, the cardiovascular system helps the body maintain a steady temperature. When the body is warm, blood vessels in the skin relax to allow heat to leave the body. When the body is cold, blood vessels in the skin narrow. This change helps the body save heat by diverting blood to deeper tissues so that less heat will escape.

❯ **Reading Check** *How does blood help the body maintain homeostasis? (See the Appendix for answers to Reading Checks.)*

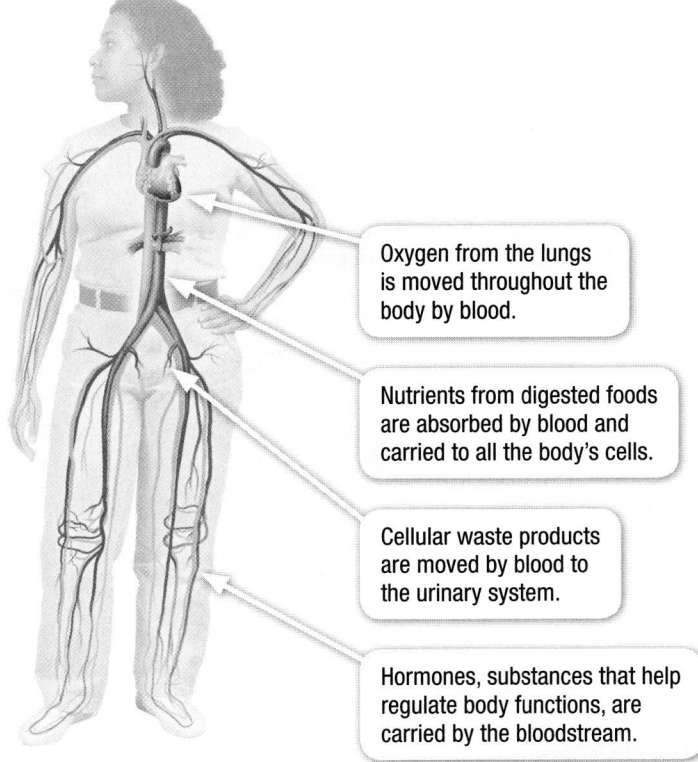

Oxygen from the lungs is moved throughout the body by blood.

Nutrients from digested foods are absorbed by blood and carried to all the body's cells.

Cellular waste products are moved by blood to the urinary system.

Hormones, substances that help regulate body functions, are carried by the bloodstream.

Figure 1 The cardiovascular system transports materials to and from every cell in the body.

The Heart

The pumping action of the heart is needed to provide enough force to move blood throughout the body. The heart is made up mostly of cardiac muscle tissue, which contracts to pump blood. **❯ The structure of the heart chambers is related to their function. The atria are thin walled because they pump blood just to the ventricles. The ventricles are thick walled because they pump blood to either the lungs or the rest of the body.**

Blood Flow Through the Heart Blood moves through two separate loops of the cardiovascular system. One loop takes blood from the right side of the heart to the lungs. There, blood picks up oxygen and gives off carbon dioxide. Blood then returns to the left side of the heart. The second loop takes blood from the left side of the heart throughout the body and then returns it to the right side of the heart. **Figure 2** summarizes the path of the blood through the heart.

cardiovascular system (KAHR dee oh VAS kyoo luhr) a collection of organs that transport blood throughout the body

atrium (AY tree uhm) a chamber that receives blood that is returning to the heart

ventricle (VEN tri kuhl) one of the two large, muscular chambers that pump blood out of the heart

pulse (PUHLS) the rhythmic pressure of the blood against the walls of a vessel, particularly an artery

Figure 2 The arrows trace the path of blood as it travels through the heart. ❯ Which veins carry oxygen-poor blood to the heart?

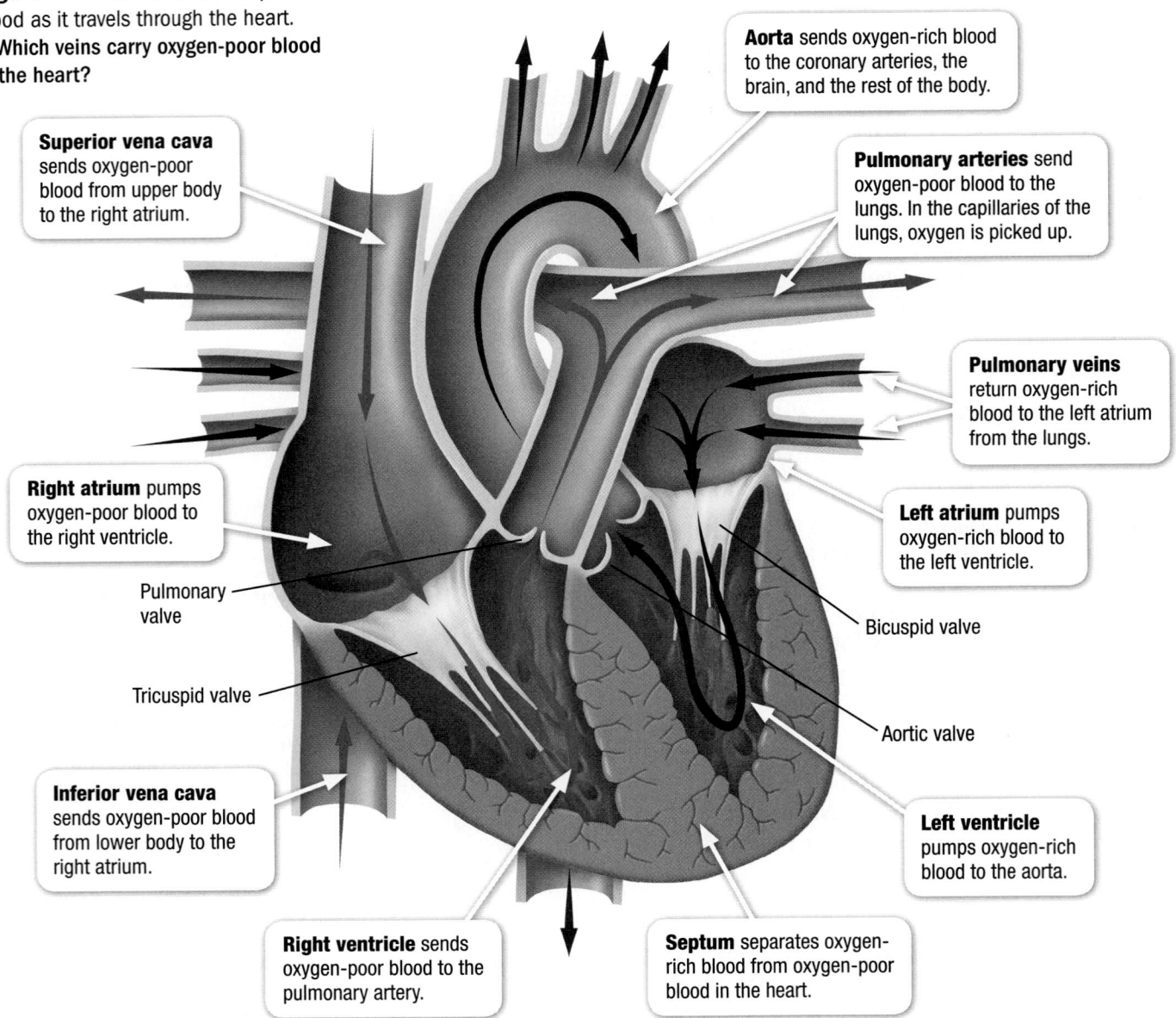

Superior vena cava sends oxygen-poor blood from upper body to the right atrium.

Aorta sends oxygen-rich blood to the coronary arteries, the brain, and the rest of the body.

Pulmonary arteries send oxygen-poor blood to the lungs. In the capillaries of the lungs, oxygen is picked up.

Pulmonary veins return oxygen-rich blood to the left atrium from the lungs.

Right atrium pumps oxygen-poor blood to the right ventricle.

Left atrium pumps oxygen-rich blood to the left ventricle.

Pulmonary valve

Bicuspid valve

Tricuspid valve

Aortic valve

Inferior vena cava sends oxygen-poor blood from lower body to the right atrium.

Left ventricle pumps oxygen-rich blood to the aorta.

Right ventricle sends oxygen-poor blood to the pulmonary artery.

Septum separates oxygen-rich blood from oxygen-poor blood in the heart.

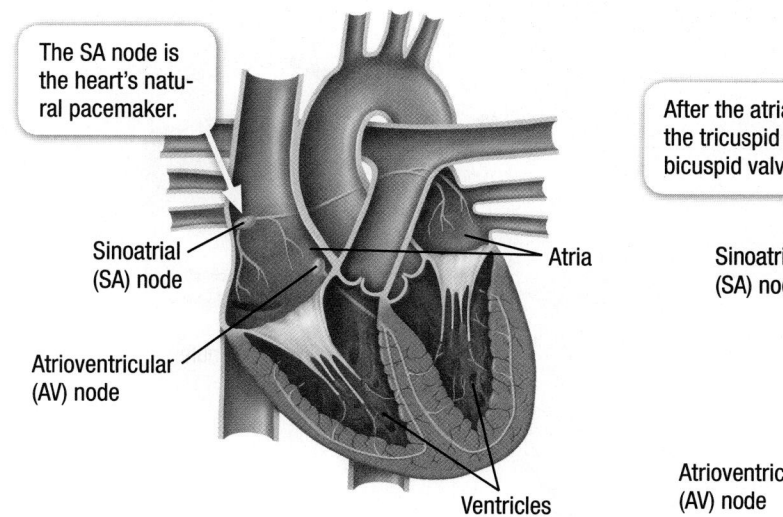

The SA node is the heart's natural pacemaker.

Sinoatrial (SA) node

Atrioventricular (AV) node

Atria

Ventricles

1 **Contraction of the Atria** The SA node signals the atria's muscle to contract. Blood is pumped from the atria into the ventricles.

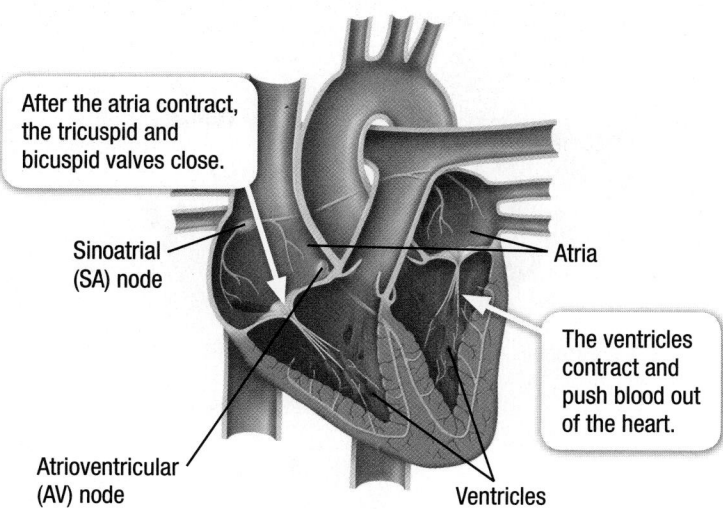

After the atria contract, the tricuspid and bicuspid valves close.

Sinoatrial (SA) node

Atrioventricular (AV) node

Atria

The ventricles contract and push blood out of the heart.

Ventricles

2 **Contraction of the Ventricles** The SA node's signal is picked up by the AV node, which signals the ventricles to contract.

The Heart's Chambers The heart has a wall that divides it into right and left sides. The **atria** (singular, *atrium*) at the top of the heart are chambers that receive blood from the body and lungs. Below the atria are the **ventricles,** chambers that pump blood away from the heart. Valves between the chambers stop blood from moving backward.

The Heartbeat Most muscle tissue contracts only when stimulated by a nerve carrying a signal from the brain. However, heart muscle is different because stimulation of its cells happens in the muscle itself. Coordinated contraction of the heart's chambers is started by a small group of cardiac muscle cells, called the *sinoatrial* (SA) *node.* The SA node is in the upper wall of the right atrium. The node "fires" electrical signals in a regular rhythm. Each signal is followed immediately by a contraction of the heart muscle that moves quickly in a wave and causes both atria to contract almost at the same time. As shown in **Figure 3,** the wave of contraction in the atria is picked up by the *atrioventricular* (AV) *node* in the ventricles. Almost one-tenth of a second after the atria contract, the AV node causes the ventricles to contract. The delay allows the atria to finish emptying blood into the ventricles before the two ventricles contract.

Heart Rate Your **pulse** is a rhythmic stretching of the blood vessels leading away from the heart. The pulse is caused by the pressure of blood pushed out of the heart's left ventricle. Each time blood rushes from the heart, the walls in the blood vessels expand. You can measure a person's pulse to find his or her heart rate—how fast or slow the heart is beating. The number of pulses per minute equals the number of heartbeats per minute. The average pulse rate ranges from 70 to 90 beats per minute for adults but goes down during sleep. During exercise, the pulse rate goes up in order to meet the body's increased need for oxygen and nutrients.

▶ **Reading Check** *What causes muscles in the ventricles to contract?*

Figure 3 A heartbeat has two phases. The opening and closing of the heart's valves during these phases give the heartbeat its familiar *"lub dup"* sound.

ACADEMIC VOCABULARY

coordinate proceeding in a matching order

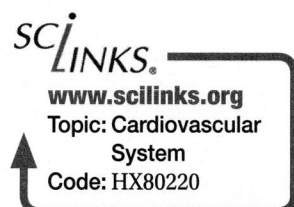

www.scilinks.org
Topic: Cardiovascular System
Code: HX80220

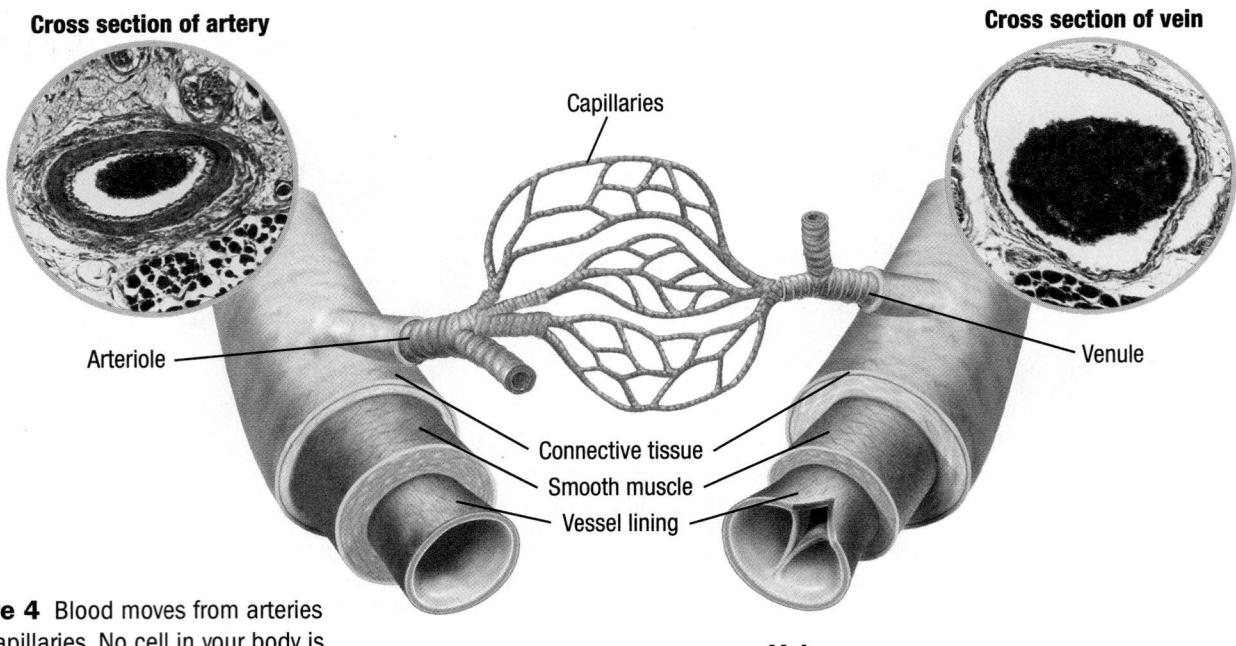

Cross section of artery

Cross section of vein

Capillaries

Arteriole

Venule

Connective tissue

Smooth muscle

Vessel lining

Artery

Vein

Figure 4 Blood moves from arteries into capillaries. No cell in your body is more than a few millimeters away from a capillary. From the capillaries, blood moves into veins.

Blood Vessels

Blood flows through the body in a network of vessels. ❯ **The structure of blood vessels relates to their function. Arteries have thick, muscular walls to withstand the force of the pumped blood. Capillaries have thin walls to allow the exchange of gases and nutrients. Veins have valves that stop blood from flowing backward.**

Arteries **Arteries** are blood vessels that carry blood away from the heart. The walls of arteries, shown in **Figure 4,** have a layer of smooth muscle that allows them to expand when blood is pumped into them. Blood passes from the arteries into smaller vessels called *arterioles*. Eventually, blood is pushed through to the capillaries.

Capillaries **Capillaries** are tiny blood vessels that allow the exchange of materials between blood and the fluid around cells. These vessels are greatly branched, forming networks of capillary beds. The exchange of materials across the walls of capillaries is possible because capillary walls are only one cell thick. Molecules can easily pass through them.

Veins From the capillaries, blood flows into small vessels called *venules* and then into veins. **Veins** are blood vessels that carry blood back to the heart. The walls of veins have a much thinner layer of smooth muscle than arterial walls. Veins are also wider than arteries. A wide blood vessel gives less resistance to blood flow than a narrower one. This size difference is important because veins are farther from the heart and do not receive the pulsing pressure that arteries do. Instead, blood is pushed through veins by muscle contractions in the arms and legs. One-way valves in veins stop blood from flowing backward during its return trip to the heart.

❯ **Reading Check** *How is blood pushed through veins?*

Blood

Blood is a connective tissue, but the material between its cells is liquid, unlike the solid materials found between cells in other kinds of connective tissue. ❯ **The key components of human blood are plasma, red blood cells, white blood cells, and platelets.**

Plasma About 45% of the total volume of blood is cells and cell fragments. The remaining 55% is **plasma,** the liquid portion of blood. Plasma is made of 90% water and 10% solutes. The solutes include nutrients, wastes, proteins, and salts. The salts in plasma have many functions, including maintaining osmotic balance and regulating the pH of the blood. Plasma proteins also have many functions. They help form blood clots, protect the body from disease, and maintain osmotic balance.

Red Blood Cells Most blood cells are **red blood cells** (RBCs), which carry oxygen. RBCs have a biconcave shape, as shown in **Figure 5.** Their interior is packed with hemoglobin. Hemoglobin is an iron-containing protein that binds to oxygen in the lungs and then carries it to the body's tissues. Mature RBCs do not have nuclei. Therefore, they cannot make proteins or repair themselves. So, the life span of a red blood cell is only about four months. New red blood cells are produced constantly by the red bone marrow.

White Blood Cells The main job of **white blood cells** is to defend the body against disease. White blood cells are larger than red blood cells and contain nuclei. There are many kinds of white blood cells, each with a different function.

Platelets Bits of cytoplasm are regularly pinched off from cells in bone marrow. These cell fragments are called **platelets.** Platelets play an important role in blood clotting. If a tear develops in a blood vessel, platelets and plasma proteins take rapid action to stop too much blood loss, which could be fatal. The steps of blood clotting are shown in **Figure 6.**

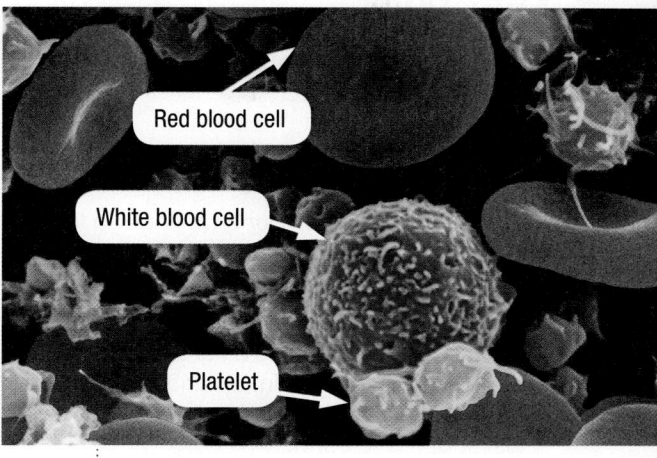

Red blood cell

White blood cell

Platelet

Figure 5 A milliliter of blood contains about 5 million red blood cells, 225,000 platelets, and 7,000 white blood cells. ❯ **How do you think the shape of a red blood cell helps with its function?**

READING TOOLBOX

Three-Panel Flip Chart Make a three panel flip chart to help you organize your notes about the heart, the blood vessels, and blood.

Figure 6 When a blood vessel is damaged, chemicals released by the damaged tissue and nearby platelets start the clotting process.

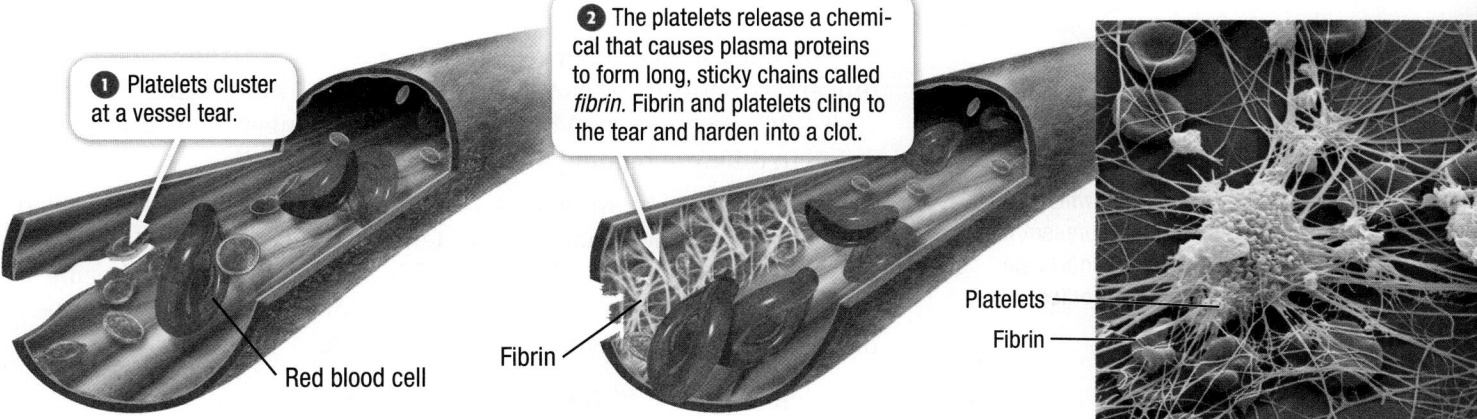

❶ Platelets cluster at a vessel tear.

❷ The platelets release a chemical that causes plasma proteins to form long, sticky chains called *fibrin.* Fibrin and platelets cling to the tear and harden into a clot.

Red blood cell

Fibrin

Platelets

Fibrin

Hands-On QuickLab

⏱ 15 min

Vein Valves

By applying pressure to your arm, you can locate the valves in the veins of your arm.

Procedure

1 Have a classmate make a fist and extend his or her arm, with the hand palm up and slightly below elbow level. Use a finger to locate a prominent vein on the inside of the forearm.

2 Gently place a second finger along the vein about 5 cm from the first finger (toward the elbow). Release the second finger, but not the first. The vein should refill partway. Use a pen to mark this point, which indicates the location of a valve. You may have to try more than one vein to locate a valve.

Analysis

1. **Identify** the direction that blood flows in the vein you chose.

2. **Propose** why the subject must make a fist and hold his or her arm slightly down.

3. **Infer** what effect standing in one place for long periods of time might have on the veins in the legs.

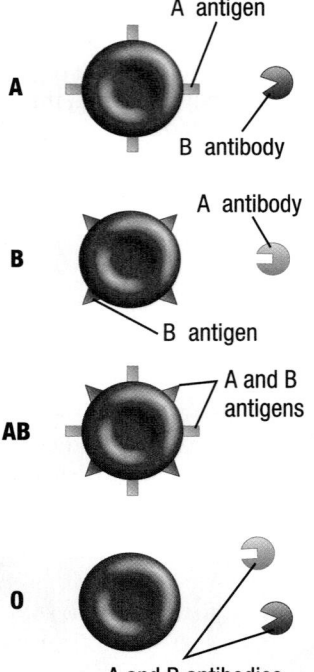

Figure 7 This figure shows which antigens and antibodies are present for each blood type. ❯ **Which blood type produces both A and B antibodies?**

Blood Types Blood type is determined by the presence or absence of markers on the surface of red blood cells. The blood types in the ABO blood group system are A, B, AB, and O. The letters *A* and *B* refer to carbohydrates on the surface of RBCs that act as antigens. Antigens are substances that can cause the immune system to react. People with type A blood have the A antigen on their RBCs. People with type B blood have the B antigen. Type AB blood has both A and B antigens, and type O blood has neither antigen.

Blood Compatibility Antibodies are defensive proteins made by the immune system. People with type A blood make antibodies against the B antigen. If a person with type A blood were given type B blood, antibodies to the B antigen would bind to the type B red blood cells. The immune system would then attack the RBCs, and they would burst. Many problems could result, including shock and kidney failure. For this reason, blood transfusion recipients must receive blood that is compatible with their own. People with type AB blood are universal recipients (they can receive any blood type) because they do not produce either A or B antibodies. Type O individuals are universal donors (they can donate blood to any blood type) because their RBCs do not carry A or B antigens. The antigens and antibodies found in different blood types are shown in **Figure 7.**

Rh Factor Another antigen on the surface of RBCs is a protein called *Rh factor*. People who have this protein are Rh⁺. Those who lack it are Rh⁻. When an Rh⁺ baby is born to an Rh⁻ mother, the mother begins to make Rh antibodies. In a future pregnancy, the antibodies may be passed to an Rh⁺ fetus and lead to fetal death.

❯ **Reading Check** *Which blood types can an A+ patient receive?*

Lymphatic System

Blood plasma is rich in proteins, so most of the fluid remains in the capillaries because of osmotic pressure. However, every time the heart pumps, some fluids are forced out of the capillaries' thin walls. The escaped fluid collects in spaces around the body's cells. This fluid is picked up by the lymphatic system and is returned to the blood supply. The **lymphatic system,** illustrated in **Figure 8,** is made up of a network of vessels, tiny bean-shaped structures called *lymph nodes,* and lymph tissue. ❯ **The lymphatic system works with the cardiovascular system by collecting fluids that leak out of capillaries and returning those fluids to the cardiovascular system.** The lymphatic system also fights infections.

Lymphatic vessels carry leaked fluid, called *lymph,* back to two major veins in the neck. This process returns the escaped fluids to the cardiovascular system. Similar to veins, lymphatic vessels have valves that stop the backflow of lymph. Lymph is pushed through the vessels when the muscles in the arms and legs contract. Lymph tissue is located in various places throughout the body, including the thymus, tonsils, spleen, and bone marrow.

The lymphatic system also acts as a key element in the immune system. Immune cells in the lymph nodes and lymphatic organs help defend the body against bacteria, viruses, other infectious microbes, and cancer cells. Many lymph nodes are found in the armpits, neck, and groin. These nodes sometimes become tender and swell when they are actively fighting infection and are filled with white blood cells. Healthcare workers are trained to detect certain kinds of infections by feeling the lymph nodes for swellings.

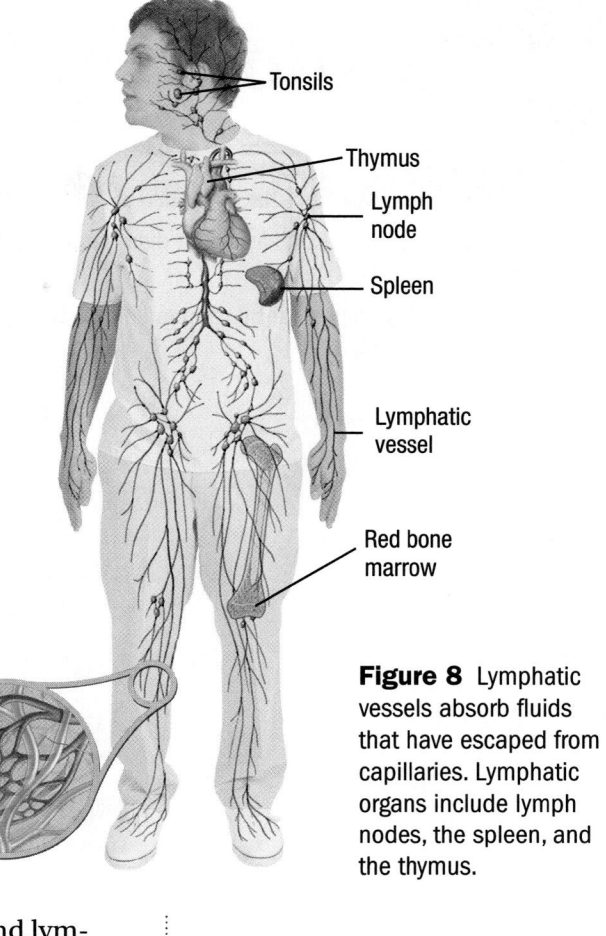

Figure 8 Lymphatic vessels absorb fluids that have escaped from capillaries. Lymphatic organs include lymph nodes, the spleen, and the thymus.

Labels: Tonsils · Thymus · Lymph node · Spleen · Lymphatic vessel · Red bone marrow

❯ **Reading Check** *What are two ways in which the cardiovascular system and the lymphatic system are related?*

lymphatic system (lim FAT ik SIS tuhm) a collection of organs whose primary function is to collect extracellular fluid and return it to the blood

---

Section 1 Review

❯ KEY IDEAS

1. **Name** the two main functions of the cardiovascular system.

2. **Compare** the four chambers of the human heart in terms of their structure and function.

3. **Relate** the structure of arteries, veins, and capillaries to their functions.

4. **Describe** the functions of the four components of blood.

5. **State** how the cardiovascular and lymphatic systems relate to each other.

CRITICAL THINKING

6. **Relating Concepts** How is the heart muscle different from other muscle tissue?

7. **Predicting Outcomes** What would happen if a person with type A blood received a transfusion of type O blood?

METHODS OF SCIENCE

8. **Making a Line Graph** Predict how a student's heart rate might change as the student wakes up in the morning, goes to school, exercises in the afternoon, and goes to bed that night. Draw a line graph showing how you predict the heart rate will change.

Cardiovascular Health

Key Ideas	Key Terms	Why It Matters
❯ What are the four main cardiovascular diseases that affect Americans? ❯ What are the most important things people can do to prevent cardiovascular disease?	blood pressure heart attack stroke	Cardiovascular disease, the number one killer of Americans, has many risk factors that can be controlled.

Diseases of the cardiovascular system kill more Americans than all other diseases combined—about a million deaths each year, or 33% of all deaths. Both your genes and your lifestyle affect your risk of developing cardiovascular disease.

Cardiovascular Disease

❯ The four main cardiovascular diseases are high blood pressure, clogged and hardened arteries, heart attack, and stroke.

High Blood Pressure **Blood pressure** is the force exerted by blood as it moves through blood vessels. A blood pressure measurement includes two numbers that are usually written as a fraction. Normal blood pressure for a young adult is about 120/80 but may be lower. Hypertension, or high blood pressure, is an elevation of one or both of these pressure readings to 140 or higher for the first number or 90 or higher for the second number. High blood pressure causes the heart to work harder than normal, so it weakens over time. Because high blood pressure damages arteries, they become less elastic. There is also an increased chance that a blood clot will break loose from a blood vessel wall. The clot could get stuck in a narrow blood vessel and shut off blood flow to part of the body. The result can be a serious condition such as a heart attack, stroke, kidney failure, or eye damage. Hypertension usually can be controlled by medication, diet, and exercise.

Figure 9 Plaque buildup causes an artery's wall to become less elastic.
❯ How would a hardened wall affect an artery's function?

Clogged and Hardened Arteries The inside walls of arteries can collect deposits of fats, cholesterol, waste products, and other materials. This buildup is plaque. Its accumulation, shown in **Figure 9,** leads to arteriosclerosis. Arteriosclerosis (ahr TIR ee OH skluh ROH sis) is the hardening and narrowing of the arteries. High blood levels of cholesterol and fats, high blood pressure, and smoking can all cause plaque to collect on artery walls. Plaque builds up slowly over time. As the plaque layer thickens, the artery narrows. So, blood pressure increases, and blood flow and oxygen supply to tissues served by the artery decrease.

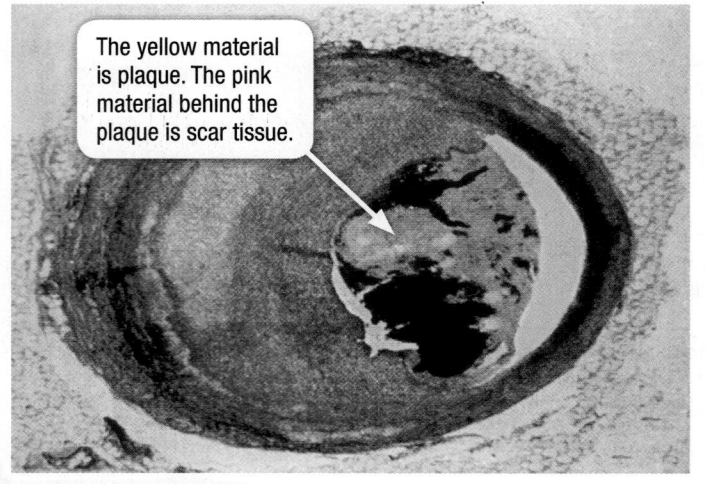

The yellow material is plaque. The pink material behind the plaque is scar tissue.

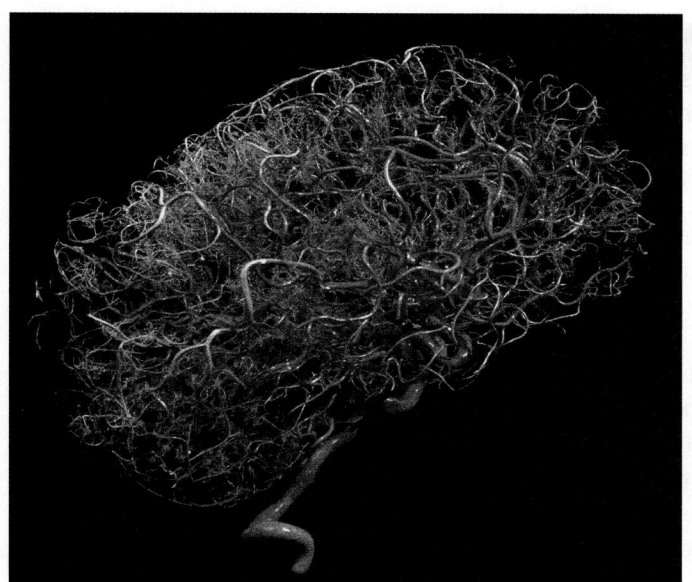

Blood vessels of the brain

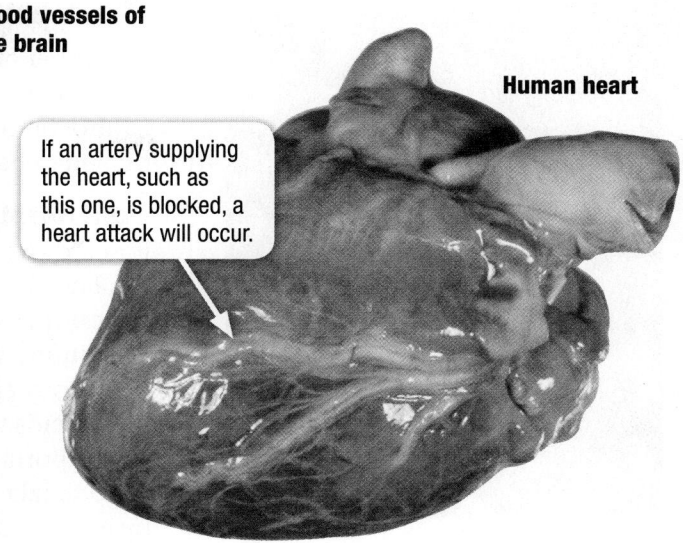

Human heart

If an artery supplying the heart, such as this one, is blocked, a heart attack will occur.

Figure 10 Heart attacks and most strokes are caused when a vessel supplying the heart or brain becomes blocked.

Blood Clots Sometimes, the body may produce a blood clot. The clot can block an artery or be carried in the blood and cut off blood flow when the clot reaches a smaller artery. Medications that lower cholesterol and blood pressure and a healthy diet are effective treatments for arteriosclerosis. However, advanced cases may require surgical removal of plaque deposits or replacement of an artery.

Heart Attack A **heart attack** occurs when the blood supply to part of the heart muscle is greatly reduced or stopped. This happens when one or more of the arteries that carry blood to the heart itself are blocked. These arteries can be seen in the wall of the heart shown in **Figure 10.** A heart attack can be caused by plaque buildup in an artery in the heart's wall. It can also happen if a blood clot forms elsewhere in the body, breaks away, and gets stuck in and blocks an artery supplying the heart. If the blood supply is cut off for more than a few minutes, cells in the affected area die from a lack of oxygen. If a large enough area of the heart is affected by the blockage, the heart attack can be fatal. Successful treatment of a heart attack depends on a fast response. Medications can be given that dissolve the clot to prevent further damage. Other treatments, such as surgery, are aimed at increasing blood flow to the heart.

Stroke A **stroke** occurs when a blood vessel that carries oxygen and other materials to the brain is blocked by a blood clot or, less commonly, bursts. As happens in a heart attack, tissues served by the blocked artery are deprived of oxygen and can quickly die. The effects of a stroke depend on the kind of stroke and the affected area of the brain. Any of the senses, motor activity, speech, memory, and other thought processes can be affected. Paralysis or weakness on one side of the body is common. Quick treatment for a stroke is critical and may involve surgery or the use of medications to dissolve the clot.

❯ **Reading Check** *Compare and contrast heart attacks with strokes.*

www.scilinks.org
Topic: Cardiovascular Problems
Code: HX80220

blood pressure the force that blood exerts on the walls of the arteries

heart attack the death of heart tissues due to a blockage of their blood supply

stroke (STROHK) a sudden loss of consciousness or paralysis that occurs when the blood flow to the brain is interrupted

Figure 11 Regular exercise is a great way to prevent cardiovascular disease.
❯ **Why do you think exercise can make your cardiovascular system healthier?**

READING TOOLBOX

Recognizing Main Ideas Read the paragraph titled "Controllable Risk Factors." Write down the main idea of this paragraph.

Preventing Cardiovascular Disease

A number of risk factors for cardiovascular disease have been found. Some of these risk factors, such as age, gender, race, and genetics, cannot be changed. But reducing controllable risk factors can lower a person's chances of developing one of these conditions.

Controllable Risk Factors Three major controllable risk factors for cardiovascular diseases are physical inactivity, high blood cholesterol levels, and recreational drug use. Regular exercise helps prevent or control diabetes, obesity, and high blood pressure. All of these conditions can lead to cardiovascular disease. Regular exercise also helps lower blood cholesterol levels. A high blood cholesterol level often leads to arteriosclerosis. High cholesterol has no symptoms, so it is important to have your cholesterol level checked to find out if you need to take measures to control it. Cholesterol levels can be reduced by eating a diet low in saturated fats, maintaining a healthy weight, and exercising regularly, as shown in **Figure 11.**

Many drugs, including alcohol and tobacco, can cause cardiovascular disease. For example, drinking alcohol raises blood pressure and increases the risk of having a stroke. Intravenous drug abuse is linked with an increased risk of stroke and heart infections. And chemicals in tobacco smoke lower the amount of oxygen in the blood, promote the development of arteriosclerosis, start clot formation, and reduce beneficial cholesterol levels.

Healthy Lifestyle ❯ **The most important ways to prevent cardiovascular disease are to maintain a healthy diet, exercise regularly, and avoid tobacco and alcohol use.** These are all practices necessary for a healthy lifestyle. Having regular medical checkups, which include screening for high blood pressure, high blood cholesterol, and diabetes, are also important ways to identify and control your risks and help you live a long and healthy life.

❯ **Reading Check** *Make a list of three changes that you can make to your lifestyle to prevent cardiovascular disease.*

Section 2 Review

❯ **KEY IDEAS**

1. **Explain** how high blood pressure and arteriosclerosis can lead to other cardiovascular diseases.
2. **Describe** how a heart attack can happen.
3. **State** the risk factors for cardiovascular disease that can be reduced by regular physical activity.

CRITICAL THINKING

4. **Inferring Relationships** Most medical professionals measure a patient's blood pressure in an artery in the upper arm. Explain why this is the best location to measure a person's blood pressure.
5. **Inferring Conclusions** Why is it important to have regular checkups by your doctor even if you feel healthy?

WRITING FOR SCIENCE

6. **Writing a List** Suppose that you have a friend who is overweight, eats a lot of junk food, and rarely exercises. Prepare a list of five things that your friend should know about his or her risk of developing cardiovascular disease. Prepare another list of five things that your friend could do to reduce his or her risk of developing one of these diseases.

Why It Matters

Living Large

Americans are getting fatter. Currently, one of every three Americans has a body weight that is more than 20% above what is considered healthy. Why is there a growing epidemic of obesity in this country? Lifestyles have changed dramatically during the last 40 years. Americans are eating more and exercising less, with serious consequences to their health.

Portion Distortion

There is no doubt that ever-increasing portion sizes served by restaurants and fast-food chains have contributed to the obesity problem. The typical combo meal (large cheeseburger, large fries, and large soda) contains an average of 1,500 Calories—that's almost an entire day's recommended caloric intake for an adult woman and two-thirds of the recommended intake for an adult man! And worst of all, almost half of those combo calories come from fat. But huge portions of high-fat foods don't jump into your mouth on their own. Ultimately, it's every person's responsibility to decide what to eat, how much, and how often.

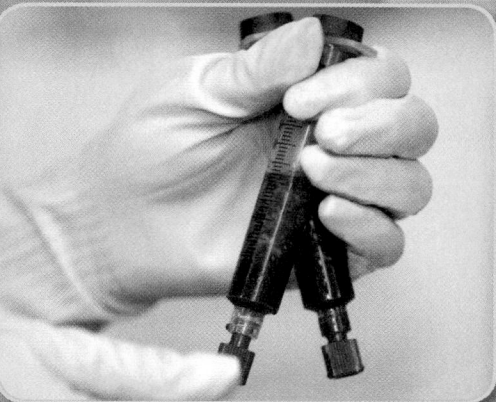

Eat Now, Liposuction Later?
These are fat cells removed during a surgical procedure called *liposuction*. Liposuction is the most popular cosmetic surgery in this country.

Research Find out the difference between subcutaneous fat and visceral fat. Which kind of fat leads to more serious health problems?

The Respiratory System

Key Ideas	Key Terms	Why It Matters
❯ What is the path that air takes from the environment into the lungs? ❯ How do the diaphragm and rib muscles work together in the process of breathing? ❯ How does the transport of oxygen differ from the transport of carbon dioxide? ❯ What are six diseases that affect the respiratory system?	pharynx larynx trachea bronchus alveolus diaphragm	The uptake of oxygen is critical to your survival. For this reason, it is important to understand how to prevent respiratory disease.

The respiratory system brings oxygen, O_2, into the body. The respiratory system also carries carbon dioxide, CO_2, the waste product of aerobic respiration, out of the body.

The Path of Air

A breath of air enters the respiratory system, as shown in **Figure 12,** through the nose or mouth. Hairs in the nose filter dust out of the air. From the nose, air passes through a muscular tube in the upper throat called the **pharynx,** which serves as a passageway for air and food. The air then moves through the **larynx,** or voice box, found in the neck. A flap of tissue that covers the opening to the larynx when you swallow food stops the food from passing into your lungs. From the larynx, the air moves into the **trachea,** a long, straight tube in the chest cavity. The trachea branches into two smaller tubes, the **bronchi,** which lead to the lungs.

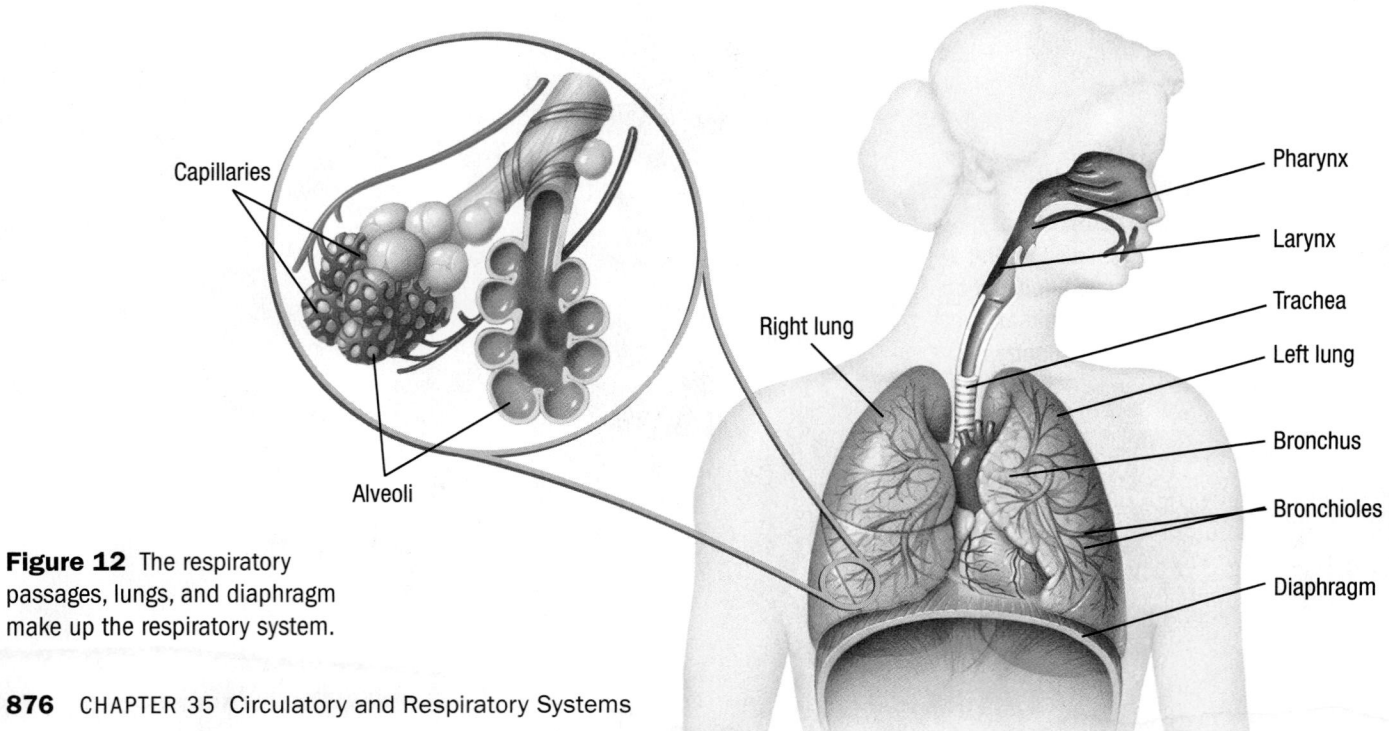

Capillaries

Right lung

Alveoli

Pharynx

Larynx

Trachea

Left lung

Bronchus

Bronchioles

Diaphragm

Figure 12 The respiratory passages, lungs, and diaphragm make up the respiratory system.

Inside a Lung Within the lung, the bronchi (singular, *bronchus*) divide into smaller and smaller tubes called *bronchioles.* The cells that line the bronchi and trachea secrete mucus that traps dust and other particles in the air. The smallest bronchioles end in clusters of tiny air sacs called **alveoli,** which are surrounded by capillaries of the cardiovascular system. The actual exchange of gases happens between the air in the alveoli and the blood in the capillaries. The lungs are suspended in the chest cavity, bounded on the sides by the ribs and on the bottom by the diaphragm. The **diaphragm** is a powerful muscle below the rib cage that drives breathing. ❯ **In summary, air enters the nasal passages, then flows through the pharynx, the larynx, the trachea, the bronchial tubes, and finally the bronchioles into the alveoli of the lungs.**

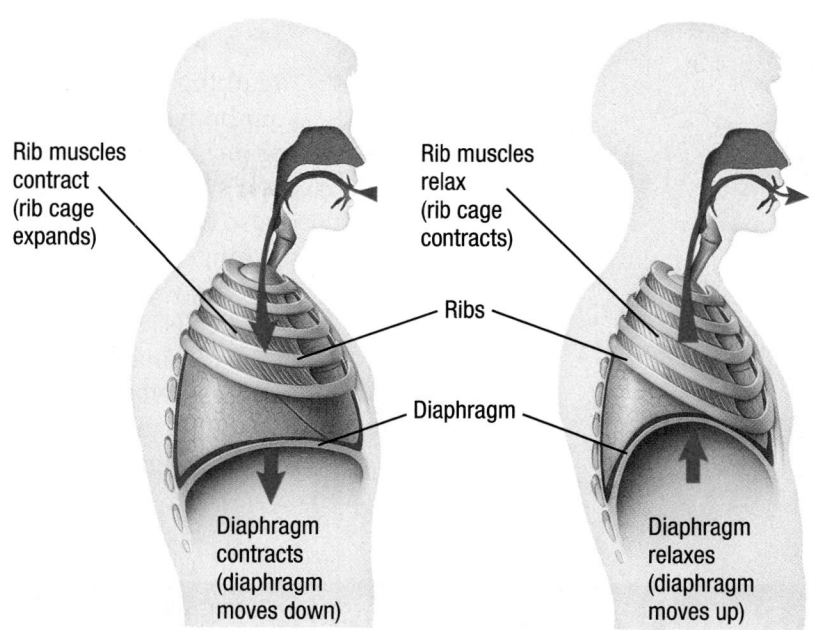

Rib muscles contract (rib cage expands)

Rib muscles relax (rib cage contracts)

Ribs

Diaphragm

Diaphragm contracts (diaphragm moves down)

Diaphragm relaxes (diaphragm moves up)

Figure 13 The diaphragm and the muscles between the ribs play a role in the movement of the chest cavity during breathing. ❯ **What occurs when the diaphragm contracts and moves downward?**

Breathing

The lungs themselves are not muscular organs that can contract and relax so that air moves in and out. Instead, air is drawn into and out of the lungs by changes in pressure in the chest cavity. As shown in **Figure 13,** these changes in pressure are brought about by movements of muscles outside the lungs—the diaphragm and the muscles between the ribs. ❯ **When the diaphragm and rib muscles contract, the chest cavity expands and air rushes in. When these muscles relax, the chest cavity returns to a resting position and air rushes out.**

Inhalation and Exhalation During inhalation, or breathing in, the diaphragm contracts and moves downward while contractions of the rib muscles move the rib cage up and out. These movements increase the volume of the chest cavity and reduce the air pressure within the cavity and within the lung's alveoli. Because air flows from a high-pressure area to a low-pressure area, air is drawn into the lungs. Exhalation, or breathing out, occurs when the diaphragm and rib-cage muscles relax. The relaxation of these muscles decreases the volume in the chest cavity, which increases the air pressure within the lungs. Because the air pressure is now higher in the lungs than in the atmosphere, air is forced out of the lungs.

Breathing Rate What controls how fast or slow you breathe? Receptors in the brain and cardiovascular system continually monitor O_2, CO_2, and H^+ (hydrogen ion) levels in the blood. For example, when CO_2 and acidity levels rise, the brain responds by sending nerve signals to the diaphragm and rib muscles that speed the rate of breathing. The opposite occurs when CO_2 and H^+ levels fall.

❯ **Reading Check** *What causes air to enter the lungs?*

pharynx (FAR ingks) the passage from the mouth to the larynx and esophagus

larynx (LAR ingks) the area of the throat that contains the vocal cords and produces vocal sounds

trachea (TRAY kee uh) the tube that connects the larynx to the lungs

bronchus (BRAHNG kuhs) one of the two tubes that connect the lungs with the trachea

alveolus (al VEE uh luhs) any of the tiny air sacs of the lungs where oxygen and carbon dioxide are exchanged

diaphragm (DIE uh fram) a dome-shaped muscle that is attached to the lower ribs and that functions as the main muscle in respiration

Gas Exchange and Transport

Breathing is the first step to getting oxygen to the billions of cells in your body. When oxygen molecules reach your alveoli, their journey has just begun. Oxygen next moves into the blood in the cardiovascular system, which carries it throughout the body. Carbon dioxide is also carried in the blood, from tissues where it is produced back to the lungs, which expel it. Oxygen is not very soluble in plasma, which is mostly water. Instead, oxygen is carried by hemoglobin inside red blood cells (RBCs). Carbon dioxide is soluble in water and is carried in the plasma. ❯ **Oxygen is transported bound to hemoglobin inside RBCs, and most carbon dioxide is carried as bicarbonate ions in the plasma.** Figure 14 summarizes the paths of O_2 and CO_2 through the body and the exchange of these gases across cell membranes.

go.hrw.com
✳ interact online
Keyword: HX8CRCF14

Transport of Oxygen and Carbon Dioxide

Figure 14 Almost all of the O_2 and about 23% of the CO_2 absorbed by the blood is attached to hemoglobin molecules inside red blood cells. The rest of the CO_2 transported by blood is dissolved in the plasma (about 7%) or carried as bicarbonate ions (about 70%).

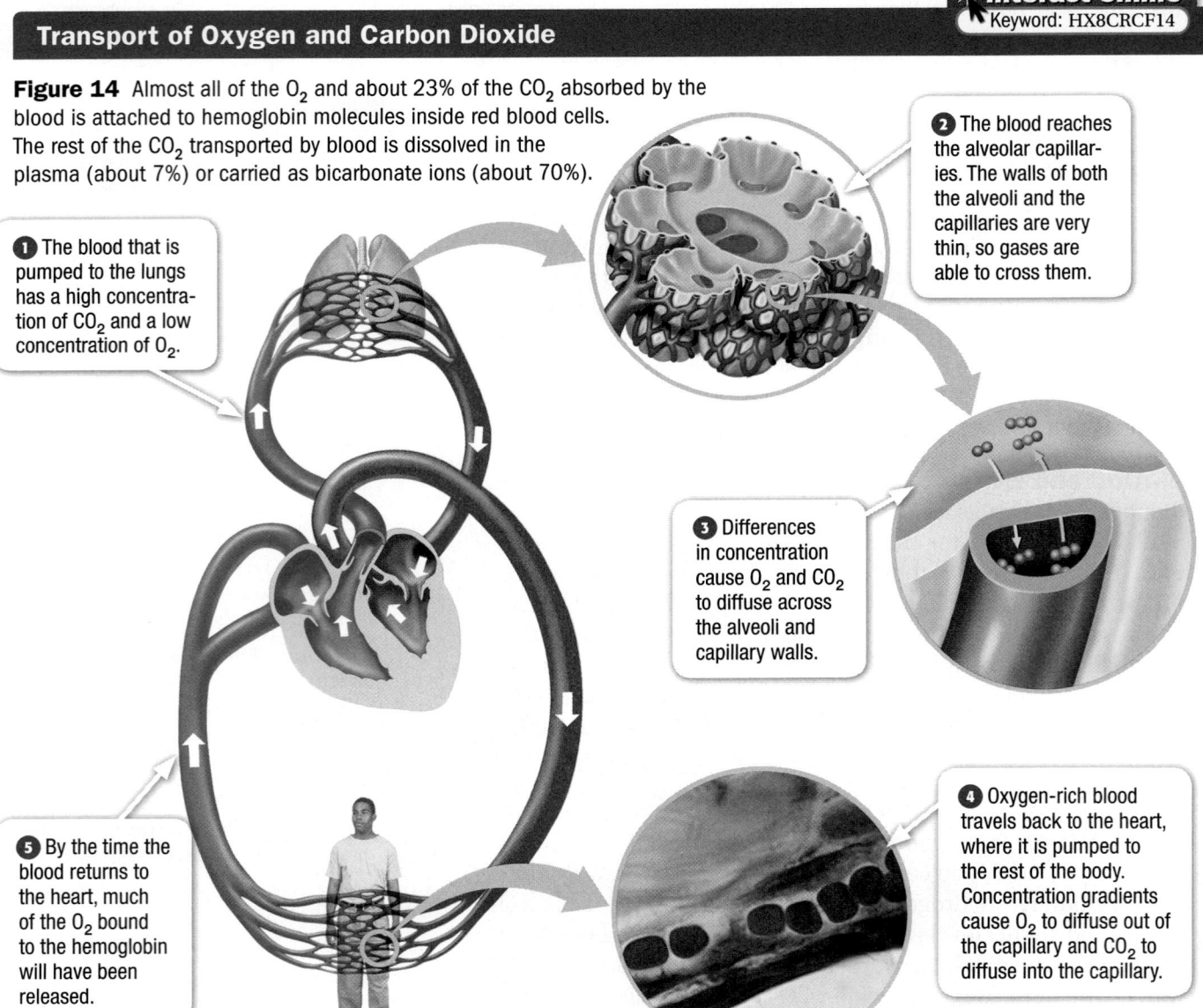

❶ The blood that is pumped to the lungs has a high concentration of CO_2 and a low concentration of O_2.

❷ The blood reaches the alveolar capillaries. The walls of both the alveoli and the capillaries are very thin, so gases are able to cross them.

❸ Differences in concentration cause O_2 and CO_2 to diffuse across the alveoli and capillary walls.

❹ Oxygen-rich blood travels back to the heart, where it is pumped to the rest of the body. Concentration gradients cause O_2 to diffuse out of the capillary and CO_2 to diffuse into the capillary.

❺ By the time the blood returns to the heart, much of the O_2 bound to the hemoglobin will have been released.

Hands-On
QuickLab

⏱ 15 min

Blood pH Homeostasis

You can use pH indicator paper, water, and baking soda to model the role of bicarbonate ions in maintaining blood pH levels in the presence of carbon dioxide.

Procedure

1. Label **one beaker** "A" and **one beaker** "B." Fill each beaker halfway with **distilled water**.

2. Add **1.4 g of baking soda** to beaker B, and stir well.

3. Use **pH indicator paper** to test and record the pH of the contents of each beaker.

4. Gently blow through a **straw** into the water in beaker A. Test and record the pH of the resulting solution. Note: blow only through your own straw.

5. Repeat step 4 for beaker B.

Analysis

1. **Describe** what happened to the pH in the two beakers during the experiment.

2. **State** the chemical name for baking soda.

3. **Propose** the chemical reaction that may have caused a change in pH in beaker A.

4. **Summarize** the effect of the baking soda on the pH of the solution in beaker B after blowing through a straw.

5. **CRITICAL THINKING** **Analyzing Information** Relate what happened in beaker B to what happens in the bloodstream.

Oxygen Exchange and Transport Each hemoglobin molecule in a RBC contains four iron atoms. Each iron atom binds with one molecule of O_2. Most hemoglobin molecules leave the lungs with a full load of O_2. In the tissues, O_2 levels are lower. Recall that materials diffuse from an area of higher concentration to an area of lower concentration. This difference in concentration causes O_2 to be <u>released</u> by the hemoglobin. O_2 diffuses out of capillaries and into cells for use during aerobic respiration. The amount of O_2 released is related to the amounts of O_2 and CO_2 in the tissues. Thus, more O_2 diffuses into tissues that are more active. Less O_2 diffuses into tissues that are less active. The result is the efficient distribution of the O_2.

Carbon Dioxide Exchange and Transport As RBCs unload O_2, the blood also absorbs CO_2 from the tissues. Most CO_2 is carried in blood as bicarbonate ions. These ions form in the presence of an enzyme that catalyzes the reaction of CO_2 and water to form carbonic acid, H_2CO_3, as shown in the equation below. The carbonic acid breaks up to form a bicarbonate ion, HCO_3^-, and a hydrogen ion, H^+:

$$H_2O + CO_2 \rightleftharpoons H_2CO_3 \rightleftharpoons HCO_3^- + H^+$$

(water in plasma)   (carbon dioxide from tissues)   (carbonic acid)   (bicarbonate ions and hydrogen ions in the blood)

When blood reaches the lungs, the reactions reverse. A bicarbonate ion and a hydrogen ion form carbonic acid, which in turn forms CO_2 and water. The CO_2 diffuses into the alveoli and is exhaled.

❯ **Reading Check** *What signals hemoglobin to release O_2?*

ACADEMIC VOCABULARY

release to make or set free

Respiratory Diseases

Respiratory diseases and disorders affect millions of Americans.
❯ **Six common diseases of the respiratory system are asthma, bronchitis, pneumonia, tuberculosis, emphysema, and lung cancer.**

Asthma Asthma is a chronic condition of the bronchioles and alveoli that is characterized by episodes called *asthma attacks*. The airways of a person with asthma are chronically inflamed and sensitive to irritants. During an attack, cells lining the airways make more mucus than usual, the airways swell, and the muscles lining the airways contract. Because these changes cause the airways to narrow, the flow of air is reduced. In severe asthma attacks, the alveoli may swell enough to break. Prescription inhalant medications, as shown in **Figure 15,** help stop an asthma attack by expanding the bronchioles. People of all ages can have asthma, which has no cure.

Bronchitis Bronchitis is an inflammation of the respiratory tract, specifically the bronchioles. Inflammation causes the cells lining the airways to make excess mucus. A person with bronchitis coughs often as his or her body works to expel the mucus. This condition can cause a feeling of tightness in the chest. It is often treated with the same kinds of medications that are used to treat asthma. Acute, or short-term, bronchitis is usually caused by a virus. It can develop from a cold. Chronic, or long-lasting, bronchitis is most often caused by cigarette smoking. It can also be caused by exposure to other irritating chemicals or fumes. Chronic bronchitis generally improves when the irritating chemical is removed from the environment.

Pneumonia Pneumonia is a condition that has many causes and is characterized by inflammation of the lungs, specifically the alveoli. Its symptoms include fever, weakness, cough, and chest pain. Most cases result from infection, usually by viruses or bacteria. Viral pneumonia is generally milder than bacterial pneumonia and usually happens as a complication of influenza. One type of pneumonia is caused by a fungus, *Pneumocystis carinii*, and mainly affects people who have AIDS, because their immune systems are weak. Pneumonia can also be caused by inhalation of various substances, including food, liquid, gases, or dust. People with other serious health problems, or those who are very young or very old, are at greatest risk of developing pneumonia.

Tuberculosis About 2 million people die of tuberculosis every year. Tuberculosis is a disease caused by the bacterium *Mycobacterium tuberculosis*. This bacterium can attack any organ, but it usually infects the lungs. Worldwide, one of every three people is infected with this bacterium, but only about 10% of people infected develop tuberculosis. The people most likely to develop tuberculosis are those who have weakened immune systems. For example, tuberculosis most commonly occurs in people who are very young, very old, or infected with HIV. The number of tuberculosis cases is currently on the rise because many strains of the tuberculosis bacterium have developed antibiotic resistance.

READING TOOLBOX

Word Parts Use the table on the Reading Toolbox page to find the definition of the word part *tuber-*. What might you expect to find on a chest X-ray of someone with tuberculosis?

Figure 15 Asthma does not have to be debilitating. It can be carefully managed so that asthma sufferers can be physically active.

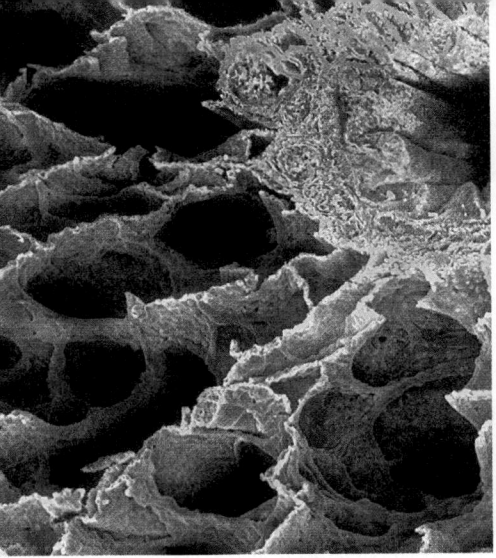
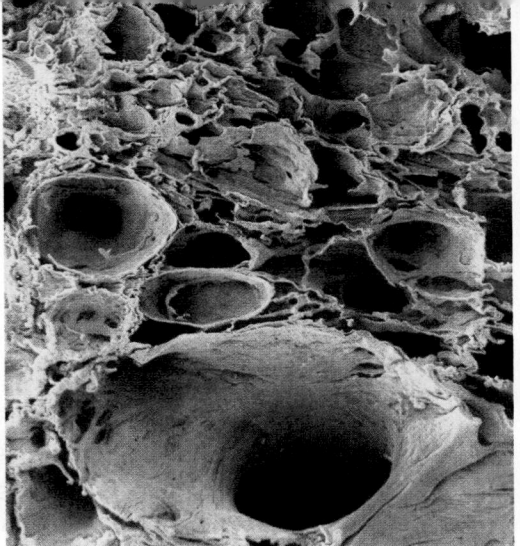
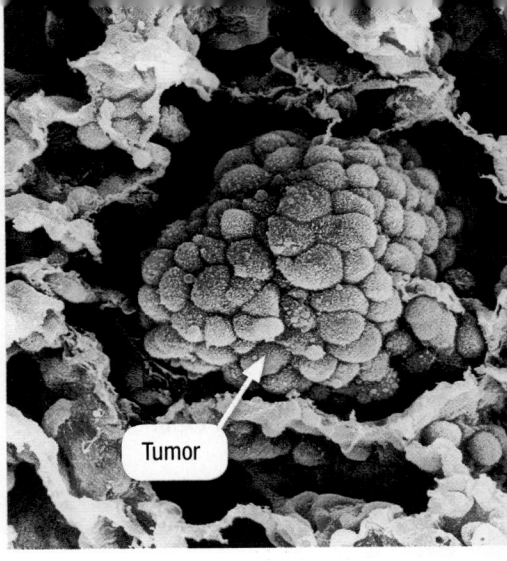

Tumor

Emphysema Emphysema is a chronic respiratory disease resulting from destruction of elastic fibers in the lungs. Smoking is the cause of up to 90% of emphysema cases. Normally, the lungs' elastic fibers allow them to expand and contract. Emphysema causes a loss of flexibility in the alveoli's walls. Over time, these walls break, and larger, less efficient air sacs are created that do not function properly in the exchange of O_2 and CO_2. Damage to the alveoli, shown in **Figure 16,** is irreversible. The damage leads to constant fatigue and breathlessness. Severely affected individuals must breathe from oxygen tanks.

Lung Cancer Lung cancer is a leading cause of death in the world today. *Cancer* is a disease characterized by abnormal cell growth. In the United States, about 28%—158,000—of all cancer deaths each year are attributed to lung cancer. Smoking is the cause of about 90% of lung cancer cases. Once cancer is found, the affected lung is sometimes removed surgically. Even with such drastic measures, lung cancer usually is not curable. Only about 15% of lung cancer victims live more than 5 years after diagnosis.

❯ **Reading Check** *Which lung diseases could be caused by smoking?*

Figure 16 The lung tissue on the far left is healthy. The lung tissue in the center came from a person who suffered from emphysema. The lung tissue on the right is cancerous. ❯ **How do the alveoli in a healthy lung compare with the alveoli in a lung with emphysema?**

SCI*LINKS*.
www.scilinks.org
Topic: Respiratory
    Disorders
Code: HX81306

Section 3 Review

❯ **KEY IDEAS**

1. **Name** the structures of the respiratory system through which air flows.
2. **Identify** the muscles that enable breathing, and explain how the actions of these muscles accomplish this task.
3. **Compare** the transport of oxygen in the blood with that of carbon dioxide.
4. **State** the causes of bronchitis, tuberculosis, and lung cancer.

CRITICAL THINKING

5. **Analyzing Information** Red blood cells are the only functioning cells in your body that lack a nucleus. How does the lack of a nucleus relate to the function and formation of a red blood cell?
6. **Comparing and Contrasting** Describe the similarities and differences between bronchitis and pneumonia.

MATH SKILLS

7. **Ratios and Percents** The world's population is roughly 6.6 billion. If one out of every three people is infected with *Mycobacterium tuberculosis* and about 10% of those infected develop tuberculosis, about how many people in the world have tuberculosis?

Chapter 35 **Lab**

Objectives

> Measure the components that make up your lung capacity, such as your tidal volume, vital capacity, and expiratory reserve volume.

> Determine your inspiratory reserve volume and your lung capacity.

> Predict how exercise will affect tidal volume, vital capacity, and lung capacity.

Materials

- spirometer
- spirometer mouthpiece

Safety

Lung Capacity

Lung capacity is the total volume of air that the lungs can hold. The lung capacity of an individual is influenced by many factors, such as gender, age, strength of diaphragm and chest muscles, and diseases.

During normal breathing, you use only a small percentage of your lung capacity. The amount of air inhaled or exhaled in a normal breath is the tidal volume. Additional air, the *inspiratory reserve volume,* can be forcefully inhaled after a normal breath. The *expiratory reserve volume* is the amount of air that can be forcefully exhaled after a normal exhalation. *Vital capacity* is the maximum amount of air that can be breathed in or out. Even after you exhale the vital capacity, a large amount of air called the *residual volume* still remains in your lungs.

In this lab, you will use a spirometer to determine your lung capacity. A spirometer is an instrument that measures the volume of air exhaled from the lungs. Then, you will use data from your classmates to predict how exercise affects lung capacity.

Procedure

Measure Air Volume

1 Copy the data table shown into your lab notebook.

2 ◆ CAUTION: **Place a clean mouthpiece in the end of a spirometer.** To measure your tidal volume, first inhale a normal breath. Then, exhale a normal breath into the spirometer through the mouthpiece. Record the volume of air exhaled in your data table. Many diseases are spread by body fluids, such as saliva. Note: do not share a spirometer mouthpiece with anyone.

3 To measure your expiratory reserve volume, inhale a normal breath and then exhale normally. Then, forcefully exhale as much air as possible into the spirometer. Record this volume.

4 To measure your vital capacity, first inhale as much as you can. Then, forcefully exhale as much air as you can into the spirometer. Record this volume.

Spirometer readings	
Tidal volume	
Expiratory reserve volume	
Inspiratory reserve volume	
Vital capacity	
Estimated residual volume	
Estimated lung capacity	

Calculate Lung Capacity

5 The data table shown contains average values for residual volume and lung capacity for young adults. Inspiratory reserve volume (IRV) can be calculated by subtracting tidal volume (TV) and expiratory reserve volume (ERV) from vital capacity (VC). The equation for this calculation is as follows:

$$IRV = VC - TV - ERV$$

Use the data in your data table and the equation above to calculate your estimated inspiratory reserve volume.

6 Lung capacity (LC) can be calculated by adding residual volume (RV) to vital capacity (VC). The equation for this calculation is as follows:

$$LC = VC + RV$$

Use the data in your data table and the value for residual volume from the table above to calculate your estimated lung capacity. Compare your estimated lung capacity to the value for lung capacity in the table above.

7 🤝 👐 Clean up your lab materials according to your teacher's instructions. Wash your hands thoroughly before leaving the lab.

Residual Volumes and Lung Capacities

	Residual Volume (mL)	Lung Capacity (mL)
Males	1,200	6,000
Females	900	4,500

Note: Athletes can have volumes 30% to 40% greater than the average for their gender.

Analyze and Conclude

1. Interpreting Data How does your expiratory reserve volume compare with your inspiratory reserve volume?

2. Interpreting Tables How do the average values for residual volume and lung capacity for young adult females compare with the average values for young adult males?

3. Analyzing Data How did your tidal volume compare with the volumes of others?

4. Recognizing Relationships Why was the value that you found for your lung capacity an estimated value?

5. SCIENTIFIC METHODS Analyzing Methods Why did you measure inspiratory reserve volume indirectly?

6. SCIENTIFIC METHODS Inferring Conclusions Why do males and athletes have greater vital capacities than females do?

7. SCIENTIFIC METHODS Justifying Conclusions Use the data from your class to justify the conclusion that exercise increases lung capacity.

SCI LINKS.
www.scilinks.org
Topic: Respiration
Code: HX81305

Extensions

8. Respiratory Disease Spirometry is the use of a spirometer to study respiratory function. Nurses and respiratory therapists use spirometers to evaluate patients who have respiratory diseases. Do research to discover how spirometry is used to distinguish different respiratory diseases. Make a chart showing what you discover.

9. Further Inquiry Write a new question that could be explored with another investigation.

Key Ideas	Key Terms

1 The Cardiovascular System

> The cardiovascular system carries nutrients, oxygen, hormones, and wastes throughout the body and distributes heat to maintain homeostasis.

> The structure of the heart chambers is related to their function. The atria are thin walled because they pump blood just to the ventricles. The ventricles are thick walled because they pump blood to either the lungs or the rest of the body.

> The structure of blood vessels relates to their function. Arteries have thick, muscular walls to withstand the force of the pumped blood. Capillaries have thin walls to allow the exchange of gases and nutrients. Veins have valves that stop blood from flowing backward.

> The key components of human blood are plasma, red blood cells, white blood cells, and platelets.

> The lymphatic system works with the cardiovascular system by collecting fluids that leak out of capillaries and returning those fluids to the cardiovascular system.

Key Terms:
cardiovascular system (865)
atrium (867)
ventricle (867)
pulse (867)
artery (868)
capillary (868)
vein (868)
plasma (869)
red blood cell (869)
white blood cell (869)
platelet (869)
lymphatic system (871)

2 Cardiovascular Health

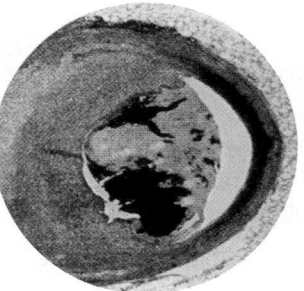

> The four main cardiovascular diseases are high blood pressure, arteriosclerosis, heart attack, and stroke.

> The most important ways to prevent cardiovascular disease are to maintain a healthy diet, exercise regularly, and avoid tobacco and alcohol use.

Key Terms:
blood pressure (872)
heart attack (873)
stroke (873)

3 The Respiratory System

> Air enters the nasal passages, then flows through the pharynx, the larynx, the trachea, the bronchial tubes, and finally the bronchioles into the alveoli of the lungs.

> When the diaphragm and rib muscles contract, the chest cavity expands and air rushes in. When these muscles relax, the chest cavity returns to a resting position and air rushes out.

> Oxygen is transported bound to hemoglobin inside red blood cells, and most carbon dioxide is transported as bicarbonate ions in the plasma.

> Six common diseases of the respiratory system are asthma, bronchitis, pneumonia, tuberculosis, emphysema, and lung cancer.

Key Terms:
pharynx (876)
larynx (876)
trachea (876)
bronchus (876)
alveolus (877)
diaphragm (877)

1. **Process Flow Chart** Draw a process flow chart that shows how gases are transported by the blood and exchanged with other body tissues.

2. **Concept Map** Make a concept that outlines the path of blood through the body. Try to include the following terms in your map: *artery, capillary, vein, lymphatic system, atrium,* and *ventricle.*

Using Key Terms

For each pair of terms, explain how the meanings of the terms differ.

3. *atrium* and *ventricle*

4. *heart attack* and *stroke*

5. *bronchus* and *alveolus*

Use all of the following terms in the same sentence.

6. *artery, capillary,* and *vein*

7. *red blood cell, white blood cell,* and *platelet*

8. *pharynx, larynx,* and *trachea*

Understanding Key Ideas

9. Most contractions of the heart are initiated or caused by
   a. all of the heart's cells initiating their own contractions.
   b. a nerve impulse traveling from the brain.
   c. the heart's pacemaker in the right atrium.
   d. the hormone epinephrine.

10. The smallest blood vessels in the body are the
    a. arteries.
    b. capillaries.
    c. lymphatic vessels.
    d. veins.

11. Blood is
    a. connective tissue.
    b. epithelial tissue.
    c. muscle tissue.
    d. not a tissue.

12. High blood pressure
    a. is a pair of pressure readings of at least 120/70.
    b. strengthens the heart and the vessels leading away from it.
    c. damages a person's cardiovascular system even when it produces no symptoms.
    d. is usually an inherited condition.

13. Both heart attacks and strokes
    a. always result in death.
    b. can always be reversed.
    c. are often treated with bypass surgery.
    d. usually involve a blocked artery.

14. Controllable risk factors for cardiovascular disease include all of the following *except*
    a. older age.
    b. cigarette smoking.
    c. elevated blood cholesterol.
    d. obesity.

15. Air moves into the lungs as a result of
    a. a diffusion gradient.
    b. the beating of cilia that line the passageways of the respiratory tract.
    c. relaxation of the muscular walls of the lungs.
    d. lower air pressure in the chest cavity and lungs than in the air outside the body.

16. Most of the carbon dioxide in the blood is carried
    a. inside red blood cells.
    b. in the plasma, as bicarbonate ion.
    c. in the plasma, as carbon dioxide.
    d. inside white blood cells.

Use the diagram to answer the following question.

17. The structure labeled "A" in the diagram at right is
    a. the pharynx.
    b. a bronchus.
    c. the trachea.
    d. the larynx.

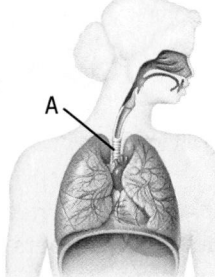

Explaining Key Ideas

18. **Name** the function of the cardiovascular system.

19. **Identify** the activities that occur as blood flows through capillaries of the cardiovascular system.

20. **State** the origin of the fluid in the lymphatic system.

21. **Evaluate** the relationship between the structure of alveoli and their function.

22. **Name** the muscles that contract and relax to produce the movements of breathing.

Using Science Graphics

The chart shows the relationship between daily salt intake and blood pressure in some humans. Use the chart to answer the following questions questions.

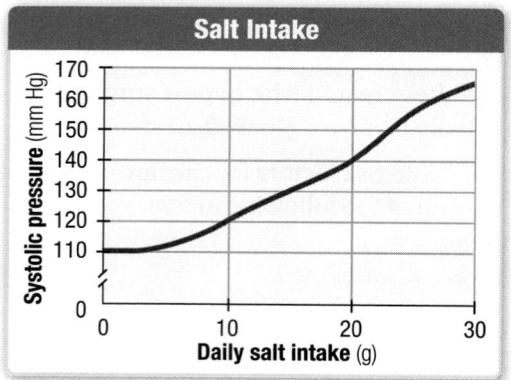

Salt Intake

23. If a person consumes about 23 g of salt per day, what would the systolic pressure most likely be?

24. What conclusions can be drawn from the chart?

Use the diagram to answer the following question.

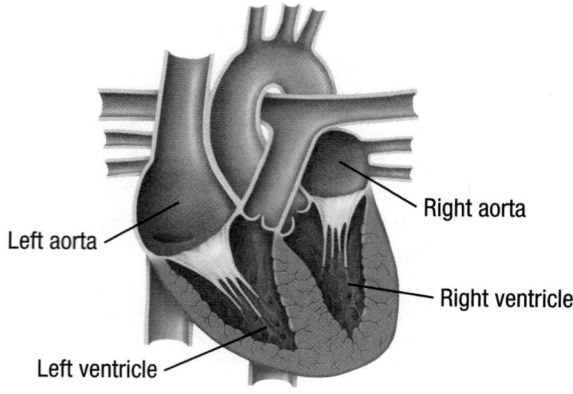

25. Relate the thickness of the muscular walls of the four chambers of the heart, shown, to their functions.

Critical Thinking

26. **Analyzing Information** Why does exchange of gases between the blood and body tissues not occur through the walls of arteries or veins?

27. **Interpreting Information** What role do cell surface markers play in blood typing?

28. **Inferring Function** How is body temperature regulated by blood vessel diameter?

29. **Comparing Structures** Relate the similarities in the components and fluids of the cardiovascular and lymphatic systems.

30. **Summarizing Information** Describe the pathway of a molecule of oxygen gas from the time it is taken into the body until it reaches the little toe on your right foot.

31. **Relating Concepts** Explain why the blood of a person who is exercising has a tendency to become more acidic.

Why It Matters

32. **Inferring Conclusions** How might the current epidemic of obesity in the United States be related to the increases in portion sizes served at restaurants?

Technology Skills

33. **Interpreting Data** Using the Centers for Disease Control and Prevention web site on the Internet, collect summary statistics on mortality from different cardiovascular and respiratory diseases. Use data for the most recent year available. Write a one-paragraph summary of the data.

Alternative Assessment

34. **Building Models** Create a model of a portion of a blood vessel that shows the blood cells, plasma, and other components. The model should be scaled as accurately as possible. Use appropriate materials and realistic colors. Include cutaways of red and white blood cells to show substances that could be found inside them. Display your model in the classroom.

Math Skills

35. **Calculating Data** Calculate the number of times a person's heart will beat if the person lives 75 years. Assume that the average heart beats 70 times per minute.

Standardized Test Prep

> **TEST TIP** Slow, deep breathing helps a person relax. If you suffer from test anxiety, focus on your breathing in order to calm down.

Science Concepts

1. In what direction does blood move when the AV node in the heart fires?
   - **A** from the atria to the veins
   - **B** from the ventricles to the atria
   - **C** from the atria to the ventricles
   - **D** from the ventricles to the arteries

2. What is the function of the lymphatic system?
   - **F** It opens two-way vessels.
   - **G** It helps the body fight infections.
   - **H** It interacts with the respiratory system.
   - **J** It transports fluids away from the heart.

3. Fibrin is a protein that does which of the following?
   - **A** transports oxygen
   - **B** helps form a blood clot
   - **C** destroys invading microorganisms
   - **D** stimulates the production of antibodies

4. Which of the following vessels have the lowest blood pressure?
   - **F** veins
   - **G** arteries
   - **H** capillaries
   - **J** arteorioles

5. Which antigens are on the red blood cells of a person with type O blood?
   - **A** O antigens
   - **B** both A and B antigens
   - **C** either A or B antigens
   - **D** neither A nor B antigens

6. Controllable risk factors for cardiovascular disease include all of the following *except*
   - **F** older age.
   - **G** being overweight.
   - **H** cigarette smoking.
   - **J** elevated blood cholesterol.

Writing Skills

7. **Short Response** Explain how concentration gradient relates to the release of O_2 by the hemoglobin molecule.

Using Science Graphics

Use the table to answer the following question.

Blood Type				
Blood type	Antigen on the red blood cell	Antibodies in plasma	Can receive blood from	Can donate blood to
A	A	B	O, A	A, AB
B	B	A	O, B	B, AB
AB	A, B	Neither A nor B	O, A, B, AB	AB
O	Neither A nor B	A, B	?	O, A, B, AB

8. Which blood types complete the blank cell in the table?
   - **F** O
   - **G** AB, O
   - **H** A, B, O
   - **J** A, B, AB, O

Use the model to answer the following questions.

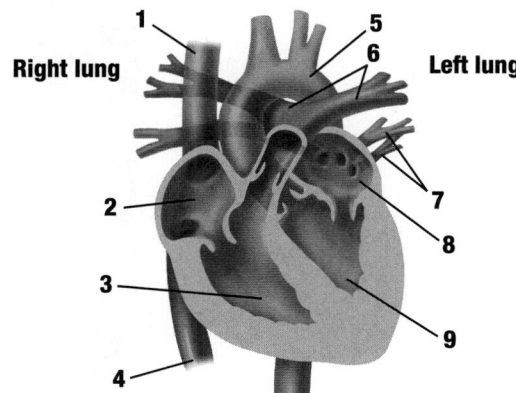

9. Which numbers point to the vessels that bring blood into the heart?
   - **A** 1, 4, and 7
   - **B** 1, 5, and 6
   - **C** 4, 5, and 6
   - **D** 5 and 6 only

10. Which number points to the chamber in which oxygen-poor blood enters the heart?
    - **F** 2
    - **G** 3
    - **H** 8
    - **J** 9

Chapter 36

Digestive and Excretory Systems

Preview

1 Nutrition
Food and Energy
Fuel for the Body
Other Essential Nutrients
Healthy Eating Habits

2 Digestion
From Food to Nutrients
Starting Digestion
Absorbing Nutrients
Removing Wastes

3 Excretion
Metabolic Wastes
Cleaning the Blood
Urinary Excretion
Kidney Failure

Why It Matters

Your digestive system converts the food that you eat into chemicals that your body can use. Your excretory system collects and removes the wastes that your cells produce in chemical reactions.

You can see what kinds of foods people eat by visiting the local food market.

Eating a variety of foods is important for a healthy diet.

The Vietnamese diet commonly includes rice or noodles at every meal.

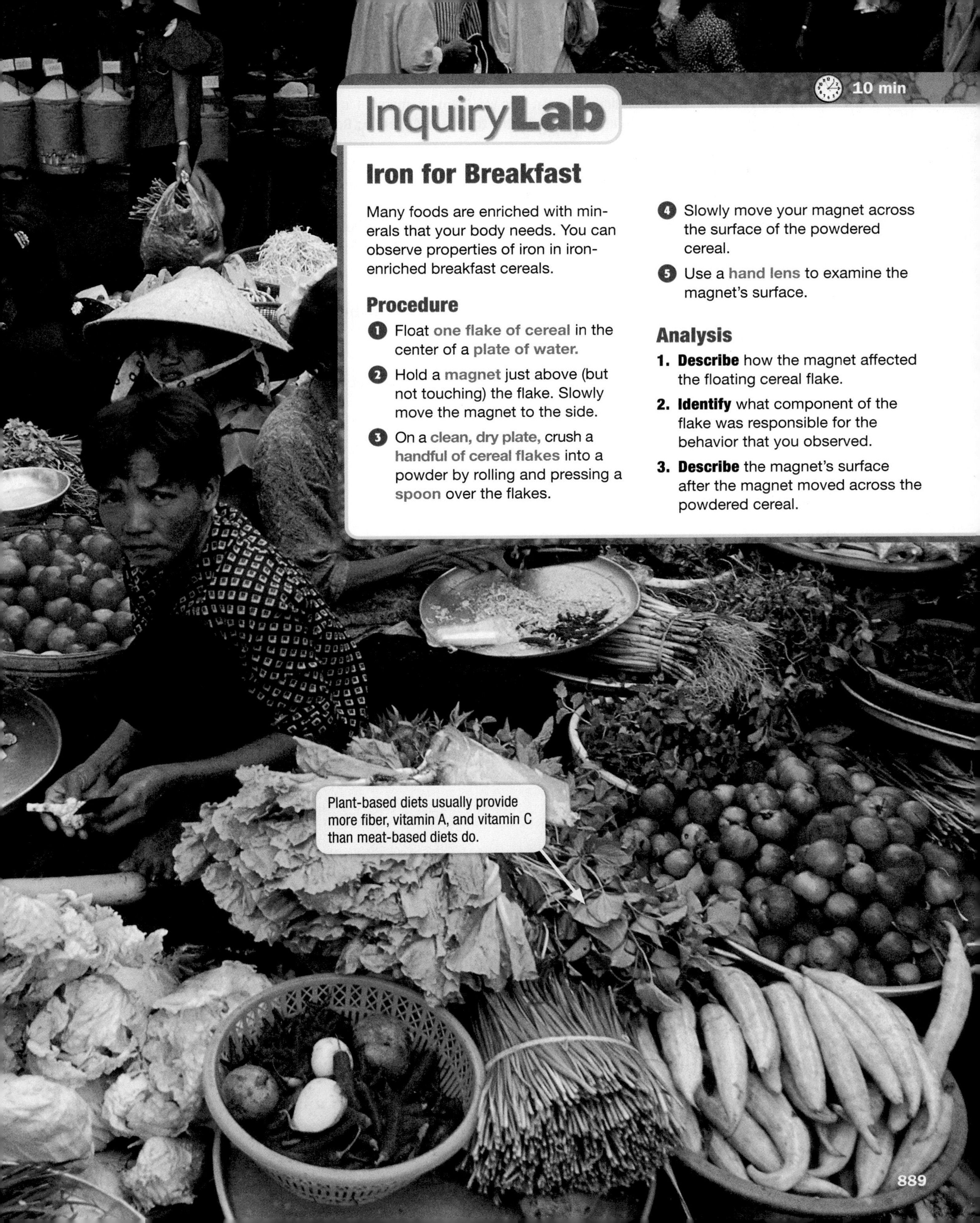

InquiryLab

Iron for Breakfast

Many foods are enriched with minerals that your body needs. You can observe properties of iron in iron-enriched breakfast cereals.

Procedure

❶ Float **one flake of cereal** in the center of a **plate of water.**

❷ Hold a **magnet** just above (but not touching) the flake. Slowly move the magnet to the side.

❸ On a **clean, dry plate,** crush a **handful of cereal flakes** into a powder by rolling and pressing a **spoon** over the flakes.

❹ Slowly move your magnet across the surface of the powdered cereal.

❺ Use a **hand lens** to examine the magnet's surface.

Analysis

1. **Describe** how the magnet affected the floating cereal flake.

2. **Identify** what component of the flake was responsible for the behavior that you observed.

3. **Describe** the magnet's surface after the magnet moved across the powdered cereal.

Plant-based diets usually provide more fiber, vitamin A, and vitamin C than meat-based diets do.

READING TOOLBOX

These reading tools can help you learn the material in this chapter. For more information on how to use these and other tools, see **Appendix: Reading and Study Skills.**

Using Words

Key-Term Fold A key-term fold is a useful tool for studying definitions of key terms in a chapter. Each tab can contain a key term on one side and the term's definition on the other.

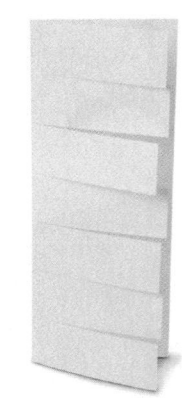

Your Turn Make a key-term fold to quiz yourself on the definitions of the key terms in this chapter.

1. Fold a sheet of lined notebook paper in half from left to right.
2. Using scissors, cut along every third line from the right edge of the paper to the center fold to make tabs.

Using Language

Classification Organizing things into groups will show their relationships to each other and to other things. Grouping is called *classification,* and another word for a group is a *class.* For example, a hammer is a tool. A hammer is not the only type of tool. Saws, drills, and screwdrivers are also tools. *Tool* is the class and *saw, drill, screwdriver,* and *hammer* are members of that class.

Classification	
Class	**Member**
food	pizza, hamburger, salad
nutrient	vitamin, mineral, carbohydrate, protein, lipid
enzyme	amylase, pepsin, lipase

Your Turn Use the table to answer the following questions.

1. List three additional members that could belong in the class *foods.*
2. Think of another class to which the members *carbohydrate, protein,* and *lipid* could belong.

Using Graphic Organizers

Pattern Puzzles A pattern puzzle is a useful tool for organizing and remembering the steps of a process. Pattern puzzles can help you remember and understand how the steps of a process fit together.

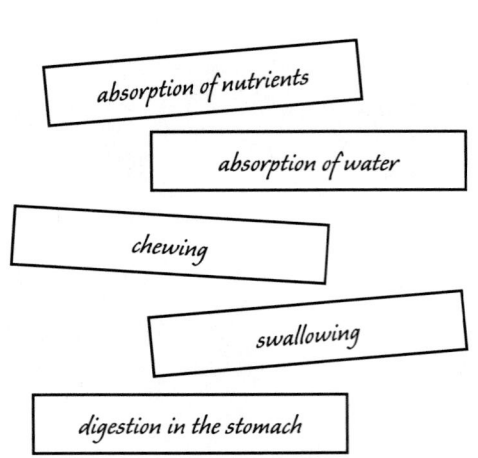

absorption of nutrients

absorption of water

chewing

swallowing

digestion in the stomach

Your Turn Use a pattern puzzle to learn the steps of digestion.

1. Write down the steps of the process on a sheet of notebook paper, one step per line. Do not number the steps.
2. Cut the paper so that there is one step per strip of paper.
3. Shuffle the paper strips so that they are out of sequence.
4. Place the strips in their proper sequence.
5. Confirm the order of the process by checking your text or class notes.

Key Ideas	Key Terms	Why It Matters
❯ How do our bodies use energy from food? ❯ What nutrients provide energy for cellular activity? ❯ What other types of nutrients are required in our diets? ❯ Why is it important to be physically active?	nutrient calorie vitamin mineral	A body cannot make many of the substances that it needs to survive, but foods can provide these substances.

In a certain sense, the saying "You are what you eat" is true. Substances in the food that you eat help build your body. They also provide the energy and materials needed for life processes. The foods that you eat provide your body with what it needs to stay healthy.

Food and Energy

A **nutrient** is a substance that the body requires for energy, growth, repair, and maintenance. Your body gets nutrients from the foods that you eat and from the beverages that you drink. Each nutrient plays a different role in keeping your body healthy.

Some nutrients have chemical bonds that release energy when the bonds are broken. A **calorie** is a unit for measuring this energy. Nutritionists use a unit called a Calorie (with a capital *C*), which is equal to 1,000 calories. The Nutrition Facts label on the outside of packages of food lists the number of Calories in the food.

Everything you do requires energy. Different activities, such as those shown in **Figure 1**, require different amounts of energy. ❯ **Even when you are not moving, your body needs energy to breathe, pump blood, and grow. The more active you are, the more Calories you burn to release energy.** When you consume more Calories than you burn, your body stores the extra energy as fat. The result is weight gain. If you consume fewer Calories than you burn, your body burns fat stores. This release of energy results in weight loss.

nutrient a substance or compound that provides nourishment (or food) or raw materials needed for life processes

calorie the amount of energy needed to raise the temperature of 1 g of water 1 °C

Figure 1 Walking and skating are two activities that use energy. ❯ Which of these activities burns more Calories?

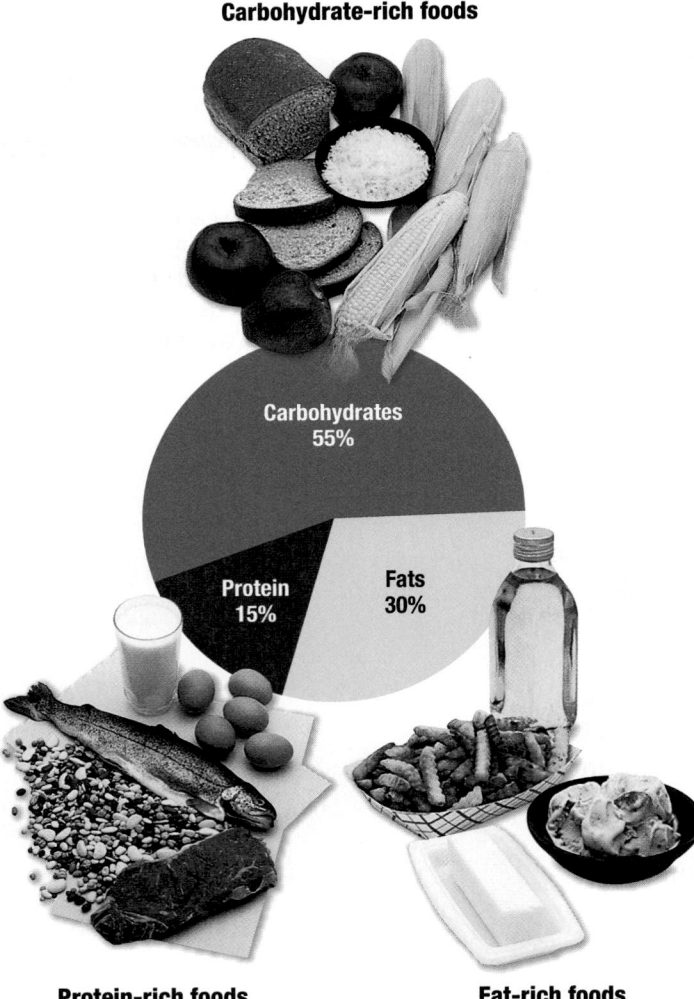

Carbohydrate-rich foods

Carbohydrates 55%

Protein 15%

Fats 30%

Protein-rich foods

Fat-rich foods

Figure 2 The percentages of the day's total calories that should come from each nutrient are shown in the graph. Most of your calories should come from foods that are high in complex carbohydrates. Limit your intake of saturated fats.

READING TOOLBOX

Classification Name a class to which the following members could belong: *glucose, sucrose, starch,* and *cellulose.*

Fuel for the Body

Three nutrients are required in large amounts by the body. ❯ **Carbohydrates, proteins, and fats provide most of the energy and building materials for the body.** These nutrients contain many chemical bonds that can be broken to release energy for activity and growth. When this energy is not used, the body builds compounds that store the energy. Most foods contain a mix of nutrients, but some foods are richer than others in a specific nutrient, as **Figure 2** shows.

Carbohydrates Recall that carbohydrates are made up of sugar molecules. Glucose is a simple sugar that cells use for energy and that can be directly absorbed into the bloodstream. Table sugar contains sucrose, two simple sugars linked together. Other simple sugars are found in fruits, honey, and onions. Complex carbohydrates, such as starch and cellulose, are long chains of many simple sugar molecules. Starches can be found in many fruits and vegetables, including cereal grains, potatoes, and corn. Cellulose is found in all foods that come from plants. Humans do not have the enzymes to break down cellulose for energy. Cellulose is a major component of fiber, which is important to the functioning of the digestive system.

Proteins Recall that proteins make up enzymes, antibodies, and muscles. The body can make only some of the 20 amino acids required to make these proteins. The rest of them, called *essential amino acids,* must be obtained directly from proteins in food. Most animal products, such as eggs, milk, fish, poultry, and beef, contain all of the essential amino acids. No single plant food contains all of the essential amino acids. But eating certain combinations of two or more plant products can supply all of the essential amino acids.

Fats Fats are one type of lipid. Lipids are used for storing energy, padding and insulating organs, making steroid hormones and cell membranes, and dissolving fat-soluble vitamins. Although lipids are essential nutrients, too much fat in the diet is known to harm several body systems. For example, a diet that is high in saturated fats may be linked to cardiovascular diseases.

Other Essential Nutrients

Many nutrients that do not provide energy are required in our diets. **Water, vitamins, and minerals contribute to many functions, such as regulating chemical reactions that release energy.** You can survive only a few days without water, but you can live several weeks without food. Your body uses water to regulate body temperature, and to transport gases, nutrients, and waste products. Vitamins and minerals are required in much smaller amounts than carbohydrates, proteins, fats, and water are.

Vitamins Vitamins are carbon-based substances that are found in small amounts in many foods. Each kind of vitamin plays different roles in metabolism, as summarized in **Figure 3.** Vitamins A, D, E, and K dissolve in fats. These vitamins are stored in body fat and can be toxic in excess amounts. Vitamins B and C dissolve in water. Excess amounts of water-soluble vitamins are excreted in urine and must be replaced by the diet. To ensure that you get a healthy amount of vitamins, you should vary your diet and eat foods rich in vitamins.

vitamin an organic compound that participates in biochemical reactions and that builds various molecules in the body

Figure 3 Different vitamins are found in various foods. The body needs each of these and other vitamins to function normally. **Which of these vitamins are needed for healthy skin?**

Important Vitamins

Vitamin	Food sources	Role	Effects of deficiency
Vitamin A (retinol)	butter, eggs, liver, carrots, green leafy vegetables, sweet potatoes	healthy eyes and skin, strong bones and teeth	infections of urinary and digestive systems, night blindness
Vitamin B$_1$ (thiamin)	most vegetables, nuts, whole grains, organ meats	nerve and heart function, carbohydrate metabolism	digestive disturbances, impaired senses
Vitamin B$_2$ (riboflavin)	fish, poultry, cheese, yeast, green vegetables 	healthy skin, tissue repair, carbohydrate metabolism	blurred vision, cataracts, cracking of skin, lesions of intestinal lining
Vitamin B$_3$ (niacin)	whole grains, fish, poultry, tomatoes, legumes, potatoes	healthy skin, carbohydrate metabolism	mental disorders, diarrhea, inflamed skin
Vitamin B$_{12}$ (cobalamin)	meat, poultry, milk, dairy products	formation of red blood cells	reduced number of red blood cells
Vitamin C (ascorbic acid)	citrus fruits, strawberries, potatoes	healthy gums and teeth, wound healing 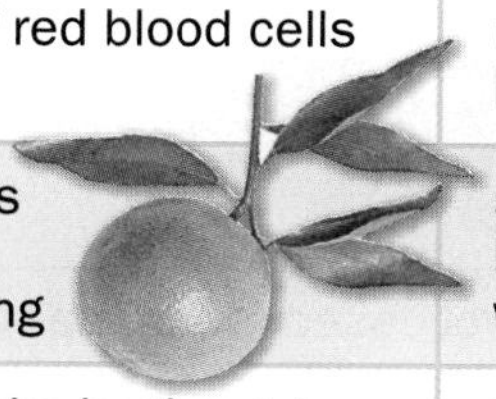	swollen and bleeding gums, loose teeth, slow-healing wounds
Vitamin D (cholecalciferol)	salmon, tuna, fish liver oils, fortified milk, cheese 	calcium uptake by the gut, strong bones and teeth	bone deformities in children, loss of muscle tone
Vitamin E (tocopherol)	vegetable oils, nuts, seeds, olives, whole grains	protects against damage by free radicals	reduced number of red blood cells, nerve tissue damage in infants
Vitamin K (phylloquinone)	leafy green vegetables, liver, cauliflower	normal blood clotting	bleeding caused by prolonged clotting time

QuickLab

 10 min

The Nutrition Facts Label

The Nutrition Facts label provides a convenient source of nutrition information about foods and can help you see how a food fits into your daily diet. The Nutrition Facts label lists the amount of Calories and nutrients per serving size. Nutrients are listed by weight and as a percentage of a 2,000 Cal diet. Daily values (DVs) are recommended daily amounts of a nutrient.

Nutrition Facts	Amount/serving	%DV*	Amount/serving	%DV*
Serv. size 2 oz (56g/ box) Servings per container 8	Total fat 1g	1%	Total carb. 43g	14%
	Saturated fat 0g	0%	Dietary fiber 2g	8%
	Trans fat 0g		Sugars 3g	
Calories 210 Fat Cal. 10	Cholesterol 0mg	0%	Protein 6g	
	Sodium 0mg	0%		

*Percent Daily Values (DV) are based on a 2,000 Calorie diet. Vitamin A 0% • Vitamin C 0% • Calcium 2% • Iron 10% Thiamin 30% • Riboflavin 10% • Niacin 15%

Analysis

1. **Calculate** the percentage of total Calories that come from fat as listed in the label shown here.

2. **CRITICAL THINKING** **Applying Information** If your diet requires 30 g of fiber, what percentage of the daily value for fiber does one serving of this food provide?

---

minerals a class of nutrients that are chemical elements that are needed for certain body processes

Minerals **Minerals** are naturally occurring inorganic substances that are not produced by living organisms. The body needs certain minerals to make certain body structures and substances, to keep nerves and muscles functioning normally, and to maintain osmotic balance. Some minerals are essential for enzyme function. Magnesium, calcium, sodium, potassium, and zinc help regulate the function of the nerves and muscles. Zinc has a role in the digestive and immune systems. Iron is needed for transporting oxygen in the blood. Selenium helps prevent chromosomes from breaking.

A few common minerals are listed in **Figure 4.** The body needs greater amounts of some minerals than of others. Trace elements are minerals present in small amounts in the body. Usually, humans get the necessary amount of a trace element directly from plants that they eat or indirectly from the meat of animals that have eaten plants. Minerals are water-soluble, so the body excretes any excess amounts.

Figure 4 This table lists many common minerals and their roles in your body.
❯ What foods should you eat for strong and healthy bones?

Common Minerals

Mineral	Food sources	Role
Sodium	table salt, processed foods, dairy products	water balance, nerve function
Potassium	meats, many fruits and vegetables, beans	fluid balance, nerve and muscle function
Calcium	milk, dairy products, tofu, legumes, dark-green leafy vegetables, shellfish, bony fish	healthy bones and teeth, nerve and muscle function, blood clotting
Iron	red meat, whole and enriched grains, dark-green vegetables, peas, beans, eggs	bone growth, metabolism, muscle contraction, oxygen transport in blood
Iodine	iodized salt, seafood	thyroid hormones, normal cell function

Healthy Eating Habits

The guidelines for healthy eating are summarized in the MyPyramid of the United States Department of Agriculture (USDA). The pyramid, shown in **Figure 5,** lists the daily number of servings needed from each food group to get a variety of nutrients in your diet. ❯ **Good nutrition must be balanced with regular physical activity to maintain a healthy body.**

Body Mass Index Healthy weights vary depending on the person, so weight recommendations are given as a range. One way to determine your healthy weight range is to calculate your body mass index, or BMI:

$$BMI = \frac{(weight\ in\ pounds)}{(height\ in\ inches)^2} \times 703$$

Adults are said to have a healthy body weight if their BMI is between 18.5 and 25.0.

Excess Body Fat Generally, adults who are overweight (BMI of 25.1–29.9) or obese (BMI of 30.0 or more) have too much body fat. Having excess body fat can increase a person's risk for many chronic diseases, such as heart disease, osteoarthritis, or type 2 diabetes.

Eating Disorders An eating disorder is a condition in which a person has an unhealthy concern for his or her body weight and shape. The person may try to control his or her weight by unhealthy means. Anorexia nervosa is an obsession with being thin that leads to extreme weight loss. Bulimia nervosa is a disorder in which frequent episodes of binge eating are usually followed by behaviors such as vomiting, using laxatives, fasting, or overexercising. Abnormal eating patterns may result in dehydration, fatigue, organ failure, and death.

❯ **Reading Check** *What is BMI? (See the Appendix for answers to Reading Checks.)*

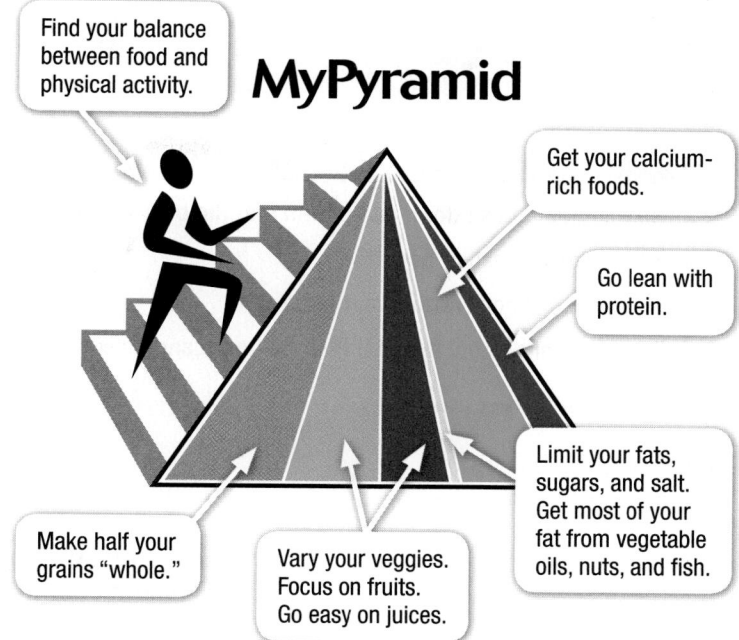

Figure 5 The MyPyramid food guidance system helps you plan your daily diet. The width of each stripe shows you the relative proportion of your diet that should be made up of foods from that group.

ACADEMIC VOCABULARY

abnormal differing from the normal or average

Section 1 Review

❯ **KEY IDEAS**

1. **List** four roles of nutrients.
2. **Compare** the functions of carbohydrates and proteins in maintaining a healthy body.
3. **Evaluate** the roles of vitamins, minerals, and water in maintaining a healthy body.

4. **Explain** how stored energy affects weight gain.

CRITICAL THINKING

5. **Real World Science** Why is eating raw plant foods recommended for high-fiber diets?
6. **Finding Evidence** A student says that obesity does not really harm your health. How would you respond to the statement?

ALTERNATIVE ASSESSMENT

7. **Menu** Create an imaginary menu of foods, including drinks and snacks, that you might eat for the next two days. List the nutrients present in each of the foods.

2 Digestion

Key Ideas	Key Terms	Why It Matters
❯ How is food broken down into a form that the body can use? ❯ Where does digestion begin? ❯ How does the body absorb nutrients? ❯ What happens to the material that the body cannot use?	digestion esophagus peristalsis pepsin villus	Your digestive system turns the foods that you eat into fuel for your body.

Imagine that you are eating your favorite meal. What is happening to the food? Before your body can use the nutrients in the food that you are eating, the large food molecules must be broken down physically and chemically. Then, the resulting smaller molecules can be absorbed into the blood and carried throughout the body.

From Food to Nutrients

The process of breaking down food into molecules that the body can use is called **digestion.** ❯ **The digestive system takes in food, breaks it down into molecules that the body can use, and gets rid of undigested molecules and waste.** As **Figure 6** shows, the digestive tract is a long, winding tube that begins at the mouth and winds through the body to the anus. Food travels more than 8 m (26 ft) through the digestive tract. The digestive system also includes the liver and pancreas. Food does not travel through the liver and pancreas, but these organs deliver secretions into the digestive tract through tubes called *ducts*.

Chemical Digestion Nutrients are broken down into smaller molecules that cells use to build new structures and new cells. The process by which chemical bonds in food are broken is chemical digestion. Carbohydrates break down into simple sugars; proteins, into amino acids; and fats, into fatty acids. Enzymes in the mouth, stomach, and small intestine aid in the chemical digestion of food.

Mechanical Digestion The physical breakdown of food is mechanical digestion. This process includes chewing food with the mouth and churning food in the stomach and small intestine. Mechanical digestion helps prepare food for chemical digestion by enzymes.

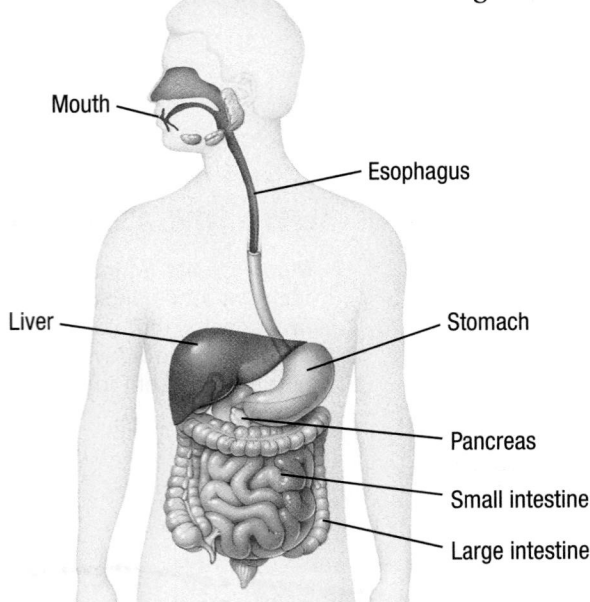

Mouth

Esophagus

Liver

Stomach

Pancreas

Small intestine

Large intestine

Figure 6 The digestive system breaks down food into individual nutrient molecules that can be absorbed into the bloodstream.

Starting Digestion

Digestion begins as soon as you put food in your mouth. ❯ **The mouth and stomach begin the process of digestion by breaking food into small particles.**

Mouth Notice in **Figure 7** that the structure of teeth helps them mechanically break down food into pieces. The tongue mixes the pieces with saliva, a watery solution. This mixture makes the food easier to swallow. Saliva contains amylases, which are enzymes that begin the chemical breakdown of starches.

Swallowing is triggered when a ball of chewed and moistened food reaches the back of the throat. The epiglottis, a flap of tissue, moves over the opening of the trachea, so that food does not enter the trachea. Instead, food moves into the **esophagus,** a long tube that connects the mouth to the stomach. The lower two-thirds of the esophagus is wrapped in sheets of smooth muscle. As **Figure 8** shows, the muscles contract in a series of rhythmic waves called **peristalsis.**

Stomach The stomach is a muscular, saclike organ located at the bottom of the esophagus. The cells of the stomach lining secrete gastric juice, which begins the chemical digestion of proteins. Gastric juice is made up of hydrochloric acid (HCl) and **pepsin,** a stomach enzyme. The acid unfolds large protein chains into single protein strands. Then, pepsin cuts these strands into smaller chains of amino acids. Pepsin is effective only in an acidic environment.

A mucous coating protects the lining of the stomach. If this coating breaks down, stomach acids eat through part of the stomach lining. The result is a painful sore called an *ulcer*. Another common problem is heartburn, which is usually caused by acid-soaked food moving back into the esophagus from the stomach. Normally, a muscular valve closes the esophagus and prevents heartburn.

Mechanical digestion also occurs in the stomach. Stomach muscles churn the food, which breaks food down to small particles and mixes them with gastric juice.

digestion the breaking down of food into chemical substances that can be used for energy

esophagus (i SAHF uh guhs) a long, straight tube that connects the pharynx to the stomach

peristalsis the series of rhythmic muscular contractions that move food through the digestive tract

pepsin an enzyme that is found in gastric juices and that helps break down proteins into smaller molecules

Figure 7 Chewing and swallowing are the first steps of digestion. ❯ **What is the tongue's role in digestion?**

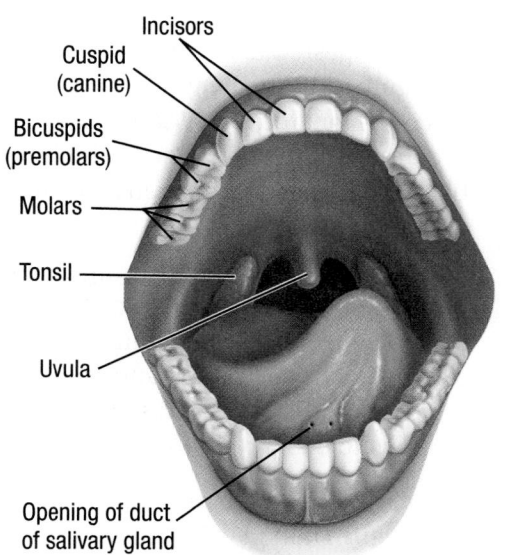

❶ Canine and incisor teeth are used to cut and tear food. Molars are used to crush and grind food.

Incisors
Cuspid (canine)
Bicuspids (premolars)
Molars
Tonsil
Uvula
Opening of duct of salivary gland

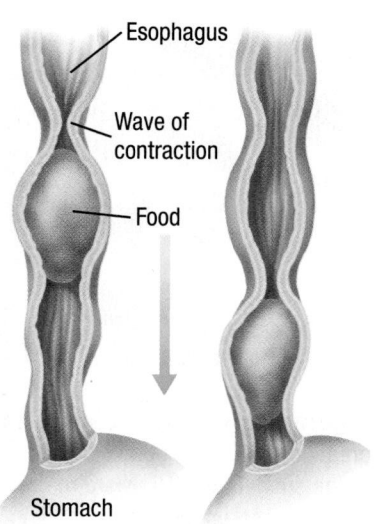

❷ The esophagus muscles narrow and squeeze the food down to the stomach. No digestion occurs in the esophagus.

Esophagus
Wave of contraction
Food
Stomach

Figure 8 Enzymes enable the chemical digestion of nutrients. The digestion of carbohydrates and proteins begins in the mouth and stomach, but the enzymes in the small intestine complete the breakdown of nutrients. ❯ **Which enzymes are help break down proteins into amino acids?**

Digestive Enzymes in the Small Intestine

Enzyme	Substrate	Digested product
Amylase (pancreas)	starch	disaccharides
Trypsin (pancreas)	proteins	peptides
Lipase (pancreas)	fat	fatty acid and glycerol
Maltase, sucrase, lactase	disaccharides	monosaccharides
Peptidase	peptides	amino acids

www.scilinks.org
Topic: Chemical
Digestion
Code: HX80267

Absorbing Nutrients

After two to six hours of churning, a valve in the stomach opens, and the food mixture moves into the small intestine. Digestive enzymes, listed in **Figure 8,** continue to break down nutrients into molecules that are small enough for the body to absorb. ❯ **Absorption of nutrients takes place primarily in the small intestine, and is aided by secretions from the liver and pancreas.**

Liver and Pancreas Both the liver and pancreas, shown in **Figure 9,** have important roles in the digestive system and in other body systems. Although food does not pass through these organs, both contribute to the process of digestion. The pancreas secretes several digestive enzymes into the small intestine. The liver secretes bile, a greenish fluid that breaks fat globules into tiny fat droplets. This process is required before fats can be chemically digested by pancreatic enzymes called *lipases.* Bile also promotes the absorption of fatty acids and the fat-soluble vitamins A, D, E, and K. The gallbladder—a green, muscular sac attached to the liver—concentrates and stores bile until it is needed in the small intestine.

Homeostasis The liver and pancreas also contribute to homeostasis by keeping a constant level of sugar in the blood. Digested food molecules in the bloodstream are transported to the liver. The liver converts extra sugar to glycogen for storage. When energy is needed, the liver breaks down the glycogen and releases glucose into the blood. The pancreas secretes hormones that regulate this conversion.

Storage In addition to storing glycogen, the liver stores fat-soluble vitamins and iron. The liver also monitors the production of cholesterol and detoxifies poisons. If it is unable to change a substance's harmful form, the liver stores the substance. Thus, toxins, including heavy metals and pesticides, accumulate in the liver.

❯ **Reading Check** *Where in the body does the digestion of fats begin?*

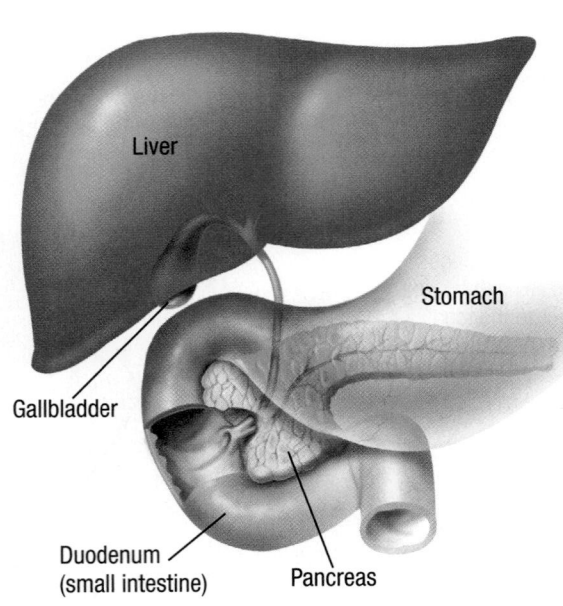

Liver

Stomach

Gallbladder

Duodenum
(small intestine)

Pancreas

Figure 9 Many organs contribute to the complete breakdown of nutrients. Food moves from the stomach to the small intestine, where many different enzymes complete the breakdown of food.

Hands-On

QuickLab

10 min

Bile Function Model

You can use a detergent and cooking oil to simulate how bile breaks up fats as part of digestion.

Procedure

1. Label **one beaker** A and **one beaker** B. Fill each beaker halfway with **water**.

2. Add **10 mL of cooking oil** to each beaker.

3. While stirring, slowly add **10 drops of dish detergent** to beaker B only. Describe what happens to the oil when the detergent is added.

Analysis

1. **Compare** the effect of dish detergent on oil with the effect of bile on fats.

2. **CRITICAL THINKING** **Inferring Conclusions** Detergents, such as bile, increase the surface area of oil. How does this characteristic help the digestive process?

Small Intestine The small intestine is a coiled tubular organ. It would be about 6 m (19.8 ft) long if stretched out. The majority of the breakdown of food occurs in the duodenum, the first part of the organ, which receives secretions. The rest of the organ contributes to the absorption of nutrients. Peristalsis continues to mix the food and to move it through the rest of the small intestine.

Fine fingerlike projections called **villi** (singular, *villus*), shown in **Figure 10,** cover the lining of the small intestine. On the outer surface of each villus are projections called *microvilli.* The villi and microvilli greatly increase the area available for the absorption of nutrients. Sugars and amino acids enter the bloodstream through capillaries in the villi. Fatty acids and glycerol enter lymphatic vessels in the villi and eventually enter the bloodstream. Blood carries these digested nutrients to cells throughout the body.

villus one of the many tiny projections from the cells in the lining of the small intestine

Figure 10 Villi, as shown in the SEM (137×) and the diagram, expand the surface area of the small intestine to allow greater absorption of nutrients. ❯ **Which nutrients enter the bloodstream through the lymphatic vessels?**

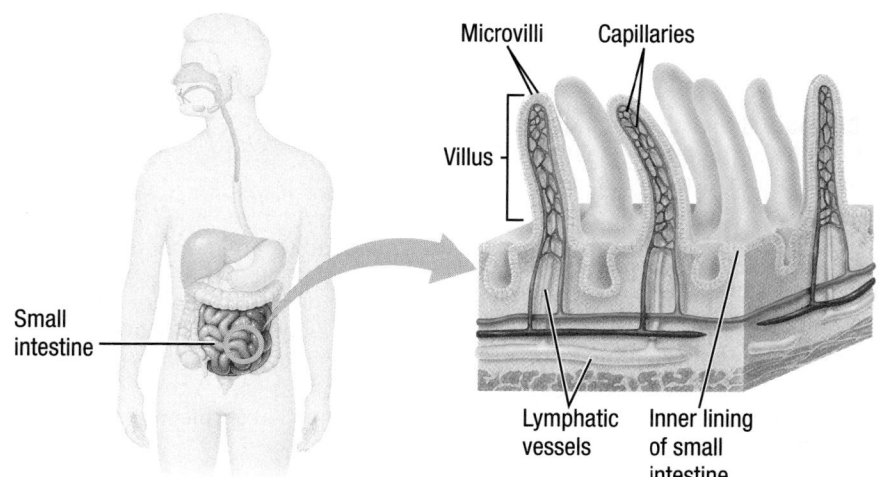

Microvilli

Capillaries

Villus

Small intestine

Lymphatic vessels

Inner lining of small intestine

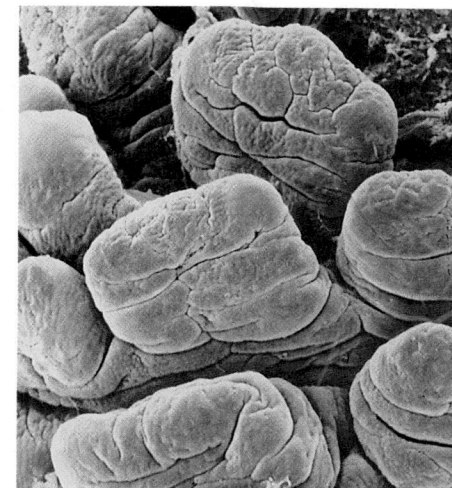

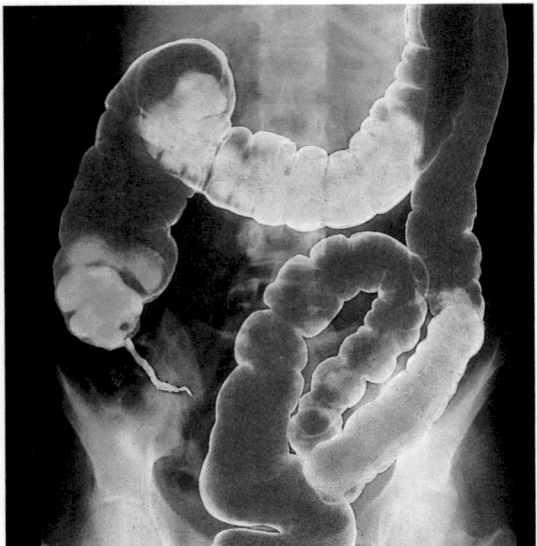

Figure 11 Stretched out, the large intestine, which appears orange in this X ray, is about 1 m (3.3 ft) long. ❯ **What does *large* refer to in this organ?**

READING TOOLBOX

Key-Term Fold On the back of your key-term fold, write a definition in your own words for the key terms in this section.

Removing Waste

A large volume of food, drink, and secretions flows through the digestive system each day. But a small amount of material leaves the body as waste. Almost all of the fluids and solids are absorbed during their passage through the small intestine. After three to six hours in the small intestines, the remaining components of food move into the large intestine. No digestion takes place in the large intestine, but mineral ions and water are absorbed through its wall.

Large intestine The diameter of the large intestine is about three times the diameter of the small intestine. The large intestine, including the colon and the rectum, would be about 1 m (3.3 ft) long if it were stretched out. It is not coiled like the small intestine. As **Figure 11** shows, the colon is composed of three relatively straight segments.

Most of the large intestine's contents are dead cells, mucus, digestive secretions, bacteria, and yeast. In humans, a thriving colony of bacteria live in the colon. These microbes synthesize vitamin K and several B vitamins, which your body cannot easily get from food. Bacteria also help transform and compact undigested materials into feces, the final waste product.

The final segment of the large intestine is the rectum. Solids pass into the rectum as a result of peristalsis in the large intestine. From the rectum, the solid feces are eliminated from the body through the anus. ❯ **All components of food that are not absorbed leave the body as wastes.** Undigested material passes through the large intestine and is expelled through the anus in 12 to 24 hours.

Water Balancing water absorption in the intestine is important. Diarrhea (watery feces) occurs when wastes rush through the large intestine before the remaining water can be absorbed. Diarrhea can lead to dehydration. Constipation (hard feces) results when food remains in the colon for a long period of time, and so too much water is absorbed from food. Hard feces are difficult to pass.

❯ **Reading Check** *What are the contents of the large intestine?*

Section 2 Review

❯ **KEY IDEAS**

1. **Explain** the purpose of the digestive system.
2. **Distinguish** between the chemical digestion that occurs in the mouth and in the stomach.
3. **Describe** the role of the small intestine.
4. **Compare** the structure and function of the small intestine with those of the large intestine.

CRITICAL THINKING

5. **Recognizing Relationships** How would the inability to make saliva affect digestion?
6. **Applying Information** How would a person's diet change after an operation to remove the gallbladder? Explain your answer.

WRITING FOR SCIENCE

7. **Report** It was once believed that stress and spicy foods caused ulcers. Recently, scientists found that the bacterium *Helicobacter pylori* causes of up to 90% of all ulcers. Research how *H. pylori* can cause ulcers to form and how these ulcers can be treated.

Why It Matters

Digestive Detours

The digestive tract enables the body to break down, absorb, and eliminate food. However, many types of problems can occur along this 26 ft–long tube.

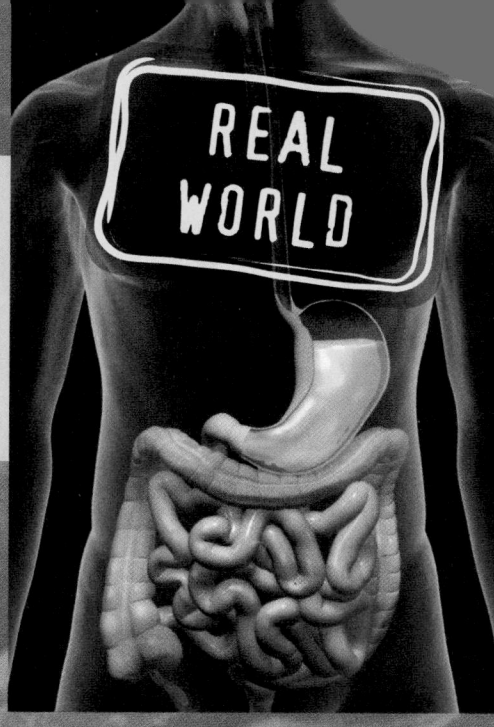

REAL WORLD

Your Own Worst Enemy

An ulcer forms when excessive stomach acids eat through the stomach wall. A hernia occurs when an internal organ protrudes through the wall of a body cavity. Appendicitis is the painful and potentially dangerous inflammation of the appendix. The appendix is a part of the large intestine that seems to serve no useful purpose in digestion.

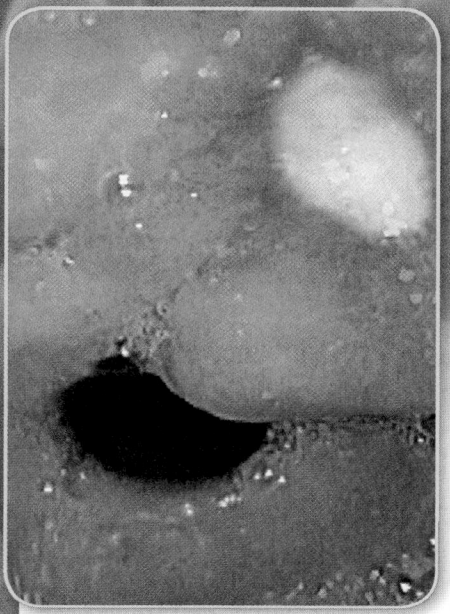

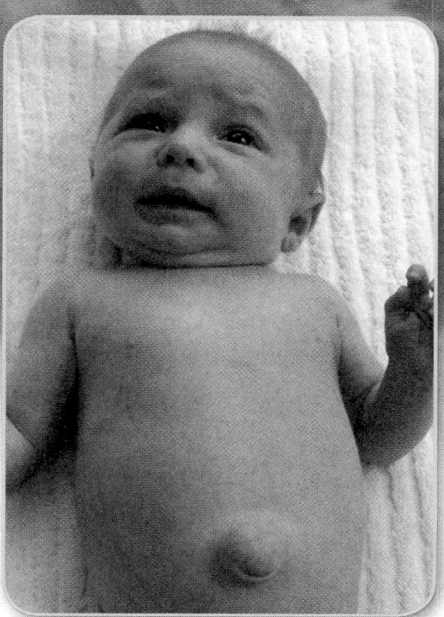

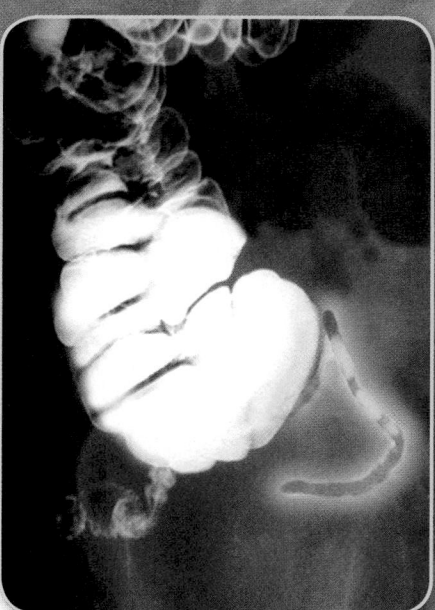

Peptic Ulcer When your stomach's protective coating breaks down, the digestive acids cause a painful sore, or ulcer. The major symptom of a peptic ulcer is stomach pain soon after eating. Sometimes, antacids can relieve this pain.

Umbilical Hernia Newborn babies commonly develop umbilical hernias when a loop of the intestine protrudes through the navel. Umbilical hernias usually heal naturally in a few years. Those that do not may require surgery.

Appendicitis An appendix is a pouchlike tube, typically 3 to 4 in. long. An elongated appendix may be a sign of appendicitis, an inflammation caused by blockage or infection of the appendix. Surgery is required to remove the appendix.

Research Find out what a volvulus is. What are the symptoms, and how is it treated?

Key Ideas	Key Terms	Why It Matters
❯ Why is excretion important? ❯ What do the kidneys do? ❯ How are metabolic wastes removed? ❯ How does kidney damage affect the body?	excretion ureter urea urinary nephron bladder urine urethra	Without your excretory system, your body would be full of cellular waste products!

Cleaning up, though not always a pleasant chore, must be done to maintain a healthy living environment. In the same way, our bodies must get rid of wastes to maintain health. The body eliminates food wastes in the form of feces. During **excretion,** the body removes wastes produced during metabolic reactions.

Metabolic Wastes

Some metabolic reactions produce toxic, nitrogen-containing wastes, such as **urea.** Excess amounts of carbon dioxide and water, the waste products of cellular respiration, can also be harmful to the body.
❯ **By removing wastes and toxic chemicals, excretion enables the body to maintain its osmotic and pH balance.**

Excretory Organs The organs involved in excretion are shown in **Figure 12.** When you sweat, your skin excretes excess water, salts, and some nitrogen wastes. Carbon dioxide is carried through the bloodstream to the lungs, where it is excreted as you exhale. The blood also carries other cellular wastes to the kidneys, the primary organs of excretion.

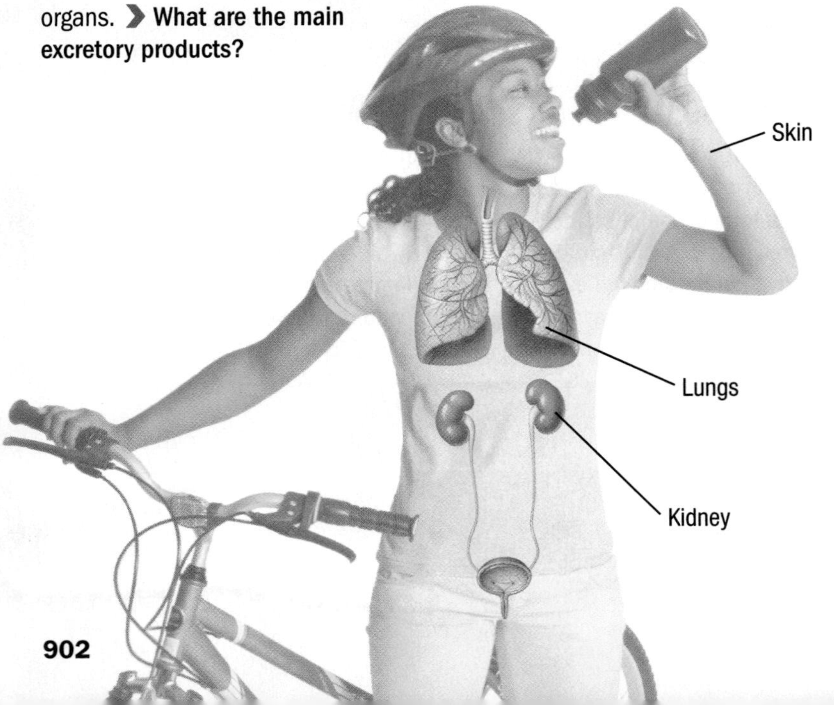

Figure 12 The lungs, the kidneys, and the skin all function as excretory organs. ❯ **What are the main excretory products?**

Skin

Lungs

Kidney

Water Most of the reactions that maintain life can take place only in water. Water absorbs and distributes heat, which helps regulate body temperature. Water also transports gases, nutrients, and wastes in and out of cells. Your body can move nutrients and wastes more efficiently when you drink enough water.

A healthy person should drink at least 2.4 L (2.5 qt) of water every day to replace the water lost through excretion. Some of your water intake can come from food. Water, juice, and low-fat milk are also healthy sources of fluid. The amount of water that you need daily is affected by your diet, by your activity level, and by how hot and humid the weather is.

Cleaning the Blood

To keep cells and organs functioning properly, the body must maintain a certain level of salts and other substances in its fluids. ❯ **The kidneys filter wastes out of the blood and balance levels of molecules.**

Kidney Structure The kidneys are a pair of fist-sized, bean-shaped, reddish brown organs that are located in the lower back. Each kidney includes roughly 1 million microscopic blood-filtering units called *nephrons*, shown in **Figure 13. Nephrons** are tiny tubes that are surrounded by a tight ball of capillaries.

Filtration At one end of the nephron is the Bowman's capsule, a cup-shaped structure. ❶ An arteriole enters this capsule and splits into a bed of capillaries called a *glomerulus*. Blood pressure forces fluid into the cup of the Bowman's capsule. ❷ This fluid, called *filtrate*, is composed of water, salt, glucose, amino acids, and urea. Blood cells, proteins, and other molecules remain in the blood because they are too large to cross the capillary membrane.

Reabsorption The filtrate passes into the renal tubules. ❸ The long, narrow tubes bend at their center to form a loop. Capillaries wrap around these tubules. ❹ Glucose, ions, and some water in the filtrate reenter the bloodstream through the capillaries. The arrangement of the renal tubules and capillaries allows the body to take back the useful molecules that were removed during filtration.

Secretion At the far end of the nephron and renal tubules, some additional substances, such as wastes and toxic materials, can pass from the blood into the filtrate. ❺ The fluid passes out of the nephron through collecting ducts, where much of the water is removed.

❯ **Reading Check** *Why aren't blood cells in the filtrate?*

excretion the process of eliminating metabolic wastes

urea the principal nitrogenous product of the metabolism of proteins that forms in the liver from amino acids and from compounds of ammonia and that is found in urine and other body fluids

nephron the functional unit of the kidney

READING TOOLBOX

Pattern Puzzles Make a pattern puzzle to learn how the nephrons clean your blood.

Figure 13 Unfiltered blood enters the kidney (left) through the renal artery. The outer region of the kidney contains many nephrons (right). Filtered blood exits the kidney through the renal vein.

go.hrw.com
✳ interact online
Keyword: HX8DGSFI3

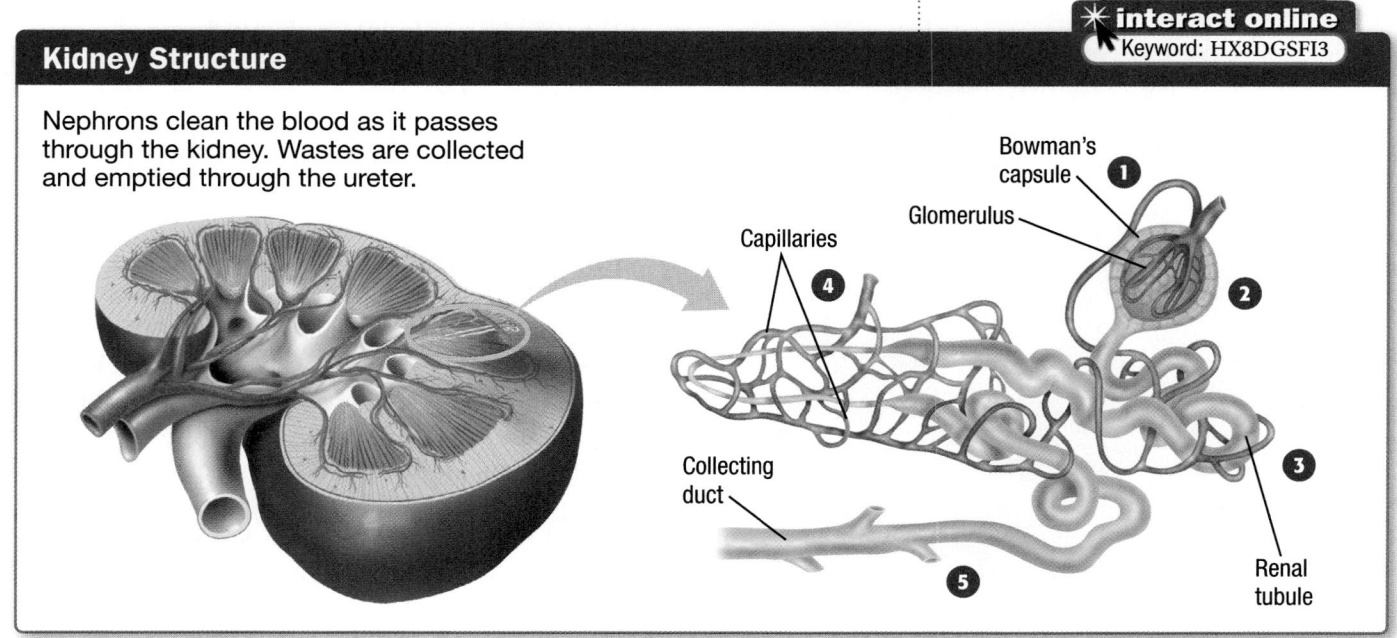

Kidney Structure

Nephrons clean the blood as it passes through the kidney. Wastes are collected and emptied through the ureter.

Capillaries

Bowman's capsule ❶

Glomerulus

❷

❹

Collecting duct

❸

❺

Renal tubule

15 min

Kidney Filtration Model

By analyzing a test solution before and after filtration, you can understand how the kidney filters blood.

Procedure

1. Prepare **three test tubes,** labeled "Protein," "Starch," and "Glucose." Put 15 drops of the **test solution** into each of the test tubes.

2. Add 15 drops of **biuret solution** to the "Protein" test tube. Add 15 drops of **Benedict's solution** to the "Glucose" test tube. Add 2 drops of **IKI solution** to the "Starch" test tube. Record your observations.

3. Pour the remaining test solution through a **filter** into a **beaker.** Using the filtered test solution, repeat steps 1 and 2.

Analysis

1. **Identify** which compounds passed through the filter. If some did not, explain why.

2. **CRITICAL THINKING** **Evaluating Models** How does the activity of the filter resemble the activity of the kidney?

Urinary Excretion

After filtration, reabsorption, and secretion in the nephron, the remaining salt, urea, and water form **urine.** ❯ **Metabolic wastes are removed from the body through the formation and excretion of urine.** The organs of urinary excretion are shown in **Figure 14.** Collecting ducts from several nephrons empty urine into areas of the kidneys that lead to the ureters.

Urinary Organs **Ureters** are two tubes of smooth muscle that carry urine from the kidney to the urinary bladder. The **urinary bladder** is a hollow, muscular sac that stores urine. The bladder gradually expands as it fills. The average bladder can hold up to about 0.6 L (0.63 qt) of urine. Urine exits the body through the **urethra.**

In females, the urethra lies in front of the vagina. In males, the urethra passes through the penis. The tube that carries sperm from the testes merges with the urethra. Both sperm and urine exit the body through the urethra.

Urination A healthy adult eliminates from about 1.5 L (1.6 qt) to 2.3 L (2.4 qt) of urine a day, depending on the volume of fluids consumed. Nerve cells in the bladder indicate when it is full. The bladder's muscular walls contract, while the rings of muscle closing off the urethra relax. The bladder then empties its contents through the urethra. In older children and adults, the brain overrides this urination reflex. So, the release of urine is delayed until a convenient time.

❯ **Reading Check** *What is a ureter?*

Figure 14 Urine exits the kidneys by way of two ureters that empty into a storage organ called the *urinary bladder.* Urine exits the body through the urethra. ❯ **What prevents the release of urine from the bladder?**

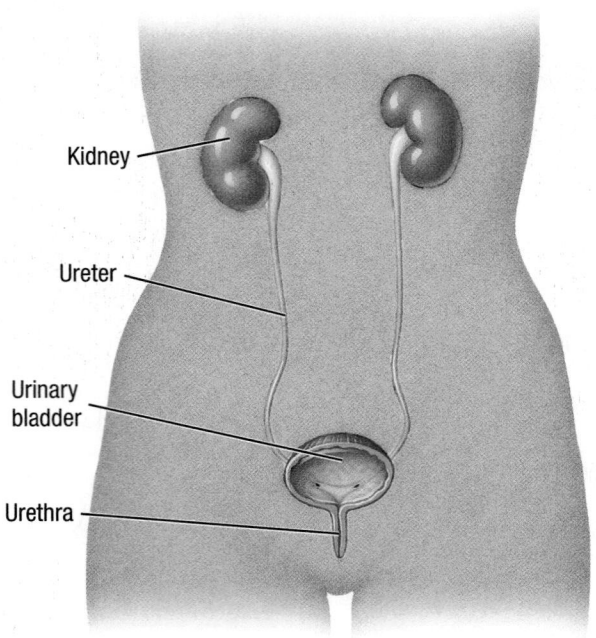

Kidney

Ureter

Urinary bladder

Urethra

Kidney Failure

The most common causes of kidney failure are infection, diabetes, high blood pressure, and damage to the kidneys by the body's own immune system. Because of their function in excretion, kidneys are often exposed to hazardous chemicals that have entered the body through the lungs, skin, or mouth. Household substances, such as paint, varnishes, furniture oils, glues, aerosol sprays, air fresheners, and lead, can damage kidneys.

❯ **Kidneys are vital to maintaining homeostasis, so damage to the kidneys may eventually become life threatening.** When kidneys fail, ions and toxic wastes, such as urea, accumulate in the blood plasma and increase to dangerous levels. If one kidney is lost in an accident or by disease, the other may do the work of both. If both kidneys fail, there are two options for treatment.

Kidney Dialysis Kidney dialysis is a procedure that uses a machine to filter the blood, as shown in **Figure 15.** Acting like nephrons, a dialysis machine filters small molecules from the blood. Some molecules are kept, and others are discarded. Dialysis is not a permanent solution to kidney failure. A single, healthy kidney can meet the homeostatic needs of the body, but no dialysis machine can. Dialysis patients must carefully manage their salt, protein, and water intake because the dialysis machine cannot regulate these blood components as well as the kidney can.

Kidney Transplant A more permanent solution to kidney failure is a kidney transplant from a healthy donor. As with all organ transplants, a major problem with kidney transplants is rejection. A transplanted organ comes from a different person, so the recipient's immune system may recognize the transplant as a foreign object and attack the organ. To reduce chances of rejection, doctors treat the recipient with drugs that suppress the activity of the immune system.

❯ **Reading Check** *What are some common causes of kidney failure?*

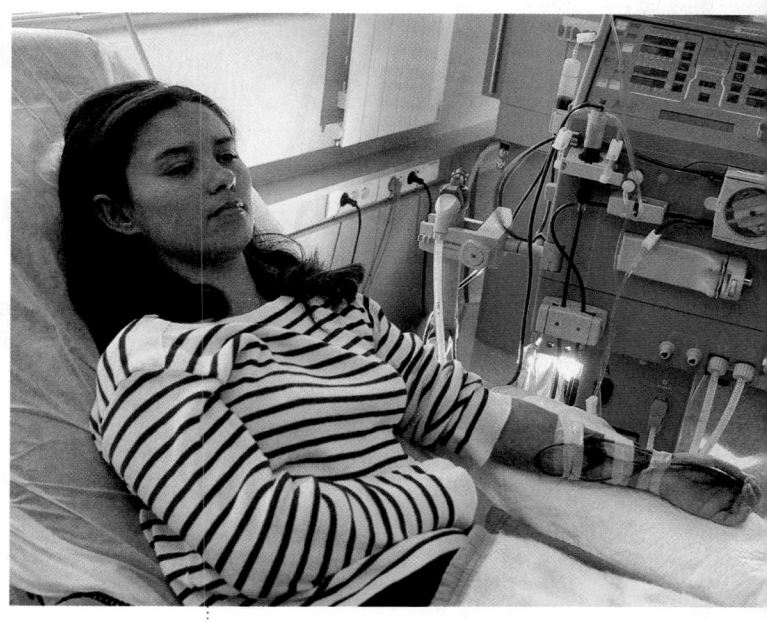

Figure 15 Kidney dialysis has prolonged the lives of many people who have damaged or diseased kidneys. Like a kidney, the dialysis machine filters urea and excess ions from the blood.

---

urine the liquid excreted by the kidneys, stored in the bladder, and passed through the urethra to the outside of the body

ureter one of the two narrow tubes that carry urine from the kidneys to the urinary bladder

urinary bladder a hollow, muscular organ that stores urine

urethra the tube that carries urine from the urinary bladder to the outside of the body

---

Section 3 Review

❯ KEY IDEAS

1. **Identify** major metabolic wastes that humans produce and the organs that eliminate the wastes from the body.

2. **List** the components of blood that are filtered into the Bowman's capsule.

3. **Summarize** how urine is stored and eliminated from the body.

4. **Describe** two treatment options if both kidneys fail.

CRITICAL THINKING

5. **Relating Concepts** Explain why a high concentration of protein in urine may indicate damaged kidneys.

WRITING FOR SCIENCE

6. **Journal** Imagine that you are a glucose molecule. Write about your journey through the kidney. Begin at the renal artery, and be sure to mention your traveling companions.

Objectives

▶ Describe the relationship between enzymes and the digestion of food molecules.

▶ Evaluate the ability of the lactase enzyme to promote lactose digestion.

▶ Infer the presence of lactose in milk and foods that contain milk.

Materials

- safety goggles
- disposable gloves
- lab apron
- lactase enzyme
- toothpicks
- spot plates
- droppers
- whole milk
- glucose solution
- glucose test strips

Safety

Lactose Digestion

Some people experience stomach and intestinal pain, bloating, and diarrhea when they eat foods that contain milk. These symptoms result from an inability to digest *lactose,* a sugar found in milk. This condition is known as *lactose intolerance*.

Lactose is a disaccharide made of one glucose unit and one galactose unit. During digestion, an enzyme called *lactase* helps break down lactose molecules into glucose and galactose molecules. People who are lactose intolerant do not produce this enzyme.

Some milk products are treated with the lactase enzyme for people who are lactose intolerant. In this lab, you will design an experiment to investigate how the lactase enzyme aids in lactose digestion. To do this, you will use glucose test strips to indicate the presence of glucose in various solutions.

Preparation

1. **SCIENTIFIC METHODS** **State the Problem** How does the lactase enzyme aid in the digestion of lactose?

2. **SCIENTIFIC METHODS** **Form a Hypothesis** Form a testable hypothesis that explains how the lactase enzyme affects milk.

Procedure

Learn About Lab Materials

1 Glucose test strips can be used to indicate the presence or absence of glucose in a solution. To use the test strip, touch the test pad to the solution being tested. After the suggested amount of time, compare the test strip to the color guide.

2 Do some research to find out how the lactase enzyme works. Discuss your findings with your lab group. In your lab report, write a summary of what you learned.

Glucose Test Results		
Solution	Result (+ or -)	Interpretation

Design an Experiment

3 Design an experiment that tests your hypothesis and that uses the materials listed for this lab. Predict what will happen during your experiment if your hypothesis is supported.

4 Write a procedure for your experiment. Identify the variables that you will control, the experimental variables, and the responding variables. Construct any tables you will need to record your data. Make a list of all the safety precautions you will take. Have your teacher approve your procedure before you begin the experiment.

Conduct Your Experiment

5 Put on safety goggles, gloves, and a lab apron.

6 CAUTION: **Handle glass slides with care. Do not touch or taste any chemicals.** Carry out your experiment. Record your observations in a data table.

7 Clean up your lab materials according to your teacher's instructions. Wash your hands before leaving the lab.

Lactose in Dairy Products

Analyze and Conclude

1. **Summarizing Information** Did the lactase enzyme have an effect on the milk?

2. **Recognizing Relationships** What is the relationship between lactose and lactase?

3. SCIENTIFIC METHODS **Interpreting Data** What role did the glucose solution play in your experiment?

4. **Drawing Conclusions** What does the lactase enzyme do to milk?

5. SCIENTIFIC METHODS **Using Evidence to Make Explanations** How do your results justify your conclusion?

6. SCIENTIFIC METHODS **Controlling Variables** Why should you test the lactase enzyme with glucose test strips?

7. **Further Inquiry** Write a new question about enzymes and digestion that could be explored with another investigation.

SC*LINKS.*

www.scilinks.org
Topic: Lactose
     Intolerance
Code: HX80845

Extensions

8. **Recognizing Patterns** What are some other food-treatment products that contain digestive enzymes?

9. **Inferring Conclusions** Why does the improper breakdown of certain food molecules cause symptoms such as stomach pain, gas, and diarrhea?

go.hrw.com
SUPER SUMMARY
Keyword: HX8DGSS

Key Ideas	Key Terms

1 Nutrition

> Your body needs energy to breathe, pump blood, and grow. The more active you are, the more Calories you burn to release energy.

> Carbohydrates, proteins, and fats provide most of the energy and building materials for the body.

> Water, vitamins and minerals contribute to many functions, such as regulating chemical reactions that release energy.

> Good nutrition must be balanced with regular physical activity to maintain a healthy body.

nutrient (891)
calorie (891)
vitamin (893)
mineral (894)

2 Digestion

> The digestive system takes in food, breaks it down into molecules that the body can use, and gets rid of undigested molecules and waste.

> The mouth, esophagus, and stomach begin the process of digestion by breaking food into small molecules.

> Absorption of nutrients takes place in the small intestine primarily, aided by secretions from the liver and pancreas.

> Components of food that are not digested leave the body as wastes.

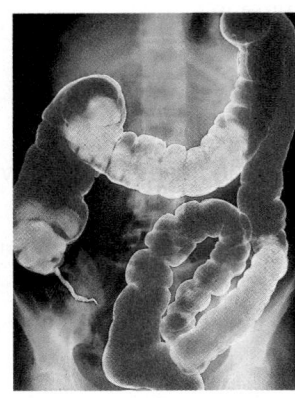

digestion (896)
esophagus (897)
peristalsis (897)
pepsin (897)
villus (899)

3 Excretion

> By removing toxic chemicals, excretion enables the body to maintain its osmotic and pH balance.

> The kidneys filter wastes out of the blood and balance levels of molecules.

> Metabolic wastes are removed from the body through the formation and excretion of urine.

> Kidneys are vital to maintaining homeostasis, so damage to kidneys may eventually become life-threatening.

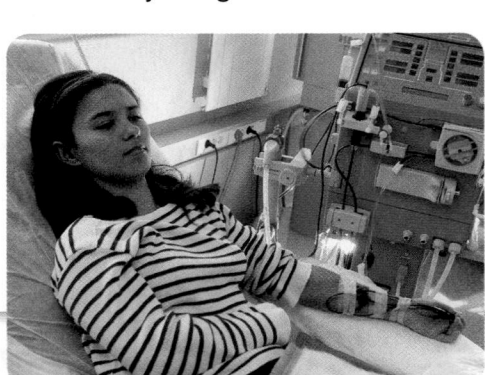

excretion (902)
urea (902)
nephron (903)
urine (904)
ureter (904)
urinary bladder (904)
urethra (904)

READING TOOLBOX

1. **Classification** Find three members of the class *fluid*.

2. 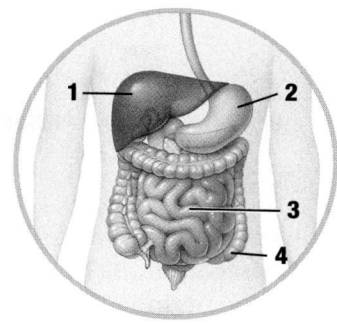 **Concept Map** Make a concept map that shows how nutrients are digested. Try to include the following words in your map: *carbohydrates, proteins, lipids, enzymes, saliva, pancreas, stomach, bile, liver, small intestine,* and *large intestine.*

Using Key Terms

3. Explain the relationship between the *esophagus* and *peristalsis.*

For each pair of terms, explain how the meanings of the terms differ.

4. *vitamin* and *mineral*

5. *urea* and *urine*

Understanding Key Ideas

6. Vitamins are organic compounds that
   a. help activate enzymes.
   b. help form cell membranes.
   c. are not obtained from food.
   d. provide energy for metabolism.

7. MyPyramid was developed by the
   a. CDC.   c. USAF.
   b. FDA.   d. USDA.

8. Enzymes in saliva begin the chemical digestion of
   a. fats.   c. vitamins.
   b. proteins.   d. carbohydrates.

9. Which of the following levels do the kidneys regulate during the filtration of blood?
   a. level of salt
   b. level of protein
   c. level of vitamin K
   d. level of blood temperature

10. Urine leaves the body through the
    a. ureter.   c. bladder.
    b. urethra.   d. intestine.

11. A kidney dialysis machine works by
    a. oxygenating the blood.
    b. reducing blood volume.
    c. increasing blood volume.
    d. removing wastes from the blood.

This image shows the organs of the digestive system. Use the image to answer the following questions.

12. Most of the end products of digestion are absorbed into the circulatory system from which structure?
    a. structure 1   c. structure 3
    b. structure 2   d. structure 4

13. What is the name of structure 4?
    a. liver   c. large intestine
    b. stomach   d. small intestine

Explaining Key Ideas

14. **Explain** how a person can eat and still lose weight.

15. **Describe** the relationship between proteins and essential amino acids.

16. **Identify** the digestive organs in which chemical digestion takes place.

17. **Summarize** the process by which carbohydrates, fats, and proteins are broken down for use by the body and by the cells.

18. **Describe** the role of water in eliminating cellular wastes.

19. **Identify** the major wastes excreted by humans, and briefly describe how each waste is eliminated from the body.

20. **Describe** the relationship between the kidney and the nephron.

21. **Explain** why kidney failure is dangerous.

Using Science Graphics

This bar graph represents the prevalence of overweight adolescents during certain time periods. Use the graph to answer the following questions.

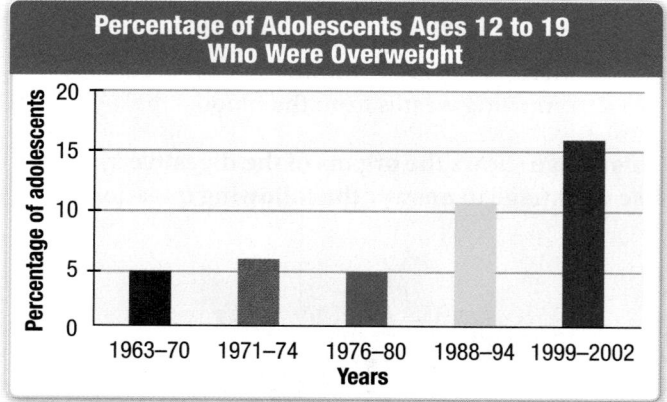

Percentage of Adolescents Ages 12 to 19 Who Were Overweight

Source: National Center for Health Statistics.

22. What is the difference between the percentage of overweight adolescents in 1999–2002 and that of overweight adolescents in 1971–1974?

23. Is the percentage of overweight adolescents increasing or decreasing?

Critical Thinking

24. **Justifying Conclusions** Your friend wants to feed her elderly grandmother more food in order to keep her healthy. Is this a good idea? Explain your answer.

25. **Analyzing Information** Why would large doses of vitamin B_{12} be less harmful than large doses of vitamin A?

26. **Inferring Conclusions** In some countries, many children suffer from a type of malnutrition called *kwashiorkor*. They have swollen stomachs and become increasingly thin until they die. Even when given rice and water, these children still die. What type of nutrients might these children lack?

27. **Predicting Patterns** A person has a small intestine that has villi but a reduced number of microvilli. Would you expect this person to be underweight or overweight? Explain your answer.

28. **Relating Concepts** Why is it important that the large intestine reabsorb water and not eliminate it?

29. **Inferring Relationships** Describe the symbiotic role of bacteria in the human intestine.

30. **Evaluating an Argument** The length of the looped tubule in the nephron varies among mammal species. A friend believes that mammals that live in water have shorter looped tubules than humans do. Do you agree or disagree? Explain your answer.

31. **Recognizing Relationships** A doctor tells a patient that the patient's urine contains a high concentration of sugar. Explain why this level of sugar may indicate damaged kidneys.

Why It Matters

32. **Research** Some hernias are present at birth. Find out what types of hernias may be acquired later in life. What are some causes of these hernias? What effect do they have on the digestive system, and how are they treated?

33. **Brochure** Appendicitis is considered a major emergency because an infected appendix can be lethal if it is not removed. Make a brochure that informs readers how appendicitis is diagnosed and treated. Include many of the common symptoms.

Alternative Assessment

34. **Animated Flipbook** Make a series of drawings showing how various substances in the blood move through the nephron.

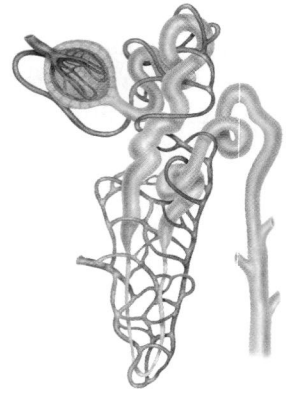

35. **Newspaper Article** Write an article that discusses diuretics (substances that increase urine excretion) for your school or local newspaper. Emphasize diuretics that most people have heard of, such as the caffeine in coffee and soft drinks.

Writing for Science

36. **Extended Response** When a person's kidneys stop functioning, urea builds up in the blood. For the urea to be removed, the person must be attached to a mechanical kidney, or dialysis machine. What happens if urea is not removed from the person's blood? Use your understanding of how a normal kidney functions to suggest a design for the major components of a dialysis machine.

Science Concepts

1. The primary function of carbohydrates is to
- **A** aid in digestion.
- **B** break down molecules.
- **C** regulate the flow of acid.
- **D** supply the body with energy.

2. Which of the following is a mineral?
- **F** fat
- **G** zinc
- **H** water
- **J** ascorbic acid

3. What type of digestion occurs when the stomach mixes food particles with gastric juice?
- **A** indigestion
- **B** physical digestion
- **C** chemical digestion
- **D** mechanical digestion

4. Which of the following nutrients are broken down in the stomach?
- **F** fats
- **G** proteins
- **H** vitamins
- **J** carbohydrates

5. The first portion of the small intestine is the
- **A** colon.
- **B** rectum.
- **C** duodenum.
- **D** esophagus.

6. How can dehydration be prevented?
- **F** by perspiring
- **G** by inhaling air
- **H** by drinking water
- **J** by not drinking water

7. lung : alveolus :: kidney :
- **A** ureter
- **B** filtrate
- **C** nephron
- **D** microvillus

Writing Skills

8. Short Response The liver and pancreas are accessory organs of the digestive tract. In what two ways do the liver and pancreas differ from other digestive organs?

Using Science Graphics

This graph shows the number of kidney transplants that were carried out during the years 1998–2001. Use the graph to answer the following questions.

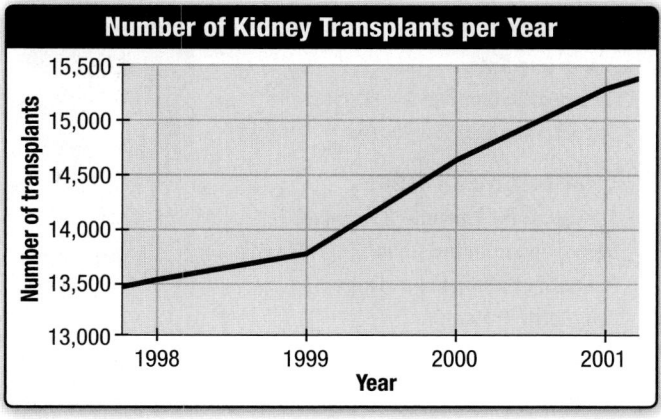

Number of Kidney Transplants per Year

9. In which year did 13,770 people receive a kidney transplant?
- **F** 1998
- **G** 1999
- **H** 2000
- **J** 2001

10. Approximately how many more people received a kidney transplant in 2001 than in 1998?
- **A** 150
- **B** 500
- **C** 1,500
- **D** 5,000

Use the image to answer the following questions.

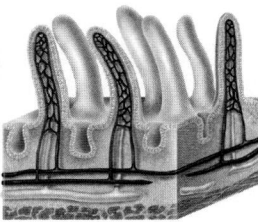

11. This structure, which is located in the small intestine, is called a
- **F** villus.
- **G** ureter.
- **H** nephron.
- **J** gallbladder.

12. What is the role of this structure?
- **A** filtration of blood
- **B** excretion of wastes
- **C** secretion of enzymes
- **D** absorption of nutrients

Chapter 37

The Body's Defenses

Preview

1 Protecting Against Disease
Preventing Entry
Nonspecific Immune Responses
Specific Immune Responses

2 Eliminating Invaders
Activating the Immune Response
Destroying Infected Cells
Removing Pathogens at Large
Long-Term Protection

3 Immune System Dysfunctions
Allergies
Autoimmune Diseases
Immune Deficiency

Why It Matters

Each day, your body is assaulted by millions of different bacteria, viruses, and other disease-causing agents. Fortunately, your body has ways to defend against these invaders. These defenses prevent you from getting sick and help heal the body if you do get sick.

Parasitic worms can invade the body and cause disease. This image shows the immune system at work against a parasite.

This microfilaria, the larval form of a parasitic worm, can infect the lymphatic system. It can enter the body through the bites of infected organisms, such as mosquitoes.

InquiryLab

⏱ 15 min

Barrier Breaking

Your skin is your first line of defense against harmful microorganisms. In this activity, you will use a protective glove to model skin.

Procedure

1. Put on **gloves** and a **lab apron**.

2. Fill a **mixing bowl** half full with **water**. Add **20 mL of vinegar** to the water. Gently swirl to mix.

3. Fill a **protective glove** half full with water. Add **several drops of bromothymol blue** to the water in the glove.

4. Knot the open end of the glove.

5. Place the glove in the bowl of water.

6. Let stand for 2 minutes. Record your observations.

7. Use **scissors** to make a 1 cm cut in one of the glove fingers. Put the glove back in the bowl.

8. Let stand for 3 to 5 minutes. Record your observations.

Analysis

1. **Describe** how the glove models skin.

2. **Explain** what happens when the glove is cut.

3. **Summarize** how cutting the glove modeled a real-world event.

This immune cell is called a *macrophage*. Macrophages are special types of white blood cells that ingest and kill disease-causing agents that enter the body.

READING TOOLBOX

These reading tools can help you learn the material in this chapter. For more information on how to use these and other tools, see **Appendix: Reading and Study Skills.**

Using Words

Word Parts Knowing the meanings of word parts can help you figure out the meanings of words that you do not know.

Your Turn Use the table to answer the following questions.

1. Define *inflammation* in your own words.
2. What do you think the word *cytotoxic* means? Use your dictionary to find out if your guess is correct.

Word Parts		
Part	**Type**	**Meaning**
in-, en-	prefix	cause, make, enable
flam	root	burn, flame
cyto-	prefix	cell
toxic	root	poison

Using Language

Mnemonics Mnemonic devices are tools that can help you memorize words, steps, concepts that go together. Use the first letter of every word you want to remember as the first letter of a new word, in a sentence that is easy to remember. For example, the trees *maple, dogwood, ash,* and *sycamore* can be remembered by the mnemonic "My Dear Aunt Sally."

Your Turn Create mnemonic devices to help you remember the following groups of words.

1. The four parts of blood: *red cells, white cells, platelets,* and *plasma*
2. The four major tissue types: *epithelial, nervous, connective,* and *muscle*

Using Graphic Organizers

Pattern Puzzles A pattern puzzle is useful for organizing and remembering the steps of a process. Pattern puzzles can help you understand how the steps of a process fit together.

Your Turn Use a pattern puzzle to learn the steps of the inflammatory immune response.

1. Write the steps of the inflammatory immune response in your own words. Write one step per line. Do not number the steps.
2. Cut the sheet of paper so that there is one step per strip of paper.
3. Shuffle the paper strips so that they are out of sequence.
4. Place the strips in their proper sequence.
5. Confirm the order of the process by checking your text or class notes.
6. Use this exercise to model another immune response.

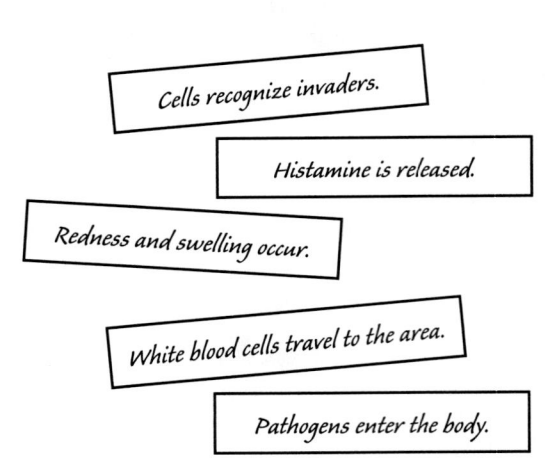

Cells recognize invaders.

Histamine is released.

Redness and swelling occur.

White blood cells travel to the area.

Pathogens enter the body.

Protecting Against Disease

Key Ideas	Key Terms	Why It Matters
❯ What physical barriers protect the human body? ❯ What are three general defense mechanisms that the body uses to fight pathogens? ❯ How does the body respond to pathogens that have infected a cell?	pathogen mucous membrane inflammation histamine antigen macrophage	To survive, the body must protect itself from infections. The body has both general and specific responses to prevent and fight infections.

Microorganisms are everywhere! Some are harmless, but others can cause illness by invading your body and infecting your cells. Disease-causing microorganisms and viruses are called **pathogens.** Your body protects against disease by preventing pathogens from entering the body, or by fighting pathogens if they do enter.

Preventing Entry

❯ **Skin and mucous membranes form strong barriers that prevent pathogens from entering the body.** Your skin is the first line of defense against pathogens. Oil makes the skin's surface acidic, which inhibits the growth of many pathogens. Sweat also contains enzymes that digest bacterial cell walls and kill the bacteria. Mucous membranes form a second barrier to pathogens. **Mucous membranes** are layers of epithelial tissue that produce a sticky, viscous fluid called *mucus.* They cover many internal body surfaces, including the linings of the digestive, respiratory, and reproductive tracts. Mucus traps pathogens before they can cause infections.

Sometimes pathogens cross one of these two physical barriers. Cuts and abrasions allow pathogens to enter through the skin. Tears in the epithelium allow pathogens to cross mucous membranes. Airborne pathogens, shown in **Figure 1,** can enter the body through the respiratory system. You can ingest pathogens via contaminated food or water. Some pathogens can cross mucous membranes of the reproductive tract during sexual contact. Sometimes, pathogens are injected directly into the bloodstream. This can occur through insect bites or through the use of contaminated needles.

❯ **Reading Check** *How do physical barriers prevent pathogens from entering the body? (See the Appendix for answers to Reading Checks.)*

pathogen a microorganism, another organism, a virus, or a protein that causes disease; an infectious agent

mucous membrane (MYOO kuhs) the layer of epithelial tissue that covers internal surfaces of the body and that secretes mucus

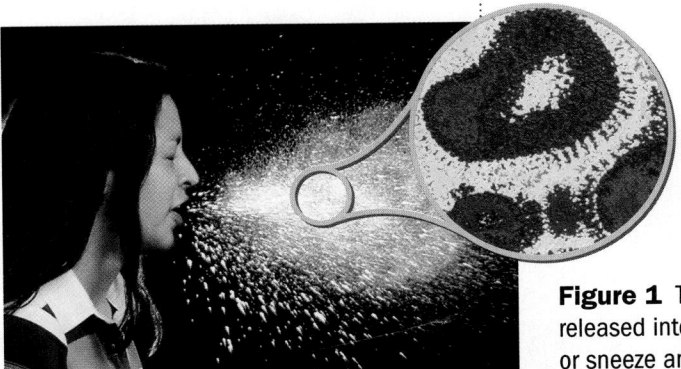

Figure 1 The flu virus can be released into the air through a cough or sneeze and can infect another person who inhales the air.

Nonspecific Immune Responses

❯ **When pathogens break through the body's physical barriers, the body quickly responds with second-line defenses. These defenses are fever, inflammation, and the activation of special proteins that kill or inhibit pathogens.** These second-line defenses depend on your body's ability to know its own cells and proteins and to separate these "self" cells and proteins from outside invaders.

Fever The body's temperature, normally 36.5 °C to 37.2 °C (97.8 °F to 99 °F), rises several degrees as the body begins to fight against an invading pathogen. High body temperature, or fever, is a common symptom of sickness. Higher temperatures are harmful to many bacterial pathogens, so fever helps the body fight infection. However, fever can be dangerous. Fever above 39 °C (103 °F) can destroy the body's cellular proteins, and fever above 41 °C (105 °F) can be fatal.

inflammation a protective response of tissues affected by disease or injury

histamine (HIS tuh MEEN) a chemical that stimulates the dilation of capillaries

antigen a substance that stimulates an immune response

macrophage an immune system cell that engulfs pathogens and other materials

Inflammation An injury or local infection stimulates inflammation, shown in **Figure 2.** During **inflammation,** chemicals and cells that attack and destroy pathogens gather around the area of injury or infection. ❶ When the skin is damaged, pathogens can enter the body. ❷ Infected or injured cells recognize the "nonself" invaders and release chemicals such as histamine. **Histamine** causes local blood vessels to dilate, which increases blood flow to the area and causes swelling and redness. ❸ White blood cells travel to the infection site to attack pathogens. The whitish liquid, or pus, connected with many infections is filled with white blood cells, dead body cells, and dead pathogens. Three types of white blood cells play a role in this response: macrophages, neutrophils, and natural killer cells. These cells are described in **Figure 3.**

Figure 2 When pathogens enter your body, an inflammatory response is triggered. ❯ **Which cells are activated by the inflammatory response?**

go.hrw.com
✳ **interact online**
Keyword: HX8IMNF2

Inflammation

❶ When skin is damaged, such as from a puncture wound, pathogens enter the body.

❷ Increased blood flow to the area causes swelling and redness.

❸ White blood cells attack and destroy the pathogens.

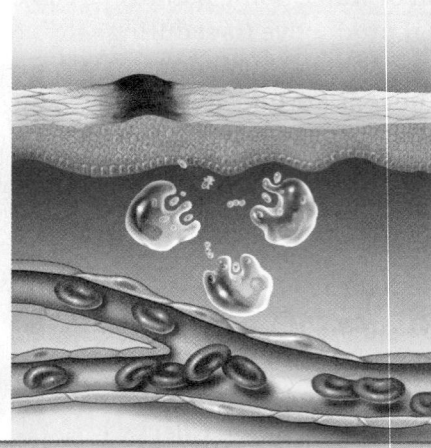

Pathogens

Capillary

White blood cells

White Blood Cells Involved in Inflammation		
Macrophage	**Neutrophil**	**Natural Killer Cell**
Target: pathogens, dead cells, and cellular debris 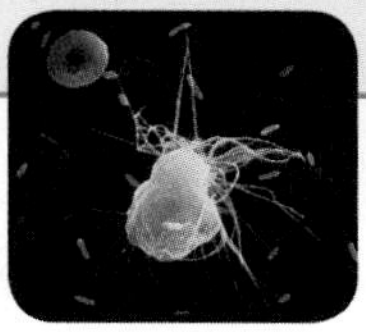	Target: pathogens 	Target: cells infected with pathogens and cancer cells 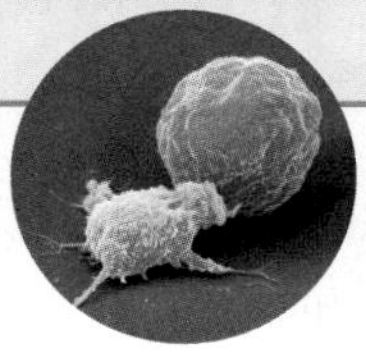
Method of action: ingests and kills pathogens	Method of action: ingests and kills pathogens	Method of action: punctures an infected cell membrane, and causes water to rush in and burst the cell
Location: lymph and fluid between cells, concentrated in the spleen and lungs	Location: blood and fluid between cells and in the walls of capillaries	Location: lymph nodes and other tissues

Protein Activation Some pathogens activate proteins that boost the body's general responses to infection. Complement proteins attack cellular pathogens, such as bacteria, by punching holes in the cell membranes and causing the contents to leak out. Interferons, another group of proteins, are released by cells infected with viruses. These proteins prevent viruses from making proteins and RNA.

Specific Immune Responses

Most pathogens are destroyed by the general, nonspecific defenses that have been looked at so far. But what happens if an invader gets past these responses? The third line of defense is the specific immune response, in which special white blood cells target a particular invader. ❯ **When a pathogen infects a cell, the body produces immune cells that specialize in detecting and destroying that specific pathogen.**

Antigen Display **Macrophages** are one type of white blood cell that destroys pathogens. Pathogens have unique proteins on their surfaces that help your body identify them as "nonself." These proteins, called **antigens,** identify the cell as foreign and start an immune response. After a macrophage or similar cell swallows up and destroys a pathogen, pieces of the pathogen that contain its antigens move to the surface of the macrophage. This "display" of antigens changes the cell surface markers on the macrophage. The antigen display alerts the immune system to an invader and the immune system cells are put into action.

Every antigen has its own receptor, which is located on the surface of an immune cell. The shape of antigen receptors allows the immune system to be specific to certain antigens. As **Figure 4** shows, antigen receptors bind to antigens that match their shape exactly, in the same way that two pieces of a puzzle fit together. The body produces a great variety of immune cells, each of which has receptors for a different antigen. This variety allows the immune system to respond to millions of different antigens.

❯ **Reading Check** *How does the body recognize "nonself" invaders?*

Figure 3 Different types of white blood cells (each shown in yellow) help defend the body against pathogens.

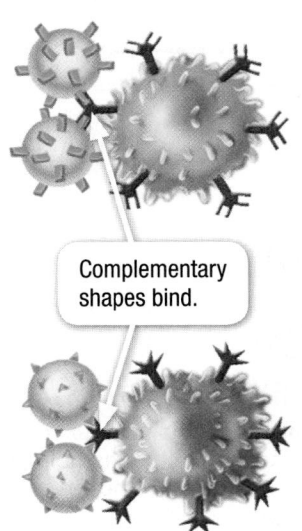

Complementary shapes bind.

Figure 4 Specific antigens (green) located on foreign cells (yellow) bind to antigen receptors (red) that are located on immune system cells (purple).

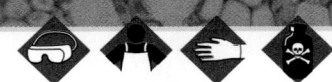

Antigen Binding

In this lab, you will observe what happens when receptors in blood-typing serum bind to the antigens on simulated red blood cells.

Procedure

1 Put on **safety goggles**, a **lab apron**, and **gloves.**

2 ☠ Use only simulated blood provided by your teacher. Place three or four drops of **type AB simulated blood** into each well of a clean **blood-typing tray.**

3 Add three drops of **anti-A blood-typing serum** to one well. Stir the mixture with a **toothpick** for 30 s.

4 Add three drops of **anti-B serum** to the other well. Stir the mixture with a new toothpick. Look for clumps separating from the mixtures.

5 Using **type O simulated blood**, repeat steps 1–4.

Analysis

1. **Determine** which blood type has antigens that are recognized by the blood-typing serums.

2. **Evaluating Results** What does the clumping of the blood mixtures indicate?

3. **CRITICAL THINKING** **Predicting Outcomes** What would happen if you used type A, type B, and type O simulated blood in the same experiment? Explain your answer.

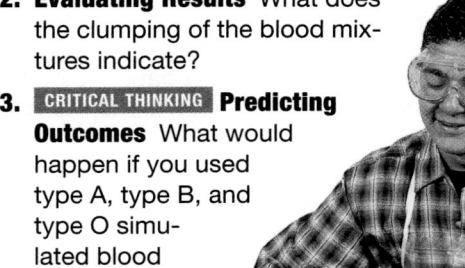

www.scilinks.org
Topic: Immune
          Systems
Code: HX80786

Two-Part Assault When a displayed antigen binds to its antigen receptor on an immune cell, another response is triggered—more immune cells are produced that have the same antigen receptor. These immune cells carry out two processes at the same time. One process destroys a person's body cells that are no longer normal. These cells may be infected by pathogens or may be other altered body cells, such as cancer cells. The other process removes extracellular pathogens, pathogens that have not entered body cells. Together, these two processes form an integrated response to an infection. These two immune processes will be described in more detail in the next section.

Section

1 Review

❯KEY IDEAS

1. **Summarize** how the skin and mucous membranes help prevent infection by a pathogen.

2. **Identify** the three general defense mechanisms that protect the body from infection.

3. **Describe** how a cell responds to pathogens.

CRITICAL THINKING

4. **Relating Concepts** Identify the process that would occur immediately if you cut your foot on a piece of glass, and describe how it would help keep the cut from getting infected.

5. **Drawing Conclusions** In the disease leukemia, abnormal white blood cells are produced. Why are people who have leukemia at greater risk for infections than other people are?

WRITING FOR SCIENCE

6. **Short Story** Imagine that you are a pathogen trying to get into a human body. Write a short story that describes the challenges that you face as you attempt to get past the body's defenses. Be sure to include at least three different types of immune system defenses.

Key Ideas	Key Terms		Why It Matters
❯ How is the specific immune response activated? ❯ How does the body eliminate intracellular pathogens? ❯ How does the body eliminate extracellular pathogens? ❯ How does the immune system protect the body from repeated infection by the same pathogen?	helper T cell cytotoxic T cell B cell plasma cell antibody	memory cell immunity vaccine	At the same time that the immune system is fighting an infection, it is creating a reserve army of cells to fight the same pathogen in the future.

The immune system consists of many types of white blood cells, including macrophages, T cells, and B cells. The first time your body meets a particular pathogen, the immune response launches an attack on the invader. The coordinated effort of all of the immune system cells not only destroys invading pathogens but also provides protection against future infection by a similar pathogen.

Activating a Specific Immune Response

As part of the body's general immune response, macrophages engulf and destroy pathogens. The result is the display of antigens on the surface of infected cells. These "altered" cells now become a target of the specific immune response. ❯ **A specialized white blood cell called a *helper T cell* activates the immune system. These cells coordinate two responses: destroying cells that have been infected by a pathogen, and cleaning up pathogens at large in the body.**

Helper T Cells Helper T cells, shown in **Figure 5,** are white blood cells that regulate the function of other cells in the immune system. Recall that helper T cells have specific antigen receptors on their surfaces that bind to specific antigens that are displayed on the surface of a macrophage. The binding of receptor to the antigen activates the helper T cell, which causes the release of chemical signals.

Activated helper T cells do not directly attack infected body cells or pathogens. Instead, they grow and divide to produce more helper T cells that have identical receptors on their surfaces. The helper T cells activate the two processes of the specific immune response: the destruction of infected cells by cytotoxic T cells and the removal of extracellular pathogens from the body by B cells.

helper T cell a white blood cell necessary for B cells to develop normal levels of antibodies

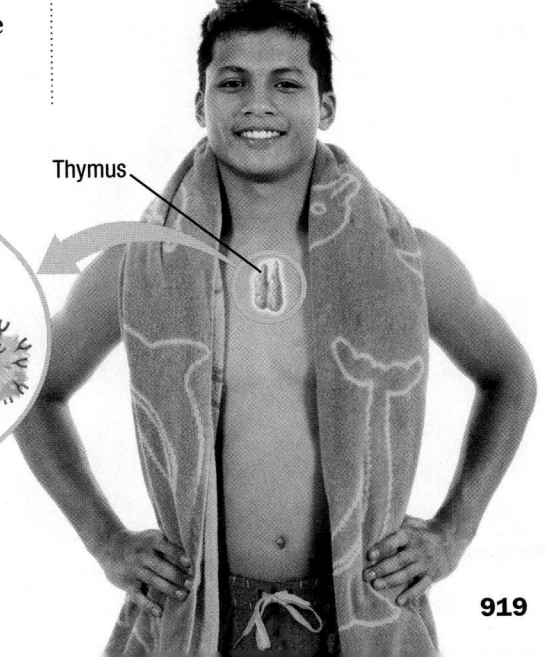

Thymus

Helper T cell

Cytotoxic T cell

Figure 5 Some white blood cells, such as helper T cells and cytotoxic T cells, are produced in bone marrow and mature in the thymus.

919

cytotoxic T cell a type of T cell that recognizes and destroys cells infected by viruses

B cell a white blood cell that matures in bones and makes antibodies

plasma cell a type of white blood cell that produces antibodies

antibody a protein that reacts to a specific antigen or that inactivates or destroys toxins

READING TOOLBOX

Pattern Puzzles Make a pattern puzzle to help you remember the steps of the immune response system.

Figure 6 When a helper T cell (blue) activates a B cell (purple), they come in close contact with each other.

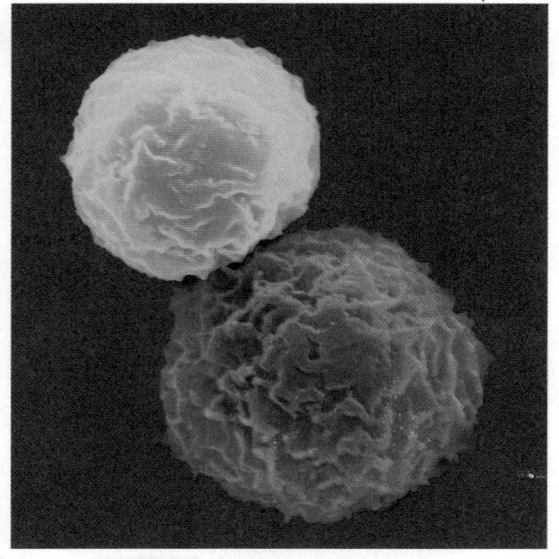

Destroying Infected Cells

Helper T cells produce chemical signals that activate the second kind of T cell, called a *cytotoxic T cell*. **Cytotoxic T cells** are white blood cells that carry pathogen-specific receptors on their surfaces. ❯ Cytotoxic T cells destroy cells that have been infected by pathogens. They can also kill cancer cells and attack foreign tissues, such as tissues that are received during an organ transplant. The cytotoxic T cell response is summarized in **Figure 7.**

Activating Cytotoxic T Cells Recall that when a body cell becomes infected by a virus, it displays specific antigens on its surface. These antigens activate matching antigen receptors on helper T cells. The activated helper T cells then turn on the production of cytotoxic T cells that will have the same antigen receptor. As a result, the new cytotoxic T cells will bind to matching antigens on the surface of infected cells. When they bind, the cytotoxic T cells release chemicals that punch holes in the membranes of the infected cells. The infected cells die when water enters them and splits them open.

Removing Pathogens at Large

Helper T cells also activate the second part of the specific immune response, which is carried out by B cells. **B cells** are white blood cells that produce proteins that bind to pathogens outside of body cells. This action tags the pathogens for destruction by macrophages. ❯ The B cell response removes extracellular pathogens from the body and prevents further infection. This response is summarized in **Figure 7.**

Activating B Cells The B cell response is triggered when B cells are activated by helper T cells, as shown in **Figure 6.** Like T cells in the T cell response, only B cells that have antigen receptors matching a specific antigen are activated. Activated B cells produce **plasma cells,** which are white blood cells that produce and release antibodies. **Antibodies** are Y-shaped protein molecules that bind to the specific antigen that they match.

Antibody Binding Antibodies are released by plasma cells and circulate in the blood and lymph fluid. When antibodies encounter extracellular pathogens that they match, they attach to the pathogens. This binding is like the specific binding of cytotoxic T cells to matching infected body cells. However, antibodies do not remain attached to the plasma cells that produced them.

Each Y-shaped antibody has two binding sites, which are located at the tips of the Ys. Antibodies can either bind to two antigens on the surface of a single pathogen cell or to single antigens on two pathogen cells. The binding of multiple antibodies to pathogens forms an antigen-antibody complex. These complexes are then destroyed by general defense mechanisms, such as macrophages or defense proteins that puncture the pathogen membranes.

❯ **Reading Check** *Which cells produce antibodies?*

Figure 7 Antigens (small green knobs), such as those from a virus (yellow), activate helper T cells. Helper T cells then activate both the intracellular response (by stimulating T cells) and the extracellular response (by stimulating B cells).

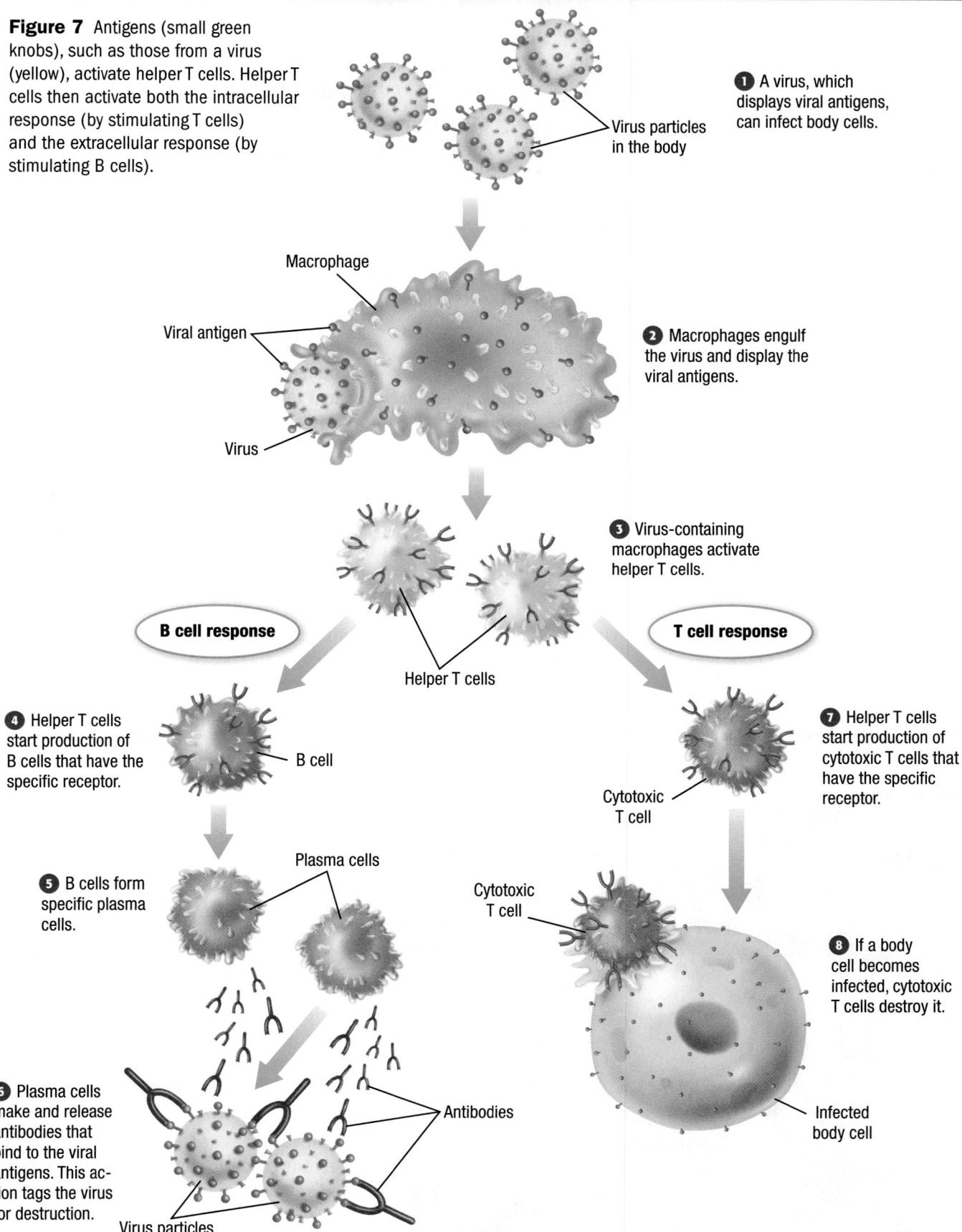

1 A virus, which displays viral antigens, can infect body cells.

Virus particles in the body

Macrophage

Viral antigen

Virus

2 Macrophages engulf the virus and display the viral antigens.

3 Virus-containing macrophages activate helper T cells.

B cell response

Helper T cells

T cell response

4 Helper T cells start production of B cells that have the specific receptor.

B cell

7 Helper T cells start production of cytotoxic T cells that have the specific receptor.

Cytotoxic T cell

5 B cells form specific plasma cells.

Plasma cells

Cytotoxic T cell

8 If a body cell becomes infected, cytotoxic T cells destroy it.

6 Plasma cells make and release antibodies that bind to the viral antigens. This action tags the virus for destruction.

Antibodies

Virus particles

Infected body cell

Long-Term Protection

When a pathogen has been destroyed, the specific T cells, plasma cells, and antibodies involved are no longer needed. But if the same pathogen invades the body again, the immune system is prepared.

Activating Memory Cells Recall that when the body first meets a pathogen, B cells make plasma cells that produce antibodies to that pathogen. At the same time, activated B cells also produce another kind of white blood cell called a *memory cell.* Like plasma cells, **memory cells** carry antigen receptors to the target antigen. These cells also continue to patrol the body's tissues, in some cases for the rest of a person's life. If the same pathogen invades the body again, the memory cells rapidly divide and produce a group of immune cells—helper T cells, cytotoxic T cells, and plasma cells. ❯ **After an immune response, memory cells continue to protect the body from pathogens the body had already encountered. An individual who recovers from an infectious disease becomes resistant to that particular pathogen.**

The secondary immune response that is started by memory cells is called *immunity.* **Immunity** is a long-lasting resistance that is usually effective only against the specific pathogen that triggered the response. This secondary response starts much more quickly than when the body first faced the pathogen. It also produces many more specialized cells. As a result, the invader is stopped before it can cause illness.

Vaccination Infection by a pathogen allows the body to gain immunity to that particular pathogen. However, the body can also become immune through the use of vaccines. A **vaccine** is a solution that contains a dead or weakened form of a pathogen. They are typically injected into the bloodstream so that the pathogens can get past the general defenses of the immune system. Vaccines are available for many serious and deadly diseases.

A vaccine triggers an immune response against a pathogen without causing symptoms. How? Vaccines carry surface antigens from the pathogen that the body recognizes as harmful. This recognition triggers the immune response and forms memory cells against the pathogen. However, the genetic material in a vaccine is weakened or destroyed so that the pathogen cannot cause illness. In this way, immunity is built against the disease without the disease occurring in the body. Future contact with the pathogen will trigger the immune system to respond.

Most vaccines are given as a shot directly into the bloodstream. This method is used so that the vaccine can get past the body's general defenses. Vaccination is shown in **Figure 8.**

memory cell an immune system B cell or T cell that does not respond the first time that it meets with an antigen or an invading cell but that recognizes and attacks the antigen or invading cell during subsequent infections

immunity the ability to resist or recover from an infectious disease

vaccine a substance prepared from killed or weakened pathogens and introduced into a body to produce immunity

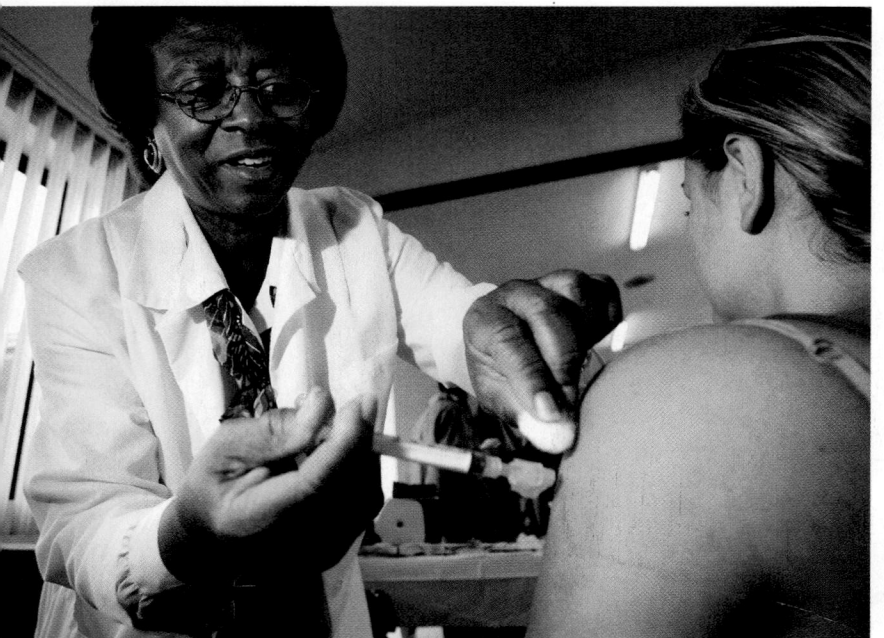

Figure 8 This young person is receiving a vaccination shot. A vaccine is produced from a killed or weakened pathogen. ❯ **Vaccines trigger which type of immune response?**

QuickLab

The Eradication of Polio

The graph shows the global incidence of polio, and the percent of the population covered by polio vaccines.

Analysis

1. **Determine** how many cases of polio were reported globally in 1980. In 2000?

2. **Determine** what percent of the population was covered by protective polio vaccine in 1980. In 2000?

3. **Describe** the relationship between the number of polio cases and the coverage by preventative vaccine.

4. **Name** the two-year period over which the greatest drop in cases occurred. Explain this decrease.

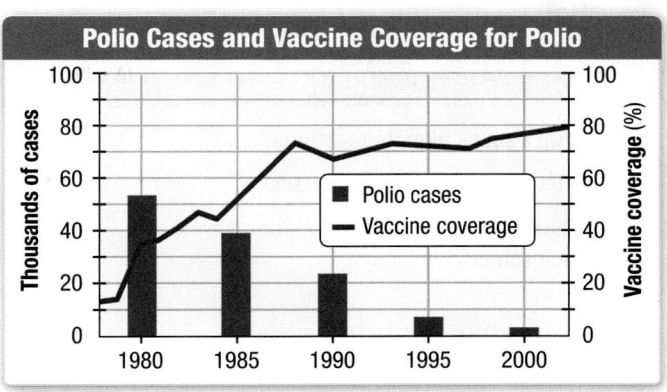

Polio Cases and Vaccine Coverage for Polio

Source: World Health Organization.

5. **CRITICAL THINKING** **Inferring Conclusions** What might cause a sudden yearly increase in the number of polio cases?

How Pathogens Evade Immunity Microorganisms have short life cycles. Several generations can be produced in as little as an hour. Also, changes in the genetic material of a microorganism often occur. These genetic changes may cause *antigen shifting,* an abrupt change in a pathogen's antigens. This process can allow a pathogen to avoid being recognized by the immune system of a person who had already become immune to the pathogen.

Influenza viruses are well known for frequent antigen shifts. New forms of the flu appear rapidly, and people at risk of serious complications from the flu must receive new vaccines annually. Human immunodeficiency virus (HIV) also undergoes antigen shifts. As a result, making a vaccine against HIV is very difficult. Antigen shifting also causes the virus to become resistant to drugs that are used to treat HIV in fection.

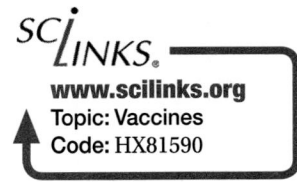

www.scilinks.org
Topic: Vaccines
Code: HX81590

❯ **Reading Check** *What causes antigen shifting?*

Section 2 Review

❯ KEY IDEAS

1. **Describe** the role of helper T cells in fighting an infection.

2. **Explain** how cytotoxic T cells destroy infected body cells.

3. **Sequence** how B cells fight an infection.

4. **Explain** how memory cells ensure immunity to a specific pathogen.

CRITICAL THINKING

5. **Drawing Conclusions** In the first vaccine developed, cowpox virus was used to protect against smallpox. This fact seems to contradict the high specificity that characterizes immune responses. What conclusion can you draw about the cowpox virus in relation to the smallpox virus?

WRITING FOR SCIENCE

6. **Short Essay** Scientists have created an effective vaccine for smallpox but have not been able to do so for HIV. What does this fact suggest about the rate of mutation of the smallpox virus? Write a short essay to explain your reasoning.

Immune System Dysfunctions

Key Ideas	Key Terms	Why It Matters
❯ What causes allergic reactions? ❯ What are autoimmune diseases? ❯ What happens when your immune system is compromised?	allergy allergen autoimmune disease AIDS HIV	Only when the immune system breaks down do we realize how important it is to our survival.

The immune system protects us from a wide variety of diseases. When the immune system malfunctions, the results are usually very serious and often fatal. Allergies, autoimmune disorders, and inherited or acquired immunodeficiency disorders are all examples of what can happen when the immune system does not work properly.

Allergies

If you suffer from hay fever, you experience an immune response to pollen antigens. **Allergies** are immune responses to antigens to which most people do not react. These weak antigens are called **allergens.** ❯ An allergic reaction is the immune system's excessive response to a normally harmless antigen. Common allergens include pollen, dust, fungal spores, the feces of dust mites, and materials found in some foods and drugs. Some allergens are shown in **Figure 9.**

In a sensitive person, exposure to an allergen causes histamine release. This event can cause swelling, redness, high mucus production, a runny or stuffy nose, and itchy eyes. Most allergy medicines contain antihistamines, drugs that prevent the action of histamine. Most allergic reactions are just uncomfortable. However, severe allergic reactions can be life threatening if they are not treated immediately.

Figure 9 These allergens cause allergies in some people. ❯ **What causes an allergic response?**

Ragweed pollen

House dust

QuickLab

Constricted Airways

During an asthma attack, muscles surrounding the airways contract and restrict airflow into the lungs.

Procedure

1. Get **three clean straws** and **three rubber bands.** Slip one rubber band near one end of a straw. Coil the rubber band around the straw so that it does not change the shape of the straw.

2. Wrap another rubber band around the end of a second straw so that the straw is slightly crushed.

3. Wrap the third rubber band around the last straw so that the straw is almost sealed.

4. Breathe through each of the straws. Only breathe through your own straws. Compare the straws in terms of how easily you can breathe through them.

Analysis

1. **Describe** what the straw and rubber band represent.

2. **State** which straw represented an unrestricted airway.

3. **Describe** how this activity models an asthma attack.

4. **CRITICAL THINKING** **Predicting Outcomes** How might you reduce the prevalence of allergen-induced asthma attacks?

Asthma Asthma is an inflammation of the respiratory tract and is often caused by an allergic reaction to particles in the air. Asthma symptoms include coughing, wheezing, and difficulty in breathing. Asthma affects nearly 20 million Americans and causes more than 4,000 deaths each year.

Other Allergies Some foods that cause allergies are eggs, peanuts, milk, and shellfish. Food allergies may cause vomiting, diarrhea, and hives. They may be so severe that they cause a person to stop breathing and go into shock. Allergies to some detergents, cosmetics, or plants such as poison ivy can cause itchy red rashes and blisters. Some people are allergic to the stings of bees and other insects. Their reaction to a sting may include hives, difficulty in breathing, and loss of consciousness.

> **Reading Check** *Why is asthma classified as an allergy?*

allergy a physical response to an antigen, which can be a common substance that produces little or no response in the general population

allergen a substance that causes an allergic reaction

Mold

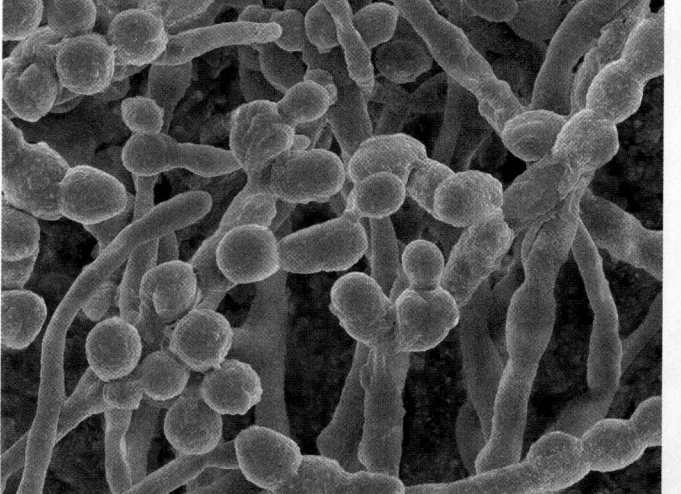

Dust mite

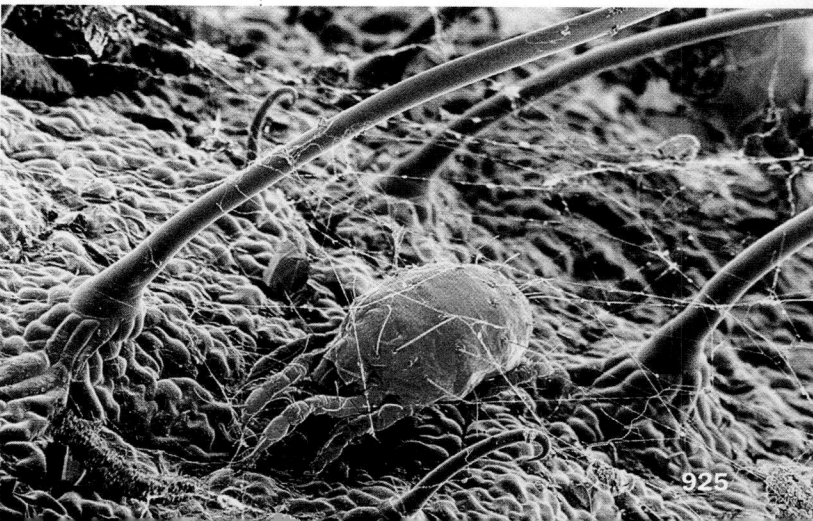

Allergies & Culture

The number of people in the United States suffering from asthma today is 1.75 times higher than in 1980. What is the reason for this trend? One interesting explanation, known as the *hygiene hypothesis,* suggests that improved sanitation conditions can lead to higher rates of asthma, allergies, and autoimmune disorders.

Immune System in Training

As sanitation conditions improve in industrialized nations, children are exposed to far fewer microorganisms. The hygiene hypothesis argues that when a child's immune system is not exposed to common microorganisms, it can become unbalanced and can trigger allergic responses to harmless substances.

The hygiene hypothesis proposes that an imbalance exists between helper T cells and cytotoxic T cells. A newborn child depends primarily on helper T cells to prevent infection. The cytotoxic T cell system grows stronger as a child is exposed to microbes in the environment. The hygiene hypothesis suggests that if a developing child is not exposed to a variety of microbes, the cytotoxic T cell system does not develop properly and helper T cells can become dominant.

T-cell

How Clean is Too Clean? As a child grows older, the overdeveloped helper T cell system can provoke an aggressive allergic response to harmless substances such as pollen or pet dander or even the body's own cells.

Research Scientists hope that they can develop new treatments to stimulate the cytotoxic T cell system and relieve the suffering of many people with asthma, allergies, and autoimmune disorders. Find out about one such treatment and report on it.

Autoimmune Diseases

The ability of the immune system to distinguish between "self" substances, which it ignores, and "nonself" molecules, which it attacks, is crucial to protecting the body from pathogens. Sometimes, the immune system loses its tolerance for "self," attacks certain cells of the body, and thus causes one of many **autoimmune diseases.** ❯ **In an autoimmune disease, the body launches an immune response, such that body cells are attacked as if they were pathogens.** Autoimmunity causes a wide range of disorders, some of which are shown in **Figure 11.** In all of these diseases, the immune system attacks the very organs that it is programmed to protect.

Common Autoimmune Disorders Diabetes is a disease in which the body does not produce or properly use the hormone insulin. This hormone allows glucose to enter body cells. Type 1 diabetes (or insulin dependent diabetes) is an example of an autoimmune disease. When a person has type 1 diabetes, the body does not produce or properly use insulin, the hormone that allows glucose to enter body cells. His or her immune cells attack the cells of the pancreas that produce insulin. As a result, he or she produces very little insulin, and the body cells starve for glucose while it accumulates in the blood. Type 1 diabetes is treated with insulin through injections or an insulin pump, shown in **Figure 10.**

Multiple sclerosis is an autoimmune disease in which the immune system targets the insulating material that covers nerves. This result is numbness, weakness, paralysis of one or more limbs, poor coordination, and vision impairment.

Autoimmune diseases affect 5% to 7% of the U.S. population and are three times more common in women than men. These diseases are not curable, but they are treatable to some extent. The causes of autoimmune diseases are not well understood but likely involve factors including genetics, environmental factors, or pathogens.

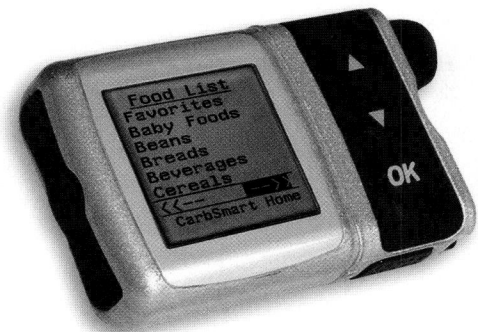

Figure 10 This insulin pump is used to treat type 1 diabetes. ❯ **How is the immune system involved in type 1 diabetes?**

---

autoimmune disease a disease in which the immune system attacks the organism's own cells

---

Examples of Autoimmune Diseases

Disease	Areas affected	Symptoms
Graves' disease	thyroid gland	weakness, irritability, heat intolerance, increased sweating, weight loss, and insomnia
Systemic lupus erythematosus (SLE)	connective tissue, joints, and kidneys	facial skin rash, painful joints, fever, fatigue, kidney problems, and weight loss
Rheumatoid arthritis	joints	severe pain, fatigue, and disabling inflammation of joints
Psoriasis	skin	dry, scaly, red skin patches
Crohn's disease	digestive system	abdominal pain, nausea, vomiting, and weight loss

Figure 11 Autoimmune diseases can affect organs and tissues in various areas of the body.

READING TOOLBOX

Mnemonics Create a mnemonic device to help you remember the types of immune system dysfunctions described in this section.

Figure 12 Family members like these two sisters are often donors for organ transplants.

Immune Deficiency

A strong immune system works so well and so quietly that we often don't realize how many times it has saved our lives. However, some people have a deficiency in which part of the immune system is missing or does not work properly. ❯ **When the immune system does not function, the body is unable to fight and survive infections by pathogens that do not cause any problems for a robust immune system.** Immune deficiencies can be inherited, acquired through infection, or even produced as an unintended side effect of a drug. They can affect antibodies, T cells, B cells, macrophages, or other substances normally produced by the immune system.

People who have immunodeficiency tend to have one infection after another. The infections are severe, and they last longer than they do in other people. Infections of the skin and the membranes lining the mouth, eyes, and digestive tract are common. The pathogens that cause infection are often ones that do not cause disease when present in the bodies of people who have healthy immune systems. Diseases caused by such agents are called *opportunistic infections.* These infections take advantage of the "opportunity" to infect a person who has a weakened immune system.

Innate Immune Deficiency Some people are born with immune deficiencies. These deficiences are usually inherited but are occasionally caused by problems during pregnancy. B cell and antibody defects are the most common kinds of innate immune deficiency. People who have these conditions are prone not only to infections but also to autoimmune disorders. Often, they do not develop immunity following vaccination. T cell defects are less common but more severe than B cell defects. Individuals fail to grow and develop normally, and they tend to develop overwhelming infections. In rare cases, neither the B cell nor the T cell response works. This condition is called *severe combined immunodeficiency (SCID).* Babies who have SCID usually develop severe or even life-threatening infections.

Immune Suppression Sometimes, there is a medical reason to suppress the immune response. For example, after having an organ transplant, a person is given drugs that suppress immune function. Because the body does not recognize the transplanted organ as "self," these drugs are needed to keep the immune system from attacking the organ. The organ transplant recipient shown in **Figure 12** will need to take immunosuppressant drugs for life. Some drugs suppress the immune system as a side effect. Chemotherapy often causes supression of the immune system. People who have suppressed immune systems are more susceptible to opportunistic infections than people with healthy immune systems.

AIDS The best-known acquired immune deficiency disease is **AIDS,** or acquired immune deficiency syndrome. In AIDS, a virus infects and kills helper T cells, shown in **Figure 13.** People who have AIDS are very susceptible to infections. Because only a few helper T cells are left in the body, neither the T cell nor the B cell response is triggered.

The virus that causes AIDS is called **HIV,** or human immunodeficiency virus. HIV is most commonly transmitted through human body fluids, such as semen, blood, and breast milk. Although HIV has been found in saliva, tears, and urine, these body fluids usually contain too few HIV particles to cause an infection. HIV is not transmitted through the air, on toilet seats, by kissing or handshaking, or by other forms of casual contact. Mosquitoes and ticks do not transmit HIV.

Once inside helper T cells, HIV is protected from the normal processes that would destroy it. The virus also uses the organelles of the host cell to produce copies of itself. Helper T cells that are loaded with HIV particles burst open, which releases large numbers of viruses into the bloodstream that can infect new cells. Initially, the immune system responds to the viruses. Antibodies to HIV can be detected in the blood. Someone whose blood contains antibodies to HIV is said to be HIV positive. As the infection progresses, the number of helper T cells decreases and the number of HIV particles increases, as shown in **Figure 13.** It takes an average of 10 years for HIV infection to progress to AIDS. AIDS is fatal in nearly every case. Currently, there is no vaccine or cure for HIV. However, some drugs can slow the progression from HIV infection to AIDS.

❯ **Reading Check** *Which immune cells does HIV destroy, and how does the virus destroy them?*

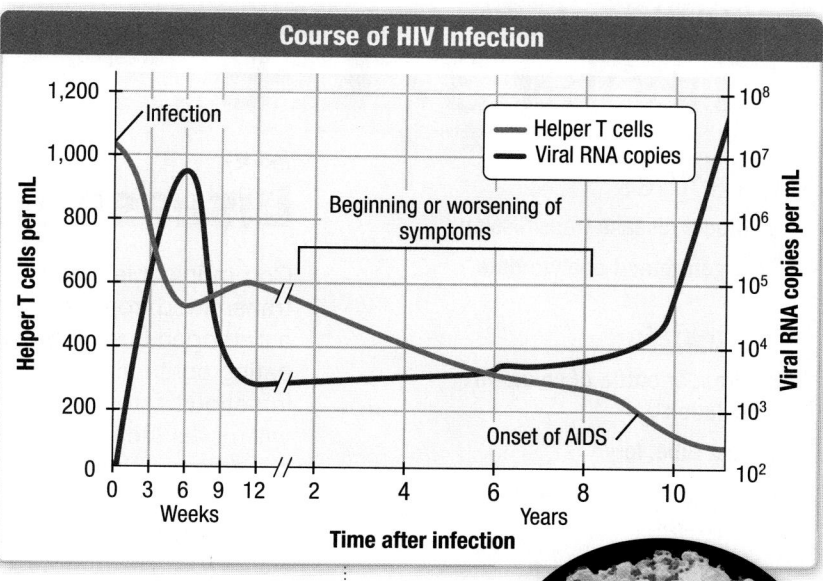

Figure 13 The graph plots the amount of helper T cells and viral RNA copies in the blood during HIV infection. In the micrograph, small HIV particles (orange) surround a helper T cell (white).

❯ **KEY IDEAS**

1. **Describe** what causes an allergic reaction.
2. **Define** what an autoimmune disease is and give an example of one.
3. **List** the causes of immune deficiency.

CRITICAL THINKING

4. **Drawing Conclusions** Would a person who has asthma be able to launch a normal immune response following exposure to an influenza virus? What about a person who has multiple sclerosis?

5. **Determining Factual Accuracy** Why are allergic reactions often referred to as inappropriate responses of the immune system? Explain your reasoning.

USING SCIENCE GRAPHICS

6. **Identifying Variables** In the graph in **Figure 13,** there are many different variables to track. Identify which variables are the dependent variables, and which are the independent variables. Describe the relationships between these variables.

Objectives
> Model disease transmission.
> Organize and analyze data.

Materials
- dropper bottle of unknown solution
- test tube, large
- dropper bottle of indophenol indicator

Safety

Disease Transmission Model

Communicable diseases are caused by pathogens and can be transmitted from one person to another. You can become infected by a pathogen in several ways, including by drinking contaminated water, eating contaminated foods, receiving contaminated blood, and inhaling infectious aerosols (droplets from coughs or sneezes). In this lab, you will model the transmission of a communicable disease. To do this, you will create a simulation of disease transmission. After the simulation, you will try to identify the person who was originally infected in the closed class population.

Procedure
Simulate Disease Transmission
1 Make two data tables similar to the ones shown.

Disease Transmission	
Round number	Partner's name

Disease Source	Names of infected person's partners		
Name of infected person	Round 1	Round 2	Round 3

2 ◈ ◈ ◈ Put on disposable gloves, a lab apron, and safety goggles.

3 ◈ ◈ **CAUTION: Do not touch or taste any chemicals. Exercise caution when working with glassware such as a test tube.** You will be given a dropper bottle of an unknown solution. When your teacher says to begin, transfer three droppersful of your solution to a clean test tube.

4 Select a partner for Round 1. Record the name of this partner in your Disease Transmission table.

5 Together, you and your partner have two test tubes. Pour the contents of one of the test tubes into the other test tube. Then, pour half of the solution back into the first test tube. You and your partner now share any pathogens either of you might have.

6 On your teacher's signal, select a new partner for Round 2. Record this partner's name in your Disease Transmission table. Repeat step 5.

7 On your teacher's signal, select a new partner for Round 3. Record this partner's name in your Disease Transmission table. Repeat step 5.

8 Add one dropperful of indophenol indicator to your test tube. "Infected" solutions will be colorless or will turn light pink. "Uninfected" solutions will turn blue. Record the results of your test.

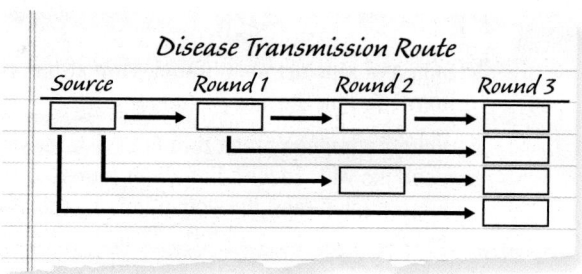

Trace the Disease Source

9 If you are infected, write your name and the name of your partner in each round on the board or on an overhead projector. Mark your infected partners. Record all of the data for your class in your Disease Source table.

10 To trace the source of the infection, cross out the names of the uninfected partners in Round 1. There should be only two names left. One is the name of the original disease carrier. To find the original disease carrier, place a sample from his or her dropper bottle in a clean test tube, and test it with indophenol indicator.

11 To show the disease transmission route, make a diagram similar to the one labeled "Disease Transmission Route." Show the original disease carrier and the people each disease carrier infected.

12 Clean up your lab materials according to your teacher's instructions. Wash your hands thoroughly before leaving the lab.

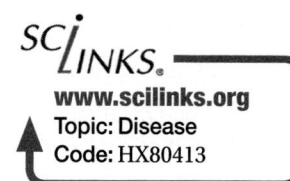

www.scilinks.org
Topic: Disease
Code: HX80413

Analyze and Conclude

1. **SCIENTIFIC METHODS** **Interpreting Data** After Round 3, how many people were infected? Express this number as a percentage of your class.

2. **Relating Concepts** What do you think the clear fluids each student started with represent? Explain your response.

3. **Drawing Conclusions** Can someone who does not show any symptoms of a disease transmit that disease? Explain.

4. **SCIENTIFIC METHODS** **Further Inquiry** Write a new question about disease transmission that could be explored with another investigation.

Extensions

5. On the Job Public health officials, such as food inspectors, research and work to prevent the spread of diseases in human populations. Do research to find out how public health officials trace the origin of communicable diseases.

Key Ideas	Key Terms

1 Protecting Against Disease

> Skin and mucous membranes form strong barriers that prevent pathogens from entering the body.

> When pathogens break through the body's physical barriers, the body quickly responds with second-line defenses—fever, inflammation, and the activation of special proteins that kill or inhibit pathogens.

> When a pathogen infects a cell, the body produces immune cells that specialize in detecing and destroying that specific pathogen.

pathogen (915)
mucous membrane (915)
inflammation (916)
histamine (916)
macrophage (917)
antigen (917)

2 Eliminating Invaders

> A specialized white blood cell called a helper T cells activates the specific immune response. These cells coordinate two responses; the destruction of cells that have been infected by a pathogen, and the removal of pathogens at large in the body.

> Cytotoxic T cells attack and kill cells that have been infected by pathogens.

> The B cell response removes extracellular pathogens from the body and prevents further infection.

> After an immune response, memory cells continue to protect the body from previously encountered pathogens.

helper T cell (919)
cytotoxic T cell (920)
B cell (920)
plasma cell (920)
antibodies (920)
memory cell (922)
immunity (922)
vaccine (922)

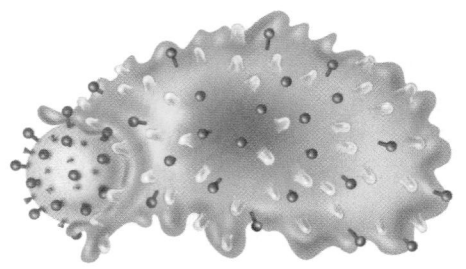

3 Immune System Dysfunctions

> An allergic reaction is an excessive immune response to a normally harmless antigen.

> In an autoimmune disease, the body launches an immune response so that body cells are attacked as if they were pathogens.

> When the immune system does not function, the body is unable to fight and survive infections by pathogens that do not cause problems for a robust immune system.

allergy (924)
allergen (924)
autoimmune disease (927)
AIDS (929)
HIV (929)

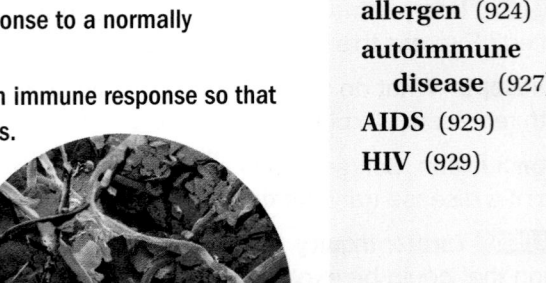

1. **Pattern Puzzles** Create a new pattern puzzle using the specific immune response as your example.

2. **Concept Map** Make a concept map that describes the immune response. Include the following terms in your map: *pathogen, macrophage, helper T cell, cytotoxic T cell, B cell, plasma cell,* and *antibody.*

Using Key Terms

For each pair of terms, explain the relationship between the meanings of the terms.

3. *pathogen* and *antigen*

4. *antibodies* and *plasma cell*

For each pair of terms, explain how the meanings of the terms differ.

5. *helper T cell* and *cytotoxic T cell*

6. *HIV* and *AIDS*

Understanding Key Ideas

7. Some white blood cells are covered with receptor proteins that recognize and bind to
   a. T cells.
   b. antigens.
   c. histamine.
   d. macrophages.

8. Vaccines are effective in preventing disease because they
   a. contain specific types of B cells and T cells.
   b. trigger an immune response without causing disease.
   c. contain antibodies directed against specific pathogens.
   d. contain pathogens to which the person is already immune.

9. Which of the following remains in the body long after an invading pathogen has been eliminated?
   a. plasma cell
   b. memory cell
   c. antibodies
   d. cytotoxic T cell

10. HIV causes AIDS by attacking and destroying
    a. B cells.
    b. helper T cells.
    c. neutrophils.
    d. natural killer cells.

11. How does the body's first line of defense work?
    a. It causes a sneezing reflex.
    b. It causes blood to clot at an injury site.
    c. It allows bacteria to live on the skin's surface.
    d. It physically blocks the entry of pathogens into the body.

12. Fever can indicate that
    a. the pathogen remains on the skin
    b. the body is responding to an infection.
    c. a pathogen has been trapped by mucous.
    d. the body has recovered from an infection.

Use the diagram to answer the following question.

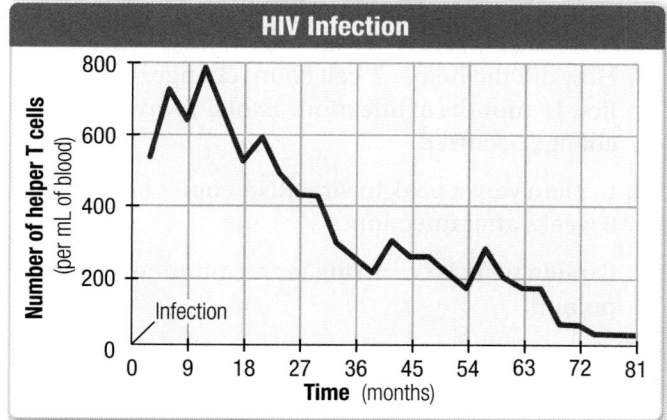

13. A diagnosis of AIDS is made when the helper T cell count is less than 200 cells per mL of blood. How many months after infection did the onset of AIDS occur?
    a. 18
    b. 39
    c. 54
    d. 69

Explaining Key Ideas

14. **Distinguish** between an autoimmune disease and an allergic reaction.

15. **Summarize** the functions of mucous membranes in the immune system.

16. **Outline** the steps of antibody production.

17. **Explain** why fever, inflammation, and protein activation responses are often referred to as the body's "second line of defense."

18. **Outline** the role of helper T cells in the immune response.

Using Science Graphics

The diagram represents helper T cells and viral RNA counts per mL of blood during HIV infection. Use the diagram to answer the following questions.

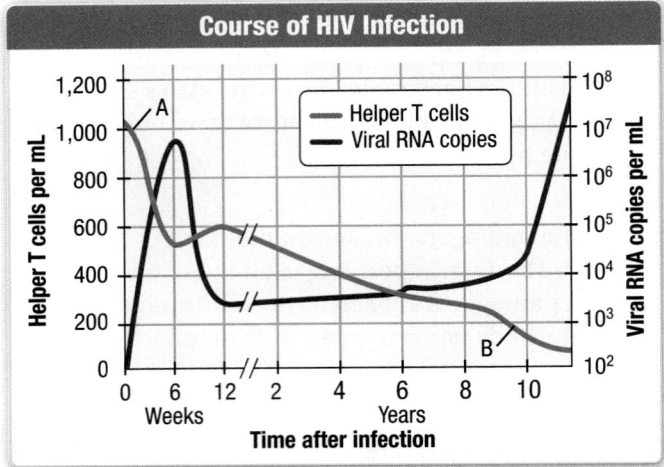

Course of HIV Infection

19. How did the helper T cell count change over the first 18 months of infection? Explain why this change occurred.

20. Explain why a peak in viral RNA copies occurs at 6 weeks after infection.

21. Explain what is occurring in the immune system at point B.

Critical Thinking

22. **Applying Information** Should a person always treat a fever with a fever-reducing drug? Explain.

23. **Making Logical Connections** A person who has a defect in the production of B cell or antibodies often does not develop immunity following vaccination. Given what you know about the immune response, explain why this problem occurs.

24. **Inferring Relationships** People who are severely burned often die from infection. Given what you know about disease transmission, explain why this is common.

25. **Making Logical Connections** Explain why it is unnecessary for a vaccine to contain a whole pathogen.

26. **Making Inferences** In rheumatic fever, a streptococcal infection stimulates the production of antibodies that react not only against the bacteria but also against surface proteins of the heart muscle. Propose a cause for this action.

27. **Relating Concepts** Plasma cells contain a large Golgi apparatus and large amounts of rough endoplasmic reticulum. How is the presence of these organelles related to the function of plasma cells?

28. **Recognizing Relationships** Explain why it might take several weeks after exposure to HIV for a person's HIV antibody test to be positive.

29. **Relating Concepts** Explain why you cannot get many diseases more than once.

30. **Relating Concepts** Explain why taking a drug that reduces fever might delay rather than speed up your recovery from an infection.

Writing for Science

31. **Career Report** Research the field of immunology, and write a report on your findings. Your report should include a job description, education and training required, kinds of employers, growth prospects, and starting salary.

Alternative Assessment

32. **Summarizing Information** Use the media center or the Internet to research three different vaccines. Make a large chart or table on poster board listing the pathogens they protect against, their effectiveness, side effects, and boosters required, if any. Present your findings to your class.

Methods of Science

33. **On the Job** As a public health official, you are sent to investigate an outbreak of a new disease. Devise an experiment to determine whether the disease has been caused by the passing of pathogens from person to person or by environmental conditions.

Science Concepts

1. Which of the following is a nonspecific defense?

  A antibody response

  B the B cell response

  C the T cell response

  D the inflammation response

2. Which of the following statements about plasma cells is true?

  F They engulf pathogens.

  G They produce antibodies.

  H They result from cytotoxic T cells.

  J They are directly stimulated by macrophages.

3. Type 1 diabetes is an example of

  A an allergic reaction.

  B a bacterial infection.

  C an autoimmune disease.

  D an infection that is related to AIDS.

4. HIV disables the immune system by

  F destroying helper T cells.

  G activating production of B cells.

  H blocking the action of macrophages.

  J destroying the production of antibodies.

5. Why are flu vaccines given each year?

  A Influenza viruses mutate often.

  B Influenza is caused by bacteria.

  C Very few memory cells are produced.

  D Macrophages cannot engulf flu viruses.

6. One common symptom of an allergic reaction to airborne antigens is

  F itchy eyes.

  G opening nasal passages.

  H reduced mucus production.

  J a weakened immune response.

7. Which cells produce antibodies and release them into the blood?

  A plasma cells   **C** macrophages

  B helper T cells   **D** cytotoxic T cells

Using Science Graphics

Use the diagram to answer the following question.

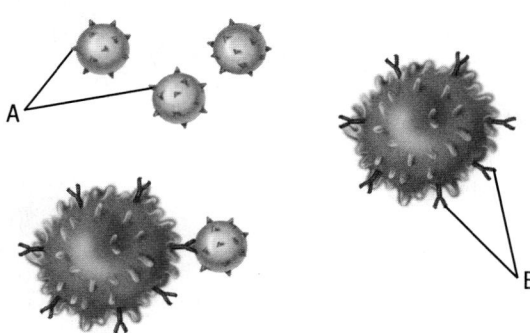

8. Why can structures A and B interact with each other?

  F They are "nonself."

  G They have matching shapes.

  H They are viral proteins.

  J They are produced by the same cells.

Use the diagram to answer the following question.

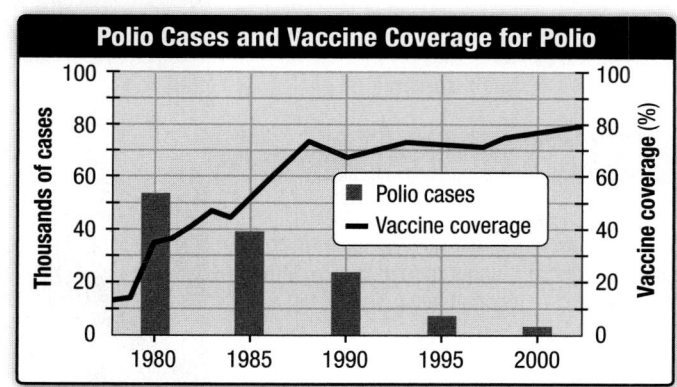

Source: World Health Organization.

9. What is the relationship between the number of polio cases and the percentage of vaccine coverage?

  A They have no relationship.

  B They have a positive relationship.

  C They have a negative relationship.

  D They have an exponential relationship.

Writing Skills

10. Short Response Under what circumstances can a child be born with HIV?

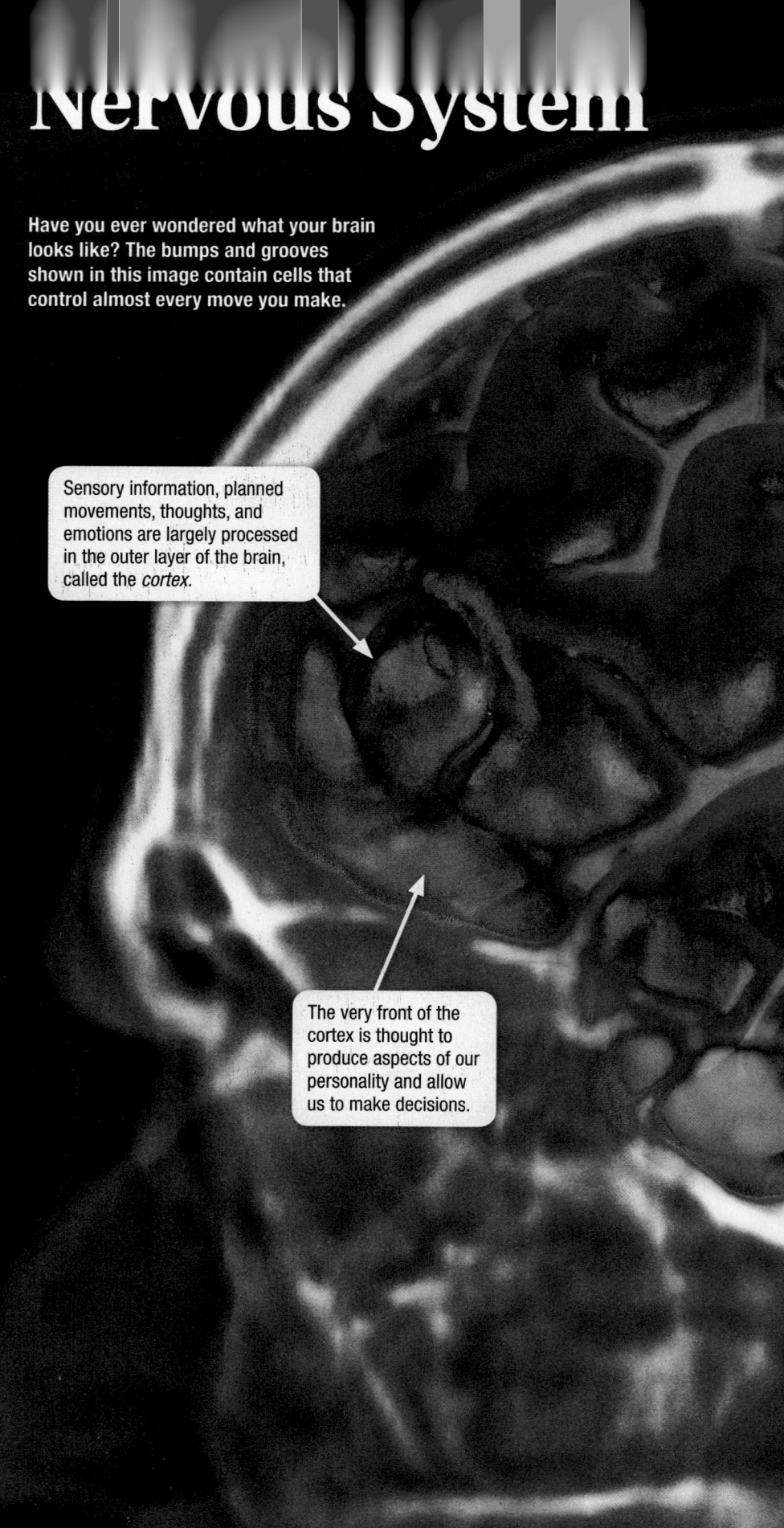

38 Nervous System

Have you ever wondered what your brain looks like? The bumps and grooves shown in this image contain cells that control almost every move you make.

Sensory information, planned movements, thoughts, and emotions are largely processed in the outer layer of the brain, called the *cortex*.

The very front of the cortex is thought to produce aspects of our personality and allow us to make decisions.

Preview

1 Structures of the Nervous System
Central Nervous System
Peripheral Nervous System
The Spinal Reflex

2 Neurons and Nerve Impulses
Our Electrical Body
Structure of Neurons
Generating a Nerve Impulse
Communication Between Neurons

3 Sensory Systems
Perception of Stimuli
Sensory Receptors
Processing Sensory Information

4 Nervous System Dysfunction
Psychoactive Drugs
Neural Changes
Nervous System Disorders

Why It Matters

The nervous system might be the most important system in our body. It allows us to do amazing things! Without our nervous system, we could not function at all.

InquiryLab

Pass It On

Nerve cells joined end to end compose a network of transmission lines that carry messages throughout your body. Traveling along these fixed paths, the nerve message is carried as a simple code of pulses.

Procedure

1. Work in teams of two. On a level desktop, stand a **single domino** up on end. Apply a slight push to the top of this domino. What happens?

2. Stand **40 dominoes** in a column. Apply a slight push to the end domino. What happened to the column of dominoes?

3. Shape a **length of kite string** into the outline of an arm and hand. Secure the shape with **tape.**

4. Set up two side-by-side columns of dominoes positioned within the arm outline.

5. Apply a slight push to the end domino of the column that is closest to the shoulder. Observe the behavior of the column.

6. Apply a slight push to the end domino of the other column, which is closest to the hand. Observe the behavior of the column.

Analysis

1. **Classify** the form of energy that the domino gains when it is stood upright.

2. **Propose** how pushing the end domino models the start of a nerve message.

3. **Explain** how the pulse traveling in each of the two side-by-side columns differs.

4. **Evaluate** whether the action of the cascading dominos is an accurate model for how nerve impulses are transmitted in the arm.

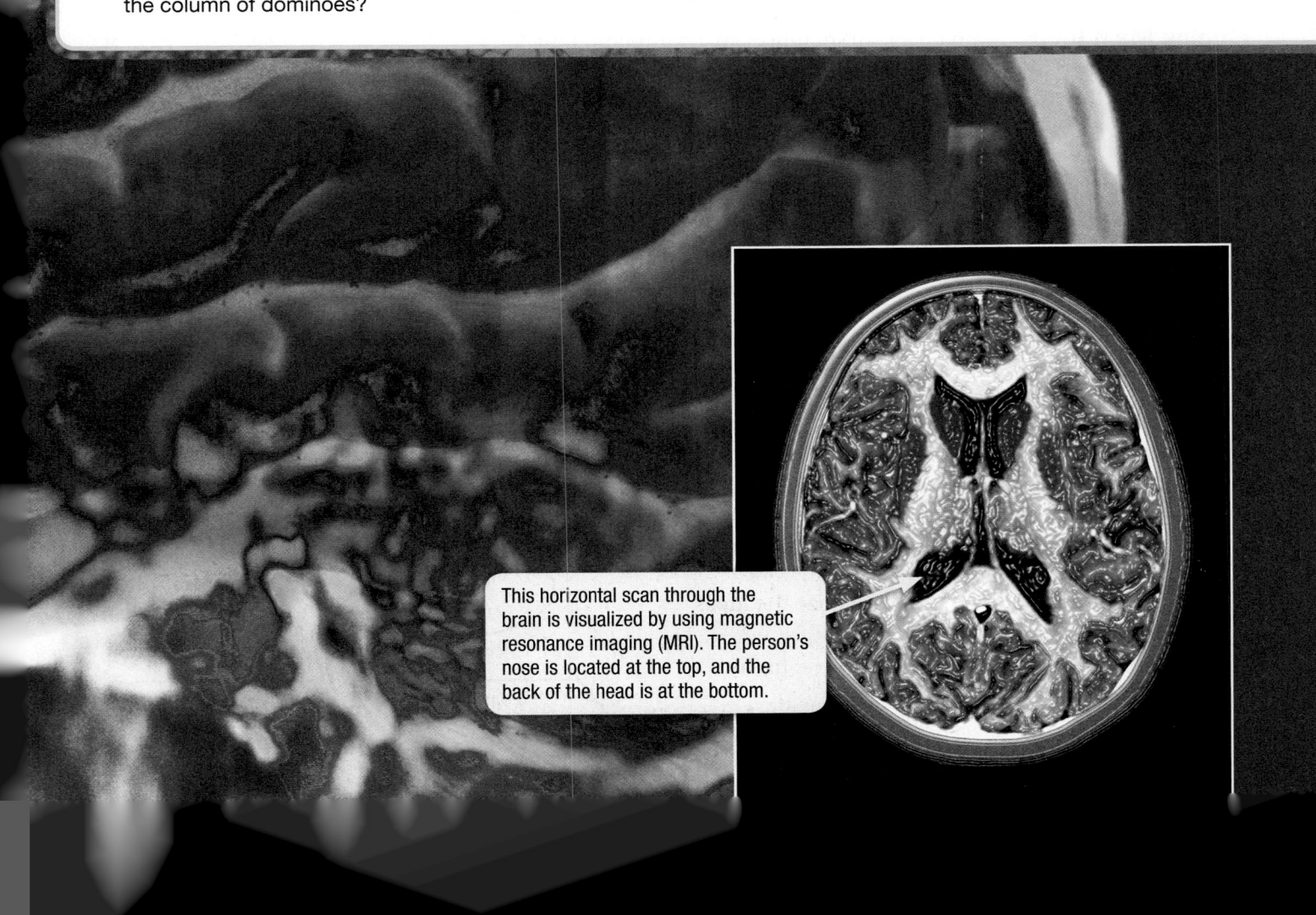

This horizontal scan through the brain is visualized by using magnetic resonance imaging (MRI). The person's nose is located at the top, and the back of the head is at the bottom.

READING TOOLBOX

These reading tools can help you learn the material in this chapter. For more information on how to use these and other tools, see **Appendix: Reading and Study Skills.**

Using Words

Key-Term Fold A key-term fold is useful for studying the definitions of key terms in a chapter. Each tab can contain a key term on one side and its definition on the other.

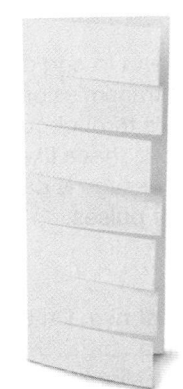

Your Turn Make a key-term fold to to help you study the definitions of the key terms in this chapter.

1. Fold a sheet of lined notebook paper in half from left to right.

2. Using scissors, cut along every third line from the right edge of the paper to the center fold to make tabs.

Using Language

Finding Main Ideas Main ideas are sentences in a paragraph that tell you what the paragraph is about. Sometimes the main idea is easy to find. Other times it may be hard to identify.

Your Turn Read the passage below and identify the main idea.

A reflex is a very fast, involuntary contraction of muscles in response to a stimulus. If you touched a hot skillet on the stove, your hand would immediately jerk away even before you sensed the pain of the hot pan. This response is an example of a reflex.

Using Graphic Organizers

Spider Map A spider map is useful for grouping details around a topic. As you read about sensory systems, look for the main ideas or characteristics about each system. Within each idea, look for details.

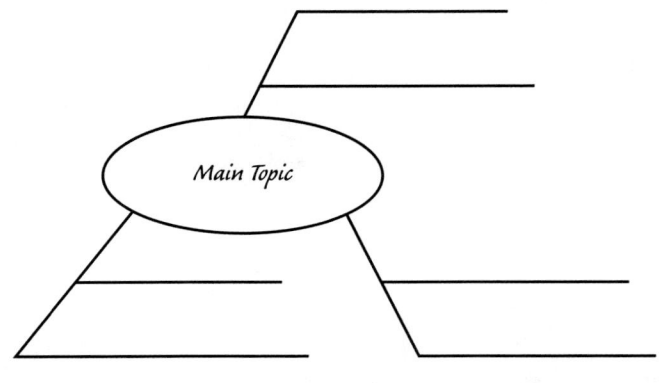

Main Topic

Your Turn Use a spider map to organize the ideas and details of each sensory system.

1. Draw a diagram like the one shown here. In the circle, write the main topic.

2. From the circle, draw legs to represent the main ideas or characteristics of the topic. Write one idea along each leg.

3. From each leg, draw horizontal lines. As you read the chapter, write details about each idea on the idea's horizontal lines. To add more details, make the legs longer and add more horizontal lines.

Structures of the Nervous System

Key Ideas	Key Terms	Why It Matters

❯ What is the function of the central nervous system?
 	
 ❯ What are the two components of the peripheral nervous system?
 	
 ❯ How is a spinal reflex generated?
	neuron
	 central nervous
	    system
	 peripheral nervous
	    system
	 brain
	
	 cerebrum
	 brainstem
	 cerebellum
	 spinal cord
	 reflex
		Your nervous system is made up of billions of nerve cells. These cells transmit signals throughout your body and allow you to carry out all of your normal activities.

The nervous system is a highly organized network of signaling cells. These signaling cells are called *neurons.* **Neurons** are nerve cells that send electrical signals in order to communicate with each other and with muscles and glands. The brain integrates and controls every action that we take. The signals of the nervous system are both electrical and chemical, and their rapid conduction in the body often occurs over long distances.

Central Nervous System

How are neurons organized in the nervous system? As **Figure 1** shows, there are two main divisions of the nervous system—the central nervous system, shown in orange, and the peripheral nervous system, shown in purple. ❯ **The central nervous system responds to internal and external information.** The **central nervous system** (CNS) is the main control center of the body, and contains the brain and spinal cord. The **peripheral nervous system** (PNS) contains specialized cells called sensory neurons and motor neurons. These cells are responsible for communicating between the CNS and the rest of the body. *Sensory neurons* send information from sense organs, such as the skin, to the CNS. *Motor neurons* send commands from the CNS to muscles and other organs, such as glands.

❯ **Reading Check** *What is a neuron? (See the Appendix for answers to Reading Checks.)*

Brain

Spinal cord

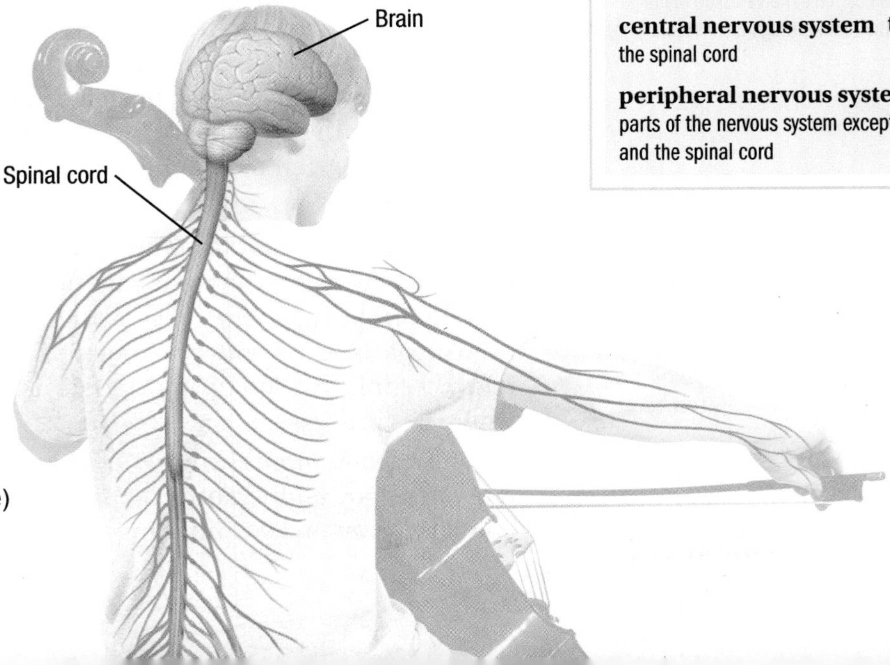

Figure 1 The central nervous system (orange) consists of the brain and the spinal cord. The peripheral nervous system (purple) branches throughout the body.

neuron (NOO RAHN) a nerve cell that is specialized to receive and conduct electrical impulses

central nervous system the brain and the spinal cord

peripheral nervous system all of the parts of the nervous system except for the brain and the spinal cord

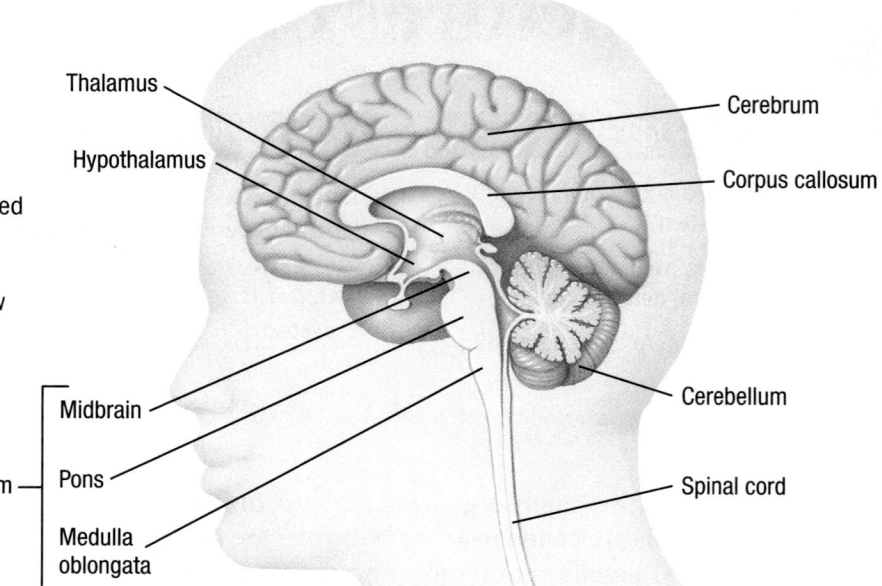

Figure 2 The cerebrum is divided into two hemispheres. This view shows the right hemisphere. The cerebral cortex and regions below the cortex are also shown.

Thalamus

Hypothalamus

Cerebrum

Corpus callosum

Cerebellum

Spinal cord

Brainstem
- Midbrain
- Pons
- Medulla oblongata

brain the mass of nervous tissue that is the main control center of the nervous system

cerebrum (suh REE brum) the upper part of the brain that receives sensation and controls movement

brainstem the stemlike portion of the brain that connects the cerebral hemispheres with the spinal cord and that maintains the necessary functions of the body, such as breathing and circulation

cerebellum (SER uh BEL uhm) a posterior portion of the brain that coordinates muscle movement and controls subconscious activities and some balance functions

spinal cord a column of nerve tissue running from the base of the brain through the vertebral column

READING TOOLBOX

Finding Main Ideas Find the main idea related to the thalamus and hypothalamus. Write a paragraph describing how these two structures are related to each other.

Brain The **brain** is the body's main processing center. Located within the skull, the brain contains about 100 billion neurons. Thoughts, feelings, emotions, behavior, perception, and memories are controlled by your brain. Your brain also enables you to learn and process information, such as the text in this book. Several parts of the brain, such as the cerebrum, the thalamus and hypothalamus, the brainstem, and the cerebellum are shown in **Figure 2.**

Cerebrum The **cerebrum** is the largest part of the brain. The folded outer surface of the cerebrum is the *cerebral cortex*, or *cortex,* which controls most sensory and motor processing in the brain. The inner areas of the cerebrum consist mostly of axons of neurons. Axons transmit signals to and from the cortex. This region also contains neurons that are involved in coordinating movements.

A long, deep groove down the center divides the cerebrum into right and left halves, or hemispheres. The cerebral hemispheres communicate through a connecting band of nerves called the *corpus callosum.* In general, the left cerebral hemisphere receives sensations from and controls movements of the right side of the body. The right cerebral hemisphere receives sensations from and controls movements of the left side of the body.

Thalamus and Hypothalamus Two structures located below the cerebrum have important roles in integrating information. The *thalamus* is a critical site for sensory processing. Sensory information from all parts of the body converges on the thalamus. The thalamus relays the information to appropriate areas of the cerebral cortex, where it is processed.

The *hypothalamus* controls feelings of hunger and thirst and regulates body temperature. It also regulates many functions of the endocrine system by controlling the secretion of many hormones.

Brainstem At the base of the brain is the brainstem. The **brainstem** consists of the midbrain, the pons, and the medulla oblongata. These structures play an important role in homeostasis. For example, the brainstem regulates vital functions, such as heart rate and breathing rate. In the medulla, most neurons carrying signals from the cerebral cortex to muscles and glands cross from one side to the other. As a result, each side of the cortex controls the opposite side of the body.

Cerebellum The **cerebellum** is located behind the brainstem, and regulates balance, posture, and movement. The cerebellum coordinates movements, such as walking, by timing the contraction of skeletal muscles. The cerebellum also responds to information about body position from the cerebrum and the spinal cord to control balance and posture. This coordination produces the action in **Figure 3.**

Spinal Cord The **spinal cord** is a thick column of nerve tissue that runs through the vertebral column and links the brain to most of the PNS. Sensory information from neurons in the PNS travels upward through the spinal cord to the brain. The brain then sends commands down through the spinal cord to the PNS in order to control the body. The spinal cord also functions in reflexes, which are simple involuntary responses to stimuli.

The spinal cord is linked to the PNS through paired spinal nerves, shown in **Figure 4.** Spinal nerves in the upper part of the spinal cord control the arms and upper body. Spinal nerves in the lower part of the spinal cord control the legs and lower body.

Each spinal nerve has a dorsal root and a ventral root. Dorsal (back) roots contain sensory neurons that carry incoming sensory information. Ventral (front) roots contain motor neurons that carry outgoing motor stimuli. **Figure 4** shows dorsal and ventral roots come together just outside the spinal cord to form the spinal nerves. The spinal cord contains a core of gray matter surrounded by white matter. Gray matter contains the cell bodies of neurons, whereas white matter contains axons.

Figure 3 The cerebellum is critical for performing intricately timed movements, such as gymnastics. ❯ **What are other functions of the cerebellum?**

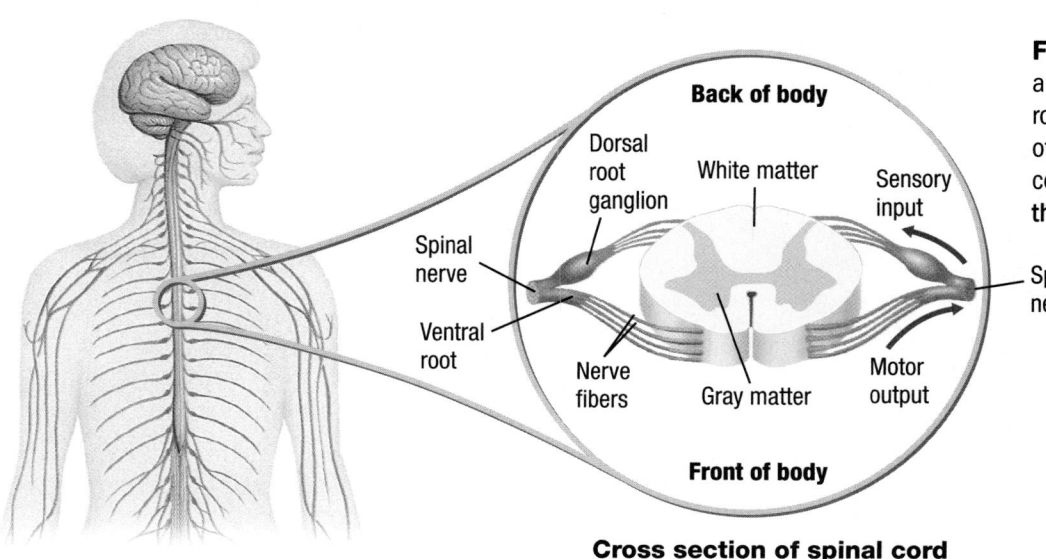

Back of body

Dorsal root ganglion

White matter

Sensory input

Spinal nerve

Ventral root

Nerve fibers

Gray matter

Motor output

Spinal nerve

Front of body

Cross section of spinal cord

Figure 4 Spinal nerves have a dorsal root and a ventral root that split away from each other as they enter the spinal cord. ❯ **What information does the dorsal root ganglion carry?**

SCILINKS.
www.scilinks.org
Topic: Autonomic Nervous System
Code: HX80126

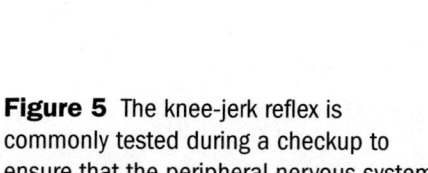

Peripheral Nervous System

› The peripheral nervous system contains sensory and motor neurons that carry information between the central nervous system and the rest of the body. The motor functions of the peripheral nervous system are grouped into two independent systems—the *autonomic nervous system* and the *somatic nervous system.*

Autonomic Nervous System Motor neurons that control smooth muscles do not require our conscious control. These neurons are part of the autonomic nervous system.

Two divisions of the autonomic nervous system maintain homeostasis by balancing the effects that each one has on the body. The parasympathetic division restores normal conditions after a change. It stimulates digestion after a meal and slows the heart rate after exercise. In contrast, the sympathetic division prepares the body for action. For example, the sympathetic division controls the "fight-or-flight" response that you experience in a stressful situation, such as having to take a pop quiz. It also increases blood flow to your heart and skeletal muscles and away from digestive activities.

Somatic Nervous System Most motor neurons that stimulate skeletal muscles are under our conscious control. For example, we choose to use our leg muscles to walk across a room. The neurons that trigger these responses are part of the somatic nervous system. It responds to signals from the environment outside the body. Some activity, such as the spinal reflex shown in **Figure 5,** is involuntary.

Figure 5 The knee-jerk reflex is commonly tested during a checkup to ensure that the peripheral nervous system and spinal cord are functioning properly.

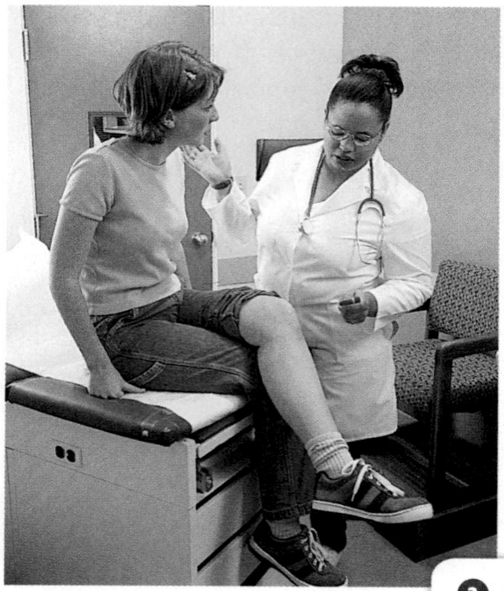

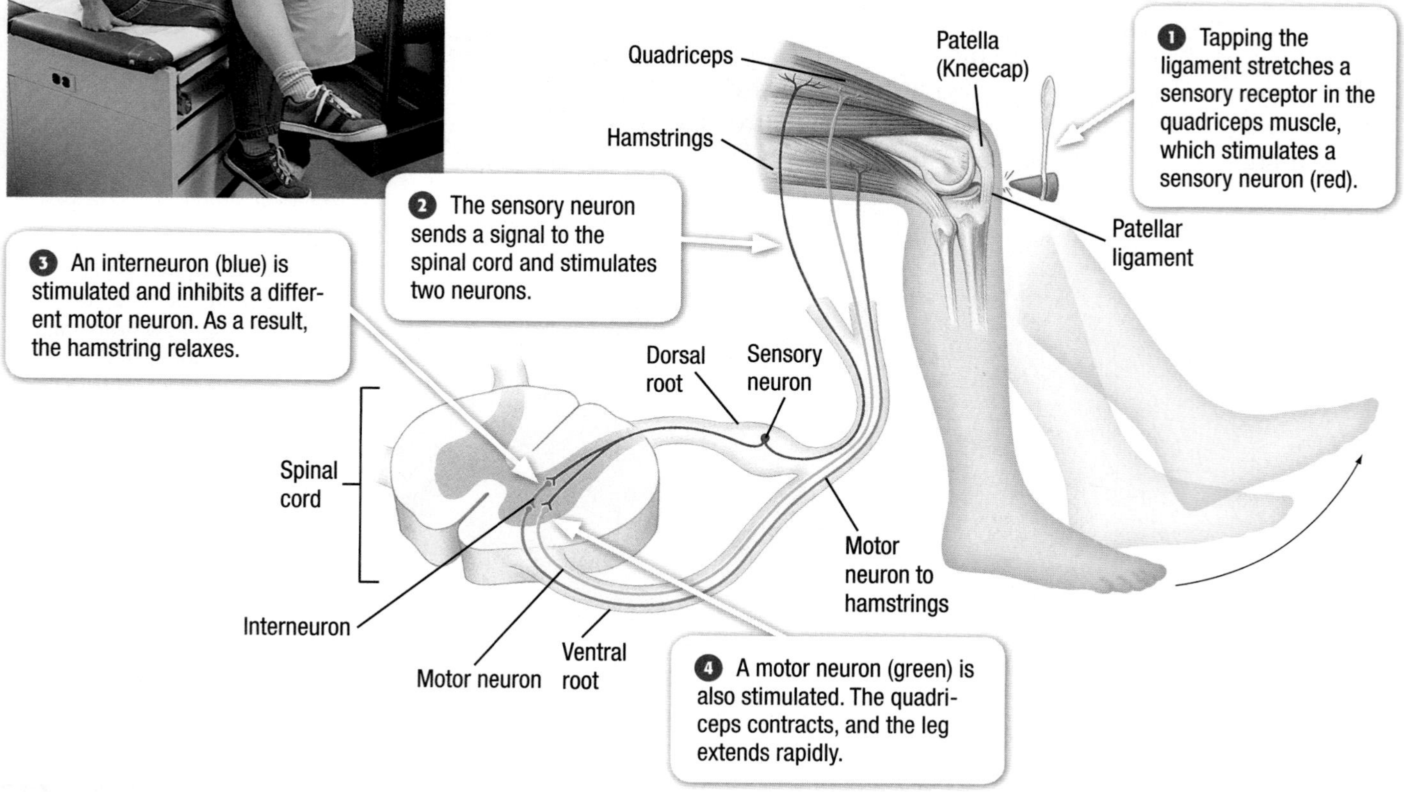

Quadriceps
Patella (Kneecap)
1 Tapping the ligament stretches a sensory receptor in the quadriceps muscle, which stimulates a sensory neuron (red).
Hamstrings
Patellar ligament
2 The sensory neuron sends a signal to the spinal cord and stimulates two neurons.
3 An interneuron (blue) is stimulated and inhibits a different motor neuron. As a result, the hamstring relaxes.
Dorsal root
Sensory neuron
Spinal cord
Motor neuron to hamstrings
Interneuron
Motor neuron
Ventral root
4 A motor neuron (green) is also stimulated. The quadriceps contracts, and the leg extends rapidly.

Knee-Jerk Reflex

A spinal reflex does not require conscious control. In this activity, you'll explore this involuntary action in the knee-jerk reflex.

Procedure

❶ Work with a partner. Assign the role of subject and researcher. The subject crosses his or her legs. The upper leg should swing freely.

❷ Upon hearing an auditory cue spoken by the researcher, the subject jerks the leg upward in a quick and controlled movement.

❸ Next, the researcher uses the side of his or her hand to gently strike a region just below the subject's kneecap. A tap applied to the correct region will produce the characteristic knee-jerk response.

❹ Once this activity is complete, exchange roles and repeat these steps.

Analysis

1. **Explain** if the movement of a jerked knee is under conscious control or unconscious control.

2. **CRITICAL THINKING** **Evaluating Results** Can the knee-jerk reflex be blocked by conscious control?

The Spinal Reflex

A **reflex** is a very fast, involuntary contraction of muscles in response to a stimulus. If you touched a hot skillet on the stove, your hand would immediately jerk away even before you sensed the pain of the hot pan. This response is an example of a spinal reflex. **❯ A spinal reflex is an involuntary movement triggered by sensory input and produced by neural circuitry limited to the spinal cord.** Your brain recognizes the stimulus that triggers a reflexive response as pain. However, the brain does not produce the signals that cause the response. A reflex protects the stimulated part of the body. It also sends information to your brain so that you can learn to avoid similar circumstances in the future. The knee-jerk reflex, shown in **Figure 5,** is another familiar example of a spinal reflex. The stimulus of the rubber mallet triggers a circuit in the spinal cord. This circuit involves sensory neurons, motor neurons, and neurons that send signals over a short distance.

reflex an involuntary and almost immediate movement in response to a stimulus

> **Reading Check** *What neurons are involved in a spinal reflex?*

Section

1 Review

❯ KEY IDEAS

1. **State** the function of the central nervous system.

2. **Describe** the major role of the peripheral nervous system.

3. **Sequence** the neurons through which a knee-jerk reflex travels.

CRITICAL THINKING

4. **Comparing Functions** Why is a spinal reflex more rapid than a voluntary movement?

5. **Relating Concepts** Name the division of the autonomic nervous system that is more active under normal conditions.

ALTERNATIVE ASSESSMENT

6. **Poster** Conduct research on split-brain surgeries, and prepare a poster illustrating the results of these procedures. Include explanations for the observed results as well as the reasons for doing split-brain surgeries.

2 Neurons and Nerve Impulses

Key Ideas	Key Terms	Why It Matters
❯ How does the body conduct electricity? ❯ How does a neuron's structure allow the neuron to send electrical signals? ❯ How is a nerve impulse generated? ❯ How do neurons communicate with each other?	dendrite axon nerve membrane potential action potential synapse neurotransmitter	Enormous amounts of information are sent through the cells of your nervous system. This information is in the form of chemical and electrical signals.

Your body has two systems that control and coordinate the functions of your body. These systems are the nervous system and the endocrine system. Both systems use chemical signals, but the nervous system sends signals more rapidly because it also uses electrical signals. Electrical signals are rapid in case your brain has an urgent message for your body. For example, a message to your leg muscles could be "Contract quickly! A speeding car is headed this way!"

Our Electrical Body

It may be hard to believe that the body sends electrical signals. How do we know that the body uses electricity to send signals? Luigi Galvani, an Italian scientist from the 18th century, first discovered that electricity could come from animal tissue. Galvani conducted an experiment using the muscles of a frog that had recently died and some metal wires. He first placed a wire in the frog's spinal cord to stabilize it. When he touched a different metal wire to the frog's leg, the leg twitched as if it were alive! He concluded that animal tissue contained a vital force that he called "animal electricity."

Alessandro Volta, another Italian scientist, believed that electricity came from metal itself. Using a different experimental procedure, Volta produced electric currents without animal tissue. He concluded that animal tissue did not produce electricity.

In a sense, both scientists were correct. Each of their conclusions was supported by the evidence they gathered. However, their conclusions were very different. Scientists now understand that Galvani's "animal electricity" was caused by the flow of ions that occurs naturally in most neurons, such as the one shown in **Figure 6.** ❯ Electrical signals in the nervous system are caused by the movement of ions across the cell membrane of neurons.

Figure 6 Purkinje cells are among the largest nerve cells in the body. ❯ **What kinds of signals do these cells send to other parts of the body?**

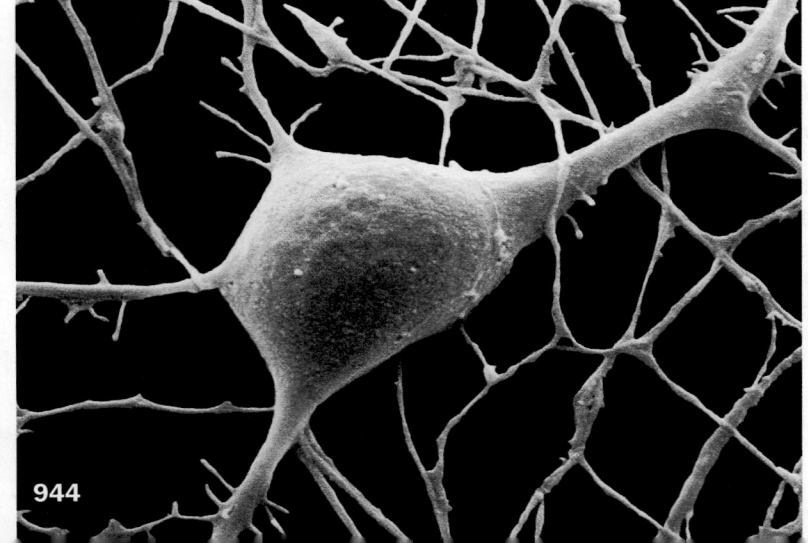

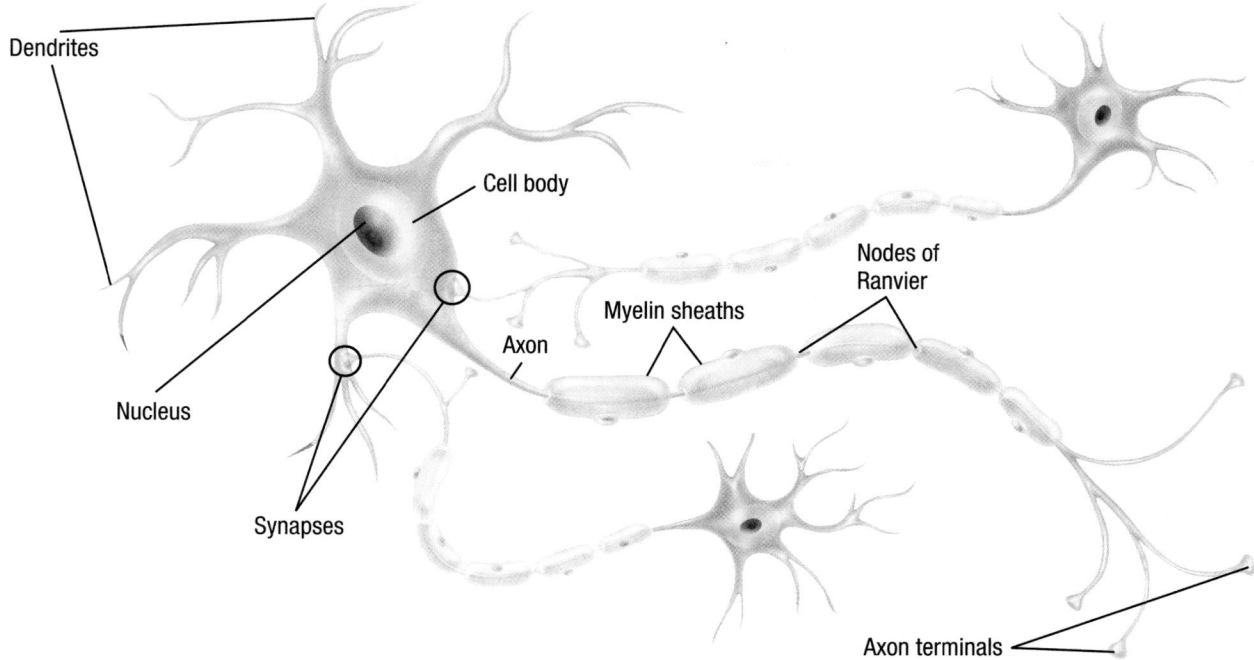

Dendrites

Cell body

Nodes of
Ranvier

Myelin sheaths

Axon

Nucleus

Synapses

Axon terminals

Structure of Neurons

The signaling network that makes up the human nervous system contains neurons. Nervous tissue consists mostly of neurons and their supporting cells.

A neuron's unique structure allows the neuron to conduct electrical signals, also called *nerve impulses.* Neurons vary greatly in form, but a typical cell is similar to the one shown in **Figure 7.** The cell body contains the cell's nucleus. **Dendrites,** which extend from the cell body, are the "antennae" of the neuron. Dendrites receive information from other cells. The neuron's cell body collects information from dendrites and relays this information to other parts of the neuron. An **axon** is a long, slender projection of the nerve cell that conducts electrical impulses away from the cell body. The ends of an axon are called *axon terminals.* A neuron communicates with other cells from its axon terminal. ❯ **A neuron's dendrites gather information from other cells, the cell body integrates this information, and the axon sends the information to other cells.**

Many axons are coated with a layer of insulation. This layer is called a *myelin sheath.* It causes nerve impulses to travel more rapidly than neurons without this insulating layer. The myelin sheath is produced by supporting cells that wrap around the axon. The layer of insulation is not continuous along the axon. The gaps between the sections of myelin are called *nodes of Ranvier.* Ions contained in the extracellular fluid can cross the axon membrane only at these gaps. Thus, the gaps are important for the conduction of nerve impulses.

Bundles of axons are called **nerves.** The arrangement of axons in a nerve is similar to a telephone cable that has many communication channels, each of which is carried by a separate wire.

❯ **Reading Check** *What part of the cell sends electrical signals?*

Figure 7 Because of its unique structure, a neuron can send electrical signals to other cells and throughout the body. ❯ **What part of a cell integrates information from other cells?**

dendrite (DEN DRIET) a cytoplasmic extension of a neuron that receives stimuli

axon (AK SAHN) an elongated extension of a neuron that carries impulses away from the cell body

nerve a collection of nerve fibers through which impulses travel between the central nervous system and other parts of the body

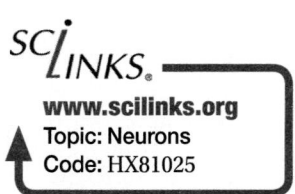

SCI*LINKS.*

www.scilinks.org
Topic: Neurons
Code: HX81025

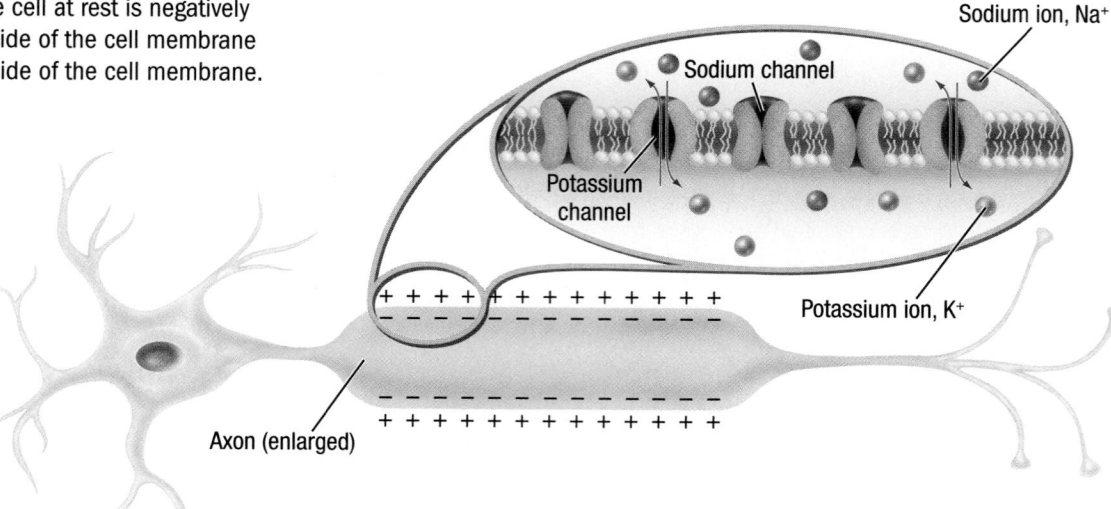

Figure 8 A nerve cell at rest is negatively charged on the inside of the cell membrane relative to the outside of the cell membrane.

Sodium ion, Na⁺

Sodium channel

Potassium channel

Potassium ion, K⁺

Axon (enlarged)

Generating a Nerve Impulse

On the inner surface of their cell membrane, all cells have an electric charge. This charge is different from the electric charge of the fluid outside the cells. The difference in electric charge between the inside of the cell and the outside of the cell is called the **membrane potential.** This difference stems from an uneven <u>distribution</u> of ions inside and outside a cell. Such a difference depends on the relative concentration of ions inside and outside the cell, the ability of the ions to cross the cell membrane, and the electric charge of the ions. When ions flow across the cell membrane, electricity is generated. This electricity is expressed as voltage, but is much smaller than the voltage of a battery.

The membrane potential of neurons and a few other kinds of cells, including muscle cells, can be altered. These changes lead to the generation of an electrical signal called an **action potential.** Neurons generate these types of nerve impulses in order to communicate. ❯ **All nerve impulses begin when the resting state of a neuron is changed by a signal from another neuron or from the environment.**

Resting Potential When a neuron is not conducting a nerve impulse, it is said to be at rest. This resting state is called the *resting potential* and is illustrated in **Figure 8.** In a typical neuron, the resting potential is negative, meaning the inside of the cell is negatively charged relative to the outside of the cell.

The resting potential is negative for many reasons. First, recall that the sodium-potassium pump actively transports more Na⁺ ions out of the cell than it pumps K⁺ ions into the cell. As a result, there are more positive ions on the outside of the cell than there are on the inside. The sodium-potassium pump is critical for maintaining the cell at rest. Second, the cell membrane allows some K⁺ ions (but not Na⁺ ions) to diffuse down their concentration gradient and out of the cell. This action removes some positive charge from the inside of the cell. Third, neurons also contain negatively charged molecules and proteins that are too large to exit the cell.

Figure 9 An action potential moves rapidly down an axon toward the axon terminal. ❯ **What event produces an action potential?**

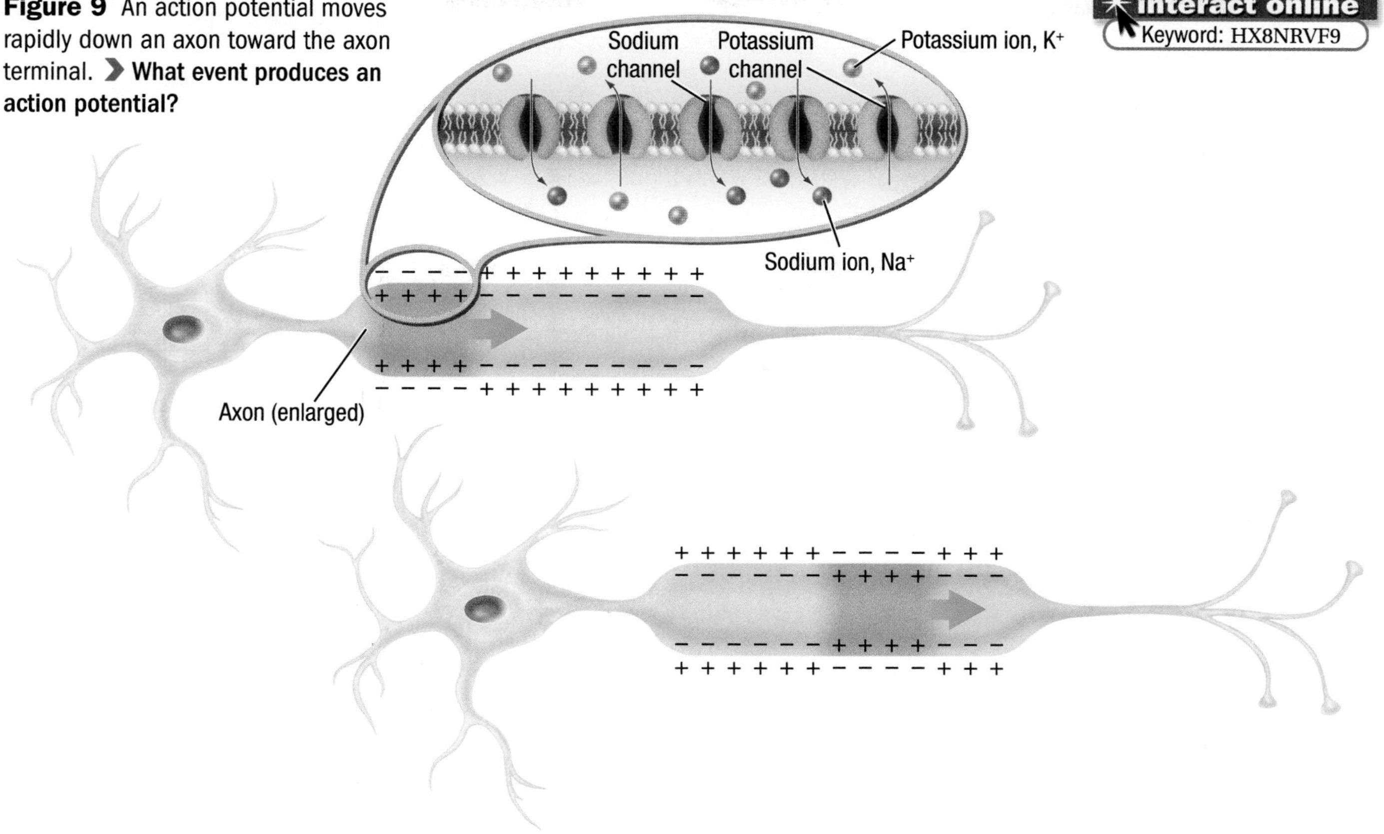

Sodium channel Potassium channel Potassium ion, K⁺

Sodium ion, Na⁺

Axon (enlarged)

Action Potential When a neuron receives a stimulus, its cell membrane changes. Some stimuli received by a neuron cause Na⁺ channels in its membrane to open. Na⁺ ions rapidly flow into the cell down their concentration gradient, and make the cell less negative on the inside. The result may be an action potential, shown in **Figure 9.**

An action potential causes a rapid change in the membrane potential to a more positive value. This sudden reversal of membrane potential begins a chain reaction. Na⁺ channels open one after another down the entire length of the axon. As each Na⁺ channel opens, Na⁺ ions flow into the cell and make the membrane more positive on the inside than on the outside. For a brief moment, the membrane potential becomes positive. Then, K⁺ channels in the membrane open, and K⁺ ions flow out of the cell. The cell membrane becomes negative, and the cell eventually returns to a resting state.

Threshold Cells receive stimuli that vary in how strong (positive) they are from nearby cells. However, a more positive stimulus will not produce a larger action potential. The action potential is "all-or-none," which means that a stimulus either will or will not produce an action potential. The critical point at which a stimulus causes an action potential is called the *threshold*. If the inward ion movement in response to a stimulus is too weak to trigger this event, an action potential will not begin. However, this weak stimulus will not be lost. It will be added to a future stimulus.

❯ **Reading Check** *What structure keeps a neuron in its resting state?*

READING TOOLBOX

Finding Main Ideas Find the main ideas of the concept of threshold. Write a short paragraph describing threshold in your own words.

QuickLab

⏱ 15 min

The Action Potential

An action potential changes the membrane potential from a negative resting value to a positive value. Once the membrane potential peaks, the value becomes negative again until the cell is at rest. This graph illustrates changes that occur in the membrane potential during an action potential. Use the graph to answer the following questions. Refer to **Figure 9** as needed.

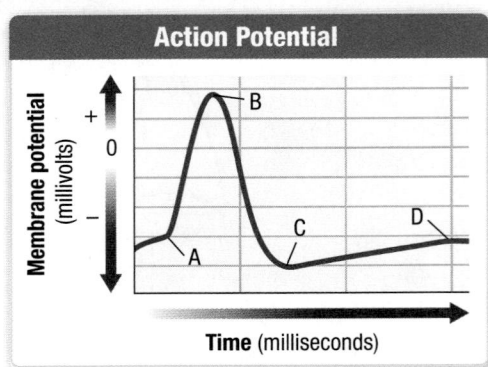

Action Potential

Membrane potential (millivolts)

Time (milliseconds)

Analysis

1. **Determine** whether the membrane potential at point A is positive or negative.

2. **Interpret** what is happening to the membrane potential at point B.

3. **CRITICAL THINKING** **Recognizing Relationships** What is the term used to describe the membrane potential at point A?

4. **CRITICAL THINKING** **Recognizing Relationships** What events cause the changes in the membrane potential that occur at point B?

---

synapse (SIN APS) the junction at which the end of the axon of a neuron meets the end of a dendrite or the cell body of another neuron or meets another cell

neurotransmitter (NOO roh TRANS MIT uhr) a chemical substance that transmits nerve impulses across a synapse

Figure 10 At this synapse, a motor neuron (green) makes contact with a muscle fiber (red).

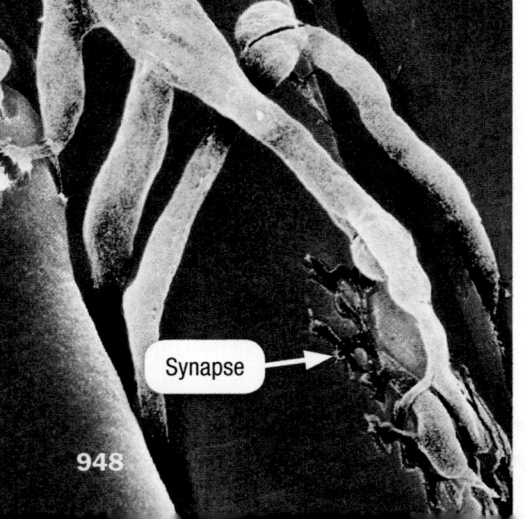

Synapse

Communication Between Neurons

A place where a neuron meets another cell is called a **synapse.**
❯ Neurons communicate with other cells at specialized junctions called synapses. Chemicals are released at synapses and can stimulate nearby cells. At synapses, neurons usually do not touch the cells they communicate with. Between an axon terminal and a receiving cell is a tiny gap called a *synaptic cleft.* At a synapse, the transmitting neuron is called a *presynaptic neuron,* and the receiving cell is called a *postsynaptic cell.* Postsynaptic cells may be neurons, muscle cells, or glands.

Neurotransmitter Release When an action potential arrives at the axon terminal of a presynaptic neuron, the electric impulse cannot cross the gap to the postsynaptic cell. Instead, the impulse triggers the release of a chemical from the presynaptic cell called a **neurotransmitter** into the gap between the two cells. Different neurotransmitters have different strengths. Some have opposing effects on each other. Recall that a stimulus does not always trigger an action potential. Likewise, a neurotransmitter does not always trigger a response in the postsynaptic cell.

Neurotransmitters are produced in the cell body of neurons and are stored inside vesicles. When an action potential reaches the axon terminal of a presynaptic neuron, vesicles fuse with the cell membrane. Then, neurotransmitter molecules are released by exocytosis.

There are many types of neurotransmitters and several ways in which they work. In the muscle shown in **Figure 10,** the presence of a neurotransmitter in a synapse between a motor neuron and a muscle cell likely causes the muscle cell to contract.

❯ **Reading Check** *How are neurotransmitters released?*

Neurotransmitter Action Neurotransmitters do not cause changes in the postsynaptic cell themselves. Once released, neurotransmitters bind to receptors on the postsynaptic cell membrane. This response is illustrated in **Figure 11.** In doing so, neurotransmitters influence whether specific ion channels will open. The flow of ions through these channels causes changes in the postsynaptic membrane potential.

A neurotransmitter may either excite or inhibit the activity of the postsynaptic cell that it binds to. For example, if positively charged ions enter the postsynaptic cell, the cell is excited and may produce an action potential. On the other hand, if positively charged ions flow out of the postsynaptic cell or if negatively charged ions enter the cell, the cell is inhibited and an action potential may be suppressed.

Neurotransmitter Removal Most neurotransmitters are cleared from the synaptic cleft very shortly after they are released. Many presynaptic neurons reabsorb neurotransmitters and use them again. At other synapses, neurotransmitters are broken down by enzymes or other chemicals. This happens, for example, at the synapses between neurons and skeletal muscle cells.

The actions of neurotransmitters are short-term. The halt of neurotransmitter activity ensures that the effect on postsynaptic cells is not prolonged. A pause between nerve impulses allows the nerve cell to reset itself. Interference with this normal start-stop pattern can have harmful effects. For example, an ingredient in many insecticides inhibits the enzyme that breaks down neurotransmitters in synapses between motor neurons and skeletal muscle cells. Thus, the muscles are constantly stimulated by too many neurotransmitter molecules in the synapse. This result kills many types of insects.

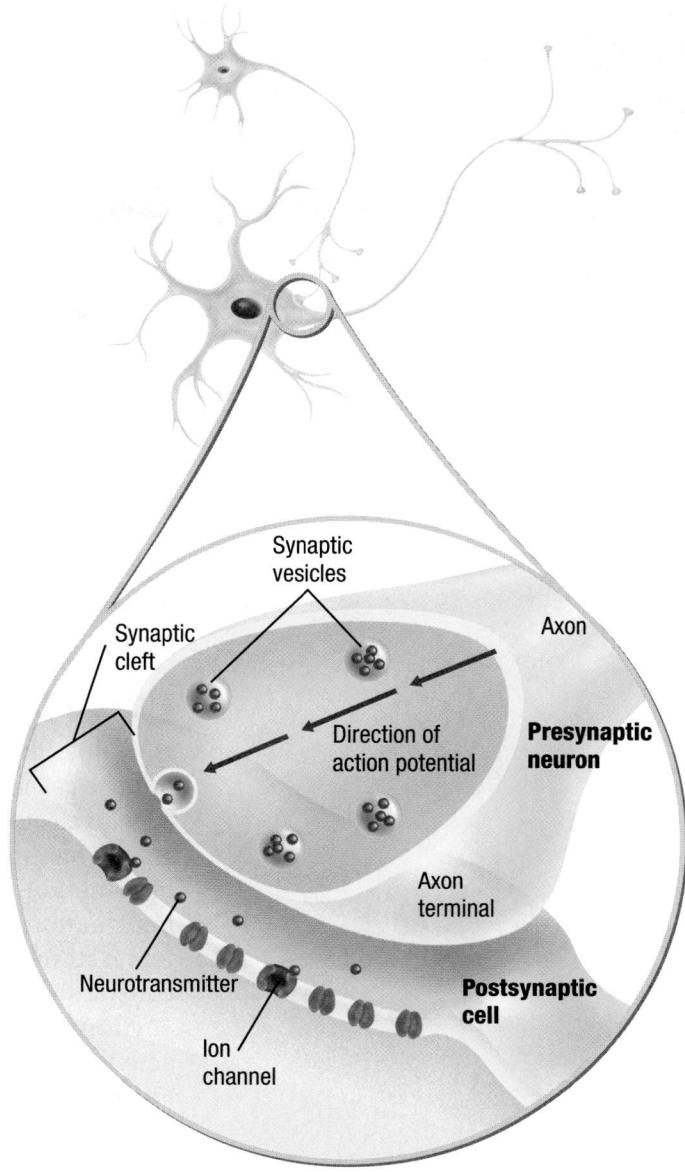

Figure 11 Neurotransmitters are released from a presynaptic neuron, diffuse across the synaptic cleft, and interact with a postsynaptic cell.

Section 2 Review

KEY IDEAS

1. **State** how the body conducts electricity.
2. **Label** the parts of a neuron.
3. **Summarize** the events that produce a nerve impulse.
4. **Summarize** the events involved in synaptic transmission.

CRITICAL THINKING

5. **Assessing Significance** How does the structure of neurons suggest how these cells form the intricate network of the nervous system that integrates and controls most of the body's activities?
6. **Predicting Outcomes** What would happen to a cell if the sodium-potassium pump stopped working?

CONNECTING KEY IDEAS

7. **Oral Report** Depression affects millions of Americans. Find out about its symptoms, causes, and treatments, including the types of drugs prescribed for it. Find out how these drugs affect the nervous system. Summarize your findings in an oral report to your class.

Sensory Systems

Key Ideas	Key Terms	Why It Matters
❯ How is sensory information detected? ❯ What are the five types of sensory receptors? ❯ Where are the sites of sensory processing in the brain?	sensory receptor retina cochlea semicircular canal taste bud	Sensory receptors collect information that is important for our survival from the internal and external environments. These receptors then send this information to the brain.

Sensory perception gives us information about the world around us—a potential danger, food, a mate, an offspring, or even something pleasurable. Perception depends on sensory receptors and regions of the brain that decode sensory stimuli.

Perception of Stimuli

How does the nervous system detect sensory stimuli? ❯ **Specialized neurons called *sensory receptors* detect sensory stimuli and convert them to electrical signals. These signals then can be interpreted by the brain.** The sensory division of the peripheral nervous system collects information about sensory stimuli in and around the body. This information is sent to the brain, which generates a motor response to the stimuli. Sensory systems also help maintain homeostasis by constantly adjusting body conditions in response to changes in the environment. Thus, while sensory perception is generally a conscious activity, the body may create a response without conscious effort. **Figure 12** illustrates several kinds of sensory perception.

❯ **Reading Check** *What types of cells are sensory receptors?*

Figure 12 Sensory receptors are located in sense organs, such as the eyes, mouth, ears, and skin. These receptors detect changes in the environment.

Taste cells detect food and drink.

Ears detect the conversation.

Pain receptors will detect an injury.

Eyes detect the sunlight.

Thermoreceptors detect the cold weather.

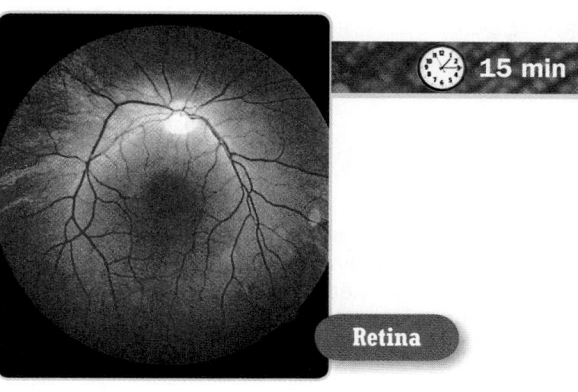

Retina

15 min

Your Blind Spot

The blind spot in your visual field corresponds to the site where the optic nerve exits the back of the eye. There are no photoreceptors at the site where the optic nerve exits. Use the procedure below to demonstrate your blind spot.

Procedure

1 On an **index card**, draw an *X* about 2.5 cm from the left side of the card by using a **pencil**. Then, draw an *O* about the same size 8 cm to the right of the *X*.

2 Hold your index card in front of you at arm's length. Close your right eye, and stare at the *O* with your left eye. Slowly move the card toward you while continuing to stare at the *O* until the *X* disappears from view.

Analysis

1. Name the two kinds of photoreceptors found in the retina.

2. Propose why you cannot see images that fall on the site where the optic nerve exits the eye.

3. CRITICAL THINKING **Relating Concepts** What is the relationship between the structure of the retina and the disappearance of the *X* on the index card?

Sensory Receptors

Although sensory receptors are located throughout the body, they are most concentrated in the sense organs—the eyes, ears, nose, mouth, and skin. **Sensory receptors** detect all forms of energy, such as heat, light, pressure, and chemicals. ❯ **The major classes of sensory receptors are photoreceptors, mechanoreceptors, chemoreceptors, pain receptors, and thermoreceptors.**

Vision Our eyes allow us to see in color and to distinguish fine details and movement. The structure of the eye is shown in **Figure 13.** Light enters the eye through the pupil and passes through the lens, a thick, transparent disk that focuses light on the retina. The **retina** is a layer of specialized cells that lines the inner surface of the eye.

The retina contains two types of *photoreceptors*— rods and cones. These cells convert light energy to electrical signals that can be interpreted by the brain. *Rods* respond best to dim light. *Cones* respond best to bright light and are stimulated by specific colors of light. The retina also contains many other neurons that process visual information. The axons of some of these cells make up the optic nerve. The optic nerve exits through the back of the eye, runs along the base of the brain to the thalamus, and later runs to the cortex for processing.

Your eyes see slightly different images. Information from both eyes is combined to produce three-dimensional vision. This process is very complex; as much as 30 % of the cerebral cortex processes visual information!

sensory receptor a specialized structure that contains the ends of sensory neurons and that responds to specific types of stimuli

retina the light-sensitive inner layer of the eye

Figure 13 Light enters the eye through the pupil and is focused on the retina, which contains photoreceptors. ❯ **Which receptors are located in the retina?**

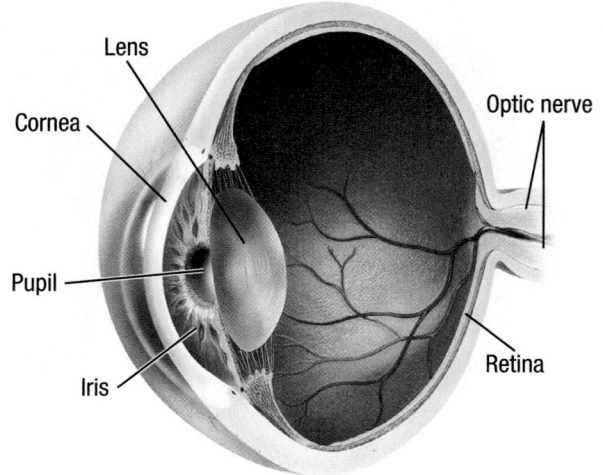

Lens

Cornea

Optic nerve

Pupil

Iris

Retina

Spider Map Recall that a spider map can be used to organize ideas. Construct a spider map based on one sensory receptor type.

ACADEMIC
VOCABULARY

generate to bring about; to produce

Figure 14 Sound waves are sent to the inner ear and are detected by mechanoreceptors in the cochlea. Other mechanoreceptors in the semicircular canals of the inner ear detect body position.

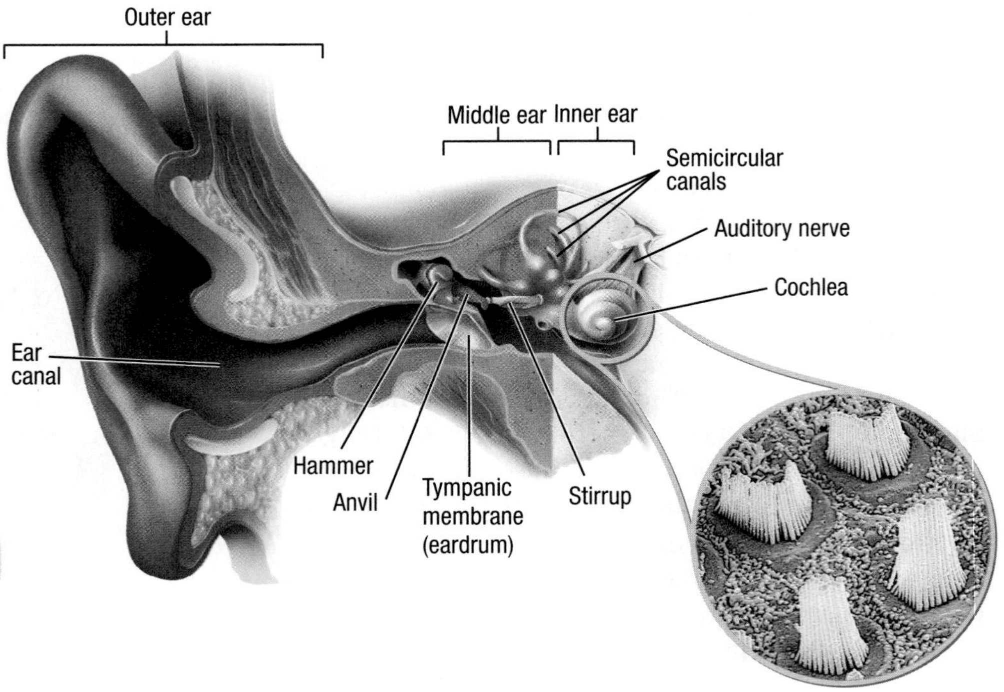

Hearing and Balance The human ear has two types of *mechanoreceptors*. One plays a role in hearing, and the other plays a role in balance. Both types of mechanoreceptors are hair cells that are in an enclosed space. These cells bend when the surrounding fluid moves. **Figure 14** shows the structure of the ear.

Hearing How do your ears allow you to hear? Sound waves enter the ear through the ear canal and strike the tympanic membrane, or eardrum. These vibrations cause the eardrum to vibrate. Behind the eardrum, three small bones of the middle ear act like a rattling chain. These bones are the hammer, the anvil, and the stirrup. They transfer the vibrations to the **cochlea,** a fluid-filled chamber within the inner ear. This chamber is coiled like a snail's shell. The cochlea contains hair cells. These hair cells rest on a membrane that vibrates when sound waves enter the cochlea. Various frequencies of sound waves cause the membrane to vibrate differently and thus stimulate the hair cells. When hair cells are stimulated, they generate action potentials in the axons of the auditory nerve. The impulses travel along the auditory nerve to the temporal lobe of the cerebral cortex. Here, the auditory information is processed.

Balance How do your ears help you maintain balance? The **semicircular canals** are another set of fluid-filled chambers in the inner ear that contain hair cells. Clusters of these hair cells respond to changes in head position relative to gravity. When your head moves, fluid in the semicircular canals also moves. Hair cells sense the strength and direction of the fluid's movement. The hair cells send electrical signals to the brain. These signals are then sent to the cerebellum along a branch of the auditory nerve. The brain processes these signals to determine the orientation and position of the head.

❯ **Reading Check** *How do hair cells detect sound waves?*

Outer ear

Middle ear Inner ear

Semicircular canals

Auditory nerve

Cochlea

Ear canal

Hammer

Anvil

Tympanic membrane (eardrum)

Stirrup

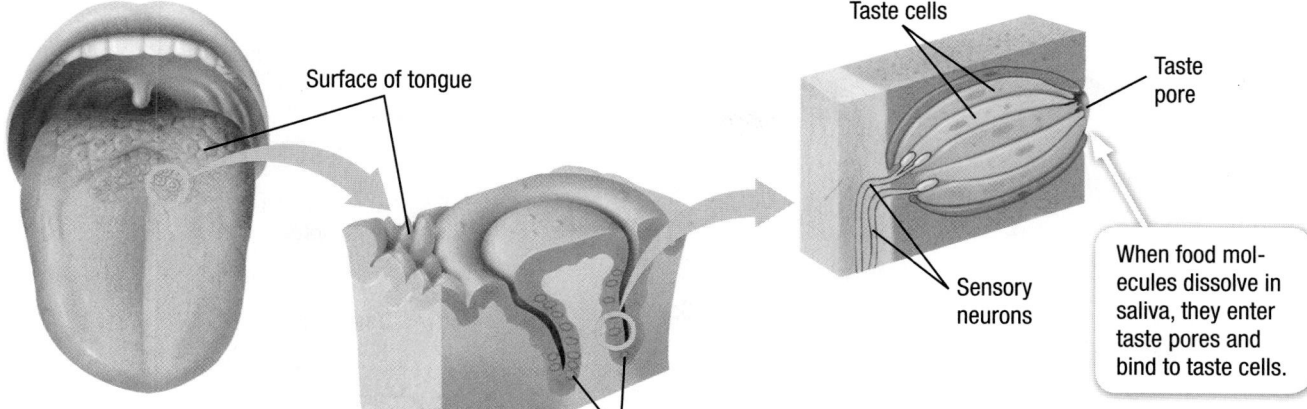

Surface of tongue

Taste buds

Taste cells

Taste pore

Sensory neurons

When food molecules dissolve in saliva, they enter taste pores and bind to taste cells.

Figure 15 The surface of the tongue contains 2,000 to 5,000 taste buds, and each taste bud is a cluster of 50 to 100 taste cells. Taste cells detect chemicals in our food. ❯ **How many types of chemicals can the tongue detect?**

Taste and Smell *Chemoreceptors* are sensory receptors that respond to chemicals. **Taste buds,** shown in **Figure 15,** detect at least five basic chemical substances: sugars (sweet), acids (sour), alkaloids (bitter), salts (salty), and proteins (savory). Food molecules dissolved in saliva flow into the taste pores and bind to taste cells, which generate nerve impulses that are sent to the brain for interpretation.

Chemicals in the air stimulate olfactory receptors, chemoreceptors located deep in your nostrils. These sensory receptors produce nerve impulses that are sent to and interpreted by the brain. When you have a bad cold and your nose is stuffed up, your food may seem to have little taste. Your ability to taste food directly depends on your ability to smell it!

Touch and Other Senses The skin is responsible for our sense of touch and our ability to quickly sense changes in the surrounding temperature. Painful sensations are also detected by the skin. The sensory receptors that detect these phenomena send nerve impulses directly to the brain. Touch and other body-related senses are collectively referred to as *somatosensation*.

Pain Receptors Pain receptors respond to potentially harmful stimuli, such as intense heat or cold and tissue damage. These receptors are nerve endings located near the surface of the skin and elsewhere in the body. Many self-protective responses, such as reflexes, are started by pain receptors.

Thermoreceptors Thermoreceptors are nerve endings that are located both in the skin and in the hypothalamus. These receptors detect changes in temperature and play an important role in homeostasis. They help keep the body temperature within its normal range.

Mechanoreceptors Throughout the body, mechanoreceptors respond to physical stimuli—such as pressure and tension—that cause the bending of tissue. Many mechanoreceptors are found in the skin, and they are concentrated in very sensitive areas, including the face, hands, fingertips, and neck.

cochlea (KAHK lee uh) a coiled tube that is found in the inner ear and that is essential to hearing

semicircular canal the fluid-filled canal in the inner ear that helps maintain balance and coordinate movements

taste bud one of many oval concentrations of sensory nerve endings on the tongue, palate, and pharynx

Top view of brain

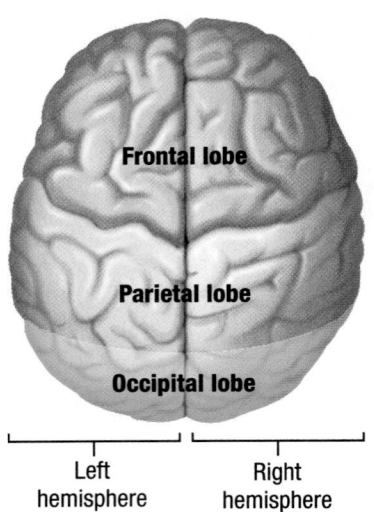

Frontal lobe

Parietal lobe

Occipital lobe

Left hemisphere   Right hemisphere

Side view of brain
(left hemisphere)

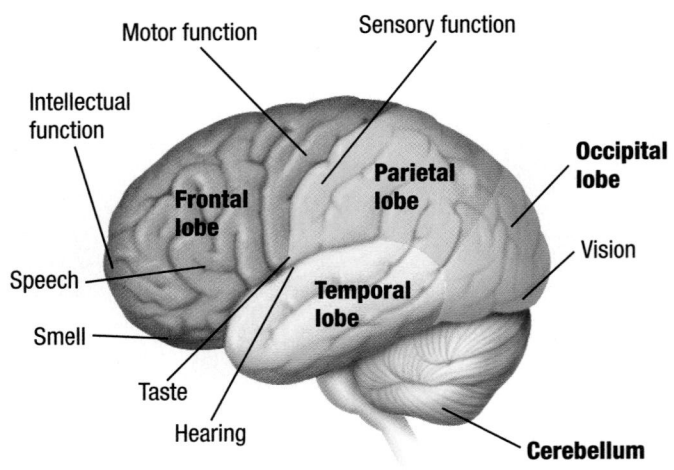

Motor function   Sensory function

Intellectual function

Frontal lobe

Parietal lobe

Occipital lobe

Speech

Smell

Temporal lobe

Vision

Taste

Hearing

Cerebellum

Figure 16 Specific areas of the cerebral cortex control different functions of the body. ❯ **Where is somatosensory information processed in the brain?**

SCI LINKS.
www.scilinks.org
Topic: Sensory Receptors
Code: HX81379

Processing of Sensory Information

Most sense organs send signals through nerves of the PNS into the CNS. The thalamus then relays this information to specific regions of the cortex. ❯ **Specialized regions of the cerebral cortex detect different sensory information.** As **Figure 16** shows, deep grooves divide the cerebral hemispheres into four general areas, or lobes: the parietal lobe, the frontal lobe, the occipital lobe, and the temporal lobe.

The parietal lobe of the cortex receives somatosensory ("body sense") stimuli. The amount of cortex devoted to a body part is proportional to the density of sensory receptors in that body part. For example, large areas of the somatosensory cortex are devoted to processing information from the hands. In the rear portion of the frontal lobe, immediately in front of the somatosensory cortex is the motor cortex. The motor cortex regulates the function of skeletal muscles. The frontal lobe also regulates intellectual function and aspects of our personality. Most visual processing occurs in the occipital lobe, located at the back of the head. The temporal lobe processes sound information.

Section 3 Review

❯ **KEY IDEAS**

1. **Describe** how sensory cues are detected and interpreted by your brain.
2. **List** the types of sensory receptors and the stimuli they respond to.
3. **Relate** the lobes of the brain to their roles in sensory perception.

CRITICAL THINKING

4. **Predicting Outcomes** What kind of a sensation do you think your brain would register if you pressed on the lids of your closed eyes? Explain your reasoning.
5. **Relating Concepts** Describe how the nervous system signals you to put on a coat on a cold day.

ALTERNATIVE ASSESSMENT

6. **Conduct an Interview** Invite an ophthalmologist or optometrist to speak about vision testing and to demonstrate how it is done. Prepare a list of the most common vision disorders, their symptoms, and the methods that are used to treat them.

Why It Matters

Your Amazing Brain

An account of a traumatic brain injury from 1848 is one of the first documented cases to show that specific areas of the brain, particularly the frontal lobe, control specific aspects of the personality and socially appropriate behavior. A railroad worker named Phineas Gage suffered a bizarre traumatic brain injury when tamping iron measuring 3 ft long was blown into his left cheek and exited the top of his skull. The accident severely damaged his frontal lobe and radically altered his personality. Neurologists today report that people with frontal lobe damage similar to Gage's experience the same type of radical personality changes.

Protecting Your Lobes

The brain is so important that it is no wonder why so many products exist to protect the brain. A properly fitted helmet can prevent most head injuries and greatly reduce the risk of traumatic brain injuries. Incorrectly fitted helmets can increase the risk of head injuries, so you should try on several helmets to find the correct size for you.

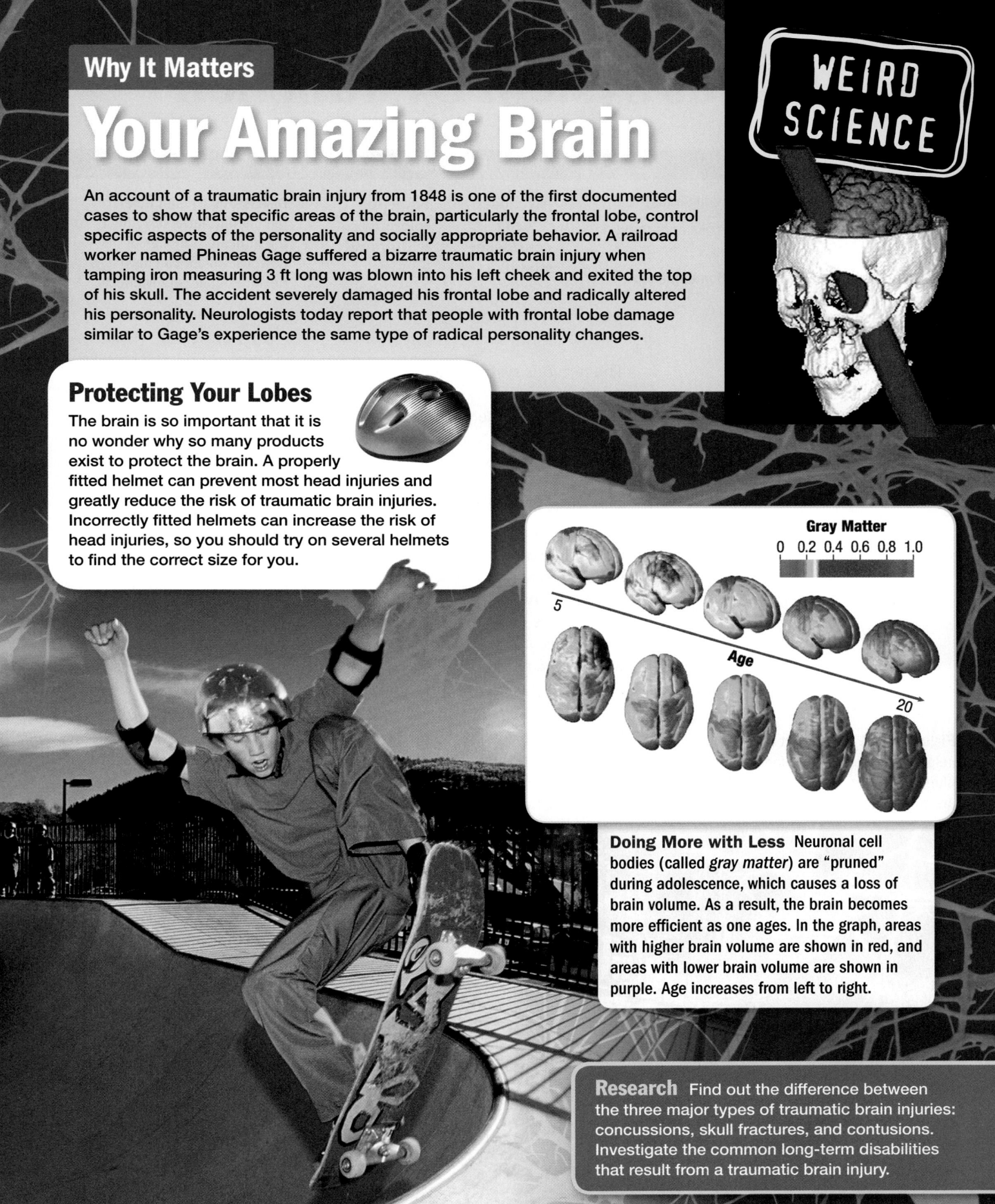

Gray Matter

0 0.2 0.4 0.6 0.8 1.0

5

Age

20

Doing More with Less Neuronal cell bodies (called *gray matter*) are "pruned" during adolescence, which causes a loss of brain volume. As a result, the brain becomes more efficient as one ages. In the graph, areas with higher brain volume are shown in red, and areas with lower brain volume are shown in purple. Age increases from left to right.

Research Find out the difference between the three major types of traumatic brain injuries: concussions, skull fractures, and contusions. Investigate the common long-term disabilities that result from a traumatic brain injury.

Nervous System Dysfunction

Key Ideas	Key Terms	Why It Matters
❯ Why are psychoactive drugs dangerous? ❯ What are the neural mechanisms underlying drug addiction? ❯ How is nervous system function damaged?	psychoactive drug addiction depressant tolerance stimulant withdrawal	Disease, injury, and other factors that adversely affect the intricate workings of the nervous system can have debilitating or deadly effects.

The nervous system is a highly complex network of neurons and their supporting cells. It regulates and coordinates nearly all of the body's activities. Because the nervous system interacts with every other system of the body, damage to or malfunctioning of any of its parts can have numerous effects.

Psychoactive Drugs

Drugs can prevent, treat, or cure many illnesses. However, drugs, whether legal or illegal, can also be misused or abused. A drug is a chemical that alters body structures or biological functions. **Psychoactive drugs** alter the functioning of the CNS. ❯ **Many psychoactive drugs produce physiological dependence and addiction when abused.** Psychoactive drugs often affect an abuser's emotional well-being, as shown in **Figure 17.** Abuse of psychoactive drugs can damage the body and, in some cases, can result in death.

Several classes of psychoactive drugs are commonly abused. **Depressants,** such as alcohol and barbiturates, generally decrease the activity of the central nervous system. High doses of depressants such as alcohol can depress respiratory functions enough to cause death. **Stimulants,** such as cocaine and nicotine, generally increase the activity of the central nervous system. Nicotine, which is found in tobacco products, increases heart rate, breathing rate, blood pressure, and overall activity level. At high doses, stimulants can be fatal.

Inhalants such as some glues are also psychoactive drugs. Inhalants cause disorientation, confusion, and memory loss. They can also cause brain and other organ damage as well as respiratory failure.

LSD and similar drugs cause sensory distortion and hallucinations. THC, found in marijuana and hashish, causes memory and judgment problems. Narcotics, such as heroin, have sedating effects that can be fatal at high doses.

❯ **Reading Check** *How do depressants cause death when they are abused?*

Figure 17 A drug addict often feels helpless. Depression and family problems often result from drug addiction. ❯ **Why are some drugs labeled "psychoactive"?**

Hands-On

Quick**Lab**

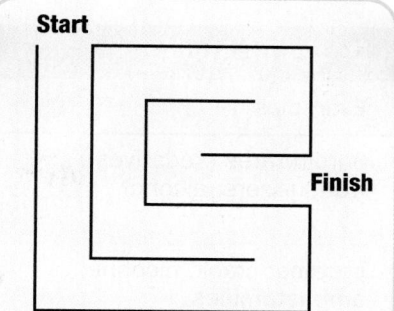

Start

Finish

⏱ 15 min

Impaired Senses

Mind-altering drugs can impair sensory perception. In this activity, you will observe how an impaired sense of vision can affect how well a task is completed.

Procedure

1 Working with a partner and using a **pencil,** measure and record how long it takes to trace a path through this maze without touching a boundary. If you make a mistake, start again. Calculate the average time for this task based on three successful completions.

2 Erase the marks, switch roles, and repeat step 1.

3 Anchor an **index card** in a small lump of **clay.** Position the card so that it blocks your direct view of the maze.

4 Position a **mirror** so that it reflects the entire maze.

5 Using only the reflection as a guide, trace a route through the maze. Calculate the average time for this task based on three successful maze completions.

6 Erase the marks, switch roles, and repeat step 5.

Analysis

1. Determine whether or not viewing the maze through a mirror affected the time needed to complete the task.

2. CRITICAL THINKING **Forming Reasoned Opinions** Does this activity accurately model impaired perception?

Nicotine Approximately 50 million Americans smoke cigarettes despite convincing evidence that smoking causes mouth cancer, heart disease, lung cancer, and emphysema. So, why do people continue to smoke?

Cigarette smoke contains nicotine, the highly addictive and very toxic stimulant found in the leaves of the tobacco plant, *Nicotiana tabacum.* In the brain, nicotine mimics the action of an important neurotransmitter by binding to its receptors. Smoking causes permanent changes in the brain. After a while, the smoker's body is unable to function properly without the effects of nicotine in his or her system. The smoker is addicted.

Alcohol Alcohol (ethanol) is a widely used and frequently abused psychoactive drug. Alcohol is a depressant that produces a sense of well-being when taken in small amounts. As more alcohol is consumed, reaction time increases. Coordination, judgment, and speech become impaired. Alcohol consumption produces a state of intoxication known as being "drunk." Drunkenness occurs as the blood-alcohol concentration increases. Blood-alcohol concentration can be measured by a breath test that detects the level of alcohol vapors in the breath. Police officers can often estimate blood-alcohol concentration by conducting coordination tests, such as the one shown in **Figure 18.**

Alcohol is absorbed into the bloodstream through the stomach and small intestine. Alcohol affects neurons throughout the brain and changes the way certain receptors work. These changes in receptors have various effects on the normal functioning of the brain.

psychoactive drug (SIE koh AK tiv) a substance that has a significant effect on the mind or on behavior

depressant a drug that reduces functional activity and produces muscular relaxation

stimulant (STIM yoo luhnt) a drug that increases the activity of the body or the activity of some part of the body

Figure 18 A driver is tested for coordination by a police officer. Alcohol alters coordination and balance.

Psychoactive Drugs of Abuse

Drug	Examples	Psychoactive effects	Health risks
Depressants	barbiturates (sedatives); tranquilizers; alcohol	decreased activity of the central nervous system	drowsiness; depression; brain or nerve damage; coma; respiratory failure
Stimulants	cocaine; crack; nicotine; amphetamines	increased activity of the central nervous system	aggressive behavior; paranoia; heart attack; high blood pressure; brain damage
Inhalants	nitrous oxide; ether; paint thinner; glue; cleaning fluid; aerosols	disorientation; confusion; memory loss	brain damage; kidney and liver damage; respiratory failure
Hallucinogens	LSD, PCP, MDMA (Ecstasy); peyote (mescaline); psilocybe mushroom	sensory distortion; anxiety; hallucinations; numbness	depression; paranoia; aggressive behavior
THC	marijuana; hashish	short-term memory loss; impaired judgment	loss of motivation
Narcotics	heroin; morphine; codeine; opium	feeling of well-being; sedation; impaired sensory perception; impaired reflexes	coma; respiratory failure

Figure 19 Psychoactive drugs are classified into broad groups based on their composition and effect on the body.

Figure 20 The opium poppy produces opium, which is used to make a wide variety of narcotic drugs.

Marijuana In addition to alcohol and nicotine, marijuana, though illegal, is a widely consumed drug. Other common drugs of abuse are featured in **Figure 19.** Marijuana and hashish come from various species of the hemp plant, *Cannabis.* The active ingredient in marijuana and hashish is commonly known as *THC.* When marijuana is either smoked or eaten, it causes disorientation, impaired judgment, short-term memory loss, and general loss of motivation. The exact mechanism by which THC affects the nervous system is unclear.

Narcotics Narcotics are a class of psychoactive drugs that are extremely addictive. They are commonly used to relieve pain and to induce sleep. Some of the most potent narcotics are derived from the poppy plant, *Papaver somniferum*, shown in **Figure 20.** The sap that oozes from the cut seed pod forms a thick, gummy substance called *opium.* Drugs derived from opium include codeine, morphine, and heroin, a more potent form of morphine. Morphine is one of the most effective pain-relieving drugs used today. Heroin addiction and abuse are among the most serious illegal-drug problems in society.

Nerve impulses generated by pain receptors travel to the spinal cord and up to the brain. After reaching the spinal cord, a pain signal can be suppressed by a class of neurotransmitters called *enkephalins.* When enkephalins bind to neurons in the spinal cord, they prevent pain signals from reaching the brain. Narcotics are useful drugs to block pain because they mimic the action of natural pain killers in our body, enkephalins. Just like our natural painkillers, narcotics bind to receptor proteins in the spinal cord and block painful sensations.

❯ **Reading Check** *Why are opiates used as pain relievers?*

Neural Changes

Addiction is a physiological or psychological dependence on a substance. ❯Addiction occurs when repeated use of a drug alters the normal functioning of neurons and synapses. With repeated exposure to a drug, an addicted person develops tolerance to the drug. **Tolerance** occurs when increasing amounts of a drug are needed to achieve desired sensations. **Withdrawal** is a set of emotional and physical symptoms caused by removing a drug from the body. Symptoms of withdrawal include vomiting, headache, and depression.

Cocaine is a highly addictive stimulant. When taken, it affects the release of dopamine from neurons in parts of the brain that play an important role in the sensation of pleasure. **Figure 21** summarizes how cocaine acts on dopamine cells. Normally, neurotransmitters released into the synapse are reabsorbed or broken down after they have stimulated postsynaptic cells. Cocaine interferes with this process. The overstimulation causes a pleasurable sensation, but eventually the number of dopamine receptors decreases with continued cocaine use. The postsynaptic cell becomes understimulated because fewer receptors exist to respond to dopamine released from the presynaptic cell. Addiction occurs because more cocaine must be taken to maintain adequate stimulation of postsynaptic cells.

❯ **Reading Check** *How does addiction change a neuron?*

www.scilinks.org
Topic: Drug Addiction
Code: HX80427

addiction a physiological or psychological dependence on a substance, such as alcohol or drugs

tolerance (TAHL uhr uhns) the condition of drug addiction in which greater amounts of a drug are needed to achieve the desired effect

withdrawal (with DRAW uhl) the set of symptoms associated with the removal of an addictive drug from the body

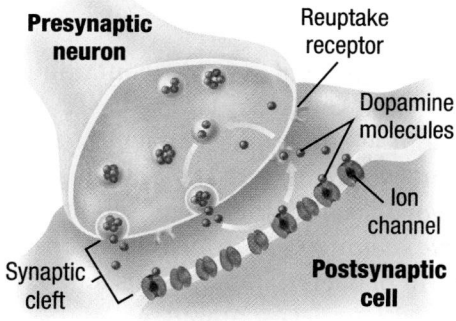

① Under normal conditions, dopamine that is released from the presynaptic neuron is reabsorbed by the same cell.

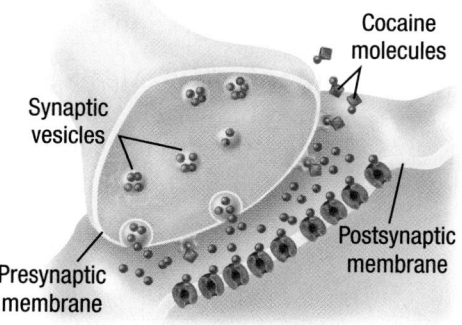

② When cocaine is used, it blocks the reabsorption of dopamine into the presynaptic cell.

Figure 21 Cocaine is addictive because it affects chemical transmission at synapses.

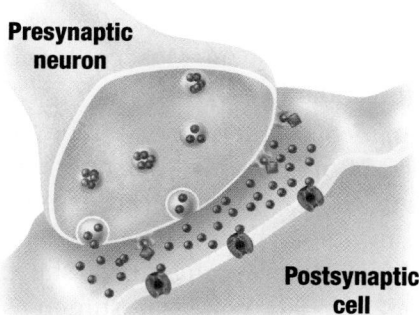

③ The number of receptors on the postsynaptic cell decreases because of the increase in dopamine in the synapse.

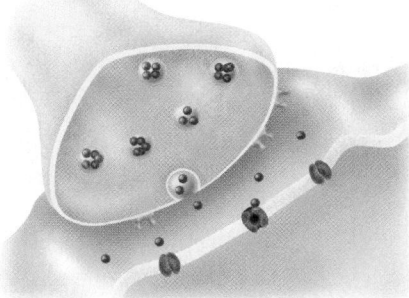

④ When cocaine is not in use, dopamine release from the presynaptic cell returns to normal. However, now the postsynaptic cell is understimulated.

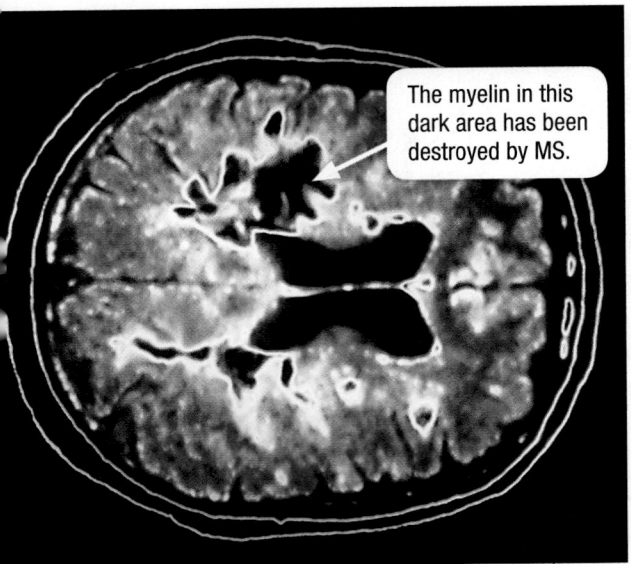
The myelin in this dark area has been destroyed by MS.

Figure 22 In multiple sclerosis, portions of some axons lose their myelin coating. As a result, the damaged neurons cannot function normally.

Figure 23 Meningococcal meningitis often occurs in crowded areas such as college dorm rooms and cafeterias.
❯ How is meningitis transmitted?

Nervous System Disorders

The brain, with its complex network of cells and its ability to process and store information, is often compared to a computer. When something in a computer malfunctions, we may notice mistakes or inconsistencies, problems accomplishing routine tasks, or even complete shutdowns. Imagine what would happen if some part of your nervous system malfunctioned! Various consequences could result. These consequences include headaches, tingling in fingers and toes, difficulty with certain kinds of movement, impaired coordination, mood changes, and fatigue. ❯ **Damage to the nervous system can occur as a result of disease, traumatic injury, or exposure to chemicals.** The broad range of symptoms illustrates how important the nervous system is to our health.

Multiple Sclerosis Multiple sclerosis (MS) is a degenerative disease of the CNS in which the myelin sheath surrounding axons is destroyed by the body's immune system. A brain damaged by MS is shown in **Figure 22.** Symptoms of the disease are generally mild and may first appear in early to middle adulthood. These symptoms include muscle weakness, difficulties with coordination and balance, fatigue, and problems with various thought processes. Some cases are mild, whereas others can involve complete paralysis. The disease seems to have a genetic basis, although environmental triggers such as viruses may play a role. There is no cure for MS. However, medications can lessen the severity of symptoms and can slow progression of the disease.

Meningitis Meningitis is an inflammation of the fluid-containing membranes that surround the brain and spinal cord. Most cases of meningitis are caused by infectious agents, typically bacteria or viruses. Bacterial meningitis is more severe than viral meningitis. Meningococcal meningitis, caused by *Neisseria meningitidis*, is the most common form of bacterial meningitis today.

Meningococcal meningitis often has a sudden onset. Its symptoms include high fever, stiff neck, and severe headache. The condition progresses rapidly and despite treatment is fatal in about 40% of cases, so early diagnosis is critical. Most cases occur in children and adolescents.

Meningococcal meningitis can be transmitted from person to person in tiny droplets of saliva or mucus. It is passed more easily among people living in crowded conditions, such as those shown in **Figure 23.** In fact, college freshmen living in dormitories have at least twice the risk of developing the disease as do people the same age not living in dormitories.

Traumatic Injury Traumatic injury to the spinal cord or brain can be disabling and even fatal. These injuries are so serious because the CNS is vital to the proper functioning of so many body systems. Also, neurons in the CNS cannot regenerate after injury.

Motor vehicle crashes are the main causes of traumatic CNS injury. Sports injuries are another important cause. Adolescents and young adults have the highest rates of these injuries. Wearing protective headgear, shown in **Figure 24,** and using other safety devices such as car seat belts are the best ways to prevent traumatic injuries.

Figure 24 Protective headgear can prevent many types of traumatic injury.
❯ How does traumatic injury produce loss of sensation throughout the body?

Spinal Cord Injury to the spinal cord usually occurs as a result of a blow to the spine that fractures or dislocates vertebrae. The spinal cord itself is rarely severed. Damage to the spinal cord occurs when vertebrae are fractured and bone fragments or other tissues crush and destroy axons in the spinal cord. This type of damage produces loss of sensation and ability in the parts of the body fed by the damaged axons. Areas below the injury may be damaged, too. Signals may not be able to cross the injured area and travel to and from the brain.

Brain Closed head injuries occur when the skull remains intact but the brain is injured when it collides with the inside of the skull. Open head injuries are far less common and can occur when an object—such as a bullet, rock, knife, or skull fragment—penetrates the brain. Mild head injuries may cause only confusion and headache. More serious injuries can <u>induce</u> seizures, lethargy, vomiting, confusion, and loss of coordination. Sometimes, complete loss of consciousness results from serious brain injury. About half of people who have a traumatic brain injury require surgery to repair or remove ruptured blood vessels or bruised tissue. These injuries could cause swelling and further damage to nearby brain tissue.

ACADEMIC VOCABULARY

induce to cause

❯ **Reading Check** *How can the majority of traumatic injuries be prevented?*

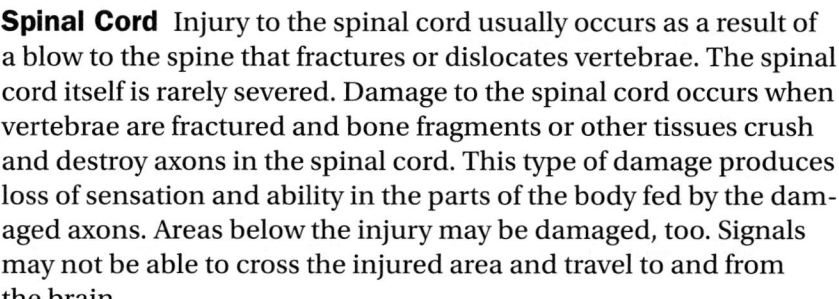

Section 4 Review

❯ **KEY IDEAS**

1. **Describe** why a psychoactive drug is considered dangerous.
2. **Summarize** how cocaine produces addiction.
3. **Describe** the major ways in which the nervous system is damaged.

CRITICAL THINKING

4. **Recognizing Relationships** What do all psychoactive drugs have in common?
5. **Justifying Conclusions** Why are college freshmen often at increased risk of developing meningococcal meningitis? What other types of situations are associated with increased risk?

MATH SKILLS

6. **Essay** Conduct Internet research on one drug of abuse. Find information on either trends over time or trends over a geographic area. Prepare a graph illustrating the data. Provide a brief written interpretation of your findings.

Objectives

▶ Determine human reaction times.

▶ Design an experiment that measures changes in reaction times.

Materials

■ meterstick

Safety

Reaction Times

When you want to move your hand, your brain must send a message all the way to the muscles in your arms. How long does that process take? In this exercise, you will work with a partner to see how quickly you can react.

In this lab, you will design an experiment to investigate reaction times and will design an experiment to investigate influences on reaction times. To do this, you will determine your reaction time under normal circumstances. Then, you will write a hypothesis about a factor that might influence your reaction time.

Preparation

1. **SCIENTIFIC METHODS** **State the Problem** What factors might influence how fast your reaction time is in response to a task?

2. **SCIENTIFIC METHODS** **Form a Hypothesis** Form a testable hypothesis that explains how a factor might influence how fast reaction time is in response to a task. Record your hypothesis.

Procedure

Calculate Reaction Times

1 Create a data table like the one shown to record reaction times.

2 Sit in a chair, and have a partner stand facing you while holding a meterstick in a vertical position.

3 Hold your thumb about 3 cm from your fingers near the bottom end of the stick. The meterstick should be positioned to fall between your thumb and fingers.

4 Tell your partner to let go of the meterstick without warning you.

A nerve cell such as this one can send very rapid signals all over your body.

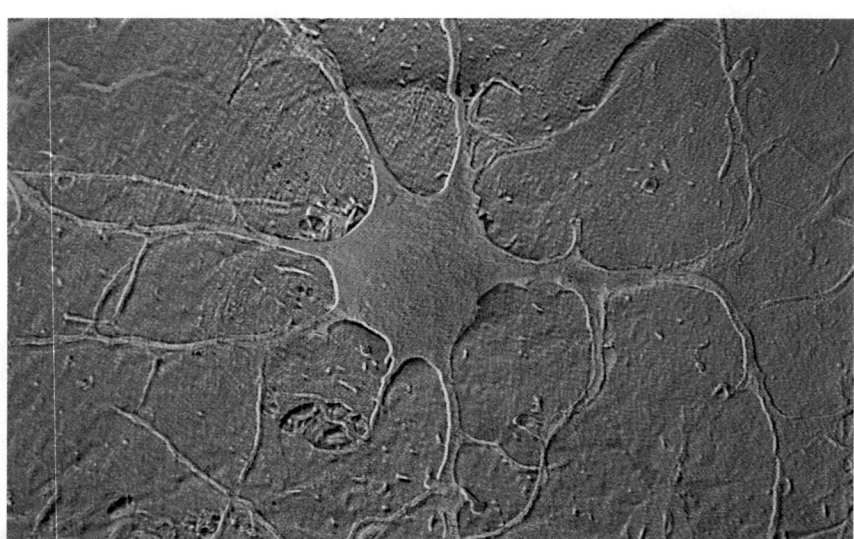

5 When your partner releases the meterstick, catch the stick by pressing your thumb and fingers together. Your partner should catch the top of the stick if it begins to tip over.

6 Record the number of centimeters that the stick dropped before you caught it. The distance that the meterstick fell can be used to evaluate your reaction time.

7 Repeat the procedure several times, and calculate the average number of centimeters that the meterstick dropped during each trial.

8 Try this procedure with your other hand. Close your eyes and have your partner say "now" when the stick is released.

9 Exchange places with your partner, and repeat the procedure.

Design an Experiment

10 Design an experiment that tests your hypothesis and that uses the materials listed for the lab. Predict what will happen during your experiment if your hypothesis is supported.

11 Write a procedure for your experiment. Identify the variables that you will control, the experimental variables, and the responding variables. Construct any tables you will need to record your data. Make a list of all the safety precautions you will take. Have your teacher approve your procedure before you begin.

Conduct Your Experiment

12 Set up your group's experiment, and collect data.

13 Clean up your lab materials according to your teacher's instructions. Wash your hands before leaving the lab.

Reaction Times		
Hand: trial number	Subject 1 reaction time (seconds, s)	Subject 2 reation time (s)
Left: 1		
Left: 2		
Left: 3		
Left: average		
Right: 1		
Right: 2		
Right: 3		
Right: average		

SCILINKS.
www.scilinks.org
Topic: Nervous System
Code: HX81023

Analyze and Conclude

1. Summarizing Results What was your fastest reaction time?

2. SCIENTIFIC METHODS Analyzing Data How does your reaction time when you use your dominant hand compare with your reaction time when you use your other hand?

3. SCIENTIFIC METHODS Drawing Conclusions Why may each hand have a different reaction time? Why may each person have a different reaction time?

4. Predicting Patterns Compile the data gathered by each lab group in your class. Can you identify any trends in the data?

5. SCIENTIFIC METHODS Analyzing Results How did the data differ in the experiment that you designed? Explain whether or not your hypothesis was supported.

Extensions

6. Predicting Outcomes Do research in the library or media center to determine how athletes can improve their reaction times. Are these methods in common practice at your school?

7. Identifying Concepts What factors can influence how fast a person reacts to a stimulus?

8. Further Inquiry Write a new question about reaction times that could be explored in another investigation.

go.hrw.com
SUPER SUMMARY
Keyword: HX8NRVS

Key Ideas	Key Terms

1 Structures of the Nervous System

> The central nervous system responds to internal and external information.

> The peripheral nervous system contains sensory and motor neurons that carry information between the central nervous system and the rest of the body.

> A spinal reflex is an involuntary movement triggered by sensory input and produced by neural circuitry limited to the spinal cord.

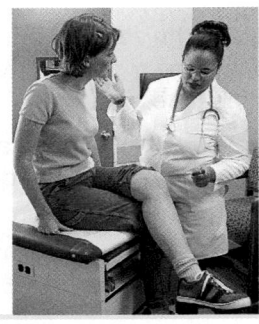

neuron (939)
central nervous system (939)
peripheral nervous system (939)
brain (940)
cerebrum (940)
brainstem (941)
cerebellum (941)
spinal cord (941)
reflex (943)

2 Neurons and Nerve Impulses

> Electrical signals in the nervous system are caused by the movement of ions across the cell membrane of neurons.

> A neuron's dendrites gather information from other cells, the cell body integrates this information, and the axon sends the information to other cells.

> All nerve impulses begin when the resting state of a neuron is changed by a signal from another neuron or from the environment.

> Neurons communicate with other cells at specialized junctions called synapses. Chemicals are released at synapses.

dendrite (945)
axon (945)
nerve (945)
membrane potential (946)
action potential (946)
synapse (948)
neurotransmitter (948)

3 Sensory Systems

> Specialized neurons called *sensory receptors* detect sensory stimuli and convert them to electrical signals. These signals then can be interpreted by the brain.

> The major classes of sensory receptors are photoreceptors, mechanoreceptors, chemoreceptors, pain receptors, and thermoreceptors.

> Specialized regions of the cortex detect different sensory information.

sensory receptor (951)
retina (951)
cochlea (952)
semicircular canal (952)
taste bud (953)

4 Nervous System Dysfunction

> Many psychoactive drugs produce physiological dependence and addiction when abused.

> Addiction occurs when repeated use of a drug alters the normal functioning of neurons and synapses.

> Damage to the nervous system can occur as a result of disease, traumatic injury, or exposure to chemicals.

psychoactive drug (956)
depressant (956)
stimulant (956)
addiction (959)
tolerance (959)
withdrawal (959)

1. **Key-Term Fold** On the back of your key-term fold, redefine each key term in your own words.

2. **Concept Map** Make a concept map that describes the structures and functions of the following terms: *spinal cord, brain, neuron, nerve, synapse,* and *neurotransmitter.*

Using Key Terms

For each pair of terms, explain how the meanings of the terms differ.

3. *resting potential* and *action potential*

4. *cochlea* and *semicircular canals*

Use each of the following terms in a separate sentence:

5. *dendrite*

6. *synapse*

Understanding Key Ideas

7. The higher thought processes of reasoning and memory occur in the
   a. cerebrum. **c.** brainstem.
   b. thalamus. **d.** cerebellum.

8. Which of the following statements about a spinal reflex is true?
   a. It is controlled by the brain.
   b. It increases blood flow to muscles.
   c. It is a voluntary contraction of muscles.
   d. It is an involuntary response to a stimulus.

9. What kinds of signals are used by the body to transmit information rapidly through the nervous system?
   a. electrical signals **c.** autonomic signals
   b. chemical signals **d.** mechanical signals

10. One type of sensory receptor that is stimulated by light is a(n)
    a. cone. **c.** olfactory receptor.
    b. retina. **d.** semicircular canal.

Use the diagram to answer the following question.

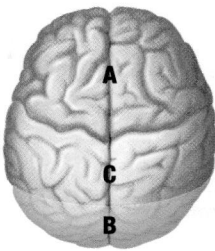 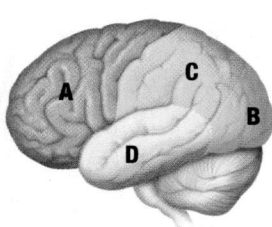

11. Which lobe of the cerebral cortex is responsible for processing visual stimuli?
    a. lobe A **c.** lobe C
    b. lobe B **d.** lobe D

12. The hallmark symptoms of multiple sclerosis are
    a. anxiety and depression.
    b. increased susceptibility to infections.
    c. loss of sensory perception in affected areas of the body.
    d. muscle weakness and decreased coordination and balance.

13. Drug tolerance results in
    a. decreased need for the drug.
    b. increased need for the drug.
    c. overstimulation of postsynaptic neurons.
    d. understimulation of postsynaptic neurons.

Explaining Key Ideas

14. **State** the role of sodium-potassium pumps in reestablishing a resting potential following an action potential.

15. **Describe** how a spinal reflex protects the body.

16. **Propose** the role of enzymes in a synaptic cleft.

17. **Distinguish** between stimulants and depressants, and give an example of each.

18. **Create** a flowchart illustrating the divisions and subdivisions of the nervous system.

19. **Classify** the two major types of traumatic spinal cord injury and traumatic head injury.

20. **Sequence** the events that occur when light enters the eye.

Using Science Graphics

Use the diagram to answer the following questions.

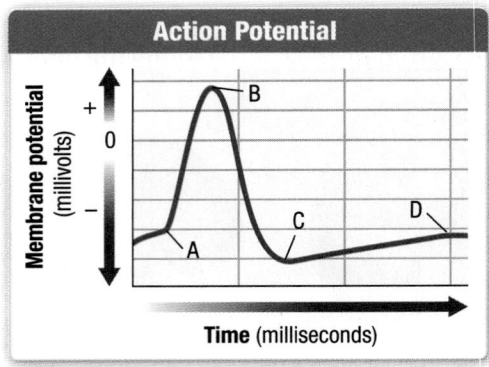

Action Potential

Membrane potential (millivolts)

+

0

–

B

A

C

D

Time (milliseconds)

21. At what point do potassium (K⁺) channels open in this neuron?
    a. point A   **c.** point C
    b. point B   **d.** point D

22. Which point corresponds to the resting potential of this neuron?
    a. point A   **c.** point C
    b. point B   **d.** point D

23. Where is the threshold of this neuron likely to be located?
    a. point A   **c.** point C
    b. point B   **d.** point D

Critical Thinking

24. Predicting Consequences A neurotransmitter is released by a presynaptic cell and opens ion channels on the postsynaptic cell. As a result, positive ions flow through these ion channels across the membrane into the postsynaptic cell. How does this event affect the postsynaptic cell?

25. Making Inferences In what ways is the brainstem like the rest of the brain, and in what ways is it like the spinal cord?

26. Making Inferences Sensory receptors help the body detect changes in the environment. Where would you expect most sensory receptors to be located?

27. Applying Concepts Why is drug addiction considered a physiological condition rather than a psychological condition?

28. Comparing Functions Why is a spinal reflex more rapid than a voluntary movement?

29. Applying Information Botulinum toxin is the most potent biological toxin known. Its single, specific effect is to bind to and destroy axonal endings at junctions between motor neurons and skeletal muscle cells. What would be the symptoms of exposure to this toxin? Explain your answer.

30. Recognizing Relationships What specific structure(s) would you expect to have some kind of defect in the eyes of a person who is color blind? How would this defect cause the color blindness? Explain your answer.

Methods of Science

31. Historical Experiment Conduct research on the Internet or in the library on the early studies of nerve function using the giant squid axon. Summarize this research in a one- to two-page report. Emphasize the selection of the organism for the studies and the equipment and procedures used.

Alternative Assessment

32. Creating a Table Conduct research on neurotransmitters to find out some of the known types of neurotransmitters, whether they are generally excitatory or inhibitory, their functions, the organs or parts of the nervous system in which they are produced and released, and at least one disorder related to the neurotransmitter. Compile this information into a table.

33. Neuron Model Create a model of a typical neuron, using common household or office materials. Label the structural components of your neuron, and include a brief description of each component's function.

Writing for Science

34. Letter Writing Currently, the cost of a dose of vaccine against *Neisseria meningitidis* approaches $100. Compose a letter to the administration of a university or college you might attend that argues for the institution to provide this vaccine at reduced cost to students. Include logical arguments and factual information to support your arguments, possibly including data on the incidence of this disease in your state.

TEST TIP When using a graph to answer a question, read the graph's title and the labels on the graph's axes. For graphs that show a change in some variable over time, keep in mind that the steepness and direction of a curve indicate the relative rate of change at a given point in time.

Science Concepts

1. The central nervous system includes
   A only the brain.
   B the brain and the spinal cord.
   C the brain, the spinal cord, and the cranial nerves.
   D the brain, the spinal cord, the cranial nerves, and the spinal nerves.

2. A typical neuron has
   F a cell body but no nucleus.
   G nuclei in each of its cellular extensions.
   H a single nucleus within the cell body.
   J a single nucleus that carries a signal to an another cell.

3. Nerve impulses sent from sensory receptors enter the brain and are routed to the appropriate area of the cerebral cortex by the
   A cerebellum.   **C** brainstem.
   B thalamus.   **D** hypothalamus.

4. Traumatic injuries that cause damage to the brain or spinal cord
   F are always life threatening.
   G cannot be repaired.
   H are most common in young children.
   J are usually fatal.

5. Which of the following is true about a spinal reflex?
   A It is a voluntary contraction of muscles.
   B It is an involuntary response to a stimulus.
   C It increases blood flow to muscles.
   D It is controlled by the brain.

6. Which cells in the body can conduct electrical signals?
   F muscle cells   **H** somatic cells
   G stem cells   **J** neurons

7. What specialized neurons detect stimuli, such as sound and light?
   A axons
   B sensory receptors
   C thalamus and hypothalamus
   D motor neurons

Math Skills

Brain Region	Total mass in grams (g)	Percentage of total mass (%)
Entire cortex	1058 g	100%
Frontal lobe	422 g	
Temporal lobe	237 g	
Parietal lobe	205 g	
Occipital lobe	194 g	

8. **Calculating Percentages** Create a table like the one shown and use the data provided to calculate the percentage of the cerebral cortex that is found in each of its lobes. What is the percentage of the frontal and parietal lobes combined?
   F 59.3%   **H** 62.3%
   G 40.7%   **J** 37.7%

Using Science Graphics

Use the diagram to answer the following questions.

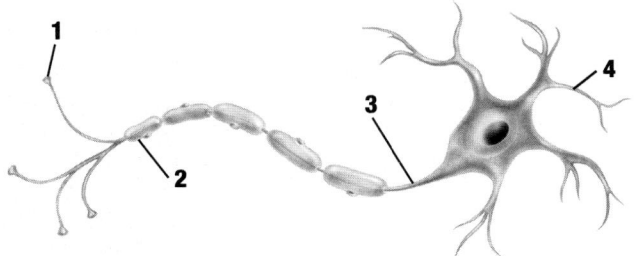

9. Which structure is a site where the neuron receives information from other neurons?
   A 1   **C** 3
   B 2   **D** 4

10. Which structure increases the speed at which the axon conducts action potentials?
    F 1   **H** 3
    G 2   **J** 4

Chapter 39

The Endocrine System

Preview

1 Hormones
What Is the Endocrine System?
Where Are Hormones Made?
Hormones and Receptors
Hormone Function
Control of Hormone Levels

2 Major Endocrine Glands
Controlling the Endocrine System
Regulating Metabolism
Responding to Stress
Regulating Reproduction

Why It Matters

Hormones are chemical messengers that regulate functions in the body such as temperature, growth, development, and response to stress.

In an emergency, the body prepares for action. Stress hormones that are involved in the fight-or-flight response raise heart rate and blood pressure and cause other changes in the body.

After a traumatic event, stress hormone levels usually return to normal. Sometimes, however, they stay high and contribute to post-traumatic stress disorder (PTSD).

PTSD can affect people of any age. In children, symptoms can include recurrent nightmares and mood changes.

InquiryLab

⏱ 10 min

Fight, Flight, or Speech?

Many people fear public speaking. Standing and speaking are not strenuous activities, so why does a person feel his or her heart race when speaking in front of other people?

Procedure

❶ While seated calmly at your desk, take your pulse for 10 s.

❷ Stand up in front of the class, and read the following statement: The endocrine system controls the body's response to stress.

❸ Return to your desk, and immediately take your pulse for 10 s.

Analysis

1. Calculate the number of beats per minute for your resting heart rate.

2. Calculate the number of beats per minute after your speech?

3. Compare the two heart rates.

4. Describe any other responses that you may have noticed as your body dealt with the stress of speaking in front of the class.

About 20% of firefighters in the United States have PTSD. Their symptoms include high blood pressure, heart problems, and sleep disorders.

READING TOOLBOX

These reading tools can help you learn the material in this chapter. For more information on how to use these and other tools, see **Appendix: Reading and Study Skills.**

Using Words

Word Parts Knowing the meanings of word parts can help you figure out the meanings of words that you do not know.

Your Turn Use the table to answer the following questions.
1. Where would you expect to find the adrenal gland?
2. How might the meanings of the word parts *endo-* and *-crine* relate to the meaning of the word *endocrine*?

Word Parts		
Word part	Type	Meaning
ad-	prefix	at, to, toward
renal	root	kidney
endo-	prefix	inside, within
crine	root	separate

Using Language

Cause and Effect In biological processes, one step leads to another step. When reading, you can often recognize these cause-and-effect relationships by words that indicate a result, such as *so, consequently, next, then,* and *as a result.*

Your Turn Identify the cause and the effect in the following sentences.
1. Some hormones cause growth. So, a person will be very tall if his or her body produces large amounts of these hormones.
2. Fear causes the production of adrenaline. As a result of the adrenaline, the heart beats faster and the body is prepared to run away.

Using FoldNotes

Booklet A booklet is a useful tool for taking notes as you read a chapter. Each page of the booklet can contain a main topic from the chapter and the details that describe the main topic.

Your Turn Make a booklet to help you organize your notes for this chapter.
1. Fold a sheet of paper in half from top to bottom.
2. Fold the sheet of paper in half again from left to right.
3. Fold the sheet of paper one more time from top to bottom.
4. Completely unfold the paper.
5. Refold the paper from top to bottom. Using scissors, cut a slit along the vertical crease in the sheet from the folded edge to the horizontal crease in the middle of the folded paper. Do not cut the entire sheet in half. Unfold the paper.
6. Fold the sheet of paper in half from left to right. While holding the bottom and top edges of the paper, push the bottom and top edges together so that the center collapses at the center slit. Fold the four flaps to form a four-page book.

Key Ideas	Key Terms	Why It Matters
❯ What are the major functions of the endocrine system? ❯ Which structures produce and release hormones? ❯ Which cells can be affected by hormones? ❯ What are two ways that hormones cause changes inside a cell? ❯ How are hormone levels in the body regulated?	hormone endocrine gland target cell second messenger feedback mechanism antagonistic hormone	The endocrine system helps the body respond to changes in the internal and external environment.

Chemical signals allow cells to communicate. Like the nervous system, the endocrine system uses chemicals to send messages to the cells of the body.

What Is the Endocrine System?

Chemical signals from the nervous system are sent along a nerve pathway and received in a fraction of a second. The endocrine system, on the other hand, sends its signals through the blood. Endocrine signals act over a longer period of time than nerve signals do. The nervous system sends messages that help the body react immediately. The endocrine system controls changes that happen in the body over a longer period of time. ❯ **The endocrine system regulates metabolism; maintains salt, water, and nutrient balance in the blood; controls the body's responses to stress; and regulates growth, development, and reproduction.**

The endocrine system sends chemical messages called *hormones* through the blood. **Hormones** are substances that are made in one part of the body and that cause changes in another part of the body. These chemical messengers cause cells to change their activities. For example, the cyclists in **Figure 1** are working hard. As they sweat, they lose water and salts. A hormone that is produced by the endocrine system causes the kidneys to produce less urine and to save water. This action helps prevent, but cannot completely prevent, dehydration. So, it is also important for the cyclists to drink plenty of fluids. Another hormone helps the body avoid losing too much salt. It causes the kidneys to filter salt from the urine and causes the sweat glands to release less salt in sweat.

hormone a substance that is made in one cell or tissue and that causes a change in another cell or tissue located in a different part of the body

Figure 1 Maintaining the water balance and the mineral balance in the blood are two functions of the endocrine system. ❯ **Why doesn't the endocrine system completely prevent water loss?**

Where Are Hormones Made?

Hormones are produced by special cells. Often, these cells are part of a *gland,* an organ that produces and releases substances. ❯ **Endocrine glands and endocrine tissues produce and release hormones.**

Endocrine and Exocrine Glands **Endocrine glands** are ductless glands that release hormones directly into the bloodstream or into the fluid around cells. The primary function of an endocrine gland is to make and release hormones. The major endocrine glands and their functions are shown in **Figure 2.**

Exocrine glands deliver nonhormonal substances through tube-like structures called *ducts.* Ducts transport substances to specific locations inside and outside the body. Sweat glands, mucous glands, and salivary glands are examples of exocrine glands. Some organs are both endocrine and exocrine glands. The pancreas acts as an exocrine gland when it delivers digestive enzymes to the small intestine through ducts. The pancreas acts as an endocrine gland when it releases hormones into the bloodstream.

Endocrine Tissues Several organs contain cells that release hormones. These organs include the brain, stomach, small intestine, kidneys, liver, and heart. Fat tissue also produces some hormones. These organs contain tissues that release hormones, but the organs have primary functions that are not part of the endocrine system.

❯ **Reading Check** *What is the difference between endocrine glands, endocrine tissues, and exocrine glands? (See the Appendix for answers to Reading Checks.)*

endocrine gland (EN doh KRIN) a ductless gland that secretes hormones into the blood

target cell a specific cell to which a hormone is directed to produce a specific effect

www.scilinks.org
Topic: Hormones
Code: HX80758

Figure 2 Endocrine glands, which secrete hormones, are located throughout the human body. Many organs that are not shown also have tissues that secrete hormones.

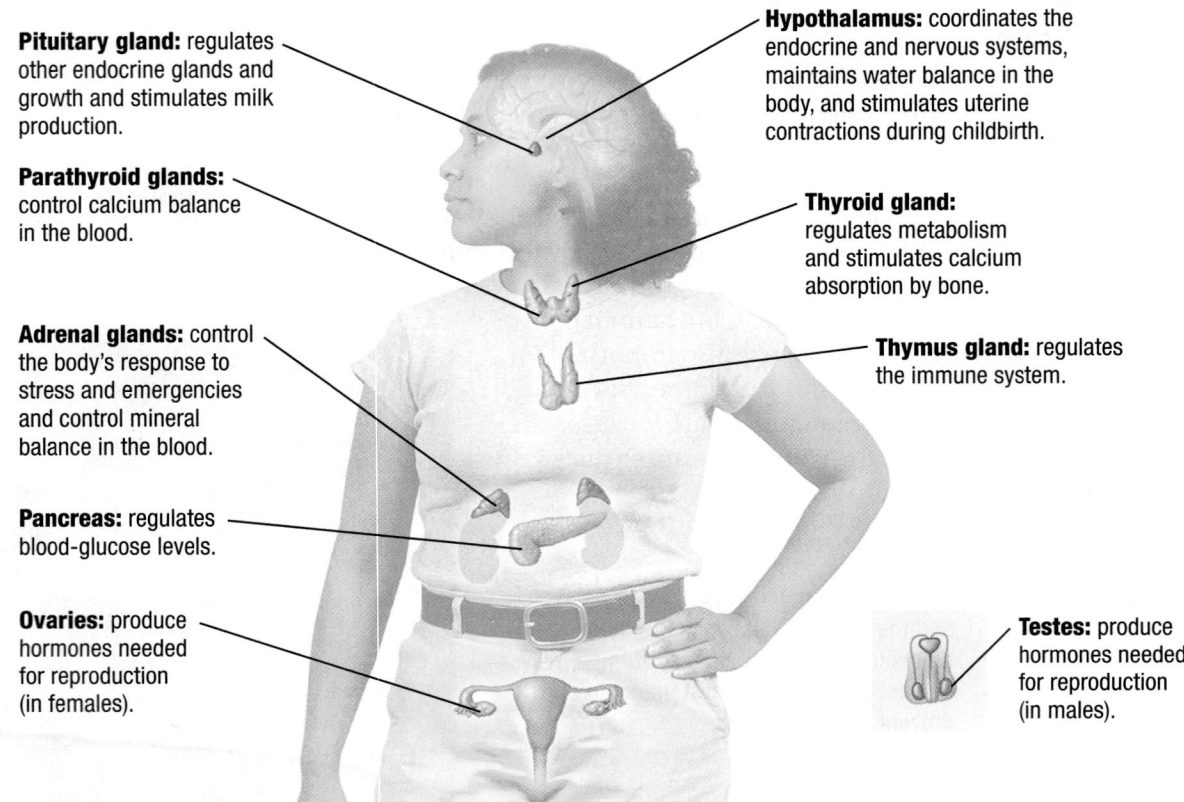

Pituitary gland: regulates other endocrine glands and growth and stimulates milk production.

Parathyroid glands: control calcium balance in the blood.

Adrenal glands: control the body's response to stress and emergencies and control mineral balance in the blood.

Pancreas: regulates blood-glucose levels.

Ovaries: produce hormones needed for reproduction (in females).

Hypothalamus: coordinates the endocrine and nervous systems, maintains water balance in the body, and stimulates uterine contractions during childbirth.

Thyroid gland: regulates metabolism and stimulates calcium absorption by bone.

Thymus gland: regulates the immune system.

Testes: produce hormones needed for reproduction (in males).

Hormones and Receptors

Because hormones circulate through the blood, they come into contact with most of the cells of the body. But hormones affect only certain cells. ❯ **Hormones can affect only cells that have receptor proteins that match the hormones.**

Types of Hormones The two main types of hormones are amino acid–based hormones and cholesterol-based hormones. Several hormonelike chemicals send messages between neighboring cells.

Amino Acid–Based Hormones Amino acid–based hormones are made of amino acids. Some are simple, and others are complex. Proteins and amino acids cannot pass through a cell membrane because they are not fat-soluble. As a result, they affect cells by attaching to proteins on the surfaces of the cells.

Cholesterol-Based Hormones The hormones in the second major group of hormones are made from cholesterol. They are called *steroid hormones*. Steroid hormones are fat-soluble, so they pass easily through cell membranes and attach to protein receptors inside the cell.

Hormonelike Substances Some chemical signals are sent from one cell directly to another and cause changes in nearby cells. These chemicals are not hormones because they do not circulate in the blood or affect cells in other parts of the body. Two examples of these substances are endorphins and prostaglandins. Endorphins work in the brain and affect emotions and pain perception. Prostaglandins are usually produced where tissues are injured. They cause pain and inflammation.

Hormone Receptors Hormones act only on target cells. **Target cells** are cells to which a hormone is directed to produce an effect. Target cells have receptor proteins. A hormone's shape matches the shape of a receptor protein like a key fits into a lock. The exact matching of hormones to receptors allows hormones to affect only certain body cells. **Figure 3** shows a hormone traveling through the bloodstream, and binding to a receptor on the surface of a target cell.

❯ **Reading Check** *How do amino acid–based and cholesterol-based hormones differ?*

Quick Lab

⏱ 20 min

Observing Solubilities

Some hormones are water-soluble, and some are not. In this lab, you will examine solubilities of different substances.

Procedure

1. Pour **75 mL of water** into a **100 mL beaker**. Add **2.5 g of gelatin**, and stir with a **spoon**. Record your observations.

2. Pour 75 mL of water into a second 100 mL beaker. Use a **dissecting pin** to puncture a **vitamin E capsule,** and squeeze the contents into the water. Stir the water, and record your observations.

3. Repeat steps 1 and 2 using **75 mL of cooking oil** instead of water. Record your observations.

Analysis

1. Which substance is water-soluble: gelatin or vitamin E?

2. Which substance is fat-soluble?

3. **CRITICAL THINKING** **Making Inferences** What is the relationship between the solubilities of hormones and whether the hormones enter their target cells or work outside of them?

Figure 3 Hormones travel through the blood to all parts of the body. However, hormones affect only cells that have receptors that match the hormones.

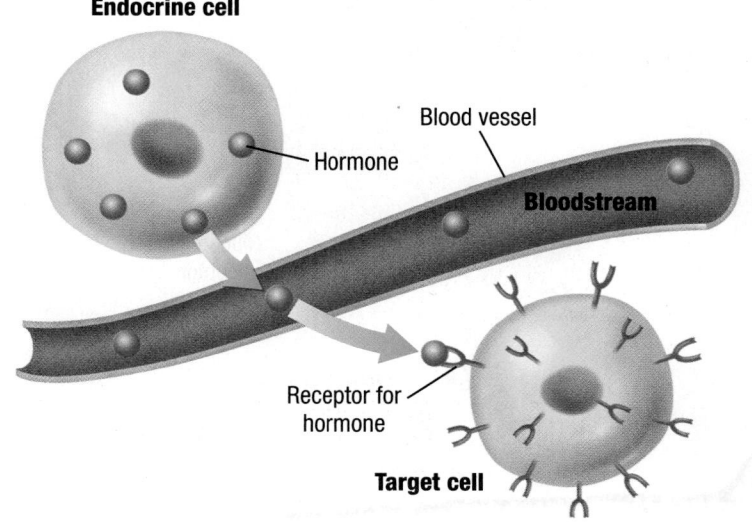

Hormone Function

The ability of a hormone to enter a target cell determines how the hormone works. ❯ **Amino acid–based hormones bind to the surface of target cells and cause changes by a second messenger system. Steroid hormones enter target cells and cause changes by direct gene activation.**

The Second Messenger System Amino acid–based hormones cannot pass through the cell membrane. They bind to receptors on the target cell's surface. The steps below and those shown in **Figure 4** explain how glucagon, a hormone released by the pancreas, works by using the second messenger system.

Step ❶ Glucagon circulates in the blood until it encounters a cell that has matching receptors on its surface. Glucagon binds to the receptor and causes the receptor to change shape.

Step ❷ The change in shape activates an enzyme that produces a second messenger. A **second messenger** is a molecule that passes the message from the hormone (first messenger) to the inside of the cell. In many cases, the second messenger is cyclic AMP (cAMP).

Step ❸ The second messenger activates or inactivates certain enzymes. One enzyme activates another enzyme, which activates another enzyme, and so on. This process is called an *enzyme cascade*. As **Figure 4** shows, cAMP activates an enzyme cascade that leads to the breakdown of glycogen into glucose.

Step ❹ Activity in the target cell is changed and glucose is produced even though glucagon never enters the cell.

> **second messenger** a molecule that is generated when a specific substance attaches to a receptor on the outside of a cell membrane, which produces a change in cellular function

Figure 4 Almost all amino acid–based hormones, such as glucagon, rely on second messengers to relay the hormone's message into the cell.

go.hrw.com
✳ interact online
Keyword: HX8ENDF4

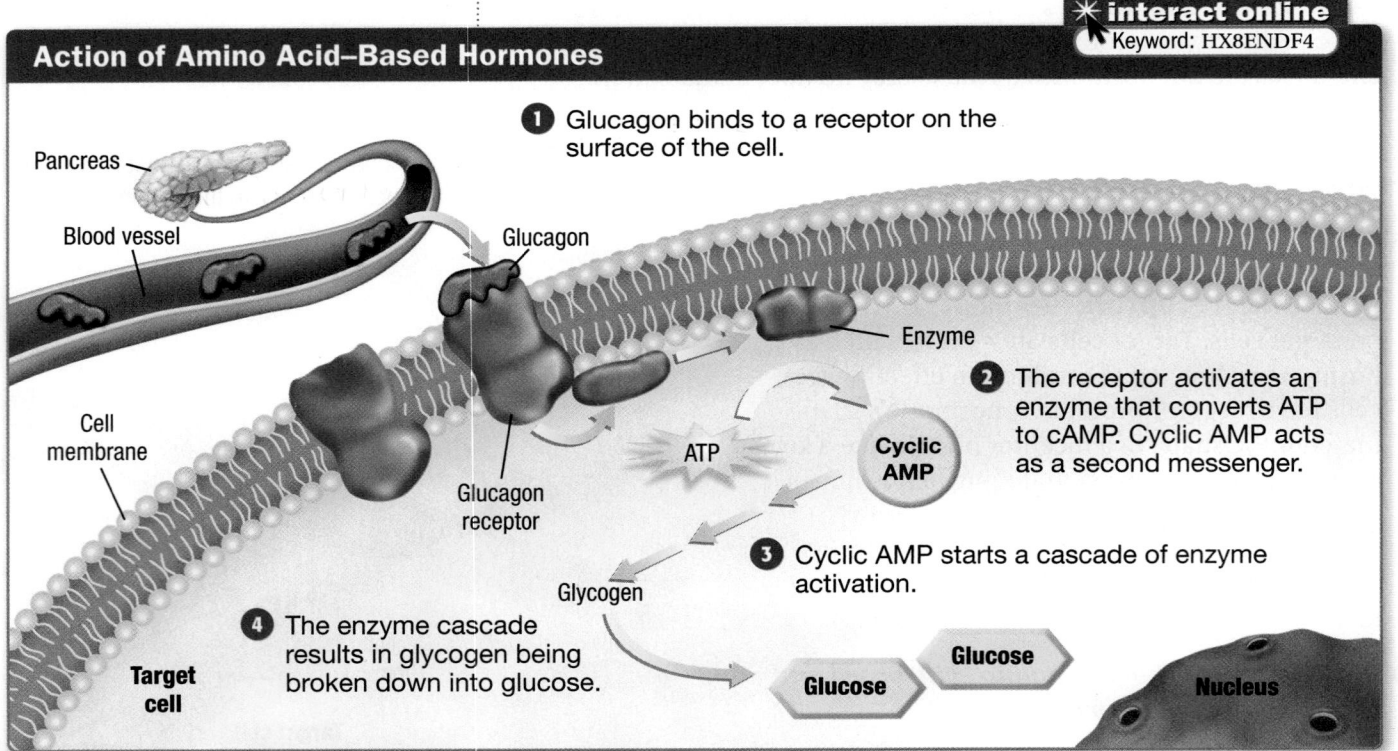

Action of Amino Acid–Based Hormones

Pancreas

Blood vessel

Glucagon

❶ Glucagon binds to a receptor on the surface of the cell.

Cell membrane

Enzyme

Glucagon receptor

ATP

Cyclic AMP

❷ The receptor activates an enzyme that converts ATP to cAMP. Cyclic AMP acts as a second messenger.

Glycogen

❸ Cyclic AMP starts a cascade of enzyme activation.

❹ The enzyme cascade results in glycogen being broken down into glucose.

Target cell

Glucose

Glucose

Nucleus

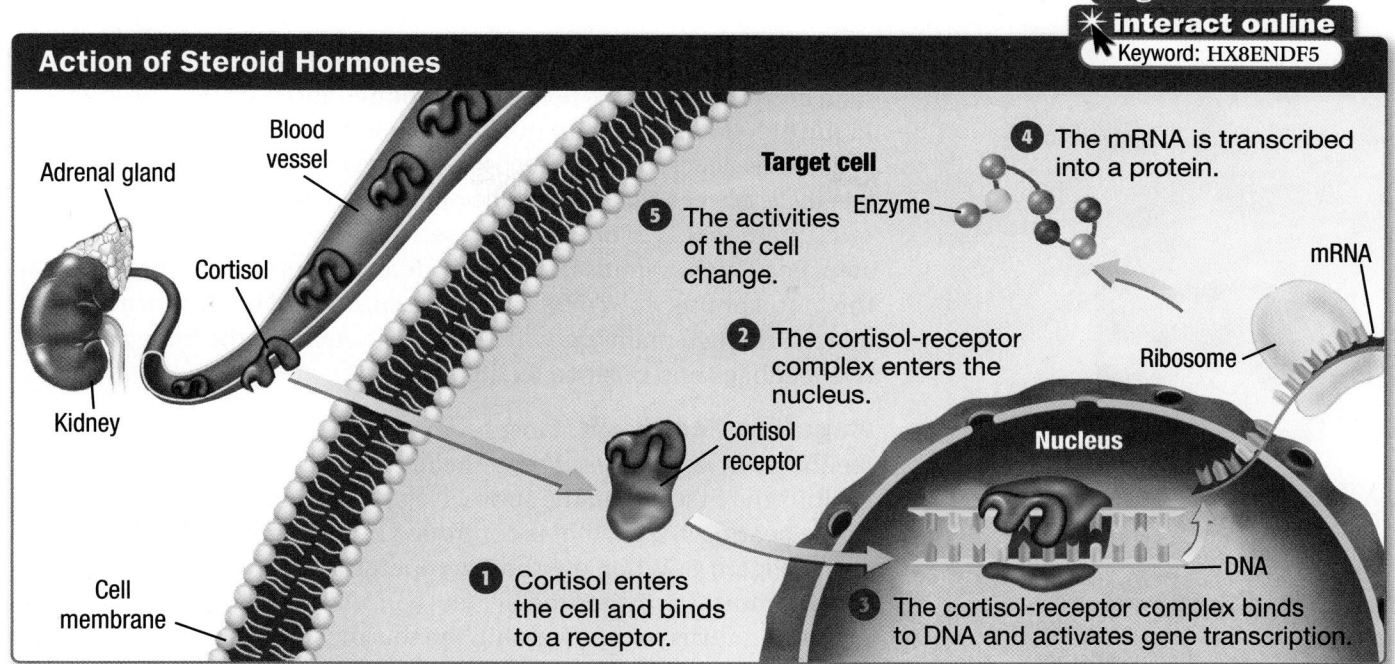

Action of Steroid Hormones

Adrenal gland

Blood vessel

Cortisol

Kidney

Cell membrane

Target cell

4 The mRNA is transcribed into a protein.

Enzyme

5 The activities of the cell change.

2 The cortisol-receptor complex enters the nucleus.

Cortisol receptor

mRNA

Ribosome

Nucleus

1 Cortisol enters the cell and binds to a receptor.

DNA

3 The cortisol-receptor complex binds to DNA and activates gene transcription.

Direct Gene Activation Cholesterol-based hormones, such as steroids, are fat-soluble. They pass through the membranes of cells that they encounter and bind to receptors inside target cells. Cortisol is a steroid hormone made in the adrenal gland. The steps below and those shown in **Figure 5** explain how cortisol causes direct changes in gene activity inside a target cell.

Step 1 Cortisol passes through the cell membrane and binds to a receptor inside the cell.

Step 2 The cortisol-receptor complex enters the nucleus of the cell and binds to DNA.

Step 3 The cortisol-receptor complex activates a gene. As a result, the gene is transcribed into a messenger RNA (mRNA). The resulting mRNA is then translated into a protein.

Step 4 The metabolic activities of the target cell are changed. For example, cortisol stimulates the production of enzymes that break down proteins and fats to make glucose.

The receptor for a hormone can be either in the cytosol or inside the nucleus of a cell. If the receptor for a steroid hormone is located in the nucleus, the hormone enters the nucleus and binds to the receptor there. When a hormone-receptor complex binds to DNA, the gene can be either activated or inactivated.

The thyroid gland produces amino acid–based hormones that are able to enter the cell. It is not currently known why thyroid hormones are able to pass through the cell membrane rather than affecting target cells by the second messenger system.

> **Reading Check** *How does glucagon cause the production of glucose in a cell?*

Figure 5 Cholesterol-based hormones, such as cortisol, pass through the cell membrane and directly activate or inactivate a gene. > **Why don't steroid hormones use second messengers?**

READING TOOLBOX

Cause and Effect Write cause-and-effect statements that describe how hormones affect target cells by the second messenger system and by direct gene activation.

Control of Hormone Levels

The body monitors the levels of hormones and hormone products in the blood and keeps them within a narrow range. ❯ **The body uses negative feedback, positive feedback, and antagonistic hormones to regulate the levels of hormones and their products.** A **feedback mechanism** is a system in which one step in a series of events controls an earlier step. Feedback systems in the body detect the amount of hormone in the blood or the amount of substances produced by the hormone's action. The two main types of feedback systems in the body are negative feedback and positive feedback.

Negative Feedback Most hormones are regulated by negative feedback. In *negative feedback,* the final step in a series of events inhibits the first step in the series. Negative feedback works like a home heating system that is controlled by a thermostat, such as the one in **Figure 6.** When the room temperature drops below a set point, the thermostat activates the heater to produce heat. When room temperature returns to the set point, the thermostat shuts off the heater. These actions maintain the room temperature within a narrow range.

How does negative feedback work in the body? High levels of a hormone stop the production of more hormone. On the other hand, low levels of a hormone cause the production of more hormone. For example, high levels of thyroid hormones in the blood stop the thyroid gland from releasing thyroid hormones. The liver also plays a role in negative feedback. When hormone levels get too high, the liver removes hormones from the blood and breaks them down. Negative feedback is illustrated in **Figure 7.**

Positive Feedback In *positive feedback,* the production of a hormone causes the release of more of the same hormone. The process continues until a specific event triggers hormone production to stop. For example, the hormone that causes the release of eggs in females works by positive feedback. Rising levels of hormones cause more hormone to be produced until an egg is released.

❯ **Reading Check** *What is the difference between negative and positive feedback mechanisms?*

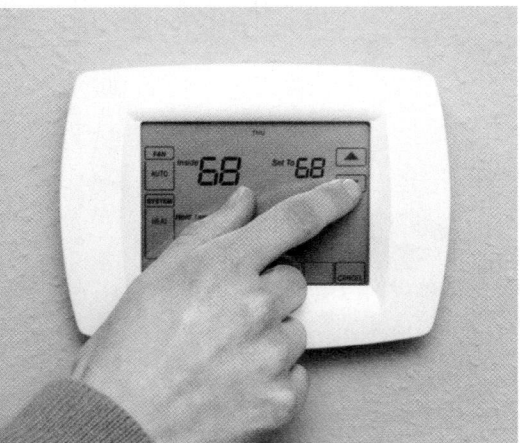

Figure 6 Like a thermostat, the endocrine system uses negative feedback to maintain homeostasis. ❯ **What would happen to the temperature of the room if a thermostat worked by positive feedback?**

ACADEMIC
VOCABULARY

specific definite or exact

Figure 7 In negative feedback, a second substance (A) stops the production of the first substance (B). In positive feedback, a second substance (A) stimulates production of the first substance (B).

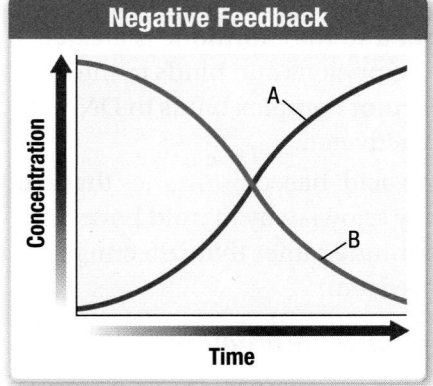

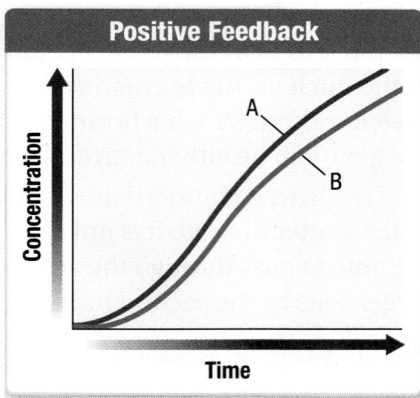

Antagonistic Hormones Some hormones work in pairs to control levels of substances. An **antagonistic hormone** counteracts the effect of another hormone. The release of each hormone is regulated by negative feedback. Insulin and glucagon are antagonistic hormones. They maintain blood-glucose levels within a narrow range, as **Figure 8** shows.

The idea of the thermostat can also apply to antagonistic hormones. Suppose that a home has a heater that turns on when the air temperature drops below a certain level and an air conditioner that turns on when the air temperature rises above a certain level. The paired functions of the heater and air conditioner, each controlled by negative feedback, would maintain a nearly constant air temperature.

Endocrine System Disorders There are three basic ways that the endocrine system can malfunction. A gland may produce too little or none of a certain hormone. A gland may produce too much of a certain hormone. Also, the body may fail to respond to a hormone.

Hyposecretion *Hyposecretion* is the production of too little or none of a hormone. If a person's body does not produce enough of a certain hormone, hormone replacement therapies can help. A large variety of hormones are now made by organisms, such as yeast, that have been genetically modified to make human hormones.

Hypersecretion In rare cases, the body may produce too much of a hormone, a process called *hypersecretion*. This can happen when a gland develops a tumor. The tumor cells grow uncontrollably and produce hormones in an uncontrolled way. This type of disorder often requires surgery to remove the tumor or affected gland.

Hormone Insensitivity Sometimes, the body produces the correct amount of hormones, but the cells are not able to respond. This type of disorder can be genetic, as in defective or missing receptors. The body can also become resistant to a hormone, so the cells stop responding to the hormone. Insensitivity disorders are sometimes managed by adjusting a person's lifestyle.

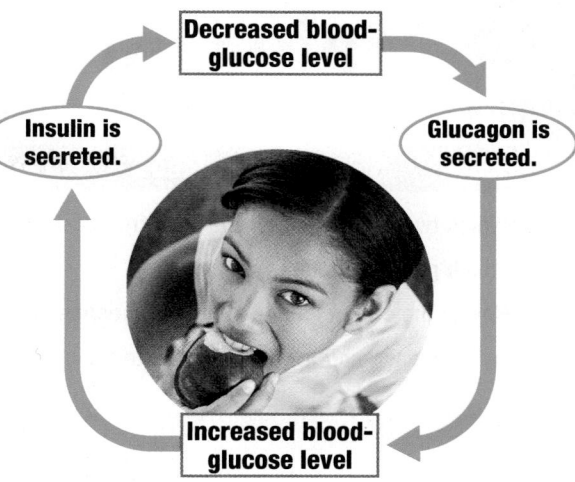

Decreased blood-glucose level

Insulin is secreted.

Glucagon is secreted.

Increased blood-glucose level

Figure 8 After eating a meal, a person's blood-glucose level increases. This increase causes the release of insulin, which lowers blood-glucose levels. After a period of time, glucose levels fall. Glucagon is released. Glucagon increases blood-glucose levels.

feedback mechanism a cycle of events in which information from one step controls or affects a previous step

antagonistic hormone a hormone that counteracts the effect of another hormone

---

Section 1 Review

> **KEY IDEAS**

1. **List** the major functions of the endocrine system.
2. **Identify** the structures that produce and release hormones.
3. **Explain** why hormones affect only certain cells.
4. **Compare** two ways that hormones cause changes inside a cell.
5. **Describe** how the endocrine system regulates hormone levels.

CRITICAL THINKING

6. **Recognizing Relationships** Which type of hormone, amino acid–based or cholesterol-based, has more possibilities for malfunction?
7. **Applying Information** During labor, oxytocin levels increase and cause stronger contractions until a certain point. What signal triggers the end of the positive feedback?

WRITING FOR SCIENCE

8. **Health Brochure** Research an endocrine disorder: hyposecretion, hypersecretion, or hormone insensitivity. Create and illustrate a health brochure for patients. In your brochure, explain the cause of the disorder, symptoms, and treatment options. Display your brochure for the class.

Major Endocrine Glands

Key Ideas	Key Terms	Why It Matters
❯ Which two glands control the endocrine system? ❯ Which glands regulate metabolism? ❯ How is the adrenal gland involved in responding to stress? ❯ Which glands and hormones regulate reproduction?	epinephrine norepinephrine androgen estrogen progesterone	The endocrine system works with the nervous system to regulate nearly all of the body's activities.

Endocrine glands are hormone-producing cells that have capillaries and lymph vessels woven through them. This structure allows glands to deliver their products easily into the blood and lymph fluid.

Controlling the Endocrine System

Two endocrine glands work with the nervous system to control the release of many hormones. Both of these glands are located at the base of the brain. ❯ **The hypothalamus and the pituitary gland work together to control the functions of the endocrine system.**

The Hypothalamus The hypothalamus (HIE poh THAL uh muhs), shown in **Figure 9,** coordinates the nervous and endocrine systems. Its functions in the nervous system include regulating the autonomic nervous system, hunger, thirst, and body temperature. The hypothalamus also produces hormones that regulate the endocrine system by controlling the release of hormones from the pituitary gland. In addition, the hypothalamus produces two hormones that are stored in and released by the posterior pituitary, oxytocin and antidiuretic hormone. Oxytocin stimulates uterine contractions during childbirth. Antidiuretic hormone (ADH) prevents dehydration by reducing the amount of water the kidneys excrete in urine.

SC*L*INKS®
www.scilinks.org
Topic: Endocrine System
Code: HX80504

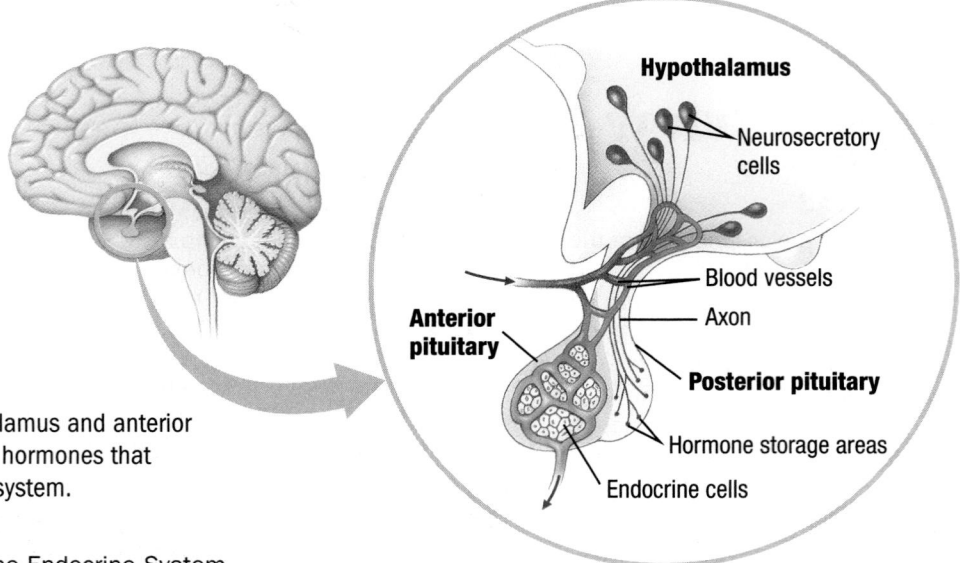

Figure 9 The hypothalamus and anterior pituitary gland produce hormones that regulate the endocrine system.

The Pituitary Gland The pituitary gland is a pea-sized gland that hangs by a short stalk directly below the hypothalamus. The anterior pituitary produces and secretes six important hormones.

Pituitary Hormones Four of the hormones that are produced by the anterior pituitary regulate hormone production in other glands. These four hormones are called *tropic hormones,* or *tropins.* The word part *tropi-* means "to turn or change." Tropins cause a change in the hormone production of other glands. The roles of these hormones are summarized in **Figure 10.**

Two pituitary hormones do not regulate the endocrine system. Growth hormone (GH) stimulates the cells of the body to grow and divide. This hormone primarily affects bones and muscles. Prolactin (PRL) stimulates milk production in women.

Pituitary Disorders Hypersecretion and hyposecretion of tropins affect the endocrine glands that are controlled by these hormones.

If the body produces too much GH during childhood, a person will be taller than average, a condition called *gigantism.* The tallest person on record is Robert Pershing Wadlow, who reached a height of 8 feet and 11 inches tall. If the body produces too much GH during adulthood, a condition called *acromegaly* results. Acromegaly causes growth in the hands, feet, jaws, and organs. If not treated, acromegaly can be fatal. If the body produces too little GH, a person can be shorter than average, a condition called *pituitary dwarfism.* If this condition is recognized early, it is easily treated by injection of synthetic growth hormone.

Hypersecretion of PRL causes women who are not breast-feeding and men to produce milk. Hyposecretion of PRL can cause a woman to be unable to breast-feed.

❯ **Reading Check** *Which hormones control the endocrine system?*

ACADEMIC
VOCABULARY

summarized explained in a brief way

Figure 10 The first four hormones listed in the table are tropins. They regulate production of hormones in other endocrine glands. ❯ **Which hormone is responsible for the difference in height of these teens?**

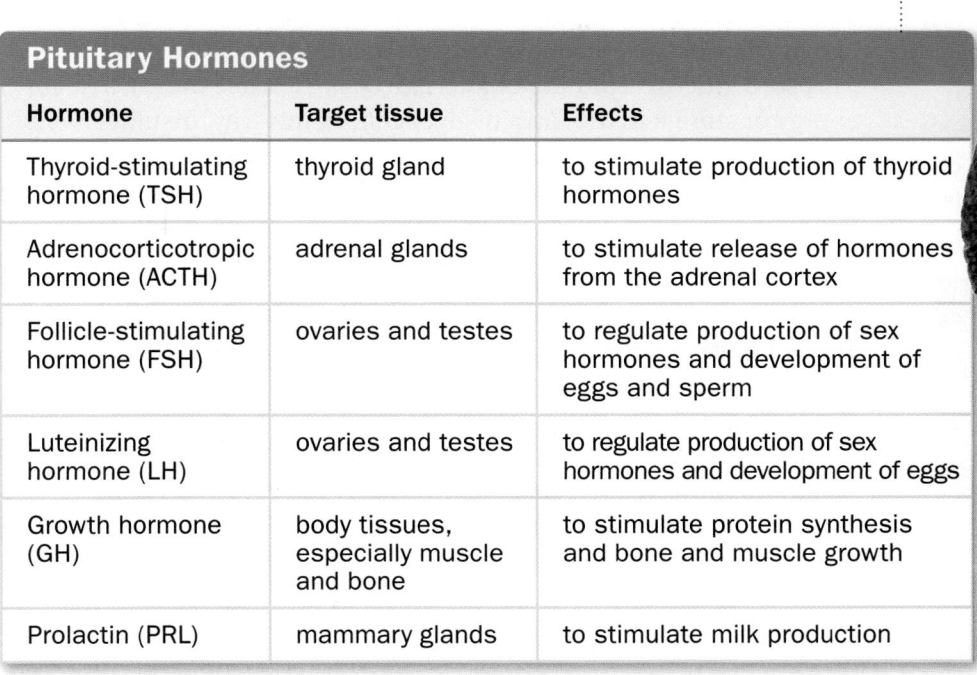

Pituitary Hormones		
Hormone	**Target tissue**	**Effects**
Thyroid-stimulating hormone (TSH)	thyroid gland	to stimulate production of thyroid hormones
Adrenocorticotropic hormone (ACTH)	adrenal glands	to stimulate release of hormones from the adrenal cortex
Follicle-stimulating hormone (FSH)	ovaries and testes	to regulate production of sex hormones and development of eggs and sperm
Luteinizing hormone (LH)	ovaries and testes	to regulate production of sex hormones and development of eggs
Growth hormone (GH)	body tissues, especially muscle and bone	to stimulate protein synthesis and bone and muscle growth
Prolactin (PRL)	mammary glands	to stimulate milk production

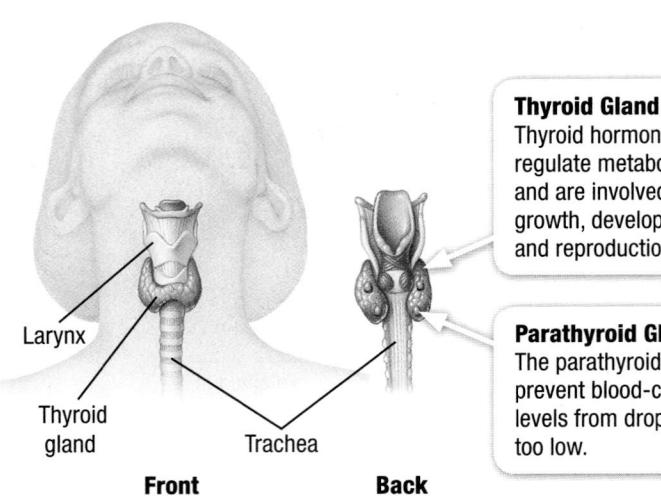

Thyroid Gland
Thyroid hormones regulate metabolic rate and are involved in growth, development, and reproduction.

Parathyroid Gland
The parathyroid glands prevent blood-calcium levels from dropping too low.

Larynx

Thyroid gland

Trachea

Front   **Back**

Figure 11 The thyroid gland, which is located in the neck, is wrapped around the trachea. The parathyroid glands are located on the back of the thyroid gland.

Figure 12 Inuits live in areas that have very little daylight in the winter months. This lack of light can disrupt production of melatonin, which leads to a mood disorder that Inuits call *arctic hysteria*.

Regulating Metabolism

❯ The thyroid gland, parathyroid glands, pancreas, and pineal gland regulate the body's metabolic processes.

The Thyroid Gland Thyroid hormones are the primary regulators of metabolic rate. They control protein production and oxygen use by cells.

Thyroid hormones are amino acid–based hormones that contain iodine. If a person's diet lacks iodine, the thyroid gland cannot function properly and becomes enlarged. Iodine deficiency has been almost eliminated in the United States because of iodized table salt. Iodine deficiency is still a problem in many parts of the world. Health organizations are working to provide iodized salt in every country.

Hypothyroidism is a condition in which the body has too little thyroid hormone. In children, it can cause stunted growth and brain damage. In adults, it can cause lack of energy, dry skin, and weight gain. *Hyperthyroidism,* too much thyroid hormone, can cause nervousness, irregular heart rate, and weight loss.

The Parathyroid Glands Calcium is a very important mineral. It is required for nerve function and muscle contraction. If there is too little calcium in the blood, the nervous system will shut down. Parathyroid hormone (PTH) is a hormone that is produced by the parathyroid glands, as **Figure 11** shows. PTH is made and released in response to falling levels of calcium in the blood. PTH raises calcium levels by causing bone cells to release calcium into the blood and by signaling the kidneys to reabsorb calcium from urine.

The Pancreas The pancreas contains clusters of cells that produce two hormones: *insulin* and *glucagon.* Insulin causes the body's cells to absorb glucose from the blood. The cells then use the glucose for energy or store it in the form of glycogen. In this way, insulin lowers blood-glucose levels. Glucagon causes liver cells to release glucose that was stored as glycogen, thus raising blood-glucose levels. Tight regulation of blood glucose is important. High blood-glucose levels can damage blood vessels and organs. If blood-glucose levels drop too low, the brain cannot function.

The Pineal Gland The pineal gland is a pea-sized gland that is located in the brain. It secretes the hormone melatonin. Melatonin regulates the body's daily sleep cycle and the *circadian rhythm.* The release of melatonin is stimulated by darkness and inhibited by light. Melatonin production can be disrupted by too much or too little light, as in arctic regions like the one shown in **Figure 12.** Abnormal production of melatonin can result in a mood disorder called *seasonal affective disorder* (SAD). Melatonin therapy is used to treat insomnia, jet lag, and certain mood disorders including SAD.

Responding to Stress

The body has two adrenal glands located above each kidney. Each adrenal gland is two glands in one. As **Figure 13** shows, an adrenal gland has an inner core, the *adrenal medulla,* and an outer layer, the *adrenal cortex.* Each part plays a role in the body's response to stress. ❯ **The adrenal medulla regulates short-term responses to stress. The adrenal cortex regulates long-term responses to stress.**

Short-Term Response The adrenal medulla releases the hormones epinephrine and norepinephrine (formerly called *adrenaline* and *noradrenaline.*) These hormones are responsible for the fight-or-flight response. **Epinephrine** increases heart rate and blood flow to the muscles and brain. It also stimulates the liver to convert glycogen to glucose, which makes more energy available to the muscles. **Norepinephrine** increases blood pressure, ensuring efficient nutrient and oxygen delivery to muscle tissues.

Long-Term Response The adrenal cortex makes several hormones called *corticosteroids* that are released in response to prolonged or severe stress. This stress can be emotional or physical. Aldosterone regulates salt concentration in the blood and raises blood pressure. Cortisol, also called *hydrocortisone,* causes the body to make glucose from fats and proteins. High levels of cortisol inhibit inflammation and suppress the immune system. Long-term stress can cause cortisol levels to remain high for long periods of time. People who are under long-term stress can face a higher risk for illness. Other effects of long-term stress on health are being studied.

Cortisol is often used to treat inflammatory disorders, such as arthritis. However, long-term use of cortisol can result in chronic high blood sugar called *steroid diabetes.* It also causes water retention and chronic high blood pressure. In addition, it causes muscle and bone loss as protein is converted to glucose for use by the body.

❯ **Reading Check** *Which hormones are part of the body's long-term response to stress?*

epinephrine (EP uh NEF rin) a hormone that stimulates the metabolism in emergencies, increases heart rate and blood flow and raises blood-glucose

norepinephrine (NAWR ep uh NEF rin) a chemical that stimulates the circulatory and respiratory systems

READING TOOLBOX

Booklet Make a booklet to organize your notes about endocrine glands. Include information about the glands that control the endocrine system, regulate metabolism, respond to stress, and control reproduction and development.

Figure 13 Each adrenal gland has two parts—the adrenal medulla and the adrenal cortex—that regulate the body's response to stress.

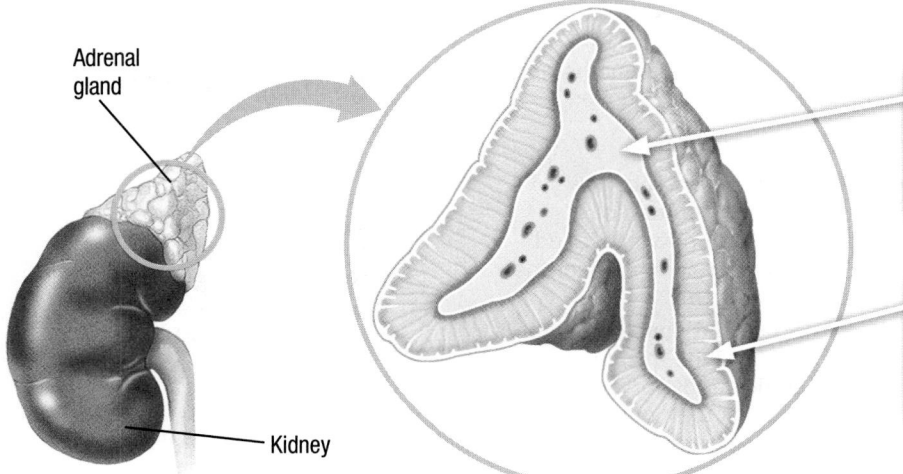

Adrenal Medulla The adrenal medulla regulates short-term responses to stress. It increases heart rate, blood pressure, blood flow to muscles, and blood-glucose levels.

Adrenal Cortex The adrenal cortex regulates long-term responses to stress by raising the levels of sugar, fats, and proteins in the blood, and by raising blood pressure.

Regulating Reproduction

❯ **Reproduction is regulated by the gonadotropins, which are released by the pituitary gland, and by sex hormones, which are released by the gonads.** These hormones regulate the development and function of the reproductive system.

Gonadotropins Gonadotropins (GOH nad oh TROH pinz) are hormones produced by the pituitary gland that regulate the function of the gonads (ovaries and testes.) Gonadotropins cause gonads to mature during puberty. The gonadotropins include follicle stimulating hormone (FSH) and luteinizing hormone (LH). Both FSH and LH stimulate the gonads to produce sex hormones. In addition, FSH stimulates egg and sperm production, and LH causes the release of mature eggs from the ovaries.

Gonads In addition to producing eggs and sperm, the gonads also produce hormones called *sex hormones.* There are three types of sex hormones: androgens, estrogen, and progesterone.

Androgens are primarily male sex hormones that are primarily produced by the testes. The main androgen is testosterone. If androgens are secreted during an embryo's development, the embryo will develop into a male. Androgens regulate the development and function of the male reproductive system. During puberty, they cause the appearance of male secondary sex characteristics.

Ovaries produce estrogen and progesterone. **Estrogen** and **progesterone** are hormones that regulate the female reproductive system. They work together to cause the development of female secondary sex characteristics, regulate the menstrual cycle, prepare the uterus for pregnancy, and maintain the uterus during pregnancy.

The adrenal cortex also produces some sex hormones. As a result, both males and females have all three sex hormones. However, the amount of these hormones produced by the adrenal glands is relatively small compared with the amount produced by the gonads.

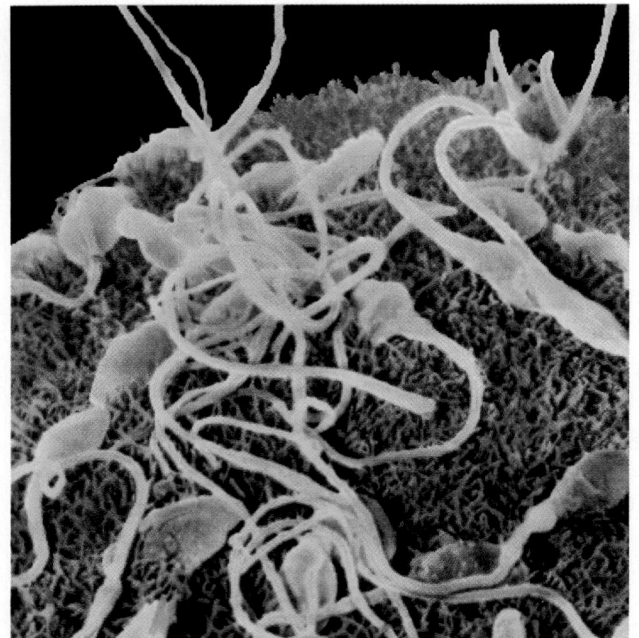

Figure 14 Sperm surround an egg before fertilization. Production of eggs and sperm is controlled by the pituitary gland and the gonads.

androgen a type of hormone that regulates the sexual development of males and stimulates development of male secondary sex characteristics

estrogen a hormone that regulates the sexual development and reproductive function of females

progesterone a steroid hormone that is secreted by the corpus luteum of the ovary, that stimulates changes in the uterus to prepare for the implantation of a fertilized egg

---

Section 2 Review

❯ KEY IDEAS

1. **Name** the two glands that control the endocrine system.
2. **Identify** four glands that are responsible for regulating metabolism.
3. **Describe** the two parts of the adrenal gland that respond to stress.
4. **Identify** the glands and hormones that regulate reproduction.

CRITICAL THINKING

5. **Applying Informaton** How might hypersecretion of parathyroid hormones, called hyperparathyroidism, affect the skeletal system?
6. **Inferring Relationships** Goiter is a swelling of the thyroid gland due to insufficient dietary iodine. Why do you think that iodine deficiency causes the thyroid gland to swell?

WRITING FOR SCIENCE

7. **Pamphlet** Imagine that you are working for a local health department. Prepare a pamphlet for middle school students that explains hormonal changes during puberty. Include information about the roles of testosterone, estrogens, and progesterone.

Diabetes

About 14.7 million Americans suffer from diabetes. Between 90% and 95% of all diagnosed cases of diabetes are type 2 diabetes. Type 2 diabetes is associated with being overweight. About 17% of American children are overweight, and about 32% of American adults are obese.

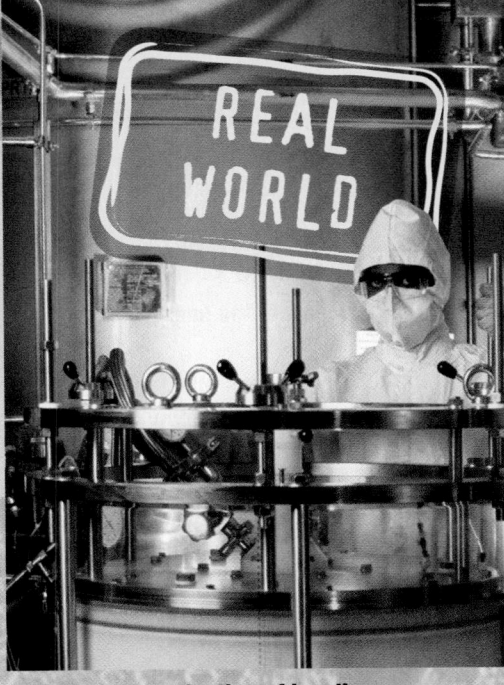

laboratory production of insulin

What is Diabetes?

There are two types of diabetes. With type 1 diabetes, the immune system destroys insulin-producing cells in the pancreas. This type of diabetes tends to run in families and often begins in childhood. Type 2 diabetes begins as insulin resistance, a disorder in which the cells of the body do not respond properly to insulin. The pancreas produces more insulin but eventually cannot produce enough to regulate blood glucose. Symptoms of diabetes include excessive thirst, increased urination, unexplained weight loss, sudden vision changes, and sores that are slow to heal.

Dangers of Diabetes If diabetes goes untreated, chronic high blood glucose can damage many parts of the body. Diabetes can lead to blindness, amputation of the feet, respiratory problems, kidney damage, heart disease, stroke, and other problems related to blood vessel and nerve damage.

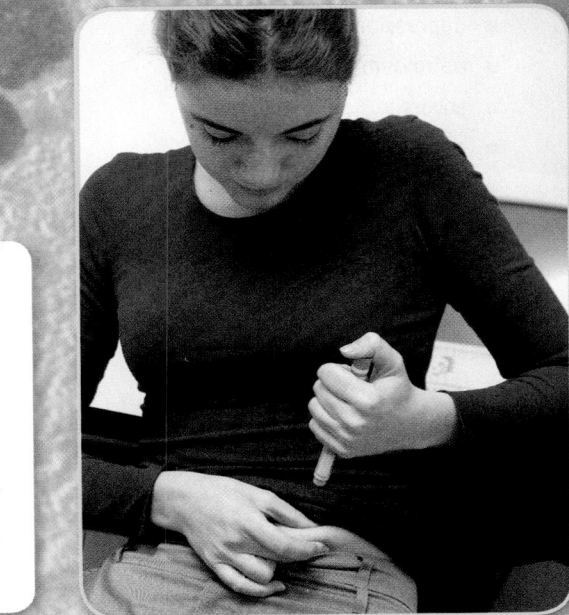

Living with Diabetes It is extremely important for people with diabetes to closely monitor their blood glucose. Type 1 diabetes can be treated with insulin injections. Exercise and a healthy diet can help prevent and manage type 2 diabetes.

Research Research the origin of the names *diabetes mellitus* and *diabetes insipidus*. Find out the difference between these two types of diabetes, and write a brief report about your findings.

Objectives

▶ Measure the heart rate of daphnia.

▶ Observe the effect of the hormone epinephrine on heart rate in daphnia.

▶ Determine the threshold concentration for the effects of epinephrine on daphnia.

Materials

- medicine dropper
- daphnia
- daphnia culture water
- depression slide
- petroleum jelly
- coverslip
- compound microscope
- watch or clock with second hand
- paper towels
- beaker, 100 mL
- graduated cylinder, 10 mL
- epinephrine solutions, 0.001%, 0.0001%, 0.00001%, and 0.000001%

Safety

Epinephrine and Heart Rate

Epinephrine is a hormone that increases blood pressure, blood-glucose level, and heart rate (HR). The lowest concentration that stimulates a response is called the *threshold concentration*.

In this lab, you will design an experiment to investigate the threshold concentration of epinephrine that affects heart rate. To do this, you will observe heart rate of the crustacean daphnia under experimental conditions that you determine.

Preparation

1. **SCIENTIFIC METHODS** **State the Problem** What is the threshold concentration of epinephrine that affects the heart rate of daphnia?

2. **SCIENTIFIC METHODS** **Form a Hypothesis** Form a testable hypothesis that explains how epinephrine might affect the heart rate of daphnia. Record your hypothesis.

Procedure

Observe Heart Rate in Daphnia

1 ◈ ◈ ◆ Put on safety goggles, gloves, and a lab apron.

2 ◆ **CAUTION: Do not touch your face while handling microorganisms.** Use a clean medicine dropper to transfer one daphnia to the well of a clean depression slide. Place a dab of petroleum jelly in the well. Add a coverslip. Observe the daphnia with a compound microscope under low power.

3 Count the daphnia's heartbeats for 10 s. Divide this number by 10 to find the HR in beats per second. Record your observations in a data table as Trial 1. Turn off the microscope light, and wait 20 s. Repeat this step two times, and record your observations as Trials 2 and 3.

4 Calculate the average HR in beats per second. Then calculate the average heartrate in beats per minute using the following formula:

$$\text{Ave HR (beats per minute)} = \text{Ave HR (beats per second)} \times 60 \text{ s/min.}$$

	Daphnia Heart Rate				
Solution	*HR (beats per second) Trial 1 (A)*	*HR (beats per second) Trial 2 (B)*	*HR (beats per second) Trial 3 (C)*	*Average HR (beats per second) [(A+B+C)/3]*	*Average HR (beats per minute)*

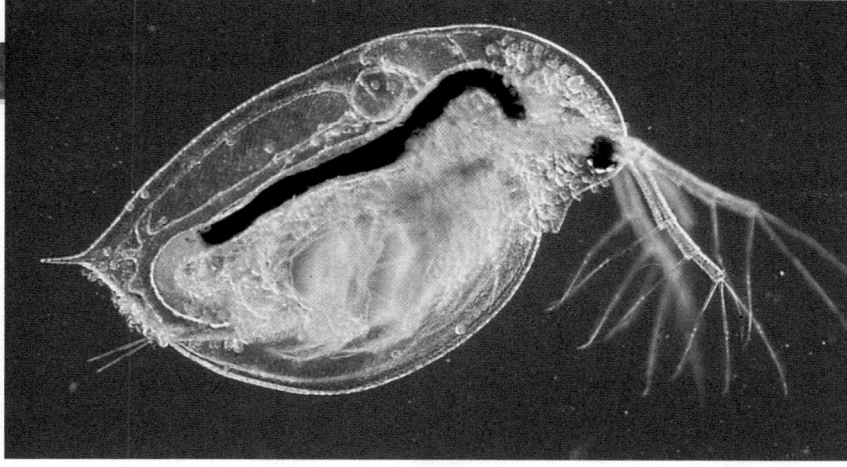

Daphnia

Design an Experiment

5 Design an experiment that tests your hypothesis and that uses the materials listed for this lab. Predict what will happen during your experiment if your hypothesis is supported.

6 CAUTION: **Handle animals carefully and with respect.** Write a procedure for your experiment. Identify the controlled variables, the experimental variables, and the responding variables. Construct any tables that you will need to record your data. Make a list of all of the safety precautions that you will take. Have your teacher approve your procedure and safety precautions before you begin.

Conduct Your Experiment

7 CAUTION: **Glassware such as coverslips and slides are fragile. Notify your teacher of broken glass or cuts.** To add a solution to a prepared slide, first place a drop of the solution at the edge of the coverslip. Then, place a piece of paper towel along the opposite edge to draw the solution under the coverslip. Wait 1 min for the solution to take effect.

8 CAUTION: **Epinephrine is toxic and is absorbed through the skin. Wear gloves at all times during this experiment. Notify your teacher of any spills.** Perform your experiment. Record your observations in a data table.

9 Clean up your lab materials according to your teacher's instructions. Wash your hands before leaving the lab.

www.scilinks.org
Topic: Hormones
Code: HX80758

Analyze and Conclude

1. **Summarizing Results** Make a graph of your data. Plot "Epinephrine concentration (%)" on the x-axis. Plot "Average heart rate (beats per minute)" on the y-axis.

2. SCIENTIFIC METHODS **Analyzing Data** Which solutions affected the heart rate of daphnia?

3. SCIENTIFIC METHODS **Interpreting Data** What was the threshold concentration of epinephrine?

4. **Making Predictions** Based on the information that you have and based on your data, predict how epinephrine concentration would affect heart rates in humans.

Extensions

5. **Inferring Relationships** Research anaphylactic shock. Explain why epinephrine is used to treat anaphylactic shock?

6. **Further Inquiry** Write a new question about hormones that could be explored with another investigation.

Chapter 39 Summary

Key Ideas	Key Terms

1 Hormones

> The endocrine system regulates metabolism; salt, water, and nutrient balance in the blood; controls the body's response to stress; and regulates growth, development, and reproduction.

> Endocrine glands and endocrine tissues produce and release hormones.

> Hormones can affect only cells that have receptor proteins that match the hormone.

> Amino acid–based hormones bind to the surface of target cells and cause changes by a second messenger system. Steroid hormones enter target cells and cause changes by direct gene activation.

> The body uses negative feedback, positive feedback, and antagonistic hormones to regulate the levels of hormones and their products.

Key Terms

hormone (971)
endocrine gland (972)
target cell (972)
second messenger (974)
feedback mechanism (976)
antagonistic hormone (977)

2 Major Endocrine Glands

> The hypothalamus and the pituitary gland work together to control the functions of the endocrine system.

> The thyroid gland, parathyroid gland, pancreas, and pineal glands regulate metabolism.

> The adrenal medulla regulates short-term responses to stress. The adrenal cortex regulates long-term responses to stress.

> Reproduction is regulated by gonadotropins, which are released by the pituitary gland, and by sex hormones, which are released by the gonads.

epinephrine (981)
norepinephrine (981)
androgen (982)
estrogen (982)
progesterone (982)

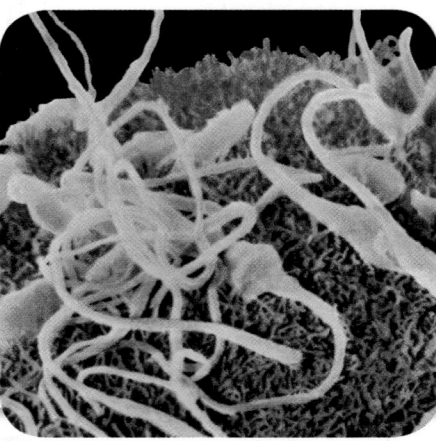

1. Booklet Use your booklet to review main ideas from this chapter. If you are confused about any of the ideas, reread the section in your textbook or talk to your teacher and then add to your notes.

2. Concept Map Make a concept map that describes the endocrine system. Try to include the following words: *hypothalamus, pituitary gland, thyroid gland, hormones, adrenal glands,* and *target cell.*

Using Key Terms

Use the following terms in the same sentence.

3. *hormone, endocrine gland,* and *target cell*

4. *adrenal gland, epinephrine,* and *norepinephrine*

For each pair of terms, explain how the meaning of the terms differ.

5. *hypothalamus* and *pituitary gland*

6. *insulin* and *glucagon*

Understanding Key Ideas

7. The endocrine system regulates all of the following processes *except*
   a. metabolism.
   b. sleep cycles.
   c. thought processes.
   d. salt and water balance.

8. Organs that release hormones into the bloodstream are
   a. exocrine glands. **c.** secretory glands.
   b. excretory glands. **d.** endocrine glands.

9. Which type of hormone causes a change in a cell by direct gene activation?
   a. antagonistic hormones
   b. cholesterol-based hormones
   c. amino acid–based hormones
   d. second messenger hormones

10. Amino acid–based hormones use cAMP as a(n)
   a. enzyme. **c.** target cell.
   b. receptor. **d.** second messenger.

11. A system in which the final step in a series of events inhibits the first step is called
   a. antagonism.
   b. positive feedback.
   c. negative feedback.
   d. endocrine feedback.

12. The hypothalamus produces hormones that are stored in the
   a. thyroid gland.
   b. hypothalamus.
   c. anterior pituitary.
   d. posterior pituitary.

13. Based on the diagram shown, patient Y probably has which of the following conditions?

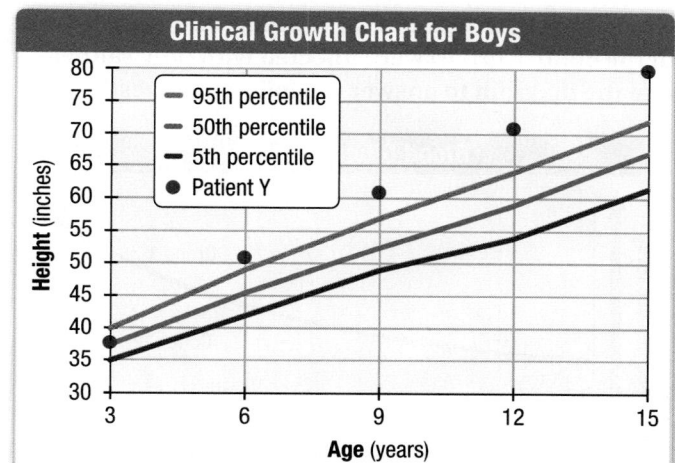

   a. gigantism
   b. acromegaly
   c. hypersecretion of TSH
   d. hyposecretion of growth hormone

14. Which organ regulates blood-glucose levels?
   a. pancreas
   b. pineal gland
   c. thyroid gland
   d. parathyroid gland

15. Which part of the adrenal gland regulates the body's short-term response to stress?
   a. adrenal cortex
   b. adrenal medulla
   c. anterior adrenal gland
   d. posterior adrenal gland

Explaining Key Ideas

16. **Describe** how an amino acid–based hormone changes a cell's activity.

17. **Summarize** the role of the parathyroid gland in regulating blood-calcium levels.

18. **Distinguish** between a positive feedback mechanism and a negative feedback mechanism.

19. **Explain** how hormones recognize their target cells.

20. **List** three major types of activities in the body that are regulated by the endocrine system.

21. **Discuss** the role of gonadotropins and sex hormones in regulating reproduction.

Using Science Graphics

The diagram shows the effects of hormone injections on blood-glucose levels in rats. Rats in groups 1 and 2 were injected with saline containing a hormone. Rats in the control group were injected with only saline. Use the diagram to answer the following question(s).

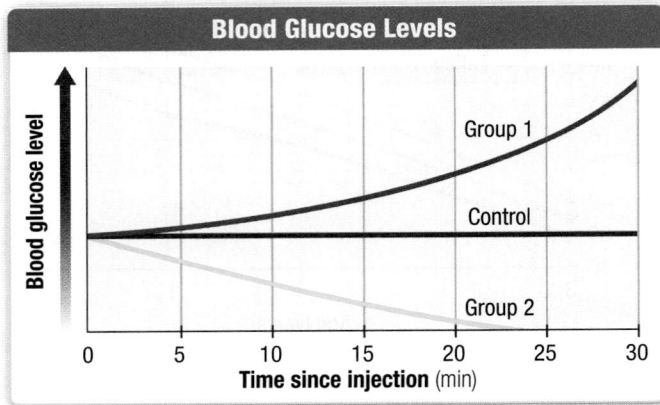

Blood Glucose Levels

22. Which hormone was likely contained in the injection that was given to rats in group 1?
    a. insulin
    b. oxytocin
    c. glucagon
    d. calcitonin

23. Which hormone was likely contained in the injection that was given to rats in group 2?
    a. insulin
    b. oxytocin
    c. glucagon
    d. calcitonin

Critical Thinking

24. **Making Predictions** X and Y are hormones. X stimulates the secretion of Y. Y exerts negative feedback on the cells that secrete X. What happens when the level of Y in the blood decreases?

25. **Applying Information** Prostaglandins are hormones that cause the body to feel pain when the body is injured. Why might it be important for the body to feel pain after an injury?

26. **Proposing Explanations** Before the discovery of the parathyroid glands, some patients who had their thyroid removed suffered muscle spasms, severe pain, and death. What might have been the cause of these deaths?

Writing for Science

27. **Summarizing** Conduct library or Internet research on the neurotransmitter hormone serotonin and its possible role in depression. Also, look for information about how SSRI (selective serotonin reuptake inhibitors) work and their effectiveness in treating depression. Write a one-page summary of your findings.

Alternative Assessment

28. **Survey** Conduct a poll of people in your school who run regularly (such as members of the track team). Ask them if they experience a runner's high, and ask them to describe it. Ask how long they have to run before they experience this effect. Also, ask if this response is strong enough to make them run more than they would otherwise. Prepare a computer presentation or poster of your findings. Include information on the role of endorphins.

Math Skills

29. **Unit Conversion** The following are normal laboratory values for blood levels of the hormones epinephrine and thyroxine: epinephrine—20 ng/ml and thyroxine—8 μg/ml. Convert the values to milligrams per milliliter.

Note: 1 mg = 1,000 μg = 1,000,000 ng

Which hormone is normally present in higher concentrations in the blood?

Science Concepts

1. If a change in the body causes more change in the same direction, the system is called
   A feedback inhibition.   **C** positive feedback.
   B negative feedback.   **D** neutral feedback.

2. Which of the following is a function of hormones?
   F making cAMP
   G causing stress
   H regulating movement
   J regulating metabolism

3. Which is produced by the testes?
   A oxytocin   **C** testosterone
   B estrogen   **D** progesterone

4. In what way do amino acid–based hormones use cyclic AMP?
   F as a receptor   **H** as a target cell
   G as a coenzyme   **J** as second messenger

Using Science Graphics

The diagram shows a feedback mechanism. Hormone A triggers cell M to release hormone B. Hormone B inhibits the release of hormone A. Use the diagram to answer the following question(s).

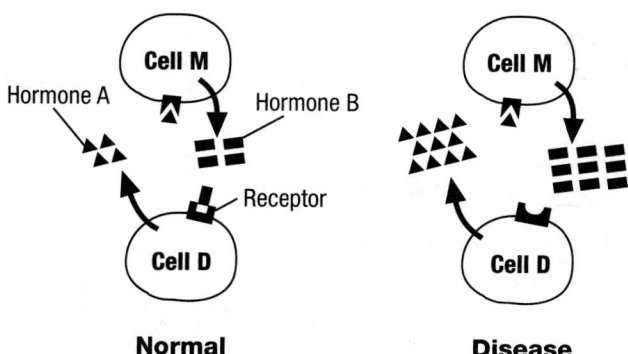

Normal   **Disease**

5. In the disease state, which structure is defective?
   A hormone A   **C** cell M receptor
   B hormone B   **D** cell D receptor

6. What happens in the disease state?
   F Cell D cannot produce hormone A.
   G Hormone A increases because of a lack of hormone B.
   H Hormone A increases because cell D cannot detect hormone B.
   J Cell M does not secrete any hormone B because cell M is not stimulated.

The diagram shows the change in blood-glucose levels after two different meals. Use the diagram to answer the following question(s).

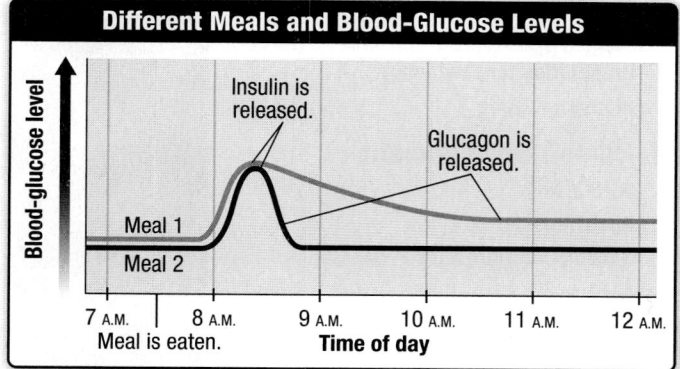

Different Meals and Blood-Glucose Levels

7. Which of the following statements is true?
   A Meal 1 causes no increase in blood glucose.
   B Meal 2 causes no increase in blood glucose.
   C Meal 1 causes a sharp decrease in blood glucose shortly after eating.
   D Meal 2 causes a sharp decrease in blood glucose shortly after eating.

8. Complex carbohydrates and proteins allow glucose to be released slowly into the bloodstream. From this information and from the diagram, what can you infer about meal 1?
   F It contains a lot of protein.
   G It contains a lot of simple sugars.
   H It will cause a large production of glucagon.
   J It includes two doughnuts and a glass of juice.

Writing Skills

9. Short Response Write a paragraph comparing the way steroid hormones affect cells with the way amino acid–based hormones affect cells.

Reproduction and Development

Preview

1 The Male Reproductive System
Sperm Production
Sperm's Path Through the Body
Semen
Sperm Delivery

2 The Female Reproductive System
Egg Production
Preparation for Pregnancy
Menstrual Cycle

3 Human Development
Fertilization
First Trimester
Second and Third Trimesters

4 Sexually Transmitted Infections
STI Transmission and Treatment
Common STIs

Why It Matters

All people start life as a single fertilized egg. Thus, the story of a fertilized egg's formation and development is the story of how your own life began.

This human fetus has been developing inside its mother for four months.

This fetus is only a little longer than 10 cm, but it is already able to hear, move, sleep, and swallow.

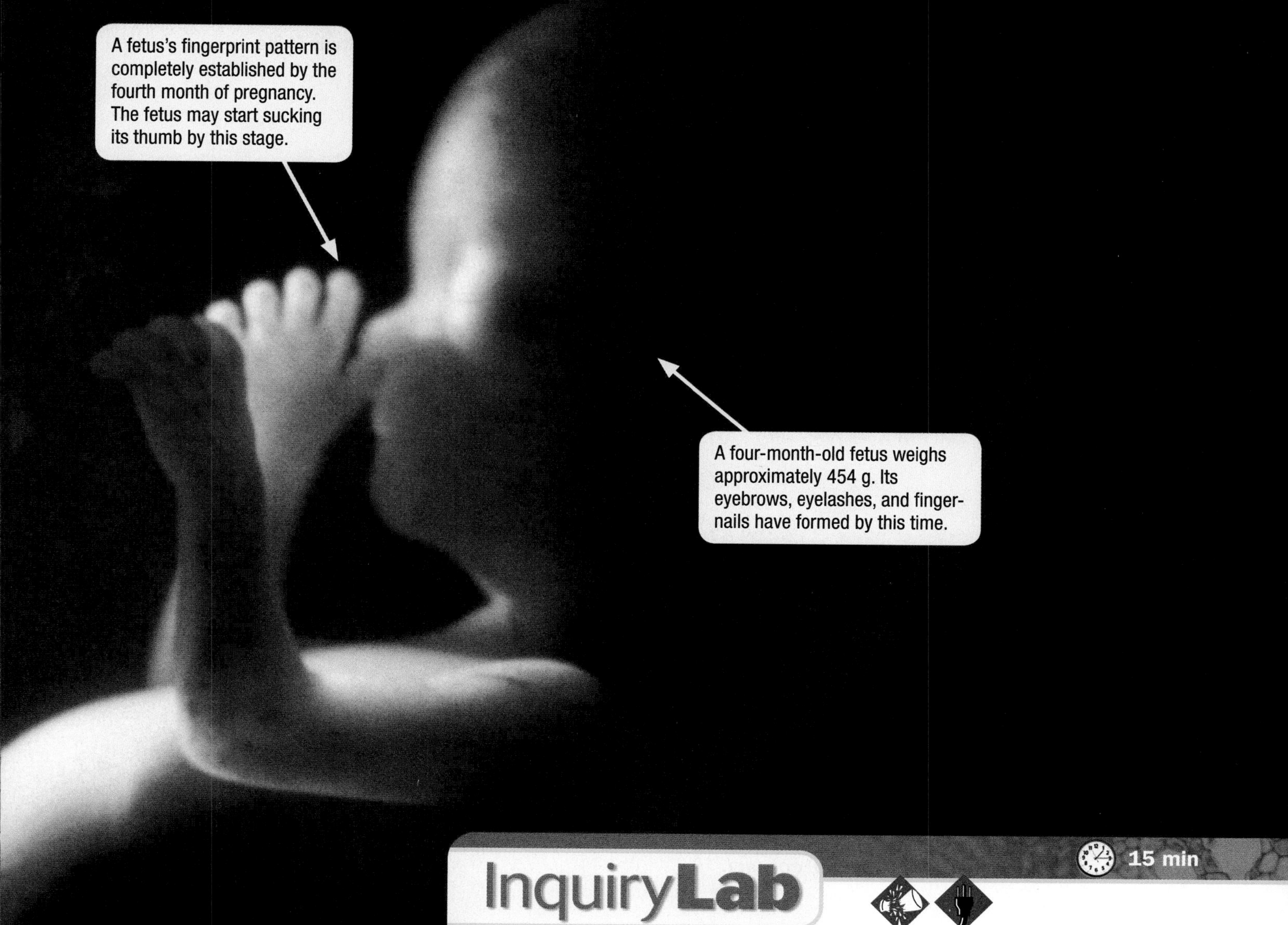

A fetus's fingerprint pattern is completely established by the fourth month of pregnancy. The fetus may start sucking its thumb by this stage.

A four-month-old fetus weighs approximately 454 g. Its eyebrows, eyelashes, and finger-nails have formed by this time.

 15 min

InquiryLab

A Closer Look at Gametes

In this lab, you will examine a mammalian ovary and sperm.

Procedure

1. Place a **human spermatozoa slide** on a **microscope** stage. Examine the smear with low power. Record what you see.

2. Switch to high power. Examine a single sperm. Draw a picture of it.

3. Place a **cross section of the ovary slide** on the microscope stage. Examine it with low power.

Locate the circular compartments that are surrounded by a distinct layer of cells.

4. Locate a separate circular mass within these chambers. The mass is the developing egg cell. Draw a picture of this cell.

Analysis

1. **Compare** the sperm cell's size with the developing egg cell's size.

2. **Explain** how the sperm cell's shape is related to its function.

READING TOOLBOX

These reading tools can help you learn the material in this chapter. For more information on how to use these and other tools, see **Appendix: Reading and Study Skills.**

Using Words

Word Families Word families are terms that share a root. The meanings of words within a family differ according to the suffixes, prefixes, and other roots which have been added to the roots.

Your Turn Use the information in the table to answer the questions below.

1. What do you think is carried through an oviduct?
2. Who do you think are more likely to get ovarian cancer, men or women?

Word Parts		
Word	**Part of speech**	**Meaning**
ovum	noun	egg
ovary	noun	organ that produces eggs
ovulate	verb	to release an egg from the ovary

Using Language

Recognizing Main Ideas A main idea is a sentence that states the main point of a paragraph. The main idea is often, but not always, one of the first few sentences of a paragraph. All the other sentences of the paragraph give support to the main idea.

Your Turn Find the main idea in the paragraph below.

Disease-causing pathogens are transmitted in many ways. Some pathogens can be passed by drinking contaminated water. Other pathogens are present in body fluids such as semen. These pathogens can be passed from one person to another through sexual contact.

Using FoldNotes

Pyramid A pyramid is a unique method for taking notes. The three sides of the pyramid can summarize information in three categories.

Your Turn Create a pyramid to summarize the development of a human fetus during the three trimesters.

1. Start with a square sheet of paper. Fold the paper in half diagonally to form a triangle.
2. Fold the triangle in half to form a smaller triangle.
3. Open the paper. The creases of the two folds will have created an X.
4. Using scissors, cut along one of the creases. Start from any corner, and stop at the center point to create two flaps.
5. Use tape or glue to attach one flap on top of the other flap.

The Male Reproductive System

Key Ideas	Key Terms	Why It Matters
❯ Where are male gametes produced? ❯ What path do sperm take to exit the body? ❯ What occurs as sperm move into the urethra? ❯ What happens to sperm after they exit the body?	testis seminiferous tubules epididymis vas deferens prostate gland semen penis	When humans reproduce, they pass their genes to their children. You have about half of your father's genes and half of your mother's genes.

Humans reproduce sexually by internal fertilization. The roles of the male reproductive system are to produce sperm and to deliver sperm to the female reproductive system.

Sperm Production

❯ The male reproductive system has two testes (testicles) that produce the male gametes, *sperm,* and the primary male sex hormone, testosterone. The **testes** are inside the *scrotum,* a sac that hangs from the body. Normal body temperature, 37 °C, is too high for proper sperm development. The temperature in the scrotum is about 3 °C lower than normal body temperature, so it is ideal for sperm production.

Seminiferous Tubules As **Figure 1** shows, testes have hundreds of compartments packed with tightly coiled tubes called **seminiferous tubules.** Sperm cells are produced through meiosis in the seminiferous tubules. Thus, human sperm cells have only 23 chromosomes (the haploid number) instead of the usual 46 chromosomes (the diploid number) found in other body cells. Two hormones released by the pituitary, luteinizing hormone (LH) and follicle-stimulating hormone (FSH), regulate the functioning of the testes. LH causes cells surrounding the seminiferous tubules to secrete testosterone. This hormone, along with FSH, stimulates sperm production. Testosterone also stimulates the growth of facial hair and other male features.

❯ **Reading Check** *Describe how hormones regulate sperm production. (See the Appendix for answers to Reading Checks.)*

testis (TES TEEZ) the primary male reproductive organ, which produces sperm cells and testosterone

seminiferous tubule (sem uh NIF uhr uhs) one of the many tubules in the testis where sperm are produced

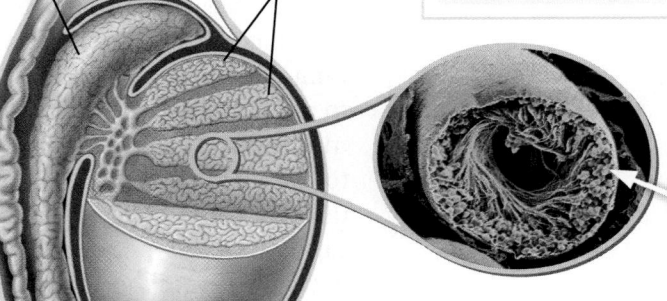

Epididymis

Seminiferous tubules

Developing sperm cells

Testis

Figure 1 Sperm are produced in the testes' seminiferous tubules. If these tubules were uncoiled, they would extend the length of six football fields!

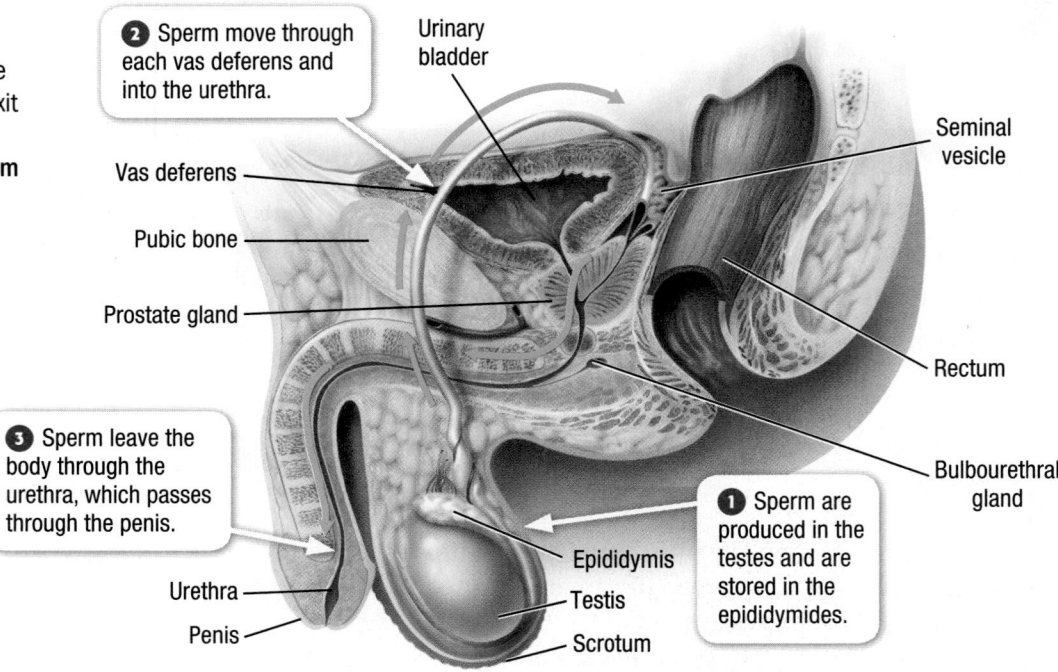

Figure 2 The arrows show the path that sperm take as they exit the body. ❯ **After leaving the testes, what structures do sperm move through?**

❷ Sperm move through each vas deferens and into the urethra.

Urinary bladder

Vas deferens

Pubic bone

Prostate gland

Seminal vesicle

Rectum

❸ Sperm leave the body through the urethra, which passes through the penis.

❶ Sperm are produced in the testes and are stored in the epididymides.

Bulbourethral gland

Epididymis

Testis

Scrotum

Urethra

Penis

Sperm's Path Through the Body

Sperm production starts during puberty and continues throughout adulthood. A typical adult male produces several hundred million sperm cells each day. The path sperm travel through the male reproductive system is illustrated in **Figure 2.** When sperm first form in the seminiferous tubules, they are not capable of swimming or of fertilizing an egg. The immature sperm travel along tubes to the epididymis. The **epididymis** is a long coiled tube attached to the top of each testis. Within each of these tubes, the sperm mature and are stored for up to two weeks. From the epididymis, sperm move to another long tube, the **vas deferens.** ❯ **The vas deferens carries sperm into the urethra. Sperm leave the body by passing through the urethra, the same duct through which urine exits the body.** A valve at the bladder-urethra connection prevents urine from entering the urethra when sperm are moving through it.

Structure of Mature Sperm As **Figure 3** shows, a mature sperm cell has a head with very little cytoplasm, a midpiece, and a long tail. Enzymes produced at the tip of the head help the sperm cell to penetrate an egg cell during fertilization. The midpiece contains many mitochondria that supply sperm with the energy they need to propel themselves through the female reproductive system. The tail of a sperm cell is a powerful flagellum that whips back and forth. This whipping motion allows the sperm cell to move. ATP produced within the mitochondria powers the movements of the tail. During fertilization, only the head of a sperm cell enters an egg. As a result, a male's mitochondria are not passed to his offspring.

❯ **Reading Check** *Why does a sperm cell need mitochondria?*

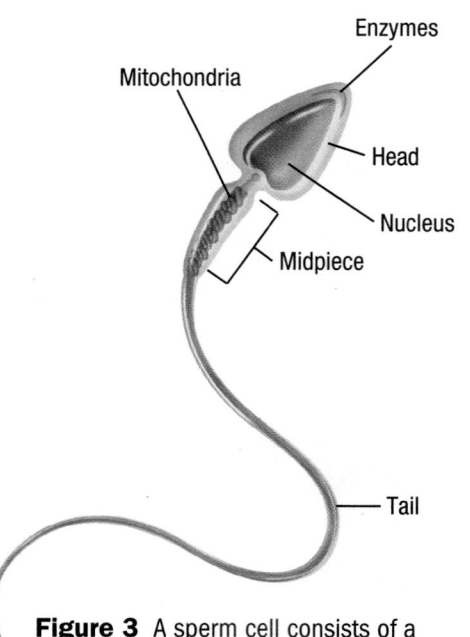

Enzymes

Mitochondria

Head

Nucleus

Midpiece

Tail

Figure 3 A sperm cell consists of a head, a midpiece, and a tail. ❯ **Which part of the sperm cell is able to fertilize an egg?**

Semen

> As sperm cells move into the urethra, they mix with fluids secreted by the seminal vesicles, the prostate gland, and the bulbourethral glands. As you can see in **Figure 4,** these fluids nourish the sperm and aid their passage through the female reproductive system. The *seminal vesicles* lie between the bladder and the rectum. These glands produce a fluid rich in sugars that sperm use for energy. The **prostate gland** is located just below the bladder. This gland secretes an alkaline fluid that helps to balance the acidic pH in the female reproductive system. Fluid from the *bulbourethral glands* neutralizes traces of acidic urine in the urethra and lubricates the path as sperm leave the body. The mixture of these fluids that are secreted with sperm is called **semen.**

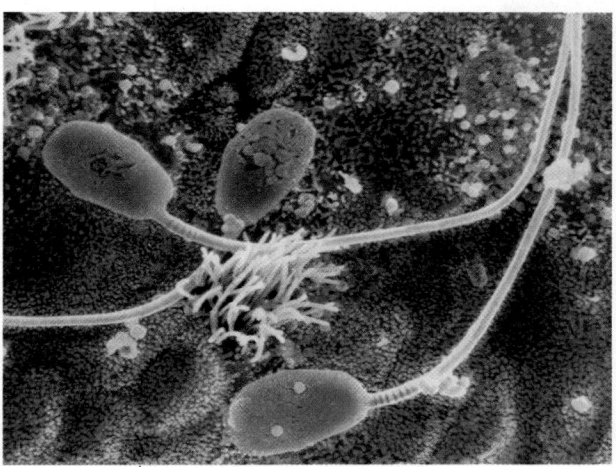

Figure 4 These sperm are swimming in a mixture of fluids that nourish, protect, and lubricate the sperm.

Sperm Delivery

The urethra passes through the **penis,** the male organ that deposits sperm into the female reproductive system during sexual intercourse. During arousal, blood flow to the penis increases. The penis contains a high volume of spongy tissue. Small spaces separate the cells of the spongy tissue. Blood collects within these spaces, which causes the penis to become erect. Muscles around each vas deferens contract, moving sperm into the urethra. The ejection of semen out of the penis through the urethra is called *ejaculation.*

> After semen is deposited in the female reproductive system, sperm swim until they encounter an egg cell or until they die. If sperm cells are unable to reach an egg, fertilization does not occur. About 3.5 mL of semen, which contains 300–400 million sperm, are expelled during ejaculation. Many sperm die in the acidic environment of the female reproductive system. In order for even one sperm cell to reach and penetrate an egg, the sperm count (sperm per mL of semen) must be high. Males with fewer than 20 million sperm per mL of semen are generally considered sterile.

> **Reading Check** *Explain why a high sperm count is necessary for fertilization.*

epididymis (ep uh DID i mis) the long, coiled tube that is on the surface of a testis and in which sperm mature

vas deferens (vas DEF uh renz) a duct through which sperm move from the epididymis to the ejaculatory duct at the base of the penis

prostate gland (PRAHS TAYT) a gland in males that contributes to the seminal fluid

semen (SEE muhn) the fluid that contains sperm and various secretions produced by the male reproductive organs

penis the male organ that transfers sperm to a female and that carries urine out of the body

---

Section 1 Review

KEY IDEAS

1. **Describe** the testes' function.
2. **State** where sperm go after leaving the epididymis.
3. **List** the components of semen.
4. **Explain** what happens to sperm when they enter a female's body.

CRITICAL THINKING

5. **Recognizing Relationships** How do secretions by exocrine glands help the delivery of sperm to the female reproductive system? Explain your reasoning.
6. **Inferring Relationships** If a male's left vas deferens is blocked by scar tissue, how will his sperm count most likey be affected? Explain your answer.

PROBLEM SOLVING

7. **Applying Concepts** Sperm cells contain many more mitochondria than most other types of cells. Why do you think sperm have such a large number of mitochondria?

The Female Reproductive System

Each month, the female reproductive system prepares for a possible pregnancy by producing a mature egg cell—the female gamete. The mature egg is called an *ovum.* If the ovum is fertilized by a sperm cell, and if the fertilized ovum implants in the uterus, a pregnancy will begin. The fertilized egg will be fed and protected through nine months of development.

Egg Production

Two **ovaries,** shown in **Figure 5,** are found within the female's abdomen. ❯ **The ovaries produce egg cells. Ovaries also secrete estrogen and progesterone, the female sex hormones.** The ovaries of a newborn female contain about 2 million immature egg cells. Egg cells have 23 chromosomes (the haploid number) because eggs, like sperm, are formed through meiosis. This process begins in the egg cells of a female before she is born, but it becomes stalled in prophase of the first meiotic division. When a female reaches puberty, the levels of sex hormone rises. This event allows meiosis to start again. However, only one egg cell completes development each month inside one of an adult female's ovaries.

Figure 5 The ovaries of the female reproductive system produce egg cells. The uterus nurtures the fetus during pregnancy.

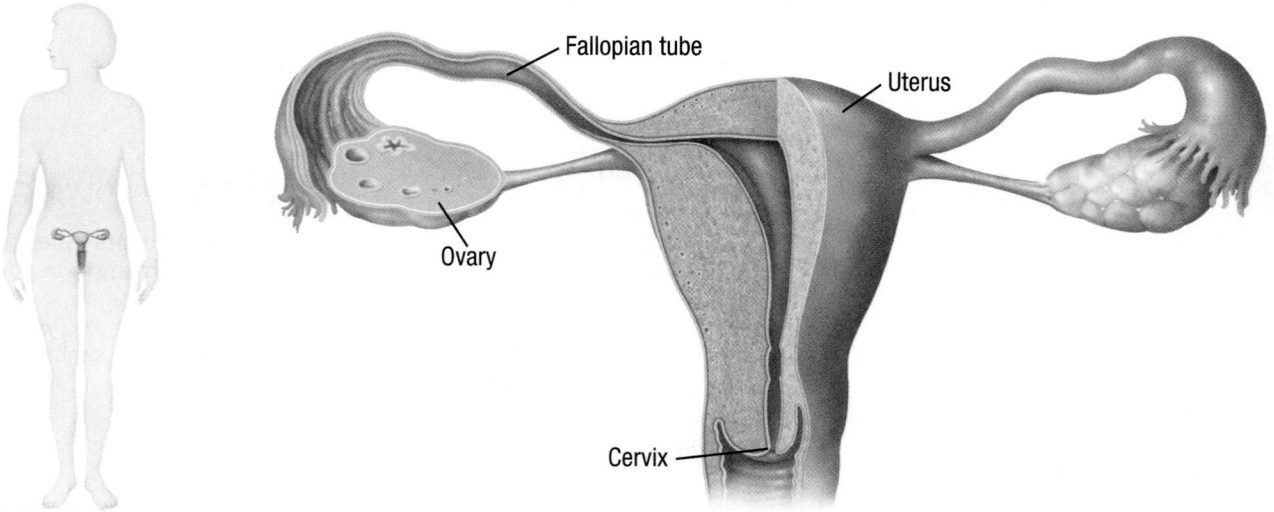

Fallopian tube

Uterus

Ovary

Cervix

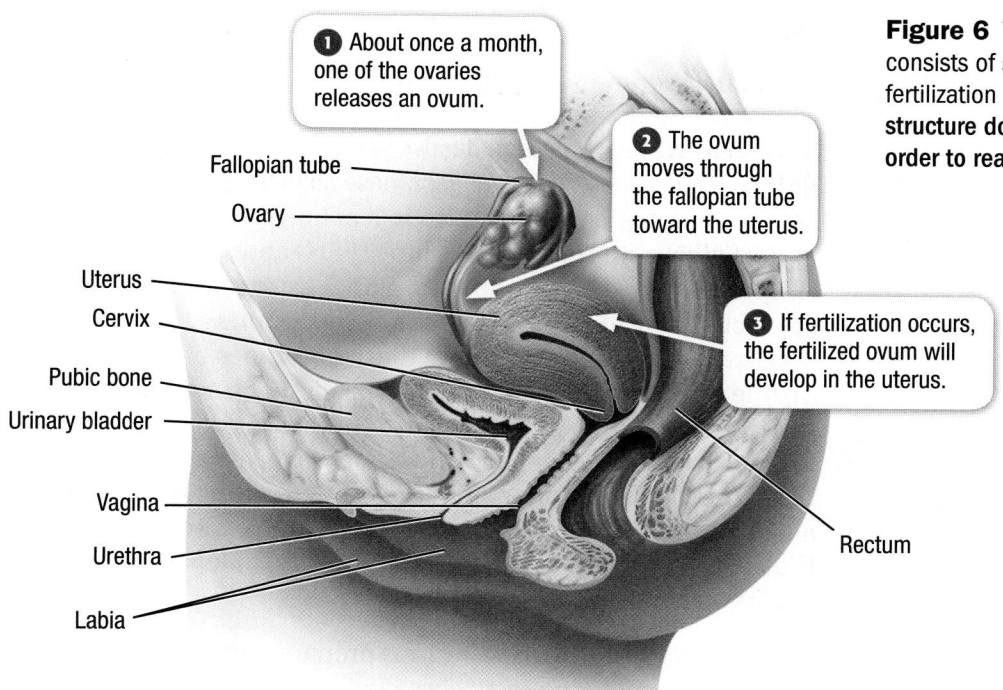

❶ About once a month, one of the ovaries releases an ovum.

❷ The ovum moves through the fallopian tube toward the uterus.

❸ If fertilization occurs, the fertilized ovum will develop in the uterus.

Fallopian tube
Ovary
Uterus
Cervix
Pubic bone
Urinary bladder
Vagina
Urethra
Labia
Rectum

Figure 6 The female reproductive system consists of several structures that enable fertilization and development. ❯ **What structure does an ovum move through in order to reach the uterus?**

The Egg's Path In contrast to the male reproductive system, which produces millions of gametes each day, the female reproductive system produces about one viable egg each month. Although a female is born with about 2 million eggs in her ovaries, only 300–400 egg cells will mature in her lifetime. When an egg cell matures, it is called an **ovum.** An ovum is about 75,000 times larger than a sperm cell and can be seen with the unaided eye.

After an ovum is released from an ovary, cilia sweep the ovum into a fallopian tube. The **fallopian tube,** shown in **Figures 5 and 6,** is a passageway through which an ovum moves from an ovary to the uterus. Rhythmic contractions of the smooth muscles lining the fallopian tube move the ovum down the tube and toward the uterus. An ovum's journey through a fallopian tube usually takes three or four days to complete. If sperm are present in the fallopian tube during this time, the ovum may become fertilized.

The Vagina and Uterus The external structures of the female reproductive system are collectively called the *vulva.* The vulva includes the *labia,* which are folds of skin and mucous membranes that cover and protect the opening of the vagina. The **vagina** is a muscular tube that leads from the vulva to the entrance to the uterus, the *cervix.* A sphincter muscle in the cervix controls the opening to the uterus. The **uterus** is a muscular, triangle-shaped organ that is about the size of a small fist. During sexual intercourse, sperm are deposited inside the vagina. If fertilization occurs, the zygote develops into a baby inside the uterus. During childbirth, a baby passes through the cervix and leaves the mother's body through the vagina.

❯ **Reading Check** *Where does an ovum become fertilized?*

ovary (OH vuh ree) an organ that produces eggs in the female reproductive system

ovum (OH vuhm) a mature egg cell

fallopian tube (fuh LOH pee uhn) a tube through which eggs move from the ovary to the uterus

vagina (vuh JIE nuh) the female reproductive organ that connects the outside of the body to the uterus and that receives sperm during reproduction

uterus (YOOT uhr uhs) in female mammals, the hollow, muscular organ in which an embryo embeds itself and develops into a fetus

Finding Main Ideas Read the first paragraph on this page. What is the main idea of that paragraph?

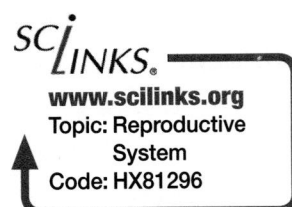
Preparation for Pregnancy

The female reproductive organs are structured to prepare a fertilized egg for development into a baby. This process is called *pregnancy.* ❯ **Throughout a female's reproductive years, her body undergoes a hormonal cycle that causes periodic changes. These changes prepare the body in the event that an egg is fertilized.** Two sets of hormones control the female cycle. Follicle-stimulating hormone (FSH) and luteinizing hormone (LH) are secreted by the pituitary gland. Estrogen and progesterone are secreted by the ovaries. All of these hormones tell the body to prepare for fertilization. Each of these hormones has a role in preparing the body for a pregnancy. If fertilization occurs, some of these hormones continue to be released. This process keeps the body from producing another egg and ovulating while a fertilized egg is developing. If fertilization does not occur, production of progesterone and estrogen slows and eventually stops. Thus, the hormonal cycle is complete for that month. After the uterine lining is shed, the cycle begins again.

The Ovarian Cycle The ovaries prepare and release an ovum in a series of events collectively called the *ovarian cycle.* This cycle has three parts: the follicular phase, ovulation, and the luteal phase. All three phases are regulated by changes in the levels of the female hormones. The release of an ovum from an ovary is called **ovulation. Figure 7** illustrates the process of ovulation. After ovulation, the ovum is drawn into the fallopian tube and begins to move toward the uterus. The lining of the uterus becomes enriched with nutrients and liquids. Although the duration of the ovarian cycle varies, the cycle generally lasts about 28 days.

ovulation (AHV yoo LAY shuhn) the release of an ovum from a follicle of the ovary

Figure 7 Ovulation occurs about midway through the 28-day ovarian cycle.
❯ **What is the function of the follicle?**

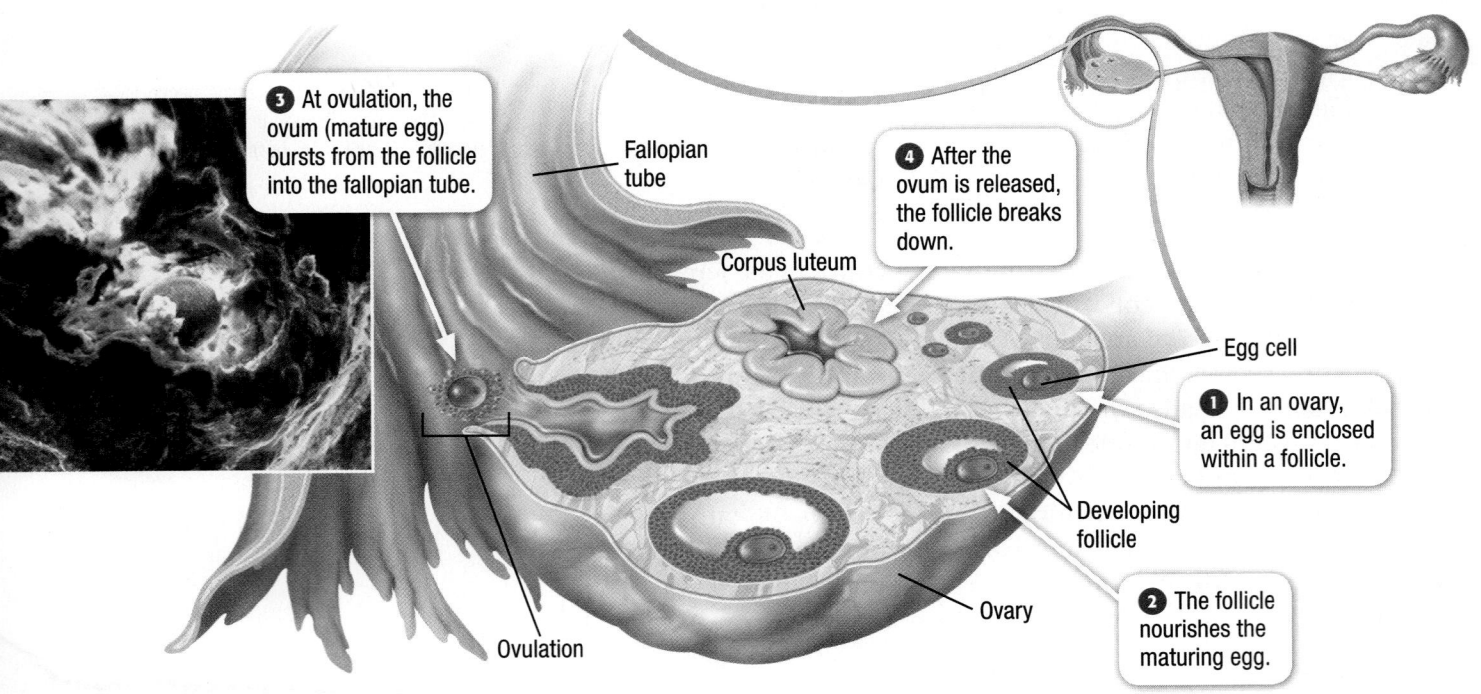

❸ At ovulation, the ovum (mature egg) bursts from the follicle into the fallopian tube.

Fallopian tube

❹ After the ovum is released, the follicle breaks down.

Corpus luteum

Egg cell

❶ In an ovary, an egg is enclosed within a follicle.

Developing follicle

Ovary

❷ The follicle nourishes the maturing egg.

Ovulation

Follicular Phase In an ovary, egg cells <u>mature</u> within follicles. A *follicle* is a cluster of cells that surrounds an immature egg cell and provides the egg with nutrients. The follicular phase, shown in **Figure 8,** marks the beginning of the ovarian cycle. Levels of hormones in the blood control the maturation of the egg. The egg begins to mature when the pituitary releases FSH into the bloodstream. FSH causes the follicle to develop and to produce estrogen. Estrogen does many things during this phase. First, it aids in the growth of the follicle. Second, it stimulates the lining of the uterus to thicken. Finally, it causes the anterior pituitary to secrete more LH. The rise in LH leads to ovulation.

Ovulation Ovulation occurs when a mature egg bursts out of a follicle. At first, a small increase in the level of estrogen slows the release of FSH from the pituitary. This kind of interaction, in which an increase in one hormone results in a decrease in another hormone, is called *negative feedback.* As the follicle nears maturity, it secretes larger and larger amounts of estrogen. The pituitary responds to the rising level of estrogen in the blood by causing the anterior pituitary gland to secrete more LH. This interaction, in which an increase in one hormone results in an increase in another hormone, is called *positive feedback.* The large amount of LH in the bloodstream causes the egg cell to complete its first meiotic division. LH also causes the follicle to burst. Ovulation occurs when the follicle bursts and the ovum is released.

Luteal Phase After ovulation, LH causes the cells of the ruptured follicle to grow and fill the cavity of the follicle. The new structure which forms is called a *corpus luteum.* Therefore, this stage of the ovarian cycle is called the *luteal phase.* The corpus luteum is a mass of follicle cells that acts like an endocrine gland. This mass of cells secretes estrogen and progesterone. These hormones turn on the growth of new blood vessels in the uterus. They also stimulate the storage of fluids and nutrients in the lining of the uterus, which causes the lining to thicken further. In addition, the estrogen and progesterone inhibit the release of more FSH and LH by the pituitary by negative feedback. Levels of FSH and LH in the blood fall, which prevents the formation of new follicles (and a second opportunity for fertilization) within a single ovarian cycle. The luteal phase lasts about 14 days. If an egg does not become embedded in the lining of the uterus during this period, the lining will be shed in a process known as *menstruation.*

> **Reading Check** *What event causes the ovarian cycle to enter the luteal phase?*

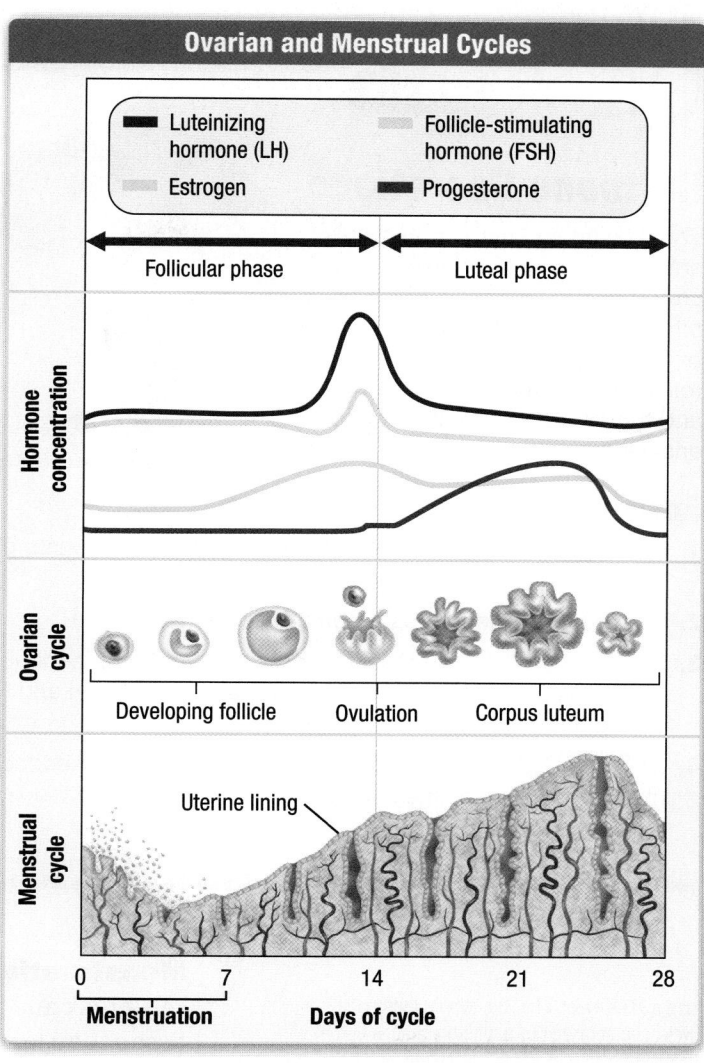

Ovarian and Menstrual Cycles

Legend:
- Luteinizing hormone (LH)
- Follicle-stimulating hormone (FSH)
- Estrogen
- Progesterone

Follicular phase | Luteal phase

Hormone concentration

Ovarian cycle — Developing follicle | Ovulation | Corpus luteum

Menstrual cycle — Uterine lining

0 | 7 | 14 | 21 | 28
Menstruation | **Days of cycle**

Figure 8 The ovarian cycle is regulated by hormones produced by the hypothalamus and the pituitary gland. The menstrual cycle is regulated by hormones produced by the follicle and the corpus luteum. ❯ **During which stage of the ovarian cycle does the corpus luteum form?**

ACADEMIC VOCABULARY

mature to reach full growth or development

QuickLab

🕐 15 min

Hormone Secretions

The ovarian and menstrual cycles are regulated by hormones secreted by the hypothalamus, the pituitary, and the ovaries. Feedback mechanisms play a major role in these cycles. Use **Figure 8** and the explanation in the text to answer the following questions.

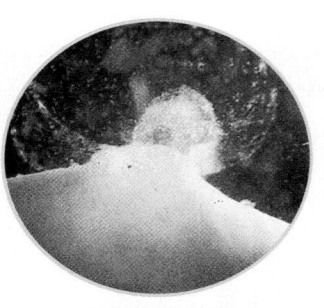

Ovulation

Analysis

1. **Identify** the hormones that are secreted in large amounts prior to ovulation.
2. **Describe** the effect of estrogen on the secretion of LH.
3. `CRITICAL THINKING` **Analyzing Concepts** What type of feedback mechanism causes a decrease in the secretion of LH and FSH during the luteal phase?
4. `CRITICAL THINKING` **Analyzing Concepts** What type of feedback mechanism causes the surge of LH secretion during the follicular phase?

menstrual cycle the female reproductive cycle, characterized by a monthly change of the lining of the uterus and the discharge of blood

menstruation the discharge of blood and discarded tissue from the uterus during the menstrual cycle

Menstrual Cycle

The series of changes that prepares the egg for fertilization is the ovarian cycle. The series of changes that prepares the uterus for a possible pregnancy is the **menstrual cycle.** The menstrual cycle lasts about 28 days and is driven by the changing levels of estrogen and progesterone during the ovarian cycle. Before ovulation, increasing levels of estrogen cause the lining of the uterus to thicken with blood vessels. This prepares the uterus for the possible implantation of a fertilized egg. The blood vessels will nourish the egg as it develops into an embryo.

After ovulation, high levels of both estrogen and progesterone cause further development and maintenance of the uterine lining. ❯ **If pregnancy does not occur, the levels of estrogen and progesterone fall. This decrease causes the lining of the uterus to be shed.** The menstrual cycle ends at the same time as the hormonal cycle ends. Both cycles then begin again. Every month, the uterus is preparing for pregnancy.

Menstruation When the lining of the uterus is shed, blood vessels break and bleeding results. A mixture of blood and discarded tissue then leaves the body through the vagina. This process, called **menstruation,** usually begins about 14 days after ovulation and lasts for three to five days. The ovarian and menstrual cycles eventually stop, usually when a woman is between the ages of 45 and 55. The end of menstruation, called *menopause,* marks the end of the childbearing phase of a woman's life.

❯ **Reading Check** *What causes menstruation to occur?*

Section 2 Review

❯ KEY IDEAS

1. **Identify** the functions of the ovaries.
2. **Summarize** the path of an egg through the female reproductive system.
3. **Compare** the roles of LH and FSH in the ovarian cycle.
4. **Explain** how the menstrual cycle is related to the ovarian cycle.

CRITICAL THINKING

5. **Recognizing Relationships** What causes the lining of the uterus to thicken and then to be shed during the menstrual cycle?
6. **Relating Concepts** How could the maturation of an egg cell in an ovary be halted?

MATH SKILLS

7. **Problem Solving** A woman does not ovulate while she is pregnant. Pregnancy generally lasts nine months. If a woman goes through three pregnancies, how many fewer mature eggs will she release in her lifetime than if she never became pregnant?

Section 3 Human Development

Key Ideas	Key Terms	Why It Matters
❯ How does fertilization occur? ❯ What important events occur in the first trimester of pregnancy? ❯ What important event occurs at the end of the third trimester of pregnancy?	embryo implantation fetus	All humans go through the same developmental stages as they change from a single fertilized egg into a complex organism composed of billions of cells.

Development begins with a single diploid cell. Billions of other cells arise from this one cell. During pregnancy, the uterus provides protection and nourishment to the developing human being.

Fertilization

If sperm are present in the female reproductive system within a few days after ovulation, fertilization may occur. To fertilize an ovum, a sperm cell must move up into a fallopian tube. ❯ **During fertilization, a sperm cell penetrates an ovum by releasing enzymes from the tip of its head. These enzymes break down the jellylike outer layers of the ovum. The head of the sperm enters the ovum, and the nuclei of the ovum and sperm fuse together.** This fusion produces a diploid cell called a *zygote*.

Cleavage and Implantation The zygote undergoes a series of mitotic divisions known as cleavage, as **Figure 9** shows. Cleavage produces many smaller cells—first two cells, then four, then eight, and so on. The resulting clump of cells is called an **embryo.** Cleavage continues as the embryo moves toward the uterus. By the time it reaches the uterus, the embryo is a hollow ball of cells called a *blastocyst.* About six days after fertilization, the blastocyst burrows into the lining of the uterus in an event called **implantation.**

embryo (EM bree OH) an organism in an early stage of development; in humans, a developing individual from first cleavage through the next eight weeks

implantation the process by which a blastocyst embeds itself in the lining of the uterus

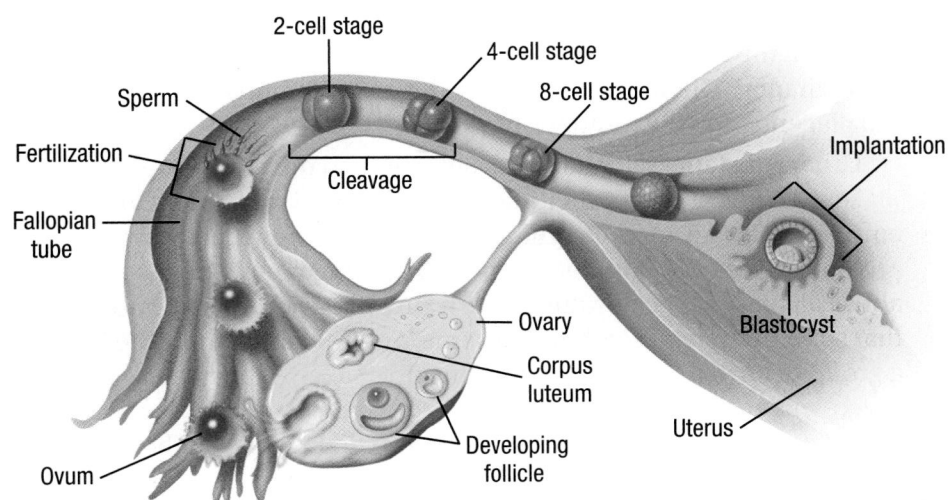

Figure 9 Fertilization, cleavage, and implantation may occur after ovulation.
❯ What has the embryo become by the time it reaches the uterus?

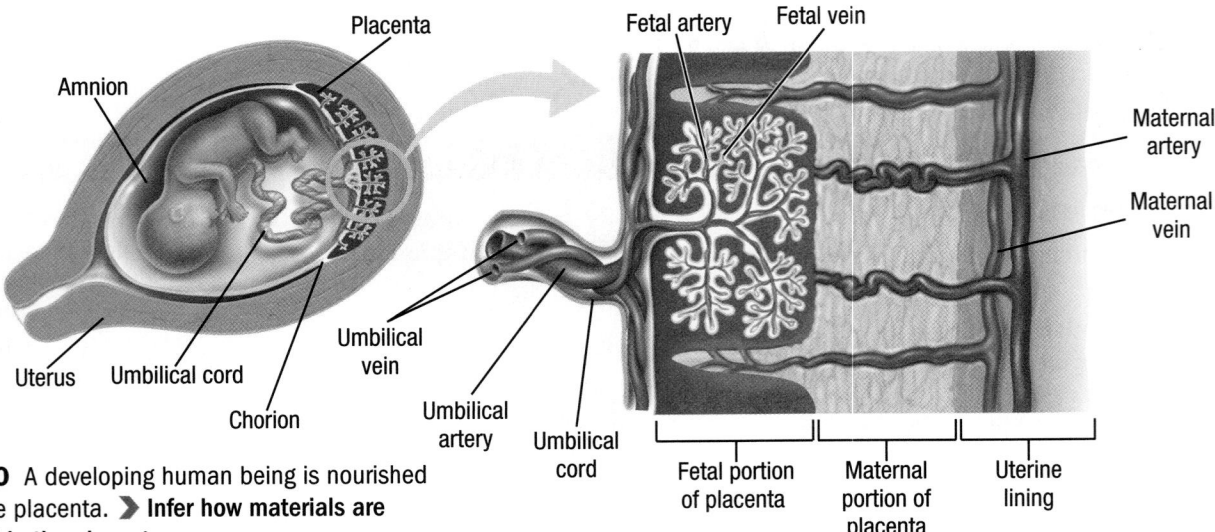

Placenta
Amnion
Fetal artery   Fetal vein
Maternal artery
Maternal vein
Uterus   Umbilical cord
Chorion
Umbilical vein
Umbilical artery   Umbilical cord
Fetal portion of placenta
Maternal portion of placenta
Uterine lining

Figure 10 A developing human being is nourished through the placenta. ❯ **Infer how materials are exchanged in the placenta.**

fetus a developing human from the end of the eighth week after fertilization until birth

READING TOOLBOX

Recognizing Main ideas How do the text heads on this page relate to the main ideas of the paragraphs following the heads? Which sentence states the main idea for each paragraph?

First Trimester

Human development takes about nine months—a period known as *gestation,* or pregnancy. Pregnancy begins when the embryo implants itself in the wall of the uterus. The nine months of pregnancy are typically divided into three *trimesters,* or three-month periods. The most important events of development occur in the first trimester. ❯ **All of the embryo's organ systems, as well as the supportive membranes that feed and protect the embryo, develop during the first trimester of pregnancy.**

Supportive Membranes Membranes that will protect and feed the embryo begin to develop very shortly after implantation. One membrane, the *amnion,* encloses and protects the embryo. Another membrane, the *chorion,* interacts with the uterus to form the placenta. The umbilical cord connects the amnion with the placenta. The placenta, shown in **Figure 10,** is the structure through which the mother feeds the embryo. The placenta forms by the third week of pregnancy. The mother's blood does not mix with the blood of the embryo. Instead, nutrients in the mother's blood diffuse through the placenta. The nutrients are carried to the embryo through blood vessels in the umbilical cord, which is fully formed by the sixth week of pregnancy. The waste products of the embryo diffuse back through the placenta into the mother's blood.

Other substances, including drugs, can also diffuse through the placenta. Thus, if the mother ingests any harmful substances, the embryo is also affected. Pregnant women who smoke may have premature births and underweight babies. Pregnant women who abuse alcohol, especially during early pregnancy, may have babies that suffer from fetal alcohol syndrome. Fetal alcohol syndrome is a group of birth defects which may include facial deformation and severe mental, behavioral, and physical retardation. All drugs that are inappropriate for infants should be avoided, or used only with a physician's prescription, throughout pregnancy.

Embryonic Development As the placenta takes shape, the inner cells of the blastocyst form the three primary tissue layers of the embryo—endoderm, mesoderm, and ectoderm. By the end of the third week, blood vessels and the digestive system begin to develop. The embryo is about 2 mm long. In the fourth week, arm and leg buds form. By the end of the fourth week, all of the major organs begin to form, and the heart begins to beat. The embryo has more than doubled its length. During the second month, the final stages of embryonic development take place. The arms and legs take shape. By the end of the second month, the embryo is about 25 mm long and weighs about 1 g.

Fetal Development From the end of the eighth week after fertilization until childbirth, the developing human is called a **fetus.** By the end of the first trimester, the sex of the fetus can be distinguished. The fetus has recognizable body features, as **Figure 11** shows. The fetus's major organ systems continue to develop.

> **Reading Check** *During which trimester do the embryo's organs begin to form?*

Hands-On

Quick Lab

 15 min

An Amniotic Shock Absorber

In this lab, you will model how amniotic fluid serves as a shock absorber for a developing fetus.

Procedure

❶ Stand a **paper clip** upright in a base of **clay**. Tap the top of the clip to see how much force is needed to topple it.

❷ Fill a **sandwich bag** with **water**. Place the clip within its clay base at the center of the water-filled bag, and seal the bag. Gently tap the bag. Does this impact topple the clip?

Analysis

1. **Compare** the parts of this model to an actual amnion.

2. **CRITICAL THINKING** **Analyzing Concepts** Explain how the water-filled bag affected the force needed to topple the paper clip.

21 weeks Hair forms on body and head. Facial features are developing.

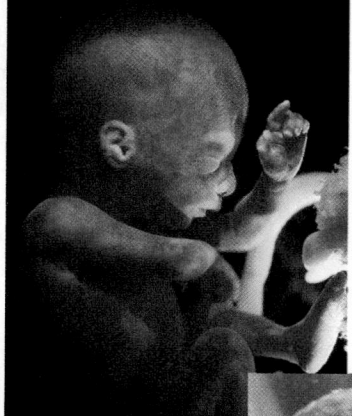

Figure 11 Near the end of the third trimester, a fetus doubles and then triples in size. **>** How does the 8-week-old fetus compare with the 12-week-old fetus?

8 weeks Major organ systems have begun to form. Limbs are forming.

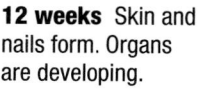

12 weeks Skin and nails form. Organs are developing.

8 months Subcutaneous tissue is forming. Fetal development nears completion.

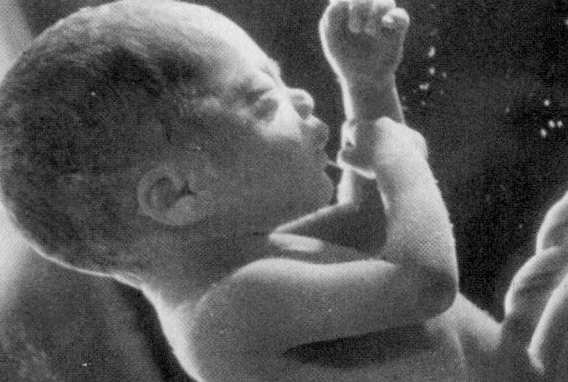

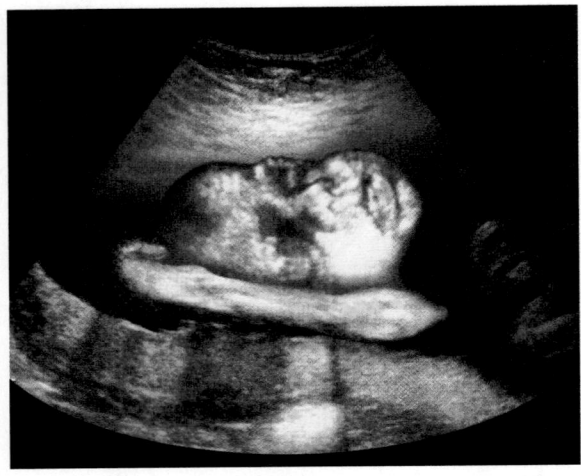

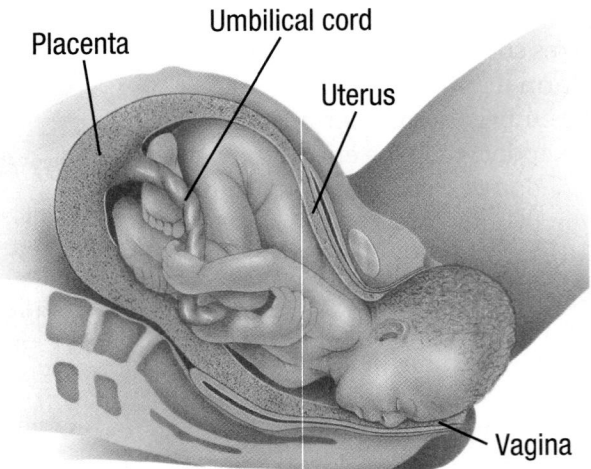

Placenta

Umbilical cord

Uterus

Vagina

Figure 12 Doctors use ultrasound imaging to monitor a fetus's growth. The fetus shown in this ultrasound (left) is near birth. During childbirth (right), the fetus exits the mother's body through the vagina. ❯ **Why is it important that the baby exit the mother head first?**

SCiLINKS.
www.scilinks.org
Topic: Before Birth
Code: HX80140

Second and Third Trimesters

During the second trimester (4–6 months) the fetus grows to about 15 cm in length. Bone development continues. Toenails and fingernails form. The brain develops and begins to control muscle responses. By the end of the fifth month, the fetus begins to move. It stretches its arms and legs, and may even suck its thumb. The mother may be able to feel these movements. The fetus has a fast heartbeat. Doctors may use ultrasound images, such as the one shown in **Figure 12,** to monitor the fetus's growth.

In the third trimester (7–9 months) the fetus gains about 2.5 kg. The brain and nerves develop. The fetus can hear, smell, and see light. The lungs mature. The fetus moves into a head down position during the ninth month, and becomes less active. ❯ **By the end of the third trimester, the fetus is able to live outside the mother's body. The fetus leaves the mother's body in a process called labor, which usually lasts several hours.** During labor, the walls of the uterus contract and expel the fetus from the uterus, as shown in **Figure 12.** The fetus leaves the mother's body through the vagina. Further contractions of the uterus expel the placenta and the umbilical cord.

❯ **Reading Check** *How does the fetus change in the third trimester?*

Section 3 Review

❯ **KEY IDEAS**

1. **Summarize** the events in development that occur during fertilization.

2. **Explain** what important events occur in the first trimester of pregnancy.

3. **Describe** the events that occur at the end of the third trimester.

CRITICAL THINKING

4. **Relating Concepts** Why can some drugs be harmful to a fetus if the mother takes them while she is pregnant?

5. **Predicting Outcomes** What might happen if more than one egg were released from the ovaries prior to fertilization?

ALTERNATIVE ASSESSMENT

6. **Sequencing Events** Draw a timeline that illustrates the developmental changes that occur during each of the three trimesters of pregnancy. Use photos, drawings, and/or charts to illustrate your timeline.

Sexually Transmitted Infections

Key Ideas	Key Terms	Why It Matters
❯ How can you avoid being infected by an STI? ❯ What are some common STIs in the United States?	genital herpes pelvic inflammatory disease	STIs are some of the most common infectious diseases in the world.

Diseases spread by sexual contact are called sexually transmitted infections (STIs). Some of the most common STIs in the United States are listed in **Figure 13.**

STI Transmission and Treatment

Disease-causing pathogens are transmitted in many ways. Pathogens present in body fluids, such as semen, can be passed from one person to another through sexual contact. STIs can be caused by both viruses and bacteria. ❯ **Abstinence is the only sure way to protect yourself from contracting an STI.** Early detection and treatment are necessary to prevent serious consequences that can result from infection. Some viral STIs can be treated with antiviral medication. Many bacterial STIs can be treated and cured with antibiotics. However, early symptoms of most bacterial STIs are very mild and often are not detected. Untreated bacterial STIs can cause sterility in both men and women.

❯ **Reading Check** *How are different kinds of STIs treated?*

Figure 13 The table shows the estimated new cases of STIs per year for the entire American population.

Sexually Transmitted Infections

Infection	New cases per year	Symptoms
Genital HPV	5,500,000	warts on genital or anal region
Trichomoniasis	5,000,000	often no symptoms in males; yellow-green vaginal discharge with strong odor in females
Chlamydia	3,000,000	painful urination and penile discharge in males; abdominal pain and vaginal discharge in females
Genital herpes	1,000,000	painful blisters around the genital region; flulike symptoms
Gonorrhea	650,000	painful urination and penile discharge in males; abdominal pain and vaginal discharge in females
Hepatitis B	120,000	flulike symptoms and yellowing of skin
Syphilis	70,000	sores on penis in males; sores in vagina or on cervix in females; fever and rash; destruction of body tissue
HIV/AIDS	40,000	immune-system failure and susceptibility to infections

Source: Centers for Disease Control and Prevention

QuickLab

 15 min

STI Rates

STIs are the most widespread type of infection in the United States. Use **Figure 13** and the explanation in the text to complete the following activities.

Analysis

1. **Draw** a bar graph showing new cases of STIs.
2. **Identify** the name of the pathogen that causes the most common STI.

3. **CRITICAL THINKING** **Predicting Patterns** Calculate the number of Americans that each of the STIs shown in **Figure 13** will infect within five years if the estimated number of new cases per year remains constant.
4. **CRITICAL THINKING** **Analyzing Data** Genital herpes is not the STI with the most new cases per year, but it is the most common STI in the United States. Suggest a possible reason for this.

SCiLINKS.
www.scilinks.org
Topic: Sexually Transmitted Diseases
Code: HX81388

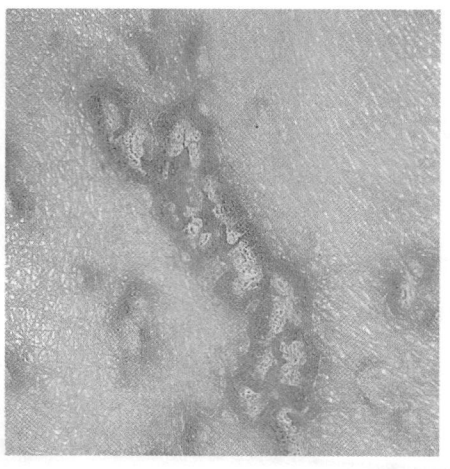

Figure 14 The blisters of genital herpes may appear on or near the genitals.

Common STIs

❭ **The most common STIs include genital herpes, genital HPV, trichomoniasis, AIDS, hepatitis B, chlamydia, and gonorrhea.** For example, around one in every five Americans has had a genital herpes infection.

Genital Herpes At a rate of 22,300 cases per 100,000 Americans, **genital herpes** is the most common STI in the United States. This STI is caused by herpes simplex virus (HSV). About 70% of genital herpes infections are caused by HSV-2. The rest are caused by HSV-1, which more commonly causes cold sores around and inside the mouth. Symptoms of genital herpes include periodic outbreaks of painful blisters, such as those shown in **Figure 14.** Symptoms may also include flulike aches and fever. Antiviral drugs can temporarily get rid of the blisters caused by genital herpes, but they cannot remove HSV from the body. Although genital herpes is not life threatening, it can have serious consequences. Women who have genital herpes have a greater risk of developing cervical cancer.

Genital HPV Human papilloma virus (HPV) causes genital warts and other symptoms. Current statistics indicate that 50% of all Americans will be infected by genital HPV at some point in their lives. Most people who are infected with HPV show no symptoms and do not know that they are infected. Some people who have HPV infections get genital warts. Some experience cell changes in the cervix, which could lead to cancer. No therapy has been shown to get rid of the virus; the infection often comes back following treatment.

Trichomoniasis Trichomoniasis is the only major STI caused by a protistan parasite rather than by a virus or a bacterium. Some men with this infection have a mild discharge and temporary irritation inside the penis. Most men, though, have no symptoms. Women with trichomoniasis often have vaginal itching and a yellow-green vaginal discharge with a strong odor. Trichomoniasis can usually be cured with medication.

AIDS AIDS is a fatal disease caused by the human immunodeficiency virus (HIV). HIV infection occurs most commonly through sexual contact. HIV attacks the immune system by destroying white blood cells. People who have AIDS usually die from infections that generally affect only people who have weakened immune systems.

Hepatitis B Of the five forms of hepatitis, form B is the most common in the United States. Like HIV, hepatitis B is a viral STI that is transmitted typically through sexual contact or contaminated needles. The virus infects the liver and damages liver cells. Any injury to the liver is a problem, because the liver fights infections and removes poisons from the body. A vaccine is <u>available</u> for hepatitis B, and can give unexposed people immunity to the virus. The vaccine also helps to treat people who have been exposed to the virus. However, the vaccine cannot cure hepatitis B.

Chlamydia and Gonorrhea Chlamydia and gonorrhea are the most common bacterial STIs in the United States. Some people show no symptoms. Some men experience painful urination, and some women experience vaginal discharge. Gonorrhea may cause pus to discharge from the penis. Chlamydia (and less often, gonorrhea) can cause scar tissue to form inside the fallopian tubes.

Pelvic Inflammatory Disease Most cases of **pelvic inflammatory disease** (PID) result from gonorrhea or chlamydia infections. A normal fallopian tube has a highly-folded lining and many spaces through which gametes can pass. The spaces in a fallopian tube of a woman who has PID may become blocked with scar tissue.

Syphilis Syphilis is a serious bacterial STI that has a low incidence level in the United States, but is still common in much of the rest of the world. Syphilis usually begins with the appearance of a small sore on the genitals a few weeks after infection. Fever and rash are also common symptoms. These symptoms disappear without treatment. Years later, however, untreated syphilis begins to destroy body tissues, including bone and skin tissue, as you can see in **Figure 15.**

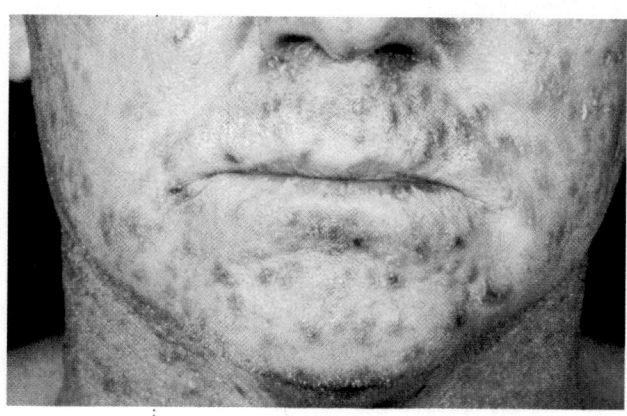

Figure 15 The sores on this man's face are caused by syphilis. Syphilis also eats away at other body tissues, including skeletal tissue.

ACADEMIC VOCABULARY

available that can be used

genital herpes a sexually transmitted infection that is caused by a herpes simplex virus

pelvic inflammatory disease a sexually transmitted infection of the upper female reproductive system, including the uterus, ovaries, fallopian tubes, and other structures

---

Section 4 Review

> **KEY IDEAS**

1. **State** the best way to avoid becoming infected by an STI.
2. **List** three symptoms of genital herpes.
3. **Identify** which bacterial STIs are the most common in the United States.

CRITICAL THINKING

4. **Making Inferences** Why is a symptomless STI just as dangerous as an STI that exhibits symptoms? Explain your answer.
5. **Applying Information** Do you think that an STI can be transmitted from a mother to her fetus? Explain your answer.

ALTERNATIVE ASSESSMENT

6. **Making Bar Graphs** Research the rate of incidence of STIs among teenagers compared to the rate of incidence in the rest of the population. Use the information you discover to construct a bar graph.

Seeing Double

Multiple births occur when two or more children are carried during the same pregnancy. In humans, the most common type of multiple births occurs when the mother gives birth to two children, which are also known as twins. About 3% of all births in the United States result in twins.

Twins in Your Genes?

There are two types of twins: identical and fraternal. While there does not seem to be any genetic basis for identical twins, fraternal twins are another matter. Women with fraternal twins in their families are more likely to give birth to fraternal twins. Also, the frequency of fraternal twinning has increased over the last 20 years, probably due to the increased use of fertility drugs.

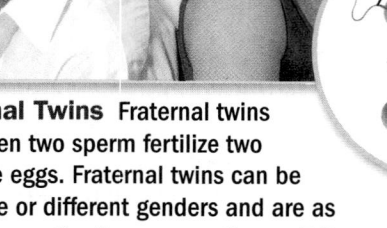

Fraternal Twins Fraternal twins form when two sperm fertilize two separate eggs. Fraternal twins can be the same or different genders and are as different genetically as any ordinary siblings.

Two sperm

Two eggs

One sperm

One egg

Embryo divides in two

Identical Twins Identical twins form when a single sperm fertilizes a single egg. The developing embryo then divides in two. Identical twins are always the same gender and are genetically identical.

Triplets While twinning is the most common type of multiple birth, other multiples do occur. About 0.1% of all births are triplets.

Research It is common for twins to develop their own language. Find out more about this occurence, which is known as cryptophasia or idioglossia.

Chapter 40 Lab

Objectives

> Analyze how different materials affect the pattern of water waves.

> Form a hypothesis about how a viscous fluid alters the wave.

Materials

- lab apron
- shallow pan
- metric ruler
- water, tap
- corn syrup
- timer
- large spoon
- various objects such as a wooden block, a domino, and paper clips

Safety

Sonography

Sonography is a medical technique that is frequently used to obtain images of a developing fetus. During this process, ultrasonic waves are directed into the uterus. Upon hitting hard surfaces, the waves reflect. These returning waves produce a distinct pattern, which is used to generate an image of the fetus. In this lab, you will explore the reflection and bending of water waves. You will use your data to develop a better understanding of sonography as a tool in prenatal observation.

Preparation

1. **SCIENTIFIC METHODS** **State the Problem** How does a viscous fluid affect the wave's pattern in a model of a sonogram?

2. **SCIENTIFIC METHODS** **Form a Hypothesis** Form a testable hypothesis that explains how corn syrup affects the wave pattern of the model.

Procedure

1. Put on a lab apron. Place a shallow pan on a flat, level surface. Carefully fill it with water to a depth of about 0.5 cm.

2. Position a spoon at one end of the tray. Keeping the spoon level over the water's surface, gently tap down once on the water. Be sure that your fingertips don't touch the water. What do you observe? Continue tapping to form a regular rhythm.

3. Place a domino or other target with a flat edge midway in the tray. Tap out a regular rhythm. What do you observe?

4. Alter the distance between the target and the spoon. Tap again.

5. Use a variety of targets with different shapes including curved and angular edges. Note how these targets affect the return wave.

6. Place several drops of corn syrup in the center of the tray. Observe how this more dense liquid affects the waves that pass through it.

7. Clean up your materials according to your teacher's instructions. Wash your hands before leaving the lab.

Analyze and Conclude

1. **Describing Observations** What happened to the wave when it struck a hard surface? Did the wave vary with the type of object?

2. **SCIENTIFIC METHODS** **Drawing Conclusions** How did the distance to the target affect the wave's return?

3. **Evaluating Models** How does this activity model the use of sonography in prenatal observation?

4. **SCIENTIFIC METHODS** **Analyzing Results** How did traveling though the corn syrup affect the wave? How might this be applied to sonography?

Key Ideas	Key Terms

1 The Male Reproductive System

> The male reproductive system has two testes that produce sperm and testosterone.

> The vas deferens carries sperm into the urethra. Sperm leave the body by passing through the urethra.

> As sperm cells move into the urethra, they mix with fluids secreted by three exocrine glands: the seminal vesicles, the prostate gland, and the bulbourethral glands.

> After the semen is deposited in the female reproductive system, sperm swim until they encounter an egg cell or until they die.

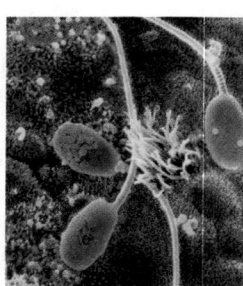

Key Terms:
testis (993)
seminiferous tubule (993)
epididymis (994)
vas deferens (994)
prostate gland (995)
semen (995)
penis (995)

2 The Female Reproductive System

> The ovaries produce egg cells. Ovaries also secrete estrogen and progesterone.

> During the reproductive years, the female body undergoes a hormonal cycle that causes periodic changes. These changes prepare the body in the event that an egg is fertilized.

> If pregnancy does not occur, levels of estrogen and progesterone fall. The decrease in these two hormones causes the lining of the uterus to be shed during menstruation.

Key Terms:
ovary (996)
ovum (997)
fallopian tube (997)
uterus (997)
vagina (997)
ovulation (998)
menstrual cycle (1000)
menstruation (1000)

3 Human Development

> When a sperm cell encounters an ovum, the sperm cell releases enzymes that break down the outer layers of the ovum. The head of the sperm enters the ovum, and the nuclei of the ovum and sperm fuse. This process, from encounter to fusion, is called fertilization.

> All of the embryo's organ systems, as well as the supportive membranes that feed and protect the embryo, develop during the first trimester of pregnancy.

> By the end of the third trimester, a fetus is able to live outside the mother's body. A baby leaves the mother's body after labor.

Key Terms:
embryo (1001)
implantation (1001)
fetus (1003)

4 Sexually Transmitted Infections

> Abstinence is the only sure way to protect yourself from contracting an STI.

> Common STIs include genital herpes, genital HPV, trichomoniasis, AIDS, hepatitis B, chlamydia, and gonorrhea.

 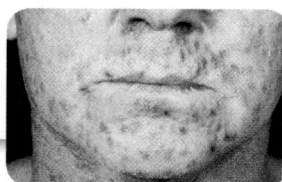

Key Terms:
genital herpes (1008)
pelvic inflammatory disease (1009)

1. **Using Words** Identify two terms from this chapter that belong to the same word family as the word *menses.*

2. **Concept Map** Make a concept map that describes the ovarian and menstrual cycles. Try to include the following words: *ovary, fallopian tube, uterus, ovarian cycle, follicle, ovulation, corpus luteum,* and *menstrual cycle.* Include additional terms in your map as you need them.

Using Key Terms

Use each of the following terms in a sentence.

3. *testis*

4. *prostate gland*

For each pair of terms, explain how the meanings of the terms differ.

5. *ovulation* and *menstruation*

6. *embryo* and *fetus*

Understanding Key Ideas

7. The pathway of sperm is from the
   a. urethra to vas deferens to testes.
   b. testes to vas deferens to epididymis.
   c. testes to epididymis to vas deferens.
   d. epididymis to urethra to vas deferens.

8. Which of the following is *not* a function of the female reproductive system?
   a. secretion of FSH
   b. maturation of eggs
   c. production of gametes
   d. nourishment of the fetus

9. What tube carries urine during excretion and semen during ejaculation?
   a. urethra
   b. fallopian tube
   c. vas deferens
   d. seminiferous tubule

10. Which of the following glands produces a fluid that lubricates the urethra for the passage of semen?
    a. prostate
    b. bulbourethral
    c. pituitary
    d. hypothalamus

11. Which of the following is the order of the steps of the ovarian cycle?
    a. ovulation, follicular phase, ovulation
    b. ovulation, follicular phase, luteal phase
    c. follicular phase, ovulation, luteal phase
    d. follicular phase, luteal phase, ovulation

12. How does a growing fetus get nourishment?
    a. through the uterus
    b. through the chorion
    c. through the placenta
    d. through the amniotic fluid

13. Which of the following has occurred by the end of the first trimester?
    a. The fetus's eyes open.
    b. The fetus sucks its thumb.
    c. The fetus "practice breathes."
    d. The fetus's heart starts beating.

14. Which is the most common STI in the United States?
    a. AIDS
    b. gonorrhea
    c. syphilis
    d. genital herpes

15. Which of the following STIs is caused by a protistan parasite?
    a. chlamydia
    b. gonorrhea
    c. genital herpes
    d. trichomoniasis

Explaining Key Ideas

16. **Describe** the role of feedback mechanisms in the maturation of an egg cell during the ovarian cycle.

17. **Outline** the process of fertilization.

18. **Identify** the common causes of pelvic inflammatory disease.

19. **Examine** the diagram and explain the roles of the structures labeled *A, B,* and *C* in the process of fertilization.

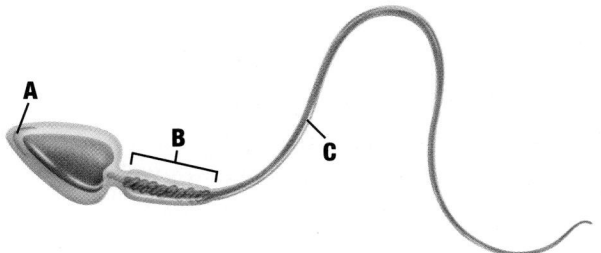

Using Science Graphics

Use the diagram and your knowledge of science to answer the following questions.

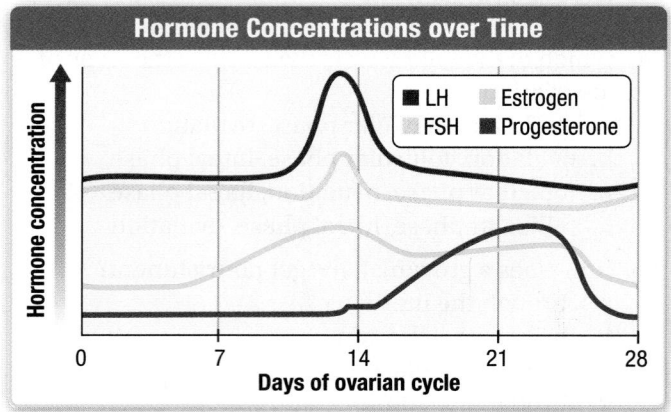

Hormone Concentrations over Time

LH ■ Estrogen
FSH Progesterone ■

Hormone concentration

Days of ovarian cycle
0   7   14   21   28

20. Approximately when during the ovarian cycle does ovulation usually occur?
  a. day 7   **c.** day 21
  b. day 14   **d.** day 28

21. What happens during the second half of the follicular phase?
  a. The concentration of LH suddenly increases and then decreases.
  b. The concentration of progesterone suddenly decreases and then increases.
  c. The concentration of FSH steadily decreases.
  d. The concentration of estrogen remains fairly constant.

22. About when during the ovarian cycle is the concentration of progesterone highest?
  a. day 7   **c.** day 23
  b. day 13   **d.** day 28

Critical Thinking

23. Making Inferences A man interested in fathering children wants to know his sperm count. He finds out that he has a sperm count of fewer than 60 million sperm in a 3.5 mL sample of semen. If you were his physician, what would you tell him about the results of the test?

24. Predicting Outcomes What do you think would happen if more than one sperm were able to fertilize an egg?

25. Inferring Relationships Why should a pregnant woman be careful to eat a healthy, well-balanced diet?

26. Evaluating Conclusions In the 1960s, many women who took a tranquilizer called thalidomide early in pregnancy gave birth to babies that had serious limb defects. Other women who took the drug later in pregnancy gave birth to normal babies. What does this tell you about the pattern of fetal development?

27. Relating Concepts After a baby is born, the umbilical cord is cut. This cut severs the baby's connection to the placenta. Why does the baby no longer need the placenta?

28. Forming Reasoned Opinions The percentage of babies surviving premature birth has increased by approximately 3 percent over the last two decades. Propose a reason for this increase.

Writing for Science

29. Writing News Articles Testicular cancer is the most common type of cancer that affects men aged 15–45. Use library or Internet resources to learn about how to perform a testicular self exam. Learn the signs and symptoms to look for during the exam. Write a short news article with your findings.

Graphing Skills

30. Graphing Human Development Use library or Internet resources to learn more about the growth processes of a developing embryo and fetus. Make a graph that displays your findings and that shows the relative size of the developing human at each month of development.

Alternative Assessment

31. Medicine and Society The increasing rate of Caesarian section deliveries in the United States is a hotly debated issue. Use library or Internet resources to learn more about what a Caesarian section is, the reasons why Caesarian sections are performed, and the risks and benefits of undergoing the surgery. Present your findings to your class, or have a classroom discussion on the issue.

32. Constructing Charts Research information on the importance of medical care throughout pregnancy. Create a chart that indicates when routine obstetric visits should take place, and the purposes of tests that are carried out at various times throughout pregnancy. Present your poster to the class.

TEST TIP If you are unsure of the correct answer to a question, cross out answers you know are wrong. Having fewer choices may help you to choose the correct answer.

Science Concepts

1. Which is true about follicle-stimulating hormone?
A It is secreted by a follicle.
B It is secreted by the pituitary gland.
C It promotes contractions of the uterus.
D It stimulates the development of the placenta.

2. Which of the following help to form the placenta?
F amnion   **H** yolk sac
G chorion   **J** umbilical cord

3. By the end of the first trimester, which of the following has occurred?
A The fetus has a full head of hair.
B The fetus uses its lungs to breathe.
C The brain of the fetus is fully formed.
D All of the organs of the fetus have begun to form.

4. What structure is a tube in which sperm mature?
F urethra
G epididymis
H vas deferens
J seminiferous tubules

5. Where does fertilization usually take place?
A cervix   **C** epididymis
B uterus   **D** fallopian tubes

6. How are semen and sperm related?
F Both are stored in the bladder.
G Sperm and semen are both gametes.
H Semen is made up of fluids and sperm.
J Both are produced in the prostate gland.

Using Science Graphics

Use the image of an ovary to answer the following question.

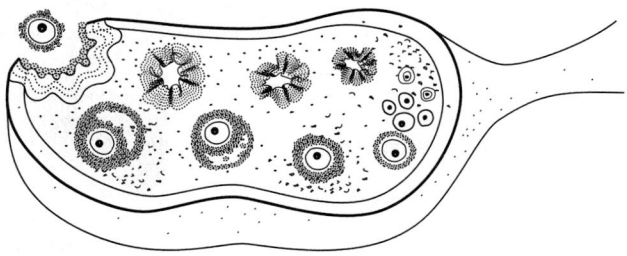

7. What event is illustrated in the picture above?
A ovulation   **C** ejaculation
B fertilization   **D** menstruation

The diagram shows the percentage of infants that are born prematurely in the United States. Use the diagram to answer the following question.

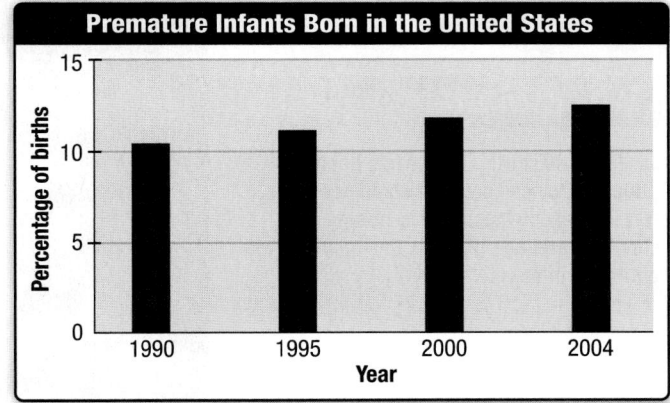

8. How has the number of infants born prematurely changed since 1990?
F The number of cases has remained stable.
G The number of cases has increased over time.
H The number of cases has decreased over time.
J The number of cases has increased and then decreased in recent years.

Writing Skills

9. Short Answer Write a short paragraph in which you describe three ways in which egg cells and sperm cells differ.

Chapter 41

Forensic Science

In a dimly lit alley, a shot is fired. One person falls to the ground. Another disappears into the night, seemingly without a trace. But believe it or not, clues are everywhere in this alley, if you know how to find them.

Preview

1 Introduction to Forensics
What Is Forensic Science?
Tools of Forensic Science

2 Inside a Crime Lab
Identification and DNA
Trace Evidence
Firearms and Toolmarks
Drugs, Alcohol, and Toxicology
Pathology
Anthropology and Entomology

3 Forensic Science in Action
At the Crime Scene
Time of Death
Cause, Mechanism, and Manner of Death
Victim and Perpetrator

Why It Matters

The science of solving crimes has become a popular subject. Forensics combines the latest investigative techniques, cutting edge technology, and age-old scientific methods with the intrigue of solving a mystery.

A crime scene can't stay taped off forever, so photographs are taken of every detail.

A Thread of Evidence

At a crime scene, even a thread may provide a clue about what happened.

Procedure

1 Press a **strip of clear tape** onto **one of three types of fabric** supplied by your teacher.

2 Peel the tape off. Repeat until you have at least **one fiber** stuck to the tape.

3 Press the tape onto a **microscope slide.**

4 Examine the slide. Trade slides with several other students, and examine those fibers.

Analysis

1. Draw the fiber on your slide and note any unique features.

2. Design a method for determining which fibers came from each of the three types of fabric.

Eyewitness evidence can be the key to finding a suspect. However, the most common cause of wrongful convictions in the United States is mistaken identity.

Why outline a body with tape? The position of a body can reveal clues about how a crime happened.

READING TOOLBOX

These reading tools can help you learn the material in this chapter. For more information on how to use these and other tools, see **Appendix: Reading and Study Skills.**

Using Words

Word Families Word families are groups of words that go together. Some word families are words that are used together to create a different meaning than the meaning of each word by itself. The table shows some examples of these words.

Word Families	
Word	**Meaning**
rigor	stiffness, hardness
livor	bluish color, like a bruise
algor	coldness
mortis	having to do with death

Your Turn Use the table to answer the following questions.

1. You probably know that the word *rigid* means "stiff." What do you think the word *livid* means?
2. Write a definition in your own words for the term *rigor mortis.*
3. How do you think algor mortis progresses after death?

Using Language

Finding Examples Concrete examples often help clarify new information. Certain words and phrases can help you recognize examples. These words include *for example, such as, like,* and *including.*

Your Turn Use what you have learned about examples to answer the following questions.

1. Find the examples in the following sentence: Evidence such as hair, skin, pollen, and glass are considered to be trace evidence.
2. Find the examples in the introductory paragraph above.

Using Graphic Organizers

Spider Maps A spider map is an effective tool for classifying the details of topics in science. A spider map divides a topic into ideas and details.

Your Turn Make a spider map to list details about each of the major sections of a crime lab.

1. Draw a diagram like the one shown here. In the circle, write the main topic.
2. From the circle, draw legs to represent each section of a crime lab. Draw one leg for each section.
3. From each leg, draw horizontal lines. As you read the chapter, write details about the sections of a crime lab on the horizontal lines. To add more details, make the legs longer and add more horizontal lines.

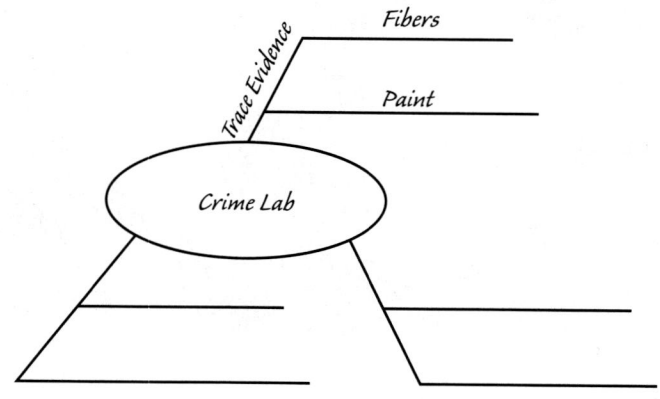

1 Introduction to Forensics

Key Ideas	Key Terms	Why It Matters
❯ What are the two major duties of forensic scientists? ❯ What are five basic types of tools used by forensic scientists?	forensic science chromatograph spectrometer	Forensic science helps to ensure that justice is achieved in a court of law.

No matter how careful a criminal may have been, some trace of evidence is almost always left at a crime scene. A footprint, a fingerprint, a hair, or just a few skin cells—whatever the evidence is, forensic scientists can find it.

What Is Forensic Science?

Forensic science is the use of science to investigate legal matters. Forensic science can be used in any type of legal matter from crime to contracts. ❯ **The two major duties of a forensic scientist are analyzing evidence and testifying in court.**

Analyze Evidence Any time two people come into contact with each other, evidence is exchanged. This idea is known as the *Locard exchange principle*. It means that when a crime is committed, some kind of evidence will always be produced. Forensic scientists analyze this evidence. In forensics, the word *identity* has two meanings. The first involves the question, What is it? The second involves the question, Whose is it? When evidence is analyzed, as **Figure 1** shows, the first step is often to find out what the evidence is. Is that ketchup or a blood stain? The next step is to identify the person to whom it belongs. Does the blood belong to the victim or to the suspect?

forensic science the use of science to investigate legal matters

Testify in Court The second major role of a forensic scientist is to provide expert testimony in court. An expert witness is someone who has education, training, or significant experience in a particular subject. Expert witnesses are allowed to give their opinion in court.

❯ **Reading Check** *What are the two meanings of the word "identity" as it relates to forensic science? (See the Appendix for answers to Reading Checks.)*

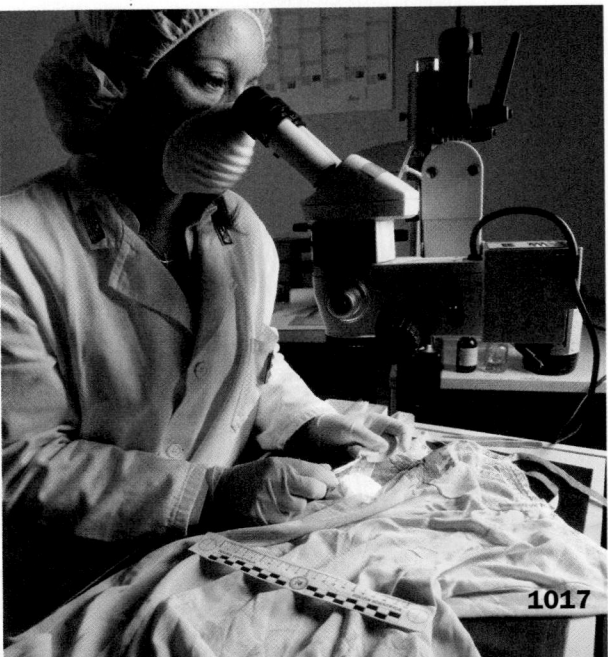

Figure 1 This forensic scientist is collecting evidence from a bloodstained garment. Evidence is photographed before it is removed. A ruler is used to show the size of the evidence in the photo.

Academic Vocabulary

portrayed shown

More Than Crime Scenes The work of forensic scientists is portrayed in television shows about crime scene investigation. But forensic scientists do more than investigate crime scenes.

Accidents and Disasters Forensic scientists, such as the ones in **Figure 2,** are often called on when a major accident or natural disaster occurs. These scientists help identify victims and look for clues to determine the cause of an accident. They also investigate fires to determine whether the fire was accidental or the work of an arsonist.

Reading Toolbox

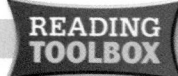

Finding Examples Search the text on this page to find examples of jobs that forensic scientists perform. Can you find more than 15 examples?

Spotting the Fake Some forensic scientists put their skills to work by verifying documents and products. These scientists detect forged signatures, money, passports, and paintings. Some identify fake designer goods; others study the details of fake credit cards. Forensic scientists can also detect altered wills and contracts.

Computer Criminals Many crimes, such as theft and fraud, are now committed electronically. Forensic computer experts can retrieve deleted data from computers, cell phones, and fax machines. These experts trace the spread of computer viruses, look for clues in the program code, and work with Internet service providers to find the programmer who wrote the virus. Forensic computer experts also work to locate hackers and try to stop Internet fraud.

› **Reading Check** ***List at least 10 things that forensic scientists do in addition to investigating crime scenes.***

Figure 2 Forensic scientists investigate plane crashes, recover bodies, and perform many duties in addition to crime scene investigation. › **What is the role of the forensic scientist investigating this plane crash site?**

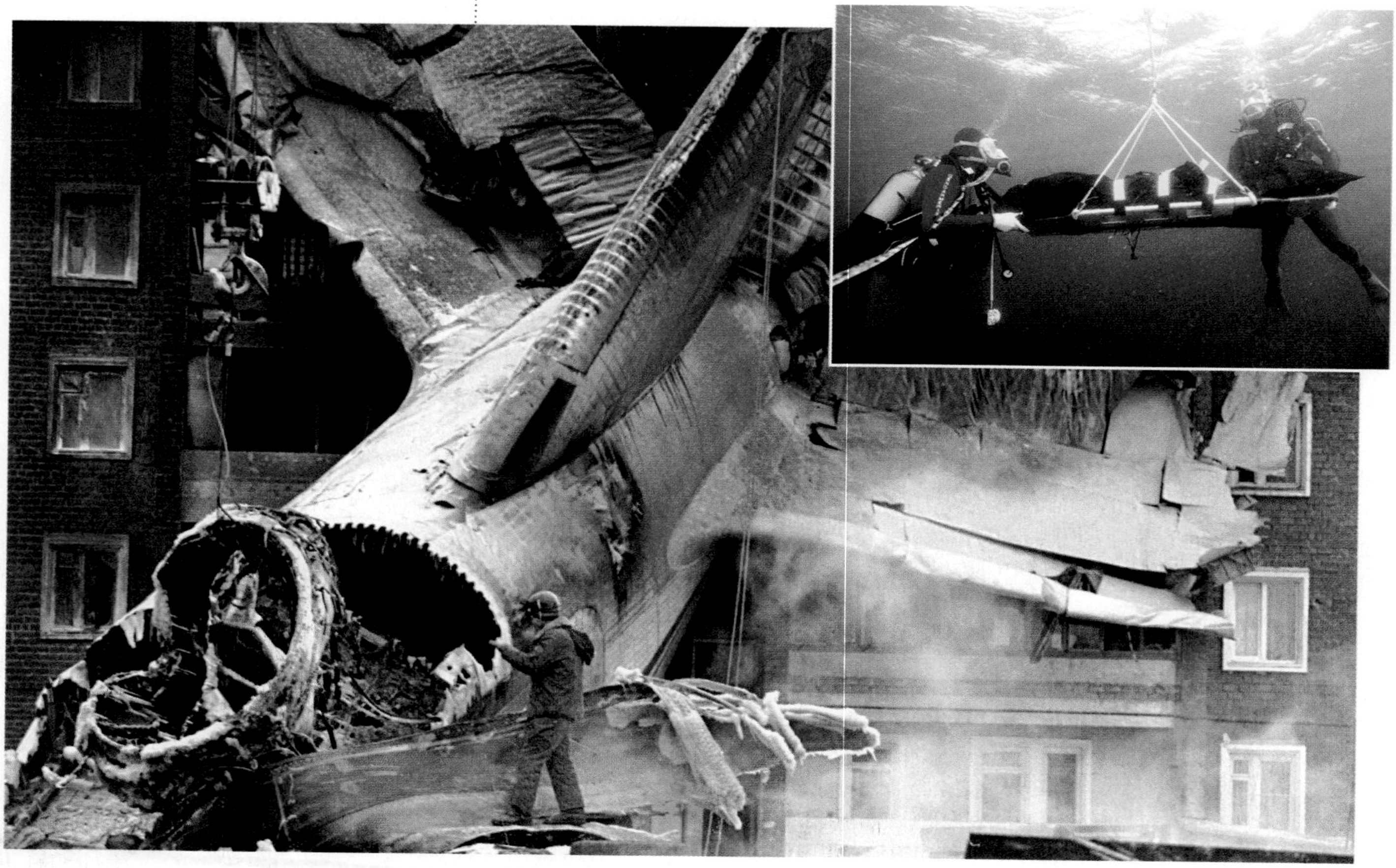

Quick**Lab**

⏱ 15 min

The Forged Signature

In this lab, you will try to identify a forged signature by using a technique that forensic document examiners use.

Procedure

1 Use a **pen** to sign your name at the top of a **piece of paper.** Sign your name again somewhere else on the paper, not directly below the first signature. Be consistent with your signature style. Do not let any classmates see where you placed the second signature.

2 Fold your paper in half, and hand it to your teacher.

3 When your teacher hands you another piece of paper, try to copy the signature at the top of the page. Be sure that you do not receive your own signature.

4 Again, fold the paper in half and hand it to your teacher.

5 When your teacher hands you a paper with three signatures, determine which of the three is the forgery. Circle differences between the signatures, such as angle, loops on letters, transitions between letters, and letter endings.

Analysis

1. **Identify** the signature that you think is the forgery. Explain your reasoning.

2. **CRITICAL THINKING** **Analyzing Methods** Can you think of other ways of comparing signatures that might make the job of detecting forged signatures easier and more precise? If possible, test your method. Did you reach a different conclusion than you did in your first experiment?

Tools of Forensic Science

One of the most important tools of forensic science is a good education. To become a forensic scientist, a person must have a bachelor's degree in forensic science, criminalistics, chemistry, biology, biochemistry, or physics. Because forensic scientists are often asked to testify in court, they need to have good communication skills. Forensic scientists also have a wide variety of external tools at their disposal. ❯ **Five basic types of tools used by forensic scientists are chemicals, microscopes, chromatographs, spectrometers, and computers.**

Crime Scene Chemistry Chemistry helps scientists find evidence that cannot be seen with the naked eye. For example, the chemicals *luminol* and *fluorescein* make bloodstains glow. A crime scene where someone has been injured or killed may appear completely clean. But these chemicals can reveal even microscopic traces of blood. Many chemicals can make fingerprints visible on different surfaces. Some can even make fingerprints glow. Another chemical detects gunshot residue. Filter paper is wiped on the skin of a victim or suspect. When the chemical is applied to the paper, the chemical turns purple anywhere lead gunshot residue is present. Forensic scientists also use chemistry to analyze drugs, alcohol, poisons, fire accelerants, and explosives.

SCI LINKS.

www.scilinks.org
Topic: Forensic
 Science
Code: HX80608

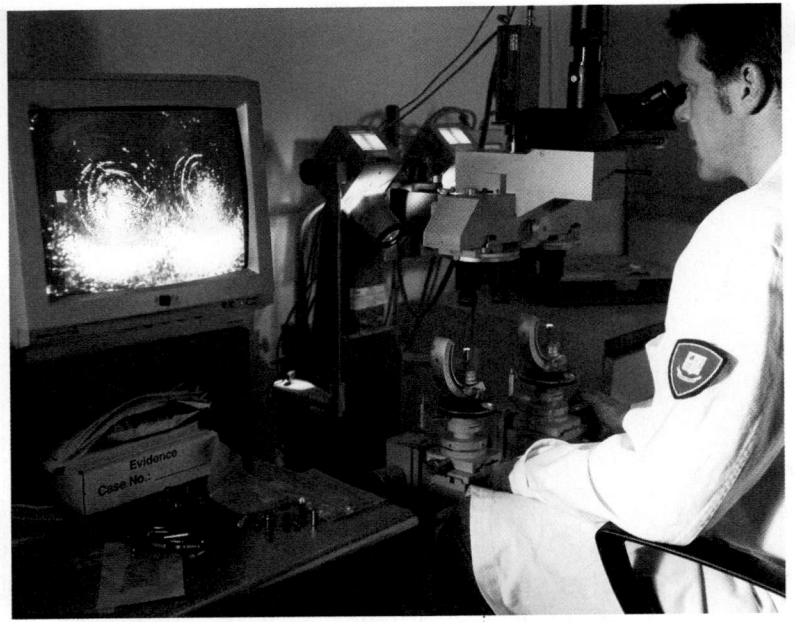

Figure 3 This scientist is using a comparison microscope to view the markings on the backs of two different bullet cartridges.

chromatograph a tool that separates chemicals based on various physical properties

spectrometer a tool that measures wavelengths of visible light or other electromagnetic radiation

Looking at Details One of the most important tools in forensic science is the microscope. Handheld lenses can be used at a crime scene to get a better look at small objects. In the lab, forensic scientists often begin examining evidence by using a light microscope. Scientists separate types of evidence that will be studied in greater detail later. A scanning electron microscope (SEM) takes a picture of the surface of extremely small objects, like grains of sand or pollen. **Figure 3** shows a comparison microscope. It allows scientists to compare small objects, such as bullets, side by side.

Identifying Substances Often, forensic scientists need to identify an unknown substance. Two tools that are often used for identifying substances are a chromatograph and a spectrometer. A **chromatograph** separates chemicals based on their physical properties, such as boiling point or molecular size. A **spectrometer** records how a substance interacts with wavelengths of electromagnetic radiation. Data from each of these tools can be used alone or can be combined to provide more information.

Organizing Information Without the help of computers, much of the work that forensic scientists do would be difficult and time consuming. Computers link to microscopes, chromatographs, and spectrometers to display results. Databases such as the Integrated Automatic Fingerprint Identification System (IAFIS) store information that forensic scientists can search through when they are trying to identify a victim or a suspect. Similar databases exist for identifying bullets, car paint samples, and DNA.

> **Reading Check** *What are three types of microscopes used by forensic scientists for examining evidence?*

Section 1 Review

> **KEY IDEAS**

1. **Identify** the two major duties of a forensic scientist.
2. **Name** three things forensic scientists investigate in addition to crime scenes.
3. **Identify** five basic types of tools that are used to examine evidence.
4. **Name** the tool that takes a picture of the surface of small objects.

CRITICAL THINKING

5. **Analyzing Methods** Which tools would you recommend using to analyze a sample of soil taken off the bottom of a suspect's shoe?
6. **Comparing Functions** If you were looking at a hair sample from a crime scene, what different information might you get from a light microscope and a scanning electron microscope?

ALTERNATIVE ASSESSMENT

7. **Examining Evidence** Use a light microscope to look at dust that has been collected from around the classroom. Take detailed notes, and make drawings of what you see. Be sure to note where each sample came from. Are there differences in the dust found in different parts of the room? How might you explain these differences?

King Tut Unmasked

BIOTECHNOLOGY

Tutankhamen, also known as King Tut, lived to be only about 19 years old. For years, many have believed that King Tut was murdered by a blow to the head. Modern forensic science now makes it possible to solve the mystery of King Tut's death and to reveal the face behind the mask.

Ancient Mystery, Modern Forensics

Because mummified corpses are fragile, any investigation into King Tutankhamen's death must be done without damaging the remains. Three teams of forensic scientists used computed tomography (CT) scans to perform a virtual autopsy of King Tut's body.

Did King Tut's face resemble the golden mask? CT scans revealed the condition of the bones and the shape of the skull. Forensic anthropologists used this information to reconstruct the face of the king, shown below. As for reconstructing the crime, scans show that King Tut's skull was not damaged and that he may have died from an infection resulting from a broken left leg.

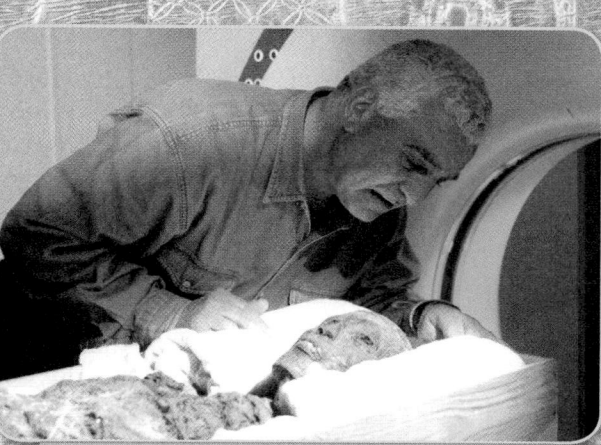

Unwrapping the Mummy Dr. Zahi Hawass, head of the Egyptian Supreme Council of Antiquities, prepares King Tut's mummy for scanning. CT scans pass hundreds of X rays through a body, which creates images of slices of the body. Computers put the slices together to make a picture.

Research Use library or Internet sources to find out about the "Iceman" discovered in the Swiss Alps in 1991. How did scientists investigate his remains? What did they learn? Write a brief report about your findings.

Key Ideas	Key Terms	Why It Matters
❯ Which two unique characteristics are used to identify a person? ❯ What are the five major types of trace evidence? ❯ What are the duties of firearms and toolmarks specialists? ❯ What kinds of information do toxicologists look for? ❯ What does a forensic pathologist do? ❯ How are anthropology and entomology related to forensic science?	ballistics toxicology pathology autopsy	In a crime lab, even the most microscopic evidence can provide clues that help solve a crime.

The size of a crime lab varies, from one or two scientists to hundreds of people on staff. Common departments, called *sections,* of a crime lab include identification, DNA analysis, trace evidence, firearms and toolmarks, toxicology, and pathology. Some investigations also require anthropology and entomology.

Identification and DNA

The Chinese used fingerprints to sign legal documents as far back as three thousand years ago. More recently, the ability to sequence DNA provides another way to identify a person. ❯ **Two unique characteristics that are used to identify people are friction ridges and DNA.**

Identification The identification section of a crime lab deals with *friction ridges*—fingerprints, palm prints, and footprints. Friction ridges are used for identification because they are unique and permanent. No two people share the same patterns of ridges. Even identical twins have unique markings in their fingerprints. From the time a fetus is 17 weeks along in development and until that person dies, friction ridges never change. Criminals have tried to remove these ridges by using chemicals and surgery, but the ridges grow back. Damage and disease can alter friction ridges, but irregularities make these prints even more unique!

Many chemicals make fingerprints visible on a variety of surfaces such as the glove in **Figure 4.** Ninhydrin is a liquid that reacts with proteins in body oils. It turns fingerprints purple on paper and on other porous surfaces. Magnetic fingerprint powder has a coating that sticks to the oil in fingerprints. Then, a magnet lifts off any excess powder. This technique produces an extremely detailed image of a fingerprint.

❯ **Reading Check** *Where are friction ridges found on the body?*

Figure 4 A burglar dropped this glove at a crime scene and probably thought that he had left no prints. He was wrong.

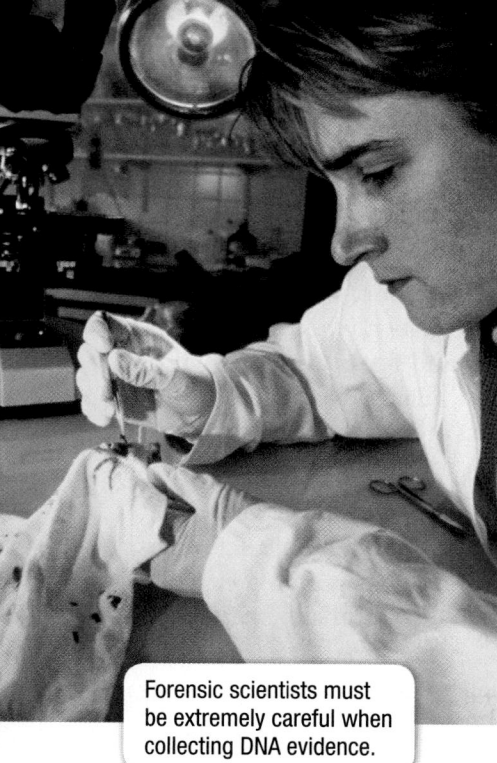

Forensic scientists must be extremely careful when collecting DNA evidence.

Samples of DNA are sorted by size using an electric current.

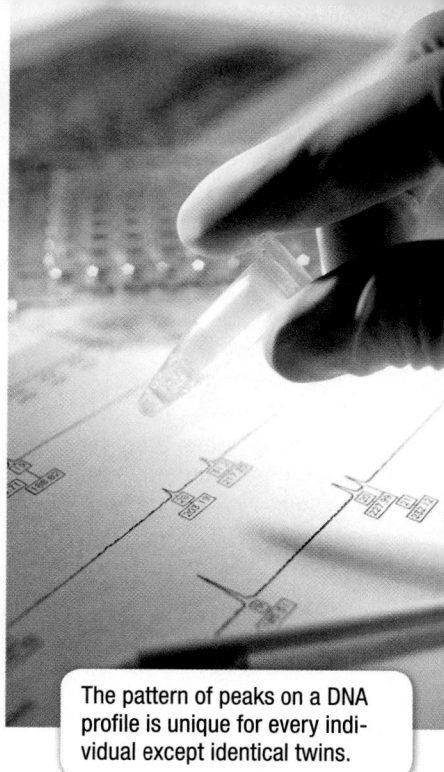

The pattern of peaks on a DNA profile is unique for every individual except identical twins.

Figure 5 Creating a DNA profile involves careful collection and analysis. Once a profile is created, it can be compared with other DNA profiles stored in CODIS, the FBI databank. ❯ **What are the advantages and concerns regarding a DNA profile databank?**

ACADEMIC VOCABULARY

analyzed studied in detail

DNA Analysis The forensic DNA (also called *forensic biology*) section of a crime lab analyzes samples containing DNA, such as blood, hair follicles, and skin cells.

Methods Sometimes only a few cells are found at a crime scene. Even these small samples can be analyzed. A technique called polymerase chain reaction *(PCR)* makes millions of copies of DNA. The DNA is then analyzed and compared, as shown in **Figure 5.** Forensic DNA analysis uses regions of repeated DNA that are slightly different in every person. The FBI uses a set of 13 regions to create a DNA profile. The Combined DNA Index System (CODIS) is a databank of DNA profiles from people convicted of felonies, from crime scene evidence, and from arrestees in some states. Unidentified DNA is entered into CODIS in order to compare it with profiles in the databank.

Uses DNA analysis can be used for more than solving crime. It can be used to identify victims of disasters, settle a paternity suit, and identify endangered species for prosecuting poachers. DNA has even been used to tag sports merchandise to prevent souvenir fraud.

Issues Contamination is a major issue when scientists work with DNA. PCR makes millions of copies of DNA, making a contaminated sample useless. Databanking DNA also raises issues. If DNA profiles from all suspects were databanked, suspects whose DNA does not match the evidence could be eliminated early in an investigation. Many people believe this could prevent innocent people from going to jail. But if DNA profiles were collected from all suspects, some people worry that this information could result in discrimination. However, the DNA regions could not reveal information about a person's characteristics.

Trace Evidence

Trace evidence is any piece of evidence that is exchanged between the criminal, the victim, or the environment. ❯ **The five major types of trace evidence are hair, fiber, glass, paint, and soil.**

- **Hair and Fiber** One advantage of hair and fiber evidence is that it does not decompose quickly. The type of fiber, whether human, animal, plant, or synthetic; color; shape; and texture suggest who or where the evidence came from. If a hair has its root, DNA from the root can be used to identify a suspect or a victim.

- **Glass** If a person breaks a piece of glass, fragments of the glass can be found in his or her clothing even after the clothing is washed. The pattern that glass creates when it is cracked can help scientists reconstruct a crime. The way that glass bends light, along with the density and color of the glass, can help investigators identify where broken glass came from.

- **Paint** The National Automotive Paint File contains over 40,000 paint samples. Crime labs use this database to match paint chips to the make, model, and year of a vehicle. The color, type, layers, and shape of a paint chip can provide a wealth of information.

- **Soil** Various types of soil have different components. When a person leaves a shoe print, the person's shoe will have small particles stuck to it. The soil from the shoe can be compared with the soil where the print was found. Tire tracks can also be important pieces of trace evidence.

- **Pollen and Other Clues** Pollen grains, like those in **Figure 6,** have unique and interesting shapes. Pollen found on a victim or a suspect can be linked with the type of plant that produced it, the areas where the plant grows, and the time of year that the pollen is produced. Other common types of trace evidence include arson debris, gunshot residue, parts of cars, cosmetics, and bits of paper.

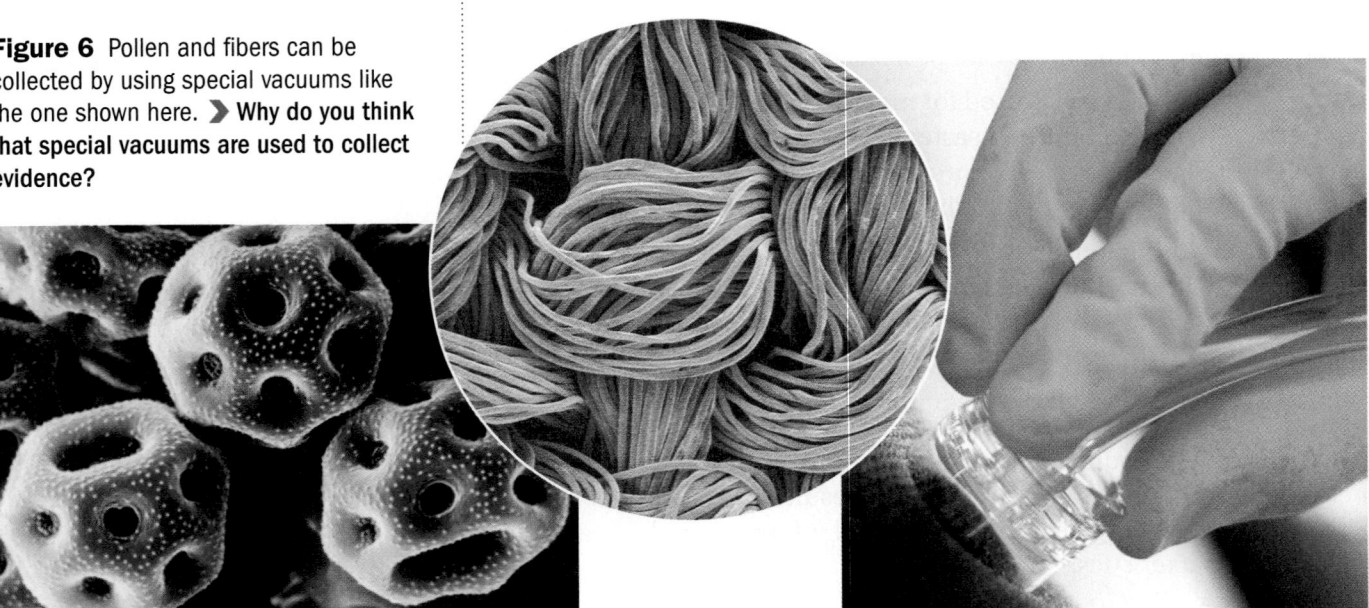

Figure 6 Pollen and fibers can be collected by using special vacuums like the one shown here. ❯ **Why do you think that special vacuums are used to collect evidence?**

QuickLab

Toolmarks Analysis

Could you work in the firearms and toolmarks section of a crime lab? Try your hand at matching toolmarks by identifying the tool that has been used on a pencil.

Procedure

1 Obtain a piece of evidence from your teacher. In this case you will obtain a **pencil** bearing unidentified toolmarks.

2 Make an exemplar to compare your evidence. Using a different pencil from your unknown sample, make a toolmark with each of the tools provided by your teacher. Label each mark.

3 Compare the unidentified toolmark on your evidence to the exemplars you made. Look for any irregularities that can help you make a positive identification.

Analysis

1. Identify the tool that was used to make the mark on your evidence.

2. **CRITICAL THINKING** **Recognizing Verifiable Facts** What conditions might make it difficult to conclude that a specific tool was used to make a particular mark?

Firearms and Toolmarks

When a weapon is used to commit a crime, the evidence is analyzed by scientists in the firearms and toolmarks section. ❯ **Firearms and toolmarks examiners study evidence from guns, ammunition, tools, toolmarks, and serial numbers, and perform crime scene reconstruction.**

Firearms When most people think of firearms analysis, they think of ballistics. **Ballistics** is the science that deals with the motion and impact of projectiles, such as bullets, missiles, and bombs. The firearms section works on evidence related to bullets and cartridge cases. When a gun is fired, unique markings are left on bullets and cartridges. No two guns make the exact same marks. Firearms experts, such as the man in **Figure 7,** use this information to compare bullets and cartridges to the gun that fired them. A national database of fired bullets and cartridge cases can also tell experts if a gun has been used in other crimes. Firearms experts also help reconstruct crime scenes by using bullet trajectories and by estimating the distance between the gun and the victim.

Toolmarks Guns are not the only weapons used by criminals. Examiners also study the marks and impressions made by other tools, such as crowbars, hammers, or pliers. These experts can figure out the type of tool that was used to steal a car or break into a house. Scientists in this section can restore serial numbers on guns, car parts, or other items to help locate the owner.

❯ **Reading Check** *Which science deals with projectiles?*

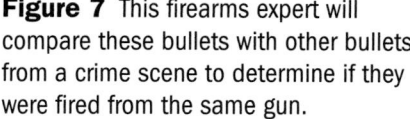

Figure 7 This firearms expert will compare these bullets with other bullets from a crime scene to determine if they were fired from the same gun.

Figure 8 Forensic scientists identify unknown substances, like the evidence above. Toxicologists test hair samples to find out if a person is using drugs or being poisoned. ❯ **If a person dies from one large dose of poison, would evidence of the poison show up in a hair sample?**

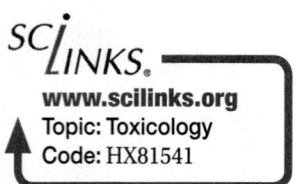

SCI
LINKS
www.scilinks.org
Topic: Toxicology
Code: HX81541

Drugs, Alcohol, and Toxicology

When a cause of death is not visible, a chemical substance might have been involved. ❯ **Forensic toxicologists analyze blood, urine, and tissue samples to detect the presence of chemicals and to determine whether a chemical was harmful or fatal.**

Forensic Toxicology Toxicology is the study of toxins and their effects on the body. A *toxin* is any substance that is physically harmful to an organism. The two main areas of forensic toxicology are antemortem and postmortem toxicology. *Antemortem* ("before death") toxicologists analyze blood, urine, and hair, as shown in **Figure 8,** from living persons. Antemortem toxicologists may test for drugs of abuse or signs that a person is being poisoned. *Postmortem* ("after death") toxicologists analyze tissue samples from a body after death. They try to determine whether a drug, a chemical, a poison, or a combination of substances was responsible for a person's death.

Forensic Alcohol When a person is arrested for driving under the influence of alcohol, that person may take a blood, urine, or breath test. Forensic scientists analyze the driver's blood or urine to determine blood alcohol content. These scientists also maintain the breath test equipment so that it accurately reports a driver's alcohol level. Forensic scientists study alcohol metabolism, analysis, and the effects of alcohol on the body in relation to driving.

Illegal Drugs The federal government has a list of drugs that are illegal to possess. When police find a substance that they suspect is a drug, forensic scientists must be able to identify the substance. These scientists analyze unknown powders, pills, liquids, and plant parts to determine whether a substance is an illegal drug. Using microscopes and spectrometers, scientists identify illegal drugs quickly and easily.

❯ **Reading Check** *What is the difference between antemortem toxicologists and postmortem toxicologists?*

Pathology

Pathology is the scientific study of disease. ❯ **Forensic pathologists perform autopsies to determine how and when a person died.** Forensic pathologists often work in a morgue, such as the one in **Figure 9,** a coroner's office, a hospital, or a funeral home.

Branches of Pathology Two types of pathology are anatomical and clinical pathology. Anatomical pathology involves studying changes in the structure of the body itself, such as visible wounds and broken bones. Clinical pathology involves looking at samples of tissue that have been removed from the body. Most forensic pathologists are experts in both anatomical and clinical pathology.

Performing an Autopsy An **autopsy** is an examination of a body after death. An autopsy is performed any time there is a question about the events that caused a person's death. An autopsy includes an external and an internal examination of a body. The external examination involves looking for signs of trauma and trace evidence. Distinguishing marks, such as birthmarks and tattoos, can be used to help identify a body.

An internal examination involves cutting the body open down the middle of the chest and abdomen and around the top of the head. All of the major organs of the body are examined, removed, and weighed. The weight of an organ can provide information about certain types of disease. Samples of blood, urine, and tissue are collected for toxicology, and samples may be taken for DNA analysis. The forensic pathologist also spends many hours at a microscope looking at thin slices of tissue from each organ to find clues about what happened to the body.

❯ **Reading Check** *What does a forensic pathologist look for during an autopsy?*

toxicology the study of toxins and their effects on the body

pathology the scientific study of disease

autopsy an examination of a body after death, usually to determine the cause of death

Figure 9 Pathologists performing an autopsy examine and weigh every major organ in the body to help determine the cause of death.

Anthropology and Entomology

A forensic team may include scientists who work in hospitals, universities, or museums. These specialists assist with a forensic investigation only when their skills are needed. Two of these specialists are anthropologists and entomologists. ❯ **Anthropology can help determine the identity of a disfigured or decomposed body. Anthropology and entomology can be used to estimate the time of death.**

Forensic Anthropology Anthropology is the study of humans, including human culture and the human body. Physical anthropologists are experts in the study of the human skeleton. Forensic anthropologists apply this skill to legal matters. As in **Figure 10,** these scientists help identify skeletal remains and bodies that cannot be recognized. They help identify victims of crimes, disasters, fires, and other tragedies that result in bodies that are difficult to identify.

When bones are found, determining whether they came from a human is important. If the bones are human, police need to know how long ago the person died. An extremely old skeleton could be part of an ancient burial ground. If the skeleton is not very old, police could have a murder to solve. A forensic anthropologist can help estimate whether skeletal remains are old or fairly recent.

By examining a skeleton, a forensic anthropologist can learn a person's sex, approximate height, age, and likely race. Some forensic anthropologists are also trained in the art of facial reconstruction. They can model how a person's face may have looked based on features of the skull. Evidence found in bones can also help determine the cause of death. Weapons or tools used on the body, some diseases, and certain injuries leave traces in bone and provide important clues.

❯ **Reading Check** *What are four things that you can learn about a person from a skeleton?*

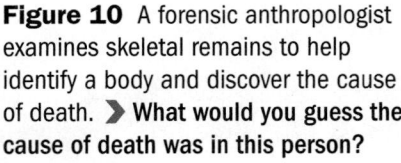

Figure 10 A forensic anthropologist examines skeletal remains to help identify a body and discover the cause of death. ❯ What would you guess the cause of death was in this person?

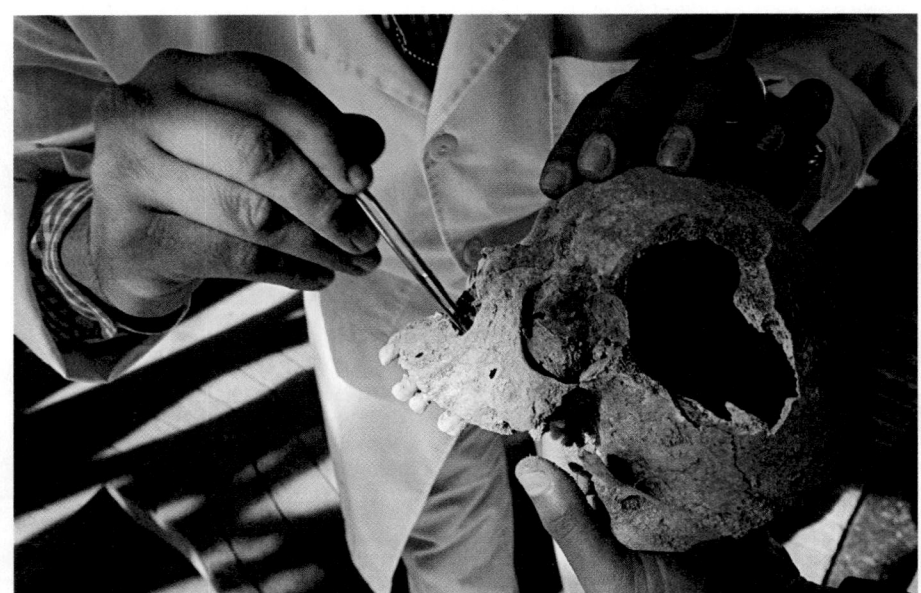

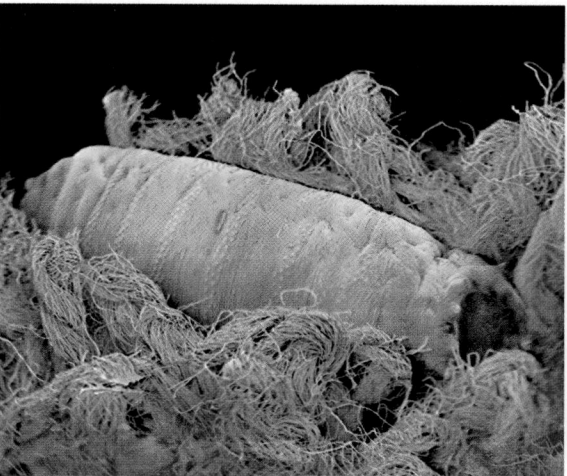
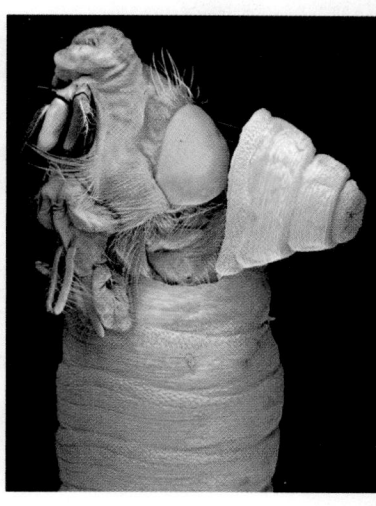

Figure 11 Blow-flies lay hundreds of eggs (left.) The life cycle of the blow-fly includes eggs, three stages of larvae, a pupa (middle and right), and an adult.

Forensic Entomology Forensic entomology applies the study of insects to legal matters. Three categories of legal matters involve insects. The first category includes insects that affect man-made structures, such as termites in buildings. The second group involves insects that contaminate food and products. The last and most well-known group includes insects that inhabit decomposing bodies.

If a body has been dead for more than a few minutes, insects can begin to gather. Insects arrive at different times. Blow flies, shown in **Figure 11,** typically arrive first. They deposit eggs around the eyes, nose, and mouth of a body. Temperature, weather, and other factors influence the growth rate of insects. The types of insects and their developmental stage when captured help the forensic entomologist estimate the time of death. Insects can also help entomologists determine where a body has been. Flies often prefer specific habitats. If a body is found outdoors with larvae from an indoor species of fly, the person may have been killed indoors and then moved. Even after a body has decomposed, insects around the body still contain evidence. The victim's DNA and chemicals that were present in the victim's body might still be recovered from an insect's digestive tract.

Section 2 Review

> **KEY IDEAS**

1. **Name** two characteristics that are unique to every person that can be used for identification.
2. **List** the five most common types of trace evidence.
3. **Identify** the duties of firearms and toolmarks specialists.
4. **Describe** the role of the forensic toxicologist.

5. **Explain** the technique used by pathologists for examining a body.
6. **Describe** how anthropology and entomology are used in forensics.

CRITICAL THINKING

7. **Making Predictions** A car is found abandoned in a pasture. Police discover a dead body in the trunk of the car. If you were the crime scene investigator, what types of evidence would you look for?

WRITING FOR SCIENCE

8. **Evidence Report** After examining the car described in the previous question, you now have to write a report to help detectives identify a suspect. Write a paragraph describing all of the evidence that you found. Include details about where and how you found each piece of evidence.

Key Ideas	Key Terms	Why It Matters
❯ What are the steps of an investigation at a crime scene? ❯ What information is used to estimate time of death? ❯ What three components describe how a person died? ❯ Which two identities must be discovered in order to solve a homicide?	rigor mortis livor mortis algor mortis	In solving a crime, forensic scientists investigate what happened, how it happened, and who was involved.

It's midnight, and you've just fallen asleep when the phone rings. You are needed at a crime scene. When you arrive, you find that the victim's head is missing. You are in for a very long night. But long nights are part of the job on a crime scene team.

At the Crime Scene

A crime scene team includes representatives from many agencies. Police, firefighters, paramedics, and crime scene investigators all have duties to perform. Police may need to chase a suspect while paramedics treat a victim. Meanwhile, the crime scene investigators can begin looking for evidence. ❯ **At a crime scene, police secure a perimeter and interview witnesses; crime scene investigators locate, mark, photograph, analyze, and collect evidence.**

Secure and Search At a crime scene, securing a perimeter as quickly as possible is extremely important. The perimeter is the outer edge of the area where investigators might be able to find evidence. Police tape is put up to keep people out so that evidence is not accidentally destroyed. The faster the perimeter is secured, the better the chances of finding evidence. Crime scene investigators search every single inch of a crime scene. Police and investigators may form a line by standing shoulder to shoulder and may slowly walk through the crime scene. In a "walk-through," each investigator is responsible for searching the area in front of him or her. Investigators may even search the whole crime scene on their hands and knees. Anything that might be evidence is marked with a numbered or lettered tag, like the ones shown in **Figure 12.**

Figure 12 This investigator is marking evidence by using numbered tags. Photographs will then be taken of every piece of evidence. ❯ **What information is preserved by photographing evidence?**

Figure 13 Some crime scene teams use lasers to analyze a bullet's path, or trajectory. Knowing the trajectory can help investigators locate stray bullets. ❯ **What other information can be discovered by analyzing bullet trajectory?**

Photograph and Document While some investigators are carefully locating and tagging evidence, other forensic specialists are busy photographing and documenting everything. Where an object was located and what position it was in can provide detectives with important clues. But a crime scene cannot stay closed forever. The only way to preserve this information is through photographs, diagrams, and very detailed notes. While investigators document evidence, police interview everyone at the scene. Anybody at or near a crime scene may have been a witness or might be a suspect. Crime scene investigators might also test suspects for gunshot residue.

Collect and Analyze Some types of analysis must be done at the crime scene. For example, fingerprints and bloodstains are often found on items that cannot be taken back to the lab, such as walls and floors. Blood-spatter analysis must also be done at the scene. Spatter patterns can be important for figuring out exactly what happened. Blood drops, trails, wipes, and spatter can reveal the location and movement of a victim or a suspect during the crime. For example, in the case of the body with the missing head, blood trails may offer a clue as to where the head might be.

Figure 13 shows how forensic scientists analyze the path of bullets at the scene. Lasers can help determine where the shooter was standing. Investigators may learn that more than one shooter was present or that the perpetrator was also being shot at. This information may mean the difference between a murder charge and a claim of self-defense. Lasers can also help locate bullets that have landed far from the crime scene. Finally, after all of the on-scene analysis is done, forensic scientists carefully collect and package evidence and take it back to the lab for even more detailed analysis.

❯ **Reading Check** *What are three types of analysis that must be done at the crime scene?*

SCI*LINKS*®

www.scilinks.org
Topic: Forensic Analysis
Code: HX80607

Time of Death

Calculating the exact time of death is impossible. However, several methods used together can provide a good estimate of the time of death. ❯ Rigor mortis, livor mortis, algor mortis, and the stages of decomposition are used to estimate the time at which a person died.

Rigor Mortis **Rigor mortis** is the stiffening of muscles after death. Rigor mortis begins in the first few hours after death. By about 12 hours, the muscles are completely stiff. The body remains stiff for about 24 hours and then slowly loosens. After about 36 hours, the muscles are completely loose again.

Livor Mortis **Livor mortis,** or *lividity,* is the settling of blood to the lowest points of the body after death. Livor mortis begins about 30 minutes after death and shows up as light red patches. After about 10 hours, the skin at the lowest points of the body are dark purple. At this time, lividity is fixed, which means that if the body is moved, some purple color will stay in the original lowest points.

Algor Mortis **Algor mortis** is the cooling of the body after death. Algor mortis is affected by many factors, such as the temperature of the environment in which the body was found. As discussed in **Figure 14,** core body temperature is used to calculate algor mortis. A body cools for 24 hours. Then chemical reactions in the body cause the body to warm up again.

Decomposition After about 24 hours, the same chemical reactions that cause the body to become warmer also cause the skin to turn green. After about 48 hours, enzymes that break down the blood cause the blood appear black. At this point, the black veins are visible through the green skin. This process is called *marbling.* Meanwhile, bacteria in the digestive system metabolize nutrients and release gases. By about 72 hours, the whole body has become bloated. Decomposition continues until all of the tissues are broken down.

READING TOOLBOX

Using Words Use information in the text to make a graph that shows the progress of rigor mortis, livor mortis, and algor mortis over the first 24 hours following death.

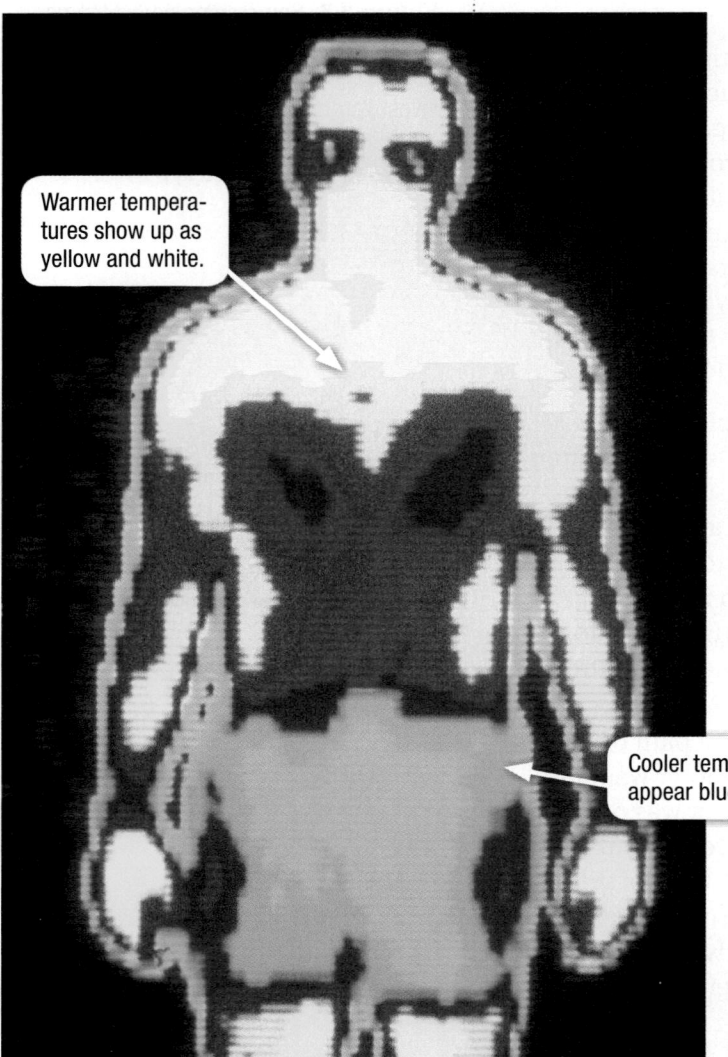

Warmer temperatures show up as yellow and white.

Cooler temperatures appear blue and green.

Figure 14 This thermogram uses color to show body temperature. Temperature varies over the surface of the body. This variation is why scientists use core body temperature in order to estimate time of death.

QuickLab

 15 min

Estimate Time of Death

A body has been found by the river. You have been called out to estimate the time of death of the victim. When you investigate the body, you find that lividity is clearly visible and rigor mortis is beginning to set in. The body temperature is very low—when measured you find that the core temperature is about 68 °F.

Analysis

1. **Estimate** how long this person has been dead based on rigor mortis and livor mortis.

2. **Estimate** the time of death using algor mortis. To calculate algor mortis, subtract the temperature of the body from 98.6 °F. Then divide the answer by 1.5. So, (98.6 − 68) ÷ 1.5 would provide an estimate of how long this person has been dead.

Postmortem Events

Post-mortem event	1 hour	3 hours	5 hours	10 hours	12 hours
Rigor mortis		beginning	obvious but not maximum		maximum rigor mortis
Livor mortis	beginning	obvious but not set		maximum lividity	
Algor mortis	~97 °F	~94 °F	~91 °F	~84 °F	~80 °F

3. **CRITICAL THINKING** **Making Inferences** How might you explain the difference in time of death estimated by using algor mortis compared with time of death estimated by using rigor mortis and livor mortis?

Cause, Mechanism, and Manner of Death

Describing how a person died is not as simple as it sounds. This description actually has three components. ❯ **The cause, the mechanism, and the manner of death describe how a person died.**

Cause The cause of death is the event that lead to the death of a person. The cause is what started the process that resulted in the death of an individual. The cause of death is the most familiar description for how a person died. For example, a cause of death might be a heart attack or a gunshot wound.

Mechanism The mechanism of death is the physiological process that resulted in death. Mechanism is a rather technical description of what happened to the body that caused the body to stop functioning. For example, in the case of a gunshot wound, the mechanism might be loss of blood, technically referred to as *exsanguination*.

Manner The manner of death falls into one of five categories: homicide, suicide, accident, natural, or undetermined. Manner of death generally describes what the intent was when a person was killed. A gunshot wound could be homicide, suicide, or accidental. If the pathologist cannot be certain what the manner of death was, it is listed as undetermined. Toxicology results often help determine the manner of death. For example, if a person was poisoned with a drug that resulted in a heart attack, the autopsy may reveal the heart attack. However, the manner of death will remain undetermined until toxicology results reveal that the heart attack was not a natural death.

rigor mortis temporary stiffness of muscles after death

livor mortis settling of blood to the lowest points in the body after death

algor mortis cooling of the body after death

Victim and Perpetrator

The victim at your crime scene is missing his head. How will you identify this person? If you cannot identify the victim, then how can you begin to guess who may have had a motive for his murder?

❯ The identities of the victim and of the perpetrator must be discovered in order to solve a homicide.

Identity of the Victim When a body is found, investigators need to find out who the victim is. Many techniques can be used to <u>establish</u> the victim's identity. Some methods are simple; others are complex. Identification often begins with a wallet or purse containing a driver's license. However, when a body has no ID, forensic scientists have to find other ways of establishing identity.

Fingerprints would be an easy way to positively identify a person. However, if the victim's fingerprints are not on file anywhere, then this information is useless. A photograph might be useful. If the person has been arrested, his or her mug shot would be on record. If not, police may take a photograph of the victim to the area where the body was discovered to find out if anyone in the area knew the victim.

When a body is badly decomposed, neither fingerprints nor photographs can be used for identification. If a person has had dental work done, dental records offer one means of identification. A skull can also be used to perform a facial reconstruction, as shown in **Figure 15.** Forensic anthropologists work with forensic artists to build a model that shows what the victim may have looked like in life.

Hair takes much longer to decompose than other tissue. Hair cells do not have a nucleus, but they do have mitochondria. Mitochondrial DNA analysis can link a person with his or her mother and the mother's relatives. If only a few drops of blood are found, the DNA profile can be compared with a sample of DNA taken from a hair brush or other item belonging to a missing person.

Figure 15 To perform a facial reconstruction, X rays are taken of the skull (left.) The X rays are used to create a computer model (middle.) Then, a forensic artist (right) uses the computer data and information about facial anatomy to build a clay model of the victim.

Identity of the Perpetrator When all of the evidence from an investigation is put together, the ultimate goal is to identify the perpetrator. A perpetrator is a person responsible for a crime. The evidence that is gathered by the police, the crime scene team, and the forensic scientists may finally lead the police to a suspect, as in **Figure 16.** Unlike scenarios shown on television, forensic scientists do not make an arrest. However, just because a suspect is in custody does not mean that a forensic scientist's job is done.

In addition to examining evidence, the second important duty of forensic scientists is to provide expert testimony in court. During a trial, attorneys for both the prosecution and the defense may bring in forensic scientists to testify. These scientists explain and interpret the evidence for the jury. Different forensic scientists may reach different conclusions. Each expert may use sound scientific principles, but he or she may interpret the data differently. Forensic scientists must be able to explain and justify their conclusions clearly, in a way that a jury can understand.

Figure 16 A forensic scientist's duties do not end just because an arrest is made. Forensic scientists also testify in court to explain the evidence and conclusions that were made. ❯ **Why might two forensic scientists interpret evidence differently?**

❯ **KEY IDEAS**

1. **Identify** the steps involved in collecting evidence at a crime scene.
2. **Explain** the difference between the cause, the manner, and the mechanism of death.
3. **Describe** some of the ways that forensic scientists determine the identity of a body.

CRITICAL THINKING

4. **Inferring Relationships** How is the cause of death related to the mechanism of death?
5. **Predicting Results** In what circumstances would a body not cool after death? Is there a circumstance in which a body might only get warmer?
6. **Drawing Conclusions** While performing an autopsy, a pathologist notices that the heart has no blood in it. What are some possible reasons for this finding?

USING SCIENCE GRAPHICS

7. **Using a Table** Imagine you have just been called to another crime scene. A body was discovered in a park near the police station. Use the table of postmortem events to estimate the time of death if the body has a core temperature of 86°F, lividity fixed, and rigor mortis at maximum.

Objectives

▶ Practice using the technique of paper chromatography to separate pigments.

▶ Determine whether a dye contains two or four pigments.

Materials

- scissors
- chromatography paper (2 strips)
- tape
- pencils (2)
- beakers, small (2)
- paper clips, small (2)
- toothpicks (2)
- pigment solutions to be tested
- water, distilled

Safety

The Counterfeit Drug

A small pharmaceutical company has been accused of illegally manufacturing and exporting a counterfeit version of a popular blood pressure medication. The Food and Drug Administration (FDA) suspects that the company manufactures its own version of the drug and labels it identically to the real drug.

The FDA, along with the Drug Enforcement Administration (DEA), has confiscated a sample of the drug. Officials need to determine whether the sample is the brand-name drug or the counterfeit version of the medication.

Officials know that the pills appear to be identical but that the pigments that are used in the brown coating differ. The coating used in the counterfeit pills contains a mixture of green and orange pigments. The coating on the genuine version contains a mixture of four different pigments. In this lab, you will use chromatography to test a sample of brown pigment to determine whether the pill that it came from is genuine or counterfeit. To make this determination, you will run a chromatogram on a control and an unknown sample of brown dye.

Procedure

❶ 👓 🧤 Put on safety goggles, gloves, and a lab apron.

❷ ⚗️ 🔷 **CAUTION: Do not use chipped or cracked glassware. Notify your teacher immediately if a piece of glassware breaks. Use extreme care when handling scissors.** Cut two lengths of chromatography paper equal to the depth of the beakers that you are using. You can check that the length is correct by taping the top of the strip of paper to a pencil and lowering the paper into the beaker, allowing the pencil to rest across the top of the beaker.

❸ Once the paper is cut to the correct length, remove it from the beaker. Leave the pencil attached to the top of the paper.

❹ Attach a paper clip to the bottom of each strip of paper in order to keep the paper hanging straight down while it is in the beaker.

❺ ☠️ **CAUTION: Dyes will stain.** Do not get any dye on your skin or your clothing. By using a toothpick, dab some of the unknown dye onto one strip of chromatography paper about 2 cm above where the water level will be in the bottom of the beaker.

❻ Allow the dye to dry for a few minutes. Repeat the dabbing process several times (at the same place on the paper each time) to build up a concentration of pigment that will yield good results.

❼ Repeat steps 5 and 6 using the control dye, which was supplied by the legitimate manufacturer of the pills.

8 Pour distilled water into each beaker to a depth of about 2 cm.

9 Make sure that the dye is above the water level and does not come into contact with the water. Refer to the photo, which shows the correct distance between the dye spot and the water level.

10 Set up the beakers, paper, pencils, and water as shown in the photo. Allow the paper to absorb water so that the water moves up the paper by capillary action and separates the pigments in the dye. This process may take several minutes.

11 When the water migrates to within a few millimeters from the top of the paper, remove the pencils and paper from each beaker.

12 Empty the water from the beaker, place the pencils back across the top of each beaker, and allow your chromatograms to dry overnight.

13 🖐 ♻ Clean up your lab materials according to your teacher's instructions. Wash your hands before leaving the lab.

Analyze and Conclude

1. Drawing Conclusions Did the unkown sample come from the genuine drug or the counterfeit drug? How can you tell?

2. Explaining Events Why do the different pigments that make up a dye separate on the chromatography paper?

3. `CRITICAL THINKING` **Analyzing Methods** Why are tests in cases like this one carried out in such a way that the analysts do not know what products they are testing?

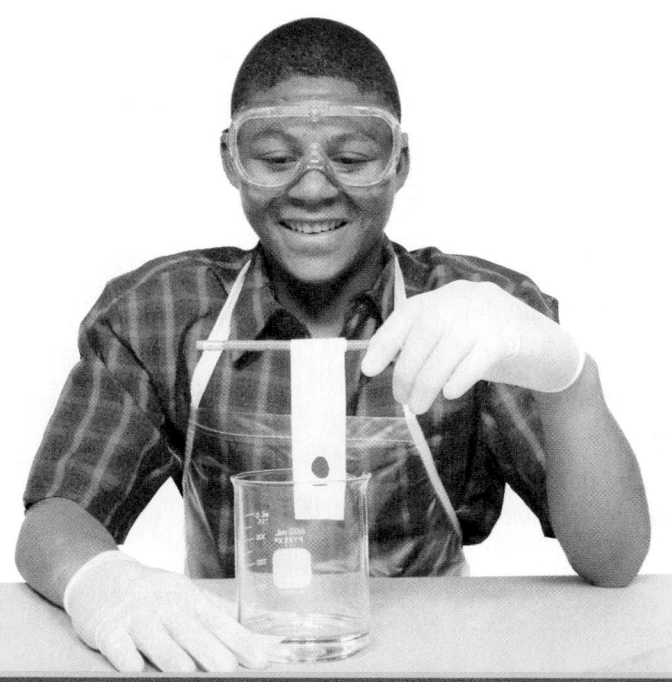

Extensions

4. Forensic Careers Research and report on careers for forensic scientists in the FDA or DEA.

Key Ideas	Key Terms

1 Introduction to Forensics

> The two major duties of a forensic scientist are analyzing evidence and testifying in court.

> Five basic types of tools used by forensic scientists are chemicals, microscopes, chromatographs, spectrometers, and computers.

forensic science (1017)
chromatograph (1020)
spectrometer (1020)

2 Inside a Crime Lab

> Two unique characteristics that are used to identify people are friction ridges and DNA.

> The five major types of trace evidence are hair, fiber, glass, paint, and soil.

> Firearms and toolmarks examiners study evidence from guns, ammunition, tools, toolmarks, and serial numbers, and perform crime scene reconstruction.

> Forensic toxicologists analyze blood, urine, and tissue samples to detect the presence of chemicals and to determine whether a chemical was harmful or fatal.

> Forensic pathologists perform autopsies to determine how and when a person died.

> Anthropology can help determine the identity of a disfigured or decomposed body. Anthropology and entomology can be used to estimate the time of death.

ballistics (1025)
toxicology (1026)
pathology (1027)
autopsy (1027)

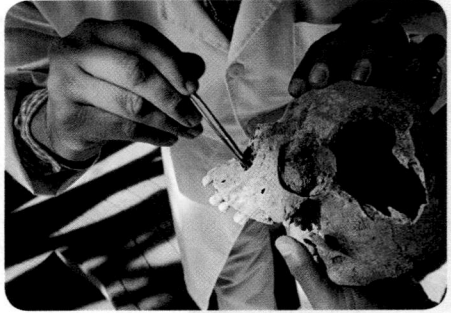

3 Forensic Science in Action

> At a crime scene, police secure a perimeter and interview witnesses; crime scene investigators locate, mark, photograph, analyze, and collect evidence.

> Rigor mortis, livor mortis, algor mortis, and the stages of decomposition are used to estimate the time at which a person died.

> The cause, the mechanism, and the manner of death describe how a person died.

> The identities of the victim and of the perpetrator must be discovered in order to solve a homicide.

rigor mortis (1032)
livor mortis (1032)
algor mortis (1032)

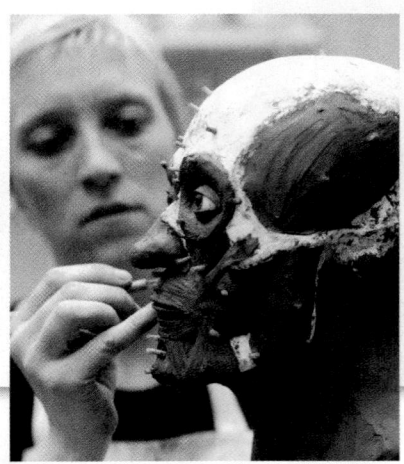

READING TOOLBOX

1. **Finding Examples** How many examples of trace evidence are described in the chapter?

2.  **Concept Map** Make a concept map that shows the sections of a crime lab and each section's function. Include the following terms in your map: *forensic science, ballistics, rigor mortis, autopsy, toxicology,* and *chromatograph.* Use additional terms as necessary.

Using Key Terms

Use each of the following terms in a separate sentence.

3. *forensic science*

4. *autopsy*

For each pair of terms, explain how the meanings of the terms differ.

5. *chromatography* and *spectroscopy*

6. *toxicology* and *pathology*

7. *livor mortis* and *algor mortis*

Understanding Key Ideas

8. What role do forensic scientists play in the legal system?
   a. They arrest criminals.
   b. They interview witnesses.
   c. They hear testimony from experts.
   d. They analyze evidence and provide expert testimony.

9. Basic tools of forensic science include all of the following *except*
   a. a microscope.
   b. a microphone.
   c. a spectrometer.
   d. a chromatograph.

10. What are the two unique characteristics used to identify people?
   a. blood type and DNA
   b. friction ridges and DNA
   c. blood type and eye color
   d. friction ridges and height

11. Evidence such as pollen and hair would be analyzed in which section of a crime lab?
   a. DNA
   b. trace
   c. toolmarks
   d. toxicology

12. *Ballistics* is defined as the
   a. study of weapons.
   b. analysis of bullets and guns.
   c. analysis of the motion of weapons.
   d. analysis of the motion and impact of projectiles.

13. Toxicologists do which of the following?
   a. perform autopsies
   b. perform crime scene reconstruction
   c. analyze tissue for the presence of DNA
   d. analyze tissue for the presence of chemicals

14. Which of the following refers to the cooling of the body after death?
   a. lividity
   b. algor mortis
   c. livor mortis
   d. rigor mortis

15. The physiological process that caused the body to stop functioning is referred to as
   a. the cause of death.
   b. the manner of death.
   c. the mechanism of death.
   d. the explanation of death.

16. Which of the following can be used to identify a badly decomposed body?
   a. tattoos
   b. fingerprints
   c. photographs
   d. dental records

Explaining Key Ideas

17. Identify three pieces of information that are determined by a forensic pathologist.

18. Explain how anthropologists and entomologists assist with homicide investigations.

19. Summarize the advantages and concerns that are involved with keeping a DNA databank.

20. Sequence the steps that a crime scene team follows on arriving at a crime scene.

Critical Thinking

21. **Analyzing Information** A driver runs into a parked car in a parking lot and leaves the scene. There are no witnesses, but investigators find paint chips on the ground and on the damaged car, as well as red plastic and sandy tire tracks. How might forensic scientists try to solve this crime?

22. **Analyzing Methods** When evidence is brought into the crime lab for analysis, forensic scientists must decide the order in which different tests will be conducted. In which order might a bloodstained garment move through the trace and DNA sections of a lab? Explain your answer.

23. **Evaluating Information** If a body were found with eggs, all three larval stages, pupae, and adult flies on and around the body, would estimating time of death be possible by using the blowfly life cycle? Explain your answer.

Using Science Graphics

The graph shows the percent change in violent crime, property crime, and murder between 2001 and 2005. Use the graph to answer the following questions.

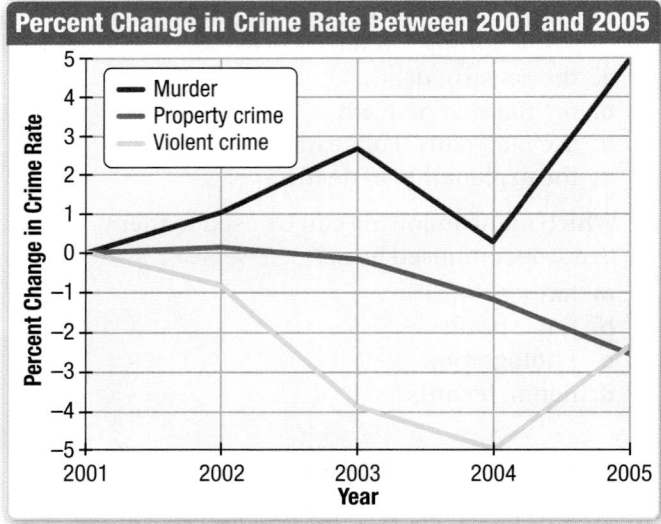

Source: FBI Uniform Crime Report, 2005

24. What was the percent change in violent crime rates between 2004 and 2005?
   a. up 5.1%
   b. up 2.5%
   c. up 4.8%
   d. down 1.6%

25. What was the overall change in property crime rates between 2001 and 2005?
   a. up 2.5%
   b. down 1.6%
   c. down 2.5%
   d. down 2.8%

The diagram shows how much time passes between each stage of a blow fly life cycle. Use the diagram to answer the following question.

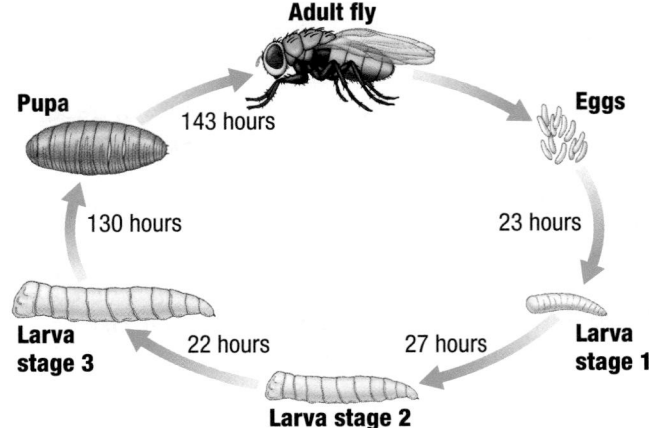

26. A body that is found with blow fly eggs and stage 1 and stage 2 larvae may have been dead for about
   a. 23 hours.
   b. 27 hours.
   c. 50 hours.
   d. 74 hours.

Methods of Science

27. **Interpreting Evidence** A dead body that is found face up in an alley is evaluated by a forensic scientist. The forensic scientist determines that the person died somewhere else face down and was transported to the alley. What evidence would you expect to find that would have led to this conclusion?

28. **Evaluating Methods** When firearms experts need to find out if a bullet found at a crime scene was fired from a particular gun, they fire another bullet from that gun into water in a large tank. Why do you think they fire the test bullet into a water tank?

Writing for Science

29. **Forming Reasoned Opinions** Do you think the FBI should keep a DNA profile for all suspects in an investigation, rather than only for convicted felons? Write a paragraph supporting your opinion.

Alternative Assessment

30. **Modeling Spatter Patterns** Design a model to demonstrate how a spatter pattern can help forensic scientists determine the location of a body. If possible, display your model for the class.

Standardized Test Prep

Science Concepts

Choose the letter of the answer choice that best answers the question.

1. In forensic science, the word identity has how many meanings?

  A one   **C** three

  B two   **D** four

2. The tool used by forensic scientists that separates chemicals based on physical properties is a

  F computer.   **H** spectrometer.

  G microscope.   **J** chromatograph.

3. Which technique makes millions of copies of DNA?

  A PCR   **C** IAFIS

  B PRC   **D** CODIS

4. Which section of a crime lab performs autopsies?

  F DNA   **H** toxicology

  G pathology   **J** anthropology

5. Which of the following is the correct order in which duties are performed at a crime scene?

  A secure, search, photograph, collect

  C search, secure, photograph, collect

  B secure, photograph, search, collect

  D secure, collect, search, photograph

Math Skills

6. Short Response Recall that algor mortis is calculated by subtracting the temperature of the corpse from 98.6 °F and then dividing the answer by 1.5. If a body is found with a core temperature of 88.6 °F, what would you estimate the time of death to be based on algor mortis?

Using Science Graphics

Use the table of postmortem events to answer the following question(s).

Postmortem Events					
Post-mortem event	1 hour	3 hours	5 hours	10 hours	12 hours
Rigor Mortis		beginning	obvious but not maximum		maximum rigor
Livor Mortis	beginning	obvious but not set		maximum lividity	
Algor Mortis	~97°F	~94°F	~91°F	~84°F	~80°F

7. What temperature would you expect in a body that is at maximum lividity and maximum rigor?

  F 80 °F   **H** 94 °F

  G 91 °F   **J** 97 °F

8. If a body is found that has early signs of rigor and livor is not set, about how long would you estimate the person has been dead?

  A 1 hour

  B 3 hours

  C 5 hours

  D 10 hours

Use the diagram of fingerprints to answer the following question(s).

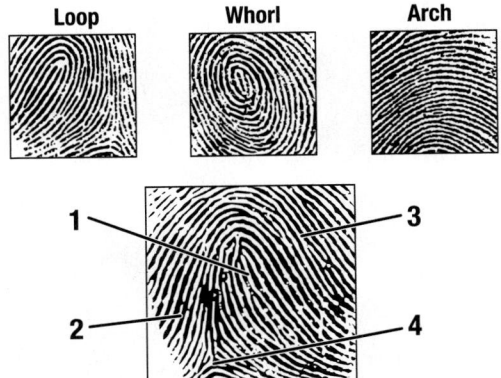

9. Label #4 points to a feature called a delta. Which fingerprint pattern contains a delta?

  F arch   **H** whorl

  G loop   **J** delta

1042

Appendix
Table of Contents

Reading and Study Skills..1044
    FoldNotes..1044
    Word Origins 1047

Science Skills 1050
    Scientific Research 1050
    Experimental Design...1052
    Microscopy..1054
    Determining Mass and Temperature...................1056
    SI Measurement..1058
    Graphing...1060

Reference 1062
    Classification..1062
    The Biologist's Periodic Table of Elements...........1064

Answers to Reading Checks.....................................1066

Glossary..1075

Index...1126

FoldNotes

FoldNotes are a useful study tool that you can use to organize concepts. One FoldNote focuses on a few main concepts. By using a FoldNote, you can learn how concepts fit together. FoldNotes are designed to make studying concepts easier, so you can remember the ideas for tests.

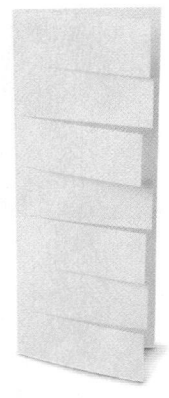

Key-Term Fold

A key-term fold is useful for studying definitions of key terms in a chapter. Each tab can contain a key term on one side and its definition on the other. Use the key-term fold to quiz yourself on the definitions of the key terms in a chapter.

❶ Fold a **sheet of lined notebook paper** in half from left to right.

❷ Using **scissors**, cut along every third line from the right edge of the paper to the center fold to make tabs.

Double-Door Fold

A double-door fold is useful when you want to compare the characteristics of two topics. The double-door fold can organize characteristics of the two topics side by side under the flaps. Similarities and differences between the two topics can then be easily identified.

❶ Fold a **sheet of paper** in half from the top to the bottom. Then, unfold the paper.

❷ Fold the top and bottom edges of the paper to the center crease.

Four-Corner Fold

A four-corner fold is useful when you want to compare the characteristics of four topics. The four-corner fold can organize the characteristics of the four topics side by side under the flaps. Similarities and differences between the four topics can then be easily identified.

❶ Fold a **sheet of paper** in half from top to bottom. Then, unfold the paper.

❷ Fold the top and bottom of the paper to the crease in the center of the paper.

❸ Fold the paper in half from side to side. Then, unfold the paper.

❹ Using **scissors**, cut the top flap creases made in step 3 to form four flaps.

Booklet

A booklet is a useful tool for taking notes as you read a chapter. Each page of the booklet can contain a main topic from the chapter. Write details of each main topic on the appropriate page to create an outline of the chapter.

1 Fold a **sheet of paper** in half from top to bottom.

2 Fold the sheet of paper in half again from left to right.

3 Fold the sheet of paper one more time from top to bottom.

4 Completely unfold the paper.

5 Refold the paper from top to bottom. Using **scissors**, cut a slit along the vertical crease of the sheet from the folded edge to the horizontal crease in the middle of the folded paper. Do not cut the entire sheet in half. Unfold the paper.

6 Fold the sheet of paper in half from left to right. While holding the bottom and top edges of the paper, push the bottom and top edges together so that the center collapses at the center slit. Fold the four flaps to form a four-page book.

Layered Book

A layered book is a useful tool for taking notes as you read a chapter. The four flaps of the layered book can summarize information into four categories. Write details of each category on the appropriate flap to create a summary of the chapter.

1 Lay one **sheet of paper** on top of **another sheet**. Slide the top sheet up so that 2 cm of the bottom sheet is showing.

2 Holding the two sheets together, fold down the top of the two sheets so that you see four 2 cm tabs along the bottom.

3 Using a stapler, staple the top of the FoldNote.

Pyramid

A pyramid provides a unique way for taking notes. The three sides of the pyramid can summarize information into three categories. Use the pyramid as a tool for studying information in a chapter.

1 Place a **sheet of paper** in front of you. Fold the lower left-hand corner of the paper diagonally to the opposite edge of the paper.

2 Cut off the tab of paper created by the fold (at the top).

3 Open the paper so that it is a square. Fold the lower right-hand corner of the paper diagonally to the opposite corner to form a triangle.

4 Open the paper. The creases of the two folds will have created an X.

5 Using **scissors**, cut along one of the creases. Start from any corner, and stop at the center point to create two flaps. Use **tape** or **glue** to attach one of the flaps on top of the other flap.

Table Fold

A table fold is a useful tool for comparing the characteristics of two or three topics. In a table fold, all topics are described in terms of the same characteristics so that you can easily make a thorough comparison.

1 Fold a **piece of paper** in half from the top to the bottom. Then, fold the paper in half again.

2 Fold the paper in thirds from side to side.

3 Unfold the paper completely. Carefully trace the fold lines by using a pen or pencil.

Tri-Fold

A tri-fold is a useful tool that helps you track your progress. By organizing the chapter topic into what you know, what you want to know, and what you learn, you can see how much you have learned after reading a chapter.

1 Fold a piece a paper in thirds from the top to the bottom.

2 Unfold the paper so that you can see the three sections. Then, turn the paper sideways so that the three sections form vertical columns.

3 Trace the fold lines by using a **pen** or **pencil**. Label the columns "Know," "Want," and "Learn."

Three-Panel Flip Chart

A three-panel flip chart is useful when you want to compare the characteristics of three topics. The three-panel flip chart can organize the characteristics of the three topics side by side under the flaps. Similarities and differences between the three topics can then be easily identified.

1 Fold a **piece of paper** in half from the top to the bottom.

2 Fold the paper in thirds from side to side. Then, unfold the paper so that you can see the three sections.

3 From the top of the paper, cut along each of the vertical fold lines to the fold in the middle of the paper. You will now have three flaps.

Two-Panel Flip Chart

A two-panel flip chart is useful when you want to compare the characteristics of two topics. The two-panel flip chart can organize the characteristics of the two topics side by side under the flaps. Similarities and differences between the two topics can then be easily identified.

1 Fold a **piece of paper** in half from the top to the bottom.

2 Fold the paper in half from side to side. Then, unfold the paper so that you can see the two sections.

3 From the top of the paper, cut along the vertical fold line to the fold in the middle of the paper. You will now have two flaps.

Word Origins

Determining the Meanings of Words

The challenge of understanding a new word can often be simplified by carefully examining the word. Many words can be divided into three parts: a prefix, root, and suffix. The prefix consists of one or more syllables placed in front of a root. The root is the main part of the word. The suffix consists of one or more syllables at the end of a root. Prefixes and suffixes modify or add to the meaning of the root. A knowledge of common prefixes, roots, and suffixes can give you clues to the meaning of unfamiliar words and can help make learning new words easier. For example, each of the word parts in **Table 1** can be combined with the root *derm* to form a word.

Table 2 lists prefixes and suffixes commonly used in biology. Each word part is followed by its common meaning, an example of a word in which the word part is used, and a definition of that word. Examine the word meaning and the example. Decide whether each word part in the first column is a prefix or suffix, depending on how the word part is used in the example.

Use **Table 1** to form five words using the root *derm*.

Table 1 Word Parts

Prefix	Root	Suffix
hypo-	derm	-ic
pachy-	derm	
	derm	-atology
	derm	-atologist
	derm	-atitis

Then, use the list of word parts and their meanings to write what you think each word that you formed means. An example is shown below.

Example: **dermatologist**

derm (root): skin
-logy (suffix): the study of
-ist (suffix): someone who practices or deals with something
dermatologist: someone who studies or deals with skin

Table 2 Word Prefixes and Suffixes

Prefix or suffix	Meaning	Example
a-	not, without	asymmetrical: not symmetrical
ab-	away, apart	abduct: move away from the middle
-able	able	viable: able to live
ad-	to, toward	adduct: move toward the middle
amphi-	both	amphibian: type of vertebrate that lives both on land and in water
ante-	before	anterior: front of an organism
anti-	against	antibiotic: substance, such as penicillin, capable of killing bacteria
arche-	ancient	Archaeopteryx: a fossilized bird
arthro-	joint	arthropod: jointed-limbed organism belonging to the phylum Arthropoda
auto-	self, same	autotrophic: able to make its own food
bi-	two	bivalve: mollusk with two shells
bio-	life	biology: the study of life
blast-	embryo	blastula: hollow ball stage in the development of an embryo
carcin-	cancer	carcinogenic: cancer-causing
cereb-	brain	cerebrum: part of the vertebrate brain
chloro-	green	chlorophyll: green pigment in plants that is needed for photosynthesis

Table 2 Word Prefixes and Suffixes, con't.

Word part	Meaning	Example
chromo-	color	chromosome: structure found in eukaryotic cells that contains DNA
chondro-	cartilage	Chondrichthyes: cartilaginous fish
circ-	around	circulatory: system for moving fluids through the body
-cide	kill	insecticide: a substance that kills insects
co-, con-	with, together	conjoined twins: identical twins physically joined by a shared portion of anatomy at birth
-cycle	circle	pericycle: layer of plant cells
cyt-	cell	cytology: the study of cells
de-	remove	dehydration: removal of water
derm-	skin	dermatology: study of the skin
di-	two	diploid: full set of chromosomes
dia-	through	dialysis: separating molecules by passing them through a membrane
ecol-	dwelling, house	ecology: the study of living things and their environments
ecto-	outer, outside	ectoderm: outer germ layer of developing embryo
-ectomy	removal	appendectomy: removal of the appendix
endo-	inner, inside	endoplasm: cytoplasm within the cell membrane
epi-	upon, over	epiphyte: plant growing upon another plant
ex-, exo-	outside of	exobiology: the search for life elsewhere in the universe
gastro-	stomach	gastropod: type of mollusk
-gen	type	genotype: genes in an organism
-gram	write or record	climatogram: report depicting the annual precipitation and temperature for an area
hemi-	half	hemisphere: half of a sphere
hetero-	different	heterozygous: different alleles inherited from parents
hist-	tissue	histology: the study of tissues
homeo-	the same	homeostasis: the maintenance of a constant condition
hydro-	water	hydroponics: growing plants in water instead of soil
hyper-	above, over	hypertension: blood pressure that is higher than normal
hypo-	below, under	hypothalamus: part of the brain located below the thalamus
-ic	of or pertaining to	hypodermic: pertaining to under the skin
inter-	between, among	interbreed: breed within a family or strain
intra-	within	intracellular: inside a cell
iso-	equal	isogenic: having the same genotype
-ist	practices or deals	biologist: someone who studies life
-logy	study of	biology: the study of life
macro-	large	macromolecule: large molecule, such as DNA or proteins
mal-	bad	malnourishment: poor nutrition

Table 2 Word Prefixes and Suffixes, con't.

Word part	Meaning	Example
mega-	large	megaspore: larger of two types of spores produced by some ferns and flowering plants
meso-	in the middle	mesoglea: jellylike material found between outer and inner layers of coelenterates
meta-	change	metamorphosis: change in form
micro-	small	microscopic: too small to be seen with unaided eye
mono-	one, single	monoploid: one set of alleles
morph-	form	morphology: study of the form of organisms
neo-	new	neonatal: newborn
nephr-	kidney	nephron: functional unit of the kidneys
neur-	neuron	neurotransmitter: chemical released by a neuron
oo-	egg	oogenesis: gamete formation in female diploid organisms
org-	living	organism: living thing
-oma	swelling	carcinoma: cancerous tumor
orth-	straight	orthodontics: the practice of straightening teeth
pachy-	thick	pachyderm: thick-skinned animal, such as an elephant
para-	near, on	parasite: organism that lives on and gets nutrients from another organism
path-	disease	pathogen: disease-causing agent
peri-	around	pericardium: membrane around the heart
photo-	light	phototropism: bending of plants toward light
phyto-	plants	phytoplankton: plankton that consists of plants
poly-	many	polypeptide: sequence of many amino acids joined together to form a protein
-pod	foot	pseudopod: false foot that projects from the main part of an amoeboid cell
pre-	before	prediction: a forecast of events before they take place
-scope	instrument used	microscope: instrument used to see very small objects
semi-	partially	semipermeable: allowing some particles to move through
-some	body	chromosome: structure found in eukaryotic cells that contains DNA
sub-	under	substrate: molecule on which an enzyme acts
super-, supra-	above	superficial: on or near the surface of a tissue or organ
syn-	with	synapse: junction of a neuron with another cell
-tomy	to cut	appendectomy: operation in which the appendix is removed
trans-	across	transformation: the transfer of genetic material from one organism to another
ur-	referring to urine	urology: study of the urinary tract
visc-	organ	viscera: internal organs of the body

Scientific Research

The Process of Science

The word *research* is derived from the French word *recherché,* which means "to investigate thoroughly." Nearly all of us have done some kind of research, but scientific research has special characteristics. At its core is systematic observation and objective recording of these observations. The goals of scientific research are the understanding of the natural world and the application of this understanding to benefit people and the world in which we live.

Science is a process of gaining knowledge about the world around us. The state of scientific knowledge is always changing. Any conclusion drawn from scientific research is subject to change if further research uncovers new information or new insights.

Scientific research is also a collaborative process. It relies on open communcation and cooperation between scientists. The results of one scientist's research are supported only when other scientists reproduce the studies and obtain the same results.

A scientist works in a greenhouse lab.

Preparation for Scientific Research

Before beginning a scientific study, it is important to learn about research that has already been conducted on the subject. Scientists learn about the latest discoveries in their fields by reading the "primary" literature on the subject. Primary literature consists of articles that are published in scientific journals and that have been reviewed by other scientists in the same field. (By comparison, textbooks, encyclopedias, and similar types of publications are referred to as "secondary" literature.) Today, many scientific journals publish online versions of their articles.

Types of Scientific Research

Scientific research typically involves asking very specific questions and then designing studies to collect answers to these questions. There are two broad styles of scientific research: experimental and observational.

In an experiment, some aspect of an organism, an object, or part of the environment is deliberately changed. The researcher then observes the effects of this change. For example, a scientist might study the effects of adding different amounts of nitrogen fertilizer to the soil in which a crop is grown.

Sometimes, it is not possible or desirable to perform an experiment. Observational research uses the senses, such as sight and hearing, to take in information. Scientific observation may also make use of instruments such as microscopes that allow us to see small things and balances that weigh objects. During scientific observation, a scientist observes but usually does not disturb or change his or her subject. For example, for a study of bird song, a scientist might quietly observe birds by recording their songs to be analyzed later in a laboratory.

The application of science for a specific purpose is referred to as *technology.* Pure scientific inquiry and research related to technology have different purposes. Scientific inquiry is conducted to advance our knowledge about the natural world. In contrast, research related to technology may be founded on prior scientific inquiry and is generally aimed at solving problems and meeting the needs of society. Scientific inquiry on the structure and function of DNA, for example, paved the way for technology that is aimed at preventing or curing diseases and improving crops.

A soil scientist surveys corn grown using environmentally-friendly methods.

A scientist sequences DNA in a lab.

Conclusions of Scientific Research

Scientific research relies upon the evaluation of hypotheses, which are testable explanations for observations. If a hypothesis cannot be tested, then it cannot be studied using the tools of science.

Scientific investigation cannot prove that a hypothesis is correct. Rather, it can provide evidence that supports a hypothesis or it can disprove the hypothesis. Hypotheses can be supported but are never proven because scientists cannot be sure that there is not another hypothesis that could better explain their results.

An example of a testable hypothesis is that poinsettia plants flower when the day length is less than 12 hours. This hypothesis about flowering was accepted until scientists discovered that poinsettias would not bloom if they were exposed to day lengths shorter than 12 hours and nights that were interrupted with a period of light. The currently accepted hypothesis is that poinsettias will flower when the length of the night is at least 12 hours.

Scientists are human. They are disappointed if a hypothesis that they favored is disproved or replaced. But scientists are bound by ethics and service to the truth. They must be truthful about their methods and results. They must open their work to the scrutiny of their peers, and they must share their work with the scientific community for the common good.

Science, Technology and Society

Science is part of society. You have read how science and technology can affect society. In a similar way, society can directly affect progress in science and in technology through laws and by giving or withholding government or private funding for research. Certain healthcare issues, such as the use of human embryonic stem cells, are subject to public debate and to governmental control. The progress made in understanding and curing certain diseases can partly depend upon funding for research.

Pure scientific inquiry often drives technological developments. Technology, in turn, enables scientists to conduct experiments that could not otherwise be done. One large difference between the two is that scientific knowledge is made freely available to the scientific community by publication in peer-reviewed scientific journals. Technology, on the other hand, is often funded by private companies. Technological advances may be closely guarded secrets, which may be patented or sold.

The use of science and technology for the benefit of society is subject to political, economic, and ethical concerns. It is the responsibility of all citizens to remain aware of these issues in order to make informed, sound decisions about science, technology, and society.

Experimental Design

Before Experiments

Scientists conduct experiments in order to explore and better understand the world around us. A key element of scientific experiments is that they address very specific questions. Scientists first ask the questions, then propose answers, and then test these possible answers using objective methods that can be repeated by other scientists.

This scientific method, as it is called, is often thought to consist of a rigid set of steps and related rules. In fact, the ways that experiments are carried out do not always fit this mold. Nevertheless, experiments must be done and explained in such a way that other scientists can repeat the procedures and obtain the same results. Producing consistent results between trials of the same experiment allows scientists to verify their conclusions.

Making Observations

An experiment always starts with an observation—something that has made someone wonder. When scientists, or any of us, wonder about something, we ask questions. How do bats catch their prey in the dark? Why do all nests from a single species of bird look the same? Why do I feel cold when I have a fever?

The questions, like these questions, are rather broad at first. But they become very focused as the investigator prepares to systematically study the subject. At this stage, scientists also typically collect and study other information on the subject, such as articles published in scientific journals.

Forming a Hypothesis

The first step a scientist takes in answering a question is to develop a possible explanation for what he or she has observed. This explanation is essentially an educated guess that is based on the evidence that the scientist has collected. The critical feature of this educated guess is that it can be tested. These educated guesses are **hypotheses.**

For example, a plant biologist (a botanist) observes that healthy plants often grow in nitrogen-rich soil. The botanist might hypothesize that nitrogen is important for plant growth. Hypotheses allow scientists to develop **predictions,** or specific expectations about what should occur if a hypothesis is true. Although it might not be worded exactly as such, a prediction takes the form of an if-then statement. The botanist might predict that if most soils do not contain a lot of nitrogen, then adding nitrogen to soil will enhance plant growth.

In addition to being testable, a scientific hypothesis must also be falsifiable. That is, an experiment is designed so that it will show the hypothesis to be false, if indeed it is. Scientists often have several alternative hypotheses that they consider when they conduct an experiment or a series of experiments.

Designing an Experiment

Next, the scientist carefully designs an experiment to test the hypothesis. He or she might grow plants in soils that contain different amounts of nitrogen. In a scientific experiment, only one factor, or *variable,* is changed. This factor that changes is the **independent variable.** The independent variable in this experiment would be the nitrogen level in the soil.

Types of Variables

Other factors must be kept constant in the experiment. These factors are **controlled variables.** Some of the variables that could affect plant growth are air temperature and the amount of rainfall and sunlight.

The factor that changes in response to a change in the independent, or tested, variable is the **dependent variable.** In the soil-nitrogen experiment, the size of plants is the dependent variable.

An experiment that has controlled variables is called a *controlled experiment.* Controlled experiments such as this one allow researchers to conclude that changes in the dependent variable are due only to changes in the independent variable.

Performing the Experiment

Once a reliable experimental design is in place, performing the experiment is often easy. It is important that researchers carefully collect data and record all of their measurements and other observations.

Analyzing Data

When an experiment has been completed, the scientist analyzes the data collected. He or she makes computations, creates tables, draws graphs, and often does statistical analyses. The primary goal of the analysis is to organize and interpret the data so that conclusions can be drawn from them. The scientist also evaluates the procedures and results for possible sources of error—human mistakes, problems with equipment, or unexpected interferences, such as bad weather.

Drawing Conclusions

The final task in an experiment is to determine whether or not the results support the tested hypothesis. If the hypothesis is supported by the findings, the researcher details the supporting evidence and notes any inconsistencies. If the hypothesis is not supported, the researcher offers possible explanations. In either case, the researcher might also discuss alternative hypotheses. These hypotheses might include new ones that have occurred to the scientist during the course of the experiments. One or more hypotheses may be falsified by the experiments, and one or more may be supported. Usually, a single hypothesis emerges that is best supported by the experimental evidence. The scientist also generally compares his or her results to those obtained by other researchers conducting related experiments.

Follow-up Experiments

Scientists usually repeat their experiments, even multiple times, to verify their findings. They also distribute their findings to other scientists, often in the form of articles published in scientific journals. The scientists may also conduct related experiments to test other hypotheses.

Microscopy

Parts of the Compound Light Microscope

- The **eyepiece** magnifies the image, usually 10x.

- The **low-power objective** further magnifies the image, up to 4x.

- The **high-power objectives** further magnify the image, from 10x to 43x.

- The **nosepiece** holds the objectives and can be turned to change from one objective to another.

- The **body tube** maintains the correct distance between the eyepiece and the objectives. This distance is usually about 25 cm, the normal distance for reading and viewing objects with the unaided eye.

- The **coarse adjustment** moves the stage up and down in large increments to allow gross positioning and focusing of the objective lens.

- The **fine adjustment** moves the stage slightly to bring the image into sharp focus.

- The **stage** supports a slide that contains the viewed specimen.

- The **stage clips** secure the slide in position for viewing.

- The **diaphragm** (not labeled), located under the stage, controls the amount of light allowed to pass through the object being viewed.

- The **light source** provides light for viewing the image. It can be either a light reflected with a mirror or an incandescent light from a small lamp. Never use reflected direct sunlight as a light source.

- The **arm** supports the body tube.

- The **base** supports the microscope.

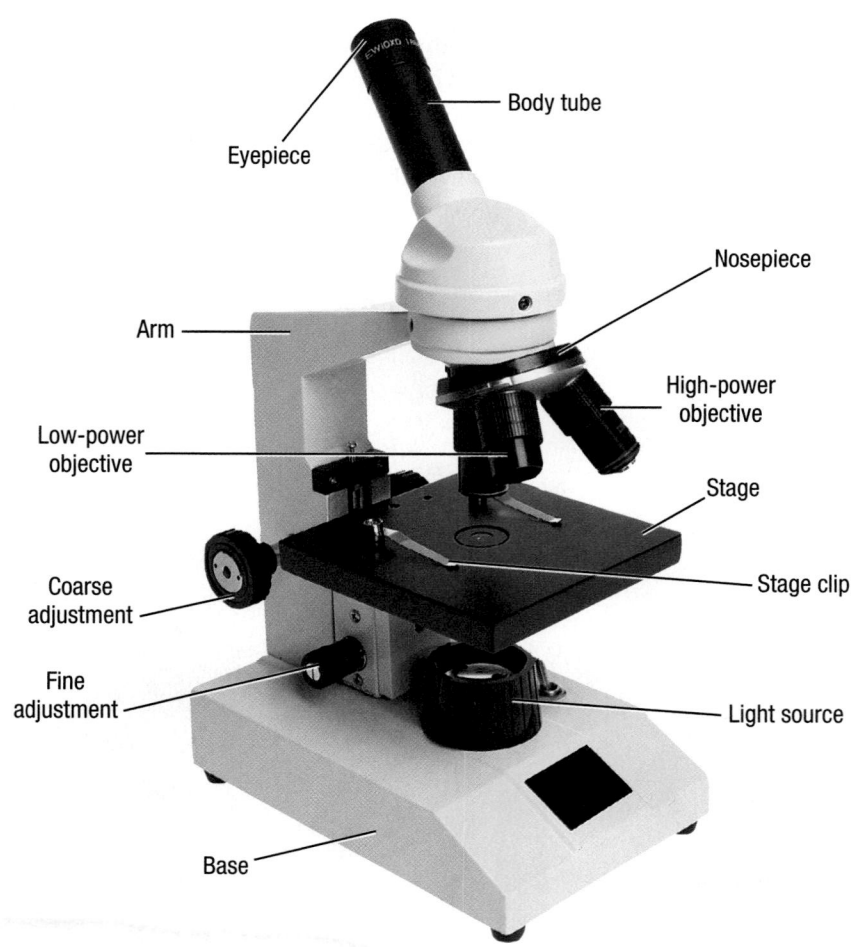

Body tube

Eyepiece

Nosepiece

Arm

High-power objective

Low-power objective

Stage

Coarse adjustment

Stage clip

Fine adjustment

Light source

Base

Proper Handling and Use of the Compound Light Microscope

1. Carry the microscope to your lab table using both hands, one supporting the base and the other holding the arm of the microscope. Hold the microscope close to your body.

2. Place the microscope on the lab table at least 5 cm from the edge of the table.

3. Check to see what type of light source the microscope has. If the microscope has a lamp, plug it in, making sure that the cord is out of the way. If the microscope has a mirror, adjust it to reflect light through the hole in the stage.

   CAUTION: If your microscope has a mirror, do not use direct sunlight as a light source. Using direct sunlight can damage your eyes.

4. Adjust the revolving nosepiece so that the low-power objective is aligned with the body tube.

5. Place a prepared slide over the hole in the stage, and secure the slide with the stage clips.

6. Look through the eyepiece, and move the diaphragm to adjust the amount of light that passes through the specimen.

7. Now look at the stage at eye level. Slowly turn the coarse adjustment to raise the stage until the objective almost touches the slide. Do not allow the objective to touch the slide.

8. While looking through the eyepiece, turn the coarse adjustment to lower the stage until the image is in focus. Never focus objectives downward. Use the fine adjustment to achieve a sharply focused image. Keep both eyes open while viewing a slide.

9. Make sure that the image is exactly in the center of your field of vision. Then switch to the high-power objective. Focus the image with the fine adjustment. Never use the coarse adjustment at high power.

10. When you are finished using the microscope, remove the slide. Clean the eyepiece and objectives with lens paper, and return the microscope to its storage area.

Procedure for Making a Wet Mount

1. Use lens paper to clean a glass slide and coverslip.

   CAUTION: Glass slides and coverslips break easily. Handle them carefully. Notify your teacher if you break a slide or coverslip.

2. Place the specimen that you wish to observe in the center of the slide.

3. Using a medicine dropper, place one drop of water on the specimen.

4. Position the coverslip so that it is at the edge of the drop of water and at a 45° angle to the slide. Make sure that the water runs along the edge of the coverslip.

5. Lower the coverslip slowly to avoid trapping air bubbles.

6. If a stain or solution will be added to a wet mount, place a drop of the staining solution on the microscope slide along one side of the coverslip. Place a small piece of paper towel on the opposite side of the coverslip to draw the stain under the coverslip.

7. As the water evaporates from the slide, add another drop of water by placing the tip of the medicine dropper next to the edge of the coverslip, just as you would when adding stains or solutions to a wet mount. If the slide is too wet, remove the excess water by using the corner of a paper towel as a blotter. Do not lift the coverslip to add or remove water.

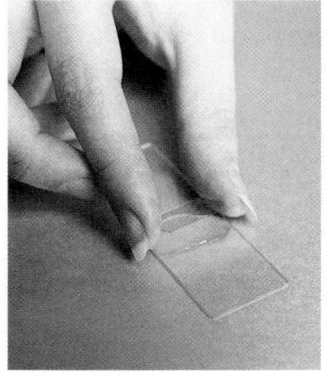
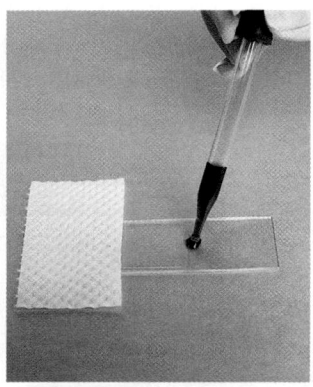

Determining Mass and Temperature

Reading a Balance

A **single-pan balance,** such as the one shown at right, has one pan and three or four beams. The scale of measure for each beam depends on the model of the balance. When an object is placed on the pan, the riders are moved along the beams until the mass on the beams equals the mass of the object in the pan.

Measuring Mass When determining the mass of a chemical or powder, use weighing or filter paper. Determine the mass of the paper, and subtract that mass from the total mass of the paper and the sample. Use the following procedure for determining an object's mass:

1. Make sure the balance is on a level surface and the pan is allowed to move freely. Position all riders at zero. If the pointer does not come to rest in the middle of the scale, calibrate the balance by using the adjustment knob (usually located under and to the left of the pan).

   CAUTION: Never place a hot object or chemical directly on a balance pan.

2. Place the object on the pan.

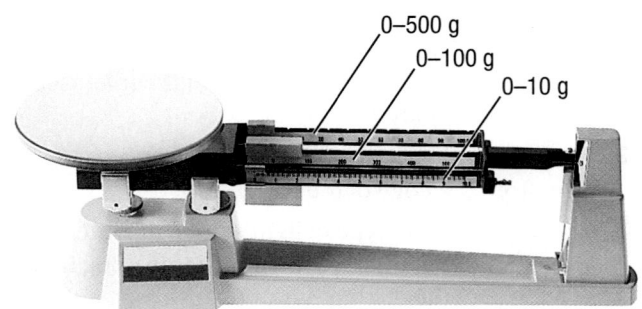

0–500 g
0–100 g
0–10 g

3. Move the largest rider along the beam to the right until it is at the last notch that does not move the pointer below the zero point in the middle of the scale.

4. Follow the same procedure with the next rider.

5. Move the smallest rider until the pointer rests at zero in the middle of the scale.

6. Add up the readings on all of the beams to determine the mass of the object.

Your Turn Complete the following exercises.

1. Determine the mass of each of the following items by using a single-pan balance:
   a. an empty 250 mL beaker
   b. 250 mL beaker filled with 100 mL of water
   c. 250 mL beaker filled with 100 mL of vegetable oil
   d. a house key
   e. a small book
   f. a paper clip or small safety pin

2. Determine the mass of each object represented by the balance readings shown.

   a.
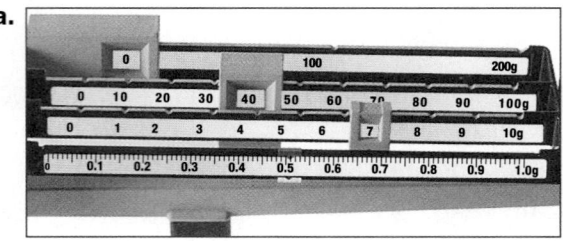

   b.
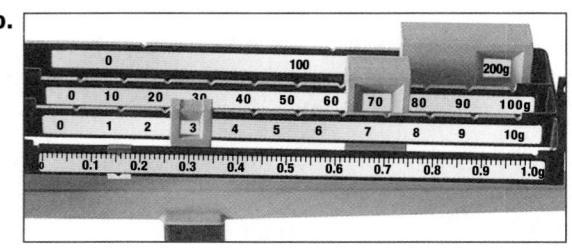

   c.
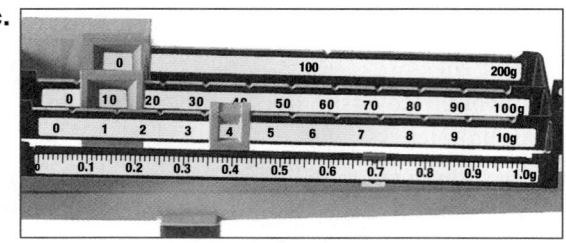

Reading a Thermometer

Many laboratory thermometers are the bulb-type shown below. The sensing bulb of the thermometer is filled with a colored liquid (alcohol) that expands when heated. When the liquid expands, it moves up the stem of the thermometer through the capillary tube. Thermometers usually measure temperature in degrees Celsius (°C).

Measuring Temperature Use the following procedure when measuring the temperature of a substance.

1. Carefully lower the bulb of the thermometer into the substance. The stem of the thermometer may rest against the side of the container, but the bulb should never rest on the bottom, where heat is being applied. If the thermometer has an adjustable clip for the side of the container, the thermometer can be suspended in the liquid.

    CAUTION: Do not hold a thermometer in your hand while measuring the temperature of a heated substance.

2. Gently rotate the thermometer in the clip. Watch the rising colored liquid in the capillary tube. When the liquid in the capillary tube stops rising, note the whole-degree increment nearest the top of the liquid column. If your thermometer is marked in whole degrees, report temperature to the nearest half degree. For example, if the top of the colored liquid column is closest to the 52 °C mark but somewhat above it, as shown at right, what is the accurate temperature reading? Because the top of the column is slightly but not halfway above the 52 °C mark, the temperature is read as 52 °C.

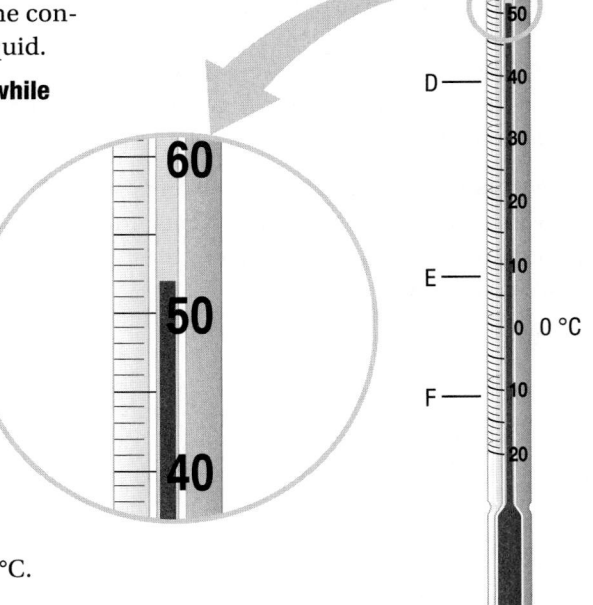

Your Turn Use the thermometer shown above to answer the following questions:

1. Identify the scale used for this thermometer.

2. Determine whether this thermometer is marked only in whole degrees or in tenths of degrees.

3. Estimate the temperature reading shown on this thermometer.

4. **Interpreting Variables** What would be the temperature reading if the top of the column were resting at each of the following points?
    a. A
    b. B
    c. C
    d. D
    e. E
    f. F

SI Measurement

SI Units

Scientists throughout the world use the metric system. The metric system is now officially known as the Système International d'Unités, or the International System of Units. It is usually referred to simply as the SI. Most measurements in this book are expressed in SI units. You will always use SI units when you take measurements in the lab.

SI Prefixes The SI is a decimal system; that is, all relationships between SI units are based on powers of 10. Most units have a prefix that indicates the relationship of a particular unit to a base unit. For example, the SI base unit for length is the meter. A meter equals 100 centimeters (cm), or 1,000 millimeters (mm). A meter also equals 0.001 kilometer (km). **Table 1** summarizes the prefixes used in SI units.

Conversion Factors Conversion between SI units requires a conversion factor. For example, to convert from meters to centimeters, you need to know the relationship between meters and centimeters.

$$1 \text{ cm} = 0.01 \text{ m} \quad \text{and} \quad 1 \text{ m} = 100 \text{ cm}$$

Table 1	SI Prefixes	
Prefix	**Symbol**	**Factor of base unit**
giga-	G	1,000,000,000
mega-	M	1,000,000
kilo-	k	1,000
hecto-	h	100
deka-	da	10
deci-	d	0.1
centi-	c	0.01
milli-	m	0.001
micro-	μ	0.000001
nano-	n	0.000000001
pico-	p	0.000000000001

If you need to convert 15.5 cm to meters, you could do either of the following:

$$15.5 \text{ cm} \times \frac{1 \text{ m}}{100 \text{ cm}} = 0.155 \text{ m}$$

or

$$15.5 \text{ cm} \times \frac{0.01 \text{ m}}{1 \text{ cm}} = 0.155 \text{ m}$$

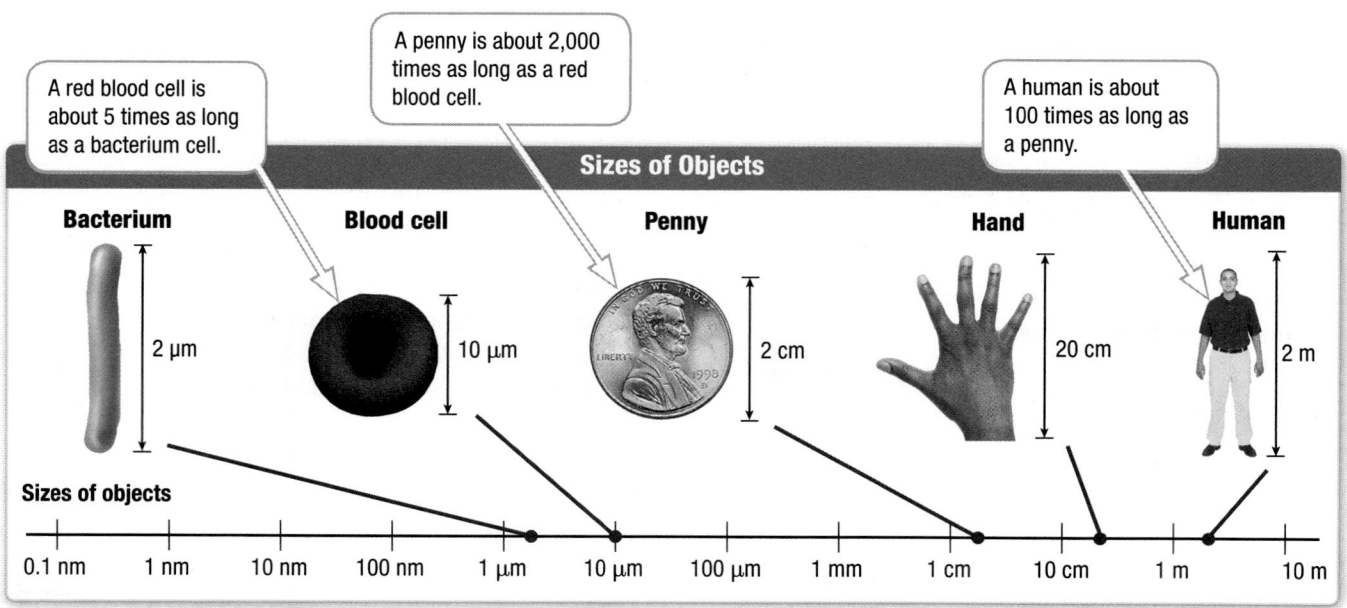

A red blood cell is about 5 times as long as a bacterium cell.

A penny is about 2,000 times as long as a red blood cell.

A human is about 100 times as long as a penny.

Sizes of Objects

Bacterium	Blood cell	Penny	Hand	Human
2 μm	10 μm	2 cm	20 cm	2 m

Sizes of objects

0.1 nm   1 nm   10 nm   100 nm   1 μm   10 μm   100 μm   1 mm   1 cm   10 cm   1 m   10 m

Base Units In this book, you will see three fundamental quantities represented by base units in SI: mass, length, and time. The base units of these quantities are the kilogram (kg), the meter (m), and the second (s). These quantities, their base units and symbols, and some unit conversions are listed in **Table 2.**

Derived Units Other quantities, such as area and liquid volume, are expressed in derived units. A derived unit is a combination of one or more base units. Like base units, derived units can be expressed by using SI prefixes. Some SI-derived units, including their symbols and common unit conversions, are listed in **Table 3.**

Table 2 Conversions for SI Base Units

Mass: unit = kilogram (kg)

1 kilogram (kg) = 1,000 g

1 gram (g) = 0.001 kg

1 milligram (mg) = 0.001 g

1 microgram (μg) = 0.000001 g

Length: unit = meter (m)

1 kilometer (km) = 1,000 m

1 meter (m) = 100 cm

1 centimeter (cm) = 0.01 m

1 millimeter (mm) = 0.001 m

1 micrometer (μm) = 0.000001 m

Time: unit = second (s)

1 minute (min) = 60 s

1 hour (h) = 3,600 s = 60 min

1 day (d) = 24 h

Table 3 Conversions for SI-Derived Units

Area: unit = square meter $\left(m^2\right)$

1 square kilometer $\left(km^2\right)$ = 100 ha

1 hectare (ha) = 10,000 m^2

1 square meter $\left(m^2\right)$ = 10,000 cm^2

1 square centimeter $\left(cm^2\right)$ = 100 mm^2

Liquid volume: unit = cubic meter $\left(m^3\right)$

1 cubic meter $\left(m^3\right)$ = 1 kL

1 kiloliter (kL) = 1,000 L

1 liter (L) = 1,000 mL

1 milliliter (mL) = 0.001 L

1 cubic centimeter $\left(cm^3\right)$ = 1 mL

Mass density: unit = kilograms per cubic meter $\left(kg/m^3\right)$

Temperature: unit = degrees Celsius (°C)

Velocity: unit = meters per second (m/s)

Temperature

Though not part of the SI, the Celsius scale is commonly used to express temperature. In the Celsius scale, 0 °C is the freezing point of water, and 100 °C is the boiling point of water. You can use the temperature scale shown below to convert between the Celsius scale and the Fahrenheit scale, which is commonly used in the United States. You can also use the following equation to convert between

degrees Celsius (T_C) and degrees Fahrenheit (T_F):

$$T_F = \frac{9}{5} T_C + 32$$

For example, to convert 0 °C to degrees Fahrenheit, perform the following calculation:

$$T_F = \frac{9}{5}\left(0\ °C\right) + 32\ °F = 0 + 32\ °F = 32\ °F$$

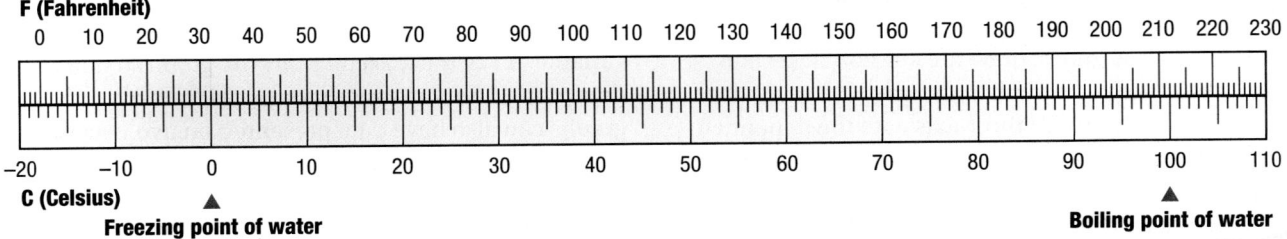

Graphing

Constructing Graphs

After finishing an experiment, scientists often illustrate experimental data in graphs. There are three main types of graphs: line graphs, bar graphs, and pie graphs. Organizing data visually helps us identify relationships between variables—factors that change.

The data table shows data collected by a researcher who has hypothesized that increased salt intake will cause an increase in blood pressure. In this experiment, the independent variable was daily salt intake. Recall that the **independent variable** is the one that is changed by the researcher. You can see in the data table that the researcher varied daily salt intake between 0 and 30 g.

Recall that the **dependent variable** is the one that is observed to determine if it is affected by changes in the independent variable. The dependent variable in this experiment was systolic pressure. You can see that in this case, an increase in salt intake corresponds to an increase in systolic pressure. These data support the hypothesis that increases in salt intake cause a rise in blood pressure.

Data Table

Systolic pressure (mm Hg)	Daily salt intake (g)
110	0
120	10
140	20
165	30

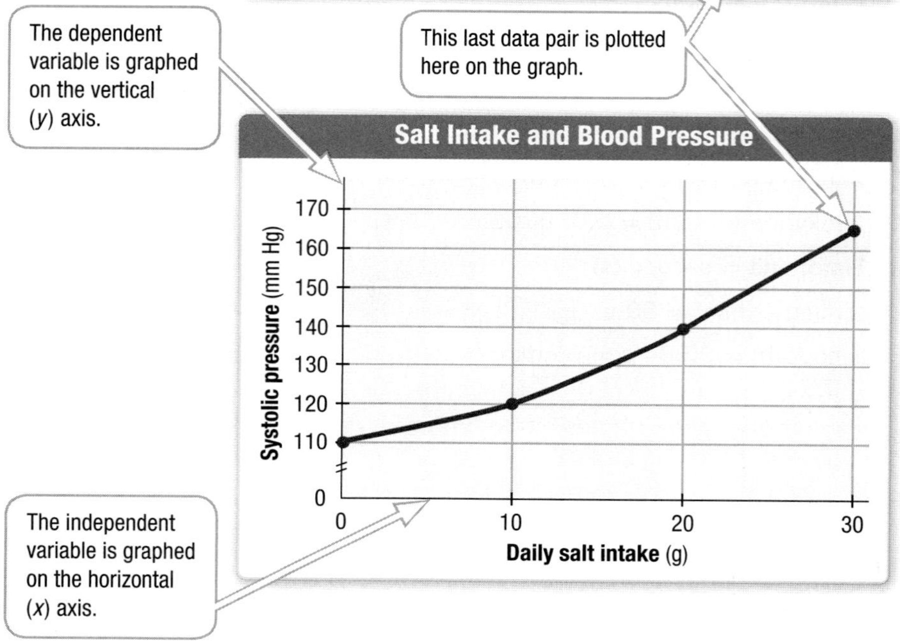

The dependent variable is graphed on the vertical (y) axis.

This last data pair is plotted here on the graph.

Salt Intake and Blood Pressure

The independent variable is graphed on the horizontal (x) axis.

Line Graphs

Line graphs, such as the one shown above, are most often used to compare or relate one or more sets of data that show continuous change. Each set of data—the independent variable and its corresponding dependent variables—is called a *data pair*.

To make a line graph, draw the horizontal (x) and vertical (y) axes of your graph. Label the y-axis with the independent variable and the x-axis with the dependent variable. (Refer to your data table to determine the scale and appropriate units for each axis). Plot each data pair, and then connect the data points to make a line, or

curve. Finally, give the graph a title that clearly indicates the relationship between the data shown by the graph.

Sometimes, line graphs can be more complex than the one shown. When a line graph has more than one line, each extra line illustrates another dependent variable. A key must accompany the graph so that the data plotted on the two or more lines are clear. Line graphs can also have data presented on two y-axes, which may have different units. In these graphs, the effect of the independent variable can be observed on two dependent variables.

Bar Graphs

Sometimes, it is not appropriate to use a line graph to represent data. A bar graph can clearly display data that are not continuous. A bar graph is a good indicator of trends if the data are taken over a sufficiently long period of time. For example, studying color variations in moths requires that data be collected over a long period of time. Even after years of study, predictions can still be difficult to make with certainty. Notice that a bar graph is also useful in comparing multiple sets of data, such as those for the light and dark moths found in the woods near Birmingham and Dorset.

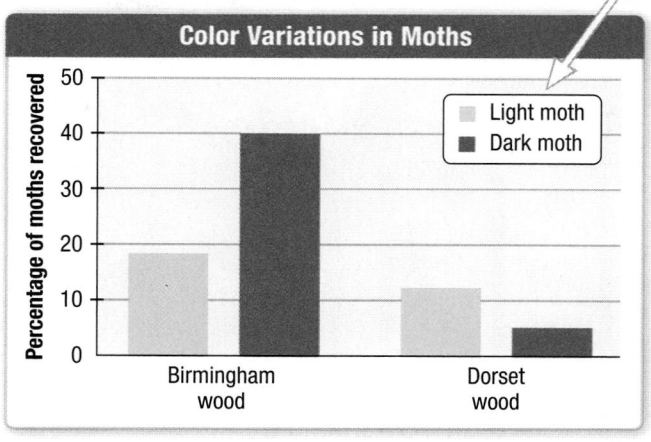

The key shows which groups are depicted.

Pie Graphs

Pie graphs are an easy way to visualize the composition of a whole. Frequently, pie graphs are made from percentage data. For example, you could create a pie graph showing the percentage of known insect species that various insect groups represent. To create a pie graph from data in a table, begin by drawing a circle to represent the whole, or total. Then, imagine dividing the circle into 100 equal sections to represent 100%. Shade in the number of consecutive sections that are represented by each group, and label the slice with the name of that group.

A source line identifies the source of the data.

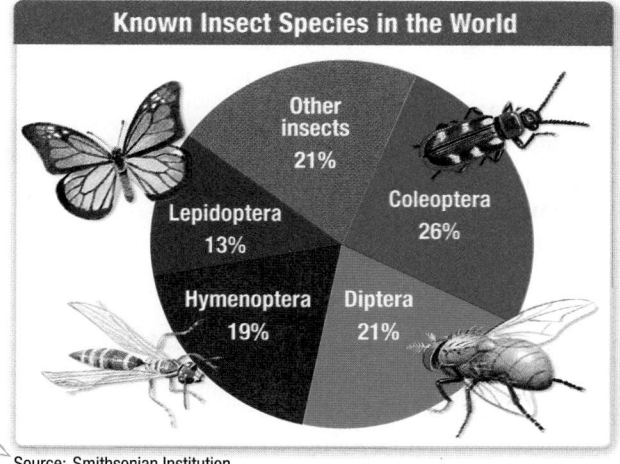

Source: Smithsonian Institution.

Using Graphs to Make Predictions

Graphs show trends in data that allow us to make predictions. For example, how might taking in 40 g of salt per day affect blood pressure? Referring to the graph of blood pressure and salt intake, you might estimate that systolic pressure could be 190 mm Hg or more. Using a trend in a range of data to estimate values beyond that range is called **extrapolation.**

Likewise, we can use graphs to estimate values that are untested but that lie *within* the range of our data. How might taking in 15 g of salt per day affect blood pressure? You might use the graph to estimate that blood

pressure would be about 130 mm Hg. Using a trend in a range of data to estimate values missing from that range is called **interpolation.**

Some data, such as the values for salt intake and blood pressure, interact in an expected way and seem to indicate a causal relationship. But beware of hastily drawing conclusions based on a graph of two variables that change together. In September, the number of school buses on the road and the number of trees turning fall colors rise. But school buses do not make leaves change color! Both are affected by the time of year.

Classification

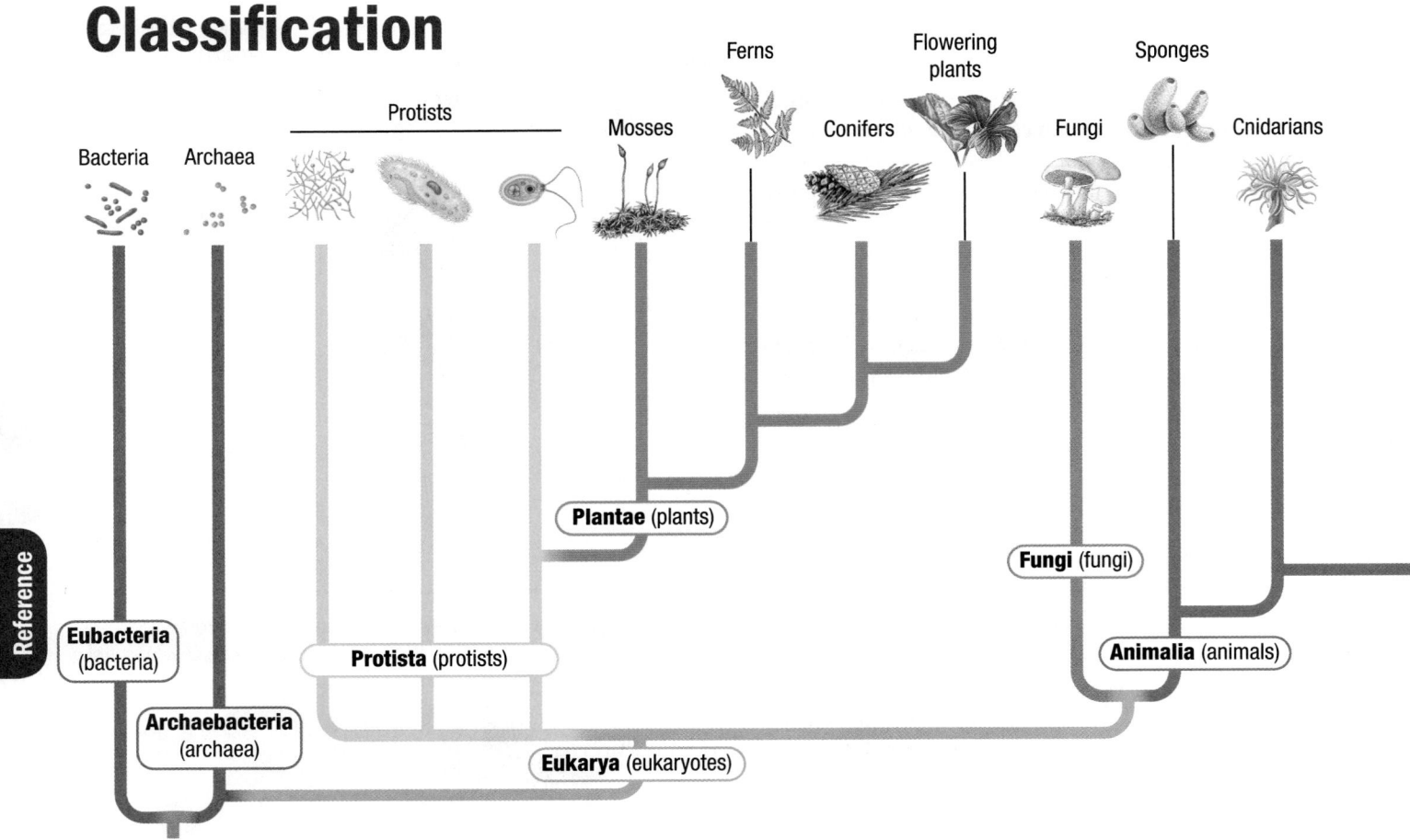

How Organisms Are Classified Like many areas of science, the classification of organisms is an active and ever-changing endeavor. Throughout history, many new taxa have been proposed, and some taxa have been reclassified. Biologists have added complexity and detail to their classification systems as they have learned more about organisms. Scientists are unlikely to discover and name all species, much less to agree on the exact relationships between all species.

Today, most biologists use and recognize the Linnaean system, shown here, which consists of three domains and six kingdoms. Also, there is general agreement on the relationships between most of the groups shown in this phylogenetic tree. However, many groupings remain the subject of strong debate and active investigation.

In particular, the relationships between protists are poorly understood, and many scientists are beginning to agree that "Protista" should no longer be considered a single, related taxon. The relationships between invertebrates, such as worms, arthropods, and mollusks, are also strongly debated. For these reasons, this phylogenetic tree does not indicate any particular relationships between these groups.

Any part of a phylogenetic tree—and any taxonomic name—may be revised when scientists gather enough evidence and agree upon revisions. In fact, the entire Linnaean system may someday be replaced with another system that is based on phylogenetic trees rather than lists and tables.

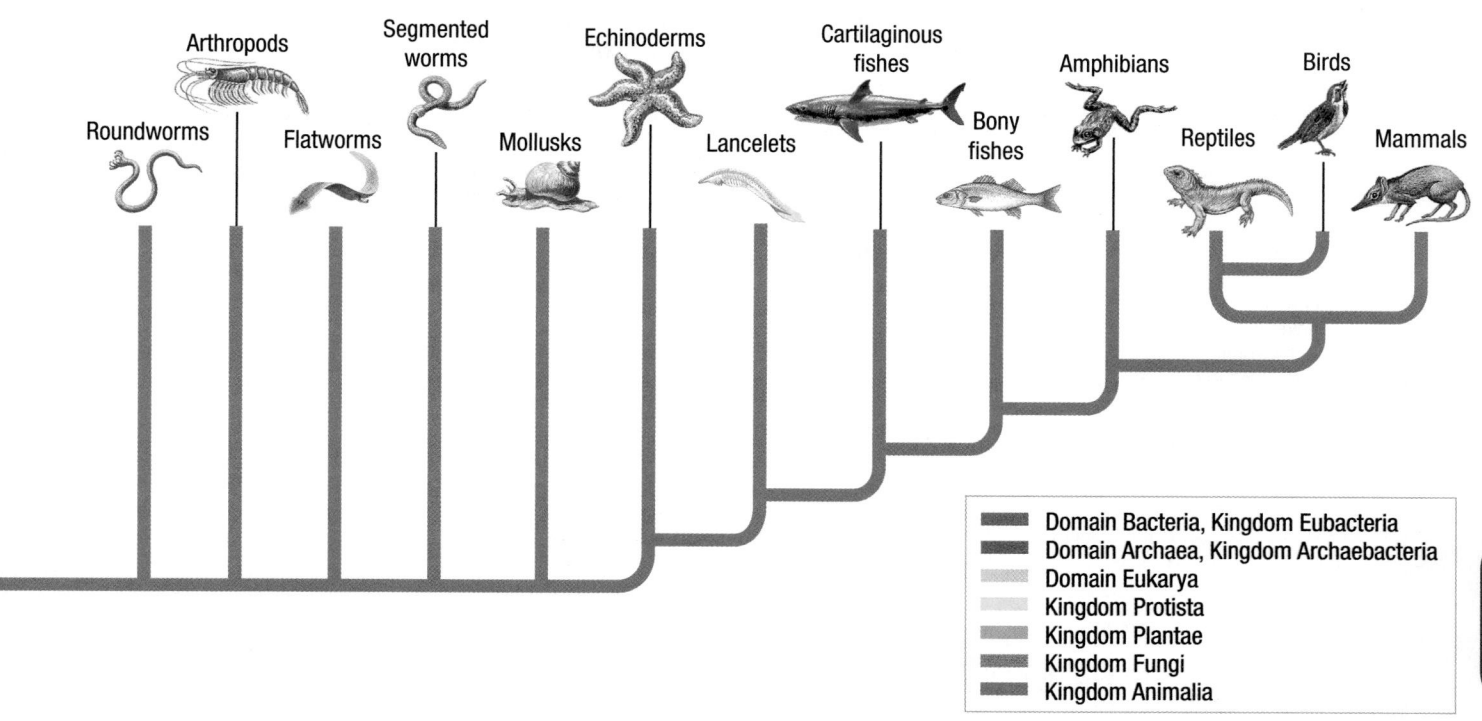

Legend:
- Domain Bacteria, Kingdom Eubacteria
- Domain Archaea, Kingdom Archaebacteria
- Domain Eukarya
- Kingdom Protista
- Kingdom Plantae
- Kingdom Fungi
- Kingdom Animalia

Characteristics of Domains and Kingdoms

Domain	Bacteria	Archaea	Eukarya			
Kingdom	Eubacteria	Archae-bacteria	Protista	Fungi	Plantae	Animalia
Example	*Streptococcus pneumoniae*	*Staphylo-thermus marinus*	paramecium	spore cap mushroom	Texas paintbrush	white-winged dove
Cell type	prokaryotic		eukaryotic			
Cell walls	cell walls with peptidoglycan	cell walls with unique lipids	cell walls in some species	cell walls with chitin	cell walls with cellulose	no cell walls
Number of cells	unicellular		unicellular or multicellular	mostly multicellular	mostly multicellular	multicellular
Nutrition	autotroph or heterotroph			heterotroph	autotroph	heterotroph

The Biologist's Periodic Table of Elements

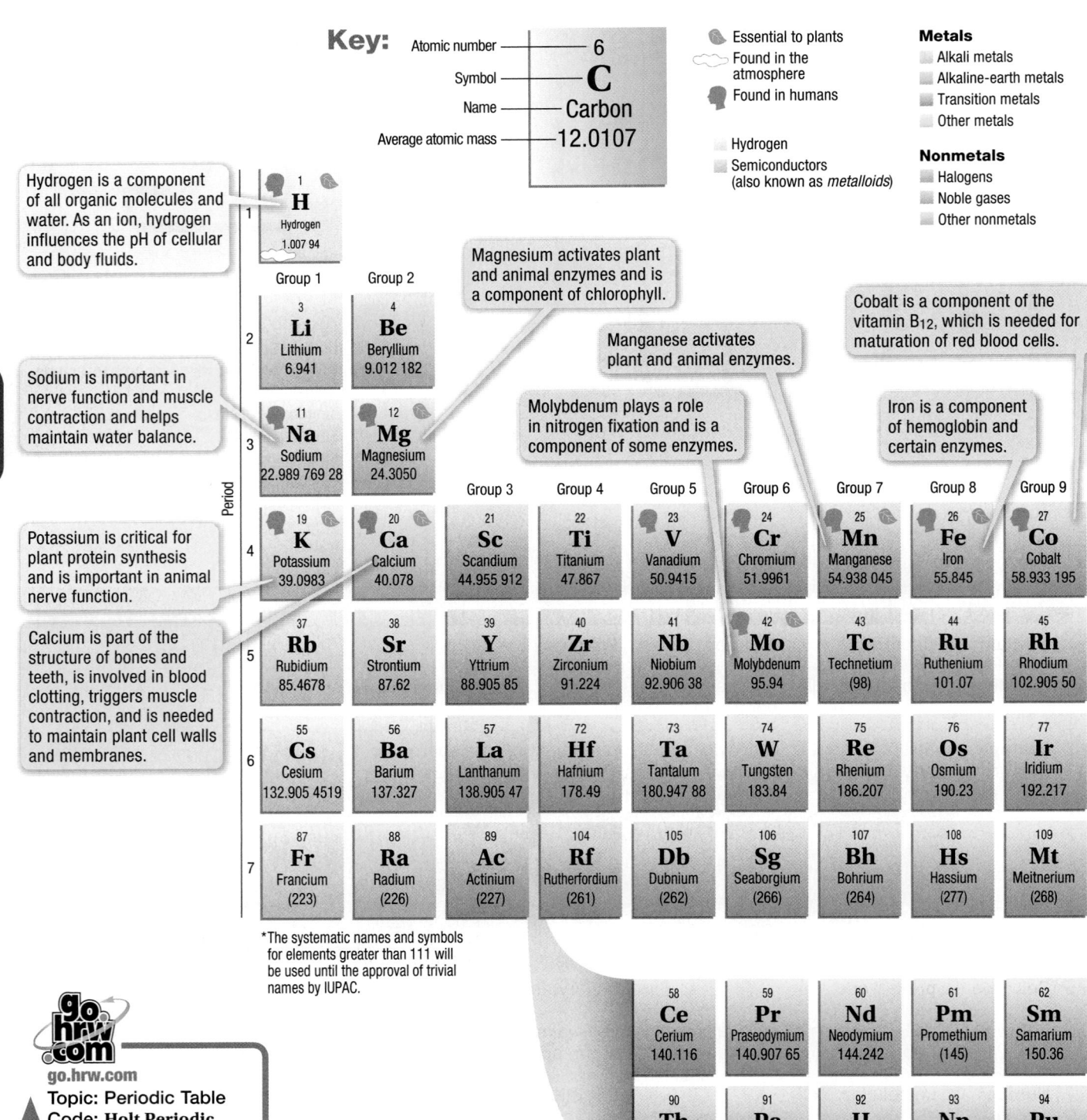

Key:

Atomic number — 6
Symbol — **C**
Name — Carbon
Average atomic mass — 12.0107

Essential to plants
Found in the atmosphere
Found in humans

Hydrogen
Semiconductors (also known as *metalloids*)

Metals
Alkali metals
Alkaline-earth metals
Transition metals
Other metals

Nonmetals
Halogens
Noble gases
Other nonmetals

Hydrogen is a component of all organic molecules and water. As an ion, hydrogen influences the pH of cellular and body fluids.

Magnesium activates plant and animal enzymes and is a component of chlorophyll.

Manganese activates plant and animal enzymes.

Cobalt is a component of the vitamin B_{12}, which is needed for maturation of red blood cells.

Sodium is important in nerve function and muscle contraction and helps maintain water balance.

Molybdenum plays a role in nitrogen fixation and is a component of some enzymes.

Iron is a component of hemoglobin and certain enzymes.

Potassium is critical for plant protein synthesis and is important in animal nerve function.

Calcium is part of the structure of bones and teeth, is involved in blood clotting, triggers muscle contraction, and is needed to maintain plant cell walls and membranes.

Period

	Group 1	Group 2	Group 3	Group 4	Group 5	Group 6	Group 7	Group 8	Group 9
1	1 **H** Hydrogen 1.007 94								
2	3 **Li** Lithium 6.941	4 **Be** Beryllium 9.012 182							
3	11 **Na** Sodium 22.989 769 28	12 **Mg** Magnesium 24.3050							
4	19 **K** Potassium 39.0983	20 **Ca** Calcium 40.078	21 **Sc** Scandium 44.955 912	22 **Ti** Titanium 47.867	23 **V** Vanadium 50.9415	24 **Cr** Chromium 51.9961	25 **Mn** Manganese 54.938 045	26 **Fe** Iron 55.845	27 **Co** Cobalt 58.933 195
5	37 **Rb** Rubidium 85.4678	38 **Sr** Strontium 87.62	39 **Y** Yttrium 88.905 85	40 **Zr** Zirconium 91.224	41 **Nb** Niobium 92.906 38	42 **Mo** Molybdenum 95.94	43 **Tc** Technetium (98)	44 **Ru** Ruthenium 101.07	45 **Rh** Rhodium 102.905 50
6	55 **Cs** Cesium 132.905 4519	56 **Ba** Barium 137.327	57 **La** Lanthanum 138.905 47	72 **Hf** Hafnium 178.49	73 **Ta** Tantalum 180.947 88	74 **W** Tungsten 183.84	75 **Re** Rhenium 186.207	76 **Os** Osmium 190.23	77 **Ir** Iridium 192.217
7	87 **Fr** Francium (223)	88 **Ra** Radium (226)	89 **Ac** Actinium (227)	104 **Rf** Rutherfordium (261)	105 **Db** Dubnium (262)	106 **Sg** Seaborgium (266)	107 **Bh** Bohrium (264)	108 **Hs** Hassium (277)	109 **Mt** Meitnerium (268)

*The systematic names and symbols for elements greater than 111 will be used until the approval of trivial names by IUPAC.

58 **Ce** Cerium 140.116	59 **Pr** Praseodymium 140.907 65	60 **Nd** Neodymium 144.242	61 **Pm** Promethium (145)	62 **Sm** Samarium 150.36
90 **Th** Thorium 232.038 06	91 **Pa** Protactinium 231.035 88	92 **U** Uranium 238.028 91	93 **Np** Neptunium (237)	94 **Pu** Plutonium (244)

go.hrw.com

go.hrw.com
Topic: Periodic Table
Code: **Holt Periodic**
Visit this site for updates to the periodic table.

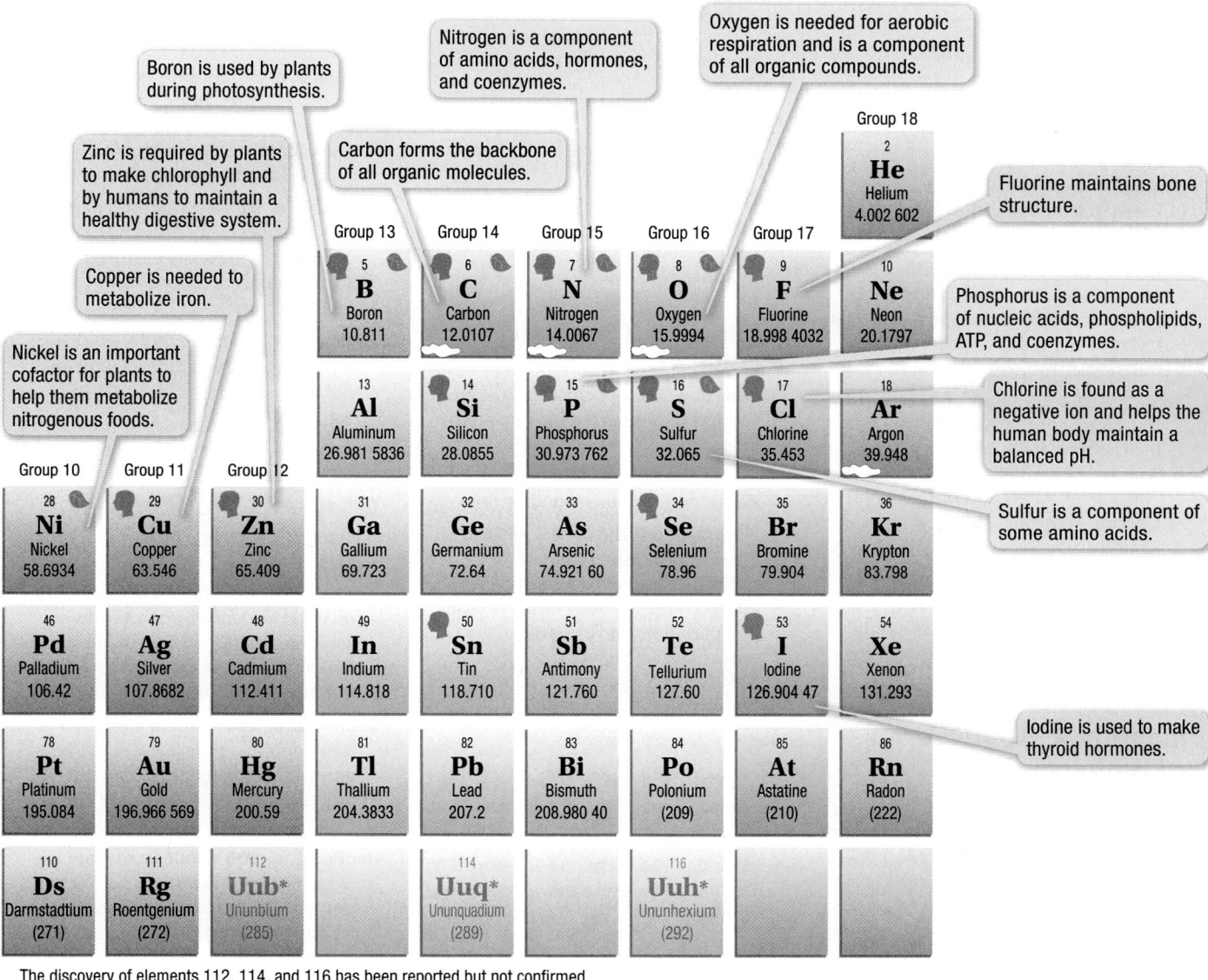

Boron is used by plants during photosynthesis.

Zinc is required by plants to make chlorophyll and by humans to maintain a healthy digestive system.

Nitrogen is a component of amino acids, hormones, and coenzymes.

Oxygen is needed for aerobic respiration and is a component of all organic compounds.

Carbon forms the backbone of all organic molecules.

Copper is needed to metabolize iron.

Nickel is an important cofactor for plants to help them metabolize nitrogenous foods.

Fluorine maintains bone structure.

Phosphorus is a component of nucleic acids, phospholipids, ATP, and coenzymes.

Chlorine is found as a negative ion and helps the human body maintain a balanced pH.

Sulfur is a component of some amino acids.

Iodine is used to make thyroid hormones.

Group 18

| 2 | He | Helium | 4.002 602 |

Group 13 — 5 B Boron 10.811
Group 14 — 6 C Carbon 12.0107
Group 15 — 7 N Nitrogen 14.0067
Group 16 — 8 O Oxygen 15.9994
Group 17 — 9 F Fluorine 18.998 4032
10 Ne Neon 20.1797

13 Al Aluminum 26.981 5836
14 Si Silicon 28.0855
15 P Phosphorus 30.973 762
16 S Sulfur 32.065
17 Cl Chlorine 35.453
18 Ar Argon 39.948

Group 10 — 28 Ni Nickel 58.6934
Group 11 — 29 Cu Copper 63.546
Group 12 — 30 Zn Zinc 65.409
31 Ga Gallium 69.723
32 Ge Germanium 72.64
33 As Arsenic 74.921 60
34 Se Selenium 78.96
35 Br Bromine 79.904
36 Kr Krypton 83.798

46 Pd Palladium 106.42
47 Ag Silver 107.8682
48 Cd Cadmium 112.411
49 In Indium 114.818
50 Sn Tin 118.710
51 Sb Antimony 121.760
52 Te Tellurium 127.60
53 I Iodine 126.904 47
54 Xe Xenon 131.293

78 Pt Platinum 195.084
79 Au Gold 196.966 569
80 Hg Mercury 200.59
81 Tl Thallium 204.3833
82 Pb Lead 207.2
83 Bi Bismuth 208.980 40
84 Po Polonium (209)
85 At Astatine (210)
86 Rn Radon (222)

110 Ds Darmstadtium (271)
111 Rg Roentgenium (272)
112 Uub* Ununbium (285)
114 Uuq* Ununquadium (289)
116 Uuh* Ununhexium (292)

The discovery of elements 112, 114, and 116 has been reported but not confirmed.

63 Eu Europium 151.964
64 Gd Gadolinium 157.25
65 Tb Terbium 158.925 35
66 Dy Dysprosium 162.500
67 Ho Holmium 164.930 32
68 Er Erbium 167.259
69 Tm Thulium 168.934 21
70 Yb Ytterbium 173.04
71 Lu Lutetium 174.967

95 Am Americium (243)
96 Cm Curium (247)
97 Bk Berkelium (247)
98 Cf Californium (251)
99 Es Einsteinium (252)
100 Fm Fermium (257)
101 Md Mendelevium (258)
102 No Nobelium (259)
103 Lr Lawrencium (262)

The atomic masses listed in this table reflect the precision of current measurements. (Each value listed in parentheses is the mass number of that radioactive element's most stable or most common isotope.)

Chapter 1 Biology and You

Section 1, p. 8 Sample answer: If a scientist falsely claims to have found a cure for a disease, people who have that disease may try to use the false cure and may be harmed.

Section 2, p. 13 Sample answer: In science, the word *theory* describes a well-tested, generally accepted principle. In general use, the word *theory* describes a good guess.

Section 3, p. 14 Most SI units have a prefix that indicates the relationship of that unit to a base unit.

Section 3, p. 15 Sterile technique is used in a lab when one is trying to avoid contaminating a specimen or is trying to grow only a certain type of microorganism.

Section 3, p. 16 Sample answer: Listen to your teacher, and follow all instructions. Read your lab procedure before beginning the lab. Always wear any needed safety equipment when working in the lab. Measure chemicals precisely. Do not use damaged or defective equipment.

Section 4, p. 19 Sample answer: Evolution is the change in inherited characteristics in a population over generations.

Chapter 2 Applications of Biology

Section 1, p. 29 It causes disease.

Section 1, p. 30 Warm water causes the copepod host to mature more quickly. As a result, the cholera bacteria also increase in number.

Section 1, p. 31 Vaccines allow one's immune system to develop resistance to a pathogen without contracting it.

Section 1, p. 32 a bionic limb

Section 2, p. 35 Relative to the eyes of other animals, lobster eyes focus light waves in a unique way. The lobster eye telescope incorporated this technology to focus X-rays, something that other telescopes cannot do.

Section 2, p. 36 DNA fingerprinting is an identification technique based on a pattern of DNA that represents the total of an organism's genetic material. It uses DNA material, such as skin cells, to identify someone.

Section 2, p. 37 Some people are concerned that eating genetically modified food may be harmful to their health.

Section 3, p. 39 A GIS allows researchers to access data from many different studies so that they can work together.

Section 3, p. 40 to help students understand the natural world through hands-on activities

Chapter 3 Chemistry of Life

Section 1, p. 51 a positively charged particle that is part of the nucleus of an atom

Section 1, p. 52 the attractive force that holds atoms or ions together

Section 1, p. 54 The partial positive charge of the H atoms in water molecules attracts the negatively charged chloride ions in salt crystals. The partial negative charge of the O atom of water molecules attracts the positively charged sodium ions in salt crystals.

Section 2, p. 59 carbon

Section 2, p. 60 a sugar

Section 2, p. 62 the order of amino acids

Section 3, p. 64 a change that occurs when the identity of the substance changes

Section 3, p. 65 their negatively charged electron clouds

Section 3, p. 67 because the shape of the active site determines which reactant will bind to the active site

Chapter 4 Ecosystems

Section 1, p. 80 Sample answer: water, sunlight, and oxygen

Section 1, p. 81 Pioneer species change the habitat so that other species can live in that habitat.

Section 1, p. 83 low latitudes

Section 1, p. 84 marine communities and estuaries

Section 2, p. 86 Consumers get their energy by eating producers or other consumers. Ultimately, all living organisms get their energy from the sun.

Section 2, p. 88 Ninety percent of the energy in a predator's prey is lost to the environment as heat as the predator burns the energy to do work, such as breathing and running.

Section 3, p. 91 Respiration is part of the carbon cycle because it is a process in which oxygen and carbon are exchanged between living organisms and their environment.

Section 3, p. 92 Bacteria breaks down N_2 into a form that other organisms can use.

Section 3, p. 93 Phosphorus is absorbed by the roots of plants.

Chapter 5 Populations and Communities

Section 1, p. 103 A zebra population consists of a group of zebras that live together and interbreed. A different zebra population lives separately from the other zebra population and does not interbreed with that population.

Section 1, p. 104 Sample answer: A population that grows exponentially grows slowly when it is small but grows quickly as it gets larger. An exponential growth curve is J shaped.

Section 1, p. 106 Biotic factors are living factors that affect a population's growth. Abiotic factors are nonliving factors that affect a population's growth.

Section 1, p. 107 by improving sanitation, controlling disease, and allowing for efficient production of food

Section 2, p. 110 Sample answer: Plants develop chemical compounds that make the plants taste terrible to the herbivores. The herbivores develop defenses against the toxic compounds so that they may eat the plants.

Section 2, p. 111 Mutualism is a relationship in which both species benefit. Commensalism is a relationship in which one species benefits and the other species is not harmed.

Section 3, p. 112 A niche is the function of a species in a community. A habitat is the place where the species lives.

Section 3, p. 113 because they usually have to compete with other species for limited resources

Section 3, p. 114 by feeding in slightly different ways or slightly different areas

Section 3, p. 115 Sample answer: Competition between species and high biodiversity contribute to the stability of an ecosystem.

Chapter 6 The Environment

Section 1, p. 125 Humans and other organisms are part of the environment and depend on resources from the environment to survive. In turn, the environment is affected by the actions of humans and other organisms.

Section 1, p. 126 It takes millions of years for natural gas to form.

Section 2, p. 129 The burning of fossil fuels releases CO_2 into the atmosphere. An increase in CO_2 in the atmosphere due to the burning of fossil fuels may be responsible for an increase in global temperatures.

Section 2, p. 130 Sample answer: runoff from roads, leaking underground septic tanks, and pesticides that run off from farms

Section 2, p. 131 Erosion causes soil to be washed away. Without soil, crops cannot be grown.

Section 2, p. 133 The zebra mussel clogs treatment facilities and causes millions of dollars in damage.

Section 3, p. 134 Restoration involves cleaning up and restoring a damaged ecosystem. Conservation involves protecting an existing ecosystem.

Section 3, p. 135 Sample answer: I can reduce resource use by using recycled materials, low-flow toilets, and low-flow shower heads.

Section 3, p. 136 by releasing less pollution into the atmosphere than the average car does

Section 3, p. 137 by having people become more aware of the problems and by motivating people to help solve the problems

Section 3, p. 138 because we can avoid damage to the environment

Chapter 7 Cell Structure

Section 1, p. 151 Hooke's microscope could magnify objects to 30 times their normal size.

Section 1, p. 153 Smaller cells can exchange substances more efficiently than larger cells of the same shape can.

Section 1, p. 154 a cellular structure on which proteins are made

Section 2, p. 157 proteins that remain in the cell, such as proteins that build new organelles or enzymes to speed chemical reactions

Section 2, p. 161 Nearly all eukaryotic cells, including plant cells, contain mitochondria.

Section 3, p. 163 long, threadlike structures that rotate quickly to move an organism through its environment

Section 3, p. 166 the process by which cells of a multicellular organism develop specialized forms and functions

Chapter 8 Cells and Their Environment

Section 1, p. 175 The cell membrane provides structural support to the cytoplasm, recognizes foreign material, communicates with other cells, and helps transport substances.

Section 1, p. 176 Small, nonpolar molecules, ions, and most polar molecules are repelled by the nonpolar interior of the lipid bilayer.

Section 2, p. 179 because its concentration is higher outside the cell than it is inside the cell

Section 2, p. 183 lipid bilayer

Section 3, p. 184 Both signals have long-distance targets. Hormones are distributed widely but affect only certain cells; nerve cells' signals are not widely distributed and instead affect cells in certain locations.

Section 3, p. 186 Transport proteins open or close in response to signals.

Chapter 9 Cellular Respiration and Photosynthesis

Section 1, p. 197 in order to maintain homeostasis

Section 1, p. 198 Solar energy powers part of the carbon cycle by providing the energy needed for autotrophs to convert carbon dioxide into glucose.

Section 1, p. 200 ATP is used as an energy source for cellular processes. When the cell needs to perform an activity, ATP can be broken down in order to release energy.

Section 2, p. 202 A chloroplast has an outer membrane and an inner membrane. The space inside the inner membrane is the stroma. Within the stroma lies the thylakoid membrane, which contains stacks of thylakoids.

Section 2, p. 205 Pigment molecules in the thylakoids of chloroplasts absorb light energy. Electrons in the pigments are excited by light and move through electron transport chains in thylakoid membranes. These chains generate both ATP and NADPH for the final stage of photosynthesis. Enzymes remove electrons from water to form O_2. These electrons replace the excited electrons that passed through the electron transport chains.

Section 2, p. 207 Temperatures that are too high or too low could inactivate enzymes that are used to perform photosynthesis, which would slow or stop the process.

Section 3, p. 209 pyruvate, ATP, and NADH

Section 3, p. 211 Glycolysis breaks down glucose into pyruvate, which is small enough to diffuse across mitochondrial membranes into the mitochondria, where the Krebs cycle takes place.

Section 3, p. 212 Electrons carried by NADH are transferred to pyruvate produced during glycolysis.

Chapter 10 Cell Growth and Division

Section 1, p. 225 A chromatid is a strand of a duplicated and condensed chromosome and is made of a single, long molecule of DNA.

Section 1, p. 226 between the two DNA copies, where a new cell membrane forms

Section 2, p. 229 G_1, S, and G_2

Section 2, p. 231 a network of several spindle fibers (microtubules)

Section 2, p. 232 a large, membrane-bound cell wall that forms across the middle of a dividing plant cell (and other cells that have cell walls)

Section 3, p. 233 protein signals within the cell; signals from other cells; environmental signals/conditions

Section 3, p. 234 The cell checks for and corrects any mistakes in the copied DNA. Proteins check that the cell is large enough to divide.

Section 3, p. 235 damage to a cell's DNA, especially genes that control the cell cycle

Chapter 11 Meiosis and Sexual Reproduction

Section 1, p. 247 Fragmentation is a kind of reproduction in which the body breaks into several pieces.

Section 1, p. 248 Germ cells produce gametes, which are reproductive cells.

Section 2, p. 251 in prophase 1

Section 2, p. 252 Meiosis produces haploid cells that contain only one set of chromosomes. Mitosis produces diploid cells that contain two sets of chromosomes.

Section 2, p. 253 Crossing-over increases genetic variation because pieces of two chromatids exchange material during meiosis.

Section 3, p. 257 One gamete is formed from one female germ cell.

Chapter 12 Mendel and Heredity

Section 1, p. 267 Mendel crossed different types of pea plants and recorded the number of each type of offspring.

Section 1, p. 268 A character is a physical feature that is inherited. A trait is one of several possible forms of a character.

Section 1, p. 269 a cross that is done to study one pair of contrasting traits

Section 1, p. 270 In the F_1 generation, all of the plants expressed the same trait for a given character. In the F_2 generation, the missing trait reappeared.

Section 2, p. 272 The blending hypothesis states that traits of offspring are always a blend of the traits from parents.

Section 2, p. 275 A dihybrid cross is a cross involving two characters.

Section 3, p. 277 Each box inside a Punnett square shows a possible genotype from a given cross.

Section 3, p. 279 1/4

Section 3, p. 280 Traits that are not expressed equally in both sexes are commonly sex-linked traits.

Section 4, p. 283 Codominance is a condition in which both alleles for the same gene are fully expressed. Incomplete dominance occurs when a phenotype that is intermediate between the two traits is expressed.

Section 4, p. 284 linked

Chapter 13 DNA, RNA, and Proteins

Section 1, p. 293 DNA

Section 1, p. 297 by weak hydrogen bonds

Section 1, p. 299 X-ray diffraction studies suggested that DNA's structure resembled a tightly coiled helix.

Section 2, p. 301 It reduces the number of replication errors.

Section 2, p. 303 Two distinct replication forks form at each start site, and replication occurs in opposite directions.

Section 3, p. 305 RNA is composed of one strand of nucleotides instead of two, and it has a ribose backbone rather than a deoxyribose backbone. In RNA, adenine pairs with uracil rather than thymine.

Section 3, p. 306 The promoter is the "start" site on a sequence of DNA.

Section 3, p. 309 Codons are the three-nucleotide sequence of mRNA that is created during transcription. An anticodon is the complementary three-nucleotide sequence that is assembled during translation.

Chapter 14 Genes in Action

Section 1, p. 319 from mutations of existing genes

Section 1, p. 321 A point mutation is often silent because the genetic code is redundant; a single nucleotide letter in a codon can change without changing the amino acid that is coded for.

Section 1, p. 323 Cancer is the uncontrolled growth of tumors, which may be caused by mutations in somatic cells.

Section 1, p. 324 When the sister chromatids in one of the parent gametes fail to separate, the gamete passes on both copies instead of one.

Section 2, p. 325 no; The expression of many genes may be turned on or off.

Section 2, p. 327 almost all parts (before and after transcription and after translation)

Section 2, p. 329 the sequence of amino acids that forms the protein

Section 3, p. 331 plants

Section 3, p. 332 Both consist of DNA or RNA, carry a small set of genes, and move around within and between genomes.

Section 3, p. 333 a DNA sequence that codes for a DNA-binding domain of a regulatory protein

Section 3, p. 334 CDK and cyclin act as the engine and gears of the protein cycle.

Chapter 15 Gene Technologies and Human Applications

Section 1, p. 345 3.2 billion base pairs (although much of human DNA is noncoding!)

Section 1, p. 346 when they are considering having children

Section 1, p. 347 because insulin is not produced by the person's body (because a gene is defective)

Section 1, p. 348 It seems to be affected by many genes as well as by the environment; we are not likely to find a simple cure.

Section 2, p. 350 a genetically modified organism, or an organism that had recombinant genes

Section 2, p. 351 to cause a plant to produce an insecticide

Section 2, p. 353 adult and embryonic

Section 2, p. 354 issues of who should get the information and what decisions should be made based on the information

Section 3, p. 355 restriction enzymes and plasmids

Section 3, p. 356 It is semisolid, so molecules can travel through it.

Section 3, p. 358 transferring genetic samples from one surface or medium to another

Section 3, p. 359 in the first step, to start copying the template sequence

Section 3, p. 360 a structure such as a virus or plasmid that can carry and transfer DNA between cells

Section 3, p. 361 identifying specific genes and mapping their locations

Section 3, p. 363 genomic and EST

Chapter 16 Evolutionary Theory

Section 1, p. 375 the development of new species over time

Section 1, p. 377 when he visited the Galápagos Islands during his voyage on the *Beagle*

Section 1, p. 379 that traits acquired during a lifetime could be passed on to offspring

Section 1, p. 381 No, natural selection is a mechanism that can cause evolution.

Section 2, p. 383 because not all organisms leave fossils and not all fossils are found

Section 2, p. 384 descent from a common ancestor

Section 2, p. 385 carefully collect and consider a great deal of data

Section 3, p. 387 small-scale genetic changes in populations (microevolution) to large-scale changes in species (macroevolution)

Chapter 17 Population Genetics and Speciation

Section 1, p. 399 We know about genetics, such as how genotype relates to phenotype.

Section 1, p. 400 because many unique combinations of alleles are possible

Section 1, p. 401 frequency of alleles

Section 1, p. 402 1 (or 100%)

Section 1, p. 403 because it is the source of variation in populations

Section 2, p. 405 migration

Section 2, p. 406 increased homozygosity

Section 2, p. 407 success in leaving future generations of offspring

Section 2, p. 408 by remaining unexpressed, recessive alleles can be inherited and yet not acted upon by selection

Section 2, p. 409 disruptive selection

Section 3, p. 411 because not all species reproduce the same way and the definition of *species* depends on why the species are being studied

Section 3, p. 413 no; It sometimes results in sterile, unhealthy, or poorly adapted offspring.

Section 3, p. 414 when it's over!

Chapter 18 Classification

Section 1, p. 423 Common names have no system.

Section 1, p. 424 He wanted to catalog all known species.

Section 1, p. 426 six

Section 2, p. 427 the field of classifying species and revising systems of classification

Section 2, p. 429 It shows relatedness and shared characters between groups of organisms.

Section 2, p. 430 Sample answer: embryonic development pattern

Section 2, p. 431 comparisons between DNA, RNA, and proteins

Section 3, p. 433 Plantae (plants) and Animalia (animals)

Section 3, p. 435 Archaebacteria and Eubacteria

Section 3, p. 437 Animalia and Fungi

Chapter 19 History of Life on Earth

Section 1, p. 447 simple organic compounds, such as amino acids, fatty acids, and other hydrocarbons

Section 1, p. 449 RNA can form spontaneously in water, and DNA cannot. RNA can also perform many functions that DNA performs in cells.

Section 2, p. 451 As layers of sedimentary rock form, layers that are older form beneath layers that are younger.

Section 2, p. 453 fossil evidence

Section 3, p. 457 Colonial organisms developed the first example of separate functions being performed by different parts in a larger unit.

Chapter 20 Bacteria and Viruses

Section 1, p. 472 Gram-negative

Section 2, p. 477 The genetic material of DNA viruses can be inserted directly into the host cell's DNA or can be used to make mRNA. The genetic material of RNA viruses must be transcribed into DNA before it can be inserted into the host cell's DNA or used to make mRNA.

Section 3, p. 482 Sample answer: Diseases can be transmitted by contact, by insect bites, through the air, in contaminated food or water, and on contaminated objects.

Section 3, p. 485 toxic viral parts, genetic information that causes infected cells to produce toxins, damage to body tissues as new viral particles burst out of cells, and the body's response to infection

Chapter 21 Protists

Section 1, p. 497 membrane-bound organelles, complex cilia and flagella, sexual reproduction with gametes, and multicellularity

Section 1, p. 499 Sample answer: In alternation of generations, there is a diploid and a haploid multicellular form of the organism. In unicellular organisms, the mature organism is haploid, and only the zygospore is diploid.

Section 2, p. 501 Protists can be grouped by their source of nutrition.

Section 2, p. 502 sporozoans

Section 2, p. 504 diatoms

Section 3, p. 507 cysts

Section 3, p. 510 They are the base of food chains, they produce deadly blooms, and they are part of corals.

Chapter 22 Fungi

Section 1, p. 523 Sexually produced spores are produced by meiosis and are genetically different from the parent. Asexually produced spores are produced by mitosis and are genetically identical to the parent.

Section 2, p. 524 Like protists, chytrids are unicellular, and they produce spores and gametes that have flagella. Like fungi, chytrids have chitin in their cell walls, they digest food outside their bodies, they form hyphae and rhizoids, and their sexual reproductive structures contain spores.

Section 2, p. 525 inside the zygosporangium

Section 2, p. 526 the ascocarp

Section 2, p. 527 the basidiocarp

Section 3, p. 530 decomposition of dead organisms

Chapter 23 Plant Diversity and Life Cycles

Section 1, p. 543 energy from the sun and carbon dioxide

Section 1, p. 545 cuticle

Section 1, p. 546 diploid

Section 2, p. 547 osmosis

Section 2, p. 549 antheridium

Section 2, p. 550 on the lower surface of fronds

Section 2, p. 551 less than 1 cm across

Section 2, p. 552 sorus

Section 3, p. 553 In gymnosperms, seeds do not develop within a fruit. In angiosperms, seeds develop within a fruit.

Section 3, p. 554 A female gametophyte develops in an ovule. A male gametophyte develops in a pollen grain.

Section 3, p. 556 ginkgo

Section 3, p. 557 It has a wing that causes it to spin like a helicopter when it falls from the tree.

Section 3, p. 558 no

Section 4, p. 559 Seeds have one cotyledon, leaves are usually long and narrow with parallel veins, and flower parts are in multiples of three.

Section 4, p. 560 It produces pollen.

Section 4, p. 561 A pollen tube allows male reproductive cells to move to the ovule.

Section 4, p. 562 brightly colored petals, sugary nectar, and strong odors

Section 4, p. 563 the ovary

Section 4, p. 564 bulbs, tubers, and stolons

Chapter 24 Seed Plant Structure and Growth

Section 1, p. 573 Dermal tissue forms the outer covering of a plant.

Section 1, p. 574 help increase water absorption

Section 1, p. 576 sieve-tube members

Section 1, p. 578 support and storage

Section 2, p. 579 anchor a plant where it grows; absorb water and mineral nutrients; store organic nutrients

Section 2, p. 580 node

Section 2, p. 583 cactus spines—protection from herbivores; tendrils—support and climbing

Section 3, p. 585 two

Section 3, p. 586 exposure to fire; passing through the digestive tract of animals

Section 3, p. 587 Primary growth increases the length or height of a plant; secondary growth increases the width of stems and roots.

Section 3, p. 588 two

Section 3, p. 589 cork cambium; vascular cambium

Chapter 25 Plant Processes

Section 1, p. 599 carbon dioxide and water

Section 1, p. 600 The cohesion of water molecules causes water molecules that are being lost through transpiration to pull on the water molecules still in the xylem.

Section 1, p. 601 The guard cells swell, and the stoma opens.

Section 1, p. 602 developing fruits

Section 2, p. 603 Hormones can stimulate or inhibit growth in a plant.

Section 2, p. 604 It grew.

Section 2, p. 605 auxin—stimulates cell elongation; gibberellins—stimulate fruit development; cytokinins—stimulate cell division; ethylene—stimulates ripening in fruit; abscisic acid—helps maintain dormancy in seeds

Section 2, p. 606 a response in which a plant grows away from a stimulus

Section 2, p. 608 day-neutral plants

Section 2, p. 610 Nastic movements are usually regulated by changes in the water content of special cells.

Chapter 26 Introduction to Animals

Section 1, p. 623 Some animals are used as food, some provide companionship to people, and some benefit humans indirectly, as in the case of bees pollinating crops.

Section 1, p. 624 find food, move to favorable environments, and avoid predators

Section 1, p. 625 Land invertebrates tend to be small because they do not have an internal skeleton to support them.

Section 1, p. 626 All vertebrates have a cranium and a backbone.

Section 2, p. 627 hydrostatic skeleton, exoskeleton, and endoskeleton

Section 2, p. 628 A gastrovascular cavity has only one opening instead of two. Food comes in and wastes go out through the same opening, and the specialized cells found in a one-way digestive tract are lacking.

Section 2, p. 629 nerve net

Section 2, p. 630 transport oxygen and nutrients to—and wastes from—the body's cells

Section 2, p. 631 sea star

Section 3, p. 632 Tissues are groups of cells that have the same structure and that work together to perform a specific function. Muscle tissue is an example of a type of tissue.

Section 3, p. 634 endoderm, ectoderm, and mesoderm

Section 3, p. 635 blastopore

Section 3, p. 636 roundworm

Section 3, p. 637 somites

Section 4, p. 639 tunicates and lancelets

Section 4, p. 641 Amphibians do not have watertight skin or eggs, so they must keep their skin and eggs moist.

Section 4, p. 643 *Archaeopteryx* had feathers on its wings and tail, and it had a fused collarbone, or wishbone.

Section 4, p. 644 Early mammals were probably small, insect-eating tree dwellers that were active at night.

Chapter 27 Simple Invertebrates

Section 1, p. 656 Sponges can shed fragments that multiply to form a new individual. Some freshwater sponges also reproduce asexually from clusters of amoebocytes.

Section 1, p. 657 The spicules of calcareous sponges are composed of calcium carbonate. The spicules of glass sponges are composed of silica. Demosponges may have skeletons made of silica spicules, spongin, both, or neither.

Section 2, p. 659 Medusas release sperm or eggs into the water. The gametes fuse and produce zygotes that develop into planulae. The planulae settle on the ocean bottom and develop into polyps. Each polyp gives rise to a colony by asexual budding. Reproductive polyps give rise asexually to male and female medusas.

Section 2, p. 661 Coral polyps secrete a skeleton of calcium carbonate that is cemented to the skeletons of neighboring polyps. When the polyps die, their skeletons remain, which forms the foundation for new polyps.

Section 3, p. 664 by diffusion

Section 3, p. 666 It protects the parasite from the host's digestive acids and enzymes.

Section 4, p. 667 It provides a surface for muscle attachment, transports nutrients to body cells, and acts as a circulatory system.

Section 4, p. 669 Sample answer: Both are intestinal parasites. Ascarids feed on food in the intestines. Hookworms feed on blood. The larvae of both parasites develop in the lung and throat tissues, are coughed up, and then travel to the intestines, where they live as adults.

Chapter 28 Mollusks and Annelids

Section 1, p. 681 A typical mollusk circulatory system includes a three-chambered heart that pumps blood in vessels that empty into spaces around body organs.

Section 1, p. 682 Gastropoda (snails and slugs), Cephalopoda (octopuses and squids), and Bivalvia (clams, oysters, and scallops)

Section 1, p. 683 Sample answer: Many gastropods scrape algae off of rocks, while sea slugs are predators that eat other mollusks.

Section 1, p. 684 Some cephalopods can eject a dark ink that makes it hard for the predators to see. They then shoot water out of their siphons, which causes them to propel through the water away from the predator.

Section 2, p. 687 An annelid's body is segmented with a head end and a tail end. Digestive, excretory, and circulatory organs are found in each segment.

Section 2, p. 690 The anticoagulants stop the host's blood from clotting. Clots would block the blood flow. The anesthetics keep the host from feeling the leech's presence and trying to remove the leech.

Chapter 29 Arthropods and Echinoderms

Section 1, p. 702 "joint footed"

Section 1, p. 704 by molting

Section 2, p. 707 the black widow and the brown recluse

Section 2, p. 709 swimmerets

Section 3, p. 713 Flying gave insects access to resources not available on land. Also, flying insects have a better chance of escaping a predator than do insects that cannot fly.

Section 3, p. 714 a dramatic change that occurs during the life cycle of some animals, including many types of insects

Section 4, p. 717 An endoskeleton allows echinoderms greater flexibility than most arthropods have.

Section 4, p. 719 The larvae of sea lilies and feather stars disperse.

Chapter 30 Fishes and Amphibians

Section 1, p. 729 Fish have evolved to live in a wide range of aquatic habitats.

Section 1, p. 730 Lateral lines enable fish to sense vibrations in the water.

Section 1, p. 731 As a fish swallows water, the water is forced over the gills and through the gills' slits. Dissolved oxygen in the water diffuses through the gill filaments into the gills' capillaries. Blood in the capillaries carries the oxygen in a single loop through the fish's body.

Section 1, p. 732 In marine fishes, fish must actively pump out excess salt. Marine fishes excrete a small amount of urine from their kidneys and a large amount of ammonia from their gills. Freshwater fishes do not pump out excess salt. Most of their excretion is in the form of urine from their kidneys.

Section 1, p. 733 At least one male fish and one female fish release gametes near one another in the water. The gametes fuse to form fertilized eggs.

Section 2, p. 734 Hagfishes are scavengers and predators, while lampreys are parasites.

Section 2, p. 735 Sample answer: cartilaginous skeletons, placoid scales, and jaws

Section 2, p. 738 Sample answer: The fins of lobe-finned fishes are fleshy, muscular structures supported by bones. Teleosts have very mobile fins that are supported by body structures called *rays*.

Section 3, p. 739 because their eggs are not watertight

Section 3, p. 740 A sound strikes the tympanic membrane. Vibrations of the tympanic membrane cause small movements that are transmitted to the fluid-filled inner ear. There, the sound vibrations are converted into nervous impulses by sensitive hair cells. These impulses are transmitted to the brain through nerves.

Section 3, p. 741 gills (usually just in larvae), lungs, and skin

Section 3, p. 743 Amphibians' hearts are more complex than the hearts of most fishes, and amphibians have double-loop rather than single-loop circulatory systems.

Section 4, p. 744 through external fertilization that takes place in water

Section 4, p. 747 Larval frogs are herbivores, while adult frogs are carnivores.

Chapter 31 Reptiles and Birds

Section 1, p. 757 They have watertight skin to keep their bodies from losing too much water. Their eggs are also watertight so that they can be laid on land. Finally, their lungs and heart are efficient at obtaining oxygen from the air and distributing it to the body tissues.

Section 1, p. 759 Reptiles are able to live only in places that are warm enough to keep their body at a functional temperature.

Section 1, p. 760 Both have double-loop circulation and separated atria. However, unlike the septum in an amphibian's heart, the septum in a reptile's heart extends down into the ventricle and almost completely divides it.

Section 1, p. 761 The shell makes up the exterior of the egg. Underneath the shell is the albumen. The albumen surrounds the amnion, which encloses the embryo, the yolk sac, the allantois, and the chorion.

Section 2, p. 762 The shell consists of two parts. The carapace is the top part of the shell, which is made of skin or horny shields. The plastron is the bottom portion and is made of bone.

Section 2, p. 765 Constrictors wrap their body around their prey and gradually squeeze tighter and tighter until the prey suffocates. Other snakes use venom to kill their prey.

Section 3, p. 767 A bird's digestive system works unusually fast because a bird must burn a large amount of energy to keep its body temperature up and have enough energy for flight.

Section 3, p. 769 short and thick in order to crush the seeds

Section 3, p. 770 Because a bird's heart has a completely divided ventricle, it is a four-chambered heart. Remnants of the sinus venosus in the right atria act as the heart's pacemaker and induce each heartbeat.

Section 3, p. 771 Birds take care to build a nest that will conceal and protect their eggs. They incubate their eggs until their eggs hatch. Then, birds provide sustenance for the hatchlings until the hatchlings are strong enough to obtain food for themselves.

Section 4, p. 774 Underwater, penguins flap their wings to propel themselves—they "fly" through the water. Penguins can also use their feet as paddles.

Chapter 32 Mammals

Section 1, p. 785 insulation, camouflage, and warning

Section 1, p. 786 mammals need more energy for their higher metabolic rate

Section 1, p. 787 canine

Section 1, p. 788 monotremes

Section 1, p. 790 running, flying, and swimming

Section 2, p. 791 Monotremes are like reptiles because they lay eggs, lack teeth, have a cloaca, and their legs sprawl to the sides of the body rather than being located directly under it.

Section 2, p. 792 kangaroo

Section 2, p. 793 placental mammals

Section 2, p. 796 food, clothing, and companionship

Section 3, p. 797 more than 50 million years ago

Section 3, p. 798 Apes lack tails and have larger brains relative to their body size.

Section 3, p. 801 bipedalism

Section 3, p. 802 Africa

Chapter 33 Animal Behavior

Section 1, p. 813 a reaction, either internal or external, to a stimulus

Section 1, p. 814 the nervous system, endocrine system, and muscular systems

Section 1, p. 815 traits that increase an individual's reproductive success and/or survival

Section 1, p. 817 Habituation allows us to become accustomed to frequent stimuli that are not threatening so that we can pay closer attention to meaningful stimuli.

Section 1, p. 819 A young animal is able to obtain food and shelter by becoming attached to a caregiver.

Section 2, p. 823 The signals produced by the sender reach the receiver in an efficient manner.

Section 2, p. 824 Chemical signals are more efficient over long distances than other types of signals are.

Section 2, p. 827 Parental care helps offspring survive. Genes can be passed on to the next generation only if the offspring survive.

Chapter 34 Skeletal, Muscular, and Integumentary Systems

Section 1, p. 840 epithelial, nervous, connective, and muscle tissue

Section 2, p. 843 pectoral girdle: shoulder blades and collar bone; pelvic girdle: ilium, ischium, and pubis

Section 2, p. 845 Osteoblasts deposit calcium and minerals as bones grow. Osteocytes are mature bone cells that make up compact bone.

Section 2, p. 846 Osteoarthritis occurs when the cartilage that covers the surface of bones wears away. Rheumatoid arthritis occurs when the immune system attacks the tissues around joints.

Section 3, p. 849 Aerobic respiration produces large amounts of ATP but is relatively slow. Anaerobic respiration is faster than aerobic respiration but produces only small amounts of ATP and causes lactic acid to build up.

Section 3, p. 850 Energy in ATP is used when myosin detaches from actin.

Section 4, p. 855 The hair bulb produces hair. The lunula produces fingernails and toenails.

Chapter 35 Circulatory and Respiratory Systems

Section 1, p. 865 by distributing heat, transporting wastes away from cells, and providing cells with the molecules that they need to stay alive

Section 1, p. 867 The wave of contraction in the atria is picked up by the atrioventricular (AV) node in the ventricles, which causes the ventricles to contract.

Section 1, p. 868 When skeletal muscles contract, they squeeze veins. The blood in the veins is then pushed toward the heart. Valves in the veins keep the blood from flowing backward.

Section 1, p. 870 types A+ and O+

Section 1, p. 871 First, the lymphatic system returns to the cardiovascular system fluids that leaked out of the capillaries. Second, both the cardiovascular and lymphatic systems contain white blood cells.

Section 2, p. 873 Heart attacks affect the heart, and strokes affect the brain. Both can cause death and have similar treatments. Heart attacks and most strokes occur when a vessel supplying the heart or brain becomes blocked. Strokes can also occur when a vessel in the brain bursts.

Section 2, p. 874 Answers may vary but may include avoiding drugs such as alcohol and tobacco, getting more exercise, and maintaining a healthy diet.

Section 3, p. 877 The diaphragm moves downward and the rib muscles draw the rib cage up and out to increase the volume of the chest cavity, which reduces the air pressure within the cavity. When air flows from a high-pressure area to a low-pressure area, air is drawn into the lungs.

Section 3, p. 879 a lower concentration of oxygen

Section 3, p. 881 asthma, bronchitis, pneumonia, emphysema, and lung cancer

Chapter 36 Digestive and Excretory Systems

Section 1, p. 895 BMI, or body mass index, is a number that relates an individual's weight and height and is used to determine a healthy weight range.

Section 2, p. 898 The digestion of fats begins in the small intestine, where the fats are acted on by lipases and by bile, which is secreted by the liver and stored in the gallbladder.

Section 2, p. 900 undigested materials, dead cells, mucus, digestive secretions, bacteria, and yeast

Section 3, p. 903 Blood cells are too large to cross the capillary membrane.

Section 3, p. 904 A ureter is a tube of smooth muscle that carriers urine from the kidney to the bladder.

Section 3, p. 905 infection, diabetes, high blood pressure, and damage to the kidneys by the body's own immune system

Chapter 37 The Body's Defenses

Section 1, p. 915 Skin prevents many pathogens from invading the body (unless there is a tear in the skin).

Section 1, p. 917 Viruses display antigens on their cell surfaces, which tells the body that the viral cells are different from "self" cells.

Section 2, p. 920 plasma cells

Section 2, p. 923 Antigen shifting is caused by the mutation of viral cells.

Section 3, p. 925 because the body is launching a strong immune response against harmless airborne particles

Section 3, p. 929 HIV destroys helper T cells by infecting them and causing them to burst open.

Chapter 38 Nervous System

Section 1, p. 939 a specialized cell in the nervous system

Section 1, p. 943 sensory neurons, motor neurons, and interneurons

Section 2, p. 945 the axon

Section 2, p. 947 the sodium-potassium pump

Section 2, p. 948 Neurotransmitters are released from synaptic vesicles at the presynaptic membrane by exocytosis.

Section 3, p. 950 specialized neurons that are located in sensory organs

Section 3, p. 952 Hair cells rest on a membrane that vibrates when sound waves enter the cochlea.

Section 4, p. 956 Depressants can slow down heart rate and breathing rate enough to cause death.

Section 4, p. 958 Opiates mimic the action of natural painkillers, endorphins.

Section 4, p. 959 Addiction affects chemical transmission at synapses.

Section 4, p. 961 Wearing protective headgear and using other safety devices, such as seat belts, can prevent many traumatic injuries.

Chapter 39 Hormones and the Endocrine System

Section 1, p. 972 Endocrine glands are organs that release hormones directly into the bloodstream. Endocrine tissues are cells that produce hormones, but they are part of organs that have primary functions that are not part of the endocrine system. Exocrine glands are organs that produce substances that are delivered through ducts.

Section 1, p. 973 Amino acid–based hormones are not fat soluble, so they work by attaching to the surface of the cell. Cholesterol-based hormones are fat soluble, so they are able to enter the cell and attach to receptors inside the cell.

Section 1, p. 975 by the second messenger system activated by the hormone glucagon and by direct gene activation stimulated by the hormone cortisol

Section 1, p. 976 Sample answer: Negative feedback results in less hormone production, and positive feedback results in more hormone production.

Section 2, p. 979 the parathyroid

Section 2, p. 981 corticosteroids, including aldosterone and cortisol

Chapter 40 Reproduction and Development

Section 1, p. 993 The anterior pituitary releases LH, which stimulates the production of testosterone. Testosterone, along with FSH, stimulates sperm production.

Section 1, p. 994 The mitochondria supply sperm with the energy that the sperm need to propel themselves through the female reproductive system.

Section 1, p. 995 Many sperm die in the acidic environment of the female reproductive system.

Section 2, p. 997 The ovum is fertilized in a fallopian tube.

Section 2, p. 999 Elevated levels of LH cause the corpus luteum to secrete estrogen and progesterone, sex hormones.

Section 2, p. 1000 If a fertilized egg does not implant on the wall of the uterus, the levels of estrogen and progesterone will fall. The thick uterine lining will no longer be maintained and will be shed.

Section 3, p. 1003 by the end of the fourth week of pregnancy

Section 3, p. 1004 The fetus gains a great deal of weight, and all of its organ systems become developed enough such that it can live outside of the mother.

Section 4, p. 1005 Some viral STDs can be treated with antiviral medication. Many bacterial STDs can be treated and cured with antibiotics.

Chapter 41 Forensics

Section 1, p. 1017 Sample answer: *Identity* refers to finding out what the evidence is and then finding out to whom the evidence belongs.

Section 1, p. 1018 Sample answer: investigating accidents, identifying bodies, investigating fires, verifying documents, detecting forged signatures, detecting forged money, investigating fake credit cards, tracking computer viruses, locating hackers, and investigating Internet fraud

Section 1, p. 1020 light microscope, scanning electron microscope, and comparison microscope

Section 2, p. 1022 hands and feet

Section 2, p. 1025 ballistics

Section 2, p. 1026 Antemortem toxicologists analyze blood, urine, and hair from living persons. Postmortem toxicologists analyze tissue samples from a body after death.

Section 2, p. 1027 Sample answer: Forensic pathologists look for evidence that explains how a person died, including signs of trauma and trace evidence. They may also look for identifying marks that help identify a body.

Section 2, p. 1028 a person's sex, approximate height, age, and likely ethnicity

Section 3, p. 1031 Sample answer: locating fingerprints and bloodstains on floors, walls, or furniture; conducting blood-spatter analysis to analyze the path of bullets

abiotic (AY bie AHT ik) describes the nonliving part of the environment, including water, rocks, light, and temperature (80)
abiótico término que describe la parte sin vida del ambiente, incluyendo el agua, las rocas, la luz y la temperatura (80)

abiotic factor (AY bie AHT ik FAK tuhr) an environmental factor that is not associated with the activities of living organisms (106)
factor abiótico un factor ambiental que no está asociado con las actividades de los seres vivos (106)

acanthodian (A kan thoh dee uhn) an early fish; the earliest known vertebrate to have jaws (640)
acantodio un pez antiguo; el primer vertebrado con mandíbulas que se conoce (640)

acid any compound that increases the number of hydronium ions when dissolved in water; acids turn blue litmus paper red and react with bases and some metals to form salts (56)
ácido cualquier compuesto que aumenta el número de iones de hidrógeno cuando se disuelve en agua; los ácidos cambian el color del papel tornasol a rojo y forman sales al reaccionar con bases y con algunos metales (56)

acid rain precipitation that has a pH below normal and has an unusually high concentration of sulfuric or nitric acids, often as a result of chemical pollution of the air from sources such as automobile exhausts and the burning of fossil fuels (128)
lluvia ácida precipitación con un pH inferior al normal, que tiene una concentración inusualmente alta de ácido sulfúrico y ácido nítrico como resultado de la contaminación química del aire por fuentes tales como los escapes de los automóviles y la quema de combustibles fósiles (128)

acoelomate (uh SEE luh MAYT) an animal that lacks a coelom, or body cavity (636)
acelomado un animal que no tiene celoma, o cavidad en el cuerpo (636)

actin (AK tin) a protein responsible for the contraction and relaxation of muscle (850)
actina una proteína responsable de la contracción y relajación de los músculos (850)

action potential a sudden change in the polarity of the membrane of a neuron, gland cell, or muscle fiber that facilitates the transmission of electrical impulses (946)
potencial de acción un cambio súbito en la polaridad de la membrana de una neurona, célula glandular o fibra muscular, el cual facilita la transmisión de impulsos eléctricos (946)

activation energy the minimum amount of energy required to start a chemical reaction (65)
energía de activación la cantidad mínima de energía que se requiere para iniciar una reacción química (65)

active site on an enzyme, the site that attaches to a substrate (66)
sitio activo el sitio en una enzima que se une al sustrato (66)

active transport the movement of chemical substances, usually across the cell membrane, against a concentration gradient; requires cells to use energy (178)
transporte activo el movimiento de sustancias químicas, normalmente a través de la membrana celular, en contra de un gradiente de concentración; requiere que la célula gaste energía (178)

adaptation (AD uhp TAY shuhn) the process of becoming adapted to an environment; an anatomical, physiological, or behavioral change that improves a population's ability to survive (381)
adaptación el proceso de adaptarse a un ambiente; un cambio anatómico, fisiológico o en la conducta que mejora la capacidad de supervivencia de una población (381)

adaptive radiation (uh DAP tiv RAY dee AY shuhn) an evolutionary pattern in which many species evolve from a single ancestral species (389, 413)
radiación adaptativa un patrón evolucionista en el cual muchas especies evolucionan a partir de una sola especie ancestral (389, 413)

addiction (uh DIK shuhn) a physiological or psychological dependence on a substance, such as alcohol or drugs (959)
adicción una dependencia fisiológica o psicológica de una sustancia, tal como el alcohol o las drogas (959)

adenine (AD uh NEEN) one of the four bases that combine with sugar and phosphate to form a nucleotide subunit of DNA; adenine pairs with thymine (297)
adenina una de las cuatro bases que se combinan con un azúcar y un fosfato para formar una de las subunidades de nucleótidos del ADN; la adenina se une a la timina (297)

adhesion (ad HEE zhuhn) the attractive force between two bodies of different substances that are in contact with each other (55)
adhesión la fuerza de atracción entre dos cuerpos de diferentes sustancias que están en contacto (55)

aerobic (er OH bik) describes a process that requires oxygen (209)
aeróbico término que describe un proceso que requiere oxígeno (209)

agar (AH GAHR) a gel-like base for culturing microbes; extracted from certain red algae (511)
agar una base parecida a un gel que se usa para cultivar microbios; se extrae de algunas algas rojas (511)

agnathan (AG nuh thuhn) a member of a class of primitive, jawless fishes (639)

agnato un miembro de una clase de peces primitivos, sin mandíbulas (639)

AIDS (AYDZ) acquired immune deficiency syndrome, a disease caused by HIV, an infection that results in an ineffective immune system (929)

SIDA síndrome de inmunodeficiencia adquirida, enfermedad causada por una infección de VIH, la cual resulta en un sistema inmunológico ineficiente (929)

alcoholic fermentation (FUHR muhn TAY shuhn) the anaerobic process by which yeasts and other microorganisms break down sugars to form carbon dioxide and ethanol (212)

fermentación alcohólica el proceso anaeróbico por medio del cual las levaduras y otros microorganismos descomponen los azúcares para formar dióxido de carbono y alcohol etílico (212)

algal bloom (AL guhl) a rapid increase in the population of algae in an aquatic ecosystem (510)

florecimiento de algas un aumento rápido de la población de algas de un ecosistema acuático (510)

algor mortis (AL guhr MAWR tis) the cooling of the body following death (1032)

algor mortis el enfriamiento del cuerpo después de la muerte (1032)

allele (uh LEEL) one of the alternative forms of a gene that governs a characteristic, such as hair color (272)

alelo una de las formas alternativas de un gene que rige un carácter, como por ejemplo, el color del cabello (272)

allergen (AL uhr juhn) a substance that causes an allergic reaction (924)

alergeno una sustancia que causa una reacción alérgica (924)

allergy (AL uhr jee) a physical response to an antigen, which can be a common substance that produces little or no response in the general population (924)

alergia una reacción física a un antígeno, el cual puede ser una sustancia común que produce una reacción ligera o que no produce ninguna reacción en la población general (924)

alternation of generations within the life cycle of an organism, the occurrence of two or more distinct forms (generations), which differ from each other in method of reproduction; usually, one generation is haploid and reproduces sexually, and the other generation is diploid and reproduces asexually (498, 546)

alternación de generaciones dentro del ciclo de vida de un organismo, la aparición de dos o más formas distintas (generaciones) que difieren entre sí en su método de reproducción; generalmente, una generación es haploide y se reproduce sexualmente, y la otra generación es diploide y se reproduce asexualmente (498, 546)

altruistic behavior (AL troo IS tik) self-sacrificing behavior that benefits another individual (827)

conducta altruista sacrificio que hace un individuo y que resulta en un beneficio para otro individuo (827)

alveolus (al VEE uh luhs) any of the tiny air sacs of the lungs where oxygen and carbon dioxide are exchanged (877)

alveolo cualquiera de las diminutas bolsas de aire de los pulmones, en donde ocurre el intercambio de oxígeno y dióxido de carbono (877)

amino acid (uh MEE noh) a compound of a class of simple organic compounds that contain a carboxyl group and an amino group and that combine to form proteins (62)

aminoácido un compuesto de una clase de compuestos orgánicos simples que contienen un grupo carboxilo y un grupo amino y que al combinarse forman proteínas (62)

ammonification (uh MAHN i fi KAY shuhn) the formation of ammonia compounds in the soil by the action of bacteria on decaying matter (92)

amonificación la formación compuestos de amoniaco en el suelo debido a la acción de las bacterias en la materia en descomposición (92)

amnion (AM nee uhn) the membrane that contains a developing embryo and its surrounding fluid (1002)

membrana amniótica la membrana que contiene al embrión en desarrollo y el líquido que lo rodea (1002)

amniotic egg (AM nee AHT ik) a type of egg that is produced by reptiles, birds, and egg-laying mammals and that contains a large amount of yolk; usually surrounded by a leathery or hard shell within which the embryo and its embryonic membranes develop (641)

huevo amniótico un tipo de huevo que es producido por los reptiles, las aves y los mamíferos que ponen huevos y que contiene una gran cantidad de yema; normalmente está rodeado por una cáscara áspera y dura, dentro de la cual se desarrollan el embrión y sus membranas embrionarias (641)

amoebocyte (uh MEE boh SIET) in sponges and other invertebrates, an amoeba-like cell that moves through the body fluids, removes wastes, and participates in other processes (657)

amebocito en las esponjas y otros invertebrados, una célula parecida a una ameba que se mueve a través de los fluidos del cuerpo, elimina desechos y participa en otros procesos (657)

anaerobic (AN uhr OH bik) describes a process that does not require oxygen (209)

anaeróbico término que describe un proceso que no requiere oxígeno (209)

analogous (uh NAL uh guhs) in comparisons of different organisms, describes features that are similar in function and appearance but not in structure or origin (428)

análogo en comparaciones de diferentes organismos, término que describe características que son similares en función y apariencia, pero no en estructura u origen (428)

anatomy (uh NAT uh mee) the bodily structure of an organism (384)

anatomía la estructura corporal de un organismo (384)

androgen (AN droh juhn) a type of hormone that regulates the sexual development of males and that stimulates development of secondary sex characteristics in males (982)

andrógeno un tipo de hormona que regula el desarrollo sexual de los machos y estimula el desarrollo de caracteres sexuales secundarios en los machos (982)

angiosperm (AN jee oh SPUHRM) a flowering plant that produces seeds within a fruit (553)

angiosperma una planta que da flores y que produce semillas dentro de la fruta (553)

antagonistic hormone (an TAG uh NIS tik) a hormone that counteracts the effect of another hormone (977)

hormona antagonista una horma que contrarresta el efecto de otra hormona (977)

anther (AN thuhr) in flowering plants, the tip of a stamen, which contains the pollen sacs where grains form (560)

antera en las plantas que dan flores, la punta del estambre, que contiene los sacos de polen donde se forman los granos (560)

antheridium (AN thuhr ID ee uhm) a reproductive structure that produces male sex cells in flowerless and seedless plants (548)

anteridio una estructura reproductiva que produce células sexuales masculinas en las plantas que no dan flores ni producen semillas (548)

antibiotic (AN tie bie AHT ik) a substance that can inhibit the growth of or kill some microorganisms (484)

antibiótico una sustancia que inhibe el crecimiento de algunos microorganismos o los mata (484)

antibody (AN ti BAHD ee) a protein that reacts to a specific antigen or that inactivates or destroys toxins (920)

anticuerpo una proteína que reacciona ante un antígeno específico o que inactiva o destruye toxinas (920)

anticodon (ANT ie KOH DAHN) a region of a tRNA molecule that consists of a sequence of three bases that is complementary to an mRNA codon (308)

anticodón una región de una molécula de ARNt formada por una secuencia de tres bases que complementan el codón del ARNm (308)

antigen (AN tuh juhn) a substance that stimulates an immune response (917)

antígeno una sustancia que estimula una respuesta inmunológica (917)

antigen shifting the production of new antigens by a virus as it mutates over time (923)

cambio antigénico la producción de antígenos nuevos por un virus cuando éste muta con el paso del tiempo (923)

apical meristem (AP i kuhl MER uh STEM) the growing region at the tips of stems and roots in plants (588)

meristemo apical la región de crecimiento en la punta de los tallos y raíces de las plantas (588)

apoptosis (AP uhp TOH sis) in multicellular organisms, a genetically controlled process that leads to the death of a cell; programmed cell death (334)

apoptosis en los organismos pluricelulares, un proceso controlado genéticamente que lleva a la muerte de una célula; la muerte programada de una célula (334)

appendage (uh PEN dij) a structure that extends from the main body, such as a limb, tentacle, fin, or wing (702)

apéndice una estructura que se extiende del cuerpo principal, como por ejemplo, una extremidad, un tentáculo, una aleta o un ala (702)

appendicular skeleton (AP uhn DIK yoo luhr) the bones of the arms and legs (843)

esqueleto apendicular los huesos de los brazos y piernas (843)

archaea (ahr KEE uh) prokaryotes (most of which are known to live in extreme environments) that are distinguished from other prokaryotes by differences in their genetics and in the makeup of their cell wall; members of the domain Archaea (singular, *archaeon*) (435)

arqueas procariotes (la mayoría de los cuales viven en ambientes extremos) que se distinguen de otros procariotes por diferencias genéticas y por la diferente composición de su pared celular; miembros del dominio Archaea (435)

archegonium (AHR kuh GOH nee uhm) a female reproductive structure of small, nonvascular plants that produces a single egg and in which fertilization and development take place (548)

arquegonio una estructura reproductiva femenina de ciertas plantas pequeñas y no vasculares, que produce un solo óvulo y en el cual ocurren la fertilización y el desarrollo (548)

artery (AHRT uhr ee) a blood vessel that carries blood away from the heart to the body's organs (868)

arteria un vaso sanguíneo que transporta sangre del corazón a los órganos del cuerpo (868)

arthritis (ahr THRIET is) inflammation of the joints that results in pain and swelling (846)

artritis inflamación de las articulaciones que causa dolor e hinchazón (846)

artificial selection the human practice of breeding animals or plants that have certain desired traits (377)
selección artificial la práctica humana de criar animales o cultivar plantas que tienen ciertos caracteres deseados (377)

ascocarp (AS koh KAHRP) the reproductive portion of an ascomycete (526)
ascocarpo la porción reproductiva de un ascomiceto (526)

ascus (AS kuhs) the spore sac where ascomycetes produce ascospores (526)
asca el saco de esporas donde los ascomicetos producen acosporas (526)

asexual reproduction (ay SEK shoo uhl) reproduction that does not involve the union of gametes and in which a single parent produces offspring that are genetically identical to the parent (247)
reproducción asexual reproducción que no involucra la unión de gametos, en la que un solo progenitor produce descendencia que es genéticamente igual al progenitor (247)

asymmetrical (AY suh ME tri kuhl) irregular in shape; without symmetry (633)
asimétrico de forma irregular; sin simetría (633)

atom the smallest unit of an element that maintains the chemical properties of that element (51)
átomo la unidad más pequeña de un elemento que conserva las propiedades químicas de ese elemento (51)

ATP adenosine triphosphate, an organic molecule that acts as the main energy source for cell processes; composed of a nitrogenous base, a sugar, and three phosphate groups (63, 198)
ATP adenosín trifosfato; molécula orgánica que funciona como la fuente principal de energía para los procesos celulares; formada por una base nitrogenada, un azúcar y tres grupos fosfato (63, 198)

ATP synthase (SIN THAYZ) an enzyme that catalyzes the synthesis of ATP (201)
ATP sintetasa una enzima que cataliza la síntesis del ATP (201)

atrioventricular node (AY tree oh ven TRIK yuh luhr NOHD) heart tissues that generate the activity that produces heartbeat (abbreviation, AV node) (867)
nodo atrioventricular tejidos del corazón que generan la actividad que produce el latido del corazón (abreviatura: nodo AV) (867)

atrium (AY tree uhm) a chamber that receives blood that is returning to the heart (867)
atrio una cámara que recibe la sangre que regresa al corazón (867)

autoimmune disease (AWT oh i MYOON) a disease in which the immune system attacks the organism's own cells (927)
enfermedad autoinmune una enfermedad en la que el sistema inmunológico ataca las células del propio organismo (927)

autonomic nervous system (AWT uh NAHM ik) the part of the nervous system that controls involuntary actions (942)
sistema nervioso autónomo la parte del sistema nervioso que controla las acciones involuntarias (942)

autopsy (AW TAHP see) an examination of a body after death, usually to determine the cause of death (1027)
autopsia un examen del cuerpo después de la muerte, generalmente para determinar la causa de la muerte (1027)

autosome (AWT uh SOHM) any chromosome that is not a sex chromosome (249)
autosoma cualquier cromosoma que no es un cromosoma sexual (249)

autotroph (AWT oh TRAHF) an organism that produces its own nutrients from inorganic substances or from the environment instead of consuming other organisms (197, 434, 437, 543)
autótrofo un organismo que produce sus propios nutrientes a partir de sustancias inorgánicas o del ambiente, en lugar de consumir otros organismos (197, 434, 437, 543)

auxin (AWK sin) a plant hormone that regulates cell elongation (604)
auxina una hormona vegetal que regula el alargamiento de las células (604)

axial skeleton (AK see uhl) the bones of the skull and vertebral column (843)
esqueleto axial los huesos del cráneo y la columna vertebral (843)

axon (AK SAHN) an elongated extension of a neuron that carries impulses away from the cell body (945)
axón una extensión alargada de una neurona que transporta impulsos hacia fuera del cuerpo de la célula (945)

bacteria (bak TIR ee uh) extremely small, single-celled organisms that usually have a cell wall and that usually reproduce by cell division (singular, *bacterium*) (435)
bacterias organismos extremadamente pequeños, unicelulares, que normalmente tienen pared celular y se reproducen por división celular (435)

bacteriophage (bak TIR ee uh FAYJ) a virus that infects bacteria (477)

    bacteriófago un virus que infecta a las bacterias (477)

barb a branch of a vane in the feather of a bird (768)

    barba una ramificación de la pluma de un ave (768)

base any compound that increases the number of hydroxide ions when dissolved in water; bases turn red litmus paper blue and react with acids to form salts (56)

    base cualquier compuesto que aumenta el número de iones de hidróxido cuando se disuelve en agua; las bases cambian el color del papel tornasol a azul y forman sales al reaccionar con ácidos (56)

base pairing rules the rules stating that in DNA cytosine pairs with guanine and adenine pairs with thymine and that in RNA cytosine pairs with guanine and adenine pairs with uracil (297)

    regla de apareamiento de las bases las reglas que establecen que en el ADN, la citosina se une a la guanina y la adenina se une a la timina, y que en el ARN, la citosina se une a la guanina y la adenina se une al uracilo (297)

basidiocarp (buh SID ee uh KAHRP) the part of a basidiomycete that produces spores (527)

    basidiocarpo la parte de un basidiomiceto que produce esporas (527)

basidium (buh SID ee uhm) a structure that produces asexual spores in basidiomycetes (527)

    basidio una estructura que produce esporas asexuales en los basidiomicetos (527)

B cell a white blood cell that matures in bones and makes antibodies (920)

    célula B un glóbulo blanco de la sangre que madura en los huesos y fabrica anticuerpos (920)

behavior an action that an individual carries out in response to a stimulus or to the environment (813)

    conducta una acción que un individuo realiza en respuesta a un estímulo o a su ambiente (813)

bell curve a symmetrical frequency curve (400)

    curva de campana una curva simétrica de frecuencia (400)

benign tumor (bi NIEN TOO muhr) an abnormal but noncancerous cell mass or growth (235)

    tumor benigno un bulto o masa de células anormal, pero que no es cancerosa (235)

bilateral symmetry (bie LAT uhr uhl SIM uh tree) a condition in which two equal halves of a body mirror each other (633)

    simetría bilateral una condición en la que dos mitades iguales de un cuerpo son imágenes de espejo una de otra (633)

binary fission (BIE nuh ree FISH uhn) a form of asexual reproduction in single-celled organisms by which one cell divides into two cells of the same size (247, 498)

    fisión binaria una forma de reproducción asexual de los organismos unicelulares, por medio de la cual la célula se divide en dos células del mismo tamaño (247, 498)

binomial nomenclature (bie NOH mee uhl NOH muhn KLAY chuhr) a system for giving each organism a two-word scientific name that consists of the genus name followed by the species name (424)

    nomenclatura binomial un sistema para darle a cada organismo un nombre científico de dos palabras, el cual está formando por el género seguido de la especie (424)

biodiversity (BIE oh duh VUHR suh tee) the variety of organisms in a given area, the genetic variation within a population, the variety of species in a community, or the variety of communities in an ecosystem (80, 132)

    biodiversidad la variedad de organismos que se encuentran en un área determinada, la variación genética dentro de una población, la variedad de especies en una comunidad o la variedad de comunidades en un ecosistema (80, 132)

biogeography (BIE oh jee AH gruh fee) the study of the geographical distribution of living organisms and fossils on Earth (383)

    biogeografía el estudio de la distribución geográfica de los seres vivos y los fósiles en la Tierra (383)

bioinformatics (BIE oh in fuhr MA tiks) the application of information technologies in biology, especially in genetics (361)

    bioinformática la aplicación de las tecnologías de la información en la biología, especialmente la genética (361)

biological species concept the principle that defines a species as a group of organisms whose members can interbreed to produce offspring (411)

    concepto de especie biológica el principio que define a una especie como un grupo de organismos que pueden producir descendencia al cruzarse entre ellos (411)

biology the scientific study of living organisms and their interactions with the environment (17)

    biología el estudio científico de los seres vivos y sus interacciones con el medio ambiente (17)

biome (BIE OHM) a large region characterized by a specific type of climate and certain types of plant and animal communities (82)

    bioma una región extensa caracterizada por un tipo de clima específico y ciertos tipos de comunidades de plantas y animales (82)

biometrics (BIE oh ME triks) the statistical analysis of biological data; especially the measurement and analysis of unique physical or behavioral characteristics to verify the identity of a person (36)

biométrica el análisis estadístico de datos biológicos, especialmente la medición y el análisis de características físicas o características de conducta únicas para verificar la identidad de una persona (36)

bioremediation (BIE oh ri MEE dee AY shuhn) the biological treatment of hazardous waste by natural or genetically engineered microorganisms (349)

bioremediación el tratamiento biológico de desechos peligrosos por medio de microorganismos naturales o modificados genéticamente (349)

biotic (bie AHT ik) describes living factors in the environment (79)

biótico término que describe los factores vivientes del ambiente (79)

biotic factor an environmental factor that is associated with or results from the activities of living organisms (106)

factor biótico un factor ambiental que está asociado con las actividades de los seres vivos o que resulta de ellas (106)

blade the broad, flat portion of a typical leaf (505, 582)

brizna la porción ancha y plana de una hoja típica (505, 582)

blastocoel (BLAS toh SEEL) the central cavity of a blastula (634)

blastocelo la cavidad central de una blástula (634)

blastocyst (BLAS toh SIST) in placental mammals, a developing embryo that consists of a hollow ball of cells surrounding an inner cell mass (1001)

blastoquistela en los mamíferos placentarios, un embrión en desarrollo que consiste en una bola hueca de células que rodean una masa de células interna (1001)

blastula (BLAS tyoo luh) in an animal, the stage of early embryonic development in which a hollow ball of cells forms; the stage before gastrulation (634)

blástula en un animal, la etapa del desarrollo embrionario temprano en la que se forma una bola hueca de células; la etapa anterior a la gastrulación (634)

blood pressure the force that blood exerts on the walls of the arteries (872)

presión sanguínea la fuerza que la sangre ejerce en las paredes de las arterias (872)

body plan an animal's shape, symmetry, and internal organization (632)

plan del cuerpo la forma, simetría y organización interna de un animal (632)

bone marrow (MAR oh) soft tissue inside bones that either produces blood cells or stores fat (844)

médula ósea el tejido blando que se encuentra en el interior de los huesos y que produce las células sanguíneas o almacena grasa (844)

brain the mass of nerve tissue that is the main control center of the nervous system (940)

encéfalo la masa de tejido nervioso que es el centro principal de control del sistema nervioso (940)

brainstem the stemlike portion of the brain that connects the cerebral hemispheres with the spinal cord and that maintains the necessary functions of the body, such as breathing and circulation (941)

tronco encefálico la porción del cerebro que tiene forma de tronco, la cual conecta los hemisferios cerebrales con la médula espinal y mantiene las funciones necesarias del cuerpo, tales como la respiración y la circulación (941)

bronchus (BRAHNG kuhs) one of the two tubes that connect the lungs with the trachea (876)

bronquio uno de los dos tubos que conectan los pulmones con la tráquea (876)

bud a shoot or flower that has immature leaves folded in the growing tip (588)

capullo un brote o flor que tiene hojas inmaduras dobladas en la punta en crecimiento (588)

budding asexual reproduction in which a part of the parent organism pinches off and forms a new organism (247)

yemación reproducción asexual en la que una parte del organismo progenitor se separa y forma un nuevo organismo (247)

buffer (BUHF uhr) a solution made from a weak acid and its conjugate base that neutralizes small amounts of acids or bases added to it (57)

búfer una solución que contiene un ácido débil y su base conjugada y que neutraliza pequeñas cantidades de ácidos y bases que se le añaden (57)

bulbourethral gland (BUHL boh yoo REE thruhl) one of the two glands in the male reproductive system that add fluid to the semen during ejaculation (995)

glándula bulbouretral una de las dos glándulas del aparato reproductor masculino que añaden líquido al semen durante la eyaculación (995)

calorie (KAL uh ree) the amount of energy needed to raise the temperature of 1 g of water 1 °C; the Calorie used to indicate the energy content of food is a kilocalorie (891)

caloría la cantidad de energía que se requiere para aumentar la temperatura de 1 g de agua en 1 °C; la Caloría que se usa para indicar el contenido energético de los alimentos es la kilocaloría (891)

Calvin cycle (KAL vin) a biochemical pathway of photosynthesis in which carbon dioxide is converted into glucose using ATP (206)

ciclo de Calvin una vía bioquímica de la fotosíntesis en la que el dióxido de carbono se convierte en glucosa usando ATP (206)

cancer a type of disorder of cell growth that results in invasion and destruction of surrounding healthy tissue by abnormal cells (235, 323)

cáncer un tipo de trastorno del crecimiento celular en el que células anormales invaden y destruyen los tejidos sanos que las rodean (235, 323)

capillary (KAP uh LER ee) a tiny blood vessel that allows an exchange between blood and cells in tissue (868)

capilar diminuto vaso sanguíneo que permite el intercambio entre la sangre y las células de los tejidos (868)

capsid a protein sheath that surrounds the nucleic acid core in a virus (477)

cápside una cubierta de proteína que rodea el centro de ácido nucleico de un virus (477)

capsule in mosses, the part that contains spores; in bacteria, a protective layer of polysaccharides around the cell wall (154)

cápsula en los musgos, la parte que contiene las esporas; en las bacterias, una capa protectora de polisacáridos que se encuentra alrededor de la pared celular (154)

carapace (KAR uh PAYS) in some crustaceans, a shieldlike plate that covers the body; in turtles and tortoises, the upper shell (762)

caparazón en algunos crustáceos, una placa parecida a un escudo que cubre el cuerpo; en las tortugas, la concha superior (762)

carbohydrate (KAHR boh HIE drayt) a class of molecules that includes sugars, starches, and fiber; contains carbon, hydrogen, and oxygen (60)

carbohidrato una clase de moléculas entre las que se incluyen azúcares, almidones y fibra; contiene carbono, hidrógeno y oxígeno (60)

carbon cycle the movement of carbon from the nonliving environment into living things and back (91)

ciclo del carbono el movimiento del carbono del ambiente sin vida a los seres vivos y de los seres vivos al ambiente (91)

cardiovascular system (KAHR dee oh VAS kyoo luhr) a collection of organs that transport blood throughout the body; the organs in this system include the heart, the arteries, and the veins (865)

aparato cardiovascular un conjunto de órganos que transportan la sangre a través del cuerpo; los órganos de este sistema incluyen al corazón, las arterias y las venas (865)

carnivore (KAHR nuh VAWR) an organism that eats animals (87)

carnívoro un organismo que se alimenta de animales (87)

carrier in biology, an individual who has one copy of a recessive autosomal allele that causes disease in the homozygous condition (323)

portador en biología, un individuo que tiene una copia de un alelo recesivo autosómico, el cual causa enfermedades en la condición homocigótica (323)

carrier protein a protein that transports substances across a cell membrane (179)

proteína transportadora una proteína que transporta sustancias a través de la membrana celular (179)

carrying capacity (kuh PAS i tee) the largest population that an environment can support at any given time (104)

capacidad de carga la población más grande que un ambiente puede sostener en cualquier momento dado (104)

cartilage (KAHRT'l IJ) a flexible and strong connective tissue (845)

cartílago un tejido conectivo flexible y fuerte (845)

caste (KAST) a group of insects in a colony that have a specific function (715)

casta un grupo de insectos en una colonia que tienen una función específica (715)

cell in biology, the smallest unit that can perform all life processes; cells are covered by a membrane and contain DNA and cytoplasm (18, 151)

célula en biología, la unidad más pequeña que puede realizar todos los procesos vitales; las células están cubiertas por una membrana y tienen ADN y citoplasma (18, 151)

cell cycle the life cycle of a cell; in eukaryotes, it consists of a cell-growth period in which DNA is synthesized and a cell-division period in which mitosis takes place (228, 334)

ciclo celular el ciclo de vida de una célula; en los eucariotes, consiste de un período de crecimiento celular en el que el ADN se sintetiza, y un período de división celular en el que ocurre la mitosis (228, 334)

cell differentiation (DIF uhr EN shee AY shuhn) the process by which a cell becomes specialized for a specific structure or function during multicellular development (333)

diferenciación celular el proceso por medio del cual una célula se especializa en una estructura o función específica durante el desarrollo pluricelular (333)

cell membrane (MEM BRAYN) a phospholipid layer that covers a cell's surface and acts as a barrier between the inside of a cell and the cell's environment (154)

membrana celular una capa de fosfolípidos que cubre la superficie de la célula y funciona como una barrera entre el interior de la célula y el ambiente de la célula (154)

cell theory the theory that states that all living things are made up of cells, that cells are the basic units of organisms, that each cell in a multicellular organism has a specific job, and that cells come only from existing cells (152)

teoría celular la teoría que establece que todos los seres vivos están formados por células, que las células son las unidades fundamentales de los organismos y que las células provienen únicamente de células existentes (152)

cellular respiration (SEL yoo luhr RES puh RAY shuhn) the process by which cells produce energy from carbohydrates; atmospheric oxygen combines with glucose to form water and carbon dioxide (198)

respiración celular el proceso por medio del cual las células producen energía a partir de los carbohidratos; el oxígeno atmosférico se combina con la glucosa para formar agua y dióxido de carbono (198)

cellulose (SEL yoo LOHS) a carbohydrate that consists of linked glucose units and that adds rigidity to the cell walls in plants, many algae, and some fungi; it is a component of dietary fiber (60, 437)

celulosa un carbohidrato compuesto por unidades de glucosa ligadas que agrega rigidez a las paredes celulares de las plantas, de muchas algas y de algunos hongos; es un componente de la fibra dietaria (60, 437)

central nervous system the brain and the spinal cord; its main function is to control the flow of information in the body (939)

sistema nervioso central el cerebro y la médula espinal; su principal función es controlar el flujo de información en el cuerpo (939)

central vacuole (VAK yoo OHL) a large cavity or sac that is found in plant cells or protozoans and that contains air or partially digested food (160)

vacuola central una cavidad o bolsa grande que se encuentra en las células vegetales o en los protozoarios y que contiene aire o alimentos parcialmente digeridos (160)

centromere (SEN troh MIR) the region of the chromosome that holds the two sister chromatids together during mitosis (225)

centrómero la región de un cromosoma que mantiene unidas las dos cromátidas hermanas durante la mitosis (225)

centrosome (SEN truh SOHM) an organelle that contains the centrioles and is the center of dynamic activity in mitosis (230)

centrosoma un organelo que contiene los centríolos y es el centro de actividad dinámica en la mitosis (230)

cephalization (SEF uh li ZAY shuhn) the concentration of nerve tissue and sensory organs at the anterior end of an organism (633)

cefalización la concentración de tejido nervioso y órganos sensoriales en la parte anterior de un organismo (633)

cephalothorax (SEF uh loh THAWR AKS) in arachnids and some crustaceans, the body part made up of the head and the thorax (701)

cefalotórax en los arácnidos y algunos crustáceos, la parte del cuerpo constituida por la cabeza y el tórax (701)

cerebellum (SER uh BEL uhm) a posterior portion of the brain that coordinates muscle movement and controls subconscious activities and some balance functions (941)

cerebelo una porción posterior del cerebro que coordina el movimiento de los músculos y controla las actividades subconscientes y algunas funciones de equilibrio (941)

cerebral ganglion (suh REE bruhl GANG glee uhn) one of a pair of nerve-cell clusters that serve as a primitive brain at the anterior end of some invertebrates, such as annelids (687)

ganglio cerebral uno de un par de conjuntos de células nerviosas que funcionan como si fueran un cerebro primitivo en la parte anterior de algunos invertebrados, tales como los anélidos (687)

cerebrum (suh REE bruhm) the upper part of the brain that receives sensation and controls movement (940)

cerebro la parte superior del encéfalo que recibe las sensaciones y controla el movimiento (940)

cervix (SUHR VIKS) the inferior portion of the uterus (997)

cuello del útero la porción inferior del útero (997)

character (KAR uhk tuhr) a recognizable inherited feature or characteristic of an organism; in Mendelian heredity, a feature that exists in one of two or more possible variations called *traits* (268)

carácter un elemento o característica heredada reconocible de un organismo; en la herencia mendeliana, una característica que existe en una de dos o más variaciones posibles llamadas *rasgos* (268)

chelicera (kuh LIS uhr uh) in arachnids, either of a pair of appendages used to attack prey (706)

quelíceros en los arácnidos, uno de los dos apéndices usados para atacar a las presas (706)

chemical bond the attractive force that holds atoms or ions together (52)

enlace químico la fuerza de atracción que mantiene unidos a los átomos o iones (52)

chemoautotroph (KEE moh AWT oh TRAHF) an organism that synthesizes organic compounds by using inorganic compounds instead of light (474)

quimioautótrofo un organismo que sintetiza compuestos orgánicos a partir de compuestos inorgánicos en lugar de la luz (474)

chemoreceptor (KEE moh ri SEP tuhr) a sensory receptor that responds to specific chemical stimuli (953)

quimiorreceptor un receptor sensorial que responde a estímulos químicos específicos (953)

chitin (KIE tin) a carbohydrate that forms part of the cell walls of fungi and part of the exoskeleton of arthropods, such as insects and crustaceans (60, 437, 521)

quitina un carbohidrato que forma parte de la pared celular de los hongos y del exoesqueleto de los artrópodos, como por ejemplo los insectos y los crustáceos (60, 437, 521)

chlorofluorocarbons (KLAWR oh FLUR uh KAWR buhnz) hydrocarbons in which some or all of the hydrogen atoms are replaced by chlorine and fluorine; used in coolants for refrigerators and air conditioners and in cleaning solvents; their use is restricted because they destroy ozone molecules in the stratosphere (abbreviation, CFCs) (128)

clorofluorocarbonos hidrocarburos en los que algunos o todos los átomos de hidrógeno son reemplazados por cloro y flúor; se usan en líquidos refrigerantes para refrigeradores y aires acondicionados y en solventes para limpieza; su uso está restringido porque destruyen las moléculas de ozono de la estratosfera (abreviatura: CFC) (128)

chlorophyll (KLAWR uh FIL) a green pigment that is present in most plant and algae cells and some bacteria, that gives plants their characteristic green color, and that absorbs light to provide energy for photosynthesis (203)

clorofila un pigmento verde presente en la mayoría de las células de las plantas y las algas y en algunas bacterias, que les da a las plantas su color verde característico y que absorbe luz para brindar energía para la fotosíntesis (203)

chloroplast (KLAWR uh PLAST) an organelle found in plant and algae cells where photosynthesis occurs (161, 543)

cloroplasto un organelo que se encuentra en las células vegetales y en las células de las algas, en el cual se lleva a cabo la fotosíntesis (161, 543)

choanocyte (koh AN uh SIET) any of the flagellate cells that line the cavities of a sponge (655)

coanocito cualquiera de las células flageladas que cubren las cavidades de una esponja (655)

chorion (KAWR ee AHN) the outer membrane that surrounds an embryo (1002)

membrana coriónica la membrana exterior que rodea al embrión (1002)

chromatid (KROH muh TID) one of the two strands of a chromosome that become visible during meiosis or mitosis (225)

cromátida una de las dos hebras de un cromosoma que se vuelve visible durante la meiosis o mitosis (225)

chromatin (KROH muh TIN) the substance that composes eukaryotic chromosomes; it consists of specific proteins, DNA, and small amounts of RNA (224)

cromatina la sustancia que compone los cromosomas eucarióticos; contiene proteínas específicas, ADN y pequeñas cantidades de ARN (224)

chromatograph (kroh MAT uh GRAF) an instrument that separates components of a chemical mixture based on physical properties as the mixture flows through a stationary medium (1020)

cromatógrafo un instrumento que separa los componentes de una mezcla química según sus propiedades físicas cuando la mezcla fluye por un medio estacionario (1020)

chromosome (KROH muh SOHM) in a eukaryotic cell, one of the structures in the nucleus that are made up of DNA and protein; in a prokaryotic cell, the main ring of DNA (224, 249, 251, 302)

cromosoma en una célula eucariótica, una de las estructuras del núcleo que está hecha de ADN y proteína; en una célula procariótica, el anillo principal de ADN (224, 249, 251, 302)

chrysalis (KRIS uh lis) the hard-shelled pupa of certain insects, such as butterflies (714)

crisálida la pupa de cubierta dura de ciertos insectos, como las mariposas (714)

circadian rhythm (suhr KAY dee uhn) a biological daily cycle (822, 980)

ritmo circadiano un ciclo biológico diario (822, 980)

clade a group of organisms that includes all of the evolutionary descendants of a common ancestral lineage (429)

clado un grupo de organismos que incluye a todos los descendientes evolutivos de un linaje ancestral en común (429)

cladistics (kluh DIS tiks) a phylogenetic classification system that uses shared derived characters and ancestry as the sole criterion for grouping taxa (428)

cladística un sistema de clasificación filogénica en el que los únicos criterios de agrupación de los taxa son los caracteres comunes derivados y la ascendencia (428)

cladogram (KLAD uh GRAM) a diagram that is based on patterns of shared, derived traits and that shows the evolutionary relationships between groups of organisms (429)

cladograma un diagrama basado en modelos de caracteres comunes derivados, que muestra las relaciones evolutivas entre grupos de organismos (429)

class a taxonomic category containing orders with common characteristics (426)

clase una categoría taxonómica que contiene órdenes con características comunes (426)

cleavage (KLEEV IJ) in biological development, a series of cell divisions that occur immediately after an egg is fertilized (634)

segmentación en el desarrollo biológico, una serie de divisiones celulares que ocurren inmediatamente después de que un óvulo es fecundado (634)

climate the average weather conditions in an area over a long period of time (82)

clima las condiciones promedio del tiempo en un área durante un largo período de tiempo (82)

cloaca (kloh AY kuh) in all vertebrates except placental mammals, a chamber in the intestine that receives materials from the digestive, reproductive, and excretory systems (791)

cloaca en todos los vertebrados excepto los mamíferos placentarios, una cámara ubicada en el intestino que recibe materiales de los aparatos digestivo, reproductor y excretor (791)

clone an organism, cell, or piece of genetic material that is genetically identical to one from which it was derived; to make a genetic duplicate (352)

clon un organismo, una célula o una muestra de material genético que es genéticamente idéntico a aquél del cual deriva; hacer un duplicado genético (352)

closed circulatory system (SUHR kyoo luh TAWR ee) a circulatory system in which the heart circulates blood through a network of vessels that form a closed loop; the blood does not leave the blood vessels, and materials diffuse across the walls of the vessels (630)

aparato circulatorio cerrado un aparato circulatorio en el que el corazón hace que la sangre circule a través de una red de vasos que forman un circuito cerrado; la sangre no sale de los vasos sanguíneos y los materiales pasan a través de las paredes de los vasos por difusión (630)

cnidocyte (NIE doh SIET) a stinging cell of a cnidarian (659)

cnidocito una célula urticante de los cnidarios (659)

cochlea (KAHK lee uh) a coiled tube that is found in the inner ear and that is essential to hearing (952)

cóclea un tubo enrollado que se encuentra en el oído interno y es esencial para poder oír (952)

codominance (koh DAHM uh nuhns) a condition in which both alleles for a gene are fully expressed (283)

codominancia una condición en la que los dos alelos de un gene están totalmente expresados (283)

codon (KOH DAHN) in DNA and mRNA, a three-nucleotide sequence that encodes an amino acid or signifies a start signal or a stop signal (307)

codón en el ADN y el ARN, una secuencia de tres nucleótidos que codifica un aminoácido o indica una señal de inicio o una señal de terminación (307)

coelom (SEE luhm) a body cavity that contains the internal organs (636, 663)

celoma una cavidad del cuerpo que contiene los órganos internos (636, 663)

coevolution (KOH ev uh LOO shuhn) the evolution of two or more species that is due to mutual influence, often in a way that makes the relationship more mutually beneficial (109)

coevolución la evolución de dos o más especies que se debe a su influencia mutua, a menudo de un modo que hace que la relación sea más mutuamente beneficiosa (109)

cohesion (coh HEE zhuhn) the force that holds molecules of a single material together (55)

cohesión la fuerza que mantiene unidas a las moléculas de un solo material (55)

colonial organism (kuh LOH nee uhl) a collection of genetically identical cells that are permanently associated but in which little or no integration of cell activities occurs (165)

organismo colonial un conjunto de células genéticamente idénticas que están asociadas permanentemente, pero en el que no se da una gran integración de las actividades celulares (165)

combustion (kuhm BUHS chuhn) the burning of a substance (91)

combustión fenómeno que ocurre cuando una sustancia se quema (91)

commensalism (kuh MEN suhl IZ uhm) a relationship between two organisms in which one organism benefits and the other is unaffected (110)

comensalismo una relación entre dos organismos en la que uno se beneficia y el otro no es afectado (110)

communication a transfer of a signal or message from one animal to another that results in some type of response (823)
comunicación la transferencia de una señal o mensaje de un animal a otro, la cual resulta en algún tipo de respuesta (823)

community a group of various species that live in the same habitat and interact with each other (79)
comunidad un grupo de varias especies que viven en el mismo hábitat e interactúan unas con otras (79)

competitive exclusion (eks KLOO zhuhn) the exclusion of one species by another due to competition (114)
exclusión competitiva la exclusión de una especie por otra debido a la competencia (114)

compound a substance made up of atoms of two or more different elements joined by chemical bonds (52)
compuesto una sustancia formada por átomos de dos o más elementos diferentes unidos por enlaces químicos (52)

compound eye an eye composed of many light detectors separated by pigment cells (703)
ojo compuesto un ojo compuesto por muchos detectores de luz separados por células de pigmentos (703)

concentration (KAHN suhn TRAY shuhn) the amount of a particular substance in a given quantity of a mixture, solution, or ore (178)
concentración la cantidad de una cierta sustancia en una cantidad determinada de mezcla, solución o mena (178)

concentration gradient a difference in the concentration of a substance across a distance (178)
gradiente de concentración una diferencia en la concentración de una sustancia a través de una distancia (178)

condensation (KAHN duhn SAY shuhn) the change of state from a gas to a liquid (90)
condensación el cambio de estado de gas a líquido (90)

conditioning (kuhn DISH uhn ing) the process of learning by association (818)
condicionamiento aprendizaje por asociación (818)

cone in plants, a seed-bearing structure; in animals, a photoreceptor within the retina that can distinguish colors and is very sensitive to bright light (550, 951)
cono en las plantas, una estructura portadora de semillas; en los animales, un fotorreceptor de la retina que distingue colores y es muy sensible a la luz brillante (550, 951)

conjugation (KAHN juh GAY shuhn) in prokaryotes, algae, and fungi, a type of sexual reproduction in which two cells join temporarily to recombine nuclear material (475)
conjugación en ciertos protozoarios, algas y hongos, un tipo de reproducción sexual en la que dos células se unen temporalmente para recombinar su material nuclear (475)

connective tissue (kuh NEKT iv) a tissue that has a lot of intracellular substance and that connects and supports other tissues (840)
tejido conectivo un tejido que tiene mucha sustancia intracelular, y que conecta y sostiene otros tejidos (840)

constrictor (kuhn STRIK tuhr) a snake that kills its prey by crushing and suffocating it (765)
boa constrictor una serpiente que aplasta y sofoca a su presa para matarla (765)

consumer an organism that eats other organisms or organic matter instead of producing its own nutrients or obtaining nutrients from inorganic sources (86)
consumidor un organismo que se alimenta de otros organismos o de materia orgánica, en lugar de producir sus propios nutrientes o de obtenerlos de fuentes inorgánicas (86)

contour feather (KAHN TOOR) one of the most external feathers that cover a bird and that help determine its shape (768)
pluma de contorno una las plumas más externas que cubren a un ave y que sirven para determinar su forma (768)

contractile vacuole (kunh TRAK til VAK yoo OHL) in protozoans, an organelle that accumulates water and then releases it periodically to maintain osmotic pressure (181)
vacuola contráctil en los protozoarios, un organelo que acumula agua y luego la libera periódicamente para mantener la presión osmótica (181)

control group in an experiment, a group that serves as a standard of comparison with another group to which the control group is identical except for one factor (11)
grupo de control en un experimento, un grupo que sirve como estándar de comparación con otro grupo, al cual el grupo de control es idéntico excepto por un factor (11)

convergent evolution (kuhn VUHR juhnt) the process by which unrelated species become more similar as they adapt to the same kind of environment (428)
evolución convergente el proceso por medio del cual especies no relacionadas se vuelven más parecidas a medida que se adaptan al mismo tipo de ambiente (428)

coral reef (KAWR uhl) a limestone ridge found in tropical climates and composed of coral fragments that are deposited around organic remains (661)
arrecife de coral una cumbre de piedra caliza ubicada en climas tropicales, formada por fragmentos de coral depositados alrededor de restos orgánicos (661)

cork the outer layer of bark of any woody plant (574)
corcho la capa externa de corteza de cualquier planta leñosa (574)

cork cambium (KAM bee uhm) a layer of tissue under the cork layer where cork cells are produced (589)

cámbium de corcho una capa de tejido que se encuentra debajo de la capa de corcho, en la cual se producen las células de corcho (589)

corpus luteum (KAWR puhs LOOT ee uhm) the structure that forms from the ruptured follicle in the ovary after ovulation; it releases hormones (999)

cuerpo lúteo la estructura que se forma a partir de los folículos rotos del ovario después de la ovulación; libera hormonas (999)

cortex (KAWR TEKS) in plants, the primary tissue located in the epidermis; in animals, the outermost portion of an organ (579)

corteza en las plantas, el tejido primario ubicado en la epidermis; en los animales, la porción externa de un órgano (579)

cotyledon (KAHT uh LEED'n) the embryonic leaf of a seed (559, 585)

cotiledón la hoja embrionaria de una semilla (559, 585)

courtship (KAWRT SHIP) behavior that leads to mating and the rearing of young (826)

cortejo conducta que lleva al apareamiento y al nacimiento de crías (826)

covalent bond (koh VAY luhnt) a bond formed when atoms share one or more pairs of electrons (52)

enlace covalente un enlace formado cuando los átomos comparten uno o más pares de electrones (52)

crossing-over the exchange of genetic material between homologous chromosomes during meiosis; can result in genetic recombination (251)

recombinación el intercambio de material genético entre cromosomas homólogos durante la meiosis; puede resultar en la recombinación genética (251)

cross-pollination (PAHL uh NAY shuhn) a reproductive process in which pollen from one plant is transferred to the stigma of another plant (268)

polinización cruzada un proceso reproductor en el que el polen de una planta es transferido al estigma de otra (268)

cuticle (KYOOT i kuhl) a waxy or fatty and watertight layer on the external wall of epidermal cells (544)

cutícula una capa cerosa o grasosa e impermeable ubicada en la pared externa de las células de la epidermis (544)

cyanobacterium (SIE uh noh bak TIR ee uhm) a bacterium that carries out photosynthesis; a blue-green alga (455)

cianobacteria una bacteria que efectúa la fotosíntesis; un alga verdiazul (455)

cytokinesis (SIET oh ki NEE sis) the division of the cytoplasm of a cell; cytokinesis follows the division of the cell's nucleus by mitosis or meiosis (229, 605)

citoquinesis la división del citoplasma de una célula; la citoquinesis ocurre después de que el núcleo de la célula se divide por mitosis o meiosis (229, 605)

cytoplasm (SIET oh PLAZ uhm) the region of the cell within the membrane that includes the fluid, the cytoskeleton, and all of the organelles except the nucleus (154)

citoplasma la región de la célula dentro de la membrana, que incluye el líquido, el citoesqueleto y los organelos, pero no el núcleo (154)

cytosine (SIET oh SEEN) one of the four bases found in DNA and RNA; cytosine pairs with guanine (297)

citosina una de las cuatro bases que se encuentran en el ADN y ARN; la citosina se une con la guanina (297)

cytoskeleton (SIET oh SKEL uh tuhn) the cytoplasmic network of protein filaments that plays an essential role in cell movement, shape, and division (156)

citoesqueleto la red citoplásmica de filamentos de proteínas que juega un papel esencial en el movimiento, forma y división de la célula (156)

cytosol (SIE tuh SAWL) the soluble portion of the cytoplasm, which includes molecules and small particles, such as ribosomes, but not the organelles covered with membranes (154)

citosol la porción soluble del citoplasma, que incluye moléculas y partículas pequeñas, tales como los ribosomas, pero no los organelos que están cubiertos por membranas (154)

cytotoxic T cell (SIE tuh TAHK sik) a type of T cell that recognizes and destroys cells infected by virus (920)

célula T citotóxica un tipo de célula T que reconoce y destruye las células infectadas por un virus (920)

day-neutral plant a plant that can develop and mature independent of the length of the days (608)

planta neutral al día una planta que se puede desarrollar y madurar independientemente de la longitud de los días (608)

decomposer (DEE kuhm POH zuhr) an organism that feeds by breaking down organic matter from dead organisms; examples include bacteria and fungi (86)

descomponedor un organismo que desintegra la materia orgánica de organismos muertos y se alimenta de ella; entre los ejemplos se encuentran las bacterias y los hongos (86)

deforestation (dee FAWR i STAY shuhn) the process of clearing forests (132)

deforestación el proceso de talar bosques (132)

dendrite (DEN DRIET) a cytoplasmic extension of a neuron that receives stimuli (945)

dendrita la extensión citoplásmica de una neurona que recibe estímulos (945)

denitrification (dee NIE truh fi KAY shuhn) the liberation of nitrogen from nitrogen-containing compounds by bacteria in the soil (92)

desnitrificación ocurre cuando las bacterias liberan nitrógeno contenido en compuestos que se encuentran en el suelo (92)

density-dependent factor a variable affected by the number of organisms present in a given area (105)

factor dependiente de la densidad una variable afectada por el número de organismos presentes en un área determinada (105)

density-independent factor a variable that affects a population regardless of the population density, such as climate (105)

factor independiente de la densidad una variable que afecta a una población independientemente de la densidad de la población, por ejemplo, el clima (105)

deoxyribose (dee AHKS ee RIE bohs) a five-carbon sugar that is a component of DNA nucleotides (296)

desoxirribosa azúcar de cinco carbonos que es un componente de los nucleótidos de ADN (296)

depressant (dee PRES uhnt) a drug that reduces functional activity and produces muscular relaxation (956)

depresor un medicamento que reduce la actividad funcional y produce relajación muscular (956)

dermal tissue (DUHR muhl TISH oo) the outer covering of a plant (573)

tejido dérmico la cubierta exterior de una planta (573)

dermatophyte (duhr MAT uh FIET) a fungus that infects the skin, hair, or nails (531)

dermatofito un hongo que infecta la piel, el cabello o las uñas (531)

dermis (DUHR mis) the layer of skin below the epidermis (853)

dermis la capa de piel que está debajo de la epidermis (853)

deuterostome (DOO tuh roh STOHM) an animal whose mouth does not derive from the blastopore and whose embryo has indeterminate cleavage (635)

deuteróstomo un animal cuya boca no se deriva del blastoporo y cuyo embrión presenta segmentación indeterminada (635)

diaphragm (DIE uh FRAM) a dome-shaped muscle that is attached to the lower ribs and that functions as the main muscle in respiration (786, 877)

diafragma un músculo en forma de cúpula que está unido a las costillas inferiores y que es el músculo principal de la respiración (786, 877)

dicot (DIE KAHT) a dicotyledonous plant; an angiosperm that has two cotyledons, net venation, and flower parts in groups of four or five (559, 585)

dicotiledónea una angiosperma con dos cotiledones, venación en forma de red y partes florales en grupos de cuatro o cinco (559, 585)

diffusion (di FYOO zhuhn) the movement of particles from regions of higher density to regions of lower density (178)

difusión el movimiento de partículas de regiones de mayor densidad a regiones de menor densidad (178)

digestion (die JES chuhn) the breaking down of food into chemical substances that can be used for energy (896)

digestión la descomposición de la comida en sustancias químicas que se usan para generar energía (896)

dihybrid cross (die HIE brid) a cross between individuals that have different alleles for the same gene (275)

cruza dihíbrida un cruzamiento entre individuos que tienen diferentes alelos para el mismo gene (275)

dikaryotic (die KAR ee AHT ik) describes a cell that has two haploid nuclei (526)

dicariótica término que describe a una célula que tiene dos núcleos haploides (526)

diploid (DIP LOYD) a cell that contains two haploid sets of chromosomes (249)

diploide una célula que contiene dos juegos de cromosomas haploides (249)

directional selection a natural selection process in which one genetic variation is selected and that causes a change in the overall genetic composition of the population (409)

selección direccional un proceso de selección natural en el cual se selecciona una variación genética que origina un cambio en la composición genética global de la población (409)

disaccharide (die SAK uh RIED) a sugar formed from two monosaccharides (60)

disacárido un azúcar formada a partir de dos monosacáridos (60)

disruptive selection a type of natural selection in which two extreme forms of a trait are selected (409)

selección disruptiva un tipo de selección natural en el cual se seleccionan dos formas extremas de un carácter (409)

distribution (DIS tri BYOO shuhn) the relative arrangement of the members of a statistical population; usually shown in a graph (400)

distribución la organización relativa de los miembros de una población estadística; normalmente se muestra en una gráfica (400)

DNA deoxyribonucleic acid, the material that contains the information that determines inherited characteristics (63, 293)

ADN ácido desoxirribonucleico, el material que contiene la información que determina las características que se heredan (63, 293)

DNA fingerprint a pattern of DNA characteristics that is unique, or nearly so, to an individual organism (347, 358)

huella de ADN un patrón de características del ADN que pertenece exclusivamente, o casi exclusivamente, a un organismo individual (347, 358)

DNA helicase (HEEL uh KAYS) an enzyme that unwinds the DNA double helix during DNA replication (301)

helicasa ADN una enzima que separa las hebras de la doble hélice del ADN durante la replicación del ADN (301)

DNA polymerase (puh LIM uhr AYS) an enzyme that catalyzes the formation of the DNA molecule (301)

polimerasa ADN una enzima que actúa como catalizadora en la formación de la molécula de ADN (301)

DNA polymorphisms (PAHL ee MAWR FIZ uhmz) variations in DNA sequences; can be used as a basis for comparing genomes (356)

polimorfismos de ADN variaciones en las secuencias de ADN; puede usarse como base para comparar genomas (356)

DNA replication (REP luh KAY shuhn) the process of making a copy of DNA (300)

replicación del ADN el proceso de hacer una copia del ADN (300)

DNA sequencing (SEE kwuhns ing) the process of determining the order of every nucleotide in a gene or genetic fragment; also referred to as *gene sequencing* (345, 359)

secuenciación de ADN el proceso de determinar el orden de cada nucleótido de un gen o un fragmento genético; también conocido como *secuenciación de genes* (345, 359)

domain in a taxonomic system based on rRNA analysis, one of the three broad groups that all living things fall into; in a protein, a functional unit that has a distinctive pattern of structural folding (329, 426)

dominio en el sistema taxonómico basado en el análisis de ARNr, uno de los tres amplios grupos al que pertenecen todos los seres vivos; en una proteína, una unidad funcional que tiene un patrón distintivo de plegamiento estructural (329, 426)

dominant (DAHM uh nuhnt) in genetics, describes an allele that is fully expressed whenever the allele is present in an individual (273)

dominante en la genética, término que describe a un alelo que se expresa por completo siempre que el alelo está presente en un individuo (273)

dormancy (DAWR muhn see) a state in which seeds, spores, bulbs, and other reproductive organs stop growth and development and reduce their metabolism, especially respiration (586, 609)

letargo un estado en el que las semillas, esporas, bulbos y otros órganos reproductores dejan de crecer y desarrollarse y reducen su metabolismo, sobre todo la respiración (586, 609)

double fertilization (FUHR'tl i ZAY shuhn) the process by which one of the two sperm nuclei fuses with the egg nucleus to produce a diploid zygote and the other fuses with the polar nuclei to produce a triploid endosperm (561)

fecundación doble el proceso por medio del cual uno de los dos núcleos de los espermatozoides se une con el núcleo del óvulo para producir un cigoto diploide, y el otro núcleo se une con el núcleo polar para producir un endosperma triploide (561)

double helix (HEE LIKS) the spiral-staircase structure characteristic of the DNA molecule (296)

doble hélice la estructura en forma de escalera en espiral característica de la molécula del ADN (296)

down feather a soft feather that covers the body of young birds and provides insulation to adult birds (768)

plumón una pluma suave que cubre el cuerpo de las crías de las aves y sirve como aislante en las aves adultas (768)

Down syndrome (SIN DROHM) a disorder caused by an extra 21st chromosome and characterized by a number of physical and mental abnormalities; also called *trisomy-21* (324)

síndrome de Down un trastorno producido por un cromosoma 21 adicional y caracterizado por una variedad de anormalidades físicas y mentales; también se llama *trisomía-21* (324)

echolocation (EK oh loh KAY shuhn) the process of using reflected sound waves to find objects; used by animals such as bats (790)

ecolocación el proceso de usar ondas de sonido reflejadas para buscar objetos; utilizado por animales tales como los murciélagos (790)

ecology (ee KAHL uh jee) the study of the interactions of living organisms with one another and with their environment (38)

ecología el estudio de las interacciones de los seres vivos entre sí mismos y entre sí mismos y su ambiente (38)

ecosystem (EE koh SIS tuhm) a community of organisms and their abiotic environment (79)

ecosistema una comunidad de organismos y su ambiente abiótico (79)

ecotourism (EK oh TUR IZ uhm) a form of tourism that supports the conservation and sustainable development of ecologically unique areas (137)

ecoturismo una forma de turismo que apoya la conservación y desarrollo sustentable de áreas ecológicamente únicas (137)

ectoparasite (EK toh PAR uh SIET) a parasite that lives on a host but does not enter the host's body (666)

ectoparásito un parásito que vive en un huésped, pero no entra al cuerpo del huésped (666)

ectothermic (EK toh THUHR mik) describes the ability of an organism to maintain its body temperature by gaining heat from the environment (759)

ectotérmico término que describe la capacidad de un organismo de mantener su temperatura corporal al obtener calor del ambiente (759)

ejaculation (ee JAK yoo LAY shuhn) the expulsion of seminal fluids from the urethra of the penis during sexual intercourse (995)

eyaculación la expulsión de fluidos seminales de la uretra del pene durante las relaciones sexuales (995)

electron (ee LEK TRAHN) a subatomic particle that has a negative charge (51)

electrón una partícula subatómica que tiene carga negativa (51)

electron cloud a region around the nucleus of an atom where electrons are likely to be found (51)

nube de electrones una región que rodea al núcleo de un átomo en la cual es probable encontrar a los electrones (51)

electron transport chain a series of molecules, found in the inner membranes of mitochondria and chloroplasts, through which electrons pass in a process that causes protons to build up on one side of the membrane (201)

cadena de transporte de electrones una serie de moléculas que se encuentran en las membranas internas de las mitocondrias y cloroplastos y a través de las cuales pasan los electrones en un proceso que hace que los protones se acumulen en un lado de la membrana (201)

electrophoresis (ee LEK troh fuh REE sis) the process by which electrically charged particles suspended in a liquid move through the liquid because of the influence of an electric field (356)

electroforesis el proceso por medio del cual las partículas con carga eléctrica que están suspendidas en un líquido se mueven por todo el líquido debido a la influencia de un campo eléctrico (356)

element a substance that cannot be separated or broken down into simpler substances by chemical means; all atoms of an element have the same atomic number (51)

elemento una sustancia que no se puede separar o descomponer en sustancias más simples por medio de métodos químicos; todos los átomos de un elemento tienen el mismo número atómico (51)

embryo (EM bree OH) in plants and animals, one of the early stages of development of an organism (555, 1001)

embrión en las plantas y los animales, un organismo en una de las primeras etapas del desarrollo (555, 1001)

embryology (EM bree AHL uh jee) the study of the development of an animal from the fertilized egg to the new adult organism; sometimes limited to the period between fertilization of the egg and hatching or birth (383)

embriología el estudio del desarrollo de un animal desde el óvulo fecundado hasta el nuevo organismo adulto; a veces se limita al período entre la fecundación del óvulo y la salida del cascarón o el nacimiento (383)

emigration (EM i GRAY shuhn) the movement of an individual or group out of its native area (104)

emigración la salida de un individuo o grupo de la región de la que es originario (104)

endocrine gland (EN doh KRIN) a ductless gland that secretes hormones into the blood (972)

glándula endocrina una glándula sin conductos que secreta hormonas a la sangre (972)

endocytosis (EN doh sie TOH sis) the process by which a cell membrane surrounds a particle and encloses the particle in a vesicle to bring the particle into the cell (183)

endocitosis el proceso por medio del cual la membrana celular rodea una partícula y la encierra en una vesícula para llevarla al interior de la célula (183)

endoparasite (EN doh PAR uh SIET) a parasite that lives inside a host's body (666)

endoparásito un parásito que vive dentro del cuerpo del huésped (666)

endoplasmic reticulum (EN doh PLAZ mik ri TIK yuh luhm) a system of membranes that is found in a cell's cytoplasm and that assists in the production, processing, and transport of proteins and in the production of lipids (158)

retículo endoplásmico un sistema de membranas que se encuentra en el citoplasma de la célula y que tiene una función en la producción, procesamiento y transporte de proteínas y en la producción de lípidos (158)

endoskeleton (EN doh SKEL uh tuhn) an internal skeleton made of bone and cartilage (627)

endoesqueleto un esqueleto interno hecho de hueso y cartílago (627)

endosperm (EN doh SPUHRM) a triploid ($3n$) tissue that develops in the seeds of angiosperms and that provides food for a developing embryo (555)

endosperma un tejido triploide ($3n$) que se desarrolla en las semillas de las angiospermas y que provee alimento para el embrión en desarrollo (555)

endospore (EN doh SPAWR) a thick-walled protective spore that forms inside a bacterial cell and resists harsh conditions (475)

endospora una espora protectiva que tiene una pared gruesa, se forma dentro de una célula bacteriana y resiste condiciones adversas (475)

endosymbiosis (EN doh SIM bie OH ses) a mutually beneficial relationship in which one organism lives within another (456)

endosimbiosis una relación mutuamente beneficiosa en la que un organismo vive dentro de otro (456)

endosymbiotic theory a theory that some cell organelles (mainly mitochondria and chloroplasts) are descended from prokaryotic cells that came to live within other cells during early evolutionary history (331)

teoría endosimbiótica una teoría según la cual los organelos celulares (principalmente las mitocondrias y los cloroplastos) descienden de células procarióticas que comenzaron a vivir dentro de otras células al comienzo de la historia evolutiva (331)

endotherm (EN duh THUHRM) an animal that can generate body heat through metabolism and can maintain a constant body temperature despite temperature changes in the animal's environment (786)

endotermo un animal que genera su propio calor corporal por medio del metabolismo y mantiene la temperatura de su cuerpo constante a pesar de que haya cambios de temperatura en el ambiente del animal (786)

endothermic (EN doh THUHR mik) describes the ability of a living thing to keep a constant body temperature by using the heat produced from metabolism (767)

endotérmico término que describe la capacidad de un ser vivo de mantener una temperatura corporal constante usando el calor producido por el metabolismo (767)

energy the capacity to do work (64)

energía la capacidad de realizar un trabajo (64)

energy pyramid a triangular diagram that shows an ecosystem's loss of energy, which results as energy passes through the ecosystem's food chain; each row in the pyramid represents a trophic (feeding) level in an ecosystem, and the area of a row represents the energy stored in that trophic level (89)

pirámide de energía un diagrama con forma de triángulo que muestra la pérdida de energía que ocurre en un ecosistema a medida que la energía pasa a través de la cadena alimenticia del ecosistema; cada hilera de la pirámide representa un nivel trófico (de alimentación) en el ecosistema, y el área de la hilera representa la energía almacenada en ese nivel trófico (89)

envelope a membranelike layer that covers the capsids of some viruses (477)

envoltura una capa similar a una membrana que cubre las cápsides de algunos virus (477)

environmental science (en VIE ruhn MENT'l) the study of the air, water, and land surrounding an organism or a community, which ranges from a small area to Earth's entire biosphere; it includes the study of the impact of humans on the environment (38, 125)

ciencias ambientales el estudio del aire, agua y tierra circundantes en relación con un organismo o comunidad, desde un área pequeña de la Tierra hasta la biosfera completa; incluye el estudio del impacto que los seres humanos tienen en el ambiente (38, 125)

enzyme (EN ziem) a molecule, either protein or RNA, that acts as a catalyst in biochemical reactions (66)

enzima una molécula, ya sea una proteína o ARN, que actúa como catalizador en las reacciones bioquímicas (66)

epidemiology (EP uh DEE mee AHL uh jee) the study of the distribution of diseases in populations and the study of factors that influence the occurrence and spread of disease (31)

epidemiología el estudio de la distribución de las enfermedades en poblaciones y el estudio de los factores que influyen en la incidencia y propagación de las enfermedades (31)

epidermis (EP uh DUHR mis) the outer surface layer of cells of a plant or animal (574, 658, 853)

epidermis la superficie externa de las células de una planta o animal (574, 658, 853)

epididymis (EP uh DID i mis) the long, coiled tube that is on the surface of a testis and in which sperm mature (994)

epidídimo el conducto largo y enrollado que se encuentra en la superficie de los testículos, en el que los espermatozoides maduran (994)

epinephrine (EP uh NEF rin) a hormone that is released by the adrenal medulla and that rapidly stimulates the metabolism in emergencies, decreases insulin secretion, and stimulates pulse and blood pressure; also called *adrenaline* (981)

epinefrina una hormona liberada por la médula suprarrenal que estimula el metabolismo rápidamente en casos de emergencia, disminuye la secreción de insulina y estimula el pulso y la presión sanguínea; también se llama *adrenalina* (981)

epithelial tissue (EP i THEE lee uhl TISH oo) tissue that covers a body surface or lines a body cavity (840)

tejido epitelial tejido que cubre una superficie corporal o recubre una cavidad corporal (840)

equilibrium (EE kwi LIB ree uhm) in biology, a state that exists when the concentration of a substance is the same throughout a space (178)

equilibrio en biología, un estado que existe cuando la concentración de una sustancia es la misma en un espacio dado (178)

era a unit of geologic time that includes two or more periods (453)

era una unidad de tiempo geológico que incluye dos o más períodos (453)

erosion (ee ROH zhuhn) a process in which the materials of Earth's surface are loosened, dissolved, or worn away and transported from one place to another by a natural agent, such as wind, water, ice, or gravity (131)

erosión un proceso por medio del cual los materiales de la superficie de la Tierra se aflojan, disuelven o desgastan y son transportados de un lugar a otro por un agente natural, como el viento, el agua, el hielo o la gravedad (131)

esophagus (i SAHF uh guhs) a long, straight tube that connects the pharynx to the stomach (897)

esófago un conducto largo y recto que conecta la faringe con el estómago (897)

estrogen (ES truh juhn) a hormone that regulates the sexual development and reproductive function of females (982)

estrógeno una hormona que regula el desarrollo sexual y la función reproductiva en las hembras (982)

estuary (ES tyoo er ee) an area where fresh water from rivers mixes with salt water from the ocean; the part of a river where the tides meet the river current (84)

estuario un área donde el agua dulce de los ríos se mezcla con el agua salada del océano; la parte de un río donde las mareas se encuentran con la corriente del río (84)

eukaryote (yoo KAR ee OHT) an organism made up of cells that have a nucleus enclosed by a membrane, multiple chromosomes, and a mitotic cycle; eukaryotes include protists, animals, plants, and fungi but not archaea or bacteria (155, 436)

eucariote un organismo cuyas células tienen un núcleo contenido en una membrana, varios cromosomas y un ciclo mitótico; entre los eucariotes se encuentran protistas, animales, plantas y hongos, pero no arqueas ni bacterias (155, 436)

evaporation (ee VAP uh RAY shuhn) the change of state from a liquid to a gas (90)

evaporación el cambio de estado de líquido a gas (90)

evolution (EV uh LOO shuhn) generally, in biology, the process of change by which new species develop from preexisting species over time; at the genetic level, the process in which inherited characteristics within populations change over time; the process defined by Darwin as "descent with modification" (19, 375)

evolución generalmente, en biología, el proceso de cambio por el cual se desarrollan nuevas especies a partir de especies preexistentes a lo largo del tiempo; a nivel genético, el proceso por el cual las características heredadas dentro de las poblaciones cambian con el tiempo; el proceso que Darwin llamó "descendencia con modificación" (19, 375)

excretion (eks KREE shuhn) the process of eliminating metabolic wastes (902)

excreción el proceso de eliminar desechos metabólicos (902)

exocrine gland (EKS oh KRIN) a gland that discharges its secretions through a duct (972)

glándula exocrina una glándula que descarga secreciones por medio de un conducto (972)

exocytosis (EK soh sie TOH sis) the process by which a substance is released from the cell through a vesicle that transports the substance to the cell surface and then fuses with the membrane to let the substance out (183)

exocitosis el proceso por medio del cual una sustancia se libera de la célula a través de una vesícula que la transporta a la superficie de la célula en donde se fusiona con la membrana para dejar salir a la sustancia (183)

exon (EK sahn) one of several nonadjacent nucleotide sequences that are part of one gene and that are transcribed, joined together, and then translated (329)

exón una de las varias secuencias de nucleótidos no adyacentes que forman parte de un gene y que se transcriben, se unen y luego se traducen (329)

exoskeleton (EKS oh SKEL uh tuhn) a hard, external, supporting structure that develops from the ectoderm (627, 702)
exoesqueleto una estructura de soporte, dura y externa, que se desarrolla a partir del ectodermo (627, 702)

experiment (ek SPER uh muhnt) a procedure that is carried out under controlled conditions to discover, demonstrate, or test a fact, theory, or general truth (11)
experimento un procedimiento que se lleva a cabo bajo condiciones controladas para descubrir, demostrar o probar un hecho, teoría o verdad general (11)

exponential growth (EKS poh NEN shuhl) logarithmic growth, or growth in which numbers increase by a certain factor in each successive time period (104, 379)
crecimiento exponencial crecimiento logarítmico o crecimiento en el que los números aumentan en función de un cierto factor en cada período de tiempo sucesivo (104, 379)

extensor (ek STEN suhr) a muscle that extends a joint (849)
extensor un músculo que extiende una articulación (849)

extinct (ek STINGKT) describes a species that has died out completely (389)
extinto término que describe a una especie que ha desaparecido por completo (389)

extinction (ek STINGK shuhn) the death of every member of a species (133, 389, 414)
extinción la muerte de todos los miembros de una especie (133, 389, 414)

eyespot an organ that is covered by pigment in some invertebrates and protozoans and that detects changes in the quantity and quality of light (504)
mancha ocular un órgano de algunos invertebrados y protozoarios que está cubierto por pigmentos y detecta cambios en la cantidad y calidad de la luz (504)

F₁ generation the first generation of offspring obtained from an experimental cross of two organisms (269)
generación F₁ la primera generación de descendencia que se obtiene de la cruza experimental de dos organismos (269)

F₂ generation the second generation of offspring, obtained from an experimental cross of two organisms; the offspring of the F₁ generation (269)
generación F₂ la segunda generación de descendencia que se obtiene de la cruza experimental de dos organismos de una generación F₁ (269)

facilitated diffusion (fuh SIL uh TAYT id di FYOO zhuhn) the transport of substances through a cell membrane along a concentration gradient with the aid of carrier proteins (179)
difusión facilitada el transporte de sustancias a través de la membrana celular de una región de mayor concentración a una de menor concentración con la ayuda de proteínas transportadoras (179)

fallopian tube (fuh LOH pee uhn) a tube through which eggs move from the ovary to the uterus (997)
trompa de Falopio un conducto a través del cual se mueven los óvulos del ovario al útero (997)

family the taxonomic category below the order and above the genus (426)
familia la categoría taxonómica debajo del orden y arriba del género (426)

fast-twitch fiber a muscle fiber that produces a large amount of force but that fatigues more quickly than a slow-twitch fiber (852)
fibra de contracción rápida una fibra muscular que produce una gran cantidad de fuerza pero que se fatiga más rápidamente que una célula de contracción lenta (852)

feedback mechanism (MEK uh NIZ uhm) a cycle of events in which information from one step controls or affects a previous step (977)
mecanismo de retroalimentación un ciclo de sucesos en el que la información de una etapa controla o afecta a una etapa anterior (977)

fermentation the breakdown of carbohydrates by enzymes, bacteria, yeasts, or mold in the absence of oxygen (212)
fermentación la descomposición de carbohidratos por enzimas, bacterias, levaduras o mohos, en ausencia de oxígeno (212)

fertilization (FUHR'tl i ZAY shuhn) the union of a male and female gamete to form a zygote (248, 554)
fecundación la unión de un gameto masculino y femenino para formar un cigoto (248, 554)

fibrous root system (FIE bruhs) a system of adventitious roots of approximately equal diameter that arise from the base of the stem of a plant (579)
sistema radicular fibroso una conjunto de raíces adventicias que tienen aproximadamente el mismo diámetro y que surgen de la base del tallo de la planta (579)

filter feeder an aquatic animal that traps food by filtering organic material from the surrounding water (624)
alimentador por filtración un animal acuático que atrapa alimento al filtrar materiales orgánicos del agua circundante (624)

fixed action pattern a highly stereotyped pattern of innate behavior that is triggered by a simple sensory cue (816)
patrón fijo de acción un patrón de conducta innata altamente estereotipado que es iniciado por un estímulo sensorial simple (816)

flagellum (fluh JEL uhm) a long, hairlike structure that grows out of a cell and enables the cell to move (162)

flagelo una estructura larga parecida a una cola, que crece hacia el exterior de una célula y le permite moverse (162)

flexor (FLEKS uhr) a muscle that bends a limb or other body part (849)

flexor un músculo que dobla una extremidad u otra parte del cuerpo (849)

flight feather a large, stiff feather that is on the wing or tail of a bird and that allows the bird to fly (768)

pluma de vuelo una pluma rígida y larga ubicada en el ala o cola de un ave, que le permite volar (768)

flower the reproductive structure of a flowering plant that usually consists of a pistil, stamens, petals, and sepals (560)

flor la estructura reproductiva de una planta que da flores, que normalmente consiste en un pistilo, estambres, pétalos y sépalos (560)

fluke (FLOOK) a parasitic flatworm of the class Trematoda (666)

trematodo un gusano plano parasítico de la clase Trematoda (666)

follicle (FAHL i kuhl) a small, narrow cavity or sac in an organ or tissue, such as the ones on the skin that contain hair roots or the ones in the ovaries that contain the developing eggs (999)

folículo una bolsa o cavidad angosta y pequeña en un órgano o tejido, como las que se encuentran en la piel y contienen las raíces de los pelos, o las que se encuentran en los ovarios y contienen los óvulos en desarrollo (999)

food chain the pathway of energy transfer through various stages as a result of the feeding patterns of a series of organisms (87)

cadena alimenticia la vía de transferencia de energía través de varias etapas, que ocurre como resultado de los patrones de alimentación de una serie de organismos (87)

food web a diagram that shows the feeding relationships between organisms in an ecosystem (87)

red alimenticia un diagrama que muestra las relaciones de alimentación entre los organismos de un ecosistema (87)

foot an appendage that some invertebrates use to move; the lower part of a vertebrate's leg (680)

pie un apéndice que algunos invertebrados usan para moverse; la parte inferior de la pierna de un vertebrado (680)

foraging (FAWR ij ing) behavior associated with seeking, obtaining, and consuming food (821)

búsqueda de alimentos conducta que se asocia con buscar, obtener y consumir alimento (821)

forensic science (fuh REN sik) the application of scientific knowledge to questions of civil and criminal law (1017)

ciencias forenses la aplicación del conocimiento científico a cuestiones de derecho civil y penal (1017)

fossil (FAHS uhl) the trace or remains of an organism that lived long ago, most commonly preserved in sedimentary rock (382)

fósil los indicios o los restos de un organismo que vivió hace mucho tiempo, comúnmente preservados en las rocas sedimentarias (382)

fossil fuel a nonrenewable energy resource formed from the remains of organisms that lived long ago; examples include oil, coal, and natural gas (126)

combustible fósil un recurso energético no renovable formado a partir de los restos de organismos que vivieron hace mucho tiempo; algunos ejemplos incluyen el petróleo, el carbón y el gas natural (126)

fossil record the history of life in the geologic past as indicated by the traces or remains of living things (382, 450)

registro fósil la historia de la vida en el pasado geológico según la indican los rastros o restos de seres vivos (382, 450)

frameshift mutation a mutation, such as the insertion or deletion of a nucleotide in a coding sequence, that results in the misreading of the code during translation because of a change in the reading frame (320)

mutación de desplazamiento del marco una mutación, tal como la inserción o supresión de un nucleoide en una secuencia de codificación, que tiene como resultado una lectura equivocada del código durante la traducción debido a un cambio en el marco de lectura (320)

frequency (FREE kwuhn see) the number of cycles or vibrations per unit of time; *also* the number of waves produced in a given amount of time (401)

frecuencia el número de ciclos o vibraciones por unidad de tiempo; *también,* el número de ondas producidas en una cantidad de tiempo determinada (401)

frond (FRAHND) the leaf of a fern or palm (550)

fronda la hoja de un helecho o palma (550)

fruit a mature plant ovary; the plant organ in which the seeds are enclosed (563)

fruta un ovario maduro de planta; el órgano de una planta donde se encuentran contenidas las semillas (563)

fundamental niche (FUHN duh MENT'l NICH) the largest ecological niche where an organism or species can live without competition (113)

nicho fundamental el nicho ecológico más grande en el que un organismo o especie vive sin experimentar competencia (113)

gamete (GAM eet) a haploid reproductive cell that unites with another haploid reproductive cell to form a zygote (248, 498)

gameto una célula reproductiva haploide que se une con otra célula reproductiva haploide para formar un cigoto (248, 498)

gametophyte (guh MEET uh FIET) in alternation of generations, the phase in which gametes are formed; a haploid individual that produces gametes (258, 499, 546)

gametofito en generaciones alternadas, la fase en la que los gametos se forman; un individuo haploide que produce gametos (258, 499, 546)

ganglion (GANG glee uhn) a mass of nerve cells (629)

ganglio una masa de células nerviosas (629)

gastrodermis (GAS troh DUHR mis) in cnidarians, the layer of cells surrounding the digestive tract (658)

gastrodermis en los cnidarios, la capa de células que rodea el tracto digestivo (658)

gastrovascular cavity (GAS troh VAS kyoo luhr) a cavity that serves both digestive and circulatory purposes in some cnidarians (628)

cavidad gastrovascular una cavidad que tiene funciones digestivas y circulatorias en algunos cnidarios (628)

gastrula (GAS troo luh) the embryo in the stage of development after the blastula; contains the embryonic germ layers (634)

gástrula el embrión en la etapa de desarrollo que sigue después de la bástula; contiene las capas germinales embrionarias (634)

gastrulation (GAS troo LAY shuhn) the transformation of the blastula into the gastrula or the formation of the embryonic germ layers (634)

gastrulación la transformación de la bástula en la gástrula o la formación de las capas germinales embrionarias (634)

gene (JEEN) the most basic physical unit of heredity; a segment of nucleic acids that codes for a functional unit of RNA and/or a protein (224, 293)

gene la unidad física más básica de la herencia; un segmento de ácidos nucleicos que codifica una unidad funcional de ARN y/o una proteína (224, 293)

gene expression (eks PRESH uhn) the manifestation of the genetic material of an organism in the form of specific traits (304)

expresión de los genes la manifestación del material genético de un organismo en forma de caracteres específicos (304)

gene flow the movement of genes into or out of a population due to interbreeding (405)

flujo de genes el movimiento de genes a una población o fuera de ella debido al entrecruzamiento (405)

gene pool the total set of genes, including all alleles, that are present in a population at any one point in time (401)

fondo común de genes el conjunto total de genes, incluyendo todos los alelos, que están presentes en una población en un momento determinado (401)

generation (JEN uhr AY shuhn) the entire group of offspring produced by a given group of parents (269)

generación el grupo completo de descendientes producido por un grupo determinado de progenitores (269)

gene technology any of a wide range of procedures that analyze, decipher, or manipulate the genetic material of organisms (350)

tecnología genética cualquiera de una gran variedad de procedimientos para analizar, descifrar o manipular el material genético de los organismos (350)

gene therapy a technique that places a gene into a cell to correct a hereditary disease or to improve the genome (347)

terapia genética una técnica que coloca un gene en una célula para corregir una enfermedad hereditaria o para mejorar el genoma (347)

genetically modified organism an organism containing genetic material that has been artificially altered so as to produce a desired characteristic (abbreviation, GMO) (350)

organismo modificado genéticamente un organismo que contiene material genético que ha sido alterado en forma artificial para producir una característica deseada (abreviatura: OMG) (350)

genetic code the rule that describes how a sequence of nucleotides, read in groups of three consecutive nucleotides (triplets) that correspond to specific amino acids, specifies the amino acid sequence of a protein (63, 307)

código genético la regla que describe la forma en que una secuencia de nucleótidos, leídos en grupos de tres nucleótidos consecutivos (triplete) que corresponden a aminoácidos específicos, especifica la secuencia de aminoácidos de una proteína (63, 307)

genetic counseling the process of testing and informing potential parents about their genetic makeup and the likelihood that they will have offspring with genetic defects or hereditary diseases (346)

orientación genética el proceso de hacer pruebas e informar a una pareja de padres potenciales acerca de su constitución genética y acerca de la posibilidad de que tengan hijos con defectos genéticos o enfermedades hereditarias (346)

genetic disorder an inherited disease or disorder that is caused by a mutation in a gene or by a chromosomal defect (280, 323)

trastorno genético una enfermedad o trastorno hereditario que es causado por una mutación en un gene o por un defecto cromosómico (280, 323)

genetic drift the random change in allele frequency in a population (405)

desviación genética el cambio aleatorio en la frecuencia de los alelos de una población (405)

genetic engineering a technology in which the genome of a living cell is modified for medical or industrial use (33, 346, 350)

ingeniería genética una tecnología en la que el genoma de una célula viva se modifica con fines médicos o industriales (33, 346, 350)

genetic equilibrium (EE kwi LIB ree uhm) a state in which the allele frequencies of a population remain in the same ratios from one generation to the next (404)

equilibrio genético un estado en el que las frecuencias de los alelos de una población permanecen en la misma proporción de generación en generación (404)

genetic library a collection of genetic sequence clones that represent all of the genes in a given genome (363)

biblioteca genética un grupo de clones de secuencia genética que representan a todos los genes de un genoma determinado (363)

genetic marker a gene whose phenotype is easily identified (362)

marcador genético un gene cuyo fenotipo se identifica fácilmente (362)

genetics (juh NET iks) the science of heredity and of the mechanisms by which traits are passed from parents to offspring (31)

genética la ciencia de la herencia y de los mecanismos por los cuales los caracteres son transmitidos de padres a hijos (31)

genital herpes (JEN i tuhl HUHR PEEZ) a sexually transmitted infection that is caused by a herpes simplex virus (1006)

herpes genital una infección de transmisión sexual causada por el virus herpes simplex (1006)

genome (JEE NOHM) the complete genetic material contained in an individual or species (31, 330)

genoma el material genético completo contenido en un individuo o especie (31, 330)

genome mapping the process of determining the relative position of genes in a genome (362)

mapeo genómico el proceso de determinar la posición relativa de los genes en un genoma (362)

genomics (juh NOH miks) the study of entire genomes, especially by using technology to compare genes within and between species (345)

genómica el estudio de genomas completos, en especial mediante el uso de tecnología para comparar genes dentro de las especies y entre ellas (345)

genotype (JEE nuh TIEP) the entire genetic makeup of an organism; *also* the combination of genes for one or more specific traits (274, 400)

genotipo la constitución genética completa de un organismo; *también,* la combinación de genes para uno o más caracteres específicos (274, 400)

genus (JEE nuhs) the level of classification that comes after family and that contains similar species (424)

género el nivel de clasificación que viene después de la familia y que contiene especies similares (424)

geologic time scale the standard method used to divide Earth's long natural history into manageable parts (453)

escala de tiempo geológico el método estándar que se usa para dividir la larga historia natural de la Tierra en partes razonables (453)

geology (jee AHL uh jee) the scientific study of the origin, history, and structure of Earth and the processes that shape Earth (379)

geología el estudio científico del origen, la historia y la estructura del planeta Tierra y los procesos que le dan forma (379)

germ cell in a multicellular organism, any reproductive cell (as opposed to a somatic cell) (248, 322, 403)

célula germinal en un organismo pluricelular, cualquier célula reproductiva (en contraposición a una célula somática) (248, 322, 403)

germination (JUHR mi NAY shuhn) the beginning of growth or development in a seed, spore, or zygote, especially after a period of inactivity (586)

germinación el comienzo del crecimiento o desarrollo de una semilla, espora o cigoto, sobre todo después de un período de inactividad (586)

gestation (jes TAY shuhn) in mammals, the process of carrying young from fertilization to birth (1002)

gestación en los mamíferos, el proceso de llevar a las crías de la fecundación al nacimiento (1002)

gestation period in mammals, the length of time between fertilization and birth (788)

período de gestación en los mamíferos, el tiempo que transcurre entre la fecundación y el nacimiento (788)

gill in aquatic animals, a respiratory structure that consists of many blood vessels surrounded by a membrane that allows for gas exchange (630, 731)

branquiaen los animales acuáticos, una estructura respiratoria que está formada por muchos vasos sanguíneos rodeados por una membrana que permite el intercambio gaseoso (630, 731)

gill slit a perforation between two gill arches through which water taken in through the mouth of a fish passes over the gills and out of the fish's body (731)

apertura branquial una perforación entre dos arcos branquiales a través de la cual el agua que un pez toma por la boca pasa sobre las branquias y hacia el exterior del cuerpo del pez (731)

gizzard (GIZ uhrd) an enlargement of the digestive tract of some invertebrates, such as annelids and insects, that grinds food; a muscular region in the digestive tract of birds that grinds and softens food (688)

molleja un alargamiento del tracto digestivo de algunos invertebrados, tales como los anélidos y los insectos, que muele la comida; una región muscular del tracto digestivo de las aves que muele y suaviza la comida (688)

global warming a gradual increase in average global temperature (128)

calentamiento global un aumento gradual de la temperatura global promedio (128)

glomerulus (gloh MER yoo luhs) a cluster of capillaries that is enclosed in a Bowman's capsule in a nephron of the kidney, where blood is filtered (903)

glomérulo un aglomerado de capilares contenidos en una cápsula de Bowman en el riñón, en los cuales se filtra la sangre (903)

glucagon (GLOO kuh GAHN) a hormone that is produced in the pancreas and that raises the blood-glucose level (980)

glucagón una hormona producida en el páncreas que aumenta el nivel de glucosa en la sangre (980)

glycolysis (glie KAHL i sis) the anaerobic breakdown of glucose to pyruvic acid, which makes a small amount of energy available to cells in the form of ATP (209)

glicólisis la descomposición anaeróbica de glucosa en ácido pirúvico, la cual hace que una pequeña cantidad de energía en forma de ATP esté disponible para las células (209)

glycoprotein (GLIE koh PROH TEEN) a protein to which carbohydrate molecules are attached (177, 477)

glicoproteína una proteína que tienen unidas moléculas de carbohidratos (177, 477)

Golgi apparatus (GOHL jee AP uh RAT uhs) a cell organelle that helps make and package materials to be transported out of the cell (158)

aparato de Golgi un organelo celular que ayuda a hacer y a empacar los materiales que serán transportados al exterior de la célula (158)

gradualism (GRA joo uhl IZ uhm) a model of evolution in which gradual change over a long period of time leads to biological diversity (389)

gradualismo un modelo de evolución en el que un cambio gradual a través de un largo período de tiempo conlleva a la diversidad biológica (389)

Gram-negative describes a type of prokaryote (eubacteria) that has a small amount of peptidoglycan in its cell wall, has an outer membrane, and is stained pink by a counterstain during Gram staining (472)

Gram negativa término que describe un tipo de procariote (eubacteria) que tiene una cantidad pequeña de péptidoglicano en su pared celular, que tiene una membrana externa y que es teñida de rosado por una contratinción durante la tinción de Gram (472)

Gram-positive describes a type of prokaryote (eubacterium) that has a large amount of peptidoglycan in its cell wall and is stained violet during Gram staining (472)

Gram positiva término que describe un tipo de procariote (eubacteria) que tiene una gran cantidad de péptidoglicano en su pared celular y que se tiñe de violeta durante la tinción de Gram (472)

Gram stain a series of dyes used to classify bacteria; depending on the chemistry of the bacterial cell wall, bacteria will either retain or lose the stain (472)

tinción de Gram una serie de colorantes que se usan para clasificar las bacterias; dependiendo de la composición química de la pared celular de las bacterias, éstas conservarán o perderán la tinción (472)

gravitropism (GRAV i TROH PIZ uhm) the growth of a plant in a particular direction in response to gravity (607)

gravitropismo el crecimiento de una planta en una determinada dirección como respuesta a la gravedad (607)

greenhouse effect the warming of the surface and lower atmosphere of Earth that occurs when carbon dioxide, water vapor, and other gases in the air absorb and reradiate infrared radiation (129)

efecto invernadero el calentamiento de la superficie terrestre y de la parte más baja de la atmósfera, el cual se produce cuando el dióxido de carbono, el vapor de agua y otros gases del aire absorben radiación infrarroja y la vuelven a irradiar (129)

ground tissue a type of plant tissue other than vascular tissue that makes up much of the inside of a plant (573)

tejido basal un tipo de tejido vegetal diferente del tejido vascular y que constituye gran parte del interior de una planta (573)

guanine (GWAH NEEN) one of the four bases that combine with sugar and phosphate to form a nucleotide subunit of DNA; guanine pairs with cytosine (297)

guanina una de las cuatro bases que se combinan con el azúcar y fosfato para formar una subunidad de nucleótidos del ADN; la guanina se une con la citosina (297)

guard cell one of a pair of specialized cells that border a stoma and regulate gas exchange (575)

célula oclusiva una de las dos células especializadas que se encuentran al borde de un estoma y regulan el intercambio gaseoso (575)

gymnosperm (JIM noh SPUHRM) a woody, vascular seed plant whose seeds are not enclosed by an ovary or fruit (553)
gimnosperma una planta leñosa vascular que produce semillas que no están contenidas en un ovario o fruto (553)

habitat the place where an organism usually lives (80, 112)
hábitat el lugar donde un organismo vive normalmente (80, 112)

half-life the time required for half of a sample of a radioactive isotope to break down by radioactive decay to form a daughter isotope (452)
vida media el tiempo que se requiere para que la mitad de una muestra de un isótopo radiactivo se descomponga por desintegración radiactiva y forme un isótopo hijo (452)

haploid (HAP LOYD) describes a cell, nucleus, or organism that has only one set of unpaired chromosomes (249)
haploide término que describe a una célula, núcleo u organismo que tiene sólo un juego de cromosomas que no están asociados en pares (249)

Hardy-Weinberg principle (HAHR dee WIEN BUHRG) the principle that states that the frequency of alleles in a population does not change unless evolutionary forces act on the population (405)
principio de Hardy-Weinberg el principio que establece que la frecuencia de alelos en una población no cambia a menos que fuerzas evolutivas actúen en la población (405)

Haversian canal (huh VUHR zhuhn) a channel containing blood vessels in compact bone tissue (845)
canal haversiano un canal que contiene vasos sanguíneos en los huesos compactos (845)

heart attack the death of heart tissues due to a blockage of their blood supply (873)
ataque cardíaco la muerte de los tejidos del corazón debido a una obstrucción de su suministro sanguíneo (873)

heartwood the nonconducting older wood in the center of a tree trunk (581)
madera de corazón la madera más vieja y que no conduce la electricidad, que se encuentra en el centro de un tronco de árbol (581)

helper T cell a white blood cell necessary for B cells to develop normal levels of antibodies (919)
célula T auxiliar un glóbulo blanco de la sangre necesario para que las células B desarrollen niveles normales de un anticuerpo (919)

herbaceous plant (huhr BAY shuhs) a plant that is soft and green instead of woody (580)
planta herbácea una planta que es suave y verde, en vez de leñosa (580)

herbivore (HUHR buh VAWR) an organism that eats only plants (87)
herbívoro un organismo que sólo come plantas (87)

heredity (huh RED i tee) the passing of genetic traits from parent to offspring (19)
herencia la transmisión de caracteres genéticos de padres a hijos (19)

heterotroph (HET uh uh TROHF) an organism that obtains organic food molecules by eating other organisms or their byproducts and that cannot synthesize organic compounds from inorganic materials (434, 474, 624)
heterótrofo un organismo que obtiene moléculas de alimento al comer otros organismos o sus productos secundarios y que no puede sintetizar compuestos orgánicos a partir de materiales inorgánicos (434, 474, 624)

heterozygous (HET uhr OH ZIE guhs) describes an individual that carries two different alleles of a gene (275)
heterocigoto término que describe un individuo que tiene dos alelos diferentes para un gene (275)

histamine (HIS tuh MEEN) a chemical that stimulates the autonomous nervous system, secretion of gastric juices, and dilation of capillaries (916)
histamina una sustancia química que estimula el sistema nervioso autónomo, la secreción de jugos gástricos y la dilatación de capilares (916)

histone (HIS TOHN) a type of protein molecule found in the chromosomes of eukaryotic cells but not prokaryotic cells (224, 302)
histona un tipo de molécula de proteína que se encuentra en los cromosomas de las células eucarióticas, pero nunca en las procarióticas (224, 302)

HIV human immunodeficiency virus, the virus that causes AIDS (929)
VIH virus de inmunodeficiencia humana; el virus que causa el SIDA (929)

holdfast the part of an alga that anchors the alga to a substrate (505)
prensa la parte de un alga que se sostiene de un sustrato (505)

homeobox (HOH mee uh BAHKS) a DNA sequence within a homeotic gene that regulates development in animals (333)
homeocaja una secuencia de ADN dentro de un gene homeótico que regula los patrones de desarrollo en los animales (333)

homeostasis (HOH mee OH STAY sis) the maintenance of a constant internal state in a changing environment; a constant internal state that is maintained in a changing environment by continually making adjustments to the internal and external environment (19)
homeostasis la capacidad de mantener un estado interno constante en un ambiente en cambio; un estado interno constante que se mantiene en un ambiente en cambio al hacer ajustes continuos al ambiente interno y externo (19)

homeotic gene (HOH mee AHD ik) a gene that controls the development of a specific adult structure (333)

gene homeótico un gene que controla el desarrollo de una estructura específica de la etapa adulta (333)

hominid (HAHM uh nid) a member of the family Hominidae of the order Primates; characterized by bipedalism, relatively long lower limbs, and lack of a tail; examples include humans and their ancestors (799)

homínido un miembro de la familia Hominidae del orden de los primates; caracterizado por ser bípedo, tener extremidades inferiores relativamente largas y no tener cola; incluye a los seres humanos y sus ancestros (799)

homologous (hoh MAHL uh guhs) describes a character that is shared by a group of species because it is inherited from a common ancestor (384)

homólogo término que describe un carácter compartido por un grupo de especies porque es heredado de un ancestro en común (384)

homologous chromosomes chromosomes that have the same sequence of genes, that have the same structure, and that pair during meiosis (249)

cromosomas homólogos cromosomas con la misma secuencia de genes, que tienen la misma estructura y que se acoplan durante la meiosis (249)

homozygous (HOH moh ZIE guhs) describes an individual that has identical alleles for a trait on both homologous chromosomes (274)

homocigoto término que describe a un individuo que tiene alelos idénticos para un carácter en los dos cromosomas homólogos (274)

hormone (HAWR MOHN) a substance that is made in one cell or tissue and that causes a change in another cell or tissue located in a different part of the body (603, 971)

hormona una sustancia que es producida en una célula o tejido, la cual causa un cambio en otra célula o tejido ubicado en una parte diferente del cuerpo (603, 971)

host an organism from which a parasite takes food or shelter (110)

huésped el organismo del cual un parásito obtiene alimento y refugio (110)

Human Genome Project a research effort to sequence and locate the entire collection of genes in human cells (345)

Proyecto del Genoma Humano un esfuerzo de investigación para determinar la secuencia y ubicación de todo el conjunto de genes de las células humanas (345)

hybrid (HIE brid) in biology, the offspring of a cross between parents that have differing traits; a cross between individuals of different species, subspecies, or varieties (268, 413)

híbrido en biología, la descendencia de una cruza entre padres que tienen características diferentes; una cruza entre individuos de especies, subespecies o variedades diferentes (268, 413)

hydrogen bond (HIE druh juhn) the intermolecular force occurring when a hydrogen atom that is bonded to a highly electronegative atom of one molecule is attracted to two unshared electrons of another molecule (54)

enlace de hidrógeno la fuerza intermolecular producida por un átomo de hidrógeno que está unido a un átomo muy electronegativo de una molécula y que experimenta atracción a dos electrones no compartidos de otra molécula (54)

hydrostatic skeleton (HIE droh STAT ik) in many invertebrates, the cavity that is filled with water and that has a support function (627)

esqueleto hidrostático la cavidad llena de agua de muchos invertebrados que tiene una función de sostén (627)

hyperthyroidism (HIE puhr THIE royd iz uhm) a condition caused by an overproduction of thyroid hormones and marked by nervousness, sleep disorders, irregular heart rate, and weight loss (980)

hipertiroidismo una enfermedad causada por la superproducción de hormonas tiroideas y caracterizada por nerviosismo, trastornos del sueño, frecuencia cardíaca irregular y pérdida de peso (980)

hypertonic (HIE puhr TAHN ik) describes a solution whose solute concentration is higher than the solute concentration inside a cell (180)

hipertónico término que describe una solución cuya concentración de soluto es más alta que la concentración del soluto en el interior de la célula (180)

hypha (HIE fuh) a nonreproductive filament of a fungus (522)

hifa un filamento no-reproductor de un hongo (522)

hypothalamus (HIE poh THAL uh muhs) the region of the brain that coordinates the activities of the nervous and endocrine systems and that controls many body activities related to homeostasis (940)

hipotálamo la región del cerebro que coordina las actividades de los sistemas nervioso y endocrino y que controla muchas actividades del cuerpo relacionadas con la homeostasis (940)

hypothesis (hie PAHTH uh sis) a testable idea or explanation that leads to scientific investigation (10)

hipótesis una idea o explicación que conlleva a la investigación científica y que se puede probar (10)

hypothyroidism (HIE poh THIE royd iz uhm) a condition caused by a deficiency of thyroid hormones and marked by fatigue, weight gain, and sensitivity to cold (980)

hipotiroidismo una condición causada por una deficiencia de las hormonas tiroideas y marcada por fatiga, aumento de peso y sensibilidad al frío (980)

hypotonic (HIE poh TAHN ik) describes a solution whose solute concentration is lower than the solute concentration inside a cell (180)
hipotónico término que describe una solución cuya concentración de soluto es más baja que la concentración del soluto en el interior de la célula (180)

immigration (IM uh GRAY shuhn) the movement of an individual or a group to a new community or region (104)
inmigración la llegada de un individuo o grupo a una nueva comunidad o región (104)

immunity (im MYOON i tee) the ability to resist or recover from an infectious disease (922)
inmunidad la capacidad de resistir una enfermedad infecciosa o recuperarse de ella (922)

implantation (IM plan TAY shuhn) the process by which a blastocyst embeds itself in the lining of the uterus; occurs about six days after fertilization (1001)
implantación el proceso por medio del cual la blastoquistela se incrusta en la cubierta interior del útero; ocurre unos seis días después de la fecundación (1001)

imprinting (im PRINT ing) learning that occurs early and quickly in a young animal's life and that cannot be changed once learned (819)
impresión aprendizaje que ocurre rápidamente al inicio de la vida de un animal joven y que una vez que se aprende no se puede cambiar (819)

inbreeding (IN BREED ing) the crossing or mating of plants or animals with close relatives (406)
endogamia el cruzamiento de plantas o animales con parientes cercanos (406)

incomplete dominance a condition in which a trait in an individual is intermediate between the phenotype of the individual's two parents because the dominant allele is unable to express itself fully (282)
dominancia incompleta una condición en la que un carácter de un individuo es intermedio entre el fenotipo de los dos padres del individuo porque el alelo dominante no puede expresarse por completo (282)

independent assortment the random distribution of the pairs of genes on different chromosomes to the gametes (253)
distribución independiente la distribución al azar de pares de genes de diferentes cromosomas a los gametos (253)

index fossil a fossil that is used to establish the age of a rock layer because the fossil is distinct, abundant, and widespread and the species that formed that fossil existed for only a short span of geologic time (451)
fósil guía un fósil que se usa para establecer la edad de una capa de roca debido a que puede diferenciarse bien de otros, es abundante y está extendido; la especie que formó ese fósil existió sólo por un corto período de tiempo geológico (451)

inflammation (IN fluh MAY shuhn) a protective response of tissues affected by disease or injury; characterized by pain, swelling, redness, and heat (916)
inflamación una reacción de protección de los tejidos afectados por una enfermedad o lesión (916)

innate behavior (in NAYT) an inherited behavior that does not depend on the environment or experience (816)
conducta innata una conducta heredada que no depende del ambiente ni de la experiencia (816)

insertion (in SUHR shuhn) the point at which a muscle is attached to a bone (849)
inserción el punto en el que un músculo está unido al hueso (849)

insulin (IN se lin) a hormone that is produced by a group of specialized cells in the pancreas and that lowers blood-glucose levels (980)
insulina una hormona que es producida por un grupo de células especializadas en el páncreas y que reduce los niveles de glucosa en la sangre (980)

internode (IN tuhr NOHD) the part of a plant stem between two consecutive nodes (580)
internodo la parte del tallo de una planta que está entre dos nodos consecutivos (580)

interphase (IN tuhr FAYZ) the period of the cell cycle during which activities such as cell growth and protein synthesis occur without visible signs of cell division (228)
interfase el período del ciclo celular durante el cual las actividades como el crecimiento celular y la síntesis de proteínas existen sin signos visibles de división celular (228)

intron (IN trahn) a nucleotide sequence that is part of a gene and that is transcribed from DNA into mRNA but not translated into amino acids (328)
intrón una secuencia de nucleótidos que es parte de un gene y que se transcribe del ADN al ARNm pero no se traduce en aminoácidos (328)

invertebrate (in VUHR tuh brit) an animal that does not have a backbone (625)
invertebrado un animal que no tiene columna vertebral (625)

involuntary muscle (in VAHL uhn TER ee) a muscle whose movement cannot be controlled voluntarily, such as the cardiac muscle (848)
músculo involuntario un músculo cuyo movimiento no se puede controlar voluntariamente, como el músculo cardíaco (848)

ion (IE AHN) an atom, radical, or molecule that has gained or lost one or more electrons and has a negative or positive charge (53)
ion un átomo, radical o molécula que ha ganado o perdido uno o más electrones y que tiene una carga negativa o positiva (53)

ionic bond (ie AHN ik) the attractive force between oppositely charged ions, which form when electrons are transferred from one atom to another (53)

enlace iónico la fuerza de atracción entre iones con cargas opuestas, que se forman cuando se transfieren electrones de un átomo a otro (53)

islets of Langerhans (IE lits UHV LAHNG uhr HAHNS) the masses of cells in the pancreas that produce insulin, glucagon, and somatostatin (980)

islotes de Langerhans las masas de células del páncreas que producen insulina, glucagón y somatostatina (980)

isotonic solution (IE soh TAHN ik) a solution whose solute concentration is equal to the solute concentration inside a cell (180)

solución isotónica una solución cuya concentración de soluto es igual a la concentración de soluto en el interior de la célula (180)

isotope (IE suh TOHP) an atom that has the same number of protons (or the same atomic number) as other atoms of the same element do but that has a different number of neutrons (and thus a different atomic mass) (51, 452)

isótopo un átomo que tiene el mismo número de protones (o el mismo número atómico) que otros átomos del mismo elemento, pero que tiene un número diferente de neutrones (y, por lo tanto, otra masa atómica) (51, 452)

Jacobson's organ (JAY kuhb suhnz) an olfactory sac that opens into the mouth and is highly developed in reptiles (759)

órgano de Jacobson una bolsa olfatoria que se abre hacia la boca y que está muy desarrollada en los reptiles (759)

keratin (KER uh tin) a hard protein that forms hair, bird feathers, nails, and horns (854)

queratina una proteína dura que forma el cabello, las plumas de las aves, las uñas y los cuernos (854)

keystone species a species that is critical to the functioning of the ecosystem in which it lives because it affects the survival and abundance of many other species in its community (114)

especie clave una especie que es crítica para el funcionamiento del ecosistema en el que vive porque afecta la supervivencia y abundancia de muchas otras especies en su comunidad (114)

kidney one of the organs that filter water and wastes from the blood, excrete products as urine, and regulate the concentration of certain substances in the blood (732)

riñón uno de los órganos que filtran el agua y los desechos de la sangre, excretan productos como orina y regulan la concentración de ciertas sustancias en la sangre (732)

kingdom the highest taxonomic category, which contains a group of similar phyla (426)

reino la categoría taxonómica más alta, que contiene un grupo de phyla similares (426)

Koch's postulates (KOHKS PAHS chuh lits) a four-stage procedure that Robert Koch formulated for identifying specific pathogens and determining the cause of a given disease (482)

postulados de Koch un procedimiento de cuatro etapas que formuló Robert Koch para identificar patógenos específicos y para determinar la causa de una determinada enfermedad (482)

Krebs cycle a series of biochemical reactions that convert pyruvic acid into carbon dioxide and water; it is the major pathway of oxidation in animal, bacterial, and plant cells, and it releases energy (210)

ciclo de Krebs una serie de reacciones bioquímicas que convierten el ácido pirúvico en dióxido de carbono y agua; es la vía principal de oxidación en las células animales, bacterianas y vegetales, y libera energía (210)

labia (LAY bee uh) liplike structures, usually referring to fleshy folds located on a female's pubis and at the opening of the vagina (997)

labia estructuras parecidas a labios, que normalmente se refieren a los pliegues carnosos que se encuentran en el pubis de una hembra a la entrada de la vagina (997)

lactic acid fermentation (FUHR muhn TAY shuhn) the chemical breakdown of carbohydrates that produces lactic acid as the main end product (212)

fermentación del ácido láctico la descomposición química de los carbohidratos que produce ácido láctico como producto final principal (212)

larynx (LAR ingks) the area of the throat that contains the vocal cords and produces vocal sounds (876)

laringe el área de la garganta que contiene las cuerdas vocales y que produce sonidos vocales (876)

lateral line a faint line visible on both sides of a fish's body that runs the length of the body and marks the location of sense organs that detect vibrations in water (730)

línea lateral una línea apenas visible que se encuentra a ambos lados del cuerpo de un pez y que recorre la longitud del cuerpo, marcando la ubicación de los órganos de los sentidos que detectan vibraciones en el agua (730)

lateral meristem (MER uh STEM) dividing tissue that runs parallel to the long axis of a stem or a root (589)
meristemo lateral tejido de división que se encuentra paralelo al eje largo de un tallo o raíz (589)

law of conservation of energy the law that states that energy cannot be created or destroyed but can be changed from one form to another (64)
ley de la conservación de la energía la ley que establece que la energía ni se crea ni se destruye, sólo se transforma de una forma a otra (64)

law of conservation of mass the law that states that mass cannot be created or destroyed in ordinary chemical and physical changes (64)
ley de la conservación de la masa la ley que establece que la masa no se crea ni se destruye por cambios químicos o físicos comunes (64)

law of independent assortment the law that states that genes separate independently of one another in meiosis (284)
ley de la distribución independiente la ley que establece que los genes se separan de manera independiente durante la meiosis (284)

leaflet one segment of a compound leaf (582)
folíolo un segmento de una hoja compuesta (582)

learning the development of behaviors through experience or practice (817)
aprendizaje el desarrollo de conductas por medio de la experiencia o práctica (817)

leukemia (loo KEE mee uh) a progressive, malignant disease of the blood-forming organs (844)
leucemia una enfermedad maligna y progresiva de los órganos de formación de la sangre (844)

lichen (LIE kuhn) a mass of fungal and algal cells that grow together in a symbiotic relationship and that are usually found on rocks or trees (528)
liquen una masa de células de hongos y de algas que crecen juntas en una relación simbiótica y que normalmente se encuentran en rocas o árboles (528)

life cycle all of the events in the growth and development of an organism until the organism reaches sexual maturity (256)
ciclo de vida todos los sucesos en el crecimiento y desarrollo de un organismo hasta que el organismo llega a su madurez sexual (256)

linked in genetics, describes two or more genes that tend to be inherited together (275, 284)
ligado en genética, término que describe dos o más genes que tienden a heredarse juntos (275, 284)

lipid (LIP id) a fat molecule or a molecule that has similar properties; examples include oils, waxes, and steroids (61)
lípido una molécula de grasa o una molécula que tiene propiedades similares; algunos ejemplos son los aceites, las ceras y los esteroides (61)

lipid bilayer (BIE LAY uhr) the basic structure of a biological membrane, composed of two layers of phospholipids (176)
bicapa de lípidos la estructura básica de la membrana biológica, formada por dos capas de fosfolípidos (176)

livor mortis (LIE VAWR MAWR tis) after death, the settling of the blood to the lowest point in the body, which causes a red to purple discoloration of the skin; also called *hypostasis* (1032)
livor mortis después de la muerte, el asentamiento de la sangre hasta el punto más bajo del cuerpo, lo que produce una decoloración violácea de la piel; también se llama *hipostasis* (1032)

logistic growth (loh JIS tik) population growth that starts with a minimum number of individuals and reaches a maximum depending on the carrying capacity of the region; described by an S-shaped curve (104)
crecimiento logístico crecimiento de la población que comienza con un número mínimo de individuos y llega al máximo dependiendo de la capacidad de carga de la región; se describe por medio de una curva en forma de S (104)

long-day plant a plant that requires a period of exposure to light that exceeds a critical length to blossom (608)
planta de día largo una planta que requiere un período de exposición a la luz que excede la longitud crítica para florecer (608)

lung the central organ of the respiratory system in which oxygen from the air is exchanged with carbon dioxide from the blood (741)
pulmón el órgano central del aparato respiratorio en el que el oxígeno del aire se intercambia con el dióxido de carbono de la sangre (741)

luteal phase (LOOT ee uhl) the menstrual stage in which the corpus luteum develops (999)
fase luteal la etapa de la menstruación en la que se desarrolla el corpus luteum (999)

lymph (LIMF) the fluid that is collected by the lymphatic vessels and nodes (871)
linfa el fluido que es recolectado por los vasos y nodos linfáticos (871)

lymphatic system (lim FAT ik) a collection of organs whose primary function is to collect extracellular fluid and return it to the blood; the organs in this system include the lymph nodes and the lymphatic vessels (871)
sistema linfático un conjunto de órganos cuya función principal es recolectar el fluido extracelular y regresarlo a la sangre; los órganos de este sistema incluyen los nodos linfáticos y los vasos linfáticos (871)

lymph node an organ that filters lymph and that is found along the lymphatic vessels (871)

nodo linfático un órgano que filtra la linfa y que se encuentra a lo largo de los vasos linfáticos (871)

lysogenic (LIE soh JEN ik) describes viral replication in which a viral genome is replicated as a provirus without destroying the host cell (478)

lisogénico término que describe la replicación viral en la que un genoma viral se replica como un provirus sin destruir la célula huésped (478)

lytic (LIT ik) describes viral replication that results in the destruction of a host cell and the release of many new virus particles (478)

lítico término que describe la replicación viral que resulta en la destrucción de una célula huésped y la liberación de muchas partículas nuevas de virus (478)

macrophage (MAK roh FAYJ) an immune system cell that engulfs pathogens and other materials (917)

macrófago una célula del sistema inmunológico que envuelve a los patógenos y otros materiales (917)

malignant tumor (muh LIG nuhnt) a cancerous mass of cells (235)

tumor maligno una masa cancerosa de células (235)

Malpighian tubule (mal PIG ee uhn) an excretory tube that opens into the back part of the intestine of most insects and certain arthropods (703)

tubo malpighiano un tubo excretorio que se abre hacia la parte trasera del intestino de la mayoría de los insectos y ciertos artrópodos (703)

mammary gland (MAM uh ree) a gland that is located in the chest of a female mammal and that secretes milk (788)

glándula mamaria una glándula que se encuentra en el pecho de los mamíferos hembra y que secreta leche (788)

mandible (MAN duh buhl) a type of mouthpart found in some arthropods and used to pierce and suck food; the lower part of the jaw (712)

mandíbula un tipo de parte de la boca que se encuentra en algunos artrópodos y que se usa para perforar y chupar la comida; la parte inferior de la quijada (712)

mantle in biology, a layer of tissue that covers the body of many invertebrates (680)

manto en biología, una capa de tejido que cubre el cuerpo de muchos invertebrados (680)

marine ecosystem (muh REEN) an ecosystem in the sea (84)

ecosistema marino un ecosistema en el mar (84)

mass extinction (ek STINGK shuhn) an episode during which large numbers of species become extinct (453)

extinción masiva un episodio durante el cual grandes cantidades de especies se extinguen (453)

mechanoreceptor (MEK uh noh ri SEP tuhr) a sensory receptor that is sensitive to mechanical pressure or distortion (952)

mecanorreceptor un receptor sensorial que es sensible a la presión o distorsión mecánica (952)

medusa (muh DOO suh) a free-swimming, jellyfish-like, and often umbrella-shaped sexual stage in the life cycle of a cnidarian; *also* a jellyfish or a hydra (658)

medusa una etapa sexual del ciclo de vida de un cnidario, que nada libremente, tiene la apariencia de un aguamala y la forma de un paraguas; *también,* un aguamala o hidra (658)

meiosis (mie OH sis) a process in cell division during which the number of chromosomes decreases to half the original number by two divisions of the nucleus, which results in the production of sex cells (gametes or spores) (250)

meiosis un proceso de división celular durante el cual el número de cromosomas disminuye a la mitad del número original por medio de dos divisiones del núcleo, lo cual resulta en la producción de células sexuales (gametos o esporas) (250)

melanin (MEL uh nin) a pigment that helps determine the color of skin, hair, eyes, fur, feathers, and scales (854)

melanina un pigmento que ayuda a determinar el color de la piel, el cabello, los ojos, el pelaje, las plumas y las escamas (854)

melanoma (MEL uh NOH muh) a tumor that starts in pigment-producing epidermal cells and that may spread quickly (856)

melanoma un tumor que comienza en las células epidérmicas que producen pigmentos y que puede expandirse rápidamente (856)

membrane potential the difference in electric potential between the two sides of a cell membrane (946)

potencial de membrana la diferencia en potencial eléctrico entre los dos lados de una membrana celular (946)

memory cell an immune system B cell or T cell that does not respond the first time that it meets with an antigen or an invading cell but that recognizes and attacks the antigen or invading cell during subsequent infections (922)

célula de memoria un célula B o una célula T del sistema inmunológico que no responde la primera vez que se encuentra con un antígeno o célula invasora, pero que reconoce y ataca al antígeno o célula invasora durante infecciones posteriores (922)

menopause (MEN uh PAWZ) the termination of the menstrual cycle; occurs between the ages of 45 and 55 (1000)

menopausia la terminación del ciclo menstrual; ocurre entre los 45 y 55 años de edad (1000)

menstruation (MEN STRAY shuhn) the discharge of blood and discarded tissue from the uterus during the menstrual cycle (999)

menstruación la descarga de sangre y tejido de desecho del útero durante el ciclo menstrual (999)

meristem (MER uh STEM) a region of undifferentiated plant cells that are capable of dividing and developing into specialized plant tissues (587)

meristemo una región de células vegetales no diferenciadas que son capaces de dividirse y desarrollarse en tejidos vegetales especializados (587)

mesoderm (MES oh DUHRM) in an embryo, the middle layer of cells that gives rise to muscles, blood, and various systems (663)

mesodermo en un embrión, la capa de células intermedia que da origen a los músculos, sangre y varios sistemas (663)

mesoglea (MES oh GLEE uh) in cnidarians, the jellylike material located between the ectoderm and the endoderm (658)

mesoglea en los cnidarios, el material gelatinoso que se ubica entre el ectodermo y el endodermo (658)

mesophyll (MES oh FIL) in leaves, the tissue between epidermal layers, where photosynthesis occurs (582)

mesofilo en las hojas, el tejido que se encuentra entre capas de epidermis, donde ocurre la fotosíntesis (582)

metabolism (muh TAB uh LIZ uhm) the sum of all chemical processes that occur in an organism (19)

metabolismo la suma de todos los procesos químicos que ocurren en un organismo (19)

metamorphosis (MET uh MAWR fuh sis) a phase in the life cycle of many animals during which a rapid change from the immature organism to the adult takes place; an example is the change from larva to adult in insects (714)

metamorfosis una fase del ciclo de vida de muchos animales durante la cual ocurre un cambio rápido del organismo inmaduro al adulto; un ejemplo es el cambio de larva a adulto en los insectos (714)

methanogen (muh THAN uh JEN) a microorganism that produces methane gas (435)

metanógeno un microorganismo que produce gas metano (435)

microarray (MIE kroh uh RAY) a device that contains, in microscopic scale, an orderly arrangement of biomolecules; a device that is used to rapidly test for the presence of a range of similar substances, such as specific DNA sequences (346, 358)

chip de ADN un aparato que contiene, a escala microscópica, una organización ordenada de biomoléculas; un aparato que se usa para probar rápidamente la presencia de una variedad de sustancias similares, como secuencias específicas de ADN (346, 358)

microfilament (MIE kroh FIL uh muhnt) a fiber found inside eukaryotic cells that is composed mainly of the protein actin and that has a role in cell structure and movement (156)

microfilamento una fibra que se encuentra dentro de las células eucarióticas, compuesta principalmente por la proteína actina, y que está relacionada con la estructura y movimiento de la célula (156)

microsphere (MIE kroh SFIR) a hollow microscopic spherical structure that is usually composed of proteins or a synthetic polymer (449)

microesfera una estructura microscópica esférica y hueca compuesta generalmente por proteínas o por un polímero sintético (449)

microtubule (MIE kroh TOO BYOOL) one of the small, tubular fibers composed of the protein tubulin that are found in the cytoplasm of eukaryotic cells, that compose the cytoskeleton, and that play a role in cell structure and movement (156)

microtúbulo una de las fibras pequeñas y tubulares compuestas de la proteína tubulina, las cuales se encuentran en el citoplasma de las células eucarióticas, forman el citoesqueleto y están involucradas en el movimiento y estructura de la célula (156)

microvillus (MIE kroh VIL uhs) a fingerlike projection from the surface of certain animal cells, such as the epithelial cells that line the intestine, that increases the cell's surface area for absorption (899)

microvillus una proyección parecida a un dedo que sale de la superficie de algunas células animales, como por ejemplo, las células epiteliales que recubren el intestino, y que aumenta el área superficial de absorción de la célula (899)

migration (mie GRAY shuhn) in general, any movement of individuals or populations from one location to another; specifically, a periodic group movement that is characteristic of a given population or species (388, 405, 822)

migración en general, cualquier movimiento de individuos o poblaciones de un lugar a otro; específicamente, un movimiento periódico en grupo que es característico de una población o especie determinada (388, 405, 822)

mineral a class of nutrients that are chemical elements that are needed for certain body processes (894)

mineral una clase de nutrientes que son elementos químicos necesarios para ciertos procesos del cuerpo (894)

missense mutation a type of point mutation that converts one codon to another such that the codon specifies a different amino acid (320)

mutación de sentido erróneo un tipo de mutación puntual que convierte a un codón en otro de manera que el codón especifica un aminoácido diferente (320)

mitochondrion (MIET oh KAHN dree uhn) in eukaryotic cells, the cell organelle that is surrounded by two membranes and that is the site of cellular respiration, which produces ATP (161)

mitocondria en las células eucarióticas, el organelo celular rodeado por dos membranas que es el lugar donde se lleva a cabo la respiración celular, la cual produce ATP (161)

mitosis (mie TOH sis) in eukaryotic cells, a process of cell division that forms two new nuclei, each of which has the same number of chromosomes (229)

mitosis en las células eucarióticas, un proceso de división celular que forma dos núcleos nuevos, cada uno de los cuales posee el mismo número de cromosomas (229)

mobile genetic element a genetic sequence that is sometimes removed or copied from one place and inserted into another within chromosomes or genomes; includes plasmids, transposons, and other elements (abbreviation, MGE) (332)

elemento genético móvil una secuencia genética que a veces se elimina o se copia de un lugar y se inserta en otro dentro de los cromosomas o genomas; incluye a los plásmidos, los transposones y otros elementos (abreviatura: EGM) (332)

mold a rapidly growing, asexually reproducing stage of some types of fungi (523)

moho una etapa de crecimiento rápido y reproducción asexual de algunos tipos de hongos (523)

molecule (MAHL i KYOOL) a group of atoms that are held together by chemical forces; a molecule is the smallest unit of matter that can exist by itself and retain all of a substance's chemical properties (52)

molécula un conjunto de átomos que se mantienen unidos por acción de las fuerzas químicas; una molécula es la unidad más pequeña de la materia capaz de existir en forma independiente y conservar todas las propiedades químicas de una sustancia (52)

mollusk (MAHL uhsk) an invertebrate that has a soft, bilaterally symmetrical body that is often enclosed in a hard shell made of calcium carbonate; examples include snails, clams, octopuses, and squids (679)

molusco un invertebrado que tiene un cuerpo blando y simétrico bilateralmente, el cual a menudo está envuelto por una concha dura hecha de carbonato de calcio; entre los ejemplos se encuentran caracoles, almejas, pulpos y calamares (679)

molting (MOHLT ing) the shedding of an exoskeleton, skin, feathers, or hair to be replaced by new parts (704)

pelechar la muda de un exoesqueleto, piel, plumas o pelo, los cuales son reemplazados por partes nuevas (704)

monocot (MAHN uh KAHT) a monocotyledonous plant; a plant that produces seeds that have only one cotyledon (559, 585)

monocotiledónea una planta que produce semillas que sólo tienen un cotiledón (559, 585)

monohybrid cross (MAHN oh HIE brid) a cross between individuals that involves one pair of contrasting traits (269)

cruza monohíbrida una cruza entre individuos que involucra un par de caracteres contrastantes (269)

monosaccharide (MAHN oh SAK uh RIED) a simple sugar that is the basic subunit of a carbohydrate (60)

monosacárido un azúcar simple que es una subunidad fundamental de los carbohidratos (60)

monotreme (MAHN oh TREEM) a mammal that lays eggs (791)

monotrema un mamífero que pone huevos (791)

morphology (mawr FAHL uh jee) the study of the structure and form of an organism (430)

morfología el estudio de la estructura y forma de un organismo (430)

motor neuron (NOO RAHN) a nerve cell that conducts nerve impulses from the central nervous system to the muscles and glands (939)

neurona motora una célula nerviosa que transmite impulsos nerviosos del sistema nervioso central a los músculos y a las glándulas (939)

mRNA messenger RNA, a single-stranded RNA molecule that encodes the information to make a protein (305)

ARNm ARNm mensajero; una molécula de ARN de una sola hebra que codifica la información para hacer una proteína (305)

mucous membrane (MYOO kuhs) the layer of epithelial tissue that covers internal surfaces of the body and that secretes mucus (915)

membrana mucosa la capa de tejido epitelial que cubre las superficies internas del cuerpo y que secreta moco (915)

multicellular (muhl ti SEL yoo luhr) describes a tissue, organ, or organism that is made of many cells (434, 624)

pluricelular término que describe a un tejido, órgano u organismo constituido por muchas células (434, 624)

multiple alleles (uh LEELZ) more than two alleles (versions of the gene) for a genetic trait (283)

alelos múltiples más de dos alelos (versiones del gene) para un carácter genético (283)

muscle fiber a multinucleate muscle cell, especially of skeletal or cardiac muscle tissue (850)

fibra muscular una célula muscular plurinucleada, sobre todo de tejido muscular esquelético o cardíaco (850)

muscle tissue the tissue made of cells that can contract and relax to produce movement (840)

tejido muscular el tejido formado por células que se contraen y relajan para producir movimiento (840)

mutation (myoo TAY shuhn) a change in the structure or amount of the genetic material of an organism (319)

mutación un cambio en la estructura o cantidad del material genético de un organismo (319)

mutualism (MYOO choo uhl IZ uhm) a relationship between two species in which both species benefit (110)

mutualismo una relación entre dos especies en la que ambas se benefician (110)

mycelium (mie SEE lee uhm) the mass of fungal filaments, or hyphae, that forms the body of a fungus (522)

micelio una masa de filamentos de hongos, o hifas, que forma el cuerpo de un hongo (522)

mycorrhiza (MIE koh RIE zuh) a symbiotic association between fungi and plant roots (528, 544)

micorriza una asociación simbiótica entre los hongos y las raíces de las plantas (528, 544)

myofibril (MIE uh FIE bruhl) a fiber that is found in striated muscle cells and that is responsible for muscle contraction (850)

miofibra una fibra que se encuentra en las células de los músculos estriados, la cual es responsable de la contracción muscular (850)

myosin (MIE oh sin) the most abundant protein in muscle tissue and the main constituent of the thick filaments of muscle fibers (850)

miosina la proteína más abundante en los tejidos musculares, la cual es el elemento constitutivo principal de los filamentos gruesos de las fibras musculares (850)

nastic movement (NAS tik) a type of plant response that is independent of the direction of a stimulus (610)

movimiento nástico un tipo de respuesta de las plantas que es independiente de la dirección del estímulo (610)

natural selection the process by which individuals that are better adapted to their environment survive and reproduce more successfully than less well adapted individuals do; a theory to explain the mechanism of evolution (380)

selección natural el proceso por medio del cual los individuos que están mejor adaptados a su ambiente sobreviven y se reproducen con más éxito que los individuos menos adaptados; una teoría que explica el mecanismo de la evolución (380)

negative feedback a change in one direction of a feedback mechanism that stops further change in that direction (842, 976, 999)

retroalimentación negativa un cambio en una dirección o un mecanismo de retroalimentación que detiene otros cambios en esa dirección (842, 976, 999)

nematocyst (NEM uh toh SIST) in cnidarians, a stinging component of a specialized cell that is used to capture prey or inject prey with a toxin (659)

nematocisto en los cnidarios, un componente urticante de una célula especializada que se usa para capturar presas o para inyectarles una toxina a las presas (659)

nephridium (nee FRID ee uhm) a tubule through which some invertebrates eliminate wastes (680)

nefridio túbulo a través del cual algunos invertebrados eliminan desechos (680)

nephron (NEF RAHN) the functional unit of the kidney (903)

nefrona la unidad funcional del riñón (903)

nerve a collection of nerve fibers through which impulses travel between the central nervous system and other parts of the body (945)

nervio un conjunto de fibras nerviosas a través de las cuales se desplazan los impulsos entre el sistema nervioso central y otras partes del cuerpo (945)

nerve net in cnidarians, a network of nerve cells that lacks a central control; impulses pass in any or all directions to produce a generalized response (629)

red de nervios en los cnidarios, una red de células nerviosas que no están sujetas a ningún control central; los impulsos pasan en cualquier dirección (o en todas las direcciones) produciendo una respuesta generalizada (629)

nervous tissue tissue of the nervous system, including neurons and their supporting cells (840)

tejido nervioso tejido del sistema nervioso que incluye las neuronas y sus células de apoyo (840)

neuron (NOO RAHN) a nerve cell that is specialized to receive and conduct electrical impulses (939)

neurona una célula nerviosa que está especializada en recibir y transmitir impulsos eléctricos (939)

neurotransmitter (NOO roh TRANS MIT uhr) a chemical substance that transmits nerve impulses across a synapse (948)

neurotransmisor una sustancia química que transmite impulsos nerviosos por una sinapsis (948)

neutron (NOO TRAHN) a subatomic particle that has no charge and that is located in the nucleus of an atom (51)

neutrón una partícula subatómica que no tiene carga y que está ubicada en el núcleo de un átomo (51)

niche (NICH) the unique position occupied by a species, both in terms of its physical use of its habitat and its function within an ecological community (113, 413)

nicho la posición única que ocupa una especie, tanto en lo que se refiere al uso de su hábitat como en cuanto a su función dentro de una comunidad ecológica (113, 413)

nictitating membrane (NIK tuh TAYT ing) a third eyelid found under the lower eyelid of many vertebrates, including birds, reptiles, and amphibians (740)
membrana nictitante un tercer párpado que se encuentra debajo del párpado inferior de algunos vertebrados, como por ejemplo, aves, reptiles y anfibios (740)

nitrification (NIE truh fi KAY shuhn) the process by which nitrites and nitrates are produced by bacteria in the soil (92)
nitrificación el proceso por medio del cual las bacterias del suelo producen nitritos y nitratos (92)

nitrogen cycle (NIE truh juhn) the cycling of nitrogen between organisms, soil, water, and the atmosphere (91)
ciclo del nitrógeno el ciclado del nitrógeno entre los organismos, el suelo, el agua y la atmósfera (91)

nitrogen fixation (NIE truh juhn fiks AY shuhn) the process by which gaseous nitrogen is converted into ammonia, a compound that organisms can use to make amino acids and other nitrogen-containing organic molecules (92)
fijación de nitrógeno el proceso por medio del cual el nitrógeno gaseoso se transforma en amoniaco, un compuesto que los organismos utilizan para elaborar aminoácidos y otras moléculas orgánicas que contienen nitrógeno (92)

node in biology, a joint between two adjacent sections in the stem of a plant where buds form and leaves or branches start to grow; usually marked by a knot or swelling (580)
nodo en biología, una articulación entre dos secciones adyacentes del tallo de una planta, donde se forman brotes y donde las hojas o ramas comienzan a crecer; normalmente marcado por un nodo o hinchazón (580)

nondisjunction (NAHN dis JUHNK shuhn) the failure of homologous chromosomes to separate during meiosis I or the failure of sister chromatids to separate during mitosis or meiosis II (324)
no-disyunción fenómeno que se produce cuando los cromosomas homólogos no se separan durante la meiosis I o cuando las cromátidas hermanas no se separan durante la meiosis II (324)

nonsense mutation a mutation that alters a gene so that a nonsense (or noncoding) codon is inserted; a mutation that usually results in the abnormal termination of an amino-acid chain during translation (321)
mutación sin sentido una mutación que altera un gene de modo que se inserta un codón sin sentido (o que no codifica); una mutación que suele tener como resultado la interrupción anormal de una cadena de aminoácidos (321)

nonvascular plant (NAHN VAHS kyuh luhr) a plant that belongs to one of the three groups of plants (liverworts, hornworts, and mosses) that lack specialized conducting tissues and true roots, stems, and leaves (544)
planta no vascular una planta que pertenece a uno de los tres grupos de plantas (hepáticas, milhojas y musgos) que carecen de tejidos transportadores especializados y de raíces, tallos y hojas verdaderos (544)

norepinephrine (NAWR EP uh NEF rin) a chemical that is both a neurotransmitter produced by the sympathetic nerve endings in the autonomic nervous system and a hormone secreted by the adrenal medulla to stimulate the functions of the circulatory and respiratory systems especially (abbreviation, NE) (981)
norepinefrina una sustancia química que es un neurotransmisor producido por las terminaciones nerviosas simpáticas en el sistema nervioso, y también una hormona secretada por la médula suprarrenal para estimular las funciones de los aparatos circulatorio y respiratorio (abreviatura: NE) (981)

normal distribution a distribution of numerical data whose graph forms a bell-shaped curve that is symmetrical about the mean (400)
distribución normal una distribución de datos numéricos cuya gráfica forma una curva en forma de campana que es simétrica respecto a la media (400)

notochord (NOHT uh KAWRD) the rod-shaped supporting axis found in the dorsal part of the embryos of all chordates, including vertebrates (638)
notocordio el eje de soporte que tiene forma de bastoncillo y está ubicado en la parte dorsal de los embriones de todos los cordados, incluyendo los vertebrados (638)

nuclear envelope (NOO klee uhr) the double membrane that surrounds the nucleus of a eukaryotic cell (157)
envoltura nuclear la doble membrana que rodea el núcleo de una célula eucariótica (157)

nucleic acid (noo KLAY ik) an organic compound, either RNA or DNA, whose molecules are made up of one or two chains of nucleotides and carry genetic information (63)
ácido nucleico un compuesto orgánico, ya sea ARN o ADN, cuyas moléculas están formadas por una o más cadenas de nucleótidos y que contiene información genética (63)

nucleolus (noo KLEE uh luhs) the part of the eukaryotic nucleus where ribosomal RNA is synthesized (157)
nucleolo la parte del núcleo eucariótico donde se sintetiza el ARN ribosomal (157)

nucleosome (NOO klee uh SOHM) a eukaryotic structural unit of chromatin that consists of DNA wound around a core of histone proteins (224)
nucleosoma una unidad estructural eucariótica de cromatina formada por ADN que rodea un núcleo de proteínas de histona (224)

nucleotide (NOO klee oh TIED) an organic compound that consists of a sugar, a phosphate, and a nitrogenous base; the basic building block of a nucleic-acid chain (63, 296)
nucleótido un compuesto orgánico formado por un azúcar, un fosfato y una base nitrogenada; el componente básico de una cadena de ácidos nucleicos (63, 296)

nucleus (NOO klee uhs) in a eukaryotic cell, a membrane-bound organelle that contains the cell's DNA and that has a role in processes such as growth, metabolism, and reproduction (155)
núcleo en una célula eucariótica, un organelo cubierto por una membrana, el cual contiene el ADN de la célula y participa en procesos tales como el crecimiento, metabolismo y reproducción (155)

nutrient (NOO tree uhnt) a substance or compound that provides nourishment (or food) or raw materials needed for life processes (891)
nutriente una sustancia o compuesto que proporciona nutrición (o alimento) o materias primas que se necesitan para llevar a cabo procesos vitales (891)

nymph (NIMF) an immature stage of some insects that is similar in function and structure to the adult (714)
ninfa una etapa inmadura de algunos insectos que es similar en función y estructura al adulto (714)

observation (AHB zuhr VAY shuhn) the process of obtaining information by using the senses; the information obtained by using the senses (10)
observación el proceso de obtener información por medio de los sentidos; la información que se obtiene al usar los sentidos (10)

omnivore (AHM ni VAWR) an organism that eats both plants and animals (87)
omnívoro un organismo que come tanto plantas como animales (87)

open circulatory system (SUHR kyoo luh TAWR ee) a type of circulatory system in which the circulatory fluid is not contained entirely within vessels; a heart pumps fluid through vessels that empty into spaces called *sinuses* (630)
aparato circulatorio abierto un tipo de aparato circulatorio en el que el fluido circulatorio no está totalmente contenido en los vasos sanguíneos; un corazón bombea fluido por los vasos sanguíneos, los cuales se vacían en espacios llamados *senos* (630)

operator (AHP uh RAY tuhr) a short sequence of viral or bacterial DNA to which a repressor binds to prevent transcription (mRNA synthesis) of the adjacent gene in an operon (326)
operador una secuencia corta de ADN viral o bacteriano a la que se une un represor para impedir la transcripción (síntesis de ARNm) del gene adyacente en un operón (326)

operculum (oh PUHR kyoo luhm) in fish, a hard plate that is attached to each side of the head, that covers gills, and that is open at the rear (736)
opérculo en los peces, una placa dura que se encuentra adherida a cada lado de la cabeza, cubre las branquias y está abierta en la parte trasera (736)

operon (AHP uhr AHN) a unit of adjacent genes that consists of functionally related structural genes and their associated regulatory genes; common in prokaryotes and phages (326)
operón una unidad de genes adyacentes formada por genes estructurales de función relacionada y sus genes reguladores asociados; es común en los procariotes y los fagos (326)

order the taxonomic category below the class and above the family (426)
orden la categoría taxonómica que se encuentra debajo de la clase y arriba de la familia (426)

organ a collection of tissues that carry out a specialized function of the body (164, 632, 841)
órgano un conjunto de tejidos que desempeñan una función especializada en el cuerpo (164, 632, 841)

organelle (AWR guh NEL) one of the small bodies that are found in the cytoplasm of a cell and that are specialized to perform a specific function (155)
organelo uno de los cuerpos pequeños que se encuentran en el citoplasma de una célula y que están especializados para llevar a cabo una función específica (155)

organism (AWR guh NIZ uhm) a living thing; anything that can carry out life processes independently (17)
organismo un ser vivo; cualquier cosa que pueda llevar a cabo procesos vitales independientemente (17)

organ system a group of organs that work together to perform body functions (165, 841)
aparato (o sistema) de órganos un grupo de órganos que trabajan en conjunto para desempeñar funciones corporales (165, 841)

origin (AWR uh jin) in anatomy, the point at which a muscle attaches to a stationary bone (849)
origen en anatomía, el punto en el que un músculo se une a un hueso estacionario (849)

osculum (AHS kyoo luhm) an opening in a sponge's body through which water exits (655)
ósculo una abertura en el cuerpo de una esponja a través de la cual el agua sale del cuerpo (655)

osmosis (ahs MOH sis) the diffusion of water or another solvent from a more dilute solution (of a solute) to a more concentrated solution (of the solute) through a membrane that is permeable to the solvent (180)
ósmosis la difusión de agua u otro solvente de una solución más diluida (de un soluto) a una solución más concentrada (del soluto) a través de una membrana que es permeable al solvente (180)

ossicle (AHS i kuhl) one of the small, calcium carbonate plates that make up the endoskeleton of an echinoderm (717)
ossículo una de las pequeñas placas de carbonato de calcio que forman el endoesqueleto de un equinodermo (717)

osteocyte (AWS tee uh SIET) a mature bone cell that maintains bone tissue (844)

osteocito una célula ósea madura que mantiene el tejido óseo (844)

osteoporosis (AHS tee OH puh ROH sis) a condition in which bones become thin and weak and break easily (845)

osteoporosis una enfermedad en la que los huesos pierden consistencia, se debilitan y se rompen fácilmente (845)

ostium (AHS tee uhm) one of the small openings in a sponge's body through which water enters (655)

ostia una de las pequeñas aberturas pequeñas del cuerpo de una esponja a través de las cuales entra el agua (655)

ovarian cycle (oh VAHR ee uhn) a series of hormone-induced changes in which the ovaries prepare and release a mature ovum each month (998)

ciclo ovárico una serie de cambios inducidos por hormonas en los cuales los ovarios preparan y liberan un óvulo maduro todos los meses (998)

ovary (OH vuh ree) in flowering plants, the lower part of a pistil that produces eggs in ovules (560, 996)

ovario en las plantas con flores, la parte inferior del pistilo que produce óvulos (560, 996)

oviparous (oh VIP uh ruhs) describes organisms that produce eggs that develop and hatch outside the body of the mother (761, 788)

ovíparo término que describe organismos que producen huevos que se desarrollan fuera del cuerpo de la madre, y cuyas crías también salen del cascarón fuera del cuerpo de la madre (761, 788)

ovoviviparous (OH voh vie VIP uh ruhs) describes organisms that produce eggs that develop and hatch inside the body of the mother (761)

ovovivíparo término que describe a organismos que producen huevos que se desarrollan dentro del cuerpo de la madre, y cuyas crías también salen del cascarón dentro del cuerpo de la madre (761)

ovulation (AHV yoo LAY shuhn) the release of an ovum from a follicle of the ovary (998)

ovulación la liberación de un óvulo de un folículo del ovario (998)

ovule (AHV YOOL) a structure in the ovary of a seed plant that contains an embryo sac and that develops into a seed after fertilization (554)

óvulo una estructura del ovario de una planta con semillas que contiene un saco embrionario y se desarrolla para convertirse en una semilla después de la fecundación (554)

ovum (OH vuhm) a mature egg cell (255, 997)

óvulo una célula sexual madura (255, 997)

palisade mesophyll (PAL uh SAYD MES oh FIL) in plants, the layer of vertically elongated cells that contains chloroplasts, that is located beneath the upper epidermis of leaves, and that participates in photosynthesis (582)

mesófilo palisada en las plantas, la capa de células alargadas verticalmente que contienen cloroplastos; está ubicada debajo de la epidermis superior de las hojas y participa en la fotosíntesis (582)

parasitism (PAR uh SIET IZ uhm) a relationship between two species in which one species, the parasite, benefits from the other species, the host, which is harmed (110)

parasitismo una relación entre dos especies en la que una, el parásito, se beneficia de la otra, el huésped, que resulta perjudicada (110)

parthenogenesis (PAHR thuh NOH JEN uh sis) reproduction in which a female gamete grows into a new individual without being fertilized by a male (247)

partenogénesis reproducción en la cual un gameto femenino se convierte en un nuevo individuo sin ser fecundado por un macho (247)

passive transport the movement of substances across a cell membrane without the use of energy by the cell (178)

transporte pasivo el movimiento de sustancias a través de una membrana celular sin que la célula tenga que usar energía (178)

pathogen (PATH uh juhn) a microorganism, another organism, a virus, or a protein that causes disease; an infectious agent (482, 915)

patógeno un microorganismo, otro organismo, un virus o una proteína que causa enfermedades; un agente infeccioso (482, 915)

pathology (puh THAHL uh jee) the scientific study of disease (1027)

patología el estudio científico de las enfermedades (1027)

pedigree (PED i GREE) a diagram that shows the occurrence of a genetic trait in several generations of a family (280)

pedigrí un diagrama que muestra la incidencia de un carácter genético en varias generaciones de una familia (280)

pedipalp (PED i PALP) in certain arthropods, one of the second pair of appendages (706)

pedipalpo en ciertos artrópodos, un segundo par de apéndices (706)

pelvic inflammatory disease (in FLAM uh TAWR ee) a sexually transmitted infection of the upper female reproductive system, including the uterus, ovaries, and fallopian tubes (1007)

enfermedad pélvica inflamatoria una infección de transmisión sexual del aparato reproductor femenino superior, que incluye el útero, los ovarios y las trompas de Falopio (1007)

penis (PEE nis) the male organ that transfers sperm to a female and that carries urine out of the body (995)

pene el órgano masculino que transfiere espermatozoides a una hembra y que lleva la orina hacia el exterior del cuerpo (995)

pepsin (PEP sin) an enzyme that is found in gastric juices and that helps break down proteins into smaller molecules (897)

pepsina una enzima que se encuentra en los jugos gástricos y que sirve para descomponer proteínas en moléculas más pequeñas (897)

peptide bond (PEP TIED) the chemical bond that forms between the carboxyl group of one amino acid and the amino group of another amino acid (62)

enlace peptídico el enlace químico que se forma entre el grupo carboxilo de un aminoácido y el grupo amino de otro aminoácido (62)

peptidoglycan (PEP ti doh GLIE kuhn) a protein-carbohydrate compound that makes the cell walls of bacteria rigid (472)

péptidoglicano un compuesto de proteína y carbohidrato que hace rígida la pared celular de las bacterias (472)

period a unit of geologic time that is longer than an epoch but shorter than an era (453)

período una unidad de tiempo geológico que es más larga que una época pero más corta que una era (453)

periosteum (PER ee AHS tee uhm) the fibrous tissue that covers bones (844)

periosteo el tejido fibroso que cubre los huesos (844)

peripheral nervous system (puh RIF uhr uhl) all of the parts of the nervous system except for the brain and the spinal cord (the central nervous system); includes the cranial nerves and nerves of the neck, chest, lower back, and pelvis (939)

sistema nervioso periférico todas las partes del sistema nervioso, excepto el encéfalo y la médula espinal (el sistema nervioso central); incluye los nervios craneales y los nervios del cuello, pecho, espalda baja y pelvis (939)

peristalsis (PER uh STAWL sis) the series of rhythmic muscular contractions that move food through the digestive tract (897)

peristalsis la serie de contracciones musculares rítmicas que mueven el alimento por el tracto digestivo (897)

petal one of the usually brightly colored, leaf-shaped parts that make up one of the rings of a flower (560)

pétalo una de las partes de una flor que normalmente tienen colores brillantes y forma de hoja, las cuales forman uno de los anillos de una flor (560)

petiole (PET ee OHL) the stalk that attaches a leaf to the stem of a plant (582)

pecíolo el pedúnculo que une una hoja al tallo de una planta (582)

P generation parental generation, the first two individuals that mate in a genetic cross (269)

generación P generación parental; los primeros dos individuos que se aparean en una cruza genética (269)

pH (PEE AYCH) a value that is used to express the acidity or alkalinity (basicity) of a system; each whole number on the scale indicates a tenfold change in acidity; a pH of 7 is neutral, a pH of less than 7 is acidic, and a pH of greater than 7 is basic (57)

pH un valor que expresa la acidez o la alcalinidad (basicidad) de un sistema; cada número entero de la escala indica un cambio de 10 veces en la acidez; un pH de 7 es neutro, un pH de menos de 7 es ácido y un pH de más de 7 es básico (57)

pharyngeal pouch (fuh RIN jee uhl) one of the lateral sacs that branch from the pharynx of chordate embryos and that may open to the outside as gill slits in adult fishes and invertebrate chordates (638)

bolsa faríngea una de las bolsas laterales que se ramifican a partir de la faringe de los embriones cordados y que puede abrirse hacia el exterior en forma de aberturas branquiales en los peces adultos y en los cordados invertebrados (638)

pharynx (FAR ingks) in flatworms, the muscular tube that leads from the mouth to the gastrovascular cavity; in animals with a digestive tract, the passage from the mouth to the larynx and esophagus (876)

faringe en los gusanos planos, el tubo muscular que va de la boca a la cavidad gastrovascular; en los animales que tienen tracto digestivo, el conducto que va de la boca a la laringe y al esófago (876)

phenotype (FEE noh TIEP) an organism's appearance or other detectable characteristic that results from the organism's genotype and the environment (274, 400)

fenotipo la apariencia de un organismo u otra característica perceptible que resulta debido al genotipo del organismo y a su ambiente (274, 400)

pheromone (FER uh MOHN) a substance that is released by the body and that causes another individual of the same species to react in a predictable way (715, 824)

feromona una sustancia que el cuerpo libera y que hace que otro individuo de la misma especia reaccione de un modo predecible (715, 824)

phloem (FLOH EM) the tissue that conducts food (sugars, amino acids, and mineral nutrients) in vascular plants (576)

floema el tejido que transporta alimento (azúcares, aminoácidos y nutrientes minerales) en las plantas vasculares (576)

phospholipid (FAHS foh LIP id) a lipid that contains phosphorus and that is a structural component in cell membranes (176)

fosfolípido un lípido que contiene fósforo y que es un componente estructural de la membrana celular (176)

phosphorus cycle (FAHS fuh ruhs) the cyclic movement of phosphorus in different chemical forms from the environment to organisms and then back to the environment (93)

ciclo del fósforo el movimiento cíclico del fósforo en diferentes formas químicas del ambiente a los organismos y de regreso al ambiente (93)

photoautotroph (FOH toh AW tuh TRAHF) an organism that uses sunlight as its source of energy for photosynthesis (474)

fotoautótrofo un organismo que utiliza la luz solar como fuente de energía para realizar la fotosíntesis (474)

photoperiodism (FOHT oh PIR ee uhd IZ uhm) the response of plants to seasonal changes in the relative length of nights and days (608)

fotoperiodismo la respuesta de las plantas a los cambios de estación durante la duración relativa de las noches y de los días (608)

photoreceptor (FOHT oh ri SEP tuhr) a sensory receptor that is sensitive to light (951)

fotorreceptor un receptor sensorial sensible a la luz (951)

photosynthesis (FOHT oh SIN thuh sis) the process by which plants, algae, and some bacteria use sunlight, carbon dioxide, and water to produce carbohydrates and oxygen (197)

fotosíntesis el proceso por medio del cual las plantas, algas y algunas bacterias utilizan la luz solar, dióxido de carbono y agua para producir carbohidratos y oxígeno (197)

phototropism (FOH toh TROH PIZ uhm) a plant growth movement that occurs in response to the direction of a source of light (607)

fototropismo un movimiento de crecimiento de las plantas que ocurre en respuesta a la dirección de una fuente de luz (607)

phylogenetic tree (FIE loh juh NET ik) a branching diagram that shows how organisms are related through evolution (428)

árbol filogenético un diagrama ramificado que muestra cómo se relacionan los organismos a través de la evolución (428)

phylogeny (fie LAHJ uh nee) the evolutionary history of a species or taxonomic group (428)

filogenia la historia evolutiva de una especie o grupo taxonómico (428)

phylum (FIE luhm) the taxonomic group below kingdom and above class (426)

phylum el grupo taxonómico que se ubica debajo del reino y arriba de la clase (426)

pigment (PIG muhnt) a substance that gives another substance or a mixture its color (203)

pigmento una sustancia que le da color a otra sustancia o mezcla (203)

pioneer species a species that colonizes an uninhabited area and that starts an ecological cycle in which many other species become established (81)

especie pionera una especie que coloniza un área deshabitada y empieza un ciclo ecológico en el cual se establecen muchas otras especies (81)

pistil (PIS til) the female reproductive part of a flower that produces seeds and consists of an ovary, style, and stigma (560)

pistilo la parte reproductora femenina de una flor, la cual produce semillas y está formada por el ovario, estilo y estigma (560)

pith the tissue that is located in the center of the stem of most vascular plants and that is used for storage (580)

médula el tejido que se ubica en el centro del tallo de la mayoría de las plantas vasculares y que se utiliza para almacenamiento (580)

placenta (pluh SEN tuh) the structure that attaches a developing fetus to the uterus and that enables the exchange of nutrients, wastes, and gases between the mother and the fetus (788)

placenta la estructura que une al feto en desarrollo con el útero y que permite el intercambio de nutrientes, desechos y gases entre la madre y el feto (788)

planula (PLAN yoo luh) the free-swimming, ciliated larva of a cnidarian (659)

plánula la larva ciliada de un cnidario, la cual nada libremente (659)

plasma (PLAZ muh) in biology, the liquid component of blood (869)

plasma en biología, el componente líquido de la sangre (869)

plasma cell a type of white blood cell that produces antibodies (920)

célula plasmática un tipo de glóbulo blanco que produce anticuerpos (920)

plasmid (PLAZ mid) a genetic structure that can replicate independently of the main chromosome(s) of a cell; usually, a circular DNA molecule in bacteria (prokaryotes) (331, 472)

plásmido una estructura genética que puede duplicarse en forma independiente del cromosoma principal o los cromosomas principales de una célula; generalmente, una molécula de ADN circular de las bacterias (procariotes) (331, 472)

plasmodium (plaz MOH dee uhm) the multinucleate cytoplasm of a slime mold that is surrounded by a membrane and that moves as a mass (506)

plasmodio el citoplasma plurinucleado de un moho de fango, el cual está rodeado por una membrana y se mueve como si fuera una masa (506)

plastron (PLAS truhn) the bottom, or ventral, portion of a turtle's shell (762)

plastrón la porción inferior, o ventral, del caparazón de una tortuga (762)

platelet (PLAYT lit) a fragment of a cell that is needed to form blood clots (869)

plaqueta el fragmento de una célula que se necesita para formar coágulos sanguíneos (869)

point mutation a mutation in which only one nucleotide or nitrogenous base in a gene is changed (320)

mutación puntual una mutación en la que sólo cambia un nucleótido o una base nitrogenada en un gene (320)

polar (POH luhr) describes a molecule in which the positive and negative charges are separated (54)

polar término que describe una molécula en la que las cargas positivas y negativas están separadas (54)

polar body one of the small cells that separate from an oocyte during meiosis, that have little cytoplasm, and that are ultimately discarded (255)

cuerpo polar una de las células pequeñas que se separan de un oocito durante la meiosis, que tienen poco citoplasma y que finalmente se descartan (255)

pollen (PAHL uhn) the tiny granules that contain the male gametophyte of seed plants (545)

polen los gránulos diminutos que contienen el gametofito masculino en las plantas con semilla (545)

pollen grain the structure that contains the male gametophyte of seed plants (554)

grano de polen la estructura que contiene el gametofito masculino en las plantas con semilla (554)

pollen tube a tubular structure that grows from a pollen grain, enters the embryo sac, and allows the male reproductive cells to move to the ovule (554)

tubo de polen una estructura tubular que crece a partir de un grano de polen, entra al saco embrionario y permite que las células reproductoras masculinas se muevan al óvulo (554)

pollination (PAWL uh NAY shuhn) the transfer of pollen from the male reproductive structures (the anthers) to the tip of a female reproductive structure (the pistil) of a flower in angiosperms or to the ovule in gymnosperms (554)

polinización la transferencia de polen de las estructuras reproductoras masculinas (las anteras) de una flor a la punta de la estructura reproductora femenina (el pistilo) en las angiospermas o al óvulo en las gimnospermas (554)

polygenic character (PAHL uh JEN ik) a character that is influenced by more than one gene (282, 400)

carácter poligénico un carácter que es influenciado por más de un gene (282, 400)

polymerase chain reaction (PAHL i muhr AYZ) a technique that is used to make many copies of selected segments of DNA (abbreviation, PCR) (357)

reacción en cadena de la polimerasa una técnica que se usa para hacer muchas réplicas de segmentos seleccionados de ADN (abreviatura: PCR, por sus siglas en inglés) (357)

polyp (PAHL ip) a form of a cnidarian that has a cylindrical, hollow body and that is usually attached to a rock or to another object (658)

pólipo una forma de un cnidario que tiene un cuerpo hueco y cilíndrico y que normalmente está unido a una roca o a otro objeto (658)

polyploidy (PAH lee PLOY dee) an abnormal condition of having more than two sets of chromosomes (324)

poliploidia la condición anormal de tener más de dos conjuntos de cromosomas (324)

polysaccharide (PAHL i SAK uh RIED) one of the carbohydrates made up of long chains of simple sugars; polysaccharides include starch, cellulose, and glycogen (60)

polisacárido uno de los carbohidratos formados por cadenas largas de azúcares simples; algunos ejemplos de polisacáridos incluyen al almidón, celulosa y glucógeno (60)

population (PAHP yoo LAY shuhn) a group of organisms of the same species that live in a specific geographical area (103, 379)

población un grupo de organismos de la misma especie que viven en un área geográfica específica (103, 379)

population genetics the study of the frequency and interaction of alleles and genes in populations (399)

genética de poblaciones el estudio de la frecuencia e interacción de los alelos y genes en las poblaciones (399)

positive feedback in a system, the mechanism by which a cycle of events establishes conditions that favor repetition of the cycle (976, 999)

retroalimentación positiva en un sistema, el mecanismo por el cual un ciclo de sucesos establece condiciones que favorecen la repetición del ciclo (976, 999)

precipitation (pree SIP uh TAY shuhn) any form of water that falls to Earth's surface from the clouds; includes rain, snow, sleet, and hail (90)

precipitación cualquier forma de agua que cae de las nubes a la superficie de la Tierra; incluye a la lluvia, nieve, aguanieve y granizo (90)

predation (pree DAY shuhn) an interaction between two organisms in which one organism, the predator, kills and feeds on the other organism, the prey (109)

depredación la interacción entre dos organismos en la que un organismo, el depredador, mata a otro organismo, la presa, y se alimenta de él (109)

pregnancy (PREG nuhn see) in developmental biology, the period of time in which a woman carries a developing human from fertilization until the birth of the baby (about 266 days, or 38 weeks); in medical practice, this period of time is measured from the first day of a woman's last menstrual period to the delivery of her baby (about 280 days, or 40 weeks) (998)

embarazo en biología del desarrollo, el período de tiempo durante el cual una mujer lleva en su interior a un ser humano en desarrollo desde la fecundación hasta el nacimiento del bebé (aproximadamente 266 días, o 38 semanas); en medicina, este período se mide desde el primer día del último período menstrual de una mujer hasta el nacimiento del bebé (aproximadamente 280 días, o 40 semanas) (998)

primary growth (PRIE MER ee) the growth that occurs as a result of cell division at the tips of stems and roots and that gives rise to primary tissue (587)

crecimiento primario el crecimiento que ocurre como resultado de la división celular en las puntas de los tallos y raíces y que da lugar al tejido primario (587)

primate (PRIE MAYT) a member of the order Primates, the group of mammals that includes humans, apes, monkeys, and prosimians; typically distinguished by a highly developed brain, forward-directed eyes and binocular vision, opposable thumbs, and varied locomotion (797)

primate un miembro del orden de los primates, el grupo de mamíferos entre los que se encuentran los seres humanos, los simios, los monos y los prosimios; normalmente se distinguen por un cerebro muy desarrollado, ojos que miran hacia delante y visión binocular, pulgares oponibles y locomoción variada (797)

primer (PRIEM uhr) a short, single-stranded fragment of DNA or RNA that is required for the initiation of DNA replication (357)

cebador un fragmento corto de una sola hebra de ADN o ARN que se requiere para iniciar la replicación del ADN (357)

prion (PRIE AHN) an infectious particle that consists only of a protein and that does not contain DNA or RNA (480)

prión una partícula infecciosa formada únicamente por una proteína y que no contiene ni ADN ni ARN (480)

probability (PRAHB uh BIL uh tee) the likelihood that a possible future event will occur in any given instance of the event; the mathematical ratio of the number of times one outcome of any event is likely to occur to the number of possible outcomes of the event (278)

probabilidad término que describe qué tan probable es que ocurra un posible evento futuro en un caso dado del evento; la proporción matemática del número de veces que es posible que ocurra un resultado de cualquier evento respecto al número de resultados posibles del evento (278)

producer (proh DOOS uhr) an organism that can make organic molecules from inorganic molecules; a photosynthetic or chemosynthetic autotroph that serves as the basic food source in an ecosystem (86)

productor un organismo que elabora moléculas orgánicas a partir de moléculas inorgánicas; un autótrofo fotosintético o quimiosintético que funciona como la fuente fundamental de alimento en un ecosistema (86)

product a substance that forms in a chemical reaction (65)

producto una sustancia que se forma en una reacción química (65)

progesterone (proh JES tuhr OHN) a steroid hormone that is secreted by the corpus luteum of the ovary, that stimulates changes in the uterus to prepare for the implantation of a fertilized egg, and that is produced by the placenta during pregnancy (982)

progesterona una hormona esteroide que es secretada por el corpus luteum del ovario, la cual estimula cambios en el útero con el fin de prepararlo para la implantación del óvulo fecundado, y que es producida por la placenta durante el embarazo (982)

proglottid (proh GLAHT id) one of the many body sections of a tapeworm; contains reproductive organs (665)

proglótido una de las muchas secciones corporales de una tenia; contiene los órganos reproductores (665)

prokaryote (proh KAR ee OHT) a single-celled organism that does not have a nucleus or membrane-bound organelles; examples are archaea and bacteria (154)

procariote un organismo unicelular que no tiene núcleo ni organelos cubiertos por una membrana, por ejemplo, las arqueas y las bacterias (154)

promoter (proh MOHT uhr) a nucleotide sequence on a DNA molecule to which an RNA polymerase molecule binds, which initiates the transcription of a specific gene (306, 326)

promotor una secuencia de nucleótidos en una molécula de ADN a la cual se une una molécula de ARN polimerasa, lo cual inicia la transcripción de un gene específico (306, 326)

prophage (PROH FAYJ) the viral genome (DNA) of a bacteriophage that has entered a bacterial cell, has become attached to the bacterial chromosome, and is replicated with the host bacterium's DNA (478)

prófago el genoma viral (ADN) de un bacteriófago que ha entrado a una célula bacteriana, se ha unido al cromosoma bacteriano y se duplica con el ADN de la bacteria huésped (478)

prostate gland (PRAHS TAYT) a gland in males that contributes to the seminal fluid (995)

glándula próstata una glándula que contribuye al fluido seminal en los machos (995)

protein (PROH TEEN) an organic compound that is made of one or more chains of amino acids and that is a principal component of all cells (62)

proteína un compuesto orgánico que está hecho de una o más cadenas de aminoácidos y que es el principal componente de todas las células (62)

protist (PROH tist) an organism that belongs to the kingdom Protista (436)

protista un organismo que pertenece al reino Protista (436)

proton (PROH TAHN) a subatomic particle that has a positive charge and that is located in the nucleus of an atom; the number of protons in the nucleus is the atomic number, which determines the identity of an element (51)

protón una partícula subatómica que tiene una carga positiva y que está ubicada en el núcleo de un átomo; el número de protones que hay en el núcleo es el número atómico, y éste determina la identidad del elemento (51)

protostome (PROHD uh STOHM) an organism whose embryonic blastopore develops into the mouth, whose coelom arises by schizocoely, and whose embryo has determinate cleavage (635)

protoestoma un organismo cuyo blastoporo embriónico se desarrolla para convertirse en la boca, cuyo celoma surge por esquizocelia y cuyo embrión tiene segmentación determinada (635)

pseudocoelom (SOO doh SEE luhm) the type of body cavity, derived from the blastocoel and referred to as a "false body cavity," that forms between the mesoderm and the endoderm in rotifers and roundworms (667)

pseudoceloma el tipo de cavidad del cuerpo que se deriva del blastocelo y se denomina "cavidad falsa del cuerpo", la cual se forma entre el mesodermo y el endodermo en los rotíferos y en los gusanos planos (667)

pseudocoelomate (SOO doh SEE luh MAYT) an animal that has a pseudocoelom, or false body cavity (636)

pseudocelomado un animal que tiene un pseudoceloma, o cavidad falsa del cuerpo (636)

pseudopodium (SOO doh POH dee uhm) a retractable, temporary cytoplasmic extension that functions in food ingestion and movement in certain amoeboid cells (502)

pseudopodio una extensión citoplásmica retráctil y temporal que tiene una función en la ingestión de alimentos y en el movimiento de algunas células ameboides (502)

psychoactive drug (SIE koh AK tiv) a substance that has a significant effect on the mind or on behavior (956)

droga psicoactiva una sustancia que tiene un efecto considerable en la mente o en el comportamiento (956)

pulmonary vein (PUHL muh NER ee) the vein that carries oxygenated blood from the lungs to the heart (743)

vena pulmonar la vena que lleva sangre oxigenada de los pulmones al corazón (743)

pulse the rhythmic pressure of the blood against the walls of a vessel, particularly an artery (867)

pulso la presión rítmica de la sangre contra las paredes de un vaso sanguíneo, particularmente de una arteria (867)

punctuated equilibrium (PUHNGK choo AYT id EE kwi LIB ree uhm) a model of evolution in which short periods of drastic change in species, including mass extinctions and rapid speciation, are separated by long periods of little or no change (389)

equilibrio puntuado un modelo de evolución en el que períodos cortos en los que ocurren cambios drásticos en una especie (incluyendo extinciones masivas y especiación rápida) están separados por períodos largos en los que ocurren muy pocos cambios o en los que no ocurre ningún cambio (389)

Punnett square (PUH nuht) a graphic used to predict the results of a genetic cross (276)

cuadro de Punnett una gráfica que se usa para predecir los resultados de una cruza genética (276)

pupa (PYOO puh) the immobile, nonfeeding stage between the larva and the adult of insects that undergoes complete metamorphosis; as a pupa, the organism is usually enclosed in a cocoon or chrysalis and undergoes important anatomical changes (714)

pupa la etapa inmóvil y que no se alimenta, entre la larva y el adulto de insectos que experimentan una metamorfosis completa; en la etapa de pupa, el organismo normalmente está encerrado en un capullo o crisálida y sufre importantes cambios anatómicos (714)

purine (PYOOR EEN) a nitrogenous base that has a double-ring structure; one of the two general categories of nitrogenous bases found in DNA and RNA; either adenine or guanine (297)

purina una base nitrogenada que tiene una estructura de anillo doble; una de las dos categorías generales de bases nitrogenadas que se encuentran en el ADN y ARN; ya sea la adenina o la guanina (297)

root hair an extension of the epidermis of a root that increases the root's surface area for absorption (574)

pelo radicular una extensión de la epidermis de una raíz, la cual aumenta el área superficial de la raíz para la absorción (574)

rough endoplasmic reticulum (EN doh PLAZ mik ri TIK yuh luhm) the portion of the endoplasmic reticulum to which ribosomes are attached (158)

retículo endoplásmico rugoso la porción del retículo endoplásmico a la que se unen los ribosomas (158)

rRNA ribosomal RNA, an organelle that contains most of the RNA in the cell and that is responsible for ribosome function (305)

ARNr ARN ribosomal; un organelo que contiene la mayor parte del ARN en la célula y que es responsable del funcionamiento de los ribosomas (305)

saprobe (SA PROHB) an organism that absorbs nutrients from dead or decaying organic matter (522)

saprofito un organismo que absorbe nutrientes de materia orgánica muerta o en descomposición (522)

sapwood the tissue of the secondary xylem that is distributed around the outside of a tree trunk and is active in transporting sap (581)

albura el tejido del xilema secundario que se distribuye en el exterior del tronco de un árbol y que tiene una función en el transporte de la savia (581)

sarcomere (SAHR koh MIR) the basic unit of contraction in skeletal and cardiac muscle (850)

sarcómero la unidad fundamental de contracción del músculo esquelético y cardíaco (850)

savanna (suh VAN uh) a plain full of grasses and scattered trees and shrubs; found in tropical and subtropical habitats and mainly in regions with a dry climate, such as East Africa (83)

sabana una planicie llena de pastizales y árboles y arbustos dispersos; se encuentra en los hábitats tropicales y subtropicales y, sobre todo, en regiones con un clima seco, como en el este de África (83)

schistosomiasis (SHIS tuh soh MIE uh sis) a disease that is caused by a parasitic blood fluke of the genus Schistosoma and that affects the skin, intestines, liver, vascular system, or other organs (666)

esquistosomiasis una enfermedad que es causada por un trematodo sanguíneo parasítico del género Schistosoma y que afecta la piel, intestinos, hígado, sistema vascular u otros órganos (666)

scrotum (SKROHT uhm) the sac that contains the testes in most male mammals (993)

escroto la bolsa que contiene los testículos en la mayoría de los mamíferos machos (993)

seminiferous tubule (sem uh NIF uhr uhs) one of the many tubules in the testis where sperm are produced (993)

túbulo seminífero uno de los muchos túbulos que hay en los testículos, en donde se producen los espermatozoides (993)

sebum (SEE buhm) the oily secretion of the sebaceous glands (854)

sebo la secreción grasosa de las glándulas sebáceas (854)

secondary growth plant growth that results from cell division in the cambia, or lateral meristems, and that causes the stems and roots to thicken (587)

crecimiento secundario crecimiento de las plantas que ocurre como resultado de la división celular en los cámbiums, o meristemos laterales, y que hace que se engruesen los tallos y las raíces (587)

second messenger a molecule that is generated when a specific substance attaches to a receptor on the outside of a cell membrane, which produces a change in cellular function (186, 974)

mensajero secundario una molécula que se genera cuando una sustancia específica se une a un receptor en el exterior de la membrana celular, lo cual produce un cambio en la función celular (186, 974)

seed a plant embryo that is enclosed in a protective coat (554)

semilla el embrión de una planta que está encerrado en una cubierta protectora (554)

semen (SEE muhn) the fluid that contains sperm and various secretions produced by the male reproductive organs (995)

semen el fluido que contiene espermatozoides y varias secreciones producidas por los órganos reproductores masculinos (995)

semicircular canal (SE mee SUHR kyuh luhr) the fluid-filled canal in the inner ear that helps maintain balance and coordinate movements (952)

canal semicircular el canal lleno de fluido ubicado en el oído interno, el cual ayuda a mantener el equilibrio y a coordinar los movimientos (952)

seminal vesicle (SEM uh nuhl VES i kuhl) one of two glandular structures in male vertebrates that hold and secrete seminal fluid (995)

vesícula seminal una de las dos estructuras glandulares en los vertebrados macho, las cuales acumulan y secretan fluido seminal (995)

sensory neuron (SEN suhr ee NOO RAHN) a neuron that carries stimuli from a sense organ to the central nervous system (939)

neurona sensorial una neurona que lleva estímulos de un órgano sensorial al sistema nervioso central (939)

sensory receptor (SEN suhr ee ri SEP tuhr) a specialized structure that contains the ends of sensory neurons and that responds to specific types of stimuli (951)

receptor sensorial una estructura especializada que contiene los extremos de las neuronas sensoriales y que responde a tipos específicos de estímulos (951)

sepal (SEE puhl) in a flower, one of the outermost rings of modified leaves that protect the flower bud (560)
sépalo en una flor, uno de los anillos más externos de hojas modificadas que protegen el capullo de la flor (560)

septum (SEP tuhm) a dividing wall, or partition, such as the wall between adjacent cells in a fungal hypha, the internal wall between adjacent segments of an annelid, and the thick wall between the right and left chambers of the heart (687, 742)
septum una pared divisoria, o partición, tal como la pared que se encuentra entre células adyacentes en las hifas de los hongos, la pared interna que se encuentra entre segmentos adyacentes de un anélido y la pared gruesa que se encuentra entre las cámaras derecha e izquierda del corazón (687, 742)

seta (SEET uh) one of the external bristles or spines that project from the body of an annelid (686)
seta una de las cerdas o espinas externas que se proyectan del cuerpo de un anélido (686)

sex chromosome one of the pair of chromosomes that determine the sex of an individual (249)
cromosoma sexual uno de los dos cromosomas que determinan el sexo de un individuo (249)

sexual reproduction reproduction in which gametes from two parents unite (248)
reproducción sexual reproducción en la que se unen los gametos de los dos progenitores (248)

sexual selection an evolutionary mechanism by which traits that increase the ability of individuals to attract or acquire mates appear with increasing frequency in a population; selection in which a mate is chosen on the basis of a particular trait or traits (406, 826)
selección sexual un mecanismo evolutivo por medio del cual los caracteres que aumentan la capacidad de los individuos de atraer o adquirir una pareja aparecen con más frecuencia en una población; selección en la que se elige una pareja con base en un carácter o caracteres particulares (406, 826)

shoot the portion of a plant that grows mostly above the ground; includes the stems and leaves (587)
brote la porción de una planta que crece principalmente sobre el suelo; incluye los tallos y las hojas (587)

short-day plant a plant that produces flowers or changes in some other way when exposed to periods of daylight that are shorter than a critical length of time (608)
planta de día corto una planta que produce flores o que experimenta algún otro cambio cuando es expuesta a períodos de luz diurna más cortos que un cierto período de tiempo crítico (608)

SI (ES IE) Le Système International d'Unités, or the International System of Units, which is the measurement system that is accepted worldwide (15)
SI Le Système International d'Unités, o el Sistema Internacional de Unidades, que es el sistema de medición que se acepta en todo el mundo (15)

sieve-tube member (SIV TOOB) one of the component cells of a sieve tube, which is found mainly in flowering plants (576)
miembro de tubo criboso una de las células componentes de un tubo criboso, las cuales se encuentran en muchas plantas que dan flores (576)

signal anything that serves to direct, guide, or warn (184, 823)
señal cualquier cosa que sirve para dirigir, guiar o advertir (184, 823)

silent mutation an alteration of genetic information that has no apparent effect on the phenotype of an organism (320)
mutación silenciosa una alteración de la información genética que no tiene un efecto aparente en el fenotipo de un organismo (320)

sink any place where a plant stores or uses organic nutrients, such as sugar or starches (602)
sumidero cualquier lugar donde una planta almacena o usa nutrientes orgánicos, tales como azúcares o almidones (602)

sinoatrial node (SIE noh AY tree uhl) a mass of cardiac muscle cells that lies at the junction of the superior vena cava with the right atrium and that initiates and regulates contraction of the heart (abbreviation, SA node) (867)
nodo sinoatrial una masa de células de músculo cardíaco que se encuentra en la unión entre la vena cava superior y el atrio derecho, y que inicia y regula la contracción del corazón (abreviatura: nodo SA) (867)

siphon (SIE fuhn) a hollow tube of bivalves used for sucking in and expelling sea water (684)
sifón un conducto hueco que los bivalvos utilizan para sorber y expulsar el agua de mar (684)

skepticism (SKEP ti SIZ uhm) a habit of mind in which a person questions the validity of accepted ideas (7)
escepticismo un hábito de la mente que hace que la persona cuestione la validez de las ideas aceptadas (7)

skin gill a transparent structure that projects from the surface of a sea star and that enables respiration (718)
branquia de la piel una estructura transparente que protege la superficie de las estrellas de mar y les permite respirar (718)

slow-twitch fiber a muscle fiber that is resistant to fatigue but that produces less force than a fast-twitch muscle fiber does (852)
fibra de contracción lenta una fibra muscular que es resistente a la fatiga pero que produce menos fuerza que una fibra muscular de contracción rápida (852)

smooth endoplasmic reticulum (EN doh PLAZ mik ri TIK yuh luhm) the portion of the endoplasmic reticulum that lacks attached ribosomes (158)

retículo endoplásmico liso la porción del retículo endoplásmico que no tiene ribosomas adjuntos (158)

sodium-potassium pump (SOH dee uhm poh TAS ee uhm) a carrier protein that uses ATP to actively transport sodium ions out of a cell and potassium ions into the cell (182)

bomba de sodio-potasio una proteína transportadora que utiliza el ATP para efectuar el transporte activo de iones de sodio hacia el exterior de la célula y de iones de potasio hacia el interior de la célula (182)

solution (suh LOO shuhn) a homogeneous mixture throughout which two or more substances are uniformly dispersed (56)

solución una mezcla homogénea en la cual dos o más sustancias se dispersan de manera uniforme (56)

somatic cell (soh MAT ik) a cell other than a gamete or germ cell; a body cell (248, 322, 403)

célula somática una célula que no es un gameto o una célula germinal; una célula del cuerpo (248, 322, 403)

somatic nervous system (soh MAT ik) the portion of the neural structure that provides nerve connections to the skin, skeleton, and muscles of the body, but not to the viscera, blood vessels, and glands (942)

sistema nervioso somático la porción de la estructura neural que provee conexiones nerviosas a la piel, al esqueleto y a los músculos del cuerpo, pero no a las vísceras, vasos sanguíneos y glándulas (942)

sorus (SOH ruhs) a cluster of spores or sporangia (552)

soro un grupo de esporas o esporangios (552)

source a part of a plant that makes sugars and other organic compounds and from which these compounds are transported to other parts of the plant (602)

fuente la parte de una planta que elabora azúcares y otros compuestos orgánicos y a partir de la cual estos compuestos se transportan a otras partes de la planta (602)

speciation (SPEE shee AY shuhn) the formation of new species as a result of evolution (387, 412)

especiación la formación de especies nuevas como resultado de la evolución (387, 412)

species (SPEE seez) a group of organisms that are closely related and can mate to produce fertile offspring; *also* the level of classification below genus and above subspecies (19, 387, 411, 426)

especie un grupo de organismos que tienen un parentesco cercano y que pueden aparearse para producir descendencia fértil; *también,* el nivel de clasificación debajo de género y arriba de subespecie (19, 387, 411, 426)

spectrometer (spek TRAHM uht uhr) an instrument that measures wavelengths and intensity of visible light or other electromagnetic radiation (1020)

espectrómetro un instrumento que mide la longitud de onda y la intensidad de la luz visible o de otra radiación electromagnética (1020)

sperm (SPUHRM) the male gamete (sex cell) (255)

espermatozoide el gameto masculino (célula sexual) (255)

spicule (SPIK YOOL) a needle of silica or calcium carbonate in the skeleton of some sponges (657)

espícula una aguja de sílice o carbonato de calcio que se encuentra en el esqueleto de algunas esponjas (657)

spinal cord (SPIE nuhl) a column of nerve tissue running from the base of the brain through the vertebral column (941)

médula espinal una columna de tejido nervioso que se origina en la base del cerebro y corre a lo largo de la columna vertebral (941)

spindle (SPIN duhl) a network of microtubules that forms during mitosis and moves chromatids to the poles (230)

huso mitótico una red de microtúbulos que se forma durante la mitosis y que mueve cromátidas a los polos (230)

spinneret (SPIN uh RET) an organ that spiders and certain insect larvae use to produce silky threads for webs and cocoons (707)

hilera un órgano que utilizan las arañas y algunas larvas de insectos para producir hilos sedosos con los que hacen redes y capullos (707)

spiracle (SPIR uh kuhl) an external opening in an insect or arthropod, used in respiration (703)

espiráculo una abertura externa de un insecto o artrópodo, que se usa en la respiración (703)

spongin (SPUHN jin) a fibrous protein that contains sulfur and composes the fibers of the skeleton of some sponges (657)

espongina una proteína fibrosa que contiene azufre y que forma las fibras del esqueleto de algunas esponjas (657)

spongy mesophyll (MES oh FIL) inside a leaf, the tissue that is made up of loosely arranged parenchyma cells that contain chloroplasts and are surrounded by air spaces that promote the diffusion of oxygen, carbon dioxide, and water throughout the leaf (583)

mesófilo esponjoso dentro de una hoja, el tejido que está formado por células de parénquima colocadas de manera poco apretada, las cuales contienen cloroplastos y están rodeadas por espacios de aire que promueven la difusión del oxígeno, dióxido de carbono y agua a través de la hoja (583)

sporangium (spoh RAN jee uhm) a specialized sac, case, capsule, or other structure that produces spores (548, 525)

esporangio una bolsa, cubierta, cápsula u otra estructura especializada que produce esporas (548, 525)

spore a reproductive cell or multicellular structure that is resistant to environmental conditions and that can develop into an adult without fusion with another cell (545)
espora una célula reproductora o estructura pluricelular que resiste las condiciones ambientales y que se puede desarrollar para convertirse en un adulto sin necesidad de fusionarse con otra célula (545)

sporophyte (SPOH ruh FIET) in plants and algae that have alternation of generations, the diploid individual or generation that produces haploid spores (258, 499, 546)
esporofito en las plantas y algas que tienen generaciones alternas, el individuo o generación diploide que produce esporas haploides (258, 499, 546)

stabilizing selection (STAY buh LIEZ ing) a type of natural selection in which the average form of a trait is favored and becomes more common (409)
selección de estabilización un tipo de selección natural en la que se favorece la forma promedio de un carácter, el cual se vuelve más común (409)

stamen (STAY muhn) the male reproductive structure of a flower that produces pollen and consists of an anther at the tip of a filament (560)
estambre la estructura reproductora masculina de una flor, que produce polen y está formada por una antera ubicada en la punta del filamento (560)

stem cell a cell that can divide repeatedly and can differentiate into specialized cell types (353, 839)
célula madre una célula que puede dividirse repetidamente y puede diferenciarse y formar tipos de células especializados (353, 839)

sticky end a single-stranded end of a double-stranded DNA molecule; can base-pair with a complementary sticky end (355)
extremo cohesivo el extremo de una hebra de la molécula de ADN de doble hebra; puede formar pares de bases con un extremo cohesivo complementario (355)

stimulant (STIM yoo luhnt) a drug that increases the activity of the body or the activity of some part of the body (956)
estimulante una droga que aumenta la actividad del cuerpo o la actividad de alguna parte del cuerpo (956)

stimulus (STIM yoo luhs) anything that causes a reaction or change in an organism or any part of an organism (813)
estímulo cualquier cosa que causa una reacción o cambio en un organismo o cualquier parte de un organismo (813)

stoma (STOH muh) one of many openings in a leaf or a stem of a plant that enable gas exchange to occur (plural, *stomata*) (575)
estoma una de las muchas aberturas de una hoja o de un tallo de una planta, la cual permite que se lleve a cabo el intercambio de gases (575)

stroke a sudden loss of consciousness or paralysis that occurs when the blood flow to the brain is interrupted (873)
ataque de apoplejía una pérdida súbita de la conciencia o parálisis que ocurre cuando se interrumpe el flujo sanguíneo al cerebro (873)

style in plants, the slender, upper part of the pistil (560)
estilo en las plantas, la parte superior y delgada del pistilo (560)

subcutaneous tissue (SUHB kyoo TAY nee uhs) the layer of cells that lies beneath the skin (853)
tejido subcutáneo la capa de células que se encuentra debajo de la piel (853)

subspecies (SUHB SPEE sheez) a taxonomic classification below species that groups organisms that live in different geographical areas, differ morphologically from other populations of the species, but can interbreed with other populations of the species (412)
subespecie una clasificación taxonómica que se ubica debajo de la especie y agrupa a organismos que viven en áreas geográficas diferentes y difieren en forma morfológica de otras poblaciones de la especie, pero tienen la capacidad de cruzarse con otras poblaciones de la especie (412)

substrate (SUHB strayt) a part, substance, or element that lies beneath and supports another part, substance, or element; the reactant in reactions catalyzed by enzymes (66)
sustrato una parte, sustancia o elemento que se encuentra debajo de otra parte, sustancia o elemento y lo sostiene; el reactivo en reacciones que son catalizadas por enzimas (66)

succession (suhk SESH uhn) the replacement of one type of community by another at a single location over a period of time (81)
sucesión el reemplazo de un tipo de comunidad por otro en un mismo lugar a lo largo de un período de tiempo (81)

swim bladder (BLAD uhr) in bony fishes, a gas-filled sac that is used to control buoyancy (730)
vejiga natatoria en los peces óseos, una bolsa llena de gas que se usa para controlar la flotabilidad (730)

symbiosis (SIM bie OH sis) a relationship in which two different organisms live in close association with each other (110, 331)
simbiosis una relación en la que dos organismos diferentes viven estrechamente asociados uno con el otro (110, 331)

synapse (SIN APS) the junction at which the end of the axon of a neuron meets the end of a dendrite or the cell body of another neuron or meets another cell (948)
sinapsis el punto en el cual el extremo del axón de una neurona se une con el extremo de una dendrita o con el cuerpo de la célula de otra neurona, o bien, se encuentra con otra célula (948)

synaptic cleft (si NAP tik KLEFT) in the nervous system, the space that separates the presynaptic and postsynaptic neuron (948)

espacio sináptico en el sistema nervioso, el espacio que separa a la neurona presináptica de la neurona postsináptica (948)

systematics (SIS tuh MAT iks) the classification of living organisms in terms of their natural relationships; it includes describing, naming, and classifying the organisms (427)

sistemática la clasificación de los seres vivos en función de sus relaciones naturales; involucra describir, nombrar y clasificar a los organismos (427)

tadpole the aquatic, fishlike larva of a frog or toad (747)

renacuajo la larva acuática, parecida a un pez, de una rana o sapo (747)

taiga (TIE guh) a region of evergreen, coniferous forest below the arctic and subarctic tundra regions (83)

taiga una región de bosques siempreverdes de coníferas, ubicado debajo de las regiones árticas y subárticas de tundra (83)

taproot a root that develops from the radicle of a plant embryo, grows vertically downward, and forms branches called *lateral roots* (579)

raíz principal una raíz que se desarrolla a partir de la radícula de un embrión vegetal, crece verticalmente hacia abajo y forma ramas llamadas *raíces laterales* (579)

target cell a specific cell to which a hormone is directed to produce a specific effect (184, 972)

célula blanco una célula específica a la que se dirige una hormona para producir un efecto específico (184, 972)

taste bud one of many oval concentrations of sensory nerve endings on the tongue, palate, and pharynx (953)

papila gustativa una de las muchas terminaciones nerviosas sensoriales que se encuentran en la lengua, paladar y faringe (953)

taxon (TAKS AHN) any named taxonomic group of any rank in the hierarchical classification of organisms; for example, family, genus, or species (423)

taxón cualquier grupo taxonómico nombrado de cualquier rango en la clasificación jerárquica de los organismos; por ejemplo: familia, género o especie (423)

taxonomy (taks AHN uh mee) the science of describing, naming, and classifying organisms (423)

taxonomía la ciencia de describir, nombrar y clasificar organismos (423)

tegument (TEG yoo muhnt) the thick, protective covering that stops endoparasites (parasites that live inside their hosts) from being digested by their host (666)

tegumento el recubrimiento protector grueso que evita que los endoparásitos (parásitos que viven dentro del cuerpo de su huésped) sean digeridos por el huésped (666)

teleost (TEL ee AHST) a group of ray-finned fishes that have a caudal fin, scales, and a swim bladder; the largest group of bony fishes (738)

teleósteo un grupo de peces con aletas rayadas que tienen una aleta caudal, escamas y una vejiga natatoria; el grupo más grande de peces óseos (738)

telomere (TEL uh MIR) the region at the tip of a chromosome; a region of repeating DNA sequences that forms one of the end points of the DNA segment that makes up a chromosome (334)

telómero la región de la punta de un cromosoma; una región de secuencias de ADN repetidas que forma uno de los extremos del segmento de ADN que compone un cromosoma (334)

temperate (TEM puhr it) describes a nonvirulent virus that rarely causes lysis in host cells (478)

atenuado término que describe a un virus no virulento que rara vez causa lisis en las células huésped (478)

temperate grassland a community (or biome) that is dominated by grasses, has few trees, and is characterized by cold winters and rainfall that is intermediate between that of a forest and a desert (83)

pradera templada una comunidad (o bioma) que está dominada por pastos, tiene pocos árboles y se caracteriza por inviernos fríos y precipitación pluvial que es intermedia entre la de un bosque y la de un desierto (83)

tendon (TEN duhn) a tough connective tissue that attaches a muscle to a bone or to another body part (849)

tendón un tejido conectivo duro que une un músculo con un hueso o con otra parte del cuerpo (849)

territorial behavior (TER uh TAWR ee uhl) behavior exhibited by an animal in defending its living space (825)

conducta territorial conducta que muestra un animal cuando defiende el espacio en el que vive (825)

test a skeletal covering that some invertebrates secrete or build (502)

encrustamiento una cubierta esquelética que secretan o elaboran algunos invertebrados (502)

testes (TES TEEZ) the primary male reproductive organs, which produce sperm cells and testosterone (singular, *testis*) (993)

testículos los principales órganos reproductores masculinos, los cuales producen espermatozoides y testosterona (993)

tetrad (TE TRAD) the four chromatids in a pair of homologous chromosomes that come together as a result of synapsis during meiosis (252)

tétrada las cuatro cromátidas que se encuentran en un par de cromosomas homólogos, las cuales vienen juntas como resultado de la sinapsis durante la meiosis (252)

thalamus (THAL uh muhs) the part of the brain that directs incoming sensory and motor signals to the proper region (940)

tálamo la parte del cerebro que dirige a la región apropiada las señales sensoriales y motoras que se reciben (940)

theory (THEE uh ree) a system of ideas that explains many related observations and is supported by a large body of evidence acquired through scientific investigation (13, 375)

teoría un sistema de ideas que explica muchas observaciones relacionadas y que está respaldado por una gran cantidad de pruebas obtenidas mediante la investigación científica (13, 375)

therapsid (thuh RAP sid) the extinct order of mammal-like reptiles that likely gave rise to mammals (644)

terápsido el orden extinto de reptiles parecidos a mamíferos que posiblemente dio origen a los mamíferos (644)

thigmotropism (THIG moh TROH PIZ uhm) a response of an organism or part of an organism to touch, such as the coiling of a vine around an object (607)

tigmotropismo la respuesta de un organismo o de una parte de un organismo al tacto, como por ejemplo, el enroscamiento de una enredadera alrededor de un objeto (607)

thorax (THAWR AKS) in higher vertebrates, the part of the body between the neck and the abdomen; in other animals, the body region behind the head; in arthropods, the mid-body region (701)

tórax en los vertebrados superiores, la parte del cuerpo que se encuentra entre el cuello y el abdomen; en otros animales, la región del cuerpo que se encuentra detrás de la cabeza; en los artrópodos, la región media del cuerpo (701)

thylakoid (THIE luh KOYD) a membrane system found within chloroplasts that contains the components for photosynthesis (202)

tilacoide un sistema de membranas que se encuentra dentro de los cloroplastos y que contiene los componentes para que se lleve a cabo la fotosíntesis (202)

thymine (THIE MEEN) one of the four bases that combine with sugar and phosphate to form a nucleotide subunit of DNA; thymine pairs with adenine (297)

timina una de las cuatro bases que se combinan con un azúcar y un fosfato para formar una subunidad de nucleótido de ADN; la timina se une a la adenina (297)

tissue (TISH oo) a group of similar cells that perform a common function (164, 632)

tejido un grupo de células similares que llevan a cabo una función común (164, 632)

tolerance (TAHL uhr uhns) the condition of drug addiction in which greater amounts of a drug are needed to achieve the desired effect (959)

tolerancia el estado de adicción a una droga en el que se necesitan mayores cantidades de la droga para obtener el efecto deseado (959)

toxicology (TAHKS i KAHL uh jee) the study of toxic substances, including their nature, effects, detection, methods of treatment, and exposure control (1026)

toxicología el estudio de las sustancias tóxicas, incluyendo su naturaleza, efectos, detección, métodos de tratamiento y control de exposición (1026)

toxin (TAHKS in) a substance that is produced by one organism and that is poisonous to other organisms (482)

toxina una sustancia que un organismo produce y que es venenosa para otros organismos (482)

trachea (TRAY kee uh) in insects, myriapods, and spiders, one of a network of air tubes; in vertebrates, the tube that connects the larynx to the lungs (703, 876)

tráquea en los insectos, miriápodos y arañas, uno de los conductos de una red de conductos de aire; en los vertebrados, el conducto que une la laringe con los pulmones (703, 876)

tracheid (TRAY kee id) a thick-walled, cylindrical cell with tapered ends that is found in xylem and that provides support and conducts water and nutrients (576)

traqueida una célula cilíndrica que tiene la pared gruesa y cuyos extremos terminan en punta, la cual se encuentra en el xilema, brinda sostén y transporta agua y nutrientes (576)

trait (TRAYT) a genetically determined characteristic (268)

carácter una característica determinada genéticamente (268)

transcription (tran SKRIP shuhn) the process of forming a nucleic acid by using another molecule as a template; particularly the process of synthesizing RNA by using one strand of a DNA molecule as a template (305)

transcripción el proceso de formar un ácido nucleico usando otra molécula como plantilla; en particular, el proceso de sintetizar ARN usando una de las hebras de la molécula de ADN como plantilla (305)

transcription factor an enzyme that is needed to begin and/or continue genetic transcription (327)

factor de transcripción una enzima que se necesita para comenzar y/ o continuar la transcripción genética (327)

transduction (trans DUHK shuhn) the transfer of a bacterial gene from one bacterium to another through a bacteriophage (475)

transducción la transferencia del gene de una bacteria de una bacteria a otra por medio de un bacteriófago (475)

transfer RNA an RNA molecule that transfers amino acids to the growing end of a polypeptide chain during translation (305)

ARN de transferencia una molécula de ARN que transfiere aminoácidos al extremo en crecimiento de una cadena de polipéptidos durante la traducción (305)

transformation (TRANS fuhr MAY shuhn) the transfer of genetic material in the form of DNA fragments from one cell to another or from one organism to another (294, 475)

transformación la transferencia de material genético en forma de fragmentos de ADN de una célula a otra o de un organismo a otro (294, 475)

transgenic organism (trans JE nik) an organism that has been transformed by the introduction of novel DNA into its genome (350)

organismo transgénico un organismo que ha sido transformado por la introducción de ADN nuevo a su genoma (350)

translation (trans LAY shuhn) the portion of protein synthesis that takes place at ribosomes and that uses the codons in mRNA molecules to specify the sequence of amino acids in polypeptide chains (305)

traducción la porción de la síntesis de proteínas que tiene lugar en los ribosomas y que usa los codones de las moléculas de ARNm para especificar la secuencia de aminoácidos en las cadenas de polipéptidos (305)

translocation (TRANS loh KAY shuhn) the movement of a segment of DNA from one chromosome to another, which results in a change in the position of the segment; *also* the movement of soluble nutrients from one part of a plant to another (602)

translocación el movimiento de un segmento de ADN de un cromosoma a otro, lo cual resulta en un cambio en la posición del segmento; *también,* el movimiento de nutrientes solubles de una parte a otra de una planta (602)

transpiration (TRAN spuh RAY shuhn) the process by which plants release water vapor into the air through stomata; *also* the release of water vapor into the air by other organisms (90, 600)

transpiración el proceso por medio del cual las plantas liberan vapor de agua al aire por medio de los estomas; *también,* la liberación de vapor de agua al aire por otros organismos (90, 600)

transposon (trans POH ZAHN) a genetic sequence that is randomly moved, in a functional unit, to new places in a genome (332)

transposón una secuencia genética que se mueve al azar, en una unidad funcional, a lugares nuevos dentro de un genoma (332)

trochophore (TRAHK on FAWR) a free-swimming, ciliated larva of many worms and some mollusks (682)

trocófora una larva ciliada de muchos gusanos y algunos moluscos, la cual nada libremente (682)

trophic level (TRAHF ik) one of the steps in a food chain or food pyramid; examples include producers and primary, secondary, and tertiary consumers (86)

nivel trófico uno de los pasos de la cadena alimenticia o de la pirámide alimenticia; entre los ejemplos se encuentran los productores y los consumidores primarios, secundarios y terciarios (86)

tropical rain forest (TRAHP i kuhl) a forest or jungle near the equator that is characterized by large amounts of rain and little variation in temperature and that contains the greatest known diversity of organisms on Earth (83)

selva tropical un bosque o jungla que se encuentra cerca del ecuador y se caracteriza por una gran cantidad de lluvia y poca variación en la temperatura, y que contiene la mayor diversidad de organismos que se conoce en la Tierra (83)

tropism (TROH PIZ uhm) the movement of all or part of an organism in response to an external stimulus, such as light or heat; movement is either toward or away from the stimulus (606)

tropismo el movimiento de un organismo o de una parte de él en respuesta a un estímulo externo, como por ejemplo, la luz o el calor; el movimiento puede ser hacia el estímulo o en sentido opuesto a él (606)

true-breeding describes organisms or genotypes that are homozygous for a specific trait and thus always produce offspring that have the same phenotype for that trait (269)

variedad pura término que describe organismos o genotipos que son homocigotos para un carácter específico y, por lo tanto, producen descendencia que tiene el mismo fenotipo para ese carácter (269)

tube foot one of many small, flexible, fluid-filled tubes that project from the body of an echinoderm and that are used in locomotion, feeding, gas exchange, and excretion (718)

pie ambulacral uno de los muchos tubos pequeños, flexibles y llenos de fluido que se proyectan a partir del cuerpo de un equinodermo y se usan en la locomoción, intercambio de gases y excreción (718)

tumor (TOO muhr) a growth that arises from normal tissue but that grows abnormally in rate and structure and lacks a function (235, 323)

tumor un bulto que surge en un tejido normal, pero que crece anormalmente en tasa y estructura, y carece de función (235, 323)

tundra (TUHN druh) a treeless plain that is located in the Arctic or Antarctic and that is characterized by very low winter temperatures; short, cool summers; and vegetation that consists of grasses, lichens, and perennial herbs (83)

tundra una llanura sin árboles situada en la región ártica o antártica y se caracteriza por temperaturas muy bajas en el invierno, veranos cortos y frescos y vegetación que consiste en pasto, líquenes y hierbas perennes (83)

tympanic membrane (tim PAN ik) the eardrum (740)

membrana timpánica el tímpano (740)

ulcer (UHL suhr) a lesion of the surface of the skin or a mucous membrane; sometimes occurs in the digestive system (897)

úlcera una lesión en la superficie de la piel o en una membrana mucosa; a veces ocurre en el aparato digestivo (897)

unicellular (YOON uh SEL yoo luhr) describes an organism that consists of a single cell (434)

unicelular término que describe a un organismo que está formado por una sola célula (434)

uracil (YOOR uh SIL) one of the four bases that combine with sugar and phosphate to form a nucleotide subunit of RNA; uracil pairs with adenine (305)

uracilo una de las cuatro bases que se combinan con un azúcar y un fosfato para formar una subunidad de nucleótido de ADN; el uracilo se une a la adenina (305)

urea (yoo REE uh) the principal nitrogenous product of the metabolism of proteins that forms in the liver from amino acids and from compounds of ammonia and that is found in urine and other body fluids (902)

urea el principal producto nitrogenado que se obtiene del metabolismo de las proteínas, se forma en el hígado a partir de aminoácidos y compuestos de amoníaco y se encuentra en la orina y otros fluidos del cuerpo (902)

ureter (yoo REET uhr) one of the two narrow tubes that carry urine from the kidneys to the urinary bladder (904)

uréter uno de los dos tubos angostos que llevan orina de los riñones a la vejiga urinaria (904)

urethra (yoo REE thruh) the tube that carries urine from the urinary bladder to the outside of the body (904)

uretra el tubo que lleva orina de la vejiga urinaria al exterior del cuerpo (904)

urinary bladder (YUR uh NER ee) a hollow, muscular organ that stores urine (904)

vejiga urinaria un órgano hueco y muscular que almacena orina (904)

urine (YUR in) the liquid excreted by the kidneys, stored in the bladder, and passed through the urethra to the outside of the body (904)

orina el líquido que excretan los riñones, se almacena en la vejiga y pasa a través de la uretra hacia el exterior del cuerpo (904)

uterus (YOOT uhr uhs) in female placental mammals, the hollow, muscular organ in which an embryo embeds itself and develops into a fetus (997)

útero en los mamíferos placentarios hembras, el órgano hueco y muscular en el que el embrión se incrusta y se desarrolla hasta convertirse en feto (997)

vaccination (VAK suh NAY shuhn) the administration of treated microorganisms into humans or animals to induce an immune response (31)

vacunación la administración a seres humanos o animales de organismos que han sido tratados para inducir una respuesta inmunológica (31)

vaccine (vak SEEN) a substance prepared from killed or weakened pathogens and introduced into a body to produce immunity (922)

vacuna una sustancia que se prepara a partir de organismos patógenos muertos o debilitados y se introduce al cuerpo para producir inmunidad (922)

vacuole (VAK yoo OHL) a fluid-filled vesicle found in the cytoplasm of plant cells or protozoans (160)

vacuola una vesícula llena de líquido que se encuentra en el citoplasma de las células vegetales o de los protozoarios (160)

vagina (vuh JIE nuh) the female reproductive organ that connects the outside of the body to the uterus and that receives sperm during reproduction (997)

vagina el canal de las hembras que se extiende de la vulva al cuello del útero y que recibe al pene durante el coito (997)

valence electron (VAY luhns) an electron that is found in the outermost shell of an atom and that determines the atom's chemical properties (52)

electrón de valencia un electrón que se encuentra en la capa más externa de un átomo y que determina las propiedades químicas del átomo (52)

vascular bundle (VAS kyuh luhr) in a plant, a strand of conducting tissue that contains both xylem and phloem (580)

haz vascular en una planta, una hebra de tejido de transporte que contiene tanto xilema como floema (580)

vascular cambium (VAS kyuh luhr KAM bee uhm) in a plant, the lateral meristem that produces secondary xylem and phloem (589)

cambio vascular en una planta, el meristemo lateral que produce xilema y floema secundarios (589)

vascular plant (VAS kyuh luhr) a plant that has a vascular system composed of xylem and phloem, specialized tissues that conduct materials from one part of the plant to another (544)

planta vascular una planta que tiene un sistema vascular formado por xilema y floema, tejidos especializados que transportan materiales de una parte de la planta a otra (544)

vascular tissue (VAS kyuh luhr) the specialized conducting tissue that is found in higher plants and that is made up mostly of xylem and phloem (573)

tejido vascular el tejido especializado de transporte que se encuentra en las plantas superiores y que está formado principalmente por xilema y floema (573)

vas deferens (vas DEF uh renz) a duct through which sperm move from the epididymis to the ejaculatory duct at the base of the penis (994)

conducto deferente un conducto a través del cual los espermatozoides se mueven del epidídimo al conducto eyaculatorio que está en la base del pene (994)

vector (VEK tuhr) in biology, any agent, such as a plasmid or a virus, that can incorporate foreign DNA and transfer that DNA from one organism to another; an intermediate host that transfers a pathogen or a parasite to another organism (360)

vector en biología, cualquier agente, como por ejemplo un plásmido o un virus, que tiene la capacidad de incorporar ADN extraño y de transferir ese ADN de un organismo a otro; un huésped intermediario que transfiere un organismo patógeno o un parásito a otro organismo (360)

vegetative reproduction (VEJ uh TAYT iv) a type of asexual reproduction in which new plants grow from nonreproductive plant parts (564)

reproducción vegetativa un tipo de reproducción asexual en el que crecen plantas nuevas a partir de partes plantas que no se reproducen (564)

vein (VAYN) in biology, a vessel that carries blood to the heart (868)

vena en biología, un vaso que lleva sangre al corazón (868)

ventricle (VEN tri kuhl) one of the two large muscular chambers that pump blood out of the heart (867)

ventrículo una de las dos cámaras musculares grandes que bombean sangre hacia el exterior del corazón (867)

vertebra (VUHR tuh bruh) one of the 33 bones in the spinal column (backbone) (626)

vértebra uno de los 33 huesos de la columna vertebral (espina dorsal) (626)

vertebrate (VUHR tuh brit) an animal that has a backbone; includes mammals, birds, reptiles, amphibians, and fish (383, 626)

vertebrado un animal que tiene columna vertebral; incluye a los mamíferos, aves, reptiles, anfibios y peces (383, 626)

vesicle (VES i kuhl) a small cavity or sac that contains materials in a eukaryotic cell; forms when part of the cell membrane surrounds the materials to be taken into the cell or transported within the cell (158)

vesícula una cavidad o bolsa pequeña que contiene materiales en una célula eucariótica; se forma cuando parte de la membrana celular rodea los materiales que van a ser llevados al interior la célula o transportados dentro de ella (158)

vessel element in plants, one of the cellular components of a xylem vessel (576)

elemento del vaso en las plantas, uno de los componentes celulares de un vaso de xilema (576)

villus (VIL uhs) one of the many tiny projections from the cells in the lining of the small intestine; increases the surface area of the lining for absorption (899)

vello una de las muchas proyecciones diminutas de las células que se encuentran en la pared interior del intestino delgado; aumenta el área superficial de la pared para absorción (899)

viroid (VIE royd) an infectious agent that consists of a small strand of RNA and that causes disease in plants (480)

viroide un agente infeccioso que está constituido por una hebra pequeña de ARN y que produce enfermedades en las plantas (480)

virulent (VIR yoo luhnt) describes a microorganism or virus that causes disease and that is highly infectious (478)

virulento término que describe a un microorganismo o virus que causa enfermedades y que es altamente infeccioso (478)

virus (VIE ruhs) a nonliving, infectious particle composed of a nucleic acid and a protein coat; it can invade and destroy a cell (332)

virus una partícula infecciosa sin vida formada por un ácido nucleico y una cubierta de proteína; puede invadir una célula y destruirla (332)

visceral mass (VIS uhr uhl) the central section of a mollusk's body that contains the mollusk's organs (680)

masa visceral la sección central del cuerpo de un molusco, la cual contiene sus órganos (680)

vitamin (VIET uh min) an organic compound that participates in biochemical reactions and that builds various molecules in the body; some vitamins are called *coenzymes* and activate specific enzymes (893)

vitamina un compuesto orgánico que participa en las reacciones bioquímicas y que forma varias moléculas en el cuerpo; algunas vitaminas se llaman *coenzimas* y activan enzimas específicas (893)

voluntary muscle (VAHL uhn TER ee) a muscle whose movement can be consciously controlled (848)

músculo voluntario un músculo cuyo movimiento se puede controlar conscientemente (848)

vulva (VUHL vuh) the external part of the female reproductive organs (997)

vulva la parte externa de los órganos reproductores femeninos (997)

water cycle the continuous movement of water between the atmosphere, the land, and the oceans (90)

ciclo del agua el movimiento continuo del agua entre la atmósfera, la tierra y los océanos (90)

water-vascular system (VAS kyuh luhr) in echinoderms, a system of canals filled with a watery fluid (718)

sistema vascular acuoso en los equinodermos, un sistema de canales que están llenos de un líquido acuoso (718)

white blood cell a type of cell in the blood that destroys bacteria, viruses, and toxic proteins and helps the body develop immunities (869)

glóbulo blanco un tipo de célula de la sangre que destruye bacterias, virus y proteínas tóxicas, y que ayuda al cuerpo a desarrollar inmunidad (869)

withdrawal (with DRAW uhl) the set of symptoms associated with the removal of an addictive drug from the body (959)

abstinencia la serie de síntomas asociados con la remoción del cuerpo de una droga adictiva (959)

xylem (ZIE luhm) the type of tissue in vascular plants that provides support and conducts water and nutrients from the roots (576)

xilema el tipo de tejido que se encuentra en las plantas vasculares, el cual provee soporte y transporta el agua y los nutrientes desde las raíces (576)

yeast (YEEST) a very small, unicellular fungus that ferments carbohydrates into alcohol and carbon dioxide; used to ferment beer and to leven bread and used as a source of vitamins and proteins (523)

levadura un hongo unicelular muy pequeño que fermenta a los carbohidratos y los convierte en alcohol y dióxido de carbono; se usa para fermentar cerveza, para hacer pan y como fuente de vitaminas y proteínas (523)

Z line the line formed by the attachment of actin filaments between two sarcomeres of a muscle fiber in striated muscle cells (850)

línea Z la línea formada por la unión de filamentos de actina entre dos sarcómeros de una fibra muscular en las células de los músculos estriados (850)

zygosporangium (ZIE goh spoh RAN jee uhm) in members of the phylum Zygomycota, a sexual structure that is formed by the fusion of two gametangia and that contains one or more zygotes that resulted from the fusion of gametes produced by the gametangia (524)

zigosporangio en los miembros del phylum Zygomycota, una estructura sexual que se forma debido a la fusión de dos gametangios y que contiene uno o más cigotos que se formaron a partir de la fusión de gametos producidos por los gametangios (524)

zygospore (ZIE GOH SPAWR) in some algae, a thick-walled protective structure that contains a zygote that resulted from the fusion of two gametes (499)

zigospora en algunas algas, una estructura protectora que tiene una pared gruesa y que contiene un cigoto que se formó a partir de la fusión de dos gametos (499)

zygote (ZIE GOHT) the cell that results from the fusion of gametes; a fertilized egg (248, 498, 1001)

cigoto la célula que resulta debido a la fusión de los gametos; el óvulo fecundado (248, 498, 1001)

Glossary · Glosario

Note: Page references followed by *f* refer to illustrative material, such as figures and tables.

A

abdomen, 701, 706, 708, 710*f*
abiotic factors, 80, 106
ABO blood groups, 283, 283*f*
abscisic acid, 605
absorption, 898, 898*f*
abstinence, 1005
acanthodians, 640. *See also* **fishes**
accidents, procedures for, 16
acid rain, 128, 140–141
acids and bases, 56–57, 56*f*
acoelomates, 636, 636*f*
acquired immune deficiency syndrome (AIDS), 880, 929, 929*f,* 1005*f,* 1007. *See also* HIV
acromegaly, 979
ACTH (adrenocorticotropic hormone), 979*f*
actin, 156, 850, 851*f*
action potentials, 946–948, 947*f,* 952
activation energy, 65, 65*f,* 66, 66*f*
activators, 327, 327*f*
active sites, 66, 67*f*
active transport, 182–183, 182*f,* 183*f*
adaptation, 380–381, 381*f*
adaptive radiation, 389
addiction, 956, 956*f,* 959, 959*f*
adenine, 296*f,* 297, 298
adenosine diphosphate (ADP), 200–201, 200*f,* 201*f,* 206*f*
adenosine triphosphate (ATP)
  in active transport, 182, 182*f*
  in aerobic respiration, 210–211, 210*f,* 211*f,* 213*f,* 849
  from cellular respiration, 198, 199*f*
  energy transfer through, 200–201, 200*f,* 201*f,* 850–851, 851*f*
  in mitochondria, 161, 161*f*
  in muscle movement, 849, 850–851, 851*f*
  in photosynthesis, 160, 204–207, 204*f,* 206*f*
  in sperm, 994
  structure of, 63, 63*f*
adenovirus, 476*f*
adhesion, 55, 55*f*
ADP (adenosine diphosphate), 200–201, 200*f,* 201*f,* 206*f*
adrenal glands, 972*f,* 975, 975*f,* 981, 981*f*
adrenaline (epinephrine), 981
adrenocorticotropic hormone (ACTH), 979*f*
adult stem cells, 839
Advanced Life Support (ALS) system, 611, 611*f*
aerobic respiration, 210–211, 210*f,* 211*f,* 213*f,* 849
aflatoxins, 531
African Americans, sickle cell anemia in, 319, 319*f*
agar, 511
aging, 333–334, 333*f,* 334*f,* 605

agnathans, 639
agriculture
  domestic mammals, 796, 796*f*
  fungi in, 530
  genetic engineering in, 33, 350–351, 350*f,* 351*f,* 354
  soil damage in, 131
AIDS, 880, 929, 929*f,* 1005*f,* 1007. *See also* HIV
air pollution, 127, 128, 128*f*
air sacs, in birds, 770, 770*f*
albinism, 280, 280*f,* 285
albumen, 761
alcohol
  alcohol resistance, 34
  birth defects from, 1002
  depressant effect of, 956–957, 958*f*
  forensics and, 1025
  high blood pressure and, 874
alcoholic fermentation, 212, 212*f*
aldosterone, 981
algae
  in anthozoans, 661
  brown, 505, 505*f*
  clams and, 685
  colonies of cells, 165, 457*f*
  green, 499, 499*f,* 505, 505*f*
  red, 505, 505*f*
algal blooms, 130, 510, 510*f*
alginate, 511
algor mortis, 1032, 1032*f*
allantois, 761
alleles
  in Drosophila, 271
  frequencies, 401–402, 401*f,* 402*f*
  heredity and, 272, 272*f*
  independent assortment of, 275, 275*f,* 284
  multiple, 283, 283*f*
  new, from mutations, 323
  random segregation of, 273
allergens, 924, 924*f,* 925*f*
allergies, 924–926, 924*f*–925*f,* 926*f*
alternation of generations, 258, 499, 546
Altman, Sidney, 449
alveoli, 877, 878*f,* 880, 881, 881*f*
amber, 451
amebic dysentery, 507
amino acid-based hormones, 974, 974*f*
amino acids
  absorption of, 899, 899*f*
  codons for, 307, 307*f*
  essential, 892
  evolution and, 384, 384*f*
  in meteorites, 448
  in mutations, 320–321, 320*f,* 321*f*
  in protein synthesis, 308–309, 308*f*–309*f*
  structure of, 62, 62*f*
ammonia, 56, 92, 92*f,* 628
ammonification, 92, 92*f*
amnion, 761, 1002
amniotic eggs, 430*f,* 641, 755, 757, 761, 761*f*
amniotic fluid, 1004
amoebas, 165, 247, 502, 502*f,* 507
amoebocytes, 656
amoeboid protists, 502, 502*f*

amphibians, 739–747
  blood circulation in, 742–743, 742*f,* 743*f*
  caecilians, 744*f,* 745
  characteristics of, 739
  evolution of, 641, 739, 745, 745*f*
  frogs and toads, 740, 740*f,* 746*f,* 747, 747*f*
  movement of, 740, 740*f*
  in the Paleozoic era, 458
  reproduction in, 739, 744, 745, 747, 747*f*
  respiration in, 741
  salamanders, 739, 739*f,* 741, 744, 744*f*
  sense organs in, 740, 740*f*
ampulla, 718, 718*f*
amylases, 897, 898*f*
anaerobic respiration, 209, 211–212, 211*f,* 212*f,* 849
analogous characteristics, 428
anaphase, 231, 231*f,* 250*f*–251*f,* 251
anatomical pathology, 1027
anatomy, evolutionary theory and, 384, 384*f. See also* **human body**
ancestral characters, 429, 431*f*
androgens, 982
angiosperms, 559–564
  evolution of, 429*f,* 545*f*
  flowers in, 560, 560*f*
  fruits in, 563, 563*f*
  kinds of, 559, 559*f*
  life cycle in, 561, 561*f*
  photoperiodism in, 608, 608*f*
  reproduction in, 554–555, 554*f,* 555*f*
  seeds in, 553
  vegetative reproduction in, 564, 564*f*
animal behavior, 813–827
  communication modes, 823–824, 823*f,* 824*f*
  cooperative, 827
  courtship, 826, 826*f*
  influences on, 814, 814*f*
  innate, 816, 816*f*
  in insects, 715, 716*f*
  learned, 817–819, 817*f,* 818*f,* 819*f*
  natural selection and, 815, 815*f*
  "nature *vs.* nurture," 814
  parental care, 827, 827*f*
  reproductive strategies, 825–827, 825*f,* 826*f,* 827*f*
  sensitive periods in, 819, 819*f*
  social, 825, 825*f*
  stimulus and response, 813, 813*f,* 818, 818*f*
  survival strategies, 821–822, 821*f,* 822*f*
  territorial, 825, 828–829
animal cells, 163*f,* 232, 232*f. See also* **eukaryotic cells**
"animalcules," 151
Animalia (kingdom), 425*f,* 434*f,* 436, 436*f*–437*f. See also* **animals**
animals
  body cavities in, 636, 636*f*
  body plans, 632–633, 633*f*
  body systems in, 627–631, 627*f,* 628*f,* 629*f,* 630*f,* 631*f*
  classification of, 434*f,* 436, 436*f*–437*f*
  early embryonic development, 634–635, 634*f,* 635*f,* 646
  emergence on land, 640–641, 640*f*

general features, 623–624
invertebrate characteristics, 625
jointed appendages in, 637, 637*f*
as multicellular organisms, 166
phylogenetic diagram of, 625, 625*f*
pollination by, 562, 562*f*
seed dispersal by, 555, 555*f*
segmentation in, 637, 637*f*
vertebrate characteristics, 626, 626*f*
annelids, 686–690
characteristics of, 686–687, 686*f*
earthworms, 637, 688–689, 689*f*
leeches, 690–691, 690*f*, 691*f*
marine worms, 688, 688*f*
anoles, 227, 227*f*, 410, 410*f*, 776–777
Anolis spp. (anoles), 410, 410*f*
anorexia nervosa, 895
antagonistic hormones, 977, 977*f*
antemortem toxicology, 1025
anterior lobe, pituitary gland, 979, 979*f*
antheridium, 548–549, 549*f*, 551–552,
551*f*–552*f*
anthers, 560, 560*f*
anthozoans, 661, 661*f*
anthrax, 487, 487*f*
anthropology, forensic, 1028, 1028*f*
antibiotic resistance, 332, 332*f*, 484, 484*f*,
880
antibiotics, 484, 529
antibodies, 870, 870*f*, 920, 921*f*
anticoagulants, 690
anticodons, 308–309, 308*f*–309*f*
antidiuretic hormone (ADH), 978, 979*f*
antigens
antibody binding of, 920, 921*f*
in blood types, 870, 870*f*
macrophages and, 917–918, 917*f*
T cells and, 920, 921*f*
in vaccines, 922
antigen shifting, 923
antihistamines, 924
ants, 518*f*–519*f*, 713, 814, 814*f*
anurans, 747. *See also* **frogs**
anus, 635, 635*f*, 900
apical meristems, 588, 588*f*
Apis mellifera (European honey bee), 424
apomixis, 255
apoptosis, 334, 334*f*
appendages, 702, 702*f*, 706–707, 706*f*, 758
appendicitis, 901, 901*f*
appendicular skeleton, 843, 843*f*
aquatic ecosystems, 84, 84*f*
arachnids, 706–707, 706*f*–707*f*, 710*f*. *See also*
spiders
archaea, 434*f*, 435, 436*f*–437*f*, 454, 471
Archaea (domain), 434, 434*f*, 435, 436*f*–437*f*.
See also **archaea**
Archaebacteria (kingdom), 433, 434*f*, 435,
436*f*–437*f*. *See also* **archaea**
Archaeopteryx, 643, 643*f*
archegonium, 548–549, 549*f*, 551–552, 551*f*,
552*f*
arithmetic growth, 378, 378*f*, 379
arteries
circulation through, 868, 868*f*

clogged and hardened, 872–873, 872*f*, 873*f*
pulmonary, 866*f*
arterioles, 868, 868*f*
arteriosclerosis, 872–873, 872*f*
arthritis, 846
arthropods, 701–709. *See also* **insects**
arachnids, 706–707, 706*f*–707*f*, 710*f*
body functions in, 703, 703*f*
classification of, 704, 705*f*
compound eyes in, 703, 703*f*
crustaceans, 702, 708–709, 708*f*–709*f*
evolutionary success of, 704
jointed appendages in, 637, 702, 702*f*
life cycle of, 704, 704*f*
in the Paleozoic era, 458
segmented body in, 701, 701*f*
artificial intelligence, 41, 41*f*
artificial selection, 377, 377*f*
ascarids, 669, 669*f*
ascocarp, 526, 526*f*
ascus (plural, *asci*), 526, 526*f*
asexual reproduction
apomixis, 255
binary fission, 247, 498
budding, 247, 247*f*, 498
cloning as, 352, 352*f*
in cnidarians, 659, 659*f*
in flatworms, 664, 664*f*
fragmentation, 247, 498
in fungi, 522–523, 525–526, 525*f*, 526*f*
parthenogenesis, 247, 255, 255*f*
in plants, 255
in protists, 498, 498*f*
in sea stars, 631, 631*f*
in sponges, 656
vegetative, 564, 564*f*
assimilation, 92, 92*f*
assistive technologies, 32, 32*f*
associative learning, 818, 818*f*
asteroids, 448, 448*f*, 460, 460*f*, 642
asthma, 880, 880*f*, 925
asymmetrical body plans, 633, 633*f*
athlete's foot, 522, 531, 856, 856*f*
atoms, 51–54, 51*f*
ATP (adenosine triphosphate)
in active transport, 182, 182*f*
in aerobic respiration, 210–211, 210*f*, 211*f*,
213*f*
from cellular respiration, 198, 199*f*
energy transfer through, 200–201, 200*f*,
201*f*
in mitochondria, 161, 161*f*
in muscle movement, 849, 851*f*
in photosynthesis, 160, 204–207, 204*f*, 206*f*
in sperm, 994
structure of, 63, 63*f*
ATP synthase, 200*f*, 201, 204*f*, 205
atria (singular, *atrium*), 742, 742*f*, 866–867,
866*f*, 867*f*
atrioventricular (AV) node, 867, 867*f*
atrophy, 852
Australopithecus, 800, 800*f*–801*f*
autoimmune diseases, 927, 927*f*, 928
automated sequencing devices, 363, 363*f*
autonomic nervous system, 942
autopsies, 1027, 1027*f*

autosomes, 249
autotrophs, 197, 437, 543
auxins, 603*f*, 604, 604*f*, 607
Avery, Oswald, 294
axial skeleton, 843, 843*f*
axons, 945, 945*f*
axon terminals, 945, 945*f*, 948

bacillus, 471, 471*f*
Bacillus thuringiensis (Bt), 33, 33*f*, 351, 354,
354*f*
bacteria, 434-435, 434*f*, 436*f*–437*f*, 471–475,
481, 483–484
antibiotic resistance in, 332, 332*f*, 484,
484*f*, 880
beneficial roles of, 351, 354, 481, 481*f*, 900
cells in, 154, 154*f*, 162, 162*f*, 165
classification of, 433, 434*f*, 435, 436*f*
in the digestive system, 900
diseases from, 483, 483*f*
energy sources of, 474, 474*f*
exponential population growth in, 104
gene regulation by operons in, 326, 326*f*
Gram staining of, 472
growth conditions for, 42–43
nitrogen fixation by, 92, 92*f*
origin of mitochondria and chloroplasts
from, 456, 456*f*
plasmids in, 331, 331*f*
reproduction and adaptation of, 475, 475*f*
shapes of, 471, 471*f*
on skin, 471
staining, 472, 472*f*, 488–489
structure of, 472–473, 472*f*, 473*f*
Bacteria (domain), 434*f*, 434–435, 436*f*–437*f*.
See also **bacteria**
bacteriophages, 295*f*, 476*f*, 477
balance, mechanoreceptors and, 952, 952*f*
bald eagles (*Haliaeetus leucocephalus*),
772–773, 773*f*
ballistics, 1025, 1025*f*
baobab trees, 584, 584*f*
barbs, 768, 768*f*
barnacles, 114, 708–709, 708*f*
base pairs
base-pairing rules, 296*f*, 297–298, 298*f*,
306
complementary, 298, 298*f*
in DNA replication, 300–301, 301*f*, 306
numbers of, 331
in RNA, 305, 305*f*
structure of, 290*f*–291*f*, 296, 296*f*
bases and acids, 56–57, 56*f*
basidia (singular, *basidium*), 527, 527*f*
basiocarps, 527, 527*f*
bats, 790, 790*f*, 794*f*
battlefield medicine, 32, 32*f*
B cells, 920, 920*f*, 921*f*, 928-292
"beads on a string," 224, 225*f*
HMS *Beagle,* 375–376, 375*f*, 376*f*
beaks, on birds, 766, 769, 769*f*
bears, 789, 789*f*, 821, 821*f*

Index

bees
classification of, 424
pollination by, 562, 562*f*
social system of, 715
waggle dance in, 716*f*
wings of, 713, 713*f*
bee sting allergies, 925
behavior, definition of, 813. *See also* **animal behavior**
bell curves, 400, 400*f*
benign tumors, 235
"bergy bits," 58
bias, in investigations, 12
bicarbonate ions, 57, 878–879
bilateral symmetry, 633, 633*f*, 636, 636*f*
bile, 898, 899
binary fission, 247, 475, 475*f*, 498
binocular vision, 797, 797*f*
binomial nomenclature, 424
biochemistry, 59–67. *See also* **atoms; water; acids and bases**
evolutionary theory and, 384, 384*f*
biodiversity, 80, 115, 132, 132*f*
biofeedback, 842. *See also* **feedback mechanisms**
biogeography, 383, 383*f*
bioinformatics, 361
biological reactions, 66–67, 66*f*, 67*f*
biological species concept, 411
biological weapons, 37, 487, 487*f*
biology, study of, 17–19, 18*f*
biomes, 82–83, 82*f*, 83*f*
biometric identification, 36, 36*f*, 37
biomimetics, 35
biomolecules, 59–63
bionics, 41, 41*f*
bioremediation, 349, 349*f*
bioterrorism, 37, 487, 487*f*
biotic factors, 79, 106
bipedalism, 799, 799*f*
bird flu, 485*f*, 486
birds, 766–775. *See also* names of specific birds
adaptations of, 768–769, 768*f*, 769*f*
behavior of, 814*f*, 817*f*, 819*f*, 820
characteristics of, 766
courtship behavior in, 826, 826*f*
endothermic metabolism in, 767
evolution of, 459, 643, 643*f*
flightless, 774, 774*f*
modern aquatic, 774–775, 774*f*
modern terrestrial, 772, 772*f*
reproduction in, 771, 771*f*
respiration and circulation in, 770, 770*f*
songs, 819
birth defects, alcohol and, 1002
birth, human, 1004, 1004*f*
bivalves, 682*f*, 685, 685*f*
bladder, urinary, 904, 904*f*
blades, of kelp, 505
blades, of leaves, 582, 582*f*
blastocoel, 634, 634*f*
blastocysts, 1001, 1001*f*
blastula, 634, 634*f*, 646, 646*f*
blending hypothesis, 272
blind spot, 951, 951*f*

blood
body temperature and, 842
bone marrow production, 844, 844*f*
calcium in, 980
components of, 869, 869*f*
gas transport and exchange, 877, 878, 878*f*
kidney filtration by, 903, 903*f*
pH of, 57
Rh factor in, 870
types, 870, 870*f*
blood-alcohol concentration, 957, 1026
blood circulation
in amphibians, 742–743, 742*f*, 743*f*
in arthropods, 703, 703*f*, 711*f*
in birds, 770, 770*f*
double-loop, 743, 743*f*
in echinoderms, 718
in fishes, 731, 731*f*
in humans, 866–867, 866*f*
in mammals, 786, 786*f*
in mollusks, 681
in reptiles, 760, 760*f*
single-loop, 731
blood clotting, 32, 869, 869*f*, 873, 873*f*
blood glucose, 927, 977, 981, 981*f*, 983, 983*f*
bloodletting, medicinal, 690
blood pressure, 872, 874, 969
blood spatter analysis, 1031
blood types, 283, 283*f*, 870, 870*f*, 918
blood vessels, 862*f*–863*f*, 868, 868*f*, 870. *See also* **arteries**
blotting processes, 358, 358*f*
blue-green algae, 455, 474
blue whales, 623*f*, 791, 822
BMI (body mass index), 895
body cavities, 636, 636*f*
body fat, 61, 61*f*, 208, 789*f*, 853
body mass index (BMI), 895
body plans
body cavities and, 636, 636*f*
embryonic development and, 634–635, 634*f*, 635*f*, 646
of flatworms, 663
of fungi, 521–522, 522*f*
of mollusks, 680, 680*f*
of roundworms, 667, 667*f*
of sponges, 655, 655*f*
symmetry of, 632–633, 633*f*
body systems, 627–631, 627*f*, 628*f*, 629*f*, 630*f*. *See also* **human body;** names of specific body systems
body temperature
after death, 1032, 1032*f*
ectothermic metabolism, 757, 758, 759, 759*f*
endothermic metabolism, 767, 786
homeostasis in, 55, 180, 842
hypothalamus and, 940
in immune response, 916
skin in, 854
body weight, 895
bone density calculations, 767
bone marrow
adult stem cells from, 353, 353*f*
functions of, 844, 844*f*, 869
lymph tissue in, 871

bones. *See also* **bone marrow**
in birds, 766, 768, 768*f*
growth of, 845
injuries and disorders, 845
joints, 846, 846*f*
structure of, 844, 844*f*
bony fins, 640, 640*f*
bony fishes, 736–738, 736*f*, 737*f*, 738*f*
book lungs, 703, 710*f*
Boston Harbor, 134, 134*f*
botulism, 483
bound ribosomes, 157, 158, 159*f*
Bowman's capsule, 903, 903*f*
brain
in annelids, 687–688, 688*f*
in cephalopods, 684
in flatworms, 663, 664*f*
in hominids, 800–801, 800*f*–801*f*
meningitis and, 960, 960*f*
MRI scans of, 936*f*–937*f*
multiple sclerosis effect on, 960, 960*f*
nicotine and, 957
sensory information processing in, 954, 954*f*
in simple *vs.* complex nervous systems, 629
structure of, 940–941, 940*f*, 941*f*
traumatic injury to, 955, 955*f*, 961
brainstem, 940*f*, 941
breathing, in humans, 877, 877*f*, 882–883. *See also* **respiration**
breeding, as artificial selection, 377, 377*f*
brittle stars, 719, 719*f*
bronchi (singular, *bronchus*), 876, 876*f*, 877
bronchioles, 876*f*, 877, 880
bronchitis, 880
brood parasitism, 814, 814*f*
brown algae, 505, 505*f*. *See also* **kelp**
brown paper test, 61
brown recluse spiders (*Loxosceles reclusa*), 707, 710*f*
Bt corn, 33, 33*f*, 351, 354, 354*f*
budding, 247, 247*f*, 498
buds, plant, 581, 588, 609, 609*f*
buffers, pH, 57
bulbourethral glands, 994*f*, 995
bulbs, 564, 564*f*
bulimia nervosa, 895
Burkitt's lymphoma, 485
bursae, 846
bursitis, 846
butterflies, 325*f*, 713–714, 714*f*, 720–721

caecilians, 744*f*, 745
caffeine, 187
calcitonin, 980
calcium, 599*f*, 845, 894, 894*f*, 980
calcium carbonate, 735
Calories, 891, 894, 894*f*
Calvin cycle, 206–207, 206*f*
cambium, 589, 589*f*
Cambrian explosion, 458

cAMP (cyclic AMP), 974, 974f
cancer. *See also names of specific cancers*
  cell production in, 235, 235f
  definition of, 235
  microarray identification of, 358
  from mutations, 322f, 323
  treatment for, 235
  viruses associated with, 485
canine teeth, 787, 787f
capillaries (blood) 868, 868f
capillary action, 597
capsids, 477, 477f
capsules, in prokaryotes, 154
carageenan, 511
carapace, 708, 762
carbohydrates
  chemistry of, 60, 60f
  digestion of, 896
  in nutrition, 892, 892f
  from photosynthesis, 160-161, 161f
carbon, 51, 51f, 52, 59-63, 452
carbon cycle, 91-92, 91f, 198, 199f
carbon dioxide
  in aerobic respiration, 210, 210f
  in the blood, 877-879, 878f
  in the carbon cycle, 91, 91f
  diffusion through cell membranes, 179
  excreted by the lungs, 902
  fixation of, 206-207, 206f
  as greenhouse gas, 129, 129f
  in photosynthesis, 206-207, 206f
Carboniferous period, 453f, 458
carcinomas, 856
cardiac muscle, 840, 840f, 848, 848f
cardiovascular disease, 872-874, 872f, 873f, 892
cardiovascular system, 865-874
  blood in, 868-870, 868f, 869f, 870f
  diseases of, 872-874, 872f, 873f, 892, 895
  function of, 865, 865f
  heart, 866-867, 866f, 867f
  lymphatic system, 871, 871f
Carnivora (order), 425f
carnivores, 87, 89, 89f
carotenoids, 203, 203f
carrier proteins, 179, 179f
carrying capacity, 105, 105f, 182
Carson, Rachel, *Silent Spring*, 137
cartilage, 845, 846
cartilaginous fishes, 735, 735f
cassowary, 427f
castes, in insects, 715
castings, earthworm, 688
CAT scans, 35, 35f
cats
  classification of, 425f
  skeletons of, 626f
CDK protein, 334
cDNA (complementary DNA), 357
Cech, Thomas, 449
cell communication, 184-186, 185f, 186f
cell cycle, 166, 228-229, 228f, 233, 233f
cell differentiation, 166, 333, 333f
cell digestion, 158
cell division. *See also* cell reproduction
  cytokinesis in, 228f, 229, 232, 232f

meiosis, 250-254, 250f-251f
mitosis, 230-231, 230f-231f
cell membranes
  active transport through, 182-183, 182f, 183f, 204f, 205
  in bacteria, 472, 473f
  cell communication and, 184-186, 185f, 186f
  homeostasis and, 175
  lipid bilayer in, 61, 176, 176f
  location of, 154, 154f
  origin of, 448
  osmosis through, 180-181, 180f, 181f
  passive transport through, 178-179, 179f
  in protein processing, 158, 159f
  transport proteins in, 176-177, 177f, 179, 179f
cell plates, 232, 232f
cell recognition, 60, 177, 477
cell reproduction, 223-226
  checkpoints in, 234, 234f
  chromosomes, 224-225, 225f
  controls on, 233, 233f
  cytokinesis, 228f, 229, 232, 232f
  definition of, 223
  eukaryotic cell cycle, 228-229, 228f
  meiosis, 250-251, 250f-251f
  mitosis, 228f, 229, 230-231, 230f-231f
  preparation for, 226, 226f
cell respiration
  aerobic, 210-211, 210f, 211f, 213f, 849
  anaerobic, 209, 211-212, 211f, 212f, 849
  in the carbon cycle, 198, 199f
  efficiency of, 213, 213f
  electron transport chain in, 211, 211f
  by fermentation, 211-212, 211f, 212f
  glycolysis in, 208-209, 209f, 213f
  Krebs cycle in, 210-211, 210f, 213f
  lab exercise on, 215
cells. *See also* cell structure, 18
  carbohydrates in, 60, 60f
  carbon compounds in, 59
  cell cycle, 228-229, 228f, 233, 233f, 334
  as characteristic of life, 18
  in colonial organisms, 165
  discovery of, 151-152
  endosymbiotic theory, 331
  energy production in, 160-161, 161f
  examples of, 152, 152f
  germ, 248, 322, 403
  levels of organization, 164-165, 164f
  lipids in, 61, 61f
  multicellularity, 165-166
  nerve, 152, 152f, 228, 629
  nucleic acids in, 63, 63f
  number in the human body, 153
  origin of first, 448-449, 449f
  plant, 160, 160f, 163f, 232, 232f
  protein processing in, 158, 159f
  proteins in, 62, 62f
  recognition of neighbors, 60, 177
  somatic, 322
  storage in, 158, 160, 160f
  surface area-to-volume ratio in, 152-153
cell size, 152-153, 223

cell structure, 148-166
  chloroplasts, 160, 160f
  cytoskeleton, 156, 156f
  endoplasmic reticulum, 158, 159f
  in eukaryotic cells, 155, 155f, 163f
  Golgi apparatus, 158, 159f
  lysosomes, 158
  mitochondria, 161, 161f
  modeling, 160
  nucleus structure, 157, 157f
  in prokaryotic cells, 154, 154f, 163f
  ribosome function, 157
  vacuoles, 160, 181, 503f, 577f
  vesicles, 158-160, 159f, 160f
cell-surface markers, 177, 177f
cell theory, 152
cell transport, 178-183
  active, 182-183, 182f, 183f
  by osmosis, 180-181, 180f, 181f
  passive, 178-179, 179f
  transport proteins, 177, 177f, 179, 179f
cellulose, 60, 437, 892
cell walls
  during cell division, 226, 226f, 232, 232f
  cellulose in, 437
  chitin in, 60, 437, 521
  in prokaryotes, 154, 154f
Cenozoic era, 453, 453f, 459, 459f
central nervous system (CNS), 939-941, 939f, 940f, 941f
central vacuoles, 160, 160f
centrioles, 230, 230f
centromeres, 225, 225f, 250f-251f, 251
centrosomes, 230, 230f
cephalization, 633
cephalopods, 682f, 684, 684f
cephalosporin, 529
cephalothorax, 706, 708-709, 709f, 710f
cerebellum, 940f, 941, 941f
cerebral cortex, 940, 954, 954f
cerebral ganglia, 687, 689, 689f
cerebrum, 940, 940f
cervical cancer, 485, 1006
cervix, 997, 997f
CFCs (chlorofluorocarbons), 128, 136
Chagas disease, 508, 508f
chain termination sequencing, 359, 359f
channel proteins, 179-180, 179f
characters, 268
Chargaff, Erwin, 298, 299f
Chase, Martha, 294-295, 295f
cheetahs (*Acinomyx jubatus*), classification of, 424f, 425f
chelicerae, 706, 706f, 710f
chelipeds, 709, 709f
chemical bonds
  breaking and forming, 65
  carbon, 59
  covalent, 52, 52f
  hydrogen, 54, 55f, 269f, 296, 297
  ionic, 53, 53f
  peptide, 62, 62f, 308-309, 308f-309f
chemical digestion, 896
chemical energy, 60, 197
chemical reactions, 65-67, 65f, 66f, 67f

chemical signals, 184, 824, 824*f*
chemoautotrophic bacteria, 474
chemoreceptors, 953, 953*f*
chemotherapy, 235
chicken pox, 485, 485*f*
chickens, genome of, 330*f*-331*f*
childbirth, 1004, 1004*f*
chimpanzees, 817, 824
chitin, 60, 437, 521, 702, 713
chlamydia, 1005*f*, 1007
chlorofluorocarbons (CFCs), 128, 136
chlorophyll, 203, 203*f*
chloroplasts
   DNA in, 331
   in endosymbiotic theory, 331, 456
   energy production in, 160, 160*f*, 161
   location of, 582, 582*f*
   origin of, 455-456, 456*f*
   photosynthesis in, 202-203, 202*f*-203*f*, 543
   structure of, 202, 202*f*-203*f*
choanocytes, 655, 655*f*
cholera, 29-30, 29*f*, 30*f*, 127, 483*f*
cholesterol, 177*f*, 874, 898
Chordata (phylum), 425*f*
chordates, 638-639, 638*f*, 639*f*. See also
   vertebrates
chorion, 761, 1002
chromatids
   in chromosome structure, 225, 225*f*
   in meiosis, 250*f*-251*f*, 251, 253
   in mitosis, 230-231, 230*f*-231*f*
chromatin, 224, 225*f*
chromatographs, 1020, 1036-1037
chromosome number, 248-249, 249*f*
chromosomes
   30 nm fiber, 225, 225*f*
   aging and, 334
   autosomes, 249
   definition of, 224, 302
   eukaryotic, 224-225, 225*f*
   genes in, 224
   homologous, 249
   in meiosis, 250-254, 250*f*-251*f*, 252*f*, 254*f*
   in mitosis, 230-231, 230*f*-231*f*
   mobile genetic elements in, 332
   mutations in, 321, 321*f*
   nondisjunction, 324, 324*f*
   polyploidy in, 324, 324*f*
   prokaryotic, 224
   replication of, 302-303, 302*f*, 334, 334*f*
   sex chromosomes, 249
chrysalis, 714, 714*f*
chytrid fungi, 524, 524*f*
cilia
   in flatworms, 665
   in mollusks, 680, 680*f*, 682*f*, 685
   in protists, 497, 502-503, 503*f*
ciliates, 502
cinchona bark, 509
circadian rhythms, 822, 822*f*, 980
circulation
   in amphibians, 742-743, 742*f*, 743*f*
   in arthropods, 703, 703*f*, 711*f*
   in birds, 770, 770*f*
   double-loop, 743, 743*f*
   in echinoderms, 718

   in fishes, 731, 731*f*
   in humans, 866-867, 866*f*
   in mammals, 786, 786*f*
   in mollusks, 681
   open *vs.* closed, 630, 630*f*, 681
   in reptiles, 760, 760*f*
   single-loop, 731
cladistics, 428*f*, 429, 429*f*, 431
cladograms, 429-430, 429*f*
clams, 685, 692-693
classes, 425*f*, 426, 426*f*
classical conditioning, 818, 818*f*
classification, 420-439, 1062-1063
   characteristics used in, 434
   cladistics, 428*f*, 429, 429*f*
   dichotomous keys, 438-439, 438*f*
   discovering new species, 432, 432*f*
   evolutionary relatedness in, 430-431, 431*f*
   Linnaean system levels, 425-426, 425*f*,
     426*f*
   mnemonic device for, 426
   by molecular sequencing, 500
   need for systems of, 423
   phylogenetics, 428, 428*f*
   scientific nomenclature, 424, 424*f*
   systematics, 427, 427*f*
   three-domain system, 434-437, 434*f*,
     436*f*-437*f*
   updating number of kingdoms in, 433,
     433*f*, 436*f*-437*f*
claws, 709, 709*f*, 758
cleavage, 634, 634*f*, 646, 1001, 1001*f*
climate
   definition of, 82
   evolution and, 799
   global warming, 128, 129, 129*f*, 510
   impact on population size, 106, 106*f*
cloaca, 746*f*, 771, 773*f*, 791
cloning, 352, 352*f*, 357, 360
closed circulatory system, 630, 630*f*
Clostridium botulinum, 483
clotting, blood, 32, 869, 869*f*, 873, 873*f*
club fungi, 527, 527*f*
club mosses, 550, 550*f*, 552
cnidarians, 658-661, 658*f*, 659*f*, 660*f*, 661*f*
cnidocytes, 658*f*, 659
CNS (central nervous system), 939-941, 939*f*,
   940*f*, 941*f*
coal, 126, 458
cocaine, 956, 958*f*, 959, 959*f*
coccus, 471, 471*f*
cochlea, 952, 952*f*
codeine, 958, 958*f*
codominance, 283
codons, 307-309, 307*f*, 308*f*-309*f*, 321
coelacanths, 738, 738*f*
coelomates, 636, 636*f*
coeloms, 636, 636*f*, 679, 686, 711*f*
coevolution, 109, 388, 388*f*
cohesion, 55
coin toss predictions, 265, 278-279, 279*f*
cold-blooded (ectothermic) metabolism,
   757, 758, 759, 759*f*
colon, 900, 900*f*
colonial organisms, 165
colonial prokaryotes, 444*f*-445*f*, 456

colorblindness, 280
Combined DNA Index System (CODIS),
   1023, 1023*f*
combustion, 91, 91*f*
commensalism, 111, 111*f*
communication
   chemical signals, 184, 824, 824*f*
   language skills, 819, 824
   by sound, 824
   by touch, 824, 824*f*
   visual signals, 823
   waggle dance in honeybees, 716*f*
communities. *See also* **biomes; ecosystems;**
   populations
   commensalism in, 111, 111*f*
   competition for resources in, 113-114,
     113*f*, 114*f*
   definition of, 79, 79*f*
   herbivore-plant interactions in, 110, 110*f*
   mutualism in, 111, 111*f*
   niches in, 112-113, 112*f*
   parasitism in, 110
   predator-prey interactions in, 109-110
   stability of, 115, 115*f*
compact bone, 844, 844*f*
companion cells, 576, 576*f*
comparison microscopes, 1020, 1020*f*
compensatory hypertrophy, 227
competition, 113-115, 113*f*, 114*f*
competitive exclusion, 114
complementary bases, 298, 298*f*
complementary DNA (cDNA), 357
complete metamorphosis, 714, 714*f*
complex carbohydrates, 892
compound eyes, 703, 703*f*
compound fractures, 845
compound leaves, 582, 582*f*
compounds, 52
concentration gradients, 178, 946
condensation, 90, 90*f*
conditioning, 818, 818*f*
cones, in eyes, 951, 951*f*
cones, in plants, 550, 550*f*, 557-558, 557*f*
conidiophores, 526, 526*f*
conifers, 429*f*, 556, 556*f*. *See also*
   gymnosperms
conjugation, 475, 475*f*, 484, 502
connective tissue, 840, 840*f*, 850, 853, 869
conservation, environmental, 134
conservation of energy, 64
conservation of mass, 64
constrictors, 765
consumers, 86, 86*f*, 88
contour feathers, 768, 768*f*
contour plowing, 131
contractile vacuoles, 160, 181, 503*f*
contraction, 850, 851*f*
control groups, 11
conus arteriosus, 742-743, 742*f*
Cooksonia, 544, 544*f*
coordination, of movement, 941, 941*f*
copepods, 29-31, 29*f*, 708, 709*f*
coralline algae, 505, 505*f*

coral reefs, 84, 84*f,* 661–662, 662*f*
corals, 510, 624–625, 631–632, 632*f,* 661–662
cork, 574, 581, 581*f*
cork cambium, 589, 589*f*
corn
  corn smut in, 531, 531*f*
  genetically modified, 33, 33*f,* 351, 354, 354*f*
  Indian, 332
corpus callosum, 940
corpus luteum, 999, 999*f*
cortex, brain, 936*f*–937*f,* 940
cortex, root, 579
cortisol, 975, 975*f,* 981
cortisone, 529
cotyledons, 559, 585, 585*f*
countercurrent flow, 731
counterfeit drugs, 1036
courtship behavior, 826, 826*f*
covalent bonds, 52, 52*f*
crabs, 100*f*–101*f,* 709, 709*f,* 820, 820*f*
crayfish, 408*f,* 709, 709*f*
Creutzfeldt-Jacob disease, 480
Crick, Francis, 296, 299, 299*f*
crime scene investigators, 1014*f*–1015*f,* 1030–1031, 1030*f,* 1031*f*
"critical biological agents," 487
crocodiles, 761, 761*f,* 763, 763*f*
Crohn's disease, 927*f*
crop, 688, 689*f,* 773*f*
crop rotation, 131
cross-fertilization, 562
crossing over, 250*f,* 251, 253, 321, 324
cross-pollination, 267–268, 267*f,* 269*f*
crustaceans, 702, 708–709, 708*f,* 709*f*
cryptosporidiosis, 508
Cryptosporidium, 508
cubes, surface area-to-volume in, 153
cutaneous respiration, 741
cuticle, plant, 544–545, 574, 582, 582*f*
Cuvier, Georges, 379
cyanobacteria, 455, 474
cycads, 556, 556*f*
cycles. *See also* **life cycles**
  Calvin, 206–207, 206*f*
  carbon, 91, 91*f,* 92, 198, 199*f*
  definition of, 747
  Krebs, 210–211, 210*f,* 213*f*
  nitrogen, 92, 92*f*
  oxygen, 91, 91*f*
  phosphorus, 93
  water, 77, 90, 90*f*
cyclic AMP (cAMP), 974, 974*f*
cyclic behavior, 822, 822*f*
cyclin, 334
cystic fibrosis, 323*f,* 407*f*
cytokinesis, 228*f,* 229, 232, 232*f*
cytokinins, 605
cytoplasm, 154, 154*f,* 156, 232
cytosine, 296*f,* 297, 298
cytoskeleton, 156, 156*f*
cytosol, 154
cytotoxic T cells, 919*f,* 920, 921*f*

Darwin, Charles
  on breeding and artificial selection, 377, 377*f*
  on courtship behavior, 826
  influence of Cuvier, Hutton, and Lyell on, 379, 379*f*
  influence of Lamarck on, 378, 378*f*
  influence of Malthus on, 379
  on natural selection, 380–381, 381*f*
  publication of *Origin of Species,* 381
  strengths and weaknesses of ideas of, 385
  voyage of HMS *Beagle,* 375–376, 375*f,* 376*f*
databases, forensic, 1020, 1023, 1024
dating methods, 451–452, 451*f,* 452*f,* 461–462
daughter cells, 232, 232*f*
daughter isotopes, 452
day-neutral plants, 608, 608*f*
DDT restrictions, 137
death, causes of, 1032–1033, 1032*f*
decapods, 709, 709*f*
decomposers, 86, 86*f*
deer ticks, 707, 707*f*
deforestation, 132, 132*f*
Deinonychus, **427***f*
deletion mutations, 320–321, 321*f*
denaturation, 357
dendrites, 945, 945*f*
denitrification, 92, 92*f*
density calculations, 767
density-dependent factors, 105
dental records, 1034
deoxyribonucleic acid (DNA). *See also* **genes**
  Avery's experiments, 294
  in bacteria, 472, 473*f*
  base pairing in, 297–298, 298*f*
  categories of, 331
  in cell cycle, 228*f,* 229
  Chargaff's observations, 298, 299*f*
  cloning, 357, 357*f*
  complementary, 357
  denaturation of, 357
  deoxyribose in, 63, 296, 296*f,* 305, 305*f*
  errors in replication of, 301, 324
  in eukaryotic cells, 155, 155*f,* 157, 157*f*
  evolution and, 384, 384*f,* 430–431, 431*f*
  extraction from wheat germ, 311
  fingerprinting, 36, 347, 347*f,* 358, 364–365
  forensic analysis of, 347, 347*f,* 1023, 1023*f*
  in forensic genealogy, 335, 335*f*
  function of, 154, 223, 224, 293
  Griffith's discovery of transformation, 294, 294*f*
  Hershey-Chase experiments, 295, 295*f*
  hybridization of, 357
  kinds of mutations in, 320–321, 320*f,* 321*f*
  mobile genetic elements in, 332
  non-coding, 328, 331, 345
  nucleotides in, 63, 63*f*
  origin of, 449
  packaging during cell division, 224–225, 225*f*
  polymorphisms, 343, 356
  in prokaryotic cells, 154, 154*f*
  recombinant, 350, 359*f,* 360, 360*f*
  repeating sequences in, 343
  replication of, 223, 226, 228, 228*f,* 229, 300–303, 300*f,* 301*f,* 302*f,* 307
  RNA compared with, 305, 305*f*
  sequencing of, 359
  size of, 303
  structure of, 63, 290*f*–291*f,* 296–297, 296*f*
  transcription factors and, 327, 327*f*
  transcription of, 304–305, 306–307, 306*f*
  Watson and Crick's model, 299, 299*f*
  X-ray diffraction of, 298–299, 299*f*
deoxyribose, 63, 296, 296*f,* 305, 305*f*
dependent variables, 11
depressants, 956, 958*f*
depth perception, 797
derived characters, 429
dermal tissue, in vascular plants, 573–575, 573*f,* 574*f,* 575*f,* 578*f*
dermatophytes, 531
dermis, 853, 854*f*
descent with modification, 375
deuterostomes, 635, 635*f*
Devonian period, 453*f,* 458*f,* 459
diabetes
  insipidus, 983
  mellitus, 927, 983, 983*f*
  steroid, 981
  type 1, 983
  type 2, 983
dialysis, kidney, 905, 905*f*
diaphragm, 786, 877, 877*f*
diatomaceous earth, 505, 511
diatoms, 504, 504*f,* 511
dichotomous keys, 438–439, 438*f*
dicots. *See also* **angiosperms**
  characteristics of, 559, 559*f*
  cotyledons in, 585, 585*f*
  vascular bundles in, 580, 580*f*
differentiation, 166, 333, 333*f,* 634, 635*f*
diffusion, 178–179, 179*f,* 188–189
digestive enzymes, 896–897, 898*f*
digestive system
  animal, 628, 628*f*
  in arthropods, 703, 703*f,* 711*f*
  in bacteria, 326, 326*f*
  in birds, 767, 773*f*
  in bony fishes, 737*f*
  in earthworms, 688, 689*f*
  in echinoderms, 718, 718*f*
  in frogs, 746*f*
  in grizzly bears, 789*f*
  in humans, 896–901, 897*f,* 898*f,* 899*f,* 900*f*
dihybrid crosses, 275, 275*f*
dikaryotic hyphae, 526, 526*f*
dinoflagellates, 500*f,* 504, 504*f,* 510, 510*f*
dinosaurs, 459, 460, 460*f,* 642, 642*f*–643*f*
diploid life cycle, 256–257, 256*f,* 257*f*
diploid phases, 249, 256–257, 256*f,* 257*f*
directional selection, 409, 409*f*
disaccharides, 60
disease transmission, 482, 482*f,* 930–931. *See also names of specific diseases*
disjunction, 324, 324*f*

disruptive selection, 409, 409*f*
distributions, 400–401, 400*f*, 401*f*
diurnal animals, 822
DNA (deoxyribonucleic acid). *See also* **genes**
  Avery's experiments, 294
  in bacteria, 472, 473*f*
  base pairing in, 297–298, 298*f*
  categories of, 331
  in cell cycle, 228*f*, 229
  Chargaff's observations, 298, 299*f*
  cloning, 357, 357*f*
  complementary, 357
  denaturation of, 357
  deoxyribose in, 63, 296, 296*f*, 305, 305*f*
  errors in replication of, 301, 324
  in eukaryotic cells, 155, 155*f*, 157, 157*f*
  evolution and, 384, 384*f*
  evolutionary relatedness and, 430–431, 431*f*
  extraction from wheat germ, 311
  fingerprinting, 36, 347, 347*f*, 358, 364–365
  forensic analysis of, 347, 347*f*, 1023, 1023*f*
  in forensic genealogy, 335, 335*f*
  function of, 154, 223, 224, 293
  Griffith's discovery of transformation, 294, 294*f*
  Hershey-Chase experiments, 295, 295*f*
  hybridization of, 357
  kinds of mutations in, 320–321, 320*f*, 321*f*
  mobile genetic elements in, 332
  non-coding, 328, 331, 345
  nucleotides in, 63, 63*f*, 296, 296*f*
  origin of, 449
  packaging during cell division, 224–225, 225*f*
  polymorphisms, 343, 356
  in prokaryotic cells, 154, 154*f*
  recombinant, 350, 359*f*, 360, 360*f*
  repeating sequences in, 343
  replication of, 223, 226, 228, 228*f*, 229, 300–303, 300*f*, 301*f*, 302*f*, 307
  RNA compared with, 305, 305*f*
  sequencing of, 359
  size of, 303
  structure of, 63, 290*f*–291*f*, 296–297, 296*f*
  transcription factors and, 327, 327*f*
  transcription of, 304–305, 306–307, 306*f*
  Watson and Crick's model, 299, 299*f*
  X-ray diffraction of, 298–299, 299*f*
DNA barcodes, 358
DNA fingerprints, 36, 347, 347*f*, 358, 364–365
DNA helicases, 301, 301*f*
DNA ligase, 360, 360*f*
DNA polymerase, 301, 301*f*
DNA sequencing, 359, 359*f*, 363, 363*f*
DNA viruses, 477
dogs, 377, 377*f*, 818, 818*f*
  genome of, 330*f*–331*f*
dolphins, 629, 817, 817*f*
domains, in classification system
  as classification level, 425*f*, 426, 426*f*
  three–domain system, 434–437, 434*f*, 436*f*–437*f*
domains, protein, 329, 329*f*
dominant alleles, 273, 281, 282

dopamine, 959, 959*f*
dormancy, 586, 609, 609*f*
dorsal nerve cord, 638–639, 638*f*
double fertilization, 561
double helix shape, 296, 296*f*
double-loop circulation, 743, 743*f*
dove, white wing, 434*f*
down feathers, 768, 768*f*
Down syndrome, 324, 324*f*
downy mildews, 506
Drosophila melanogaster, 271, 271*f*, 362, 362*f*, 410
  genome of, 330*f*-331*f*
drug addiction, 956, 956*f*
drug use and abuse
  cardiovascular disease and, 874
  counterfeit drugs, 1036
  forensic science and, 1025
  neural changes from, 959, 959*f*
  during pregnancy, 1002
  psychoactive drugs, 956–958, 958*f*
duckbill platypus, 788, 791, 791*f*
ducks, 61, 61*f*, 769, 769*f*, 775
duodenum, 899
duplication mutations, 321, 321*f*

eagles, 772–773, 773*f*
ears
  in amphibians, 740, 740*f*
  communication and, 824, 824*f*
  in fishes, 730
  mechanoreceptors, 952, 952*f*
  in reptiles, 758
  structure of, 952, 952*f*
earthworms, 637, 688–689, 689*f*
eating disorders, 895
echidnas, 788, 791, 791*f*
echinoderms, 717–719, 717*f*, 718*f*, 719*f*
echolocation, 790
E. coli *(Escherichia coli)*
  as ancient organism, 454*f*
  diseases from, 483*f*
  E. coli O157:H7, 473
  gene regulation by operons in, 326, 326*f*
  genome compared with that of *Salmonella,* 332
  structure of, 162*f*, 473, 473*f*
  vitamin K production by, 481
ecosystems, 76–93
  abiotic factors in, 80, 82
  aquatic, 84, 84*f*
  biodiversity in, 80, 115
  carbon and oxygen cycles in, 91, 91*f*
  closed, 94–95
  coevolution in, 109, 388, 388*f*
  communities, 79, 79*f*
  definition of, 79
  disruption of, 132–133, 132*f*, 133*f*
  energy pyramid in, 88–89, 88*f*, 89*f*
  fires and, 85*f*
  nitrogen cycle in, 92, 92*f*
  phosphorus cycle in, 93

  population growth models in, 104–105, 104*f*, 105*f*
  populations in, 103
  role of fungi in, 522
  stability of, 115, 115*f*
  succession in, 81, 81*f*
  terrestrial biomes, 82–83, 82*f*, 83*f*
  trophic levels in, 86–87, 86*f*, 87*f*
  water cycle in, 90, 90*f*
ecotourism, 137, 137*f*
ectoderm, 634, 635*f*, 1003
ectoparasites, 666
ectothermic metabolism, 757, 758, 759, 759*f*
eggs, human, 982*f*, 996–999, 996*f*, 997*f*, 998*f*
ejaculation, 995
electrical signals, 944
electromagnetic radiation, 203, 203*f*
electron carriers, 63, 201*f*, 203, 210
electron clouds, 51, 51*f*, 52*f*
electrons, 51–52, 51*f*, 203
electron transport chain
  in aerobic respiration, 211, 211*f*
  in cellular respiration, 201, 201*f*
  in photosynthesis, 204–205, 204*f*
electrophoresis, 336–337, 356, 356*f*, 358*f*
elements, 51
elephantiasis, 669, 669*f*
embryology, 383
embryonic stem cells, 353, 839, 839*f*
embryonic structures, 383
embryos
  development of, 634–635, 634*f*, 635*f*, 646
  in humans, 1001, 1001*f*
  in plants, 555, 561*f*, 585–586, 585*f*, 586*f*
emerging diseases, 486
emphysema, 881, 881*f*
emus, 769, 774
endangered species, 39
endocrine glands, 972, 972*f*
endocrine system. *See also* **hormones**
  disorders of, 977, 979–981
  feedback mechanisms in, 976–977, 976*f*, 977*f*
  glands and tissues in, 972, 972*f*
  growth and reproduction control by, 982, 982*f*
  metabolism control by, 980–981, 980*f*, 981*f*
  nervous system control, 978–979, 978*f*, 979*f*
  target cells, 973, 973*f*
endocytosis, 183, 183*f*
endoderm, 634, 635*f*, 1003
endoparasites, 666
endoplasmic reticulum (ER), 158, 159*f*
endorphins, 977
endoskeletons, 627, 717, 730, 758
endosperm, 555, 561*f*
endospore formation, 475, 475*f*
endosymbiosis, 456, 456*f*
endosymbiotic theory, 331
endothermic metabolism, 767, 786, 842
energy
  activation, 65–66, 65*f*, 66*f*
  from aerobic respiration, 210–211, 210*f*, 211*f*, 213*f*

from anaerobic respiration, 212–213, 212*f*, 213*f*
from carbohydrates, 60
carriers, 63
chemical, 60, 64–65, 197
conservation of, 64
flow of, in ecosystems, 86–89, 86*f*, 87*f*, 88*f*, 89*f*
from glycolysis, 208–209, 209*f*, 213*f*
from lipids, 61
from metabolism of food, 67
from photosynthesis, 197, 202–205, 202*f*–203*f*, 204*f*
production in cells, 160–161, 161*f*
transferring, 63, 200–201, 200*f*, 201*f*
usable, 64
energy pyramid, 88–89, 88*f*, 89*f*
enhancers, 327, 327*f*
enkephalins, 958
entomology, forensic, 1029, 1029*f*
envelopes, virus, 477, 477*f*
environment, 122–139. *See also* **ecosystems**
air pollution, 127, 128, 128*f*
cars of the future, 139, 139*f*
conservation and restoration of, 134, 134*f*
ecosystem disruption, 132–133, 132*f*, 133*f*
environmental awareness, 137, 137*f*
gene regulation in prokaryotes and, 326
genetically engineered bioremediation microbes, 349, 349*f*
global warming, 128, 129, 129*f*
health and, 127
humans and, 125
planning for the future, 138, 138*f*
protists and, 510, 510*f*
resources in, 126, 126*f*, 135
soil damage, 131
technological innovation, 39, 136, 136*f*
water pollution, 130, 130*f*
environmental clubs, 40, 40*f*
environmental stimulus
nastic movements in plants, 610, 610*f*
plant tropisms, 606–607, 606*f*, 607*f*
seasonal responses of plants, 608–609, 608*f*, 609*f*
enzymes. *See also names of specific enzymes*
action of, 66, 67*f*
in cell membranes, 177, 177*f*, 186
in detergents, 68–69
digestive, 896–897, 898*f*
in lysosomes, 158, 160
in protein processing, 158
restriction, 355–356, 355*f*, 360, 360*f*
RNA as, 449
second messenger activation of, 186, 186*f*, 974, 974*f*
in transcription and translation, 329
Ephedra, 556
epidemiology, 31
epidermis
of cnidarians, 658
of humans, 853, 854*f*
of plants, 574, 574*f*, 579, 582, 582*f*
epididymis, 993*f*, 994, 994*f*
epiglottis, 897
epinephrine, 981, 984–985

epithelial tissue, 840, 840*f*, 853
Epstein-Barr virus, 485
equilibrium, 81, 178
ergotism, 532, 532*f*
erosion, 131
Escherichia coli (E. coli)
as ancient organism, 454*f*
diseases from, 483*f*
E. coli O157:H7, 473
gene regulation by operons in, 326, 326*f*
genome compared with that of *Salmonella,* 332
structure of, 162*f*, 473, 473*f*
vitamin K production by, 481
esophagus, 896*f*, 897, 897*f*
essential amino acids, 892
EST (expressed sequence tag) library, 363
estrogen, 982, 996, 999–1000, 999*f*
estuaries, 84
ethanol cars, 139, 139*f*
ethical issues
in biometric identification, 37
in cloning, 37, 352
in diagnosing genetic disorders, 354
in DNA databanking, 1023
in experimentation, 8, 11
in human genome research, 348
safety of GMOs, 37, 354, 354*f*
in stem cell research, 353
Ethical Legal and Social Implications (ELSI), 348
ethylene, 605–606, 605*f*
Eubacteria (kingdom), 433, 434*f*, 435, 436*f*–437*f*. *See also* **bacteria**
Euglena, 504, 504*f*
euglenoids, 151*f*, 504, 504*f*,
Eukarya (domain), 434*f*, 435–437, 436*f*–437*f*. *See also* **eukaryotes**
eukaryotes. *See also* **eukaryotic cells**
characteristics of, 434*f*, 435–436
major groups of, 434*f*, 436–437, 436*f*–437*f*
structure of, 155, 155*f*
eukaryotic cells
aging and, 333–334
animal cell structure, 163*f*
cell cycle in, 228–229, 228*f*
chloroplasts in, 160, 160*f*, 455
cytoskeleton in, 156, 156*f*
diversity in, 163, 163*f*
DNA replication in, 302–303, 302*f*
gene regulation in, 327–329, 327*f*, 328*f*
mitochondria in, 161, 161*f*, 455
non-coding DNA in, 328, 331, 345
nucleus in, 157, 157*f*
plant cell structure, 163*f*
preparation for cell division in, 226
protein processing in, 158, 159*f*
reproduction controls, 233–234, 233*f*, 234*f*
ribosomes in, 157
storage in, 158, 160, 160*f*
structure of, 155, 155*f*, 163*f*
evaporation, 90, 90*f*
evolution. *See also* **evolutionary theory**
of amphibians, 641, 739, 745, 745*f*
analyzing relatedness in, 430–431, 431*f*
of behavior, 815, 815*f*

of birds, 459, 643, 643*f*
body segmentation and, 637
as characteristic of life, 19
of chordates, 638–639, 638*f*, 639*f*
coevolution, 109, 388, 388*f*
convergent, 388, 428
definition of, 375
extinction and, 414
of fishes, 640, 640*f*
of fungi, 524
gradualism in, 389, 389*f*
of herbivores, 110, 110*f*
of hominids, 800–802, 801*f*–802*f*, 803*f*
of humans, 799–803, 799*f*, 800*f*–801*f*, 802*f*, 803*f*
on islands, 803
macroevolution, 388–389, 389*f*
of mammals, 644, 644*f*
microevolution, 388
of mitochondria and chloroplasts, 456, 456*f*
natural selection and, 407–408, 408*f*
in the Paleozoic era, 458–459, 458*f*
of plants from green algae, 544*f*–545*f*
of populations, not individuals, 380–381, 381*f*, 386
in Precambrian time, 454–457, 454*f*, 455*f*, 456*f*
punctuated equilibrium in, 389, 389*f*
of reptiles, 641, 641*f*
sexual selection and, 406, 406*f*
speciation and, 387, 387*f*
unpredictability of, 387
evolutionary theory, 373–389
anatomy and, 384, 384*f*
biochemistry and, 384
biogeography and, 383, 383*f*
breeding and artificial selection, 377, 377*f*
embryonic structures and, 383
fossil record and, 382–383, 382*f*
influence of Lamarck on, 378, 378*f*
influence of population growth patterns on, 379
modern synthesis of, 386
natural selection in, 380–381, 380*f*, 381*f*, 387, 390–391
population growth pattern in, 378, 378*f*, 379
publication of, 381
rate of geologic change and, 379, 379*f*
speciation, 387, 387*f*
strengths and weaknesses of Darwin's, 385
updates to, 386–387
voyage of HMS *Beagle* and, 375–376, 375*f*, 376*f*
exchange principle, 1017
excretion
animal excretory systems, 628, 628*f*
in arthropods, 703, 703*f*
in birds, 773*f*
in echinoderms, 718, 718*f*
in fishes, 732, 732*f*
in humans, 900–905, 902*f*, 903*f*, 904*f*, 905*f*
in mollusks, 680, 680*f*
in protists, 503*f*
excurrent siphons, 692, 693*f*

exercise, 852, 852*f*, 874. *See also* **physical activity**
exhalation, 877, 877*f*, 902
exocrine glands, 972
exocytosis, 183, 183*f*, 503*f*, 948
exons, 328, 328*f*
exoskeletons, 627, 627*f*, 702, 702*f*
experiments, 11, 1052–1053
expert testimony, 1017, 1035
expiratory reserve volume (ERV), 882
exponential growth, 104, 104*f*, 378, 378*f*, 379
expressed sequence tag (EST) library, 363
exsanguination, 1033
extensors, 849, 849*f*
extinction, 133, 389, 414, 414*f*, 644. *See also* **mass extinction**
extremophiles, 435, 471
eyes
  in amphibians, 740, 748
  in birds, 772–773
  blind spot in, 951, 951*f*
  in cephalopods, 684
  color in, 400*f*
  compound, 703, 703*f*
  in fishes, 730
  occipital lobe processing and, 954, 954*f*
  photoreceptors in, 951, 951*f*
  placement of, in primates, 797, 797*f*
  in reptiles, 758–759, 759*f*
  structure of, 951, 951*f*
eyespots, 485*f*, 504

F1 generation, 269
F2 generation, 269
facilitated diffusion, 179–180, 179*f*
FADH2, 210–211, 210*f*, 211*f*, 213
fallopian tubes, 996*f*, 997, 997*f*, 1007
family, 425*f*, 426, 426*f*
fangs, 706–707, 706*f*, 710*f*, 764*f*
fast-food meals, 875
fast-twitch muscle fibers, 852
fats, 61, 61*f*, 208, 789*f*, 853, 892
fatty acids, 899
feathers, 61, 61*f*, 429, 643, 643*f*, 768, 768*f*
feedback mechanisms, 976–977, 976*f*, 977*f*
feeding
  in arthropods, 703, 703*f*, 712, 712*f*
  foraging behavior, 821, 821*f*
feet, bird, 769, 769*f*, 772, 775
Felidae (family), 425*f*
female reproductive system, 996–1000
  cleavage and implantation in, 1001, 1001*f*
  egg production in, 996–997, 996*f*
  menstrual cycle in, 1000
  ovarian cycle in, 998–999, 998*f*, 999*f*
  structure of, 997, 997*f*
fermentation, 211–212, 211*f*, 213*f*, 533
ferns, 429*f*, 550–552, 550*f*, 551*f*, 552*f*
fertilization
  in amphibians, 744, 747
  in arthropods, 704

  in birds, 771
  cross-fertilization, 562
  double, 561
  in fishes, 733, 733*f*
  gametes in, 248, 248*f*
  genetic variation from, 253–254, 254*f*
  in humans, 982*f*, 995, 1001, 1001*f*
  in reptiles, 761
  in seed plants, 554, 560, 561*f*
  self-fertilization, 562
fetal alcohol syndrome, 1002
fetus, 990*f*–991*f*, 1003–1004, 1003*f*
fevers, 916
fiber, dietary, 892
fibers, in forensics, 1024, 1024*f*
fibrous root systems, 579, 579*f*
field guides, using, 435
"fight-or-flight" response, 942, 968*f*–969*f*, 981
filial (F) generation, 269, 269*f*
filter feeders, 624, 638*f*, 656, 685
finches, Galápagos, 375, 375*f*, 410
fingernails, 855
fingerprints
  DNA, 36, 347, 347*f*, 358, 364–365
  in forensic science, 1020, 1022, 1022*f*
  formation of, 855
fins, 640, 640*f*, 730, 737*f*
firearms, 1025, 1025*f*
fires, ecosystems and, 85*f*
first gap phase (G1), 228*f*, 229
fishes, 729–738
  bony, 736–738, 736*f*, 737*f*, 738*f*
  cartilaginous, 735, 735*f*
  endoskeleton in, 730
  evolution of, 640, 640*f*
  excretion in, 732, 732*f*
  jawless, 458, 639, 734, 734*f*
  movement in, 730
  in the Paleozoic era, 458
  reproduction in, 733, 733*f*
  respiration and circulation in, 731, 731*f*
  sensory organs in, 730, 730*f*
fixed action patterns, 816, 816*f*
flagella (singular, *flagellum*)
  in bacteria, 220*f*, 473*f*
  in prokaryotes, 162, 162*f*
  in protists, 497, 502, 504
  in sperm, 994, 994*f*
  in sponges, 655
flagellates, 502, 502*f*
flatworms, 663–666
  characteristics of, 663–664, 664*f*
  flukes, 666, 666*f*
  nervous system in, 629, 629*f*, 664*f*
  reproduction in, 664, 664*f*
  tapeworms, 663, 665, 665*f*
  turbellarians, 664*f*, 665
flexors, 849, 849*f*
flies, 712*f*, 713
flight
  by bats, 790, 790*f*
  by birds, 643, 755*f*, 768, 768*f*
  by insects, 713, 713*f*
flight feathers, 768
flowering plants. *See* **angiosperms**

flowers, 557*f*, 560–562, 560*f*, 561*f*, 609
flukes, 666, 666*f*
fluorescein, 1019
flu viruses, 476*f*, 485–486, 485*f*, 880, 923
FoldNotes, 1044–1046
follicles, 999, 999*f*
follicle-stimulating hormone (FSH), 979*f*, 993, 998–999, 999*f*
follicular phase, 999, 999*f*
food allergies, 925
food chains, 87
food guide pyramid. *See* **MyPyramid**
food labels, 891, 894
food vacuoles, 160
food webs, 87, 87*f*, 94–95, 510
foot, mollusk, 680, 692
foraging behavior, 821, 821*f*
foraminiferans, 501*f*
forensic anthropology, 1028, 1028*f*
forensic entomology, 1029, 1029*f*
forensic genealogy, 335, 335*f*
forensic science, 1014–1035
  anthropology in, 1028, 1028*f*
  ballistics, 1025, 1025*f*
  blood alcohol content and, 1025
  cause, mechanism, and manner of death, 1033
  crime scene analysis, 1014*f*–1015*f*, 1030–1031, 1030*f*, 1031*f*
  DNA analysis in, 36, 347, 347*f*, 1023, 1023*f*
  entomology in, 1029, 1029*f*
  expert testimony in, 1017, 1035
  fingerprint identification in, 1022, 1022*f*
  and King Tut, 1021, 1021*f*
  lab on, 1036–1037
  overview, 1017
  pathology, 1027, 1027*f*
  time of death in, 1032–1033, 1032*f*
  toolmarks in, 1025
  tools used in, 1019–1020, 1020*f*
  toxicology in, 1025, 1025*f*, 1033
  trace evidence in, 1024, 1024*f*
  uses of, 1018, 1018*f*
  victim identification, 1034, 1034*f*
forensic toxicology, 1025, 1025*f*
forests, 83, 83*f*, 458*f*
forged signatures, 1019
fossil fuels
  air pollution from, 128, 128*f*
  carbon dioxide from, 91
  as nonrenewable resource, 126, 126*f*
  origin of, 458
fossil record, 379, 379*f*, 382–383, 382*f*, 450
fossils, 382, 382*f*
  formation of, 450, 450*f*
  fungi, 524
  hominid, 799–802, 800*f*–801*f*, 803, 803*f*
  index, 451
  lancelet, 639
  oldest known, 455, 456
  types of, 451
fractures, 845
fragmentation, 247, 498
frameshift mutations, 320
frameshifts, 320
Franklin, Rosalind, 298–299, 299*f*

fraternal twins, 1008, 1008*f*
freshwater ecosystems, 84, 84*f*
friction ridges, 855, 1022
frogs. *See also* **amphibians**
  anatomy of, 746*f*
  lab exercise on, 748–749
  mutations in, 316*f*–317*f*
  skeletons of, 740
  speciation in, 413, 413*f*
  tadpoles, 334, 747, 747*f*, 748*f*
  tympanic membranes in, 740, 740*f*
fronds, 550, 550*f*
frontal lobe, 954, 954*f*
fruit flies, 271, 271f, 362, 362f. *See also* ***Drosophila melanogaster***
  genome of, 330*f*–331*f*
  hox genes in, 333*f*
fruits, 563, 563*f*, 578, 605–606, 605*f*, 893*f*, 894*f*, 895*f*
FSH (follicle-stimulating hormone), 979*f*, 993, 998–999, 999*f*
fuel cell cars, 139, 139*f*
fundamental niche, 113
fungi, 518–531
  characteristics of, 436, 521–522
  chytrid, 524, 524*f*
  classification of, 434*f*, 436, 436*f*–437*f*
  club, 527, 527*f*
  as decomposers, 530, 530*f*
  diseases from, 531, 531*f*
  haploid life cycle in, 258, 258*f*
  imperfect, 522, 523
  industrial uses of, 529, 529*f*
  in lichens, 510, 528, 528*f*
  multicellular, 166*f*
  in mycorrhizae, 458, 528, 528*f*, 530, 544
  in the Paleozoic era, 458
  pneumonia from, 880
  reproduction in, 522–523, 522*f*
  sac, 526, 526*f*
  in skin disorders, 856, 856*f*
  zygote, 525, 525*f*
Fungi (kingdom), 434*f*, 436, 436*f*–437*f*. *See also* **fungi**
fungus-like protists, 506, 506*f*

G1/G2 checkpoints, 234, 234*f*
Galápagos Island finches, 375, 375*f*
gallbladder, 898, 898*f*
Galvani, Luigi, 944
gametes, 248, 248*f*, 272*f*, 273, 498
gametophytes
  generation, 499
  haploid life cycle in, 258, 258*f*
  in nonvascular plants, 548–549, 548*f*, 549*f*
  in plant life cycles, 546, 546*f*
  in seedless vascular plants, 550–552, 551*f*, 552*f*
  in seed plants, 554, 554*f*, 557, 557*f*, 561*f*
ganglia (singular, *ganglion*), 629
ganja, 956, 958*f*

gases, 129, 129*f*, 727, 730. *See also* **gas transport and exchange**
gasohol, 529
gas transport and exchange
  in echinoderms, 718
  in human respiratory system, 877, 878, 878*f*
  in plants, 575, 575*f*, 582*f*, 583
gastric juice, 897
gastrodermis, 658
gastropods, 451*f*, 682*f*, 683, 683*f*
gastrovascular cavity, 628, 628*f*
gastrula, 634–635, 634*f*, 635*f*, 646, 647*f*
gastrulation, 634, 634*f*
geckos, 227, 227*f*, 758, 759*f*
gel electrophoresis, 336–337, 356, 356*f*, 358*f*
gels, 336
genealogy, 335, 335*f*
gene expression
  codons in, 307, 307*f*
  complexities of, 310
  factors regulating, 325, 325*f*
  gene technologies in, 351, 351*f*
  hormones and, 975, 975*f*
  overview of, 304–305, 304*f*
  RNA types in, 305
  RNA *vs.* DNA, 305, 305*f*
  transcription, 304–305, 306–307, 306*f*
  translation, 304–305, 304*f*, 308–309, 308*f*–309*f*
gene flow, 405
gene pool, 401
generations, 269
gene rearrangements, 321
gene regulation
  cell differentiation and, 333, 333*f*
  definition of, 325
  in eukaryotes, 327–329, 327*f*, 328*f*
  factors in, 325, 325*f*
  in prokaryotes, 326, 326*f*
  by regulatory proteins, 329
  by transcription factors, 327, 327*f*
genes. *See also* **alleles**
  associated, 362
  definition of, 224, 293
  DNA in, 293
  homeotic, 333, 333*f*
  independent assortment of, 275, 275*f*, 284
  jumping, 332
  linked, 275, 284
  multiple alleles, 283, 283*f*
  mutation types in, 320–321, 320*f*
  number in human genome, 345
  processing RNA after transcription, 328, 328*f*
  promoters, 306
  sequencing, 345, 363, 363*f*
  sex-linked, 280
  in sexual reproduction, 248
gene technologies
  in bioremediation, 349, 349*f*
  blotting processes, 358, 358*f*
  cloning, 352, 352*f*
  data management in, 361, 363
  definition of, 350
  denaturation, 357

in disease diagnosis and treatment, 346–347, 346*f*
  DNA polymorphisms, 356
  DNA sequencing, 359, 359*f*, 363, 363*f*
  ethical issues in, 37, 348, 350, 352, 353, 354, 354*f*
  future work in, 39, 348
  gene cloning and recombination, 360, 360*f*
  genetically modified organisms, 33, 350–351, 350*f*, 354
  genome mapping, 362, 362*f*
  genome sequence assembly, 363
  hybridization, 357
  manipulating cell interactions in, 351, 351*f*
  polymerase chain reaction, 357, 357*f*, 1023
  property laws and, 354
  restriction enzymes in, 355, 355*f*
  tissue culture in, 351, 351*f*
  using stem cells, 353, 353*f*
gene therapy, 347, 351
genetically modified organisms (GMOs), 33, 350–351, 350*f*, 354
genetic code, 63, 307, 307*f*, 330. *See also* **genomes**
genetic counseling, 346
genetic disorders
  albinism, 280–281, 280*f*, 281*f*
  diagnosing and preventing, 346, 354
  Down syndrome, 324, 324*f*
  eczema, 856, 856*f*
  examples of, 323, 323*f*
  gene therapy, 347, 351
  natural selection and, 408
  pedigree analysis of, 280–281, 280*f*, 281*f*
  recessive, 323
  risk assessment of, 407
genetic drift, 388, 405, 406, 406*f*, 415
genetic engineering. *See also* **gene technologies**
  in bioremediation, 349, 349*f*
  of *Bt* corn, 33, 33*f*, 351, 354, 354*f*
  definition of, 346, 350
  ethical issues in, 37, 350, 354, 354*f*
  and GMOs, 350, 351
  of human proteins, 351, 360
  of vaccines, 346
genetic equilibrium, 404–405, 404*f*
genetic libraries, 363
genetic markers, 362, 362*f*
genetics. *See also* **heredity**
  Avery's experiments in, 294
  chromosome sorting errors, 324, 324*f*
  definition of, 31, 267
  Griffith's discovery of transformation, 294, 294*f*
  Hershey-Chase experiments in, 295, 295*f*
  phenotypic variation, 400, 400*f*
  role of genes in, 293
genetic switches, 325, 329, 334*f*
genetic variation
  allele frequency, 401–402, 401*f*, 402*f*
  gene pools, 401
  genetic equilibrium, 404–405, 404*f*
  meiosis and, 253–254, 254*f*

Index

genetic variation (*continued*)
  natural selection and, 407–408, 408*f*
  phenotypic variation, 400, 400*f*
  population genetics, 399
  population size and, 406, 406*f*
  sources of, 403
genital herpes, 485, 1005*f*, 1006, 1006*f*
genital HPV, 1005*f*, 1006
genital warts, 1006
genomes. *See also* **human genome**
  of cell organelles, 331
  data management of, 361, 363
  definition of, 31, 330
  mapping of, 362, 362*f*
  rearrangement of materials in, 332
  sequence assembly, 363
  sizes of, 331
  universal code of, 330, 330*f*–331*f*
genomic imprinting, 352
genomic libraries, 363
genomics, 345–348
  disease and, 346, 347
  future work in, 348
  individual identification through, 347
  pharmacogenomics, 347
genotypes, 274, 274*f*, 402, 402*f*, 408
genus (plural, *genera*), 424, 425*f*, 426, 426*f*
geographic information systems (GIS), 39
geologic time scale, 453, 453*f*
geology, influence on Darwin, 379, 379*f*
geometric growth, 378, 378*f*, 379
germ cells, 248, 322, 403
germination, 586–587, 586*f*, 605, 609
gestation, 1001–1004, 1001*f*, 1002*f*, 1003*f*, 1004*f*
gestation period, 788
giardiasis, 507, 507*f*
gibberellins, 605, 605*f*
gill covers, 736
gills
  in arthropods, 703
  in fishes, 731, 731*f*
  in mollusks, 681, 681*f*, 685
  respiration through, 630, 630*f*
  in salamanders, 744
gill slits, 731, 731*f*
ginkgo, 556, 556*f*
GIS (geographic information systems), 39
gizzards, 688, 689*f*, 711*f*, 773*f*
glaciers, 58, 81, 81*f*
glands, endocrine, 972, 972*f*
global positioning system (GPS), 15
global warming, 128, 129, 129*f*, 510
glomerulus, 903, 903*f*
"glow" gene, 342*f*–343*f*, 350*f*, 351
glucagon, 974*f*, 977, 977*f*, 980
glucose
  in blood, 898, 977, 977*f*
  cell transport of, 182
  chemical structure of, 60, 60*f*
  diabetes and, 983, 983*f*
  energy from, 67
  in foods, 892
  glycolysis of, 208–209, 209*f*, 213*f*
  in muscle movement, 849
glue inhalants, 956, 958*f*

glycerol, 899
glycogen, 60, 898, 980
glycolysis, 208–209, 209*f*, 213*f*
glycoproteins, 177, 177*f*, 477
GMOs (genetically modified organisms), 33, 350–351, 350*f*, 354
gnetophytes, 556, 556*f*
Golgi apparatus, 158, 159*f*
gonads, 982
gonorrhea, 1005*f*, 1007
Goodall, Jane, 817
gorillas, 799*f*, 824
gradualism, 389, 389*f*
Gram-negative bacteria, 472, 472*f*, 473*f*
Gram-positive bacteria, 472, 472*f*
Gram stain, 472, 472*f*
grandchildren, as sign of evolutionary fitness, 407
graphing, 1060–1061
grasshoppers
  anatomy of, 711*f*
  exoskeleton molting, 704*f*
  life cycle of, 714, 714*f*
  mouthparts, 712*f*
  nervous system, 629, 629*f*
grasslands, 83, 83*f*
Grave's disease, 927*f*
gravitropisms, 607, 607*f*
gray matter, 941, 941*f*
Great Barrier Reef, 625
green algae, 499, 499*f*, 505, 505*f*
greenhouse effect, 123, 129, 129*f*
green sulfur bacteria, 474
Griffith, Frederick, 294, 294*f*
grizzly bears (*Ursus arctos*), 789, 789*f*, 821, 821*f*
ground pines (club mosses), 550, 550*f*, 552
ground tissue, 573, 573*f*, 578, 578*f*
growth hormones, 603–606, 603*f*, 604*f*, 605*f*, 979*f*
growth rings, clam, 692, 693*f*
guanine, 296*f*, 297, 298
guard cells, 575, 575*f*, 582*f*, 601, 601*f*
gunpowder detection, 1019
gymnosperms
  cotyledons in, 585, 585*f*
  evolution of, 545*f*
  kinds of, 556, 556*f*
  life cycle of, 557–558, 557*f*
  reproduction in, 554–555, 554*f*, 555*f*
  seeds of, 553, 553*f*, 554*f*

habitat, 112, 127, 132, 132*f*, 133*f*
habituation, 817
hagfishes, 734, 734*f*
hair, 644, 785, 855, 1024
hair cells, in ears, 952
hair follicles, 854*f*, 855
Haldane, John B. S., 447
half-life, 452, 452*f*
Hanta virus, 486
haploid life cycle, 258, 258*f*

haploid phases, 249, 250*f*–251*f*, 251–252, 252*f*
Hardy, G. H., 404
Hardy-Weinberg principle, 404–405, 404*f*
hashish, 956, 958, 958*f*
Haversian canals, 844*f*, 845
headgear, 955, 955*f*, 961, 961*f*
healing, 223, 223*f*, 233, 233*f*
health. *See also names of specific diseases and disorders*
  assistive technologies, 32, 32*f*
  battlefield medicine, 32, 32*f*
  cholera research and, 29–30, 29*f*, 30*f*
  eradication of specific diseases, 31
  future challenges in, 29
  Human Genome Project and, 31, 345
hearing
  in amphibians, 740, 740*f*
  in communication, 824, 824*f*
  ear structure, 952, 952*f*
  in fishes, 730
  mechanoreceptors, 952, 952*f*
  in reptiles, 758
  temporal lobe processing of, 954, 954*f*
heart. *See also* **cardiovascular disease**
  in amphibians, 641, 742, 742*f*
  in birds, 770, 770*f*
  in fishes, 731, 731*f*
  heart attacks, 873, 873*f*
  in humans, 866–867, 866*f*, 867*f*
  in mammals, 786, 786*f*
  in reptiles, 760, 760*f*
heartburn, 897
heart rate, 867, 968, 984–985
heartwood, 581, 581*f*
heartworms, 669, 669*f*
heat-sensing, in snakes, 759
height, factors in, 284
helicases, 301, 301*f*
Helicobacter pylori, 7, 483*f*
heliotropisms, 606*f*, 607, 607*f*
helmets, 955, 955*f*, 961, 961*f*
helper T cells
  HIV and, 929, 929*f*
  in immune response, 919–920, 919*f*, 920*f*, 921*f*
hemispheres, brain, 940
hemoglobin
  evolution and, 384, 384*f*
  oxygen transport in, 878–879, 878*f*
  in red blood cells, 869
  in sickle cell anemia, 319
hemophilia, 323*f*, 351
hepatitis B, 485, 485*f*, 1005*f*, 1007
herbaceous plants, 580, 580*f*
herbivores, 87, 89, 89*f*, 110
heredity, 19, 267–284. *See also* **genetics**
  characters and traits in, 268, 268*f*
  codominance, 283
  definition of, 19
  dominant and recessive alleles, 273
  environmental conditions and, 284
  genotype and phenotype, 274, 274*f*
  homozygous *vs.* heterozygous, 274*f*, 275
  incomplete dominance, 282–283
  Lamarckian inheritance, 378, 378*f*

Index

Mendelian theory of, 272–275, 272*f*, 274*f*, 275*f*
Mendel's pea plant experiments, 267–270, 267*f*, 268*f*, 269*f*
multiple alleles, 283, 283*f*
of mutations, 322
origin of, 449
pedigrees, 280–281, 281*f*
phenotypic variation, 400, 400*f*
polygenic, 282
probability in, 278–279, 278*f*, 279*f*
Punnett squares in, 276–277, 276*f*
random segregation of alleles, 273
hernias, 901, 901*f*
heroin, 956, 958, 958*f*, 958*t*
herpes, 1005*f*, 1006, 1006*f*
herpes simplex virus (HSV), 1006
Hershey, Alfred, 294–295, 295*f*
Hershey-Chase experiments, 295, 295*f*
heterotrophs, 437, 474, 474*f*, 521, 624
heterozygous crosses, 276*f*, 277
heterozygous individuals, 274*f*, 275
HGP (Human Genome Project), 31, 345
hibernation, 822, 981
high blood pressure, 872
high-latitude biomes, 83
hirudin, 690–691
Hirudo medicinalis, 691
histamine, 916, 924
histograms, 401, 401*f*
histones, 224, 225*f*, 302
histoplasmosis, 531, 928
history of life, 444–460
dating methods in, 451–452, 451*f*, 452*f*
eukaryotic life, 455
first cells, 448–449, 449*f*
first organic molecules, 447, 447*f*
formation of oxygen, 455
fossil record and, 450, 450*f*
geologic time scale, 453, 453*f*
location of first life, 448, 448*f*
multicellular organisms, 455, 455*f*, 456–457
origin of mitochondria and chloroplasts, 456, 456*f*
Paleozoic era, 453, 453*f*, 458–459, 458*f*
in Pre-Cambrian time, 454–457, 454*f*, 455*f*, 456*f*
prokaryotic life, 454–455, 454*f*
HIV (human immunodeficiency virus)
antigenic shifting in, 923
course of infection, 929*f*
pneumonia and, 880
prevalence of, 1005*f*
shape of virus, 477, 477*f*
symptoms of, 1005*f*, 1007
transmission of, 915, 929
tuberculosis and, 880
viral reproduction, 479*f*
holdfasts, 505
homeobox genes, 333, 333*f*
homeostasis, 191
biofeedback in, 842
in blood pH, 879
in body temperature, 842
cell membranes and, 175

as characteristic of life, 19
definition of, 842
energy for, 197
enzymes in, 66
liver and pancreas in, 898
sensory systems and, 950, 953
stomata in, 601, 601*f*
vesicles in, 158
homeotic genes, 333, 333*f*
hominids, 799–803, 799*f*, 800*f*–801*f*, 803*f*
Homo erectus, 801, 801*f*
Homo ergaster, 801, 801*f*
Homo floresiensis, 801, 801*f*, 803, 803*f*
Homo habilis, 801, 801*f*
homologous chromosomes, 249, 250*f*–251*f*, 251, 253
homologous structures, 383, 384, 384*f*
Homo sapiens, 426*f*, 802. *See also* **humans**
homozygous crosses, 276*f*, 277
homozygous individuals, 274*f*, 275
Hooke, Robert, 151
hookworms, 668, 668*f*
hormones, 971–977. *See also names of specific hormones*
adrenal, 981
amino acid–based, 974, 974*f*
antagonistic, 977, 977*f*
diffusion through the cell membrane, 179
endocrine glands and, 972, 972*f*
feedback mechanisms, 976–977, 976*f*, 977*f*
functions of, 971
gonad, 982
hormone-receptor interactions, 973–975, 973*f*, 974*f*, 975*f*
pancreatic, 980
parathyroid, 980
pineal, 981
pituitary, 979, 979*f*, 982, 993, 998
plant, 603–606, 603*f*, 604*f*, 605*f*
as signal molecules, 184
steroid, 975, 975*f*
target cells, 184, 973, 973*f*
thyroid, 975, 980, 982
hornworts, 548, 548*f*
horseshoe crabs, 707, 707*f*
horsetails, 550, 550*f*, 552
hosts
in gene recombination, 360, 360*f*
in parasitism, 110
hox **sequence,** 333, 333*f*
HPV (human papilloma virus), 485, 485*f*, 1005*f*, 1006
human body. *See also under specific systems*
blood in, 868–870, 868*f*, 869*f*, 870*f*
chromosome number in, 248, 249*f*
circulatory system, 866–867, 866*f*
digestive system, 896–901, 896*f*, 897*f*, 898*f*, 899*f*
endocrine system, 971–977, 972*f*, 976*f*, 977*f*
female reproductive system, 996–1000, 996*f*, 997*f*, 998*f*, 999*f*
heart, 866–867, 866*f*, 867*f*
integumentary system, 853–856, 854*f*, 856*f*
levels of organization in, 839–841, 839*f*, 840*f*, 841*f*

lymphatic system, 871, 871*f*
male reproductive system, 993–995, 993*f*, 994*f*, 995*f*
muscular system, 848–852, 848*f*, 849*f*, 851*f*
nervous system, 936–961, 939*f*
during pregnancy, 1001–1004, 1001*f*, 1002*f*, 1003*f*, 1004*f*
respiratory system, 876–881, 876*f*, 877*f*, 878*f*, 881*f*
skeletal system, 843–846, 843*f*, 844*f*, 846*f*
tissue types in, 840, 840*f*
urinary system, 902–905, 902*f*, 903*f*, 904*f*, 905*f*
human evolution, 799–803, 799*f*, 800*f*–801*f*, 802*f*, 803*f*
human genome
ethical issues in research, 348
future work in, 348
Human Genome Project, 31, 345
mapping of, 362, 362*f*
non-coding genes in, 345
number of genes in, 345
similarity to other genomes, 330, 330*f*–331*f*, 345
Human Genome Project (HGP), 31, 345
human immunodeficiency virus (HIV)
antigenic shifting in, 923
course of infection, 929*f*
pneumonia and, 880
prevalence of, 1005*f*
shape of virus, 477, 477*f*
symptoms of, 1005*f*, 1007
transmission of, 915, 929
tuberculosis and, 880
viral reproduction, 479*f*
human papilloma virus (HPV), 485, 485*f*, 1005*f*, 1006
human population growth, 107–108, 107*f*, 108*f*, 125
humans, classification of, 425*f*, 426*f*. *See also Homo sapiens*
hummingbirds, 562, 754*f*–755*f*, 769, 769*f*
Huntington disease, 323*f*
Hutton, James, 379
hybrid cars, 136, 139, 139*f*
hybridization, 268, 357, 413
hydras
asexual reproduction in, 247*f*
behavior of, 671
movement of, 660, 660*f*
nerve net in, 629, 629*f*
hydrochloric acid, 56, 897
hydrogen bonds, 54–55, 54*f*, 296*f*, 297
hydrogen ion pumps, 201, 201*f*, 204*f*, 205, 211
hydrogen ions
in acids and bases, 56–57, 56*f*
in aerobic respiration, 210–211, 210*f*, 211*f*
in ATP energy transfer, 200–201, 200*f*, 201*f*
breathing rate and, 877
hydroponic plants, 611*f*, 612–613
hydrostatic skeletons, 627, 627*f*
hydrothermal vents, 448, 448*f*
hydrozoans, 660, 660*f*
hypertension (high blood pressure), 872
hyperthyroidism, 980
hypertonic solutions, 180, 180*f*

Index

hyphae (singular, *hypha*), 522, 525*f*, 526, 526*f*
hyperthyroidism, 980
hypothalamus, 940, 972*f*, 978–979, 978*f*
hypotheses (singular, *hypothesis*), 6, 10
hypothyroidism, 980
hypotonic solutions, 180–181, 180*f*, 181*f*

icebergs, 58, 58*f*
identical twins, 1008, 1008*f*
identity, in forensics, 1017, 1034–1035, 1034*f*, 1035*f*
immune deficiency, 928–929, 928*f*, 929*f*
immune system, 915–929
  activation of, 919
  allergies and, 924–926, 924*f*, 925*f*, 926*f*
  autoimmune diseases, 927, 927*f*
  destroying infected cells, 920, 921*f*
  immune deficiency, 928–929, 928*f*, 929*f*
  long-term protection by, 922–923
  lymphatic system and, 871
  non-specific responses, 916–917, 916*f*, 917*f*
  physical barriers in, 915
  removing pathogens, 920, 921*f*
  skin in, 854, 915
  specific responses, 917–918, 917*f*
immunity, 922
immunosuppression, 928
impacts, asteroid, 448, 460, 460*f*, 642
imperfect fungi, 522, 523
implantation, 1001, 1001*f*
imprinting, 819, 819*f*
inbreeding, 406
incisors, 787, 787*f*, 897*f*
incomplete dominance, 282–283
incomplete flowers, 560
incomplete metamorphosis, 714, 714*f*
incubation of eggs, 771
incurrent siphons, 692, 693*f*
independent assortment, 254, 254*f*, 275, 275*f*, 284
independent variables, 11
index fossils, 451
Indian corn, 332
infectious diseases, spread of, 127, 930–931
inferences, scientific, 373, 382
infertility, from STIs, 1007
inflammation, 880, 916, 916*f*, 917*f*, 925
influenza viruses, 476*f*, 485–486, 485*f*, 880, 923
inhalants, 956, 958*f*
inhalation, 877, 877*f*
innate behavior, 816, 816*f*
insecticides, 949
insects, 712–715
  exoskeletons in, 627, 627*f*
  in forensic entomology, 1029, 1029*f*
  grasshopper structure, 711*f*
  jointed appendages in, 702, 702*f*
  life cycle of, 714, 714*f*
  mandibles in, 712, 712*f*

  in the Paleozoic era, 458
  pollination by, 562, 562*f*
  segmented body in, 701, 701*f*
  social systems of, 715
insect sting allergies, 925
insertion, in muscle attachment, 849
insertion mutations, 320
insight, 377
inspiratory reserve volume, 882
insulin
  diabetes and, 927, 983, 983*f*
  glucagon and, 977, 977*f*, 980
  produced by genetically engineered organisms, 34, 347, 360, 360*f*
Integrated Automatic Fingerprinting Identification Systems (IAFIS), 1020
integumentary system, 853–856, 854*f*
intellectual property (IP), 354
interdependence, 19
intermediate fibers, 156
intermediate forms, 382*f*, 383
International System of Units (SI), 14, 14*f*, 20–21, 1058–1059
internodes, 580, 580*f*
interphase, 228–229, 228*f*
intravenous drug use, 874
introns, 328, 328*f*, 331
invasive species, 133, 133*f*
inversion mutations, 321, 321*f*
invertebrates
  chordate, 639, 639*f*
  digestive and excretory systems in, 628, 628*f*
  general characteristics of, 625
  in phylogenetic diagram, 625*f*
involuntary (smooth) muscle, 840, 840*f*, 848, 848*f*
iodide salts, 980
ion excretion, 732, 732*f*
ionic bonds, 53, 53*f*
ions, 56, 56*f*, 946–947, 946*f*, 947*f*
iris scans, 36, 36*f*
iron, 879, 889, 894, 894*f*, 898
islands, natural selection on, 803, 803*f*
islets of Langerhans, 980
isopods, 708, 708*f*
isotonic solutions, 180, 180*f*
isotopes, 51, 452, 452*f*

Jacobson's organ, 759, 764*f*
jawless fishes, 458, 639, 734, 734*f*
jellyfish, 627, 627*f*, 629, 660
jointed appendages, 637, 637*f*, 702, 702*f*, 706–707, 706*f*,
joints, 846, 846*f*
jumping genes, 332
Jurassic period, 453*f*, 642

kangaroos, 106, 792
Katrina, Hurricane, 335
kelp, 115, 500*f*, 501*f*, 505
keratin, 310, 854, 854*f*, 855
keystone species, 115, 115*f*
kidneys
  blood filtration by, 903–904, 903*f*
  dialysis, 905, 905*f*
  in fishes, 732
  function of, 902, 902*f*
  kidney failure, 905
  transplant, 905
kingdoms, 425*f*, 426, 426*f*, 433, 434*f*
kleptoparasitism, 113
knee-jerk reflex, 942–943, 942*f*
knockout mice, 847, 847*f*
Koch's postulates, 482, 482*f*
Krebs cycle, 210–211, 210*f*, 213*f*
Krebs, Hans, 210
krill, 708
K–T extinction, 459, 460, 460*f*

labia, 997, 997*f*
labor, 1004
lab safety, 16
lac **operon,** 326, 326*f*
lactase, 906
lactic acid, 212, 212*f*, 849, 857–858
lactose, 60, 60*f*, 326, 326*f*, 906–907
lactose intolerance, 906
ladders, in electrophoresis, 356
Lamarckian inheritance, 378, 378*f*
Lamarck, Jean Baptiste, 378
lampreys, 734, 734*f*
lancelets, 638*f*, 639
landmines, 716
land plants, evolution of, 429*f*
language, 819, 824
large intestine, 900, 900*f*
largest known organism, 527
larvae
  annelid, 686, 687
  arthropod, 701, 708, 714, 714*f*
  cnidarian, 659, 659*f*
  echinoderm, 718
  flatworm, 666, 666*f*
  mollusk, 682, 682*f*
  sponge, 656, 656*f*
larynx, 876, 876*f*
lasers, 1031, 1031*f*
lateral line, 730, 730*f*, 736
lateral meristems, 589, 589*f*
latitude, ecosystems and, 82
law of conservation of energy, 64
law of conservation of mass, 64
law of independent assortment, 275, 275*f*, 284
law of segregation, 273, 279
law of superposition, 451, 451*f*

laws of heredity, 386
laws, scientific, 8
leaflets, 582, 582*f*
learned behavior, 816–819, 817*f,* 818*f,* 819*f*
leaves
  attached at nodes, 580, 580*f*
  simple *vs.* compound, 582, 582*f*
  specialized, 580, 583, 583*f*
  stomata on, 575, 575*f,* 582*f,* 583, 601
  structure of, 582–583, 582*f*
  tissue functions in, 578*f*
  transpiration from, 600–601, 600*f,* 601*f*
  in vascular plants, 577*f*
leeches, 690–691, 690*f,* 691*f*
Leeuwenhoek, Anton van, 151
Leishmania, 502, 502*f*
lemurs, 782*f*–783*f,* 798, 827, 827*f*
lens, 951, 951*f*
leopards (*Panthera pardus***),** classification of, 424f, 425*f*
leukemia, 845
LH (luteinizing hormone)*,* 993, 998–999, 999*f*
lichens, 510, 528, 528*f*
life, characteristics of, 18–19, 149
life cycles
  of angiosperms, 561, 561*f*
  of arthropods, 704, 704*f*
  of basic plants, 546, 546*f*
  of club fungi, 527, 527*f*
  of cnidarians, 659, 659*f*
  definition of, 256
  diploid, 256–257, 256*f,* 257*f*
  of flukes, 666, 666*f*
  of gymnosperms, 557, 557*f*
  haploid, 258, 258*f*
  of insects, 714, 714*f*
  of mosses, 549, 549*f*
  of protists, 498–499, 498*f,* 499*f*
  of sac fungi, 526, 526*f*
  of seedless vascular plants, 551, 551*f*
  of viruses, 478, 478*f,* 479*f*
  of zygote fungi, 525, 525*f*
ligaments, 846
light energy, 202–205, 203*f,* 204*f,* 207
lineages, 389
linear growth, 378, 378*f,* 379
linkage mapping, 362, 362*f*
linked genes, 275, 284
Linnaeus, Carl, 424–425, 425*f*
lions (*Panthera leo***),** 424*f,* 815, 851*f*
lipid bilayer, 176, 176*f,* 177*f*
lipids, 61, 448, 892. *See also* **fats**
liposuction, 875
liver, 485, 898, 898*f,* 976, 1007
liver cancer, 485
liverworts, 548, 548*f*
lividity, 1032
livor mortis, 1032
lizards
  characteristics of, 765
  color changes in, 765, 776–777
  ectothermic metabolism in, 759, 759*f*
  regeneration in, 227, 227*f*
  reproduction in, 761
  saltwater, 101*f*

lobe-finned fishes, 738, 738*f*
lobster-eye telescope, 35
lobsters, 709, 709*f*
lock-and-key enzyme action, 66, 67*f*
locomotion. *See also* **movement**
  in annelids, 688, 689*f*
  in cephalopods, 684
  in flatworms, 665
  jointed appendages and, 637
  in mammals, 790
  in mollusks, 680, 680*f,* 683
  muscles and, 624
  in protists, 502, 502*f,* 504
  in reptiles, 758
logistic growth, 105, 105*f*
long-day plants, 608, 608*f*
looped domains, 225, 225*f*
Lorenz, Konrad, 819
LSD, 956, 958*f*
luminol, 1019
lung cancer, 235, 881, 881*f*
lungfishes, 731, 738
lungs
  in amphibians, 641, 741
  in birds, 770, 770*f*
  capacity, 882–883
  excretion by, 902, 902*f*
  in humans, 876*f,* 877, 877*f*
  in mollusks, 681
  in reptiles, 760, 760*f*
lunula, 855
lupus, 927*f*
luteal phase, 999, 999*f*
luteinizing hormone (LH**),** 993, 998–999, 999*f*
lycophytes (club mosses**),** 550, 550*f,* 552
Lyell, Charles, 379
Lyme disease, 483*f,* 486, 707
lymph, 871, 871*f*
lymphatic system, 871, 871*f*
lymph nodes, 871, 871*f*
lysogenic cycle, 478, 478*f*
lysosomes, 158, 160
lytic cycle, 478, 478*f*

macroevolution, 388–389, 389*f*
macronucleus, 503*f*
macrophages, 912*f*–913*f,* 916–917, 917*f*
mad cow disease, 480, 480*f*
madreporite, 718, 718*f*
magnesium, 599*f,* 894
magnetic powder, 1022
malaria, 509, 509*f*
male reproductive system, 993–995, 993*f,* 994*f,* 995*f*
malignant tumors, 235
Malpighian tubules, 703
Malthus, Thomas, 379
mammals, 782–803. *See also* **hominids; primates**
  domestic, 796, 796*f*
  evolution of, 644, 644*f*

  key characteristics of, 785, 786, 790, 790*f,* 804–805
  marsupials, 788, 788*f,* 792, 792*f*
  monkeys, 798, 798*f*
  monotremes, 788, 791, 791*f*
  parental care in, 788, 788*f*
  placental, 788, 788*f,* 793, 793*f,* 794*f*–795*f*
  reproduction in, 787
  specialized teeth in, 787, 787*f*
mammary glands, 644, 785, 788, 791
mandibles, 709, 712, 712*f*
manner of death, 1033
mantle, in mollusks, 680, 692
Mantophasmatodea, 432*f*
mapping, genome, 362, 362*f*
marbling, in forensics, 1032
marijuana, 956, 958, 958*f*
marine ecosystems, 84, 84*f*
marine worms, 688, 688*f*
marsupials, 788, 788*f,* 792, 792*f*
mass, conservation of, 64
mass extinction
  definition of, 453
  during the Devonian period, 459
  at the end of the Ordovician period, 459
  at the end of the Permian period, 457
  geologic time scale and, 453, 453*f*
  K-T extinction, 459, 460, 460*f*
  in the Paleozoic era, 459
  in Pre-Cambrian times, 457
mate selection
  attracting mates, 820, 820*f*
  courtship behavior, 826, 826*f*
  evolution and, 406, 406*f*
  microevolution and, 388
matter, 51–54, 51*f,* 52*f,* 53*f,* 54*f,* 64
measles, 485*f*
measurement systems, 14, 14*f,* 20–21
mechanical digestion, 896, 897
mechanoreceptors, 952–953, 952*f*
medulla oblongata, 940*f,* 941
medusa forms, 658, 658*f,* 659*f*
meiosis, 250–254
  alleles in, 272*f,* 273
  diploid life cycle, 256–257, 256*f,* 257*f*
  genetic variation in, 253–254, 254*f*
  haploid life cycle, 258, 258*f*
  in humans, 996
  independent assortment in, 254, 254*f*
  mitosis compared with, 252, 252*f*
  mutations during, 321
  in plant life cycles, 546, 546*f*
  stages of, 250–251, 250*f*–251*f*
melanin, 854, 855
melanomas, 322, 322*f,* 856, 856*f*
melatonin, 981, 981*f*
membrane potentials, 946–948, 946*f,* 947*f*
membrane pumps, 182, 182*f,* 204*f,* 205
memory cells, 922
Mendel, Gregor Johann
  first pea plant experiments, 267–270, 267*f,* 268*f,* 269*f*
  heredity theory of, 272–275, 272*f,* 274*f,* 275*f*
  laws of heredity, 386
  life of, 267

Index

Mendel, Gregor Johann (*continued*)
ratios in results of, 270
second pea plant experiments, 275, 275*f*
meningitis, 483*f*, 960, 960*f*
meningococcal meningitis, 960, 960*f*
menopause, 1000
menstrual cycle, 999*f*, 1000
menstruation, 999*f*, 1000
meristems, 236, 587–589, 587*f*, 588*f*, 589*f*
merozoite, 509
mesoderm, 634, 635*f*, 663, 1003
mesoglea, 658, 659
mesophyll, 582, 582*f*
Mesozoic era, 453, 453*f*, 459
messenger RNA (mRNA), 305–307, 306*f*, 307*f*
metabolism, 19
chemical reactions in, 67
endocrine system control of, 980–981, 980*f*, 981*f*
photosynthesis and respiration, 198, 199*f*
metamorphosis, 714, 714*f*, 720–721, 747, 747*f*
metaphase
in meiosis, 250*f*–251*f*, 251
in mitosis, 230*f*, 231, 234, 234*f*
metastasis, 235
methanogens, 435
metric system, 14, 14*f*, 20–21
mice (*Mus musculus*), *hox* genes in, 333*f*
microarrays, 346, 346*f*, 358
microevolution, 388, 399
microfilaments, 156
micronucleus, 503*f*
microscopes, 15, 151, 1020, 1020*f*, 1054–1055
microspheres, 449
microtubules, 156, 229, 230, 230*f*
microvilli, 899, 899*f*
midbrain, 940*f*, 941
migration, 388, 405, 822
Miller, Stanley, 447
Miller-Urey experiment, 447, 447*f*
mineralized fossils, 451, 451*f*. See also **fossils**
minerals, 599*f*, 894, 894*f*. See also names of specific minerals
missense mutations, 320
mites, 623*f*, 707, 707*f*, 925*f*
mitochondria
ATP energy reactions in, 201, 201*f*
DNA in, 331, 335
in endosymbiotic theory, 331
origin of, 455–456, 456*f*
in sperm, 994, 994*f*
structure of, 161, 161*f*
mitosis
checkpoint, 234, 234*f*
in eukaryotic cell cycles, 228*f*, 229
meiosis compared with, 252, 252*f*
in plant life cycles, 546, 546*f*
stages of, 230–231, 230*f*–231*f*, 236
mobile genetic elements, 332
modern synthesis of evolutionary theory, 386. See also **evolutionary theory**
molars, 787, 787*f*, 897*f*

molds, 523, 925*f*
"molecular clocks," 431, 431*f*
molecular evidence, 430–431
molecular sequencing, 500
molecules, 52
Molina, Mario, 136
mollusks, 679–685
bivalves, 682*f*, 685, 685*f*
cephalopods, 682*f*, 684, 684*f*
characteristics of, 679, 679*f*
diversity of, 682, 682*f*
gastropods, 682*f*, 683, 683*f*
organ systems in, 680–681, 680*f*, 681*f*, 682*f*
origin of name, 679
reproduction in, 682, 682*f*
molting, 704, 708, 714, 714*f*
monarch butterflies, 354, 354*f*
monkeys, 798. See also **primates**
monocots. See also **angiosperms**
characteristics of, 559, 559*f*
cotyledons in, 585, 585*f*
roots in, 579, 579*f*
seed lab exercise, 590–591
vascular bundles in, 580, 580*f*
monohybrid crosses, 269, 276*f*, 277
monosaccharides, 60
monotremes, 788, 791, 791*f*
morphine, 958, 958*f*
morphological evidence, 430
mosquitos, 509, 509*f*, 712*f*, 713
mosses, 429*f*, 547–549, 547*f*, 548*f*, 549*f*
moths, 713
motor cortex, 954, 954*f*
motor neurons, 939, 942*f*
mouse-ear cress, genome of, 330*f*–331*f*
movement
of amphibians, 740, 740*f*
of animals, 624
of annelids, 688, 689*f*
of cephalopods, 684
of cnidarians, 659
coordination of, 941, 941*f*
of crustaceans, 709
of fishes, 730
by flagella, 162, 162*f*, 504
of flatworms, 665
of mammals, 790
of mollusks, 680, 680*f*, 683
muscles and, 849, 849*f*
nastic, in plants, 610, 610*f*
of plant spores, 545
of protists, 502, 502*f*, 504
of reptiles, 758–759, 759*f*
mRNA (messenger RNA), 305–307, 306*f*, 307*f*
mucous membranes, 915
mucus, 877, 880, 915
mules, 796
multicellular organisms
aging and, 333–334, 333*f*, 334*f*
animals as, 624
eukaryotes as, 166, 436
interdependence of cells in, 165–166, 166*f*
levels of organization in, 164–165, 164*f*
sexual reproduction in multicellular protists, 499, 499*f*
stromatolites, 455, 455*f*

multiple alleles, 283, 283*f*
multiple sclerosis (MS), 927, 960, 960*f*
multipotent cells, 353
mumps, 485*f*
Münch, Ernst, 602, 602*f*
muscle cells, 163
muscle cramps, 852
muscle fatigue, 849, 857–858
muscle fibers, 850, 852
muscles, 848–852
contraction of, 850, 851*f*
exercise and, 852, 852*f*
in flatworms, 663
injuries in, 852
in mollusks, 685, 685*f*
movement and, 849, 849*f*
myostatin and, 847, 847*f*
respiration in, 849
tissue structure, 850
types of, 840, 840*f*, 848, 848*f*, 852
mushrooms, 434*f*, 522, 522*f*, 529–530, 530*f*. See also **fungi**
Mus musculus (house mouse), *hox* genes in, 333*f*
mussels, 114, 115
mutants, 319. See also **mutations**
mutations, 319–324
cancer from, 322*f*, 323
chromosomal, 321
effects of, 319–321, 320*f*
in frogs, 316*f*–317*f*
in fruit flies, 271, 271*f*
genetic disorders from, 323, 323*f*
genetic variation from, 403, 405
inheritance of, 322
microevolution and, 388
modeling, 321
as "molecular clock," 431, 431*f*
and single nucleotide polymorphisms (SNPs), 356
types of, 320–321, 320*f*, 321*f*
mutualism, 100*f*–101*f*, 111, 111*f*
mycelium, 522, 522*f*
Mycobacterium tuberculosis, 483, 483*f*, 880
mycorrhizae, 458, 528, 528*f*, 530, 544
myelin sheaths, 945, 945*f*, 960, 960*f*
myofibrils, 850, 851*f*
myosin, 850, 851*f*
myostatin, 847, 847*f*
MyPyramid, 895, 895*f*

nacre, 685
NAD+ (nicotinamide adenine dinucleotide), 201, 201*f*
NADH, 210–211, 210*f*, 211*f*, 212–213, 212*f*
NADPH, 204*f*, 205–206, 205*f*
nails, 855
nanometers, 480
nanotechnology, 34, 34*f*
narcotics, 956, 958, 958*f*
nastic movements, 610, 610*f*
National Automotive Paint database, 1024

natural gas, 126
natural killer cells, 916, 917*f*
natural selection. *See also* **evolutionary theory**
animal behavior and, 815, 815*f*
chance variations and, 387
genetic change from, 405
limitations of, 408
modeling exercise, 387, 390–391
patterns of, 409, 409*f*
role in evolution, 407
steps in, 380–381, 380*f*, 381*f*
"nature *vs.* nurture," 814
nauplius, 708
nautiluses, 684, 684*f*
Neanderthals, 802
necrotizing fasciitis, 483
negative feedback, 976, 976*f*
negative tropisms, 606
Neisseria meningitides, 483*f*, 960
nematocysts, 658*f*, 659, 683
nematodes, genome of, 330*f*-331*f*
nephridia, 680, 680*f*, 686
nephrons, 903, 903*f*
nerve cells, 152, 152*f*, 228, 629
nerve nets, 629, 629*f*, 659
nerves, 944–945, 944*f*, 945*f*
"nervousness," 942
nervous system. *See also* **nervous system, human**
in annelids, 687
behavior and, 814
in echinoderms, 718, 718*f*
in flatworms, 664*f*
in insects, 711*f*
simple *vs.* complex, 629, 629*f*
nervous system, human, 936–961
brain, 936*f*-937*f*, 940–941, 940*f*, 941*f*
disorders of, 960–961, 960*f*
electrical signals in, 944, 944*f*
endocrine control of, 978–979, 978*f*, 979*f*
nerve impulse generation, 946–947, 946*f*, 947*f*
neuron communication, 948–949, 948*f*, 949*f*
psychoactive drugs and, 956–958, 958*f*
reaction times, 962–963
sensory systems, 950–954, 951*f*, 952*f*, 953*f*
spinal cord, 941, 941*f*
nervous tissue, 840, 840*f*
nests, bird, 771
neurons
in the brain, 940–941
communication between, 948–949, 948*f*, 949*f*
function of, 939
presynaptic, 948
postsynaptic, 948–949, 949*f*, 959, 959*f*
sensory receptors, 950–953, 950*f*, 951*f*, 952*f*, 953*f*
structure of, 944*f*, 945, 945*f*
neuropeptides, 977
neurosecretory cells, 978
neurotransmitters, 948–949, 949*f*, 959, 959*f*
neutrons, 51
neutrophils, 916, 917*f*

Neversink Pit (Alabama), 122*f*-123*f*
New Guinea, "lost world" in, 38, 38*f*
niches, 112–113, 112*f*, 413
nicotinamide adenine dinucleotide (NAD+), 201, 201*f*
nicotine, 956–957
nictitating membranes, 740, 748
ninhydrin, 1022
nitric acid, 128
nitrification, 92, 92*f*
nitrogen, 92, 92*f*, 599*f*
nitrogen cycle, 92, 92*f*
nitrogen fixation, 92, 92*f*
nitrogenous bases
base-pairing rules, 296*f*, 297–298, 298*f*, 306
complementary, 298, 298*f*
in DNA replication, 300–301, 301*f*, 306
numbers of, 331
in RNA, 305, 305*f*
structure of, 290*f*-291*f*, 296, 296*f*
noctural animals, 822, 822*f*
nodes, in stems, 580, 580*f*
nodes of Ranvier, 945, 945*f*
non-coding sequences, 328, 331, 345
nondisjunction, 324
nonrandom mating, 406
nonrenewable resources, 126, 126*f*
nonsense mutations, 321
non-sulfur bacteria, 474
nonvascular plants, 544, 547–549, 547*f*, 548*f*, 549*f*
norepinephrine (noradrenaline), 981
normal distribution, 400, 400*f*
northern blot process, 358
notochords, 638, 638*f*, 734, 734*f*
nuclear envelope, 157, 157*f*
nuclear pores, 157, 157*f*
nuclear waste dumps, 349, 349*f*
nucleic acids, 63, 294. *See also* **DNA; RNA**
nucleoid, 472
nucleolus, 157, 157*f*
nucleosomes, 224–225, 225*f*
nucleotides, 63, 63*f*, 296, 296*f*
nucleus, atomic, 51, 51*f*
nucleus, cell, 155, 155*f*, 157, 157*f*, 503*f*
nudibranchs, 683, 683*f*
nutrients, definition of, 891
nutrition, 891–895
carbohydrates, 892, 892*f*, 896
energy from food, 891–892
fats, 892, 892*f*
healthy eating habits, 895, 895*f*
minerals, 894, 894*f*
proteins, 892, 892*f*
vitamins, 893, 893*f*
"Nutrition Facts" labels, 891, 894
nymphs, insect, 714, 714*f*

obesity, 875, 875*f*, 895
observations, 10
occipital lobe, 954, 954*f*

octopuses, 620*f*-621*f*, 681, 684, 684*f*
oil, 61, 126, 458
oil glands, 804
oil spills, 349, 349*f*
olfactory receptors, 953
oligochaetes, 688–689, 689*f*
omnivores, 87
On the Origin of Species (Darwin), 381
Oparin, Aleksandr I., 447
open circulatory system, 630, 630*f*, 681
operant conditioning, 818
operator sites, 326, 326*f*
opercula (singular, *operculum*), 736
operons, 326, 326*f*
opium, 958, 958*f*
opossums, 788, 788*f*, 792, 822
opportunistic infections, 928
optic nerve, 951, 951*f*
optimal foraging, 821
orders, 425*f*, 426, 426*f*
Ordovician period, 453*f*, 459
organelles, 155, 155*f*, 331
organic compounds, 59–63, 447, 447*f*, 602, 602*f*
organs, 164, 164*f*, 632, 841. *See also under specific organs*
organ systems, 164*f*, 165, 841, 841*f*. *See also under specific systems*
organ transplants, 839, 845, 905, 928
origin, in muscle attachment, 849
osculum, 655, 655*f*
osmosis
cell transport by, 180–181, 180*f*, 181*f*
root water from, 600, 600*f*
water balance in fishes, 732
ossicles, 717
osteoblasts, 845
osteocytes, 844, 844*f*
osteoporosis, 845
ostia (singular, *ostium*), 655
outgroups, 429
ovarian cycle, 998–999, 998*f*, 999*f*
ovaries
egg production in, 631
in flowers, 560, 560*f*
hormone production in, 972*f*
in humans, 996, 996*f*, 997*f*, 998–999, 998*f*
overproduction, 380, 381*f*
overweight, 895. *See also* **obesity**
oviparous organisms, 761, 788
ovoviviparous organisms, 761
ovulation, 998–999, 998*f*, 999*f*
ovules, 554, 557, 557*f*, 560–561, 561*f*
ovum (plural, *ova*), 256, 997, 998, 998*f*
owls, 767*f*, 772, 786, 822, 822*f*
oxygen
in aerobic respiration, 211, 211*f*
in the blood, 877–879, 878*f*
in carbon and oxygen cycles, 91, 91*f*
combustion and, 91
from cyanobacteria, 455
diffusion through the cell membrane, 179, 179*f*
formation of atmospheric, 455
mass extinction from rise of, 457
oxygen cycle, 91

oxygen (*continued*)
from protists, 510
oxytocin, 979*f*
oysters, 685
ozone layer, 128, 136, 447, 455

pain receptors, 953, 958
paint, 1024
paint brush, Texas, 434*f*
paired fins, 737*f*, 738
Paleozoic era, 453, 453*f*, 458–459, 458*f*
palisade layer, 582, 582*f*
pancreas, 898, 898*f*, 972*f*, 974, 974*f*, 980, 983
Panthera pardus (leopard), 424*f*, 425*f*
Panthera spp. (leopards and lions), classification of, 424*f*, 425*f*
paramecium, 425*f*, 434*f*, 503, 503*f*
Paranthropus, 800, 801*f*
parapodia, 688
parasites
flatworms, 663, 665–666, 665*f*
flukes, 666, 666*f*
fungi, 522, 524
identifying, 670, 670*f*
lampreys, 734, 734*f*
leeches, 690
preventing infections, 670
protists, 502
roundworms, 668–669, 668*f*, 669*f*
tapeworms, 663, 665, 665*f*
trichomoniasis from, 1006
parasitism, 110, 113, 814, 814*f*
parasympathetic division, 942
parathyroid glands, 972*f*, 980, 980*f*
parathyroid hormone (PTH), 980
parental care
in birds, 771, 771*f*
in insects, 715
in mammals, 788, 788*f*, 792
as reproductive strategy, 827, 827*f*
in reptiles, 761, 761*f*, 763
parental (P) generation, 269, 269*f*
parent isotopes, 452
parietal lobe, 954, 954*f*
parsimony, principle of, 431
parthenogenesis, 247, 255, 255*f*
passive transport, 178–180, 179*f*
patents, 354
pathogens
antigen shifting in, 923
definition of, 915
immune response to, 919–920, 921*f*
immunity to, 922
Koch's postulates and, 482, 482*f*
pathology, 1027, 1027*f*
Pavlov, Ivan, 818, 818*f*
PCR (polymerase chain reaction), 357, 357*f*, 1023
pea plants, 267–270, 267*f*, 268, 268*f*, 269*f*
pearls, 685
pedigrees, 280–281, 281*f*
pedipalps, 706–707, 710*f*

pelvic inflammatory disease (PID), 1007
penguins, 106, 766, 771, 774, 774*f*
penicillin, 529
penis, 994*f*, 995
pepsin, 897
peptic ulcers, 901, 901*f*
peptide bonds, 62, 62*f*, 308–309, 308*f*–309*f*
peptidoglycan, 472, 473*f*
percentage calculations, 237
percolation, 90, 90*f*
periodic table of the elements, 1064–1065*f*
periosteum, 844, 844*f*
peripheral nervous system (PNS), 939, 939*f*, 941–942, 941*f*, 942*f*
peristalsis, 897, 897*f*, 899, 900
permeability, 176, 176*f*, 186
Permian extinction, 459
petals, 560, 560*f*
petioles, 582, 582*f*
P generation, 269
pH, 56–57, 56*f*, 66, 68, 878–879
phages, 295*f*, 476*f*, 477
pharmaceuticals, 133, 1036
pharmacogenomics, 347
pharyngeal pouches, 638, 638*f*
pharynx, 876, 876*f*
phenotypes, 274, 274*f*, 400, 400*f*, 408
pheromones, 715, 824, 824*f*
phloem
in leaves, 582, 582*f*
primary *vs.* secondary, 589, 589*f*
in stems, 580–581, 581*f*
structure of, 576, 576*f*, 580*f*
translocation in, 602, 602*f*
phosphates
in ATP energy transfer, 182, 182*f*, 200–201
in DNA, 290*f*–291*f*, 296, 296*f*
in phosphorus cycle, 93
phospholipids, 61, 176, 176*f*
phosphorus cycle, 93, 599*f*. See also phosphates
photoautotrophic bacteria, 474
photographs, 1014*f*, 1031
photoperiodism, 608, 608*f*
photoreceptors, 951, 951*f*
photosynthesis, 202–207
in bacteria, 474
in carbon and oxygen cycles, 91, 91*f*
chemical equation for, 199*f*
in chloroplasts, 543
electron transport chains in, 204–205, 204*f*
factors affecting, 202
leaf structure and, 582, 582*f*
light energy and, 202–203, 202*f*–203*f*
origin of atmospheric oxygen from, 455
in protists, 504–505, 504*f*, 505*f*
respiration and, 198, 199*f*
in stems, 583
stomata and, 575
sugar production in, 206–207, 206*f*
phototropisms, 606*f*, 607, 607*f*
phyla (singular, *phylum*), 425*f*, 426, 426*f*, 625
phylogenetics, 411, 428, 428*f*
phylogenetic species concept, 411
phylogenetic trees, 422, 428–429, 428*f*, 429*f*, 625, 625*f*, 705*f*, 793*f*

phylogeny, 428, 428*f*
physical activity, 891, 895. *See also* **exercise**
physical mapping, 362, 362*f*
phytoplankton, 88*f*, 504, 504*f*
PID (pelvic inflammatory disease), 1007
pigments, 202*f*–203*f*, 203
pili, 162, 162*f*, 473*f*, 475*f*
pimples, 856
pineal gland, 980
pinworms, 668, 668*f*
pioneer species, 81, 81*f*
pistils, 560, 560*f*
pitcher plants, 584, 584*f*
pith, 580–581, 580*f*
pituitary gland
anterior, 978, 978*f*, 979
growth and development control by, 979, 982
hormones from, 979, 979*f*, 982, 993, 998
location of, 972*f*, 978*f*
nervous system control by, 978, 978*f*
posterior, 978, 978*f*, 979
placenta, 788, 1002, 1002*f*, 1004*f*
placental mammals, 788, 788*f*, 793, 793*f*, 794*f*–795*f*
placoderms, 640
plague, 487
planarians (*Dugesia*), 664, 664*f*
plankton, 460, 505, 510
Plantae (kingdom), 434*f*, 436, 436*f*–437*f*
plant cells, 160, 160*f*, 163*f*, 232, 232*f*
plants
albinism in, 285
alternation of generations, 258, 499, 546
basic life cycle of, 546, 546*f*
cells in, 160, 160*f*, 163*f*, 232, 232*f*
cladogram of, 429*f*
cuticles in, 544–545
dermal tissue in, 573–575, 573*f*, 574*f*, 575*f*, 578*f*
diversity in, 565, 565*f*
embryos in, 555, 561*f*, 585–586, 585*f*, 586*f*
establishment on land, 544–545, 544*f*–545*f*
evolution from green algae, 505
extreme, 584, 584*f*
germination of, 586–587, 586*f*, 605, 609
ground tissue in, 573, 573*f*, 578, 578*f*
hormones in, 603–606, 603*f*, 604*f*, 605*f*
hydroponic, 612–613
leaves in, 582–583, 582*f*, 583*f*
meristems, 587, 587*f*
microscope exercise on, 167
as multicellular organisms, 166
nastic movements in, 610, 610*f*
nutrient requirements by, 599, 599*f*
overview of, 434*f*, 436, 543
in the Paleozoic era, 458, 458*f*
primary and secondary growth in, 587–589, 588*f*, 589*f*
roots, 574, 578*f*, 579, 579*f*
seasonal responses of, 608–609, 608*f*, 609*f*
signaling in, 184
in space, 611, 611*f*
stems, 580–581, 580*f*, 581*f*

translocation of organic compounds, 602, 602*f*

transpiration in, 600–601, 600*f*, 601*f*

tropisms in, 606–607, 606*f*, 607*f*

vascular tissue in, 573, 573*f*, 576, 576*f*, 578*f*

wilting of, 181*f*

planulae (singular, *planula*), 659

plaque, 872, 872*f*

plasma, blood

carbon dioxide transport in, 878, 878*f*

cells in, 920, 921*f*

composition of, 869, 869*f*

plasmids, 331–332, 331*f*, 360, 360*f*, 484

plasmodium, 506

Plasmodium, 509, 509*f*

plastron, 762

platelets, blood, 869, 869*f*

platypus, 788, 791, 791*f*

pluripotent cells, 353

Pneumocystis carinii, 880

pneumonia, 880

point mutations, 320

poisons

accumulation in the liver, 898

in bacteria, 483

in cnidarians, 659, 660

in fungi, 531

in scorpions, 707

in snakes, 765

in spiders, 707, 710*f*

polar biomes, 82–83, 82*f*, 83*f*

polar body, 257, 257*f*

polarity, 54, 54*f*, 176, 176*f*

polio, 485, 923

pollen

allergies to, 924*f*

in angiosperms, 561*f*

dispersal of, 545

in forensics, 1024, 1024*f*

in gymnosperms, 554, 554*f*

pollen grains, 245

pollen tubes, 554, 554*f*, 561, 561*f*

pollination, 554, 555*f*, 561–562, 561*f*, 562*f*

pollution

air, 127, 128, 128*f*

health effects of, 127

ozone layer damage from, 128, 136

water, 130, 130*f*

polychaetes, 688, 688*f*

polygenic characters, 282, 400, 400*f*

polymerase chain reaction (PCR), 357, 357*f*, 1023

polymerases

DNA, 301, 301*f*

RNA, 306, 306*f*, 327*f*, 329

polymorphisms, 356

polynomials, in classification, 424

polypeptides, from RNA translation, 308–309, 308*f*–309*f*

polyp forms, 658, 658*f*, 659*f*

polyploidy, 324, 324*f*, 413

polysaccharides, 60

pons, 940*f*, 941

population genetics

definition of, 399

divergence in, 412

forces of genetic change, 405

genetic drift, 388, 405–406, 415

genetic equilibrium, 404–405, 404*f*

genetic variation and change, 401–402, 402*f*

phenotypic variation, 400–401, 400*f*, 401*f*

population size and, 406, 406*f*

role of natural selection in, 407–409, 408*f*, 409*f*

sources of genetic variation, 403

population growth

evolution and, 378, 378*f*, 379

exponential, 104, 104*f*, 378, 378*f*, 379

of humans, 125

logistic, 105, 105*f*

populations, 103–108. *See also* **population growth**

definition of, 103

factors in size of, 106, 106*f*

genetic drift in, 388, 405, 415

human, 107–108, 107*f*, 108*f*, 125, 125*f*

lab exercise, 116–117

microevolution in, 388

migration and, 104

natural selection in, 380–381, 381*f*, 387, 390–391

separation of, 376, 387, 387*f*

portion sizes, 875

Portuguese man-of-war colonies (*Physalia*), 660

positive feedback, 976*f*, 977

positive tropisms, 606, 606*f*

postanal tails, 638*f*, 639

posterior pituitary, 979

postmortem toxicology, 1025

postsynaptic cells, 948–949, 949*f*, 959, 959*f*

potassium, 599*f*, 894, 894*f*

potatoes, 506, 580

Precambrian time, 453–457, 453*f*, 454*f*, 456*f*, 457*f*

precipitation, 90, 90*f*

predation, definition of, 109

predators

in communities, 79, 79*f*, 109

ecosystem stability and, 115

foraging behavior in, 821, 821*f*

impact on population sizes, 106

prefixes, in units, 14, 14*f*

pregnancy

cleavage and implantation in, 1001, 1001*f*

first trimester, 1002–1003, 1002*f*, 1003*f*

preparation for, 998–999, 998*f*, 999*f*

second trimester, 1004

third trimester, 1004, 1004*f*

premolars, 787, 787*f*

pressure-flow model, in plants, 602, 602*f*

presynaptic neurons, 948–949, 949*f*, 959*f*

prey, 79, 79*f*, 109

primary growth, in plants, 587–588, 588*f*, 589*f*

primary structure of proteins, 62, 329, 329*f*

primary tissues, 587, 589*f*

primates

apes, 798, 798*f*

characteristics of, 794*f*, 797, 797*f*

hominids, 799–802, 799*f*, 800*f*–801*f*, 802*f*

lemurs, 798

monkeys, 798

tarsiers, 797, 797*f*, 798

Primates (order), 426*f*, 797

primers, 357

prions, 480, 480*f*

probability, 278–279, 278*f*, 279*f*

probes, 357

problem solving, 817, 817*f*

producers, 86, 86*f*, 88–89, 89*f*

products, reaction, 64–65

progesterone, 982, 996, 999–1000, 999*f*

proglottids, 665, 665*f*

prokaryotes, 154, 433, 456, 471, 471*f*. *See also* **prokaryotic cells**

prokaryotic cells

DNA replication in, 302, 302*f*

gene regulation in, 326, 326*f*

origin of mitochondria and chloroplasts from, 456, 456*f*

plasmids in, 331, 331*f*

in Pre-Cambrian time, 454–455

preparation for cell division in, 226, 226*f*

structure of, 154, 154*f*, 162, 162*f*

prolactin, 979

promoters, 306, 306*f*, 326–327, 326*f*, 327*f*

prophage, 478, 478*f*

prophase, 230, 231*f*, 250*f*–251*f*, 251

prostaglandins, 977

prostate gland, 994*f*, 995

proteases, 68

protein activation, 917

protein fibers, in cells, 156, 156*f*, 230

proteins

active domains on, 329, 329*f*

amino acids in, 62, 62*f*

carrier, 179, 179*f*

in the cell cycle, 334

cell maintenance by, 223

in cell membranes, 176–177, 177*f*

in cell transport, 179, 179*f*, 180, 182, 182*f*

constructed from RNA translation, 304–305, 304*f*, 308–309, 308*f*–309*f*

Cro, 329

in the cytoskeleton, 156, 156*f*

detection of, 317, 336–337

dietary, 892

digestion of, 897

DNA helicases, 301, 301*f*

domains on, 329, 329*f*

in the endoplasmic reticulum, 158, 159*f*

folding and structure of, 62, 329, 329*f*

in gene expression, 329, 329*f*

genes, 293

histones, 302, 224, 225*f*

in immune response, 917

in mutations, 320–321, 320*f*, 321*f*

origin of first, 448–449, 449*f*

production in cells, 157, 158, 159*f*

regulatory, 329

roles in cells, 156, 158, 176, 179, 223, 329, 334, 917

separation by electrophoresis, 336–337

size of, 329

sorting, after translation, 328–329

structure of, 62, 329, 329*f*

proteins (*continued*)
  subunits, 329
  in vesicles, 158, 159*f*
protein sorting, 328-329
protein test strips, 317
proteomics, 351
Protista (kingdom), 434*f*, 437, 436*f*-437*f*. *See also* **protists**
protists, 494-511
  alternation of generations, 258, 499, 546
  animal-like, 502-503, 502*f*, 503*f*
  characteristics of, 434*f*, 437, 497
  classification of, 433, 434*f*, 436, 436*f*-437*f*, 500
  contractile vacuoles in, 160
  disease and, 507-509, 507*f*, 508*f*, 509*f*
  environment and, 510, 510*f*
  fungus-like, 506, 506*f*
  industrial uses of, 511
  light responses of, 512-513
  methods of obtaining nutrients in, 501, 501*f*
  multicellular, 166, 166*f*, 456-457
  plant-like, 504-505, 504*f*, 505*f*
  reproduction in, 498-499, 498*f*, 499*f*
protons, 51
protostomes, 635, 635*f*
provirus, 478, 478*f*
pseudocoelom, 636, 636*f*, 667
pseudocoelomates, 636, 636*f*
pseudopodia, 502, 502*f*
psoriasis, 856, 856*f*, 927*f*
psychoactive drugs, 956-959, 958*f*, 959*f*, 1025
pteropods, 683
pterosaurs, 641
PTH (parathyroid hormone), 980
pulmonary arteries, 866*f*
pulmonary veins, 743, 743*f*, 866*f*
pulse, 867, 968, 984-985
pumps, membrane, 182, 182*f*, 204*f*
punctuated equilibrium, 389, 389*f*
Punnett squares, 276-277, 276*f*
pupa, 714, 714*f*
pupils, 951, 951*f*
purines, 296*f*, 297
Purkinje cells, 944*f*
purple sulfur bacteria, 474
pygmy elephants, 803
pyridines, 296*f*, 297
pyruvate, 209, 209*f*, 210, 210*f*

qualitative experiments, 11
quantitative experiments, 11
Quaternary period, 453, 453*f*
quaternary structure of proteins, 62
quinine, 509

rabbits, in Australia, 103
radial symmetry, 633, 633*f*, 658, 718, 718*f*
radiation pattern of divergence, 410, 413
radioactive decay, 452, 452*f*
radioactive waste, 349, 349*f*
radioisotopes, 452, 452*f*
radiometric dating, 452, 452*f*
radula, 679*f*, 680, 680*f*
rain forests, 83, 83*f*
Rana **spp.** (frogs), evolution in, 413
randomness, 254, 273
range of movement, 702
Raptor Rehabilitation Center (Kentucky), 40, 40*f*
rats, 803
ravens, 817, 871*f*
ray-finned fishes, 738
rays, 733, 735, 735*f*
RBCs (red blood cells)
  blood typing and, 918
  photograph of, 862*f*-863*f*
  in sickle cell anemia, 319, 319*f*
  structure and function of, 869, 869*f*
reactants, 64-65
reaction times, 962-963
reading frames, 320-321
realized niche, 113, 113*f*
reasoning, 817, 817*f*
receptor proteins
  in cell membranes, 177, 177*f*, 185-186, 185*f*, 186*f*
  in nerve impulses, 949, 949*f*
receptors, 973, 973*f*
recessive alleles, 273, 281
recombinant DNA, 350, 350*f*, 360, 360*f*
recombination, 324
rectum, 900
recycling resources, 108, 108*f*, 135
red algae, 505, 505*f*
red blood cells (RBCs)
  blood typing and, 918
  photograph of, 862*f*-863*f*
  in sickle cell anemia, 319, 319*f*
  structure and function of, 869, 869*f*
red bone marrow, 844, 844*f*
red tide, 510, 510*f*
reflexes, 942-943, 942*f*, 953
regeneration, 227, 227*f*, 656
regulatory proteins, 329
relative dating, 451, 451*f*, 461-462
relative humidity, 601, 601*f*
remote data collection, 15
renal tubules, 903, 903*f*
renewable resources, 126, 126*f*
replication bubbles, 302*f*, 303
replication forks, 300-302, 300*f*, 301*f*, 302*f*
replication of DNA, 300-303, 300*f*, 301*f*, 302*f*, 307
repressors, 327, 327*f*
reproduction, 19, 244-258. *See also* **asexual reproduction; reproduction, human; sexual reproduction**
  in amphibians, 739, 744, 745, 747, 747*f*

  in angiosperms, 554-555, 554*f*, 555*f*
  in annelids, 687, 689*f*
  in birds, 771, 771*f*
  in bony fishes, 737*f*
  as characteristic of life, 19
  in diatoms, 504
  in fishes, 733, 733*f*
  in flatworms, 664, 664*f*
  in fungi, 522-523, 522*f*
  in gymnosperms, 557-558, 557*f*
  haploid life cycle, 258, 258*f*
  in insects, 711*f*
  in mammals, 787, 791, 792, 793
  mate selection, 388, 820, 820*f*, 826, 826*f*
  in mollusks, 682, 682*f*
  nonrandom mating, 405-406
  in nonvascular plants, 548-549, 549*f*
  in protists, 498-499, 498*f*, 499*f*, 503*f*
  reproductive strategies, 825-827, 825*f*, 826*f*, 827*f*
  in reptiles, 761, 761*f*, 763, 764*f*, 765
  in seedless vascular plants, 551, 551*f*
  in seed plants, 554-555, 554*f*, 555*f*, 561, 561*f*
  in sponges, 656, 656*f*
  vegetative, 564, 564*f*
  in viruses, 478, 478*f*, 479*f*
reproduction, human, 993-1004
  birth, 1004, 1004*f*
  cleavage and implantation in, 1001, 1001*f*
  female reproductive system, 996-1000, 996*f*, 997*f*, 998*f*, 999*f*
  fertilization, 982*f*, 995, 1001, 1001*f*
  first trimester, 1002-1003, 1002*f*, 1003*f*
  male reproductive system, 993-995, 993*f*, 994*f*, 995*f*
  second trimester, 1004
  third trimester, 1004, 1004*f*
reproductive isolation, 412-413, 412*f*, 413*f*
reproductive strategies, 825-827, 825*f*, 826*f*, 827*f*
reptiles, 757-765
  characteristics of, 757, 757*f*
  evolution of, 641, 641*f*
  in the Mesozoic era, 459
  movement and response in, 758-759, 758*f*, 759*f*
  respiration and circulation in, 760, 760*f*
resources
  competition for, 113-114, 113*f*, 114*f*
  recycling, 108, 108*f*, 135
  use of, 126, 126*f*, 135
respiration. *See also* **cell respiration; respiratory system**
  aerobic, 210-211, 210*f*, 211*f*, 213*f*, 849
  anaerobic, 209, 211-212, 211*f*, 212*f*
  in carbon and oxygen cycles, 91, 91*f*
  cutaneous, 741
respiratory system, 876-881
  in amphibians, 741
  anaerobic, 849
  in animals, 630, 630*f*
  in arthropods, 703, 703*f*, 710*f*
  in birds, 770, 770*f*
  breathing, 877, 877*f*
  diseases of, 880-881, 880*f*, 881*f*

in earthworms, 689*f*
in echinoderms, 718, 718*f*
in fishes, 731, 731*f*
in flatworms, 664
in humans, 876–881, 876*f*, 877*f*, 878*f*, 881*f*
in mammals, 786
in mollusks, 681
in reptiles, 760, 760*f*
response
behavior and, 813, 813*f*, 818, 818*f*
to environment, 19
resting potential, 946, 964*f*
restoration, environmental, 134, 134*f*
restriction enzymes, 355–356, 355*f*, 360, 360*f*
restriction fragment length polymorphisms (RFLPs), 356
restriction sites, 355–356
retina, 951, 951*f*
retroviruses, 332, 477, 477*f*
reuse of resources, 135
RFLPs (restriction fragment length polymorphisms), 356
rheumatoid arthritis, 846, 927*f*
Rh factor, 870
rhizoids, 522
rhizomes, 550
Rhizopus, 525
ribonucleic acid (RNA)
codons in, 307, 307*f*
DNA compared with, 305, 305*f*
in DNA transcription, 304–307, 306*f*
origin of, 449, 449*f*
processing after transcription, 328, 328*f*
ribose in, 63, 305, 305*f*
splicing of, 328, 328*f*
translation of, 304–305, 304*f*, 308–309, 308*f*–309*f*
types of, 305
in viroids, 480
ribose, 63, 305, 305*f*
ribosomal RNA (rRNA), 305, 331
ribosomes
formation of, 157
free *vs.* bound, 157
function of, 157, 158, 159*f*
location of, 154, 154*f*, 155*f*
protein synthesis in, 308–309, 308*f*–309*f*
RNA in, 305
ribozymes, 449
rigor mortis, 1032
ring canal, 718, 718*f*
rings, tree, 589, 589*f*
ringworm, 522, 531, 531*f*
RNA (ribonucleic acid)
codons in, 307, 307*f*
DNA compared with, 305, 305*f*
in DNA transcription, 304–307, 306*f*
origin of, 449, 449*f*
processing after transcription, 328, 328*f*
ribose in, 63, 305, 305*f*
splicing of, 328, 328*f*
translation of, 304–305, 304*f*, 308–309, 308*f*–309*f*
types of, 305
in viroids, 480

RNA polymerase, 306, 306*f*, 327*f*, 329
RNA viruses, 477, 477*f*
robots, 41, 41*f*
rods, in eyes, 951, 951*f*
roots
embryonic, 585, 585*f*
epidermal cells on, 574
osmosis of water in, 600, 600*f*
root caps, 579
root hairs, 574, 579
root tips, 579
structure of, 579, 579*f*
tissue functions in, 578*f*, 579
rough endoplasmic reticulum, 158, 159*f*
roundworms, 667–670, 667*f*, 668*f*, 669*f*
rRNA (ribosomal RNA), 305, 331

sac fungi, 526, 526*f*
SAD (seasonal affective disorder), 981
safety precautions, 16
salamanders
acid rain and, 140
characteristics of, 739, 739*f*, 744, 744*f*
gills in, 630, 630*f*
reproduction in, 744, 744*f*
respiration of, 741
Salem witch trials, 532, 532*f*
saliva, 897
Salmonella, 332
salts, 53–54, 53*f*, 54*f*, 732, 732*f*
saprobes, 522
sapwood, 581, 581*f*
sarcomeres, 850, 851*f*
Sarcosuchus imperator, 645, 645*f*
SARS (Sudden Acute Respiratory Syndrome), 486
satellite data, 15, 30*f*
satellite tagging, 39, 39*f*
savannas, 83
scales
on bony fishes, 737*f*
in gymnosperms, 557*f*, 558
on reptiles, 757, 757*f*
on sharks, 735
scanning electron microscope (SEM), 1020
schistosomiasis, 666
Schleiden, Matthias, 152
Schwann, Theodor, 152
SCID (severe combined immunodeficiency), 928
science
ethics and, 8 (*See also* **ethical issues**)
human population size and, 107
reasons for studying, 9
research in, 1050–1051
scientific investigations, 10–13, 13*f*
scientific thought, 7
universal laws in, 8
scientific claims, 9
scientific names, 424, 424*f*
scientific nomenclature, 424, 424*f*
scientific theories, 13, 375

SCNT (somatic–cell nuclear transfer), 352–353
scorpions, 706–707, 706*f*
scrotum, 993
scrubbers, 136
scyphozoans, 660
sea anemones, 652*f*–653*f*, 661, 661*f*
sea cucumbers, 719, 719*f*
sea lilies, 719
sea otters, 115, 115*f*
sea slugs, 681*f*, 683
seasonal affective disorder (SAD), 981
seasonal behaviors, 822
seasonal responses, 608–609, 608*f*, 609*f*
sea stars
anatomy of, 718*f*
asexual reproduction in, 247, 631, 631*f*
below breathing holes in ice, 698*f*–699*f*
characteristics of, 717–718, 717*f*
as deuterostomes, 635, 635*f*
regeneration in, 227, 227*f*
sea urchins, 719, 719*f*
seaweed, chloroplasts in, 160, 160*f*. See also **algae; kelp**
sebum, 854
secondary growth, 587, 589, 589*f*
secondary structure of proteins, 62
secondary tissues, 587, 589*f*
second gap phase (G2), 228*f*, 229
second messengers, 186, 186*f*, 974, 974*f*
securing perimeters, 1030
seed coats, 555
seedless plants, 547–552
nonvascular, 547–549, 547*f*, 548*f*, 549*f*
vascular, 550–552, 550*f*, 551*f*, 552*f*
seed plants, 553–564
angiosperms, 559–564, 559*f*, 560*f*, 561*f*, 562*f*, 564*f*
evolution of, 429, 429*f*
gymnosperms, 553–558, 554*f*, 556*f*, 557*f*
reproduction in, 554–555, 554*f*, 555*f*
types of, 429, 429*f*, 553
seeds
cotyledons in, 559, 585, 585*f*
dispersal of, 555, 555*f*
effects of acid rain on, 140–141
fertilization of, 554, 554*f*, 560, 561*f*
germination of, 586–587, 586*f*, 605, 609
hormones in, 603, 603*f*, 605
segmented bodies
in annelids, 686–687, 686*f*
in arthropods, 701, 701*f*, 715
benefits of, 637, 637*f*
segregation, law of, 273, 279
selenium, dietary, 894
self-fertilization, 562
self-pollination, 268, 269*f*
self-recognition, in sponges, 656
SEM (scanning electron microscope), 1020
semen, 995, 995*f*
semicircular canals, 952, 952*f*
seminal receptacle, 711*f*
seminal vesicles, 995
seminiferous tubules, 993, 993*f*
sensory neurons, 939, 942*f*
sensory receptors, 950–953, 951*f*, 952*f*, 953*f*

Index

sensory systems, 950–954. *See also* **ears; eyes**
in amphibians, 740, 740*f*
chemoreceptors, 953, 953*f*
for echolocation, 790, 790*f*
in fishes, 730, 730*f*
information processing, 954, 954*f*
mechanoreceptors, 952, 952*f*
perception of stimuli, 950, 950*f*
photoreceptors, 951, 951*f*
in reptiles, 758–759, 759*f*
somatosensation, 953
sepals, 560, 560*f*
septa
in annelids, 687
in fungi, 522, 522*f*
septum, heart, 742
sequence assembly, 363
sessile organisms, 708–709, 708*f*
setae, 686, 686*f*
severe combined immunodeficiency
(SCID), 928
sex chromosomes, 249
sex determination, 249, 335
sex-linked genes, 280
sexually transmitted infections (STIs), 508,
1005–1007, 1005*f*, 1006*f*, 1007*f*. *See also*
names of specific infections
sexual reproduction
advantages of, 248, 253
in angiosperms, 561–562, 561*f*, 562*f*
chromosome number and, 248–249, 249*f*
in cnidarians, 659, 659*f*
diploid life cycle, 256–257, 256*f*, 257*f*
evolution and, 406
in fishes, 733, 733*f*
in flatworms, 664, 664*f*
in fungi, 522–523, 525–527, 525*f*, 526*f*, 527*f*
meiosis in, 250–254, 250*f*–251*f*, 252*f*, 254*f*
overview of, 248, 248*f*, 631
in protists, 499, 499*f*
in sponges, 656, 656*f*
sexual selection
attraction, 820, 820*f*
courtship behavior, 826, 826*f*
evolution and, 406, 406*f*
microevolution and, 388
shared characters, 429
sharks, 730, 733, 735
shark skin, 27
shells, 679, 679*f*, 685, 685*f*
shingles, 485, 485*f*
shin splints, 852
shoots, 585–587, 586*f*, 604, 604*f*
short-day plants, 608, 608*f*
shotgun sequencing method, 363
SI (International System of Units), 14, 14*f*,
20–21, 1058–1059
sickle cell anemia, 319, 319*f*, 323*f*
sieve-tube members, 576, 576*f*, 602, 602*f*
sight, 823, 823*f*. *See also* **eyes**
signal molecules, 184–186, 185*f*, 186*f*
silent mutations, 320
Silent Spring (Carson), 137
simple carbohydrates, 60, 892
simple diffusion, 179, 179*f*

single-loop circulation, 731
single nucleotide polymorphisms (SNPs),
356
sinks, in plants, 602
sinoatrial (SA) node, 867, 867*f*
siphons, 684
sister chromatids, 230–231, 230*f*-231*f*
skates, 733, 735
skeletal muscle, 840, 840*f*, 848, 848*f*
skeletons. *See also* **bones**
in amphibians, 740, 745, 745*f*, 746*f*
appendicular, 843, 843*f*
axial, 843, 843*f*
in birds, 768, 768*f*
cytoskeletons, 156, 156*f*
endoskeletons, 627, 717, 730, 758
in fishes, 730
forensic anthropology and, 1028, 1028*f*
in humans, 843–846, 843*f*, 844*f*, 846*f*
hydrostatic, 627, 627*f*
in invertebrates, 627, 627*f*
in sponges, 657
skepticism, 7
skin
in amphibians, 741
disorders of, 856, 856*f*
in echinoderms, 717
in humans, 853–854, 854*f*
immune function of, 854, 915
in reptiles, 757, 757*f*, 763
respiration through, 741
sense of touch, 953
skin cells, 152*f*
in temperature regulation, 854
skin cancer, 856, 856*f*
Skinner, B. F., 818
SLE (systemic lupus erythematosus), 927*f*
sleep disorders, 981
slime molds
cell grouping in, 165
examples of, 500*f*, 506*f*
genome of, 330*f*-331*f*
nutrient absorption by, 501*f*
reproduction by, 506
research uses of, 511
slow-twitch muscle fibers, 852
small intestine, 899, 899*f*
smallpox, 31, 487
smears, in electrophoresis, 356
smelling, 759, 772, 953
smoking
cardiovascular disease from, 874
chronic bronchitis from, 880
emphysema from, 881, 881*f*
lung cancer from, 235, 881, 881*f*
nicotine in, 956–957
during pregnancy, 1002
smooth endoplasmic reticulum, 158
smooth muscle, 840, 840*f*, 848, 848*f*
smut, corn, 531, 531*f*
snails
brown-lipped or grovesnails, 676*f*-677*f*
characteristics of, 683, 683*f*
courtship behavior in, 826, 826*f*
white-lipped or garden snails, 396*f*-397*f*

snakes, 255, 759, 761, 764*f*, 765. *See also*
names of specific snakes
SNPs (single nucleotide polymorphisms),
356
social behavior, 825, 825*f*
sodium, 53, 53*f*, 54*f*, 179, 179*f*, 894, 894*f*
sodium chloride, 53–54, 53*f*, 54*f*
sodium hydroxide, 56
sodium-potassium pump, 182, 182*f*,
946–947, 946*f*, 947*f*
soil, 131, 1024
solar panels, 136, 136*f*
solar-powered cars, 139, 139*f*
solubility, 54, 54*f*, 974
solutions, 56
somatic-cell nuclear transfer (SCNT),
352–353
somatic cells, 248, 322–323, 322*f*, 403
somatic nervous system, 942, 942*f*
somatosensation, 953–954
somites, 637
sonography, 1004, 1004*f*, 1009
sori (singular, *sorus*), 552
sorting signals, 329
sources, in plants, 602
Southern blot process, 358, 358*f*
space, plants in, 611, 611*f*
spawning, 733, 733*f*
speciation, 399, 412
species
biological species concept, 411
chromosome number in, 248–249, 249*f*
in classification system, 425*f*, 426, 426*f*
definition of, 19, 387, 411
discovering new, 432, 432*f*
extinction of, 414, 414*f*
formation of new, 412–413, 412*f*, 413*f*
invasive, 133, 133*f*
natural selection in, 380–381, 381*f*
pioneer, 81, 81*f*
spectrometers, 1020
sperm
definition of, 256
delivery of, 995
fertilization by, 982*f*, 1001
path through the body, 994, 994*f*
production of, 993, 993*f*
semen and, 995, 995*f*
structure of, 994, 994*f*
sperm packets, 704
spicules, 655*f*, 657
spiders. *See also names of specific spiders*
anatomy of, 710*f*
characteristics of, 706–707, 706*f*
effect of caffeine on, 187, 187*f*
reproduction in, 244*f*-245*f*
web-building behavior in, 187, 187*f*, 816,
816*f*
spinal cord, 941, 941*f*, 961
spinal nerves, 941, 941*f*
spinal reflex, 942–943, 942*f*
spindles, 230, 230*f*-231*f*, 250*f*-251*f*, 251
spines, 583, 583*f*, 764*f*
spinnerets, 707, 710*f*
spiny fishes, 640. *See also* **fishes**
spiracles, 703, 703*f*

Index

spirillum, 471, 471*f*
spirometers, 882
spleen, 871, 871*f*
sponges, 655–657
  asymmetrical body plan in, 633, 633*f*, 655, 655*f*
  classification of, 425*f*, 433, 433*f*, 657
  feeding by, 656
  lack of movement in, 624
  reproduction of, 656, 656*f*
  skeletons, 657
  types of, 657, 657*f*
spongin, 657
spongy bone, 844, 844*f*
spongy layer, 582*f*, 583
sporangium, 525, 525*f*, 548–549, 549*f*
spores
  in amoebas, 165
  in bacteria, 475, 475*f*
  in mosses, 549, 549*f*
  in plants, 545, 548*f*
  in seedless vascular plants, 551–552, 551*f*
  in seed plants, 557, 557*f*, 561*f*
sporophyte generation, 499
sporophytes
  diploid life cycle in, 258, 258*f*
  in nonvascular plants, 548–549, 548*f*, 549*f*
  in plant life cycles, 546, 546*f*
  in seedless vascular plants, 550–551, 551*f*
  in seed plants, 554–555, 557, 557*f*, 561*f*
sporozoans, 502
sporozoite, 509
sprains, 846
sprouting, 585–586, 585*f*, 586*f*
squids, 684, 684*f*
stabilizing selection, 409, 409*f*
stalking predators, 821
stamens, 560, 560*f*
Staphylococcus aureus, 332*f*, 483*f*
Staphylothermus marinus, 434*f*
starch, dietary, 60, 892
starfish (sea stars)
  anatomy of, 718*f*
  asexual reproduction in, 247, 631, 631*f*
  basket stars, 719
  characteristics of, 717–718, 717*f*
  as deuterostomes, 635, 635*f*
  regeneration in, 227, 227*f*
stem cells, 37, 353, 353*f*, 839, 839*f*
stems, 578*f*, 580–581, 580*f*, 581*f*
sterile technique, 15, 42
sterility, from STIs, 1005
steroid hormones, 61, 975, 975*f*
sticky ends, 355, 355*f*, 360*f*
stimulants, 956, 958*f*
stimulus, 813, 813*f*, 818, 818*f*, 947
stipes, 505
STIs (sexually transmitted infections), 508, 1005–1007, 1005*f*, 1006*f*, 1007*f*. *See also names of specific STIs*
stolons, 564, 564*f*
stomach, 789*f*, 896*f*, 897
stomata (singular, *stoma*), 575, 575*f*, 582*f*, 583, 601, 601*f*
stop codons, 308–309, 308*f*–309*f*
strata, sediment, 451, 451*f*, 461

Streptococcus pneumoniae, 434*f*
stress, 968*f*–969*f*, 981
stress fractures, 845
strokes, 873, 873*f*, 874
stromatolites, 455, 455*f*
subcutaneous tissue, 853, 854*f*
submarine engineering, 34
subspecies, 412
substrates, enzyme, 66, 67*f*
subunits, of proteins, 329
succession, 81, 81*f*
suckers, 665, 665*f*, 690, 690*f*
sucrose, 60, 892
sugars. *See also* **glucose;** *names of specific sugars*
  absorption of, 899, 899*f*
  in cell membrane, 177
  chemical structure of, 60, 60*f*
  diabetes and, 983, 983*f*
  in DNA, 290*f*–291*f*, 296, 296*f*
  in foods, 60, 60*f*, 892
  homeostasis of, in blood, 898, 980
  production of, 206–207, 206*f*
  translocation within plants, 602, 602*f*
sulfuric acid, 128
sunburn, 334, 334*f*
SuperCroc, 645, 645*f*
superposition, law of, 451, 451*f*
surface area–to-volume ratio, 152–153, 188–189, 223
survival strategies, 821–822, 821*f*, 822*f*
sweat, 854, 902, 915
sweat glands, 804, 854*f*
swim bladders, 34, 730, 736
swimmerets, 709
swimming, 730, 774, 774*f*
symbionts, 505
symbiosis, 111, 111*f*, 331
symmetry
  bilateral, 178, 633, 633*f*, 636, 636*f*, 718
  radial, 633, 633*f*, 658, 717–718, 718*f*
sympathetic division, 942
synapses, 948, 948*f*
synaptic cleft, 948–949, 949*f*
synthesis phase, 228*f*, 229
syphilis, 1005*f*, 1007, 1007*f*
systematics, 427, 427*f*, 430
systemic lupus erythematosus (SLE), 927*f*

tadpoles, 747, 747*f*, 748*f*
taiga, 83, 83*f*
tails, postanal, 638*f*, 639
talons, 769, 772–773
tanning, 854
tapeworms, 663, 665, 665*f*
taproot systems, 579, 579*f*
target cells, 184–185, 185*f*, 973, 973*f*
tarsiers, 797, 797*f*, 798
taste buds, 730, 730*f*, 953, 953*f*
taxon (plural, *taxa*), 423
taxonomy, definition of, 423. *See also* **classification**

Tay-Sachs disease, 323*f*
T cells
  in AIDS, 929, 929*f*
  cytotoxic, 919*f*, 920, 921*f*
  defects in, 928
  helper, 919–920, 919*f*, 920*f*, 921*f*
teeth
  human, 897, 897*f*
  in mammals, 787, 787*f*, 789*f*
  in sharks, 735
teguments, 666
teleosts, 738
telomeres, 334
telophase, 231, 231*f*, 250*f*–251*f*, 251
temperate biomes, 82–83, 83*f*
temperate viruses, 478
temperature. *See also* **body temperature**
  cholera and, 30, 30*f*
  enzymes and, 66
  microbial growth and, 42–43
  phenotype and, 284, 284*f*
  photosynthesis and, 207
  plant growth and, 609, 609*f*
temporal lobe, 954, 954*f*
tendinitis, 852
tendons, 849, 849*f*
tendrils, 583, 583*f*, 607, 607*f*
tennis elbow, 852
ten percent rule, 88, 88*f*
termites, 510, 715
terracing, 131
terrestrial biomes, 82–83, 82*f*, 83*f*
territorial behavior, 825, 828–829
Tertiary period, 453*f*, 644
tertiary structure of proteins, 62
testcrosses, 277
testes, 631, 972*f*, 993, 993*f*
testosterone, 982, 993
tetanus, 483*f*
tetrads, 252
Texas paint brush, 434*f*
thalamus, 940
THC, 956, 958*f*
theories, scientific, 6, 13, 375
therapsids, 459, 644
thermometers, 1057
thermoreceptors, 953
theropods, 427*f*, 642, 642*f*–643*f*
thigmotropisms, 607, 607*f*
thorax, 701, 701*f*, 711*f*
thrush, 531
thylakoid membrane, 204, 204*f*
thylakoids, 202–203, 202*f*–203*f*
thymine, 296*f*, 297, 298
thymus gland, 871, 871*f*, 919*f*, 972*f*
thyroid gland, 972*f*, 980, 980*f*
  disorders of, 980
  hormones of, 980
thyroid-stimulating hormone, 979*f*
tidal volume, 882
Tiktaalik roseae, 640*f*
time of death, 1032–1033, 1032*f*
tissue culture, 351, 351*f*
tissues
  differentiation in embryos, 634, 635*f*
  as level of organization, 164, 164*f*

tissues (*continued*)
    plant, 573–578
    symmetry and, 632
    types of, 840, 840*f*
tobacco
    cardiovascular disease and, 874
    chronic bronchitis from, 880
    emphysema from, 881, 881*f*
    lung cancer from, 235, 881, 881*f*
    nicotine in, 956–957
    during pregnancy, 1002
tolerance, drug, 959
tongue, 746*f*, 953*f*
tonsils, 871, 871*f*
tortoises, 761, 762, 762*f*
totipotent cells, 353
touch, 953
toxicology, 1026, 1026*f*, 1033
toxins. *See also* **poisons**
    accumulation in the liver, 898
    in bacteria, 483
    in cnidarians, 659, 660
    definition of, 1026
    in fungi, 531
    in scorpions, 707
    in snakes, 765
    in spiders, 707, 710*f*
toxoplasmosis, 508
trace evidence, 1024, 1024*f*
trachea, 703, 703*f*, 876, 876*f*
tracheids, 576
traits, 268, 280–282, 281*f*
transcription
    gene expression and, 304–305
    gene regulation of, 327, 327*f*
    replication compared to, 307
    RNA processing after, 328, 328*f*
    steps in, 306, 306*f*
transcription factors, 327, 327*f*
transduction, 475, 475*f*
transfer RNA (tRNA), 305, 308–309,
    308*f*–309*f*, 331
transformation, of genotype, 294, 475
transgenic organisms, 350, 350*f*
translation, 304–305, 304*f*, 308–309,
    308*f*–309*f*
translocation, 602, 602*f*
translocation mutations, 321, 321*f*
transpiration, 90, 90*f*, 600–601, 600*f*, 601*f*
transplants, organ, 839, 845, 905, 928
transport, cell, 178–183
    active, 182–183, 182*f*, 183*f*
    by osmosis, 180–181, 180*f*, 181*f*
    passive, 178–179, 179*f*
transport proteins, 177, 177*f*, 179, 179*f*
transposons, 332
trees, 581, 581*f*, 589, 589*f*, 608–609. *See also*
    names of specific trees
trichocyst, 503, 503*f*
Trichomonas vaginalis, 508, 508*f*
trichomoniasis, 508, 508*f*, 1005*f*, 1006
triploid phases, 561, 561*f*
tRNA (transfer RNA), 305, 308–309,
    308*f*–309*f*, 331
trochophores, 682, 682*f*, 686, 687
trophic levels, 86–87, 86*f*, 87*f*

tropic hormones, 979
tropical biomes, 82–83, 83*f*
tropisms, 606–607, 606*f*, 607*f*
true-breeding plants, 269, 269*f*
Trypanosoma cruzi, 508, 508*f*
T2 bacteriophages, 476*f*, 477
tuataras, 763, 763*f*
tube feet, 718, 718*f*
tuberculosis, 483–484, 483*f*, 880
tubers, 564, 564*f*
tubeworms, 688
tubulin, 156
tumors, 235, 235*f*, 323
tundra, 83
tunicates, 639, 639*f*
turbellarians, 664, 664*f*
turtles, 760–762, 760*f*, 762*f*
Tut, King, 1021, 1021*f*
twins, 1008, 1008*f*
tympanic membranes, 740, 740*f*
Tyrannosaurus rex, 642, 642*f*–643*f*

ulcers, 7, 483*f*, 897, 901, 901*f*
ultrasound imaging, 1004, 1004*f*, 1009
ultraviolet radiation (UV radiation), 234–
    235, 854, 856
Ulva, life cycle of, 499*f*
umbilical cord, 1002, 1004*f*
umbilical hernias, 901, 901*f*
umbo, 692, 693*f*
ungulates, 794*f*
unicellular organisms, 165
units, 14, 14*f*, 20–21
universal laws, 8
uracil, 305, 305*f*, 306
ureters, 904, 904*f*
urethra, 904, 904*f*
Urey, Harold, 447
urinary bladder, 904, 904*f*
urination, 904
urine, 732, 903–904, 903*f*, 904*f*
uropods, 709
uterus, 997, 997*f*, 1000, 1004*f*
UV radiation, 234–235, 854, 856

vaccines, 31, 346, 529, 922–923
vacuoles, 160, 160*f*, 181, 503*f*, 577*f*
vagina, 997, 997*f*
valence electrons, 52
varicella-zoster virus, 485, 485*f*
vascular bundles, 580, 580*f*, 582, 582*f*, 589*f*
vascular cambium, 589, 589*f*
vascular plants. *See also* **seed plants;**
    vascular tissue
    evolution of, 429, 429*f*, 544–545, 544*f*–545*f*
    seedless, 550–552, 550*f*, 551*f*, 552*f*
    structure of, 577*f*
vascular tissue
    in leaves, 582, 582*f*

    in roots, 579
    secondary growth and, 589, 589*f*
    in stems, 580–581, 580*f*, 581*f*
    translocation in, 544, 602, 602*f*
    transpiration and, 600–601, 600*f*, 601*f*
    types of, 576, 576*f*
vas deferens, 994, 994*f*, 995
vectors, 360, 360*f*
vegetative reproduction, 564, 564*f*
veins, 582, 582*f*, 868, 868*f*, 870
ventricles, 742, 742*f*, 866–867, 866*f*, 867*f*
venules, 868, 868*f*
Venus flytraps, 583, 583*f*, 596*f*–597*f*, 610,
    610*f*
vertebrae, 626
vertebrates
    complex nervous systems in, 629, 629*f*
    as deuterostomes, 635, 635*f*
    earliest, 639
    embryology of, 383
    evolution of, 383, 384, 384*f*
    general characteristics of, 383, 626, 626*f*
    homologous structures in, 384, 384*f*
    in the Paleozoic era, 458
vesicles
    in cell transport, 183, 183*f*
    in protein processing, 158, 159*f*
    seminal, 995
    in storage and maintenance, 158, 160,
    160*f*
vessel elements, 576
villi (singular, *villus*), 899, 899*f*
Virchow, Rudolph, 152
viroids, 480
viruses, 476–480
    bacteriophages, 295, 295*f*, 476*f*, 477
    beneficial roles of, 481
    diseases from, 485, 485*f*
    DNA *vs.* RNA, 477, 477*f*
    infecting bacteria, 468*f*–469*f*
    as nonliving, 476
    rearrangement of genetic material by, 332
    reproduction of, 478, 478*f*, 479*f*
    shapes of, 476*f*, 477
    structure of, 477, 477*f*
    temperate, 478
    virulent, 478
visceral mass, 680
vision
    in amphibians, 740, 748
    in birds, 772–773
    blind spot in, 951, 951*f*
    in cephalopods, 684
    in color, 400*f*
    compound eyes, 703, 703*f*
    eye placement in primates, 797, 797*f*
    eye structure, 951, 951*f*
    in fishes, 730
    occipital lobe processing and, 954, 954*f*
    photoreceptors and, 951, 951*f*
    in reptiles, 758–759, 759*f*
visual signals, 823
vital capacity, 882
vitamins
    absorption of, 898
    in large intestine, 481, 900

overview of, 893, 893*f*
    parathyroid hormone and, 980
vitamin D, 893*f*, 980
vitamin K, 481, 893*f*, 900
Volta, Alessandro, 944
voluntary (skeletal) muscle, 840, 840*f*, 848, 848*f*
vulva, 997, 997*f*

Wallace, Alfred Russel, 381
warblers, 114, 114*f*
waste recycling, 108, 108*f*, 135
water, 55–58. *See also* **water transport**
    acids and bases in, 56–57, 56*f*
    adhesion in, 55, 55*f*
    cell transport of, 180–181, 180*f*, 181*f*
    cohesion in, 55, 55*f*, 600
    contamination of, 127
    cycle, 77, 90, 90*f*
    dissolved gases in, 727
    drinking, 30
    floating ice, 55, 55*f*
    as greenhouse gas, 129, 129*f*
    hydrogen bonds in, 54, 54*f*, 55
    in the intestine, 900
    molecular structure of, 52, 52*f*
    need for, 893, 902
    in photosynthesis reaction, 204, 204*f*
    in plants, 55, 55*f*, 600–602, 600*f*, 601*f*, 602*f*
    polarity of, 54, 54*f*
    properties of, 55, 55*f*
water birds, 769, 769*f*, 775, 775*f*
water cycle, 77, 90, 90*f*
water lily leaves, 574, 574*f*, 583
water molds, 506, 506*f*
water pollution, 130, 130*f*
water-soluble vitamins, 893
water transport
    by capillary action, 597
    in cells, 180–181, 180*f*, 181*f*
    in nonvascular plants, 547
    transpiration process, 600–601, 600*f*, 601*f*
    in vascular plants, 575–576, 575*f*, 576*f*
water-vascular system, 718
Watson, James, 296, 299, 299*f*
waxes, 61, 61*f*
webbed feet, 775
weight, body, 895
Weinberg, Wilhelm, 404
Went, Frits, 604
West Nile virus, 485*f*
wetlands, 84, 84*f*
whales, 382*f*, 794*f*, 822, 824
whelks, 683
white blood cells
    B cells, 920, 920*f*, 921*f*
    cytotoxic T cells, 919*f*, 920, 921*f*
    helper T cells, 919, 919*f*, 920*f*
    in inflammation, 916, 916*f*, 917*f*
    in leukemia, 845
    macrophages, 912*f*–913*f*, 916–917, 917*f*
    natural killer cells, 916, 917*f*

    neutrophils, 916, 917*f*
    overview, 869, 869*f*
    shapes of, 152
white matter, 941, 941*f*
white wing dove, 431*f*
Wilkins, Maurice, 298–299
wind dispersal, 555, 555*f*
wings, insect, 713, 713*f*
wishbone, 643, 768*f*
withdrawal, drug, 959
woodpeckers, 769, 771
woody stems, 581, 581*f*, 589, 589*f*
word origins (prefixes and suffixes), 1047–1049
wrasses, evolution in, 412*f*

X chromosome, 249, 362, 362*f*
xylem
    in leaves, 582, 582f
    primary *vs.* secondary, 589, 589f
    in stems, 580–581, 580f
    structure of, 576, 576f, 581f

Y chromosome, 249, 335
yeast infections, 531
yeasts, 116–117, 523, 529, 533
yellow bone marrow, 844, 844*f*
yellow perch *(Perca flavens),* 737*f*, 738
yolk sac, 761

zebra fish, genome of, 330*f*-331*f*
zebra mussels, 133, 133*f*
zinc, 894, 894*f*
Z lines, 850, 851*f*
zygomycetes, 525, 525*f*
zygosporangium, 525, 525*f*
zygospores, 499
zygote fungi, 525, 525*f*
zygotes
    definition of, 498
    human, 1001
    in multicellular protists, 499
    in seed plants, 557, 557*f*, 561, 561*f*
    from sexual reproduction, 248, 248*f*

Credits

Photography

LABS (bkgd) Brand X/SuperStock; **UNIT OPENERS** (bkgd), (border) Royalty-Free/Getty Images; **UNIT 1** (section borders) Michael Melford/Royalty-Free/Getty Images; **UNITS 2–4** (section borders) Royalty-Free/Creatas Images; **UNITS 5–6** (section borders) PhotoDisc/Veer; **UNIT 7** (section borders) Brand X/SuperStock; **UNIT 8** (section borders) Dynamic Graphics/Jupiter Images; **UNIT 9** (section borders) Digital Archive Japan/Alamy

COVER AND TITLE © Frank Lane/Parfitt/Getty Images; iv (Gaul) Sam Dudgeon/HRW; (Haig) Rick Friedman/World Picture News; (Moorehead) Sam Dudgeon/HRW; (Lumsden) Paul Draper/HRW; (Zavaleta) © Robert Houser; v (Govind) Andy Christiansen/HRW; vii (b) Barbara Strnadova/Photo Researchers, Inc.; viii (tl) James M. Bell/Photo Researchers, Inc.; (bl) Stephen Alvarez/National Geographic Image Collection; ix (b) ABPL/Daryl Balfour/Animals Animals/Earth Scenes; x (cl) Dr. Linda Stannard, UCT/Photo Researchers, Inc.; xi (t) Joe Outland/Alamy; (bl) Dr. Paul Andrews, University of Dundee/Photo Researchers, Inc.; xii (tl) Andrew Leonard/Photo Researchers, Inc.; xiii (cr) Toni Angermayer/Photo Researchers, Inc.; xiv (b) Steve Axford; xv (tr) Steve & Dave Maslowski/Photo Researchers, Inc.; (bc) PhotoDisc/Getty Images; (br) PhotoDisc/Getty Images; xvi (bl) Art Wolfe/Photo Researchers, Inc.; xvii (tr) Creatas/SuperStock; (bl) Lourens Smak/Alamy; xviii (l) Sam Dudgeon/HRW; xix (br) Michael Donne, University of Manchester/Photo Researchers, Inc.; xx (tr) Dr. Arthur Tucker/Photo Researchers, Inc.; xxi (tc) Rod Planck/Photo Researchers, Inc.; xxii (tr) Sam Dudgeon/HRW; xxiii (cr) Phototake Inc./Alamy; (b) Victoria Smith/HRW; xxv (br) Sam Dudgeon/HRW; 2 (bl) Bill Curtsinger/National Geographic Image Collection; (br) Katherine Feng/Globio/Minden Pictures; (tl) Royalty-Free/Corbis; 2A Bill Hatcher/National Geographic Image Collection; 2B (bl) Meul/ARCO/Nature Picture Library; (tr) (cl) Bettmann/Corbis; (cr) Time & Life Pictures/Getty Images; 3 (tl) (cr) Sam Dudgeon/HRW; (cl) Age Fotostock/SuperStock

CHAPTER 1: 4–5 Frans Lanting/Minden Pictures; 7 (tr) Deep Light Productions/Photo Researchers, Inc.; (bc) P. Hawtin/University of Southhampton/Photo Researchers, Inc.; 8 (tr) National Optical Astronomy Observatories/Photo Researchers, Inc.; (tl) David Tipling/Nature Picture Library; 9 (tr) Victoria Smith/HRW; 10 (bl) Georgette Douwma/Nature Picture Library; 11 (tr) Sam Dudgeon/HRW; 12 (bl) Millard H. Sharp/Photo Researchers, Inc.; (br) AP Photo/Marcio Jose Sanchez; 13 (tr) Royalty-Free/Corbis; 14 (r) Sam Dudgeon/HRW; (cl) PhotoDisc/Getty Images; (cr), 15 (tr) Victoria Smith/HRW; 16 (tl) Carsten Peter/National Geographic Image Collection; 17 (bl) Phil Schermeister/National Geographic Image Collection; 18 (bl) Stephen Alvarez/National Geographic Image Collection; (tr) Paul Nicklen/National Geographic Image Collection; (c) Douglas Faulkner/Photo Researchers, Inc.; (bkgd) Michael Martin/Photo Researchers, Inc.; 19 (tr) Gabe Palmer/Alamy; 20 Victoria Smith/HRW; 22 (b) Stephen Alvarez/National Geographic Image Collection; (t) P. Hawtin/University of Southhampton/Photo Researchers, Inc.; (tc) Sam Dudgeon/HRW; (bc) PhotoDisc/Getty Images

CHAPTER 2: 26–27 Roger Harris/Photo Researchers, Inc.; 29 (b) James M. Bell/Photo Researchers, Inc.; 30 (b) Jeremy Horner/Corbis; (cl) Amit Dave/NewsCom; 31 (tr) Sam Dudgeon/HRW; 32 (tl) epa/Corbis; (tr) Vo Trung Dung/Corbis Sygma; 33 (bl) Taxi/Getty Images; (br) Don Farrall/Photographer's Choice RF/Getty Images; 34 (bl) Peter Menzel/Photo Researchers, Inc.; 35 (b) ORNL/Photo Researchers, Inc.; 36 (br) Eric Miller/Getty Images; (bl) Mark Maio/King-Holmes/Photo Researchers, Inc.; 37 (tr) Getty Images; 38 (cl), (br), (cr) David Brabyn/Sipa Photos/NewsCom; 39 (t) Mike Johnson. All rights reserved.; 30 (tl) Courtesy of Dr. Rita Colwell; 40 (t) Andrew Dunn; 41 (tr) Yuriko Nakao/NewsCom; (bl) Jim Sulley/NewsCom; (c) Volker Steger/Photo Researchers, Inc.; (bkgd) Royalty-Free/Corbis; 43 (tr) Sam Dudgeon/HRW; 44 (t) Amit Dave/NewsCom; (c) David Brabyn/NewsCom; (b) Don Farrall/Photographer's Choice RF/Getty Images; 46 (tc) AP Photo/Katsumi Kasahara

CHAPTER 3: 48–49 Daniel Boschung/zefa/Corbis; 51 (bl) Victoria Smith/HRW; 52 (tc) blickwinkel/Alamy; 53 (br) Sergio Purtell/Foca/HRW; 55 (b) Botanica/The Garden Picture Library; 56 (b-all) Sam Dudgeon/HRW; 57 (t) Victoria Smith/HRW; 58 (tr) O.S.F./Animals Animals/Earth Scenes; (cl) Bernard, George/Animals Animals/Earth Scenes; (t-bkgd) PhotoDisc/Getty Images; (cr) Layne Kennedy/Corbis; (b-bkgd) Bernhard Edmaier/SPL/Photo Researchers, Inc.; 59 (br) Andrew Holt/Alamy; (bl) Andy Christiansen/HRW; 60 (bc) Sam Dudgeon/HRW; 61 (t) Sam Dudgeon/HRW; (bl) Suzanne Danegger/NHPA; (br) Tony Hamblin; Frank Lane Picture Agency/Corbis; 62 (br) SuperStock; 64 (b) Victor Ruiz Caballero/AP/Wide World Photos; 68 Sam Dudgeon/HRW; 70 (t) Victoria Smith/HRW; (c) Botanica/The Garden Picture Library; (b) Victor Ruiz Caballero/AP/Wide World Photos; 74 (br) A ROOM WITH VIEWS/Alamy; (bl) FRANS LANTING/Minden Pictures; 74A Doug Perrine/Nature Picture Library; 74B (bl) Mark Moffett/Minden Pictures; (tl) Brand X Pictures; (tr) Royalty-Free/Corbis; (cl) Erich Hartmann/Magnum Photos; (cr) Iain Masterton/Alamy; 75 (tl, cr) Robert Houser; (cl) Heidi & Hans-Jurgen Koch/Minden Pictures

CHAPTER 4: 76–77 Ingo Arndt/Nature Picture Library; 79 (b) Kim Taylor/Nature Picture Library; 80 (t) Sam Dudgeon/HRW Photo; 81 (l) Ken M. Johns, The National Audubon Society Collection/Photo Researchers; (c) Glenn M. Oliver/Visuals Unlimited; (r) ER Degginger/Color-Pic, Inc.; 82–83 (t) Michael DeYoung/Corbis; 83 (tc) Brenda Tharp/Photo Researchers, Inc.; (tr) ER Degginger/Color-Pic, Inc.; 84 (tl) Tamara Dormier/Seapics; (tr) Mark Conlin/Seapics; 85 (b-bkgd) Jan Baks/Alamy; (tr) Paul Chesley/National Geographic/Getty Images; (t-bkgd) Victoria Smith/HRW; (c) Roger W. Archibald/Animals Animals/Earth Scenes; 86 (l) blickwinkel/Alamy; (cl) B.A.E. Inc./Alamy; (cr) James Carmichael, Jr./NHPA; (r) Tom Vezo/VIREO; 88 (t) Michael Keller/Corbis; 89 (t) Brian Wheeler/VIREO; (c) D. Robert & Lorri Franz/Corbis; (b) Jason Brindel Photography/Alamy Photos; 93, 94, 95 Sam Dudgeon/HRW; 96 (t) Kim Taylor/Nature Picture Library; (b) Michael Keller/Corbis

CHAPTER 5: 100–101 Tui De Roy/Minden Pictures; 103 (b) ABPL/Balfour, Daryl/Animals Animals/Earth Scenes; 104 (t) Terry Andrewartha/Nature Picture Library; 105 (b) Frans Lanting/Minden Pictures; 106 (b) Fritz Polking/Peter Arnold, Inc.; 107 (t-bkgd) Janine Wiedel Photolibrary/Alamy; 108 (cl) Yoshikazu Tsuno/AFP/Getty Images; (b-bkgd) SETBOUN/Corbis; (tr) Iain Masterton/Alamy; (t-bkgd) Corbis/PunchStock; 109 (b) Mitsuaki Iwago/Minden Pictures; 110 (tc) Patti Murray/Animals Animals/Earth Scenes; 111 (tl) Doug Perrine/Nature Picture Library; (tr) Clay Perry/Corbis; 112 (b) Ilene MacDonald/Alamy; 114 (tl) Robert Royse/VIREO; (tcl) John Dunning/VIREO; (tc) Bob Steele/VIREO; (tcr) Rob & Ann Simpson/VIREO; (tr) Arthur Morris/VIREO; 115 (t) James D. Watt/Seapics; 117 (tl) Victoria Smith/HRW; (tr) Dr. David B. Fankhouser; 118 (t) Frans Lanting/Minden Pictures; (c) Doug Perrine/Nature Picture Library; (b) James D. Watt/Seapics

CHAPTER 6: 122–123 George Steinmetz/Corbis; 123 (br) Victoria Smith/HRW; 125 (br) Cameron Davidson/Getty Images; 126 (br) George Steinmetz/Corbis; (bl) Lester Lefkowitz/Corbis; 127 (tr) Sam Dudgeon/HRW; 128 (b) China Photos/Getty Images; 131 (tr) Victoria Smith/HRW; 132 (b) Peter Oxford/Nature Picture Library; 133 (tl) Will Meinderts/Foto Natura/Minden Pictures; (tr) Shin Yoshino/Minden Pictures; 134 (b) Royalty-free/Robert Harding; 135 (tr) Victoria Smith/HRW; 136 (bl) Courtesy Cliff Lerner/HRW; (br) Richard Price/Getty Images; 137 (t) Stuart Westmorland/Corbis; 138 (tr) Image entitled "Fresh Kills Future Parkland" used with permission of the New York City Department of City Planning. All rights reserved; (tl) Louie Psihoyos/Corbis; 139 (cr) Handout-Obvio!/Reuters/Corbis; (tr) Reuters/Corbis; (b) Issei Kato/Reuters/Corbis; (bkgd) Royalty-Free/Corbis; 141 (tr) Sam Dudgeon/HRW; 142 (br) Royalty-free/Robert Harding; (c) Shin Yoshino/Minden Pictures; (tr) Lester Lefkowitz/Corbis; 146 (bl) PHOTOTAKE Inc./Alamy; (br) Andrew Syred/Photo Researchers, Inc.; 146A James Cavallini/Photo Researchers, Inc.; 146B (bl) Jennifer C. Waters/Photo Researchers, Inc.; (tl) Kevin Collins/Visuals Unlimited; (tr) PhotoDisc/Getty Images; (cl) Gary D. Gaugler/Photo Researchers, Inc.; (cr) Paula Lerner/Aurora; 147 (tl, cr) Andy Christiansen/HRW; (cl) Don W. Fawcett/Photo Researchers, Inc.

CHAPTER 7: 148–149 Volker Steger/Christian Bardele/Photo Researchers, Inc.;149 (tr) Victoria Smith/HRW;151 (bc) Michael Newman/Photo Edit; (br) Michael Abbey/Visuals Unlimited;152 (br) Andrew Syred/Photo Researchers, Inc.; (c) Laude Nuridsany & Marie Perennou/Photo Researchers, Inc.; (tr) Thomas Deerinck/Visuals Unlimited; (bl), (bkgd) Francois Paquet-Durand/Photo Researchers, Inc.;154 (cr) CNRI/Photo Researchers, Inc.;155 (tl) Dr. Donald Fawcett/Visuals Unlimited;157 (tr) Don Fawcett/Visuals Unlimited;159 (tr), (cr) R. Boldender/D. Fawcett/Visuals Unlimited; (br) Professor Birgit H. Satir;160 (br) Dr. Jeremy Burgess/Photo Researchers, Inc.; 161 (tr) Dr. Don Fawcett/Visuals Unlimited; 162 (bl) Dr. Linda Stannard, UCT/Photo Researchers, Inc.; 164 (cl) Dr. George Chapman/Visuals Unlimited; (c) Clouds Hill Imaging Ltd./Corbis; (cr) Gentl & Hyers/Botanica/Jupiter Images; (bl) Photo Insolite Realite/SPL/Photo Researchers, Inc.; 166 (tl) Lawrence Naylor/Photo Researchers, Inc.; (cl) Eddy Marissen/Foto Natura/Minden Pictures; (tr) Age FotoStock/SuperStock; (br) IT Stock International/Jupiter Images; 167 (tr) E.R. Degginger/Color-Pic, Inc.; 168 (br) Eddy Marissen/Foto Natura/Minden Pictures; (tr) Michael Newman/Photo Edit

CHAPTER 8: 172–173 CNRI/Photo Researchers, Inc.; 173 (cr) Runk/Schoenberger/Grant Heilman Photography; 175 (b) Marc Chamberlain/Seapics; 178 (b) Keith Levit/Alamy; 180 (all) Dr. David M. Phillips/Visuals Unlimited; 181 (t) Sam Dudgeon/HRW; 184 (b) Nigel Cattlin/Photo Researchers, Inc.; 184 (b) Bob Daemmrich/PhotoEdit, Inc.; 185 (t) Kevin Schafer/Corbis; 187 (cl, cr) NASA/SPL/Photo Researchers, Inc.; (tr) Meul/ARCO/Nature Picture Library; (tl) PhotoDisc/Getty Images; (bkgd) Dr. Jeremy Burgess/SPL/Photo Researchers, Inc.; (br) Lourens Smak/Alamy; 188 (bl) WARD'S Natural Science; (br) Sam Dudgeon/HRW; 190 (t) Marc Chamberlain/Seapics; (c) Keith Levit/Alamy; (b) Bob Daemmrich/PhotoEdit, Inc.

CHAPTER 9: 194–195 Frans Lanting/Minden Pictures; 195 (tr) Sam Dudgeon/HRW; 197 (br) Terry W. Eggers/Corbis; 198 (tr) Victoria Smith/HRW; 199 (cr) Michael Newman/PhotoEdit; (cl) Royalty-Free/Corbis; 200 (br) Troy and Mary Parlee/Alamy; 202 (bl) Copyright Dorling Kindersley; 207 (tl) Richard Cummins/Corbis; (tr) Wolfgang Kaehler/Corbis; 208 John Henley/Corbis; 213 (tl) Mike Powell/Allsport Concepts/Getty Images; (tc) David Madison/Getty Images; 214 (bkgd), (tr), (cr) Roger Ressmeyer/Corbis; (b) James Marshall/Corbis; 215 (bl) Victoria Smith/HRW; 216 (t) Richard Cummins/Corbis; (b) David Madison/Getty Images; (t) Troy and Mary Parlee/Alamy

Researchers, Inc.; 459 Jonathan Blair/Corbis; 460 (tr) Reuters/Corbis; (c) Chris Butler/Photo Researchers, Inc.; (bkgd) Robert Harding Picture Library Ltd./Alamy; (b) Mark Garlick/Photo Researchers, Inc.; 461 Victoria Smith/HRW; 462 (t) Breck P. Kent/Animals Animals-Earth Scenes; (c) Theo Allofs/Corbis; (b) Jonathan Blair/Corbis; 466 (bl) FLIP NICKLIN/Minden Pictures; (br) Scimat/ Photo Researchers, Inc.; 466A Steve Gschmeissner/ Photo Researchers, Inc.; 466B (tl) Steve Axford; (tr) POPPERFOTO/Alamy; (cl) Bettmann/Corbis; (cr) Photo by Erskine Palmer/Time Magazine/Time & Life Pictures/ Getty Images; 467 (tl, cr) Sam Dudgeon/HRW; (cl) Pat O'Hara/Corbis

CHAPTER 20: 468–469 Eye of Science/Photo Researchers, Inc.; 471 (br) CNRI/Photo Researchers, Inc.; (bc) CDC/Photo Researchers, Inc.; (bl) Andrew Syred/ Photo Researchers, Inc.; 472 (bl) Science VU/Visuals Unlimited; (br) George J. Wilder/Visuals Unlimited; 473 (tr) Dr. T.J. Beveridge/Visuals Unlimited; 474 (tr) Victoria Smith/HRW; (cl), (bl) E. Weber/Visuals Unlimited; 475 (tl) Dr. Linda Stannard/Photo Researchers, Inc.; (tc) Dr. Dennis Kunkel/Phototake-All rights reserved; (tr) A.B. Dowsett/Photo Researchers, Inc.; 476 (tr) NIBSC/SPL/ Photo Researchers; (cl) Dr. O. Bradfute/Peter Arnold, Inc.; (cr) E.O.S./Gelderglom/Photo Researchers, Inc.; (bl) Lee D. Simon/Photo Researchers, Inc.; 479 (tr) Eye of Science/Photo Researchers, Inc.; 480 Carsten Rehder/dpa/Corbis; 481 Lester Lefkowitz/Corbis; 482 (cl) CNRI/Science Photo Library/Photo Researchers; (cl) Hank Morgan/Photo Researchers; (br) CNRI/Science Photo Library/Photo Researchers; 483 (t) David Scharf/ Photo Researchers, Inc.; (c) CNRI/Photo Researchers, Inc.; (b) Dr. Dennis Kunkel/Visuals Unlimited; 485 (tr) Dr. M.A. Ansary/Photo Researchers, Inc.; 487 (bkgd) Dennis Kunkel/Phototake-All rights reserved; 489 (b) Sam Dudgeon/HRW; (tr) Steve Allen/Photo Researchers, Inc.; (cr) Scott Camazine/Photo Researchers, Inc.; (bl) AFP/Getty Images; (cl) Visuals Unlimited/Corbis; 490 (c) NIBSC/SPL/Photo Researchers; (t) Science VU/Visuals Unlimited; (b) Lester Lefkowitz/Corbis

CHAPTER 21: 494–495 Phototake Inc./Alamy; 495 (tr) Dennis MacDonald/PhotoEdit, Inc.; 497 (br) Scott Camazine/Photo Researchers, Inc.; (bl) Randy Morse/ Seapics; 498 (br) Microfield Scientific Ltd./SPL/Photo Researchers, Inc.; 499 (cr) Andrew J. Martinez/Photo Researchers, Inc.; 500 (tl) Steve Gschmeissner/SPL/ Photo Researchers; (tc) Matt Meadows/Peter Arnold; (tr) Gregory Ochocki/Photo Researchers; 501 (bl) Phillip Colla/Seapics; (bc) Dwight R. Kuhn; (br) Eric V. Grave/Photo Researchers, Inc.; 502 (bl) Dr. Stanley Flegler/Visuals Unlimited; (br) SPL/Photo Researchers, Inc.; 503 (tr) Dr. Dennis Kunkel/Visuals Unlimited; (cl) Dennis Kunkel/Phototake; (br) Dr. Karl Aufderheide/ Visuals Unlimited; 504 (bl) Steve Gschmeissner/Photo Researchers, Inc.; (bc) SPL/Photo Researchers, Inc.; (br) Dennis Kunkel/Phototake; 505 (bc) Linda Sims/Visuals Unlimited; (br) Wildscape/Alamy; (bl) Gary R. Robinson/ Visuals Unlimited; (t) Kent Wood; 506 (tl) Gregory G. Dimijian, M.D./Photo Researchers, Inc.; (tr) Fred Rhoades/Mycena Consulting; 507 (t) Professors P.M. Motta & F.M. Magliocca/SPL/Photo Researchers; 508 (bl) Sinclair Stammers/Photo Researchers, Inc.; (br) Dr. David M. Phillips/Visuals Unlimited; 509 (c) REUTERS/Corinne Dufka; (tr) Jack Clark/Animals Animals/Earth Scenes; (br) AP Photo/Eugene Hoshiko; (bkgd-t) iStockphoto.com/ Luba Nel; 510 (bl) Bill Bachman/Photo Researchers, Inc.; 511 (t) Royalty Free/Corbis; 512 (bl) Victoria Smith/HRW (br) Phototake Inc./Alamy; 513 (t) Sam Dudgeon/HRW; 514 (t) Scott Camazine/Photo Researchers, Inc.; (c) Linda Sims/Visuals Unlimited; (b) Professors P.M. Motta & F.M. Magliocca/SPL/Photo Researchers

CHAPTER 22: 518–519 Mark Moffett/Minden Pictures; 519 (tr) James Noble/Corbis; 521 (bcr, br) Steve Axford; (bl) David M. Dennis/Tom Stack; (cl) geogphotos/Alamy;

523 (tr) E. R. Degginger/Color-Pic, Inc.; (tl) Barry Runk/ Grant Heilman Photography; 524 (bl) John Taylor/Visuals Unlimited; 525 (cr) Andrew Syred/Science Photo Library/ Photo Researchers; 527 (br) Frans Lanting/Minden Pictures; 528 (tl) V. Ahmadjian/Visuals Unlimited; (tc, tr) National Geographic Image Collection/Stephen & Sylvia Duran Sharnoff; 529 (br) Victoria Smith/HRW; (bl) Dr. Paul A. Zahl/Photo Researchers; 530 (t) B. Runk/S. Schoenberger/Grant Heilman Photography -- All rights reserved.; (b) Wolfgang Kaehler/Corbis; 531 (tc) Mediscan/Visuals Unlimited; (tr) SPL/Photo Researchers, Inc.; (tl) Visuals Unlimited/Inga Spence; 532 (tr) Holt Studios/Photo Researchers, Inc.; (cr) Robert Day/Courtesy of Birmingham Repertory Theatre and The Touring Consortium/(l-r) Sara Beharrell, Leah Muller, Bethan Cecil and Maria Golledge; (bl) Robert Day/Courtesy of Birmingham Repertory Theatre and The Touring Consortium/(l-r) Michelle Tate, Leah Muller, Maria Golledge and Bethan Cecil; (bkgd) Tony Baker/ Photonica/Getty Images; 533 (tr) Victoria Smith/HRW; 534 (b) Victoria Smith/HRW; (t) Steve Axford; (c) National Geographic Image Collection/Stephen & Sylvia Duran Sharnoff; 538 (bl) SA Team/Foto Natura/Minden Pictures; (br) Stockbyte; 538A CuboImages srl/Alamy; 538B (bl) imagebroker/Alamy; (tl) Egyptian National Museum, Cairo, Egypt/SuperStock; (cl) National Museum of American History, Smithsonian Institution, Washington, DC, neg. no 73-11287; (tr) Royalty-Free/Corbis; (cr) Topham/The Image Works; 539 (tl) Harvard University News Office; (cr) Rick Friedman/World Picture News; (cl) Susumu Nishinaga/Photo Researchers, Inc.

CHAPTER 23: 540–541 Pete Oxford/Minden Pictures; 543 (b) Adrian Thomas/SPL/Photo Researchers, Inc.; 544 (tl) Courtesy of Hans Steur; (bl) H. Taylor/OSF/Animals Animals/Earth Scenes; (br) Dani/Jeske/Animals Animals/ Earth Scenes; 545 (bl) age fotostock/SuperStock; (br) age fotostock/SuperStock; (tr) Sam Dudgeon/HRW; 547 (b) Darrell Gulin/Corbis; 548 (tl) Ed Reschke/Peter Arnold, Inc.; (tc) B. Runk/S. Schoenberger/Grant Heilman Photography, Inc.; (tr) B. Runk/S. Schoenberger/Grant Heilman Photography, Inc.; 550 (tl) Runk/Schoenberger/ Grant Heilman Photography; (bl) Adam Jones/Photo Researchers, Inc.; (br) Tom Dietrich/Getty Images; 552 (tr) Ed Reschke/Peter Arnold, Inc.; 553 (bl) Geoff Kidd/ SPL/Photo Researchers, Inc.; (br) Nigel Cattlin/Photo Researchers, Inc.; 554 (cr) N.H. [Dan] Cheatham/DRK Photo; (cl) Peter Chadwick Dorling Kindersley; (tr) William E. Ferguson; (tl) Robert J. Erwin/Photo Researchers, Inc.; (cl) Peter Chadwick Dorling Kindersley; 555 (bc) B. Runk/ S. Schoenberger/Grant Heilman Photography, Inc.; (br) Barry Runk/Grant Heilman Photography, Inc.; (br) Steve & Dave Maslowski/Photo Researchers, Inc.; (bl) Dick Canby/ DRK Photo; 556 (tc) Dr. Carleton Ray/Photo Researchers, Inc.; (bl) Thomas Wiewandt/Visions of America/Corbis; (br) E. Webber/Visuals Unlimited; (bc) Robert & Linda Mitchell; 558 (tr) Dr. E.R. Degginger/Animals Animals/Earth Scenes; 560 (tr) Sam Dudgeon/HRW; 562 (br) Merlin D. Tuttle/Bat Conservation International; (bc) Joanna McCarthy/Getty Images; (bl) Bob Gibbons, The National Audubon Society Collection/Photo Researchers; (cr) Martha Cooper/Peter Arnold, Inc.; 563 (br) PunchStock; (tr) photocuisine/Corbis; 564 (tr) George Bernard/Animals Animals/Earth Scenes; (tl) Brand X Pictures; (tc) Paul Hein/Unicorn; 565 (bl) Pat Anderson/Visuals Unlimited; (cl) David Sieren/Visuals Unlimited; (br) Runk/Schoenberger/ Grant Heilman Photography; (cr) Dr. E.R. Degginger; 566 (cr) Adam Jones/Photo Researchers, Inc.

CHAPTER 24: 570–571 Phil Schermeister/Corbis; 574 (cr) Lefever/Grushow/Grant Heilman Photography; (tr) E.R. Degginger/Color-Pic, Inc.; (tl) Cindy Kassab/Corbis; 575 (tr) Photodisc/Getty Images (bl) Sam Dudgeon/HRW; (br) Larry Mellichamp/Visuals Unlimited; 576 (br) Runk/ Shoenberger/Grant Heilman Photography; 577 (tr) Dorling Kindersley; (cr) CuboImages srl/Alamy; 579 (br) Herb

Charles Ohlmeyer; (bl) R. Calentine/Visuals Unlimited; (bc) Dwight Kuhn; 580 (cl), (r) Runk/Schoenberger/Grant Heilman Photography; (cr) Royalty-Free/Corbis; (l) PhotoDisc/Getty Images; 581 (cr) Sam Dudgeon/HRW; 583 (tl) Peter Johnson/Corbis; (tr) Donald Specker/Animals Animals-Earth Scenes; 584 (bl) Gallo Images/Corbis; (c) Mark Moffett/Minden Pictures; (br) Martin Harvey/Corbis; (tr) Oxford Scientific/Jupiter Images; (bkgd) Clouds Hill Imaging Ltd./Corbis; 588 (cr) Robert P. Comport/Animals Animals-Earth Scenes; (cl) Robert & Linda Mitchell; (br) Tim Fuller/HRW Photo; (bl) R.F. Evert; 590 (bl) Sam Dudgeon/HRW; 591 (t), (b) Michael P. Gadomski/Photo Researchers, Inc.; 592 (c) Peter Johnson/Corbis; 592 (t) Cindy Kassab/Corbis; 592 (b) Tim Fuller/HRW Photo

CHAPTER 25: 596–597 David Maitland/Getty Images; 599 (br) PhotoDisc/Getty Images; 601 (br) Larry Mellichamp/Visuals Unlimited; 603 (bl), (bc), (br) Bruce Iverson; 605 (tr) Wally Eberhart/Visuals Unlimited; (tl) Courtesy of Valent BioSciences Corporation; 606 (tr) Sam Dudgeon/HRW; (bl) Cathlyn Melloan/Getty Images; 607 (tc) Ed Reschke/Peter Arnold, Inc.; (tr) Joel Arrington/Visuals Unlimited; (tr) Peter Miller/Getty Images; 609 (br) Sally A. Morgan; Ecoscene/Corbis; (bl) Royalty Free/Corbis; 610 (cl) D. Heuclin/Peter Arnold, Inc.; (tr), (cr) Christi Carter/Grant Heilman Photography, Inc.; (tl) Barry Rice/Visuals Unlimited; 611 (bl) Raymond M. Wheeler, Ph.D./Kennedy Space Center and pictured: Gregory D. Goins, Ph.D.; (cr) NASA; (tr) Royalty-Free/Corbis; (bkgd) NASA/Hubble Heritage Team; 612 (bl) Sam Dudgeon/ HRW; 614 (tr) Larry Mellichamp/Visuals Unlimited; (cl) PhotoDisc/Getty Images; (bc) Barry Rice/Visuals Unlimited; 618 (br) Monica Delmasso/Photographer's Choice/Getty Images; (bl) Fred Bavendam/Minden Pictures; 618A Steve Bloom Images/Alamy; 618B (cr) Time & Life Pictures/Getty Images; (tr) John James Audubon/Collection of The New York Historical Society/ Accession # 1863.17.159; (cl) M. Gunther/BIOS/Peter Arnold, Inc.; (bl) Pete Oxford/Minden Pictures; 619 (tl), (cr) Patrick Greene/National Geographic Image Collection; (cl) Karl Ammann/Digital Vision/Getty Images

CHAPTER 26: 620–621 Fred Bavendam/Minden Pictures; 623 (br) Mark Moffett/Minden Pictures; (bl) Flip Nicklin/Minden Pictures; 624 Age Fotostock/SuperStock; 626 (tr) Robert Maier/Animals Animals-Earth Scenes; 627 (br) Art Wolfe/Tony Stone Images; (bl) Norbert Wu/ Minden Pictures; 628 Sergio Purtell/Foca/HRW; 630 (tl) Fabio Liverani/Nature Picture Library; 631 (tl) Georgette Douwma/Nature Picture Library; (tr) Meul/ARCO/Nature Picture Library; 632 Norbert Wu/Minden Pictures; 633 (bl) Joyce and Frank Burek/Animals Animals-Earth Scenes; (bc) Purestock/SuperStock; (br) Michael and Patricia Fogden/Minden Pictures; 637 (tr) Konrad Wothe/Minden Pictures; (cr) Ingo Arndt/Nature Picture Library; 639 Royalty-Free/Corbis; 640 (tr) Mike Parry/Minden Pictures; (bl) James L. Amos/Photo Researchers, Inc.; 641 Zigmund Leszczynski/Animals Animals-Earth Scenes; 643 (tr) S. Nielsen/DRK Photo; 644 Frans Lanting/Minden Pictures; 645 (tr), (cr) Mike Hettwer; (bkgd) W. Cody/Corbis; 645 (b) Don Foley/Foley Media; 646 Victoria Smith/HRW; 647 (t) Georgette Douwma/Photo Researchers, Inc.; 648 (c) Michael and Patricia Fogden/Minden Pictures; (t) Mark Moffett/Minden Pictures; (b) Zigmund Leszczynski/ Animals Animals-Earth Scenes

CHAPTER 27: 652–653 Jeff Rotman/Nature Picture Library; 657 (tl) David J. Wrobel/Biological Photo Service; (tc) Neil G. McDaniel/NASC/Photo Researchers, Inc.; (tr) Runk/Schoenberger/Grant Heilman Photography; (cl) Cabisco/Visuals Unlimited; (c) Manfred Kage/Peter Arnold, Inc.; (cr) Robert & Linda Mitchell; 659 (tl) Robert Brons/ Biological Photo Service; (tr) Biodisc/Visuals Unlimited; 660 (tr) Victoria Smith/HRW; (bl) T.E. Adams/Visuals Unlimited; 661 (tl) Stuart Westmorland/Getty Images; (tr) Neil McDaniel/Photo Researchers; 662 (tr) Altrendo/ Getty Images; (cr) SuperStock, Inc./SuperStock; (b) Age

Smith/HRW; 884 (tl) Dr. Dennis Kunkel/Visuals Unlimited; (cr) GJLP/Photo Researchers, Inc.; (br) Reuters/Corbis

CHAPTER 36: 888–889 Anders Blomqvist/Lonely Planet Images; 891 (bc) Scott Markewitz/Getty Images; (bl) Photodisc/gettyimages; 892 (tl), (cl), (cr) Dominic Oldershaw; 893 (c), (br), (bl) Sergio Purtell/Foca/HRW; 894 (br) Royalty Free/Corbis; (bc) PhotoDisc/Getty Images; 895 (tr) U. S. Department of Agriculture/MyPyramid.gov; (tr) U. S. Department of Agriculture/MyPyramid.gov; 899 (tr) Sam Dudgeon/HRW; (br) Prof. P. Motta/Dept. of Anatomy/University "La Sapienza", Rome/Photo Researchers, Inc.; 900 (tl) CNRI/SPL/Photo Researchers, Inc.; 901 (cl) David M. Martin, M.D./Photo Researchers, Inc.; (cr) Scott Camazine/SPL/Photo Researchers, Inc.; (c) Bubbles Photolibrary/Alamy; (tr) Argosy Publishing; (bkgd) Biophoto Associates/Photo Researchers, Inc.; 902 (bl) Victoria Smith/HRW; 904 (tr) Victoria Smith/HRW; 905 (tr) BSIP/Phototake; 908 (tl) Sergio Purtell/Foca/HRW; (cr) CNRI/SPL/Photo Researchers, Inc.; (br) BSIP/Phototake; 909 (tr) Tim Fuller/HRW

CHAPTER 37: 912–913 Eye of Science/Photo Researchers, Inc.; 915 (bc) A. Davidhazy/Custom Medical Stock Photo; (br) Gopal Murti/Phototake, Inc./Alamy; 917 (tl), (tc) Dr. Dennis Kunkel/Phototake; (tr) Meckes/Ottawa/Photo Researchers, Inc.; 918 (tr) Sam Dudgeon/HRW; 919 (br) Victoria Smith/HRW; 920 (bl) Dennis Kunkel/Phototake; 922 (bl) David McNew/Getty Images; 924 (bl) Sam Dudgeon/HRW; (br) Peter Arnold, Inc./Alamy; (bc) SciMAT/Photo Researchers, Inc.; 925 (br) Derek Berwin/Getty Images; (bl) Dennis Kunkel/Phototake; (tr) Victoria Smith/HRW; 926 (cr) Science Pictures Ltd/Photo Researchers, Inc.; (bl) Steve Jems/Photo Researchers, Inc.; (tr) Brand X Pictures; (bkgd) Luca DiCecco/Alamy; 927 (tr) Animas Corp; 928 (bl) AP Photo/Damian Dovarganes; (cr) NIBSC/Photo Researchers, Inc.; 930 (cl) Tim Fuller/HRW; 932 (tc) A. Davidhazy/Custom Medical Stock Photo; (bc) SciMAT/Photo Researchers, Inc.

CHAPTER 38: 936–937 Mike Agliolo/Photo Researchers, Inc.; 937 (br) Neil Borden/Photo Researchers, Inc.; 941 Jim Cummins/Taxi/Getty Images; 942 (cl) Tim Fuller/HRW Photo; 944 (b) David McCarthy/Photo Researchers, Inc.; 948 (bl) David McCarthy/Photo Researchers, Inc.; 950 (bl) RubberBall/Alamy; (br) Mike Chew/Corbis; 951 (t) A.L. Blum/Visuals Unlimited; 952 (br) Susumu Nishinaga/Photo Researchers, Inc.; (bl) IT Stock Free/SuperStock; 955 (cr) Jay Geidd/National Institute of Mental Health; (tr) From H. Damasio, T. Grabowski, R. Frank, A.M. Galaburda & A.R. Damasio (1994) The Return of Phineas Gage: clues about the brain from a famous patient, Science, 264, 1102–1105; 955 (bl) WireImageStock/Masterfile; (bkgd) Dr. Dennis Kunkel/Visuals Unlimited; (cl), 956 Royalty-Free/Corbis; 957 (br) Royalty-Free/Corbis; 958 (t) Scott Camazine/Photo Researchers, Inc.; (b) Charles Gupton/Corbis; 961 (tr) David Stoecklein/Corbis; 962 (b) Dr. David Scott/Phototake; 964 (b) David Stoecklein/Corbis; (tr) Tim Fuller/HRW Photo; (cl) David McCarthy/Photo Researchers, Inc.

CHAPTER 39: 968–969 (all) Derek Berwin/Getty Images; 971 (br) Bob Daemmrich/The Image Works; 972 (bc) Sam Dudgeon/HRW; 976 (tl) Victoria Smith/HRW; 977 (tr) Royalty Free/Corbis; 979 (br) David Kelly Crow/PhotoEdit, Inc.; 981 (tr) Bryan & Cherry Alexander/Photo Researchers, Inc.; 982 (tl) Y. Nikas/Photo Researchers, Inc. 983 (cr) BSIP/Phototake; (bl) Justin Hayworth/Duluth News Tribune/AP/Wide World Photos; 983 (c) Justin Hayworth/Duluth News Tribune/AP/Wide World Photos; (bkgd) CNRI/Photo Researchers, Inc.; 983 (tr) Volker Steger/SPL/Photo Researchers, Inc.; 985 (t) M.I. Walker/Photo Researchers; 986 (tr) Royalty Free/Corbis; (br) Y. Nikas/Photo Researchers, Inc.

CHAPTER 40: 990–991 OSF/Derek Bromhall/Animals Animals-Earth Scenes; 993 (br) CNRI/Photo Researchers, Inc.; 995 (tr) Professor P. Motta, Dept. of Anatomy, Rome University/Photo Researchers, Inc.; 998 (bl) Professors P.M. Motta & J. Van Blerkom/Photo Researchers, Inc.; 1000 (t) C. Edelmann/La Villette/SS/Photo Researchers, Inc.; 1003 (tl), (bl) Lennart Nilsson/Albert Bonniers Förlag; (tr) D. Bromhall/OSF/Animals Animals-Earth Scenes; (br) Petit Format/Nestle/Photo Researchers, Inc.; 1004 (tr) Zephyr/Photo Researchers, Inc.; 1006 (bl) SPL/Custom Medical Stock Photo; 1007 (t) NMSB/Custom Medical Stock Photo; 1008 (cl) Big Cheese Photo/Royalty-Free/Getty Images; (b) Robert W. Ginn/Photo Edit; (cr) Tony Freeman/Photo Edit; (tr) Dr. Najeeb Layyous/Photo Researchers, Inc.; (bkgd) P. Motta/G. Macchiarelli/S. Nottola/Photo Researchers, Inc.; 1010 (tr) Professor P. Motta, Dept. of Anatomy, Rome University/Photo Researchers, Inc.; (tr) D. Bromhall/OSF/Animals Animals-Earth Scenes

CHAPTER 41: 1014–1015 Karen Moskowitz/Stone/Getty Images; 1017 (br) Mauro Fermriello/Photo Researchers, Inc.; 1018 (bl) Anatoly Maltsev/epa/Corbis; (cr) Alexis Rosenfeld/Photo Researchers, Inc.; 1019 Victoria Smith/HRW; 1020 Mauro Fermariello/Photo Researchers, Inc.; 1021 (bkgd) Gianni Dagli Orti/Corbis; (tr) Archivo Iconographico, S.A./Corbis; (cr) Supreme Council of Antiquities/epa/Corbis; (bl) Kenneth Garrett/National Geographic Society; 1022 James King-Holmes/Photo Researchers, Inc.; 1023 (tl) Dr. Jurgen Scriba/Photo Researchers, Inc.; (tc) Andrew Brookes/Corbis; (tr) Tek Image/Photo Researchers, Inc.; 1024 (bc) Microscan/Phototake; (bl) D. Phillips/Photo Researchers, Inc.; (br) Mauro Fermariello/Photo Researchers, Inc.; 1025 (tr) Victoria Smith/HRW; (br) Steve Liss/Corbis; 1026 (tr) Dr. Jurgen Scriba/Photo Researchers, Inc.; (tl) William F. Campbell/Time Life Pictures/Getty Images; 1027 Julie Plasencia/San Francisco Chronicle/Corbis; 1028 Karen Kasmauski/Corbis; 1029 (tl), (tc), (tr) Volker Steger/Photo Researchers, Inc.; 1030 AP Photo/Mary Altaffer; 1031 Sam Yeh/AFP/Getty Images; 1032 Keith/Custom Medical Stock Photo; 1034 (bc) 3D4Medicalcom/Getty Images; (bl) Silvia Otte/Photonica/Getty Images; 1035 (br) Michael Donne, University of Manchester/Photo Researchers, Inc.; (tr) Royalty-Free/Corbis; (tl) Mike Karlsson/On Scene Photos; 1037 Victoria Smith/HRW; 1038 (t) Karen Kasmauski/Corbis; (b) Michael Donne, University of Manchester/Photo Researchers, Inc.; 1050 (bl) Rob Melnychuk/gettyimages; 1051 (tl) Scott Bauer/Agricultural Research Service, USDA; (tr) Tek Image/Photo Researchers, Inc. 1052 (t) LWA-Dann Tardif/Corbis; 1053 (b) Victoria Smith/HRW; 1054 (b) Sergio Purtell/Foca/HRW; 1055 (bc), (br) Sergio Purtell/Foca/HRW; 1056 (all) Sergio Purtell/Foca/HRW; 1058 (cl) Dr. Dennis Kunkel/Phototake; (c), (cr), (br) Sam Dudgeon/HRW; 1063 (animalia) Myron Jay Dorf/Corbis; (Eubacteria) © Gary D. Gaugler/Photo Researchers, Inc.; (archaebacteria) Wolfgang Baumeister/Science Photo Library/Photo Researchers, Inc.; (protista) Dr. Dennis Kunkel/PhotoTake; (fungi) Rod Planck/Photo Researchers Inc.; (plantae) Adam Jones/Photo Researchers Inc.

HRW Staff

The people who contributed to **Holt Biology** are listed below. They represent editorial, design, production, emedia, marketing, and permissions.

David Alvarado, Karen Arneson, Wesley M. Bain, Kimberly Barr, Soojinn Choi, Martize Cross, Eddie Dawson, Julie Dervin, Lydia Doty, Paul Draper, Sam Dudgeon, Sally Garland, Diana Goetting, Mark Grayson, Frieda Gress, Angela Hemmeter, Timothy Hovde, Jevara Jackson, Simon Key, Jane A. Kirschman, Liz Kline, Michelle Kwan, Denise Mahoney, Richard Metzger, Cathy Murphy, Mercedes Newman, Erin O'Bryant, Cathy Paré, Jenny Patton, Peter Reid, Raegan Remington, Diana Rodriguez, Karen Ross, Michelle Rumpf-Dike, Kathryn Selke, Chris Smith, Victoria Smith, Dawn Marie Spinozza, Jeff Streber, Amy Taulman, Jeannie Taylor, Kathy Towns, David Trevino, Bob Tucek, Heather Tucek, Kira J. Watkins, Aimee Wiley

Biologist's Periodic Table of Elements

Key:

Atomic number — 6
Symbol — **C**
Name — Carbon
Average atomic mass — 12.0107

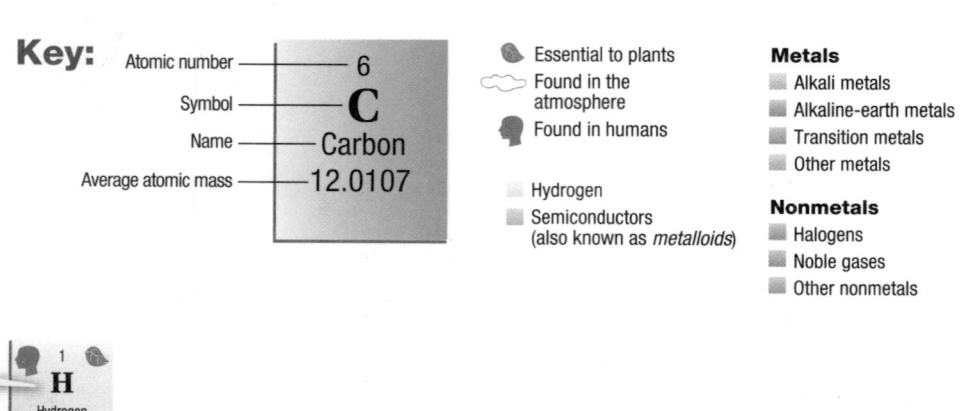

- Essential to plants
- Found in the atmosphere
- Found in humans

- Hydrogen
- Semiconductors (also known as *metalloids*)

Metals
- Alkali metals
- Alkaline-earth metals
- Transition metals
- Other metals

Nonmetals
- Halogens
- Noble gases
- Other nonmetals

Hydrogen is a component of all organic molecules and water. As an ion, hydrogen influences the pH of cellular and body fluids.

Magnesium activates plant and animal enzymes and is a component of chlorophyll.

Manganese activates plant and animal enzymes.

Cobalt is a component of the vitamin B_{12}, which is needed for maturation of red blood cells.

Sodium is important in nerve function and muscle contraction and helps maintain water balance.

Molybdenum plays a role in nitrogen fixation and is a component of some enzymes.

Iron is a component of hemoglobin and certain enzymes.

Potassium is critical for plant protein synthesis and is important in animal nerve function.

Calcium is part of the structure of bones and teeth, is involved in blood clotting, triggers muscle contraction, and is needed to maintain plant cell walls and membranes.

	Group 1	Group 2		Group 3	Group 4	Group 5	Group 6	Group 7	Group 8	Group 9
1	1 **H** Hydrogen 1.007 94									
2	3 **Li** Lithium 6.941	4 **Be** Beryllium 9.012 182								
3	11 **Na** Sodium 22.989 769 28	12 **Mg** Magnesium 24.3050								
4	19 **K** Potassium 39.0983	20 **Ca** Calcium 40.078		21 **Sc** Scandium 44.955 912	22 **Ti** Titanium 47.867	23 **V** Vanadium 50.9415	24 **Cr** Chromium 51.9961	25 **Mn** Manganese 54.938 045	26 **Fe** Iron 55.845	27 **Co** Cobalt 58.933 195
5	37 **Rb** Rubidium 85.4678	38 **Sr** Strontium 87.62		39 **Y** Yttrium 88.905 85	40 **Zr** Zirconium 91.224	41 **Nb** Niobium 92.906 38	42 **Mo** Molybdenum 95.94	43 **Tc** Technetium (98)	44 **Ru** Ruthenium 101.07	45 **Rh** Rhodium 102.905 50
6	55 **Cs** Cesium 132.905 4519	56 **Ba** Barium 137.327		57 **La** Lanthanum 138.905 47	72 **Hf** Hafnium 178.49	73 **Ta** Tantalum 180.947 88	74 **W** Tungsten 183.84	75 **Re** Rhenium 186.207	76 **Os** Osmium 190.23	77 **Ir** Iridium 192.217
7	87 **Fr** Francium (223)	88 **Ra** Radium (226)		89 **Ac** Actinium (227)	104 **Rf** Rutherfordium (261)	105 **Db** Dubnium (262)	106 **Sg** Seaborgium (266)	107 **Bh** Bohrium (264)	108 **Hs** Hassium (277)	109 **Mt** Meitnerium (268)

*The systematic names and symbols for elements greater than 111 will be used until the approval of trivial names by IUPAC.

58 **Ce** Cerium 140.116	59 **Pr** Praseodymium 140.907 65	60 **Nd** Neodymium 144.242	61 **Pm** Promethium (145)	62 **Sm** Samarium 150.36
90 **Th** Thorium 232.038 06	91 **Pa** Protactinium 231.035 88	92 **U** Uranium 238.028 91	93 **Np** Neptunium (237)	94 **Pu** Plutonium (244)

Period